Annual Abstract
of Statistics

No 149
2013 Edition
Compiled by: Dandy Booksellers

Contacts

For information about the content of this publication, contact
Dandy Booksellers: Tel 020 7624 2993
Email: dandybooksellers@btconnect.com

Publications orders

To obtain the print version of this publication, please contact Dandy
Booksellers
Tel: 0207 624 2993
Email: dandybooksellers@btconnect.com
Fax: 0207 624 5049
Post: Unit 3&4, 31-33 Priory Park Road
       London, NW6 7UP
Web: www.dandybooksellers.com

Contents

Page:

Units of measurement
Introduction

1: Area

1.1	Standard Area Measurement for UK Local Authority Districts	4

2: Parliamentary elections

2.1	Parliamentary elections	13
2.2	Parliamentary by-elections	13
2.3	Devolved assembly elections (Wales and Scotland)	14
2.4	Devolved assembly elections (Northern Ireland)	14

3: International Development

3.1a	Total Gross Public Expenditure on Development	20
3.1b	DFID Expenditure on Development	20
3.1c	Non-DFID Public Expenditure on Development	21
3.2a	Total DFID Expenditure and GPEX by Recipient Country (Africa)	22
3.2b	Total DFID Expenditure and GPEX by Recipient Country (Americas)	26
3.2c	Total DFID Expenditure and GPEX by Recipient Country (Asia)	29
3.2d	Total DFID Expenditure and GPEX by Recipient Country (Europe)	32
3.2e	Total DFID Expenditure and GPEX by Recipient Country (Pacific)	34
3.3	DFID Bilateral Expenditure by Input Sector Code	36

4: Labour Market

4.1	Labour Force Summary by sex: United Kingdom	47
4.2	Employment: Full-time, part-time and temporary workers	48
4.3	Employment: by sex and age: United Kingdom	58
4.4	All in employment by industry sector	60
4.5a	International comparisons	63
4.5b	Labour disputes	63
4.6	Civil Service employment; regional (GOR) distribution by government department	64
4.7	Unemployment by sex, age and duration	67
4.8	Regional labour market summary (employment, unemployment, economic activity, inactivity)	80
4.9	Claimant count rates: by region	81
4.10	Claimant count by Unitary and Local Authority	82
4.11a	Weekly pay - Gross (£) - For all employee jobs by Industry: United Kingdom, 2012	89
4.11b	Hourly pay - Gross (£) - For all employee jobs by Industry: United Kingdom, 2012	92
4.12a	Weekly pay - Gross (£) - For all employee jobs: United Kingdom, 2012	95
4.12b	Hourly pay - Excluding overtime (£) - For all employee jobs: United Kingdom, 2012	96
4.13	Average weekly earnings: main industrial sectors, Great Britain	99
4.14a	Average Weekly Earnings By Industry (Not Seasonally Adjusted)	100
4.14b	Average Weekly Earnings - regular pay	106
4.14c	Average Weekly Earnings - bonus pay	112
4.14d	Average Weekly Earnings in the public sector for selected activities (Not Seasonally Adjusted)	118
4.15a	Weekly pay - Gross (£) - For all employee jobs by age group and occupation: United Kingdom, 2012	119
4.15b	Hourly pay - Gross (£) - For all employee jobs by age group and occupation: United Kingdom, 2012	123
4.16	Median weekly and hourly earnings of full-time employees by age group: United Kingdom	127
4.17	Trade Unions	129

5: Social Protection

5.1	National Insurance Fund (Great Britain and Northern Ireland)	137
5.2	Persons who paid National Insurance contributions in a tax year: by sex	138
5.3	Main Features of National Insurance Contributions (NCIS)	139
5.4	Social Security Benefit Rates	141
5.5	Number of persons claiming benefits: Caseloads by age group, thousands	157
5.6	Jobseeker's Allowance claimants: by benefit entitlement: Great Britain	158
5.7	Employment and Support Allowance and Incapacity Benefit claimants: by sex, age and duration of spell	159
5.8	Attendance allowance - cases in payment: Age and gender of claimant Great Britain	160
5.9a	Families and children receiving Child Benefit, in each country and English Region	161
5.9b	Families receiving Child Benefit nationally, in each country and English Region	162
5.10	Child Tax Credit or Working Tax Credit elements and thresholds	163
5.11	Number of families and children with Child Tax Credit or Working Tax Credit, by level of award	164
5.12	Widows' Allowance (excluding bereavement payment): by type of benefit Great Britain	165
5.13	Bereavement Allowance (excluding bereavement payment): by sex, type of benefit and age of widow/er Great Britain	166
5.14	Contributory and non-contributory retirement pensions: by sex and age of claimant Great Britain and Overseas	167
5.15a	War pensions: estimated number of pensioners, Great Britain	168
5.15b	War Pensions in payment by type of pension, gender and financial year end	168

Contents

Page:

5: Social Protection

5.16	Income support by statistical group: number of claimants receiving weekly payment	168
5.17	Pension Credit: number of claimants	169
5.18	Income support: average weekly amounts of benefit	169
5.19	Pension Credit: average weekly amounts of benefit	169

6: External trade and investment

6.1	Trade in goods	178
6.2	Sales of products manufactured in the United Kingdom by Industry Division	178
6.3	United Kingdom exports: by commodity	179
6.4	United Kingdom imports: by commodity	180
6.5	United Kingdom exports: by area	181
6.6	United Kingdom imports: by area	183
6.7	Total International Trade in Services all industries (excluding travel, transport and banking) analysed by product	185
6.8	Total International Trade in Services (excluding travel, transport and banking) analysed by continents and countries	186
6.9	Summary of balance of payments	188
6.10	Summary of balance of payments: balances (credits less debits)	189
6.11	Balance of payments: current account	190
6.12	Balance of payments: financial account and investment income summary of international investment position, financial account and investment income	192
6.13	Net foreign direct investment flows abroad analysed by area and main country	193
6.14	FDI international investment position abroad analysed by area and main country	195
6.15	Earnings from foreign direct investment abroad analysed by area and main country	197
6.16	Foreign direct investment flows into the UK analysed by area and main country	199
6.17	FDI International positions in the UK analysed by area and main country	200
6.18	Earnings from foreign direct investment in the UK analysed by area and main country	201

7: Research and development

7.1a	R&D performed in the UK in each sector according to source of funding	205
7.1b	Expenditure on research and development in the UK by sector of performance	206
7.2	Gross central government expenditure on research and development	207
7.3	Government funding of net R&D by socio-economic objectives - percentage share	207
7.4	Expenditure on civil and defence R&D performed in UK businesses: broad product groups	208
7.5a	Sources of funds for R&D performed in UK businesses	209
7.5b	Sources of funds for R&D performed in UK businesses: civil and defence	210

8: Personal income, expenditure & wealth

8.1	Distribution of total income before and after tax by gender	214
8.2	Summary of the effects of taxes and benefits, by household type	216
8.3	Income and source of income	217
8.4	Household expenditure based on the FES classification	218
8.5	Percentage of households with durable goods	219

9: Lifestyles

9.1	Expenditure by the Department for Culture, Media and Sport	223
9.2	Estimates of Average Issue Readership of National Daily Newspapers	225
9.3	Employment in the Creative Economy	225
9.4	Selected activities performed in free time: by age	226
9.5	Films	226
9.6	Box office top 20 films released in the UK and Republic of Ireland, 2011	227
9.7	Full year accommodation usage figures by visitors from overseas	228
9.8	International tourism	229
9.9	Holidays abroad: by destination	229
9.10	All Tourism	230
9.11	All Tourism in Great Britain	230
9.12	Gambling	231
9.13	Most Popular Boy and Girl Baby Names in England and Wales, 2011	233
9.14a	Libraries overview (Great Britain)	234
9.14b	Proportion who have visited a public library in the last year - area-level breakdown	234
9.14c	Proportion who have visited a public library in the last year - demographic breakdown	235
9.15	Museums and galleries overview (adults)	235
9.16	Participation in voluntary activities	236
9.17	UK residents' visits to friends and relatives abroad: by destination	236
9.18	The Internet	237
9.19	Radio Listening	238

Page:

10: Environment

10.1	Atmospheric emissions	248
10.2	Road Transport Emissions by Pollutant	249
10.3	UK Greenhouse Gas Emissions , headline results	249
10.4	Greenhouse Gas Emissions Bridging Table	250
10.5	Estimated emissions of carbon dioxide (CO2)	250
10.6	Estimated emissions of methane (CH4)	251
10.7	Estimated emissions of nitrous oxide (N2O)	251
10.8	Material flow account for the United Kingdom	252
10.9	Annual rainfall: by region	253
10.10	UK Annual Weather Summary	253
10.11	Summary of River Basin district ecological and chemical status	254
10.12	Overall status of rivers & canals in Scotland	254
10.13	Monthly reservoir stocks for England & Wales	255
10.14a	Water industry turnover and current cost profit/(loss) before taxation by company	255
10.14b	Water Industry return on capital measured by average regulatory capital value (RCV) by company	256
10.15	Overall summary of pollution incident results by region, medium and incident category	257
10.16a	2012 mandatory compliance results for bathing waters in the UK	258
10.16b	2012 guideline compliance results for bathing waters in the UK	259
10.17	Estimated abstractions from all surface and groundwater sources: by purpose	259
10.18	Estimates of remaining recoverable oil & gas reserves and resources	260
10.19a	Local Authority Collected Waste (England)	261
10.19b	Waste managed by type and year (Wales)	261
10.19c	Household waste WasteDataFlow Scotland	262
10.19d	Municipal waste sent for recycling & composting, KPI(e), and landfilled, KPI(f), for Northern Ireland	263
10.19d	Household waste sent for recycling and composting, KPI(a), for Northern Ireland	264
10.19d	Household waste landfilled, KPI(b), and generated per household, KPI(h), and per capita, KPI(p), in Northern Ireland	265
10.20a	Amounts of different materials from household sources collected for recycling (including reuse) by collection method, England	265
10.20b	Total Household recycling by material and source, Wales	266
10.20c	Waste Collections in Scotland	268
10.20d	Material types collected for recycling (inc composting) in Northern Ireland	271
10.21	Survey of Local Authority Noise Enforcement Activity (England and Wales)	273
10.22	Government revenues from environmental taxes	274

11: Housing

11.1a	Dwelling stock: by tenure, England	277
11.1b	Dwelling stock: by tenure, Wales	278
11.1c	Dwelling stock: by tenure, Scotland	279
11.1d	Dwelling stock: by tenure, Northern Ireland	280
11.2	Type of Accommodation by Tenure Great Britain	281
11.3	House building: permanent dwellings completed, by tenure and country	282
11.4a	Housebuilding: permanent dwellings completed, by house and flat, number of bedroom and tenure, England	284
11.4b	Housebuilding completions: by number of bedrooms	285
11.5	Mortgage possession workload in the county courts of England and Wales	285
11.6	Mortgage arrears and repossessions	286
11.7	Households in temporary accommodation, by type of accommodation, England	287
11.8	Homeless Households in temporary accommodation at the end of the period	289
11.9	Households in temporary accommodation by accommodation type: Scotland	289

12: Banking and Finance

12.1a	Central bank's balance sheet - Bank of England 'Bank return' - Amounts outstanding of consolidated Issue and Banking department liabilities	293
12.1b	Central bank's balance sheet - Bank of England 'Bank return' - Amounts outstanding of consolidated Issue and Banking Department assets	294
12.1c	Central bank's balance sheet - Bank of England 'Bank return' - Amounts outstanding of Issue Department liabilities	295
12.1d	Central bank's balance sheet - Bank of England 'Bank return' - Amounts outstanding of Issue Department assets	296
12.1e	Central bank's balance sheet - Bank of England 'Bank return' - Amounts outstanding of Banking Department liabilities	297
12.1f	Central bank's balance sheet - Bank of England 'Bank return' - Amounts outstanding of Banking Department assets	298
12.2a	Annual clearing volumes and values	299
12.2b	Average daily clearing volumes and values	300
12.2c	Bacs volumes and values	301
12.2d	CHAPS volumes and values	302
12.2e	CHAPS value band analysis	303
12.2f	Faster Payments volumes and values	304
12.2g	Inter-bank cheque volumes and values	305
12.2h	Inter-bank credit volumes and values	306
12.2i	Inter-bank clearing values: UK summary	307
12.2j	Inter-bank clearing volumes: UK summary	308
12.3a	Monetary financial institutions (excluding central bank): Balance sheet - Amounts outstanding of sterling liabilities	309
12.3b	Monetary financial institutions (excluding central bank): Balance sheet - Amounts outstanding of foreign currency liabilities (including euro)	311
12.3c	Monetary financial institutions (excluding central bank): Balance sheet - Amounts outstanding of sterling assets	313

Contents

Page:

12: Banking and Finance

12.3d	Monetary financial institutions (excluding central bank): Balance sheet - Amounts outstanding of foreign currency assets (including euro)	316
12.3e	Monetary financial institutions (excluding central bank): Balance sheet - Changes in sterling liabilities	318
12.3f	Monetary financial institutions (excluding central bank): Balance sheet - Changes in foreign currency liabilities (including euro)	320
12.3g	Monetary financial institutions (excluding central bank): Balance sheet - Changes in sterling assets	322
12.3h	Monetary financial institutions (excluding central bank): Balance sheet - Changes in foreign currency assets (including euro)	325
12.4a	Industrial analysis of monetary financial institutions lending to UK residents - Amounts outstanding of lending in sterling	327
12.4b	Industrial analysis of monetary financial institutions lending to UK residents - Amounts outstanding of lending in all currencies	333
12.4c	Industrial analysis of monetary financial institutions lending to UK residents - Amounts outstanding of facilities granted in sterling	339
12.4d	Industrial analysis of monetary financial institutions lending to UK residents - Amounts outstanding of facilities granted in all currencies	345
12.5a	Industrial analysis of monetary financial institutions deposits from UK residents - Amounts outstanding of deposit liabilities (including under repo) in sterling	351
12.5b	Industrial analysis of monetary financial institutions deposits from UK residents - Amounts outstanding of deposit liabilities (including under repo) in sterling and other currencies	356
12.6a	Components of M4 - Amounts outstanding	361
12.6b	Components of M4 - Changes	362
12.7	Counterparts to changes in M4: alternative presentation	363
12.8	Selected retail banks' base rate	365
12.9	Average three month sterling money market rates	366
12.10	Average Foreign Exchange rates	370
12.11	Average zero coupon yields	374
12.12	Consumer credit excluding student loans	377
12.13a	Investment trusts' assets & liabilities at market values	378
12.13b	Unit trusts & property unit trusts' assets & liabilities at market values	379
12.14	Self-administered pension funds' balance sheet at market values combined public and private sector	380
12.15a	Insurance companies' assets & liabilities at market values long-term funds	382
12.15b	Insurance companies' assets & liabilities at market values general funds	384
12.16a	Individual insolvencies	386
12.16b	Insolvencies, Scotland	386
12.16c	Insolvencies, Northern Ireland	387
12.17a	Company liquidations	388
12.17b	Company Insolvencies, Scotland	388
12.17c	Company Insolvencies, Northern Ireland	389
12.18a	Monetary financial institutions consolidated balance sheet - Amounts outstanding of liabilities	390
12.18b	Monetary financial institutions consolidated balance sheet - Amounts outstanding of assets	391
12.18c	Monetary financial institutions consolidated balance sheet - Changes in liabilities	392
12.18d	Monetary financial institutions consolidated balance sheet - Changes in assets	393
12.19	Selected interest rates, exchange rates and security prices	394
12.20	Mergers and Acquisitions in the UK by other UK Companies: Category of Expenditure	396

13: Service industry

13.1a	Retail Trade, except of motor vehicles and motorcycles	399
13.1b	Retail trade, except of motor vehicles and motorcycles - Turnover	400
13.2	Retail trade: index numbers of value and volume of sales	401
13.3	Wholesale and retail trade and repair of motor vehicles and motorcycles	402
13.4	Accommodation and food service activities	403

14: Defence

14.1	United Kingdom defence expenditure by commododity block	412
14.2	Intake to UK Regular Forces by Service and sex	413
14.3a	Number of vessels in the Royal Navy and Royal Fleet Auxiliary and Squadrons in Fleet Air Arm	414
14.3b	Number of regiments, infantry battalions & major headquarters, in the Regular and Territorial Army	415
14.3c	Number of squadrons in the Royal Air Force and the Royal Auxiliary Air Force	416
14.3d	Number of regiments and squadrons in selected Joint Units	417
14.4	Outflow from UK Regular Forces by Service and sex	418
14.5	United Kingdom Armed Forces full-time trained strength and requirement	419
14.6a	Civilian personnel	420
14.6b	Civilian personnel by budgetary area and grade equivalent	421
14.7a	Land holdings by country and whether owned, leased or with legal rights	422
14.7b	Service family accommodation in the United Kingdom	423
14.8a	Location of Service and civilian personnel in the United Kingdom	424
14.8b	Global locations of Service and civilian personnel	425
14.9a	UK regular Armed Forces deaths by service, year of occurrence, numbers, age and gender standardised rates	427
14.9b	UK regular Armed Forces deaths by service, numbers, Standardised Mortality Ratios (SMR)	427
14.10a	Military Search and Rescue - UK & Overseas callouts, incidents and persons moved	428
14.10b	Search and Rescue Helicopters - UK & Overseas callouts by unit	430
14.10c	Search and Rescue Helicopters - UK & Overseas callouts by assistance type	431
14.10d	Strength of uniformed UK medical staff	431
14.11	Number of vessels boarded by the Royal Navy Fishery Protection Squadron within British fishing limits and convictions arising from these boardings	432

Page:

15: Population and vital statistics

15.1	Population summary: by country and sex	438
15.2a	Population projections by the Office for National Statistics United Kingdom	439
15.2b	Population projections by the Office for National Statistics England & Wales	441
15.2c	Population projections by the Office for National Statistics Scotland	443
15.2d	Population projections by the Office for National Statistics Northern Ireland	445
15.3a	Mid-2012 Population Estimates: United Kingdom; estimated resident population by single year of age and sex	447
15.3b	Population projections by the Office for National Statistics United Kingdom	448
15.3c	Mid-2012 Population Estimates: England and Wales; estimated resident population by single year of age and sex	454
15.3d	Population projections by the Office for National Statistics England and Wales	455
15.3e	Mid-2012 Population Estimates: Scotland; estimated resident population by single year of age and sex	467
15.3f	Population projections by the Office for National Statistics Scotland	468
15.3g	Mid-2012 Population Estimates: Northern Ireland; estimated resident population by single year of age and sex	474
15.3h	Population projections by the Office for National Statistics Northern Ireland	475
15.4	Families by family type and presence of children	481
15.5	Geographical distribution of the population	482
15.6	Comparing the Broad Ethnic groups for England and Wales	490
15.7	Long-Term International Migration, Citizenship	491
15.8	Long-Term International Migration, Country of Last or Next Residence	494
15.9	Grants of settlement by country of nationality and category and in-country refusals of settlement	498
15.10	Asylum applications and initial decisions for main applicants, by country of nationality	502
15.11	Previous marital status and manner of solemnisation (numbers and percentages)	506
15.12	Duration of marriage at divorce by age of wife at marriage	507
15.13	Duration of marriage at divorce by age of husband at marriage	513
15.14	Live births by local authority of usual residence of mother, numbers, sex, General Fertility Rates and Total Fertility Rates	515
15.15	Live births by age of mother and registration type	522
15.16	Legal abortions: by country of procedure and (i) age, (ii) gestation weeks, (iii) procedure, (iv) parity, (v) previous abortions, (vi) grounds and (vii) principal medical condition for abortions performed under ground E	525
15.17	Death rates per 1,000 population: by age and sex	526
15.18	Stillbirth and infant death rates: England and Wales age at death	527
15.19	Interim life tables	529
15.20a	Adoptions by date of entry in Adopted Children Register (numbers and percentages): sex and age	530
15.20b	Adoptions by age of child and relationship of the adopter(s)	531
15.20c	Adoptions - Northern Ireland	531

16: Health

16.1a	NHS Hospital and Community Health Services: Qualified ambulance service staff and support to ambulance service staff	536
16.1b	NHS Labour Turnover and Stability Analysis Welsh Ambulance Trust	536
16.1c	Ambulance staff by Type: Scotland	537
16.1d	Ambulance Staff by Type: Northern Ireland	537
16.2	Hospital and primary care services: Scotland	538
16.3	Hospital and general health services: Northern Ireland	541
16.4	NHS Hospital & Community Health Service (HCHS) and General Practice workforce as at 30 September each specified year England	544
16.5	Staffing summary: Wales	545
16.6	Deaths: underlying cause, sex and age-group, summary	546
16.7a	Notifications of infectious diseases: England and Wales	547
16.7b	Notifications of infectious diseases: Scotland	547
16.7c	Notifications of Infectious diseases: Northern Ireland	548
16.8a	Work-related and occupational respiratory disease: estimated number of cases reported by chest physicians to SWORD and by occupational physicians to OPRA by sex and diagnostic category	549
16.8b	Work-related mental ill-health: estimated number of cases reported by psychiatrists to SOSMI and by occupational physicians to OPRA, by sex and diagnostic category	549
16.8c	Work-related skin disease: estimated number of cases reported by dermatologists to EPIDERM and by occupational physicians to OPRA, by sex and diagnostic category	549
16.8d	Work-related musculoskeletal disorders: estimated number of cases reported by rheumatologists to MOSS and by occupational physicians to OPRA, by sex and diagnostic category	550
16.9	Deaths due to occupationally related lung disease Great Britain	550
16.10	Reported injuries to employees and the self-employed, by detailed industry and severity of injury	551

17: Prices

17.1	Producer prices index	557
17.2	Producer prices index of output	560
17.3	Internal purchasing power of the pound (based on RPI)	563
17.4	CPI: Detailed figures by division	564
17.5	Retail Prices Index United Kingdom	565
17.6	Tax and Price Index United Kingdom	566
17.7	Index of Producer Prices of Agricultural Products - Total Inputs, UK	567
17.8	Index of Producer Prices of Agricultural Products - Total Outputs, UK	568
17.9	Harmonised Indicies of Consumer Prices (HICPs) - International comparisons: EU countries: Percentage change over 12 months	569

Contents

18: Production

18.1	Production and Construction Industries	579
18.2	UK Manufacturer's Sales by Industry	585
18.3	United Kingdom - number of local units in vat and/or paye based enterprises	591
18.4	Production of primary fuels	594
18.5	Total inland energy consumption	594
18.6	Coal: supply and demand	595
18.7	Fuel input and gas output: gas consumption	595
18.8	Electricity: generation, supply and consumption	596
18.9	Electricity: plant capacity and demand	597
18.10	Electricity: fuel used in generation	598
18.11	Indigenous petroleum production, refinery receipts, imports and exports of oil	598
18.12	Throughput of crude and process oils and output of refined products from refineries	599
18.13	Deliveries of petroleum products for inland consumption	600
18.14	Iron and steel: summary of steel supplies, deliveries and stocks	601
18.15	Iron and steel: iron ore, manganese ore, pig iron and iron and steel scrap	602
18.16	Iron and steel: furnaces and production of steel	603
18.17	Fertilisers - UK consumption	603
18.18a	United Kingdom production of minerals	604
18.18b	Minerals produced in Northern Ireland, the Isle of Man, Guernsey and Jersey	605
18.19a	Building materials and components, Bricks - Production, Deliveries and Stocks	606
18.19b	Building materials and components, Concrete Blocks - Production, Deliveries and Stocks	607
18.19c	Building materials and components, Other Building Materials	608
18.19d	Building materials and components, Slate - Production, Deliveries and Stocks	609
18.19e	Building materials and components, Cement & Clinker - Production, Deliveries and Stocks	610
18.19f	Building materials and components, Sales of Sand and Gravel in Great Britain	611
18.20	Volume of construction output in Great Britain: constant prices, seasonally adjusted - by sector	612
18.21	Value of orders for new construction obtained by main contractors in Great Britain: current prices - by sector	612
18.22	Total engineering	613
18.23	Manufacture of fabricated metal products and machinery and equipment n.e.c	614
18.24	Alcoholic drink	615
18.25	Tobacco products: released for home consumption	615

19: National Accounts

19.1	UK national and domestic product Main aggregates: index numbers and values Current prices and chained volume measures	621
19.2	UK gross domestic product and national income Current prices	623
19.3	UK gross domestic product Chained volume measures	625
19.4	Output and capital formation: by industry Gross value added at current basic prices	626
19.5	Gross value added at basic prices: by industry Chained volume indices	630
19.6	Non-financial corporations ESA95 sector S.11 - Allocation of Primary Income Accounts	632
19.7	Non-financial corporations ESA95 sector S.11 - Secondary Distribution of Income Account	632
19.8	Private non-financial corporations ESA95 sectors S.11002 National controlled and S.11003 Foreign controlled - Allocation of Primary Income Accounts	633
19.9	Private non-financial corporations ESA95 sectors S.11002 National controlled and S.11003 Foreign controlled - Secondary Distribution of Income Account	633
19.10	Households and non-profit institutions serving households ESA95 sectors S.14 and S.15 - Allocation of Primary Income Accounts	634
19.11	Households and non-profit institutions serving households ESA95 sectors S.14 and S.15 - Secondary Distribution of Income Account	635
19.12	Households and non-profit institutions serving households ESA95 sectors S.14 and S.15	636
19.13	The sector accounts: key economic indicators	637
19.14	Household final consumption expenditure: classified by purpose at current market prices	638
19.15	Household final consumption expenditure: classified by purpose Chained volume measures	639
19.16	Individual consumption expenditure at current market prices by households, non-profit institutions serving households and general government	640
19.17	Individual consumption expenditure by households, NPISH and general government Chained volume measures Classified by function (COICOP/COPNI/COFOG)	642
19.18	Change in inventories at chained volume measures	644
19.19	Gross fixed capital formation at current purchasers' prices Analysis by broad sector and type of asset, total economy	645
19.20	Gross fixed capital formation at current purchasers' prices Analysis by type of asset, total economy	645
19.21	Gross fixed capital formation Chained volume measures, total economy: analysis by broad sector and type of asset	646
19.22	Gross fixed capital formation Chained volume measures, total economy: analysis by type of asset	646

20: Education

20.1	Number of schools, by type of school - time series	653
20.2	Full-time and part-time pupils by age, gender and school type	654
20.3	Pupil: teacher ratios (PTRs) and pupil: adult ratios (PARs) within schools, by type of school -time series	655
20.4	Pupils with statements of Special Educational Needs (SEN)	656
20.5	GCE, GCSE, SCE/NQ and vocational qualifications obtained by pupils and students - time series	657
20.6	Qualifications obtained by students on HE courses at HEIs in the UK by gender, subject area and level of qualification obtained	658
20.7	Qualifications obtained by students on HE courses at HEIs in the UK by gender, level of qualification obtained, mode of study and domicile	662
20.8	Students in further and higher education, UK time series	663

Page:

20: Education

20.9	Students in higher education by level, mode of study, gender and subject group	664
20.10	Qualified teachers by type of school and gender - time series	665

21: Crime and Justice

21.1a	Police officer strength in England and Wales by police force area	673
21.1b	Special constable strength, and joiners/leavers by police force area, gender and ethnicity	674
21.1c	Police forces strength: by country and sex	675
21.1d	Number of Police Officers (Full-time Equivalent) in Scotland by Police Force and Deployment	675
21.2	Prison Population International Comparisons with other EU Countries	676
21.3	Police recorded crime statistics by offence group	678
21.4	Offenders convicted and sentenced at all courts	684
21.5	Persons cautioned for summary offences (excluding motoring) by offence, sex and age	699
21.6a	Persons aged 10 to under 12 convicted and sentenced at all courts	702
21.6b	Persons aged 12 to under 15 convicted and sentenced at all courts	704
21.6c	Persons aged 15 to under 18 convicted and sentenced at all courts	708
21.6d	Persons aged 18 to under 21 convicted and sentenced at all courts	713
21.6e	Persons aged 21 or over convicted and sentenced at all courts	720
21.7	Persons cautioned for indictable offences by offences, sex and age	727
21.8	Persons sentenced to immediate custody at all courts by offence, sex, length of sentence and average sentence length	734
21.9a	Persons sentenced to life imprisonment by sex and age	744
21.9b	Persons sentenced to determinate and indeterminate custodial sentences custody by age group, sex & type of sentence	745
21.10	Prison receptions and population in custody, England and Wales	748
21.11	Prison population under immediate custodial sentence by age and offence, England and Wales	749
21.12	Crimes recorded by the police, Scotland	752
21.13	People with a charge proved by main crime/offence, Scotland	753
21.14	People with a charge proved by type of court, Scotland	754
21.15	People with a charge proved by main penalty, Scotland	755
21.16	People with a charge proved by main penalty, gender and age, Scotland	756
21.17a	Average daily population in penal establishments by type of custody	757
21.17b	Average daily population of sentenced offenders by sentence length	758
21.17c	Receptions to penal establishments by type of custody	759
21.18	Scottish Police Service Statement of Comprehensive Net Expenditure	760
21.19	Number of recorded crimes, Northern Ireland	761
21.20	Average Northern Ireland prison population, by sex, prisoner type and age	762

22: Transport

22.1	Average number of trips (trip rates) by purpose and main mode: Great Britain	768
22.2	Domestic freight transport: by mode:	769
22.3	Passenger transport: by mode	770
22.4	Motor vehicle traffic (vehicle kilometres) by road class in Great Britain	770
22.5	Road lengths (kilometres) by road type in Great Britain	771
22.6	Road traffic (vehicle kilometres) by vehicle type in Great Britain	771
22.7	Cars licensed by propulsion / fuel type, Great Britain	772
22.8	Motor vehicles registered for the first time by tax class: Great Britain	773
22.9a	Practical car test pass rates by gender, Great Britain	773
22.9b	Practical motorcycle test (Module 1) pass rates by gender, Great Britain	774
22.9c	Practical motorcycle test1 (Module 2) pass rates by gender, Great Britain	774
22.9d	Practical large goods vehicle (LGV) test rates by gender, Great Britain	774
22.9e	Practical passenger carrying vehicle (PCV) test rates by gender, Great Britain	775
22.10	Full car driving licence holders by age and gender, England	776
22.11a	Household car availability, Great Britain	777
22.11b	Household car ownership by region and rural-urban classification, Great Britain	777
22.12	Vehicles currently licensed by taxation group, Northern Ireland	778
22.13	Motor vehicles registered for the first time in NI by vehicle type	779
22.14	Vehicle kilometres on local bus services by metropolitan area status and country, Great Britain	780
22.15	Local bus fares index by metropolitan area status and country, Great Britain	780
22.16	Reported road accident casualties by road user type and severity	781
22.17a	Goods lifted and goods moved by mode of working: by GB HGVs in the UK	782
22.17b	Goods moved by type and weight of vehicle: by GB HGVs in the UK	782
22.17c	Goods moved by commodity	783
22.18a	Goods lifted by type and weight of vehicle:by GB HGVs in UK	783
22.18b	Goods lifted by commodity	784
22.19a	Passenger journeys by sector - National Rail, Great Britain	785
22.19b	Passenger revenue by sector - National Rail, Great Britain	786
22.19c	Passenger kilometres by sector - National Rail, Great Britain	787
22.19d	Infrastructure on the railways - National Rail Network, Great Britain	788
22.19e	Number of stations or stops on light rail and trams by system, England	789
22.19f	London Underground statistics	789
22.19g	Glasgow Underground statistics	790
22.20a	Freight moved	790
22.20b	Freight lifted	791

Contents

Page:

22: Transport

22.21	Railways: permanent way and rolling stock, Northern Ireland	791
22.22	Operating statistics of railways, Northern Ireland	792
22.23	Main Outputs of UK Airlines in Tonne-kilometres Available and Used	793
22.24a	Air Transport Movements by Type and Nationality of Operator	794
22.24b	Air Passengers by Type and Nationality of Operator	795
22.25	Scheduled and Non-Scheduled Services All services	797
22.26a	Aircraft Movements	798
22.26b	Terminal and Transit Passengers 2012 Comparison with the Previous Year	800
22.26c	Freight by Type and Nationality of Operator	802
22.26d	Mail by Type and Nationality of Operator	804

23: Government Finance

23.1	Sector analysis of key fiscal balances, United Kingdom	810
23.2	Public sector transactions and fiscal balances, United Kingdom	811
23.3	Public sector net debt, United Kingdom	812
23.4a	Central government surplus on current budget and net borrowing	813
23.4b	Central government surplus on current budget and net borrowing - Monthly	815
23.5	National Loans Fund: assets and liabilities	816
23.6a	Taxes paid by UK residents to general government and the European Union - Generation of Income	817
23.6b	Taxes paid by UK residents to general government and the European Union - Secondary Distribution of Income	818
23.7	Central Government borrowing and repayment of debt	819
23.8	Central government net cash requirement on own account (receipts and outlays on a cash basis)	821
23.9	HM Revenue and Customs receipts	822
23.10	Income tax personal allowances and reliefs	826
23.11	Rates of Income Tax	827
23.12	Non-domestic rating in England & Wales	828
23.13	Revenue expenditure of local authorities	829
23.14	Financing of revenue expenditure, England and Wales	831
23.15	Financing of capital expenditure	832
23.16a	Capital receipts: all services, England 2nd provisional outturn	833
23.16b	Capital expenditure: all services, England 2nd provisional outturn	834
23.17	Capital outturn expenditure, by service	835
23.18	Expenditure of local authorities, Scotland	836
23.19a	Local Government revenue income by source, Scotland	838
23.19b	Total Capital Expenditure and Financing, Scotland	838
23.20	Subjective analysis of General Fund Revenue Income, Scotland	839
23.21	Expenditure of local authorities , Northern Ireland	840

24: Agriculture

24.1	Production and income account at current prices; United Kingdom	845
24.2	Output and input of volume indices; United Kingdom	847
24.3	Agricultural land use	848
24.4a	Estimated quantity of crops and grass harvested	848
24.4b	Fruit: Home production marketed	849
24.4c	Field vegetables: Home production marketed	850
24.5	Crop areas and livestock numbers	851
24.6	Forestry	852
24.7	Sales for food of agricultural produce and livestock	853
24.8	Organic and In Conversion Livestock Numbers in the UK	853
24.9	Number of organic producers and/or processors time series	854
24.10a	Organic and In-conversion Land	854
24.10b	Organic and In-conversion Land use in England	855
24.11	Average weekly and hourly earnings and hours of full-time male agricultural workers	856
24.12	Median weekly and hourly earnings and hours of agricultural workers by type	856
24.13	Agricultural labour force on commercial holdings	857
24.14	Summary of UK fishing industry	858
24.15	UK Fishing Fleet	859
24.16	Estimated household food consumption	860

Sources: 863

Units of measurement

Length

1 millimetre (mm)	= 0.03937 inch	
1 centimetre (cm)	= 10 millimetres	= 0.3937 inch
1 metre (m)	= 1,000 millimetres	= 1.094 yards
1 kilometre (km)	= 1,000 metres	= 0.6214 mile
1 inch (in.)		= 25.40 millimetres or 2.540 centimetres
1 foot (ft.)	= 12 inches	= 0.3048 metre
1 yard (yd.)	= 3 feet	= 0.9144 metre
1 mile	= 1,760 yards	= 1.609 kilometres

Area

1 square millimetre (mm2)		= 0.001550 square inch
1 square metre (m2)	= one million square millimetres	= 1.196 square yards
1 hectare (ha)	= 10,000 square metres	= 2.471 acres
1 square kilometre (km2)	= one million square metres	= 247.1 acres
1 square inch (sq. in.)		= 645.2 square millimetres or 6.452 square centimetres
1 square foot (sq. ft.)	= 144 square inches	= 0.09290 square metre or 929.0 square centimetres
1 square yard (sq. yd.)	= 9 square feet	= 0.8361 square metre
1 acre	= 4,840 square yards	= 4,046 square metres or 0.4047 hectare
1 square mile (sq. mile)	= 640 acres	= 2.590 square kilometres or 259.0 hectares

Volume

1 cubic centimetre (cm3)		= 0.06102 cubic inch
1 cubic decimetre (dm3)	= 1,000 cubic centimetres	= 0.03531 cubic foot
1 cubic metre (m3)	= one million cubic centimetres	= 1.308 cubic yards
1 cubic inch (cu.in.)		=16.39 cubic centimetres
1 cubic foot (cu. ft.)	= 1,728 cubic inches	= 0.02832 cubic metre or 28.32 cubic decimetres
1 cubic yard (cu. yd.)	= 27 cubic feet	= 0.7646 cubic metre

Capacity

1 litre (l)	= 1 cubic decimetre	= 0.2200 gallon
1 hectolitre (hl)	= 100 litres	= 22.00 gallons
1 pint		= 0.5682 litre
1 quart	= 2 pints	= 1.137 litres
1 gallon	= 8 pints	= 4.546 litres
1 bulk barrel	= 36 gallons (gal.)	= 1.637 hectolitres

Weight

1 gram (g)		= 0.03527 ounce avoirdupois
1 hectogram (hg)	= 100 grams	= 3.527 ounces or 0.2205 pound
1 kilogram (kg)	= 1,000 grams or 10 hectograms	= 2.205 pounds
1 tonne (t)	= 1,000 kilograms	= 1.102 short tons or 0.9842 long ton
1 ounce avoirdupois (oz.)	= 437.5 grains	= 28.35 grams
1 pound avoirdupois (lb.)	= 16 ounces	= 0.4536 kilogram
1 hundredweight (cwt.)	= 112 pounds	= 50.80 kilograms
1 short ton	= 2,000 pounds	= 907.2 kilograms or 0.9072 tonne
1 long ton (referred to as ton)	= 2,240 pounds	= 1,016 kilograms or 1.016 tonnes
1 ounce troy	= 480 grains	= 31.10 grams

Energy

British thermal unit (Btu)	= 0.2520 kilocalorie (kcal) = 1.055 kilojoule (kj)
Therm	= 105 British thermal units = 25,200 kcal = 105,506 kj
Megawatt hour (MWh)	= 106 watt hours (Wh)
Gigawatt hour (GWh)	= 106 kilowatt hours = 34,121 therms

Food and drink

Butter	23,310 litres milk	= 1 tonne butter (average)
Cheese	10,070 litres milk	= 1 tonne cheese
Condensed milk	2,550 litres milk	= 1 tonne full cream condensed milk
	2,953 litres skimmed milk	= 1 tonne skimmed condensed milk
Milk	1 million litres	= 1,030 tonnes
Milk powder	8,054 litres milk	= 1 tonne full cream milk powder
	10,740 litres skimmed milk	= 1 tonne skimmed milk powder
Eggs	17,126 eggs	= 1 tonne (approximate)
Sugar	100 tonnes sugar beet	= 92 tonnes refined sugar
	100 tonnes cane sugar	= 96 tonnes refined sugar

Shipping

Gross tonnage	= The total volume of all the enclosed spaces of a vessel, the unit of measurement being a 'ton' of 100 cubic feet.
Deadweight tonnage	= Deadweight tonnage is the total weight in tons of 2,240 lb. that a ship can legally carry, that is the total weight of cargo, bunkers, stores and crew.

Introduction

Welcome to the 2013 edition of the Annual Abstract of Statistics. This compendium draws together statistics from a wide range of official and other authoritative sources.

Dandy Booksellers have sourced and formatted these tables under instruction from various government departments/ organisations

Regional information, supplementary to the national figures in Annual Abstract, appear in Regional Trends online. The latest edition of Regional Trends is available electronically on the ONS website free of charge. This can be accessed at:

http://www.ons.gov.uk/ons/rel/regional-trends/regional-trends/no--43--2011-edition/index.html

Current data for many of the series appearing in this Annual Abstract are contained in other ONS publications, such as Economic & Labour Market Review, Population Trends, Health Statistics Quarterly and Financial Statistics. These titles can be purchased through Dandy Booksellers.

Other ONS publications which contain related data are the Monthly Digest of Statistics and Social Trends.

These publications can be found at:
http://www.ons.gov.uk

The name (and telephone number, where this is available) of the organisation providing the statistics are shown under each table. In addition, a list of Sources is given at the back of the book, which sets out the official publications or other sources to which further reference can be made.

Identification codes

The four-letter identification code at the top of each data column, or at the side of each row is the ONS reference for this series of data on their database. Please quote the relevant code if you contact them requiring any further information about the data. On some tables it is not possible to include these codes, so please quote the table number in these cases.

Definitions and classification

Time series
So far as possible annual totals are given throughout, but quarterly or monthly figures are given where these are more suitable to the type of series.

Explanatory notes

Most sections are preceded by explanatory notes which should be read in conjunction with the tables. Definitions and explanatory notes for many of the terms occurring in the Annual Abstract are also given in the Annual Supplement to the Monthly Digest of Statistics, published in the January edition. Detailed notes on items which appear in both the Annual Abstract and Financial Statistics are given in an annual supplement to the latter entitled Financial Statistics Explanatory Handbook. The original sources listed in the Sources may also be consulted.

Standard Industrial Classification

A Standard Industrial Classification (SIC) was first introduced into the UK in 1948 for use in classifying business establishments and other statistical units by the type of economic activity in which they are engaged. The classification provides a framework for the collection, tabulation, presentation and analysis of data about economic activities. Its use promotes uniformity of data collected by various government departments and agencies.

Since 1948 the classification has been revised in 1958, 1968, 1980, 1992, 2003 and 2007. One of the principal objectives of the 1980 revision was to eliminate differences from the activity classification issued by the Statistical Office of the European Communities (Eurostat) and entitled 'Nomenclature générale des activités économiques dans les Communautés Européennes', usually abbreviated to NACE.

In 1990 the European Communities introduced a new statistical classification of economic activities (NACE Rev 1) by regulation. The regulation made it obligatory for the UK to introduce a new Standard Industrial Classification SIC(92), based on NACE Rev 1. UK SIC(92) was based exactly on NACE Rev 1 but, where it was thought necessary or helpful, a fifth digit was added to form subclasses of the NACE 1 four digit system. Classification systems need to be revised periodically because, over time, new products, processes and industries emerge. In January 2003 a minor revision of NACE Rev 1, known as NACE Rev 1.1, was published in the Official Journal of the European Communities.

Consequently, the UK was obliged to introduce a new Standard Industrial Classification, SIC(2003) consistent with NACE Rev 1.1. The UK took the opportunity of the 2003 revision also to update the national Subclasses. Full details are available in UK Standard Industrial Classification of Economic Activities 2003 and the Indexes to the UK Standard Industrial Classification of Economic Activities 2003. These are the most recent that are currently used. The most up to date version is the UK Standard Industrial Classification of Economic activities 2007 (SIC2007). It will be implemented in five stages and came into effect on 1 January 2008.

• For reference year 2008, the Annual Business Inquiry (parts 1 & 2) will be based on SIC 2007

• PRODCOM will also be based on SIC 2007 from reference year 2008

• Other annual outputs will be based on SIC 2007 from reference year 2009, unless otherwise determined by regulation

• Quarterly and monthly surveys will be based on SIC 2007 from the first reference period in 2010, unless otherwise determined by regulation

• National Accounts will move to SIC 2007 in September 2011

Symbols and conventions used

Change of basis
Where consecutive figures have been compiled on different bases and are not strictly comparable, a footnote is added indicating the nature of the difference.

Geographic coverage
Statistics relate mainly to the UK. Where figures relate to other areas, this is indicated on the table.

Units of measurement
The various units of measurement used are listed after the Contents.

Rounding of figures
In tables where figures have been rounded to the nearest final digit, the constituent items may not add up exactly to the total.

Symbols
The following symbols have been used throughout:

.. = not available or not applicable (also information supressed to avoid disclosure)

- = nil or less than half the final digit shown

Office for National Statistics online:
www.ons.gov.uk
Web-based access to time series, cross-sectional data and metadata from across the Government Statistical Service (GSS), is available using the site search function from the homepage. Download many datasets, in whole or in part, or consult directory information for all GSS statistical resources, including censuses, surveys, periodicals and enquiry services. Information is posted as PDF electronic documents or in XLS and CSV formats, compatible with most spreadsheet packages.

Contact point
Dandy Books welcomes any feedback on the content of the Annual Abstract, including comments on the format of the data and the selection of topics. Comments and requests for general information should be addressed to:

Dandy Booksellers
Unit 3&4
31-33 Priory Park Road
London
NW6 7UP
or
enquiries@dandybooksellers.com

04 November 2014

this page is intentionally blank

Area

Chapter 1

Area

The United Kingdom (UK) comprises Great Britain and Northern Ireland. Great Britain comprises England, Wales and Scotland.

Physical Features

The United Kingdom (UK) constitutes the greater part of the British Isles. The largest of the islands is Great Britain. The next largest comprises Northern Ireland and the Irish Republic. Western Scotland is fringed by the large island chain known as the Hebrides, and to the north east of the Scottish mainland are the Orkney and Shetland Islands. All these, along with the Isle of Wight, Anglesey and the Isles of Scilly, form part of the UK, but the Isle of Man, in the Irish Sea and the Channel Islands, between Great Britain and France are largely self-governing and are not part of the UK. The UK is one of the 27 member states of the European Union. With an area of about 243 000 sq km (about 94 000 sq miles), the UK is just under 1 000 km (about 600 miles) from the south coast to the extreme north of Scotland and just under 500 km (around 300 miles) across at the widest point.

- Highest mountain: Ben Nevis, in the highlands of Scotland, at 1 343 m (4 406 ft)
- Longest river: the Severn, 354 km (220 miles) long, which rises in central Wales and flows through Shrewsbury, Worcester and Gloucester in England to the Bristol Channel
- Largest lake: Lough Neagh, Northern Ireland, at 396 sq km (153 sq miles)
- Deepest lake: Loch Morar in the Highlands of Scotland, 310 m (1 017 ft) deep
- Highest waterfall: Eas a'Chual Aluinn, from Glas Bheinn, in the highlands of Scotland, with a drop of 200 m (660 ft)
- Deepest cave: Ogof Ffynnon Ddu, Wales, at 308 m (1 010 ft) deep
- Most northerly point on the British mainland: Dunnet Head, north-east Scotland
- Most southerly point on the British mainland: Lizard Point, Cornwall
- Closest point to mainland continental Europe: Dover, Kent. The Channel Tunnel, which links England and France, is a little over 50 km (31 miles) long, of which nearly 38 km (24 miles) are actually under the Channel

Area Measurements

I'd like to get area figures for all the local authorities in the UK. Where do I look?

UK Standard Area Measurements (SAM) are now available as downloadable Excel spreadsheets for a variety of administrative areas. The two questions below, show some statistics taken from SAM 2013 (Extent of the Realm figures)

Which is the largest local authority in the UK?

- The largest anywhere in the UK is Highland (Scotland), at 2648436.34HA.
- The largest in England is Northumberland, at 507835.00HA.
- The largest in Wales is Powys, at 519543.65HA.
- The largest in Northern Ireland is Fermanagh, at 187125.95HA

Which is the smallest local authority in the UK?

- The smallest anywhere in the UK is the City of London, at 314.94HA.
- The smallest in Scotland is Dundee City, at 6222.59HA.
- The smallest in Wales is Blaenau Gwent, at 10872.81HA.
- The smallest in Northern Ireland is North Down, at 8150.19HA.

UK Standard Area Measurements (SAM)

About UK Standard Area Measurements (SAM)

The SAM product provides a definitive list of measurements for administrative, health, Census, electoral and other geographic areas in the UK. SAM will change annually for some geographies, but for others it will be 'frozen' for several years.

The land measurement figures provided are defined by topographic boundaries (coastline and inland water), where available.

Measurements are reviewed annually and include information up to the end of December.

The measurements have been produced in conjunction with the following UK government statistical organisations and independent mapping agencies: National Records of Scotland; Northern Ireland Statistics and Research Agency; Office for National Statistics; Ordnance Survey®; Land & Property Services and Ordnance Survey of Northern Ireland®.

The SAM User Guide explains differences in methodology and base mapping between these agencies.

Product details

If you have any queries about this dataset, please contact:

ONS Geography Customer Services
Office for National Statistics
Segensworth Road
Titchfield
Fareham
Hampshire
PO15 5RR

Tel: 01329 444 971
Email: ons.geography@ons.gov.uk

1.1 Standard Area Measurement for UK Loal Authority Districts as at 31/12/2012

	Code as at December 2012[1]	Extent of the realm (Km^2)	Area to mean high water (Km^2)	Inland water (Km^2)	Land only (Km^2)
United Kingdom	K02000001	248542	244166	1664	242502
Great Britain	K03000001	234412	230037	1097	228940
England	E92000001	132948	130449	152	130297
Hartlepool	E06000001	98	94	0	94
Middlesbrough	E06000002	55	54	0	54
Redcar and Cleveland	E06000003	254	245	0	245
Stockton-on-Tees	E06000004	210	204	0	204
Darlington	E06000005	197	197	0	197
Halton	E06000006	90	79	0	79
Warrington	E06000007	182	181	0	181
Blackburn with Darwen	E06000008	137	137	0	137
Blackpool	E06000009	43	35	0	35
Kingston upon Hull, City of	E06000010	81	71	0	71
East Riding of Yorkshire	E06000011	2495	2406	1	2405
North East Lincolnshire	E06000012	204	192	0	192
North Lincolnshire	E06000013	876	846	0	846
York	E06000014	272	272	0	272
Derby	E06000015	78	78	0	78
Leicester	E06000016	73	73	0	73
Rutland	E06000017	394	394	12	382
Nottingham	E06000018	75	75	0	75
Herefordshire, County of	E06000019	2180	2180	0	2180
Telford and Wrekin	E06000020	290	290	0	290
Stoke-on-Trent	E06000021	93	93	0	93
Bath and North East Somerset	E06000022	351	351	5	346
Bristol, City of	E06000023	235	110	0	110
North Somerset	E06000024	391	375	1	374
South Gloucestershire	E06000025	537	497	0	497
Plymouth	E06000026	84	80	0	80
Torbay	E06000027	119	63	0	63
Bournemouth	E06000028	47	46	0	46
Poole	E06000029	75	65	0	65
Swindon	E06000030	230	230	0	230
Peterborough	E06000031	343	343	0	343
Luton	E06000032	43	43	0	43
Southend-on-Sea	E06000033	68	42	0	42
Thurrock	E06000034	184	163	0	163
Medway	E06000035	269	192	0	192
Bracknell Forest	E06000036	109	109	0	109
West Berkshire	E06000037	704	704	0	704
Reading	E06000038	40	40	0	40
Slough	E06000039	33	33	0	33
Windsor and Maidenhead	E06000040	198	198	2	197
Wokingham	E06000041	179	179	0	179
Milton Keynes	E06000042	309	309	0	309
Brighton and Hove	E06000043	85	83	0	83
Portsmouth	E06000044	60	40	0	40
Southampton	E06000045	56	50	0	50
Isle of Wight	E06000046	395	380	0	380
County Durham	E06000047	2233	2232	6	2226
Northumberland	E06000048	5078	5026	12	5014
Cheshire East	E06000049	1166	1166	0	1166
Cheshire West and Chester	E06000050	941	917	0	917
Shropshire	E06000051	3197	3197	0	3197
Cornwall	E06000052	3613	3550	4	3546
Isles of Scilly	E06000053	23	16	0	16
Wiltshire	E06000054	3255	3255	0	3255
Bedford	E06000055	476	476	0	476
Central Bedfordshire	E06000056	716	716	0	716

1.1 Standard Area Measurement for UK Loal Authority Districts as at 31/12/2012

	Code as at December 2012[1]	Extent of the realm (Km^2)	Area to mean high water (Km^2)	Inland water (Km^2)	Land only (Km^2)
Aylesbury Vale	E07000004	903	903	0	903
Chiltern	E07000005	196	196	0	196
South Bucks	E07000006	141	141	0	141
Wycombe	E07000007	325	325	0	325
Cambridge	E07000008	41	41	0	41
East Cambridgeshire	E07000009	652	651	0	651
Fenland	E07000010	547	546	0	546
Huntingdonshire	E07000011	913	912	6	906
South Cambridgeshire	E07000012	902	902	0	902
Allerdale	E07000026	1321	1258	16	1242
Barrow-in-Furness	E07000027	132	78	0	78
Carlisle	E07000028	1054	1039	0	1039
Copeland	E07000029	776	738	6	732
Eden	E07000030	2156	2156	14	2142
South Lakeland	E07000031	1743	1553	19	1534
Amber Valley	E07000032	265	265	0	265
Bolsover	E07000033	160	160	0	160
Chesterfield	E07000034	66	66	0	66
Derbyshire Dales	E07000035	795	795	3	792
Erewash	E07000036	110	110	0	110
High Peak	E07000037	540	540	1	539
North East Derbyshire	E07000038	276	276	0	276
South Derbyshire	E07000039	338	338	0	338
East Devon	E07000040	824	814	0	814
Exeter	E07000041	48	47	0	47
Mid Devon	E07000042	913	913	0	913
North Devon	E07000043	1105	1086	0	1086
South Hams	E07000044	905	886	0	886
Teignbridge	E07000045	681	674	0	674
Torridge	E07000046	996	985	1	984
West Devon	E07000047	1165	1161	1	1160
Christchurch	E07000048	52	50	0	50
East Dorset	E07000049	354	354	0	354
North Dorset	E07000050	609	609	0	609
Purbeck	E07000051	428	404	0	404
West Dorset	E07000052	1087	1081	0	1081
Weymouth and Portland	E07000053	43	42	0	42
Eastbourne	E07000061	46	44	0	44
Hastings	E07000062	31	30	0	30
Lewes	E07000063	294	292	0	292
Rother	E07000064	518	512	2	509
Wealden	E07000065	836	835	2	833
Basildon	E07000066	110	110	0	110
Braintree	E07000067	612	612	0	612
Brentwood	E07000068	153	153	0	153
Castle Point	E07000069	64	45	0	45
Chelmsford	E07000070	343	342	3	339
Colchester	E07000071	347	333	4	329
Epping Forest	E07000072	339	339	0	339
Harlow	E07000073	31	31	0	31
Maldon	E07000074	427	359	0	359
Rochford	E07000075	263	169	0	169
Tendring	E07000076	366	338	0	338
Uttlesford	E07000077	641	641	0	641
Cheltenham	E07000078	47	47	0	47
Cotswold	E07000079	1165	1165	0	1165
Forest of Dean	E07000080	561	527	0	527
Gloucester	E07000081	41	41	0	41
Stroud	E07000082	476	461	0	461
Tewkesbury	E07000083	415	414	0	414
Basingstoke and Deane	E07000084	634	634	0	634
East Hampshire	E07000085	514	514	0	514

1.1 Standard Area Measurement for UK Loal Authority Districts as at 31/12/2012

	Code as at December 2012[1]	Extent of the realm (Km^2)	Area to mean high water (Km^2)	Inland water (Km^2)	Land only (Km^2)
Eastleigh	E07000086	85	80	0	80
Fareham	E07000087	78	74	0	74
Gosport	E07000088	28	25	0	25
Hart	E07000089	215	215	0	215
Havant	E07000090	79	55	0	55
New Forest	E07000091	777	753	0	753
Rushmoor	E07000092	39	39	0	39
Test Valley	E07000093	628	628	0	628
Winchester	E07000094	661	661	0	661
Broxbourne	E07000095	51	51	0	51
Dacorum	E07000096	212	212	0	212
East Hertfordshire	E07000097	476	476	0	476
Hertsmere	E07000098	101	101	0	101
North Hertfordshire	E07000099	375	375	0	375
Stevenage	E07000101	26	26	0	26
Three Rivers	E07000102	89	89	0	89
Watford	E07000103	21	21	0	21
Ashford	E07000105	581	581	0	581
Canterbury	E07000106	321	309	0	309
Dartford	E07000107	76	73	0	73
Dover	E07000108	321	315	0	315
Gravesham	E07000109	105	99	0	99
Maidstone	E07000110	393	393	0	393
Sevenoaks	E07000111	370	370	1	369
Shepway	E07000112	365	357	0	357
Swale	E07000113	422	373	0	373
Thanet	E07000114	112	103	0	103
Tonbridge and Malling	E07000115	241	240	0	240
Tunbridge Wells	E07000116	331	331	0	331
Burnley	E07000117	111	111	0	111
Chorley	E07000118	203	203	0	203
Fylde	E07000119	183	166	0	166
Hyndburn	E07000120	73	73	0	73
Lancaster	E07000121	654	576	0	576
Pendle	E07000122	169	169	0	169
Preston	E07000123	143	142	0	142
Ribble Valley	E07000124	584	584	1	583
Rossendale	E07000125	138	138	0	138
South Ribble	E07000126	115	113	0	113
West Lancashire	E07000127	381	347	0	347
Wyre	E07000128	329	283	0	283
Blaby	E07000129	130	130	0	130
Charnwood	E07000130	279	279	0	279
Harborough	E07000131	593	593	1	592
Hinckley and Bosworth	E07000132	297	297	0	297
Melton	E07000133	481	481	0	481
North West Leicestershire	E07000134	279	279	0	279
Oadby and Wigston	E07000135	24	24	0	24
Boston	E07000136	397	364	0	364
East Lindsey	E07000137	1832	1765	0	1765
Lincoln	E07000138	36	36	0	36
North Kesteven	E07000139	922	922	0	922
South Holland	E07000140	815	745	0	745
South Kesteven	E07000141	943	943	0	943
West Lindsey	E07000142	1158	1156	0	1156
Breckland	E07000143	1305	1305	0	1305
Broadland	E07000144	553	552	0	552
Great Yarmouth	E07000145	182	174	0	174
King's Lynn and West Norfolk	E07000146	1529	1438	0	1438
North Norfolk	E07000147	991	965	2	963
Norwich	E07000148	41	39	0	39
South Norfolk	E07000149	909	908	0	908

1.1 Standard Area Measurement for UK Loal Authority Districts as at 31/12/2012

	Code as at December 2012[1]	Extent of the realm (Km^2)	Area to mean high water (Km^2)	Inland water (Km^2)	Land only (Km^2)
Corby	E07000150	80	80	0	80
Daventry	E07000151	666	666	3	663
East Northamptonshire	E07000152	510	510	0	510
Kettering	E07000153	233	233	0	233
Northampton	E07000154	81	81	0	81
South Northamptonshire	E07000155	634	634	0	634
Wellingborough	E07000156	163	163	0	163
Craven	E07000163	1179	1179	1	1177
Hambleton	E07000164	1311	1311	0	1311
Harrogate	E07000165	1309	1309	1	1308
Richmondshire	E07000166	1319	1319	0	1319
Ryedale	E07000167	1507	1507	0	1507
Scarborough	E07000168	827	817	0	817
Selby	E07000169	602	599	0	599
Ashfield	E07000170	110	110	0	110
Bassetlaw	E07000171	639	638	0	638
Broxtowe	E07000172	80	80	0	80
Gedling	E07000173	120	120	0	120
Mansfield	E07000174	77	77	0	77
Newark and Sherwood	E07000175	652	651	0	651
Rushcliffe	E07000176	409	409	0	409
Cherwell	E07000177	589	589	0	589
Oxford	E07000178	46	46	0	46
South Oxfordshire	E07000179	679	679	0	679
Vale of White Horse	E07000180	579	579	1	578
West Oxfordshire	E07000181	714	714	0	714
Mendip	E07000187	739	739	0	739
Sedgemoor	E07000188	606	564	0	564
South Somerset	E07000189	959	959	0	959
Taunton Deane	E07000190	463	462	0	462
West Somerset	E07000191	747	727	1	725
Cannock Chase	E07000192	79	79	0	79
East Staffordshire	E07000193	390	390	3	387
Lichfield	E07000194	331	331	0	331
Newcastle-under-Lyme	E07000195	211	211	0	211
South Staffordshire	E07000196	407	407	0	407
Stafford	E07000197	598	598	0	598
Staffordshire Moorlands	E07000198	576	576	0	576
Tamworth	E07000199	31	31	0	31
Babergh	E07000200	612	595	1	594
Forest Heath	E07000201	378	378	0	378
Ipswich	E07000202	40	39	0	39
Mid Suffolk	E07000203	871	871	0	871
St Edmundsbury	E07000204	657	657	0	657
Suffolk Coastal	E07000205	921	891	0	891
Waveney	E07000206	375	370	0	370
Elmbridge	E07000207	96	96	1	95
Epsom and Ewell	E07000208	34	34	0	34
Guildford	E07000209	271	271	0	271
Mole Valley	E07000210	258	258	0	258
Reigate and Banstead	E07000211	129	129	0	129
Runnymede	E07000212	78	78	0	78
Spelthorne	E07000213	51	51	6	45
Surrey Heath	E07000214	95	95	0	95
Tandridge	E07000215	248	248	0	248
Waverley	E07000216	345	345	0	345
Woking	E07000217	64	64	0	64
North Warwickshire	E07000218	284	284	0	284
Nuneaton and Bedworth	E07000219	79	79	0	79
Rugby	E07000220	354	354	2	351
Stratford-on-Avon	E07000221	978	978	0	978
Warwick	E07000222	283	283	0	283

1.1 Standard Area Measurement for UK Loal Authority Districts as at 31/12/2012

	Code as at December 2012[1]	Extent of the realm (Km^2)	Area to mean high water (Km^2)	Inland water (Km^2)	Land only (Km^2)
Adur	E07000223	44	42	0	42
Arun	E07000224	224	221	0	221
Chichester	E07000225	812	786	0	786
Crawley	E07000226	45	45	0	45
Horsham	E07000227	531	530	0	530
Mid Sussex	E07000228	334	334	0	334
Worthing	E07000229	34	32	0	32
Bromsgrove	E07000234	217	217	0	217
Malvern Hills	E07000235	577	577	0	577
Redditch	E07000236	54	54	0	54
Worcester	E07000237	33	33	0	33
Wychavon	E07000238	664	664	0	664
Wyre Forest	E07000239	195	195	0	195
St Albans	E07000240	161	161	0	161
Welwyn Hatfield	E07000241	130	130	0	130
Bolton	E08000001	140	140	0	140
Bury	E08000002	99	99	0	99
Manchester	E08000003	116	116	0	116
Oldham	E08000004	142	142	0	142
Rochdale	E08000005	158	158	0	158
Salford	E08000006	97	97	0	97
Stockport	E08000007	126	126	0	126
Tameside	E08000008	103	103	0	103
Trafford	E08000009	106	106	0	106
Wigan	E08000010	188	188	0	188
Knowsley	E08000011	86	86	0	86
Liverpool	E08000012	134	112	0	112
St. Helens	E08000013	136	136	0	136
Sefton	E08000014	205	153	0	153
Wirral	E08000015	256	157	0	157
Barnsley	E08000016	329	329	0	329
Doncaster	E08000017	569	568	0	568
Rotherham	E08000018	287	287	0	287
Sheffield	E08000019	368	368	0	368
Gateshead	E08000020	144	142	0	142
Newcastle upon Tyne	E08000021	115	113	0	113
North Tyneside	E08000022	85	82	0	82
South Tyneside	E08000023	67	64	0	64
Sunderland	E08000024	140	137	0	137
Birmingham	E08000025	268	268	0	268
Coventry	E08000026	99	99	0	99
Dudley	E08000027	98	98	0	98
Sandwell	E08000028	86	86	0	86
Solihull	E08000029	178	178	0	178
Walsall	E08000030	104	104	0	104
Wolverhampton	E08000031	69	69	0	69
Bradford	E08000032	366	366	0	366
Calderdale	E08000033	364	364	0	364
Kirklees	E08000034	409	409	0	409
Leeds	E08000035	552	552	0	552
Wakefield	E08000036	339	339	0	339
City of London	E09000001	3	3	0	3
Barking and Dagenham	E09000002	38	36	0	36
Barnet	E09000003	87	87	0	87
Bexley	E09000004	64	61	0	61
Brent	E09000005	43	43	0	43
Bromley	E09000006	150	150	0	150
Camden	E09000007	22	22	0	22
Croydon	E09000008	86	86	0	86
Ealing	E09000009	56	56	0	56
Enfield	E09000010	82	82	1	81
Greenwich	E09000011	50	47	0	47

1.1 Standard Area Measurement for UK Loal Authority Districts as at 31/12/2012

	Code as at December 2012[1]	Extent of the realm (Km^2)	Area to mean high water (Km^2)	Inland water (Km^2)	Land only (Km^2)
Hackney	E09000012	19	19	0	19
Hammersmith and Fulham	E09000013	17	16	0	16
Haringey	E09000014	30	30	0	30
Harrow	E09000015	50	50	0	50
Havering	E09000016	114	112	0	112
Hillingdon	E09000017	116	116	0	116
Hounslow	E09000018	57	56	0	56
Islington	E09000019	15	15	0	15
Kensington and Chelsea	E09000020	12	12	0	12
Kingston upon Thames	E09000021	37	37	0	37
Lambeth	E09000022	27	27	0	27
Lewisham	E09000023	35	35	0	35
Merton	E09000024	38	38	0	38
Newham	E09000025	39	36	0	36
Redbridge	E09000026	56	56	0	56
Richmond upon Thames	E09000027	59	57	0	57
Southwark	E09000028	30	29	0	29
Sutton	E09000029	44	44	0	44
Tower Hamlets	E09000030	22	20	0	20
Waltham Forest	E09000031	39	39	0	39
Wandsworth	E09000032	35	34	0	34
Westminster	E09000033	22	21	0	21
Scotland	S92000003	80240	78808	900	77907
Clackmannanshire	S12000005	164	159	0	159
Dumfries and Galloway	S12000006	6676	6437	11	6426
East Ayrshire	S12000008	1270	1270	8	1262
East Lothian	S12000010	701	679	0	679
East Renfrewshire	S12000011	174	174	0	174
Eilean Siar	S12000013	3269	3100	41	3059
Falkirk	S12000014	315	297	0	297
Fife	S12000015	1374	1325	0	1325
Highland	S12000017	26484	26162	506	25656
Inverclyde	S12000018	174	162	2	160
Midlothian	S12000019	355	355	2	354
Moray	S12000020	2257	2238	0	2238
North Ayrshire	S12000021	904	885	0	885
Orkney Islands	S12000023	1086	1013	25	989
Perth and Kinross	S12000024	5419	5384	98	5286
Scottish Borders	S12000026	4743	4739	7	4732
Shetland Islands	S12000027	1657	1468	1	1467
South Ayrshire	S12000028	1235	1224	2	1222
South Lanarkshire	S12000029	1774	1774	2	1772
Stirling	S12000030	2255	2253	66	2187
Aberdeen City	S12000033	206	186	0	186
Aberdeenshire	S12000034	6339	6318	5	6313
Argyll and Bute	S12000035	7164	7008	99	6909
City of Edinburgh	S12000036	273	263	0	263
Renfrewshire	S12000038	269	261	0	261
West Dunbartonshire	S12000039	183	177	19	159
West Lothian	S12000040	432	429	1	428
Angus	S12000041	2204	2185	4	2182
Dundee City	S12000042	62	60	0	60
North Lanarkshire	S12000044	472	472	2	470
East Dunbartonshire	S12000045	174	174	0	174
Glasgow City	S12000046	176	175	0	175

1.1 Standard Area Measurement for UK Loal Authority Districts as at 31/12/2012

	Code as at December 2012[1]	Extent of the realm (Km²)	Area to mean high water (Km²)	Inland water (Km²)	Land only (Km²)
Wales	W92000004	21225	20780	45	20736
Isle of Anglesey	W06000001	749	714	3	711
Gwynedd	W06000002	2622	2548	13	2535
Conwy	W06000003	1153	1130	4	1126
Denbighshire	W06000004	846	839	2	837
Flintshire	W06000005	489	437	0	437
Wrexham	W06000006	504	504	0	504
Ceredigion	W06000008	1806	1789	3	1786
Pembrokeshire	W06000009	1650	1619	0	1619
Carmarthenshire	W06000010	2439	2371	1	2370
Swansea	W06000011	421	380	0	380
Neath Port Talbot	W06000012	452	442	1	441
Bridgend	W06000013	255	251	0	251
The Vale of Glamorgan	W06000014	340	331	0	331
Cardiff	W06000015	149	140	0	140
Rhondda Cynon Taf	W06000016	424	424	0	424
Caerphilly	W06000018	277	277	0	277
Blaenau Gwent	W06000019	109	109	0	109
Torfaen	W06000020	126	126	1	126
Monmouthshire	W06000021	886	850	1	849
Newport	W06000022	218	191	0	191
Powys	W06000023	5195	5195	15	5181
Merthyr Tydfil	W06000024	112	112	1	111
Northern Ireland	N92000002	14130	14130	568	13562
Derry	95A	380	380	0	379
Limavady	95B	586	586	0	585
Coleraine	95C	484	484	1	483
Ballymoney	95D	418	418	0	418
Moyle	95E	494	494	0	494
Larne	95F	336	336	1	335
Ballymena	95G	632	632	2	630
Magherafelt	95H	573	573	9	563
Cookstown	95I	622	622	109	513
Strabane	95J	859	859	1	858
Omagh	95K	1130	1130	1	1129
Fermanagh	95L	1871	1871	154	1718
Dungannon	95M	784	784	12	771
Craigavon	95N	378	378	100	279
Armagh	95O	671	671	2	668
Newry and Mourne	95P	901	901	4	897
Banbridge	95Q	453	453	1	452
Down	95R	648	648	4	644
Lisburn	95S	447	447	5	442
Antrim	95T	577	577	156	421
Newtownabbey	95U	151	151	0	150
Carrickfergus	95V	82	82	1	81
North Down	95W	82	82	1	81
Ards	95X	378	378	1	377
Castlereagh	95Y	85	85	0	85
Belfast	95Z	110	110	1	109

Source: Standard Area Measurement for UK Local Authority Districts as at 31/12/2012

1. Area codes implemented from 1 January 2011; in line with the GSS Coding and Naming policy

Figures have been rounded to the nearest whole number

Parliamentary elections

Chapter 2

Parliamentary elections

This chapter covers parliamentary elections, by-elections and devolved assembly elections in the UK, Wales, Scotland and Northern Ireland.

Parliamentary elections (Table 2.1)

Information is supplied on the total electorate, average electorate and valid votes as a percentage of electorate. The number of seats by party is also listed.

Parliamentary by-elections (Table 2.2)

Information can be found on the votes recorded for each party and General Elections and subsequent by-elections between General Elections.

Devolved assembly elections (Tables 2.3 and 2.4)

Table 2.2 provides information on the devolved assembly elections in Wales and Scotland, listing information on the total electorate, average electorate and valid votes as a percentage of electorate. The number of seats by party is also listed. Table 2.4 provides information on the devolved assembly elections in Northern Ireland, listing information on the total electorate, average electorate and valid votes as a percentage of electorate. The number of seats by party is also listed.

2.1 Parliamentary elections[1]

United Kingdom

Thousands and percentages

		15-Oct 1964	31-Mar 1966	18-Jun 1970[1]	28-Feb 1974		10-Oct 1974	03-May 1979	09-Jun 1983	11-Jun 1987	09-Apr 1992	01-May 1997	07-Jun 2001	05-May 2005	06-May 2010
United Kingdom															
Electorate	DZ5P	35894	35957	39615	40256	DZ6V	40256	41573	42704	43666	43719	43846	44403	44246	45597
Average-electors per seat	DZ5T	57	57.1	62.9	63.4	DZ6R	63.4	65.5	66.7	67.2	67.2	66.5	67.4	68.5	70.1
Valid votes counted	DZ5X	27657	27265	28345	31340	DZ6N	29189	31221	30671	32530	33614	31286	26367	27149	29688
As percentage of electorate	DZ63	77.1	75.8	71.5	77.9	DZ6J	72.5	75.1	71.8	74.5	76.7	71.4	59.4	61.4	65.1
England and Wales															
Electorate	DZ5Q	31610	31695	34931	35509	DZ6W	35509	36695	37708	38568	38648	38719	39228	39266	40565
Average-electors per seat	DZ5U	57.8	57.9	63.9	64.3	DZ6S	64.3	66.5	67.2	68.8	68.8	68	68.9	69	70.8
Valid votes counted	DZ5Y	24384	24116	24877	27735	DZ6O	25729	27609	27082	28832	29897	27679	23243	24097	26548
As percentage of electorate	DZ64	77.1	76.1	71.2	78.1	DZ6K	72.5	75.2	71.8	74.8	77.5	71.5	59.3	61.4	65.4
Scotland															
Electorate	DZ5R	3393	3360	3659	3705	DZ6X	3705	3837	3934	3995	3929	3949	3984	3840	3863
Average-electors per seat	DZ5V	47.8	47.3	51.5	52.2	DZ6T	52.2	54	54.6	55.5	54.6	54.8	55.3	65.1	65.5
Valid votes counted	DZ5Z	2635	2553	2688	2887	DZ6P	2758	2917	2825	2968	2931	2817	2313	2334	2466
As percentage of electorate	DZ65	77.6	76	73.5	77.9	DZ6L	74.5	76	71.8	74.3	74.2	71.3	58.1	60.8	63.8
Northern Ireland															
Electorate	DZ5S	891	902	1025	1027	DZ6Y	1037	1028	1050	1090	1141	1178	1191	1140	1169
Average-electors per seat	DZ5W	74.2	75.2	85.4	85.6	DZ6U	86.4	85.6	61.8	64.1	67.1	65.4	66.2	63.3	65
Valid votes counted	DZ62	638	596	779	718	DZ6Q	702	696	765	730	785	791	810	718	674
As percentage of electorate	DZ66	71.7	66.1	76	69.9	DZ6M	67.7	67.7	72.9	67	68.8	67.1	68	62.9	57.6
Members of Parliament elected: (numbers)	DZV7	630	630	630	635	DZV8	635	635	650	650	651	659	659	646	650
Conservative	DZ67	303	253	330	296	DZ6D	276	339	396	375	336	165	166	198	306
Labour	DZ68	317	363	287	301	DZ6E	319	268	209	229	271	418	412	355	258
Liberal Democrat[2]	DZ69	9	12	6	14	DZ6F	13	11	23	22	20	46	52	62	57
Scottish National Party	DZ6A	–	–	1	7	DZ6G	11	2	2	3	3	6	5	6	6
Plaid Cymru	DZ6B	–	–	–	2	DZ6H	3	2	2	3	4	4	4	3	3
Other[3]	DZ6C	1	2	6	15	DZ6I	13	13	18	18	17	20	20	22	20

1 The Representation of the People Act 1969 lowered the minimum voting age from 21 to 18 years with effect from 16 February 1970.
2 Liberal before 1992. The figures for 1983 and 1987 include six and five MPs respectively who were elected for the Social Democratic Party.
3 Including the Speaker.

Source: British Electoral Facts 1832-2012
Plymouth University for the Electoral Commission: 01752 233207

2.2 Parliamentary by-elections

United Kingdom

	May 1997 - June 2001	General[1,2] Election May 1997	June 2001 - November 2004	General[1] Election June 2001	May 2005 - November 2009	General[1] Election May 2005	May 2010- June 2014	General[1] Election May 2010
Numbers of by-elections	17		6		14		18	
Votes recorded								
By party (percentages)								
Conservative	27	25.1	17.7	21.2	27.7	25.7	15.6	23.2
Labour	29.7	40.1	40.8	58.3	29.3	35.7	39.1	42.7
Liberal Democrat	22.1	14.4	31.3	13.7	20	20.6	9.5	17.8
Scottish National Party	6	4.1	-	-	9.5	6.2	1.9	1.2
Plaid Cymru	2.5	2.3	2.7	2.1	0.4	0.1	0.4	0.3
UKIP[3]							11.1	
Other	12.7	14.1	7.4	4.7	13	11.7	22.5	14.8
Total votes recorded (percentages)	100	100	100	100	100	100	100	100
(thousands)	435	723	140	205	436	586		

Source: Plymouth University for the Electoral Commission: 01752 233207

1 Votes recorded in the same seats in the previous General Election.
2 Proportions of 'other' votes inflated by the fact that votes were cast for the retiring Speaker as 'The Speaker seeking re-election' and not as a party.

The Bradford West by-election of 29th March 2012 was won by the Respect candidate whose votes were included under "other"
3 figures for UKIP only recorded for by-elections since 2010

2.3 Devolved assembly elections

Wales and Scotland

Thousands and percentages

		06-May 1999	01-May 2003	03-May 2007	05-May 2011
Welsh Assembly					
Electorate	E28K	2205	2230	2248	2290
Average-electors per seat[1]	E28N	55.1	55.7	56.2	57.2
Valid votes counted	E28Q	1023	850	978	949
As percentage of electorate	E28T	46.4	38.1	43.5	41.5
Members elected:[2] (numbers)	E2XI	60	60	60	60
Conservative	E2WG	9	11	12	14
Labour	E2WU	28	30	26	30
Liberal Democrat	E2WW	6	6	6	5
Plaid Cymru	E2X3	17	12	15	11
Other	E2WY	–	1	1	-
Scottish Parliament					
Electorate	E28L	4024	3879	3899	3951
Average-electors per seat[1]	E28O	55.1	53.1	53.4	54.1
Valid votes counted	E28R	2342	1916	2017	1989
As percentage of electorate	E28U	58.2	49.4	51.7	50.3
Members elected:[3] (numbers)	E2XJ	129	129	129	129
Conservative	E2WH	18	18	17	15
Labour	E2WV	56	50	46	37
Liberal Democrat	E2WX	17	17	16	5
Scottish National Party	E2X4	35	27	47	69
Other	E2WZ	3	17	3	3

1 This is the average in each first-past-the-post constituency. Additional members are then elected on the basis of a regional 'list' vote.
2 Comprising 40 from constituencies and 20 from the regional 'list'.
3 Comprising 73 from constituencies and 56 from the regional 'list'.

Sources: British Electoral Facts 1832-2012;
Plymouth University for the Electoral Commission: 01752 233207

2.4 Devolved assembly elections

Northern Ireland

Thousands and percentages

		25-Jun 1998	26-Nov 2003	08-Mar 2007	05-May 2011
Electorate	E28M	1179	1098	1108	1210
Average-electors per seat[1]	E28P	65.5	61	61.6	67.2
Valid votes counted	E28S	810	692	692	662
As percentage of electorate	E28V	68.7	63	63	55.7
Members elected: (numbers)	E2XK	108	108	108	108
Alliance Party	E2X5	6	6	7	8
SDLP	E2X6	24	18	16	14
Sinn Fein	E2X7	18	24	28	29
Democratic Unionist Party	E2X8	20	30	36	38
UK Unionist Party	E2X9	5	1	–	-
Ulster Unionist Party	E2XA	28	27	18	16
Other	E2X2	7	2	3	3

1 This is the average in each Westminster constituency. Six members are
elected by single transferable vote (STV) in each constituency.

Sources: British Electoral Facts 1832-2012;
Plymouth University for the Electoral Commission: 01752233207

International development

Chapter 3

International development

Overseas development assistance

The Department for International Development (DFID) is the UK Government Department with lead responsibility for overseas development. DFID's aim is to eliminate poverty in poorer countries through achievement of the Millennium Development Goals (MDG's) by 2015. Statistics relating to international development are published on a financial year basis and on a calendar year basis. Statistics on a calendar year basis allow comparisons of aid expenditure with other donor countries. Aid flows can be measured before (gross) or after (net) deductions of repayments of principal on past loans. These tables show only the gross figures.

Aid is provided in two main ways: Bilateral funding is provided directly to partner countries while multilateral funding is provided through international organisations.

Funds can only be classified as multilateral if they are channelled through an organisation on a list in the OECD –

Development Assistance Committee (DAC) Statistical Reporting Directives – which identifies all multilateral organisations. This list also highlights some bodies that might appear to be multilateral but are actually bilateral (in particular this latter category includes some international non-governmental organisations such as the International Committee of the Red Cross and some Public-Private Partnerships). The DAC list of multilaterals is updated annually based on members nominations; organisations must be engaged in development work to be classified as multilateral aid channels although money may be classified as bilateral while a case is being made for a new multilateral organisation to be recognised.

While core funding to multilateral organisations is always classified as multilateral expenditure, additional funding channelled through multilaterals is often classified as bilateral expenditure. This would be the case in circumstances where a DFID country office transfers some money to a multilateral organisation (for example UN agency) for a particular programme in that country (or region). That is where DFID has control over what the money is being spent on and/or where it is being spent. Likewise, if DFID responds to an emergency appeal from an agency for a particular country or area, the funds will be allocated as bilateral spend to that country or region. As a result, some organisations, such as UN agencies have some of their DFID funding classified as bilateral and some as multilateral.

Bilateral assistance takes various forms:

Financial Aid – Poverty Reduction Budget Support (PRBS) – Funds provided to developing countries for them to spend in support of their expenditure programmes whose long-term objective is to reduce poverty; funds are spent using the overseas governments' own financial management, procurement and accountability systems to increase ownership and long term sustainability. PRBS can take the form of a general contribution to the overall budget – general budget support – or support with a more restricted focus which is earmarked for a specific sector – sector budget support.

Other Financial Aid – Funding of projects and programmes such as Sector Wide Programmes not classified as PRBS. Financial aid in its broader sense covers all bilateral aid expenditure other than technical cooperation and administrative costs but in SID we separately categorise this further.

Technical Co-operation – Activities designed to enhance the knowledge, intellectual skills, technical expertise or the productive capability of people in recipient countries. It also covers funding of services which contribute to the design or implementation of development projects and programmes.

This assistance is mainly delivered through research and development, the use of consultants, training (generally overseas partners visiting the UK or elsewhere for a training programme) and employment of 'other Personnel' (non-DFID experts on fixed term contracts). This latter category is growing less significant over time as existing contracted staff reach the end of their assignments.

Bilateral Aid Delivered Through a Multilateral Organisation – This category covers funding that is channelled through a multilateral organisation and DFID has control over the country, sector or theme that the funds will be spent on. For example, where a DFID country office transfers money to a multilateral organisation for a particular piece of work in that country. This also includes aid delivered through multi donor funds such as the United Nations Central Emergency Response Fund (CERF).

Bilateral Aid Delivered Through a Non-Governmental Organisation (NGO) – This category covers support to the international development work of UK and international not for profit organisations such as NGOs or Civil Society Organisations. This covers Partnership Programme Arrangements (PPAs), the Civil Society Challenge Fund and other grants.

Other Bilateral Aid – This category includes any aid not elsewhere classified such as funding to other donors for shared development purposes. More information on all of the above aid types is provided in the Glossary.

Humanitarian Assistance – Provides food, aid and other humanitarian assistance including shelter, medical care and advice in emergency situations and their aftermath. Work of the conflict pools is also included.

DFID Debt Relief – This includes sums for debt relief on DFID aid loans and cancellation of debt under the Commonwealth Debt Initiative (CDI). The non-CDI DFID debt relief is reported on the basis of the 'benefit to the recipient country'. This means that figures shown represent the money available to the country in the year in question that would otherwise have been spent on debt servicing. The CDI debt cancellation is reported on a 'lump sum' basis where all outstanding amounts on a loan are shown at the time the agreement to cancel is made.

CDC Gross Investments – **CDC Group PLC** is wholly government owned. Its investments must have a clear development objective. The net amount (that is equity purchase less equity sales) of

CDC investments in official development assistance (ODA)-eligible countries is reported as ODA and the gross amount (that is equity purchase only) is reported in GPEX.

Non-DFID Debt Relief – Comprises CDC Debt and ECGD Debt. CDC has a portfolio of loans to governments which can become eligible for debt relief under the Heavily Indebted Poor Countries (HIPC) or other debt relief deals. In 2005/06 £90 million of debts owed to CDC were reorganised. Export Credit Guarantee Department (ECGD) is the UK's official export credit agency providing insurance for exporters against the main risks in selling overseas and guarantees to banks providing export finance. It also negotiates debt relief arrangements on commercial debt.

The Foreign and Commonwealth Office (FCO) contributes to UK GPEX in a number of ways:

The FCO Strategic Programme Fund supports a range of the UK government's international goals. Where the programme funds projects which meet the required OECD definition these projects are included in UK GPEX statistics.

The FCO supports the British Council through grant-in-aid funding. This funding goes to support a range of initiatives including building the capacity and quality of English language teaching; supporting education systems; and using cultural exchange to improve economic welfare. UK GPEX statistics include the proportion of this work which is clearly focussed on delivering economic welfare and development in ODA eligible countries.

The British Council also manages, on behalf of the FCO, the Chevening Scholarships programme, which provides funding for postgraduate students or researchers from developing countries to study in UK universities. Funding from this scheme to students from ODA eligible countries are included in UK ODA and GPEX statistics.

The FCO makes annual contributions to UN and Commonwealth organisations. A proportion of these contributions are allowed to score as ODA in line with Annex 2 of the DAC Statistical Reporting Directives.

In addition to contributing directly to the Conflict Pool (see below) the FCO is also responsible for the UK contribution to the UN Department for Peacekeeping Operations (UNDPKO). In line with DAC rules 6 per cent of donor funding to UNDPKO is allowed to score as ODA. FCO also funds other bilateral peacekeeping missions including the Organisation for Security and Cooperation in Europe (OSCE) and the European Security and Defence Policy (ESDP) civilian missions; a proportion of which is reported as bilateral GPEX.

The Conflict Pool (CP) –is governed and jointly managed by DFID, the FCO and the Ministry of Defence (MoD) to bring together the UK government's development, diplomatic and defence interest and expertise to ensure a coherent response to conflict prevention. Some of the CP's expenditure is ODA eligible. All CP funds disbursed through DFID are included in GPEX and appear in these statistics as part of DFID expenditure. The remaining figures comprise the aggregate of FCO and MOD spending. Data on the ODA eligible CP funds disbursed by the FCO and MOD are collected by DFID in liaison with programme officers in the relevant departments.

Other –includes contributions from other government departments including: Department of Energy and Climate Change; Department of Health; Department for Environment, Food & Rural

Affairs; Department for Culture, Media and Sport; Scottish Government; and the Welsh Assembly Government. It also includes estimates of the UK Border Agency's costs of supporting refugees in the UK; as well as estimates of gift aid to NGOs and other official funding to NGOs.

Further details on the UK's development assistance can be found in the Department for International Developments publication Statistics on International Development which can be found on the website www.dfid.gov.uk

Comparisons are available in the OECD Development Assistance Committee's annual report.

3.1a Total Gross Public Expenditure on Development 2007/08 - 2011/12

£ thousand

	2007/08	2008/09	2009/10	2010/11	2011/12 [1]
Total GPEX					
Total Bilateral GPEX	3 517 389	4 333 951	4 765 735	5 311 859	5 178 611
Total Multilateral GPEX	2 246 995	2 600 365	2 748 766	3 461 939	3 461 684
Of which Total Multilateral European Commission	*1 200 319*	*1 407 901*	*1 424 089*	*1 431 849*	*1 355 553*
Total Multilateral World Bank	*493 387*	*573 652*	*559 785*	*926 713*	*1 038 568*
Total Multilateral UN Agencies	*296 940*	*308 154*	*278 619*	*417 317*	*434 462*
Total Multilateral Other Organisations	*256 348*	*310 659*	*486 273*	*686 060*	*633 102*
Total Admin	262 731	249 000	252 101	233 208	309 292
TOTAL GPEX ON DEVELOPMENT	**6 027 115**	**7 183 316**	**7 766 602**	**9 007 006**	**8 949 587**
of which: DFID Programme					
DFID Bilateral Programme	2 957 909	3 283 996	3 958 263	4 248 018	4 204 114
DFID Multilateral Programme	1 990 184	2 277 358	2 436 338	3 221 673	3 257 724
DFID Admin	247 683	237 899	234 398	219 457	220 352
TOTAL DFID PROGRAMME	**5 195 776**	**5 799 253**	**6 628 999**	**7 689 149**	**7 682 191**

1. Section 2 shows a reconciliation of 2011/12 GPEX and 2011/12 ODA

3.1b DFID Expenditure on Development 2007/08-2011/12

£thousands

	2007/08	2008/09	2009/10	2010/11	2011/12
DFID Bilateral Programme [1]					
Poverty Reduction Budget Support	635 083	648 668	634 101	643 671	536 662
of which					
General Budget Support	*366 453*	*392 748*	*383 150*	*360 467*	*242 290*
Sector Budget Support	*268 631*	*255 920*	*250 951*	*283 204*	*294 372*
Other Financial Aid	456 657	516 431	518 817	550 728	544 778
Technical Co-operation	474 287	514 235	419 911	467 939	527 907
Bilateral Aid Delivered though a Multilateral Organisation [2]	576 809	656 448	1 264 716	1 465 789	1 404 592
Bilateral Aid Delivered through a NGO	300 515	462 597	599 434	626 752	739 558
of which:					
Partnership Programme Agreements	*89 695*	*108 928*	*128 823*	*115 347*	*119 625*
Other CSO's	*210 820*	*353 669*	*470 612*	*511 405*	*619 933*
Other Bilateral Aid [3]	12 399	17 030	34 668	76 009	81 372
Humanitarian Assistance	430 773	449 163	434 556	350 669	354 293
DFID Debt Relief	71 386	19 425	52 061	66 460	14 954
Total DFID Bilateral Programme	**2 957 909**	**3 283 996**	**3 958 263**	**4 248 018**	**4 204 114**
DFID Multilateral Programme					
European Comission	991 408	1 153 892	1 186 303	1 268 563	1 220 076
World Bank	493 387	573 652	559 785	926 713	1 038 568
United Nations	249 854	251 903	216 315	355 337	376 708
Other Multilateral	255 535	297 911	473 934	671 061	622 373
Total DFID Multilateral Programme	**1 990 184**	**2 277 358**	**2 436 338**	**3 221 673**	**3 257 724**
Total DFID Programme (excl. Admin)	**4 948 093**	**5 561 355**	**6 394 601**	**7 475 391**	**7 461 839**
DFID Administration	247 683	237 899	234 398	219 457	220 352
Total DFID Programme	**5 195 776**	**5 799 253**	**6 628 999**	**7 689 149**	**7 682 191**

1. Descriptions of aid types given in Section 2 and in the Glossary
2. This covers aid provided through multilateral organisations where the recipient country, region, sector, theme or specific project are known.
3. Other Bilateral Aid covers bilateral aid that does not fit into any other category.

3.1c Non-DFID Public Expenditure on Development 2007/08 -2011/12

£ thousand

	2007/08	2008/09	2009/10	2010/11	2011/12
BILATERAL AID FROM OTHER UK OFFICIAL SOURCES					
CDC Gross Investments [1]	360 821	436 028	354 436	416 181	284 267
of which Net Investments	*-500053*	*167 456*	*221 556*	*218 173*	*42 247*
Debt Relief	3 760	280 337	7 237	54 297	91 004
Foreign & Commonwealth Office	117 591	122 963	142 269	162 000	210 113
of which					
Bilateral Programme	*86 944*	*72 280*	*74 023*	*61 648*	*86 593*
Bilateral Peacekeeping [7]	*..*	*9 500*	*23 311*	*23 982*	*31 670*
British Council	*30 647*	*41 183*	*44 935*	*76 371*	*91 849*
Conflict Pool	17 173	97 357	103 645	98 362	88 581
Department of Environment & Climate Change	-	50 000	105 413	255 051	143 655
of which the Environmental Transformation Fund	*-*	*50 000*	*100 000*	*250 000*	*130 922*
UK Border Agency Costs of Supporting Refugees in the UK [2]	-	-	7 355	11 700	20 427
Scottish Government	3 898	5 829	5 298	9 275	10 001
Gift Aid for NGOs [3]	43 672	43 857	43 891	47 109	65 000
Colonial Pensions [1,4]	3 897	3 732	4 321	3 200	2 913
Other [5]	*8 668*	9 850	33 606	6 665	58 536
Total Bilateral Aid from other UK Official Sources	**559 480**	**1 049 954**	**807 472**	**1 063 841**	**974 497**
MULTILATERAL AID FROM OTHER UK OFFICIAL SOURCES					
European Commission [1,6]	208 911	254 008	237 786	163 286	135 476
Global Environmental Assistance	139	7 102	5 414	5 614	-
UN Agencies	47 086	56 252	62 304	61 980	57 753
Commonwealth	674	711	726	740	824
Other Multilateral Organisations	-	4 935	6 200	8 645	9 905
Total Multilateral Aid from other UK Official Sources	**256 811**	**323 007**	**312 428**	**240 265**	**203 959**
TOTAL AID FROM OTHER UK OFFICIAL SOURCES excluding Administration	**816 291**	**1 372 962**	**1 119 900**	**1 304 106**	**1 178 456**
Other UK Official Sources Administration	15 048	11 101	17 703	13 751	88 940
Total AID FROM OTHER UK OFFICIAL SOURCES	**831 339**	**1 384 063**	**1 137 603**	**1 317 857**	**1 267 396**

1. Some of these flows are not ODA eligible, e.g. only net CDC flows are included in ODA. The rest of the information in this table is included in ODA.

2. These costs were included for the first time in 2009/10 to improve international comparability. They have not been estimated retrospectively. This estimate is produced on a calendar year basis.

3. Gift Aid figure estimated based on ongoing methodological work. Further methodological development to take place in 2013.

4. Prior to the 2009/10 edition of SID, these costs were classified as DFID Bilateral Expenditure.

5. Includes Department for Health; Department for Environment, Food & Rural Affairs; Department for Culture, Media & Sport; Department for Business, Innovation and Skills; and the Welsh Assembly. This also includes other official funding to UK NGOs.

6. Prior to 2007/08 aid to Romania and Bulgaria who joined the EU in 2007 was attributed to DFID. Since 2007/08 these sums have become part of the UK's total contribution to the EU and cannot be attributed directly to DFID.

7. This expenditure will be reported under the 'Conflict Pool' in future publications as the Peacekeeping Budget is funded from the Conflict Pool settlement. The FCO manages HMG's Peacekeeping Budget on behalf of DFID, FCO and the MOD.

3.2a Total DFID Expenditure and GPEX by Recipient Country (Africa) 2007/08 - 2011/12[1]

£ thousand

		Financial Aid												
		General Poverty Reduction Budget Support	Sector Poverty Reduction Budget Support	Other Financial Aid[5]	Technical Cooperation	Bilateral aid delivered through a Multilateral	Bilateral aid Delivered through an NGO	Other Bilateral Aid[2]	Humanitarian Assistance	DFID Debt Relief	Total DFID Bilateral Programme	Aid from other UK Official Sources[5]	Total Bilateral Gross Public Expenditure	UK Imputed Multilateral Shares[3]
Africa: North of Sahara														
Algeria	2007/08	-	-	-	-	-	-	-	-	-	-	285	285	6 492
	2008/09	-	-	-	-	-	-	-	-	-	-	1 169	1 169	1 560
	2009/10	-	-	-	-	-	-	-	230	-	230	2 314	2 545	6 479
	2010/11	-	-	-	-	-	-	-	-	-	-	1 481	1 481	10 173
	2011/12	-	-	-	-	-	-	-	-	-	-	1 533	1 533	..
Egypt	2007/08	-	-	-	-	-	-	-	-	-	-	2 135	2 135	14 376
	2008/09	-	-	-	-	-	-	-	-	-	-	6 529	6 529	15 065
	2009/10	-	-	-	-	-	-	-	-	-	-	23 666	23 666	18 728
	2010/11	-	-	-	-	-	-	-	-	-	-	10 843	10 843	29 033
	2011/12	-	-	-	-	100	-	-	-	-	100	12 951	13 051	..
Libyan Arab Republic	2007/08	-	-	-	-	-	-	-	-	-	-	146	146	200
	2008/09	-	-	-	-	-	-	-	-	-	-	630	630	691
	2009/10	-	-	-	-	-	-	-	-	-	-	1 187	1 187	75
	2010/11	-	-	-	-	-	-	-	28	-	28	1 020	1 048	1 833
	2011/12	-	-	-	2 107	156	-	-	5 305	-	7 568	6 245	13 813	..
Morocco	2007/08	-	-	-	-	-	-	-	-	-	-	169	169	19 838
	2008/09	-	-	-	-	-	-	-	-	-	-	3 693	3 693	23 343
	2009/10	-	-	-	-	-	-	-	-	-	-	3 040	3 040	18 444
	2010/11	-	-	-	-	-	-	-	-	-	-	2 137	2 137	23 527
	2011/12	-	-	-	-	-	-	-	-	-	-	3 659	3 659	..
Tunisia	2007/08	-	-	-	-	-	-	-	-	-	-	58	58	10 501
	2008/09	-	-	-	-	-	-	-	-	-	-	807	807	10 899
	2009/10	-	-	-	-	-	-	-	-	-	-	2 446	2 446	10 225
	2010/11	-	-	-	-	-	-	-	-	-	-	1 633	1 633	13 083
	2011/12	-	-	-	-	48	-	-	-	-	48	6 102	6 150	..
North of Sahara Regional	2007/08	-	-	-	-	-	-	-	-	-	-	5	5	2 238
	2008/09	-	-	-	124	510	-	-	-	-	634	7 114	7 748	4 635
	2009/10	-	-	-	31	397	-	-	-	-	429	-	429	26 086
	2010/11	-	-	-	-	-	-	-	10 249	-	10 249	-	10 249	21 469
	2011/12	-	-	-	-	-	-	-	-	-	-	126	126	..
Total North of Sahara	**2007/08**	-	-	-	-	-	-	-	-	-	-	**2 797**	**2 797**	**53 645**
	2008/09	-	-	-	**124**	**510**	-	-	-	-	**634**	**19 942**	**20 576**	**56 192**
	2009/10	-	-	-	**31**	**397**	-	-	**230**	-	**659**	**32 653**	**33 312**	**80 037**
	2010/11	-	-	-	-	-	-	-	**10 277**	-	**10 277**	**17 113**	**27 391**	**99 117**
	2011/12	-	-	-	**2 107**	**304**	-	-	**5 305**	-	**7 716**	**30 615**	**38 331**	**..**
Africa: South of Sahara														
Angola	2007/08	-	-	-	137	2 525	703	-	956	-	4 322	391	4 712	7 917
	2008/09	-	-	-	114	465	1 638	-	1 048	-	3 265	164	3 428	12 619
	2009/10	-	-	-	176	2 350	866	-	348	-	3 741	78	3 818	2 450
	2010/11	-	-	-	-	-29	502	-	-	-	473	8 999	9 472	10 845
	2011/12	-	-	-	-	-	-	-	-	-	-	336	336	..
Benin[4]	2007/08	-	-	-	-	-	-	-	-	-	-	-	-	10 911
	2008/09	-	-	-	-	-	-	-	-	-	-	-	-	15 666
	2009/10	-	-	-	-	-	-	-	-	-	-	17	17	14 537
	2010/11	-	-	-	-	3 257	-	-	66	-	3 323	-	3 323	25 873
	2011/12	-	-	-	-	-	-	-	26	-	26		26	..
Botswana	2007/08	-	-	-	-	-	-	-	-	-	-	171	171	754
	2008/09	-	-	-	-	-	-	-	-	-	-	484	484	873
	2009/10	-	-	-	-	-	-	-	-	-	-	594	594	8 128
	2010/11	-	-	-	-	-	-	-	-	-	-	684	684	1 865
	2011/12	-	-	-	-	-	-	-	-	-	-	1 146	1 146	..
Burkina Faso	2007/08	-	-	-	-	-	9	-	-	-	9	-	9	16 761
	2008/09	-	-	-	-	-	127	-	-	-	127	-	127	46 482
	2009/10	-	-	-	-	-	131	-	1 269	-	1 400	-	1 400	19 637
	2010/11	-	-	-	-	-	-	-	-	-	-	142	142	36 099
	2011/12	-	-	-	-	-	-	-	-	-	-	510	510	..
Burundi[4]	2007/08	-	-	-	503	685	120	227	3 618	-	5 153	1 500	6 653	12 176
	2008/09	-	-	-	2 611	484	1 891	410	5 024	-	10 421	-	10 421	12 767
	2009/10	-	-	3 004	1 086	2 530	1 963	410	3 995	-	12 988	15	13 003	15 052
	2010/11	-	-	2 790	741	1 539	4 161	406	1 299	-	10 936	24	10 960	16 800
	2011/12	-	-	2 206	890	1 051	4 915	-	-	-	9 062	36	9 098	..
Cameroon	2007/08	-	-	-	71	1 098	449	-	-	-	1 619	395	2 013	13 826
	2008/09	-	-	-	28	5 618	1 204	-	-	-	6 850	1 057	7 907	16 148
	2009/10	-	-	-	-	-	240	-	-	-	240	709	949	21 193
	2010/11	-	-	-	-	319	-62	-	-	-	257	576	833	25 182
	2011/12	-	-	-	-	508	8	-	-	-	516	414	930	..
Cape Verde	2007/08	-	-	-	-	-	-	-	-	130	130	-	130	1 703
	2008/09	-	-	-	-	-	-	-	-	449	449	-	449	7 338
	2009/10	-	-	-	-	-	-	-	71	456	527	-	527	2 368
	2010/11	-	-	-	-	-	-	-	-	581	581	-	581	3 966
	2011/12	-	-	-	-	-	-	-	-	620	620	31	651	..
Central African Republic	2007/08	-	-	-	-	-	-	300	834	-	1 134	-	1 134	6 062
	2008/09	-	-	-	-	-	-	-	3 615	-	3 615	-	3 615	5 745
	2009/10	-	-	-	-	-	-	-	2 706	-	2 706	-	2 706	13 136
	2010/11	-	-	-	-	1 268	-	-	-	24	1 291	456	1 747	10 125
	2011/12	-	-	-	-	-	-	-	-	-	-	-	-	..
Chad[4]	2007/08	-	-	-	-	-	-	-	5 140	-	5 140	-	5 140	11 779
	2008/09	-	-	-	-	-	-	-	6 331	-	6 331	-	6 331	6 978
	2009/10	-	-	-	-	900	-	-	4 893	-	5 793	-	5 793	12 526
	2010/11	-	-	-	-	-	-	-	149	-	149	10	159	22 484
	2011/12	-	-	-	-	-	-	-	66	-	66		66	..

3.2a Total DFID Expenditure and GPEX by Recipient Country (Africa) 2007/08 - 2011/12[1]

£ thousand

| | | Financial Aid | | | | | | | | | | | |
		General Poverty Reduction Budget Support	Sector Poverty Reduction Budget Support	Other Financial Aid [5]	Technical Cooperation	Bilateral aid delivered through a Multilateral	Bilateral aid Delivered through an NGO	Other Bilateral Aid [2]	Humanitarian Assistance	DFID Debt Relief	Total DFID Bilateral Programme	Aid from other UK Official Sources [5]	Total Bilateral Gross Public Expenditure	UK Imputed Multilateral Shares [3]
Comoros	2007/08	-	-	-	-	-	-	-	-	-	-	-	-	890
	2008/09	-	-	-	-	-	-	-	-	-	-	-	-	734
	2009/10	-	-	-	-	-	-	-	-	-	-	-	-	3 831
	2010/11	-	-	-	-	-	-	-	-	-	-	79	79	2 472
	2011/12	-	-	-	-	-	-	-	-	-	-	75	75	..
Congo	2007/08	-	-	-	-	-	61	-	-	-	61	-	61	7 069
	2008/09	-	-	-	-	-	9	-	-	-	9	-	9	7 709
	2009/10	-	-	-	-	-	-	-	1 181	-	1 181	-	1 181	3 508
	2010/11	-	-	-	-	-	-	-	750	40 750	41 500	50 238	50 238	6 429
	2011/12	-	-	-	-	-	-	-	-	-	-	-	-	..
Congo (Dem Rep) [4]	2007/08	-	-	0	1 098	11 642	21 829	1 693	46 156	293	82 711	199	82 910	35 226
	2008/09	-	-	-	3 551	21 899	28 737	6 751	32 778	176	93 892	5 753	99 645	38 602
	2009/10	-	-	2	3 994	34 848	25 117	4 116	40 979	-	109 055	7 728	116 783	68 987
	2010/11	-	-	-	8 992	38 487	32 980	5 425	47 089	-	132 973	910	133 883	88 195
	2011/12	-	-	-	20 296	46 127	49 458	2 976	27 002	-	145 859	93 453	239 312	..
Cote d'Ivoire	2007/08	-	-	-	-	-	42	-	530	-	572	210	782	11 327
	2008/09	-	-	-	-	-	-	-	-	-	-	180	180	28 421
	2009/10	-	-	-	-	-	-	-	360	-	360	256	616	23 714
	2010/11	-	-	-	-	-	-	-	-	-	-	16 880	16 880	21 432
	2011/12	-	-	-	-	-	-	-	7 950	-	7 950	495	8 445	..
Djibouti	2007/08	-	-	-	-	176	-	-	-	-	176	-	176	3 012
	2008/09	-	-	-	-	-	-	-	-	-	-	-	-	2 408
	2009/10	-	-	-	-	-	-	-	443	-	443	1 504	1 947	771
	2010/11	-	-	-	-	-	-	-	-	-	-	3	3	2 331
	2011/12	-	-	-	-	-	-	-	-	-	-	20	20	..
Equatorial Guinea	2007/08	-	-	-	-	-	-	-	-	-	-	-	-	892
	2008/09	-	-	-	-	-	-	-	-	-	-	-	-	278
	2009/10	-	-	-	-	-	-	-	-	-	-	-	-	531
	2010/11	-	-	-	-	-	-	-	-	-	-	-	-	134
	2011/12	-	-	-	-	-	-	-	-	-	-	-	-	..
Eritrea [4]	2007/08	-	-	-	-	-	-	-	3 367	-	3 367	131	3 498	7 382
	2008/09	-	-	-	-	-	-	-	3 692	-	3 692	357	4 049	2 857
	2009/10	-	-	-	-	-	-	-	3 176	-	3 176	47	3 222	9 734
	2010/11	-	-	-	-	-	-	-	4 187	-	4 187	270	4 457	5 380
	2011/12	-	-	-	-	-	-	-	3 686	-	3 686	29	3 715	..
Ethiopia [4]	2007/08	-	111 607	17 719	1 083	1 419	2 690	-	5 000	-	139 519	492	140 011	94 186
	2008/09	-	105 184	16 248	1 930	4 860	3 600	-	33 699	-	165 521	3 086	168 607	61 574
	2009/10	-	93 030	39 895	1 920	13 738	1 094	1 000	63 609	-	214 286	1 401	215 688	76 226
	2010/11	-	94 700	95 501	5 374	42 004	1 085	5 989	5 900	-	250 553	1 342	251 895	105 665
	2011/12	-	132 800	65 000	4 222	57 612	1 447	6 500	56 850	-	324 430	1 359	325 789	..
Gabon	2007/08	-	-	-	-	-	-	-	-	-	-	-	-	816
	2008/09	-	-	-	-	-	-	-	-	-	-	-	-	479
	2009/10	-	-	-	-	-	-	-	-	-	-	-	-	1 390
	2010/11	-	-	-	-	-	-	-	-	-	-	106	106	2 585
	2011/12	-	-	-	-	-	-	-	-	-	-	126	126	..
Gambia [4]	2007/08	-	-	-	1 535	317	560	-	-	-	2 412	43	2 455	1 799
	2008/09	-	-	-	1 617	1	800	-	-	49	2 467	106	2 573	923
	2009/10	-	-	-	1 458	-1	643	-	59	-	2 159	83	2 243	2 237
	2010/11	-	-	-	852	-	192	-	-	-	1 044	10	1 054	7 945
	2011/12	-	-	-	487	-	94	-	-	-	581	4 805	5 386	..
Ghana	2007/08	56 469	10 000	15 767	2 530	5 747	1 269	-	426	-	92 208	868	93 076	25 130
	2008/09	59 548	18 000	12 830	1 905	2 746	2 638	-	1 781	-	99 448	4 279	103 728	54 288
	2009/10	48 000	24 210	11 203	1 748	1 387	2 965	-	404	-	89 917	6 832	96 749	38 282
	2010/11	36 000	25 000	7 275	3 255	11 233	4 430	-	-	-	87 192	8 280	95 471	52 059
	2011/12	12 290	46 000	3 988	11 310	2 568	4 023	-	-	-	80 178	3 748	83 927	..
Guinea	2007/08	-	-	-	-	-	46	-	155	22	223	44	267	11 877
	2008/09	-	-	-	-	-	434	-	246	-	680	271	951	1 789
	2009/10	-	-	-	-	-	120	-	629	-	749	139	888	1 778
	2010/11	-	-	-	-	2 658	-	-	-	7	2 666	-	2 666	2 684
	2011/12	-	-	-	-	-	-	-	-	-	-	192	192	..
Guinea-Bissau	2007/08	-	-	-	-	-	-	-	1	-	1	-	1	6 219
	2008/09	-	-	-	-	-	-	-	42	-	42	25	67	3 657
	2009/10	-	-	-	-	-	-	-	-	-	-	85	85	4 381
	2010/11	-	-	-	-	-	-	-	-	-	-	47	47	4 761
	2011/12	-	-	-	-	-	-	-	-	-	-	75	75	..
Kenya [4]	2007/08	-	-	10 922	6 777	13 170	7 280	1 464	4 735	-	44 348	7 786	52 135	34 433
	2008/09	-	-	12 152	8 194	35 572	30 618	-	15 795	-	102 331	7 498	109 829	4 921
	2009/10	-	-	7 651	7 006	10 375	23 872	1 600	13 716	-	64 219	11 466	75 685	50 032
	2010/11	-	-	451	11 671	25 401	24 041	2 000	5 536	-	69 099	4 750	73 849	67 636
	2011/12	-	-	1 425	10 027	24 776	38 750	396	22 740	-	98 115	9 216	107 331	..
Lesotho [4]	2007/08	-	-	350	2 625	516	406	-	-	-	3 896	13	3 908	6 303
	2008/09	-	-	698	2 750	1 550	333	-	-	878	6 209	82	6 292	3 607
	2009/10	-	-	818	1 759	250	1 242	-	83	923	5 075	45	5 120	4 579
	2010/11	-	-	30	335	436	1 215	-	-	920	2 935	10	2 946	14 246
	2011/12	-	-	-	-	-	1 790	-	-	1 093	2 883	80	2 963	..
Liberia [4]	2007/08	-	-	2 000	1 735	-	928	612	2 332	-	7 606	1	7 608	27 897
	2008/09	-	-	2 166	1 557	1 250	3 421	-	4 757	3 548	16 698	329	17 027	7 859
	2009/10	-	-	165	2 151	4 910	4 000	-	739	-	11 965	611	12 576	17 865
	2010/11	-	-	4 000	214	6 220	80	-	1 000	-	11 514	3 530	15 044	17 005
	2011/12	-	-	3 000	-	5 000	-	-	10 959	-	18 959	100	19 059	..

23

3.2a Total DFID Expenditure and GPEX by Recipient Country (Africa) 2007/08 - 2011/12[1]

£ thousand

| | | Financial Aid | | | | | | | | | | | | |
		General Poverty Reduction Budget Support	Sector Poverty Reduction Budget Support	Other Financial Aid[5]	Technical Cooperation	Bilateral aid delivered through a Multilateral	Bilateral aid Delivered through an NGO	Other Bilateral Aid[2]	Humanitarian Assistance	DFID Debt Relief	Total DFID Bilateral Programme	Aid from other UK Official Sources[5]	Total Bilateral Gross Public Expenditure	UK Imputed Multilateral Shares[3]
Madagascar	2007/08	-	-	-	-	587	40	-	851	-	1 477	66	1 543	14 812
	2008/09	-	-	-	-	9 029	-	-	311	-	9 341	904	10 245	51 072
	2009/10	-	-	-	-	-	-	-	2 521	-	2 521	-	2 521	2 636
	2010/11	-	-	-	-	6 869	-	-	-29	-	6 840	375	7 215	11 328
	2011/12	-	-	-	-	-	-	-	-	-	-	505	505	..
Malawi[4]	2007/08	22 000	19 267	15 635	3 469	3 379	3 534	-	1 946	184	69 415	3 204	72 619	10 938
	2008/09	22 000	20 420	20 360	2 863	5 973	5 032	-	451	-	77 100	4 921	82 021	14 390
	2009/10	24 000	17 514	22 524	1 939	2 088	4 835	11	943	-	73 853	3 517	77 370	29 400
	2010/11	19 000	26 659	13 727	2 366	920	6 767	284	901	-	70 624	5 810	76 434	40 549
	2011/12	-	14 000	22 614	2 965	6 636	7 133	43	8 491	-	61 882	4 470	66 351	..
Mali	2007/08	-	-	-	-	-	-	-	-	-	-	-	-	14 873
	2008/09	-	-	-	-	1 104	-	-	-	-	1 104	-	1 104	38 671
	2009/10	-	-	-	-	-	-	-	-	-	-	37	37	27 881
	2010/11	-	-	-	3	1 042	-	-	-	-	1 045	30	1 076	14 640
	2011/12	-	-	-	-	-	-	-	-	-	-	15	15	..
Mauritania	2007/08	-	-	-	-	59	-	-	-4	38	93	-	93	4 100
	2008/09	-	-	-	-	-	-	-	-	-	-	-	-	2 254
	2009/10	-	-	-	-	-	-	-	325	-	325	497	822	643
	2010/11	-	-	-	-	363	-	-	-	-	363	-	-	4 721
	2011/12	-	-	-	-	-	-	-	-	-	-	904	904	..
Mauritius	2007/08	-	-	-	-	-	-	-	-	-	-	60	60	8 031
	2008/09	-	-	-	-	-	-	-	-	-	-	332	332	4 932
	2009/10	-	-	-	-	-	-	-	-	-	-	13 513	13 513	13 068
	2010/11	-	-	-	-	-	-	-	-	-	-	4 625	4 625	2 128
	2011/12	-	-	-	-	-	-	-	-	-	-	8 734	8 734	..
Mayotte	2007/08	-	-	-	-	-	-	-	-	-	-	-	-	1 979
	2008/09	-	-	-	-	-	-	-	-	-	-	-	-	-
	2009/10	-	-	-	-	-	-	-	-	-	-	-	-	-
	2010/11	-	-	-	-	-	-	-	-	-	-	-	-	-
	2011/12	-	-	-	-	-	-	-	-	-	-	-	-	-
Mozambique[4]	2007/08	41 000	-	20 391	3 613	300	2 123	-	183	-30	67 580	218	67 799	28 499
	2008/09	42 000	14 481	1 307	3 688	401	1 647	-	1 971	-	65 495	869	66 365	50 397
	2009/10	44 000	16 860	66	4 184	619	1 925	-	237	-	67 891	410	68 301	13 788
	2010/11	48 205	28 556	2 658	3 571	9 617	1 141	-	500	-	94 248	568	94 815	41 569
	2011/12	48 000	21 367	8 000	4 479	1 930	1 151	-	750	-	85 677	678	86 354	..
Namibia	2007/08	-	-	-	49	-	319	-	50	-	418	34	452	5 425
	2008/09	-	-	280	12	70	173	-	-	-	535	221	755	2 924
	2009/10	-	-	-	-	-	-	-	195	-	195	178	373	609
	2010/11	-	-	-	-	-	-	-	-	-	-	362	362	14 384
	2011/12	-	-	-	-	-	-	-	-	-	-	153	153	..
Niger[4]	2007/08	-	-	-	-	-	-	522	1 519	-	2 041	-	2 041	7 119
	2008/09	-	986	-	-	2 007	-	-	4 553	-	7 546	-	7 546	29 577
	2009/10	-	868	-	-	-	-	-	4 275	-	5 143	-	5 143	6 052
	2010/11	-	-	-	-	1 737	958	-	5	-	2 700	-	2 700	16 213
	2011/12	-	33	-	-	-	9	-	-	-	42	-	42	..
Nigeria	2007/08	-	-	2 480	57 733	11 225	12 401	-	942	-	84 780	72 941	157 722	34 534
	2008/09	-	-	2 106	97 155	5 406	4 806	-	551	-	110 025	21 612	131 637	54 211
	2009/10	-	-	160	94 327	15 379	3 499	-	860	-	114 226	16 369	130 594	88 405
	2010/11	-	-	57	104 200	16 903	4 091	16 700	-	-	141 952	39 063	181 015	52 330
	2011/12	-	-	40	127 159	24 343	5 879	4 368	-	-	161 789	44 405	206 194	..
Rwanda[4]	2007/08	33 000	5 000	3 446	2 835	6 674	1 355	-	305	-	52 616	153	52 769	10 524
	2008/09	33 000	2 180	9 270	2 697	21 126	1 800	-	8	-	70 081	489	70 570	25 417
	2009/10	33 000	5 680	4 001	4 306	5 068	711	-	-	-	52 766	936	53 702	23 407
	2010/11	35 750	10 540	9 716	16 330	16 877	121	567	-	-	89 901	998	90 898	46 524
	2011/12	37 000	23 172	9 981	3 340	100	1 838	567	-	-	75 997	942	76 939	..
Sao Tome & Principe	2007/08	-	-	-	-	-	-	-	-	-	-	-	-	768
	2008/09	-	-	-	-	-	-	-	-	-	-	-	-	687
	2009/10	-	-	-	-	-	-	-	-	-	-	-	-	2 079
	2010/11	-	-	-	-	487	-	-	-	-	487	-	-	342
	2011/12	-	-	-	-	-	-	-	-	-	-	-	-	..
Senegal	2007/08	-	-	-	-	1 029	23	-	37	-	1 090	3 458	4 548	9 731
	2008/09	-	-	-	-	-	163	-	-	-	163	415	578	22 862
	2009/10	-	-	-	-	-	137	-	-	-1,140	-1,002	3 981	2 978	20 152
	2010/11	-	-	-	-	-	-	-	-	-	-	1 005	1 492	19 179
	2011/12	-	-	-	-	-	-	-	-	-	-	1 614	1 614	..
Seychelles	2007/08	-	-	-	-	-	-	-	-	-	-	17	17	17
	2008/09	-	-	-	-	-	-	-	-	-	-	39	39	26
	2009/10	-	-	-	-	-	-	-	-	-	-	38	38	2 317
	2010/11	-	-	-	-	-	-	-	-	-	-	28	28	231
	2011/12	-	-	-	-	-	-	-	-	-	-	72	72	..
Sierra Leone[4]	2007/08	13 000	-	2 743	16 685	18 671	2 850	31	-	76	54 056	3 649	57 705	8 456
	2008/09	20 000	-	114	15 394	5 405	5 063	-	1 794	-	47 770	582	48 352	9 499
	2009/10	12 150	-	7 559	12 338	8 154	4 243	-	213	-	44 655	2 030	46 686	5 528
	2010/11	8 000	-	12 647	12 447	14 192	3 998	-	7	-	51 291	2 270	53 561	21 642
	2011/12	12 500	-	3 240	9 896	23 147	3 795	-	-	-	52 578	704	53 282	..
Somalia[4]	2007/08	-	-	-	237	7 624	4 057	121	13 675	-	25 714	86	25 799	9 229
	2008/09	-	-	-	227	9 376	5 579	-	18 288	-	33 471	129	33 600	12 192
	2009/10	-	-	-	361	8 110	4 061	-	31 900	-	44 431	744	45 176	10 380
	2010/11	-	-	-	454	10 595	5 156	-	29 855	-	46 060	1 529	47 588	8 746
	2011/12	-	-	-	202	12 467	9 721	-	79 093	-	101 483	2 359	103 842	..
South Africa	2007/08	-	-	-	21 067	2 681	3 477	-	74	-	27 300	61 777	89.076	19 736
	2008/09	-	-	-	23 600	1 677	14 626	-[2]	776	-	40 679	37 877	78 556	13 822
	2009/10	-	-	3 000	9 957	400	7 914	-	-7	-	21 265	18 139	39 404	16 009
	2010/11	-	-	4 000	6 880	1 061	5 274	-	196	-	17 411	33 965	51 376	29 147
	2011/12	-	-	4 000	8 015	-	7 324	-	-	-	19 339	3 902	23 241	..

3.2a Total DFID Expenditure and GPEX by Recipient Country (Africa) 2007/08 - 2011/12[1]

£ thousand

| | | Financial Aid | | | | | | | | | | | | |
		General Poverty Reduction Budget Support	Sector Poverty Reduction Budget Support	Other Financial Aid[5]	Technical Cooperation	Bilateral aid delivered through a Multilateral	Bilateral aid Delivered through an NGO	Other Bilateral Aid[2]	Humanitarian Assistance	DFID Debt Relief	Total DFID Bilateral Programme	Aid from other UK Official Sources[5]	Total Bilateral Gross Public Expenditure	UK Imputed Multilateral Shares[3]
South Sudan [4,6]	2011/12	-	-	-	16 415	38 899	5 278	956	17 955	-	79 503	503	80 005	..
St Helena &	2007/08	-	-	13 084	4 440	10	16	-	-	-	17 550	40	17 591	213
Dependencies	2008/09	-	-	29 150	6 092	460	35	-	-	-	35 738	-	35 738	-
	2009/10	-	-	20 377	2 228	-	97	-	-	-	22 701	40	22 741	-
	2010/11	-	-	24 885	6 033	-	132	-	-	-	31 050	627	31 677	-
	2011/12	-	-	64 435	3 697	-	90	-	-	-	68 223	191	68 414	..
Sudan [4]	2007/08	-	-	1	9 430	29 334	4 304	351	91 245	-	134 666	4 037	138 702	25 304
	2008/09	-	-	-	14 644	32 358	6 212	-	52 574	-	105 787	4 157	109 945	23 435
	2009/10	-	-	-	10 350	67 991	7 280	895	59 062	-	145 578	3 711	149 289	15 694
	2010/11	-	-	-	16 478	22 535	4 752	912	83 529	-	128 206	4 907	133 113	27 805
	2011/12	-	-	-	6 480	11 058	7 972	196	6 901	-	32 607	2 909	35 515	..
Swaziland	2007/08	-	-	-	1	-	-	-	2 152	-	2 154	25	2 178	2 510
	2008/09	-	-	-	-	-	-	-	997	-	997	32	1 029	3 554
	2009/10	-	-	-	-	-	-	-	195	-	195	50	244	3 533
	2010/11	-	-	-	-	-	-	-	-	-	-	11	11	5 015
	2011/12	-	-	-	-	-	-	-	-	-	-	23	23	..
Tanzania [4]	2007/08	105 000	-	8 717	1 735	3 458	3 030	-	460	-	122 400	2 953	125 353	42 354
	2008/09	103 500	-	11 651	501	11 275	4 864	-	550	-	132 341	9 958	142 299	52 243
	2009/10	103 500	-	12 785	2 869	9 715	5 719	815	8 245	-	143 648	2 381	146 029	93 424
	2010/11	103 512	-	8 449	8 514	17 811	5 358	445	1 956	-	146 045	3 726	149 771	87 596
	2011/12	80000	-	17 850	9 000	8 150	16 334	7 630	-	-	138 964	9 804	148 768	..
Togo	2007/08	-	-	-	-	-	150	-	-	-	150	30	180	8 335
	2008/09	-	-	-	-	-	67	-	-	-	67	4 859	4 926	11 212
	2009/10	-	-	-	-	-	-	-	-	-	-	6 668	6 668	8 090
	2010/11	-	-	-	-	-	-	-	-	13 076	13 076	20	13 096	15 136
	2011/12	-	-	-	-	-	-	-	-	-	-	1 202	1 202	..
Uganda [4]	2007/08	35 000	-	4 595	4 244	2 462	8 026	530	14 059	-	68 915	8 316	77 231	38 577
	2008/09	35 000	-	7 815	2 903	5 574	3 747	125	15 508	-	70 672	1 458	72 131	44 763
	2009/10	32 500	-	5 313	2 801	15 722	1 915	1 313	8 477	-	68 041	10 090	78 131	45 817
	2010/11	27 200	-	11 455	4 563	44 839	1 896	4 450	-	-	94 402	1 618	96 020	35 868
	2011/12	20 000	5 000	8 916	7 505	21 496	4 687	6 000	2 966	-	76 571	4 805	81 376	..
Zambia [4]	2007/08	28 000	-	5 670	2 928	906	2 422	-	1 462	-	41 388	554	41 942	10 806
	2008/09	27 700	-	7 487	2 847	758	4 128	-	3 671	-	46 590	2 876	49 466	43 326
	2009/10	36 000	-	7 192	2 163	726	1 692	769	18	615	49 176	1 177	50 353	11 417
	2010/11	32 800	-	4 767	1 947	3 769	3 354	5 270	6	-	51 912	1 070	52 982	18 779
	2011/12	12 500	-	4 462	5 736	8 586	5 596	5 788	-	-	42 668	2 684	45 352	..
Zimbabwe [4]	2007/08	-	-	-27	2 030	12 670	5 631	4 974	17 987	-	43 266	3 394	46 660	7 894
	2008/09	-	-	-	6 310	15 571	12 099	-	21 004	1 063	56 048	1 285	57 332	2 647
	2009/10	-	-	-	18 100	20 442	8 218	-	18 646	1 167	66 572	3 751	70 323	8 127
	2010/11	-	-	-	20 498	38 674	5 272	2 000	2 081	-	68 526	4 770	73 296	10 185
	2011/12	-	-	-	27 910	53 836	4 029	2 629	-	-	88 403	3 154	91 557	..
East African	2007/08	-	-	-	-	-	-	-	-	-	-	508	508	-
Community	2008/09	-	-	-	180	209	-	-	-	-	389	475	864	-
	2009/10	-	-	-	64	1 491	-	-	-	-	1 555	559	2 115	-
	2010/11	-	-	-	-	840	-	-	-	-	840	419	419	-
	2011/12	-	-	-	-	60	-	-	-	-	60	65	125	..
Southern Africa	2007/08	-	-	-	399	259	2 509	-	0	-	3 167	-	3 167	-
Dev Comm	2008/09	-	-	-	149	1 100	8 658	-	150	-	10 057	-	10 057	-
(SADC)	2009/10	-	-	-	-	2 000	5 275	-	-	-	7 275	-	7 275	-
	2010/11	-	-	-	-	1 200	10 643	2 800	-	-	14 643	-	14 643	-
	2011/12	-	-	-	-	-	4 800	-	-	-	4 800	168	4 968	..
South of Sahara	2007/08	-	-	-	3 072	76 072	146	-	-	4 750	84 041	100	84 141	38 790
regional	2008/09	-	-	32	5 844	3 783	4 082	500	4 892	-	19 134	67	19 200	39 742
	2009/10	-	-	650	5 364	47 155	5 842	2 285	17 075	-	78 370	686	79 057	68 949
	2010/11	-	-	3 053	6 497	49 988	8 213	199	-	-	67 950	252	68 202	42 212
	2011/12	-	-	3 000	5 296	8 037	4 587	-	2 724	-	23 644	28 132	51 776	..
Total South of	2007/08	333 469	145 875	123 491	152 063	214 694	92 807	10 826	220 194	5 464	1 298 883	177 864	1 476 746	719 902
Sahara	2008/09	342 748	161 252	133 665	209 364	207 108	158 231	7 786	236 858	6 163	1 463 174	117 227	1 580 402	898 575
	2009/10	333 150	158 163	146 365	192 648	276 347	125 616	13 213	291 836	2 022	1 539 360	121 113	1 660 472	934 277
	2010/11	310 467	185 454	205 460	242 213	393 112	135 751	47 445	184 984	55 358	1 760 245	205 393	1 965 639	1 120 466
	2011/12	222 290	242 372	222 158	285 327	356 386	190 709	38 047	248 159	1 713	1 807 161	239 342	2 046 503	..
Africa regional	2007/08	-	-	32	9 597	30 625	5 515	-	1 028	-	46 796	25 783	72 579	58 766
	2008/09	-	-	2	6 013	36 976	17 480	142	3 671	4 759	69 043	91 322	160 365	1 130
	2009/10	-	-	5 500	6 594	55 997	23 587	7 475	1 527	6 785	107 463	112 986	220 449	144 407
	2010/11	-	-	6 500	6 374	44 383	22 487	424	16 471	-	96 640	24 382	121 022	38 581
	2011/12	-	-	-	10 625	30 037	22 292	6 998	6 865	-	76 817	17 412	94 229	..
Total Africa	2007/08	333 469	145 875	123 523	161 660	245 319	98 321	10 826	221 222	5 464	1 345 679	206 443	1 552 123	832 313
	2008/09	342 748	161 252	133 667	215 501	244 594	175 711	7 928	240 530	10 922	1 532 652	228 491	1 761 343	955 897
	2009/10	333 150	158 163	151 865	199 273	332 740	149 203	20 688	293 593	8 807	1 647 482	266 751	1 914 233	1 158 720
	2010/11	310 467	185 454	211 960	248 588	437 496	158 238	47 869	211 732	55 358	1 867 162	246 889	2 114 051	1 258 164
	2011/12	222 290	242 372	222 158	298 059	386 727	213 000	45 046	260 329	1 713	1 891 694	287 369	2 179 063	..

1. Descriptions of aid types given in Section 2.
2. Other Bilateral Aid covers bilateral aid not elsewhere classified.
3. Details on DFID Imputed Multilateral Shares are in Section 2; 2011/12 data are not yet available.
4. Low Income Country. Income groups are classified using 2010 GNI per capita thresholds.
5. Pension payments have been reclassified from "Other Financial Aid" to "Aid from other UK Official Sources". This is consistent with the classification of spending under Department Expenditure Limits (DEL) agreed with Treasury.
6. South Sudan expenditure information reported in 2011/12 for the first time, following independence in 2011.

3.2b Total DFID Expenditure and GPEX by Recipient Country (Americas) 2007/08 - 2011/12[1]

£ thousand

		General Poverty Reduction Budget Support	Sector Poverty Reduction Budget Support	Other Financial Aid [5]	Technical Cooperation	Bilateral aid delivered through a Multilateral	Bilateral aid Delivered through an NGO	Other Bilateral Aid [2]	Humanitarian Assistance	DFID Debt Relief	Total DFID Bilateral Programme	Aid from other UK Official Sources [5]	Total Bilateral Gross Public Expenditure	UK Imputed Multilateral Shares [3]
North and Central America														
Costa Rica	2007/08	-	-	-	-	-	-	-	-	-	-	57	57	203
	2008/09	-	-	-	-	-	-	-	-	-	-	356	356	883
	2009/10	-	-	-	-	-	-	-	-	-	-	1 640	1 640	958
	2010/11	-	-	-	-	-	-	-	-	-	-	497	497	1 613
	2011/12											234	234	..
Cuba	2007/08	-	-	-	-	-	-	-	-	-	-	91	91	822
	2008/09	-	-	-	-	-	-	-	-	-	-	132	132	471
	2009/10	-	-	-	-	-	-	-	250	-	250	362	612	4 685
	2010/11	-	-	-	-	-	-	-	-	-	-	250	250	2 030
	2011/12											272	272	..
El Salvador	2007/08	-	-	-	-	-	-	-	-	-	-	-	-	297
	2008/09	-	-	-	-	-	-	-	-	-	-	39	39	626
	2009/10	-	-	-	-	-	-	-	372	-	372	21	393	6 419
	2010/11	-	-	-	-	-	-	-	-	-	-	-	-	4 866
	2011/12											10	10	..
Guatemala	2007/08	-	-	-	-	-	225	-	-	-	225	119	344	3 380
	2008/09	-	-	-	-	-	256	-	-	-	256	36	292	2 221
	2009/10	-	-	-	-	-	194	-	744	-	938	228	1 167	5 413
	2010/11	-	-	-	-	-	-	-	100	-	100	-	100	4 888
	2011/12											95	95	..
Haiti	2007/08	-	-	-	-	-	-	-	-	-	-	-	-	14 378
	2008/09	-	-	-	-	-	-	-	824	-	824	-	824	8 691
	2009/10	-	-	-	71	-	-	-	15 044	-	15 114	703	15 817	38 477
	2010/11	-	-	-	1	7 089	341	-	6 934	1 706	16 071	23	16 094	43 543
	2011/12					1 255	533		2 459		4 246	24	4 270	..
Honduras	2007/08	-	-	-	-	-	-	-	-	-	-	-	-	3 045
	2008/09	-	-	-	-	-	-	-	-	-	-	18	18	12 146
	2009/10	-	-	-	-	-	111	-	189	-	300	4	304	3 153
	2010/11	-	-	-	-	-	-	-	-	-	-	16 286	16 286	11 633
	2011/12											20	20	..
Mexico	2007/08	-	-	-	-	-	-	-	65	-	65	1 105	1 170	957
	2008/09	-	-	-	-	-	-	-	80	-	80	3 633	3 713	2 107
	2009/10	-	-	-	-	-	-	-	-	-	-	7 593	7 593	1 986
	2010/11	-	-	-	-	-	-	-	-	-	-	6 093	6 093	5 967
	2011/12											5 050	5 050	..
Nicaragua	2007/08	1 450	1 000	-	785	566	258	-	100	-	4 158	599	4 757	3 341
	2008/09	-	-	-	712	843	44	-	2 255	-	3 854	18	3 872	7 123
	2009/10	-	-	-	194	2 276	30	995	307	-	3 802	26	3 829	5 604
	2010/11	-	-	-	-	2 000	-	2 695	-	-	4 695	-	4 695	8 077
	2011/12											29	29	..
Panama	2007/08	-	-	-	-	-	-	-	-	-	-	25	25	776
	2008/09	-	-	-	-	-	-	-	-	-	-	20	20	271
	2009/10	-	-	-	-	-	-	-	-	-	-	48	48	1 592
	2010/11	-	-	-	-	-	-	-	-	-	-	26	26	241
	2011/12											202	202	..
North & Central	2007/08	-	-	-	-	31	-	-	-	-	31	-	31	7 637
America	2008/09	-	-	-	-	110	-	-	-	-	110	-	110	1 831
	2009/10	-	-	-	-	-53	-	-	-	-	-53	-	-53	6 748
	2010/11	-	-	-	-	-	-	-	-	-	-	84	84	1 499
	2011/12											3 427	3 427	..
Total North and	2007/08	1 450	1 000	-	785	597	483	-	166	-	4 480	1 995	6 475	34 835
Central America	2008/09	-	-	-	712	953	300	-	3 158	-	5 123	4 252	9 375	36 370
	2009/10	-	-	-	265	2 222	336	995	16 905	-	20 723	10 626	31 349	75 033
	2010/11	-	-	-	1	9 089	341	2 695	7 034	1 706	20 866	23 259	44 125	84 356
	2011/12	1 450	-	-	-	1 255	533	-	2 459	-	4 246	9 362	13 609	..
Caribbean														
Anguilla	2007/08	-	-	-	-	-	-	-	-	-	-	113	113	381
	2008/09	-	-	-	-	-	-	-	-	-	-	28	28	-
	2009/10	-	-	-	-	-	-	-	-	-	-	136	136	..
	2010/11	-	-	-	-	-	-	-	-	-	-	58	58	..
	2011/12											400	400	..
Antigua &	2007/08	-	-	-	-	-	-	-	-	-	-	3	3	52
Barbuda	2008/09	-	-	-	-	-	-	-	-	-	-	11	11	-
	2009/10	-	-	-	-	-	-	-	-	-	-	4	4	514
	2010/11	-	-	-	-	-	-	-	-	-	-	3	3	1 313
	2011/12											2	2	..
Barbados	2007/08	-	-	-	-	-	-	-	-	-	-	1 249	1 249	1 214
	2008/09	-	-	-	-	-	-	-	-	-	-	97	97	845
	2009/10	-	-	-	-	-	-	-	-	-	-	290	290	277
	2010/11	-	-	-	-	-	-	-	-	-	-	52	52	2 196
	2011/12											-	-	..
Belize	2007/08	-	-	-	-	-	-2	-	-	646	644	26	670	878
	2008/09	-	-	-	-	-	8	-	-	-	8	45	53	878
	2009/10	-	-	-	-	-	-	-	-	-	-	33	33	3 060
	2010/11	-	-	-	-	-	-	-	-	-	-	51	51	3 514
	2011/12											378	378	..
Dominica	2007/08	-	-	-	-	-	-	-	-	541	541	1	542	1 832
	2008/09	-	-	-	-	-	-	-	-	-	-	134	134	439
	2009/10	-	-	-	-	-	-	-	-	-	-	1	1	7
	2010/11	-	-	-	-	-	-	-	-	-	-	195	195	778
	2011/12											34	34	..

3.2b Total DFID Expenditure and GPEX by Recipient Country (Americas) 2007/08 - 2011/12[1]

£ thousand

| | | Financial Aid | | | | | | | | | | | | |
		General Poverty Reduction Budget Support	Sector Poverty Reduction Budget Support	Other Financial Aid[5]	Technical Cooperation	Bilateral aid delivered through a Multilateral	Bilateral aid Delivered through an NGO	Other Bilateral Aid[2]	Humanitarian Assistance	DFID Debt Relief	Total DFID Bilateral Programme	Aid from other UK Official Sources[5]	Total Bilateral Gross Public Expenditure	UK Imputed Multilateral Shares[3]
Dominican Republic	2007/08	-	-	-	-	-	-	-	-	-	-	56	56	3 208
	2008/09	-	-	-	-	-	-	-	-	-	-	818	818	1 532
	2009/10	-	-	-	-	-	-	-	-	-	-	64	64	4 917
	2010/11	-	-	-	-	-	-	-	-	-	-	36	36	14 744
	2011/12											157	157	..
Grenada	2007/08	-	-	-	-	-	-	-	-	56	56	2	57	1 118
	2008/09	-	-	-	-	-	-	-	-	-	-	12	12	411
	2009/10	-	-	-	-	-	-	-	-	-	-	16	16	862
	2010/11	-	-	-	-	-	-	-	-	-	-	1	1	745
	2011/12											1	1	..
Guyana	2007/08	-	-	1 327	707	681	68	-	-	-	2 783	156	2 939	7 034
	2008/09	-	-	922	1 139	341	70	-	-	-	2 472	168	2 640	2 432
	2009/10	-	-	462	432	600	88	-	-	47	1 629	97	1 726	3 037
	2010/11	-	-	-	9	11 591	0	-	-	-	11 600	45	11 645	4 865
	2011/12											107	107	..
Jamaica	2007/08	-	-	2 383	69	288	191	-	-	2 714	5 646	486	6 132	5 890
	2008/09	-	-	2 430	756	-	167	-	-	-	3 352	875	4 227	8 351
	2009/10	-	-	748	720	64	251	-	-	-	1 783	1 929	3 711	2 825
	2010/11	-	-	986	769	1 067	-	-	-	-	2 822	613	3 435	7 314
	2011/12	-	-	2 400	-	3 167	750	-	-	-	6 317	1 413	7 730	..
Montserrat	2007/08	-	-	15 448	1 693	-	20	-	3	-	17 164	131	17 295	634
	2008/09	-	-	15 043	1 132	-	101	-	0	-	16 276	107	16 383	-
	2009/10	-	-	19 798	968	-	-	-	-	-	20 766	61	20 827	2
	2010/11	-	-	18 763	317	-	-	-	-	-	19 080	119	19 199	6
	2011/12	-	-	23 834	534	-	-	-	-	-	24 368	205	24 573	..
St Kitts - Nevis	2007/08	-	-	-	-	-	-	-	-	-	-	6	6	1 260
	2008/09	-	-	-	-	-	-	-	-	-	-	1	1	742
	2009/10	-	-	-	-	-	-	-	-	-	-	1	1	1 424
	2010/11	-	-	-	-	-	-	-	-	-	-	1	1	2 811
	2011/12	-	-	-	-	-	-	-	-	-	-	0	0	..
St. Lucia	2007/08	-	-	-	-	-	-	-	-	-	-	4	4	993
	2008/09	-	-	-	-	-	-	-	-	-	-	38	38	768
	2009/10	-	-	-	-	-	-	-	-	-	-	8	8	134
	2010/11	-	-	-	-	213	-	-	-	-	213	11	224	513
	2011/12	-	-	-	-	-4	-	-	-	-	-4	33	29	..
St. Vincent & Grenadines	2007/08	-	-	-	-	-	-	-	-	263	263	1	264	1 498
	2008/09	-	-	-	-	-	-	-	-	-	-	9	9	347
	2009/10	-	-	-	-	-	-	-	-	-	-	0	0	219
	2010/11	-	-	-	-	-	-	-	-	-	-	10	10	990
	2011/12	-	-	-	-	-	-	-	-	-	-	44	44	..
Suriname	2007/08	-	-	-	-	-	-	-	-	-	-	-	-	1 017
	2008/09	-	-	-	-	-	-	-	-	-	-	-	-	329
	2009/10	-	-	-	-	-	-	-	-	-	-	-	-	2 176
	2010/11	-	-	-	-	-	-	-	-	-	-	-	-	389
	2011/12	-	-	-	-	-	-	-	-	-	-	-	-	..
Trinidad and Tobago	2007/08	-	-	-	-	-	-	-	-	-	-	64	64	868
	2008/09	-	-	-	-	-	-	-	-	-	-	464	464	972
	2009/10	-	-	-	-	-	-	-	-	-	-	282	282	1 320
	2010/11	-	-	-	-	-	-	-	-	-	-	157	157	4 826
	2011/12	-	-	-	-	-	-	-	-	-	-	-	-	..
Turks and Caicos Islands	2007/08	-	-	-	1	-	70	-	-	107	178	162	340	386
	2008/09	-	-	1 000	-	-	-	-	-	-	1 000	-	1 000	-
	2009/10	-	-	4 000	520	-	-	-	170	-	4 690	-	4 690	-
	2010/11	-	-	-	581	-	110	-	-	-	691	-	691	-
	2011/12	-	-	160	1 694	-	208	-	-	-	2 061		2 061	..
Windward Islands	2007/08	-	-	-	61	887	-	-	-	-	948	-	948	-
	2008/09	-	-	-	71	108	-	-	-	-	179	-	179	-
	2009/10	-	-	-	21	-	-	-	-	-	21	-	21	-
	2010/11	-	-	-	-	-	-	-	-	-	-	-	-	-
	2011/12	-	-	-	-	-	-	-	-	-	-	95	95	-
Caribbean regional	2007/08	-	-	-	1 280	300	122	27	4 291	-	6 020	122	6 142	-
	2008/09	-	-	217	1 749	355	19	-	7 979	-	10 319	1 557	11 876	-
	2009/10	-	-	411	1 828	13 096	375	-	-4 750	-	10 960	34	10 994	153
	2010/11	-	-	-	603	7 449	609	475	340	-	9 476	281	9 757	4 210
	2011/12	-	-	-	591	9 107	243	526	78	-	10 545	162	10 707	..
Overseas Territories (cross territory programmes)	2007/08	-	-	70	51	251	378	-	251	-	1 001	-	1 001	-
	2008/09	-	-	54	197	163	368	-	21	-	804	-	804	-
	2009/10	-	-	53	625	336	217	-	-	-	1 231	-	1 231	-
	2010/11	-	-	220	866	210	565	-	-	-	1 861	-	1 861	-
	2011/12	-	-	182	1 113	479	482	-	-	-	2 256	28	2 284	..
Total Caribbean	2007/08	-	-	19 229	3 861	2 407	847	27	4 545	4 327	35 243	2 581	37 824	28 261
	2008/09	-	-	19 666	5 044	966	733	-	8 001	-	34 411	4 362	38 773	18 044
	2009/10	-	-	25 472	5 114	14 096	932	-	-4 580	47	41 081	2 955	44 036	20 927
	2010/11	-	-	19 969	3 145	20 530	1 284	475	340	-	45 742	1 632	47 374	49 214
	2011/12	-	-	26 576	3 932	12 749	1 683	526	78	-	45 543	3 061	48 604	..
South America Argentina	2007/08	-	-	-	-	-	-	-	-	-	-	479	479	1 522
	2008/09	-	-	-	-	-	-	-	-	-	-	574	574	1 145
	2009/10	-	-	-	-	-	-	-	-	-	-	916	916	1 835
	2010/11	-	-	-	-	-	-	-	-	-	-	350	350	3 662
	2011/12	-	-	-	-	-	-	-	-	-	-	1 217	1 217	..

3.2b Total DFID Expenditure and GPEX by Recipient Country (Americas) 2007/08 - 2011/12[1]

£ thousand

| | | Financial Aid | | | | | | | | | | | | |
		General Poverty Reduction Budget Support	Sector Poverty Reduction Budget Support	Other Financial Aid [5]	Technical Cooperation	Bilateral aid delivered through a Multilateral	Bilateral aid Delivered through an NGO	Other Bilateral Aid [2]	Humanitarian Assistance	DFID Debt Relief	Total DFID Bilateral Programme	Aid from other UK Official Sources [5]	Total Bilateral Gross Public Expenditure	UK Imputed Multilateral Shares [3]
Bolivia	2007/08	-	-	-	95	-	392	-	-	-	487	75	562	8 797
	2008/09	-	-	-	42	897	344	-	-	-	1 283	93	1 376	3 951
	2009/10	-	-	-	-	-	-	-	-	-	-	262	262	7 630
	2010/11	-	-	-	-	-	-	-	-	-	-	54	54	7 950
	2011/12	-	-	-	-	-	-	-	-	-	-	148	148	..
Brazil	2007/08	-	-	-	93	-	343	-	-	-	436	1 096	1 532	506
	2008/09	-	-	-	291	-	569	-	-	-	860	6 737	7 597	2 622
	2009/10	-	-	216	424	-	286	-	-	-	927	9 895	10 823	4 262
	2010/11	-	-	134	24	-	-	-	-	-	158	29 533	29 691	3 492
	2011/12	-	-	-	-	-	-	-	-	-	-	36 595	36 595	..
Chile	2007/08	-	-	-	-	-	-	-	-	-	-	18	18	4 947
	2008/09	-	-	-	-	-	-	-	-	-	-	264	264	720
	2009/10	-	-	-	-	-	-	-	250	-	250	383	633	238
	2010/11	-	-	-	-	-	-	-	67	-	67	110	178	1 473
	2011/12	-	-	-	-	-	-	-	-	-	-	564	564	..
Colombia	2007/08	-	-	-14	-	-	273	-	-	-	259	485	744	3 172
	2008/09	-	-	-	-	-	219	-	-	-	219	1 617	1 836	4 154
	2009/10	-	-	-	-	-	-	-	1 269	-	1 269	4 915	6 184	3 626
	2010/11	-	-	-	-	-	-	-	-	-	-	1 709	1 709	11 575
	2011/12	-	-	-	-	-	-	-	-	-	-	3 976	3 976	..
Ecuador	2007/08	-	-	-	-	-	67	-	-	-	67	24	91	2 544
	2008/09	-	-	-348	-	-	102	-	-	-	-246	105	-141	5 061
	2009/10	-	-	-245	-	-	97	-	-	-	-147	20	-127	4 530
	2010/11	-	-	-	-	-	-	-	-	-	-	124	124	2 148
	2011/12	-	-	-	-	-	-	-	-	-	-	173	173	..
Paraguay	2007/08	-	-	-	-	-	-	-	-	-	-	-	-	600
	2008/09	-	-	-	-	-	-	-	-	-	-	36	36	5 588
	2009/10	-	-	-	-	-	-	-	-	-	-	27	27	651
	2010/11	-	-	-	-	-	-	-	-	-	-	7	7	1 823
	2011/12	-	-	-	-	-	-	-	-	-	-	47	47	..
Peru	2007/08	-	-	-	-	-	687	-	750	-	1 437	2 292	3 729	4 107
	2008/09	-	-	-	-40	-	510	-	21	-	492	1 424	1 915	1 163
	2009/10	-	-	-	-	-	311	-	-	-	311	412	723	9 839
	2010/11	-	-	-	-	-	-	-	-	-	-	718	718	2 694
	2011/12	-	-	-	-	-	-	-	-	-	-	557	557	..
Uruguay	2007/08	-	-	-	-	-	-	-	-	-	-	55	55	2 185
	2008/09	-	-	-	-	-	-	-	-	-	-	80	80	383
	2009/10	-	-	-	-	-	-	-	-	-	-	26	26	202
	2010/11	-	-	-	-	-	-	-	-	-	-	43	43	233
	2011/12	-	-	-	-	-	-	-	-	-	-	97	97	..
Venezuela	2007/08	-	-	-	-	-	-	-	-	-	-	59	59	1 138
	2008/09	-	-	-	-	-	-	-	-	-	-	285	285	1 259
	2009/10	-	-	-	-	-	-	-	-	-	-	1 384	1 384	1 782
	2010/11	-	-	-	-	-	-	-	-	-	-	705	705	467
	2011/12	-	-	-	-	-	-	-	-	-	-	798	798	..
Latin America Regional	2007/08	-	-	-	2 321	3 960	795	-	-	-	7 077	9 149	16 226	6 417
	2008/09	-	-	-	2 759	2 401	654	-	82	-	5 895	16	5 911	6 714
	2009/10	-	-	-	99	-71	248	-	-	-	276	2 350	2 626	3 763
	2010/11	-	-	-	-	-	-	-	-	-	-	219	219	11 405
	2011/12	-	-	-	-	-	-	-	-	-	-	112	112	..
Total South America	2007/08	-	-	-14	2 510	3 960	2 558	-	750	-	9 764	13 731	23 495	35 935
	2008/09	-	-	-348	3 051	3 298	2 399	-	103	-	8 503	11 230	19 733	32 760
	2009/10	-	-	-28	524	-71	942	-	1 519	-	2 886	20 590	23 476	38 359
	2010/11	-	-	134	24	-	-	-	67	-	225	33 573	33 797	46 921
	2011/12	-	-	-	-	-	-	-	-	-	-	44 284	44 284	..
Americas regional	2007/08	-	-	-	-	-	-	-	749	-	749	2	751	20 149
	2008/09	-	-	-	-	-	-	-	-	-	-	7 495	7 495	6 166
	2009/10	-	-	-	-	-	-	-	-	-	-	-	-	18 736
	2010/11	-	-	-	-	-	-	-	-	-	-	6 738	6 738	30 535
	2011/12	-	-	-	-	-	-	-	-	-	-	146	146	..
Total Americas	2007/08	1 450	1 000	19 215	7 156	6 964	3 887	27	6 210	4 327	50 237	18 309	68 545	119 180
	2008/09	-	-	19 319	8 807	5 217	3 432	-	11 262	-	48 036	27 339	75 376	93 340
	2009/10	-	-	25 444	5 903	16 248	2 209	995	13 844	47	64 690	34 171	98 861	153 055
	2010/11	-	-	25 803	3 170	29 618	1 624	3 170	7 442	1 706	66 833	65 202	132 035	211 026
	2011/12	-	-	26 576	3 932	14 004	2 215	526	2 537	-	49 789	56 853	106 642	..

1. Descriptions of aid types given in Section 2.
2. Other Bilateral Aid covers bilateral aid not elsewhere classified.
3. Details on DFID Imputed Multilateral Shares are in Section 2; 2010/11 data are not yet available.
4. Low Income Country. Income groups are classified using 2007 GNI per capita thresholds.
5. Pension payments have been reclassified from "Other Financial Aid" to "Aid from other UK Official Sources". This is consistent with the classification of spending under Department Expenditure Limits (DEL) agreed with Treasury.

3.2c Total DFID Expenditure and GPEX by Recipient Country (Asia) 2007/08 - 2011/12[1]

£ thousand

| | | Financial Aid | | | | | | | | | | | | |
		General Poverty Reduction Budget Support	Sector Poverty Reduction Budget Support	Other Financial Aid [5]	Technical Cooperation	Bilateral aid delivered through a Multilateral	Bilateral aid Delivered through an NGO	Other Bilateral Aid [2]	Humanitarian Assistance	DFID Debt Relief	Total DFID Bilateral Programme	Aid from other UK Official Sources [5]	Total Bilateral Gross Public Expenditure	UK Imputed Multilateral Shares [3]
Asia: Middle East														
Iran	2007/08	-	-	-	-	-	-	-	-	-	-	245	245	1 028
	2008/09	-	-	-	-	-	-	-	-	-	-	919	919	2 051
	2009/10	-	-	-	-	-	-	-	-	-	-	466	466	1 200
	2010/11	-	-	-	-	-	-	-	-	-	-	-	-	2 057
	2011/12	-	-	-	-	-	-	-	-	-	-	435	435	..
Iraq	2007/08	-	-	69	18 643	-	874	-17	19 958	-	39 527	1 122	40 649	9 180
	2008/09	-	-	81	15 509	-	1 223	-	16 000	-	32 812	304 665	337 477	14 012
	2009/10	-	-	-	10 009	600	1 981	-	7 648	-	20 238	9 767	30 005	7 865
	2010/11	-	-	-	4 859	2 650	-10	-	2 800	-	10 299	5 277	15 576	6 202
	2011/12	-	-	-	1 887	1 200	-	-	-	-	3 087	4 505	7 592	..
Jordan	2007/08	-	-	-	-	-	-	-	100	-	100	155	255	9 184
	2008/09	-	-	-	-	-	-	-	-	-	-	2 454	2 454	8 603
	2009/10	-	-	-	-	-	-	-	-	-	-	974	974	8 571
	2010/11	-	-	178	-	-	-	-	-	-	178	1 619	1 797	10 911
	2011/12	-	-	-	-	-	-	-	-	-	-	2 523	2 523	..
Lebanon	2007/08	-	-	-	-	-	100	-	68	-	169	102	271	9 371
	2008/09	-	-	-	-	-	39	-	-	-	39	1 364	1 403	9 177
	2009/10	-	-	-	-	-	-	-	-	-	-	3 450	3 450	5 880
	2010/11	-	-	-	-	-	-	-	-	-	-	2 565	2 565	7 859
	2011/12	-	-	-	-	-	-	-	-	-	-	2 064	2 064	..
Oman	2007/08	-	-	-	-	-	-	-	-	-	-	83	83	43
	2008/09	-	-	-	-	-	-	-	-	-	-	308	308	33
	2009/10	-	-	-	-	-	-	-	-	-	-	410	410	25
	2010/11	-	-	-	-	-	-	-	-	-	-	602	602	20
	2011/12	-	-	-	-	-	-	-	-	-	-	-	-	..
Saudi Arabia	2007/08	-	-	-	-	-	-	-	-	-	-	380	380	-
	2008/09	-	-	-	-	-	-	-	-	-	-	-	-	-
	2009/10	-	-	-	-	-	-	-	-	-	-	-	-	-
	2010/11	-	-	-	-	-	-	-	-	-	-	-	-	-
	2011/12	-	-	-	-	-	-	-	-	-	-	-	-	-
Syria	2007/08	-	-	-	-	-	-	-	-	-	-	46	46	4 568
	2008/09	-	-	-	-	-	-	-	-	-	-	1 263	1 263	2 979
	2009/10	-	-	-	-	-	-	-	490	-	490	672	1 162	6 313
	2010/11	-	-	-	-	-	-	-	-	-	-	1 260	1 260	9 810
	2011/12	-	-	-	-	-	-	-	2 011	-	2 011	2 018	4 029	..
West Bank &	2007/08	-	-	22 718	2 161	20 000	71	-	84	-	45 033	158	45 191	61 499
Gaza	2008/09	-	-	896	3 621	23 950	-	-	12 847	-	41 314	1 243	42 557	50 933
	2009/10	-	-	340	3 952	38 500	-	-	14 838	-	57 630	4 973	62 603	72 818
	2010/11	-	-	1 000	5 018	36 751	216	-	3 587	-	46 572	5 214	51 786	77 309
	2011/12	-	-	48	2 384	49 163	1 135	-	236	-	52 966	3 455	56 421	..
Yemen [4]	2007/08	-	-	-	815	10 347	7	-	830	-	11 999	280	12 279	6 673
	2008/09	-	-	1 050	3 402	13 053	-	-	1 710	-	19 215	1 098	20 313	9 216
	2009/10	-	-	17 038	863	3 613	40	982	7 241	-	29 778	882	30 660	12 986
	2010/11	-	-	30 193	1 972	10 225	123	1 172	7 429	-	51 113	2 598	53 711	21 851
	2011/12	-	-	9 000	327	4 055	210	750	19 957	-	34 299	1 721	36 020	..
Middle East,	2007/08	-	-	-	189	525	-	-	2 585	-	3 299	426	3 725	2 445
Regional	2008/09	-	-	-	-	976	75	-	-	-	1 051	14 594	15 645	979
	2009/10	-	-	-	55	2 653	1 135	-	-	-	3 843	69	3 912	2 202
	2010/11	-	-	-	-	2 852	968	-	-	-	3 820	2 883	6 703	7 234
	2011/12	-	-	-	8	6 897	210	-	-	-	7 114	32	7 147	..
Total Middle	2007/08	-	-	22 787	21 807	30 872	1 052	-17	23 625	-	100 126	2 997	103 123	103 991
East	2008/09	-	-	2 027	22 532	37 979	1 336	-	30 557	-	94 431	327 909	422 340	97 982
	2009/10	-	-	17 378	14 880	45 367	3 156	982	30 217	-	111 979	21 663	133 642	117 860
	2010/11	-	-	31 371	11 849	52 477	1 298	1 172	13 816	-	111 983	22 018	134 001	143 252
	2011/12	-	-	9 048	4 606	61 316	1 555	750	22 204	-	99 478	16 753	116 231	..
Asia: South														
Afghanistan [4]	2007/08	-	-	55 000	19 109	8 511	18 002	-	8 304	-	108 926	37 891	146 818	34 460
	2008/09	-	-	71 881	21 618	28 877	4 538	933	19 607	-	147 455	50 231	197 687	25 181
	2009/10	-	-	74 698	28 146	8 486	14 036	840	7 160	-	133 367	72 334	205 701	45 755
	2010/11	-	-	19 458	29 019	37 120	11 026	-	503	-	97 185	75 126	172 311	55 968
	2011/12	-	-	5 672	27 625	95 488	13 127	-	4 219	-	146 131	79 178	225 309	..
Bangladesh [4]	2007/08	-	-	34 791	24 596	32 701	23 963	-	13 341	-	129 392	333	129 725	42 624
	2008/09	-	-	20 568	38 111	15 107	50 916	916	7 324	-	132 941	2 745	135 686	86 475
	2009/10	-	-	31 914	33 881	15 009	63 524	3 258	1 222	-	148 808	2 368	151 176	25 863
	2010/11	-	-	27 325	28 733	44 409	64 976	5 476	3 472	-	174 391	4 174	178 565	79 981
	2011/12	-	-	30 000	28 272	72 138	82 843	5 482	539	-	219 273	4 379	223 652	..
Bhutan	2007/08	-	-	-	-	-	-	-	-	-	-	-	-	1 886
	2008/09	-	-	-	-	-	-	-	-	-	-	-	-	629
	2009/10	-	-	-	-	-	-	-	71	-	71	-	71	1 102
	2010/11	-	-	-	-	-	-	-	-	-	-	-	-	4 437
	2011/12	-	-	-	-	-	-	-	-	-	-	-	-	..
Burma [4]	2007/08	-	-	-	34	5 934	1 744	-	1 068	-	8 780	136	8 915	7 195
	2008/09	-	-	-	1 894	7 115	1 987	-	45 666	-	56 661	940	57 601	5 583
	2009/10	-	-	-	1 409	13 726	9 978	-	3 061	-	28 175	844	29 019	5 403
	2010/11	-	-	-	1 092	20 689	5 088	-	4 616	-	31 485	1 053	32 538	13 113
	2011/12	-	-	-	1 015	25 099	7 507	-	2 528	-	36 150	1 179	37 329	..
India	2007/08	-	54 000	142 888	16 905	53 722	6 874	-	1 013	-	275 402	37 349	312 751	89 414
	2008/09	-	54 000	194 292	17 871	27 673	2 807	-	386	-	297 028	105 211	402 239	73 974
	2009/10	-	52 000	177 152	19 360	42 023	4 584	-	-	-	295 119	61 371	356 490	35 761
	2010/11	-	46 000	185 226	26 016	15 802	5 892	-	-	-	278 936	149 148	428 084	273 161
	2011/12	-	-	220 451	29 469	30 269	4 170	-	-	-	284 359	87 030	371 389	..

3.2c Total DFID Expenditure and GPEX by Recipient Country (Asia) 2007/08 - 2011/12[1]

£ thousand

		General Poverty Reduction Budget Support	Sector Poverty Reduction Budget Support	Other Financial Aid [5]	Technical Cooperation	Bilateral aid delivered through a Multilateral	Bilateral aid Delivered through an NGO	Other Bilateral Aid [2]	Humanitarian Assistance	DFID Debt Relief	Total DFID Bilateral Programme	Aid from other UK Official Sources [5]	Total Bilateral Gross Public Expenditure	UK Imputed Multilateral Shares [3]
Maldives	2007/08	-	-	-	-	-	-	-	-	-	-	44	44	539
	2008/09	-	-	-	-	-	-	-	-	-	-	58	58	1 285
	2009/10	-	-	150	-	-	-	-	-	-	150	94	244	784
	2010/11	-	-	-	-	-	-	-	-	-	-	170	170	1 478
	2011/12	-	-	-	-	-	-	-	-	-	-	177	177	
Nepal [4]	2007/08	-	18 006	12 710	12 722	2 495	7 962	-	800	-	54 694	580	55 274	19 008
	2008/09	-	9 018	6 858	14 965	5 123	13 859	-	5 596	2 579	57 999	519	58 518	11 048
	2009/10	-	5 239	12 247	16 496	15 415	7 350	1 020	6 013	3 082	66 862	1 625	68 487	15 231
	2010/11	-	7 000	5 603	20 295	14 985	9 653	873	25	3 391	61 825	1 168	62 993	27 723
	2011/12	-	14 000	6 897	24 262	11 143	10 896	6	-	3 477	70 682	708	71 389	..
Pakistan	2007/08	10 000	38 000	4 916	8 283	12 642	5 101	150	7 866	-	86 958	1 188	88 145	58 547
	2008/09	30 000	25 700	26 977	8 082	13 994	4 416	-	10 775	-	119 942	9 771	129 713	20 570
	2009/10	30 000	22 500	7 029	6 617	21 645	23 164	-	29 444	-	140 398	10 846	151 244	102 099
	2010/11	30 000	32 500	28 075	11 129	11 459	7 059	-	82 715	-	202 937	8 923	211 860	69 800
	2011/12	-	38 000	15 500	15 330	77 920	5 596	-	59 337	-	211 682	13 167	224 849	..
Sri Lanka	2007/08	-	-	-	-	-	226	-	1 819	-232	1 813	1 895	3 708	6 413
	2008/09	-	-	-	-	-	-60	-	3 038	-	2 978	574	3 552	17 595
	2009/10	-	-	-	49	-	139	-	12 872	-	13 061	3 293	16 354	14 153
	2010/11	-	-	-	-	-	-	-	1 375	-	1 375	2 993	4 367	17 795
	2011/12	-	-	-	860	-	-	-	2	-	863	2 695	3 557	..
South & Central Asia	2007/08	-	-	-	-	-	-	-	-	-	-	-	-	751
	2008/09	-	-	-	2 442	86	-	-	927	-	3 455	10 146	13 601	179
	2009/10	-	-	-	1 706	-	-	-	-	-	1 706	1 050	2 757	1 101
	2010/11	-	-	-	78	-	-	-	-	-	78	728	806	2 714
	2011/12	-	-	-	34	-	-	-	-	-	34	1 598	1 632	..
Total South Asia	2007/08	10 000	110 006	250 306	81 650	116 003	63 872	150	34 209	-232	665 964	79 415	745 380	260 838
	2008/09	30 000	88 718	320 576	104 983	97 974	78 462	1 849	93 319	2 579	818 460	180 195	998 655	242 518
	2009/10	30 000	79 739	303 190	107 665	116 303	122 776	5 118	59 844	3 082	827 717	153 826	981 543	247 251
	2010/11	30 000	85 500	265 687	116 421	144 463	103 694	6 349	92 707	3 391	848 211	243 484	1 091 695	546 170
	2011/12	-	52 000	278 521	126 867	312 056	124 140	5 488	66 625	3 477	969 174	190 111	1 159 285	..
Asia: Far East														
Brunei	2007/08	-	-	-	-	-	-	-	-	-	-	3	3	-
	2008/09	-	-	-	-	-	-	-	-	-	-	3	3	-
	2009/10	-	-	-	-	-	-	-	-	-	-	3	3	-
	2010/11	-	-	-	-	-	-	-	-	-	-	-	-	-
	2011/12	-	-	-	-	-	-	-	-	-	-	-	-	-
Cambodia [4]	2007/08	1 534	-	2 200	1 273	4 933	1 084	1 373	405	-	12 802	223	13 025	8 927
	2008/09	-	-	2 857	2 019	9 215	680	2 904	49	-	17 725	1 279	19 003	9 086
	2009/10	-	-	1 200	2 391	6 280	795	5 205	-	-	15 871	402	16 273	4 521
	2010/11	-	-	-	1 390	13 217	51	4 798	-	-	19 456	538	19 993	21 200
	2011/12	-	-	-	2 586	8 000	-	1 059	-	-	11 645	994	12 638	..
China	2007/08	-	-	22 967	4 602	8 500	2 727	-	-	-	38 796	44 947	83 743	7 390
	2008/09	-	-	19 255	6 776	10 442	1 705	-	2 118	-	40 296	78 091	118 387	12 678
	2009/10	-	-	14 014	3 494	14 420	1 281	198	1 104	-	34 512	56 283	90 796	23 529
	2010/11	-	-	11 388	2 505	7 020	1 286	231	440	-	22 871	56 634	79 505	24 503
	2011/12	-	-	-747	128	-	110	-	-	-	-508	55 797	55 289	..
East Timor	2007/08	-	-	-	-	1 153	113	-	55	-	1 321	-	1 321	3 335
	2008/09	-	-	-	-	2 057	72	-	-	-	2 129	21	2 150	1 713
	2009/10	-	-	-	-	-	-	-	-	-	-	20	20	1 404
	2010/11	-	-	-	-	1 145	-	-	-	-	1 145	-	1 145	7 537
	2011/12	-	-	-	-	-	-	-	-	-	-	75	75	..
Indonesia	2007/08	-	-	5 730	563	8 636	1 952	-	15 329	-	32 210	504	32 715	20 010
	2008/09	-	-	4 562	462	15 130	1 404	-	15 106	-	36 665	20 733	57 397	24 482
	2009/10	-	-	756	430	15 613	2 630	-	5 628	-	25 058	8 110	33 167	25 929
	2010/11	-	-	3 318	779	3 000	2 470	-	592	-	10 159	22 762	32 921	17 359
	2011/12	-	-	2 716	1 422	-	3 251	4 965	-	-	12 355	10 782	23 137	..
Japan	2007/08	-	-	-	-	-	-	-	-	-	-	-	-	-
	2008/09	-	-	-	-	-	-	-	-	-	-	-	-	-
	2009/10	-	-	-	-	-	-	-	-	-	-	-	-	-
	2010/11	-	-	-	-	-	-	-	1 380	-	1 380	-	1 380	-
	2011/12	-	-	-	-	-	-	-	-	-	-	-	-	-
Korea (North)	2007/08	-	-	-	-	-	-	-	649	-	649	83	732	1 361
	2008/09	-	-	-	-	-	-	-	-	-	-	185	185	935
	2009/10	-	-	-	-	-	-	-	2 822	-	2 822	32	2 853	1 309
	2010/11	-	-	-	-	-	-	-	-	-	-	264	264	4 832
	2011/12	-	-	-	-	-	-	-	-	-	-	620	620	..
Laos [4]	2007/08	-	-	-	-	-	220	-	209	-	429	-	429	4 289
	2008/09	-	-	-	-	-	145	-	100	-	245	-	245	5 733
	2009/10	-	-	-	-	-	153	-	567	-	720	-	720	2 878
	2010/11	-	-	-	58	-	-	-	-	-	58	-	58	11 248
	2011/12	-	-	-	1 206	-	-	-	-	-	1 206	-	1 206	..
Malaysia	2007/08	-	-	-	-	-	-	-	-	-	-	10 500	10 500	239
	2008/09	-	-	-	-	-	-	-	-	-	-	11 922	11 922	995
	2009/10	-	-	-	-	-	-	-	-	-	-	2 929	2 929	393
	2010/11	-	-	-	-	-	-	-	-	-	-	2 742	2 742	1 556
	2011/12	-	-	-	-	-	-	-	-	-	-	5 177	5 177	..
Mongolia	2007/08	-	-	-	-	481	-	-	225	-	706	138	844	3 458
	2008/09	-	-	-	-	2 508	-	-	307	-	2 815	354	3 170	1 509
	2009/10	-	-	-	-	-	-	-	331	-	331	306	637	2 402
	2010/11	-	-	-	-	1 969	-	-	375	-	2 344	163	2 507	6 488
	2011/12	-	-	-	-	-	-	-	477	-	477	181	658	..

3.2c Total DFID Expenditure and GPEX by Recipient Country (Asia) 2007/08 - 2011/12[1]

£ thousand

| | | Financial Aid | | | | | | | | | | | |
		General Poverty Reduction Budget Support	Sector Poverty Reduction Budget Support	Other Financial Aid [5]	Technical Cooperation	Bilateral aid delivered through a Multilateral	Bilateral aid Delivered through an NGO	Other Bilateral Aid [2]	Humanitarian Assistance	DFID Debt Relief	Total DFID Bilateral Programme	Aid from other UK Official Sources [5]	Total Bilateral Gross Public Expenditure	UK Imputed Multilateral Shares [3]
Philippines	2007/08	-	-	12	11	-	299	-	-	-	321	475	796	3 434
	2008/09	-	-	-5	12	-	13	-	-	-	20	823	844	4 837
	2009/10	-	-	-2	9	-	-	-	2 271	-	2 278	2 402	4 680	9 434
	2010/11	-	-	-	-	-	-	-	-	-	-	564	564	13 079
	2011/12	-	-	-	-	-	-	-	-	-	-	1 561	1 561	..
Singapore	2007/08	-	-	-	-	-	-	-	-	-	-	29	29	-
	2008/09	-	-	-	-	-	-	-	-	-	-	26	26	-
	2009/10	-	-	-	-	-	-	-	-	-	-	31	31	-
	2010/11	-	-	-	-	-	-	-	-	-	-	-	-	..
	2011/12	-	-	-	-	-	-	-	-	-	-	-	-	..
Thailand	2007/08	-	-	-	-	-	-	-	-	-	-	101	101	2 376
	2008/09	-	-	-	-	-	-	-	-	-	-	1 207	1 207	2 261
	2009/10	-	-	-	-	-	52	-	-	-	52	6 326	6 378	4 496
	2010/11	-	-	-	-	-	52	-	-	-	-	4 667	4 667	3 741
	2011/12	-	-	-	-	-	-	-	-	-	-	2 864	2 864	..
Vietnam	2007/08	20 000	11 750	5 861	360	8 836	2 958	-	-	1 203	50 968	422	51 390	42 453
	2008/09	20 000	5 950	2 762	233	20 858	2 047	-	-	3 205	55 055	1 616	56 671	65 532
	2009/10	20 000	9 550	710	359	19 325	233	-	-	4 140	54 317	1 343	55 660	60 281
	2010/11	20 000	9 750	1 007	566	19 220	94	-	-	4 742	55 378	3 107	58 485	87 161
	2011/12	20 000	-	1 602	1 387	8 810	350	-	-	5 264	37 413	4 009	41 422	..
Far East Regional	2007/08	-	-	-	-	-	-	-	-	-	-	-	-	62
	2008/09	-	-	-	-	803	-	-	-	-	803	-	803	-
	2009/10	-	-	-	-	-	-	-	-	-	-	-	-	-
	2010/11	-	-	-	-	-	-	-	-	-	-	-	-	2 787
	2011/12	-	-	-	-	-	-	-	-	-	-	-	-	..
Total Far East Asia	2007/08	21 534	11 750	36 771	6 808	32 538	9 352	1 373	16 648	1 428	138 202	57 425	195 627	97 333
	2008/09	20 000	5 950	29 430	9 503	61 014	6 067	2 904	17 374	3 513	155 754	116 259	272 012	129 762
	2009/10	20 000	9 550	16 678	6 684	55 638	5 144	5 404	12 392	4 471	135 961	78 187	214 148	136 574
	2010/11	20 000	9 750	15 713	5 298	45 571	3 901	5 029	2 412	5 117	112 790	91 441	204 231	201 490
	2011/12	20 000	-	3 571	6 730	16 810	3 712	6 024	-	5 741	62 588	82 060	144 648	..
Asia: Central Asian Republics														
Kazakhstan	2007/08	-	-	-	-	-	-	-	-	-	-	328	328	2 765
	2008/09	-	-	-	-	-	-	-	-	-	-	2 996	2 996	1 634
	2009/10	-	-	-	-	-	-	-	-	-	-	4 446	4 446	1 813
	2010/11	-	-	-	-	-	-	-	-	-	-	1 113	1 113	5 190
	2011/12	-	-	-	-	-	-	-	-	-	-	2 199	2 199	..
Kyrgyzstan [4]	2007/08	-	-	1 019	2 119	2 579	82	-	57	-	5 856	53	5 908	2 933
	2008/09	-	-	1 000	862	6 772	22	-	703	-	9 359	1 324	10 683	5 736
	2009/10	-	-	1 000	198	3 010	-	186	-	-	4 395	229	4 624	5 265
	2010/11	-	-	980	290	1 053	998	-	-	-	3 321	231	3 552	11 716
	2011/12	-	-	2 000	378	2 548	42	-	-	-	4 968	857	5 824	..
Tajikistan [4]	2007/08	-	-	-	609	1 901	-	-	730	-	3 240	100	3 340	5 844
	2008/09	-	-	3	1 372	2 627	-	-	1 092	-	5 093	278	5 372	3 031
	2009/10	-	-	0	570	3 547	221	-	511	-	4 849	205	5 054	4 958
	2010/11	-	-	-	489	8 150	168	800	94	-	9 701	718	10 419	11 247
	2011/12	-	-	-	70	4 224	-	3 000	12	-	7 306	96	7 402	..
Turkmenistan	2007/08	-	-	-	-	-	-	-	-	-	-	118	118	868
	2008/09	-	-	-	-	-	-	-	-	-	-	218	218	752
	2009/10	-	-	-	-	-	-	-	-	-	-	218	218	137
	2010/11	-	-	-	-	-	-	-	-	-	-	39	39	2 718
	2011/12	-	-	-	-	-	-	-	-	-	-	150	150	..
Uzbekistan	2007/08	-	-	-	-	-	-	-	-	-	-	24	24	2 006
	2008/09	-	-	-	-	-	-	-	-	-	-	551	551	4 746
	2009/10	-	-	-	-	-	-	-	-	-	-	1 183	1 183	8 639
	2010/11	-	-	-	-	-	-	-	-	-	-	797	797	9 252
	2011/12	-	-	-	-	-	-	-	-	-	-	859	859	..
Central Asia Regional	2007/08	-	-	-	-	-	-	-	-	-	-	-	-	1 931
	2008/09	-	-	-	-	18	-	-	-	-	18	-	18	2 656
	2009/10	-	-	-	-	-	-	-	-	-	-	-	-	3 901
	2010/11	-	-	-	-	-	-	-	-	-	-	-	-	3 866
	2011/12	-	-	-	-	-	-	-	-	-	-	-	-	..
Total Central Asian Republics	2007/08	-	-	1 019	2 728	4 480	82	-	787	-	9 095	623	9 718	16 349
	2008/09	-	-	1 003	2 234	9 416	22	-	1 795	-	14 470	5 367	19 837	18 556
	2009/10	-	-	1 000	768	6 557	221	186	511	-	9 244	6 281	15 525	24 713
	2010/11	-	-	980	780	9 203	1 166	800	94	-	13 022	2 897	15 920	43 989
	2011/12	-	-	2 000	448	6 772	42	3 000	12	-	12 274	4 161	16 434	..
Asia Regional	2007/08	-	-	-	3 139	10 274	2 195	-	1 582	-	17 190	45 491	62 680	7 874
	2008/09	-	-	584	0	1 099	2 962	-	0	-	4 644	16 206	20 851	7 161
	2009/10	-	-	-	320	1 832	1 869	-	222	-	4 243	4 452	8 695	36 112
	2010/11	-	-	-	1 205	5 812	420	-	-	-	7 437	16 693	24 130	26 266
	2011/12	-	-	-	3 452	16 433	1 130	80	-	-	21 095	5 876	26 971	..
Total Asia	2007/08	31 534	121 756	310 882	116 131	194 168	76 552	1 506	76 852	1 196	930 577	185 951	1 116 528	486 384
	2008/09	50 000	94 668	353 620	139 252	207 482	88 848	4 753	143 045	6 092	1 087 760	645 936	1 733 696	495 978
	2009/10	50 000	89 289	338 246	130 317	225 697	133 166	11 691	103 187	7 553	1 089 144	264 409	1 353 553	562 511
	2010/11	50 000	95 250	313 750	135 553	257 527	110 479	13 349	109 028	8 508	1 093 443	376 534	1 469 977	961 167
	2011/12	20 000	52 000	293 140	142 103	413 386	130 578	15 342	88 841	9 218	1 164 608	298 961	1 463 569	

1. Descriptions of aid types given in Section 2.
2. Other Bilateral Aid covers bilateral aid not elsewhere classified.
3. Details on DFID Imputed Multilateral Shares are in Section 2; 2011/12 data are not yet available.
4. Low Income Country. Income groups are classified using 2010 GNI per capita thresholds
5. Pension payments have been reclassified from "Other Financial Aid" to "Aid from other UK Official Sources". This is consistent with the classification of spending under Department Expenditure Limits (DEL) agreed with Treasury.

3.2d Total DFID Expenditure and GPEX by Recipient Country (Europe) 2007/08 - 2011/12 [1]

£ thousand

	year	General Poverty Reduction Budget Support	Sector Poverty Reduction Budget Support	Other Financial Aid [5]	Technical Cooperation	Bilateral aid delivered through a Multilateral	Bilateral aid Delivered through an NGO	Other Bilateral Aid [2]	Humanitarian Assistance	DFID Debt Relief	Total DFID Bilateral Programme	Aid from other UK Official Sources [5]	Total Bilateral Gross Public Expenditure	UK Imputed Multilateral Shares [3]
Europe														
Albania	2007/08	-	-	-	872	500	142	-	-	-	1 514	1 173	2 688	6 402
	2008/09	-	-	-	356	180	149	-	-	-	686	831	1 516	10 774
	2009/10	-	-	-	-	-	143	-	-	-	143	720	863	9 096
	2010/11	-	-	-	-	-	-	-	-	-	-	537	537	12 912
	2011/12	-	-	-	-	-	-	-	-	-	-	696	696	..
Armenia	2007/08	-	-	900	1 347		-	-	541	295	3 082	74	3 156	8 571
	2008/09	-	-	200	1 492		246	-	-	860	2 798	407	3 204	4 030
	2009/10	-	-	-	-		-	-	24	-	24	380	404	14 359
	2010/11	-	-	-	-		-	-	-	-	-	405	405	4 898
	2011/12	-	-	-	-		-	-	-	-	-	358	358	..
Azerbaijan	2007/08	-	-	-	-	-	-	-	-	-	-	173	173	2 981
	2008/09	-	-	-	-	-	-	-	-	-	-	1 033	1 033	8 296
	2009/10	-	-	-	-	-	-	-	-	-	-	918	918	5 378
	2010/11	-	-	-	-	-	-	-	-	-	-	559	559	7 269
	2011/12	-	-	-	-	-	-	-	-	-	-	978	978	..
Belarus	2007/08	-	-	-	-	-	-	-	-	-	-	408	408	1 372
	2008/09	-	-	-	-	-	-	-	-	-	-	601	601	1 394
	2009/10	-	-	-	-	-	-	-	-	-	-	392	392	2 058
	2010/11	-	-	-	-	-	-	-	-	-	-	238	238	3 768
	2011/12	-	-	-	-	-	-	-	-	-	-	127	127	..
Bosnia-	2007/08	-	-	-	4 306	333	266	-	-	-	4 905	549	5 454	9 173
Herzegovina	2008/09	-	-	750	3 025	321	16	-	-	-	4 112	988	5 100	8 490
	2009/10	-	-	750	1 405	43	182	-	-	-	2 379	2 737	5 116	12 862
	2010/11	-	-	947	2 750	149	20	-	-	-	3 866	2 207	6 073	23 015
	2011/12	-	-	-	-	-	-	-	-	-	-	2 285	2 285	..
Croatia	2007/08	-	-	-	-	-	-	-	-	-	-	524	524	10 352
	2008/09	-	-	-	-	-	-	-	-	-	-	779	779	14 018
	2009/10	-	-	-	-	-	-	-	-	-	-	1 200	1 200	17 029
	2010/11	-	-	-	-	-	-	-	-	-	-	679	679	21 283
	2011/12	-	-	-	-	-	-	-	-	-	-	-	-	..
Cyprus	2007/08	-	-	-	-	-	-	-	-	-	-	3	3	-
	2008/09	-	-	-	-	-	-	-	-	-	-	2	-	-
	2009/10	-	-	-	-	-	-	-	-	-	-	2	2	-
	2010/11	-	-	-	-	-	-	-	-	-	-	-	-	-
	2011/12	-	-	-	-	-	-	-	-	-	-	-	-	..
Georgia	2007/08	-	-	-	2 327	-	150	-	-	-23	2 454	130	2 584	6 214
	2008/09	-	-	1 500	2 342	-	-	-	3 199	784	7 825	408	8 234	20 314
	2009/10	-	-	-	165	-	-	-	948	-	1 113	2 037	3 149	21 665
	2010/11	-	-	-	-	-	-	-	-	-	-	2 223	2 223	18 583
	2011/12	-	-	-	-	-	-	-	-	-	-	2 221	2 221	..
Gibraltar	2007/08	-	-	-	-	-	-	-	-	-	-	-	-	-
	2008/09	-	-	-	-	-	-	-	-	-	-	-	-	-
	2009/10	-	-	-	-	-	-	-	-	-	-	-	-	-
	2010/11	-	-	-	-	-	-	-	-	-	-	-	-	-
	2011/12	-	-	-	-	-	-	-	-	-	-	-	-	..
Macedonia	2007/08	-	-	-	-	-	-	-	-	-	-	964	964	4 889
(FYR of)	2008/09	-	-	-	-	-	-	-	-	-	-	1 181	1 181	6 035
	2009/10	-	-	-	-	-	-	-	-	-	-	1 250	1 250	9 616
	2010/11	-	-	-	-	-	-	-	-	-	-	743	743	13 538
	2011/12	-	-	-	-	-	-	-	-	-	-	1 017	1 017	..
Moldova	2007/08	-	-	-	1 241	326	111	2	40	70	1 790	153	1 942	10 701
	2008/09	-	-	-	1 824	2 706	114	-	-	176	4 820	433	5 253	9 270
	2009/10	-	3 500	-	1 216	157	122	-	140	297	5 432	415	5 847	10 090
	2010/11	-	2 500	-	2 396	480	57	-	26	365	5 825	169	5 994	38 444
	2011/12	-	-	-	-	-	-	-	-	378	378	196	574	..
Russian	2007/08	-	-	-	301	-	72	-	-	-	373	-	373	-
Federation	2008/09	-	-	-	-	-	190	-	-	-	190	-	190	-
	2009/10	-	-	-	7	1 259	242	-	-	-	1 507	535	2 042	-
	2010/11	-	-	-	-	1 134	135	-	-	-	1 269	-	1 269	-
	2011/12	-	-	-	-	-	-	-	-	-	-	-	-	..
Serbia	2007/08	-	-	450	1 456	764	134	-	-	-	2 803	687	3 491	26 685
	2008/09	-	-	144	1 638	896	192	-	-	-	2 869	1 018	3 888	41 081
	2009/10	-	-	326	545	648	202	-	-	-	1 721	3 685	5 406	22 438
	2010/11	-	-	291	8	377	277	55	-	-	1 008	1 830	2 837	28 945
	2011/12	-	-	-	-	-	-	-28	-	-	-28	2 370	2 342	..
Kosovo	2007/08	-	-	-	2 775	345	80	-	-	-	3 200	197	3 397	-
	2008/09	-	-	154	2 891	250	8	-	-	-	3 304	364	3 668	-
	2009/10	-	-	-	2 729	50	243	-	-	-	3 022	4 294	7 316	27 348
	2010/11	-	-	1 000	1 857	6	438	-	-	-	3 301	3 547	6 848	24 135
	2011/12	-	-	-	3 230	244	326	-	-	-	3 799	4 022	7 821	..
Montenegro	2007/08	-	-	-	-	-	-	-	-	-	-	143	143	4 019
	2008/09	-	-	-	-	-	-	-	-	-	-	407	407	2 665
	2009/10	-	-	-	-	-	-	-	-	-	-	292	292	3 887
	2010/11	-	-	-	-	-	-	-	-	-	-	135	135	4 817
	2011/12	-	-	-	-	-	-	-	-	-	-	333	333	..
States of ex	2007/08	-	-	-	-	-	-	-	-	-	-	-	-	729
Yugoslavia	2008/09	-	-	-	-	-	-	-	-	-	-	-	-	23
	2009/10	-	-	-	-	-	-	-	-	-	-	-	-	-
	2010/11	-	-	-	-	-	-	-	-	-	-	-	-	233
	2011/12	-	-	-	-	-	-	-	-	-	-	-	-	..

3.2d Total DFID Expenditure and GPEX by Recipient Country (Europe) 2007/08 - 2011/12 [1]

£ thousand

| | year | Financial Aid | | | Technical Cooperation | Bilateral aid delivered through a Multilateral | Bilateral aid Delivered through an NGO | Other Bilateral Aid [2] | Humanitarian Assistance | DFID Debt Relief | Total DFID Bilateral Programme | Aid from other UK Official Sources [5] | Total Bilateral Gross Public Expenditure | UK Imputed Multilateral Shares [3] |
		General Poverty Reduction Budget Support	Sector Poverty Reduction Budget Support	Other Financial Aid [5]										
Turkey	2007/08	-	-	444	-	-	-	-	-	-	444	882	1 326	46 747
	2008/09	-	-	105	-	-	-	-	-	-	105	2 859	2 964	155 971
	2009/10	-	-	-	-	-	-	-	-	-	-	1 743	1 743	63 260
	2010/11	-	-	-	-	-	-	-	-	-	-	2 429	2 429	95 661
	2011/12	-	-	-	-	-	-	-	425	-	425	5 302	5 727	..
Ukraine	2007/08	-	-	-	2 739	334	13	-	-	-	3 086	350	3 436	18 086
	2008/09	-	-	-	153	-	126	-	-	-	279	608	887	14 088
	2009/10	-	-	-	-	-	34	-	-	-	34	1 633	1 667	20 939
	2010/11	-	-	-	-	-	9	-	-	-	9	543	552	22 349
	2011/12	-	-	-	-	-	18	-	-	-	18	1 359	1 377	..
Balkan Regional	2007/08	-	-	-	446	2 000	289	-	-	-	2 735	1 365	4 100	-
	2008/09	-	-	-	371	2 847	178	-	-	-	3 397	7 483	10 880	-
	2009/10	-	-	-	300	1 650	-	-	-	-	1 950	122	2 071	-
	2010/11	-	-	-	20	2 497	-	-	-	-	2 517	91	2 608	-
	2011/12	-	-	-	-	-	-	-	-	-	-	-	-	..
Europe regional	2007/08	-	-	-	1 520	773	2 236	-	82	-	4 612	724	5 336	27 573
	2008/09	-	-	-	1 764	1 462	269	-	-	-	3 495	-	3 495	27 515
	2009/10	-	-	-	1 156	2 142	179	2	49	-	3 527	1 970	5 497	46 480
	2010/11	-	-	1	-	60	-	13	-	-	74	-	74	56 887
	2011/12	-	-	-	-	-	-	14	-	-	14	121	135	..
Total Europe	2007/08	-	-	1 794	19 330	5 375	3 493	2	663	342	30 998	8 498	39 496	184 495
	2008/09	-	-	2 853	15 855	8 662	1 490	-	3 199	1 821	33 880	19 404	53 284	323 966
	2009/10	-	3 500	1 076	7 522	5 949	1 346	2	1 161	297	20 853	24 321	45 174	286 505
	2010/11	-	2 500	2 239	7 030	4 703	937	68	26	365	17 868	16 335	34 203	376 737
	2011/12	-	-		3 230	244	344	-14	425	378	4 607	21 385	25 992	..

1. Descriptions of aid types given in Section 2.
2. Other Bilateral Aid covers bilateral aid not elsewhere classified.
3. Details on DFID Imputed Multilateral Shares are in Section 2; 2011/12 data are not yet available.
4. Low Income Country. Income groups are classified using 2010 GNI per capita thresholds
5. Pension payments have been reclassified from "Other Financial Aid" to "Aid from other UK Official Sources". This is consistent with the classification of spending under Department Expenditure Limits (DEL) agreed with Treasury.

3.2e Total DFID Expenditure and GPEX by Recipient Country (Pacific) 2007/08 - 2011/12 [1]

£ thousand

		Financial Aid												
		General Poverty Reduction Budget Support	Sector Poverty Reduction Budget Support	Other Financial Aid [5]	Technical Cooperation	Bilateral aid delivered through a Multilateral	Bilateral aid Delivered through an NGO	Other Bilateral Aid [2]	Humanitarian Assistance	DFID Debt Relief	Total DFID Bilateral Programme	Aid from other UK Official Sources [5]	Total Bilateral Gross Public Expenditure	UK Imputed Multilateral Shares [3]
Cook Islands	2007/08	-	-	-	-	-	-	-	-	-	-	-	-	96
	2008/09	-	-	-	-	-	-	-	-	-	-	-	-	35
	2009/10	-	-	-	-	-	-	-	-	-	-	-	-	113
	2010/11	-	-	-	-	-	-	-	-	-	-	-	-	53
	2011/12	-	-	-	-	-	-	-	-	-	-	..	..	..
Fiji	2007/08	-	-	-	-	-	-	-	-	-	-	315	315	925
	2008/09	-	-	-	-	-	-	-	-	-	-	409	409	2 165
	2009/10	-	-	-	-	-	-	-	-	-	-	373	373	609
	2010/11	-	-	-	-	-	-	-	-	-	-	243	243	1 992
	2011/12	-	-	-	-	-	-	-	-	-	-	231	231	..
Kiribati	2007/08	-	-	-	-	-	-	-	-	-	-	20	20	212
	2008/09	-	-	-	-	-	-	-	-	-	-	18	18	72
	2009/10	-	-	-	-	-	-	-	-	-	-	22	22	629
	2010/11	-	-	-	-	-	-	-	-	-	-	36	36	708
	2011/12	-	-	-	-	-	-	-	-	-	-	16	16	..
Marshall Islands	2007/08	-	-	-	-	-	-	-	-	-	-	-	-	174
	2008/09	-	-	-	-	-	-	-	-	-	-	-	-	39
	2009/10	-	-	-	-	-	-	-	-	-	-	-	-	536
	2010/11	-	-	-	-	-	-	-	-	-	-	-	-	128
	2011/12	-	-	-	-	-	-	-	-	-	-	11	11	..
Micronesia, Federal States	2007/08	-	-	-	-	-	-	-	-	-	-	-	-	204
	2008/09	-	-	-	-	-	-	-	-	-	-	-	-	58
	2009/10	-	-	-	-	-	-	-	-	-	-	-	-	887
	2010/11	-	-	-	-	-	-	-	-	-	-	-	-	..
	2011/12	-	-	-	-	-	-	-	-	-	-	-	-	..
Nauru	2007/08	-	-	-	-	-	-	-	-	-	-	-	-	74
	2008/09	-	-	-	-	-	-	-	-	-	-	-	-	16
	2009/10	-	-	-	-	-	-	-	-	-	-	-	-	300
	2010/11	-	-	-	-	-	-	-	-	-	-	8	8	..
	2011/12	-	-	-	-	-	-	-	-	-	-	-	-	..
Niue	2007/08	-	-	-	-	-	-	-	-	-	-	-	-	3
	2008/09	-	-	-	-	-	-	-	-	-	-	-	-	-
	2009/10	-	-	-	-	-	-	-	-	-	-	-	-	402
	2010/11	-	-	-	-	-	-	-	-	-	-	-	-	3
	2011/12	-	-	-	-	-	-	-	-	-	-	-	-	..
Palau	2007/08	-	-	-	-	-	-	-	-	-	-	-	-	87
	2008/09	-	-	-	-	-	-	-	-	-	-	55	55	20
	2009/10	-	-	-	-	-	-	-	-	-	-	-	-	296
	2010/11	-	-	-	-	-	-	-	-	-	-	12	12	..
	2011/12	-	-	-	-	-	-	-	-	-	-	-	-	..
Papua New Guinea [4]	2007/08	-	-	-	-	-	322	-	-	-	-	322	561	883	8 645
	2008/09	-	-	-	-	-	279	-	-	-	-	279	302	582	2 550
	2009/10	-	-	-	-	-	97	-	-	-	-	97	431	528	3 346
	2010/11	-	-	-	-	-	-	-	-	-	-	-	814	814	9 731
	2011/12	-	-	-	-	-	-	-	-	-	-	-	301	301	..
Pitcairn Islands	2007/08	-	-	1 125	92	-	242	-	-	-	-	1 460	3	1 462	-
	2008/09	-	-	1 821	219	-	75	-	-	-	-	2 115	1	2 116	-
	2009/10	-	-	1 745	3	-	42	-	-	-	-	1 790	-	1 790	..
	2010/11	-	-	2 235	212	-	-	-	-	-	-	2 447	39	2 486	..
	2011/12	-	-	2 738	36	-	-	-	-	-	-	2 774	-	2 774	..
Samoa [4]	2007/08	-	-	-	-	-	-	-	-	-	-	-	-	-	648
	2008/09	-	-	-	-	-	-	-	-	111	111	-	111	573
	2009/10	-	-	-	-	-	-	-	100	115	215	-	215	2 065
	2010/11	-	-	-	-	-	-	-	-	150	150	-	150	3 806
	2011/12	-	-	-	-	-	-	-	-	170	170	85	254	..
Solomon Islands [4]	2007/08	-	-	-	-	-	-	-	-	-	-	-	134	134	1 467
	2008/09	-	-	-	-	-	-	-	-	-	-	-	137	137	253
	2009/10	-	-	-	-	-	-	-	-	-	-	-	146	146	1 316
	2010/11	-	-	-	-	-	-	-	-	-	-	-	144	144	3 793
	2011/12	-	-	-	-	-	-	-	-	-	-	-	139	139	..
Tokelau	2007/08	-	-	-	-	-	-	-	-	-	-	-	-	-
	2008/09	-	-	-	-	-	-	-	-	-	-	-	-	-
	2009/10	-	-	-	-	-	-	-	-	-	-	-	-	14
	2010/11	-	-	-	-	-	-	-	-	-	-	-	-	9
	2011/12	-	-	-	-	-	-	-	-	-	-	-	-	..
Tonga	2007/08	-	-	-	-	-	-	-	-	-	-	-	-	330
	2008/09	-	-	-	-	-	-	-	-	-	-	277	277	251
	2009/10	-	-	-	-	-	-	-	-	-	-	6	6	214
	2010/11	-	-	-	-	-	-	-	-	-	-	99	99	1 462
	2011/12	-	-	-	-	-	-	-	-	-	-	34	34	..
Tuvalu	2007/08	-	-	-	-	-	-	-	-	-	-	-	-	67
	2008/09	-	-	-	-	-	-	-	-	-	-	-	-	47
	2009/10	-	-	-	-	-	-	-	-	-	-	-	-	548
	2010/11	-	-	-	-	-	-	-	-	-	-	28	28	219
	2011/12	-	-	-	-	-	-	-	-	-	-	51	51	..
Vanuatu [4]	2007/08	-	-	-	-	-	-	-	-	-	-	19	19	497
	2008/09	-	-	-	-	-	-	-	-	33	33	18	51	112
	2009/10	-	-	-	-	-	-	-	-	40	40	22	62	1 070
	2010/11	-	-	-	-	-	-	-	-	42	42	17	58	60
	2011/12	-	-	-	-	-	-	-	-	42	42	31	73	..
Wallis & Fortuna	2007/08	-	-	-	-	-	-	-	-	-	-	-	-	1 574
	2008/09	-	-	-	-	-	-	-	-	-	-	-	-	-
	2009/10	-	-	-	-	-	-	-	-	-	-	-	-	-
	2010/11	-	-	-	-	-	-	-	-	-	-	-	-	-
	2011/12	-	-	-	-	-	-	-	-	-	-	-	-	..

3.2e Total DFID Expenditure and GPEX by Recipient Country (Pacific) 2007/08 - 2011/12[1]

£ thousand

		General Poverty Reduction Budget Support	Sector Poverty Reduction Budget Support	Other Financial Aid [5]	Technical Cooperation	Bilateral aid delivered through a Multilateral	Bilateral aid Delivered through an NGO	Other Bilateral Aid [2]	Humanitarian Assistance	DFID Debt Relief	Total DFID Bilateral Programme	Aid from other UK Official Sources [5]	Total Bilateral Gross Public Expenditure	UK Imputed Multilateral Shares [3]
			Financial Aid											
South Pacific Regional	2007/08	-	-	-	7	-	-	-	-	-	7	-	7	-
	2008/09	-	-	-	156	-	95	-	-	-	251	-	251	-
	2009/10	-	-	-	-	-	-	-	-	-	-	-	-	-
	2010/11	-	-	-	-	-	-	-	-	-	-	-	-	-
	2011/12	-	-	-	-	-	-	-	-	-	-	60	60	..
Oceania Regional	2007/08	-	-	-	-	-	-	-	-	-	-	3	3	3 990
	2008/09	-	-	-	-	-	-	-	-	-	-	-	-	475
	2009/10	-	-	-	-	-	-	-	-	-	-	-	-	3 535
	2010/11	-	-	-	-	-	-	-	-	-	-	103	103	7 391
	2011/12	-	-	-	-	-	-	-	-	-	-	101	101	..
Total Pacific	2007/08	-	-	1 125	99	-	564	-	-	-	1 788	1 054	2 842	18 993
	2008/09	-	-	1 821	375	-	449	-	-	144	2 790	1 217	4 007	6 666
	2009/10	-	-	1 745	3	-	139	-	100	155	2 142	1 001	3 142	15 882
	2010/11	-	-	2 235	212	-	-	-	-	191	2 638	1 542	4 180	29 355
	2011/12	-	-	2 738	36	-	-	-	-	212	2 986	1 060	4 046	..

1. Descriptions of aid types given in Section 2.
2. Other Bilateral Aid covers bilateral aid not elsewhere classified
3. Details on DFID Imputed Multilateral Shares are in Section 2; 2011/12 data are not yet available.
4. Low Income Country. Income groups are classified using 2010 GNI per capita thresholds.
5. Pension payments have been reclassified from "Other Financial Aid" to "Aid from other UK Official Sources". This is consistent with the classification of spending under Department Expenditure Limits (DEL) agreed with Treasury.

3.3 DFID Bilateral Expenditure by Input Sector Code 2007/08 to 2011/12

£ thousand

Input Sector Code	2007/08	2008/09	2009/10	2010/11	2011/12
Education:					
11010 Education Poverty Reduction Budget Support	100 605	105 319	155 629	152 581	90,301
11020 Education Unallocable/Unspecified	-	281	1 489	8 718	51,403
11110 Education Policy and Administrative Management	78 577	63 585	53 549	68 527	122,537
11120 Facilities and Training Education	31 945	43 243	34 929	31 044	44,756
11130 Teacher Training	2 338	9 891	14 135	17 775	15,879
11220 Primary Education	113 980	179 650	111 045	210 797	231,124
11230 Basic Life Skills for Youth and Adults Education	8 612	11 248	3 749	10 933	11,426
11240 Pre-School	1 383	1 164	4 717	4 337	3,717
11320 Secondary Education	22 207	11 784	8 040	27 059	28,089
11330 Vocational Training	587	4 411	4 820	8 588	6,609
11420 Higher Education	1 323	20 075	2 677	20 237	19,267
11430 Advanced Technical and Managerial Training	46	323	269	312	281
Education Total	**361 603**	**450 973**	**395 049**	**560 907**	**625 389**
Health:					
12010 Health Poverty Reduction Budget Support	111 499	105 679	111 811	100 327	57,306
12020 Health Unallocable/Unspecified	-	1 827	2 585	3 712	13,504
12110 Health Policy and Administrative Management	42 888	48 784	46 829	58 667	43,590
12220 Basic Health Care	75 595	99 652	91 566	74 650	105,712
12240 Basic Nutrition	9 486	12 927	19 365	23 715	37,505
12250 Infectious Disease Control	99 722	69 169	61 487	73 853	146,612
12261 Health Education	16 297	19 842	19 919	26 392	31,717
12262 Malaria Control	-	35 060	42 295	101 393	86,181
12263 Tuberculosis Control	-	12 802	13 577	44 187	10,051
12281 Health Personnel Development	8 709	10 918	10 368	7 773	12,295
13010 Population Policy and Administrative Management	2 843	2 619	2 949	7 092	6,063
13021 Reproductive Health Care	18 621	36 466	43 196	47 962	108,852
13022 Maternal and Neonatal Health	34 394	61 645	49 376	49 987	121,362
13030 Family Planning	-	8 075	15 252	31 082	43,767
13041 HIV/AIDS including STD Prevention	134 229	147 863	122 036	119 094	69,002
13042 HIV/AIDS including STD Treatment and Care	-	10 113	24 002	52 717	27,331
13081 Personnel Development for Population and Reproductive Health	-	1 490	6 676	7 506	8,332
Health Total	**554 284**	**684 931**	**683 289**	**830 109**	**929 182**
Social Infrastructure and Services:					
16011 Social Protection	45 458	68 656	156 911	186 531	103,647
16012 Social Other	33 841	22 893	27 923	48 714	83,879
16020 Employment Policy & Admin Management	-	150	623	2 956	2,924
16030 Housing Policy and Admin Management	5 463	2 764	623	73	594
16040 Low-cost Housing	-	564	2 226	1 706	5,693
16070 Poverty Reduction Budget Support-Social infrastructure and services	16 250	18 647	23 319	18 273	12,940
52010 Food Aid and Food Security Programmes	35 830	51 148	26 468	52 145	50,622
Social Infrastructure and Services Total	**136 842**	**164 822**	**238 093**	**310 396**	**260 300**
Water Supply and Sanitation:					
14010 Water Resources Policy and Administrative Management	13 359	7 484	20 611	14 317	20,655
14015 Water Resources Protection	-	384	1 323	2 335	5,216
14020 Water Supply and Sanitation Large Systems	50	4 415	3 081	4 869	9,175
14021 Water Supply – Large Systems	-	-	54	4 039	5,100
14030 Basic Drinking Water	47 585	59 799	55 820	63 219	73,031
14031 Basic drinking water supply	-	-	72	964	891
14032 Basic sanitation	-	-	88	1 466	7,605
14040 River Development	17	1 359	5 439	3 688	1,360
14050 Waste Management and Disposal	-	110	2 900	2 669	2,519
14060 Water Poverty Reduction Budget Support	10 610	13 325	15 556	13 271	8,255
14070 Water Unallocable/Unspecified	-	484	718	868	6,976
14081 Education and Training	8	1 108	250	354	1,408
Water Supply and Sanitation Total	**71 629**	**88 467**	**105 912**	**112 061**	**142 191**
Government and Civil Society:					
15010 Government Poverty Reduction Budget Support	75 895	111 246	137 078	115 004	58,494
15020 Government Unallocated/ Unspecified	-	11 017	26 082	52 166	37,876
15110 Economic and Development Policy/Planning	200 057	135 931	114 791	121 076	90,314
15121 Public Sector Financial Management	127 843	118 112	113 514	105 996	132,449
15122 Corruption - Public Sector Financial Management	370	7 908	13 182	17 719	18,010
15130 Legal and Judicial Development	18 025	19 147	18 469	17 351	18,158

3.3 DFID Bilateral Expenditure by Input Sector Code 2007/08 to 2011/12

£ thousand

Input Sector Code	2007/08	2008/09	2009/10	2010/11	2011/12
15141 National Government Administration	14 368	21 657	16 791	30 876	33,736
15142 Local Government Administration	32 943	36 803	42 417	36 266	57,607
15150 Strengthening Civil Society	153 268	172 757	89 251	116 792	121,683
15161 Elections	21 680	30 456	18 539	33 880	28,920
15162 Human Rights	12 308	11 591	9 084	10 688	10,284
15163 Free Flow of Information	25	2 956	7 419	9 997	10,144
15164 Women's Equality Organisations and Institutions	-	3 748	6 138	12 306	11,742
15171 Culture and Recreation	-	-	143	82	
15172 Statistical Capacity Building	18 147	12 262	27 935	40 395	31,102
15173 Narcotics Control	30	-	46	53	24
15210 Security System Management and Reform	14 430	13 050	13 338	19 285	27,065
15220 Civilian Peace-Building, Conflict Prevention and Resolution	66 941	61 327	39 409	20 497	21,597
15230 Post-Conflict Peace-Building (UN)	-	2 627	5 689	6 520	5,719
15240 Reintegration and SALW Control	-	1 343	6 377	4 683	754
15250 Land Mine Clearance	8 401	16 444	9 907	9 902	11,720
15261 Child Soldiers (Prevention and Demobilisation)	-	375	261	141	159
Government and Civil Society Total	**764 733**	**790 756**	**715 860**	**781 674**	**727 557**
Economic:					
Economic Infrastructure					
21010 Transport Policy and Administrative Management	28 675	37 973	39 007	65 697	42,208
21021 Road Transport: Excluding Rural Feeder Roads	-	623	36 408	37 096	26,548
21022 Road Transport: Rural Feeder Roads	-	9 868	8 745	15 224	17,222
21031 Other Transport	69	12 295	12 832	5 755	22,965
22010 Communications Policy and Administrative Management	11 009	8 190	8 150	6 065	1,680
22020 Telecommunications	-	73	9 439	8 596	8,892
22030 Radio/Television/Print Media: Communications	-	788	1 872	64	38
22040 Information and Communication Technology (ICT)	-	28	519	2 055	655
23010 Energy Policy and Administrative Management	28 015	22 815	23 993	35 208	12,887
23020 Power Generation/Non-Renewable Sources: Energy	-	23	7 439	11 809	9,760
23030 Power Generation/Renewable Sources: Energy	-	5 023	23 513	30 633	3,956
24010 Financial Policy and Administrative Management	93 991	30 268	24 223	26 098	27,913
24020 Monetary Institutions	-	1 593	205 870	1 319	3,111
24030 Formal Sector Financial Intermediaries	-	4 528	6 239	10 968	12,825
24040 Informal/Semi-Formal Financial Intermediaries	-	4 105	6 250	7 449	6,764
24081 Education/Training in Banking and Financial Services	-	1 297	2 382	2 471	4,877
25010 Business Support Services and Institutions	28	2 912	16 947	29 087	25,071
25020 Privatisation	26 399	17 009	5 765	7 896	5,479
Production Sectors					
31110 Agriculture Policy and Administrative Management	22 739	27 519	43 937	38 879	34,080
31120 Agricultural Development	4 755	18 122	26 089	18 023	37,625
31130 Agricultural Land Resources	19 996	11 972	7 555	11 033	4,115
31163 Livestock: Agriculture	3 108	4 914	3 231	2 281	2,895
31191 Agricultural Services	-	82	1 287	865	2,766
31210 Forestry Policy and Administrative Management	2 423	10 901	16 583	30 650	4,910
31220 Forestry Development	4 930	10 962	15 320	28 989	4,351
31310 Fishing Policy and Administrative Management	1 329	1 025	2 368	3 046	1,838
31320 Fishery Development	543	330	201	265	0
32110 Industrial Policy and Administrative Management	-	45	548	1 068	1,632
32120 Industrial Development	945	126	934	2 034	2,816
32130 Small and Medium-Sized Enterprises (SME): Development	31 006	31 730	24 765	30 011	25,575
32210 Mineral/Mining Policy and Administrative Management	2 775	1 101	679	369	8,663
32310 Construction Policy and Administrative Management	2 653	101	105	939	2,503
32350 Production Poverty Reduction Budget Support	32 718	34 501	34 237	30 984	18,803
33110 Trade Policy and Administrative Management	31 299	35 267	34 430	30 713	19,204
33120 Trade Facilitation	-	4 015	29 745	40 024	11,613
33130 Regional Trade Agreements (RTAs)	-	160	3 865	6 792	4,191
33140 Multilateral Trade Negotiations	-	1 982	741	120	273
33181 Trade Education/Training	-	31	360	613	838
33210 Tourism Policy and Administrative Management	-	13	829	1 272	2,215
43050 Non-Agricultural Alternative Development	252	211	550	818	1,692
Development Planning					
43020 Poverty Reduction Budget Support for Econ. Infrastructure & Dev. Planning	71 286	83 370	108 985	67 825	42,162
43030 Urban Development and Management	25 371	28 476	16 626	30 362	19,907
43040 Rural Development	48 633	55 536	51 502	68 083	55,302
Economic Total	**494 945**	**526 925**	**865 063**	**749 546**	**542 821**

3.3 DFID Bilateral Expenditure by Input Sector Code 2007/08 to 2011/12

£ thousand

Input Sector Code	2007/08	2008/09	2009/10	2010/11	2011/12
Environment Protection:					
41010 Environmental Policy and Administrative Management	11 192	11 587	15 071	16 512	9,506
41031 Bio-Diversity	206	1 533	1 869	198	3,264
41032 Climate Change	6 914	30 043	54 926	2 191	30,997
41033 Desertification	431	108	624	101 790	
41040 Site Preservation	-	10	15	242	
41050 Flood Prevention/Control	-	472	188	22	898
41060 Environment: Poverty Reduction Budget Support	1 275	2 990	3 359	377	1,418
41070 Environment Unallocable/Unspecified	-	217	38	1 846	3,104
41081 Environmental Education/ Training	17 720	4 737	1 804	1 905	2,591
41090 Climate Change - Low Carbon Emissions					55,772
41092 Climate Change - Cross Cutting					2,811
41093 Climate Change - Adaptation					99,048
74010 Disaster Prevention and Preparedness	-	8 838	21 450	10 142	7,896
Environment Protection Total	**37 738**	**60 536**	**99 344**	**135 226**	**217 304**
Research:					
80010 Economic Research	8 016	12 182	9 784	12 651	16,350
80011 Education Research	2 012	3 549	3 076	1 775	2,884
80012 Health Research	47 985	48 900	66 816	46 997	49,312
80013 Water Supply and Sanitation Research	66	1 622	908	2 064	1,502
80014 Governance Research	4 120	17 247	9 923	6 825	11,836
80015 Social Research	9 231	10 774	11 529	12 257	8,327
80016 Humanitarian Research	601	772	939	1 185	1,163
80017 Renewable Natural Resources Research	26 827	29 978	20 000	7 603	6,139
80018 Environment Research	5 858	4 538	5 044	6 883	8,968
80019 Energy Research	-	26	17	817	1,037
80020 Agricultural Research	-	3 141	11 397	19 624	22,073
80021 Forestry Research	-	17	403	269	54
80022 Fishery Research	-		70	169	
80023 Technological Research and Development	549	3 284	2 436	1 541	1,210
80024 Unspecified/Unallocated Research	-	3 191	3 983	7 442	9,253
Research Total	**105 264**	**139 222**	**146 325**	**128 103**	**140 109**
Humanitarian Assistance:					
72010 Material Relief Assistance and Services	302 165	174 831	232 635	198 368	157,678
72040 Emergency Food Aid	11 591	80 354	96 986	68 862	106,548
72050 Relief Coordination, Protection and Support Services	169	46 535	56 769	61 763	38,336
73010 Reconstruction Relief and Rehabilitation	823	15 674	50 861	27 996	47,043
Humanitarian Assistance Total	**314 749**	**317 395**	**437 250**	**356 989**	**349 604**
Non Sector Allocable:					
11110 Education policy and administrative management					
15220 Civilian peace-building, conflict preventiona and resolution					
74010 Disaster prevention and preparedness					
10000 DFID Administrative Costs	-	-	-	220	
88889 Multilateral Capacity Building and Administration	-	1 893	27 836	17 850	42,463
88890 Multilateral Institutions: Secondees to & Staffing of	-	485	1 163	1,838	4,673
60010 Action Relating to Debt	86 025	19 619	50 992	66 483	15,110
90010 Programme Partnership Agreements	-		129 557	116 100	91,508
91010 Administrative Costs of Donors	53	902	559	1 236	
92000 Support to Non-Governmental Organisations (NGOs)	-	1 784	36 422	50 815	101,785
93020 Aid to Refugees in Recipient Countries	25 281	19 479	2 348	9 164	2,344
88888 Multilateral Core Contribution					
99820 Promotion of Development Awareness	2 453	15 279	28 372	19 300	11,775
Others					
Non Sector Allocable Total	**113 812**	**59 440**	**277 249**	**283 006**	**269 658**

1. '-' means nil
   '0' means less than half the final digit shown
   '..' means not available
   'n/a' means not applicable
2. Figures are rounded to the nearest unit, therefore they may not add exactly to the rounded totals.
3. Negative amounts reflect accounting adjustments.

Labour market

Chapter 4

Labour Market

Labour Force Survey

Background

The Labour Force Survey (LFS) is the largest regular household survey in the UK. LFS interviews are conducted continuously throughout the year. In any three-month period, nationally representative samples of approximately 110,000 people aged 16 and over in around 50,000 households are interviewed. Each household is interviewed five times, at three-monthly intervals. The initial interview is done face-to-face by an interviewer visiting the address, except for residents north of the Caledonian Canal in Scotland. The other interviews are done by telephone wherever possible. The survey asks a series of questions about respondents' personal circumstances and their labour market activity. Most questions refer to activity in the week before the interview.

The LFS collects information on a sample of the population. To convert this information to give estimates for the population, the data must be grossed. This is achieved by calculating weighting factors (often referred to simply as weights) which can be applied to each sampled individual in such a way that the weighted-up results match estimates or projections of the total population in terms of age distribution, sex, and region of residence. There is a considerable amount of ongoing research to improve methodologies. Whenever methodologies are implemented the estimates may be revised.

The concepts and definitions used in the LFS are agreed by the International Labour Organisation (ILO) – an agency of the United Nations. The definitions are used by European Union member countries and members of the Organisation for Economic Co-operation and Development (OECD). The LFS was carried out every two years from 1973 to 1983. The ILO definition was first used in 1984. This was also the first year in which the survey was conducted on an annual basis with results available for every spring quarter (representing an average of the period from March to May). The survey moved to a continuous basis in spring 1992 in Great Britain and in winter 1994/95 in Northern Ireland, with average quarterly results published four times a year for seasonal quarters: spring (March to May), summer (June to August), autumn (September to November) and winter (December to February). From April 1998, results are published 12 times a year for the average of three consecutive months.

Strengths and limitations of the LFS

The LFS produces coherent labour market information on the basis of internationally standard concepts and definitions. It is a rich source of data on a wide variety of labour market and personal characteristics. It is the most suitable source for making comparisons between countries. The LFS is designed so that households interviewed in each three month period constitute a representative sample of UK households. The survey covers those living in private households and nurses in

National Health Service accommodation. Students living in halls of residence have been included since 1992, as information about them is collected at their parents' address.

However the LFS has its limitations. It is a sample survey and is therefore subject to sampling variability. The survey does not include people living in institutions such as hostels, hotels, boarding houses, mobile home sites or residential homes. 'Proxy' reporting (when members of the household are not present at the interview, another member of the household answers the questions on their behalf) can affect the quality of information on topics such as earnings, hours worked, benefit receipt and qualifications. Around a third of interviews are conducted 'by proxy', usually by a spouse or partner but sometimes by a parent or other near relation. LFS estimates are also potentially affected by non-response.

Sampling Variability

Survey estimates are prone to sampling variability. The easiest way to explain this concept is by example. In the September to November 1997 period, ILO unemployment in Great Britain (seasonally adjusted) stood at 1,847,000. If we drew another sample for the same period we could get a different result, perhaps 1,900,000 or 1,820,000.

In theory, we could draw many samples, and each would give a different result. This is because each sample would be made up of different people who would give different answers to the questions. The spread of these results is the sampling variability. Sampling variability is determined by a number of factors including the sample size, the variability of the population from which the sample is drawn and the sample design. Once we know the sampling variability we can calculate a range of values about the sample estimate that represents the expected variation with a given level of assurance. This is called a confidence interval. For a 95 per cent confidence interval we expect that in 95 per cent of the samples (19 times out of 20) the confidence interval will contain the true value that would be obtained by surveying the entire population. For the example given above, we can be 95 per cent confident that the true value was in the range 1,791,000 to 1,903,000.

Unreliable estimates

Estimates of small numbers have relatively wide confidence intervals making them unreliable. For this reason, the Office for National Statistics (ONS) does not currently publish LFS estimates below 10,000.

Non-response

All surveys are subject to non-response – that is respondents in the sample who either refuse to take part in the survey or who cannot be contacted. Non-response can introduce bias to a survey, particularly if the people not responding have characteristics that are different from those who do respond.

The LFS has a response rate of around 65 per cent to the first interview, and over 90 per cent of those who are interviewed once go on to complete all five interviews. These are relatively high levels for a household survey.

Any bias from non-response is minimised by weighting the results. Weighting (or grossing) converts sample data to represent the full population. In the LFS, the data are weighted separately by age, sex and area of residence to population estimates based on the census. Weighting also adjusts for people not in the survey and thus minimises non-response bias.

LFS concepts and definitions

Discouraged worker - A sub-group of the economically inactive population who said although they would like a job their main reason for not seeking work was because they believed there were no jobs available.

Economically active – People aged 16 and over who are either in employment or unemployed.

Economic activity rate – The number of people who are in employment or unemployed expressed as a percentage of the relevant population.

Economically inactive – People who are neither in employment nor unemployed. These include those who want a job but have not been seeking work in the last four weeks, those who want a job and are seeking work but not available to start, and those who do not want a job.

Employment – People aged 16 and over who did at least one hour of paid work in the reference week (as an employee or self-employed), those who had a job that they were temporarily away from, those on government-supported training and employment programmes, and those doing unpaid family work.

Employees – The division between employees and self employed is based on survey respondents' own assessment of their employment status.

Full Time – The classification of employees, self-employed and unpaid family workers in their main job as full-time or part-time is on the basis of self-assessment. However, people on government supported employment and training programmes that are at college in the reference week are classified, by convention, as part-time.

Government -supported training and employment programmes – Comprise all people aged 16 and over participating in one of the government's employment and training programmes (Youth Training, Training for Work and Community Action), together with those on similar programmes administered by Training and Enterprise Councils in England and Wales, or Local Enterprise Companies in Scotland.

Hours worked – Respondents to the LFS are asked a series of questions enabling the identification of both their usual hours and their actual hours. Total hours include overtime (paid and unpaid) and exclude lunch breaks.

Actual Hours Worked – Actual hours worked statistics measure how many hours were actually worked. These statistics are directly affected by changes in the number of people in employment and in the number of hours that individual works.

Usual Hours Worked – Usual hours worked statistics measure how many hours people usually work per week. Compared with actual hours worked, they are not affected by absences and so can provide a better measure of normal working patterns.

Unemployment – The number of unemployed people in the UK is measured through the LFS following the internationally agreed definition recommended by the International Labour Organisation (ILO), an agency of the United Nations.

Unemployed people are:

Without a job, have actively sought work in the last four weeks and are available to start work in the next two weeks, or

Out of work, have found a job and are waiting to start in the next two weeks

Unemployment (rate) – The number of unemployed people expressed as a percentage of the relevant economically active population.

Unemployment (duration) – The duration of respondents unemployment is defined as the shorter of the following two periods:

Duration of active search for work

Length of time since employment

Part-time – see full-time.

Second jobs – Jobs which LFS respondents hold in addition to a main full-time or part-time job.

Self-employment – See Employees.

Temporary employees – In the LFS these are defined as those employees who say that their main job is non permanent in one of the following ways: fixed period contract, agency temping, casual work, seasonal work or other temporary work.

Unpaid family workers – Persons doing unpaid work for a business they own or for a business that a relative owns.

International Employment Comparisons

All employment rates for European Union (EU) countries published by Eurostat (including the rate for the UK) are based on the population aged 15–64. The rates for Canada and Japan are also based on the population aged 15–64, but the rate for the US is for those aged 16–64. The employment rate for the UK published by ONS is based on the working age population aged 16–64 (men) and 16–59 (women) and therefore takes into account both the current school leaving age and state pension ages.

The unemployment rate published by Eurostat for most EU countries (but not for the UK), are calculated by extrapolating from the most recent LFS data using monthly registered unemployment data. A standard population basis (15–74) is used by Eurostat except for Spain and the UK (16–74). The unemployment rate for the US is based on those aged 16 and over, but the rates for Canada and Japan are for those aged 15 and over. All unemployment rates are seasonally adjusted.

The unemployment rate for the UK published by Eurostat is based on the population aged 16–74 while the unemployment rate for the UK published by ONS is based on those aged 16 and over. There are other minor definitional differences.

Jobseekers allowance claimant count

This is a count of all those people who are claiming Jobseeker's Allowance (JSA) at Jobcentre Plus local offices. People claiming JSA must declare that they are:

- out of work
- capable of work
- available for work
- actively seeking work

during the week in which the claim is made.
All people claiming JSA on the day of the monthly count are included in the claimant count, irrespective of whether they are actually receiving benefits. Also see table 5.6 in Social protection chapter.

Annual Survey of Hours and Earnings

The Annual Survey of Hours and Earnings (ASHE) is based on a one per cent sample of employee jobs taken from HM Revenue & Customs (HMRC) PAYE records. Information on earnings and paid hours worked is obtained from employers and treated confidentially. ASHE does not cover the self-employed nor does it cover employees not paid during the reference period.

The headline statistics for ASHE are based on the median rather than the mean. The median is the value below which 50 per cent of employees fall. It is ONS's preferred measure of average earnings as it is less affected by a relatively small number of very high earners and the skewed distribution of earnings. It therefore gives a better indication of typical pay than the mean.

The earnings information presented relates to gross pay before tax, National Insurance or other deductions, and excludes payments in kind. With the exception of annual earnings, the results are restricted to earnings relating to the survey pay period and so exclude payments of arrears from another period made during the survey period; any payments due as a result of a pay settlement but not yet paid at the time of the survey will also be excluded.

More detailed information is available on the National Statistics web site at:

www.statistics.gov.uk/StatBase/Product.asp?vlnk=13101

Average Weekly Earnings

The Average Weekly Earnings (AWE) indicator measures changes in the level of earnings in Great Britain. Average earnings are calculated as the total wages and salaries paid by firms, divided by the number of employees paid. It is given as a level, in pounds per employee per week. Annual growth rates are derived from the level of average weekly earnings.

The AWE data are now published on a SIC 2007 basis, and the historic time series have been re-estimated as a result. For more information, see the article available at:

www.statistics.gov.uk/downloads/theme_labour/average-week-earnings-sic2007.pdf

AWE is based on the Monthly wages and Salaries Survey (MWSS). As such, it is a timely indicator of changes in the level of earnings. The survey does not cover businesses with fewer than 20 employees; an adjustment is made to AWE to reflect these businesses. Note that the survey does not include Northern Ireland.

Unlike the previous measure of average earnings (the Average Earnings Index), changes in the composition of the workforce have an impact on AWE. If a high-paying sector of the economy employs more people, other things staying the same, average earnings will increase.

Average Weekly Earnings, like AEI before it, is a measure based on earnings per employee. If the number of paid hours worked per employee change, average earnings will also change.

Trade unions

The statistics relate to all organisations of workers known to the Certification Officer with head offices in Great Britain that fall within the appropriate definition of a trade union in the Trade Union and Labour Relations (Consolidation) Act 1992. Included in the data are home and overseas membership figures of contributory and non-contributory members. Employment status of members is not provided and the figures may therefore include some people who are self-employed, unemployed or retired.

4.1 Labour Force Summary by Sex: United Kingdom

United Kingdom
(thousands) seasonally
adjusted

		LFS household population[1]		Headline indicators					
				Employment		Unemployment		Inactivity	
				Level	Rate[2]	Level	Rate[3]	Level	Rate[4]
		All aged 16 & over	All aged 16 to 64	All aged 16 & over	All aged 16 to 64	All aged 16 & over	All aged 16 & over	All aged 16 to 64	All aged 16 to 64
People		MGSL	LF2O	MGRZ	LF24	MGSC	MGSX	LF2M	LF2S
	Aug-Oct 2010	49,895	40,026	29,109	70.6	2,484	7.9	9,301	23.2
	Aug-Oct 2011	50,258	40,171	29,102	70.3	2,637	8.3	9,321	23.2
	Nov-Jan 2012	50,350	40,177	29,141	70.4	2,652	8.3	9,274	23.1
	Feb-Apr 2012	50,442	40,183	29,324	70.7	2,599	8.1	9,193	22.9
	May-Jul 2012	50,532	40,187	29,560	71.2	2,592	8.1	9,013	22.4
	Aug-Oct 2012	**50,625**	**40,204**	**29,601**	**71.2**	**2,510**	**7.8**	**9,072**	**22.6**
	Change on quarter	*92*	*17*	*40*	*0.1*	*-82*	*-0.2*	*60*	*0.1*
	Change %	*0.2*	*0.0*	*0.1*		*-3.2*		*0.7*	
	Change on year	*367*	*33*	*499*	*0.9*	*-128*	*-0.5*	*-249*	*-0.6*
	Change %	*0.7*	*0.1*	*1.7*		*-4.8*		*-2.7*	
Men		MGSM	YBTG	MGSA	MGSV	MGSD	MGSY	YBSO	YBTM
	Aug-Oct 2010	24,366	19,936	15,620	75.8	1,450	8.5	3,386	17.0
	Aug-Oct 2011	24,555	20,003	15,569	75.2	1,533	9.0	3,445	17.2
	Nov-Jan 2012	24,606	20,009	15,591	75.4	1,530	8.9	3,416	17.1
	Feb-Apr 2012	24,656	20,014	15,739	75.9	1,482	8.6	3,366	16.8
	May-Jul 2012	24,706	20,018	15,847	76.3	1,491	8.6	3,269	16.3
	Aug-Oct 2012	**24,757**	**20,029**	**15,901**	**76.5**	**1,430**	**8.3**	**3,299**	**16.5**
	Change on quarter	*50*	*11*	*54*	*0.2*	*-61*	*-0.3*	*30*	*0.1*
	Change %	*0.2*	*0.1*	*0.3*		*-4.1*		*0.9*	
	Change on year	*202*	*26*	*332*	*1.3*	*-103*	*-0.7*	*-146*	*-0.8*
	Change %	*0.8*	*0.1*	*2.1*		*-6.7*		*-4.2*	
Women		MGSN	LF2P	MGSB	LF25	MGSE	MGSZ	LF2N	LF2T
	Aug-Oct 2010	25,530	20,090	13,489	65.4	1,034	7.1	5,914	29.4
	Aug-Oct 2011	25,703	20,168	13,533	65.5	1,104	7.5	5,876	29.1
	Nov-Jan 2012	25,744	20,168	13,550	65.4	1,122	7.6	5,858	29.0
	Feb-Apr 2012	25,785	20,169	13,585	65.6	1,117	7.6	5,827	28.9
	May-Jul 2012	25,826	20,169	13,713	66.1	1,101	7.4	5,744	28.5
	Aug-Oct 2012	**25,868**	**20,175**	**13,700**	**66.1**	**1,080**	**7.3**	**5,773**	**28.6**
	Change on quarter	*42*	*6*	*-13*	*-0.1*	*-21*	*-0.1*	*29*	*0.1*
	Change %	*0.2*	*0.0*	*-0.1*		*-1.9*		*0.5*	
	Change on year	*165*	*7*	*166*	*0.6*	*-25*	*-0.2*	*-103*	*-0.5*
	Change %	*0.6*	*0.0*	*1.2*		*-2.2*		*-1.7*	

Source: Labour Force Survey
Labour market statistics enquiries: labour.market@ons.gov.uk

1. The Labour Force Survey (LFS) is a survey of the population of private households, student halls of residence and NHS accommodation.
2. The headline employment rate is the number of people aged 16 to 64 in employment divided by the population aged 16 to 64.
3. The headline unemployment rate is the number of unemployed people (aged 16+) divided by the economically active population (aged 16+). The economically active population is defined as those in employment plus those who are unemployed.
4. The headline inactivity rate is the number of economically inactive people aged 16 to 64 divided by the population aged 16 to 64.

Note on headline employment, unemployment and inactivity rates

The headline employment and inactivity rates are based on the population aged 16 to 64 but the headline unemployment rate is based on the economically active population aged 16 and over. The employment and inactivity rates for those aged 16 and over are affected by the inclusion of the retired population in the denominators and are therefore less meaningful than the rates for those aged from 16 to 64. However, for the unemployment rate for those aged 16 and over, no such effect occurs as the denominator for the unemployment rate is the economically active population which only includes people in work or actively seeking and able to work.

Note on headline employment, unemployment and inactivity levels

The headline employment and unemployment levels are for those aged 16 and over; they measure all people in work or actively seeking and able to work. However, the headline inactivity level is for those aged 16 to 64. The inactivity level for those aged 16 and over is less meaningful as it includes elderly people who have retired from the labour force.

4.2: Full-time, part-time and temporary workers

United Kingdom (thousands) seasonally adjusted

	All in employment					Full-time and part-time workers[1]						Total workers with second jobs
	Total	Employees	Self employed	Unpaid family workers	Government supported training & employment programmes[2]	Total people working full-time	Total people working part-time	Employees working full-time	Employees working part-time	Self-employed people working full-time	Self-employed people working part-time	
	1	2	3	4	5	6	7	8	9	10	11	12
All Persons	MGRZ	MGRN	MGRQ	MGRT	MGRW	YCBE	YCBH	YCBK	YCBN	YCBQ	YCBT	YCBW
Nov-Jan 2003	28,048	24,476	3,381	91	100	20,900	7,148	18,242	6,234	2,592	789	1,164
Dec-Feb 2003	28,024	24,431	3,402	88	103	20,844	7,181	18,172	6,259	2,607	795	1,135
Jan-Mar 2003	28,064	24,467	3,419	84	94	20,841	7,223	18,178	6,289	2,604	815	1,131
Feb-Apr 2003	28,105	24,449	3,478	87	91	20,844	7,262	18,141	6,308	2,643	836	1,135
Mar-May 2003	28,160	24,454	3,528	86	92	20,882	7,278	18,146	6,309	2,677	850	1,132
Apr-Jun 2003	28,188	24,457	3,551	88	92	20,918	7,269	18,138	6,319	2,718	833	1,108
May-Jul 2003	28,194	24,438	3,566	99	91	20,939	7,256	18,140	6,298	2,733	834	1,100
Jun-Aug 2003	28,187	24,374	3,611	101	102	20,913	7,275	18,066	6,308	2,773	837	1,103
Jul-Sep 2003	28,214	24,352	3,647	108	107	20,935	7,279	18,066	6,286	2,791	856	1,115
Aug-Oct 2003	28,243	24,381	3,656	101	105	20,944	7,300	18,070	6,311	2,796	860	1,113
Sep-Nov 2003	28,252	24,408	3,635	101	109	20,957	7,295	18,078	6,329	2,802	833	1,099
Oct-Dec 2003	28,264	24,420	3,638	99	107	20,945	7,319	18,065	6,355	2,804	834	1,111
Nov-Jan 2004	28,356	24,513	3,630	101	111	20,994	7,362	18,125	6,388	2,795	836	1,096
Dec-Feb 2004	28,394	24,559	3,622	107	107	21,004	7,391	18,147	6,412	2,787	835	1,105
Jan-Mar 2004	28,415	24,585	3,608	104	118	21,001	7,415	18,158	6,426	2,768	839	1,108
Feb-Apr 2004	28,404	24,553	3,622	108	122	21,011	7,393	18,144	6,409	2,791	831	1,103
Mar-May 2004	28,420	24,573	3,620	101	127	21,033	7,388	18,181	6,392	2,772	847	1,074
Apr-Jun 2004	28,425	24,539	3,665	97	123	21,061	7,364	18,159	6,380	2,821	844	1,070
May-Jul 2004	28,419	24,565	3,635	89	130	21,058	7,361	18,193	6,372	2,788	847	1,074
Jun-Aug 2004	28,433	24,587	3,627	87	132	21,073	7,360	18,205	6,383	2,788	839	1,075
Jul-Sep 2004	28,467	24,667	3,582	90	129	21,121	7,346	18,275	6,392	2,768	814	1,059
Aug-Oct 2004	28,491	24,651	3,616	94	130	21,175	7,316	18,294	6,358	2,801	814	1,045
Sep-Nov 2004	28,568	24,717	3,624	94	133	21,267	7,301	18,385	6,332	2,801	823	1,069
Oct-Dec 2004	28,615	24,777	3,615	97	125	21,314	7,301	18,446	6,331	2,790	825	1,054
Nov-Jan 2005	28,663	24,845	3,596	98	123	21,365	7,298	18,511	6,335	2,777	819	1,065
Dec-Feb 2005	28,727	24,883	3,612	105	127	21,441	7,286	18,569	6,314	2,792	820	1,063
Jan-Mar 2005	28,719	24,889	3,597	104	128	21,439	7,280	18,569	6,320	2,788	809	1,060
Feb-Apr 2005	28,687	24,860	3,602	103	122	21,400	7,287	18,528	6,332	2,791	812	1,064
Mar-May 2005	28,706	24,859	3,630	102	115	21,378	7,328	18,483	6,376	2,813	817	1,080
Apr-Jun 2005	28,726	24,904	3,609	99	114	21,392	7,334	18,510	6,394	2,800	809	1,075
May-Jul 2005	28,776	24,951	3,618	95	112	21,442	7,335	18,553	6,398	2,810	808	1,068
Jun-Aug 2005	28,826	25,003	3,629	85	108	21,515	7,310	18,641	6,361	2,803	826	1,063
Jul-Sep 2005	28,845	24,990	3,658	90	107	21,543	7,301	18,647	6,344	2,823	834	1,068
Aug-Oct 2005	28,827	24,995	3,637	92	103	21,541	7,285	18,665	6,329	2,805	832	1,059
Sep-Nov 2005	28,786	24,921	3,669	92	103	21,513	7,273	18,619	6,303	2,822	848	1,034
Oct-Dec 2005	28,788	24,915	3,674	90	110	21,533	7,255	18,635	6,279	2,824	849	1,028
Nov-Jan 2006	28,837	24,957	3,682	92	106	21,566	7,270	18,660	6,297	2,832	850	1,036
Dec-Feb 2006	28,889	25,002	3,704	88	96	21,582	7,307	18,673	6,329	2,841	863	1,044
Jan-Mar 2006	28,946	25,052	3,711	88	95	21,607	7,339	18,686	6,366	2,854	857	1,028
Feb-Apr 2006	28,982	25,077	3,727	84	93	21,658	7,324	18,728	6,349	2,863	863	1,031
Mar-May 2006	28,959	25,087	3,690	86	96	21,644	7,315	18,742	6,344	2,842	849	1,021
Apr-Jun 2006	28,999	25,115	3,699	91	94	21,641	7,358	18,736	6,379	2,843	856	1,044
May-Jul 2006	29,030	25,128	3,714	98	90	21,666	7,364	18,754	6,374	2,847	867	1,048
Jun-Aug 2006	29,110	25,182	3,736	105	87	21,717	7,394	18,781	6,401	2,869	867	1,056
Jul-Sep 2006	29,066	25,107	3,756	105	98	21,655	7,411	18,721	6,386	2,864	892	1,064
Aug-Oct 2006	29,072	25,090	3,783	98	102	21,601	7,472	18,656	6,434	2,877	905	1,063
Sep-Nov 2006	29,078	25,089	3,773	101	116	21,631	7,447	18,677	6,412	2,883	890	1,054
Oct-Dec 2006	29,089	25,107	3,774	102	106	21,634	7,455	18,684	6,423	2,884	891	1,075
Nov-Jan 2007	29,072	25,070	3,794	100	108	21,637	7,435	18,658	6,412	2,912	883	1,069
Dec-Feb 2007	29,045	25,039	3,801	99	106	21,632	7,413	18,656	6,383	2,909	892	1,073
Jan-Mar 2007	29,064	25,054	3,807	102	102	21,639	7,425	18,678	6,376	2,895	911	1,072
Feb-Apr 2007	29,098	25,092	3,806	100	100	21,679	7,419	18,723	6,369	2,892	913	1,091
Mar-May 2007	29,178	25,191	3,785	98	104	21,775	7,403	18,820	6,371	2,893	892	1,096
Apr-Jun 2007	29,178	25,184	3,785	97	111	21,774	7,403	18,823	6,361	2,891	894	1,103
May-Jul 2007	29,205	25,191	3,794	103	118	21,795	7,410	18,853	6,337	2,882	912	1,110
Jun-Aug 2007	29,222	25,194	3,813	102	113	21,817	7,405	18,866	6,327	2,889	924	1,111
Jul-Sep 2007	29,262	25,239	3,813	98	111	21,855	7,406	18,907	6,332	2,887	926	1,098
Aug-Oct 2007	29,313	25,275	3,829	97	111	21,902	7,410	18,941	6,335	2,901	928	1,110
Sep-Nov 2007	29,362	25,325	3,824	104	110	21,916	7,446	18,962	6,363	2,887	937	1,111
Oct-Dec 2007	29,408	25,372	3,816	106	114	21,935	7,474	18,977	6,395	2,884	931	1,118
Nov-Jan 2008	29,437	25,390	3,826	109	112	21,935	7,502	18,977	6,414	2,884	942	1,107
Dec-Feb 2008	29,499	25,402	3,870	109	118	21,983	7,516	18,971	6,431	2,937	933	1,121
Jan-Mar 2008	29,510	25,428	3,858	108	117	21,988	7,522	18,991	6,437	2,930	928	1,102
Feb-Apr 2008	29,528	25,466	3,830	114	118	22,010	7,518	19,016	6,450	2,923	907	1,117
Mar-May 2008	29,572	25,503	3,836	114	119	22,077	7,494	19,084	6,419	2,924	912	1,112
Apr-Jun 2008	29,536	25,481	3,835	109	110	22,032	7,504	19,039	6,442	2,927	908	1,127
May-Jul 2008	29,508	25,467	3,830	99	111	22,019	7,489	19,034	6,433	2,922	908	1,123
Jun-Aug 2008	29,418	25,418	3,805	90	105	21,924	7,494	18,977	6,441	2,895	909	1,115
Jul-Sep 2008	29,386	25,391	3,796	92	106	21,904	7,482	18,958	6,434	2,897	899	1,121
Aug-Oct 2008	29,346	25,365	3,782	92	106	21,854	7,492	18,928	6,437	2,877	906	1,123
Sep-Nov 2008	29,361	25,355	3,811	92	103	21,802	7,558	18,875	6,480	2,884	927	1,140
Oct-Dec 2008	29,329	25,332	3,803	94	99	21,793	7,535	18,870	6,462	2,878	925	1,131
Nov-Jan 2009	29,328	25,325	3,816	88	99	21,784	7,544	18,849	6,476	2,894	922	1,147
Dec-Feb 2009	29,228	25,244	3,797	85	103	21,686	7,542	18,734	6,510	2,894	903	1,150
Jan-Mar 2009	29,172	25,164	3,821	86	102	21,610	7,562	18,656	6,508	2,898	922	1,161
Feb-Apr 2009	29,078	25,053	3,834	87	104	21,559	7,520	18,612	6,441	2,890	945	1,151
Mar-May 2009	28,970	24,940	3,831	98	101	21,432	7,539	18,512	6,429	2,871	960	1,137
Apr-Jun 2009	28,900	24,886	3,817	94	103	21,326	7,575	18,423	6,462	2,847	971	1,121
May-Jul 2009	28,831	24,809	3,830	88	104	21,266	7,566	18,342	6,467	2,871	959	1,111
Jun-Aug 2009	28,875	24,815	3,865	85	111	21,286	7,589	18,331	6,484	2,899	966	1,133
Jul-Sep 2009	28,867	24,828	3,851	78	110	21,226	7,641	18,295	6,532	2,878	973	1,136
Aug-Oct 2009	28,885	24,842	3,856	84	104	21,190	7,695	18,251	6,591	2,890	966	1,141

4.2: Full-time, part-time and temporary workers

	All in employment					Full-time and part-time workers[1]						Total
	Total	Employees	Self employed	Unpaid family workers	Government supported training & employment programmes[2]	Total people working full-time	Total people working part-time	Employees working full-time	Employees working part-time	Self-employed people working full-time	Self-employed people working part-time	Total workers with second jobs
	1	2	3	4	5	6	7	8	9	10	11	12
Sep-Nov 2009	28,895	24,842	3,868	76	108	21,193	7,702	18,271	6,571	2,876	992	1,125
Oct-Dec 2009	28,901	24,819	3,882	87	114	21,199	7,703	18,256	6,563	2,892	989	1,125
Nov-Jan 2010	28,843	24,769	3,871	85	118	21,131	7,712	18,203	6,566	2,878	993	1,090
Dec-Feb 2010	28,823	24,732	3,881	91	119	21,137	7,686	18,196	6,537	2,892	989	1,076
Jan-Mar 2010	28,807	24,669	3,927	90	121	21,086	7,722	18,117	6,552	2,920	1,007	1,062
Feb-Apr 2010	28,842	24,679	3,948	90	124	21,075	7,767	18,095	6,584	2,931	1,017	1,092
Mar-May 2010	28,930	24,776	3,933	92	128	21,109	7,821	18,143	6,634	2,912	1,021	1,128
Apr-Jun 2010	28,975	24,831	3,924	89	131	21,143	7,832	18,178	6,653	2,908	1,015	1,134
May-Jul 2010	29,118	24,919	3,962	100	137	21,189	7,929	18,199	6,721	2,927	1,034	1,125
Jun-Aug 2010	29,128	24,921	3,963	110	134	21,162	7,966	18,163	6,757	2,937	1,026	1,117
Jul-Sep 2010	29,173	24,920	4,016	106	132	21,186	7,987	18,163	6,757	2,965	1,051	1,113
Aug-Oct 2010	29,109	24,920	3,958	101	131	21,149	7,961	18,180	6,740	2,915	1,043	1,110
Sep-Nov 2010	29,086	24,884	3,976	94	132	21,154	7,933	18,174	6,709	2,924	1,052	1,110
Oct-Dec 2010	29,120	24,929	3,976	92	123	21,197	7,923	18,233	6,696	2,913	1,062	1,119
Nov-Jan 2011	29,167	24,952	3,990	97	128	21,243	7,925	18,287	6,665	2,903	1,087	1,149
Dec-Feb 2011	29,242	25,019	4,003	96	124	21,310	7,932	18,362	6,657	2,902	1,101	1,166
Jan-Mar 2011	29,229	25,050	3,960	97	122	21,301	7,928	18,385	6,665	2,870	1,090	1,156
Feb-Apr 2011	29,228	25,036	3,986	91	114	21,287	7,941	18,363	6,673	2,879	1,107	1,142
Mar-May 2011	29,248	25,060	3,997	89	101	21,303	7,945	18,390	6,670	2,874	1,123	1,139
Apr-Jun 2011	29,224	25,054	3,984	93	94	21,328	7,896	18,397	6,656	2,891	1,093	1,131
May-Jul 2011	29,130	24,986	3,970	89	86	21,325	7,805	18,393	6,593	2,897	1,073	1,129
Jun-Aug 2011	29,080	24,882	4,013	101	83	21,305	7,776	18,340	6,542	2,926	1,087	1,119
Jul-Sep 2011	29,063	24,788	4,079	107	89	21,259	7,803	18,265	6,523	2,948	1,130	1,133
Aug-Oct 2011	29,102	24,773	4,126	111	92	21,271	7,831	18,212	6,561	3,005	1,121	1,138
Sep-Nov 2011	29,128	24,802	4,115	112	99	21,261	7,867	18,214	6,588	2,985	1,130	1,141
Oct-Dec 2011	29,146	24,868	4,075	108	94	21,260	7,886	18,244	6,624	2,962	1,113	1,125
Nov-Jan 2012	29,141	24,847	4,084	107	104	21,250	7,892	18,234	6,613	2,964	1,120	1,116
Dec-Feb 2012	29,210	24,865	4,132	97	116	21,255	7,955	18,221	6,645	2,977	1,155	1,140
Jan-Mar 2012	29,274	24,892	4,163	97	123	21,275	7,999	18,235	6,657	2,981	1,182	1,141
Feb-Apr 2012	29,324	24,927	4,171	98	128	21,335	7,989	18,277	6,650	2,998	1,173	1,138
Mar-May 2012	29,378	24,962	4,161	110	145	21,374	8,004	18,296	6,666	3,006	1,156	1,130
Apr-Jun 2012	29,476	25,020	4,202	109	144	21,405	8,070	18,308	6,712	3,020	1,182	1,124
May-Jul 2012	29,560	25,071	4,223	113	152	21,438	8,123	18,328	6,743	3,017	1,206	1,118
Jun-Aug 2012	29,590	25,124	4,196	112	158	21,462	8,129	18,386	6,738	2,988	1,209	1,119
Jul-Sep 2012	29,576	25,107	4,191	112	166	21,456	8,120	18,373	6,735	2,987	1,204	1,107
Aug-Oct 2012	29,601	25,118	4,200	111	171	21,482	8,119	18,376	6,743	3,010	1,191	1,122
Sep-Nov 2012	29,681	25,201	4,203	111	165	21,574	8,106	18,468	6,733	3,015	1,188	1,120
Oct-Dec 2012	**29,730**	**25,241**	**4,215**	**111**	**163**	**21,654**	**8,076**	**18,540**	**6,701**	**3,021**	**1,194**	**1,148**
Change on qtr	*154*	*133*	*25*	*-1*	*-3*	*197*	*-43*	*167*	*-34*	*34*	*-10*	*41*
Change %	*0.5*	*0.5*	*0.6*	*-0.6*	*-2.0*	*0.9*	*-0.5*	*0.9*	*-0.5*	*1.1*	*-0.8*	*3.7*
Change on year	*584*	*373*	*140*	*3*	*69*	*394*	*190*	*296*	*77*	*59*	*80*	*23*
Change %	*2.0*	*1.5*	*3.4*	*2.5*	*72.8*	*1.9*	*2.4*	*1.6*	*1.2*	*2.0*	*7.2*	*2.1*
Male	MGSA	MGRO	MGRR	MGRU	MGRX	YCBF	YCBI	YCBL	YCBO	YCBR	YCBU	YCBX
Nov-Jan 2003	15,206	12,637	2,475	33	62	13,654	1,552	11,463	1,174	2,147	328	483
Dec-Feb 2003	15,166	12,586	2,487	30	64	13,606	1,560	11,411	1,174	2,152	335	467
Jan-Mar 2003	15,183	12,609	2,491	27	56	13,617	1,565	11,426	1,183	2,152	339	458
Feb-Apr 2003	15,219	12,598	2,537	29	55	13,641	1,578	11,412	1,187	2,188	349	459
Mar-May 2003	15,263	12,607	2,571	30	55	13,676	1,588	11,421	1,187	2,215	357	460
Apr-Jun 2003	15,295	12,613	2,597	32	53	13,706	1,589	11,413	1,200	2,252	345	454
May-Jul 2003	15,292	12,586	2,616	39	51	13,707	1,585	11,395	1,191	2,269	347	444
Jun-Aug 2003	15,280	12,554	2,632	37	59	13,699	1,581	11,366	1,187	2,286	346	459
Jul-Sep 2003	15,288	12,524	2,663	40	61	13,721	1,568	11,358	1,166	2,313	349	463
Aug-Oct 2003	15,275	12,516	2,659	38	61	13,704	1,571	11,342	1,175	2,311	348	468
Sep-Nov 2003	15,269	12,511	2,657	38	63	13,715	1,554	11,348	1,163	2,319	338	463
Oct-Dec 2003	15,264	12,502	2,664	38	60	13,704	1,560	11,337	1,165	2,320	344	467
Nov-Jan 2004	15,309	12,548	2,658	40	64	13,735	1,574	11,369	1,179	2,318	340	462
Dec-Feb 2004	15,342	12,568	2,669	43	63	13,759	1,584	11,384	1,184	2,327	341	469
Jan-Mar 2004	15,362	12,611	2,639	44	68	13,750	1,612	11,400	1,211	2,297	342	472
Feb-Apr 2004	15,357	12,583	2,658	44	71	13,742	1,615	11,375	1,208	2,313	345	469
Mar-May 2004	15,379	12,607	2,656	41	75	13,743	1,636	11,390	1,217	2,302	354	454
Apr-Jun 2004	15,369	12,567	2,689	41	72	13,739	1,629	11,351	1,216	2,337	352	449
May-Jul 2004	15,380	12,597	2,673	36	74	13,749	1,631	11,389	1,208	2,312	361	451
Jun-Aug 2004	15,390	12,613	2,672	33	71	13,753	1,637	11,391	1,222	2,310	362	454
Jul-Sep 2004	15,406	12,656	2,641	34	76	13,765	1,641	11,421	1,235	2,295	346	452
Aug-Oct 2004	15,408	12,634	2,663	34	77	13,776	1,632	11,407	1,226	2,319	344	447
Sep-Nov 2004	15,444	12,657	2,668	38	81	13,827	1,617	11,444	1,213	2,329	339	461
Oct-Dec 2004	15,465	12,689	2,663	38	76	13,830	1,635	11,460	1,229	2,321	343	451
Nov-Jan 2005	15,489	12,730	2,646	40	73	13,839	1,651	11,479	1,251	2,311	336	454
Dec-Feb 2005	15,499	12,740	2,645	42	72	13,849	1,650	11,495	1,246	2,307	338	448
Jan-Mar 2005	15,514	12,761	2,640	42	70	13,859	1,655	11,509	1,252	2,301	339	453
Feb-Apr 2005	15,501	12,736	2,652	42	70	13,841	1,660	11,477	1,259	2,313	339	456
Mar-May 2005	15,492	12,714	2,669	40	69	13,838	1,654	11,453	1,261	2,332	336	466
Apr-Jun 2005	15,509	12,749	2,652	37	71	13,863	1,646	11,483	1,266	2,326	326	462
May-Jul 2005	15,521	12,763	2,652	35	70	13,878	1,643	11,502	1,261	2,325	327	463
Jun-Aug 2005	15,535	12,783	2,652	33	66	13,897	1,637	11,544	1,239	2,307	345	464
Jul-Sep 2005	15,551	12,785	2,672	32	63	13,912	1,639	11,543	1,241	2,323	348	458
Aug-Oct 2005	15,550	12,792	2,666	32	59	13,909	1,640	11,555	1,238	2,314	352	451
Sep-Nov 2005	15,543	12,768	2,686	30	59	13,893	1,650	11,520	1,247	2,331	356	435
Oct-Dec 2005	15,546	12,756	2,699	29	62	13,888	1,658	11,509	1,247	2,336	363	445

4.2: Full-time, part-time and temporary workers

United Kingdom (thousands) seasonally adjusted

	All in employment					Full-time and part-time workers[1]						Total workers with second jobs
	Total	Employees	Self employed	Unpaid family workers	Government supported training & employment programmes[2]	Total people working full-time	Total people working part-time	Employees working full-time	Employees working part-time	Self-employed people working full-time	Self-employed people working part-time	
	1	2	3	4	5	6	7	8	9	10	11	12
Nov-Jan 2006	15,577	12,776	2,709	32	60	13,923	1,654	11,532	1,244	2,346	363	455
Dec-Feb 2006	15,588	12,789	2,709	30	60	13,920	1,667	11,533	1,257	2,343	366	457
Jan-Mar 2006	15,582	12,802	2,689	31	59	13,927	1,655	11,548	1,254	2,335	354	440
Feb-Apr 2006	15,629	12,839	2,701	30	58	13,973	1,656	11,578	1,261	2,353	348	442
Mar-May 2006	15,612	12,834	2,687	33	58	13,948	1,664	11,563	1,271	2,347	340	433
Apr-Jun 2006	15,625	12,845	2,689	36	55	13,949	1,676	11,565	1,280	2,346	342	448
May-Jul 2006	15,655	12,875	2,689	38	54	13,970	1,685	11,591	1,284	2,338	351	452
Jun-Aug 2006	15,693	12,900	2,701	42	49	14,014	1,678	11,622	1,279	2,351	351	448
Jul-Sep 2006	15,709	12,887	2,721	43	59	13,996	1,713	11,594	1,293	2,356	364	454
Aug-Oct 2006	15,708	12,871	2,735	43	60	13,965	1,743	11,556	1,316	2,364	371	455
Sep-Nov 2006	15,709	12,855	2,744	40	69	13,987	1,722	11,564	1,292	2,378	366	448
Oct-Dec 2006	15,715	12,877	2,736	41	60	13,999	1,715	11,583	1,294	2,375	361	461
Nov-Jan 2007	15,724	12,861	2,762	39	63	14,017	1,707	11,569	1,292	2,406	355	445
Dec-Feb 2007	15,719	12,863	2,757	40	59	14,006	1,713	11,573	1,290	2,392	365	459
Jan-Mar 2007	15,727	12,864	2,763	42	57	13,991	1,735	11,564	1,301	2,388	375	461
Feb-Apr 2007	15,749	12,891	2,761	39	57	14,018	1,730	11,600	1,291	2,381	380	459
Mar-May 2007	15,813	12,957	2,759	38	60	14,087	1,726	11,668	1,289	2,382	377	455
Apr-Jun 2007	15,803	12,941	2,763	36	63	14,074	1,729	11,657	1,285	2,380	383	456
May-Jul 2007	15,809	12,943	2,760	37	69	14,071	1,737	11,667	1,276	2,367	393	459
Jun-Aug 2007	15,820	12,960	2,759	39	62	14,086	1,734	11,673	1,287	2,377	383	455
Jul-Sep 2007	15,841	12,994	2,748	39	60	14,090	1,751	11,693	1,301	2,362	386	449
Aug-Oct 2007	15,862	13,000	2,769	37	56	14,127	1,734	11,710	1,289	2,385	384	458
Sep-Nov 2007	15,894	13,024	2,771	38	61	14,126	1,768	11,711	1,314	2,374	397	454
Oct-Dec 2007	15,898	13,020	2,775	39	64	14,126	1,772	11,695	1,325	2,384	391	448
Nov-Jan 2008	15,912	13,032	2,774	38	67	14,119	1,793	11,685	1,348	2,385	389	451
Dec-Feb 2008	15,942	13,018	2,809	39	75	14,138	1,804	11,669	1,350	2,421	389	460
Jan-Mar 2008	15,959	13,037	2,808	38	75	14,156	1,803	11,696	1,341	2,416	393	450
Feb-Apr 2008	15,977	13,073	2,792	41	71	14,171	1,806	11,723	1,350	2,403	389	457
Mar-May 2008	15,976	13,071	2,796	40	69	14,199	1,777	11,750	1,322	2,406	390	458
Apr-Jun 2008	15,964	13,066	2,794	39	64	14,157	1,808	11,709	1,357	2,408	387	463
May-Jul 2008	15,938	13,056	2,782	36	64	14,119	1,819	11,682	1,374	2,400	382	452
Jun-Aug 2008	15,876	13,020	2,761	31	64	14,045	1,831	11,638	1,382	2,375	386	451
Jul-Sep 2008	15,859	13,009	2,755	31	64	14,025	1,834	11,621	1,389	2,374	381	457
Aug-Oct 2008	15,818	12,987	2,730	33	67	13,973	1,844	11,592	1,395	2,350	381	453
Sep-Nov 2008	15,830	12,974	2,753	37	65	13,985	1,845	11,586	1,388	2,369	384	471
Oct-Dec 2008	15,814	12,954	2,756	41	64	13,954	1,860	11,557	1,398	2,370	386	469
Nov-Jan 2009	15,793	12,932	2,762	37	61	13,925	1,867	11,523	1,409	2,379	383	477
Dec-Feb 2009	15,732	12,889	2,749	32	62	13,876	1,857	11,465	1,425	2,379	371	481
Jan-Mar 2009	15,694	12,848	2,757	30	59	13,849	1,845	11,438	1,410	2,379	378	491
Feb-Apr 2009	15,636	12,784	2,760	32	60	13,786	1,850	11,380	1,405	2,374	386	499
Mar-May 2009	15,543	12,694	2,757	36	57	13,669	1,874	11,286	1,408	2,353	404	488
Apr-Jun 2009	15,475	12,639	2,738	39	59	13,587	1,887	11,228	1,411	2,324	414	482
May-Jul 2009	15,427	12,591	2,741	36	60	13,569	1,858	11,199	1,391	2,337	404	480
Jun-Aug 2009	15,423	12,579	2,749	34	61	13,562	1,861	11,171	1,408	2,355	394	492
Jul-Sep 2009	15,401	12,581	2,728	30	62	13,551	1,850	11,181	1,401	2,338	389	489
Aug-Oct 2009	15,402	12,556	2,753	33	59	13,540	1,862	11,151	1,405	2,359	395	494
Sep-Nov 2009	15,400	12,571	2,738	33	57	13,524	1,876	11,161	1,410	2,337	401	482
Oct-Dec 2009	15,398	12,550	2,750	37	61	13,514	1,884	11,142	1,408	2,344	406	485
Nov-Jan 2010	15,356	12,510	2,749	36	61	13,459	1,897	11,094	1,416	2,338	411	466
Dec-Feb 2010	15,360	12,512	2,746	40	63	13,467	1,893	11,100	1,412	2,339	407	456
Jan-Mar 2010	15,354	12,488	2,760	40	66	13,441	1,913	11,063	1,425	2,350	410	432
Feb-Apr 2010	15,378	12,502	2,766	41	69	13,457	1,921	11,071	1,431	2,356	410	452
Mar-May 2010	15,458	12,569	2,771	42	76	13,504	1,953	11,121	1,448	2,351	420	476
Apr-Jun 2010	15,497	12,607	2,774	41	76	13,519	1,978	11,131	1,476	2,355	419	474
May-Jul 2010	15,595	12,664	2,804	43	85	13,585	2,010	11,183	1,481	2,365	438	465
Jun-Aug 2010	15,610	12,664	2,820	44	83	13,575	2,035	11,157	1,506	2,379	441	460
Jul-Sep 2010	15,655	12,682	2,844	44	85	13,591	2,064	11,156	1,526	2,396	448	465
Aug-Oct 2010	15,620	12,698	2,795	44	84	13,555	2,065	11,176	1,522	2,347	448	460
Sep-Nov 2010	15,619	12,692	2,810	34	84	13,566	2,053	11,180	1,512	2,355	456	462
Oct-Dec 2010	15,644	12,722	2,812	34	76	13,594	2,050	11,206	1,516	2,357	455	470
Nov-Jan 2011	15,653	12,740	2,798	34	81	13,624	2,029	11,253	1,487	2,342	456	489
Dec-Feb 2011	15,670	12,754	2,807	32	77	13,661	2,009	11,296	1,458	2,341	467	506
Jan-Mar 2011	15,643	12,753	2,784	31	75	13,630	2,013	11,292	1,461	2,315	469	492
Feb-Apr 2011	15,695	12,782	2,816	27	70	13,647	2,048	11,291	1,491	2,337	479	485
Mar-May 2011	15,688	12,781	2,818	32	58	13,643	2,045	11,301	1,479	2,325	493	487
Apr-Jun 2011	15,675	12,758	2,825	37	55	13,638	2,036	11,280	1,478	2,340	485	487
May-Jul 2011	15,604	12,704	2,817	37	46	13,599	2,005	11,242	1,462	2,340	477	493
Jun-Aug 2011	15,564	12,652	2,825	41	46	13,607	1,957	11,234	1,418	2,353	472	478
Jul-Sep 2011	15,543	12,585	2,869	43	45	13,577	1,966	11,178	1,407	2,376	493	486
Aug-Oct 2011	15,569	12,577	2,904	41	46	13,588	1,981	11,137	1,440	2,423	482	492
Sep-Nov 2011	15,598	12,602	2,900	43	53	13,580	2,018	11,139	1,463	2,409	491	490
Oct-Dec 2011	15,603	12,647	2,862	41	53	13,582	2,022	11,169	1,478	2,382	480	479
Nov-Jan 2012	15,591	12,627	2,864	41	59	13,570	2,021	11,156	1,471	2,384	480	463
Dec-Feb 2012	15,660	12,665	2,894	36	65	13,579	2,081	11,143	1,522	2,399	495	487
Jan-Mar 2012	15,695	12,673	2,907	43	72	13,585	2,110	11,146	1,527	2,399	507	485
Feb-Apr 2012	15,739	12,697	2,920	45	77	13,615	2,124	11,156	1,541	2,418	502	489
Mar-May 2012	15,781	12,705	2,935	47	94	13,653	2,128	11,164	1,541	2,441	493	487
Apr-Jun 2012	15,838	12,743	2,963	41	91	13,687	2,151	11,178	1,565	2,460	503	490
May-Jul 2012	15,847	12,745	2,964	42	97	13,721	2,127	11,196	1,548	2,461	503	478
Jun-Aug 2012	15,875	12,777	2,950	46	102	13,733	2,142	11,236	1,541	2,436	514	479
Jul-Sep 2012	15,877	12,772	2,946	49	111	13,740	2,137	11,237	1,534	2,431	514	468
Aug-Oct 2012	15,901	12,777	2,960	47	117	13,780	2,121	11,259	1,519	2,448	512	466
Sep-Nov 2012	15,929	12,842	2,930	46	112	13,816	2,113	11,317	1,524	2,434	496	454
Oct-Dec 2012	**15,932**	**12,852**	**2,926**	**45**	**110**	**13,832**	**2,100**	**11,338**	**1,514**	**2,429**	**497**	**457**

4.2: Full-time, part-time and temporary workers

United Kingdom (thousands) seasonally adjusted

	All in employment					Full-time and part-time workers[1]						Total workers with second jobs
	Total	Employees	Self employed	Unpaid family workers	Government supported training & employment programmes[2]	Total people working full-time	Total people working part-time	Employees working full-time	Employees working part-time	Self-employed people working full-time	Self-employed people working part-time	
	1	2	3	4	5	6	7	8	9	10	11	12
Change on qtr	55	80	-19	-4	-1	93	-37	100	-20	-2	-17	-11
Change %	0.3	0.6	-0.7	-8.9	-0.8	0.7	-1.7	0.9	-1.3	-0.1	-3.4	-2.3
Change on year	329	205	64	4	57	251	79	169	35	47	17	-21
Change %	2.1	1.6	2.2	10.4	106.0	1.8	3.9	1.5	2.4	2.0	3.6	-4.5
Female	MGSB	MGRP	MGRS	MGRV	MGRY	YCBG	YCBJ	YCBM	YCBP	YCBS	YCBV	YCBY
Nov-Jan 2003	12,841	11,839	906	58	38	7,246	5,596	6,780	5,060	444	461	681
Dec-Feb 2003	12,859	11,845	915	58	40	7,238	5,621	6,761	5,085	456	460	668
Jan-Mar 2003	12,882	11,858	928	57	38	7,224	5,657	6,751	5,107	452	476	673
Feb-Apr 2003	12,886	11,851	941	58	36	7,203	5,683	6,729	5,122	454	487	676
Mar-May 2003	12,897	11,847	956	56	38	7,206	5,691	6,725	5,122	462	494	673
Apr-Jun 2003	12,893	11,844	954	56	39	7,212	5,681	6,725	5,119	466	488	655
May-Jul 2003	12,902	11,851	950	61	40	7,231	5,671	6,744	5,107	463	487	657
Jun-Aug 2003	12,907	11,820	979	65	43	7,214	5,693	6,699	5,121	487	492	644
Jul-Sep 2003	12,926	11,828	985	68	46	7,214	5,712	6,709	5,119	478	506	653
Aug-Oct 2003	12,969	11,865	997	63	44	7,240	5,729	6,728	5,136	485	512	646
Sep-Nov 2003	12,983	11,897	978	63	45	7,242	5,741	6,730	5,166	484	494	636
Oct-Dec 2003	12,999	11,918	974	61	47	7,240	5,759	6,728	5,190	484	490	644
Nov-Jan 2004	13,047	11,965	973	61	48	7,259	5,787	6,756	5,209	477	496	634
Dec-Feb 2004	13,052	11,991	953	63	45	7,245	5,807	6,763	5,228	459	494	636
Jan-Mar 2004	13,053	11,974	968	61	50	7,251	5,802	6,759	5,216	471	497	636
Feb-Apr 2004	13,047	11,969	963	64	51	7,269	5,778	6,768	5,201	477	486	634
Mar-May 2004	13,041	11,966	964	60	52	7,290	5,752	6,791	5,175	471	493	620
Apr-Jun 2004	13,056	11,973	977	57	51	7,322	5,735	6,808	5,165	484	492	621
May-Jul 2004	13,039	11,968	962	53	57	7,309	5,730	6,804	5,164	476	486	623
Jun-Aug 2004	13,043	11,974	955	54	61	7,320	5,723	6,814	5,160	477	477	621
Jul-Sep 2004	13,061	12,011	941	55	53	7,356	5,705	6,854	5,157	473	469	607
Aug-Oct 2004	13,083	12,018	953	60	53	7,399	5,684	6,886	5,131	483	470	598
Sep-Nov 2004	13,124	12,060	956	56	51	7,440	5,684	6,941	5,119	472	485	609
Oct-Dec 2004	13,150	12,088	952	60	50	7,484	5,666	6,986	5,103	470	482	603
Nov-Jan 2005	13,174	12,116	949	58	51	7,526	5,647	7,032	5,084	466	483	611
Dec-Feb 2005	13,228	12,143	967	63	55	7,592	5,636	7,075	5,069	485	482	615
Jan-Mar 2005	13,205	12,128	957	62	58	7,580	5,625	7,060	5,068	487	470	607
Feb-Apr 2005	13,186	12,123	950	61	52	7,559	5,628	7,051	5,073	477	473	609
Mar-May 2005	13,214	12,145	961	63	46	7,540	5,674	7,030	5,115	480	480	615
Apr-Jun 2005	13,217	12,155	957	62	43	7,529	5,688	7,028	5,128	473	483	613
May-Jul 2005	13,256	12,188	966	60	42	7,564	5,691	7,051	5,137	485	481	604
Jun-Aug 2005	13,291	12,220	977	52	42	7,618	5,673	7,098	5,122	496	481	599
Jul-Sep 2005	13,294	12,205	986	58	44	7,631	5,662	7,103	5,102	500	486	610
Aug-Oct 2005	13,277	12,202	971	60	43	7,632	5,645	7,110	5,092	492	480	608
Sep-Nov 2005	13,243	12,154	983	62	44	7,620	5,624	7,098	5,055	491	492	599
Oct-Dec 2005	13,242	12,159	975	61	48	7,645	5,597	7,126	5,032	488	486	583
Nov-Jan 2006	13,260	12,181	973	60	46	7,644	5,616	7,128	5,053	486	487	581
Dec-Feb 2006	13,301	12,213	995	58	35	7,662	5,639	7,141	5,072	498	497	587
Jan-Mar 2006	13,364	12,250	1,021	58	36	7,680	5,685	7,139	5,111	518	503	588
Feb-Apr 2006	13,353	12,238	1,025	54	35	7,684	5,669	7,150	5,088	510	516	589
Mar-May 2006	13,347	12,252	1,003	53	39	7,695	5,651	7,179	5,073	494	509	587
Apr-Jun 2006	13,374	12,270	1,010	54	39	7,692	5,682	7,172	5,098	496	514	596
May-Jul 2006	13,375	12,253	1,025	60	36	7,696	5,679	7,163	5,090	509	516	596
Jun-Aug 2006	13,418	12,282	1,035	63	38	7,702	5,715	7,160	5,122	518	516	608
Jul-Sep 2006	13,357	12,220	1,036	62	39	7,659	5,698	7,127	5,093	508	528	610
Aug-Oct 2006	13,364	12,219	1,048	55	42	7,636	5,728	7,101	5,118	513	535	608
Sep-Nov 2006	13,369	12,233	1,029	60	47	7,644	5,725	7,113	5,120	505	524	606
Oct-Dec 2006	13,375	12,230	1,038	60	46	7,635	5,740	7,102	5,128	509	530	614
Nov-Jan 2007	13,348	12,209	1,033	62	45	7,620	5,728	7,089	5,121	505	527	623
Dec-Feb 2007	13,326	12,176	1,044	59	47	7,626	5,701	7,083	5,093	518	527	614
Jan-Mar 2007	13,337	12,189	1,043	60	45	7,648	5,689	7,114	5,075	507	536	611
Feb-Apr 2007	13,350	12,201	1,045	61	42	7,661	5,689	7,123	5,079	511	533	631
Mar-May 2007	13,365	12,233	1,026	60	45	7,687	5,677	7,151	5,082	511	515	640
Apr-Jun 2007	13,375	12,243	1,023	61	49	7,701	5,674	7,166	5,077	511	512	647
May-Jul 2007	13,397	12,248	1,034	65	49	7,724	5,673	7,186	5,062	515	519	651
Jun-Aug 2007	13,402	12,233	1,054	63	51	7,731	5,671	7,193	5,040	512	541	656
Jul-Sep 2007	13,421	12,245	1,066	59	51	7,765	5,656	7,214	5,031	525	541	648
Aug-Oct 2007	13,451	12,276	1,060	60	55	7,775	5,676	7,230	5,045	517	544	652
Sep-Nov 2007	13,468	12,300	1,053	66	49	7,790	5,678	7,251	5,049	513	540	657
Oct-Dec 2007	13,510	12,352	1,041	67	50	7,809	5,701	7,282	5,070	500	541	670
Nov-Jan 2008	13,525	12,358	1,052	70	45	7,817	5,709	7,292	5,066	499	553	656
Dec-Feb 2008	13,557	12,384	1,061	70	42	7,845	5,712	7,303	5,082	516	545	662
Jan-Mar 2008	13,552	12,391	1,049	69	42	7,833	5,719	7,295	5,095	515	535	652
Feb-Apr 2008	13,551	12,393	1,039	73	46	7,839	5,712	7,293	5,100	520	518	660
Mar-May 2008	13,596	12,432	1,040	74	50	7,878	5,718	7,335	5,097	519	522	654
Apr-Jun 2008	13,571	12,415	1,041	70	46	7,875	5,696	7,330	5,085	520	521	664
May-Jul 2008	13,570	12,411	1,048	63	47	7,900	5,670	7,352	5,059	523	526	671
Jun-Aug 2008	13,542	12,398	1,044	59	41	7,879	5,663	7,340	5,059	520	524	664
Jul-Sep 2008	13,527	12,382	1,042	61	42	7,879	5,648	7,337	5,045	523	518	664
Aug-Oct 2008	13,528	12,378	1,052	59	39	7,881	5,647	7,335	5,043	527	525	670
Sep-Nov 2008	13,531	12,381	1,058	55	37	7,818	5,714	7,288	5,092	515	543	669
Oct-Dec 2008	13,514	12,378	1,047	54	36	7,839	5,675	7,313	5,065	507	539	662
Nov-Jan 2009	13,536	12,393	1,054	51	38	7,859	5,677	7,327	5,066	515	539	670
Dec-Feb 2009	13,496	12,354	1,048	52	41	7,810	5,686	7,269	5,085	516	532	669

4.2: Full-time, part-time and temporary workers

United Kingdom (thousands) seasonally adjusted

	All in employment					Full-time and part-time workers[1]						Total workers with second jobs
	Total	Employees	Self employed	Unpaid family workers	Government supported training & employment programmes[2]	Total people working full-time	Total people working part-time	Employees working full-time	Employees working part-time	Self-employed people working full-time	Self-employed people working part-time	
	1	2	3	4	5	6	7	8	9	10	11	12
Jan-Mar 2009	13,478	12,316	1,064	55	43	7,762	5,716	7,219	5,098	519	545	669
Feb-Apr 2009	13,442	12,269	1,074	55	44	7,772	5,670	7,233	5,036	516	558	653
Mar-May 2009	13,427	12,247	1,074	62	45	7,763	5,664	7,226	5,021	518	556	650
Apr-Jun 2009	13,426	12,247	1,079	56	44	7,738	5,687	7,195	5,052	523	556	638
May-Jul 2009	13,404	12,219	1,089	53	44	7,696	5,708	7,142	5,076	533	555	630
Jun-Aug 2009	13,452	12,235	1,115	51	50	7,725	5,728	7,159	5,076	543	572	641
Jul-Sep 2009	13,466	12,246	1,123	48	48	7,675	5,791	7,115	5,132	539	584	648
Aug-Oct 2009	13,483	12,286	1,102	50	44	7,651	5,832	7,101	5,186	531	571	647
Sep-Nov 2009	13,495	12,271	1,130	44	51	7,669	5,826	7,111	5,160	539	591	643
Oct-Dec 2009	13,504	12,269	1,132	50	53	7,685	5,819	7,114	5,155	549	583	641
Nov-Jan 2010	13,488	12,260	1,122	49	57	7,672	5,816	7,109	5,151	540	582	624
Dec-Feb 2010	13,463	12,220	1,135	51	56	7,670	5,793	7,096	5,125	553	582	620
Jan-Mar 2010	13,453	12,181	1,167	50	55	7,644	5,809	7,054	5,126	570	598	630
Feb-Apr 2010	13,464	12,177	1,182	49	55	7,618	5,846	7,024	5,153	575	608	640
Mar-May 2010	13,473	12,208	1,162	51	52	7,605	5,868	7,022	5,186	561	601	652
Apr-Jun 2010	13,477	12,224	1,150	48	55	7,623	5,854	7,047	5,177	553	597	659
May-Jul 2010	13,522	12,256	1,158	57	52	7,604	5,918	7,016	5,240	562	596	660
Jun-Aug 2010	13,518	12,257	1,143	67	50	7,587	5,931	7,006	5,251	558	585	657
Jul-Sep 2010	13,518	12,237	1,172	62	47	7,595	5,923	7,006	5,231	569	603	648
Aug-Oct 2010	13,489	12,222	1,163	57	47	7,593	5,896	7,004	5,218	569	595	650
Sep-Nov 2010	13,467	12,192	1,166	61	49	7,587	5,880	6,994	5,198	570	596	648
Oct-Dec 2010	13,477	12,207	1,164	58	48	7,604	5,873	7,027	5,180	556	608	649
Nov-Jan 2011	13,515	12,212	1,192	63	48	7,619	5,896	7,035	5,177	561	631	660
Dec-Feb 2011	13,572	12,264	1,196	65	47	7,649	5,923	7,066	5,199	562	634	660
Jan-Mar 2011	13,586	12,296	1,176	67	47	7,672	5,915	7,093	5,203	555	622	663
Feb-Apr 2011	13,533	12,254	1,171	64	44	7,640	5,893	7,073	5,182	542	628	657
Mar-May 2011	13,560	12,279	1,180	58	43	7,660	5,900	7,089	5,191	549	630	652
Apr-Jun 2011	13,549	12,296	1,159	56	39	7,690	5,860	7,117	5,178	551	608	644
May-Jul 2011	13,526	12,282	1,152	52	40	7,726	5,799	7,151	5,131	557	595	636
Jun-Aug 2011	13,516	12,231	1,188	60	37	7,698	5,818	7,106	5,125	573	615	641
Jul-Sep 2011	13,520	12,203	1,209	64	44	7,682	5,838	7,087	5,117	572	637	647
Aug-Oct 2011	13,533	12,196	1,222	70	46	7,683	5,850	7,075	5,121	582	640	646
Sep-Nov 2011	13,530	12,200	1,216	69	46	7,682	5,849	7,075	5,125	576	640	652
Oct-Dec 2011	13,543	12,220	1,213	68	41	7,678	5,865	7,075	5,146	580	634	646
Nov-Jan 2012	13,550	12,220	1,220	66	45	7,680	5,871	7,078	5,142	580	640	654
Dec-Feb 2012	13,551	12,201	1,238	61	51	7,676	5,874	7,078	5,123	578	661	654
Jan-Mar 2012	13,579	12,219	1,256	54	51	7,691	5,889	7,089	5,130	582	675	656
Feb-Apr 2012	13,585	12,230	1,251	53	51	7,720	5,865	7,120	5,110	580	671	650
Mar-May 2012	13,597	12,257	1,227	63	51	7,721	5,876	7,132	5,124	564	663	644
Apr-Jun 2012	13,637	12,278	1,239	68	53	7,719	5,919	7,131	5,147	559	679	634
May-Jul 2012	13,713	12,327	1,259	72	55	7,717	5,996	7,132	5,195	556	703	640
Jun-Aug 2012	13,715	12,347	1,246	66	56	7,729	5,986	7,150	5,197	552	695	640
Jul-Sep 2012	13,699	12,336	1,245	63	56	7,717	5,982	7,135	5,200	556	689	640
Aug-Oct 2012	13,700	12,341	1,241	64	54	7,702	5,998	7,117	5,224	562	679	656
Sep-Nov 2012	13,751	12,359	1,273	65	54	7,758	5,993	7,151	5,208	581	692	666
Oct-Dec 2012	**13,797**	**12,389**	**1,289**	**66**	**53**	**7,821**	**5,976**	**7,202**	**5,187**	**592**	**697**	**691**
Change on qtr	*98*	*53*	*44*	*4*	*-2*	*105*	*-6*	*67*	*-13*	*36*	*8*	*52*
Change %	*0.7*	*0.4*	*3.5*	*6.0*	*-4.4*	*1.4*	*-0.1*	*0.9*	*-0.3*	*6.5*	*1.1*	*8.1*
Change on year	*255*	*168*	*76*	*-1*	*12*	*143*	*111*	*127*	*41*	*12*	*63*	*45*
Change %	*1.9*	*1.4*	*6.2*	*-2.2*	*29.7*	*1.9*	*1.9*	*1.8*	*0.8*	*2.1*	*10.0*	*6.9*

	Temporary employees (reasons for temporary working)						Part-time workers (reasons for working part-time)[3]					
	Total	Total as % of all employees	Could not find permanent job	% that could not find permanent job	Did not want permanent job	Had a contract with period of training	Some other reason	Total[4]	Could not find full-time job	% that could not find full-time job	Did not want full-time job	Ill or disabled	Student or at school
	13	14	15	16	17	18	19	20	21	22	23	24	25
All Persons	YCBZ	YCCC	YCCF	YCCI	YCCL	YCCO	YCCR	YCCU	YCCX	YCDA	YCDD	YCDG	YCDJ
Nov-Jan 2003	1,551	6.3	409	26.4	467	92	583	7,023	554	7.9	5,169	132	1,138
Dec-Feb 2003	1,535	6.3	412	26.8	449	89	585	7,054	554	7.9	5,207	136	1,125
Jan-Mar 2003	1,519	6.2	398	26.2	455	87	579	7,104	559	7.9	5,229	139	1,143
Feb-Apr 2003	1,518	6.2	401	26.4	464	75	577	7,144	569	8.0	5,257	139	1,144
Mar-May 2003	1,506	6.2	406	27.0	459	73	568	7,159	581	8.1	5,248	146	1,150
Apr-Jun 2003	1,493	6.1	403	27.0	459	79	552	7,151	577	8.1	5,249	149	1,140
May-Jul 2003	1,486	6.1	393	26.4	453	82	558	7,132	563	7.9	5,250	146	1,138
Jun-Aug 2003	1,476	6.1	382	25.9	452	89	553	7,145	564	7.9	5,259	149	1,135
Jul-Sep 2003	1,523	6.3	393	25.8	463	93	574	7,143	566	7.9	5,262	156	1,125
Aug-Oct 2003	1,555	6.4	409	26.3	470	95	581	7,172	573	8.0	5,266	163	1,134
Sep-Nov 2003	1,539	6.3	403	26.2	454	87	595	7,162	570	8.0	5,255	171	1,139
Oct-Dec 2003	1,530	6.3	399	26.1	444	85	601	7,186	565	7.9	5,280	178	1,134
Nov-Jan 2004	1,519	6.2	405	26.7	435	82	598	7,223	563	7.8	5,299	180	1,151
Dec-Feb 2004	1,516	6.2	404	26.7	436	87	588	7,247	560	7.7	5,318	186	1,154
Jan-Mar 2004	1,507	6.1	405	26.9	431	86	585	7,265	570	7.8	5,313	188	1,165
Feb-Apr 2004	1,503	6.1	394	26.2	434	86	588	7,240	568	7.8	5,289	185	1,168
Mar-May 2004	1,490	6.1	386	25.9	439	82	582	7,240	545	7.5	5,317	183	1,163
Apr-Jun 2004	1,510	6.2	390	25.8	440	89	591	7,224	533	7.4	5,327	182	1,150
May-Jul 2004	1,499	6.1	393	26.2	428	88	591	7,219	543	7.5	5,312	178	1,155

4.2: Full-time, part-time and temporary workers

United Kingdom (thousands) seasonally adjusted

	Temporary employees (reasons for temporary working)							Part-time workers (reasons for working part-time)[3]					
	Total	Total as % of all employees	Could not find permanent job	% that could not find permanent job	Did not want permanent job	Had a contract with period of training	Some other reason	Total[4]	Could not find full-time job	% that could not find full-time job	Did not want full-time job	Ill or disabled	Student or at school
	13	14	15	16	17	18	19	20	21	22	23	24	25
Jun-Aug 2004	1,535	6.2	385	25.1	431	92	627	7,221	547	7.6	5,306	176	1,163
Jul-Sep 2004	1,515	6.1	377	24.9	422	100	617	7,208	555	7.7	5,282	170	1,168
Aug-Oct 2004	1,519	6.2	371	24.4	421	103	624	7,173	555	7.7	5,246	171	1,169
Sep-Nov 2004	1,488	6.0	362	24.4	414	111	600	7,155	537	7.5	5,242	171	1,174
Oct-Dec 2004	1,507	6.1	364	24.2	430	116	596	7,154	537	7.5	5,246	166	1,175
Nov-Jan 2005	1,500	6.0	357	23.8	427	113	603	7,154	538	7.5	5,239	166	1,182
Dec-Feb 2005	1,502	6.0	357	23.7	419	113	614	7,134	549	7.7	5,228	166	1,161
Jan-Mar 2005	1,466	5.9	357	24.3	404	102	603	7,129	568	8.0	5,209	166	1,153
Feb-Apr 2005	1,444	5.8	357	24.7	385	104	599	7,143	563	7.9	5,225	176	1,146
Mar-May 2005	1,445	5.8	357	24.7	382	105	602	7,193	585	8.1	5,258	168	1,151
Apr-Jun 2005	1,450	5.8	356	24.5	387	98	609	7,202	588	8.2	5,243	165	1,173
May-Jul 2005	1,474	5.9	355	24.1	402	107	610	7,206	592	8.2	5,234	160	1,186
Jun-Aug 2005	1,471	5.9	378	25.7	397	100	596	7,188	589	8.2	5,234	165	1,164
Jul-Sep 2005	1,480	5.9	392	26.5	395	104	589	7,179	597	8.3	5,234	168	1,152
Aug-Oct 2005	1,433	5.7	386	26.9	388	100	559	7,162	593	8.3	5,226	170	1,143
Sep-Nov 2005	1,419	5.7	370	26.1	378	102	569	7,151	612	8.6	5,212	167	1,127
Oct-Dec 2005	1,387	5.6	347	25.0	375	94	572	7,126	604	8.5	5,206	168	1,113
Nov-Jan 2006	1,430	5.7	363	25.4	388	104	574	7,147	610	8.5	5,210	168	1,122
Dec-Feb 2006	1,450	5.8	363	25.0	402	102	583	7,191	618	8.6	5,217	177	1,141
Jan-Mar 2006	1,485	5.9	373	25.1	411	115	586	7,222	618	8.6	5,239	174	1,148
Feb-Apr 2006	1,484	5.9	369	24.8	418	115	583	7,213	617	8.6	5,229	171	1,157
Mar-May 2006	1,478	5.9	368	24.9	414	114	581	7,193	610	8.5	5,211	170	1,162
Apr-Jun 2006	1,463	5.8	369	25.2	419	110	565	7,234	623	8.6	5,225	170	1,178
May-Jul 2006	1,441	5.7	359	24.9	417	99	567	7,241	632	8.7	5,213	175	1,186
Jun-Aug 2006	1,468	5.8	362	24.7	434	96	576	7,268	644	8.9	5,215	184	1,198
Jul-Sep 2006	1,462	5.8	365	25.0	434	93	570	7,280	645	8.9	5,206	186	1,211
Aug-Oct 2006	1,476	5.9	383	26.0	429	88	576	7,340	659	9.0	5,238	187	1,217
Sep-Nov 2006	1,495	6.0	390	26.1	438	94	573	7,302	662	9.1	5,217	189	1,190
Oct-Dec 2006	1,510	6.0	391	25.9	448	92	579	7,311	663	9.1	5,221	193	1,192
Nov-Jan 2007	1,527	6.1	398	26.1	443	105	581	7,295	666	9.1	5,213	197	1,178
Dec-Feb 2007	1,520	6.1	396	26.1	441	106	578	7,275	645	8.9	5,232	191	1,171
Jan-Mar 2007	1,533	6.1	402	26.2	436	113	582	7,287	659	9.0	5,235	188	1,173
Feb-Apr 2007	1,513	6.0	401	26.5	427	104	581	7,283	669	9.2	5,242	177	1,162
Mar-May 2007	1,514	6.0	406	26.8	423	100	584	7,264	685	9.4	5,222	176	1,151
Apr-Jun 2007	1,506	6.0	415	27.5	411	97	584	7,255	683	9.4	5,224	174	1,141
May-Jul 2007	1,500	6.0	409	27.3	414	91	586	7,250	696	9.6	5,199	179	1,141
Jun-Aug 2007	1,488	5.9	403	27.1	417	86	581	7,251	696	9.6	5,217	164	1,139
Jul-Sep 2007	1,478	5.9	390	26.4	421	83	583	7,260	692	9.5	5,227	169	1,137
Aug-Oct 2007	1,458	5.8	383	26.2	421	84	570	7,262	698	9.6	5,226	167	1,134
Sep-Nov 2007	1,475	5.8	379	25.7	432	82	581	7,299	694	9.5	5,255	172	1,146
Oct-Dec 2007	1,491	5.9	380	25.5	447	80	583	7,324	725	9.9	5,229	170	1,160
Nov-Jan 2008	1,470	5.8	366	24.9	440	78	586	7,357	733	10.0	5,244	173	1,168
Dec-Feb 2008	1,443	5.7	362	25.1	429	83	569	7,365	724	9.8	5,245	177	1,178
Jan-Mar 2008	1,428	5.6	359	25.1	429	84	556	7,365	701	9.5	5,262	183	1,175
Feb-Apr 2008	1,438	5.6	357	24.8	433	85	563	7,358	690	9.4	5,246	185	1,192
Mar-May 2008	1,420	5.6	356	25.1	407	83	575	7,331	670	9.1	5,249	193	1,171
Apr-Jun 2008	1,397	5.5	345	24.7	407	84	560	7,350	683	9.3	5,247	203	1,175
May-Jul 2008	1,384	5.4	351	25.3	392	87	554	7,341	689	9.4	5,229	213	1,168
Jun-Aug 2008	1,376	5.4	351	25.5	401	82	542	7,350	701	9.5	5,254	213	1,145
Jul-Sep 2008	1,376	5.4	358	26.0	397	88	534	7,333	712	9.7	5,241	205	1,134
Aug-Oct 2008	1,361	5.4	348	25.5	403	83	528	7,342	727	9.9	5,244	195	1,133
Sep-Nov 2008	1,396	5.5	362	25.9	398	84	552	7,405	748	10.1	5,273	198	1,143
Oct-Dec 2008	1,404	5.5	380	27.1	389	86	549	7,386	768	10.4	5,241	197	1,135
Nov-Jan 2009	1,417	5.6	396	27.9	388	91	542	7,399	808	10.9	5,220	191	1,136
Dec-Feb 2009	1,420	5.6	419	29.5	385	84	533	7,414	844	11.4	5,220	183	1,125
Jan-Mar 2009	1,425	5.7	420	29.5	388	82	534	7,431	869	11.7	5,226	184	1,114
Feb-Apr 2009	1,416	5.7	419	29.6	381	86	530	7,386	893	12.1	5,167	190	1,095
Mar-May 2009	1,407	5.6	417	29.6	388	90	513	7,389	935	12.7	5,132	193	1,088
Apr-Jun 2009	1,435	5.8	429	29.9	392	88	527	7,433	966	13.0	5,130	189	1,096
May-Jul 2009	1,430	5.8	442	30.9	372	84	532	7,427	972	13.1	5,138	178	1,087
Jun-Aug 2009	1,430	5.8	445	31.2	374	89	521	7,450	975	13.1	5,141	183	1,102
Jul-Sep 2009	1,440	5.8	462	32.1	372	84	521	7,506	996	13.3	5,160	187	1,118
Aug-Oct 2009	1,434	5.8	467	32.5	367	86	515	7,557	1,011	13.4	5,165	189	1,149
Sep-Nov 2009	1,438	5.8	489	34.0	366	76	507	7,562	1,029	13.6	5,160	183	1,146
Oct-Dec 2009	1,445	5.8	498	34.5	362	77	508	7,552	1,027	13.6	5,159	187	1,138
Nov-Jan 2010	1,449	5.9	499	34.4	370	76	505	7,561	1,038	13.7	5,158	184	1,138
Dec-Feb 2010	1,474	6.0	511	34.7	364	82	516	7,526	1,043	13.9	5,121	179	1,142
Jan-Mar 2010	1,474	6.0	510	34.6	366	79	520	7,559	1,066	14.1	5,146	167	1,136
Feb-Apr 2010	1,490	6.0	536	36.0	362	81	512	7,601	1,083	14.2	5,171	172	1,132
Mar-May 2010	1,528	6.2	549	35.9	376	79	524	7,653	1,072	14.0	5,227	167	1,146
Apr-Jun 2010	1,559	6.3	565	36.2	378	81	535	7,667	1,072	14.0	5,254	172	1,130
May-Jul 2010	1,565	6.3	568	36.3	380	81	536	7,755	1,110	14.3	5,265	170	1,169
Jun-Aug 2010	1,569	6.3	591	37.7	367	87	524	7,784	1,130	14.5	5,258	169	1,181
Jul-Sep 2010	1,571	6.3	597	38.0	363	87	524	7,808	1,148	14.7	5,268	162	1,181
Aug-Oct 2010	1,584	6.4	588	37.1	370	92	534	7,783	1,167	15.0	5,270	164	1,129
Sep-Nov 2010	1,571	6.3	587	37.4	354	94	537	7,761	1,165	15.0	5,295	172	1,077
Oct-Dec 2010	1,544	6.2	579	37.5	339	95	531	7,759	1,181	15.2	5,271	164	1,091
Nov-Jan 2011	1,559	6.2	579	37.2	339	93	548	7,754	1,170	15.1	5,299	164	1,067
Dec-Feb 2011	1,565	6.3	570	36.4	349	94	551	7,758	1,172	15.1	5,307	172	1,050
Jan-Mar 2011	1,586	6.3	576	36.3	358	100	552	7,755	1,182	15.2	5,288	181	1,051
Feb-Apr 2011	1,589	6.3	580	36.5	357	93	559	7,779	1,220	15.7	5,262	184	1,060
Mar-May 2011	1,590	6.3	577	36.3	365	90	558	7,791	1,259	16.2	5,251	181	1,048
Apr-Jun 2011	1,591	6.3	600	37.7	358	86	547	7,747	1,263	16.3	5,212	180	1,034
May-Jul 2011	1,551	6.2	577	37.2	348	85	541	7,665	1,281	16.7	5,131	179	1,013

4.2: Full-time, part-time and temporary workers

United Kingdom (thousands) seasonally adjusted

	Temporary employees (reasons for temporary working)							Part-time workers (reasons for working part-time)[3]					
	Total	Total as % of all employees	Could not find permanent job	% that could not find permanent job	Did not want permanent job	Had a contract with period of training	Some other reason	Total[4]	Could not find full-time job	% that could not find full-time job	Did not want full-time job	Ill or disabled	Student or at school
	13	14	15	16	17	18	19	20	21	22	23	24	25
Jun-Aug 2011	1,520	6.1	585	38.5	312	81	541	7,629	1,268	16.6	5,125	178	1,007
Jul-Sep 2011	1,508	6.1	583	38.7	318	85	522	7,654	1,269	16.6	5,132	186	1,016
Aug-Oct 2011	1,523	6.1	602	39.5	324	85	512	7,683	1,280	16.7	5,154	183	1,019
Sep-Nov 2011	1,551	6.3	593	38.2	351	90	517	7,719	1,315	17.0	5,144	183	1,032
Oct-Dec 2011	1,549	6.2	606	39.1	346	91	506	7,739	1,349	17.4	5,136	188	1,023
Nov-Jan 2012	1,556	6.3	613	39.4	339	96	508	7,736	1,386	17.9	5,114	189	1,004
Dec-Feb 2012	1,575	6.3	631	40.0	344	95	506	7,800	1,398	17.9	5,148	182	1,026
Jan-Mar 2012	1,564	6.3	619	39.6	336	89	520	7,839	1,406	17.9	5,167	189	1,030
Feb-Apr 2012	1,550	6.2	608	39.2	331	94	517	7,822	1,400	17.9	5,149	190	1,034
Mar-May 2012	1,562	6.3	632	40.4	320	93	518	7,819	1,397	17.9	5,152	190	1,032
Apr-Jun 2012	1,580	6.3	631	39.9	323	101	526	7,891	1,422	18.0	5,186	183	1,051
May-Jul 2012	1,628	6.5	658	40.4	335	100	535	7,947	1,424	17.9	5,250	177	1,047
Jun-Aug 2012	1,621	6.5	649	40.0	334	100	538	7,946	1,411	17.8	5,256	178	1,054
Jul-Sep 2012	1,615	6.4	655	40.5	323	93	543	7,939	1,411	17.8	5,263	177	1,037
Aug-Oct 2012	1,620	6.4	650	40.1	325	93	552	7,935	1,405	17.7	5,273	184	1,018
Sep-Nov 2012	1,650	6.5	654	39.7	341	91	564	7,920	1,388	17.5	5,279	181	1,014
Oct-Dec 2012	**1,659**	**6.6**	**661**	**39.9**	**338**	**97**	**563**	**7,895**	**1,381**	**17.5**	**5,272**	**183**	**996**
Change on qtr	*43*	*0.1*	*6*	*-0.7*	*14*	*3*	*20*	*-44*	*-31*	*-0.3*	*9*	*6*	*-41*
Change %	*2.7*		*1.0*		*4.4*	*3.6*	*3.6*	*-0.6*	*-2.2*		*0.2*	*3.4*	*-4.0*
Change on year	*109*	*0.3*	*55*	*0.8*	*-8*	*6*	*57*	*156*	*32*	*0.1*	*136*	*-5*	*-26*
Change %	*7.1*		*9.1*		*-2.4*	*6.4*	*11.2*	*2.0*	*2.3*		*2.6*	*-2.4*	*-2.6*
Male	YCCA	YCCD	YCCG	YCCJ	YCCM	YCCP	YCCS	YCCV	YCCY	YCDB	YCDE	YCDH	YCDK
Nov-Jan 2003	690	5.5	224	32.5	185	41	240	1,502	236	15.7	689	61	505
Dec-Feb 2003	684	5.4	228	33.3	179	38	239	1,510	244	16.2	696	62	497
Jan-Mar 2003	684	5.4	223	32.7	184	38	238	1,522	243	16.0	700	64	505
Feb-Apr 2003	688	5.5	226	32.9	188	34	240	1,535	246	16.0	710	66	504
Mar-May 2003	685	5.4	226	33.0	188	34	237	1,543	250	16.2	717	66	502
Apr-Jun 2003	686	5.4	224	32.7	193	36	233	1,545	256	16.6	717	67	495
May-Jul 2003	691	5.5	221	31.9	191	40	239	1,538	250	16.2	715	68	494
Jun-Aug 2003	694	5.5	223	32.1	185	42	244	1,533	251	16.4	712	69	488
Jul-Sep 2003	707	5.6	220	31.2	185	41	260	1,516	253	16.7	700	72	478
Aug-Oct 2003	710	5.7	223	31.4	186	40	262	1,523	247	16.2	703	73	487
Sep-Nov 2003	707	5.6	226	32.0	178	37	265	1,501	250	16.7	688	71	483
Oct-Dec 2003	712	5.7	231	32.4	179	35	268	1,509	245	16.2	701	74	480
Nov-Jan 2004	707	5.6	236	33.3	172	33	266	1,519	249	16.4	704	76	482
Dec-Feb 2004	709	5.6	234	33.0	174	37	264	1,525	251	16.5	706	76	484
Jan-Mar 2004	698	5.5	233	33.3	168	37	260	1,553	265	17.1	718	73	488
Feb-Apr 2004	700	5.6	221	31.6	176	41	261	1,553	259	16.7	726	71	488
Mar-May 2004	695	5.5	221	31.8	178	41	256	1,571	253	16.1	742	72	496
Apr-Jun 2004	702	5.6	224	31.9	174	44	260	1,568	244	15.6	745	73	497
May-Jul 2004	701	5.6	227	32.4	172	43	258	1,569	243	15.5	751	69	498
Jun-Aug 2004	743	5.9	224	30.2	184	49	285	1,584	245	15.5	761	67	501
Jul-Sep 2004	723	5.7	218	30.2	175	55	274	1,581	246	15.5	762	64	501
Aug-Oct 2004	718	5.7	218	30.3	171	52	277	1,570	244	15.5	753	66	499
Sep-Nov 2004	691	5.5	209	30.2	169	51	262	1,551	232	14.9	742	69	500
Oct-Dec 2004	715	5.6	212	29.7	187	52	264	1,571	230	14.7	756	66	509
Nov-Jan 2005	709	5.6	203	28.6	187	54	265	1,587	228	14.4	754	65	529
Dec-Feb 2005	706	5.5	202	28.6	177	52	276	1,583	225	14.2	768	66	512
Jan-Mar 2005	697	5.5	202	28.9	175	52	268	1,591	232	14.6	768	69	510
Feb-Apr 2005	692	5.4	206	29.7	170	53	265	1,598	229	14.4	772	76	506
Mar-May 2005	691	5.4	211	30.5	161	57	263	1,597	236	14.8	766	72	510
Apr-Jun 2005	695	5.5	210	30.2	169	56	261	1,592	236	14.8	754	73	512
May-Jul 2005	696	5.5	208	29.8	174	60	254	1,589	242	15.2	747	73	512
Jun-Aug 2005	682	5.3	212	31.1	175	58	237	1,585	228	14.4	756	75	512
Jul-Sep 2005	684	5.3	213	31.1	169	59	243	1,590	228	14.4	770	76	506
Aug-Oct 2005	671	5.2	206	30.7	170	56	239	1,590	234	14.7	772	77	496
Sep-Nov 2005	663	5.2	202	30.5	166	51	243	1,603	248	15.5	778	76	490
Oct-Dec 2005	652	5.1	195	29.8	165	43	249	1,610	247	15.3	785	77	489
Nov-Jan 2006	655	5.1	196	29.9	164	50	245	1,607	245	15.2	784	75	489
Dec-Feb 2006	663	5.2	191	28.8	169	55	248	1,622	251	15.5	786	76	497
Jan-Mar 2006	669	5.2	192	28.8	169	61	247	1,608	247	15.4	777	76	495
Feb-Apr 2006	673	5.2	195	29.0	177	56	246	1,609	248	15.4	775	72	503
Mar-May 2006	670	5.2	188	28.1	175	55	252	1,611	249	15.5	774	73	503
Apr-Jun 2006	659	5.1	188	28.6	175	53	242	1,623	256	15.8	770	70	518
May-Jul 2006	650	5.0	181	27.8	170	48	250	1,635	258	15.8	771	74	523
Jun-Aug 2006	667	5.2	187	28.0	174	47	259	1,629	265	16.2	758	76	520
Jul-Sep 2006	671	5.2	194	28.9	175	47	255	1,658	272	16.4	767	74	533
Aug-Oct 2006	690	5.4	206	29.8	178	46	261	1,686	281	16.7	786	74	531
Sep-Nov 2006	705	5.5	211	30.0	184	50	260	1,658	281	17.0	779	75	510
Oct-Dec 2006	710	5.5	214	30.1	187	49	261	1,655	279	16.9	784	78	504
Nov-Jan 2007	716	5.6	210	29.3	188	57	262	1,647	281	17.1	769	83	503
Dec-Feb 2007	708	5.5	213	30.1	187	52	256	1,655	268	16.2	786	81	508
Jan-Mar 2007	718	5.6	215	29.9	185	55	263	1,676	276	16.4	797	81	512
Feb-Apr 2007	701	5.4	212	30.2	178	49	262	1,670	274	16.4	798	80	508
Mar-May 2007	702	5.4	220	31.4	176	43	263	1,666	279	16.8	802	76	498
Apr-Jun 2007	698	5.4	223	31.9	174	40	260	1,668	280	16.8	821	75	480
May-Jul 2007	696	5.4	220	31.6	179	39	258	1,669	284	17.0	831	79	463
Jun-Aug 2007	698	5.4	218	31.2	187	38	255	1,670	292	17.5	826	69	470
Jul-Sep 2007	686	5.3	207	30.2	191	37	251	1,687	293	17.4	828	72	480

4.2: Full-time, part-time and temporary workers

United Kingdom (thousands) seasonally adjusted

	Temporary employees (reasons for temporary working)							Part-time workers (reasons for working part-time)[3]					
	Total	Total as % of all employees	Could not find permanent job	% that could not find permanent job	Did not want permanent job	Had a contract with period of training	Some other reason	Total[4]	Could not find full-time job	% that could not find full-time job	Did not want full-time job	Ill or disabled	Student or at school
	13	14	15	16	17	18	19	20	21	22	23	24	25
Aug-Oct 2007	671	5.2	202	30.1	188	38	243	1,673	292	17.4	814	71	484
Sep-Nov 2007	687	5.3	203	29.6	193	42	248	1,710	288	16.8	831	71	508
Oct-Dec 2007	699	5.4	201	28.8	195	45	258	1,716	290	16.9	834	70	508
Nov-Jan 2008	689	5.3	189	27.4	192	44	265	1,737	290	16.7	855	68	511
Dec-Feb 2008	667	5.1	183	27.4	183	44	258	1,739	292	16.8	855	68	510
Jan-Mar 2008	660	5.1	183	27.7	185	41	251	1,734	288	16.6	858	68	506
Feb-Apr 2008	661	5.1	181	27.4	185	42	253	1,738	286	16.4	859	72	505
Mar-May 2008	654	5.0	180	27.6	168	44	261	1,711	270	15.8	858	77	490
Apr-Jun 2008	633	4.8	176	27.8	162	46	249	1,744	276	15.8	865	77	510
May-Jul 2008	619	4.7	184	29.6	147	48	241	1,756	292	16.6	857	81	512
Jun-Aug 2008	618	4.8	180	29.0	155	44	240	1,768	305	17.2	856	82	513
Jul-Sep 2008	635	4.9	185	29.1	157	47	246	1,769	316	17.8	857	80	503
Aug-Oct 2008	628	4.8	176	28.1	169	42	241	1,775	321	18.1	854	79	507
Sep-Nov 2008	636	4.9	186	29.2	156	42	252	1,772	332	18.7	844	79	501
Oct-Dec 2008	641	4.9	195	30.5	153	42	250	1,784	353	19.8	837	80	497
Nov-Jan 2009	660	5.1	215	32.6	155	48	242	1,793	376	21.0	829	77	494
Dec-Feb 2009	663	5.1	227	34.2	160	38	239	1,796	385	21.5	828	79	490
Jan-Mar 2009	666	5.2	231	34.6	158	38	239	1,788	393	22.0	820	78	484
Feb-Apr 2009	668	5.2	231	34.6	157	40	240	1,791	405	22.6	812	79	476
Mar-May 2009	658	5.2	223	33.8	156	47	233	1,812	427	23.6	806	83	477
Apr-Jun 2009	683	5.4	230	33.7	161	46	246	1,825	445	24.4	796	80	481
May-Jul 2009	689	5.5	233	33.8	155	45	256	1,795	442	24.6	790	72	474
Jun-Aug 2009	681	5.4	236	34.7	151	47	246	1,802	431	23.9	800	70	480
Jul-Sep 2009	674	5.4	243	36.0	146	44	241	1,790	433	24.2	784	78	477
Aug-Oct 2009	675	5.4	247	36.6	140	50	238	1,800	434	24.1	778	78	492
Sep-Nov 2009	690	5.5	264	38.3	146	43	237	1,812	448	24.7	785	76	486
Oct-Dec 2009	698	5.6	272	39.0	147	42	237	1,815	447	24.6	797	77	478
Nov-Jan 2010	689	5.5	262	38.1	149	41	237	1,827	451	24.7	809	74	476
Dec-Feb 2010	713	5.7	276	38.7	151	46	241	1,819	457	25.1	798	71	479
Jan-Mar 2010	709	5.7	270	38.0	152	43	245	1,835	466	25.4	805	68	484
Feb-Apr 2010	715	5.7	284	39.7	152	42	238	1,840	467	25.4	802	68	493
Mar-May 2010	733	5.8	291	39.7	159	41	243	1,868	464	24.8	828	63	503
Apr-Jun 2010	755	6.0	302	39.9	163	40	251	1,894	471	24.9	845	71	497
May-Jul 2010	756	6.0	302	39.9	160	41	253	1,919	481	25.1	842	70	513
Jun-Aug 2010	761	6.0	317	41.6	157	45	242	1,947	490	25.1	847	77	519
Jul-Sep 2010	757	6.0	321	42.5	148	46	241	1,974	502	25.4	857	71	527
Aug-Oct 2010	761	6.0	315	41.4	154	50	242	1,970	520	26.4	866	72	498
Sep-Nov 2010	749	5.9	306	40.8	150	53	240	1,968	519	26.4	873	77	483
Oct-Dec 2010	728	5.7	296	40.7	148	54	230	1,971	520	26.4	875	73	488
Nov-Jan 2011	744	5.8	303	40.7	146	51	244	1,944	511	26.3	874	72	470
Dec-Feb 2011	745	5.8	297	39.9	147	51	248	1,925	511	26.6	866	75	453
Jan-Mar 2011	752	5.9	301	40.0	148	56	248	1,930	525	27.2	863	80	440
Feb-Apr 2011	766	6.0	312	40.8	147	50	256	1,970	543	27.6	872	83	453
Mar-May 2011	766	6.0	311	40.6	150	47	258	1,971	558	28.3	880	75	439
Apr-Jun 2011	780	6.1	324	41.6	150	45	260	1,962	565	28.8	871	72	435
May-Jul 2011	756	6.0	306	40.4	152	46	253	1,939	579	29.9	854	70	417
Jun-Aug 2011	740	5.9	310	41.9	133	42	255	1,889	565	29.9	832	67	410
Jul-Sep 2011	733	5.8	306	41.8	137	43	246	1,900	556	29.3	845	66	415
Aug-Oct 2011	731	5.8	311	42.6	134	42	244	1,922	562	29.2	850	67	424
Sep-Nov 2011	735	5.8	303	41.3	149	42	241	1,954	577	29.5	853	67	437
Oct-Dec 2011	737	5.8	315	42.8	143	42	238	1,959	594	30.3	846	69	433
Nov-Jan 2012	739	5.9	319	43.1	140	44	236	1,951	606	31.1	836	72	424
Dec-Feb 2012	743	5.9	331	44.6	137	44	231	2,017	625	31.0	856	72	450
Jan-Mar 2012	744	5.9	324	43.5	138	43	239	2,034	637	31.3	861	72	453
Feb-Apr 2012	741	5.8	311	42.0	138	45	246	2,043	643	31.5	858	74	452
Mar-May 2012	734	5.8	322	43.9	133	44	235	2,033	638	31.4	853	76	449
Apr-Jun 2012	735	5.8	319	43.4	132	48	237	2,067	654	31.7	864	75	454
May-Jul 2012	753	5.9	336	44.6	131	50	236	2,050	645	31.4	869	70	449
Jun-Aug 2012	750	5.9	327	43.6	132	51	240	2,055	632	30.7	879	73	451
Jul-Sep 2012	758	5.9	335	44.2	126	47	250	2,049	637	31.1	880	69	442
Aug-Oct 2012	764	6.0	337	44.1	125	47	255	2,031	634	31.2	889	68	418
Sep-Nov 2012	782	6.1	347	44.3	131	42	262	2,021	632	31.3	885	62	415
Oct-Dec 2012	**797**	**6.2**	**362**	**45.4**	**135**	**44**	**256**	**2,011**	**640**	**31.8**	**877**	**66**	**400**
Change on qtr	*39*	*0.3*	*26*	*1.1*	*10*	*-3*	*6*	*-38*	*3*	*0.7*	*-3*	*-3*	*-41*
Change %	*5.1*		*7.8*		*7.7*	*-7.1*	*2.5*	*-1.8*	*0.5*		*-0.4*	*-4.2*	*-9.3*
Change on year	*60*	*0.4*	*46*	*2.6*	*-8*	*2*	*19*	*52*	*45*	*1.5*	*31*	*-3*	*-32*
Change %	*8.1*		*14.7*		*-5.4*	*5.0*	*7.9*	*2.7*	*7.6*		*3.6*	*-4.2*	*-7.5*
Female	YCCB	YCCE	YCCH	YCCK	YCCN	YCCQ	YCCT	YCCW	YCCZ	YCDC	YCDF	YCDI	YCDL
Nov-Jan 2003	861	7.3	185	21.5	282	51	343	5,521	318	5.8	4,480	72	633
Dec-Feb 2003	850	7.2	184	21.6	270	51	346	5,544	310	5.6	4,511	75	627
Jan-Mar 2003	836	7.0	174	20.9	271	49	341	5,582	316	5.7	4,528	75	638
Feb-Apr 2003	830	7.0	175	21.1	276	41	337	5,609	323	5.8	4,547	73	641
Mar-May 2003	821	6.9	180	22.0	271	39	330	5,616	331	5.9	4,531	80	649
Apr-Jun 2003	807	6.8	179	22.2	266	43	319	5,606	322	5.7	4,532	82	645
May-Jul 2003	795	6.7	172	21.7	261	43	319	5,594	313	5.6	4,534	79	645
Jun-Aug 2003	782	6.6	159	20.4	266	47	309	5,612	312	5.6	4,547	81	647
Jul-Sep 2003	816	6.9	172	21.1	279	52	313	5,627	313	5.6	4,562	84	647
Aug-Oct 2003	845	7.1	187	22.1	284	55	319	5,649	326	5.8	4,563	90	647
Sep-Nov 2003	833	7.0	177	21.2	276	51	330	5,661	320	5.6	4,566	100	656

4.2: Full-time, part-time and temporary workers

United Kingdom (thousands) seasonally adjusted

	Temporary employees (reasons for temporary working)							Part-time workers (reasons for working part-time)[3]					
	Total	Total as % of all employees	Could not find permanent job	% that could not find permanent job	Did not want permanent job	Had a contract with period of training	Some other reason	Total[4]	Could not find full-time job	% that could not find full-time job	Did not want full-time job	Ill or disabled	Student or at school
	13	14	15	16	17	18	19	20	21	22	23	24	25
Oct-Dec 2003	817	6.9	168	20.6	265	50	333	5,677	320	5.6	4,579	103	654
Nov-Jan 2004	812	6.8	169	20.9	263	49	331	5,705	314	5.5	4,596	104	670
Dec-Feb 2004	808	6.7	170	21.1	262	50	325	5,722	310	5.4	4,612	110	670
Jan-Mar 2004	809	6.8	172	21.3	263	49	325	5,712	304	5.3	4,596	114	677
Feb-Apr 2004	803	6.7	173	21.5	258	45	327	5,687	309	5.4	4,563	114	680
Mar-May 2004	795	6.6	166	20.9	261	41	326	5,669	292	5.2	4,576	111	668
Apr-Jun 2004	809	6.8	167	20.6	266	45	330	5,656	289	5.1	4,583	109	653
May-Jul 2004	798	6.7	166	20.7	256	44	333	5,650	300	5.3	4,561	110	657
Jun-Aug 2004	792	6.6	160	20.2	247	43	342	5,637	302	5.4	4,545	109	661
Jul-Sep 2004	793	6.6	158	20.0	247	44	343	5,627	309	5.5	4,520	106	667
Aug-Oct 2004	801	6.7	153	19.1	250	51	347	5,602	311	5.6	4,493	105	669
Sep-Nov 2004	796	6.6	153	19.3	245	60	338	5,604	305	5.4	4,500	102	674
Oct-Dec 2004	792	6.5	152	19.2	243	64	333	5,582	307	5.5	4,490	100	666
Nov-Jan 2005	790	6.5	154	19.5	240	58	338	5,567	310	5.6	4,485	101	653
Dec-Feb 2005	796	6.6	155	19.4	242	62	338	5,551	323	5.8	4,460	100	649
Jan-Mar 2005	769	6.3	155	20.1	229	51	334	5,538	336	6.1	4,441	97	643
Feb-Apr 2005	752	6.2	151	20.1	215	51	335	5,545	333	6.0	4,453	99	640
Mar-May 2005	755	6.2	146	19.3	221	48	340	5,595	349	6.2	4,493	96	642
Apr-Jun 2005	755	6.2	146	19.3	218	42	349	5,611	351	6.3	4,489	92	661
May-Jul 2005	778	6.4	147	18.9	228	47	356	5,618	350	6.2	4,487	87	674
Jun-Aug 2005	789	6.5	165	21.0	222	42	359	5,603	361	6.4	4,478	91	651
Jul-Sep 2005	796	6.5	180	22.6	226	45	346	5,590	369	6.6	4,463	92	646
Aug-Oct 2005	762	6.2	179	23.5	218	44	320	5,572	359	6.4	4,454	93	647
Sep-Nov 2005	756	6.2	168	22.2	212	51	325	5,548	364	6.6	4,434	92	637
Oct-Dec 2005	735	6.0	152	20.7	209	51	323	5,516	357	6.5	4,421	92	624
Nov-Jan 2006	775	6.4	168	21.6	224	54	329	5,540	365	6.6	4,425	93	633
Dec-Feb 2006	787	6.4	172	21.8	233	47	335	5,569	368	6.6	4,431	101	644
Jan-Mar 2006	815	6.7	180	22.1	242	54	339	5,614	371	6.6	4,462	98	652
Feb-Apr 2006	811	6.6	174	21.4	241	59	337	5,604	369	6.6	4,454	99	654
Mar-May 2006	808	6.6	180	22.3	239	59	330	5,582	360	6.5	4,437	97	659
Apr-Jun 2006	804	6.6	181	22.5	244	56	322	5,612	368	6.6	4,455	101	661
May-Jul 2006	791	6.5	178	22.5	246	51	316	5,607	374	6.7	4,442	101	663
Jun-Aug 2006	800	6.5	175	21.9	260	48	317	5,639	379	6.7	4,456	108	677
Jul-Sep 2006	791	6.5	171	21.7	258	46	315	5,622	373	6.6	4,439	112	678
Aug-Oct 2006	786	6.4	178	22.6	252	42	315	5,653	378	6.7	4,451	113	686
Sep-Nov 2006	790	6.5	179	22.7	254	44	313	5,644	380	6.7	4,438	114	680
Oct-Dec 2006	799	6.5	178	22.2	261	43	318	5,655	384	6.8	4,436	115	688
Nov-Jan 2007	811	6.6	188	23.2	255	48	320	5,649	386	6.8	4,444	115	675
Dec-Feb 2007	812	6.7	183	22.5	254	54	322	5,620	377	6.7	4,445	110	663
Jan-Mar 2007	815	6.7	187	23.0	251	58	319	5,611	384	6.8	4,438	107	661
Feb-Apr 2007	812	6.7	190	23.4	249	55	318	5,612	395	7.0	4,444	97	654
Mar-May 2007	812	6.6	186	22.9	248	57	321	5,598	406	7.2	4,419	100	652
Apr-Jun 2007	809	6.6	192	23.7	237	56	324	5,588	403	7.2	4,403	99	661
May-Jul 2007	805	6.6	189	23.5	235	53	329	5,581	413	7.4	4,369	101	678
Jun-Aug 2007	790	6.5	185	23.4	230	48	327	5,581	404	7.2	4,391	95	669
Jul-Sep 2007	792	6.5	183	23.2	230	46	332	5,573	399	7.2	4,399	97	656
Aug-Oct 2007	786	6.4	180	22.9	233	45	327	5,589	406	7.3	4,412	97	649
Sep-Nov 2007	787	6.4	176	22.3	239	40	333	5,589	406	7.3	4,424	102	638
Oct-Dec 2007	791	6.4	179	22.6	252	35	325	5,608	435	7.8	4,395	100	652
Nov-Jan 2008	781	6.3	177	22.7	248	34	321	5,620	443	7.9	4,389	105	657
Dec-Feb 2008	776	6.3	179	23.1	246	39	311	5,627	432	7.7	4,390	109	668
Jan-Mar 2008	768	6.2	176	22.9	244	43	305	5,630	413	7.3	4,404	115	670
Feb-Apr 2008	777	6.3	176	22.7	248	43	310	5,619	404	7.2	4,387	113	687
Mar-May 2008	767	6.2	176	22.9	239	39	314	5,619	401	7.1	4,392	117	681
Apr-Jun 2008	763	6.1	169	22.2	245	38	312	5,606	406	7.2	4,382	125	665
May-Jul 2008	765	6.2	167	21.9	245	40	312	5,585	397	7.1	4,373	132	655
Jun-Aug 2008	757	6.1	171	22.6	246	38	302	5,582	396	7.1	4,398	131	631
Jul-Sep 2008	741	6.0	173	23.3	239	41	288	5,564	397	7.1	4,384	125	631
Aug-Oct 2008	733	5.9	171	23.4	234	41	287	5,567	406	7.3	4,390	116	626
Sep-Nov 2008	760	6.1	176	23.1	242	42	300	5,634	416	7.4	4,429	119	643
Oct-Dec 2008	763	6.2	185	24.3	236	43	299	5,602	415	7.4	4,403	117	638
Nov-Jan 2009	757	6.1	180	23.8	234	44	299	5,606	432	7.7	4,391	113	642
Dec-Feb 2009	757	6.1	192	25.4	225	46	294	5,618	459	8.2	4,392	105	635
Jan-Mar 2009	758	6.2	189	25.0	230	44	295	5,643	476	8.4	4,406	106	630
Feb-Apr 2009	747	6.1	188	25.1	224	46	289	5,595	488	8.7	4,355	110	619
Mar-May 2009	749	6.1	194	25.9	232	43	280	5,577	508	9.1	4,326	110	612
Apr-Jun 2009	752	6.1	198	26.4	231	42	281	5,608	521	9.3	4,334	109	615
May-Jul 2009	740	6.1	209	28.2	218	38	276	5,632	530	9.4	4,348	106	614
Jun-Aug 2009	749	6.1	209	27.9	223	41	275	5,648	544	9.6	4,341	113	622
Jul-Sep 2009	766	6.3	220	28.7	226	40	280	5,716	563	9.9	4,376	108	641
Aug-Oct 2009	759	6.2	219	28.9	227	36	277	5,757	578	10.0	4,387	111	657
Sep-Nov 2009	748	6.1	225	30.1	220	33	270	5,750	581	10.1	4,376	107	660
Oct-Dec 2009	747	6.1	226	30.2	215	35	272	5,737	580	10.1	4,362	110	659
Nov-Jan 2010	760	6.2	236	31.1	221	35	268	5,734	587	10.2	4,349	110	661
Dec-Feb 2010	761	6.2	236	31.0	213	37	275	5,707	586	10.3	4,323	108	664
Jan-Mar 2010	765	6.3	240	31.3	214	36	275	5,724	600	10.5	4,341	99	652
Feb-Apr 2010	775	6.4	252	32.5	210	39	274	5,761	616	10.7	4,370	104	639
Mar-May 2010	795	6.5	258	32.4	217	38	282	5,786	609	10.5	4,399	104	643
Apr-Jun 2010	804	6.6	263	32.7	216	41	284	5,773	601	10.4	4,409	101	633
May-Jul 2010	809	6.6	266	32.9	220	40	283	5,835	628	10.8	4,423	99	656
Jun-Aug 2010	808	6.6	274	33.9	210	42	282	5,836	641	11.0	4,411	92	662
Jul-Sep 2010	814	6.7	276	33.9	214	41	283	5,834	646	11.1	4,411	91	653
Aug-Oct 2010	823	6.7	273	33.1	216	43	292	5,813	647	11.1	4,404	92	631
Sep-Nov 2010	822	6.7	282	34.2	204	41	296	5,793	646	11.1	4,421	94	594

4.2: Full-time, part-time and temporary workers

United Kingdom (thousands) seasonally adjusted

	Temporary employees (reasons for temporary working)							Part-time workers (reasons for working part-time)[3]					
	Total	Total as % of all employees	Could not find permanent job	% that could not find permanent job	Did not want permanent job	Had a contract with period of training	Some other reason	Total[4]	Could not find full-time job	% that could not find full-time job	Did not want full-time job	Ill or disabled	Student or at school
	13	14	15	16	17	18	19	20	21	22	23	24	25
Oct-Dec 2010	816	6.7	283	34.6	191	42	301	5,788	661	11.4	4,395	91	603
Nov-Jan 2011	816	6.7	277	33.9	193	42	304	5,810	660	11.4	4,425	92	596
Dec-Feb 2011	820	6.7	273	33.3	202	43	303	5,833	661	11.3	4,441	97	598
Jan-Mar 2011	834	6.8	275	33.0	211	44	304	5,825	658	11.3	4,425	100	611
Feb-Apr 2011	823	6.7	268	32.5	210	43	303	5,809	677	11.7	4,390	101	608
Mar-May 2011	824	6.7	267	32.4	215	43	299	5,820	701	12.0	4,371	106	608
Apr-Jun 2011	811	6.6	276	34.0	208	41	287	5,785	698	12.1	4,342	108	599
May-Jul 2011	795	6.5	272	34.2	196	39	288	5,726	702	12.3	4,277	109	597
Jun-Aug 2011	780	6.4	275	35.3	180	39	287	5,740	703	12.3	4,293	112	597
Jul-Sep 2011	775	6.4	277	35.7	181	41	276	5,754	713	12.4	4,286	120	601
Aug-Oct 2011	793	6.5	291	36.7	190	43	268	5,762	718	12.5	4,304	116	594
Sep-Nov 2011	816	6.7	290	35.5	203	48	276	5,764	738	12.8	4,291	116	595
Oct-Dec 2011	812	6.6	291	35.8	203	49	269	5,780	755	13.1	4,290	119	590
Nov-Jan 2012	817	6.7	295	36.1	198	52	272	5,784	780	13.5	4,277	118	580
Dec-Feb 2012	832	6.8	299	36.0	207	50	275	5,784	773	13.4	4,292	110	576
Jan-Mar 2012	820	6.7	296	36.1	197	46	281	5,804	769	13.3	4,306	117	577
Feb-Apr 2012	810	6.6	296	36.6	194	48	271	5,780	757	13.1	4,291	115	582
Mar-May 2012	828	6.8	310	37.4	187	49	283	5,785	758	13.1	4,299	114	583
Apr-Jun 2012	845	6.9	312	36.9	191	53	290	5,824	768	13.2	4,322	109	597
May-Jul 2012	875	7.1	322	36.8	204	50	299	5,897	779	13.2	4,382	107	599
Jun-Aug 2012	871	7.1	322	36.9	202	49	298	5,891	780	13.2	4,377	104	603
Jul-Sep 2012	857	6.9	319	37.3	198	46	293	5,890	774	13.1	4,383	108	596
Aug-Oct 2012	856	6.9	313	36.6	200	45	297	5,904	771	13.1	4,384	116	600
Sep-Nov 2012	868	7.0	307	35.4	210	49	302	5,899	756	12.8	4,393	119	599
Oct-Dec 2012	**862**	**7.0**	**300**	**34.8**	**202**	**53**	**306**	**5,883**	**741**	**12.6**	**4,395**	**117**	**596**
Change on qtr	*5*	*0.0*	*-20*	*-2.5*	*5*	*7*	*13*	*-7*	*-34*	*-0.6*	*12*	*9*	*0*
Change %	*0.5*		*-6.2*		*2.3*	*14.4*	*4.5*	*-0.1*	*-4.3*		*0.3*	*8.3*	*0.0*
Change on year	*50*	*0.3*	*9*	*-1.0*	*-1*	*4*	*38*	*103*	*-14*	*-0.5*	*105*	*-2*	*6*
Change %	*6.1*		*3.0*		*-0.3*	*7.6*	*14.1*	*1.8*	*-1.8*		*2.4*	*-1.4*	*1.0*

Relationship between columns: 1= 2+3+4+5; 1=6+7; 2=8+9; 3=10+11; 13=15+17+18+19; 20=21+23+24+25 ; 20=9+11 ;14=13/2; 16=15/13; 22=21/20

1. The split between full-time and part-time employment is based on respondents' self-classification.

2. This series does not include all people on these programmes; it only includes those engaging in any form of work, work experience or work-related training.

3. These series cover Employees and Self-employed only. These series include some temporary employees recorded in columns 13 to 19.

4. The total includes those who did not give a reason for working part-time and it therefore does not equal the sum of columns 21, 23, 24 and 25.

.. Data not available.

Source: Labour Force Survey
Labour market statistics enquiries: labour.market@ons.gov.uk

Data taken from Labour Market Statistics, February 2013 : http://www.ons.gov.uk/ons/rel/lms/labour-market-statistics/february-2013/table-emp01.xls

Further information

The Labour Force Survey is a survey of the population of private households, student halls of residence and NHS accommodation

4.3 Employment: by sex and age: United Kingdom

United Kingdom (thousands) seasonally adjusted

	Aged 16 and over						Aged 16-64					
	Employment		Unemployment		Inactivity		Employment		Unemployment		Inactivity	
	Level	Rate	Level	Rate	Level	Rate	Level	Rate	Level	Rate	Level	Rate
People	MGRZ	MGSR	MGSC	MGSX	MGSI	YBTC	LF2G	LF24	LF2I	LF2Q	LF2M	LF2S
Oct-Dec 2010	29,120	58.3	2,477	7.8	18,359	36.8	28,243	70.5	2,457	8.0	9,358	23.4
Oct-Dec 2011	29,146	57.9	2,657	8.4	18,517	36.8	28,272	70.4	2,630	8.5	9,273	23.1
Jan-Mar 2012	29,274	58.1	2,610	8.2	18,527	36.8	28,384	70.6	2,582	8.3	9,214	22.9
Apr-Jun 2012	29,476	58.4	2,564	8.0	18,463	36.6	28,544	71.0	2,544	8.2	9,098	22.6
Jul-Sep 2012	29,576	58.5	2,514	7.8	18,504	36.6	28,631	71.2	2,494	8.0	9,073	22.6
Oct-Dec 2012	**29,730**	**58.7**	**2,501**	**7.8**	**18,456**	**36.4**	**28,757**	**71.5**	**2,479**	**7.9**	**8,979**	**22.3**
Change on quarter	*154*	*0.2*	*-14*	*-0.1*	*-48*	*-0.2*	*126*	*0.3*	*-15*	*-0.1*	*-94*	*-0.2*
Change %	*0.5*		*-0.5*		*-0.3*		*0.4*		*-0.6*		*-1.0*	
Change on year	*584*	*0.7*	*-156*	*-0.6*	*-62*	*-0.4*	*485*	*1.1*	*-152*	*-0.6*	*-294*	*-0.8*
Change %	*2.0*		*-5.9*		*-0.3*		*1.7*		*-5.8*		*-3.2*	
Men	MGSA	MGSS	MGSD	MGSY	MGSJ	YBTD	YBSF	MGSV	YBSI	YBTJ	YBSO	YBTM
Oct-Dec 2010	15,644	64.1	1,451	8.5	7,303	29.9	15,117	75.8	1,436	8.7	3,397	17.0
Oct-Dec 2011	15,603	63.5	1,537	9.0	7,449	30.3	15,077	75.4	1,520	9.2	3,410	17.0
Jan-Mar 2012	15,695	63.7	1,494	8.7	7,450	30.2	15,159	75.8	1,475	8.9	3,378	16.9
Apr-Jun 2012	15,838	64.1	1,464	8.5	7,387	29.9	15,265	76.3	1,453	8.7	3,299	16.5
Jul-Sep 2012	15,877	64.2	1,426	8.2	7,437	30.1	15,312	76.5	1,412	8.4	3,301	16.5
Oct-Dec 2012	**15,932**	**64.3**	**1,410**	**8.1**	**7,448**	**30.0**	**15,339**	**76.6**	**1,392**	**8.3**	**3,304**	**16.5**
Change on quarter	*55*	*0.1*	*-16*	*-0.1*	*11*	*0.0*	*28*	*0.1*	*-20*	*-0.1*	*3*	*0.0*
Change %	*0.3*		*-1.1*		*0.1*		*0.2*		*-1.4*		*0.1*	
Change on year	*329*	*0.8*	*-127*	*-0.8*	*-1*	*-0.3*	*262*	*1.2*	*-128*	*-0.8*	*-106*	*-0.6*
Change %	*2.1*		*-8.3*		*0.0*		*1.7*		*-8.4*		*-3.1*	
Women	MGSB	MGST	MGSE	MGSZ	MGSK	YBTE	LF2H	LF25	LF2J	LF2R	LF2N	LF2T
Oct-Dec 2010	13,477	52.7	1,026	7.1	11,057	43.3	13,126	65.3	1,021	7.2	5,961	29.6
Oct-Dec 2011	13,543	52.6	1,120	7.6	11,068	43.0	13,194	65.4	1,110	7.8	5,863	29.1
Jan-Mar 2012	13,579	52.7	1,116	7.6	11,076	43.0	13,225	65.6	1,106	7.7	5,837	28.9
Apr-Jun 2012	13,637	52.8	1,099	7.5	11,076	42.9	13,279	65.8	1,091	7.6	5,798	28.7
Jul-Sep 2012	13,699	53.0	1,089	7.4	11,066	42.8	13,319	66.0	1,082	7.5	5,772	28.6
Oct-Dec 2012	**13,797**	**53.3**	**1,091**	**7.3**	**11,008**	**42.5**	**13,417**	**66.5**	**1,087**	**7.5**	**5,675**	**28.1**
Change on quarter	*98*	*0.3*	*2*	*0.0*	*-59*	*-0.3*	*98*	*0.5*	*5*	*0.0*	*-97*	*-0.5*
Change %	*0.7*		*0.2*		*-0.5*		*0.7*		*0.4*		*-1.7*	
Change on year	*255*	*0.6*	*-29*	*-0.3*	*-61*	*-0.5*	*223*	*1.1*	*-23*	*-0.3*	*-188*	*-0.9*
Change %	*1.9*		*-2.6*		*-0.5*		*1.7*		*-2.1*		*-3.2*	

	Aged 16-17						Aged 18-24					
	Employment		Unemployment		Inactivity		Employment		Unemployment		Inactivity	
	Level	Rate	Level	Rate	Level	Rate	Level	Rate	Level	Rate	Level	Rate
People	YBTO	YBUA	YBVH	YBVK	YCAS	LWEX	YBTR	YBUD	YBVN	YBVQ	YCAV	LWFA
Oct-Dec 2010	353	23.4	211	37.4	941	62.5	3,390	58.2	745	18.0	1,689	29.0
Oct-Dec 2011	345	23.4	211	37.9	921	62.4	3,295	56.6	822	20.0	1,703	29.3
Jan-Mar 2012	346	23.5	206	37.3	919	62.5	3,304	56.8	810	19.7	1,701	29.2
Apr-Jun 2012	352	24.0	203	36.5	912	62.2	3,338	57.5	809	19.5	1,663	28.6
Jul-Sep 2012	359	24.5	189	34.5	916	62.6	3,327	57.4	774	18.9	1,699	29.3
Oct-Dec 2012	**327**	**22.3**	**197**	**37.6**	**941**	**64.2**	**3,388**	**58.6**	**776**	**18.6**	**1,620**	**28.0**
Change on quarter	*-32*	*-2.2*	*8*	*3.1*	*25*	*1.7*	*62*	*1.2*	*3*	*-0.2*	*-79*	*-1.3*
Change %	*-9.0*		*4.1*		*2.7*		*1.9*		*0.4*		*-4.6*	
Change on year	*-18*	*-1.1*	*-14*	*-0.3*	*20*	*1.9*	*93*	*2.0*	*-45*	*-1.3*	*-84*	*-1.3*
Change %	*-5.3*		*-6.4*		*2.2*		*2.8*		*-5.5*		*-4.9*	
Men	YBTP	YBUB	YBVI	YBVL	YCAT	LWEY	YBTS	YBUE	YBVO	YBVR	YCAW	LWFB
Oct-Dec 2010	162	21.0	112	40.9	497	64.5	1,802	60.8	439	19.6	724	24.4
Oct-Dec 2011	159	21.0	109	40.7	488	64.5	1,691	57.2	514	23.3	751	25.4
Jan-Mar 2012	165	21.9	106	39.1	482	64.0	1,702	57.6	504	22.9	747	25.3
Apr-Jun 2012	164	21.9	103	38.6	484	64.4	1,723	58.4	505	22.7	722	24.5
Jul-Sep 2012	159	21.1	93	37.0	498	66.4	1,726	58.6	473	21.5	745	25.3
Oct-Dec 2012	**140**	**18.6**	**108**	**43.6**	**502**	**66.9**	**1,744**	**59.4**	**462**	**20.9**	**730**	**24.9**
Change on quarter	*-19*	*-2.5*	*15*	*6.6*	*4*	*0.5*	*18*	*0.8*	*-11*	*-0.6*	*-15*	*-0.4*
Change %	*-11.9*		*16.2*		*0.7*		*1.1*		*-2.4*		*-2.0*	
Change on year	*-19*	*-2.4*	*-1*	*3.0*	*14*	*2.4*	*54*	*2.2*	*-53*	*-2.4*	*-21*	*-0.5*
Change %	*-12.1*		*-0.7*		*2.8*		*3.2*		*-10.2*		*-2.8*	
Women	YBTQ	YBUC	YBVJ	YBVM	YCAU	LWEZ	YBTT	YBUF	YBVP	YBVS	YCAX	LWFC
Oct-Dec 2010	191	26.0	99	34.2	443	60.4	1,588	55.6	305	16.1	964	33.7
Oct-Dec 2011	186	25.8	102	35.4	433	60.1	1,604	56.0	308	16.1	952	33.2
Jan-Mar 2012	181	25.2	99	35.4	438	60.9	1,602	56.0	306	16.0	954	33.3
Apr-Jun 2012	188	26.2	100	34.7	428	59.9	1,615	56.5	304	15.9	941	32.9
Jul-Sep 2012	200	28.0	96	32.5	418	58.5	1,601	56.1	301	15.8	954	33.4
Oct-Dec 2012	**187**	**26.1**	**89**	**32.3**	**439**	**61.4**	**1,644**	**57.7**	**315**	**16.1**	**890**	**31.2**
Change on quarter	*-14*	*-1.9*	*-7*	*-0.2*	*21*	*2.9*	*43*	*1.7*	*14*	*0.3*	*-64*	*-2.2*
Change %	*-6.7*		*-7.6*		*5.0*		*2.7*		*4.7*		*-6.7*	
Change on year	*1*	*0.3*	*-13*	*-3.1*	*6*	*1.3*	*40*	*1.7*	*7*	*0.0*	*-62*	*-2.0*
Change %	*0.5*		*-12.6*		*1.5*		*2.5*		*2.3*		*-6.6*	

Source: Labour Force Survey

Labour market statistics enquiries: labour.market@ons.gov.uk

4.3 Employment: by sex and age: United Kingdom

United Kingdom (thousands) seasonally adjusted

	Aged 25-34						Aged 35-49					
	Employment		Unemployment		Inactivity		Employment		Unemployment		Inactivity	
	Level	Rate	Level	Rate	Level	Rate	Level	Rate	Level	Rate	Level	Rate
People	YBTU	YBUG	YCGM	YCGP	YCAY	LWFD	YBTX	YBUJ	YCGS	YCGV	YCBB	LWFG
Oct-Dec 2010	6,428	78.8	512	7.4	1,215	14.9	10,753	81.0	627	5.5	1,895	14.3
Oct-Dec 2011	6,529	77.9	575	8.1	1,281	15.3	10,695	81.4	624	5.5	1,819	13.8
Jan-Mar 2012	6,601	78.2	566	7.9	1,273	15.1	10,684	81.6	609	5.4	1,806	13.8
Apr-Jun 2012	6,661	78.4	555	7.7	1,278	15.0	10,691	81.9	594	5.3	1,775	13.6
Jul-Sep 2012	6,730	78.7	555	7.6	1,264	14.8	10,679	82.0	600	5.3	1,741	13.4
Oct-Dec 2012	**6,781**	**78.8**	**539**	**7.4**	**1,284**	**14.9**	**10,637**	**82.0**	**600**	**5.3**	**1,741**	**13.4**
Change on quarter	*51*	*0.1*	*-16*	*-0.3*	*21*	*0.1*	*-41*	*-0.1*	*0*	*0.0*	*0*	*0.0*
Change %	*0.8*		*-2.9*		*1.6*		*-0.4*		*0.0*		*0.0*	
Change on year	*252*	*1.0*	*-37*	*-0.7*	*3*	*-0.4*	*-58*	*0.6*	*-25*	*-0.2*	*-77*	*-0.4*
Change %	*3.9*		*-6.4*		*0.2*		*-0.5*		*-4.0*		*-4.2*	
Men	YBTV	YBUH	YCGN	YCGQ	YCAZ	LWFE	YBTY	YBUK	YCGT	YCGW	YCBC	LWFH
Oct-Dec 2010	3,537	85.9	293	7.7	288	7.0	5,671	86.5	348	5.8	534	8.2
Oct-Dec 2011	3,594	84.7	317	8.1	330	7.8	5,673	87.4	327	5.4	492	7.6
Jan-Mar 2012	3,652	85.5	302	7.6	316	7.4	5,667	87.5	314	5.2	493	7.6
Apr-Jun 2012	3,701	86.1	295	7.4	303	7.0	5,681	88.0	309	5.2	466	7.2
Jul-Sep 2012	3,723	86.0	296	7.4	310	7.2	5,681	88.3	303	5.1	453	7.0
Oct-Dec 2012	**3,761**	**86.3**	**291**	**7.2**	**308**	**7.1**	**5,645**	**88.0**	**291**	**4.9**	**482**	**7.5**
Change on quarter	*38*	*0.3*	*-5*	*-0.2*	*-2*	*-0.1*	*-36*	*-0.3*	*-12*	*-0.2*	*29*	*0.5*
Change %	*1.0*		*-1.9*		*-0.7*		*-0.6*		*-4.0*		*6.3*	
Change on year	*167*	*1.5*	*-27*	*-0.9*	*-21*	*-0.7*	*-28*	*0.6*	*-36*	*-0.5*	*-10*	*-0.1*
Change %	*4.6*		*-8.4*		*-6.5*		*-0.5*		*-11.0*		*-2.0*	
Women	YBTW	YBUI	YCGO	YCGR	YCBA	LWFF	YBTZ	YBUL	YCGU	YCGX	YCBD	LWFI
Oct-Dec 2010	2,892	71.6	219	7.1	927	22.9	5,081	75.6	279	5.2	1,361	20.2
Oct-Dec 2011	2,935	70.8	258	8.1	952	23.0	5,022	75.6	298	5.6	1,327	20.0
Jan-Mar 2012	2,950	70.7	263	8.2	957	23.0	5,016	75.7	295	5.6	1,313	19.8
Apr-Jun 2012	2,960	70.6	260	8.1	975	23.2	5,011	75.9	285	5.4	1,309	19.8
Jul-Sep 2012	3,007	71.3	259	7.9	953	22.6	4,997	75.9	297	5.6	1,288	19.6
Oct-Dec 2012	**3,021**	**71.2**	**248**	**7.6**	**976**	**23.0**	**4,992**	**76.1**	**309**	**5.8**	**1,259**	**19.2**
Change on quarter	*13*	*-0.1*	*-11*	*-0.3*	*23*	*0.4*	*-6*	*0.2*	*12*	*0.2*	*-29*	*-0.4*
Change %	*0.4*		*-4.1*		*2.4*		*-0.1*		*4.0*		*-2.2*	
Change on year	*85*	*0.3*	*-10*	*-0.5*	*24*	*0.0*	*-30*	*0.5*	*11*	*0.2*	*-68*	*-0.8*
Change %	*2.9*		*-3.9*		*2.5*		*-0.6*		*3.7*		*-5.1*	

	Aged 50-64						Age 65+					
	Employment		Unemployment		Inactivity		Employment		Unemployment		Inactivity	
	Level	Rate	Level	Rate	Level	Rate	Level	Rate	Level	Rate	Level	Rate
People	LF26	LF2U	LF28	LF2E	LF2A	LF2W	LFK4	LFK6	K5HU	K5HW	LFL4	LFL6
Oct-Dec 2010	7,320	64.8	362	4.7	3,618	32.0	877	8.9	20	2.2	9,001	90.9
Oct-Dec 2011	7,408	65.2	398	5.1	3,549	31.3	874	8.6	26	2.9	9,244	91.1
Jan-Mar 2012	7,449	65.6	391	5.0	3,515	31.0	890	8.7	28	3.1	9,312	91.0
Apr-Jun 2012	7,502	66.1	384	4.9	3,470	30.6	931	9.0	20	2.1	9,366	90.8
Jul-Sep 2012	7,537	66.3	377	4.8	3,453	30.4	945	9.1	20	2.1	9,431	90.7
Oct-Dec 2012	**7,623**	**67.0**	**367**	**4.6**	**3,393**	**29.8**	**973**	**9.3**	**22**	**2.2**	**9,476**	**90.5**
Change on quarter	*87*	*0.7*	*-10*	*-0.2*	*-60*	*-0.6*	*28*	*0.2*	*2*	*0.1*	*46*	*-0.2*
Change %	*1.2*		*-2.6*		*-1.7*		*3.0*		*8.3*		*0.5*	
Change on year	*216*	*1.7*	*-31*	*-0.5*	*-156*	*-1.4*	*99*	*0.7*	*-5*	*-0.7*	*232*	*-0.6*
Change %	*2.9*		*-7.8*		*-4.4*		*11.4*		*-17.4*		*2.5*	
Men	MGUX	YBUN	MGVM	MGXF	MGWB	LWFK	MGVA	YBUQ	MGVP	MGXI	MGWE	LWFN
Oct-Dec 2010	3,946	71.2	244	5.8	1,353	24.4	526	11.8	15	2.7	3,906	87.8
Oct-Dec 2011	3,961	71.2	253	6.0	1,349	24.3	526	11.5	17	3.1	4,039	88.2
Jan-Mar 2012	3,974	71.4	248	5.9	1,340	24.1	536	11.6	19	3.4	4,073	88.0
Apr-Jun 2012	3,996	71.9	241	5.7	1,324	23.8	573	12.3	12	2.0	4,088	87.5
Jul-Sep 2012	4,023	72.3	247	5.8	1,295	23.3	565	12.0	13	2.3	4,136	87.7
Oct-Dec 2012	**4,049**	**72.7**	**241**	**5.6**	**1,282**	**23.0**	**593**	**12.5**	**18**	**2.9**	**4,144**	**87.1**
Change on quarter	*26*	*0.4*	*-6*	*-0.2*	*-13*	*-0.3*	*28*	*0.5*	*5*	*0.6*	*8*	*-0.6*
Change %	*0.6*		*-2.5*		*-1.0*		*4.9*		*33.7*		*0.2*	
Change on year	*89*	*1.5*	*-12*	*-0.4*	*-67*	*-1.2*	*67*	*1.0*	*1*	*-0.2*	*104*	*-1.0*
Change %	*2.2*		*-4.8*		*-5.0*		*12.8*		*5.6*		*2.6*	
Women	LF27	LF2V	LF29	LF2F	LF2B	LF2X	LFK5	LFK7	K5HV	K5HX	LFL5	LFL7
Oct-Dec 2010	3,374	58.6	118	3.4	2,266	39.4	351	6.4	*	*	5,096	93.5
Oct-Dec 2011	3,447	59.5	145	4.0	2,199	38.0	348	6.3	*	*	5,205	93.6
Jan-Mar 2012	3,475	60.0	143	3.9	2,175	37.5	354	6.3	*	*	5,240	93.5
Apr-Jun 2012	3,506	60.5	143	3.9	2,145	37.0	358	6.3	*	*	5,277	93.5
Jul-Sep 2012	3,513	60.6	130	3.6	2,158	37.2	380	6.7	*	*	5,295	93.2
Oct-Dec 2012	**3,574**	**61.5**	**126**	**3.4**	**2,111**	**36.3**	**380**	**6.7**	*	*	**5,333**	**93.3**
Change on quarter	*61*	*0.9*	*-3*	*-0.1*	*-48*	*-0.9*	*0*	*0.0*	*	*	*38*	*0.1*
Change %	*1.7*		*-2.6*		*-2.2*		*0.1*		*		*0.7*	
Change on year	*127*	*2.0*	*-19*	*-0.6*	*-89*	*-1.7*	*32*	*0.4*	*	*	*128*	*-0.3*
Change %	*3.7*		*-13.0*		*-4.0*		*9.2*		*		*2.5*	

Source: Labour Force Survey

Data taken from Labour Market Statistics, February 2013 : http://www.ons.gov.uk/ons/rel/lms/labour-market-statistics/february-2013/table-a01.xls   Labour market statistics enquiries: labour.market@ons.gov.uk

4.4: All in employment by industry sector

United Kingdom (thousands) not seasonally adjusted

Standard Industrial Classification (SIC) 2007 [1]

People

	All in employment[2]	Public sector[3]	Private sector	A Agriculture, forestry & fishing	B,D,E Mining, energy and water supply	C Manufacturing	F Construction	G Wholesale, retail & repair of motor vehicles	H Transport & storage	I Accommodation and food services	J Information & communication	K Financial & insurance activities	L Real estate activities	M Professional, scientific & technical activities	N Administrative & support services	O Public admin & defence; social security	P Education	Q Human health & social work activities	R,S,T Other services
Jan-Mar 2003	27,966	6,550	21,274	272	377	3,647	2,160	4,213	1,544	1,309	1,004	1,251	205	1,691	1,263	1,857	2,534	3,167	1,402
Apr-Jun 2003	28,127	6,538	21,403	260	369	3,598	2,215	4,214	1,584	1,276	1,009	1,249	207	1,721	1,228	1,862	2,581	3,212	1,476
Jul-Sep 2003	28,325	6,556	21,627	276	379	3,505	2,296	4,285	1,540	1,339	1,033	1,270	216	1,715	1,268	1,877	2,545	3,233	1,486
Oct-Dec 2003	28,316	6,646	21,524	270	358	3,424	2,277	4,387	1,526	1,315	1,026	1,237	208	1,744	1,239	1,883	2,594	3,275	1,478
Jan-Mar 2004	28,327	6,768	21,423	260	368	3,379	2,295	4,240	1,517	1,331	1,044	1,215	228	1,753	1,253	1,882	2,695	3,327	1,460
Apr-Jun 2004	28,361	6,819	21,421	263	376	3,312	2,310	4,243	1,514	1,319	1,045	1,205	244	1,719	1,265	1,888	2,717	3,392	1,465
Jul-Sep 2004	28,577	6,853	21,605	273	409	3,384	2,370	4,250	1,521	1,335	1,048	1,200	234	1,692	1,297	1,945	2,668	3,408	1,455
Oct-Dec 2004	28,668	6,859	21,660	271	400	3,364	2,399	4,324	1,531	1,304	1,027	1,190	242	1,719	1,319	1,917	2,711	3,409	1,452
Jan-Mar 2005	28,635	6,932	21,554	288	399	3,294	2,392	4,249	1,530	1,303	1,025	1,217	224	1,732	1,346	1,945	2,725	3,456	1,411
Apr-Jun 2005	28,658	6,894	21,644	283	397	3,322	2,378	4,207	1,553	1,320	1,011	1,208	239	1,751	1,332	1,930	2,759	3,465	1,429
Jul-Sep 2005	28,953	6,992	21,846	282	404	3,302	2,453	4,235	1,570	1,283	1,021	1,286	248	1,778	1,320	1,973	2,709	3,556	1,446
Oct-Dec 2005	28,844	7,007	21,720	287	413	3,244	2,405	4,196	1,586	1,270	1,019	1,278	256	1,813	1,294	1,957	2,744	3,543	1,442
Jan-Mar 2006	28,863	7,095	21,667	272	402	3,225	2,425	4,156	1,556	1,290	1,011	1,268	252	1,828	1,270	2,009	2,823	3,558	1,421
Apr-Jun 2006	28,923	7,060	21,751	267	412	3,267	2,455	4,111	1,546	1,343	1,021	1,255	262	1,800	1,274	1,978	2,836	3,560	1,442
Jul-Sep 2006	29,174	6,980	22,087	291	422	3,260	2,505	4,146	1,565	1,384	1,042	1,249	247	1,818	1,316	1,959	2,745	3,608	1,525
Oct-Dec 2006	29,151	6,901	22,130	301	433	3,214	2,536	4,189	1,576	1,330	1,054	1,266	246	1,817	1,322	1,951	2,797	3,499	1,504
Jan-Mar 2007	28,976	6,914	21,949	287	447	3,195	2,519	4,109	1,558	1,323	1,052	1,259	255	1,867	1,297	1,968	2,782	3,478	1,469
Apr-Jun 2007	29,096	6,942	22,031	293	461	3,260	2,535	4,022	1,549	1,371	1,046	1,267	244	1,874	1,338	1,970	2,805	3,435	1,510
Jul-Sep 2007	29,370	6,868	22,363	295	465	3,247	2,549	4,076	1,547	1,407	1,058	1,300	265	1,902	1,420	1,974	2,763	3,478	1,508
Oct-Dec 2007	29,475	6,964	22,368	305	457	3,193	2,528	4,172	1,565	1,396	1,015	1,306	278	1,944	1,388	1,979	2,819	3,503	1,512
Jan-Mar 2008	29,417	6,992	22,280	332	448	3,124	2,523	4,164	1,592	1,381	1,019	1,282	262	1,930	1,385	1,993	2,828	3,538	1,505
Apr-Jun 2008	29,448	7,046	22,250	319	443	3,065	2,501	4,176	1,577	1,352	1,028	1,280	253	1,957	1,403	2,017	2,841	3,610	1,511
Jul-Sep 2008	29,497	6,980	22,380	311	460	3,046	2,573	4,230	1,593	1,351	1,059	1,266	258	1,909	1,393	2,012	2,785	3,615	1,524
Oct-Dec 2008	29,399	7,108	22,155	305	505	2,958	2,553	4,204	1,610	1,329	1,030	1,241	250	1,841	1,336	2,016	2,828	3,716	1,572
Jan-Mar 2009	29,074	7,165	21,771	320	486	2,831	2,470	4,088	1,556	1,317	1,027	1,224	272	1,833	1,300	1,990	2,897	3,739	1,566
Apr-Jun 2009	28,809	7,179	21,489	309	480	2,752	2,375	3,972	1,496	1,352	1,007	1,233	266	1,872	1,293	1,950	2,904	3,706	1,572
Jul-Sep 2009	28,972	7,216	21,609	327	488	2,790	2,302	4,015	1,450	1,420	1,011	1,243	263	1,880	1,290	1,960	2,937	3,744	1,586
Oct-Dec 2009	28,964	7,260	21,554	321	478	2,777	2,303	3,998	1,444	1,399	1,005	1,218	252	1,875	1,315	1,928	3,019	3,812	1,567
Jan-Mar 2010	28,712	7,192	21,341	334	467	2,791	2,201	3,920	1,448	1,381	1,002	1,207	261	1,872	1,305	1,915	3,036	3,787	1,537
Apr-Jun 2010	28,901	7,264	21,440	339	458	2,854	2,203	3,979	1,432	1,452	969	1,172	260	1,883	1,312	1,910	3,104	3,810	1,521
Jul-Sep 2010	29,279	7,240	21,828	367	470	2,868	2,228	4,083	1,474	1,492	1,036	1,165	299	1,840	1,327	1,909	3,095	3,787	1,583
Oct-Dec 2010	29,182	7,219	21,781	365	485	2,882	2,230	4,052	1,427	1,418	1,023	1,168	297	1,872	1,367	1,853	3,093	3,849	1,541
Jan-Mar 2011	29,134	7,254	21,688	355	494	2,840	2,201	4,004	1,442	1,407	1,052	1,176	296	1,847	1,287	1,860	3,095	3,932	1,527
Apr-Jun 2011	29,157	7,125	21,870	341	518	2,849	2,188	4,021	1,435	1,446	1,068	1,171	304	1,840	1,309	1,830	3,103	3,897	1,574
Jul-Sep 2011	29,171	6,953	22,068	367	516	2,824	2,227	3,990	1,417	1,488	1,054	1,190	298	1,876	1,327	1,839	2,959	3,947	1,628
Oct-Dec 2011	29,205	6,916	22,132	354	525	2,868	2,165	4,054	1,420	1,487	1,079	1,214	290	1,885	1,340	1,852	2,991	3,895	1,569
Jan-Mar 2012	29,178	6,898	22,077	372	533	2,835	2,141	3,993	1,421	1,426	1,118	1,198	331	1,893	1,357	1,835	3,061	3,832	1,542
Apr-Jun 2012	29,414	6,798	22,394	352	531	2,907	2,165	4,081	1,406	1,483	1,093	1,228	326	1,933	1,348	1,794	3,055	3,838	1,562
Jul-Sep 2012	29,692	6,839	22,608	355	547	2,922	2,170	4,108	1,448	1,514	1,106	1,218	328	1,974	1,363	1,818	2,997	3,918	1,596
Oct-Dec 2012	29,794	6,933	22,623	316	517	2,897	2,145	4,080	1,471	1,510	1,139	1,167	344	1,959	1,365	1,814	3,117	3,961	1,578
Change on year	293	170	96	-12	-22	-176	49	181	-2	22	-7	9	-21	-21	-50	55	121	93	86
Change %	1.1	2.7	0.5	-4.1	-5.5	-4.6	2.3	4.5	-0.1	1.7	-0.7	0.7	-9.4	-1.2	-3.8	3.1	5.0	3.0	6.5

4.4: All in employment by industry sector

United Kingdom (thousands) not seasonally adjusted

Standard Industrial Classification (SIC) 2007 [1]

	All in employment [2]	Public sector [3]	Private sector	Agriculture forestry & fishing (A)	Mining, energy and water supply (B,D,E)	Manufacturing (C)	Construction (F)	Wholesale, retail & repair of motor vehicles (G)	Transport & storage (H)	Accommodation and food services (I)	Information & communication (J)	Financial & insurance activities (K)	Real estate activities (L)	Professional, scientific & technical activities (M)	Administrative & support services (N)	Public admin & defence; social security (O)	Education (P)	Human health & social work activities (Q)	Other services (R,S,T)
Men																			
Jan-Mar 2003	**15,106**	**2,378**	**12,649**	**207**	**299**	**2,775**	**1,899**	**2,084**	**1,237**	**563**	**693**	**621**	**101**	**953**	**676**	**964**	**719**	**640**	**629**
Apr-Jun 2003	15,252	2,372	12,779	195	299	2,742	1,940	2,119	1,277	560	690	620	105	970	681	968	731	644	668
Jul-Sep 2003	15,377	2,374	12,929	210	298	2,659	2,004	2,162	1,251	589	709	629	106	977	707	956	739	654	689
Oct-Dec 2003	15,302	2,387	12,838	203	280	2,612	1,990	2,214	1,241	571	714	614	103	1,000	686	954	746	652	676
Jan-Mar 2004	15,289	2,431	12,787	198	289	2,589	2,009	2,120	1,247	578	723	605	114	993	700	981	787	657	650
Apr-Jun 2004	15,323	2,449	12,803	200	293	2,528	2,016	2,145	1,241	593	729	593	127	984	704	976	768	705	667
Jul-Sep 2004	15,492	2,460	12,964	199	320	2,595	2,072	2,154	1,241	598	733	587	124	954	720	999	756	718	667
Oct-Dec 2004	15,504	2,412	13,011	196	320	2,581	2,085	2,199	1,251	581	714	584	129	973	730	972	748	737	655
Jan-Mar 2005	15,443	2,478	12,882	209	315	2,521	2,076	2,128	1,237	593	715	610	117	986	735	994	753	755	639
Apr-Jun 2005	15,461	2,464	12,927	200	316	2,538	2,062	2,131	1,250	600	713	611	127	997	741	973	764	753	638
Jul-Sep 2005	15,635	2,528	13,036	201	318	2,528	2,133	2,141	1,274	568	721	638	127	993	754	1,009	768	748	650
Oct-Dec 2005	15,585	2,521	12,992	213	323	2,485	2,098	2,113	1,292	585	717	638	132	1,024	735	993	781	738	643
Jan-Mar 2006	15,513	2,552	12,894	198	337	2,479	2,101	2,080	1,255	589	722	640	134	1,022	712	1,010	806	752	629
Apr-Jun 2006	15,575	2,522	12,988	199	320	2,495	2,123	2,086	1,257	608	727	640	144	998	705	989	814	748	664
Jul-Sep 2006	15,791	2,504	13,223	217	321	2,479	2,179	2,144	1,260	634	741	631	124	1,027	710	991	782	775	713
Oct-Dec 2006	15,757	2,440	13,253	220	326	2,450	2,207	2,160	1,256	584	750	647	130	1,023	732	985	792	728	689
Jan-Mar 2007	15,657	2,426	13,172	203	335	2,438	2,205	2,137	1,237	591	756	664	125	1,023	733	996	767	713	662
Apr-Jun 2007	15,750	2,447	13,231	207	344	2,492	2,209	2,086	1,238	623	748	660	116	1,023	768	986	784	705	685
Jul-Sep 2007	15,923	2,410	13,437	213	357	2,449	2,237	2,105	1,239	653	754	683	127	1,050	823	997	780	699	688
Oct-Dec 2007	15,943	2,431	13,435	208	361	2,414	2,219	2,131	1,260	653	712	704	134	1,064	819	1,013	795	716	680
Jan-Mar 2008	15,885	2,470	13,335	221	355	2,364	2,196	2,131	1,284	635	721	693	130	1,059	800	1,032	783	752	667
Apr-Jun 2008	15,909	2,496	13,332	220	349	2,340	2,173	2,143	1,265	637	730	675	131	1,080	819	1,046	778	796	660
Jul-Sep 2008	15,944	2,475	13,388	217	347	2,302	2,241	2,178	1,266	624	752	650	142	1,065	800	1,030	738	801	705
Oct-Dec 2008	15,861	2,526	13,257	218	368	2,239	2,225	2,164	1,282	617	743	633	137	1,022	771	1,021	775	826	716
Jan-Mar 2009	15,618	2,561	12,979	246	407	2,128	2,204	2,104	1,246	605	719	627	132	1,069	713	997	801	824	719
Apr-Jun 2009	15,417	2,547	12,791	239	389	2,085	2,120	2,057	1,199	621	713	639	123	1,104	709	980	787	809	711
Jul-Sep 2009	15,482	2,561	12,834	251	382	2,113	2,059	2,091	1,163	648	722	646	122	1,093	693	991	827	802	725
Oct-Dec 2009	15,434	2,569	12,782	245	387	2,108	2,065	2,070	1,165	636	719	639	114	1,065	703	989	864	816	719
Jan-Mar 2010	15,282	2,523	12,660	251	380	2,139	1,967	2,038	1,171	647	706	631	118	1,091	703	979	853	788	693
Apr-Jun 2010	15,455	2,569	12,775	262	376	2,194	1,959	2,093	1,153	683	688	626	113	1,093	720	999	862	806	698
Jul-Sep 2010	15,736	2,593	13,016	282	370	2,200	1,989	2,157	1,167	687	746	628	131	1,069	755	990	871	801	736
Oct-Dec 2010	15,678	2,573	13,002	281	378	2,203	1,985	2,144	1,127	669	747	644	129	1,096	784	946	840	848	701
Jan-Mar 2011	15,569	2,571	12,890	269	392	2,168	1,947	2,111	1,160	643	755	650	131	1,091	721	959	845	849	693
Apr-Jun 2011	15,637	2,537	13,012	261	410	2,160	1,932	2,107	1,164	652	766	649	142	1,101	748	909	885	857	723
Jul-Sep 2011	15,624	2,443	13,104	270	426	2,159	1,997	2,079	1,141	680	752	654	153	1,105	738	902	837	845	759
Oct-Dec 2011	15,636	2,428	13,130	260	420	2,189	1,934	2,123	1,145	711	788	659	149	1,104	730	920	832	840	711
Jan-Mar 2012	15,619	2,421	13,089	269	422	2,145	1,905	2,091	1,152	678	810	640	176	1,117	740	911	865	819	694
Apr-Jun 2012	15,804	2,359	13,311	256	433	2,198	1,924	2,155	1,135	672	801	665	162	1,144	746	890	868	833	733
Jul-Sep 2012	15,961	2,387	13,415	256	440	2,215	1,939	2,162	1,168	680	803	677	156	1,152	753	922	851	837	744
Oct-Dec 2012	15,962	2,404	13,407	236	404	2,192	1,914	2,158	1,183	674	813	646	164	1,139	763	951	898	852	722
Change on year	*167*	*91*	*64*	*-3*	*-18*	*-105*	*53*	*84*	*2*	*27*	*7*	*12*	*-16*	*-10*	*-50*	*64*	*36*	*44*	*48*
Change %	*1.1*	*4.0*	*0.5*	*-1.3*	*-5.8*	*-3.7*	*2.9*	*4.2*	*0.1*	*5.1*	*1.1*	*1.9*	*-13.6*	*-1.0*	*-6.8*	*7.2*	*5.3*	*7.4*	*8.2*

4.4: All in employment by industry sector

United Kingdom (thousands) not seasonally adjusted

Standard Industrial Classification (SIC) 2007 [1]

	All in employment [2]	Public sector [3]	Private sector	Agriculture, forestry & fishing	Mining, energy and water supply	Manufacturing	Construction	Wholesale, retail & repair of motor vehicles	Transport & storage	Accommod-ation and food services	Information & communication	Financial & insurance activities	Real estate activities	Professional, scientific & technical activities	Administrative & support services	Public admin & defence; social security	Education	Human health & social work activities	Other services
				A	B, D, E	C	F	G	H	I	J	K	L	M	N	O	P	Q	R, S, T
Women																			
Jan-Mar 2003	**12,860**	**4,172**	**8,624**	**65**	**78**	**871**	**261**	**2,129**	**307**	**747**	**311**	**630**	**103**	**738**	**586**	**894**	**1,815**	**2,527**	**773**
Apr-Jun 2003	12,875	4,166	8,624	65	70	856	276	2,095	307	716	319	629	102	750	547	895	1,850	2,569	808
Jul-Sep 2003	12,948	4,182	8,698	65	81	846	292	2,123	289	751	324	640	109	737	561	921	1,806	2,580	797
Oct-Dec 2003	13,014	4,260	8,686	68	78	812	287	2,173	284	743	312	623	105	744	553	929	1,849	2,623	802
Jan-Mar 2004	13,038	4,336	8,636	62	79	790	286	2,120	270	753	321	610	114	760	552	901	1,908	2,669	809
Apr-Jun 2004	13,038	4,370	8,618	63	83	785	294	2,098	273	726	317	612	117	735	560	912	1,948	2,687	798
Jul-Sep 2004	13,085	4,393	8,640	74	88	789	297	2,095	280	737	316	612	111	738	577	946	1,912	2,690	788
Oct-Dec 2004	13,165	4,447	8,649	75	85	782	314	2,124	281	722	313	606	113	746	589	945	1,963	2,671	797
Jan-Mar 2005	13,191	4,454	8,672	79	83	773	316	2,121	293	711	309	607	107	746	611	951	1,971	2,701	772
Apr-Jun 2005	13,196	4,430	8,717	83	78	784	316	2,076	303	719	298	597	113	755	592	957	1,995	2,711	791
Jul-Sep 2005	13,319	4,465	8,811	82	81	774	320	2,094	296	715	299	648	121	785	566	964	1,941	2,808	796
Oct-Dec 2005	13,259	4,486	8,727	74	76	759	307	2,083	294	685	302	640	124	790	559	964	1,963	2,805	798
Jan-Mar 2006	13,350	4,542	8,773	75	82	746	324	2,076	301	701	289	628	118	806	558	1,000	2,017	2,807	792
Apr-Jun 2006	13,348	4,538	8,764	67	91	772	332	2,025	289	734	294	615	118	802	569	989	2,022	2,812	778
Jul-Sep 2006	13,383	4,477	8,865	75	95	781	325	2,001	305	750	301	619	122	790	605	968	1,962	2,834	812
Oct-Dec 2006	13,394	4,461	8,877	81	98	764	329	2,028	320	745	303	619	116	795	591	966	2,005	2,771	816
Jan-Mar 2007	13,319	4,487	8,776	84	103	757	314	1,972	320	732	296	595	130	844	564	971	2,016	2,765	807
Apr-Jun 2007	13,346	4,494	8,800	86	104	768	325	1,972	311	748	299	607	127	851	570	985	2,021	2,730	825
Jul-Sep 2007	13,447	4,458	8,926	83	105	797	311	1,971	308	754	305	617	138	852	598	977	1,982	2,779	820
Oct-Dec 2007	13,532	4,534	8,932	97	102	779	309	2,040	305	742	303	602	144	880	568	966	2,025	2,787	832
Jan-Mar 2008	13,531	4,522	8,945	111	99	761	328	2,034	308	745	298	589	132	871	585	962	2,045	2,785	838
Apr-Jun 2008	13,539	4,550	8,918	96	96	725	328	2,033	312	715	299	605	121	877	584	972	2,064	2,814	851
Jul-Sep 2008	13,554	4,505	8,992	94	92	744	332	2,052	327	727	307	617	116	844	593	983	2,047	2,814	819
Oct-Dec 2008	13,538	4,582	8,898	87	97	719	327	2,040	329	712	288	608	114	818	565	996	2,053	2,891	856
Jan-Mar 2009	13,456	4,604	8,792	75	97	704	266	1,984	311	712	307	597	140	764	587	994	2,096	2,914	847
Apr-Jun 2009	13,391	4,632	8,698	71	98	667	255	1,915	298	731	293	594	143	768	584	971	2,117	2,897	861
Jul-Sep 2009	13,490	4,656	8,775	76	101	667	243	1,924	287	772	289	597	142	786	597	970	2,110	2,942	861
Oct-Dec 2009	13,531	4,692	8,771	76	97	669	238	1,928	279	762	286	579	138	810	613	939	2,155	2,996	848
Jan-Mar 2010	13,431	4,669	8,682	83	91	653	235	1,882	277	734	295	575	143	782	602	935	2,183	2,999	845
Apr-Jun 2010	13,446	4,695	8,665	77	88	660	244	1,885	279	769	281	546	147	790	591	911	2,242	3,004	823
Jul-Sep 2010	13,544	4,646	8,812	85	92	667	240	1,927	307	805	290	537	168	772	572	919	2,224	2,986	847
Oct-Dec 2010	13,504	4,646	8,779	83	94	679	245	1,908	300	749	275	525	168	775	583	907	2,253	3,001	840
Jan-Mar 2011	13,565	4,683	8,797	86	84	673	254	1,893	281	764	298	526	165	755	566	902	2,250	3,083	835
Apr-Jun 2011	13,520	4,588	8,858	80	92	688	256	1,914	271	795	301	523	162	739	561	920	2,218	3,040	850
Jul-Sep 2011	13,546	4,510	8,964	98	96	665	230	1,911	276	807	302	536	145	771	588	937	2,122	3,102	869
Oct-Dec 2011	13,569	4,488	9,002	94	103	680	231	1,931	275	776	291	555	141	781	610	932	2,158	3,056	858
Jan-Mar 2012	13,559	4,477	8,988	103	100	690	235	1,902	270	748	308	558	155	776	617	924	2,196	3,013	847
Apr-Jun 2012	13,610	4,439	9,083	95	96	709	241	1,926	271	810	292	562	165	789	602	904	2,187	3,005	829
Jul-Sep 2012	13,730	4,452	9,193	99	107	707	230	1,947	280	834	304	540	172	822	610	896	2,146	3,080	852
Oct-Dec 2012	13,832	4,530	9,216	80	113	705	232	1,921	288	835	326	522	181	820	603	862	2,218	3,110	856
Change on year	*125*	*80*	*33*	*-9*	*-4*	*-71*	*-4*	*97*	*-3*	*-6*	*-15*	*-3*	*-6*	*-11*	*-1*	*-9*	*85*	*49*	*38*
Change %	*1.0*	*2.0*	*0.4*	*-12.0*	*-4.6*	*-7.5*	*-1.5*	*4.8*	*-1.1*	*-0.7*	*-4.6*	*-0.5*	*-5.1*	*-1.5*	*-0.1*	*-1.0*	*4.9*	*2.0*	*5.1*

Source: Labour Force Survey

1 The breakdown by industry sector for Q1 2009 onwards is not entirely consistent with those of previous quarters. This is because:
(a) LFS data on industrial activity were coded directly to SIC 1992 for all quarters up to and including Q4 2008 and then mapped to the new industrial classification, SIC 2007, according to the assumed relationship between the two classifications;
(b) data for Q1 2009 onwards have been coded directly to SIC 2007; and
(c) a new, automatic coding tool was introduced in January 2009.

The effect of these changes on the time series was significant for some of the industry sectors shown. Consequently some adjustments have been made to the pre-2009 estimates to account for the estimated combined effects of the new classification and the new coding tool. This also means that the pre-2009 estimates in this table are not the same as those obtained from LFS microdata. More information and analysis of these effects are available in the Labour Force Survey User Guide (Volume 1) and from Labour Force Assessment Branch (tel 01633 455839 or email labour.market.assessment@ons.gov.uk).

2 Includes people with workplace outside UK and those who did not state their industry.

3 In the LFS the distinction between public and private sector is based on respondents' views about the organisation for which they work. The public sector estimates provided here do not correspond to the official Public Sector Employment estimates which are based on National Accounts definitions.

Data taken from Labour Market Statistics, February 2013 : http://www.ons.gov.uk/ons/rel/lms/labour-market-statistics/february-2013/table-emp13.xls

4.5a International comparisons

		Latest period	Employment rate (%)[1][2]	Change on year %			Latest Period	Unemployment rate (%)[3]	Change on period %[6]	Change on year %
As published by EUROSTAT: (not seasonally adjusted)					**As published by EUROSTAT on 1 February 2013 (seasonally adjusted)**					
European Union (EU)					**European Union (EU)**					
Austria	YXSN	Jul-Sep 12	73.6	0.6	Austria	ZXDS	Dec 12	4.3	-0.1	0.1
Belgium	YXSO	Jul-Sep 12	62.1	0.4	Belgium	ZXDI	Dec 12	7.5	0.0	0.4
Bulgaria	A495	Jul-Sep 12	60.6	0.7	Bulgaria	A492	Dec 12	12.3	-0.1	0.5
Cyprus	A4AC	Jul-Sep 12	64.6	-2.5	Cyprus	A4AN	Dec 12	14.7	0.5	5.0
Czech Republic	A4AD	Jul-Sep 12	67.1	1.0	Czech Republic	A4AO	Dec 12	7.5	0.1	0.8
Denmark	YXSP	Jul-Sep 12	72.8	-1.0	Denmark	ZXDJ	Dec 12	8.0	0.1	0.3
Estonia	A4AE	Jul-Sep 12	68.1	0.9	Estonia	A4AP	Nov 12	9.9	0.2	-2.2
Finland	YXSQ	Jul-Sep 12	70.7	0.4	Finland	ZXDU	Dec 12	7.7	0.0	0.1
France	YXSR	Jul-Sep 12	64.4	0.1	France	ZXDN	Dec 12	10.6	0.1	0.7
Germany	YXSS	Jul-Sep 12	73.2	0.4	Germany	ZXDK	Dec 12	5.3	0.0	-0.3
Greece	YXST	Jul-Sep 12	51.0	-4.4	Greece	ZXDL	Oct 12	26.8	0.6	7.1
Hungary	A4AF	Jul-Sep 12	58.2	1.8	Hungary	A4AQ	Nov 12	10.9	0.0	0.1
Ireland	YXSU	Jul-Sep 12	59.0	0.2	Ireland	ZXDO	Dec 12	14.7	0.0	-0.3
Italy	YXSV	Jul-Sep 12	56.9	0.0	Italy	ZXDP	Dec 12	11.2	0.0	1.7
Latvia	A4AG	Jul-Sep 12	64.5	2.8	Latvia	A4AR	2012 Q3	14.1	-1.6	-1.6
Lithuania	A4AH	Jul-Sep 12	63.3	2.5	Lithuania	A4AS	Dec 12	12.3	-0.4	-1.4
Luxembourg	YXSW	Jul-Sep 12	66.6	1.6	Luxembourg	ZXDQ	Dec 12	5.3	0.1	0.4
Malta	A4AI	Jul-Sep 12	59.6	1.5	Malta	A4AT	Dec 12	6.7	-0.2	0.2
Netherlands	YXSX	Jul-Sep 12	75.3	0.2	Netherlands	ZXDR	Dec 12	5.8	0.2	0.9
Poland	A4AJ	Jul-Sep 12	60.2	0.0	Poland	A4AU	Dec 12	10.6	0.1	0.7
Portugal	YXSY	Jul-Sep 12	62.0	-2.5	Portugal	ZXDT	Dec 12	16.5	0.2	1.9
Romania	A494	Jul-Sep 12	60.8	1.7	Romania	A48Z	Dec 12	6.5	-0.2	-1.0
Slovak Republic	A4AK	Jul-Sep 12	60.1	0.2	Slovak Republic	A4AV	Dec 12	14.7	0.2	0.8
Slovenia	A4AL	Jul-Sep 12	64.3	-0.8	Slovenia	A4AW	Dec 12	10.0	0.2	1.4
Spain	YXSZ	Jul-Sep 12	55.6	-2.3	Spain	ZXDM	Dec 12	26.1	-0.1	2.9
Sweden	YXTA	Jul-Sep 12	75.6	0.2	Sweden	ZXDV	Dec 12	7.8	-0.3	0.3
United Kingdom	ANZ6	Jul-Sep 12	70.5	1.0	United Kingdom[4]	ZXDW	Oct 12	7.8	0.0	-0.6
Total EU[5]	**A496**	**Jul-Sep 12**	**64.6**	**0.0**	**Total EU[5]**	**A493**	**Dec 12**	**10.7**	**0.0**	**0.7**
Eurozone[5]	YXTC	Jul-Sep 12	64.1	-0.4	Eurozone[5]	ZXDH	Dec 12	11.7	0.0	1.0
As published by national statistical offices					**As published by national statistical offices (seasonally adjusted)**					
Canada (NSA)	IUUK	Oct-Dec 12	72.4	0.6	Canada	ZXDZ	Jan 13	7.0	-0.1	-0.5
Japan (NSA)	YXTF	Oct-Dec 12	70.9	0.4	Japan	ZXDY	Dec 12	4.2	0.1	-0.3
United Kingdom (SA)	LF24	Oct-Dec 12	71.5	1.1	United Kingdom[4]	MGSX	Oct-Dec 12	7.8	-0.1	-0.6
United States (NSA)	YXTE	Oct-Dec 12	67.4	0.6	United States	ZXDX	Jan 13	7.9	0.1	-0.4

Sources: Eurostat, national statistical offices.
Labour market statistics enquiries: labour.market@ons.gov.uk

1. The UK employment rate shown in the lower part of the table - as published by the Office for National Statistics - is seasonally adjusted; all other employment rates are unadjusted.

2. All employment rates for EU countries published by EUROSTAT (including the rate for the UK) are based on the population aged 15-64. The rates for Canada and Japan are also based on the population aged 15-64, but the rate for the US is for those aged 16-64. The employment rate for the UK published by the Office for National Statistics is based on the population aged 16-64.

3. Unemployment rates published by EUROSTAT for most EU countries (but not for the UK), are calculated by extrapolating from the most recent LFS data using monthly registered unemployment data. A standard population basis (15-74) is used by EUROSTAT except for Spain, Italy and the UK (16-74). The unemployment rate for the US is based on those aged 16 and over, but the rates for Canada and Japan are for those aged 15 and over. All unemployment rates are seasonally adjusted.

4. The unemployment rate for the UK published by EUROSTAT is based on the population aged 16-74 but the unemployment rate for the UK published by the Office for National Statistics is based on those aged 16 and over. There are other minor definitional differences.

5. The "Total EU" series consist of all 27 EU countries. The Eurozone figures consist of the following EU countries: Austria, Belgium, Cyprus, Estonia, Finland, France, Germany, Greece, Ireland, Italy, Luxembourg, Malta, Netherlands, Portugal, Slovak Republic, Slovenia and Spain.

6. Change on previous month except "Latvia" and "United Kingdom as published by national statistical office" (change on previous quarter).

Data taken from Labour Market Statistics, February 2013 : http://www.ons.gov.uk/ons/rel/lms/labour-market-statistics/february-2013/table-a01.xls

4.5b Labour disputes

United Kingdom, not seasonally adjusted

		Working days lost (thousands) [1,2]	Working days lost in the Public Sector (thousands)[1,2]	Working days lost in the Private Sector (thousands)[1,2]	Number of stoppages[3,4]	Number of stoppages in the Public Sector [4]	Number of stoppages in the Private Sector [4]	Workers involved (thousands)[1,3]
		1	2	3	4	5	6	7
		BBFW	F8XZ	F8Y2	BLUU	F8Y3	F8Y4	BLUT
2010 Dec		7	2	5	15	7	8	4
2011 Dec		7	2	5	15	7	8	7
2012 Jan		21	14	7	11	6	5	18
Feb		5	0	5	10	1	9	2
Mar		29	24	5	11	6	5	29
Apr		6	5	1	11	7	4	3
May		112	106	6	20	11	9	126
Jun		35	23	12	18	8	10	41
Jul		7	6	1	17	11	6	3
Aug		10	9	1	15	8	7	8
Sep		8	4	4	12	6	6	6
Oct		3	1	3	18	7	11	3
Nov		9	6	3	18	7	11	8
Dec	(p)	4	1	3	16	7	9	3
Cumulative totals 12 months to:								
Dec 11		1,390	1,276	113	149	88	61	1,530
Dec 12	(p)	248	198	51	128	63	65	235

Relationship between columns 1=2+3; 4=5+6

Source: ONS Labour Disputes Inquiry
Labour disputes enquiries 01633 456724

1. Estimates of working days lost and workers involved are shown to the nearest thousand. Unrounded estimates of less than 500 therefore round to zero.
2. Due to rounding the working days lost for the public and private sectors may not add up to the total working days lost
3. The latest 12 month cumulative totals for the figures in these columns will not necessarily equal the sum of the 12 months as some disputes continue for over one month. These disputes appear in each month's data, but only once in the total.
4. These series exclude disputes which do not result in a stoppage of work, those involving fewer than ten workers or lasting less than one day unless the total number of working days lost in the dispute is 100 or more.

Data taken from Labour Market Statistics, February 2013 : http://www.ons.gov.uk/ons/rel/lms/labour-market-statistics/february-2013/table-a01.xls

4.6 Civil Service employment; regional (GOR) distribution by government department[1,2]

All employees

	North West	North East	Yorkshire and the Humber	West Midlands	East Midlands	East of England	London	South East	South West	Scotland	Wales	Northern Ireland	Overseas	Not reported
31 March 2012														
Attorney General's Departments														
Attorney General's Office	0	0	0	0	0	0	40	0	0	0	0	0	0	0
Crown Prosecution Service	1,080	410	910	730	500	560	1,800	820	430	0	410	0	10	0
Crown Prosecution Service Inspectorate	0	0	10	0	0	0	30	0	0	0	0	0	0	0
Serious Fraud Office	0	0	0	0	0	0	310	0	0	0	0	0	0	0
Treasury Solicitor	0	0	0	0	0	0	990	0	0	0	0	0	0	0
Business, Innovation and Skills														
Business, Innovation and Skills (excl. agencies)	50	60	250	20	20	30	2,410	10	10	40	60	0	0	0
Advisory Conciliation and Arbitration Service	120	70	70	60	60	50	240	50	50	70	50	0	0	0
Companies House	0	0	0	0	0	0	10	0	0	30	930	20	0	0
Insolvency Service	250	80	160	460	90	200	420	150	160	30	80	0	0	0
Land Registry	640	430	250	450	620	250	290	20	1,270	0	450	0	0	0
Met Office	10	0	20	20	50	40	60	80	1,460	110	20	10	30	..
National Measurement Office	0	0	0	0	0	0	70	0	0	0	0	0	0	0
Office of Fair Trading	0	0	0	0	0	0	560	0	0	..	0	0	0	0
Office of Gas and Electricity Market	0	0	0	0	0	0	530	0	0	30	..	0	0	0
Ordnance Survey	30	10	20	20	20	30	20	840	20	30	20	0	0	0
Skills Funding Agency	130	80	100	490	50	50	180	120	70	0	0	0	0	0
UK Intellectual Property Office	0	0	0	0	0	0	40	0	0	0	850	0	0	0
UK Space Agency	0	0	0	0	0	0	10	0	30	0	0	0	0	0
Cabinet Office														
Cabinet Office (excl. agencies)	0	0	10	0	0	80	1,510	20	..	0	0	0	0	0
Other Cabinet Office agencies														
Central Office of Information	10	10	10	10	10	10	300	0	10	..	..	0	0	0
Office of the Parliamentary Counsel	0	0	0	0	0	0	110	0	0	0	0	0	0	0
Government Procurement Service	190	0	..	0	..	90	..	..	..	..	0	0	0	0
Chancellor's other departments														
Debt Management Office	0	0	0	0	0	0	110	0	0	0	0	0	0	0
Government Actuary's Department	0	0	0	0	0	0	120	0	0	0	0	0	0	0
National Savings and Investments	10	10	0	..	..	10	90	30	0	10	0	0	0	0
Charity Commission														
Charity Commission	170	0	0	0	0	0	70	0	110	0	10	0	..	0
Communities and Local Government														
Department for Communities and Local Government (excl. agencies)	80	40	50	70	30	80	1,390	30	80	0	0	0	0	40
Fire Service College	0	0	0	0	0	0	0	0	180	0	0	0	0	0
Planning Inspectorate	0	0	0	0	0	0	0	0	640	0	40	0	0	0
Queen Elizabeth II Conference Centre	0	0	0	0	0	0	40	0	0	0	0	0	0	0
Culture, Media and Sport														
Department for Culture Media and Sport	0	0	0	0	0	0	460	0	0	0	0	0	0	0
Royal Parks	0	0	0	0	0	0	130	0	0	0	0	0	0	0
Defence														
Ministry of Defence[4]	2,000	340	3,150	3,060	1,940	4,550	3,950	9,790	15,150	4,610	1,010	1,620	1,950	280
Defence Support Group	0	0	120	1,010	..	100	..	90	690	90	550	10	100	0
Defence Science and Technology Laboratory	0	0	0	0	10	10	10	2,020	1,680	0	0	0	0	0
Royal Fleet Auxiliary[4]	0	0	0	0	0	0	0	0	0	0	0	0	0	2,030
UK Hydrographic Office	0	0	0	0	0	0	0	10	1,030	..	0	0	..	0
Education														
Department for Education	230	400	460	180	0	0	1,520	0	0	0	0	0	0	0
Energy and Climate Change														
Department for Energy and Climate Change	0	0	..	0	0	0	1,220	0	0	90	0	0	0	0

4.6 Civil Service employment; regional (GOR) distribution by government department[1,2]

All employees

Headcount

	North West	North East	Yorkshire and the Humber	West Midlands	East Midlands	East of England	London	South East	South West	Scotland	Wales	Northern Ireland	Overseas	Not reported
Environment, Food and Rural Affairs														
Department for Environment Food and Rural Affairs (excl. agencies)	20	60	350	20	10	20	1,530	10	130	0	0	0	0	10
Animal Health and Veterinary Laboratories Agency	190	50	80	400	110	100	60	850	320	150	220	0	0	0
Centre for Environment Fisheries and Aquaculture Science	..	0	..	0	0	400	0	0	140	0	0	0	0	0
Food and Environment Research Agency	10	..	720	30	..	50	20	20	50	0	..	0	0	0
Office of Water Services	0	0	0	170	0	0	10	0	0	0	0	0	0	0
Rural Payments Agency	870	300	400	40	30	40	10	470	390	0	..	10	0	0
Veterinary Medicines Directorate	0	0	0	0	0	0	0	150	0	0	0	0	0	0
ESTYN														
ESTYN	0	0	0	0	0	0	0	0	0	0	100	0	0	0
Food Standards Agency														
Food Standards Agency	90	20	210	100	80	130	220	90	90	160	100	40	..	20
Foreign and Commonwealth Office														
Foreign and Commonwealth Office (excl. agencies)	0	0	0	0	0	0	3,150	840	0	0	0	0	2,570	0
Wilton Park Executive Agency	0	0	0	0	0	0	0	70	0	0	0	0	0	0
Health														
Department of Health (excl. agencies)	60	10	750	10	10	10	1,410	30	10	0	0	0	0	60
Medicines and Healthcare Products Regulatory Agency	..	0	20	0	0	30	840	0	0	0	0	0	0	0
HM Revenue and Customs														
HM Revenue and Customs	13,080	12,950	5,040	4,160	3,730	4,190	7,820	4,990	2,960	9,840	4,070	1,970	0	170
Valuation Office	420	210	420	320	250	290	710	460	310	50	270	0	0	70
HM Treasury														
HM Treasury	0	0	0	0	0	30	1,040	0	0	0	0	0	0	0
Asset Protection Agency	0	0	0	0	0	0	30	0	0	0	0	0	0	0
Office for Budget Responsibility	0	0	0	0	0	0	20	0	0	0	0	0	0	0
Home Office														
Home Office (excl. agencies)[3]	560	120	300	260	60	960	4,920	2,790	200	240	140	70	140	10
Criminal Records Bureau	510	0	0	0	0	0	0	0	0	0	0	0	0	..
Identity and Passport Service	1,110	670	30	10	10	460	580	20	20	180	180	180	0	10
National Fraud Authority	0	0	0	0	0	0	40	0	0	0	0	0	0	0
UK Border Agency[3]	2,030	160	1,920	430	120	230	5,620	480	110	270	210	50	..	..
International Development														
Department for International Development	0	0	0	0	0	0	710	0	0	510	0	0	500	0
Justice														
Ministry of Justice (excl. agencies)	210	30	120	180	70	10	2,440	30	30	370	760	0	0	0
Her Majesty's Courts and Tribunals Service	2,900	1,060	1,950	2,070	1,770	1,330	4,710	1,980	1,280	290	1,160	0	0	160
National Archives	0	0	0	0	0	..	630	0	0	0	0	0	0	0
National Offender Management Service	5,640	3,500	5,400	3,950	4,750	4,620	5,250	7,780	3,670	0	1,020	0	0	0
Office of the Public Guardian	0	0	0	340	110	0	80	0	0	0	0	0	0	0
UK Supreme Court	0	0	0	0	0	0	50	0	0	0	0	0	0	0
Northern Ireland Office														
Northern Ireland Office	0	0	0	0	0	0	50	0	0	0	0	40	0	0
Office for Standards in Education														
Office for Standards in Education	490	0	0	0	340	0	270	0	330	0	0	0	0	0
Office of Qualifications and Examinations Regulation														
Ofqual	0	0	0	160	0	0	0	0	0	0	0	10	0	0
Scottish Government														

4.6 Civil Service employment; regional (GOR) distribution by government department[1,2]

All employees

Headcount

	North West	North East	Yorkshire and the Humber	West Midlands	East Midlands	East of England	London	South East	South West	Scotland	Wales	Northern Ireland	Overseas	Not reported
Scottish Government (excl. agencies)	0	0	0	0	0	0	0	0	0	5,180	0	0	10	20
Crown Office and Procurator Fiscal Service	0	0	0	0	0	0	0	0	0	1,570	0	0	0	90
Disclosure Scotland	0	0	0	0	0	0	0	0	0	180	0	0	0	0
National Records of Scotland	0	0	0	0	0	0	0	0	0	400	0	0	0	0
Education Scotland	0	0	0	0	0	0	0	0	0	300	0	0	0	0
Historic Scotland	0	0	0	0	0	0	0	0	0	1,040	0	0	0	0
Office of Accountant in Bankruptcy	0	0	0	0	0	0	0	0	0	160	0	0	0	0
Office of the Scottish Charity Regulator	0	0	0	0	0	0	0	0	0	50	0	0	0	0
Registers of Scotland	0	0	0	0	0	0	0	0	0	1,160	0	0	0	0
Scottish Court Service	0	0	0	0	0	0	0	0	0	1,200	0	0	0	260
Scottish Housing Regulator	0	0	0	0	0	0	0	0	0	50	0	0	0	0
Scottish Prison Service	0	0	0	0	0	0	0	0	0	4,180	0	0	0	0
Scottish Public Pensions Agency	0	0	0	0	0	0	0	0	0	260	0	0	0	0
Student Awards Agency	0	0	0	0	0	0	0	0	0	160	0	0	0	0
Transport Scotland	0	0	0	0	0	0	0	0	0	380	0	0	0	0
Scotland Office														
Scotland Office	0	0	0	0	0	0	20	0	0	70	0	0	10	0
Security and Intelligence Services														
Security and Intelligence Services	0	0	0	0	0	0	0	0	5,440	0	0	0	0	0
Transport														
Department for Transport (excl. agencies)	0	10	10	..	20	0	1,440	190	10	0	0	0	..	0
Driver and Vehicle Licensing Agency	160	70	90	90	120	150	120	110	140	120	5,090	0	0	0
Driving Standards Agency	200	370	170	190	430	220	270	250	150	160	140	0	0	30
Government Car and Despatch Agency	..	0	..	0	0	10	140	20	0	0	10	0	0	0
Highways Agency	450	30	440	880	120	450	110	590	360	0	0	0	0	60
Maritime and Coastguard Agency	40	20	50	0	..	60	20	430	130	180	140	30	0	0
Office of Rail Regulation	20	..	20	10	..	..	200	10	10	10	..	0	..	..
Vehicle and Operator Services Agency	230	70	240	180	130	200	130	230	360	170	270	0	0	0
Vehicle Certification Agency	0	0	0	0	50	0	0	..	100	0	0	0	10	0
United Kingdom Statistics Authority														
United Kingdom Statistics Authority	0	0	0	0	0	0	30	2,030	..	0	1,600	0	0	0
UK Export Finance														
UK Export Finance	0	0	0	0	0	0	180	0	0	0	..	0	0	0
Wales Office														
Wales Office	0	0	0	0	0	0	40	0	0	0	20	0	0	0
Welsh Government														
Welsh Government	0	0	0	0	0	0	10	0	0	0	5,310	0	20	0
Work and Pensions														
Department for Work and Pensions	19,560	10,150	10,950	8,670	6,070	5,400	10,480	6,350	5,340	10,330	6,510	..	0	150
The Health and Safety Executive	1,390	70	360	150	480	160	210	170	120	270	110	0	0	0
Child Maintenance and Enforcement Commission	1,720	1,240	400	1,230	110	200	80	1,070	1,350	1,530	100	0	0	0
											0	0	0	0
Total employment	56,960	33,100	36,010	30,620	22,380	25,860	74,670	46,570	46,590	46,260	31,970	4,050	5,340	3,450

Source: Annual Civil Service Employment Survey

1 Numbers are rounded to the nearest ten, and cells containing between one and five employees are represented by "..".

2 Workplace postcode data are used to derive geographical information.

3 On 1 March 2012, Border Force, which had been part of UK Border Agency, transferred to Home Office Headquarters, a movement of approximately 8000 employees.

4 National Identity is unknown for all MOD employees as this is not held on their systems.

4.7: Unemployment by sex, age and duration

United Kingdom (thousands) seasonally adjusted

	All aged 16 & over							All aged 16 - 64						
	All	Rate (%)[+]	Up to 6 months	Over 6 and up to 12 months	All over 12 months	% over 12 months	All over 24 months	All	Rate (%)[+]	Up to 6 months	Over 6 and up to 12 months	All over 12 months	% over 12 months	All over 24 months
	1	2	3	4	5	6	7	8	9	10	11	12	13	14
All Persons	MGSC	MGSX	YBWF	YBWG	YBWH	YBWI	YBWL	LF2I	LF2Q	LF2Y	LF32	LF34	LF36	LF38
Nov-Jan 2004	1,443	4.8	906	228	309	21.4	148	1,429	4.9	896	226	307	21.5	144
Dec-Feb 2004	1,438	4.8	916	215	307	21.4	146	1,426	4.9	910	213	303	21.2	143
Jan-Mar 2004	1,436	4.8	904	225	307	21.4	143	1,423	4.9	896	225	303	21.3	141
Feb-Apr 2004	1,439	4.8	913	228	298	20.7	146	1,427	4.9	909	228	290	20.3	142
Mar-May 2004	1,436	4.8	912	232	293	20.4	138	1,423	4.9	907	231	285	20.1	134
Apr-Jun 2004	1,439	4.8	926	227	286	19.9	132	1,428	4.9	918	226	284	19.9	130
May-Jul 2004	1,426	4.8	918	220	288	20.2	124	1,417	4.8	912	219	285	20.1	122
Jun-Aug 2004	1,407	4.7	918	216	273	19.4	119	1,398	4.8	913	216	269	19.3	117
Jul-Sep 2004	1,403	4.7	917	210	277	19.8	125	1,394	4.8	913	208	272	19.5	123
Aug-Oct 2004	1,398	4.7	911	210	276	19.7	128	1,388	4.7	906	209	272	19.6	126
Sep-Nov 2004	1,410	4.7	908	215	287	20.4	135	1,396	4.7	901	213	282	20.2	132
Oct-Dec 2004	1,427	4.7	922	227	279	19.5	131	1,412	4.8	912	225	275	19.5	127
Nov-Jan 2005	1,428	4.7	926	221	281	19.7	133	1,413	4.8	917	219	277	19.6	129
Dec-Feb 2005	1,449	4.8	927	224	299	20.6	140	1,435	4.8	919	223	294	20.5	137
Jan-Mar 2005	1,419	4.7	908	215	296	20.9	137	1,406	4.8	901	215	291	20.7	135
Feb-Apr 2005	1,422	4.7	909	214	299	21.0	133	1,409	4.8	903	214	292	20.7	131
Mar-May 2005	1,437	4.8	918	214	304	21.2	139	1,426	4.8	915	213	297	20.8	136
Apr-Jun 2005	1,439	4.8	912	215	313	21.7	143	1,428	4.8	904	213	310	21.7	139
May-Jul 2005	1,426	4.7	902	217	306	21.5	141	1,413	4.8	896	216	301	21.3	137
Jun-Aug 2005	1,423	4.7	894	232	298	20.9	138	1,411	4.8	888	230	293	20.8	135
Jul-Sep 2005	1,439	4.8	908	242	290	20.1	134	1,424	4.8	901	241	282	19.8	130
Aug-Oct 2005	1,503	5.0	951	255	297	19.8	147	1,489	5.0	942	254	294	19.7	144
Sep-Nov 2005	1,542	5.1	971	252	319	20.7	159	1,524	5.1	963	250	311	20.4	154
Oct-Dec 2005	1,572	5.2	987	254	331	21.1	163	1,556	5.2	979	251	326	21.0	157
Nov-Jan 2006	1,555	5.1	970	259	326	21.0	163	1,539	5.2	960	255	324	21.1	159
Dec-Feb 2006	1,587	5.2	984	272	332	20.9	161	1,573	5.3	977	269	327	20.8	157
Jan-Mar 2006	1,607	5.3	988	281	339	21.1	164	1,592	5.3	981	278	334	20.9	159
Feb-Apr 2006	1,635	5.3	1,010	279	347	21.2	161	1,621	5.4	1,007	276	339	20.9	157
Mar-May 2006	1,665	5.4	1,015	296	354	21.3	171	1,651	5.5	1,010	293	347	21.0	167
Apr-Jun 2006	1,686	5.5	1,025	300	361	21.4	169	1,672	5.6	1,016	297	359	21.5	166
May-Jul 2006	1,700	5.5	1,023	304	373	21.9	174	1,683	5.6	1,012	301	369	21.9	171
Jun-Aug 2006	1,692	5.5	1,024	301	366	21.7	165	1,677	5.6	1,016	297	364	21.7	163
Jul-Sep 2006	1,696	5.5	1,017	289	389	23.0	181	1,680	5.6	1,011	286	383	22.8	178
Aug-Oct 2006	1,694	5.5	1,014	293	387	22.8	181	1,682	5.6	1,009	291	382	22.7	178
Sep-Nov 2006	1,677	5.5	1,004	283	390	23.2	184	1,665	5.5	1,000	282	383	23.0	180
Oct-Dec 2006	1,705	5.5	1,023	286	396	23.3	187	1,694	5.6	1,016	285	394	23.2	185
Nov-Jan 2007	1,704	5.5	1,030	275	399	23.4	184	1,693	5.6	1,021	274	397	23.5	181
Dec-Feb 2007	1,707	5.6	1,041	269	397	23.2	178	1,696	5.6	1,034	267	395	23.3	176
Jan-Mar 2007	1,701	5.5	1,033	277	391	23.0	178	1,687	5.6	1,026	275	386	22.9	174
Feb-Apr 2007	1,688	5.5	1,011	277	400	23.7	176	1,673	5.5	1,006	276	391	23.4	172
Mar-May 2007	1,663	5.4	996	269	397	23.9	180	1,648	5.5	990	269	389	23.6	176
Apr-Jun 2007	1,655	5.4	999	262	394	23.8	175	1,638	5.4	989	260	389	23.8	171
May-Jul 2007	1,643	5.3	988	261	393	23.9	178	1,628	5.4	981	260	387	23.8	175
Jun-Aug 2007	1,645	5.3	987	266	392	23.8	175	1,631	5.4	981	264	385	23.6	171
Jul-Sep 2007	1,650	5.3	991	268	391	23.7	176	1,638	5.4	984	268	385	23.5	173
Aug-Oct 2007	1,631	5.3	988	260	383	23.5	176	1,619	5.3	980	260	380	23.4	173
Sep-Nov 2007	1,636	5.3	987	258	392	23.9	176	1,624	5.4	982	257	385	23.7	173
Oct-Dec 2007	1,610	5.2	970	256	383	23.8	169	1,601	5.3	965	254	381	23.8	167
Nov-Jan 2008	1,619	5.2	977	261	381	23.5	179	1,608	5.3	969	258	381	23.7	177
Dec-Feb 2008	1,620	5.2	957	274	388	24.0	189	1,607	5.3	950	271	386	24.0	187
Jan-Mar 2008	1,618	5.2	954	267	396	24.5	198	1,605	5.3	949	264	392	24.4	195
Feb-Apr 2008	1,660	5.3	985	265	409	24.6	197	1,643	5.4	979	262	402	24.5	195
Mar-May 2008	1,614	5.2	949	262	403	25.0	190	1,599	5.2	943	258	398	24.9	189
Apr-Jun 2008	1,674	5.4	989	271	413	24.7	191	1,659	5.4	981	268	411	24.8	189
May-Jul 2008	1,719	5.5	1,011	275	433	25.2	204	1,706	5.6	1,006	271	428	25.1	202
Jun-Aug 2008	1,788	5.7	1,073	275	440	24.6	205	1,771	5.8	1,066	270	436	24.6	203
Jul-Sep 2008	1,836	5.9	1,110	285	440	24.0	202	1,817	6.0	1,101	282	434	23.9	201
Aug-Oct 2008	1,873	6.0	1,148	288	437	23.3	200	1,853	6.1	1,135	285	433	23.4	198
Sep-Nov 2008	1,943	6.2	1,192	313	438	22.5	198	1,924	6.3	1,181	311	432	22.4	195
Oct-Dec 2008	2,003	6.4	1,226	324	453	22.6	210	1,986	6.5	1,215	319	452	22.7	208
Nov-Jan 2009	2,059	6.6	1,255	345	459	22.3	207	2,044	6.7	1,244	341	459	22.4	205
Dec-Feb 2009	2,123	6.8	1,287	355	481	22.7	222	2,105	6.9	1,276	351	478	22.7	218
Jan-Mar 2009	2,225	7.1	1,336	382	507	22.8	231	2,206	7.2	1,327	379	501	22.7	228
Feb-Apr 2009	2,283	7.3	1,358	404	521	22.8	235	2,265	7.4	1,350	401	514	22.7	232
Mar-May 2009	2,377	7.6	1,408	437	532	22.4	236	2,359	7.7	1,400	433	526	22.3	234
Apr-Jun 2009	2,435	7.8	1,411	476	549	22.5	239	2,415	7.9	1,399	472	543	22.5	234
May-Jul 2009	2,469	7.9	1,398	492	579	23.4	245	2,446	8.0	1,387	488	571	23.3	240
Jun-Aug 2009	2,473	7.9	1,348	515	610	24.7	252	2,454	8.0	1,340	513	601	24.5	246
Jul-Sep 2009	2,462	7.9	1,296	536	629	25.6	236	2,437	8.0	1,287	532	618	25.4	229
Aug-Oct 2009	2,469	7.9	1,285	562	622	25.2	236	2,444	8.0	1,273	557	614	25.1	230
Sep-Nov 2009	2,442	7.8	1,248	559	634	26.0	235	2,415	7.9	1,237	551	627	26.0	230
Oct-Dec 2009	2,438	7.8	1,245	533	659	27.0	246	2,416	7.9	1,234	527	655	27.1	242
Nov-Jan 2010	2,428	7.8	1,197	548	682	28.1	246	2,403	7.9	1,184	541	678	28.2	241
Dec-Feb 2010	2,486	7.9	1,206	552	727	29.3	271	2,462	8.1	1,196	547	719	29.2	265
Jan-Mar 2010	2,512	8.0	1,206	542	764	30.4	283	2,487	8.2	1,198	537	752	30.2	276
Feb-Apr 2010	2,494	8.0	1,186	525	783	31.4	294	2,471	8.1	1,179	521	771	31.2	287
Mar-May 2010	2,491	7.9	1,176	518	797	32.0	302	2,469	8.1	1,169	514	785	31.8	295
Apr-Jun 2010	2,471	7.9	1,166	508	797	32.3	314	2,452	8.0	1,158	504	790	32.2	307
May-Jul 2010	2,475	7.8	1,187	489	799	32.3	321	2,456	8.0	1,179	486	791	32.2	314
Jun-Aug 2010	2,455	7.8	1,168	468	819	33.4	333	2,435	7.9	1,160	465	810	33.3	327
Jul-Sep 2010	2,442	7.7	1,181	445	816	33.4	328	2,424	7.9	1,176	443	805	33.2	323
Aug-Oct 2010	2,484	7.9	1,189	461	835	33.6	333	2,467	8.0	1,185	457	826	33.5	328
Sep-Nov 2010	2,476	7.8	1,204	441	831	33.6	335	2,455	8.0	1,197	436	822	33.5	328
Oct-Dec 2010	2,477	7.8	1,197	451	829	33.5	339	2,457	8.0	1,187	448	822	33.5	332

4.7: Unemployment by sex, age and duration

United Kingdom (thousands) seasonally adjusted

	All aged 16 & over							All aged 16 - 64						
	All	Rate (%)+	Up to 6 months	Over 6 and up to 12 months	All over 12 months	% over 12 months	All over 24 months	All	Rate (%)+	Up to 6 months	Over 6 and up to 12 months	All over 12 months	% over 12 months	All over 24 months
	1	2	3	4	5	6	7	8	9	10	11	12	13	14
Nov-Jan 2011	2,507	7.9	1,213	451	843	33.6	346	2,487	8.1	1,204	449	834	33.5	339
Dec-Feb 2011	2,471	7.8	1,190	439	842	34.1	369	2,454	8.0	1,183	437	834	34.0	363
Jan-Mar 2011	2,460	7.8	1,173	437	850	34.5	386	2,443	7.9	1,169	435	838	34.3	381
Feb-Apr 2011	2,436	7.7	1,177	429	829	34.0	385	2,418	7.9	1,170	428	821	33.9	380
Mar-May 2011	2,470	7.8	1,218	442	809	32.8	383	2,452	8.0	1,213	443	796	32.5	378
Apr-Jun 2011	2,513	7.9	1,246	432	835	33.2	405	2,495	8.1	1,238	430	827	33.1	402
May-Jul 2011	2,531	8.0	1,236	444	851	33.6	415	2,509	8.2	1,227	442	840	33.5	411
Jun-Aug 2011	2,577	8.1	1,241	469	868	33.7	423	2,555	8.3	1,233	464	858	33.6	418
Jul-Sep 2011	2,624	8.3	1,260	497	868	33.1	421	2,598	8.4	1,248	492	857	33.0	416
Aug-Oct 2011	2,637	8.3	1,276	495	867	32.9	429	2,608	8.5	1,261	490	857	32.9	424
Sep-Nov 2011	2,675	8.4	1,306	512	858	32.1	424	2,647	8.6	1,289	506	852	32.2	419
Oct-Dec 2011	2,657	8.4	1,289	510	858	32.3	423	2,630	8.5	1,273	504	853	32.4	418
Nov-Jan 2012	2,652	8.3	1,289	510	853	32.1	405	2,628	8.5	1,274	506	848	32.3	400
Dec-Feb 2012	2,634	8.3	1,251	504	879	33.4	421	2,610	8.4	1,238	502	871	33.4	414
Jan-Mar 2012	2,610	8.2	1,215	515	881	33.8	426	2,582	8.3	1,204	510	867	33.6	419
Feb-Apr 2012	2,599	8.1	1,195	523	882	33.9	434	2,572	8.3	1,182	518	872	33.9	429
Mar-May 2012	2,577	8.1	1,183	511	883	34.3	443	2,554	8.2	1,173	506	875	34.3	440
Apr-Jun 2012	2,564	8.0	1,180	502	882	34.4	422	2,544	8.2	1,172	496	875	34.4	417
May-Jul 2012	2,592	8.1	1,184	504	904	34.9	443	2,569	8.2	1,179	499	891	34.7	435
Jun-Aug 2012	2,528	7.9	1,167	464	897	35.5	444	2,507	8.0	1,163	461	883	35.2	437
Jul-Sep 2012	2,514	7.8	1,168	452	894	35.5	443	2,494	8.0	1,164	450	880	35.3	436
Aug-Oct 2012	2,510	7.8	1,165	442	904	36.0	449	2,490	8.0	1,159	439	892	35.8	444
Sep-Nov 2012	2,493	7.7	1,177	424	892	35.8	435	2,469	7.9	1,168	420	882	35.7	429
Oct-Dec 2012	**2,503**	**7.8**	**1,186**	**437**	**880**	**35.1**	**442**	**2,481**	**7.9**	**1,175**	**434**	**872**	**35.1**	**436**
Change on qtr	*-11*	*-0.1*	*18*	*-15*	*-14*	*-0.4*	*0*	*-13*	*-0.1*	*11*	*-16*	*-8*	*-0.2*	*0*
Change %	*-0.5*		*1.5*	*-3.3*	*-1.6*		*0.0*	*-0.5*		*1.0*	*-3.5*	*-1.0*		*0.0*
Change on year	*-154*	*-0.6*	*-103*	*-72*	*22*	*2.8*	*20*	*-149*	*-0.6*	*-98*	*-69*	*18*	*2.7*	*18*
Change %	*-5.8*		*-8.0*	*-14.2*	*2.5*		*4.7*	*-5.7*		*-7.7*	*-13.8*	*2.1*		*4.3*
Male	MGSD	MGSY	MGYK	MGYM	MGYO	YBWJ	YBWM	YBSI	YBTJ	YBWP	YBWS	YBWV	YBWY	YBXB
Nov-Jan 2004	865	5.3	497	148	219	25.3	115	855	5.4	492	148	214	25.1	111
Dec-Feb 2004	855	5.3	504	138	213	25.0	107	846	5.3	500	137	209	24.7	105
Jan-Mar 2004	844	5.2	491	142	210	24.9	101	833	5.3	485	142	206	24.8	99
Feb-Apr 2004	844	5.2	498	142	204	24.2	103	834	5.3	493	142	200	23.9	101
Mar-May 2004	830	5.1	491	142	198	23.9	100	820	5.2	485	141	194	23.7	98
Apr-Jun 2004	845	5.2	503	141	201	23.8	100	837	5.3	499	140	198	23.6	97
May-Jul 2004	835	5.1	495	137	202	24.2	94	828	5.2	492	136	200	24.1	92
Jun-Aug 2004	831	5.1	500	138	192	23.1	89	823	5.2	496	138	189	23.0	86
Jul-Sep 2004	818	5.0	495	133	190	23.2	93	811	5.1	491	132	187	23.1	91
Aug-Oct 2004	807	5.0	487	133	187	23.2	94	800	5.0	482	132	185	23.2	93
Sep-Nov 2004	834	5.1	494	140	200	24.0	104	823	5.2	488	138	196	23.9	101
Oct-Dec 2004	841	5.2	500	147	194	23.1	101	830	5.2	495	145	190	22.9	98
Nov-Jan 2005	844	5.2	505	143	195	23.2	101	832	5.2	500	142	190	22.9	98
Dec-Feb 2005	847	5.2	498	144	205	24.3	101	837	5.2	492	142	202	24.2	99
Jan-Mar 2005	838	5.1	492	140	206	24.6	99	828	5.2	487	139	202	24.4	97
Feb-Apr 2005	836	5.1	486	143	206	24.7	98	826	5.2	481	142	202	24.5	96
Mar-May 2005	842	5.2	492	139	210	24.9	103	834	5.2	489	138	206	24.7	101
Apr-Jun 2005	837	5.1	483	137	217	25.9	105	830	5.2	479	136	214	25.8	102
May-Jul 2005	840	5.1	488	136	216	25.8	104	831	5.2	484	134	213	25.6	101
Jun-Aug 2005	847	5.2	493	140	215	25.3	103	838	5.2	488	139	211	25.2	101
Jul-Sep 2005	848	5.2	499	145	203	24.0	99	839	5.2	494	145	200	23.8	96
Aug-Oct 2005	890	5.4	533	145	212	23.8	109	881	5.5	528	145	209	23.7	106
Sep-Nov 2005	910	5.5	538	145	227	25.0	120	898	5.6	533	143	221	24.6	115
Oct-Dec 2005	932	5.7	545	146	241	25.8	124	920	5.7	541	144	234	25.5	119
Nov-Jan 2006	897	5.4	510	157	230	25.6	118	885	5.5	506	155	224	25.4	114
Dec-Feb 2006	918	5.6	525	163	230	25.1	115	908	5.6	522	161	225	24.8	111
Jan-Mar 2006	937	5.7	533	168	237	25.2	119	927	5.7	529	166	232	25.0	115
Feb-Apr 2006	952	5.7	548	159	245	25.8	119	942	5.8	546	157	240	25.4	115
Mar-May 2006	973	5.9	543	172	258	26.5	129	963	5.9	538	170	255	26.5	126
Apr-Jun 2006	976	5.9	541	175	259	26.5	125	965	6.0	536	173	256	26.5	122
May-Jul 2006	980	5.9	538	180	262	26.7	127	968	6.0	531	178	259	26.8	125
Jun-Aug 2006	971	5.8	544	179	248	25.5	116	961	5.9	539	176	246	25.6	114
Jul-Sep 2006	983	5.9	543	173	267	27.2	131	970	6.0	538	170	262	27.1	128
Aug-Oct 2006	983	5.9	540	177	266	27.1	132	973	6.0	536	175	262	26.9	129
Sep-Nov 2006	960	5.8	532	169	259	27.0	129	949	5.8	527	167	254	26.8	126
Oct-Dec 2006	978	5.9	541	169	268	27.4	132	971	6.0	537	169	265	27.3	129
Nov-Jan 2007	974	5.8	537	163	275	28.2	129	966	5.9	533	162	271	28.1	127
Dec-Feb 2007	980	5.9	545	156	278	28.4	127	971	6.0	541	154	276	28.4	125
Jan-Mar 2007	975	5.8	539	165	272	27.9	126	965	5.9	535	162	268	27.7	123
Feb-Apr 2007	972	5.8	531	164	277	28.5	126	960	5.9	527	162	271	28.3	122
Mar-May 2007	956	5.7	521	162	273	28.6	130	945	5.8	516	161	268	28.4	127
Apr-Jun 2007	945	5.6	522	152	270	28.6	124	932	5.7	517	152	264	28.3	120
May-Jul 2007	940	5.6	521	153	267	28.4	126	930	5.7	516	152	261	28.1	123
Jun-Aug 2007	940	5.6	520	153	267	28.4	124	930	5.7	515	153	262	28.2	121
Jul-Sep 2007	941	5.6	521	156	264	28.0	126	933	5.7	516	156	261	28.0	124
Aug-Oct 2007	925	5.5	511	155	260	28.1	130	916	5.6	505	154	256	28.0	127
Sep-Nov 2007	933	5.5	513	152	267	28.6	130	924	5.6	509	152	263	28.5	127
Oct-Dec 2007	917	5.5	505	152	259	28.3	122	911	5.6	503	150	257	28.2	120
Nov-Jan 2008	934	5.5	520	152	262	28.0	130	926	5.6	517	150	259	27.9	128
Dec-Feb 2008	938	5.6	509	163	266	28.3	140	929	5.6	506	161	263	28.3	138
Jan-Mar 2008	939	5.6	509	157	272	29.0	146	929	5.6	505	156	269	28.9	144
Feb-Apr 2008	948	5.6	515	155	277	29.3	142	936	5.7	509	153	274	29.3	141
Mar-May 2008	938	5.5	511	151	276	29.4	138	927	5.6	505	149	273	29.4	137
Apr-Jun 2008	981	5.8	534	158	289	29.5	142	971	5.9	530	155	286	29.4	139

4.7: Unemployment by sex, age and duration

United Kingdom (thousands) seasonally adjusted

	All aged 16 & over							All aged 16 - 64						
	All	Rate (%)+	Up to 6 months	Over 6 and up to 12 months	All over 12 months	% over 12 months	All over 24 months	All	Rate (%)+	Up to 6 months	Over 6 and up to 12 months	All over 12 months	% over 12 months	All over 24 months
	1	2	3	4	5	6	7	8	9	10	11	12	13	14
May-Jul 2008	1,012	6.0	546	163	303	30.0	150	1,002	6.1	543	160	300	29.9	148
Jun-Aug 2008	1,054	6.2	581	163	310	29.4	149	1,042	6.3	575	159	308	29.6	148
Jul-Sep 2008	1,083	6.4	612	164	306	28.3	147	1,068	6.5	603	162	303	28.4	146
Aug-Oct 2008	1,110	6.6	647	163	300	27.0	143	1,095	6.6	637	160	297	27.2	142
Sep-Nov 2008	1,158	6.8	678	183	297	25.7	139	1,144	6.9	669	181	294	25.7	138
Oct-Dec 2008	1,201	7.1	700	191	310	25.8	151	1,190	7.2	693	189	308	25.9	150
Nov-Jan 2009	1,237	7.3	719	204	314	25.4	148	1,226	7.4	714	202	311	25.3	147
Dec-Feb 2009	1,276	7.5	742	209	325	25.5	157	1,264	7.6	736	207	321	25.4	156
Jan-Mar 2009	1,342	7.9	776	227	338	25.2	160	1,328	8.0	769	224	335	25.2	159
Feb-Apr 2009	1,383	8.1	795	248	341	24.7	164	1,370	8.3	788	244	338	24.7	162
Mar-May 2009	1,454	8.6	837	272	345	23.7	166	1,442	8.7	831	268	343	23.8	165
Apr-Jun 2009	1,494	8.8	837	303	354	23.7	164	1,480	9.0	830	300	350	23.7	161
May-Jul 2009	1,527	9.0	825	318	383	25.1	172	1,510	9.2	817	315	378	25.0	169
Jun-Aug 2009	1,538	9.1	787	343	408	26.6	180	1,522	9.2	779	341	402	26.4	176
Jul-Sep 2009	1,526	9.0	743	362	421	27.6	167	1,508	9.2	735	359	414	27.5	162
Aug-Oct 2009	1,529	9.0	731	382	416	27.2	166	1,509	9.2	723	377	409	27.1	161
Sep-Nov 2009	1,499	8.9	713	369	416	27.8	162	1,479	9.0	705	363	410	27.8	158
Oct-Dec 2009	1,487	8.8	706	343	438	29.5	170	1,472	9.0	699	339	433	29.5	167
Nov-Jan 2010	1,498	8.9	685	353	460	30.7	173	1,481	9.0	678	349	454	30.7	170
Dec-Feb 2010	1,522	9.0	672	352	497	32.6	192	1,504	9.2	666	348	490	32.6	188
Jan-Mar 2010	1,544	9.1	672	350	522	33.8	203	1,525	9.3	665	345	515	33.8	199
Feb-Apr 2010	1,523	9.0	651	335	536	35.2	211	1,506	9.2	646	332	529	35.1	207
Mar-May 2010	1,500	8.8	636	321	543	36.2	216	1,483	9.0	630	317	536	36.1	211
Apr-Jun 2010	1,478	8.7	623	308	547	37.0	223	1,464	8.9	618	305	541	36.9	218
May-Jul 2010	1,462	8.6	627	287	548	37.5	226	1,448	8.8	622	284	543	37.5	222
Jun-Aug 2010	1,440	8.4	615	267	558	38.8	235	1,426	8.6	609	265	553	38.8	231
Jul-Sep 2010	1,426	8.3	626	249	551	38.7	236	1,411	8.5	621	246	545	38.6	233
Aug-Oct 2010	1,450	8.5	635	257	559	38.5	239	1,436	8.7	631	253	552	38.5	236
Sep-Nov 2010	1,462	8.6	646	253	563	38.5	235	1,446	8.7	641	249	555	38.4	230
Oct-Dec 2010	1,451	8.5	636	256	559	38.5	237	1,436	8.7	632	253	551	38.4	232
Nov-Jan 2011	1,471	8.6	642	263	565	38.4	241	1,457	8.8	640	262	555	38.1	235
Dec-Feb 2011	1,444	8.4	628	252	564	39.1	262	1,432	8.6	625	249	557	38.9	258
Jan-Mar 2011	1,433	8.4	614	250	569	39.7	272	1,421	8.6	611	248	562	39.5	269
Feb-Apr 2011	1,420	8.3	621	245	554	39.0	278	1,407	8.5	616	243	548	38.9	274
Mar-May 2011	1,436	8.4	636	259	540	37.6	279	1,423	8.6	632	259	531	37.3	275
Apr-Jun 2011	1,458	8.5	659	245	554	38.0	288	1,447	8.7	655	244	547	37.8	286
May-Jul 2011	1,465	8.6	654	256	555	37.9	296	1,451	8.8	649	254	548	37.8	293
Jun-Aug 2011	1,502	8.8	672	266	565	37.6	302	1,489	9.0	668	262	559	37.5	299
Jul-Sep 2011	1,531	9.0	688	281	562	36.7	303	1,516	9.2	683	277	556	36.7	300
Aug-Oct 2011	1,533	9.0	694	280	559	36.5	306	1,517	9.2	687	277	553	36.4	301
Sep-Nov 2011	1,547	9.0	700	290	556	36.0	295	1,530	9.2	693	287	550	36.0	292
Oct-Dec 2011	1,537	9.0	694	289	554	36.0	291	1,520	9.2	687	285	548	36.0	286
Nov-Jan 2012	1,530	8.9	699	287	544	35.5	270	1,515	9.1	694	284	537	35.4	265
Dec-Feb 2012	1,506	8.8	667	286	553	36.7	285	1,490	9.0	661	284	545	36.6	279
Jan-Mar 2012	1,494	8.7	648	294	552	37.0	291	1,475	8.9	641	290	544	36.9	286
Feb-Apr 2012	1,482	8.6	629	297	556	37.5	299	1,464	8.8	620	294	550	37.5	295
Mar-May 2012	1,475	8.5	636	283	556	37.7	299	1,461	8.8	630	279	551	37.8	297
Apr-Jun 2012	1,464	8.5	627	280	558	38.1	286	1,453	8.7	625	276	552	38.0	281
May-Jul 2012	1,491	8.6	631	289	570	38.3	301	1,476	8.8	629	285	563	38.1	295
Jun-Aug 2012	1,444	8.3	623	263	558	38.7	303	1,430	8.5	619	260	551	38.5	297
Jul-Sep 2012	1,426	8.2	611	265	549	38.5	301	1,412	8.4	607	262	543	38.4	297
Aug-Oct 2012	1,430	8.3	609	262	559	39.1	311	1,413	8.4	603	258	553	39.1	307
Sep-Nov 2012	1,408	8.1	606	243	559	39.7	303	1,389	8.3	599	240	550	39.6	298
Oct-Dec 2012	**1,412**	**8.1**	**614**	**241**	**557**	**39.4**	**306**	**1,394**	**8.3**	**608**	**239**	**547**	**39.2**	**300**
Change on qtr	*-14*	*-0.1*	*2*	*-24*	*8*	*0.9*	*5*	*-18*	*-0.1*	*1*	*-23*	*4*	*0.8*	*3*
Change %	*-1.0*		*0.4*	*-9.1*	*1.4*		*1.6*	*-1.3*		*0.1*	*-8.9*	*0.8*		*1.0*
Change on year	*-125*	*-0.8*	*-81*	*-48*	*3*	*3.4*	*15*	*-126*	*-0.8*	*-79*	*-46*	*-1*	*3.2*	*13*
Change %	*-8.2*		*-11.6*	*-16.5*	*0.5*		*5.2*	*-8.3*		*-11.5*	*-16.3*	*-0.1*		*4.6*
Female	MGSE	MGSZ	MGYL	MGYN	MGYP	YBWK	YBWN	LF2J	LF2R	LF2Z	LF33	LF35	LF37	LF39
Nov-Jan 2004	578	4.2	408	79	90	15.6	33	575	4.3	404	78	93	16.1	32
Dec-Feb 2004	583	4.3	412	77	94	16.1	39	580	4.3	410	77	93	16.1	38
Jan-Mar 2004	592	4.3	412	83	97	16.4	42	590	4.4	411	83	96	16.3	41
Feb-Apr 2004	595	4.4	415	86	94	15.8	43	593	4.4	416	86	91	15.3	42
Mar-May 2004	606	4.4	422	90	95	15.6	37	604	4.5	422	90	91	15.1	37
Apr-Jun 2004	594	4.3	423	86	85	14.2	33	591	4.4	419	86	86	14.6	33
May-Jul 2004	591	4.3	423	83	85	14.4	30	588	4.4	420	83	86	14.6	30
Jun-Aug 2004	577	4.2	418	78	81	14.0	31	574	4.3	416	78	80	14.0	31
Jul-Sep 2004	586	4.3	422	76	87	14.9	32	583	4.3	422	76	85	14.6	32
Aug-Oct 2004	591	4.3	425	77	89	15.1	34	588	4.4	424	77	87	14.8	33
Sep-Nov 2004	576	4.2	414	75	87	15.1	31	573	4.2	413	75	85	14.9	31
Oct-Dec 2004	585	4.3	421	80	84	14.4	29	582	4.3	417	80	85	14.7	29
Nov-Jan 2005	584	4.2	421	78	85	14.6	32	581	4.3	417	77	86	14.8	31
Dec-Feb 2005	602	4.4	428	80	93	15.5	40	599	4.4	427	80	92	15.3	39
Jan-Mar 2005	581	4.2	416	76	90	15.5	38	578	4.3	414	75	89	15.3	37
Feb-Apr 2005	586	4.3	422	71	92	15.8	35	583	4.3	422	71	89	15.4	35
Mar-May 2005	595	4.3	426	75	94	15.9	36	592	4.4	426	75	91	15.3	35
Apr-Jun 2005	602	4.4	429	77	96	15.9	37	599	4.4	425	77	96	16.1	37
May-Jul 2005	586	4.2	414	81	90	15.4	37	582	4.3	412	81	89	15.2	36
Jun-Aug 2005	576	4.2	401	92	83	14.4	35	572	4.2	400	91	81	14.2	34
Jul-Sep 2005	591	4.3	409	96	86	14.6	35	585	4.3	407	96	83	14.1	35
Aug-Oct 2005	613	4.4	418	110	85	13.9	38	609	4.5	415	109	85	13.9	38
Sep-Nov 2005	632	4.6	433	107	92	14.6	39	626	4.6	429	107	90	14.4	39

4.7: Unemployment by sex, age and duration

United Kingdom (thousands) seasonally adjusted

| | All aged 16 & over | | | | | | | All aged 16 - 64 | | | | | | |
	All	Rate (%)[+]	Up to 6 months	Over 6 and up to 12 months	All over 12 months	% over 12 months	All over 24 months	All	Rate (%)[+]	Up to 6 months	Over 6 and up to 12 months	All over 12 months	% over 12 months	All over 24 months
	1	2	3	4	5	6	7	8	9	10	11	12	13	14
Oct-Dec 2005	641	4.6	442	108	90	14.1	39	637	4.7	438	107	92	14.4	38
Nov-Jan 2006	658	4.7	460	101	97	14.7	45	653	4.8	454	100	99	15.2	45
Dec-Feb 2006	669	4.8	458	109	102	15.2	46	665	4.8	455	108	102	15.4	46
Jan-Mar 2006	670	4.8	455	113	102	15.2	44	666	4.8	452	112	102	15.3	44
Feb-Apr 2006	683	4.9	462	120	101	14.8	42	679	4.9	461	119	99	14.5	42
Mar-May 2006	692	4.9	472	124	96	13.9	42	688	5.0	472	124	93	13.5	41
Apr-Jun 2006	710	5.0	484	125	102	14.3	44	706	5.1	480	124	102	14.5	44
May-Jul 2006	720	5.1	485	124	111	15.4	47	715	5.2	481	124	109	15.3	46
Jun-Aug 2006	721	5.1	480	122	118	16.4	49	716	5.2	477	121	118	16.5	49
Jul-Sep 2006	713	5.1	474	116	122	17.2	50	710	5.1	473	116	120	16.9	50
Aug-Oct 2006	711	5.0	474	116	121	17.0	49	709	5.1	473	116	121	17.0	49
Sep-Nov 2006	718	5.1	473	114	130	18.2	55	716	5.2	473	114	128	17.9	55
Oct-Dec 2006	726	5.1	481	116	129	17.7	56	723	5.2	478	116	129	17.9	55
Nov-Jan 2007	730	5.2	493	113	125	17.1	55	727	5.3	489	112	127	17.4	54
Dec-Feb 2007	727	5.2	496	113	118	16.3	51	725	5.2	493	113	119	16.5	51
Jan-Mar 2007	726	5.2	494	112	119	16.4	51	722	5.2	491	113	118	16.4	51
Feb-Apr 2007	717	5.1	480	113	123	17.2	50	713	5.2	479	114	120	16.8	50
Mar-May 2007	708	5.0	476	108	124	17.5	50	703	5.1	474	108	121	17.2	49
Apr-Jun 2007	710	5.0	477	110	124	17.4	51	706	5.1	472	108	126	17.8	51
May-Jul 2007	703	5.0	468	109	127	18.0	53	698	5.0	465	108	126	18.0	52
Jun-Aug 2007	705	5.0	467	113	125	17.7	52	701	5.1	466	112	123	17.6	51
Jul-Sep 2007	709	5.0	470	112	127	18.0	50	705	5.1	469	112	125	17.7	49
Aug-Oct 2007	707	5.0	477	106	124	17.5	47	703	5.1	474	105	124	17.6	46
Sep-Nov 2007	704	5.0	474	105	125	17.7	47	701	5.0	473	105	122	17.4	46
Oct-Dec 2007	693	4.9	465	104	124	17.9	47	690	4.9	462	104	124	18.0	47
Nov-Jan 2008	684	4.8	456	109	119	17.4	49	682	4.9	451	108	122	17.9	48
Dec-Feb 2008	682	4.8	449	111	122	18.0	50	678	4.8	445	110	124	18.2	49
Jan-Mar 2008	680	4.8	445	110	124	18.3	52	676	4.8	444	109	124	18.3	52
Feb-Apr 2008	712	5.0	470	110	132	18.5	54	707	5.0	470	109	128	18.2	54
Mar-May 2008	676	4.7	438	111	127	18.9	52	672	4.8	437	110	125	18.6	52
Apr-Jun 2008	692	4.9	455	113	124	17.9	49	688	4.9	451	112	125	18.2	49
May-Jul 2008	707	5.0	465	113	129	18.3	54	703	5.0	464	112	128	18.2	54
Jun-Aug 2008	734	5.1	492	112	129	17.6	56	729	5.2	491	111	128	17.5	55
Jul-Sep 2008	753	5.3	498	121	134	17.8	56	749	5.3	498	120	131	17.5	55
Aug-Oct 2008	764	5.3	501	125	137	18.0	57	759	5.4	498	125	136	17.9	56
Sep-Nov 2008	785	5.5	514	130	141	17.9	59	780	5.5	512	130	138	17.7	58
Oct-Dec 2008	801	5.6	526	132	143	17.9	59	796	5.7	522	131	143	18.0	58
Nov-Jan 2009	822	5.7	536	141	145	17.6	59	817	5.8	530	139	148	18.1	58
Dec-Feb 2009	847	5.9	545	146	156	18.4	65	841	6.0	540	145	156	18.6	62
Jan-Mar 2009	884	6.2	560	155	169	19.1	71	879	6.2	558	155	166	18.9	69
Feb-Apr 2009	899	6.3	563	156	180	20.0	71	894	6.4	562	157	176	19.6	70
Mar-May 2009	923	6.4	571	165	187	20.3	70	917	6.5	569	165	183	19.9	69
Apr-Jun 2009	941	6.6	574	173	194	20.6	75	935	6.6	570	172	193	20.7	74
May-Jul 2009	941	6.6	572	173	195	20.8	73	936	6.7	570	173	193	20.6	71
Jun-Aug 2009	936	6.5	562	172	202	21.6	72	931	6.6	561	172	199	21.4	70
Jul-Sep 2009	936	6.5	554	174	208	22.2	68	930	6.6	552	174	204	21.9	67
Aug-Oct 2009	941	6.5	553	181	207	22.0	70	935	6.6	550	180	205	21.9	69
Sep-Nov 2009	942	6.5	535	190	218	23.1	73	936	6.6	531	188	217	23.2	72
Oct-Dec 2009	951	6.6	540	190	221	23.2	76	944	6.7	535	188	221	23.4	74
Nov-Jan 2010	930	6.4	513	195	222	23.9	73	922	6.5	506	192	224	24.3	71
Dec-Feb 2010	964	6.7	534	200	231	23.9	79	958	6.8	530	199	229	23.9	77
Jan-Mar 2010	969	6.7	534	193	242	25.0	80	962	6.8	533	193	237	24.6	77
Feb-Apr 2010	971	6.7	534	190	247	25.5	83	965	6.8	533	190	242	25.1	80
Mar-May 2010	991	6.9	540	197	254	25.6	86	986	7.0	539	197	249	25.3	84
Apr-Jun 2010	994	6.9	543	200	250	25.2	90	988	7.0	540	199	249	25.2	89
May-Jul 2010	1,013	7.0	560	202	251	24.8	94	1,008	7.1	557	202	248	24.6	93
Jun-Aug 2010	1,014	7.0	553	201	261	25.7	98	1,009	7.1	551	201	257	25.5	97
Jul-Sep 2010	1,017	7.0	555	197	264	26.0	92	1,013	7.1	555	197	260	25.7	91
Aug-Oct 2010	1,034	7.1	554	204	276	26.7	94	1,031	7.3	554	204	274	26.5	93
Sep-Nov 2010	1,014	7.0	559	188	268	26.4	99	1,010	7.1	556	187	267	26.4	98
Oct-Dec 2010	1,026	7.1	561	195	270	26.3	102	1,021	7.2	555	194	271	26.5	101
Nov-Jan 2011	1,037	7.1	571	188	278	26.8	105	1,030	7.3	564	187	279	27.1	103
Dec-Feb 2011	1,028	7.0	562	187	278	27.1	107	1,022	7.2	558	188	277	27.0	106
Jan-Mar 2011	1,027	7.0	559	187	281	27.4	113	1,022	7.2	558	187	277	27.1	112
Feb-Apr 2011	1,016	7.0	556	184	275	27.1	107	1,011	7.1	554	185	273	27.0	106
Mar-May 2011	1,034	7.1	582	183	269	26.0	104	1,029	7.2	580	184	265	25.8	103
Apr-Jun 2011	1,055	7.2	587	187	281	26.6	117	1,048	7.4	583	186	279	26.6	116
May-Jul 2011	1,065	7.3	582	188	296	27.8	119	1,058	7.4	578	188	292	27.6	117
Jun-Aug 2011	1,075	7.4	569	203	303	28.2	121	1,066	7.5	565	202	299	28.1	119
Jul-Sep 2011	1,093	7.5	572	216	306	28.0	119	1,081	7.6	565	215	301	27.8	117
Aug-Oct 2011	1,104	7.5	582	215	307	27.8	123	1,091	7.6	574	213	304	27.9	122
Sep-Nov 2011	1,129	7.7	605	221	302	26.7	128	1,117	7.8	597	219	301	27.0	128
Oct-Dec 2011	1,120	7.6	595	221	304	27.2	132	1,110	7.8	586	218	306	27.5	131
Nov-Jan 2012	1,122	7.6	590	224	309	27.5	135	1,113	7.8	581	222	311	28.0	135
Dec-Feb 2012	1,128	7.7	584	218	327	29.0	136	1,120	7.8	577	218	326	29.1	135
Jan-Mar 2012	1,116	7.6	566	221	329	29.4	135	1,106	7.7	563	220	323	29.2	133
Feb-Apr 2012	1,117	7.6	566	225	326	29.2	135	1,108	7.7	562	224	322	29.1	134
Mar-May 2012	1,103	7.5	547	228	328	29.7	144	1,094	7.6	543	226	324	29.6	143
Apr-Jun 2012	1,099	7.5	553	222	324	29.5	136	1,091	7.6	547	220	323	29.6	136
May-Jul 2012	1,101	7.4	553	215	333	30.3	142	1,093	7.6	551	214	328	30.0	140
Jun-Aug 2012	1,084	7.3	544	201	338	31.2	141	1,077	7.5	544	201	332	30.8	140
Jul-Sep 2012	1,089	7.4	557	187	345	31.7	142	1,082	7.5	557	188	337	31.2	140
Aug-Oct 2012	1,080	7.3	555	180	344	31.9	138	1,076	7.5	556	181	339	31.5	137
Sep-Nov 2012	1,085	7.3	571	180	333	30.7	132	1,080	7.5	568	180	332	30.7	130
Oct-Dec 2012	**1,091**	**7.3**	**572**	**196**	**323**	**29.6**	**137**	**1,088**	**7.5**	**568**	**195**	**325**	**29.9**	**136**

4.7: Unemployment by sex, age and duration

United Kingdom (thousands) seasonally adjusted

	All aged 16 & over							All aged 16 - 64						
	All	Rate (%)[+]	Up to 6 months	Over 6 and up to 12 months	All over 12 months	% over 12 months	All over 24 months	All	Rate (%)[+]	Up to 6 months	Over 6 and up to 12 months	All over 12 months	% over 12 months	All over 24 months
	1	2	3	4	5	6	7	8	9	10	11	12	13	14
Change on qtr	3	0.0	16	9	-22	-2.1	-5	5	0.0	10	8	-13	-1.3	-3
Change %	0.2		2.8	4.9	-6.4		-3.5	0.5		1.9	4.1	-3.7		-2.4
Change on year	-28	-0.3	-22	-25	19	2.4	5	-23	-0.3	-19	-23	19	2.3	5
Change %	-2.5		-3.7	-11.2	6.2		3.6	-2.0		-3.2	-10.5	6.2		3.7

	16-17							18-24						
	All	Rate (%)[+]	Up to 6 months	Over 6 and up to 12 months	All over 12 months	% over 12 months	All over 24 months	All	Rate (%)[+]	Up to 6 months	Over 6 and up to 12 months	All over 12 months	% over 12 months	All over 24 months
	15	16	17	18	19	20	21	22	23	24	25	26	27	28
All Persons	YBVH	YBVK	YBXD	YBXG	YBXJ	YBXM	YBXP	YBVN	YBVQ	YBXS	YBXV	YBXY	YBYB	YBYE
Nov-Jan 2004	169	20.8	129	25	15	8.9	*	389	10.0	276	60	53	13.7	20
Dec-Feb 2004	171	21.3	135	25	12	7.0	*	395	10.1	281	61	53	13.5	21
Jan-Mar 2004	174	21.4	135	29	10	5.6	*	401	10.2	283	60	58	14.5	23
Feb-Apr 2004	178	21.9	140	29	10	5.5	*	401	10.2	284	61	56	14.0	23
Mar-May 2004	176	21.5	136	29	10	5.8	*	391	9.9	278	62	50	12.9	18
Apr-Jun 2004	173	21.5	135	27	11	6.3	*	404	10.3	288	66	50	12.3	17
May-Jul 2004	177	21.7	139	29	9	5.2	*	403	10.3	288	63	52	12.9	15
Jun-Aug 2004	177	21.5	137	29	11	6.2	*	407	10.4	293	60	54	13.3	15
Jul-Sep 2004	184	22.1	145	29	11	5.9	*	408	10.4	296	57	56	13.6	18
Aug-Oct 2004	175	21.1	139	25	11	6.1	*	407	10.4	293	59	55	13.5	19
Sep-Nov 2004	174	21.2	142	23	9	5.3	*	416	10.5	297	60	58	14.1	22
Oct-Dec 2004	169	20.8	138	24	7	4.2	*	431	10.9	306	69	56	12.9	18
Nov-Jan 2005	175	21.3	142	24	9	5.0	*	426	10.7	306	64	56	13.0	18
Dec-Feb 2005	176	21.5	142	25	9	5.2	*	435	10.9	315	63	58	13.2	19
Jan-Mar 2005	180	22.1	146	23	12	6.7	*	409	10.4	297	55	57	13.9	19
Feb-Apr 2005	175	21.8	143	22	11	6.1	*	415	10.5	298	58	59	14.2	21
Mar-May 2005	176	21.8	140	25	12	6.5	*	429	10.9	310	58	61	14.2	24
Apr-Jun 2005	176	21.9	139	24	13	7.4	*	437	11.0	312	58	66	15.2	28
May-Jul 2005	175	21.7	139	25	12	6.7	*	425	10.7	303	59	63	14.7	26
Jun-Aug 2005	175	22.3	137	27	11	6.2	*	428	10.8	294	68	66	15.5	28
Jul-Sep 2005	174	22.3	134	28	12	6.7	*	436	10.9	297	75	63	14.6	27
Aug-Oct 2005	182	23.8	139	31	11	6.2	*	472	11.8	323	79	70	14.7	30
Sep-Nov 2005	178	23.8	138	27	13	7.5	*	473	11.8	318	80	74	15.7	34
Oct-Dec 2005	185	25.1	145	29	11	6.0	*	480	12.0	322	83	75	15.7	35
Nov-Jan 2006	190	25.5	146	30	13	6.7	*	462	11.5	306	86	70	15.1	36
Dec-Feb 2006	190	25.3	146	33	11	5.9	*	469	11.6	318	82	69	14.7	31
Jan-Mar 2006	182	24.7	136	33	13	7.2	*	478	11.7	325	81	71	15.0	33
Feb-Apr 2006	183	24.3	134	35	14	7.6	*	488	11.9	344	73	72	14.7	29
Mar-May 2006	182	24.5	131	39	12	6.4	*	503	12.3	343	81	80	15.9	34
Apr-Jun 2006	178	24.0	129	35	14	7.8	*	518	12.6	353	85	80	15.4	33
May-Jul 2006	173	23.6	126	31	16	9.1	*	533	12.9	355	89	89	16.7	35
Jun-Aug 2006	171	23.4	127	25	19	10.9	*	522	12.5	349	93	81	15.5	30
Jul-Sep 2006	183	24.9	141	25	16	9.0	*	520	12.5	340	94	87	16.7	32
Aug-Oct 2006	184	25.1	144	24	16	8.6	*	510	12.3	329	100	81	15.8	32
Sep-Nov 2006	187	25.1	143	27	17	9.1	*	490	11.9	333	84	72	14.8	29
Oct-Dec 2006	187	24.9	144	27	16	8.5	*	511	12.3	357	80	74	14.5	28
Nov-Jan 2007	188	25.4	146	27	14	7.7	*	513	12.4	362	73	78	15.2	29
Dec-Feb 2007	192	26.2	149	29	15	7.6	*	519	12.5	360	70	88	16.9	31
Jan-Mar 2007	191	26.3	149	28	14	7.4	*	520	12.5	352	78	89	17.2	32
Feb-Apr 2007	188	25.9	146	27	15	8.0	*	523	12.6	345	86	92	17.5	28
Mar-May 2007	190	26.5	149	26	15	8.0	*	527	12.7	350	88	90	17.0	30
Apr-Jun 2007	195	27.4	152	29	14	7.4	*	520	12.5	342	85	93	17.8	30
May-Jul 2007	208	28.3	158	30	20	9.7	*	503	12.1	334	79	89	17.7	32
Jun-Aug 2007	206	28.0	152	35	19	9.2	*	507	12.2	338	74	95	18.7	36
Jul-Sep 2007	215	29.1	156	37	22	10.0	*	496	11.9	333	72	91	18.3	34
Aug-Oct 2007	204	27.6	148	41	14	7.1	*	493	11.8	331	69	94	19.1	35
Sep-Nov 2007	195	26.2	143	37	15	7.7	*	500	12.0	332	71	96	19.3	33
Oct-Dec 2007	188	25.0	138	34	16	8.6	*	497	11.9	328	71	97	19.6	37
Nov-Jan 2008	178	24.2	132	31	14	7.9	*	506	12.1	338	71	97	19.2	41
Dec-Feb 2008	176	24.2	130	33	13	7.3	*	503	12.0	336	75	92	18.4	40
Jan-Mar 2008	174	24.2	129	33	12	7.1	*	513	12.2	342	73	97	19.0	43
Feb-Apr 2008	182	24.8	135	34	13	7.3	*	515	12.3	343	66	107	20.7	41
Mar-May 2008	183	25.2	135	36	13	6.9	*	503	12.0	328	68	107	21.2	40
Apr-Jun 2008	187	26.0	145	32	11	5.7	*	526	12.6	346	75	105	20.0	36
May-Jul 2008	186	25.8	143	31	12	6.5	*	541	12.9	357	80	105	19.3	39
Jun-Aug 2008	190	26.4	152	27	11	5.9	*	556	13.3	363	82	111	20.0	40
Jul-Sep 2008	187	26.3	146	29	12	6.5	*	578	13.7	386	83	109	18.9	39
Aug-Oct 2008	189	27.0	152	25	12	6.6	*	591	14.0	399	93	98	16.6	35
Sep-Nov 2008	194	27.7	148	30	16	8.4	*	610	14.5	408	101	102	16.6	36
Oct-Dec 2008	193	28.2	145	32	16	8.2	*	619	14.7	410	104	105	16.9	37
Nov-Jan 2009	199	28.7	144	38	17	8.3	*	626	14.9	411	112	104	16.6	39
Dec-Feb 2009	188	27.7	136	35	17	8.9	*	633	15.2	414	112	107	16.9	40
Jan-Mar 2009	197	29.3	144	32	22	11.0	*	677	16.2	434	125	118	17.4	46
Feb-Apr 2009	188	29.0	134	33	22	11.5	*	698	16.8	435	131	132	18.9	51
Mar-May 2009	200	30.8	145	35	20	10.2	*	731	17.5	456	139	136	18.6	51
Apr-Jun 2009	206	32.0	145	39	21	10.4	*	719	17.3	431	146	143	19.8	51
May-Jul 2009	219	34.7	156	42	21	9.4	*	725	17.5	419	151	156	21.5	56
Jun-Aug 2009	210	33.9	142	45	23	11.1	*	729	17.6	411	157	160	22.0	57
Jul-Sep 2009	203	33.2	135	42	26	12.8	*	738	17.9	410	156	172	23.3	55
Aug-Oct 2009	197	32.3	128	40	29	14.5	*	741	18.1	426	153	163	21.9	51

4.7: Unemployment by sex, age and duration

United Kingdom (thousands) seasonally adjusted

	16-17							18-24						
	All	Rate (%)[+]	Up to 6 months	Over 6 and up to 12 months	All over 12 months	% over 12 months	All over 24 months	All	Rate (%)[+]	Up to 6 months	Over 6 and up to 12 months	All over 12 months	% over 12 months	All over 24 months
	15	16	17	18	19	20	21	22	23	24	25	26	27	28
Sep-Nov 2009	198	32.6	128	41	29	14.7	*	712	17.5	409	147	156	21.9	52
Oct-Dec 2009	196	33.0	130	37	29	14.6	*	712	17.4	411	142	159	22.3	53
Nov-Jan 2010	198	33.7	133	38	26	13.3	*	711	17.5	395	147	168	23.7	50
Dec-Feb 2010	198	34.1	133	35	30	15.1	*	725	17.8	393	158	174	24.1	59
Jan-Mar 2010	204	34.7	135	43	26	12.7	*	740	18.1	388	162	190	25.7	66
Feb-Apr 2010	215	36.2	141	48	25	11.8	*	729	17.7	380	154	195	26.8	72
Mar-May 2010	219	36.2	142	53	24	10.8	*	723	17.6	379	148	196	27.0	72
Apr-Jun 2010	197	33.5	131	44	22	11.3	*	732	17.8	404	141	187	25.5	74
May-Jul 2010	190	32.8	129	39	22	11.4	*	733	17.7	410	130	193	26.3	72
Jun-Aug 2010	181	31.6	123	33	24	13.2	*	740	17.8	407	126	208	28.1	72
Jul-Sep 2010	190	33.4	126	36	28	14.6	*	711	17.1	402	118	191	26.8	66
Aug-Oct 2010	208	35.7	138	40	30	14.4	*	732	17.6	402	131	198	27.1	69
Sep-Nov 2010	204	36.5	144	36	25	12.2	*	736	17.9	400	134	202	27.5	71
Oct-Dec 2010	211	37.4	151	35	25	12.0	*	745	18.0	395	141	208	27.9	76
Nov-Jan 2011	213	37.2	148	37	28	13.0	*	756	18.2	414	143	199	26.3	70
Dec-Feb 2011	214	37.3	149	39	26	12.2	*	743	17.9	410	135	198	26.6	76
Jan-Mar 2011	209	37.1	146	37	26	12.4	*	726	17.7	393	135	198	27.3	82
Feb-Apr 2011	204	36.2	140	39	26	12.6	*	700	17.1	393	122	186	26.5	82
Mar-May 2011	205	36.7	136	42	26	12.7	*	720	17.5	409	131	180	25.0	78
Apr-Jun 2011	208	37.1	143	39	25	12.2	*	749	18.2	418	129	201	26.9	93
May-Jul 2011	205	37.3	138	39	27	13.4	*	775	18.9	422	136	217	28.0	92
Jun-Aug 2011	208	37.6	136	41	31	14.7	*	790	19.2	416	146	228	28.8	98
Jul-Sep 2011	216	39.2	135	45	35	16.4	*	800	19.6	421	156	223	27.9	88
Aug-Oct 2011	211	39.0	134	45	32	15.2	*	815	19.8	430	158	226	27.8	98
Sep-Nov 2011	213	38.3	132	45	36	16.8	*	826	20.0	453	163	210	25.5	92
Oct-Dec 2011	211	37.9	132	46	33	15.5	*	822	20.0	443	166	213	25.9	94
Nov-Jan 2012	217	39.2	135	46	36	16.7	*	821	20.0	440	165	216	26.4	89
Dec-Feb 2012	212	38.1	135	45	32	15.2	*	812	19.8	416	169	227	28.0	96
Jan-Mar 2012	206	37.3	130	43	32	15.7	*	810	19.7	412	168	231	28.5	99
Feb-Apr 2012	202	36.6	133	40	30	14.7	*	808	19.7	405	180	223	27.6	97
Mar-May 2012	202	36.6	134	38	30	14.8	*	816	19.8	398	179	239	29.2	111
Apr-Jun 2012	203	36.5	135	38	29	14.3	*	809	19.5	396	176	236	29.2	98
May-Jul 2012	201	36.8	134	39	27	13.7	*	816	19.6	398	170	249	30.4	103
Jun-Aug 2012	193	35.5	126	37	30	15.4	*	764	18.5	383	140	241	31.5	105
Jul-Sep 2012	189	34.5	122	34	34	17.9	*	774	18.9	397	144	232	30.0	103
Aug-Oct 2012	198	36.3	128	35	35	17.6	*	747	18.2	381	135	231	30.9	101
Sep-Nov 2012	196	36.7	129	35	32	16.5	*	763	18.4	398	131	233	30.6	90
Oct-Dec 2012	**197**	**37.6**	**131**	**38**	**29**	**14.5**	*	**778**	**18.6**	**399**	**131**	**248**	**31.8**	**102**
Change on qtr	*8*	*3.1*	*9*	*4*	*-5*	*-3.4*	*	*4*	*-0.2*	*1*	*-12*	*15*	*1.8*	*-2*
Change %	*4.2*		*7.6*	*11.6*	*-15.5*		*	*0.5*		*0.3*	*-8.6*	*6.5*		*-1.8*
Change on year	*-13*	*-0.3*	*-1*	*-8*	*-4*	*-1.0*	*	*-44*	*-1.3*	*-44*	*-35*	*35*	*6.0*	*7*
Change %	*-6.4*		*-0.6*	*-18.2*	*-12.6*		*	*-5.4*		*-10.0*	*-21.0*	*16.4*		*7.8*
Male	YBVI	YBVL	YBXE	YBXH	YBXK	YBXN	YBXQ	YBVO	YBVR	YBXT	YBXW	YBXZ	YBYC	YBYF
Nov-Jan 2004	97	23.9	74	14	9	9.2	*	233	11.2	151	44	38	16.1	14
Dec-Feb 2004	95	23.9	75	14	7	7.1	*	238	11.4	157	43	38	15.9	15
Jan-Mar 2004	95	23.9	74	16	6	6.4	*	240	11.4	155	42	43	17.9	16
Feb-Apr 2004	99	24.8	76	17	6	6.3	*	235	11.2	154	40	40	17.2	17
Mar-May 2004	102	24.7	77	19	6	6.0	*	217	10.3	145	38	35	16.1	14
Apr-Jun 2004	98	24.2	74	18	6	6.4	*	232	11.0	158	39	36	15.4	13
May-Jul 2004	104	25.4	79	20	5	4.8	*	232	11.0	157	37	38	16.3	11
Jun-Aug 2004	104	25.2	78	20	7	6.3	*	239	11.3	161	40	39	16.1	11
Jul-Sep 2004	111	26.2	83	20	7	6.5	*	233	11.1	157	38	38	16.2	13
Aug-Oct 2004	99	24.1	77	16	6	6.3	*	233	11.1	156	39	38	16.4	15
Sep-Nov 2004	97	24.0	77	15	5	5.5	*	251	11.9	167	42	42	16.8	17
Oct-Dec 2004	93	23.0	74	15	4	4.0	*	260	12.2	176	43	41	15.7	15
Nov-Jan 2005	93	22.6	73	14	6	6.2	*	263	12.4	182	39	42	16.0	15
Dec-Feb 2005	95	23.0	74	15	6	6.4	*	265	12.4	184	36	45	16.9	16
Jan-Mar 2005	97	23.5	75	12	9	9.5	*	254	11.9	176	34	44	17.5	16
Feb-Apr 2005	96	23.8	75	13	7	7.7	*	253	11.9	172	37	44	17.6	18
Mar-May 2005	94	23.3	72	14	8	8.4	*	265	12.5	180	39	47	17.7	20
Apr-Jun 2005	100	24.7	74	18	8	8.3	*	263	12.3	175	38	51	19.4	24
May-Jul 2005	100	24.6	75	17	8	8.0	*	261	12.2	174	38	49	18.8	21
Jun-Aug 2005	102	26.2	78	16	8	7.9	*	262	12.2	168	41	52	19.9	23
Jul-Sep 2005	103	26.4	79	15	9	8.4	*	268	12.5	173	47	48	18.0	21
Aug-Oct 2005	109	29.0	84	17	9	8.0	*	292	13.4	191	49	52	17.7	25
Sep-Nov 2005	101	27.4	75	16	10	9.5	*	293	13.5	188	49	56	19.2	28
Oct-Dec 2005	102	28.1	76	17	9	8.6	*	300	13.8	192	53	56	18.6	29
Nov-Jan 2006	104	28.5	75	20	9	8.2	*	274	12.7	171	53	50	18.3	28
Dec-Feb 2006	110	29.9	83	20	8	7.2	*	284	13.0	181	53	49	17.3	25
Jan-Mar 2006	111	30.5	81	21	9	8.2	*	288	13.2	183	51	55	18.9	28
Feb-Apr 2006	111	29.6	78	22	11	9.5	*	302	13.8	204	43	55	18.3	25
Mar-May 2006	111	29.9	77	25	9	7.8	*	303	13.8	194	47	61	20.3	30
Apr-Jun 2006	104	28.1	73	21	10	9.3	*	311	14.2	198	52	62	19.9	28
May-Jul 2006	100	27.2	70	19	10	10.5	*	315	14.2	190	57	69	21.9	32
Jun-Aug 2006	95	26.3	67	16	12	12.4	*	308	13.8	190	58	61	19.8	27
Jul-Sep 2006	104	28.6	75	18	11	10.4	*	312	13.9	187	60	65	20.8	30
Aug-Oct 2006	104	28.6	76	17	11	10.4	*	308	13.8	186	64	59	19.0	28
Sep-Nov 2006	108	29.2	79	19	10	9.6	*	295	13.3	189	54	51	17.4	24
Oct-Dec 2006	107	29.0	79	18	10	9.1	*	306	13.7	202	50	54	17.6	23
Nov-Jan 2007	108	29.7	80	18	10	9.0	*	307	13.6	201	47	59	19.2	22
Dec-Feb 2007	107	29.6	79	18	10	9.7	*	310	13.8	201	44	65	20.9	23
Jan-Mar 2007	106	29.2	79	17	10	9.0	*	309	13.7	195	51	63	20.4	23
Feb-Apr 2007	101	28.0	77	15	10	9.8	*	316	14.0	192	58	66	21.0	22

4.7: Unemployment by sex, age and duration

United Kingdom (thousands) seasonally adjusted

	16-17							18-24						
	All	Rate (%)[+]	Up to 6 months	Over 6 and up to 12 months	All over 12 months	% over 12 months	All over 24 months	All	Rate (%)[+]	Up to 6 months	Over 6 and up to 12 months	All over 12 months	% over 12 months	All over 24 months
	15	16	17	18	19	20	21	22	23	24	25	26	27	28
Mar-May 2007	106	29.6	81	15	11	10.0	*	315	13.9	193	58	65	20.5	23
Apr-Jun 2007	108	30.9	82	15	10	9.6	*	314	13.9	191	55	68	21.8	23
May-Jul 2007	116	32.1	86	18	12	10.5	*	298	13.4	185	50	63	21.2	25
Jun-Aug 2007	114	31.2	83	21	11	9.6	*	305	13.7	188	48	69	22.6	28
Jul-Sep 2007	116	31.4	80	23	13	11.5	*	302	13.5	191	45	65	21.7	27
Aug-Oct 2007	115	30.7	80	27	8	7.1	*	297	13.3	188	42	67	22.7	29
Sep-Nov 2007	110	28.8	78	22	10	9.4	*	300	13.4	188	44	68	22.6	28
Oct-Dec 2007	110	28.8	79	20	11	10.3	*	298	13.3	183	45	69	23.2	32
Nov-Jan 2008	103	27.2	73	19	12	11.3	*	306	13.6	190	46	71	23.1	35
Dec-Feb 2008	101	27.3	71	22	9	8.7	*	312	13.8	194	47	70	22.5	36
Jan-Mar 2008	98	26.7	69	22	8	8.4	*	320	14.1	200	46	74	23.1	39
Feb-Apr 2008	102	27.9	73	19	9	8.8	*	315	14.0	197	41	76	24.1	35
Mar-May 2008	101	28.2	75	18	9	8.6	*	307	13.6	188	44	75	24.3	32
Apr-Jun 2008	100	28.0	76	15	8	8.0	*	329	14.6	203	50	76	23.1	29
May-Jul 2008	101	27.8	77	16	7	7.4	*	344	15.2	215	53	76	22.0	30
Jun-Aug 2008	101	27.7	80	14	6	6.2	*	354	15.6	222	52	80	22.6	30
Jul-Sep 2008	102	27.9	84	12	6	5.9	*	363	16.0	230	54	79	21.9	29
Aug-Oct 2008	102	28.3	85	11	6	5.7	*	369	16.3	234	62	73	19.9	25
Sep-Nov 2008	106	29.7	82	16	8	8.0	*	380	16.7	238	66	76	19.9	26
Oct-Dec 2008	104	29.7	76	19	8	7.9	*	388	17.0	241	69	78	20.1	27
Nov-Jan 2009	107	30.6	76	21	10	9.3	*	395	17.3	244	74	78	19.8	29
Dec-Feb 2009	103	30.1	74	18	11	11.0	*	398	17.8	246	77	75	18.9	29
Jan-Mar 2009	108	31.8	79	14	14	13.4	*	418	18.7	253	83	82	19.5	34
Feb-Apr 2009	101	31.0	69	19	13	12.7	*	429	19.2	257	86	87	20.2	39
Mar-May 2009	110	33.7	76	20	13	11.9	*	451	20.1	271	92	89	19.6	39
Apr-Jun 2009	117	36.5	78	24	15	12.5	*	450	20.0	259	97	94	20.9	39
May-Jul 2009	121	38.7	80	26	15	12.5	*	464	20.7	251	103	110	23.7	44
Jun-Aug 2009	118	38.6	77	27	15	12.6	*	464	20.8	236	111	117	25.2	45
Jul-Sep 2009	108	37.2	68	26	14	12.7	*	465	21.0	231	110	123	26.4	42
Aug-Oct 2009	106	36.8	67	24	16	14.7	*	464	21.1	240	111	113	24.4	36
Sep-Nov 2009	109	39.1	69	26	14	12.9	*	439	20.1	229	99	111	25.4	40
Oct-Dec 2009	108	39.1	70	23	15	13.6	*	437	20.1	226	93	118	27.1	40
Nov-Jan 2010	109	39.9	72	23	13	11.9	*	436	20.1	215	92	129	29.6	41
Dec-Feb 2010	109	40.0	72	21	16	14.5	*	441	20.3	211	101	129	29.2	45
Jan-Mar 2010	115	41.5	74	28	14	11.9	*	455	20.8	212	104	140	30.7	52
Feb-Apr 2010	121	42.5	76	32	13	10.6	*	448	20.3	206	99	143	32.0	56
Mar-May 2010	123	41.5	75	34	14	11.1	*	439	19.9	202	92	145	33.0	57
Apr-Jun 2010	106	37.0	67	26	14	12.8	*	439	19.9	213	89	137	31.3	57
May-Jul 2010	103	36.5	68	22	13	12.7	*	433	19.4	213	81	139	32.1	55
Jun-Aug 2010	96	34.5	64	17	14	15.0	*	438	19.6	219	72	147	33.6	55
Jul-Sep 2010	101	36.6	65	21	16	15.8	*	414	18.4	219	65	130	31.5	49
Aug-Oct 2010	105	38.1	67	22	16	15.2	*	429	19.1	223	73	133	31.0	49
Sep-Nov 2010	108	39.6	74	19	15	13.5	*	436	19.5	219	80	137	31.4	47
Oct-Dec 2010	112	40.9	78	19	14	12.6	*	439	19.6	217	82	141	32.1	47
Nov-Jan 2011	116	40.7	77	21	18	15.3	*	438	19.6	220	87	131	29.9	43
Dec-Feb 2011	112	41.4	78	21	14	12.4	*	435	19.5	222	84	130	29.8	48
Jan-Mar 2011	107	40.4	75	18	15	13.5	*	434	19.7	214	86	134	30.7	54
Feb-Apr 2011	107	40.4	72	20	16	14.8	*	431	19.4	223	79	129	30.0	59
Mar-May 2011	107	40.3	66	25	17	15.5	*	438	19.7	230	85	122	27.9	56
Apr-Jun 2011	111	41.4	70	23	18	15.8	*	448	20.2	236	79	133	29.7	64
May-Jul 2011	107	41.9	67	22	18	17.0	*	458	20.8	230	86	142	31.0	65
Jun-Aug 2011	112	42.1	68	23	21	18.4	*	477	21.7	235	88	154	32.3	72
Jul-Sep 2011	119	44.5	72	25	22	18.3	*	488	22.3	245	95	148	30.4	67
Aug-Oct 2011	114	43.3	69	25	20	17.4	*	502	22.9	253	97	152	30.3	74
Sep-Nov 2011	111	41.7	64	23	24	21.1	*	509	23.2	268	101	140	27.5	67
Oct-Dec 2011	109	40.7	65	23	20	18.6	*	514	23.3	260	106	147	28.7	71
Nov-Jan 2012	117	43.7	71	23	22	19.0	*	516	23.5	263	104	149	28.9	64
Dec-Feb 2012	111	40.7	70	22	19	17.1	*	511	23.1	246	110	155	30.4	72
Jan-Mar 2012	106	39.1	67	21	18	17.0	*	504	22.9	239	107	158	31.3	73
Feb-Apr 2012	102	38.0	67	19	16	15.8	*	503	22.9	233	114	156	30.9	74
Mar-May 2012	105	38.8	73	16	16	15.0	*	509	23.0	228	114	167	32.9	80
Apr-Jun 2012	103	38.6	73	15	15	14.5	*	505	22.7	229	112	163	32.3	71
May-Jul 2012	98	37.7	70	17	10	10.3	*	506	22.6	227	112	168	33.1	74
Jun-Aug 2012	95	37.5	63	19	13	14.0	*	469	21.3	218	89	162	34.5	73
Jul-Sep 2012	93	37.0	59	20	14	15.2	*	473	21.5	224	91	158	33.4	71
Aug-Oct 2012	101	39.4	65	19	17	16.9	*	458	20.7	214	86	158	34.4	70
Sep-Nov 2012	104	41.8	69	19	16	15.3	*	461	20.8	213	84	165	35.7	66
Oct-Dec 2012	**108**	**43.6**	**70**	**21**	**17**	**15.7**	*	**462**	**20.9**	**211**	**80**	**171**	**37.1**	**71**
Change on qtr	*15*	*6.6*	*11*	*1*	*3*	*0.6*	*	*-11*	*-0.6*	*-13*	*-11*	*13*	*3.6*	*1*
Change %	*16.3*		*18.2*	*7.6*	*20.6*		*	*-2.3*		*-5.8*	*-12.1*	*8.4*		*0.8*
Change on year	*-1*	*3.0*	*5*	*-2*	*-3*	*-2.9*	*	*-52*	*-2.4*	*-50*	*-26*	*24*	*8.4*	*0*
Change %	*-0.6*		*7.0*	*-8.5*	*-16.2*		*	*-10.1*		*-19.1*	*-24.5*	*16.2*		*0.6*
Female	YBVJ	YBVM	YBXF	YBXI	YBXL	YBXO	YBXR	YBVP	YBVS	YBXU	YBXX	YBYA	YBYD	YBYG
Nov-Jan 2004	72	17.8	55	11	6	8.5	*	156	8.6	125	15	16	10.0	7
Dec-Feb 2004	76	18.7	60	11	5	6.9	*	157	8.6	124	17	15	9.8	6
Jan-Mar 2004	79	19.0	61	14	4	4.7	*	161	8.8	128	18	15	9.4	7
Feb-Apr 2004	79	19.2	63	12	4	4.6	*	166	9.1	129	21	16	9.5	6
Mar-May 2004	74	18.2	59	10	4	5.5	*	174	9.5	134	25	15	8.8	5
Apr-Jun 2004	75	18.7	61	9	5	6.2	*	172	9.4	130	27	14	8.2	5
May-Jul 2004	73	17.9	60	9	4	5.9	*	171	9.4	130	26	14	8.2	4
Jun-Aug 2004	73	17.7	60	9	4	6.0	*	168	9.3	131	21	16	9.4	4
Jul-Sep 2004	74	17.8	61	9	4	5.1	*	175	9.6	139	19	18	10.1	5
Aug-Oct 2004	76	18.1	62	9	4	5.9	*	173	9.5	137	19	17	9.6	4

4.7: Unemployment by sex, age and duration

United Kingdom (thousands) seasonally adjusted

	16-17							18-24						
	All	Rate (%)[+]	Up to 6 months	Over 6 and up to 12 months	All over 12 months	% over 12 months	All over 24 months	All	Rate (%)[+]	Up to 6 months	Over 6 and up to 12 months	All over 12 months	% over 12 months	All over 24 months
	15	16	17	18	19	20	21	22	23	24	25	26	27	28
Sep-Nov 2004	76	18.5	65	8	4	4.9	*	165	9.0	130	18	16	9.8	4
Oct-Dec 2004	77	18.8	64	9	3	4.4	*	170	9.3	129	26	15	8.8	3
Nov-Jan 2005	82	20.1	69	10	3	3.7	*	163	8.9	125	25	13	8.2	3
Dec-Feb 2005	81	19.9	69	10	3	3.8	*	170	9.2	131	27	13	7.5	2
Jan-Mar 2005	84	20.7	70	10	3	3.4	*	155	8.5	121	22	13	8.1	3
Feb-Apr 2005	80	19.9	68	9	3	4.3	*	162	8.9	126	21	14	8.9	2
Mar-May 2005	82	20.3	68	10	4	4.4	*	164	9.0	131	19	14	8.6	4
Apr-Jun 2005	76	19.1	65	6	5	6.1	*	173	9.5	137	21	15	8.8	4
May-Jul 2005	75	18.9	64	8	4	4.9	*	164	9.0	129	21	14	8.3	5
Jun-Aug 2005	73	18.4	59	11	3	3.9	*	167	9.1	125	27	14	8.6	5
Jul-Sep 2005	72	18.3	56	13	3	4.2	*	168	9.2	124	28	15	9.1	5
Aug-Oct 2005	73	18.8	56	15	2	3.4	*	180	9.8	132	30	18	9.9	6
Sep-Nov 2005	76	20.3	62	10	4	4.8	*	180	9.8	130	31	18	10.1	5
Oct-Dec 2005	83	22.2	70	11	2	2.9	*	180	9.8	130	30	19	10.8	6
Nov-Jan 2006	86	22.6	71	11	4	4.9	*	188	10.1	135	33	20	10.5	8
Dec-Feb 2006	79	20.9	63	13	3	4.1	*	185	9.9	137	28	19	10.5	6
Jan-Mar 2006	71	18.9	55	12	4	5.5	*	189	10.0	142	30	17	8.9	5
Feb-Apr 2006	72	19.1	55	13	3	4.5	*	187	9.9	140	30	17	8.9	3
Mar-May 2006	71	19.1	54	14	3	4.1	*	200	10.5	148	34	18	9.1	5
Apr-Jun 2006	74	19.9	56	13	4	5.6	*	206	10.8	156	33	18	8.6	4
May-Jul 2006	73	20.0	56	12	5	7.3	*	218	11.4	166	32	20	9.1	4
Jun-Aug 2006	76	20.6	61	8	7	9.0	*	214	11.1	159	35	20	9.4	3
Jul-Sep 2006	79	21.3	66	7	6	7.1	*	208	10.9	153	33	22	10.5	3
Aug-Oct 2006	80	21.7	68	7	5	6.3	*	201	10.5	143	36	22	10.9	4
Sep-Nov 2006	79	21.1	64	8	7	8.3	*	195	10.3	144	30	21	10.8	5
Oct-Dec 2006	80	20.9	64	9	6	7.8	*	205	10.7	155	30	20	9.8	6
Nov-Jan 2007	80	21.2	66	10	5	5.9	*	206	10.8	161	26	19	9.2	7
Dec-Feb 2007	85	22.8	70	11	4	4.9	*	209	11.0	159	26	23	11.1	8
Jan-Mar 2007	85	23.4	70	10	4	5.3	*	211	11.1	157	28	26	12.4	8
Feb-Apr 2007	86	23.8	69	13	5	5.8	*	208	10.9	154	29	25	12.3	7
Mar-May 2007	84	23.4	68	11	5	5.5	*	212	11.1	157	30	25	11.9	7
Apr-Jun 2007	87	24.0	70	13	4	4.7	*	207	10.8	152	31	24	11.7	7
May-Jul 2007	93	24.7	72	13	8	8.8	*	205	10.7	149	30	26	12.6	7
Jun-Aug 2007	92	24.9	69	15	8	8.6	*	202	10.5	150	26	26	12.9	8
Jul-Sep 2007	99	26.9	76	14	8	8.3	*	194	10.1	142	26	25	13.1	7
Aug-Oct 2007	89	24.4	68	15	6	7.0	*	197	10.2	143	27	27	13.6	7
Sep-Nov 2007	85	23.4	65	15	5	5.6	*	199	10.3	144	27	28	14.2	5
Oct-Dec 2007	77	21.1	59	14	5	6.2	*	198	10.3	145	26	28	14.3	5
Nov-Jan 2008	74	21.1	60	12	2	3.2	*	199	10.3	149	25	26	13.1	6
Dec-Feb 2008	75	21.1	59	11	4	5.3	*	191	9.9	141	28	22	11.6	4
Jan-Mar 2008	75	21.6	60	11	4	5.3	*	193	10.0	142	27	23	12.2	5
Feb-Apr 2008	81	21.8	61	15	4	5.3	*	201	10.4	145	25	31	15.3	6
Mar-May 2008	82	22.3	60	18	4	4.7	*	196	10.1	140	23	32	16.4	8
Apr-Jun 2008	87	24.0	68	16	3	3.1	*	197	10.2	143	25	29	14.6	7
May-Jul 2008	85	23.9	66	15	5	5.4	*	198	10.2	142	27	29	14.6	9
Jun-Aug 2008	89	25.1	71	13	5	5.6	*	202	10.5	142	30	31	15.3	10
Jul-Sep 2008	85	24.6	62	17	6	7.1	*	215	11.1	156	29	30	13.8	10
Aug-Oct 2008	88	25.6	66	15	7	7.6	*	222	11.5	165	32	25	11.1	10
Sep-Nov 2008	88	25.6	66	13	8	9.0	*	231	11.8	170	34	26	11.3	11
Oct-Dec 2008	89	26.7	69	13	8	8.5	*	232	11.9	169	36	27	11.6	11
Nov-Jan 2009	93	26.8	69	17	7	7.2	*	231	11.9	167	38	26	11.1	10
Dec-Feb 2009	85	25.3	62	17	5	6.3	*	235	12.2	167	35	32	13.6	11
Jan-Mar 2009	89	26.7	65	18	7	8.2	*	259	13.4	180	42	36	14.1	12
Feb-Apr 2009	87	27.1	65	14	9	10.1	*	269	13.9	178	45	45	16.9	13
Mar-May 2009	90	27.9	69	14	7	8.0	*	279	14.5	185	47	47	16.9	12
Apr-Jun 2009	89	27.5	67	15	7	7.6	*	270	14.1	172	49	49	18.0	13
May-Jul 2009	98	30.7	76	17	5	5.6	*	261	13.8	168	48	46	17.5	12
Jun-Aug 2009	92	29.2	65	18	8	9.2	*	265	13.9	175	46	44	16.5	12
Jul-Sep 2009	95	29.6	67	15	12	12.9	*	273	14.3	178	46	49	18.0	14
Aug-Oct 2009	90	28.3	62	16	13	14.2	*	277	14.7	186	42	49	17.8	15
Sep-Nov 2009	90	27.2	59	16	15	16.8	*	273	14.4	180	48	45	16.4	12
Oct-Dec 2009	88	27.7	60	14	14	15.9	*	275	14.4	186	49	40	14.7	13
Nov-Jan 2010	89	28.4	61	15	13	15.0	*	275	14.5	181	55	39	14.3	10
Dec-Feb 2010	89	28.8	61	14	14	15.9	*	284	14.9	182	57	46	16.0	13
Jan-Mar 2010	89	28.7	61	15	12	13.8	*	285	14.9	176	58	50	17.7	14
Feb-Apr 2010	94	30.4	65	16	13	13.4	*	281	14.7	174	55	52	18.5	16
Mar-May 2010	96	31.1	67	19	10	10.5	*	284	14.9	177	56	50	17.8	15
Apr-Jun 2010	91	30.2	64	19	9	9.4	*	293	15.3	191	52	49	16.8	16
May-Jul 2010	87	29.3	61	17	9	9.9	*	300	15.6	198	49	54	17.8	17
Jun-Aug 2010	85	29.0	59	16	9	11.2	*	302	15.6	188	54	60	19.9	17
Jul-Sep 2010	88	30.3	61	16	12	13.2	*	297	15.5	183	53	60	20.3	17
Aug-Oct 2010	103	33.5	71	18	14	13.7	*	302	15.9	179	58	65	21.5	20
Sep-Nov 2010	97	33.6	70	16	10	10.9	*	300	16.1	181	54	65	21.7	25
Oct-Dec 2010	99	34.2	73	16	11	11.2	*	305	16.1	179	59	67	21.9	29
Nov-Jan 2011	97	33.6	71	16	10	10.3	*	318	16.6	194	56	68	21.4	27
Dec-Feb 2011	102	33.7	72	18	12	11.9	*	307	16.1	187	52	68	22.2	28
Jan-Mar 2011	102	34.2	72	19	11	11.1	*	292	15.4	179	48	65	22.2	27
Feb-Apr 2011	97	32.5	68	19	10	10.0	*	270	14.4	170	43	57	21.1	23
Mar-May 2011	97	33.4	70	18	9	9.7	*	282	14.9	179	46	58	20.5	22
Apr-Jun 2011	96	33.1	73	16	8	8.1	*	301	15.8	182	50	68	22.7	29
May-Jul 2011	97	33.3	71	17	9	9.5	*	317	16.6	192	50	75	23.7	26
Jun-Aug 2011	96	33.5	67	19	10	10.4	*	312	16.4	182	57	73	23.5	26
Jul-Sep 2011	97	34.3	63	20	14	14.1	*	312	16.4	176	61	75	24.0	22
Aug-Oct 2011	97	34.8	64	20	12	12.6	*	312	16.2	177	61	74	23.7	24
Sep-Nov 2011	102	35.1	68	22	12	12.0	*	317	16.4	185	62	71	22.2	25
Oct-Dec 2011	102	35.4	66	23	12	12.2	*	308	16.1	182	60	65	21.2	23

4.7: Unemployment by sex, age and duration

United Kingdom (thousands) seasonally adjusted

	16-17							18-24					
	All	Rate (%)[+]	Up to 6 months	Over 6 and up to 12 months	All over 12 months	% over 12 months	All over 24 months	All	Rate (%)[+]	Up to 6 months	Over 6 and up to 12 months	All over 12 months	% over 12 months	All over 24 months
	15	16	17	18	19	20	21	22	23	24	25	26	27	28
Nov-Jan 2012	100	35.0	64	23	14	14.0	*	305	16.0	177	61	67	22.0	25
Dec-Feb 2012	101	35.6	64	24	13	13.0	*	302	15.8	170	60	72	24.0	24
Jan-Mar 2012	99	35.4	63	22	14	14.3	*	306	16.0	173	60	73	23.9	25
Feb-Apr 2012	100	35.3	66	21	14	13.5	*	305	16.0	172	66	67	22.1	23
Mar-May 2012	97	34.4	61	22	14	14.7	*	308	16.1	171	66	71	23.2	31
Apr-Jun 2012	100	34.7	62	23	14	14.0	*	304	15.9	167	64	73	24.0	27
May-Jul 2012	103	35.9	64	22	17	16.9	*	310	16.1	171	58	81	26.1	29
Jun-Aug 2012	98	33.8	63	18	16	16.7	*	295	15.4	165	50	79	26.8	33
Jul-Sep 2012	96	32.5	62	14	20	20.5	*	301	15.8	174	53	74	24.7	33
Aug-Oct 2012	97	33.6	63	16	18	18.3	*	289	15.2	167	49	73	25.2	32
Sep-Nov 2012	92	32.2	60	16	16	17.8	*	302	15.6	186	47	68	22.7	24
Oct-Dec 2012	**89**	**32.2**	**61**	**17**	**12**	**13.0**	*	**315**	**16.1**	**188**	**51**	**76**	**24.1**	**30**
Change on qtr	-7	-0.2	-2	2	-8	-7.5	*	15	0.3	14	-1	2	-0.5	-2
Change %	-7.5		-2.5	17.1	-41.3		*	4.9		8.1	-2.7	2.6		-7.5
Change on year	-13	-3.1	-5	-6	-1	0.8	*	8	0.0	5	-9	11	3.0	7
Change %	-12.5		-8.1	-27.9	-6.8		*	2.4		3.0	-14.8	16.8		29.3

	25-49							50 and over					
	All	Rate (%)[+]	Up to 6 months	Over 6 and up to 12 months	All over 12 months	% over 12 months	All over 24 months	All	Rate (%)[+]	Up to 6 months	Over 6 and up to 12 months	All over 12 months	% over 12 months	All over 24 months
	29	30	31	32	33	34	35	36	37	38	39	40	41	42
All Persons	MGVI	MGXB	YBYH	YBYK	YBYN	YBYQ	YBYT	YBVT	YBVW	YBYW	YBYZ	YBZC	YBZF	YBZI
Nov-Jan 2004	672	3.8	397	108	168	24.9	83	212	2.9	104	35	73	34.5	46
Dec-Feb 2004	658	3.7	397	95	165	25.1	79	214	2.9	103	34	77	35.9	46
Jan-Mar 2004	646	3.7	381	103	163	25.2	74	215	2.9	105	33	77	35.7	45
Feb-Apr 2004	642	3.6	380	104	158	24.7	76	218	2.9	110	34	74	34.0	45
Mar-May 2004	652	3.7	387	105	160	24.6	76	217	2.9	111	35	72	33.0	43
Apr-Jun 2004	650	3.7	393	99	158	24.3	74	212	2.8	110	35	67	31.5	40
May-Jul 2004	633	3.6	381	93	159	25.1	70	213	2.8	111	35	67	31.6	39
Jun-Aug 2004	624	3.5	381	98	146	23.4	66	199	2.7	107	29	62	31.2	38
Jul-Sep 2004	608	3.4	370	94	145	23.8	67	203	2.7	106	31	66	32.4	39
Aug-Oct 2004	616	3.5	376	97	142	23.1	67	200	2.7	103	29	68	33.9	42
Sep-Nov 2004	614	3.5	367	97	149	24.3	70	207	2.7	101	35	70	34.1	44
Oct-Dec 2004	617	3.5	373	99	145	23.5	69	210	2.8	105	34	71	33.7	45
Nov-Jan 2005	617	3.5	372	100	145	23.4	71	210	2.8	105	33	72	34.2	45
Dec-Feb 2005	624	3.5	366	106	152	24.4	75	214	2.8	103	31	80	37.3	46
Jan-Mar 2005	617	3.5	365	106	146	23.7	71	212	2.8	100	31	81	38.0	47
Feb-Apr 2005	623	3.5	372	103	149	23.9	67	209	2.7	97	32	80	38.4	44
Mar-May 2005	630	3.5	377	100	153	24.2	72	201	2.6	92	30	79	39.2	43
Apr-Jun 2005	620	3.5	366	101	153	24.7	67	207	2.7	95	31	80	38.7	48
May-Jul 2005	616	3.5	362	101	152	24.8	67	210	2.8	98	32	80	37.9	47
Jun-Aug 2005	605	3.4	364	103	138	22.9	60	215	2.8	99	33	82	38.2	48
Jul-Sep 2005	613	3.4	373	104	136	22.2	60	216	2.8	103	35	79	36.4	46
Aug-Oct 2005	629	3.5	383	108	138	21.9	64	221	2.9	105	36	79	35.8	51
Sep-Nov 2005	664	3.7	409	107	148	22.2	68	228	3.0	106	38	84	36.8	56
Oct-Dec 2005	679	3.8	414	106	159	23.4	71	227	2.9	105	37	86	37.7	57
Nov-Jan 2006	679	3.8	413	105	160	23.6	72	225	2.9	105	37	84	37.2	55
Dec-Feb 2006	708	4.0	417	121	170	24.0	77	221	2.8	102	36	82	37.3	53
Jan-Mar 2006	722	4.0	425	129	167	23.2	75	226	2.9	102	37	87	38.5	56
Feb-Apr 2006	732	4.1	421	136	174	23.8	79	232	3.0	111	34	87	37.3	53
Mar-May 2006	743	4.1	420	139	184	24.7	88	237	3.0	121	37	79	33.4	48
Apr-Jun 2006	755	4.2	422	140	193	25.6	91	236	3.0	120	41	74	31.4	44
May-Jul 2006	755	4.2	424	141	190	25.2	90	238	3.0	117	44	78	32.7	48
Jun-Aug 2006	754	4.2	427	142	185	24.5	84	245	3.1	122	42	82	33.3	50
Jul-Sep 2006	744	4.1	418	129	198	26.6	92	248	3.1	119	41	88	35.7	55
Aug-Oct 2006	758	4.2	424	132	202	26.7	91	242	3.1	117	37	88	36.4	57
Sep-Nov 2006	767	4.3	426	135	206	26.9	93	233	3.0	102	37	94	40.3	61
Oct-Dec 2006	773	4.3	412	144	217	28.1	102	233	3.0	110	34	89	38.3	57
Nov-Jan 2007	765	4.3	406	141	219	28.6	101	238	3.0	116	35	88	37.0	54
Dec-Feb 2007	756	4.2	409	131	216	28.6	100	241	3.0	123	39	78	32.4	46
Jan-Mar 2007	745	4.1	410	128	208	27.9	100	245	3.1	121	44	80	32.7	46
Feb-Apr 2007	724	4.0	393	122	209	28.8	99	253	3.2	128	41	84	33.3	47
Mar-May 2007	699	3.9	383	115	200	28.6	101	247	3.1	114	40	92	37.4	48
Apr-Jun 2007	690	3.8	388	106	196	28.4	95	249	3.1	117	42	91	36.4	48
May-Jul 2007	685	3.8	383	108	193	28.2	96	247	3.1	113	43	91	36.8	48
Jun-Aug 2007	690	3.8	382	118	190	27.6	89	242	3.0	115	39	88	36.2	48
Jul-Sep 2007	696	3.9	387	123	186	26.7	89	244	3.0	115	36	92	37.9	51
Aug-Oct 2007	695	3.9	394	115	186	26.7	91	239	3.0	115	35	89	37.3	49
Sep-Nov 2007	702	3.9	396	115	191	27.2	91	240	3.0	116	35	90	37.4	52
Oct-Dec 2007	692	3.8	392	113	187	27.1	90	233	2.9	113	38	82	35.3	43
Nov-Jan 2008	705	3.9	394	123	188	26.6	96	230	2.9	112	37	82	35.6	43
Dec-Feb 2008	706	3.9	384	126	196	27.8	102	235	2.9	108	40	87	37.0	48
Jan-Mar 2008	702	3.9	378	125	199	28.3	101	231	2.8	106	37	88	38.2	52
Feb-Apr 2008	720	4.0	396	124	200	27.8	101	242	3.0	112	41	89	36.8	52
Mar-May 2008	701	3.9	381	121	200	28.5	99	227	2.8	105	37	84	37.0	50
Apr-Jun 2008	723	4.0	388	127	208	28.8	102	238	2.9	110	38	90	37.7	52
May-Jul 2008	747	4.1	402	126	219	29.4	108	245	3.0	109	39	97	39.5	57
Jun-Aug 2008	782	4.3	439	121	222	28.4	109	260	3.2	118	46	95	36.7	56
Jul-Sep 2008	801	4.4	450	124	227	28.3	111	270	3.3	129	49	92	34.2	53
Aug-Oct 2008	813	4.5	454	125	234	28.8	111	280	3.4	143	44	93	33.2	54

4.7: Unemployment by sex, age and duration

United Kingdom (thousands) seasonally adjusted

	25-49							50 and over						
	All	Rate (%)+	Up to 6 months	Over 6 and up to 12 months	All over 12 months	% over 12 months	All over 24 months	All	Rate (%)+	Up to 6 months	Over 6 and up to 12 months	All over 12 months	% over 12 months	All over 24 months
	29	30	31	32	33	34	35	36	37	38	39	40	41	42
Sep-Nov 2008	843	4.7	480	139	224	26.6	109	295	3.6	155	44	96	32.5	53
Oct-Dec 2008	880	4.8	510	140	230	26.2	113	310	3.8	161	47	102	32.9	60
Nov-Jan 2009	919	5.0	536	144	239	26.0	114	314	3.8	164	51	99	31.5	56
Dec-Feb 2009	967	5.3	567	149	252	26.0	118	335	4.1	170	59	105	31.5	64
Jan-Mar 2009	1,005	5.5	581	164	260	25.8	122	346	4.2	177	61	108	31.1	62
Feb-Apr 2009	1,034	5.7	604	179	251	24.3	117	362	4.3	186	61	116	31.9	64
Mar-May 2009	1,089	6.0	625	197	267	24.5	126	357	4.3	182	66	109	30.5	58
Apr-Jun 2009	1,140	6.3	647	220	273	24.0	127	371	4.4	188	71	112	30.1	58
May-Jul 2009	1,151	6.3	634	226	291	25.3	133	373	4.5	189	73	111	29.8	55
Jun-Aug 2009	1,157	6.4	613	233	310	26.8	137	378	4.5	182	79	117	30.9	57
Jul-Sep 2009	1,147	6.3	586	249	312	27.2	124	374	4.5	166	89	119	31.9	56
Aug-Oct 2009	1,149	6.3	570	267	312	27.1	126	383	4.6	161	103	119	31.2	59
Sep-Nov 2009	1,143	6.3	548	270	325	28.4	121	388	4.6	163	101	124	32.0	61
Oct-Dec 2009	1,140	6.2	536	262	342	30.0	129	391	4.6	168	92	130	33.3	65
Nov-Jan 2010	1,129	6.2	511	267	351	31.1	130	390	4.6	158	96	136	35.0	66
Dec-Feb 2010	1,175	6.5	522	269	384	32.7	150	388	4.6	158	91	139	35.9	63
Jan-Mar 2010	1,183	6.5	532	248	403	34.0	153	386	4.6	150	90	145	37.7	64
Feb-Apr 2010	1,176	6.5	524	244	408	34.7	154	374	4.4	141	78	155	41.4	66
Mar-May 2010	1,160	6.4	510	241	409	35.3	155	388	4.6	144	75	169	43.4	74
Apr-Jun 2010	1,149	6.3	483	247	419	36.4	167	393	4.6	147	76	170	43.2	71
May-Jul 2010	1,154	6.3	495	245	414	35.9	170	398	4.6	152	75	171	42.9	76
Jun-Aug 2010	1,142	6.2	484	236	422	37.0	177	392	4.6	154	73	165	42.2	82
Jul-Sep 2010	1,149	6.3	501	223	426	37.1	183	393	4.6	153	69	171	43.6	78
Aug-Oct 2010	1,151	6.3	496	220	435	37.8	187	393	4.6	152	69	172	43.7	76
Sep-Nov 2010	1,151	6.3	509	204	438	38.1	185	385	4.5	151	68	166	43.1	75
Oct-Dec 2010	1,139	6.2	503	201	435	38.2	184	382	4.5	148	74	161	42.0	77
Nov-Jan 2011	1,151	6.3	505	199	448	38.9	196	387	4.5	146	73	168	43.5	78
Dec-Feb 2011	1,130	6.2	491	195	445	39.3	210	385	4.4	141	70	174	45.3	82
Jan-Mar 2011	1,130	6.2	484	201	446	39.4	210	394	4.6	150	65	180	45.6	91
Feb-Apr 2011	1,137	6.2	491	203	443	39.0	204	394	4.6	154	65	174	44.3	95
Mar-May 2011	1,152	6.3	514	203	435	37.7	205	393	4.5	159	66	168	42.8	97
Apr-Jun 2011	1,168	6.3	522	200	447	38.2	209	388	4.5	163	64	161	41.5	98
May-Jul 2011	1,165	6.3	518	202	446	38.3	218	386	4.5	158	67	160	41.6	101
Jun-Aug 2011	1,193	6.5	532	209	452	37.9	222	386	4.5	156	72	158	40.8	99
Jul-Sep 2011	1,197	6.5	539	218	440	36.8	227	412	4.8	165	77	170	41.2	105
Aug-Oct 2011	1,200	6.5	544	219	437	36.4	230	412	4.8	168	72	172	41.7	99
Sep-Nov 2011	1,204	6.5	548	227	429	35.7	222	433	5.0	173	77	183	42.3	105
Oct-Dec 2011	1,200	6.5	551	224	425	35.4	215	424	4.9	164	73	188	44.3	111
Nov-Jan 2012	1,188	6.4	545	227	416	35.0	204	426	4.9	169	73	184	43.2	111
Dec-Feb 2012	1,181	6.4	525	226	430	36.4	208	429	4.9	176	63	189	44.2	118
Jan-Mar 2012	1,175	6.4	511	234	430	36.6	209	419	4.8	162	69	188	44.9	117
Feb-Apr 2012	1,167	6.3	497	231	440	37.7	214	421	4.8	160	73	189	44.9	121
Mar-May 2012	1,152	6.2	489	222	441	38.3	222	407	4.6	162	71	174	42.6	108
Apr-Jun 2012	1,149	6.2	490	221	438	38.2	218	403	4.6	159	66	178	44.2	103
May-Jul 2012	1,162	6.3	506	220	436	37.5	222	413	4.7	147	75	192	46.4	113
Jun-Aug 2012	1,162	6.3	514	217	430	37.0	222	410	4.6	143	70	196	47.9	115
Jul-Sep 2012	1,155	6.2	515	204	436	37.7	222	397	4.5	134	70	192	48.4	115
Aug-Oct 2012	1,165	6.3	514	207	444	38.1	234	400	4.5	140	65	194	48.7	112
Sep-Nov 2012	1,138	6.1	507	191	439	38.6	232	396	4.4	142	66	188	47.5	108
Oct-Dec 2012	**1,139**	**6.1**	**510**	**203**	**426**	**37.4**	**234**	**389**	**4.3**	**147**	**65**	**177**	**45.6**	**104**
Change on qtr	*-15*	*-0.1*	*-5*	*-1*	*-9*	*-0.3*	*11*	*-8*	*-0.1*	*12*	*-5*	*-15*	*-2.8*	*-12*
Change %	*-1.3*		*-1.0*	*-0.5*	*-2.1*		*5.2*	*-2.0*		*9.3*	*-7.7*	*-7.7*		*-10.2*
Change on year	*-61*	*-0.4*	*-41*	*-21*	*2*	*2.0*	*19*	*-35*	*-0.5*	*-17*	*-8*	*-11*	*1.2*	*-8*
Change %	*-5.0*		*-7.4*	*-9.5*	*0.4*		*8.8*	*-8.4*		*-10.4*	*-10.4*	*-5.9*		*-6.9*
Male	MGVJ	MGXC	YBYI	YBYL	YBYO	YBYR	YBYU	YBVU	YBVX	YBYX	YBZA	YBZD	YBZG	YBZJ
Nov-Jan 2004	395	4.1	210	68	117	29.6	62	140	3.4	62	22	56	39.8	39
Dec-Feb 2004	381	4.0	209	60	112	29.4	56	140	3.4	63	21	56	40.3	36
Jan-Mar 2004	366	3.8	198	63	105	28.6	49	142	3.4	65	21	56	39.6	35
Feb-Apr 2004	361	3.8	194	63	103	28.7	51	150	3.6	73	23	54	36.2	34
Mar-May 2004	363	3.8	197	62	104	28.6	52	148	3.5	72	23	53	35.8	34
Apr-Jun 2004	368	3.9	200	60	108	29.3	55	146	3.5	71	24	51	35.1	32
May-Jul 2004	358	3.8	191	59	107	30.0	51	141	3.3	68	21	52	37.0	32
Jun-Aug 2004	353	3.7	195	59	99	28.0	48	134	3.2	66	20	48	35.9	30
Jul-Sep 2004	338	3.6	187	55	95	28.2	50	137	3.3	67	20	50	36.2	30
Aug-Oct 2004	337	3.5	187	58	92	27.4	48	137	3.3	67	20	50	36.5	31
Sep-Nov 2004	344	3.6	183	61	101	29.3	53	141	3.3	67	22	52	36.7	33
Oct-Dec 2004	347	3.6	184	66	96	27.8	52	141	3.3	66	22	53	37.7	35
Nov-Jan 2005	349	3.7	184	69	96	27.5	52	138	3.3	66	21	51	37.2	33
Dec-Feb 2005	344	3.6	174	70	100	29.0	51	143	3.4	66	22	55	38.3	33
Jan-Mar 2005	343	3.6	175	69	98	28.6	49	144	3.4	66	24	54	37.7	33
Feb-Apr 2005	347	3.6	181	67	100	28.7	47	140	3.3	59	26	55	39.2	32
Mar-May 2005	348	3.7	186	61	101	28.9	50	134	3.1	55	24	54	40.5	32
Apr-Jun 2005	341	3.6	181	58	102	29.8	46	132	3.1	53	24	56	42.3	35
May-Jul 2005	342	3.6	182	57	103	30.1	48	137	3.2	57	23	57	41.2	35
Jun-Aug 2005	341	3.6	188	58	95	27.9	43	143	3.3	59	24	59	41.6	36
Jul-Sep 2005	337	3.5	189	59	89	26.5	41	140	3.3	58	25	57	40.9	35
Aug-Oct 2005	347	3.6	199	57	92	26.4	44	142	3.3	60	22	60	42.2	40
Sep-Nov 2005	367	3.8	214	56	97	26.4	46	148	3.4	60	24	64	43.3	46
Oct-Dec 2005	380	4.0	217	54	109	28.8	50	150	3.4	61	22	67	44.6	45
Nov-Jan 2006	372	3.9	206	58	108	28.9	49	147	3.4	58	26	63	43.0	41
Dec-Feb 2006	382	4.0	205	67	111	29.0	51	142	3.3	57	23	62	43.8	38
Jan-Mar 2006	397	4.1	217	72	108	27.1	49	141	3.3	52	23	65	46.3	43
Feb-Apr 2006	401	4.1	213	73	114	28.5	51	139	3.2	53	21	65	47.1	43

4.7: Unemployment by sex, age and duration

United Kingdom (thousands) seasonally adjusted

	25-49							50 and over					
	All	Rate (%)+	Up to 6 months	Over 6 and up to 12 months	All over 12 months	% over 12 months	All over 24 months	All	Rate (%)+	Up to 6 months	Over 6 and up to 12 months	All over 12 months	% over 12 months	All over 24 months
	29	30	31	32	33	34	35	36	37	38	39	40	41	42
Mar-May 2006	414	4.3	209	75	129	31.1	60	145	3.3	62	24	59	40.7	39
Apr-Jun 2006	415	4.3	207	76	132	31.8	62	145	3.3	64	26	55	38.1	35
May-Jul 2006	417	4.3	211	77	128	30.8	61	148	3.4	67	27	54	36.5	34
Jun-Aug 2006	414	4.3	217	79	118	28.5	54	155	3.5	71	26	57	37.2	35
Jul-Sep 2006	406	4.2	210	67	128	31.5	61	160	3.7	70	27	63	39.4	40
Aug-Oct 2006	412	4.2	210	71	131	31.7	62	159	3.6	68	25	66	41.6	43
Sep-Nov 2006	411	4.2	210	72	129	31.5	59	147	3.3	54	24	68	46.6	46
Oct-Dec 2006	419	4.3	201	79	139	33.2	67	147	3.3	59	22	65	44.6	42
Nov-Jan 2007	411	4.2	194	76	140	34.1	66	149	3.4	61	22	66	44.2	40
Dec-Feb 2007	412	4.3	196	70	146	35.4	70	151	3.4	69	24	58	38.1	35
Jan-Mar 2007	403	4.2	193	69	140	34.9	67	158	3.6	71	28	59	37.4	36
Feb-Apr 2007	391	4.0	186	65	140	35.8	67	164	3.7	77	26	61	37.2	36
Mar-May 2007	376	3.9	179	66	131	34.8	70	158	3.6	68	23	67	42.5	36
Apr-Jun 2007	362	3.7	179	58	125	34.6	64	161	3.6	71	24	67	41.2	36
May-Jul 2007	368	3.8	183	58	127	34.4	64	159	3.6	67	27	65	41.0	36
Jun-Aug 2007	366	3.8	180	60	126	34.3	60	154	3.5	68	25	61	39.7	34
Jul-Sep 2007	367	3.8	184	63	120	32.8	61	157	3.5	66	26	65	41.2	36
Aug-Oct 2007	361	3.7	181	61	120	33.1	65	152	3.4	62	25	64	42.5	36
Sep-Nov 2007	366	3.8	183	61	122	33.3	62	156	3.5	63	26	67	42.9	39
Oct-Dec 2007	360	3.7	183	59	118	32.9	58	149	3.3	60	28	61	40.8	32
Nov-Jan 2008	372	3.8	194	61	118	31.6	63	152	3.4	64	27	62	40.5	32
Dec-Feb 2008	372	3.8	182	66	124	33.3	67	153	3.4	61	29	63	41.1	37
Jan-Mar 2008	372	3.8	180	65	127	34.1	66	148	3.3	61	24	63	42.4	40
Feb-Apr 2008	380	3.9	184	67	129	33.8	66	151	3.3	60	27	64	42.3	41
Mar-May 2008	379	3.9	187	64	128	33.8	67	151	3.3	61	26	64	42.6	39
Apr-Jun 2008	395	4.1	194	67	134	33.8	71	157	3.4	61	25	71	45.4	42
May-Jul 2008	404	4.1	193	70	141	34.9	73	164	3.6	61	24	79	48.1	48
Jun-Aug 2008	430	4.4	214	67	149	34.7	75	170	3.7	65	30	75	44.1	45
Jul-Sep 2008	441	4.5	224	67	150	34.1	76	175	3.8	74	31	70	40.1	41
Aug-Oct 2008	454	4.7	241	64	150	33.0	76	185	4.0	87	27	71	38.4	41
Sep-Nov 2008	475	4.9	257	75	143	30.1	76	197	4.3	102	25	71	35.7	38
Oct-Dec 2008	498	5.1	276	73	149	30.0	80	212	4.6	107	30	74	35.1	44
Nov-Jan 2009	524	5.3	294	75	156	29.7	79	211	4.6	106	35	70	33.3	40
Dec-Feb 2009	548	5.6	312	74	162	29.6	80	227	4.9	110	41	76	33.6	47
Jan-Mar 2009	576	5.9	327	87	162	28.2	81	240	5.2	116	44	80	33.3	45
Feb-Apr 2009	601	6.1	345	99	157	26.1	77	252	5.4	124	44	85	33.6	48
Mar-May 2009	638	6.5	366	111	162	25.4	83	255	5.5	124	49	82	32.0	44
Apr-Jun 2009	665	6.8	373	130	162	24.3	80	263	5.7	127	51	84	32.0	45
May-Jul 2009	678	6.9	369	135	175	25.8	85	264	5.7	125	55	83	31.6	43
Jun-Aug 2009	684	7.0	349	149	186	27.2	89	272	5.8	125	56	91	33.5	46
Jul-Sep 2009	686	7.0	332	159	195	28.4	82	268	5.8	111	66	90	33.7	43
Aug-Oct 2009	682	7.0	315	171	196	28.7	84	276	5.9	110	75	91	32.9	45
Sep-Nov 2009	677	6.9	307	170	200	29.6	77	275	5.9	108	75	91	33.1	45
Oct-Dec 2009	670	6.9	298	161	211	31.5	84	272	5.9	112	66	94	34.7	46
Nov-Jan 2010	678	6.9	291	169	218	32.2	85	276	5.9	106	69	100	36.3	47
Dec-Feb 2010	699	7.2	284	165	250	35.7	100	272	5.8	104	65	103	37.7	47
Jan-Mar 2010	702	7.2	286	156	261	37.2	102	271	5.8	101	63	107	39.6	49
Feb-Apr 2010	691	7.1	275	149	266	38.5	105	263	5.6	94	56	114	43.2	51
Mar-May 2010	670	6.9	262	142	267	39.8	106	268	5.7	97	53	118	44.0	53
Apr-Jun 2010	663	6.8	248	139	276	41.6	114	269	5.7	95	54	120	44.6	51
May-Jul 2010	655	6.7	247	132	275	42.0	116	271	5.7	99	52	121	44.5	55
Jun-Aug 2010	646	6.6	237	132	277	42.9	119	261	5.5	95	46	120	45.9	60
Jul-Sep 2010	644	6.6	246	120	277	43.1	128	267	5.6	96	43	127	47.8	58
Aug-Oct 2010	650	6.6	250	116	284	43.6	134	266	5.7	94	46	126	47.3	55
Sep-Nov 2010	653	6.6	258	108	287	43.9	130	265	5.6	95	46	125	47.1	57
Oct-Dec 2010	641	6.5	250	106	285	44.5	130	259	5.5	91	49	118	45.6	58
Nov-Jan 2011	653	6.6	252	108	293	44.9	138	264	5.6	92	48	124	46.8	58
Dec-Feb 2011	634	6.4	240	101	294	46.4	153	262	5.5	88	47	127	48.4	60
Jan-Mar 2011	625	6.3	231	103	291	46.5	151	266	5.6	93	43	130	48.9	66
Feb-Apr 2011	619	6.3	233	102	283	45.8	147	263	5.5	93	44	126	47.7	70
Mar-May 2011	627	6.3	246	106	276	44.0	147	264	5.5	94	44	126	47.7	74
Apr-Jun 2011	640	6.5	253	101	285	44.6	149	259	5.4	99	42	118	45.5	73
May-Jul 2011	644	6.5	260	104	280	43.5	152	256	5.4	97	44	115	44.8	75
Jun-Aug 2011	658	6.6	272	107	279	42.5	155	255	5.4	97	48	110	43.3	71
Jul-Sep 2011	652	6.6	273	109	270	41.5	157	272	5.8	98	52	122	44.7	75
Aug-Oct 2011	647	6.5	271	111	265	40.9	159	269	5.7	100	47	122	45.4	71
Sep-Nov 2011	647	6.5	268	116	263	40.6	150	280	5.9	100	49	131	46.7	75
Oct-Dec 2011	644	6.5	275	115	253	39.4	139	270	5.7	93	44	133	49.2	78
Nov-Jan 2012	627	6.3	266	116	245	39.1	129	270	5.7	100	43	127	47.0	76
Dec-Feb 2012	617	6.2	254	116	247	40.1	128	267	5.6	97	38	131	49.2	85
Jan-Mar 2012	616	6.2	249	121	247	40.0	132	267	5.6	94	44	130	48.6	85
Feb-Apr 2012	613	6.2	240	117	255	41.6	136	264	5.5	88	47	129	48.8	89
Mar-May 2012	607	6.1	241	107	259	42.6	144	253	5.3	94	45	114	44.9	75
Apr-Jun 2012	604	6.1	236	111	258	42.6	141	252	5.2	89	42	122	48.3	73
May-Jul 2012	625	6.2	252	110	263	42.0	146	263	5.4	83	50	130	49.6	81
Jun-Aug 2012	611	6.1	255	106	249	40.8	145	269	5.6	87	48	134	49.9	85
Jul-Sep 2012	599	6.0	250	104	245	41.0	143	261	5.4	79	51	131	50.3	87
Aug-Oct 2012	604	6.0	246	109	249	41.2	154	266	5.5	84	46	136	50.9	86
Sep-Nov 2012	579	5.8	240	95	244	42.2	154	264	5.4	84	46	134	50.9	81
Oct-Dec 2012	582	5.8	244	94	244	41.9	159	259	5.3	89	46	124	48.0	73
Change on qtr	-17	-0.2	-6	-10	-1	1.0	15	-2	-0.1	10	-5	-7	-2.3	-13
Change %	-2.8		-2.4	-9.2	-0.6		10.8	-0.6		13.2	-10.2	-5.2		-15.5
Change on year	-62	-0.7	-31	-21	-9	2.6	20	-11	-0.4	-4	1	-8	-1.1	-5
Change %	-9.6		-11.4	-18.2	-3.7		14.1	-4.1		-4.3	3.1	-6.4		-6.6

4.7: Unemployment by sex, age and duration

United Kingdom (thousands) seasonally adjusted

	25-49							50 and over						
	All	Rate (%)[+]	Up to 6 months	Over 6 and up to 12 months	All over 12 months	% over 12 months	All over 24 months	All	Rate (%)[+]	Up to 6 months	Over 6 and up to 12 months	All over 12 months	% over 12 months	All over 24 months
	29	30	31	32	33	34	35	36	37	38	39	40	41	42
Female	MGVK	MGXD	YBYJ	YBYM	YBYP	YBYS	YBYV	YBVV	YBVY	YBYY	YBZB	YBZE	YBZH	YBZK
Nov-Jan 2004	277	3.4	187	40	51	18.4	20	72	2.2	42	13	17	24.3	7
Dec-Feb 2004	277	3.4	189	35	53	19.1	23	73	2.2	40	13	20	27.7	9
Jan-Mar 2004	281	3.5	183	40	58	20.6	25	72	2.2	40	12	20	28.1	10
Feb-Apr 2004	282	3.5	185	41	55	19.5	25	68	2.1	37	11	20	29.2	11
Mar-May 2004	289	3.6	190	43	57	19.5	23	69	2.1	39	12	19	27.0	9
Apr-Jun 2004	282	3.5	192	39	50	17.9	19	66	2.0	39	11	15	23.4	9
May-Jul 2004	275	3.4	189	34	52	18.8	18	72	2.2	44	13	15	21.1	7
Jun-Aug 2004	271	3.3	186	38	47	17.3	18	64	2.0	41	9	14	21.4	8
Jul-Sep 2004	271	3.3	183	38	50	18.4	17	66	2.0	39	10	16	24.4	10
Aug-Oct 2004	279	3.4	189	40	50	18.0	18	63	1.9	36	9	18	28.3	11
Sep-Nov 2004	270	3.3	185	36	48	18.0	16	65	2.0	34	13	19	28.6	10
Oct-Dec 2004	270	3.3	189	32	49	18.0	17	69	2.1	39	12	18	25.5	10
Nov-Jan 2005	268	3.3	188	31	48	18.1	18	72	2.2	40	12	20	28.6	12
Dec-Feb 2005	280	3.4	192	35	52	18.7	24	71	2.1	37	9	25	35.2	13
Jan-Mar 2005	274	3.3	190	36	48	17.7	22	68	2.0	34	8	26	38.6	14
Feb-Apr 2005	276	3.4	191	36	49	17.9	21	69	2.1	37	6	25	36.6	12
Mar-May 2005	282	3.4	191	39	52	18.4	21	67	2.0	37	6	25	36.6	11
Apr-Jun 2005	279	3.4	184	43	52	18.6	21	74	2.2	42	8	24	32.4	12
May-Jul 2005	274	3.3	180	44	50	18.1	20	73	2.2	41	9	23	31.6	12
Jun-Aug 2005	264	3.2	176	45	43	16.4	16	72	2.1	40	9	23	31.6	12
Jul-Sep 2005	276	3.3	184	45	47	16.9	18	76	2.2	44	10	21	28.2	10
Aug-Oct 2005	281	3.4	184	51	46	16.4	21	79	2.3	46	14	19	24.2	11
Sep-Nov 2005	297	3.6	195	51	51	17.0	23	80	2.4	46	14	20	24.6	11
Oct-Dec 2005	299	3.6	198	52	50	16.6	21	78	2.3	44	14	19	24.4	11
Nov-Jan 2006	306	3.7	207	47	53	17.2	23	78	2.3	47	11	20	26.2	15
Dec-Feb 2006	326	3.9	213	54	59	18.0	26	79	2.3	45	13	20	25.6	14
Jan-Mar 2006	325	3.9	208	57	60	18.4	27	85	2.5	50	13	22	25.5	13
Feb-Apr 2006	331	4.0	208	63	60	18.2	28	93	2.7	59	13	21	22.7	10
Mar-May 2006	329	4.0	211	64	55	16.7	27	91	2.6	59	13	20	21.7	9
Apr-Jun 2006	340	4.1	215	64	61	18.0	29	90	2.6	56	15	19	20.8	10
May-Jul 2006	338	4.1	213	63	62	18.3	29	91	2.6	49	17	24	26.5	14
Jun-Aug 2006	340	4.1	210	63	67	19.7	30	90	2.6	51	15	24	26.7	15
Jul-Sep 2006	339	4.1	207	62	70	20.6	31	88	2.5	49	14	25	28.8	15
Aug-Oct 2006	346	4.2	214	61	71	20.6	29	84	2.4	50	12	22	26.5	14
Sep-Nov 2006	356	4.3	216	63	77	21.6	34	87	2.5	48	13	26	29.8	15
Oct-Dec 2006	354	4.3	211	65	78	22.0	34	87	2.5	51	12	24	27.8	15
Nov-Jan 2007	355	4.3	212	64	79	22.2	36	89	2.5	54	13	22	24.8	13
Dec-Feb 2007	344	4.2	213	61	70	20.5	31	90	2.6	54	15	20	22.8	12
Jan-Mar 2007	342	4.1	216	59	67	19.7	32	87	2.5	50	16	21	24.2	11
Feb-Apr 2007	333	4.0	207	57	69	20.8	31	90	2.6	51	15	23	26.0	11
Mar-May 2007	323	3.9	204	49	69	21.4	30	89	2.5	46	17	25	28.3	12
Apr-Jun 2007	329	4.0	209	48	71	21.7	31	88	2.5	46	18	24	27.6	12
May-Jul 2007	317	3.8	200	50	67	21.1	32	88	2.5	46	16	26	29.3	13
Jun-Aug 2007	324	3.9	201	58	65	19.9	29	87	2.5	47	14	26	30.2	14
Jul-Sep 2007	329	4.0	203	60	66	20.0	28	87	2.5	49	10	28	31.9	15
Aug-Oct 2007	333	4.0	213	54	66	19.9	26	87	2.5	53	10	25	28.2	14
Sep-Nov 2007	336	4.0	213	54	69	20.5	29	84	2.4	52	9	23	27.0	13
Oct-Dec 2007	332	4.0	209	54	69	20.8	31	84	2.4	52	10	22	25.8	11
Nov-Jan 2008	332	4.0	200	62	70	21.1	33	78	2.2	48	10	20	26.1	11
Dec-Feb 2008	334	4.0	201	61	72	21.6	36	82	2.3	47	11	24	29.3	11
Jan-Mar 2008	329	3.9	198	59	72	21.7	35	82	2.3	45	12	25	30.8	12
Feb-Apr 2008	340	4.1	212	57	71	21.0	35	91	2.5	52	14	25	27.7	12
Mar-May 2008	323	3.9	194	57	72	22.2	33	76	2.1	44	12	20	25.9	11
Apr-Jun 2008	327	3.9	194	60	74	22.6	31	80	2.2	50	13	18	22.7	10
May-Jul 2008	343	4.1	209	56	78	22.8	35	81	2.2	48	15	18	21.7	10
Jun-Aug 2008	352	4.2	225	54	73	20.8	35	90	2.5	53	16	20	22.8	11
Jul-Sep 2008	359	4.3	226	57	76	21.3	35	94	2.6	55	18	22	23.4	11
Aug-Oct 2008	359	4.3	213	61	84	23.4	35	95	2.6	56	17	22	23.2	13
Sep-Nov 2008	369	4.4	223	64	81	22.1	33	98	2.7	54	19	25	26.0	15
Oct-Dec 2008	382	4.6	235	67	81	21.2	33	98	2.7	54	17	28	28.2	16
Nov-Jan 2009	395	4.7	242	70	84	21.2	35	103	2.8	58	16	29	27.8	16
Dec-Feb 2009	419	5.0	255	75	89	21.4	38	108	3.0	61	18	29	27.1	17
Jan-Mar 2009	429	5.1	254	78	97	22.6	42	106	2.9	61	18	28	26.1	16
Feb-Apr 2009	433	5.2	259	80	94	21.8	40	110	3.0	62	17	31	28.2	16
Mar-May 2009	451	5.4	259	87	106	23.4	42	102	2.8	58	17	27	26.5	14
Apr-Jun 2009	475	5.6	274	90	111	23.4	47	108	2.9	61	19	27	25.4	13
May-Jul 2009	473	5.6	265	91	116	24.6	48	109	2.9	64	18	28	25.4	12
Jun-Aug 2009	473	5.6	265	84	124	26.2	48	106	2.8	57	23	26	24.2	11
Jul-Sep 2009	462	5.5	254	90	118	25.5	42	106	2.9	55	23	29	27.3	13
Aug-Oct 2009	467	5.5	255	96	116	24.9	41	107	2.9	50	28	29	26.8	14
Sep-Nov 2009	466	5.5	241	100	125	26.7	44	114	3.0	54	26	33	29.4	17
Oct-Dec 2009	469	5.5	238	101	131	27.9	46	118	3.1	56	26	36	30.2	19
Nov-Jan 2010	451	5.3	220	98	133	29.5	46	114	3.0	51	27	36	31.8	19
Dec-Feb 2010	476	5.6	238	104	134	28.2	51	116	3.1	54	25	37	31.8	16
Jan-Mar 2010	481	5.7	247	92	141	29.4	51	115	3.0	50	27	38	33.2	15
Feb-Apr 2010	485	5.8	249	95	141	29.1	49	111	2.9	47	23	41	37.3	16
Mar-May 2010	490	5.8	248	99	143	29.1	49	120	3.2	47	22	51	42.2	21
Apr-Jun 2010	486	5.8	236	107	143	29.4	53	124	3.3	52	22	50	40.0	20
May-Jul 2010	499	5.9	248	112	139	27.9	55	127	3.3	53	24	50	39.5	21
Jun-Aug 2010	496	5.9	247	104	145	29.2	58	131	3.4	59	26	46	34.9	22
Jul-Sep 2010	505	6.0	254	102	148	29.4	56	126	3.3	57	25	44	34.9	20
Aug-Oct 2010	501	5.9	246	104	151	30.1	53	127	3.3	58	23	46	36.3	21
Sep-Nov 2010	498	5.9	251	96	151	30.4	55	120	3.1	57	22	41	34.2	18
Oct-Dec 2010	498	5.9	253	95	150	30.0	54	123	3.2	56	24	43	34.5	19

4.7: Unemployment by sex, age and duration

United Kingdom (thousands) seasonally adjusted

	25-49							50 and over						
	All	Rate (%)[+]	Up to 6 months	Over 6 and up to 12 months	All over 12 months	% over 12 months	All over 24 months	All	Rate (%)[+]	Up to 6 months	Over 6 and up to 12 months	All over 12 months	% over 12 months	All over 24 months
	29	30	31	32	33	34	35	36	37	38	39	40	41	42
Nov-Jan 2011	499	5.9	253	91	155	31.1	58	123	3.2	54	25	45	36.5	19
Dec-Feb 2011	496	5.8	251	94	150	30.3	57	123	3.2	52	23	48	38.7	22
Jan-Mar 2011	505	5.9	253	98	155	30.7	59	128	3.3	56	22	50	38.8	25
Feb-Apr 2011	519	6.1	257	101	160	30.8	57	131	3.4	61	21	49	37.3	25
Mar-May 2011	525	6.2	268	98	159	30.3	58	129	3.3	64	22	43	33.0	23
Apr-Jun 2011	529	6.2	269	99	161	30.5	61	129	3.3	64	22	43	33.4	25
May-Jul 2011	522	6.1	258	98	166	31.8	65	129	3.3	61	23	46	35.3	26
Jun-Aug 2011	535	6.3	260	102	172	32.2	67	131	3.4	59	25	47	36.0	28
Jul-Sep 2011	545	6.4	266	109	169	31.1	69	139	3.5	66	25	48	34.3	29
Aug-Oct 2011	553	6.5	273	108	172	31.1	72	143	3.6	68	25	49	34.6	28
Sep-Nov 2011	557	6.6	280	110	167	29.9	72	153	3.9	73	28	52	34.3	30
Oct-Dec 2011	556	6.5	276	109	171	30.8	76	154	3.9	70	28	55	35.9	33
Nov-Jan 2012	561	6.6	279	111	171	30.4	75	156	3.9	69	29	57	36.7	35
Dec-Feb 2012	564	6.6	271	109	183	32.5	79	162	4.1	79	25	58	35.9	33
Jan-Mar 2012	559	6.6	263	113	183	32.8	77	152	3.8	68	26	58	38.2	32
Feb-Apr 2012	555	6.5	257	113	185	33.3	78	158	3.9	71	26	60	38.3	32
Mar-May 2012	544	6.4	247	115	182	33.5	79	154	3.9	68	26	60	38.8	33
Apr-Jun 2012	544	6.4	253	110	181	33.2	77	151	3.8	70	24	56	37.4	29
May-Jul 2012	537	6.3	254	110	173	32.3	77	151	3.7	64	25	62	40.9	32
Jun-Aug 2012	551	6.4	259	111	181	32.9	76	140	3.5	57	22	62	44.1	30
Jul-Sep 2012	556	6.5	265	100	190	34.2	79	136	3.4	55	20	61	44.7	29
Aug-Oct 2012	561	6.5	268	98	195	34.7	80	133	3.3	56	18	59	44.1	26
Sep-Nov 2012	558	6.5	267	97	195	34.8	78	132	3.3	58	20	54	40.8	27
Oct-Dec 2012	**557**	**6.5**	**266**	**109**	**182**	**32.7**	**75**	**130**	**3.2**	**58**	**19**	**53**	**40.7**	**30**
Change on qtr	*1*	*0.0*	*1*	*8*	*-8*	*-1.5*	*-4*	*-6*	*-0.2*	*2*	*0*	*-8*	*-4.0*	*2*
Change %	*0.3*		*0.3*	*8.4*	*-4.2*		*-5.0*	*-4.6*		*3.7*	*-1.3*	*-13.2*		*6.0*
Change on year	*1*	*0.0*	*-9*	*0*	*11*	*1.9*	*-1*	*-24*	*-0.7*	*-13*	*-9*	*-3*	*4.8*	*-2*
Change %	*0.2*		*-3.4*	*-0.4*	*6.5*		*-1.0*	*-15.8*		*-18.3*	*-31.4*	*-4.6*		*-7.5*

Relationship between columns: 1=3+4+5; 8=10+11+12.

Source: Labour Force Survey,
Labour Market Statistics
Labour market statistics enquiries: labour.market@ons.gov.uk

[+] Denominator = economically active for that age group.

* Sample size too small for reliable estimate.

.. Data not available.

Further information

The Labour Force Survey is a survey of the population of private households, student halls of residence and NHS accommodation

4.8 Regional labour market summary (employment, unemployment, economic activity, inactivity)

Thousands, seasonally adjusted

Headline estimates for October to December 2012

	Economically active		Employment		Unemployment		Economically inactive	
	Aged 16+	Aged 16-64	Aged 16+	Aged 16-64	Aged 16+	Aged 16+	Aged 16-64	Aged 16-64
	Level	Rate (%)[2]	Level	Rate (%)[2]	Level	Rate (%)[3]	Level	Rate (%)[2]
	1	2	3	4	5	6	7	8
North East	1,297	75.1	1,172	67.7	125	9.7	422	24.9
North West	3,477	76.3	3,182	69.8	295	8.5	1,051	23.7
Yorkshire and The Humber	2,740	77.3	2,495	70.2	245	8.9	786	22.7
East Midlands	2,303	77.6	2,125	71.4	178	7.7	645	22.4
West Midlands	2,758	77.7	2,521	70.8	238	8.6	764	22.3
East of England	3,122	80.4	2,910	74.8	212	6.8	730	19.6
London	4,291	76.9	3,929	70.3	362	8.4	1,257	23.1
South East	4,534	80.3	4,238	75.0	295	6.5	1,067	19.7
South West	2,703	79.2	2,553	74.7	150	5.5	681	20.8
England	**27,225**	**78.1**	**25,125**	**71.9**	**2,100**	**7.7**	**7,403**	**21.9**
Wales	1,471	75.2	1,344	68.6	127	8.6	470	24.8
Scotland	2,667	76.7	2,461	70.7	206	7.7	791	23.3
Great Britain	**31,364**	**77.8**	**28,931**	**71.6**	**2,433**	**7.8**	**8,664**	**22.2**
Northern Ireland	867	72.8	799	67.0	68	7.8	316	27.2
United Kingdom	**32,230**	**77.7**	**29,730**	**71.5**	**2,501**	**7.8**	**8,979**	**22.3**

Change on quarter (change since July to September 2012)[4]

	Economically active		Employment		Unemployment		Economically inactive	
	Aged 16+	Aged 16-64	Aged 16+	Aged 16-64	Aged 16+	Aged 16+	Aged 16-64	Aged 16-64
	Level	Rate (%)[2]	Level	Rate (%)[2]	Level	Rate (%)[3]	Level	Rate (%)[2]
North East	-5	-0.1	-3	-0.1	-2	-0.1	3	0.1
North West	1	-0.1	-2	-0.1	2	0.1	3	0.1
Yorkshire and The Humber	20	0.4	21	0.4	-1	-0.1	-13	-0.4
East Midlands	5	0.0	5	0.0	-1	0.0	0	0.0
West Midlands	45	1.3	42	1.2	3	0.0	-44	-1.3
East of England	8	0.0	9	0.1	0	0.0	-1	0.0
London	35	0.5	45	0.6	-10	-0.3	-23	-0.5
South East	56	0.5	50	0.4	6	0.1	-29	-0.5
South West	11	0.2	17	0.3	-6	-0.2	-5	-0.2
England	**175**	**0.3**	**184**	**0.4**	**-8**	**-0.1**	**-109**	**-0.3**
Wales	-8	-0.1	-14	-0.4	6	0.4	3	0.1
Scotland	-23	-0.3	-11	0.1	-13	-0.4	9	0.3
Great Britain	**144**	**0.3**	**159**	**0.3**	**-15**	**-0.1**	**-97**	**-0.3**
Northern Ireland	-4	-0.3	-6	-0.4	1	0.2	4	0.3
United Kingdom	**140**	**0.2**	**154**	**0.3**	**-14**	**-0.1**	**-94**	**-0.2**

Change on year (change since October to December 2011)

	Economically active		Employment		Unemployment		Economically inactive	
	Aged 16+	Aged 16-64	Aged 16+	Aged 16-64	Aged 16+	Aged 16+	Aged 16-64	Aged 16-64
	Level	Rate (%)[2]	Level	Rate (%)[2]	Level	Rate (%)[3]	Level	Rate (%)[2]
North East	2	0.3	21	1.4	-19	-1.5	-5	-0.3
North West	18	0.5	44	1.1	-26	-0.8	-24	-0.5
Yorkshire and The Humber	60	1.6	78	2.1	-18	-0.9	-55	-1.6
East Midlands	6	-0.1	15	0.2	-9	-0.4	2	0.1
West Midlands	101	2.6	107	2.7	-6	-0.6	-93	-2.6
East of England	37	0.0	39	0.1	-2	-0.1	3	0.0
London	138	1.7	192	2.8	-54	-1.6	-87	-1.7
South East	82	1.0	65	0.7	17	0.3	-53	-1.0
South West	9	0.4	24	0.8	-15	-0.6	-13	-0.4
England	**452**	**1.0**	**584**	**1.4**	**-131**	**-0.6**	**-324**	**-1.0**
Wales	-6	-0.1	0	0.2	-6	-0.4	2	0.1
Scotland	-23	-0.8	2	-0.1	-25	-0.9	27	0.8
Great Britain	**424**	**0.8**	**586**	**1.2**	**-162**	**-0.6**	**-296**	**-0.8**
Northern Ireland	4	0.0	-2	-0.5	6	0.7	2	0.0
United Kingdom	**428**	**0.8**	**584**	**1.1**	**-156**	**-0.6**	**-294**	**-0.8**

Relationship between columns: 1=3+5

1. Labour Force Survey is tabulated by region of residence.

2. Denominator = all persons aged 16 to 64.

3. Denominator = Total economically active.

4. Quarter on quarter changes at regional level are particularly subject to sampling variability and should be interpreted in the context of changes over several quarters rather than in isolation.

Source: Labour Force Survey
Labour Market Statistics
Labour market statistics enquiries: labour.market@ons.gov.uk

4.9 claimant count rates: by region

ONS Crown Copyright Reserved [from Nomis on 1 August 2014]

Sex: Total
Rate: Workplace-based estimates

Area		January 2002 - December 2002 (inclusive)		January 2003 - December 2003 (inclusive)		January 2004 - December 2004 (inclusive)		January 2005 - December 2005 (inclusive)	
		number	rate	number	rate	number	rate	number	rate
England	E92000001	761,175	2.9	754,375	2.8	690,317	2.6	706,092	2.6
United Kingdom	K02000001	946,650	3.0	933,050	3.0	853,342	2.7	861,775	2.7
North East	E12000001	57,942	5.0	52,808	4.5	46,275	3.9	45,942	3.8
North West	E12000002	118,117	3.5	111,650	3.3	99,200	2.8	101,242	2.9
Yorkshire and The Humber	E12000003	88,808	3.6	83,708	3.3	73,400	2.8	76,017	2.9
East Midlands	E12000004	58,683	2.8	58,875	2.8	52,483	2.5	54,083	2.5
West Midlands	E12000005	93,708	3.5	94,675	3.5	88,258	3.2	93,958	3.4
East	E12000006	56,558	2.0	58,067	2.1	55,408	2.0	58,100	2.1
London	E12000007	166,017	3.5	170,692	3.6	162,750	3.4	162,950	3.4
South East	E12000008	71,242	1.6	75,558	1.7	70,675	1.6	71,625	1.6
South West	E12000009	50,100	1.9	48,342	1.8	41,867	1.6	42,175	1.6
Wales	W92000004	47,067	3.5	44,600	3.3	40,208	3.0	41,200	2.9
Scotland	S92000003	101,975	3.8	99,500	3.7	92,000	3.4	85,892	3.1
Northern Ireland	N92000002	36,433	4.4	34,575	4.1	30,817	3.6	28,592	3.3

Area		January 2006 - December 2006 (inclusive)		January 2007 - December 2007 (inclusive)		January 2008 - December 2008 (inclusive)		January 2009 - December 2009 (inclusive)	
		number	rate	number	rate	number	rate	number	rate
England	E92000001	785,550	2.9	723,100	2.6	754,108	2.7	1,275,583	4.6
United Kingdom	K02000001	944,967	2.9	864,467	2.6	906,083	2.7	1,527,683	4.6
North East	E12000001	50,233	4.0	49,275	4.0	53,717	4.3	83,775	6.7
North West	E12000002	115,550	3.3	110,092	3.1	119,708	3.4	191,708	5.3
Yorkshire and The Humber	E12000003	87,358	3.3	81,158	3.1	88,033	3.3	149,817	5.6
East Midlands	E12000004	61,975	2.8	58,483	2.6	61,408	2.7	108,300	4.8
West Midlands	E12000005	108,325	3.8	102,525	3.7	106,167	3.8	173,775	6.2
East	E12000006	65,583	2.2	61,225	2.1	63,625	2.2	115,992	3.9
London	E12000007	166,833	3.4	145,450	3.0	137,658	2.7	211,150	4.2
South East	E12000008	81,675	1.8	71,950	1.6	76,942	1.7	149,225	3.3
South West	E12000009	48,017	1.8	42,942	1.6	46,850	1.7	91,842	3.3
Wales	W92000004	44,217	3.1	40,692	2.8	45,517	3.2	77,133	5.3
Scotland	S92000003	87,258	3.1	76,300	2.7	78,633	2.8	125,958	4.5
Northern Ireland	N92000002	27,875	3.2	24,375	2.8	27,825	3.1	49,008	5.5

Area		January 2010 - December 2010 (inclusive)		January 2011 - December 2011 (inclusive)		January 2012 - December 2012 (inclusive)	
		number	rate	number	rate	number	rate
England	E92000001	1,230,708	4.4	1,258,225	4.5	1,301,508	4.6
United Kingdom	K02000001	1,496,358	4.6	1,534,408	4.7	1,585,492	4.7
North East	E12000001	81,417	6.5	85,367	7.0	93,400	7.7
North West	E12000002	184,017	5.2	190,200	5.4	200,292	5.6
Yorkshire and The Humber	E12000003	148,008	5.6	153,267	5.8	164,067	6.2
East Midlands	E12000004	101,492	4.5	103,142	4.5	108,842	4.7
West Midlands	E12000005	163,667	5.9	164,025	6.0	164,992	5.9
East	E12000006	111,067	3.8	111,800	3.8	115,075	3.8
London	E12000007	217,283	4.3	228,000	4.5	226,683	4.3
South East	E12000008	139,858	3.1	137,242	3.0	139,308	3.0
South West	E12000009	83,900	3.0	85,183	3.1	88,850	3.2
Wales	W92000004	73,192	5.1	74,850	5.2	79,592	5.6
Scotland	S92000003	135,733	5.0	141,508	5.1	141,442	5.1
Northern Ireland	N92000002	56,725	6.2	59,825	6.6	62,950	7.1

Seasonally adjusted
Rate figures from 2012 onwards are calculates using mid-2012 workforce estimates

4.10 Claimant count[1] by Unitary and Local Authority

not seasonally adjusted

		CLAIMANT COUNT ON 13th DECEMBER 2012						Change on year					
		Levels			Percentage of Pop[2]			Levels			Percentage[2]		
		Men	Women	People	Men	Women	People	Men	Women	People	Men	Women	People
		1	2	3	4	5	6	7	8	9	10	11	12
K02000001	**UNITED KINGDOM**	1,002,240	520,982	1,523,222	4.9	2.5	3.7	-54,367	8,740	-45,627	-0.3	0.0	-0.1
E12000001	**NORTH EAST**	63,399	29,865	93,264	7.6	3.5	5.5	1,199	2,691	3,890	0.1	0.3	0.2
E06000047	**County Durham**	10,790	5,197	15,987	6.6	3.1	4.8	505	537	1,042	0.3	0.3	0.3
E06000005	**Darlington**	2,466	1,192	3,658	7.5	3.5	5.5	48	97	145	0.1	0.3	0.2
E06000001	**Hartlepool**	3,190	1,525	4,715	11.1	5.1	8.0	50	214	264	0.2	0.7	0.5
E06000002	**Middlesbrough**	5,254	2,365	7,619	11.8	5.2	8.5	267	288	555	0.6	0.6	0.6
E06000048	**Northumberland**	5,785	2,897	8,682	5.9	2.9	4.4	230	310	540	0.2	0.3	0.3
E06000003	**Redcar and Cleveland**	3,953	1,825	5,778	9.6	4.2	6.8	113	167	280	0.3	0.4	0.3
E06000004	**Stockton-on-Tees**	4,919	2,205	7,124	8.0	3.5	5.7	151	187	338	0.2	0.3	0.3
E11000004	**Tyne and Wear**	27,042	12,659	39,701	7.5	3.5	5.5	-165	891	726	0.0	0.2	0.1
E08000020	Gateshead	4,500	2,068	6,568	7.0	3.2	5.1	33	199	232	0.1	0.3	0.2
E08000021	Newcastle upon Tyne	6,625	3,007	9,632	6.7	3.2	5.0	-139	233	94	-0.1	0.2	0.0
E08000022	North Tyneside	4,262	1,974	6,236	6.7	3.0	4.8	-144	140	-4	-0.2	0.2	0.0
E08000023	South Tyneside	4,877	2,371	7,248	10.4	4.9	7.6	307	211	518	0.7	0.4	0.5
E08000024	Sunderland	6,778	3,239	10,017	7.6	3.5	5.6	-222	108	-114	-0.3	0.1	-0.1
E12000002	**NORTH WEST**	129,071	62,403	191,474	5.7	2.7	4.2	-6,411	1,652	-4,759	-0.3	0.1	-0.1
E06000008	**Blackburn with Darwen**	2,998	1,272	4,270	6.3	2.7	4.5	44	-16	28	0.1	0.0	0.0
E06000009	**Blackpool**	4,215	1,881	6,096	9.4	4.2	6.8	1	29	30	0.0	0.1	0.0
E06000049	**Cheshire East**	3,656	1,771	5,427	3.2	1.5	2.3	-353	-143	-496	-0.3	-0.1	-0.2
E06000050	**Cheshire West and Chester**	4,281	2,106	6,387	4.1	2.0	3.0	-423	-12	-435	-0.4	0.0	-0.2
E06000006	**Halton**	2,677	1,408	4,085	6.6	3.4	5.0	-201	44	-157	-0.5	0.1	-0.2
E06000007	**Warrington**	2,963	1,422	4,385	4.5	2.2	3.3	-175	68	-107	-0.3	0.1	-0.1
E10000006	**Cumbria**	5,804	2,634	8,438	3.7	1.7	2.7	-323	-62	-385	-0.2	0.0	-0.1
E07000026	Allerdale	1,303	598	1,901	4.4	2.0	3.2	-42	16	-26	-0.1	0.1	0.0
E07000027	Barrow-in-Furness	1,214	547	1,761	5.5	2.5	4.0	-104	-40	-144	-0.5	-0.2	-0.3
E07000028	Carlisle	1,398	670	2,068	4.1	1.9	3.0	18	49	67	0.1	0.1	0.1
E07000029	Copeland	1,069	431	1,500	4.6	1.9	3.3	-118	-39	-157	-0.5	-0.2	-0.3
E07000030	Eden	253	125	378	1.6	0.8	1.2	-22	-16	-38	-0.1	-0.1	-0.1
E07000031	South Lakeland	567	263	830	1.8	0.8	1.3	-55	-32	-87	-0.2	-0.1	-0.1
E11000001	**Greater Manchester**	55,148	26,911	82,059	6.3	3.1	4.7	-1,568	1,653	85	-0.2	0.2	0.0
E08000001	Bolton	5,575	2,734	8,309	6.3	3.1	4.7	-122	168	46	-0.1	0.2	0.0
E08000002	Bury	3,229	1,489	4,718	5.5	2.5	4.0	6	43	49	0.0	0.1	0.0
E08000003	Manchester	13,288	6,491	19,779	7.3	3.7	5.5	-155	554	399	-0.1	0.3	0.1
E08000004	Oldham	4,898	2,678	7,576	7.0	3.7	5.3	-158	265	107	-0.2	0.4	0.1
E08000005	Rochdale	4,648	2,430	7,078	6.9	3.5	5.2	-424	20	-404	-0.6	0.0	-0.3
E08000006	Salford	5,486	2,641	8,127	6.9	3.5	5.2	-230	319	89	-0.3	0.4	0.1
E08000007	Stockport	4,019	1,708	5,727	4.5	1.9	3.2	-202	-103	-305	-0.2	-0.1	-0.2
K08000008	Tameside	4,598	2,318	6,916	6.5	3.2	4.9	-240	156	-84	-0.3	0.2	-0.1
E08000009	Trafford	3,051	1,391	4,442	4.2	1.9	3.1	-133	-30	-163	-0.2	0.0	-0.1
E08000010	Wigan	6,356	3,031	9,387	6.1	2.9	4.6	90	261	351	0.1	0.3	0.2
E10000017	**Lancashire**	15,283	7,355	22,638	4.1	2.0	3.0	-995	98	-897	-0.3	0.0	-0.1
E07000117	Burnley	1,734	922	2,656	6.3	3.3	4.8	-76	56	-20	-0.3	0.2	0.0
E07000118	Chorley	1,151	549	1,700	3.2	1.6	2.4	-142	19	-123	-0.4	0.1	-0.2
E07000119	Fylde	703	329	1,032	3.1	1.4	2.3	39	9	48	0.2	0.0	0.1
E07000120	Hyndburn	1,334	600	1,934	5.2	2.4	3.8	2	30	32	0.0	0.1	0.1
E07000121	Lancaster	1,865	869	2,734	4.3	1.9	3.1	-136	-19	-155	-0.3	0.0	-0.2
E07000122	Pendle	1,362	670	2,032	4.8	2.3	3.6	-115	7	-108	-0.4	0.0	-0.2
E07000123	Preston	2,150	994	3,144	4.5	2.2	3.4	-265	-89	-354	-0.6	-0.2	-0.4
E07000124	Ribble Valley	329	168	497	1.9	0.9	1.4	-32	-9	-41	-0.2	-0.1	-0.1
E07000125	Rossendale	1,035	489	1,524	4.7	2.2	3.4	-109	6	-103	-0.5	0.0	-0.2
E07000126	South Ribble	950	511	1,461	2.8	1.5	2.1	-57	48	-9	-0.2	0.1	0.0
E07000127	West Lancashire	1,543	729	2,272	4.5	2.0	3.3	-39	-2	-41	-0.1	0.0	-0.1
E07000128	Wyre	1,127	525	1,652	3.6	1.6	2.6	-65	42	-23	-0.2	0.1	0.0
E11000002	**Merseyside**	32,046	15,643	47,689	7.2	3.4	5.3	-2,418	-7	-2,425	-0.5	0.0	-0.3
E08000011	Knowsley	3,812	2,117	5,929	8.5	4.3	6.3	-341	4	-337	-0.8	0.0	-0.4
E08000012	Liverpool	13,435	6,695	20,130	8.3	4.2	6.3	-968	91	-877	-0.6	0.1	-0.3
E08000014	Sefton	5,677	2,670	8,347	6.9	3.1	4.9	-340	26	-314	-0.4	0.0	-0.2
E08000013	St. Helens	3,671	1,753	5,424	6.6	3.1	4.9	-143	73	-70	-0.3	0.1	-0.1
E08000015	Wirral	5,451	2,408	7,859	5.6	2.4	3.9	-626	-201	-827	-0.6	-0.2	-0.4
E12000003	**YORKSHIRE AND THE HUMBER**	106,987	52,521	159,508	6.3	3.1	4.7	-3,739	3,332	-407	-0.2	0.2	0.0

4.10 Claimant count[1] by Unitary and Local Authority

not seasonally adjusted

		CLAIMANT COUNT ON 13th DECEMBER 2012						Change on year					
		Levels			Percentage of Pop[2]			Levels			Percentage[2]		
		Men	Women	People	Men	Women	People	Men	Women	People	Men	Women	People
		1	2	3	4	5	6	7	8	9	10	11	12
E06000011	**East Riding of Yorkshire**	4,614	2,216	6,830	4.5	2.1	3.3	-291	-45	-336	-0.3	0.0	-0.2
E06000010	**Kingston upon Hull, City of**	10,261	4,687	14,948	11.7	5.6	8.7	-156	351	195	-0.2	0.4	0.1
E06000012	**North East Lincolnshire**	4,220	2,078	6,298	8.4	4.1	6.2	-486	13	-473	-1.0	0.0	-0.5
E06000013	**North Lincolnshire**	3,039	1,569	4,608	5.7	3.0	4.3	-377	88	-289	-0.7	0.2	-0.3
E06000014	**York**	1,921	929	2,850	2.9	1.4	2.2	-401	-104	-505	-0.6	-0.2	-0.4
E10000023	**North Yorkshire**	5,735	3,050	8,785	3.0	1.6	2.4	-766	-294	-1,060	-0.4	-0.2	-0.3
E07000163	Craven	439	223	662	2.7	1.3	2.0	-42	-20	-62	-0.3	-0.1	-0.2
E07000164	Hambleton	572	347	919	2.1	1.3	1.7	-115	-39	-154	-0.4	-0.1	-0.3
E07000165	Harrogate	979	545	1,524	2.0	1.1	1.5	-385	-121	-506	-0.8	-0.2	-0.5
E07000166	Richmondshire	356	222	578	1.8	1.5	1.7	-29	-35	-64	-0.1	-0.2	-0.2
E07000167	Ryedale	429	266	695	2.7	1.7	2.2	24	-1	23	0.2	0.0	0.1
E07000168	Scarborough	2,172	967	3,139	6.7	2.9	4.8	-2	21	19	0.0	0.1	0.0
E07000169	Selby	788	480	1,268	3.0	1.8	2.3	-217	-99	-316	-0.8	-0.4	-0.6
E11000003	**South Yorkshire**	29,029	14,045	43,074	6.7	3.2	4.9	-559	1,198	639	-0.1	0.3	0.1
E08000016	Barnsley	4,931	2,548	7,479	6.7	3.4	5.0	150	367	517	0.2	0.5	0.3
E08000017	Doncaster	6,583	3,473	10,056	6.8	3.6	5.2	-177	391	214	-0.2	0.4	0.1
E08000018	Rotherham	5,778	2,803	8,581	7.1	3.4	5.3	83	247	330	0.1	0.3	0.2
E08000019	Sheffield	11,737	5,221	16,958	6.4	2.9	4.6	-615	193	-422	-0.3	0.1	-0.1
E11000006	**West Yorkshire**	48,168	23,947	72,115	6.7	3.3	5.0	-703	2,125	1,422	-0.1	0.3	0.1
E08000032	Bradford	12,741	6,691	19,432	7.7	4.0	5.9	-23	872	849	0.0	0.5	0.3
E08000033	Calderdale	4,326	2,193	6,519	6.6	3.3	5.0	-174	135	-39	-0.3	0.2	0.0
E08000034	Kirklees	8,550	4,176	12,726	6.3	3.1	4.7	57	251	308	0.0	0.2	0.1
E08000035	Leeds	16,496	7,791	24,287	6.6	3.1	4.8	-483	581	98	-0.2	0.2	0.0
E08000036	Wakefield	6,055	3,096	9,151	5.8	2.9	4.3	-80	286	206	-0.1	0.3	0.1
E12000004	**EAST MIDLANDS**	66,785	35,641	102,426	4.6	2.4	3.5	-4,195	757	-3,438	-0.3	0.1	-0.1
E06000015	**Derby**	5,014	2,663	7,677	6.2	3.3	4.8	-474	79	-395	-0.6	0.1	-0.2
E06000016	**Leicester**	7,842	4,313	12,155	7.1	3.9	5.5	-336	298	-38	-0.3	0.3	0.0
E06000018	**Nottingham**	9,027	4,441	13,468	8.3	4.3	6.3	-371	241	-130	-0.3	0.2	-0.1
E06000017	**Rutland**	188	103	291	1.6	0.9	1.3	-11	-14	-25	-0.1	-0.1	-0.1
E10000007	**Derbyshire**	9,438	4,962	14,400	3.9	2.0	2.9	-1,383	-316	-1,699	-0.6	-0.1	-0.3
E07000032	Amber Valley	1,440	796	2,236	3.7	2.0	2.9	-294	-51	-345	-0.8	-0.1	-0.4
E07000033	Bolsover	898	561	1,459	3.7	2.3	3.0	-239	-71	-310	-1.0	-0.3	-0.6
E07000034	Chesterfield	1,753	811	2,564	5.3	2.4	3.9	-175	-28	-203	-0.5	-0.1	-0.3
E07000035	Derbyshire Dales	422	233	655	1.9	1.1	1.5	-85	-27	-112	-0.4	-0.1	-0.3
E07000036	Erewash	1,784	916	2,700	5.0	2.5	3.7	-275	-70	-345	-0.8	-0.2	-0.5
E07000037	High Peak	1,164	570	1,734	4.0	1.9	3.0	-79	-31	-110	-0.3	-0.1	-0.2
E07000038	North East Derbyshire	1,205	575	1,780	3.9	1.9	2.9	-166	-53	-219	-0.5	-0.2	-0.4
E07000039	South Derbyshire	772	500	1,272	2.5	1.6	2.1	-70	15	-55	-0.2	0.0	-0.1
E10000018	**Leicestershire**	5,787	3,268	9,055	2.8	1.6	2.2	-381	-117	-498	-0.2	-0.1	-0.1
E07000129	Blaby	752	444	1,196	2.5	1.5	2.0	-12	-2	-14	0.0	0.0	0.0
E07000130	Charnwood	1,521	835	2,356	2.7	1.5	2.1	-197	-21	-218	-0.4	0.0	-0.2
E07000131	Harborough	460	252	712	1.7	0.9	1.3	-93	-68	-161	-0.3	-0.3	-0.3
E07000132	Hinckley and Bosworth	976	584	1,560	2.9	1.7	2.3	-92	-19	-111	-0.3	-0.1	-0.2
E07000133	Melton	422	258	680	2.6	1.6	2.1	-14	21	7	-0.1	0.1	0.0
E07000134	North West Leicestershire	1,057	587	1,644	3.6	2.0	2.8	49	12	61	0.2	0.0	0.1
E07000135	Oadby and Wigston	599	308	907	3.5	1.7	2.6	-22	-40	-62	-0.1	-0.2	-0.2
E10000019	**Lincolnshire**	9,524	4,956	14,480	4.4	2.2	3.3	-441	77	-364	-0.2	0.0	-0.1
E07000136	Boston	758	458	1,216	3.8	2.2	3.0	-124	0	-124	-0.6	0.0	-0.3
E07000137	East Lindsey	2,191	1,138	3,329	5.6	2.8	4.2	-64	41	-23	-0.2	0.1	0.0
E07000138	Lincoln	2,189	991	3,180	6.9	3.0	4.9	-7	129	122	0.0	0.4	0.2
E07000139	North Kesteven	833	458	1,291	2.5	1.4	1.9	-91	4	-87	-0.3	0.0	-0.1
E07000140	South Holland	874	524	1,398	3.3	1.9	2.6	-77	-42	-119	-0.3	-0.2	-0.2
E07000141	South Kesteven	1,336	696	2,032	3.3	1.6	2.4	-35	-50	-85	-0.1	-0.1	-0.1
E07000142	West Lindsey	1,343	691	2,034	5.0	2.4	3.7	-43	-5	-48	-0.2	0.0	-0.1
E10000021	**Northamptonshire**	9,505	5,381	14,886	4.3	2.4	3.3	27	511	538	0.0	0.2	0.1
E07000150	Corby	1,223	756	1,979	6.1	3.7	4.9	89	178	267	0.4	0.9	0.7
E07000151	Daventry	718	416	1,134	2.9	1.7	2.3	76	0	76	0.3	0.0	0.2
E07000152	East Northamptonshire	890	538	1,428	3.3	1.9	2.6	-13	55	42	0.0	0.2	0.1
E07000153	Kettering	1,436	782	2,218	4.8	2.6	3.7	16	97	113	0.1	0.3	0.2
E07000154	Northampton	3,504	1,925	5,429	5.0	2.7	3.9	-32	173	141	0.0	0.2	0.1

4.10 Claimant count[1] by Unitary and Local Authority

not seasonally adjusted

		CLAIMANT COUNT ON 13th DECEMBER 2012						Change on year					
		Levels			Percentage of Pop[2]			Levels			Percentage[2]		
		Men	Women	People	Men	Women	People	Men	Women	People	Men	Women	People
		1	2	3	4	5	6	7	8	9	10	11	12
E07000155	South Northamptonshire	405	254	659	1.5	0.9	1.2	-83	-5	-88	-0.3	0.0	-0.2
E07000156	Wellingborough	1,329	710	2,039	5.6	2.9	4.2	-26	13	-13	-0.1	0.1	0.0
E10000024	**Nottinghamshire**	10,460	5,554	16,014	4.2	2.2	3.2	-825	-2	-827	-0.3	0.0	-0.2
E07000170	Ashfield	1,990	1,087	3,077	5.3	2.8	4.0	-163	5	-158	-0.4	0.0	-0.2
E07000171	Bassetlaw	1,464	787	2,251	4.0	2.2	3.1	-181	-39	-220	-0.5	-0.1	-0.3
E07000172	Broxtowe	1,410	752	2,162	4.0	2.1	3.0	-221	-60	-281	-0.6	-0.2	-0.4
E07000173	Gedling	1,634	782	2,416	4.6	2.1	3.3	-109	-67	-176	-0.3	-0.2	-0.2
E07000174	Mansfield	1,836	977	2,813	5.4	2.9	4.2	-75	125	50	-0.2	0.4	0.1
E07000175	Newark and Sherwood	1,243	709	1,952	3.5	2.0	2.7	26	108	134	0.1	0.3	0.2
E07000176	Rushcliffe	883	460	1,343	2.5	1.3	1.9	-102	-74	-176	-0.3	-0.2	-0.3
E12000005	**WEST MIDLANDS**	**102,656**	**54,392**	**157,048**	**5.8**	**3.1**	**4.4**	**-9,195**	**993**	**-8,202**	**-0.5**	**0.1**	**-0.2**
E06000019	**Herefordshire, County of**	1,641	891	2,532	2.9	1.6	2.2	-122	-16	-138	-0.2	0.0	-0.1
E06000051	**Shropshire**	3,050	1,592	4,642	3.2	1.7	2.4	-263	-1	-264	-0.3	0.0	-0.1
E06000021	**Stoke-on-Trent**	5,261	2,552	7,813	6.4	3.2	4.8	-435	189	-246	-0.5	0.2	-0.2
E06000020	**Telford and Wrekin**	2,772	1,640	4,412	5.1	3.0	4.1	-272	230	-42	-0.5	0.4	0.0
E10000028	**Staffordshire**	8,591	4,721	13,312	3.2	1.8	2.5	-1,069	-230	-1,299	-0.4	-0.1	-0.2
E07000192	Cannock Chase	1,391	744	2,135	4.4	2.3	3.4	-80	-12	-92	-0.3	0.0	-0.1
E07000193	East Staffordshire	1,084	611	1,695	2.9	1.7	2.3	-170	-37	-207	-0.5	-0.1	-0.3
E07000194	Lichfield	772	493	1,265	2.4	1.6	2.0	-202	-38	-240	-0.6	-0.1	-0.4
E07000195	Newcastle-under-Lyme	1,363	748	2,111	3.4	1.9	2.6	-214	-41	-255	-0.5	-0.1	-0.3
E07000196	South Staffordshire	1,083	563	1,646	3.2	1.7	2.4	-84	-17	-101	-0.2	0.0	-0.1
E07000197	Stafford	1,161	599	1,760	2.7	1.5	2.1	-66	28	-38	-0.2	0.1	0.0
E07000198	Staffordshire Moorlands	833	407	1,240	2.8	1.3	2.0	-12	-72	-84	0.0	-0.2	-0.1
E07000199	Tamworth	904	556	1,460	3.7	2.2	2.9	-241	-41	-282	-1.0	-0.2	-0.6
E10000031	**Warwickshire**	4,815	2,679	7,494	2.8	1.5	2.2	-679	-101	-780	-0.4	-0.1	-0.2
E07000218	North Warwickshire	523	362	885	2.7	1.8	2.2	-108	17	-91	-0.5	0.1	-0.2
E07000219	Nuneaton and Bedworth	1,793	985	2,778	4.5	2.4	3.5	-132	-12	-144	-0.3	0.0	-0.2
E07000220	Rugby	794	494	1,288	2.5	1.6	2.0	-68	8	-60	-0.2	0.0	-0.1
E07000221	Stratford-on-Avon	573	301	874	1.6	0.8	1.2	-161	-41	-202	-0.4	-0.1	-0.3
E07000222	Warwick	1,132	537	1,669	2.4	1.2	1.8	-210	-73	-283	-0.5	-0.2	-0.3
E11000005	**West Midlands (Metropolitan County)**	69,971	37,018	106,989	8.1	4.2	6.1	-5,795	1,237	-4,558	-0.7	0.1	-0.3
E08000025	Birmingham	31,686	16,393	48,079	9.3	4.7	7.0	-3,322	295	-3,027	-1.0	0.1	-0.4
E08000026	Coventry	6,187	3,213	9,400	5.9	3.1	4.5	-620	-53	-673	-0.6	-0.1	-0.3
E08000027	Dudley	6,708	3,356	10,064	6.9	3.4	5.2	-141	223	82	-0.1	0.2	0.0
E08000028	Sandwell	8,624	4,722	13,346	8.8	4.8	6.8	-452	320	-132	-0.5	0.3	-0.1
E08000029	Solihull	2,657	1,473	4,130	4.2	2.3	3.2	-576	-16	-592	-0.9	0.0	-0.5
E08000030	Walsall	6,416	3,569	9,985	7.7	4.3	6.0	-547	107	-440	-0.7	0.1	-0.3
E08000031	Wolverhampton	7,693	4,292	11,985	9.6	5.4	7.5	-137	361	224	-0.2	0.5	0.1
E10000034	**Worcestershire**	6,555	3,299	9,854	3.7	1.8	2.8	-560	-315	-875	-0.3	-0.2	-0.2
E07000234	Bromsgrove	828	393	1,221	2.8	1.4	2.1	-30	-46	-76	-0.1	-0.2	-0.1
E07000235	Malvern Hills	599	322	921	2.8	1.4	2.1	-92	-14	-106	-0.4	-0.1	-0.2
E07000236	Redditch	1,122	653	1,775	4.1	2.3	3.2	-209	-48	-257	-0.8	-0.2	-0.5
E07000237	Worcester	1,403	672	2,075	4.3	2.1	3.2	-222	-73	-295	-0.7	-0.2	-0.5
E07000238	Wychavon	1,102	572	1,674	3.1	1.6	2.3	-34	-35	-69	-0.1	-0.1	-0.1
E07000239	Wyre Forest	1,501	687	2,188	5.0	2.3	3.6	27	-99	-72	0.1	-0.3	-0.1
E12000006	**EAST OF ENGLAND**	**70,027**	**39,246**	**109,273**	**3.8**	**2.1**	**2.9**	**-4,433**	**-509**	**-4,942**	**-0.2**	**0.0**	**-0.1**
E06000055	**Bedford**	2,500	1,484	3,984	5.0	2.9	3.9	-168	70	-98	-0.3	0.1	-0.1
E06000056	**Central Bedfordshire**	2,398	1,388	3,786	2.9	1.7	2.3	-331	-102	-433	-0.4	-0.1	-0.3
E06000032	**Luton**	3,263	2,028	5,291	4.8	3.1	4.0	-615	-257	-872	-0.9	-0.4	-0.7
E06000031	**Peterborough**	3,520	2,201	5,721	5.9	3.7	4.8	105	386	491	0.2	0.6	0.4
E06000033	**Southend-on-Sea**	3,360	1,645	5,005	6.1	3.0	4.5	-274	-64	-338	-0.5	-0.1	-0.3
E06000034	**Thurrock**	2,380	1,581	3,961	4.6	3.0	3.8	-146	-4	-150	-0.3	0.0	-0.1
E10000003	**Cambridgeshire**	5,317	3,007	8,324	2.6	1.5	2.0	-249	12	-237	-0.1	0.0	-0.1
E07000008	Cambridge	1,103	542	1,645	2.3	1.3	1.8	-54	21	-33	-0.1	0.0	0.0
E07000009	East Cambridgeshire	662	414	1,076	2.5	1.5	2.0	-38	-16	-54	-0.1	-0.1	-0.1
E07000010	Fenland	1,269	786	2,055	4.3	2.6	3.5	-66	14	-52	-0.2	0.0	-0.1
E07000011	Huntingdonshire	1,484	800	2,284	2.7	1.5	2.1	-49	-33	-82	-0.1	-0.1	-0.1
E07000012	South Cambridgeshire	799	465	1,264	1.7	1.0	1.3	-42	26	-16	-0.1	0.1	0.0
E10000012	**Essex**	16,348	9,512	25,860	3.8	2.1	2.9	-840	-257	-1,097	-0.2	-0.1	-0.1

4.10 Claimant count[1] by Unitary and Local Authority

not seasonally adjusted

		CLAIMANT COUNT ON 13th DECEMBER 2012						Change on year					
		Levels			Percentage of Pop[2]			Levels			Percentage[2]		
		Men	Women	People	Men	Women	People	Men	Women	People	Men	Women	People
		1	2	3	4	5	6	7	8	9	10	11	12
E07000066	Basildon	2,761	1,712	4,473	5.1	3.0	4.0	-4	161	157	0.0	0.3	0.1
E07000067	Braintree	1,559	998	2,557	3.4	2.1	2.7	-22	51	29	0.0	0.1	0.0
E07000068	Brentwood	532	331	863	2.3	1.4	1.9	-61	-44	-105	-0.3	-0.2	-0.2
E07000069	Castle Point	1,023	546	1,569	3.8	2.0	2.9	19	-41	-22	0.1	-0.2	0.0
E07000070	Chelmsford	1,696	948	2,644	3.1	1.7	2.4	-96	-89	-185	-0.2	-0.2	-0.2
E07000071	Colchester	2,023	1,062	3,085	3.6	1.9	2.7	-162	-79	-241	-0.3	-0.1	-0.2
E07000072	Epping Forest	1,287	881	2,168	3.3	2.2	2.7	-90	-65	-155	-0.2	-0.2	-0.2
E07000073	Harlow	1,458	888	2,346	5.6	3.3	4.4	-117	-11	-128	-0.5	0.0	-0.2
E07000074	Maldon	561	304	865	2.9	1.6	2.3	-20	-23	-43	-0.1	-0.1	-0.1
E07000075	Rochford	690	424	1,114	2.7	1.6	2.2	8	-25	-17	0.0	-0.1	0.0
E07000076	Tendring	2,295	1,139	3,434	6.1	2.8	4.4	-221	-81	-302	-0.6	-0.2	-0.4
E07000077	Uttlesford	463	279	742	1.9	1.1	1.5	-74	-11	-85	-0.3	0.0	-0.2
E10000015	**Hertfordshire**	10,597	6,278	16,875	3.0	1.7	2.3	-876	-202	-1,078	-0.2	-0.1	-0.1
E07000095	Broxbourne	1,141	771	1,912	3.9	2.5	3.2	-66	-33	-99	-0.2	-0.1	-0.2
E07000096	Dacorum	1,191	785	1,976	2.6	1.7	2.1	-265	-62	-327	-0.6	-0.1	-0.4
E07000097	East Hertfordshire	1,007	592	1,599	2.3	1.3	1.8	-90	-48	-138	-0.2	-0.1	-0.2
E07000098	Hertsmere	875	601	1,476	2.8	1.8	2.3	-78	46	-32	-0.3	0.1	-0.1
E07000099	North Hertfordshire	1,237	699	1,936	3.1	1.7	2.4	5	41	46	0.0	0.1	0.1
E07000100	St Albans	924	508	1,432	2.1	1.1	1.6	-121	-8	-129	-0.3	0.0	-0.1
E07000101	Stevenage	1,401	769	2,170	5.1	2.8	3.9	-15	11	-4	-0.1	0.0	0.0
E07000102	Three Rivers	648	362	1,010	2.4	1.3	1.8	-46	-97	-143	-0.2	-0.3	-0.3
E07000103	Watford	1,114	614	1,728	3.7	2.0	2.8	-44	2	-42	-0.1	0.0	-0.1
E07000104	Welwyn Hatfield	1,059	577	1,636	2.9	1.6	2.2	-156	-54	-210	-0.4	-0.1	-0.3
E10000020	**Norfolk**	11,867	5,702	17,569	4.5	2.1	3.3	-400	-5	-405	-0.2	0.0	-0.1
E07000143	Breckland	1,407	764	2,171	3.5	1.9	2.7	-39	-15	-54	-0.1	0.0	-0.1
E07000144	Broadland	932	431	1,363	2.5	1.1	1.8	-53	-27	-80	-0.1	-0.1	-0.1
E07000145	Great Yarmouth	2,645	1,269	3,914	8.9	4.3	6.6	-43	63	20	-0.1	0.2	0.0
E07000146	King's Lynn and West Norfolk	1,844	961	2,805	4.2	2.1	3.2	-28	6	-22	-0.1	0.0	0.0
E07000147	North Norfolk	993	486	1,479	3.5	1.7	2.6	-36	-55	-91	-0.1	-0.2	-0.2
E07000148	Norwich	3,039	1,285	4,324	6.7	2.8	4.7	-167	45	-122	-0.4	0.1	-0.1
E07000149	South Norfolk	1,007	506	1,513	2.7	1.3	2.0	-34	-22	-56	-0.1	-0.1	-0.1
E10000029	**Suffolk**	8,477	4,420	12,897	3.8	2.0	2.9	-639	-86	-725	-0.3	0.0	-0.2
E07000200	Babergh	786	460	1,246	3.0	1.7	2.4	-43	32	-11	-0.2	0.1	0.0
E07000201	Forest Heath	582	310	892	2.9	1.6	2.3	-19	26	7	-0.1	0.1	0.0
E07000202	Ipswich	2,615	1,232	3,847	5.9	2.8	4.4	-295	-65	-360	-0.7	-0.1	-0.4
E07000203	Mid Suffolk	687	416	1,103	2.3	1.4	1.8	-57	-24	-81	-0.2	-0.1	-0.1
E07000204	St Edmundsbury	975	585	1,560	2.7	1.7	2.2	-96	32	-64	-0.3	0.1	-0.1
E07000205	Suffolk Coastal	842	436	1,278	2.3	1.2	1.7	-110	-69	-179	-0.3	-0.2	-0.2
E07000206	Waveney	1,990	981	2,971	6.0	2.9	4.4	-19	-18	-37	-0.1	-0.1	-0.1
E12000007	**LONDON**	**131,124**	**88,167**	**219,291**	**4.6**	**3.1**	**3.9**	**-12,261**	**-2,121**	**-14,382**	**-0.4**	**-0.1**	**-0.3**
E13000001	**Inner London**	62,498	41,303	103,801	5.3	3.5	4.4	-6,052	-1,534	-7,586	-0.5	-0.1	-0.3
E09000007	Camden	3,075	1,999	5,074	3.9	2.5	3.2	-293	-231	-524	-0.4	-0.3	-0.3
E09000001	City of London	72	43	115	2.2	1.8	2.0	-9	13	4	-0.3	0.5	0.1
E09000012	Hackney	5,946	3,943	9,889	6.7	4.4	5.5	-847	-340	-1,187	-1.0	-0.4	-0.7
E09000013	Hammersmith and Fulham	2,783	1,987	4,770	4.2	2.9	3.5	-289	-46	-335	-0.4	-0.1	-0.2
E09000014	Haringey	5,787	3,833	9,620	6.4	4.2	5.3	-753	-133	-886	-0.8	-0.1	-0.5
E09000019	Islington	4,121	2,630	6,751	5.4	3.4	4.3	-250	-208	-458	-0.3	-0.3	-0.3
E09000020	Kensington and Chelsea	1,737	1,185	2,922	3.1	2.1	2.6	-261	-138	-399	-0.5	-0.2	-0.3
E09000022	Lambeth	6,878	4,691	11,569	6.0	4.2	5.1	-551	-5	-556	-0.5	0.0	-0.2
E09000023	Lewisham	6,042	4,010	10,052	6.4	4.1	5.2	-472	-43	-515	-0.5	0.0	-0.3
E09000025	Newham	6,653	4,367	11,020	5.7	4.3	5.0	-467	-86	-553	-0.4	-0.1	-0.3
E09000028	Southwark	6,245	4,197	10,442	5.9	3.9	4.9	-658	-25	-683	-0.6	0.0	-0.3
E09000030	Tower Hamlets	6,637	3,995	10,632	6.7	4.4	5.6	-508	-21	-529	-0.5	0.0	-0.3
E09000032	Wandsworth	3,729	2,496	6,225	3.3	2.1	2.7	-274	-68	-342	-0.2	-0.1	-0.1
E09000033	Westminster	2,793	1,927	4,720	3.3	2.5	2.9	-420	-203	-623	-0.5	-0.3	-0.4
E13000002	**Outer London**	68,626	46,864	115,490	4.2	2.8	3.5	-6,209	-587	-6,796	-0.4	0.0	-0.2
E09000002	Barking and Dagenham	4,178	2,953	7,131	7.2	4.8	6.0	-373	-32	-405	-0.6	-0.1	-0.3
E09000003	Barnet	3,819	2,752	6,571	3.3	2.3	2.8	-306	-88	-394	-0.3	-0.1	-0.2
E09000004	Bexley	2,587	1,798	4,385	3.6	2.4	3.0	-303	9	-294	-0.4	0.0	-0.2
E09000005	Brent	5,939	3,730	9,669	5.4	3.5	4.5	-101	192	91	-0.1	0.2	0.0
E09000006	Bromley	3,392	2,137	5,529	3.5	2.1	2.8	-386	-126	-512	-0.4	-0.1	-0.3
E09000008	Croydon	5,901	4,019	9,920	5.0	3.2	4.1	-768	-128	-896	-0.7	-0.1	-0.4
E09000009	Ealing	5,153	3,338	8,491	4.4	2.9	3.6	-422	-118	-540	-0.4	-0.1	-0.2
E09000010	Enfield	5,709	4,440	10,149	5.8	4.2	5.0	-591	19	-572	-0.6	0.0	-0.3

4.10 Claimant count[1] by Unitary and Local Authority

not seasonally adjusted

		CLAIMANT COUNT ON 13th DECEMBER 2012						Change on year					
		Levels			Percentage of Pop[2]			Levels			Percentage[2]		
		Men	Women	People	Men	Women	People	Men	Women	People	Men	Women	People
		1	2	3	4	5	6	7	8	9	10	11	12
E09000011	Greenwich	4,751	3,143	7,894	5.5	3.6	4.5	-195	43	-152	-0.2	0.0	-0.1
E09000015	Harrow	2,137	1,566	3,703	2.7	2.0	2.3	-413	-68	-481	-0.5	-0.1	-0.3
E09000016	Havering	3,108	2,198	5,306	4.2	2.9	3.5	-239	114	-125	-0.3	0.1	-0.1
E09000017	Hillingdon	2,891	1,920	4,811	3.2	2.1	2.6	-285	-94	-379	-0.3	-0.1	-0.2
E09000018	Hounslow	2,931	1,978	4,909	3.3	2.3	2.8	-364	-73	-437	-0.4	-0.1	-0.2
E09000021	Kingston upon Thames	1,184	804	1,988	2.2	1.5	1.8	-63	15	-48	-0.1	0.0	0.0
E09000024	Merton	2,226	1,514	3,740	3.2	2.2	2.7	-246	2	-244	-0.4	0.0	-0.2
E09000026	Redbridge	3,865	2,717	6,582	4.2	2.9	3.6	-473	-131	-604	-0.5	-0.1	-0.3
E09000027	Richmond upon Thames	1,162	773	1,935	1.9	1.2	1.5	-61	-5	-66	-0.1	0.0	-0.1
E09000029	Sutton	2,005	1,344	3,349	3.3	2.1	2.7	-192	-4	-196	-0.3	0.0	-0.2
E09000031	Waltham Forest	5,688	3,740	9,428	6.3	4.2	5.3	-428	-114	-542	-0.5	-0.1	-0.3
E12000008	**SOUTH EAST**	**86,404**	**45,473**	**131,877**	**3.1**	**1.6**	**2.4**	**-7,043**	**-1,103**	**-8,146**	**-0.3**	**0.0**	**-0.1**
E06000036	**Bracknell Forest**	971	585	1,556	2.5	1.5	2.0	-124	30	-94	-0.3	0.1	-0.1
E06000043	**Brighton and Hove**	3,974	2,083	6,057	4.1	2.2	3.1	-344	-130	-474	-0.4	-0.1	-0.2
E06000046	**Isle of Wight**	2,475	1,226	3,701	6.0	2.9	4.5	2	27	29	0.0	0.1	0.0
E06000035	**Medway**	4,350	2,305	6,655	5.0	2.7	3.8	-391	-101	-492	-0.4	-0.1	-0.3
E06000042	**Milton Keynes**	3,202	1,907	5,109	3.9	2.3	3.1	-798	-251	-1,049	-1.0	-0.3	-0.6
E06000044	**Portsmouth**	3,361	1,665	5,026	4.6	2.5	3.6	-193	23	-170	-0.3	0.0	-0.1
E06000038	**Reading**	2,345	1,241	3,586	4.3	2.4	3.3	-94	37	-57	-0.2	0.1	-0.1
E06000039	**Slough**	2,080	1,276	3,356	4.4	2.7	3.6	-78	105	27	-0.2	0.2	0.0
E06000045	**Southampton**	3,589	1,687	5,276	4.3	2.1	3.2	-454	1	-453	-0.5	0.0	-0.3
E06000037	**West Berkshire**	1,046	574	1,620	2.1	1.2	1.6	-104	37	-67	-0.2	0.1	-0.1
E06000040	**Windsor and Maidenhead**	1,108	595	1,703	2.4	1.3	1.8	-91	-10	-101	-0.2	0.0	-0.1
E06000041	**Wokingham**	839	467	1,306	1.7	0.9	1.3	-128	0	-128	-0.3	0.0	-0.1
E10000002	**Buckinghamshire**	3,849	2,159	6,008	2.4	1.3	1.9	-93	84	-9	-0.1	0.1	0.0
E07000004	Aylesbury Vale	1,253	694	1,947	2.2	1.2	1.7	-52	-2	-54	-0.1	0.0	0.0
E07000005	Chiltern	566	339	905	2.1	1.2	1.6	-34	31	-3	-0.1	0.1	0.0
E07000006	South Bucks	379	242	621	1.9	1.2	1.5	-15	27	12	-0.1	0.1	0.0
E07000007	Wycombe	1,651	884	2,535	3.0	1.6	2.3	8	28	36	0.0	0.1	0.0
E10000011	**East Sussex**	6,333	3,125	9,458	4.1	1.9	3.0	-335	46	-289	-0.2	0.0	-0.1
E07000061	Eastbourne	1,452	666	2,118	4.9	2.2	3.5	-80	-23	-103	-0.3	-0.1	-0.2
E07000062	Hastings	2,258	1,003	3,261	7.9	3.4	5.6	-118	24	-94	-0.4	0.1	-0.2
E07000063	Lewes	865	479	1,344	3.0	1.6	2.3	-73	-8	-81	-0.3	0.0	-0.1
E07000064	Rother	930	530	1,460	3.8	2.0	2.9	-21	26	5	-0.1	0.1	0.0
E07000065	Wealden	828	447	1,275	1.9	1.0	1.4	-43	27	-16	-0.1	0.1	0.0
E10000014	**Hampshire**	10,293	5,316	15,609	2.5	1.3	1.9	-596	-258	-854	-0.1	-0.1	-0.1
E07000084	Basingstoke and Deane	1,352	742	2,094	2.5	1.3	1.9	-23	-78	-101	0.0	-0.1	-0.1
E07000085	East Hampshire	671	372	1,043	1.9	1.0	1.4	24	-8	16	0.1	0.0	0.0
E07000086	Eastleigh	904	489	1,393	2.3	1.2	1.7	-190	-75	-265	-0.5	-0.2	-0.3
E07000087	Fareham	743	377	1,120	2.2	1.1	1.6	-53	5	-48	-0.2	0.0	-0.1
E07000088	Gosport	1,033	509	1,542	4.0	1.9	2.9	-86	10	-76	-0.3	0.0	-0.1
E07000089	Hart	408	238	646	1.4	0.8	1.1	-53	-5	-58	-0.2	0.0	-0.1
E07000090	Havant	1,641	765	2,406	4.6	2.1	3.3	-73	-31	-104	-0.2	-0.1	-0.1
E07000091	New Forest	1,243	622	1,865	2.5	1.2	1.8	-19	2	-17	0.0	0.0	0.0
E07000092	Rushmoor	975	528	1,503	3.0	1.7	2.4	-87	-35	-122	-0.3	-0.1	-0.2
E07000093	Test Valley	723	368	1,091	2.0	1.0	1.5	-26	-59	-85	-0.1	-0.2	-0.1
E07000094	Winchester	600	306	906	1.7	0.8	1.2	-10	16	6	0.0	0.0	0.0
E10000016	**Kent**	18,329	9,418	27,747	4.0	2.0	3.0	-1,235	-86	-1,321	-0.3	0.0	-0.1
E07000105	Ashford	1,243	658	1,901	3.5	1.7	2.6	-34	1	-33	-0.1	0.0	0.0
E07000106	Canterbury	1,577	694	2,271	3.3	1.4	2.3	-86	-94	-180	-0.2	-0.2	-0.2
E07000107	Dartford	1,064	642	1,706	3.4	2.0	2.7	-109	-62	-171	-0.3	-0.2	-0.3
E07000108	Dover	1,733	892	2,625	5.1	2.6	3.8	-61	85	24	-0.2	0.2	0.0
E07000109	Gravesham	1,569	860	2,429	4.9	2.6	3.8	-213	-87	-300	-0.7	-0.3	-0.5
E07000110	Maidstone	1,531	816	2,347	3.1	1.6	2.4	-120	-51	-171	-0.2	-0.1	-0.2
E07000111	Sevenoaks	743	437	1,180	2.1	1.2	1.7	-95	-30	-125	-0.3	-0.1	-0.2
E07000112	Shepway	1,814	916	2,730	5.5	2.8	4.1	-157	79	-78	-0.5	0.2	-0.1
E07000113	Swale	2,248	1,107	3,355	5.2	2.6	3.9	-51	-28	-79	-0.1	-0.1	-0.1
E07000114	Thanet	3,245	1,570	4,815	8.3	3.8	6.0	-80	128	48	-0.2	0.3	0.1
E07000115	Tonbridge and Malling	940	494	1,434	2.5	1.3	1.9	-78	4	-74	-0.2	0.0	-0.1
E07000116	Tunbridge Wells	622	332	954	1.7	0.9	1.3	-151	-31	-182	-0.4	-0.1	-0.3
E10000025	**Oxfordshire**	4,323	2,239	6,562	2.0	1.1	1.5	-791	-258	-1,049	-0.4	-0.1	-0.2
E07000177	Cherwell	849	465	1,314	1.8	1.0	1.4	-163	-82	-245	-0.4	-0.2	-0.3
E07000178	Oxford	1,624	757	2,381	3.0	1.4	2.2	-250	-100	-350	-0.5	-0.2	-0.3

4.10 Claimant count[1] by Unitary and Local Authority

not seasonally adjusted

		CLAIMANT COUNT ON 13th DECEMBER 2012						Change on year					
		Levels			Percentage of Pop[2]			Levels			Percentage[2]		
		Men	Women	People	Men	Women	People	Men	Women	People	Men	Women	People
		1	2	3	4	5	6	7	8	9	10	11	12
E07000179	South Oxfordshire	635	387	1,022	1.5	0.9	1.2	-157	-31	-188	-0.4	-0.1	-0.2
E07000180	Vale of White Horse	636	330	966	1.6	0.9	1.3	-171	-49	-220	-0.4	-0.1	-0.3
E07000181	West Oxfordshire	579	300	879	1.7	0.9	1.3	-50	4	-46	-0.2	0.0	-0.1
E10000030	**Surrey**	7,136	4,006	11,142	2.0	1.1	1.5	-567	-243	-810	-0.2	-0.1	-0.1
E07000207	Elmbridge	704	371	1,075	1.8	0.9	1.3	-67	-10	-77	-0.2	0.0	-0.1
E07000208	Epsom and Ewell	480	291	771	2.1	1.2	1.6	-3	-15	-18	0.0	-0.1	0.0
E07000209	Guildford	918	516	1,434	2.0	1.1	1.6	-76	-16	-92	-0.2	0.0	-0.1
E07000210	Mole Valley	442	238	680	1.7	0.9	1.3	-11	-9	-20	0.0	0.0	0.0
E07000211	Reigate and Banstead	972	569	1,541	2.2	1.3	1.7	-51	-18	-69	-0.1	0.0	-0.1
E07000212	Runnymede	494	283	777	1.9	1.1	1.5	-59	-17	-76	-0.2	-0.1	-0.1
E07000213	Spelthorne	730	430	1,160	2.4	1.4	1.9	-109	-76	-185	-0.4	-0.2	-0.3
E07000214	Surrey Heath	562	302	864	2.0	1.1	1.6	-38	-41	-79	-0.1	-0.1	-0.1
E07000215	Tandridge	531	340	871	2.1	1.3	1.7	-34	14	-20	-0.1	0.1	0.0
E07000216	Waverley	624	340	964	1.7	0.9	1.3	-66	-21	-87	-0.2	-0.1	-0.1
E07000217	Woking	679	326	1,005	2.1	1.0	1.6	-53	-34	-87	-0.2	-0.1	-0.1
E10000032	**West Sussex**	6,801	3,599	10,400	2.8	1.4	2.1	-629	-156	-785	-0.3	-0.1	-0.2
E07000223	Adur	607	346	953	3.3	1.8	2.6	-56	-1	-57	-0.3	0.0	-0.2
E07000224	Arun	1,485	735	2,220	3.5	1.6	2.6	-116	-63	-179	-0.3	-0.1	-0.2
E07000225	Chichester	910	508	1,418	2.8	1.5	2.1	-7	13	6	0.0	0.0	0.0
E07000226	Crawley	1,146	731	1,877	3.2	2.0	2.6	-209	-22	-231	-0.6	-0.1	-0.3
E07000227	Horsham	817	379	1,196	2.1	0.9	1.5	-85	-79	-164	-0.2	-0.2	-0.2
E07000228	Mid Sussex	609	334	943	1.4	0.8	1.1	-132	-9	-141	-0.3	0.0	-0.2
E07000229	Worthing	1,227	566	1,793	3.9	1.7	2.8	-24	5	-19	-0.1	0.0	0.0
E12000009	**SOUTH WEST**	**56,068**	**28,438**	**84,506**	**3.4**	**1.7**	**2.5**	**-4,549**	**-288**	**-4,837**	**-0.3**	**0.0**	**-0.1**
E06000022	**Bath and North East Somerset**	1,520	701	2,221	2.7	1.2	1.9	-57	-15	-72	-0.1	0.0	-0.1
E06000028	**Bournemouth**	2,507	1,135	3,642	4.0	1.9	3.0	-53	-27	-80	-0.1	0.0	-0.1
E06000023	**Bristol, City of**	7,845	3,974	11,819	5.3	2.8	4.0	-665	144	-521	-0.4	0.1	-0.2
E06000052	**Cornwall**	6,585	3,370	9,955	4.1	2.0	3.0	-270	5	-265	-0.2	0.0	-0.1
E06000053	**Isles of Scilly**	7	6	13	1.0	0.9	1.0	6	1	7	0.9	0.1	0.5
E06000024	**North Somerset**	2,183	1,100	3,283	3.6	1.8	2.7	66	62	128	0.1	0.1	0.1
E06000026	**Plymouth**	3,965	1,822	5,787	4.6	2.2	3.4	-494	-115	-609	-0.6	-0.1	-0.4
E06000029	**Poole**	1,102	589	1,691	2.4	1.3	1.8	-156	-36	-192	-0.3	-0.1	-0.2
E06000025	**South Gloucestershire**	2,173	1,259	3,432	2.6	1.5	2.0	-178	62	-116	-0.2	0.1	-0.1
E06000030	**Swindon**	2,389	1,472	3,861	3.4	2.1	2.8	-758	-97	-855	-1.1	-0.1	-0.6
E06000027	**Torbay**	2,279	1,093	3,372	6.0	2.7	4.3	-268	22	-246	-0.7	0.1	-0.3
E06000054	**Wiltshire**	3,630	1,964	5,594	2.4	1.3	1.9	-294	-10	-304	-0.2	0.0	-0.1
E10000008	**Devon**	6,211	3,062	9,273	2.8	1.3	2.0	-639	-282	-921	-0.3	-0.1	-0.2
E07000040	East Devon	785	402	1,187	2.1	1.0	1.6	-180	-84	-264	-0.5	-0.2	-0.4
E07000041	Exeter	1,270	601	1,871	3.2	1.5	2.3	-266	-49	-315	-0.7	-0.1	-0.4
E07000042	Mid Devon	609	278	887	2.6	1.2	1.9	1	-27	-26	0.0	-0.1	-0.1
E07000043	North Devon	920	421	1,341	3.3	1.5	2.4	-32	-32	-64	-0.1	-0.1	-0.1
E07000044	South Hams	475	274	749	1.9	1.1	1.5	-58	-41	-99	-0.2	-0.2	-0.2
E07000045	Teignbridge	986	520	1,506	2.7	1.4	2.0	-74	-33	-107	-0.2	-0.1	-0.1
E07000046	Torridge	788	360	1,148	4.2	1.8	3.0	5	4	9	0.0	0.0	0.0
E07000047	West Devon	378	206	584	2.4	1.3	1.8	-35	-20	-55	-0.2	-0.1	-0.2
E10000009	**Dorset**	2,618	1,374	3,992	2.2	1.1	1.7	-276	-4	-280	-0.2	0.0	-0.1
E07000048	Christchurch	311	147	458	2.4	1.1	1.7	-39	12	-27	-0.3	0.1	-0.1
E07000049	East Dorset	421	218	639	1.8	0.9	1.3	14	-20	-6	0.1	-0.1	0.0
E07000050	North Dorset	311	188	499	1.5	0.9	1.2	-64	9	-55	-0.3	0.0	-0.1
E07000051	Purbeck	264	159	423	2.0	1.2	1.6	-13	-7	-20	-0.1	-0.1	-0.1
E07000052	West Dorset	469	268	737	1.7	0.9	1.3	-70	4	-66	-0.3	0.0	-0.1
E07000053	Weymouth and Portland	842	394	1,236	4.1	2.0	3.0	-104	-2	-106	-0.5	0.0	-0.3
E10000013	**Gloucestershire**	6,530	3,301	9,831	3.5	1.7	2.6	-17	131	114	0.0	0.1	0.0
E07000078	Cheltenham	1,586	734	2,320	4.1	1.9	3.0	25	24	49	0.1	0.1	0.1
E07000079	Cotswold	471	221	692	1.9	0.9	1.4	11	-47	-36	0.0	-0.2	-0.1
E07000080	Forest of Dean	850	443	1,293	3.3	1.7	2.5	-58	9	-49	-0.2	0.0	-0.1
E07000081	Gloucester	2,009	1,046	3,055	5.1	2.6	3.8	28	104	132	0.1	0.3	0.2
E07000082	Stroud	971	477	1,448	2.8	1.4	2.1	64	25	89	0.2	0.1	0.1
E07000083	Tewkesbury	643	380	1,023	2.6	1.5	2.0	-87	16	-71	-0.3	0.1	-0.1
E10000027	**Somerset**	4,524	2,216	6,740	2.8	1.4	2.1	-496	-129	-625	-0.3	-0.1	-0.2
E07000187	Mendip	776	405	1,181	2.3	1.2	1.7	-246	-66	-312	-0.7	-0.2	-0.5
E07000188	Sedgemoor	1,264	686	1,950	3.6	1.9	2.8	-167	-43	-210	-0.5	-0.1	-0.3

4.10 Claimant count[1] by Unitary and Local Authority

not seasonally adjusted

		CLAIMANT COUNT ON 13th DECEMBER 2012						Change on year					
		Levels			Percentage of Pop[2]			Levels			Percentage[2]		
		Men	Women	People	Men	Women	People	Men	Women	People	Men	Women	People
		1	2	3	4	5	6	7	8	9	10	11	12
E07000189	South Somerset	1,115	507	1,622	2.3	1.0	1.7	-65	-29	-94	-0.1	-0.1	-0.1
E07000190	Taunton Deane	1,047	481	1,528	3.1	1.4	2.2	-17	20	3	-0.1	0.1	0.0
E07000191	West Somerset	322	137	459	3.4	1.4	2.3	-1	-11	-12	0.0	-0.1	-0.1
W92000004	**WALES**	**52,283**	**25,194**	**77,477**	**5.4**	**2.6**	**4.0**	**-1,257**	**2,022**	**765**	**-0.1**	**0.2**	**0.0**
W06000001	Isle of Anglesey	1,291	627	1,918	6.1	3.0	4.5	27	69	96	0.1	0.3	0.2
W06000002	Gwynedd	1,730	821	2,551	4.6	2.2	3.4	-60	109	49	-0.2	0.3	0.1
W06000003	Conwy	1,835	803	2,638	5.5	2.3	3.9	-72	66	-6	-0.2	0.2	0.0
W06000004	Denbighshire	1,618	785	2,403	5.7	2.7	4.2	-115	71	-44	-0.4	0.2	-0.1
W06000005	Flintshire	1,914	1,086	3,000	4.0	2.2	3.1	-171	8	-163	-0.4	0.0	-0.2
W06000006	Wrexham	2,285	1,089	3,374	5.3	2.5	3.9	-48	91	43	-0.1	0.2	0.0
W06000023	Powys	1,306	637	1,943	3.3	1.6	2.4	-54	6	-48	-0.1	0.0	-0.1
W06000008	Ceredigion	675	279	954	2.8	1.2	2.0	-39	-33	-72	-0.2	-0.1	-0.1
W06000009	Pembrokeshire	1,811	765	2,576	5.0	2.0	3.5	21	-16	5	0.1	0.0	0.0
W06000010	Carmarthenshire	2,325	1,142	3,467	4.2	2.0	3.1	-85	95	10	-0.2	0.2	0.0
W06000011	Swansea	3,272	1,528	4,800	4.2	2.0	3.1	-96	102	6	-0.1	0.1	0.0
W06000012	Neath Port Talbot	1,977	1,008	2,985	4.5	2.3	3.4	10	74	84	0.0	0.2	0.1
W06000013	Bridgend	2,258	1,106	3,364	5.1	2.5	3.8	-178	59	-119	-0.4	0.1	-0.1
W06000014	The Vale of Glamorgan	1,842	796	2,638	4.7	2.0	3.3	-301	-35	-336	-0.8	-0.1	-0.4
W06000015	Cardiff	7,108	3,181	10,289	6.0	2.7	4.3	-324	308	-16	-0.3	0.3	0.0
W06000016	Rhondda Cynon Taf	4,784	2,351	7,135	6.5	3.1	4.8	-140	183	43	-0.2	0.2	0.0
W06000024	Merthyr Tydfil	1,538	767	2,305	8.2	4.0	6.1	-112	61	-51	-0.6	0.3	-0.1
W06000018	Caerphilly	3,978	2,117	6,095	7.1	3.7	5.3	15	293	308	0.0	0.5	0.3
W06000019	Blaenau Gwent	2,253	1,151	3,404	10.1	5.1	7.6	68	73	141	0.3	0.3	0.3
W06000020	Torfaen	2,036	981	3,017	7.2	3.4	5.2	79	136	215	0.3	0.5	0.4
W06000021	Monmouthshire	930	470	1,400	3.3	1.7	2.5	135	65	200	0.5	0.2	0.4
W06000022	Newport	3,517	1,704	5,221	7.7	3.6	5.6	183	237	420	0.4	0.5	0.5
S92000003	**SCOTLAND**	**91,904**	**41,599**	**133,503**	**5.4**	**2.4**	**3.9**	**-5,748**	**117**	**-5,631**	**-0.3**	**0.0**	**-0.2**
S12000033	Aberdeen City	2,044	947	2,991	2.6	1.3	2.0	-335	-68	-403	-0.4	-0.1	-0.3
S12000034	Aberdeenshire	1,245	629	1,874	1.6	0.8	1.2	-246	-106	-352	-0.3	-0.1	-0.2
S12000041	Angus	1,435	638	2,073	4.3	1.8	3.0	-118	-64	-182	-0.4	-0.2	-0.3
S12000035	Argyll & Bute	1,247	581	1,828	4.4	2.1	3.3	-136	-32	-168	-0.5	-0.1	-0.3
S12000005	Clackmannanshire	1,122	579	1,701	6.8	3.5	5.1	-138	15	-123	-0.8	0.1	-0.4
S12000006	Dumfries & Galloway	2,238	1,116	3,354	5.1	2.4	3.7	84	43	127	0.2	0.1	0.1
S12000042	Dundee City	3,860	1,434	5,294	8.3	2.9	5.5	-6	-14	-20	0.0	0.0	0.0
S12000008	East Ayrshire	3,143	1,403	4,546	8.3	3.5	5.8	-98	-3	-101	-0.3	0.0	-0.1
S12000009	East Dunbartonshire	1,084	471	1,555	3.4	1.4	2.4	-188	-38	-226	-0.6	-0.1	-0.3
S12000010	East Lothian	1,273	659	1,932	4.3	2.1	3.1	-141	16	-125	-0.5	0.1	-0.2
S12000011	East Renfrewshire	838	397	1,235	3.1	1.4	2.2	-86	-13	-99	-0.3	0.0	-0.2
S12000036	Edinburgh, City of	7,267	3,296	10,563	4.2	1.8	3.0	-500	-54	-554	-0.3	0.0	-0.2
S12000013	Na h-Eileanan an Iar	334	127	461	4.1	1.6	2.9	-37	-33	-70	-0.5	-0.4	-0.4
S12000014	Falkirk	2,950	1,384	4,334	6.0	2.7	4.3	-132	106	-26	-0.3	0.2	0.0
S12000015	Fife	6,468	3,069	9,537	5.6	2.5	4.0	-715	-10	-725	-0.6	0.0	-0.3
S12000043	Glasgow City	15,993	6,927	22,920	7.7	3.3	5.5	-779	-59	-838	-0.4	0.0	-0.2
S12000017	Highland	2,761	1,352	4,113	3.9	1.9	2.9	-78	79	1	-0.1	0.1	0.0
S12000018	Inverclyde	1,536	734	2,270	6.2	2.8	4.5	-243	8	-235	-1.0	0.0	-0.5
S12000019	Midlothian	1,404	650	2,054	5.6	2.4	3.9	-40	68	28	-0.2	0.2	0.1
S12000020	Moray	846	428	1,274	3.0	1.6	2.3	-139	-12	-151	-0.5	0.0	-0.3
S12000021	North Ayrshire	3,813	1,800	5,613	9.3	4.0	6.6	96	149	245	0.2	0.3	0.3
S12000044	North Lanarkshire	7,725	3,491	11,216	7.4	3.2	5.3	-506	30	-476	-0.5	0.0	-0.2
S12000023	Orkney Islands	112	64	176	1.8	1.0	1.4	-51	-33	-84	-0.8	-0.5	-0.7
S12000024	Perth & Kinross	1,394	598	1,992	2.9	1.3	2.1	-177	-58	-235	-0.4	-0.1	-0.2
S12000038	Renfrewshire	3,594	1,498	5,092	6.6	2.6	4.6	-219	0	-219	-0.4	0.0	-0.2
S12000026	Scottish Borders	1,366	618	1,984	4.0	1.7	2.8	-73	21	-52	-0.2	0.1	-0.1
S12000027	Shetland Islands	151	64	215	2.0	0.9	1.5	32	-3	29	0.4	0.0	0.2
S12000028	South Ayrshire	2,110	961	3,071	6.2	2.7	4.4	-66	69	3	-0.2	0.2	0.0
S12000029	South Lanarkshire	6,026	2,741	8,767	6.1	2.6	4.3	-277	68	-209	-0.3	0.1	-0.1
S12000030	Stirling	1,281	585	1,866	4.5	1.9	3.2	-90	8	-82	-0.3	0.0	-0.1
S12000039	West Dunbartonshire	2,548	1,043	3,591	8.9	3.4	6.1	-75	-29	-104	-0.3	-0.1	-0.2
S12000040	West Lothian	2,696	1,315	4,011	4.8	2.3	3.5	-271	66	-205	-0.5	0.1	-0.2

Relationship between columns = 3=1+2; 9=7+8

Source: Jobcentre Plus administrative system

1. Count of claimants of Jobseeker's Allowance.

Labour market statistics enquiries: labour.market@ons.gov.uk

2. Percentages of population aged from 16 to 64. For England and Wales and their component areas are based on the 2011 Census. Estimates for Scotland and its component areas are based on mid-year 2011 population estimates. The estimate for the UK is based on a combination of these estimates plus mid-year 2011 population estimates for Northern Ireland consistent with the 2001 Census.

NB. These are different from the national and regional claimant count rates shown in Table HI05 - 7 and of other headline indicators. See Concepts and Definitions.

More detailed estimates and time series are available from Nomis at:

http://www.nomisweb.co.uk

Table 4.11a Weekly pay - Gross (£) - For all employee jobs[a] by Industry: United Kingdom, 2012

Description	Code	Number of jobs[b] (thousand)	Median	Annual % change	Mean	Annual % change	Percentiles 10	20	25	30	40	60	70	75	80	90
ALL EMPLOYEES		24,203	405.8	1.5	491.3	0.8	121.1	207.2	246.4	279.7	341.2	482.3	574.9	629.4	693.4	893.5
All Industries and Services		24,198	405.8	1.5	491.3	0.9	121.1	207.3	246.4	279.7	341.2	482.3	574.9	629.4	693.4	893.5
All Index of Production Industries		2,690	505.7	1.7	581.5	1.9	268.0	329.5	357.1	383.4	440.8	576.9	658.2	704.0	761.8	955.5
All Manufacturing		2,339	496.0	2.1	569.1	2.4	262.5	324.2	351.0	377.8	433.1	566.5	645.0	689.9	744.1	923.3
All Service Industries		20,548	385.7	1.3	476.6	0.7	109.8	187.1	227.2	260.0	322.5	461.7	557.8	613.0	679.3	881.6
AGRICULTURE, FORESTRY AND FISHING	A	127	330.1	-2.0	362.4	-1.0	111.9	191.4	227.2	257.0	295.7	379.8	430.8	465.2	499.3	609.9
Crop and animal production, hunting and related service activities	1	117	327.4	-2.0	355.0	-1.4	109.7	181.3	219.2	250.3	291.0	374.8	420.2	461.5	492.4	597.8
Forestry and logging	2	8	446.4	9.0	466.8	4.9	x	260.2	302.0	317.2	381.0	514.7	552.9	x	x	x
Fishing and aquaculture	3	x	330.3	-0.6	381.2	8.6	x	x	x	x	x	350.8	x	x	x	x
MINING AND QUARRYING	B	43	718.4	-3.3	837.0	-5.5	377.9	461.0	508.2	549.4	633.7	809.9	924.4	998.2	1,105.2	x
Mining of coal and lignite	5	7	827.2	2.7	837.9	-0.7	x	592.9	663.9	721.4	753.0	889.6	921.9	x	x	x
Extraction of crude petroleum and natural gas	6	10	1,106.5	3.3	1,271.4	1.1	627.0	743.2	766.7	798.5	1,001.9	1,226.7	x	x	x	x
Mining of metal ores	7	..														
Other mining and quarrying	8	14	487.8	-11.4	547.3	-12.2	327.1	380.7	399.9	411.6	451.6	538.3	609.5	670.2	688.1	x
Mining support service activities	9	13	719.6	-9.6	827.2	-11.1	x	480.6	537.8	557.4	653.1	820.0	906.8	x	x	x
MANUFACTURING	C	2,339	496.0	2.1	569.1	2.4	262.5	324.2	351.0	377.8	433.1	566.5	645.0	689.9	744.1	923.3
Manufacture of food products	10	331	382.7	-0.7	466.2	-2.5	228.0	267.5	284.3	304.8	339.6	438.7	512.6	553.6	602.3	752.7
Manufacture of beverages	11	39	560.6	-0.9	632.1	-0.1	337.3	424.7	450.2	475.0	514.2	635.2	706.6	765.4	803.9	x
Manufacture of tobacco products	12	5	800.7	9.0	821.4	2.4	x	681.1	705.6	728.9	782.2	826.2	851.3	x	x	x
Manufacture of textiles	13	40	352.5	-4.2	420.3	-1.9	209.7	248.0	267.5	280.4	314.8	387.3	445.1	466.1	528.4	x
Manufacture of wearing apparel	14	18	270.9	-6.5	340.8	-4.1	119.9	149.0	177.1	212.7	242.8	322.2	397.2	459.5	x	x
Manufacture of leather and related products	15	9	332.8	-9.3	404.1	-11.2	x	235.9	258.6	279.8	296.8	419.6	496.4	x	x	x
Manufacture of wood and of products of wood and cork, except furniture; manufacture of articles of straw and plaiting materials	16	52	402.7	3.2	444.4	2.4	243.2	290.0	310.3	320.3	350.9	434.8	498.0	537.1	567.0	x
Manufacture of paper and paper products	17	59	491.0	0.7	556.2	0.7	270.1	341.1	364.9	393.0	437.7	555.6	616.5	651.1	689.1	x
Printing and reproduction of recorded media	18	96	448.3	-2.5	502.6	-1.8	212.7	297.5	323.5	348.4	398.4	499.7	571.7	603.3	646.8	x
Manufacture of coke and refined petroleum products	19	10	878.9		987.9	51.7	362.7	546.0	603.8	646.4	797.8	950.7	x	x	x	x
Manufacture of chemicals and chemical products	20	97	555.7	1.0	623.4	1.7	274.0	351.0	378.5	420.9	482.0	611.6	694.7	749.2	804.1	1,047.6
Manufacture of basic pharmaceutical products and pharmaceutical preparations	21	63	653.1	6.2	768.9	5.5	363.4	438.2	471.4	504.1	594.1	742.6	845.7	921.8	1,000.5	x
Manufacture of rubber and plastic products	22	152	411.6	-0.1	489.2	-0.3	258.0	300.0	317.2	337.8	372.9	469.2	536.6	574.9	619.2	746.8
Manufacture of other non-metallic mineral products	23	78	486.7	1.3	559.1	5.4	268.1	321.2	351.9	379.5	425.7	548.8	630.1	657.4	689.9	789.8
Manufacture of basic metals	24	85	607.2	7.1	641.6	8.6	350.8	425.9	456.4	486.8	561.9	654.7	731.7	787.0	822.6	965.1
Manufacture of fabricated metal products, except machinery and equipment	25	261	468.3	-0.6	522.1	1.1	265.2	325.2	353.2	373.9	416.1	526.0	592.3	633.6	677.5	810.4
Manufacture of computer, electronic and optical products	26	132	574.9	0.0	651.4	0.4	292.7	359.9	385.0	412.6	493.1	662.1	747.0	787.5	851.4	1,055.1
Manufacture of electrical equipment	27	99	450.3	1.7	523.2	-0.7	268.8	308.4	335.5	352.0	402.4	519.7	594.5	633.7	688.1	851.8
Manufacture of machinery and equipment n.e.c.	28	207	548.5	4.1	617.2	4.2	318.4	376.7	400.0	431.2	489.4	611.1	689.9	728.7	775.5	953.5
Manufacture of motor vehicles, trailers and semi-trailers	29	151	567.1	-1.2	638.6	1.0	320.1	389.8	423.1	456.3	521.4	645.3	733.6	776.7	850.5	1,014.2
Manufacture of other transport equipment	30	160	663.2	4.5	744.2	8.1	404.2	491.2	518.8	553.3	613.4	713.6	783.7	825.8	881.8	1,067.2
Manufacture of furniture	31	55	396.1	1.3	454.9	1.2	239.7	277.9	300.1	320.0	359.5	438.6	497.6	526.3	598.1	x
Other manufacturing	32	64	430.0	6.9	498.5	5.0	236.9	292.5	309.2	336.7	386.4	480.8	552.0	611.2	663.1	x
Repair and installation of machinery and equipment	33	78	590.1	-0.4	681.4	4.4	308.9	381.7	417.7	452.5	504.8	663.5	774.6	839.6	913.0	x
ELECTRICITY, GAS, STEAM AND AIR CONDITIONING SUPPLY	D	171	610.6	4.2	692.7	0.4	315.9	371.8	414.9	462.4	558.0	693.6	819.4	871.5	941.0	1,156.9
Electricity, gas, steam and air conditioning supply	35	171	610.6	4.2	692.7	0.4	315.9	371.8	414.9	462.4	558.0	693.6	819.4	871.5	941.0	1,156.9
WATER SUPPLY; SEWERAGE, WASTE MANAGEMENT AND REMEDIATION ACTIVITIES	E	137	509.8	4.0	573.4	3.1	287.5	351.8	375.7	401.2	450.1	569.6	643.7	676.8	727.1	880.0
Water collection, treatment and supply	36	39	552.3	-1.2	596.0	-4.2	323.1	396.8	435.2	453.5	502.9	616.4	667.4	706.8	730.3	x
Sewerage	37	12	507.5	13.2	529.3	3.1	268.3	333.2	352.0	382.0	440.9	540.1	595.4	629.3	x	x
Waste collection, treatment and disposal activities; materials recovery	38	83	485.0	5.0	566.6	5.4	282.9	334.2	364.2	383.0	430.7	548.8	632.7	672.8	731.6	x
Remediation activities and other waste management services	39	x	477.2	38.0	657.4	76.4	x	x	x	x	428.2	x	x	x	x	x

Table 4.11a Weekly pay - Gross (£) - For all employee jobs[a] by Industry: United Kingdom, 2012

Description	Code	Number of jobs[b] (thousand)	Median	Annual % change	Mean	Annual % change	Percentiles 10	20	25	30	40	60	70	75	80	90
CONSTRUCTION	F	833	505.8	0.4	582.5	1.3	230.5	338.9	369.3	400.0	453.0	574.9	657.2	704.6	767.0	972.0
Construction of buildings	41	260	545.5	5.0	647.8	3.4	251.4	345.0	385.4	416.5	479.1	621.8	725.1	793.0	881.6	1,138.0
Civil engineering	42	155	524.4	-2.9	619.7	-0.8	287.5	370.5	400.0	420.0	470.0	598.7	695.0	744.7	805.2	1,001.9
Specialised construction activities	43	418	486.0	-0.3	528.0	-0.1	208.0	319.6	350.9	378.3	432.7	538.1	600.0	650.0	699.4	855.8
WHOLESALE AND RETAIL TRADE; REPAIR OF MOTOR VEHICLES AND MOTORCYCLES	G	3,625	297.1	2.4	370.9	0.9	94.6	136.6	161.6	191.6	251.1	346.7	415.5	460.0	513.3	700.2
Wholesale and retail trade and repair of motor vehicles and motorcycles	45	408	385.0	-0.8	441.8	0.0	191.5	265.6	285.0	301.8	345.0	433.2	486.9	518.0	562.6	716.9
Wholesale trade, except of motor vehicles and motorcycles	46	947	431.5	1.9	538.8	-0.6	230.0	291.8	315.2	336.4	378.4	491.2	574.9	632.4	702.5	954.2
Retail trade, except of motor vehicles and motorcycles	47	2,270	227.2	0.8	288.1	1.9	76.7	109.4	124.6	139.8	179.2	269.1	318.2	349.4	392.3	557.4
TRANSPORTATION AND STORAGE	H	1,051	486.9	3.7	549.1	3.8	273.2	341.1	369.3	393.7	435.7	540.0	607.2	649.2	705.9	884.6
Land transport and transport via pipelines	49	445	496.2	3.6	528.5	3.3	266.2	347.8	375.5	400.3	444.6	545.8	603.8	637.0	688.8	834.3
Water transport	50	11	505.3	9.6	588.1	10.0	x	319.2	345.0	393.5	450.3	557.4	x	x	x	x
Air transport	51	74	557.6	-7.3	710.5	-1.1	284.6	355.5	406.2	433.7	485.5	677.3	761.7	817.5	935.0	x
Warehousing and support activities for transportation	52	307	516.3	5.4	599.1	4.2	288.0	341.8	369.4	394.0	453.7	581.2	665.6	714.9	790.0	1,018.1
Postal and courier activities	53	214	428.7	5.0	462.4	4.9	250.8	325.5	348.6	379.9	398.7	465.5	510.0	537.9	576.2	679.4
ACCOMMODATION AND FOOD SERVICE ACTIVITIES	I	1,211	202.0	2.1	240.1	0.9	54.2	91.2	103.7	120.6	154.4	245.7	287.5	312.3	344.4	443.0
Accommodation	55	280	253.4	2.3	286.6	-1.1	70.1	119.6	145.1	172.5	222.2	282.8	318.4	343.9	373.5	480.7
Food and beverage service activities	56	931	182.4	0.3	226.1	1.6	51.8	85.0	97.4	110.8	142.7	227.4	273.6	300.6	331.2	429.0
INFORMATION AND COMMUNICATION	J	939	632.5	3.1	731.1	1.7	268.6	376.5	421.6	468.4	551.5	719.6	837.5	907.8	986.7	1,289.1
Publishing activities	58	152	494.1	1.5	589.3	-0.8	x	287.5	328.7	361.1	421.6	580.6	658.5	716.7	804.9	1,015.4
Motion picture, video and television programme production, sound recording and music publishing activities	59	53	480.3	-16.5	633.8	-6.3	102.2	209.8	291.8	330.8	403.2	540.5	672.4	747.4	846.0	x
Programming and broadcasting activities	60	40	670.3	-10.3	791.0	-13.7	379.3	460.8	502.7	547.4	613.8	742.8	813.5	855.4	925.5	x
Telecommunications	61	210	657.6	9.6	737.6	6.5	325.2	450.4	491.5	530.8	594.1	720.2	817.2	879.5	956.9	1,201.8
Computer programming, consultancy and related activities	62	422	674.6	-1.0	775.7	0.4	284.2	397.7	449.9	493.1	576.0	775.6	908.1	972.6	1,077.4	1,392.2
Information service activities	63	63	694.6	1.6	795.8	2.5	325.3	396.6	453.5	506.7	597.0	818.0	917.5	981.6	1,056.3	x
FINANCIAL AND INSURANCE ACTIVITIES	K	1,060	574.9	-0.9	803.1	-3.6	268.1	332.6	359.9	393.5	474.5	700.0	864.0	976.1	1,119.1	1,595.4
Financial service activities, except insurance and pension funding	64	564	571.2	0.0	807.0	-3.7	261.7	325.1	353.3	386.3	464.4	711.3	890.9	996.6	1,138.5	1,603.5
Insurance, reinsurance and pension funding, except compulsory social security	65	142	544.7	1.0	749.7	2.8	284.7	343.3	363.6	397.2	466.1	657.2	785.8	881.6	1,015.9	1,448.5
Activities auxiliary to financial services and insurance activities	66	354	589.0	-4.4	818.3	-5.5	268.3	342.4	371.8	406.6	486.5	708.8	862.5	971.7	1,130.6	1,629.0
REAL ESTATE ACTIVITIES	L	295	422.1	1.9	492.3	1.5	147.5	252.9	294.0	322.5	373.9	479.6	550.2	588.3	636.9	835.9
Real estate activities	68	295	422.1	1.9	492.3	1.5	147.5	252.9	294.0	322.5	373.9	479.6	550.2	588.3	636.9	835.9
PROFESSIONAL, SCIENTIFIC AND TECHNICAL ACTIVITIES	M	1,483	548.1	0.6	671.0	-1.5	199.2	306.6	346.1	384.6	466.5	632.4	747.4	815.7	900.8	1,230.3
Legal and accounting activities	69	477	517.5	5.8	656.6	2.9	202.1	290.4	325.7	356.4	427.7	613.3	728.3	795.8	878.3	1,284.1
Activities of head offices; management consultancy activities	70	278	554.3	-8.1	719.2	-12.2	163.4	280.9	333.4	372.2	451.4	636.5	776.1	862.4	973.1	1,423.8
Architectural and engineering activities; technical testing and analysis	71	367	584.7	-0.3	678.7	0.4	268.3	368.9	407.8	445.5	517.8	666.1	772.5	838.9	918.3	1,154.1
Scientific research and development	72	122	674.3	2.4	828.4	1.4	383.3	476.2	514.0	538.4	611.6	761.5	871.1	934.2	1,012.7	x
Advertising and market research	73	110	482.9	-1.2	632.2	-2.2	116.4	270.6	325.8	364.1	421.8	574.9	697.3	766.6	831.8	x
Other professional, scientific and technical activities	74	83	449.6	2.0	515.7	-0.4	115.9	183.3	230.0	280.2	363.4	518.7	623.0	697.7	766.5	x
Veterinary activities	75	48	368.7	5.9	435.1	0.6	130.3	218.2	237.5	262.4	303.4	440.8	535.8	592.6	656.8	x
ADMINISTRATIVE AND SUPPORT SERVICE ACTIVITIES	N	1,395	311.1	2.7	374.4	0.6	81.5	138.3	173.9	211.3	264.3	364.1	431.7	479.1	527.0	693.6
Rental and leasing activities	77	116	415.1	2.7	469.1	1.0	166.0	288.8	313.0	332.1	366.3	474.4	529.0	569.2	622.5	811.2
Employment activities	78	487	291.2	5.5	357.6	2.1	105.0	170.0	200.0	225.8	255.4	338.3	394.7	434.2	482.8	632.5
Travel agency, tour operator and other reservation service and related activities	79	75	364.4	1.4	476.2	2.7	167.1	239.6	261.7	281.3	325.8	419.6	498.3	553.2	614.4	x
Security and investigation activities	80	95	383.4	2.3	406.7	0.7	125.3	242.7	280.1	300.3	346.6	434.0	482.1	508.8	538.8	640.5

Table 4.11a Weekly pay - Gross (£) - For all employee jobs[a] by Industry: United Kingdom, 2012

Description	Code	Number of jobs[b] (thousand)	Median	Annual % change	Mean	Annual % change	Percentiles 10	20	25	30	40	60	70	75	80	90
Services to buildings and landscape activities	81	391	194.0	-4.5	271.2	-2.3	60.8	76.0	88.2	99.7	135.3	268.3	330.0	370.0	423.4	586.4
Office administrative, office support and other business support activities	82	232	383.3	2.5	490.0	1.7	138.0	232.4	260.0	280.1	329.0	453.4	530.2	586.6	670.8	925.6
PUBLIC ADMINISTRATION AND DEFENCE; COMPULSORY SOCIAL SECURITY	O	1,335	529.4	2.8	562.0	1.3	245.2	337.9	366.5	398.6	463.5	590.9	664.8	709.8	755.3	900.9
Public administration and defence; compulsory social security	84	1,335	529.4	2.8	562.0	1.3	245.2	337.9	366.5	398.6	463.5	590.9	664.8	709.8	755.3	900.9
EDUCATION	P	3,776	408.2	1.5	450.5	0.7	96.3	178.2	215.6	253.5	328.9	486.6	586.4	645.1	696.3	834.4
Education	85	3,776	408.2	1.5	450.5	0.7	96.3	178.2	215.6	253.5	328.9	486.6	586.4	645.1	696.3	834.4
HUMAN HEALTH AND SOCIAL WORK ACTIVITIES	Q	3,474	369.9	1.4	459.7	1.0	135.5	203.3	233.5	260.8	315.1	437.7	529.4	577.7	636.7	807.7
Human health activities	86	2,258	440.5	1.7	537.8	1.2	173.1	255.2	288.3	321.9	377.4	524.2	608.8	655.2	717.5	917.5
Residential care activities	87	607	266.1	1.8	309.6	2.6	109.4	157.3	178.1	199.9	234.9	302.9	347.0	376.2	418.5	546.7
Social work activities without accommodation	88	609	275.3	1.0	319.5	-1.1	87.0	141.0	164.0	187.1	236.3	324.3	391.0	425.9	473.7	591.2
ARTS, ENTERTAINMENT AND RECREATION	R	462	279.5	-0.6	363.6	3.4	39.4	96.9	126.7	155.6	219.9	332.5	398.7	441.4	494.9	670.8
Creative, arts and entertainment activities	90	41	439.7	2.6	483.6	-1.6	92.0	177.4	258.4	295.3	360.9	498.6	574.9	614.9	663.2	x
Libraries, archives, museums and other cultural activities	91	56	403.7	3.7	430.1	2.4	x	205.6	247.1	289.4	347.5	465.8	517.9	559.6	590.9	x
Gambling and betting activities	92	103	288.2	5.1	350.1	6.9	104.7	167.3	193.0	207.5	251.5	323.8	373.1	403.8	429.0	x
Sports activities and amusement and recreation activities	93	263	223.5	-5.7	336.1	4.7	26.2	55.4	78.4	104.5	155.4	285.0	348.6	382.5	435.9	624.9
OTHER SERVICE ACTIVITIES	S	389	325.2	-0.3	394.2	0.8	94.9	144.0	174.5	201.4	260.4	400.3	460.0	501.6	560.6	746.1
Activities of membership organisations	94	188	401.5	2.9	441.6	2.2	69.4	156.0	197.9	242.2	323.6	449.0	522.0	565.8	622.5	818.9
Repair of computers and personal and household goods	95	26	430.0	-0.3	532.0	2.1	237.5	287.5	303.9	343.7	395.4	505.1	568.6	580.4	659.7	x
Other personal service activities	96	175	249.3	-5.7	322.7	-1.2	97.3	125.5	145.9	168.0	208.2	300.0	371.8	405.8	453.8	607.1
ACTIVITIES OF HOUSEHOLDS AS EMPLOYERS; UNDIFFERENTIATED GOODS- AND SERVICES-PRODUCING ACTIVITIES OF HOUSEHOLDS FOR OWN USE	T	52	135.0	-1.6	190.5	5.3	28.0	48.4	62.5	71.2	102.0	182.7	234.9	279.9	318.1	x
Activities of households as employers of domestic personnel	97	52	135.0	-1.6	190.5	5.3	28.0	48.4	62.5	71.2	102.0	182.7	234.9	279.9	318.1	x
Undifferentiated goods- and services-producing activities of private households for own use	98	:														
ACTIVITIES OF EXTRATERRITORIAL ORGANISATIONS AND BODIES	U	x	586.9		562.3		x	x	x	x	x	x	x	x	x	x
Activities of extraterritorial organisations and bodies	99	x	586.9		562.3		x	x	x	x	x	x	x	x	x	x
NOT CLASSIFIED		5	x		x		x	x	x	x	137.1	x	x	x	x	x

a Employees on adult rates whose pay for the survey pay-period was not affected by absence.
b Figures for Number of Jobs are for indicative purposes only and should not be considered an accurate estimate of employee job counts.
KEY - The colour coding indicates the quality of each estimate; jobs, median, mean and percentiles but not the annual percentage change.
The quality of an estimate is measured by its coefficient of variation (CV), which is the ratio of the standard error of an estimate to the estimate.
Source: Annual Survey of Hours and Earnings, Office for National Statistics.

Key
CV <= 5%
CV > 5% and <= 10%
CV > 10% and <= 20%
x = unreliable CV > 20% or unavailable
.. = disclosive
: = not applicable
- = nil or negligible

Table 4.11b Hourly pay - Gross (£) - For all employee jobs[a] by Industry: United Kingdom, 2012

Description	Code	Number of jobs[b] (thousand)	Median	Annual % change	Mean	Annual % change	Percentiles 10	20	25	30	40	60	70	75	80	90
ALL EMPLOYEES		24,203	11.28	1.3	14.84	0.9	6.47	7.42	7.96	8.51	9.77	13.29	15.80	17.42	19.17	25.00
All Industries and Services		24,198	11.28	1.3	14.84	0.9	6.47	7.42	7.96	8.51	9.77	13.30	15.80	17.42	19.17	25.00
All Index of Production Industries		2,690	12.45	2.5	14.82	2.3	7.25	8.51	9.12	9.71	10.96	14.27	16.43	17.71	19.26	24.58
All Manufacturing		2,339	12.18	2.4	14.50	2.8	7.14	8.36	8.96	9.50	10.77	13.96	16.04	17.32	18.92	23.75
All Service Industries		20,548	11.10	1.7	14.88	0.6	6.38	7.25	7.76	8.31	9.57	13.15	15.75	17.44	19.23	25.14
AGRICULTURE, FORESTRY AND FISHING	A	127	8.38	-1.5	9.78	-0.4	6.25	6.77	7.00	7.24	7.76	9.17	10.24	10.89	11.98	14.45
Crop and animal production, hunting and related service activities	1	117	8.21	-1.6	9.53	-0.9	6.25	6.74	7.00	7.15	7.62	8.96	9.97	10.50	11.61	13.80
Forestry and logging	2	8	12.32	6.6	13.74	8.2	x	9.69	10.30	10.30	11.03	13.65	14.89	x	x	x
Fishing and aquaculture	3	x	8.58	7.6	10.24	7.2	x	x	x	x	x	x	x	x	x	x
MINING AND QUARRYING	B	43	17.28	-1.7	20.08	-2.2	9.15	10.61	11.30	11.96	14.36	20.00	23.58	25.43	28.63	x
Mining of coal and lignite	5	7	14.66	0.8	16.89	-2.3	x	11.90	12.73	13.13	14.13	15.38	x	x	x	x
Extraction of crude petroleum and natural gas	6	10	29.12	3.7	34.95	4.5	17.96	20.30	21.03	21.68	27.53	32.74	x	x	x	x
Mining of metal ores	7	..														
Other mining and quarrying	8	14	10.68	-7.6	12.56	-9.2	7.75	8.68	9.05	9.42	10.07	11.68	x	x	17.34	x
Mining support service activities	9	13	19.09	-0.9	20.88	-6.2	9.88	11.71	13.71	14.16	15.38	21.54	24.45	x	x	x
MANUFACTURING	C	2,339	12.18	2.4	14.50	2.8	7.14	8.36	8.96	9.50	10.77	13.96	16.04	17.32	18.92	23.75
Manufacture of food products	10	331	9.22	1.5	11.77	-1.6	6.36	6.98	7.26	7.62	8.31	10.34	12.02	13.13	14.39	19.14
Manufacture of beverages	11	39	14.16	3.4	16.45	1.3	9.18	10.84	11.24	11.85	12.79	16.06	17.92	19.56	21.09	x
Manufacture of tobacco products	12	5	20.61	1.2	21.68	1.8	x	18.75	18.95	19.16	19.97	21.32	22.70	x	x	x
Manufacture of textiles	13	40	9.03	0.2	11.17	0.6	6.27	6.84	7.17	7.54	8.18	10.11	11.26	12.11	13.57	x
Manufacture of wearing apparel	14	18	8.09	0.4	10.58	-1.6	6.08	6.22	6.45	6.79	7.14	9.10	10.56	x	x	x
Manufacture of leather and related products	15	9	8.68	-1.9	11.15	-5.3	6.44	7.04	7.38	7.75	8.43	10.76	x	x	x	x
Manufacture of wood and of products of wood and cork, except furniture; manufacture of articles of straw and plaiting materials	16	52	9.45	0.2	10.93	0.8	6.58	7.44	7.84	8.12	8.69	10.35	11.36	11.90	12.69	x
Manufacture of paper and paper products	17	59	12.27	1.0	14.26	1.1	7.48	8.81	9.41	10.13	11.17	13.80	15.49	16.93	17.85	x
Printing and reproduction of recorded media	18	96	11.33	-2.3	13.41	0.1	7.06	8.04	8.76	9.28	10.14	12.70	14.35	15.34	16.65	20.95
Manufacture of coke and refined petroleum products	19	10	23.06		25.28	39.8	x	12.93	14.80	16.67	20.52	25.00	x	x	x	x
Manufacture of chemicals and chemical products	20	97	14.31	1.7	16.54	2.3	7.68	9.38	10.12	10.91	12.63	16.09	18.18	19.58	21.11	28.02
Manufacture of basic pharmaceutical products and pharmaceutical preparations	21	63	16.98	5.6	20.34	3.7	9.44	11.76	12.37	13.31	15.56	19.57	22.55	24.56	26.95	x
Manufacture of rubber and plastic products	22	152	10.26	2.5	12.39	1.2	6.90	7.70	8.05	8.52	9.29	11.44	13.15	14.23	15.33	19.29
Manufacture of other non-metallic mineral products	23	78	11.35	1.8	14.06	6.4	7.19	8.41	8.88	9.31	10.20	12.90	15.44	16.33	17.73	x
Manufacture of basic metals	24	85	15.26	11.5	16.13	12.0	8.71	10.60	11.35	12.22	13.71	16.66	18.39	19.53	21.04	24.64
Manufacture of fabricated metal products, except machinery and equipment	25	261	11.25	-0.6	12.90	1.0	7.21	8.41	8.98	9.35	10.38	12.50	13.97	14.99	16.03	19.56
Manufacture of computer, electronic and optical products	26	132	14.91	0.4	17.16	1.5	7.91	9.45	10.20	10.70	12.87	16.77	19.48	20.58	22.71	28.31
Manufacture of electrical equipment	27	99	11.59	4.1	13.48	-0.1	7.24	8.22	8.88	9.27	10.46	12.97	14.63	15.87	17.20	21.79
Manufacture of machinery and equipment n.e.c.	28	207	13.41	4.0	15.49	4.5	8.19	9.55	10.09	10.67	12.01	15.04	17.01	18.20	19.46	24.39
Manufacture of motor vehicles, trailers and semi-trailers	29	151	14.37	0.4	15.89	0.1	8.27	9.88	10.58	11.46	12.99	15.96	18.55	19.48	20.86	24.07
Manufacture of other transport equipment	30	160	16.90	6.4	18.98	7.3	10.51	12.30	13.02	13.89	15.28	18.28	19.78	21.37	22.89	28.04
Manufacture of furniture	31	55	9.72	0.4	11.58	1.8	6.47	7.27	7.66	8.03	8.95	10.79	11.91	12.68	13.96	x
Other manufacturing	32	64	11.00	7.3	13.27	4.0	7.07	7.94	8.32	8.83	9.99	12.25	13.95	16.06	17.56	x
Repair and installation of machinery and equipment	33	78	14.34	2.1	16.65	4.4	8.43	9.91	10.58	11.25	12.38	16.29	18.02	19.54	21.56	x
ELECTRICITY, GAS, STEAM AND AIR CONDITIONING SUPPLY	D	171	16.38	5.0	18.64	0.4	9.19	10.45	11.47	12.37	14.84	18.13	20.69	22.84	24.69	30.79
Electricity, gas, steam and air conditioning supply	35	171	16.38	5.0	18.64	0.4	9.19	10.45	11.47	12.37	14.84	18.13	20.69	22.84	24.69	30.79
WATER SUPPLY; SEWERAGE, WASTE MANAGEMENT AND REMEDIATION ACTIVITIES	E	137	11.99	4.2	14.09	2.4	7.50	8.69	9.28	9.80	10.75	13.25	15.23	16.54	17.67	22.32
Water collection, treatment and supply	36	39	14.52	1.6	15.76	-3.5	9.18	10.66	11.50	11.86	13.07	15.87	17.13	17.65	19.08	x
Sewerage	37	12	11.71	2.0	13.35	1.4	7.57	9.01	9.23	9.76	10.25	12.45	13.55	x	x	x
Waste collection, treatment and disposal activities; materials recovery	38	83	10.97	5.9	13.40	4.0	7.27	8.23	8.60	9.18	10.00	12.19	13.86	15.13	17.17	x

Table 4.11b   Hourly pay - Gross (£) - For all employee jobs[a] by Industry: United Kingdom, 2012

Description	Code	Number of jobs[b] (thousand)	Median	Annual % change	Mean	Annual % change	Percentiles									
							10	20	25	30	40	60	70	75	80	90
Remediation activities and other waste management services	39	x	x		16.92	75.7	x	x	x	x	11.22	x	x	x	x	x
CONSTRUCTION	F	833	12.46	2.7	14.83	2.4	7.72	9.02	9.67	10.18	11.27	13.73	15.42	16.77	18.39	23.80
Construction of buildings	41	260	13.42	5.1	16.77	3.5	7.98	9.46	10.04	10.62	11.96	15.22	17.94	19.75	21.98	29.36
Civil engineering	42	155	12.23	0.1	15.01	2.7	8.00	9.33	9.80	10.36	11.19	13.55	15.53	17.08	18.70	23.95
Specialised construction activities	43	418	12.02	0.5	13.55	0.7	7.50	8.78	9.34	9.96	10.97	13.14	14.50	15.23	16.46	20.18
WHOLESALE AND RETAIL TRADE; REPAIR OF MOTOR VEHICLES AND MOTORCYCLES	G	3,625	8.20	1.9	11.56	0.9	6.14	6.50	6.70	6.90	7.48	9.12	10.56	11.65	12.97	18.26
Wholesale and retail trade and repair of motor vehicles and motorcycles	45	408	9.51	0.5	11.38	-0.2	6.18	6.90	7.30	7.72	8.58	10.47	11.79	12.50	13.38	17.24
Wholesale trade, except of motor vehicles and motorcycles	46	947	10.81	1.6	14.25	-0.9	6.85	7.74	8.17	8.62	9.57	12.36	14.73	16.29	18.26	25.25
Retail trade, except of motor vehicles and motorcycles	47	2,270	7.35	2.6	10.11	2.2	6.08	6.30	6.48	6.62	6.91	7.97	8.83	9.46	10.40	14.46
TRANSPORTATION AND STORAGE	H	1,051	11.25	1.6	13.67	2.9	7.69	8.74	9.28	9.71	10.30	12.56	14.43	15.64	17.49	23.81
Land transport and transport via pipelines	49	445	10.87	1.8	12.62	2.6	7.46	8.36	8.75	9.15	10.00	12.10	13.71	14.78	16.18	21.98
Water transport	50	11	13.40	17.5	16.27	10.8	7.92	8.47	8.75	10.27	12.20	14.35	x	x	x	x
Air transport	51	74	17.39	-4.1	21.44	1.3	9.65	11.23	11.87	12.86	14.60	19.25	23.86	25.30	28.15	x
Warehousing and support activities for transportation	52	307	12.31	4.3	15.11	4.9	7.69	8.75	9.32	9.83	11.04	13.99	16.18	17.77	20.07	26.38
Postal and courier activities	53	214	10.35	3.6	11.57	1.1	7.85	9.48	9.74	9.84	10.10	10.91	11.70	12.19	12.94	15.73
ACCOMMODATION AND FOOD SERVICE ACTIVITIES	I	1,211	6.50	1.6	8.40	0.6	5.42	x	x	6.08	6.24	7.00	7.58	8.01	8.68	11.20
Accommodation	55	280	6.90	2.2	9.00	-2.5	6.07	x	6.08	6.15	6.47	7.45	8.15	8.77	9.51	12.63
Food and beverage service activities	56	931	6.49	3.2	8.19	1.6	5.16	x	x	6.08	6.20	6.89	7.47	7.86	8.46	10.80
INFORMATION AND COMMUNICATION	J	939	17.15	3.8	20.50	2.1	8.32	10.73	11.98	13.10	15.23	19.31	22.34	24.18	26.53	34.73
Publishing activities	58	152	14.24	3.2	18.60	0.5	6.85	9.15	9.96	10.52	12.31	16.54	18.88	20.55	22.48	29.08
Motion picture, video and television programme production, sound recording and music publishing activities	59	53	12.52	-22.3	18.57	-7.4	6.08	6.89	7.69	8.97	10.88	15.00	17.97	19.92	22.18	x
Programming and broadcasting activities	60	40	19.18	1.8	22.62	-6.7	11.69	13.47	14.86	15.68	17.22	20.75	23.22	24.41	26.28	x
Telecommunications	61	210	17.23	9.9	19.57	7.3	9.28	12.09	13.35	14.56	15.62	18.67	20.83	22.44	24.37	30.71
Computer programming, consultancy and related activities	62	422	18.33	-0.7	21.44	0.7	8.69	11.50	12.72	13.80	15.81	21.00	24.28	26.43	28.85	37.45
Information service activities	63	63	18.12	-0.7	21.68	2.7	9.30	11.43	12.50	13.88	15.90	21.34	24.59	26.06	28.81	x
FINANCIAL AND INSURANCE ACTIVITIES	K	1,060	16.36	-1.3	23.42	-4.1	8.65	10.01	10.73	11.60	13.58	19.94	24.62	27.66	31.68	44.86
Financial service activities, except insurance and pension funding	64	564	16.23	-1.2	23.86	-4.6	8.68	10.00	10.73	11.51	13.51	20.41	25.35	28.28	32.29	45.41
Insurance, reinsurance and pension funding, except compulsory social security	65	142	15.72	2.1	21.71	2.3	8.83	9.93	10.81	11.67	13.28	18.78	22.99	25.40	28.66	40.69
Activities auxiliary to financial services and insurance activities	66	354	16.69	-4.1	23.43	-5.4	8.48	10.07	10.74	11.67	13.69	19.93	24.41	27.36	31.73	45.27
REAL ESTATE ACTIVITIES	L	295	11.80	1.4	14.67	1.8	7.10	8.41	8.91	9.45	10.47	13.35	15.11	16.30	17.68	23.82
Real estate activities	68	295	11.80	1.4	14.67	1.8	7.10	8.41	8.91	9.45	10.47	13.35	15.11	16.30	17.68	23.82
PROFESSIONAL, SCIENTIFIC AND TECHNICAL ACTIVITIES	M	1,483	15.32	-0.1	19.50	-1.4	7.79	9.59	10.37	11.26	13.20	17.53	20.56	22.49	24.76	34.17
Legal and accounting activities	69	477	15.29	3.6	20.04	2.5	7.97	9.52	10.22	11.00	13.13	17.77	20.80	22.78	25.21	36.72
Activities of head offices; management consultancy activities	70	278	14.91	-8.8	20.65	-11.3	7.22	9.07	9.87	10.55	12.63	17.50	21.29	23.44	26.29	39.35
Architectural and engineering activities; technical testing and analysis	71	367	15.80	0.6	18.50	1.0	8.62	10.39	11.33	12.00	13.88	17.81	20.44	22.36	24.20	30.56
Scientific research and development	72	122	18.19	1.7	22.58	0.7	10.95	12.85	13.84	14.56	16.39	20.64	23.37	25.26	27.72	x
Advertising and market research	73	110	13.42	-3.4	19.12	-5.3	7.26	9.00	9.99	10.73	11.95	15.81	19.17	20.80	23.00	x
Other professional, scientific and technical activities	74	83	13.15	4.8	16.17	1.5	6.81	8.24	8.96	9.86	11.24	14.96	17.45	19.37	20.85	x
Veterinary activities	75	48	10.62	4.7	13.23	1.0	6.75	7.51	7.91	8.33	9.40	12.97	15.44	16.30	18.28	x
ADMINISTRATIVE AND SUPPORT SERVICE ACTIVITIES	N	1,395	8.58	3.5	11.51	1.9	6.08	6.43	6.67	7.00	7.75	9.71	11.28	12.44	13.83	18.69
Rental and leasing activities	77	116	10.00	1.4	11.95	1.8	6.33	7.50	7.90	8.19	8.97	11.01	12.31	13.39	14.89	20.34
Employment activities	78	487	8.69	8.6	11.02	3.8	6.08	6.46	6.75	7.12	7.89	9.77	11.47	12.50	13.93	18.37

Table 4.11b   Hourly pay - Gross (£) - For all employee jobs[a] by Industry: United Kingdom, 2012

Description	Code	Number of jobs[b] (thousand)	Median	Annual % change	Mean	Annual % change	Percentiles 10	20	25	30	40	60	70	75	80	90
Travel agency, tour operator and other reservation service and related activities	79	75	10.25	4.7	13.94	5.3	6.97	7.55	8.01	8.38	9.32	11.58	13.69	14.80	15.85	x
Security and investigation activities	80	95	8.48	1.3	9.85	-0.1	6.45	6.99	7.20	7.46	7.96	9.10	10.22	10.70	11.11	14.27
Services to buildings and landscape activities	81	391	7.01	0.1	9.99	-0.8	x	6.08	6.11	6.25	6.52	7.71	8.82	9.65	10.62	14.60
Office administrative, office support and other business support activities	82	232	10.50	2.5	14.30	1.3	6.50	7.43	7.85	8.23	9.29	12.37	14.30	15.70	17.98	24.31
PUBLIC ADMINISTRATION AND DEFENCE; COMPULSORY SOCIAL SECURITY	O	1,335	14.34	2.2	15.76	0.7	9.03	10.10	10.79	11.58	12.92	15.67	17.50	18.47	19.59	23.19
Public administration and defence; compulsory social security	84	1,335	14.34	2.2	15.76	0.7	9.03	10.10	10.79	11.58	12.92	15.67	17.50	18.47	19.59	23.19
EDUCATION	P	3,776	13.40	2.1	16.02	0.5	7.10	8.18	8.75	9.49	11.15	16.04	18.82	20.50	22.03	26.93
Education	85	3,776	13.40	2.1	16.02	0.5	7.10	8.18	8.75	9.49	11.15	16.04	18.82	20.50	22.03	26.93
HUMAN HEALTH AND SOCIAL WORK ACTIVITIES	Q	3,474	11.62	2.1	14.65	1.1	6.77	7.76	8.28	8.82	10.06	13.69	15.82	17.22	18.34	22.79
Human health activities	86	2,258	14.13	0.7	16.90	1.4	8.10	9.30	9.89	10.76	12.24	15.97	17.80	18.97	20.52	25.71
Residential care activities	87	607	7.76	1.0	9.66	1.4	6.15	6.43	6.58	6.79	7.22	8.54	9.73	10.63	11.64	14.43
Social work activities without accommodation	88	609	8.86	-0.5	10.96	-0.2	6.27	6.81	7.08	7.40	8.03	10.10	11.74	12.66	13.91	17.23
ARTS, ENTERTAINMENT AND RECREATION	R	462	8.72	1.3	12.76	5.1	6.08	6.42	6.69	7.02	7.81	9.88	11.51	12.73	14.37	19.35
Creative, arts and entertainment activities	90	41	12.50	1.9	15.03	-1.1	6.70	7.70	8.09	8.94	11.23	13.97	15.95	17.06	18.07	x
Libraries, archives, museums and other cultural activities	91	56	11.49	2.9	13.40	1.2	6.58	7.77	8.28	8.96	10.33	12.54	14.27	15.40	16.26	x
Gambling and betting activities	92	103	7.82	2.7	10.53	5.6	6.15	6.37	6.56	6.75	7.39	8.48	9.40	9.89	10.67	x
Sports activities and amusement and recreation activities	93	263	8.50	4.2	13.30	8.4	6.08	6.20	6.47	6.75	7.50	9.50	10.92	12.27	14.08	20.00
OTHER SERVICE ACTIVITIES	S	389	10.00	1.0	13.03	2.4	6.08	6.74	7.04	7.50	8.55	11.34	13.22	14.46	15.84	21.55
Activities of membership organisations	94	188	11.75	0.2	15.17	2.6	6.71	7.92	8.40	9.05	10.41	13.36	15.56	16.76	18.64	23.65
Repair of computers and personal and household goods	95	26	11.12	-1.8	13.93	-0.9	6.81	7.67	8.11	8.84	10.03	12.47	14.59	15.40	16.85	x
Other personal service activities	96	175	7.96	-0.6	10.64	2.5	6.08	6.14	6.30	6.52	7.09	8.96	10.31	11.09	12.22	16.62
ACTIVITIES OF HOUSEHOLDS AS EMPLOYERS; UNDIFFERENTIATED GOODS- AND SERVICES-PRODUCING ACTIVITIES OF HOUSEHOLDS FOR OWN USE	T	52	8.50	1.7	9.49	3.9	6.81	7.45	7.54	7.76	8.02	9.00	9.68	10.00	10.41	x
Activities of households as employers of domestic personnel	97	52	8.50	1.7	9.49	3.9	6.81	7.45	7.54	7.76	8.02	9.00	9.68	10.00	10.41	x
Undifferentiated goods- and services-producing activities of private households for own use	98	:														
ACTIVITIES OF EXTRATERRITORIAL ORGANISATIONS AND BODIES	U	x	15.78		15.82	9.6	x	x	x	x	x	x	x	x	x	x
Activities of extraterritorial organisations and bodies	99	x	15.78		15.82	9.6	x	x	x	x	x	x	x	x	x	x
NOT CLASSIFIED		5	8.35	-58.4	11.06	-42.4	x	6.10	6.38	7.02	7.46	9.24	x	x	x	x

a Employees on adult rates whose pay for the survey pay-period was not affected by absence.

b Figures for Number of Jobs are for indicative purposes only and should not be considered an accurate estimate of employee job counts.

KEY - The colour coding indicates the quality of each estimate; jobs, median, mean and percentiles but not the annual percentage change.

The quality of an estimate is measured by its coefficient of variation (CV), which is the ratio of the standard error of an estimate to the estimate.

Source: Annual Survey of Hours and Earnings, Office for National Statistics.

Key
CV <= 5%
CV > 5% and <= 10%
CV > 10% and <= 20%
x = unreliable
CV > 20% or unavailable
.. = disclosive
: = not applicable
- = nil or negligible

4.12a Weekly pay - Gross (£) - For all employee jobs[a]: United Kingdom, 2012

Description	Number of jobs[b] (thousand)	Median	Annual % change	Mean	Annual % change	Percentiles									
						10	20	25	30	40	60	70	75	80	90
All Employees	24,203	405.8	1.5	491.3	0.8	121.1	207.2	246.4	279.7	341.2	482.3	574.9	629.4	693.4	893.5
Male	12,281	498.1	1.0	596.9	0.2	199.7	297.4	330.2	361.9	426.0	575.1	671.0	728.3	800.6	1,048.7
Female	11,922	319.7	2.1	382.4	1.9	94.3	148.9	178.5	208.0	263.9	381.4	459.5	509.7	568.1	728.7
Full-Time	17,322	506.1	1.6	607.8	0.8	282.1	335.0	360.0	385.2	442.3	577.0	665.4	714.8	779.4	1,001.9
Part-Time	6,881	155.2	1.5	197.7	0.2	48.6	81.8	96.7	108.0	132.9	182.4	216.7	239.5	268.7	384.9
Male Full-Time	10,570	546.0	1.4	660.7	0.4	300.0	359.2	386.8	416.4	479.1	619.6	712.0	769.8	845.4	1,100.3
Male Part-Time	1,711	145.8	2.3	203.0	-1.9	43.6	74.1	87.7	99.4	123.4	170.8	205.5	230.0	260.0	394.0
Female Full-Time	6,752	448.9	2.0	525.1	1.9	262.3	307.7	328.3	348.7	395.8	516.2	591.3	638.0	689.1	845.1
Femail Part-Time	5,170	158.7	1.3	196.0	1.0	50.4	85.0	98.3	110.6	135.3	185.9	219.5	242.3	271.6	382.1

Soure: Annual Survey of Hours and Earnings, Office for National Statistics

a Employees on adult rates whose pay for the survey pay-period was not affected by absence.
b Figures for Number of Jobs are for indicative purposes only and should not be considered an accurate estimate of employee job counts.
KEY - The colour coding indicates the quality of each estimate; jobs, median, mean and percentiles but not the annual percentage change.
The quality of an estimate is measured by its coefficient of variation (CV), which is the ratio of the standard error of an estimate to the estimate.
Source: Annual Survey of Hours and Earnings, Office for National Statistics.

4.12b Hourly pay - Excluding overtime (£) - For all employee jobs[a]: United Kingdom, 2012

Description	Code	Number of jobs[b] (thousand)	Median	Annual % change	Mean	Annual % change	Percentiles 10	20	25	30	40	60	70	75	80	90
ALL EMPLOYEES		24,203	11.23	1.4	14.88	0.9	6.45	7.40	7.92	8.49	9.73	13.22	15.72	17.37	19.16	24.99
All Industries and Services		24,198	11.23	1.5	14.89	0.9	6.45	7.40	7.92	8.49	9.73	13.22	15.72	17.37	19.16	24.99
All Index of Production Industries		2,690	12.20	2.1	14.78	2.2	7.15	8.38	8.98	9.51	10.76	14.07	16.27	17.58	19.17	24.53
All Manufacturing		2,339	11.97	3.1	14.45	2.7	7.02	8.20	8.80	9.35	10.56	13.72	15.84	17.20	18.75	23.74
All Service Industries		20,548	11.06	1.6	14.94	0.6	6.36	7.24	7.74	8.28	9.54	13.13	15.70	17.42	19.21	25.11
AGRICULTURE, FORESTRY AND FISHING	A	127	8.11	-1.5	9.68	-0.1	6.15	6.71	6.91	7.11	7.61	8.82	10.00	10.68	11.88	14.45
Crop and animal production, hunting and related service activities	1	117	8.00	-1.4	9.41	-0.6	6.13	6.66	6.81	7.00	7.50	8.52	9.62	10.23	11.47	13.80
Forestry and logging	2	8	12.30	11.9	13.72	8.6	x	9.69	10.29	10.30	11.03	13.64	14.89	x	x	x
Fishing and aquaculture	3	x	8.25	4.2	10.14	8.2	x	x	x	x	x	x	x	x	x	x
MINING AND QUARRYING	B	43	17.38	0.4	20.51	-2.2	9.03	10.30	10.77	11.78	13.28	20.00	23.41	25.23	28.63	x
Mining of coal and lignite	5	7	13.21	-5.3	17.09	-5.2	x	11.22	11.87	12.04	12.48	15.25	x	x	x	x
Extraction of crude petroleum and natural gas	6	10	29.12	3.2	34.95	4.0	17.96	20.30	21.03	21.68	27.53	32.74	x	x	x	x
Mining of metal ores	7	..														
Other mining and quarrying	8	14	10.60	-5.4	12.53	-9.1	7.32	8.36	8.82	9.07	9.88	11.54	x	x	x	x
Mining support service activities	9	13	18.81	-0.9	21.03	-5.5	9.88	11.32	12.51	13.70	15.30	21.54	24.45	x	x	x
MANUFACTURING	C	2,339	11.97	3.1	14.45	2.7	7.02	8.20	8.80	9.35	10.56	13.72	15.84	17.20	18.75	23.74
Manufacture of food products	10	331	9.01	1.4	11.74	-1.8	6.31	6.84	7.13	7.49	8.14	10.17	11.88	12.96	14.33	18.91
Manufacture of beverages	11	39	14.12	4.4	16.43	0.8	8.88	10.75	11.06	11.82	12.70	15.96	17.88	19.10	21.11	x
Manufacture of tobacco products	12	5	20.09	-1.3	21.28	1.9	x	17.81	18.62	18.90	19.68	20.88	22.48	x	x	x
Manufacture of textiles	13	40	9.02	1.6	11.14	0.8	6.18	6.77	6.99	7.51	8.15	10.07	11.25	12.14	13.44	x
Manufacture of wearing apparel	14	18	7.94	-1.5	10.56	-1.6	6.08	6.19	6.42	6.79	7.14	8.82	10.56	x	x	x
Manufacture of leather and related products	15	9	8.66	-0.7	11.13	-5.3	6.44	6.99	7.34	7.58	8.25	10.52	x	x	x	x
Manufacture of wood and of products of wood and cork, except furniture; manufacture of articles of straw and plaiting materials	16	52	9.17	-0.1	10.84	0.5	6.50	7.41	7.70	8.00	8.58	10.03	11.21	11.59	12.61	x
Manufacture of paper and paper products	17	59	12.06	0.3	14.22	1.2	7.43	8.72	9.31	9.90	11.01	13.69	15.26	16.68	17.51	x
Printing and reproduction of recorded media	18	96	11.18	-2.8	13.34	0.5	7.00	8.00	8.51	9.00	10.00	12.44	14.29	15.33	16.40	21.01
Manufacture of coke and refined petroleum products	19	10	23.06	101.4	25.22	39.3	x	12.65	14.80	16.67	20.29	24.57	x	x	x	x
Manufacture of chemicals and chemical products	20	97	14.14	1.5	16.55	2.4	7.62	9.26	10.06	10.71	12.53	15.89	18.14	19.42	21.11	28.11
Manufacture of basic pharmaceutical products and pharmaceutical preparations	21	63	16.84	4.6	20.33	3.6	9.44	11.51	12.34	13.17	15.31	19.39	22.50	24.54	27.01	x
Manufacture of rubber and plastic products	22	152	10.09	2.0	12.38	1.2	6.82	7.62	7.99	8.38	9.16	11.36	13.02	14.11	15.33	19.29
Manufacture of other non-metallic mineral products	23	78	11.22	1.8	14.07	6.7	7.06	8.22	8.72	9.20	10.10	12.77	15.36	16.33	17.66	x
Manufacture of basic metals	24	85	15.11	13.0	16.14	12.2	8.66	10.36	11.13	12.05	13.49	16.60	18.22	19.47	21.04	24.67
Manufacture of fabricated metal products, except machinery and equipment	25	261	10.99	1.0	12.70	0.7	7.12	8.17	8.75	9.20	10.06	12.03	13.48	14.51	15.72	19.51
Manufacture of computer, electronic and optical products	26	132	14.76	1.2	17.17	1.4	7.88	9.36	10.06	10.64	12.61	16.64	19.39	20.44	22.47	28.31
Manufacture of electrical equipment	27	99	11.32	3.3	13.48	0.0	7.15	8.18	8.80	9.19	10.36	12.77	14.56	15.86	17.15	21.70
Manufacture of machinery and equipment n.e.c.	28	207	13.06	3.8	15.37	4.1	8.08	9.37	9.95	10.50	11.65	14.64	16.67	18.10	19.36	24.32
Manufacture of motor vehicles, trailers and semi-trailers	29	151	14.25	1.2	15.77	-0.3	8.16	9.71	10.44	11.25	12.80	15.59	18.41	19.16	20.55	24.26
Manufacture of other transport equipment	30	160	16.80	6.9	19.04	7.5	10.23	11.96	12.68	13.58	15.02	18.17	19.69	21.38	22.90	28.04
Manufacture of furniture	31	55	9.52	0.5	11.50	1.7	6.40	7.24	7.57	8.00	8.95	10.53	11.72	12.41	13.81	x
Other manufacturing	32	64	10.93	8.5	13.27	4.2	6.98	7.86	8.24	8.74	9.99	12.08	14.00	15.85	17.57	x
Repair and installation of machinery and equipment	33	78	14.15	3.5	16.54	4.5	8.37	9.68	10.36	10.85	12.26	16.01	17.99	19.41	21.56	x
ELECTRICITY, GAS, STEAM AND AIR CONDITIONING SUPPLY	D	171	16.29	4.8	18.44	0.9	9.14	10.35	11.41	12.26	14.63	17.70	20.37	22.69	24.57	30.32
Electricity, gas, steam and air conditioning supply	35	171	16.29	4.8	18.44	0.9	9.14	10.35	11.41	12.26	14.63	17.70	20.37	22.69	24.57	30.32
WATER SUPPLY; SEWERAGE, WASTE MANAGEMENT AND REMEDIATION ACTIVITIES	E	137	11.82	4.7	14.02	2.0	7.39	8.45	9.04	9.50	10.54	13.04	15.01	16.34	17.63	22.29
Water collection, treatment and supply	36	39	14.27	3.8	15.72	-3.6	8.87	10.63	11.33	11.82	12.98	15.62	16.99	17.65	19.08	x
Sewerage	37	12	11.73	3.7	13.54	2.8	7.48	8.83	9.24	9.45	10.27	12.45	13.55	x	x	x
Waste collection, treatment and disposal activities; materials recovery	38	83	10.60	4.3	13.25	2.9	7.09	8.00	8.35	8.75	9.72	11.88	13.39	14.88	16.73	x
Remediation activities and other waste management services	39	x	x		x		x	x	x	x	11.22	x	x	x	x	x

4.12b Hourly pay - Excluding overtime (£) - For all employee jobs[a]: United Kingdom, 2012

Description	Code	Number of jobs[b] (thousand)	Median	Annual % change	Mean	Annual % change	Percentiles 10	20	25	30	40	60	70	75	80	90
CONSTRUCTION	F	833	12.28	2.3	14.78	2.4	7.67	9.00	9.56	10.00	11.15	13.54	15.19	16.56	18.25	23.80
Construction of buildings	41	260	13.24	5.0	16.78	3.5	7.94	9.34	10.00	10.50	11.79	15.00	17.90	19.71	21.98	29.36
Civil engineering	42	155	12.04	0.0	15.01	2.7	7.98	9.23	9.69	10.26	11.09	13.46	15.30	17.00	18.58	24.00
Specialised construction activities	43	418	11.98	1.1	13.43	0.8	7.48	8.71	9.25	9.82	10.84	12.95	14.36	15.03	16.15	20.05
WHOLESALE AND RETAIL TRADE; REPAIR OF MOTOR VEHICLES AND MOTORCYCLES	G	3,625	8.17	1.9	11.64	1.0	6.12	6.50	6.70	6.90	7.46	9.10	10.54	11.61	12.92	18.26
Wholesale and retail trade and repair of motor vehicles and motorcycles	45	408	9.46	0.9	11.36	-0.2	6.13	6.85	7.25	7.69	8.52	10.36	11.63	12.43	13.29	17.25
Wholesale trade, except of motor vehicles and motorcycles	46	947	10.73	1.6	14.29	-1.0	6.77	7.67	8.11	8.53	9.49	12.27	14.63	16.15	18.26	25.23
Retail trade, except of motor vehicles and motorcycles	47	2,270	7.36	2.7	10.22	2.5	6.08	6.30	6.47	6.62	6.92	7.97	8.84	9.50	10.44	14.46
TRANSPORTATION AND STORAGE	H	1,051	11.22	1.9	13.79	3.4	7.59	8.67	9.18	9.66	10.25	12.53	14.37	15.58	17.50	23.69
Land transport and transport via pipelines	49	445	10.75	1.2	12.62	2.3	7.29	8.22	8.65	9.03	9.86	12.00	13.55	14.77	16.07	21.96
Water transport	50	11	13.40	21.1	16.23	11.2	7.92	8.47	8.75	10.27	12.20	14.01	x	x	x	x
Air transport	51	74	17.41	-3.3	21.52	1.2	9.64	11.25	11.84	12.80	14.51	19.26	23.81	25.30	28.15	x
Warehousing and support activities for transportation	52	307	12.21	4.4	15.16	5.4	7.67	8.62	9.18	9.72	10.85	13.96	16.19	17.80	20.24	26.30
Postal and courier activities	53	214	10.36	3.6	11.80	2.6	7.92	9.57	9.82	9.84	10.10	10.99	11.83	12.33	13.08	15.69
ACCOMMODATION AND FOOD SERVICE ACTIVITIES	I	1,211	6.50	1.7	8.40	0.6	5.40	x	x	6.08	6.23	7.00	7.58	8.00	8.68	11.20
Accommodation	55	280	6.90	2.4	9.02	-2.6	6.07	x	6.08	6.15	6.46	7.45	8.15	8.78	9.51	12.63
Food and beverage service activities	56	931	6.48	3.2	8.19	1.7	5.16	x	x	6.08	6.20	6.87	7.47	7.86	8.46	10.77
INFORMATION AND COMMUNICATION	J	939	17.10	4.3	20.50	2.0	8.26	10.69	11.97	13.03	15.02	19.21	22.30	24.13	26.46	34.74
Publishing activities	58	152	14.21	3.0	18.61	0.5	6.85	9.15	9.96	10.48	12.30	16.54	18.88	20.55	22.48	29.08
Motion picture, video and television programme production, sound recording and music publishing activities	59	53	12.51	-22.0	18.50	-7.5	6.08	6.89	7.69	8.92	10.86	15.00	17.81	19.79	21.93	x
Programming and broadcasting activities	60	40	19.04	1.7	22.59	-7.4	11.69	13.47	14.86	15.64	17.11	20.71	23.02	24.25	26.23	x
Telecommunications	61	210	17.09	10.6	19.54	7.2	9.20	12.01	13.33	14.50	15.32	18.46	20.66	22.36	24.11	30.71
Computer programming, consultancy and related activities	62	422	18.25	-1.1	21.45	0.7	8.67	11.49	12.59	13.69	15.77	20.89	24.28	26.28	28.82	37.45
Information service activities	63	63	18.12	-0.5	21.70	2.6	9.24	11.36	12.50	13.87	15.86	21.34	24.59	26.06	28.81	x
FINANCIAL AND INSURANCE ACTIVITIES	K	1,060	16.26	-1.6	23.48	-4.2	8.60	9.96	10.67	11.54	13.51	19.93	24.60	27.47	31.50	44.80
Financial service activities, except insurance and pension funding	64	564	16.18	-1.4	23.93	-4.6	8.63	9.95	10.64	11.48	13.44	20.36	25.30	28.22	32.23	45.41
Insurance, reinsurance and pension funding, except compulsory social security	65	142	15.63	1.9	21.71	2.1	8.72	9.90	10.69	11.50	13.22	18.70	22.69	25.33	28.59	40.69
Activities auxiliary to financial services and insurance activities	66	354	16.69	-3.9	23.49	-5.5	8.43	10.01	10.72	11.66	13.69	19.93	24.53	27.36	31.68	45.10
REAL ESTATE ACTIVITIES	L	295	11.79	1.4	14.69	1.7	7.10	8.37	8.87	9.44	10.46	13.29	15.07	16.29	17.65	23.80
Real estate activities	68	295	11.79	1.4	14.69	1.7	7.10	8.37	8.87	9.44	10.46	13.29	15.07	16.29	17.65	23.80
PROFESSIONAL, SCIENTIFIC AND TECHNICAL ACTIVITIES	M	1,483	15.23	-0.5	19.55	-1.3	7.76	9.58	10.31	11.23	13.17	17.51	20.57	22.50	24.75	34.18
Legal and accounting activities	69	477	15.22	3.3	20.05	2.5	7.98	9.51	10.22	10.96	13.13	17.71	20.79	22.75	25.16	36.72
Activities of head offices; management consultancy activities	70	278	14.86	-9.2	20.82	-11.0	7.19	9.01	9.80	10.54	12.71	17.50	21.41	23.53	26.34	39.47
Architectural and engineering activities; technical testing and analysis	71	367	15.62	0.5	18.51	1.1	8.57	10.27	11.22	11.96	13.84	17.71	20.44	22.32	24.24	30.56
Scientific research and development	72	122	18.21	1.8	22.73	1.0	10.70	12.83	13.79	14.63	16.41	20.64	23.41	25.15	27.76	x
Advertising and market research	73	110	13.42	-3.4	19.16	-5.4	7.21	9.00	9.99	10.73	11.95	15.81	19.17	20.80	23.00	x
Other professional, scientific and technical activities	74	83	13.14	5.1	16.19	1.4	6.75	8.18	8.96	9.85	11.16	14.87	17.45	19.29	20.95	x
Veterinary activities	75	48	10.42	2.9	13.26	1.1	6.70	7.50	7.90	8.32	9.41	12.78	15.44	16.30	18.26	x
ADMINISTRATIVE AND SUPPORT SERVICE ACTIVITIES	N	1,395	8.52	3.7	11.50	2.1	6.08	6.40	6.64	7.00	7.71	9.66	11.21	12.35	13.75	18.57
Rental and leasing activities	77	116	9.89	2.5	11.91	2.1	6.30	7.39	7.78	8.11	8.87	10.77	12.28	13.40	14.81	20.34
Employment activities	78	487	8.57	7.1	11.03	4.0	6.08	6.40	6.70	7.02	7.81	9.69	11.37	12.38	13.88	18.37
Travel agency, tour operator and other reservation service and related activities	79	75	10.23	4.6	13.92	5.5	6.97	7.54	8.00	8.39	9.32	11.60	13.57	14.80	15.87	x
Security and investigation activities	80	95	8.48	1.6	9.83	0.0	6.43	6.97	7.20	7.44	7.95	9.11	10.20	10.73	11.10	14.23

4.12b Hourly pay - Excluding overtime (£) - For all employee jobs[a]: United Kingdom, 2012

Description	Code	Number of jobs[b] (thousand)	Median	Annual % change	Mean	Annual % change	Percentiles 10	20	25	30	40	60	70	75	80	90
Services to buildings and landscape activities	81	391	7.00	0.0	9.91	-0.7	x	6.08	6.10	6.24	6.50	7.70	8.76	9.61	10.56	14.42
Office administrative, office support and other business support activities	82	232	10.48	2.3	14.32	1.3	6.50	7.42	7.81	8.19	9.21	12.29	14.26	15.58	17.88	24.15
PUBLIC ADMINISTRATION AND DEFENCE; COMPULSORY SOCIAL SECURITY	O	1,335	14.31	2.3	15.70	0.5	8.98	10.06	10.76	11.57	12.89	15.66	17.50	18.32	19.49	23.14
Public administration and defence; compulsory social security	84	1,335	14.31	2.3	15.70	0.5	8.98	10.06	10.76	11.57	12.89	15.66	17.50	18.32	19.49	23.14
EDUCATION	P	3,776	13.39	2.1	16.08	0.4	7.09	8.16	8.73	9.47	11.15	16.03	18.81	20.49	22.01	26.93
Education	85	3,776	13.39	2.1	16.08	0.4	7.09	8.16	8.73	9.47	11.15	16.03	18.81	20.49	22.01	26.93
HUMAN HEALTH AND SOCIAL WORK ACTIVITIES	Q	3,474	11.64	2.0	14.67	1.2	6.77	7.75	8.28	8.82	10.07	13.72	15.84	17.23	18.34	22.82
Human health activities	86	2,258	14.13	0.7	16.88	1.6	8.09	9.29	9.88	10.76	12.31	16.00	17.80	18.96	20.52	25.67
Residential care activities	87	607	7.75	1.1	9.70	1.4	6.14	6.41	6.57	6.78	7.20	8.50	9.74	10.72	11.67	14.54
Social work activities without accommodation	88	609	8.89	-0.2	11.02	-0.3	6.27	6.81	7.09	7.39	8.03	10.14	11.76	12.70	13.94	17.23
ARTS, ENTERTAINMENT AND RECREATION	R	462	8.68	1.4	12.87	5.0	6.08	6.39	6.65	7.00	7.76	9.82	11.50	12.66	14.37	19.32
Creative, arts and entertainment activities	90	41	12.45	2.2	15.03	-1.2	6.70	7.58	8.10	8.91	11.08	13.80	15.95	17.06	18.07	x
Libraries, archives, museums and other cultural activities	91	56	11.43	2.6	13.41	1.0	6.54	7.77	8.28	8.94	10.23	12.51	14.26	15.22	16.17	x
Gambling and betting activities	92	103	7.71	1.1	10.67	5.1	6.10	6.25	6.45	6.62	7.34	8.42	9.36	9.81	10.66	x
Sports activities and amusement and recreation activities	93	263	8.49	4.5	13.37	8.3	6.08	6.20	6.46	6.73	7.49	9.47	10.94	12.18	14.01	20.00
OTHER SERVICE ACTIVITIES	S	389	10.00	1.5	13.04	2.4	6.08	6.70	7.01	7.50	8.55	11.31	13.16	14.45	15.85	21.50
Activities of membership organisations	94	188	11.75	0.1	15.18	2.5	6.70	7.92	8.40	9.07	10.41	13.39	15.47	16.74	18.67	23.58
Repair of computers and personal and household goods	95	26	10.97	-1.8	13.91	-0.7	6.81	7.67	8.10	8.69	9.98	12.42	14.57	15.40	16.85	x
Other personal service activities	96	175	7.89	-1.3	10.63	2.5	6.08	6.12	6.29	6.50	7.04	8.96	10.29	11.05	12.24	16.62
ACTIVITIES OF HOUSEHOLDS AS EMPLOYERS; UNDIFFERENTIATED GOODS- AND SERVICES-PRODUCING ACTIVITIES OF HOUSEHOLDS FOR OWN USE	T	52	8.50	0.9	9.48	3.4	6.81	7.45	7.54	7.75	8.02	9.00	9.68	10.00	10.48	x
Activities of households as employers of domestic personnel	97	52	8.50	0.9	9.48	3.4	6.81	7.45	7.54	7.75	8.02	9.00	9.68	10.00	10.48	x
Undifferentiated goods- and services-producing activities of private households for own use	98	:														
ACTIVITIES OF EXTRATERRITORIAL ORGANISATIONS AND BODIES	U	x	15.78		15.78	9.4	x	x	x	x	x	x	x	x	x	x
Activities of extraterritorial organisations and bodies	99	x	15.78		15.78	9.4	x	x	x	x	x	x	x	x	x	x
NOT CLASSIFIED		5	8.35	-58.4	11.03	-42.6	x	6.10	6.38	7.02	7.46	9.24	x	x	x	x

Soure: Annual Survey of Hours and Earnings, Office for National Statistics

a Employees on adult rates whose pay for the survey pay-period was not affected by absence.
b Figures for Number of Jobs are for indicative purposes only and should not be considered an accurate estimate of employee job counts.
KEY - The colour coding indicates the quality of each estimate; jobs, median, mean and percentiles but not the annual percentage change.
The quality of an estimate is measured by its coefficient of variation (CV), which is the ratio of the standard error of an estimate to the estimate.
Source: Annual Survey of Hours and Earnings, Office for National Statistics.

Key
CV <= 5%
CV > 5% and <= 10%
CV > 10% and <= 20%
x = unreliable CV > 20% or unavailable
.. = disclosive
: = not applicable
- = nil or negligible

4.13 Average weekly earnings: main industrial sectors Great Britain

Great Britain
Standard Industrial Classification 2007

	Whole economy		Manufacturing		Construction		Services		Distribution Hotels and Restuarants	
	Actual	Seasonally adjusted	Actual	Seasonally adjusted	Actual	Seasonally adjusted	Actual	Seasonally adjusted	Actual	Seasonally adjusted
	KA46	KAB9	K55I	K5CA	K55L	K5CD	K55O	K5BZ	K55R	K5CG
2000	318	318	369	369	378	377	303	303	215	215
2001	335	334	383	382	407	407	320	320	223	223
2002	345	345	397	396	418	417	331	330	232	232
2003	356	356	412	411	436	436	342	341	237	237
2004	372	371	431	431	448	448	358	357	245	245
2005	389	388	447	446	461	461	375	375	254	254
2006	407	407	464	464	490	490	393	392	263	263
2007	427	426	483	482	522	522	413	412	279	279
2008	443	441	498	497	531	531	429	428	286	286
2009	442	441	503	503	536	535	427	427	290	290
2010	452	451	525	524	535	535	437	436	297	296
2011	463	463	532	532	542	542	450	449	300	300
2012	470	469	542	541	545	544	456	455	307	306

	Finance and Business Industries		Private Sector		Public Sector		Private Sector Excl Financial Services	
	Actual	Seasonally adjusted	Actual	Seasonally adjusted	Actual	Seasonally adjusted	Actual	Seasonally adjusted
	K55U	K5C4	KA4O	KAC4	KA4R	KAC7	KA4U	KAD8
2000	389	391	319	319	314	313	314	313
2001	417	418	335	335	331	329	331	329
2002	423	424	345	345	344	342	344	342
2003	434	434	355	355	360	358	360	358
2004	458	458	371	370	376	374	375	374
2005	485	485	387	387	396	394	395	394
2006	519	518	406	406	410	408	410	408
2007	546	544	428	428	424	421	424	421
2008	573	570	443	442	439	436	438	436
2009	552	553	439	438	452	451	450	448
2010	576	575	448	447	465	464	458	458
2011	610	610	459	459	477	477	466	465
2012	612	612	466	465	485	483	473	473

Source: Office for National Statistics: 01633 456780

4.14a Average Weekly Earnings by Industry (Not Seasonally Adjusted)

	Agriculture, Forestry and Fishing (A)			Mining and Quarrying (B)			Manufacturing - Food Products, Beverages and Tobacco (C1)			Manufacturing - Textiles, Leather and Clothing (C2)		
	Average Weekly Earnings	of which		Average Weekly Earnings	Of which		Average Weekly Earnings	Of which		Average Weekly Earnings	Of which	
		Bonuses	Arrears		Bonuses	Arrears		Bonuses	Arrears		Bonuses	Arrears
CDID	K57A	K57B	K57C	K57D	K57E	K57F	K57G	K57H	K57I	K57J	K57K	K57L
2009 Jan	339	8	0	1044	128	1	456	10	0	339	14	0
2009 Feb	332	12	0	1022	88	4	457	17	0	344	15	0
2009 Mar	341	7	2	1311	379	6	518	71	1	349	22	0
2009 Apr	330	3	0	1044	98	0	462	16	0	346	15	0
2009 May	342	2	0	989	52	0	456	9	0	340	11	1
2009 Jun	337	2	0	996	59	1	459	14	0	361	36	0
2009 Jul	330	11	0	992	46	0	459	16	2	336	9	0
2009 Aug	330	3	0	995	62	0	441	6	0	335	6	0
2009 Sep	346	9	0	988	40	2	463	21	1	335	9	0
2009 Oct	335	5	1	1002	56	0	448	9	0	344	8	0
2009 Nov	347	4	0	993	47	6	449	11	0	357	15	0
2009 Dec	376	31	0	1045	95	1	514	36	0	375	33	0
2010 Jan	343	4	0	1021	112	0	487	9	0	367	20	0
2010 Feb	358	26	0	1092	152	1	471	14	0	357	18	1
2010 Mar	360	17	0	1583	639	0	581	106	0	400	39	15
2010 Apr	340	7	0	1001	72	0	487	24	0	362	12	0
2010 May	322	2	0	966	51	0	462	8	0	360	12	0
2010 Jun	328	2	0	968	48	1	473	12	1	359	8	0
2010 Jul	336	4	0	971	36	3	465	12	0	369	14	0
2010 Aug	331	12	0	979	45	1	461	6	1	366	10	0
2010 Sep	328	4	0	976	59	0	482	32	0	361	6	0
2010 Oct	373	28	0	966	43	0	463	8	0	366	12	0
2010 Nov	365	8	0	975	53	2	461	7	1	363	9	0
2010 Dec	407	54	0	1029	115	0	510	47	1	370	20	0
2011 Jan	333	5	0	1052	110	0	466	6	3	364	14	0
2011 Feb	326	4	0	1093	173	1	464	11	0	361	15	0
2011 Mar	364	16	0	1584	657	1	550	86	0	386	39	1
2011 Apr	339	2	0	1066	133	0	502	30	0	361	13	0
2011 May	322	2	0	1026	66	1	464	6	0	363	8	0
2011 Jun	312	1	0	1013	56	0	472	14	0	366	10	0
2011 Jul	340	25	0	1057	97	1	458	5	0	363	8	0
2011 Aug	333	11	0	993	36	0	463	5	0	360	6	0
2011 Sep	317	2	0	1006	48	0	499	34	1	366	9	0
2011 Oct	337	11	0	1002	34	0	462	5	0	368	8	0
2011 Nov	330	6	0	1017	40	1	471	4	0	372	10	0
2011 Dec	378	39	0	1063	98	1	510	32	0	381	23	0
2012 Jan	329	3	0	1241	259	7	463	8	0	358	8	0
2012 Feb	333	7	0	1132	159	0	466	10	0	372	18	0
2012 Mar	345	18	0	1525	546	2	514	47	0	371	20	0
2012 Apr	319	3	0	1123	134	0	476	15	1	363	10	0
2012 May	319	5	0	1060	60	0	473	12	1	370	10	0
2012 Jun	328	3	0	1025	54	0	480	12	0	373	16	0
2012 Jul	349	14	0	1028	57	0	469	8	0	384	14	0
2012 Aug	342	8	0	1013	36	0	468	4	0	378	9	0
2012 Sep	340	6	0	1017	35	1	493	23	0	384	11	0
2012 Oct	333	4	1	1030	42	3	475	11	0	382	10	0
2012 Nov	339	5	0	1061	59	5	468	4	0	391	17	0
2012 Dec (r)	364	28	2	1065	82	4	505	27	0	398	29	0
2013 Jan (p)	339	6	0	1209	227	0	469	8	0	382	10	0

p = Provisional
r = Revised
All figures are in pounds (£)

Source: Monthly Wages & Salaries Survey

Earnings enquiries: 01633 456773

4.14a Average Weekly Earnings by Industry (Not Seasonally Adjusted)

CDID	Manufacturing - Chemicals and Man-made Fibres (C3) Average Weekly Earnings	Of which Bonuses	Arrears	Manufacturing - Basic Metals and Metal Products (C4) Average Weekly Earnings	Of which Bonuses	Arrears	Manufacturing - Engineering and Allied Industries (C5) Average Weekly Earnings	Of which Bonuses	Arrears	Other Manufacturing (C6) Average Weekly Earnings	Of which Bonuses	Arrears
	K57M	K57N	K57O	K57P	K57Q	K57R	K57S	K57T	K57U	K57V	K57W	K57X
2009 Jan	578	15	1	491	18	0	546	17	1	452	11	1
2009 Feb	595	36	1	491	23	0	563	34	1	449	10	0
2009 Mar	730	157	0	510	41	0	591	59	1	470	29	1
2009 Apr	690	110	0	495	21	1	562	28	1	453	12	0
2009 May	610	12	0	485	13	0	545	16	1	456	12	0
2009 Jun	639	23	1	500	17	0	544	13	1	461	11	0
2009 Jul	623	14	0	490	20	0	540	12	1	456	11	0
2009 Aug	609	7	0	481	8	0	544	10	3	455	10	0
2009 Sep	611	8	0	486	6	0	544	10	0	459	10	0
2009 Oct	614	12	0	492	10	0	552	9	0	463	12	0
2009 Nov	615	11	2	510	23	0	554	10	0	463	10	0
2009 Dec	663	48	0	513	23	0	576	28	0	476	22	0
2010 Jan	639	26	0	502	19	0	557	12	0	469	10	0
2010 Feb	673	62	1	529	24	2	577	31	1	477	20	0
2010 Mar	823	207	0	591	89	1	627	70	1	505	45	0
2010 Apr	670	61	1	528	25	0	582	24	1	470	11	0
2010 May	634	21	0	524	19	0	572	15	1	467	9	0
2010 Jun	635	15	1	523	21	1	569	11	1	472	11	0
2010 Jul	637	14	1	531	22	1	568	13	1	476	16	0
2010 Aug	622	11	0	513	10	0	569	10	0	468	9	0
2010 Sep	623	11	1	520	8	4	568	7	0	471	10	0
2010 Oct	650	18	1	524	20	0	572	11	0	475	13	1
2010 Nov	657	15	1	517	9	0	576	11	1	475	13	0
2010 Dec	682	35	0	512	14	0	594	29	1	485	26	0
2011 Jan	661	28	0	524	21	2	595	28	0	467	11	0
2011 Feb	661	27	0	515	15	1	591	31	1	478	21	0
2011 Mar	959	324	1	563	54	0	640	70	3	502	42	1
2011 Apr	698	68	1	525	22	0	596	30	1	471	15	0
2011 May	665	16	1	533	22	0	582	17	2	468	9	1
2011 Jun	664	18	1	530	14	0	592	24	1	471	14	0
2011 Jul	679	29	1	543	24	1	582	15	1	476	15	1
2011 Aug	661	11	1	519	7	1	573	9	1	470	9	0
2011 Sep	666	22	2	521	7	0	578	10	1	471	8	0
2011 Oct	656	14	1	533	16	1	584	9	5	473	12	0
2011 Nov	662	12	3	525	13	1	595	13	4	479	15	0
2011 Dec	688	36	4	528	29	1	597	24	2	490	26	0
2012 Jan	677	26	10	531	20	0	595	20	1	473	14	0
2012 Feb	668	25	2	526	16	0	614	42	1	478	17	0
2012 Mar	907	265	0	555	39	0	645	66	1	515	46	1
2012 Apr	736	85	1	556	37	1	610	27	2	488	20	0
2012 May	675	19	1	543	24	1	602	18	1	482	13	0
2012 Jun	683	24	1	532	21	0	615	28	1	482	13	1
2012 Jul	683	22	4	539	21	0	603	17	0	478	12	0
2012 Aug	678	19	1	516	8	0	597	13	1	479	10	0
2012 Sep	668	13	1	518	9	0	593	7	4	481	10	0
2012 Oct	674	17	0	522	12	0	598	8	1	482	13	0
2012 Nov	689	17	2	529	14	2	601	15	1	488	15	0
2012 Dec (r)	722	36	1	536	24	4	611	27	0	494	23	0
2013 Jan (p)	709	22	6	531	14	6	605	19	0	483	12	0

p = Provisional
r = Revised
All figures are in pounds (£)

Source: Monthly Wages & Salaries Survey

Earnings enquiries: 01633 456773

4.14a Average Weekly Earnings by Industry (Not Seasonally Adjusted)

	Electricity, Gas and Water Supply (D , E)			Construction (F)			Wholesale Trade (G46)			Retail Trade and Repairs (G45 & G47)		
	Average Weekly Earnings	Of which Bonuses	Arrears	Average Weekly Earnings	Of which Bonuses	Arrears	Average Weekly Earnings	Of which Bonuses	Arrears	Average Weekly Earnings	Of which Bonuses	Arrears
CDID	K57Y	K57Z	K582	K583	K584	K585	K586	K587	K588	K589	K58A	K58B
2009 Jan	577	16	0	530	13	0	518	51	0	252	11	0
2009 Feb	581	21	0	528	14	0	528	61	0	258	18	0
2009 Mar	639	72	0	559	41	0	537	69	2	265	24	0
2009 Apr	599	40	0	535	19	0	497	35	0	258	17	0
2009 May	589	24	0	525	12	0	494	30	0	257	15	0
2009 Jun	636	66	1	526	17	0	498	33	0	260	18	0
2009 Jul	618	47	3	530	17	0	494	31	0	258	16	0
2009 Aug	588	19	0	524	12	0	491	28	0	256	13	0
2009 Sep	590	19	0	531	16	0	493	27	0	254	10	0
2009 Oct	592	20	0	537	15	0	497	28	0	256	14	0
2009 Nov	606	25	1	543	22	0	507	37	0	250	12	0
2009 Dec	594	18	1	559	38	1	523	50	0	250	11	0
2010 Jan	595	20	1	540	15	0	512	42	1	258	13	0
2010 Feb	601	22	1	537	14	0	523	58	0	266	22	0
2010 Mar	670	83	2	592	67	0	610	136	2	294	46	0
2010 Apr	608	31	1	535	12	1	503	34	0	270	23	0
2010 May	595	21	0	527	12	0	496	29	0	261	14	0
2010 Jun	661	81	3	531	14	0	497	32	0	267	16	0
2010 Jul	621	29	4	525	14	0	501	34	0	265	15	0
2010 Aug	599	22	2	515	9	0	489	27	0	261	11	0
2010 Sep	600	21	3	531	19	0	489	25	0	260	8	0
2010 Oct	606	21	1	526	8	0	490	29	0	257	12	0
2010 Nov	613	26	1	531	15	0	490	29	0	258	12	0
2010 Dec	622	36	1	532	25	0	516	58	0	256	12	0
2011 Jan	608	27	1	539	14	0	510	43	0	263	12	0
2011 Feb	606	24	3	546	21	1	504	45	0	265	19	0
2011 Mar	646	81	1	583	55	0	565	99	0	286	38	0
2011 Apr	617	43	1	530	14	0	503	37	0	272	18	0
2011 May	584	17	5	530	11	0	501	30	1	270	16	0
2011 Jun	656	90	3	543	18	0	522	53	1	272	20	0
2011 Jul	640	69	0	535	12	0	519	48	1	267	16	0
2011 Aug	596	31	2	528	9	0	507	38	0	262	10	0
2011 Sep	596	20	2	542	19	0	501	30	0	260	9	0
2011 Oct	601	18	1	535	12	0	511	34	0	264	13	0
2011 Nov	611	21	6	546	21	0	505	27	1	261	11	0
2011 Dec	616	25	3	545	27	0	540	61	0	258	10	0
2012 Jan	608	24	0	539	13	0	538	56	0	265	12	0
2012 Feb	608	32	1	540	14	0	533	54	0	279	28	0
2012 Mar	665	87	1	589	50	3	585	103	1	288	34	0
2012 Apr	625	36	0	544	16	0	527	42	0	274	18	1
2012 May	602	17	2	548	13	0	527	39	1	274	16	0
2012 Jun	667	80	1	554	22	0	543	54	0	276	16	0
2012 Jul	647	60	2	545	16	0	534	43	1	272	15	0
2012 Aug	600	15	1	526	8	0	532	43	0	271	15	0
2012 Sep	605	17	2	538	18	0	524	34	0	267	10	0
2012 Oct	619	19	5	536	15	0	535	38	1	271	15	0
2012 Nov	626	24	2	542	17	0	528	31	1	267	14	0
2012 Dec (r)	621	22	1	540	25	0	542	49	1	266	14	0
2013 Jan (p)	610	20	0	528	12	1	555	54	0	269	13	0

p = Provisional
r = Revised
All figures are in pounds (£)

Source: Monthly Wages & Salaries Survey

Earnings enquiries: 01633 456773

4.14a   Average Weekly Earnings by Industry (Not Seasonally Adjusted)

CDID	Transport and Storage (H) Average Weekly Earnings	Of which Bonuses	Of which Arrears	Accommodation and Food Service Activities (I) Average Weekly Earnings	Of which Bonuses	Of which Arrears	Information and Communication (J) Average Weekly Earnings	Of which Bonuses	Of which Arrears	Financial & Insurance Activities (K) Average Weekly Earnings	Of which Bonuses	Of which Arrears
	K58F	K58G	K58H	K58C	K58D	K58E	K5E9	K5EA	K5EB	K58I	K58J	K58K
2009 Jan	480	7	0	206	2	0	710	60	2	1033	365	1
2009 Feb	477	6	4	215	7	0	752	94	1	1229	554	1
2009 Mar	490	19	3	213	5	0	803	145	1	1170	496	2
2009 Apr	494	19	0	212	3	0	747	80	1	803	115	12
2009 May	542	63	0	217	6	0	729	66	0	760	78	1
2009 Jun	500	20	0	211	3	0	749	91	0	846	166	3
2009 Jul	484	6	1	214	3	0	713	63	0	755	71	1
2009 Aug	486	4	0	211	2	0	725	72	0	749	61	2
2009 Sep	492	7	0	210	2	0	719	62	0	785	96	1
2009 Oct	487	5	1	212	3	0	696	48	1	754	61	2
2009 Nov	485	5	1	213	6	0	693	50	0	780	68	14
2009 Dec	503	15	1	219	5	0	704	66	0	922	227	1
2010 Jan	488	5	0	213	4	0	713	59	1	984	283	1
2010 Feb	491	8	2	222	8	0	746	95	1	1694	975	10
2010 Mar	517	29	1	221	7	0	827	169	1	1438	714	2
2010 Apr	497	9	2	217	4	0	704	46	2	789	71	1
2010 May	496	8	1	221	8	0	725	59	1	887	162	2
2010 Jun	521	32	1	215	3	0	782	114	1	975	239	5
2010 Jul	500	6	1	215	4	0	728	55	0	804	60	2
2010 Aug	499	4	0	223	3	0	736	58	6	780	47	1
2010 Sep	501	3	0	221	3	0	728	54	2	839	112	1
2010 Oct	503	6	0	226	4	0	722	45	1	793	57	1
2010 Nov	507	6	1	220	7	0	729	48	1	787	54	1
2010 Dec	515	10	1	222	7	0	745	66	0	878	138	0
2011 Jan	507	7	0	219	5	0	759	72	2	1235	473	0
2011 Feb	506	7	0	226	9	0	771	83	1	1662	901	1
2011 Mar	527	31	1	225	8	0	867	180	1	1541	783	2
2011 Apr	516	14	1	223	5	0	743	56	1	850	86	0
2011 May	515	10	1	227	8	0	755	61	1	892	121	1
2011 Jun	518	14	3	224	3	1	816	129	1	1064	296	1
2011 Jul	523	18	2	225	6	1	752	62	1	878	114	1
2011 Aug	512	6	1	223	3	0	791	97	1	815	50	2
2011 Sep	512	5	2	222	4	0	746	52	1	871	105	1
2011 Oct	511	5	1	223	5	1	754	65	1	830	51	1
2011 Nov	522	6	7	227	9	1	754	58	0	825	47	0
2011 Dec	526	10	2	229	8	0	756	65	1	903	121	0
2012 Jan	517	8	0	231	6	0	771	83	1	1093	325	0
2012 Feb	529	17	0	236	11	0	792	98	1	1488	713	2
2012 Mar	539	26	0	228	7	0	870	171	2	1505	728	3
2012 Apr	538	17	1	228	5	1	766	71	1	897	117	0
2012 May	533	9	1	232	8	0	777	80	2	875	95	1
2012 Jun	553	27	2	230	4	0	826	137	2	1000	225	3
2012 Jul	534	6	1	232	5	0	778	81	1	861	88	0
2012 Aug	548	18	1	233	4	0	788	82	1	842	67	1
2012 Sep	538	12	0	230	3	0	777	71	3	856	85	1
2012 Oct	538	13	1	227	5	0	755	51	1	819	47	1
2012 Nov	533	7	2	231	6	0	775	66	1	819	41	1
2012 Dec (r)	555	23	2	235	8	1	765	56	1	899	115	0
2013 Jan (p)	532	9	0	224	5	1	786	76	2	1138	358	1

p = Provisional
r = Revised
All figures are in pounds (£)

Source: Monthly Wages & Salaries Survey

Earnings enquiries: 01633 456773

4.14a Average Weekly Earnings by Industry (Not Seasonally Adjusted)

CDID	Real Estate Activities (L) Average Weekly Earnings	Of which Bonuses	Arrears	Professional, Scientific & Technical Activities (M) Average Weekly Earnings	Of which Bonuses	Arrears	Administrative and Support Service Activities (N) Average Weekly Earnings	Of which Bonuses	Arrears	Public Administration (O) Average Weekly Earnings	Of which Bonuses	Arrears
	K58L	K58M	K58N	K5EC	K5ED	K5EE	K5EF	K5EG	K5EH	K58O	K58P	K58Q
2009 Jan	449	22	1	632	30	2	341	14	0	502	1	2
2009 Feb	430	16	0	638	30	1	337	12	0	524	3	16
2009 Mar	483	62	1	670	65	0	345	17	0	505	1	4
2009 Apr	450	22	3	632	27	0	344	10	0	508	1	1
2009 May	439	17	0	629	21	0	345	12	0	512	1	3
2009 Jun	439	22	1	633	25	1	344	7	0	507	1	2
2009 Jul	459	43	0	637	30	0	346	11	0	508	3	7
2009 Aug	433	24	0	620	15	0	346	9	0	513	3	2
2009 Sep	449	29	1	619	14	0	333	7	0	505	1	1
2009 Oct	453	30	1	628	21	0	336	9	0	508	1	7
2009 Nov	460	35	1	626	17	1	334	8	0	514	3	3
2009 Dec	471	42	0	653	42	1	335	11	0	520	10	2
2010 Jan	456	28	0	637	23	1	343	11	0	521	1	1
2010 Feb	456	15	1	652	37	1	333	13	0	521	1	1
2010 Mar	521	83	0	719	96	3	353	23	0	521	2	1
2010 Apr	451	15	0	648	28	0	342	12	0	522	1	0
2010 May	454	14	0	635	18	0	341	9	0	522	2	0
2010 Jun	463	24	0	641	22	1	334	8	0	524	3	1
2010 Jul	481	34	3	634	31	1	339	15	0	532	3	1
2010 Aug	466	27	0	635	20	1	332	10	0	535	11	0
2010 Sep	468	27	1	636	18	1	330	9	0	528	1	1
2010 Oct	473	30	0	645	28	1	334	11	0	529	1	0
2010 Nov	474	30	0	655	31	1	329	9	0	533	3	1
2010 Dec	484	34	0	685	56	1	331	14	0	537	8	0
2011 Jan	493	34	1	658	29	0	338	13	0	536	1	0
2011 Feb	484	26	1	671	35	1	329	12	0	534	2	0
2011 Mar	534	70	1	777	143	1	352	33	0	537	4	0
2011 Apr	500	34	0	667	28	0	326	13	0	537	2	0
2011 May	490	27	0	671	31	0	330	8	0	537	2	0
2011 Jun	512	48	0	669	33	0	340	14	0	542	6	0
2011 Jul	506	42	1	696	56	0	344	16	0	539	5	0
2011 Aug	491	35	0	658	21	1	340	13	0	545	11	0
2011 Sep	484	28	0	661	18	0	332	9	0	545	1	0
2011 Oct	494	36	0	676	29	0	339	11	0	538	1	0
2011 Nov	507	43	3	682	35	1	335	10	0	537	2	0
2011 Dec	517	49	1	709	58	0	355	24	0	540	6	0
2012 Jan	493	30	0	682	38	1	351	12	0	535	1	0
2012 Feb	504	39	0	695	49	1	353	13	0	538	1	0
2012 Mar	612	142	0	785	134	1	381	39	0	541	2	0
2012 Apr	505	34	0	692	41	0	351	13	0	545	0	0
2012 May	494	32	0	680	30	0	350	10	0	543	1	0
2012 Jun	518	52	0	685	29	0	348	10	0	550	5	0
2012 Jul	521	56	0	708	61	1	352	12	0	551	5	0
2012 Aug	488	29	0	674	26	1	353	9	0	547	3	0
2012 Sep	502	38	1	666	23	1	347	9	0	554	7	1
2012 Oct	504	41	0	661	24	1	350	10	0	547	2	1
2012 Nov	501	38	0	667	28	1	348	8	0	544	2	0
2012 Dec (r)	515	54	0	706	71	1	360	21	0	543	2	2
2013 Jan (p)	506	49	2	650	20	0	348	11	0	547	1	1

p = Provisional
r = Revised
All figures are in pounds (£)

Source: Monthly Wages & Salaries Survey

Earnings enquiries: 01633 456773

4.14a Average Weekly Earnings by Industry (Not Seasonally Adjusted)

CDID	Education (P) Average Weekly Earnings	Of which Bonuses	Of which Arrears	Health and Social Work (Q) Average Weekly Earnings	Of which Bonuses	Of which Arrears	Arts, Entertainment and Recreation (R) Average Weekly Earnings	Of which Bonuses	Of which Arrears	Other Service Activities (S) Average Weekly Earnings	Of which Bonuses	Of which Arrears
	K58R	K58S	K58T	K58U	K58V	K58W	K5EI	K5EJ	K5EK	K58X	K58Y	K58Z
2009 Jan	391	1	3	387	1	1	293	10	1	380	23	2
2009 Feb	390	1	1	384	1	0	291	9	0	376	16	0
2009 Mar	388	1	1	385	1	1	301	18	0	387	28	0
2009 Apr	393	1	1	392	0	0	303	10	6	382	13	0
2009 May	392	1	0	394	1	1	295	7	0	367	13	0
2009 Jun	394	1	0	396	0	0	308	12	0	361	10	0
2009 Jul	398	1	1	391	0	0	305	14	0	368	11	0
2009 Aug	399	1	0	386	0	0	297	7	0	366	10	0
2009 Sep	402	1	0	390	0	0	295	5	1	362	6	0
2009 Oct	401	1	4	391	1	1	300	9	3	365	7	1
2009 Nov	396	1	1	390	1	0	312	19	0	370	11	1
2009 Dec	398	1	2	393	1	0	317	22	1	378	12	0
2010 Jan	393	1	1	388	1	0	322	17	0	401	16	0
2010 Feb	392	1	0	392	1	0	307	9	0	368	14	0
2010 Mar	393	2	0	390	1	0	333	35	0	411	63	1
2010 Apr	395	1	0	397	0	0	302	8	0	365	15	0
2010 May	394	1	0	398	0	0	304	8	0	353	11	0
2010 Jun	394	1	0	399	0	0	309	11	1	360	8	1
2010 Jul	397	2	0	396	0	0	319	10	1	356	7	0
2010 Aug	398	1	0	395	0	0	325	10	0	359	11	0
2010 Sep	404	1	1	397	0	0	323	6	0	352	8	0
2010 Oct	401	1	1	396	0	0	315	5	0	345	8	0
2010 Nov	400	1	1	398	0	0	317	8	0	354	13	0
2010 Dec	401	1	0	398	1	0	328	15	0	353	10	0
2011 Jan	397	0	0	398	0	0	329	13	0	351	14	1
2011 Feb	398	0	1	399	1	1	319	15	1	362	17	1
2011 Mar	401	2	0	398	1	0	331	23	0	401	50	1
2011 Apr	404	1	0	400	1	0	314	9	0	364	12	0
2011 May	401	1	0	401	0	0	311	10	2	356	10	1
2011 Jun	401	1	0	402	0	0	312	9	0	359	8	1
2011 Jul	402	1	0	400	1	0	320	13	0	364	11	1
2011 Aug	407	1	0	398	0	0	326	17	0	359	8	1
2011 Sep	409	1	0	400	1	0	322	12	0	358	8	0
2011 Oct	404	1	0	399	1	0	312	5	0	360	7	0
2011 Nov	402	1	0	401	0	0	322	9	0	367	14	1
2011 Dec	402	2	0	402	1	0	337	13	0	369	14	0
2012 Jan	396	0	0	402	0	0	340	16	0	356	15	1
2012 Feb	396	1	0	403	1	0	330	7	0	354	19	0
2012 Mar	398	1	0	403	2	0	338	26	0	354	22	0
2012 Apr	400	1	0	404	0	0	329	10	1	348	12	0
2012 May	399	1	0	407	0	0	332	10	0	347	12	0
2012 Jun	402	1	0	404	0	0	360	24	0	352	15	0
2012 Jul	402	1	0	405	1	0	344	11	1	348	13	0
2012 Aug	409	1	0	404	1	0	356	10	0	351	13	0
2012 Sep	411	1	0	403	1	0	360	13	0	339	7	0
2012 Oct	407	0	0	404	1	0	348	6	0	337	9	0
2012 Nov	406	0	0	406	0	0	354	13	0	346	13	0
2012 Dec (r)	407	1	1	407	1	0	370	14	0	350	14	0
2013 Jan (p)	402	1	1	407	0	0	368	17	0	348	13	0

p = Provisional
r = Revised
All figures are in pounds (£)

Source: Monthly Wages & Salaries Survey

Earnings enquiries: 01633 456773

4.14b Average Weekly Earnings - regular pay [1]

Seasonally adjusted   Great Britain

Standard Industrial Classification (2007)

	Whole Economy			Private sector [3][4]			Public sector [3][4]		
		% changes year on year			% changes year on year			% changes year on year	
	Weekly Earnings (£)	Single month	3 month average [2]	Weekly Earnings (£)	Single month	3 month average [2]	Weekly Earnings (£)	Single month	3 month average [2]
	KAI7	KAI8	KAI9	KAJ2	KAJ3	KAJ4	KAJ5	KAJ6	KAJ7
Jan 01	309	3.6		306	3.7		319	3.0	
Feb 01	309	3.7		307	3.8		321	2.8	
Mar 01	311	4.5	3.9	308	4.6	4.1	323	4.3	3.4
Apr 01	313	5.4	4.5	310	5.2	4.5	325	6.3	4.4
May 01	314	4.9	4.9	310	4.6	4.8	327	6.2	5.6
Jun 01	314	4.9	5.1	311	4.8	4.8	328	5.7	6.1
Jul 01	316	5.4	5.1	313	5.1	4.8	330	6.4	6.1
Aug 01	319	5.6	5.3	315	5.3	5.1	332	6.6	6.2
Sep 01	319	4.8	5.2	316	4.4	5.0	331	6.2	6.4
Oct 01	320	4.8	5.0	317	4.4	4.7	333	6.2	6.3
Nov 01	321	4.8	4.8	319	4.7	4.5	332	5.3	5.9
Dec 01	322	4.5	4.7	319	4.2	4.4	333	5.6	5.7
Jan 02	323	4.5	4.6	320	4.4	4.4	335	4.8	5.2
Feb 02	325	5.2	4.7	323	5.4	4.6	335	4.5	4.9
Mar 02	326	4.8	4.8	323	4.9	4.9	337	4.4	4.5
Apr 02	327	4.2	4.7	324	4.3	4.8	337	3.7	4.2
May 02	327	4.1	4.4	324	4.2	4.5	339	3.6	3.9
Jun 02	329	4.5	4.3	326	4.7	4.4	340	3.6	3.6
Jul 02	329	4.0	4.2	326	4.0	4.3	343	4.0	3.7
Aug 02	328	3.1	3.9	326	3.2	4.0	340	2.3	3.3
Sep 02	329	3.4	3.5	326	3.4	3.5	342	3.3	3.2
Oct 02	330	3.2	3.2	326	3.0	3.2	344	3.5	3.0
Nov 02	331	3.0	3.2	327	2.7	3.0	346	4.2	3.6
Dec 02	331	2.9	3.0	326	2.4	2.7	348	4.5	4.0
Jan 03	334	3.4	3.1	330	3.2	2.8	349	4.2	4.3
Feb 03	335	2.9	3.1	331	2.5	2.7	350	4.3	4.3
Mar 03	335	2.9	3.1	331	2.4	2.7	351	4.3	4.3
Apr 03	337	3.0	3.0	332	2.6	2.5	353	4.6	4.4
May 03	337	3.3	3.1	333	3.0	2.7	352	4.1	4.3
Jun 03	338	2.9	3.1	334	2.3	2.6	356	4.6	4.4
Jul 03	339	2.9	3.0	334	2.4	2.6	359	4.7	4.4
Aug 03	340	3.6	3.1	334	2.7	2.5	362	6.4	5.2
Sep 03	341	3.6	3.4	336	3.0	2.7	362	5.6	5.6
Oct 03	342	3.7	3.6	337	3.2	3.0	361	5.0	5.7
Nov 03	344	3.8	3.7	338	3.4	3.2	363	4.8	5.1
Dec 03	345	4.3	3.9	340	4.1	3.6	364	4.7	4.8
Jan 04	345	3.4	3.8	340	3.1	3.5	364	4.3	4.6
Feb 04	346	3.3	3.7	340	2.8	3.3	366	4.7	4.6
Mar 04	347	3.4	3.4	341	3.1	3.0	367	4.4	4.5
Apr 04	348	3.5	3.4	343	3.2	3.0	369	4.6	4.6
May 04	350	3.6	3.5	344	3.2	3.2	370	5.0	4.7
Jun 04	351	3.7	3.6	345	3.4	3.3	372	4.5	4.7
Jul 04	352	3.8	3.7	346	3.7	3.4	373	3.9	4.4
Aug 04	353	3.9	3.8	348	4.0	3.7	375	3.6	4.0
Sep 04	354	3.6	3.8	348	3.5	3.7	376	4.1	3.9
Oct 04	356	3.9	3.8	350	3.7	3.8	378	4.6	4.1
Nov 04	356	3.7	3.8	350	3.5	3.6	379	4.5	4.4
Dec 04	359	4.1	3.9	354	4.1	3.8	379	4.1	4.4
Jan 05	360	4.2	4.0	353	3.9	3.8	382	5.0	4.5
Feb 05	360	4.2	4.1	354	4.2	4.0	382	4.3	4.5
Mar 05	362	4.4	4.3	356	4.2	4.1	386	5.3	4.9
Apr 05	363	4.3	4.3	357	4.0	4.1	389	5.4	5.0
May 05	364	4.2	4.3	357	3.7	4.0	391	5.7	5.4
Jun 05	365	4.2	4.2	358	3.9	3.9	391	5.2	5.4
Jul 05	367	4.4	4.3	361	4.2	3.9	392	5.2	5.4
Aug 05	369	4.4	4.3	362	4.1	4.1	394	5.0	5.1
Sep 05	370	4.6	4.5	363	4.4	4.2	396	5.2	5.1
Oct 05	371	4.2	4.4	364	4.0	4.2	397	5.1	5.1
Nov 05	372	4.2	4.3	364	4.0	4.1	399	5.2	5.2
Dec 05	372	3.7	4.0	365	3.3	3.8	400	5.5	5.3
Jan 06	374	4.1	4.0	367	4.0	3.8	400	4.7	5.1
Feb 06	375	4.2	4.0	368	4.0	3.7	402	5.3	5.2
Mar 06	376	3.8	4.1	370	4.0	4.0	400	3.6	4.5
Apr 06	377	3.7	3.9	371	4.0	4.0	400	3.1	4.0
May 06	379	4.0	3.8	373	4.5	4.1	401	2.6	3.1
Jun 06	381	4.2	4.0	374	4.5	4.3	404	3.4	3.0
Jul 06	381	3.6	3.9	374	3.7	4.2	406	3.5	3.2
Aug 06	381	3.4	3.7	375	3.6	3.9	405	2.9	3.3
Sep 06	383	3.5	3.5	377	3.9	3.7	406	2.7	3.0
Oct 06	386	4.0	3.7	380	4.4	4.0	408	2.8	2.8
Nov 06	386	4.0	3.8	380	4.4	4.2	410	2.8	2.8
Dec 06	388	4.1	4.0	382	4.5	4.4	411	3.0	2.8
Jan 07	388	3.7	4.0	381	3.8	4.2	414	3.7	3.1
Feb 07	390	3.8	3.9	384	4.1	4.1	413	2.7	3.1
Mar 07	392	4.2	3.9	386	4.3	4.1	415	3.7	3.3
Apr 07	392	4.0	4.0	386	4.2	4.2	414	3.3	3.2
May 07	395	4.2	4.1	389	4.4	4.3	416	3.7	3.5

4.14b Average Weekly Earnings - regular pay [1]

Seasonally adjusted

Standard Industrial Classification (2007)

Great Britain

	Whole Economy			Private sector [3][4]			Public sector [3][4]		
		% changes year on year				% changes year on year			% changes year on year
	Weekly Earnings (£)	Single month	3 month average [2]	Weekly Earnings (£)	Single month	3 month average [2]	Weekly Earnings (£)	Single month	3 month average [2]
	KAI7	KAI8	KAI9	KAJ2	KAJ3	KAJ4	KAJ5	KAJ6	KAJ7
Jun 07	397	4.2	4.1	391	4.5	4.4	417	3.2	3.4
Jul 07	398	4.6	4.3	393	5.1	4.7	417	2.8	3.2
Aug 07	400	4.9	4.6	395	5.2	4.9	419	3.5	3.2
Sep 07	400	4.5	4.7	395	4.8	5.1	420	3.3	3.2
Oct 07	401	3.9	4.4	395	4.1	4.7	421	3.2	3.3
Nov 07	403	4.2	4.2	397	4.5	4.5	422	3.1	3.2
Dec 07	403	4.0	4.0	397	4.1	4.3	425	3.4	3.2
Jan 08	404	4.1	4.1	398	4.5	4.4	426	2.9	3.1
Feb 08	406	4.2	4.1	401	4.4	4.3	428	3.7	3.3
Mar 08	408	4.1	4.1	402	4.1	4.3	430	3.8	3.4
Apr 08	411	4.8	4.4	405	4.8	4.4	432	4.4	4.0
May 08	409	3.8	4.2	404	3.7	4.2	431	3.7	4.0
Jun 08	411	3.5	4.0	405	3.7	4.1	429	2.9	3.7
Jul 08	412	3.4	3.6	406	3.2	3.5	434	4.0	3.6
Aug 08	413	3.3	3.4	407	3.1	3.3	434	3.6	3.5
Sep 08	414	3.3	3.3	408	3.1	3.2	436	3.8	3.8
Oct 08	415	3.6	3.4	409	3.6	3.3	436	3.6	3.6
Nov 08	416	3.2	3.4	410	3.1	3.3	437	3.6	3.6
Dec 08	416	3.2	3.3	410	3.1	3.2	438	3.0	3.4
Jan 09	416	2.8	3.1	409	2.8	3.0	439	3.0	3.2
Feb 09	417	2.6	2.8	410	2.4	2.7	442	3.1	3.0
Mar 09	417	2.1	2.5	410	2.2	2.4	439	2.0	2.7
Apr 09	418	1.8	2.2	411	1.5	2.0	444	2.8	2.6
May 09	419	2.3	2.1	411	1.9	1.9	446	3.4	2.7
Jun 09	419	2.0	2.0	411	1.4	1.6	448	4.4	3.5
Jul 09	418	1.4	1.9	408	0.6	1.3	450	3.8	3.8
Aug 09	418	1.3	1.6	409	0.4	0.8	452	4.0	4.0
Sep 09	419	1.4	1.4	410	0.5	0.5	452	3.7	3.8
Oct 09	419	1.0	1.2	410	0.1	0.3	453	3.7	3.8
Nov 09	420	1.0	1.1	410	0.0	0.2	455	3.9	3.8
Dec 09	421	1.3	1.1	412	0.4	0.2	455	3.9	3.9
Jan 10	423	1.8	1.4	413	1.0	0.5	457	4.0	3.9
Feb 10	423	1.5	1.5	412	0.6	0.7	458	3.8	3.9
Mar 10	425	2.0	1.8	416	1.3	0.9	457	4.0	4.0
Apr 10	424	1.4	1.7	414	0.6	0.8	459	3.4	3.7
May 10	424	1.2	1.6	413	0.4	0.8	462	3.5	3.6
Jun 10	425	1.4	1.3	414	0.8	0.6	459	2.6	3.1
Jul 10	427	2.2	1.6	417	2.0	1.1	461	2.3	2.8
Aug 10	428	2.3	2.0	418	2.4	1.7	460	1.9	2.2
Sep 10	429	2.2	2.2	418	2.0	2.2	463	2.5	2.2
Oct 10	429	2.3	2.3	419	2.2	2.2	464	2.5	2.3
Nov 10	430	2.4	2.3	419	2.4	2.2	465	2.4	2.4
Dec 10	430	2.0	2.3	419	1.8	2.1	467	2.5	2.5
Jan 11	433	2.3	2.3	422	2.1	2.1	468	2.5	2.5
Feb 11	432	2.2	2.2	421	2.1	2.0	468	2.2	2.4
Mar 11	433	1.8	2.1	421	1.4	1.9	470	2.8	2.5
Apr 11	433	2.2	2.0	422	2.1	1.9	469	2.2	2.4
May 11	434	2.4	2.1	424	2.6	2.1	470	1.8	2.3
Jun 11	434	2.2	2.3	423	2.2	2.3	470	2.3	2.1
Jul 11	434	1.7	2.1	424	1.8	2.2	469	1.8	2.0
Aug 11	435	1.6	1.8	425	1.5	1.8	470	2.1	2.1
Sep 11	436	1.8	1.7	426	1.9	1.7	472	1.9	2.0
Oct 11	438	2.0	1.8	427	2.1	1.8	473	2.0	2.0
Nov 11 (r)	438	1.8	1.9	428	2.0	2.0	473	1.7	1.9
Dec 11 (r)	439	2.0	1.9	429	2.3	2.1	473	1.4	1.7
Jan 12 (r)	438	1.1	1.7	428	1.4	1.9	472	0.8	1.3
Feb 12	439	1.7	1.6	430	2.0	1.9	474	1.2	1.1
Mar 12	441	1.9	1.6	431	2.3	1.9	475	1.2	1.1 (r)
Apr 12	441	1.7	1.8	431	2.0	2.1	476	1.3	1.2
May 12	442	1.8	1.8	432	2.0	2.1	477	1.5	1.3
Jun 12	443	2.0	1.8	433	2.2	2.1	480	2.2	1.7
Jul 12	443	1.9	1.9	433	1.9	2.0	481	2.6	2.1
Aug 12	444	2.1	2.0	434	2.1	2.1	484	2.9	2.6
Sep 12	443	1.6	1.9	433	1.6	1.9	482	2.1	2.6
Oct 12	443	1.3	1.7	433	1.4	1.7	482	1.8	2.3
Nov 12	444	1.4	1.4	434 (r)	1.5	1.5	482	1.8	1.9
Dec 12 (r)	444	1.3	1.3	434	1.3	1.4	482	1.8	1.8
Jan 13 (p)	**442**	**1.0**	**1.2**	**432**	**0.9**	**1.2**	**481**	**2.0**	**1.8**

1. Estimates of regular pay exclude bonuses and arrears of pay.

Source: Monthly Wages & Salaries Survey

2. The three month average figures are the changes in the average seasonally adjusted values for the three months ending with the relevant month compared with the same period a year earlier.

Earnings enquiries: 01633 456773

1. Estimates of regular pay exclude bonuses and arrears of pay.

2. The three month average figures are the changes in the average seasonally adjusted values for the three months ending with the relevant month compared with the same period a year earlier.

3. From July 2009 Royal Bank of Scotland Group plc and Lloyds Banking Group plc are classified to the public sector; previously they are in the private sector.

4. Between June 2010 and May 2012 English Further Education Corporations and Sixth Form College Corporations are classified to the public sector. Before June 2010 and after May 2012 they are classified to the private sector.

4.14b Average Weekly Earnings - regular pay [1]

Seasonally adjusted

Great Britain

Standard Industrial Classification (2007)

	Services, SIC 2007 sections G-S			Finance and business services, SIC 2007 sections K-N			Public sector excluding financial services [4]		
	Weekly Earnings (£)	% changes year on year		Weekly Earnings (£)	% changes year on year		Weekly Earnings (£)	% changes year on year	
		Single month	3 month average [2]		Single month	3 month average [2]		Single month	3 month average [2]
	K5DL	K5DM	K5DN	K5DO	K5DP	K5DQ	KAK6	KAK7	KAK8
Jan 01	293	3.7		360	5.0		319	3.0	
Feb 01	294	3.6		358	4.8		321	2.8	
Mar 01	296	4.9	4.0	362	6.3	5.3	322	4.3	3.4
Apr 01	298	6.1	4.8	364	7.3	6.1	325	6.2	4.4
May 01	298	5.2	5.4	366	5.3	6.3	327	6.1	5.5
Jun 01	300	5.3	5.5	368	6.1	6.3	328	5.6	6.0
Jul 01	301	5.5	5.3	370	5.7	5.7	329	6.3	6.0
Aug 01	303	5.7	5.5	373	6.9	6.2	332	6.6	6.2
Sep 01	303	4.9	5.3	371	4.1	5.5	331	6.1	6.3
Oct 01	304	4.9	5.2	372	3.9	4.9	333	6.1	6.3
Nov 01	306	5.1	5.0	378	5.4	4.5	332	5.2	5.8
Dec 01	306	4.8	5.0	377	4.3	4.5	333	5.5	5.6
Jan 02	308	5.0	5.0	377	4.6	4.8	334	4.7	5.1
Feb 02	310	5.7	5.2	381	6.4	5.1	335	4.4	4.9
Mar 02	311	5.4	5.3	381	5.2	5.4	336	4.3	4.5
Apr 02	312	4.7	5.2	382	4.8	5.5	337	3.7	4.1
May 02	312	4.5	4.8	380	3.8	4.6	338	3.6	3.8
Jun 02	314	4.9	4.7	383	4.1	4.3	340	3.6	3.6
Jul 02	314	4.4	4.6	383	3.5	3.8	342	4.0	3.7
Aug 02	313	3.3	4.2	382	2.5	3.4	340	2.3	3.3
Sep 02	314	3.6	3.8	384	3.5	3.2	342	3.3	3.2
Oct 02	315	3.5	3.5	385	3.6	3.2	344	3.4	3.0
Nov 02	316	3.2	3.4	387	2.5	3.2	346	4.1	3.6
Dec 02	316	3.0	3.2	382	1.3	2.4	347	4.5	4.0
Jan 03	319	3.7	3.3	390	3.4	2.4	348	4.2	4.3
Feb 03	320	3.1	3.3	392	2.9	2.5	350	4.3	4.3
Mar 03	321	2.9	3.3	392	2.9	3.1	351	4.3	4.3
Apr 03	322	3.3	3.1	393	3.0	2.9	352	4.6	4.4
May 03	323	3.5	3.3	395	3.9	3.3	352	4.1	4.3
Jun 03	324	2.9	3.2	393	2.7	3.2	355	4.6	4.4
Jul 03	324	3.2	3.2	393	2.7	3.1	359	4.7	4.4
Aug 03	326	4.0	3.4	393	2.8	2.7	362	6.4	5.2
Sep 03	326	3.9	3.7	395	2.8	2.8	361	5.6	5.6
Oct 03	328	4.0	4.0	398	3.3	3.0	361	5.0	5.7
Nov 03	329	4.0	4.0	398	3.0	3.1	363	4.8	5.2
Dec 03	330	4.6	4.2	399	4.4	3.6	364	4.7	4.9
Jan 04	330	3.5	4.0	399	2.5	3.3	363	4.3	4.6
Feb 04	331	3.3	3.8	398	1.7	2.8	366	4.7	4.6
Mar 04	331	3.3	3.4	400	2.1	2.1	367	4.5	4.5
Apr 04	333	3.6	3.4	402	2.1	2.0	369	4.6	4.6
May 04	334	3.7	3.5	405	2.6	2.3	370	5.0	4.7
Jun 04	336	3.8	3.7	404	2.6	2.5	371	4.5	4.7
Jul 04	337	3.9	3.8	405	3.0	2.8	372	3.9	4.4
Aug 04	338	3.9	3.8	407	3.6	3.1	375	3.6	4.0
Sep 04	339	3.9	3.9	409	3.4	3.3	376	4.1	3.9
Oct 04	341	4.2	4.0	410	3.1	3.4	378	4.6	4.1
Nov 04	342	3.9	4.0	411	3.2	3.2	379	4.5	4.4
Dec 04	345	4.5	4.2	415	4.1	3.5	379	4.0	4.4
Jan 05	345	4.4	4.2	416	4.2	3.8	382	5.0	4.5
Feb 05	346	4.7	4.5	420	5.5	4.6	382	4.3	4.5
Mar 05	348	5.1	4.7	422	5.4	5.0	386	5.3	4.9
Apr 05	349	4.8	4.8	423	5.2	5.4	388	5.3	5.0
May 05	350	4.7	4.8	424	4.5	5.0	391	5.7	5.4
Jun 05	351	4.7	4.7	423	4.7	4.8	390	5.2	5.4
Jul 05	354	5.0	4.8	429	5.9	5.0	392	5.2	5.4
Aug 05	355	4.8	4.8	429	5.3	5.3	394	5.1	5.1
Sep 05	356	5.0	4.9	430	5.3	5.5	396	5.2	5.1
Oct 05	356	4.4	4.7	430	4.9	5.1	397	5.1	5.1
Nov 05	357	4.5	4.6	431	4.7	5.0	398	5.2	5.2
Dec 05	358	3.8	4.2	430	3.5	4.4	399	5.5	5.3
Jan 06	360	4.4	4.2	435	4.5	4.2	400	4.7	5.1
Feb 06	360	4.1	4.1	433	3.1	3.7	402	5.4	5.2
Mar 06	361	3.8	4.1	439	4.0	3.8	400	3.6	4.5
Apr 06	362	3.6	3.8	439	3.9	3.7	400	3.1	4.0
May 06	363	3.7	3.7	440	4.0	4.0	401	2.6	3.1
Jun 06	366	4.1	3.8	443	4.9	4.3	404	3.4	3.0
Jul 06	366	3.4	3.7	443	3.3	4.0	405	3.5	3.2
Aug 06	366	3.3	3.6	445	3.8	4.0	405	2.9	3.3
Sep 06	368	3.4	3.3	446	3.6	3.6	406	2.7	3.0
Oct 06	370	4.0	3.5	447	4.0	3.8	408	2.8	2.8
Nov 06	371	4.0	3.8	448	3.9	3.8	409	2.8	2.8
Dec 06	373	4.2	4.1	451	5.0	4.3	411	3.0	2.9
Jan 07	372	3.5	3.9	444	2.2	3.7	414	3.7	3.1
Feb 07	375	4.1	3.9	450	4.0	3.7	413	2.7	3.1
Mar 07	376	4.1	3.9	452	3.1	3.1	414	3.7	3.3
Apr 07	377	4.2	4.1	455	3.7	3.6	413	3.3	3.2
May 07	380	4.6	4.3	459	4.2	3.6	415	3.6	3.5

4.14b Average Weekly Earnings - regular pay [1]

Seasonally adjusted

Great Britain

Standard Industrial Classification (2007)

	Services, SIC 2007 sections G-S			Finance and business services, SIC 2007 sections K-N			Public sector excluding financial services [4]		
	Weekly Earnings (£)	% changes year on year		Weekly Earnings (£)	% changes year on year		Weekly Earnings (£)	% changes year on year	
		Single month	3 month average [2]		Single month	3 month average [2]		Single month	3 month average [2]
	K5DL	K5DM	K5DN	K5DO	K5DP	K5DQ	KAK6	KAK7	KAK8
Jun 07	381	4.3	4.4	461	4.0	3.9	416	3.1	3.3
Jul 07	382	4.5	4.5	463	4.5	4.2	417	2.8	3.2
Aug 07	384	4.9	4.6	464	4.1	4.2	419	3.5	3.1
Sep 07	385	4.6	4.6	467	4.8	4.5	420	3.3	3.2
Oct 07	385	3.9	4.4	468	4.6	4.5	421	3.1	3.3
Nov 07	387	4.3	4.3	471	5.3	4.9	422	3.1	3.2
Dec 07	388	4.0	4.1	472	4.7	4.8	425	3.4	3.2
Jan 08	389	4.3	4.2	470	5.8	5.2	426	2.8	3.1
Feb 08	390	4.1	4.1	475	5.5	5.3	428	3.6	3.3
Mar 08	393	4.3	4.2	476	5.2	5.5	430	3.8	3.4
Apr 08	395	4.9	4.4	479	5.2	5.3	431	4.4	3.9
May 08	394	3.7	4.3	477	4.0	4.8	431	3.7	4.0
Jun 08	395	3.5	4.0	482	4.7	4.6	428	2.9	3.7
Jul 08	396	3.7	3.6	486	5.1	4.6	434	4.1	3.6
Aug 08	398	3.6	3.6	489	5.4	5.1	434	3.5	3.5
Sep 08	399	3.6	3.7	489	4.7	5.1	435	3.8	3.8
Oct 08	400	3.9	3.7	490	4.7	4.9	436	3.5	3.6
Nov 08	400	3.3	3.6	490	4.0	4.4	437	3.6	3.6
Dec 08	401	3.3	3.5	488	3.4	4.0	438	3.0	3.4
Jan 09	400	3.0	3.2	490	4.3	3.9	439	3.0	3.2
Feb 09	402	3.1	3.1	491	3.4	3.7	441	3.1	3.1
Mar 09	402	2.3	2.8	493	3.6	3.8	439	2.0	2.7
Apr 09	403	2.0	2.5	494	3.1	3.4	443	2.8	2.6
May 09	404	2.6	2.3	495	3.6	3.4	445	3.3	2.7
Jun 09	404	2.4	2.3	494	2.5	3.1	447	4.3	3.5
Jul 09	404	1.8	2.3	494	1.6	2.6	446	2.9	3.5
Aug 09	403	1.4	1.9	495	1.3	1.8	447	3.1	3.4
Sep 09	405	1.5	1.6	495	1.2	1.3	448	2.8	2.9
Oct 09	404	1.1	1.3	495	1.0	1.1	448	2.9	2.9
Nov 09	405	1.1	1.2	498	1.6	1.2	450	2.8	2.8
Dec 09	405	1.2	1.1	498	2.0	1.5	450	2.8	2.8
Jan 10	408	1.8	1.4	501	2.2	1.9	452	2.9	2.9
Feb 10	407	1.2	1.4	498	1.3	1.8	453	2.7	2.8
Mar 10	409	1.8	1.6	506	2.7	2.1	452	3.0	2.9
Apr 10	408	1.2	1.4	503	1.9	2.0	454	2.5	2.7
May 10	409	1.1	1.4	504	2.0	2.2	456	2.4	2.6
Jun 10	409	1.2	1.2	504	1.8	1.9	453	1.5	2.1
Jul 10	412	2.1	1.5	511	3.5	2.4	455	2.1	2.0
Aug 10	413	2.3	1.9	514	3.8	3.1	454	1.5	1.7
Sep 10	414	2.3	2.3	515	4.2	3.8	458	2.2	1.9
Oct 10	414	2.4	2.4	517	4.6	4.2	458	2.2	2.0
Nov 10	415	2.6	2.5	518	4.2	4.3	460	2.3	2.3
Dec 10	416	2.5	2.5	523	5.0	4.6	461	2.4	2.3
Jan 11	419	2.7	2.6	528	5.5	4.9	463	2.5	2.4
Feb 11	418	2.6	2.6	525	5.5	5.3	462	2.0	2.3
Mar 11	418	2.2	2.5	525	3.7	4.9	464	2.6	2.4
Apr 11	419	2.7	2.5	527	4.8	4.7	463	1.9	2.2
May 11	420	2.8	2.5	531	5.4	4.6	463	1.6	2.0
Jun 11	420	2.5	2.7	531	5.4	5.2	463	2.1	1.8
Jul 11	420	1.9	2.4	531	3.8	4.8	463	1.6	1.8
Aug 11	420	1.7	2.0	530	3.0	4.1	463	2.0	1.9
Sep 11	422	1.9	1.8	533	3.4	3.4	465	1.6	1.7
Oct 11	423	2.2	1.9	537	3.9	3.4	465	1.5	1.7
Nov 11 (r)	424	2.0	2.0	536	3.5	3.6	465	1.1	1.4
Dec 11 (r)	424	2.1	2.1	541	3.4	3.6	465	0.8	1.1
Jan 12 (r)	423	1.2	1.8	537	1.7	2.9	465	0.5	0.8
Feb 12	425	1.8	1.7	540	2.9	2.7 (r)	466	0.8	0.7 (r)
Mar 12	426	1.9	1.6	543	3.4	2.7 (r)	467	0.7	0.6
Apr 12	426	1.6	1.8	542	2.8	3.0	467	1.0	0.8
May 12	427	1.6	1.7	541	1.9	2.7	468	1.1	0.9
Jun 12	428	1.9	1.7	543	2.3	2.3	472	2.0	1.4
Jul 12	428	1.9	1.8	540	1.8	2.0	474	2.6	1.9
Aug 12	429	2.3	2.0	543	2.6	2.2	475	2.5	2.4
Sep 12	429	1.6	1.9	541	1.6	2.0	475	2.0	2.4
Oct 12	429	1.3	1.7	539	0.2	1.4	475	2.0	2.2
Nov 12	430	1.5	1.5	539 (r)	0.5	0.8	474	2.0	2.0
Dec 12 (r)	430	1.3	1.4	539	-0.4	0.1	474	1.9	2.0
Jan 13 (p)	**428**	**1.1**	**1.3**	**537**	**-0.1**	**0.0**	**474**	**2.0**	**2.0**

1. Estimates of regular pay exclude bonuses and arrears of pay.

Source: Monthly Wages & Salaries Survey

2. The three month average figures are the changes in the average seasonally adjusted values for the three months ending with the relevant month compared with the same period a year earlier.

Earnings enquiries: 01633 456773

1. Estimates of regular pay exclude bonuses and arrears of pay.

2. The three month average figures are the changes in the average seasonally adjusted values for the three months ending with the relevant month compared with the same period a year earlier.

3. From July 2009 Royal Bank of Scotland Group plc and Lloyds Banking Group plc are classified to the public sector; previously they are in the private sector.

4. Between June 2010 and May 2012 English Further Education Corporations and Sixth Form College Corporations are classified to the public sector. Before June 2010 and after May 2012 they are classified to the private sector.

4.14b Average Weekly Earnings - regular pay [1]

Seasonally adjusted   Great Britain

Standard Industrial Classification (2007)

	Manufacturing, SIC 2007 section C			Construction, SIC 2007 section F			Wholesaling, retailing, hotels & restaurants, SIC 2007 sections G & I		
	Weekly Earnings (£)	% changes year on year		Weekly Earnings (£)	% changes year on year		Weekly Earnings (£)	% changes year on year	
		Single month	3 month average [2]		Single month	3 month average [2]		Single month	3 month average [2]
	K5DU	K5DV	K5DW	K5DX	K5DY	K5DZ	K5E2	K5E3	K5E4
Jan 01	364	3.4		377	7.9		205	2.4	
Feb 01	365	3.8		373	6.4		206	3.0	
Mar 01	366	3.6	3.6	381	8.1	7.5	206	4.1	3.2
Apr 01	368	3.7	3.7	381	8.4	7.6	207	3.5	3.5
May 01	368	4.1	3.8	383	8.7	8.4	206	1.9	3.2
Jun 01	368	4.3	4.0	388	7.2	8.1	208	3.4	2.9
Jul 01	369	4.4	4.3	395	9.2	8.4	209	4.4	3.2
Aug 01	370	4.6	4.4	390	8.6	8.4	210	4.3	4.0
Sep 01	372	4.3	4.4	392	8.6	8.8	210	3.1	3.9
Oct 01	373	4.3	4.4	395	7.5	8.2	210	2.9	3.4
Nov 01	375	4.1	4.3	397	6.8	7.6	211	2.7	2.9
Dec 01	375	4.1	4.2	397	5.8	6.7	210	2.6	2.7
Jan 02	377	3.7	4.0	391	3.7	5.4	211	3.1	2.8
Feb 02	379	3.9	3.9	399	7.0	5.5	213	3.4	3.0
Mar 02	378	3.4	3.6	396	4.1	4.9	214	3.9	3.5
Apr 02	381	3.4	3.6	397	4.1	5.0	215	3.9	3.7
May 02	383	4.2	3.7	398	3.8	4.0	216	4.7	4.2
Jun 02	384	4.2	3.9	400	3.0	3.6	219	5.6	4.7
Jul 02	385	4.5	4.3	401	1.7	2.8	219	4.6	5.0
Aug 02	386	4.1	4.3	393	0.8	1.8	219	4.3	4.8
Sep 02	385	3.6	4.1	400	1.9	1.5	219	4.2	4.4
Oct 02	387	3.5	3.7	398	0.9	1.2	219	4.2	4.2
Nov 02	386	2.9	3.3	407	2.5	1.8	220	4.1	4.1
Dec 02	389	3.7	3.4	404	1.8	1.7	219	4.1	4.1
Jan 03	389	3.1	3.2	408	4.5	2.9	223	5.4	4.5
Feb 03	390	2.9	3.2	411	3.0	3.1	221	4.1	4.5
Mar 03	389	2.9	3.0	414	4.5	4.0	221	3.2	4.2
Apr 03	392	2.9	2.9	413	4.1	3.9	222	3.4	3.6
May 03	394	2.8	2.9	411	3.5	4.0	223	3.5	3.4
Jun 03	396	3.0	2.9	419	4.9	4.2	223	1.6	2.8
Jul 03	397	2.9	2.9	416	3.6	4.0	222	1.5	2.2
Aug 03	398	3.2	3.1	409	4.0	4.2	223	1.6	1.6
Sep 03	401	4.0	3.4	420	5.0	4.2	224	2.1	1.8
Oct 03	401	3.6	3.6	420	5.3	4.8	223	1.8	1.9
Nov 03	402	4.3	4.0	423	4.0	4.8	224	2.1	2.0
Dec 03	405	4.1	4.0	427	5.8	5.0	226	3.2	2.4
Jan 04	406	4.4	4.2	427	4.6	4.8	226	1.7	2.3
Feb 04	407	4.5	4.3	427	3.8	4.7	227	2.6	2.5
Mar 04	410	5.2	4.7	434	4.8	4.4	227	2.8	2.4
Apr 04	409	4.4	4.7	431	4.3	4.3	229	3.3	2.9
May 04	412	4.6	4.8	431	4.7	4.6	230	3.1	3.1
Jun 04	414	4.6	4.5	427	1.9	3.6	231	3.7	3.4
Jul 04	416	4.9	4.7	429	3.1	3.2	232	4.2	3.7
Aug 04	417	4.7	4.7	427	4.4	3.1	232	4.1	4.0
Sep 04	418	4.4	4.7	427	1.7	3.1	232	3.8	4.0
Oct 04	421	5.0	4.7	423	0.7	2.3	234	4.7	4.2
Nov 04	422	4.8	4.7	428	1.2	1.2	234	4.2	4.2
Dec 04	421	3.9	4.6	429	0.3	0.7	236	4.5	4.5
Jan 05	422	4.0	4.2	439	2.9	1.5	237	4.5	4.4
Feb 05	423	3.9	3.9	425	-0.4	0.9	237	4.5	4.5
Mar 05	426	3.9	3.9	428	-1.4	0.4	238	4.6	4.5
Apr 05	427	4.5	4.1	431	0.0	-0.6	239	4.1	4.4
May 05	427	3.7	4.0	432	0.3	-0.4	237	2.9	3.9
Jun 05	428	3.6	3.9	434	1.7	0.7	239	3.3	3.5
Jul 05	430	3.4	3.5	436	1.7	1.2	240	3.6	3.3
Aug 05	432	3.7	3.6	437	2.4	1.9	242	4.6	3.8
Sep 05	434	3.7	3.6	444	4.1	2.7	241	4.0	4.1
Oct 05	434	3.2	3.5	446	5.5	4.0	244	4.3	4.3
Nov 05	435	3.1	3.3	451	5.5	5.0	244	4.6	4.3
Dec 05	437	3.7	3.3	446	4.0	5.0	244	3.4	4.1
Jan 06	436	3.3	3.4	453	3.0	4.2	245	3.7	3.9
Feb 06	442	4.5	3.8	455	7.2	4.7	246	3.5	3.5
Mar 06	441	3.5	3.8	456	6.4	5.5	245	3.1	3.4
Apr 06	443	3.7	3.9	459	6.5	6.7	245	2.6	3.1
May 06	446	4.3	3.8	466	7.8	6.9	248	4.5	3.4
Jun 06	444	3.6	3.9	470	8.1	7.5	248	3.8	3.7
Jul 06	442	2.7	3.5	473	8.6	8.2	248	3.5	3.9
Aug 06	446	3.2	3.2	463	5.8	7.5	248	2.3	3.2
Sep 06	448	3.4	3.1	473	6.5	6.9	250	3.7	3.2
Oct 06	450	3.7	3.4	474	6.3	6.2	253	3.6	3.2
Nov 06	451	3.7	3.6	475	5.3	6.0	255	4.3	3.9
Dec 06	450	3.0	3.5	476	6.6	6.1	256	4.8	4.2
Jan 07	456	4.6	3.8	476	5.3	5.8	254	3.5	4.2
Feb 07	457	3.4	3.7	471	3.4	5.1	257	4.7	4.3
Mar 07	460	4.5	4.2	481	5.5	4.7	258	5.2	4.5
Apr 07	457	3.3	3.7	478	4.2	4.4	260	5.9	5.3
May 07	459	2.9	3.6	480	3.1	4.2	260	4.8	5.3

4.14b Average Weekly Earnings - regular pay [1]

Seasonally adjusted

Standard Industrial Classification (2007)

Great Britain

	Manufacturing, SIC 2007 section C			Construction, SIC 2007 section F			Wholesaling, retailing, hotels & restaurants, SIC 2007 sections G & I		
	Weekly Earnings (£)	% changes year on year		Weekly Earnings (£)	% changes year on year		Weekly Earnings (£)	% changes year on year	
		Single month	3 month average [2]		Single month	3 month average [2]		Single month	3 month average [2]
	K5DU	K5DV	K5DW	K5DX	K5DY	K5DZ	K5E2	K5E3	K5E4
Jun 07	461	3.7	3.3	488	3.9	3.7	261	5.3	5.3
Jul 07	462	4.7	3.8	506	7.0	4.7	262	5.6	5.2
Aug 07	462	3.6	4.0	502	8.5	6.5	263	6.2	5.7
Sep 07	463	3.2	3.8	509	7.7	7.7	263	5.0	5.6
Oct 07	464	3.2	3.3	502	5.8	7.3	264	4.4	5.2
Nov 07	464	3.0	3.1	506	6.4	6.6	264	3.7	4.3
Dec 07	465	3.3	3.2	503	5.7	6.0	263	2.8	3.6
Jan 08	469	2.8	3.0	494	3.8	5.3	265	4.4	3.6
Feb 08	472	3.3	3.1	502	6.6	5.3	265	3.0	3.4
Mar 08	472	2.5	2.8	498	3.5	4.6	268	3.7	3.7
Apr 08	474	3.6	3.1	507	6.1	5.4	271	4.2	3.6
May 08	474	3.3	3.2	505	5.3	5.0	269	3.5	3.8
Jun 08	475	3.1	3.4	512	5.0	5.5	268	2.9	3.6
Jul 08	476	3.0	3.2	510	0.7	3.6	267	2.0	2.8
Aug 08	476	2.9	3.0	498	-0.8	1.6	269	2.1	2.3
Sep 08	476	2.9	2.9	510	0.2	0.0	270	2.9	2.3
Oct 08	477	2.8	2.9	515	2.7	0.7	269	2.2	2.4
Nov 08	480	3.5	3.1	514	1.7	1.6	268	1.5	2.2
Dec 08	480	3.2	3.2	511	1.8	2.1	271	2.9	2.2
Jan 09	479	2.1	2.9	517	4.6	2.7	271	2.2	2.2
Feb 09	478	1.2	2.2	514	2.4	2.9	274	3.4	2.8
Mar 09	478	1.3	1.5	517	4.0	3.7	272	1.7	2.4
Apr 09	480	1.3	1.3	516	1.7	2.7	271	0.1	1.7
May 09	481	1.6	1.4	513	1.6	2.4	272	1.1	0.9
Jun 09	484	2.0	1.6	509	-0.6	0.9	272	1.3	0.8
Jul 09	480	0.8	1.4	513	0.7	0.5	273	2.0	1.4
Aug 09	484	1.7	1.5	512	2.9	0.9	272	1.3	1.5
Sep 09	486	2.1	1.5	515	0.9	1.5	274	1.2	1.5
Oct 09	488	2.2	2.0	522	1.2	1.7	275	1.9	1.4
Nov 09	488	1.6	2.0	521	1.3	1.1	274	2.2	1.8
Dec 09	499	4.0	2.6	521	1.8	1.4	276	1.9	2.0
Jan 10	499	4.2	3.3	525	1.4	1.5	275	1.7	1.9
Feb 10	500	4.8	4.3	523	1.8	1.7	277	1.1	1.6
Mar 10	504	5.4	4.8	524	1.4	1.5	279	2.4	1.7
Apr 10	502	4.5	4.9	522	1.2	1.5	277	2.1	1.9
May 10	501	4.1	4.7	515	0.4	1.0	275	1.4	2.0
Jun 10	502	3.7	4.1	517	1.6	1.1	278	2.2	1.9
Jul 10	501	4.4	4.1	511	-0.3	0.6	278	2.1	1.9
Aug 10	504	4.3	4.1	506	-1.1	0.0	279	2.6	2.3
Sep 10	504	3.7	4.1	512	-0.5	-0.7	279	2.0	2.2
Oct 10	504	3.3	3.7	517	-0.8	-0.8	278	1.3	2.0
Nov 10	504	3.2	3.4	516	-1.0	-0.8	278	1.6	1.6
Dec 10	505	1.2	2.5	507	-2.7	-1.5	277	0.5	1.1
Jan 11	506	1.5	2.0	524	0.0	-1.2	279	1.4	1.1
Feb 11	506	1.0	1.2	524	0.3	-0.8	278	0.4	0.8
Mar 11	507	0.6	1.1	527	0.5	0.3	278	-0.1	0.6
Apr 11	507	1.0	0.9	516	-1.2	-0.1	281	1.6	0.6
May 11	508	1.2	0.9	519	0.6	0.0	282	2.3	1.3
Jun 11	508	1.2	1.1	525	1.4	0.3	281	1.0	1.6
Jul 11	510	1.7	1.4	522	2.1	1.4	281	0.8	1.4
Aug 11	510	1.2	1.4	519	2.6	2.0	281	0.6	0.8
Sep 11	513	1.8	1.6	522	2.0	2.2	281	0.6	0.7
Oct 11	512	1.6	1.5	522	0.9	1.8	283	1.7	1.0
Nov 11 (r)	514	2.1	1.8	524	1.7	1.5	284	2.1	1.5
Dec 11 (r)	513	1.6	1.8	518	2.2	1.6	284	2.4	2.1
Jan 12 (r)	513	1.3	1.7	526	0.3	1.4	285	2.2	2.2
Feb 12	515	1.8	1.6	525	0.2	0.9	286	2.8	2.5
Mar 12	517	1.9	1.7 (r)	536	1.7	0.7	286	2.6	2.6 (r)
Apr 12	518	2.3	2.0	528	2.3	1.4	286	1.7	2.4
May 12	520	2.5	2.2	535	3.1	2.4	287	1.9	2.1
Jun 12	520	2.3	2.3	532	1.3	2.2	289	3.1	2.2
Jul 12	521	2.2	2.3	529	1.3	1.9	289	2.9	2.6
Aug 12	522	2.2	2.2	518	-0.3	0.8	288	2.5	2.8
Sep 12	521	1.7	2.0	520	-0.4	0.2	288	2.6	2.7
Oct 12	522	2.0	2.0	521	-0.2	-0.3	289	2.2	2.4
Nov 12	521	1.4	1.7	524	0.0	-0.2	291	2.3	2.4
Dec 12 (r)	524	2.1	1.8	515	-0.5	-0.2	290	2.0	2.1
Jan 13 (p)	**524**	**2.2**	**1.9**	**515**	**-2.0**	**-0.9**	**288**	**0.7**	**1.6**

1. Estimates of regular pay exclude bonuses and arrears of pay.

Source: Monthly Wages & Salaries Survey

2. The three month average figures are the changes in the average seasonally adjusted values for the three months ending with the relevant month compared with the same period a year earlier.

Earnings enquiries: 01633 456773

1. Estimates of regular pay exclude bonuses and arrears of pay.

2. The three month average figures are the changes in the average seasonally adjusted values for the three months ending with the relevant month compared with the same period a year earlier.

3. From July 2009 Royal Bank of Scotland Group plc and Lloyds Banking Group plc are classified to the public sector; previously they are in the private sector.

4. Between June 2010 and May 2012 English Further Education Corporations and Sixth Form College Corporations are classified to the public sector. Before June 2010 and after May 2012 they are classified to the private sector.

4.14c Average Weekly Earnings - bonus pay

Seasonally adjusted

Standard Industrial Classification (2007)

Great Britain

	Whole Economy			Private sector [2][3]			Public sector [2][3]		
	Weekly Earnings (£)	% changes year on year		Weekly Earnings (£)	% changes year on year		Weekly Earnings (£)	% changes year on year	
		Single month	3 month average [1]		Single month	3 month average [1]		Single month	3 month average [1]
	KAF4	KAF5	KAF6	KAF7	KAF8	KAF9	KAG2	KAG3	KAG4
Jan 01	20	41.7		24	42.2		3	-30.8	
Feb 01	21	67.6		25	68.4		3	-17.3	
Mar 01	20	6.5	34.1	24	6.6	34.5	3	-24.5	-24.6
Apr 01	20	13.9	24.7	24	16.9	26.0	3	-39.8	-27.7
May 01	19	5.6	8.6	23	6.3	9.7	3	-10.0	-26.2
Jun 01	20	28.2	15.3	25	30.0	17.1	3	-14.1	-23.2
Jul 01	18	-5.0	8.5	22	-4.0	9.7	3	-31.1	-18.9
Aug 01	18	-8.4	3.3	22	-8.7	4.1	3	10.9	-14.9
Sep 01	18	-5.5	-6.3	22	-5.0	-5.9	3	-18.3	-16.3
Oct 01	19	4.4	-3.4	22	6.1	-2.9	3	-20.1	-11.3
Nov 01	18	-6.2	-2.6	22	-5.3	-1.7	2	-29.3	-22.7
Dec 01	18	-11.6	-4.9	22	-10.7	-3.8	1	-24.4	-24.7
Jan 02	18	-8.2	-8.7	22	-8.6	-8.3	3	-0.6	-17.0
Feb 02	18	-14.1	-11.3	21	-14.2	-11.2	4	8.7	-0.9
Mar 02	17	-15.6	-12.7	21	-15.5	-12.8	3	7.2	5.1
Apr 02	18	-10.2	-13.3	22	-9.4	-13.1	4	30.0	14.5
May 02	18	-6.0	-10.7	22	-7.4	-10.8	4	21.4	19.0
Jun 02	18	-10.8	-9.0	22	-11.1	-9.3	3	5.8	18.9
Jul 02	18	1.0	-5.5	22	1.0	-6.1	3	26.3	17.7
Aug 02	18	0.8	-3.3	22	1.8	-3.1	2	-9.6	7.6
Sep 02	18	-1.9	-0.1	22	-2.2	0.2	3	22.6	13.3
Oct 02	17	-5.8	-2.4	21	-5.2	-1.9	3	21.8	11.8
Nov 02	18	-3.1	-3.6	21	-3.2	-3.6	3	33.5	25.7
Dec 02	18	-3.8	-4.3	21	-4.5	-4.3	3	182.3	54.3
Jan 03	16	-14.4	-7.1	19	-13.2	-7.0	3	-12.5	35.1
Feb 03	17	-3.0	-7.1	21	-1.5	-6.5	3	-20.9	10.0
Mar 03	20	18.9	0.1	25	21.0	1.6	3	-11.0	-15.0
Apr 03	16	-11.3	1.3	20	-8.6	3.3	3	-19.8	-17.4
May 03	17	-8.9	-0.8	20	-6.9	1.5	3	-28.5	-20.1
Jun 03	17	-3.5	-7.9	21	-4.0	-6.5	4	38.4	-5.8
Jul 03	18	-2.3	-4.9	22	0.2	-3.6	3	-9.6	-2.2
Aug 03	17	-7.8	-4.5	21	-7.4	-3.8	3	27.7	17.1
Sep 03	18	0.5	-3.2	22	2.3	-1.7	3	-8.6	0.5
Oct 03	20	14.3	2.2	25	17.3	3.8	3	-8.5	1.0
Nov 03	18	0.6	5.1	22	3.1	7.5	2	-28.7	-15.2
Dec 03	18	-0.6	4.8	21	0.7	7.0	3	3.4	-11.6
Jan 04	20	25.6	7.9	24	25.1	9.1	3	16.4	-4.0
Feb 04	17	-1.0	7.4	21	-1.4	7.7	3	3.1	7.5
Mar 04	21	3.2	8.5	25	2.6	8.0	3	14.8	11.4
Apr 04	21	33.9	10.9	26	31.9	10.2	3	6.8	8.3
May 04	20	20.6	17.9	27	32.9	21.0	3	11.0	10.9
Jun 04	20	13.7	22.4	24	15.9	26.7	3	-20.8	-4.0
Jul 04	20	10.5	14.8	24	10.7	19.5	3	-4.4	-7.2
Aug 04	20	19.7	14.6	24	18.5	14.9	3	9.1	-7.2
Sep 04	22	20.7	16.9	26	18.1	15.7	3	-2.5	0.7
Oct 04	24	18.0	19.4	29	17.4	18.0	3	2.8	3.1
Nov 04	22	24.2	20.8	27	22.1	19.1	3	38.6	10.9
Dec 04	22	24.3	22.0	27	25.4	21.4	3	10.1	15.4
Jan 05	22	10.1	19.2	27	9.8	18.8	3	-2.4	12.9
Feb 05	22	26.0	19.7	26	26.4	20.0	3	7.2	4.8
Mar 05	21	1.8	11.8	26	1.9	11.9	3	-9.1	-1.8
Apr 05	22	4.7	9.8	27	3.8	9.6	4	18.8	5.0
May 05	22	10.4	5.6	27	-0.4	1.7	4	21.6	9.5
Jun 05	21	8.3	7.7	26	8.2	3.7	4	10.2	16.6
Jul 05	22	12.6	10.4	27	10.8	6.0	4	38.0	22.6
Aug 05	25	24.4	15.2	30	24.4	14.5	4	32.5	26.4
Sep 05	24	9.1	15.2	28	8.1	14.3	5	55.1	41.6
Oct 05	23	-1.1	10.2	28	-1.5	9.6	5	53.4	46.6
Nov 05	25	11.9	6.5	30	12.0	6.0	4	23.1	43.4
Dec 05	25	14.9	8.3	31	13.9	7.9	5	34.2	36.6
Jan 06	22	-0.1	8.9	26	-1.1	8.3	6	70.1	42.3
Feb 06	27	26.4	13.7	33	25.8	12.8	5	53.4	52.1
Mar 06	26	23.7	16.6	32	22.8	15.7	5	52.2	58.6
Apr 06	26	16.6	22.2	31	14.5	20.9	5	36.8	46.9
May 06	26	16.5	18.9	31	16.2	17.8	5	37.4	41.7
Jun 06	28	32.8	21.8	34	31.1	20.5	5	27.9	34.0
Jul 06	28	27.0	25.3	34	26.4	24.6	5	19.4	27.9
Aug 06	27	8.1	21.9	33	8.0	21.2	5	7.8	17.8
Sep 06	25	6.3	13.4	29	4.5	12.6	4	-18.7	2.0
Oct 06	26	11.5	8.6	32	11.3	7.9	6	20.8	3.4
Nov 06	27	8.2	8.6	33	8.5	8.1	3	-20.4	-5.2
Dec 06	32	27.1	15.7	39	28.5	16.2	5	7.4	3.8
Jan 07	29	34.6	22.8	35	34.5	23.4	4	-22.8	-12.2
Feb 07	37	35.0	32.2	45	35.3	32.8	3	-29.8	-15.7
Mar 07	28	7.8	25.4	34	7.3	25.3	5	11.1	-14.4
Apr 07	28	10.2	17.9	34	9.5	17.7	5	4.0	-5.0

4.14c Average Weekly Earnings - bonus pay

Seasonally adjusted   Great Britain

Standard Industrial Classification (2007)

	Whole Economy			Private sector [2][3]			Public sector [2][3]		
	Weekly Earnings (£)	% changes year on year		Weekly Earnings (£)	% changes year on year		Weekly Earnings (£)	% changes year on year	
		Single month	3 month average [1]		Single month	3 month average [1]		Single month	3 month average [1]
	KAF4	KAF5	KAF6	KAF7	KAF8	KAF9	KAG2	KAG3	KAG4
May 07	29	10.3	9.4	35	14.2	10.3	5	8.4	7.8
Jun 07	29	4.4	8.2	35	3.1	8.7	6	23.3	11.7
Jul 07	30	6.1	6.8	36	6.2	7.6	5	3.5	11.6
Aug 07	30	10.7	7.0	36	11.4	6.8	5	3.6	10.1
Sep 07	34	36.4	17.1	40	36.6	17.3	5	27.6	10.3
Oct 07	30	14.4	20.2	36	15.5	20.7	3	-49.6	-11.5
Nov 07	32	17.1	22.4	39	17.1	22.7	5	55.0	-0.4
Dec 07	29	-8.4	6.7	36	-8.6	6.9	5	-6.4	-10.1
Jan 08	29	0.2	2.3	36	0.5	2.3	4	-5.6	9.6
Feb 08	39	7.3	0.1	48	6.5	-0.2	5	41.7	6.9
Mar 08	31	8.4	5.4	37	8.8	5.4	4	-29.5	-2.8
Apr 08	31	8.9	8.1	37	9.4	8.1	4	-24.4	-10.0
May 08	32	12.8	10.1	42	19.3	12.5	5	-8.1	-20.6
Jun 08	30	0.8	7.4	36	2.8	10.5	5	-10.8	-14.2
Jul 08	30	-1.0	4.1	36	-1.0	6.9	6	20.9	-0.2
Aug 08	29	-3.0	-1.1	35	-2.8	-0.3	6	19.6	8.7
Sep 08	30	-12.9	-6.0	36	-11.5	-5.3	6	16.5	19.0
Oct 08	30	0.9	-5.4	37	0.7	-4.7	5	79.4	32.1
Nov 08	26	-17.3	-10.1	32	-17.7	-9.7	6	22.3	33.1
Dec 08	27	-6.4	-7.8	33	-6.8	-8.1	6	21.4	35.1
Jan 09	26	-10.6	-11.6	32	-10.1	-11.7	6	36.8	26.3
Feb 09	20	-50.3	-25.3	23	-50.8	-25.4	5	0.7	18.5
Mar 09	18	-42.1	-36.0	22	-41.0	-35.7	7	73.3	33.7
Apr 09	30	-3.1	-33.4	36	-4.4	-33.6	5	38.0	34.1
May 09	26	-20.7	-21.9	30	-28.7	-24.8	4	-11.5	29.1
Jun 09	21	-28.9	-17.5	32	-12.7	-15.8	4	-23.0	-1.9
Jul 09	24	-18.5	-22.6	31	-14.9	-19.3	4	-38.0	-25.0
Aug 09	25	-12.8	-20.1	32	-10.8	-12.8	4	-38.1	-33.4
Sep 09	25	-17.2	-16.2	30	-15.6	-13.8	6	10.2	-22.6
Oct 09	25	-17.2	-15.7	30	-17.1	-14.5	5	-4.6	-11.4
Nov 09	26	1.3	-11.6	33	3.1	-10.4	5	-21.7	-5.8
Dec 09	28	2.8	-4.8	34	2.5	-4.4	4	-30.7	-19.5
Jan 10	22	-15.7	-3.8	28	-14.1	-2.8	6	10.4	-14.4
Feb 10	29	46.5	7.9	35	49.0	8.8	5	6.3	-5.4
Mar 10	26	44.3	20.2	32	44.2	21.6	5	-28.8	-5.9
Apr 10	24	-18.7	17.0	30	-17.0	18.7	5	-4.8	-10.8
May 10	26	0.1	3.2	34	14.4	9.1	5	20.4	-7.6
Jun 10	24	13.9	-3.4	28	-12.2	-5.8	5	22.5	11.1
Jul 10	22	-8.4	1.3	29	-6.4	-1.7	5	28.9	23.7
Aug 10	24	-5.8	-0.8	29	-8.4	-9.0	5	45.4	31.9
Sep 10	26	4.5	-3.2	32	6.2	-3.0	5	-18.7	11.7
Oct 10	25	2.5	0.3	31	2.5	0.0	6	26.3	12.2
Nov 10	25	-3.9	0.9	31	-4.2	1.3	6	20.6	7.1
Dec 10	26	-9.1	-3.7	32	-8.1	-3.5	5	34.2	26.6
Jan 11	30	37.7	6.2	38	39.2	7.0	5	-18.0	8.4
Feb 11	27	-5.6	5.3	33	-5.5	6.3	6	15.3	7.0
Mar 11	27	7.1	11.2	34	6.2	11.5	7	47.7	12.1
Apr 11	27	10.9	3.6	33	12.2	3.8	5	3.8	21.3
May 11	26	3.0	6.9	34	-0.3	5.7	5	-5.8	13.9
Jun 11	30	24.2	12.5	36	28.6	12.5	6	19.1	5.4
Jul 11	31	38.4	21.0	37	28.1	17.5	16	239.9	81.0
Aug 11	28	17.9	26.6	35	19.5	25.3	5	-5.4	81.5
Sep 11	27	3.6	19.1	33	2.5	16.2	6	11.0	78.6
Oct 11	27	7.9	9.6	34	8.6	9.9	3	-44.4	-15.2
Nov 11 (r)	27	6.5	6.0	33	6.3	5.8	5	-13.2	-17.6
Dec 11 (r)	26	3.5	6.0	33	3.1	6.0	5	-7.1	-22.6
Jan 12 (r)	27	-12.4	-1.5	33	-13.8	-2.3	7	34.1	3.5
Feb 12	25	-6.5	-5.6 (r)	31	-7.0	-6.4 (r)	5	-22.0	-0.1 (r)
Mar 12	26	-4.3	-7.9 (r)	32	-4.7	-8.8 (r)	5	-21.0	-6.0 (r)
Apr 12	31	15.6	1.5	38	15.0	1.1	5	-3.5	-16.2
May 12	27	3.7	4.9	34	0.4	3.5	5	9.2	-6.8
Jun 12	28	-7.0	3.7	34	-4.5	3.4	5	-13.1	-3.1
Jul 12	29	-5.7	-3.3	36	-2.1	-2.1	6	-63.8	-39.5
Aug 12	30	6.7	-2.2	36	4.3	-0.8	7	32.4	-35.3
Sep 12	29	6.9	2.4	34	4.7	2.2	7	25.4	-27.6
Oct 12	28	0.2	4.6	33	-2.9	2.0	7	111.6	49.2
Nov 12 (r)	27	0.7	2.6	33	-1.1	0.2	5	7.9	40.5
Dec 12 (r)	27	1.3	0.7	32	-1.4	-1.8	8	54.7	52.0
Jan 13 (p)	27	0.9	0.9	33	-1.0	-1.2	7	7.0	21.5

Source: Monthly Wages & Salaries Survey

Earnings enquiries: 01633 456773

1. The three month average figures are the changes in the average seasonally adjusted values for the three months ending with the relevant month compared with the same period a year earlier.

2. From July 2009 Royal Bank of Scotland Group plc and Lloyds Banking Group plc are classified to the public sector; previously they are in the private sector.

3. Between June 2010 and May 2012 English Further Education Corporations and Sixth Form College Corporations are classified to the public sector. Before June 2010 and after May 2012 they are classified to the private sector.

4.14c Average Weekly Earnings - bonus pay

Seasonally adjusted

Great Britain

Standard Industrial Classification (2007)

	Services, SIC 2007 sections G-S			Finance and business services, SIC 2007 sections K-N			Public sector excluding financial services [3]		
	Weekly Earnings (£)	% changes year on year		Weekly Earnings (£)	% changes year on year		Weekly Earnings (£)	% changes year on year	
		Single month	3 month average [1]		Single month	3 month average [1]		Single month	3 month average [1]
	K5CS	K5CT	K5CU	K5CV	K5CW	K5CX	KAH3	KAH4	KAH5
Jan 01	21	52.8		50	78.6		2	-31.9	
Feb 01	22	75.5		50	97.3		3	-17.2	
Mar 01	21	3.2	37.4	49	3.4	47.6	2	-24.4	-24.8
Apr 01	22	30.4	30.6	50	25.9	32.3	2	-45.0	-30.5
May 01	20	8.7	13.2	45	-1.4	8.4	2	-10.5	-29.6
Jun 01	21	31.8	22.9	69	51.8	25.4	2	-14.2	-27.2
Jul 01	19	-5.0	10.5	42	-2.3	16.3	2	-32.0	-19.6
Aug 01	19	-12.1	2.7	42	-16.6	10.2	2	9.3	-15.6
Sep 01	19	-8.3	-8.5	44	-0.1	-6.8	2	-18.7	-17.1
Oct 01	19	5.5	-5.5	44	5.8	-4.4	2	-20.5	-11.9
Nov 01	19	-7.2	-3.7	42	-14.0	-3.3	2	-29.9	-23.1
Dec 01	19	-12.5	-5.4	43	-17.1	-9.3	1	-26.0	-25.4
Jan 02	19	-8.8	-9.6	42	-15.9	-15.7	2	-3.1	-18.6
Feb 02	19	-13.4	-11.6	42	-15.0	-16.0	2	-10.4	-10.3
Mar 02	16	-22.2	-14.7	36	-26.7	-19.2	2	1.7	-4.1
Apr 02	19	-13.0	-16.1	39	-20.8	-20.8	3	14.6	1.4
May 02	19	-6.0	-13.8	40	-9.8	-19.4	3	20.5	12.1
Jun 02	18	-12.9	-10.7	41	-41.2	-26.4	2	5.1	13.6
Jul 02	19	1.2	-6.2	44	4.5	-19.8	2	24.0	16.5
Aug 02	19	1.4	-3.8	41	-2.6	-18.0	2	-11.4	6.0
Sep 02	19	-0.9	0.6	44	-1.4	0.2	2	21.8	11.6
Oct 02	18	-4.4	-1.3	41	-6.5	-3.5	2	21.2	10.6
Nov 02	19	-2.2	-2.5	41	-2.1	-3.3	2	32.3	24.9
Dec 02	18	-5.6	-4.1	38	-9.6	-6.1	2	174.7	52.5
Jan 03	16	-19.4	-9.1	31	-24.9	-12.2	2	-14.5	33.3
Feb 03	18	-5.3	-10.2	41	-2.4	-12.2	2	-9.1	15.6
Mar 03	18	14.1	-4.6	42	14.5	-5.1	2	-13.8	-12.5
Apr 03	17	-10.4	-1.3	38	-3.7	2.4	2	-24.4	-16.1
May 03	17	-9.5	-2.8	39	-3.1	2.2	2	-29.4	-22.9
Jun 03	18	-4.4	-8.1	37	-9.0	-5.3	3	36.6	-8.3
Jul 03	18	-4.2	-6.1	40	-10.0	-7.5	2	-12.5	-4.0
Aug 03	17	-9.8	-6.2	38	-7.7	-9.0	2	24.2	14.4
Sep 03	18	-4.3	-6.1	38	-12.5	-10.1	2	-10.3	-2.1
Oct 03	20	12.3	-0.8	47	14.3	-2.2	2	-9.8	-0.9
Nov 03	18	-2.9	1.5	42	2.6	1.1	2	-30.7	-16.9
Dec 03	18	-2.2	2.3	31	-18.9	-0.3	2	1.2	-13.5
Jan 04	20	28.0	6.6	49	56.9	10.5	2	14.6	-6.3
Feb 04	18	-0.8	7.4	38	-7.0	6.9	2	-0.5	4.8
Mar 04	20	10.9	12.1	50	20.9	20.7	2	11.1	8.3
Apr 04	23	37.1	15.3	54	44.1	18.6	2	6.5	5.7
May 04	20	16.1	21.0	54	39.6	34.5	2	9.5	9.1
Jun 04	20	14.0	22.3	47	27.7	37.2	2	-21.7	-5.0
Jul 04	20	10.1	13.4	50	26.0	31.1	2	-5.3	-8.3
Aug 04	20	19.2	14.3	38	0.4	18.1	2	7.6	-8.3
Sep 04	22	22.4	17.2	47	22.1	16.4	2	-4.9	-0.9
Oct 04	24	20.2	20.6	65	38.9	21.9	2	-0.2	0.8
Nov 04	23	25.2	22.5	51	22.8	28.5	2	34.7	7.7
Dec 04	22	26.5	23.8	53	70.4	41.5	2	8.3	12.5
Jan 05	22	9.7	20.0	55	11.0	30.2	2	-3.7	10.9
Feb 05	22	24.6	19.8	51	32.9	33.7	2	4.2	2.8
Mar 05	21	3.2	11.9	52	4.4	14.7	2	-5.1	-1.7
Apr 05	23	-0.4	8.0	54	0.0	10.4	2	11.9	3.4
May 05	23	13.3	5.0	51	-6.6	-0.9	2	14.8	6.8
Jun 05	22	8.9	6.9	60	27.4	6.0	2	4.4	10.1
Jul 05	23	12.5	11.5	54	7.7	8.7	3	32.9	16.7
Aug 05	26	27.2	16.2	67	76.7	33.9	3	27.4	21.0
Sep 05	24	8.2	15.8	64	37.7	37.5	3	50.8	36.7
Oct 05	23	-2.8	10.0	60	-8.2	27.6	3	53.1	43.2
Nov 05	26	13.3	6.0	67	31.6	17.5	3	19.5	40.8
Dec 05	26	14.8	8.1	62	16.6	11.6	3	30.3	34.0
Jan 06	22	-0.7	9.2	57	4.5	17.3	4	71.9	40.2
Feb 06	28	26.5	13.5	65	28.0	16.1	4	74.5	58.0
Mar 06	27	28.7	18.0	71	35.7	22.5	3	49.5	65.3
Apr 06	26	14.7	23.1	70	28.7	30.8	3	36.3	53.0
May 06	27	18.8	20.5	71	39.0	34.4	3	35.4	40.1
Jun 06	29	34.8	22.6	96	60.5	43.4	3	25.7	32.4
Jul 06	30	31.7	28.4	82	51.6	50.9	3	17.4	25.8
Aug 06	28	7.9	23.9	77	15.5	41.2	3	6.7	16.0
Sep 06	24	2.8	13.7	62	-4.1	19.2	2	-21.5	0.0
Oct 06	26	9.4	6.7	73	23.1	11.3	4	18.0	1.3
Nov 06	28	9.5	7.3	80	19.3	12.6	2	-21.6	-7.2
Dec 06	35	37.6	19.1	107	72.9	38.1	3	4.6	1.8
Jan 07	30	37.0	27.6	82	43.0	44.4	3	-25.4	-14.5
Feb 07	38	36.0	36.8	84	28.0	47.7	3	-24.6	-16.4
Mar 07	29	6.9	26.0	75	4.7	23.8	3	-1.4	-17.9
Apr 07	29	10.7	18.1	78	11.0	14.2	3	-3.4	-10.6

4.14c Average Weekly Earnings - bonus pay

Seasonally adjusted   Great Britain

Standard Industrial Classification (2007)

	Services, SIC 2007 sections G-S			Finance and business services, SIC 2007 sections K-N			Public sector excluding financial services [3]		
	Weekly Earnings (£)	% changes year on year		Weekly Earnings (£)	% changes year on year		Weekly Earnings (£)	% changes year on year	
		Single month	3 month average [1]		Single month	3 month average [1]		Single month	3 month average [1]
	K5CS	K5CT	K5CU	K5CV	K5CW	K5CX	KAH3	KAH4	KAH5
May 07	29	9.1	8.9	75	5.9	7.2	3	5.9	0.4
Jun 07	30	1.1	6.8	75	-22.3	-4.0	4	19.7	7.3
Jul 07	31	3.7	4.5	78	-5.0	-8.6	3	0.8	8.7
Aug 07	31	10.2	4.9	80	4.2	-8.8	3	1.2	7.1
Sep 07	34	39.7	16.6	92	49.6	13.5	3	24.2	7.4
Oct 07	30	18.2	22.1	74	1.4	16.4	2	-50.7	-14.1
Nov 07	32	14.1	23.4	79	-1.9	14.0	3	54.0	-3.0
Dec 07	30	-16.5	3.1	75	-29.8	-12.4	3	-9.6	-12.6
Jan 08	30	-0.2	-2.1	80	-1.4	-12.8	3	-8.2	7.0
Feb 08	41	8.7	-2.5	87	4.4	-10.8	2	-13.8	-10.5
Mar 08	32	9.1	6.1	83	11.4	4.6	2	-40.7	-21.7
Apr 08	32	8.3	8.7	80	2.3	5.9	3	0.9	-18.2
May 08	33	10.9	9.4	94	25.5	12.9	3	-9.3	-16.4
Jun 08	30	2.4	7.2	91	22.1	16.5	3	-14.7	-8.2
Jul 08	30	-1.1	4.0	79	2.3	16.5	4	20.0	-2.2
Aug 08	30	-2.5	-0.4	74	-8.4	5.0	4	18.2	6.7
Sep 08	30	-12.9	-5.7	83	-10.1	-5.7	3	15.7	18.0
Oct 08	31	2.8	-4.5	88	18.8	-0.8	3	80.1	31.8
Nov 08	27	-15.5	-8.8	63	-20.1	-4.6	4	27.9	35.6
Dec 08	29	-2.5	-5.3	81	7.3	1.6	3	16.3	36.0
Jan 09	27	-7.8	-8.8	77	-4.1	-5.8	2	-6.7	13.7
Feb 09	20	-51.6	-24.2	44	-49.4	-16.8	4	59.9	22.3
Mar 09	18	-43.3	-36.3	47	-43.2	-32.8	4	95.8	45.0
Apr 09	31	-2.5	-34.2	87	9.1	-28.7	5	50.6	65.1
May 09	26	-19.9	-21.9	55	-41.1	-26.2	3	-13.3	36.6
Jun 09	21	-30.4	-17.4	54	-40.9	-25.9	2	-26.1	3.6
Jul 09	25	-17.2	-22.4	64	-19.0	-34.4	2	-46.1	-29.8
Aug 09	26	-13.8	-20.5	68	-7.9	-23.8	2	-54.5	-43.1
Sep 09	25	-14.5	-15.2	60	-27.6	-18.6	3	-11.2	-38.0
Oct 09	25	-19.1	-15.8	64	-27.8	-21.7	2	-39.8	-35.6
Nov 09	27	-0.6	-11.9	68	7.3	-18.3	2	-53.5	-35.8
Dec 09	29	0.8	-6.8	84	3.7	-7.3	2	-44.0	-46.2
Jan 10	23	-17.3	-5.6	61	-20.3	-3.7	2	-4.7	-38.4
Feb 10	29	47.7	6.5	75	69.3	8.9	2	-54.9	-38.8
Mar 10	26	43.7	19.2	65	38.2	19.5	4	16.8	-16.5
Apr 10	25	-18.8	16.8	65	-24.6	15.3	1	-70.9	-39.5
May 10	26	-0.7	2.5	83	49.8	12.8	2	-26.9	-30.9
Jun 10	25	16.8	-3.1	68	25.4	10.1	2	-14.9	-45.2
Jul 10	24	-6.8	2.3	61	-5.3	21.8	2	-23.8	-22.0
Aug 10	24	-6.4	0.2	67	-1.2	5.1	2	6.5	-11.9
Sep 10	26	3.3	-3.4	73	21.3	4.5	2	-46.6	-26.5
Oct 10	26	1.9	-0.5	71	11.5	10.1	2	-0.4	-19.5
Nov 10	26	-2.0	1.0	71	4.7	12.2	2	-6.4	-22.3
Dec 10	26	-11.1	-4.0	68	-18.5	-2.3	2	-7.3	-4.6
Jan 11	32	40.0	6.8	96	55.7	10.3	1	-38.2	-18.6
Feb 11	28	-5.9	5.1	74	-1.5	8.0	2	12.4	-13.2
Mar 11	28	9.2	12.5	77	17.6	22.1	2	-58.2	-37.8
Apr 11	27	9.6	3.8	76	15.5	10.0	2	47.6	-22.1
May 11	27	2.7	7.1	79	-4.6	8.3	2	-20.5	-29.6
Jun 11	31	25.2	12.3	91	33.8	13.5	1	-44.2	-11.9
Jul 11	33	40.5	22.2	89	47.0	22.5	2	16.7	-18.4
Aug 11	29	20.5	28.6	73	8.7	29.3	2	1.6	-10.9
Sep 11	27	3.7	21.0	73	-0.6	17.0	2	0.1	5.8
Oct 11	29	11.7	11.8	74	3.6	3.8	1	-42.3	-15.1
Nov 11 (r)	28	5.7	7.0	76	7.6	3.5	2	-1.8	-16.4
Dec 11 (r)	27	5.6	7.6	72	5.3	5.5	1	-17.5	-21.6
Jan 12 (r)	27	-13.7	-1.7	72	-25.1	-6.4	3	82.9	16.7
Feb 12	26	-6.7	-5.6 (r)	63	-14.1	-13.0 (r)	1	-29.8	5.1 (r)
Mar 12	27	-3.5	-8.2 (r)	73	-4.9	-15.5 (r)	1	-15.9	5.5 (r)
Apr 12	32	18.2	2.6	93	22.6	1.3	1	-30.9	-25.9
May 12	27	2.8	5.8	69	-13.0	1.4	2	7.6	-14.7
Jun 12	28	-8.6	3.6	71	-22.0	-5.3	2	52.5	1.7
Jul 12	31	-7.2	-4.7	80	-10.3	-15.2	2	1.4	16.1
Aug 12	31	7.6	-3.0	81	11.3	-8.3	1	-33.8	-0.3
Sep 12	30	10.6	3.0	70	-4.1	-1.7	2	44.0	2.4
Oct 12	28	-0.9	5.7	68	-7.4	-0.1	3	151.0	40.4
Nov 12 (r)	28	0.9	3.4	66	-13.2	-8.3	2	8.5	58.3
Dec 12 (r)	28	2.8	0.9	72	0.9	-6.7	2	68.0	66.9
Jan 13 (p)	28	1.4	1.7	71	-0.7	-4.5	2	-20.7	10.6

Source: Monthly Wages & Salaries Survey

Earnings enquiries: 01633 456773

1. The three month average figures are the changes in the average seasonally adjusted values for the three months ending with the relevant month compared with the same period a year earlier.

2. From July 2009 Royal Bank of Scotland Group plc and Lloyds Banking Group plc are classified to the public sector; previously they are in the private sector.

3. Between June 2010 and May 2012 English Further Education Corporations and Sixth Form College Corporations are classified to the public sector. Before June 2010 and after May 2012 they are classified to the private sector.

4.14c Average Weekly Earnings - bonus pay

Seasonally adjusted

Standard Industrial Classification (2007)

Great Britain

	Manufacturing, SIC 2007 section C			Construction, SIC 2007 section F			Wholesaling, retailing, hotels & restaurants, SIC 2007 sections G & I		
	Weekly Earnings (£)	% changes year on year		Weekly Earnings (£)	% changes year on year		Weekly Earnings (£)	% changes year on year	
		Single month	3 month average [1]		Single month	3 month average [1]		Single month	3 month average [1]
	K5D3	K5D4	K5D5	K5D6	K5D7	K5D8	K5D9	K5DA	K5DB
Jan 01	15	-17.4		21	24.8		14	16.0	
Feb 01	16	30.5		18	-19.5		15	15.4	
Mar 01	14	20.3	7.1	15	-0.9	-0.8	17	32.5	21.3
Apr 01	14	-35.7	-3.2	20	10.6	-4.9	16	26.2	24.6
May 01	15	-11.3	-14.1	21	13.0	8.1	17	34.1	30.9
Jun 01	15	-5.7	-19.3	28	52.1	25.4	15	17.3	25.9
Jul 01	14	-12.2	-9.8	21	15.7	27.0	15	7.0	19.0
Aug 01	15	-3.8	-7.3	24	30.4	32.9	17	14.6	12.9
Sep 01	15	-4.7	-7.0	22	6.4	17.1	16	19.0	13.5
Oct 01	15	-3.3	-3.9	23	12.4	15.9	14	-2.1	10.4
Nov 01	14	-9.3	-5.8	23	8.9	9.2	16	8.4	8.2
Dec 01	15	-5.2	-6.0	19	-17.6	0.4	15	5.1	3.9
Jan 02	13	-10.6	-8.4	16	-24.6	-11.3	16	12.2	8.5
Feb 02	14	-11.5	-9.1	20	6.8	-12.8	15	-2.1	4.9
Mar 02	15	6.4	-5.5	20	35.4	2.5	15	-9.0	-0.1
Apr 02	15	6.7	0.1	27	39.7	27.0	15	-4.0	-5.1
May 02	14	-6.5	2.1	19	-10.4	19.7	16	-4.8	-5.9
Jun 02	16	7.7	2.5	21	-25.3	-2.1	17	11.4	0.5
Jul 02	14	0.3	0.5	21	2.6	-12.5	14	-5.8	0.0
Aug 02	14	-5.9	0.7	23	-3.0	-10.0	16	-8.9	-1.5
Sep 02	14	-5.2	-3.6	20	-5.9	-2.2	16	-2.6	-5.8
Oct 02	14	-4.3	-5.1	17	-25.1	-11.3	16	13.1	-0.2
Nov 02	15	3.2	-2.1	17	-26.7	-19.5	16	-1.3	2.6
Dec 02	15	4.8	1.2	19	-1.2	-18.5	15	-2.3	2.8
Jan 03	16	16.9	8.0	21	36.2	-1.1	16	-0.4	-1.3
Feb 03	17	25.9	15.6	20	2.5	10.9	15	2.7	-0.1
Mar 03	16	5.6	15.8	24	18.5	17.8	14	-5.0	-0.9
Apr 03	13	-11.3	6.4	20	-27.4	-4.9	12	-20.2	-7.7
May 03	16	14.8	2.9	17	-11.1	-8.9	13	-19.6	-15.1
Jun 03	13	-16.8	-5.1	19	-10.7	-17.6	14	-16.6	-18.8
Jul 03	17	16.5	4.0	19	-9.3	-10.3	15	2.9	-11.7
Aug 03	17	24.9	7.1	20	-13.5	-11.3	13	-15.2	-10.1
Sep 03	16	11.1	17.4	22	9.5	-4.9	14	-9.1	-7.4
Oct 03	16	11.3	15.7	24	40.2	9.4	15	-5.8	-10.0
Nov 03	19	31.0	18.0	22	29.8	25.4	13	-16.7	-10.6
Dec 03	15	-3.7	12.7	21	8.7	25.5	18	21.0	-0.9
Jan 04	17	8.5	11.7	21	-3.5	10.3	14	-12.2	-3.1
Feb 04	14	-18.1	-5.0	20	1.7	2.1	15	0.3	2.8
Mar 04	16	-0.3	-3.8	23	-2.7	-1.6	14	-4.3	-5.6
Apr 04	16	23.8	-0.3	21	5.4	1.2	15	24.4	5.8
May 04	19	19.8	13.7	25	51.7	15.0	14	9.3	9.0
Jun 04	16	24.6	22.5	20	7.2	19.9	15	6.3	13.0
Jul 04	17	3.1	15.1	22	12.6	22.6	15	1.3	5.4
Aug 04	18	6.8	10.5	18	-10.7	2.8	15	14.3	7.1
Sep 04	20	27.7	12.2	15	-32.9	-11.5	17	17.7	10.9
Oct 04	19	16.4	16.7	18	-23.4	-22.8	15	-1.5	9.9
Nov 04	17	-12.0	9.0	26	21.5	-12.3	15	11.2	8.9
Dec 04	22	45.2	13.9	20	-1.7	-2.0	16	-13.8	-2.6
Jan 05	18	7.8	11.1	24	14.6	11.6	16	13.7	2.0
Feb 05	17	19.9	23.7	23	14.0	8.9	16	4.3	0.1
Mar 05	17	5.6	10.7	25	10.1	12.8	13	-4.7	4.5
Apr 05	19	16.2	13.7	24	15.4	13.1	15	-0.9	-0.3
May 05	17	-11.7	2.5	26	4.5	9.7	15	8.1	0.8
Jun 05	16	-0.4	0.6	23	16.2	11.5	14	-2.3	1.5
Jul 05	18	6.8	-2.1	24	10.0	9.8	14	-4.0	0.5
Aug 05	19	1.6	2.7	20	11.4	12.5	14	-5.5	-4.0
Sep 05	17	-16.6	-3.3	21	42.4	19.4	15	-9.4	-6.4
Oct 05	18	-4.4	-6.8	25	34.9	28.9	15	2.3	-4.4
Nov 05	19	13.5	-3.3	26	-0.8	21.1	15	0.0	-2.7
Dec 05	19	-11.2	-1.6	25	21.3	16.3	17	5.0	2.5
Jan 06	19	6.9	2.0	25	7.5	8.4	15	-5.5	-0.2
Feb 06	21	22.5	4.7	27	17.2	15.1	13	-15.4	-5.3
Mar 06	19	12.9	14.0	23	-8.6	5.0	15	13.6	-3.4
Apr 06	21	11.0	15.3	25	1.6	3.0	15	-3.7	-2.8
May 06	19	14.4	12.7	25	-5.8	-4.4	14	-7.2	0.3
Jun 06	20	20.2	15.0	27	15.9	3.4	15	5.2	-2.1
Jul 06	19	2.8	12.1	27	16.2	8.2	17	18.9	5.3
Aug 06	18	-1.8	6.5	28	39.0	22.9	15	3.9	9.3
Sep 06	21	25.0	8.1	21	-0.7	17.6	15	-1.5	6.9
Oct 06	24	36.6	19.5	26	3.5	12.8	15	0.4	0.9
Nov 06	20	0.9	20.1	23	-11.8	-3.3	15	1.5	0.1
Dec 06	20	2.8	12.8	25	1.2	-2.5	16	-4.2	-0.9
Jan 07	21	9.8	4.5	25	-2.0	-4.3	16	9.7	2.1
Feb 07	22	4.3	5.6	46	67.3	23.5	17	27.4	9.8
Mar 07	21	7.8	7.2	25	9.2	26.4	19	27.8	21.4
Apr 07	21	1.5	4.5	30	20.8	34.1	18	24.9	26.7

4.14c Average Weekly Earnings - bonus pay

Seasonally adjusted

Great Britain

Standard Industrial Classification (2007)

	Manufacturing, SIC 2007 section C			Construction, SIC 2007 section F			Wholesaling, retailing, hotels & restaurants, SIC 2007 sections G & I		
	Weekly Earnings (£)	% changes year on year		Weekly Earnings (£)	% changes year on year		Weekly Earnings (£)	% changes year on year	
		Single month	3 month average [1]		Single month	3 month average [1]		Single month	3 month average [1]
	K5D3	K5D4	K5D5	K5D6	K5D7	K5D8	K5D9	K5DA	K5DB
May 07	22	17.4	8.7	31	25.8	18.8	19	37.0	29.8
Jun 07	24	21.8	13.4	36	33.0	26.7	21	37.4	33.1
Jul 07	23	24.7	21.3	29	5.8	21.3	21	20.8	31.2
Aug 07	23	23.4	23.3	28	1.1	13.1	18	20.3	26.0
Sep 07	23	10.9	19.3	33	56.6	18.2	21	40.4	26.9
Oct 07	23	-5.6	8.2	30	16.3	22.1	22	42.2	34.3
Nov 07	24	23.8	8.7	33	45.4	38.1	20	30.3	37.6
Dec 07	24	23.2	12.4	35	37.7	32.7	19	22.8	31.6
Jan 08	22	2.8	16.2	32	28.3	36.9	18	7.6	19.9
Feb 08	23	3.4	9.4	31	-32.3	1.8	19	10.2	13.4
Mar 08	19	-6.1	0.2	27	7.6	-6.0	20	5.6	7.7
Apr 08	24	14.0	3.8	27	-10.2	-15.7	20	8.5	8.0
May 08	34	54.2	21.6	28	-10.8	-5.2	20	4.1	6.0
Jun 08	24	2.3	23.3	23	-34.8	-19.5	19	-10.3	0.3
Jul 08	27	16.5	23.7	24	-17.7	-21.9	19	-8.2	-5.0
Aug 08	22	-3.4	5.2	26	-5.6	-20.7	17	-3.0	-7.4
Sep 08	22	-5.7	2.6	29	-13.8	-12.5	16	-21.5	-11.3
Oct 08	24	5.5	-1.2	23	-21.8	-13.9	16	-26.4	-17.8
Nov 08	19	-20.2	-7.1	22	-33.6	-23.2	18	-6.5	-18.5
Dec 08	21	-11.8	-9.1	21	-39.9	-32.2	17	-12.4	-15.5
Jan 09	21	-3.7	-12.2	18	-42.6	-38.7	19	5.7	-4.7
Feb 09	19	-18.4	-11.4	20	-34.9	-39.2	18	-1.1	-2.9
Mar 09	21	9.8	-4.8	23	-15.5	-31.8	16	-19.8	-5.6
Apr 09	25	5.4	-1.5	26	-3.1	-18.7	17	-13.4	-11.7
May 09	20	-40.8	-14.0	18	-33.6	-17.6	17	-13.7	-15.7
Jun 09	19	-21.3	-21.8	20	-15.1	-17.6	17	-9.4	-12.3
Jul 09	18	-33.5	-33.0	20	-16.9	-22.5	17	-11.8	-11.7
Aug 09	19	-12.2	-23.2	20	-23.3	-18.6	18	4.1	-5.9
Sep 09	19	-10.8	-20.0	18	-35.5	-25.8	17	5.2	-1.2
Oct 09	18	-25.8	-16.6	22	-7.7	-23.1	17	9.9	6.3
Nov 09	21	8.6	-10.5	22	-0.2	-16.2	17	-5.4	2.8
Dec 09	21	-3.9	-8.3	21	-0.9	-3.1	17	0.0	1.1
Jan 10	20	-3.8	0.1	22	19.5	5.5	19	-1.1	-2.2
Feb 10	22	17.8	2.7	20	-1.9	5.1	20	8.6	2.5
Mar 10	22	3.3	5.2	22	-3.1	4.0	22	37.7	14.0
Apr 10	19	-22.3	-2.5	17	-33.5	-14.1	20	15.1	19.8
May 10	20	-0.2	-7.4	19	2.5	-13.2	17	-0.9	16.8
Jun 10	16	-16.9	-13.7	15	-24.3	-20.3	16	-6.2	2.7
Jul 10	22	23.2	1.6	19	-3.4	-8.6	17	3.6	-1.2
Aug 10	23	22.0	9.1	18	-8.7	-12.1	17	-4.0	-2.3
Sep 10	21	9.0	17.9	18	-2.9	-5.1	18	3.2	0.8
Oct 10	25	41.9	23.8	15	-29.2	-14.3	18	1.4	0.1
Nov 10	21	-0.3	15.7	16	-29.6	-21.5	19	8.4	4.4
Dec 10	23	9.8	15.9	18	-13.0	-24.1	19	12.2	7.3
Jan 11	24	16.1	8.4	19	-12.0	-18.3	17	-6.7	4.4
Feb 11	21	-3.8	7.1	23	15.3	-3.6	16	-20.1	-5.7
Mar 11	22	-1.0	3.4	19	-16.8	-5.2	18	-20.8	-16.3
Apr 11	23	16.4	3.4	19	13.6	2.7	18	-9.5	-17.0
May 11	21	2.6	5.6	18	-4.8	-4.0	19	8.8	-8.4
Jun 11	22	37.5	17.4	20	33.4	12.6	23	44.0	12.5
Jul 11	23	1.0	11.5	17	-10.4	3.9	21	21.7	24.3
Aug 11	21	-10.5	6.1	18	0.2	5.8	19	8.8	24.2
Sep 11	23	8.9	-0.5	19	7.2	-1.2	19	8.3	12.9
Oct 11	21	-17.8	-7.3	22	46.1	16.2	19	8.9	8.6
Nov 11 (r)	23	7.3	-1.6	22	40.1	29.9	18	-4.1	4.2
Dec 11 (r)	22	-4.1	-5.7	19	7.9	30.2	20	2.4	2.2
Jan 12 (r)	22	-7.9	-1.9	18	-4.5	12.9	20	15.5	4.3
Feb 12	23	11.5	-0.6 (r)	16	-29.6	-10.3 (r)	21	30.6	15.3 (r)
Mar 12	18	-15.6	-4.3 (r)	17	-9.8	-15.6 (r)	17	-4.9	13.2 (r)
Apr 12	24	4.2	-0.1	23	15.7	-9.0	18	3.4	9.0
May 12	25	20.7	2.9	21	17.7	7.9	21	10.1	3.0
Jun 12	25	15.5	13.2	24	18.1	17.2	20	-12.5	-0.6
Jul 12	22	-4.2	10.4	22	26.8	20.7	19	-11.3	-5.3
Aug 12	27	30.7	13.6	18	-2.2	14.1	24	27.7	0.0
Sep 12	19	-16.6	2.5	18	-8.2	4.8	22	12.1	8.8
Oct 12	22	3.6	5.2	26	17.9	3.4	21	10.6	16.7
Nov 12 (r)	25	8.9	-1.6	17	-20.2	-3.1	20	12.2	11.6
Dec 12 (r)	21	-4.4	2.8	18	-8.2	-3.1	20	0.2	7.5
Jan 13 (p)	19	-10.4	-1.8	17	-8.7	-12.7	20	-0.3	3.8

Source: Monthly Wages & Salaries Survey

Earnings enquiries: 01633 456773

1. The three month average figures are the changes in the average seasonally adjusted values for the three months ending with the relevant month compared with the same period a year earlier.

2. From July 2009 Royal Bank of Scotland Group plc and Lloyds Banking Group plc are classified to the public sector; previously they are in the private sector.

3. Between June 2010 and May 2012 English Further Education Corporations and Sixth Form College Corporations are classified to the public sector. Before June 2010 and after May 2012 they are classified to the private sector.

4.14d Average Weekly Earnings in the public sector for selected activities (Not Seasonally Adjusted)

CDID	Public Administration (Public Sector) (O)			Education (Public Sector) (P)			Health and Social Work (Public Sector) (Q)			Arts, Entertainment and Recreation (Public Sector) (R)		
	Average Weekly Earnings	Of which		Average Weekly Earnings	Of which		Average Weekly Earnings	Of which		Average Weekly Earnings	Of which	
		Bonuses	Arrears		Bonuses	Arrears		Bonuses	Arrears		Bonuses	Arrears
	K5BE	K5BF	K5BG	K5BH	K5BI	K5BJ	K5BK	K5BL	K5BM	K5BN	K5BO	K5BP
2009 Jan	503	1	2	364	0	4	491	0	1	392	0	0
2009 Feb	526	3	16	361	0	1	494	0	0	400	0	5
2009 Mar	506	1	4	358	1	1	496	0	1	400	0	3
2009 Apr	510	1	1	367	1	1	508	0	0	403	1	0
2009 May	511	1	3	365	0	0	510	0	1	406	0	1
2009 Jun	505	1	2	366	1	0	513	0	1	415	10	1
2009 Jul	506	3	8	368	1	1	507	0	0	400	1	0
2009 Aug	511	3	2	370	1	0	500	0	0	416	10	0
2009 Sep	503	1	1	373	1	0	504	0	0	415	4	4
2009 Oct	508	1	7	376	1	5	505	0	1	403	1	1
2009 Nov	514	3	3	371	1	1	509	0	0	415	1	2
2009 Dec	521	11	2	374	1	2	507	0	0	414	4	2
2010 Jan	520	1	1	369	0	0	505	0	0	415	0	4
2010 Feb	520	1	1	371	0	0	509	0	0	412	0	0
2010 Mar	521	2	1	371	1	0	502	0	0	409	1	0
2010 Apr	522	1	0	374	1	0	516	0	0	413	1	0
2010 May	521	2	0	372	0	0	522	0	0	418	9	0
2010 Jun	524	3	1	371	0	0	524	0	0	420	11	0
2010 Jul	530	3	1	373	1	0	521	0	0	412	6	2
2010 Aug	535	11	0	374	1	0	514	0	0	414	1	0
2010 Sep	528	1	1	380	1	1	520	0	0	416	0	0
2010 Oct	529	1	0	378	0	1	520	0	0	418	0	0
2010 Nov	534	3	1	379	0	1	522	0	0	420	0	2
2010 Dec	538	8	0	381	1	0	525	0	0	424	2	0
2011 Jan	537	1	0	377	0	0	527	0	0	427	2	0
2011 Feb	535	2	0	378	0	0	527	0	0	423	0	0
2011 Mar	534	1	0	381	0	0	527	0	0	430	0	0
2011 Apr	537	1	0	384	0	1	530	0	1	433	5	0
2011 May	538	1	0	378	0	0	532	0	0	458	29	1
2011 Jun	542	6	0	379	0	0	534	0	0	428	3	0
2011 Jul	539	5	0	380	1	0	528	0	0	421	0	0
2011 Aug	545	11	0	383	0	0	524	0	0	424	4	0
2011 Sep	545	1	0	384	0	0	528	0	0	418	0	0
2011 Oct	538	1	0	381	1	0	529	0	0	419	0	0
2011 Nov	537	2	0	380	0	1	533	0	0	423	1	1
2011 Dec	540	6	0	379	0	0	533	0	0	427	0	0
2012 Jan	535	1	0	375	0	0	534	0	0	435	1	0
2012 Feb	538	1	0	377	0	0	537	0	0	463	0	0
2012 Mar	541	2	0	377	0	0	536	0	0	462	0	0
2012 Apr	545	0	0	381	0	0	540	0	0	463	1	1
2012 May	543	1	0	379	0	0	543	0	0	501	44	0
2012 Jun	550	5	0	381	0	0	541	0	0	463	5	0
2012 Jul	551	5	0	382	1	0	542	0	0	461	0	2
2012 Aug	547	3	0	387	0	0	536	0	0	455	0	0
2012 Sep	554	7	1	388	0	0	537	0	0	437	3	1
2012 Oct	547	2	1	385	0	0	536	0	0	462	41	0
2012 Nov	544	2	0	385	0	0	538	0	0	442	1	2
2012 Dec	543	2	2	385	0	0	537	0	0	444	5	0

p = Provisional

r = Revised

All figures are in pounds (£)

Table 4.15a Weekly pay - Gross (£) - For all employee jobs[a] by age group and occupation: United Kingdom, 2012

Description	Code	Number of jobs[b] (thousand)	Median	Annual percentage change	Mean	Annual percentage change	Percentiles 10	20	25	30	40	60	70	75	80	90
All employees		24,203	405.8	1.5	491.3	0.8	121.1	207.2	246.4	279.7	341.2	482.3	574.9	629.4	693.4	893.5
18-21		1,274	174.2	-0.7	192.2	1.5	45.0	73.0	86.1	100.6	133.8	217.2	252.7	269.9	289.2	345.0
22-29		4,108	361.3	1.9	394.3	1.5	136.8	227.2	255.4	278.9	320.0	412.4	470.9	503.0	540.0	650.9
30-39		5,550	479.1	1.1	544.0	0.3	160.0	267.2	306.2	340.4	406.0	558.1	645.9	692.6	752.4	944.1
40-49		6,471	468.5	1.9	565.6	0.5	148.0	243.2	284.7	322.6	391.6	557.4	657.1	713.3	784.5	1,025.8
50-59		4,872	430.8	0.8	538.4	1.3	142.6	230.0	265.1	299.2	362.8	515.6	615.7	677.9	748.1	976.8
60+		1,747	318.9	2.6	405.4	2.2	78.1	130.5	156.8	186.5	252.0	386.3	467.6	520.4	584.2	795.6
18-21 ALL OCCUPATIONS		1,274	174.2	-0.7	192.2	1.5	45.0	73.0	86.1	100.6	133.8	217.2	252.7	269.9	289.2	345.0
18-21 Managers, directors and senior officials	1	14	303.9	-0.9	304.8	0.0	x	201.5	234.9	251.4	274.1	317.9	335.9	377.3	394.5	470.1
18-21 Corporate managers and directors	11	9	318.0	0.9	329.1	-0.1	x	255.6	268.8	280.4	305.0	326.0	366.9	384.0	x	x
18-21 Other managers and proprietors	12	x	x		256.2	1.6	x	x	x	x	x	x	x	x	x	x
18-21 Professional occupations	2	24	348.0	21.1	340.2	12.3	x	x	244.3	262.3	306.6	373.5	415.0	440.7	456.3	538.5
18-21 Science, research, engineering and technology professionals	21	10	306.6	-0.2	325.6	-8.7	x	x	242.6	285.1	302.7	325.1	360.4	x	x	x
18-21 Health professionals	22	6	354.6		352.3	17.1	x	x	x	x	x	408.3	471.1	x	x	x
18-21 Teaching and educational professionals	23	x	x		x		x	x	x	x	x	x	x	x	x	x
18-21 Business, media and public service professionals	24	x	x		416.5	46.3	x	x	x	x	x	x	x	x	x	x
18-21 Associate professional and technical occupations	3	77	282.6	13.4	317.0	31.6	50.1	122.6	151.3	211.9	250.3	309.1	348.5	373.9	390.8	477.2
18-21 Science, engineering and technology associate professionals	31	21	303.4	-0.7	304.4	0.8	x	238.4	247.7	254.8	286.9	323.7	349.6	366.8	378.7	x
18-21 Health and social care associate professionals	32	9	x		160.8	-23.2	x	x	x	x	x	x	x	x	x	x
18-21 Protective service occupations	33	x	453.8	-4.0	478.4	12.4	x	x	x	x	x	x	x	x	x	x
18-21 Culture, media and sports occupations	34	14	215.3		x		x	x	x	x	x	243.2	269.3	x	x	x
18-21 Business and public service associate professionals	35	31	307.7	30.5	307.7	33.7	x	185.9	220.4	243.3	277.2	345.0	380.0	402.6	420.1	x
18-21 Administrative and secretarial occupations	4	113	250.0	0.5	234.7	0.9	71.7	120.9	145.4	181.2	223.2	272.7	293.7	305.1	324.6	364.3
18-21 Administrative occupations	41	94	257.4	1.8	239.2	0.0	72.7	127.2	159.6	189.3	230.0	277.9	297.0	309.5	325.8	364.5
18-21 Secretarial and related occupations	42	20	218.5	-2.5	212.9	5.3	64.5	100.6	114.4	139.1	188.5	251.0	270.8	287.3	294.6	x
18-21 Skilled trades occupations	5	79	294.1	-1.4	314.3	0.0	180.4	216.1	230.8	246.8	272.9	313.4	350.2	370.3	398.9	477.8
18-21 Skilled agricultural and related trades	51	x	266.4	15.7	266.4	13.5	x	x	x	x	286.0	x	x	x	x	x
18-21 Skilled metal, electrical and electronic trades	52	35	337.3	3.6	366.9	4.3	199.4	250.7	267.7	277.7	308.9	370.8	404.5	445.3	471.8	x
18-21 Skilled construction and building trades	53	13	281.6	-7.6	311.1	-4.3	x	231.7	247.9	256.6	272.7	300.0	328.7	352.4	x	x
18-21 Textiles, printing and other skilled trades	54	28	254.5	-5.2	255.6	-5.6	109.9	180.7	191.6	203.7	224.0	278.8	294.3	308.2	316.1	x
18-21 Caring, leisure and other service occupations	6	167	208.3	3.6	199.0	3.9	46.8	96.3	122.2	146.0	180.7	236.3	252.9	264.7	279.0	314.9
18-21 Caring personal service occupations	61	123	216.4	4.6	204.5	4.4	50.7	115.0	138.8	160.7	193.9	240.1	256.5	266.3	279.7	314.9
18-21 Leisure, travel and related personal service occupations	62	44	180.9	-3.2	183.7	1.6	34.1	71.4	85.0	102.9	145.3	205.0	243.3	254.3	269.6	x
18-21 Sales and customer service occupations	7	354	119.0	-1.3	142.6	-1.4	45.0	63.4	73.0	81.0	97.7	144.0	179.1	201.6	228.0	275.2
18-21 Sales occupations	71	307	111.1	-3.2	133.4	-2.0	42.0	60.1	69.1	78.5	92.8	133.7	163.6	182.5	207.4	259.3
18-21 Customer service occupations	72	47	201.9	10.5	202.5	4.4	63.7	98.8	109.9	124.4	163.7	246.3	266.4	275.9	289.4	321.0
18-21 Process, plant and machine operatives	8	36	262.5	-2.6	269.3	-4.0	114.0	156.1	194.4	218.6	243.6	280.3	309.8	328.7	346.2	428.5
18-21 Process, plant and machine operatives	81	28	269.3	-0.8	278.2	-4.5	129.0	195.3	218.5	234.8	252.2	282.4	315.0	329.7	347.9	432.5
18-21 Transport and mobile machine drivers and operatives	82	8	x		236.9	0.2	x	x	x	x	138.6	x	x	x	x	x
18-21 Elementary occupations	9	410	130.0	4.6	154.7	3.3	33.9	58.4	67.9	78.3	102.2	163.5	208.9	228.2	248.6	301.3
18-21 Elementary trades and related occupations	91	33	274.5	11.8	281.4	4.9	135.0	197.3	211.3	229.3	255.3	301.5	323.1	340.7	349.8	x
18-21 Elementary administration and service occupations	92	377	121.6	6.6	143.7	3.3	33.0	54.1	63.4	73.2	96.6	150.5	187.9	213.3	232.4	283.0
22-29 ALL OCCUPATIONS		4,108	361.3	1.9	394.3	1.5	136.8	227.2	255.4	278.9	320.0	412.4	470.9	503.0	540.0	650.9
22-29 Managers, directors and senior officials	1	201	446.5	2.7	525.1	0.3	272.7	321.4	340.0	354.6	396.0	496.3	556.7	596.7	678.0	869.7
22-29 Corporate managers and directors	11	153	469.5	0.7	558.7	-0.8	272.6	325.8	345.0	364.1	416.0	524.4	592.9	659.4	746.7	948.5
22-29 Other managers and proprietors	12	48	390.4	4.6	418.2	6.5	270.0	313.3	326.4	345.0	364.1	423.9	479.1	495.3	512.9	x
22-29 Professional occupations	2	802	532.7	1.5	557.5	1.7	336.8	413.7	440.8	457.9	498.3	574.9	617.1	650.6	686.5	805.0
22-29 Science, research, engineering and technology professionals	21	193	555.8	2.6	585.2	1.3	364.2	430.5	450.4	478.9	515.5	594.3	639.8	674.6	719.0	828.8
22-29 Health professionals	22	176	541.1	0.6	565.5	0.6	347.7	433.9	455.3	476.5	508.9	580.2	629.1	652.8	695.9	852.3
22-29 Teaching and educational professionals	23	205	487.5	-0.5	483.6	0.3	254.0	401.5	413.7	421.6	454.5	519.4	560.4	583.9	604.7	673.1
22-29 Business, media and public service professionals	24	229	555.8	4.4	594.1	2.9	344.2	416.9	442.1	469.2	507.9	603.1	654.7	691.9	734.6	862.4
22-29 Associate professional and technical occupations	3	628	457.4	3.8	497.3	4.9	276.5	335.4	355.9	379.3	418.7	500.0	550.8	575.0	611.6	724.2
22-29 Science, engineering and technology associate professionals	31	119	424.6	2.7	446.1	0.9	283.5	322.9	337.6	355.7	383.4	460.0	503.6	529.8	558.1	647.5
22-29 Health and social care associate professionals	32	49	390.9	10.0	365.1	7.0	99.7	182.4	240.4	293.6	350.0	425.1	454.3	472.3	503.5	x
22-29 Protective service occupations	33	58	576.2	3.1	583.2	3.4	385.6	485.1	509.0	526.2	553.7	599.2	636.7	661.9	681.3	x
22-29 Culture, media and sports occupations	34	60	379.1	5.3	509.1	20.2	x	235.0	270.9	294.9	338.3	416.5	460.0	479.1	506.5	x
22-29 Business and public service associate professionals	35	343	474.4	4.7	517.1	3.7	307.7	354.5	379.3	392.7	431.2	517.5	574.9	599.8	638.0	782.0
22-29 Administrative and secretarial occupations	4	510	336.0	1.4	346.8	0.4	164.4	246.1	270.7	286.6	310.4	358.6	392.9	412.4	439.4	517.5
22-29 Administrative occupations	41	429	341.7	1.9	355.3	0.8	183.1	262.5	279.9	295.4	316.2	364.1	399.6	420.4	443.1	521.4

119

Table 4.15a Weekly pay - Gross (£) - For all employee jobs[a] by age group and occupation: United Kingdom, 2012

Description	Code	Number of jobs[b] (thousand)	Median	Annual percentage change	Mean	Annual percentage change	Percentiles									
							10	20	25	30	40	60	70	75	80	90
22-29 Secretarial and related occupations	42	81	292.4	-2.4	301.3	-1.4	121.0	172.9	203.9	226.3	263.7	325.8	358.2	383.8	403.0	484.6
22-29 Skilled trades occupations	5	347	396.4	0.2	424.4	0.0	253.7	294.8	314.0	329.6	365.1	434.2	482.1	509.3	542.8	634.8
22-29 Skilled agricultural and related trades	51	15	327.3	8.6	340.8	5.4	211.7	273.1	285.6	290.0	315.0	349.6	372.0	384.4	x	x
22-29 Skilled metal, electrical and electronic trades	52	163	453.7	-0.5	484.1	0.5	294.2	340.4	364.4	376.2	413.2	498.3	547.6	573.0	602.6	704.1
22-29 Skilled construction and building trades	53	65	432.6	1.5	452.5	-0.1	293.3	337.5	356.7	369.8	402.6	465.6	502.8	529.9	552.5	x
22-29 Textiles, printing and other skilled trades	54	104	320.1	2.3	324.7	1.5	178.6	243.6	262.5	272.5	294.8	345.0	374.9	387.0	405.3	460.2
22-29 Caring, leisure and other service occupations	6	400	253.3	-0.7	255.1	-1.3	100.2	148.8	169.2	188.7	225.2	281.0	311.6	328.4	346.2	409.6
22-29 Caring personal service occupations	61	319	252.3	-0.2	252.7	-1.2	99.6	147.2	167.6	187.4	223.3	279.0	307.7	325.2	343.2	404.8
22-29 Leisure, travel and related personal service occupations	62	81	259.1	-2.2	264.6	-1.6	103.5	151.9	179.3	195.7	231.9	293.1	325.4	342.1	358.7	428.9
22-29 Sales and customer service occupations	7	504	249.4	1.3	248.7	0.4	93.6	127.3	146.6	165.6	212.0	277.7	305.3	323.1	342.5	403.3
22-29 Sales occupations	71	374	221.9	-1.2	227.7	-0.1	84.7	114.1	128.9	145.7	182.4	255.3	286.0	300.0	319.7	379.1
22-29 Customer service occupations	72	131	303.9	1.3	308.7	3.1	150.7	214.5	244.0	258.7	281.3	325.8	352.4	366.3	385.7	462.4
22-29 Process, plant and machine operatives	8	200	350.0	0.0	373.5	-0.5	215.1	258.4	271.6	288.4	317.6	383.3	421.3	450.0	484.0	588.5
22-29 Process, plant and machine operatives	81	134	335.4	-1.9	365.8	-0.2	227.4	254.1	267.4	281.6	310.0	370.6	405.9	436.3	466.1	572.6
22-29 Transport and mobile machine drivers and operatives	82	66	376.6	2.9	389.3	-0.9	170.2	267.9	287.5	306.1	344.5	404.4	445.6	475.1	507.0	604.1
22-29 Elementary occupations	9	517	249.1	3.9	249.3	3.2	71.4	115.5	136.5	160.6	215.7	279.0	314.8	334.4	356.0	421.7
22-29 Elementary trades and related occupations	91	77	320.0	3.2	331.0	1.9	186.7	246.0	258.6	270.9	297.5	347.2	374.6	393.9	415.0	484.6
22-29 Elementary administration and service occupations	92	440	234.0	4.8	235.1	3.6	64.6	104.4	121.6	144.1	194.6	262.4	296.9	318.9	340.9	409.2
30-39 ALL OCCUPATIONS		5,550	479.1	1.1	544.0	0.3	160.0	267.2	306.2	340.4	406.0	558.1	645.9	692.6	752.4	944.1
30-39 Managers, directors and senior officials	1	568	695.9	1.0	850.1	-1.8	342.5	435.7	479.1	517.2	603.9	797.6	952.5	1,046.4	1,149.9	1,547.6
30-39 Corporate managers and directors	11	472	750.7	3.1	905.4	-1.3	357.3	468.1	513.8	558.7	654.3	857.7	1,023.4	1,119.8	1,242.9	1,623.4
30-39 Other managers and proprietors	12	96	498.3	-6.9	578.4	-5.2	287.5	350.8	370.8	392.1	455.7	557.7	632.4	679.4	730.2	907.8
30-39 Professional occupations	2	1,447	662.7	1.1	706.3	0.5	342.2	459.0	505.0	541.2	604.7	722.5	794.4	841.7	897.8	1,090.5
30-39 Science, research, engineering and technology professionals	21	359	711.6	1.0	770.4	0.2	445.3	538.6	575.2	604.8	662.1	779.1	859.0	903.3	957.2	1,149.9
30-39 Health professionals	22	345	601.3	2.7	673.2	3.3	277.1	402.0	439.1	482.1	543.3	661.7	747.5	808.8	888.8	1,156.8
30-39 Teaching and educational professionals	23	365	655.1	0.0	612.6	-0.1	254.4	405.3	446.4	502.2	585.4	700.2	742.5	773.6	798.1	897.8
30-39 Business, media and public service professionals	24	378	683.7	1.9	766.4	-1.1	412.5	499.9	536.6	567.0	621.8	754.6	843.0	896.4	958.8	1,211.1
30-39 Associate professional and technical occupations	3	964	576.2	1.7	629.4	-0.1	304.5	402.5	432.6	463.1	522.6	633.6	702.5	743.7	796.1	979.8
30-39 Science, engineering and technology associate professionals	31	160	534.3	2.9	561.2	-0.5	319.0	398.6	421.7	444.8	482.1	574.9	626.9	664.6	698.5	838.8
30-39 Health and social care associate professionals	32	81	444.2	6.3	441.7	8.0	161.3	262.9	308.4	350.0	406.3	488.1	529.4	552.7	587.6	683.9
30-39 Protective service occupations	33	138	668.7	0.9	680.5	2.3	476.6	555.9	565.9	588.6	626.8	705.2	745.0	773.7	809.8	907.2
30-39 Culture, media and sports occupations	34	61	479.1	-3.8	494.0	-9.1	111.3	243.6	305.0	350.8	414.8	542.3	609.0	632.4	670.8	x
30-39 Business and public service associate professionals	35	525	595.9	1.8	681.3	-1.1	330.4	410.5	440.8	479.1	535.7	670.8	747.4	798.1	874.6	1,119.7
30-39 Administrative and secretarial occupations	4	610	357.7	1.4	380.5	-0.1	143.7	210.0	244.3	272.5	321.7	398.6	441.6	474.1	505.7	619.5
30-39 Administrative occupations	41	508	364.1	0.9	390.5	-0.6	150.5	224.7	256.9	287.4	328.9	404.5	449.6	480.2	513.3	626.9
30-39 Secretarial and related occupations	42	102	314.9	6.0	330.9	2.8	122.6	157.0	180.0	209.4	259.6	360.5	405.0	429.9	470.5	581.4
30-39 Skilled trades occupations	5	406	454.3	-1.1	488.1	-1.4	267.7	326.0	350.0	368.5	411.8	502.8	566.4	598.9	636.0	749.4
30-39 Skilled agricultural and related trades	51	22	343.7	-3.3	356.2	-3.7	199.5	282.4	297.4	306.0	327.2	363.7	383.8	395.4	423.7	x
30-39 Skilled metal, electrical and electronic trades	52	211	525.0	0.3	560.8	-0.4	341.9	399.0	420.0	435.9	479.9	575.3	632.3	664.1	701.2	827.5
30-39 Skilled construction and building trades	53	61	466.1	-0.8	505.8	-3.2	300.2	362.2	386.1	404.1	434.5	503.4	556.0	582.9	627.3	x
30-39 Textiles, printing and other skilled trades	54	111	345.0	-2.1	366.6	-0.6	156.2	243.9	267.9	286.1	317.0	377.1	423.1	445.7	479.9	598.4
30-39 Caring, leisure and other service occupations	6	423	248.7	-0.1	269.0	-1.4	97.3	139.9	156.4	178.4	215.2	286.5	329.4	352.5	381.4	457.4
30-39 Caring personal service occupations	61	354	240.6	-1.0	258.5	-1.2	96.9	138.1	154.4	174.9	209.1	277.6	315.4	340.4	365.3	432.9
30-39 Leisure, travel and related personal service occupations	62	69	301.3	-1.1	322.9	-1.6	100.5	148.8	166.4	202.5	255.4	341.2	402.0	431.9	469.6	570.9
30-39 Sales and customer service occupations	7	347	268.3	2.5	296.8	-0.6	101.7	134.7	153.0	176.9	226.7	310.6	354.0	381.2	411.6	511.3
30-39 Sales occupations	71	237	232.5	0.3	259.8	-1.7	96.0	121.2	132.5	145.4	182.8	272.0	311.8	336.6	362.7	450.5
30-39 Customer service occupations	72	110	348.5	1.2	376.1	1.4	155.0	215.7	243.7	265.5	314.4	387.7	436.9	460.9	499.0	590.3
30-39 Process, plant and machine operatives	8	288	405.9	-2.3	436.8	-0.7	237.7	286.2	305.9	326.8	364.9	458.3	511.1	539.6	570.0	678.1
30-39 Process, plant and machine operatives	81	162	382.9	-4.6	426.5	-1.7	243.2	277.0	292.7	310.9	344.7	431.1	486.8	518.6	557.0	681.7
30-39 Transport and mobile machine drivers and operatives	82	127	435.7	-0.6	449.9	0.6	225.9	304.0	332.7	354.7	393.6	489.3	533.4	558.3	587.5	671.3
30-39 Elementary occupations	9	496	264.5	3.4	270.1	2.7	64.4	102.7	124.8	151.4	217.9	306.8	349.4	374.7	400.5	484.5
30-39 Elementary trades and related occupations	91	67	338.0	-1.1	348.6	-3.3	185.1	245.2	260.8	278.2	309.7	369.4	399.1	416.0	449.4	525.1
30-39 Elementary administration and service occupations	92	429	247.6	4.8	257.8	4.4	60.8	97.3	112.0	132.6	188.7	293.1	335.9	363.2	392.7	477.0
40-49 ALL OCCUPATIONS		6,471	468.5	1.9	565.6	0.5	148.0	243.2	284.7	322.6	391.6	557.4	657.1	713.3	784.5	1,025.8
40-49 Managers, directors and senior officials	1	775	766.6	-2.4	968.5	-2.3	334.5	460.0	513.0	567.4	664.6	902.1	1,069.2	1,179.9	1,332.9	1,770.6
40-49 Corporate managers and directors	11	659	808.0	-3.3	1,018.4	-2.3	345.0	481.3	548.0	601.6	698.5	962.5	1,133.2	1,249.9	1,418.0	1,860.7

Table 4.15a Weekly pay - Gross (£) - For all employee jobs[a] by age group and occupation: United Kingdom, 2012

Description	Code	Number of jobs[b] (thousand)	Median	Annual percentage change	Mean	Annual percentage change	Percentiles									
							10	20	25	30	40	60	70	75	80	90
40-49 Other managers and proprietors	12	116	574.9	-0.4	684.2	-4.7	292.5	374.8	405.1	444.4	512.2	647.5	755.9	810.9	878.2	1,153.7
40-49 Professional occupations	2	1,421	688.7	1.4	754.6	0.2	315.7	447.2	503.6	548.6	623.9	757.9	846.4	893.6	965.1	1,219.8
40-49 Science, research, engineering and technology professionals	21	322	787.5	2.2	852.1	2.1	479.1	596.9	629.4	664.0	722.6	859.3	938.1	994.9	1,066.9	1,294.4
40-49 Health professionals	22	393	607.5	2.5	720.1	1.3	265.7	377.1	423.6	466.5	536.2	669.8	746.0	782.6	862.7	1,383.3
40-49 Teaching and educational professionals	23	375	679.3	0.0	655.5	-0.1	224.7	385.3	438.0	499.1	604.7	729.5	806.0	846.4	877.2	1,034.1
40-49 Business, media and public service professionals	24	331	697.7	-1.2	813.0	-2.5	374.5	491.1	539.0	578.7	634.0	793.1	895.2	958.2	1,045.1	1,330.2
40-49 Associate professional and technical occupations	3	961	600.5	1.4	675.6	0.4	300.1	401.0	441.4	475.0	538.7	671.3	754.8	801.2	864.0	1,076.3
40-49 Science, engineering and technology associate professionals	31	158	553.2	-0.6	582.5	-1.3	290.2	374.6	403.7	443.9	499.8	606.5	660.8	697.5	736.8	884.5
40-49 Health and social care associate professionals	32	101	439.0	1.3	441.4	0.3	166.0	263.7	312.4	343.4	392.2	481.3	529.7	559.1	591.5	701.8
40-49 Protective service occupations	33	150	727.9	0.7	745.2	1.5	495.6	565.9	586.2	623.3	692.4	779.7	828.2	860.2	892.0	1,001.9
40-49 Culture, media and sports occupations	34	45	474.8	4.4	494.3	-11.6	x	x	x	301.2	381.1	543.9	614.7	661.3	718.1	x
40-49 Business and public service associate professionals	35	508	625.6	1.6	746.6	0.8	337.3	422.2	460.0	490.9	557.4	705.3	803.5	874.4	960.2	1,274.5
40-49 Administrative and secretarial occupations	4	789	342.9	1.2	374.8	-1.3	141.2	197.3	226.1	254.1	299.5	382.8	434.4	465.2	502.6	631.1
40-49 Administrative occupations	41	620	352.2	0.7	388.7	-1.8	146.4	212.8	242.0	269.3	315.1	392.0	443.9	476.3	512.3	647.1
40-49 Secretarial and related occupations	42	169	293.0	2.2	324.0	1.5	121.2	162.4	186.7	203.0	252.3	337.6	389.5	417.8	464.5	573.9
40-49 Skilled trades occupations	5	489	488.2	0.4	520.3	-0.1	259.9	342.0	371.0	394.0	440.8	538.0	597.2	633.6	678.1	806.7
40-49 Skilled agricultural and related trades	51	28	364.9	3.8	388.3	-0.8	259.6	293.7	301.7	310.9	334.0	386.7	437.1	466.0	483.2	x
40-49 Skilled metal, electrical and electronic trades	52	261	559.7	1.4	597.9	0.7	369.2	423.4	447.9	468.7	513.5	605.1	663.0	702.7	735.9	876.6
40-49 Skilled construction and building trades	53	84	497.2	-1.7	541.6	-2.4	344.0	386.7	404.3	420.0	457.6	529.9	581.3	630.6	679.0	817.5
40-49 Textiles, printing and other skilled trades	54	117	327.6	-4.6	362.8	-0.1	145.6	202.7	227.9	248.5	294.7	383.3	423.1	450.6	491.3	597.9
40-49 Caring, leisure and other service occupations	6	620	251.2	-1.0	274.9	-0.5	97.6	146.2	165.2	185.2	217.7	291.2	331.5	357.7	383.1	463.0
40-49 Caring personal service occupations	61	528	246.8	0.1	264.3	0.6	98.4	146.0	164.4	183.7	214.7	283.6	323.6	347.1	371.4	435.4
40-49 Leisure, travel and related personal service occupations	62	92	293.1	-5.8	335.7	-5.7	97.3	149.4	174.6	197.8	239.0	342.7	412.5	454.6	506.9	651.1
40-49 Sales and customer service occupations	7	360	240.9	0.8	281.7	-1.6	100.4	130.0	143.8	162.4	196.4	281.5	329.4	355.9	392.5	517.9
40-49 Sales occupations	71	260	204.3	-4.1	243.4	-2.6	96.0	117.0	131.3	143.4	173.3	243.2	280.7	305.5	332.6	441.8
40-49 Customer service occupations	72	101	345.0	5.4	380.8	0.3	136.7	196.4	237.2	259.7	307.3	384.8	435.5	466.4	520.4	638.5
40-49 Process, plant and machine operatives	8	415	443.4	-0.4	473.9	0.9	253.4	314.2	337.7	360.6	400.0	492.2	548.1	577.5	610.9	741.3
40-49 Process, plant and machine operatives	81	191	426.2	-0.7	458.2	-1.1	241.3	284.1	314.2	332.8	380.7	472.8	527.2	560.8	598.6	717.4
40-49 Transport and mobile machine drivers and operatives	82	224	458.1	-0.1	487.3	2.5	270.1	337.0	358.4	375.3	416.7	511.2	562.8	588.0	620.1	753.9
40-49 Elementary occupations	9	641	247.7	0.2	264.1	0.5	57.6	97.0	115.2	136.3	190.5	299.3	347.8	374.9	404.8	495.1
40-49 Elementary trades and related occupations	91	82	358.4	0.5	383.2	-0.9	221.5	261.4	273.7	291.2	329.4	393.3	445.5	475.0	509.2	581.0
40-49 Elementary administration and service occupations	92	559	220.6	-0.4	246.7	1.3	51.8	88.7	103.4	121.3	164.4	276.9	330.7	356.2	390.6	473.5
50-59 ALL OCCUPATIONS		4,872	430.8	0.8	538.4	1.3	142.6	230.0	265.1	299.2	362.8	515.6	615.7	677.9	748.1	976.8
50-59 Managers, directors and senior officials	1	558	775.4	3.4	1,004.7	5.4	296.5	440.8	498.3	557.7	664.1	911.2	1,093.6	1,215.3	1,379.9	1,875.4
50-59 Corporate managers and directors	11	465	829.8	3.1	1,065.6	5.0	304.8	463.0	529.4	590.3	703.7	978.9	1,172.2	1,302.9	1,468.9	1,933.6
50-59 Other managers and proprietors	12	93	586.1	2.7	701.0	2.8	280.1	369.1	409.3	441.9	523.7	665.4	774.4	840.4	918.6	x
50-59 Professional occupations	2	1,012	688.5	0.4	743.8	-0.5	288.9	427.1	481.9	531.7	615.7	755.6	833.9	877.3	949.0	1,170.8
50-59 Science, research, engineering and technology professionals	21	198	770.8	0.5	848.8	1.4	460.0	573.7	607.2	653.8	709.7	856.9	944.3	1,005.1	1,073.5	1,286.8
50-59 Health professionals	22	285	584.8	0.2	709.6	-1.2	241.8	349.5	407.6	442.7	524.2	655.2	738.8	774.4	830.9	1,130.4
50-59 Teaching and educational professionals	23	314	704.4	-1.1	699.3	-1.3	227.9	409.9	469.7	548.2	655.4	774.9	837.5	871.7	916.1	1,069.6
50-59 Business, media and public service professionals	24	215	668.0	-0.4	757.2	-1.3	326.4	453.4	490.8	544.2	609.3	750.1	846.0	897.1	979.7	1,231.3
50-59 Associate professional and technical occupations	3	583	554.4	1.5	613.3	-0.2	261.8	360.8	398.1	429.8	490.2	616.3	696.3	747.0	799.6	994.5
50-59 Science, engineering and technology associate professionals	31	115	540.1	-1.6	567.9	-2.0	302.1	366.5	392.7	429.7	485.4	589.4	655.2	687.1	730.4	871.8
50-59 Health and social care associate professionals	32	84	409.2	-2.0	421.2	-2.8	171.3	250.9	295.6	317.7	365.6	459.4	511.1	530.1	572.6	663.8
50-59 Protective service occupations	33	51	696.1	3.2	693.2	4.3	388.3	503.9	556.3	565.9	615.7	753.6	794.9	831.6	866.8	x
50-59 Culture, media and sports occupations	34	24	399.1	-3.3	465.6	-4.9	36.9	x	x	x	x	463.1	567.0	663.4	723.3	x
50-59 Business and public service associate professionals	35	308	590.3	2.7	681.1	0.4	315.1	402.4	437.8	464.4	526.4	666.9	747.4	804.0	862.4	1,138.0
50-59 Administrative and secretarial occupations	4	722	334.6	1.0	366.6	0.6	140.9	199.1	226.1	252.7	299.6	372.1	417.8	446.2	485.7	598.8
50-59 Administrative occupations	41	544	350.3	1.5	382.5	0.8	149.6	214.7	244.7	271.2	314.0	385.0	431.3	460.0	498.9	611.5
50-59 Secretarial and related occupations	42	178	290.1	0.7	318.0	0.4	123.0	161.9	185.6	207.0	252.1	326.7	366.5	400.0	429.3	550.3
50-59 Skilled trades occupations	5	372	482.2	0.7	510.0	0.5	252.7	330.9	360.0	386.8	431.1	536.6	591.7	625.6	662.4	785.4
50-59 Skilled agricultural and related trades	51	21	328.8	-2.0	349.0	-0.3	x	251.5	273.5	290.0	308.5	359.7	387.3	401.5	424.1	x
50-59 Skilled metal, electrical and electronic trades	52	208	558.6	3.4	586.6	0.8	355.1	415.3	440.9	466.7	515.7	602.4	652.6	688.6	725.9	836.5
50-59 Skilled construction and building trades	53	61	480.8	-0.3	523.9	-1.7	346.3	395.8	412.3	422.1	451.0	520.2	568.0	592.4	626.3	797.6
50-59 Textiles, printing and other skilled trades	54	81	319.2	1.2	346.2	0.6	143.4	210.6	228.8	248.4	281.8	349.7	392.7	415.0	453.0	559.9

Table 4.15a Weekly pay - Gross (£) - For all employee jobs[a] by age group and occupation: United Kingdom, 2012

Description	Code	Number of jobs[b] (thousand)	Median	Annual percentage change	Mean	Annual percentage change	Percentiles 10	20	25	30	40	60	70	75	80	90
50-59 Caring, leisure and other service occupations	6	484	269.0	2.7	285.5	0.8	104.0	157.2	176.1	197.8	234.9	305.6	344.4	366.5	393.2	473.9
50-59 Caring personal service occupations	61	403	265.4	2.1	279.1	0.0	105.2	158.1	177.2	198.4	233.1	301.1	339.3	362.9	385.3	454.7
50-59 Leisure, travel and related personal service occupations	62	80	293.2	3.9	317.5	3.4	97.3	145.8	170.6	188.8	248.0	327.1	367.8	414.5	453.4	565.3
50-59 Sales and customer service occupations	7	302	216.6	1.9	255.4	1.6	98.6	127.7	140.3	153.2	182.8	255.8	296.9	320.9	351.1	449.0
50-59 Sales occupations	71	228	189.4	-1.6	223.5	0.5	94.3	121.9	129.4	140.5	163.4	223.8	258.6	281.7	306.6	378.9
50-59 Customer service occupations	72	74	316.7	3.3	353.6	4.5	140.4	190.5	217.4	243.7	276.6	354.7	395.0	429.1	482.2	619.7
50-59 Process, plant and machine operatives	8	340	424.3	0.9	453.2	1.3	237.3	291.7	315.0	334.7	380.0	474.0	527.2	560.8	593.0	706.5
50-59 Process, plant and machine operatives	81	162	407.2	0.5	448.8	1.4	236.4	280.5	300.5	318.8	363.9	461.9	522.3	558.1	594.0	707.6
50-59 Transport and mobile machine drivers and operatives	82	178	435.5	0.6	457.2	1.2	241.6	305.1	326.9	349.6	394.9	481.7	531.5	563.8	590.4	703.9
50-59 Elementary occupations	9	499	242.8	-1.3	257.7	-1.3	60.4	95.8	114.0	134.1	187.6	288.8	338.6	366.6	398.7	476.9
50-59 Elementary trades and related occupations	91	61	347.0	-0.9	368.2	-2.4	214.1	255.5	272.2	290.2	317.3	382.6	424.1	451.6	474.6	557.1
50-59 Elementary administration and service occupations	92	438	217.1	-2.4	242.3	-0.8	53.2	88.0	103.5	121.9	162.8	266.0	319.8	348.4	385.6	466.2
60+ ALL OCCUPATIONS		1,747	318.9	2.6	405.4	2.2	78.1	130.5	156.8	186.5	252.0	386.3	467.6	520.4	584.2	795.6
60+ Managers, directors and senior officials	1	175	581.7	1.2	779.3	4.4	217.0	299.0	345.0	399.9	490.9	705.6	866.8	977.5	1,111.8	1,533.2
60+ Corporate managers and directors	11	139	615.9	3.0	824.9	3.3	214.1	300.0	362.4	421.6	516.0	767.5	937.5	1,053.0	1,170.9	1,608.5
60+ Other managers and proprietors	12	36	495.4	6.3	601.1	7.9	223.8	290.0	315.0	345.0	416.3	580.7	650.0	705.3	761.1	x
60+ Professional occupations	2	278	540.9	1.9	625.5	-0.4	139.6	255.2	302.8	353.9	447.7	649.7	742.1	799.8	877.9	1,150.6
60+ Science, research, engineering and technology professionals	21	47	718.6	11.9	754.4	4.4	306.5	455.7	511.2	539.7	637.7	775.0	878.7	931.0	998.6	x
60+ Health professionals	22	67	436.7	-3.5	602.1	-5.6	160.1	251.9	274.2	304.7	375.3	509.0	609.1	660.5	769.3	x
60+ Teaching and educational professionals	23	98	506.9	4.7	569.6	-0.8	82.4	162.1	215.6	252.3	365.3	647.4	715.9	785.4	871.7	1,097.4
60+ Business, media and public service professionals	24	66	574.9	0.0	639.7	-0.1	215.4	335.0	394.0	435.7	497.0	657.9	738.0	791.0	871.4	x
60+ Associate professional and technical occupations	3	164	456.2	3.7	505.6	3.3	126.4	230.0	274.1	321.0	390.1	533.1	600.0	651.7	703.8	904.3
60+ Science, engineering and technology associate professionals	31	33	472.5	7.6	499.4	6.2	198.0	293.9	331.3	364.2	427.8	528.8	587.6	625.2	679.3	x
60+ Health and social care associate professionals	32	22	311.0	11.1	318.9	-5.3	55.5	x	150.0	168.7	248.2	368.6	426.7	452.6	484.7	x
60+ Protective service occupations	33	8	476.2	15.3	484.7	2.8	x	345.1	363.5	366.8	401.4	514.4	546.7	x	x	x
60+ Culture, media and sports occupations	34	10	x		302.8	24.8	x	x	x	x	x	x	x	x	x	x
60+ Business and public service associate professionals	35	92	527.3	5.2	575.7	1.1	168.5	261.7	310.9	358.9	435.2	590.5	672.4	723.2	814.6	1,079.3
60+ Administrative and secretarial occupations	4	281	251.8	3.5	285.2	2.8	67.1	119.3	139.4	158.4	201.0	309.5	353.2	383.3	417.8	538.8
60+ Administrative occupations	41	201	262.7	4.6	290.7	3.5	59.8	120.2	141.4	160.9	210.0	322.5	364.2	394.7	422.9	538.5
60+ Secretarial and related occupations	42	80	223.4	-2.0	271.2	0.9	80.0	117.8	133.6	149.0	184.0	272.7	326.4	353.9	399.9	543.0
60+ Skilled trades occupations	5	138	435.0	1.5	454.3	1.2	176.6	281.9	316.4	346.6	392.4	470.9	525.1	559.5	601.6	734.3
60+ Skilled agricultural and related trades	51	11	278.7	3.9	279.5	6.0	x	141.0	x	174.4	252.5	311.0	340.5	373.0	x	x
60+ Skilled metal, electrical and electronic trades	52	75	496.3	0.5	530.2	-0.3	305.8	380.9	398.7	424.4	456.8	530.5	590.0	616.9	667.6	782.9
60+ Skilled construction and building trades	53	24	452.5	-4.2	489.6	0.0	298.7	364.8	378.9	401.4	427.5	472.4	520.5	541.2	604.4	x
60+ Textiles, printing and other skilled trades	54	28	285.8	9.5	294.1	4.3	97.6	125.8	154.7	177.0	222.4	307.3	345.9	371.1	391.0	x
60+ Caring, leisure and other service occupations	6	176	209.1	1.4	232.2	0.3	61.7	102.2	121.3	135.9	171.7	251.2	298.3	325.5	356.2	434.6
60+ Caring personal service occupations	61	132	208.0	-0.3	229.5	-0.1	65.4	109.6	126.9	142.3	174.4	245.3	290.3	314.2	345.0	418.9
60+ Leisure, travel and related personal service occupations	62	44	215.8	11.8	240.2	1.3	52.0	89.9	102.4	116.9	159.9	273.6	329.3	359.9	386.0	x
60+ Sales and customer service occupations	7	131	154.8	4.5	195.8	5.8	67.7	92.8	101.1	112.2	131.7	182.7	223.4	245.3	277.1	376.8
60+ Sales occupations	71	105	145.4	3.8	184.7	6.9	67.2	91.3	100.0	107.9	126.5	173.0	208.1	229.3	251.8	345.5
60+ Customer service occupations	72	25	210.7	2.9	242.0	0.3	68.9	98.7	119.5	130.2	157.5	253.8	317.3	346.5	371.0	x
60+ Process, plant and machine operatives	8	167	332.8	-1.8	353.2	0.1	107.6	172.8	208.6	243.2	290.6	384.5	442.5	475.6	508.3	599.1
60+ Process, plant and machine operatives	81	54	331.8	-3.4	361.2	-0.7	135.7	222.5	244.3	269.5	301.7	373.6	432.6	465.3	497.6	593.4
60+ Transport and mobile machine drivers and operatives	82	114	333.5	0.3	349.4	0.5	97.3	156.9	188.8	228.2	284.8	394.5	450.0	481.2	514.2	600.0
60+ Elementary occupations	9	239	149.2	-7.3	199.3	-1.2	40.9	63.6	76.0	87.5	114.0	205.6	267.7	301.2	333.2	410.2
60+ Elementary trades and related occupations	91	24	313.7	0.3	323.7	2.0	111.1	186.2	235.9	256.5	282.5	347.6	375.4	394.0	422.9	x
60+ Elementary administration and service occupations	92	215	135.1	-3.5	185.2	-1.0	39.5	60.8	69.8	81.0	106.6	182.0	245.0	273.6	311.6	395.9
Not Classified																

a Employees on adult rates whose pay for the survey pay-period was not affected by absence.

b Figures for Number of Jobs are for indicative purposes only and should not be considered an accurate estimate of employee job counts.

KEY - The colour coding indicates the quality of each estimate; jobs, median, mean and percentiles but not the annual percentage change.

The quality of an estimate is measured by its coefficient of variation (CV), which is the ratio of the standard error of an estimate to the estimate.

Source: Annual Survey of Hours and Earnings, Office for National Statistics.

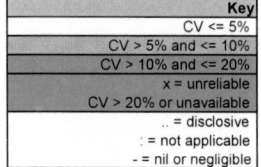

Key	
CV <= 5%	
CV > 5% and <= 10%	
CV > 10% and <= 20%	
x = unreliable CV > 20% or unavailable	
.. = disclosive	
: = not applicable	
- = nil or negligible	

Table 4.15b   Hourly pay - Gross (£) - For all employee jobs[a] by age group and occupation: United Kingdom, 2012

Description	Code	Number of jobs[b] (thousand)	Median	Annual percentage change	Mean	Annual percentage change	Percentiles 10	20	25	30	40	60	70	75	80	90
All employees		24,203	11.28	1.3	14.84	0.9	6.47	7.42	7.96	8.51	9.77	13.29	15.80	17.42	19.17	25.00
18-21		1,274	6.57	1.7	7.47	3.1	5.22	6.08	6.08	6.09	6.29	6.96	7.48	7.78	8.18	9.63
22-29		4,108	9.60	1.4	11.38	1.3	6.32	7.02	7.41	7.78	8.62	10.87	12.54	13.50	14.55	17.67
30-39		5,550	13.16	1.7	15.79	0.2	7.00	8.33	9.01	9.75	11.27	15.26	17.66	19.02	20.76	26.25
40-49		6,471	12.88	1.9	16.66	0.4	6.95	8.20	8.85	9.54	11.03	15.23	17.99	19.68	21.63	28.28
50-59		4,872	12.08	0.9	16.13	1.3	6.82	7.97	8.52	9.10	10.43	14.25	17.17	18.81	20.79	27.44
60+		1,747	10.20	2.0	14.16	2.5	6.46	7.20	7.64	8.10	9.09	11.84	14.14	15.81	17.91	24.49
18-21 ALL OCCUPATIONS		1,274	6.57	1.7	7.47	3.1	5.22	6.08	6.08	6.09	6.29	6.96	7.48	7.78	8.18	9.63
18-21 Managers, directors and senior officials	1	14	7.92	10.0	8.51	4.9	x	6.51	6.62	6.78	7.24	8.14	8.99	9.22	9.74	11.88
18-21 Corporate managers and directors	11	9	8.15	5.5	8.57	1.7	x	6.54	6.79	7.06	7.91	8.68	9.20	9.35	x	x
18-21 Other managers and proprietors	12	x	7.05	7.6	8.37	13.7	x	x	x	x	6.75	x	x	x	x	x
18-21 Professional occupations	2	24	10.05	11.7	10.80	5.6	6.84	7.92	8.18	8.39	9.12	11.38	12.73	12.80	14.01	17.34
18-21 Science, research, engineering and technology professionals	21	10	8.43	3.4	9.50	-3.9	x	x	7.63	7.92	8.29	9.06	x	x	x	x
18-21 Health professionals	22	6	10.31	-6.4	10.98	5.9	x	x	8.70	8.89	12.09	x	x	x	x	x
18-21 Teaching and educational professionals	23	x	13.69		12.90	9.3	x	x	x	x	x	x	x	x	x	x
18-21 Business, media and public service professionals	24	x	11.39	24.1	12.37	28.1	x	x	x	x	10.73	11.76	x	x	x	x
18-21 Associate professional and technical occupations	3	77	8.36	8.3	10.53	22.9	6.28	6.85	7.14	7.43	7.85	9.05	10.00	10.27	11.15	13.23
18-21 Science, engineering and technology associate professionals	31	21	8.25	1.0	8.77	-1.8	6.54	7.01	7.28	7.49	7.80	9.12	9.62	9.95	10.13	x
18-21 Health and social care associate professionals	32	9	8.54	7.5	9.51	14.4	x	7.64	7.72	7.99	8.25	8.78	9.59	9.99	x	x
18-21 Protective service occupations	33	x	12.01	-3.7	11.63	-3.8	x	x	x	x	x	x	x	x	x	x
18-21 Culture, media and sports occupations	34	14	7.66	2.3	x		6.08	6.20	6.55	6.70	7.25	8.61	9.70	x	x	x
18-21 Business and public service associate professionals	35	31	8.33	13.9	9.48	16.5	6.25	6.61	6.96	7.15	7.73	9.00	10.30	10.85	11.52	x
18-21 Administrative and secretarial occupations	4	113	7.60	3.7	7.84	-0.4	5.91	6.23	6.43	6.62	7.02	7.99	8.54	8.92	9.29	10.25
18-21 Administrative occupations	41	94	7.69	3.1	7.95	-1.1	5.99	6.29	6.55	6.70	7.22	8.07	8.69	9.04	9.40	10.36
18-21 Secretarial and related occupations	42	20	6.80	2.9	7.31	3.0	5.53	x	6.08	6.25	6.50	7.48	7.81	8.22	8.46	x
18-21 Skilled trades occupations	5	79	7.37	1.3	8.16	2.5	5.53	6.10	6.29	6.50	6.83	7.81	8.57	9.14	9.81	11.16
18-21 Skilled agricultural and related trades	51	x	6.73	1.7	6.92	0.2	x	x	x	x	x	7.12	x	x	x	x
18-21 Skilled metal, electrical and electronic trades	52	35	8.40	5.2	9.02	5.8	5.42	6.43	6.66	6.96	7.57	9.12	9.93	10.41	10.97	x
18-21 Skilled construction and building trades	53	13	7.66	0.6	8.03	-2.3	x	6.26	6.33	6.54	7.00	8.09	8.72	9.02	x	x
18-21 Textiles, printing and other skilled trades	54	28	6.73	1.0	7.16	0.9	5.76	x	6.10	6.17	6.45	7.05	7.36	7.46	7.66	x
18-21 Caring, leisure and other service occupations	6	167	6.63	0.3	7.12	2.5	5.48	x	6.08	6.18	6.39	7.03	7.54	7.81	8.16	9.50
18-21 Caring personal service occupations	61	123	6.70	0.2	7.14	1.7	5.91	6.08	6.14	6.22	6.46	7.06	7.57	7.85	8.14	9.60
18-21 Leisure, travel and related personal service occupations	62	44	6.46	0.4	7.07	4.5	5.00	5.52	5.93	6.08	6.25	6.97	7.35	7.64	8.17	x
18-21 Sales and customer service occupations	7	354	6.51	2.0	6.90	0.9	5.46	x	6.08	6.14	6.30	6.75	7.00	7.21	7.48	8.28
18-21 Sales occupations	71	307	6.50	2.0	6.79	0.8	5.41	x	6.08	6.10	6.29	6.72	6.95	7.12	7.36	8.09
18-21 Customer service occupations	72	47	6.74	0.6	7.46	2.2	6.08	6.22	6.25	6.25	6.47	7.21	7.67	7.95	8.15	x
18-21 Process, plant and machine operatives	8	36	6.93	2.0	7.60	-0.7	5.98	x	6.08	6.16	6.50	7.32	7.86	8.24	8.80	9.98
18-21 Process, plant and machine operatives	81	28	7.00	2.0	7.64	0.6	6.04	6.08	6.12	6.28	6.54	7.35	7.85	8.22	8.77	10.18
18-21 Transport and mobile machine drivers and operatives	82	8	6.50	0.1	7.42	-6.5	x	x	6.00	6.08	6.08	6.99	7.93	x	x	x
18-21 Elementary occupations	9	410	6.12	2.0	6.66	2.6	5.00	5.43	5.80	6.00	6.08	6.30	6.66	6.93	7.22	8.15
18-21 Elementary trades and related occupations	91	33	7.09	9.1	7.57	6.6	5.99	6.09	6.17	6.40	6.78	7.47	7.72	8.22	8.72	x
18-21 Elementary administration and service occupations	92	377	6.10	1.7	6.52	2.1	5.00	5.33	5.62	5.99	6.08	6.25	6.50	6.75	7.03	7.92
22-29 ALL OCCUPATIONS		4,108	9.60	1.4	11.38	1.3	6.32	7.02	7.41	7.78	8.62	10.87	12.54	13.50	14.55	17.67
22-29 Managers, directors and senior officials	1	201	11.45	3.9	13.68	0.4	7.22	8.13	8.47	8.87	10.03	12.75	14.50	15.79	17.50	24.08
22-29 Corporate managers and directors	11	153	12.17	0.1	14.73	0.1	7.25	8.27	8.68	9.27	10.67	13.71	15.84	17.59	20.03	26.07
22-29 Other managers and proprietors	12	48	9.68	6.9	10.51	4.0	7.15	7.68	8.00	8.31	8.83	10.54	11.91	12.27	13.34	x
22-29 Professional occupations	2	802	15.19	1.0	15.95	1.1	10.26	12.03	12.71	13.19	14.17	16.30	17.65	18.62	19.71	22.79
22-29 Science, research, engineering and technology professionals	21	193	14.52	1.2	15.39	1.0	9.81	11.33	12.01	12.57	13.59	15.62	16.89	17.76	18.80	21.46
22-29 Health professionals	22	176	14.67	1.3	15.52	1.0	10.83	12.12	12.59	13.06	13.90	15.49	16.50	17.51	18.89	21.66
22-29 Teaching and educational professionals	23	205	16.55	0.1	16.54	-0.6	11.73	13.34	13.76	14.40	15.24	17.47	18.61	19.39	20.20	23.09
22-29 Business, media and public service professionals	24	229	15.13	3.0	16.36	2.8	9.71	11.50	12.03	12.78	13.87	16.28	17.88	19.16	20.79	24.13
22-29 Associate professional and technical occupations	3	628	12.22	2.2	13.60	3.6	8.16	9.23	9.74	10.22	11.17	13.29	14.44	15.29	16.11	19.15
22-29 Science, engineering and technology associate professionals	31	119	11.02	0.7	11.73	0.5	7.72	8.62	8.98	9.35	10.17	11.98	12.86	13.44	14.31	16.43
22-29 Health and social care associate professionals	32	49	11.00	4.8	11.59	1.3	7.74	8.49	8.91	9.22	10.22	11.59	12.35	12.77	13.62	x
22-29 Protective service occupations	33	58	14.36	2.1	14.65	2.6	10.98	12.86	13.13	13.19	13.87	15.11	15.67	15.98	16.67	x
22-29 Culture, media and sports occupations	34	60	11.15	7.5	15.81	22.7	7.19	8.35	8.87	9.32	10.20	11.94	12.94	13.43	14.41	x
22-29 Business and public service associate professionals	35	343	12.69	4.1	13.99	2.3	8.43	9.58	10.05	10.50	11.50	13.89	15.32	16.20	17.10	21.43
22-29 Administrative and secretarial occupations	4	510	9.21	0.9	10.14	0.9	6.90	7.58	7.91	8.17	8.67	9.82	10.67	11.16	11.82	14.02
22-29 Administrative occupations	41	429	9.34	1.2	10.27	1.2	7.08	7.77	8.03	8.29	8.83	9.96	10.80	11.27	11.97	14.14

Table 4.15b Hourly pay - Gross (£) - For all employee jobs[a] by age group and occupation: United Kingdom, 2012

Description	Code	Number of jobs[b] (thousand)	Median	Annual percentage change	Mean	Annual percentage change	Percentiles 10	20	25	30	40	60	70	75	80	90
22-29 Secretarial and related occupations	42	81	8.38	-1.6	9.41	-0.7	6.30	6.77	7.00	7.23	7.82	9.01	9.77	10.37	10.87	12.91
22-29 Skilled trades occupations	5	347	9.50	-0.3	10.40	-0.3	6.75	7.34	7.67	8.00	8.72	10.42	11.48	12.17	12.78	14.98
22-29 Skilled agricultural and related trades	51	15	7.96	6.1	8.48	4.0	6.55	6.95	7.07	7.23	7.64	8.55	9.15	9.27	9.56	x
22-29 Skilled metal, electrical and electronic trades	52	163	10.89	0.0	11.58	0.5	7.30	8.38	8.67	9.10	10.00	12.00	13.15	13.80	14.57	16.41
22-29 Skilled construction and building trades	53	65	10.46	0.7	10.95	-0.8	7.50	8.25	8.72	9.02	9.91	11.10	11.99	12.30	12.73	x
22-29 Textiles, printing and other skilled trades	54	104	7.66	2.2	8.32	0.5	6.25	6.71	6.92	7.00	7.30	8.14	8.90	9.26	9.61	10.85
22-29 Caring, leisure and other service occupations	6	400	7.80	0.2	8.34	-0.6	6.18	6.51	6.73	6.91	7.35	8.25	8.93	9.32	9.79	11.36
22-29 Caring personal service occupations	61	319	7.81	0.1	8.33	-0.3	6.20	6.53	6.74	6.95	7.39	8.30	8.99	9.41	9.87	11.37
22-29 Leisure, travel and related personal service occupations	62	81	7.68	0.4	8.38	-2.0	6.11	6.37	6.62	6.81	7.25	8.16	8.74	9.10	9.58	11.25
22-29 Sales and customer service occupations	7	504	7.32	1.1	8.23	0.2	6.10	6.34	6.50	6.64	6.95	7.80	8.41	8.80	9.26	10.82
22-29 Sales occupations	71	374	7.04	1.4	7.88	0.2	6.08	6.26	6.40	6.50	6.75	7.43	7.91	8.23	8.62	10.06
22-29 Customer service occupations	72	131	8.46	1.1	9.10	0.7	6.30	6.95	7.19	7.43	7.95	9.01	9.63	9.96	10.51	12.19
22-29 Process, plant and machine operatives	8	200	8.31	0.2	9.17	0.2	6.16	6.66	6.87	7.17	7.74	9.00	9.78	10.22	10.84	12.67
22-29 Process, plant and machine operatives	81	134	8.20	1.0	9.10	1.6	6.11	6.54	6.79	7.08	7.61	9.00	9.76	10.24	10.88	12.67
22-29 Transport and mobile machine drivers and operatives	82	66	8.54	-1.5	9.30	-2.4	6.24	6.75	7.08	7.37	8.00	9.07	9.78	10.21	10.66	x
22-29 Elementary occupations	9	517	7.00	4.1	7.83	2.8	6.08	6.10	6.19	6.28	6.55	7.45	8.02	8.42	8.91	10.14
22-29 Elementary trades and related occupations	91	77	7.63	2.1	8.20	2.1	6.08	6.48	6.71	6.91	7.31	8.00	8.66	9.00	9.39	10.58
22-29 Elementary administration and service occupations	92	440	6.83	3.6	7.74	3.0	6.08	6.08	6.14	6.25	6.50	7.27	7.91	8.29	8.76	10.05
30-39 ALL OCCUPATIONS		**5,550**	**13.16**	**1.7**	**15.79**	**0.2**	**7.00**	**8.33**	**9.01**	**9.75**	**11.27**	**15.26**	**17.66**	**19.02**	**20.76**	**26.25**
30-39 Managers, directors and senior officials	1	568	18.40	1.0	22.66	-1.4	9.04	11.24	12.41	13.53	15.84	21.20	25.46	27.96	31.53	42.55
30-39 Corporate managers and directors	11	472	19.90	2.7	24.26	-0.8	9.61	12.40	13.63	14.67	17.36	23.03	27.29	30.22	33.58	45.21
30-39 Other managers and proprietors	12	96	12.50	-6.9	15.03	-5.4	7.95	9.06	9.58	10.16	11.30	14.07	16.45	17.79	19.05	x
30-39 Professional occupations	2	1,447	19.24	1.1	20.93	0.6	12.56	14.65	15.54	16.35	17.83	21.11	23.09	24.47	25.99	31.34
30-39 Science, research, engineering and technology professionals	21	359	19.08	1.3	20.52	0.5	12.29	14.56	15.41	16.31	17.72	20.76	22.60	23.84	25.34	30.04
30-39 Health professionals	22	345	17.61	1.7	20.26	3.6	12.52	14.13	14.64	15.30	16.51	18.96	21.22	22.66	24.86	31.96
30-39 Teaching and educational professionals	23	365	21.49	0.1	21.59	0.5	13.83	16.80	17.90	18.65	20.15	22.73	24.52	25.67	27.00	30.76
30-39 Business, media and public service professionals	24	378	18.94	2.3	21.38	-1.4	12.00	14.30	15.08	15.91	17.28	20.72	23.19	24.53	26.33	33.83
30-39 Associate professional and technical occupations	3	964	15.43	0.8	17.36	-1.1	9.82	11.47	12.22	12.90	14.22	16.83	18.49	19.63	20.91	25.87
30-39 Science, engineering and technology associate professionals	31	160	14.04	1.5	15.05	-0.2	9.19	10.69	11.26	11.84	12.87	15.28	16.41	17.32	18.28	21.56
30-39 Health and social care associate professionals	32	81	12.60	2.6	13.56	2.0	8.50	9.76	10.26	10.93	11.84	13.90	14.82	15.32	16.07	18.46
30-39 Protective service occupations	33	138	16.62	1.1	16.90	1.6	12.92	13.99	14.50	14.92	15.72	17.55	18.31	18.80	19.47	21.51
30-39 Culture, media and sports occupations	34	61	14.06	-4.4	15.53	-7.8	8.98	10.35	10.82	11.50	12.96	15.59	17.03	18.13	19.32	x
30-39 Business and public service associate professionals	35	525	16.21	0.6	18.94	-1.8	10.00	11.66	12.44	13.25	14.67	17.98	20.29	21.76	23.65	30.92
30-39 Administrative and secretarial occupations	4	610	10.46	0.9	11.98	0.2	7.47	8.33	8.72	9.06	9.74	11.39	12.59	13.29	14.17	17.43
30-39 Administrative occupations	41	508	10.61	0.7	12.13	0.0	7.59	8.50	8.85	9.19	9.83	11.51	12.76	13.43	14.37	17.65
30-39 Secretarial and related occupations	42	102	9.91	3.1	11.20	1.6	6.88	7.64	8.12	8.46	9.19	10.62	11.77	12.59	13.29	16.27
30-39 Skilled trades occupations	5	406	11.09	0.1	12.04	-0.8	7.12	8.17	8.63	9.09	10.12	12.04	13.37	14.13	14.96	17.73
30-39 Skilled agricultural and related trades	51	22	8.85	-1.0	9.52	0.8	6.77	7.47	7.57	7.87	8.36	9.46	10.10	10.60	11.19	x
30-39 Skilled metal, electrical and electronic trades	52	211	12.51	-0.2	13.40	0.3	8.54	9.77	10.39	10.82	11.60	13.62	14.72	15.65	16.63	19.28
30-39 Skilled construction and building trades	53	61	11.30	-0.7	12.22	-2.3	8.17	9.00	9.50	9.97	10.62	12.15	13.34	13.88	14.38	x
30-39 Textiles, printing and other skilled trades	54	111	8.43	-1.4	9.60	-1.2	6.28	6.90	7.10	7.35	7.98	9.10	10.12	10.70	11.41	14.00
30-39 Caring, leisure and other service occupations	6	423	8.49	-0.2	9.43	-1.2	6.36	6.89	7.13	7.37	7.86	9.21	10.04	10.62	11.21	13.18
30-39 Caring personal service occupations	61	354	8.37	-0.2	9.18	-1.0	6.38	6.89	7.12	7.34	7.81	9.04	9.85	10.35	11.00	12.49
30-39 Leisure, travel and related personal service occupations	62	69	9.20	1.6	10.64	-2.0	6.23	6.89	7.25	7.55	8.34	9.92	11.28	12.46	13.29	x
30-39 Sales and customer service occupations	7	347	8.03	1.3	9.71	-1.0	6.18	6.50	6.71	6.92	7.45	8.84	9.79	10.35	11.16	13.76
30-39 Sales occupations	71	237	7.41	3.0	8.88	-1.2	6.10	6.38	6.50	6.67	6.97	7.94	8.65	9.10	9.64	11.93
30-39 Customer service occupations	72	110	10.01	1.0	11.29	-0.8	6.66	7.67	8.06	8.48	9.40	10.87	11.84	12.74	13.45	15.64
30-39 Process, plant and machine operatives	8	288	9.56	0.6	10.44	0.7	6.50	7.30	7.66	8.04	8.76	10.29	11.26	11.91	12.60	15.00
30-39 Process, plant and machine operatives	81	162	9.34	-0.8	10.49	0.0	6.42	7.15	7.50	7.79	8.53	10.19	11.51	12.28	13.09	15.33
30-39 Transport and mobile machine drivers and operatives	82	127	9.70	1.5	10.38	1.5	6.69	7.55	8.00	8.38	9.00	10.34	11.09	11.53	12.11	14.04
30-39 Elementary occupations	9	496	7.50	2.9	8.63	1.6	6.08	6.21	6.38	6.52	7.00	8.11	8.96	9.47	9.98	11.45
30-39 Elementary trades and related occupations	91	67	8.07	-0.8	8.81	-2.0	6.10	6.58	6.84	7.14	7.61	8.68	9.46	9.89	10.31	12.06
30-39 Elementary administration and service occupations	92	429	7.40	3.2	8.59	2.5	6.08	6.18	6.32	6.50	6.90	8.03	8.83	9.39	9.91	11.35
40-49 ALL OCCUPATIONS		**6,471**	**12.88**	**1.9**	**16.66**	**0.4**	**6.95**	**8.20**	**8.85**	**9.54**	**11.03**	**15.23**	**17.99**	**19.68**	**21.63**	**28.28**
40-49 Managers, directors and senior officials	1	775	20.44	-2.0	26.03	-1.9	9.49	12.27	13.60	14.87	17.50	24.31	28.73	31.40	35.90	47.91
40-49 Corporate managers and directors	11	659	21.73	-2.1	27.39	-1.6	9.87	12.99	14.40	15.79	18.67	25.76	30.09	33.49	37.77	50.34

Table 4.15b Hourly pay - Gross (£) - For all employee jobs[a] by age group and occupation: United Kingdom, 2012

Description	Code	Number of jobs[b] (thousand)	Median	Annual percentage change	Mean	Annual percentage change	Percentiles 10	20	25	30	40	60	70	75	80	90
40-49 Other managers and proprietors	12	116	14.89	-4.4	18.33	-6.0	8.58	10.19	10.98	11.64	13.24	17.30	19.72	21.58	23.46	31.17
40-49 Professional occupations	2	1,421	20.50	1.4	22.90	0.2	12.99	15.36	16.25	17.12	18.64	22.29	24.54	26.06	28.12	35.04
40-49 Science, research, engineering and technology professionals	21	322	21.28	2.9	22.95	2.3	13.49	16.01	16.92	17.83	19.45	23.15	24.99	26.48	28.27	33.84
40-49 Health professionals	22	393	18.03	0.2	22.36	0.7	12.57	14.31	15.02	15.72	17.25	19.71	21.35	22.76	24.65	38.66
40-49 Teaching and educational professionals	23	375	22.49	0.0	23.29	0.1	14.17	17.30	18.60	19.19	21.11	24.19	26.22	27.56	28.98	33.23
40-49 Business, media and public service professionals	24	331	19.76	-0.2	23.09	-2.3	12.28	14.83	15.69	16.43	17.88	21.82	24.57	26.39	28.82	36.56
40-49 Associate professional and technical occupations	3	961	16.13	1.0	18.71	-0.1	9.84	11.79	12.55	13.19	14.65	17.93	19.73	20.88	22.34	28.61
40-49 Science, engineering and technology associate professionals	31	158	14.53	0.7	15.62	-0.8	8.87	10.36	10.95	11.65	13.15	15.78	17.21	18.27	19.25	22.65
40-49 Health and social care associate professionals	32	101	12.84	0.6	13.94	2.4	8.87	10.22	10.74	11.08	11.97	13.93	15.26	15.98	17.18	18.57
40-49 Protective service occupations	33	150	18.12	0.0	18.25	0.5	12.99	14.41	14.85	15.65	17.48	19.28	20.24	20.81	21.50	23.53
40-49 Culture, media and sports occupations	34	45	14.91	2.4	17.23	-9.0	8.71	10.46	11.50	12.14	13.23	16.78	18.50	19.72	20.31	x
40-49 Business and public service associate professionals	35	508	17.05	0.7	20.81	-0.3	10.30	12.27	12.91	13.80	15.35	19.05	21.89	23.51	26.05	34.91
40-49 Administrative and secretarial occupations	4	789	10.34	0.2	12.09	-1.4	7.42	8.27	8.64	8.95	9.64	11.24	12.46	13.24	14.13	17.48
40-49 Administrative occupations	41	620	10.50	-0.1	12.30	-2.0	7.55	8.47	8.82	9.11	9.76	11.50	12.67	13.48	14.31	17.77
40-49 Secretarial and related occupations	42	169	9.71	1.4	11.22	1.4	7.03	7.73	8.02	8.34	8.98	10.67	11.49	12.31	13.37	16.75
40-49 Skilled trades occupations	5	489	11.84	0.3	12.92	0.2	7.45	8.77	9.34	9.85	10.84	12.84	14.16	14.99	15.86	18.84
40-49 Skilled agricultural and related trades	51	28	9.40	2.3	10.04	-3.4	6.65	7.35	7.54	8.22	8.76	9.91	10.63	11.10	12.16	x
40-49 Skilled metal, electrical and electronic trades	52	261	13.27	1.9	14.20	1.0	9.18	10.38	10.95	11.35	12.22	14.39	15.52	16.37	17.32	20.61
40-49 Skilled construction and building trades	53	84	12.08	-3.1	13.04	-2.5	8.97	9.80	10.10	10.50	11.39	12.82	13.66	14.27	15.15	17.85
40-49 Textiles, printing and other skilled trades	54	117	8.73	0.2	10.20	1.4	6.25	7.00	7.25	7.52	8.01	9.43	10.50	11.09	11.94	14.74
40-49 Caring, leisure and other service occupations	6	620	8.66	0.9	9.65	0.0	6.50	7.02	7.26	7.50	8.03	9.29	10.16	10.70	11.28	13.16
40-49 Caring personal service occupations	61	528	8.61	0.8	9.33	0.5	6.53	7.03	7.26	7.50	8.02	9.23	10.02	10.51	11.07	12.48
40-49 Leisure, travel and related personal service occupations	62	92	8.89	-0.5	11.40	-2.1	6.40	7.00	7.26	7.50	8.15	9.99	11.55	12.71	14.25	x
40-49 Sales and customer service occupations	7	360	7.61	1.8	9.54	-1.0	6.14	6.42	6.55	6.71	7.04	8.38	9.27	9.87	10.75	13.84
40-49 Sales occupations	71	260	7.05	0.0	8.58	-1.7	6.08	6.30	6.43	6.54	6.77	7.53	8.23	8.64	9.13	11.47
40-49 Customer service occupations	72	101	9.89	1.6	11.68	-0.1	6.47	7.52	7.96	8.43	9.09	10.80	12.26	13.05	14.17	16.97
40-49 Process, plant and machine operatives	8	415	10.00	0.1	11.10	1.4	6.81	7.80	8.19	8.54	9.31	10.85	11.89	12.59	13.55	16.33
40-49 Process, plant and machine operatives	81	191	10.29	0.9	11.31	1.1	6.50	7.59	8.08	8.50	9.33	11.18	12.40	13.27	14.22	16.92
40-49 Transport and mobile machine drivers and operatives	82	224	9.89	1.0	10.94	1.7	7.07	8.00	8.28	8.58	9.27	10.61	11.55	12.13	13.00	15.72
40-49 Elementary occupations	9	641	7.51	1.1	8.80	0.2	6.08	6.25	6.43	6.58	7.02	8.16	9.02	9.60	10.09	11.64
40-49 Elementary trades and related occupations	91	82	8.62	-0.2	9.51	-0.5	6.24	6.77	7.04	7.31	8.04	9.45	10.41	10.96	11.65	13.41
40-49 Elementary administration and service occupations	92	559	7.39	1.6	8.65	0.5	6.08	6.20	6.37	6.50	6.96	7.99	8.82	9.39	9.89	11.23
50-59 ALL OCCUPATIONS		4,872	12.08	0.9	16.13	1.3	6.82	7.97	8.52	9.10	10.43	14.25	17.17	18.81	20.79	27.44
50-59 Managers, directors and senior officials	1	558	20.92	4.2	27.31	5.9	9.07	12.17	13.51	14.84	17.66	24.61	29.46	32.95	37.30	50.98
50-59 Corporate managers and directors	11	465	22.24	3.3	28.96	5.6	9.44	12.77	14.31	15.93	18.89	26.19	31.50	35.31	39.44	53.06
50-59 Other managers and proprietors	12	93	15.49	3.3	19.08	2.6	8.16	10.16	11.09	11.97	13.82	17.66	21.19	22.46	24.55	x
50-59 Professional occupations	2	1,012	20.52	-0.4	22.95	-1.3	12.69	15.19	16.24	17.24	18.74	22.29	24.60	26.18	28.26	34.54
50-59 Science, research, engineering and technology professionals	21	198	20.63	0.5	22.66	0.0	12.93	15.54	16.50	17.44	19.01	22.67	24.95	26.36	28.43	33.96
50-59 Health professionals	22	285	18.16	0.6	22.66	-1.9	12.52	14.13	14.82	15.71	17.28	19.71	20.92	22.32	23.85	35.82
50-59 Teaching and educational professionals	23	314	23.31	-2.5	24.60	-1.6	15.20	18.64	19.32	20.40	21.72	25.18	27.36	28.87	30.30	34.91
50-59 Business, media and public service professionals	24	215	18.79	1.4	21.62	-0.9	10.88	13.75	14.86	15.81	17.23	20.58	23.20	24.80	27.08	33.66
50-59 Associate professional and technical occupations	3	583	15.16	0.9	17.44	-0.7	9.25	10.95	11.71	12.36	13.75	16.77	18.82	19.86	21.28	26.62
50-59 Science, engineering and technology associate professionals	31	115	14.41	0.7	15.26	-1.8	8.72	10.06	10.72	11.55	12.84	15.63	16.97	17.90	19.10	21.84
50-59 Health and social care associate professionals	32	84	12.37	-2.7	13.44	-3.0	8.61	9.78	10.17	10.63	11.40	13.51	14.47	15.60	16.46	18.47
50-59 Protective service occupations	33	51	17.69	-2.3	17.67	0.5	10.96	13.60	14.39	14.60	15.79	19.18	19.94	20.74	21.65	x
50-59 Culture, media and sports occupations	34	24	15.00	5.6	18.53	0.6	8.06	10.53	11.60	12.31	13.53	16.60	19.50	20.00	21.46	x
50-59 Business and public service associate professionals	35	308	16.06	1.6	19.14	-0.2	9.76	11.68	12.46	13.00	14.52	18.10	20.32	21.75	23.78	31.13
50-59 Administrative and secretarial occupations	4	722	10.18	1.6	11.86	0.9	7.40	8.25	8.57	8.85	9.57	11.09	12.08	12.79	13.67	16.88
50-59 Administrative occupations	41	544	10.36	1.9	12.13	1.2	7.63	8.46	8.81	9.09	9.76	11.27	12.40	13.14	13.91	17.11
50-59 Secretarial and related occupations	42	178	9.50	-1.1	10.96	0.2	7.00	7.70	8.00	8.27	8.82	10.18	11.14	11.59	12.47	15.99
50-59 Skilled trades occupations	5	372	11.96	2.7	12.92	0.9	7.48	8.78	9.38	9.91	10.85	13.00	14.38	15.04	15.88	18.70
50-59 Skilled agricultural and related trades	51	21	8.86	0.3	9.76	3.2	6.49	7.19	7.53	7.88	8.31	9.67	10.14	10.51	10.80	x
50-59 Skilled metal, electrical and electronic trades	52	208	13.33	2.1	14.14	1.5	9.06	10.37	11.00	11.53	12.46	14.50	15.55	16.24	17.30	19.91
50-59 Skilled construction and building trades	53	61	12.12	1.0	12.92	-1.4	9.15	10.00	10.28	10.54	11.37	12.87	13.80	14.48	15.18	17.60
50-59 Textiles, printing and other skilled trades	54	81	8.72	2.3	10.02	-0.1	6.46	7.00	7.31	7.51	8.12	9.35	10.14	10.70	11.42	14.13

Table 4.15b Hourly pay - Gross (£) - For all employee jobs[a] by age group and occupation: United Kingdom, 2012

Description	Code	Number of jobs[b] (thousand)	Median	Annual percentage change	Mean	Annual percentage change	Percentiles 10	20	25	30	40	60	70	75	80	90
50-59 Caring, leisure and other service occupations	6	484	8.80	0.4	9.72	-0.2	6.57	7.19	7.46	7.67	8.22	9.49	10.31	10.88	11.41	13.22
50-59 Caring personal service occupations	61	403	8.80	-0.3	9.55	-1.1	6.63	7.24	7.48	7.72	8.23	9.48	10.28	10.82	11.31	12.92
50-59 Leisure, travel and related personal service occupations	62	80	8.73	2.9	10.55	3.3	6.35	7.00	7.25	7.54	8.14	9.55	10.58	11.31	12.01	15.73
50-59 Sales and customer service occupations	7	302	7.28	1.8	8.91	1.0	6.10	6.30	6.45	6.58	6.85	7.86	8.75	9.22	9.91	12.27
50-59 Sales occupations	71	228	6.97	1.9	8.10	0.6	6.08	6.25	6.36	6.48	6.71	7.33	7.87	8.22	8.75	10.28
50-59 Customer service occupations	72	74	9.49	1.5	11.07	2.0	6.25	6.87	7.33	7.83	8.81	10.41	11.62	12.40	13.43	16.20
50-59 Process, plant and machine operatives	8	340	9.81	1.0	10.88	1.4	6.70	7.50	7.86	8.20	8.97	10.67	11.77	12.43	13.35	16.02
50-59 Process, plant and machine operatives	81	162	10.07	2.3	11.28	1.9	6.61	7.42	7.76	8.14	9.00	11.21	12.42	13.48	14.27	17.25
50-59 Transport and mobile machine drivers and operatives	82	178	9.68	0.8	10.55	1.0	6.77	7.51	7.97	8.28	8.96	10.34	11.23	11.79	12.50	14.81
50-59 Elementary occupations	9	499	7.50	0.5	8.73	0.4	6.08	6.29	6.47	6.62	7.02	8.01	8.82	9.39	10.03	11.63
50-59 Elementary trades and related occupations	91	61	8.34	-1.2	9.31	-0.2	6.17	6.69	7.01	7.30	7.83	9.00	10.07	10.55	11.15	13.08
50-59 Elementary administration and service occupations	92	438	7.40	1.3	8.62	0.6	6.08	6.26	6.42	6.55	6.98	7.93	8.65	9.18	9.89	11.45
60+ ALL OCCUPATIONS		1,747	10.20	2.0	14.16	2.5	6.46	7.20	7.64	8.10	9.09	11.84	14.14	15.81	17.91	24.49
60+ Managers, directors and senior officials	1	175	17.31	6.2	22.92	5.1	8.20	10.00	10.88	12.08	14.33	20.52	25.02	28.11	32.18	43.07
60+ Corporate managers and directors	11	139	18.81	8.3	24.30	4.9	8.25	10.26	11.62	12.73	15.18	22.59	26.99	30.00	33.53	44.61
60+ Other managers and proprietors	12	36	14.10	3.8	17.58	4.9	7.93	8.89	9.65	10.02	11.72	16.22	18.16	19.72	x	x
60+ Professional occupations	2	278	20.38	1.9	22.83	-0.2	12.00	14.38	15.77	16.81	18.39	22.31	25.00	26.78	28.76	37.24
60+ Science, research, engineering and technology professionals	21	47	20.66	11.5	22.06	4.7	12.34	14.81	15.58	16.32	18.68	22.38	24.44	25.55	26.56	x
60+ Health professionals	22	67	17.62	-0.8	23.26	-1.5	11.87	13.85	14.13	14.94	16.69	19.23	21.33	22.76	25.68	x
60+ Teaching and educational professionals	23	98	23.51	0.2	25.72	1.1	14.99	18.26	18.82	20.16	21.68	25.62	28.17	29.66	31.59	x
60+ Business, media and public service professionals	24	66	17.90	0.1	20.07	-2.3	10.87	12.50	13.45	14.56	16.65	19.43	22.00	23.57	25.59	x
60+ Associate professional and technical occupations	3	164	13.97	5.4	16.41	4.6	8.42	9.97	10.57	11.22	12.49	15.31	17.44	18.66	20.05	26.58
60+ Science, engineering and technology associate professionals	31	33	13.36	9.2	14.52	6.5	8.62	9.57	10.17	10.72	12.23	14.28	15.32	16.33	17.38	x
60+ Health and social care associate professionals	32	22	11.50	-1.8	12.51	-3.9	7.47	8.56	8.96	9.40	10.47	12.28	13.91	14.29	14.99	x
60+ Protective service occupations	33	8	13.92	7.7	13.84	4.0	x	9.75	10.75	11.24	12.63	14.65	15.50	x	x	x
60+ Culture, media and sports occupations	34	10	11.96	11.0	14.38	8.2	x	8.44	9.06	9.99	10.67	14.26	16.49	x	x	x
60+ Business and public service associate professionals	35	92	15.25	3.7	18.29	4.8	8.87	10.79	11.49	12.30	13.60	17.27	19.51	20.92	23.12	30.10
60+ Administrative and secretarial occupations	4	281	9.76	1.7	11.36	2.2	7.09	7.91	8.20	8.55	9.12	10.56	11.59	12.32	13.25	16.32
60+ Administrative occupations	41	201	9.88	2.7	11.37	2.0	7.10	7.95	8.22	8.62	9.22	10.60	11.68	12.44	13.26	16.34
60+ Secretarial and related occupations	42	80	9.59	1.1	11.33	2.7	7.02	7.78	8.07	8.49	8.95	10.43	11.36	12.06	13.23	16.24
60+ Skilled trades occupations	5	138	11.06	0.5	12.18	0.0	7.15	8.26	8.74	9.22	10.20	11.97	13.13	13.83	14.85	17.38
60+ Skilled agricultural and related trades	51	11	8.06	-2.1	8.84	1.9	6.29	6.60	6.78	7.01	7.70	8.67	8.95	9.79	x	x
60+ Skilled metal, electrical and electronic trades	52	75	12.28	0.3	13.28	-0.5	8.69	9.83	10.26	10.77	11.49	13.31	14.51	15.26	16.00	19.06
60+ Skilled construction and building trades	53	24	11.51	-0.9	12.41	0.0	8.81	9.49	10.00	10.38	11.00	12.00	12.53	13.23	14.96	x
60+ Textiles, printing and other skilled trades	54	28	8.17	2.1	9.57	0.5	6.49	7.00	7.16	7.37	7.88	8.66	9.28	9.82	10.22	x
60+ Caring, leisure and other service occupations	6	176	8.64	0.8	9.41	0.4	6.40	7.00	7.25	7.51	8.01	9.19	9.94	10.30	11.05	12.76
60+ Caring personal service occupations	61	132	8.67	-0.5	9.37	0.1	6.50	7.10	7.35	7.59	8.09	9.25	9.97	10.31	11.04	12.72
60+ Leisure, travel and related personal service occupations	62	44	8.43	5.4	9.53	1.3	6.22	6.62	7.00	7.25	7.94	8.98	9.88	10.21	11.04	x
60+ Sales and customer service occupations	7	131	6.98	2.8	8.37	5.0	6.09	6.26	6.40	6.50	6.69	7.38	8.05	8.51	9.10	10.99
60+ Sales occupations	71	105	6.84	2.4	8.04	5.3	6.08	6.25	6.36	6.46	6.64	7.15	7.58	8.00	8.44	9.99
60+ Customer service occupations	72	25	8.32	2.2	9.63	3.7	6.25	6.37	6.58	6.82	7.60	9.19	9.97	10.60	10.95	x
60+ Process, plant and machine operatives	8	167	8.70	2.2	9.72	1.1	6.25	6.82	7.14	7.50	8.08	9.49	10.15	10.66	11.17	13.11
60+ Process, plant and machine operatives	81	54	8.92	-0.8	10.13	-0.4	6.40	6.88	7.27	7.59	8.24	9.88	10.99	11.51	12.29	14.83
60+ Transport and mobile machine drivers and operatives	82	114	8.58	2.2	9.53	1.9	6.20	6.79	7.06	7.46	8.00	9.30	10.00	10.38	10.75	12.34
60+ Elementary occupations	9	239	7.10	-0.7	8.28	0.5	6.08	6.23	6.36	6.50	6.77	7.60	8.20	8.66	9.18	10.53
60+ Elementary trades and related occupations	91	24	8.16	1.9	9.19	2.8	6.37	6.76	6.86	7.10	7.64	8.93	9.35	10.00	10.64	x
60+ Elementary administration and service occupations	92	215	7.03	-0.2	8.12	0.2	6.08	6.20	6.30	6.45	6.70	7.49	8.03	8.48	8.92	10.26
Not Classified																

a Employees on adult rates whose pay for the survey pay-period was not affected by absence.

b Figures for Number of Jobs are for indicative purposes only and should not be considered an accurate estimate of employee job counts.

KEY - The colour coding indicates the quality of each estimate; jobs, median, mean and percentiles but not the annual percentage change.

The quality of an estimate is measured by its coefficient of variation (CV), which is the ratio of the standard error of an estimate to the estimate.

Source: Annual Survey of Hours and Earnings, Office for National Statistics.

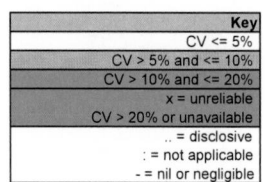

Key	
CV <= 5%	
CV > 5% and <= 10%	
CV > 10% and <= 20%	
x = unreliable	
CV > 20% or unavailable	
.. = disclosive	
: = not applicable	
- = nil or negligible	

4.16 Median[1] weekly and hourly earnings of full-time employees[2] by age group: United Kingdom April 2006 to 2012

	18-21	22-29	30-39	40-49	50-59	60+
Median gross weekly earnings						
All	**JRG9**	**JRH2**	**JRH3**	**JRH4**	**JEH5**	**JRH6**
2006	250.6	376.5	496.1	502.5	465.4	400.0
2007	265.5	387.8	509.0	517.3	479.1	418.7
2008	271.6	400.0	532.7	539.9	504.1	437.5
2009	277.5	407.1	541.8	550.5	514.0	446.3
2010	277.4	411.2	547.8	559.6	528.2	457.3
2011	277.8	406.6	553.7	564.7	531.8	466.1
2012	279.7	412.0	557.7	573.1	535.9	476.1
Men	**JRH8**	**JRH9**	**JRI2**	**JRI3**	**JRI4**	**JRI5**
2006	261.5	390.6	525.0	558.7	516.0	421.6
2007	275.9	402.5	539.0	574.9	534.4	440.9
2008	280.0	416.7	566.3	599.1	563.6	462.6
2009	285.7	421.6	571.1	605.2	569.7	469.0
2010	285.9	421.2	573.7	613.7	582.7	483.0
2011	288.2	413.7	574.9	618.9	586.7	496.3
2012	295.4	420.6	574.9	622.9	598.2	508.3
Women	**JRI7**	**JRI8**	**JRI9**	**JRJ2**	**JRJ3**	**JRJ4**
2006	240.4	362.7	444.0	410.2	385.0	343.7
2007	254.3	374.1	460.6	420.3	395.6	356.1
2008	258.8	384.7	480.9	437.3	419.7	376.4
2009	268.3	392.9	497.9	457.7	432.8	382.1
2010	268.3	401.3	507.9	472.2	440.9	389.0
2011	264.7	398.5	519.4	477.1	449.1	399.6
2012	266.3	402.5	527.0	484.4	446.0	407.4
Median hourly earnings (excluding overtime)						
All	**JRJ6**	**JRJ7**	**JRJ8**	**JRJ9**	**JRK2**	**JRK3**
2006	6.31	9.50	12.43	12.49	11.50	9.72
2007	6.60	9.80	12.77	12.77	11.87	10.09
2008	6.75	10.12	13.34	13.31	12.53	10.57
2009	7.00	10.43	13.82	13.83	12.95	10.97
2010	7.00	10.34	13.91	14.01	13.19	11.18
2011	6.97	10.23	14.07	14.16	13.34	11.46
2012	7.00	10.34	14.23	14.37	13.55	11.83

4.16 Median[1] weekly and hourly earnings of full-time employees[2] by age group: United Kingdom April 2006 to 2012

	18-21	22-29	30-39	40-49	50-59	60+
Men	JRK5	JRK6	JRK7	JRK8	JRK9	JRL2
2006	6.37	9.51	12.78	13.46	12.28	9.96
2007	6.65	9.80	13.10	13.77	12.79	10.31
2008	6.85	10.13	13.70	14.37	13.52	10.89
2009	7.09	10.45	14.15	14.95	13.91	11.25
2010	7.05	10.26	14.07	14.95	14.25	11.50
2011	7.07	10.08	14.14	15.14	14.31	11.84
2012	7.24	10.22	14.28	15.27	14.68	12.15
Women	JRL4	JRL5	JRL6	JRL7	JRL8	JRL9
2006	6.24	9.48	11.87	10.95	10.24	9.17
2007	6.55	9.79	12.28	11.14	10.54	9.48
2008	6.64	10.12	12.78	11.57	11.10	9.82
2009	6.93	10.40	13.29	12.21	11.52	10.23
2010	6.90	10.48	13.66	12.54	11.84	10.40
2011	6.76	10.45	13.99	12.77	12.02	10.64
2012	6.82	10.53	14.18	12.93	11.99	10.99

1. Median values are less affected by extremes of earnings at either ends of the scale with half the employees earning above the stated amount and half below.
2. Data relate to full-time employees on adult rates whose pay for the survey pay-period was not affected by absence.

Source: Annual Survey of Hours and Earnings: 01633 456 120

Labour market

4.17 Trade Unions

Trade unions: distribution by size

Number of Members	Number of Unions	Membership	Number of Unions		Membership of all Unions	
			Per cent	Cumulative Per cent	Per cent	Cumulative Per cent
Under 100	28	986	17.0	17.0	0.0	0.0
100-499	33	8,924	19.9	36.9	0.1	0.1
500-999	13	9,856	7.8	44.7	0.1	0.2
1,000-2,499	21	33,384	12.7	57.4	0.5	0.7
2,500-4,999	18	62,344	10.8	68.2	0.9	1.6
5,000-9,999	11	82,334	6.6	74.8	1.1	2.7
10,000-14,999	2	24,255	1.2	76.0	0.3	3.0
15,000-24,999	12	248,769	7.2	83.2	3.5	6.5
25,000-49,999	11	385,826	6.6	89.8	5.4	11.9
50,000-99,999	4	267,441	2.4	92.2	3.7	15.6
100,000-249,999	5	799,489	3.0	95.2	11.1	26.7
250,000 and over	8	5,273,807	4.8	100.0	73.3	100.0
Total	166	7,197,415	100	100	100	100

The recorded trade union membership of 7,197,415, in 2012-13, compares to 7,261,210 reported in the previous period. This indicates a decrease of 63,795 members or 0.88%. The total recorded membership of around 7.2 million compares with a peak of 13.2 million in 1979, a fall of about 45%.

The following table shows unions whose membership has increased or decreased by 10,000 or more since the previous reporting period.

Trade Union: Changes in Membership

	Total Membership (000's)		
	2011-2012	2010-2011	% changes
Increases			
National Association of Schoolmasters Union of Women Teachers	338,688	326,810	+3.6%
Union of Shop Distributive and Allied Workers	412,441	398,859	+3.4%
National Union of Teachers	386,668	375,042	+3.1%
Decreases			
Public and Commercial Service Union	280,547	292,091	-4.0%
UNISON: The Public Service Union	1,317,500	1,374,500	-4.2%
Union of Construction, Allied Trades and Technicians	83,760	110,559	-24.2%

The annual returns submitted by unions to the Certification Officer require each union to provide figures for both total membership and members who pay contributions. There can be significant differences between these figures. This is usually the result of total membership figures including retired and unemployed members, members on long term sick and maternity/child care leave and those on career breaks. The returns submitted by unions during this reporting period show that the total number of contributing members was around 90.5% of the total number of members. This compares with a figure of 89.4% in the preceding year.

Source: Certification Officer Annual Report

this page is intentionally blank

Social protection

Chapter 5

Social Protection

(Tables 5.2 to 5.11, 5.13 and 5.15 to 5.19)

Tables 5.2 to 5.6, 5.9 to 5.11 and 5.13 to 5.19 give details of contributors and beneficiaries under the National Insurance and Industrial Injury Acts, supplementary benefits and war pensions.

There are four classes of National Insurance Contributions (NICs):

Class 1 Earnings-related contributions paid on earnings from employment. Employees pay primary Class 1 contributions and employers pay secondary Class 1 contributions. Payment of Class 1 contributions builds up entitlement to contributory benefits which include Basic State Pension; Additional State Pension (State Earnings Related Pension Scheme SERPS and from April 2002, State Second Pension, S2P); Contribution Based Jobseeker's Allowance; Bereavement Benefits; Incapacity Benefit; and the new Employment and Support Allowance.

Primary class 1 contributions stop at State Pension age, but not Class 1 secondary contributions paid by employers. There are reduced contribution rates where the employee contracts out of S2P (previously SERPS). They still receive a Basic State Pension but an Occupational or Personal Pension instead of the Additional State Second Pension.

Class 2 Flat rate contributions paid by the self-employed whose profits are above the small earnings exception. Payment of Class 2 contributions builds up entitlement to the contributory benefits which include Basic State Pension; Bereavement Benefits; Maternity Allowance; Incapacity Benefit; and the Employment and Support Allowance, but not Additional State Second Pension or Contribution Based Jobseeker's Allowance (JSA).

Class 2 contributions stop at State Pension age.

Class 3 Flat rate voluntary contributions, which can be paid by someone whose contribution record is insufficient. Payment of Class 3 contributions builds up entitlement to contributory benefits which include Basic State Pension and Bereavement Benefits. (Tables 5.2 to 5.11, 5.13 and 5.15 to 5.19) Tables 5.2 to 5.6, 5.9 to 5.11 and 5.13 to 5.19 give details of contributors and beneficiaries under the National Insurance and Industrial Injury Acts, supplementary benefits and war pensions.

Class 4 Profit-related contributions paid by the self employed in addition to Class 2 contributions. Class 4 contributions stop at State Pension age. Under some circumstances people who are not in employment do not have to make voluntary contributions to accrue a qualifying year for Basic State Pension.

Home Responsibilities Protection

Home Responsibilities Protection (HRP) was introduced to help to protect the basic State Pension of those precluded from regular employment because they are caring for children or a sick or disabled person at home. To be entitled to HRP, a person must have been precluded from regular employment for a full tax year. HRP reduces the amount of qualifying years a person would otherwise need for a Basic State Pension. The scheme ceased on the 6th April 2010 and has been replaced by new weekly credits which can be claimed if qualifying criteria are met.

National Insurance Credits

In addition to paying, or being treated as having paid contributions, a person can be credited with National Insurance contributions (NIC) credits. Contribution credits help to protect people's rights to State Retirement Pension and other Social Security Benefits.

A person is likely to be entitled to contributions credits if they are: a student in full time education or training, in receipt of Jobseeker's Allowance, unable to work due to sickness or disability, entitled to Statutory Maternity Pay or Statutory Adoption Pay, or they have received Carer's Allowance.

Credits are automatically awarded for men aged 60 to 65 provided they are not liable to pay Class 1 or 2 NICs, and to young people for the tax years containing their 16th, 17th and 18th birthdays.

Jobseeker's Allowance (Table 5.6)

Jobseeker's Allowance (JSA) replaced Unemployment Benefit and Income Support for unemployed claimants on 7 October 1996. It is a unified benefit with two routes of entry: contribution-based, which depends mainly upon National Insurance contributions, and income-based, which depends mainly upon a means test. Some claimants can qualify by either route. In practice they receive income-based JSA but have an underlying entitlement to the contribution based element.

Employment and Support Allowance, Invalidity Benefit and Incapacity Benefit (Table 5.7)

Incapacity Benefit replaced Sickness Benefit and Invalidity Benefit from 13 April 1995. The first condition for entitlement to these contributory benefits is that the claimants are incapable of work because of illness or disablement. The second is that they satisfy the contribution conditions, which depend on contributions paid as an employed (Class 1) or self-employed person (Class 2). Under Sickness and Invalidity Benefits the contribution conditions were automatically treated as satisfied if a person was incapable of work because of an industrial accident or prescribed disease. Under Incapacity Benefit those who do not satisfy the contribution conditions do not have them treated as satisfied. Class 1A contributions paid by employers are in respect of the benefit of cars provided for the private use of employees, and the free fuel provided for private use. These contributions do not provide any type of benefit cover.

Since 6 April 1983, most people working for an employer and paying National Insurance contributions as employed persons receive Statutory Sick Pay (SSP) from their employer when they are off work sick. Until 5 April 1986 SSP was payable for a maximum of eight weeks, since this date SSP has been payable for 28 weeks. People who do not work for an employer, and employees who are excluded from the SSP scheme, or those who have run out of SSP before reaching the maximum of 28 weeks and are still sick, can claim benefit. Any period of SSP is excluded from the tables.

Spells of incapacity of three days or less do not count as periods of interruption of employment and are excluded from the tables. Exceptions are where people are receiving regular weekly treatment by dialysis or treatment by radiotherapy, chemotherapy or plasmapheresis where two days in any six consecutive days make up a period of interruption of employment, and those whose incapacity for work ends within three days of the end of SSP entitlement.

At the beginning of a period of incapacity, benefit is subject to three waiting days, except where there was an earlier spell of incapacity of more than three days in the previous eight weeks. Employees entitled to SSP for less than 28 weeks and who are still sick can get Sickness Benefit or Incapacity Benefit Short Term (Low) until they reach a total of 28 weeks provided they satisfy the conditions.

After 28 weeks of SSP and/or Sickness Benefit (SB), Invalidity Benefit (IVB) was payable up to pension age for as long as the incapacity lasted. From pension age, IVB was paid at the person's State Pension rate, until entitlement ceased when SP was paid, or until deemed pension age (70 for a man, 65 for a woman). People who were on Sickness or Invalidity Benefit on 12 April 1995 were automatically transferred to Incapacity Benefit, payable on the same basis as before.

For people on Incapacity Benefit under State Pension age there are two short-term rates: the lower rate is paid for the first 28 weeks of sickness and the higher rate for weeks 29 to 52. From week 53 the Long Term rate Incapacity Benefit is payable. The Short Term rate Incapacity Benefit is based on State Pension entitlement for people over State Pension age and is paid for up to a year if incapacity began before pension age.

The long-term rate of Incapacity Benefit applies to people under State Pension age who have been sick for more than a year. People with a terminal illness, or who are receiving the higher rate care component of Disability Living Allowance, will get the Long Term rate. The Long Term rate is not paid for people over pension age.

Under Incapacity Benefit, for the first 28 weeks of incapacity, people previously in work will be assessed on the 'own occupation' test – the claimant's ability to do their own job. Otherwise, incapacity will be based on a personal capability assessment, which will assess ability to carry out a range of work-related activities. The test will apply after 28 weeks of incapacity or from the start of the claim for people who did not previously have a job. Certain people will be exempted from this test.

The tables exclude all men aged over 65 and women aged over 60 who are in receipt of State Pension, and all people over deemed pension age (70 for a man and 65 for a woman), members of the armed forces, mariners while at sea, and married women and certain widows who have chosen not to be insured for sickness benefit. The tables include a number of individuals who were unemployed prior to incapacity.

The Short Term (Higher) and Long Term rates of Incapacity Benefit are treated as taxable income. There were transitional provisions for people who were on Sickness or Invalidity Benefit on 12 April 1995. They were automatically transferred to Incapacity Benefit, payable on the same basis as before. Former IVB recipients continue to get Additional Pension entitlement, but frozen at 1994 levels. Also their IVB is not subject to tax. If they were over State Pension age on 12 April 1995 they may get Incapacity Benefit for up to five years beyond pension age.

Employment and Support Allowance (ESA) replaced Incapacity Benefit and Income Support paid on the grounds of incapacity for new claims from 27 October 2008. ESA consists of two phases. The first, the assessment phase rate, is paid for the first 13 weeks of the claim whilst a decision is made on the claimants capability through the 'Work Capability Asessment'. The second, or main phase begins after 14 weeks, but only if the 'Work Capability Assesment' has deemed the claimants illness or disability as a limitation on their ability to work.

Within the main phase there are two groups, 'The Work Related Activity Group' and 'The Support Group'. If a claimant is placed in the first, they are expected to take part in work focused interviews with a personal advisor. They will be given support to help them prepare for work and on gaining work will receive a work related activity component in addition to their basic rate. If the claimant is placed in the second group due to their illness or disability having a severe effect upon their ability to work, the claimant will not be expected to work at all, but can do so on a voluntary basis. These claimants will receive a support component in addition to their basic rate.

Child Benefits (Table 5.9a and 5.9b)

Child Benefit (CB) is paid to those responsible for children (aged under 16) or qualifying young people. The latter includes:
a) a person under the age of 19 in full-time non-advanced education or (from April 2006) on certain approved vocational training programmes
b) a person who is aged 19 who began their course of full-time, non-advanced education or approved training before reaching age 19 (note: those reaching 19 up to 9 April 2006 ceased to qualify on their 19th birthday)
c) a person who has reached the age of 16 until the 31 August following their 16th birthday
d) a person aged 16 or 17 who has left education and training who is registered with the Careers service or with Connexions and is awaiting a placement in employment or training for the limited period of up to 20 weeks from the date they left education or training. Entitlement for a qualifying young person continues until the terminal date following the date they leave full-time education or approved training. The terminal dates are at the end of August, November, February and May (there is a slight variation for Scotland). Entitlement is also maintained for a person who is entered for external examinations connected with their course throughout the period between a person leaving education or training and completing those examinations. Entitlement in all cases ceases when a person reaches the age of 20.

Guardian's Allowance is an additional allowance for people bringing up a child because one or both of their parents has died. They must be getting Child Benefit (CB) for the child. The table shows the number of families in the UK in receipt of CB. The numbers shown in the table are estimates based on a random 5 per cent sample of awards current at 31 August, and are therefore subject to sampling error. The figures take no account of new claims, or revisions to claims that were received or processed after 31 August, even if they are backdated to start before 31 August.

Child and Working Tax Credits (New Tax Credits) (Table 5.10 and 5.11)

Child and Working Tax Credits (CTC and WTC) replaced Working Families' Tax Credit (WFTC) from 6th April 2003. CTC and WTC are claimed by individuals, or jointly by couples, whether or not they have children.

CTC provides support to families for the children (up to the 31 August after their 16th birthday) and the 'qualifying' young people (in full-time non-advanced education until their 19th birthday) for which they are responsible. It is paid in addition to CB.

WTC tops up the earnings of families on low or moderate incomes. People working for at least 16 hours a week can claim it if they: (a) are responsible for at least one child or qualifying young person, (b) have a disability which puts them at a disadvantage in getting a job or, (c) in the first year of work, having returned to work aged at least 50 after a period of at least six months receiving out-of-work benefits. Other adults also qualify if they are aged at least 25 and work for at least 30 hours a week.

Widow's Benefit and Bereavement Benefit (Table 5.12 and 5.13)

Widow's Benefit is payable to women widowed on or after 11 April 1988 and up to and including 8 April 2001. There are three types of Widow's Benefits: Widow's Payment, Widowed Mother's Allowance and Widow's Pension. Women widowed before 11 April 1988 continue to receive Widow's Benefit based on the rules that existed before that date. Bereavement Benefit was introduced on 9 April 2001 as a replacement for Widow's Benefit, payable to both men and women widowed on or after 9 April 2001. There are three types of Bereavement Benefits available: Bereavement Payment, Widowed Parent's Allowance and Bereavement Allowance.

5.1 National Insurance Fund (Great Britain and Northern Ireland)

Years ended 31 March

£ million

		2001 /02	2002 /03	2003 /04	2004 /05	2005 /06	2006 /07	2007 /08	2008 /09	2009 /10	2010 /11	2011 /12
Receipts												
Opening balance	KJFB	19868	24177	27267	27816	29804	34940	39243	50288	53046	48457	43164[3]
Contributions	JXVM	58050	59658	59827	62863	67786	69599	77224	74453	73817	74182	78424
State Scheme Premiums[1]	C59W	..	194	147	115	117	76	79	67	52	47	37
Grant from Consolidated Fund	KOTF	..	..	..	..	..	..	..	..	..	..	..
Compensation for SSP/SMP	KJQM	710	775	1346	1470	1392	1197	1919	1626	1684	2052	3009
Transfers from Great Britian	KOTG	110	350	260	270	185	630	452	505	395	125	145
Income from investments	KJFE	1146	1457	1292	1288	1399	1867	2453	1957	237	204	189
Other receipts	KJFF	67	80	82	72	66	54	57	50	49	47	46
Redundancy receipts	KIBQ	22	24	28	32	38	43	37	39	40	49	49
Total	JYJO	79972	86716	90249	93926	100787	108406	121464	128985	129320	125163	125063
Expenditure												
Total benefits	JYJP	54550	54201	56255	58572	61304	63695	67443	70487	75410	77800	82358
Jobseeker's Allowance (Contributory)	LUQW	478	519	512	455	497	493	435	703	1106	812	758
Incapacity	JYXL	7074	7104	7116	6910	7028	7009	6945	6600	6177	5599	4981
Maternity	KETY	57	70	128	153	128	180	250	320	343	343	367
Bereavement Benefits	KEWU	1132	1142	1033	946	903	826	759	683	647	615	605
Guardian's allowances and Child's special allowance[2]	KJFK	2	2	2	1	2	2	2	2	2	2	2
State pensions	JYJV	45677	45240	47339	49979	52578	55053	58921	61301	66442	69347	74111
Other payments	KAAZ	29	27	34	30	33	40	61	97	126	149	150
Administration	KABE	873	1280	1794	1521	1464	1473	1430	1326	1401	1420	1125
Transfers to Northern Ireland	KABF	110	350	260	270	185	630	452	505	395	125	145
Redundancy payments	KIBR	232	255	243	222	295	248	215	428	531	446	407
Personal Pensions	C59X	..	3336	3847	3508	2566	3076	2557	2629	2623	2314	2139
Total	JYJU	55795	59449	62433	64123	65847	69161	72027	74594	79793	81172	84790
Accumulated funds	KABH	24177	27267	27816	29804	34940	39245	50288	53046	48457	42834[3]	38594

1 State Scheme Premiums are payable in respect of employed persons who cease to be covered, in certain circumstances, by a contracted out pension scheme.
2 Includes Child's special allowance for Northern Ireland
3 opening balance has been restated based on analysis of prior year data as better management information has become available

Sources: HM Revenue and Customs
https://www.gov.uk/government/uploads/system/uploads/attachment_data/file/229082/1107.pdf
Department for Work and Pensions:01253 856123 Ext 62436

5.2 Persons[1] who paid National Insurance contributions[2,3] in a tax year:4 by sex

Millions

United Kingdom

		Total					Men					Women			
		2005 /06	2006 /07	2007 /08	2008 /09		2005 /06	2006 /07	2007 /08	2008 /09		2005 /06	2006 /07	2007 /08	2008 /09
Total	KABI	29.02	28.91	28.98	29.39	KEYF	15.89	15.8	15.82	15.97	KEYP	13.13	13.08	13.17	13.42
Class 1	KABJ	24.5	24.5	24.77	25.21	KEYG	13.03	13.49	13.16	13.39	KEYQ	11.47	11.47	11.61	11.82
Not contracted out[5]	KABK	17.47	17.88	18.54	18.73	KEYH	9.69	9.64	10.35	10.43	KEYR	7.79	7.93	8.19	8.30
Contracted out	KABL	7.03	6.62	6.23	6.48	KEYI	3.35	3.34	2.81	2.96	KEYS	3.68	3.54	3.42	3.52
Mixed contracted in/out[6]	KABM	1.18	1.1	1.06	1.10	KEYJ	0.5	0.52	0.43	0.43	KEYT	0.68	0.63	0.63	0.67
Class 1 Reduced rate (including standard rate)	KABO	0.04	0.03	0.02	0.02	KEYL	–	–	–	–	KEYV	0.04	0.03	0.02	0.02
Class 2 exclusively[7]	KABP	2.38	2.4	2.36	2.32	KEYM	1.8	1.77	1.75	1.69	KEYW	0.59	0.6	0.62	0.63
Mixed Class 1 and Class 2	KABQ	0.71	0.7	0.7	0.69	KEYN	0.47	0.46	0.45	0.44	KEYX	0.24	0.25	0.25	0.26
Class 3 exclusively[8]	KABR	0.16	0.13	0.07	0.05	KEYO	0.07	0.06	0.03	0.02	KEYY	0.09	0.07	0.04	0.03
Mixed Class 1, 2 and 3[9]	I6CH	0.06	0.05	0.01	0.01	I6CK	0.02	0.02	–	–	I6CN	0.03	0.03	0.01	–

1 Based on all persons making contributions and not only if they have a qualifying year.
2 Estimates obtained from DWP Infor mation Directorate: Lifetime Labour Market Data Tabulation Tool which uses a 1% sample of the National Insurance Recording System (NIRS2) summer 2010 extract.
3 Components may not sum to totals as a result of rounding.
4 The tax year commences on 6 April and ends on 5 April the following year.

5 Includes those persons with an Appropriate Personal Pension (such persons pay contributions at the not contracted out rate but then receive a rebate paid directly to their scheme).
6 Not included in the above rows.
7 Persons who paid a mixture of Class 2 contributions and others are not included in this category.
8 Persons who paid a mixture of Class 3 contributions and others are not included in this category.
9 Persons with a mixture of class 1,2 or 3 contributions.
Source: HM:Revenue and Customs:020 7147 3045
Department for Work and Pensions;
Information Directorate

Contributions and Qualifying Years People contributing (Thousands) : Contribution type by Gender

Time Series=APR2011

	Total	Gender	
		Female	Male
	People contributing (Thousands)	People contributing (Thousands)	People contributing (Thousands)
Total	28,557	13,157	15,399
Contribution type			
Class 1 only - Contracted In	18,894	8,331	10,562
Class 1 only - Contracted Out	5,853	3,336	2,517
Class 1 only - Contracted Out and In	909	560	349
Reduced Rate	3	3	
Class 1 and Class 2	617	243	375
Class 2 only	2,264	676	1,588
Class 3 only	16	8	-
Combinations of class 1 2 or 3	* 1	-	-
No contributions	-	-	-

DEFINITIONS AND CONVENTIONS: "*" Figures are subject to a high degree of sampling error and should only be used as a guide"-" Nil or Negligible; "." Not applicable.
Caseload figures are rounded to the nearest thousand and displayed in thousands. Totals may not sum due to rounding.
Figures for the two most up-to-date releases should be regarded as provisional and may be subject to changes in future releases.
As these statistics are taken from a 1% sample, they are subject to sampling variation. The Quality document at http://statistics.dwp.gov.uk/asd/index.php?page=stpp_cq contains details of indicative confidence intervals. *SOURCE:* DWP Information Governance and Security Directorate: Lifetime Labour Market Database (L2) 1% sample of the National Insurance Recording System (NIRS2)

5.3 Main Features of National Insurance Contributions (NCIS) 1999-2000 to 2013-14

	Rate in 1999-2000	Rate in 2000-2001	Rate in 2001-2002	Rate in 2002-2003	Rate in 2003-2004	Rate in 2004-2005	Rate in 2005-2006	Rate in 2006-2007	Rate in 2007-2008	Rate in 2008-2009	Rate in 2009-2010	Rate in 2010-11	Rate in 2011-12	Rate in 2012-13 (10)	Rate in 2013-14 (10)
Class 1															
Lower earnings limit (LEL) – a week	£66	£67	£72	£75	£77	£79	£82	£84	£87	£90	£95	£97	£102	£107	£109
Primary threshold (PT) – a week	-	£76	£87	£89	£89	£91	£94	£97	£100	£105	£110	£110	£139	£146	£149
Secondary threshold (ST) – a week	£83	£84	£87	£89	£89	£91	£94	£97	£100	£105	£110	£110	£136	£144	£148
Upper accruals Point (UAP) – a week (1)	-	-	-	-	-	-	-	-	-	-	£770	£770	£770	£770	£770
Upper earnings limit (UEL) – a week (2)	£500	£535	£575	£585	£595	£610	£630	£645	£670	£770	£844	£844	£817	£817	£797
Primary contributions (employee)															
Main contribution rate (PT to UEL) (3)	10.0%	10.0%	10.0%	10.0%	11.0%	11.0%	11.0%	11.0%	11.0%	11.0%	11.0%	11.0%	12.0%	12.0%	12.0%
Additional contribution rate (above UEL)	-	-	-	-	1.0%	1.0%	1.0%	1.0%	1.0%	1.0%	1.0%	1.0%	2.0%	2.0%	2.0%
Contracted out rebate (LEL to UAP/UEL) (4) (5)	1.6%	1.6%	1.6%	1.6%	1.6%	1.6%	1.6%	1.6%	1.6%	1.6%	1.6%	1.6%	1.6%	1.4%	1.4%
Reduced rate for married women and widow optants (6)	3.85%	3.85%	3.85%	3.85%	4.85%	4.85%	4.85%	4.85%	4.85%	4.85%	4.85%	4.85%	5.85%	5.85%	5.85%
Secondary contributions (employer)															
Contribution rate (above ST)	12.2%	12.2%	11.9%	11.8%	12.8%	12.8%	12.8%	12.8%	12.8%	12.8%	12.8%	12.8%	13.8%	13.8%	13.8%
Contracted out rebate (LEL to UAP/UEL) (5)															
- COSRS	3.0%	3.0%	3.0%	3.5%	3.5%	3.5%	3.5%	3.5%	3.7%	3.7%	3.7%	3.7%	3.7%	3.4%	3.4%
- COMPS (7)	0.6%	0.6%	0.6%	1.0%	1.0%	1.0%	1.0%	1.0%	1.4%	1.4%	1.4%	1.4%	1.4%	-	-
Class 1A and 1B															
Contribution rate (8)	12.2%	12.2%	11.9%	11.8%	12.8%	12.8%	12.8%	12.8%	12.8%	12.8%	12.8%	12.8%	13.8%	13.8%	13.8%
Class 2															
Flat-rate contribution – a week	£6.55	£2.00	£2.00	£2.00	£2.00	£2.05	£2.10	£2.10	£2.20	£2.30	£2.40	£2.40	£2.50	£2.65	£2.70
Small earnings exception – a year	£3,770	£3,825	£3,955	£4,025	£4,095	£4,215	£4,345	£4,465	£4,635	£4,825	£5,075	£5,075	£5,315	£5,595	£5,725
Class 3															
Flat-rate contribution – a week (9)	£6.45	£6.55	£6.75	£6.85	£6.95	£7.15	£7.35	£7.55	£7.80	£8.10	£12.05	£12.05	£12.60	£13.25	£13.55
Class 4															
Lower profits limit (LPL) – a year	£7,530	£4,385	£4,535	£4,615	£4,615	£4,745	£4,895	£5,035	£5,225	£5,435	£5,715	£5,715	£7,225	£7,605	£7,755
Upper profits limit (UPL) – a year (2)	£26,000	£27,820	£29,900	£30,420	£30,940	£31,720	£32,760	£33,540	£34,840	£40,040	£43,875	£43,875	£42,475	£42,475	£41,450
Main contribution rate (LPL to UPL)	6%	7%	7%	7%	8%	8%	8%	8%	8%	8%	8%	8%	9%	9%	9%
Additional contribution rate (above UPL)	-	-	-	-	1%	1%	1%	1%	1%	1%	1%	1%	2%	2%	2%

Source: HM Revenue and Customs. Table updated March 2013

(1) The upper accruals point was introduced in April 2009.
(2) From April 2009 the upper earnings limit and upper profits limit were aligned to the income tax higher rate threshold.
(3) Between LEL and UEL for 1999-2000.
(4) For Appropriate Personal Pension Schemes (APPS) both employer and employee pay NICs at the full contracted-out rate and in the following tax year on submission of the end-of-year returns HMRC pay an age related rebate direct to the schemes. The employee's share of this rebate is 1.6%.
(5) Up to and including 2008-09, the rebate applies between the LEL and the UEL. From 2009-10 onwards the rebate applies between the LEL and UAP.
(6) Married women opting to pay contributions at the reduced rate earn no entitlement to contributory National Insurance benefits as a result of these contributions. No women have been allowed to exercise this option since 1977.
(7) For employers operating a COMPS, in addition to the reduction shown in secondary Class 1 contributions, in the following tax year on submission of end-of-year returns, HMRC pay an additional "top-up" rebate direct to the scheme. As with APPS, this rebate is age related. COMPs are abolished from 2012-13 onwards.
(8) From April 2000 the Class 1A liability for employers was extended from company cars and fuel to include other taxable benefits not already attracting a Class 1 liability. Class 1A and Class 1B contributions are paid in the year following accrual.
(9) Class 3 contribution rules changed in 2009-10 to allow those reaching state pension age before April 2015 with 20 qualifying years to purchase up to 6 additional years.
(10) From 2012-13 the default indexation assumption for NICs is CPI (excluding the secondary threshold).

Additional notes on National Insurance Contributions can be found on the following page

5.3

Main Features of National Insurance Contributions (NCIS)
1999-2000 to 2013-14

Notes:

Class 1 National Insurance Contributions (NICs)

Class 1 NICs are earnings related contributions paid by employed earners who are below State Pension age (65 for men, 60 for women) and their employers. The contributions are paid at either the contracted-out rate or the not contracted-out rate. The contracted-out rate is payable only where the employee is a member of a contracted-out occupational scheme in place of State Second Pension (formerly SERPS). Class 1 NICs are collected by HMRC along with income tax under the Pay As You Earn (PAYE) scheme.

Class 1A National Insurance Contributions (NICs)

Class 1A NICs are paid only by employers on the value of most taxable benefits-in-kind provided to employees, such as private use of company cars and fuel, private medical insurance, accommodation and loan benefits. They do not give any benefit rights.

Class 1B National Insurance Contributions (NICs)

Class 1B NICs were introduced on 6 April 1999. Like Class 1A they are also paid only by employers and cover PAYE Settlement Agreements (PSA) under which employers agree to meet the income tax liability arising on a restricted range of benefits. Class 1B is payable on the value of the items included in the PSA that would otherwise attract a Class 1 or Class 1A liability and the value of the income tax met by the employer. They do not give any benefit rights.

Class 2 National Insurance Contributions (NICs)

Class 2 contributions are a flat rate weekly liability payable by all self-employed people over 16 (up to State Pension age) unless they have applied for and been granted a "small earnings exception" (SEE) because their earnings from self-employment are expected to be low, although they may still pay if they choose to. Class 2 NICs can be paid up to six years after the tax year in which they are due. Class 4 NICS may also have to be paid if their profits for the year are over the lower profits limit (see below).

Class 3 National Insurance Contributions (NICs)

Class 3 NICs may be paid voluntarily by people aged 16 and over (but below State Pension age) to help them qualify for State Pension and Bereavement Benefits if their contribution record would not otherwise be sufficient. Contributions are flat rate and can be paid up to six years after the year in which they are due.

Class 4 National Insurance Contributions (NICs)

Class 4 NICS are paid by the self-employed whose profits are above the lower profits limit. They are profit related and do not count for any benefits themselves.

5.4 The Department for Work and Pensions - Social Security Benefit Up-rating

Schedule of proposed benefit rates from April 2012

(Weekly rates unless otherwise shown)	RATES 2011	RATES 2012
ATTENDANCE ALLOWANCE		
higher rate	73.60	77.45
lower rate	49.30	51.85
BEREAVEMENT BENEFIT		
Bereavement payment (lump sum)	2000.00	2000.00
Widowed parent's allowance	100.70	105.95
Bereavement Allowance		
standard rate	100.70	105.95
age-related		
age 54	93.65	98.53
53	86.60	91.12
52	79.55	83.70
51	72.50	76.28
50	65.46	68.87
49	58.41	61.45
48	51.36	54.03
47	44.31	46.62
46	37.26	39.20
45	30.21	31.79

CAPITAL LIMITS - rules common to Income Support, income based Jobseeker's Allowance, income-related Employment and Support Allowance, Pension Credit, Housing Benefit and Council Tax Benefit unless stated otherwise

upper limit	16000.00	16000.00
upper limit - Pension Credit guarantee credit and those getting Housing Benefit /Council Tax Benefit and Pension Credit guarantee credit	No limit	No limit
Amount disregarded - all benefits except Pension Credit and Housing Benefit and Council Tax benefit for those above the qualifying age for Guarantee Credit	6000.00	6000.00
Amount disregarded - Pension Credit and Housing Benefit and Council Tax Benefit for those above the qualifying age for Pension Credit	10000.00	10000.00
child disregard (not Pension Credit or Employment and Support Allowance)	3000.00	3000.00
amount disregarded (living in RC/NH)	10000.00	10000.00

Tariff income
   £1 for every £250, or part thereof, between the amount of
   capital disregarded and the capital upper limit

Tariff income - Pension Credit and HB/CTB where claimant/ partner is over Guarantee Credit qualifying age
   £1 for every £500, or part thereof, between the amount of
   capital disregarded and capital upper limit

5.4 The Department for Work and Pensions - Social Security Benefit Up-rating

Schedule of proposed benefit rates from April 2012

(Weekly rates unless otherwise shown)	RATES 2011	RATES 2012
CARER'S ALLOWANCE	55.55	58.45
COUNCIL TAX BENEFIT		
Personal allowances		
single		
18 to 24	53.45	56.25
25 or over	67.50	71.00
entitled to main phase ESA	67.50	71.00
lone parent	67.50	71.00
couple	105.95	111.45
dependent children	62.33	64.99
pensioner		
single/lone parent has attained the qualifying age for Pension Credit but under 65.	137.35	142.70
couple – one or both has attained the qualifying age for Pension Credit but both under 65	209.70	217.90
single / lone parent - 65 and over	157.90	161.25
couple - one or both 65 and over	236.80	241.65
Premiums		
family	17.40	17.40
family (lone parent rate)	22.20	22.20
disability		
single	28.85	30.35
couple	41.10	43.25
enhanced disability		
single	14.05	14.80
disabled child	21.63	22.89
couple	20.25	21.30
severe disability		
single	55.30	58.20
couple (lower rate)	55.30	58.20
couple (higher rate)	110.60	116.40
disabled child	53.62	56.63

5.4 The Department for Work and Pensions - Social Security Benefit Up-rating

Schedule of proposed benefit rates from April 2012

(Weekly rates unless otherwise shown)	RATES 2011	RATES 2012
carer	31.00	32.60
ESA components		
work-related activity	26.75	28.15
support	32.35	34.05
Alternative maximum Council Tax Benefit		
	25% of Council Tax	25% of Council Tax
second adult on IS, JSA(IB), ESA(IR) or Pension Credit		
	100% of Council Tax	100% of Council Tax
first adult(s) student(s)		
second adult's gross income :		
	15% of Council Tax	15% of Council Tax
- under £180.00		
	7.5% of Council Tax	7.5% of Council Tax
- £180.00 to £234.99		

DEDUCTIONS - rules common to Income Support, Jobseeker's Allowance, Employment and Support Allowance, Pension Credit, Housing Benefit and Council tax benefit unless stated otherwise

Non-dependant deductions from housing benefit and from IS, JSA(IB), ESA(IR) and Pension Credit		
aged 25 and over in receipt of IS and JSA(IB), in receipt of main phase ESA(IR), aged 18 or over, not in remunerative work	9.40	11.45
aged 18 or over and in remunerative work		
- gross income: less than £124.00	9.40	11.45
- gross income: £124 to £182.99	21.55	26.25
- gross income: £183 to £237.99	29.60	36.10
- gross income: £238 to £315.99	48.45	59.05
- gross income: £316 to £393.99	55.20	67.25
- gross income: £394 and above	60.60	73.85
Non-dependant deductions from council tax benefit		
aged 18 or over and in remunerative work		
- gross income: £394 or more	8.60	9.90
- gross income: £316 - £393.99	7.20	8.25
- gross income: £183 - £315.99	5.70	6.55
- gross income less than £183	2.85	3.30
others,aged 18 or over	2.85	3.30

5.4 The Department for Work and Pensions - Social Security Benefit Up-rating

Schedule of proposed benefit rates from April 2012

(Weekly rates unless otherwise shown)	RATES 2011	RATES 2012
Deductions from housing benefit		
Service charges for fuel		
heating	21.55	25.50
hot water	2.50	2.95
lighting	1.75	2.05
cooking	2.50	2.95
Amount ineligible for meals		
three or more meals a day		
single claimant	24.05	25.30
each person in family aged 16 or over	24.05	25.30
each child under 16	12.15	12.80
less than three meals a day		
single claimant	16.00	16.85
each person in family aged 16 or over	16.00	16.85
each child under 16	8.05	8.45
breakfast only - claimant and each member of the family	2.95	3.10
Amount for personal expenses (not HB/CTB)	22.60	23.25
Third party deductions from IS, JSA(IB), ESA(IR) and Pension Credit for;		
arrears of housing, fuel and water costs council tax etc. and deductions for ELDS and ILS.	3.40	3.55
child support, contribution towards maintenance (CTM)		
standard deduction	6.80	7.10
lower deduction	3.40	3.55
arrears of Community Charge		
court order against claimant	3.40	3.55
court order against couple	5.30	5.60
fine or compensation order		
standard rate	5.00	5.00
lower rate	3.40	3.55
Maximum deduction rates for recovery of overpayments (not CTB/JSA(C)/ESA(C))		
ordinary overpayments	10.20	10.65
where claimant convicted of fraud	13.60	17.75
Deductions from JSA(C) and ESA (C)		
Arrears of Comm. Charge, Council Tax, fines & overpayment recovery		
Age 16 - 24	17.81	18.75
Age 25 +	22.50	23.66
Max. dedn for arrears of Child Maintenance (CTM)		
Age 16 - 24	17.81	18.75
Age 25 +	22.50	23.66

5.4 The Department for Work and Pensions - Social Security Benefit Up-rating

Schedule of proposed benefit rates from April 2012

(Weekly rates unless otherwise shown)	RATES 2011	RATES 2012
DEPENDENCY INCREASES		
Adult dependency increases for spouse or person looking after after children - payable with;		
State Pension on own insurance (Cat A or B)	58.80	61.85
long term Incapacity Benefit ISCS Group 13 Type 5	54.75	57.60
Severe Disablement Allowance	32.90	34.60
Carers Allowance	32.70	34.40
short-term Incapacity Benefit (over state pension age)	52.70	55.45
short-term Incapacity Benefit (under State Pension age)	42.65	44.85
Child Dependency Increases - payable with;		
State Pension; Widowed Mothers/Parents Allowance; short-term Incapacity benefit - higher rate or over state pension age; long-term Incapacity Benefit; Carer's Allowance; Severe Disablement Allowance; Industrial Death Benefit (higher rate);	11.35	11.35
NB - The rate of child dependency increase is adjusted where it is payable for the eldest child for whom child benefit is also paid. The weekly rate in such cases is reduced by the difference (less £3.65) between the ChB rates for the eldest and subsequent children.	8.10	8.10
DISABILITY LIVING ALLOWANCE		
Care Component		
Highest	73.60	77.45
Middle	49.30	51.85
Lowest	19.55	20.55
Mobility Component		
Higher	51.40	54.05
Lower	19.55	20.55
DISREGARDS		
Housing Benefit and Council Tax Benefit		
Earnings disregards		
standard (single claimant)	5.00	5.00
couple	10.00	10.00
higher (special occupations/circumstances)	20.00	20.00
lone parent	25.00	25.00
childcare charges	175.00	175.00
childcare charges (2 or more children)	300.00	300.00
permitted work higher	95.00	97.50
permitted work lower	20.00	20.00

5.4 The Department for Work and Pensions - Social Security Benefit Up-rating

Schedule of proposed benefit rates from April 2012

(Weekly rates unless otherwise shown)	RATES 2011	RATES 2012
Other Income disregards		
adult maintenance disregard	15.00	15.00
war disablement pension and war widows pension	10.00	10.00
widowed mothers/parents allowance	15.00	15.00
Armed Forces Compensation Scheme	10.00	10.00
student loan	10.00	10.00
student's covenanted income	5.00	5.00
income from boarders (plus 50% of the balance)	20.00	20.00
additional earnings disregard	17.10	17.10
income from subtenants (£20 fixed from April 08)	20.00	20.00
Income Support, income-based Jobseeker's Allowance, income-related Employment and Support Allowance and Pension Credit		
Earnings disregards		
standard (single claimant)	5.00	5.00
couple	10.00	10.00
higher (special occupations/circumstances)	20.00	20.00
Other Income disregards		
war disablement pension and war widows pension	10.00	10.00
widowed mothers/parents allowance	10.00	10.00
Armed Forces Compensation Scheme	10.00	10.00
student loan (not Pension Credit)	10.00	10.00
student's covenanted income (not Pension Credit)	5.00	5.00
income from boarders (plus 50% of the balance)	20.00	20.00
income from subtenants (£20 fixed from April 08)	20.00	20.00

EARNINGS RULES

	2011	2012
Carers Allowance	100.00	100.00
Limit of earnings from councillor's allowance	95.00	97.50
Permitted work earnings limit - higher	95.00	97.50
- lower	20.00	20.00
Industrial injuries unemployability supplement permitted earnings level (annual amount)	4940.00	5070.00
Earnings level at which adult dependency (ADI) increases are affected with:		
short-term incapacity benefit where claimant is		
(a) under state pension age	42.65	44.85
(b) over state pension age	52.70	55.45

5.4 The Department for Work and Pensions - Social Security Benefit Up-rating

Schedule of proposed benefit rates from April 2012

(Weekly rates unless otherwise shown)	RATES 2011	RATES 2012
state pension, long term incapacity benefit, severe disablement allowance, unemployability supplement - payable when dependant		
(a) is living with claimant	67.50	71.00
(b) still qualifies for the tapered earnings rule	45.09	45.09
Earnings level at which ADI is affected when dependent is not living with claimant;		
state pension,	58.80	61.85
long-term incapacity benefit,	54.75	57.60
unemployability supplement,	55.55	58.45
severe disablement allowance	32.90	34.60
Carers allowance	32.70	34.40
Earnings level at which child dependency increases are affected		
for first child	205.00	215.00
additional amount for each subsequent child	27.00	28.00
Pension income threshold for incapacity benefit	85.00	85.00
Pension income threshold for contributory Employment Support Allowance	85.00	85.00

EMPLOYMENT AND SUPPORT ALLOWANCE

Personal Allowances		
Single		
under 25	53.45	56.25
25 or over	67.50	71.00
lone parent		
under 18	53.45	56.25
18 or over	67.50	71.00
couple		
both under 18	53.45	56.25
both under 18 with child	80.75	84.95
both under 18 (main phase)	67.50	71.00
both under 18 with child (main phase)	105.95	111.45
one 18 or over, one under 18 (certain conditions apply)	105.95	111.45
both over 18	105.95	111.45
claimant under 25, partner under 18	53.45	56.25
claimant 25 or over, partner under 18	67.50	71.00
claimant (main phase), partner under 18	67.50	71.00

5.4 The Department for Work and Pensions - Social Security Benefit Up-rating

Schedule of proposed benefit rates from April 2012

(Weekly rates unless otherwise shown)	RATES 2011	RATES 2012
Premiums		
enhanced disability		
single	14.05	14.80
couple	20.25	21.30
severe disability		
single	55.30	58.20
couple (lower rate)	55.30	58.20
couple (higher rate)	110.60	116.40
carer	31.00	32.60
pensioner		
single with WRAC	43.10	43.55
single with support component	37.50	37.65
single with no component	69.85	71.70
couple with WRAC	77.00	78.30
couple with support component	71.40	72.40
couple with no component	103.75	106.45
Components		
Work-related Activity	26.75	28.15
Support	32.35	34.05
HOUSING BENEFIT		
Personal allowances		
single		
under 25	53.45	56.25
25 or over	67.50	71.00
entitled to main phase ESA	67.50	71.00
lone parent		
under 18	53.45	56.25
18 or over	67.50	71.00
entitled to main phase ESA	67.50	71.00
couple		
both under 18	80.75	84.95
one or both 18 or over	105.95	111.45
claimant entitled to main phase ESA	105.95	111.45
dependent children	62.33	64.99

5.4 The Department for Work and Pensions - Social Security Benefit Up-rating

Schedule of proposed benefit rates from April 2012

(Weekly rates unless otherwise shown)	RATES 2011	RATES 2012
pensioner		
single/lone parent has attained the qualifying age for Pension Credit but under 65.	137.35	142.70
couple – one or both has attained the qualifying age for Pension Credit but both under 65	209.70	217.90
single / lone parent - 65 and over	157.90	161.25
couple - one or both 65 and over	236.80	241.65
Premiums		
family	17.40	17.40
family (lone parent rate)	22.20	22.20
disability		
single	28.85	30.35
couple	41.10	43.25
enhanced disability		
single	14.05	14.80
disabled child	21.63	22.89
couple	20.25	21.30
severe disability		
single	55.30	58.20
couple (lower rate)	55.30	58.20
couple (higher rate)	110.60	116.40
disabled child	53.62	56.63
carer	31.00	32.60
ESA components		
work-related activity	26.75	28.15
support	32.35	34.05

INCAPACITY BENEFIT

	RATES 2011	RATES 2012
Long-term Incapacity Benefit	94.25	99.15
Short-term Incapacity Benefit (under state pension age)		
lower rate	71.10	74.80
higher rate	84.15	88.55
Short-term Incapacity Benefit (over state pension age)		
lower rate	90.45	95.15
higher rate	94.25	99.15

5.4 The Department for Work and Pensions - Social Security Benefit Up-rating

Schedule of proposed benefit rates from April 2012

(Weekly rates unless otherwise shown)	RATES 2011	RATES 2012
Increase of Long-term Incapacity Benefit for age		
higher rate	13.80	11.70
lower rate	5.60	5.90
Invalidity Allowance (Transitional)		
higher rate	13.80	11.70
middle rate	7.10	5.90
lower rate	5.60	5.90
INCOME SUPPORT		
Personal Allowances		
single		
under 25	53.45	56.25
25 or over	67.50	71.00
lone parent		
under 18	53.45	56.25
18 or over	67.50	71.00
couple		
both under 18	53.45	56.25
both under 18 - higher rate	80.75	84.95
one under 18, one under 25	53.45	56.25
one under 18, one 25 and over	67.50	71.00
both 18 or over	105.95	111.45
dependent children	62.33	64.99
Premiums		
family / lone parent	17.40	17.40
pensioner (applies to couples only)	103.75	106.45
disability		
single	28.85	30.35
couple	41.10	43.25
enhanced disability		
single	14.05	14.80
disabled child	21.63	22.89
couple	20.25	21.30
severe disability		
single	55.30	58.20
couple (lower rate)	55.30	58.20
couple (higher rate)	110.60	116.40

5.4 The Department for Work and Pensions - Social Security Benefit Up-rating

Schedule of proposed benefit rates from April 2012

(Weekly rates unless otherwise shown)	RATES 2011	RATES 2012
disabled child	53.62	56.63
carer	31.00	32.60
Relevant sum for strikers	36.00	38.00

INDUSTRIAL DEATH BENEFIT

	RATES 2011	RATES 2012
Widow's pension		
higher rate	102.15	107.45
lower rate	30.65	32.24
Widower's pension	102.15	107.45

INDUSTRIAL INJURIES DISABLEMENT BENEFIT

	RATES 2011	RATES 2012
18 and over, or under 18 with dependants		
100%	150.30	158.10
90%	135.27	142.29
80%	120.24	126.48
70%	105.21	110.67
60%	90.18	94.86
50%	75.15	79.05
40%	60.12	63.24
30%	45.09	47.43
20%	30.06	31.62
Under 18		
100%	92.10	96.90
90%	82.89	87.21
80%	73.68	77.52
70%	64.47	67.83
60%	55.26	58.14
50%	46.05	48.45
40%	36.84	38.76
30%	27.63	29.07
20%	18.42	19.38
Maximum life gratuity (lump sum)	9980.00	10500.00
Unemployability Supplement	92.90	97.75
increase for early incapacity		
higher rate	19.25	20.25
middle rate	12.40	13.00
lower rate	6.20	6.50
Maximum reduced earnings allowance	60.12	63.24

5.4 The Department for Work and Pensions - Social Security Benefit Up-rating

Schedule of proposed benefit rates from April 2012

(Weekly rates unless otherwise shown)	RATES 2011	RATES 2012
Maximum retirement allowance	15.03	15.81
Constant attendance allowance		
exceptional rate	120.40	126.60
intermediate rate	90.30	94.95
normal maximum rate	60.20	63.30
part-time rate	30.10	31.65
Exceptionally severe disablement allowance	60.20	63.30
JOBSEEKER'S ALLOWANCE		
Contribution based JSA - Personal rates		
under 25	53.45	56.25
25 or over	67.50	71.00
Income-based JSA - personal allowances		
under 25	53.45	56.25
25 or over	67.50	71.00
lone parent		
under 18	53.45	56.25
18 or over	67.50	71.00
couple		
both under 18	53.45	56.25
both under 18 - higher rate	80.75	84.95
one under 18, one under 25	53.45	56.25
one under 18, one 25 and over	67.50	71.00
both 18 or over	105.95	111.45
dependent children	62.33	64.99
Premiums		
family / lone parent	17.40	17.40
pensioner		
single	69.85	71.70
couple	103.75	106.45
disability		
single	28.85	30.35
couple	41.10	43.25
enhanced disability		
single	14.05	14.80
disabled child	21.63	22.89
couple	20.25	21.30

5.4 The Department for Work and Pensions - Social Security Benefit Up-rating

Schedule of proposed benefit rates from April 2012

(Weekly rates unless otherwise shown)	RATES 2011	RATES 2012
severe disability		
single	55.30	58.20
couple (lower rate)	55.30	58.20
couple (higher rate)	110.60	116.40
disabled child	53.62	56.63
carer	31.00	32.60
Prescribed sum for strikers	36.00	38.00
MATERNITY ALLOWANCE		
Standard rate	128.73	135.45
MA threshold	30.00	30.00
PENSION CREDIT		
Standard minimum guarantee		
single	137.35	142.70
couple	209.70	217.90
Additional amount for severe disability		
single	55.30	58.20
couple (one qualifies)	55.30	58.20
couple (both qualify)	110.60	116.40
Additional amount for carers	31.00	32.60
Savings credit		
threshold - single	103.15	111.80
threshold - couple	164.55	178.35
maximum - single	20.52	18.54
maximum - couple	27.09	23.73
Amount for claimant and first spouse in polygamous marriage	209.70	217.90
Additional amount for additional spouse	72.35	75.20
Non-State Pensions (for Pension Credit purposes)		
	Increase	
Statutory minimum increase to non-state pensions	by:	5.20%

PNEUMOCONIOSIS, BYSSINOSIS, AND MISCELLANEOUS DISEASES SCHEME AND THE WORKMEN'S COMPENSATION (SUPPLEMENTATION)

	RATES 2011	RATES 2012
Total disablement allowance and major incapacity allowance (maximum)	150.30	158.10

5.4 The Department for Work and Pensions - Social Security Benefit Up-rating

Schedule of proposed benefit rates from April 2012

(Weekly rates unless otherwise shown)	RATES 2011	RATES 2012
Partial disablement allowance	55.55	58.45
Unemployability supplement	92.90	97.75
increases for early incapacity -		
higher rate	19.25	20.25
middle rate	12.40	13.00
lower rate	6.20	6.50
Constant attendance allowance		
exceptional rate	120.40	126.60
intermediate rate	90.30	94.95
normal maximum rate	60.20	63.30
part-time rate	30.10	31.65
Exceptionally severe disablement allowance	60.20	63.30
Lesser incapacity allowance		
maximum rate of allowance	55.55	58.45
based on loss of earnings over	73.60	77.45

SEVERE DISABLEMENT ALLOWANCE

Basic rate	62.95	69.00
Age-related addition (from Dec 90)		
Higher rate	13.80	11.70
Middle rate	7.10	5.90
Lower rate	5.60	5.90

STATE PENSION

Category A or B	102.15	107.45
Category B(lower) - spouse or civil partner's insurance	61.20	64.40
Category C or D - non-contributory	61.20	64.40
Additional pension	Increase by:	5.20%

Increments to:-

Basic pension	Increase by:	5.20%
Additional pension	Increase by:	5.20%
Graduated Retirement Benefit (GRB)	Increase by:	5.20%
Inheritable lump sum	Increase by:	5.20%

5.4 The Department for Work and Pensions - Social Security Benefit Up-rating

Schedule of proposed benefit rates from April 2012

(Weekly rates unless otherwise shown)	RATES 2011	RATES 2012
Contracted-out Deduction from AP in respect of pre-April 1988 contracted-out earnings	Nil	Nil
Contracted-out Deduction from AP in respect of contracted-out earnings from April 1988 to 1997	Increase by:	3.00%
Graduated Retirement Benefit (unit)	0.1189	0.1251
Increase of long term incapacity for age	Increase by:	5.20%
Addition at age 80	0.25	0.25
Increase of Long-term incapacity for age		
higher rate	19.25	20.25
lower rate	9.65	10.15
Invalidity Allowance (Transitional) for State Pension recipients		
higher rate	19.25	20.25
middle rate	12.40	13.00
lower rate	6.20	6.50
STATUTORY ADOPTION PAY		
Earnings threshold	102.00	107.00
Standard Rate	128.73	135.45
STATUTORY MATERNITY PAY		
Earnings threshold	102.00	107.00
Standard rate	128.73	135.45
STATUTORY PATERNITY PAY		
Earnings threshold	102.00	107.00
Standard Rate	128.73	135.45
ADDITIONAL STATUTORY PATERNITY PAY		
Earnings threshold	102.00	107.00
Standard Rate	128.73	135.45
STATUTORY SICK PAY		
Earnings threshold	102.00	107.00
Standard rate	81.60	85.85

5.4 The Department for Work and Pensions - Social Security Benefit Up-rating

Schedule of proposed benefit rates from April 2012

(Weekly rates unless otherwise shown)	RATES 2011	RATES 2012
WIDOW'S BENEFIT		
Widowed mother's allowance	100.70	105.95
Widow's pension		
standard rate	100.70	105.95
age-related		
age 54 (49)	93.65	98.53
53 (48)	86.60	91.12
52 (47)	79.55	83.70
51 (46)	72.50	76.28
50 (45)	65.46	68.87
49 (44)	58.41	61.45
48 (43)	51.36	54.03
47 (42)	44.31	46.62
46 (41)	37.26	39.20
45 (40)	30.21	31.79

Note: For deaths occurring before 11 April 1988 refer to age-points shown in brackets.

Source: Department for Work and Pensions

5.5 Number of persons claiming benefits: Caseloads by age group, thousands

	2001/02 Outturn	2002/03 Outturn	2003/04 Outturn	2004/05 Outturn	2005/06 Outturn	2006/07 Outturn	2007/08 Outturn	2008/09 Outturn	2009/10 Outturn	2010/11 Outturn	2011/12 Outturn
Benefits directed at Children											
Attendance Allowance (in payment)	-	-	-	-	-	-	-	-	-	-	-
Child Benefit & One Parent Benefit	6,991	7,042	-	-	-	-	-	-	-	-	-
number of children covered	12,600	12,622	-	-	-	-	-	-	-	-	-
Disability Living Allowance	239	258	270	279	286	292	300	310	322	331	339
of which in payment	239	258	270	279	286	292	300	310	322	331	339
of which entitlement without payment	-	-	-	-	-	-	-	-	-	-	-
Mobility Allowance	-	-	-	-	-	-	-	-	-	-	-
Benefits Directed at People of Working Age	-	-	-	-	-	-	-	-	-	-	-
Attendance Allowance (in payment)	-	-	-	-	-	-	-	-	-	-	-
Bereavement Benefits	214	227	203	180	163	147	129	117	108	101	95
Carer's Allowance	408	433	455	467	475	485	496	519	550	584	615
of which in payment	-	-	386	407	422	432	442	462	491	523	558
of which entitlement without payment	-	-	69	60	53	52	54	57	59	61	57
Christmas Bonus - non-contributory	1,635	1,719	1,854	1,921	1,912	1,920	2,003	3,164	3,246	3,227	3,212
Council Tax Benefit	2,293	2,268	2,358	2,473	2,603	2,570	2,533	2,566	2,940	3,172	3,254
Disability Living Allowance	1,410	1,491	1,553	1,596	1,627	1,657	1,692	1,733	1,780	1,819	1,847
of which in payment	1,396	1,477	1,539	1,582	1,612	1,641	1,676	1,715	1,761	1,800	1,828
of which entitlement without payment	14	14	14	14	15	16	16	17	19	19	20
Disability Working Allowance	-	-	-	-	-	-	-	-	-	-	-
Employment and Support Allowance	-	-	-	-	-	-	-	136	391	579	811
of which contributory	-	-	-	-	-	-	-	59	145	199	262
of which contributory and income-based	-	-	-	-	-	-	-	6	22	38	59
of which income-based	-	-	-	-	-	-	-	56	168	275	424
of which credits only	-	-	-	-	-	-	-	16	56	67	65
Family Credit	-	-	-	-	-	-	-	-	-	-	-
Housing Benefit	2,209	2,194	2,267	2,387	2,495	2,518	2,527	2,625	2,981	3,224	3,356
Incapacity Benefit, Invalidity Benefit & Sickness Benefit	2,427	2,483	2,504	2,510	2,475	2,443	2,415	2,332	2,031	1,827	1,577
of which in payment	1,572	1,586	1,570	1,543	1,500	1,456	1,413	1,346	1,177	1,054	909
of which credits only	856	898	934	967	975	987	1,002	986	854	773	668
Income Support	2,235	2,213	2,218	2,187	2,142	2,135	2,117	2,087	1,935	1,803	1,619
Industrial Injuries Disablement Benefit	-	-	192	187	182	176	170	163	156	146	145
Jobseeker's Allowance	932	920	898	819	870	927	818	1,025	1,538	1,415	1,515
of which contributory	178	190	185	158	165	157	142	244	321	234	212
of which contributory and income-based	20	19	18	14	15	15	13	21	30	22	19
of which income-based	666	646	631	588	632	691	609	695	1,072	1,069	1,207
of which credits only	67	65	64	59	58	64	54	66	114	91	77
Maternity Allowance	17	15	22	26	29	27	44	54	56	54	57
Mobility Allowance	-	-	-	-	-	-	-	-	-	-	-
Personal Independence Payment	-	-	-	-	-	-	-	-	-	-	-
of which in payment	-	-	-	-	-	-	-	-	-	-	-
of which entitlement without payment	-	-	-	-	-	-	-	-	-	-	-
Severe Disablement Allowance	326	289	274	260	246	234	221	210	200	191	135
Statutory Maternity Pay	82	86	104	137	154	154	197	248	253	274	273
Unemployment Benefit	-	-	-	-	-	-	-	-	-	-	-
Benefits Directed at Pensioners											
Attendance Allowance	1,495	1,510	1,547	1,589	1,629	1,666	1,700	1,737	1,776	1,782	1,756
of which in payment	1,296	1,304	1,343	1,400	1,445	1,489	1,528	1,568	1,607	1,619	1,597
of which entitlement without payment	199	206	204	189	184	177	172	169	169	163	160
Bereavement Benefits	29	29	27	26	23	21	19	14	11	10	11
Carer's Allowance	-	-	178	235	279	319	356	388	411	420	417
of which in payment	-	-	20	22	24	26	28	30	31	30	26
of which entitlement without payment	-	-	158	213	255	292	327	357	381	390	391
Christmas Bonus - contributory	12,014	12,002	12,232	12,302	12,387	12,586	12,728	11,754	12,123	15,466	15,547
Council Tax Benefit	2,371	2,357	2,335	2,442	2,426	2,510	2,535	2,592	2,631	2,633	2,620
Disability Living Allowance	719	741	784	826	864	903	949	991	1,031	1,055	1,066
of which in payment	715	736	779	821	859	897	942	984	1,023	1,046	1,057
of which entitlement without payment	4	5	5	5	5	6	6	7	8	9	9
Housing Benefit	1,637	1,612	1,546	1,554	1,491	1,503	1,509	1,541	1,566	1,574	1,576
Incapacity Benefit, Invalidity Benefit & Sickness Benefit	2	-	-	-	-	-	-	-	-	-	-
of which in payment	2	-	-	-	-	-	-	-	-	-	-
of which credits only	-	-	-	-	-	-	-	-	-	-	-
Industrial Injuries Disablement Benefit	-	-	150	153	156	159	171	172	176	187	185
Income Support	1,750	1,776	-	-	-	-	-	-	-	-	-
Mobility Allowance	-	-	-	-	-	-	-	-	-	-	-
Over-75 TV Licence	3,859	3,790	3,839	3,892	3,965	3,982	3,993	4,079	4,206	4,236	4,277
Pension Credit	-	-	1,979	2,594	2,700	2,729	2,732	2,724	2,736	2,718	2,649

5.5 Number of persons claiming benefits: Caseloads by age group, thousands

	2001/02 Outturn	2002/03 Outturn	2003/04 Outturn	2004/05 Outturn	2005/06 Outturn	2006/07 Outturn	2007/08 Outturn	2008/09 Outturn	2009/10 Outturn	2010/11 Outturn	2011/12 Outturn
Personal Independence Payment	-	-	-	-	-	-	-	-	-	-	-
of which in payment	-	-	-	-	-	-	-	-	-	-	-
of which entitlement without payment	-	-	-	-	-	-	-	-	-	-	-
State Pension	11,095	11,195	11,320	11,477	11,585	11,715	11,938	12,160	12,410	12,566	12,667
of which contributory	11,095	11,195	11,320	11,477	11,585	11,715	11,938	12,160	12,410	12,566	12,667
of which basic element	11,018	11,102	11,231	11,384	11,492	11,617	11,837	12,053	12,285	12,460	12,556
of which earnings-related element ("Additional Pension", "SERPS" or "S2P")	6,589	6,851	7,122	7,425	7,700	7,963	8,324	8,673	9,052	9,320	9,549
of which Graduated Retirement Benefit	8,834	8,961	9,117	9,296	9,439	9,594	9,842	10,087	10,358	10,563	10,702
of which lump sums (covering all contributory elements)	-	-	-	-	-	8	24	46	58	66	63
of which Single Tier Pension (excluding protected payments)											
of which Single Tier Protected Payments (including inherited elements)											
of which non-contributory ("Category D")	23	24	23	23	23	23	25	26	28	29	33
Severe Disablement Allowance	41	41	41	42	42	42	42	41	40	39	85
Winter Fuel Payments	11,202	11,358	11,486	11,430	11,555	11,750	12,123	12,421	12,681	12,783	12,686

Sources: Department for Work and Pensions;

5.6 Jobseeker's Allowance[1,2,3] claimants: by benefit entitlement Great Britain

As at May Thousands

All Persons

		2001	2002	2003	2004	2005	2006	2007	2008	2009	2010	2011	2012
All with benefit - total	KXDX	818.7	790.4	797.9	699.6	728.3	812	730.8	718	1316.4	1237.3	1298.3	1377
Contribution-based JSA only	KXDY	141.9	155.3	160.4	131	139.5	134.6	113.6	127.8	341.8	205.3	182.7	159.5
Contribution based JSA & income-based JSA	KXDZ	17.6	18.5	18.1	13.5	13.5	13	11.9	12.8	34.6	21.1	19.9	16.8
Income-based JSA only payment	KXEA	659.2	616.6	619.4	555.1	575.3	664.5	605.3	577.4	940	1010.9	1096	1201.7
No benefit in payment	KXEB	90.4	87.0	87.9	77.8	72.4	83.9	76.4	69.9	126.6	117.3	105.8	107.2
Total	KXEC	909.1	877.4	885.8	777.4	800.7	895.9	807.4	788	1443	1354.6	1404	1484

Males

		2001	2002	2003	2004	2005	2006	2007	2008	2009	2010	2011	2012
All with benefit - total	KXED	636.4	606.2	605.6	527.2	545.3	606.8	537.8	529.9	978.9	890.9	879.8	930
Contribution-based JSA only	KXEE	100.8	110.8	114.1	93.8	99.5	95.8	79.6	90.6	248.7	143.4	118.9	103.5
Contribution based JSA & income-based JSA	KXEF	16.2	16.7	15.9	12.3	12.6	12	10.7	11.7	31.2	18.1	16.9	13.7
Income-based JSA only payment	KXEG	519.4	478.7	475.6	421.1	433.2	498.9	447.5	427.6	698.9	729.5	744	812.8
No benefit in payment	KXEH	59.7	59.5	60.3	52.7	49.8	56.6	51.7	46.7	88.8	82.2	69.3	71.6
Total	KXEI	696.1	665.7	665.9	580	595.1	663.4	589.6	576.7	1067.7	973.1	949.1	1002

Females

		2001	2002	2003	2004	2005	2006	2007	2008	2009	2010	2011	2012
All with benefit - total	KXEJ	182.3	184.2	192.3	172.4	182.9	205.3	193	188.1	337.6	346.4	418.4	447
Contribution-based JSA only	KXEK	41.0	44.5	46.3	37.2	40	38.7	34	37.2	93.1	61.9	63.7	56
Contribution based JSA & income-based JSA	KXEL	1.5	1.8	2.2	1.2	0.8	1	1.2	1.2	3.4	3.0	3	3.1
Income-based JSA only payment	KXEM	139.8	137.9	143.8	134	142.1	165.5	157.8	149.8	241.1	281.4	351.7	387.9
No benefit in payment	KXEN	30.7	27.5	27.6	25	22.6	27.2	24.8	23.2	37.7	35.1	36.5	35.5
Total	KXEO	213.1	211.7	219.8	197.4	205.5	232.5	217.8	211.3	375.3	381.5	455	482.5

Sources: Department for Work and Pensions;
Information Directorate

1. Jobseeker's Allowance (JSA) has two routes of entry: contrbution-based which depends mainly upon national insurance contributions and income-based which depends mainly on a means test. Some claimants can qualify by either route. In practice they receive income-based JSA but have an under lying entitlement to the contribution-based element.

2 Figures are given at May each year and have been derived by applying 5% proportions to 100% totals taken from the DWP 100% Work and Pensions Longitudinal Study (WPLS).

3 Figures are rounded to the nearest hundred and quoted in thousands. They may not sum due to rounding.

5.7 Employment and Support Allowance and Incapacity Benefit[1,2,3] claimants: by sex, age and duration of spell
Great Britain and Overseas (excluding Northern Ireland).

At end of May

Thousands

		2000	2001	2002	2003	2004	2005	2006	2007	2008[4]	2009	2010	2011	2012
Males														
All durations: All ages	KJJA	1481.64	1512.24	1526.17	1525.02	1517.62	1492.38	1455.52	1428.65	1399.58	1419.43	1409.10	1358.24	1,312.25
Under 20	KJJB	11.3	11.33	21.79	21.81	22.04	21.45	19.95	18.66	17.25	18.09	17.33	15.6	15.66
20-29	KJJC	122.62	129.02	133.83	138.54	142.68	143.24	141.8	146.07	149.47	159.1	160.91	156.22	156.71
30-39	KJJD	232.51	245.71	250.79	254.3	253.32	245.61	233.7	224.29	215.51	215.95	213.57	201.58	195.39
40-49	KJJE	287.37	298.04	304.47	311.85	318.04	320.77	319.77	320.24	319.22	330.96	335.93	328.57	319.31
50-59	KJJF	474.44	482.18	478.01	472.03	463.37	451.93	439.54	418.26	404.76	405.59	403.61	391.96	384.28
60-64	KJJG	353.22	345.87	337.22	326.45	318.12	309.36	300.73	301.1	293.33	289.57	277.30	263.8	240.26
65 and over	KJJH	0.17	0.09	0.05	0.05	0.05	0.04	0.02	0.03	0.04	0.17	0.46	0.48	0.60
Unknown													0.04	0.03
Over six months: All ages	KJJI	1311.22	1338.11	1346.8	1359.53	1359.08	1347.43	1323.2	1291.32	1266.8	1253.91	1251.24	1213.77	1,050.73
Under 20	KJJJ	4.99	3.52	6.91	13.4	13.78	13.51	12.85	11.7	10.9	10.42	10.50	9.29	9.46
20-29	KJJK	90.06	94.86	96.61	105.72	110.85	114.57	115.21	117.83	121.9	124.5	128.76	125.36	115.47
30-39	KJJL	195.96	207.75	213.19	217.05	217.81	213.91	205.36	195.22	188.25	182.41	180.52	170.92	145.09
40-49	KJJM	253.84	264.41	271.25	278.53	285.9	290.72	291.36	289.94	289.72	293.13	298.29	294.15	249.83
50-59	KJJN	431.52	439.78	438.55	434.04	427.06	418.6	409.46	387.76	374.75	368.48	367.26	360.03	311.58
60-64	KJJO	334.73	327.73	320.26	310.75	303.64	296.1	288.93	288.85	281.25	274.93	265.52	253.54	218.74
65 and over	KJJP	0.14	0.06	0.03	0.03	0.04	0.02	0.02	0.03	0.03	0.05	0.39	0.43	0.53
Unknown													0.04	0.03
Females														
All durations: All ages	KJJQ	870.14	908.03	944.44	969.44	990.84	998.2	994.33	988.93	982.33	998.74	1007.13	1026.38	1,037.34
Under 20	KJJR	14.62	13.68	21.51	21.49	21.48	20.51	18.92	17.86	16.79	15.68	14.54	13.05	13.01
20-29	KJJS	91.03	92.79	96.66	100.78	105.02	108.61	109.73	114.42	117.91	121.5	122.82	121.54	121.56
30-39	KJJT	165.07	172.04	175.37	177.7	177.91	173.45	167.36	162.39	156.95	156.85	157.74	157.34	155.59
40-49	KJJU	231.94	243.27	252.82	262.2	270.9	276.62	279.32	283.45	285.84	296.87	305.06	305.31	299.72
50-59	KJJV	367.23	386.21	398.06	407.24	415.52	418.99	418.99	410.8	404.82	407.82	406.97	401.12	397.31
60 and over	KJJW	0.26	0.04	0.03	0.03	0.02	0.02	0.02	0.02	0.02	0.02	0.01	27.98	50.13
Unknown													0.03	0.02
Over six months: All ages	KJJX	761.08	795.67	825.25	858.03	880.52	894.57	896.33	885.69	881.41	882.94	888.73	905.11	817.68
Under 20	KJJY	6.94	4.74	7.41	12.35	12.4	12.1	11.13	10.2	9.55	8.75	8.15	7.16	7.31
20-29	KJJZ	69.35	70.88	72.32	79.63	84.02	88.98	90.99	93.6	97.24	99.15	100.81	99.22	90.34
30-39	KJKA	141.41	148.19	151.59	154.19	154.95	152.48	148	142.28	137.59	134.9	134.29	131.11	116.57
40-49	KJKB	205.6	216.19	225.65	234.71	243.52	250.11	253.5	255.99	258.74	263.7	269.48	269.38	234.09
50-59	KJKC	337.54	355.64	368.25	377.12	385.61	390.88	392.69	383.6	378.27	376.43	375.99	371.76	322.89
60 and over	KJKD	0.26	0.04	0.03	0.03	0.02	0.02	0.02	0.02	0.02	0.02	0.02	26.45	46.46
Unknown													0.03	0.02
Unknown Gender														
All durations	EW44	0.74	0.62	0.54	0.44	0.31	0.26	0.15	0.13	0.11	0.23	3.86	-	-
Over 6 months	EW45	0.33	0.28	0.29	0.21	0.16	0.13	0.1	0.09	0.09	0.1	3.67	-	-

Source: Department for Work and Pensions Information, Governance and Security Directorate

Definitions and conventions. Caseload figures are rounded to the nearest ten and displayed in thousands. Totals may not sum due to rounding.
1 See chapter text. Figures are given at May each year.
2 Table includes Employment and Support Allowance and Incapacity Benefit ONLY claimants and not those claiming Severe Disablement Allowance (SDA).
3 From 27th October 2008, new claims to Incapacity Benefit can also be allocated, on incapacity grounds, to the newly introduced Employment and Support Allowance (ESA).
4 Due to rounding errors several figures have been revised for May 2008.
5 2011 figures provided by IGS in relation to FOI 2013-2248 therefore 'Unknown' categories are different to previous years but match IGS published information on IB and ESA

5.8 Attendance allowance - cases in payment[1]: Age and gender of claimant Great Britain

At May each year   Thousands

		2004	2005	2006	2007	2008	2009	2010	2011	2012
Males: All ages	JT9Z	418.5	436.9	459.5	478.4	497.2	516.5	531.5	530.00	526.1
Unknown age	JTA2	–	–	–	–	–	–	–	0.02	0.02
65 - 69	JTA3	21.4	22	22.3	22.8	23.5	24.4	24.8	23.8	23.3
70 - 74	JTA4	59.8	61.6	64.2	66.8	70.2	73.7	74.9	71.9	68.8
75 - 79	JTA5	103.8	104.2	104.8	106.3	109.1	112.4	114.9	113.7	112.3
80 - 84	JTA6	121.7	125.3	130.4	133.1	135.4	137.8	139.9	137.6	135.3
85 - 89	JTA7	70.1	78.7	89.4	98.5	107.7	116	118.1	118.00	117.0
90 and over	JTA8	41.7	45.1	48.4	50.8	51.2	52.2	58.9	65.00	69.4
Females: All ages	JTA9	958.9	982.6	1006.2	1029.1	1049.5	1069.3	1082.8	1069.1	1047.5
Unknown age	JTB2	–	–	–	–	–	–	–	0.03	0.02
65 - 69	JTB3	27.3	27.7	28.3	28.4	29.1	30	30.3	28.7	27.2
70 - 74	JTB4	91.5	92	93.6	96.4	99.6	103.5	104.5	99.7	93.9
75 - 79	JTB5	190.9	189.1	186.8	185.8	186.7	188.4	188.4	182.2	176.5
80 - 84	JTB6	282.5	282	279.4	278.3	277.7	277.7	277.0	269.2	259.8
85 - 89	JTB7	204.7	221.4	241.6	259.3	276.7	290.9	286.6	279.8	271.7
90 and over	JTB8	162	170.4	176.4	180.9	179.6	178.8	196.0	209.6	218.5

1 Totals show the number of people in receipt of allowance, and exclude people
with entitlement where the payment has been suspended, for example if they are in hospital.

Sources: Department for Work and Pensions;
Information Directorate

5.9a: Families and children receiving Child Benefit, in each country and English Region, 2003 to 2012

Thousands

Time Series	United Kingdom [1]	Great Britain	England and Wales	England	North East	North West	Yorkshire and the Humber	East Midlands	West Midlands	East	London	South East	South West	Wales	Scotland	Northern Ireland	Foreign and not known
	Number of families and children				England												
Area Codes [2]	K02000001	K03000001	K04000001	E92000001	E12000001	E12000002	E12000003	E12000004	E12000005	E12000006	E12000007	E12000008	E12000009	W92000004	S92000003	N92000002	n/a
Number of families																	
August 2003	7,246,335	7,000,770	6,394,870	6,037,500	318,470	861,775	619,630	517,590	663,400	653,695	876,120	956,080	570,735	357,370	605,900	225,885	19,675
August 2004	7,296,495	7,055,160	6,448,355	6,087,500	317,515	863,070	622,065	520,870	667,175	660,390	894,090	965,480	576,845	360,855	606,805	226,850	14,485
August 2005	7,315,165	7,074,665	6,470,575	6,110,190	315,855	860,660	622,475	522,195	667,565	664,155	909,045	970,225	578,015	360,385	604,085	226,800	13,705
August 2006	7,413,475	7,129,720	6,528,205	6,168,010	316,665	864,650	626,740	527,105	672,220	671,850	926,055	981,015	581,705	360,195	601,515	230,140	53,615
August 2007	7,475,035	7,212,565	6,605,270	6,241,895	318,020	869,475	631,995	535,775	678,300	683,780	937,480	995,990	591,085	363,375	607,290	230,825	31,650
August 2008	7,582,990	7,320,990	6,708,080	6,341,345	319,815	876,795	640,670	543,350	686,910	696,485	964,180	1,013,595	599,550	366,735	612,910	233,830	28,165
August 2009	7,769,880	7,485,730	6,864,935	6,492,290	324,525	892,240	653,645	554,925	701,070	713,455	1,002,815	1,038,010	611,600	372,650	620,795	238,605	45,545
August 2010	7,841,675	7,557,305	6,935,695	6,562,705	324,265	894,940	657,700	559,645	705,640	723,030	1,028,265	1,051,885	617,340	372,985	621,615	240,985	43,385
August 2011	7,884,760	7,600,115	6,979,465	6,606,285	323,155	895,670	659,240	561,885	708,325	730,180	1,044,355	1,061,870	621,605	373,180	620,650	242,310	42,335
August 2012	7,920,495	7,641,575	7,022,780	6,650,070	321,310	895,845	661,370	564,385	711,110	737,485	1,061,620	1,071,795	625,145	372,705	618,795	243,185	35,735
Number of children																	
August 2003	13,138,075	12,670,975	11,625,050	10,983,290	552,970	1,549,900	1,116,630	934,450	1,219,985	1,200,175	1,613,235	1,754,585	1,041,360	641,755	1,045,925	439,870	27,230
August 2004	13,096,760	12,635,505	11,600,380	10,960,280	544,840	1,534,595	1,109,155	930,920	1,214,695	1,200,175	1,632,425	1,752,995	1,040,475	640,100	1,035,125	435,690	25,565
August 2005	13,111,665	12,654,135	11,626,490	10,988,765	540,940	1,528,255	1,109,150	932,310	1,215,315	1,204,750	1,658,755	1,758,520	1,040,780	637,725	1,027,640	431,995	25,535
August 2006	13,233,320	12,706,365	11,685,995	11,050,975	540,980	1,529,585	1,113,190	936,980	1,219,915	1,212,530	1,686,375	1,768,965	1,042,445	635,020	1,020,370	435,485	91,475
August 2007	13,267,355	12,778,460	11,754,415	11,117,770	540,610	1,529,060	1,117,760	946,090	1,225,025	1,225,485	1,699,215	1,782,530	1,052,000	636,645	1,024,045	433,370	55,525
August 2008	13,340,565	12,857,555	11,831,255	11,194,420	539,840	1,528,890	1,124,420	951,000	1,231,190	1,235,400	1,732,120	1,795,225	1,056,340	636,835	1,026,300	434,390	48,625
August 2009	13,604,375	13,088,240	12,054,140	11,409,950	546,125	1,549,625	1,143,245	967,010	1,251,900	1,258,520	1,794,220	1,827,530	1,071,775	644,190	1,034,095	440,570	75,565
August 2010	13,685,250	13,170,155	12,138,365	11,495,395	544,775	1,551,080	1,147,440	971,690	1,257,180	1,269,870	1,831,965	1,843,465	1,077,930	642,965	1,031,795	443,110	71,985
August 2011	13,721,160	13,207,465	12,179,715	11,537,505	542,680	1,549,475	1,148,450	973,310	1,259,770	1,276,525	1,853,670	1,852,950	1,080,680	642,210	1,027,750	444,285	69,410
August 2012	13,771,635	13,267,355	12,243,960	11,602,370	540,060	1,550,880	1,153,480	976,870	1,265,765	1,284,980	1,880,560	1,865,335	1,084,435	641,590	1,023,390	445,220	59,055

Source: HM Revenue and Customs

Footnotes
[1] Includes Foreign and not known
[2] Area codes implemented from 1 January 2011; in line with the new GSS Coding and Naming policy.

5.9b: Families receiving Child Benefit nationally, in each country and English Region, August 2012

Area names	Area Codes [1]	Number of families, by size						Total	Number of children in these families, by age			
		Total	One child	Two children	Three children	Four children	Five or more children		Under 5	5-10	11-15	16 and over
United Kingdom [2]	K02000001	7,920,495	3,748,230	2,945,290	901,685	239,055	86,235	13,771,635	3,883,470	4,313,775	3,600,345	1,974,045
Great Britain	K03000001	7,641,575	3,622,570	2,844,885	862,865	228,260	82,995	13,267,355	3,743,375	4,159,970	3,469,445	1,894,560
England and Wales	K04000001	7,022,780	3,307,530	2,619,820	801,345	214,715	79,375	12,243,960	3,459,220	3,835,100	3,185,935	1,763,710
England	E92000001	6,650,070	3,128,505	2,482,140	759,450	204,155	75,815	11,602,370	3,285,055	3,637,730	3,013,655	1,665,935
North East	E12000001	321,310	162,105	115,295	32,680	8,265	2,970	540,060	149,205	167,585	142,585	80,690
North West	E12000002	895,845	434,745	321,965	100,370	27,900	10,865	1,550,880	431,715	483,855	405,495	229,810
Yorkshire and the Humber	E12000003	661,370	314,515	242,765	74,295	21,685	8,115	1,153,480	326,470	361,890	299,330	165,795
East Midlands	E12000004	564,385	267,000	212,785	62,565	16,150	5,890	976,870	271,280	303,650	258,990	142,950
West Midlands	E12000005	711,110	330,955	258,625	84,805	25,775	10,950	1,265,765	353,285	396,820	331,440	184,215
East	E12000006	737,485	336,330	290,210	84,190	20,485	6,270	1,284,980	358,385	401,215	338,880	186,500
London	E12000007	1,061,620	507,695	370,615	128,595	37,820	16,895	1,880,560	577,040	603,225	455,755	244,540
South East	E12000008	1,071,795	487,090	425,025	122,090	29,105	8,480	1,865,335	520,345	585,440	490,555	269,000
South West	E12000009	625,145	288,075	244,855	69,860	16,975	5,380	1,084,435	297,330	334,055	290,615	162,435
Wales	W92000004	372,705	179,025	137,680	41,890	10,560	3,555	641,590	174,165	197,370	172,280	97,775
Scotland	S92000003	618,795	315,040	225,065	61,525	13,545	3,620	1,023,390	284,155	324,870	283,515	130,850
Northern Ireland	N92000002	243,185	106,635	88,105	35,445	10,005	3,000	445,220	122,865	135,245	116,200	70,915
Foreign and not known	n/a	35,735	19,030	12,305	3,375	790	240	59,055	17,230	18,560	14,700	8,570

Source: HM Revenue and Customs

Footnotes
[1] Area codes implemented from 1 January 2011; in line with the new GSS Coding and Naming policy.
[2] Includes Foreign and not known.

5.10 Child Tax Credit or Working Tax Credit elements and thresholds

Annual rate (£), except where specified

	2004-05	2005-06	2006-07	2007-08	2008-09	2009-10	2010-11	2011-12	2012-13
Child Tax Credit									
Family element	545	545	545	545	545	545	545	545	545
Child element[2]	1,625	1,690	1,765	1,845	2,085	2,235	2,300	2,555	2,690
Disabled child additional element[3]	2,215	2,285	2,350	2,440	2,540	2,670	2,715	2,800	2,950
Severely disabled child additional element[4]	890	920	945	980	1,020	1,075	1,095	1,130	1,190
Working Tax Credit									
Basic element	1,570	1,620	1,665	1,730	1,800	1,890	1,920	1,920	1,920
Couples and lone parent element	1,545	1,595	1,640	1,700	1,770	1,860	1,890	1,950	1,950
30 hour element[5]	640	660	680	705	735	775	790	790	790
Disabled worker element	2,100	2,165	2,225	2,310	2,405	2,530	2,570	2,650	2,790
Severely disabled adult element	890	920	945	980	1,020	1,075	1,095	1,130	1,190
50+ return to work payment[6]									
16 but less than 30 hours per week	1,075	1,110	1,140	1,185	1,235	1,300	1,320	1,65	N/A
at least 30 hours per week	1,610	1,660	1,705	1,770	1,840	1,935	1,965	2,030	N/A
Childcare element									
Maximum eligible costs allowed (£ per week)									
Eligible costs incurred for 1 child	135	175	175	175	175	175	175	175	175
Eligible costs incurred for 2+ children	200	300	300	300	300	300	300	300	300
Percentage of eligible costs covered	*70%*	*70%*	*80%*	*80%*	*80%*	*80%*	*80%*	70%	70%
Common features									
First income threshold[7]	5,060	5,220	5,220	5,220	6,420	6,420	6,420	6,420	6,420
First withdrawal rate	*37%*	*37%*	*37%*	*37%*	*39%*	*39%*	*39%*	*41%*	*41%*
Second income threshold[8]	50,000	50,000	50,000	50,000	50,000	50,000	50,000	40,000	..
First income threshold for those entitled to Child Tax Credit only[9]	13,480	13,910	14,155	14,495	15,575	16,040	16,190	15,860	15,860
Income increase disregard	2,500	2,500	25,000	25,000	25,000	25,000	25,000	10,000	10,000
Minimum award payable	26	26	26	26	26	26	26	26	26

Source: HM Treasury

1 Payable to families for any period during which they have one or more children aged under 1.

2 Payable for each child up to 31 August after their 16th birthday, and for each young person for any period in which they are aged under 20 (under 19 to 2005-06) and in full-time non-advanced education, or under 18 and in their first 20 weeks of registration with the Careers service or Connexions.

3 Payable in addition to the child element for each disabled child.

4 Payable in addition to the disabled child element for each severely disabled child.

5 Payable for any period during which normal hours worked (for a couple, summed over the two partners) is at least 30 per week.

6 Payable for each qualifying adult for the first 12 months following a return to work.

7 Income is net of pension contributions, and excludes Child Benefit, Housing benefit, Council tax benefit, maintenance and the first £300 of family income other than from work or benefits. The award is reduced by the excess of income over the first threshold, multiplied by the first withdrawal rate.

8 For those entitled to the Child Tax Credit, the award is reduced only down to the family element, plus the baby addition where relevant, less the excess of income over the second threshold multiplied by the second withdrawal rate.

9 Those also receiving Income Support, income-based Jobseeker's Allowance or Pension Credit are passported to maximum award with no tapering.

N/A The 50-plus element of the Working Tax Credit ended on 6 April 2012.

.. From 6 April 2012, the second income threshold has been removed and so the family element is no longer protected. Instead, the family element will be reduced at a rate of 41% immediately after all other credits have been withdrawn. This means that some people who received the family element in 2011-2012 may receive nothing in 2012-2013.

5.11: Number of families and children with Child Tax Credit or Working Tax Credit, by level of award

Thousands

	New Area Codes [1]	Total out-of-work families	In-work families				Total in receipt (out-of-work and in-work families)	Number of children in recipient families		
			With children			With no children		Total out-of-work families	In-work families	
			Receiving WTC and CTC	Receiving CTC only	Of which, lone parents	Receiving WTC only			Receiving WTC and CTC	Receiving CTC only
United Kingdom [2]	K02000001	1,484	1,849	777	1,114	512	4,622	2,835	3,289	1,581
Great Britain	K03000001	1,422	1,784	747	1,075	493	4,446	2,718	3,174	1,516
England and Wales	K04000001	1,309	1,643	688	974	441	4,081	2,520	2,945	1,400
England	E92000001	1,232	1,548	647	916	410	3,837	2,375	2,781	1,316
North East	E12000001	71	82	32	53	30	215	132	139	62
North West	E12000002	182	239	88	145	75	585	346	426	176
Yorkshire and the Humber	E12000003	130	178	72	98	53	432	252	322	143
East Midlands	E12000004	97	138	65	80	40	340	188	243	131
West Midlands	E12000005	146	182	76	99	48	452	292	338	156
East	E12000006	114	149	73	89	33	370	219	264	152
London	E12000007	248	239	71	143	46	604	488	447	144
South East	E12000008	149	199	95	125	43	485	285	351	199
South West	E12000009	93	143	75	84	43	353	175	251	154
Wales	W92000004	77	95	41	58	31	244	145	164	83
Scotland	S92000003	113	141	59	101	52	365	197	229	117
Northern Ireland	N92000002	54	62	28	38	18	162	100	111	60
Foreign and not known	n/a	9	2	1	2	1	13	17	3	3

[1] New area codes to be implemented from 1 January 2011; in line with the new GSS Coding and Naming policy.
[2] Includes Foreign and not known

Source: HM Revenue and Customs

5.12 Widows' Allowance (excluding bereavement payment[1,2,3]): by type of benefit Great Britain

Number in receipt of widows benefit as at May each year

Thousands

		2005	2006	2007	2008	2009	2010	2011	2012
All Widows' Benefit (excluding bereavement allowance)									
All ages	KJGA	139	117.7	96.89	77.9	62.14	50.75	44	38
Unknown Age	EW4O	–	–	0.02	–	–	–	–	–
18 - 24	EW4P	–	–	–	–	–	–	–	–
25 - 29	EW4Q	0.1	0.1	0.04	0.02	0.01	–	–	–
30 - 34	EW4R	0.8	0.5	0.32	0.2	0.13	0.08	0.05	0.02
35 - 39	EW4S	2.9	2.1	1.53	1.08	0.74	0.50	0.34	0.22
40 - 44	EW4T	6.1	4.9	3.93	3.04	2.31	1.72	1.22	0.84
45 - 49	EW4U	11	9.1	7.58	6.26	5.14	4.20	3.38	2.71
50 - 54	EW4V	26.9	21.8	17.69	14.42	11.72	9.76	8.09	6.77
55 - 59	EW4W	66.9	57.3	45.78	36.86	30.37	24.62	20.00	16.31
60 - 64	EW4X	24.3	21.8	20.01	16.01	11.71	9.86	10.93	11.13
Widowed parents' allowance - with dependant children									
All ages	KJGG	23.2	19	15.6	12.6	9.98	7.91	6.11	4.61
Unknown Age	EW4Y	–	–	–	–	–	–	–	–
18 - 24	EW4Z	–	–	–	–	–	–	–	–
25 - 29	EW52	0.1	0.1	0.03	0.02	0.01	–	–	–
30 - 34	EW53	0.8	0.5	0.31	0.19	0.12	0.07	0.04	0.02
35 - 39	EW54	2.8	2.1	1.49	1.05	0.72	0.49	0.32	0.21
40 - 44	EW55	5.7	4.6	3.75	2.92	2.23	1.65	1.18	0.80
45 - 49	EW56	6.7	5.6	4.71	3.87	3.13	2.61	2.04	1.56
50 - 54	EW57	4.8	4.1	3.58	3.1	2.53	2.08	1.68	1.32
55 - 59	EW58	2	1.8	1.57	1.33	1.13	0.92	0.75	0.62
60 - 64	EW59	0.3	0.2	0.17	0.13	0.1	0.09	0.09	0.08
Widowed parents' allowance - without dependant children									
All ages	KJGM	1.1	0.8	0.69	0.54	0.46	0.39	0.28	0.22
Unknown Age	EW5A	–	–	–	–	–	–	–	–
18 - 24	EW5B	–	–	–	–	–	–	–	–
25 - 29	EW5C	–	–	–	–	–	–	–	–
30 - 34	EW5D	–	–	0.01	0.01	0.01	0.01	–	–
35 - 39	EW5E	0.1	0.1	0.04	0.03	0.02	0.02	0.01	0.01
40 - 44	EW5F	0.2	0.2	0.13	0.09	0.07	0.06	0.04	0.03
45 - 49	EW5G	0.3	0.2	0.21	0.17	0.15	0.12	0.09	0.07
50 - 54	EW5H	0.3	0.2	0.17	0.13	0.13	0.12	0.08	0.06
55 - 59	EW5I	0.2	0.1	0.11	0.1	0.07	0.06	0.04	0.04
60 - 64	EW5J	–	–	0.02	0.01	0.01	0.01	0.01	0.01
Age-related bereavement allowance									
All ages	KJGS	96.6	84	70.13	57.37	46.58	38.55	34.2	30.16
Unknown Age	EW5K	–	–	0.01	–	–	–	–	–
18 - 24	EW5L	–	–	–	–	–	–	–	–
25 - 29	EW5M	–	–	–	–	–	–	–	–
30 - 34	EW5N	–	–	–	–	–	–	–	–
35 - 39	EW5O	–	–	–	–	–	–	–	–
40 - 44	EW5P	0.2	0.1	0.06	0.03	0.01	–	–	–
45 - 49	EW5Q	4	3.3	2.66	2.23	1.86	1.47	1.24	1.08
50 - 54	EW5R	21.4	17.2	13.75	11.08	9.01	7.55	6.32	5.39
55 - 59	EW5S	59	50.9	40.57	32.61	26.83	21.74	17.71	14.44
60 - 64	EW5T	12	12.5	13.08	11.42	8.87	7.78	6.92	9.25
Bereavement allowance (Not age related)									
All ages	KJGW	18.1	13.9	10.47	7.39	5.12	3.90	3.41	3.02
Unknown Age	EW5U	–	–	–	–	–	–	–	–
18 - 24	EW5V	–	–	–	–	–	–	–	–
25 - 29	EW5W	–	–	–	–	–	–	–	–
30 - 34	EW5X	–	–	–	–	–	–	–	–
35 - 39	EW5Y	–	–	–	–	–	–	–	–
40 - 44	EW5Z	–	–	–	–	–	–	–	–
45 - 49	EW62	–	–	–	–	–	–	–	–
50 - 54	EW63	0.5	0.3	0.2	0.11	0.05	0.01	0.01	–
55 - 59	EW64	5.6	4.4	3.53	2.82	2.33	1.90	1.5	1.22
60 - 64	EW65	12	9.1	6.74	4.45	2.74	1.98	1.91	1.79

Sources: DWP Information, Governance and Security, Work and Pensions Longitudinal Study.

1 "-" Nil or Negligible; "." Not applicable; Caseload figures are rounded to the nearest ten; Some additional disclosure control has also been applied. Average amounts are shown as pounds per week and rounded to the nearest penny. Totals may not sum due to rounding.
2 Caseload (Thousands) All Claimants of Widows Benefit are female. No new claims for WA have been accepted since April 2001 when it was replaced by Bereavement Allowance
3 Figures include overseas cases.

STATE PENSION AGE: The age at which women reach State Pension age is gradually increasing from 60 to 65 between April 2010 and April 2016 to November 2018. Under current legislation, State Pension age for men and women is planned to increase to: 66 between November 2018 and October 2020; 67 between 2034 and 2036; 68 between 2044 and 2046. This will introduce a small increase to the number of working age benefit recipients and a small reduction to the number of pension age recipients. Figures from May 2010 onwards reflect this change. For more information see http://statistics.dwp.gov.uk/asd/espa.pdf.

5.13 Bereavement Allowance[1,2] (excluding bereavement payment): by sex, type of benefit and age of widow/er Great Britain.

Thousands

		Males						Females				
		2008	2009	2010	2011	2012		2008	2009	2010	2011	2012
All Bereavement Benefit (excluding bereavement allowance)												
All ages	WLSX	17.82	18.6	18.67	18.59	18.78	WLTC	42.04	43.32	44.64	46.18	47.40
18 - 24	EVW9	–	–	–	–	.	EVY2	0.08	0.06	0.04	0.05	0.05
25 - 29	EVX2	0.06	0.06	0.05	0.06	0.05	EVY3	0.53	0.53	0.52	0.48	0.47
30 - 34	EVX3	0.25	0.25	0.26	0.24	0.25	EVY4	1.66	1.68	1.71	1.67	1.69
35 - 39	EVX4	1.11	1.06	0.99	0.88	0.84	EVY5	4.31	4.3	4.27	4.01	3.86
40 - 44	EVX5	2.5	2.47	2.32	2.13	2.15	EVY6	7.33	7.61	7.74	7.77	7.76
45 - 49	EVX6	3.69	3.92	3.98	4.00	3.92	EVY7	9.54	10.22	10.78	11.09	11.30
50 - 54	EVX7	3.51	3.68	3.77	3.82	3.97	EVY8	9.1	9.64	10.3	10.58	10.76
55 - 59	EVX8	3.33	3.38	3.42	3.41	3.53	EVY9	9.49	9.28	9.18	9.38	9.51
60 - 64	EVX9	3.36	3.77	3.87	4.05	4.08	EVZ2	–	–	0.11	1.15	1.99
Widowed parents' allowance - with dependant children												
All ages	WLUD	11.51	11.81	11.78	11.58	11.68	WLUH	29.18	31.08	32.47	33.27	33.90
18 - 24	EVZ3	–	–	–	–	.	EW24	0.08	0.06	0.04	0.05	0.05
25 - 29	EVZ4	0.06	0.06	0.05	0.06	0.05	EW25	0.52	0.53	0.52	0.48	0.46
30 - 34	EVZ5	0.25	0.25	0.26	0.24	0.25	EW26	1.64	1.66	1.7	1.66	1.68
35 - 39	EVZ6	1.11	1.06	0.99	0.88	0.84	EW27	4.27	4.26	4.24	3.98	3.85
40 - 44	EVZ7	2.49	2.46	2.31	2.12	2.15	EW28	7.25	7.54	7.69	0.73	7.73
45 - 49	EVZ8	3.26	3.39	3.47	3.51	3.41	EW29	7.99	8.7	9.22	9.56	9.81
50 - 54	EVZ9	2.48	2.62	2.67	2.7	2.86	EW2A	5.29	5.97	6.58	6.97	7.12
55 - 59	EW22	1.32	1.38	1.42	1.45	1.46	EW2B	2.14	2.36	2.47	2.69	2.93
60 - 64	EW23	0.54	0.59	0.61	0.63	0.66	EW2C	–	–	0.01	0.14	0.25
Widowed parents' allowance - without dependant children												
All ages	WLVK	0.04	0.04	0.04	0.03	0.03	WMMR	0.32	0.28	0.25	0.21	0.18
18 - 24	EW2D	–	–	–	–	.	EW2M	–	–	–	–	.
25 - 29	EW2E	–	–	–	–	.	EW2N	0.01	0.01	–	–	.
30 - 34	EW2F	–	–	–	–	.	EW2O	0.02	0.02	0.01	0.01	0.01
35 - 39	EW2G	–	–	–	–	.	EW2P	0.04	0.04	0.03	0.02	0.01
40 - 44	EW2H	0.01	0.01	0.01	0.01	0.01	EW2Q	0.08	0.06	0.05	0.04	0.04
45 - 49	EW2I	0.01	0.01	0.01	0.01	0.01	EW2R	0.09	0.08	0.07	0.06	0.06
50 - 54	EW2J	0.01	0.01	0.01	0.01	.	EW2S	0.05	0.05	0.04	0.05	0.04
55 - 59	EW2K	–	0.01	0.01	0.01	.	EW2T	0.04	0.03	0.03	0.02	0.01
60 - 64	EW2L	–	–	–	–	.	EW2U	–	–	–	–	.
Age-related bereavement allowance												
All ages	WMOB	1.59	1.74	1.76	1.75	1.75	WMOC	5.76	5.59	5.63	5.51	5.53
18 - 24	EW2V	–	–	–	–	.	EW36	–	–	–	–	.
25 - 29	EW2W	–	–	–	–	.	EW37	–	–	–	–	.
30 - 34	EW2X	–	–	–	–	.	EW38	–	–	–	–	.
35 - 39	EW2Y	–	–	–	–	.	EW39	–	–	–	–	.
40 - 44	EW2Z	–	–	–	–	.	EW3A	–	–	–	–	.
45 - 49	EW32	0.42	0.52	0.5	0.49	0.49	EW3B	1.46	1.45	1.48	1.46	1.43
50 - 54	EW33	1.03	1.06	1.1	1.11	1.11	EW3C	3.76	3.62	3.67	3.56	3.60
55 - 59	EW34	0.14	0.16	0.16	0.15	0.15	EW3D	0.54	0.52	0.47	0.49	0.51
60 - 64	EW35	–	–	–	–	.	EW3E	–	–	–	–	.
Bereavement allowance (not age related)												
All ages	WMOX	4.68	5.01	5.09	5.22	5.33	WMOY	6.77	6.36	6.3	7.19	7.80
18 - 24	EW3F	–	–	–	–	.	EW3O	–	–	–	–	.
25 - 29	EW3G	–	–	–	–	.	EW3P	–	–	–	–	.
30 - 34	EW3H	–	–	–	–	.	EW3Q	–	–	–	–	.
35 - 39	EW3I	–	–	–	–	.	EW3R	–	–	–	–	.
40 - 44	EW3J	–	–	–	–	.	EW3S	–	–	–	–	.
45 - 49	EW3K	–	–	–	–	.	EW3T	–	–	–	–	.
50 - 54	EW3L	–	–	–	–	.	EW3U	–	–	–	–	.
55 - 59	EW3M	1.86	1.83	1.83	1.8	1.91	EW3V	6.77	6.36	6.2	6.18	6.06
60 - 64	EW3N	2.81	3.18	3.26	3.42	3.42	EW3W	–	–	0.1	1.00	1.73

1 Figures include overseas cases.

2 Figures are given at May each year and are taken from the DWP 100%   Work and Pensions Longitudinal Study (WPLS).

Sources: DWP Information, Governance and Security, Work and Pensions Longitudinal Study

"-" Nil or Negligible; "." Not applicable; Caseload figures are rounded to the nearest ten; Some additional disclosure control has also been applied. Average amounts are shown as pounds per week and rounded to the nearest penny. Totals may not sum due to rounding.

Notes:

Type of BA *The category 'WPA with dependants' will include clients getting paid at the personal rate only due to the introduction of of Child Tax Credits in April 2003. To obtain figures for those who still receive Child Dependency Increases, under the transitional protection arrangements, use the 'type of dependant' option.*

STATE PENSION AGE: The age at which women reach State Pension age is gradually increasing from 60 to 65 between April 2010 and April 2016 to November 2018. Under current legislation, State Pension age for men and women is planned to increase to: 66 between November 2018 and October 2020; 67 between 2034 and 2036; 68 between 2044 and 2046. This will introduce a small increase to the number of working age benefit recipients and a small reduction to the number of pension age recipients. Figures from May 2010 onwards reflect this change. For more information see http://statistics.dwp.gov.uk/asd/espa.pdf.

5.14 Contributory and non-contributory retirement pensions:[1,2] by sex and age of claimant Great Britain and Overseas.

At May each year.   Thousands and percentages

		2003	2004	2005	2006	2007	2008	2009	2010	2011	2012
Men:											
Age-groups:											
65-69	KJSB	1,330.18	1354.3	1364.1	1341.5	1332.77	1350.61	1389.85	1,441.17	1,498.78	1,629.37
Percentage	KJSC	*31.55*	31.6	31.4	30.6	30.03	29.84	29.99	*30.28*	*30.77*	*32.14*
70-74	KJSD	1,136.59	1140.3	1150	1160.1	1177.96	1205.7	1232.97	1,252.63	1249.42	1,256.65
Percentage	KJSE	*26.95*	26.6	26.5	26.5	26.54	26.63	26.61	*26.32*	*25.65*	*24.79*
75-79	KJSF	867.13	875	887.1	903	918.47	932.17	942.03	958.54	975.17	996.90
Percentage	KJSG	*20.56*	20.4	20.4	20.6	20.7	20.59	20.33	*20.14*	*20.02*	*19.67*
80-84	KJSH	565.32	593.7	593.3	596.9	604.74	614.77	627.28	644.94	663.35	680.67
Percentage	KJSI	*13.41*	13.9	13.7	13.6	13.63	13.58	13.54	*13.55*	*13.62*	*13.43*
85-89	KJSJ	225.86	221.4	246.4	273.1	296.36	317.9	335.49	340.87	348.51	357.78
Percentage	KJSK	*5.36*	5.2	5.7	6.2	6.68	7.02	7.24	*7.16*	*7.16*	*7.06*
90 and over	KJSL	90.59	95.5	100.2	103.6	106.13	105.33	105.62	120.82	135.62	147.15
Percentage	KJSM	*2.15*	2.2	2.3	2.4	2.39	2.33	2.28	*2.54*	*2.79*	*2.90*
Unknown age	EW3Y	1.00	0.8	1.1	1.2	1.45	0.19	0.24	0.23	0.27	0.27
Percentage	EW3Z	*0.02*	–	–	–	–	–	–	–	-	-
Total all ages	KJSA	4,216.74	4281.1	4342.2	4379.5	4437.99	4526.79	4633.62	4,759.36	4871.26	5068.96
Women:											
Age-groups:											
60-64	KJSO	1,402.74	1451.3	1498.7	1524	1628.19	1695.88	1734.92	1,747.21	1621.44	1391.16
Percentage	KJSP	*19.88*	20.3	20.8	21	21.98	22.47	22.62	*22.45*	*20.94*	*18.07*
65-69	KJSQ	1,429.68	1452.7	1464.2	1453.1	1456.08	1484.8	1527.47	1,576.10	1632.12	1768.96
Percentage	KJSR	*20.27*	20.4	20.3	20	19.65	19.67	19.91	*20.25*	*21.1*	*22.98*
70-74	KJSS	1,329.08	1319.2	1314.5	1312.7	1322.14	1343.22	1366.91	1,382.42	1377.54	1385.36
Percentage	KJST	*18.84*	18.5	18.2	18.1	17.85	17.8	17.82	*17.77*	*17.79*	*18.00*
75-79	KJSU	1,161.86	1156.7	1158.6	1165.5	1168.86	1170.01	1166.2	1,168.83	1172.33	1185.64
Percentage	KJSV	*16.47*	16.2	16.1	16	15.78	15.5	15.2	*15.02*	*15.14*	*15.40*
80-84	KJSW	939.41	973.9	951.6	933.3	923.7	919.11	921.01	931.08	942.31	950.53
Percentage	KJSX	*13.32*	13.6	13.2	12.9	12.47	12.18	12.01	*11.97*	*12.17*	*12.35*
85-89	KJSY	491.33	473.1	511	552.7	587.91	621.15	643.5	634.29	628.71	626.68
Percentage	KJSZ	*6.96*	6.6	7.1	7.6	7.94	8.23	8.39	*8.15*	*8.12*	*8.14*
90 and over	KJTA	298.76	307.2	314.9	319.4	319.9	313.66	310.07	341.10	370.18	389.38
Percentage	KJTB	*4.23*	4.3	4.4	4.4	4.32	4.16	4.04	*4.38*	*4.78*	*5.06*
Unknown age	EW42	2.01	1.1	1.3	1.5	1.67	0.37	0.38	0.35	0.35	0.35
Percentage	EW43	*0.03*	–	–	–	–	–	–	–	-	-
Total all ages	KJSN	7,054.88	7135.1	7214.7	7262.3	7408.44	7548.2	7670.44	7,781.39	7744.98	7698.12

Source: DWP Information, Governance and Security, Work and Pensions Longitudinal Study.

1 See chapter text.

2 Caseloads include both contributory and non-contributory state pensioners.

"-" Nil or Negligible; "." Not applicable; Caseload figures are rounded to the nearest ten; Some additional disclosure control has also been applied. Average amounts are shown as pounds per week and rounded to the nearest penny. Totals may not sum due to rounding.

STATE PENSION AGE: *The age at which women reach State Pension age is gradually increasing from 60 to 65 between April 2010 and April 2016 to November 2018. Under current legislation, State Pension age for men and women is planned to increase to: 66 between November 2018 and October 2020; 67 between 2034 and 2036; 68 between 2044 and 2046. This will introduce a small increase to the number of working age benefit recipients and a small reduction to the number of pension age recipients. Figures from May 2010 onwards reflect this change. For more information see http://statistics.dwp.gov.uk/asd/espa.pdf.*

5.15a War pensions: estimated number of pensioners[1]
Great Britain

At 31 March each year   Thousands

		2001	2002	2003	2004	2005	'2006[2]	2007	2008	2009	2010	2011	2012
Disablement	KADH	231.62	221.8	212.18	201.55	191.75	182.8	173.85	165.17	157.13	148.95	141.72	134.43
Widows and dependants	KADI	52.71	50.98	48.61	46.04	43.55	41.05	38.69	36.1	33.62	31.45	29.20	27.11
Total	KADG	284.33	272.78	260.79	247.59	235.3	223.85	212.54	201.27	190.75	180.40	170.92	161.54

1 See chapter text. From 1914 war, 1939 war and later service.
2 The discontinuity between 2005 and 2006 is due to improvements in data processing.

Source: Ministry of Defence/DASA (Health Information): 01225 468599

5.15b War Pensions in payment by type of pension, gender and financial year end, 31 March 2008 to 31 March 2012, numbers

	Awards in payment at:				
	31-Mar-08	31-Mar-09	31-Mar-10	31-Mar-11	31-Mar-12
ALL IN PAYMENT	**201,265**	**190,745**	**180,400**	**170,910**	**161,535**
Men	**158,455**	**150,655**	**142,770**	**135,740**	**128,720**
Women	**42,810**	**40,090**	**37,630**	**35,175**	**32,820**
Disablement Pensioners	**165,165**	**157,125**	**148,945**	**141,715**	**134,430**
Men	157,780	150,005	142,135	135,120	128,130
Women	7,385	7,120	6,810	6,595	6,305
War Widow(er)s	**35,235**	**32,790**	**30,655**	**28,425**	**26,375**
Men	70	70	75	75	80
Women	35,165	32,715	30,580	28,350	26,295
Other Pensioners	**865**	**830**	**795**	**770**	**730**
Men	605	580	555	540	510
Women	260	255	240	230	220

Source: Ministry of Defence/DASA (Health Information): 01225 468599

5.16 Income support[1],[2] by statistical group[3]: number of claimants receiving weekly payment

Great Britain   Thousands[4]

		2004	2005	2006	2007	2008	2009	2010	2011	2012
All income support claimants (including MIG from 2003)[5]	F8YY	2204.7	2150.8	2125.1	2128.4	2102.3	1990.0	1852.3	1703.2	1417.1
Incapacity Benefits	F8YZ	1214.2	1202.8	1191.7	1193.5	1191.4	1097.0	996.6	924.9	654.13
Lone Parent	F8Z2	823.3	789.3	774.9	765.6	738.6	720.5	679.2	595.4	577.08
Carer	F8Z3	79.9	80.5	81.7	84.3	87.3	93.8	103.9	115.7	129.75
Others on Income Related Benefits	F8Z4	87.3	78.1	76.8	84.9	85.0	78.9	72.7	67.2	56.1

Sources: DWP Information, Governance and Security, Work and Pensions Longitudinal Study

1 Figures are given at May each year and are taken from the DWP 100% Work and Pensions Longitudinal Study (WPLS).
2 From 27th October 2008, new claims to Income Support can also be allocated, on incapacity grounds, to the newly introduced Employment and Support Allowance (ESA).
3 Statistical Group is a hierarchical variable. A person who fits into more than one category will only appear in the top-most one for which they are eligible. These statistical groups differ from the groups shown in the 5% sample tables. Lone Parents are defined as claimants on Income Support with child under 16 and no partner. Lone Parent Obligations were introduced from 24th November 2008 affecting the eligibility criteria based on the age of the youngest child. For more information see
http://83.244.183.180/100pc/is/tabtool_is.html.
4 Figures are rounded to the nearest hundred and quoted in thousands.
5 Totals may not sum due to rounding.
"-" Nil or Negligible; "." Not applicable; Caseload figures are rounded to the nearest ten; Some additional disclosure control has also been applied.

STATE PENSION AGE: The age at which women reach State Pension age is gradually increasing from 60 to 65 between April 2010 and April 2016 to November 2018. Under current legislation, State Pension age for men and women is planned to increase to: 66 between November 2018 and October 2020; 67 between 2034 and 2036; 68 between 2044 and 2046. This will introduce a small increase to the number of working age benefit recipients and a small reduction to the number of pension age recipients. Figures from May 2010 onwards reflect this change. For more information see http://statistics.dwp.gov.uk/asd/espa.pdf.

5.17 Pension Credit[1]: number of claimants

Great Britain
End of May

		2005	2006	2007	2008	2009	2010	2011	Thousands[2] 2012
All Pension Credit	**F8Z5**	2682.7	2717.4	2733.5	2719.1	2730.6	2734.2	2674.7	2541.5
Guarantee Credit Only	**F8Z6**	767.3	775.6	805.7	882.1	925.7	954.4	937	1015.9
Guarantee Credit and Savings Credit	**F8Z7**	1321.7	1343.2	1330.1	1246.2	1205.2	1202.4	1148.1	964.3
Savings Credit	**F8Z8**	593.7	598.6	597.7	590.8	599.6	577.4	589.6	561.4

1 Source: DWP 100% Work and Pensions Longitudinal study (WPLS).

2 Figures are rounded to the nearest hundred and expressed in thousands.

Source: DWP Information, Governance and Security, Work and Pensions Longitudinal Study.

Caseload - number of claimants (Thousands) - Pension Credit was introduced on 6 October 2003 and replaced Minimum Income Guarantee (Income Support for people aged 60 or over). The vast majority of people who were previously in receipt of the Minimum Income Guarantee transferred to Pension Credit in October 2003. These Pension Credit statistics are produced on a different basis to the Early Estimates. The latter are more timely but operational processing times mean that a number of claim commencements and terminations are not reflected in them.

Type of Pension Credit - Certain aspects of the April 2012 uprating for Pension Credit were applied to the administrative computer system in advance, before the February 2012 statistics were extracted. Hence, the statistics in February 2012 show the Pension Credit type based on 2012/13 rates. However, the amounts in payment had not been adjusted and claimants were still being paid the correct rate of benefit, based on 2011/12 rates.

5.18 Income support: average weekly amounts of benefit[1,2,3]

Great Britain
As at May

		2004	2005	2006	2007	2008	2009	2010	2011	£ per week 2012
All income support claimants	**F8ZF**	91.14	85.89	83.54	82.45	82.55	85.17	85.01	84.88	83.93
Incapacity benefits[4]	**F8ZG**	77.84	77.12	78.35	80.04	81.85	89.22	91.81	93.66	93.69
Lone Parent[4]	**F8ZH**	114.96	102.85	94.88	89.70	87.37	82.79	79.02	75.94	76.54
Carer[4]	**F8ZI**	77.22	73.03	71.13	70.82	70.21	71.85	70.90	69.94	72.23
Others on income related benefits[4]	**F8ZJ**	64.24	62.81	62.78	62.47	63.02	66.35	67.87	68.82	73.19

1 Figures are given at May each year and are taken from the DWP 100% Work and Pensions Longitudinal Study (WPLS).

Source: DWP Information, Governance and Security, Work and Pensions Longitudinal Study.

2 The amount of Income Support is affected by the introduction in April 2003 of Child Tax Credit. From that date there were no new child dependency increases awarded to IS claimants, although existing CDIs were transitionally protected.

3 Average amounts are shown as pounds per week and rounded to the nearest penny.

4 Statistical Group is a hierarchical variable. A person who fits into more than one category will only appear in the top-most one for which they are eligible. These statistical groups differ from the groups shown in the 5% sample tables. Lone Parents are defined as claimants on Income Support with child under 16 and no partner. Lone Parent Obligations were introduced from 24th November 2008 affecting the eligibility criteria based on the age of the youngest child. For more information see http://83.244.183.180/100pc/is/tabtool_is.html.

5.19 Pension Credit: average weekly amounts of benefit1

Great Britain
As at May

		2005	2006	2007	2008	2009	2010	2011	£ per week[2] 2012
All Pension Credit	**F8ZA**	43.62	46.75	50.04	52.69	55.56	57.39	57.74	57.60
Guarantee Credit Only	**F8ZB**	75.43	79.56	83.74	85.07	88.86	90.73	92.51	90.12
Guarantee Credit and Savings Credit	**F8ZC**	39.87	43.11	46.11	48.29	50.81	51.75	52.04	50.26
Savings Credit only	**F8ZD**	10.83	12.39	13.36	13.62	13.71	14.01	13.57	11.36

1 Figures are given in each May and are taken from the DWP 100% Work and Pensions Longitudinal Study (WPLS).

2 Average amounts are shown as pounds per week and rounded to the nearest penny.

Source: DWP Information, Governance and Security, Work and Pensions Longitudinal Study.

Certain aspects of the April 2012 uprating for Pension Credit were applied to the administrative computer system in advance, before the February 2012 statistics were extracted. Hence, the statistics in February 2012 show the Pension Credit type based on 2012/13 rates. However, the amounts in payment had not been adjusted and claimants were still being paid the correct rate of benefit, based on 2011/12 rates.

STATE PENSION AGE: The age at which women reach State Pension age is gradually increasing from 60 to 65 between April 2010 and April 2016 to November 2018. Under current legislation, State Pension age for men and women is planned to increase to: 66 between November 2018 and October 2020; 67 between 2034 and 2036; 68 between 2044 and 2046. This will introduce a small increase to the number of working age benefit recipients and a small reduction to the number of pension age recipients. Figures from May 2010 onwards reflect this change. For more information see http://statistics.dwp.gov.uk/asd/espa.pdf.

this page is intentionally blank

External trade and investment

Chapter 6

External trade and investment

External trade (Table 6.1 and 6.3 to 6.6)

The statistics in this section are on the basis of Balance of Payments (BoP). They are compiled from information provided to HM Revenue and Customs (HMRC) by importers and exporters on the basis of Overseas Trade Statistics (OTS) which values exports 'f.o.b.' (free on board) and imports 'c.i.f.' (including insurance and freight). In addition to deducting these freight costs and insurance premiums from the OTS figures, coverage adjustments are made to convert the OTS data to a BoP basis. Adjustments are also made to the level of all exports and European Union (EU) imports to take account of estimated under-recording. The adjustments are set out and described in the annual United Kingdom *Balance of Payments Pink Book* (Office for National Statistics (ONS)). These adjustments are made to conform to the definitions in the 5th edition of the IMF Balance of Payments Manual.

Aggregate estimates of trade in goods, seasonally adjusted and on a BoP basis, are published monthly in the ONS statistical bulletin UK Trade. More detailed figures are available from time series data on the ONS website (www.ons.gov.uk) and are also published in the *Monthly Review of External Trade Statistics.* Detailed figures for EU and non-EU trade on an OTS basis are published in *Overseas trade statistics: United Kingdom trade with the European Community and the world* (HMRC).

A fuller description of how trade statistics are compiled can be found in Statistics on Trade in Goods (Government Statistical Service Methodological Series) available at: www.statistics.gov.uk/STATBASE/Product.asp?vlnk=14943

Overseas Trade Statistics

HMRC provide accurate and up to date information via the website: www.uktradeinfo.com
They also produce publications entitled 'Overseas Trade Statistics'.

Import penetration and export sales ratios (Table 6.2)

The ratios were first introduced in the August 1977 edition of *Economic Trends* in an article entitled 'The Home and Export Performance of United Kingdom Industries'. The article described the conceptual and methodological problems involved in measuring such variables as import penetration.

The industries are grouped according to the 2007 Standard Industrial Classification at 2-digit level.

Table 19.2a lists total UK manufacturers' sales, and tables 19.2b to 19.2e list the four different sets of ratios defined as follows:

Ratio 1:   percentage ratio of imports to home demand

Ratio 2:   percentage ratio of imports to home demand plus exports

Ratio 3:   percentage ratio of exports to total manufacturers' sales

Ratio 4:   percentage ratio of exports to total manufacturers' sales plus imports

Home demand is defined as total manufacturers' sales plus imports minus exports. This is only an approximate estimate as different sources are used for the total manufacturers' sales and the import and export data. Total manufacturers' sales are determined by the Products of the European Community inquiry and import and export data are provided by HMRC.

Ratio 1 is commonly used to describe the import penetration of the home market. Allowance is made for the extent of a domestic industry's involvement in export markets by using Ratio 2; this reduces as exports increase.

Similarly, Ratio 3 is the measure normally used to relate exports to total sales by UK producers and Ratio 4 makes an allowance for the extent to which imports of the same product are coming into the UK.

Table 6.3 to 6.6

The series are now available as datasets in the UK Trade release, which is updated monthly

International trade in services (Tables 6.7 and 6.8)

These data relate to overseas trade in services and cover both production and non-production industries (excluding the public sector). In terms of the types of services traded these include royalties, various forms of consultancy, computing and telecommunications services, advertising and market research and other business services. A separate inquiry covers the film and television industries. The surveys cover receipts from the provision of services to residents of other countries (exports) and payments to residents of other countries for services rendered (imports).

Sources of data

The International Trade in Services (ITIS) surveys (which consist of a quarterly component addressed to the largest businesses and an annual component for the remainder) are based on a sample of companies derived from the Inter-departmental Business Register in addition to a reference list and from 2007 onwards a sample of approximately 5000 contributors from the Annual Business Inquiry (ABI). The companies are asked to show the amounts for their imports and exports against the geographical area to which they were paid or from which they were received, irrespective of where they were first earned.

The purpose of the ITIS survey is to record international transactions which impact on the UK's BoP. Exports and imports of goods are generally excluded, as they will have been counted in the estimate for trade in goods. However earnings from third country trade – that is, from arranging the sale of goods between two countries other than the UK and where the goods never physically enter the UK (known as merchanting) – are included. Earnings from commodity trading are also included. Together, these two comprise trade related services.

Royalties are a large part of the total trade in services collected in the ITIS survey. These cover transactions for items such as printed matter, sound recordings, performing rights, patents, licences, trademarks, designs, copyrights, manufacturing rights, the use of technical know-how and technical assistance.

Balance of Payments (Tables 6.9 to 6.12)

Tables 6.9 to 6.12 are derived from *United Kingdom Balance of Payments: The Pink Book* 2012 edition. The following general notes to the tables provide brief definitions and explanations of the figures and terms used. Further notes are included in the Pink Book.

Summary of Balance of Payments

The BoP consists of the current account, the capital account, the financial account and the International Investment Position (IIP). The current account consists of trade in goods and services, income, and current transfers. Income consists of investment income and compensation of employees. The capital account mainly consists of capital transfers and the financial account covers financial transactions. The IIP covers balance sheet levels of UK external assets and liabilities. Every credit entry in the balance of payments accounts should, in theory, be matched by a corresponding debit entry so that total current, capital and financial account credits should be equal to, and therefore offset by, total debits. In practice there is a discrepancy termed net errors and omissions.

Current account

Trade in goods

The goods account covers exports and imports of goods. Imports of motor cars from Japan, for example, are recorded as debits in the trade in goods account, whereas exports of vehicles manufactured in the UK are recorded as credits. Trade in goods forms a component of the expenditure measure of gross domestic product (GDP).

Trade in services

The services account covers exports and imports of services, for example civil aviation. Passenger tickets for travel on UK aircraft sold abroad, for example, are recorded as credits in the services account, whereas the purchases of airline tickets from foreign airlines by UK passengers are recorded as debits. Trade in services, along with trade in goods, forms a component of the expenditure measure of GDP.

Income

The income account consists of compensation of employees and investment income and is dominated by the latter. Compensation of employees covers employment income from cross-border and seasonal workers which is less significant in the UK than in other countries. Investment income covers earnings (for example, profits, dividends and interest payments and receipts) arising from cross-border investment in financial assets and liabilities. For example, earnings on foreign bonds and shares held by financial institutions based in the UK are recorded as credits in the investment income account, whereas earnings on UK company securities held abroad are recorded as investment income debits. Investment income forms a component of gross national income (GNI) but not GDP.

Current transfers

Current transfers are composed of central government transfers (for example, taxes and payments to and receipts from, the EU) and other transfers (for example gifts in cash or kind received by private individuals from abroad or receipts from the EU where the UK government acts as an agent for the ultimate beneficiary of the transfer). Current transfers do not form a component either of GDP or of GNI. For example, payments to the UK farming industry under the EU Agricultural Guarantee Fund are recorded as credits in the current transfers account, while payments of EU agricultural levies by the UK farming industry are recorded as debits in the current transfers account.

Capital account

Capital account transactions involve transfers of ownership of fixed assets, transfers of funds associated with acquisition or disposal of fixed assets and cancellation of liabilities by creditors without any counterparts being received in return. The main components are migrants transfers, EU transfers relating to fixed capital formation (regional development fund and agricultural guidance fund) and debt forgiveness. Funds brought into the UK by new immigrants would, for example, be recorded as credits in the capital account, while funds sent abroad by UK residents emigrating to other countries would be recorded as debits in the capital account. The size of capital account transactions are quite minor compared with the current and financial accounts.

Financial account

While investment income covers earnings arising from cross-border investments in financial assets and liabilities, the financial account of the balance of payments covers the flows of such investments. Earnings on foreign bonds and shares held by financial institutions based in the UK are, for example, recorded as credits in the investment income account, but the acquisition of such foreign securities by UK-based financial institutions are recorded as net debits in the financial account or portfolio investment abroad. Similarly, the acquisitions of UK company securities held by foreign residents are recorded in the financial account as net credits or portfolio investment in the UK.

International Investment Position

While the financial account covers the flows of foreign investments and financial assets and liabilities, the IIP records the levels of external assets and liabilities. While the acquisition of foreign securities by UK-based financial institutions are recorded in the financial account as net debits, the total holdings of foreign securities by UK-based financial institutions are recorded as levels of UK external assets. Similarly, the holdings of UK company securities held by foreign residents are recorded as levels of UK liabilities.

Foreign direct investment (Tables 6.13 to 6.18)

Direct investment refers to investment that adds to, deducts from, or acquires a lasting interest in an enterprise operating in an economy other than that of the investor – the investor's purpose being to have an effective voice in the management of the enterprise. (For the purposes of the statistical inquiry, an effective voice is taken as equivalent to a holding of 10 per cent or more in the foreign enterprise.) Other investments in which the investor does not have an effective voice in the management of the enterprise are mainly portfolio investments and these are not covered here.

Direct investment is a financial concept and is not the same as capital expenditure on fixed assets. It covers only the money invested in a related concern by the parent company and the concern will then decide how to use the money. A related concern may also raise money locally without reference to the parent company.

The investment figures are published on a net basis; that is they consist of investments net of disinvestments by a company into its foreign subsidiaries, associate companies and branches.

Definitional changes from 1997

The new European System of Accounts (ESA(95)) definitions were introduced from the 1997 estimates. The changes were as follows:

i.   Previously, for the measurement of direct investment, an effective voice in the management of an enterprise was taken as the equivalent of a 20 per cent shareholding. This is now 10 per cent

ii.   The Channel Islands and the Isle of Man have been excluded from the definition of the economic territory of the UK. Prior to 1987 these islands were considered to be part of the UK

iii.   Interest received or paid was replaced by interest accrued in the figures on earnings from direct investment. There is deemed to be little or no impact arising from this definitional change on the estimates

A further change caused by the move to ESA(95) is that withholding taxes payable on direct investment earnings are now measured. Earnings were shown gross of these taxes in the Balance of Payments 2005 Pink Book. However, for the purposes of this business monitor earnings are calculated net of tax, as before.

New register sources available from 1998 have led to revisions of the figures from that year onwards. These sources gave an improved estimate of the population satisfying the criteria for foreign direct investment.

From the 2005 surveys new data sources have allowed the inclusion of data for the previously excluded Private Property (outward & inward surveys) and Public Corporations (outward surveys) sectors. From the 2006 surveys the tax data previously excluded from the FDI surveys are now also included in the final earnings figures for both the outward & inward surveys. This now means that there are no coherence issues between the FDI annual surveys and the quarterly Balance of Payments figures as published in the latest Balance of Payments Pink Book.

Definitional changes have been introduced from 1997 and the register changes from 1998. Data prior to these years have not been reworked in Tables 6.13 to 6.18. For clarity, the Offshore Islands are identified separately on the tables. Breaks in the series for the other definitional changes are not quantified but are relatively small. More detailed information on the effect of these changes appears in the business monitor MA4 – Foreign Direct Investment 2002, which was published in February 2003 and is available from the ONS website.

Country allocation

The analysis of inward investment is based on the country of ownership of the immediate parent company. Thus, inward investment in a UK company may be attributed to the country of the intervening overseas subsidiary, rather than the country of the ultimate parent. Similarly, the country analysis of outward investment is based on the country of ownership of the immediate subsidiary; for example, to the extent that overseas investment in the UK is channelled through holding companies in the Netherlands, the underlying flow of investment from this country is overstated and the inflow from originating countries is understated.

Further information

More detailed statistics on foreign direct investment are available on request from Richard Tonkin, Office for National Statistics, International Transactions Branch, Room 2.364, Government Buildings, Cardiff Road, Newport, South Wales, United Kingdom, NP10 8XG. Telephone: +44 (0)1633 456082, fax: +44 (0)1633 812855, email Richard.tonkin@ons.gov.uk

6.1 Trade in goods[1]
United Kingdom
Balance of payments basis

£million and indices (2006=100)

		2000	2001	2002	2003	2004	2005	2006	2007	2008	2009	2010	2011	2012
Value (£ million)														
Exports of goods	BOKG	187,936	189,093	186,524	188,320	190,874	211,608	243,633	220,858	252,086	227,645	266,079	299,073	300,456
Imports of goods	BOKH	220,912	230,305	234,229	236,927	251,774	280,197	319,945	310,612	345,202	310,010	363,278	399,303	406,799
Balance on trade in goods	BOKI	-32,976	-41,212	-47,705	-48,607	-60,900	-68,589	-76,312	-89,754	-93,116	-82,365	-97,199	-100,230	-106,343
Price index numbers														
Exports of goods	BQKR	95	94	94	96	96	100	103	103	114	117	124	116	115
Imports of goods	BQKS	100	99	97	96	96	100	104	105	114	118	125	116	115
Terms of trade[2]	BQKT	95	95	97	100	100	100	99	99	100	100	99	101	100
Volume index numbers														
Exports of goods	BQKU	90	92	91	91	92	100	112	100	91	80	89	116	118
Imports of goods	BQKV	78	82	86	87	94	100	110	107	96	84	93	111	115

Source: Office for National Statistics: 01633 456294

1 Statistics of trade in goods on a balance of payments basis are obtained by making certain adjustments in respect of valuation and coverage to the statistics recorded in the Overseas Trade Statistics. These adjustments are described in detail in The Pink Book.
2 Export price index as a percentage of the import price index.

6.2 Sales of products manufactured in the United Kingdom by Industry Division

		S - Suppressed as disclosive
		£ Thousands
Industry	Division[1]	2011
Other mining and quarrying	8	2,348,023
Manufacture of food products	10	60,663,124
Manufacture of beverages	11	12,875,926
Manufacture of tobacco products	12	1,672,839
Manufacture of textiles	13	4,047,168
Manufacture of wearing apparel	14	1,490,960
Manufacture of leather and related products	15	618,239
Manufacture of wood and of products of wood and cork, except furniture; manufacture of articles of straw and plaiting materials	16	5,577,606
Manufacture of paper and paper products	17	S
Printing and reproduction of recorded media	18	8,927,210
Manufacture of chemicals and chemical products	20	S
Manufacture of basic pharmaceutical products and pharmaceutical preparations	21	13,901,544
Manufacture of rubber and plastic products	22	S
Manufacture of other non-metallic mineral products	23	10,249,359
Manufacture of fabricated metal products, except machinery and equipment	25	S
Manufacture of computer, electronic and optical products	26	12,857,258
Manufacture of electrical equipment	27	11,864,709
Manufacture of machinery and equipment n.e.c.	28	S
Manufacture of motor vehicles, trailers and semi-trailers	29	38,446,099
Manufacture of other transport equipment	30	21,392,793
Manufacture of furniture	31	S
Other manufacturing	32	S
Repair and installation of machinery and equipment	33	12,589,466
Publishing activities	58	N/A*
Total		337,144,227

Source: Office for National Statistics

[1] Division 07 (Mining of metal ores), Division 19 (manufacture of coke and refined petroleum products) and Division 24 (Manufacture of basic metals) do not form part of this analysis.

*** data for division 30 excludes SIC(07) 30400 Manufacture of military fighting machines

2011 data are final estimates

Tables 6.2b, c, d and e are no longer included in this publication. The import penetration and export sales ratios are no longer published by the ONS as a result of potential data differences with trade data which feed into the ratios.

6.3 United Kingdom exports: by commodity[1,2]

Seasonally adjusted

£ million

		2002	2003	2004	2005	2006	2007	2008	2009	2010	2011	2012
0. Food and live animals	BOGG	5703	6491	6475	6568	6776	7382	8712	9180	10130	11103	10888
01. Meat and meat preparations	BOGS	516	607	668	730	755	835	1169	1252	1406	1677	1595
02. Dairy products and eggs	BQMS	627	761	781	719	712	808	886	835	1038	1248	1169
04 & 08. Cereals and animal feeding stuffs	BQMT	1446	1688	1554	1558	1593	1793	2301	2379	2588	2763	2780
05. Vegetables and fruit	BQMU	437	480	513	519	585	608	694	760	815	882	848
1. Beverages and tobacco	BQMZ	4307	4410	4123	4105	4178	4371	5045	5367	5960	6982	6930
11. Beverages	BQNB	3325	3485	3360	3490	3718	4070	4598	4966	5636	6839	6856
12. Tobacco	BQOW	982	925	763	615	460	301	447	401	324	143	74
2. Crude materials	BQOX	2647	3076	3570	3754	4628	5191	6263	4810	6926	8575	8004
of which:												
24. Wood, lumber and cork	BQOY	80	107	116	131	147	143	125	83	111	113	110
25. Pulp and waste paper	BQOZ	106	180	244	283	338	415	478	354	543	623	543
26. Textile fibres	BQPA	472	492	522	517	544	497	540	571	675	782	822
28. Metal ores	BQPB	930	1196	1608	1716	2420	2901	3676	2524	4120	5095	4533
3. Fuels	BOPN	16031	16578	17929	21613	25360	24393	35474	26974	35139	42762	44023
33. Petroleum and petroleum products	ELBL	14348	14623	16241	19906	23230	22451	31928	24611	31329	38039	39684
32, 34 & 35. Coal, gas and electricity	BOQI	1683	1955	1688	1707	2130	1942	3546	2363	3810	4723	4339
4. Animal and vegetable oils and fats	BQPI	211	267	207	236	273	326	360	375	422	440	482
5. Chemicals	ENDG	28415	31433	32070	33467	37204	38934	43895	47013	50916	53176	52950
of which:												
51. Organic chemicals	BQPJ	5708	6081	6051	6718	8014	7600	8395	9090	8859	9187	8999
52. Inorganic chemicals	BQPK	1370	1462	1546	1559	2144	2829	2985	2837	3487	3018	2890
53. Colouring materials	CSCE	1585	1631	1634	1638	1603	1669	1841	1690	1954	2165	1999
54. Medicinal products	BQPL	10101	11919	12347	12349	13794	14576	17340	20499	22362	22881	23459
55. Toilet preparations	CSCF	2827	3128	3111	3227	3446	3689	3947	4134	4298	4845	4852
57 & 58. Plastics	BQQA	3532	3710	3855	4308	4448	4613	4863	4396	5318	5870	5626
6. Manufactures classified chiefly by material	BQQB	21673	22836	24163	25966	27149	29361	32432	24557	29255	34917	32433
of which:												
63. Wood and cork manufactures	BQQC	270	323	291	255	273	273	243	220	224	253	267
64. Paper and paperboard manufactures	BQQD	2022	2101	1999	2047	2016	2124	2345	2282	2341	2376	2293
65. Textile manufactures	BQQE	2853	2963	2853	2654	2682	2594	2600	2374	2599	2791	2738
67. Iron and steel	BQQF	2922	3325	4252	5196	5136	6021	6862	4584	5033	6045	5759
68. Non-ferrous metals	BQQG	2355	2244	2893	3284	4295	5786	6865	3972	5842	8602	6817
69. Metal manufactures	BQQH	3667	3774	3864	4074	4523	4669	5057	4263	4520	4849	4933
7. Machinery and transport equipment[3]	BQQI	84540	79804	78533	89591	110602	82507	89049	79428	92736	103519	104561
71-716, 72, 73 & 74. Mechanical machinery	BQQK	22738	24279	23850	25857	28261	28964	32259	29324	32857	38596	39411
716, 75, 76 & 77. Electrical machinery	BQQL	38774	30705	28685	37212	55515	24033	25139	24085	25770	26190	24276
78. Road vehicles	BQQM	16343	17506	18523	19485	19346	21081	22482	17029	23373	27420	28949
79. Other transport equipment	BQQN	6685	7314	7475	7037	7480	8429	9169	8990	10736	11313	11925
8. Miscellaneous manufactures[3]	BQQO	22014	22575	22978	25236	26140	26694	28606	27844	31446	33751	35920
of which:												
84. Clothing	CSCN	2511	2713	2735	2717	2880	3062	3307	3431	3666	4218	4461
85. Footwear	CSCP	453	427	420	471	522	543	621	722	853	932	1034
87 & 88. Scientific and photographic	BQQQ	7229	7295	7055	7262	7351	7059	8052	8288	9290	10192	10382
9. Other commodities and transactions	BOQL	1033	817	815	1070	1435	1366	2321	2587	2778	3848	4265
Total United Kingdom exports	BOKG	186574	188287	190863	211606	243745	220525	252157	228135	265708	299073	300456

Source: Office for National Statistics: 01633 456294

1 The numbers on the left hand side of the table refer to the code numbers of the Standard International Trade Classification, Revision 3, which was introduced in January 1988.
2 Balance of payments consistent basis.
3 Sections 7 and 8 are shown by broad economic category in table G2 of the Monthly Review of External Trade Statistics.

6.4 United Kingdom imports: by commodity[1,2]

Seasonally adjusted

£ million

		2002	2003	2004	2005	2006	2007	2008	2009	2010	2011	2012
0. Food and live animals	BQQR	14884	16464	17224	18606	19881	21354	25320	26362	27174	29498	30077
of which:												
01. Meat and meat preparations	BQQS	2796	3268	3444	3622	3813	3991	4616	4919	5006	5629	5634
02. Dairy products and eggs	BQQT	1292	1502	1610	1701	1814	1838	2288	2320	2429	2547	2615
04 & 08. Cereals and animal feeding stuffs	BQQU	1990	2233	2315	2369	2504	2919	3815	3932	3973	4154	4639
05. Vegetables and fruit	BQQV	4281	4662	4783	5299	5820	6229	7070	7059	7458	7921	7907
1. Beverages and tobacco	BQQW	4505	4738	4944	5107	5215	5354	5816	5961	6296	6492	6475
11. Beverages	EGAT	3031	3239	3479	3629	3715	3869	4301	4367	4613	4885	5035
12. Tobacco	EMAI	1474	1499	1465	1478	1500	1485	1515	1594	1683	1607	1440
2. Crude materials	ENVB	5427	5528	5721	6136	7143	8661	9612	6562	9148	10460	9407
of which:												
24. Wood, lumber and cork	ENVC	1238	1366	1338	1359	1459	1805	1407	1168	1465	1430	1504
25. Pulp and waste paper	EQAH	488	489	480	477	514	516	612	452	596	629	521
26. Textile fibres	EQAP	362	339	340	316	301	322	338	290	360	466	391
28. Metalores	EHAA	1449	1430	1648	2001	2682	3771	4656	2256	3899	4761	3996
3. Fuels	BQAT	10288	12316	17560	26002	31065	32307	49024	35476	44923	61928	65289
33. Petroleum and petroleum products	ENXO	9220	11237	15317	22065	26126	27149	38429	28037	36048	49550	53844
32, 34 & 35. Coal, gas and electricity	BPBI	1068	1079	2243	3937	4939	5158	10595	7439	8875	12378	11445
4. Animal and vegetable oils and fats	EHAB	539	614	622	642	775	897	1397	1052	1128	1493	1413
5. Chemicals	ENGA	24008	26152	27948	29231	31834	34678	37977	39029	44756	48920	49440
of which:												
51. Organic chemicals	EHAC	5676	6106	6807	7188	7718	8666	8465	8284	9398	10115	10106
52. Inorganic chemicals	EHAE	1071	1093	1367	1508	2131	2696	2761	2743	2952	3618	3198
53. Colouring materials	CSCR	953	1004	1060	1074	1093	1157	1227	1144	1253	1325	1364
54. Medicinal products	EHAF	7294	8193	8378	8511	9190	9932	11072	13224	15244	16356	17681
55. Toilet preparations	CSCS	2502	2746	2883	3037	3347	3449	3925	4167	4416	4665	4757
57 & 58. Plastics	EHAG	4067	4405	4753	5043	5426	5698	6229	5566	6848	7753	7543
6. Manufactures classified chiefly by material	EHAH	28360	29606	31989	33161	36521	39787	41944	35922	43591	49223	49904
of which:												
63. Wood and cork manufactures	EHAI	1437	1449	1586	1506	1580	1738	1728	1477	1664	1690	1663
64. Paper and paperboard manufactures	EHAJ	4585	4749	4845	4825	5055	5246	5491	5510	5898	6032	5704
65. Textile manufactures	EHAK	4152	4091	4128	3848	4031	4086	4080	3821	4290	4615	4539
67. Iron and steel	EHAL	3050	3239	4202	4405	4998	5944	6569	3858	5162	6501	6186
68. Non-ferrous metals	EHAM	2827	3005	3283	3593	4987	6253	6440	6355	8681	10163	12567
69. Metal manufactures	EHAN	4505	4769	4982	5359	5872	6565	6988	5978	6878	7556	7606
7. Machinery and transport equipment[3]	EHAO	107629	101458	103977	117279	140313	117627	120908	107335	129235	129023	131324
71 - 716, 72, 73 & 74. Mechanical machinery	EHAQ	18916	18960	19737	21863	22689	25566	29107	24429	28781	32851	34368
716, 75, 76 & 77. Electrical machinery	EHAR	49950	43639	45539	55575	75264	46068	47248	44574	50998	51268	50664
78. Road vehicles	EHAS	28469	29909	30768	31543	32887	36580	33916	26185	33664	36779	36600
79. Other transport equipment	EHAT	10294	8950	7933	8298	9473	9413	10637	12147	15792	8125	9692
8. Miscellaneous manufactures[3]	EHAU	36848	38138	39878	42285	45256	47965	51080	50111	54764	58744	59686
of which:												
84. Clothing	CSDR	9787	10304	10665	11310	11968	12374	13219	13862	14847	16186	15846
85. Footwear	CSDS	2367	2376	2449	2565	2708	2681	2841	3098	3606	3703	3862
87 & 88. Scientific and photographic	EHAW	7050	7053	7265	7421	7682	7542	8443	8502	9114	9582	10109
9. Other commodities and transactions	BQAW	1446	1606	1800	1843	2145	2373	3161	3166	3202	3522	3784
Total United Kingdom imports	BOKH	233934	236620	251663	280292	320148	311003	346239	310976	364217	399303	406799

Source: Office for National Statistics: 01633 456294

1 The numbers on the left hand side of the table refer to the code numbers of the Standard International Trade Classification, Revision 3, which was introduced in January 1988.
2 Balance of payments consistent basis.
3 Sections 7 and 8 are shown by broad economic category in table G2 of the Monthly Review of External Trade Statistics.

6.5 United Kingdom exports: by area[1]
Seasonally adjusted

		2002	2003	2004	2005	2006	2007	2008	2009	2010	2011	£ million 2012
European Union:[2]	LGCK	114863	111475	111825	121675	152709	127880	142055	124879	142009	159056	151150
EMU members:	QAKW	104359	101164	101076	110049	136780	114836	127190	111914	125575	140560	134437
Austria	CHMY	1262	1265	1098	1335	1690	1377	1474	1293	1461	1694	1563
Belgium & Luxembourg	CHNQ	10571	11401	10530	11413	14768	12113	13652	11093	13603	16252	14590
Cyprus	BQGN	271	314	321	355	1047	415	538	620	562	694	479
Finland	CHMZ	1445	1495	1364	1520	1820	1957	1912	1325	1497	1657	1556
France	ENYL	18787	18926	18593	19963	29111	18116	18122	17227	19201	21998	20976
Germany	ENYO	22097	20853	21702	23060	27246	24710	28003	24306	27877	32564	32491
Greece	CHNT	1200	1250	1408	1371	1473	1356	1664	1625	1378	1202	909
Irish Republic	CHNS	15441	12250	14159	16320	17264	17791	19168	15960	16907	17897	17430
Italy	CHNO	8520	8623	8415	8806	9497	9189	9417	8359	8839	10020	8078
Malta	BQGY	225	256	257	239	320	363	450	401	392	450	403
Netherlands	CHNP	14035	13628	12045	12734	16685	15102	19951	18228	21218	23566	25046
Portugal	CHNU	1519	1455	1582	1702	2343	1483	1645	1545	1837	1754	1374
Slovakia	BQHB	200	234	223	259	275	380	455	379	466	553	535
Slovenia	BQHE	181	159	160	168	195	204	223	176	219	241	218
Spain	CHNV	8505	8962	9113	10689	12574	10052	10295	9237	9925	9739	8498
Non-EMU members:[2]	BQIA	10604	10404	10855	11741	16401	13272	15086	13105	16627	18775	17004
of which:												
Bulgaria	WYUF	133	152	155	220	226	202	252	198	249	327	310
Czech Rep	FKML	1034	1008	979	1080	1578	1403	1552	1445	1822	1923	1835
Denmark	CHNR	2735	2187	2048	2322	3867	2180	2595	2479	2752	3015	2701
Estonia	AUEV	100	93	106	115	472	228	221	140	193	279	291
Hungary	QALC	753	858	940	838	840	861	1012	851	1082	1187	1103
Latvia	BQGQ	76	112	91	101	587	145	169	109	168	236	257
Lithuania	BQGU	149	188	142	167	236	311	282	172	225	269	378
Poland	ERDR	1317	1463	1423	1658	2798	2372	3021	2801	3797	4321	3438
Romania	WMDB	429	510	609	646	609	664	754	686	782	951	951
Sweden	CHNA	3878	3833	4362	4594	5188	4906	5228	4224	5557	6267	5740
Other Western Europe:	HCJD	6689	6843	7248	9907	9376	9351	10880	9722	12242	13566	14918
of which:												
Iceland	EPLW	133	144	170	176	189	201	188	128	132	149	191
Norway	EPLX	1786	1945	2003	2256	2164	2730	2881	2834	3120	3399	3645
Switzerland	EPLV	3262	2879	2934	5079	4251	3828	4711	3971	5222	5466	6754
Turkey	EOBA	1357	1692	1960	2198	2467	2345	2599	2365	3253	3936	3687
North America:	HBZQ	31909	32646	32430	34669	36521	36067	39424	37970	43111	45715	46374
of which:												
Canada	EOBC	3087	3211	3308	3247	3850	3265	3240	3325	4132	4752	4155
Mexico	EPJX	697	681	622	632	732	763	901	749	953	1006	1130
USA inc Puerto Rica	J9C5	28125	28754	28499	30790	31938	32038	35262	33896	37985	39881	41089

6.5 United Kingdom exports: by area[1]

Seasonally adjusted

£ million

		2002	2003	2004	2005	2006	2007	2008	2009	2010	2011	2012
Other OECD countries:	HCII	7492	7809	8209	8560	8686	8642	9952	9033	10471	12350	15183
of which:												
Australia	EPMA	2123	2284	2451	2572	2480	2577	3102	2953	3368	4393	4736
Japan	EOBD	3582	3694	3852	3893	4092	3850	3911	3565	4344	4728	4922
New Zealand	EPMB	309	349	418	415	374	359	388	350	414	541	614
South Korea	ERDM	1478	1473	1479	1675	1740	1852	2551	2165	2345	2688	4911
Oil exporting countries:	HDII	6168	7637	7975	10997	9186	9674	11660	11495	12569	13715	15317
of which:												
Brunei	QALF	61	125	67	43	80	862	64	61	159	56	52
UAE inc Dubai	J8YH	1578	2053	2685	5520	3613	2744	3822	3659	4066	4864	5366
Indonesia	FKMR	330	458	403	378	316	294	395	366	462	672	656
Kuwait	QATB	315	384	355	435	443	456	546	470	553	525	613
Nigeria	QATE	706	745	772	815	829	1003	1517	1309	1423	1612	1503
Saudi Arabia	ERDI	1376	1823	1606	1583	1664	1846	2211	2359	2492	2697	3088
Rest of the World	HCHW	19453	21877	23176	25798	27267	28911	38186	35036	45306	54671	57514
of which:												
Brazil	FKMO	879	819	801	842	908	1066	1693	1785	2219	2470	2663
China	ERDN	1484	1906	2366	2795	3254	3764	5054	5389	7623	9298	10543
Egypt	QALL	460	459	669	544	577	686	944	1005	1201	1104	960
Hong Kong	ERDG	2480	2467	2624	3074	2849	2645	3659	3732	4463	5382	5373
India	ERDJ	1743	2263	2233	2788	2688	2951	4116	2941	4074	5699	4665
Israel	ERDL	1419	1355	1390	1343	1305	1235	1338	1142	1391	1654	1547
Malaysia	ERDK	872	1022	994	1081	879	947	1130	1050	1274	1485	1537
Pakistan	FKMU	228	284	345	461	490	427	478	478	462	534	562
Philippines	FKMX	359	380	317	272	239	247	241	268	284	292	331
Russia	ERDQ	989	1408	1472	1855	2049	2792	4266	2398	3602	5012	5588
Singapore	ERDH	1438	1568	1707	2071	2307	2437	2807	2950	3453	3822	4481
South Africa	EPME	1581	1751	1876	2064	2172	2147	2649	2250	2894	3465	3675
Taiwan	ERDP	841	890	951	939	908	932	887	794	1118	1388	1152
Thailand	ERDO	530	569	636	632	564	598	758	913	1139	1419	2001

Source: Office for National Statistics: 01633 456294

1 Balance of payments consistent basis.
2 Includes Austria, Belgium, Bulgaria, Cyprus, Czech Republic, Denmark, Estonia, Finland, France, Germany, Greece, Hungary, Irish Republic, Italy, Latvia, Lithuania, Luxemburg, Malta, Netherlands, Poland, Portugal, Romania, Slovakia, Slovenia, Spain and Sweden.

6.6 United Kingdom imports: by area[1,2]

Seasonally adjusted

£ million

		2002	2003	2004	2005	2006	2007	2008	2009	2010	2011	2012
European Union:[3]	LGDC	137012	137419	142678	158349	184457	170192	181967	162752	186064	202349	205820
EMU members	QAKX	124337	123749	127569	140428	160608	150243	158844	140956	159330	171477	173597
Austria	CHNB	2397	2779	2357	2470	2785	2495	2355	2282	2636	2954	2605
Belgium & Luxembourg	CHNY	13101	13081	13731	15038	18066	15717	17294	15629	18017	20078	18902
Cyprus	BQGO	246	253	208	273	1717	196	155	123	106	140	162
Finland	CHNC	2791	2665	2341	2433	3078	2622	2800	2114	2165	2453	2170
France	ENYP	20823	20404	20171	22050	26808	21962	23312	20449	21574	23077	22521
Germany	ENYS	32472	33694	35444	39195	42053	44677	44934	40004	46419	50457	52539
Greece	CHOB	595	645	665	718	814	648	667	558	703	671	681
Irish Republic	CHOA	13230	9928	10152	10411	10748	11353	12299	12435	12870	13079	12897
Italy	CHNW	10680	11486	12211	12692	12903	13333	14208	12319	13944	14091	14307
Malta	BQGZ	170	186	184	179	168	179	136	106	170	168	129
Netherlands	CHNX	16161	16708	18228	20473	22513	23210	26000	21958	26450	28592	31257
Portugal	CHOC	1761	1967	1928	2022	3180	1514	1747	1424	1748	1801	1742
Slovakia	BQHC	211	260	263	373	847	1275	1633	1604	1620	1513	1569
Slovenia	BQHN	173	171	171	204	753	318	321	251	357	362	342
Spain	CHOD	9204	9258	9136	11532	12049	10505	10832	9573	10385	11817	11542
Non-EMU members:[3]	BQIB	12997	13934	15488	18286	25975	20188	23274	21923	26900	31096	32455
of which:												
Bulgaria	WYUT	117	126	150	173	200	239	215	183	231	289	286
Czech Rep	FKMM	1250	1416	1292	1881	2961	2987	3607	3338	3992	4247	4466
Denmark	CHNZ	3606	3403	3370	4417	6542	3450	3941	3838	4117	6090	5867
Estonia	BQGL	322	264	379	365	2126	239	151	127	166	224	232
Hungary	QALD	847	1119	1585	1862	2362	2379	2545	2541	3250	3091	2634
Latvia	BQGR	476	517	691	718	800	627	420	339	439	446	404
Lithuania	BQGV	264	287	271	279	284	310	359	370	550	607	825
Poland	ERED	1267	1547	1835	2322	3677	3702	4328	4671	6106	7089	7403
Romania	WMDC	522	683	788	802	830	944	813	790	1240	1287	1277
Sweden	CHND	4326	4572	5127	5467	6193	5311	6895	5726	6809	7726	9061
Other Western Europe:	HBTS	12963	13561	16024	20376	23515	24669	32873	26877	34431	39008	37793
of which:												
Iceland	EPMW	301	303	361	350	404	418	465	489	433	417	392
Norway	EPMX	5512	6622	8734	12430	14659	14586	21961	16202	21057	25219	22359
Switzerland	EPMV	4762	3814	3488	3855	4327	4800	5326	5316	7432	7595	9029
Turkey	EOBU	2239	2664	3308	3558	3952	4688	4954	4665	5350	5569	5762
North America:	HCRB	29164	27073	26639	26610	30632	31950	32028	29429	33802	36056	36216
of which:												
Canada	EOBW	3513	3653	4164	4138	4895	5789	5722	4461	5770	6152	5549
Mexico	EPJY	489	477	398	431	427	554	782	757	1032	1087	722
USA inc Puerto Rica	J9C6	25161	22943	22077	22041	25310	25606	25524	24211	26998	28795	29919

6.6 United Kingdom imports: by area[1,2]

Seasonally adjusted

		2002	2003	2004	2005	2006	2007	2008	2009	2010	2011	£ million 2012
Other OECD countries:	HDJQ	12909	12893	13513	14280	13515	13743	15182	12567	13830	14817	15113
of which:												
Australia	EPNA	1643	1734	1825	2059	2072	2190	2382	2224	2316	2445	2425
Japan	EOBX	8041	8066	8050	8602	7802	7908	8542	6666	8106	8881	8542
New Zealand	EPNB	515	547	575	585	598	656	750	819	844	872	894
South Korea	ERDY	2710	2546	3063	3034	3043	2989	3508	2858	2564	2619	3252
Oil exporting countries:	HCPC	3847	4084	4980	6275	7232	6657	8200	7858	11608	16604	18964
of which:												
Brunei	QALG	34	54	65	28	72	50	28	48	20	32	58
UAE inc Dubai	J8YI	729	1025	1056	1288	1007	1012	956	1126	1632	1893	2187
Indonesia	FKMS	1084	975	981	920	1026	1009	1219	1238	1390	1352	1281
Kuwait	QATC	281	342	419	394	785	761	1123	763	1033	1523	1521
Nigeria	QATF	66	62	91	134	192	316	921	645	889	2312	3995
Saudi Arabia	ERDU	685	727	1193	1836	1273	893	688	610	766	1060	1693
Rest of the World	HCIF	38039	41590	47829	54402	60797	63792	75989	71493	84482	90469	92893
of which:												
Brazil	FKMP	1377	1499	1581	1777	1924	2060	2657	2564	3110	2730	2457
China	ERDZ	6897	8525	10606	13233	15473	18876	23435	24615	30637	31532	31510
Egypt	QALM	409	426	491	334	659	535	647	687	659	827	650
Hong Kong	ERDS	5651	5574	5840	6687	7417	6987	8165	7753	8172	7640	7410
India	ERDV	1797	2076	2295	2768	3115	3734	4529	4618	5812	6097	6203
Israel	ERDX	857	839	912	995	952	1046	1172	1098	1566	2272	2422
Malaysia	ERDW	1758	1891	2052	1827	1909	1702	1891	1664	1838	1779	1722
Pakistan	FKMV	473	519	553	484	508	493	637	700	809	886	846
Philippines	FKMY	967	722	666	722	742	720	636	396	526	480	455
Russia	EREC	1944	2451	3530	5058	5760	5438	6981	4648	5259	7466	8459
Singapore	ERDT	1970	2694	3424	3872	3775	4086	4044	3587	4145	3887	3740
South Africa	EPNE	2718	2986	3317	4000	3933	3143	4789	3851	4426	2955	3313
Taiwan	EREB	2438	2234	2379	2261	2372	2413	2629	2267	3117	3496	3972
Thailand	EREA	1585	1673	1794	1746	1951	2020	2452	2321	2683	2598	2627

Source: Office for National Statistics: 01633 456294

1 See chapter text.

2 Balance of payments consistent basis.

3 Includes Austria, Belguim, Bulgaria, Cyprus, Czech Republic, Denmark, Estonia, Finland, France, Germany, Greece, Hungary, Irish Republic, Italy, Latvia, Lithuania, Luxemburg, Malta, Netherlands, Poland, Portugal, Romania, Slovakia, Slovenia, Spain and Sweden.

6.7 Total International Trade in Services all industries (excluding travel, transport and banking) analysed by product 2010 - 2012

£ million

	Exports			Imports			Balances		
	2010	2011	2012	2010	2011	2012	2010	2011	2012
Agricultural, Mining and On-site Processing Services									
Agricultural	69	28	37	14	78	22	55	-50	15
Mining	243	151	181	46	28	28	197	122	153
Waste treatment and depollution	7	14	9	4	15	18	3	-	-9
Other on-site processing services	647	727	874	155	206	228	493	521	646
Total Agricultural, Mining and On-site Processing Services	**966**	**920**	**1,102**	**219**	**327**	**296**	**747**	**593**	**806**
Business and Professional Services									
Accountancy, auditing, bookkeeping and tax consulting services	1,111	1,118	1,170	409	475	666	702	642	503
Advertising	2,392	2,749	2,838	1,821	1,598	1,664	572	1,151	1,173
Management consulting	1,563	1,641	1,893	853	653	693	710	989	1,200
Public relations services	438	437	393	178	183	121	260	254	272
Recruitment	787	722	931	406	236	299	382	486	632
Other business management	1,622	1,781	2,214	1,288	1,361	1,637	334	420	577
Legal services	3,267	3,510	3,835	654	601	877	2,613	2,910	2,958
Market research and public opinion polling	526	552	641	368	413	385	158	138	257
Operational leasing services	362	367	327	462	354	477	-100	12	-150
Procurement	157	152	188	276	239	262	-119	-87	-75
Property management	157	155	218	34	44	42	123	111	175
Research and development	5,683	5,736	5,559	4,217	4,025	3,523	1,465	1,711	2,037
Services between related enterprises	12,482	13,758	17,308	6,892	7,996	9,027	5,590	5,762	8,282
Other business and professional services	2,931	3,592	4,573	1,520	1,847	2,179	1,410	1,745	2,394
Total Business and Professional Services	**33,478**	**36,270**	**42,088**	**19,378**	**20,026**	**21,853**	**14,100**	**16,245**	**20,235**
Communications Services									
Postal and courier	809	812	916	413	372	486	396	440	430
Telecommunications	4,818	4,656	5,397	4,148	3,467	3,606	670	1,189	1,792
Total Communications Services	**5,627**	**5,468**	**6,313**	**4,561**	**3,840**	**4,092**	**1,066**	**1,628**	**2,222**
Computer and Information Services									
Computers	6,654	7,279	7,674	3,784	3,688	4,200	2,869	3,591	3,474
News agency services	435	416	397	65	38	38	370	378	359
Publishing services	513	615	638	80	107	91	433	508	547
Other information provision services	638	887	868	230	434	444	408	453	424
Total Computer and Information Services	**8,240**	**9,196**	**9,578**	**4,160**	**4,267**	**4,774**	**4,080**	**4,930**	**4,804**
Construction Goods and Services									
Construction in the UK	103	133	170	521	378	783	-418	-245	-613
Construction outside the UK	1,053	1,471	1,452	475	502	491	578	969	961
Total Construction Goods and Services	**1,156**	**1,604**	**1,622**	**996**	**880**	**1,274**	**160**	**724**	**348**
Financial Services									
Financial	9,318	9,847	11,629	1,477	1,903	1,826	7,841	7,944	9,803
Insurance Services									
Insurance Claims	2,253	2,494	3,009				2,253	2,494	3,009
Insurance Premiums				894	502	671	-894	-502	-671
Merchanting and Other Trade related Services									
Merchanting	3,712	7,635	3,025	133	329	306	3,579	7,305	2,719
Other trade - related services	1,059	964	975	517	634	569	543	329	405
Total Merchanting and Other Trade related Services	**4,771**	**8,598**	**4,000**	**649**	**964**	**875**	**4,122**	**7,634**	**3,124**
Personal, Cultural and Recreational Services									
Audio- Visual and related services	1,784	1,863	1,678	362	346	410	1,422	1,518	1,268
Health Services	59	65	38	58	32	20	1	32	18
Training and educational services	454	279	321	41	43	58	414	237	263
Other personal, cultural and recreational services	578	453	418	175	162	119	403	291	299
Total Personal, Cultural and Recreational Services	**2,875**	**2,660**	**2,456**	**635**	**582**	**607**	**2,240**	**2,078**	**1,849**
Royalties and Licenses									
Use of franchise and similar rights fees	2,408	2,129	2,527	1,784	1,590	1,625	624	539	902
Other royalties and license fees	7,160	6,660	5,495	3,811	4,980	3,882	3,349	1,680	1,613
Purchases and sales of franchises and similar rights	490	191	212	229	212	91	262	-21	121
Purchases and sales of other royalties and licenses	800	1,086	1,500	1,008	870	1,275	-209	216	225
Total Royalties and Licenses	**10,858**	**10,066**	**9,733**	**6,832**	**7,652**	**6,872**	**4,026**	**2,414**	**2,861**
Technical services									
Architectural	378	369	351	25	30	37	354	339	314
Engineering	4,850	5,409	5,627	1,123	1,113	1,503	3,727	4,296	4,124
Surveying	183	250	203	69	125	96	115	125	107
Other technical services	1,724	1,345	1,652	522	512	642	1,203	833	1,010
Total Technical Services	**7,136**	**7,373**	**7,834**	**1,738**	**1,779**	**2,279**	**5,398**	**5,594**	**5,555**
Other Trade in Services									
Other trade in services	2,844	2,815	4,465	535	844	979	2,309	1,971	3,487
World Total	**89,523**	**97,311**	**103,828**	**42,074**	**43,564**	**46,399**	**47,449**	**53,746**	**57,430**

Source: Office for National Statistics

- Denotes nil or less than £500,000

.. Denotes disclosive data

6.8 Total International Trade in Services (excluding travel, transport and banking) analysed by continents and countries 2010 - 2012

£ million

	Exports			Imports			Balances		
	2010	2011	2012	2010	2011	2012	2010	2011	2012
Europe									
European Union (EU)									
Austria	640	641	340	194	198	158	446	444	183
Belgium	1,287	1,399	1,596	987	943	1,007	300	456	589
Bulgaria	68	73	77	38	86	37	30	-13	40
Cyprus	190	272	301	74	129	110	116	143	191
Czech Republic	218	322	313	125	160	144	93	162	168
Denmark	1,224	1,158	1,237	412	444	441	812	714	796
Estonia	26	29	38	12	15	15	14	14	22
Finland	869	755	719	226	195	211	643	560	508
France	3,920	4,061	4,547	2,973	3,395	3,518	948	667	1,029
Germany	5,158	5,471	6,018	4,111	3,760	4,102	1,046	1,710	1,915
Greece	487	564	434	100	102	122	387	462	312
Hungary	313	341	342	238	225	238	75	116	104
Irish Republic	5,398	6,094	6,346	2,154	1,873	2,597	3,244	4,221	3,748
Italy	1,859	1,904	1,928	1,278	1,191	1,415	581	713	513
Latvia	26	36	32	9	11	9	17	25	24
Lithuania	26	45	29	20	50	20	6	-5	9
Luxembourg	1,112	1,704	1,683	1,102	1,191	1,182	11	514	501
Malta	134	227	183	37	62	37	96	165	146
Netherlands	4,701	4,838	5,373	1,680	1,494	1,657	3,021	3,344	3,717
Poland	557	739	636	320	394	407	236	344	229
Portugal	318	323	289	131	154	156	187	168	133
Romania	171	170	211	55	70	94	116	100	117
Slovakia	202	378	199	45	34	48	156	344	151
Slovenia	..	..	..	..	..	..	25	.. ..	
Spain	1,680	1,589	1,791	1,026	911	1,056	653	678	735
Sweden	1,666	1,816	1,686	1,116	1,403	1,381	550	413	305
EU Institutions	..	..	..	..	..	..	6	.. ..	
Total European Union (EU)	**32,289**	**35,071**	**36,497**	**18,473**	**18,592**	**20,281**	**13,816**	**16,479**	**16,217**
European Free Trade Association (EFTA)									
Iceland	76	69	84	9	73	14	67	-4	69
Liechtenstein	35	40	55	6	6	3	29	34	52
Norway	1,692	1,463	1,723	507	470	441	1,185	993	1,282
Switzerland	5,979	6,001	6,248	1,664	1,301	1,307	4,316	4,700	4,941
Total EFTA	**7,783**	**7,572**	**8,109**	**2,186**	**1,850**	**1,765**	**5,597**	**5,722**	**6,344**
Other Europe									
Russia	566	753	754	283	342	210	283	411	544
Channel Islands	1,391	1,339	2,073	206	244	255	1,185	1,095	1,818
Isle of Man	80	65	68	12	22	12	68	43	56
Turkey	491	647	549	92	107	121	399	541	429
Rest of Europe	378	1,030	900	137	163	223	240	868	677
Europe Unallocated	2,285	2,431	3,013	1,007	1,006	1,326	1,279	1,425	1,687
Total Europe	**45,262**	**48,909**	**51,963**	**22,395**	**22,325**	**24,192**	**22,867**	**26,583**	**27,771**
America									
Brazil	373	556	743	160	183	183	213	373	560
Canada	1,154	1,362	1,368	636	975	583	518	387	785
Mexico	194	175	171	71	54	59	123	121	112
USA	19,411	20,670	22,759	9,344	9,471	10,654	10,067	11,200	12,104
Rest of America	2,954	3,299	3,184	858	425	599	2,096	2,874	2,585
America Unallocated	646	666	580	93	109	114	554	557	466
Total America	**24,732**	**26,729**	**28,805**	**11,162**	**11,217**	**12,193**	**13,570**	**15,512**	**16,612**
Asia									
China	920	1,007	1,183	342	325	427	578	682	757
Hong Kong	525	578	757	337	610	637	188	-31	120
India	767	1,087	717	1,151	1,355	1,241	-385	-268	-524
Indonesia	112	108	141	21	30	25	91	77	116
Israel	400	549	433	269	348	333	131	201	100
Japan	1,659	2,056	1,995	1,627	2,793	1,579	33	-737	417

6.8 Total International Trade in Services (excluding travel, transport and banking) analysed by continents and countries 2010 - 2012

£ million

	Exports			Imports			Balances		
	2010	2011	2012	2010	2011	2012	2010	2011	2012
Malaysia	339	391	413	86	111	88	253	280	325
Pakistan	93	103	103	31	23	40	61	79	63
Philippines	60	70	84	81	81	124	-21	-11	-40
Saudi Arabia	2,204	1,525	3,483	77	156	322	2,127	1,369	3,162
Singapore	2,501	2,547	1,346	885	900	1,070	1,617	1,647	275
South Korea	481	480	626	133	158	201	347	322	425
Taiwan	288	388	387	51	47	72	236	341	316
Thailand	183	185	213	75	51	56	108	134	157
Rest of Asia	2,944	3,382	3,616	1,019	924	1,005	1,925	2,458	2,611
Asia Unallocated	663	989	786	403	337	588	260	652	198
Total Asia	**14,137**	**15,445**	**16,284**	**6,589**	**8,250**	**7,807**	**7,548**	**7,195**	**8,477**
Australasia and Oceania									
Australia	1,435	1,642	1,785	674	744	855	761	898	931
New Zealand	115	89	154	42	42	46	73	47	109
Rest of Australia and Oceania	106	162	224	19	27	13	86	135	211
Oceania Unallocated	10	14	21	8	4	5	2	10	16
Total Australasia and Oceania	**1,665**	**1,907**	**2,185**	**743**	**816**	**918**	**922**	**1,090**	**1,266**
Africa									
Nigeria	496	543	507	94	50	140	402	492	367
South Africa	807	868	1,127	305	253	307	502	615	820
Rest of Africa	2,004	2,539	2,453	464	410	371	1,541	2,129	2,082
Africa Unallocated	192	244	326	195	183	279	-2	61	47
Total Africa	**3,499**	**4,194**	**4,412**	**1,058**	**897**	**1,097**	**2,441**	**3,297**	**3,316**
Total Unallocated	..	..	180	..	..	192	..	..	-12
International Organisations	..	..	-	..	..	-	..	..	-
TOTAL INTERNATIONAL TRADE IN SERVICES	89,523	97,311	103,828	42,074	43,564	46,399	47,449	53,746	57,430

Source: Office for National Statistics

- Denotes nil or less than £500,000
.. Denotes disclosive data
The sum of constituent items may not always agree exactly with the totals shown due to rounding

See background notes for geographical groupings

6.9 Summary of balance of payments in 2011

£ million

	Credits	Debits
1. Current account		
A. Goods and services	492 646	516 609
1. Goods	298 987	399 330
2. Services	193 659	117 279
2.1. Transportation	23 120	19 951
2.2. Travel	21 888	31 830
2.3. Communications	6 465	4 704
2.4. Construction	1 653	1 065
2.5. Insurance	10 210	2 197
2.6. Financial	50 833	12 170
2.7. Computer and information	9 167	3 993
2.8. Royalties and licence fees	8 848	6 654
2.9. Other business	56 126	30 246
2.10. Personal, cultural and recreational	2 877	640
2.11. Government	2 472	3 829
B. Income	188 668	171 535
1. Compensation of employees	1 121	1 293
2. Investment income	187 547	170 242
2.1 Direct investment	96 513	47 659
2.2 Portfolio investment	51 526	68 348
2.3 Other investment	38 747	54 235
2.4 Reserve assets	761	
C. Current transfers	17 290	39 506
1. General government	3 438	19 855
2. Other sectors	13 852	19 651
Total current account	**698 604**	**727 650**
2. Capital and financial accounts		
A. Capital account	5 565	2 121
1. Capital transfers	4 151	1 119
2. Acquisition/disposal of non-produced, non-financial assets	1 414	1 002
B. Financial account	202 314	186 445
1. Direct investment	33 672	66 837
Abroad		66 837
1.1. Equity capital		39 975
1.2. Reinvested earnings		34 599
1.3. Other capital[1]		−7 737
In United Kingdom	33 672	
1.1. Equity capital	28 849	
1.2. Reinvested earnings	4 205	
1.3. Other capital[2]	618	
2. Portfolio investment	−18 206	22 410
Assets		22 410
2.1. Equity securities		−25 032
2.2. Debt securities		47 442
Liabilities	−18 206	
2.1. Equity securities	3 333	
2.2. Debt securities	−21 539	
3. Financial derivatives (net)		−16 030
4. Other investment	186 848	108 280
Assets		108 280
4.1 Trade credits		−33
4.2 Loans		13 796
4.3 Currency and deposits		92 519
4.4 Other assets		1 998
Liabilities	186 848	
4.1. Trade credits	−	
4.2. Loans	113 077	
4.3. Currency and deposits	73 494	
4.4. Other liabilities	277	
5. Reserve assets		4 948
5.1. Monetary gold		−
5.2. Special drawing rights		333
5.3. Reserve position in the IMF		445
5.4. Foreign exchange		4 306
5.5. Other claims		−136
Total capital and financial accounts	**207 879**	**188 566**
Total current, capital and financial accounts	**906 483**	**916 216**
Net errors and omissions	9 733	

Source: Office for National Statistics - United Kingdom Balance of Payments 2012

1 Other capital transaction on direct investment abroad represents claims on affiliated enterprises less liabilities to affiliated enterprises

2 Other capital transactions on direct investment in the United Kingdom represents liabilities to direct investors less claims on direct investors.

6.10 Summary of balance of payments: balances (credits less debits)[1]
United Kingdom

£ million

					Current account							
	Trade in goods	Trade in services	Total goods and services	Compensati-on of employees	Investment income	Total income	Current transfers	Current balance	Current balance as % of GDP[1]	Capital account	Financial account	Net errors & omissions
	LQCT	KTMS	KTMY	KTMP	HMBM	HMBP	KTNF	HBOG	AA6H	FKMJ	HBNT	HHDH
1946	−101	−274	−375	−20	76	56	166	−153	..	−21	181	−7
1947	−358	−197	−555	−19	140	121	123	−311	..	−21	552	−220
1948	−152	−64	−216	−20	223	203	96	83	0.7	−17	−58	−8
1949	−137	−43	−180	−20	206	186	29	35	0.3	−12	−103	80
1950	−54	−4	−58	−21	378	357	39	338	2.6	−10	−447	119
1951	−692	32	−660	−21	322	301	29	−330	−2.3	−15	426	−81
1952	−272	123	−149	−22	231	209	169	229	1.4	−15	−229	15
1953	−244	123	−121	−25	207	182	143	204	1.2	−13	−177	−14
1954	−210	115	−95	−27	227	200	55	160	0.9	−13	−174	27
1955	−315	42	−273	−27	149	122	43	−108	−0.6	−15	34	89
1956	50	26	76	−30	203	173	2	251	1.2	−13	−250	12
1957	−29	121	92	−32	223	191	−5	278	1.3	−13	−313	48
1958	34	119	153	−34	261	227	4	384	1.7	−10	−411	37
1959	−116	118	2	−37	233	196	−	198	0.8	−5	−68	−125
1960	−404	39	−365	−35	201	166	−6	−205	−0.8	−6	−7	218
1961	−144	51	−93	−35	223	188	−9	86	0.3	−12	23	−97
1962	−104	50	−54	−37	301	264	−14	196	0.7	−12	−195	11
1963	−123	4	−119	−38	364	326	−37	170	0.6	−16	−30	−124
1964	−551	−34	−585	−33	365	332	−74	−327	−1.0	−17	392	−48
1965	−263	−66	−329	−34	405	371	−75	−33	−0.1	−18	49	2
1966	−111	44	−67	−39	358	319	−91	161	0.4	−19	22	−164
1967	−601	157	−444	−39	354	315	−118	−247	−0.6	−25	179	93
1968	−708	341	−367	−48	303	255	−119	−231	−0.5	−26	688	−431
1969	−214	392	178	−47	468	421	−109	490	1.0	−23	−794	327
1970	−18	455	437	−56	527	471	−89	819	1.6	−22	−818	21
1971	205	617	822	−63	454	391	−90	1 123	2.0	−23	−1 330	230
1972	−736	722	−14	−52	350	298	−142	142	0.2	−35	477	−584
1973	−2 573	907	−1 666	−68	970	902	−336	−1 100	−1.5	−39	1 031	108
1974	−5 241	1 292	−3 949	−92	1 010	918	−302	−3 333	−4.0	−34	3 185	182
1975	−3 245	1 708	−1 537	−102	257	155	−313	−1 695	−1.6	−36	1 569	162
1976	−3 930	2 872	−1 058	−140	760	620	−534	−972	−0.8	−12	507	477
1977	−2 271	3 704	1 433	−152	−678	−830	−889	−286	−0.2	11	−3 286	3 561
1978	−1 534	4 215	2 681	−140	−300	−440	−1 420	821	0.5	−79	−2 655	1 913
1979	−3 326	4 573	1 247	−130	−342	−472	−1 777	−1 002	−0.5	−103	864	241
1980	1 329	4 414	5 743	−82	−2 268	−2 350	−1 653	1 740	0.8	−4	−2 157	421
1981	3 238	4 776	8 014	−66	−1 883	−1 949	−1 219	4 846	1.9	−79	−5 312	545
1982	1 879	4 261	6 140	−95	−2 336	−2 431	−1 476	2 233	0.8	6	−1 233	−1 006
1983	−1 618	5 406	3 788	−89	−1 050	−1 139	−1 391	1 258	0.4	75	−3 287	1 954
1984	−5 409	6 101	692	−94	−326	−420	−1 566	−1 294	−0.4	107	−7 130	8 317
1985	−3 416	8 499	5 083	−120	−2 609	−2 729	−2 924	−570	−0.2	185	−1 657	2 042
1986	−9 617	8 182	−1 435	−156	71	−85	−2 094	−3 614	−0.9	135	−122	3 601
1987	−11 698	9 163	−2 535	−174	−855	−1 029	−3 437	−7 001	−1.6	333	10 606	−3 938
1988	−21 553	7 506	−14 047	−64	−1 438	−1 502	−3 293	−18 842	−3.9	235	16 989	1 618
1989	−24 724	7 543	−17 181	−138	−2 683	−2 821	−4 228	−24 230	−4.6	270	13 614	10 346
1990	−18 707	8 879	−9 828	−110	−5 085	−5 195	−4 802	−19 825	−3.5	497	22 272	−2 944
1991	−10 223	9 106	−1 117	−63	−6 266	−6 329	−999	−8 445	−1.4	290	7 855	300
1992	−13 050	9 706	−3 344	−49	−1 786	−1 835	−5 228	−10 407	−1.7	421	16 311	−6 325
1993	−13 066	12 086	−980	35	−3 420	−3 385	−5 056	−9 421	−1.4	309	22 278	−13 166
1994	−11 126	12 632	1 506	−170	523	353	−5 187	−3 328	−0.5	33	−3 240	6 535
1995	−12 023	16 195	4 172	−296	−1 669	−1 965	−7 363	−5 156	−0.7	533	−1 717	6 340
1996	−13 722	17 249	3 527	93	−3 494	−3 401	−4 539	−4 413	−0.6	1 260	−940	4 093
1997	−12 169	18 048	5 879	83	−1 225	−1 142	−5 525	−788	−0.1	958	−7 294	7 124
1998	−21 632	16 194	−5 438	−10	10 292	10 282	−8 171	−3 327	−0.4	489	4 480	−1 642
1999	−28 889	15 403	−13 486	201	−4 211	−4 010	−7 322	−24 818	−2.7	747	29 505	−5 434
2000	−32 903	14 951	−17 952	150	−447	−297	−9 775	−28 024	−2.9	1 703	23 133	3 188
2001	−40 976	17 797	−23 179	66	5 785	5 851	−6 515	−23 843	−2.3	1 318	27 194	−4 669
2002	−47 360	18 254	−29 106	67	15 498	15 565	−8 870	−22 411	−2.1	932	16 204	5 275
2003	−48 333	22 556	−25 777	59	16 113	16 172	−9 834	−19 439	−1.7	1 466	22 561	−4 588
2004	−60 800	27 808	−32 992	−494	18 110	17 616	−10 276	−25 652	−2.1	2 064	29 463	−5 875
2005	−68 686	33 248	−35 438	−610	21 969	21 359	−11 849	−25 928	−2.1	1 503	35 235	−10 810
2006	−76 403	41 419	−34 984	−958	8 720	7 762	−11 876	−39 098	−2.9	975	33 976	4 147
2007	−90 478	52 858	−37 620	−734	19 741	19 007	−13 546	−32 159	−2.3	2 566	24 982	4 611
2008	−94 082	61 028	−33 054	−715	33 121	32 406	−13 765	−14 413	−1.0	3 241	25 985	−14 813
2009	−82 841	62 239	−20 602	−259	18 250	17 991	−15 126	−17 737	−1.3	3 637	22 650	−8 550
2010	−98 509	67 007	−31 502	−389	15 017	14 628	−20 410	−37 284	−2.5	3 704	28 277	5 303
2011	−100 343	76 380	−23 963	−172	17 305	17 133	−22 216	−29 046	−1.9	3 444	15 869	9 733

1 Using series YBHA: GDP at current market prices.

Source: Office for National Statistics - United Kingdom Balance of Payments 2012

6.11 Balance of payments: current account

United Kingdom

£ million

		1990	1991	1992	1993	1994	1995	1996	1997	1998	1999	2000
Credits												
Exports of goods and services												
Exports of goods	LQAD	102 313	103 939	107 863	122 229	135 143	153 577	167 196	171 966	164 025	166 109	187 898
Exports of services	KTMQ	36 706	37 768	41 271	47 868	52 944	59 051	64 934	67 630	70 849	76 864	82 386
Total exports of goods and services	KTMW	139 019	141 707	149 134	170 097	188 087	212 628	232 130	239 596	234 874	242 973	270 284
Income												
Compensation of employees	KTMN	543	551	551	595	681	887	911	1 007	840	960	1 032
Investment income	HMBN	76 353	73 652	65 168	70 944	72 585	85 490	89 794	93 360	102 548	100 733	131 902
Total income	HMBQ	76 896	74 203	65 719	71 539	73 266	86 377	90 705	94 367	103 388	101 693	132 934
Current transfers												
General government	FJUM	2 050	4 892	2 180	2 826	2 138	1 730	2 828	2 393	1 767	3 542	2 465
Other sectors	FJUN	5 724	7 234	9 945	9 085	8 918	10 213	11 372	11 646	11 446	9 056	8 882
Total current transfers	KTND	7 774	12 126	12 125	11 911	11 056	11 943	14 200	14 039	13 213	12 598	11 347
Total	HBOE	**223 689**	**228 036**	**226 978**	**253 547**	**272 409**	**310 948**	**337 035**	**348 002**	**351 475**	**357 264**	**414 565**
Debits												
Imports of goods and services												
Imports of goods	LQBL	121 020	114 162	120 913	135 295	146 269	165 600	180 918	184 135	185 657	194 998	220 801
Imports of services	KTMR	27 827	28 662	31 565	35 782	40 312	42 856	47 685	49 582	54 655	61 461	67 435
Total imports of goods and services	KTMX	148 847	142 824	152 478	171 077	186 581	208 456	228 603	233 717	240 312	256 459	288 236
Income												
Compensation of employees	KTMO	653	614	600	560	851	1 183	818	924	850	759	882
Investment income	HMBO	81 438	79 918	66 954	74 364	72 062	87 159	93 288	94 585	92 256	104 944	132 349
Total income	HMBR	82 091	80 532	67 554	74 924	72 913	88 342	94 106	95 509	93 106	105 703	133 231
Current transfers												
General government	FJUO	1 995	3 218	3 506	4 156	4 795	4 811	5 081	5 087	6 585	7 271	7 778
Other sectors	FJUP	10 581	9 907	13 847	12 811	11 448	14 495	13 658	14 477	14 799	12 649	13 344
Total current transfers	KTNE	12 576	13 125	17 353	16 967	16 243	19 306	18 739	19 564	21 384	19 920	21 122
Total	HBOF	**243 514**	**236 481**	**237 385**	**262 968**	**275 737**	**316 104**	**341 448**	**348 790**	**354 802**	**382 082**	**442 589**
Balances												
Trade in goods and services												
Trade in goods	LQCT	−18 707	−10 223	−13 050	−13 066	−11 126	−12 023	−13 722	−12 169	−21 632	−28 889	−32 903
Trade in services	KTMS	8 879	9 106	9 706	12 086	12 632	16 195	17 249	18 048	16 194	15 403	14 951
Total trade in goods and services	KTMY	−9 828	−1 117	−3 344	−980	1 506	4 172	3 527	5 879	−5 438	−13 486	−17 952
Income												
Compensation of employees	KTMP	−110	−63	−49	35	−170	−296	93	83	−10	201	150
Investment income	HMBM	−5 085	−6 266	−1 786	−3 420	523	−1 669	−3 494	−1 225	10 292	−4 211	−447
Total income	HMBP	−5 195	−6 329	−1 835	−3 385	353	−1 965	−3 401	−1 142	10 282	−4 010	−297
Current transfers												
General government	FJUQ	55	1 674	−1 326	−1 330	−2 657	−3 081	−2 253	−2 694	−4 818	−3 729	−5 313
Other sectors	FJUR	−4 857	−2 673	−3 902	−3 726	−2 530	−4 282	−2 286	−2 831	−3 353	−3 593	−4 462
Total current transfers	KTNF	−4 802	−999	−5 228	−5 056	−5 187	−7 363	−4 539	−5 525	−8 171	−7 322	−9 775
Total (Current balance)	HBOG	**−19 825**	**−8 445**	**−10 407**	**−9 421**	**−3 328**	**−5 156**	**−4 413**	**−788**	**−3 327**	**−24 818**	**−28 024**

6.11 Balance of payments: current account

United Kingdom

£ million

		2001	2002	2003	2004	2005	2006	2007	2008	2009	2010	2011
Credits												
Exports of goods and services												
Exports of goods	LQAD	189 067	186 574	188 287	190 863	211 606	243 745	220 525	252 157	228 135	265 708	298 987
Exports of services	KTMQ	89 208	94 053	105 434	115 415	128 818	144 462	159 591	177 413	176 026	182 177	193 659
Total exports of goods and services	KTMW	278 275	280 627	293 721	306 278	340 424	388 207	380 116	429 570	404 161	447 885	492 646
Income												
Compensation of employees	KTMN	1 087	1 121	1 116	931	974	938	984	1 046	1 176	1 097	1 121
Investment income	HMBN	137 447	120 543	122 069	137 380	185 640	237 505	291 614	262 842	167 724	159 369	187 547
Total income	HMBQ	138 534	121 664	123 185	138 311	186 614	238 443	292 598	263 888	168 900	160 466	188 668
Current transfers												
General government	FJUM	4 991	3 663	3 968	4 177	4 294	4 383	4 318	5 652	6 205	3 866	3 438
Other sectors	FJUN	8 391	10 129	10 861	11 894	14 065	19 055	12 363	17 647	15 020	13 367	13 852
Total current transfers	KTND	13 382	13 792	14 829	16 071	18 359	23 438	16 681	23 299	21 225	17 233	17 290
Total	HBOE	**430 191**	**416 083**	**431 735**	**460 660**	**545 397**	**650 088**	**689 395**	**716 757**	**594 286**	**625 584**	**698 604**
Debits												
Imports of goods and services												
Imports of goods	LQBL	230 043	233 934	236 620	251 663	280 292	320 148	311 003	346 239	310 976	364 217	399 330
Imports of services	KTMR	71 411	75 799	82 878	87 607	95 570	103 043	106 733	116 385	113 787	115 170	117 279
Total imports of goods and services	KTMX	301 454	309 733	319 498	339 270	375 862	423 191	417 736	462 624	424 763	479 387	516 609
Income												
Compensation of employees	KTMO	1 021	1 054	1 057	1 425	1 584	1 896	1 718	1 761	1 435	1 486	1 293
Investment income	HMBO	131 662	105 045	105 956	119 270	163 671	228 785	271 873	229 721	149 474	144 352	170 242
Total income	HMBR	132 683	106 099	107 013	120 695	165 255	230 681	273 591	231 482	150 909	145 838	171 535
Current transfers												
General government	FJUO	7 340	9 085	10 657	12 225	13 637	13 874	14 082	14 714	17 665	18 662	19 855
Other sectors	FJUP	12 557	13 577	14 006	14 122	16 571	21 440	16 145	22 350	18 686	18 981	19 651
Total current transfers	KTNE	19 897	22 662	24 663	26 347	30 208	35 314	30 227	37 064	36 351	37 643	39 506
Total	HBOF	**454 034**	**438 494**	**451 174**	**486 312**	**571 325**	**689 186**	**721 554**	**731 170**	**612 023**	**662 868**	**727 650**
Balances												
Trade in goods and services												
Trade in goods	LQCT	−40 976	−47 360	−48 333	−60 800	−68 686	−76 403	−90 478	−94 082	−82 841	−98 509	−100 343
Trade in services	KTMS	17 797	18 254	22 556	27 808	33 248	41 419	52 858	61 028	62 239	67 007	76 380
Total trade in goods and services	KTMY	−23 179	−29 106	−25 777	−32 992	−35 438	−34 984	−37 620	−33 054	−20 602	−31 502	−23 963
Income												
Compensation of employees	KTMP	66	67	59	−494	−610	−958	−734	−715	−259	−389	−172
Investment income	HMBM	5 785	15 498	16 113	18 110	21 969	8 720	19 741	33 121	18 250	15 017	17 305
Total income	HMBP	5 851	15 565	16 172	17 616	21 359	7 762	19 007	32 406	17 991	14 628	17 133
Current transfers												
General government	FJUQ	−2 349	−5 422	−6 689	−8 048	−9 343	−9 491	−9 764	−9 062	−11 460	−14 796	−16 417
Other sectors	FJUR	−4 166	−3 448	−3 145	−2 228	−2 506	−2 385	−3 782	−4 703	−3 666	−5 614	−5 799
Total current transfers	KTNF	−6 515	−8 870	−9 834	−10 276	−11 849	−11 876	−13 546	−13 765	−15 126	−20 410	−22 216
Total (Current balance)	HBOG	**−23 843**	**−22 411**	**−19 439**	**−25 652**	**−25 928**	**−39 098**	**−32 159**	**−14 413**	**−17 737**	**−37 284**	**−29 046**

Source: Office for National Statistics - United Kingdom Balance of Payments 2012

6.12 Balance of payments: financial account and investment income
summary of international investment position,financial account and investment income

£ billion

		2001	2002	2003	2004	2005	2006	2007	2008	2009	2010	2011
Investment abroad												
International investment position												
Direct investment	HBWD	616.9	637.2	691.1	678.1	705.9	733.1	899.8	1 068.7	975.3	1 039.2	1 119.7
Portfolio investment	HHZZ	937.4	844.0	935.8	1 092.1	1 360.9	1 531.0	1 689.7	1 664.3	1 875.3	2 070.3	2 082.2
Financial derivatives	JX96	..	..	..	709.4	820.1	853.7	1 378.1	4 040.2	2 176.4	2 962.8	3 617.8
Other investment	HLXV	1 521.9	1 545.2	1 813.7	2 118.0	2 714.8	2 916.6	3 744.5	4 180.6	3 511.2	3 780.6	4 066.6
Reserve assets	LTEB	25.6	25.5	23.8	23.2	24.7	22.9	26.7	36.3	40.1	49.7	56.8
Total	HBQA	**3 101.9**	**3 051.9**	**3 464.5**	**4 620.8**	**5 626.4**	**6 057.4**	**7 738.8**	**10 990.1**	**8 578.3**	**9 902.7**	**10 943.1**
Financial account transactions												
Direct investment	-HJYP	42.8	35.0	40.9	51.5	44.0	45.0	162.6	99.6	25.2	25.6	66.8
Portfolio investment	-HHZC	86.6	1.0	36.3	141.0	151.0	138.8	91.5	−123.2	164.7	76.8	22.4
Financial derivatives (net)	-ZPNN	−8.4	−1.0	5.4	6.8	−5.8	−20.6	27.0	121.7	−29.1	−32.8	−16.0
Other investment	-XBMM	170.7	70.4	260.4	325.2	506.3	395.9	742.4	−613.0	−354.9	224.1	108.3
Reserve assets	-LTCV	−3.1	−0.5	−1.6	0.2	0.7	−0.4	1.2	−1.3	5.8	6.1	4.9
Total	-HBNR	**288.5**	**105.0**	**341.4**	**524.7**	**696.1**	**558.7**	**1 024.7**	**−516.2**	**−188.3**	**299.8**	**186.4**
Investment income												
Direct investment	HJYW	46.7	51.5	55.1	63.3	79.2	83.6	91.4	69.5	67.9	79.2	96.5
Portfolio investment	HLYX	34.9	32.5	32.5	36.7	45.4	55.1	66.1	67.5	54.6	47.1	51.5
Other investment	AIOP	54.9	35.8	33.6	36.7	60.4	98.1	133.5	125.1	44.4	32.4	38.7
Reserve assets	HHCB	1.0	0.8	0.8	0.7	0.7	0.6	0.6	0.8	0.8	0.7	0.8
Total	HMBN	**137.4**	**120.5**	**122.1**	**137.4**	**185.6**	**237.5**	**291.6**	**262.8**	**167.7**	**159.4**	**187.5**
Investment in the UK												
International investment position												
Direct investment	HBWI	363.5	340.6	355.5	383.3	494.2	577.3	613.8	660.4	681.8	742.7	775.4
Portfolio investment	HLXW	1 013.2	925.3	1 082.9	1 227.9	1 461.7	1 703.5	1 945.7	1 980.2	2 397.0	2 509.2	2 446.9
Financial derivatives	JX97	..	..	..	715.0	831.1	890.5	1 392.2	3 915.3	2 096.8	2 895.0	3 554.9
Other investment	HLYD	1 861.9	1 898.0	2 135.2	2 511.8	3 109.0	3 270.0	4 115.6	4 518.1	3 791.0	4 047.2	4 362.3
Total	HBQB	**3 238.5**	**3 163.9**	**3 573.6**	**4 838.1**	**5 896.0**	**6 441.2**	**8 067.3**	**11 073.9**	**8 966.7**	**10 194.1**	**11 139.6**
Financial account transactions												
Direct investment	HJYU	37.3	16.8	16.8	31.2	97.8	84.9	100.0	48.4	49.0	32.8	33.7
Portfolio investment	HHZF	40.8	49.7	105.6	97.3	129.0	152.5	217.9	200.6	191.5	77.9	−18.2
Other investment	XBMN	237.6	54.6	241.5	425.6	504.5	355.3	731.8	−739.2	−406.1	217.4	186.8
Total	HBNS	**315.7**	**121.2**	**364.0**	**554.2**	**731.3**	**592.7**	**1 049.7**	**−490.2**	**−165.7**	**328.1**	**202.3**
Investment income												
Direct investment	HJYX	21.4	16.0	21.9	27.6	36.2	51.6	45.1	3.1	26.6	37.1	47.7
Portfolio investment	HLZC	36.1	33.3	32.9	38.7	47.6	57.6	66.8	74.5	60.0	60.2	68.3
Other investment	HLZN	74.1	55.7	51.1	52.9	79.9	119.6	160.0	152.1	63.0	47.1	54.2
Total	HMBO	**131.7**	**105.0**	**106.0**	**119.3**	**163.7**	**228.8**	**271.9**	**229.7**	**149.5**	**144.4**	**170.2**
Net investment												
International investment position												
Direct investment	HBWQ	253.5	296.6	335.6	294.7	211.7	155.8	285.9	408.4	293.5	296.5	344.2
Portfolio investment	CGNH	−75.7	−81.3	−147.0	−135.8	−100.8	−172.4	−255.9	−315.9	−521.8	−438.9	−364.7
Financial derivatives	JX98	..	..	..	−5.6	−11.0	−36.8	−14.1	124.9	79.6	67.8	62.9
Other investment	CGNG	−339.9	−352.8	−321.5	−393.9	−394.2	−353.4	−371.0	−337.5	−279.8	−266.6	−295.7
Reserve assets	LTEB	25.6	25.5	23.8	23.2	24.7	22.9	26.7	36.3	40.1	49.7	56.8
Net investment position	HBQC	**−136.5**	**−112.0**	**−109.2**	**−217.3**	**−269.6**	**−383.8**	**−328.4**	**−83.8**	**−388.3**	**−291.4**	**−196.4**
Financial account transactions												
Direct investment	HJYV	−5.5	−18.3	−24.1	−20.3	53.8	39.9	−62.7	−51.2	23.8	7.2	−33.2
Portfolio investment	HHZD	−45.7	48.7	69.4	−43.7	−21.9	13.7	126.4	323.8	26.8	1.1	−40.6
Financial derivatives	ZPNN	8.4	1.0	−5.4	−6.8	5.8	20.6	−27.0	−121.7	29.1	32.8	16.0
Other investment	HHYR	66.9	−15.7	−18.9	100.4	−1.8	−40.6	−10.6	−126.2	−51.2	−6.7	78.6
Reserve assets	LTCV	3.1	0.5	1.6	−0.2	−0.7	0.4	−1.2	1.3	−5.8	−6.1	−4.9
Net transactions	HBNT	**27.2**	**16.2**	**22.6**	**29.5**	**35.2**	**34.0**	**25.0**	**26.0**	**22.6**	**28.3**	**15.9**
Investment income												
Direct investment	HJYE	25.3	35.5	33.2	35.7	43.0	32.0	46.3	66.4	41.4	42.1	48.9
Portfolio investment	HLZX	−1.2	−0.8	−0.4	−2.0	−2.2	−2.4	−0.7	−7.0	−5.4	−13.1	−16.8
Other investment	CGNA	−19.3	−20.0	−17.5	−16.3	−19.5	−21.5	−26.5	−27.1	−18.5	−14.7	−15.5
Reserve assets	HHCB	1.0	0.8	0.8	0.7	0.7	0.6	0.6	0.8	0.8	0.7	0.8
Net earnings	HMBM	**5.8**	**15.5**	**16.1**	**18.1**	**22.0**	**8.7**	**19.7**	**33.1**	**18.2**	**15.0**	**17.3**

Source: Office for National Statistics - United Kingdom Balance of Payments 2012

6.13 Net foreign direct investment flows abroad analysed by area and main country, 2003 to 2012[1,2]

£ million

	2003	2004	2005	2006	2007	2008	2009	2010	2011	2012
EUROPE	**16,600**	**10,814**	**12,105**	**16,899**	**90,683**	**50,863**	**15,690**	**11,374**	**27,312**	**-705**
EU	13,417	11,917	13,337	4,038	69,836	47,298	-7,047	9,761	15,856	-8,987
AUSTRIA	165	1,322	-301	-94	110	-159	-154	2,389	-16	-434
BELGIUM	..	-544	970	-4,356	1,037	1,656	-1,307	7,594	5,575	-1,484
BULGARIA	..	0	11	-5	..	43	11	-80	-1	14
CYPRUS	-53	18	69	98	365	294	63	-290	-184	-85
CZECH REPUBLIC	142	23	24	-160	59	371	-105	-182	-80	832
DENMARK	-53	569	391	1,529	539	2,774	-2,170	511	-240	99
ESTONIA	4	21	2	3	-3	-20	38	9	0	9
FINLAND	99	-37	707	106	268	63	-95	-41	-393	44
FRANCE	6,627	793	3,138	1,175	4,536	5,979	-1,248	3,382	1,823	2,417
GERMANY	1,552	-366	-479	3,186	2,260	2,268	3,186	-1,644	444	-344
GREECE	229	-253	63	15	286	362	-366	33	-230	-89
HUNGARY	527	336	1,821	39	88	164	76	85	50	64
IRISH REPUBLIC	985	3,325	-1,181	5,161	3,995	-2,098	3,530	-7,731	3,260	1,250
ITALY	500	667	191	-397	2,904	463	-3,801	362	-92	-1,008
LATVIA	0	1	-1	4	65	142	-51	-19	-24	35
LITHUANIA	..	1	-4	1	..	..	..	3	6	3
LUXEMBOURG	1,313	-1,022	-1,213	-14,131	25,453	6,094	4,874	5,820	7,947	-535
MALTA	58	178	142	891	-1,952	..	..	..	..	..
NETHERLANDS	728	4,805	4,821	1,350	22,176	11,056	-14,072	-638	-1,194	-6,545
POLAND	4	182	150	397	-500	-128	1,261	73	134	291
PORTUGAL	308	444	603	314	278	341	277	576	104	53
ROMANIA	56	11	101	40	117	211	27	22	61	-10
SLOVAKIA	-11	18	21	18	90	104	-29	-17	23	32
SLOVENIA	37	-5	-5	14	9	12	9	..	..	..
SPAIN	626	1,131	564	2,177	4,155	12,974	1,628	2,148	-566	-617
SWEDEN	794	299	2,732	6,669	3,501	3,155	1,314	-2,025	-454	-2,480
EFTA	2,313	-6,667	547	6,926	3,620	2,476	4,550	1,468	1,834	5,510
of which										
NORWAY	-274	367	-831	3	1,060	1,556	1,693	-759	1,045	1,398
SWITZERLAND	2,591	-7,007	1,330	6,948	2,653	1,054	2,956	2,221	791	4,124
OTHER EUROPEAN COUNTRIES	870	5,564	-1,779	5,935	17,227	1,088	18,188	145	9,621	2,773
of which										
RUSSIA	2,030	1,831	349	-13	1,334	3,919	-353	-1,859	467	-1,314
UK OFFSHORE ISLANDS[3]	-1,031	3,528	-2,341	5,023	14,752	-4,278	17,848	1,036	8,468	3,348
THE AMERICAS	**15,959**	**24,321**	**20,689**	**19,100**	**53,837**	**33,574**	**-2,218**	**-13,814**	**14,675**	**11,775**
of which										
BERMUDA	-2,613	6,242	653	908	2,082	3,913	-2,160	-479	-1,238	-6
BRAZIL	786	386	48	354	791	832	525	1,605	1,723	777
CANADA	2,521	1,143	3,372	8,130	15,468	-1,075	-2,732	-8,528	1,372	5,726
CHILE	290	675	790	25	110	-315	59	204	469	21
COLOMBIA	78	225	-687	315	126	157	311	402	-769	3
MEXICO	261	1,386	168	334	128	409	57	503	1,015	566
PANAMA	58	12	27	7	-18	-4	60	40	36	25
USA	19,300	9,732	15,041	-1,803	30,820	27,568	7,851	-9,025	12,055	5,304
ASIA	**3,601**	**7,689**	**5,399**	**7,992**	**7,734**	**6,364**	**8,575**	**8,401**	**20,526**	**8,281**
NEAR & MIDDLE EAST COUNTRIES	82	486	398	1,219	2,044	2,884	1,330	-1,136	4,754	2,482
of which										
GULF ARABIAN COUNTRIES	-85	293	577	329	482	544	1,424	830	167	1,362
OTHER ASIAN COUNTRIES	3,518	7,203	5,001	6,773	5,689	3,480	7,245	9,538	15,772	5,799
of which										
CHINA	309	539	598	374	1,138	290	343	797	1,311	908
HONG KONG	1,285	5,303	1,547	1,674	1,503	305	1,798	2,180	3,475	4,138
INDIA	193	274	616	104	650	437	695	1,856	7,090	360
INDONESIA	481	-289	-116	196	-140	-68	594	1,021	3,308	564
JAPAN	338	37	247	440	1,141	-140	923	-568	1,996	31
MALAYSIA	277	428	244	241	216	321	337	603	585	243
SINGAPORE	-449	-161	-508	2,621	-1,265	183	-582	392	-4,733	-1,061
SOUTH KOREA	332	278	2,247	679	488	810	566	833	411	616
THAILAND	155	181	228	536	3	192	331	154	178	149

6.13 Net foreign direct investment flows abroad analysed by area and main country, 2003 to 2012[1,2]

£ million

	2003	2004	2005	2006	2007	2008	2009	2010	2011	2012
AUSTRALASIA & OCEANIA	**-1,524**	**1,026**	**423**	**3,132**	**2,149**	**7,662**	**-3,543**	**11,704**	**803**	**2,442**
of which										
AUSTRALIA	-492	408	444	2,743	2,012	6,590	-4,625	11,487	338	2,411
NEW ZEALAND	-1,017	258	-56	405	125	126	1,078	156	373	-71
AFRICA	**3,454**	**5,863**	**5,843**	**-235**	**4,726**	**881**	**6,590**	**7,822**	**-3,186**	**4,716**
of which										
KENYA	58	47	73	62	97	67	115	195	63	-6
NIGERIA	19	-44	-108	44	56	273	763	228	354	90
SOUTH AFRICA	2,222	3,840	4,368	1,466	1,734	1,317	994	2,459	1,814	5,087
ZIMBABWE	37	91	18	8	4	-6	1	12	25	18
WORLD TOTAL	**38,088**	**49,713**	**44,458**	**46,887**	**159,129**	**99,322**	**25,094**	**25,486**	**60,130**	**26,509**
OECD	37,030	18,355	35,305	21,276	125,975	83,393	1,164	7,674	36,119	11,761
CENTRAL & EASTERN EUROPE [4]	156	36	158	76	0	53	40	-26	-3	16

1 Net foreign direct investment includes unremitted profits.

2 A negative sign before values indicates a net disinvestment abroad (i.e. a decrease in the amount due to the UK).

3 The UK Offshore Islands consist of the Channel Islands & the Isle of Man, excluded from the definition of the economic territory of the UK from 1997

4 Central & Eastern Europe prior to 2007 includes data for Bulgaria and Romania.

.. Indicates data are disclosive.

.- Indicates nil returns.

Source: Office for National Statistics

6.14 FDI international investment position abroad analysed by area and main country, end 2003 to end 2012[1]

£ million

	2003	2004	2005	2006	2007	2008	2009	2010	2011	2012
EUROPE	**408,881**	**382,104**	**387,324**	**402,593**	**527,997**	**600,375**	**552,235**	**612,848**	**614,775**	**590,050**
EU	355,045	348,576	339,691	314,481	412,024	513,506	477,747	539,683	533,266	513,491
AUSTRIA	3,339	4,102	4,005	2,402	2,579	2,707	3,746	1,054	999	459
BELGIUM	8,662	7,828	13,492	4,380	6,887	11,207	14,615	41,128	38,027	37,731
BULGARIA	81	22	53	46	46	143	117	104	88	53
CYPRUS	80	64	59	561	683	363	498	560	643	1,744
CZECH REPUBLIC	954	793	823	523	632	1,011	510	533	438	1,346
DENMARK	3,021	5,256	5,090	7,782	6,220	10,809	6,995	7,940	7,152	8,089
ESTONIA	21	78	7	-1	7	25	33	62	86	65
FINLAND	588	695	2,465	1,287	2,329	609	396	1,190	1,533	519
FRANCE	31,460	35,313	47,348	36,327	39,598	42,111	39,944	54,841	53,459	54,438
GERMANY	13,486	12,164	20,753	17,602	19,766	30,550	26,896	22,476	20,482	19,186
GREECE	460	456	625	562	864	1,047	910	2,028	1,417	1,431
HUNGARY	1,722	1,506	2,491	1,795	1,870	2,136	697	635	1,007	1,070
IRISH REPUBLIC	29,989	29,059	26,824	26,432	25,362	30,529	34,859	40,927	44,844	41,441
ITALY	10,178	11,322	10,872	7,924	12,786	10,734	11,689	11,971	11,708	15,372
LATVIA	13	25	22	27	..	95	1	-26	48	72
LITHUANIA	16	22	16	6	11	..	25	..	41	44
LUXEMBOURG	79,208	81,709	97,260	62,355	95,915	137,065	124,582	140,457	137,410	139,642
MALTA	264	1,528	-459	2,399	3,263	..	1,467	824	333	1,695
NETHERLANDS	146,345	131,143	64,511	92,783	138,769	160,172	146,027	145,279	144,966	126,238
POLAND	2,900	2,316	1,974	2,519	2,078	2,914	3,723	3,647	3,796	4,041
PORTUGAL	973	1,664	2,702	3,167	3,366	3,528	3,311	3,665	3,014	2,824
ROMANIA	257	260	356	247	402	675	558	549	530	588
SLOVAKIA	332	103	93	136	184	392	253	262	275	211
SLOVENIA	128	54	3	53	..	52	52	..	320	65
SPAIN	9,460	11,318	25,604	25,233	30,879	37,105	32,552	35,836	37,343	36,954
SWEDEN	11,108	9,776	12,702	17,935	17,388	26,069	23,289	23,305	23,309	17,778
EFTA	27,187	14,468	12,933	12,637	17,745	20,119	25,927	26,373	23,761	24,210
of which										
NORWAY	4,900	4,934	4,498	2,116	2,370	3,927	5,310	5,532	4,664	5,019
SWITZERLAND	21,913	9,104	7,979	10,239	15,124	15,790	20,202	20,813	19,071	19,168
OTHER EUROPEAN COUNTRIES	26,649	19,060	34,700	75,475	98,228	66,750	48,561	46,792	57,747	52,349
of which										
RUSSIA	777	1,627	1,814	6,054	7,182	10,380	10,042	10,019	7,863	6,166
UK OFFSHORE ISLANDS[2]	22,717	15,678	29,954	65,814	86,482	49,921	31,225	29,483	41,723	35,557
THE AMERICAS	**178,599**	**182,091**	**216,343**	**256,423**	**292,687**	**354,745**	**300,175**	**265,351**	**286,481**	**300,410**
of which										
BERMUDA	1,554	7,561	10,604	13,889	13,839	24,027	15,707	16,123	15,625	15,144
BRAZIL	2,532	3,922	3,220	2,824	3,717	6,502	4,602	6,442	14,113	11,422
CANADA	8,537	8,922	12,812	19,188	28,980	29,216	28,879	32,546	27,602	33,289
CHILE	1,919	2,133	2,814	563	439	320	226	506	744	794
COLOMBIA	2,434	1,874	1,132	985	1,109	1,520	1,975	2,553	439	703
MEXICO	1,431	2,461	2,860	2,337	3,791	3,548	2,489	3,088	5,007	4,381
PANAMA	153	132	166	..	..	168	182	183	297	..
USA	150,021	140,321	164,405	180,629	202,117	246,063	224,957	184,788	205,481	205,102
ASIA	**43,118**	**47,311**	**54,919**	**54,377**	**60,887**	**77,412**	**80,647**	**105,706**	**121,635**	**117,735**
NEAR & MIDDLE EAST COUNTRIES	1,559	3,008	3,733	6,874	9,984	14,690	18,514	24,084	28,544	30,504
of which										
GULF ARABIAN COUNTRIES	1,211	2,062	3,013	4,756	6,320	8,926	12,800	16,153	20,598	22,324
OTHER ASIAN COUNTRIES	41,559	44,303	51,187	47,503	50,903	62,723	62,133	81,622	93,091	87,231
of which										
CHINA	1,809	1,882	2,685	2,228	2,719	4,571	4,446	5,760	6,337	7,099
HONG KONG	17,221	19,165	20,432	22,256	25,517	28,666	24,342	27,675	31,015	35,839
INDIA	1,555	1,682	2,126	1,977	2,942	3,475	9,287	10,890	13,618	6,040
INDONESIA	1,309	1,178	1,168	982	825	1,035	1,848	2,651	5,457	3,580
JAPAN	2,361	5,829	6,076	2,485	592	1,901	2,943	2,588	5,833	5,413
MALAYSIA	1,476	1,592	1,455	1,174	1,233	891	884	1,364	1,736	2,117
SINGAPORE	9,510	6,610	7,144	6,684	6,220	10,479	6,284	7,969	9,538	9,192
SOUTH KOREA	1,339	1,218	4,586	3,763	4,457	3,048	3,243	4,160	4,403	3,526
THAILAND	1,357	947	1,281	1,407	1,456	1,708	1,201	1,288	1,363	1,441

6.14 FDI international investment position abroad analysed by area and main country, end 2003 to end 2012[1]

£ million

	2003	2004	2005	2006	2007	2008	2009	2010	2011	2012
AUSTRALASIA & OCEANIA	**17,486**	**16,888**	**16,694**	**12,665**	**16,173**	**19,930**	**18,893**	**32,051**	**37,161**	**42,502**
of which										
AUSTRALIA	16,283	14,586	14,627	11,571	15,391	18,024	16,091	31,490	36,201	42,585
NEW ZEALAND	1,060	1,459	1,176	923	682	580	1,509	457	641	-529
AFRICA	**17,039**	**17,350**	**20,834**	**15,105**	**18,516**	**21,104**	**29,548**	**30,143**	**30,848**	**37,349**
of which										
KENYA	285	238	281	313	331	372	396	474	579	533
NIGERIA	1,028	950	924	1,011	744	1,349	2,071	1,858	2,175	1,942
SOUTH AFRICA	11,250	10,964	13,733	8,255	9,533	10,994	14,404	10,245	10,609	13,428
ZIMBABWE	48	103	50	58	32	35	29	15	14	31
WORLD TOTAL	**665,123**	**645,744**	**696,113**	**741,163**	**916,261**	**1,073,613**	**981,481**	**1,046,098**	**1,090,900**	**1,088,046**
OECD	563,769	537,109	561,694	547,303	684,619	837,804	785,854	827,827	845,859	834,616
CENTRAL & EASTERN EUROPE[3]	560	534	640	515	65	275	312	239	245	183

1 A negative sign before values indicates a net disinvestment abroad (ie a decrease in the amount due to the UK).

2 The UK Offshore Islands consist of the Channel Islands & the Isle of Man, excluded from the definition of the economic territory of the UK from 1997.

3 Central & Eastern Europe prior to 2007 includes data for Bulgaria and Romania.

.. Indicates data are disclosive.
.- Indicates nil returns.

Source: Office for National Statistics

6.15 Earnings from foreign direct investment abroad analysed by area and main country, 2003 to 2012[1]

£ million

	2003	2004	2005	2006	2007	2008	2009	2010	2011	2012
EUROPE	**26,857**	**25,782**	**32,186**	**38,957**	**44,062**	**43,598**	**34,944**	**30,867**	**45,661**	**30,805**
EU	23,114	20,708	23,904	28,337	34,284	37,521	28,673	20,889	35,899	21,683
AUSTRIA	317	296	301	186	247	169	259	139	0	-77
BELGIUM	324	653	818	875	1,312	1,568	1,443	1,171	1,853	1,561
BULGARIA	..	0	9	3	-9	-3	5	0	8	..
CYPRUS	20	22	37	171	366	92	57	-8	-58	154
CZECH REPUBLIC	165	110	108	-64	72	-134	-127	-70	42	212
DENMARK	197	272	387	411	580	530	216	628	586	487
ESTONIA	9	3	..	11	5	6	26	17	23	12
FINLAND	103	112	103	69	281	131	120	184	218	99
FRANCE	1,714	2,107	2,957	3,344	3,007	1,769	1,437	3,419	3,531	2,381
GERMANY	1,592	2,328	2,685	2,189	2,890	3,116	2,732	1,492	1,649	..
GREECE	120	102	160	151	223	102	208	-51	19	-71
HUNGARY	241	202	295	83	96	77	32	22	94	112
IRISH REPUBLIC	2,197	2,461	2,835	2,525	3,049	1,879	-2,747	-10,064	-756	..
ITALY	639	708	732	696	837	311	32	630	251	154
LATVIA	0	0	..	5	4	-18	-26	..	..	..
LITHUANIA	0	0	-	-	2	-	0	2	4	3
LUXEMBOURG	1,500	2,191	4,006	7,626	8,030	13,185	11,547	10,357	12,002	7,288
MALTA	41	60	31	-185	-56	50	334	27	-21	119
NETHERLANDS	11,691	6,651	5,344	7,251	9,725	9,460	8,210	9,743	12,658	7,864
POLAND	290	218	293	373	256	414	693	363	486	625
PORTUGAL	175	191	297	234	264	271	155	292	38	..
ROMANIA	76	19	26	43	76	111	92	12	66	..
SLOVAKIA	..	..	34	24	103	20	22	37	42	26
SLOVENIA	..	..	17	5	11	14	5	..	..	..
SPAIN	576	694	1,023	918	1,021	1,083	764	-53	463	-1,966
SWEDEN	959	1,271	1,395	1,395	1,896	3,325	3,187	2,475	2,715	..
EFTA	1,761	2,382	3,334	3,759	4,987	4,765	3,311	5,577	5,183	4,644
of which										
NORWAY	319	297	937	345	296	578	577	537	515	805
SWITZERLAND	1,441	2,084	2,396	3,411	4,377	3,872	2,460	4,849	4,667	3,845
OTHER EUROPEAN COUNTRIES	1,982	2,692	4,948	6,861	4,791	1,312	2,959	4,401	4,578	4,478
of which										
RUSSIA	345	841	1,681	1,715	1,180	1,811	1,492	1,584	2,996	2,581
UK OFFSHORE ISLANDS[2]	1,332	1,602	3,017	4,580	3,138	-993	707	2,401	1,058	1,498
THE AMERICAS	**17,586**	**21,113**	**26,585**	**26,461**	**28,527**	**9,871**	**13,450**	**21,476**	**26,635**	**19,119**
of which										
BERMUDA	1,254	1,629	1,561	..	1,557	1,558	1,178	2,338	1,450	2,194
BRAZIL	291	652	866	577	712	725	1,225	1,063	1,303	1,123
CANADA	1,055	1,340	1,895	1,769	1,653	-2,501	-477	468	-42	968
CHILE	273	820	1,164	771	777	678	531	125	322	98
COLOMBIA	234	379	414	274	190	320	137	280	..	45
MEXICO	207	485	536	531	563	293	260	545	1,364	787
PANAMA	55	44	50	23	42	..	65	53	83	61
USA	12,723	14,332	18,244	17,112	19,110	6,034	8,865	14,634	20,127	11,931
ASIA	**5,108**	**8,001**	**10,975**	**11,621**	**11,389**	**9,129**	**11,917**	**15,901**	**18,952**	**18,966**
NEAR & MIDDLE EAST COUNTRIES	461	692	1,053	1,430	2,563	2,341	1,744	2,049	2,704	2,838
of which										
GULF ARABIAN COUNTRIES	370	549	688	717	983	405	868	773	975	1,373
OTHER ASIAN COUNTRIES	4,647	7,309	9,922	10,191	8,826	6,788	10,173	13,852	16,248	16,129
of which										
CHINA	278	370	580	445	504	265	579	815	821	1,118
HONG KONG	1,083	2,541	3,553	3,786	4,163	1,448	1,316	3,119	4,362	5,273
INDIA	511	427	626	715	798	690	1,046	1,647	1,794	1,442
INDONESIA	184	155	226	336	153	105	420	562	1,091	825
JAPAN	332	440	482	388	145	304	344	284	366	391
MALAYSIA	477	525	508	494	595	526	731	810	592	625
SINGAPORE	911	1,651	2,510	2,285	478	1,663	2,553	2,469	3,267	3,303
SOUTH KOREA	237	340	683	532	519	536	568	907	609	505
THAILAND	160	159	171	-121	23	-132	199	221	222	269

6.15 Earnings from foreign direct investment abroad analysed by area and main country, 2003 to 2012[1]

£ million

	2003	2004	2005	2006	2007	2008	2009	2010	2011	2012
AUSTRALASIA & OCEANIA	**2,022**	**3,623**	**3,157**	**3,065**	**3,716**	**3,134**	**4,323**	**6,007**	**2,359**	**4,390**
of which										
AUSTRALIA	1,518	3,108	2,681	2,665	3,294	2,734	3,843	5,545	2,044	4,049
NEW ZEALAND	478	279	359	388	379	329	402	371	209	209
AFRICA	2,959	3,958	5,764	3,488	4,548	3,765	3,298	6,084	6,355	6,936
of which										
KENYA	81	64	70	88	89	100	141	174	144	..
NIGERIA	122	153	197	133	78	212	108	660	1,045	1,275
SOUTH AFRICA	1,693	2,706	3,768	1,620	2,236	1,143	1,199	2,588	2,596	2,934
ZIMBABWE	43	87	16	10	6	-5	-4	5	23	23
WORLD TOTAL	**54,531**	**62,476**	**78,667**	**83,591**	**92,242**	**69,500**	**67,942**	**80,334**	**99,962**	**80,217**
OECD	41,353	43,453	52,138	55,675	64,794	50,006	45,802	49,160	66,062	45,081
CENTRAL & EASTERN EUROPE[3]	195	74	76	62	-11	25	28	-3	0	-11

1 Net earnings equal profits of foreign branches plus United Kingdom companies' receipts of interest and their share of profits of foreign subsidiaries and associates. Earnings are after deduction of provisions for depreciation and foreign taxes on profits, dividends and interest.

2 The UK Offshore Islands consist of the Channel Islands & the Isle of Man, excluded from the definition of the economic territory of the UK from 1997.

3 Central & Eastern Europe prior to 2007 includes data for Bulgaria and Romania.

A negative sign before values indicates a net disinvestment abroad (ie a decrease in the amount due to the UK).

.. Indicates data are disclosive.
.- Indicates nil returns.

Source: Office for National Statistics

6.16 Foreign direct investment flows into the United Kingdom analysed by area and main country, 2003 to 2012[1,2]

£ million

	2003	2004	2005	2006	2007	2008	2009	2010	2011	2012
EUROPE	**7,013**	**29,901**	**80,087**	**53,837**	**49,752**	**25,258**	**32,075**	**355**	**12,736**	**16,549**
EU	5,505	26,384	71,034	47,698	39,348	24,122	25,739	-6,574	17,688	17,450
AUSTRIA	8	-31	171	-61	183	-170	-42	84	971	-105
BELGIUM	218	1,542	23	670	317	-547	367	146	9,057	9,627
BULGARIA	..	..	..	..	1	..	..	..	..	-11
CYPRUS	0	0	7	18	75	30	19	47	97	178
CZECH REPUBLIC	0	0	-	..	1	1	..	0	-2	1
DENMARK	321	-11	-1,246	13	-18	1,577	-414	-209	79	463
ESTONIA	-	-	-	-	-	..	-	..	..	..
FINLAND	26	32	238	44	21	-25	131	64	63	50
FRANCE	414	1,703	9,643	2,356	-1,931	-2,682	18,952	-4,523	592	1,389
GERMANY	1,437	11,131	7,279	5,566	16,616	4,454	5,473	2,711	-4,171	2,079
GREECE	33	13	14	17	17	11	74	197	99	-33
HUNGARY	0	..	1	3	1	-	0	0	1	..
IRISH REPUBLIC	206	936	723	816	829	811	92	1,238	-240	-177
ITALY	-468	1,327	-42	282	288	-282	-655	146	399	788
LATVIA	..	-	..	..	0	..	-	-	-	..
LITHUANIA	-	..	0	0	-	-	..	..	..	..
LUXEMBOURG	-105	-115	151	221	4,349	972	6,382	-3,490	-4,729	799
MALTA	0	0	1	2	6	1	-14	4	27	36
NETHERLANDS	2,452	1,226	50,366	13,715	2,471	17,668	-9,977	-4,216	12,068	2,131
POLAND	0	0	1	50	-29	7	0	2	4	-2
PORTUGAL	..	..	-6	9	123	-79	15	44	20	85
ROMANIA	..	-34	..	..	4	-	..	..	1	0
SLOVAKIA	..	..	..	..	1	..	..	..	..	..
SLOVENIA	..	..	..	..	3	-	..	..	0	..
SPAIN	518	..	3,297	23,457	16,139	1,807	5,287	889	2,553	-297
SWEDEN	406	-14	393	508	-117	575	56	294	803	405
EFTA	1,408	3,016	9,050	5,321	8,793	-4,082	1,973	2,567	-2,396	-279
of which										
NORWAY	-179	-798	927	171	423	265	-116	216	27	184
SWITZERLAND	1,411	3,488	7,405	4,786	8,159	-3,094	1,839	1,876	-2,000	-554
OTHER EUROPEAN COUNTRIES	100	501	3	817	1,611	5,219	4,363	4,362	-2,555	-623
of which										
RUSSIA	..	..	..	..	332	1,769	1	..	190	38
UK OFFSHORE ISLANDS[3]	32	476	-60	733	1,248	4,208	4,255	3,984	-2,717	-833
THE AMERICAS	**3,396**	**-4,792**	**17,422**	**17,242**	**32,460**	**18,614**	**16,774**	**28,636**	**11,621**	**15,117**
of which										
BRAZIL	4	..	6	..	2	1	..	..	1	5
CANADA	-325	683	1,632	3,509	799	343	-1,265	3,680	-231	652
USA	2,676	-5,727	15,589	12,313	27,975	18,135	15,175	22,829	12,268	12,118
ASIA	**-449**	**4,081**	**-4,168**	**11,806**	**9,938**	**4,026**	**-2,330**	**5,324**	**2,842**	**3,580**
NEAR & MIDDLE EAST COUNTRIES	-34	384	736	5,034	-979	-635	274	335	-895	-489
OTHER ASIAN COUNTRIES	-415	3,697	-4,904	6,772	10,919	4,662	-2,604	4,988	3,738	4,068
of which										
CHINA	2	-26	13	12	16	-20	123	9	..	193
HONG KONG	63	..	315	92	-1,919	737	-152	2,995	2,004	588
INDIA	7	-15	138	265	151	2,638	20	48	563	240
JAPAN	-543	817	-5,575	3,726	5,816	796	-2,750	-90	1,288	1,740
SINGAPORE	-76	14	46	..	6,749	268	136	1	-467	149
SOUTH KOREA	-20	193	175	-85	5	247	11	..	38	206
AUSTRALASIA & OCEANIA	**310**	**1,420**	**3,396**	**1,869**	**540**	**-104**	**2,450**	**-2,388**	**1,609**	**303**
of which										
AUSTRALIA	309	1,412	3,396	1,479	588	-66	2,471	-2,392	1,597	291
NEW ZEALAND	2	8	-	54	-48	-20	-20	4	9	2
AFRICA	**7**	**-43**	**66**	**131**	**459**	**1,083**	**18**	**181**	**75**	**-115**
of which										
SOUTH AFRICA	21	-35	25	101	438	..	31	35	81	-148
WORLD TOTAL	**10,276**	**30,566**	**96,803**	**84,885**	**93,148**	**48,875**	**48,986**	**32,106**	**28,883**	**35,433**
OECD	8,984	26,762	95,187	73,961	83,165	39,384	41,296	21,921	30,096	32,001
CENTRAL & EASTERN EUROPE [4]	4	-32	..	6	1	..	..	0	..	..

1. Net foreign direct investment includes unremitted profits.
2. A negative sign before values indicates a net disinvestment abroad (i.e. a decrease in the amount due to the UK).
3. The UK Offshore Islands consist of the Channel Islands & the Isle of Man, excluded from the definition of the economic territory of the UK from 1997.
4. Central & Eastern Europe prior to 2007 includes data for Bulgaria and Romania.
.. Indicates data are disclosive.
- Indicates nil returns.

Source: Office for National Statistics

6.17 FDI International positions in the United Kingdom analysed by area and main country, 2003 to 2012[1]

£ million

	2003	2004	2005	2006	2007	2008	2009	2010	2011	2012
EUROPE	**158,903**	**181,198**	**277,027**	**332,077**	**354,382**	**389,925**	**416,484**	**417,201**	**447,608**	**543,704**
EU	142,273	161,395	244,392	299,906	308,996	335,526	362,673	353,741	371,932	466,550
AUSTRIA	349	366	561	848	1,030	840	935	1,076	2,435	4,346
BELGIUM	1,987	4,338	4,481	5,609	4,545	4,121	4,341	7,846	16,177	32,264
BULGARIA	..	..	..	..	..	..	..	..	..	25
CYPRUS	67	78	100	162	437	494	316	2,307	2,536	3,971
CZECH REPUBLIC	9	6	3	..	8	18	1	7	26	47
DENMARK	2,086	2,359	1,404	4,344	5,530	8,706	5,357	3,140	3,710	5,904
ESTONIA	-	-	-	-	..	..	-	..	..	..
FINLAND	946	886	756	817	708	736	753	780	875	2,050
FRANCE	36,565	41,100	56,309	59,998	54,303	51,838	73,534	67,241	61,236	78,447
GERMANY	32,260	39,300	51,469	54,382	64,558	71,755	67,784	51,677	50,046	65,176
GREECE	86	100	103	121	174	221	456	668	805	678
HUNGARY	9	12	9	12	12	20	5	10	14	14
IRISH REPUBLIC	4,769	5,021	7,146	8,186	8,839	10,204	10,886	9,524	11,013	13,952
ITALY	4,580	6,708	6,122	4,482	4,901	6,258	4,854	753	2,106	8,818
LATVIA	..	-	..	..	..	..	-	-	-	..
LITHUANIA	..	..	-	-	-	-	-	-	-	1
LUXEMBOURG	5,627	5,963	7,880	16,021	20,399	26,833	48,756	58,233	47,941	54,806
MALTA	21	5	12	12	62	69	48	172	292	1,052
NETHERLANDS	46,876	47,579	95,579	119,843	110,903	137,248	110,878	112,291	126,715	144,105
POLAND	10	7	21	96	75	76	16	26	98	75
PORTUGAL	115	113	111	122	222	308	600	892	302	513
ROMANIA	..	..	..	..	..	..	..	..	11	8
SLOVAKIA	..	..	-	-	..	..	..	..	..	3
SLOVENIA	..	..	..	..	9	13	..	7	0	20
SPAIN	3,344	4,536	8,782	20,658	27,876	11,178	26,781	33,344	40,447	41,953
SWEDEN	2,527	2,849	3,467	4,113	4,312	4,453	6,265	3,680	5,141	7,825
EFTA	13,758	15,752	25,033	22,358	32,570	29,931	29,654	35,771	41,470	40,521
of which										
NORWAY	831	242	1,085	969	1,522	1,789	1,776	1,723	2,400	4,988
SWITZERLAND	12,439	14,685	21,624	19,033	28,936	26,783	26,885	33,043	36,140	34,373
OTHER EUROPEAN COUNTRIES	2,872	4,051	7,602	9,813	12,816	24,468	24,158	27,689	34,205	36,634
of which										
RUSSIA	..	..	..	..	179	1,581	743	1,200	1,343	1,218
UK OFFSHORE ISLANDS[2]	2,361	3,500	7,059	9,111	11,963	22,026	23,025	26,120	32,183	27,691
THE AMERICAS	**145,973**	**140,090**	**174,037**	**200,709**	**202,062**	**209,792**	**208,475**	**242,270**	**263,464**	**311,705**
of which										
BRAZIL	5	..	77	134	21	9	..	..	17	21
CANADA	11,176	12,108	15,587	19,369	20,835	21,333	19,535	19,259	18,028	14,877
USA	130,512	122,069	149,759	170,880	167,008	168,689	170,206	198,163	219,181	269,479
ASIA	**19,869**	**24,800**	**24,101**	**39,436**	**53,166**	**50,419**	**42,521**	**54,791**	**66,426**	**69,408**
NEAR & MIDDLE EAST COUNTRIES	1,627	2,765	2,970	10,160	6,449	5,389	3,780	4,498	5,137	4,469
OTHER ASIAN COUNTRIES	18,242	22,035	21,131	29,275	46,717	45,030	38,741	50,293	61,289	64,939
of which										
CHINA	102	119	111	99	202	427	618	378	780	1,170
HONG KONG	..	..	..	..	..	..	6,641	9,579	20,504	10,528
INDIA	194	164	518	798	1,376	3,591	1,900	2,846	2,921	2,068
JAPAN	11,949	12,300	10,513	14,766	25,479	30,643	24,646	27,638	31,512	41,610
SINGAPORE	830	925	1,034	4,046	12,197	1,555	3,526	6,115	3,829	4,434
SOUTH KOREA	635	635	638	798	779	914	703	2,867	953	2,595
AUSTRALASIA & OCEANIA	**14,336**	**16,804**	**12,537**	**7,623**	**9,412**	**8,122**	**12,705**	**9,721**	**12,941**	**9,608**
of which										
AUSTRALIA	14,160	16,631	12,313	7,093	8,974	7,842	12,466	9,478	11,926	9,043
NEW ZEALAND	158	153	224	428	430	279	239	239	289	550
AFRICA	**560**	**530**	**510**	**469**	**1,397**	**2,115**	**1,088**	**1,574**	**2,220**	**2,026**
of which										
SOUTH AFRICA	387	296	186	130	900	1,600	501	570	1,124	835
WORLD TOTAL	**339,641**	**363,422**	**488,212**	**580,313**	**620,419**	**660,373**	**681,273**	**725,557**	**792,660**	**936,452**
OECD	324,491	340,870	458,185	535,218	564,201	594,466	619,512	644,444	690,293	840,386
CENTRAL & EASTERN EUROPE [3]	34	..	..	..	6	..	..	..	..	2

1. A negative sign before values indicates a net disinvestment abroad (ie a decrease in the amount due to the UK).

2. The UK Offshore Islands consist of the Channel Islands & the Isle of Man, excluded from the definition of the economic territory of the UK from 1997.

3. Central & Eastern Europe prior to 2007 includes data for Bulgaria and Romania.

.. Indicates data are disclosive

- Indicates nil returns.

Source: Office for National Statistics

6.18 Earnings from foreign direct investment in the United Kingdom analysed by area and main country, 2003 to 2012[1]

£ million

	2003	2004	2005	2006	2007	2008	2009	2010	2011	2012
EUROPE	**10,158**	**12,676**	**17,592**	**27,447**	**26,174**	**-17,381**	**9,438**	**20,481**	**21,139**	**20,778**
EU	9,010	11,330	15,278	22,919	24,144	-3,729	9,817	15,301	17,607	20,302
AUSTRIA	111	61	60	207	211	-45	85	112	171	99
BELGIUM	165	269	367	646	577	286	-218	488	1,020	2,267
BULGARIA	0	..	-	-	..	..	..	..	..	..
CYPRUS	24	20	24	44	66	57	33	147	124	185
CZECH REPUBLIC	0	0	0	..	1	1	..	0	18	3
DENMARK	305	311	326	204	-70	-175	-257	91	-91	108
ESTONIA	-	-	-	-	..	..	-	..	..	0
FINLAND	36	62	61	93	181	50	96	98	76	206
FRANCE	2,743	3,842	5,121	5,329	3,489	1,351	9,249	4,670	5,119	4,578
GERMANY	1,754	2,900	4,037	4,541	5,789	-823	-1,902	4,945	3,778	2,902
GREECE	4	-4	49	70	104	212	193	338	67	-27
HUNGARY	0	0	1	3	1	..	..	1	1	1
IRISH REPUBLIC	578	471	724	1,012	1,202	-132	-1,785	-2,598	333	10
ITALY	174	408	483	477	577	466	430	269	174	1,021
LATVIA	..	-	..	..	..	..	-	-	-	..
LITHUANIA	-	..	1	1	-	-	-	-	-	0
LUXEMBOURG	196	289	214	79	463	619	937	1,500	699	1,918
MALTA	0	0	0	3	7	28	22	46	47	95
NETHERLANDS	2,405	2,585	2,800	7,283	8,393	-7,297	-464	2,962	4,180	3,673
POLAND	0	0	1	8	6	3	1	2	4	11
PORTUGAL	49	47	30	48	54	50	42	52	-66	102
ROMANIA	..	..	..	..	..	..	..	..	1	1
SLOVAKIA	..	..	5	5	3	..	..	..	..	0
SLOVENIA	..	..	..	..	..	..	..	0	1	1
SPAIN	298	37	773	2,536	2,696	1,255	3,023	1,636	1,359	2,415
SWEDEN	167	21	182	316	386	368	337	541	592	610
EFTA	822	849	1,495	3,366	264	-16,382	-2,352	1,029	1,419	-1,937
of which										
NORWAY	0	-20	82	169	194	262	15	29	215	348
SWITZERLAND	794	819	1,320	2,933	-286	-15,112	-2,411	528	821	-2,380
OTHER EUROPEAN COUNTRIES	326	497	819	1,162	1,767	2,731	1,975	4,152	2,113	2,412
of which										
RUSSIA	..	..	..	..	7	-77	-14	40	101	27
UK OFFSHORE ISLANDS[2]	287	468	757	1,107	1,752	2,891	1,939	4,090	2,001	2,149
THE AMERICAS	**10,013**	**12,278**	**16,460**	**20,154**	**17,158**	**21,033**	**18,584**	**17,333**	**20,121**	**18,303**
of which										
BRAZIL	..	1	-4	-4	6	-6	..	32	9	17
CANADA	639	1,021	1,348	1,458	-250	-2,856	350	912	453	922
USA	9,054	10,981	14,156	16,828	15,060	22,518	16,931	14,993	17,920	15,538
ASIA	**-781**	**168**	**937**	**2,710**	**447**	**-1,316**	**-3,631**	**-202**	**2,835**	**3,697**
NEAR & MIDDLE EAST COUNTRIES	114	188	354	564	237	216	101	135	483	503
OTHER ASIAN COUNTRIES	-895	-19	583	2,145	210	-1,533	-3,731	-337	2,352	3,195
of which										
CHINA	..	8	-63	-35	17	-38	34	25	31	100
HONG KONG	-456	..	..	-597	..	-337	-89	549	55	606
INDIA	55	-2	65	132	140	261	89	161	700	225
JAPAN	-538	608	1,089	1,956	-216	-2,000	-3,979	-1,646	394	1,889
SINGAPORE	62	32	85	259	609	166	-213	-64	821	162
SOUTH KOREA	-54	23	72	104	125	134	59	116	49	87

6.18 Earnings from foreign direct investment in the United Kingdom analysed by area and main country, 2003 to 2012[1]

£ million

	2003	2004	2005	2006	2007	2008	2009	2010	2011	2012
AUSTRALASIA & OCEANIA	**835**	**695**	**535**	**1,259**	**1,222**	**613**	**2,143**	**-30**	**140**	**-82**
of which										
AUSTRALIA	802	690	521	876	1,196	629	2,152	-47	154	-117
NEW ZEALAND	4	5	13	46	25	-13	-4	18	6	26
AFRICA	**59**	**59**	**65**	**80**	**137**	**166**	**47**	**51**	**152**	**25**
of which										
SOUTH AFRICA	50	26	25	31	82	126	67	23	82	45
WORLD TOTAL	**20,283**	**25,876**	**35,588**	**51,650**	**45,138**	**3,113**	**26,581**	**37,631**	**44,388**	**42,721**
OECD	19,715	25,471	33,927	47,476	40,242	-1,792	22,914	30,470	37,463	36,446
CENTRAL & EASTERN EUROPE[3]	1	1	..	..	1	..	..	0	..	0

1. Net earnings equal profits of foreign branches plus United Kingdom companies' receipts of interest and their share of profits of foreign subsidiaries and associates. Earnings are after deduction of provisions for depreciation and foreign taxes on profits, dividends and interest.
2. The UK Offshore Islands consist of the Channel Islands & the Isle of Man, excluded from the definition of the economic territory of the UK from 1997.
3. Central & Eastern Europe prior to 2007 includes data for Bulgaria and Romania.
4. A negative sign before values indicates a net disinvestment abroad (i.e. a decrease in the amount due to the UK).

.. Indicates data are disclosive.
- Indicates nil returns.

Source: Office for National Statistics

Research and development

Chapter 7

Research and development

(Tables 7.1 to 7.5)

Research and experimental development (R&D) is defined for statistical purposes as 'creative work undertaken on a systematic basis in order to increase the stock of knowledge, including knowledge of man, culture and society, and the use of this stock of knowledge to devise new applications'.

R&D is financed and carried out mainly by businesses, the Government, and institutions of higher education. A small amount is performed by non-profit-making bodies. Gross Expenditure on R&D (GERD) is an indicator of the total amount of R&D performed within the UK: it has been approximately 2 per cent of GDP in recent years. Detailed figures are reported each year in a statistical bulletin published in March. Table 7.1 shows the main components of GERD.

ONS conducts an annual survey of expenditure and employment on R&D performed by government, and of government funding of R&D. The survey collects data for the reference period along with future estimates. Until 1993 the detailed results were reported in the *Annual Review of Government Funded R&D*. From 1997 the results have appeared in the Science, Engineering and Technology (SET) Statistics published by the Department for Business, Innovation and Skills (BIS). Table 7.2 gives some broad totals for gross expenditure by government (expenditure before deducting funds received by government for R&D). Table 7.3 gives a breakdown of net expenditure (receipts are deducted).

The ONS conducts an annual survey of R&D in business. Tables 7.4 and 7.5 give a summary of the main trends up to 2011. The latest set of results from the survey became available in a statistical bulletin dated 1 December.

Statistics on expenditure and employment on R&D in higher education institutions (HEIs) are based on information collected by Higher Education Funding Councils and the Higher Education Statistics Agency (HESA). In 1994 a new methodology was introduced to estimate expenditure on R&D in HEIs. This is based on the allocation of various Funding Council Grants. Full details of the new methodology are contained in science, engineering and technology (SET) Statistics available on the BIS website at: www.bis.gov.uk/policies/science/science-funding/set-stats

The most comprehensive international comparisons of resources devoted to R&D appear in Main Science and Technology Indicators published by the Organisation for Economic Co-operation and Development (OECD). The Statistical Office of the European Union and the United Nations also compile R&D statistics based on figures supplied by member states.

To make international comparisons more reliable the OECD have published a series of manuals giving guidance on how to measure various components of R&D inputs and outputs. The most important of these is the Frascati Manual, which defines R&D and recommends how resources for R&D should be measured. The UK follows the Frascati Manual as far as possible.

For information on available aggregated data on Research and Development please contact Mark Williams on 01633 456728 (e-mail Mark.Williams@ons.gsi.gov.uk).

7.1a R&D PERFORMED IN THE UK IN EACH SECTOR ACCORDING TO SOURCE OF FUNDING, 2011

CURRENT PRICES	Sector carrying out the work						£ million
	Government	Research Councils	Higher Education	Business Enterprise	Private Non-Profit	Total	Abroad
Sector providing the funds							
Government	977	86	406	1,601	68	3,138	531
Research Councils	47	819	1,979	11	86	2,942	188
Higher Education Funding Council	-	-	2,257	-	-	2,257	-
Higher Education	2	11	290	-	14	317	-
Business Enterprise	203	26	284	11,957	85	12,556	2,003
Private Non-Profit	3	47	987	104	165	1,306	-
Abroad	77	51	923	3,734	79	4,864	-
TOTAL	1,308	1,040	7,127	17,408	496	27,380	-
of which:							
Civil	1,151	1,040	7,091	15,562	494	25,338	-
Defence	158	-	35	1,847	2	2,042	-

Source: Office for National Statistics

- denotes nil, figures unavailable or too small to display.

Please note, as of 27th March 2013, there have been minor corrections made to the estimates for civil and defence expenditure.

7.1b Expenditure on research and development in the UK by sector of performance: 2004 to 2011

£ million

		2004	2005	2006	2007	2008	2009	2010	2011
Sector carrying out the work									
Current prices									
TOTAL	**GLBA**	20,242	22,106	22,993	24,696 [†]	25,345	25,632	26,179	27,380
Government[1]	**GLBK**	1,240	1,238	1,252	1,320	1,348	1,406	1,371	1,308
Research Councils	**DMRS**	930	1,051	1,061	1,034	1,041	1,097	1,141	1,040
Business Enterprise[1]	**GLBL**	12,662	13,734	14,144	15,676	15,814	15,532 [†]	16,053	17,408
Higher Education	**GLBM**	5,004	5,580	6,022	6,119 [†]	6,545	6,931	6,962	7,127
Private Non-Profit	**GLBN**	406	502	513	546 [†]	595	666	652	496
As % of GDP		1.67	1.72	1.70	1.72	1.78	1.81	1.77	1.79

	2004	2005	2006	2007	2008	2009	2010	2011
Sector carrying out the work								
Constant prices (2011 prices)								
TOTAL	23,867	25,482	25,811	27,049	27,022	26,923	26,738	27,380
Government[1]	1,462	1,427	1,405	1,446	1,437	1,477	1,400	1,308
Research Councils	1,097	1,212	1,191	1,133	1,110	1,152	1,165	1,040
Business Enterprise[1]	14,929	15,832	15,878	17,169	16,861	16,314	16,396	17,408
Higher Education	5,900	6,432	6,760	6,702	6,978	7,280	7,111	7,127
Private Non-Profit	479	579	576	598	634	700	666	496

Source: Office for National Statistics

1. On 1 July 2001, the Government research agency, the Defence Evaluation and Research Agency (DERA) was disestablished and two new organisations were created. Around a quarter of DERA remained within Ministry of Defence (MOD) as a Government agency whilst the remaining three quarters became a Private limited company (PLC). As a PLC its R&D activities are now classified and included within the Business sector.

[†] crosses denote earliest data revision.

7.2 Gross central government expenditure on research and development

United Kingdom

£ million

	2006/07		2007/08r		2008/09r		2009/10r		2010/11r		2011/12	
	Intra-mural	Extra-mural[1]	Intra-mural[2]	Extra-mural	Intra-mural	Extra-mural	Intra-mural	Extra-mural	Intra-mural	Extra-mural	Intra-mural	Extra-mural
Defence	361	1851	279	1941	262	1812	288	1551	226	1556	158	1190
Research councils	1051	2135	1034	2005	1041	2297	1097	2434	1141	2414	1040	2440
Higher education institutes	-	2085	-	2234	-	2227	-	2395	-	2303	-	2257
Other programmes	309	881	410	1019	419	1064	421	1276	400	1236	418	1410
Total (excluding NHS)	1721	6952	1723	7199	1722	7400	1806	7656	1767	7509	1616	7297

1. Extramural Includes work performed overseas and excludes monies spent with other government departments.
2. From 2007/08 expenditure data no longer includes VAT.
r - revised data

Source: Office for National Statistics 01633 456763

7.3 Government funding of net R&D by socio-economic objectives, percentage share: 2007 to 2012

Current prices

£ million

	2007	2008	2009	2010	2011	2012
TOTAL	8,825	9,107	9,371	9,260	9,002	8,953

%

	2007	2008	2009	2010	2011	2012
TOTAL	100	100	100	100	100	100
Agriculture	3	3	4	3	4	4
Industrial production and technology	-	1	2	1	-	-
Energy	1	1	1	1	1	1
Transport, telecommunication, other infrastructure	1	1	1	1	1	1
Environment	2	3	3	3	3	3
Health	17	18	19	21	21	21
Education	1	1	1	1	-	-
Exploration and exploitation of the earth	3	3	3	3	3	3
General advancement of knowledge: R&D financed from General University Funds	25	24	26	25	25	24
Exploration and exploitation of space	2	2	2	2	3	3
Defence	24	22	19	18	15	16
Culture, recreation, religion and mass media	2	2	2	2	2	2
Political and social systems, structures and processes	1	2	2	2	1	2
General advancement of knowledge: R&D financed from other sources	18	18	17	18	19	18

Source: Office for National Statistics

- denotes nil or figures unavailable.

7.4 Expenditure on civil and Defence R&D performed in UK businesses: Broad product groups, 2009 to 2012

£ million

		Civil					Defence			
		2009	2010	2011	2012		2009	2010	2011	2012
CURRENT PRICES										
TOTAL	DLBV	13,646	14,392 †	15,699	15,518	DLBW	1,886	1,653 †	1,769	1,588
Manufacturing	DLEP	9,484	10,036 †	10,835	10,741	DLEX	1,746	1,549 †	1,631	1,495
Chemicals	DLEQ	..	..	..	..	DLEY	..	..	..	..
Mechanical engineering	DLER	450	456 †	520	568	DLEZ	516	446	572	527
Electrical machinery	DLES	867	751 †	847	1,060	DLFA	408	393 †	353	271
Transport equipment	DLET	..	..	..	..	DLFB	..	..	..	..
Aerospace	DLEU	905	1,018 †	1,036	1,167	DLFC	560	419 †	402	350
Other manufacturing	DLEV	1,136	1,168 †	1,399	1,380	DLFD	115	127	82 †	107
Services	DLEW	3,811	4,016	4,437 †	..	DLFE	140	104	138	..
Other: Total	LDIL	350	.. †	426	..	LDJJ	-	..	-	..
Agriculture, hunting & forestry; Fishing	LDIN	111	102	133	..	LDJL	-	-	-	..
Extractive industries	LDIS	140	152	195 †	..	LDKF	-	-	-	..
Electricity, gas & water supply; Waste management	LDJB	75	..	68 †	..	LDKG	-	..	-	..
Construction	LDJG	24	..	31 †	..	LDKS	-	..	-	..

	Civil				Defence			
	2009	2010	2011	2012	2009	2010	2011	2012
CONSTANT PRICES								
TOTAL	14,577	14,983	15,977	15,518	2,015	1,721	1,800	1,588
Manufacturing	10,131	10,448	11,027	10,741	1,865	1,613	1,660	1,495
Chemicals	..	..	..	..	..	..	..	..
Mechanical engineering	481	475	529	568	551	464	582	527
Electrical machinery	926	782	862	1,060	436	409	359	271
Transport equipment	..	..	..	..	..	..	..	..
Aerospace	967	1,060	1,054	1,167	598	436	409	350
Other manufacturing	1,214	1,216	1,424	1,380	123	132	83	107
Services	4,071	4,181	4,515	..	150	108	140	..
Other: Total	374	..	434	..	-	..	-	..
Agriculture, hunting & forestry; Fishing	119	106	135	..	-	-	-	..
Extractive industries	150	158	198	..	-	-	-	..
Electricity, gas & water supply; Waste management	80	..	69	..	-	..	-	..
Construction	26	..	32	..	-	..	-	..

Source: Office for National Statistics

- denotes nil, figures unavailable or too small to display.

.. denotes disclosive figures.

† crosses denote earliest data revision.

7.5a Sources of funds for R&D performed in UK businesses 2009 to 2012

CURRENT PRICES

		2009	2010	2011	2012
£ Million					
TOTAL	**DLBX**	**15,532**	**16,045** [†]	**17,468**	**17,107**
UK Government	DLDO	1,324	1,407 [†]	1,506	1,348
Overseas total of which:	DLHK	3,458	3,789 [†]	3,939	4,030
EC Programmes	DLDQ	47	62 [†]	56	42
All other funding from abroad	DLDS	3,411	3,727 [†]	3,884	3,988
Other UK Business	DLDU	698	718 [†]	594	367
Own funds	DLDW	10,047	10,129 [†]	11,306	11,299
Other	DLDY	4	3	122 [†]	62

	2009	2010	2011	2012
Per cent				
TOTAL	**100**	**100**	**100**	**100**
UK Government	9	9	9	8
Overseas total of which:	22	24	23 [†]	24
EC Programmes	-	-	-	-
All other funding from abroad	22	23	22 [†]	23
Other UK Business	4	4 [†]	3	2
Own funds	65	63	65	66
Other	-	-	1	-

Source: Office for National Statistics

1. - denotes nil, figures unavailable or too small to display.
2. [†] crosses denote earliest data revision.
3. The sum of percentages may be more or less than 100 due to rounding.
4. 'Other' includes funds from UK Private Non-Profit organisations and Higher Education establishments, and from 2011, international organisations.

7.5b Sources of funds for R&D performed in UK businesses: Civil and defence, 2009 to 2012

£ million

		Civil					Defence			
		2009	2010	2011	2012		2009	2010	2011	2012
UK Government	DLFG	350	410 †	394	294	DLFN	974	996 †	1,112	1,055
Overseas total of which:	DLHS	3,206	3,584 †	3,791	3,867	DLIF	251	205	148 †	163
EC Programmes	DLFH	45	60 †	53	40	DLFO	2	2	3	2
All other funding from abroad	DLFI	3,161	3,524 †	3,738	3,828	DLFP	250	203	146 †	160
Other UK Business	DLFJ	..	607 †	485	295	DLFQ	..	111	109 †	72
Own	DLFK	9,503	9,787	10,951 †	11,000	DLFR	545	341 †	355	299
Other	DLFL	..	3	78 †	62	DLFS	..	1	44	1
TOTAL	DLBV	13,646	14,392 †	15,699	15,518	DLBW	1,886	1,653 †	1,769	1,588

Source: Office for National Statistics

1. - denotes nil, figures unavailable or too small to display.
2. .. denotes disclosive figures.
3. † crosses denote earliest data revision.
4. 'Other' includes funds from UK Private Non-Profit organisations and Higher Education establishments, and from 2011, international organisations.

Income and wealth

Chapter 8

Personal income, expenditure and wealth

Distribution of total incomes (Table 8.1)

The information shown in Table 8.1 comes from the Survey of Personal Incomes 2010/11. This is an annual survey covering approximately 600,000 individuals across the whole of the UK. It is based on administrative data held by HM Revenue & Customs (HMRC) on individuals who could be liable for tax.

The table relates only to those individuals who are taxpayers. The distributions only cover incomes as computed for tax purposes, and above a level which for each year corresponds approximately to the single person's allowance. Incomes below these levels are not shown because the information about them is incomplete.

Some components of investment income (for example interest and dividends), from which tax has been deducted at source, are not always held on HMRC business systems. Estimates of missing bank and building society interest and dividends from UK companies are included in these tables. The missing investment income is distributed to cases, so that the population as a whole has amounts consistent with evidence from other sources. For example, amounts of tax accounted for by deposit takers and the tendency to hold interest-bearing accounts as indicated by household surveys.

Superannuation contributions are estimated and included in total income. They have been distributed among earners in the Survey of Personal Incomes sample, by a method consistent with information about the number of employees who are contracted in or out of the State Earnings Related Pension Scheme (SERPS) and the proportion of their earnings contributed. When comparing results of these surveys across years, it should be noted that the Survey of Personal Incomes is not a longitudinal survey. However, sample sizes have increased in recent years to increase precision.

Average incomes of households (Table 8.2)

Original income is the total income in cash of all the members of the household before receipt of Related Pension Scheme (SERPS) and the proportion of their earnings contributed. When comparing results of these surveys across years, it should be noted that the Survey of Personal Incomes is not a longitudinal survey. However, sample sizes have increased in recent years to increase precision.

Average incomes of households (Table 8.2)

Original income is the total income in cash of all the members of the household before receipt of state benefits or the deduction of taxes. It includes income from employment, self-employment, investment income and occupational pensions. Gross income is original income plus cash benefits received from government (retirement pensions, child benefit, and so on). Disposal income is the income available for consumption; it is equal to gross income less direct taxes (which include income tax, national insurance contributions, and council tax). By further allowing for taxes paid on goods and services purchased, such as VAT, an estimate of post-tax income is derived. These income figures are derived from estimates made by the Office for National Statistics (ONS) based largely on information from the Living Costs and Food Survey (LFC) and published each year on the ONS website.

In Table 8.2, a retired household is defined as one where the combined income of retired members amounts to at least half the total gross income of the household; where a retired person is defined as anyone who describes themselves as retired, or anyone over the minimum National Insurance (NI) pension age describing themselves as 'unoccupied' or 'sick or injured but not intending to seek work.

Children are defined as persons aged under 16 or between 16 and 18, unmarried and receiving full-time non-advanced further education.

Living Costs and Food Survey (Tables 8.3–8.5)

The Living Costs and Food Survey (LCF) is a sample survey of 12,566 private households in the UK, with an achieved response of around 5,825 private households in 2009. The LCF sample is representative of all regions of the UK and of different types of households. The survey is continuous, with interviews spread evenly over the year to ensure that estimates are not biased by seasonal variation. The survey results show how households spend their money; how much goes on food, clothing and so on, how spending patterns vary depending upon income, household composition, and regional location of households. From January 2006 the survey has been conducted on a calendar-year basis, therefore the latest results refer to the January to December 2009 period.

One of the main purposes of the LCF is to define the 'basket of goods' for the Retail Prices Index (RPI) and the Consumer Prices Index (CPI). The RPI has a vital role in the up rating of state pensions and welfare benefits, while the CPI is a key instrument of the Government's monetary policy. Information from the survey is also a major source for estimates of household expenditure in the UK National Accounts. In addition, many other government departments use LCF data as a basis for policy making, for example in the areas of housing and transport. The Department for Environment, Food and Rural Affairs (Defra) uses LCF data to report on trends in food consumption and nutrient intake within the UK. Users of the LCF outside government include independent research institutes, academic researchers and business and market researchers. Like all surveys based on a sample of the population, its results are subject to sampling variability and potentially to some bias due to non-response. The results of the survey are published in an annual report the latest being The Family Spending 2013 edition. The report includes a list of definitions used in the survey, items on which information is collected, and a brief account of the fieldwork procedure.

8.1 Distribution of total income before and after tax by gender, 2010-11

Taxpayers only

Numbers: thousands; Amounts: £ million

Range of total income (lower limit) £	Total							
	Before tax, by range of total income before tax				After tax, by range of total income after tax			
	No. of taxpayers	Total income before tax	Total tax	Total income after tax	No. of taxpayers	Total income before tax	Total tax	Total income after tax
6,475	622	4,190	28	4,160	767	5,210	44	5,170
7,000	1,130	8,460	209	8,250	1,350	10,500	314	10,100
8,000	2,240	20,300	969	19,400	2,720	26,100	1,470	24,700
10,000	2,810	30,900	1,870	29,000	3,470	41,000	2,910	38,100
12,000	3,910	52,700	4,610	48,100	4,570	68,300	6,740	61,500
15,000	5,440	94,600	10,700	83,900	5,870	116,000	14,300	102,000
20,000	6,880	168,000	23,100	145,000	6,520	185,000	26,900	159,000
30,000	5,640	214,000	33,100	181,000	4,530	204,000	34,600	169,000
50,000	1,370	79,400	16,100	63,300	834	63,900	15,600	48,400
70,000	651	53,600	13,500	40,100	365	42,100	12,300	29,800
100,000	319	38,400	11,400	27,000	173	30,800	10,300	20,500
150,000	116	19,800	6,550	13,300	49	13,400	5,050	8,340
200,000	77	18,600	6,800	11,800	33	13,200	5,300	7,940
300,000	43	16,100	6,450	9,650	18	11,800	4,890	6,910
500,000	23	15,500	6,420	9,050	10	11,200	4,740	6,470
1,000,000	10	22,300	9,730	12,600	4	14,200	6,090	8,070
All ranges	31,300	857,000	152,000	706,000	31,300	857,000	152,000	706,000

Range of total income (lower limit) £	Male							
	Before tax, by range of total income before tax				After tax, by range of total income after tax			
	No. of taxpayers	Total income before tax	Total tax	Total income after tax	No. of taxpayers	Total income before tax	Total tax	Total income after tax
6,475	267	1,790	12	1,780	328	2,220	19	2,200
7,000	450	3,370	85	3,280	541	4,180	129	4,050
8,000	918	8,340	392	7,950	1,120	10,800	599	10,200
10,000	1,260	13,800	801	13,000	1,570	18,600	1,280	17,300
12,000	1,860	25,100	2,130	23,000	2,280	34,100	3,310	30,800
15,000	2,890	50,500	5,680	44,800	3,280	64,900	7,950	57,000
20,000	4,120	101,000	13,900	87,400	4,080	116,000	16,900	99,300
30,000	3,680	140,000	21,700	118,000	3,060	139,000	23,800	115,000
50,000	1,000	58,100	11,900	46,200	637	48,900	12,000	37,000
70,000	500	41,300	10,400	30,900	291	33,600	9,880	23,700
100,000	256	30,900	9,190	21,700	144	25,700	8,640	17,100
150,000	96	16,500	5,440	11,000	42	11,500	4,340	7,180
200,000	66	15,900	5,810	10,100	29	11,700	4,700	7,030
300,000	38	14,200	5,670	8,490	16	10,700	4,430	6,250
500,000	20	14,000	5,810	8,220	9	10,400	4,410	6,000
1,000,000	9	20,600	9,070	11,500	4	13,000	5,670	7,340
All ranges	17,400	556,000	108,000	448,000	17,400	556,000	108,000	448,000

8.1 Distribution of total income before and after tax by gender, 2010-11

Taxpayers only

Numbers: thousands; Amounts: £ million

Range of total income (lower limit) £	Female							
	Before tax, by range of total income before tax				After tax, by range of total income after tax			
	No. of taxpayers	Total income before tax	Total tax	Total income after tax	No. of taxpayers	Total income before tax	Total tax	Total income after tax
6,475	355	2,390	16	2,380	439	2,990	25	2,960
7,000	679	5,090	123	4,970	813	6,280	185	6,090
8,000	1,330	12,000	577	11,400	1,600	15,300	868	14,500
10,000	1,550	17,100	1,070	16,000	1,890	22,400	1,640	20,800
12,000	2,050	27,600	2,470	25,100	2,290	34,200	3,430	30,700
15,000	2,540	44,100	5,070	39,100	2,590	51,000	6,330	44,700
20,000	2,750	67,000	9,200	57,800	2,440	69,200	10,000	59,200
30,000	1,960	73,700	11,300	62,400	1,470	64,900	10,800	54,100
50,000	373	21,300	4,280	17,100	197	15,000	3,610	11,400
70,000	151	12,300	3,070	9,260	74	8,460	2,440	6,020
100,000	63	7,580	2,230	5,350	29	5,130	1,700	3,430
150,000	20	3,350	1,110	2,240	7	1,870	710	1,160
200,000	11	2,710	992	1,720	4	1,520	604	915
300,000	5	1,940	776	1,160	2	1,120	464	660
500,000	2	1,440	605	830	1	805	337	468
1,000,000	1	1,690	656	1,030	-	1,150	421	729
All ranges	13,800	301,000	43,600	258,000	13,800	301,000	43,600	258,000

Source: Survey of Personal Incomes 2010-11
Table updated December 2012

Notes on the Table
Distribution of total income before and after tax by gender, 2010-11

1. This table only covers individuals with some liability to tax.

2. It should be noted that individuals may not necessarily fall into the same total income range for before and after tax breakdowns. Total income before tax is used to assign people to an income range for columns 2 to 5, whereas total income after the deduction of tax is used to assign individuals to an income band for columns 6 to 9.

3. For more information about the SPI and symbols used in this table, please refer to Personal Income Statistics release 2010-11

8.2: Summary of the effects of taxes and benefits, by household type,[1] 2011/12

	Retired households					Non-Retired households		
	1 adult Men	1 adult Women	All 1 adult	2 or more adults		1 adult Men[2]	1 adult Women[2]	All 1 adult[2]
Average per household (£ per year)								
Original income	6 835	5 445	5 862	16 685		23 412	17 345	20 984
plus Cash benefits	8 796	9 008	8 944	12 101		2 760	3 179	2 928
Gross income	15 632	14 453	14 806	28 786		26 172	20 524	23 912
less Direct taxes and employees' NIC	1 751	1 382	1 493	3 952		5 939	4 427	5 334
Disposable income	13 880	13 071	13 313	24 833		20 233	16 097	18 577
Equivalised disposable [3] income	20 788	19 606	19 960	24 303		30 349	24 145	27 866
less Indirect taxes	2 711	2 195	2 349	5 371		3 557	3 351	3 475
Post-tax income	11 169	10 876	10 964	19 462		16 675	12 746	15 103
plus Benefits in kind	4 498	4 851	4 745	7 204		1 580	1 750	1 648
Final income	15 667	15 727	15 709	26 666		18 256	14 496	16 751

	Non-Retired households							
	2 adults[2]	3 or more adults[2]	1 adult with children	2 adults with 1 child	2 adults with 2 children	2 adults with 3 or more children	3 or more adults with children	All house-holds
Average per household (£ per year)								
Original income	45 618	50 499	9 762	48 222	49 304	41 308	47 024	31 477
plus Cash benefits	2 635	4 030	11 104	3 478	4 419	9 326	8 143	5 979
Gross income	48 253	54 529	20 866	51 700	53 723	50 635	55 166	37 456
less Direct taxes and employees' NIC	11 097	10 926	1 598	11 518	12 048	9 146	9 573	7 428
Disposable income	37 156	43 603	19 268	40 181	41 675	41 489	45 594	30 027
Equivalised disposable income	37 156	29 739	18 830	32 646	28 762	23 974	24 651	28 155
less Indirect taxes	6 486	8 606	3 730	6 650	7 085	7 314	9 292	5 518
Post-tax income	30 669	34 997	15 538	33 531	34 590	34 175	36 302	24 509
plus Benefits in kind	3 353	7 482	11 229	7 836	13 543	21 194	15 672	6 787
Final income	34 022	42 479	26 768	41 368	48 132	55 369	51 974	31 297

Source: Office for National Statistics

Notes:
1 See Further Analysis and Methodology section for definitions of retired households, adults and children.
2 Without children.
3 Using the modified-OECD scale.

8.3 Income and source of income, 1970 to 2012

United Kingdom

	Weighted number of house- holds	Number of house- holds in the sample	Weekly household income[1]				Source of income					
			Current prices		Constant prices[2]		Wages and salaries	Self employ- ment	Invest- ments	Annuities and pensions[3]	Social security benefits[4]	Other sources
			Dispo- sable	Gross	Dispo- sable	Gross						
	(000s)	Number	£	£	£	£	Percentage of gross weekly household income					
1970		6,390	28	34	282	340	77	7	4	3	9	1
1980		6,940	115	140	337	412	75	6	3	3	13	1
1990		7,050	258	317	443	545	67	10	6	5	11	1
1995-96		6,800	307	381	436	541	64	9	5	7	14	2
1996-97		6,420	325	397	451	551	65	9	4	7	14	1
1997-98		6,410	343	421	469	575	67	8	4	7	13	1
1998-99[5]	24,660	6,630	371	457	499	615	68	8	4	7	12	1
1999-2000	25,340	7,100	391	480	520	638	66	10	5	7	12	1
2000-01	25,030	6,640	409	503	540	663	67	9	4	7	12	1
2001-02[6]	24,450	7,470	447	547	581	711	68	8	4	7	12	1
2002-03	24,350	6,930	453	552	583	710	68	8	3	7	12	1
2003-04	24,670	7,050	464	570	588	723	67	9	3	7	13	1
2004-05	24,430	6,800	489	601	611	751	68	8	3	7	13	1
2005-06	24,800	6,790	500	616	612	754	67	8	3	7	13	1
2006[7]	24,790	6,650	521	642	626	771	67	9	3	7	12	1
2006[8]	25,440	6,650	515	635	619	763	67	9	3	7	13	1
2007	25,350	6,140	534	659	627	774	67	8	4	7	13	1
2008	25,690	5,850	582	713	659	808	67	9	4	7	12	1
2009	25,980	5,830	558	683	619	757	66	8	3	8	14	1
2010	26,320	5,260	578	700	621	752	65	10	2	8	14	1
2011	26,110	5,690	587	713	603	733	66	7	2	9	14	1
2012	26,410	5,600	597	720	597	720	65	8	3	9	14	1

1 Does not include imputed income from owner-occupied and rent-free households.

2 Constant prices have been deflated using the CPI All Items Index for years from 1998. Before 1988, the index is based on modelled or indicative data.

3 Other than social security benefits.

4 Excluding housing benefit and council tax benefit (rates rebate in Northern Ireland) and their predecessors in earlier years - see Appendix B.

5 Based on weighted data from 1998-99 onwards

6 From 2001-02 onwards, weighting is based on the population estimates from the 2001 Census.

7 From 1998-99 to this version of 2006, figures shown are based on weighted data using non-response weights based on the 1991 Census and population figures from the 1991 and 2001 Censuses.

8 From this version of 2006, figures shown are based on weighted data using updated weights, with non-response weights and population figures based on the 2001 Census.

ONS, Family Spending 2012, © Crown copyright 2013

8.4 Household expenditure based on the FES classification, 1999-00 to 2011

at 2011 prices[1]

United Kingdom

Year	1999 -2000	2000 -01	2001[3] -02	2002 -03	2003 -04	2004 -05	2005 -06	2006[4]	2006[5]	2007	2008	2009	2010	2011
Weighted number of households (thousands)	25,330	25,030	24,450	24,350	24,670	24,430	24,800	24,790	25,440	25,350	25,690	25,980	26,320	26,110
Total number of households in sample	7,100	6,640	7,470	6,930	7,050	6,800	6,790	6,650	6,650	6,140	5,850	5,830	5,260	5,690
Total number of persons	16,790	15,930	18,120	16,590	16,970	16,260	16,090	15,850	15,850	14,650	13,830	13,740	12,180	13,430
Average number of persons per household	2.3	2.4	2.4	2.3	2.4	2.4	2.4	2.4	2.3	2.4	2.4	2.3	2.3	2.4

Commodity or service	Average weekly household expenditure (£)													
1 Housing (net)[6]	80.60	87.70	89.10	88.40	90.10	95.90	98.50	99.00	98.80	104.70	102.90	93.80	89.80	88.70
2 Fuel and power	16.00	16.30	15.90	15.50	15.40	15.70	16.90	18.90	18.70	19.50	20.70	23.40	22.50	22.10
3 Food and non-alcoholic drinks	84.30	85.00	83.70	85.20	83.70	84.20	82.70	83.50	82.70	81.20	81.60	83.20	81.60	80.10
4 Alcoholic drink	21.60	20.60	19.30	19.60	19.00	18.50	18.00	17.60	17.50	16.70	14.70	15.40	15.20	14.70
5 Tobacco	8.50	8.30	7.40	7.20	7.00	6.20	5.50	5.50	5.50	5.20	5.00	4.80	4.90	4.70
6 Clothing and footwear	29.60	30.20	30.20	29.10	28.90	29.40	27.30	27.20	26.80	24.60	23.20	22.70	24.30	21.50
7 Household goods	43.40	44.80	44.70	44.80	45.20	44.50	40.80	40.90	40.40	39.40	37.20	35.00	37.50	31.70
8 Household services	26.70	30.10	31.90	30.90	32.00	32.90	33.00	31.60	31.40	30.10	29.80	29.40	30.10	28.20
9 Personal goods and services	19.60	20.20	20.20	20.20	20.80	20.00	20.60	20.90	20.80	20.30	18.80	19.40	18.30	18.70
10 Motoring	74.30	75.60	78.30	81.70	80.40	78.30	77.70	74.10	72.60	70.60	69.60	66.10	66.70	68.00
11 Fares and other travel costs	13.00	13.00	12.60	12.90	12.40	11.80	13.50	13.20	13.10	12.40	15.60	12.10	14.40	11.70
12 Leisure goods	26.20	27.10	26.60	27.10	27.60	26.80	23.70	23.30	23.00	22.90	20.80	20.30	19.90	18.00
13 Leisure services	62.10	69.50	70.20	71.00	70.90	74.50	76.70	78.70	77.50	70.20	72.10	69.80	66.10	71.10
14 Miscellaneous	2.00	1.00	2.50	2.60	2.50	2.50	2.60	2.50	2.50	2.20	2.20	2.20	2.40	2.10
1-14 All expenditure groups	508.20	529.50	532.70	536.30	536.00	541.20	537.60	537.00	531.20	520.00	514.30	497.60	493.70	481.20

Average weekly expenditure per person (£) All expenditure groups	220.90	225.00	225.20	225.20	227.40	226.70	226.80	227.10	227.20	220.70	218.20	212.70	211.80	204.40

	Average weekly household income (£)[7]													
Gross income (£)	679	690	731	732	735	751	750	762	753	751	781	751	737	713
Disposable income (£)	553	562	598	601	598	611	609	619	612	608	637	614	608	587

Figures are based on FES data between 1984 and 2000-01, EFS data between 2000-01 and 2007, and LCF thereafter.

1 Figures have been deflated to 2011 prices using the RPI All Items Index.

2 From this version of 1995-96, figures are shown based on weighted data, including children's expenditure. Weighting is based on the population figures from the 1991 and 2001 Censuses.

3 From 2001-02 onwards, commodities and services are based on COICOP codes broadly mapped to FES.

4 From 1995-96 to this version of 2006, figures shown are based on weighted data using non-response weights based on the 1991 Census and population figures from the 1991 and 2001 Censuses.

5 From this version of 2006, figures shown are based on weighted data using updated weights, with non-response weights figures based on the 2001 Census.

6 An improvement to the imputation of mortgage interest payments has been implemented for 2006 data onwards. Also, an error was discovered in the derivation of mortgage capital repayments which was leading to double counting; this has been amended for 2006 data onwards. These changes may lead to a slight discontinuity between 2006 and earlier years.

7 Does not include imputed income from owner-occupied and rent-free households.

ONS, Family Spending 2011, © Crown copyright 2012

8.5 Percentage of households with durable goods 1998/99 to 2011

United Kingdom

	Car/ van	Central heating[1]	Washing machine	Tumble dryer	Dish-washer	Micro-wave	Tele-phone	Mobile phone	DVD Player	Home computer	Internet connection
1998-99[2]	72	89	92	51	23	79	95	27	--	33	10
1999-2000	71	90	91	52	23	80	95	44	--	38	19
2000-01	72	91	93	53	25	84	93	47	--	44	32
2001-02[3]	74	92	93	54	27	86	94	64	--	49	39
2002-03	74	93	94	56	29	87	94	70	31	55	45
2003-04	75	94	94	57	31	89	92	76	50	58	49
2004-05	75	95	95	58	33	90	93	78	67	62	53
2005-06	74	94	95	58	35	91	92	79	79	65	55
2006[4]	76	95	96	59	38	91	91	80	83	67	59
2006[5]	74	95	96	59	37	91	91	79	83	67	58
2007	75	95	96	57	37	91	89	78	86	70	61
2008	74	95	96	59	37	92	90	79	88	72	66
2009	76	95	96	58	39	93	88	81	90	75	71
2010	75	96	96	57	40	92	87	80	88	77	73
2011	75	96	97	56	41	92	88	87	88	79	77

-- Data not available

1 Full or partial

2 From this version of 1998-99, figures shown are based on weighted data and including children's expenditure.

3 From 2001-02 onwards, weighting is based on the population figures from the 2001 census.

4 From 1998-99 to this version of 2006, figures shown are based on weighted data using non-response weights based on the 1991 Census and population figures from the 1991 and 2001 Census.

5 From this version of 2006, figures shown are based on weighted data using updated weights, with non-response weights and population figures based on the 2001 Census

ONS, Family Spending 2011, © Crown copyright 2012

this page is intentionally blank

Lifestyles

Chapter 9

Lifestyles

Expenditure by the Department for Culture, Media and Sport (Table 9.1)
The figures in this table are taken from the department's Annual Report and are outturn figures for each of the headings shown (later figures are the estimated outturn). The department's planned expenditure for future years is also shown.

International tourism and holidays abroad (Tables 9.8 and 9.9)
The figures in these tables are compiled using data from the International Passenger Survey (IPS). A holiday abroad is a visit made for holiday purposes. Business trips and visits to friends and relatives are excluded.

Domestic tourism (Table 9.10)
The figures in this table are compiled using data from the UK Tourism Survey (UKTS) and represent trips of one or more nights away from home. The UKTS changed survey methodology in 2000 and 2005. Data from 1995 to 1999 were reworked to allow comparisons to be made with 2000 to 2004 data. Data for 2004 should be used and interpreted with caution. Data for 2005 is not comparable with previous years.

Gambling (Table 9.12)
The National Lottery figures in this table are the latest figures released by The National Lottery Commission at the time of going to press. They represent ticket sales (money staked1) for each of the games which comprise the lottery. The figures have been adjusted to real terms using the Retail Prices Index (RPI).
The National Lottery started on the 19 November 1994 with the first instant ticket being sold in March 1995. The sum of the individual games may not agree exactly with the figures for total sales which also include the Easy Play games which started in 1998 but were dropped in 1999.
The other gambling figures in this table are obtained from the Gambling Commission (formerly the Gaming Board) and HM Revenue & Customs (HMRC). The figures have been adjusted to real terms using the Retail Prices Index (RPI).

9.1 Expenditure by the Department for Culture, Media and Sport

£'000

	2006-07 Outturn	2007-08 Outturn	2008-09 Outturn	2009-10 Outturn	2010-11 outturn	2011-12 outturn	2012-13 outturn	2013-14 Plans	2014-15 Plans
Resource DEL									
Support for the Museums and Galleries sector	4,532	12,619	4,230	4,170	3,831	13,336	12,664	16,621	17,180
Museums and Galleries sponsored bodies	342,921	334,044	278,988	357,425	361,853	306,816	359,754	406,016	378,597
Libraries sponsored bodies	100,913	99,452	104,277	103,587	106,243	113,172	110,753	114,024	113,274
Museums, libraries and archives council	48,525	59,804	61,838	58,376	64,474	43,741	8,632	-	124
Support for the Arts sector	2,074	3,088	(1,273)	(3,821)	(1,737)	2,373	(53,218)	(66,107)	(60,893)
Arts and culture bodies	387,109	402,293	413,791	420,612	420,204	380,835	446,545	447,244	449,902
Support for the Sports sector	2,583	8,525	2,203	8,801	1,098	5,394	6,847	6,395	13,370
Sport sponsored bodies	111,731	141,744	161,154	151,945	148,362	136,077	144,942	121,961	119,503
Ceremonial and support for the Heritage sector	16,654	19,064	20,633	18,555	22,200	13,946	22,161	14,980	14,281
Heritage sponsored bodies	161,239	141,608	151,149	151,825	144,270	130,737	97,567	97,999	97,423
The Royal Parks	17,851	18,999	20,092	18,487	15,759	17,162	16,955	15,575	14,846
Support for the Tourism sector	1,925	1,985	2,230	127	2,362	16	70	–	–
Tourism sponsored bodies	52,980	53,848	52,985	50,450	39,479	45,494	47,824	31,381	29,195
Support for the Broadcasting and Media sector	1,154	4,417	2,722	2,624	1,561	3,218	15,161	11,397	7,106
Broadcasting and Media sponsored bodies	120,039	118,109	129,542	136,260	138,139	170,893	183,593	98,319	97,204
Administration and Research	53,910	53,309	56,476	56,448	53,406	58,429	51,679	53,354	33,828
Support for horseracing and the Gambling Sector	(11,015)	(11,518)	(5,121)	(3,732)	(4,020)	2,700	(1,560)	(1,445)	–
Grant to the National Lottery Commission	8,415	12,502	6,490	4,974	4,917	4,974	1,714	3216	815
Gambling Commission	14,126	4,108	1,437	827	(810)	(252)	245	1,175	1,234
Olympics – legacy programmes	154	459	(67)	524	13,022	65,868	501,628	2,192	–
London 2012	20,249	24,130	(2,703)	(35,363)	(18,700)	45,399	1,575,240	168,776	–
Government Equalities Office	-	5,969	10,333	13,998	11,611	7,080	15,283	21,375	20,333
Equality and Human Rights Commission (EHRC)	-	74,129	59,395	55,700	52,800	42,982	26,683	32,526	25,118
Spectrum management receipts	-	–	–	–	–	–	(60,142)	(62,300)	(62,600)
Total Resoirce DEL	1,458,069	1,582,687	1,530,801	1,572,799	1,580,324	1,610,390	3,531,020	1,534,674	1,309,840

9.1 Expenditure by the Department for Culture, Media and Sport

£'000

	2006-07 Outturn	2007-08 Outturn	2008-09 Outturn	2009-10 Outturn	2010-11 Outturn	2011-12 Outturn	2012-13 Outturn	2013-14 Plans	2014-15 Plans
Total Resource DEL	1,458,069	1,582,687	1,530,801	1,572,799	1,580,324	1,610,390	3,531,020	1,534,674	1,309,840
Of which:									
Staff Costs	508,044	632,674	585,335	604,087	606,177	648,611	594,034	247,279	212,025
Purchase of goods and services	754,022	817,214	852,475	795,638	745,002	931,655	849,340	624,450	518,644
Income from sales of goods and services	(354,510)	(400,225)	(435,149)	(371,751)	(364,397)	(402,992)	(273,532)	(19,270)	-
Current grants to local government (net)	25,174	48,672	91,378	38,415	57,507	(26,931)	10,603	–	–
Current grants to persons and non-profit (net)	497,304	575,071	580,437	649,477	606,302	585,540	786,028	496,185	497,321
Current grants abroad (net)	(649)	(12,410)	906	493	823	136	-	51	-
Subsidies to public corporations	-	-	-	-	82,590	74,880	522,976	1,691	1,677
Rentals	-	-	-	-	800	6,346	3,545	-	-
Depreciation[1]	101,589	107,081	28,571	115,617	109,300	114,120	1,443,884	296,000	176,200
Change in pension scheme liabilities[2]	-	-	-	-	100	471	12	-	-
Other resource	(72,905)	(185,390)	(173,152)	(259,177)	(263,880)	(321,446)	(405,870)	(111,712)	(96,027)
Resource AME									
British Broadcasting Corporation and other broadcasting and media sponsored bodies	2,797,000	2,962,800	2,868,987	3,020,000	3,121,360	2,607,337	3,061,145	3,179,759	3,392,531
New and adjustments to existing provisions and impairments	3,375	11,273	17,293	41,730	303,698	(98,473)	(12,437)	576	-
Release of Provisions	(4,357)	(4,944)	(3,902)	(2,646)	(6,041)	(20,372)	(39,548)	-	-
Museums and Galleries Sponsored bodies	-	-	-	-	(44,810)	-	25,325	27,066	-
Libraries sponsored bodies	-	-	-	-	-	-	3	3	-
Arts and culture bodies	-	-	-	-	-	-	-	5,005	-
Sport sponsored bodies	-	(50)	-	-	-	-	4,061	724	-
The Royal Parks	-	-	-	-	-	-	702	165	-
Tourism sponsored bodies	-	-	-	-	-	-	1,937	140	-
Gambling levy bodies	-	-	-	-	-	(30,535)	(10,268)	-	-
Horseracing and gambling bodies	-	-	-	-	-	-	472	-	-
Equality and Human Rights Commission (EHRC)	-	-	-	-	-	86	68	-	-
London 2012	-	-	-	-	-	-	-142	-	-
Lottery Grants	837,047	882,351	1,010,728	100,814	994,845	1,334,509	1,449,621	932,084	932,084
Total Resource AME	3,633,065	3,851,430	3,893,106	4,059,898	4,369,052	3,792,552	4,480,939	4,145,522	4,324,615
Of which: Staff Costs	916,000	1,097,800	974,130	1,248,000	1,053,000	1,199,758	889,527	1,040,458	1,070,067
Purchase of goods and services	2,411,000	2,375,000	2,410,870	2,279,000	2,630,510	1,973,067	2,844,775	2,609,837	2,821,444
Change in pension scheme liabilities[2]	-	-	-	-	-	-	162,231	-	-
Income from sales of goods and services	-	-	-	-	-	-	(328,808)	-	-
Rentals	-	-	-	-	-	-	80,775	-	-
Current grants to local government (net)	49,014	43,953	102,440	79,898	73,666	57,497	20,812	89,110	89,110
Current grants to persons and non-profit (net)	735,187	729,672	784,288	784,245	761,179	961,726	557,133	842,974	842,974
Depreciation[1]	35,000	35,000	84,787	93,000	69,585	124,644	237,369	197,302	176,020
Take up of provisions	7,028	12,911	17,283	41,771	292,898	(96,968)	592,197	576	-
Release of provision	(8,010)	(6,632)	(3,892)	(2,687)	(6,041)	(16,345)	(40,604)	-	-
Unwinding of discount rate on pension scheme liabilities[2]	-	-	-	-	-	560,222	557,712	-	-
Other resource	(512,154)	(436,274)	(476,800)	(463,329)	(505,745)	(971,049)	(1,092,180)	(634,735)	(675.000)
Total Resource Budget	5,091,134	5,434,117	5,423,907	5,632,697	5,949,376	5,402,942	8,011,959	5,680,196	5,634,455
Of which:Depreciation[2]	136,589	142,081	113,358	208,617	178,885	238,764	1,681,253	493,302	352,220

1 Depreciation includes impairments.

2 Pension schemes report under IAS 19 Employee Benefits accounting requirements. These figures, therefore, include cash payments made and contributions received, as well as certain non-cash items.

9.2 Estimates of Average Issue Readership of National Daily Newspapers
rolling 12 months' periods ending

000's

		2009 Mar	2009 Jun	2009 Sep	2009 Dec	2010 Mar	2010 Jun	2010 Sep	2010 Dec	2011 Mar	2011 Jun	2011 Sept	2011 Dec	2012 Mar	2012 Jun	2012 Sep	2012 Dec	2013 Mar
The Sun	WSDV	7,870	7,860	7,798	7,761	7,751	7,694	7,700	7,722	7,722	7,683	7,652	7,480	7,331	7,244	7,084	7,007	6,707
Daily Mail	WSEI	4,949	4,846	4,936	4,934	4,881	4,896	4,739	4,741	4,775	4,622	4,561	4,455	4,426	4,385	4,320	4,258	4,245
Daily Mirror/Daily Record	WSEH	4,555	4,608	4,476	4,404	4,288	4,170	4,004	3,947	4,026	3,997	4,114	4,053	4,046	3,995	3,849	3,773	3,614
Daily Mirror	WSEM	3,489	3,566	3,477	3,425	3,381	3,244	3,117	3,087	3,163	3,163	3,251	3,200	3,196	3,178	3,062	2,995	2,856
The Daily Telegraph	WSEN	1,887	1,843	1,834	1,905	1,840	1,796	1,751	1,680	1,693	1,688	1,584	1,562	1,468	1,387	1,394	1,346	1,352
The Times	WSES	1,770	1,801	1,802	1,773	1,768	1,673	1,613	1,571	1,552	1,486	1,435	1,385	1,359	1,302	1,310	1,311	1,300
Daily Express	WSEP	1,557	1,624	1,546	1,577	1,617	1,586	1,551	1,565	1,504	1,457	1,439	1,417	1,329	1,304	1,265	1,192	1,157
Daily Star	WSEQ	1,451	1,471	1,598	1,577	1,529	1,463	1,423	1,427	1,488	1,498	1,506	1,452	1,409	1,439	1,421	1,358	1,279
The Guardian	WSET	1,206	1,205	1,142	1,147	1,124	1,132	1,130	1,103	1,154	1,143	1,119	1,120	1,058	1,081	1,062	1,050	1,027
i		-	-	-	-	-	-	-	-	-	-	-	-	-	564	561	612	579
The Independent	WSEU	649	679	636	671	635	607	556	532	562	535	541	530	533	537	506	490	443
Financial Times	WSEY	417	430	433	434	418	404	391	364	367	344	325	317	301	300	285	319	312
Any national morning	WSEZ	20,918	20,817	20,609	20,574	20,404	20,207	19,841	19,690	19,751	19,481	19,391	19,124	18,679	18,466	18,069	17,825	17,403

Source: National Readership Surveys Ltd.

9.3 Employment in the Creative Economy in 2011
By Group

Group	Employees in the Creative Economy	Self Employed in the Creative Economy	Employment in Creative Industries	Creative Jobs outside of the Creative Industries	Employment in the Creative Economy
1. Advertising and marketing	394,000	73,000	147,000	320,000	468,000
2. Architecture	91,000	30,000	93,000	28,000	121,000
3. Crafts	58,000	46,000	9,000	95,000	104,000
4. Design: product, graphic and fashion design	85,000	66,000	100,000	51,000	151,000
5. Film, TV, video, radio and photography	140,000	92,000	209,000	23,000	232,000
6. IT, software and computer services	596,000	113,000	482,000	226,000	709,000
7. Publishing	175,000	61,000	207,000	28,000	236,000
8. Museums, galleries and libraries	107,000	5,000	90,000	22,000	113,000
9. Music, performing and visual arts	76,000	198,000	212,000	62,000	274,000
Total	1,722,000	684,000	1,551,000	856,000	2,407,000
Wider UK Economy Total	-	-	-	-	29,935,000

1: Source – Annual Population Survey 2012
2: Figures have been rounded to the nearest thousand, and therefore estimates may not sum across rows or columns to equal totals

9.4 Selected activities performed in free time[1]: by age, 2012/13 England

Percentages

	16–24	25–44	45–64	65–74	75 and over	All aged 16 and over
Watch TV	84.1	88.6	91.6	92.5	93.9	89.8
Spend time with friends/family	88.6	87.7	86.8	87.0	84.8	87.2
Listen to music	88.3	80.7	76.7	70.5	67.5	78.2
Shopping	71.6	77.1	74.9	78.4	76.4	75.7
Eat out at restaurants	70.5	74.7	74.8	73.7	66.8	73.2
Read	53.7	68.4	73.7	76.3	74.6	69.3
Days out or visits to places	59.7	71.3	69.3	72.7	57.5	67.8
Internet/emailing	80.4	80.1	66.3	48.6	22.7	67.0
Sport/exercise	65.1	62.2	55.7	49.4	34.4	56.6
Go to cinema	73.3	63.3	49.7	36.1	25.0	54.0
Go to pubs/bars/clubs	58.2	56.4	51.5	39.0	26.3	50.4

Source: Taking Part: The National Survey of Culture, Leisure and Sport, Department for Culture, Media and Sport

1 Respondents were shown a list of activities and asked to pick the things they did in their free time.

9.5 Films

United Kingdom

Numbers and £ million

	Production of UK films[1,4]		Expenditure on feature films (Expressed in 2012 Pounds)			
	Films produced in the UK (numbers)	Production costs (current prices)	UK box office	Video[2] rental	Video[2] retail[3]	Video on Demand
	KWGD	KWGE	KWHU	KWHV	KWHW	
1998	83	389	547	437	453	33
1999	92	507	563	408	451	40
2000	80	578	583	444	601	50
2001	74	379	645	494	821	65
2002	119	551	755	494	1,175	63
2003	198	1,119	742	462	1,392	68
2004	173	875	770	476	1,557	73
2005	174	582	770	389	1,399	74
2006	139	826	762	327	1,302	67
2007	136	836	821	280	1,440	75
2008	143	721.6 [4]	850	265	1,454	101
2009	163	1123.0 [4]	944	263	1,311	127
2010	141	1292.8 [4]	988	253	1,267	145
2011	166	1274.0 [4]	1,040	246	1,165	162

Source:BFI RSU analysis, BVA, Official Charts Company, Attentional, IHS

1 Includes films with a production budget of £500,000 or more.

2 Video includes only rental and retail of physical discs, and does not include downloads.

3 In 2005 the British Video Association changed its methodology for producing market value which has necessitated a change to historical figures quoted.

4. Prior to 2010, the Research and Statistics Unit tracked all features shooting in the UK with a minimum budget of £500,000. However, evidence from a variety of sources (data on British film certification and the 2008 UK Film Council report Low and Micro-Budget Film Production in the UK) revealed a substantial number of films produced below this budget level. In order to broaden the evidence base, production tracking was extended to include feature films with budgets under £500,000 and data was collected from 2008 onwards.

9.6 Box office top 20 films released in the UK and Republic of Ireland, 2011

Rank	Title	Country of Origin	Box Office Gross (£millions)	Distributor
1	Harry Potter and the Deathly Hallows Part 2	UK/USA	73.09	Warner Bros
2	The King's Speech	UK	45.68	Momentum
3	The Inbetweeners Movie	UK	45.03	Entertainment
4	Pirates of the Caribbean: On Stranger Tides	UK/USA	32.92	Walt Disney
5	The Hangover Part II	USA	32.83	Warner Bros
6	The Twilight Saga: Breaking Dawn – Part 1	USA	30.77	eOne Films
7	Transformers: Dark of the Moon	USA	28.11	Paramount
8	Sherlock Holmes: A Game of Shadows*	UK/USA	26.23	Warner Bros
9	Bridesmaids	USA	23.02	Universal
10	Arthur Christmas*	UK/USA	20.84	Sony Pictures
11	Rise of the Planet of the Apes	USA	20.77	20th Century Fox
12	Johnny English Reborn*	UK/USA	20.63	Universal
13	Tangled	USA	20.47	Walt Disney
14	Fast & Furious 5	USA	18.52	Universal
15	Mission: Impossible – Ghost Protocol*	USA	17.99	Paramount
16	The Smurfs*	USA	17.25	Sony Pictures
17	Kung Fu Panda 2	USA	16.87	Paramount
18	The Adventures of Tintin: The Secret of the Unicorn*	USA/NZ	16.30	Paramount
19	Black Swan	USA	16.19	20th Century Fox
20	Gnomeo & Juliet	UK/USA	15.82	eOne Films

Source: Rentrak EDI, RSU analysis

Box office gross =cumulative total up to 12 February 2012

Films with an asterisk * were still on sale on 12 February 2012

9.7 Full year accommodation usage figures by visitors from overseas for 2004 - 2012

Data	Accommodation	Year								
		2004	2005	2006	2007	2008	2009	2010	2011	2012
Total Visits (000s)	All staying visits	25,677	28,038	30,654	30,871	30,142	28,208	28,300	29,197	29,282
	Bed & Breakfast	1,177	1,221	1,242	1,174	1,118	1,065	1,083	996	1,003
	Camping/mobile home	295	381	425	394	298	333	312	302	284
	Free guest with relatives or friends	10,174	11,144	12,081	11,944	12,056	11,165	10,570	10,646	10,811
	Holiday village/Centre	37	60	44	67	59	77	41	49	59
	Hostel/university/school	949	1,096	1,167	1,203	1,138	1,218	1,102	1,180	1,174
	Hotel/guest house	11,451	12,465	13,939	14,156	13,472	13,001	13,841	14,446	14,406
	Other	1,815	1,855	2,143	2,073	1,930	1,470	1,518	1,360	1,439
	Own home	413	412	466	446	418	385	358	392	364
	Paying guest family or friends house	610	616	595	567	650	461	465	577	537
	Rented house	740	806	832	836	868	934	882	958	1,002
Total Nights (000s)	All staying visits	227,406	249,181	273,417	251,522	245,775	229,391	227,960	234,363	230,149
	Bed & Breakfast	8,576	7,840	7,411	7,078	6,500	5,804	6,341	5,639	5,307
	Camping/mobile home	3,015	4,705	4,350	4,182	2,988	3,296	2,904	3,229	2,757
	Free guest with relatives or friends	113,736	121,487	133,209	121,272	122,898	111,947	107,642	108,703	107,575
	Holiday village/Centre	222	346	336	576	329	448	321	321	393
	Hostel/university/school	16,757	17,863	21,103	15,680	15,443	16,775	16,305	18,670	18,236
	Hotel/guest house	45,291	51,069	57,540	57,174	55,133	54,246	58,741	60,365	60,081
	Other	5,546	7,078	6,930	6,452	6,597	4,397	4,982	4,990	4,635
	Own home	4,638	5,507	7,895	5,169	5,110	4,524	5,068	5,625	4,895
	Paying guest family or friends house	8,807	8,716	9,692	8,240	7,961	5,423	5,148	6,574	7,433
	Rented house	20,818	24,570	24,950	25,695	22,817	22,362	20,482	20,237	18,838
Total Spend (£m)	All staying visits	12,798	14,011	15,759	15,699	16,058	16,354	16,649	17,666	18,245
	Bed & Breakfast	481	511	512	488	470	459	522	470	457
	Camping/mobile home	97	112	142	146	111	144	129	128	111
	Free guest with relatives or friends	3,822	3,972	4,498	4,207	4,501	4,425	4,254	4,371	4,515
	Holiday village/Centre	9	12	17	27	22	27	23	23	27
	Hostel/university/school	739	848	937	829	813	1,055	1,004	1,122	1,083
	Hotel/guest house	5,826	6,547	7,580	7,916	7,914	7,773	8,577	9,138	9,626
	Other	263	308	245	328	337	328	272	307	265
	Own home	354	357	412	402	429	531	354	377	505
	Paying guest family or friends house	345	393	439	385	379	364	340	426	475
	Rented house	861	951	977	971	1,084	1,245	1,172	1,305	1,181
Sample	All staying visits	37,321	39,977	40,410	36,432	31,854	41,952	41,948	38,144	37,666
	Bed & Breakfast	1,570	1,617	1,471	1,266	1,137	1,469	1,518	1,252	1,224
	Camping/mobile home	250	322	339	320	298	363	378	379	325
	Free guest with relatives or friends	15,167	16,363	16,256	14,386	12,831	16,976	16,003	14,233	14,207
	Holiday village/Centre	45	64	53	59	46	99	49	55	82
	Hostel/university/school	1,232	1,372	1,348	1,261	1,153	1,616	1,510	1,382	1,381
	Hotel/guest house	18,716	19,971	20,585	18,560	15,641	20,885	21,998	19,765	19,458
	Other	965	893	910	864	873	1,008	1,033	1,136	1,174
	Own home	730	744	740	645	522	656	637	545	594
	Paying guest family or friends house	562	599	527	487	507	529	538	637	548
	Rented house	1,101	1,161	1,164	1,034	973	1,457	1,397	1,291	1,334

International Passenger Survey, Office for National Statistics

9.8 International tourism[1]

Thousands and £ million

	Visits to the UK by overseas residents (thousands)	Spending in the UK by overseas residents		Visits overseas by UK residents (thousands)	Spending overseas by UK residents	
		Current prices	Constant 1995 prices		Current prices	Constant 1995 prices
	GMAA	GMAK	CQPR	GMAF	GMAM	CQPS
2000	25207	12806	11,102	56837	24250	27,281
2001	22832	11305	9,528	58281	25332	27,710
2002	24392	11737	9,641	59498	26962	29,311
2003	24874	11856	9,451	61334	28550	28,677
2004	27755	13047	10,146	64194	30285	30,444
2005	29970	14248	10,714	66441	32154	30,954
2006	32713	16002	11,641	69536	34411	30,904
2007	32778	15960	11,389	69450	35013	32,477
2008	31888	16323	11,276	69011	36838	28,657
2009	29889	16592	11,032	58614	31694	22,673
2010	29803	16899	10,644	55562	31820	22,116
2011	30798	17998	10,870	56836	31701	20,569
2012	31,084	18,640	10,842	56,538	32,450	22,024

1 See chapter text

Sources: International Passenger Survey
Office for National Statistics;
01633 456032

9.9 Holidays abroad:[1] by destination

Percentages

		1991	2001	2002	2003	2004	2005	2006	2007	2008	2009	2010	2011	2012
Spain	JTKC	21.3	27.9	28.5	29.8	28.4	27.2	27.8	26.5	26.6	26.5	25.9	25.8	27.0
France	JTKD	25.8	18.3	19	18.1	17.3	16.6	15.9	16.7	16.7	18.6	18.3	17.4	17.2
Greece	JTKF	7.6	7.8	7	6.6	5.7	5.1	5.0	5.0	4.2	4.4	4.8	4.8	4.5
USA	JTKE	6.8	6.3	5.4	5.5	6.1	6.0	5.1	5.2	5.4	5.4	4.9	5.2	5.2
Italy	JTKG	3.5	4.3	4.6	5	5	5.4	5.4	5.6	5.2	4.7	4.6	4.5	5.0
Irish Republic	JTKI	3	4.1	4.1	3.7	3.8	3.8	4.0	3.3	3.2	3.2	2.5	2.9	2.3
Portugal	JTKH	4.8	3.6	4	4	3.5	3.6	3.7	4.1	4.8	4.1	4.4	4.5	4.5
Cyprus	JTKL	2.4	3.5	3	2.7	2.6	2.8	2.4	2.4	2.4	2.1	2.1	2.2	2.0
Netherlands	JTKK	3.5	2.6	2.8	2.6	2.6	2.5	2.7	2.4	2.1	2.2	2.2	2.6	2.6
Turkey	JTKJ	0.7	2	2.2	2.3	2.3	2.7	2.7	2.8	3.7	3.5	4.7	3.7	3.3
Belgium	JTKM	2.1	2.1	2	2.2	1.8	1.9	2.0	2.2	2.0	1.9	1.7	2	2.5
Germany	JTKN	2.7	1.4	1.5	1.2	1.6	1.7	1.7	2.0	1.9	1.7	1.7	2.2	2.0
Austria	JTKP	2.4	1.1	1.4	1.1	1.4	1.3	1.2	1.2	1.4	1.4	1.5	1	1.1
Malta	JTKO	1.7	1	1			1.1	1.0	0.9	0.9	0.8	1.0	1	1.0
Other countries	JTKQ	11.8	13.8	13.6	14.2	16.8	18.4	20	19.6	19.5	19.5	19.6	20.2	13.3

1 See chapter text.

Sources: International Passenger Survey, Office for National Statistics;
01633 456032

9.10 All Tourism

	2007	2008	2009	2010	2011	2012	2013
TRIPS (millions)	119.854	114.442	122.537	115.711	126.635	126.019	122.905
BEDNIGHTS (millions)	382.055	367.635	387.448	361.398	387.329	388.24	373.607
EXPENDITURE (£ millions)	£20,234	£20,168	£20,971	£19,797	£22,666	£23,976	23,294
Av. Trip Length	3.19	3.21	3.16	3.12	3.06	3.08	3.04
Av. £ / Night	£53	£55	£54	£55	£59	£62	£62
Av. £ / Trip	£169	£176	£171	£171	£179	£190	£190

latest results are provisional and subject to minor changed in subsequent months due to trip-takers returning from late trips. Pre-2012 results are based on full year data so will not change

All expenditure figures are in historic prices

9.11 All Tourism in Great Britain

	TRIPS				NIGHTS				SPEND			
	GB	England	Scotland	Wales	GB	England	Scotland	Wales	GB	England	Scotland	Wales
		Millions				Millions				Millions		
All Tourism - 2011	126.64	104.28	13.36	9.70	387.3	306.8	45.6	34.9	£22,666	£17,914	£3,018	£1,734
All Tourism - 2012	126.02	104.46	12.75	9.60	388.2	310.2	43.3	34.7	£23,976	£19,497	£2,891	£1,588
PURPOSE												
Leisure	102.83	84.91	10.20	8.29	332.1	263.4	37.0	31.7	£18,846	£15,198	£2,297	£1,351
Holiday (total)	83.14	67.47	8.72	7.46	282.4	220.7	32.0	29.6	£16,765	£13,457	£2,063	£1,245
Holiday / pleasure / leisure	57.70	45.99	6.17	5.91	203.1	156.2	22.5	24.4	£13,763	£11,007	£1,684	£1,072
Visiting friends & relatives – mainly holiday	25.45	21.48	2.55	1.54	79.3	64.5	9.6	5.2	£3,001	£2,450	£379	£173
Visiting friends & relatives – mainly other	19.69	17.44	1.48	0.83	49.7	42.7	5.0	2.0	£2,082	£1,742	£234	£106
Visiting friends or relatives (total)	45.14	38.92	4.03	2.37	129.0	107.2	14.6	7.3	£5,083	£4,192	£613	£279
Business (total)	19.57	16.49	2.18	1.12	45.8	38.0	5.5	2.3	£4,603	£3,859	£541	£202
Business travel	18.94	15.90	2.15	1.10	44.5	36.8	5.4	2.2	£4,486	£3,750	£537	£199

The GB Tourist 2012

British residents made an estimated 126 million trips in Great Britain in 2012, representing 388 million bed nights and £24 billion in spending.

Holidays are the main purpose of trips taken, accounting for two thirds (66%) of trips taken and are even more important in terms of nights (73%) and spending (70%).

Visits to friends and relatives (VFR) for mainly holiday trips account for one in five trips and nights away (20%) but are less important in terms of spending (13%).

Business and work is the main purpose for around one in seven trips (16%) accounting for one in nine nights (12%). These are higher spending trips, accounting for a fifth (19%) of all tourism spending.

Friends' and relatives' homes (including owned second homes) are a widely used type of accommodation accounting for almost four in ten of all trips (37%). This reflects not only visits to friends and relatives as such, but also holidays spent staying with friends and relatives. With no real accommodation costs, trips staying at friends' and relatives' homes account for only a fifth (20%) of spending on all tourism trips.

Commercial accommodation is used on almost three-fifths of trips (59%), but these trips represent a much higher share of spending (77%). Commercial accommodation is mainly serviced (40% of trips) where trips tend to be shorter in duration (29% of nights) but higher spending (54%). Hotels and motels account for 34% of trips and 45% of spend; Guest houses and B&Bs account for 5% of trips and 8% of spend.

Self catering rented accommodation is used on a lower volume of trips (17%), but these trips are longer (26% of nights) and slightly above average in terms of spending (22%).

The car is the dominant form of transport with 73% of trips using a private car for the longest part of the journey from home to the destination.

Firm bookings are made before more than half of all trips (54%), but this figure reflects the high level of staying at friends and relatives' homes and using personal transport, where advance booking is less relevant. Firm bookings are made for 74% of all trips which involve staying in commercial accommodation.

Large cities/large towns (40%) are the major destinations of tourism trips, followed by small towns (24%), the seaside (19%) and countryside/villages (19%).

9.12 Gambling[1]

United Kingdom

£ million[2] and numbers

		1999 /00	2000 /01	2001 /02	2002 /03	2003 /04	2004 /05	2005 /06	2006 /07	2007 /08	2008 /09	2009 /10	2010 /11	2011 /12
Money staked on gambling														
National Lottery -Total[3]	C229	5,450	5,315	5,029	4,670	4,614	4,757	5,000	4,911	4,966	5,149	5,477	5824.7	6503.3
Lotto including on-line	C3PU	4,641	4,416	4,038	3,479	3,225	3,225	3,021	2,858	2,752	2,698	2,661	2,667	2475
Instants[4]	C3PV	612	590	606	592	641	729	804	943	1,109	1,221	1,340	1,436	1,726
Thunderball	C3PW	197	257	254	287	351	343	355	329	309	297	286	356	331
Lottery Extra[5]	C3PX	..	51	131	90	78	77	57	12	0	-	-	-	-
HotPicks	C3PY	..	..	..	222	244	219	228	222	210	211	210	206	200
Euromillions	C3Q2	..	..	..	..	15	104	427	464	476	618	881	1,056	1,666
Daily Play	C3Q3	..	..	..	..	45	59	54	49	50	50	49	46	4.3
Dream number[6]		..	..	..	..	..	..	..	59	59	54	50	39	-
Number operating in GB:														
Casinos	JE55	118	117	122	126	131	138	140	138	144	145	141	149	146
betting shops[7]	JE5B	..	..	..	..	..	..	..	..	8,800	8,862	8,822	9,067	9128

1 See chapter text.

2 Adjusted to real terms using the Retail Prices Index.

3 Includes Easy Play tickets which are not shown separately.

4 From 2003/04 includes Inter-active Instant Win Games

5 Discontinued July 2006

6 Started July 2006

7 The Gambling Commission started regulating the betting industry from 1 September 2007, the number of betting shops is an ABB estimate.

Sources: National Lottery Commission;

Gambling Commission: 0121 230 6666;

Department for Culture, Media and Sport: 020 7211 6451

	General Remote Data (£m) - turnover and gross gambling yield				
	2008/09	**2009/10**	**2010/11**	**2011/12**	**2012/13**
Betting Turnover	10,263.69	10,825.64	12,999.82	14,098.91	19,550.74
GGY	640.77	460.85	492.25	563.96	752.54
Betting Exchange Turnover	n/a	n/a	n/a	n/a	n/a
GGY	142.54	146.91	145.93	46.04	32.51
Bingo Turnover	3.94	20.44	26.24	28.17	33.78
GGY	0.47	1.51	2.19	2.03	2.46
Casino Turnover	950.07	685.49	340.57	512.25	861.39
GGY	33.08	22.95	12.69	20.23	41.66
Pool Betting Turnover	n/a	n/a	n/a	154.11	184.73
GGY	n/a	n/a	n/a	77.92	103.45

	Betting Data (£m) - turnover and gross gambling yield				
	2008/09	**2009/10**	**2010/11**	**2011/12**	**2012/13**
Cricket Turnover	n/a	n/a	n/a	320.77	333.44
GGY	n/a	n/a	n/a	6.16	9.23
Dogs Turnover	n/a	83.79	71.50	59.33	90.93
GGY	n/a	11.06	9.44	5.83	8.05
Financials Turnover	n/a	n/a	n/a	205.41	314.47
GGY	n/a	n/a	n/a	2.73	8.96
Football Turnover	n/a	4,130.06	5,402.97	5,396.85	7,770.87
GGY	n/a	172.19	271.19	281.23	377.22
Golf Turnover	n/a	n/a	n/a	52.25	60.18
GGY	n/a	n/a	n/a	2.50	1.17
Horses Turnover	n/a	2,402.45	2,441.95	1,956.56	1,902.73
GGY	n/a	201.29	105.97	92.21	112.83
Tennis Turnover	n/a	n/a	n/a	2,071.02	3,948.78
GGY	n/a	n/a	n/a	68.81	121.61
Other Turnover	n/a	4,209.34	5,083.39	4,190.83	5,314.05
GGY	n/a	223.22	251.59	228.44	249.42

9.12 Gambling[1]

Casino Data (£m) - turnover and gross gambling yield						
		2008/09	2009/10	2010/11	2011/12	2012/13
Card Game	Turnover	n/a	48.90	43.71	27.84	56.26
	GGY	n/a	1.47	1.59	1.10	2.55
Peer to Peer	Turnover	n/a	0.78	0.01	0.02	0.00
	GGY	n/a	0.78	0.01	0.01	0.00
Slots	Turnover	n/a	86.08	102.18	200.50	384.54
	GGY	n/a	5.11	6.24	12.44	24.68
Table Game	Turnover	n/a	508.21	144.16	238.00	404.72
	GGY	n/a	13.41	3.24	4.95	10.32
Other	Turnover	n/a	41.52	50.50	45.89	15.87
	GGY	n/a	2.18	1.61	1.73	4.10

Gambling Software Income (£m)						
		2008/09	2009/10	2010/11	2011/12	2012/13
Game	Sales	n/a	n/a	n/a	3.85	3.64
	Shared Income	n/a	n/a	n/a	14.87	15.18
	Total Revenue	n/a	n/a	n/a	18.73	18.81
Platform	Sales	n/a	n/a	n/a	65.89	62.91
	Shared Income	n/a	n/a	n/a	20.93	19.59
	Total Revenue	n/a	n/a	n/a	86.83	82.50
Other	Sales	n/a	n/a	n/a	1.72	0.65
	Shared Income	n/a	n/a	n/a	0.73	2.32
	Total Revenue	n/a	n/a	n/a	2.45	2.97

Number of employees					
	at 31 Mar 2009	at 31 Mar 2010	at 31 Mar 2011	at 31 Mar 2012	at 31 Mar 2013
Number of employees	n/a	7,496	6,438	5,832	4,732

Accounts					
	2008/09	2009/10	2010/11	2011/12	2012/13
Customer accounts	16.14	16.57	14.92	15.18	16.53
Active customer accounts	4.92	4.19	3.50	3.99	4.66
New player registrations	4.22	3.95	3.31	3.83	4.62
Funds held in customer accounts (£m)	281.02	256.76	265.95	147.13	185.09

Social responsibility data					
	2008/09	2009/10	2010/11	2011/12	2012/13
Self-exclusions	46,359	40,358	33,953	34,321	37,746
Known breaches of self-exclusion	7,198	7,480	2,533	2,317	2,031
Number of individuals who cancelled their self-exclusion after minimum period	1,540	1,525	1,581	1,508	1,984
Challenged when attempting to gamble but unable to prove age	159	109	74		
Challenged having gambled but unable to prove age				188	432

Notes on the data in this section:

1. All years above refer to the period April-March unless otherwise stated.
2. The betting exchange sector saw a large decrease from April 2009-March 2010 to April 2011-March 2012. This is a result of Betfair moving its' previously Commission regulated business offshore during quarter 1 of 2011/12.
3. In 2008/09, betting data was not collected on individual sports. It wasn't until 2011/12 when the Commission collected data onthe full list of sports in the table above. Between 2009/10 and 2010/11 data on cricket, financials, golf and tenniswere captured under under 'Other'. Similarly, casino data was not collected on individual games in 2008/09.
4. The decrease in employee numbers is in part due to the clarification of operators on the classification of staff directly associated with remote gambling activities.
5. Customers will often have accounts with more than one operator and therefore the datain the accounts table above relates to accounts rather than the individuals holding those accounts.
6. The number of people who have self excluded and the number of people who have cancelled their self exclusion may be lower than these figures as individuals may have self excluded from more than one site or operator and therefore been counted more than once. The number of breaches represents the number of separate incidents, rather than the number of individuals. The majority of the figures in the 'known breaches / attempted breaches of self exclusion' field are incidents where a customer has attempted to breach their self exclusion but has been successfully detected and prevented from gambling by the operator.
7. As of October 2011, the question 'challenged when attempting to gamble but unable to prove age' and the guidance issued in association with this question changed to 'challenged having gambled and unable to prove age'.
8. The Commission began collecting data on gambling software licence holders in 2011.
9. Shared Income includes income generated from gambling software provided to organisations for which royalties are received.
10. The above data only relates to operators licensed by the Commission.
11. In previous publications, headcount figures were averaged dependent upon the number of returns submitted within the reporting period. This publication however uses the figures detailed on the latest regulatory return submitted before the reporting date.

9.13 Most Popular Boy and Girl Baby Names in England and Wales [1], 2011

Rank	Boys Name	Rank	Boys Name	Rank	Girls Name	Rank	Girls Name
1	HARRY	51	TOBY	1	AMELIA	51	AMY
2	OLIVER	52	HARVEY	2	OLIVIA	52	AMBER
3	JACK	53	MICHAEL	3	LILY	53	GRACIE *
4	ALFIE	54	NATHAN	4	JESSICA	54	AMELIE *
5	CHARLIE	55	HARLEY *	5	EMILY	55	ROSIE
6	THOMAS	56	KAI	6	SOPHIE	56	LEAH
7	JACOB	57	DAVID	7	RUBY	57	KATIE
8	JAMES	58	AARON	8	GRACE	58	MAYA *
9	JOSHUA	59	ALEX	9	AVA *	59	ELEANOR
10	WILLIAM	60	CHARLES	10	ISABELLA	59	GEORGIA
11	ETHAN	61	AIDEN *	11	EVIE	61	EMILIA *
12	GEORGE	62	LEON	12	CHLOE	62	ELIZA *
13	RILEY *	63	MOHAMMAD	13	MIA	63	FAITH *
14	DANIEL	64	LUCA *	14	POPPY	63	BETHANY
15	SAMUEL	65	TOMMY *	15	ISLA *	65	EVELYN *
16	NOAH *	66	FINLAY *	16	ELLA	66	ISABEL
17	OSCAR	67	JENSON *	17	ISABELLE	67	ANNA
18	JOSEPH	68	ARTHUR *	18	SOPHIA	68	HOLLIE
19	MOHAMMED	69	LOUIS	19	FREYA	69	BELLA *
19	MAX	70	RHYS	20	DAISY	70	PAIGE
21	DYLAN	71	OWEN	21	CHARLOTTE	71	HARRIET
22	MUHAMMAD	72	REUBEN *	22	MAISIE	72	ESME *
23	ALEXANDER	73	OLLIE *	23	LUCY	73	ZARA *
24	ARCHIE	74	LOUIE *	24	PHOEBE	74	LEXIE *
25	BENJAMIN	74	GABRIEL *	25	SCARLETT *	75	WILLOW *
26	LUCAS	76	BOBBY *	26	HOLLY	76	ROSE *
27	LEO *	77	CAMERON	27	LILLY *	77	MADISON
28	HENRY	78	DEXTER *	28	ELLIE	78	JULIA *
29	JAKE	79	BLAKE *	29	MEGAN	79	ANNABELLE *
30	LOGAN *	80	STANLEY *	30	LAYLA *	80	ISOBEL
31	TYLER	81	KIAN	31	LOLA *	81	NIAMH
32	JAYDEN *	82	EVAN *	32	IMOGEN	82	MADDISON *
33	ISAAC	83	JUDE *	33	EVA *	83	MARTHA *
34	FINLEY *	84	FRANKIE *	34	SUMMER *	84	SKYE *
35	MASON	85	ELLIOT	35	MILLIE	85	LAUREN
36	RYAN	86	HAYDEN *	36	SIENNA *	86	CAITLIN
37	HARRISON	87	ASHTON *	37	ALICE	87	ELSIE *
38	ADAM	88	JOEL	38	ABIGAIL	88	KEIRA *
39	LEWIS	89	CALEB *	39	ERIN	89	REBECCA
40	EDWARD	90	BAILEY	40	LACEY *	90	SARAH
41	LUKE	91	ELIJAH *	41	HANNAH	91	HEIDI *
42	FREDDIE *	92	TAYLOR	42	JASMINE	92	ZOE
43	MATTHEW	93	ROBERT	43	FLORENCE *	93	MARIA *
44	LIAM	94	KAYDEN *	44	ELIZABETH	93	MARYAM *
45	ZACHARY	95	KYLE	45	LEXI *	95	AISHA *
46	CALLUM	96	FREDERICK *	46	MOLLY	96	TIA
47	SEBASTIAN *	97	BEN	47	SOFIA *	97	NICOLE
48	CONNOR	98	REECE	48	MATILDA *	98	KAYLA *
49	JAMIE	99	JACKSON *	49	EMMA	99	FRANCESCA
50	THEO *	100	JOHN	50	BROOKE	100	LYDIA

Notes:

These rankings have been produced using the exact spelling of the name given at birth registration. Similar names with different spellings have been counted separately.

Births where the name was not stated have been excluded from these figures. Of the 352,939 baby girls in the 2011 dataset, 8 were excluded for this reason.

* denotes new entry to top 100

Source: Office for National Statistics

9.14a Libraries overview
Great Britain

	2005/06	2006/07	2007/08	2008/09	2009/10	2010/11	Percentages 2011/12
	%	% (1)	% (1)	% (1)	% (1)	% (1)	% (1)
Has visited a public library in the last year [2]	48.2	46.1	45.0	41.1	39.4	**39.7**	**38.8**
Frequency of attendance [2]							
1-2 times a year	10.4	10.3	10.5	8.9	7.9	**8.9**	**8.4**
3-4 times a year	13.4	12.9	13.0	11.4	10.9	**11.6**	**12.2**
At least once a month	16.4	15.7	14.9	13.3	12.8	**13.4**	**12.4**
At least once a week	7.9	7.2	6.7	5.9	5.4	**5.8**	**5.7**
Has not visited	51.8	53.9	55.0	60.5	63.0	**60.3**	**61.2**

Notes

(1) Figures in bold indicate a significant change from 2005/06.

(2) Figures exclude people who have visited a library for the purposes of paid work or academic study

Source: DCMS Taking Part Survey 2012/13 Q1

https://www.gov.uk/government/statistics/taking-part-2012-13-quarter-1-statistical-release

9.14b Proportion who have visited a public library in the last year - area-level breakdown

	2005/06	2006/07	2007/08	2008/09	2009/10	2010/11	Percentages 2011/12
	%	% (1)	% (1)	% (1)	% (1)	% (1)	% (1)
Index of deprivation							
1- Most deprived	N/A	N/A	N/A	N/A	37.6	39.8	37.3
2	N/A	N/A	N/A	N/A	32.8	38.2	37.0
3	N/A	N/A	N/A	N/A	38.3	39.2	39.2
4	N/A	N/A	N/A	N/A	36.1	41.2	39.1
5	N/A	N/A	N/A	N/A	42.1	38.4	40.6
6	N/A	N/A	N/A	N/A	38.7	36.4	38.3
7	N/A	N/A	N/A	N/A	39.9	40.7	40.4
8	N/A	N/A	N/A	N/A	34.6	40.1	33.8
9	N/A	N/A	N/A	N/A	45.4	**38.7**	42.2
10- Least deprived	N/A	N/A	N/A	N/A	46.3	43.5	39.8
Region							
North East	44.9	43.9	40.1	37.1	42.9	**38.8**	**36.3**
North West	46.9	46.2	45.0	42.1	41.4	**43.0**	**37.5**
Yorkshire and The Humber	42.1	40.5	36.6	33.7	30.0	**33.6**	**33.4**
East Midlands	44.7	42.9	44.3	38.8	42.7	**35.8**	**37.7**
West Midlands	47.6	47.1	43.5	39.3	38.0	**36.6**	**40.1**
East of England	50.5	47.5	45.5	42.9	39.5	**42.4**	**41.2**
London	52.6	49.2	49.5	43.6	38.1	**43.1**	**43.1**
South East	51.0	48.3	48.5	44.5	43.5	**40.5**	**37.4**
South West	47.9	45.1	45.5	41.8	38.8	**38.8**	**40.0**
Urban	48.5	46.5	45.6	41.6	40.1	**40.0**	**39.2**
Rural	47.1	44.7	42.8	38.9	36.5	**38.2**	**36.9**
ACORN							
Wealthy Achievers	50.9	48.9	47.4	42.1	39.9	**40.7**	**40.6**
Urban Prosperity	57.3	51.0	52.0	41.8	42.6	**43.9**	**41.9**
Comfortably Off	48.5	46.4	44.2	41.9	41.9	**38.2**	**37.9**
Moderate Means	45.3	45.0	42.4	41.5	37.7	**41.3**	**38.9**
Hard-pressed	40.9	39.8	41.0	37.5	33.9	**36.9**	**35.8**
Unclassified	61.7	50.0	62.7	46.9	*	*	*
All	48.2	46.1	45.0	41.1	39.4	**39.7**	**38.8**

Notes

(1) Figures in bold indicate a significant change from 2005/06.

(2) Index of deprivation data not available pre-2009/10. For Index of Deprivation data, figures in bold indicate a significant change from 2009/10.

(3) *= N too small to report

Source: DCMS Taking Part Survey 2012/13 Q1

https://www.gov.uk/government/statistics/taking-part-2012-13-quarter-1-statistical-release

9.14c Proportion who have visited a public library in the last year - demographic breakdown

percentages

	2005/06	2006/07	2007/08	2008/09	2009/10	2010/11	2011/12
		%	%	%	%	%	%
	%	(1)	(1)	(1)	(1)	(1)	(1)
Age							
16-24	51.0	47.1	45.4	42.8	40.0	**34.4**	**34.5**
25-44	51.2	50.2	49.5	43.7	40.9	**44.6**	**44.0**
45-64	45.7	44.3	42.1	38.8	39.5	**36.0**	**36.1**
65-74	46.7	44.4	44.7	42.0	39.3	44.3	**35.8**
75+	42.3	37.1	37.6	35.0	32.9	**37.1**	38.9
Sex							
Male	43.8	42.1	40.2	35.3	35.5	**34.3**	**33.6**
Female	52.3	49.9	49.6	46.5	43.2	**44.8**	**43.8**
NS-SEC							
Upper socio-economic group	52.1	50.2	48.0	43.3	43.1	**43.9**	**42.3**
Lower socio-economic group	40.1	38.1	38.7	35.1	32.3	**33.6**	**33.5**
Employment status							
Not working	49.7	46.7	46.6	44.0	42.4	**42.9**	**41.7**
Working	47.2	45.7	44.0	39.0	37.4	**37.5**	**36.8**
Tenure							
Owners	48.7	46.4	44.8	41.1	39.8	**40.1**	**39.2**
Social rented sector	41.9	40.5	42.2	39.0	36.8	**37.0**	**37.2**
Private rented sector	53.3	51.0	49.2	43.0	39.8	**40.2**	**38.7**
Ethnicity							
White	47.2	44.9	43.6	40.1	37.9	**38.3**	**37.8**
Black or ethnic minority	57.5	56.7	57.9	50.2	50.6	**50.0**	**46.5**
Religion							
No religion	46.8	45.5	45.3	40.1	35.2	**37.8**	**36.8**
Christian	47.3	44.8	43.7	40.3	39.7	**39.2**	**38.8**
Other religion	58.2	58.9	57.1	52.7	53.0	**48.2**	**44.4**
Long-standing illness or disability							
No	50.0	48.0	46.0	42.1	40.4	**40.1**	**39.2**
Yes	43.8	41.5	42.4	38.4	36.8	**38.5**	**37.9**
All	48.2	46.1	45.0	41.1	39.4	**39.7**	**38.8**

Notes

(1) Figures in bold indicate a significant change from 2005/06.

Source: DCMS Taking Part Survey 2012/13 Q1

https://www.gov.uk/government/statistics/taking-part-2012-13-quarter-1-statistical-release

9.15 Museums and galleries overview (adults)

Great Britain

Percentages

	2006 /07	2007 /08	2008 /09	2009 /10	2010 /11	2011 /12
Has visited a museum, gallery in the last year	41.5	**43.5**	44.5	**46.0**	**46.3**	48.9
Frequency of attendance						
At least once a week	**0.4**	0.3	0.4	0.4	**0.5**	0.5
Less often than once a week but at least once a month	2.8	3.2	2.9	3.6	**3.6**	3.4
Less often than once a month but at least 3-4 times a year	12.9	13.8	13.9	14.1	**14.7**	15.3
1-2 times a year	25.3	26.3	26.1	**27.9**	**27.4**	29.6
Never	58.5	**56.5**	56.7	54.0	**53.7**	51.1

Source DCMS

(1) Figures in bold indicate a significant change from 2005/06.

(2) Figures exclude people who have for the purposes of paid work or academic study

9.16 Participation in voluntary activities, 2003 to 2012/13
England

Percentages

	At least once a month						
	2003/04	2005/06	2007/08[4]	2008/09[4]	2009/10[4]	2010/11[4]	2012/13[5]
Informal volunteering[1]	37	37	35	35	29	29	36
Formal volunteering[2]	28	29	27	26	25	25	29
Any volunteering[3]	**50**	**50**	**48**	**47**	**42**	**41**	**49**
	At least once in last year						
Informal volunteering	63	68	64	62	54	55	62
Formal volunteering	42	44	43	41	40	39	44
Any volunteering	**73**	**76**	**73**	**71**	**66**	**65**	**72**

1 Informal volunteering: Giving unpaid help as an individual to people who are not relatives.

2 Formal volunteering: Giving unpaid help through groups, clubs or organisations to benefit other people or

3 Participated in either formal or informal volunteering.

4. Source: Citizenship Survey: 2010-11 (April 2010-March 2011), England, Department for Communities and Local Government, http://www.communities.gov.uk/documents/statistics/pdf/1992885.pdf

5. Source: Community Life Survey 2012 to 2013

9.17 UK residents' visits to friends and relatives[1] abroad:by destination

United Kingdom

Percentages[2]

	1999	2003	2006	2009	2011	2012
Irish Republic	19	16	15	14	13	10
France	12	13	11	11	10	10
Poland	1	1	6	9	9	9
Spain	6	9	9	8	7	8
Germany	7	6	6	5	5	5
USA	9	7	6	5	5	4
India	3	3	3	4	4	4
Italy	3	4	4	4	3	4
Netherlands	5	4	3	3	3	3
Pakistan	2	3	3	3	3	3
Other countries	34	34	35	36	39	39
All destinations (=100%) (millions)	6.6	8.5	12.0	11.6	11.6	11.8

Source: International Passenger Survey, Office for National Statistics

1 As a proportion of all visits to friends and relatives taken abroad by residents of the UK. Excludes business trips and other miscellaneous visits.

2 Percentages may not add up to 100 per cent due to rounding.

9.18: The Internet

Internet activities by age group and sex, 2012 %

	16-24	25-34	35-44	45-54	55-64	65+	Men	Women	All
Sending/receiving emails	83	87	87	77	69	41	74	72	73
Finding information about goods and services	71	83	81	74	66	34	69	65	67
Buying goods or services over the Internet	79	87	84	72	61	32	68	67	67
Social networking, for example Facebook or Twitter	87	78	62	40	24	10	48	48	48
Internet banking	43	69	65	52	43	18	51	44	47
Reading or downloading online news, newspapers or news magazines	58	66	59	49	38	20	51	44	47
Using services related to travel or travel related accommodation	41	57	55	51	42	22	47	41	44
Playing or downloading games, images, films, or music	67	60	46	36	27	12	43	37	40
Listening to web radio or watching web television	56	55	48	37	27	12	44	32	38
Uploading self-created content for example text, photos, music, videos, etc	60	50	45	32	22	11	36	35	35
Posting messages to chat sites, blogs, forums, or instant messaging	60	56	41	28	18	7	35	32	33
Telephoning or making video calls over the Internet	45	49	40	31	23	11	33	31	32
Selling goods or services, for example eBay	27	36	31	22	15	5	24	20	22
Making a medical appointment	7	15	12	12	11	4	11	9	10
Creating websites or blogs	16	11	7	5	1	1	7	6	6

Base: Adults (aged 16+) in Great Britain   Source: Office for National Statistics

Purchases made over the Internet, in the last 12 months, by age group and sex, 2012 %

	16-24	25-34	35-44	45-54	55-64	65+	Men	Women	All
Clothes, sports goods	52	56	59	46	31	13	39	44	42
Household goods	28	54	56	39	31	16	38	36	37
Other travel arrangements	26	46	45	38	32	15	36	31	33
Holiday accommodation	18	41	42	39	35	16	34	29	32
Tickets for events	36	45	44	38	27	9	33	31	32
Books, magazines, newspapers	22	34	38	34	30	13	26	30	28
Music	33	32	34	24	16	6	26	21	23
Films	24	27	28	17	12	3	20	16	18
Electronic equipment	24	28	22	20	13	4	23	13	18
Share purchases, insurance policies etc	14	25	27	22	16	5	21	15	18
Food or groceries	10	30	29	20	11	5	15	20	17
Telecommunication services	12	23	21	17	11	6	20	10	15
Video games software and upgrades	26	24	20	11	3	1	20	8	14
Other computer software and upgrades	20	20	19	14	11	5	19	10	14
Computer hardware	13	13	13	10	10	2	14	6	10
E-learning material	6	10	10	6	3	1	6	6	6
Medicine	2	4	5	8	7	3	4	5	5

Adults (aged 16+) in Great Britain   Source: Office for National Statistics

Households with Internet access, 2008 to 2012 %

Year	
2008	65
2009	70
2010	73
2011	77
2012	80

All GB households   Source: Office for National Statistics

9.19 Radio Listening

	Adult (15+) Population '000	Weekly Reach '000's	Weekly Reach %	Average Hours Per Head	Average Hours Per Listener	Total Hours ('000's)	Share of Listening %
Quarterly Summary of Radio Listening - Survey Period ending 23rd June 2013							
ALL RADIO	**53205**	**48319**	**91%**	**19.3**	**21.3**	**1028389**	**100.0%**
ALL BBC	**53205**	**35880**	**67%**	**10.4**	**15.5**	**554730**	**53.90%**
BBC Local/Regional	53205	9536	18%	1.6	8.9	84963	8.30%
ALL COMMERCIAL	53205	35064	66%	8.4	12.8	449411	43.70%
All National Commercial[1]	53205	17702	33%	2.6	7.7	137005	13.30%
All Local Commercial (National TSA)	53205	27866	52%	5.9	11.2	213406	30.40%
All BBC Network Radio[1]	53205	32635	61%	8.8	14.4	469767	45.70%
BBC Radio 1	53205	11018	21%	1.3	6.4	70440	6.80%
BBC Radio 2	53205	15443	29%	3.3	11.5	176874	17.20%
BBC Radio 3	53205	1995	4%	0.2	6	11911	1.20%
BBC Radio 4	53205	10978	21%	2.3	11.4	124714	12.10%
BBC Radio 4 (including 4 Extra)	53205	11266	21%	2.5	11.9	134167	13.00%
BBC Radio 4 Extra	53205	1565	3%	0.2	6	9453	0.90%
BBC Radio FIVE LIVE	53205	6040	11%	0.8	7	42391	4.10%
BBC Radio FIVE LIVE (inc SPORTS EXTRA)	53205	6324	12%	0.9	7.3	45916	4.50%
FIVE LIVE SPORTS EXTRA	53205	947	2%	0.1	3.7	3525	0.30%
BBC 6 Music	53205	1792	3%	0.3	8.9	15923	1.50%
1Xtra from the BBC	53205	1114	2%	0.1	4.8	5302	0.50%
BBC Asian Network UK	53205	587	1%	0.1	5.5	3228	0.3%
BBC World Service	53205	1355	3%	0.1	4.4	6006	0.60%

1. Audiences in local analogue areas excluded from 'All BBC Network Radio' and 'All National Commercial' totals.

STATION SUMMARY ANALYSIS - RAJAR REPORTING PERIOD 2013 Q1
(Report 1690) All Radio, Total Sample
Quarterly Weighted Data

		Age Group of Respondent						
	Total	10-14	15-24	25-34	35-44	45-54	55-64	65+
Unw. Sample	25387	689	2607	2943	3772	4266	4455	6655
Est. Pop'n	55805	3453	8181	8585	8494	8905	7286	10902
ALL RADIO								
Weekly Reach 000s	50395	3111	6952	7578	7855	8395	6776	9729
Weekly Reach %	90.3	90.1	85	88.3	92.5	94.3	93	89.2
Total Hours	1065377	31081	109523	139473	159980	198005	172061	255253
Average Hours Per Head	19.09	9	13.39	16.25	18.83	22.24	23.62	23.41
Average Hours Per Listener	21.14	9.99	15.75	18.41	20.37	23.59	25.39	26.24

Environment

Chapter 10

Environment

Air emissions (Table 10.2 to 10.8)

Emissions of air pollutants arise from a wide variety of sources. The National Atmospheric Emissions Inventory (NAEI) is prepared annually for the Government and the devolved administrations by AEA Energy and Environment, with the work being co-ordinated by the Department of Energy and Climate Change (DECC). Information is available for a range of point sources including the most significant polluters. However, a different approach has to be taken for diffuse sources such as transport and domestic emissions, where this type of information is not available. Estimates for these are derived from statistical information and from research on emission factors for stationary and mobile sources. Although for any given year considerable uncertainties surround the emission estimates for each pollutant, trends over time are likely to be more reliable.

UK national emission estimates are updated annually and any developments in methodology are applied retrospectively to earlier years. Adjustments in the methodology are made to accommodate new technical information and to improve international comparability.

Three different classification systems are used in the tables presented here; a National Accounts basis (Table 10.2), the format required by the Inter-governmental Panel on Climate Change (IPCC) (Table 10.3) and the National Communications (NC) categories (Tables 10.5-10.7).

The NC source categories are detailed below together with details of the main sources of these emissions:

Energy supply total: Power stations, refineries, manufacture of solid fuels and other energy industries, solid fuel transformation, exploration, production and transport of oils, offshore oil and gas – venting and flaring, power stations - FGD, coal mining and handling, and exploration, production and transport of gas.

Business total: Iron and steel – combustion, other industrial combustion, miscellaneous industrial and commercial combustion, energy recovery from waste fuels, refrigeration and air conditioning, foams, fire fighting, solvents, one components foams, and electronics, electrical insulation and sporting goods.

Transport total: Civil aviation (domestic, landing and take off, and cruise), passenger cars, light duty vehicles, buses, HGVs, mopeds & motorcycles, LPG emissions (all vehicles), other road vehicle engines, railways, railways – stationary combustion, national navigation, fishing vessels, military aircraft and shipping, and aircraft – support vehicles.

Residential total: Residential combustion, use of non aerosol consumer products, accidental vehicle fires, and aerosols and metered dose inhalers.

Agriculture total: Stationary and mobile combustion, breakdown of pesticides, enteric fermentation (cattle, sheep, goats, horses, pigs, and deer), wastes (cattle, sheep, goats, horses, pigs, poultry, and deer), manure liquid systems, manure solid storage and dry lot, other manure management, direct soil emission, and field burning of agricultural wastes.

Industrial process total: Sinter production, cement production, lime production, limestone and dolomite use, soda ash production and use, fletton bricks, ammonia production, iron and steel, nitric acid production, adipic acid production, other – chemical industry, halocarbon production, and magnesiun cover gas.

Land-use change: Forest land remaining forest land, forest land biomass burning, land converted to forest land, direct N2O emissions from N fertilisation of forest land, cropland liming, cropland remaining cropland, cropland biomass burning, land converted to cropland, N2O emissions from disturbance associated with land-use conversion to cropland, grassland biomass burning, grassland liming, grassland remaining grassland, land converted to grassland, wetlands remaining wetland, Non-CO2 emissions from drainage of soils and wetlands, settlements biomass burning, land converted to settlements, and harvested wood.

Waste management total: Landfill, waste-water handling, and waste incineration.

Atmospheric emissions on a National Accounts basis (Table 10.2)

The air and energy accounts are produced for ONS by AEA Technology plc based on data compiled for the National Atmospheric Emissions Inventory (NAEI)7 and UK Greenhouse Gas Inventory (GHGI)8. Every year a programme of development work is undertaken to optimise the methodologies employed in compiling the accounts. Assessments in previous years have indicated that a number of splits used to apportion road transport source data to more than one industry should be reviewed. The results of this review have been implemented in the 2011 UK Environmental Accounts for reference period 2009 and years back to 1990.

The industry breakdown used in the accounts has moved to using the Standard Industrial Classification 2007 (SIC 2007). Historically, the accounts were based on Environmental Accounts codes (EAcodes) based on SIC 2003. This change will allow the accounts which are broken down by industry to be more readily compared with other economic statistics. A methodology article that outlines this change in more detail was published on the ONS website in May 2011: http//www.statistics.gov.uk/cci/article.asp?id=2694. As a result while names given to the breakdown maybe similar they are not necessarily the same.

The National Accounts figures in Table 10.2 differ from those on an IPCC basis, in that they include estimated emissions from fuels purchased by UK resident households and companies either at home or abroad (including emissions from UK international shipping and aircraft operators), and exclude emissions in the UK resulting from the activities of non-residents. This allows for a more consistent comparison with key National Accounts indicators such as Gross Domestic Product (GDP).

Greenhouse gases include carbon dioxide, methane, nitrous oxide, hydro-fluorocarbons, perfluorocarbons and sulphur hexafluoride which are expressed in thousand tonnes of carbon dioxide equivalent.

Acid rain precursors include sulphur dioxide, nitrogen oxides and ammonia which are expressed as thousand tonnes of sulphur dioxide equivalent.

Estimated total emissions of greenhouse gases on an IPCC basis (Table 10.3)

The IPCC classification is used to report greenhouse gas emissions under the UN Framework Convention on Climate Change (UNFCCC) and includes Land Use Change and all emissions from Domestic aviation and shipping, but excludes International aviation and shipping bunkers. Estimates of the relative contribution to global warming of the main greenhouse gases, or classes of gases, are presented weighted by their global warming potential.

Greenhouse gas emissions bridging table (Table 10.4)
National Accounts measure to UNFCCC measure

The air and energy accounts are produced for ONS by AEA Technology plc based on data compiled for the National Atmospheric Emissions Inventory (NAEI)7 and UK Greenhouse Gas Inventory (GHGI)8. Every year a programme of development work is undertaken to optimise the methodologies employed in compiling the accounts. Assessments in previous years have indicated that a number of splits used to apportion road transport source data to more than one industry should be reviewed. The results of this review have been implemented in the 2011 UK Environmental Accounts for reference period 2009 and years back to 1990.

There are a number of formats for the reporting and recording of atmospheric emissions data, including those used by the Department of Energy and Climate Change (DECC) for reporting greenhouse gases under UNFCCC and the Kyoto Protocol, and for reporting air pollutant emissions to the UN Economic Commission for Europe (UNECE), which differ from the National Accounts consistent measure published by the Office for National Statistics (ONS).
Differences between the National Accounts measure and those for reporting under UNFCCC and the Kyoto Protocol, following the guidance of the IPCC, are shown in Table 10.4.

Emissions of carbon dioxide (Table 10.5)

Carbon dioxide is the main man-made contributor to global warming. The UK contributes about 2 per cent to global man-made emissions which, according to the IPCC, was estimated to be 38 billion tonnes of carbon dioxide in 2004. Carbon dioxide emissions accounted for about 84 per cent of the UK's man-made greenhouse gas emissions in 2009.

Emissions of methane (Table 10.6)

Weighted by global warming potential, methane accounted for about 8 per cent of the UK's greenhouse gas emissions in 2009. Methane emissions, excluding those from natural sources, were 61 per cent below 1990 levels. In 2009, the main sources of methane emissions were agriculture (41 per cent of the total) and landfill sites (37 per cent). Emissions from landfill have reduced by 72 per cent and emissions from agriculture by 19 per cent since 1990.

Emissions of nitrous oxide (Table 10.7)

Weighted by global warming potential, nitrous oxide emissions accounted for about 6 per cent of the UK's man-made greenhouse gas emissions in 2009. Nitrous oxide emissions fell by 49 per cent between 1990 and 2009. The largest reductions were in emissions from adipic acid production between 1998 and 1999 (down 95 per cent). This leaves agriculture as the main source in 2009, accounting for 79 per cent of emissions, mainly from agricultural soils.

Annual rainfall (Table 10.9)

Regional rainfall is derived by the Met Office's National Climate Information Centre for the National Hydrological Monitoring Programme at the Centre for Ecology and Hydrology. These monthly area rainfalls are based initially on a subset of rain gauges (circa 350) but are updated after four to five months with figures using the majority of the UK's rain gauge network.
The regions of England shown in this table correspond to the original nine English regions of the National Rivers Authority (NRA). The NRA became part of the Environment Agency on its creation in April 1996. The figures in this table relate to the country of Wales, not the Environment Agency Welsh Region.

UK weather summary (Table 10.10)

For 2010, initial averages use data available from about 200 observing sites available on 1 January 2011. They represent an initial assessment of the weather that was experienced across the UK during 2010 and how it compares with the 1961 to 1990 average.
For all other years, final averages use quality controlled data from the UK climate network of observing stations. They show the Met Office's best assessment of the weather that was experienced across the UK during the years and how it compares with the 1961 to 1990 average. The columns headed 'Anom' (anomaly) show the difference from, or percentage of, the 1961 to 1990 long-term average.

Biological and chemical quality of rivers and canals (Table 10.11)

The chemical quality of river and canal waters is monitored in a series of separate national surveys in England, Wales and Northern Ireland. The General Quality Assessment Headline Indicator (GQAHI) and General Quality Assessment (GQA) schemes are used in surveys to provide a rigorous and objective method for assessing the basic chemical quality of rivers and canals. In England the GQAHI survey is based on two determinants: dissolved oxygen and ammoniacal nitrogen. In previous years this assessment included biochemical oxygen demand however in 2007 this was removed from the assessment and the historic data recalculated. In Wales the GQA assessment is based on three determinants: dissolved oxygen, biochemical oxygen demand and ammoniacal nitrogen. The GQA grades river stretches into six categories (A-F) of chemical quality, and these in turn have been grouped into four broader groups: good (classes A and B), fair (C and D), poor (E) and bad (F)

To provide a more comprehensive picture of the health of rivers and canals, biological testing has also been carried out. The biological grading is based on the monitoring of tiny animals (invertebrates) which live in or on the bed of the river. Research has shown that there is a relationship between species composition and water quality. Using a procedure known as the River Invertebrate Prediction and Classification System, species groups recorded at a site were compared with those which would be expected to be present in the absence of pollution, allowing for the different environmental characteristics in different parts of the country. Two different summary statistics (known as ecological quality indices) were calculated and then the biological quality was assigned to one of six bands based on a combination of these two statistics.

From 2008, Northern Ireland uses a different classification system than that which was previously used. A unit of area known as a water body is now the classification unit rather than discrete stretches of individual rivers.

Water Framework Directive (WFD) classifications are based on chemical, physical and ecological parameters (referred to as quality elements). The indicators recorded here are just some of the WFD quality elements that are monitored in river water bodies.

It should be noted that the monitoring network only covers selected stretches which the Environment Agency are required to monitor. In England and Wales 32,000 km of river network are monitored out of an estimated total river length of 150,000 km. No canals are classified in Northern Ireland.

Biological and chemical quality of rivers and canals Scotland (Table 10.12)

Scotland's previous classification schemes focused on describing the pollution levels of the water environment. As required by the Water Framework Directive, the new classification scheme for surface waters now assesses:

• the quality of the aquatic ecosystems within rivers, lochs, estuaries and coastal waters

• the extent to which they have been adversely affected by the full range of pressures on the water environment – from water resources and physical habitat to pollution and invasive non-native species

This new scheme which started in 2007 assesses the condition of each river, loch, estuary and coastal water and assigns it a 'status' from of high, good, moderate, poor to bad.

The results on the current condition of our rivers, lochs, estuaries, coasts and ground waters are based primarily on monitoring data collected during 2007. However, as the new monitoring programmes have only been in place for one year, the Scottish Environment Protection Agency (SEPA) has supplemented the limited new monitoring data with data from previous assessments (where relevant and available). This is to ensure the classification results reflect the best current understanding of the status of the water environment. As more monitoring data are collected, SEPA expects its confidence in classification to progressively increase over the next five years.

Prior to 2007, river and canal water quality was based on the Scottish River Classification Scheme of 20 June 1997, which combined chemical, biological, nutrient and aesthetic quality using the following classes: excellent (A1), good (A2), fair (B), poor (C) and seriously polluted (D). The figures in the table are rounded to the nearest 10 km and may not sum to totals.

During 2000 a new digitised river network (DRN) was developed, based on 1:50,000 ordnance survey data digitised by the Institute of Hydrology. The DRN ensures consistency between all SEPA areas and includes the Scottish Islands which were not previously covered. Data based on this network were published for the first time in the 2004 edition of Annual Abstract of Statistics and are not consistent with data published previously. The DRN includes:

• All mainland and island rivers with a catchment area of 10 km2 or more. This is known as the 'baseline network'

• Mainland and island stream stretches with a catchment of less than 10 km2 which are classified as fair, poor or seriously polluted and have been monitored. These are added to the baseline network to give a 'classification network'

It is intended that future emphasis will be placed on the baseline network, which will be the reportable network for the purposes of the European Commission Water Framework Directive. Efforts to improve the quality of the downgraded smaller streams will continue, but once this has been sustainably achieved, their monitoring may be reduced. Many of these streams are the subject of current attention because of their influence on the quality of larger classification Network Rivers.

Using the DRN scheme, data for every routine sampling point are automatically applied to an identified river stretch of predetermined length. The loss in total river length in moving to the DRN (that is despite the first time inclusion of Island Rivers) arises mainly from the exclusion from classification of thousands of small remote headwater streams which were never monitored, but assumed to be of excellent quality. The smaller reduction in length of downgraded waters arises mainly from using 1:50,000 maps for the DRN; in the former system lengths were hand measured from 1:10,000 maps, so more minor channel bends were included.

Reservoir stocks in England and Wales (Table 10.13)
Data are collected for a network of major reservoirs (or reservoir groups) in England and Wales for the National Hydrological Monitoring Programme at the Centre for Ecology and Hydrology. Figures of usable capacity are supplied by the Water PLCs and the Environment Agency at the start of each month and are aggregated to provide an index of the total reservoir stocks for England and Wales.

Water industry expenditure (Table 10.14)
The data is taken from the annual regulatory accounts (and the June return submission to Ofwat) of water and sewerage companies and water companies of England and Wales.

Operating expenditure includes: employment costs, power, Environment Agency charges, bulk supply imports, general overheads, customer services, scientific services, local authority rates, local authority sewerage agencies, materials and consumables, charge for bad and doubtful debts, current cost depreciation and the infrastructure renewals charge.

Capital expenditure figures represent all capital additions (both maintenance and enhancement) but exclude infrastructure renewals expenditure. Figures quoted are before deducting grants and contributions, typically received from developers. Adopted assets at nil cost are not included.

Water pollution incidents (Table 10.15)
The Environment Agency responds to complaints and reported incidents of pollution in England and Wales. Each incident is then logged and categorised according to its severity. The category describes the impact of each incident on water, land and air. The impact of an incident on each medium is considered and reported separately. If no impact has occurred for a particular medium, the incident is reported as a category 4. Before 1999, the reporting system was used only for water pollution incidents; thus the total number of substantiated incidents was lower, as it did not include incidents not relating to the water environment.

Bathing waters (Table 10.16)

Under the EC Bathing Water Directive 76/160/EEC, 11 physical, chemical and microbiological parameters are measured including total and faecal coliforms which are generally considered to be the most important indicators of the extent to which water is contaminated by sewage. The mandatory value for total coliforms is 10,000 per 100 ml, and for faecal coliforms 2,000 per 100 ml. For a bathing water to comply with the coliform standards, the Directive requires that at least 95 per cent of samples taken for each of these parameters over the bathing season are less than or equal to the mandatory values. In the UK a minimum of 20 samples are normally taken at each site. In practice this means that where 20 samples are taken, a maximum of only one sample may exceed the mandatory value for the bathing water to comply, and where less than 20 samples are taken none may exceed the mandatory value for the bathing water to comply.

The bathing water season is from mid-May to end-September in England and Wales, but shorter in Scotland and Northern Ireland. Bathing waters which are closed for the season are excluded for that year.

The table shows Environment Agency regions for England and Wales, the boundaries of which are based on river catchment areas and not county borders. In particular, the figures shown for Wales are the Environment Agency Welsh Region, the boundary of which does not coincide with the boundary of Wales.

Surface and groundwater abstractions (Table 10.17)

Significant changes in the way data is collected and/or reported were made in 1991 (due to the Water Resources Act 1991) and 1999 (commission of National Abstraction Licensing Database). Figures are therefore not strictly comparable with those in previous/intervening years. From 1999, data have been stored and retrieved from one system nationally and are therefore more accurate and reliable. Some regions report licensed and actual abstracts for financial rather than calendar years. As figures represent an average for the whole year expressed as daily amounts, differences between amounts reported for financial and calendar years are small.

Under the Water Act 2003, abstraction of less than 20 m3/day became exempt from the requirement to hold a licence as of 1 April 2005. As a result over 22,000 licences were deregulated, mainly for agricultural or private water supply purposes. However, due to the small volumes involved, this has had a minimal affect on the estimated licensed and actual abstraction totals.

The following changes have occurred in the classification of individual sources:
• Spray irrigation: this category includes small amounts of non-agricultural spray irrigation
• Mineral washing: from 1999 this was not reported as a separate category; licences for 'Mineral washing' are now contained in 'Other industry'
• Private water supply: this was shown as separate category from 1992 and includes private abstractions for domestic use and individual households
• Fish farming, cress growing, amenity ponds: includes amenity ponds, but excludes miscellaneous from 1991

Estimates of remaining recoverable oil and gas reserves (Table 10.18)

Only a small proportion of the estimated remaining recoverable reserves of oil and gas are known with any degree of certainty. The latest oil and gas data for 2008 shows that the upper range of total UK oil reserves was estimated to be around 2.7 billion tonnes, while UK gas reserves were around 1950 billion cubic metres. Of these, proven reserves of oil were 0.4 billion tonnes and proven reserves of gas were 292 billion cubic metres. Compared with a year earlier, proven reserves were 9.7 per cent lower for oil and 14.9per cent lower for gas.

Local authority collected (Table 10.19)

Local authority collected includes household and non-household waste that is collected and disposed of by local authorities. It includes regular household collections, specific recycling collections, and special collections of bulky items, waste received at civic amenity sites, and waste collected from non-household sources that come under the control of local authorities.

Amounts of different materials from household sources collected for recycling (Table 10.20)

Household recycling includes those materials collected for recycling, composting or reuse by local authorities and those collected from household sources by 'private/voluntary' organisations where this material comes under the possession or control of local authorities. It includes residual waste from the household stream which was diverted for recycling by sorting or further treatment.

'Bring sites' are facilities where members of the public can bring recyclable materials (such as paper, glass, cans, textiles, shoes, etc). These are often located at supermarkets or similar locations, but exclude civic amenity sites.

'Civic Amenity sites' refers to household waste collected at sites provided by local authorities for the disposal of excess household and garden waste free of charge, as required by the Refuse Disposal (Amenity) Act 1978. These are also known as Household Waste Recycling Centres.

Material flows (Table 10.22)

Economy-wide material flow accounts record the total mass of natural resources and products that are used by the UK economy, either directly in the production and distribution of products and services, or indirectly through the movement of materials which are displaced in order for production to take place.

The direct movement of materials into the economy derives primarily from domestic extraction. This covers: biomass (agricultural harvest, timber, fish and animal grazing); fossil fuel extraction (such as coal, crude oil and natural gas); mineral extraction (metal ores, industrial minerals such as pottery clay; and construction material such as crushed rock, sand and gravel). This domestic extraction is supplemented by the imports of products, which may be raw materials such as unprocessed agricultural products, but can also be semi-manufactured or finished products. In a similar way the UK produces exports of raw materials, semi-manufactured and finished goods which can be viewed as inputs to the production and consumption of overseas economies.

Indirect flows of natural resources consist of the unused material resulting from domestic extraction, such as mining and quarrying overburden and the soil removed during construction and dredging activities. They also include the movement of used and unused material overseas which is associated with the production and delivery of imports. Water, except for that included directly in products, is excluded.

There are three main indicators used to measure inputs. The Direct Material Input measures the input of used materials into the economy that is all materials which are of economic value and are used in production and consumption activities (including the production of exports). Domestic Material Consumption measures the total amount of material directly used in the economy that is it includes imports but excludes exports. The Total Material Requirement (TMR) measures the total material basis of the economy that is the total primary resource requirements of all the production and consumption activities. It includes not only the direct use of resources for producing exports, but also indirect flows from the production of imports and the indirect flows associated with domestic extraction. Although TMR is widely favoured as a resource use indicator, the estimates of indirect flows are less reliable than those for materials directly used by the economy, and the indicator therefore needs to be considered alongside other indicators.

Between 2007 and 20082 the quantity of natural resources used by the UK economy, known as domestic material consumption, fell by 67 million tonnes (9.9 per cent) to 613 million tonnes. This is the largest recorded fall since records began in 1970. It follows 10 years where resource use has remained broadly unchanged. This means that, with rising levels of economic activity, UK material productivity has been increasing.

The fall in domestic material consumption mainly reflects decreases in the domestic extraction of minerals, with a decrease of 57 million tonnes (19.3 per cent) driven by a sharp fall in the extraction of primary aggregates – crushed stone, sand and gravel – as demand was impacted by the economic downturn. Imports of minerals also fell in 2008, by 10.9 per cent.

Much of the period 1990 to 2007 had seen strong economic growth in the UK and material productivity increased, with material use falling in relation to the level of economic activity. This in part reflects the increasing importance of the service industries in the UK economy. Gross Domestic Product overall continued to increase in 2008 (by 0.5 per cent) and material use fell. The fall in demand for primary aggregates coincides with the contraction in output of the construction industry in 2008.

10.1 Atmospheric emissions[1] 2011

	Total greenhouse gas emissions	Carbon Dioxide (CO2)	Methane (CH4)	Nitrous Oxide (N2O)	Hydrofluoro-carbons (HFCs)	Perfluoro-carbons (PFCs)	Sulphur hexafluoride (SF6)
Thousand tonnes CO2 equivalent							
Agriculture, forestry and fishing	53 148	6 206	17 769	29 141	33	–	–
Mining and quarrying	21 579	17 956	3 233	382	9	–	–
Manufacturing	97 763	95 009	337	875	1 037	319	187
Electricity, gas, steam & air conditioning supply; water supply, sewerage, waste management activities & remediation services	183 994	161 677	19 593	2 220	77	6	421
Construction	10 109	9 425	17	331	336	–	–
Wholesale & retail trade; repair of motor vehicles & motorcycles	16 676	12 092	9	127	4 448	–	–
Transport & storage; information & communication	91 305	89 524	173	845	764	–	–
Accommodation and food services	3 009	2 388	4	22	595	–	–
Financial and insurance activities	230	129	–	15	86	–	–
Real estate activities; professional scientific & technical activities; administration & support service activities	5 292	4 501	5	35	751	–	–
Public administration & defence; compulsory social security	6 275	6 001	7	54	213	–	–
Education	3 366	3 117	5	21	223	–	–
Human health and social work activities	4 704	4 343	9	9	343	–	–
Arts, entertainment and recreation; other service activities	2 409	2 174	3	16	215	–	–
Activities of households as employers; undifferentiated goods & services-producing activities of households for own use	230	228	1	1	–	–	–
Consumer expenditure	134 678	128 197	557	559	5 365	–	–
Total	634 765	542 966	41 722	34 652	14 493	325	607
of which, emissions from road transport[2]	113 241	112 323	61	858	–	–	–

	Total acid rain precursors	Sulphur Dioxide (SO2)	Nitrogen Oxides (NOx)	Ammonia (NH3)
Thousand tonnes SO2 equivalent				
Agriculture, forestry and fishing	473	–	24	448
Mining and quarrying	55	8	47	–
Manufacturing	280	149	121	10
Electricity, gas, steam & air conditioning supply; water supply, sewerage, waste management activities & remediation services	369	168	174	28
Construction	33	–	33	–
Wholesale & retail trade; repair of motor vehicles & motorcycles	31	–	30	–
Transport & storage; information & communication	591	157	433	1
Accommodation and food services	3	–	3	–
Financial and insurance activities	1	–	1	–
Real estate activities; professional scientific & technical activities; administrative & support service activities	9	–	9	–
Public administration and defence; compulsory social security	34	6	21	7
Education	10	6	4	–
Human health and social work activities	5	1	5	–
Arts, entertainment and recreation; other service activities	11	1	3	7
Activities of households as employers; undifferentiated goods & services-producing activities of households for own use	–	–	–	–
Consumer expenditure	197	34	121	42
Total (excluding Natural World)	2 101	529	1 028	544
of which, emissions from road transport[2]	257	–	239	17

	Thousand tonnes						Tonnes		
	PM10[3]	PM2.5[3]	CO	NMVOC[4]	Benzene	Butadiene	Lead	Cadmium	Mercury
Agriculture, forestry and fishing	21.09	7.94	69.69	82.79	0.14	0.05	0.43	0.04	0.02
Mining and quarrying	7.91	3.67	31.22	85.06	0.43	–	0.32	0.05	0.02
Manufacturing	22.93	14.20	544.41	266.37	1.18	0.37	44.75	1.73	2.91
Electricity, gas, steam & air conditioning supply; water supply, sewerage, waste management activities & remediation services	7.38	4.55	92.50	65.57	1.49	0.06	4.03	0.19	1.74
Construction	4.78	3.67	189.67	50.57	0.55	0.16	0.28	0.04	0.01
Wholesale & retail trade; repair of motor vehicles & motorcycles	2.98	2.15	22.22	39.86	0.11	0.05	1.75	0.04	0.01
Transport & storage; information & communication	41.79	38.47	124.00	33.59	3.17	0.43	3.61	1.58	0.10
Accommodation and food services	0.30	0.26	2.79	0.77	0.02	–	0.02	–	–
Financial and insurance activities	0.11	0.10	0.65	0.25	–	–	0.01	–	–
Real estate activities; professional scientific & technical activities; administration & support service activities	0.87	0.69	22.00	1.92	0.08	0.03	0.05	0.01	–
Public administration & defence: compulsory social security	1.07	0.96	25.78	2.74	0.18	0.03	0.16	0.03	0.01
Education	0.65	0.34	3.35	0.32	0.01	–	0.83	0.01	0.07
Human health and social work activities	0.27	0.22	5.04	1.16	0.02	–	0.02	0.01	–
Arts, entertainment and recreation; other service activities	0.37	0.27	5.86	2.12	0.02	0.01	0.10	0.01	0.65
Activities of households as employers; undifferentiated goods & services-producing activities of households for own use	–	–	48.49	2.94	0.20	0.04	–	–	–
Consumer expenditure	34.52	22.08	1 012.26	201.53	3.07	0.59	5.07	0.39	0.19
Total (excluding Natural World)	147.02	99.57	2 199.92	837.56	10.67	1.82	61.46	4.14	5.72
of which, emissions from road transport[2]	23.86	17.15	739.80	44.13	2.15	0.76	1.56	0.37	–

1 Components may not sum to totals due to rounding.
2 Includes emissions from fuel sources which are used by road vehicles (eg HGVs, LGVs, cars and motorcycles) across all industries.
3 PM10 is particulate matter arising from various sources including fuel combustion, quarrying and construction, and formation of 'secondary' particles in the atmosphere from reactions involving other pollutants - sulphur dioxide, nitrogen oxides, ammonia and NMVOCs.
4 Non-methane Volatile Compounds, including benzene and 1,3-butadiene.

Source: AEA Energy & Environment, ONS

10.2 Road Transport[1] Emissions by Pollutant, 1998 to 2011

UK resident basis
All weights in thousand tonnes unless otherwise specified
Greenhouse gases are made up of carbon dioxide, methane and nitrous oxide. Weight in carbon dioxide equivalent
Acid rain precursors are made of sulphur dioxide, nitrogen oxides and ammonia. Weight in sulphur dioxide equivalent

Pollutant	1998	1999	2000	2001	2002	2003	2004	2005	2006	2007	2008	2009	2010	2011
Greenhouse gases	118,445.27	119,372.78	118,490.45	118,183.09	120,505.78	120,106.50	120,813.90	121,347.82	122,004.10	123,532.77	119,441.38	115,642.66	115,011.83	113,240.98
of which														
Carbon dioxide	116,582.78	117,566.86	116,768.20	116,584.75	118,995.79	118,695.49	119,482.26	120,095.44	120,806.19	122,382.91	118,461.68	114,741.78	114,115.06	112,322.65
Methane	380.02	346.10	300.18	260.81	232.69	206.82	184.12	165.54	149.77	133.32	115.34	83.19	70.15	60.82
Nitrous oxide	1,482.46	1,459.82	1,422.07	1,337.54	1,277.30	1,204.19	1,147.52	1,086.84	1,048.15	1,016.54	864.36	817.69	826.62	857.51
Acid rain precursors	646.68	601.77	560.31	530.75	500.38	470.83	448.31	425.37	408.60	389.44	362.24	299.47	280.63	257.07
of which	0.00	0.00	0.00	0.00	0.00	0.00	0.00	0.00	0.00	0.00	0.00	0.00	0.00	0.00
Sulphur dioxide	22.80	13.63	5.93	3.39	3.04	3.00	2.73	2.39	2.11	1.69	1.05	0.48	0.48	0.45
Nitrogen Oxides as NO_2	597.52	557.81	510.19	486.23	458.86	432.69	412.80	392.83	378.40	361.99	338.36	277.23	260.77	239.43
Ammonia	26.36	30.33	44.19	41.13	38.49	35.14	32.79	30.15	28.09	25.75	22.83	21.75	19.38	17.19
PM_{10}	39.39	38.89	34.88	34.27	33.15	32.41	31.73	30.83	29.97	29.10	27.74	26.39	25.62	23.86
$PM_{2.5}$	32.07	31.50	27.71	27.09	25.92	25.16	24.44	23.61	22.72	21.85	20.63	19.46	18.81	17.15
Carbon monoxide	4,809.31	4,437.23	3,852.10	3,464.91	3,089.71	2,756.14	2,456.05	2,139.13	1,883.18	1,602.53	1,431.96	1,071.33	906.07	739.80
Non Methane VOC	543.30	473.79	394.52	350.36	293.81	242.51	199.77	164.33	137.92	113.79	95.62	66.23	54.15	44.13
Benzene	20.82	19.75	12.22	12.20	11.47	10.65	9.68	8.46	7.38	6.04	5.17	3.65	2.85	2.15
1,3-Butadiene	7.89	6.98	5.88	4.99	4.26	3.64	3.12	2.68	2.36	2.02	1.80	1.12	0.93	0.76
Cadmium (tonnes)	0.40	0.40	0.40	0.40	0.40	0.40	0.41	0.41	0.41	0.41	0.39	0.38	0.38	0.37
Lead (tonnes)	573.99	301.87	2.20	2.01	1.97	1.97	1.99	2.06	2.07	1.71	1.64	1.59	1.58	1.56
Mercury (tonnes)	0.00	0.00	0.00	0.00	0.00	0.00	0.00	0.00	0.00	0.00	0.00	0.00	0.00	0.00

Source: Ricardo-AEA, ONS

[1] Emissions from fuel sources which are used by road vehicles across industry groups.

For any further information about road transport and associated emissions please contact us at environment.accounts@ons.gsi.gov.uk

10.3: UK Greenhouse Gas Emissions 1997-2011, headline results

Greenhouse gas emissions: actual emissions in tonnes

	Units (tonnes)	1997	1998	1999	2000	2001	2002	2003	2004	2005	2006	2007	2008	2009	2010	2011
Net CO_2 emissions (emissions minus removals)	Million	548.6	552.5	544.6	552.2	562.3	545.1	555.6	556.2	552.8	552.3	544.9	527.3	477.9	495.2	454.0
Methane (CH_4)	Million	4.4	4.3	4.0	3.7	3.6	3.5	3.3	3.1	3.0	2.9	2.8	2.8	2.7	2.5	2.5
Nitrous Oxide (N_2O)	Million	0.2	0.2	0.2	0.2	0.1	0.1	0.1	0.1	0.1	0.1	0.1	0.1	0.1	0.1	0.1
Hydrofluorocarbons (HFC)	Thousand	3.80	4.33	3.92	4.48	5.09	5.54	6.22	6.47	6.96	7.37	7.55	7.91	8.10	8.24	8.36
Perfluorocarbons (PFC)	Thousand	0.05	0.05	0.05	0.06	0.05	0.04	0.04	0.05	0.04	0.04	0.03	0.03	0.02	0.03	0.05
Sulphur hexafluoride (SF_6)	Thousand	0.05	0.05	0.06	0.07	0.06	0.06	0.05	0.04	0.04	0.03	0.03	0.02	0.02	0.03	0.02

Greenhouse gas emissions: weighted by global warming potential (million tonnes carbon dioxide equivalent)

	Baseline	1997	1998	1999	2000	2001	2002	2003	2004	2005	2006	2007	2008	2009	2010	2011
Net CO_2 emissions (emissions minus removals)		548.6	552.5	544.6	552.2	562.3	545.1	555.6	556.2	552.8	552.3	544.9	527.3	477.9	495.2	454.0
Methane (CH_4)		93.4	90.0	83.8	78.2	74.8	74.0	69.3	65.1	62.3	61.2	59.2	58.0	55.7	52.5	51.7
Nitrous Oxide (N_2O)		59.9	59.8	49.2	48.3	45.6	43.8	43.3	43.8	42.9	40.8	40.0	39.0	36.8	37.7	36.3
Hydrofluorocarbons (HFC)		18.9	16.7	9.9	8.8	9.7	10.1	11.2	10.4	11.2	11.9	12.2	12.7	13.1	13.5	13.8
Perfluorocarbons (PFC)		0.4	0.4	0.4	0.5	0.4	0.3	0.3	0.3	0.3	0.3	0.2	0.2	0.1	0.2	0.3
Sulphur hexafluoride (SF_6)		1.2	1.3	1.4	1.8	1.4	1.4	1.3	1.0	1.0	0.7	0.7	0.6	0.6	0.6	0.6
Kyoto greenhouse gas basket	779.9 [r]	722.1 [r]	721.1 [r]	690.2 [r]	692.2 [r]	697.6 [r]	678.9 [r]	685.3 [r]	682.3 [r]	676.3 [r]	673.2 [r]	663.7 [r]	644.2 [r]	590.7 [r]	606.2 [r]	563.2 [r]

Notes:

1. Figures for each individual gas include the Land Use, Land-Use Change and Forestry sector (LULUCF). These emissions cover the UK and Crown Dependencies, but exclude emissions from UK Overseas Territories.

2. Kyoto basket total differs slightly from sum of individual pollutants above as the basket uses a narrower definition for the Land Use, Land-Use Change and Forestry sector (LULUCF) and has a slightly different geographical coverage. This includes emissions from the UK, Crown Dependencies and UK Overseas Territories, as well as emissions from flights between the UK, Crown Dependencies, and Overseas Territories. A detailed breakdown is shown in Table 2.

3. Kyoto base year consists of emissions of CO_2, CH_4 and N_2O in 1990, and of HFCs, PFCs and SF_6 in 1995. Includes an allowance for net emissions from LULUCF in 1990.

4. The entire time series is revised each year to take account of methodological improvements in the UK emissions inventory.

5. Emissions in the bottom table are presented as carbon dioxide equivalent in line with international reporting and carbon trading. To convert Carbon dioxide into carbon equivalents, divide figures by 44/12.

6. Figures shown do not include any adjustment for the effect of the EU Emissions Trading Scheme (EUETS), which was introduced in 2005.

r The Kyoto greenhouse gas basket figures were revised on the 27th March 2014 to correct a minor error.

10.4 Greenhouse Gas Emissions Bridging Table

UK [56 9]   Thousand tonnes CO_2 equivalent

	1990	1995	2000	2005	2009	2010	2011
Greenhouse gases[2] - CO2,CH4,N20,HFCs,PFCs and SF6							
Environmental Account	806,495.10	754,413.29	734,054.65	739,458.45	651,531.46	671,151.72	634,765.31
less							
Bunker emissions[3]	24,508.64	28,488.91	37,190.85	43,148.47	43,263.61	40,450.07	42,856.41
CO2 biomass[4]	3,105.25	5,353.38	7,158.98	12,533.04	18,340.49	20,610.00	21,937.85
Cross-boundary [5]	11,717.26	11,984.23	16,107.42	25,793.61	13,544.94	16,363.71	17,585.39
plus							
Crown Dependencies[6]	1,737.26	1,884.01	1,863.20	1,579.29	1,612.49	1,583.58	1,562.14
Land, Land-Use Change and Forestry (LULUCF) [7]	4,038.92	3,322.21	486.90	-2,526.33	-3,723.48	-3,575.90	-3,215.94
DECC reported (Excluding Overseas Territories)[8 9]	772,940.12	713,793.00	675,947.51	657,036.29	574,271.43	591,735.62	550,731.86
plus							
Overseas Territories (including net emissions from land use change/forestry)	1,865.81	1,811.71	1,965.96	2,302.15	2,294.75	2,378.23	2,416.61
UNFCCC reported in the UK Greenhouse Gas Inventory [8]	774,805.94	715,604.71	677,913.47	659,338.45	576,566.18	594,113.85	553,148.47
Kyoto greenhouse gas basket (baseline taken from the Assigned Amount Report)[8 9]	769,697.73	710,952.85	675,249.88	659,016.25	576,838.04	593,961.29	552,550.83

Source: Ricardo-AEA, DECC, ONS

1 United Nations Framework Convention on Climate Change http://unfccc.int/2860.php
2 Carbon dioxide, methane, nitrous oxide, hydrofluorocarbons, perfluorocarbons and sulphur hexafluoride expressed as thousand tonnes of carbon dioxide equivalent
3 Bunker emissions includes UK aviation and shipping to overseas territories and international destinations
4 Emissions arising from wood, straw, biogases and poultry litter combustion for energy production
5 Emissions generated by UK households and business transport and travel abroad, net of emissions generated by non-residents travel and transport in the UK
6 Emissions of Crown dependancies; Guernsey, Jersey, Isle of Man.
7 Emissions from deforestation, soils and changes in forest and other woody biomass.
8 https://www.gov.uk/government/publications/final-uk-emissions-estimates
9 This is the UK total for the sum of the 6 individual pollutants and differs slightly from the Kyoto greenhouse gas basket totals which uses a narrower definition of Land use, Land Use Change and Forestry and includes emissions from UK Overseas Territories (Gibraltar, the Falkland Islands, the Cayman Islands, Montserrat, Bermuda)

10.5 Estimated emissions of carbon dioxide (CO_2), 1990-2011

Geographical coverage: United Kingdom and Crown Dependencies

Units: Million tonnes   Million tonnes, as CO2

NC Category	1990	1997	1998	1999	2000	2001	2002	2003	2004	2005	2006	2007	2008	2009	2010	2011
By source																
Energy Supply Total	241.5	197.8	203.0	192.9	203.1	213.2	210.9	218.2	217.4	217.3	224.4	219.2	212.7	189.7	195.5	182.0
Business Total	113.7	105.7	105.4	107.6	108.2	107.4	96.6	98.8	97.2	97.6	94.6	92.9	88.4	77.1	77.2	72.7
Transport Total	119.6	125.8	124.8	125.9	124.9	125.0	127.5	127.1	128.3	129.2	129.7	132.7	125.5	120.7	119.1	117.4
Public Total Residential	13.1	13.4	12.4	12.2	11.5	11.9	10.2	10.2	11.1	11.0	10.0	9.3	9.9	9.7	10.5	9.7
Total Agriculture Total	79.0	85.0	86.9	86.7	87.1	89.3	86.1	87.0	88.4	84.3	81.7	78.1	79.9	74.8	86.6	66.5
Industrial Process Total	5.2	5.3	5.1	5.1	4.8	4.8	4.8	4.8	4.6	4.6	4.3	4.1	4.1	4.0	4.1	4.2
Land Use Change Total	16.7	15.6	15.8	15.8	15.2	14.1	13.4	14.3	14.7	15.0	14.7	14.3	15.6	14.1	9.3	9.5
Waste Management Total	1.0	-0.5	-1.5	-2.0	-3.0	-4.0	-4.9	-5.1	-6.0	-6.5	-7.0	-7.4	-7.6	-7.7	-8.0	-8.2
	1.3	0.5	0.5	0.5	0.5	0.5	0.5	0.5	0.4	0.4	0.3	0.3	0.3	0.3	0.3	0.3
Grand Total	**591.1**	**548.6**	**552.5**	**544.6**	**552.2**	**562.3**	**545.1**	**555.6**	**556.2**	**552.8**	**552.3**	**544.9**	**527.3**	**477.9**	**495.2**	**454.0**

Notes:
1. The entire time series is revised each year to take account of methodological improvements in the UK emissions inventory.
2. These figures include emissions from the UK and Crown Dependencies, but exclude emissions from Overseas Territories.

10.6: Estimated emissions of methane (CH$_4$), 1999-2011

Geographical coverage: United Kingdom and Crown Dependencies
Units: Thousand tonnes   Thousand tonnes

NC Category	1999	2000	2001	2002	2003	2004	2005	2006	2007	2008	2009	2010	2011
By source													
Energy Supply Total	722.7	656.6	607.2	584.7	522.8	511.2	445.1	413.3	392.6	373.8	370.6	359.5	350.8
Business Total	8.1	8.2	8.2	7.8	8.3	7.7	7.5	7.2	7.1	6.8	6.1	6.5	6.3
Transport Total	16.8	14.7	12.7	11.5	10.2	9.2	8.5	7.7	7.1	6.1	4.5	3.9	3.4
Public Total Residential	1.2	1.1	1.2	1.0	1.0	1.1	1.1	1.0	0.9	0.9	0.9	1.0	0.9
Total Agriculture Total	42.7	32.4	29.1	24.1	22.4	21.3	19.2	19.8	21.5	22.6	21.5	24.2	22.2
Industrial Process Total	1,301.3	1,246.1	1,177.0	1,152.4	1,147.2	1,154.8	1,135.3	1,129.4	1,107.3	1,083.0	1,065.2	1,066.7	1,060.0
Land Use Change Total	6.1	5.6	5.5	5.6	6.4	5.9	5.1	5.1	5.5	4.3	4.6	4.8	4.3
Waste Management Total	1.0	1.9	1.7	1.9	3.2	2.0	2.4	2.3	2.6	2.2	2.1	2.0	2.1
	1,889.9	1,759.2	1,718.8	1,735.0	1,580.2	1,387.7	1,341.1	1,330.2	1,273.3	1,260.3	1,178.6	1,031.5	1,011.2
Grand Total	**3,989.8**	**3,725.8**	**3,561.3**	**3,524.0**	**3,301.6**	**3,100.9**	**2,965.1**	**2,916.0**	**2,817.8**	**2,760.0**	**2,654.1**	**2,500.0**	**2,461.3**

Notes:
1. The entire time series is revised each year to take account of methodological improvements in the UK emissions inventory.
2. These figures include emissions from the UK and Crown Dependencies, but exclude emissions from Overseas Territories.

10.7: Estimated emissions of nitrous oxide (N$_2$O), 1997-2011

Geographical coverage: United Kingdom and Crown Dependencies
Units: Thousand tonnes   Thousand tonnes

NC Category	1997	1998	1999	2000	2001	2002	2003	2004	2005	2006	2007	2008	2009	2010	2011
By source															
Energy Supply Total	5.0	5.2	4.7	5.1	5.4	5.4	5.5	5.3	5.5	5.7	5.2	4.9	4.5	4.5	4.6
Business Total	4.3	4.1	4.1	4.1	4.1	4.1	4.0	3.9	4.1	3.9	4.0	3.6	2.9	3.0	2.6
Transport Total	5.2	5.1	5.0	4.9	4.6	4.5	4.3	4.1	4.0	3.9	3.8	3.2	3.0	3.1	3.2
Public Total Residential	0.1	0.1	0.1	0.1	0.1	0.0	0.0	0.0	0.0	0.0	0.0	0.0	0.0	0.0	0.0
Total Agriculture Total	0.7	0.7	0.7	0.6	0.6	0.5	0.5	0.4	0.4	0.4	0.4	0.4	0.4	0.4	0.4
Industrial Process Total	122.8	121.3	119.8	115.9	109.7	110.7	109.0	108.7	108.2	103.3	100.1	99.2	97.7	100.0	99.4
Land Use Change Total	48.5	49.4	17.5	18.1	15.7	9.1	9.6	12.3	9.7	7.8	9.1	8.2	4.0	4.4	0.8
Waste Management Total	2.8	2.8	2.8	2.7	2.7	2.6	2.7	2.5	2.5	2.5	2.5	2.4	2.4	2.3	2.2
	4.0	4.1	4.1	4.3	4.2	4.2	4.1	4.0	4.0	4.0	4.0	3.8	3.9	3.9	3.9
Grand Total	**193.4**	**192.8**	**158.9**	**155.7**	**147.0**	**141.2**	**139.6**	**141.4**	**138.4**	**131.5**	**129.1**	**125.8**	**118.8**	**121.6**	**117.1**

Notes:
1. The entire time series is revised each year to take account of methodological improvements in the UK emissions inventory.
2. hese figures include emissions from the UK and Crown Dependencies, but exclude emissions from Overseas Territories.

10.8 Material flow account for the United Kingdom, 1986 to 2011

Million tonnes

	1986	1989	1990	1995	2000	2001	2002	2003	2004	2005	2006	2007	2008	2009	2010	2011
Domestic extraction																
Biomass																
Agricultural harvest	48.62	45.94	46.25	46.75	51.03	45.23	50.72	48.17	48.71	47.55	45.57	42.75	49.05	47.94	45.30	51.48
Timber	5.21	6.43	6.35	7.56	7.79	7.90	7.77	8.05	8.29	8.52	8.42	9.02	8.42	8.62	9.72	10.02
Animal grazing	47.02	47.38	47.24	45.19	42.80	43.43	43.10	43.81	43.22	43.42	44.14	43.94	44.72	43.86	43.76	40.61
Fish	0.86	0.91	0.82	1.01	0.90	0.91	0.87	0.82	0.86	0.84	0.80	0.79	0.78	0.77	0.81	0.79
Total biomass	101.70	100.66	100.66	100.51	102.51	97.47	102.47	100.84	101.09	100.33	98.92	96.50	102.95	101.19	99.59	102.90
Minerals																
Ores	0.61	0.33	0.32	0.16	0.00	0.00	0.00	0.00	0.00	0.00	0.00	0.00	0.00	0.00	0.00	0.00
Clay	22.23	24.57	21.15	18.25	14.94	14.14	13.93	14.22	14.50	14.22	13.44	13.14	11.01	7.23	8.04	8.54
Other industrial minerals	11.02	11.66	10.87	9.65	8.31	8.64	8.36	8.70	8.45	8.56	7.97	8.06	7.98	8.59	9.09	9.14
Sand and gravel	116.15	142.76	128.15	106.08	105.72	105.25	98.26	95.28	102.34	98.81	97.28	98.15	90.25	69.98	65.77	68.08
Crushed stone	168.29	221.26	212.31	199.83	176.12	182.79	172.56	169.62	174.66	168.93	172.56	175.82	152.33	124.96	125.51	124.15
Total minerals	318.30	400.57	372.80	333.96	305.09	310.81	293.10	287.82	299.95	290.53	291.25	295.16	261.57	210.75	208.41	209.90
Fossil fuels																
Coal	108.10	101.13	94.40	53.04	31.20	31.93	29.99	28.28	25.10	20.50	18.52	17.01	18.05	17.87	18.42	18.34
Natural gas	38.78	38.45	42.45	70.76	108.40	105.87	103.65	102.93	96.41	88.22	80.01	72.12	69.68	59.74	57.19	45.29
Crude oil	127.07	91.81	91.62	129.90	126.04	116.68	115.94	106.07	95.37	84.72	76.58	76.58	71.67	68.20	62.96	51.97
Total fossil fuels	273.95	231.40	228.46	253.70	265.64	254.48	249.58	237.28	216.88	193.44	175.11	165.71	159.40	145.81	138.57	115.60
Total domestic extraction	693.95	732.62	701.92	688.16	673.24	662.76	645.15	625.94	617.92	584.30	565.28	557.36	523.92	457.75	446.57	428.40
Imports																
Biomass	34.64	38.37	38.93	41.33	46.08	49.56	50.10	52.90	53.63	53.91	55.76	53.91	52.15	49.42	51.39	50.42
Minerals	35.17	49.73	43.33	53.21	52.91	54.65	55.27	56.69	60.55	58.04	59.56	62.89	56.77	38.24	46.33	48.27
Fossil fuels	80.17	80.46	94.94	81.75	93.16	109.17	105.29	113.30	138.36	148.16	159.11	159.10	152.38	148.59	148.02	162.52
Other Products	9.30	10.40	9.92	11.29	16.42	16.84	15.18	15.80	18.26	16.92	17.17	17.04	16.61	14.86	16.55	16.73
Total imports	159.28	178.96	187.12	187.59	208.57	230.21	225.85	238.69	270.80	277.02	291.60	292.94	277.90	251.12	262.29	277.93
Exports																
Biomass	15.09	13.88	13.93	15.75	18.12	13.84	15.68	20.67	19.11	20.00	21.25	21.36	21.45	20.13	22.40	21.94
Minerals	20.99	23.67	25.76	39.49	44.43	42.74	41.79	44.46	47.73	47.98	49.87	49.27	47.40	37.19	39.39	40.67
Fossil fuels	109.78	61.16	72.19	110.59	125.03	127.54	129.79	113.53	108.69	97.35	93.76	90.40	88.70	87.84	95.69	92.22
Other Products	6.50	7.55	5.42	7.59	9.03	8.83	8.60	8.94	8.69	9.42	8.51	9.54	8.70	7.72	7.72	7.10
Total exports	152.36	106.26	117.30	173.43	196.60	192.95	195.87	187.59	184.21	174.75	173.39	170.57	166.25	152.89	165.19	161.93
Domestic Material Consumption (domestic extraction + imports - exports)	700.97	805.41	771.82	703.45	686.00	700.91	675.64	678.01	705.15	687.31	684.26	680.19	635.96	556.41	544.15	544.80
of which																
biomass	121.26	125.15	125.66	126.09	130.46	133.19	136.88	133.07	135.62	134.24	133.43	129.05	133.65	130.48	128.59	131.38
minerals	332.48	426.64	390.37	347.68	313.57	322.72	306.59	300.06	312.77	300.59	300.94	308.78	270.94	211.80	215.35	217.50
fossil fuels	244.33	250.69	251.21	224.86	233.77	236.11	225.08	237.05	246.56	244.25	240.46	234.40	223.07	206.56	190.89	185.90
Indirect flows																
From domestic extraction (excl soil erosion)	630.13	727.62	702.78	641.37	586.88	593.80	577.91	563.14	561.64	531.35	499.52	504.98	504.89	479.72	491.07	498.15
of which																
unused biomass	38.21	37.07	36.85	37.34	40.57	35.12	40.00	38.45	38.80	37.84	36.01	33.85	39.23	38.03	35.92	39.62
fossil fuels	269.08	329.04	319.00	282.16	233.80	244.36	228.23	211.81	206.40	179.72	150.87	152.21	161.42	164.73	172.55	172.63
Minerals and ores	124.45	155.85	144.39	120.58	104.47	103.32	100.57	100.25	103.68	101.18	99.62	105.26	91.73	71.04	73.18	75.16
soil excavation and	198.39	205.67	202.54	201.28	208.04	211.00	209.11	212.62	212.75	212.61	213.02	213.66	212.52	205.92	209.42	210.74
From production of raw materials and semi-natural products imported	435.03	459.83	457.02	526.77	504.73	665.72	600.72	638.55	644.41	708.67	745.89	716.31	662.46	546.10	439.10	525.61
Other Indicators																
Physical Trade Balance (imports-exports)	6.91	72.70	69.82	14.16	11.97	37.26	29.98	51.10	86.59	102.27	118.21	122.37	111.65	98.22	97.09	116.00
Direct Material Input (domestic extraction + imports)	853.33	911.67	889.12	876.88	882.61	893.86	871.50	865.59	889.36	862.07	857.65	850.76	802.21	709.30	709.34	706.73
TOTAL MATERIAL REQUIREMENT (direct material input + indirect flows)	1918.49	2099.12	2048.92	2045.02	1974.22	2153.38	2050.14	2067.28	2095.41	2102.09	2103.06	2072.05	1969.56	1735.12	1639.51	1730.50

1. Components may not sum to totals due to rounding
2. Indirect flows from domestic extraction relate to unused material which is moved during extraction, such as overburden from mining and quarrying. It does not represent the raw material use embedded in the import of manufactured products.
3. A positive physical trade balance indicates a net import of material into the UK. This calculation of the PTB differs from the National Accounts formula (exports - imports) because flows of materials and products are considered the inverse of the flows of money recorded in the National Accounts.
For more information please email: environment.accounts@ons.gsi.gov.uk
Source: ONS

10.9 Annual rainfall: by region

United Kingdom

Millimetres and percentages

Region		1971 - 2000[2] rainfall average (= 100%) millimetres	1999	2000	2001	2002	2003	2004	2005	2006	2007	2008	2009	2010	2011	2012
United Kingdom	JSJB	1084	114	123	97	118	83	112	100	109	111	120	112	88	108	123
North West	JSJC	1177	111	132	94	121	85	116	96	114	110	126	113	84	116	136
Northumbria	JSJD	831	106	132	106	124	80	120	111	101	105	135	116	105	104	144
Severn Trent[1]	JSJE	759	120	132	104	119	81	110	92	103	123	121	103	84	74	139
Yorkshire	JSJF	814	110	136	100	126	82	114	96	110	115	130	105	91	89	143
Anglian	JSJG	603	113	129	124	118	86	115	89	102	118	116	99	97	73	138
Thames	JSLK	700	111	137	116	128	81	103	79	106	118	115	104	87	79	134
Southern	JSLL	782	105	148	114	129	85	97	79	101	106	108	109	94	81	130
Wessex	JSLM	866	118	136	100	132	83	98	89	100	113	116	107	80	84	140
South West	JSLN	1208	113	128	92	121	78	99	90	92	110	112	110	83	86	133
England	JSLO	819	113	133	105	123	83	109	91	103	114	120	107	89	87	137
Wales	JSLP	1373	116	133	98	119	83	108	95	107	108	121	109	82	94	124
Scotland	JSLQ	1440	116	113	91	112	84	117	110	114	109	120	117	87	131	112
Northern Ireland	JSLR	1111	111	110	81	127	84	98	96	104	99	114	114	94	115	107

Sources: Met Office; National Hydrological Monitoring Programme, Centre for Ecology and Hydrology

1. The regions of England shown in this table correspond to the original nine English regions of the National Rivers Authority (NRA); the NRA became part of the Environment Agency upon its creation in April 1996.
The exception to this is the Severn Trent region, part of which (the upper Severn) lies in Wales.
2 . 1971-2000 averages have been derived using arithmetic averages of Met Office areal rainfall.

10.10 UK Annual Weather Summary

	Max Temp		Min Temp		Mean Temp		Sunshine		Rainfall	
	Actual (degrees celsius)	Anomaly (degrees celsius)	Actual (degrees celsius)	Anomaly (degrees celsius)	Actual (degrees celsius)	Anomaly (degrees celsius)	Actual (hours/ day)	Anomaly (%)	Actual (mm)	Anomaly (%)
	WLRL	WLRM	WLRO	WLRP	WLRR	WLRS	WLRX	WLRY	WLSH	WLSI
1989	13.1	1.2	5.5	0.7	9.3	1.0	1563.8	116.9	1018.5	92.6
1990	13.1	1.2	5.8	0.9	9.4	1.1	1490.7	111.4	1172.8	106.7
1991	12.1	0.3	5.1	0.2	8.6	0.3	1302.0	97.3	998.2	90.8
1992	12.3	0.4	5.2	0.4	8.7	0.4	1290.8	96.5	1186.8	107.9
1993	11.8	-0.1	5.0	0.1	8.4	0.0	1218.6	91.1	1121.1	102.0
1994	12.4	0.5	5.5	0.6	8.9	0.6	1366.9	102.2	1184.7	107.7
1995	13.0	1.1	5.4	0.6	9.2	0.9	1588.5	118.7	1023.7	93.1
1996	11.7	-0.1	4.7	-0.1	8.2	-0.2	1403.5	104.9	916.6	83.4
1997	13.1	1.3	5.8	1.0	9.4	1.1	1430.3	106.9	1024.0	93.1
1998	12.6	0.8	5.8	1.0	9.1	0.8	1268.4	94.8	1265.1	115.1
1999	13.0	1.1	5.9	1.0	9.4	1.1	1419.4	106.1	1239.1	112.5
2000	12.7	0.8	5.6	0.8	9.1	0.8	1367.5	102.2	1337.3	121.5
2001	12.4	0.6	5.3	0.5	8.8	0.5	1411.9	105.5	1052.8	95.5
2002	13.0	1.1	6.0	1.2	9.5	1.2	1304.0	97.5	1283.7	116.5
2003	13.5	1.6	5.6	0.7	9.5	1.2	1587.4	118.7	904.2	82.0
2004	13.0	1.2	6.0	1.2	9.5	1.2	1361.4	101.8	1210.1	110.1
2005	13.1	1.2	5.9	1.1	9.5	1.1	1399.2	104.6	1083.0	98.4
2006	13.4	1.5	6.1	1.3	9.7	1.4	1495.9	111.8	1175.9	106.8
2007	13.3	1.4	6.0	1.1	9.6	1.3	1450.7	108.4	1197.1	108.8
2008	12.7	0.8	5.5	0.6	9.1	0.7	1388.8	103.8	1295.0	117.7
2009	12.8	1.0	5.6	0.7	9.2	0.9	1467.4	109.7	1213.3	110.2
2010	11.7	-0.1	4.2	-0.6	8.0	-0.4	1456.0	108.8	950.5	86.4
2011	13.5	1.5	6.0	1.2	9.6	1.3	1406.2	105.0	1172.5	107
2012	12.4	0.5	5.2	0.4	8.8	0.4	1340.5	100	1334.8	121

Source: Met Office

10.11 Summary of River Basin District Ecological and Chemical Status 2009-2012

	Percent of surface water bodies are at good chemical status or better			
River Basin District	2009	2010	2011	2012
Solway Tweed	50	89	89	88
Northumbria	50	68	72	68
Humber	77	79	83	77
Anglian	85	89	92	87
Thames	75	76	79	74
South East	88	91	93	88
South West	77	80	83	84
Severn	78	83	88	82
Dee	75	92	92	87
North West	70	75	72	71

	Percent of surface water bodies are at good ecological status/potential or better			
River Basin District	2009	2010	2011	2012
Solway Tweed	44	43	45	48
Northumbria	43	41	43	40
Humber	18	16	17	18
Anglian	18	19	18	18
Thames	23	22	22	18
South East	19	15	16	15
South West	33	31	34	32
Severn	29	30	30	30
Dee	28	26	30	30
North West	30	31	30	29

Source: Environment Agency

Improvements measureed in terms of the number of water bodies meeting good standards

10.12 Overall status of rivers & canals in Scotland, 2011

	High	Max EP	Good	Good EP	Moderate	Moderate EP	Poor	Poor EP	Bad	Bad EP
No. of river water bodies	182	-	977	135	499	56	290	61	120	72
Length of river water bodies (km)	1370.5	-	10002.1	1274.6	6253.4	520.3	2997.3	611.4	1320.4	774.3
% of length of river water bodies	5.5%	0.0%	39.8%	5.1%	24.9%	2.1%	11.9%	2.4%	5.3%	3.1%

Water Quality 2011

	High	Good	Moderate	Poor	Bad
No. of river water bodies	838	762	412	64	5
Length of river water bodies (km)	8775.9	7975.6	4822.4	706.2	55.1
% of length of river water bodies	39.3%	35.7%	21.6%	3.2%	0.2%

Source: Scottish Environment Protection Agency

10.13 Monthly reservoir stocks for England & Wales[1]

Percentages

		2000	2001	2002	2003	2004	2005	2006	2007	2008	2009	2010	2011	2012
January	JTAS	95.9	94.4	93.7	95.0	93.8	92.3	88.7	93.7	95.7	95.3	92.4	89.8	90.4
February	JTAT	97.4	95.0	95.5	92.1	92.1	92.1	91.2	96.7	95.6	93.4	91.8	93.7	92.0
March	JTAU	95.2	95.5	94.5	92.3	94.4	93.6	96.2	95.2	97.3	94.5	94.1	92.2	89.2
April	JTAV	97.0	96.7	91.9	88.6	94.7	95.0	93.4	91.9	95.1	92.0	91.9	88.9	94.0
May	JTAW	95.7	91.9	97.0	93.1	90.5	93.0	94.4	91.1	92.6	93.3	86.2	87.4	93.6
June	JTAX	93.8	85.1	94.9	87.0	84.8	85.6	88.4	94.4	90.6	88.6	79.0	86.7	97.8
July	JTAY	88.5	80.7	91.1	81.1	78.5	77.9	77.2	93.5	92.0	91.1	77.3	84.7	96.8
August	JTAZ	83.2	77.9	85.9	69.9	82.4	71.5	70.7	88.3	92.5	89.7	75.5	79.9	96.0
September	JTBA	88.0	77.0	77.3	60.4	84.2	67.4	67.8	86.1	90.9	84.0	81.1	81.0	95.3
October	JTBB	95.2	85.5	82.9	53.0	87.5	77.2	80.0	81.2	93.8	82.3	82.0	80.0	94.3
November	JTBC	96.7	87.9	91.8	60.9	86.2	83.8	89.8	82.4	93.1	93.0	86.9	79.7	95.8
December	JTBD	94.8	86.5	95.1	79.9	91.2	85.9	92.2	89.8	92.4	90.6	84.3	88.6	97.6

1 Reservoir stocks are the percentage of useable capacity based on a representative
selection of reservoirs; the percentages relate to the end of each month.

Sources: Water PLCs;
Environment Agency;
National Hydrological Monitoring Programme, Centre for Ecology and Hydrology: 01491 838800

10.14a Water Industry Turnover and current cost profit/(loss) before taxation by company[1]

2012-13 prices

	Turnover			Current cost profit/(loss) before tax		
	2010-11	2011-12	2012-13	2010-11	2011-12	2012-13
	£m	£m	£m	£m	£m	£m
Water and sewerage companies						
Anglian	1,166.0	1,158.3	1,147.0	202.6	185.9	160.1
Dŵr Cymru	722.7	708.7	707.6	117.0	81.7	118.6
Northumbrian	707.8	724.4	730.1	183.8	169.9	172.8
Severn Trent	1,482.4	1,483.4	1,492.2	414.3	351.0	310.7
South West	480.0	486.1	496.4	214.8	178.5	193.6
Southern	693.7	733.2	773.1	(41.8)	94.9	141.9
Thames	1,728.6	1,723.0	1,758.9	245.8	178.8	82.6
United Utilities	1,627.6	1,601.7	1,622.9	396.0	237.5	284.9
Wessex	475.7	476.8	486.6	186.4	138.8	133.4
Yorkshire	928.8	912.6	927.0	163.4	32.8	138.8
Total water and sewerage companies	10,013.3	10,008.3	10,141.8	2,082.3	1,649.8	1,737.4
Water only companies						
Affinity Water [2]	296.1	297.7	292.3	22.1	65.9	44.6
Bristol	105.4	108.6	112.3	11.2	8.5	12.6
Cambridge[3]	21.8	21.7	21.6	7.8	6.8	5.2
Dee Valley	23.0	22.7	22.7	0.2	0.8	1.1
Portsmouth	38.3	37.8	36.2	(0.6)	1.1	2.2
Sembcorp Bournemouth	43.7	43.7	43.1	10.2	8.7	9.7
South East	199.5	201.6	204.0	33.5	25.9	28.5
South Staffordshire	91.3	90.4	92.3	5.8	6.7	8.3
Sutton & East Surrey	57.3	57.6	57.5	1.2	2.2	4.2
Total water only companies	876.4	881.7	882.0	91.4	126.7	116.5
Industry	10,889.7	10,889.9	11,023.8	2,173.7	1,776.5	1,853.9

Notes:
1. Numbers may not add because of rounding.
2. As of 1 October 2012, Affinity Water is the new name for the combined Veolia companies (previously Veolia Water Central, Veolia Water East and Veolia Water South East).
3. With effect from 1 April 2013, South Staffordshire Water PLC will replace Cambridge Water PLC as the Water Undertaker for its Area.

10.14b Water Industry Return on capital measured by average regulatory capital value (RCV) by company[1]

2012-13 prices	Average regulatory capital value			Post tax return on RCV		
	2010-11	2011-12	2012-13	2010-11	2011-12	2012-13
	£m	£m	£m	%	%	%
Water and sewerage companies						
Anglian	6,149.4	6,273.2	6,456.2	5.4	5.3	4.2
Dŵr Cymru	4,166.7	4,214.6	4,256.8	5.6	5.6	5.2
Northumbrian	3,462.0	3,550.8	3,646.9	5.2	5.7	5.2
Severn Trent	7,144.1	7,189.0	7,223.9	6.1	5.8	6.7
South West	2,839.2	2,859.5	2,870.4	5.5	5.4	5.0
Southern	3,892.5	4,025.1	4,158.3	1.8	3.2	4.4
Thames	9,037.8	9,741.7	10,443.1	6.1	6.3	4.3
United Utilities	8,559.6	8,738.9	9,039.1	5.2	5.0	4.8
Wessex	2,514.8	2,553.2	2,636.3	6.4	6.6	6.0
Yorkshire	5,131.0	5,274.4	5,452.1	5.5	5.1	4.9
Total water and sewerage companies	**52,897.1**	**54,420.4**	**56,183.0**	**5.4**	**5.4**	**5.0**
Water only companies						
Affinity Water [2]	983.6	969.7	962.7	2.1	6.7	5.5
Bristol	318.0	343.1	371.3	4.2	4.5	4.9
Cambridge[3]	64.8	69.2	70.6	7.2	6.8	6.7
Dee Valley	64.5	66.5	70.4	6.2	7.6	6.1
Portsmouth	122.4	119.5	117.9	2.8	4.3	4.2
Sembcorp Bournemouth	152.7	148.8	145.7	6.7	7.6	7.8
South East	950.9	980.7	1,008.1	6.1	6.2	6.3
South Staffordshire	247.1	253.8	257.8	6.4	6.1	6.2
Sutton & East Surrey	191.6	200.2	206.4	6.1	6.3	5.7
Total water only companies	**3,095.7**	**3,151.4**	**3,211.1**	**4.6**	**6.2**	**5.8**
Industry	**55,992.7**	**57,571.8**	**59,394.1**	**5.4**	**5.5**	**5.0**

Notes:

1. Numbers may not add because of rounding.

2. As of 1 October 2012, Affinity Water is the new name for the combined Veolia companies (previously Veolia Water Central, Veolia Water East and Veolia Water South East).

3. With effect from 1 April 2013, South Staffordshire Water PLC will replace Cambridge Water PLC as the Water Undertaker for its Area.

10.15 Overall summary of pollution incident results by region, medium and incident category 2012

Water	Anglian	EA Wales	Midlands	North East	North West	South East	South West	Total
Cat 1	6	11	7	8	4	11	5	52
Cat 2	34	59	37	38	31	63	47	309
Cat 3	1166	956	1294	1155	952	2284	1103	8910
Cat 4	1613	1844	2432	2153	1032	3908	1178	14160
Total	2819	2870	3770	3354	2019	6266	2333	23431
							Cat 1 & 2 Total	**361**

Land	Anglian	EA Wales	Midlands	North East	North West	South East	South West	Total
Cat 1	0	2	2	0	1	4	0	9
Cat 2	7	33	21	10	20	25	17	133
Cat 3	731	895	796	960	461	1482	748	6073
Cat 4	2081	1940	2951	2384	1537	4755	1568	17216
Total	2819	2870	3770	3354	2019	6266	2333	23431
							Cat 1 & 2 Total	**142**

Air	Anglian	EA Wales	Midlands	North East	North West	South East	South West	Total
Cat 1	0	1	1	0	3	0	0	5
Cat 2	8	25	65	10	6	24	20	158
Cat 3	750	826	827	860	371	1116	564	5314
Cat 4	2061	2018	2877	2484	1639	5126	1749	17954
Total	2819	2870	3770	3354	2019	6266	2333	23431
							Cat 1 & 2 Total	**163**

Source: Environmental Agency

"Contains Environment Agency information © Environment Agency and database right"

Note:

Please note that this data refers to substantiated, completed (ie: not ongoing) environmental pollution incidents. Category 1 classifies incidents as having a major environmental impact, Category 2 significant, Category 3 minor and Category 4 is no environmental impact

10.16a 2012 mandatory compliance[1] results for bathing waters in the UK

Coastal Bathing Waters (results for 2011 are in brackets)

Region *	Mandatory Pass	Fail	Total	Compliance%
North East	47(54)	7 (0)	54 (54)	87.0 (100)
Anglian	40 (40)	0 (0)	40 (40)	100 (100)
South East	90 (89)	0 (1)	90 (90)	100 (98.9)
South West	177 (189)	16 (2)	193 (191)	91.7 (99)
North West	24 (24)	6 (6)	30 (30)	80.0 (80.0)
England	**378 (396)**	**29 (9)**	**407 (405)**	**92.9 (97.8)**
Wales	**97 (87)**	**3 (1)**	**100 (88)**	**97.0 (98.9)**
Scotland	**78 (76)**	**2 (4)**	**80 (80)**	**97.5 (95)**
Northern Ireland	**22 (24)**	**1 (0)**	**23 (24)**	**95.7 (100)**
UK COASTAL WATERS	**575 (583)**	**35 (14)**	**610 (597)**	**94.3 (97.7)**

Inland Bathing Waters (results for 2011 are in brackets)

Region*	Mandatory Pass	Fail	Total	Compliance %
South East	6 (6)	0 (0)	6 (6)	100 (100)
North West	3 (3)	0 (0)	3 (3)	100 (100)
England	**9 (9)**	**0 (0)**	**9 (9)**	**100 (100)**
Scotland	**3 (3)**	**0 (0)**	**3 (3)**	**100 (100)**
UK INLAND WATERS	**12 (12)**	**0 (0)**	**12 (12)**	**100 (100)**

[1] Figures shown are for compliance with the mandatory microbiological standards set by the EC Bathing Water Directive (76/160/EEC)

* Environment Agency operational regions

10.16b 2012 guideline[2] compliance results for bathing waters in the UK

Coastal Bathing Waters   (results for 2011 are in brackets)

Region *	Guideline Pass	Fail	Total	Compliance %
North East	25 (49)	29 (5)	54 (54)	46.3 (90.7)
Anglian	33 (36)	7 (4)	40 (40)	82.5 (90.0)
South East	62 (66)	28 (24)	90 (90)	68.9 (73.3)
South West	117 (162)	76 (29)	193 (191)	60.6 (84.8)
North West	3 (9)	27 (21)	30 (30)	10.0 (30.0)
England	**240 (322)**	**167 (83)**	**407 (405)**	**59.0 (79.5)**
Wales	**75 (78)**	**25 (10)**	**100 (88)**	**75.0 (88.6)**
Scotland	**32 (39)**	**48 (41)**	**80 (80)**	**40.0 (48.8)**
Northern Ireland	**16 (20)**	**7 (4)**	**23 (24)**	**69.6 (83.3)**
UK COASTAL WATERS	**363 (459)**	**247 (138)**	**610 (597)**	**59.5 (76.9)**

Inland Bathing Waters   (Results for 2011 are in brackets)

Region *	Guideline Pass	Fail	Total	Compliance %
South East	2 (3)	4 (3)	6 (6)	33.3 (50)
North West	1 (3)	2 (0)	3 (3)	33.3 (100)
England	**3 (6)**	**6 (3)**	**9 (9)**	**33.3 (66.7)**
Scotland	**0 (1)**	**3 (2)**	**3 (3)**	**0 (33.3)**
UK INLAND WATERS	**3 (7)**	**9 (5)**	**12 (12)**	**25.0 (58.3)**

2 Figures for 2011 are for compliance with the tightest guideline microbiological standards set by the EC Bathing Water Directive (76/160/EEC).   The figures for 2012 show compliance with the equivalent single standard that will be used during the transitional period from 2012 - 2014 as the revised Directive (2006/7/EC) is implemented.

* Environment Agency operational regions

10.17 Estimated abstractions from all surface and groundwater sources: by purpose[1]

England and Wales — million cubic metres

		2000	2001	2002	2003	2004	2005	2006	2007	2008	2009	2010	2011	2012
Public water supply	JZLA	6,218	5,923	6,183	6,036	6,298	6,342	6,207	5,979	5,944	5,768	5,977	5,829	5,844
Spray irrigation	JZLB	106	94	91	116	83	81	101	58	58	86	106	117	49
Agriculture (excl spray irrigation)	JZLC	57	40	44	49	44	22	18	26	14	17	24	26	25
Electricity supply industry[2]	JZLD	11,546	11,777	12,938	11,555	11,189	10,956	11,737	11,856	12,128	10,977	10,868	10,716	13,309
Other industry[3]	JZLE	1,989	1,743	1,784	2,160	2,409	2,314	2,379	1,886	1,814	2,065	1,815	1,737	2,011
Fish farming, cress growing, amenity ponds	JYXG	1,724	1,700	1,173	1,241	1,490	1,334	1,322	1,245	1,043	953	1,059	848	974
Private water supply	JZLG	37	32	20	15	10	9	14	11	9	9	8	9	10
Other	JZLH	204	40	28	27	28	22	32	41	27	28	22	22	27
Total	JZLI	21,880	21,348	22,259	21,199	21,552	21,080	21,809	21,105	21,036	19,899	19,875	19,304	22,251

1 See chapter text.

Source: Environment Agency

2 Increased electricity supply abstraction from 2002 due to issue of 2 new abstraction licences

3 Three abstraction licences in 2003 re-assigned to "other industry" from "electricty supply"

10.18 Estimates of remaining recoverable oil & gas reserves and resources, 2001-2011

United Kingdom

	2001	2002	2003	2004	2005	2006	2007	2008	2009	2010	2011
OIL (million tonnes)											
Discovered reserves											
Proven	605.00	595.00	571.00	533.00	516.00	479.00	452.00	408.00	378.00	373.84	413.12
Probable	350.00	325.00	286.00	283.00	300.00	298.00	328.00	361.00	390.00	376.71	374.39
Proven plus Probable	955.00	920.00	857.00	816.00	816.00	776.00	780.00	770.00	769.00	750.55	787.52
Possible	475.00	425.00	410.00	512.00	451.00	478.00	399.00	360.00	343.00	342.31	318.52
Maximum	1,430.00	1,345.00	1,267.00	1,328.00	1,267.00	1,254.00	1,179.00	1,130.00	1,112.00	1,092.86	1,106.04
Range of undiscovered resources											
Lower	205.00	272.00	323.00	396.00	346.00	438.00	379.00	454.00	397.00	475.00	422.00
Upper	1,930.00	1,770.00	1,826.00	1,830.00	1,581.00	1,637.00	1,577.00	1,561.00	1,477.00	1,374.00	1,321.00
Range of total reserves and resources											
Lower[1]	810.00	867.00	894.00	929.00	862.00	917.00	831.00	862.00	775.00	848.84	835.12
Upper[2]	3,360.00	3,115.00	3,093.00	3,158.00	2,848.00	2,891.00	2,756.00	2,691.00	2,589.00	2,466.86	2,427.04
Expected level of reserves[3]											
Opening stocks	1,010.00	955.00	920.00	857.00	816.00	816.00	776.00	780.00	770.00	769.00	750.55
Extraction[4]	-116.68	-115.94	-106.07	-95.37	-84.72	-76.58	-76.83	-71.66	-68.20	-62.96	-51.97
Other volume changes	61.68	80.94	43.07	54.37	84.72	36.58	80.83	61.66	67.20	44.51	88.93
Closing stocks	955.00	920.00	857.00	816.00	816.00	776.00	780.00	770.00	769.00	750.55	787.52
GAS (billion cubic metres)											
	2001	2002	2003	2004	2005	2006	2007	2008	2009	2010	2011
Discovered reserves											
Proven	655.00	630.00	590.00	531.00	481.00	412.00	343.00	292.00	256.00	252.59	246.03
Probable	445.00	370.00	315.00	296.00	247.00	272.00	304.00	309.00	308.00	267.29	246.48
Proven plus Probable	1,100.00	1,000.00	905.00	826.00	728.00	684.00	647.00	601.00	564.00	519.88	492.52
Possible	395.00	330.00	336.00	343.00	278.00	283.00	293.00	306.00	276.00	261.43	216.44
Maximum	1,495.00	1,330.00	1,241.00	1,169.00	1,006.00	967.00	940.00	907.00	840.00	781.30	708.96
Range of undiscovered resources											
Lower	290.00	238.00	279.00	293.00	226.00	301.00	280.00	319.00	300.00	363.00	353.00
Upper	1,680.00	1,386.00	1,259.00	1,245.00	1,035.00	1,049.00	1,039.00	1,043.00	949.00	1,021.00	977.00
Range of total reserves and resources											
Lower[1]	945.00	868.00	869.00	824.00	707.00	713.00	623.00	611.00	556.00	615.59	599.03
Upper[2]	3,175.00	2,716.00	2,500.00	2,414.00	2,041.00	2,016.00	1,979.00	1,950.00	1,789.00	1,802.30	1,685.96
Expected level of reserves[3]											
Opening stocks	1,195.00	1,100.00	1,000.00	905.00	826.00	728.00	684.00	647.00	601.00	564.00	519.88
Extraction[4]	-104.50	-102.10	-101.90	-95.00	-86.40	-77.80	-70.45	-68.20	-57.26	-54.53	-42.94
Other volume changes	9.50	2.10	6.90	16.00	-11.60	33.80	33.45	22.20	20.26	10.40	15.58
Closing stocks	1,100.00	1,000.00	905.00	826.00	728.00	684.00	647.00	601.00	564.00	519.88	492.52

All data refer to end of year.   Sources: ONS, DECC

Components may not sum to totals due to rounding.

1. The lower end of the range of total reserves and resources has been calculated as the sum of proven reserves and the lower end of the range of undiscovered resources.

2. The upper end of the range of total reserves and resources is the sum of proven, probable and possible reserves and the upper end of the range of undiscovered resources.

3. Expected reserves are the sum of proven and probable reserves.

4. The negative of extraction is shown here for the purposes of the calculation only. Of itself, extraction should be considered as a positive value.

10.19a Local Authority Collected Waste (England) 2000/01 to 2011/12

England and Regions

Thousand tonnes

Household waste from:	2000/01	2001/02	2002/03	2003/04	2004/05	2005/06	England 2006/07r	2007/08	2008/09r	2009/10	2010/11	2011/12
Regular household collection	16,655	16,683	16,528	16,066	15,470	14,616	14,050	13,046	12,076	11,432	11,048	10,586
Other household sources	1,381	1,277	1,351	1,244	1,205	1,314	1,173	1,073	1,026	1,070	1,047	997
Civic amenity sites	4,234	4,367	4,213	3,616	3,198	2,726	2,576	2,434	2,086	1,765	1,635	1,470
Household recycling	2,809	3,197	3,740	4,521	5,785	6,796	7,976	8,735	9,146	9,398	9,724	9,846
Total household	**25,079**	**25,524**	**25,832**	**25,448**	**25,658**	**25,454**	**25,775**	**25,287**	**24,334**	**23,666**	**23,454**	**22,899**
Non household sources (excl. recycling)	2,342	2,656	2,730	2,650	2,795	2,289	2,408	2,250	2,063	1,999	1,882	1,654
Non household recycling	636	724	832	1,016	1,167	1,003	961	969	936	877	864	866
Total LA collected waste	**28,057**	**28,905**	**29,394**	**29,114**	**29,619**	**28,745**	**29,144**	**28,506**	**27,334**	**26,541**	**26,200**	**25,419**

There has been a revision to 2008/09 to include asbestos in "Other household sources" instead of "Non household sources".
2010/11 data has been revised slightly due to data issues.
Source: Department for Environment, Food & Rural Affairs

10.19b Waste managed by type and year (Wales) (a)

Thousand tonnes

	2008-09	2009-10	2010-11	2011-12	2012-13
Composted	214	233	264	291	285
Recycled	433	443	471	493	531
Incineration	32	35	38	51	72
Landfill	1,035	931	826	710	641
Other (b)	12	16	14	15	36
Total	**1,724**	**1,659**	**1,613**	**1,560**	**1,565**

Source: WasteDataFlow

(a) Includes household and non-household waste. Excluding abandoned vehicles.

(b) Includes refuse derived fuel, and mechanical biological treatment (MBT)

10.19c Household waste WasteDataFlow data 2012 CALENDAR YEAR[1]

2011

Local Authority	HOUSEHOLD WASTE[2] Arisings (tonnes)	HOUSEHOLD WASTE Recycled / Composted[1] (tonnes)	Percentage HOUSEHOLD WASTE Recycled / Composted (%)	HOUSEHOLD WASTE Recovered (tonnes)[3]	Percentage HOUSEHOLD WASTE Recovery (%)	HOUSEHOLD WASTE Landfilled (tonnes)[4]	Percentage HOUSEHOLD WASTE Landfilled (%)	Percentage HOUSEHOLD WASTE Recycled / Composted (%)
Aberdeen	97,242	36,242	37.3	12	0.0	60,988	62.7	35.7
Aberdeenshire	134,708	47,889	35.6	0	0.0	86,819	64.4	33.6
Angus	60,803	24,393	40.1	3,564	5.9	32,846	54.0	41.8
Argyll and Bute	48,509	15,291	31.5	5,558	11.5	27,660	57.0	29.6
Clackmannanshire	27,737	16,348	58.9	1,443	5.2	9,945	35.9	52.0
Dumfries and Galloway	77,709	17,231	22.2	34,708	44.7	23,702	30.5	21.5
Dundee	70,103	20,794	29.7	14,653	20.9	34,655	49.4	32.4
East Ayrshire	58,793	26,107	44.4	0	0.0	32,685	55.6	46.8
East Dunbartonshire	55,233	21,368	38.7	0	0.0	33,865	61.3	37.7
East Lothian	52,346	23,461	44.8	4,686	9.0	24,200	46.2	44.1
East Renfrewshire	43,986	23,829	54.2	0	0.0	20,162	45.8	53.2
Edinburgh	187,741	68,896	36.7	0	0.0	118,845	63.3	31.1
Eilean Siar	14,299	4,251	29.7	0	0.0	10,069	70.4	26.5
Falkirk	76,111	41,979	55.2	1,870	2.5	32,262	42.4	52.7
Fife	195,595	103,303	52.8	0	0.0	92,292	47.2	54.0
Glasgow	234,209	69,113	29.5	0	0.0	165,096	70.5	26.7
Highland	126,183	55,938	44.3	812	0.6	69,436	55.0	44.5
Inverclyde	33,248	16,844	50.7	612	1.8	15,793	47.5	41.2
Midlothian	42,701	19,339	45.3	0	0.0	23,362	54.7	47.2
Moray	49,883	25,905	51.9	0	0.0	23,979	48.1	44.6
North Ayrshire	62,729	32,479	51.8	358	0.6	29,752	47.4	51.8
North Lanarkshire	155,838	62,013	39.8	0	0.0	93,826	60.2	39.4
Orkney	10,233	2,301	22.5	4,875	47.6	2,721	26.6	30.1
Perth and Kinross	75,015	41,253	55.0	0	0.0	33,761	45.0	52.3
Renfrewshire	82,126	31,911	38.9	3,177	3.9	47,050	57.3	42.3
Scottish Borders	52,861	22,648	42.8	777	1.5	29,440	55.7	46.3
Shetland Islands	10,865	1,464	13.5	7,596	69.9	1,799	16.6	16.7
South Ayrshire	57,627	27,351	47.5	0	0.0	30,275	52.5	48.2
South Lanarkshire	151,923	56,799	37.4	0	0.0	95,124	62.6	35.3
Stirling	43,190	24,052	55.7	689	1.6	17,009	39.4	53.5
West Dunbartonshire	38,944	17,193	44.1	130	0.3	21,622	55.5	45.0
West Lothian	72,345	31,129	43.0	93	0.1	41,167	56.9	43.6
TOTAL SCOTLAND	**2,500,836**	**1,029,109**	**41.2**	**85,613**	**3.4**	**1,382,208**	**55.3**	**40.1**

[1] All the figures are calculated according to the Zero Waste Plan - guidance for local authorities

[2] Household waste is waste generated by households (see full definition in par 1.2 of the Zero Waste Plan - guidance for local authorities).

[3] Recovery is the fate of waste material not reused, recycled or landfilled. It includes household waste treated by incineration, mechanical biological and heat treatment. Recovery includes any Incinerator Bottom Ash and Metals recycled as a result of treatment, and excludes the residue from incineration which is landfilled. Recovery also excludes any weight loss during the treatment process.

[4] Includes household waste disposed of instead of being recycled and residues from incineration that are landfilled.

[5] LACMSW = Local authority collected municipal solid waste.

Please note local authorities report stockpiled materials in the quarter when the material is sent to reprocessors to avoid discrepancies with the total arisings. The figures are accurate at the time of publication. However the data may be updated if further revisions are necessary.

10.19d Municipal waste sent for recycling & composting, KPI(e), and landfilled, KPI(f), for Northern Ireland, 2011/12

	KPI(j)						KPI (e)		KPI(f)
Area	Municipal waste arisings (tonnes)	Municipal dry recycling (tonnes)	Municipal composting (tonnes)	Total municipal dry recyling & composting (tonnes)	Municipal dry recycling rate	Municipal composting rate	Municipal waste sent for recycling (inc composting) as a % of municipal waste arisings	Municipal waste landfilled (tonnes)	Municipal waste landfilled as a % of total municipal waste arisings
arc21									
Antrim	35,186	10,321	8,406	**18,727**	29.3%	23.9%	53.2%	16,001	45.5%
Ards	42,435	7,665	8,527	**16,192**	18.1%	20.1%	38.2%	26,080	61.5%
Ballymena	31,926	6,108	6,114	**12,222**	19.1%	19.2%	38.3%	19,693	61.7%
Belfast	148,866	23,607	16,445	**40,052**	15.9%	11.0%	26.9%	105,500	70.9%
Carrickfergus	24,272	7,129	4,049	**11,178**	29.4%	16.7%	46.1%	13,093	53.9%
Castlereagh	31,004	6,413	6,707	**13,120**	20.7%	21.6%	42.3%	17,468	56.3%
Down	32,635	6,079	4,026	**10,106**	18.6%	12.3%	31.0%	22,414	68.7%
Larne	20,396	6,776	4,042	**10,818**	33.2%	19.8%	53.0%	8,743	42.9%
Lisburn	58,637	11,576	11,873	**23,448**	19.7%	20.2%	40.0%	34,481	58.8%
Newtownabbey	45,212	8,445	9,931	**18,377**	18.7%	22.0%	40.6%	25,689	56.8%
North Down	47,404	12,242	8,748	**20,990**	25.8%	18.5%	44.3%	26,075	55.0%
All arc21	**517,972**	**106,362**	**88,869**	**195,231**	**20.5%**	**17.2%**	**37.7%**	**315,238**	**60.9%**
NWRWMG									
Ballymoney	15,720	3,333	2,194	**5,527**	21.2%	14.0%	35.2%	9,970	63.4%
Coleraine	35,261	9,033	4,310	**13,342**	25.6%	12.2%	37.8%	20,155	57.2%
Derry	55,984	15,109	1,553	**16,662**	27.0%	2.8%	29.8%	39,166	70.0%
Limavady	17,255	4,467	1,843	**6,311**	25.9%	10.7%	36.6%	9,919	57.5%
Magherafelt	24,507	8,459	6,030	**14,489**	34.5%	24.6%	59.1%	6,841	27.9%
Moyle	9,544	2,628	1,049	**3,678**	27.5%	11.0%	38.5%	5,676	59.5%
Strabane	18,856	5,035	945	**5,981**	26.7%	5.0%	31.7%	11,926	63.2%
All NWRWMG	**177,128**	**48,065**	**17,924**	**65,989**	**27.1%**	**10.1%**	**37.3%**	**103,654**	**58.5%**
SWaMP2008									
Armagh	28,687	7,286	5,174	**12,460**	25.4%	18.0%	43.4%	14,145	49.3%
Banbridge	26,709	5,842	8,398	**14,240**	21.9%	31.4%	53.3%	12,060	45.2%
Cookstown	20,160	4,410	3,882	**8,293**	21.9%	19.3%	41.1%	11,753	58.3%
Craigavon	47,916	11,530	8,139	**19,669**	24.1%	17.0%	41.0%	14,017	29.3%
Dungannon	29,374	6,045	5,483	**11,528**	20.6%	18.7%	39.2%	16,881	57.5%
Fermanagh	29,477	8,231	2,663	**10,894**	27.9%	9.0%	37.0%	18,403	62.4%
Newry & Mourne	46,589	9,270	5,870	**15,140**	19.9%	12.6%	32.5%	31,109	66.8%
Omagh	25,480	6,786	4,112	**10,898**	26.6%	16.1%	42.8%	14,212	55.8%
All SWaMP2008	**254,392**	**59,401**	**43,721**	**103,122**	**23.4%**	**17.2%**	**40.5%**	**132,580**	**52.1%**
Northern Ireland	**949,491**	**213,828**	**150,514**	**364,342**	**22.5%**	**15.9%**	**38.4%**	**551,472**	**58.1%**

Source: NIEA

Note: Rates calculated by dividing total tonnage of municipal waste sent for recycling, composting and landfill by total municipal waste arisings.

Note: The tonnages of recycled (including composted) and landfilled waste may not always equal the waste arisings because the recycling measures were defined to capture outputs from recovery processes which excludes reuse.

Note: The percentage of recycled (including composted) and landfilled waste may not always equal 100% because the recycling measures were defined to capture outputs from recovery processes which excludes reuse.

Data revised from previous publication.

10.19d Household waste sent for recycling and composting, KPI(a), for Northern Ireland, 2011/12

Area	Household waste arisings (tonnes)	Household dry recycling (tonnes)	Household composting (tonnes)	Total household dry recyling & composting (tonnes)	Household dry recycling rate	Household composting rate	KPI (a) Household waste sent for recycling (inc composting) as a % of household waste arisings
arc21							
Antrim	29,360	6,056	8,406	14,462	20.6%	28.6%	49.3%
Ards	38,618	7,385	8,527	15,912	19.1%	22.1%	41.2%
Ballymena	28,811	4,843	6,114	10,957	16.8%	21.2%	38.0%
Belfast	121,203	22,408	16,034	38,442	18.5%	13.2%	31.7%
Carrickfergus	19,231	3,824	4,049	7,873	19.9%	21.1%	40.9%
Castlereagh	29,144	5,586	6,706	12,292	19.2%	23.0%	42.2%
Down	30,091	6,014	3,930	9,943	20.0%	13.1%	33.0%
Larne	17,007	4,603	4,042	8,645	27.1%	23.8%	50.8%
Lisburn	53,052	9,633	11,873	21,505	18.2%	22.4%	40.5%
Newtownabbey	41,414	8,211	9,783	17,994	19.8%	23.6%	43.4%
North Down	38,909	8,942	8,563	17,505	23.0%	22.0%	45.0%
All arc21	**446,839**	**87,505**	**88,026**	**175,531**	**19.6%**	**19.7%**	**39.3%**
NWRWMG							
Ballymoney	13,878	2,825	2,194	5,019	20.4%	15.8%	36.2%
Coleraine	31,079	8,053	4,310	12,363	25.9%	13.9%	39.8%
Derry	49,087	12,596	1,553	14,149	25.7%	3.2%	28.8%
Limavady	16,275	4,088	1,843	5,931	25.1%	11.3%	36.4%
Magherafelt	21,583	6,963	6,030	12,993	32.3%	27.9%	60.2%
Moyle	8,506	2,458	1,049	3,507	28.9%	12.3%	41.2%
Strabane	17,325	4,878	945	5,823	28.2%	5.5%	33.6%
All NWRWMG	**157,733**	**41,862**	**17,924**	**59,786**	**26.5%**	**11.4%**	**37.9%**
SWaMP2008							
Armagh	25,567	5,837	5,015	10,852	22.8%	19.6%	42.4%
Banbridge	24,583	4,525	8,260	12,785	18.4%	33.6%	52.0%
Cookstown	17,787	3,411	3,882	7,294	19.2%	21.8%	41.0%
Craigavon	44,360	11,179	8,139	19,319	25.2%	18.3%	43.5%
Dungannon	27,513	5,965	5,483	11,448	21.7%	19.9%	41.6%
Fermanagh	25,857	6,501	2,663	9,164	25.1%	10.3%	35.4%
Newry & Mourne	40,777	9,259	5,868	15,127	22.7%	14.4%	37.1%
Omagh	23,133	5,916	4,112	10,028	25.6%	17.8%	43.4%
All SWaMP2008	**229,576**	**52,595**	**43,422**	**96,017**	**22.9%**	**18.9%**	**41.8%**
Northern Ireland	**834,149**	**181,961**	**149,373**	**331,334**	**21.8%**	**17.9%**	**39.7%**

Source: NIEA

Note: Rates calculated by dividing total tonnage of household waste sent for recycling and composting by total household waste arisings.

Note: The tonnages of recycled (including composted) and landfilled waste may not always equal the waste arisings because the recycling measures were defined to capture outputs from recovery processes which excludes reuse.

Note: The percentage of recycled (including composted) and landfilled waste may not always equal 100% because the recycling measures were defined to capture outputs from recovery processes which excludes reuse.

Data revised from previous publication.

10.19d Household waste landfilled, KPI(b), and generated per household, KPI(h), and per capita, KPI(p), in Northern Ireland, 2011/12

		KPI (b)		KPI(h)		KPI(p)
Area	Household waste landfilled (tonnes)	Household waste landfilled as a % of household waste arisings	Estimated households (March 2012)	Annual household waste collected per household (tonnes)	Estimated population (2011)	Annual household waste collected per capita (kilogrammes)
arc21						
Antrim	14,480	49.3%	20,937	1.402	53,428	550
Ards	22,565	58.4%	33,920	1.138	78,078	495
Ballymena	17,843	61.9%	25,640	1.120	64,044	450
Belfast	80,280	66.2%	127,394	0.951	280,962	431
Carrickfergus	11,358	59.1%	16,313	1.179	39,114	492
Castlereagh	16,459	56.5%	28,967	1.006	67,242	433
Down	20,043	66.6%	28,057	1.072	69,731	432
Larne	7,635	44.9%	14,261	1.193	32,180	528
Lisburn	30,909	58.3%	48,438	1.095	120,165	441
Newtownabbey	22,412	54.1%	35,626	1.162	85,139	486
North Down	21,097	54.2%	34,865	1.116	78,937	493
All arc21	**265,080**	**59.3%**	**414,418**	**1.078**	**969,020**	**461**
NWRWMG						
Ballymoney	8,664	62.4%	12,197	1.138	31,224	444
Coleraine	17,198	55.3%	27,338	1.137	59,067	526
Derry	34,845	71.0%	40,397	1.215	107,877	455
Limavady	9,366	57.5%	12,817	1.270	33,536	485
Magherafelt	5,875	27.2%	16,209	1.332	45,038	479
Moyle	4,838	56.9%	7,851	1.083	17,050	499
Strabane	10,644	61.4%	15,460	1.121	39,843	435
All NWRWMG	**91,429**	**58.0%**	**132,269**	**1.193**	**333,635**	**473**
SWaMP2008						
Armagh	12,821	50.1%	22,676	1.127	59,340	431
Banbridge	11,411	46.4%	19,624	1.253	48,339	509
Cookstown	10,382	58.4%	13,940	1.276	37,013	481
Craigavon	12,451	28.1%	38,301	1.158	93,023	477
Dungannon	15,176	55.2%	21,777	1.263	57,852	476
Fermanagh	16,529	63.9%	27,326	0.946	61,805	418
Newry & Mourne	25,325	62.1%	34,292	1.189	99,480	410
Omagh	12,748	55.1%	20,307	1.139	51,356	450
All SWaMP2008	**116,843**	**50.9%**	**198,243**	**1.158**	**508,208**	**452**
Northern Ireland	**473,353**	**56.7%**	**744,930**	**1.120**	**1,810,863**	**461**

Source: NIEA, NISRA, DSD

Note: Rates calculated by dividing total tonnage of household waste sent to landfill by total household waste arisings.
Note: The tonnages of recycled (including composted) and landfilled waste may not always equal the waste arisings because the recycling measures were defined to capture outputs from recovery processes which excludes reuse.
Note: The percentage of recycled (including composted) and landfilled waste may not always equal 100% because the recycling measures were defined to capture outputs from recovery processes which excludes reuse.
Data revised from previous publication.

10.20a Amounts of different materials from household sources collected for recycling (including reuse) by collection method 2011/12, England

(Thousand tonnes)

	Paper & Card	Glass	Compost	Scrap & White Goods	Textiles	Cans	Plastic	Co-mingled	Other	Total
Kerbside	834.5	369.3	2,860.0	11.8	15.0	50.6	57.7	2,417.3	20.6	6,636.6
Bring site collection	106.9	209.2	12.9	1.6	51.0	5.2	11.7	19	7.9	425.5
Civic amenity site collection	196.8	42.8	1,012.5	466.3	43.5	5.9	29.5	3.4	710.6	2,511.3
Private/voluntary collection schemes*	0.5	0.2	125.5	0.1	-	0.0	0.1	15.2	84.4	226.0
Total	1,138.7	621.4	4,010.9	479.7	109.5	61.7	98.9	2,454.9	823.5	9,799.4

Sources: WasteDataFlow, Department for Environment Food and Rural affairs

* Based on Includes street sweepings, street recycling bins, gully waste, community skips and household green waste collected by private/voluntary schemes

2 Total amount of household waste collected for recycling is greater than that sent for recycling as some material is subsequently rejected during sorting or by the reprocessor.

10.20b Total Houshold recycling by material and source, Wales

Materials	Kerbside collection (tonnes)					
	2006-07	2007-08	2008-09	2009-10	2010-11	2011-12
All paper and Card	69,581.5	84,592.8	61,161.1	60,908.1	58,790.1	59670.6
Ferrous food & beverage cans (1)	5,857.0	7,808.7	7,083.2	6,193.9	5,846.2	5927.8
Food (6)	0.0	0.0	0.0	15,957.1	35,486.5	62216.1
Garden waste (2)	63,409.7	85,402.8	107,069.8	118,959.4	138,226.2	137393.0
Glass	28,052.1	36,709.5	33,393.1	32,321.5	29,956.7	30280.5
Miscellaneous	24,201.4	28,276.3	78,314.4	102,333.6	119,930.2	132460.5
Non-ferrous metal	321.3	888.4	486.4	393.7	564.2	752.8
Other ferrous metal (3)	750.7	559.8	50.1	78.6	67.0	82.2
Plastics	9,569.5	12,740.8	9,105.2	8,094.2	11,267.0	13663.1
Textiles and shoes	807.2	725.7	726.1	622.7	631.1	690.5
WEEE (4)	1,723.9	1,690.1	1,532.6	1,340.5	1,466.6	356.4
Wood	423.6	574.1	69.2	9.1	124.8	318.6
TOTAL	204,697.7	259,969.0	298,991.2	347,212.4	402,356.7	443812.1

Materials	Bring and Civic Amenity sites (tonnes)[5]					
	2006-07	2007-08	2008-09	2009-10	2010-11	2011-12
All paper and Card	33,116.0	32,994.4	31,282.1	28,596.9	24,816.0	22154.5
Ferrous food & beverage cans (1)	1,323.2	884.5	753.6	843.5	748.2	559.3
Food (6)	0.0	0.0	0.0	0.0	275.9	0.0
Garden waste (2)	61,864.9	62,988.0	63,381.3	61,667.5	58,991.5	56222.8
Glass	18,815.5	20,613.1	20,283.4	19,256.6	17,213.5	16366.0
Miscellaneous	6,235.5	18,033.3	10,227.8	15,675.3	15,694.2	92309.3
Non-ferrous metal	52.2	70.8	61.3	141.2	26.3	56.5
Other ferrous metal (3)	23,078.6	21,460.4	17,076.9	16,895.6	16,110.8	14411.0
Plastics	3,855.9	3,844.6	4,390.6	4,499.5	5,240.5	5678.1
Textiles and shoes	3,876.9	4,292.6	4,771.4	5,323.1	5,484.8	5615.8
WEEE (4)	13,484.0	17,016.0	19,627.8	21,539.1	21,558.4	18451.1
Wood	39,696.3	46,557.9	53,673.2	52,615.6	53,621.0	54471.0
TOTAL	205,398.9	228,755.6	225,529.4	227,054.0	219,780.9	286295.5

Materials	Total Kerbside, Bring and Civic Amenity sites (tonnes)					
	2006-07	2007-08	2008-09	2009-10	2010-11	2011-12
All paper and Card	102,697.5	117,587.2	92,443.2	89,505.0	83,606.1	81825.2
Ferrous food & beverage cans (1)	7,180.2	8,693.2	7,836.8	7,037.4	6,594.4	6487.1
Food (6)	0.0	0.0	0.0	15,957.1	35,762.5	62216.1
Garden waste (2)	125,274.6	148,390.9	170,451.2	180,626.9	197,217.7	193615.8
Glass	46,867.6	57,322.6	53,676.5	51,578.1	47,170.1	46646.6
Miscellaneous	30,436.9	46,309.5	88,542.2	118,008.9	135,624.4	224769.8
Non-ferrous metal	373.4	959.3	547.7	535.0	590.5	809.3
Other ferrous metal (3)	23,829.3	22,020.2	17,127.0	16,974.2	16,177.8	14493.1
Plastics	13,425.3	16,585.4	13,495.8	12,593.8	16,507.5	19341.2
Textiles and shoes	4,684.1	5,018.3	5,497.5	5,945.8	6,115.8	6306.3
WEEE (4)	15,207.9	18,706.1	21,160.4	22,879.6	23,025.0	18807.5
Wood	40,119.9	47,132.0	53,742.3	52,624.7	53,745.8	54789.7
TOTAL	410,096.6	488,724.6	524,520.6	574,266.4	622,137.6	730107.6

10.20b Total Houshold recycling by material and source, Wales

Materials	Voluntary/Private collection/Other (tonnes)					
	2006-07	2007-08	2008-09	2009-10	2010-11	2011-12
All paper and Card	1,652.6	914.2	297.5	87.1	73.0	44.6
Ferrous food & beverage cans (1)	242.7	95.2	30.3	0.0	0.0	2.2
Food (6)	0.0	0.0	0.0	0.0	0.0	0.0
Garden waste (2)	3,165.8	6,238.1	5,165.5	7,582.7	863.9	0.0
Glass	977.4	328.2	109.1	0.3	0.4	140.3
Miscellaneous	1,710.8	2,024.7	2,628.3	3,700.9	2,981.3	4565.4
Non-ferrous metal	14.2	1.4	0.0	0.0	0.0	0.0
Other ferrous metal (3)	65.6	9.5	22.1	38.6	2.0	138.4
Plastics	268.4	123.5	47.0	0.0	0.0	2.3
Textiles and shoes	385.6	434.2	354.6	519.7	543.0	120.9
WEEE (4)	198.1	125.3	333.3	206.0	284.7	108.6
Wood	57.4	21.4	227.2	69.4	398.7	412.2
TOTAL	8,738.7	10,315.8	9,214.8	12,204.8	5,147.1	5534.9

Materials	Total household recycled / composted (tonnes)					
	2006-07	2007-08	2008-09	2009-10	2010-11	2011-12
All paper and Card	104,350.1	118,501.5	92,740.6	89,592.0	83,679.1	81869.8
Ferrous food & beverage cans (1)	7,422.8	8,788.4	7,867.0	7,037.4	6,594.4	6489.2
Food (6)	0.0	0.0	0.0	15,957.1	35,762.5	62216.1
Garden waste (2)	128,440.4	154,629.0	175,616.7	188,209.6	198,081.7	193615.8
Glass	47,845.0	57,650.8	53,785.6	51,578.4	47,170.5	46786.8
Miscellaneous	32,147.7	48,334.2	91,170.5	121,709.8	138,605.8	229335.2
Non-ferrous metal	387.7	960.7	547.7	535.0	590.5	809.3
Other ferrous metal (3)	23,894.9	22,029.7	17,149.0	17,012.8	16,179.8	14631.5
Plastics	13,693.7	16,708.9	13,542.8	12,593.8	16,507.5	19343.6
Textiles and shoes	5,069.8	5,452.5	5,852.0	6,465.6	6,658.9	6427.2
WEEE (4)	15,406.0	18,831.3	21,493.8	23,085.6	23,309.7	18916.1
Wood	40,177.3	47,153.5	53,969.6	52,694.2	54,144.5	55201.9
TOTAL	418,835.3	499,040.4	533,735.3	586,471.2	627,284.7	735642.5

1. Includes mixed cans
2. Includes mixed food and garden waste
3. Includes scrap metal
4. Waste Electronic and Electrical Equipment
5. Includes Small element of Street Recycling Bins
6 food waste that is seperatly collected only

10.20c Waste Collections in Scotland - Kerbside Collections 2012

Tonnage collected

Kerbside Collection	Collected for Recycling	Collected for Reuse
Green glass	6801.105	0
Brown glass	2362.406	0
Clear glass	8132.541	0
Mixed glass	23222.56	0
Paper	23059.026	0
Card	4164.716	0
Books	0	0
Mixed paper & card	36250.536	0
Steel cans	724.86	0
Aluminium cans	208.11	0
Mixed cans	1490.064	0
Plastics	897.13	0
Mixed Plastic Bottles	2034.181	0
PET [1]	0	0
HDPE [2]	0	0
PVC [3]	0	0
LDPE [4]	0	0
PP [5]	0	0
PS [6]	0	0
OTHER PLASTICS [7]	71.86	0
Green garden waste only	171103.24	0
Waste food only	7848.4	0
Mixed garden and food waste	72504.74	0
Wood for composting	0	0
Other compostable waste	11176.66	0
Wood	400.46	0
Chipboard and mdf	0	0
Composite wood materials	1074.18	0
WEEE - Large Domestic App	46.27	0
WEEE - Small Domestic App	224.03	0
WEEE - Cathode Ray Tubes	0	0
WEEE - Flourescent tubes and other light bulbs	0	0
WEEE - Fridges & Freezers	707.4	23.27
Other Scrap metal	694.72	0
Automotive batteries	0	0
Post consumer, non automotive batteries	5.94	0
Car tyres	0	0
Van tyres	0	0
Large vehicle tyres	0	0
Mixed tyres	0	0
Furniture	480.84	1142.53
Rubble	0	0
Soil	0	0
Plasterboard	0	0
Vegetable Oil	0	0
Mineral Oil	0	0
Aluminium foil	0	0
Aerosols	0	0
Bric-a-brac	28.46	0
Composite food and beverage cartons	15.22	0
Fire extinguishers	0	0
Gas bottles	0	0
Ink & toner cartridges	0	0
Mattresses	0	597.96
Paint	0	0
Textiles & footwear	317.63	93.82
Video tapes, DVDs and CDs	0	0
Yellow Pages	0	0
Other materials	201.3	0
Bicycles	0	0
Co mingled materials	185325.719	0
Absorbent Hygiene Products (AHP)	0	0
Carpets	0	0

Source: www.wastedataflow.org

Data is subject to change. Only included for the selected authorities and periods if returns have been completed.

10.20c Waste Collections in Scotland - Civic Amenity Site Collections

		Tonnage collected
Civic Amenity Site Collection	**Collected for Recycling**	**Collected for Reuse**
Green glass	2440.41	0
Brown glass	1070.39	0
Clear glass	2937.12	0
Mixed glass	679.05	0
Plasterboard	803.99	0
Wood for composting	86.66	0
Paper	1810.27	0
Card	9953.23	0
Books	138.26	54.74
Mixed paper & card	1271.46	0
Steel cans	27.10	0
Aluminium cans	10.58	0
Mixed cans	354.08	0
Plastics	645.57	0
Mixed Plastic Bottles	1036.55	0
PET [1]	0	0
HDPE [2]	3.36	0
PVC [3]	0	0
LDPE [4]	0	0
PP [5]	0	0
PS [6]	0	0
OTHER PLASTICS [7]	195.83	0
Green garden waste only	70037.42	0
Waste food only	0	0
Mixed garden and food waste	0	0
Other compostable waste	0	0
Wood	53680.76	0
Chipboard and mdf	9330.12	0
Composite wood materials	4582.24	0
WEEE - Large Domestic App	6343.49	0
WEEE - Small Domestic App	11260.56	0
WEEE - Cathode Ray Tubes	8048.25	0
WEEE - Flourescent tubes and other light bulbs	44.82	0
WEEE - Fridges & Freezers	5278.18	40.41
Other Scrap metal	21673.46	0
Automotive batteries	307.03	0
Post consumer, non automotive batteries	64.05	0
Car tyres	136.98	0
Van tyres	0	0
Large vehicle tyres	0	0
Mixed tyres	1027.82	0
Furniture	731.18	540.84
Rubble	87164.91	1186.40
Soil	12392.96	559.94
Vegetable Oil	51.91	0
Mineral Oil	497.67	0
Aluminium foil	0	0
Aerosols	0	0
Bric-a-brac	44.21	0
Composite food and beverage cartons	31.59	0
Fire extinguishers	0	0
Gas bottles	192.45	19.19
Ink & toner cartridges	0.70	0
Mattresses	484.45	31.82
Paint	35.24	44.62
Textiles & footwear	2495.88	643.21
Video tapes, DVDs and CDs	3.89	0
Yellow Pages	0	0
Other materials	2600.91	3.12
Bicycles	289.44	38.94
Co mingled materials	5592.59	17.99
Absorbent Hygiene Products (AHP)	0	0
Carpets	309.96	0

Source: www.wastedataflow.org

Data is subject to change. Only included for the selected authorities and periods if returns have been completed.

10.20c Waste Collections in Scotland- Bring Site Collections 2012

Tonnage collected

Bring Site Collection	Collected for Recycling	Collected for Reuse
Green glass	12065.45	0
Brown glass	4182.16	0
Clear glass	13011.37	0
Mixed glass	11704.47	0
Paper	13714.93	0
Card	3707.36	0
Books	222.57	48.18
Mixed paper & card	2818.85	0
Steel cans	624.90	0
Aluminium cans	184.80	0
Mixed cans	402.48	0
Plastics	119.45	0
Mixed Plastic Bottles	2221.15	0
PET [1]	0	0
HDPE [2]	0	0
PVC [3]	0	0
LDPE [4]	0	0
PP [5]	0	0
PS [6]	0	0
OTHER PLASTICS [7]	14.10	0
Green garden waste only	10085.21	0
Waste food only	353.42	0
Mixed garden and food waste	0.00	0
Wood for composting	1367.63	0
Other compostable waste	580.06	0
Wood	1631.32	0
Chipboard and mdf	0	0
Composite wood materials	0	0
WEEE - Large Domestic App	688.24	0
WEEE - Small Domestic App	771.91	32.88
WEEE - Cathode Ray Tubes	606.16	0
WEEE - Flourescent tubes and other light bulbs	7.33	0
WEEE - Fridges & Freezers	413.19	0
Other Scrap metal	1495.16	0
Automotive batteries	16.24	0
Post consumer, non automotive batteries	20.96	0
Car tyres	0	0
Van tyres	0	0
Large vehicle tyres	0	0
Mixed tyres	177.46	0
Furniture	730.05	0
Rubble	6289.63	0
Soil	1977.55	0
Plasterboard	0	0
Vegetable Oil	10.27	0
Mineral Oil	56.86	0
Aluminium foil	0	0
Aerosols	0	0
Bric-a-brac	0	47.27
Composite food and beverage cartons	46.04	0
Fire extinguishers	0	0
Gas bottles	29.41	0
Ink & toner cartridges	0	0
Mattresses	0	0
Paint	0	0
Textiles & footwear	9457.39	871.91
Video tapes, DVDs and CDs	2.61	0
Yellow Pages	0	0
Other materials	81.86	0
Bicycles	4.83	23.41
Co mingled materials	4254.00	154.46
Absorbent Hygiene Products (AHP)	0	0
Carpets	0	0

Source: www.wastedataflow.org

Data is subject to change. Only included for the selected authorities and periods if returns have been completed.

10.20d Material types collected for recycling (inc composting) at kerbside in Northern Ireland, 2011/12

Unit: Tonnes

Area	Glass	Metal	Paper and card	Plastic	Compostable (excluding all wood)	WEEE	Other waste collected	All recycled materials collected
arc21								
Antrim	0	119	1,935	204	4,055	0	2	6,315
Ards	0	191	3,280	340	6,099	0	0	9,910
Ballymena	952	164	2,139	295	4,554	0	22	8,126
Belfast	977	611	9,251	1,142	11,945	0	69	23,996
Carrickfergus	713	120	1,075	198	3,570	0	19	5,695
Castlereagh	835	226	2,313	345	5,776	64	22	9,581
Down	0	128	2,406	260	2,887	0	0	5,681
Larne	285	88	1,481	152	2,801	0	0	4,808
Lisburn	0	290	4,725	500	10,113	0	0	15,627
Newtownabbey	1,701	270	2,529	498	7,362	0	35	12,396
North Down	0	219	3,601	377	6,555	0	0	10,753
All arc21	**5,464**	**2,426**	**34,736**	**4,311**	**65,717**	**64**	**170**	**112,887**
NWRWMG								
Ballymoney	50	97	1,189	255	1,252	0	140	2,983
Coleraine	325	303	2,544	471	0	0	197	3,839
Derry	585	347	4,273	820	0	87	466	6,578
Limavady	132	115	1,301	224	930	0	312	3,014
Magherafelt	329	133	1,851	450	3,771	0	248	6,783
Moyle	99	85	762	155	524	0	69	1,693
Strabane	0	127	1,775	304	0	0	201	2,407
All NWRWMG	**1,520**	**1,208**	**13,695**	**2,679**	**6,476**	**87**	**1,632**	**27,298**
SWaMP2008								
Armagh	920	170	1,409	311	3,639	0	27	6,476
Banbridge	681	129	1,101	212	6,066	0	29	8,219
Cookstown	0	115	1,686	319	1,430	0	184	3,734
Craigavon	0	153	4,474	458	4,572	0	180	9,836
Dungannon	0	182	2,718	514	3,285	0	194	6,893
Fermanagh	707	255	3,195	1,111	0	0	289	5,557
Newry & Mourne	0	163	4,706	488	3,241	0	361	8,960
Omagh	0	162	2,326	476	2,138	0	166	6,267
All SWaMP2008	**2,309**	**1,328**	**21,616**	**3,888**	**24,370**	**0**	**1,430**	**54,941**
Northern Ireland	**9,293**	**4,962**	**70,047**	**10,879**	**96,563**	**152**	**3,232**	**195,126**

Source: NIEA

Material types collected for recycling (inc composting) at bring sites in Northern Ireland, 2011/12

Unit: Tonnes

Area	Glass	Metal	Paper and card	Plastic	Compostable (excluding all wood)	WEEE	Other waste collected	All recycled materials collected
arc21								
Antrim	87	17	1	0	0	0	6	110
Ards	620	1	0	0	0	0	24	645
Ballymena	129	3	69	0	0	0	36	237
Belfast	792	1	231	4	0	0	91	1,119
Carrickfergus	84	2	98	0	0	0	25	209
Castlereagh	168	2	11	1	0	0	17	199
Down	774	9	1	0	0	0	17	802
Larne	178	1	0	0	0	0	22	202
Lisburn	561	1	8	0	0	0	17	587
Newtownabbey	62	2	6	0	0	0	2	72
North Down	765	1	26	0	0	0	10	802
All arc21	**4,221**	**39**	**451**	**5**	**0**	**0**	**267**	**4,984**
NWRWMG								
Ballymoney	152	0	8	0	0	0	15	175
Coleraine	174	1	29	0	0	0	27	230
Derry	250	4	0	0	0	0	17	271
Limavady	228	0	0	0	0	0	20	249
Magherafelt	29	0	0	0	0	0	15	44
Moyle	116	1	6	0	0	0	28	151
Strabane	367	8	80	0	0	0	15	469
All NWRWMG	**1,316**	**14**	**122**	**0**	**0**	**0**	**137**	**1,589**
SWaMP2008								
Armagh	48	1	100	0	0	0	8	157
Banbridge	0	0	1	0	0	0	57	58
Cookstown	251	2	4	0	0	0	37	295
Craigavon	421	1	0	0	0	0	31	453
Dungannon	255	1	0	0	0	0	54	310
Fermanagh	352	1	0	0	0	0	44	397
Newry & Mourne	594	7	45	0	0	0	82	727
Omagh	291	1	1	0	0	0	33	326
All SWaMP2008	**2,212**	**14**	**150**	**0**	**0**	**0**	**347**	**2,723**
Northern Ireland	**7,749**	**67**	**723**	**5**	**0**	**0**	**751**	**9,295**

Source: NIEA

Material types collected for recycling (inc composting) at civic amenity sites in Northern Ireland, 2011/12

Unit: Tonnes

Area	Glass	Metal	Paper and card	Plastic	Compostable (excluding all wood)	WEEE	Other waste collected	All recycled materials collected
arc21								
Antrim	308	348	204	69	4,351	436	6,223	**11,940**
Ards	443	412	222	0	2,428	658	1,341	**5,504**
Ballymena	0	184	181	0	1,560	285	1,651	**3,862**
Belfast	1,067	1,115	1,128	94	4,088	1,504	3,761	**12,757**
Carrickfergus	42	142	80	0	485	239	4,293	**5,281**
Castlereagh	187	200	306	6	932	291	1,377	**3,298**
Down	210	251	107	0	1,043	428	735	**2,773**
Larne	115	253	190	5	1,241	344	2,554	**4,700**
Lisburn	291	452	224	22	1,760	792	3,563	**7,104**
Newtownabbey	180	339	358	14	2,421	614	1,257	**5,183**
North Down	421	540	275	90	2,049	711	4,793	**8,880**
All arc21	**3,265**	**4,236**	**3,274**	**299**	**22,358**	**6,301**	**31,548**	**71,281**
NWRWMG								
Ballymoney	71	112	78	0	942	160	848	**2,211**
Coleraine	225	226	323	0	4,310	415	1,621	**7,120**
Derry	277	348	440	0	1,679	676	3,509	**6,928**
Limavady	85	36	404	140	914	153	450	**2,182**
Magherafelt	133	138	265	11	2,259	240	1,750	**4,796**
Moyle	9	16	0	0	526	78	151	**779**
Strabane	115	117	63	0	945	149	626	**2,015**
All NWRWMG	**915**	**993**	**1,574**	**152**	**11,574**	**1,871**	**8,954**	**26,033**
SWaMP2008								
Armagh	161	232	650	41	1,376	303	2,196	**4,959**
Banbridge	387	221	645	50	2,194	353	1,532	**5,382**
Cookstown	94	123	221	64	2,007	215	1,658	**4,381**
Craigavon	258	497	457	94	3,567	703	1,403	**6,979**
Dungannon	181	206	237	77	2,198	349	903	**4,150**
Fermanagh	92	346	4	212	2,663	387	1,695	**5,401**
Newry & Mourne	431	378	421	118	2,627	566	1,251	**5,793**
Omagh	233	280	523	73	1,974	361	1,957	**5,401**
All SWaMP2008	**1,837**	**2,282**	**3,158**	**731**	**18,607**	**3,238**	**12,594**	**42,446**
Northern Ireland	**6,017**	**7,511**	**8,006**	**1,181**	**52,539**	**11,409**	**53,097**	**139,760**

Source: NIEA

10.21 Survey of Local Authority Noise Enforcement Activity 2011/12

England and Wales

Data represents 140 (40%) of local authorities

	INDUSTRY		COMMERCE / LEISURE			RESIDENTIAL			CONSTRUCTION ETC	VME's	TOTAL'S	
	Agricultural Premises	Industrial / Warehousing / Distribution Premises	"On"-licensed Premises e.g. Pubs, Clubs, Restaurants	Commercial Premises e.g. Offices, Shops, Public transport	Leisure Premises e.g. Sports Facilities, Funfairs	Single Family House / Bungalow	Flats / Maisonettes	Other Residential e.g. Hostels, HMOs, Boarding Schools	Construction / Demolition Sites	Vehicles, Machinery and Equipment in Streets	TOTAL OF ALL COLUMNS	TOTAL OF ALL COMPLAINTS [4]
COMPLAINTS												
Number of Noise Complaints Received in Year	703	2,248	8,409	8,515	2,704	78,648	22,011	1,984	6,210	6,865	143,733	155,889
Number of Noise Complaints Resolved in Year	622	1,743	7,076	7,733	2,325	66,250	19,204	1,449	5,694	6,431	122,679	137,212
Number of Noise Incidents Complained-of	575	1,752	6,335	6,692	2,118	64,124	18,905	1,728	4,778	4,949	113,450	126,071
Incidents Confirmed as Potentially Actionable [1,2]	216	673	2,868	2,617	772	27,224	8,242	676	2,074	1,397	46,993	-
STATUTORY NUISANCES REMEDIED WITHOUT A NOTICE [3,5]												
Nuisance Ceased and Not Likely to Recur	29	65	336	378	85	2,609	717	60	305	230	4,969	-
Referred to Other Services	11	50	133	73	38	543	391	24	58	93	1,421	-
Resolved Informally	53	288	1,129	890	264	7,951	2,523	207	806	409	14,550	-
No Action Possible	29	68	344	230	137	3,548	1,122	62	164	131	5,845	-
NOTICES SERVED [5]												
S.80 EPA 1990 Abatement Notice	7	19	292	308	34	1,708	580	59	30	144	3,213	4,136
S.60 & S.61 CoPA 1974 Control of Construction Noise	-	-	-	-	-	-	-	-	451	9	460	503
Noise Act 1996 Warning Notice	-	-			-	41	25	2	-	-	68	91
Noise Act 1996 Fixed Penalty	-	-			-	2	1		-	-	3	3
S.80(4A) EPA 1990 Fixed Penalty (Lond)						6	3				9	9
APPEALS AGAINST NOTICES [5]												
Number of Appeals Allowed in Whole or in Part		2				1					3	-
PROSECUTIONS BEGUN [5]												
Breach of Abatement Notice			43	14	5	198	123	4	4	9	400	1,500
Breach of Restriction on, or Prior Consent for, Construction Noise	-	-	-	-	-	-	-	-	9		9	10
Noise Act 1996	-	-			-				-	-	0	0
Convictions Gained	1		5	6	4	68	33		10		127	-
OTHER REMEDIES [5]												
Nuisance Remedied by the LA in Default			11	3		81	12			1	41	149	205
Number of Seizures		1	1	3		81	69	3			158	-

1. Incidents Confirmed as Potentially Actionable includes all those 'triggers' giving rise to formal enforcement power (described previously as "incidents confirmed as statutory nuisances etc")

2. The sum of actions taken to resolve nuisances may exceed the Incidents Confirmed as Potentially Actionable figure because not all local authorities could provide data on

3. "Nuisances" here means statutory nuisances

4. The Total of all Complaints column includes noise activity unaccounted for in previous columns

5. Figures reported from 2005-06 may seem lower than previous years as they have not been subject to a 'grossing' calculation. Before 2005-06, where responding authorities were not able to provide data on the questions concerning outcome of noise incidents, estimates were made by pro-rating on number of noise incidents complained of

Source: Chartered Institute of Environmental Health.

Website: http://www.cieh.org

10.22 Government revenues from environmental taxes, 2001 to 2012

United Kingdom   £ million

		2001	2002	2003	2004	2005	2006	2007	2008	2009	2010	2011	2012
Energy		**26,575**	**26,984**	**27,582**	**28,638**	**28,548**	**28,712**	**30,012**	**30,288**	**30,941**	**32,878**	**33,455**	**33,164**
Duty on hydrocarbon oils	GTAP	22,046	22,070	22,476	23,412	23,346	23,448	24,512	24,790	25,894	27,013	26,923	26,703
including													
Unleaded petrol1,3	KI26	1,906	-	-	-	-	-	-	-	-	-	-	-
Leaded petrol/LRP2	KI27	650	103	69	67	20	15	13	10	9	10	11	9
Ultra low sulphur petrol	KI28	10,117	12,624	12,183	12,160	11,688	11,299	11,313	11,114	11,175	11,001	10,642	10,080
Diesel3	KI29	65	-	-	-	-	-	-	-	-	-	-	-
Ultra low sulphur diesel	KI2A	8,492	9,029	9,523	10,168	10,829	11,228	12,146	12,284	12,683	13,923	14,382	14,695
Vat on duty	CMYA	3,858	3,862	3,933	4,097	4,086	4,103	4,290	4,285	3,884	4,727	5,385	5,341
Fossil fuel levy	CIQY	86	32	-	-	-	-	-	-	-	-	-	-
Climate change levy	LSNT	585	825	828	756	747	711	690	717	693	666	675	648
Renewable energy obligations	EP89	-	195	345	373	369	450	520	496	470	472	472	472
Gas levy	GTAZ	-	-	-	-	-	-	-	-	-	-	-	-
Road vehicles		**4,102**	**4,294**	**4,720**	**4,763**	**4,762**	**5,010**	**5,387**	**5,528**	**5,634**	**5,844**	**5,824**	**5,877**
Vehicle excise duty	CMXZ	4,102	4,294	4,720	4,763	4,762	5,010	5,384	5,524	5,630	5,840	5,820	5,873
NI Driver Vehicle Agency	IY9N	-	-	-	-	-	-	3	4	4	4	4	4
Other environmental taxes		**1,326**	**1,568**	**1,728**	**2,080**	**2,074**	**2,231**	**3,363**	**3,469**	**3,433**	**4,260**	**5,000**	**5,427**
Air passenger duty	CWAA	824	814	781	856	896	961	1,883	1,876	1,800	2,094	2,605	2,766
Landfill tax	BKOF	502	541	607	672	733	804	877	954	842	1,065	1,090	1,077
Aggregates Levy	MDUQ	-	213	340	328	327	321	339	334	275	289	289	270
Rail Franchise Premia	LITT	-	-	-	205	98	125	244	285	496	792	993	1,293
Boat Licences	NSNP	-	-	-	-	-	-	-	-	-	-	-	-
Fishing Licences	NRQB	-	-	-	19	20	20	20	20	20	20	23	21
Total environmental taxes	JKVW	32,003	32,846	34,030	35,481	35,384	35,953	38,762	39,285	40,008	42,982	44,279	44,468
As a percentage of total taxes and social contributions													
Total Environmental Taxes	JKVX	8.6	8.7	8.6	8.4	7.8	7.4	7.6	7.5	8.3	8.3	8.1	8.1
As a percentage of Gross Domestic Product (GDP)													
Energy		2.6	2.5	2.4	2.4	2.3	2.2	2.1	2.1	2.2	2.2	2.2	2.2
Road Vehicles		0.4	0.4	0.4	0.4	0.4	0.4	0.4	0.4	0.4	0.4	0.4	0.4
Other		0.1	0.1	0.2	0.2	0.2	0.2	0.2	0.2	0.2	0.3	0.3	0.4
Total Environmental Taxes	JKVY	3.1	3.1	3.0	3.0	2.8	2.7	2.7	2.7	2.9	2.9	2.9	2.9

Source: ONS, Department for Energy and Climate Change

1 Unleaded petrol includes super unleaded petrol.
2 Lead Replacement Petrol (the alternative to 4-Star petrol introduced in 2000) is lead-free.
3 Duty incentives have concentrated production on ultra low sulphur varieties.

Housing

Chapter 11

Housing

Permanent dwellings (Table 11.1, 11.3)

Local housing authorities include: the Commission for the New Towns and New Towns Development Corporations; Communities Scotland; and the Northern Ireland Housing Executive. The figures shown for housing associations include dwellings provided by housing associations other than the Communities Scotland and the Northern Ireland Housing Executive and include those provided or authorised by government departments for the families of police, prison staff, the Armed Forces and certain other services.

Mortgage possession actions by region (Table 11.6)

The table shows mortgage possession actions in the county courts of England and Wales and excludes a small number of mortgage actions in the High Court.

A claimant begins an action for an order for possession of a property by issuing a claim in the county court, either by using the Possession Claim Online system or locally through a county court. In mortgage possession cases, the usual procedure is for the claim being issued to be given a hearing date before a district judge. The court, following a judicial hearing, may grant an order for possession immediately. This entitles the claimants to apply for a warrant to have the defendant evicted. However, even where a warrant for possession is issued, the parties can still negotiate a compromise to prevent eviction.

Frequently the court grants the claimant possession but suspends the operation of the order. Provided the defendant complies with the terms of suspension, which usually require the defendant to pay the current mortgage instalments plus some of the accrued arrears, the possession order cannot be enforced.

The mortgage possession figures do not indicate how many houses have actually been repossessed through the courts. Repossessions can occur without a court order being made while not all court orders result in repossession.

A new mortgage pre-action protocol (MPAP), approved by the Master of the Rolls, was introduced for possession claims in the County Courts with effect from 19 November 2008. The MPAP gives clear guidance on what the courts expect lenders and borrowers to have done prior to a claim being issued.

Evidence from administrative records from Qtr4 2008 suggests that this date coincided with a fall of around 50% in the daily and weekly numbers of new mortgage repossession claims being issued in the courts.

It therefore seems highly likely that the launch of the MPAP has led to a fall in the number of new claims being issued since introduction of MPAP (19th November to 31st December 2008).

Mortgage possession orders are typically made (where necessary) around 8 weeks after the corresponding claims are issued. For this reason, the impact of the MPAP is yet to have visible effect on the statistics on possession orders made.

At this early stage is not clear to what extent the launch of the MPAP has led to a permanent fall in the numbers of new mortgage possession claims being issued, as opposed to some merely being postponed. This will become clearer as statistics for 2009 become available.

Households in Temporary Accommodation under homelessness provisions (Tables 11.7, 11.8, 11.9)

Comprises households in accommodation arranged by local authorities pending enquiries or after being accepted as owed a main homeless duty under the 1996 Act (includes residual cases awaiting re-housing under the 1985 Act). Excludes "homeless at home" cases. The data shown for Wales includes "homeless at home" cases.

11.1a Dwelling stock: by tenure[1], England

Thousands of dwellings

31 March [3]	Owner Occupied	Rented Privately or with a job or business	Rented from Private Registered Providers	Rented from Local Authorities	Other public sector dwellings	All Dwellings
1999	14,408	2,086	1,146	3,178	110	20,927
2000	14,600	2,089	1,273	3,012	101	21,075
2001	14,735	2,133	1,424	2,812	103	21,207
2002	14,846	2,197	1,492	2,706	112	21,354
2003 [4]	14,752	2,549	1,651	2,457	104	21,513
2004 [4]	14,986	2,578	1,702	2,335	83	21,684
2005 [4]	15,100	2,720	1,802	2,166	82	21,870
2006 [4]	15,052	2,987	1,865	2,087	82	22,073
2007 [4]	15,093	3,182	1,951	1,987	75	22,288
2008 [4]	15,067	3,443	2,056	1,870	74	22,511
2009 [4]	14,968	3,705	2,128	1,820	74	22,694
2010 [4]	14,895	3,912	2,180	1,786	66	22,839
2011 [4]	14,827	4,105	2,255	1,726	63	22,976
2012 [4] R P	14,757	4,286	2,304	1,689	75	23,111

1. For detailed definitions of all tenures, see Definitions of housing terms in Housing Statistics home page.
2. Figures for census years are based on census output.
3. Series from 1992 to 2001 for England has been adjusted so that the 2001 total dwelling estimate matches the 2001 Census.
   Estimates from 2002 are based on local authority and housing association dwelling counts, the Labour Force Survey
   and, from 2003, the English Housing Survey.
   Estimates may not be strictly comparable between periods.
4. From 2003 the figures for owner-occupied and the private rental sector for England have been produced using a new
   improved methodology as detailed in the dwelling stock release. Previous to this vacancy was not accounted for.
5. Insuffcient data was available at time of publication to produce the owner occupied and private rental tenure split for 2013.
   This will be updated when data becomes available

R- Revised from previous publication
P - Provisional

Contact: 0303 44 41864
E-Mail: housing.statistics@communities.gsi.gov.uk

Source:
For stock calculation see Notes and Definitions

Data for earlier years are less reliable and definitions
may not be consistent throughout the series
Stock estimates are expressed to the nearest thousand
but should not be regarded as accurate to the last digit
Components may not sum to totals due to rounding

11.1b Dwelling stock: by tenure[1,2], Wales

Thousands of dwellings

	Owner Occupied	Rented Privately or with a job or business	Rented from Housing Associations	Rented from Local Authorities	All Dwellings
31 March					
1999 [5]	926	84	52	197	1,259
2000 [5]	914	106	54	193	1,267
2001 [5]	941	90	55	188	1,275
2002 [5]	957	89	57	183	1,285
2003 [5]	966	97	57	176	1,296
2004 [5]	980	103	64	160	1,307
2005 [5]	990	108	65	156	1,319
2006 [5]	998	113	66	154	1,331
2007 [5]	1,002	122	67	153	1,343
2008 [5]	1,001	135	89	130	1,355
2009 [5]	989	157	107	113	1,366
2010 [5]	983	171	110	111	1,375
2011 [5]	980	181	134	89	1,384
2012 [5 R]	976	191	135	88	1,389

1. For detailed definitions of all tenures, see Definitions of housing terms in Housing Statistics home page.

2. Owner-occupied tenure includes owner-occupied, intermediate and other.

3. April data for census years are based on census output.

4. Data for years 1969 to 1990 sourced from Department of Environment publications:
   Housing and Construction Statistics, 1967-1979, 1977-1987,1980-1990 and 1990-1997.

5. The tenure split between owner-occupied and privately rented dwellings has been calculated from 1997 onwards using information from the Labour Force Survey. These figures were revised in January 2011 following a re-weighting of the Labour Force Survey data.

R - Revised

P - Provisional

Contact: 0303 44 41864

E-Mail: housing.statistics@communities.gsi.gov.uk

Source:

Welsh Assembly Government

These data are produced and published separately by the Welsh Assembly Government, and although the figures in this table are correct at the time of its latest update they may be superseded before the next update.

Data for earlier years are less reliable and definitions may not be consistent throughout the series. Stock estimates are expressed to the nearest thousand but should not be regarded as accurate to the last digit.

Components may not sum to totals due to rounding.

11.1c Dwelling stock: by tenure[1,2,3,4,5], Scotland

Thousands of dwellings

	Owner Occupied	Rented Privately or with a job or business	Rented from Housing Associations	Rented from Local Authorities	All Dwellings
31 December[4]					
1999	1,435	155	131	583	**2,303**
2000	1,472	155	137	557	**2,322**
31 March[4]					
2001 [R]	1,451	170	139	553	**2,312**
2002 [R]	1,477	179	143	531	**2,329**
2003 [R]	1,512	180	238	416	**2,347**
2004 [R]	1,542	184	251	389	**2,367**
2005 [R]	1,554	207	251	374	**2,387**
2006 [R]	1,569	225	251	362	**2,406**
2007 [R]	1,588	233	261	346	**2,428**
2008 [R]	1,589	263	269	330	**2,451**
2009 [R]	1,612	263	268	326	**2,469**
2010 [R]	1,600	287	272	323	**2,482**
2011 [R]	1,595	305	275	320	**2,495**
2012 [P]	1,589	322	277	319	**2,508**

1. For detailed definitions of all tenures, see Definitions of housing terms in Housing Statistics home page
2. April data for census years are based on census output
3. Data for years 1969 to 1989 sourced from Department of Environment publications:
   Housing and Construction Statistics, 1967-1979, 1977-1987,1980-1990 and 1990-1997.
4. Estimates from 1990 onwards are based on the Census (1991, 2001, 2011), council tax records and exemptions,
   social sector stock counts, and private tenure splits from the Scottish Household Survey and are not strictly comparable
   with earlier figures. These are not all collected for the same timescales and may not be exact counts, even rounded
   to the nearest thousand.
5. In order to include vacant private sector dwellings in table 107, estimates for vacant private sector stock in the Scottish
   statistics have been apportioned according to the % of occupied dwellings for the private sector tenures.

R- Revised from previous publication
P- Provisional

Source:
Scottish Government
These data are produced and published separately by the Scottish Government, and although the figures in this table are correct at the time of its latest update they may be superseded before the next update.

Contact: 0303 44 41864
E-Mail: housing.statistics@communities.gsi.gov.uk

Data for earlier years are less reliable and definitions may not be consistent throughout the series.
Stock estimates are expressed to the nearest thousand but should not be regarded as accurate to the last digit.
Components may not sum to totals due to rounding.

11.1d Dwelling stock: by tenure[1], Northern Ireland

Thousands of dwellings

	Owner Occupied	Rented Privately or with a job or business	Rented from Housing Associations	Rented from Local Authorities	All Dwellings
31 December[3]					
1999	455	32	17	131	636
2000	488	37	19	129	674
31 March					
2002 [4]	481	47	20	120	668
2003 [4]	491	54	21	113	679
2004 [4]	501	61	22	100	684
2005 [4]	505	68	22	102	698
2006 [4]	508	76	23	99	706
2007 [4]	523	69	24	97	713
2008 [4]	524	83	26	97	730
2009 [4]	517	97	28	96	737
2010 [4]	521	106	29	96	752
2011 [4]	512	121	30	95	759
2012 [4P]	514	121	31	93	759

1. For detailed definitions of all tenures, see Definitions of housing terms in Housing Statistics home page
2. April data for census years are based on census output.
3. Data for years 1980 to 1997 sourced from Department of Environment publications: Housing and Construction Statistics, 1980-1990 and 1990-1997.
4. To include estimates for vacant dwellings, stock figures from Northern Ireland Housing Statistics 2011/12 table 1.3 have been apportioned according to the % of occupied dwellings for each of the tenures given in table 1.3

R- Revised from previous publication
P- Provisional

Source:
Department for Social Development (NI)

These data are produced and published separately by the Northern Ireland Department for Social Development, and although the figures in this table are correct at the time of its latest update they may be superseded before the next update.

Contact: 0303 44 41864
E-Mail: housing.statistics@communities.gsi.gov.uk

Data for earlier years are less reliable and definitions may not be consistent throughout the series.
Stock estimates are expressed to the nearest thousand but should not be regarded as accurate to the last digit.
Components may not sum to totals due to rounding.

11.2 Type of Accommodation by Tenure, 2011 Great Britain

Table 4.4   **(a) Type of accommodation by tenure**
                  (b) Tenure by type of accommodation

Households   *Great Britain: 2011[1]*

Tenure		Type of accommodation[2]							Weighted base (000's) =100%	Unweighted sample[7]
		Detached house	Semi-detached house	Terraced house	All houses	Purpose-built flat or maisonette	Converted flat or maisonette/ rooms	All flats/ rooms		
(a)										
Owner occupied, owned outright	%	38	33	20	92	7	1	8	*8,060*	*3,030*
Owner occupied, with mortgage	%	29	35	27	91	8	1	9	*8,829*	*2,580*
All owners	%	33	34	24	91	8	1	9	*16,888*	*5,610*
Rented from council[3]	%	1	29	30	59	39	2	41	*2,480*	*700*
Rented from housing association[4]	%	2	24	29	54	42	4	46	*2,360*	*680*
Social sector tenants	%	1	26	29	56	41	3	44	*4,840*	*1,370*
Rented privately, unfurnished[5]	%	12	21	34	67	20	13	33	*3,044*	*770*
Rented privately, furnished	%	6	13	20	39	41	21	61	*732*	*160*
Private renters[6]	%	10	20	31	61	24	15	39	*3,776*	*920*
Total	%	24	30	26	80	16	3	20	*25,505*	*7,910*
(b)									Total	
		%	%	%	%	%	%	%	%	
Owner occupied, owned outright		51	34	25	36	14	10	13	32	
Owner occupied, with mortgage		42	40	36	39	17	11	16	35	
All owners		93	74	61	75	31	21	29	66	
Rented from council[3]		0	9	11	7	23	5	20	10	
Rented from housing association[4]		1	7	10	6	24	10	22	9	
Social sector tenants		1	16	21	13	47	16	42	19	
Rented privately, unfurnished[5]		6	8	16	10	15	46	20	12	
Rented privately, furnished		1	1	2	1	7	17	9	3	
Private renters[6]		7	10	18	11	22	63	29	15	
Weighted base (000's) =100%		*6,085*	*7,753*	*6,634*	*20,473*	*4,168*	*865*	*5,032*	*25,505*	
Unweighted sample[7]		*2,170*	*2,480*	*2,000*	*6,660*	*1,070*	*190*	*1,250*	*7,910*	

1   Results for 2011 include longitudinal data (see Appendix B).
2   Tables for type of accommodation exclude households living in caravans.
3   Council includes local authorities.
4   Since 1996, housing associations are more correctly described as Registered Social Landlords (RSLs).
5   Unfurnished includes the answer 'partly furnished'.
6   Tenants whose accommodation goes with the job of someone in the household have been allocated to 'rented privately'. Squatters are also included.
7   All unweighted bases are rounded to the nearest 10.

Source: General Lifestyle Survey, Office for National Statistics

11.3 House building: permanent dwellings completed, by tenure[1] and country

Number of dwellings

	Financial Year	United Kingdom	England	Wales	Scotland	Northern Ireland
All Dwellings	1991-92	191,250	155,130	9,980	18,790	7,350
	1992-93	178,420	142,460	9,400	18,990	7,560
	1993-94	186,850	147,710	9,870	22,110	7,160
	1994-95	195,580	157,970	9,070	21,810	6,730
	1995-96	197,710	154,600	9,170	24,690	9,250
	1996-97	185,940	146,250	10,090	20,700	8,910
	1997-98	190,760	149,560	8,430	22,590	10,180
	1998-99	178,290	140,260	7,740	20,660	9,640
	1999-00	184,010	141,800	8,710	23,110	10,400
	2000-01	175,370	133,260	8,330	22,110	11,670
	2001-02	174,200	129,870	8,270	22,570	13,490
	2002-03	183,210	137,740	8,310	22,750	14,420
	2003-04	190,590	143,960	8,300	23,820	14,510
	2004-05	206,620	155,890	8,490	26,470	15,770
	2005-06 [2]	214,000	163,400	8,250	24,950	17,410
	2006-07 [2]	219,070	167,680	9,330	24,260	17,800
	2007-08	218,530	170,610	8,660	25,790	13,480
	2008-09	178,780	140,990	7,120	20,950	9,720
	2009-10	152,940	119,910	6,170	17,110	9,750
	2010-11	137,400	107,870	5,510	16,380	7,640
	2011-12	145,930	117,600	5,580	15,960	6,800
Private Enterprise	1991-92	160,250	132,050	7,170	15,480	5,550
	1992-93	143,980	115,910	6,690	15,620	5,760
	1993-94	146,750	116,050	6,650	18,310	5,730
	1994-95	155,290	125,740	6,300	17,890	5,350
	1995-96	156,540	123,620	6,880	19,200	6,850
	1996-97	153,450	121,170	7,520	17,490	7,270
	1997-98	160,680	127,840	6,490	17,980	8,370
	1998-99	154,560	121,190	6,440	18,780	8,140
	1999-00	160,520	124,470	7,860	19,070	9,120
	2000-01	152,740	116,640	7,390	18,200	10,510
	2001-02	153,580	115,700	7,490	18,310	12,070
	2002-03	164,300	124,460	7,520	18,940	13,390
	2003-04	172,360	130,100	7,860	20,450	13,950
	2004-05	184,500	139,130	7,990	22,440	14,940
	2005-06 [2]	189,700	144,940	7,880	20,250	16,630
	2006-07 [2]	192,170	145,680	8,990	21,030	16,470
	2007-08	189,660	147,170	8,320	21,660	12,510
	2008-09	144,920	113,800	6,430	16,040	8,650
	2009-10	117,970	93,030	5,290	11,120	8,530
	2010-11	104,730	83,180	4,510	10,660	6,380
	2011-12	108,990	88,500	4,750	10,070	5,680
Housing Associations	1991-92	21,090	15,970	2,470	1,810	840
	1992-93	30,010	23,970	2,590	2,600	850
	1993-94	36,580	30,210	3,010	2,820	550
	1994-95	37,240	31,380	2,570	2,790	500
	1995-96	38,170	30,230	2,130	4,780	1,040
	1996-97	30,950	24,630	2,550	2,960	810
	1997-98	28,550	21,400	1,940	4,490	730
	1998-99	22,870	18,890	1,270	1,750	960
	1999-00	23,170	17,270	850	3,960	1,090
	2000-01	22,250	16,430	900	3,800	1,110
	2001-02	20,400	14,100	710	4,200	1,390
	2002-03	18,610	13,080	780	3,720	1,030
	2003-04	18,020	13,670	420	3,370	560
	2004-05	21,990	16,660	480	4,020	830
	2005-06 [2]	23,990	18,160	350	4,700	780
	2006-07 [2]	26,650	21,750	350	3,230	1,330
	2007-08	28,630	23,220	340	4,100	970
	2008-09	33,040	26,690	690	4,580	1,070
	2009-10	34,190	26,520	880	5,580	1,210

11.3 House building: permanent dwellings completed, by tenure[1] and country

Number of dwellings

	Financial Year	United Kingdom	England	Wales	Scotland	Northern Ireland
	2010-11	30,920	23,550	990	5,110	1,270
	2011-12	33,900	27,170	830	4,780	1,120
Local	**1991-92**	9,900	7,110	330	1,500	960
Authorities	**1992-93**	4,420	2,580	120	770	950
	1993-94	3,530	1,450	210	980	890
	1994-95	3,060	850	200	1,130	880
	1995-96	3,010	760	160	720	1,360
	1996-97	1,540	450	20	240	820
	1997-98	1,520	320	-	110	1,080
	1998-99	870	180	30	120	540
	1999-00	320	60	-	70	190
	2000-01	380	180	50	110	50
	2001-02	230	60	70	70	30
	2002-03	300	200	10	90	-
	2003-04	210	190	20	-	-
	2004-05	130	100	30	-	-
	2005-06 [2]	320	300	20	-	-
	2006-07 [2]	260	250	-	10	-
	2007-08	250	220	10	30	-
	2008-09	830	490	-	340	-
	2009-10	780	370	-	410	-
	2010-11	1,760	1,140	-	610	-
	2011-12	3,080	1,960	-	1,110	-

1. For detailed definitions of all tenures see definitions of housing terms on Housing Statistics home page

2. Figures from October 2005 to March 2007 in England are missing a small number of starts and completions that were inspected by independent approved inspectors. These data are included from June 2007

Totals may not equal the sum of component parts due to rounding to the nearest 10

- Less than 5 dwellings

P Figure provisional and subject to revision

R Revised from previous release

.. Not available

Contact:
Telephone: 0303 444 3139
Email: housing.statistics@communities.gsi.gov.uk

Source:
P2 returns from local authorities
National House-Building Council (NHBC)
Approved inspector data returns
Welsh Assembly Government
Scottish Government
Department for Social Development (NI),
Northern Ireland Housing Executive,
Local Authority Building Control (NI)

11.4a Housebuilding: permanent dwellings completed, by house and flat, number of bedroom and tenure[1], ENGLAND

Percentage of all dwellings

Financial Year		1999 /00	2000 /01	2001 /02[2]	2002 /03[2]	2003 /04[2]	2004 /05[2]	2005 /06[2]	2006 /07[2]	2007 /08[2]	2008 /09[2]	2009 /10[2]	2010 /11[2]	2011 /12[2]
Private Enterprise														
Houses	1 bedroom	1	1	-	-	-	-	-		-	0	1	1	1
	2 bedrooms	14	13	9	9	8	7	6	6	7	8	8	9	10
	3 bedrooms	35	33	30	29	28	28	26	27	26	25	28	33	32
	4 or more bedrooms	35	36	39	36	31	25	22	22	21	21	24	27	26
	All	85	83	78	74	67	60	55	56	55	54	60	70	69
Flats	1 bedroom	4	4	6	5	7	9	9	9	9	12	11	6	8
	2 bedrooms	10	12	15	19	24	30	35	34	35	33	28	23	22
	3 bedrooms	1	1	1	1	1	1	1	1	1	1	1	1	1
	4 or more bedrooms	-	-	-	-	-	-	-	-	-	0	0	0	0
	All	15	17	22	26	33	40	45	44	45	46	40	30	31
Houses and flats	1 bedroom	5	5	6	6	8	9	9	9	10	12	11	7	8
	2 bedrooms	24	24	24	28	32	37	41	40	41	41	35	33	32
	3 bedrooms	36	35	31	30	29	29	28	28	27	26	29	34	33
	4 or more bedrooms	35	36	39	36	32	25	22	22	22	21	25	27	27
	All	100	100	100	100	100	100	100	100	100	100	100	100	100
Housing Associations														
Houses	1 bedroom	4	3	2	2	1	1	1	0	0	0	1	1	0
	2 bedrooms	32	29	29	24	23	19	18	15	15	17	16	19	21
	3 bedrooms	30	27	28	27	24	22	19	16	15	17	19	23	24
	4 or more bedrooms	4	4	5	8	6	5	4	3	3	3	5	6	5
	All	71	63	64	62	54	47	42	34	34	37	40	50	51
Flats	1 bedroom	15	17	15	14	13	17	18	23	18	17	17	13	11
	2 bedrooms	12	17	20	22	31	34	38	41	45	44	38	34	33
	3 bedrooms	2	3	1	2	1	2	2	1	2	2	3	3	4
	4 or more bedrooms	-	-	-	1	1	0	-	0	1	-	1	1	1
	All	29	37	36	39	46	53	58	66	66	63	60	50	49
Houses and flats	1 bedroom	20	19	17	17	14	18	19	24	18	17	18	14	12
	2 bedrooms	44	46	49	45	54	52	56	56	60	61	54	54	54
	3 bedrooms	32	30	28	29	25	24	21	17	18	18	22	26	28
	4 or more bedrooms	5	5	5	9	7	5	4	3	4	4	6	7	6
	All	100	100	100	100	100	100	100	100	100	100	100	100	100
All tenures														
Houses	1 bedroom	1	1	0	1	0	0	0		0	0	1	1	1
	2 bedrooms	17	15	11.0	10	9	8	8	8	8	10	10	12	13
	3 bedrooms	34	32	28	29	28	27	26	25	25	23	25	30	30
	4 or more bedrooms	31	32	37	34	30	23	20	20	19	16	19	22	21
	All	83	80	77	73	66	59	54	53	52	50	55	65	64
Flats	1 bedroom	6	6	6	6	8	10	10	11	11	13	12	8	9
	2 bedrooms	10	12	15	19	24	30	35	35	36	36	31	26	25
	3 bedrooms	1	2	1	1	1	1	1	1	1	1	1	1	2
	4 or more bedrooms	0	0	0	-	-	0	0	0	0	-	0	0	0
	All	17.0	20.0	23.0	27	34	41	46	47	48	50	45	35	36
Houses and flats	1 bedroom	7	7	7	6	8	10	10	11	11	13	13	8	9
	2 bedrooms	26	27	25	29	33	38	42	42	44	46	40	38	38
	3 bedrooms	35	34	31	30	29	28	27	27	26	24	27	32	32
	4 or more bedrooms	32	32	37	34	30	23	21	20	19	17	20	22	21
	All	100	100	100	100	100	100	100	100	100	100	100	100	100

1. For detailed definitions of all tenures, see Definitions of housing terms in Housing Statistics home page
2. Figures for 2001/02 onwards are based on NHBC data only, so there is some degree of variability owing to partial coverage.
3. The England worksheet and charts have been corrected following initial publication.

Contact:

Telephone: 0303 444 3139
E-Mail: housing.statistics@communities.gsi.gov.uk

11.4b Housebuilding completions: by number of bedrooms

Percentages

		1998 /99	1999 /00	2000 /01	2001 /02	2002 /03	2003 /04	2004 /05	2005 /06	2006 /07	2007 /08	2008 /09	2009 /10	2010 /11	2011 /12
Wales[1]															
1 bedroom	JUWO	3	5	5	4	6	6	7	9	11	10	16	11	10	11
2 bedrooms	JUWP	21	19	18	19	18	20	21	27	28	30	33	33	29	28
3 bedrooms	JUWQ	46	43	42	39	35	37	35	35	33	33	30	36	39	36
4 or more bedrooms	JUWR	30	34	34	38	41	37	37	30	28	27	22	20	22	25
All houses and flats	JUWS	100	100	100	100	100	100	100	100	100	100	100	100	100	100

Sources: Communities and Local Government;

Welsh Government

1 Figures for all years for Wales are based on the reports of local authority building inspectors and the National House Building Council (NHBC). It does not include information from other private approved inspector.

11.5 Mortgage possession workload in the county courts of England and Wales, 2001- 2012

Year	Quarter	Claims Issued	Orders that came from unique claims			Warrants that came from unique claims	Repossessions by county court bailiffs that came from unique claims	Properties taken into possession[2]
			Outright	Suspended	Total			
2001		65,555	17,696	28,116	45,812	26,279	11,637	18,200
2002		62,862	16,116	24,314	40,430	22,914	8,654	12,000
2003		65,373	16,046	23,738	39,784	20,691	6,566	8,500
2004		76,993	19,578	25,778	45,356	22,366	6,924	8,200
2005		114,733	31,879	37,043	68,922	34,833	12,567	14,500
2006		131,248	44,819	43,199	88,018	46,968	20,635	21,000
2007		137,725	49,180	41,474	90,654	50,622	23,501	25,900
2008		142,741	59,669	52,094	111,763	62,071	35,392	40,000
2009		93,533	39,289	32,946	72,235	49,643	32,208	48,300
2010		75,431	30,473	26,495	56,968	37,695	23,425	38,100
2011		73,181	28,227	26,991	55,218	38,883	25,185	37,100
2012		59,877	22,649	21,664	44,313	32,290	19,557	34,000
2008	Q1	40,873	13,996	12,203	26,199	15,579	7,874	8,500
	Q2	39,072	15,338	14,248	29,586	16,970	9,057	10,000
	Q3	38,047	15,652	13,632	29,284	16,174	9,943	11,100
	Q4	24,749	14,683	12,011	26,694	13,348	8,518	10,400
2009	Q1	23,968	8,823	7,699	16,522	13,785	9,222	13,000
	Q2	26,419	10,319	8,723	19,042	12,918	7,983	12,000
	Q3	24,938	11,765	9,350	21,115	12,944	8,076	12,400
	Q4	18,208	8,382	7,174	15,556	9,996	6,927	10,900
2010	Q1	18,805	7,624	6,470	14,094	9,881	6,839	10,800
	Q2	18,395	7,369	6,188	13,557	9,490	5,877	9,800
	Q3	20,384	8,212	7,168	15,380	9,771	5,848	9,300
	Q4	17,847	7,268	6,669	13,937	8,553	4,861	8,200
2011	Q1	19,608	7,556	6,994	14,550	10,408	6,496	9,600
	Q2	18,339	6,884	6,688	13,572	9,882	6,124	9,300
	Q3	18,763	7,348	7,109	14,457	9,673	7,148	9,500
	Q4	16,471	6,439	6,200	12,639	8,920	5,417	8,700
2012	Q1	16,963	6,321	6,432	12,753	9,092	6,017	9,600
	Q2	14,615	5,709	5,592	11,301	7,927	4,797	8,500
	Q3	14,168	5,216	4,920	10,136	7,728	4,630	8,200
	Q4 (r)	14,131	5,403	4,720	10,123	7,543	4,113	7,700

Source:

HM Courts and Tribunals Service CaseMan, Possession Claim OnLine (PCOL) and Council of Mortgage Lenders (CML)

Notes:

[1] Data relating to 1999 onwards are sourced from county court administrative systems and exclude duplicate observations. Data prior to 1999 are sourced from manual counts made by court staff and represent the number of orders rather than claims leading to an order (all claims in which the first order is made during the period).

[2] Council of Mortgage Lenders (CML) statistics for the latest quarter are unavailable prior to this bulletin being published as the MoJ does not have pre-release access to them. Please also note this figure relates to repossessions made in the United Kingdom whereas all other statistics in this bulletin relate to England and Wales. It should also be noted that these figures are rounded by the CML to the nearest hundred. Please see the CML website http://www.cml.org.uk/cml/statistics for more information about these statistics.

11.6 Mortgage arrears and repossessions

Year	2001	2002	2003	2004	2005	2006	2007	2008	2009	2010	2011	2012
Number of mortgages at year end (000s)	11,251	11,368	11,452	11,515	11,608	11,746	11,852	11,667	11,504	11,478	11,384	11,284
Repossessions during year	18,200	12,000	8,500	8,200	14,500	21,000	25,900	40,000	48,900	38,500	37,300	33,900
Cases in mortgage arrears												
12+ months arrears	19,700	16,500	12,600	11,000	15,000	15,700	15,300	29,500	69,500	63,700	54,400	48,500
6 - 12 months arrears	43,200	34,100	31,000	29,900	38,600	34,900	40,500	72,000	93,900	80,500	72,200	69,900
3 - 6 months arrears	81,400	66,600	55,800	60,500	69,400	64,900	71,700	117,400	112,400	103,300	99,000	97,200
3 - 5 months arrears	–	–	–	–	–	–	–	–	–	–	–	–
2 months arrears	–	–	–	–	–	–	–	–	–	–	–	–

Sources:

Compendium of Housing Finance Statistics & Housing Finance, Council of Mortgage Lenders; Janet Ford, Roof (figures for 2 & 3-5 months arrears for years 1985 to 1994).

Notes: Properties taken into possession include those voluntarily surrendered. The CML 3-6, 6-12 & 12+ months arrears figures are for the end of the year. The Janet Ford survey figures for 2 & 3-5 months arrears are for March of the year. Her survey of mortgage arrears figures has now been discontinued from publication following the introduction of the CML 3-6 months arrears series. Changes in the mortgage rate have the effect of changing monthly repayments and hence the number of months in arrears which a given amount represents.

11.7 Households in temporary accommodation[1], by type of accommodation, at the end of each quarter, England

Number and percentage of total households in TA (%)

Year	Qtr	Total in TA (Seasonally Adjusted)	Total in TA (Not Seasonally Adjusted)	Total in TA: of which with Children[4]	Total in TA: Total number of children[5]	B&B hotels[2]: Total	B&B: with Children[4]	B&B: % of Total TA	B&B: with Children and resident for more than 6 weeks	B&B: accommodated pending review/appeal	Hostels (incl women's refuges): Total	Hostels: of which with Children[4]	Hostels: % of Total TA	LA/HA stock[6]: Total	LA/HA: of which with Children[4]	LA/HA: % of Total TA	Leased from Private Sector by LA or HA[6]: Total	Leased: of which with Children[4]	Leased: % of Total TA	Other Private Sector[2] (inc private landlord): Total	Other: of which with Children[4]	Other: % of Total TA	Of which: in temporary accommodation in another local authority district	Cases where homelessness main duty accepted	of which with Children[4]	All cases including "decision pending"[3]	of which with Children[4]
1999	Q1	56,550	56,580	..	..	6,570	..	12%	..	..	9,840	..	17%	18,600	..	33%	16,210	..	29%	5,360	..	9%	5,170	6,110	..	10,820	..
	Q2	58,430	58,430	..	..	7,700	..	13%	..	..	10,210	..	17%	18,740	..	32%	15,030	..	26%	6,750	..	12%	6,280	6,500	..	11,160	..
	Q3	60,660	61,450	..	..	8,240	..	13%	..	..	9,960	..	16%	20,330	..	33%	15,300	..	25%	7,620	..	12%	6,260	6,780	..	11,420	..
	Q4	62,770	62,180	..	..	8,000	..	13%	..	..	9,660	..	16%	20,330	..	33%	16,280	..	26%	7,910	..	13%	6,220	6,440	..	10,450	..
2000	Q1	65,130	65,170	..	..	8,680	..	13%	..	..	10,300	..	16%	21,380	..	33%	17,060	..	26%	7,750	..	12%	5,870	6,580	..	11,150	..
	Q2	67,750	67,520	..	..	8,910	..	13%	..	..	10,320	..	15%	22,490	..	33%	19,720	..	29%	6,080	..	9%	5,660	6,370	..	11,270	..
	Q3	71,070	71,860	..	..	9,420	..	13%	..	..	10,460	..	15%	23,700	..	33%	18,570	..	26%	9,710	..	14%	6,120	7,160	..	12,570	..
	Q4	73,690	73,080	..	..	9,870	..	14%	..	..	10,790	..	15%	24,320	..	33%	21,610	..	30%	6,490	..	9%	5,470	7,610	..	12,220	..
2001	Q1	75,160	75,200	..	..	10,860	..	14%	..	..	10,610	..	14%	25,480	..	34%	21,900	..	29%	6,350	..	8%	6,150	8,420	..	12,730	..
	Q2	76,120	75,920	..	..	11,390	..	15%	..	..	10,320	..	14%	25,450	..	34%	21,970	..	29%	6,790	..	9%	7,440	8,870	..	13,240	..
	Q3	77,020	77,800	..	..	12,220	..	16%	..	..	11,280	..	14%	25,930	..	33%	20,050	..	26%	8,320	..	11%	8,240	8,090	..	11,820	..
	Q4	78,120	77,510	..	..	11,860	..	15%	..	..	10,680	..	14%	26,570	..	34%	20,600	..	27%	7,800	..	10%	8,460	8,600	..	12,000	..
2002	Q1	80,200	80,200	54,660	..	12,710	6,960	16%	..	..	9,570	5,540	12%	27,760	19,160	35%	20,660	17,070	26%	9,510	5,930	12%	9,670	8,620	..	11,990	3,320
	Q2	81,810	81,660	58,870	..	12,720	6,820	16%	..	..	9,770	6,030	12%	28,470	21,360	35%	22,610	18,570	28%	8,090	6,090	10%	8,190	8,890	..	12,440	4,450
	Q3	84,260	85,010	61,740	..	13,950	6,970	16%	..	..	9,720	6,280	11%	28,870	21,130	34%	23,840	20,600	28%	8,620	6,760	10%	11,550	10,390	..	14,440	6,760
	Q4	85,320	85,140	60,310	..	13,240	5,870	16%	3,050	..	9,640	5,760	11%	27,580	20,380	32%	25,940	21,630	30%	8,740	6,660	10%	12,310	9,760	..	14,800	5,830
2003	Q1	89,100	89,040	61,510	..	12,440	5,240	14%	2,910	..	10,060	6,040	11%	28,260	19,700	32%	28,370	23,240	32%	9,920	7,310	11%	11,470	10,580	..	16,280	7,550
	Q2	91,970	91,870	65,040	..	11,390	3,940	12%	2,120	..	10,420	6,360	11%	27,590	19,900	30%	31,460	26,620	34%	11,010	8,220	12%	10,880	13,310	..	19,380	9,410
	Q3	93,730	94,440	67,260	..	10,310	3,200	11%	1,590	..	10,790	6,450	11%	27,560	19,650	29%	35,140	29,960	37%	10,640	8,020	11%	9,880	15,370	..	23,060	10,140
	Q4	95,120	94,610	67,540	..	8,420	1,730	9%	940	..	10,370	6,060	11%	27,470	19,460	29%	38,740	33,340	41%	9,620	6,950	10%	10,440	17,500	..	23,070	10,990
2004	Q1	97,820	97,680	70,580	..	7,090	820	7%	30	..	10,780	6,280	11%	27,880	20,120	29%	42,390	36,400	43%	9,540	6,980	10%	9,850	15,870	..	21,940	11,610
	Q2	99,570	99,530	71,640	121,590	7,250	1,100	7%	60	..	10,580	6,090	11%	27,960	20,070	28%	42,640	35,900	43%	11,140	8,480	11%	9,480	17,030	..	23,000	13,230
	Q3	100,650	101,300	72,510	122,530	7,460	1,420	7%	180	..	10,380	5,960	10%	28,220	20,070	28%	43,720	36,660	43%	11,530	8,420	11%	10,030	17,100	..	23,200	13,400
	Q4	101,470	101,030	72,800	124,630	6,450	820	6%	100	..	10,060	5,660	10%	27,730	19,730	27%	46,140	38,750	46%	10,640	7,840	11%	8,610	16,100	..	20,930	11,880
2005	Q1	101,260	101,070	72,670	125,860	6,780	1,180	7%	110	..	10,280	5,840	10%	26,630	18,610	26%	46,530	39,180	46%	10,860	7,890	11%	11,660	15,290	..	20,910	12,850
	Q2	100,990	100,970	72,810	124,900	6,290	1,300	6%	130	50	9,870	5,440	10%	27,440	19,070	27%	46,990	39,600	47%	10,380	7,390	10%	11,790	16,020	10,470	..	..
	Q3	100,420	101,020	74,180	127,990	6,100	1,470	6%	150	40	10,020	5,410	10%	25,030	17,610	25%	48,860	41,500	48%	11,020	8,200	11%	13,430	15,140	10,270	..	..
	Q4	99,110	98,730	72,920	127,620	4,950	820	5%	140	30	9,230	5,000	9%	24,220	17,110	25%	49,910	42,310	51%	10,420	7,700	11%	10,700	11,570	7,840	..	..
2006	Q1	96,580	96,370	71,560	127,650	5,150	1,020	5%	110	30	9,010	4,960	9%	22,350	16,080	23%	49,670	41,960	52%	10,200	7,550	11%	11,080	11,010	7,210	..	..
	Q2	93,910	93,910	69,790	130,470	4,900	1,050	5%	110	50	8,930	4,820	10%	20,800	14,880	22%	49,320	41,740	53%	9,980	7,300	11%	11,590	10,210	6,920	..	..
	Q3	92,530	93,090	69,500	129,340	4,900	1,100	5%	120	40	8,460	4,450	9%	20,180	14,840	22%	49,710	41,980	53%	9,850	7,140	11%	11,620	9,720	6,550	..	..
	Q4	89,870	89,510	65,770	122,080	4,210	640	5%	110	40	7,840	3,950	9%	18,840	13,930	21%	48,850	40,130	55%	9,770	7,120	11%	9,950	8,470	5,740	..	..
2007	Q1	87,310	87,120	65,210	125,430	4,310	980	5%	80	30	7,640	4,030	9%	18,040	13,510	21%	45,600	38,600	52%	11,540	8,090	13%	10,130	8,780	5,910	..	..
	Q2	84,890	84,900	64,020	117,340	4,070	940	5%	100	30	7,230	3,890	9%	17,240	12,970	20%	44,610	37,920	53%	11,750	8,290	14%	10,490	9,150	6,280	..	..
	Q3	82,220	82,750	62,830	117,090	4,090	900	5%	130	30	7,180	3,850	9%	16,490	12,410	20%	43,430	37,100	52%	11,570	8,580	14%	11,130	9,540	6,300	..	..
	Q4	79,880	79,500	59,990	112,260	3,530	700	4%	120	20	6,620	3,490	8%	15,910	11,780	20%	41,730	35,380	52%	11,710	8,640	15%	10,820	8,080	5,510	..	..
2008	Q1	77,670	77,510	59,230	110,360	3,840	1,030	5%	160	30	6,450	3,580	8%	14,740	11,080	19%	40,480	34,610	52%	12,000	8,930	13%	10,200	7,470	5,180	..	..
	Q2	74,650	74,690	57,210	107,050	3,440	1,030	5%	180	30	6,020	3,350	8%	14,030	10,660	19%	41,130	34,900	55%	10,070	7,270	13%	8,720	7,890	5,630	..	..
	Q3	71,640	72,130	55,850	104,640	3,230	940	4%	160	30	5,800	3,190	8%	13,420	10,240	19%	39,990	34,390	55%	9,710	7,090	13%	7,620	6,740	4,520	..	..
	Q4	67,920	67,480	52,290	98,880	2,560	520	4%	100	20	5,250	2,830	8%	11,930	8,990	18%	38,790	33,560	57%	8,950	6,400	13%	7,360	6,070	4,030	..	..

11.7 Households in temporary accommodation[1], by type of accommodation, at the end of each quarter, England

Year	Quarter	Total in TA (Temporary Accommodation)				Bed and breakfast hotels[2]					Hostels (including women's refuges)			Local Authority or Housing Association (LA/HA) stock[6]			Leased from the Private Sector by an LA or HA[6]			Other Private Sector[2] accommodation (inc private landlord)				Duty owed, but no accommodation has been secured[3]		
		(Seasonally Adjusted)	(Not Seasonally) Adjusted	of which with Children[4]	Total number of children[5]	Total	Percentage of Total TA	with Children[4]	of which: resident for more than 6 weeks	of which: accommodated pending review/appeal	Total	Percentage of Total TA	of which with Children[4]	Total	Percentage of Total TA	of which with Children[4]	Total	Percentage of Total TA	of which with Children[4]	Total	Percentage of Total TA	of which with Children[4]	Of which: in temporary accommodation in another local authority district	Cases where homelessness main duty accepted	of which with Children[4]	All cases including "decision pending"[4]
2009	Q1	64,090	64,000	49,030	92,590	2,450	4%	470	70	10	5,170	8%	2,740	10,480	16%	7,800	37,450	59%	32,050	8,460	13%	5,970	7,960	5,560	3,740	..
	Q2	60,160	60,230	45,940	87,030	2,150	4%	510	80	20	4,710	8%	2,430	9,520	16%	6,970	35,920	60%	30,620	7,930	13%	5,410	7,880	4,560	2,940	..
	Q3	56,460	56,920	43,400	82,780	2,050	4%	510	130	20	4,480	8%	2,330	8,780	15%	6,390	34,130	60%	29,090	7,490	13%	5,080	6,550	4,350	2,770	..
	Q4	53,870	53,370	40,560	77,990	1,880	4%	400	120	10	4,150	8%	2,150	8,180	15%	5,950	32,430	61%	27,540	6,730	13%	4,520	5,780	4,150	2,540	..
2010	Q1	51,350	51,310	39,200	74,610	2,050	4%	630	100	10	4,240	8%	2,270	7,790	15%	5,790	30,920	60%	26,310	6,320	12%	4,210	5,430	3,710	2,320	..
	Q2	50,290	50,400	37,940	72,590	2,410	5%	740	160	10	4,320	9%	2,380	7,650	15%	5,570	29,820	59%	25,210	6,200	12%	4,040	5,630	3,780	2,510	..
	Q3	49,250	49,680	37,620	71,460	2,660	5%	930	140	10	4,360	9%	2,440	7,610	15%	5,480	28,740	58%	24,570	6,320	13%	4,200	5,880	4,100	2,700	..
	Q4	48,540	48,010	36,230	69,050	2,310	5%	660	150	10	4,160	9%	2,270	7,430	15%	5,440	27,730	58%	23,620	6,380	13%	4,250	5,810	4,410	2,970	..
2011	Q1	48,240	48,240	36,640	69,660	2,750	6%	1,030	200	10	4,250	9%	2,330	7,490	16%	5,500	26,960	56%	23,170	6,790	14%	4,620	6,300	4,770	3,270	..
	Q2	48,200	48,330	35,950	68,770	3,120	6%	1,210	240	20	4,370	9%	2,340	7,570	16%	5,460	26,240	54%	22,170	7,050	15%	4,780	6,290	4,770	3,420	..
	Q3	48,680	49,100	36,680	69,850	3,370	7%	1,340	310	40	4,380	9%	2,370	7,890	16%	5,810	26,380	54%	22,250	7,090	14%	4,910	6,850	5,110	3,590	..
	Q4	49,500	48,920	36,600	69,460	3,170	6%	1,310	450	60	4,310	9%	2,380	7,990	16%	5,840	26,080	53%	21,800	7,370	15%	5,280	7,350	5,490	3,550	..
2012	Q1	50,420	50,430	37,190	70,090	3,960	8%	1,660	480	60	4,360	9%	2,350	8,270	16%	6,000	26,040	52%	21,490	7,810	15%	5,690	7,870	5,400	3,860	..
	Q2 R	51,470	51,630	39,470	73,890	4,230	8%	1,900	680	70	4,350	8%	2,610	8,600	17%	6,470	25,960	50%	22,240	8,500	16%	6,250	8,170	5,500	3,830	..
	Q3 R	52,530	52,960	40,090	75,460	4,120	8%	1,920	870	90	4,390	8%	2,690	8,930	17%	6,730	26,290	50%	21,880	9,230	17%	6,860	8,520	5,560	4,080	..
	Q4 R	53,780	53,140	40,830	76,740	3,820	7%	1,600	770	90	4,280	8%	2,610	9,090	17%	6,830	26,310	50%	22,490	9,630	18%	7,300	9,270	5,690	3,950	..

Notes: 1 Households in accommodation arranged by local authorities pending enquiries or after being accepted as homeless under the 1996 Act (includes residual cases awaiting re-housing under the 1985 Act).

2 From 2002 Q1, some self-contained accommodation in Annex-style units previously recorded under B&B is now more appropriately attributed to Private Sector Accommodation. The Homelessness (Suitability of Accommodation) (England) Order 2003 came into force on 1 April 2004. This prohibits the use of B&B accommodation for families except in an emergency and even then for no longer than six weeks.

3 "Duty owed, but no accommodation has been secured" are households accepted as owed a main duty but able to remain in their existing accommodation for the immediate future. Cases in the final two columns include those households awaiting a decision on their application. Since Q2 2005, this can only apply once an appeal has been accepted as owed a main duty.

4 Includes expectant mothers with no other dependent children.

5 Includes expected children.

6 Housing Association (HA) - this was previously known as "Registered Social Landlord".

R Revised Data

P Provisional Data

Totals may not equal the sum of components because of rounding.

Source: DCLG P1E Homelessness returns (quarterly)

Contact:
Telephone: 0303 4443510 or 0303 4441258
E-mail: homelessnessstats@communities.gsi.gov.uk

11.8 Homeless Households in temporary accommodation at the end of the period - as at 31 March each year (a) (b): Wales

Number of households

		2000-01 Annual	2001-02 Annual	2002-03 Annual	2003-04 Annual	2004-05 Annual	2005-06 Annual	2006-07 Annual	2007-08 Annual	2008-09 Annual	2009-10 Annual	2010-11 Annual	2011-12 Annual
Total accommodated at the end of quarter	Private sector accommodation (c)	200	130	175	255	415	505	710	900	1070	1050	1080	1065
	Public sector accommodation (d)	375	395	455	355	460	615	575	445	415	390	435	380
	Hostels and women's refuges	150	195	230	310	310	450	405	475	510	400	415	485
	Bed and breakfast	80	125	300	690	760	595	380	280	255	235	240	310
	Other (e)	10	30	110	145	170	300	230	190	105	*	*	5
	Homeless at home	265	430	220	1130	1230	980	855	585	465	415	470	525
	Accommodation type unknown	.	.	.	.	.	.	.	.	.	.	.	.
Total accommodated at the end of quarter		1080	1310	1490	2890	3350	3440	3150	2880	2815	2490	2640	2770

Source: Welsh Government - Statutory Homelessness data collection from local authorities

(a) All the figures are rounded independently to the nearest 5 to protect the identity of individuals. As a result, there may be a difference between the sum of the constituent items and the total.

(b) Under Part VII of the Housing Act 1996

(c) Includes households placed directly with a private sector landlord, private sector accommodation leased by local authorities and private sector accommodation leased by registered social landlords.

(d) Includes local authority stock and registered social landlord stock on assured shorthold tenancies

(e) Prior to the April to June quarter 2009 the 'Other' category was used by some local authorities who were unable to were unable to distinguish the exact accommodation type for all households in temporary accommodation. Following a validation exercise all authorities are now able to provide this information.

* The data item is disclosive or not sufficiently robust for publication

11.9 Households in temporary accommodation by accommodation type: Scotland

All households		Social sector accommodation[1]		Hostel		Bed & Breakfast		Other[2]		Total	
		Number	%	Number	%	Number	%	Number	%	Number	%
2002	as at 31 March	2,152	52	1,363	33	569	14	69	2	4,153	100
	as at 30 June	2,392	54	1,260	29	653	15	115	3	4,420	100
	as at 30 September	2,471	53	1,324	28	706	15	203	4	4,704	100
	as at 31 December	2,643	52	1,389	28	879	17	136	3	5,047	100
2003	as at 31 March	2,984	55	1,380	26	898	17	141	3	5,403	100
	as at 30 June	3,224	58	1,218	22	986	18	112	2	5,540	100
	as at 30 September	3,329	56	1,519	25	1,061	18	85	1	5,994	100
	as at 31 December	3,475	56	1,601	26	983	16	116	2	6,175	100
2004	as at 31 March	3,537	55	1,586	25	1,190	18	132	2	6,445	100
	as at 30 June	3,754	56	1,514	23	1,273	19	105	2	6,646	100
	as at 30 September	3,894	56	1,590	23	1,331	19	110	2	6,925	100
	as at 31 December	4,071	59	1,521	22	1,243	18	117	2	6,952	100
2005	as at 31 March	4,136	57	1,490	20	1,516	21	159	2	7,301	100
	as at 30 June	4,324	59	1,340	18	1,413	19	264	4	7,341	100
	as at 30 September	4,606	60	1,320	17	1,424	19	333	4	7,683	100
	as at 31 December	4,525	60	1,295	17	1,323	18	356	5	7,499	100
2006	as at 31 March	4,747	59	1,328	17	1,494	19	416	5	7,985	100
	as at 30 June	4,732	60	1,342	17	1,362	17	452	6	7,888	100
	as at 30 September	4,880	60	1,301	16	1,491	18	439	5	8,111	100
	as at 31 December	4,981	62	1,235	15	1,391	17	482	6	8,089	100
2007	as at 31 March	5,164	60	1,242	14	1,528	18	643	7	8,577	100
	as at 30 June	5,075	60	1,170	14	1,588	19	690	8	8,523	100
	as at 30 September	5,104	61	1,134	13	1,492	18	671	8	8,401	100
	as at 31 December	5,460	63	1,104	13	1,348	16	721	8	8,633	100
2008	as at 31 March[3]	6,134	64	1,079	11	1,609	17	713	7	9,535	100
	as at 30 June	6,079	62	1,064	11	1,791	18	815	8	9,749	100
	as at 30 September	6,131	62	1,058	11	1,780	18	848	9	9,817	100
	as at 31 December	5,931	62	1,019	11	1,662	17	924	10	9,536	100
2009	as at 31 March	6,355	63	994	10	1,748	17	956	10	10,053	100
	as at 30 June	6,294	62	1,186	12	1,654	16	1,072	11	10,206	100
	as at 30 September	6,438	62	1,221	12	1,584	15	1,100	11	10,343	100
	as at 31 December	6,378	62	1,234	12	1,515	15	1,151	11	10,278	100
2010	as at 31 March	6,775	63	1,217	11	1,765	16	972	9	10,729	100
	as at 30 June	6,938	62	1,267	11	1,940	17	958	9	11,103	100
	as at 30 September	7,124	63	1,369	12	1,673	15	1,098	10	11,264	100
	as at 31 December	7,272	66	1,339	12	1,418	13	1,066	10	11,095	100
2011	as at 31 March	7,215	64	1,371	12	1,544	14	1,124	10	11,254	100
	as at 30 June	7,443	67	1,349	12	1,414	13	953	9	11,159	100
	as at 30 September	7,382	67	1,329	12	1,433	13	916	8	11,060	100
	as at 31 December	7,102	66	1,310	12	1,232	12	1,041	10	10,685	100
2012	as at 31 March	7,093	66	1,333	12	1,281	12	1,043	10	10,750	100
	as at 30 June	7,106	68	1,190	11	1,205	12	965	9	10,466	100
	as at 30 September	7,146	68	1,333	13	1,090	10	977	9	10,546	100
	as at 31 December	6,920	67	1,292	13	1,063	10	977	10	10,252	100

1. Includes Glasgow Housing Association stock from 2003, and all other housing associations from June 2005 onward.

2. The category 'other' includes mainly private landlords. Prior to June 1999 the figures may also include an unknown number of local authority-owned chalets or mobile homes.

3. From 31 March 2008 there is a break in comparability in numbers in temporary accommodation in Glasgow-see notes page.

this page is intentionally blank

Banking, insurance

Chapter 12

Banking, insurance

Bank lending to, and bank deposits from, UK residents
(Tables 12.4 and 12.5)

These are series statistics based on the Standard Industrial Classification (SIC) 1992 (which was revised slightly in 2003).

Table 12.4. Until the third quarter of 2007, the analysis of lending covered loans, advances (including under reverse repos), finance leasing, acceptances and facilities (all in Sterling and other currencies) provided by reporting banks to their UK resident non-bank non-building society customers, as well as bank holdings of sterling and euro commercial paper issued by these resident customers. Following a review of statistical data collected, acceptances and holdings of sterling and euro commercial paper are no longer collected at the industry level detail with effect from fourth quarter 2007 data. Total lending therefore reflects loans and advances (including under reverse repos) only, from fourth quarter 2007 data.

Table 12.5 includes borrowing under sale and repo. Adjustments for transit items are not included. Figures for both tables are supplied by monthly reporting banks and grossed to cover quarterly reporters. Following the transition of building societies' statistical reporting from the Financial Services Authority to the Bank of England on 1st January 2008, both tables will include data reported by building societies from the first quarter of 2008 onwards. They exclude lending to building societies and to residents of the Channel Islands and Isle of Man.

Consumer credit (Excluding Student Loans)
(Table 12.12)

Following an ONS review in August 1997, data for 'other specialist lenders' were improved and revised back to January 1995. Total outstanding consumer credit was revised upwards by £2.6bn. Flows were break adjusted. Monthly data are available for lending by retailers from January 1997 but are not available for lending by insurance companies. The missing monthly data have been interpolated from quarterly data.

Within total consumer credit (excluding student loans) outstanding, credit card lending had been underestimated and 'other' consumer credit overestimated prior to January 1999 as a result of a longstanding inconsistency. The credit card element had previously covered sterling credit card lending to the UK household sector by only UK banks and building societies. Credit card lending by other specialist lenders and retailers (where they finance lending themselves) could not be separately identified and so was included within the 'other' consumer credit component.

From January 1999 onwards this inconsistency has been corrected, as credit card lending by other specialist lenders can be separately identified. As a result, data from January 1999 onwards for credit card lending and for 'other' consumer credit are not directly comparable with those for earlier periods. The change affects all three measures of credit card lending (gross, net and amounts outstanding), with an equal offsetting change to 'other' consumer credit. In non-seasonally adjusted terms, gross credit card lending was on average around £800 million per month higher since January 1999, whilst the amount outstanding of credit card debt was boosted by £4.8 billion in January 1999. The changes to net credit card lending are much smaller in absolute terms, with no discernible change to trend.

From November 2006, the Bank of England ceased to update the separate data on consumer credit provided by other specialist lenders, retailers, and insurance companies, previously contained in Table A5.6 of Monetary and Financial Statistics. The final month for which separate data are available on the Bank's Statistical Interactive Database is November 2006. The three categories have been merged into "other consumer credit lenders".

Prior to January 2008, building societies' lending was unsecured lending to individuals including sterling bridging loans (prior to October 1998 this was class 3 lending to individuals). Building societies gross lending through overdrafts is no longer included from January 2008.

http://www.bankofengland.co.uk/boeapps/iadb/newintermed.asp

12.1a Central bank's balance sheet - Bank of England 'Bank return'

£ millions   Not seasonally adjusted

Amounts outstanding of consolidated Issue and Banking department liabilities

RPW	Notes in circulation	Reserve balances	Short-term open market operations	of which: one week sterling	fine-tuning sterling	other maturity within maintenance period sterling	Foreign currency public securities issued	Cash ratio deposits	Other liabilities	Total liabilities
	B55A (a)	B56A (a)	B9R6	B9R8	B58A (a)	BV79	B59A (a)	B62A (a)	B63A (a)	B75A (a)
2012 Jul 04	56,797	229,604	-	-	-	-	3,891	2,419	67,738	360,450
11	56,838	231,803	-	-	-	-	3,898	2,419	67,763	362,721
18	56,788	237,557	-	-	-	-	3,885	2,419	64,872	365,522
25	57,207	242,432	-	-	-	-	3,923	2,419	66,584	372,565
Aug 01	57,413	246,060	-	-	-	-	3,894	2,419	66,163	375,949
08	57,362	248,181	-	-	-	-	3,874	2,419	66,510	378,346
15	57,188	251,906	-	-	-	-	3,861	2,419	65,641	381,014
22	57,347	255,586	-	-	-	-	3,834	2,419	65,804	384,990
29	57,682	256,543	-	-	-	-	3,829	2,419	66,255	386,729
Sep 05	57,553	260,246	-	-	-	-	3,811	2,419	66,968	390,996
12	57,237	259,831	-	-	-	-	3,765	2,419	69,841	393,093
19	56,958	262,639	-	-	-	-	3,737	2,419	70,487	396,239
26	57,064	266,460	-	-	-	-	3,753	2,419	69,811	399,508
Oct 03	57,345	269,072	-	-	-	-	3,773	2,419	69,478	402,087
10	57,083	272,143	-	-	-	-	3,783	2,419	69,195	404,623
17	57,138	275,186	-	-	-	-	3,748	2,419	69,347	407,839
24	57,292	277,247	-	-	-	-	3,778	2,419	70,264	411,001
31	57,670	280,715	-	-	-	-	3,759	2,419	69,305	413,868
Nov 07	57,531	281,894	-	-	-	-	3,786	2,419	68,841	414,472
14	57,602	281,161	-	-	-	-	3,820	2,419	69,453	414,455
21	57,537	281,745	-	-	-	-	3,796	2,419	68,845	414,343
28	57,962	280,236	-	-	-	-	3,784	2,419	70,438	414,839
Dec 05	58,445	279,609	-	-	-	-	3,760	2,483	70,254	414,552
12	58,803	277,013	-	-	-	-	3,754	2,483	73,047	415,099
19	59,774	274,966	-	-	-	-	3,716	2,483	73,672	414,611
26	60,621	271,149	-	-	-	-	3,738	2,483	72,390	410,381
2013 Jan 02	60,085	271,426	-	-	-	-	3,712	2,483	72,517	410,223
09	57,954	276,817	-	-	-	-	3,776	2,483	68,823	409,852
16	57,146	278,180	-	-	-	-	3,778	2,483	68,266	409,853
23	57,046	273,214	-	-	-	-	3,814	2,483	68,788	405,346
30	57,169	272,248	-	-	-	-	3,825	2,483	68,793	404,517
Feb 06	57,194	272,056	-	-	-	-	3,857	2,479	68,824	404,410
13	57,176	278,027	-	-	-	-	3,882	2,479	62,489	404,054
20	57,242	279,727	-	-	-	-	3,943	2,479	60,836	404,228
27	57,661	279,399	-	-	-	-	3,987	2,479	58,905	402,431
Mar 06	57,766	280,508	-	-	-	-	4,006	2,479	58,059	402,819
13	57,880	276,655	-	-	-	-	5,383	2,479	63,169	405,567
20	58,018	278,781	-	-	-	-	4,006	2,479	60,396	403,680
27	59,083	278,830	-	-	-	-	4,009	2,479	59,660	404,061
Apr 03	59,587	281,182	-	-	-	-	4,006	2,479	56,542	403,797
10	58,676	286,481	-	-	-	-	3,936	2,479	52,397	403,969
17	58,356	286,447	-	-	-	-	3,961	2,479	52,828	404,071
24	58,508	286,409	-	-	-	-	3,953	2,479	52,508	403,858
May 01	58,972	286,412	-	-	-	-	3,874	2,479	51,643	403,381
08	59,237	289,882	-	-	-	-	3,877	2,479	47,493	402,968
15	58,754	289,598	-	-	-	-	3,962	2,479	47,987	402,779
22	58,889	289,286	-	-	-	-	4,009	2,468	49,642	404,294
29	59,512	288,739	-	-	-	-	3,984	2,468	49,068	403,771
Jun 05	59,132	287,898	-	-	-	-	3,913	4,013	48,448	403,404
12	59,110	289,955	-	-	-	-	3,836	4,013	46,472	403,386
19	59,101	290,587	-	-	-	-	3,846	4,013	46,673	404,220
26	59,264	290,518	-	-	-	-	3,915	4,013	46,382	404,092

Notes to table
(a) Following Bank of England money market reform on 18 May 2006 the Bank of England 'Bank Return' was changed. This series forms part of the new Bank Return, with data starting on 24 May 2006. More information on changes made to the Bank's monetary policy operations and their impact on published data can be found in 'The implications of money market reform for data published in Monetary and Financial Statistics' in the June 2006 issue of Bank of England: Monetary and Financial Statistics.

12.1b Central bank's balance sheet - Bank of England 'Bank return'

£ millions   Not seasonally adjusted

Amounts outstanding of consolidated Issue and Banking Department assets

RPW	Short-term open market operations	of which: one week sterling reverse repo	of which: fine-tuning sterling reverse repo	of which: other maturity within maintenance period reverse repo	Longer-term sterling reverse repo	Ways and Means advances to HM government	Bonds and other securities acquired via market transactions	Other assets	Total assets
	B66A (b)	B67A (b)	B68A (b)	BL59	B69A (b)	B72A (b)(c)	B73A (b)(d)	B74A (b)	B75A (b)
2012 Jul 04	-	-	-	-	5,835	370	13,638	340,607	360,450
11	-	-	-	-	5,835	370	13,646	342,871	362,721
18	-	-	-	-	5,700	370	13,664	345,787	365,522
25	-	-	-	-	9,875	370	13,693	348,627	372,565
Aug 01	-	-	-	-	9,875	370	13,690	352,014	375,949
08	-	-	-	-	9,875	370	13,555	354,546	378,346
15	-	-	-	-	9,875	370	13,510	357,259	381,014
22	-	-	-	-	11,115	370	13,519	359,986	384,990
29	-	-	-	-	11,115	370	13,526	361,718	386,729
Sep 05	-	-	-	-	11,115	370	13,558	365,954	390,996
12	-	-	-	-	11,115	370	13,467	368,142	393,093
19	-	-	-	-	11,330	370	13,460	371,080	396,239
26	-	-	-	-	11,480	370	13,479	374,179	399,508
Oct 03	-	-	-	-	11,480	370	13,502	376,736	402,087
10	-	-	-	-	11,480	370	13,497	379,276	404,623
17	-	-	-	-	11,285	370	13,462	382,722	407,839
24	-	-	-	-	11,285	370	13,475	385,872	411,001
31	-	-	-	-	11,285	370	13,483	388,730	413,868
Nov 07	-	-	-	-	11,285	370	13,508	389,309	414,472
14	-	-	-	-	11,285	370	13,532	389,269	414,455
21	-	-	-	-	11,265	370	13,485	389,223	414,343
28	-	-	-	-	11,265	370	13,509	389,695	414,839
Dec 05	-	-	-	-	11,265	370	13,436	389,481	414,552
12	-	-	-	-	11,265	370	13,390	390,075	415,099
19	-	-	-	-	11,055	370	13,346	389,840	414,611
26	-	-	-	-	6,055	370	13,376	390,580	410,381
2013 Jan 02	-	-	-	-	6,055	370	13,319	390,480	410,223
09	-	-	-	-	6,055	370	13,096	390,332	409,852
16	-	-	-	-	6,050	370	13,136	390,298	409,853
23	-	-	-	-	1,875	370	13,168	389,933	405,346
30	-	-	-	-	1,875	370	13,184	389,088	404,517
Feb 06	-	-	-	-	1,875	370	13,208	388,958	404,410
13	-	-	-	-	1,875	370	13,195	388,614	404,054
20	-	-	-	-	2,085	370	13,248	388,525	404,228
27	-	-	-	-	585	370	13,285	388,191	402,431
Mar 06	-	-	-	-	585	370	13,185	388,679	402,819
13	-	-	-	-	585	370	13,958	390,654	405,567
20	-	-	-	-	585	370	13,464	389,262	403,680
27	-	-	-	-	435	370	13,474	389,782	404,061
Apr 03	-	-	-	-	435	370	13,480	389,512	403,797
10	-	-	-	-	435	370	13,373	389,791	403,969
17	-	-	-	-	440	370	13,411	389,850	404,071
24	-	-	-	-	440	370	13,381	389,667	403,858
May 01	-	-	-	-	440	370	13,360	389,211	403,381
08	-	-	-	-	440	370	13,331	388,827	402,968
15	-	-	-	-	440	370	13,314	388,656	402,779
22	-	-	-	-	335	370	13,363	390,226	404,294
29	-	-	-	-	335	370	13,357	389,709	403,771
Jun 05	-	-	-	-	335	370	13,271	389,429	403,404
12	-	-	-	-	335	370	13,210	389,472	403,386
19	-	-	-	-	325	370	14,038	389,487	404,220
26	-	-	-	-	325	370	14,500	388,897	404,092

Notes to table

(b) Following Bank of England money market reform on 18 May 2006 the Bank of England 'Bank Return' was changed. This series forms part of the new Bank Return, with data starting on 24 May 2006. More information on changes made to the Bank's monetary policy operations and their impact on published data can be found in `The implications of money market reform for data published in Monetary and Financial Statistics' in the June 2006 issue of Bank of England: Monetary and Financial Statistics.

(c) The Debt Management Office announced on 24 January 2008 that HM Treasury had instructed an initial part repayment of the Ways and Means balance, with a payment to the Bank of England of £4.0bn, which is first shown in this table on 30 January 2008. The Ways and Means facility is the central government's overdraft facility at the Bank of England.

(d) As part of the Bank of England's reformed framework for implementing monetary policy, the Bank announced in May 2006 its intention to conduct open market operations to make outright purchases of gilts and high-quality foreign currency government bonds. The first of these gilt-purchase open market operations took place in January 2008.

12.1c Central bank's balance sheet - Bank of England 'Bank return'

£ millions   Not seasonally adjusted

Amounts outstanding of Issue Department liabilities

RPW	Notes in circulation AEFA (e)	Notes in Banking Department AEFB (e)(f)	Total liabilities BL37 (e)
2012 Jul 04	56,797	-	56,797
11	56,838	-	56,838
18	56,788	-	56,788
25	57,207	-	57,207
Aug 01	57,413	-	57,413
08	57,362	-	57,362
15	57,188	-	57,188
22	57,347	-	57,347
29	57,682	-	57,682
Sep 05	57,553	-	57,553
12	57,237	-	57,237
19	56,958	-	56,958
26	57,064	-	57,064
Oct 03	57,345	-	57,345
10	57,083	-	57,083
17	57,138	-	57,138
24	57,292	-	57,292
31	57,670	-	57,670
Nov 07	57,531	-	57,531
14	57,602	-	57,602
21	57,537	-	57,537
28	57,962	-	57,962
Dec 05	58,445	-	58,445
12	58,803	-	58,803
19	59,774	-	59,774
26	60,621	-	60,621
2013 Jan 02	60,085	-	60,085
09	57,954	-	57,954
16	57,146	-	57,146
23	57,046	-	57,046
30	57,169	-	57,169
Feb 06	57,194	-	57,194
13	57,176	-	57,176
20	57,242	-	57,242
27	57,661	-	57,661
Mar 06	57,766	-	57,766
13	57,880	-	57,880
20	58,018	-	58,018
27	59,083	-	59,083
Apr 03	59,587	-	59,587
10	58,676	-	58,676
17	58,356	-	58,356
24	58,508	-	58,508
May 01	58,972	-	58,972
08	59,237	-	59,237
15	58,754	-	58,754
22	58,889	-	58,889
29	59,512	-	59,512
Jun 05	59,132	-	59,132
12	59,110	-	59,110
19	59,101	-	59,101
26	59,264	-	59,264

Notes to table

(e) Following Bank of England money market reform on 18 May 2006 the Bank of England 'Bank Return' was changed. This series forms part of the new Bank Return, with data starting on 24 May 2006. More information on changes made to the Bank's monetary policy operations and their impact on published data can be found in `The implications of money market reform for data published in Monetary and Financial Statistics' in the June 2006 issue of Bank of England: Monetary and Financial Statistics.

(f) On 1 August 2006, the Bank ceased using 'Notes in Banking Department' in the Issue Department balance sheet as a balancing item to ensure that the total liabilities of Issue Department were rounded-up to the nearest £10 million. Consequently, the total liabilities of Issue Department are now equal to 'Notes in circulation', which are notes that have been issued and paid for. The entry for `Notes in Banking Department' does not reflect the value of physical notes held on Bank premises.

12.1d Central bank's balance sheet - Bank of England 'Bank return'

£ millions   Not seasonally adjusted

Amounts outstanding of Issue Department assets

RPW	Short-term open market operations	of which: one week sterling reverse repo	of which: fine-tuning sterling reverse repo	Longer-term sterling reverse repo	Ways and Means advances to HM government	Bonds and other securities acquired via market transactions	Other assets	Total assets
	BL29 (g)	BL32 (g)	BL33 (g)	BL34 (g)	B54A (g)(h)	BL35 (g)(i)	BL36 (g)	BL37 (g)
2012 Jul 04	-	-	-	225	370	5,071	51,131	56,797
11	-	-	-	225	370	5,071	51,172	56,838
18	-	-	-	25	370	5,071	51,322	56,788
25	-	-	-	25	370	5,071	51,741	57,207
Aug 01	-	-	-	25	370	5,071	51,947	57,413
08	-	-	-	25	370	5,071	51,896	57,362
15	-	-	-	25	370	5,071	51,722	57,188
22	-	-	-	5	370	5,071	51,901	57,347
29	-	-	-	5	370	5,071	52,236	57,682
Sep 05	-	-	-	5	370	5,088	52,090	57,553
12	-	-	-	5	370	5,088	51,774	57,237
19	-	-	-	55	370	5,088	51,445	56,958
26	-	-	-	55	370	5,088	51,552	57,064
Oct 03	-	-	-	55	370	5,088	51,832	57,345
10	-	-	-	55	370	5,088	51,570	57,083
17	-	-	-	60	370	5,088	51,621	57,138
24	-	-	-	60	370	5,088	51,774	57,292
31	-	-	-	60	370	5,088	52,152	57,670
Nov 07	-	-	-	60	370	5,088	52,014	57,531
14	-	-	-	60	370	5,088	52,084	57,602
21	-	-	-	65	370	5,088	52,014	57,537
28	-	-	-	65	370	5,088	52,439	57,962
Dec 05	-	-	-	65	370	4,990	53,020	58,445
12	-	-	-	65	370	4,990	53,378	58,803
19	-	-	-	20	370	4,990	54,393	59,774
26	-	-	-	20	370	4,990	55,241	60,621
2013 Jan 02	-	-	-	20	370	4,990	54,705	60,085
09	-	-	-	20	370	4,990	52,574	57,954
16	-	-	-	15	370	4,990	51,771	57,146
23	-	-	-	15	370	4,990	51,671	57,046
30	-	-	-	15	370	4,990	51,794	57,169
Feb 06	-	-	-	15	370	4,990	51,818	57,194
13	-	-	-	15	370	4,990	51,801	57,176
20	-	-	-	15	370	4,990	51,867	57,242
27	-	-	-	15	370	4,990	52,286	57,661
Mar 06	-	-	-	15	370	4,893	52,488	57,766
13	-	-	-	15	370	4,893	52,603	57,880
20	-	-	-	5	370	4,893	52,750	58,018
27	-	-	-	5	370	4,893	53,816	59,083
Apr 03	-	-	-	5	370	4,893	54,319	59,587
10	-	-	-	5	370	4,893	53,408	58,676
17	-	-	-	5	370	4,893	53,088	58,356
24	-	-	-	5	370	4,893	53,240	58,508
May 01	-	-	-	5	370	4,893	53,704	58,972
08	-	-	-	5	370	4,893	53,969	59,237
15	-	-	-	5	370	4,893	53,486	58,754
22	-	-	-	-	370	4,893	53,626	58,889
29	-	-	-	-	370	4,893	54,249	59,512
Jun 05	-	-	-	-	370	4,847	53,915	59,132
12	-	-	-	-	370	4,847	53,893	59,110
19	-	-	-	-	370	4,847	53,884	59,101
26	-	-	-	-	370	4,847	54,047	59,264

Notes to table

(g) Following Bank of England money market reform on 18 May 2006 the Bank of England 'Bank Return' was changed. This series forms part of the new Bank Return, with data starting on 24 May 2006. More information on changes made to the Bank's monetary policy operations and their impact on published data can be found in `The implications of money market reform for data published in Monetary and Financial Statistics' in the June 2006 issue of Bank of England: Monetary and Financial Statistics.

(h) The Debt Management Office announced on 24 January 2008 that HM Treasury had instructed an initial part repayment of the Ways and Means balance, with a payment to the Bank of England of £4.0bn, which is first shown in this table on 30 January 2008. The Ways and Means facility is the central government's overdraft facility at the Bank of England.

(i) As part of the Bank of England's reformed framework for implementing monetary policy, the Bank announced in May 2006 its intention to conduct open market operations to make outright purchases of gilts and high-quality foreign currency government bonds. The first of these gilt-purchase open market operations took place in January 2008.

12.1e Central bank's balance sheet - Bank of England 'Bank return'

£ millions   Not seasonally adjusted

Amounts outstanding of Banking Department liabilities

RPW	Reserve balances	Short-term open market operations	of which: one week sterling	of which: fine-tuning sterling	of which: other maturity within maintenance period sterling	Foreign currency public securities issued	Cash ratio deposits	Other liabilities	Total liabilities
	BL38 (j)	B9R5	B9R7	BL42 (j)	BV78	BL43 (j)	BL44 (j)	BL45 (j)	BL56 (j)
2012 Jul 04	229,604	-	-	-	-	3,891	2,419	118,869	354,784
11	231,803	-	-	-	-	3,898	2,419	118,934	357,055
18	237,557	-	-	-	-	3,885	2,419	116,194	360,056
25	242,432	-	-	-	-	3,923	2,419	118,325	367,099
Aug 01	246,060	-	-	-	-	3,894	2,419	118,110	370,483
08	248,181	-	-	-	-	3,874	2,419	118,406	372,880
15	251,906	-	-	-	-	3,861	2,419	117,362	375,548
22	255,586	-	-	-	-	3,834	2,419	117,704	379,544
29	256,543	-	-	-	-	3,829	2,419	118,491	381,283
Sep 05	260,246	-	-	-	-	3,811	2,419	119,057	385,533
12	259,831	-	-	-	-	3,765	2,419	121,615	387,630
19	262,639	-	-	-	-	3,737	2,419	121,932	390,727
26	266,460	-	-	-	-	3,753	2,419	121,363	393,995
Oct 03	269,072	-	-	-	-	3,773	2,419	121,310	396,575
10	272,143	-	-	-	-	3,783	2,419	120,765	399,110
17	275,186	-	-	-	-	3,748	2,419	120,968	402,321
24	277,247	-	-	-	-	3,778	2,419	122,038	405,484
31	280,715	-	-	-	-	3,759	2,419	121,457	408,350
Nov 07	281,894	-	-	-	-	3,786	2,419	120,855	408,954
14	281,161	-	-	-	-	3,820	2,419	121,537	408,937
21	281,745	-	-	-	-	3,796	2,419	120,859	408,820
28	280,236	-	-	-	-	3,784	2,419	122,876	409,316
Dec 05	279,609	-	-	-	-	3,760	2,483	123,275	409,126
12	277,013	-	-	-	-	3,754	2,483	126,424	409,674
19	274,966	-	-	-	-	3,716	2,483	128,066	409,231
26	271,149	-	-	-	-	3,738	2,483	127,631	405,001
2013 Jan 02	271,426	-	-	-	-	3,712	2,483	127,221	404,843
09	276,817	-	-	-	-	3,776	2,483	121,396	404,472
16	278,180	-	-	-	-	3,778	2,483	120,037	404,478
23	273,214	-	-	-	-	3,814	2,483	120,459	399,971
30	272,248	-	-	-	-	3,825	2,483	120,587	399,142
Feb 06	272,056	-	-	-	-	3,857	2,479	120,642	399,035
13	278,027	-	-	-	-	3,882	2,479	114,291	398,679
20	279,727	-	-	-	-	3,943	2,479	112,703	398,852
27	279,399	-	-	-	-	3,987	2,479	111,191	397,056
Mar 06	280,508	-	-	-	-	4,006	2,479	110,547	397,541
13	276,655	-	-	-	-	5,383	2,479	115,772	400,289
20	278,781	-	-	-	-	4,006	2,479	113,146	398,413
27	278,830	-	-	-	-	4,009	2,479	113,475	398,794
Apr 03	281,182	-	-	-	-	4,006	2,479	110,862	398,529
10	286,481	-	-	-	-	3,936	2,479	105,805	398,701
17	286,447	-	-	-	-	3,961	2,479	105,916	398,803
24	286,409	-	-	-	-	3,953	2,479	105,749	398,590
May 01	286,412	-	-	-	-	3,874	2,479	105,347	398,113
08	289,882	-	-	-	-	3,877	2,479	101,462	397,700
15	289,598	-	-	-	-	3,962	2,479	101,473	397,511
22	289,286	-	-	-	-	4,009	2,468	103,268	399,031
29	288,739	-	-	-	-	3,984	2,468	103,317	398,508
Jun 05	287,898	-	-	-	-	3,913	4,013	102,363	398,187
12	289,955	-	-	-	-	3,836	4,013	100,365	398,169
19	290,587	-	-	-	-	3,846	4,013	100,557	399,003
26	290,518	-	-	-	-	3,915	4,013	100,429	398,875

Notes to table

(j) Following Bank of England money market reform on 18 May 2006 the Bank of England 'Bank Return' was changed. This series forms part of the new Bank Return, with data starting on 24 May 2006. More information on changes made to the Bank's monetary policy operations and their impact on published data can be found in `The implications of money market reform for data published in Monetary and Financial Statistics' in the June 2006 issue of Bank of England: Monetary and Financial Statistics.

© Bank of England. Requests for copyright, please email srdd_editor@bankofengland.co.uk or telephone +44 (0)20 7601 5432.

12.1f Central bank's balance sheet - Bank of England 'Bank return'

£ millions   Not seasonally adjusted

Amounts outstanding of Banking Department assets

| | Short-term open market operations | of which: | | | Longer-term sterling reverse repo | Bonds and other securities acquired via market transactions | Bank of England notes | Other assets | Total assets |
| | | one week sterling reverse repo | fine-tuning sterling reverse repo | other maturity within maintenance period reverse repo | | | | | |
RPW	BL48 (k)	BL49 (k)	BL52 (k)	BL98	B3J2	BL53 (k)	BL54 (k)(l)	BL55 (k)	BL56 (k)
2012 Jul 04	-	-	-	-	5,610	8,567	-	340,607	354,784
11	-	-	-	-	5,610	8,575	-	342,871	357,055
18	-	-	-	-	5,675	8,593	-	345,787	360,056
25	-	-	-	-	9,850	8,622	-	348,627	367,099
Aug 01	-	-	-	-	9,850	8,619	-	352,014	370,483
08	-	-	-	-	9,850	8,484	-	354,546	372,880
15	-	-	-	-	9,850	8,439	-	357,259	375,548
22	-	-	-	-	11,110	8,448	-	359,986	379,544
29	-	-	-	-	11,110	8,455	-	361,718	381,283
Sep 05	-	-	-	-	11,110	8,470	-	365,954	385,533
12	-	-	-	-	11,110	8,379	-	368,142	387,630
19	-	-	-	-	11,275	8,372	-	371,080	390,727
26	-	-	-	-	11,425	8,391	-	374,179	393,995
Oct 03	-	-	-	-	11,425	8,414	-	376,736	396,575
10	-	-	-	-	11,425	8,410	-	379,276	399,110
17	-	-	-	-	11,225	8,374	-	382,722	402,321
24	-	-	-	-	11,225	8,387	-	385,872	405,484
31	-	-	-	-	11,225	8,395	-	388,730	408,350
Nov 07	-	-	-	-	11,225	8,420	-	389,309	408,954
14	-	-	-	-	11,225	8,444	-	389,269	408,937
21	-	-	-	-	11,200	8,397	-	389,223	408,820
28	-	-	-	-	11,200	8,421	-	389,695	409,316
Dec 05	-	-	-	-	11,200	8,446	-	389,481	409,126
12	-	-	-	-	11,200	8,400	-	390,075	409,674
19	-	-	-	-	11,035	8,356	-	389,840	409,231
26	-	-	-	-	6,035	8,386	-	390,580	405,001
2013 Jan 02	-	-	-	-	6,035	8,328	-	390,480	404,843
09	-	-	-	-	6,035	8,105	-	390,332	404,472
16	-	-	-	-	6,035	8,145	-	390,298	404,478
23	-	-	-	-	1,860	8,177	-	389,933	399,971
30	-	-	-	-	1,860	8,194	-	389,088	399,142
Feb 06	-	-	-	-	1,860	8,217	-	388,958	399,035
13	-	-	-	-	1,860	8,205	-	388,614	398,679
20	-	-	-	-	2,070	8,258	-	388,525	398,852
27	-	-	-	-	570	8,295	-	388,191	397,056
Mar 06	-	-	-	-	570	8,292	-	388,679	397,541
13	-	-	-	-	570	9,065	-	390,654	400,289
20	-	-	-	-	580	8,571	-	389,262	398,413
27	-	-	-	-	430	8,581	-	389,782	398,794
Apr 03	-	-	-	-	430	8,587	-	389,512	398,529
10	-	-	-	-	430	8,480	-	389,791	398,701
17	-	-	-	-	435	8,518	-	389,850	398,803
24	-	-	-	-	435	8,488	-	389,667	398,590
May 01	-	-	-	-	435	8,467	-	389,211	398,113
08	-	-	-	-	435	8,438	-	388,827	397,700
15	-	-	-	-	435	8,421	-	388,656	397,511
22	-	-	-	-	335	8,470	-	390,226	399,031
29	-	-	-	-	335	8,464	-	389,709	398,508
Jun 05	-	-	-	-	335	8,423	-	389,429	398,187
12	-	-	-	-	335	8,362	-	389,472	398,169
19	-	-	-	-	325	9,191	-	389,487	399,003
26	-	-	-	-	325	9,653	-	388,897	398,875

Notes to table

(k) Following Bank of England money market reform on 18 May 2006 the Bank of England 'Bank Return' was changed. This series forms part of the new Bank Return, with data starting on 24 May 2006. More information on changes made to the Bank's monetary policy operations and their impact on published data can be found in 'The implications of money market reform for data published in Monetary and Financial Statistics' in the June 2006 issue of Bank of England: Monetary and Financial Statistics.

(l) On 1 August 2006, the Bank ceased using 'Notes in Banking Department' in the Issue Department balance sheet as a balancing item to ensure that the total liabilities of Issue Department were rounded-up to the nearest £10 million. Consequently, the total liabilities of Issue Department are now equal to 'Notes in circulation', which are notes that have been issued and paid for. The entry for 'Notes in Banking Department' does not reflect the value of physical notes held on Bank premises.

12.2a Annual clearing volumes and values

Clearing volumes thousands

	Annual volumes		
	2012	**2013**	**Change 2013 on 2012 %**
Bacs			
Standing orders	17,074	18,409	8%
Bacs Direct Credits	2,182,667	2,151,714	-1%
Direct Debits	3,416,651	3,524,905	3%
Total	**5,616,392**	**5,695,028**	**1%**
CHAPS Clearing Company			
CHAPS	33,936	34,976	3%
Total	**33,936**	**34,976**	**3%**
Faster Payments Scheme			
Standing Order Payments	299,630	312,995	4%
Single Immediate Payments	379,844	502,025	32%
Forward Dated Payments	129,829	150,381	16%
Return Payments	1,788	2,228	25%
Total	**811,090**	**967,629**	**19%**
Cheque and Credit Clearing Company			
Cheques exchanged in Great Britain	597,076	525,295	-12%
Euro debits exchanged in Great Britain	165	131	-21%
Credits (paper bank giro credits) exchanged in Great Britain	46,927	40,569	-14%
Total	**644,168**	**565,995**	**-12%**
Currency Clearing: US Dollar	31.0	26.9	-13%
Total all Clearing Companies	**7,105,617**	**7,263,655**	**2%**

Clearing values £ millions

	Annual values		
	2012	**2013**	**Change 2013 on 2012 %**
Bacs			
Standing orders and Bacs Direct Credits	3,036,714	3,103,579	2%
Direct Debits	1,075,507	1,115,065	4%
Total	**4,112,222**	**4,218,644**	**3%**
CHAPS Clearing Company			
CHAPS	71,716,857	70,138,927	-2%
Total	**71,716,857**	**70,138,927**	**-2%**
Faster Payments Scheme			
Standing Order Payments	80,009	88,885	11%
Single Immediate Payments	328,685	423,571	29%
Forward Dated Payments	208,252	257,794	24%
Return Payments	965	1,111	15%
Total	**617,911**	**771,361**	**25%**
Cheque and Credit Clearing Company			
Cheques exchanged in Great Britain	601,256	535,513	-11%
Euro debits exchanged in Great Britain	1,188	1,166	-11%
Credits (paper bank giro credits) exchanged in Great Britain	23,802	21,109	-2%
Total	**626,247**	**557,787**	**-11%**
Currency Clearing: US Dollar	**407**	**328**	**-20%**
Total all Clearing Companies	**77,073,644**	**75,687,047**	**-2%**

Source: UK Payments Administration Ltd

(a) Totals, averages and percentages are calculated using unrounded data. The values of all euro and US Dollar clearings are shown as £ sterling equivalent.

(b) There were 253 clearing days in 2013 and 252 in 2012. In terms of the Faster Payments Scheme there were 253 clearing days and 365 calendar days in 2013. Please note that the number of processing days varies between payment types.

(c) A description of the United Kingdom payment clearings together with more comprehensive statistics over a longer period is available from the Information Management team. These data are published annually in UK Payment Statistics; the 2013 edition will be available in May 2014.

For further information please contact Information Management
(Telephone: 020 3217 8720, E-Mail: inform@paymentscouncil.org.uk)

12.2b Average daily clearing volumes and values

Average clearing volumes thousands

	Peak daily volumes		Average daily volumes	
	2012	2013	2012	2013
Bacs				
Standing orders	28,411}	34,794}	68	73
Bacs Direct			8,661	8,505
Credits Direct	77,394	78,542	13,558	13,932
Debits **Total**			**22,287**	**22,510**
CHAPS				
Retail and commercial	187	210	107.1	108.9
(MT103) Wholesale financial	44	45	27.5	29.3
(MT202) **Total**			**134.7**	**138.2**
Faster Payments				
Scheme Standing Order	8,431	9,210	1,189.0	1,237.1
Payments Single	3,742	5,599	1,040.7	1,375.4
Immediate Payments	1,534	1,770	355.7	412.0
Forward Dated Payments	49	137	4.9	6.1
Return Payments				
Cheque and Credit Clearing Company				
Cheques exchanged in Great Britain	3,529	3,430	2,369	2,076
Euro debits exchanged in Great Britain	1.6	1.0	0.7	0.5
Credits (paper bank giro credits) exchanged in Great Britain	386	341	186	160
Total			**2,556**	**2,237**

Average clearing values

	Average values			
	Daily £ millions		Per item £	
	2012	2013	2012	2013
Bacs				
Standing orders and Bacs Direct	12,050	12,267	1,380	1,430
Credits Direct Debits	4,268	4,407	315	316
Total	**16,318**	**16,674**	**732**	**741**
CHAPS				
Retail and commercial	63,193	61,303	589,877	562,828
(MT103) Wholesale financial	221,397	215,926	8,040,384	7,363,128
(MT202) **Total**	**284,591**	**277,229**	**2,113,318**	**2,005,341**
Faster Payments				
Scheme Standing Order	317.5	351.3	267	284
Payments Single	898.0^	1,160.5	865	844
Immediate Payments	569.0^	706.3	1,604	1,714
Forward Dated Payments	2.6	3.0	540	499
Return Payments			**762**	**797**
Total				
Cheque and Credit Clearing Company	2,386	2,117	1,007	1,019
Cheques exchanged in Great Britain	4.7	4.6	7,186	8,923
Euro debits exchanged in Great Britain	94	83	507	520
Credits (paper bank giro credits) exchanged in Great Britain				
Total	**2,485**	**2,205**	**972**	**985**
Total all Clearing			**10,847**	**10,420**
Companies				

Source: UK Payments Administration Ltd

There were 252 clearing days in 2012 and 253 in 2013.

12.2c Bacs volumes and values

Annual volumes thousands

	Standing orders		Bacs Direct Credits		Bacs Euro Credits		Direct Debits		Total volumes	
	Number	% Change	Number	% Change	Number	% Change	Number	% Change	Number	% Change
2003	288,443	5.6	1,341,945	14.4	54	45.0	2,429,915	6.2	4,060,357	8.7
2004	301,879	4.7	1,710,673	27.5	84	55.5	2,589,934	6.6	4,602,570	13.4
2005	318,022	5.3	2,093,859	22.4	12	48.6	2,722,245	5.1	5,134,250	11.6
2006	332,245	4.5	2,171,586	3.7	157	25.9	2,857,761	5.0	5,361,749	4.4
2007	347,347	4.5	2,233,106	2.8	181	15.8	2,296,474	3.7	5,544,109	3.4
2008	323,843	-6.8	2,254,875	1.0	176	-3.2	3,076,857	3.8	5,655,751	2.0
2009	199,759	-38.3	2,289,813	1.5	193	10.0	3,149,153	2.3	5,638,919	-0.3
2010	150,307	-24.8	2,292,942	0.1	143	26.0	3,229,338	2.5	5,672,730	0.6
2011	123,652	-17.7	2,270,987	-1.0			3,322,360	2.9	5,716,999	0.8
2012	17,074	-86.2	2,182,667	-3.9			3,416,651	2.8	5,616,392	-1.8
2013	18,409	8%	2,151,714	-1.0			3,524,905	3.0	5,695,028	1.0

Average values £ millions

	Bacs Direct Credits [a]		Bacs Euro Credits		Direct Debits		Total volumes	
	Number	% Change	Number	% Change	Number	% Change	Number	% Change
2003	1,910,251	8.3	1,924	53.9	662,192	7.3	2,574,367	8.1
2004	2,131,031	11.6	2,040	6.0	750,381	13.3	2,883,452	12.0
2005	2,350,644	10.3	2,524	23.7	797,039	6.2	3,150,207	9.3
2006	2,581,682	9.8	2,819	11.7	844,832	6.0	3,429,333	8.9
2007	2,808,349	8.8	3,965	40.6	883,592	4.6	3,695,906	7.8
2008	3,006,159	7.0	4,806	21.2	935,356	5.9	3,946,321	6.8
2009	2,969,711	-1.2	5,255	9.3	885,708	-5.3	3,860,674	-2.2
2010	3,111,218	4.8	3,033	-42.3	948,137	7.0	4,062,388	5.2
2011	3,318,536	6.7			1,044,677	10.2	4,363,214	7.4
2012	3,036,714	-8.5			1,075,507	3.0	4,112,222	-5.8
2013	3,103,579	2.0			1,115,065	4.0	4,218,644	3.0

Source: UK Payments Administration Ltd

(a) Values represent standing orders and Bacs Direct Credits combined

Bacs has 16 members and is responsible for the processing of bulk payments through its two principle payment schemes; Direct Debit and Bacs Direct Credit.

The Euro Debit Credit Service ceased operation on 29 October 2010

12.2d CHAPS volumes and values

Annual volumes thousands

	CHAPS Sterling [a]		CHAPS Euro						Total volumes [a]	
			Domestic (a)		Target					
					Transmitted to		Received from			
	Number	% Change	Number	% Change	Number	% Change	Number	% Change	Number	% Change
2003	27,215	6.5	1,399	13.1	2,904	19.2	1,685	4.7	33,202	7.6
2004	28,322	4.1	1,378	-1.5	3,314	14.1	1,849	9.7	34,862	5.0
2005	29,686	4.8	1,484	7.7	3,597	8.6	1,988	7.5	36,756	5.4
2006	33,030	11.3	1,461	-1.6	4,115	14.4	2,080	4.6	40,686	10.7
2007	35,588	7.7	1,455	-0.3	4,263	3.6	2,229	7.1	43,535	7.0
2008	34,606	-2.8	220	-84.9	379	-91.1	593	-73.4	35,797	-17.8
2009	31,926	-7.7							31,926	-10.8
2010	32,169	0.8							32,169	0.8
2011	34,024	5.8							34,024	5.8
2012	33,936	-0.3							33,936	-0.3
2013	34,976	3.0							34,976	3.0

Annual Values £ millions

	CHAPS Sterling [a]		CHAPS Euro (sterling equivalent)						Total values [a]	
			Domestic (a)		Target					
					Transmitted to		Received from			
	Number	% Change	Number	% Change	Number	% Change	Number	% Change	Number	% Change
2003	51,613,456	-0.5	5,114,198	22.7	15,924,879	21.5	15,923,974	21.5	88,576,506	7.7
2004	52,347,525	1.4	4,509,924	-11.8	17,238,602	8.2	17,238,737	8.3	91,334,788	3.1
2005	52,671,592	0.6	6,069,146	34.6	19,180,194	11.3	19,179,273	11.3	97,100,206	6.3
2006	59,437,370	12.8	7,365,558	21.4	21,415,027	11.7	21,419,195	11.7	109,637,149	12.9
2007	69,352,322	16.7	6,781,942	-7.9	25,266,729	18.0	25,268,856	18.0	126,669,848	15.5
2008	73,625,908	6.2	574,610	-91.5	4,413,570	-82.5	4,403,022	-82.6	83,017,110	-34.5
2009	64,616,956	-12.2							64,616,956	-22.2
2010	61,587,609	-4.7							61,587,609	-4.7
2011	63,876,772	3.7							63,876,772	3.7
2012	71,716,857	12.3							71,716,857	12.3
2013	70,138,927	-2.0							70,138,927	-2.0

Source: UK Payments Administration Ltd

(a) NewCHAPS was launched on 27 August 2001 and since his date CHAPS Sterling and CHAPS Euro Domestic figures include all CHAPS traffic

The CHAPS Scheme enables same-day bank-to-bank payments in sterling and has 20 direct participants

CHAPS Sterling came into operation on 9 February 1984 and provides an inter-bank electronic sterling transfer service on the basis of same-day settlement with guaranteed payment. Initially, CHAPS Sterling was limited to payments of £10,000 and above, but this minimum threshold was progressively reduced (to £7,000 in July 1988, £5,000 in February 1990, and £1,000 in January 1992) and removed completely in January 1993. From April 1996 CHAPS has operated a Real-Time Gross Settlement (RTGS) system with each payment settled individually in real time across settlement accounts at the Bank of England. After the closure of the CHAPS Euro service, CHAPS Sterling was renamed back to CHAPS.

CHAPS Euro was in operation between 4 January 1999 and 16 May 2008. It provided an RTGS system carrying euro payments between CHAPS Euro members and to institutions addressable across the TARGET infrastructure. Domestic euro payments were those exchanged between members of the CHAPS Euro scheme and settled across accounts at the Bank of England whereas TARGET payments were those cross border payments settled across the European Central Bank's interlinking system which connected the 19 euro RTGS systems.

For further information please contact Information Management
(Telephone: 020 3217 8720, E-Mail: inform@paymentscouncil.org.uk)

12.2e CHAPS value band analysis: 2013

Annual volume thousands				**Annual value**	CHAPS £ millions	
	CHAPS					
Upper Value (£/€)	Number	% of total		Upper Value (£/€)	Value	% of total
100,000	27,216	77.8		100,000	367,425	0.5
300,000	3,590	10.3		300,000	629,756	0.9
1,000,000	1,927	5.5		1,000,000	1,099,207	1.6
3,000,000	906	2.6		3,000,000	1,631,923	2.3
10,000,000	634	1.8		10,000,000	3,608,505	5.1
30,000,000	345	1		30,000,000	6,123,175	8.7
100,000,000	222	0.6		100,000,000	12,528,444	17.9
300,000,000	97	0.3		300,000,000	16,548,477	23.6
1,000,000,000	32	0.1		1,000,000,000	16,769,088	23.9
100,000,000,000	6	..		100,000,000,000	10,832,927	15.4
Total	**34,976**			**Total**	**70,138,927**	

The Bank of England and SWIFT provide services to CHAPS Co in operation of the CHAPS system. The Bank of England provides the real-time gross settlement process and SWIFT provides the secure communications network.

Source: UK Payments Administration Ltd

12.2f Faster Payments volumes and values

Annual volumes thousands

	Standing Order Payments		Single Immediate Payments		Forward Dated Payments		Return Payments		Total volumes[a]	
	Number	% Change	Number	% Change	Number	% Change	Number	% Change	Number	% Change
2003										
2004										
2005										
2006										
2007										
2008	37,574	*	36,325	*	8,708	*	182	*	82,789	*
2009	156,865	*	109,337	*	27,912	*	673	*	294,787	*
2010	203,055	29.4	181,195	65.7	40,632	45.6	880	30.6	425,761	44.4
2011	235,654	16.1	237,718	31.2	50,861	25.2	1,092	24.2	525,325	23.4
2012	299,630	27.1	379,844	59.8	129,829	155.3	1,788	63.6	811,090	54.4
2013	312,995	4.0	502,025	32.0	150,381	16.0	2,228	25.0	967,629	19.0

Annual values £ millions

	Standing Order Payments		Single Immediate Payments		Forward Dated Payments		Return Payments		Total values[a]	
	Value	% Change	Value	% Change	Value	% Change	Value	% Change	Value	% Change
2003										
2004										
2005										
2006										
2007										
2008	3,341	*	22,015	*	7,473	*	42	*	32,871	*
2009	26,527	*	59,015	*	20,544	*	136	*	106,223	*
2010	38,963	46.9	92,847	57.3	32,193	56.7	208	52.9	164,211	54.6
2011	50,206	28.9	135,101	45.5	49,429	53.5	308	47.9	235,044	43.1
2012	80,009	59.4	328,685	143.3	208,252	321.3	965	213.0	617,911	162.9
2013	88,885	11.0	423,571	29.0	257,794	24.0	1,111	15.0	771,361	25.0

Source: UK Payments Administration Ltd

[a] The UK Faster Payments Service was launched on 27 May 2008.

The Faster Payments Service enables electronic payments, typically made via the internet or phone, to be processed in hours rather than days. 10 banks and building societies operated in the service in 2013.

Single Immediate Payments are spontaneous payments typically originated electronically, e.g. by internet or telephone banking. Payments of up to a current limit of £100,000, can be made all day, every day, and are not restricted to Monday to Friday.

Standing Order Payments are fixed amount, pre-mandated beneficiary payments, repeated at regular intervals, up to a current limit of £100,000. This same day payment type is available Monday – Friday, excluding non-banking days.

Forward Dated Payments are input typically via internet or telephone banking, but post-dated, i.e, diarised by the Payer. The payments can be for variable amounts with no pre-mandated beneficiary, up to a current limit of £100,000. Unlike Standing Order payments they are not restricted to Monday – Friday.

12.2g Inter-bank cheque volumes and values

Annual volumes thousands

	Exchanged in Great Britain					Total volumes	
	Cheques			**Euro debits**			
	Number	% Change		Number	% Change	Number	% Change
2003	1,519,117	-6.3		759	3.6	1,519,876	-6.3
2004	1,423,742	-6.3		724	-4.6	1,424,465	-6.3
2005	1,325,762	-6.9		637	-12.0	1,326,399	-6.9
2006	1,237,401	-6.7		586	-7.9	1,237,987	-6.7
2007	1,124,869	-9.1		531	-9.5	1,125,400	-9.1
2008	1,007,379	-10.4		445	-16.1	1,007,824	-10.4
2009	875,533	-13.1		351	-21.2	875,884	-13.1
2010	775,643	-11.4		279	-20.5	775,922	-11.4
2011	682,082	-12.1		223	-20.1	682,305	-12.1
2012	597,076	-12.5		165	-25.7	597,241	-12.5
2013	525,295	-12.0		131	-21.0	525,426	-12.0

Annual values £ millions

	Exchanged in Great Britain					Total values	
	Cheques			**Euro debits**			
	Value	% Change		Value	% Change	Value	% Change
2003	1,240,685	-3.2		3,898	13.8	1,244,583	-3.1
2004	1,210,057	-2.5		3,456	-11.4	1,213,513	-2.5
2005	1,152,256	-4.8		3,206	-7.2	1,155,462	-4.8
2006	1,171,062	1.6		3,111	-3.0	1,174,174	1.6
2007	1,156,684	-1.2		2,970	-4.6	1,159,653	-1.2
2008	1,075,694	-7.0		2,980	0.4	1,078,674	-7.0
2009	870,591	-19.1		2,993	0.4	873,584	-19.0
2010	761,081	-12.6		1,767	-41.0	762,848	-12.7
2011	675,706	-11.2		1,559	-11.8	677,266	-11.2
2012	601,256	-11.0		1,188	-23.9	602,444	-11.0
2013	535,513	-11.0		1,166	-2.0	536,679	-11.0

Source: UK Payments Administration Ltd

The Cheque & Credit Clearing Company was established in 1985 and took over responsibility for managing the operation of the two bulk paper clearings for England and Wales.

From December 1996 the Cheque and Credit Clearing Company also took over responsibility for managing the operation of the inter-bank clearings in Scotland. The clearing of cheque and credit payments in Northern Ireland is managed by the Belfast Bankers' Clearing Company Limited (BBCCL)

Inter-branch clearing volumes (i.e. items cleared between branches of the same bank) are shown separately. These data are less comprehensive due to changes in agency arrangements and individual member processing policies, for example, the increased use of electronic processing methods. It is likely, therefore, that a proportion of inter-branch transactions are not included in these totals.

In-house volumes (i.e. payments between different accounts held at the same branch of a financial institution) are shown separately.

Comparable statistics prior to 2003 are available from Information Management.
(Telephone: 020 3217 8720, E-Mail: inform@paymentscouncil.org.uk)

12.2h Inter-bank credit volumes and values

Annual volumes thousands

	Exchanged in Great Britain		Total volumes	
	Number	% Change	Number	% Change
2003	140,792	-6.4	140,792	-6.4
2004	132,899	-5.6	132,899	-5.6
2005	123,280	-7.2	123,280	-7.2
2006	108,309	-12.1	108,309	-12.1
2007	96,290	-11.1	96,290	-11.1
2008	86,442	-10.2	86,442	-10.2
2009	73,686	-14.8	73,686	-14.8
2010	61,662	-16.3	61,662	-16.3
2011	53,934	-12.5	53,934	-12.5
2012	46,927	-12.9	46,927	-12.9
2013	40,569	-14.0	40,569	-14.0

Annual values £ millions

	Exchanged in Great Britain		Total values	
	Value	% Change	Value	% Change
2003	74,366	-7.6	74,366	-7.6
2004	68,261	-8.2	68,261	-8.2
2005	61,844	-9.4	61,844	-9.4
2006	59,309	-4.1	59,309	-4.1
2007	57,347	-3.3	57,347	-3.3
2008	51,641	-9.9	51,641	-9.9
2009	41,624	-19.4	41,624	-19.4
2010	32,312	-22.4	32,312	-22.4
2011	27,990	-13.4	27,990	-13.4
2012	23,802	-15.0	23,802	-15.0
2013	21,109	-11.0	21,109	-11.0

Source: UK Payments Administration Ltd

The Cheque & Credit Clearing Company was established in 1985 and took over responsibility for managing the operation of the two bulk paper clearings for England and Wales.

From December 1996 the Cheque and Credit Clearing Company also took over responsibility for managing the operation of the inter-bank clearings in Scotland. The clearing of cheque and credit payments in Northern Ireland is managed by the Belfast Bankers' Clearing Company Limited (BBCCL)

Inter-branch clearing volumes (i.e. items cleared between branches of the same bank) are shown separately. These data are less comprehensive due to changes in agency arrangements and individual member processing policies, for example, the increased use of electronic processing methods. It is likely, therefore, that a proportion of inter-branch transactions are not included in these totals.

In-house volumes (i.e. payments between different accounts held at the same branch of a financial institution) are shown separately.

Comparable statistics prior to 2003 are available from Information Management.
(Telephone: 020 3217 8720, E-Mail: inform@paymentscouncil.org.uk)

12.2i Inter-bank clearing values: UK summary £ billions

	Total bulk paper clearings inter-bank cheque and credit				Bulk electronic clearings	
	Great Britain	Northern Ireland[a]	Total		Bacs	
	Value	Value	Value	% Change	Value	% Change
2003	1,318	29	1,348	-3.4	2,574	8.1
2004	1,282	28	1,310	-2.8	2,883	12.0
2005	1,217	27	1,244	-5.0	3,150	9.3
2006	1,234	27	1,261	1.3	3,429	8.9
2007	1,217	27	1,244	-1.3	3,696	7.8
2008	1,130	45	1,175	-5.5	3,946	6.8
2009	915	36	952	-19.0	3,861	-2.2
2010	795	31	826	-13.2	4,062	5.2
2011	705	27	733	-11.3	4,363	7.4
2012	626	25	652	-11.0	4,112	-5.8
2013	558	23	581	-10.9	4,219	2.6

	Total bulk clearings		Same-day clearings				Grand total all UK inter-bank clearings	
			CHAPS		Faster Payments[b]			
	Value	% Change	Value	% Change	Value	% Change	Value	% Change
2003	3,922	3.9	88,577	7.7			92,499	7.5
2004	4,193	6.9	91,335	3.1			95,528	3.3
2005	4,394	4.8	97,100	6.3			101,494	6.2
2006	4,690	6.7	109,637	12.9			114,327	12.6
2007	4,940	5.3	126,670	15.5			131,609	15.1
2008	5,122	3.7	83,017	-34.5	33	*	88,172	-33.0
2009	4,812	-6.0	64,617	-22.2	106	*	69,535	-21.1
2010	4,888	1.6	61,588	-4.7	164	54.6	66,640	-4.2
2011	5,096	4.3	63,877	3.7	235	43.1	69,208	3.9
2012	4,764	-6.5	71,717	12.3	618	162.9	77,099	11.4
2013	4,799	0.7	70,139	-2.2	771	24.8	75,710	-1.8

Source: UK Payments Administration Ltd

[a] The clearing of cheque and credit payments in Northern Ireland is managed by the Belfast Bankers' Clearing Company (BBCC). Figures from 2002 – 2007 are estimated, but those for 2008 onwards were provided by the BBCC.

[b] CHAPS Euro ceased operation on 16 May 2008

[c] The Faster Payments Service was launched on 27 may 2008

12.2j Inter-bank clearing volumes: UK summary millions

	Total bulk paper clearings inter-bank cheque and credit				Bulk electronic clearings	
	Great Britain	Northern Ireland[a]	Total		Bacs	
	Number	Number	Number	% Change	Number	% Change
2003	1,660.6	44.1	1,704.7	-6.2	4,060.4	8.7
2004	1,557.4	41.3	1,598.7	-6.2	4,602.6	13.4
2005	1,449.7	38.4	1,488.1	-6.9	5,134.3	11.6
2006	1,346.3	35.7	1,382.0	-7.1	5,361.7	4.4
2007	1,221.7	32.4	1,254.1	-9.3	5,544.1	3.4
2008	1,094.3	25.1	1,119.4	-10.7	5,655.8	2.0
2009	949.6	22.4	972.0	-13.2	5,638.9	-0.3
2010	837.6	20.2	857.8	-11.8	5,672.7	0.6
2011	736.2	18.7	754.9	-12.0	5,717.0	0.8
2012	644.2	16.8	661.0	-12.4	5,616.4	-1.8
2013	566.0	15.2	581.2	-12.1	5,695.0	1.4

	Total bulk clearings		Same-day clearings				Grand total all UK inter-bank clearings	
			CHAPS		Faster Payments[b]			
	Number	% Change	Number	% Change	Number	% Change	Number	% Change
2003	5,765.1	3.8	33.2	7.6			5,798.3	3.8
2004	6,201.2	7.6	34.9	5.0			6,236.1	7.6
2005	6,622.4	6.8	36.8	5.4			6,659.1	6.8
2006	6,743.8	1.8	40.7	10.7			6,784.4	1.9
2007	6,798.2	0.8	43.5	7.0			6,841.8	0.8
2008	6,775.2	-0.3	35.8	-17.8	82.8	*	6,893.7	0.8
2009	6,610.9	-2.4	31.9	-10.8	294.8	*	6,937.6	0.6
2010	6,530.5	-1.2	32.2	0.8	425.8	44.4	6,988.4	0.7
2011	6,471.9	-0.9	34.0	5.8	525.3	23.4	7,031.3	0.6
2012	6,277.4	-3.0	33.9	-0.3	811.1	54.4	7,122.4	1.3
2013	6,276.2	..	35.0	3.1	967.6	19.3	7,278.8	2.2

Source: UK Payments Administration Ltd

[a] The clearing of cheque and credit payments in Northern Ireland is managed by the Belfast Bankers' Clearing Companyn(BBCC). Figures from 2003 – 2007 are estimated, but those for 2008 onwards were provided by the BBCC.

[b] CHAPS Euro ceased operation on 16 May 2008.

[c] The Faster Payments Service was launched on 27 May 2008.

12.3a Monetary financial institutions (excluding central bank): Balance sheet

£ millions   Not seasonally adjusted

Amounts outstanding of sterling liabilities

	Notes outstanding and cash loaded cards	Sight deposits					Time deposits						
		UK MFIs	of which intragroup banks	UK public sector	Other UK residents	Non-residents	UK MFIs	of which intragroup banks	UK public sector	Other UK residents	of which SAYE	of which cash ISAs	Non-residents
RPM	B3LM	B3GL	B8ZC	B3MM	B3NM	B3OM	B3HL	B8ZE	B3PM	B3QM	B3RM	B3SM	B3TM
2011 Nov	6,032	178,813	157,184	11,086	892,949	125,935	253,543	239,893	17,167	995,753	1,160	191,672	243,550
Dec	6,217	174,809	155,793	11,593	886,874	133,398	258,448	245,411	16,644	988,585	1,156	191,644	248,747
2012 Jan	5,995	184,061	162,155	12,574	880,412	127,873	254,557 (b)	240,060 (b)	16,214	984,797 (f)	1,169	191,879	244,536
Feb	5,967	189,063	166,096	11,477	877,626	125,599	261,572	246,672	15,312	950,302	1,188	192,343	257,853
Mar	6,031	197,694	176,744	10,533	897,318	126,944	245,705	231,585	13,363	956,906	1,178	195,572	253,589
Apr	5,972	197,648	177,494	12,815	882,020	121,550	254,693	239,623	16,936 (e)	976,694 (g)(h)	1,195	203,814	253,440
May	6,146	211,991	191,550	12,512	882,274	127,692	253,971	239,476	18,004	981,254	1,218	207,429	252,489
Jun	6,186	221,796	201,093	12,111	909,806 (a)	133,659	259,702	245,424	18,385	939,283	1,206	208,773	250,596
Jul	6,238	216,902	195,866	13,325	905,427	129,332	263,046	248,095	18,749	931,744	1,208	209,406	264,761
Aug	6,299	216,895	195,640	12,363	912,463	130,798	262,702	249,547	19,516	928,601	1,043	210,288	260,807
Sep	6,373	225,242	204,665	12,656	925,344	134,457	269,906	256,448	19,639	922,014	1,036	210,673	255,081
Oct	6,395	174,369	154,645	12,869	924,505	139,514	273,951	261,201	18,951	912,800 (i)	1,031	210,815	249,209
Nov	6,433	167,163	148,104	13,310	941,695	130,202	276,964	265,487	18,750	898,752	1,055	210,781	253,452
Dec	6,685	181,298	161,685	13,643	951,840	135,251	281,824	269,950	18,548	912,703	1,102	210,728	248,001
2013 Jan	6,386	184,901	165,678	15,100	952,010	131,272	281,191 (c)	269,069 (c)	18,705	898,564	1,132	210,720	239,076 (l)
Feb	6,340	193,924	173,803	16,123	964,164	140,514	274,993	262,827	17,789	896,905 (j)	1,143	210,995	234,390
Mar	6,460	191,194	172,069	12,491	987,102	130,909	272,414	259,143	15,896	887,863	1,128	213,544	235,578
Apr	6,443	198,427	177,406	14,940	978,145	126,971	286,294	273,867	18,491	883,549	1,141	221,899	234,778
May	6,538	208,690	190,089	14,111	983,445	133,836	284,486	272,159	19,556	879,500	1,174	224,054	230,125
Jun	6,764	212,376	194,879	13,663	999,197	142,652	288,101	275,987	20,012	872,963	1,182	224,809	221,273
Jul	6,518	206,604	187,937	14,172	1,001,659	136,036	291,824	280,412	20,928	872,433 (k)	1,182	225,042	221,612
Aug	6,520	211,825	193,324	14,417	1,013,348	134,012	284,256	273,064	20,495	874,454	1,114	225,557	212,371
Sep	6,621	225,781	206,927	14,424	1,029,192	140,523	307,027 (d)	296,833 (d)	20,219	871,381	1,104	225,537	209,340
Oct	6,598	231,647	213,032	14,653	1,033,977	138,808	311,693	301,076	19,584	864,022	1,175	225,109	206,285

12.3a Monetary financial institutions (excluding central bank): Balance sheet

£ millions

Amounts outstanding of sterling liabilities Not seasonally adjusted

RPM	UK MFIs	of which intragroup banks	Sale and repurchase agreements UK public sector	Other UK residents	Non-residents	Acceptances granted	CDs and other paper issued CDs and Commercial paper	Bonds with maturity of up to and incl. 5 years	Bonds with maturity of greater than 5 years	Total	Total sterling deposits	Sterling items in suspense and transmission	Net derivatives	Accrued amounts payable	Sterling capital and other internal funds	Total sterling liabilities
	B3IL	B3ZA	B3UM	B3VM	B3WM	B3XM	B2TL	B6OI	B2TM	B3YM	B3ZM	B3GN	B3HN	B3IN	B3JN	B3KN
2011 Nov	101,016	71,430	2,980	102,314	43,895	603	69,295	53,816 (m)	41,260 (n)	164,371	3,133,975	43,540	-22,883	30,594	527,215	3,718,474
Dec	104,636	82,296	2,607	94,006	38,132	478	67,913	44,526	41,880	154,319	3,113,275	29,223	-24,870	30,070	516,777	3,670,691
2012 Jan	81,967	57,516	7,633	112,194	37,585	438	80,182	37,740	50,637	168,558	3,113,399	52,865	-45,703	28,638	513,430	3,668,625
Feb	81,221	55,436	5,895	115,748	45,281	425	84,816	37,756	53,481	176,054	3,113,429	53,886	-46,845	28,321	502,824	3,657,561
Mar	75,045	57,947	2,153	94,580	62,061	433	84,721	33,634	56,053	174,408	3,110,734	51,215	-55,370	27,148	515,067	3,654,825
Apr	83,024	61,457	5,789	107,549	54,633	374	84,461	30,547	56,935	171,943	3,139,109	50,672	-63,750	25,848	523,566	3,681,418
May	84,808	63,052	11,080	108,494	51,203	361	86,080	30,481	54,892	171,453	3,167,587	47,439	-17,145	27,146	477,780	3,708,952
Jun	83,569	62,402	7,211	105,132	58,298	343	81,244	29,470	56,832	167,546	3,167,438	52,421	-31,258	26,985	468,039	3,689,811
Jul	87,373	61,844	7,779	113,489	61,297	306	84,502	28,777	56,262	169,542	3,183,072	47,377	-28,142	27,666	430,500 (p)	3,666,711
Aug	93,819	65,001	8,841	115,946	57,388	374	86,223	28,107	49,104 (o)	163,434	3,183,947	47,929	-47,028	26,420	440,599	3,658,167
Sep	92,194	63,672	5,706	118,296	66,104	349	85,428	27,280	47,642	160,351	3,207,339	52,750	-51,370	26,403	454,505	3,696,000
Oct	98,157	66,490	5,418	121,137	62,693	342	84,793	26,848	47,294	158,934	3,152,850	40,991	-29,520	26,689	445,856	3,643,260
Nov	98,127	63,542	6,935	113,641	67,611	341	81,966	26,003	44,846	152,815	3,139,758	53,853	-21,861	26,771	438,396 (q)	3,643,350
Dec	91,676	61,120	3,591	109,564	62,803	341	78,571	25,273	45,288	149,132	3,160,216	26,281	-24,957	25,869	443,471	3,637,564
2013 Jan	79,787	58,196	7,799	125,282	73,318	315	77,822	26,189	45,389	149,400	3,156,720	51,424	-6,819	27,362	435,031	3,670,103
Feb	81,799	57,301	10,785	119,712	63,678	315	76,109	26,245	46,391	148,744	3,163,835	44,707	24,111	26,622	424,942 (r)	3,690,558
Mar	70,271	47,415	4,661	102,964	60,369	320	77,011	24,948	45,888	147,847	3,119,879	50,417	-161	26,613	440,862	3,644,071
Apr	65,882	43,038	4,813	115,009	68,735	319	78,128	24,489	46,096	148,713	3,145,067	43,930	-942	22,724	441,399 (s)	3,658,621
May	68,594	41,259	5,361	115,194	67,606	305	79,704	26,203	44,373	150,280	3,161,089	47,032	3,877	21,806	429,946	3,670,289
Jun	63,066	41,283	5,301	107,570	58,630	258	79,684	25,039	45,110	149,833	3,154,896	49,844	16,135	22,808	412,951	3,663,398
Jul	66,316	42,748	9,896	115,827	64,952	252	75,672	25,684	44,995	146,351	3,168,862	38,715	18,687	20,158	412,937	3,665,877
Aug	64,660	40,852	5,653	124,257	55,892	118	72,645	25,253	44,469	142,367	3,158,126	44,196	11	21,078	415,481	3,645,411
Sep	68,514	46,261	2,255	124,418	61,852	130	72,386	25,497	44,704	142,587	3,217,643	45,750	-13,478	19,244	392,842 (t)	3,668,623
Oct	67,806	42,900	6,425	125,305	57,825	130	68,778	25,433	44,552	138,763	3,216,922	46,804	611	19,246	397,311	3,687,492

Source: Bank of England

Notes to table

Movements in amounts outstanding can reflect breaks in data series as well as underlying flows. For changes data, users are recommended to refer directly to the appropriate series or data tables. Further explanation can be found at: www.bankofengland.co.uk/statistics/iadb/notesiadb/Changes_flows_growth_rates.aspx.

(a) Due to a change in accounting treatment at one reporting institution, the amounts outstanding increased by £7bn. This effect has been adjusted out of the flows for June 2012.

(b) Due to improvements in reporting at two institutions, the amounts outstanding decreased by £8bn. This effect has been adjusted out of the flows for January 2012.

(c) Due to a change in the reporting population, the amounts outstanding decreased by £3bn The effect has been adjusted out of the flows for January 2013.

(d) Due to improvements in reporting at one institution, the amounts outstanding increased by £12bn. The effect has been adjusted out of the flows for September 2013.

(e) Due to improvements in reporting at one institution, the amounts outstanding increased by £1bn. This effect has been adjusted out of the flows for April 2012.

(f) Due to a change in accounting treatment at one reporting institution, the amounts outstanding increased by £12bn. This effect has been adjusted out of the flows for January 2012.

(g) Due to improvements in reporting at one institution, the amounts outstanding increased by £5bn. This effect has been adjusted out of the flows for April 2012.

(h) Due to a change in treatment at one reporting institution, the amounts outstanding increased by £5bn. This effect has been adjusted out of the flows for April 2012.

(i) Due to a change in treatment at one reporting institution, the amounts outstanding decreased by £5bn. This effect has been adjusted out of the flows for October 2012.

(j) Due to improvements in reporting at one institution, the amounts outstanding increased by £6bn. This effect has been adjusted out of the flows for February 2013.

(k) Due to improvements in reporting at one institution, the amounts outstanding increased by £8bn. This effect has been adjusted out of the flows for July 2013.

(l) Due to a change in the reporting population, the amounts outstanding decreased by £3bn The effect has been adjusted out of the flows for January 2013.

(m) Due to improvements in reporting at one institution, the amounts outstanding decreased by £4bn. This effect has been adjusted out of the flows for November 2011.

(n) Due to improvements in reporting at one institution, the amounts outstanding increased by £4bn. This effect has been adjusted out of the flows for November 2011.

(o) Due to improvements in reporting at one institution, the amounts outstanding decreased by £7bn. This effect has been adjusted out of the flows for August 2012.

(p) Due to improvements in reporting at one institution, the amounts outstanding decreased by £22bn. The effect has been adjusted out of the flows for July 2012.

(q) Due to improvements in reporting at one institution, this series has decreased by £12bn for November 2012.

(r) Due to improvements in reporting at one institution, the amounts outstanding increased by £5bn. This effect has been adjusted out of the flows for February 2013.

(s) Due to improvements in reporting at one institution, the amounts outstanding decreased by £6bn. The effect has been adjusted out of the flows for April 2013.

(t) Due to improvements in reporting at one institution, the amounts outstanding decreased by £8bn. The effect has been adjusted out of the flows for September 2013.

12.3b Monetary financial institutions (excluding central bank): Balance sheet

£ millions Not seasonally adjusted

Amounts outstanding of foreign currency liabilities (including euro)

RPM	Sight and time deposits					Acceptances granted	Sale and repurchase agreements				
	UK MFIs	of which intragroup banks	UK public sector	Other UK residents	Non-residents		UK MFIs	of which intragroup banks	UK public sector	Other UK residents	Non-residents
	B3JL	B8ZM	B2UP	B2UV	B3NN	B3KQ	B3KL	B8ZK	B3PN	B3QN	B3RN
2011 Nov	199,819	135,187	1,373	274,611	2,286,836	1,968	191,527	119,729	8,616	80,926	597,967
Dec	191,532	128,180	1,309	259,449	2,292,510	2,162	163,061	108,446	2,730	76,604	501,628
2012 Jan	192,857	127,009	1,432	254,645	2,231,775	2,147	181,318	119,442	3,256	79,549	562,232
Feb	211,918	148,370	1,595	246,869	2,203,054 (u)	2,008	171,014	105,226	4,143	86,639	586,506
Mar	211,704	152,333	1,576	252,946	2,206,915	1,929	152,087	93,986	4,406	94,854	544,005
Apr	210,695	149,758	1,837	262,537	2,063,390 (v)	1,866	158,187	95,534	4,677	94,281	600,663
May	202,120	135,685	1,853	262,566	2,087,139	1,719	156,862	90,848	6,187	100,111	596,233
Jun	202,830	138,232	2,049	260,703	2,063,347 (w)	1,919	156,892	94,237	5,539	91,676	530,181 (ab)
Jul	198,922	132,546	1,879	265,842	2,018,093	1,881	163,609	94,573	6,274	99,028	525,342
Aug	195,205	128,375	1,811	253,995	2,011,692	1,656	155,239	85,740	4,883	96,832	535,175 (ac)
Sep	202,205	138,923	1,599	253,024	2,023,455	1,508	153,792	86,722	1,940	103,324	508,377
Oct	192,621	128,799	1,449	246,323	1,974,360	1,604	154,414	83,275	1,425	111,539	523,543
Nov	193,887	131,587	1,529	250,548	2,024,857 (x)(y)	1,908	142,215	76,742	1,859	111,795	521,133
Dec	198,457	138,565	1,368	263,904	2,008,277	1,635	128,811	70,770	2,393	107,059	498,943
2013 Jan	192,866	131,839	1,388	258,861	2,059,018 (z)	1,787	147,193	80,467	1,207	123,004	537,923
Feb	195,487	130,073	1,427	262,944	2,081,070	1,582	142,081	72,185	3,203	128,975	585,517
Mar	186,073	122,349	1,473	272,095	2,042,578	1,644	136,881	72,727	833	134,188	557,240
Apr	194,230	128,543	1,683	284,547	2,014,601	1,782	140,382	76,282	1,370	132,856	595,194
May	188,931	122,046	1,479	284,959	1,997,227	1,682	141,258	76,181	1,652	151,179	603,752
Jun	191,423	124,706	1,344	284,954	1,958,376 (aa)	2,102	137,827	74,655	1,438	147,178	592,276
Jul	192,354	124,235	1,364	290,654	1,907,997	2,158	139,358	74,701	1,263	140,216	565,674
Aug	180,384	114,751	1,356	280,071	1,831,876	2,138	129,127	70,079	1,010	140,479	561,275
Sep	182,092	120,182	1,370	255,071	1,791,653	2,063	117,818	63,740	669	127,884	520,252
Oct	191,436	128,419	1,431	256,459	1,820,521	2,269	130,452	75,243	1,468	122,856	518,760

12.3b Monetary financial institutions (excluding central bank): Balance sheet

£ millions Not seasonally adjusted

Amounts outstanding of foreign currency liabilities (including euro)

RPM	CDs and Commercial paper	Bonds with maturity of up to and incl. 5 years	Bonds with maturity of greater than 5 years	Total	Total foreign currency deposits	Items in suspense and transmission	Net derivatives	Accrued amounts payable	Capital and other internal funds	Total foreign currency liabilities	Total liabilities
	B2TP	B6OK	B2TQ	B3SN	B3TN	B3UN	B3VN	B3WN	B3XN	B3YN	B3ZN
2011 Nov	124,728	308,896	254,210	687,833	4,331,475	306,300	29,291	53,380	79,952	4,800,399	8,518,873
Dec	115,250	298,223	251,390	664,864	4,155,848	129,764	27,631	48,277	94,515	4,456,034	8,126,726
2012 Jan	130,763	295,255	249,267	675,285	4,184,496	251,008	39,360	43,459	150,555	4,668,878	8,337,503
Feb	133,600	294,279	249,667 (ad)	677,546	4,191,293	272,297	51,644	41,356	153,928	4,710,518	8,368,079
Mar	126,683	281,332	249,168	657,183	4,127,605	252,672	62,823	38,497	144,823	4,626,421	8,281,246
Apr	124,472	271,223	243,276	638,971	4,037,103	226,505	75,319	40,934	142,069	4,521,930	8,203,348
May	123,832	263,267	243,981	631,081	4,045,871	250,734	34,171	43,291	176,735	4,550,803	8,259,754
Jun	120,906	260,777	240,821	622,504	3,937,640	213,971	58,566	44,078	178,768	4,433,023	8,122,835
Jul	127,266	251,068	238,696	617,029	3,897,898	219,259	51,310	43,276	207,371 (ak)	4,419,115	8,085,826
Aug	122,047	249,219	238,969	610,234	3,866,722	193,776	56,139	43,618	199,451	4,359,706	8,017,873
Sep	115,116	243,930	236,994	596,041	3,845,264	246,552	57,697	44,049	193,190	4,386,753	8,082,753
Oct	110,548	237,899	235,807	584,254	3,791,533	186,442	35,767	42,790	206,753	4,263,285	7,906,545
Nov	111,376	236,056	232,228	579,659	3,829,389	203,785 (ae)	15,690 (af)	44,048	204,163	4,297,076	7,940,426
Dec	107,117	233,947	233,086	574,150	3,784,999	95,923	21,692	41,054	217,077	4,160,746	7,798,310
2013 Jan	122,148	233,742	230,982	586,872	3,910,118	257,195	5,210	45,037	214,636	4,432,196	8,102,299
Feb	121,493	231,218	235,393	588,104	3,990,390	250,516	-24,889	30,649 (ai)	227,915	4,474,583	8,165,141
Mar	117,454	224,299	233,296	575,049	3,908,055	229,118	-8,765	30,204	232,261	4,390,873	8,034,945
Apr	116,472	220,815	226,812	564,099	3,930,745	255,869	815 (ag)	20,209 (aj)	214,544 (al)	4,422,182	8,080,803
May	122,126	218,326	226,022	566,474	3,938,594	241,150	-5,922	21,157	215,862	4,410,840	8,081,129
Jun	111,089	209,081	220,056	540,226	3,857,144	218,796	-35,822 (ah)	21,136	222,477	4,283,732	7,947,130
Jul	118,448	211,170	224,621	554,239	3,795,276	199,587	-33,076	20,052	228,349	4,210,188	7,876,066
Aug	114,170	202,791	216,531	533,491	3,661,207	195,823	-16,142	21,390	213,541	4,075,819	7,721,230
Sep	105,419	194,043	212,795	512,257	3,511,130	218,490	-1,172	20,017	226,978 (am)	3,975,443	7,644,066
Oct	105,055	199,922	213,018	517,995	3,563,648	233,015	-18,345	19,677	220,426	4,018,421	7,705,913

Source: Bank of England

Notes to table

Movements in amounts outstanding can reflect breaks in data series as well as underlying flows. For changes data, users are recommended to refer directly to the appropriate series or data tables. Further explanation can be found at: www.bankofengland.co.uk/statistics/Pages/iadb/notesiadb/Changes_flows_growth_rates.aspx.

(u) Due to improvements in reporting at one institution, the amounts outstanding decreased by £3bn. This effect has been adjusted out of the flows for February 2012.

(v) Due to improvements in reporting at one institution, the amounts outstanding decreased by £19bn. This effect has been adjusted out of the flows for April 2012.

(w) Due to a reclassification by one reporting institution, the amounts outstanding increased by £3bn. This effect has been adjusted out of the flows for June 2012.

(x) Due to a change in accounting treatment at one reporting institution, the amounts outstanding increased by £3bn. This effect has been adjusted out of the flows for November 2012.

(y) Due to a change in accounting treatment at one reporting institution, the amounts outstanding increased by £8bn. This effect has been adjusted out of the flows for November 2012.

(z) Due to a change in accounting treatment at one reporting institution, the amounts outstanding decreased by £8bn. This effect has been adjusted out of the flows for January 2013.

(aa) Due to a change in treatment at one reporting institution, the amounts outstanding increased by £11bn. The effect has been adjusted out of the flows for June 2013.

(ab) Due to a reclassification by one reporting institution, the amounts outstanding decreased by £3bn. This effect has been adjusted out of the flows for June 2012.

(ac) Due to improvements in reporting at one institution, the amounts outstanding increased by £5bn. This effect has been adjusted out of the flows for August 2012.

(ad) Due to improvements in reporting at one institution, the amounts outstanding increased by £3bn. This effect has been adjusted out of the flows for February 2012.

(ae) Due to a change in accounting treatment at one reporting institution, the amounts outstanding decreased by £9bn. This effect has been adjusted out of the flows for November 2012.

(af) Due to a change in accounting treatment at one reporting institution, the amounts outstanding decreased by £11bn. This effect has been adjusted out of the flows for November 2012.

(ag) Due to improvements in reporting at one institution, the amounts outstanding decreased by £12bn. The effect has been adjusted out of the flows for April 2013.

(ah) Due to a change in treatment at one reporting institution, the amounts outstanding increased by £11bn. The effect has been adjusted out of the flows for June 2013.

(ai) Due to improvements in reporting at one institution, the amounts outstanding decreased by £8bn. The effect has been adjusted out of the flows for February 2013.

(aj) Due to improvements in reporting at one institution, the amounts outstanding decreased by £8bn. The effect has been adjusted out of the flows for April 2013.

(ak) Due to improvements in reporting at one institution, the amounts outstanding increased by £26bn. The effect has been adjusted out of the flows for July 2012.

(al) Due to improvements in reporting at one institution, the amounts outstanding increased by £11bn. The effect has been adjusted out of the flows for April 2013.

(am) Due to improvements in reporting at one institution, the amounts outstanding increased by £8bn. The effect has been adjusted out of the flows for September 2013.

12.3c Monetary financial institutions (excluding central bank): Balance sheet

£ millions   Not seasonally adjusted

Amounts outstanding of sterling assets

RPM	Notes coin	With UK central bank		Loans					Acceptances granted			
		Cash ratio deposits	Other	UK MFIs	of which intragroup banks	UK MFIs CDs	UK MFIs commercial paper	Non-residents	UK MFIs	UK public sector	Other UK residents	Non-residents
	B3UO	B3VO	B3WO	B3NL	B8ZI	B3OL	B3PL	B3XO	B3QL	B3YO	B3ZO	B3GP
2011 Nov	9,103	2,390	168,791	426,032	396,700	11,917	20	127,809	2	-	471	131
Dec	10,642	2,385	174,595	428,005	401,327	9,330	61	119,093	2	-	389	87
2012 Jan	9,015	2,385	194,250	430,994 (az)	402,456 (az)	10,582	139	127,036	2	-	354	82
Feb	8,974	2,386	207,828	443,256	412,929	10,989	169	118,937	2	-	343	80
Mar	8,990	2,386	218,387	437,474	407,765	10,685	168	124,330	2	-	350	81
Apr	8,777	2,386	236,182	445,924	417,295	9,777	162	116,925	5	-	297	73
May	9,847	2,386	238,336	462,244	430,758	9,758	150	116,002	4	-	285	72
Jun	9,235	2,420	239,792	477,645	446,110	9,342	130	121,494	4	-	268	71
Jul	9,764	2,420	253,331	476,695	443,729	9,327	130	114,970	5	-	244	56
Aug	10,189	2,420	263,782	476,907	444,258	8,581	85	114,133	6	-	311	57
Sep	9,595	2,420	272,477	491,438	459,915	8,498	75	119,200	10	-	283	57
Oct	10,067	2,421	282,400	446,044	413,859	7,389	198	117,408	10	-	277	55
Nov	9,912	2,424	281,025	441,983	411,598	6,684	61	118,672	10	-	275	56
Dec	11,180	2,483	269,271	461,309	429,453	5,981	22	115,907	10	-	277	54
2013 Jan	9,806	2,480	275,632	463,776	434,007	6,025	22	114,455	10	-	256	49
Feb	9,851	2,480	273,572	465,603	436,281	6,557	43	116,586	10	-	260	45
Mar	10,706	2,468	277,823	462,130	431,031	6,734	8	105,180	23	-	255	42
Apr	9,696	2,464	285,025	480,544	450,799	7,003	10	103,454	28	-	253	38
May	9,693	2,597	287,157	489,504	461,488	6,977	14	108,478	27	-	241	37
Jun	9,253	4,013	283,826	498,292	471,966	6,939	17	112,727	20	-	200	38
Jul	9,301	4,013	292,476	495,172	469,628	6,670	22	108,360	20	-	196	37
Aug	9,762	4,013	289,419	492,878	467,110	6,554	22	112,308	20	-	83	15
Sep	9,020	4,013	289,689	531,176 (ba)	505,782 (ba)	6,023	22	110,360	29	-	88	13
Oct	9,529	4,013	300,457	543,788	516,957	5,466	22	108,198	29	-	83	18

12.3c Monetary financial institutions (excluding central bank): Balance sheet

£ millions

Not seasonally adjusted

Amounts outstanding of sterling assets

	Bills				Sales and repurchase agreements					Advances		
	Treasury bills	UK MFIs bills	Other UK residents	Non-residents	UK MFIs	of which intragroup banks	UK public sector	Other UK residents	Non-residents	UK public sector	Other UK residents	Non-residents
RPM	B3HP	B3RL	B3IP	B3JP	B3SL	B8ZG	B3KP	B3LP	B3MP	B2UK	B3OP	B3PP
2011 Nov	15,278	4	202	16,213	90,548	71,907	186	105,407	50,392	7,779	1,918,199	85,773
Dec	13,676	4	238	15,315	96,014	82,510	1,157	107,404	42,293	7,897	1,910,101	86,584
2012 Jan	12,339	5	232	14,528	76,966	57,510	493	100,255	48,295	7,716	1,922,388 (bb)	85,312
Feb	10,313	4	277	15,988	76,091	55,357	500	107,572	46,882	7,839	1,919,220	84,725
Mar	10,949	6	310	15,569	71,453	57,884	201	98,954	50,469	7,861	1,923,201	84,860
Apr	8,888	6	276	18,459	81,494	61,436	411	101,588	54,601	8,257	1,926,064 (bc)	89,185
May	11,574	8	288	16,302	82,449	62,914	1,967	100,696	51,605	7,928	1,916,923	83,909
Jun	10,448	5	399	15,575	77,373	62,229	40	111,180	48,862	7,831	1,921,311 (bd)	86,779
Jul	9,683	6	326	15,342	77,615	61,673	284	102,229	49,677	8,215	1,924,261	87,729
Aug	10,054	5	293	14,925	80,849	64,726	14	106,831	50,943	7,956	1,922,489	84,608
Sep	9,994	5	425	14,831	77,396	63,418	218	114,633	54,323	8,208	1,919,766	80,057
Oct	9,365	4	283	14,010	84,482	66,231	1,166	109,134	50,840	8,163	1,911,566 (be)	77,083
Nov	8,479	3	300	14,634	84,703	63,286	311	118,438	49,168	8,015	1,907,689 (bf)	77,526
Dec	8,408	6	328	4,453	84,062	60,877	9	121,160	48,530	7,943	1,919,203	77,865
2013 Jan	7,658	7	270	4,435	78,533	57,924	295	120,787	53,641	7,998	1,912,943 (bg)	76,198
Feb	7,782	6	265	4,345	78,548	57,019	692	118,889	50,459	7,970	1,909,404	75,972
Mar	8,628	5	341	4,143	68,431	47,152	23	113,918	46,846	7,992	1,904,547	73,143
Apr	6,956	6	363	4,135	63,421	42,733	42	121,028	47,839	8,039	1,885,407	74,132
May	8,437	6	351	3,963	65,060	41,198	289	124,298	45,117	7,948	1,878,209	75,499
Jun	8,097	6	458	3,914	60,825	41,016	755	121,264	47,438	7,916	1,873,749	74,260
Jul	7,102	5	246	3,828	62,487	42,457	421	116,693	45,300	7,807	1,884,061	74,324
Aug	6,516	5	271	3,878	61,095	40,504	104	121,642	44,329	7,671	1,889,636	70,120
Sep	7,184	24	255	3,776	66,630	45,875	1,019	129,839	40,431	7,879	1,891,063	70,810
Oct	6,279	2	264	4,169	64,317	42,515	1,102	118,411	43,196	8,325	1,895,744	71,738

12.3c Monetary financial institutions (excluding central bank): Balance sheet

£ millions   Not seasonally adjusted

Amounts outstanding of sterling assets

RPM	UK government bonds B3QP	Other UK public sector B3RP	Investments UK MFIs B3TL	Other UK residents B3SP	Non-residents B3TP	Items in suspense and collection B3UP	Accrued amounts receivable B3VP	Other assets B3WP	Total sterling assets B3XP
2011 Nov	115,147	338	80,831	348,661	37,571	49,752	27,028	19,122	3,715,094
Dec	109,182	347	74,441	344,297	38,181	28,946	24,237	20,531	3,665,434
2012 Jan	101,486	344	72,951	331,993	38,663	56,598	23,168	23,021	3,691,592
Feb	100,196	213	72,173	309,196	39,830	52,447	23,194	22,988	3,682,614
Mar	103,189	196	72,388	303,916	43,222	49,519	21,301	23,843	3,684,257
Apr	95,921	197	71,889	300,120	44,194	45,972	21,798	23,095	3,712,922
May	103,980	220	73,672	293,331	43,176	48,939	22,790	23,521	3,722,360
Jun	104,510	221	74,439	257,374	44,306	56,933	21,399	24,378	3,723,764
Jul	102,643	222	74,024	252,664	46,565	52,198	20,209	24,327	3,715,162
Aug	96,356	233	74,198	251,574	47,848	46,686	21,021	24,835	3,718,186
Sep	94,299	220	74,488	251,544	49,218	58,247	19,615	25,140	3,756,679
Oct	90,979	207	75,915	255,732	50,196	43,150	19,156	25,053	3,692,753
Nov	94,152	238	76,687	257,124 (bh)	50,870	47,218	19,470	25,380	3,701,507
Dec	91,158	253	83,955	267,892	43,723	24,566	18,643	25,867	3,694,518
2013 Jan	93,854	238	83,688	258,801	48,606	50,924	19,617	25,642	3,716,645
Feb	92,547	233	84,080	267,602 (bi)(bj)	46,523	45,058	18,934	25,929	3,710,246
Mar	96,221	289	84,508	264,552	45,981	48,555	17,428	26,005	3,676,928
Apr	95,939	235	85,278	261,881	52,240	41,482	16,530	26,024	3,679,492
May	97,707	193	85,022	258,090	50,447	46,906	16,707	25,689	3,694,664
Jun	100,196	227	84,794	255,542	43,607	50,185	19,088	25,883	3,693,527
Jul	107,785	188	84,469	258,168	43,443	35,171	19,923	23,201	3,690,887
Aug	106,726	172	83,845	259,900	40,877	41,495	19,177	22,697	3,695,232
Sep	109,834	172	84,259	257,299	40,283	44,654	18,773	23,088	3,747,705
Oct	117,326	-125	83,752	250,050	42,304	44,810	18,133	23,083	3,764,483

Source: Bank of England

Notes to table

Movements in amounts outstanding can reflect breaks in data series as well as underlying flows. For changes data, users are recommended to refer directly to the appropriate series or data tables. Further explanation can be found at: www.bankofengland.co.uk/statistics/Pages/iadb/notesiadb/Changes_flows_growth_rates.aspx.

(az) Due to improvements in reporting at two institutions, the amounts outstanding decreased by £8bn. This effect has been adjusted out of the flows for January 2012.
(ba) Due to improvements in reporting at one institution, the amounts outstanding increased by £12bn. The effect has been adjusted out of the flows for September 2013.
(bb) Due to a change in accounting treatment at one reporting institution, the amounts outstanding increased by £12bn. This effect has been adjusted out of the flows for January 2012.
(bc) Due to a change in treatment at one reporting institution, the amounts outstanding increased by £5bn. This effect has been adjusted out of the flows for April 2012.
(bd) Due to a change in accounting treatment at one reporting institution, the amounts outstanding increased by £7bn. This effect has been adjusted out of the flows for June 2012.
(be) Due to a change in treatment at one reporting institution, the amounts outstanding decreased by £5bn. This effect has been adjusted out of the flows for October 2012.
(bf) Due to improvements in reporting at one institution, the amounts outstanding decreased by £4bn. This effect has been adjusted out of the flows for November 2012.
(bg) Due to a change in the reporting population, the amounts outstanding decreased by £8bn. The effect has been adjusted out of the flows for January 2013.
(bh) Due to improvements in reporting at one institution, the amounts outstanding increased by £4bn. This effect has been adjusted out of the flows for November 2012.
(bi) Due to improvements in reporting at one institution, the amounts outstanding increased by £6bn. This effect has been adjusted out of the flows for February 2013.
(bj) Due to improvements in reporting at one institution, the amounts outstanding increased by £5bn. This effect has been adjusted out of the flows for February 2013.

12.3d Monetary financial institutions (excluding central bank): Balance sheet

£ millions   Not seasonally adjusted

Amounts outstanding of foreign currency assets (including euro)

	Loans and advances						Sale and repurchase agreements					Acceptances granted	Total bills
	UK MFIs	of which intragroup banks	UK MFIs' CDs etc.	UK public sector	Other UK residents	Non-residents	UK MFIs	of which intragroup banks	UK public sector	Other UK residents	Non-residents		
RPM	B3UL	B8ZQ	B3VL	B2UN	B3ZP	B2UH	B3WL	B8ZO	B3HQ	B3IQ	B3JQ	B3KQ	B3LQ
2011 Nov	203,670	135,935	5,169	150	248,110	2,221,537	191,026	119,274	1,853	180,502	681,157	1,968	41,289
Dec	197,654	129,014	4,162	103	242,442	2,192,835	163,746	108,454	1,186	158,502	599,685	2,162	38,813
2012 Jan	197,657	128,761	3,820	125	247,864	2,180,345	183,811	119,477	484	164,997	631,216	2,147	41,519
Feb	214,561	149,618	3,760	136	241,999	2,149,457 (bl)	174,685	105,283	741	173,966	646,846	2,008	43,345
Mar	215,153	153,302	3,661	127	248,236	2,166,659	153,559	93,998	632	167,499	612,944	1,929	41,328
Apr	217,178	151,872	3,223	128	245,566	2,068,392 (bm)	162,299	95,900	792	171,045	648,377	1,866	51,236
May	205,233	137,618	2,649	125	244,539	2,098,910	159,195	90,892	584	173,980	654,941	1,719	42,116
Jun	208,141	139,595	2,609	117	235,958	2,076,211	161,377	94,204	642	161,146	617,302	1,919	43,681
Jul	205,919	134,777	2,092	128	233,135	2,022,066	162,180	94,254	359	169,222	620,491	1,881	47,228
Aug	199,192	130,548	1,812	132	228,214	2,018,245	155,390	85,501	644	155,246	605,842	1,656	45,979
Sep	205,754	139,212	1,550	130	238,153	1,979,404	152,688	86,753	941	150,627	598,572	1,508	46,439
Oct	196,415	128,956	1,830	119	227,271	1,927,505	144,603	83,076	790	142,914	609,754	1,604	46,797
Nov	197,888	131,804	2,380	122	234,856 (bk)	1,929,427	136,635	76,755	192	148,304	605,122	1,908	53,101
Dec	203,784	139,886	2,284	105	245,505	1,936,943	123,923	70,804	809	144,443	578,338	1,635	51,635
2013 Jan	198,682	135,017	2,616	114	251,858	1,969,180	142,015	80,351	450	166,378	624,862	1,787	49,747
Feb	198,559	131,383	2,946	112	264,887	1,980,793	137,117	72,232	778	172,708	677,335	1,582	50,880
Mar	188,479	123,383	2,936	137	271,148	1,954,853	127,908	72,711	815	174,378	671,014	1,644	48,391
Apr	198,790	129,402	3,397	117	274,343	1,933,271	134,022	76,850	1,256	175,183	689,782	1,782	47,964
May	191,727	123,145	3,643	75	289,675	1,898,902	133,758	76,440	1,408	182,333	703,454	1,682	48,943
Jun	187,308	125,831	3,746	60	254,393	1,883,952	133,230	74,648	1,563	170,564	678,184	2,102	44,012
Jul	191,876	124,921	3,922	66	254,341	1,840,435	135,219	74,776	1,720	162,410	673,046	2,158	45,657
Aug	180,390	115,279	4,060	56	245,093	1,755,892	124,958	70,230	1,536	163,480	654,487	2,138	43,203
Sep	180,721	120,127	4,006	74	232,541	1,703,061	111,842	63,945	1,285	159,167	621,311	2,063	38,003
Oct	190,472	128,436	3,989	107	236,325	1,681,195	125,481	75,294	1,262	157,117	621,350	2,269	37,508

12.3d Monetary financial institutions (excluding central bank): Balance sheet

£ millions Not seasonally adjusted

Amounts outstanding of foreign currency assets (including euro)

RPM	Investments — UK government bonds	Investments — Other UK public sector	Investments — UK MFIs	Investments — Other UK residents	Investments — Non-residents	Items in suspense and collection	Accrued amounts receivable	Other assets	Total foreign currency assets	Total assets	Holdings of own sterling acceptances	Holdings of own foreign currency acceptances
	B3MQ	B3NQ	B3XL	B3OQ	B3PQ	B3QQ	B3RQ	B3SQ	B3TQ	B3UQ	B3IM	B3JM
2011 Nov	62	1	27,889	66,004	555,671	274,907	49,157	53,636	4,803,756	8,518,851	45	1,213
Dec	65	7	24,776	64,154 (bn)	548,090	124,029	47,914	50,947	4,461,270	8,126,703	45	1,294
2012 Jan	200	9	26,212	60,277	551,497	254,225	46,760	52,725	4,645,891	8,337,482	40	1,179
Feb	180	6	27,414	58,730	574,734	276,190	44,241	52,448	4,685,445	8,368,059	43	844
Mar	230	5	24,651	59,999	554,312	255,642	44,319	46,088	4,596,970	8,281,227	45	858
Apr	238	8	26,413	57,988	521,308	252,514	45,059	46,782	4,490,410	8,203,333	50	1,262
May	240	14	24,023	61,640	516,250	252,272	49,842	49,110	4,537,382	8,259,743	56	1,159
Jun	147	11	22,604	55,598	506,621	207,788	48,539	48,652	4,399,062	8,122,827	57	1,449
Jul	152	10	23,279	53,313	508,876	220,322	51,034	48,952	4,370,638	8,085,800	58	1,624
Aug	146	12	23,433	53,065	520,044	192,805	45,547	52,240	4,299,643	8,017,829	44	1,546
Sep	139	12	23,378	53,750	535,005	241,107	44,147	52,707	4,326,012	8,082,691	52	1,707
Oct	161	6	20,481	54,226	557,954	185,069	42,471	53,749	4,213,719	7,906,472	57	2,031
Nov	165	7	22,626	52,698	554,614	202,984 (bp)	41,926	53,883	4,238,835	7,940,342	81	1,939
Dec	163	12	21,658	49,701	557,353	94,211	38,176	53,017	4,103,696	7,798,214	81	1,980
2013 Jan	136	11	21,735	51,232	553,192 (bo)	258,680	39,409	53,504	4,385,589	8,102,234	80	2,059
Feb	44	9	21,414	49,985	557,509	254,111	24,601 (bq)	59,492	4,454,860	8,165,106	78	2,119
Mar	114	8	19,370	50,123	536,214	222,237	25,489	62,757	4,358,014	8,034,941	79	2,427
Apr	21	8	20,140	50,227	535,590	257,199	18,204 (br)	60,008	4,401,307	8,080,799	79	1,278
May	-	7	19,774	53,119	540,977	240,474	19,763	56,748	4,386,462	8,081,126	60	1,349
Jun	-	17	20,039	52,967	515,839	224,195	18,958	52,470	4,253,599	7,947,126	71	1,262
Jul	-	15	19,411	53,753	523,363	196,034	17,877	63,871	4,185,174	7,876,062	78	1,346
Aug	-	2	18,658	54,854	504,834	194,277	18,605	59,472	4,025,993	7,721,225	84	1,291
Sep	1	-	17,788	53,713	484,175	213,801	16,876	55,929	3,896,356	7,644,061	93	1,191
Oct	63	-	18,768	53,639	509,751	228,813	17,014	56,302	3,941,425	7,705,908		1,344

Source: Bank of England

Notes to table

Movements in amounts outstanding can reflect breaks in data series as well as underlying flows. For changes data, users are recommended to refer directly to the appropriate series or data tables. Further explanation can be found at: www.bankofengland.co.uk/statistics/Pages/iadb/notesiadb/Changes_flows_growth_rates.aspx.

(bk) Due to a change in accounting treatment at one reporting institution, the amounts outstanding increased by £8bn. This effect has been adjusted out of the flows for November 2012.
(bl) Due to improvements in reporting at one institution, the amounts outstanding decreased by £3bn. This effect has been adjusted out of the flows for February 2012.
(bm) Due to improvements in reporting at one institution, the amounts outstanding decreased by £9bn. This effect has been adjusted out of the flows for April 2012.
(bn) Due to improvements in reporting at one institution, the amounts outstanding decreased by £3bn. This effect has been adjusted out of the flows for December 2011.
(bo) Due to a change in accounting treatment at one reporting institution, the amounts outstanding decreased by £8bn. This effect has been adjusted out of the flows for January 2013.
(bp) Due to a change in accounting treatment at one reporting institution, the amounts outstanding decreased by £9bn. This effect has been adjusted out of the flows for November 2012.
(bq) Due to improvements in reporting at one institution, the amounts outstanding decreased by £8bn. The effect has been adjusted out of the flows for February 2013
(br) Due to improvements in reporting at one institution, the amounts outstanding decreased by £6bn. The effect has been adjusted out of the flows for April 2013.

12.3e Monetary financial institutions (excluding central bank): Balance sheet

£ millions

Not seasonally adjusted

Changes in sterling liabilities

RPM	Notes outstanding & cash loaded cards	Sight deposits UK MFIs	of which intragroup banks	UK public sector	Other UK residents	Non-residents	UK MFIs	of which intragroup banks	Time deposits UK public sector	Other UK residents	of which SAYE	of which cash ISAs	Non-residents
	B4IJ	B4GA	B8ZD	B4CF	B4BH	B4DD	B4HA	B8ZF	B4DF	B4CH	B4FH	B4DH	B4ED
2011 Nov	136	11,794	12,705	-365	10,854	-10,615	-2,538	-2,225	-259	-7,723	-58	-28	-4,011
Dec	184	-4,527	-1,391	507	-6,389	7,987	4,905	5,518	-523	-7,168	-4	-29	5,197
2012 Jan	-221	9,042	6,363	981	-6,772	-5,525	3,608	2,149	-430	-16,229	13	235	-4,211
Feb	-29	5,002	3,941	-1,097	-2,787	-2,274	7,016	6,612	-902	-34,495	19	464	13,317
Mar	65	8,630	10,648	-944	19,692	1,345	-15,867	-15,087	-1,949	5,918	-10	3,230	-4,264
Apr	-59	575	751	2,282	-15,275	-4,660	8,891	7,998	2,070	10,765	17	8,242	748
May	174	14,343	14,056	-303	269	6,752	-722	-146	1,067	2,060	23	3,614	1,549
Jun	40	9,805	9,543	-401	20,859	5,554	5,731	5,948	382	-41,981	-11	1,344	-1,938
Jul	53	-4,894	-5,227	1,214	-4,379	-4,327	3,343	2,671	364	-7,539	1	634	14,165
Aug	61	-7	-226	-962	6,146	1,466	-344	1,452	767	-3,160	-165	882	-3,048
Sep	74	8,346	9,025	293	12,882	3,759	7,204	6,901	123	-6,587	-6	384	-5,378
Oct	22	-50,872	-50,020	214	-839	5,091	4,045	4,753	-689	-4,314	-5	143	-5,871
Nov	38	-7,594	-6,541	208	17,409	-9,559	3,013	4,287	-201	-13,648	23	-34	4,243
Dec	252	13,784	13,581	333	10,495	5,049	4,860	4,462	-201	13,951	47	-53	-5,451
2013 Jan	-299	3,604	3,993	1,457	-172	-5,068	2,569	2,378	157	-13,905	30	-9	-4,701
Feb	-46	9,023	8,124	1,023	11,389	9,242	-6,199	-6,242	-917	-6,747	11	275	-4,685
Mar	121	-2,728	-2,477	-3,631	22,983	-9,605	-1,831	-2,936	-1,892	-9,753	-15	2,549	1,124
Apr	-17	7,233	5,337	2,449	-7,768	-2,093	13,881	14,723	2,595	-4,301	14	8,355	112
May	95	10,263	12,683	-829	5,300	6,864	-1,808	-1,708	1,065	-4,049	32	2,155	-4,443
Jun	226	3,686	4,790	-448	14,803	8,816	3,615	3,828	455	-5,675	8	755	-8,642
Jul	-246	-5,773	-6,942	508	3,278	-6,616	3,723	4,425	917	-9,887	-	233	339
Aug	2	5,222	5,387	246	10,289	-943	-7,568	-7,348	-434	1,814	-68	433	-5,425
Sep	101	13,956	13,604	7	15,841	6,525	11,271	12,269	-276	-3,173	-9	-19	-2,668
Oct	-23	5,867	6,104	228	2,314	-1,715	4,666	4,244	-635	-4,888	71	-429	-3,055

12.3e Monetary financial institutions (excluding central bank): Balance sheet

£ millions   Not seasonally adjusted

Changes in sterling liabilities

RPM	UK MFIs	of which intragroup banks	Liabilities under sale and repurchase agreements — UK public sector	Other UK residents	Non-residents	Acceptances granted	CDs and other paper issued — CDs and Commercial paper	Bonds with maturity of up to and incl. 5 years	Bonds with maturity of greater than 5 years	Total	Total sterling deposits	Sterling items in suspense and transmission	Net derivatives	Accrued amounts payable	Sterling capital and other internal funds	Total sterling liabilities
	B4IA	B8ZB	B4EF	B4EH	B4FD	B4BK	B2SU	B6OH	B2TK	B4EJ	B4FJ	B4AK	B4GJ	B4CJ	B4DJ	B4JJ
2011 Nov	-15,473	-10,330	-842	1,175	9,114	-1	-3,824	-13,115	571	-16,367	-25,259	-8,922	17,938	-510	7,829	-8,789
Dec	3,619	10,865	-373	-8,605	-5,763	-126	-1,382	-9,290	620	-10,051	-21,312	-13,835	-1,987	-720	-11,498	-49,168
2012 Jan	-22,669	-24,779	5,026	18,189	-547	-39	12,269	-6,786	3,099	8,581	-10,994	23,642	-20,832	-998	-7,297	-16,701
Feb	-745	-2,080	-1,738	3,554	7,697	-13	4,634	17	2,856	7,507	41	1,001	-1,143	-316	-9,038	-9,485
Mar	-6,176	2,510	-3,742	-21,168	16,780	9	-95	-4,123	2,572	-1,645	-3,382	-993	-8,522	-1,212	12,055	-1,989
Apr	7,979	3,510	3,636	12,968	-7,428	-59	-260	-3,087	726	-2,621	19,873	-543	-8,380	-1,300	17,309	26,900
May	1,784	1,595	5,291	945	-3,430	-13	-642	-66	218	-490	29,103	-1,858	46,604	1,298	-49,098	26,224
Jun	-1,239	-650	-3,868	-3,362	7,095	-19	-4,835	-1,011	1,940	-3,907	-7,288	4,982	-14,013	-162	-8,631	-25,072
Jul	3,804	-558	568	8,357	2,998	-37	3,257	-691	-570	1,996	15,633	-5,045	3,116	682	-8,628	5,811
Aug	6,445	3,158	1,062	2,457	-3,909	69	1,722	-672	-326	724	7,707	805	-18,886	-1,803	9,234	-2,882
Sep	-1,625	-1,329	-3,135	2,349	8,716	-25	-795	-826	-1,462	-3,083	23,840	4,821	-4,343	-17	15,554	39,928
Oct	5,963	2,818	-287	2,841	-3,411	-7	-636	709	-424	-351	-48,488	-10,262	21,850	286	-19,058	-55,650
Nov	-30	-2,948	1,517	-7,495	4,918	-1	-2,827	-845	-2,447	-6,119	-13,339	12,862	11,359	-33	-10,057	-4,849
Dec	-6,451	-2,422	-3,344	-4,077	-4,808	-	-3,394	-730	474	-3,650	20,491	-27,572	-3,096	-832	5,909	44,991
2013 Jan	-11,889	-2,924	4,208	15,718	10,515	-26	-750	916	101	267	2,733	25,145	17,913	1,710	-2,212	8,711
Feb	2,012	-894	2,986	-5,570	-9,640	1	-1,713	56	1,002	-655	1,262	-6,716	30,931	-711	-16,009	-47,624
Mar	-11,528	-9,886	-6,124	-16,748	-3,309	5	902	-1,297	-502	-898	-43,936	5,716	-24,272	227	14,520	19,519
Apr	-4,390	-4,377	152	12,045	8,366	-1	1,117	-348	207	977	29,256	-6,487	-4,525	-3,402	4,694	16,234
May	2,712	-1,780	548	185	-1,129	-14	1,576	1,715	-1,723	1,567	16,232	3,102	4,819	-918	-7,096	675
Jun	-5,527	24	-60	-7,624	-8,976	-47	-20	-1,164	737	-447	-6,070	2,811	12,257	1,002	-9,552	-2,932
Jul	3,249	1,465	4,595	8,257	6,321	-5	-4,012	645	-114	-3,482	5,425	-11,129	2,980	-2,650	2,688	-10,085
Aug	-1,656	-2,004	-4,243	8,430	-9,059	4	-3,027	430	-526	-3,984	-7,308	5,481	-18,677	270	10,146	20,710
Sep	4,552	5,409	-3,397	161	5,960	12	-259	244	235	219	48,990	434	-13,488	-1,005	-14,322	16,385
Oct	-476	-3,361	4,170	887	-4,260	-1	-3,608	-64	-152	-3,824	-721	1,054	14,089	1	1,985	

Source: Bank of England

Explanatory Notes (http://www.bankofengland.co.uk/statistics/Pages/iadb/notesiadb/MFIs_exICB.aspx)

12.3f Monetary financial institutions (excluding central bank): Balance sheet

£ millions   Not seasonally adjusted

Changes in foreign currency liabilities (including euro)

RPM	Sight and time deposits					Acceptances granted	Sale and repurchase agreements				
	UK MFIs	of which intragroup banks	UK public sector	Other UK residents	Non-residents		UK MFIs	of which intragroup banks	UK public sector	Other UK residents	Non-residents
	B4GB	B8ZN	B2VP	B2VV	B2VJ	B4HM	B4HB	B8ZL	B4GG	B4GI	B4HE
2011 Nov	-26,634	-24,164	196	-13	9,713	36	5,278	1,303	-432	-10,476	-634
Dec	-4,902	-5,955	-66	-14,527	7,655	184	-26,701	-9,688	-5,816	-5,852	-97,075
2012 Jan	3,814	518	145	-945	-28,983	17	20,614	12,367	543	4,218	73,667
Feb	19,023	21,371	174	-6,466	-16,326	-120	-9,976	-14,591	887	7,118	29,170
Mar	467	4,493	-16	6,675	10,525	-76	-18,332	-10,919	289	8,560	-40,871
Apr	2,855	190	291	14,595	-87,346	-39	8,894	3,410	363	1,195	66,112
May	-10,523	-15,334	-43	-6,567	-20,625	-199	-3,131	-5,188	1,545	4,775	-20,062
Jun	1,340	2,985	217	497	-13,284	220	702	3,542	-671	-8,173	-57,306
Jul	-1,006	-3,599	-156	7,566	-22,874	-32	8,958	1,966	862	9,034	-488
Aug	-3,614	-4,060	-14	-10,543	-1,109	-212	-9,317	-8,991	-1,436	-3,014	7,609
Sep	7,921	11,203	-193	1,207	27,798	-131	-787	1,244	-2,961	6,749	-22,080
Oct	-10,701	-10,927	-155	-7,518	-58,087	92	-162	-4,043	-533	7,608	13,582
Nov	-263	2,037	72	3,283	29,719	298	-12,915	-7,046	420	-495	-4,624
Dec	4,944	7,344	-153	14,466	-7,597	-262	-12,955	-5,933	537	-4,615	-18,934
2013 Jan	-11,311	-10,816	-9	-12,148	-500	120	13,637	6,768	-1,258	11,778	25,554
Feb	-935	-4,282	-4	-3,099	-28,776	-251	-7,646	-9,445	1,989	3,246	32,486
Mar	-7,283	-6,352	49	10,570	-19,956	71	-3,316	1,571	-2,352	6,943	-24,201
Apr	12,343	7,179	239	10,200	-3,144	165	4,257	3,898	548	175	47,406
May	-7,632	-8,102	-235	-4,466	-48,166	-126	-147	-1,003	274	15,800	-1,543
Jun	2,068	2,363	-135	716	-58,853	405	-3,775	-1,681	-221	-4,332	-12,443
Jul	-1,157	-1,991	14	-1,709	-68,451	47	-475	-1,103	-198	-8,982	-31,346
Aug	-8,034	-7,530	17	-4,391	-36,069	18	-6,951	-2,836	-223	3,555	7,693
Sep	6,137	8,512	61	-16,564	24,809	-12	-7,924	-4,659	-318	-8,546	-22,449
Oct	7,751	7,123	50	-849	12,907	193	11,431	10,843	794	-6,368	-6,240

12.3f Monetary financial institutions (excluding central bank): Balance sheet

£ millions   Not seasonally adjusted

Changes in foreign currency liabilities (including euro)

RPM	CDs and Commercial paper	CDs and other paper issued — Bonds with maturity of up to and incl. 5 years	Bonds with maturity of greater than 5 years	Total	Total foreign currency deposits	Items in suspense and transmission	Net derivatives	Accrued amounts payable	Capital and other internal funds	Total foreign currency liabilities	Total liabilities
	B2TN	B6OJ	B2TO	B4CM	B4DM	B4GM	B4EM	B4AM	B4BM	B4FM	B4JM
2011 Nov	-578	-20,596	-871	-22,044	-45,011	47,549	-36,838	-1,462	19,067	-16,695	-25,484
Dec	-9,053	-9,603	-688	-19,344	-166,444	-175,618	388	-4,634	13,208	-333,099	-382,267
2012 Jan	17,264	665	693	18,621	91,711	121,994	12,617	2,150	45,644	274,117	257,417
Feb	2,953	1,920	-1,830	3,043	26,528	20,105	11,554	-2,240	4,164	60,111	50,626
Mar	-6,611	-11,823	569	-17,865	-50,643	-19,019	11,236	-2,809	-9,576	-70,811	-72,801
Apr	228	-5,514	-2,434	-7,720	-798	-23,499	12,965	2,676	-7,475	-16,131	10,769
May	-2,469	-11,941	-1,539	-15,950	-70,779	25,726	-40,673	2,530	28,110	-55,086	-28,862
Jun	-2,391	-1,148	-2,424	-5,963	-82,420	-37,467	23,506	698	8,891	-86,793	-111,865
Jul	8,200	-6,278	1,647	3,569	5,435	8,326	-5,122	-434	-11,737	-3,532	2,279
Aug	-4,988	-3,864	-31	-8,883	-30,534	-26,405	4,324	212	-7,839	-60,242	-63,124
Sep	-6,138	-5,348	-2,778	-14,265	3,259	52,544	1,430	381	-1,256	56,358	96,286
Oct	-5,230	-5,752	-3,719	-14,701	-70,572	-61,347	-22,109	-1,388	29,639	-125,777	-181,426
Nov	141	-2,858	-4,719	-7,436	8,058	31,393	1,156	1,160	-24,164	17,603	18,432
Dec	-3,891	-1,138	1,421	-3,608	-28,177	-108,092	6,092	-2,765	12,824	-120,119	-124,968
2013 Jan	11,710	-7,027	-9,605	-4,923	20,940	156,339	-14,641	3,405	-4,547	161,495	206,486
Feb	-4,256	-7,175	439	-10,991	-13,982	-7,755	-29,712	-1,948	4,820	-48,576	-39,865
Mar	-3,249	-4,436	1,990	-5,695	-45,170	-19,152	16,152	-266	5,056	-43,380	-91,004
Apr	738	-885	-4,398	-4,545	67,645	26,745	19,280	-1,045	-22,791	89,834	109,353
May	3,405	-5,143	-3,299	-5,037	-51,280	-16,021	-6,285	869	5,121	-67,596	-51,362
Jun	-10,990	-9,785	-6,121	-26,896	-103,467	-22,575	-13,067	172	15,004	-123,932	-123,258
Jul	6,479	-419	1,419	7,479	-104,776	-21,529	3,727	-1,261	14,298	-109,542	-112,473
Aug	-1,718	-2,920	-2,396	-7,034	-51,419	-955	15,065	1,569	-5,243	-40,983	-51,068
Sep	-4,816	-1,990	1,690	-5,116	-29,922	24,611	12,885	-1,194	7,775	14,155	34,865
Oct	-1,336	4,050	-1,914	800	20,468	13,212	-16,335	-449	-13,212	3,685	20,070

Source: Bank of England

Explanatory Notes (http://www.bankofengland.co.uk/statistics/Pages/iadb/notesiadb/MFIs_exICB.aspx)

12.3g Monetary financial institutions (excluding central bank): Balance sheet

£ millions   Not seasonally adjusted

Changes in sterling assets

RPM	Notes and coin	With UK central bank		Loans					Acceptances granted			
		Cash ratio deposits	Other	UK MFIs	of which intragroup banks	UK MFIs' CDs etc	UK MFIs commercial paper	Non-residents	UK MFIs	UK public sector	Other UK residents	Non-residents
	B4II	B3YR	B3ZR	B4DC	B8ZJ	B4JB	B4BC	B4BD	B4EC	B4FF	B3TR	B4GD
2011 Nov	388	12	22,728	10,529	10,563	-722	-63	-3,250	-	-	2	-3
Dec	1,540	-5	5,805	2,083	4,627	-2,587	41	-8,825	-	-	-82	-44
2012 Jan	-1,628	-	19,654	10,489	8,629	1,252	78	7,943	-	-	-35	-4
Feb	-41	1	13,578	12,263	10,473	408	30	-8,099	-	-	-11	-2
Mar	16	-	10,559	-5,793	-5,165	-304	-2	5,393	3	-	8	1
Apr	-213	1	17,795	8,449	9,530	-909	-6	-6,644	-	-	-54	-8
May	1,070	-1	2,154	15,521	13,463	-19	-12	-122	-	-	-12	-1
Jun	-613	34	1,456	15,358	15,352	-416	-20	5,837	-	-	-18	-1
Jul	529	-	13,540	-945	-2,381	-15	-	-6,524	1	-	-23	-15
Aug	425	-	10,450	211	529	-746	-45	428	1	-	67	1
Sep	-594	-	8,695	14,530	15,656	-83	-10	5,067	4	-	-29	-
Oct	472	2	9,924	-45,302	-46,056	-1,110	124	-1,792	-	-	-6	-2
Nov	-155	3	-1,375	-4,070	-2,261	-705	-137	1,247	-	-	-2	1
Dec	1,268	59	-11,754	19,324	17,855	-703	-39	-2,765	-	-	2	-2
2013 Jan	-1,375	-	6,361	2,738	4,569	44	21	-1,452	-	-	-21	-5
Feb	45	-	-2,060	1,987	2,435	532	-35	2,131	-	-	5	4
Mar	855	-11	4,251	-3,452	-5,227	177	2	-11,407	13	-	-5	-3
Apr	-1,009	-	7,201	18,466	19,768	269	4	-1,726	5	-	-2	-4
May	-3	134	2,132	8,959	10,688	-27	3	5,024	-	-	-13	-2
Jun	-440	1,416	-3,331	8,787	10,479	-38	5	4,249	-8	-	-41	1
Jul	48	-	8,650	-3,120	-2,338	-269		-4,367	-	-	-4	-1
Aug	461	-	-3,057	-2,295	-2,518	-115		4,036	-	-	3	1
Sep	-742	-	270	26,805	27,151	-531		-1,929	9	-	5	-2
Oct	509	-	10,768	12,611	11,195	-557		-2,162	-	-	-5	5

12.3g Monetary financial institutions (excluding central bank): Balance sheet

£ millions Not seasonally adjusted

Changes in sterling assets

RPM	Bills Treasury bills	Bills UK MFIs bills	Bills Other UK	Bills Non-residents	Claims under sale and repurchase agreements UK MFIs	of which intragroup banks	UK public sector	Other UK residents	Non-residents	Advances UK public sector	Other UK residents	Non-residents
	B4BA	B4IB	B4HG	B4IC	B4FA	B8ZH	B4BF	B4AH	B4CD	B2VK	B2VQ	B4HC
2011 Nov	-1,028	-	-9	-568	-15,000	-10,180	-334	-9,266	3,875	-125	-2,989	2,349
Dec	-1,602	-	36	-897	5,466	10,603	971	1,538	-8,100	96	-6,631	976
2012 Jan	-1,337	1	-6	-788	-19,048	-25,000	-664	-7,150	6,002	-180	301	-1,270
Feb	-2,027	-1	45	1,460	-875	-2,153	7	7,317	-1,412	123	-2,144	-584
Mar	636	2	32	-419	-4,639	2,527	-299	-8,618	3,586	22	4,070	342
Apr	-2,061	-	-34	2,891	10,042	3,552	210	2,634	4,133	397	2,094	4,909
May	2,685	2	12	-2,158	955	1,479	1,556	-893	-2,996	-329	-7,382	-5,699
Jun	-1,288	-2	111	-727	-5,076	-685	-1,928	10,485	-2,743	-81	-1,666	2,849
Jul	-765	-	-73	-232	242	-557	244	-8,951	815	218	3,837	977
Aug	371	-1	-33	-417	3,233	3,053	-270	4,602	1,266	-259	-1,113	-4,359
Sep	-60	1	132	-95	-3,004	-1,308	204	7,802	3,379	204	-1,601	-4,524
Oct	-629	-1	-142	-821	7,085	2,812	948	-5,499	-3,482	-44	-921	-2,872
Nov	-886	-1	17	624	221	-2,945	-855	9,304	-1,673	-148	2,033	541
Dec	-71	2	28	-10,180	-641	-2,409	-302	2,722	-638	-71	12,316	362
2013 Jan	85	2	-58	-18	-5,529	-2,953	285	-373	5,111	86	2,730	-1,189
Feb	124	-1	-5	16	15	-905	398	-1,898	-3,181	-28	-2,101	-278
Mar	846	-1	76	-202	-10,117	-9,867	-669	-4,971	-3,614	-40	-13,201	-3,176
Apr	-1,672	1	22	-8	-5,010	-4,419	18	7,110	994	47	-6,163	1,242
May	1,481	-	-12	-172	1,639	-1,535	247	3,270	-2,722	-91	-3,535	1,717
Jun	-340	-	107	-49	-4,235	-182	466	-3,034	2,320	-32	5,455	-1,152
Jul	-995	-1	-212	-86	1,662	1,442	-334	-4,571	-2,138	-108	9,454	130
Aug	-587	-	25	50	-1,392	-1,953	-317	4,949	-971	-136	2,122	-2,538
Sep	667	19	-16	-103	5,536	5,371	915	8,196	-3,898	208	5,576	1,117
Oct	-905	-22	9	394	-2,313	-3,360	83	-11,427	2,765	447		995

12.3g Monetary financial institutions (excluding central bank): Balance sheet

£ millions   Not seasonally adjusted

Changes in sterling assets

RPM	UK government bonds	Other UK public sector	Investments UK MFIs	Other UK residents	Non-residents	Items in suspense and collection	Accrued amounts receivable	Other assets	Total sterling assets
	B4CA	B4IE	B4CC	B4IG	B4JC	B4BJ	B4HI	B4JI	B4AJ
2011 Nov	-6,091	12	-2,162	-473	-5,494	-4,553	1,409	61	-10,764
Dec	-7,923	9	-6,738	-4,831	554	-20,805	-2,793	1,377	-51,372
2012 Jan	-7,474	-2	-1,930	-13,939	560	27,652	-1,069	-227	17,182
Feb	93	-132	-852	-24,013	1,626	-4,150	27	-34	-7,399
Mar	3,694	-17	231	-5,218	3,345	-2,928	-1,895	838	2,642
Apr	-7,684	1	-439	-4,122	1,387	-3,547	132	-748	28,608
May	4,573	24	1,946	-5,671	-2,241	4,343	389	425	8,124
Jun	801	1	607	-36,906	1,440	7,994	-1,298	478	-5,334
Jul	-2,869	1	-624	-6,728	2,063	-4,735	-1,191	-52	-11,274
Aug	-5,525	11	26	-2,771	2,003	-5,221	812	508	3,654
Sep	-1,046	-13	213	1,373	-398	11,538	-1,405	305	40,589
Oct	-2,728	-13	1,271	3,522	859	-13,656	-698	-87	-55,597
Nov	3,062	31	606	-3,412	263	4,068	560	331	9,492
Dec	-2,662	15	4,526	10,671	-4,599	-22,652	-757	488	-6,052
2013 Jan	4,624	-15	-362	-9,406	4,974	26,358	1,083	-111	34,568
Feb	-1,062	-5	329	-3,007	-3,883	-5,866	-654	287	-18,143
Mar	1,945	56	436	-4,125	-401	3,498	-1,284	76	-34,532
Apr	-1,345	-54	634	-3,415	6,643	-6,814	-475	21	7,941
May	4,425	-43	-236	-3,645	-1,433	5,425	178	-335	19,738
Jun	5,026	34	95	12	-5,707	3,278	2,381	194	6,428
Jul	7,112	-39	-529	1,251	-282	-15,014	69	-628	-8,316
Aug	1,002	-16	-276	2,913	-1,544	5,724	-146	-504	14,726
Sep	2,405	-	372	-3,588	805	3,159	-405	391	41,787
Oct	6,776	-297	-626	-9,428	1,590	156	-640	-5	14,295

Explanatory Notes (http://www.bankofengland.co.uk/statistics/Pages/iadb/notesiadb/MFIs_exlCB.aspx)

Source: Bank of England

12.3h Monetary financial institutions (excluding central bank): Balance sheet

£ millions

Not seasonally adjusted

Changes in foreign currency assets (including euro)

| RPM | Loans and advances | | | | | | Claims under sale and repurchase agreements | | | | | Acceptances granted | Total Bills |
| | UK MFIs | of which intragroup banks | UK MFIs' CDs etc. | UK public sector | Other UK residents | Non-residents | UK MFIs | of which intragroup banks | UK public sector | Other UK residents | Non-residents | | |
	B4EB	B8ZR	B4AF	B2VN	B2VT	B2VH	B4FB	B8ZP	B4EG	B4EI	B4FE	B4HM	B4GL
2011 Nov	-19,875	-24,520	90	27	-10,340	-13,502	8,378	1,165	-807	3,494	6,292	36	-9,984
Dec	-3,436	-5,983	-936	-47	-4,838	-20,487	-25,518	-9,213	-665	-22,642	-81,016	184	-2,561
2012 Jan	2,555	1,446	-308	24	9,194	16,231	22,274	12,398	-694	8,419	40,091	17	3,136
Feb	16,813	20,872	-81	10	-4,313	-21,925	-8,917	-14,591	264	9,243	22,120	-120	2,461
Mar	1,312	4,215	-87	-8	6,683	22,032	-19,906	-10,972	-103	-6,488	-31,490	-76	-1,852
Apr	5,678	1,469	-385	3	2,010	-49,780	11,610	3,782	170	6,622	45,027	-39	10,587
May	-13,262	-15,497	-558	-2	-8,790	-3,482	-5,105	-5,453	-217	952	-11,140	-199	-10,152
Jun	3,477	2,417	-49	-8	-5,882	-11,735	2,903	3,446	63	-12,105	-31,278	220	1,955
Jul	764	-2,707	-465	11	-1,156	-26,527	3,002	1,692	-285	9,468	9,284	-32	3,709
Aug	-6,661	-4,122	-291	4	-3,627	-3,880	-6,636	-8,915	281	-14,051	-11,695	-212	-1,139
Sep	7,449	9,326	-266	-	12,100	-27,560	-682	1,527	297	-3,207	-1,895	-131	653
Oct	-10,456	-11,120	269	-12	-11,558	-57,365	-8,846	-4,279	-157	-8,383	9,794	92	283
Nov	-231	2,098	537	3	-1,227	-8,099	-8,588	-6,850	-600	4,892	-6,654	298	6,196
Dec	6,186	8,329	-101	-16	12,216	13,499	-12,721	-5,922	617	-2,642	-22,221	-262	-1,146
2013 Jan	-11,041	-9,033	255	8	377	-25,705	13,650	6,609	-385	17,168	31,816	120	-3,089
Feb	-3,141	-5,638	311	-3	4,940	-33,742	-7,507	-9,285	326	3,159	35,040	-251	842
Mar	-8,125	-6,611	27	25	7,970	-5,234	-7,520	1,504	52	3,817	-570	71	-1,981
Apr	11,765	7,033	468	-19	8,481	1,791	7,251	4,486	440	2,920	29,919	165	101
May	-9,420	-7,878	212	-42	10,352	-61,195	-1,787	-1,323	142	4,780	2,918	-126	374
Jun	-4,751	2,397	91	-16	-25,376	-19,090	-834	-1,949	151	-12,209	-26,383	405	-5,007
Jul	2,381	-2,441	118	5	-2,841	-60,854	181	-1,021	124	10,352	-11,317	47	1,152
Aug	-7,574	-7,057	224	-9	-3,935	-45,247	-7,132	-2,745	-140	4,826	-4,237	18	-1,496
Sep	6,241	8,206	32	20	-4,647	7,301	-9,792	-4,570	-223	343	-11,872	-12	-4,056
Oct	8,160	7,190	-55	32	1,725	-36,812	12,497	10,679	-38	-3,652	-5,702	193	-845

12.3h Monetary financial institutions (excluding central bank): Balance sheet

£ millions | Not seasonally adjusted

Changes in foreign currency assets (including euro)

RPM	UK government bonds	Other UK public sector	Investments UK MFIs	Other UK residents	Non-residents	Items in suspense and collection	Accrued amounts receivable	Other assets	Total foreign currency assets	Total assets	Holdings of own sterling acceptances	Holdings of own foreign currency acceptances
	B4EA	B4CG	B4AG	B4CI	B4DE	B4JL	B4FL	B4HL	B4IL	B4IM	B3VR	B3XR
2011 Nov	-2	1	-3,554	-1,676	10,077	17,305	-1,542	854	-14,728	-25,492	2	113
Dec	2	5	-2,800	1,196	-12,321	-151,058	-1,163	-2,817	-330,917	-382,289	-	66
2012 Jan	138	3	760	-2,940	6,635	132,533	-409	2,558	240,216	257,397	-5	-93
Feb	-18	-3	1,152	-1,262	22,539	22,386	-2,435	125	58,039	50,640	3	-326
Mar	50	-1	-2,681	1,412	-18,499	-19,604	143	-6,267	-75,429	-72,788	1	16
Apr	13	4	186	-1,062	-22,902	-28,859	1,835	1,439	-17,843	10,766	5	421
May	-9	6	-2,522	1,999	-15,447	26,813	3,352	780	-36,985	-28,862	6	-154
Jun	-90	-3	-1,401	-5,473	-3,333	-43,497	-762	485	-106,513	-111,847	2	310
Jul	5	-1	1,082	-1,918	-1,802	15,310	2,764	313	13,524	2,250	-	175
Aug	-4	2	95	28	9,986	-27,581	-5,155	3,723	-66,814	-63,160	-14	-62
Sep	-4	1	-15	1,141	18,650	49,064	-933	1,027	55,688	96,277	-	182
Oct	22	-7	-3,053	318	20,477	-57,212	-1,010	961	-125,840	-181,437	8	322
Nov	3	1	2,002	-1,810	-8,549	30,731	86	-77	8,913	18,406	5	-100
Dec	-1	5	8	-2,374	1,308	-108,224	-2,334	-729	-118,934	-124,986	23	55
2013 Jan	-30	-1	-730	234	-10,096	158,940	516	-63	171,945	206,512	1	47
Feb	-96	-2	-627	-2,533	-10,942	-8,787	-2,985	4,283	-21,714	-39,857	-1	-11
Mar	70	-1	-1,811	444	-18,484	-29,679	1,075	3,406	-56,449	-90,982	-2	312
Apr	-92	1	888	818	588	37,480	-75	-1,501	101,390	109,331	1	-1,113
May	-21	-2	-600	2,001	3,782	-19,575	1,274	-4,152	-71,083	-51,345	-	40
Jun	-	10	222	-209	-14,942	-16,582	-834	-4,282	-129,635	-123,207	-19	-86
Jul	-	-2	-880	-165	1,071	-30,574	-1,229	8,970	-104,167	-112,483	12	83
Aug	-	-13	-345	2,156	-2,789	2,286	1,082	-3,441	-65,765	-51,039	6	-29
Sep	1	-2	-441	621	-12,377	24,768	-1,177	-1,668	-6,939	34,849	7	-50
Oct	62	-	812	-517	16,777	13,080	-7	45	5,754	20,048	9	144

Source: Bank of England

Explanatory Notes (http://www.bankofengland.co.uk/statistics/Pages/iadb/notesiadb/MFIs_exICB.aspx)

12.4a Industrial analysis of monetary financial institutions lending to UK residents

£ millions Not seasonally adjusted

Amounts outstanding of lending in sterling

RPM	Agriculture, hunting and forestry	Fishing	Mining and quarrying	Manufacturing Food, beverages and tobacco	Textiles, wearing apparel and leather	Pulp, paper, and printing	Chemicals, pharmaceuticals, rubber and plastics	Non-metallic mineral products and metals	Machinery, equipment and transport equipment	Electrical, medical and optical equipment	Other manufacturing	Total	Electricity, gas and water supply Electricity, gas steam and air conditioning	Water collection and sewerage	Waste management services related and remediation activities	Total
	TBUC	TBUD	TBUE	TBUG	TBUH	TBUI	TBUJ	TBUK	TBUL	TBUM	TBUN	TBUF	TBUO	TBUP	B3F9	B3FN
2012 Jan	11,922	276	1,914	5,854	633	1,504	2,403	2,818	4,407	1,774	2,826	22,218	4,888	2,011	1,642	8,541
Feb	11,892	266	1,851	6,216	654	1,527	2,465	2,871	4,540	1,832	2,831	22,937	4,857	1,971	1,663	8,490
Mar	12,113	265	1,816	5,615	624	1,455	2,425	2,942	4,645	1,825	2,755	22,286	4,763	1,993	1,618	8,374
Apr	12,248	256	2,434	5,935	632	1,552	2,490	3,066	4,755	1,900	2,811	23,142	4,748	2,091	1,724	8,563
May	12,410	254	1,998	5,555	624	1,538	2,488	3,158	5,010	1,958	2,763	23,095	4,648	2,018	1,708	8,373
Jun	12,547	252	1,873	5,989	664	1,844	2,562	3,226	4,911	1,941	2,720	23,858	4,779	2,397	1,748	8,924
Jul	12,764	256	1,909	5,472	660	1,870	2,564	3,196	4,913	1,948	2,860	23,484	4,923	2,509	1,736	9,169
Aug	12,879	255	1,709	5,145	637	1,813	2,568	3,326	5,133	1,942	2,925	23,489	4,834	2,394	1,742	8,969
Sep	13,054	259	1,617	5,065	630	1,777	2,680	3,174	4,891	1,840	2,901	22,958	4,909	2,472	1,763	9,144
Oct	13,231	284	1,657	5,166	607	1,560	2,563	3,147	5,249	1,900	2,932	23,125	5,071	2,498	1,737	9,306
Nov	13,305	266	1,592	5,485	582	1,718	2,548	3,131	5,374	1,811	2,799	23,448	5,178	2,535	1,648	9,361
Dec	13,004	257	1,466	5,483	559	1,712	2,417	3,011	5,349	1,862	2,556	22,950	5,496	2,519	1,795	9,810
2013 Jan	13,231	246	1,352	5,112	577	1,698	2,565	3,098	5,310	1,941	2,720	23,021	5,636	2,516	1,835	9,987
Feb	13,394	242	1,479	4,899	574	1,689	2,278	3,143	5,490	1,725	2,654	22,453	5,601	1,809	1,863	9,272
Mar	13,509	243	1,561	5,188	582	1,811	2,231	3,161	5,401	2,041	2,636	23,051	5,324	2,358	1,882	9,564
Apr	13,667	238	1,514	5,131	600	1,725	2,311	3,200	5,200	1,690	2,611	22,468	4,952	2,334	1,882	9,167
May	13,846	241	1,427	4,496	584	1,850	2,232	3,242	5,090	1,587	2,773	21,854	5,007	2,310	1,886	9,203
Jun	14,036	241	2,308	4,429	596	1,826	2,166	3,512	4,712 (a)	1,611	2,724	21,573 (a)	4,961	2,259	1,856	9,076
Jul	14,296	240	2,317	4,387	564	1,802	2,236	3,554	4,295	1,629	2,710	21,179	5,653	2,259	1,867	9,779
Aug	14,416	237	2,276	4,322	562	1,818	2,281	3,551	4,230	1,734	2,669	21,167	5,548	2,227	1,859	9,634
Sep	14,563	236	2,581	4,318	551	1,988	2,156	3,345	4,447	1,659	2,681	21,145	6,217	2,511	1,789	10,518
Oct	14,709	234	2,647	4,407	564	1,954	2,316	3,430	4,474	1,601	2,680	21,426	6,415	2,551	1,887	10,853
Nov	14,880	232	2,792	5,274	551	1,911	2,304	3,407	4,375	1,628	2,502	21,951	6,500	2,552	1,861	10,913
Dec	14,243	227	2,773	5,703	538	1,980	2,322	3,176	4,289	1,455	2,477	21,939	7,889	2,609	1,937	12,434

12.4a Industrial analysis of monetary financial institutions lending to UK residents

£ millions   Not seasonally adjusted

Amounts outstanding of lending in sterling

RPM		Development of buildings	Construction					Wholesale and retail trade				Accommodation and food service activities	Transport, storage and communication		
			Construction of commercial buildings	Construction of domestic buildings	Civil Engineering	Other construction activities	Total	Wholesale and retail trade and repair of motor vehicles and motorcycles	Wholesale trade, excluding motor vehicles and motor cycles	Retail trade excluding motor vehicles and motor cycles	Total		Transportation and storage	Information and communication	Total
		B7EB	B3I6	B3LX	B4PK	B4PX	TBUQ	TBUS	TBUT	TBUU	TBUR	TBUV	B5PK	B5PR	TBUW
2012	Jan	33,622	4,022	5,968	2,975	7,847	54,434	10,125	10,307	16,696	37,129	28,895	15,244	10,973	26,217
	Feb	33,670	4,057	5,779	3,050	7,913	54,470	10,619	10,282	16,775	37,676	28,719	15,031	11,232	26,262
	Mar	33,367	4,021	5,592	2,873	8,072	53,925	10,130	10,207	17,086	37,423	28,905	15,263	10,614	25,877
	Apr	33,288	4,021	5,573	2,984	8,169	54,015	10,035	10,353	16,797	37,185	28,444	15,239	10,350	25,590
	May	33,139	4,052	5,525	3,114	8,159	53,989	9,656	10,207	16,745	36,607	28,383	14,671	10,387	25,057
	Jun	33,001	3,941	4,762	2,991	8,107	52,802	9,603	10,222	16,959	36,784	28,240	14,044	10,612	24,656
	Jul	32,907	4,041	4,931	3,058	8,014	52,952	9,896	10,291	16,693	36,879	27,888	14,434	10,485	24,919
	Aug	32,673	4,069	4,979	3,125	7,900	52,745	10,149	10,266	16,472	36,887	27,682	13,992	10,412	24,404
	Sep	32,261	4,153	4,914	3,147	7,894	52,369	9,858	10,351	16,929	37,138	27,636	14,619	10,327	24,947
	Oct	31,822	4,610	4,852	3,194	7,601	52,079	9,719	10,263	16,522	36,505	27,451	14,211	10,648	24,859
	Nov	31,545	4,298	4,760	3,151	7,535	51,290	9,202	10,309	16,515	36,026	27,326	14,051	10,557	24,608
	Dec	31,982	3,968	4,465	2,900	7,687	51,001	9,619	10,025	15,537	35,181	27,328	13,058	10,526	23,584
2013	Jan	31,734	4,033	4,731	3,175	7,869	51,542	10,230	10,275	15,961	36,466	27,442	13,362	10,756	24,117
	Feb	31,751	4,166	4,850	3,262	7,731	51,759	10,669	10,291	15,909	36,870	26,851	12,976	10,097	23,073
	Mar	31,357	4,163	4,639	3,257	7,606	51,022	10,146	10,163	16,055	36,363	26,797	12,859	10,507	23,366
	Apr	30,565	4,226	4,624	3,048	7,507	49,969	9,943	10,376	15,705	36,025	24,494	12,953	9,853	22,806
	May	30,505	4,148	4,556	3,090	7,499	49,797	9,926	10,209	15,533	35,668	24,313	12,906	9,671	22,577
	Jun	30,437	3,849	4,100	2,770	7,313	48,469	10,375 (e)	10,027	15,558	35,960 (e)	24,367	12,770	9,066	21,836
	Jul	30,206	4,035	4,105	2,998	7,278	48,622	10,591	10,000	15,563	36,154	24,304	12,716	9,233	21,950
	Aug	29,912	4,138	4,193	3,056	7,275	48,575	10,153	10,359	15,516	36,029	24,189	12,690	9,242	21,931
	Sep	29,769	4,228	4,229	3,089	7,264	48,578	8,944 (f)	10,772	15,753	35,469 (f)	23,854	12,557	9,336	21,893
	Oct	29,696	4,592	4,208	3,145	6,926	48,567	8,718	10,637	15,661	35,016	23,548	12,820	10,267	23,087
	Nov	35,194 (b)	5,585 (c)	4,349	3,171	6,120 (d)	54,419 (b)	8,764	10,840	16,067	35,672	25,188 (g)	12,810	10,301	23,111
	Dec	34,040	5,170	4,005	2,416	5,833	51,465	8,827	10,956	15,950	35,733	24,740	12,678	10,930	23,608

12.4a Industrial analysis of monetary financial institutions lending to UK residents

£ millions   Not seasonally adjusted

Amounts outstanding of lending in sterling

| | Real estate, professional services and support activities | | | | Public administration and defence | Education | Human health and social work | Recreational, personal and community service activities | | | Financial leasing corporations | Financial intermediation (excluding insurance and pension funds) | | | |
	Buying, selling and renting of real estate	Professional, scientific and technical activities	Administrative and support services	Total				Recreational, cultural and sporting activities	Personal and community service activities	Total		Non-bank credit grantors excluding credit unions and SPVs	Credit unions	Factoring corporations	Mortgage and housing credit corporations excluding SPVs
RPM	TBUY	B6PD	B6PO	TBUX	TBVD	TBVE	TBVF	TBVH	TBVG	B6PT	TBVJ	TBVK	TBVL	TBVM	TBVN
2012 Jan	180,915	17,371	14,781	213,068	8,187	11,281	21,245	7,186	3,834	11,020	27,429	14,478	1	6,308	59,356
Feb	179,563	17,581	13,741	210,885	8,425	11,337	21,315	7,125	3,818	10,943	27,290	14,498	2	6,390	59,230
Mar	178,661	17,238	13,679	209,578	7,957	11,484	21,429	7,166	3,810	10,976	27,386	14,424	2	6,725	59,789
Apr	177,438	16,741	13,647	207,827	8,222	11,409	21,384	7,054	3,764	10,819	26,949	14,071	2	6,711	57,199
May	176,208 (h)	16,465	13,247	205,920 (h)	9,848	11,374	21,419	6,958	3,783	10,741	27,590	14,240	2	6,793	56,380
Jun	174,731	16,149	12,980	203,859	7,826	11,445	21,424	7,013	3,784	10,797	27,598	14,063	2	6,832	56,856
Jul	174,321	16,550	12,821	203,692	8,084	11,508	21,459	7,058	3,740	10,798	27,589	13,983	1	6,845	56,362
Aug	173,449	16,159	12,809	202,416	7,808	11,537	21,322	7,014	3,692	10,707	27,196	13,823	1	6,932	55,066
Sep	171,887	16,319	12,499	200,705	8,064	11,460	21,416	6,995	3,669	10,663	27,483	13,490	2	7,128	55,187
Oct	170,204	16,300	13,453	199,956	8,992	11,478	21,354	6,537	3,708	10,246	27,166	12,866	1	6,970	54,097
Nov	169,198 (i)	15,884	13,033	198,114 (i)	8,081	11,581	21,262	6,517	3,645	10,162	27,021	12,670	2	6,997	53,478
Dec	169,529 (j)	15,133	13,096	197,758 (j)	7,742	12,049	21,536	6,429	3,624	10,053	26,048	12,703	2	7,283	51,446
2013 Jan	168,760	15,469	13,813	198,042	8,029	11,939	21,158	6,319	3,691	10,010	25,560	12,497	1	6,838	51,416
Feb	167,924	15,588	14,361 (m)	197,873 (m)	8,391	11,780	20,907	6,415	3,672	10,087	25,385	12,353	1	7,137	51,522
Mar	165,929	15,525	14,217	195,670	7,656	11,884	20,974	6,786	3,586	10,373	24,917	12,443	2	7,436	51,543
Apr	162,660	15,101	14,274	192,035	7,703	11,609	21,099	6,273	3,578	9,851	24,319	12,477	1	7,338	54,499
May	162,102	15,052	14,758	191,912	7,974	11,431	21,010	6,353	3,549	9,902	23,958	12,311	-	7,633	55,385
Jun	161,347	15,077	14,801	191,226	8,418	11,494	21,008	5,868	3,506	9,374	23,909	12,193	5	8,183	55,586
Jul	159,293	15,469	15,050	189,812	8,022	11,292	20,951	5,884	3,497	9,381	23,412	12,063	-	7,905	55,974
Aug	156,471 (k)	15,714	15,152	187,337 (k)	7,733	11,331	20,773	5,831	3,478	9,308	22,421	12,106	1	8,015	55,745
Sep	155,518	15,860	15,309	186,687	8,733	11,247	20,908	5,913	3,481	9,394	22,555	12,283	1	7,680	55,937
Oct	154,169	16,080	15,049	185,298	8,916	11,274	20,835	6,022	3,482	9,504	21,989	12,362	1	8,004	55,029
Nov	144,172 (l)	14,360 (d)	19,077 (n)	177,609 (n)(o)	8,075	11,191	20,804	5,992	3,273	9,265	22,214	12,317	1	4,753 (p)	51,656 (q)
Dec	143,394	13,866	20,018	177,277	7,723	10,911	20,585	5,990	3,244	9,234	22,552	12,551	1	4,828	50,446 (r)

12.4a Industrial analysis of monetary financial institutions lending to UK residents

£ millions   Not seasonally adjusted

Amounts outstanding of lending in sterling

RPM	Investment and unit trusts excluding money market mutual funds	Money market mutual funds	Financial intermediation (excluding insurance and pension funds)						Insurance companies & pension funds			Fund management activities	Activities auxiliary to financial intermediation			Total
			Bank holding companies	Securities dealers	SPVs related to securitisation	Other financial intermediaries	Total	of which intragroup activity	Insurance companies	Pension funds	Total		Central clearing counterparties	Other auxiliary activities	Total	
	TBVO	TBVP	TBVQ	TBVR	B6PY	TBVS	TBVI	B3U8	B3V6	B3W4	TBVT	TBVU	B7FX	B8FD	TBVV	B8FJ
2012 Jan	6,176	121	27,630	20,069	16,891	149,383 (s)	327,842 (s)	139,779 (s)	16,687	10,780	27,468	23,774	63,402	2,991	66,393	90,167
Feb	5,906	108	26,280	24,896	17,329	142,653	324,582	133,543	16,562	10,860	27,422	24,125	72,414	2,932	75,347	99,472
Mar	6,584	110	24,121	29,841	19,375	142,932	331,287	134,075	15,128	9,699	24,827	24,466	65,179	2,673	67,852	92,318
Apr	6,430	109	23,410	33,968	15,946	153,140 (t)	337,935 (t)	144,037 (t)	16,731	9,623	26,353	24,442	64,372	2,771	67,143	91,586
May	6,606	112	24,101	30,924	16,242	148,773	331,762	139,513	16,085	10,804	26,888	25,718	61,113	2,959	64,072	89,790
Jun	7,077	109	21,488	30,422	18,356	148,296	331,100	139,135	15,018	11,083	26,101	25,334	72,007	2,656	74,663	99,997
Jul	7,141	109	21,485	29,168	18,492	149,272	330,448	140,544	15,355	9,777	25,131	28,568	62,204	2,948	65,152	93,721
Aug	7,504	109	21,478	31,131	18,027	150,823	332,091	141,931	14,084	10,076	24,160	29,017	65,832	2,690	68,522	97,539
Sep	7,058	109	23,195	26,492	18,410	153,939	332,482	144,319	14,241	10,227	24,468	29,266	71,330	2,453	73,783	103,049
Oct	6,750	109	24,357	26,635	19,349	148,538 (u)	326,837 (u)	139,433 (u)	13,749	10,699	24,447	30,178	63,808	2,704	66,512	96,690
Nov	7,612	110	28,732	29,694	18,577	142,694 (v)	327,587 (v)	133,260 (v)	13,452	10,802	24,254	32,953	67,942	2,819	70,761	103,714
Dec	6,629	60	28,810	20,744	19,245	158,347	331,317	149,874	10,016 (z)	10,267	20,283 (z)	33,856	83,864 (ab)	3,192	87,055 (ab)	120,911 (ab)
2013 Jan	6,867	62	30,069	20,246	19,925	162,151 (w)	335,632 (w)	154,147 (w)	10,053	11,118	21,171	35,305	74,710	3,746	78,457	113,762
Feb	9,078	101	32,872	23,143	18,814	158,418	338,824	149,188	9,075	11,259	20,334	37,790	68,298	3,051	71,349	109,139
Mar	7,058	62	35,944	19,108	18,816	150,135	327,462	141,552	9,164	14,563	23,726	38,615	68,344	3,115	71,460	110,075
Apr	6,649	62	29,432	20,206	18,824	146,343	320,150	138,554	8,818	14,203	23,021	39,847	71,987	3,482	75,469	115,316
May	6,547	62	24,385	20,467	18,692	147,028	316,468	139,508	9,166	13,340	22,506	38,702	74,400	3,290	77,690	116,392
Jun	7,284	64	24,499	19,931	18,516	144,791	314,961	137,565	9,257	13,544	22,801	38,994	67,903	3,148	71,051	110,045
Jul	7,707	65	29,796	21,441	19,694	146,075 (x)	324,133	138,813 (x)	8,340	12,738	21,078	40,238	61,693	3,208	64,901	105,139
Aug	8,262	60	33,102	20,527	19,903	146,810	326,952	139,710	7,456	12,557	20,012	42,355	69,439	3,416	72,855	115,210
Sep	8,503	62	35,483	18,571	19,459	146,607	327,140	140,187	7,076 (aa)	13,504	20,580 (aa)	43,248	73,219	5,314	78,533	121,782
Oct	7,659	62	35,415	20,893	19,637	148,334	329,386	141,502	7,635	13,022	20,657	44,746	63,098 (ac)	3,249 (ad)	66,347	111,093
Nov	7,648	62	35,427	21,851	20,044	147,682 (p)	323,655 (q)(y)	140,861 (p)	7,765	12,939	20,704	45,741	63,093	3,098	66,191	111,931
Dec	8,636	63	35,779	22,716	20,073	126,358	304,005 (r)	119,400	11,850	11,673	23,522	47,094	50,823	3,075	53,898	100,992

12.4a Industrial analysis of monetary financial institutions lending to UK residents

£ millions   Not seasonally adjusted

Amounts outstanding of lending in sterling

RPM	Total financial and non-financial businesses	Individuals and individual trusts			Total UK residents
		Lending secured on dwellings inc. bridging finance	Other loans and advances	Total	
	Z949	TBVX	TBVY	TBVW	TBUA
2012 Jan	901,822	1,012,808	116,215	1,129,022	2,030,844
Feb	906,944	1,013,073	115,113	1,128,187	2,035,130
Mar	900,842	1,014,683	114,691	1,129,374	2,030,216
Apr	907,410	1,015,318	113,591	1,128,909	2,036,319 (t)
May	897,910	1,016,459	113,144	1,129,603	2,027,513
Jun	902,483	1,024,612 (af)	113,267	1,137,879 (af)	2,040,362
Jul	895,060	1,027,097	112,833	1,139,929	2,034,990
Aug	896,601	1,028,158	112,531	1,140,689	2,037,290
Sep	901,429	1,028,886	112,512	1,141,397	2,042,826
Oct	888,499	1,029,692	111,837	1,141,530	2,030,029 (u)
Nov	891,976	1,030,879	111,598	1,142,477	2,034,453 (j)(v)
Dec	906,230	1,029,317 (ag)	112,768	1,142,085 (ag)	2,048,315 (am)
2013 Jan	907,146	1,029,535	105,342 (aj)(ak)	1,134,877 (aj)(ak)	2,042,022 (aj)(am)
Feb	902,727 (m)	1,028,904	105,324	1,134,228	2,036,955 (m)
Mar	893,297	1,028,609	104,575	1,133,184	2,026,481
Apr	881,132	1,028,356	105,028	1,133,384	2,014,516
May	876,521	1,029,108	105,114	1,134,222	2,010,743
Jun	867,191	1,030,938	105,554	1,136,492	2,003,683
Jul	868,650 (ae)	1,032,668	107,664 (al)	1,140,332 (al)	2,008,982 (ae)(al)
Aug	877,111	1,034,121	107,881	1,142,003	2,019,113
Sep	885,308	1,035,329	109,162	1,144,491	2,029,799
Oct	877,050	1,038,101	108,583	1,146,684	2,023,734
Nov	872,393 (p)(q)	1,042,057 (ah)(ai)	108,915	1,150,972 (ah)(ai)	2,023,366 (p)(q)(ai)
Dec	841,412 (r)	1,043,121	108,865	1,151,986	1,993,398 (r)

Source: Bank of England

12.4a Industrial analysis of monetary financial institutions lending to UK residents

£ millions   Not seasonally adjusted

Movements in amounts outstanding can reflect breaks in data series as well as underlying flows. For changes data, users are recommended to refer directly to the appropriate series or data tables.
www.bankofengland.co.uk/statistics/Pages/iadb/notesiadb/Changes_flows_growth_rates.aspx.

(a) Due to improvements in reporting at one institution, the amounts outstanding decreased by £0.7bn. This effect has been adjusted out of the flows for June 2013.

(b) Due to improvements in reporting at one institution, the amounts outstanding increased by £6bn. This effect has been adjusted out of the flows for November 2013.

(c) Due to improvements in reporting at one institution, the amounts outstanding increased by £1bn. This effect has been adjusted out of the flows for November 2013.

(d) Due to improvements in reporting at one institution, the amounts outstanding decreased by £1bn. This effect has been adjusted out of the flows for November 2013.

(e) Due to improvements in reporting at one institution, the amounts outstanding increased by £0.4bn. This effect has been adjusted out of the flows for June 2013.

(f) Due to a reclassification by one reporting institution, the amounts outstanding decreased by £1bn. This effect has been adjusted out of the flows for September 2013.

(g) Due to improvements in reporting at one institution, the amounts outstanding increased by £2bn. This effect has been adjusted out of the flows for November 2013.

(h) Due to improvements in reporting at one institution, the amounts outstanding decreased by £0.6bn. This effect has been adjusted out of the flows for May 2012.

(i) Following a sale of loans by one reporting institution, the amounts outstanding decreased by £0.5bn. This effect has been adjusted out of the flows for November 2012.

(j) Due to a change in the reporting population, this series has increased by £1bn. The effect has been adjusted out of the flows for December 2012.

(k) Due to loan transfers out of the UK MFI population, the amounts outstanding decreased by £2bn. This effect has been adjusted out of the flows for August 2013.

(l) Due to improvements in reporting at one institution, the amounts outstanding decreased by £7bn. This effect has been adjusted out of the flows for November 2013.

(m) Due to a reclassification at one institution, the amounts outstanding increased by £0.6bn. This effect has been adjusted out of the flows for February 2013.

(n) Due to a restructuring at one reporting institution, the amounts outstanding increased by £3bn. This effect has been adjusted out of the flows for November 2013.

(o) Due to improvements in reporting at one institution, the amounts outstanding decreased by £8bn. This effect has been adjusted out of the flows for November 2013.

(p) Due to a restructuring at one reporting institution, the amounts outstanding decreased by £3bn. This effect has been adjusted out of the flows for November 2013.

(q) Due to improvements in reporting at one institution, the amounts outstanding decreased by £1bn. This effect has been adjusted out of the flows for November 2013.

(r) Due to improvements in reporting at one institution, the amounts outstanding decreased by £2bn. This effect has been adjusted out of the flows for December 2013.

(s) Due to a change in accounting treatment at one reporting institution, the amounts outstanding increased by £12bn. The effect has been adjusted out of the flows for January 2012.

(t) Due to a change in treatment at one reporting institution, the amounts outstanding increased by £5bn. This effect has been adjusted out of the flows for April 2012.

(u) Due to a change in treatment at one reporting institution, the amounts outstanding decreased by £5bn. This effect has been adjusted out of the flows for October 2012.

(v) Due to improvements in reporting at one institution, the amounts outstanding decreased by £4bn. This effect has been adjusted out of the flows for November 2012.

(w) Due to a restructuring at one reporting institution the amounts outstanding decreased by £2bn. This effect has been adjusted out of the flows for January 2013.

(x) Due to improvements in reporting at one institution, the amounts outstanding increased by £2bn. This effect has been adjusted out of the flows for July 2013.

(y) Due to a restructuring at one reporting institution, the amounts outstanding decreased by £6bn. This effect has been adjusted out of the flows for November 2013.

(z) Due to a change in the reporting population, this series has decreased by £3bn. The effect has been adjusted out of the flows for December 2012.

(aa) Due to a reclassification by one reporting institution, the amounts outstanding increased by £1bn. This effect has been adjusted out of the flows for September 2013.

(ab) Due to a change in the reporting population, this series has increased by £8bn. The effect has been adjusted out of the flows for December 2012.

(ac) Due to improvements in reporting at one institution, the amounts outstanding increased by £2bn. This effect has been adjusted out of the flows for October 2013.

(ad) Due to improvements in reporting at one institution, the amounts outstanding decreased by £2bn. This effect has been adjusted out of the flows for October 2013.

(ae) Due to improvements in reporting at one institution, the amounts outstanding increased by £5bn. This effect has been adjusted out of the flows for July 2013.

(af) Due to a change in accounting treatment at one reporting institution, the amounts outstanding increased by £7bn. This effect has been adjusted out of the flows for June 2012.

(ag) Due to a change in the reporting population, this series has decreased by £2bn. The effect has been adjusted out of the flows for December 2012.

(ah) Due to improvements in reporting at one institution, the amounts outstanding increased by £1bn. This effect has been adjusted out of the flows for November 2013.

(ai) Following a purchase of loans by one reporting institution, the amounts outstanding increased by £2bn. This effect has been adjusted out of the flows for November 2013.

(aj) Due to a change in the reporting population, the amounts outstanding decreased by £8bn. The effect has been adjusted out of the flows for January 2013.

(ak) Due to a restructuring at one reporting institution the amounts outstanding increased by £1bn. This effect has been adjusted out of the flows for January 2013.

(al) Following a purchase of loans by one reporting institution, the amounts outstanding increased by £2bn. This effect has been adjusted out of the flows for July 2013.

(am) Due to a change in the reporting population, this series has increased by £4bn. The effect has been adjusted out of the flows for December 2012.

(an) Due to a restructuring at one reporting institution the amounts outstanding decreased by £1bn. This effect has been adjusted out of the flows for January 2013.

12.4b Industrial analysis of monetary financial institutions lending to UK residents

£ millions   Not seasonally adjusted

Amounts outstanding of lending in all currencies

RPM	Agriculture, hunting and forestry	Fishing	Mining and quarrying	Manufacturing									Electricity, gas and water supply			
				Food, beverages and tobacco	Textiles, wearing apparel and leather	Pulp, paper, and printing	Chemicals, pharmaceuticals, rubber and plastics	Non-metallic mineral products and metals	Machinery, equipment and transport equipment	Electrical, medical and optical equipment	Other manufacturing	Total	Electricity, gas steam and air conditioning	Water collection and sewerage	Waste management related services and remediation activities	Total
	TBSC	TBSD	TBSE	TBSG	TBSH	TBSI	TBSJ	TBSK	TBSL	TBSM	TBSN	TBSF	TBSO	TBSP	B3FA	B3FO
2012 Jan	12,225	286	7,094	7,507	982	2,056	4,505	4,709	6,820	3,942	4,328	34,848	6,096	2,067	1,690	9,854
Feb	12,209	277	6,060	7,723	986	1,911	4,995	4,577	6,759	3,852	3,852	35,077	6,110	2,063	1,715	9,889
Mar	12,440	276	6,125	6,994	959	1,858	5,136	4,572	6,772	3,763	4,076	34,129	5,938	2,048	1,681	9,667
Apr	12,574	276	7,457	7,278	964	1,980	5,073	4,656	6,661	3,888	4,063	34,562	5,916	2,145	1,808	9,869
May	12,719	268	6,112	6,970	973	1,982	4,391	4,775	7,043	4,010	4,041	34,185	5,857	2,068	1,780	9,705
Jun	12,837	267	6,055	7,256	972	2,740	4,630	4,844	7,359	4,128	4,080	36,010	5,901	2,449	1,810	10,160
Jul	13,051	275	5,872	6,607	1,100	2,806	4,188	4,717	7,178	4,066	3,975	34,636	6,114	2,564	1,801	10,479
Aug	13,154	276	5,774	6,245	1,073	2,545	4,246	4,962	7,416	4,089	4,032	34,608	6,000	2,446	1,787	10,233
Sep	13,317	281	5,936	6,064	1,051	2,492	4,346	4,704	7,396	3,884	3,940	33,877	6,012	2,523	1,813	10,348
Oct	13,500	306	6,198	6,054	1,022	2,167	4,510	4,697	7,651	3,905	4,013	34,019	6,097	2,549	1,786	10,433
Nov	13,585	292	5,731	6,519	993	2,486	4,278	4,746	7,820	3,811	3,946	34,598	6,584	2,587	1,740	10,911
Dec	13,258	285	4,736	6,957	949	2,389	4,130	4,566	7,961	3,932	3,673	34,558	6,315	2,571	1,927	10,813
2013 Jan	13,477	259	4,929	6,354	992	2,373	4,707	4,614	7,804	4,118	3,718	34,681	6,517	2,570	1,917	11,004
Feb	13,659	255	5,257	6,143	1,000	2,385	4,415	4,718	8,060	3,854	3,558	34,133	6,526	1,814	1,984	10,323
Mar	13,752	254	6,923	6,377	1,019	2,505	3,919	4,910	7,887	4,190	3,574	34,381	6,216	2,362	2,055	10,633
Apr	13,928	254	6,724	6,115	1,037	2,350	4,442	4,693	7,794	3,860	3,508	33,799	5,794	2,339	1,975	10,107
May	14,087	246	5,121	5,425	1,020	2,542	4,697	4,737	7,872	3,752	3,667	33,712	5,930	2,314	1,949	10,193
Jun	14,252	246	5,937	5,366	1,039	2,515	4,594	4,959	7,073 (ba)	3,770	3,615	32,932 (ba)	5,803	2,280	1,941	10,025
Jul	14,514	245	6,239	5,650	1,015	2,415	5,238	5,066	7,024	3,920	3,583	33,911	6,660	2,281	2,023	10,964
Aug	14,642	241	5,757	5,336	986	2,401	5,142	5,028	6,657	3,861	3,516	32,928	6,547	2,248	1,968	10,763
Sep	14,767	240	5,516	5,598	954	2,682	4,884	4,721	6,953	3,649	3,468	32,908	6,818	2,532	1,884	11,234
Oct	14,948	238	5,993	5,480	969	2,451	5,038	4,823	7,038	3,774	3,565	33,137	6,967	2,572	1,975	11,514
Nov	15,156	236	5,866	6,189	927	2,429	4,936	4,582	6,582	3,614	3,228	32,487	7,108	2,572	1,914	11,595
Dec	14,469	232	5,674	6,864	866	2,538	4,645	4,457	6,648	3,359	3,224	32,601	8,541	2,628	1,985	13,154

12.4b Industrial analysis of monetary financial institutions lending to UK residents

£ millions   Not seasonally adjusted

Amounts outstanding of lending in all currencies

| | Construction | | | | | | Wholesale and retail trade | | | | Accommodation and food service activities | Transport, storage and communication | | |
	Development of buildings	Construction of commercial buildings	Construction of domestic buildings	Civil Engineering	Other construction activities	Total	Wholesale and retail trade and repair of motor vehicles and motorcycles	Wholesale trade, excluding motor vehicles and motor cycles	Retail trade excluding motor vehicles and motor cycles	Total		Transportation and storage	Information and communication	Total
RPM	**B7EC**	**B3I7**	**B3LY**	**B4PL**	**B4PY**	**TBSQ**	**TBSS**	**TBST**	**TBSU**	**TBSR**	**TBSV**	**B5PL**	**B5PS**	**TBSW**
2012 Jan	34,032	4,099	5,987	3,102	8,023	55,244	10,450	13,177	18,307	41,935	29,341	20,948	13,850	34,799
Feb	34,084	4,136	5,793	3,177	8,092	55,283	11,118	13,173	18,020	42,311	29,164	20,058	14,117	34,174
Mar	33,746	4,099	5,593	2,979	8,225	54,642	10,764	13,131	18,662	42,558	29,343	20,403	13,362	33,765
Apr	33,663	4,098	5,574	3,089	8,319	54,744	10,670	13,135	18,053	41,858	28,879	20,410	13,076	33,486
May	33,533	4,131	5,526	3,220	8,323	54,733	10,611	13,169	18,171	41,951	28,790	19,901	13,426	33,327
Jun	33,372	4,019	4,764	3,086	8,259	53,499	10,191	13,216	18,241	41,649	28,620	19,330	13,926	33,255
Jul	33,271	4,121	4,932	3,148	8,175	53,648	10,574	13,699	18,015	42,288	28,267	19,584	13,799	33,383
Aug	33,017	4,151	4,980	3,213	8,108	53,470	10,829	13,729	17,930	42,488	28,060	18,949	13,705	32,654
Sep	32,617	4,199	4,915	3,204	8,126	53,061	10,358	13,478	18,408	42,244	28,036	20,038	13,466	33,504
Oct	32,166	4,658	4,853	3,249	7,789	52,715	10,279	13,375	17,895	41,548	27,957	19,629	13,916	33,546
Nov	31,871	4,344	4,762	3,206	7,712	51,895	9,571	13,842	18,041	41,453	27,772	19,425	13,891	33,316
Dec	32,312	4,028	4,465	2,983	7,852	51,640	9,926	13,367	17,110	40,403	27,639	18,000	13,331	31,331
2013 Jan	32,079	4,095	4,732	3,244	8,100	52,249	10,496	13,605	17,406	41,507	27,758	18,201	13,711	31,911
Feb	32,099	4,228	4,851	3,343	7,900	52,421	10,917	13,613	17,332	41,861	27,138	17,676	13,095	30,772
Mar	31,690	4,225	4,640	3,340	7,736	51,631	10,356	13,591	17,509	41,457	27,104	17,470	13,449	30,919
Apr	30,896	4,288	4,624	3,133	7,645	50,585	10,148	14,097	17,266	41,511	24,771	17,546	13,280	30,826
May	30,836	4,211	4,556	3,183	7,626	50,412	10,129	13,694	16,978	40,801	24,585	17,655	12,322	29,977
Jun	30,776	3,912	4,101	2,877	7,450	49,116	11,090 (be)	13,741	16,905	41,736 (be)	24,653	16,735	11,868	28,603
Jul	30,550	4,099	4,105	3,129	7,516	49,400	11,128	14,132	17,095	42,355	24,655	16,398	12,005	28,403
Aug	30,234	4,234	4,194	3,172	7,440	49,274	10,655	13,896	17,188	41,739	24,536	16,424	11,705	28,129
Sep	30,082	4,318	4,229	3,197	7,461	49,287	9,358 (bf)	14,613	17,269	41,239 (bf)	24,188	16,295	11,810	28,105
Oct	30,001	4,665	4,208	3,274	7,123	49,271	9,132	14,386	17,167	40,685	23,864	16,565	12,782	29,347
Nov	35,877 (bb)	5,644 (bc)	4,350	3,260	6,280 (bd)	55,410 (bb)	9,169	14,574	17,668	41,411	25,467 (bg)	16,013	12,921	28,934
Dec	34,509	5,247	4,006	2,505	5,995	52,261	9,340	14,424	17,729	41,494	25,064	16,019	14,032	30,052

12.4b Industrial analysis of monetary financial institutions lending to UK residents

£ millions

Not seasonally adjusted

Amounts outstanding of lending in all currencies

| | Real estate, professional services and support activities | | | | Public administration and defence | Education | Human health and social work | Recreational, personal and community service activities | | | Financial intermediation (excluding insurance and pension funds) | | | | |
| | Buying, selling and renting of real estate | Professional, scientific and technical activities | Administrative and support services | Total | | | | Recreational, cultural and sporting activities | Personal and community service activities | Total | Financial leasing corporations | Non-bank credit grantors excluding credit unions and SPVs | Credit unions | Factoring corporations | Mortgage and housing credit corporations excluding SPVs |
RPM	TBSY	B6PE	B6PP	TBSX	TBTD	TBTE	TBTF	TBTH	TBTG	B6H5	TBTJ	TBTK	TBTL	TBTM	TBTN
2012 Jan	184,078	19,930	17,906	221,914	8,689	11,413	21,448	7,744	3,995	11,739	36,171	16,371	1	6,885	59,780
Feb	182,739	20,071	16,641	219,451	9,188	11,468	21,511	7,696	3,983	11,679	35,887	16,413	2	6,922	59,662
Mar	181,867	19,579	16,465	217,912	8,600	11,564	21,636	7,761	3,946	11,707	35,806	16,330	2	7,246	60,208
Apr	180,636	18,977	16,550	216,164	9,024	11,483	21,601	7,541	3,888	11,429	34,964	15,910	2	7,298	57,602
May	179,460 (bh)	18,726	16,517	214,703 (bh)	10,437	11,459	21,639	7,391	3,912	11,303	36,292	15,974	2	7,385	56,809
Jun	177,814	18,687	16,609	213,110	8,416	11,531	21,649	7,438	3,905	11,343	35,310	15,806	3	7,559	57,278
Jul	177,299	18,417	17,104	212,821	8,466	11,599	21,692	7,457	3,853	11,309	34,278	15,593	2	7,563	57,165
Aug	176,295	17,998	17,237	211,530	8,483	11,653	21,555	7,415	3,807	11,222	33,665	15,393	2	7,581	55,432
Sep	174,797	18,488	16,867	210,152	9,038	11,591	21,611	7,419	3,776	11,195	33,741	15,054	2	7,590	55,631
Oct	173,097	18,334	17,646	209,077	9,807	11,604	21,547	6,953	3,819	10,772	33,343	14,391	2	7,394	54,507
Nov	172,099 (bi)	18,170	16,743	207,011 (bi)	8,306	11,729	21,458	6,933	3,762	10,696	32,909	13,646	2	7,404	53,887
Dec	172,478 (bj)	17,525	16,766	206,770 (bj)	8,565	12,178	21,727	6,853	3,748	10,601	31,639	13,787	2	7,992	51,830
2013 Jan	171,809	17,957	17,029	206,794	8,493	12,049	21,349	6,759	3,830	10,590	31,089	13,511	2	7,319	51,807
Feb	170,937	18,100	18,378 (bm)	207,415 (bm)	9,184	11,882	21,103	6,865	3,803	10,668	31,043	13,374	2	7,537	51,931
Mar	168,928	18,080	18,097	205,105	8,526	12,000	21,164	7,224	3,719	10,943	30,117	13,455	2	7,874	51,949
Apr	165,654	17,688	18,106	201,448	9,008	11,725	21,304	6,701	3,714	10,415	29,368	12,737	1	7,733	54,905
May	165,109	17,724	18,808	201,640	9,398	11,548	21,223	6,808	3,682	10,491	29,016	12,539	1	8,039	55,790
Jun	164,435	18,224	18,983	201,642	9,979	11,605	21,186	6,528	3,624	10,152	28,699	12,349	6	8,750	55,964
Jul	162,362	18,202	19,488	200,052	9,748	11,380	21,135	6,659	3,612	10,271	28,230	12,372	1	8,321	56,370
Aug	159,319 (bk)	18,497	19,299	197,116 (bk)	9,276	11,605	20,958	6,561	3,589	10,149	26,975	12,293	1	8,385	56,119
Sep	158,304	18,514	19,225	196,043	10,043	11,354	21,058	6,578	3,592	10,170	26,807	12,423	1	8,052	56,285
Oct	156,596	18,675	18,792	194,062	10,232	11,352	20,977	6,643	3,593	10,236	26,184	12,503	1	8,398	55,376
Nov	146,058 (bl)	16,447 (bd)	22,904 (bn)	185,409 (bn)(bo)	9,449	11,246	20,945	6,412	3,381	9,793	26,315	12,492	1	5,147 (bq)	52,017 (bq)
Dec	145,135	15,813	23,663	184,612	9,879	10,969	20,740	6,376	3,349	9,725	26,160	12,787	1	5,302	50,786 (br)

12.4b Industrial analysis of monetary financial institutions lending to UK residents

£ millions   Not seasonally adjusted

Amounts outstanding of lending in all currencies

RPM	Investment and unit trusts excluding money market mutual funds	Money market mutual funds	Bank holding companies	Securities dealers	SPVs related to securitisation	Other financial intermediaries	of which intragroup activity	Total	Insurance companies	Pension funds	Total
				Financial intermediation (excluding insurance and pension funds)					Insurance companies & pension funds		
	TBTO	TBTP	TBTQ	TBTR	B6PZ	TBTS	B3U9	TBTI	B3V7	B3W5	TBTT
2012 Jan	15,168	338	31,737	121,407	18,534	263,116 (bu)	226,051 (bu)	569,507 (bu)	21,815	11,540	33,355
Feb	14,451	379	31,010	128,471	18,829	254,694	216,333	566,718	20,668	11,743	32,412
Mar	14,209	365	29,029	131,915	20,841	258,400	220,972	574,351	19,015	11,006	30,021
Apr	16,397	350	28,215	143,690 (bt)	17,345	270,401 (bv)	232,814 (bv)	592,174 (bt)(bv)	20,941	10,705	31,646
May	17,729	430	29,466	143,586	17,533	267,719	228,930	592,927	20,479	11,898	32,377
Jun	14,226	359	26,214	137,496	18,847	263,418	226,385	576,515	19,452	12,363	31,815
Jul	16,195	255	24,101	145,291	19,830	281,244	225,932	581,516	19,415	10,697	30,112
Aug	16,316	265	24,110	144,641	19,511	253,099	218,235	570,015	18,077	11,044	29,122
Sep	14,502	196	26,632	144,755	19,919	254,721	220,410	572,744	18,046	11,161	29,207
Oct	16,312	190	27,305	139,828	20,854	247,097 (bw)	214,173 (bw)	561,223 (bw)	17,330	11,353	28,683
Nov	16,006	201	31,983	145,260	20,322	245,492 (bx)	210,968 (bx)	567,113 (bx)	17,187	11,531	28,718
Dec	15,219	167	35,034	130,470	20,635	263,445 (by)	231,478 (cb)	570,219 (by)	13,599 (by)	10,976	24,574 (by)
2013 Jan	16,674	138	36,388	138,457	21,537	270,987 (bz)	239,672 (bz)	587,908 (bz)	13,491	11,773	25,264
Feb	18,581	162	39,285	146,400	19,956	271,204	238,559	599,475	12,602	11,870	24,471
Mar	18,356	114	43,419	148,059	20,062	258,971	227,429	592,377	12,786	15,662	28,448
Apr	24,591	141	36,875	153,536	20,008	258,187	228,251	598,081	11,600	15,091	26,692
May	17,845	136	31,694	170,801	19,823	259,290	230,697	604,974	12,597	14,050	26,648
Jun	19,962	106	31,591	155,505	19,585	245,915	217,564	578,433	12,558	14,218	26,776
Jul	20,952	133	36,468	152,882	20,600	239,693 (ca)	221,647 (cc)	576,022	11,503	13,407	24,909
Aug	19,238	154	39,283	149,153	20,837	235,271	218,266	567,708	10,500	13,292	23,793
Sep	21,051	143	42,726	133,127	20,889	226,313	210,721	547,817	10,187 (ce)	14,329	24,516 (ce)
Oct	21,263	140	44,701	138,469	21,081	228,405	213,284	556,521	10,412	13,671	24,083
Nov	14,885 (bs)	116	42,204	143,684	21,420	226,951 (bp)	210,945 (bp)	545,233 (bq)(bs)(cd)	10,943	13,586	24,529
Dec	16,171	107	44,363	139,675	21,351	201,474	185,640	518,179 (br)	14,292	12,174	26,466

12.4b Industrial analysis of monetary financial institutions lending to UK residents

£ millions   Not seasonally adjusted

Amounts outstanding of lending in all currencies

	Fund management activities	Activities auxiliary to financial intermediation			Total	Total financial and non-financial businesses	Individuals and individual trusts			Total UK residents
		Central clearing counterparties	Other auxiliary activities	Total			Lending secured on dwellings inc. bridging finance	Other loans and advances	Total	
RPM	TBTU	B3X2	B8FE	TBTV	B5H8	Z92T	TBTX	TBTY	TBTW	TBSA
2012 Jan	56,137	149,566	4,180	153,745	209,882	1,313,572	1,013,391	117,342	1,130,733	2,444,305
Feb	57,501	163,087	4,642	167,728	225,229	1,322,099	1,013,654	116,214	1,129,868	2,451,966
Mar	57,696	155,176	4,026	159,202	216,898	1,315,634	1,015,281	115,787	1,131,068	2,446,702
Apr	63,396	138,628 (ch)	4,055	142,683 (ch)	206,079 (ch)	1,323,305	1,015,993	114,544	1,130,536	2,453,842 (bv)
May	66,218	127,904	4,720	132,624	198,842	1,315,476	1,017,148	114,117	1,131,265	2,446,741
Jun	63,308	134,445	4,161	138,606	201,913	1,298,644	1,025,330 (cm)	114,192	1,139,522 (cm)	2,438,166
Jul	61,911	130,191	4,793	134,984	196,895	1,296,311	1,027,753	113,770	1,141,523	2,437,833
Aug	61,026	129,462	4,494	133,956	194,982	1,279,279	1,028,818	113,428	1,142,247	2,421,525
Sep	61,134	138,100	4,387	142,486	203,620	1,289,762	1,029,552	113,363	1,142,915	2,432,677
Oct	57,210	122,985	4,967	127,952	185,162	1,258,095	1,030,343	112,684	1,143,027	2,401,122 (bw)
Nov	73,899 (cf)	120,775	4,687	125,462	199,361 (cf)	1,273,945	1,031,536	112,445	1,143,981	2,417,927 (bi)(bx)(cf)
Dec	73,837	147,671 (ci)	4,934	152,605 (ci)	226,442 (ci)	1,295,740	1,029,910 (cb)	113,527	1,143,437 (cb)	2,439,177 (cs)
2013 Jan	82,048	146,799	5,440	152,239	234,287	1,324,509	1,030,138	106,174 (cp)(cq)	1,136,313 (cp)(cq)	2,460,822 (cp)(ct)
Feb	88,189	146,640	4,929	151,568	239,757	1,339,773 (bm)	1,029,509	106,157	1,135,666	2,475,439 (bm)
Mar	91,560	146,117	5,034	151,151	242,711	1,338,328	1,029,204	105,426	1,134,631	2,472,958
Apr	91,907	142,183	5,359	147,542	239,449	1,330,628	1,028,955	105,832	1,134,787	2,465,415
May	94,195	154,236	5,121	159,357	253,552	1,348,607	1,029,707	105,920	1,135,627	2,484,234
Jun	86,030	144,030	5,017	149,047	235,077	1,302,352	1,031,523	106,383	1,137,906	2,440,258
Jul	86,119	130,543	4,932	135,474	221,593	1,285,796 (cl)	1,033,249	108,473 (cr)	1,141,723 (cr)	2,427,519
Aug	91,222	140,963	5,126	146,088	237,311	1,285,924	1,034,692	108,662	1,143,354	2,429,278
Sep	91,504	149,348	7,720	157,068	248,572	1,277,057	1,035,877	109,931	1,145,808	2,422,866
Oct	89,425	140,124 (cj)	5,166 (ck)	145,290	234,715	1,271,175	1,038,641	109,319	1,147,960	2,419,135
Nov	92,638 (cg)	145,113	4,650	149,763	242,401 (cg)	1,265,568 (bp)(bq)	1,042,602 (cn)(co)	109,642	1,152,244 (cn)(co)	2,417,812 (bp)(bq)(co)
Dec	95,773	128,442	4,970	133,412	229,185	1,224,756 (br)	1,043,652	109,620	1,153,272	2,378,027 (br)

Source: Bank of England

12.4b Industrial analysis of monetary financial institutions lending to UK residents

£ millions   Not seasonally adjusted

Amounts outstanding of lending in all currencies

Notes to table

Movements in amounts outstanding can reflect breaks in data series as well as underlying flows. For changes data, users are recommended to refer directly to the appropriate series or data tables. Further explanation can be found at: www.bankofengland.co.uk/statistics/Pages/iadb/notesiadb/Changes_flows_growth_rates.aspx.

(ba) Due to improvements in reporting at one institution, the amounts outstanding decreased by £1bn. This effect has been adjusted out of the flows for June 2013.

(bb) Due to improvements in reporting at one institution, the amounts outstanding increased by £6bn. This effect has been adjusted out of the flows for November 2013.

(bc) Due to improvements in reporting at one institution, the amounts outstanding increased by £1bn. This effect has been adjusted out of the flows for November 2013.

(bd) Due to improvements in reporting at one institution, the amounts outstanding decreased by £1bn. This effect has been adjusted out of the flows for November 2013.

(be) Due to improvements in reporting at one institution, the amounts outstanding increased by £0.7bn. This effect has been adjusted out of the flows for June 2013.

(bf) Due to a reclassification by one reporting institution, the amounts outstanding decreased by £1bn. This effect has been adjusted out of the flows for September 2013.

(bg) Due to improvements in reporting at one institution, the amounts outstanding increased by £2bn. This effect has been adjusted out of the flows for November 2013.

(bh) Due to improvements in reporting at one institution, the amounts outstanding decreased by £0.6bn. This effect has been adjusted out of the flows for May 2012.

(bi) Following a sale of loans by one reporting institution, the amounts outstanding decreased by £0.5bn. This effect has been adjusted out of the flows for November 2012.

(bj) Due to a change in the reporting population, this series has increased by £1bn. The effect has been adjusted out of the flows for December 2012.

(bk) Due to loan transfers out of the UK MFI population, the amounts outstanding decreased by £2bn. This effect has been adjusted out of the flows for August 2013.

(bl) Due to improvements in reporting at one institution, the amounts outstanding decreased by £7bn. This effect has been adjusted out of the flows for November 2013.

(bm) Due to a reclassification at one institution, the amounts outstanding increased by £0.6bn. This effect has been adjusted out of the flows for February 2013.

(bn) Due to a restructuring at one reporting institution, the amounts outstanding increased by £3bn. This effect has been adjusted out of the flows for November 2013.

(bo) Due to improvements in reporting at one institution, the amounts outstanding decreased by £8bn. This effect has been adjusted out of the flows for November 2013.

(bp) Due to a restructuring at one reporting institution, the amounts outstanding decreased by £3bn. This effect has been adjusted out of the flows for November 2013.

(bq) Due to improvements in reporting at one institution, the amounts outstanding decreased by £1bn. This effect has been adjusted out of the flows for November 2013.

(br) Due to improvements in reporting at one institution, the amounts outstanding decreased by £2bn. This effect has been adjusted out of the flows for December 2013.

(bs) Due to improvements in reporting at one institution, the amounts outstanding decreased by £4bn. This effect has been adjusted out of the flows for November 2013.

(bt) Due to changes in the reporting population, the amounts outstanding increased by £11bn. This effect has been adjusted out of the flows for April 2012.

(bu) Due to a change in accounting treatment at one reporting institution, the amounts outstanding increased by £12bn. The effect has been adjusted out of the flows for January 2012.

(bv) Due to a change in treatment at one reporting institution, the amounts outstanding increased by £50bn. This effect has been adjusted out of the flows for April 2012.

(bw) Due to a change in treatment at one reporting institution, the amounts outstanding decreased by £55bn. This effect has been adjusted out of the flows for October 2012.

(bx) Due to improvements in reporting at one institution, the amounts outstanding decreased by £4bn. This effect has been adjusted out of the flows for November 2012.

(by) Due to a change in the reporting population, this series has decreased by £3bn. The effect has been adjusted out of the flows for December 2012.

(bz) Due to a restructuring at one reporting institution the amounts outstanding decreased by £2bn. This effect has been adjusted out of the flows for January 2013.

(ca) Due to improvements in reporting at one institution, the amounts outstanding decreased by £2bn. This effect has been adjusted out of the flows for July 2013.

(cb) Due to a change in the reporting population, this series has decreased by £2bn. The effect has been adjusted out of the flows for December 2012.

(cc) Due to improvements in reporting at one institution, the amounts outstanding increased by £2bn. This effect has been adjusted out of the flows for July 2013.

(cd) Due to a restructuring at one reporting institution, the amounts outstanding decreased by £6bn. This effect has been adjusted out of the flows for November 2013.

(ce) Due to a reclassification by one reporting institution, the amounts outstanding increased by £1bn. This effect has been adjusted out of the flows for November 2012.

(cf) Due to a change in accounting treatment at one reporting institution, the amounts outstanding increased by £8bn. This effect has been adjusted out of the flows for September 2013.

(cg) Due to improvements in reporting at one institution, the amounts outstanding increased by £4bn. This effect has been adjusted out of the flows for November 2013.

(ch) Due to changes in the reporting population, the amounts outstanding decreased by £11bn. This effect has been adjusted out of the flows for April 2012.

(ci) Due to a change in the reporting population, this series has increased by £12bn. The effect has been adjusted out of the flows for December 2012.

(cj) Due to improvements in reporting at one institution, the amounts outstanding increased by £2bn. This effect has been adjusted out of the flows for October 2013.

(ck) Due to improvements in reporting at one institution, the amounts outstanding decreased by £2bn. This effect has been adjusted out of the flows for October 2013.

(cl) Due to improvements in reporting at one institution, the amounts outstanding decreased by £4bn. This effect has been adjusted out of the flows for July 2013.

(cm) Due to a change in accounting treatment at one reporting institution, the amounts outstanding increased by £7bn. This effect has been adjusted out of the flows for June 2012.

(cn) Due to improvements in reporting at one institution, the amounts outstanding increased by £1bn. This effect has been adjusted out of the flows for November 2013.

(co) Following a purchase of loans by one reporting institution, the amounts outstanding increased by £2bn. This effect has been adjusted out of the flows for November 2013.

(cp) Due to a change in the reporting population, the amounts outstanding decreased by £8bn. The effect has been adjusted out of the flows for January 2013.

(cq) Due to a restructuring at one reporting institution the amounts outstanding increased by £1bn. This effect has been adjusted out of the flows for January 2013.

(cr) Following a purchase of loans by one reporting institution, the amounts outstanding increased by £2bn. This effect has been adjusted out of the flows for July 2013.

(cs) Due to a change in the reporting population, this series has increased by £5bn. The effect has been adjusted out of the flows for December 2012.

(ct) Due to a restructuring at one reporting institution the amounts outstanding decreased by £1bn. This effect has been adjusted out of the flows for January 2013.

12.4c Industrial analysis of monetary financial institutions lending to UK residents

£ millions Not seasonally adjusted

Amounts outstanding of facilities granted in sterling

| | Agriculture, hunting and forestry | Fishing | Mining and quarrying | Manufacturing | | | | | | | | | Electricity, gas and water supply | | | |
				Food, beverages and tobacco	Textiles, wearing apparel and leather	Pulp, paper, and printing	Chemicals, pharmaceuticals, rubber and plastics	Non-metallic mineral products and metals	Machinery, equipment and transport equipment	Electrical, medical and optical equipment	Other manufacturing	Total	Electricity, gas steam and air conditioning	Water collection and sewerage	Waste management related services and remediation activities	Total
RPM	TCCC	TCCD	TCCE	TCCG	TCCH	TCCI	TCCJ	TCCK	TCCL	TCCM	TCCN	TCCF	TCCO	TCCP	B3FE	B3FS
2012 Jan	14,884	311	2,908	9,076	999	2,512	5,949	4,231	8,146	2,725	3,820	37,457	10,250	4,704	1,964	16,918
Feb	14,817	303	2,447	9,600	1,022	2,650	6,132	4,248	8,327	2,776	3,724	38,479	10,705	4,652	2,135	17,492
Mar	15,017	304	2,477	9,143	968	2,597	6,100	4,301	8,779	2,757	3,678	38,322	9,792	4,702	2,050	16,545
Apr	14,959	293	3,038	9,430	945	2,741	6,111	4,444	8,413	2,894	3,795	38,772	9,663	4,555	2,157	16,376
May	15,026	298	2,650	8,932	964	2,714	6,187	4,424	8,743	2,939	3,737	38,640	9,619	4,529	2,122	16,271
Jun	15,105	298	2,500	9,578	991	2,736	6,343	4,645	8,597	2,915	3,736	39,541	9,640	4,905	2,296	16,840
Jul	15,335	296	2,435	8,884	980	2,674	6,418	4,507	8,872	2,900	3,831	39,065	10,058	4,994	2,262	17,314
Aug	15,468	325	2,378	8,716	926	2,653	6,410	4,806	9,261	3,050	3,996	39,818	10,184	4,919	2,220	17,323
Sep	15,669	335	2,184	8,754	926	2,634	6,883	4,660	9,113	2,807	3,963	39,741	10,088	5,124	2,244	17,456
Oct	15,763	343	2,333	8,598	898	2,595	7,338	4,533	9,007	2,834	3,972	39,776	10,458	5,248	2,243	17,950
Nov	15,756	319	2,325	8,737	890	2,550	7,242	4,659	9,106	2,734	3,852	39,770	10,302	5,285	2,176	17,763
Dec	16,038	297	2,389	8,470	865	2,429	7,105	4,669	9,091	2,866	3,579	39,073	10,311	5,350	2,338	17,999
2013 Jan	16,113	289	2,169	8,092	882	2,467	6,300	4,557	9,060	2,978	3,623	37,960	10,340	5,242	2,394	17,976
Feb	16,204	280	2,337	7,900	865	2,443	5,978	4,449	9,235	2,772	3,584	37,226	10,431	4,506	2,519	17,456
Mar	16,313	284	2,413	8,011	874	2,537	7,360	4,524	9,052	3,103	3,734	39,195	10,044	5,090	2,606	17,740
Apr	16,428	272	2,347	8,209	860	2,482	7,477	4,749	8,768	2,871	3,681	39,096	9,962	5,175	2,641	17,778
May	16,572	276	2,454	7,771	842	2,503	7,304	4,822	8,762	2,756	3,833	38,593	10,022	5,175	2,675	17,872
Jun	16,723	272	3,410	7,547	852	2,456	7,181	4,749	8,523 (cu)	2,754	3,983	38,044 (cu)	10,109	5,153	2,698	17,960
Jul	16,872	269	3,384	7,572	810	2,403	7,432	4,738	8,383	2,763	4,046	38,148	10,953	5,214	2,723	18,890
Aug	16,993	266	3,383	7,398	822	2,418	7,928	4,868	8,396	2,781	4,003	38,614	10,996	5,185	2,617	18,798
Sep	17,171	268	3,529	7,480	783	2,626	7,329	4,753	8,697	2,618	3,996	38,283	11,181	5,330	2,482	18,994
Oct	17,301	268	3,542	7,526	850	2,695	7,536	4,808	8,723	2,619	4,002	38,760	11,372	5,386	2,583	19,341
Nov	17,414	267	3,716	8,369	866	2,555	7,570	4,841	8,600	2,637	3,859	39,297	11,479	5,411	2,593	19,483
Dec	17,400	274	3,752	8,684	816	2,512	6,834	4,696	8,277	2,556	3,948	38,323	12,662	5,455	2,939	21,056

12.4c Industrial analysis of monetary financial institutions lending to UK residents

£ millions   Not seasonally adjusted

Amounts outstanding of facilities granted in sterling

	Development of buildings	Construction: Construction of commercial buildings	Construction: Construction of domestic buildings	Construction: Civil Engineering	Construction: Other construction activities	Construction: Total	Wholesale and retail trade: Wholesale and retail trade and repair of motor vehicles and motorcycles	Wholesale and retail trade: Wholesale trade, excluding motor vehicles and motor cycles	Wholesale and retail trade: Retail trade excluding motor vehicles and motor cycles	Wholesale and retail trade: Total	Accommodation and food service activities	Transport, storage and communication: Transportation and storage	Transport, storage and communication: Information and communication	Transport, storage and communication: Total
RPM	B7EG	B3ID	B4PC	B4PP	B5QH	TCCQ	TCCS	TCCT	TCCU	TCCR	TCCV	B5PP	B5PW	TCCW
2012 Jan	38,298	4,992	9,139	5,091	10,317	67,837	12,066	15,111	24,845	52,023	31,900	21,497	14,803	36,300
Feb	38,372	5,007	8,819	5,133	10,228	67,559	12,595	15,100	24,513	52,208	31,848	21,351	15,150	36,501
Mar	38,066	5,005	8,597	4,781	10,285	66,733	11,994	15,137	24,695	51,826	32,160	21,896	14,670	36,566
Apr	37,887	4,936	8,464	4,886	10,331	66,504	11,842	15,132	24,380	51,354	31,687	20,907	14,177	35,083
May	37,647	4,865	8,425	4,874	10,362	66,173	11,442	14,948	24,323	50,713	31,498	20,321	14,091	34,412
Jun	37,528	4,861	8,233	4,776	10,207	65,604	11,521	15,231	24,382	51,135	31,404	19,555	14,305	33,860
Jul	37,435	4,850	8,249	4,934	10,149	65,617	11,799	15,232	24,652	51,682	31,173	19,966	14,062	34,028
Aug	37,110	4,858	8,240	5,156	10,148	65,512	12,108	15,191	24,065	51,364	30,770	19,889	13,797	33,686
Sep	36,807	4,876	7,976	5,082	10,002	64,743	11,740	15,142	24,709	51,591	30,896	20,817	13,862	34,679
Oct	36,358	5,608	7,497	5,051	9,773	64,286	11,682	15,176	24,149	51,008	30,669	20,537	14,272	34,809
Nov	36,072	5,182	7,384	5,103	9,765	63,505	11,014	15,268	24,281	50,563	30,359	20,462	14,335	34,796
Dec	36,519	5,079	7,372	4,976	10,008	63,955	11,276	14,891	23,412	49,579	30,391	19,314	14,051	33,365
2013 Jan	36,190	5,108	7,691	5,175	10,048	64,212	11,910	14,911	23,779	50,600	30,390	19,124	14,089	33,213
Feb	36,247	5,111	7,641	5,120	9,860	63,979	12,495	15,054	23,699	51,248	29,815	18,384	14,174	32,558
Mar	35,780	5,119	7,466	4,955	9,919	63,239	11,916	14,899	23,591	50,405	29,631	18,844	14,469	33,314
Apr	34,968	5,222	7,381	4,873	9,717	62,162	11,775	15,713	23,727	51,215	27,521	18,835	13,641	32,476
May	34,909	5,134	7,355	4,826	9,688	61,912	11,685	15,564	23,591	50,840	27,305	18,725	13,394	32,119
Jun	34,866	4,972	7,274	4,763	9,511	61,386	12,126 (cy)	15,527	23,324	50,978 (cy)	27,220	18,890	13,062	31,952
Jul	34,593	5,061	7,051	4,734	9,451	60,890	12,433	15,047	23,118	50,597	27,225	18,938	13,612	32,551
Aug	34,298	5,195	7,173	4,717	9,516	60,900	12,069	15,677	22,634	50,379	27,176	18,812	13,424	32,235
Sep	34,065	5,276	7,279	4,657	9,477	60,754	10,894 (cz)	15,624	22,895	49,600 (cz)	27,010	19,125	13,753	32,879
Oct	34,472	5,598	7,193	4,941	9,052	61,256	10,747	15,624	22,706	49,076	26,675	19,228	13,864	33,092
Nov	41,106 (cv)	7,071 (cw)	7,287	4,953	7,950 (cx)	68,367 (cv)	10,776	15,855	23,057	49,688	28,313 (da)	19,203	14,086	33,289
Dec	39,867	6,577	7,301	4,543	7,688	65,976	10,672	16,009	23,155	49,836	27,856	19,952	14,899	34,851

12.4c Industrial analysis of monetary financial institutions lending to UK residents

£ millions   Not seasonally adjusted

Amounts outstanding of facilities granted in sterling

| RPM | Buying, selling and renting of real estate | Real estate, professional services and support activities | | | Public administration and defence | Education | Human health and social work | Recreational, personal and community service activities | | | Financial intermediation (excluding insurance and pension funds) | | | | |
| | | Professional, scientific and technical activities | Administrative and support services | Total | | | | Recreational, cultural and sporting activities | Personal and community service activities | Total | Financial leasing corporations | Non-bank credit grantors excluding credit unions and SPVs | Credit unions | Factoring corporations | Mortgage and housing credit corporations excluding SPVs |
	TCCY	B6PH	B3S2	TCCX	TCDD	TCDE	TCDF	TCDH	TCDG	B3SR	TCDJ	TCDK	TCDL	TCDM	TCDN
2012 Jan	203,750	23,172	20,782	247,704	10,787	14,072	24,796	9,055	4,795	13,850	30,249	15,430	8	6,637	60,711
Feb	202,311	22,876	20,277	245,464	11,019	14,120	24,869	8,981	4,746	13,727	30,052	15,475	5	6,726	60,588
Mar	202,238	22,972	19,830	245,039	10,503	14,183	25,004	8,893	4,784	13,676	30,223	15,221	6	7,057	61,133
Apr	200,111	22,494	19,363	241,968	10,442	14,143	25,101	8,602	4,608	13,210	29,926	14,768	5	6,943	58,575
May	198,753 (db)	22,191	19,617	240,561 (db)	11,980	14,123	25,072	8,713	4,619	13,332	30,415	14,876	5	6,997	57,756
Jun	196,811	21,910	19,779	238,500	9,977	14,157	25,219	8,657	4,578	13,235	30,289	14,772	6	7,203	58,040
Jul	195,878	21,829	19,513	237,221	10,202	13,882	25,188	8,722	4,511	13,234	30,320	14,635	3	7,085	57,556
Aug	194,770	21,519	19,694	235,983	9,912	13,862	25,102	8,611	4,452	13,063	29,444	14,675	3	7,162	56,261
Sep	193,583	21,489	19,666	234,738	10,181	13,777	25,135	8,629	4,444	13,073	30,221	14,260	3	7,333	56,351
Oct	193,215	21,503	20,106	234,824	11,222	13,825	25,291	8,112	4,542	12,654	29,940	13,554	3	7,277	55,290
Nov	191,128 (dc)	21,007	19,001	231,136 (dc)	10,465	13,899	25,202	8,038	4,398	12,436	29,728	13,455	3	7,268	54,652
Dec	191,736 (dd)	20,320	19,098	231,153 (dd)	10,149	14,345	25,321	8,336	4,328	12,664	27,950	13,618	3	7,571	52,624
2013 Jan	190,181	20,321	19,685	230,187	10,357	14,345	25,003	8,217	4,408	12,626	27,486	13,520	2	7,068	52,581
Feb	189,251	20,501	20,443 (dg)	230,194 (dg)	10,612	14,111	24,617	8,392	4,414	12,806	27,376	13,436	3	7,432	52,640
Mar	186,994	20,620	20,193	227,808	10,121	14,029	24,735	8,361	4,319	12,680	26,865	13,348	3	7,793	52,637
Apr	183,599	20,714	20,234	224,547	9,725	13,917	24,821	7,758	4,271	12,029	26,406	13,358	2	7,645	55,613
May	182,289	20,568	21,002	223,859	10,099	13,757	24,716	7,833	4,246	12,079	26,023	13,282	2	7,923	56,505
Jun	181,694	20,814	21,069	223,576	10,629	13,734	24,690	7,311	4,206	11,517	25,943	13,103	6	8,415	56,711
Jul	179,755	20,623	21,373	221,751	10,112	13,378	24,523	7,250	4,251	11,501	25,408	13,075	2	8,137	57,061
Aug	176,692 (de)	20,548	21,604	218,843 (de)	9,706	13,457	24,467	7,387	4,297	11,685	24,362	13,280	2	8,242	56,850
Sep	175,783	20,905	21,766	218,453	10,756	13,349	24,466	7,417	4,318	11,735	24,453	13,409	2	7,917	57,048
Oct	174,722	21,285	21,918	217,925	10,773	13,263	24,300	7,497	4,277	11,774	23,902	13,431	2	8,275	56,076
Nov	164,024 (df)	19,612 (cx)	25,824 (dh)	209,460 (dh)(di)	9,914	13,123	23,924	7,394	4,045	11,439	24,155	14,146	2	5,004 (dk)	52,655 (dk)
Dec	163,324	20,018	26,262	209,605	9,254	12,660	23,399	7,448	3,920	11,369	24,406	14,233	2	5,104	51,450 (dl)

12.4c Industrial analysis of monetary financial institutions lending to UK residents

£ millions   Not seasonally adjusted

Amounts outstanding of facilities granted in sterling

RPM	Investment and unit trusts excluding money market mutual funds	Money market mutual funds	Financial intermediation (excluding insurance and pension funds)						Insurance companies & pension funds		
			Bank holding companies	Securities dealers	SPVs related to securitisation	Other financial intermediaries	of which intragroup activity	Total	Insurance companies	Pension funds	Total
	TCDO	TCDP	TCDQ	TCDR	B8EX	TCDS	B7FF	TCDI	B7FK	B3W9	TCDT
2012 Jan	8,367	122	27,685	20,565	20,408	155,046 (dm)	139,884 (dm)	345,229 (dm)	20,720	11,422	32,142
Feb	8,088	110	26,378	25,460	20,940	147,953	133,649	341,775	20,746	11,504	32,250
Mar	8,888	112	24,219	30,337	22,968	148,016	134,178	348,178	19,303	10,329	29,632
Apr	8,377	111	23,510	34,935	19,526	157,232 (dn)	144,142 (dn)	353,908 (dn)	20,879	10,257	31,135
May	8,501	115	24,199	31,489	19,870	153,658	139,700	347,882	20,413	11,445	31,858
Jun	9,153	113	21,586	30,886	21,438	153,151	139,311	346,636	19,533	11,717	31,250
Jul	9,273	112	21,583	29,667	20,870	154,076	140,715	345,180	19,670	10,382	30,052
Aug	9,599	113	21,576	31,578	20,641	154,092	142,091	345,143	18,505	10,679	29,183
Sep	9,283	113	23,296	27,149	20,909	158,684	144,637	347,601	18,534	10,836	29,370
Oct	8,754	112	24,457	27,198	21,801	153,339 (do)	139,752 (do)	341,725 (do)	18,302	11,255	29,556
Nov	9,577	112	28,779	30,378	21,051	147,596 (dp)	133,548 (dp)	342,600 (dp)	18,210	11,371	29,581
Dec	8,821	63	28,857	21,463	20,895	163,008	149,955	344,872	14,569 (dt)	10,858	25,426 (dt)
2013 Jan	9,532	64	30,115	20,882	21,447	167,051 (dq)	154,367 (dq)	349,748 (dq)	14,590	11,711	26,301
Feb	11,242	104	32,918	23,746	20,410	163,005	149,405	352,313	13,526	11,809	25,335
Mar	9,369	66	35,988	19,736	20,388	154,679	141,714	340,871	13,469	15,126	28,595
Apr	8,830	65	29,473	20,337	20,468	151,013	138,761	333,709	13,131	14,744	27,875
May	8,638	65	24,424	21,043	20,299	151,754	139,754	329,958	13,209	13,899	27,108
Jun	9,472	66	24,535	20,552	20,164	149,571	137,757	328,539	13,014	14,148	27,162
Jul	9,940	67	29,830	22,066	21,365	151,087 (dr)	139,004 (dr)	338,036	11,949	13,339	25,288
Aug	10,287	63	33,134	21,087	21,407	151,991	139,923	340,706	10,998	13,183	24,181
Sep	10,463	64	35,512	19,211	21,092	151,757	140,384	340,927	10,534 (du)	14,124	24,658 (du)
Oct	9,707	64	35,443	21,503	21,225	153,594	141,693	343,222	11,071	13,634	24,705
Nov	9,833	65	35,454	22,469	21,601	152,590 (dj)	141,054 (dj)	337,975 (dk)(ds)	11,490	13,564	25,054
Dec	11,084	66	35,802	23,354	21,386	131,266	119,639	318,152 (dl)	15,560	12,311	27,871

12.4c Industrial analysis of monetary financial institutions lending to UK residents

£ millions   Not seasonally adjusted

Amounts outstanding of facilities granted in sterling

RPM	Fund management activities	Activities auxiliary to financial intermediation				Total financial and non-financial businesses	Individuals and individual trusts			Total UK residents
		Other			Total		Lending secured on dwellings inc. bridging finance	Other loans and advances	Total	
		Central clearing counterparties	Other auxiliary activities	Total						
	TCDU	B3X6	B3Y4	TCDV	B8FO	Z94D	TCDX	TCDY	TCDW	TCCA
2012 Jan	24,598	63,411	4,331	67,741	92,339	1,041,458	1,066,661	167,796	1,234,456	2,275,914
Feb	24,862	72,423	4,211	76,634	101,496	1,046,375	1,067,069	166,801	1,232,870	2,279,245
Mar	25,152	65,188	4,093	69,281	94,432	1,040,598	1,067,078	166,695	1,233,773	2,274,371
Apr	25,160	64,381	4,098	68,478	93,638	1,041,611	1,068,916	165,447	1,234,363	2,275,974 (dn)
May	26,396	61,121	3,935	65,057	91,453	1,031,942	1,069,692	165,193	1,234,885	2,266,827
Jun	26,007	72,015	3,949	75,964	101,971	1,037,232	1,076,865 (dz)	165,753	1,242,618 (dz)	2,279,850
Jul	29,336	62,224	4,049	66,273	95,609	1,027,512	1,078,794	165,239	1,244,032	2,271,544
Aug	29,739	65,841	3,763	69,604	99,343	1,028,237	1,078,511	165,011	1,243,522	2,271,758
Sep	30,077	71,339	3,524	74,863	104,940	1,036,109	1,078,802	165,125	1,243,926	2,280,035
Oct	31,044	63,814	3,624	67,438	98,482	1,024,516	1,078,834	164,480	1,243,314	2,267,830 (do)
Nov	33,877	67,949	3,923	71,871	105,749	1,026,224	1,080,443	164,577	1,245,020	2,271,244 (dc)(dp)
Dec	34,707	83,872 (dv)	4,237	88,109 (dv)	122,816 (dv)	1,039,833	1,078,041 (ea)	165,755	1,243,796 (ea)	2,283,628 (eg)
2013 Jan	36,053	74,719	4,865	79,584	115,637	1,037,127	1,081,567	159,078 (ed)(ee)	1,240,645 (ed)(ee)	2,277,772 (ed)(eh)
Feb	38,542	68,298	4,062	72,360	110,902	1,031,994 (dg)	1,080,763	159,288	1,240,051	2,272,045 (dg)
Mar	39,323	68,345	4,216	72,560	111,883	1,023,257	1,084,354	159,119	1,243,473	2,266,730
Apr	40,556	71,987	4,437	76,424	116,980	1,012,900	1,084,410	159,478	1,243,888	2,256,788
May	39,397	74,400	4,096	78,496	117,894	1,007,414	1,084,719	160,088	1,244,808	2,252,222
Jun	39,673	67,905	4,022	71,928	111,601	999,394	1,087,611	160,609	1,248,221	2,247,614
Jul	40,957	61,694	3,942	65,636	106,593	1,000,009 (dy)	1,089,650	162,714 (ef)	1,252,364 (ef)	2,252,373
Aug	43,066	69,439	4,217	73,656	116,722	1,008,509	1,091,354	163,302	1,254,656	2,263,165
Sep	43,978	73,219	6,050	79,269	123,247	1,016,079	1,093,039	164,224	1,257,263	2,273,342
Oct	45,387	63,098 (dw)	3,982 (dx)	67,080	112,467	1,007,741	1,096,774	163,863	1,260,636	2,268,377
Nov	46,415	63,093	3,841	66,935	113,349	1,004,072 (dj)(dk)	1,102,019 (eb)(ec)	164,258	1,266,277 (eb)(ec)	2,270,350 (dj)(dk)(ec)
Dec	47,828	50,823	3,886	54,709	102,537	974,171 (dl)	1,102,649	163,624	1,266,273	2,240,444 (dl)

Source: Bank of England

12.4c Industrial analysis of monetary financial institutions lending to UK residents

£ millions   Not seasonally adjusted

Amounts outstanding of facilities granted in sterling

Notes to table

Movements in amounts outstanding can reflect breaks in data series as well as underlying flows.   For changes data, users are recommended to refer directly to the appropriate series or data tables.   Further explanation can be found at: www.bankofengland.co.uk/statistics/Pages/iadb/notesiadb/Changes_flows_growth_rates.aspx.

(cu) Due to improvements in reporting at one institution, the amounts outstanding decreased by £0.7bn. This effect has been adjusted out of the flows for June 2013.

(cv) Due to improvements in reporting at one institution, the amounts outstanding increased by £6bn. This effect has been adjusted out of the flows for November 2013.

(cw) Due to improvements in reporting at one institution, the amounts outstanding increased by £1bn. This effect has been adjusted out of the flows for November 2013.

(cx) Due to improvements in reporting at one institution, the amounts outstanding decreased by £1bn. This effect has been adjusted out of the flows for November 2013.

(cy) Due to improvements in reporting at one institution, the amounts outstanding increased by £0.4bn. This effect has been adjusted out of the flows for June 2013.

(cz) Due to a reclassification by one reporting institution, the amounts outstanding decreased by £1bn. This effect has been adjusted out of the flows for September 2013.

(da) Due to improvements in reporting at one institution, the amounts outstanding increased by £2bn. This effect has been adjusted out of the flows for November 2013.

(db) Due to improvements in reporting at one institution, the amounts outstanding decreased by £0.6bn. This effect has been adjusted out of the flows for May 2012.

(dc) Following a sale of loans by one reporting institution, the amounts outstanding decreased by £0.5bn. This effect has been adjusted out of the flows for November 2012.

(dd) Due to a change in the reporting population, this series has increased by £1bn. The effect has been adjusted out of the flows for December 2012.

(de) Due to loan transfers out of the UK MFI population, the amounts outstanding decreased by £2bn. This effect has been adjusted out of the flows for August 2013.

(df) Due to improvements in reporting at one institution, the amounts outstanding decreased by £7bn. This effect has been adjusted out of the flows for November 2013.

(dg) Due to a reclassification at one institution, the amounts outstanding increased by £0.6bn. This effect has been adjusted out of the flows for February 2013.

(dh) Due to improvements in reporting at one institution, the amounts outstanding increased by £3bn. This effect has been adjusted out of the flows for November 2013.

(di) Due to improvements in reporting at one institution, the amounts outstanding decreased by £8bn. This effect has been adjusted out of the flows for November 2013.

(dj) Due to a restructuring at one reporting institution, the amounts outstanding increased by £3bn. This effect has been adjusted out of the flows for November 2013.

(dk) Due to improvements in reporting at one institution, the amounts outstanding decreased by £1bn. This effect has been adjusted out of the flows for November 2013.

(dl) Due to improvements in reporting at one institution, the amounts outstanding decreased by £2bn. This effect has been adjusted out of the flows for December 2013.

(dm) Due to a change in accounting treatment at one reporting institution, the amounts outstanding increased by £12bn. The effect has been adjusted out of the flows for January 2012.

(dn) Due to a change in treatment at one reporting institution, the amounts outstanding increased by £5bn. This effect has been adjusted out of the flows for April 2012.

(do) Due to a change in treatment at one reporting institution, the amounts outstanding decreased by £5bn. This effect has been adjusted out of the flows for October 2012.

(dp) Due to improvements in reporting at one institution, the amounts outstanding decreased by £4bn. This effect has been adjusted out of the flows for November 2012.

(dq) Due to a restructuring at one reporting institution the amounts outstanding decreased by £2bn. This effect has been adjusted out of the flows for January 2013.

(dr) Due to improvements in reporting at one institution, the amounts outstanding increased by £2bn. This effect has been adjusted out of the flows for July 2013.

(ds) Due to a restructuring at one institution, the amounts outstanding decreased by £6bn. This effect has been adjusted out of the flows for November 2013.

(dt) Due to a change in the reporting population, this series has decreased by £3bn. The effect has been adjusted out of the flows for December 2012.

(du) Due to a reclassification by one reporting institution, the amounts outstanding increased by £1bn. This effect has been adjusted out of the flows for September 2013.

(dv) Due to a change in the reporting population, this series has increased by £8bn. The effect has been adjusted out of the flows for December 2012.

(dw) Due to improvements in reporting at one institution, the amounts outstanding increased by £2bn. This effect has been adjusted out of the flows for October 2013.

(dx) Due to improvements in reporting at one institution, the amounts outstanding decreased by £2bn. This effect has been adjusted out of the flows for October 2013.

(dy) Due to improvements in reporting at one institution, the amounts outstanding increased by £5bn. This effect has been adjusted out of the flows for July 2013.

(dz) Due to a change in accounting treatment at one reporting institution, the amounts outstanding increased by £7bn. This effect has been adjusted out of the flows for June 2012.

(ea) Due to a change in the reporting population, this series has decreased by £2bn. The effect has been adjusted out of the flows for December 2012.

(eb) Due to improvements in reporting at one institution, the amounts outstanding increased by £1bn. This effect has been adjusted out of the flows for November 2013.

(ec) Following a purchase of loans by one reporting institution, the amounts outstanding increased by £2bn. This effect has been adjusted out of the flows for November 2013.

(ed) Due to a change in the reporting population, the amounts outstanding decreased by £8bn. The effect has been adjusted out of the flows for January 2013.

(ee) Due to a restructuring at one reporting institution the amounts outstanding increased by £1bn. This effect has been adjusted out of the flows for January 2013.

(ef) Following a purchase of loans by one reporting institution, the amounts outstanding increased by £2bn. This effect has been adjusted out of the flows for July 2013.

(eg) Due to a change in the reporting population, this series has increased by £4bn. The effect has been adjusted out of the flows for December 2012.

(eh) Due to a restructuring at one reporting institution the amounts outstanding decreased by £1bn. This effect has been adjusted out of the flows for January 2013.

12.4d Industrial analysis of monetary financial institutions lending to UK residents

£ millions   Not seasonally adjusted

Amounts outstanding of facilities granted in all currencies

RPM	Agriculture, hunting and forestry	Fishing	Mining and quarrying	Manufacturing									Electricity, gas and water supply			Total
				Food, beverages and tobacco	Textiles, wearing apparel and leather	Pulp, paper, and printing	Chemicals, pharmaceuticals, rubber and plastics	Non-metallic mineral products and metals	Machinery, equipment and transport equipment	Electrical, medical and optical equipment	Other manufacturing	Total	Electricity, gas steam and air conditioning	Water collection and sewerage	Waste management related services and remediation activities	
	TCAC	TCAD	TCAE	TCAG	TCAH	TCAI	TCAJ	TCAK	TCAL	TCAM	TCAN	TCAF	TCAO	TCAP	B3FF	B3FT
2012 Jan	15,391	321	22,747	17,392	1,869	4,321	14,199	8,355	13,714	6,172	6,415	72,437	16,318	5,329	2,328	23,975
Feb	15,298	314	21,164	17,236	1,702	4,285	14,568	8,533	13,543	5,911	6,137	71,915	16,744	5,239	2,489	24,472
Mar	15,512	315	21,691	17,041	1,669	4,269	14,917	8,535	13,937	5,816	5,686	71,868	16,070	5,290	2,432	23,792
Apr	15,430	313	22,349	17,123	1,614	4,352	14,281	8,592	13,230	5,916	5,707	70,814	15,646	5,029	2,427	23,102
May	15,510	312	22,060	17,171	1,650	4,398	13,831	8,587	13,516	6,123	5,692	70,968	15,773	4,997	2,355	23,124
Jun	15,602	313	21,683	17,548	1,642	4,442	14,752	8,739	13,869	6,068	5,732	72,793	15,322	5,396	2,523	23,240
Jul	15,816	315	21,106	17,016	1,713	4,466	14,211	8,561	14,132	6,020	5,583	71,702	16,333	5,483	2,510	24,326
Aug	15,935	346	21,455	17,061	1,623	4,300	13,854	8,991	14,646	6,166	5,703	72,343	16,516	5,410	2,457	24,383
Sep	16,099	357	21,314	17,057	1,603	4,217	14,519	8,793	14,821	5,821	5,629	72,459	16,197	5,594	2,485	24,276
Oct	16,178	366	21,640	16,867	1,585	4,157	14,652	8,670	14,409	5,795	5,661	71,797	16,695	5,673	2,502	24,870
Nov	16,188	345	21,839	17,120	1,569	4,138	14,499	8,537	14,728	5,701	5,633	71,925	17,211	5,730	2,491	25,432
Dec	16,425	326	21,828	16,227	1,506	3,887	14,238	8,582	14,868	5,790	5,346	70,445	16,344	5,749	2,679	24,772
2013 Jan	16,478	309	22,276	16,413	1,556	3,969	14,104	8,414	14,804	5,965	5,250	70,476	16,256	5,670	2,692	24,617
Feb	16,557	298	23,693	16,220	1,483	3,974	13,936	8,447	15,143	5,813	5,150	70,167	16,570	5,137	2,858	24,565
Mar	16,676	303	26,042	16,377	1,482	4,063	14,891	8,663	14,852	6,081	5,323	71,733	16,103	5,606	2,985	24,694
Apr	16,770	294	25,089	16,024	1,478	3,918	15,346	8,270	14,740	5,937	5,177	70,889	15,867	5,581	2,932	24,379
May	16,920	288	25,810	15,920	1,485	3,949	15,585	8,704	14,782	5,789	5,285	71,500	16,021	5,559	2,915	24,495
Jun	17,065	284	26,533	15,824	1,511	3,889	15,794	8,458	13,875 (ei)	5,824	5,444	70,620 (ei)	16,110	5,582	2,951	24,643
Jul	17,219	281	26,943	16,183	1,483	3,714	16,207	8,520	13,978	5,922	5,487	71,494	17,828	5,647	3,051	26,526
Aug	17,365	277	25,472	16,032	1,502	3,602	16,412	8,466	13,704	5,728	5,409	70,854	19,160	5,611	2,906	27,677
Sep	17,511	279	24,395	15,993	1,423	3,898	15,465	8,206	14,007	5,382	5,306	69,679	19,091	5,735	2,816	27,642
Oct	17,654	278	25,260	15,939	1,522	3,860	15,975	8,279	14,126	5,561	5,379	70,640	18,883	5,813	2,925	27,620
Nov	17,771	276	24,856	16,308	1,549	3,779	15,907	8,318	13,863	5,467	5,079	70,269	18,568	5,816	2,898	27,282
Dec	17,746	284	25,394	16,048	1,440	3,757	14,864	8,089	13,781	5,383	5,219	68,581	19,640	5,800	3,232	28,672

12.4d Industrial analysis of monetary financial institutions lending to UK residents

£ millions   Not seasonally adjusted

Amounts outstanding of facilities granted in all currencies

	Development of buildings	Construction				Total	Wholesale and retail trade				Accommodation and food service activities	Transport, storage and communication			Total
		Construction of commercial buildings	Construction of domestic buildings	Civil Engineering	Other construction activities		Wholesale and retail trade and repair of motor vehicles and motorcycles	Wholesale trade, excluding motor vehicles and motor cycles	Retail trade excluding motor vehicles and motor cycles	Total		Transportation and storage	Information and communication	
RPM	B7EH	B3IE	B4PD	B3KK	B5PC	TCAQ	TCAS	TCAT	TCAU	TCAR	TCAV	B3NF	B5PX	TCAW
2012 Jan	40,171	5,402	9,547	5,405	10,747	71,272	13,163	20,641	30,859	64,662	33,752	29,539	26,698	56,237
Feb	40,153	5,387	9,197	5,443	10,662	70,841	13,820	20,606	30,038	64,464	33,673	28,696	27,303	55,999
Mar	39,797	5,371	8,954	5,085	10,707	69,914	13,328	21,055	30,611	64,993	33,840	29,460	26,514	55,974
Apr	39,671	5,292	8,756	5,179	10,724	69,622	13,254	21,177	30,022	64,452	33,198	28,105	25,964	54,069
May	39,175	5,253	8,704	5,165	10,769	69,066	13,072	21,010	30,018	64,101	33,207	27,875	25,993	53,868
Jun	39,077	5,276	8,548	5,054	10,605	68,560	12,723	21,358	29,776	63,856	33,024	27,357	26,553	53,911
Jul	38,947	5,221	8,561	5,203	10,546	68,477	13,185	21,727	30,309	65,222	32,804	27,418	26,281	53,699
Aug	38,673	5,242	8,538	5,419	10,495	68,367	13,502	21,952	29,809	65,264	32,387	27,159	26,104	53,264
Sep	38,578	5,224	8,406	5,312	10,489	68,008	13,031	21,604	30,232	64,868	32,578	28,684	25,911	54,595
Oct	38,008	6,105	7,782	5,272	10,203	67,370	12,910	21,532	29,506	63,948	32,321	28,683	26,322	55,004
Nov	37,613	5,810	7,582	5,332	10,161	66,498	12,009	22,140	29,863	64,013	32,078	28,782	26,382	55,164
Dec	38,081	5,726	7,607	5,256	10,430	67,100	12,125	21,350	29,124	62,599	31,859	26,990	25,207	52,197
2013 Jan	37,633	5,792	7,917	5,382	10,526	67,250	12,759	21,106	29,489	63,354	31,951	26,610	25,243	51,853
Feb	37,548	5,755	7,850	5,269	10,276	66,699	13,369	20,953	29,639	63,961	31,393	26,339	25,635	51,974
Mar	37,214	5,715	7,683	5,128	10,310	66,049	12,746	21,212	29,145	63,103	31,069	26,761	25,735	52,496
Apr	36,333	5,832	7,588	5,055	10,113	64,921	12,658	22,058	29,364	64,080	29,101	26,525	26,971	53,496
May	36,076	5,750	7,562	5,019	10,093	64,499	12,737	21,835	29,184	63,756	28,880	26,655	25,967	52,622
Jun	36,102	5,679	7,510	4,971	9,942	64,203	14,012 (em)	22,446	28,956	65,413 (em)	28,803	26,054	25,961	52,015
Jul	35,869	5,746	7,281	4,939	9,937	63,771	13,811	22,270	28,809	64,890	28,900	26,322	26,758	53,080
Aug	35,543	5,721	7,350	4,911	9,929	63,453	13,491	22,106	27,599	63,195	28,758	26,117	26,094	52,210
Sep	35,232	5,738	7,457	4,843	9,931	63,201	12,037 (en)	22,556	28,137	62,730 (en)	28,611	26,478	25,964	52,442
Oct	35,378	6,044	7,367	5,131	9,503	63,423	11,856	22,280	27,843	61,979	28,297	25,992	26,017	52,009
Nov	42,403 (ej)	7,506 (ek)	7,463	5,204	8,373 (el)	70,949 (ej)	11,756	22,424	28,388	62,567	29,799 (eo)	25,820	26,096	51,916
Dec	41,079	7,228	7,497	5,050	7,953	68,807	11,722	22,631	28,961	63,314	29,388	26,630	27,230	53,861

12.4d Industrial analysis of monetary financial institutions lending to UK residents

£ millions   Not seasonally adjusted

Amounts outstanding of facilities granted in all currencies

RPM	Real estate, professional services and support activities — Buying, selling and renting of real estate	Real estate — Professional, scientific and technical activities	Real estate — Administrative and support services	Real estate — Total	Public administration and defence	Education	Human health and social work	Recreational, personal and community service activities — Recreational, cultural and sporting activities	Recreational — Personal and community service activities	Recreational — Total	Financial intermediation (excluding insurance and pension funds) — Financial leasing corporations	Financial — Non-bank credit grantors excluding credit unions and SPVs	Financial — Credit unions	Financial — Factoring corporations	Financial — Mortgage and housing credit corporations excluding SPVs
	TCAY	B3QF	B3S3	TCAX	TCBD	TCBE	TCBF	TCBH	TCBG	B3T2	TCBJ	TCBK	TCBL	TCBM	TCBN
2012 Jan	208,530	27,932	26,724	263,186	11,340	14,225	25,367	10,544	5,398	15,942	39,641	17,684	9	7,288	61,259
Feb	207,161	27,414	26,210	260,786	11,802	14,273	25,431	10,539	5,281	15,821	39,313	18,228	6	7,334	61,145
Mar	207,010	27,437	25,875	260,322	11,166	14,304	25,561	10,469	5,303	15,772	38,719	18,090	6	7,631	61,681
Apr	204,707	26,853	25,010	256,570	11,264	14,243	25,661	10,031	5,075	15,106	38,012	17,832	6	7,576	59,110
May	203,330 (ep)	26,530	25,659	255,520 (ep)	12,590	14,238	25,617	10,099	5,056	15,154	39,197	17,381	6	7,643	58,317
Jun	201,281	26,718	26,253	254,252	10,587	14,268	25,769	9,998	5,046	15,044	38,075	17,326	7	7,981	58,585
Jul	200,159	25,756	26,828	252,742	10,625	13,997	25,722	10,043	4,958	15,002	37,129	17,026	4	7,864	58,481
Aug	199,201	25,764	26,978	251,943	10,609	14,004	25,611	9,942	4,910	14,852	36,594	17,000	3	7,888	56,757
Sep	198,430	26,013	26,917	251,359	11,175	13,927	25,603	10,063	4,905	14,968	36,541	16,711	4	7,849	56,927
Oct	197,740	25,993	27,097	250,829	12,057	13,969	25,847	9,510	5,010	14,520	36,179	15,944	3	7,772	55,822
Nov	195,746 (eq)	25,692	25,154	246,592 (eq)	10,719	14,063	25,557	9,372	4,877	14,249	35,680	15,293	4	7,740	55,187
Dec	196,376 (er)	25,225	25,700	247,301 (er)	10,999	14,486	25,686	9,747	4,845	14,591	33,579	15,217	4	8,343	53,134
2013 Jan	194,970	25,651	26,105	246,726	10,849	14,470	25,366	9,583	4,963	14,546	33,053	14,998	3	7,605	53,100
Feb	194,195	25,948	27,933 (eu)	248,077 (eu)	11,433	14,237	24,981	9,802	4,960	14,763	33,076	14,930	3	7,885	53,197
Mar	191,832	26,068	27,536	245,436	11,021	14,166	25,091	9,956	4,845	14,801	32,104	14,900	4	8,280	53,187
Apr	188,076	26,244	27,500	241,820	11,057	14,052	25,192	9,029	4,873	13,901	31,494	14,168	3	8,098	56,165
May	186,801	25,981	29,136	241,918	11,551	13,891	25,110	9,397	4,824	14,221	31,122	14,086	3	8,374	57,058
Jun	186,296	26,826	29,302	242,425	12,219	13,866	25,081	8,800	4,779	13,578	30,774	14,045	7	9,031	57,233
Jul	184,306	26,089	29,992	240,388	11,864	13,501	24,935	8,860	4,780	13,640	30,266	14,178	3	8,595	57,597
Aug	181,132 (es)	26,072	29,898	237,102 (es)	11,274	13,764	24,866	9,103	4,670	13,773	28,953	14,102	3	8,687	57,364
Sep	180,168	26,272	29,696	236,136	12,224	13,489	24,861	8,945	4,691	13,636	28,740	14,215	3	8,373	57,621
Oct	179,057	26,693	29,526	235,276	12,115	13,362	24,643	8,981	4,606	13,587	28,162	14,072	3	8,746	56,639
Nov	167,903 (et)	24,802 (el)	33,458 (ev)	226,163 (ev)(ew)	12,484	13,198	24,269	8,679	4,370	13,049	28,315	14,862	3	5,493 (ex)	53,230 (ey)
Dec	167,479	25,815	32,942	226,237	11,435	12,732	23,750	8,701	4,240	12,940	28,066	14,987	3	5,660	51,995 (ez)

12.4d Industrial analysis of monetary financial institutions lending to UK residents

£ millions   Not seasonally adjusted

Amounts outstanding of facilities granted in all currencies

RPM	Investment and unit trusts excluding money market mutual funds	Money market mutual funds	Financial intermediation (excluding insurance and pension funds)						Insurance companies & pension funds			Fund management activities	Activities auxiliary to financial intermediation			Total
			Bank holding companies	Securities dealers	SPVs related to securitisation	Other financial intermediaries	of which intragroup activity	Total	Insurance companies	Pension funds	Total		Other		Total	
													Central clearing counterparties	Other auxiliary activities		
	TCBO	TCBP	TCBQ	TCBR	B7FB	TCBS	B7FG	TCBI	B7FL	B7FQ	TCBT	TCBU	B3X7	B3Y5	TCBV	B3Z2
2012 Jan	18,909	339	31,795	122,537	22,330	283,378 (fc)	226,341 (fc)	605,169 (fc)	28,315	12,304	40,620	58,240	149,759	6,164	155,923	214,163
Feb	18,237	381	31,111	129,650	22,699	274,768	218,415	602,872	27,522	12,505	40,027	59,479	163,290	6,676	169,966	229,445
Mar	18,186	366	29,143	133,073	24,693	277,727	223,031	609,315	25,992	11,755	37,747	59,641	155,375	6,202	161,578	221,219
Apr	19,619	352	28,318	145,507 (fb)	21,185	288,598 (fd)	234,990 (fd)	626,116 (fb)(fd)	27,991	11,457	39,448	65,327	138,808 (fp)	6,031	144,839 (fp)	210,166 (fp)
May	21,065	432	29,584	144,915	21,427	286,704	231,297	626,670	27,863	12,657	40,520	68,173	128,080	6,414	134,494	202,668
Jun	17,598	362	26,330	138,667	22,179	282,260	228,569	609,369	27,226	13,114	40,340	65,136	134,610	6,356	140,966	206,102
Jul	19,670	258	24,216	146,299	22,452	280,326	228,131	613,725	26,883	11,419	38,302	63,857	130,386	6,773	137,159	201,016
Aug	19,649	270	24,224	145,644	22,367	270,299	220,444	600,694	25,771	11,765	37,535	62,891	129,651	6,471	136,122	199,013
Sep	18,090	200	26,752	146,218	22,656	272,855	220,900	604,802	25,644	11,888	37,532	63,082	138,303	6,381	144,684	207,765
Oct	19,744	193	27,429	141,117	23,546	264,810 (fe)	214,660 (fe)	592,560 (fe)	25,161	12,043	37,204	59,138	123,156	6,754	129,910	189,049
Nov	19,341	203	32,039	146,807	23,037	263,610 (ff)	211,441 (ff)	598,941 (ff)	25,191	12,233	37,424	75,937 (fn)	121,074	6,665	127,739	203,676 (fm)
Dec	19,314	169	35,095	132,191	22,529	280,899 (fg)	231,771 (fg)	600,473 (fg)	21,242 (fg)	11,704	32,946 (fg)	75,850	148,773 (fq)	6,859	155,632 (fq)	231,482 (fq)
2013 Jan	20,640	140	36,448	140,012	23,309	289,183 (fh)	239,974 (fh)	618,492 (fh)	21,266	12,504	33,771	84,022	147,867	7,413	155,280	239,302
Feb	22,127	165	39,345	148,045	21,811	289,303	238,860	629,885	20,526	12,609	33,135	90,171	147,765	6,782	154,547	244,718
Mar	22,300	117	43,480	149,692	21,892	276,216	227,685	622,171	20,452	16,352	36,804	93,558	147,307	6,968	154,275	247,833
Apr	28,671	144	36,930	155,269	21,906	275,861	228,547	628,709	19,301	15,758	35,059	93,781	143,326	7,238	150,564	244,345
May	21,671	139	31,747	173,583	21,689	276,317	230,997	635,788	20,088	14,736	34,823	96,072	155,084	6,824	161,908	257,980
Jun	23,876	108	31,642	157,557	21,492	262,839	217,785	608,605	19,507	14,948	34,456	87,915	144,755	6,825	151,579	239,495
Jul	25,074	135	36,516	154,662	22,532	257,005 (fi)	221,869 (fk)	606,563	18,340	14,134	32,475	88,021	131,755	6,703	138,458	226,479
Aug	23,235	157	39,329	150,670	22,593	252,345	218,503	597,437	17,105	14,013	31,118	93,067	141,456	6,879	148,334	241,401
Sep	24,996	145	42,769	134,833	22,765	243,094	210,940	577,553	16,885 (fm)	15,135	32,020 (fm)	93,578	149,667	9,242	158,909	252,487
Oct	25,297	142	44,742	140,072	22,914	245,022	213,490	585,812	16,937	14,469	31,406	91,583	140,424 (fr)	6,849 (fs)	147,273	238,857
Nov	18,755 (fa)	119	42,246	145,276	23,219	242,759 (ex)	211,288 (ex)	574,277 (ey)(fa)(fl)	17,703	14,397	32,100	94,551 (fo)	145,439	6,241	151,680	246,231 (fo)
Dec	20,453	110	44,400	141,256	22,902	217,061	185,879	546,894 (ez)	20,999	12,996	33,995	97,722	128,747	6,611	135,359	233,081

12.4d Industrial analysis of monetary financial institutions lending to UK residents

£ millions   Not seasonally adjusted

Amounts outstanding of facilities granted in all currencies

	Total financial and non-financial businesses	Individuals and individual trusts			Total UK residents
		Lending secured on dwellings inc. bridging finance	Other loans and advances	Total	
RPM	Z94H	TCBX	TCBY	TCBW	TCAA
2012 Jan	1,550,806	1,067,244	169,074	1,236,318	2,787,124
Feb	1,558,597	1,066,649	168,046	1,234,695	2,793,292
Mar	1,553,306	1,067,676	167,949	1,235,624	2,788,930
Apr	1,551,921	1,069,652	166,553	1,236,205	2,788,125 (fd)
May	1,545,193	1,070,387	166,235	1,236,623	2,781,815
Jun	1,528,713	1,077,593 (fu)	166,753	1,244,347 (fu)	2,773,060
Jul	1,524,598	1,079,461	166,251	1,245,712	2,770,310
Aug	1,508,006	1,079,183	165,977	1,245,160	2,753,167
Sep	1,521,685	1,079,476	166,045	1,245,521	2,767,206
Oct	1,489,529	1,079,511	165,397	1,244,908	2,734,438 (fe)
Nov	1,504,702	1,081,109	165,497	1,246,606	2,751,308 (eq)(ff)(fm)
Dec	1,525,514	1,078,643 (ff)	166,578	1,245,221 (ff)	2,770,735 (ga)
2013 Jan	1,552,084	1,082,180	159,969 (fx)(fy)	1,242,149 (fx)(fy)	2,794,233 (fx)(gb)
Feb	1,570,536 (eu)	1,081,375	160,178	1,241,552	2,812,088 (eu)
Mar	1,569,488	1,084,956	160,021	1,244,977	2,814,465
Apr	1,563,156	1,085,017	160,326	1,245,343	2,808,499
May	1,584,051	1,085,326	160,936	1,246,261	2,830,312
Jun	1,539,303	1,088,203	161,488	1,249,691	2,788,994
Jul	1,522,946 (ft)	1,090,237	163,578 (fz)	1,253,815 (fz)	2,776,761
Aug	1,519,997	1,091,971	164,140	1,256,111	2,776,108
Sep	1,508,895	1,093,595	165,069	1,258,664	2,767,559
Oct	1,502,219	1,097,320	164,663	1,261,983	2,764,202
Nov	1,497,256 (ex)(ey)	1,102,571 (fv)(fw)	165,048	1,267,619 (fv)(fw)	2,764,876 (ex)(ey)(fw)
Dec	1,457,110 (ez)	1,103,189	164,442	1,267,632	2,724,742 (ez)

Source: Bank of England

12.4d Industrial analysis of monetary financial institutions lending to UK residents

£ millions   Not seasonally adjusted

Amounts outstanding of facilities granted in all currencies

Notes to table

Movements in amounts outstanding can reflect breaks in data series as well as underlying flows. For changes data, users are recommended to refer directly to the appropriate series or data tables. Further explanation can be found at: www.bankofengland.co.uk/statistics/Pages/iadb/notesiadb/Changes_flows_growth_rates.aspx.

(ei) Due to improvements in reporting at one institution, the amounts outstanding decreased by £1bn. This effect has been adjusted out of the flows for June 2013.
(ej) Due to improvements in reporting at one institution, the amounts outstanding increased by £6bn. This effect has been adjusted out of the flows for November 2013.
(ek) Due to improvements in reporting at one institution, the amounts outstanding increased by £1bn. This effect has been adjusted out of the flows for November 2013.
(el) Due to improvements in reporting at one institution, the amounts outstanding decreased by £1bn. This effect has been adjusted out of the flows for November 2013.
(em) Due to improvements in reporting at one institution, the amounts outstanding increased by £0.7bn. This effect has been adjusted out of the flows for June 2013.
(en) Due to a reclassification by one reporting institution, the amounts outstanding decreased by £1bn. This effect has been adjusted out of the flows for September 2013.
(eo) Due to improvements in reporting at one institution, the amounts outstanding increased by £2bn. This effect has been adjusted out of the flows for November 2013.
(ep) Due to improvements in reporting at one institution, the amounts outstanding decreased by £0.6bn. This effect has been adjusted out of the flows for May 2012.
(eq) Following a sale of loans by one reporting institution, the amounts outstanding decreased by £0.5bn. This effect has been adjusted out of the flows for November 2012.
(er) Due to a change in the reporting population, this series has increased by £1bn. The effect has been adjusted out of the flows for December 2012.
(es) Due to loan transfers out of the UK MFI population, the amounts outstanding decreased by £2bn. This effect has been adjusted out of the flows for August 2013.
(et) Due to improvements in reporting at one institution, the amounts outstanding decreased by £7bn. This effect has been adjusted out of the flows for November 2013.
(eu) Due to a reclassification at one institution, the amounts outstanding increased by £0.6bn. This effect has been adjusted out of the flows for February 2013.
(ev) Due to a restructuring at one reporting institution, the amounts outstanding increased by £3bn. This effect has been adjusted out of the flows for November 2013.
(ew) Due to improvements in reporting at one institution, the amounts outstanding decreased by £8bn. This effect has been adjusted out of the flows for November 2013.
(ex) Due to a restructuring at one reporting institution, the amounts outstanding decreased by £3bn. This effect has been adjusted out of the flows for November 2013.
(ey) Due to improvements in reporting at one institution, the amounts outstanding decreased by £1bn. This effect has been adjusted out of the flows for November 2013.
(ez) Due to improvements in reporting at one institution, the amounts outstanding decreased by £2bn. This effect has been adjusted out of the flows for December 2013.
(fa) Due to improvements in reporting at one institution, the amounts outstanding decreased by £4bn. This effect has been adjusted out of the flows for November 2013.
(fb) Due to changes in the reporting population, the amounts outstanding increased by £11bn. This effect has been adjusted out of the flows for April 2012.
(fc) Due to a change in accounting treatment at one reporting institution, the amounts outstanding increased by £12bn. The effect has been adjusted out of the flows for January 2012.
(fd) Due to a change in treatment at one reporting institution, the amounts outstanding increased by £5bn. This effect has been adjusted out of the flows for April 2012.
(fe) Due to a change in treatment at one reporting institution, the amounts outstanding decreased by £5bn. This effect has been adjusted out of the flows for October 2012.
(ff) Due to improvements in reporting at one institution, the amounts outstanding decreased by £4bn. This effect has been adjusted out of the flows for November 2012.
(fg) Due to a change in the reporting population, this series has decreased by £3bn. The effect has been adjusted out of the flows for December 2012.
(fh) Due to a restructuring at one reporting institution the amounts outstanding decreased by £2bn. This effect has been adjusted out of the flows for January 2013.
(fi) Due to a change in the reporting population, this series has decreased by £2bn. The effect has been adjusted out of the flows for July 2013.
(fj) Due to improvements in reporting at one institution, the amounts outstanding decreased by £2bn. The effect has been adjusted out of the flows for December 2012.
(fk) Due to improvements in reporting at one institution, the amounts outstanding increased by £2bn. This effect has been adjusted out of the flows for July 2013.
(fl) Due to a restructuring at one reporting institution, the amounts outstanding decreased by £6bn. This effect has been adjusted out of the flows for November 2013.
(fm) Due to a reclassification by one reporting institution, the amounts outstanding increased by £1bn. This effect has been adjusted out of the flows for September 2013.
(fn) Due to a change in accounting treatment at one reporting institution, the amounts outstanding increased by £8bn. This effect has been adjusted out of the flows for November 2012.
(fo) Due to improvements in reporting at one institution, the amounts outstanding increased by £4bn. This effect has been adjusted out of the flows for November 2013.
(fp) Due to changes in the reporting population, the amounts outstanding decreased by £11bn. This effect has been adjusted out of the flows for April 2012.
(fq) Due to a change in the reporting population, this series has increased by £12bn. The effect has been adjusted out of the flows for December 2012.
(fr) Due to improvements in reporting at one institution, the amounts outstanding increased by £2bn. The effect has been adjusted out of the flows for December 2012.
(fs) Due to improvements in reporting at one institution, the amounts outstanding decreased by £2bn. This effect has been adjusted out of the flows for October 2013.
(ft) Due to improvements in reporting at one institution, the amounts outstanding decreased by £4bn. This effect has been adjusted out of the flows for October 2013.
(fu) Due to a change in accounting treatment at one reporting institution, the amounts outstanding increased by £7bn. This effect has been adjusted out of the flows for July 2013.
(fv) Due to improvements in reporting at one institution, the amounts outstanding increased by £1bn. This effect has been adjusted out of the flows for November 2013.
(fw) Following a purchase of loans by one reporting institution, the amounts outstanding increased by £2bn. This effect has been adjusted out of the flows for June 2012.
(fx) Due to a change in the reporting population, the amounts outstanding decreased by £8bn. The effect has been adjusted out of the flows for January 2013.
(fy) Due to a restructuring at one reporting institution the amounts outstanding increased by £1bn. This effect has been adjusted out of the flows for July 2013.
(fz) Following a purchase of loans by one reporting institution, this series has increased by £5bn. The effect has been adjusted out of the flows for December 2012.
(ga) Due to a change in the reporting population, the amounts outstanding increased by £2bn. The effect has been adjusted out of the flows for December 2012.
(gb) Due to a restructuring at one reporting institution the amounts outstanding decreased by £1bn. This effect has been adjusted out of the flows for January 2013.

12.5a Industrial analysis of monetary financial institutions deposits from UK residents

£ millions   Not seasonally adjusted

| | Agriculture, hunting and forestry | Fishing | Mining and quarrying | Manufacturing | | | | | | | | | Electricity, gas and water supply | | | |
				Food, beverages and tobacco	Textiles, wearing apparel and leather	Pulp, paper, and printing	Chemicals, pharmaceuticals, rubber and plastics	Non-metallic mineral products and metals	Machinery, equipment and transport equipment	Electrical, medical and optical equipment	Other manufacturing	Total	Electricity, gas steam and air conditioning	Water collection and sewerage	Waste management related services and remediation activities	Total
RPM	TDCB	TDCC	TDCD	TDCF	TDCG	TDCH	TDCI	TDCJ	TDCK	TDCL	TDCM	TDCE	TDCN	TDCO	BE2M	B3FI
2012 Jan	5,626	255	4,466	2,718	833	1,480	4,794	4,389	5,718	3,663	3,208	26,803	4,296	2,891	991	8,178
Feb	5,525	293	3,503	2,805	825	1,527	5,216	4,244	5,539	3,880	3,260	27,297	4,511	2,764	1,033	8,308
Mar	5,441	280	3,165	3,027	801	1,627	5,537	4,390	5,846	3,965	3,233	28,425	4,423	2,656	926	8,006
Apr	5,316	258	3,137	2,821	802	1,651	5,128	4,447	5,727	3,944	3,054	27,574	4,330	2,640	985	7,955
May	5,241	256	3,489	2,852	847	1,618	4,726	4,377	6,421	3,970	3,084	27,895	4,089	2,628	1,027	7,743
Jun	5,193	252	3,700	2,838	850	1,601	4,852	4,301	6,586	3,895	3,010	27,933	4,207	2,711	999	7,918
Jul	4,981	229	4,043	3,015	875	1,596	4,394	4,301	6,723	3,920	2,859	27,683	4,314	2,342	946	7,602
Aug	4,970	303	3,025	3,245	897	1,616	4,183	4,352	6,537	4,102	3,282	28,214	3,867	2,292	965	7,124
Sep	5,086	300	2,935	3,112	892	1,572	4,186	4,581	6,731	3,854	3,224	28,152	3,806	2,257	923	6,985
Oct	5,128	285	2,664	3,429	923	1,499	4,193	4,621	6,225	3,926	3,421	28,235	4,131	2,421	942	7,494
Nov	5,130	290	2,626	3,346	936	1,650	4,584	4,637	6,188	3,927	3,684	28,951	3,987	2,631	1,001	7,619
Dec	6,073	276	4,208	3,277	950	1,761	4,800	4,713	7,632	4,032	3,494	30,658	3,905	2,445	1,115	7,464
2013 Jan	5,822	264	4,725	2,996	924	1,506	4,900	4,758	7,855	4,115	3,569	30,623	3,649	2,861	1,112	7,623
Feb	5,711	296	4,870	3,240	893	1,543	4,093	4,363	7,767	4,145	3,656	29,701	4,019	2,745	1,119	7,883
Mar	5,685	286	5,640	3,300	894	1,757	4,250	4,457	7,498	4,282	3,341	29,781	4,186	3,128	1,200	8,513
Apr	5,559	248	5,456	3,543	899	1,546	3,835	4,650	7,088	4,361	3,350	29,272	4,470	2,735	1,132	8,337
May	5,523	243	5,414	3,220	916	1,527	4,163	4,538	7,236	4,496	3,270	29,367	4,517	2,913	1,153	8,583
Jun	5,446	205	5,691	3,290	888	1,462	3,732	4,530	7,629	4,159	3,248	28,949	4,166	2,873	1,187	8,226
Jul	5,411	195	5,007	2,758	907	1,439	3,626	4,527	7,993	4,173	3,432	28,854	3,762	2,845	1,292	7,900
Aug	5,348	186	4,306	2,943	920	1,373	4,213	4,500	7,900	4,056	3,570	29,477	3,975	2,554	1,289	7,817
Sep	5,393	192	4,601	3,179	906	1,366	4,313	4,703	7,552	4,176	3,625	29,820	4,224	2,473	1,249	7,946
Oct	5,247	202	4,528	2,874	924	1,367	4,649	4,821	7,587	3,999	3,648	29,868	4,347	2,365	1,246	7,958
Nov	5,271	239	4,811	3,047	975	1,403	4,509	4,852	7,471	4,063	3,668	29,986	4,649	2,402	1,259	8,310
Dec	6,248	220	4,454	3,545	1,004	1,415	6,075	4,877	8,611	4,138	3,561	33,227	4,270	2,432	1,335	8,037

12.5a Industrial analysis of monetary financial institutions deposits from UK residents

£ millions   Not seasonally adjusted

| | Development of buildings | Construction | | | | | Wholesale and retail trade | | | | Accommodation and food service activities | Transport, storage and communication | | |
| | | Construction of commercial buildings | Construction of domestic buildings | Civil Engineering | Other construction activities | Total | Wholesale and retail trade and repair of motor vehicles and motorcycles | Wholesale trade, excluding motor vehicles and motor cycles | Retail trade excluding motor vehicles and motor cycles | Total | | Transportation and storage | Information and communication | Total |
RPM	B3FW	B7EK	B3LS	B3JO	B4PS	TDCP	TDCR	TDCS	TDCT	TDCQ	TDCU	B5PF	B3NI	TDCV
2012 Jan	5,877	2,307	1,528	3,812	7,965	21,488	4,209	10,880	11,259	26,348	4,917	10,245	19,426	29,671
Feb	5,783	2,346	1,519	3,678	7,923	21,249	4,468	10,872	11,179	26,518	5,270	11,307	19,869	31,176
Mar	5,504 (a)	2,318	1,659	3,915	8,320	21,715 (a)	4,614	11,290	10,460	26,364	5,346	10,252	20,383	30,635
Apr	5,579	2,293	1,625	3,831	8,283	21,612	4,484	11,106	10,904	26,494	5,411	10,321	20,308	30,629
May	5,427	2,250	1,681	3,774	8,253	21,385	4,550	11,757	11,327	27,634	5,433	10,414	20,155	30,568
Jun	5,856	2,304	1,873	3,877	8,134	22,043	4,375	11,459	11,109	26,943	5,243	10,022	20,079	30,101
Jul	5,736	2,101	1,689	3,675	8,206	21,408	4,506	11,952	11,228	27,686	5,923	9,878	20,471	30,350
Aug	5,911	2,137	1,738	3,774	8,270	21,829	4,630	11,734	11,128	27,491	6,273	9,834	18,807	28,641
Sep	5,908	2,126	1,785	3,721	8,324	21,864	4,522	11,279	10,849	26,649	6,073	9,877	20,261	30,138
Oct	5,931	2,659	1,844	3,821	8,567	22,822	4,596	12,056	11,739	28,390	6,018	9,991	20,070	30,061
Nov	5,924	2,567	1,882	4,006	8,578	22,958	4,605	11,978	11,832	28,415	5,906	10,460	21,529	31,989
Dec	6,266	2,556	2,260	4,222	8,777	24,081	4,448	12,409	13,939	30,796	5,825	9,896	20,053	29,948
2013 Jan	6,263	2,361	1,832	3,857	8,389	22,702	4,346	11,727	12,180	28,253	5,395	10,214	24,320	34,535
Feb	6,276	2,304	1,850	3,859	8,180	22,469	4,597	11,690	12,369	28,656	5,499	11,417	23,648	35,065
Mar	6,763	2,496	1,935	4,024	8,613	23,831	3,889	11,787	11,570	27,245	5,466	11,205	22,474	33,679
Apr	6,402	2,495	1,924	4,055	8,678	23,554	4,029	11,654	12,228	27,911	5,629	11,015	21,733	32,749
May	6,416	2,440	2,022	4,124	8,674	23,676	4,133	12,087	12,936	29,156	5,951	11,700	21,520	33,219
Jun	6,762	2,525	2,370	4,134	8,898	24,690	4,035	12,103	12,231	28,369	5,912	11,626	21,481	33,107
Jul	6,719	2,465	2,124	4,113	8,987	24,407	4,259	12,334	13,590	30,182	6,556	11,150	22,336	33,486
Aug	6,620	2,575	2,254	4,334	9,044	24,825	4,473	12,379	13,215	30,067	6,630	11,027	21,179	32,206
Sep	6,687	2,639	2,230	4,190	9,274	25,020	4,269	12,219	12,861	29,349	6,640	11,405	21,196	32,602
Oct	6,294	3,466 (b)	2,267	4,453	8,562 (c)	25,042	4,220	12,572	12,567	29,358	6,695	11,943	20,208	32,152
Nov	6,598	3,427	2,349	4,624	8,774	25,772	4,193	12,640	13,465	30,298	6,612	11,506	20,301	31,807
Dec	6,762	3,535	2,761	5,113	8,891	27,061	4,129	12,936	16,516	33,582	6,672	11,023	20,477	31,500

12.5a Industrial analysis of monetary financial institutions deposits from UK residents

£ millions   Not seasonally adjusted

| | Real estate, professional services and support activities | | | | Public administration and defence | Education | Human health and social work | Recreational, personal and community service activities | | | Financial intermediation (excluding insurance and pension funds) | | | | | | |
	Buying, selling and renting of real estate	Professional, scientific and technical activities	Administrative and support services	Total				Recreational, cultural and sporting activities	Personal and community service activities	Total	Financial leasing corporations	Non-bank credit grantors excluding credit unions and SPVs	Credit unions	Factoring corporations	Mortgage and housing credit corporations excluding SPVs	Investment and unit trusts excluding money market mutual funds	Money market mutual funds
RPM	TDCX	B3ON	B6PK	TDCW	TDDB	TDDC	TDDD	TDDF	TDDE	B3S6	TDDH	TDDI	TDDJ	TDDK	TDDL	TDDM	TDDN
2012 Jan	27,919	48,264	18,555	94,738	32,075	15,483	15,847	10,636	16,153	26,790	3,887	6,951	704	865	15,686	25,153	267
Feb	26,889	47,717	18,699	93,305	27,942	15,431	15,915	10,556	16,331	26,887	4,105	7,032	718	726	15,270	25,261	358
Mar	29,735	50,362	18,998	99,095	22,315	15,050	15,314	10,654	16,614	27,268	3,930	8,165	735	1,041	15,141	25,553	190
Apr	28,891	50,058	18,882	97,830	30,798 (h)	16,301	16,751	10,896	16,689	27,585	3,770	8,023	758	1,155	14,325	24,788	218
May	28,944	52,021	19,887	100,852	36,739	16,951	17,231	10,789	16,518	27,307	4,121	2,891 (i)	761	980	14,063	23,749	352
Jun	30,988	51,559	19,506	102,053	32,870	16,346	17,553	10,782	16,667	27,449	4,204	3,194	761	960	14,238	24,451	163
Jul	29,172	51,054	19,558	99,785	35,140	15,456	17,148	10,891	16,524	27,415	4,283	3,159	772	888	14,597	23,465	534
Aug	28,741	53,027	19,505	101,272	36,268	15,918	17,267	11,057	16,503	27,561	4,193	2,902	780	915	13,678	23,914	215
Sep	31,707	54,472	19,440	105,620	33,428	17,550	17,101	10,832	16,382	27,213	4,296	2,742	783	867	13,751	23,236	301
Oct	29,481	52,302	19,942	101,724	32,666	17,676	17,374	10,675	16,533	27,208	4,206	2,897	810	875	13,873	24,478	261
Nov	28,944	52,743	19,733	101,421	34,575	17,090	17,839	10,465	16,499	26,964	4,509	1,934	798	877	13,821	23,332	251
Dec	31,731	50,670	20,030	102,431	31,398	16,771	17,126	10,295	16,079	26,374	4,415	2,162	800	859	14,253	23,010	400
2013 Jan	29,410	51,537	20,177	101,124	36,999	17,833	16,930	10,405	16,195	26,600	4,424	1,997	815	817	14,438	23,446	247
Feb	29,430	51,892	20,254	101,576	39,910	17,674	17,286	10,686	16,210	26,896	4,462	1,972	829	799	14,106	23,552	278
Mar	32,242	52,842	20,654	105,738	29,929	16,977	15,754	10,609	16,450	27,060	4,331	2,076	830	995	14,045	24,420	236
Apr	30,967	54,184	20,348	105,499	34,448	17,929	15,860	10,863	16,533	27,396	4,047	1,805	837	1,058	14,369	23,326	237
May	29,861	55,079	21,096	106,036	34,923	18,766	16,185	10,941	16,600	27,541	4,358	2,627	838	990	14,087	23,784	284
Jun	32,250	56,783	21,354	110,387	34,995	18,359	16,327	10,826	16,550	27,376	4,227	2,352	828	1,184	14,143	25,050	295
Jul	30,801	56,097	21,608	108,506	41,078	17,401	16,108	10,851	16,837	27,688	4,204	2,431	848	1,163	14,690	24,373	336
Aug	30,637	55,827	21,350	107,814	36,431	17,507	16,115	11,252	16,625	27,878	4,059	2,461	859	1,082	14,617	31,538	338
Sep	33,601	56,273	21,556	111,430	32,736	18,934	15,688	10,854	16,792	27,646	4,399	2,442	882	1,050	14,527	30,406	307
Oct	31,705	62,360 (d)	18,162 (f)	112,228	36,276	19,408	16,047	10,949	17,061	28,010	4,073	2,315	909	892	14,573	30,982	300
Nov	32,319	62,301 (e)	18,832 (g)	113,452	34,408	18,314	16,163	10,963	17,082	28,044	4,758	2,499	874	949	14,235	30,877	298
Dec	34,887	59,140	19,359	113,385	30,389	17,286	15,902	10,951	17,037	27,989	4,583	2,380	881	1,004	14,517	24,010	316

12.5a Industrial analysis of monetary financial institutions deposits from UK residents

£ millions Not seasonally adjusted

	Bank holding companies	Securities dealers	SPVs related to securitisation	Other financial intermediaries	of which intragroup activity	Total	Insurance companies	Pension funds	Total	Fund management activities	Central clearing counterparties	Other auxiliary activities	Total	Total	Total financial and non-financial businesses	Individuals and individuals trusts	Total UK residents
				Financial intermediation (excluding insurance and pension funds)			Insurance companies & pension funds				Activities auxiliary to financial intermediation — Other						
RPM	TDDO	TDDP	B3T5	TDDQ	B3U3	TDDG	B7FI	B3VH	TDDR	TDDS	B7FT	B7FY	TDDT	B3Y8	Z945	TDDU	TDCA
2012 Jan	20,397	29,890	293,457	131,866 (m)	105,054 (m)	529,122 (m)	29,629	20,372	50,001	61,056	81,487	11,327	92,815	153,871	1,045,680	968,143	2,013,823
Feb	18,789	30,191	268,644	117,742	91,627	488,837	28,959	19,865	48,824	55,917	88,949	11,402	100,351	156,267	1,002,548	973,810	1,976,357
Mar	18,845	34,719	261,016	124,479	97,925	493,815	30,924	20,172	51,096	60,677	65,088	11,482	76,570	137,248	990,577	984,273	1,974,850
Apr	18,123	40,986	262,315	123,984 (n)	98,169 (n)	498,445 (n)	29,628	19,813	49,441	61,081	75,318	11,752	87,070	148,151	1,013,688	988,113	2,001,801 (n)
May	20,884	36,728	264,989 (k)	123,394	97,662	492,913	29,380	19,809	49,189	61,235	79,850	11,805	91,655	152,890	1,023,717	989,898	2,013,616
Jun	21,424	38,000	225,992	125,702	98,743	459,088	32,064	19,317	51,381	63,151	76,369	12,323	88,692	151,843	987,910	1,004,019 (w)	1,991,929
Jul	22,565	39,340	222,392	119,466	93,064	451,460	32,333	18,713	51,046	64,881	79,937	12,828	92,766	157,647	985,001	1,005,512	1,990,513
Aug	22,285	41,058	218,394	121,169	93,321	449,503	30,553	17,798	48,351	65,172	84,313	11,667	95,980	161,151	985,161	1,012,568	1,997,730
Sep	19,385	40,291	216,682	122,088	94,099	444,423	29,594	19,732	49,326	66,524	85,588	11,948	97,536	164,060	986,904	1,016,751	2,003,655
Oct	18,014	39,492	213,327	115,777 (o)	88,155 (o)	434,011 (o)	28,240	19,829	48,069	68,072	87,727	12,278	100,005	168,077	977,902	1,017,777	1,995,680 (o)
Nov	17,743	39,677	214,167	112,415	86,174	429,523	28,799	20,104	48,903	64,945	79,180	13,228	92,409	157,353	967,552	1,025,530	1,993,082
Dec	17,619	35,794	212,366	136,545	109,921	448,223	26,789 (t)	19,535	46,325 (t)	60,662	79,367 (v)	13,212	92,579 (v)	153,240 (v)	981,219	1,028,670	2,009,889 (y)
2013 Jan	17,750	34,677	199,009	137,914	111,321	435,534	27,472	20,313	47,784	61,616	94,950	13,281	108,231	169,847	992,592	1,024,868	2,017,460
Feb	18,420	33,651	196,845	135,371	109,643	430,285	26,262	25,974 (u)	52,236 (u)	61,903	91,960	13,148	105,108	167,010	993,024 (u)	1,032,454	2,025,478 (u)
Mar	18,162	34,802	192,409	134,820	108,086	427,126	27,627	26,404	54,030	62,695	73,856	13,519	87,375	150,070	966,809	1,044,168	2,010,977
Apr	13,730	37,470	188,038	129,447	104,142	414,364	26,359	26,732	53,091	66,697	81,750	13,929	95,679	162,376	969,677	1,045,271	2,014,947
May	11,530	37,502	188,769	128,804	103,171	413,575	26,437	26,176	52,612	62,100	80,120	13,687	93,806	155,906	966,678	1,050,490	2,017,167
Jun	9,288	35,240	187,968	135,602	108,730	416,178	27,152	26,633	53,785	61,003	73,262	13,689	86,950	147,953	965,956	1,052,750	2,018,706
Jul	16,274 (j)	35,552	186,818	136,531 (p)	110,867 (p)	423,219 (s)	25,158	25,974	51,133	60,754	81,128	13,936	95,064	155,818	982,948 (s)	1,051,967	2,034,914 (s)
Aug	16,768	35,292	185,352	140,889	114,922	433,256	24,923	25,995	50,918	62,727	86,905	13,627	100,532	163,259	994,040	1,058,745 (x)	2,052,785
Sep	17,972	33,759	185,593	139,973	114,107	431,308	25,575	26,833	52,408	66,164	89,653	14,558	104,211	170,375	1,002,086	1,059,803	2,061,889
Oct	22,002	37,560	179,772	132,298	106,131	425,675	22,842	26,982	49,824	67,231	92,843	13,391	106,234	173,465	1,001,983	1,062,167	2,064,150
Nov	21,127	38,436	182,162	127,859 (q)	101,399 (q)	424,074 (q)	23,505	26,353	49,858	70,169	89,450	12,243	101,693	171,862	999,282 (q)	1,069,366	2,068,648 (q)
Dec	21,170	32,549	177,626 (l)	124,251 (r)	96,843 (r)	403,288	24,861	25,980	50,841	65,181	65,670	12,641	78,311	143,492	953,574	1,068,133	2,021,708

Source: Bank of England

12.5a Industrial analysis of monetary financial institutions deposits from UK residents

£ millions   Not seasonally adjusted

Notes to table

Movements in amounts outstanding can reflect breaks in data series as well as underlying flows.   For changes data, users are recommended to refer directly to the appropriate series or data tables.
www.bankofengland.co.uk/statistics/Pages/iadb/notesiadb/Changes_flows_growth_rates.aspx.

(a) Due to improvements in reporting at one institution, the amounts outstanding decreased by £0.5bn. This effect has been adjusted out of the flows for March 2012.
(b) Due to improvements in reporting at one institution, the amounts outstanding increased by £1bn. This effect has been adjusted out of the flows for October 2013.
(c) Due to improvements in reporting at one institution, the amounts outstanding decreased by £1bn. This effect has been adjusted out of the flows for October 2013.
(d) Due to improvements in reporting at one institution, the amounts outstanding increased by £4bn. This effect has been adjusted out of the flows for October 2013.
(e) Due to improvements in reporting at one institution, the amounts outstanding decreased by £1bn. This effect has been adjusted out of the flows for November 2013.
(f) Due to improvements in reporting at one institution, the amounts outstanding decreased by £4bn. This effect has been adjusted out of the flows for October 2013.
(g) Due to improvements in reporting at one institution, the amounts outstanding increased by £1bn. This effect has been adjusted out of the flows for November 2013.
(h) Due to improvements in reporting at one institution, the amounts outstanding increased by £2bn. This effect has been adjusted out of the flows for April 2012.
(i) Due to a reclassification by one reporting institution from non-bank credit grantors to SPVs, the amounts outstanding decreased by £5bn. This effect has been adjusted out of the flows for May 2012.
(j) Due to improvements in reporting at one institution, the amounts outstanding increased by £7bn. This effect has been adjusted out of the flows for July 2013.
(k) Due to a reclassification by one reporting institution from non-bank credit grantors to SPVs, the amounts outstanding increased by £5bn. This effect has been adjusted out of the flows for May 2012.
(l) Due to improvements in reporting at one institution, the amounts outstanding increased by £1bn. This effect has been adjusted out of the flows for December 2013.
(m) Due to a change in accounting treatment at one reporting institution, the amounts outstanding increased by £12bn. The effect has been adjusted out of the flows for January 2012.
(n) Due to a change in treatment at one reporting institution, the amounts outstanding increased by £5bn. This effect has been adjusted out of the flows for April 2012.
(o) Due to a change in treatment at one reporting institution, the amounts outstanding decreased by £5bn. This effect has been adjusted out of the flows for October 2012.
(p) Due to improvements in reporting at one institution, the amounts outstanding increased by £2bn. This effect has been adjusted out of the flows for July 2013.
(q) Due to improvements in reporting at one institution, the amounts outstanding decreased by £3bn. This effect has been adjusted out of the flows for November 2013.
(r) Due to improvements in reporting at one institution, the amounts outstanding increased by £1bn. This effect has been adjusted out of the flows for December 2013.
(s) Due to improvements in reporting at one institution, the amounts outstanding increased by £9bn. This effect has been adjusted out of the flows for July 2013.
(t) Due to a change in the reporting population, this series has decreased by £3bn. The effect has been adjusted out of the flows for December 2012.
(u) Due to improvements in reporting at one institution, the amounts outstanding increased by £6bn. This effect has been adjusted out of the flows for February 2013.
(v) Due to a change in the reporting population, this series has increased by £7bn. The effect has been adjusted out of the flows for December 2012.
(w) Due to a change in accounting treatment at one reporting institution, the amounts outstanding increased by £7bn. This effect has been adjusted out of the flows for June 2012.
(x) Due to improvements in reporting at one institution, the amounts outstanding increased by £1bn. This effect has been adjusted out of the flows for August 2013.
(y) Due to a change in the reporting population, this series has increased by £4bn. The effect has been adjusted out of the flows for December 2012.

12.5b Industrial analysis of monetary financial institutions deposits from UK residents

£ millions   Not seasonally adjusted

Amounts outstanding of deposit liabilities (including under repo) in sterling and other currencies

	Agriculture, hunting and forestry	Fishing	Mining and quarrying	Manufacturing									Electricity, gas and water supply			
				Food, beverages and tobacco	Textiles, wearing apparel and leather	Pulp, paper, and printing	Chemicals, pharmaceuticals, rubber and plastics	Non-metallic mineral products and metals	Machinery, equipment and transport equipment	Electrical, medical and optical equipment	Other manufacturing	Total	Electricity, gas steam and air conditioning	Water collection and sewerage	Waste management related services and remediation activities	Total
RPM	TDAB	TDAC	TDAD	TDAF	TDAG	TDAH	TDAI	TDAJ	TDAK	TDAL	TDAM	TDAE	TDAN	TDAO	BE2N	B3FJ
2012 Jan	5,870	264	11,937	4,439	1,098	1,748	7,090	5,412	7,484	6,791	3,933	37,994	5,421	2,903	1,067	9,391
Feb	5,682	302	11,371	4,228	1,106	1,829	7,632	5,199	7,152	6,930	4,094	38,169	5,661	2,778	1,132	9,572
Mar	5,620	288	12,403	4,534	1,092	1,861	8,136	5,539	7,436	6,992	3,926	39,515	5,608	2,667	1,114	9,389
Apr	5,498	267	11,265	3,956	1,153	1,885	8,051	5,488	7,565	7,006	3,750	38,855	6,069	2,649	1,158	9,876
May	5,391	264	15,827	4,637	1,167	1,869	9,755	5,363	8,312	7,313	4,037	42,452	5,626	2,634	1,199	9,459
Jun	5,354	263	14,712	4,410	1,146	1,833	9,574	5,302	9,711	7,100	3,672	42,749	5,843	2,728	1,124	9,696
Jul	5,125	240	14,080	4,231	1,163	1,902	7,473	5,245	8,696	7,139	3,687	39,537	5,853	2,363	1,102	9,318
Aug	5,114	316	12,586	4,380	1,190	1,835	7,107	5,398	8,791	7,629	3,989	40,319	5,460	2,311	1,058	8,829
Sep	5,235	315	12,448	4,053	1,177	1,811	7,543	5,449	9,012	7,408	4,252	40,705	5,267	2,275	1,014	8,556
Oct	5,292	302	11,688	4,284	1,209	1,739	7,521	5,484	8,690	7,538	4,334	40,799	5,442	2,440	1,027	8,908
Nov	5,308	309	13,104	4,203	1,241	1,890	8,029	5,488	9,022	7,245	4,476	41,594	5,618	2,664	1,106	9,388
Dec	6,360	286	15,659	4,707	1,278	2,006	8,172	5,690	11,214	7,742	4,167	44,977	4,664 (ap)	2,489	1,214	8,367 (ap)
2013 Jan	6,056	274	14,284	3,925	1,243	1,784	7,676	5,928	10,065	7,952	4,648	43,221	4,556	2,876	1,241	8,673
Feb	5,977	304	17,852	4,134	1,225	1,799	7,565	5,480	10,131	8,102	4,609	43,045	4,999	2,774	1,254	9,027
Mar	5,977	294	17,865	4,429	1,234	2,037	7,296	5,413	10,201	8,480	4,596	43,686	5,054	3,142	1,303	9,498
Apr	5,685	256	17,307	4,415	1,228	1,841	6,511	5,555	9,482	8,196	4,445	41,672	5,537	2,750	1,220	9,507
May	5,654	250	17,948	4,812	1,259	1,960	6,735	5,592	9,902	8,412	4,443	43,115	5,447	2,927	1,231	9,606
Jun	5,586	213	16,161	4,859	1,218	2,002	7,044	5,501	10,954	8,187	4,033	43,799	4,953	2,894	1,318	9,165
Jul	5,543	203	16,893	4,485	1,128	1,930	6,866	5,585	10,640	7,920	4,400	42,954	4,690	2,872	1,489	9,051
Aug	5,495	192	17,822	4,236	1,155	1,902	7,216	5,580	10,168	7,986	4,364	42,607	4,602	2,586	1,417	8,605
Sep	5,518	201	17,682	5,125	1,158	1,796	7,640	5,781	9,620	8,544	4,443	44,107	4,814	2,501	1,391	8,706
Oct	5,377	210	18,039	4,037	1,203	1,803	8,406	6,033	9,976	7,485	4,300	43,242	5,015	2,384	1,382	8,781
Nov	5,430	251	20,707	4,143	1,235	1,933	7,189	5,836	9,823	8,037	4,424	42,619	5,472	2,427	1,436	9,335
Dec	6,473	232	14,995	4,789	1,275	1,995	8,478	5,960	11,866	7,458	4,281	46,100	5,393	2,453	1,506	9,352

12.5b Industrial analysis of monetary financial institutions deposits from UK residents

£ millions   Not seasonally adjusted

Amounts outstanding of deposit liabilities (including under repo) in sterling and other currencies

RPM	Development of buildings	Construction					Wholesale and retail trade				Accommodation and food service activities	Transport, storage and communication		
		Construction of commercial buildings	Construction of domestic buildings	Civil Engineering	Other construction activities	Total	Wholesale and retail trade and repair of motor vehicles and motorcycles	Wholesale trade, excluding motor vehicles and motor cycles	Retail trade excluding motor vehicles and motor cycles	Total		Transportation and storage	Information and communication	Total
	B3FX	B7EL	B3LT	B4PG	B4PT	TDAP	TDAR	TDAS	TDAT	TDAQ	TDAU	B5PG	B3NJ	TDAV
2012 Jan	6,337	2,489	1,536	3,932	8,158	22,453	5,077	14,625	12,834	32,536	5,093	12,355	22,989	35,343
Feb	5,808	2,501	1,527	3,800	8,038	21,676	5,362	14,528	12,368	32,258	5,455	13,689	23,257	36,946
Mar	5,527 (aq)	2,541	1,668	4,032	8,433	22,201 (aq)	5,752	14,846	11,728	32,326	5,500	12,672	24,180	36,852
Apr	5,601	2,515	1,637	3,956	8,381	22,089	5,203	14,526	12,343	32,071	5,610	12,834	23,715	36,549
May	5,460	2,470	1,691	3,884	8,387	21,893	5,205	15,104	12,989	33,298	5,621	12,950	23,664	36,614
Jun	5,886	2,498	1,883	3,995	8,349	22,611	5,090	15,066	12,628	32,784	5,455	12,685	24,975	37,660
Jul	5,760	2,216	1,699	3,783	8,324	21,783	4,869	15,788	12,712	33,369	6,130	12,537	24,851	37,388
Aug	5,937	2,277	1,748	3,897	8,407	22,265	4,991	15,968	12,572	33,531	6,538	12,707	22,844	35,551
Sep	5,936	2,244	1,794	3,835	8,457	22,267	4,927	15,422	12,216	32,565	6,317	12,984	24,076	37,060
Oct	5,956	2,780	1,853	3,938	8,746	23,273	4,916	16,235	13,029	34,180	6,198	13,090	24,556	37,646
Nov	5,947	2,683	1,891	4,142	8,699	23,362	4,921	16,429 (at)	13,243	34,593 (at)	6,182	13,819	26,017	39,836
Dec	6,294	2,675	2,277	4,373	8,929	24,548	4,770	17,112	15,355	37,237	6,159	13,326	24,861	38,187
2013 Jan	6,288	2,459	1,841	3,999	8,604	23,192	4,600	16,111	13,686	34,396	5,734	13,792	28,847	42,639
Feb	6,301	2,435	1,858	4,014	8,344	22,953	4,890	16,792	13,498	35,180	5,814	15,727	28,553	44,280
Mar	6,802	2,622	1,943	4,170	8,790	24,326	4,174	17,062	12,588	33,824	5,841	14,198	26,781	40,979
Apr	6,431	2,598	1,932	4,196	8,860	24,018	4,413	16,894	13,428	34,734	5,964	13,896	26,109	40,005
May	6,443	2,557	2,029	4,283	8,838	24,151	4,406	16,669	14,078	35,153	6,340	16,539	25,783	42,322
Jun	6,790	2,663	2,378	4,258	9,059	25,147	4,351	16,630	13,617	34,598	6,265	15,075	26,152	41,227
Jul	6,744	2,599	2,132	4,290	9,207	24,971	4,497	17,119	14,944	36,559	6,903	14,414	27,930	42,345
Aug	6,655	2,694	2,261	4,503	9,203	25,316	4,728	17,173	14,409	36,310	6,982	14,427	26,466	40,894
Sep	6,724	2,755	2,238	4,347	9,431	25,495	4,541	17,069	14,141	35,751	7,005	14,625	26,108	40,734
Oct	6,336	3,580 (ar)	2,276	4,624	8,716 (as)	25,531	4,580	17,464	13,923	35,967	7,022	15,029	24,998	40,027
Nov	6,640	3,500	2,357	4,797	8,932	26,225	4,471	17,912	14,780	37,164	7,147	14,405	25,278	39,683
Dec	6,798	3,612	2,769	5,280	9,046	27,504	4,441	17,899	17,748	40,089	7,244	15,270	24,927	40,197

12.5b Industrial analysis of monetary financial institutions deposits from UK residents

£ millions   Not seasonally adjusted

Amounts outstanding of deposit liabilities (including under repo) in sterling and other currencies

	Real estate, professional services and support activities				Public administration and defence	Education	Human health and social work	Recreational, personal and community service activities			Financial intermediation (excluding insurance and pension funds)							
	Buying, selling and renting of real estate	Professional, scientific and technical activities	Administrative and support services	Total				Recreational, cultural and sporting activities	Personal and community service activities	Total	Financial leasing corporations	Non-bank credit grantors excluding credit unions and SPVs	Credit unions	Factoring corporations	Mortgage and housing credit corporations excluding SPVs	Investment and unit trusts excluding money market mutual funds	Money market mutual funds	Bank holding companies
RPM	TDAX	B3TK	B6PL	TDAW	TDBB	TDBC	TDBD	TDBF	TDBE	B3S7	TDBH	TDBI	TDBJ	TDBK	TDBL	TDBM	TDBN	TDBO
2012 Jan	29,375	54,518	28,016	111,909	36,710	15,971	16,412	11,527	16,668	28,195	4,565	7,626	705	961	16,287	34,209	620	37,370
Feb	28,393	54,160	28,163	110,715	33,608	15,907	16,449	11,504	16,863	28,366	4,825	7,707	718	784	16,065	36,336	704	35,035
Mar	31,259	56,691	28,432	116,382	28,229	15,554	15,837	11,604	17,147	28,751	4,702	8,789	735	1,100	15,997	36,652	360	36,052
Apr	30,245	56,738	28,310	115,294	37,297 (az)	16,804	17,310	11,859	17,235	29,094	4,415	8,564	764	1,231	15,025	34,379	562	36,363
May	30,299	58,162	29,505	117,966	44,748	17,443	17,770	11,775	17,036	28,811	5,395	3,476 (ba)	767	1,046	14,616	34,241	588	37,441
Jun	32,402	57,905	29,085	119,391	40,196	16,849	18,100	11,763	17,191	28,954	5,018	3,860	761	1,011	14,830	32,480	364	38,497
Jul	30,533	57,642	29,802	117,977	43,234	15,940	17,706	11,950	16,995	28,946	5,049	3,681	772	942	15,623	32,025	893	38,225
Aug	30,208	60,065	29,069	119,342	42,932	16,439	17,842	12,006	17,029	29,034	4,995	3,448	780	946	14,595	34,276	590	37,508
Sep	32,250	60,839	28,832	121,921	36,981	18,067	17,669	11,791	16,904	28,695	4,988	3,254	783	911	14,581	33,205	695	32,582
Oct	29,991	58,517	29,138	117,646	35,557	18,258	17,969	11,694	17,032	28,726	4,855	3,393	810	910	14,467	35,255	710	31,171
Nov	29,518	58,870	28,877	117,265	37,989	17,676	18,445	11,446	16,986	28,431	5,275	2,519	798	914	14,539	32,567	1,022	31,340
Dec	32,339	57,660	30,229 (aw)	120,227 (aw)	35,184	17,455	17,731	11,384	16,637	28,022	5,096	3,002	800	896	16,025	35,622	651	33,351
2013 Jan	30,027	58,403	31,349	119,779	39,591	18,496	17,463	11,599	16,722	28,321	5,160	2,455	815	853	16,367	38,594	1,325	34,185
Feb	30,095	59,164	31,934	121,192	44,552	18,387	17,838	11,866	16,792	28,658	5,191	2,465	829	877	15,933	40,914	704	34,109
Mar	32,878	59,787	31,582	124,247	32,154	17,648	16,357	11,788	17,025	28,814	5,048	2,551	830	1,030	15,806	39,851	714	37,195
Apr	31,614	61,331	30,924	123,869	37,440	18,649	16,478	12,169	17,159	29,327	4,769	2,264	837	1,110	16,102	39,930	606	32,150
May	30,503	62,826	32,215	125,544	37,942	19,521	16,789	12,377	17,296	29,673	5,016	3,191	838	1,084	15,726	42,370	454	27,690
Jun	32,855	67,817	32,995	133,667	37,657	19,068	16,960	12,330	17,228	29,557	4,922	2,960	828	1,244	15,655	45,882	406	25,336
Jul	31,505	65,652	33,257	130,413	43,587	18,122	16,758	12,256	17,586	29,841	4,943	2,920	848	1,212	16,255	45,638	503	36,245 (bc)
Aug	31,327	65,187	32,779	129,292	38,684	18,235	16,806	12,536	17,313	29,849	4,655	2,967	859	1,148	15,976	54,794	639	37,363
Sep	34,286	63,381	26,311	123,978	34,676	19,670	16,340	12,110	17,474	29,584	5,012	2,894	882	1,093	15,721	48,447	388	40,099
Oct	32,410	69,518 (au)	22,618 (ax)	124,545	39,101	20,148	16,681	12,264	17,756	30,020	4,678	2,797	909	935	15,629	47,835	487	44,448
Nov	33,063	69,690 (av)	22,793 (ay)	125,545	37,649	19,080	16,937	12,320	17,800	30,119	5,332	3,024	874	991	15,395	45,214 (bb)	440	42,365
Dec	35,573	67,179	23,097	125,849	33,907	18,089	16,716	12,305	17,736	30,041	5,205	2,836	881	1,064	15,458	37,270	544	41,582

12.5b Industrial analysis of monetary financial institutions deposits from UK residents

£ millions   Not seasonally adjusted

Amounts outstanding of deposit liabilities (including under repo) in sterling and other currencies

	Securities dealers	SPVs related to securitisation	Financial intermediation (excluding insurance and pension funds) Other financial intermediaries	of which intragroup activity	Total	Insurance companies	Pension funds	Total	Fund management activities	Activities auxiliary to financial intermediation Central clearing counterparties	Other auxiliary activities	Total	Total	Total financial and non-financial businesses	Individuals and individual trusts	Total UK residents
RPM	TDBP	B3T6	TDBQ	B3U4	TDBG	B3V2	B7FO	TDBR	TDBS	B7FU	B7FZ	TDBT	B5H5	Z8ZX	TDBU	TDAA
2012 Jan	110,119	294,989	197,601 (bh)	156,647 (bh)	705,051 (bh)	36,515	22,641	59,156	115,037	114,874	16,172	131,046	246,083	1,380,367	972,337	2,352,704
Feb	107,430	270,041	184,040	144,155	663,686	35,808	22,150	57,958	110,603	122,563	16,310	138,873	249,476	1,337,595	978,009	2,315,604
Mar	111,425	262,715	192,790	153,615	671,316	37,681	22,513	60,194	116,384	107,189	16,543	123,733	240,117	1,340,475	988,158	2,328,633
Apr	133,833 (bd)	264,396	196,457 (bi)	156,894 (bi)	695,987 (bd)(bi)	36,608	22,177	58,785	120,139	103,267 (bv)	17,134	120,401 (bv)	240,540 (bv)	1,373,190	991,942	2,365,132 (bi)
May	128,159	267,097 (bf)	197,790	157,377	690,615	36,060	22,143	58,203	117,202	109,088	17,891	126,979	244,180	1,390,556	993,776	2,384,333
Jun	121,264	227,947	199,509	158,184	645,541	38,900	22,090	60,990	113,582	110,821	18,068	128,888	242,470	1,343,776	1,007,891 (by)	2,351,667
Jul	133,427	224,209	193,109	152,639	647,956	39,332	21,398	60,730	115,445	120,433	18,903	139,336	254,782	1,354,241	1,009,295	2,363,535
Aug	129,529	220,170	191,813	148,181	638,652	37,055	19,954	57,009	112,772	122,023	17,732	139,755	252,527	1,338,825	1,016,425	2,355,251
Sep	135,632	218,528	194,080	152,007	639,238	35,968	22,557	58,525	116,069	122,669	17,734	140,404	256,473	1,343,036	1,020,505	2,363,541
Oct	129,175	215,152	187,231 (bj)	145,362 (bj)	623,128 (bj)	34,444	22,252	56,696	119,217	131,609	17,820	149,429	268,647	1,334,913	1,021,503	2,356,416 (bj)
Nov	126,772	216,007	189,524	149,566	621,278	35,062	22,494	57,556	116,262	122,330	18,511	140,841	257,103	1,329,418	1,029,395	2,358,813 (at)
Dec	111,221 (be)	213,863	209,966 (bk)	170,533 (bo)	630,492 (bq)	33,089 (bs)	22,887	55,976 (bs)	112,618	133,924 (bw)	18,451	152,375 (bw)	264,993 (bw)	1,351,861	1,032,753	2,384,614 (ca)
2013 Jan	109,023	200,407	212,014	174,502	621,199	33,943	22,764	56,706	117,921	156,355	18,715	175,070	292,991	1,373,015	1,028,905	2,401,920
Feb	109,523	198,314	208,469	172,087 (bp)	617,330	33,026	28,355 (bt)	61,382 (bt)	121,061	151,700	18,902	170,602	291,663	1,385,435 (bt)	1,036,592	2,422,027 (bt)
Mar	115,626	193,818	209,164	171,062	621,635	34,904	28,918	63,822	125,396	139,337	19,446	158,783	284,180	1,371,145	1,048,312	2,419,457
Apr	124,085	189,414	203,561	166,189	614,828	33,380	29,364	62,745	127,299	155,024 (bx)	20,154	175,178 (bx)	302,477 (bx)	1,384,961 (bx)	1,050,442	2,435,403 (bx)
May	128,686	190,268	201,868	164,993	617,193	33,728	28,968	62,695	126,704	160,326	19,829	180,154	306,858	1,400,755	1,055,682	2,456,437
Jun	126,732	189,285	202,068	164,127	615,316	35,459	29,666	65,125	124,203	152,028	19,821	171,849	296,052	1,395,567	1,058,054	2,453,621
Jul	125,808	188,082	200,727 (bl)	164,176 (br)	623,182 (br)	33,718	29,059	62,777	128,264	152,601	20,173	172,774	301,038	1,411,142 (br)	1,057,268	2,468,410 (br)
Aug	121,064	186,693	205,291	167,341	631,451	32,923	28,514	61,436	133,624	149,073	19,470	168,543	302,167	1,412,145	1,063,555 (bz)	2,475,700
Sep	96,416	187,391	201,308	164,492	599,651	33,276	29,328	62,604	131,932	158,406	20,168	178,574	310,507	1,382,207	1,064,676	2,446,884
Oct	101,980	181,622	193,684	156,857	595,003	31,207	29,330	60,537	129,723	160,489	19,022	179,511	309,234	1,379,467	1,067,133	2,446,600
Nov	105,753	183,813	187,276 (bm)	151,027 (bm)	590,477 (bb)(bm)	31,518	28,932	60,450	132,664 (bu)	163,726	17,890	181,617	314,280 (bu)	1,383,099 (bm)	1,074,374	2,457,473 (bm)
Dec	102,265	179,341 (bg)	183,315 (bn)	145,137 (bn)	569,760	31,710	28,404	60,114	128,710	131,209	17,966	149,175	277,884	1,324,547	1,073,092	2,397,638

Source: Bank of England

12.5b Industrial analysis of monetary financial institutions deposits from UK residents

£ millions   Not seasonally adjusted

Amounts outstanding of deposit liabilities (including under repo) in sterling and other currencies

Notes to table

Movements in amounts outstanding can reflect breaks in data series as well as underlying flows. For changes data, users are recommended to refer directly to the appropriate series or data tables. www.bankofengland.co.uk/statistics/Pages/iadb/notesiadb/Changes_flows_growth_rates.aspx.

(ap) Due to a change in the reporting population, this series has decreased by £0.6bn. The effect has been adjusted out of the flows for December 2012.
(aq) Due to improvements in reporting at one institution, the amounts outstanding decreased by £0.5bn. This effect has been adjusted out of the flows for March 2012.
(ar) Due to improvements in reporting at one institution, the amounts outstanding increased by £1bn. This effect has been adjusted out of the flows for October 2013.
(as) Due to improvements in reporting at one institution, the amounts outstanding decreased by £1bn. This effect has been adjusted out of the flows for October 2013.
(at) Due to improvements in reporting at one institution, the amounts outstanding increased by £0.5bn. This effect has been adjusted out of the flows for November 2012.
(au) Due to improvements in reporting at one institution, the amounts outstanding increased by £4bn. This effect has been adjusted out of the flows for October 2013.
(av) Due to improvements in reporting at one institution, the amounts outstanding decreased by £1bn. This effect has been adjusted out of the flows for November 2013.
(aw) Due to a change in the reporting population, this series has increased by £0.8bn. The effect has been adjusted out of the flows for December 2012.
(ax) Due to improvements in reporting at one institution, the amounts outstanding decreased by £4bn. This effect has been adjusted out of the flows for October 2013.
(ay) Due to improvements in reporting at one institution, the amounts outstanding increased by £1bn. This effect has been adjusted out of the flows for November 2013.
(az) Due to improvements in reporting at one institution, the amounts outstanding increased by £2bn. This effect has been adjusted out of the flows for April 2012.
(ba) Due to a reclassification by one reporting institution from non-bank credit grantors to SPVs, the amounts outstanding decreased by £5bn. This effect has been adjusted out of the flows for May 2012.
(bb) Due to improvements in reporting at one institution, the amounts outstanding decreased by £2bn. This effect has been adjusted out of the flows for November 2013.
(bc) Due to improvements in reporting at one institution, the amounts outstanding increased by £12bn. This effect has been adjusted out of the flows for July 2013.
(bd) Due to changes in the reporting population, the amounts outstanding increased by £7bn. This effect has been adjusted out of the flows for April 2012.
(be) Due to a change in the reporting population, this series has decreased by £4bn. The effect has been adjusted out of the flows for December 2012.
(bf) Due to a reclassification by one reporting institution from non-bank credit grantors to SPVs, the amounts outstanding increased by £5bn. This effect has been adjusted out of the flows for May 2012.
(bg) Due to improvements in reporting at one institution, the amounts outstanding increased by £1bn. This effect has been adjusted out of the flows for December 2013.
(bh) Due to a change in accounting treatment at one reporting institution, the amounts outstanding increased by £12bn. The effect has been adjusted out of the flows for January 2012.
(bi) Due to improvements in reporting at one institution, the amounts outstanding increased by £5bn. This effect has been adjusted out of the flows for April 2012.
(bj) Due to a change in treatment at one reporting institution, the amounts outstanding decreased by £5bn. This effect has been adjusted out of the flows for October 2012.
(bk) Due to a change in the reporting population, this series has decreased by £8bn. The effect has been adjusted out of the flows for December 2012.
(bl) Due to improvements in reporting at one institution, the amounts outstanding increased by £2bn. This effect has been adjusted out of the flows for July 2013.
(bm) Due to improvements in reporting at one institution, the amounts outstanding increased by £3bn. This effect has been adjusted out of the flows for November 2013.
(bn) Due to improvements in reporting at one institution, the amounts outstanding decreased by £1bn. This effect has been adjusted out of the flows for December 2013.
(bo) Due to a change in the reporting population, this series has decreased by £9bn. The effect has been adjusted out of the flows for December 2012.
(bp) Due to improvements in reporting at one institution, the amounts outstanding increased by £1bn. This effect has been adjusted out of the flows for February 2013.
(bq) Due to a change in the reporting population, this series has decreased by £12bn. The effect has been adjusted out of the flows for December 2012.
(br) Due to improvements in reporting at one institution, the amounts outstanding increased by £14bn. This effect has been adjusted out of the flows for July 2013.
(bs) Due to a change in the reporting population, this series has decreased by £3bn. The effect has been adjusted out of the flows for December 2012.
(bt) Due to improvements in reporting at one institution, the amounts outstanding increased by £6bn. This effect has been adjusted out of the flows for February 2013.
(bu) Due to improvements in reporting at one institution, the amounts outstanding increased by £2bn. This effect has been adjusted out of the flows for November 2013.
(bv) Due to changes in the reporting population, the amounts outstanding decreased by £7bn. This effect has been adjusted out of the flows for April 2012.
(bw) Due to a change in the reporting population, this series has increased by £17bn. The effect has been adjusted out of the flows for December 2012.
(bx) Due to improvements in reporting at one institution, the amounts outstanding increased by £7bn. The effect has been adjusted out of the flows for April 2013.
(by) Due to a change in accounting treatment at one reporting institution, the amounts outstanding increased by £7bn. This effect has been adjusted out of the flows for June 2012.
(bz) Due to improvements in reporting at one institution, the amounts outstanding increased by £1bn. This effect has been adjusted out of the flows for August 2013.
(ca) Due to a change in the reporting population, this series has increased by £2bn. The effect has been adjusted out of the flows for December 2012.

12.6a Components of M4

£ millions   Seasonally adjusted

Amounts outstanding

| | Retail deposits and cash in M4 | | | Wholesale deposits in M4 | | M4 | M3 |
| | Deposits | Notes and coin | Total | Deposits | of which repos | | (estimate of EMU aggregate for the UK) |
LPM	B3SF	VQJO	VQWK (a)	VRGP	VZZQ	AUYN	VWYZ
2011 Dec	1,211,891 (b)	53,468	1,265,360 (b)	821,964	101,563	2,088,402	2,270,811
2012 Jan	1,214,390	54,198	1,268,588	828,206 (d)	110,692	2,106,259 (d)	2,290,288
Feb	1,219,481	54,466	1,273,947	797,838	118,133	2,077,387	2,266,129
Mar	1,223,132	54,577	1,277,709	786,777	94,555	2,060,572	2,266,159
Apr	1,224,785	54,384	1,279,169	803,678 (e)(f)	106,712	2,080,434 (e)(f)	2,274,411
May	1,229,933	54,947	1,284,879	805,709	108,557	2,088,597	2,290,671
Jun	1,240,639 (c)	55,282	1,295,921 (c)	774,559	106,773	2,060,090 (c)	2,273,993
Jul	1,246,329	55,561	1,301,890	770,650	112,681	2,068,435	2,293,842
Aug	1,259,216	55,648	1,314,864	766,777	115,769	2,076,691	2,290,629
Sep	1,263,033	55,719	1,318,752	758,165	117,276	2,079,179	2,297,604
Oct	1,270,268	55,911	1,326,179	747,835 (g)	117,238	2,076,382 (g)	2,299,418
Nov	1,276,737	56,105	1,332,842	735,152	109,095	2,071,108	2,300,338
Dec	1,278,541	56,525	1,335,066	752,086	120,601	2,090,939	2,335,374
2013 Jan	1,288,627	56,764	1,345,391	749,526	120,524	2,105,553	2,355,569
Feb	1,295,590	57,117	1,352,707	749,258 (h)	115,560	2,108,173 (h)	2,366,289
Mar	1,298,064	56,744	1,354,808	731,923	107,620	2,083,967	2,360,384
Apr	1,301,028	57,672	1,358,700	729,767	116,921	2,087,820	2,365,341
May	1,312,137	58,024	1,370,161	725,131	115,565	2,090,912	2,380,936
Jun	1,317,490	58,166	1,375,656	722,728	113,799	2,090,789	2,392,542
Jul	1,324,288	58,804	1,383,092	733,684 (i)	117,432	2,112,841 (i)	2,407,302
Aug	1,329,284	58,848	1,388,132	744,584	121,024	2,127,135	2,417,517
Sep	1,333,007	59,676	1,392,683	743,859	120,213	2,138,963	2,387,895
Oct	1,340,298	59,509	1,399,808	737,293	116,361	2,140,862	2,391,795
Nov	1,348,677	59,195	1,407,872	732,148 (j)	114,882	2,139,400 (j)	2,401,476

Notes to table   Source: Bank of England

Movements in amounts outstanding can reflect breaks in data series as well as underlying flows. For changes and growth rates data, users are recommended to refer directly to the appropriate series or data tables. Further details can be found at to www.bankofengland.co.uk/statistics/Pages/iadb/notesiadb/Changes_flows_growth_rates.aspx

(a) A minor change was made to the definition of Retail M4 in October 2007. From October data onwards, non-interest-bearing bank deposits are only included in Retail M4 when reporters identify them explicitly as being taken from retail sources. There was also a change to the reporting population in October 2007. Together these led to a break in the amount outstanding of Retail M4 in October 2007. The effect of this has been removed from the flows data.

(b) Due to improvements in reporting at one institution, the amounts outstanding increased by £2bn. This effect has been adjusted out of the flows for December 2011.

(c) Due to a change in accounting treatment at one reporting institution, the amounts outstanding increased by £7bn. This effect has been adjusted out of the flows for June 2012.

(d) Due to a change in accounting treatment at one reporting institution, the amounts outstanding increased by £12bn. This effect has been adjusted out of the flows for January 2012.

(e) Due to improvements in reporting at one institution, the amounts outstanding increased by £5bn. This effect has been adjusted out of the flows for April 2012.

(f) Due to a change in treatment at one reporting institution, the amounts outstanding increased by £5bn. This effect has been adjusted out of the flows for April 2012.

(g) Due to a change in treatment at one reporting institution, the amounts outstanding decreased by £5bn. This effect has been adjusted out of the flows for October 2012.

(h) Due to improvements in reporting at one institution, the amounts outstanding increased by £6bn. This effect has been adjusted out of the flows for February 2013.

(i) Due to improvements in reporting at one institution, the amounts outstanding increased by £8bn. This effect has been adjusted out of the flows for July 2013.

(j) Due to a restructuring at one reporting institution, the amounts outstanding decreased by £3bn. This effect has been adjusted out of the flows for November 2013.

Explanatory notes

12.6b Components of M4

£ millions   Not seasonally adjusted

Changes

| LPM | Retail deposits and cash in M4 | | | Wholesale deposits in M4 | | M4 | M3 (estimate of EMU aggregate for the UK) |
	Deposits	Notes and coin	Total	Deposits	of which repos		
	VRLW	VQLU	VQZA	VRLR	VWDN	AUZI	VWXK
2011 Dec	13,482	751	14,233	-34,195	-8,605	-19,962	-45,444
2012 Jan	-10,116	-1,645	-11,761	3,854	18,189	-7,907	8,194
Feb	5,864	274	6,138	-33,530	3,554	-27,393	-25,709
Mar	18,930	1,149	20,079	-16,131	-21,168	3,948	17,770
Apr	-782	-296	-1,079	7,805	12,968	6,726	17,138
May	2,725	160	2,885	-3,573	945	-688	8,010
Jun	7,089	1,031	8,120	-35,916	-3,362	-27,796	-27,103
Jul	-2,407	-427	-2,834	338	8,357	-2,496	16,074
Aug	12,394	444	12,839	-1,975	2,457	10,863	-9,931
Sep	8,360	210	8,570	-4,751	2,349	3,819	21,360
Oct	3,044	-432	2,612	-2,404	2,841	208	-1,531
Nov	9,295	1,493	10,788	-9,258	-7,495	1,530	1,363
Dec	7,316	950	8,267	7,463	-4,077	15,730	21,418
2013 Jan	-3,287	-1,947	-5,234	6,017	15,718	783	6,562
Feb	7,941	411	8,352	-9,580	-5,570	-1,228	-2,385
Mar	17,012	1,514	18,527	-21,535	-16,748	-3,008	12,128
Apr	-323	-559	-882	-419	12,045	-1,301	11,549
May	9,065	1,299	10,364	-6,257	185	4,107	20,036
Jun	8,036	402	8,438	-6,517	-7,624	1,921	1,042
Jul	-1,266	-386	-1,652	4,469	8,257	2,817	-9,056
Aug	3,883	495	4,378	15,335	8,592	19,713	15,906
Sep	7,283	303	7,586	2,302	-1	9,888	-5,918
Oct	1,620	-274	1,346	-3,120	887	-1,774	-9,481
Nov	11,945	1,114	13,060	-1,325	-3,640	11,735	23,986

Notes to table

Source: Bank of England

12.7 Counterparts to changes in M4: alternative presentation

£ millions   Not seasonally adjusted

Changes

| | Public sector net cash requirement (PSNCR) | M4 private sector net purchases (-) of Central Government debt | | | | | | M4 private sector net purchases of other public sector debt | | | |
		Gilts	Sterling treasury bills	Tax instruments	National Savings	Other	Total	Local government debt (-)	Public corporation debt (-)	Other public sector purchases of M4 private sector debt (+)	Total
LPM	ABEN	AVBY	VQLK	VQLG	VQLJ	VQLI	RCMD	VQLL	VQLO	VQLQ	AVBV
2011 Dec	24,817	-8,954	-8,389	-10	-170	-2,942	-20,465	-49	-	597	548
2012 Jan	-16,788	4,109	1,905	2	104	17,990	24,109	62	-	633	695
Feb	6,917	-3,467	1,108	59	197	4,644	2,541	-79	-	-563	-642
Mar	28,297	26,755	-2,906	-5	575	-21,217	3,202	-235	-	-762	-997
Apr	-8,384	-10,349	2,338	-17	77	12,209	4,259	-960	-	1,044	84
May	11,364	-11,836	3,670	-2	190	-423	-8,402	63	-	492	555
Jun	20,201	3,634	-8,273	-21	-107	-14,701	-19,468	-209	-	782	573
Jul	-5,750	-1,737	3,184	-12	165	16,049	17,650	147	-	-94	53
Aug	9,597	3,092	2,851	-6	331	-2,439	3,830	-1,499	-	377	-1,122
Sep	21,790	-3,616	2,344	-12	132	-1,159	-2,311	112	-	45	157
Oct	4,132	-2,813	3,132	11	4	14,339	14,674	-80	-	-418	-498
Nov	12,376	-7,615	1,436	21	87	-7,072	-13,143	210	-	-91	119
Dec	22,839	8,074	243	-27	-32	-16,583	-8,326	-253	-	26	-227
2013 Jan	-17,571	-6,854	-213	-10	7	26,232	19,162	-180	-	255	75
Feb	1,826	-4,976	241	38	-172	3,637	-1,231	179	-	-881	-702
Mar	27,445	30,832	-4,166	41	-11	-25,006	1,690	602	-	-1,924	-1,322
Apr	-4,187	-14,348	378	-57	-529	2,007	-12,549	-1,098	-	4,106	3,008
May	9,541	-62	2,198	-28	-570	388	1,926	-486	-	-231	-717
Jun	12,848	-13,879	2,406	-21	-664	1,675	-10,483	-25	-	-752	-777
Jul	-8,825	-3,577	2,793	10	-519	10,623	9,329	-306	-	-30	-336
Aug	9,249	-3,941	570	-58	-179	-7,043	-10,651	128	-	-901	-773
Sep	15,011	-10,213	-706	-35	-35	3,883	-7,106	-276	-	-683	-959
Oct	-4,785	-6,063	2,508	-21	-230	14,184	10,378	134	-	55	189
Nov	12,034	6,173	1,535	-14	-93	490	8,090	147	-	-637	-490

£ millions   Not seasonally adjusted

Changes

| | Purchases of public sector net debt (-) | External and foreign currency finance of public sector | | | | Public sector contribution | M4 lending | | | |
		Non-residents' purchases of gilts (-)	Non-residents' purchases of £TBs (-)	Other	Total		Loans	of which reverse repos	Investments	Total
LPM	VQLN	VQCZ	VRME	VQOC	VQDC	VWZL (a)	VYAJ	VWDP	VYAP	AVBS (b)
2011 Dec	-19,917	10,663	1,342	-12,294	-289	4,611	-7,100	1,538	-4,894	-11,995
2012 Jan	24,804	-9,414	446	5,077	-3,891	4,125	-6,015	-7,157	-13,967	-19,983
Feb	1,899	4,659	-286	4,258	8,632	17,448	3,138	7,324	-24,136	-20,998
Mar	2,205	1,730	-2,325	197	-399	30,103	-4,815	-8,618	-5,277	-10,092
Apr	4,343	1,257	1,208	302	2,768	-1,273	3,976	2,634	-4,133	-157
May	-7,847	1,603	536	1,460	3,599	7,116	-5,800	-893	-5,704	-11,505
Jun	-18,895	7,128	-1,508	-4,878	742	2,047	10,316	10,485	-36,911	-26,594
Jul	17,703	-9,371	409	3,139	-5,823	6,130	-4,740	-8,951	-6,810	-11,551
Aug	2,708	-5,572	336	-1,836	-7,071	5,234	1,095	4,602	-2,780	-1,685
Sep	-2,155	-1,839	362	-3,584	-5,062	14,573	7,704	7,802	1,375	9,079
Oct	14,175	-4,317	1,299	-1,844	-4,861	13,446	-6,656	-5,499	3,486	-3,170
Nov	-13,024	-2,319	1,110	2,612	1,403	755	8,145	9,304	-3,416	4,728
Dec	-8,553	-15,444	1,439	642	-13,364	922	17,337	2,722	10,674	28,011
2013 Jan	19,238	-1,560	1,137	-1,885	-2,309	-642	2,129	-373	-9,405	-7,276
Feb	-1,934	-7,488	-124	4,877	-2,735	-2,843	-4,929	-1,898	-3,014	-7,943
Mar	368	-8,275	-1,239	-3,684	-13,197	14,616	-8,732	-4,971	-4,151	-12,883
Apr	-9,540	3,907	659	-446	4,120	-9,607	-6,776	7,110	-3,421	-10,197
May	1,209	-6,871	870	1,522	-4,479	6,271	-2,013	3,270	-3,643	-5,656
Jun	-11,260	2,607	582	-669	2,520	4,108	-5,440	-3,034	11	-5,429
Jul	8,993	-1,252	1,040	1,008	796	964	-1,745	-4,571	1,251	-495
Aug	-11,424	6,057	128	-462	5,723	3,548	14,348	5,009	2,913	17,260
Sep	-8,066	-2,476	338	-683	-2,821	4,124	12,151	8,137	-3,588	8,563
Oct	10,567	-929	204	622	-102	5,680	-6,114	-11,427	-9,778	-15,892
Nov	7,600	-15,935	513	2,201	-13,221	6,414	5,903	2,741	2,501	8,404

12.7 Counterparts to changes in M4: alternative presentation

£ millions   Not seasonally adjusted

Changes

LPM	External and foreign currency flows			Total external counterparts	Net non-deposit £ liabilities (-)	M4
	Net sterling deposits from non-residents (-)	Net foreign currency liabilities (-)	Total			
	B69P	**B72P**	**AVBW**	**VQLP**	**VWZV**	**AUZI**
2011 Dec	-24,092	1,718	**-22,374**	-22,663	9,796	**-19,962**
2012 Jan	17,398	-34,222	**-16,824**	-20,715	24,774	**-7,907**
Feb	-29,372	-1,944	**-31,316**	-22,684	7,474	**-27,393**
Mar	-2,579	-4,705	**-7,284**	-7,683	-8,780	**3,948**
Apr	16,169	-1,818	**14,351**	17,119	-6,194	**6,726**
May	-17,977	18,038	**61**	3,659	3,639	**-688**
Jun	-1,285	-20,310	**-21,594**	-20,852	18,345	**-27,796**
Jul	-18,750	17,010	**-1,739**	-7,562	4,663	**-2,496**
Aug	792	-6,992	**-6,199**	-13,271	13,514	**10,863**
Sep	-4,918	-852	**-5,770**	-10,832	-14,063	**3,819**
Oct	-8,407	-162	**-8,570**	-13,431	-1,498	**208**
Nov	2,277	-9,051	**-6,774**	-5,372	2,821	**1,530**
Dec	-13,539	985	**-12,554**	-25,918	-648	**15,730**
2013 Jan	11,904	10,473	**22,378**	20,069	-13,677	**783**
Feb	-5,561	26,857	**21,296**	18,561	-11,738	**-1,228**
Mar	-3,161	-11,981	**-15,143**	-28,340	10,402	**-3,008**
Apr	511	11,151	**11,662**	15,782	6,841	**-1,301**
May	-1,786	-3,374	**-5,160**	-9,640	8,653	**4,107**
Jun	9,981	-6,280	**3,701**	6,221	-459	**1,921**
Jul	-4,473	5,178	**705**	1,500	1,643	**2,817**
Aug	12,572	-24,821	**-12,248**	-6,525	11,153	**19,713**
Sep	-11,364	-21,248	**-32,612**	-35,434	29,813	**9,888**
Oct	18,270	2,581	**20,851**	20,748	-12,413	**-1,774**
Nov	-1,620	-10,624	**-12,244**	-25,464	9,161	**11,735**

Notes to table   Source: Bank of England

[a] Net sterling lending to the public sector includes holdings of coin. Coin is a liability of Central Government and therefore outside of the MFIs' consolidated balance sheet. Holdings of coin are a component of M4 and are therefore included here in order to reconcile the counterparts.

[b] M4 lending may be affected by securitisations and loan transfers up to December 2009 and loan transfers from January 2010. Please see www.bankofengland.co.uk/statistics/documents/ms/articles/art1feb10.pdf for more details.

12.8 Selected retail banks' base rate
Daily average of 4 UK Banks' base rates

Date of change	New rate	Date of change	New rate	Date of change	New rate
09-Jan-86	12.5	17-Sep-92	10.5	05-Jul-07	5.75
19-Mar-86	11.5	18-Sep-92	10	06-Dec-07	5.5
08-Apr-86	11.13	22-Sep-92	9	07-Feb-08	5.25
09-Apr-86	11	16-Oct-92	8.25	10-Apr-08	5
21-Apr-86	10.5	19-Oct-92	8	08-Oct-08	4.5
23-May-86	10.25	13-Nov-92	7	06-Nov-08	3
27-May-86	10	26-Jan-93	6	04-Dec-08	2
14-Oct-86	10.5	23-Nov-93	5.5	08-Jan-09	1.5
15-Oct-86	11	08-Feb-94	5.25	05-Feb-09	1
10-Mar-87	10.5	12-Sep-94	5.75	05-Mar-09	0.5
18-Mar-87	10.25	07-Dec-94	6.25	04-Jan-10	0.5
19-Mar-87	10	02-Feb-95	6.63	31-Dec-10	0.5
28-Apr-87	9.88	03-Feb-95	6.75	04-Jan-11	0.5
29-Apr-87	9.5	13-Dec-95	6.5	30-Dec-11	0.5
11-May-87	9	18-Jan-96	6.25	03-Jan-12	0.5
06-Aug-87	9.25	08-Mar-96	6	31-Dec-12	0.5
07-Aug-87	10	06-Jun-96	5.75		
23-Oct-87	9.88	30-Oct-96	5.94		
26-Oct-87	9.5	31-Oct-96	6		
04-Nov-87	9.38	06-May-97	6.25		
05-Nov-87	9	06-Jun-97	6.44		
04-Dec-87	8.5	09-Jun-97	6.5		
02-Feb-88	9	10-Jul-97	6.75		
17-Mar-88	8.63	07-Aug-97	7		
18-Mar-88	8.5	06-Nov-97	7.25		
11-Apr-88	8	04-Jun-98	7.5		
17-May-88	7.88	08-Oct-98	7.25		
18-May-88	7.5	06-Nov-98	6.75		
02-Jun-88	7.75	10-Dec-98	6.25		
03-Jun-88	8	07-Jan-99	6		
06-Jun-88	8.25	04-Feb-99	5.5		
07-Jun-88	8.5	08-Apr-99	5.25		
22-Jun-88	8.88	10-Jun-99	5		
23-Jun-88	9	08-Sep-99	5.19		
28-Jun-88	9.25	10-Sep-99	5.25		
29-Jun-88	9.5	04-Nov-99	5.5		
04-Jul-88	9.88	14-Jan-00	5.75		
05-Jul-88	10	10-Feb-00	6		
18-Jul-88	10.38	08-Feb-01	5.75		
19-Jul-88	10.5	05-Apr-01	5.5		
08-Aug-88	10.88	10-May-01	5.25		
09-Aug-88	11	02-Aug-01	5		
25-Aug-88	11.75	18-Sep-01	4.75		
26-Aug-88	12	04-Oct-01	4.5		
25-Nov-88	13	08-Nov-01	4		
24-May-89	14	07-Feb-03	3.75		
05-Oct-89	15	11-Jul-03	3.5		
08-Oct-90	14	06-Nov-03	3.75		
13-Feb-91	13.5	05-Feb-04	4		
27-Feb-91	13	07-May-04	4.25		
22-Mar-91	12.5	10-Jun-04	4.5		
12-Apr-91	12	05-Aug-04	4.75		
24-May-91	11.5	04-Aug-05	4.5		
12-Jul-91	11	03-Aug-06	4.75		
04-Sep-91	10.5	09-Nov-06	5		
05-May-92	10	11-Jan-07	5.25		
16-Sep-92	12	10-May-07	5.5		

1 Data obtained from Barclays Bank, Lloyds/TSB Bank, HSBC Bank and National Westminster Bank whose rates are used to compile this series.

2 Where all the rates did not change on the same day a spread is shown.

Source: Bank of England: 020 7601 3644

12.9 Average three month sterling money market rates

Monthly average rate of discount, 3 month Treasury bills, Sterling **IUMAAJNB**		Monthly average of Eligible bills discount rate, 3 month (a) **IUMAAJND**		Monthly average Sterling 3 month mean interbank lending rate **IUMAAMIJ**		Monthly average of Sterling certificates of deposit interest rate, 3 months, mean offer/bid **IUMAVCDA**	
31-Jan-98	6.8426	31-Jan-98	7.28	31-Jan-98	7.4762	31-Jan-98	7.44
28-Feb-98	6.8778	28-Feb-98	7.24	28-Feb-98	7.4595	28-Feb-98	7.42
31-Mar-98	6.9513	31-Mar-98	7.25	31-Mar-98	7.4774	31-Mar-98	7.43
30-Apr-98	7.0027	30-Apr-98	7.24	30-Apr-98	7.437	30-Apr-98	7.4
31-May-98	7.01	31-May-98	7.2	31-May-98	7.4069	31-May-98	7.37
30-Jun-98	7.2916	30-Jun-98	7.42	30-Jun-98	7.6258	30-Jun-98	7.59
31-Jul-98	7.219	31-Jul-98	7.49	31-Jul-98	7.7088	31-Jul-98	7.66
31-Aug-98	7.194	31-Aug-98	7.4	31-Aug-98	7.6558	31-Aug-98	7.61
30-Sep-98	6.9448	30-Sep-98	7.2	30-Sep-98	7.3825	30-Sep-98	7.34
31-Oct-98	6.5383	31-Oct-98	6.91	31-Oct-98	7.1352	31-Oct-98	7.09
30-Nov-98	6.3118	30-Nov-98	6.52	30-Nov-98	6.8881	30-Nov-98	6.82
31-Dec-98	5.7172	31-Dec-98	6.05	31-Dec-98	6.3817	31-Dec-98	6.32
31-Jan-99	5.2781	31-Jan-99	5.63	31-Jan-99	5.7985	31-Jan-99	5.74
28-Feb-99	5.0407	28-Feb-99	5.28	28-Feb-99	5.4328	28-Feb-99	5.38
31-Mar-99	4.9192	31-Mar-99	5.11	31-Mar-99	5.303	31-Mar-99	5.26
30-Apr-99	4.9003	30-Apr-99	5.02	30-Apr-99	5.2313	30-Apr-99	5.19
31-May-99	4.9302	31-May-99	5.08	31-May-99	5.2482	31-May-99	5.22
30-Jun-99	4.7598	30-Jun-99	4.94	30-Jun-99	5.1234	30-Jun-99	5.09
31-Jul-99	4.7596	31-Jul-99	4.89	31-Jul-99	5.0657	31-Jul-99	5.03
31-Aug-99	4.8495	31-Aug-99	4.94	31-Aug-99	5.1795	31-Aug-99	5.14
30-Sep-99	5.1223	30-Sep-99	5.16	30-Sep-99	5.3168	30-Sep-99	5.28
31-Oct-99	5.2315	31-Oct-99	5.42	31-Oct-99	5.9388	31-Oct-99	5.86
30-Nov-99	5.2018	30-Nov-99	5.43	30-Nov-99	5.7824	30-Nov-99	5.72
31-Dec-99	5.4637	31-Dec-99	5.59	31-Dec-99	5.9656	31-Dec-99	5.89
31-Jan-00	5.7218	31-Jan-00	5.9	31-Jan-00	6.0578	31-Jan-00	6.02
29-Feb-00	5.8346	29-Feb-00	6.01	29-Feb-00	6.1492	29-Feb-00	6.1
31-Mar-00	5.8582	31-Mar-00	5.98	31-Mar-00	6.1458	31-Mar-00	6.09
30-Apr-00	5.9178	30-Apr-00	6.05	30-Apr-00	6.2129	30-Apr-00	6.17
31-May-00	5.9501	31-May-00	6.09	31-May-00	6.2289	31-May-00	6.19
30-Jun-00	5.8535	30-Jun-00	6.03	30-Jun-00	6.1423	30-Jun-00	6.1
31-Jul-00	5.8333	31-Jul-00	5.97	31-Jul-00	6.1146	31-Jul-00	6.08
31-Aug-00	5.8103	31-Aug-00	5.97	31-Aug-00	6.1365	31-Aug-00	6.09
30-Sep-00	5.7798	30-Sep-00	5.95	30-Sep-00	6.1191	30-Sep-00	6.08
31-Oct-00	5.7482	31-Oct-00	5.92	31-Oct-00	6.081	31-Oct-00	6.05
30-Nov-00	5.6833	30-Nov-00	5.88	30-Nov-00	6.0007	30-Nov-00	5.98
31-Dec-00	5.6229	31-Dec-00	5.78	31-Dec-00	5.8882	31-Dec-00	5.85
31-Jan-01	5.4852	31-Jan-01	5.64	31-Jan-01	5.7642	31-Jan-01	5.73
28-Feb-01	5.4582	28-Feb-01	5.56	28-Feb-01	5.6854	28-Feb-01	5.66
31-Mar-01	5.2286	31-Mar-01	5.37	31-Mar-01	5.473	31-Mar-01	5.44
30-Apr-01	5.1158	30-Apr-01	5.21	30-Apr-01	5.3323	30-Apr-01	5.3
31-May-01	4.9765	31-May-01	5.06	31-May-01	5.1727	31-May-01	5.15
30-Jun-01	4.991	30-Jun-01	5.08	30-Jun-01	5.189	30-Jun-01	5.16
31-Jul-01	5.0052	31-Jul-01	5.07	31-Jul-01	5.1917	31-Jul-01	5.17
31-Aug-01	4.7198	31-Aug-01	4.82	31-Aug-01	4.9269	31-Aug-01	4.9
30-Sep-01	4.4297	30-Sep-01	4.57	30-Sep-01	4.6485	30-Sep-01	4.62
31-Oct-01	4.1567	31-Oct-01	4.26	31-Oct-01	4.3594	31-Oct-01	4.33
30-Nov-01	3.7799	30-Nov-01	3.85	30-Nov-01	3.9326	30-Nov-01	3.91
31-Dec-01	3.8296	31-Dec-01	3.88	31-Dec-01	3.9852	31-Dec-01	3.96
31-Jan-02	3.8321	31-Jan-02	3.91	31-Jan-02	3.978	31-Jan-02	3.96
28-Feb-02	3.868	28-Feb-02	3.92	28-Feb-02	3.9805	28-Feb-02	3.96
31-Mar-02	3.9672	31-Mar-02	3.99	31-Mar-02	4.0609	31-Mar-02	4.04
30-Apr-02	3.9693	30-Apr-02	4.04	30-Apr-02	4.1086	30-Apr-02	4.08
31-May-02	3.9525	31-May-02	4.01	31-May-02	4.0795	31-May-02	4.06
30-Jun-02	3.9767	30-Jun-02	4.04	30-Jun-02	4.112	30-Jun-02	4.09

12.9 Average three month sterling money market rates

Monthly average rate of discount, 3 month Treasury bills, Sterling IUMAAJNB		Monthly average of Eligible bills discount rate, 3 month (a) IUMAAJND		Monthly average Sterling 3 month mean interbank lending rate IUMAAMIJ		Monthly average of Sterling certificates of deposit interest rate, 3 months, mean offer/bid IUMAVCDA	
31-Jul-02	3.8408	31-Jul-02	3.94	31-Jul-02	3.9925	31-Jul-02	3.97
31-Aug-02	3.7663	31-Aug-02	3.86	31-Aug-02	3.9174	31-Aug-02	3.9
30-Sep-02	3.7861	30-Sep-02	3.86	30-Sep-02	3.9315	30-Sep-02	3.91
31-Oct-02	3.7509	31-Oct-02	3.82	31-Oct-02	3.9015	31-Oct-02	3.88
30-Nov-02	3.8033	30-Nov-02	3.84	30-Nov-02	3.9091	30-Nov-02	3.89
31-Dec-02	3.8418	31-Dec-02	3.71	31-Dec-02	3.9488	31-Dec-02	3.93
31-Jan-03	3.7993	31-Jan-03	3.87	31-Jan-03	3.9132	31-Jan-03	3.9
28-Feb-03	3.4993	28-Feb-03	3.65	28-Feb-03	3.6888	28-Feb-03	3.68
31-Mar-03	3.4721	31-Mar-03	3.54	31-Mar-03	3.5838	31-Mar-03	3.57
30-Apr-03	3.4537	30-Apr-03	3.52	30-Apr-03	3.576	30-Apr-03	3.57
31-May-03	3.4366	31-May-03	3.52	31-May-03	3.5665	31-May-03	3.56
30-Jun-03	3.4724	30-Jun-03	3.45	30-Jun-03	3.5702	30-Jun-03	3.56
31-Jul-03	3.3119	31-Jul-03	3.39	31-Jul-03	3.42	31-Jul-03	3.41
31-Aug-03	3.3998	31-Aug-03	3.42	31-Aug-03	3.4518	31-Aug-03	3.44
30-Sep-03	3.5239	30-Sep-03	3.59	30-Sep-03	3.6311	30-Sep-03	3.62
31-Oct-03	3.6514	31-Oct-03	3.69	31-Oct-03	3.727	31-Oct-03	3.72
30-Nov-03	3.808	30-Nov-03	3.88	30-Nov-03	3.9085	30-Nov-03	3.9
31-Dec-03	3.8298	31-Dec-03	3.9	31-Dec-03	3.949	31-Dec-03	3.94
31-Jan-04	3.8983	31-Jan-04	3.94	31-Jan-04	3.986	31-Jan-04	3.98
29-Feb-04	3.9788	29-Feb-04	4.06	29-Feb-04	4.101	29-Feb-04	4.09
31-Mar-04	4.1025	31-Mar-04	4.19	31-Mar-04	4.2328	31-Mar-04	4.22
30-Apr-04	4.1862	30-Apr-04	4.28	30-Apr-04	4.3288	30-Apr-04	4.32
31-May-04	4.34	31-May-04	4.42	31-May-04	4.4555	31-May-04	4.45
30-Jun-04	4.5793	30-Jun-04	4.68	30-Jun-04	4.7305	30-Jun-04	4.72
31-Jul-04	4.6424	31-Jul-04	4.75	31-Jul-04	4.7859	31-Jul-04	4.79
31-Aug-04	4.7218	31-Aug-04	4.85	31-Aug-04	4.8938	31-Aug-04	4.89
30-Sep-04	4.6937	30-Sep-04	4.83	30-Sep-04	4.8743	30-Sep-04	4.87
31-Oct-04	4.679	31-Oct-04	4.79	31-Oct-04	4.8336	31-Oct-04	4.83
30-Nov-04	4.6578	30-Nov-04	4.78	30-Nov-04	4.8159	30-Nov-04	4.81
31-Dec-04	4.677	31-Dec-04	4.77	31-Dec-04	4.8057	31-Dec-04	4.8
31-Jan-05	4.6568	31-Jan-05	4.75	31-Jan-05	4.8045	31-Jan-05	4.8
28-Feb-05	4.6858	28-Feb-05	4.78	28-Feb-05	4.822	28-Feb-05	4.82
31-Mar-05	4.7691	31-Mar-05	4.88	31-Mar-05	4.9186	31-Mar-05	4.91
30-Apr-05	4.7047	30-Apr-05	4.84	30-Apr-05	4.8756	30-Apr-05	4.86
31-May-05	4.6618	31-May-05	4.8	31-May-05	4.8253	31-May-05	4.82
30-Jun-05	4.6175	30-Jun-05	4.76	30-Jun-05	4.7777	30-Jun-05	4.78
31-Jul-05	4.4609	31-Jul-05	4.57	31-Jul-05	4.5948	31-Jul-05	4.6
31-Aug-05	4.4057	31-Aug-05	4.51	31-Aug-05	4.533	31-Aug-05	4.53
30-Sep-05	4.4037	30-Sep-05	-	30-Sep-05	4.5359	30-Sep-05	4.54
31-Oct-05	4.402	31-Oct-05	-	31-Oct-05	4.525	31-Oct-05	4.52
30-Nov-05	4.4169	30-Nov-05	-	30-Nov-05	4.5614	30-Nov-05	4.56
31-Dec-05	4.4287	31-Dec-05	-	31-Dec-05	4.587	31-Dec-05	4.58
31-Jan-06	4.3906	31-Jan-06	-	31-Jan-06	4.5369	31-Jan-06	4.54
28-Feb-06	4.3839	28-Feb-06	-	28-Feb-06	4.5203	28-Feb-06	4.52
31-Mar-06	4.3956	31-Mar-06	-	31-Mar-06	4.5263	31-Mar-06	4.53
30-Apr-06	4.4196	30-Apr-06	-	30-Apr-06	4.5725	30-Apr-06	4.57
31-May-06	4.5012	31-May-06	-	31-May-06	4.6519	31-May-06	4.65
30-Jun-06	4.5414	30-Jun-06	-	30-Jun-06	4.6927	30-Jun-06	4.69
31-Jul-06	4.534	31-Jul-06	-	31-Jul-06	4.6838	31-Jul-06	4.68
31-Aug-06	4.7544	31-Aug-06	-	31-Aug-06	4.8968	31-Aug-06	4.89
30-Sep-06	4.8359	30-Sep-06	-	30-Sep-06	4.9819	30-Sep-06	4.98
31-Oct-06	4.9357	31-Oct-06	-	31-Oct-06	5.0909	31-Oct-06	5.09
30-Nov-06	5.0095	30-Nov-06	-	30-Nov-06	5.1791	30-Nov-06	5.18
31-Dec-06	5.0759	31-Dec-06	-	31-Dec-06	5.2453	31-Dec-06	5.24

12.9 Average three month sterling money market rates

	Monthly average rate of discount, 3 month Treasury bills, Sterling IUMAAJNB		Monthly average of Eligible bills discount rate, 3 month (a) IUMAAJND		Monthly average Sterling 3 month mean interbank lending rate IUMAAMIJ		Monthly average of Sterling certificates of deposit interest rate, 3 months, mean offer/bid IUMAVCDA
31-Jan-07	5.304	31-Jan-07	-	31-Jan-07	5.4545	31-Jan-07	5.45
28-Feb-07	5.3393	28-Feb-07	-	28-Feb-07	5.5248	28-Feb-07	5.51
31-Mar-07	5.3274	31-Mar-07	-	31-Mar-07	5.5041	31-Mar-07	5.52
30-Apr-07	5.4329	30-Apr-07	-	30-Apr-07	5.6058	30-Apr-07	5.69
31-May-07	5.5516	31-May-07	-	31-May-07	5.7221	31-May-07	5.84
30-Jun-07	5.6702	30-Jun-07	-	30-Jun-07	5.8348	30-Jun-07	5.94
31-Jul-07	5.7742	31-Jul-07	-	31-Jul-07	5.9789	31-Jul-07	6.11
31-Aug-07	5.7943	31-Aug-07	-	31-Aug-07	6.3389	31-Aug-07	6.35
30-Sep-07	5.6896	30-Sep-07	-	30-Sep-07	6.5813	30-Sep-07	6.54
31-Oct-07	5.6058	31-Oct-07	-	31-Oct-07	6.2122	31-Oct-07	6.21
30-Nov-07	5.4986	30-Nov-07	-	30-Nov-07	6.3564	30-Nov-07	6.34
31-Dec-07	5.3034	31-Dec-07	-	31-Dec-07	6.3542	31-Dec-07	6.35
31-Jan-08	5.1215	31-Jan-08	-	31-Jan-08	5.6071	31-Jan-08	5.61
29-Feb-08	5.0178	29-Feb-08	-	29-Feb-08	5.6083	29-Feb-08	5.6
31-Mar-08	4.8835	31-Mar-08	-	31-Mar-08	5.8555	31-Mar-08	5.85
30-Apr-08	4.8258	30-Apr-08	-	30-Apr-08	5.8961	30-Apr-08	5.89
31-May-08	4.9496	31-May-08	-	31-May-08	5.7933	31-May-08	5.79
30-Jun-08	5.1138	30-Jun-08	-	30-Jun-08	5.9002	30-Jun-08	5.89
31-Jul-08	5.0843	31-Jul-08	-	31-Jul-08	5.803	31-Jul-08	5.8
31-Aug-08	4.9539	31-Aug-08	-	31-Aug-08	5.7588	31-Aug-08	5.75
30-Sep-08	4.7425	30-Sep-08	-	30-Sep-08	5.8698	30-Sep-08	5.86
31-Oct-08	3.6788	31-Oct-08	-	31-Oct-08	6.1772	31-Oct-08	6.16
30-Nov-08	1.9948	30-Nov-08	-	30-Nov-08	4.3955	30-Nov-08	4.4
31-Dec-08	1.2875	31-Dec-08	-	31-Dec-08	3.2143	31-Dec-08	3.21
31-Jan-09	0.8945	31-Jan-09	-	31-Jan-09	2.28	31-Jan-09	2.29
28-Feb-09	0.7177	28-Feb-09	-	28-Feb-09	2.0758	28-Feb-09	2.06
31-Mar-09	0.6035	31-Mar-09	-	31-Mar-09	1.8273	31-Mar-09	1.79
30-Apr-09	0.625	30-Apr-09	-	30-Apr-09	1.4838	30-Apr-09	1.43
31-May-09	0.5271	31-May-09	-	31-May-09	1.3026	31-May-09	1.27
30-Jun-09	0.5037	30-Jun-09	-	30-Jun-09	1.2057	30-Jun-09	1.14
31-Jul-09	0.4397	31-Jul-09	-	31-Jul-09	1.0293	31-Jul-09	0.92
31-Aug-09	0.3946	31-Aug-09	-	31-Aug-09	0.7963	31-Aug-09	0.69
30-Sep-09	0.3761	30-Sep-09	-	30-Sep-09	0.617	30-Sep-09	0.51
31-Oct-09	0.4315	31-Oct-09	-	31-Oct-09	0.5636	31-Oct-09	0.5
30-Nov-09	0.4459	30-Nov-09	-	30-Nov-09	0.5976	30-Nov-09	0.58
31-Dec-09	0.3587	31-Dec-09	-	31-Dec-09	0.6071	31-Dec-09	0.58
31-Jan-10	0.4874	31-Jan-10	-	31-Jan-10	0.6013	31-Jan-10	0.58
28-Feb-10	0.4878	28-Feb-10	-	28-Feb-10	0.5995	28-Feb-10	0.58
31-Mar-10	0.5109	31-Mar-10	-	31-Mar-10	0.6002	31-Mar-10	0.6
30-Apr-10	0.5083	30-Apr-10	-	30-Apr-10	0.6	30-Apr-10	0.63
31-May-10	0.4976	31-May-10	-	31-May-10	0.6645	31-May-10	0.68
30-Jun-10	0.4839	30-Jun-10	-	30-Jun-10	0.7045	30-Jun-10	0.77
31-Jul-10	0.498	31-Jul-10	-	31-Jul-10	0.75	31-Jul-10	0.78
31-Aug-10	0.4945	31-Aug-10	-	31-Aug-10	0.75	31-Aug-10	0.7655
30-Sep-10	0.4966	30-Sep-10	-	30-Sep-10	0.7545	30-Sep-10	0.725
31-Oct-10	0.5061	31-Oct-10	-	31-Oct-10	0.75	31-Oct-10	0.725
30-Nov-10	0.4935	30-Nov-10	-	30-Nov-10	0.75	30-Nov-10	0.725
31-Dec-10	0.4913	31-Dec-10	-	31-Dec-10	0.755	31-Dec-10	0.7655
31-Jan-11	0.5055	31-Jan-11	-	31-Jan-11	0.7785	31-Jan-11	0.825
28-Feb-11	0.5363	28-Feb-11	-	28-Feb-11	0.775	28-Feb-11	0.825
31-Mar-11	0.5603	31-Mar-11	-	31-Mar-11	0.7811	31-Mar-11	0.8315
30-Apr-11	0.5676	30-Apr-11	-	30-Apr-11	0.8	30-Apr-11	0.875
31-May-11	0.5265	31-May-11	-	31-May-11	0.8	31-May-11	0.875
30-Jun-11	0.5174	30-Jun-11	-	30-Jun-11	0.8464	30-Jun-11	0.875

12.9 Average three month sterling money market rates

Monthly average rate of discount, 3 month Treasury bills, Sterling IUMAAJNB		Monthly average of Eligible bills discount rate, 3 month (a) IUMAAJND		Monthly average Sterling 3 month mean interbank lending rate IUMAAMIJ		Monthly average of Sterling certificates of deposit interest rate, 3 months, mean offer/bid IUMAVCDA	
31-Jul-11	0.4996	31-Jul-11	-	31-Jul-11	0.86	31-Jul-11	0.875
31-Aug-11	0.4531	31-Aug-11	-	31-Aug-11	0.8873	31-Aug-11	0.9114
30-Sep-11	0.4649	30-Sep-11	-	30-Sep-11	0.9664	30-Sep-11	1.0077
31-Oct-11	0.4608	31-Oct-11	-	31-Oct-11	1.0179	31-Oct-11	1.0593
30-Nov-11	0.4387	30-Nov-11	-	30-Nov-11	1.0511	30-Nov-11	1.0968
31-Dec-11	0.2996	31-Dec-11	-	31-Dec-11	1.0878	31-Dec-11	1.15
31-Jan-12	0.3239	31-Jan-12	-	31-Jan-12	1.1086	31-Jan-12	1.175
29-Feb-12	0.3912	29-Feb-12	-	29-Feb-12	1.0971	29-Feb-12	1.156
31-Mar-12	0.4248	31-Mar-12	-	31-Mar-12	1.0752	31-Mar-12	1.1164
30-Apr-12	0.4236	30-Apr-12	-	30-Apr-12	1.0558	30-Apr-12	1.0992
31-May-12	0.3561	31-May-12	-	31-May-12	1.0143	31-May-12	1.0891
30-Jun-12	0.3422	30-Jun-12	-	30-Jun-12	0.9658	30-Jun-12	1.0376
31-Jul-12	0.2943	31-Jul-12	-	31-Jul-12	0.8627	31-Jul-12	0.8691
31-Aug-12	0.2398	31-Aug-12	-	31-Aug-12	0.7048	31-Aug-12	0.7405
30-Sep-12	0.2478	30-Sep-12	-	30-Sep-12	0.6418	30-Sep-12	0.6825
31-Oct-12	0.2368	31-Oct-12	-	31-Oct-12	0.535	31-Oct-12	0.575
30-Nov-12	0.2243	30-Nov-12	-	30-Nov-12	0.5034	30-Nov-12	0.575
31-Dec-12	0.249	31-Dec-12	-	31-Dec-12	0.5	31-Dec-12	0.575
31-Jan-13	0.2677	31-Jan-13	-	31-Jan-13	0.4927	31-Jan-13	0.575
28-Feb-13	0.3147	28-Feb-13	-	28-Feb-13	0.49	28-Feb-13	0.575
31-Mar-13	0.3391	31-Mar-13	-	31-Mar-13	0.4865	31-Mar-13	0.5655
30-Apr-13	0.3447	30-Apr-13	-	30-Apr-13	0.485	30-Apr-13	0.5731
31-May-13	0.3065	31-May-13	-	31-May-13	0.485	31-May-13	0.5512
30-Jun-13	0.3066	30-Jun-13	-	30-Jun-13	0.485	30-Jun-13	0.525
31-Jul-13	0.3124	31-Jul-13	-	31-Jul-13	0.4839	31-Jul-13	0.525
31-Aug-13	0.2812	31-Aug-13	-	31-Aug-13	0.485	31-Aug-13	0.525
30-Sep-13	0.289	30-Sep-13	-	30-Sep-13	0.4931	30-Sep-13	0.525
31-Oct-13	0.3141	31-Oct-13	-	31-Oct-13	0.495	31-Oct-13	0.525
30-Nov-13	0.2865	30-Nov-13	-	30-Nov-13	0.5017	30-Nov-13	0.5512
31-Dec-13	0.2555	31-Dec-13	-	31-Dec-13	0.5335	31-Dec-13	0.575

Notes:

Source: Bank of England

Data

The Bank of England does not warrant, or accept responsibility/liability for, the accuracy/completeness of content, or loss/damage, whether direct, indirect or consequential, which may arise from reliance on said data. We reserve the right to change information published, including timing and methods used. We give no assurance that data currently published will be in the future.

(a) This series discontinued at end of August 2005

12.10 Average Foreign Exchange rates

Monthly average Old IMF-based Effective exchange rate index, Sterling (a) (1990 average = 100) XUMAGBG		Monthly average Effective exchange rate index, Sterling (Jan 2005 = 100) XUMABK67		Monthly average Spot exchange rate, US$ into Sterling XUMAUSS		Monthly average Spot exchange rate, Euro into Sterling XUMAERS	
31-Jan-99	99.57	31-Jan-99	96.2115	31-Jan-99	1.6509	31-Jan-99	1.4236
28-Feb-99	100.84	28-Feb-99	97.0376	28-Feb-99	1.6276	28-Feb-99	1.4534
31-Mar-99	102.84	31-Mar-99	98.6792	31-Mar-99	1.622	31-Mar-99	1.4902
30-Apr-99	103.36	30-Apr-99	98.7026	30-Apr-99	1.6105	30-Apr-99	1.5051
31-May-99	104.25	31-May-99	99.4914	31-May-99	1.6154	31-May-99	1.5185
30-Jun-99	104.71	30-Jun-99	99.4638	30-Jun-99	1.595	30-Jun-99	1.5374
31-Jul-99	103.45	31-Jul-99	98.279	31-Jul-99	1.5747	31-Jul-99	1.5204
31-Aug-99	103.34	31-Aug-99	98.5198	31-Aug-99	1.6073	31-Aug-99	1.5146
30-Sep-99	104.7	30-Sep-99	99.6949	30-Sep-99	1.6243	30-Sep-99	1.5458
31-Oct-99	105.37	31-Oct-99	100.554	31-Oct-99	1.6572	31-Oct-99	1.5491
30-Nov-99	105.74	30-Nov-99	100.4651	30-Nov-99	1.6214	30-Nov-99	1.5706
31-Dec-99	106.68	31-Dec-99	101.0815	31-Dec-99	1.6132	31-Dec-99	1.5953
31-Jan-00	108.55	31-Jan-00	102.688	31-Jan-00	1.6402	31-Jan-00	1.6201
29-Feb-00	108.44	29-Feb-00	102.3277	29-Feb-00	1.5998	29-Feb-00	1.6266
31-Mar-00	108.41	31-Mar-00	102.1212	31-Mar-00	1.5802	31-Mar-00	1.6377
30-Apr-00	110.06	30-Apr-00	103.4755	30-Apr-00	1.5837	30-Apr-00	1.673
31-May-00	108.52	31-May-00	101.5188	31-May-00	1.5075	31-May-00	1.6655
30-Jun-00	104.64	30-Jun-00	98.4742	30-Jun-00	1.5089	30-Jun-00	1.5882
31-Jul-00	105.63	31-Jul-00	99.2483	31-Jul-00	1.5088	31-Jul-00	1.6052
31-Aug-00	107.38	31-Aug-00	100.3681	31-Aug-00	1.491	31-Aug-00	1.6478
30-Sep-00	106.21	30-Sep-00	98.9249	30-Sep-00	1.4355	30-Sep-00	1.6471
31-Oct-00	109.19	31-Oct-00	101.5257	31-Oct-00	1.4511	31-Oct-00	1.6994
30-Nov-00	107.27	30-Nov-00	99.8475	30-Nov-00	1.4256	30-Nov-00	1.6664
31-Dec-00	106.39	31-Dec-00	99.5963	31-Dec-00	1.4625	31-Dec-00	1.6302
31-Jan-01	104.43	31-Jan-01	98.3668	31-Jan-01	1.4769	31-Jan-01	1.5753
28-Feb-01	104.14	28-Feb-01	97.869	28-Feb-01	1.4529	28-Feb-01	1.5786
31-Mar-01	105.02	31-Mar-01	98.5867	31-Mar-01	1.4454	31-Mar-01	1.5901
30-Apr-01	105.85	30-Apr-01	99.2021	30-Apr-01	1.435	30-Apr-01	1.6084
31-May-01	106.56	31-May-01	99.5458	31-May-01	1.4259	31-May-01	1.6304
30-Jun-01	106.77	30-Jun-01	99.3859	30-Jun-01	1.4014	30-Jun-01	1.6434
31-Jul-01	107.18	31-Jul-01	99.9109	31-Jul-01	1.4139	31-Jul-01	1.6433
31-Aug-01	105.09	31-Aug-01	98.5728	31-Aug-01	1.4365	31-Aug-01	1.5955
30-Sep-01	106.08	30-Sep-01	99.7406	30-Sep-01	1.4635	30-Sep-01	1.606
31-Oct-01	105.78	31-Oct-01	99.4889	31-Oct-01	1.4517	31-Oct-01	1.6024
30-Nov-01	106.14	30-Nov-01	99.5935	30-Nov-01	1.4358	30-Nov-01	1.6166
31-Dec-01	106.49	31-Dec-01	100.2141	31-Dec-01	1.4409	31-Dec-01	1.6151
31-Jan-02	106.9	31-Jan-02	100.3782	31-Jan-02	1.4323	31-Jan-02	1.6222
28-Feb-02	107.36	28-Feb-02	100.6146	28-Feb-02	1.4231	28-Feb-02	1.6348
31-Mar-02	106.48	31-Mar-02	99.9212	31-Mar-02	1.4225	31-Mar-02	1.6224
30-Apr-02	107.13	30-Apr-02	100.642	30-Apr-02	1.4434	30-Apr-02	1.6282
31-May-02	105.32	31-May-02	99.2558	31-May-02	1.4593	31-May-02	1.5914
30-Jun-02	103.58	30-Jun-02	98.0717	30-Jun-02	1.4863	30-Jun-02	1.5515
31-Jul-02	105.29	31-Jul-02	100.1987	31-Jul-02	1.5546	31-Jul-02	1.5665
31-Aug-02	105.38	31-Aug-02	100.1439	31-Aug-02	1.5377	31-Aug-02	1.5723
30-Sep-02	106.46	30-Sep-02	101.2767	30-Sep-02	1.5561	30-Sep-02	1.5861
31-Oct-02	106.67	31-Oct-02	101.4791	31-Oct-02	1.5574	31-Oct-02	1.5868
30-Nov-02	105.87	30-Nov-02	100.9087	30-Nov-02	1.5723	30-Nov-02	1.5694
31-Dec-02	105.48	31-Dec-02	100.671	31-Dec-02	1.5863	31-Dec-02	1.5566
31-Jan-03	104.04	31-Jan-03	99.7744	31-Jan-03	1.6169	31-Jan-03	1.5222
28-Feb-03	102.42	28-Feb-03	98.389	28-Feb-03	1.6085	28-Feb-03	1.4924
31-Mar-03	100.6	31-Mar-03	96.7263	31-Mar-03	1.5836	31-Mar-03	1.4649
30-Apr-03	99.8	30-Apr-03	95.9595	30-Apr-03	1.5747	30-Apr-03	1.4505
31-May-03	97.9	31-May-03	94.8061	31-May-03	1.623	31-May-03	1.403
30-Jun-03	99.64	30-Jun-03	96.5395	30-Jun-03	1.6606	30-Jun-03	1.4234
31-Jul-03	99.4	31-Jul-03	95.9989	31-Jul-03	1.6242	31-Jul-03	1.4277

12.10 Average Foreign Exchange rates

Monthly average Old IMF-based Effective exchange rate index, Sterling (a) (1990 average = 100) XUMAGBG		Monthly average Effective exchange rate index, Sterling (Jan 2005 = 100) XUMABK67		Monthly average Spot exchange rate, US$ into Sterling XUMAUSS		Monthly average Spot exchange rate, Euro into Sterling XUMAERS	
31-Aug-03	99.01	31-Aug-03	95.4177	31-Aug-03	1.595	31-Aug-03	1.4286
30-Sep-03	99.24	30-Sep-03	95.7447	30-Sep-03	1.6131	30-Sep-03	1.4338
31-Oct-03	99.82	31-Oct-03	96.806	31-Oct-03	1.6787	31-Oct-03	1.4334
30-Nov-03	100.42	30-Nov-03	97.4128	30-Nov-03	1.6901	30-Nov-03	1.4426
31-Dec-03	100.29	31-Dec-03	97.8787	31-Dec-03	1.7507	31-Dec-03	1.4246
31-Jan-04	102.38	31-Jan-04	100.1801	31-Jan-04	1.8234	31-Jan-04	1.4447
29-Feb-04	104.84	29-Feb-04	102.5014	29-Feb-04	1.8673	29-Feb-04	1.4774
31-Mar-04	104.99	31-Mar-04	102.2094	31-Mar-04	1.8267	31-Mar-04	1.489
30-Apr-04	105.18	30-Apr-04	102.1832	30-Apr-04	1.8005	30-Apr-04	1.5022
31-May-04	104.63	31-May-04	101.7671	31-May-04	1.7876	31-May-04	1.4894
30-Jun-04	105.8	30-Jun-04	103.0614	30-Jun-04	1.8275	30-Jun-04	1.505
31-Jul-04	105.89	31-Jul-04	103.1619	31-Jul-04	1.8429	31-Jul-04	1.5023
31-Aug-04	105.16	31-Aug-04	102.4197	31-Aug-04	1.8216	31-Aug-04	1.4933
30-Sep-04	103.32	30-Sep-04	100.707	30-Sep-04	1.7922	30-Sep-04	1.4676
31-Oct-04	102.17	31-Oct-04	99.822	31-Oct-04	1.8065	31-Oct-04	1.4455
30-Nov-04	101.73	30-Nov-04	99.7376	30-Nov-04	1.8603	30-Nov-04	1.4311
31-Dec-04	103.15	31-Dec-04	101.2844	31-Dec-04	1.9275	31-Dec-04	1.4401
31-Jan-05	102.1	31-Jan-05	100	31-Jan-05	1.8764	31-Jan-05	1.4331
28-Feb-05	103.29	28-Feb-05	100.9806	28-Feb-05	1.8871	28-Feb-05	1.4499
31-Mar-05	103.21	31-Mar-05	101.0593	31-Mar-05	1.9078	31-Mar-05	1.444
30-Apr-05	104.38	30-Apr-05	102.0037	30-Apr-05	1.896	30-Apr-05	1.4652
31-May-05	103.55	31-May-05	100.9914	31-May-05	1.8538	31-May-05	1.4611
30-Jun-05	104.92	30-Jun-05	101.7605	30-Jun-05	1.8179	30-Jun-05	1.4952
31-Jul-05	102.14	31-Jul-05	98.8204	31-Jul-05	1.7509	31-Jul-05	1.4547
31-Aug-05	102.85	31-Aug-05	99.7065	31-Aug-05	1.7943	31-Aug-05	1.4592
30-Sep-05	103.91	30-Sep-05	100.6524	30-Sep-05	1.8081	30-Sep-05	1.4761
31-Oct-05	103.09	31-Oct-05	99.6445	31-Oct-05	1.764	31-Oct-05	1.4674
30-Nov-05	103.16	30-Nov-05	99.4096	30-Nov-05	1.7341	30-Nov-05	1.4719
31-Dec-05	103.32	31-Dec-05	99.4991	31-Dec-05	1.7462	31-Dec-05	1.4725
31-Jan-06	102.67	31-Jan-06	99.054	31-Jan-06	1.7678	31-Jan-06	1.4582
28-Feb-06	102.83	28-Feb-06	98.917	28-Feb-06	1.747	28-Feb-06	1.4637
31-Mar-06	102.09	31-Mar-06	98.3522	31-Mar-06	1.7435	31-Mar-06	1.45
30-Apr-06	101.87	30-Apr-06	98.3606	30-Apr-06	1.7685	30-Apr-06	1.4402
31-May-06	104.14	31-May-06	101.2341	31-May-06	1.8702	31-May-06	1.4637
30-Jun-06	-	30-Jun-06	100.903	30-Jun-06	1.8428	30-Jun-06	1.456
31-Jul-06	-	31-Jul-06	100.8868	31-Jul-06	1.8447	31-Jul-06	1.454
31-Aug-06	-	31-Aug-06	102.9004	31-Aug-06	1.8944	31-Aug-06	1.4785
30-Sep-06	-	30-Sep-06	102.9568	30-Sep-06	1.8847	30-Sep-06	1.4811
31-Oct-06	-	31-Oct-06	103.0901	31-Oct-06	1.8755	31-Oct-06	1.4869
30-Nov-06	-	30-Nov-06	103.4105	30-Nov-06	1.9119	30-Nov-06	1.4834
31-Dec-06	-	31-Dec-06	104.464	31-Dec-06	1.9633	31-Dec-06	1.486
31-Jan-07	-	31-Jan-07	105.4954	31-Jan-07	1.9587	31-Jan-07	1.5079
28-Feb-07	-	28-Feb-07	104.9552	28-Feb-07	1.9581	28-Feb-07	1.4969
31-Mar-07	-	31-Mar-07	103.4989	31-Mar-07	1.9471	31-Mar-07	1.4703
30-Apr-07	-	30-Apr-07	104.2158	30-Apr-07	1.9909	30-Apr-07	1.4713
31-May-07	-	31-May-07	103.8536	31-May-07	1.9836	31-May-07	1.4677
30-Jun-07	-	30-Jun-07	104.4457	30-Jun-07	1.9864	30-Jun-07	1.4805
31-Jul-07	-	31-Jul-07	105.1846	31-Jul-07	2.0338	31-Jul-07	1.4821
31-Aug-07	-	31-Aug-07	104.4866	31-Aug-07	2.0111	31-Aug-07	1.4762
30-Sep-07	-	30-Sep-07	103.2664	30-Sep-07	2.0185	30-Sep-07	1.4515
31-Oct-07	-	31-Oct-07	102.7813	31-Oct-07	2.0446	31-Oct-07	1.437
30-Nov-07	-	30-Nov-07	101.8841	30-Nov-07	2.0701	30-Nov-07	1.4106
31-Dec-07	-	31-Dec-07	99.9266	31-Dec-07	2.0185	31-Dec-07	1.3863
31-Jan-08	-	31-Jan-08	96.6397	31-Jan-08	1.9698	31-Jan-08	1.3383
29-Feb-08	-	29-Feb-08	96.156	29-Feb-08	1.9638	29-Feb-08	1.3316

12.10 Average Foreign Exchange rates

Monthly average Old IMF-based Effective exchange rate index, Sterling (a) (1990 average = 100) XUMAGBG		Monthly average Effective exchange rate index, Sterling (Jan 2005 = 100) XUMABK67		Monthly average Spot exchange rate, US$ into Sterling XUMAUSS		Monthly average Spot exchange rate, Euro into Sterling XUMAERS	
31-Mar-08	-	31-Mar-08	94.8008	31-Mar-08	2.0032	31-Mar-08	1.2897
30-Apr-08	-	30-Apr-08	93.0255	30-Apr-08	1.9817	30-Apr-08	1.258
31-May-08	-	31-May-08	93.0212	31-May-08	1.9641	31-May-08	1.2633
30-Jun-08	-	30-Jun-08	93.1397	30-Jun-08	1.9658	30-Jun-08	1.2636
31-Jul-08	-	31-Jul-08	93.2716	31-Jul-08	1.988	31-Jul-08	1.2615
31-Aug-08	-	31-Aug-08	91.6657	31-Aug-08	1.8889	31-Aug-08	1.2614
30-Sep-08	-	30-Sep-08	89.9816	30-Sep-08	1.7986	30-Sep-08	1.2531
31-Oct-08	-	31-Oct-08	89.5079	31-Oct-08	1.69	31-Oct-08	1.2718
30-Nov-08	-	30-Nov-08	83.6639	30-Nov-08	1.5338	30-Nov-08	1.2041
31-Dec-08	-	31-Dec-08	78.3393	31-Dec-08	1.4859	31-Dec-08	1.1043
31-Jan-09	-	31-Jan-09	77.1736	31-Jan-09	1.4452	31-Jan-09	1.0919
28-Feb-09	-	28-Feb-09	79.0023	28-Feb-09	1.4411	28-Feb-09	1.1264
31-Mar-09	-	31-Mar-09	77.0751	31-Mar-09	1.4174	31-Mar-09	1.0867
30-Apr-09	-	30-Apr-09	79.0293	30-Apr-09	1.4715	30-Apr-09	1.1157
31-May-09	-	31-May-09	80.6024	31-May-09	1.5429	31-May-09	1.1295
30-Jun-09	-	30-Jun-09	84.1282	30-Jun-09	1.6366	30-Jun-09	1.1682
31-Jul-09	-	31-Jul-09	83.7104	31-Jul-09	1.6366	31-Jul-09	1.1622
31-Aug-09	-	31-Aug-09	83.6118	31-Aug-09	1.6539	31-Aug-09	1.1597
30-Sep-09	-	30-Sep-09	81.2979	30-Sep-09	1.6328	30-Sep-09	1.1212
31-Oct-09	-	31-Oct-09	79.5413	31-Oct-09	1.6199	31-Oct-09	1.0928
30-Nov-09	-	30-Nov-09	81.1074	30-Nov-09	1.6597	30-Nov-09	1.1126
31-Dec-09	-	31-Dec-09	80.4758	31-Dec-09	1.6239	31-Dec-09	1.1127
31-Jan-10	-	31-Jan-10	81.0391	31-Jan-10	1.6162	31-Jan-10	1.1327
28-Feb-10	-	28-Feb-10	80.3291	28-Feb-10	1.5615	28-Feb-10	1.1415
31-Mar-10	-	31-Mar-10	77.5459	31-Mar-10	1.5053	31-Mar-10	1.1092
30-Apr-10	-	30-Apr-10	79.4288	30-Apr-10	1.534	30-Apr-10	1.1436
31-May-10	-	31-May-10	79.3189	31-May-10	1.4627	31-May-10	1.1685
30-Jun-10	-	30-Jun-10	81.1195	30-Jun-10	1.4761	30-Jun-10	1.2082
31-Jul-10	-	31-Jul-10	81.4716	31-Jul-10	1.5299	31-Jul-10	1.1959
31-Aug-10	-	31-Aug-10	82.6642	31-Aug-10	1.566	31-Aug-10	1.2132
30-Sep-10	-	30-Sep-10	81.2366	30-Sep-10	1.5578	30-Sep-10	1.1901
31-Oct-10	-	31-Oct-10	79.5008	31-Oct-10	1.5862	31-Oct-10	1.1412
30-Nov-10	-	30-Nov-10	80.9631	30-Nov-10	1.5961	30-Nov-10	1.1701
31-Dec-10	-	31-Dec-10	80.4556	31-Dec-10	1.5603	31-Dec-10	1.1802
31-Jan-11	-	31-Jan-11	80.7578	31-Jan-11	1.5795	31-Jan-11	1.1817
28-Feb-11	-	28-Feb-11	81.543	28-Feb-11	1.613	28-Feb-11	1.1815
31-Mar-11	-	31-Mar-11	80.3101	31-Mar-11	1.6159	31-Mar-11	1.1527
30-Apr-11	-	30-Apr-11	79.7423	30-Apr-11	1.6345	30-Apr-11	1.1331
31-May-11	-	31-May-11	79.8363	31-May-11	1.6312	31-May-11	1.1403
30-Jun-11	-	30-Jun-11	78.9371	30-Jun-11	1.6214	30-Jun-11	1.1261
31-Jul-11	-	31-Jul-11	78.813	31-Jul-11	1.6145	31-Jul-11	1.1308
31-Aug-11	-	31-Aug-11	79.6825	31-Aug-11	1.6348	31-Aug-11	1.1422
30-Sep-11	-	30-Sep-11	79.297	30-Sep-11	1.5783	30-Sep-11	1.147
31-Oct-11	-	31-Oct-11	79.5689	31-Oct-11	1.576	31-Oct-11	1.1487
30-Nov-11	-	30-Nov-11	80.5031	30-Nov-11	1.5804	30-Nov-11	1.1659
31-Dec-11	-	31-Dec-11	80.9179	31-Dec-11	1.5585	31-Dec-11	1.1843
31-Jan-12	-	31-Jan-12	81.1171	31-Jan-12	1.551	31-Jan-12	1.2034
29-Feb-12	-	29-Feb-12	81.0071	29-Feb-12	1.5802	29-Feb-12	1.1941
31-Mar-12	-	31-Mar-12	81.4323	31-Mar-12	1.5823	31-Mar-12	1.1981
30-Apr-12	-	30-Apr-12	82.5765	30-Apr-12	1.6014	30-Apr-12	1.2161
31-May-12	-	31-May-12	83.8001	31-May-12	1.5905	31-May-12	1.244
30-Jun-12	-	30-Jun-12	83.0735	30-Jun-12	1.5571	30-Jun-12	1.2416
31-Jul-12	-	31-Jul-12	83.9724	31-Jul-12	1.5589	31-Jul-12	1.2688
31-Aug-12	-	31-Aug-12	83.9862	31-Aug-12	1.5719	31-Aug-12	1.2676
30-Sep-12	-	30-Sep-12	84.2131	30-Sep-12	1.6116	30-Sep-12	1.2524

12.10 Average Foreign Exchange rates

Monthly average Old IMF-based Effective exchange rate index, Sterling (a) (1990 average = 100) XUMAGBG		Monthly average Effective exchange rate index, Sterling (Jan 2005 = 100) XUMABK67		Monthly average Spot exchange rate, US$ into Sterling XUMAUSS		Monthly average Spot exchange rate, Euro into Sterling XUMAERS	
31-Oct-12	-	31-Oct-12	83.6155	31-Oct-12	1.6079	31-Oct-12	1.2393
30-Nov-12	-	30-Nov-12	83.67	30-Nov-12	1.5961	30-Nov-12	1.244
31-Dec-12	-	31-Dec-12	83.5805	31-Dec-12	1.6144	31-Dec-12	1.231
31-Jan-13	-	31-Jan-13	82.2038	31-Jan-13	1.5957	31-Jan-13	1.2
28-Feb-13	-	28-Feb-13	79.7501	28-Feb-13	1.5478	28-Feb-13	1.1594
31-Mar-13	-	31-Mar-13	79.1204	31-Mar-13	1.5076	31-Mar-13	1.1634
30-Apr-13	-	30-Apr-13	80.1669	30-Apr-13	1.5316	30-Apr-13	1.175
31-May-13	-	31-May-13	80.4728	31-May-13	1.5285	31-May-13	1.1777
30-Jun-13	-	30-Jun-13	81.0462	30-Jun-13	1.5478	30-Jun-13	1.174
31-Jul-13	-	31-Jul-13	80.0174	31-Jul-13	1.5172	31-Jul-13	1.16
31-Aug-13	-	31-Aug-13	81.0454	31-Aug-13	1.5507	31-Aug-13	1.1649
30-Sep-13	-	30-Sep-13	82.7985	30-Sep-13	1.5865	30-Sep-13	1.1883
31-Oct-13	-	31-Oct-13	82.7444	31-Oct-13	1.6094	31-Oct-13	1.1797
30-Nov-13	-	30-Nov-13	83.6352	30-Nov-13	1.6104	30-Nov-13	1.1938
31-Dec-13	-	31-Dec-13	84.5249	31-Dec-13	1.6375	31-Dec-13	1.1947

(a) This series was discontinued in May 2006

12.11 Average zero coupon yields

End month level of yield from British Government Securities, 5 year Nominal Zero Coupon IUMSNZC [a] [b]		End month level of yield from British Government Securities, 10 year Nominal Zero Coupon IUMMNZC [a] [b]		End month level of yield from British Government Securities, 20 year Nominal Zero Coupon IUMLNZC [a] [b]		Monthly average yield from British Government Securities, 10 year Real Zero Coupon IUMAMRZC [a] [b]		Monthly average yield from British Government Securities, 20 year Real Zero Coupon IUMALRZC [a] [b]	
31-Jan-98	6.1285	31-Jan-98	5.9443	31-Jan-98	5.9454	31-Jan-98	3.1008	31-Jan-98	3.0604
28-Feb-98	6.2125	28-Feb-98	5.9791	28-Feb-98	5.8968	28-Feb-98	3.0619	28-Feb-98	3.0535
31-Mar-98	6.0446	31-Mar-98	5.7766	31-Mar-98	5.6711	31-Mar-98	2.9972	31-Mar-98	2.9798
30-Apr-98	5.9082	30-Apr-98	5.723	30-Apr-98	5.6691	30-Apr-98	2.9076	30-Apr-98	2.8509
31-May-98	5.8198	31-May-98	5.5868	31-May-98	5.5322	31-May-98	2.9233	31-May-98	2.8326
30-Jun-98	6.157	30-Jun-98	5.6548	30-Jun-98	5.4298	30-Jun-98	2.8456	30-Jun-98	2.6277
31-Jul-98	6.0474	31-Jul-98	5.5784	31-Jul-98	5.3983	31-Jul-98	2.7725	31-Jul-98	2.5805
31-Aug-98	5.532	31-Aug-98	5.1976	31-Aug-98	5.1123	31-Aug-98	2.6515	31-Aug-98	2.5302
30-Sep-98	5.0376	30-Sep-98	4.792	30-Sep-98	4.6574	30-Sep-98	2.5949	30-Sep-98	2.4889
31-Oct-98	4.9727	31-Oct-98	4.9951	31-Oct-98	4.9385	31-Oct-98	2.6653	31-Oct-98	2.5875
30-Nov-98	4.7206	30-Nov-98	4.5992	30-Nov-98	4.4848	30-Nov-98	2.4118	30-Nov-98	2.3753
31-Dec-98	4.3719	31-Dec-98	4.3204	31-Dec-98	4.38	31-Dec-98	2.1233	31-Dec-98	2.1487
31-Jan-99	4.198	31-Jan-99	4.1264	31-Jan-99	4.2935	31-Jan-99	2.0044	31-Jan-99	2.0654
28-Feb-99	4.6468	28-Feb-99	4.5624	28-Feb-99	4.5413	28-Feb-99	1.8996	28-Feb-99	1.9769
31-Mar-99	4.5823	31-Mar-99	4.5323	31-Mar-99	4.5472	31-Mar-99	1.8371	31-Mar-99	1.9171
30-Apr-99	4.8102	30-Apr-99	4.6291	30-Apr-99	4.5427	30-Apr-99	1.6793	30-Apr-99	1.8048
31-May-99	5.0702	31-May-99	4.9183	31-May-99	4.7684	31-May-99	1.9009	31-May-99	1.9803
30-Jun-99	5.4032	30-Jun-99	5.1012	30-Jun-99	4.58	30-Jun-99	1.8806	30-Jun-99	1.9628
31-Jul-99	5.7292	31-Jul-99	5.3649	31-Jul-99	4.6066	31-Jul-99	1.8961	31-Jul-99	2.0007
31-Aug-99	5.7076	31-Aug-99	5.168	31-Aug-99	4.4194	31-Aug-99	2.2085	31-Aug-99	2.1526
30-Sep-99	6.1497	30-Sep-99	5.6269	30-Sep-99	4.6545	30-Sep-99	2.3324	30-Sep-99	2.273
31-Oct-99	6.0228	31-Oct-99	5.379	31-Oct-99	4.2998	31-Oct-99	2.2768	31-Oct-99	2.2287
30-Nov-99	5.9641	30-Nov-99	5.1532	30-Nov-99	4.107	30-Nov-99	2.0636	30-Nov-99	1.9276
31-Dec-99	6.0376	31-Dec-99	5.3756	31-Dec-99	4.3647	31-Dec-99	1.9953	31-Dec-99	1.8803
31-Jan-00	6.2861	31-Jan-00	5.6139	31-Jan-00	4.479	31-Jan-00	2.1092	31-Jan-00	2.0073
29-Feb-00	6.0103	29-Feb-00	5.335	29-Feb-00	4.3632	29-Feb-00	2.1685	29-Feb-00	1.9533
31-Mar-00	5.8575	31-Mar-00	5.1478	31-Mar-00	4.3495	31-Mar-00	2.0489	31-Mar-00	1.7809
30-Apr-00	5.7047	30-Apr-00	5.0977	30-Apr-00	4.2623	30-Apr-00	2.0737	30-Apr-00	1.8364
31-May-00	5.6958	31-May-00	5.0513	31-May-00	4.3045	31-May-00	2.1386	31-May-00	1.9033
30-Jun-00	5.595	30-Jun-00	5.0731	30-Jun-00	4.3797	30-Jun-00	2.1202	30-Jun-00	1.8707
31-Jul-00	5.6384	31-Jul-00	5.1357	31-Jul-00	4.4363	31-Jul-00	2.1409	31-Jul-00	1.8992
31-Aug-00	5.6807	31-Aug-00	5.2491	31-Aug-00	4.5683	31-Aug-00	2.2278	31-Aug-00	1.9479
30-Sep-00	5.5287	30-Sep-00	5.1367	30-Sep-00	4.6199	30-Sep-00	2.2736	30-Sep-00	1.9532
31-Oct-00	5.4743	31-Oct-00	5.0874	31-Oct-00	4.5168	31-Oct-00	2.3268	31-Oct-00	1.9916
30-Nov-00	5.1547	30-Nov-00	4.7891	30-Nov-00	4.2618	30-Nov-00	2.3179	30-Nov-00	1.9296
31-Dec-00	5.083	31-Dec-00	4.7809	31-Dec-00	4.291	31-Dec-00	2.2104	31-Dec-00	1.8589
31-Jan-01	4.978	31-Jan-01	4.6718	31-Jan-01	4.3694	31-Jan-01	2.2154	31-Jan-01	1.8684
28-Feb-01	4.9824	28-Feb-01	4.7079	28-Feb-01	4.378	28-Feb-01	2.2144	28-Feb-01	1.8523
31-Mar-01	4.8425	31-Mar-01	4.7218	31-Mar-01	4.5984	31-Mar-01	2.2702	31-Mar-01	1.9601
30-Apr-01	5.126	30-Apr-01	5.065	30-Apr-01	4.8872	30-Apr-01	2.5368	30-Apr-01	2.2434
31-May-01	5.2777	31-May-01	5.1627	31-May-01	5.0197	31-May-01	2.5735	31-May-01	2.3112
30-Jun-01	5.4376	30-Jun-01	5.2329	30-Jun-01	5.0078	30-Jun-01	2.5725	30-Jun-01	2.2817
31-Jul-01	5.1702	31-Jul-01	5.0002	31-Jul-01	4.7653	31-Jul-01	2.5826	31-Jul-01	2.2629
31-Aug-01	4.9746	31-Aug-01	4.8652	31-Aug-01	4.682	31-Aug-01	2.3919	31-Aug-01	2.1494
30-Sep-01	4.8735	30-Sep-01	4.9172	30-Sep-01	4.8559	30-Sep-01	2.4992	30-Sep-01	2.3047
31-Oct-01	4.5126	31-Oct-01	4.5368	31-Oct-01	4.4576	31-Oct-01	2.5713	31-Oct-01	2.3376
30-Nov-01	4.6523	30-Nov-01	4.6479	30-Nov-01	4.5089	30-Nov-01	2.3844	30-Nov-01	2.1178
31-Dec-01	5.0788	31-Dec-01	5.0326	31-Dec-01	4.782	31-Dec-01	2.5171	31-Dec-01	2.2145
31-Jan-02	4.9044	31-Jan-02	4.8138	31-Jan-02	4.6689	31-Jan-02	2.4923	31-Jan-02	2.2395
28-Feb-02	4.9428	28-Feb-02	4.923	28-Feb-02	4.7928	28-Feb-02	2.4722	28-Feb-02	2.2767
31-Mar-02	5.3046	31-Mar-02	5.2456	31-Mar-02	5.0823	31-Mar-02	2.5074	31-Mar-02	2.3014
30-Apr-02	5.1522	30-Apr-02	5.1553	30-Apr-02	5.0257	30-Apr-02	2.4157	30-Apr-02	2.2401
31-May-02	5.2156	31-May-02	5.2282	31-May-02	5.1364	31-May-02	2.4142	31-May-02	2.2421
30-Jun-02	5.0148	30-Jun-02	4.9715	30-Jun-02	4.8164	30-Jun-02	2.3162	30-Jun-02	2.1556
31-Jul-02	4.7231	31-Jul-02	4.9201	31-Jul-02	4.8015	31-Jul-02	2.409	31-Jul-02	2.2475
31-Aug-02	4.4976	31-Aug-02	4.6394	31-Aug-02	4.4857	31-Aug-02	2.3109	31-Aug-02	2.1482
30-Sep-02	4.1825	30-Sep-02	4.412	30-Sep-02	4.3797	30-Sep-02	2.1834	30-Sep-02	2.0609
31-Oct-02	4.3315	31-Oct-02	4.5992	31-Oct-02	4.5466	31-Oct-02	2.3919	31-Oct-02	2.236
30-Nov-02	4.5062	30-Nov-02	4.6898	30-Nov-02	4.6549	30-Nov-02	2.3853	30-Nov-02	2.2838
31-Dec-02	4.1583	31-Dec-02	4.3967	31-Dec-02	4.4607	31-Dec-02	2.3083	31-Dec-02	2.2482
31-Jan-03	4.0136	31-Jan-03	4.2807	31-Jan-03	4.374	31-Jan-03	2.0797	31-Jan-03	2.0936
28-Feb-03	3.7987	28-Feb-03	4.227	28-Feb-03	4.4687	28-Feb-03	1.787	28-Feb-03	1.979
31-Mar-03	3.9584	31-Mar-03	4.3549	31-Mar-03	4.5931	31-Mar-03	1.8418	31-Mar-03	2.0679
30-Apr-03	4.0086	30-Apr-03	4.4202	30-Apr-03	4.6491	30-Apr-03	1.9411	30-Apr-03	2.1236
31-May-03	3.7737	31-May-03	4.1579	31-May-03	4.4323	31-May-03	1.7954	31-May-03	2.0315
30-Jun-03	3.8401	30-Jun-03	4.2698	30-Jun-03	4.6015	30-Jun-03	1.6503	30-Jun-03	1.9703

12.11 Average zero coupon yields

End month level of yield from British Government Securities, 5 year Nominal Zero Coupon IUMSNZC [a] [b]		End month level of yield from British Government Securities, 10 year Nominal Zero Coupon IUMMNZC [a] [b]		End month level of yield from British Government Securities, 20 year Nominal Zero Coupon IUMLNZC [a] [b]		Monthly average yield from British Government Securities, 10 year Real Zero Coupon IUMAMRZC [a] [b]		Monthly average yield from British Government Securities, 20 year Real Zero Coupon IUMALRZC [a] [b]	
31-Jul-03	4.2291	31-Jul-03	4.6075	31-Jul-03	4.8344	31-Jul-03	1.8311	31-Jul-03	2.1601
31-Aug-03	4.4574	31-Aug-03	4.6562	31-Aug-03	4.6988	31-Aug-03	1.9459	31-Aug-03	2.141
30-Sep-03	4.3404	30-Sep-03	4.5844	30-Sep-03	4.6736	30-Sep-03	2.0465	30-Sep-03	2.1819
31-Oct-03	4.9274	31-Oct-03	5.0093	31-Oct-03	4.859	31-Oct-03	2.1484	31-Oct-03	2.2234
30-Nov-03	4.911	30-Nov-03	5.0473	30-Nov-03	4.8909	30-Nov-03	2.2143	30-Nov-03	2.2058
31-Dec-03	4.612	31-Dec-03	4.7733	31-Dec-03	4.7034	31-Dec-03	2.034	31-Dec-03	2.0784
31-Jan-04	4.7324	31-Jan-04	4.8572	31-Jan-04	4.7485	31-Jan-04	1.9359	31-Jan-04	1.9606
29-Feb-04	4.5996	29-Feb-04	4.735	29-Feb-04	4.7232	29-Feb-04	1.959	29-Feb-04	1.901
31-Mar-04	4.6154	31-Mar-04	4.7184	31-Mar-04	4.6453	31-Mar-04	1.8077	31-Mar-04	1.7684
30-Apr-04	4.8491	30-Apr-04	4.9564	30-Apr-04	4.839	30-Apr-04	1.9295	30-Apr-04	1.848
31-May-04	5.1163	31-May-04	5.1062	31-May-04	4.8917	31-May-04	2.0517	31-May-04	1.8784
30-Jun-04	5.039	30-Jun-04	5.0587	30-Jun-04	4.84	30-Jun-04	2.1008	30-Jun-04	1.8799
31-Jul-04	5.0958	31-Jul-04	5.0518	31-Jul-04	4.7933	31-Jul-04	2.0733	31-Jul-04	1.8713
31-Aug-04	4.8585	31-Aug-04	4.881	31-Aug-04	4.6547	31-Aug-04	2.0347	31-Aug-04	1.8228
30-Sep-04	4.7433	30-Sep-04	4.7878	30-Sep-04	4.6312	30-Sep-04	1.9736	30-Sep-04	1.798
31-Oct-04	4.6267	31-Oct-04	4.7002	31-Oct-04	4.5693	31-Oct-04	1.8877	31-Oct-04	1.7646
30-Nov-04	4.473	30-Nov-04	4.5606	30-Nov-04	4.4453	30-Nov-04	1.8755	30-Nov-04	1.7059
31-Dec-04	4.4287	31-Dec-04	4.4872	31-Dec-04	4.4097	31-Dec-04	1.7552	31-Dec-04	1.5992
31-Jan-05	4.4769	31-Jan-05	4.5419	31-Jan-05	4.4811	31-Jan-05	1.7474	31-Jan-05	1.5862
28-Feb-05	4.6761	28-Feb-05	4.6514	28-Feb-05	4.5249	28-Feb-05	1.77	28-Feb-05	1.5918
31-Mar-05	4.6106	31-Mar-05	4.6357	31-Mar-05	4.5618	31-Mar-05	1.874	31-Mar-05	1.7246
30-Apr-05	4.444	30-Apr-05	4.4735	30-Apr-05	4.4264	30-Apr-05	1.7638	30-Apr-05	1.6408
31-May-05	4.2051	31-May-05	4.2823	31-May-05	4.3326	31-May-05	1.6959	31-May-05	1.5704
30-Jun-05	4.0387	30-Jun-05	4.1519	30-Jun-05	4.2073	30-Jun-05	1.6498	30-Jun-05	1.5324
31-Jul-05	4.2154	31-Jul-05	4.2892	31-Jul-05	4.3179	31-Jul-05	1.6469	31-Jul-05	1.5442
31-Aug-05	4.0641	31-Aug-05	4.1248	31-Aug-05	4.1705	31-Aug-05	1.6095	31-Aug-05	1.4945
30-Sep-05	4.1884	30-Sep-05	4.2489	30-Sep-05	4.2336	30-Sep-05	1.5097	30-Sep-05	1.4043
31-Oct-05	4.2874	31-Oct-05	4.2833	31-Oct-05	4.238	31-Oct-05	1.5665	31-Oct-05	1.3974
30-Nov-05	4.2061	30-Nov-05	4.1685	30-Nov-05	4.0854	30-Nov-05	1.541	30-Nov-05	1.2925
31-Dec-05	4.1019	31-Dec-05	4.0505	31-Dec-05	3.9626	31-Dec-05	1.4668	31-Dec-05	1.2015
31-Jan-06	4.172	31-Jan-06	4.0817	31-Jan-06	3.8631	31-Jan-06	1.2921	31-Jan-06	0.9687
28-Feb-06	4.2134	28-Feb-06	4.1211	28-Feb-06	3.9088	28-Feb-06	1.3237	28-Feb-06	0.9897
31-Mar-06	4.3946	31-Mar-06	4.3444	31-Mar-06	4.1388	31-Mar-06	1.4135	31-Mar-06	1.1011
30-Apr-06	4.6102	30-Apr-06	4.5855	30-Apr-06	4.3286	30-Apr-06	1.542	30-Apr-06	1.2818
31-May-06	4.6302	31-May-06	4.5395	31-May-06	4.2978	31-May-06	1.6291	31-May-06	1.3321
30-Jun-06	4.7356	30-Jun-06	4.6536	30-Jun-06	4.4151	30-Jun-06	1.6832	30-Jun-06	1.3862
31-Jul-06	4.6631	31-Jul-06	4.5482	31-Jul-06	4.2984	31-Jul-06	1.6457	31-Jul-06	1.3078
31-Aug-06	4.6343	31-Aug-06	4.4391	31-Aug-06	4.163	31-Aug-06	1.5515	31-Aug-06	1.2077
30-Sep-06	4.6412	30-Sep-06	4.4471	30-Sep-06	4.1548	30-Sep-06	1.4912	30-Sep-06	1.1173
31-Oct-06	4.6979	31-Oct-06	4.4201	31-Oct-06	4.0629	31-Oct-06	1.5738	31-Oct-06	1.1275
30-Nov-06	4.6926	30-Nov-06	4.4113	30-Nov-06	4.0858	30-Nov-06	1.4736	30-Nov-06	1.0294
31-Dec-06	4.9131	31-Dec-06	4.6318	31-Dec-06	4.2526	31-Dec-06	1.5561	31-Dec-06	1.1073
31-Jan-07	5.1482	31-Jan-07	4.855	31-Jan-07	4.4219	31-Jan-07	1.7849	31-Jan-07	1.2302
28-Feb-07	4.9735	28-Feb-07	4.6791	28-Feb-07	4.3078	28-Feb-07	1.7983	28-Feb-07	1.2474
31-Mar-07	5.1338	31-Mar-07	4.8548	31-Mar-07	4.4697	31-Mar-07	1.7002	31-Mar-07	1.1947
30-Apr-07	5.194	30-Apr-07	4.9284	30-Apr-07	4.5536	30-Apr-07	1.9068	30-Apr-07	1.3595
31-May-07	5.448	31-May-07	5.1283	31-May-07	4.6951	31-May-07	2.0466	31-May-07	1.4583
30-Jun-07	5.6348	30-Jun-07	5.3604	30-Jun-07	4.8891	30-Jun-07	2.2101	30-Jun-07	1.5415
31-Jul-07	5.3529	31-Jul-07	5.1173	31-Jul-07	4.6572	31-Jul-07	2.1934	31-Jul-07	1.5156
31-Aug-07	5.1209	31-Aug-07	4.9347	31-Aug-07	4.5484	31-Aug-07	1.9666	31-Aug-07	1.3126
30-Sep-07	4.9798	30-Sep-07	4.9495	30-Sep-07	4.6447	30-Sep-07	1.7894	30-Sep-07	1.2421
31-Oct-07	4.9395	31-Oct-07	4.8667	31-Oct-07	4.5916	31-Oct-07	1.7455	31-Oct-07	1.2495
30-Nov-07	4.5718	30-Nov-07	4.6361	30-Nov-07	4.5157	30-Nov-07	1.4823	30-Nov-07	1.095
31-Dec-07	4.4137	31-Dec-07	4.5151	31-Dec-07	4.3859	31-Dec-07	1.4983	31-Dec-07	1.0845
31-Jan-08	4.2964	31-Jan-08	4.4877	31-Jan-08	4.4193	31-Jan-08	1.3032	31-Jan-08	0.9192
29-Feb-08	4.1991	29-Feb-08	4.5274	29-Feb-08	4.503	29-Feb-08	1.3276	29-Feb-08	1.0259
31-Mar-08	3.9541	31-Mar-08	4.424	31-Mar-08	4.6048	31-Mar-08	1.0236	31-Mar-08	0.8844
30-Apr-08	4.4429	30-Apr-08	4.733	30-Apr-08	4.7139	30-Apr-08	1.2032	30-Apr-08	1.0184
31-May-08	4.94	31-May-08	4.9984	31-May-08	4.8293	31-May-08	1.3612	31-May-08	0.9959
30-Jun-08	5.1659	30-Jun-08	5.1663	30-Jun-08	4.8995	30-Jun-08	1.3581	30-Jun-08	0.8405
31-Jul-08	4.7675	31-Jul-08	4.8448	31-Jul-08	4.7434	31-Jul-08	1.2887	31-Jul-08	0.8261
31-Aug-08	4.4108	31-Aug-08	4.5222	31-Aug-08	4.5953	31-Aug-08	1.1652	31-Aug-08	0.6719
30-Sep-08	4.208	30-Sep-08	4.5137	30-Sep-08	4.6924	30-Sep-08	1.2511	30-Sep-08	0.7995
31-Oct-08	3.9697	31-Oct-08	4.713	31-Oct-08	4.9258	31-Oct-08	2.0565	31-Oct-08	1.3285
30-Nov-08	3.3664	30-Nov-08	4.0317	30-Nov-08	4.5731	30-Nov-08	2.58	30-Nov-08	1.3657
31-Dec-08	2.708	31-Dec-08	3.4126	31-Dec-08	4.066	31-Dec-08	2.1901	31-Dec-08	1.2361

12.11 Average zero coupon yields

End month level of yield from British Government Securities, 5 year Nominal Zero Coupon IUMSNZC [a] [b]		End month level of yield from British Government Securities, 10 year Nominal Zero Coupon IUMMNZC [a] [b]		End month level of yield from British Government Securities, 20 year Nominal Zero Coupon IUMLNZC [a] [b]		Monthly average yield from British Government Securities, 10 year Real Zero Coupon IUMAMRZC [a] [b]		Monthly average yield from British Government Securities, 20 year Real Zero Coupon IUMALRZC [a] [b]	
31-Jan-09	2.8834	31-Jan-09	4.0861	31-Jan-09	4.7012	31-Jan-09	1.5257	31-Jan-09	1.052
28-Feb-09	2.6227	28-Feb-09	3.8159	28-Feb-09	4.7151	28-Feb-09	1.2501	28-Feb-09	1.1934
31-Mar-09	2.4459	31-Mar-09	3.311	31-Mar-09	4.2558	31-Mar-09	1.1902	31-Mar-09	1.1852
30-Apr-09	2.594	30-Apr-09	3.6361	30-Apr-09	4.5822	30-Apr-09	1.0832	30-Apr-09	1.1448
31-May-09	2.7154	31-May-09	3.8141	31-May-09	4.7127	31-May-09	1.0904	31-May-09	1.0545
30-Jun-09	2.9717	30-Jun-09	3.703	30-Jun-09	4.5708	30-Jun-09	1.0821	30-Jun-09	1.0074
31-Jul-09	3.083	31-Jul-09	3.9125	31-Jul-09	4.7431	31-Jul-09	1.2285	31-Jul-09	0.9964
31-Aug-09	2.6877	31-Aug-09	3.6313	31-Aug-09	4.1118	31-Aug-09	1.1562	31-Aug-09	0.8698
30-Sep-09	2.6807	30-Sep-09	3.7123	30-Sep-09	4.1499	30-Sep-09	1.0559	30-Sep-09	0.8862
31-Oct-09	2.7662	31-Oct-09	3.7684	31-Oct-09	4.2789	31-Oct-09	0.703	31-Oct-09	0.7436
30-Nov-09	2.6607	30-Nov-09	3.6987	30-Nov-09	4.2359	30-Nov-09	0.774	30-Nov-09	0.7106
31-Dec-09	2.9821	31-Dec-09	4.203	31-Dec-09	4.5939	31-Dec-09	0.8046	31-Dec-09	0.7645
31-Jan-10	2.9411	31-Jan-10	4.1135	31-Jan-10	4.5279	31-Jan-10	0.8237	31-Jan-10	0.8421
28-Feb-10	2.7834	28-Feb-10	4.2373	28-Feb-10	4.7692	28-Feb-10	0.9608	28-Feb-10	1.0657
31-Mar-10	2.7852	31-Mar-10	4.1764	31-Mar-10	4.6577	31-Mar-10	0.8276	31-Mar-10	0.9801
30-Apr-10	2.7534	30-Apr-10	4.1034	30-Apr-10	4.6279	30-Apr-10	0.7118	30-Apr-10	0.9024
31-May-10	2.4101	31-May-10	3.7919	31-May-10	4.4818	31-May-10	0.7264	31-May-10	0.9331
30-Jun-10	2.2133	30-Jun-10	3.5853	30-Jun-10	4.3767	30-Jun-10	0.7631	30-Jun-10	0.9715
31-Jul-10	2.2281	31-Jul-10	3.5691	31-Jul-10	4.4956	31-Jul-10	0.8433	31-Jul-10	1.0381
31-Aug-10	1.7575	31-Aug-10	3.0217	31-Aug-10	3.9415	31-Aug-10	0.6535	31-Aug-10	0.9004
30-Sep-10	1.813	30-Sep-10	3.1512	30-Sep-10	4.0071	30-Sep-10	0.4628	30-Sep-10	0.7343
31-Oct-10	1.878	31-Oct-10	3.3042	31-Oct-10	4.3031	31-Oct-10	0.3775	31-Oct-10	0.7099
30-Nov-10	2.0313	30-Nov-10	3.4591	30-Nov-10	4.4002	30-Nov-10	0.4815	30-Nov-10	0.8143
31-Dec-10	2.314	31-Dec-10	3.6174	31-Dec-10	4.3314	31-Dec-10	0.6754	31-Dec-10	0.8243
31-Jan-11	2.5858	31-Jan-11	3.8827	31-Jan-11	4.5822	31-Jan-11	0.6353	31-Jan-11	0.8637
28-Feb-11	2.6508	28-Feb-11	3.8872	28-Feb-11	4.5184	28-Feb-11	0.7203	28-Feb-11	0.8809
31-Mar-11	2.6575	31-Mar-11	3.8974	31-Mar-11	4.5078	31-Mar-11	0.5424	31-Mar-11	0.8003
30-Apr-11	2.4534	30-Apr-11	3.7116	30-Apr-11	4.3435	30-Apr-11	0.5699	30-Apr-11	0.8156
31-May-11	2.2507	31-May-11	3.5655	31-May-11	4.3125	31-May-11	0.4104	31-May-11	0.793
30-Jun-11	2.2036	30-Jun-11	3.6665	30-Jun-11	4.4964	30-Jun-11	0.2576	30-Jun-11	0.6595
31-Jul-11	1.7512	31-Jul-11	3.1755	31-Jul-11	4.2227	31-Jul-11	0.1927	31-Jul-11	0.5845
31-Aug-11	1.6065	31-Aug-11	2.9038	31-Aug-11	4.0173	31-Aug-11	-0.1442	31-Aug-11	0.4083
30-Sep-11	1.4048	30-Sep-11	2.5096	30-Sep-11	3.5397	30-Sep-11	-0.2071	30-Sep-11	0.3008
31-Oct-11	1.3719	31-Oct-11	2.5642	31-Oct-11	3.4276	31-Oct-11	-0.1245	31-Oct-11	0.337
30-Nov-11	1.2752	30-Nov-11	2.4275	30-Nov-11	3.1294	30-Nov-11	-0.3177	30-Nov-11	0.1173
31-Dec-11	1.001	31-Dec-11	2.105	31-Dec-11	3.0454	31-Dec-11	-0.475	31-Dec-11	-0.0286
31-Jan-12	0.9544	31-Jan-12	2.0983	31-Jan-12	3.0189	31-Jan-12	-0.5915	31-Jan-12	-0.1548
29-Feb-12	1.001	29-Feb-12	2.2582	29-Feb-12	3.2967	29-Feb-12	-0.5785	29-Feb-12	-0.0236
31-Mar-12	1.0698	31-Mar-12	2.3289	31-Mar-12	3.447	31-Mar-12	-0.5281	31-Mar-12	0.0341
30-Apr-12	1.1164	30-Apr-12	2.2516	30-Apr-12	3.3938	30-Apr-12	-0.5759	30-Apr-12	-0.0135
31-May-12	0.6748	31-May-12	1.673	31-May-12	2.8994	31-May-12	-0.6844	31-May-12	-0.0644
30-Jun-12	0.8284	30-Jun-12	1.8661	30-Jun-12	2.9815	30-Jun-12	-0.5935	30-Jun-12	-0.0546
31-Jul-12	0.566	31-Jul-12	1.6099	31-Jul-12	2.7932	31-Jul-12	-0.6427	31-Jul-12	-0.0304
31-Aug-12	0.5849	31-Aug-12	1.6346	31-Aug-12	2.8217	31-Aug-12	-0.6944	31-Aug-12	-0.023
30-Sep-12	0.6798	30-Sep-12	1.6958	30-Sep-12	2.9454	30-Sep-12	-0.6639	30-Sep-12	0.0775
31-Oct-12	0.8255	31-Oct-12	1.879	31-Oct-12	3.0256	31-Oct-12	-0.5872	31-Oct-12	0.1513
30-Nov-12	0.8264	30-Nov-12	1.794	30-Nov-12	2.9544	30-Nov-12	-0.6283	30-Nov-12	0.0967
31-Dec-12	0.8853	31-Dec-12	1.8782	31-Dec-12	3.023	31-Dec-12	-0.7274	31-Dec-12	-0.011
31-Jan-13	1.098	31-Jan-13	2.2055	31-Jan-13	3.3222	31-Jan-13	-0.825	31-Jan-13	-0.0952
28-Feb-13	0.9145	28-Feb-13	2.1054	28-Feb-13	3.2498	28-Feb-13	-1.01	28-Feb-13	-0.1883
31-Mar-13	0.7439	31-Mar-13	1.8933	31-Mar-13	3.0961	31-Mar-13	-1.2531	31-Mar-13	-0.3
30-Apr-13	0.73	30-Apr-13	1.7929	30-Apr-13	2.9541	30-Apr-13	-1.3223	30-Apr-13	-0.4891
31-May-13	1.02	31-May-13	2.1641	31-May-13	3.2631	31-May-13	-1.0738	31-May-13	-0.3514
30-Jun-13	1.3933	30-Jun-13	2.618	30-Jun-13	3.5337	30-Jun-13	-0.6377	30-Jun-13	-0.1279
31-Jul-13	1.2511	31-Jul-13	2.5513	31-Jul-13	3.5392	31-Jul-13	-0.5794	31-Jul-13	-0.0071
31-Aug-13	1.5644	31-Aug-13	2.8265	31-Aug-13	3.6373	31-Aug-13	-0.3798	31-Aug-13	0.0923
30-Sep-13	1.5498	30-Sep-13	2.7601	30-Sep-13	3.5437	30-Sep-13	-0.2206	30-Sep-13	0.1506
31-Oct-13	1.5122	31-Oct-13	2.7053	31-Oct-13	3.4942	31-Oct-13	-0.3819	31-Oct-13	0.0185
30-Nov-13	1.6323	30-Nov-13	2.8783	30-Nov-13	3.6515	30-Nov-13	-0.2983	30-Nov-13	0.0607
31-Dec-13	1.9931	31-Dec-13	3.1577	31-Dec-13	3.7316	31-Dec-13	-0.1979	31-Dec-13	0.1006

Source: Bank of England

Notes:

[a] Calculated by the Bank of England using the Variable Roughness Penalty (VRP) model

[b] There have been small revisions to the UK government VRP curves (nominal, real and inflation) going back to the beginning of November 1998. (30 Nov 1998)

12.12 Consumer credit excluding student loans

£ millions   Not seasonally adjusted

Net lending - monthly changes

LPM	MFIs	of which: mutuals	Other consumer credit lenders	Total	of which: credit card	other
	VVXP (s)	B3VC (s)	B4TH (s)	B3PT	VZQS	B4TV
2011 Jan	-961	46	-576	-1,537	-896	-641
Feb	-419	11	-375	-794	-201	-593
Mar	-230	43	187	-43	-326	283
Apr	317	33	-26	291	773	-481
May	21	51	-236	-215	55	-270
Jun	328	46	-7	321	246	75
Jul	-208	89	-115	-322	141	-463
Aug	488	89	-191	298	262	36
Sep	-193	11	432	239	236	3
Oct	-125	27	-25	-150	-154	4
Nov	225	34	167	392	376	17
Dec	-326	40	231	-94	718	-812
2012 Jan	-878	10	-203	-1,081	-969	-112
Feb	-970	5	-245	-1,215	-518	-697
Mar	-188	23	755	566	-22	589
Apr	-19	55	41	22	192	-169
May	-178	48	180	2	-19	21
Jun	205	22	407	612	568	45
Jul	-25	73	70	45	-218	263
Aug	-337	46	-66	-404	227	-630
Sep	635	26	830	1,465	424	1,040
Oct	-572	28	127	-445	-343	-102

Source: Bank of England

Notes to table
(s) These series may be affected by securitisations and loan transfers up to December 2009 and loan transfers from January 2010

12.13a INVESTMENT TRUSTS' ASSETS & LIABILITIES AT MARKET VALUES

£ million at end of year

		2001	2002	2003	2004	2005	2006	2007	2008	2009	2010	2011
ASSETS												
British government securities denominated in sterling	RLLT	645	470	302	466	768	533	715	628	585	466	681
Index-linked	AFIS	65	0	0	0	0	0	0	0	0	8	95
Other than index-linked	K5HJ	580	470	302	466	768	533	715	628	585	458	586
British government securities denominated in foreign currency	CBPP	0	0	0	0	0	0	0	0	0	0	0
UK local authority securities	AHBR	1	0	0	0	0	0	0	0	0	0	0
Other UK public sector investments	AHBS	5	5	5	0	0	0	0	0	0	0	0
UK ordinary shares												
Quoted	AHBM	28,955	18,509	22,403	22,598	24,021	21,843	21,848	13,428	16,297	17,547	17,329
Unquoted	AHBQ	1,383	966	889	1,343	1,016	1,027	1,186	938	1,349	1,336	1,437
Overseas ordinary shares	AHCC	19,476	14,453	20,294	18,967	23,065	21,659	25,795	18,385	23,865	29,341	29,083
Other corporate securities												
UK[1]	CBGZ	1,516	946	1,079	1,270	673	1,071	1,259	813	665	560	529
Overseas[2]	CBHA	1,143	458	603	682	937	741	1,038	623	939	1,304	1,344
Authorised unit trust units	AHBT	26	47	79	149	140	24	0	28	33	42	76
Overseas government securities	AHBY	399	137	122	33	168	4	151	410	256	410	254
UK land, existing buildings and new construction work	CBHB	375	532	498	39	117	252	154	142	141	197	1,522
Other UK and overseas assets[3]	AMSE	1,012	1,224	1,760	1,665	2,359	2,898	3,462	3,684	3,824	4,618	5,439
TOTAL	**AHBD**	54,936	37,747	48,034	47,212	53,264	50,052	55,608	39,079	47,954	55,821	57,694
Total short term assets	CBGX	3,169	2,626	2,535	3,100	3,032	2,138	3,303	3,397	2,522	2,174	2,893
TOTAL ASSETS	**CBGW**	58,105	40,373	50,569	50,312	56,296	52,190	58,911	42,476	50,476	57,995	60,587
LIABILITIES												
Borrowing from UK and overseas banks	CBHD	4,174	3,376	3,207	2,797	2,771	2,900	2,708	2,553	2,216	2,359	2,897
Other UK liabilities	CBHG	2,362	1,326	1,189	843	670	952	988	1,012	1,062	1,123	914
Other overseas liabilities	CBHI	28	19	0	0	0	2	0	225	185	186	126
Capital issues	CBHK	8,796	8,711	9,873	8,210	7,155	5,492	5,659	3,834	3,627	3,361	4,395
TOTAL LIABILITIES	**CBHO**	15,360	13,432	14,269	11,850	10,596	9,346	9,355	7,624	7,090	7,029	8,332
TOTAL NET ASSETS	**CBHM**	42,745	26,941	36,300	38,462	45,700	42,844	49,556	34,852	43,386	50,966	52,255

1 Includes UK corporate bonds and preference shares.
2 Includes overseas bonds and preference shares.
3 Includes other UK mutual funds, overseas mutual funds, other UK fixed assets, overseas fixed assets, direct investment and other UK & overseas assets not elsewhere classified.

Source: Office for National Statistics

12.13b UNIT TRUSTS & PROPERTY UNIT TRUSTS' ASSETS & LIABILITIES AT MARKET VALUES

£ million at end of year

		2001	2002	2003	2004	2005	2006	2007	2008	2009	2010	2011
ASSETS												
British government securities denominated in sterling	CBHT	4,690	7,077	9,125	9,768	25,181	31,603	32,120	33,466	29,331	33,306	37,116
Ordinary shares												
UK	RLIB	103,704	82,851	116,407	130,230	157,149	185,637	195,009	143,550	167,401	204,616	179,940
Overseas	RLIC	71,329	63,152	75,074	81,034	105,443	127,409	142,211	113,667	150,863	200,028	187,714
Other corporate securities												
UK[1]	CBHU	16,318	21,152	23,972	22,467	29,293	29,876	30,626	30,174	36,646	52,786	52,735
Overseas[2]	CBHV	4,113	5,916	9,840	13,142	16,057	25,617	30,029	30,442	43,301	49,098	48,388
Overseas government securities	CBHW	1,749	3,278	2,267	2,347	3,412	3,532	3,880	5,754	5,810	9,251	14,797
UK land, existing buildings and new construction work	RLIE	2,078	4,026	5,125	5,909	9,623	12,781	12,480	8,518	7,248	9,484	13,220
Other UK and overseas assets[3]	CBHX †	8,551	10,151	10,940	14,261	22,327	29,765	38,707	42,670	49,417	60,029	66,640
Total short term assets *of which:*	CBHS	8,995	8,928	12,090	11,497	16,417	20,653	27,969	35,224	37,263	48,382	45,001
Derivative assets with UK and overseas counterparties[4]	KUU5	666	719	4,028	2,099	4,745	4,552	7,271	13,151	17,132	25,944	18,168
TOTAL ASSETS	CBHR †	**221,527**	**206,531**	**264,840**	**290,655**	**384,902**	**466,873**	**513,031**	**443,465**	**527,280**	**666,980**	**645,551**
LIABILITIES												
Borrowing from UK and overseas banks	RLLF	537	314	425	413	1,456	2,544	2,603	3,486	1,541	991	1,992
Other UK borrowing	RLLH	59	35	85	27	130	16	36	80	26	74	350
Other overseas borrowing	RLLI	13	29	26	1	1	0	0	0	54	0	0
Derivative liabilities with UK and overseas counterparties[4]	KUU6	410	270	2,169	1,611	2,814	3,701	6,382	11,890	15,294	23,676	17,464
Creditors, provisions and other liabilities[4]	KUU7	1,083	1,337	1,289	1,835	2,425	3,370	2,562	3,442	5,524	7,228	14,087
Liability attributable to unit and share holders	RLLG †	219,425	204,546	260,846	286,768	378,076	457,242	501,448	424,567	504,841	635,011	611,658
TOTAL LIABILITIES	RLLE †	**221,527**	**206,531**	**264,840**	**290,655**	**384,902**	**466,873**	**513,031**	**443,465**	**527,280**	**666,980**	**645,551**

1 Includes UK corporate bonds and preference shares.
2 Includes overseas bonds and preference shares.
3 Includes British government foreign currency securities, UK local authority securities, other UK public sector investments, UK and overseas mutual funds, other UK fixed assets, overseas fixed assets, direct investment and other UK & overseas assets not elsewhere classified.
4 New series from 2011. Estimates available back to 2000.

Source: Office for National Statistics

12.14 SELF-ADMINISTERED PENSION FUNDS' BALANCE SHEET AT MARKET VALUES COMBINED PUBLIC AND PRIVATE SECTOR[1]

£ million at end of year

		2001	2002	2003	2004	2005	2006	2007	2008	2009	2010	2011
British government securities denominated in sterling	AHVK	83,754	84,461	88,803	87,579	94,325	104,910	113,617	98,577	108,871	122,007	167,372
Index-linked	AHWC	46,335	47,173	52,041	46,333	48,821	53,858	64,797	58,564	70,317	83,016	110,808
Other than index-linked	J8Y5	37,419	37,288	36,762	41,246	45,504	51,052	48,820	40,013	38,554	38,991	56,564
British government securities denominated in foreign currency	RYEX	14	37	0	44	45	27	42	4	126	89	1,287
UK local authority investments	AHVO	125	42	8	4	4	2	5	0	2	274	113
Other UK public sector investments	JE5J	459	731	639	656	846	1,118	1,351	1,259	2,347	2,911	1,703
TOTAL PUBLIC SECTOR SECURITIES	**RYHC**	**84,352**	**85,271**	**89,450**	**88,283**	**95,220**	**106,057**	**115,015**	**99,840**	**111,346**	**125,281**	**170,475**
UK corporate bonds	JX62	22,138	30,351	36,918	42,871	47,912	54,626	57,306	55,741	64,351	59,469	61,586
Sterling	GQFT	21,589	29,984	36,415	42,151	47,061	53,190	55,550	53,765	62,073	57,086	59,322
Foreign currency	GQFU	549	367	503	720	851	1,436	1,756	1,976	2,278	2,383	2,264
UK ordinary shares	AHVP	260,696	186,437	186,426	180,561	199,199	208,473	152,048	110,571	116,710	121,882	108,631
UK preference shares	J8YF	163	99	164	156	153	276	235	775	833	16	11
Overseas corporate securities	JRS8	139,674	115,778	138,215	156,278	203,562	224,514	215,068	175,747	214,230	222,751	211,562
Bonds	RLPF	11,689	11,119	12,301	15,794	19,891	30,867	44,387	47,612	57,920	60,826	61,129
Ordinary shares	AHVR	127,893	104,392	125,740	140,282	183,060	192,978	169,598	127,525	155,577	161,043	149,638
Preference shares	RLPC	92	267	174	202	611	669	1,083	610	733	882	795
Mutual fund investments	JRS9	82,009	77,372	117,834	144,265	192,033	215,218	254,936	211,724	286,493	369,955	385,337
UK	J8Y7	65,011	60,288	97,218	115,622	150,316	168,635	194,833	148,798	203,523	266,058	264,652
Unit trust units	JX63	50,841	47,083	77,468	86,005	105,429	115,872	147,536	110,558	148,642	178,027	172,120
Other[2]	JX64	14,170	13,205	19,750	29,617	44,887	52,763	47,297	38,240	54,881	88,031	92,532
Overseas	JE4P	16,998	17,084	20,616	28,643	41,717	46,583	60,103	62,926	82,970	103,897	120,685
TOTAL CORPORATE SECURITIES	**RYHN**	**504,680**	**410,037**	**479,557**	**524,131**	**642,859**	**703,107**	**679,593**	**554,558**	**682,617**	**774,073**	**767,127**
Overseas government securities	AHVT	20,383	16,031	16,340	15,075	19,037	21,776	22,434	21,527	16,900	17,335	21,424
Loans and mortgages	JRT4	20	144	35	44	9	42	417	518	1,768	2,343	1,656
UK	JE5E	3	0	35	44	6	6	12	0	116	81	77
Overseas	AHVZ	17	144	0	0	3	36	405	518	1,652	2,262	1,579
Fixed assets	JRT5	31,082	31,825	30,775	30,676	31,742	34,608	30,466	22,892	24,957	30,159	32,991
UK	JE5F	30,622	31,662	30,621	30,554	31,616	34,435	30,306	22,818	24,718	28,991	32,178
Overseas	GOLB	460	163	154	122	126	173	160	74	239	1,168	813
Holdings in insurance managed funds	RYHS	45,145	40,593	43,063	67,936	86,336	92,387	103,610	86,541	70,318	80,613	93,823
Other UK and overseas assets not elsewhere classified	J8YA	5,410	5,845	14,327	17,071	21,423	31,234	41,455	45,301	51,100	69,419	81,562
TOTAL OTHER INVESTMENTS	**RYHW**	**102,040**	**94,438**	**104,540**	**130,802**	**158,547**	**180,047**	**198,382**	**176,779**	**165,043**	**199,869**	**231,456**
TOTAL LONGER TERM INVESTMENTS	**RYHX**	**691,072**	**589,746**	**673,547**	**743,216**	**896,626**	**989,211**	**992,990**	**831,177**	**959,006**	**1,099,223**	**1,169,058**

1 Data from the pension funds surveys are of lower quality than equivalent data from other institutional groups because of the difficulties in constructing a suitable sampling frame of pension funds for the surveys.
2 Includes UK investment trust securities, open-ended investment companies and other UK mutual funds.

Source: Office for National Statistics

12.14 SELF-ADMINISTERED PENSION FUNDS' BALANCE SHEET AT MARKET VALUES COMBINED PUBLIC AND PRIVATE SECTOR[1]

continued

£ million at end of year

		2001	2002	2003	2004	2005	2006	2007	2008	2009	2010	2011
Cash in hand	GNOR	0	0	0	0	0	0	0	0	0	0	0
Balances with banks and building societies in UK	JX5Q	17,162	15,079	16,103	16,216	17,789	22,823	25,974	20,133	23,054	23,736	23,854
Sterling	JX5S	15,040	14,094	14,349	14,064	15,510	20,211	22,615	16,802	19,099	20,043	20,159
Foreign currency	JX5U	2,122	985	1,754	2,152	2,279	2,612	3,359	3,331	3,955	3,693	3,695
Balances with overseas banks	GNOW	259	226	249	287	361	525	807	351	134	197	72
Other liquid deposits	GNOX	1,016	992	1,883	1,782	3,010	3,891	5,392	4,300	12,431	9,631	11,956
Certificates of deposit issued by banks and building societies in UK	IX8H	1,374	1,109	2,063	1,678	2,649	4,932	8,156	6,480	2,269	2,472	6,498
Money market instruments issued by HM Treasury	IX9J	862	771	206	69	89	22	304	548	1,709	1,109	1,734
UK local authority debt	AHVF	296	365	276	337	270	221	205	323	210	116	157
Commercial paper issued by UK companies	GQFR	672	322	197	175	476	401	857	367	664	1,135	993
Other UK money market instruments	GOZR	200	275	497	1,428	883	1,174	1,893	1,959	2,822	3,416	3,936
Money market instruments issued by non-resident businesses	GOZS	418	735	441	413	384	449	1,279	911	963	2,067	3,709
Other UK and overseas short-term assets not elsewhere classified	JX5W	550	760	721	1,365	1,854	1,898	1,304	3,474	3,113	3,644	2,311
TOTAL	RKIG	22,809	20,634	22,636	23,750	27,765	36,336	46,171	38,846	47,369	47,523	55,220
Amounts outstanding from stockbrokers and securities dealers	RYIL	3,829	4,584	5,383	8,939	18,879	24,812	28,297	30,536	11,281	7,145	8,241
Income accrued on investments and rents	RYIM	2,230	1,792	2,256	1,921	1,970	2,303	2,744	2,576	2,714	2,761	2,930
Amounts outstanding from HMRC	RYIN	51	30	22	28	29	16	15	23	32	37	53
Other debtors and assets	RYIO	2,418	3,660	15,794	22,838	25,006	35,224	22,454	24,565	21,464	13,159	8,902
TOTAL	RYIP	8,528	10,066	23,455	33,726	45,884	62,355	53,510	57,700	35,491	23,102	20,126
Derivative assets with UK counterparties	JRO3	3,050	1,775	3,089	10,235	22,157	24,357	29,789	35,194	61,862	99,420	170,170
Derivative assets with overseas counterparties	GOJU	753	696	561	2,962	2,668	5,995	8,652	5,835	20,534	19,803	29,445
TOTAL SHORT TERM ASSETS	RYIQ	35,140	33,171	49,741	70,673	98,474	129,043	138,122	137,575	165,256	189,848	274,961
TOTAL ASSETS	RYIR	726,212	622,917	723,288	813,889	995,100	1,118,254	1,131,112	968,752	1,124,262	1,289,071	1,444,019
Borrowing[3]	GQED	1,466	2,380	5,216	8,133	11,678	14,661	16,180	4,461	3,859	2,830	3,361
Amounts owed to stockbrokers and securities dealers	RYIS	4,138	4,424	5,472	9,248	18,722	25,954	33,965	37,912	13,707	7,312	9,688
Pensions due but not paid	RYIT	481	173	248	138	86	285	220	167	280	271	300
Derivative liabilities with UK counterparties	JRP9	722	1,282	1,817	7,873	16,818	17,231	26,187	27,533	37,689	78,322	147,217
Derivative liabilities with overseas counterparties	GKGR	738	392	437	3,082	2,785	7,036	11,275	6,335	41,110	37,345	42,712
Other creditors provisions and liabilities	RYIU	4,734	3,028	16,008	22,107	24,834	36,208	18,327	20,577	21,603	18,889	9,905
MARKET VALUE OF PENSION FUNDS (assets of funds less liabilities)	AHVA	713,933	611,238	694,090	763,308	920,177	1,016,879	1,024,958	871,767	1,006,014	1,144,102	1,230,836
TOTAL LIABILITIES	RYIR	726,212	622,917	723,288	813,889	995,100	1,118,254	1,131,112	968,752	1,124,262	1,289,071	1,444,019

1 Data from the pension funds surveys are of lower quality than equivalent data from other institutional groups because of the difficulties in constructing a suitable sampling frame of pension funds for the surveys.

Source: Office for National Statistics

3 Previously published at lower levels of aggregation. These have been removed to avoid the disclosure of confidential data.

12.15a INSURANCE COMPANIES' ASSETS & LIABILITIES AT MARKET VALUES LONG-TERM FUNDS

£ million at end of year

		2001	2002	2003	2004	2005	2006	2007	2008	2009	2010	2011
British government securities denominated in sterling	AHNJ	119,513	131,305	142,920	157,019	161,906	161,641	158,694	166,879	167,247	182,506	205,223
Index-linked	AHQI	19,195	22,359	23,186	28,673	33,722	41,104	45,902	54,387	57,157	66,115	78,354
Other than index-linked	J5HZ	100,318	108,946	119,734	128,346	128,184	120,537	112,792	112,492	110,090	116,391	126,869
British government securities denominated in foreign currency	RGBV	1	36	56	0	206	12	0	0	0	0	0
UK local authority investments	AHNN	1,407	1,427	1,547	2,044	1,840	1,614	998	776	655	768	813
Other public sector investments	RGCS	205	308	613	254	801	651	634	872	1,461	2,189	2,207
TOTAL PUBLIC SECTOR SECURITIES	**RYEK**	**121,126**	**133,076**	**145,136**	**159,317**	**164,753**	**163,918**	**160,326**	**168,527**	**169,363**	**185,463**	**208,243**
UK corporate bonds	IFLF	120,183	146,190	151,703	150,884	165,918	159,073	159,273	159,789	160,532	158,987	163,348
Sterling	IFLG	119,685	142,019	146,410	144,280	158,995	150,907	153,694	154,525	155,184	156,477	160,842
Foreign currency	IFLH	498	4,171	5,293	6,604	6,923	8,166	5,579	5,264	5,348	2,510	2,506
UK ordinary shares	IFLI	308,190	228,497	235,601	237,610	273,679	299,717	293,655	188,430	209,992	207,971	177,480
UK preference shares	RLOL	1,553	1,306	1,126	1,198	1,228	1,231	983	724	624	648	536
Overseas corporate securities	IFLJ	127,259	110,738	110,193	130,098	165,452	194,997	234,388	219,957	266,280	278,930	262,823
Bonds	RLOP	23,277	30,242	32,507	40,281	45,970	57,774	69,696	85,077	111,866	112,338	115,744
Ordinary shares	AHNQ	103,544	80,213	77,501	89,654	119,207	136,652	163,249	134,211	153,500	165,216	145,932
Preference shares	RLOM	438	283	185	163	275	571	1,443	669	914	1,376	1,147
Mutual fund investments[1]	IFLK	79,867	73,685	89,523	108,019	168,896	192,516	222,081	186,950	230,247	259,457	265,750
TOTAL CORPORATE SECURITIES	**RYEO**	**637,052**	**560,416**	**588,146**	**627,809**	**775,173**	**847,534**	**910,380**	**755,850**	**867,675**	**905,993**	**869,937**
Overseas government securities	AHNS	21,285	19,762	20,561	20,161	16,065	21,078	25,787	29,053	24,601	25,363	23,727
Other UK and overseas assets[2]	JX8D	67,384	66,835	77,739	89,063	83,665	92,326	99,316	76,139	67,531	74,900	81,916
TOTAL OTHER INVESTMENTS	**RYER**	**88,669**	**86,597**	**98,300**	**109,224**	**99,730**	**113,404**	**125,103**	**105,192**	**92,132**	**100,263**	**105,643**
TOTAL LONGER TERM INVESTMENTS	**RYES**	**846,847**	**780,089**	**831,582**	**896,350**	**1,039,656**	**1,124,856**	**1,195,809**	**1,029,569**	**1,129,170**	**1,191,719**	**1,183,823**

1 Includes UK unit trust units, investment trust securities, open-ended investment companies, other UK mutual funds & oveseas mutual funds.
2 Includes UK and overseas loans, fixed assets and other assets not elsewhere classified.

Source: Office for National Statistics

12.15a INSURANCE COMPANIES' ASSETS & LIABILITIES AT MARKET VALUES LONG-TERM FUNDS

continued

£ million at end of year

		2001	2002	2003	2004	2005	2006	2007	2008	2009	2010	2011
Cash in hand	HLGW	1	0	29	15	29	0	0	0	0	0	0
Balances with banks and building societies in UK	JX2C	35,217	29,750	26,527	28,018	31,606	34,454	48,619	51,139	44,483	34,026	34,998
Sterling	JX3R	32,250	28,505	24,928	26,116	30,221	32,653	45,948	47,456	42,097	32,387	32,698
Foreign currency	JX3T	2,967	1,245	1,599	1,902	1,385	1,801	2,671	3,683	2,386	1,639	2,300
Balances with overseas banks	HLHB	962	1,266	1,067	1,086	1,454	1,022	1,484	2,816	3,758	2,766	1,726
Other liquid deposits	HLHC	2,668	3,170	787	1,522	1,215	333	678	1,638	12,385	14,076	15,891
Certificates of deposit issued by banks and building societies in UK	AHND	14,049	15,910	19,344	18,733	14,200	17,256	15,177	11,401	8,177	8,622	6,158
Money market instruments issued by HM Treasury	RGBM	242	10	334	534	537	685	785	179	1,344	509	1,392
UK local authority debt	AHNF	0	0	0	0	0	0	0	0	0	0	0
Commercial paper issued by UK	JF77	2,568	3,555	3,512	2,884	5,130	2,714	2,723	2,268	1,806	646	891
Other UK money market instruments	HLHL	1,421	984	1,562	1,997	2,670	3,538	3,071	3,159	2,959	3,208	5,501
Money market instruments issued by non-resident businesses	HLHM	1,167	218	1,990	952	1,681	405	859	689	1,755	2,956	1,530
Other UK and overseas short-term not elsewhere classified (excl	JX2E	1,624	1,855	1,525	2,615	10,432	10,749	20,965	19,555	10,076	5,232	6,159
Net balance due to/from stockbrokers and/or securities dealers	RGBU	163	577	176	-228	-1,052	-345	140	-399	-1,159	-834	-1,245
TOTAL SHORT TERM ASSETS (excluding dervatives)	**RYEW**	**60,082**	**57,295**	**56,853**	**58,128**	**67,902**	**70,811**	**94,501**	**92,445**	**85,584**	**71,207**	**73,001**
Derivative assets with UK and overseas counterparties	IFKX	7,788	5,795	4,545	3,743	5,739	5,937	5,205	17,892	10,317	12,399	24,060
Other debtors	RYPF	21,700	28,147	28,548	23,028	19,694	44,923	51,373	37,342	33,162	30,366	28,806
TOTAL CURRENT ASSETS	**RFXF**	**89,570**	**91,237**	**89,946**	**84,899**	**93,335**	**121,671**	**151,079**	**147,679**	**129,063**	**113,972**	**125,867**
Agents' balances and outstanding premiums (net)												
UK	RYPA	844	1,883	635	269	500	669	738	535	467	515	554
Overseas	RYPB	40	49	73	106	-103	-136	-177	0	1	3	3
Reinsurance balances (net)												
UK	RYPC	-329	3,683	3,187	2,965	2,607	3,462	-413	-1,000	3,817	-838	-1,147
Overseas	RYPD	65	758	825	415	929	1,105	836	-7,355	-8,232	-6,020	-6,035
Outstanding interest, dividends and rents (net)	RYPH	5,585	6,244	6,866	7,476	7,897	7,330	8,690	9,256	9,158	8,591	8,511
TOTAL OTHER ASSETS	**RFXM**	**6,205**	**12,617**	**11,586**	**11,231**	**11,830**	**12,430**	**9,674**	**1,436**	**5,211**	**2,251**	**1,886**
TOTAL ASSETS (excluding direct investment)	**RFXN**	**942,622**	**883,943**	**933,114**	**992,480**	**1,144,821**	**1,258,957**	**1,356,562**	**1,178,684**	**1,263,444**	**1,307,942**	**1,311,576**
Borrowing from banks and building societies in UK	JX2G	8,810	5,390	4,164	5,362	5,043	2,867	3,801	5,089	3,305	2,099	1,980
Other UK borrowing	ICXU	5,330	6,974	10,923	8,381	9,030	9,537	6,699	4,832	5,460	8,112	8,730
Overseas borrowing	RGDD	81	800	530	793	1,151	1,965	1,926	2,546	2,101	2,331	1,374
TOTAL BORROWING	**AHNI**	**14,221**	**13,164**	**15,617**	**14,536**	**15,224**	**14,369**	**12,426**	**12,467**	**10,866**	**12,542**	**12,084**
TOTAL NET ASSETS	**RGGR**	**928,401**	**870,779**	**917,497**	**977,944**	**1,129,597**	**1,244,588**	**1,344,136**	**1,166,217**	**1,252,578**	**1,295,400**	**1,299,492**

Source: Office for National Statistics

12.15b INSURANCE COMPANIES' ASSETS & LIABILITIES AT MARKET VALUES
GENERAL FUNDS

£ million at end of year

		2001	2002	2003	2004	2005	2006	2007	2008	2009	2010	2011
British government securities denominated in sterling	AHMJ	15,064	18,390	19,645	19,662	19,818	19,296	16,026	18,441	16,969	13,631	13,384
Index-linked	AHMZ	525	733	453	345	538	603	297	1,622	1,991	1,731	1,724
Other than index-linked	J8EX	14,539	17,657	19,192	19,317	19,280	18,693	15,729	16,819	14,978	11,900	11,660
British government securities denominated in foreign currency	RYMQ	0	0	0	35	12	72	69	3	0	0	..
UK local authority investments	AHMN	6	10	10	49	44	0	3	0	0	0	..
Other public sector investments	RYMU	50	6	3	54	6	0	10	0	65	249	..
TOTAL PUBLIC SECTOR SECURITIES	**RYMV**	**15,120**	**18,406**	**19,658**	**19,800**	**19,880**	**19,368**	**16,108**	**18,444**	**17,034**	**13,880**	**13,907**
UK corporate bonds	IFVV	5,590	6,699	7,233	9,826	10,815	11,797	13,397	12,060	13,550	10,487	10,817
Sterling	IFVW	5,582	6,687	7,067	9,637	9,932	11,057	12,647	11,009	12,288	9,544	10,217
Foreign currency	IFVX	8	12	166	189	883	740	750	1,051	1,262	943	600
UK ordinary shares	IFVY	10,113	6,755	6,548	8,724	9,864	10,138	9,006	10,501	9,963	9,525	8,435
UK preference shares	RLOT	185	192	143	54	40	9	44	29	26	26	25
Overseas corporate securities	IFVZ	6,402	7,394	7,124	11,520	12,645	18,636	14,773	20,258	23,002	17,594	18,636
Bonds	RLOX	3,714	5,436	5,473	9,762	10,866	16,128	12,872	18,081	21,017	15,847	16,939
Ordinary shares	AHMQ	2,653	1,924	1,638	1,758	1,779	2,507	1,901	2,175	1,976	1,741	1,692
Preference shares	RLOU	35	34	13	0	0	1	0	2	9	6	5
Mutual fund investments [1]	IFWA	1,285	2,901	1,563	2,470	1,270	1,256	1,780	1,911	3,498	4,878	5,802
TOTAL CORPORATE SECURITIES	**RYNF**	**23,575**	**23,941**	**22,611**	**32,594**	**34,634**	**41,836**	**39,000**	**44,759**	**50,039**	**42,510**	**43,715**
Overseas government securities	AHMS	7,134	7,156	5,720	6,662	7,341	8,035	4,869	8,505	7,204	5,126	5,524
Other UK and overseas assets [2]	JX8E	3,698	2,859	3,335	4,451	6,362	6,746	7,059	8,269	7,338	9,158	9,938
TOTAL OTHER INVESTMENTS	**RYNO**	**10,832**	**10,015**	**9,055**	**11,113**	**13,703**	**14,781**	**11,928**	**16,774**	**14,542**	**14,284**	**15,462**
TOTAL LONGER TERM INVESTMENTS	**RYNP**	**49,527**	**52,362**	**51,324**	**63,507**	**68,217**	**75,985**	**67,036**	**79,977**	**81,615**	**70,674**	**73,084**

.. Suppressed to avoid the disclosure of confidential data.

Source: Office for National Statistics

1 Includes UK unit trust units, investment trust securities, open-ended
investment companies, other UK mutual funds & overseas mutual funds.
2 Includes UK and overseas loans, fixed assets and other assets not elsewhere classified.

12.15b INSURANCE COMPANIES' ASSETS & LIABILITIES AT MARKET VALUES GENERAL FUNDS

continued

£ million at end of year

		2001	2002	2003	2004	2005	2006	2007	2008	2009	2010	2011
Cash in hand	HLMN	49	0	12	23	63	0	0	0	0	0	0
Balances with banks and building societies in UK	JX3H	7,034	10,309	12,683	18,051	9,116	9,327	8,949	9,871	10,227	7,961	7,619
Sterling	JX43	6,493	9,280	11,257	16,485	7,952	6,501	6,907	8,170	8,763	6,730	6,532
Foreign currency	JX45	541	1,029	1,426	1,566	1,164	2,826	2,042	1,701	1,464	1,231	1,087
Balances with overseas banks	HLMS	544	370	700	1,523	1,116	1,031	1,015	1,250	1,138	981	1,150
Other liquid deposits	HLMT	46	93	103	204	70	396	375	869	2,476	3,326	2,916
Certificates of deposit issued by banks and building societies in UK	IX8K	3,687	4,800	3,486	6,808	8,402	7,708	8,264	7,775	2,002	558	843
Money market instruments issued by HM Treasury	ICWI	42	172	20	444	1,670	379	342	708	979	327	237
UK local authority debt	AHMF	0	0	3	0	0	0	0	0	0	0	0
Commercial paper issued by UK companies	JF75	377	399	607	441	610	732	2,682	1,640	1,630	275	281
Other UK money market instruments	HLNC	114	500	1,209	160	139	68	90	278	346	359	360
Money market instruments issued by non-resident businesses	HLND	452	957	1,239	1,619	2,429	3,516	3,261	2,277	2,321	545	745
Other UK and overseas short-term assets not elsewhere classified (excl derivatives)	JX2I	20	229	171	138	2,992	1,733	612	1,576	718	725	933
Net balance due to/from stockbrokers and/or securities dealers	RYMA	0	-105	-160	-61	3	-66	25	891	52	90	26
TOTAL SHORT TERM ASSETS (excluding derivatives)	**RYME**	**12,365**	**17,724**	**20,073**	**29,350**	**26,610**	**24,824**	**25,615**	**27,135**	**21,889**	**15,147**	**15,110**
Derivative assets with UK and overseas counterparties	IFVJ	15	487	104	122	44	45	208	685	455	906	629
Other debtors	RKAC	8,035	13,581	12,273	11,462	12,405	15,814	19,096	17,189	10,785	11,064	10,683
TOTAL CURRENT ASSETS	**RKAE**	**20,415**	**31,792**	**32,450**	**40,934**	**39,059**	**40,683**	**44,919**	**45,009**	**33,129**	**27,117**	**26,422**
Agents' balances and outstanding premiums (net)												
UK	RYMF	7,299	8,081	8,390	8,450	7,991	9,060	8,216	9,022	8,171	8,470	8,222
Overseas	RYMG	153	342	816	1,385	572	480	575	55	73	-15	-200
Reinsurance balances (net)												
UK	RYMH	705	1,182	698	942	934	1,290	1,164	1,092	1,730	-165	-258
Overseas	RYMI	-216	-113	-14	-919	-1,501	-48	-23	537	491	375	921
Outstanding interest, dividends and rents (net)	RYPN	1,021	856	982	1,156	905	1,067	1,255	1,108	958	765	726
TOTAL OTHER ASSETS	**RKAK**	**8,962**	**10,348**	**10,872**	**11,014**	**8,901**	**11,849**	**11,187**	**11,814**	**11,423**	**9,430**	**9,411**
TOTAL ASSETS (excluding direct investment)	**RKAL**	**78,904**	**94,502**	**94,646**	**115,455**	**116,177**	**128,517**	**123,142**	**136,800**	**126,167**	**107,221**	**108,917**
Borrowing from banks and building societies in UK	JX3J	481	1,384	2,046	4,519	893	3,148	675	343	744	621	606
Other UK borrowing	IFHX	10,621	10,472	9,342	10,261	11,080	10,445	10,885	13,179	9,965	9,835	8,991
Overseas borrowing	RYMD	1,964	2,916	2,918	2,476	2,817	5,459	7,037	6,692	4,893	3,975	4,684
TOTAL BORROWING	**AHMI**	**13,066**	**14,772**	**14,306**	**17,256**	**14,790**	**19,052**	**18,597**	**20,214**	**15,602**	**14,431**	**14,281**
TOTAL NET ASSETS	**RKAQ**	**65,838**	**79,730**	**80,340**	**98,199**	**101,387**	**109,465**	**104,545**	**116,586**	**110,565**	**92,790**	**94,636**

Source: Office for National Statistics

12.16a Individual insolvencies

England & Wales

		Not Seasonally Adjusted		
Year	Total	Bankruptcy Orders[4]	Debt Relief Orders[1]	Individual Voluntary Arrangements[2]
2003	35,604	28,021	:	7,583
2004	46,652	35,898	:	10,753
2005	67,584	47,291	:	20,293
2006	107,288	62,956	:	44,332
2007	106,645	64,480	:	42,165
2008	106,544	67,428	:	39,116
2009	134,142	74,670	11,831	47,641
2010	135,045	59,173	25,179	50,693
2011	119,941	41,876	29,009	49,056
2012	r 109,629	31,756	r 31,179	46,694

p Provisional.

: Not applicable

r Revised, reflecting changes to the raw data, or updates to the seasonally adjusted series.

[1] Debt Relief Orders (DROs) came into effect on 6 April 2009 as an alternative route into personal insolvency.

In April 2011 a change was introduced to the legislation to allow those who have built up value in a pension scheme to apply for debt relief under these provisions.

[2] Including Deeds of Arrangement

[3] See "Notes to Editors" paragraph 11 regarding seasonal adjustment of Bankruptcy Orders series.

[4] Figures from Q2 2011 based on the date the court order was granted

12.16b Insolvencies

Scotland

		not seasonally adjusted	
		Individuals[1]	
Year	Total	Sequestrations (No. of LILA[2])	Protected Trust Deeds
2003	8,780	3,328	5,452
2004	9,321	3,297	6,024
2005	11,897	5,033	6,864
2006	13,789	5,566	8,223
2007	13,924	6,331	7,593
2008	19,991	12,449 (7,133)	7,542
2009	23,541	14,415 (8,775)	9,126
2010	20,344	11,906 (6,801)	8,438
2011	19,650	11,128 (4,812)	8,522
2012	18,392	9,620 (3,883)	8,772

p Provisional   r Revised.

[1] Source: Accountant in Bankruptcy (AiB). Latest News Release http://www.aib.gov.uk/scottish-insolvency-statistics-quarter-4-2012-13

[2] On 1 April 2008, Part 1 of the Bankruptcy and Diligence etc. (Scotland) Act 2007 came into force making significant changes to some aspects of bankruptcy, debt relief and debt enforcement in Scotland. This included the introduction of the new route into bankruptcy for people with low income and low assets (LILA). Of the number or sequestrations, individuals who meet LILA criteria are shown in brackets

[3] Source: Companies House.

[4] Including those companies which had previously been in administration or other insolvency procedure

12.16c Insolvencies
Northern Ireland

not seasonally adjusted

| Year | | Individuals[1] | | |
	Total	Bankruptcy Orders	Debt Relief Orders[4]	Individual Voluntary Arrangements
2003	835	517	:	318
2004	1,115	666	:	449
2005	1,454	821	:	633
2006	1,809	1,035	:	774
2007	1,338	898	:	440
2008	1,638	1,079	:	559
2009	1,958	1,236	:	722
2010	2,323	1,321	:	1,002
2011	2,839	1,615	112	1,112
2012	r 3,189	r 1,452	506	1,231

p Provisional

r Revised

.. Not available

: Not applicable

[1] Source: Department for Enterprise, Trade and Investment, Northern Ireland (DETINI)

[2] Source: Companies House

[3] Including those companies which had previously been in administration or other insolvency procedure

[4] Debt Relief Orders (DROs) came into effect on 30 June 2011 as an alternative route into personal insolvency.

12.17a Company liquidations[1]

England & Wales

		Not Seasonally Adjusted	
Year	Total	Compulsory Liquidations[3]	Creditors' Voluntary Liquidations[2]
2003	14,184	5,234	8,950
2004	12,192	4,584	7,608
2005	12,893	5,233	7,660
2006	13,137	5,418	7,719
2007	12,507	5,165	7,342
2008	15,535	5,494	10,041
2009	19,077	5,643	13,434
2010	16,045	4,792	11,253
2011	16,886	5,003	11,883
2012	16,138	4,243	11,895

p Provisional.

r Revised, reflecting changes to the raw data, or updates to the seasonally adjusted series.

[1] Including partnerships.

[2] Where the Creditors' Voluntary Liquidation is the first insolvency procedure entered into

[3] Figures from Q2 2011 based on the date the court winding-up order was granted

12.17b Company Insolvencies

Scotland

not seasonally adjusted

		Companies[3]	
Year	Total	Compulsory Liquidations	Creditors' Voluntary Liquidations[4]
2003	631	436	195
2004	621	431	190
2005	569	420	149
2006	549	416	133
2007	539	439	100
2008	524	437	87
2009	584	432	152
2010	1,041	735	306
2011	1,237	918	319
2012	1,199	926	273

p Provisional   r Revised.

[1] Source: Accountant in Bankruptcy (AiB).
Latest News Release http://www.aib.gov.uk/scottish-insolvency-statistics-quarter-4-2012-13

[2] On 1 April 2008, Part 1 of the Bankruptcy and Diligence etc. (Scotland) Act 2007 came into force making significant changes to some aspects of bankruptcy, debt relief and debt enforcement in Scotland. This included the introduction of the new route into bankruptcy for people with low income and low assets (LILA). Of the number or sequestrations, individuals who meet LILA criteria are shown in brackets

[3] Source: Companies House.

[4] Including those companies which had previously been in administration or other insolvency procedure

12.17c Company Insolvencies

Northern Ireland

not seasonally adjusted

Year	Companies		
	Total	Compulsory Liquidations[1]	Creditors' Voluntary Liquidations[2,3]
2003	142	95	47
2004	121	76	45
2005	138	85	53
2006	128	78	50
2007	164	122	42
2008	209	158	51
2009	247	164	83
2010	382	250	132
2011	344	208	136
2012	r 410	r 252	158

p Provisional

r Revised

.. Not available

: Not applicable

[1] Source: Department for Enterprise, Trade and Investment, Northern Ireland (DETINI)

[2] Source: Companies House

[3] Including those companies which had previously been in administration or other insolvency procedure

[4] Debt Relief Orders (DROs) came into effect on 30 June 2011 as an alternative route into personal insolvency.

12.18a Monetary financial institutions consolidated balance sheet

£ millions   Not seasonally adjusted

Amounts outstanding of liabilities

	Currency, deposits and money market instruments						Financial derivatives (net)		Other securities issued		Other liabilities		Total liabilities/ assets
	Private sector		Public sector		Non-residents								
	Sterling	Foreign currency	Sterling	Foreign currency	Sterling	Foreign currency	Sterling	Foreign currency	Sterling	Foreign currency	Sterling	Foreign currency	
LPM	VYAX	VYAY	VYAZ	VYBA	VYBB	VYBC	VWKM	VWKN	VWKO	VWKP	VWKQ	VWKR	VYBF
2012 May	2,084,412	444,041	50,969	8,374	479,386	2,976,278	-17,145	33,481	54,892	243,981	563,172	220,115	7,141,957
Jun	2,063,680 (ar)	433,507	46,057	7,918	487,312	2,885,465	20,136 (bc)	58,044	56,832	240,821	498,260 (bh)	222,939	7,020,972
Jul	2,060,968	442,754	46,769	8,557	503,258	2,832,812	30,565	50,481	56,262	238,696	461,359 (bi)	250,746 (bp)	6,983,225
Aug	2,072,672	428,323	48,835	7,003	500,101	2,831,064 (ax)	10,955	55,856	49,104 (bg)	238,969	470,319	243,146	6,956,346
Sep	2,076,513	432,723	45,661	3,835	507,712	2,809,267	4,118	57,688	47,642	236,994	484,219	237,302	6,943,677
Oct	2,070,864 (as)	434,304	43,949	3,135	508,093	2,768,242	22,863	35,767	47,294	235,807	475,797	249,595	6,895,708
Nov	2,071,815	437,223	45,572	3,777	507,175	2,815,552 (ay)(az)	33,450	15,688	44,846	232,228	468,382 (bj)	248,271	6,923,978
Dec	2,087,273	444,370	41,350	4,278	503,103	2,772,029	20,490	21,837	45,288	233,086	472,480	258,201	6,903,784
2013 Jan	2,087,161	455,787	47,225	3,074	494,896 (aw)	2,872,253 (ba)	34,877	5,580	45,389	230,982	465,545	259,752	7,002,521
Feb	2,091,797 (at)	465,996	49,442	5,040	494,655	2,938,402	65,294	-24,995	46,391	235,393	454,767 (bk)	258,655 (bq)	7,080,836
Mar	2,089,167	481,862	36,839	2,690	479,242	2,870,131	44,019	-9,147	45,888	233,296	470,633	262,531	7,007,152
Apr	2,086,679	488,550	43,328	3,445	482,745	2,870,674	43,579	723 (bd)	46,096	226,812	467,358 (bl)	234,825 (br)(bs)	6,994,814
May	2,090,881	508,466	43,223	3,564	486,728	2,867,277	34,197	-5,911	44,373	226,022	454,868	237,081	6,990,768
Jun	2,093,068	501,058	45,688	3,185	476,449	2,798,449 (bb)	33,144	-35,673 (be)	45,110	220,056	438,876	243,678	6,863,086
Jul	2,104,334 (au)	500,905	50,443	3,079	473,821	2,732,942	33,073	-32,615	44,995	224,621	436,242	248,472	6,820,312
Aug	2,125,279	488,004	46,816	2,973	456,431	2,641,632	6,000	-16,008	44,469	216,531	440,220	234,982	6,687,329
Sep	2,135,788	448,414	44,413	2,394	462,859	2,548,474	-8,715	-941	44,704	212,795	415,178 (bm)	247,038 (bt)	6,552,402
Oct	2,134,356	445,845	46,893	3,227	448,135	2,579,852	3,641	-18,222	44,552	213,039	419,465	240,392	6,561,174
Nov	2,144,499	450,544	45,464	3,715	453,912	2,516,729	-9,000	-8,459	44,468	214,099	414,210	259,309	6,529,490
Dec	2,101,361	437,070	42,118	4,107	466,508	2,470,774	-12,032	-9,771	43,939	206,575	412,229	256,893	6,419,770
2014 Jan	2,117,666 (av)	440,425	52,564	4,029	471,153	2,496,022	-11,404	-6,333 (bf)	43,428	200,902	458,682 (bn)(bo)	228,225 (bu)	6,495,359 (av)(bf)(bn)(bo)(bu)
Feb	2,138,257	451,795	52,197	4,732	457,909	2,454,399	-14,317	763	42,818	202,494	482,004	192,794	6,465,844
Mar	2,103,639	432,111	46,533	5,395	457,545	2,446,317	-8,795	-11,589	42,794	200,085	469,304	201,764	6,385,103
Apr	2,096,790	433,595	45,720	3,820	446,705	2,441,549	-25,232	-3,261	42,475	203,788	473,347	199,696	6,358,992

Source: Bank of England

Notes to table

Movements in amounts outstanding can reflect breaks in data series as well as underlying flows. For changes data, users are recommended to refer directly to the appropriate series or data tables. Further explanation can be found at:
www.bankofengland.co.uk/statistics/Pages/iadb/notesiadb/Changes_flows_growth_rates.aspx.

(ar) Due to a change in accounting treatment at one reporting institution, the amounts outstanding increased by £7bn. This effect has been adjusted out of the flows for June 2012.

(as) Due to a change in accounting treatment at one reporting institution, the amounts outstanding decreased by £5bn. This effect has been adjusted out of the flows for October 2012.

(at) Due to a change in accounting treatment at one reporting institution, the amounts outstanding increased by £6bn. This effect has been adjusted out of the flows for February 2013.

(au) Due to improvements in reporting at one institution, the amounts outstanding increased by £8bn. This effect has been adjusted out of the flows for July 2013.

(av) Due to a change in treatment at one institution, the amounts outstanding increased by £19bn. The effect has been adjusted out of the flows for January 2014.

(aw) Due to a change in the reporting population, the amounts outstanding decreased by £3bn. The effect has been adjusted out of the flows for January 2013.

(ax) Due to improvements in reporting at one institution, the amounts outstanding decreased by £5bn. This effect has been adjusted out of the flows for August 2012.

(ay) Due to a change in accounting treatment at one reporting institution, the amounts outstanding increased by £3bn. This effect has been adjusted out of the flows for November 2012.

(az) Due to a change in accounting treatment at one reporting institution, the amounts outstanding increased by £8bn. This effect has been adjusted out of the flows for November 2012.

(ba) Due to a change in accounting treatment at one reporting institution, the amounts outstanding decreased by £8bn. This effect has been adjusted out of the flows for January 2013.

(bb) Due to a change in treatment at one reporting institution, the amounts outstanding increased by £11bn. The effect has been adjusted out of the flows for June 2013.

(bc) Due to improvements in reporting at one institution, the amounts outstanding increased by £55bn. This effect has been adjusted out of the flows for June 2012.

(bd) Due to improvements in reporting at one institution, the amounts outstanding decreased by £12bn. The effect has been adjusted out of the flows for April 2013.

(be) Due to a restructuring at one reporting institution, the amounts outstanding decreased by £11bn. The effect has been adjusted out of the flows for November 2012.

(bf) Due to improvements in reporting at one institution, the amounts outstanding decreased by £13bn. The effect has been adjusted out of the flows for June 2013.

(bg) Due to improvements in reporting at one institution, the amounts outstanding decreased by £18bn. This effect has been adjusted out of the flows for January 2014.

(bh) Due to improvements in reporting at one institution, the amounts outstanding decreased by £7bn. This effect has been adjusted out of the flows for August 2012.

(bi) Due to improvements in reporting at one institution, the amounts outstanding decreased by £55bn. This effect has been adjusted out of the flows for June 2012.

(bj) Due to improvements in reporting at one institution, the amounts outstanding decreased by £22bn. The effect has been adjusted out of the flows for July 2012.

(bk) Due to improvements in reporting at one institution, this series has decreased by £12bn for November 2012.

(bl) Due to improvements in reporting at one institution, the amounts outstanding increased by £5bn. This effect has been adjusted out of the flows for February 2013.

(bm) Due to improvements in reporting at one institution, the amounts outstanding decreased by £6bn. The effect has been adjusted out of the flows for April 2013.

(bn) Due to improvements in reporting at one institution, the amounts outstanding decreased by £8bn. The effect has been adjusted out of the flows for September 2013.

(bo) Due to improvements in reporting at one institution, the amounts outstanding increased by £18bn. The effect has been adjusted out of the flows for January 2014.

(bp) Due to improvements in reporting at one institution, the amounts outstanding increased by £26bn. The effect has been adjusted out of the flows for July 2012.

(bq) Due to improvements in reporting at one institution, the amounts outstanding decreased by £8bn. The effect has been adjusted out of the flows for February 2013

(br) Due to improvements in reporting at one institution, the amounts outstanding increased by £11bn. The effect has been adjusted out of the flows for April 2013.

(bs) Due to improvements in reporting at one institution, the amounts outstanding decreased by £8bn. The effect has been adjusted out of the flows for April 2013.

(bt) Due to improvements in reporting at one institution, the amounts outstanding increased by £8bn. The effect has been adjusted out of the flows for September 2013.

(bu) Due to a restructuring at one reporting institution, the amounts outstanding increased by £13bn. The effect has been adjusted out of the flows for January 2014.

12.18b Monetary financial institutions consolidated balance sheet

£ millions   Not seasonally adjusted

Amounts outstanding of assets

	Loans						Securities (other than financial derivatives)						Other assets	
	Private sector		Public sector		Non-residents		Private sector		Public sector		Non-residents			
	Sterling	Foreign currency	Sterling	Foreign currency	Sterling	Foreign currency	Sterling	Foreign currency	Sterling	Foreign currency	Sterling	Foreign currency	Sterling	Foreign currency
LPM	VYBG	VYBH	VYBI	VYBJ	VYBK	VYBL	VYBM	VYBN	VYBO	VYBP	VYBQ	VYBR	VYBS	VYBT
2012 May	2,016,838	425,971	22,258	709	267,325	2,832,290	293,576	61,640	471,371	254	43,556	520,486	110,053	75,632
Jun	2,033,225 (bv)	405,285	19,090	759	272,271	2,772,340	257,615	55,598	465,540	158	44,679	510,815	110,254	73,343
Jul	2,027,596	410,532	18,968	487	267,448	2,725,175	252,826	53,313	480,792	162	46,900	513,029	109,510	76,488
Aug	2,028,017	391,012	18,800	775	263,970	2,706,349	251,728	53,065	486,628	158	48,176	524,193	111,594	71,882
Sep	2,034,445	395,679	19,223	1,071	267,372	2,658,780	251,699	53,750	490,535	152	49,535	539,127	110,821	71,487
Oct	2,020,493 (bw)	374,659	19,451	909	258,666	2,618,280	255,853	54,226	498,419	167	50,501	562,076	112,155	69,855
Nov	2,022,596 (bx)	389,149 (cc)	17,573	314	259,362	2,622,529	257,241 (cd)	52,698	505,592	172	51,171	558,740	113,457	73,384
Dec	2,039,009	396,183	16,831	914	246,242	2,603,912	268,013	49,701	490,264	175	44,023	561,435	120,371	66,710
2013 Jan	2,033,173 (by)	424,552	16,444	564	248,494	2,679,524	258,923	51,232	492,550	147	48,900	557,142 (ci)	120,950	69,926
Feb	2,026,750	442,983	16,928	890	246,488	2,748,334	267,718 (ce)(cf)	49,985	494,357	53	46,811	561,548	120,713	57,277 (cj)
Mar	2,016,645	448,213	17,135	952	228,816	2,713,118	264,642	50,123	501,632	122	46,267	540,513	120,215	58,756
Apr	2,003,806	454,057	15,589	1,373	228,736	2,710,246	261,967	50,227	505,596	29	52,522	539,807	119,581	51,278 (ck)
May	2,000,758	475,471	17,306	1,483	232,227	2,686,375	258,092	53,119	496,913	7	50,865	545,226	119,494	53,432
Jun	1,994,394	438,196	17,435	1,623	237,729	2,637,951	255,543	52,967	488,631	17	44,022	520,102	122,236	52,241
Jul	1,997,505	420,039	16,001	1,786	230,858	2,598,733	258,168	53,753	498,639	15	43,858	527,678	120,615	52,666
Aug	2,008,057	411,218	14,907	1,591	230,639	2,489,672	259,900	54,854	492,817	2	41,289	509,267	119,159	53,956
Sep	2,019,430	392,819	16,685	1,359	224,858	2,393,271	257,299	53,713	492,922	1	40,694	488,830	119,336	51,185
Oct	2,012,761	395,492	15,966	1,370	226,730	2,373,396	249,717	53,639	505,032	63	42,732	514,771	118,635	50,871
Nov	2,012,915	393,482	14,767	1,428	229,335	2,332,948	252,170	52,409	505,807	83	43,097	521,360	120,737	48,951
Dec	1,984,026	381,250	13,351	2,214	230,884	2,301,474	245,988	52,551	497,773	61	41,140	498,946	119,673	50,439
2014 Jan	1,992,653 (bz)(ca)(cb)	392,492	15,406	3,515	239,066	2,348,558	246,572 (ca)(cg)	46,103 (ch)	509,854	74	48,050	486,000	116,826	50,190
Feb	1,995,734	381,393	16,836	2,953	248,045	2,330,716	238,326	45,461	511,401	76	47,536	477,833	118,937	50,596
Mar	1,948,672	362,527	17,596	2,381	243,815	2,341,461	234,654	46,220	500,619	87	47,739	472,507	116,680	50,144
Apr	1,933,512	377,129	16,574	2,136	233,911	2,326,212	232,676	45,254	504,642	91	44,924	476,225	115,898	49,808

Source: Bank of England

Notes to table

Movements in amounts outstanding can reflect breaks in data series as well as underlying flows. For changes data, users are recommended to refer directly to the appropriate series or data tables. Further explanation can be found at:
www.bankofengland.co.uk/statistics/Pages/iadb/notesiadb/Changes_flows_growth_rates.aspx.

(bv) Due to a change in accounting treatment at one reporting institution, the amounts outstanding increased by £7bn. This effect has been adjusted out of the flows for June 2012.
(bw) Due to a change in treatment at one reporting institution, the amounts outstanding decreased by £5bn. This effect has been adjusted out of the flows for October 2012.
(bx) Due to improvements in reporting at one institution, the amounts outstanding decreased by £4bn. This effect has been adjusted out of the flows for November 2012.
(by) Due to a change in the reporting population, the amounts outstanding decreased by £8bn. The effect has been adjusted out of the flows for January 2013.
(bz) Due to a change in treatment at one institution, the amounts outstanding increased by £19bn. This effect has been adjusted out of the flows for January 2014.
(ca) Due to improvements in reporting at one institution, the amounts outstanding decreased by £4bn. This effect has been adjusted out of the flows for January 2014.
(cb) Due to improvements in reporting at one institution, the amounts outstanding increased by £2bn. This effect has been adjusted out of the flows for January 2014.
(cc) Due to a change in accounting treatment at one reporting institution, the amounts outstanding increased by £8bn. This effect has been adjusted out of the flows for November 2012.
(cd) Due to improvements in reporting at one institution, the amounts outstanding increased by £4bn. This effect has been adjusted out of the flows for November 2012.
(ce) Due to improvements in reporting at one institution, the amounts outstanding increased by £6bn. This effect has been adjusted out of the flows for February 2013.
(cf) Due to improvements in reporting at one institution, the amounts outstanding increased by £5bn. This effect has been adjusted out of the flows for February 2014.
(cg) Due to improvements in reporting at one institution, the amounts outstanding increased by £4bn. This effect has been adjusted out of the flows for January 2014.
(ch) Due to improvements in reporting at one institution, the amounts outstanding decreased by £3bn. This effect has been adjusted out of the flows for January 2014.
(ci) Due to a change in accounting treatment at one reporting institution, the amounts outstanding decreased by £8bn. This effect has been adjusted out of the flows for January 2013.
(cj) Due to improvements in reporting at one institution, the amounts outstanding decreased by £8bn. The effect has been adjusted out of the flows for February 2013
(ck) Due to improvements in reporting at one institution, the amounts outstanding decreased by £6bn. The effect has been adjusted out of the flows for April 2013.

12.18c Monetary financial institutions consolidated balance sheet

£ millions Not seasonally adjusted

Changes in liabilities

	Currency, deposits and money market instruments						Financial derivatives (net)		Other securities issued		Other liabilities		Total liabilities/assets
	Private sector		Public sector		Non-residents								
LPM	Sterling	Foreign currency	Sterling	Foreign currency	Sterling	Foreign currency	Sterling	Foreign currency	Sterling	Foreign currency	Sterling	Foreign currency	
	VYAA	VYAB	VYAC	VYAD	VYAE	VYAF	VWKG	VWKH	VWKI	VWKJ	VWKK	VWKL	VYAI
2012 May	-210	-3,965	5,981	1,503	3,808	-49,097	46,605	-41,054	218	-1,539	-48,220	31,293	-54,678
Jun	-27,335	-7,741	-4,912	-458	7,492	-70,310	-17,667	23,656	1,940	-2,422	-2,783	9,406	-91,133
Jul	-2,541	14,423	712	789	15,988	-22,027	10,429	-5,336	-570	1,647	-15,259	-11,865	-13,611
Aug	10,834	-14,968	2,066	-1,547	-2,235	-240	-19,610	4,846	-326	-33	8,434	-7,946	-20,726
Sep	3,802	6,322	-3,173	-3,169	8,019	-855	-6,837	1,702	-1,462	-2,778	21,643	-1,087	22,126
Oct	223	233	-1,712	-726	644	-51,939	18,744	-22,123	-424	-3,719	-15,817	28,115	-48,502
Nov	1,507	908	1,391	618	-1,205	22,965	14,287	1,132	-2,447	-4,719	-13,189	-23,127	-1,880
Dec	15,698	8,750	-4,222	509	-4,121	-30,291	-12,960	6,228	474	1,421	17,391	9,828	8,704
2013 Jan	771	-1,816	5,876	-1,328	-4,640	28,269	14,162	-14,523	101	-9,605	78	-1,588	15,756
Feb	-1,240	-890	2,216	1,912	-257	-5,449	30,417	-30,214	1,002	439	-19,911	3,182	-18,793
Mar	-3,026	19,688	-12,603	-2,321	-15,360	-43,091	-21,276	15,911	-502	1,990	11,053	4,768	-44,769
Apr	-1,284	7,060	6,489	794	6,295	37,834	-4,183	19,568	207	-4,398	-3,127	-24,251	41,005
May	4,122	12,028	-105	76	4,172	-47,569	-9,439	-6,206	-1,723	-3,299	2,123	6,244	-39,577
Jun	1,935	-7,180	2,466	-387	-10,111	-90,122	-1,053	-12,933	737	-6,121	3,666	15,689	-103,415
Jul	2,803	-10,300	4,754	-142	-2,608	-90,680	357	3,997	-114	1,419	-2,403	12,299	-80,619
Aug	19,681	-1,891	-3,627	-38	-12,542	-33,524	-27,073	14,795	-526	-2,396	15,718	-3,002	-34,424
Sep	9,876	-25,885	-2,403	-499	6,915	-6,410	-14,715	13,023	235	1,690	-15,329	5,694	-27,820
Oct	-1,300	-6,410	2,480	812	-14,908	9,272	12,356	-16,467	-152	-1,893	-827	-13,043	-30,079
Nov	12,624	14,055	-1,780	556	5,908	-20,717	-12,541	8,849	-52	3,059	4,591	25,981	40,533
Dec	-42,197	-11,612	-3,446	408	11,047	-34,512	-3,282	-1,250	-528	-7,015	12,971	-3,782	-83,199
2014 Jan	187	1,428	10,446	-61	4,731	35,678	-980	8,984	-511	-5,072	36,419	-43,512	47,737
Feb	20,664	16,744	-343	720	-12,596	-21,054	-2,913	6,691	-610	2,314	25,348	-37,841	-2,877
Mar	-34,575	-19,636	-5,664	655	-412	-16,339	5,523	-12,164	-24	-3,041	-6,848	9,835	-82,690
Apr	-7,166	5,266	-814	-1,544	-10,980	17,023	-16,437	7,999	-320	5,325	2,309	-1,708	-1,046

Source: Bank of England

12.18d Monetary financial institutions consolidated balance sheet

£ millions Not seasonally adjusted

Changes in assets

	Loans						Securities (other than financial derivatives)						Other assets	
	Private sector		Public sector		Non-residents		Private sector		Public sector		Non-residents			
	Sterling	Foreign currency	Sterling	Foreign currency	Sterling	Foreign currency	Sterling	Foreign currency	Sterling	Foreign currency	Sterling	Foreign currency	Sterling	Foreign currency
LPM	VYAJ	VYAK	VYAL	VYAM	VYAN	VYAO	VYAP	VYAQ	VYAR	VYAS	VYAT	VYAU	VYAV	VYAW
2012 May	-5,800	-9,018	3,960	-220	-11,414	-24,021	-5,704	1,999	9,123	-3	-2,263	-15,449	2,242	1,892
Jun	6,267	-17,044	-3,315	55	5,263	-41,195	-32,861	-5,472	420	-93	1,437	-3,323	-165	-1,106
Jul	-4,740	8,392	-288	-274	-4,795	-13,235	-6,810	-1,918	7,097	3	2,022	-1,864	-737	3,536
Aug	1,095	-17,900	-168	285	-3,451	-15,145	-2,780	29	7,451	-2	1,997	9,966	2,011	-4,112
Sep	7,704	8,754	376	297	3,496	-29,864	1,375	1,141	11,019	4	-407	18,647	-719	310
Oct	-6,656	-22,409	228	-169	-8,591	-47,498	3,486	318	11,501	15	846	20,462	1,005	-1,041
Nov	8,145	5,093	-1,878	-598	834	-8,428	-3,416	-1,810	3,981	4	257	-8,587	1,471	3,051
Dec	17,337	9,739	-741	600	-13,045	-7,717	10,674	-2,374	-2,610	5	-4,596	1,261	4,257	-4,085
2013 Jan	2,129	17,341	478	-377	2,291	1,085	-9,405	234	4,752	-31	4,965	-10,335	664	1,964
Feb	-4,929	6,833	485	323	-1,927	3,939	-3,014	-2,533	-1,114	-98	-3,900	-10,960	-230	-1,667
Mar	-8,732	9,169	146	78	-18,128	-8,244	-4,151	444	1,858	69	-491	-18,363	-234	1,811
Apr	-6,777	12,871	-1,546	421	183	33,140	-3,421	818	-1,573	-91	6,614	457	-235	144
May	-2,014	13,663	1,716	100	3,841	-62,871	-3,643	2,001	4,445	-23	-1,653	3,635	-167	1,392
Jun	-5,441	-37,801	129	135	5,590	-53,749	11	-209	6,436	10	-5,665	-14,461	2,858	-1,259
Jul	-1,745	-13,203	-1,434	129	-6,801	-62,934	1,251	-165	7,146	-2	-366	591	-440	-2,645
Aug	14,348	458	-1,094	-149	1,562	-52,985	2,913	2,156	987	-13	-1,507	-2,540	-756	2,196
Sep	12,151	-4,932	1,777	-203	-5,434	-15,099	-3,588	620	-60	-1	816	-12,897	165	-1,134
Oct	-5,974	-1,071	-669	-5	1,874	-40,375	-9,761	-517	8,879	62	1,603	16,609	-758	25
Nov	6,089	4,952	-1,308	82	2,589	-581	2,517	-300	5,950	22	1,487	17,879	2,175	-1,018
Dec	-25,214	-10,173	-1,481	786	2,607	-19,702	-6,118	428	621	-22	-1,282	-24,317	-1,136	1,805
2014 Jan	-8,448	9,801	2,054	1,337	8,107	38,793	-198	-3,092	2,936	12	1,433	-2,820	484	-2,662
Feb	4,633	-6,780	1,432	-574	8,944	2,209	-8,651	-121	2,157	4	-187	-8,970	2,130	897
Mar	-45,316	-19,781	685	-585	-4,281	4,335	-3,569	597	-6,681	11	126	-5,475	-2,156	-601
Apr	-13,201	18,235	-1,022	-228	-10,695	6,797	-2,070	-545	618	5	-2,727	4,513	-814	87

Source: Bank of England

12.19 Selected interest rates, exchange rates and security prices

Monthly average of 4 UK Banks' base rates IUMAAMIH [a]		Monthly average rate of discount, 3 month Treasury bills, Sterling IUMAAJNB		Monthly average yield from British Government Securities, 20 year Nominal Par Yield IUMALNPY [b] [c]		Monthly average Spot exchange rate, US$ into Sterling XUMAUSS	
31-Jan-06	4.5	31-Jan-06	4.3906	31-Jan-06	3.9287	31-Jan-06	1.7678
28-Feb-06	4.5	28-Feb-06	4.3839	28-Feb-06	3.9954	28-Feb-06	1.747
31-Mar-06	4.5	31-Mar-06	4.3956	31-Mar-06	4.151	31-Mar-06	1.7435
30-Apr-06	4.5	30-Apr-06	4.4196	30-Apr-06	4.3575	30-Apr-06	1.7685
31-May-06	4.5	31-May-06	4.5012	31-May-06	4.4361	31-May-06	1.8702
30-Jun-06	4.5	30-Jun-06	4.5414	30-Jun-06	4.4775	30-Jun-06	1.8428
31-Jul-06	4.5	31-Jul-06	4.534	31-Jul-06	4.4631	31-Jul-06	1.8447
31-Aug-06	4.73	31-Aug-06	4.7544	31-Aug-06	4.4259	31-Aug-06	1.8944
30-Sep-06	4.75	30-Sep-06	4.8359	30-Sep-06	4.3032	30-Sep-06	1.8847
31-Oct-06	4.75	31-Oct-06	4.9357	31-Oct-06	4.3287	31-Oct-06	1.8755
30-Nov-06	4.93	30-Nov-06	5.0095	30-Nov-06	4.2572	30-Nov-06	1.9119
31-Dec-06	5	31-Dec-06	5.0759	31-Dec-06	4.3351	31-Dec-06	1.9633
31-Jan-07	5.17	31-Jan-07	5.304	31-Jan-07	4.5131	31-Jan-07	1.9587
28-Feb-07	5.25	28-Feb-07	5.3393	28-Feb-07	4.5597	28-Feb-07	1.9581
31-Mar-07	5.25	31-Mar-07	5.3274	31-Mar-07	4.5195	31-Mar-07	1.9471
30-Apr-07	5.25	30-Apr-07	5.4329	30-Apr-07	4.735	30-Apr-07	1.9909
31-May-07	5.43	31-May-07	5.5516	31-May-07	4.8163	31-May-07	1.9836
30-Jun-07	5.5	30-Jun-07	5.6702	30-Jun-07	5.0696	30-Jun-07	1.9864
31-Jul-07	5.72	31-Jul-07	5.7742	31-Jul-07	5.026	31-Jul-07	2.0338
31-Aug-07	5.75	31-Aug-07	5.7943	31-Aug-07	4.8049	31-Aug-07	2.0111
30-Sep-07	5.75	30-Sep-07	5.6896	30-Sep-07	4.7407	30-Sep-07	2.0185
31-Oct-07	5.75	31-Oct-07	5.6058	31-Oct-07	4.7394	31-Oct-07	2.0446
30-Nov-07	5.75	30-Nov-07	5.4986	30-Nov-07	4.5924	30-Nov-07	2.0701
31-Dec-07	5.54	31-Dec-07	5.3034	31-Dec-07	4.5916	31-Dec-07	2.0185
31-Jan-08	5.5	31-Jan-08	5.1215	31-Jan-08	4.4578	31-Jan-08	1.9698
29-Feb-08	5.3	29-Feb-08	5.0178	29-Feb-08	4.6173	29-Feb-08	1.9638
31-Mar-08	5.25	31-Mar-08	4.8835	31-Mar-08	4.5401	31-Mar-08	2.0032
30-Apr-08	5.08	30-Apr-08	4.8258	30-Apr-08	4.7315	30-Apr-08	1.9817
31-May-08	5	31-May-08	4.9496	31-May-08	4.8539	31-May-08	1.9641
30-Jun-08	5	30-Jun-08	5.1138	30-Jun-08	5.0261	30-Jun-08	1.9658
31-Jul-08	5	31-Jul-08	5.0843	31-Jul-08	4.9391	31-Jul-08	1.988
31-Aug-08	5	31-Aug-08	4.9539	31-Aug-08	4.7438	31-Aug-08	1.8889
30-Sep-08	5	30-Sep-08	4.7425	30-Sep-08	4.6619	30-Sep-08	1.7986
31-Oct-08	4.61	31-Oct-08	3.6788	31-Oct-08	4.7579	31-Oct-08	1.69
30-Nov-08	3.23	30-Nov-08	1.9948	30-Nov-08	4.6898	30-Nov-08	1.5338
31-Dec-08	2.14	31-Dec-08	1.2875	31-Dec-08	4.1461	31-Dec-08	1.4859
31-Jan-09	1.6	31-Jan-09	0.8945	31-Jan-09	4.2758	31-Jan-09	1.4452
28-Feb-09	1.08	28-Feb-09	0.7177	28-Feb-09	4.3394	28-Feb-09	1.4411
31-Mar-09	0.57	31-Mar-09	0.6035	31-Mar-09	4.007	31-Mar-09	1.4174
30-Apr-09	0.5	30-Apr-09	0.625	30-Apr-09	4.2419	30-Apr-09	1.4715
31-May-09	0.5	31-May-09	0.5271	31-May-09	4.3752	31-May-09	1.5429
30-Jun-09	0.5	30-Jun-09	0.5037	30-Jun-09	4.471	30-Jun-09	1.6366
31-Jul-09	0.5	31-Jul-09	0.4397	31-Jul-09	4.4588	31-Jul-09	1.6366
31-Aug-09	0.5	31-Aug-09	0.3946	31-Aug-09	4.2164	31-Aug-09	1.6539
30-Sep-09	0.5	30-Sep-09	0.3761	30-Sep-09	4.0688	30-Sep-09	1.6328
31-Oct-09	0.5	31-Oct-09	0.4315	31-Oct-09	4.05	31-Oct-09	1.6199
30-Nov-09	0.5	30-Nov-09	0.4459	30-Nov-09	4.2177	30-Nov-09	1.6597
31-Dec-09	0.5	31-Dec-09	0.3587	31-Dec-09	4.3306	31-Dec-09	1.6239
31-Jan-10	0.5	31-Jan-10	0.4874	31-Jan-10	4.4152	31-Jan-10	1.6162
28-Feb-10	0.5	28-Feb-10	0.4878	28-Feb-10	4.5205	28-Feb-10	1.5615

12.19 Selected interest rates, exchange rates and security prices

Monthly average of 4 UK Banks' base rates IUMAAMIH [a]		Monthly average rate of discount, 3 month Treasury bills, Sterling IUMAAJNB		Monthly average yield from British Government Securities, 20 year Nominal Par Yield IUMALNPY [b] [c]		Monthly average Spot exchange rate, US$ into Sterling XUMAUSS	
31-Mar-10	0.5	31-Mar-10	0.5109	31-Mar-10	4.5714	31-Mar-10	1.5053
30-Apr-10	0.5	30-Apr-10	0.5083	30-Apr-10	4.5595	30-Apr-10	1.534
31-May-10	0.5	31-May-10	0.4976	31-May-10	4.3169	31-May-10	1.4627
30-Jun-10	0.5	30-Jun-10	0.4839	30-Jun-10	4.2209	30-Jun-10	1.4761
31-Jul-10	0.5	31-Jul-10	0.498	31-Jul-10	4.1894	31-Jul-10	1.5299
31-Aug-10	0.5	31-Aug-10	0.4945	31-Aug-10	3.9953	31-Aug-10	1.566
30-Sep-10	0.5	30-Sep-10	0.4966	30-Sep-10	3.9092	30-Sep-10	1.5578
31-Oct-10	0.5	31-Oct-10	0.5061	31-Oct-10	3.8942	31-Oct-10	1.5862
30-Nov-10	0.5	30-Nov-10	0.4935	30-Nov-10	4.1251	30-Nov-10	1.5961
31-Dec-10	0.5	31-Dec-10	0.4913	31-Dec-10	4.2728	31-Dec-10	1.5603
31-Jan-11	0.5	31-Jan-11	0.5055	31-Jan-11	4.3331	31-Jan-11	1.5795
28-Feb-11	0.5	28-Feb-11	0.5363	28-Feb-11	4.4094	28-Feb-11	1.613
31-Mar-11	0.5	31-Mar-11	0.5603	31-Mar-11	4.2967	31-Mar-11	1.6159
30-Apr-11	0.5	30-Apr-11	0.5676	30-Apr-11	4.2921	30-Apr-11	1.6345
31-May-11	0.5	31-May-11	0.5265	31-May-11	4.1373	31-May-11	1.6312
30-Jun-11	0.5	30-Jun-11	0.5174	30-Jun-11	4.1299	30-Jun-11	1.6214
31-Jul-11	0.5	31-Jul-11	0.4996	31-Jul-11	4.1021	31-Jul-11	1.6145
31-Aug-11	0.5	31-Aug-11	0.4531	31-Aug-11	3.7258	31-Aug-11	1.6348
30-Sep-11	0.5	30-Sep-11	0.4649	30-Sep-11	3.4218	30-Sep-11	1.5783
31-Oct-11	0.5	31-Oct-11	0.4608	31-Oct-11	3.251	31-Oct-11	1.576
30-Nov-11	0.5	30-Nov-11	0.4387	30-Nov-11	3.0191	30-Nov-11	1.5804
31-Dec-11	0.5	31-Dec-11	0.2996	31-Dec-11	2.9759	31-Dec-11	1.5585
31-Jan-12	0.5	31-Jan-12	0.2677	31-Jan-12	2.8955	31-Jan-12	1.551
29-Feb-12	0.5	29-Feb-12	0.3147	29-Feb-12	3.0994	29-Feb-12	1.5802
31-Mar-12	0.5	31-Mar-12	0.3391	31-Mar-12	3.1896	31-Mar-12	1.5823
30-Apr-12	0.5	30-Apr-12	0.3447	30-Apr-12	3.1417	30-Apr-12	1.6014
31-May-12	0.5	31-May-12	0.3065	31-May-12	2.9235	31-May-12	1.5905
30-Jun-12	0.5	30-Jun-12	0.3066	30-Jun-12	2.7365	30-Jun-12	1.5571
31-Jul-12	0.5	31-Jul-12	0.3124	31-Jul-12	2.6509	31-Jul-12	1.5589
31-Aug-12	0.5	31-Aug-12	0.2812	31-Aug-12	2.6509	31-Aug-12	1.5719
30-Sep-12	0.5	30-Sep-12	0.289	30-Sep-12	2.7516	30-Sep-12	1.6116
31-Oct-12	0.5	31-Oct-12	0.3141	31-Oct-12	2.7981	31-Oct-12	1.6079
30-Nov-12	0.5	30-Nov-12	0.2865	30-Nov-12	2.7866	30-Nov-12	1.5961
31-Dec-12	0.5	31-Dec-12	0.2555	31-Dec-12	2.8438	31-Dec-12	1.6144

Notes:

[a] Data obtained from Barclays Bank, Lloyds Bank, HSBC, and National Westminster Bank whose rates are used to compile this series. Where all the rates did not change on the same day a spread is shown.

[b] Calculated using the Variable Roughness Penalty (VRP) model.

[c] The monthly average figure is calculated using the available daily observations within each month.

12.20 Mergers and Acquisitions in the UK by other UK Companies: Category of Expenditure

£ million

	Expenditure					Percentage of Expenditure		
		Cash						
	Total	Independent Companies	Subsidiaries	Issues of Ordinary Shares[2]	Issues of Fixed Interest Securities[2]	Cash	Issues of Ordinary Shares	Issues of Fixed Interest Securities
	DUCM	DWVW	DWVX	AIHD	AIHE	DWVY	DWVZ	DWWA
Annual								
2003	18,679	8,956	7,183	1,667	873	86	9	5
2004	31,408	12,080	7,822	10,338	1,168	63	33	4
2005	25,134	13,425	8,510	2,768	431	87	11	2
2006	28,511	..	8,131	..	335	..	..	2
2007	26,778	13,671	6,507	4,909	1,691	76	18	6
2008	36,469	31,333	2,851	1,910	375	94	5	1
2009	12,195	2,937	709	8,435	114	30	69	1
2010[1]	12,605	6,175	4,520	1,560	350	85	12	3
2011	8,089	4,432	2,667	719	271	87	10	4
2012	3,413	1,937	789	419	268	82	10	8
Quarterly								
2009 Q2	729	130	150	437	12	38	60	2
2009 Q3	1,886	1,409	214	254	9	87	13	–
2009 Q4	1,374	1,066	217	45	46	94	3	3
2010 Q1[1]	1,361	765	525	58	13	95	4	1
2010 Q2	2,032	986	714	275	57	83	14	3
2010 Q3	2,949	1,165	814	839	131	68	28	4
2010 Q4	6,263	3,259	2,467	388	149	92	6	2
2011 Q1	1,500	552	651	240	57	80	16	4
2011 Q2	3,346	2,355	704	204	83	92	6	2
2011 Q3	1,452	828	462	75	87	89	5	6
2011 Q4	1,791	697	850	200	44	87	11	2
2012 Q1	1,070	518	199	323	30	67	30	3
2012 Q2	1,041	575	269	54	143	81	5	14
2012 Q3	610	409	100	8	93	84	1	15
2012 Q4	692	435	221	34	2	95	5	–
2013 Q1	2,825	567	2,216	26	16	98	1	1

† indicates earliest revision, if any
– indicates data is zero or less than £0.5m
Disclosive data indicated by ..

1 The deal identification threshold has been increased from Q1 2010 from £0.1m to £1.0m and as a consequence there may be a discontinuity in the number and value of transactions reported.
2 Issued to the vendor company as payment.

Source: Mergers and Acquisitions Surveys, Office for National Statistics

Service industry

Chapter 13

Service industry

Annual Business Inquiry (Tables 13.1, 13.3 and 13.4)

The Annual Business Inquiry (ABI) estimates cover all UK businesses registered for Value Added Tax (VAT) and/or Pay As You Earn (PAYE). The businesses are classified to the 2007 Standard Industrial Classification (SIC(2007)) headings listed in the tables. The ABI obtains details on these businesses from the Office for National Statistics (ONS) Inter-Departmental Business Register (IDBR).

As with all its statistical inquiries, ONS is concerned to minimise the form-filling burden of individual contributors and as such the ABI is a sample inquiry. The sample was designed as a stratified random sample of about 66,600 businesses; the inquiry population is stratified by SIC(2007) and employment using the information from the register.

The inquiry results are grossed up to the total population so that they relate to all active UK businesses on the IDBR for the sectors covered.

The results meet a wide range of needs for government, economic analysts and the business community at large. In official statistics the inquiry is an important source for the national accounts and input-output tables, and also provides weights for the indices of production and producer prices. Additionally, inquiry results enable the UK to meet statistical requirements of the European Union.

Data from 1995 and 1996 were calculated on a different basis from those for 1997 and later years. In order to provide a link between the two data series, the 1995 and 1996 data were subsequently reworked to provide estimates on a consistent basis.

Revised ABI results down to SIC(2007) 4 digit class level for 1995–2007, giving both analysis and tabular detail, are available from the ONS website at: www.statistics.gov.uk, with further extracts and bespoke analyses available on request. This service replaces existing publications.

Retail trade: index numbers of value and volume (Table 13.2)

The main purpose of the Retail Sales Inquiry (RSI) is to provide up-to-date information on short period movements in the level of retail sales. In principle, the RSI covers the retail activity of every business classified in the retail sector (Division 52 of the 2007 Standard Industrial Classification (SIC(2007)) in Great Britain. A business will be classified to the retail sector if its main activity is one of the individual 4 digit SIC categories within Division 52. The retail activity of a business is then defined by its retail turnover, that is the sale of all retail goods (note that petrol, for example, is not a retail good).

The RSI is compiled from the information returned to the statutory inquiries into the distribution and services sector. The inquiry is addressed to a stratified sample of 5,000 businesses classified to the retail sector, the stratification being by 'type of store' (the individual 4 digit SIC categories within Division 52) and by size. The sample structure is designed to ensure that the inquiry estimates are as accurate as possible. In terms of the selection, this means that:

• each of the individual 4 digit SIC categories are represented – their coverage depending upon the relative size of the category and the variability of the data

• within each 4 digit SIC category the larger retailers tend to be fully enumerated with decreasing proportions of medium and smaller retailers

The structure of the inquiry is updated periodically by reference to the more comprehensive results of the Annual Business Inquiry (ABI). The monthly inquiry also incorporates a rotation element for the smallest retailers. This helps to spread the burden more fairly, as well as improving the representativeness between successive benchmarks.

13.1a Retail Trade, except of motor vehicles and motorcycles

Description	Year	Number of enterprises	Total turnover inc VAT	VAT in total turnover	Total retail turnover	Total non-retail turnover	Total Turnover	Approximate total output at basic prices (Gross Margin)	Approximate gross value added at basic prices	Total purchases	Purchase of energy and water products for own consumption
		Number	£ million	£ million	£ million	£ million	£ million	£ million	£ million	£ million	£ million
Retail trade, except of motor vehicles and motorcycles	2008	194,677	346,002	34,257	325,847	20,155	311,745	107,483	65,123	246,237	3,527
	2009	187,890	350,269	30,951	331,256	19,013	319,318	112,756	69,924	249,058	3,625
	2010	187,230	367,446	35,315	347,144	20,303	332,131	115,484	71,500	261,676	3,289
	2011	189,110	384,773	43,542	363,012	21,761	341,231	114,767	70,757	270,382	3,562

Description	Year	Purchase of goods and materials	Purchases of goods bought for resale	Payments for hiring, leasing or renting plant, machinery and vehicles	Commercial insurance premiums paid	Purchases of road transport services	Purchases of telecommunication services	Purchases of computer and related services	Purchases of advertising and marketing services	Payments to sub-contractors
		£ million	£ million	£ million	£ million	£ million	£ million	£ million	£ million	£ million
Retail trade, except of motor vehicles and motorcycles	2008	4,119	203,752	609	940	2,898	556	967	4,155	1,186
	2009	5,065	206,152	714	948	2,795	576	995	4,070	1,175
	2010	5,489	217,595	650	878	2,614	533	1,021	4,401	1,276
	2011	4,803	226,214	636	934	2,631	562	1,122	4,605	1,247

Description	Year	Other services purchased	Total taxes, duties and levies pad	National non-domestic (business rates)	Other amounts paid for taxes, duties and levies	Total employment - point in time [1]	Total number of full-time employees - point in time [1]	Total number of part-time employees - point in time [1]	Total employment - average during the year [1]	Total number of full-time employees - average during the year [1]	Total number of part-time employees - average during the year [1]
		£ million	£ million	£ million	£ million	Thousand	Thousand	Thousand	Thousand	Thousand	Thousand
Retail trade, except of motor vehicles and motorcycles	2008	23,528	6,498	5,218	1,280	3,054	1,335	1,618	3,106	1,358	1,646
	2009	22,941	6,843	5,462	1,381	3,086	1,271	1,625	3,151	1,306	1,656
	2010	23,931	7,130	5,651	1,479	3,016	1,285	1,603	3,040	1,296	1,616
	2011	24,066	7,859	6,116	1,743	3,027	1,260	1,628	3,054	1,250	1,665

Description	Year	Total employment costs	Gross wages and salaries - including redundancy and severance	Social Security costs	Total net capital expenditure - inc NYIP	Total acquisitions - inc NYIP	Total disposals - inc NYIP	Total stocks and work in progress - value at end of year	Total stocks and work in progress - value at beginning of year	Total stocks and work in progress - increase during year
		£ million	£ million	£ million	£ million	£ million	£ million	£ million	£ million	£ million
Retail trade, except of motor vehicles and motorcycles	2008	38,466	34,712	3,754	9,069	10,495	1,426	26,110	25,519	591
	2009	38,914	35,126	3,788	7,784	9,113	1,330	26,539	25,759	781
	2010	39,816	35,763	4,053	6,149	9,258	3,108	28,743	26,425	2,317
	2011	41,544	37,530	4,014	8,716	10,548	1,832	30,438	29,054	1,384

Notes:

1. *Total employment - point in time* and *Total employment - average during the year* which are from the Business Register and Employment Survey (BRES). Changes in the treatment of working owners in the 2010 and 2011 BRES have led to a discontinuity between the 2010 and 2011 BRES employment estimate and earlier years. Care should be taken when making comparisons between employment in 2010 and 2011 and that in any earlier years. More detail about the discontinuity can be found on the BRES webpages.

13.1b - Retail trade, except of motor vehicles and motorcycles

	2008	2009	£ million (Inclusive of VAT) 2010	2011
TOTAL TURNOVER	**346,002**	**350,269**	**367,446**	**384,773**
RETAIL TURNOVER	**325,847**	**331,256**	**347,144**	**363,012**
Fruit (including fresh, chilled, dried, frozen, canned and processed)	5,949	6,469	6,821	7,631
Vegetables (including fresh, chilled, dried, frozen canned and processed)	10,070	9,949	10,533	10,632
Meat (including fresh, chilled, smoked, frozen, canned and processed)	17,243	17,855	17,909	19,290
Fish, crustaceans and molluscs (including fresh, chilled, smoked, frozen, canned and processed)	2,936	2,989	2,978	3,284
Bakery products and cereals (including rice and pasta products)	15,816	16,719	17,875	18,796
Sugar, jam, honey, chocolate and confectionery (including ice-cream)	8,192	8,618	8,844	8,666
Alcoholic drink	14,965	15,609	16,618	17,370
Non-alcoholic beverages (including tea, coffee, fruit drinks and vegetable drinks)	7,793	7,756	8,018	9,155
Tobacco (excluding smokers requisites e.g. pipes, lighters etc)	10,343	11,411	11,369	11,804
Milk, cheese and eggs (including yoghurts and cream)	10,813	11,562	10,918	11,173
Oils and fats (including butter and margarine)	1,488	1,440	1,444	1,608
Food products not elsewhere classified (including sauces, herbs spices, soups)	4,969	5,149	4,427	4,512
Pharmaceutical products	3,519	3,636	3,946	4,399
National Health Receipts	11,479	11,792	12,067	11,520
Other medical products and therapeutic appliances and equipment	3,822	3,213	4,210	3,625
Other appliances, articles and products for personal care	12,596	13,148	14,109	15,099
Other articles of clothing, accessories for making clothing	3,011	2,505	3,395	3,854
Garments	34,121	35,556	36,706	38,010
Footwear (excluding sports shoes)	6,858	7,685	7,458	7,734
Travel goods and other personal effects not elsewhere classified	1,512	1,722	2,352	2,469
Household textiles (including furnishing fabrics, curtains etc)	4,368	4,535	4,862	4,202
Household and personal appliances whether electric or not	6,362	6,736	6,917	7,294
Glassware, tableware and household utensils (including non-electric)	2,768	2,824	2,754	3,374
Furniture and furnishings	13,839	13,226	12,313	13,453
Audio and visual equipment (including radios, televisions and video recorders)	6,215	6,016	6,245	5,360
Recording material for pictures and sound (including audio and video tapes, blank and pre recorded records etc)	3,622	3,052	2,787	2,547
Information processing equipment (including printers, software, calculators and typewriters)	4,423	4,384	4,530	5,439
Decorating and DIY supplies	6,176	6,820	7,319	7,617
Tools and equipment for house and garden	3,131	2,964	3,088	3,564
Books	2,497	2,623	2,648	2,553
Newspapers and periodicals	3,971	3,405	3,947	3,617
Stationery and drawing materials and miscellaneous printed matter	4,446	4,423	4,025	4,441
Carpets and other floor coverings (excluding bathroom mats, rush and door mats)	3,493	2,840	2,824	3,177
Photographic and cinematographic equipment and optical instruments	2,274	1,854	1,625	1,662
Telephone and telefax equipment (including mobile phones)	3,264	3,249	3,143	3,657
Jewellery, silverware and plate; watches and clocks	5,091	5,693	6,045	6,371
Works of art and antiques (including furniture, floor coverings and jewellery)	1,391	1,347	1,756	1,496
Equipment and accessories for sport, camping, recreation and musical instruments	4,019	4,416	4,864	5,143
Spare parts and accessories for all types of vehicle and sales of bicycles	1,159	924	1,148	993
Games, toys, hobbies (including video game software, video game computers that plug into the tv, video-games cassettes and CD-ROM'S)	7,961	7,484	7,514	7,486
Other goods not elsewhere classified (including sale of new postage stamps and sales of liquid and solid fuels)	4,307	5,007	5,896	5,881
Non-durable household goods (including household cleaning, maintenance products) & paper products and other non-durable household goods	4,942	5,280	4,727	4,910
Natural or artificial plants and flowers	4,192	2,973	3,609	4,022
Pets and related products (including pet food)	3,601	3,884	3,896	4,156
Petrol, diesel, lubricating oil and other petroleum products	30,840	30,515	36,664	39,968

Source: Annual Business Survey (ABS)

The following symbols and abbreviations are used throughout the ABS releases;

*   Information suppressed to avoid disclosure

..   not available

-   nil or less than half the level of rounding

The sum of constituent items in tables may not always agree exactly with the totals shown due to rounding.

13.2 Retail trade: index numbers of value and volume of sales[1]

Great Britain

Non-seasonally adjusted

		Sales in 2012 £ thousand	2002	2003	2004	2005	2006	2007	2008	2009	2010	2011	2012
Value													
All retailing	J5AH	351,100,470	79.2	81.3	85.2	86.3	89.5	93.1	96.6	97.4	100	105.2	107.6
Large	J5AI	277,566,648	72.5	76.2	80.1	81.6	85.4	89.6	93.9	95.5	100	105.3	108.1
Small	J5AJ	73,533,804	104	100.4	103.9	103.4	104.7	106	106.7	104.3	100	104.8	105.7
All retailing excluding automotive fuel	J43S	310,808,322	81	82.7	86.5	87.5	89.6	92.8	95.7	97.6	100	103.6	106.3
Predominantly food stores	EAFS	145,675,897	73.4	76.2	79.2	81.8	84.7	88.3	93.4	98.4	100	104.4	107.3
Predominantly non-food stores	EAFT	145,097,278	89.2	90.7	94.9	94.4	95.8	98.7	99.1	97.6	100	101.5	103.1
Non specialised predominantly non-food stores	EAGE	28,283,177	85	86.9	88.7	88.4	90.9	94.4	91.9	93.5	100	104	110.3
Textile, clothing, footwear and leather	EAFU	42,700,527	79.6	82.5	86.7	87.5	91.5	94	93.8	94.9	100	103.7	105.3
Household goods stores	EAFV	30,104,415	107.8	107.3	111.1	107.5	108.2	112	109.6	104.1	100	97.7	96.8
Other specialised non-food stores	EAFW	44,009,159	87.3	88.7	94.6	95.1	94	96.2	101	97.8	100	100.7	101.2
Non-store retailing	J596	20,035,147	74.3	67.8	74.8	74.7	76.3	79.5	84.8	90.4	100	114.9	125.9
Automotive fuel	J43H	40,292,148	63.2	69.6	73.5	76	88.9	95.2	104.5	95.5	100	119.2	118.9
Volume													
All retailing	J5DD	351,100,470	85.3	87.9	92.5	93.8	96.9	99.6	100.2	100.6	100	100.6	101.6
All retailing excluding automotive fuel	J448	310,808,322	83.8	86.2	91.1	92.9	95.2	97.8	98.9	99.6	100	100.2	101.5
Predominantly food stores	EAGW	145,675,897	91.1	93.7	97.1	99.1	100.6	101.3	100.7	101.6	100	99.1	98.9
Predominantly non-food stores	EAGX	145,097,278	79.8	82.7	88.5	90	93	97	98.8	98.6	100	99.8	101.4
Non specialised predominantly non-food stores	EAHI	28,283,177	78.6	81.8	85.3	86.6	90.2	94.1	92.6	94.3	100	103	110.2
Textile, clothing, footwear and leather	EAGY	42,700,527	63.7	67.6	73.3	76.3	81.8	85.8	88.9	94.9	100	100.9	101.4
Household goods stores	EAGZ	30,104,415	94.9	97.7	104	103.6	107.3	112.6	112	105.8	100	96.6	95.7
Other specialised non-food stores	EAHA	44,009,159	86.2	87.9	94.7	96.3	95.5	98.5	102.8	99.5	100	99.1	100.2
Non-store retailing	J5CL	20,035,147	67.9	62.9	70.7	71.8	74.4	78.4	84.4	91.2	100	113.6	125.2
Automotive fuel	J43V	40,292,148	100	106.2	106.4	101.6	112.7	117.1	112.7	110.5	100	104.5	102.1

Weekly average (2010=100)

Source: Office for National Statistics

1 See chapter text.

Please note that the indices have been re-referenced so the value of 100 is in 2010 rather than 2006 as previously shown

13.3 Wholesale and retail trade and repair of motor vehicles and motorcycles

Standard Industrial Classification (Revised 2007) Section Division Group Class Subclass	Description	Year	Number of enterprises	Total Turnover	Total motor trades turnover	Total non motor trades turnover	Approximate total output at basic prices (Gross Margin)	Approximate gross value added at basic prices	Total purchases	Purchase of energy and water products for own consumption	Purchase of goods and materials	Purchases of parts used solely in repair and servicing activities
			Number	£ million	£ million	£ million	£ million	£ million	£ million	£ million	£ million	£ million
45	Wholesale and retail trade and repair of motor vehicles and motorcycles	2008	67,683	135,669	133,093	2,576	31,531	20,957	115,372	1,068	1,432	8,227
		2009	66,372	125,764	122,885	2,879	27,858	18,348	105,457	842	1,206	7,240
		2010	66,239	132,077	129,128	2,949	32,308	22,150	111,243	866	1,481	6,667
		2011	67,299	137,762	133,538	4,224	34,311	23,493	115,611	1,056	1,637	8,370

Standard Industrial Classification (Revised 2007) Section Division Group Class Subclass	Description	Year	Purchases of goods bought for resale	Payments for hiring, leasing or renting plant, machinery and vehicles	Commercial insurance premiums paid	Purchases of road transport services	Purchases of telecommunication services	Purchases of computer and related services	Purchases of advertising and marketing services	Payments to sub-contractors	Other services purchased	Total taxes, duties and levies pad
			£ million	£ million	£ million	£ million	£ million	£ million	£ million	£ million	£ million	£ million
45	Wholesale and retail trade and repair of motor vehicles and motorcycles	2008	96,539	229	456	534	272	331	1,940	655	3,690	925
		2009	88,674	202	426	592	227	324	1,646	525	3,554	983
		2010	94,386	212	441	603	231	338	1,977	531	3,511	926
		2011	96,374	233	491	613	234	370	1,718	758	3,759	991

Standard Industrial Classification (Revised 2007) Section Division Group Class Subclass	Description	Year	National non-domestic (business rates)	Other amounts paid for taxes, duties and levies	Total employment - point in time [1]	Total number of full-time employees - point in time [1]	Total number of part-time employees - point in time [1]	Total employment - average during the year [1]	Total number of full-time employees - average during the year [1]	Total number of part-time employees - average during the year [1]	Total employment costs	Gross wages and salaries - including redundancy and severance payments
			£ million	£ million	Thousand	Thousand	Thousand	Thousand	Thousand	Thousand	£ million	£ million
45	Wholesale and retail trade and repair of motor vehicles and motorcycles	2008	596	328	532	422	63	535	425	64	10,925	9,657
		2009	688	295	503	387	62	541	423	64	10,445	9,212
		2010	566	361	511	407	66	510	401	71	10,439	9,257
		2011	701	290	523	409	70	536	421	71	10,666	9,379

Standard Industrial Classification (Revised 2007) Section Division Group Class Subclass	Description	Year	Social Security costs	Total net capital expenditure - inc NYIP	Total acquisitions - inc NYIP	Total disposals - inc NYIP	Total stocks and work in progress - value at end of year	Total stocks and work in progress - value at beginning of year	Total stocks and work in progress - increase during year
			£ million	£ million	£ million	£ million	£ million	£ million	£ million
45	Wholesale and retail trade and repair of motor vehicles and motorcycles	2008	1,268	1,044	2,110	1,066	16,136	15,402	735
		2009	1,233	885	1,669	784	13,624	15,545	-1,921
		2010	1,182	1,035	1,747	711	15,008	13,640	1,368
		2011	1,287	1,311	2,114	803	16,401	15,063	1,338

Source: Annual Business Survey (ABS)

The following symbols and abbreviations are used throughout the ABS releases;
*   Information suppressed to avoid disclosure
.. not available
-   nil or less than half the level of rounding

The sum of constituent items in tables may not always agree exactly with the totals shown due to rounding.

Notes:

1. *Total employment - point in time* and *Total employment - average during the year* which are from the Business Register and Employment Survey (BRES). Changes in the treatment of working owners in the 2010 and 2011 BRES have led to a discontinuity between the 2010 and 2011 BRES employment estimates and earlier years. Care should be taken when making comparisons between employment in 2010 and 2011 and that in any earlier years. More detail about the discontinuity can be found on the BRES webpages.

13.4 Accommodation and food service activities

Standard Industrial Classification (Revised 2007) Section Division Group Class Subclass	Description	Year	Number of enterprises	Total turnover inc VAT	VAT in total turnover	Total Turnover	Approximate total output at basic prices (Gross Margin)	Approximate gross value added at basic prices	Total purchases	Purchase of energy and water products for own consumption	Purchase of goods and materials
			Number	£ million	£ million	£ million	£ million	£ million	£ million	£ million	£ million
I	Accommodation and food service activities	2009	129,112	75,756	9,561	66,195	54,349	29,375	36,745	2,384	12,002
		2010	127,844	78,994	10,648	68,346	56,078	31,435	36,883	2,292	11,556
		2011	130,336	84,432	12,286	72,147	60,118	34,948	37,268	2,377	12,017
55	Accommodation	2009	15,157	19,654	2,419	17,235	15,859	9,231	7,973	822	1,871
		2010	15,075	20,412	2,762	17,650	16,098	9,087	8,603	841	2,034
		2011	15,159	21,970	3,303	18,667	17,080	9,836	8,870	788	1,974
55.1	Hotels and similar accommodation	2009	9,687	15,610	1,986	13,624	12,751	7,439	6,171	658	1,510
		2010	9,559	15,755	2,262	13,493	12,586	7,102	6,399	643	1,653
		2011	9,575	16,919	2,700	14,219	13,285	7,587	6,625	583	1,504
55.2	Holiday and other short stay accommodation	2009	3,351	1,367	148	1,219	1,111	661	554	60	99
		2010	3,318	1,783	181	1,603	1,351	846	776	57	81
		2011	3,297	1,935	256	1,679	1,510	833	866	83	196
55.20/1	Holiday centre and villages	2009	728	680	81	598	502	281	315	28	40
		2010	723	901	106	795	663	438	362	31	39
		2011	720	1,148	155	994	824	545	454	36	71
55.20/2	Youth Hostels	2009	88	99	11	89	86	42	47	4	8
		2010	90	123	15	108	106	54	54	5	10
		2011	107	104	15	89	88	48	41	6	13
55.20/9	Other holiday and other collective accommodation (not including holiday centres and villages or youth hostels) n.e.c	2009	2,535	588	56	531	523	337	191	28	51
		2010	2,505	759	60	699	581	354	360	22	33
		2011	2,470	683	86	597	598	240	370	42	112
55.3	Camping grounds, recreational vehicle parks and trailer parks	2009	1,711	2,506	276	2,230	1,852	1,033	1,184	95	253
		2010	1,735	2,622	297	2,325	1,961	1,031	1,307	129	294
		2011	1,774	2,905	336	2,569	2,092	1,309	1,288	107	264
55.9	Other accommodation	2009	408	171	8	162	145	98	64	9	9
		2010	463	252	23	229	200	108	121	12	6
		2011	513	210	11	200	193	108	92	14	11
56	Food and beverage service activities	2009	113,955	56,102	7,142	48,960	38,490	20,144	28,772	1,563	10,131
		2010	112,769	58,582	7,885	50,696	39,980	22,348	28,281	1,451	9,523
		2011	115,177	62,463	8,982	53,480	43,039	25,111	28,397	1,590	10,043
56.1	Restaurants and mobile food service activities	2009	61,192	25,763	3,105	22,658	19,212	9,910	12,765	756	5,038
		2010	61,387	26,598	3,581	23,017	19,132	10,407	12,623	714	4,744
		2011	63,712	29,771	4,405	25,366	21,894	12,194	13,244	855	5,648
56.10/1	Licensed restaurants	2009	23,219	11,967	1,488	10,479	9,104	4,496	6,002	385	2,473
		2010	23,245	11,668	1,616	10,052	8,794	4,744	5,314	340	2,156
		2011	24,894	13,851	2,105	11,746	10,264	5,811	5,975	405	2,518
56.10/2	Unlicensed restaurants and cafes	2009	10,882	8,335	1,047	7,289	5,714	3,104	4,170	199	1,354
		2010	11,208	7,972	1,080	6,893	5,365	2,880	4,015	170	1,313
		2011	11,711	9,604	1,436	8,168	6,625	3,669	4,517	200	1,695
56.10/3	Take away food shops and mobile food stands	2009	27,091	5,461	570	4,890	4,394	2,310	2,593	172	1,212
		2010	26,934	6,958	886	6,072	4,973	2,783	3,294	204	1,275
		2011	27,107	6,315	863	5,452	5,004	2,713	2,752	250	1,436
56.2	Event catering and other food service activities	2009	7,049	7,830	1,019	6,811	6,156	2,786	4,029	69	2,888
		2010	7,031	8,957	987	7,971	7,060	4,003	3,970	86	2,337
		2011	7,967	10,052	1,163	8,889	7,836	4,629	4,264	88	2,228
56.21	Event catering activities	2009	6,070	7,128	989	6,139	5,579	2,505	3,636	54	2,670
		2010	5,767	8,231	943	7,289	6,475	3,710	3,581	76	2,124
		2011	6,267	9,284	1,111	8,173	7,307	4,329	3,842	81	2,083
56.29	Other food service activities	2009	979	703	31	672	577	281	393	16	218
		2010	1,264	726	44	682	585	293	389	10	212
		2011	1,700	768	52	716	529	300	422	7	145
56.3	Beverage serving activities	2009	45,714	22,509	3,017	19,491	13,123	7,448	11,979	737	2,205
		2010	44,351	23,026	3,317	19,709	13,789	7,938	11,688	651	2,442
		2011	43,498	22,640	3,415	19,225	13,309	8,289	10,889	646	2,167
56.30/1	Licensed Clubs	2009	9,487	3,440	458	2,981	1,707	886	2,093	135	239
		2010	9,250	3,089	445	2,644	1,739	862	1,779	88	204
		2011	8,955	2,485	354	2,131	1,307	791	1,338	82	131
56.30/2	Public houses and bars	2009	36,227	19,069	2,559	16,510	11,416	6,562	9,886	602	1,966
		2010	35,101	19,937	2,872	17,065	12,050	7,076	9,909	563	2,238
		2011	34,543	20,155	3,061	17,094	12,003	7,498	9,551	565	2,036

The following symbols and abbreviations are used throughout the ABS releases;

*   Information suppressed to avoid disclosure

..   not available

-   nil or less than half the level of rounding

Source: Annual Business Survey (ABS)

The sum of constituent items in tables may not always agree exactly with the totals shown due to rounding.

Notes:

    1. *Total employment - point in time* and *Total employment - average during the year* which are from the Business Register and Employment Survey (BRES). Changes in the treatment of working owners in the 2010 and 2011 BRES have led to a discontinuity between the 2010 and 2011 BRES employment estimates and earlier years. Care should be taken when making comparisons between employment in 2010 and 2011 and that in any earlier years. More detail about the discontinuity can be found on the BRES webpages.

13.4 Accommodation and food service activities

Standard Industrial Classification (Revised 2007) Section Division Group Class Subclass	Description	Year	Purchases of goods bought for resale	Payments for hiring, leasing or renting plant, machinery and vehicles	Commercial insurance premiums paid	Purchases of road transport services	Purchases of telecommunication services	Purchases of computer and related services	Purchases of advertising and marketing services	Payments to sub-contractors	Other services purchased
			£ million	£ million	£ million	£ million	£ million	£ million	£ million	£ million	£ million
I	Accommodation and food service activities	2009	11,745	333	451	202	224	231	872	461	7,840
		2010	12,197	441	479	225	268	227	931	516	7,750
		2011	12,025	355	497	214	219	218	970	804	7,573
55	Accommodation	2009	1,340	85	171	33	78	110	378	164	2,922
		2010	1,590	60	188	45	86	116	453	202	2,988
		2011	1,621	69	188	49	74	106	460	260	3,281
55.1	Hotels and similar accommodation	2009	857	55	128	17	60	90	243	85	2,470
		2010	914	48	139	16	60	91	276	102	2,458
		2011	924	56	133	26	54	80	313	172	2,780
55.2	Holiday and other short stay accommodation	2009	102	3	16	5	8	6	42	28	184
		2010	271	4	14	13	8	7	71	26	222
		2011	188	7	21	10	8	7	62	49	234
55.20/1	Holiday centre and villages	2009	93	1	5	1	1	3	19	20	104
		2010	137	1	7	3	2	2	25	18	98
		2011	175	2	9	3	2	2	25	27	101
55.20/2	Youth Hostels	2009	3	1	1	1	1	-	2	2	24
		2010	2	2	1	2	1	1	4	1	26
		2011	1	1	1	1	1	1	2	1	14
55.20/9	Other holiday and other collective accommodation (not including holiday centres and villages or youth hostels) n.e.c	2009	6	1	10	3	6	3	21	7	56
		2010	132	2	7	8	5	5	42	6	98
		2011	11	4	10	6	5	4	35	22	119
55.3	Camping grounds, recreational vehicle parks and trailer parks	2009	364	27	25	10	10	11	92	46	251
		2010	377	7	32	15	16	14	103	38	282
		2011	503	6	33	12	11	13	83	36	220
55.9	Other accommodation	2009	17	-	1	-	1	2	2	5	18
		2010	28	-	3	1	2	4	3	36	26
		2011	6	-	2	2	1	6	2	2	47
56	Food and beverage service activities	2009	10,405	248	281	169	145	121	493	297	4,918
		2010	10,607	381	291	180	182	111	478	314	4,762
		2011	10,403	285	309	165	145	112	510	544	4,292
56.1	Restaurants and mobile food service activities	2009	3,458	125	136	100	62	53	318	92	2,627
		2010	3,874	74	132	100	104	53	332	115	2,380
		2011	3,484	68	142	93	71	64	362	110	2,347
56.10/1	Licensed restaurants	2009	1,391	94	69	40	33	31	118	32	1,335
		2010	1,257	37	62	34	62	29	106	49	1,183
		2011	1,506	36	68	26	36	34	123	41	1,181
56.10/2	Unlicensed restaurants and cafes	2009	1,559	14	35	47	14	12	152	47	737
		2010	1,520	18	34	52	17	14	165	52	661
		2011	1,533	15	38	54	15	18	179	53	717
56.10/3	Take away food shops and mobile food stands	2009	508	17	32	13	15	10	48	12	554
		2010	1,098	19	36	14	26	10	61	14	536
		2011	445	16	36	12	20	11	60	16	449
56.2	Event catering and other food service activities	2009	660	38	18	16	15	17	21	24	265
		2010	913	143	27	22	18	17	39	45	322
		2011	1,057	156	26	28	20	16	43	137	466
56.21	Event catering activities	2009	563	30	14	8	13	15	15	23	231
		2010	816	132	23	11	15	16	31	43	293
		2011	864	147	23	21	18	15	37	135	420
56.29	Other food service activities	2009	97	7	4	8	2	1	6	1	34
		2010	97	12	4	11	3	1	8	2	30
		2011	193	9	3	7	2	1	6	2	46
56.3	Beverage serving activities	2009	6,287	86	127	54	69	51	154	182	2,027
		2010	5,820	164	132	58	59	41	108	154	2,060
		2011	5,862	61	141	44	54	33	105	297	1,479
56.30/1	Licensed Clubs	2009	1,271	17	23	3	15	9	26	57	299
		2010	899	22	26	3	9	6	15	49	458
		2011	822	10	25	2	6	4	11	53	193
56.30/2	Public houses and bars	2009	5,017	68	104	51	54	43	128	125	1,728
		2010	4,921	142	106	55	50	35	93	105	1,602
		2011	5,040	51	116	42	48	29	94	244	1,286

The following symbols and abbreviations are used throughout the ABS releases;

Source: Annual Business Survey (ABS)

*   Information suppressed to avoid disclosure

..   not available

-   nil or less than half the level of rounding

The sum of constituent items in tables may not always agree exactly with the totals shown due to rounding.

Notes:

1. *Total employment - point in time* and *Total employment - average during the year* which are from the Business Register and Employment Survey (BRES). Changes in the treatment of working owners in the 2010 and 2011 BRES have led to a discontinuity between the 2010 and 2011 BRES employment estimates and earlier years. Care should be taken when making comparisons between employment in 2010 and 2011 and that in any earlier years. More detail about the discontinuity can be found on the BRES webpages.

13.4 Accommodation and food service activities

Standard Industrial Classification (Revised 2007) Section Division Group Class Subclass	Description	Year	Total taxes, duties and levies pad	National non-domestic (business rates)	Other amounts paid for taxes, duties and levies	Total employment - point in time (1)	Total number of full-time employees - point in time (1)	Total number of part-time employees - point in time (1)	Total employment - average during the year (1)	Total number of full-time employees - average during the year (1)	Total number of part-time employees - average during the year (1)
			£ million	£ million	£ million	Thousand	Thousand	Thousand	Thousand	Thousand	Thousand
I	Accommodation and food service activities	2009	2,168	2,023	146	1,927	791	1,014	1,821	725	974
		2010	2,173	1,982	191	1,869	805	991	1,855	797	984
		2011	2,352	2,182	170	1,936	821	1,026	1,869	792	987
55	Accommodation	2009	638	618	20	394	221	157	361	205	140
		2010	664	637	27	388	214	162	377	208	157
		2011	777	738	39	429	239	177	407	227	167
55.1	Hotels and similar accommodation	2009	549	534	14	327	182	131	298	173	113
		2010	553	534	18	321	175	135	316	172	135
		2011	650	616	34	358	198	149	342	191	141
55.2	Holiday and other short stay accommodation	2009	33	30	2	30	16	13	29	13	14
		2010	46	40	5	29	15	12	26	14	11
		2011	57	56	1	33	17	15	30	15	14
55.20/1	Holiday centre and villages	2009	19	19	-	15	8	7	15	7	8
		2010	28	26	2	16	8	7	14	7	6
		2011	41	40	1	18	9	9	16	8	8
55.20/2	Youth Hostels	2009	-	-	-	3	2	1	2	1	1
		2010	1	1	-	3	2	1	2	1	1
		2011	1	1	-	3	2	1	3	2	1
55.20/9	Other holiday and other collective accommodation (not including holiday centres and villages or youth hostels) n.e.c	2009	13	11	2	12	6	5	11	5	5
		2010	17	14	3	11	5	4	10	5	4
		2011	15	15	-	12	6	5	11	6	5
55.3	Camping grounds, recreational vehicle parks and trailer parks	2009	55	52	2	34	22	11	31	18	12
		2010	63	60	3	*	*	*	*	*	*
		2011	69	65	4	34	21	12	31	19	11
55.9	Other accommodation	2009	2	2	1	3	2	1	3	2	1
		2010	3	3	1	*	*	*	*	*	*
		2011	2	1	1	4	2	2	4	2	2
56	Food and beverage service activities	2009	1,530	1,404	126	1,533	570	857	1,460	520	835
		2010	1,509	1,344	165	1,481	591	829	1,478	589	827
		2011	1,575	1,444	131	1,507	582	849	1,461	565	821
56.1	Restaurants and mobile food service activities	2009	712	690	22	741	287	392	649	243	344
		2010	746	700	45	705	302	369	684	300	349
		2011	808	765	43	767	311	409	765	316	402
56.10/1	Licensed restaurants	2009	336	329	7	371	149	190	324	126	167
		2010	351	335	16	343	155	174	333	154	165
		2011	428	411	17	373	161	195	373	163	192
56.10/2	Unlicensed restaurants and cafes	2009	229	217	12	206	86	108	179	73	95
		2010	211	194	17	202	89	106	196	89	100
		2011	247	230	18	215	89	116	214	91	114
56.10/3	Take away food shops and mobile food stands	2009	146	144	2	165	52	94	146	44	82
		2010	184	172	12	161	57	88	156	57	84
		2011	133	125	9	179	61	98	178	62	96
56.2	Event catering and other food service activities	2009	36	34	2	210	114	90	235	124	105
		2010	46	37	9	227	98	127	253	104	147
		2011	67	57	10	231	106	123	212	99	111
56.21	Event catering activities	2009	27	26	1	198	108	85	223	119	98
		2010	39	30	9	211	91	119	236	96	138
		2011	59	49	9	213	98	113	195	91	102
56.29	Other food service activities	2009	10	8	1	12	6	6	12	5	6
		2010	7	6	-	16	8	8	17	8	9
		2011	8	8	-	18	8	10	17	7	9
56.3	Beverage serving activities	2009	782	681	101	581	169	375	576	153	386
		2010	718	607	110	549	191	334	540	185	331
		2011	699	621	78	509	165	318	484	150	307
56.30/1	Licensed Clubs	2009	86	80	6	120	28	83	120	25	85
		2010	79	68	11	111	30	74	109	29	73
		2011	67	64	3	97	24	65	93	22	63
56.30/2	Public houses and bars	2009	696	601	95	461	141	293	456	127	301
		2010	638	539	99	439	162	260	431	157	258
		2011	633	558	75	412	140	253	391	128	244

The following symbols and abbreviations are used throughout the ABS releases;

* Information suppressed to avoid disclosure

.. not available

- nil or less than half the level of rounding

Source: Annual Business Survey (ABS)

The sum of constituent items in tables may not always agree exactly with the totals shown due to rounding.

Notes:

1. *Total employment - point in time* and *Total employment - average during the year* which are from the Business Register and Employment Survey (BRES). Changes in the treatment of working owners in the 2010 and 2011 BRES have led to a discontinuity between the 2010 and 2011 BRES employment estimates and earlier years. Care should be taken when making comparisons between employment in 2010 and 2011 and that in any earlier years. More detail about the discontinuity can be found on the BRES webpages.

13.4 Accommodation and food service activities

Standard Industrial Classification (Revised 2007) Section Division Group Class Subclass	Description	Year	Total employment costs	Gross wages and salaries including redundancy and severance payments	Social Security costs	Total net capital expenditure - inc NYIP	Total acquisitions - inc NYIP	Total disposals - inc NYIP	Total stocks and work in progress - value at end of year	Total stocks and work in progress - value at beginning of year	Total stocks and work in progress - increase during year
			£ million	£ million	£ million	£ million	£ million	£ million	£ million	£ million	£ million
I	Accommodation and food service activities	2009	19,012	17,628	1,383	3,443	3,803	360	1,318	1,303	15
		2010	19,074	17,663	1,411	2,807	3,804	997	1,481	1,403	79
		2011	19,962	18,473	1,488	3,688	4,713	1,025	1,487	1,362	126
55	Accommodation	2009	4,724	4,314	409	1,628	1,728	100	359	391	-32
		2010	5,075	4,648	427	1,301	1,489	188	488	445	43
		2011	5,369	4,935	435	1,415	1,640	225	496	440	57
55.1	Hotels and similar accommodation	2009	3,942	3,605	337	1,390	1,433	43	181	197	-15
		2010	4,173	3,829	343	936	1,072	136	250	231	20
		2011	4,462	4,107	356	945	1,135	190	190	172	18
55.2	Holiday and other short stay accommodation	2009	289	263	25	50	67	17	24	29	-5
		2010	339	312	27	186	214	28	75	66	9
		2011	385	351	34	181	199	17	69	58	12
55.20/1	Holiday centre and villages	2009	152	139	13	43	47	4	20	23	-3
		2010	177	163	14	109	119	10	42	37	5
		2011	239	218	21	*	*	*	45	44	-
55.20/2	Youth Hostels	2009	41	37	4	-	3	3	1	-	-
		2010	44	40	4	5	6	1	1	1	-
		2011	37	33	4	*	*	*	-	1	-
55.20/9	Other holiday and other collective accommodation (not including holiday centres and villages or youth hostels) n.e.c	2009	96	87	9	6	17	10	4	5	-2
		2010	118	109	9	72	88	16	32	28	4
		2011	110	100	10	90	98	8	24	13	11
55.3	Camping grounds, recreational vehicle parks and trailer parks	2009	448	404	44	138	*	*	153	164	-11
		2010	495	443	51	160	181	21	159	145	14
		2011	473	433	40	227	244	16	236	210	26
55.9	Other accommodation	2009	46	42	4	50	*	*	1	1	-
		2010	69	63	6	19	22	4	3	3	-
		2011	49	44	5	62	63	1	1	1	-
56	Food and beverage service activities	2009	14,288	13,314	974	1,815	2,075	260	959	912	47
		2010	13,998	13,015	984	1,507	2,316	809	993	958	35
		2011	14,593	13,539	1,054	2,273	3,074	801	991	922	69
56.1	Restaurants and mobile food service activities	2009	6,460	6,029	431	1,104	1,250	146	437	408	29
		2010	6,306	5,879	427	998	1,185	187	429	402	27
		2011	6,875	6,405	470	1,582	1,704	123	420	373	47
56.10/1	Licensed restaurants	2009	3,430	3,206	224	657	757	100	260	240	20
		2010	3,175	2,962	214	464	509	46	173	160	13
		2011	3,617	3,358	260	1,110	1,178	68	264	227	37
56.10/2	Unlicensed restaurants and cafes	2009	1,813	1,681	132	326	342	16	89	94	-4
		2010	1,655	1,534	121	270	387	117	83	75	7
		2011	1,951	1,816	135	365	401	35	97	90	7
56.10/3	Take away food shops and mobile food stands	2009	1,216	1,142	75	121	151	30	88	75	13
		2010	1,476	1,384	92	264	288	24	173	166	7
		2011	1,307	1,231	76	106	126	20	59	55	4
56.2	Event catering and other food service activities	2009	2,952	2,711	241	44	49	5	103	98	5
		2010	3,149	2,916	233	135	176	41	126	122	4
		2011	3,231	2,972	259	175	189	14	153	147	6
56.21	Event catering activities	2009	2,782	2,554	228	33	37	4	87	84	3
		2010	2,957	2,741	216	117	155	38	111	107	4
		2011	3,019	2,784	235	116	129	13	132	132	-
56.29	Other food service activities	2009	170	158	13	11	12	1	16	14	2
		2010	192	175	17	18	21	2	15	15	-
		2011	211	187	24	59	60	1	21	15	6
56.3	Beverage serving activities	2009	4,876	4,574	302	667	776	109	419	406	13
		2010	4,543	4,219	324	374	955	581	438	434	5
		2011	4,487	4,163	324	516	1,180	665	418	402	16
56.30/1	Licensed Clubs	2009	885	832	53	147	156	9	110	110	-
		2010	733	684	49	72	203	130	102	98	3
		2011	624	582	43	124	205	80	83	84	-1
56.30/2	Public houses and bars	2009	3,991	3,742	249	520	620	100	310	296	14
		2010	3,810	3,536	274	301	752	451	337	335	1
		2011	3,863	3,581	281	391	976	584	335	318	17

Source: Annual Business Survey (ABS)

The following symbols and abbreviations are used throughout the ABS releases;
* Information suppressed to avoid disclosure
.. not available
- nil or less than half the level of rounding

The sum of constituent items in tables may not always agree exactly with the totals shown due to rounding.

Notes:
1. *Total employment - point in time* and *Total employment - average during the year* which are from the Business Register and Employment Survey (BRES). Changes in the treatment of working owners in the 2010 and 2011 BRES have led to a discontinuity between the 2010 and 2011 BRES employment estimates and earlier years. Care should be taken when making comparisons between employment in 2010 and 2011 and that in any earlier years. More detail about the discontinuity can be found on the BRES webpages.

Defence

Chapter 14

Defence

This section includes figures on Defence expenditure, on the size and role of the Armed Forces and on related support activities. Much of the material used in this section can be found in UK Defence Statistics 2012

Table 14.1 United Kingdom Defence Expenditure by Commodity Block

From 2011/12 the MOD reports expenditure against Commodity Blocks and these headings, although similar in some instances, are not directly comparable to the previously used Resource DEL and Capital DEL categories. This table shows a breakdown of Resource and Capital DEL, and AME by Commodity Block. Under Clear Line of Sight (CLoS), the main MOD expenditure categories are now presented as Commodity Blocks. This provides a more meaningful description of the Department's planned and actual spend, which enables a clearer understanding of the MOD's plans and expenditure over the Spending Review period.

Please refer to the Resource Accounting & Budgeting section of UKDS 2012 to view important information relating to the introduction of the International Financial Reporting Standard (IFRS), the implementation of the Clear Line of Sight (CLoS) Alignment project and recent accounting changes for 2011/12, which have led to presentational changes to the reporting of MOD accounts.

Prior to 2011/12, when Commodity Block reporting was first introduced, information contained in this table was reported in Table 1.3a of UK Defence Statistics 2012.

The data are derived directly from the MOD Departmental Resource Accounts .

Table 14.2 Intake to UK Regular Forces by Service and sex
Women accounted for 8.7 per cent of the intake to UK Regular Forces in 2011/12, which represents a gradual decline since 2006/07. This decrease is not uniform across the Officers and Other Ranks with all Services having an increase in the percentage of Officer intake from 15.8 per cent in 2010/11 to 16.8 per cent in 2011/12, notably in the RAF where 36.3 per cent of the 2011/12 intake were female.

The percentage of female intake in the Other Ranks has increased slightly from 7.9 per cent in 2010/11 to 8.1 per cent in 2011/12. When compared to 2010/11, the Naval Service and Army has seen an increase whereas the RAF have decreased.

Table 14.3 provides information on the formation of the United Kingdom's Armed Forces

Table 14.3a shows the number of submarines and ships in the Royal Navy and Royal Fleet Auxiliary, Royal Marine Commando units, squadrons of helicopters and fixed-wing aircraft in the Fleet Air Arm, and Reserve Units at 1 April 2012. The figures show overall unit numbers only; they do not reflect the level of readiness at which the unit is held which changes throughout the year.

Table 14.3b shows the numbers of Regiments and Infantry battalions in the Regular and Territorial Army; and Corps, Divisional and Brigade headquarters. Key points - The number of combat arms regiments in the Army was unchanged between April 2010 and April 2012, when there were 46 Regular Army and 18 Territorial Army combat arms regiments. The number of combat support regiments has increased slightly with an increase in the number of Regular Army Engineers regiments offsetting a fall in the number of Regular Army Signals Regiments. At 1 April 2012 there were 39 Regular Army and 17 Territorial combat support regiments.

Table 14.3c shows the number of squadrons in the Royal Air Force (RAF) and the Royal Auxiliary Air Force (RAuxAF), and units in the RAF Regiment. Key point - here has been a slight fall in the number of RAF squadrons.

Table 14.3d shows the number of regiments and squadrons in the Special Forces, Joint Helicopter Command and Joint Force Harrier. Key points - The number of Joint Forces Squadrons reduced by two between April 2010 and April 2012 due to the disbanding of the Joint Harrier Force Squadrons.

Table 14.4 Outflow from UK Regular Forces by Service and sex
Females as a percentage of total outflow decreased to 8.3 per cent during 2011/12 from 8.8 per cent in 2010/11 and has fallen from 9.7 per cent in 2000/01. Total outflow of females has been fairly stable since 2006/07 in both the Officers and Other Ranks. Females as a proportion of outflow has increased during 2011/12 in the Naval Service and decreased in the Army and the RAF. Naval Service female outflow rose by 0.2 percentage points to 10.1 per cent; Army fell by 0.6 percentage points to 6.3 per cent and RAF fell by 1.4 percentage points to 13.1 per cent.

Table 14.5 United Kingdom Armed Forces Full-time trained strength and requirement, at 1 April each year
The full-time trained strength of the UK Armed Forces was 170,010 at 1 April 2012, down 6,840 (3.9 per cent) since 1 April 2011 and down 20,260 (10.6 per cent) since 1 April 2000.

The requirement for the UK's full-time trained Armed Forces decreased from 198,160 in 2000 to 185,920 in 2006 and 174,840 in 2012. The rate of decrease has been greatest in the RAF, followed by the Naval Service and least in the Army. Contrasting with the other Services, and the Army other ranks, the requirement for Army officers increased between 2011 and 2012, and at 13,480 was higher than it was in 2000.

The deficit between strength and requirement of full-time trained Armed Forces has decreased from 7,880 at 1 April 2000 to 4,830 at 1 April 2012. The deficit at 1 April 2012 is mainly due to a deficit of 4,720 Other Ranks. Officers were also in deficit in 2012, having reduced in strength by 1,150 since 1 April 2011 against a slightly increased requirement. This is the first time that Officers have been in overall deficit since 2005. The largest deficit as a percentage of requirement is in the Naval Service, where the strength has fallen faster than the requirement in the last year.

Table 14.6a Civilian personnel, at 1 April each year
The full-time trained strength of the UK Armed Forces was 170,010 at 1 April 2012, down 6,840 (3.9 per cent) since 1 April 2011 and down 20,260 (10.6 per cent) since 1 April 2000.

The requirement for the UK's full-time trained Armed Forces decreased from 198,160 in 2000 to 185,920 in 2006 and 174,840 in 2012. The rate of decrease has been greatest in the RAF, followed by the Naval Service and least in the Army. Contrasting with the other Services, and the Army other ranks, the requirement for Army officers increased between 2011 and 2012, and at 13,480 was higher than it was in 2000.

The deficit between strength and requirement of full-time trained Armed Forces has decreased from 7,880 at 1 April 2000 to 4,830 at 1 April 2012. The deficit at 1 April 2012 is mainly due to a deficit of 4,720 Other Ranks. Officers were also in deficit in 2012, having reduced in strength by 1,150 since 1 April 2011 against a slightly increased requirement. This is the first time that Officers have been in overall deficit since 2005. The largest deficit as a percentage of requirement is in the Naval Service, where the strength has fallen faster than the requirement in the last year.

Table 14.6b Civilian personnel by budgetary area and grade equivalent, at 1 April each year
A budgetary area is defined as higher level groupings of the Top Level Budgetary areas combined together to allow consistent presentation of data across multiple time periods. Although constituent TLBs in areas such as centralised support and logistic support services have changed in structure across the period, the budgetary area groupings remain the same across the period. The budgetary areas for Navy Command, Land Forces and Air Command each represent individual Service areas. While Defence Equipment & Support covers the departments logistic support systems, with remaining TLB areas falling to Centre covering centralised support services.

As directed by policy deriving from the Strategic Defence and Security Review (SDSR), personnel reductions under the SDSR are set to continue until 2020 from the baseline start point of April 2010. Between 2010 (the start of the current SDSR rundown exercise) and 2012, the total FTE strength of MOD civilian personnel fell by 17.3 per cent. Decreases have been seen within each individual Service Command over this period, with the largest proportionate decrease of 24.5 per cent seen in Air Command and the smallest proportionate decrease of 12.8 per cent in Defence Equipment & Support.

Between 2000 and the start of the current SDSR rundown exercise in 2010, the total FTE strength of MOD civilian personnel fell by 29.2 per cent and between 2000 and 2012 the total FTE strength of MOD civilian personnel fell by 41.5 per cent. Decreases have been seen within each individual Service Command between 2000 and 2012, with the largest proportionate decrease of 43.5 per cent seen in Air Command, while Navy Command and Land Forces showed decreases of similar proportions, by 40.4 per cent and 38.0 per cent respectively. Defence Equipment & Support, decreased significantly by 60.0 per cent across the whole period.

Table 14.7a Land holdings by country and whether owned, leased or with legal rights, at 1 April each year
Table 14.7a shows the area of MOD holdings by country. These holdings include land declared as surplus to defence requirements. A thousand hectares is 3.86 square miles.

Table 14.7b Service Family Accommodation in the United Kingdom, at 31 March each year
The Defence Infrastructure Organisation's Directorate of Operations Accommodation is responsible for Service Family Accommodation (SFA) in the UK, having assumed responsibility for Northern Ireland from 1 April 2008. At 31st March 2012 it managed some 49,000 properties. The planned reduction in UK Permanent Holdings has seen around 300 properties disposed of in the last year which has been partially offset by the procurement of 200 additional properties.

Vacant Properties
There are about 6,500 vacant properties in the UK. A number of these are awaiting incoming deployments particularly from units relocating from Germany, modernisation or disposal, whilst the remainder are available to let or are already under offer to Service families.

The apparent increase in the percentage of properties which are vacant between 2011 and 2012 is explained by uncertainty over the Future Footprint Strategy which has resulted in SFA, previously earmarked for disposal, being retained in certain areas including Scotland and Northern Ireland.

Number of Occupants
DIO Ops Accommodation provides SFA for entitled Service personnel in accordance with Tri-Service Accommodation Regulations, as well as for other entitled/eligible personnel, and for core welfare purposes. SFA can also be utilised for other defence purposes such as Single Living Accommodation.

DIO Ops Accommodation also reports on the number of Substitute Service Family Accommodation (SSFA) properties occupied by entitled Service personnel, i.e. those who would otherwise occupy SFA were it available when and where required. SSFA is private property, is not part of DIO Ops Housing stock, and is provided under contract.

At 1 April 2012 there were around 42,600 entitled and eligible occupants in England, Wales and Scotland in SFA, to which must be added 1,780 in SSFA.

Table 14.8a Location of Service and civilian personnel in the United Kingdom, at 1 April each year
The strength of UK-based civilian personnel has reduced from 67,610 in 2011 to 57,220 in 2012, a decrease of 15.4 per cent. The total strength of MOD service personnel based in Northern Ireland has continued to reduce, falling by 6.8 per cent since last year. Since 2000, the number of Service personnel stationed in Northern Ireland has been reduced by 55.4 per cent, from 8,390 to 3,740, whilst the civilian strength has fallen by 50.6 per cent during the same period from 3,250 to 1,610. The South East Region has the largest population of UK Service personnel, with 43,330, although the South West has the largest population of civilians, with 21,690.

Table 14.8b Global locations of Service and civilian personnel, at 1 April each year
At 1 April 2012, 87.3 per cent of UK Service and 80.6 per cent of MOD civilian personnel were stationed in the UK. The number of UK military personnel stationed overseas has decreased from 37,200 in 2000 to 22,440 in 2012, a decrease of 39.7 per cent. At the same time the number of UK civilian personnel stationed overseas has decreased from 16,800 in 2000 to 11,270 in 2012, a decrease of 32.9 per cent. The percentage of UK military personnel stationed overseas has fallen from 17.4 per cent in 2000 to 12.5 per cent in 2012. Over the same period, the percentage of UK civilian personnel stationed overseas has risen from 13.9 per cent in 2000 to 15.9 per cent in 2012.

Despite the numbers stationed there falling for at least the sixth year in succession, the Germany/Belgium/Netherlands region has the second largest population of MOD personnel after the UK, with 17,480 Service and 5,950 civilians. This amounts to 77.9 per cent of UK military personnel stationed overseas and 52.8 per cent of UK civilian personnel stationed overseas.

Table 14.9a UK regular Armed Forces deaths by Service, Year of occurrence 2004-2012, numbers, age and gender standardised rates
In 2012, there were 129 deaths in the regular Armed Forces. Of these, 19 deaths were in the Naval Service, 95 in the Army and 15 in the RAF. In 2012 the mortality rate for the UK Armed Forces was 71 per 100,000. This was an increase on the 10 year low rate of seen in 2011.

Table 14.10a UK & Overseas Callouts, Incidents and Persons Moved, 2004 to 2012
Table 14.10a shows the number of incidents, callouts and persons moved each year between 2004 and 2013. Between 2004 and 2009 the number of callouts increased year-on-year. Callout numbers peaked in 2009, and since then the number of callouts fell year-on-year.

14.10b Search and Rescue Helicopters - UK & Overseas Callouts and Persons Moved by Unit
This data focuses on SAR helicopter callouts, excluding Mountain Rescue Teams.
Table 14.10b presents the number of callouts by unit and number of Persons moved by Unit between 2004 and 2012. The unit with the highest number of callouts during 2012 was RAF Valley, with 300, closely followed by HMS Gannet with 298. This is the second year in a row that RAF Valley has had the highest number of callouts in a year, although it has been among the top three units with the highest number of callouts for the past five years. HMS Gannet moved the highest number of persons during 2012 with 285, followed by RAF Valley with 284. For the past four years HMS Gannet and RAF Valley have been the two units with the highest number of persons moved.
RAF Wattisham moved the lowest number of persons of the UK units during 2012, with 80.

14.10c Search and Rescue Helicopters: UK & Overseas Callouts by Assistance Type, 2004 to 2012
14.10c presents callout numbers by assistance type between 2004 and 2012. The assistance type with the largest number of callouts during 2012 was Medrescue, representing 45% of all helicopter callouts. Most of the other callout types have very low numbers. The second half of the table shows the number of persons moved by assistance type between 2004 and 2012. In 2012, 56% of persons moved were for Medrescue, a similar proportion to recent years.

14.10d Strength of United Kingdom Medical Staff
The figures shown in 14.10d are for regular personnel only and therefore do not represent the strength of either Reserve or veterinarian personnel.

14.11 Number of vessels boarded by the Royal Navy Fishery Protection Squadron within British fishing limits and convictions arising from these boardings each financial year

This table shows the activities of the Royal Navy Fishery Protection Squadron operating within British fishery limits under contract to the Marine Maritime Organisation (MMO). Boardings carried out by vessels of the Scottish Executive Environment Directorate and the Department of Agriculture and Rural Development for Northern Ireland are not included. The data in this Table are outside the scope of National Statistics since they have not been put forward for assessment by the UK Statistics Authority.

Convictions arising from Royal Navy boardings are convictions of infringements detected by the Royal Navy Fishery Protection vessels in that year operating under contract to DEFRA. Figures may change retrospectively as some cases may not be heard in court until a year or more after the initial Royal Navy boarding.

in financial year 08/09, the Marine and Fisheries Agency introduced the Fisheries Administration Penalty (FAP). This has streamlined the penalty process, and has removed the necessity for most of the crews of vessels that would previously have been sent to Court from actually having to attend Court, where they would probably have been convicted. Convictions from 2008/09 onwards are based on the number of offences addressed by the Courts that resulted in a Court conviction, not the number of fishing vessel crews that attended Court. That is, the same fishing vessel crew could be required to attend Court for one or more offences to be heard and each offence would count separately.

In 2011/12 1,408 vessels were boarded by the Royal Navy Fisheries Protection Squadron, the highest figure in the last six years. This had resulted in 17 court convictions by the time the information was available.

14.1 United Kingdom Defence Expenditure by Commodity Block

Inclusive of non-recoverable VAT at Current Prices (£ million)

	Outturn 2011/12
Defence Spending	**37 169**
Departmental Expenditure Limits (DEL)	**46 994**
Cash Resource DEL	**37 980**
Personnel Costs	12 846
of which: Service Personnel Costs[1]	10 101
Civilian Personnel Costs[2]	2 745
Infrastructure Costs[3]	4 580
Inventory Consumption[4]	2 535
Equipment Support Costs[5]	6 256
Other Costs & Services[6]	1 850
Receipts & Other Income[7]	-1 327
Depreciation & Impairment[8]	9 825
Cash Release of Provisions[9]	348
Research & Development Costs[10]	833
Conflict Pool	46
Arm's Length Bodies[11]	187
Capital DEL[12]	**9 014**
Single Use Military Equipment[13]	5 284
Other (Fiscal)[14]	3 883
Asset/Estate Disposal Costs	- 150
New Loans and Loan Repayments	- 5
Arm's Length Bodies	2
Annually Managed Expenditure (AME)[15]	**967** [r]
Depreciation & Impairment	510
Provisions	- 460
Cash Release of Provisions	- 345
Movement on Fair Value of Financial Instruments	347
War Pensions Benefits	916

Source: Defence Economics (Defence Expenditure Analysis) and Defence Resources

1. Military and other ranks pay and other allowances; SCAPE; Employer's National Insurance Contributions (ERNIC).

2. Civilian pay and other allowances; pension contributions; Employer's National Insurance Contributions (ERNIC).

3. Property management; service charges; IT & communications costs; utilities costs.

4. Munitions; stores; fuel (marine & aviation); clothing; other materials consumed e.g. stationary, sundries, general stores, etc.

5. Equipment support costs, including leases & hire charges for plant, machinery and transport.

6. Travel & subsistence; professional services & fees; training.

7. Receipts from various sources; costs recoveries; dividends; interest.

8. Depreciation & impairments on Non-Current Assets (Property, SUME, dual purpose).

9. Nuclear and non nuclear provisions e.g. staff redundancies, legal costs, environmental, etc.

10. Research and Development expenditure is incurred mainly for the future benefit of the Department. Such expenditure is primarily incurred on the development of new Single Use Military Equipment (SUME), and on the improvement of the effectiveness and capability of existing SUME.

11. Army Benevolent Fund; Council of Reserve Forces and Cadet Associations; Royal Hospital Chelsea; National Army Museum; RAF Museum; National Museum of the Royal Navy; Commonwealth War Graves Commission.

12. Expenditure on the acquisition of Non-Current Assets.

13. Single Use Military Equipment (SUME) are assets which only have a military use, such as tanks and fighter aircraft. Dual use items (those that also have a civilian use) are recorded under the Other category.

14. Expenditure on Property, Plant and dual use military equipment that could be used by civilian organisations for the production of goods and services.

15. The 2011/12 AME figures have been revised following the removal from the total of Capital AME, which is a balance sheet movement which is not voted or included in the outturn.

14.2 Intake[1] to UK Regular Forces by Service and sex

	2000/01	2006/07	2007/08	2008/09	2009/10	2010/11	2011/12
All Services	**23 020**	**20 100**	**21 350**	**23 190**	**21 500**	**12 730**	**14 800**
Percentage female	*11.3%*	*10.0%*	*9.9%*	*9.2%*	*8.9%*	*8.8%*	*8.7%*
Officers	**1 760**	**1 660**	**1 720**	**1 690**	**1 580**	**1 360**	**1 070**
of which female	350	330	300	300	250	210	180
Percentage female	*19.9%*	*19.9%*	*17.4%*	*18.0%*	*15.8%*	*15.8%*	*16.8%*
Other Ranks	**21 260**	**18 440**	**19 630**	**21 500**	**19 920**	**11 370**	**13 730**
of which female	2 260	1 680	1 820	1 830	1 660	900	1 110
Percentage female	*10.6%*	*9.1%*	*9.3%*	*8.5%*	*8.4%*	*7.9%*	*8.1%*
Naval Service	**4 620**	**3 890**	**4 040**	**4 240**	**4 130**	**2 550**	**2 220**
Percentage female	*13.7%*	*12.2%*	*12.1%*	*10.5%*	*9.4%*	*6.7%*	*8.3%*
Officers	**450**	**330**	**380**	**310**	**390**	**300**	**280**
of which female	80	50	60	50	50	30	40
Percentage female	*18.5%*	*14.9%*	*16.0%*	*16.9%*	*13.0%*	*9.4%*	*13.5%*
Other Ranks	**4 180**	**3 560**	**3 660**	**3 930**	**3 740**	**2 250**	**1 940**
of which female	550	420	430	390	340	140	150
Percentage female	*13.2%*	*11.9%*	*11.7%*	*9.9%*	*9.0%*	*6.3%*	*7.5%*
Army [2]	**14 770**	**14 300**	**14 290**	**14 660**	**13 910**	**8 760**	**11 190**
Percentage female	*9.0%*	*8.0%*	*7.8%*	*6.9%*	*6.8%*	*8.1%*	*8.3%*
Officers	**870**	**900**	**940**	**840**	**790**	**780**	**710**
of which female	170	170	150	130	120	120	110
Percentage female	*19.2%*	*19.3%*	*15.8%*	*15.3%*	*15.0%*	*14.8%*	*16.0%*
Other Ranks	**13 900**	**13 400**	**13 350**	**13 820**	**13 120**	**7 980**	**10 480**
of which female	1 160	970	960	890	830	590	810
Percentage female	*8.3%*	*7.2%*	*7.2%*	*6.4%*	*6.3%*	*7.4%*	*7.7%*
Royal Air Force	**3 630**	**1 900**	**3 020**	**4 300**	**3 460**	**1 410**	**1 390**
Percentage female	*18.0%*	*20.9%*	*17.1%*	*15.8%*	*16.7%*	*16.7%*	*13.1%*
Officers	**440**	**430**	**410**	**540**	**400**	**280**	**80**
of which female	100	110	90	120	80	70	30
Percentage female	*22.8%*	*25.0%*	*22.4%*	*22.9%*	*20.3%*	*25.3%*	*36.3%*
Other Ranks	**3 190**	**1 470**	**2 620**	**3 760**	**3 070**	**1 140**	**1 310**
of which female	560	290	430	560	500	170	150
Percentage female	*17.4%*	*19.8%*	*16.3%*	*14.8%*	*16.3%*	*14.6%*	*11.7%*

Source: DASA(Quad-Service)

1.

Figures show intake to UK Regular Forces, both trained and untrained, which comprises new entrants, re-entrants, direct trained entrants (including professionally qualified officers) and intake from the reserves. They exclude all movements within the Regular Forces; including flows from untrained to trained strength, transfers between Services and flows from ranks to officer due to promotion.

2. From 2009/10 Army intake figures include transfers from the Gurkhas to the UK Regular Forces.

Data from the Joint Personnel Administration System for the period 1 May 2009 to 1 October 2011 have been reviewed and finalised, therefore some figures may differ from previous publications.

This table is a National Statistic (Latest figures http://www.dasa.mod.uk).

Table 14.3a Number of Vessels in the Royal Navy and Royal Fleet Auxiliary, and Squadrons in the Fleet Air Arm, at 1 April each year

Royal Navy submarines		2000	2006	2007	2008	2009	2010	2011	2012
Trident / Polaris	Vessels	4	4	4	4	4	4	4	4
Fleet	Vessels	12	10	9 [1]	9	8 [2]	7 [3]	7	7 [4]

Royal Navy ships		2000	2006	2007	2008	2009	2010	2011	2012
Aircraft Carriers	Vessels	3	2	2	2	2	2	- [5, 6]	-
Landing Platform Docks / Helicopter	Vessels	3	3	3	3	3	3	4 [6]	4
Destroyers	Vessels	11	8	8	8	7 [7]	6 [8]	6 [9]	5 [10]
Frigates	Vessels	21	17	17	17	17	17	15 [11]	13 [12]
Mine countermeasures vessels	Vessels	21	16	16	16	16	16	15 [13]	15
Patrol ships and craft	Vessels	23	22	22	22 [14]	22	22	22	22
Survey ships	Vessels	6	5	5	5	5	4 [15]	4	4
Ice patrol ships	Vessels	1	1	1	1	1	1 [16]	1 [16]	2 [17]

Royal Fleet Auxiliary Service		2000	2006	2007	2008	2009	2010	2011	2012
Tankers	Vessels	7	10	10	8 [18]	6 [19]	6	5 [20]	5
Fleet replenishment ships	Vessels	4	2	2	2	4 [19]	4	3 [21]	3
Primary Casualty Receiving Ship[22]	Vessels	1	1	1	1	1	1	1	1
Landing ships	Vessels	5	3	4 [23]	4 [24]	4	4	3 [25]	3
Forward repair ships	Vessels	1	1	1	1	1	1	1	1
Roll-on Roll-off vessels[26]	Vessels	2	6	6	6	6	6	6	6

Royal Marines		2000	2006	2007	2008	2009	2010	2011	2012
RM Commando	Commandos	3	3	3	3	3	3	3	3
Command Support Group	Commandos	1	1	1	1	1	1	1	1
Infantry Battalion	Battalion	-	-	-	1 [27]	1	1	1	1
Logistic unit	Regiments	1	1	1	1	1	1	1	1
Artillery unit	Regiments	1	1	1	1	1	1	1	1
Engineer unit	Squadrons	1	1	1	1	1	1	1	1
Nuclear Guarding and Fleet Security	Squadrons	1	3	3	3	3	4 [28]	4	4
Assault (landing craft)	Squadrons	3	4	4	4	4	4	4	4

Naval Aircraft		2000	2006	2007	2008	2009	2010	2011	2012
Fixed Wing Aircraft	Squadrons	1	1	1	1	1	1	- [29]	-
Helicopters	Squadrons	9	6	7	7	7	7	7	7

Reserve Units		2000	2006	2007	2008	2009	2010	2011	2012
Royal Navy Reserve Units	Units	..	14	14	14	14	14	14	14
Royal Marine Reserve Units	Units	..	5	5	5	5	5	5	5

Source: MOD Finance & Military Capability

1. HMS Sovereign was withdrawn from service during the year.

2. HMS Superb was withdrawn from service during the year.

3. HMS Trafalgar and HMS Sceptre were withdrawn from service during the year. HMS Astute undergoing sea trials.

4. Reducing to 6 HMS TURBULENT decommissions in 2012.

5. HMS Ark Royal withdrawn from service.

6. HMS Illustrious converted into an Landing Platform Helicopter.

7. HMS Southampton was withdrawn from service during the year.

8. HMS Exeter and HMS Nottingham were withdrawn from service during the year. HMS Daring entered full service during 2010.

9. HMS Dauntless entered service and HMS Manchester was withdrawn from service during the year.

10. HMS DIAMOND entered service, HMS GLOUCESTER and HMS LIVERPOOL was decommissioned.

11. HMS Chatham and HMS Campbeltown were withdrawn from service during the year.

12. HMS CUMBERLAND and HMS CORNWALL were decommissioned in year.

13. HMS WALNEY was withdrawn from service during the year.

14. HMS Clyde entered service during the year. HMS Dumbarton Castle was withdrawn from service.

15. HMS Roebuck was withdrawn from service during the year.

16. HMS Endurance non-operational while options for her repair or replacement were considered.

17. HMS Endurance non-operational while options for her repair or replacement were considered. Replaced on an operational basis by HMS

18. RFA Brambleleaf and RFA Oakleaf were withdrawn from service during the year.

19. Two vessels re-categorised as Fleet Replenishment ships to reflect their primary role.

20. RFA Fort George was withdrawn from service during the year.

21. RFA Bayleaf was withdrawn from service during the year.

22. Also known as Aviation training ship, as vessel has both these roles.

23. RFA Largs Bay and RFA Cardigan Bay entered service during the year. RFA Sir Galahad was withdrawn from service.

24. RFA Lyme Bay entered service during the year. RFA Sir Bedivere was withdrawn from service.

25. RFA Largs Bay was sold to Australia in January 2011 as a result of SDSR10.

26. Commercially owned vessels that are leased to the Royal Navy for training and operations as required.

27. 1 Rifles became part of 3 Commando Brigade on 1 April 2008.

28. Fleet Protection Group Royal Marines expanded by one squadron (P Sqn) during Mar-Sep 10.

29. The Harrier was withdrawn as a result of SDSR10. Royal Navy fixed wing aviation will resume when Joint Combat Aircraft is introduced into service

14.3b Number of Regiments, Infantry battalions & Major Headquarters, in the Regular & Territorial Army, at 1 April each year

Combat arms			2000		2006	2007	2008	2009	2010	2011	2012
Armour											
	Regular Army	Regiments	10		10	10	10	10	10	10	10
	Territorial Army	Regiments	4		4	4	4	4	4	4	4
Infantry											
	Regular Army	Battalions	40		36	36	36	36	36	36	36
	Territorial Army	Battalions	15		15	14	14	14	14	14	14
	Home Service Forces	Battalions	7		-	-	-	-	-	-	-

Combat support			2000		2006	2007	2008	2009	2010	2011	2012
Artillery											
	Regular Army[1]	Regiments	15		14	14	14	14	14	14	14
	Territorial Army[2]	Regiments	7		7	7	7	7	7	7	7
Engineers											
	Regular Army	Regiments	11		11	11	11	11	12 [3]	12	14
	Territorial Army	Regiments	6		6	6	6	6	5	5	5
Signals											
	Regular Army	Regiments	11		11	12	12	12	12	12	11
	Territorial Army	Regiments	11		11	11	11	5 [4]	5	5	5

Combat service support			2000		2006	2007	2008	2009	2010	2011	2012
Equipment support											
	Regular Army	Battalions	7		7	7	7	7	7	7	7
	Territorial Army	Battalions	4		4	4	2 [5]	2	2	2	2
Logistics											
	Regular Army	Regiments	22		17	17	17	17	17	17	17
	Territorial Army	Regiments	17		15	17	17	17	17	17	17
Medical Regiments / Field Hospitals											
	Regular Army	Number	8		11	8	8	8	9	9	9
	Territorial Army	Number	15		15	15	15	15	15	15	15

Corps, Division & Brigade HQ			2000		2006	2007	2008	2009	2010	2011	2012
NATO Corps HQ			1		1	1	1	1	1	1	1
Division / District HQ:											
	deployable		2		2	2	2	2	2	2	2
	non-deployable		4		5	5	5	5	5	5	5
Brigade HQ:											
	deployable		7		8	8	7	7	7	7	7
	non-deployable		15		10	9	9	9	10	10	10

Source: Army General Staff

1. Excludes 14th Regiment Royal Artillery.

2. Includes the Honourable Artillery Company.

3. 101 Engr Regt (EOD) has now been 'regularised' under Op ENTIRETY, in order to support ongoing operations in Afghanistan.

4. As a result of Planning Round 2009, six R Signals Regts (V) were removed from the force structure.

5. Restructuring of Royal Electrical and Mechanical Engineers was announced in 2008.

This table is a National Statistic.

14.3c Number of Squadrons in the Royal Air Force and the Royal Auxiliary Air Force, at 1 April each year

Excludes Operational Conversion Units which train qualified aircrew for different aircraft types.

This table is a National Statistic.

Regular Air Force		2000	2006	2007	2008	2009	2010	2011	2012
Multi-roled Fast Jet Squadrons [1,2]	Squadrons	17	13	13	11	11	10 [3]	10 [4]	8 [5]
Maritime patrol	Squadrons	3	3	2	2	2	2	2	- [6]
ISTAR (inc Airborne Early Warning)	Squadrons	2	3 [2]	3	4	4	4	4	5 [7]
Air transport / Air Refuelling	Squadrons	8	8	8	8	8	8	7 [8]	7
Search and Rescue	Squadrons	2	2	2	2	2	2	2	2
RAF FP Wg	HQs	..	6	6	7	7	8	8	8
RAF Ground based air defence [9]	Squadrons	*	3	2	-	-	-	-	-
RAF Regiment Field [9]	Squadrons	*	6	6	7	7	8	8	8
RAF Regt (Jt CBRN) [10]	Squadrons	-	-	1	1	1	1	1	-
Defence CBRN Wing [10]	HQ	-	-	-	-	-	-	-	1
	Squadrons	-	-	-	-	-	-	-	2
Tactical Provost Wg	HQ	-	1	1	1	1	1	1	1
	Squadrons	-	2	1	1	1	1	1	1
Specialist Policing Wg [11]	HQ	-	1	1	1	1	1	1	1
	Squadrons	-	3	3	3	3	3	3	3
General Policing Wg [11]	HQ	-	1	1	1	1	1	1	1
	Squadrons	-	4	4	4	4	4	4	4
Tactical Communications Wg [12]	Squadrons		4	4	4	4	4	4	4

Auxiliary Air Force		2000	2006	2007	2008	2009	2010	2011	2012
Air Movements	Squadrons	1	1	1	1	1	1	1	1
Aeromedical [13]	Squadrons	2	2	2	2	2	2	2	2
HQ Augmentation	Squadrons	1	1	1	1	1	1	1	
Intelligence	Squadrons	2	2	2	2	2	2	2	2
Photographic Interpretation	Squadrons	1	1	1	1	1	1	1	1
Public Relations	Squadrons	1	1	1	1	1	1	1	1
Meteorological	Squadrons	1	1	1	1	1	1	1	1
RAuxAF Regt Field	Squadrons	4	4	3	3	3	3	3	3
FP Operations Support	Squadrons	4	4	4	4	4	4	4	4
Tactical Provost	Squadrons	-	1	1	1	1	1	1	1
RAuxAF Regt Chemical, Biological, Radiological and Nuclear	Squadrons	-	1	1	1	1	1	1	1

Source: MOD Finance & Military Capability

1. Excludes Joint Force Harrier squadrons.

2. From 2006, four Air Defence squadrons amalgamated with Strike/Attack, Offensive support and Reconnaissance squadrons to form multi-roled fast jet squadrons.
   One Reconnaissance squadron was reroled ISTAR. One squadron was disbanded.

3. 43 Sqn was stood down on 1 July 2009

4. 6 Sqn (Typhoon) stood up 6 Sep 2010. 111 Sqn (Tornado F3) stood down 22 Mar 2011.

5. 13 Sqn and 14 Sqn (both Tornado GR4) were disbanded on 1 Jun 2011. (See further footnote below on 14 Sqn)

6. 201 Sqn and 120 Sqn were disbanded on 26 May 2011

7. 14 Sqn was subsequently stood up on 14 October 2011. This unit replaced the flight within 5 Sqn operating the R1 Shadow aircraft

8. 70 Sqn disbanded 10 Sep 2010.

9. Delivery of Ground based air defence has been vested with the Army since 2008. The remaining 2 squadrons were combined on 1 Apr 08 to provide a 7th Field Sqn (15 Sqn RAF Regt).

10. Defence CBRN Wing was established on 14 Dec 2011 on the disbandment of the Joint CBRN Regiment

11. Project DARWIN1 and Project BEAGLE re-brigaded Specialist Policing assets under Specialist Policing Wg in 2006. The project also rebrigaded General Policing assets under General Policing Wing; this was not recognised in previous iterations of this table.

12. TCW has existed as a formed unit since 1969 and are currently subordinate to 90 Signals Unit at RAF Leeming.

13. Includes Air Transportable Surgical.

14.3d Number of Regiments and Squadrons in selected Joint Units, at 1 April each year

Excludes Operational Conversion Units which train qualified aircrew for different aircraft types.

This table is a National Statistic.

Joint Units		2006	2007	2008	2009	2010	2011	2012
Special Forces								
Special Air Service	Regiments	1	1	1	1	1	1	1
Special Air Service - Territorial Army	Regiments	2	2	2	2	2	2	2
Special Boat Service	Squadrons[1]	4	4	4	4	4	4	4
Special Forces Support Group Battalion	Battalions	1 [2]	1	1	1	1	1	1
Joint Nuclear Biological Chemical	Regiments	1	1	1	1	1	1	- [3]
Joint Helicopter Command		2006	2007	2008	2009	2010	2011	2012
Royal Navy Helicopter	Squadrons[1]	4	4	4	4	4	4	4
Army Aviation[4]	Regiments	5	5	5	5	5	5	5
Army Aviation - Territorial Army	Regiments	1	2 [5]	2	1 [6]	1	1	1
Royal Air Force Helicopter	Squadrons[1]	5	5	6 [7]	6	6	6	6
Royal Auxiliary Air Force[8]	Squadrons[1]	1	1	1	1	1	1	1
Joint Special Forces Air Wing	Unit	1	1	1	1	1	1	1
Joint Force Harrier		2006	2007	2008	2009	2010	2011	2012
Royal Navy	Squadrons[1]	1	2	2	2	1 [9]	- [10]	-
Royal Air Force	Squadrons[1]	2	2	2	2	1 [11]	- [12]	-

Source: MOD Finance & Military Capability

1. The term "squadron" has different meanings among the three Services

2. The Special Forces Support Group was formed as a result of the Ministerial Announcement on 16 Dec 2004 as part of The Future Army Structure. It is a Tri-Service Unit based on 1 PARA, to provide specialist support to Special Forces.

3 The JNBC regiment disbanded on the formation of the Defence CBRN Wing on 14 Dec 2011.

4. These figures exclude the School of Army Aviation, 667 (D&T) Sqn and 657 Sqn and three independent Army Air Corps flights (7, 25 and 29 Flts).

5. 6 Regt AAC(V) formed on 1 April 2007.

6. 7 Regt AAC(V) was disbanded 31 March 09.

7. Reflects the standing up of 78 Sqn RAF to accommodate the endorsed increase in Merlin Mk3 crews and aircraft.

8. Helicopter Support Squadron provides a pool of trained personnel to provide combat service support to the Support Helicopter Force in training and on operations in times of crisis and war.

9. On the reduction in the Joint Force Harrier force from 1 April 2010, the Fleet Air Arm Strike Wing was counted as 1 Sqn.

10 800 RNAS was disbanded on 28 January 2011.

11 20 Sqn was disbanded 31 March 2010.

12 1 Sqn was disbanded on 28 January 2011.

14.4 Outflow[1] from UK Regular Forces by Service and sex

	2000/01	2006/07	2007/08	2008/09	2009/10	2010/11	2011/12
All Services [2]	**24 950**	**25 320 ‖**	**24 760**	**21 650**	**18 270**	**18 140**	**21 370**
of which female	2 430	2 180 ‖	2 190	1 900	1 440	1 590	1 770
percentage female	*9.7*	*8.6 ‖*	*8.9*	*8.8*	*7.9*	*8.8*	*8.3*
Officers: total	**2 290**	**2 690 ‖**	**2 740**	**2 380**	**1 880**	**1 930**	**2 560**
of which female	260	300 ‖	340	300	220	240	290
percentage female	*11.1*	*11.0 ‖*	*12.4*	*12.7*	*11.5*	*12.2*	*11.5*
Other ranks: total	**22 650**	**22 630 ‖**	**22 020**	**19 270**	**16 390**	**16 200**	**18 810**
of which female	2 180	1 890 ‖	1 860	1 600	1 220	1 350	1 480
percentage female	*9.6*	*8.3 ‖*	*8.4*	*8.3*	*7.5*	*8.3*	*7.9*
Naval Service	**5 040**	**4 400**	**4 330**	**4 440**	**3 720**	**3 630**	**4 320**
of which female	550	500	460	460	340	360	440
percentage female	*11.0*	*11.3*	*10.7*	*10.3*	*9.1*	*9.9*	*10.1*
Officers: total	**480**	**500**	**570**	**520**	**440**	**460**	**570**
of which female	40	50	40	50	50	50	60
percentage female	*9.1*	*10.0*	*7.7*	*9.6*	*11.2*	*10.1*	*11.1*
Other ranks: total	**4 550**	**3 900**	**3 760**	**3 920**	**3 280**	**3 170**	**3 750**
of which female	510	450	420	410	290	310	380
percentage female	*11.2*	*11.5*	*11.2*	*10.4*	*8.8*	*9.9*	*10.0*
Army [2]	**15 230**	**15 770 ‖**	**15 280**	**13 080**	**11 560**	**11 500**	**13 200**
of which female	1 330	1 110 ‖	1 080	920	690	790	830
percentage female	*8.8*	*7.0 ‖*	*7.1*	*7.1*	*6.0*	*6.9*	*6.3*
Officers: total	**1 150**	**1 330 ‖**	**1 380**	**1 210**	**980**	**990**	**1 240**
of which female	160	140 ‖	180	160	100	120	120
percentage female	*13.4*	*10.8 ‖*	*12.9*	*13.1*	*9.9*	*12.3*	*9.6*
Other ranks: total	**14 080**	**14 440 ‖**	**13 900**	**11 870**	**10 580**	**10 510**	**11 960**
of which female	1 180	960 ‖	900	760	600	670	710
percentage female	*8.4*	*6.7 ‖*	*6.5*	*6.4*	*5.6*	*6.4*	*5.9*
RAF	**4 680**	**5 150**	**5 150**	**4 120**	**2 990**	**3 010**	**3 850**
of which female	540	580	650	520	410	440	510
percentage female	*11.6*	*11.2*	*12.6*	*12.5*	*13.6*	*14.5*	*13.1*
Officers: total	**660**	**860**	**790**	**650**	**460**	**490**	**740**
of which female	60	100	120	90	70	70	110
percentage female	*8.5*	*11.7*	*14.9*	*14.3*	*15.3*	*13.9*	*15.1*
Other ranks: total	**4 020**	**4 290**	**4 360**	**3 470**	**2 530**	**2 520**	**3 110**
of which female	490	480	530	420	340	370	390
percentage female	*12.1*	*11.1*	*12.2*	*12.2*	*13.3*	*14.6*	*12.7*

Source: DASA(Quad-Service)

1. Figures show outflow from UK Regular Forces, both trained and untrained, including personnel leaving the Services, deaths, recalled reservists on release and outflow to the Home Service battalions of the Royal Irish Regiment (which disbanded on 31 March 2008). They do not include promotion from ranks to officers or flows between Services and are not comparable with gains to trained strength figures which include promotion from ranks to officers.

2. Outflow figures up to and including 2006/07 include the net flow of between 100 and 200 personnel from the Regular Army to Long Term Absentee (LTA). Outflow figures from 2007/08 do not include this net flow to LTA.

Data from the Joint Personnel Administration System for the period 1 May 2009 to 1 October 2011 have been reviewed and finalised, therefore some figures may differ from previous publications.

This table is a National Statistic.

14.5 United Kingdom Armed Forces Full-time trained strength[1] and requirement, at 1 April each year

	2000		2006	2007	2008	2009	2010	2011	2012
All Services									
Requirement	198 160		185 920	183 610	179 270	178 860	178 750	179 250	174 840
Strength[2]	190 270		183 170	177 430	173 530	174 170	177 890	176 860	170 010
Surplus/Deficit	-7 880		-2 750	-6 190	-5 740	-4 690	- 860	-2 400	-4 830
Surplus/Deficit as % of requirement	*-4.0*		*-1.5*	*-3.4*	*-3.2*	*-2.6*	*-0.5*	*-1.3*	*-2.8*
Naval Service									
Requirement	39 860		36 830	36 800	36 260	35 760	35 790	35 700	34 800
Strength[2]	38 880		35 620	34 830	35 050	35 020	35 500	35 420	33 290
Surplus/Deficit	- 990		-1 220	-1 970	-1 210	- 740	- 290	- 280	-1 510
Surplus/Deficit as % of requirement	*-2.5*		*-3.3*	*-5.3*	*-3.3*	*-2.1*	*-0.8*	*-0.8*	*-4.3*
Army									
Requirement	106 400		101 800	101 800	101 800	101 790	102 160	102 210	101 210
Strength[2]	100 190		100 620	99 080	98 070	99 510	102 260	101 340	98 600
Surplus/Deficit	-6 210		-1 180	-2 720	-3 730	-2 280	100	- 870	-2 610
Surplus/Deficit as % of requirement	*-5.8*		*-1.2*	*-2.7*	*-3.7*	*-2.2*	*0.1*	*-0.8*	*-2.6*
Royal Air Force									
Requirement	51 900		47 290	45 020	41 210	41 310	40 800	41 340	38 830
Strength[2]	51 210		46 940	43 510	40 400	39 640	40 130	40 090	38 120
Surplus/Deficit	- 690		- 350	-1 500	- 800	-1 670	- 670	-1 250	- 700
Surplus/Deficit as % of requirement	*-1.3*		*-0.7*	*-3.3*	*-1.9*	*-4.1*	*-1.7*	*-3.0*	*-1.8*

Source: DASA(Quad-Service)

1. The Full-Time Trained Strength of the UK Armed Forces is defined as comprising of trained UK Regular Forces, trained Gurkhas and elements of the FTRS (Full Time Reserve Service) personnel. It does not include mobilised reservists.

2. From 1 April 2010 some elements of the FTRS are excluded. For a full description of FTRS please refer to the Glossary of Terms and Abbreviations at the end of UK Defence Statistics

Data from the Joint Personnel Administration System for 2010 and 2011 have been reviewed and finalised, therefore some figures may differ from previous publications.

This table is a National Statistic (Latest figures http://www.dasa.mod.uk/index.php?pub=MPR).

14.6a Civilian personnel[1], at 1 April each year

Thousands: FTE

	2000	2006[2]	2007	2008[2]	2009	2010	2011	2012[2]
Civilian Level 0[1]	**121.3**	**103.4**	**97.7**	**89.5**	**86.6**	**85.8**	**83.1** [e]	**71.0** [e]
Civilian Level 1[1]	91.9	78.1	73.8	69.0	66.4	65.9	63.1	54.5
Trading Funds	14.5	10.7	10.1	9.2	9.6	9.7	9.4	7.1
Locally engaged civilians	14.8	14.5	13.8	11.2	10.5	10.2	10.6 [e]	9.4 [e]
Civilian Level 1[1] - Permanent	**88.2**	**74.7**	**70.5**	**66.0**	**63.6**	**63.3**	**60.7**	**52.5**
Non-industrial	64.9	60.5	57.5	54.3	52.7	52.4	50.2	43.9
Industrial	23.3	14.2	13.0	11.7	11.0	10.9	10.5	8.6
Civilian Level 1[1] - Casual[3]	**1.3**	**1.1**	**0.9**	**0.8**	**0.5**	**0.3**	**0.1**	**0.0**
Non-industrial	0.9	0.8	0.6	0.4	0.4	0.2	0.0	0.0
Industrial	0.4	0.3	0.3	0.4	0.1	0.1	0.1	0.0
Civilian Level 1[1] - RFA	**2.4**	**2.3**	**2.4**	**2.3**	**2.3**	**2.3**	**2.4**	**2.0**
Trading Funds	**14.5**	**10.7**	**10.1**	**9.2**	**9.6**	**9.7**	**9.4**	**7.1**
Permanent	14.2	10.6	9.9	9.1	9.5	9.6	9.3	7.0
Casual[3]	0.3	0.1	0.1	0.1	0.1	0.1	0.1	0.1
Locally engaged civilians	**14.8**	**14.5**	**13.8**	**11.2**	**10.5**	**10.2**	**10.6** [e]	**9.4** [e]

Source: DASA(Quad-Service)

1. Civilian Level 0 - This contains all those at level 1 plus Trading Funds and Locally Engaged Civilians.
   Civilian Level 1 - Permanent and casual civilian personnel and Royal Fleet Auxiliaries, but exclides Trading Funds and Locally engaged Civilians.

2. The following changes have affected the continuity of the civilian data: In 2001 the QinetiQ portion of the Defence Evaluation and Research Agency (8,000) was established as a private company. At 1 April 2008 the Defence Aviation Repair Agency and the Army Base Repair Organisation merged to form the Defence Support Group and around 1,000 personnel transferred to the Vector Aerospace Corporation. In October 2011 responsibility for management of the Meteorological Office personnel (1,900) transferred to Department for Business, Innovation and Skills (BIS).

3. Casual personnel are usually engaged for less than 12 months.

This table is a National Statistic. These statistics have previously been published in the Quarterly Civilian Personnel Report (QCPR). This is a quarterly publication and the latest figures can be found here (http://www.dasa.mod.uk/index.php?pub=QCPR).

14.6b Civilian personnel[1] by budgetary area and grade equivalent[2], at 1 April each year

FTE

Grade	2000	2006[3]	2007	2008[3]	2009	2010	2011	2012[3]
Civilian Level 0[1]	**121 280**	**103 380**	**97 690**	**89 500**	**86 620**	**85 850**	**83 060** ᵉ	**71 010** ᵉ
Senior Civil Service and Equivalent[4]	310	310	280	300	300	290	270	240
Pay Band B	2 240	2 740	2 450	2 450	2 440	2 470	2 430	2 210
Pay Band C	15 230	17 310	16 840	16 540	16 800	16 630	16 680	15 170
Pay Band D	14 900	13 500	12 170	10 990	10 580	10 440	9 930	8 890
Pay Band E	33 020	27 220	25 590	23 490	22 800	22 440	20 870	17 370
Other non-industrial[5]	90	170	790	940	110	300	10	40
Industrial	23 670	14 540	13 300	12 060	11 100	11 010	10 580	8 600
Trading Funds	14 550	10 700	10 060	9 210	9 630	9 730	9 350	7 110
Royal Fleet Auxiliary	2 420	2 340	2 360	2 270	2 300	2 330	2 360	2 000
Locally engaged civilians	14 850	14 540	13 840	11 240	10 550	10 200	10 580 ᵉ	9 390 ᵉ
Navy Command	**6 440**	**5 290**	**5 230**	**4 600**	**4 640**	**4 760**	**4 700**	**3 990**
Pay Band C and above	660	640	580	500	510	540	530	500
Pay Band D and below	2 370	1 700	1 640	1 260	1 280	1 320	1 250	1 020
Other non-industrial[5]	-	-	30	30	-	10	10	10
Industrial	990	610	620	540	550	570	540	470
Royal Fleet Auxiliary	2 420	2 340	2 360	2 270	2 300	2 330	2 360	2 000
Land Forces	**22 090**	**18 650**	**17 960**	**17 180**	**16 490**	**16 480**	**14 920**	**13 160**
Pay Band C and above	3 300	3 590	3 340	3 290	3 420	3 450	3 170	2 950
Pay Band D and below	12 960	9 830	8 930	8 390	8 370	8 270	7 530	6 490
Other non-industrial[5]	10	30	400	520	80	150	-	-
Industrial	5 820	5 200	5 300	4 970	4 630	4 610	4 230	3 720
Air Command	**11 570**	**10 770**	**8 980**	**8 710**	**8 560**	**8 660**	**8 430**	**6 540**
Pay Band C and above	1 250	1 190	1 060	1 070	1 120	1 150	1 180	1 060
Pay Band D and below	5 820	5 550	4 870	4 580	4 600	4 660	4 480	3 710
Other non-industrial[5]	10	10	70	80	10	-	-	-
Industrial	4 480	4 020	2 980	2 980	2 830	2 850	2 760	1 770
Defence Equipment & Support[6]	**35 210**	**22 490**	**20 880**	**18 010**	**16 740**	**16 150**	**15 750** ʳ	**14 090**
Pay Band C and above	8 080	8 970	8 710	8 430	8 520	8 410	8 610 ʳ	7 860
Pay Band D and below	15 610	9 560	8 490	6 710	5 800	5 410	4 950 ʳ	4 300
Other non-industrial[5]	60	40	60	70	10	20	-	10
Industrial	11 470	3 920	3 620	2 790	2 400	2 310	2 190 ʳ	1 920
Centre	**16 570**	**20 720**	**20 530**	**20 260**	**19 890**	**19 770**	**19 320** ʳ	**16 720**
Pay Band C and above	4 490	5 860	5 760	5 930	5 900	5 790	5 890 ʳ	5 240
Pay Band D and below	11 170	13 990	13 760	13 440	13 290	13 210	12 580 ʳ	10 730
Other non-industrial[5]	-	80	240	230	10	100	-	20
Industrial	910	790	780	660	680	670	860 ʳ	720
Unknown[7]	**-**	**210**	**190**	**290**	**130**	**100**	**10**	**10**
Pay Band C and above	-	130	110	60	80	60	-	-
Pay Band D and below	-	80	80	100	40	30	10	10
Other non-industrial[5]	-	10	-	10	10	10	-	-
Industrial	-	-	-	120	10	-	-	-

Source: DASA(Quad-Service)

1. Civilian Level 0 - This contains all those at Level 1 plus Trading Funds and Locally Engaged Civilians. This will be used for external reporting, including the Quarterly Civilian Personnel Report, UKDS, and Parliamentary Business.

2. Grade equivalent is shown in terms of the broader banding structure and is based on paid grade.

3. The following changes have affected the continuity of the civilian data: In 2001 the QinetiQ portion of the Defence Evaluation and Research Agency (8,000) was established as a private company. At 1 April 2008 the Defence Aviation Repair Agency and the Army Base Repair Organisation merged to form the Defence Support Group and around 1,000 personnel transferred to the Vector Aerospace Corporation. In October 2011 responsibility for management of the Meteorological Office personnel (1,900) transferred to Department for Business, Innovation and Skills (BIS).

4. Includes personnel outside the Senior Civil Service but of equivalent grade, primarily Senior Medical Specialists.

5. Includes industrial personnel on temporary promotion to non-industrial grades and personnel for whom no grade information is available.

6. Defence Equipment & Support formed in 2007 by merging the Defence Logistics Organisation and Defence Procurement Agency. For consistency information in this table has been merged across the series between 2000 and 2006.

7. Personnel for whom no Top Level Budget (TLB) information is available are included in this section of the table.

14.7a Land holdings by country and whether owned, leased or with legal rights, at 1 April each year in thousand hectares

	2000	2006	2007	2008	2009 [1]	2010 [1]		2011 [2]	2012
Land & foreshore holdings and Rights held[3]	363.3	365.6	365.6	373.4	372.0	371.0	||	435.3	434.1
Land and foreshore holdings	238.5	240.7	240.7	240.3	239.0	238.0	||	230.4	229.1
Freehold	219.9	220.4	220.4	220.0	219.0	218.0	||	209.8	208.8
Leasehold	18.6	20.3	20.3	20.3	20.0	20.0	||	20.6	20.3
Rights held[3]	124.8	124.9	124.9	133.1	133.0	133.0	||	204.9	204.9
England	226.3	224.2	224.2	223.9	223.0	221.0	||	263.3	262.4
Land and foreshore holdings	191.8	189.8	189.8	189.5	188.0	187.0	||	179.1	178.2
Freehold	176.2	172.5	172.5	172.2	171.0	170.0	||	164.5	163.8
Leasehold	15.6	17.3	17.3	17.3	17.0	17.0	||	14.6	14.4
Rights held[3]	34.5	34.4	34.4	34.4	34.0	34.0	||	84.1	84.1
Wales	23.0	22.9	22.9	22.9	23.0	23.0	||	23.4	23.4
Land and foreshore holdings	20.8	20.7	20.7	20.7	21.0	21.0	||	20.1	20.1
Freehold	20.6	20.5	20.5	20.5	21.0	21.0	||	19.8	19.8
Leasehold	0.2	0.2	0.2	0.2	-	-	||	0.3	0.3
Rights held[3]	2.2	2.2	2.2	2.2	2.0	2.0	||	3.3	3.3
Scotland	110.7	115.3	115.3	123.5	124.0	124.0	||	146.4	146.4
Land and foreshore holdings	22.7	27.2	27.2	27.2	28.0	28.0	||	28.9	28.9
Freehold	20.2	24.6	24.6	24.6	25.0	25.0	||	23.5	23.5
Leasehold	2.5	2.6	2.6	2.6	3.0	3.0	||	5.4	5.4
Rights held[3]	88.0	88.1	88.1	96.3	96.0	96.0	||	117.4	117.5
Northern Ireland	3.3	3.2	3.2	3.2	3.0	3.0	||	2.2	1.9
Land and foreshore holdings	3.2	3.1	3.1	3.1	3.0	3.0	||	2.2	1.8
Freehold	2.9	2.8	2.8	2.8	3.0	3.0	||	2.0	1.7
Leasehold	0.3	0.3	0.3	0.3	-	-	||	0.2	0.1
Rights held[3]	0.1	0.1	0.1	0.1	-	-	||	-	-
Land and foreshore holdings	238.5	240.7	240.7	240.3	239.0	238.0	||	230.4 [4]	229.1
Land	219.9	222.1ʳ	222.1ʳ	221.7	221.0	220.0	||	..	..
England	176.6	174.5	174.5	174.2	173.0	172.0	||	..	..
Wales	19.7	19.7	19.7	19.7	20.0	20.0	||	..	..
Scotland	20.6	25.0	25.0	24.9	25.0	25.0	||	..	..
Northern Ireland	3.0	2.9	2.9	2.9	3.0	3.0	||	..	..
Foreshore	18.6	18.6	18.6	18.6	18.0	18.0	||	..	..
England	15.3	15.3	15.3	15.3	15.0	15.0	||	..	..
Wales	1.0	1.0	1.0	1.0	1.0	1.0	||	..	..
Scotland	2.1	2.1	2.1	2.1	2.0	2.0	||	..	..
Northern Ireland	0.2	0.2	0.2	0.2	-	-	||	..	..

Source: MOD Defence Infrastructure Organisation

1. The figures presented for years 2009 and 2010 were rounded to the nearest thousand hectares.

2. Data from 2011 has been compiled using a new spatial dataset which allows for greater accuracy in the measurement of the estate, because of this new dataset comparable figures for earlier years are not available. Figures have been rounded to the nearest hundred hectares

3. Rights held are Land and foreshore that are not owned by, or leased to MOD, but over which the Department has limited rights undergrants and rights

4. Separate figures for land and foreshore are no longer recorded

These holdings include land declared as surplus to defence requirements.
A thousand hectares is 3.86 square miles.
This table is a National Statistic.

14.7b Service Family Accommodation in the United Kingdom, at 31 March each year in thousands of dwellings

Permanent holdings

Thousands

	2000	2006	2007	2008	2009	2010	2011	2012
United Kingdom	**64.8**	**51.8**	**51.1**	**51.2**	**49.9**	**49.1**	**49.1**	**49.0**
England & Wales	55.9	45.1	44.9	45.2	44.9	44.1	44.2	44.0
Scotland	5.7	3.8	3.5	3.6	3.2	3.2	3.2	3.3
Northern Ireland	3.2	2.9	2.7	2.4	1.8	1.8	1.7	1.7

Vacant accommodation

Thousands

	2000	2006	2007	2008	2009	2010	2011	2012
United Kingdom	**14.7**	**9.5**	**10.1**	**10.5**	**8.4**	**7.3**	**6.0**	**6.5**
England & Wales	12.6	7.9	8.2	8.1	7.3	6.1	5.0	5.0
Scotland	1.7	0.8	0.8	0.9	0.6	0.6	0.5	0.7
Northern Ireland	0.4	0.8	1.1	1.5	0.5	0.6	0.5	0.8

Vacant properties as a percentage of all dwellings

Percentage

	2000	2006	2007	2008	2009	2010	2011	2012
United Kingdom	**23**	**18**	**20**	**21**	**17**	**15**	**12**	**13**
England & Wales	23	18	18	18	16	14	11	11
Scotland	30	21	23	25	19	18	16	24
Northern Ireland	13	28	41	63	28	34	29	40

Source: MOD Defence Infrastructure Organisation

14.8a Location of Service and civilian personnel [1,2] in the United Kingdom, at 1 April each year

FTE

	2000 [3]	2006	2007	2008	2009	2010	2011	2012
United Kingdom	**267 700**	**248 710**	**239 460**	**231 350**	**233 290**	**236 710**	**229 400**	**214 190**
Service	170 300	165 710	161 360	158 450	162 670	166 100	161 790	156 970
Civilian	97 410	83 000	78 110	72 900	70 620	70 610	67 610	57 220
England	**222 560**	**211 870**	**207 550**	**202 710**	**204 400**	**207 890**	**201 320**	**188 810**
Service	143 040	142 130	141 360	140 120	143 540	146 950	142 860	139 260
Civilian	79 520	69 740	66 200	62 590	60 860	60 940	58 450	49 560
Wales	**8 260**	**6 320**	**5 010**	**4 800**	**4 730**	**4 900**	**4 580**	**4 150**
Service	3 220	3 260	2 590	2 630	2 720	2 930	2 820	2 780
Civilian	5 040	3 050	2 420	2 170	2 010	1 970	1 760	1 370
Scotland	**24 680**	**20 440**	**19 190**	**17 960**	**17 880**	**17 840**	**17 630**	**15 880**
Service	15 080	13 520	12 640	11 960	12 020	12 080	12 090	11 190
Civilian	9 600	6 920	6 550	5 990	5 860	5 760	5 540	4 690
Northern Ireland	**11 640**	**10 080**	**7 700**	**5 880**	**6 280**	**6 080**	**5 870**	**5 350**
Service	8 390	6 800	4 770	3 730	4 390	4 140	4 010	3 740
Civilian	3 250	3 290	2 940	2 150	1 890	1 930	1 850	1 610

Source: DASA(Quad-Service)

Service and Civilian personnel[1,2] by Region

FTE

	Service			Civilian		
	2011	2012	% change	2011	2012	% change
United Kingdom	**161 790**	**156 970**	**-3.0**	**67 610**	**57 220**	**-15.4**
England	**142 860**	**139 260**	**-2.5**	**58 450**	**49 560**	**-15.2**
East of England	18 210	17 350	-4.7	5 510	4 600	-16.5
East Midlands	9 080	8 420	-7.3	2 380	1 900	-19.9
London	6 020	5 400	-10.4	4 570	3 960	-13.4
North East	1 420	1 400	-1.4	450	330	-25.1
North West	2 100	2 160	2.7	2 250	1 900	-15.6
South East	42 490	43 330	2.0	13 400	11 550	-13.8
South West	41 540	39 040	-6.0	21 690	18 100	-16.5
West Midlands	6 900	6 570	-4.8	4 490	3 970	-11.5
Yorkshire and The Humber	15 110	15 600	3.2	3 720	3 230	-13.2
Wales	**2 820**	**2 780**	**-1.5**	**1 760**	**1 370**	**-22.4**
Scotland	**12 090**	**11 190**	**-7.5**	**5 540**	**4 690**	**-15.3**
Northern Ireland	**4 010**	**3 740**	**-6.8**	**1 850**	**1 610**	**-13.3**

Source: DASA(Quad-Service)

1. Service personnel figures are for UK Regular Forces based in the UK. They include all trained and untrained Personnel and exclude Gurkhas, Full Time Reserve Service personnel and mobilised reservists.

2. Civilian personnel includes Trading Fund staff and exclude RFAs and LECs.

3. 2000 figures are as at 1 July.

Data from the Joint Personnel Administration System for 2010 and 2011 have been reviewed and finalised, therefore some figures may differ from previous publications.

14.8b Global locations of Service[1] and civilian personnel[2,3], at 1 April each year

Number: FTE

		2000 [4]	2006	2007	2008	2009	2010	2011	2 012
Global Total		**333 960** [r]	**299 220**	**288 360**	**276 410**	**275 220**	**277 560**	**269 420** [e]	**250 810** [e]
	Service	213 220	195 850	190 670	186 910	188 600	191 710	186 360	179 800
	Civilian Level 0	120 740	103 380	97 690	89 500	86 620	85 850	83 060 [e]	71 010 [e]
United Kingdom Total		**267 700**	**248 710**	**239 460**	**231 350**	**233 290**	**236 710**	**229 390**	**214 190**
	Service	170 300	165 710	161 360	158 450	162 670	166 100	161 790	156 970
	Civilian	97 410	83 000	78 110	72 900	70 620	70 610	67 610	57 220
Overseas Total		**54 000** [r]	**45 640**	**44 320**	**41 270** [r]	**38 240** [r]	**37 650** [r]	**36 910** [re]	**33 710** [e]
	Service	37 200	28 540	27 980	27 590	25 350	25 260	24 230	22 440
	Civilian	16 800 [r]	17 110	16 340	13 680 [r]	12 890 [r]	12 400 [r]	12 680 [re]	11 270 [e]
EUROPE (exc. UK)		..	**40 330**	**39 370**	**36 800**	**33 670**	**33 000**	**31 300**	**29 050** [e]
Germany / Belgium / Netherlands[5]	Service	20 190	22 590	22 380	22 310	19 760	19 720	18 760	17 480
	Civilian	..	8 740	8 860	7 980	7 560	7 190	6 590	5 950 [e]
Balkans[6]	Service	6 030	30	50	20	20	-	10	-
	Civilian	..	660	700	210	190	20	10	20
Cyprus	Service	3 510	3 040	2 950	2 780	2 910	2 880	2 830	2 590
	Civilian	..	3 230	2 280	1 850	1 640	1 610	1 570	1 670
Gibraltar	Service	550	340	310	280	260	270	260	230
	Civilian	..	1 010	1 190	750	730	730	750	650 [e]
Remainder	Service	1 290	550	500	470	470	440	390	350
	Civilian	..	120	160	160	140	150	140	110
ASIA (EXC. MIDDLE EAST)		..	**1 130**	**1 340**	**1 430**	**1 600**	**1 920**	**2 080** [e]	**2 110** [e]
	Service	970	280	220	260	260	260	280	260
	Civilian	..	850	1 110	1 170	1 340	1 660	1 800 [e]	1 860 [e]
NORTH AFRICA / MIDDLE EAST		..	**1 910**	**1 450**	**960**	**730**	**460**	**500**	**430**
	Service	1 300	420	310	360	370	380	420	340
	Civilian	..	1 490	1 140	600	360	80	80	90
SUB SAHARAN AFRICA		..	**560**	**610**	**650**	**680**	**690**	**1 540**	**890**
of which:									
Kenya[7]	Service	-	30	30	30	80	90	140	180
	Civilian	..	170	180	230	320	360	1 190	640
Sierra Leone	Service	-	90	90	80	60	30	30	20
	Civilian	..	230	220	220	150	150	130	-

Continued on the next page

14.8b Global locations of Service[1] and civilian personnel[2,3], at 1 April each year

		2000 [4]	2006	2007	2008	2009	2010	2011	2 012
NORTH AMERICA		..	**870**	**860**	**880**	**920**	**990**	**980**	**990** [e]
of which:									
United States	Service	910	410	390	420	470	520	550	560
	Civilian	..	180	180	180	160	160	150	150 [e]
Canada	Service	1 610	260	270	270	270	270	270	270
	Civilian	..	20	10	10	10	50	10	10
CENTRAL AMERICA / CARIBBEAN		..	**240**	**250**	**260**	**250**	**240**	**240**	**70**
	Service	-	80	80	80	70	70	70	10
	Civilian	..	160	170	180	180	170	160	60
SOUTH AMERICA		..	**20**	**20**	**20**	**20**	**20**	**20**	**20**
	Service	-	10	10	10	10	10	10	10
	Civilian	..	-	10	10	10	10	10	10
SOUTH ATLANTIC		..	**390**	**360**	**190**	**310**	**270**	**180**	**80** [e]
of which:									
Falkland Islands	Service	780	310	290	130	250	220	120	50
	Civilian	..	60	60	50	50	40	40	30 [e]
OCEANIA		..	**50**	**70**	**80**	**60**	**60**	**70**	**70**
	Service	20	50	50	60	50	50	50	60
	Civilian	..	-	10	20	20	10	20	10
Unallocated		-	**2 530**	**2 210**	**1 520** [r]	**1 390** [r]	**860** [r]	**760** [r]	**910**
	Service	5 720	1 600	1 330	880	580	350	340	390
	Civilian	4 080 [r]	930	880	650 [r]	800 [r]	520 [r]	420 [r]	520
Royal Fleet Auxiliaries Civilian		**2 450**	**2 340**	**2 360**	**2 270**	**2 300**	**2 330**	**2 360**	**2 000**

Source: DASA(Quad-Service)

1. Service personnel figures are for UK Regular Forces. They include all trained and untrained Personnel and exclude Gurkhas, Full Time Reserve Service personnel and mobilised reservists.

2. Civilian Level 0 - This contains all those at Level 1 plus Trading Funds and Locally Engaged Civilians.

   Civilian Level 1 - Permanent and casual civilian personnel and Royal Fleet Auxiliaries, but excludes Trading Funds and Locally Engaged Civilians.

3. UK civilian totals include Trading Fund personnel but exclude RFA and LEC personnel and those with an unknown location. Overseas civilian includes LEC personnel.

4. Detailed break down of LEC data for 2000 are not available. The "Overseas Total" for year 2000 subsumes the total LEC figure. 2000 figures as at 1 July.

5. As data for locally engaged civilians cannot be separated for Germany, Belgium and the Netherlands, these countries are grouped together.

6. Consists of Bosnia-Herzegovina, Croatia, the Former Yugoslav Republic of Macedonia, Kosovo, Montenegro, Serbia.

7. The increase in civilian numbers in 2011 reflects the additional requirements for locally engaged civilian to support military exercises.

r The overseas and unallocated groupings have changed since previous years to bring it in to line with the groupings used in Quarterly Location Statistics publication (QLS). As a result, the figures have been revised for the time series to correspond with the new groupings where possible.

Data from the Joint Personnel Administration System for 2010 and 2011 have been reviewed and finalised, therefore some figures may differ from previous publications. Please see Chapter 2 introduction for more details.

14.9a UK regular Armed Forces deaths by Service, Year of occurrence 2004-2012, numbers, age and gender standardised rates[1]

Year	All		Naval Service		Army		RAF	
	Number	Rate	Number	Rate	Number	Rate	Number	Rate
2004	170	82	37	92	96	75	37	67
2005	160	82	27	69	93	90	40	72
2006	191	98	33	85	111	94	47	91
2007	204	106	27	74	145	128	32	73
2008	137	74	40	110	79	74	18	37
2009	205	107	23	58	158	133	24	55
2010	187	97	30	78	136	116	21	50
2011	132	69	19	52	98	89	15	33
2012	129	71	19	55	95	89	15	42

[1] Rates have been age and gender standardised to the 2013 Armed Forces population, expressed per 100,000 strength.

Source: UK Defence Statistics 2014, Ministry of Defence

14.9b UK regular Armed Forces deaths by Service, 2004-2012[1], numbers, Standardised Mortality Ratios[2] (SMR) (95% confidence intervals (CI))

Cause	All			Naval Service			Army			RAF		
	Number	SMR	(95% CI)	Number	SMR	(95% CI)	Number	SMR	(95% CI)	Number	SMR	(95% CI)
2004	170	76	(65-88)	37	82	(59-113)	96	86	(70-105)	37	55	(40-76)
2005		75	(64-88)	27	62	(41-91)	93	88	(71-107)	40	62	(46-85)
2006	191	87	(76-101)	33	73	(52-103)	111	100	(83-120)	47	75	(57-100)
2007	204	96	(84-110)	27	61	(40-89)	145	132	(112-155)	32	55	(39-78)
2008	137	65	(55-76)	40	89	(65-122)	79	72	(58-90)	18	32	(19-50)
2009	205	99	(86-113)	23	53	(33-79)	158	146	(125-170)	24	43	(28-64)
2010	187	94	(81-108)	30	71	(50-102)	136	131	(111-155)	21	39	(24-60)
2011	132	r 71	(60-84)	19	4	(29-76)	98	0	(82-122)	15	3	(17-50)
2012	129	r 75	(63-90)	19	r 53 r	(32-82)	95	r 105	(86-128)	15	r 34	(19-56)

[1] Change in how UK deaths collated, prior to 2006 includes deaths occurred in year, post 2006 includes deaths registered in the year

[2] Standardised mortality ratios have been age and gender standardised.
'r' indicates a change in previously published data

Source: UK Defence Statistics 2014, Ministry of Defence

14.10a Military Search and Rescue - UK & Overseas Callouts, Incidents and Persons Moved, 2004 to 2012

	Incidents			Callouts			Persons Moved		
	All[2]	UK	Overseas[2]	All[2]	UK	Overseas[2]	All[2]	UK	Overseas[2]
2004	1,564	1,504	60	1,711	1,638	73	1,449	1,414	35
2005	1,641	1,584	57	1,766	1,702	64	1,431	1,384	47
2006	1,767	1,703	64	1,948	1,875	73	1,538	1,463	75
2007	1,877	1,803	74	2,065	1,973	92	1,817	1,767	50
2008	2,025	1,941	84	2,179	2,083	96	1,763	1,607	156
2009	2,262	2,191	71	2,418	2,337	81	1,873	1,810	63
2010	1,960	1,901	59	2,050	1,983	67	1,647	1,605	42
2011	1,864	1,801	63	1,921	1,856	65	1,560	1,501	59
2012	1,774 r	1,733	41 r	1,879 r	1,837	42 r	1,550 r	1,522	28 r

2. The numbers of callouts and persons moved in Cyprus and the Falkland Islands have been revised, due to additional data being received for 2012

Source: UK Defence Statistics 2014, Ministry of Defence

14.10b Callouts and persons moved by UK Military Search and Rescue units: 2001 - 2011

Time series tables are no longer published for Fixed Wing, Ships, MRT or Military/Civilian split. Data for 2012 data is only available for Helicopters.

Callouts	UK Total	Helicopters			MRT	Fixed wing aircraft		Ships		Civilian	Military
		RN	RAF	Other		Nimrod	Other				
2001	1 763	502	1 115	-	91	54	1	-		1 660	103
2002	1 684	436	1 122	-	79	46	1	-		1 586	98
2003	1 714	424	1 173	-	80	37	-	-		1 618	96
2004	1 638	453	1 079	-	67	37	2	-		1 538	100
2005	1 702	478	1 114	-	73	37	-	-		1 610	92
2006	1 875	497	1 258	1	86	32	1	-		1 785	90
2007	1 973	592	1 258	-	102	21	-	-		1 892	81
2008	2 083	586	1 377	-	91	29	-	-		2 028	55
2009	2 337	758	1 479	-	86	13	1	-		2 268	69
2010	1 983	639	1 282	-	59	3	-	-		1 944	39
2011	1 856	542	1 257	-	57	-	-	-		1 815	41

Source: DASA(Price Indices)

Search and Rescue Helicopters - UK & Overseas Callouts by Unit, 2004 to 2012

	RAF Boulmer	RAF Lossiemouth	RAF Leconfield	RAF Valley	RAF Chivenor	RAF Wattisham	RAF UK Total	RNAS Culdrose	HMS Gannet	RN Total	UK Other	UK Total	Cyprus	Falklands	Overseas Total
2004	166	190	136	230	216	137	1,075	203	250	453	4	1,532	46	21	67
2005	144	200	135	218	281	131	1,109	211	267	478	5	1,592	39	24	63
2006	206	217	147	225	293	163	1,251	228	269	497	8	1,756	35	38	73
2007	170	188	222	234	256	183	1,253	231	359	590	7	1,850	53	39	92
2008	211	275	232	222	262	174	1,376	204	382	586	1	1,963	30	66	96
2009	214	236	204	322	340	162	1,478	311	447	758	1	2,237	36	45	81
2010	193	175	174	268	339	133	1,282	260	379	639	0	1,921	29	38	67
2011	181	207	168	276	267	157	1,256	244	298	542	1	1,799	24	41	65
2012	141	216	129	300	266	160	1,212	251	298	549	0	1,761	20	22	42

Source: UK Defence Statistics, ARCC Database

14.10b Callouts and persons moved by UK Military Search and Rescue units: 2001 - 2011
Continued

Time series tables are no longer published for Fixed Wing, Ships, MRT or Military/Civilian split. Data for 2012 data is only available for Helicopters.

Persons moved

	UK Total	RN	RAF	Other	MRT	Nimrod	Other	Ships	Civilian	Military
		Helicopters				Fixed wing aircraft		Ships		
2001	1 182	386	781	-	15	-	-	-	1 139	43
2002	1 224	314	900	-	10	-	-	-	1 181	43
2003	1 273	320	922	-	31	-	-	-	1 206	67
2004	1 412	416	978	-	17	-	1	-	1 355	57
2005	1 384	380	907	-	97	-	-	-	1 315	69
2006	1 463	479	968	-	16	-	-	-	1 409	54
2007	1 767	507	1 219	-	41	-	-	-	1 710	57
2008	1 607	516	1,062	-	29	-	-	-	1 565	42
2009	1 810	656	1 135	-	19	-	-	-	1 761	49
2010	1 605	539	1 047	-	19	-	-	-	1 575	30
2011	1 501	459	1 030	-	12	-	-	-	1 475	26

Source: DASA(Price Indices)

Search and Rescue Helicopters - UK & Overseas Persons Moved by Unit, 2004 to 2012

	RAF Boulmer	RAF Lossiemouth	RAF Leconfield	RAF Valley	RAF Chivenor	RAF Wattisham	RAF UK Total	RNAS Culdrose	HMS Gannet	RN Total	UK Other	UK Total	Cyprus	Falklands	Overseas Total
2004	134	199	114	196	248	75	966	205	211	416	12	1,394	9	26	35
2005	136	181	94	195	216	83	905	154	226	380	2	1,287	17	30	47
2006	132	180	125	202	213	110	962	176	303	479	6	1,447	5	70	75
2007	136	160	315	236	224	122	1,193	220	286	506	27	1,726	11	39	50
2008	185	199	163	217	211	87	1,062	169	347	516	0	1,578	5	151	156
2009	149	171	132	296	304	82	1,134	278	378	656	1	1,791	9	54	63
2010	169	156	120	263	256	83	1,047	215	324	539	0	1,586	5	37	42
2011	121	239	125	246	203	96	1,030	219	240	459	0	1,489	15	44	59
2012	129	205	97	284	187	80	982	235	285	520	0	1,502	3	25	28

Source: UK Defence Statistics; ARCC Database

14.10c Search and Rescue Helicopters: UK & Overseas Callouts by Assistance Type, 2004 to 2012

	2004	2005	2006	2007	2008	2009	2010	2011	2012
Rescue	118	115	100	106	99	97	105	87	81
Search-Rescue[7]	0	0	0	30	33	75	40	30	39
Medrescue	602	675	751	703	744	914	839	843	808
Search-Medrescue[7]	0	0	0	38	55	59	61	53	46
Medtransfer	195	157	191	209	229	224	210	182	169
Recovery	26	30	33	15	29	19	13	14	21
Search-Recovery[7]	0	0	0	2	8	16	7	7	8
Transfer	19	28	24	18	16	15	12	10	9
Civil Aid	31	22	23	41	26	17	20	10	5
Search	248	246	289	284	291	297	189	202	178
Top Cover	35	38	28	35	15	28	22	24	19
Assist	42	29	33	25	27	34	31	20	35
Search-Assist[7]	0	0	0	37	53	49	19	27	36
Recall	178	183	222	212	277	280	243	224	221
Not Required	58	98	83	113	80	104	88	94	97
False Alarm	15	10	9	25	31	36	29	10	9
Hoax	8	6	10	12	15	11	15	7	3
Precaution	10	4	8	5	1	2	9	6	5
Aborted	12	14	25	27	23	34	33	9	9
Search-Aborted[7]	0	0	0	5	8	7	3	5	5
Total Callouts	1,597	1,655	1,829	1,942	2,060	2,318	1,988	1,864	1,803

Search and Rescue Helicopters: UK & Overseas Persons Moved by Assistance Type, 2004 to 2012

	2004	2005	2006	2007	2008	2009	2010	2011	2012
Rescue	490	322	407	575	383	289	290	301	287
Search-Rescue[7]	0	0	0	56	70	155	82	55	100
Medrescue	683	791	852	839	821	1,026	917	910	860
Search-Medrescue[7]	0	0	0	56	65	70	68	59	48
Medtransfer	204	159	192	212	243	238	227	190	185
Recovery	30	30	39	16	28	22	15	14	27
Search-Recovery[7]	0	0	0	2	9	20	8	7	10
Transfer	22	32	32	20	115	34	21	12	13
Total Persons Moved	1,429	1,334	1,522	1,776	1,734	1,854	1,628	1,548	1,530

7.There was a change in callout classification in 2007. Prior to 2007, 'Search-Rescue' was included in 'Rescue', 'Search-Medrescue' was included in 'Medrescue', 'Search-Recovery' was included in 'Recovery', 'Search-Asssist' was included in 'Assist' and 'Search-Aborted' was included in 'Aborted'

Source: UK Defence Statistics; ARCC Database

14.10d Strength of uniformed United Kingdom medical staff[1]

As at 1 April

Numbers

		2000	2001	2002	2003	2004	2005	2006	2007 [6]	2008 [7]	2009	2010
Qualified doctors:[2]												
Naval Service	KDMA	210	220	220	230	240	260	260	290	280	360	300
Army[3]	KDMB	460	470	490	550	600	610	650	550	600	490	490
Royal Air Force	KDMC	180	180	180	190	200	220	230	220	230	180	230
All Services	KDMD	860	870	890	970	1,040	1,090	1,140	1,060	1,110	1,040	1,020
Qualified dentists:[2]												
Naval Service	KDME	60	60	60	60	60	60	60	50	60	50	50
Army[3]	KDMF	140	150	140	150	150	150	140	130	130	110	110
Royal Air Force	KDMG	80	80	70	70	80	70	70	60	60	50	60
All Services	KDMH	280	290	280	270	290	280	270	240	250	220	210
Support staff:[4]												
Naval Service[5]	KDMI	1,000	1,030	1,010	1,060	1,110	1,110	1,120	1,130	1,280	1,150	1,110
Nursing services[5]	ZBTL	210	210	220	250	280	290	300	300	300	310	270
Support[5]	ZBTM	790	820	790	810	840	820	820	830	980	840	840
Army[3]	KDMJ	3,210	3,260	3,320	3,410	3,560	..	..	3,000	4,070	3,490	3,350
Nursing services[3,4,5]	ZBTN	570	610	650	710	770	770	800	790	960	950	800
Support[3]	ZBTO	2,640	2,650	2,670	2,700	2,800	..	..	2,210	3,110	2,540	2,540
Royal Air Force	KDMK	1,460	1,480	1,500	1,600	1,680	1,660	1,550	1,340	1,380	1,250	1,350
Nursing services[5]	ZBTP	400	420	450	470	480	510	480	490	440	460	520
Support	ZBTQ	1,060	1,070	1,050	1,130	1,200	1,160	1,070	850	940	790	820
All Services	KDML	5,760	5,800	5,930	6,180	6,440	..	..	..	..	..	..

Source:DASA:0207 2181429/HQ Surgeon General, Pers Div, Manning (from 2009)

1 Includes staff employed at units (including ships) and in hospitals.

2 The Medical and Dental Officers exclude Late Entry personnel. From 2007-10 'Qualified' Doctors refers to personnel who hold a basic registrable qualification but may not necessarily have completed their career directed professional training, and as such may not necessarily be fully trained in their speciality. From 2009-10, Dental Officers refers only to fully qualified Dentists.

3 Due to a change in source data, Army figures prior to 2005 cannot be verified.

4 'Support staff' from 2007 includes all medical support staff collated by the Defence Medical Services Dept (from 2009 onwards, HQ Surgeon General) in their tri-service manning return; trained and in-training. 2010 figures for Army Healthcare Assistants were not provided and so are not included in the 'Support' total shown. From 1999, 'Support Staff' figures are split so that nurses are separate from other support staff.

5 From 2007, includes trained and untrained.

6 Figures from 2007-2008 provided by Defence Medical Services Department. Figures from 2009-10 provided by HQ Surgeon General.

7 2008-10 support figures include all support staff both trained and untrained.

Strength of uniformed United Kingdom medical staff 2011 - 2012

	2011	2012
Qualified Doctors	588	575
Qualified Dentists	245	244
Nursing Services	1,329	1,461
Support Staff	4,038	4,000
Total	6,200	6,280

Source: Headquarters of the Surgeon General

figures are for Regular personnel only and therefore do not represent the strength of either Reserve or veterinarian personnel.

14.11 Number of vessels boarded by the Royal Navy Fishery Protection Squadron within British fishing limits and convictions arising from these boardings each financial year

	2000/01	2006/07	2007/08	2008/09	2009/10	2010/11	2011/12
Vessels boarded	**1 603**	**1 335**	**1 309**	**1 102**	**1 201**	**1 399**	**1 408**
by sea areas¹:							
North Sea	627	343	367	306	338	411	417
Bristol Channel, Celtic Sea, English Channel, Irish Sea and Western Approaches	976	992	942	796	863	988	991

Source: Marine Management Organisation

Convictions Arising from Royal Navy Boardings

	2000/01	2006/07	2007/08	2008/09	2009/10	2010/11	2011/12
Convictions arising from boardings²	**48**	**53**	**57**	**30**	**10**	**29**	**17**
by nationality:							
Belgium	4	10	19	5	3	1	2
Denmark	3	-	-	-	-	-	
Eire	4	10	6	-	1	3	3
Faeroes	3	-	-	-	-	-	
France	8	14	16	12	1	14	6
Germany	-	-	-	-	-	2	
Netherlands	6	4	-	2	-	3	2
Spain	-	-	-	3	1	1	2
United Kingdom	20	15	16	8	4	5	2

Source: Marine Management Organisation

1. The Faroes, Rockall and West of Scotland are not covered by the Royal Navy Fishery Protection Squadron
2. From 2008/09, these figures include Fisheries Administration Penalties.

The data in this Table are outside the scope of National Statistics since they have not been put forward for assessment by the UK Statistics Authority.

Population and vital statistics

Chapter 15

Population and Vital Statistics

This section begins with a summary of population figures for the United Kingdom and constituent countries for 1851 to 2031 and for Great Britain from 1801 (Table 15.1). Table 15.2 analyses the components of population change. Table 15.3 gives details of the national sex and age structures for years up to the present date, with projected figures up to the year 2026. Legal marital condition of the population is shown in Table 15.4. The distribution of population at regional and local levels is summarised in Table 15.5.

In the main, historical series relate to census information, while mid-year estimates, which make allowance for under-enumeration in the census, are given for the recent past and the present (from 1961 onwards).

Population
(Tables 15.1 - 15.3)

Figures shown in these tables relate to the population enumerated at successive censuses, (up to 1951), mid-year estimates (from 1961 to 2008) and population projections (up to 2031). Further information can be found on the National Statistics website www.ons.gov.uk.

Population projections are 2012-based and were published by the Office for National Statistics on 21st October 2009. Further information can be found at www.ons.gov.uk

Definition of resident population

The estimated resident population of an area includes all people who usually live there, whatever their nationality. Members of HM and US Armed Forces in England and Wales are included on a residential basis wherever possible. HM Forces stationed outside England and Wales are not included. Students are taken to be resident at their term time address.

The projections of the resident population of the United Kingdom and constituent countries were prepared by the National Statistics Centre for Demography within ONS, in consultation with the Registrars General, as a common framework for use in national planning in a number of different fields. New projections are made every second year on assumptions regarding future fertility, mortality and migration which seem most appropriate on the basis of the statistical evidence available at the time. The population projections in Tables 15.1 -15.3 are based on the estimates of the population of the United Kingdom at mid-2008 made by the Registrars General.

Marital condition (de jure): estimated population
(Table 15.4)

This table shows population estimates by marital status

Geographical distribution of the population
(Table 15.5)

The population enumerated in the censuses for 1911-1951, and the mid-year population estimates for later years, are provided for standard regions of the United Kingdom, for metropolitan areas, for broad groupings of local authority districts by type within England and Wales, and for some of the larger cities. Projections of future sub-national population levels are prepared from time to time by the Registrar General, but are not shown in this publication.

Migration into and out of the United Kingdom
(Tables 15.7 - 15.8)

A long-term international migrant is defined as a person who changes his or her country of usual residence for a period of at least a year,so that the country of destination effectively becomes the country of usual residence.

The main source of long-term international migration data is the International Passenger Survey (IPS). This is a continuous voluntary sample survey that provides information on passengers entering and leaving the UK by the principal air, sea and tunnel routes. Being a sample survey, the IPS is subject to some uncertainty; therefore it should be noted that long-term international migration estimates, in particular the difference between inflow and outflow, may be subject to large sampling errors. The IPS excludes routes between the Channel Islands and Isle of Man and the rest of the world.

The IPS data are supplemented with four types of additional information in order to provide a full picture of total long-term international migration, known as Long-Term International Migration or LTIM:

1. The IPS is based on intentions to migrate and intentions are liable to change. Adjustments are made for visitor switchers (those who intend to stay in the UK or abroad for less than one year but subsequently stay for longer and become migrants) and for migrant switchers (those who intend to stay in the UK or abroad for one year or more but then return earlier so are no longer migrants). These adjustments are primarily based on IPS data but for years prior to 2001, Home Office data on short-term visitors who were subsequently granted an extension of stay for a year or longer for other reasons have been incorporated.

2. Home Office data on applications for asylum and dependants of asylum seekers entering the UK are used to estimate inflows of asylum seekers and dependants not already captured by the I PS. In addition, Home Office data on removals and refusals are used to estimate outflows of failed asylum seekers not identified by the IPS.

3. Migration flows between the UK and the Irish Republic were added to the data to 2007 as the IPS did not cover this route until recently. These flows were obtained mainly from the Quarterly National Household Survey and were agreed between the Irish Central Statistics Office and ONS. From 2008 onwards, estimates of migration between the UK and Irish Republic come from the IPS.

4. Migration flows to and from Northern Ireland are added to the IPS data for Great Britain from 2008 onwards. These flows are obtained from the Irish Quarterly National Household Survey (from CSO Ireland) and health card registration data (from Northern Ireland Statistics Research Agency (NISRA)). These data are now deemed a better source for Northern Irish flows than IPS data. Prior to 2008, estimates of migration to and from Northern Ireland came from the IPS.

Grants for settlement in the United Kingdom
(Table 15.9)

This table presents in geographic regions, the statistics of individual countries of nationality, arranged alphabetically within each region. The figures are on a different basis from those derived from IPS (Tables 15.9 and 15.10) and relate only to people subject to immigration control. Persons granted settlement are allowed to stay indefinitely in the United Kingdom. They exclude temporary migrants such as students and generally relate only to non-EEA nationals. Settlement can occur several years after entry to the country.

Applications received for asylum in the United Kingdom, excluding dependants
(Table 15.10)

This table shows statistics of applications for asylum in the United Kingdom. Figures are shown for the main applicant nationalities by geographic region. The basis of assessing asylum applications, and hence of deciding whether to grant asylum in the United Kingdom, is the 1951 United Nations Convention on Refugees.

Marriages
(Table 15.11)

The figures in this table relate to marriages solemnised in England and Wales. They take no account of the growing trend towards marrying abroad.

Births
(Tables 15.14 –15.16)

For Scotland and Northern Ireland the number of births relate to those registered during the year. For England and Wales the figures up to and including 1930-32 are for those registered, while later figures relate to births occurring in each year.

All data for England and Wales and for Scotland include births occurring in those countries to mothers not usually resident in them. Data for Northern Ireland, and hence UK, prior to 1981 include births occurring in Northern Ireland to non-resident mothers; from 1981, such births are excluded.

Deaths
(Tables 15.17 - 15.18)

The figures relate to the number of deaths registered during each calendar year.

Infant and maternal mortality
(Table 15.18)

On 1 October 1992 the legal definition of a stillbirth was altered from a baby born dead after 28 completed weeks gestation or more, to one born after 24 completed weeks of gestation or more. The 258 stillbirths of 24 to 27 weeks gestation that which occurred between 1 October and 31 December 1992 are excluded from this table.

Life tables
(Table 15.19)

The current set of interim life tables are constructed from the estimated populations in 2010-2012 and corresponding data on births, infant deaths and deaths by individual age registered in those years.

Adoptions
(Table 15.20)

The figures shown within these tables relate to the date the adoption was entered in the Adopted Children Register. Figures based on the date of court order are available for England and Wales in the volumes Adoptions in England and Wales, Marriages in England and Wales and Divorces in England and Wales available on the National Statistics website www.statistics.gov.uk.

15.1 Population summary: by country and sex

Thousands

	United Kingdom			England and Wales			Wales	Scotland			Northern Ireland		
	Persons	Males	Females	Persons	Males	Females	Persons	Persons	Males	Females	Persons	Males	Females
Enumerated population: census figures													
1801	..	..	..	8,893	4,255	4,638	587	1,608	739	869	..	..	..
1851	22,259	10,855	11,404	17,928	8,781	9,146	1,163	2,889	1,376	1,513	1,442	698	745
1901	38,237	18,492	19,745	32,528	15,729	16,799	2,013	4,472	2,174	2,298	1,237	590	647
1911	42,082	20,357	21,725	36,070	17,446	18,625	2,421	4,761	2,309	2,452	1,251	603	648
1921 [1]	44,027	21,033	22,994	37,887	18,075	19,811	2,656	4,882	2,348	2,535	1,258	610	648
1931 [1]	46,038	22,060	23,978	39,952	19,133	20,819	2,593	4,843	2,326	2,517	1,243	601	642
1951	50,225	24,118	26,107	43,758	21,016	22,742	2,599	5,096	2,434	2,662	1,371	668	703
1961	52,709	25,481	27,228	46,105	22,304	23,801	2,644	5,179	2,483	2,697	1,425	694	731
Resident population: mid-year estimates													
	DYAY	BBAB	BBAC	BBAD	BBAE	BBAF	KGJM	BBAG	BBAH	BBAI	BBAJ	BBAK	BBAL
1973	56,223	27,332	28,891	49,459	24,061	25,399	2,773	5,234	2,515	2,719	1,530	756	774
1974	56,236	27,349	28,887	49,468	24,075	25,393	2,785	5,241	2,519	2,722	1,527	755	772
1975	56,226	27,361	28,865	49,470	24,091	25,378	2,795	5,232	2,516	2,716	1,524	753	770
1976	56,216	27,360	28,856	49,459	24,089	25,370	2,799	5,233	2,517	2,716	1,524	754	769
1977	56,190	27,345	28,845	49,440	24,076	25,364	2,801	5,226	2,515	2,711	1,523	754	769
1978	56,178	27,330	28,848	49,443	24,067	25,375	2,804	5,212	2,509	2,704	1,523	754	770
1979	56,240	27,373	28,867	49,508	24,113	25,395	2,810	5,204	2,505	2,699	1,528	755	773
1980	56,330	27,411	28,919	49,603	24,156	25,448	2,816	5,194	2,501	2,693	1,533	755	778
1981	56,357	27,412	28,946	49,634	24,160	25,474	2,813	5,180	2,495	2,685	1,543	757	786
1982	56,291	27,364	28,927	49,582	24,119	25,462	2,804	5,165	2,487	2,677	1,545	757	788
1983	56,316	27,371	28,944	49,617	24,133	25,484	2,803	5,148	2,479	2,669	1,551	759	792
1984	56,409	27,421	28,989	49,713	24,185	25,528	2,801	5,139	2,475	2,664	1,557	761	796
1985	56,554	27,489	29,065	49,861	24,254	25,606	2,803	5,128	2,470	2,658	1,565	765	800
1986	56,684	27,542	29,142	49,999	24,311	25,687	2,811	5,112	2,462	2,649	1,574	768	805
1987	56,804	27,599	29,205	50,123	24,371	25,752	2,823	5,099	2,455	2,644	1,582	773	809
1988	56,916	27,652	29,265	50,254	24,434	25,820	2,841	5,077	2,444	2,633	1,585	774	812
1989	57,076	27,729	29,348	50,408	24,510	25,898	2,855	5,078	2,443	2,635	1,590	776	814
1990	57,237	27,819	29,419	50,561	24,597	25,964	2,862	5,081	2,444	2,637	1,596	778	818
1991	57,439	27,909	29,530	50,748	24,681	26,067	2,873	5,083	2,445	2,639	1,607	783	824
1992	57,585	27,977	29,608	50,876	24,739	26,136	2,878	5,086	2,445	2,640	1,623	792	831
1993	57,714	28,039	29,675	50,986	24,793	26,193	2,884	5,092	2,448	2,644	1,636	798	837
1994	57,862	28,108	29,754	51,116	24,853	26,263	2,887	5,102	2,453	2,649	1,644	802	842
1995	58,025	28,204	29,821	51,272	24,946	26,326	2,889	5,104	2,453	2,650	1,649	804	845
1996	58,164	28,287	29,877	51,410	25,030	26,381	2,891	5,092	2,447	2,645	1,662	810	851
1997	58,314	28,371	29,943	51,560	25,113	26,446	2,895	5,083	2,442	2,641	1,671	816	856
1998	58,475	28,458	30,017	51,720	25,201	26,519	2,900	5,077	2,439	2,638	1,678	819	859
1999	58,684	28,578	30,106	51,933	25,323	26,610	2,901	5,072	2,437	2,635	1,679	818	861
2000	58,886	28,690	30,196	52,140	25,438	26,702	2,907	5,063	2,432	2,631	1,683	820	862
2001	59,113	28,832	30,281	52,360	25,574	26,786	2,910	5,064	2,434	2,630	1,689	824	865
2002	59,319	28,961	30,358	52,567	25,700	26,867	2,918	5,055	2,432	2,623	1,697	829	868
2003	59,552	29,104	30,448	52,792	25,837	26,955	2,929	5,057	2,435	2,623	1,703	833	870
2004	59,842	29,274	30,568	53,053	25,991	27,062	2,943	5,078	2,446	2,632	1,710	836	874
2005	60,235	29,493	30,742	53,416	26,193	27,224	2,950	5,095	2,456	2,639	1,724	844	880
2006	60,584	29,689	30,895	53,726	26,366	27,359	2,962	5,117	2,469	2,647	1,742	853	888
2007	60,986	29,918	31,068	54,082	26,570	27,512	2,976	5,144	2,486	2,659	1,759	862	897
2009	61,792	30,374	31,418	54,809	26,980	27,829	2,999	5,194	2,515	2,679	1,789	879	910
2010	62,262	30,643	31,619	55,240	27,229	28,012	3,006	5,222	2,530	2,692	1,799	884	915
2011	63,285	31,097	32,188	56,171	27,638	28,533	3,064	5,300	2,570	2,730	1,814	889	925
2012	63,705	31,315	32,389	56,567	27,843	28,724	3,074	5,313	2,577	2,736	1,823	894	929
Resident population: projections (mid-year)[2]													
	C59J	C59K	C59L	C59M	C59N	C59O	C59P	C59Q	C59R	C59S	C59T	C59U	C59V
2016	65,386	32,244	33,143	58,139	28,710	29,430	3,119	5,386	2,619	2,767	1,861	915	946
2021	67,550	33,414	34,136	60,143	29,793	30,351	3,181	5,497	2,680	2,817	1,910	942	968
2026	69,575	34,497	35,078	62,019	30,795	31,224	3,238	5,606	2,739	2,867	1,950	963	987
2031	71,380	35,457	35,922	63,702	31,689	32,013	3,283	5,698	2,789	2,909	1,980	979	1,001

1 Figures for Northern Ireland are estimated. The population at the Census of 1926 was 1,257 thousand (608 thousand males and 648 thousand females).

2 These projections are 2012-based.

Sources: Office for National Statistics: 01329 444661;
National Records of Scotland
Northern Ireland Statistics and Research Agency;

15.2a Population projections by the Office for National Statistics

United Kingdom
PERSONS, thousands

2012-based Principal projection

Components of change (mid-year to mid-year), total fertility rate and expectation of life at birth based on the mortality rates for the year

	2012 -2013	2013 -2014	2014 -2015	2015 -2016	2016 -2017	2017 -2018	2018 -2019	2019 -2020	2020 -2021	2021 -2022	2022 -2023	2023 -2024	2024 -2025	2025 -2026	2026 -2027	2027 -2028
Population at start	63,705	64,087	64,511	64,938	65,386	65,825	66,266	66,697	67,126	67,550	67,969	68,382	68,788	69,186	69,575	69,955
Births	799	807	810	813	815	817	817	816	815	813	812	809	807	805	803	801
Deaths	582	549	548	548	548	549	551	553	556	559	564	569	574	581	588	595
Natural change	218	258	262	265	267	268	266	263	259	254	248	241	233	224	215	206
Net migration	165	166	165	184	171	174	165	165	165	165	165	165	165	165	165	165
Total change	382	424	427	449	438	442	431	428	424	419	413	406	398	389	380	371
Population at end	64,087	64,511	64,938	65,386	65,825	66,266	66,697	67,126	67,550	67,969	68,382	68,788	69,186	69,575	69,955	70,325
Annual growth rate	0.60%	0.66%	0.66%	0.69%	0.67%	0.67%	0.65%	0.64%	0.63%	0.62%	0.61%	0.59%	0.58%	0.56%	0.55%	0.53%
Total fertility rate (TFR)	1.88	1.89	1.89	1.89	1.89	1.89	1.89	1.89	1.89	1.89	1.89	1.89	1.89	1.89	1.89	1.89
EOLB Males	78.7	79.4	79.7	80.0	80.3	80.5	80.8	81.0	81.3	81.5	81.7	81.9	82.1	82.3	82.5	82.7
Females	82.4	83.2	83.5	83.7	83.9	84.1	84.4	84.6	84.8	85.0	85.2	85.3	85.5	85.7	85.9	86.0

2012-based Principal projection — Annual averages for longer-term projections

Components of change (mid-year to mid-year), total fertility rate and expectation of life at birth based on the mortality rates for the year

	2028 -2029	2029 -2030	2030 -2031	2031 -2032	2032 -2033	2033 -2034	2034 -2035	2035 -2036	2036 -2037	2037 -2041	2041 -2046	2046 -2051	2051 -2056	2056 -2061	2061 -2062
Population at start	70,325	70,686	71,037	71,380	71,713	72,037	72,355	72,666	72,971	73,272	74,450	75,879	77,234	78,489	79,671
Births	799	798	797	797	798	799	802	806	811	825	848	859	860	859	860
Deaths	603	611	620	629	638	647	656	666	675	696	727	753	774	788	792
Natural change	196	186	177	168	160	152	146	140	136	129	121	106	86	71	69
Net migration	165	165	165	165	165	165	165	165	165	165	165	165	165	165	165
Total change	361	351	342	333	325	317	311	305	301	294	286	271	251	236	234
Population at end	70,686	71,037	71,380	71,713	72,037	72,355	72,666	72,971	73,272	74,450	75,879	77,234	78,489	79,671	79,904
Annual growth rate	0.51%	0.50%	0.48%	0.47%	0.45%	0.44%	0.43%	0.42%	0.41%	0.40%	0.38%	0.35%	0.32%	0.30%	0.29%
Total fertility rate (TFR)	1.89	1.89	1.89	1.89	1.89	1.89	1.89	1.89	1.89	1.89	1.89	1.89	1.89	1.89	1.89
EOLB Males	82.9	83.0	83.2	83.3	83.5	83.6	83.8	83.9	84.0	84.4	84.9	85.6	86.2	86.8	87.2
Females	86.2	86.3	86.5	86.6	86.8	86.9	87.0	87.2	87.3	87.6	88.1	88.7	89.3	89.9	90.3

15.2a Population projections by the Office for National Statistics

United Kingdom
PERSONS, thousands

Annual averages for longer-term projections

	2062 -2066	2066 -2071	2071 -2076	2076 -2081	2081 -2086	2086 -2087	2087 -2092	2092 -2102	2102 -2112
Population at start	79,904	80,855	82,114	83,455	84,831	86,193	86,463	87,808	90,554
Births	864	876	891	903	908	910	913	923	944
Deaths	792	789	788	793	801	806	809	814	831
Natural change	73	87	103	110	107	105	104	110	113
Net migration	165	165	165	165	165	165	165	165	165
Total change	238	252	268	275	272	270	269	275	278
Population at end	80,855	82,114	83,455	84,831	86,193	86,463	87,808	90,554	93,332
Annual growth rate	0.30%	0.31%	0.32%	0.33%	0.32%	0.31%	0.31%	0.31%	0.30%
Total fertility rate (TFR)	1.89	1.89	1.89	1.89	1.89	1.89	1.89	1.89	1.89
EOLB Males	87.5	88.1	88.7	89.4	90.0	90.4	90.7	91.7	92.9
Females	90.5	91.1	91.7	92.2	92.8	93.2	93.5	94.4	95.6

Note: Figures may not add exactly due to rounding.

* Children under 16. Working age and pensionable age populations based on state pension age (SPA) for given year.
Between 2012 and 2018, SPA will change from 65 years for men and 61 years for women, to 65 years for both sexes.
Then between 2019 and 2020, SPA will change from 65 years to 66 years for both men and women. Between 2034 and 2046,
SPA will increase in two stages from 66 years to 68 years for both sexes. This is based on SPA under the 2011 Pensions Act.
** This is consistent with the age-group definitions used in ONS Labour Market Statistics.

15.2b Population projections by the Office for National Statistics

England & Wales
PERSONS, thousands

2012-based
Principal projection

Components of change (mid-year to mid-year), total fertility rate
and expectation of life at birth based on the mortality rates for the year

	2012 -2013	2013 -2014	2014 -2015	2015 -2016	2016 -2017	2017 -2018	2018 -2019	2019 -2020	2020 -2021	2021 -2022	2022 -2023	2023 -2024	2024 -2025	2025 -2026	2026 -2027	2027 -2028
Population at start	56,558	56,927	57,323	57,721	58,139	58,546	58,956	59,355	59,751	60,143	60,531	60,913	61,289	61,658	62,019	62,372
Births	718	725	727	730	732	732	733	732	731	729	727	726	724	722	720	718
Deaths	511	482	481	481	481	482	483	485	488	491	495	499	504	510	516	523
Natural change	207	244	247	249	251	251	249	247	243	238	233	226	219	212	204	195
Net migration	152	153	151	170	157	159	150	150	150	150	150	150	150	150	150	150
Total change	359	396	398	419	407	410	399	396	392	388	382	376	369	361	353	345
Population at end	56,927	57,323	57,721	58,139	58,546	58,956	59,355	59,751	60,143	60,531	60,913	61,289	61,658	62,019	62,372	62,717
Annual growth rate	0.63%	0.70%	0.69%	0.73%	0.70%	0.70%	0.68%	0.67%	0.66%	0.64%	0.63%	0.62%	0.60%	0.59%	0.57%	0.55%
Total fertility rate (TFR)	1.90	1.91	1.91	1.91	1.91	1.91	1.90	1.90	1.90	1.90	1.90	1.90	1.90	1.90	1.90	1.90
EOLB Males	78.9	79.7	80.0	80.3	80.5	80.8	81.1	81.3	81.5	81.8	82.0	82.2	82.4	82.6	82.8	82.9
Females	82.6	83.4	83.7	83.9	84.1	84.4	84.6	84.8	85.0	85.2	85.4	85.6	85.7	85.9	86.1	86.2

2012-based
Principal projection

Components of change (mid-year to mid-year), total fertility rate
and expectation of life at birth based on the mortality rates for the year

	2028 -2029	2029 -2030	2030 -2031	2031 -2032	2032 -2033	2033 -2034	2034 -2035	2035 -2036	2036 -2037
Population at start	62,717	63,053	63,382	63,702	64,015	64,320	64,619	64,913	65,202
Births	717	716	716	716	717	719	722	726	731
Deaths	530	537	545	553	561	570	578	586	595
Natural change	187	179	171	163	156	150	144	140	136
Net migration	150	150	150	150	150	150	150	150	150
Total change	337	328	320	313	305	299	294	289	285
Population at end	63,053	63,382	63,702	64,015	64,320	64,619	64,913	65,202	65,487
Annual growth rate	0.54%	0.52%	0.51%	0.49%	0.48%	0.47%	0.45%	0.45%	0.44%
Total fertility rate (TFR)	1.90	1.90	1.90	1.90	1.90	1.90	1.90	1.90	1.90
EOLB Males	83.1	83.3	83.4	83.6	83.7	83.9	84.0	84.1	84.3
Females	86.4	86.6	86.7	86.8	87.0	87.1	87.2	87.4	87.5

Annual averages for
longer-term projections

	2037 -2041	2041 -2046	2046 -2051	2051 -2056	2056 -2061	2061 -2062
Population at start	65,487	66,606	67,971	69,270	70,477	71,616
Births	744	765	776	777	777	779
Deaths	613	642	666	685	698	703
Natural change	130	123	110	92	78	76
Net migration	150	150	150	150	150	150
Total change	280	273	260	241	228	225
Population at end	66,606	67,971	69,270	70,477	71,616	71,842
Annual growth rate	0.42%	0.41%	0.38%	0.35%	0.32%	0.31%
Total fertility rate (TFR)	1.90	1.90	1.90	1.90	1.90	1.90
EOLB Males	84.6	85.1	85.8	86.4	87.0	87.4
Females	87.8	88.3	88.9	89.5	90.1	90.4

15.2b Population projections by the Office for National Statistics

England & Wales
PERSONS, thousands

Annual averages for longer-term projections

	2062 -2066	2066 -2071	2071 -2076	2076 -2081	2081 -2086	2086 -2087	2087 -2092	2092 -2102	2102 -2112
Population at start	71,842	72,757	73,965	75,247	76,560	77,860	78,118	79,402	82,019
Births	783	794	809	820	825	828	830	841	861
Deaths	703	702	702	707	715	720	723	729	746
Natural change	79	92	107	113	111	108	107	112	115
Net migration	150	150	150	150	150	150	150	150	150
Total change	229	242	256	263	260	257	257	262	264
Population at end	72,757	73,965	75,247	76,560	77,860	78,118	79,402	82,019	84,659
Annual growth rate	0.32%	0.33%	0.34%	0.35%	0.34%	0.33%	0.33%	0.32%	0.32%
Total fertility rate (TFR)	1.90	1.90	1.90	1.90	1.90	1.90	1.90	1.90	1.90
EOLB Males	87.7	88.3	88.9	89.5	90.1	90.5	90.9	91.8	93.1
Females	90.7	91.2	91.8	92.4	93.0	93.3	93.7	94.6	95.7

Note: Figures may not add exactly due to rounding.
* Children under 16. Working age and pensionable age populations based on state pension age (SPA) for given year.
Between 2012 and 2018, SPA will change from 65 years for men and 61 years for women, to 65 years for both sexes.
Then between 2019 and 2020, SPA will change from 65 years to 66 years for both men and women. Between 2034 and 2046,
SPA will increase in two stages from 66 years to 68 years for both sexes. This is based on SPA under the 2011 Pensions Act.
** This is consistent with the age-group definitions used in ONS Labour Market Statistics.

15.2c Population projections by the Office for National Statistics

Scotland
PERSONS, thousands

2012-based
Principal projection

Components of change (mid-year to mid-year), total fertility rate and expectation of life at birth based on the mortality rates for the year

	2012 -2013	2013 -2014	2014 -2015	2015 -2016	2016 -2017	2017 -2018	2018 -2019	2019 -2020	2020 -2021	2021 -2022	2022 -2023	2023 -2024	2024 -2025	2025 -2026	2026 -2027	2027 -2028
Population at start	5,314	5,328	5,346	5,365	5,386	5,407	5,429	5,452	5,474	5,497	5,520	5,542	5,564	5,585	5,606	5,626
Births	57	57	58	59	59	60	60	60	60	61	61	61	60	60	60	60
Deaths	56	53	53	53	53	53	53	53	53	54	54	54	55	55	56	56
Natural change	1	5	5	6	6	7	7	7	7	7	7	6	6	5	5	4
Net migration	13	14	14	14	15	15	16	16	16	16	16	16	16	16	16	16
Total change	14	18	19	20	21	22	23	23	23	23	22	22	21	21	20	19
Population at end	5,328	5,346	5,365	5,386	5,407	5,429	5,452	5,474	5,497	5,520	5,542	5,564	5,585	5,606	5,626	5,645
Annual growth rate	0.27%	0.34%	0.36%	0.38%	0.40%	0.41%	0.42%	0.42%	0.41%	0.41%	0.40%	0.39%	0.38%	0.37%	0.36%	0.34%
Total fertility rate (TFR)	1.64	1.64	1.65	1.67	1.68	1.68	1.69	1.69	1.70	1.70	1.71	1.71	1.72	1.73	1.73	1.74
EOLB Males	76.5	77.2	77.5	77.7	78.0	78.3	78.5	78.8	79.0	79.3	79.5	79.7	79.9	80.1	80.3	80.5
Females	80.4	81.4	81.6	81.8	82.1	82.3	82.5	82.7	82.9	83.1	83.3	83.5	83.6	83.8	84.0	84.1

2012-based
Principal projection

Annual averages for longer-term projections

Components of change (mid-year to mid-year), total fertility rate and expectation of life at birth based on the mortality rates for the year

	2028 -2029	2029 -2030	2030 -2031	2031 -2032	2032 -2033	2033 -2034	2034 -2035	2035 -2036	2036 -2037	2037 -2041	2041 -2046	2046 -2051	2051 -2056	2056 -2061	2061 -2062
Population at start	5,645	5,664	5,681	5,698	5,714	5,728	5,742	5,756	5,768	5,780	5,826	5,877	5,925	5,972	6,019
Births	60	59	59	59	58	58	58	58	58	59	60	61	61	61	61
Deaths	57	57	58	58	59	60	60	61	62	63	65	67	67	67	67
Natural change	3	2	1	0	-1	-2	-2	-3	-3	-4	-5	-6	-6	-6	-6
Net migration	16	16	16	16	16	16	16	16	16	16	16	16	16	16	16
Total change	18	18	17	16	15	14	13	13	12	11	10	10	9	9	10
Population at end	5,664	5,681	5,698	5,714	5,728	5,742	5,756	5,768	5,780	5,826	5,877	5,925	5,972	6,019	6,029
Annual growth rate	0.33%	0.31%	0.29%	0.28%	0.26%	0.24%	0.23%	0.22%	0.21%	0.19%	0.18%	0.16%	0.16%	0.16%	0.16%
Total fertility rate (TFR)	1.74	1.75	1.75	1.75	1.75	1.75	1.75	1.75	1.75	1.75	1.75	1.75	1.75	1.75	1.75
EOLB Males	80.7	80.8	81.0	81.2	81.3	81.5	81.6	81.8	81.9	82.2	82.9	83.6	84.2	84.9	85.3
Females	84.3	84.5	84.6	84.8	84.9	85.0	85.2	85.3	85.4	85.8	86.3	86.9	87.6	88.2	88.6

15.2c Population projections by the Office for National Statistics

Scotland
PERSONS, thousands

Annual averages for longer-term projections

	2062 -2066	2066 -2071	2071 -2076	2076 -2081	2081 -2086	2086 -2087	2087 -2092	2092 -2102	2102 -2112
Population at start	6,029	6,069	6,126	6,188	6,254	6,319	6,332	6,396	6,532
Births	61	61	61	62	62	62	62	62	63
Deaths	66	65	64	64	65	65	65	64	64
Natural change	-5	-4	-3	-2	-2	-3	-3	-2	-1
Net migration	16	16	16	16	16	16	16	16	16
Total change	10	11	13	13	13	13	13	14	14
Population at end	6,069	6,126	6,188	6,254	6,319	6,332	6,396	6,532	6,674
Annual growth rate	0.17%	0.19%	0.20%	0.21%	0.21%	0.20%	0.20%	0.21%	0.22%
Total fertility rate (TFR)	1.75	1.75	1.75	1.75	1.75	1.75	1.75	1.75	1.75
EOLB Males	85.7	86.3	86.9	87.6	88.3	88.7	89.1	90.1	91.4
Females	88.9	89.4	90.0	90.7	91.3	91.7	92.0	93.0	94.2

Note: Figures may not add exactly due to rounding.
* Children under 16. Working age and pensionable age populations based on state pension age (SPA) for given year
Between 2012 and 2018, SPA will change from 65 years for men and 61 years for women, to 65 years for both sexes.
Then between 2019 and 2020, SPA will change from 65 years to 66 years for both men and women. Between 2034 and 2046,
SPA will increase in two stages from 66 years to 68 years for both sexes. This is based on SPA under the 2011 Pensions Act.
** This is consistent with the age-group definitions used in ONS Labour Market Statistics.

15.2d Population projections by the Office for National Statistics

Northern Ireland
PERSONS, thousands

2012-based
Principal projection

Components of change (mid-year to mid-year), total fertility rate
and expectation of life at birth based on the mortality rates for the year

	2012 -2013	2013 -2014	2014 -2015	2015 -2016	2016 -2017	2017 -2018	2018 -2019	2019 -2020	2020 -2021	2021 -2022	2022 -2023	2023 -2024	2024 -2025	2025 -2026	2026 -2027	2027 -2028
Population at start	1,824	1,832	1,842	1,852	1,861	1,871	1,881	1,891	1,900	1,910	1,918	1,927	1,935	1,943	1,950	1,957
Births	25	25	25	25	25	24	24	24	24	24	24	23	23	23	23	22
Deaths	15	14	14	14	14	14	15	15	15	15	15	15	15	16	16	16
Natural change	10	10	10	10	10	10	10	10	9	9	8	8	8	7	7	6
Net migration	-1	-1	-1	-0	-0	-0	0	0	0	0	0	0	0	0	0	0
Total change	9	10	10	10	10	10	10	10	9	9	8	8	8	7	7	6
Population at end	1,832	1,842	1,852	1,861	1,871	1,881	1,891	1,900	1,910	1,918	1,927	1,935	1,943	1,950	1,957	1,963
Annual growth rate	0.48%	0.52%	0.52%	0.53%	0.53%	0.53%	0.52%	0.50%	0.49%	0.46%	0.44%	0.42%	0.40%	0.37%	0.35%	0.33%
Total fertility rate (TFR)	1.98	1.98	1.99	1.99	2.00	2.00	2.00	2.00	2.00	2.00	2.00	2.00	2.00	2.00	2.00	2.00
EOLB Males	77.9	78.5	78.8	79.1	79.4	79.7	79.9	80.2	80.4	80.7	80.9	81.1	81.3	81.5	81.7	81.9
Females	81.9	82.7	82.9	83.2	83.4	83.6	83.8	84.0	84.2	84.4	84.6	84.8	85.0	85.2	85.4	85.5

2012-based
Principal projection

Components of change (mid-year to mid-year), total fertility rate
and expectation of life at birth based on the mortality rates for the year

Annual averages for longer-term projections

	2028 -2029	2029 -2030	2030 -2031	2031 -2032	2032 -2033	2033 -2034	2034 -2035	2035 -2036	2036 -2037	2037 -2041	2041 -2046	2046 -2051	2051 -2056	2056 -2061	2061 -2062
Population at start	1,963	1,969	1,975	1,980	1,985	1,989	1,993	1,997	2,001	2,005	2,018	2,032	2,039	2,040	2,035
Births	22	22	22	22	22	22	22	22	22	22	23	23	22	21	21
Deaths	16	17	17	17	17	18	18	18	18	19	20	21	22	22	23
Natural change	6	6	5	5	4	4	4	4	4	3	3	2	0	-1	-1
Net migration	0	0	0	0	0	0	0	0	0	0	0	0	0	0	0
Total change	6	6	5	5	4	4	4	4	4	3	3	2	0	-1	-1
Population at end	1,969	1,975	1,980	1,985	1,989	1,993	1,997	2,001	2,005	2,018	2,032	2,039	2,040	2,035	2,034
Annual growth rate	0.30%	0.28%	0.26%	0.24%	0.23%	0.21%	0.20%	0.19%	0.18%	0.17%	0.14%	0.08%	0.01%	-0.05%	-0.07%
Total fertility rate (TFR)	2.00	2.00	2.00	2.00	2.00	2.00	2.00	2.00	2.00	2.00	2.00	2.00	2.00	2.00	2.00
EOLB Males	82.1	82.2	82.4	82.6	82.7	82.9	83.0	83.1	83.3	83.6	84.2	84.8	85.5	86.1	86.5
Females	85.7	85.8	86.0	86.1	86.3	86.4	86.5	86.7	86.8	87.1	87.6	88.2	88.8	89.4	89.8

15.2d Population projections by the Office for National Statistics

Northern Ireland
PERSONS, thousands

	2062 -2066	2066 -2071	2071 -2076	2076 -2081	2081 -2086	2086 -2087	2087 -2092	2092 -2102	2102 -2112
Population at start	2,034	2,028	2,023	2,020	2,017	2,014	2,014	2,010	2,004
Births	21	21	21	21	21	21	20	20	20
Deaths	22	22	22	22	22	21	21	21	21
Natural change	-1	-1	-1	-0	-1	-1	-1	-1	-1
Net migration	0	0	0	0	0	0	0	0	0
Total change	-1	-1	-1	-0	-1	-1	-1	-1	-1
Population at end	2,028	2,023	2,020	2,017	2,014	2,014	2,010	2,004	1,998
Annual growth rate	-0.07%	-0.05%	-0.03%	-0.02%	-0.03%	-0.04%	-0.04%	-0.03%	-0.03%
Total fertility rate (TFR)	2.00	2.00	2.00	2.00	2.00	2.00	2.00	2.00	2.00
EOLB Males	86.9	87.4	88.1	88.7	89.4	89.8	90.2	91.1	92.4
Females	90.1	90.6	91.2	91.8	92.4	92.7	93.1	94.0	95.1

Note: Figures may not add exactly due to rounding.

* Children under 16. Working age and pensionable age populations based on state pension age (SPA) for given year.
Between 2012 and 2018, SPA will change from 65 years for men and 61 years for women, to 65 years for both sexes.
Then between 2019 and 2020, SPA will change from 65 years to 66 years for both men and women. Between 2034 and 2046,
SPA will increase in two stages from 66 years to 68 years for both sexes. This is based on SPA under the 2011 Pensions Act.

** This is consistent with the age-group definitions used in ONS Labour Market Statistics.

15.3a Mid-2012 Population Estimates: United Kingdom; estimated resident population by single year of age and sex

Thousands

Age	Persons	Males	Females	Age	Persons	Males	Females
All ages	63,705.0	31,315.1	32,390.0				
0-4	3,996.4	2,045.2	1,951.2	45-49	4,685.7	2,312.8	2,372.9
0	816.0	418.1	397.9	45	939.2	465.1	474.2
1	806.7	413.1	393.6	46	939.1	462.7	476.3
2	793.3	405.5	387.7	47	947.5	467.1	480.4
3	786.4	402.1	384.3	48	939.2	463.1	476.1
4	794.0	406.5	387.6	49	920.8	454.8	465.9
5-9	3,641.0	1,864.2	1,776.8	50-54	4,235.8	2,097.9	2,137.9
5	767.9	393.4	374.4	50	901.5	446.6	454.9
6	752.1	384.6	367.5	51	872.2	432.0	440.1
7	722.5	369.7	352.8	52	838.0	415.0	423.1
8	709.6	363.4	346.2	53	821.0	406.5	414.5
9	689.0	353.1	335.9	54	803.1	397.7	405.3
10-14	3,576.4	1,831.3	1,745.0	55-59	3,684.2	1,819.8	1,864.4
10	677.9	347.2	330.7	55	774.8	383.3	391.5
11	696.5	355.8	340.7	56	748.3	370.4	377.9
12	715.3	366.8	348.5	57	721.6	356.4	365.1
13	738.3	378.2	360.1	58	724.0	356.8	367.2
14	748.4	383.4	365.1	59	715.5	352.8	362.6
15-19	3,926.6	2,013.2	1,913.3	60-64	3,624.4	1,776.2	1,848.2
15	769.8	394.4	375.4	60	695.8	341.9	353.9
16	769.3	396.8	372.6	61	701.8	344.5	357.3
17	771.3	396.1	375.2	62	716.4	350.5	365.9
18	802.0	411.3	390.7	63	735.3	360.3	375.0
19	814.0	414.6	399.4	64	775.1	379.0	396.2
20-24	4,332.2	2,191.5	2,140.7	65-69	3,345.1	1,626.0	1,719.0
20	848.8	428.4	420.4	65	840.0	410.9	429.1
21	875.6	446.5	429.1	66	650.8	317.3	333.5
22	867.3	442.3	425.0	67	632.1	306.9	325.2
23	864.7	436.0	428.7	68	631.6	306.7	324.9
24	875.9	438.4	437.5	69	590.5	284.3	306.3
25-29	4,317.8	2,152.1	2,165.8	70-74	2,475.9	1,170.2	1,305.8
25	858.1	425.7	432.4	70	530.1	253.2	276.8
26	868.0	434.9	433.0	71	479.3	227.0	252.3
27	873.2	437.0	436.2	72	496.2	234.5	261.7
28	854.4	425.5	428.9	73	491.8	231.2	260.6
29	864.2	428.9	435.3	74	478.5	224.2	254.3
30-34	4,239.9	2,109.2	2,130.7	75-79	2,046.9	928.8	1,118.1
30	865.7	428.6	437.1	75	455.0	211.0	244.0
31	874.1	434.2	439.9	76	433.3	198.6	234.7
32	875.7	435.4	440.2	77	412.2	187.3	224.9
33	840.1	419.3	420.8	78	382.4	171.3	211.1
34	784.3	391.6	392.7	79	363.9	160.5	203.4
35-39	4,036.4	2,008.7	2,027.7	80-84	1,533.7	637.5	896.1
35	772.4	386.5	385.9	80	353.5	153.4	200.1
36	787.9	392.2	395.7	81	335.3	142.3	193.1
37	803.2	399.5	403.7	82	310.9	128.3	182.6
38	817.8	405.9	412.0	83	281.3	113.9	167.3
39	854.9	424.6	430.3	84	252.7	99.7	153.0
40-44	4,567.3	2,253.7	2,313.6	85-89	925.9	335.6	590.4
40	892.5	442.7	449.8	85	230.8	89.4	141.3
41	922.4	454.3	468.1	86	208.6	78.2	130.4
42	901.8	444.7	457.1	87	183.9	66.2	117.7
43	924.9	455.6	469.2	88	162.2	55.8	106.3
44	925.7	456.4	469.3	89	140.6	46.0	94.6
				90 and over	513.4	141.2	372.3

Note: Figures may not add exactly due to rounding.

Sources: Office for National Statistics, National Records of Scotland, Northern Ireland Statistics and Research Agency.

15.3b Population projections by the Office for National Statistics

United Kingdom

PERSONS, thousands

2012-based

Principal projection

Projected populations at mid-years by age last birthday

Ages	2012	2013	2014	2015	2016	2017	2018	2019	2020	2021	2022	2023	2024	2025	2026	2027	2028	2029	2030	2031	2032
Thousands																					
0-14	11,214	11,278	11,360	11,466	11,599	11,748	11,887	12,002	12,103	12,172	12,223	12,244	12,270	12,285	12,283	12,268	12,270	12,262	12,250	12,234	12,217
15-29	12,577	12,588	12,596	12,558	12,510	12,442	12,360	12,293	12,223	12,160	12,129	12,147	12,159	12,203	12,261	12,325	12,391	12,473	12,581	12,709	12,857
30-44	12,844	12,778	12,711	12,693	12,663	12,658	12,719	12,819	12,951	13,122	13,295	13,433	13,516	13,538	13,562	13,596	13,609	13,618	13,581	13,526	13,457
45-59	12,606	12,775	12,940	13,087	13,231	13,321	13,347	13,322	13,267	13,166	13,023	12,876	12,768	12,691	12,624	12,551	12,495	12,437	12,426	12,397	12,396
60-74	9,445	9,562	9,688	9,813	9,985	10,140	10,271	10,388	10,524	10,680	10,705	10,810	10,971	11,159	11,354	11,556	11,730	11,897	12,045	12,190	12,284
75 & over	5,020	5,106	5,216	5,319	5,399	5,517	5,682	5,874	6,058	6,249	6,595	6,872	7,104	7,309	7,491	7,657	7,830	7,999	8,155	8,324	8,503
All ages	63,705	64,087	64,511	64,938	65,386	65,825	66,266	66,697	67,126	67,550	67,969	68,382	68,788	69,186	69,575	69,955	70,325	70,686	71,037	71,380	71,713
Percentages																					
0-14	17.6	17.6	17.6	17.7	17.7	17.8	17.9	18.0	18.0	18.0	18.0	17.9	17.8	17.8	17.7	17.5	17.4	17.3	17.2	17.1	17.0
15-29	19.7	19.6	19.5	19.3	19.1	18.9	18.7	18.4	18.2	18.0	17.8	17.8	17.7	17.6	17.6	17.6	17.6	17.6	17.7	17.8	17.9
30-44	20.2	19.9	19.7	19.5	19.4	19.2	19.2	19.2	19.3	19.4	19.6	19.6	19.6	19.6	19.5	19.4	19.4	19.3	19.1	18.9	18.8
45-59	19.8	19.9	20.1	20.2	20.2	20.2	20.1	20.0	19.8	19.5	19.2	18.8	18.6	18.3	18.1	17.9	17.8	17.6	17.5	17.4	17.3
60-74	14.8	14.9	15.0	15.1	15.3	15.4	15.5	15.6	15.7	15.8	15.7	15.8	15.9	16.1	16.3	16.5	16.7	16.8	17.0	17.1	17.1
75 & over	7.9	8.0	8.1	8.2	8.3	8.4	8.6	8.8	9.0	9.3	9.7	10.0	10.3	10.6	10.8	10.9	11.1	11.3	11.5	11.7	11.9
All ages	100.0	100.0	100.0	100.0	100.0	100.0	100.0	100.0	100.0	100.0	100.0	100.0	100.0	100.0	100.0	100.0	100.0	100.0	100.0	100.0	100.0
Mean age	40.1	40.2	40.3	40.4	40.5	40.7	40.8	41.0	41.1	41.2	41.4	41.5	41.7	41.8	42.0	42.1	42.3	42.4	42.6	42.7	42.8
Median age	39.7	39.9	40.0	40.0	40.1	40.1	40.1	40.2	40.4	40.5	40.6	40.8	40.9	41.0	41.2	41.3	41.5	41.6	41.8	41.9	42.1

15.3b Population projections by the Office for National Statistics

United Kingdom
PERSONS, thousands

Ages	Projected populations at mid-years by age last birthday											Annual averages for longer-term projections								
	2033	2034	2035	2036	2037	2041	2046	2051	2056	2061	2062	2066	2071	2076	2081	2086	2087	2092	2102	2112
Thousands																				
0-14	12,198	12,182	12,169	12,161	12,159	12,228	12,472	12,768	12,960	13,018	13,021	13,040	13,120	13,282	13,479	13,644	13,669	13,765	13,934	14,216
15-29	12,993	13,109	13,210	13,279	13,330	13,392	13,345	13,272	13,341	13,586	13,647	13,883	14,075	14,134	14,158	14,239	14,265	14,440	14,790	14,959
30-44	13,373	13,309	13,240	13,180	13,151	13,288	13,740	14,311	14,427	14,384	14,368	14,317	14,389	14,638	14,937	15,132	15,153	15,198	15,332	15,707
45-59	12,458	12,560	12,693	12,863	13,035	13,308	13,285	12,960	13,084	13,544	13,691	14,116	14,243	14,212	14,157	14,240	14,279	14,559	15,026	15,120
60-74	12,318	12,303	12,260	12,175	12,052	11,737	11,600	12,093	12,545	12,555	12,497	12,285	12,458	12,939	13,514	13,667	13,664	13,663	13,808	14,420
75 & over	8,695	8,892	9,093	9,312	9,546	10,497	11,438	11,830	12,132	12,584	12,680	13,213	13,828	14,250	14,587	15,272	15,432	16,183	17,665	18,909
All ages	72,037	72,355	72,666	72,971	73,272	74,450	75,879	77,234	78,489	79,671	79,904	80,855	82,114	83,455	84,831	86,193	86,463	87,808	90,554	93,332
Percentages																				
0-14	16.9	16.8	16.7	16.7	16.6	16.4	16.4	16.5	16.5	16.3	16.3	16.1	16.0	15.9	15.9	15.8	15.8	15.7	15.4	15.2
15-29	18.0	18.1	18.2	18.2	18.2	18.0	17.6	17.2	17.0	17.1	17.1	17.2	17.1	16.9	16.7	16.5	16.5	16.4	16.3	16.0
30-44	18.6	18.4	18.2	18.1	17.9	17.8	18.1	18.5	18.4	18.1	18.0	17.7	17.5	17.5	17.6	17.6	17.5	17.3	16.9	16.8
45-59	17.3	17.4	17.5	17.6	17.8	17.9	17.5	16.8	16.7	17.0	17.1	17.5	17.3	17.0	16.7	16.5	16.5	16.6	16.6	16.2
60-74	17.1	17.0	16.9	16.7	16.4	15.8	15.3	15.7	16.0	15.8	15.6	15.2	15.2	15.5	15.9	15.9	15.8	15.6	15.2	15.5
75 & over	12.1	12.3	12.5	12.8	13.0	14.1	15.1	15.3	15.5	15.8	15.9	16.3	16.8	17.1	17.2	17.7	17.8	18.4	19.5	20.3
All ages	100.0	100.0	100.0	100.0	100.0	100.0	100.0	100.0	100.0	100.0	100.0	100.0	100.0	100.0	100.0	100.0	100.0	100.0	100.0	100.0
Mean age	43.0	43.1	43.2	43.3	43.4	43.8	44.1	44.4	44.6	44.9	44.9	45.1	45.4	45.6	45.9	46.2	46.2	46.5	47.1	47.7
Median age	42.3	42.4	42.6	42.7	42.8	43.1	43.0	43.1	43.4	43.8	43.9	44.2	44.4	44.7	44.8	45.1	45.1	45.5	46.2	46.7

Note: Figures may not add exactly due to rounding.
* Children under 16. Working age and pensionable age populations based on state pension age (SPA) for given year.
Between 2012 and 2018, SPA will change from 65 years for men and 61 years for women, to 65 years for both sexes.
Then between 2019 and 2020, SPA will change from 65 years to 66 years for both men and women. Between 2034 and 2046,
SPA will increase in two stages from 66 years to 68 years for both sexes. This is based on SPA under the 2011 Pensions Act.
** This is consistent with the age-group definitions used in ONS Labour Market Statistics.

15.3b Population projections by the Office for National Statistics

United Kingdom
MALES, thousands

2012-based
Principal projection

Projected populations at mid-years by age last birthday

Ages	2012	2013	2014	2015	2016	2017	2018	2019	2020	2021	2022	2023	2024	2025	2026	2027	2028	2029	2030	2031	2032
Thousands																					
0-14	5,741	5,774	5,816	5,871	5,940	6,016	6,087	6,147	6,199	6,235	6,261	6,272	6,286	6,295	6,294	6,286	6,287	6,283	6,277	6,269	6,260
15-29	6,357	6,380	6,399	6,393	6,380	6,360	6,330	6,302	6,267	6,236	6,227	6,238	6,244	6,266	6,293	6,327	6,361	6,403	6,458	6,525	6,601
30-44	6,371	6,340	6,310	6,307	6,302	6,302	6,340	6,401	6,483	6,585	6,680	6,763	6,820	6,850	6,882	6,918	6,943	6,962	6,957	6,939	6,919
45-59	6,231	6,309	6,386	6,453	6,518	6,559	6,570	6,555	6,526	6,475	6,405	6,333	6,283	6,246	6,214	6,175	6,149	6,124	6,125	6,121	6,123
60-74	4,572	4,630	4,692	4,754	4,840	4,916	4,980	5,036	5,103	5,178	5,191	5,242	5,319	5,410	5,504	5,602	5,685	5,763	5,832	5,899	5,944
75 &over	2,043	2,099	2,161	2,219	2,265	2,329	2,415	2,514	2,608	2,705	2,875	3,011	3,124	3,223	3,310	3,390	3,472	3,552	3,625	3,704	3,788
All ages	31,315	31,532	31,764	31,998	32,244	32,482	32,722	32,955	33,186	33,414	33,639	33,860	34,077	34,289	34,497	34,699	34,896	35,088	35,275	35,457	35,635
Percentages																					
0-14	18.3	18.3	18.3	18.3	18.4	18.5	18.6	18.7	18.7	18.7	18.6	18.5	18.4	18.4	18.2	18.1	18.0	17.9	17.8	17.7	17.6
15-29	20.3	20.2	20.1	20.0	19.8	19.6	19.3	19.1	18.9	18.7	18.5	18.4	18.3	18.3	18.2	18.2	18.2	18.2	18.3	18.4	18.5
30-44	20.3	20.1	19.9	19.7	19.5	19.4	19.4	19.4	19.5	19.7	19.9	20.0	20.0	20.0	19.9	19.9	19.9	19.8	19.7	19.6	19.4
45-59	19.9	20.0	20.1	20.2	20.2	20.2	20.1	19.9	19.7	19.4	19.0	18.7	18.4	18.2	18.0	17.8	17.6	17.5	17.4	17.3	17.2
60-74	14.6	14.7	14.8	14.9	15.0	15.1	15.2	15.3	15.4	15.5	15.4	15.5	15.6	15.8	16.0	16.1	16.3	16.4	16.5	16.6	16.7
75 &over	6.5	6.7	6.8	6.9	7.0	7.2	7.4	7.6	7.9	8.1	8.5	8.9	9.2	9.4	9.6	9.8	10.0	10.1	10.3	10.4	10.6
All ages	100.0	100.0	100.0	100.0	100.0	100.0	100.0	100.0	100.0	100.0	100.0	100.0	100.0	100.0	100.0	100.0	100.0	100.0	100.0	100.0	100.0
Mean age	39.0	39.1	39.3	39.4	39.5	39.7	39.8	40.0	40.1	40.3	40.4	40.5	40.7	40.8	41.0	41.1	41.3	41.4	41.6	41.7	41.8
Median age	38.7	38.7	38.8	38.8	38.8	38.9	38.9	39.1	39.2	39.3	39.4	39.5	39.6	39.8	39.9	40.0	40.2	40.3	40.5	40.7	40.8

15.3b Population projections by the Office for National Statistics

United Kingdom
MALES, thousands

Projected populations at mid-years by age last birthday

Annual averages for longer-term projections

Ages	2033	2034	2035	2036	2037	2041	2046	2051	2056	2061	2062	2066	2071	2076	2081	2086	2087	2092	2102	2112
Thousands																				
0-14	6,251	6,242	6,235	6,231	6,230	6,266	6,391	6,543	6,641	6,671	6,673	6,682	6,724	6,806	6,907	6,992	7,005	7,054	7,141	7,285
15-29	6,671	6,730	6,783	6,819	6,845	6,879	6,855	6,818	6,853	6,979	7,011	7,132	7,230	7,261	7,273	7,315	7,328	7,418	7,597	7,685
30-44	6,887	6,861	6,827	6,798	6,789	6,860	7,094	7,388	7,451	7,430	7,421	7,396	7,434	7,562	7,716	7,816	7,827	7,851	7,920	8,113
45-59	6,162	6,224	6,306	6,407	6,502	6,706	6,769	6,640	6,711	6,951	7,026	7,246	7,315	7,301	7,275	7,319	7,340	7,485	7,726	7,778
60-74	5,960	5,951	5,930	5,888	5,830	5,687	5,645	5,944	6,243	6,321	6,306	6,222	6,321	6,573	6,869	6,954	6,953	6,958	7,041	7,360
75 &over	3,878	3,970	4,063	4,165	4,274	4,711	5,139	5,314	5,457	5,686	5,736	6,043	6,414	6,681	6,895	7,272	7,359	7,760	8,528	9,163
All ages	35,808	35,977	36,144	36,308	36,470	37,108	37,893	38,647	39,357	40,037	40,172	40,721	41,437	42,185	42,936	43,668	43,812	44,525	45,954	47,384
Percentages																				
0-14	17.5	17.4	17.3	17.2	17.1	16.9	16.9	16.9	16.9	16.7	16.6	16.4	16.2	16.1	16.1	16.0	16.0	15.8	15.5	15.4
15-29	18.6	18.7	18.8	18.8	18.8	18.5	18.1	17.6	17.4	17.4	17.5	17.5	17.4	17.2	16.9	16.8	16.7	16.7	16.5	16.2
30-44	19.2	19.1	18.9	18.7	18.6	18.5	18.7	19.1	18.9	18.6	18.5	18.2	17.9	17.9	18.0	17.9	17.9	17.6	17.2	17.1
45-59	17.2	17.3	17.4	17.6	17.8	18.1	17.9	17.2	17.1	17.4	17.5	17.8	17.7	17.3	16.9	16.8	16.8	16.8	16.8	16.4
60-74	16.6	16.5	16.4	16.2	16.0	15.3	14.9	15.4	15.9	15.8	15.7	15.3	15.3	15.6	16.0	15.9	15.9	15.6	15.3	15.5
75 &over	10.8	11.0	11.2	11.5	11.7	12.7	13.6	13.8	13.9	14.2	14.3	14.8	15.5	15.8	16.1	16.7	16.8	17.4	18.6	19.3
All ages	100.0	100.0	100.0	100.0	100.0	100.0	100.0	100.0	100.0	100.0	100.0	100.0	100.0	100.0	100.0	100.0	100.0	100.0	100.0	100.0
Mean age	41.9	42.1	42.2	42.3	42.4	42.8	43.1	43.4	43.7	43.9	44.0	44.2	44.6	44.9	45.2	45.5	45.6	45.9	46.6	47.2
Median age	41.0	41.1	41.3	41.4	41.5	41.8	41.7	42.0	42.4	42.9	42.9	43.3	43.6	43.9	44.1	44.4	44.5	44.9	45.6	46.2

Note: Figures may not add exactly due to rounding.

* Children under 16. Working age and pensionable age populations based on state pension age (SPA) for given year.
Between 2012 and 2018, SPA will change from 65 years for men and 61 years for women, to 65 years for both sexes.
Then between 2019 and 2020, SPA will change from 65 years to 66 years for both men and women. Between 2034 and 2046,
SPA will increase in two stages from 66 years to 68 years for both sexes. This is based on SPA under the 2011 Pensions Act.
** This is consistent with the age-group definitions used in ONS Labour Market Statistics.

15.3b Population projections by the Office for National Statistics

United Kingdom
FEMALES, thousands

2012-based
Principal projection

Projected populations at mid-years by age last birthday

Ages	2012	2013	2014	2015	2016	2017	2018	2019	2020	2021	2022	2023	2024	2025	2026	2027	2028	2029	2030	2031	2032
Thousands																					
0-14	5,473	5,504	5,543	5,595	5,659	5,731	5,799	5,855	5,904	5,937	5,962	5,972	5,984	5,990	5,989	5,982	5,983	5,979	5,973	5,965	5,957
15-29	6,220	6,208	6,197	6,166	6,130	6,082	6,030	5,991	5,955	5,924	5,902	5,909	5,915	5,938	5,968	5,999	6,030	6,070	6,122	6,184	6,256
30-44	6,472	6,439	6,402	6,386	6,361	6,356	6,379	6,417	6,468	6,537	6,614	6,670	6,695	6,688	6,680	6,677	6,666	6,655	6,624	6,587	6,538
45-59	6,375	6,466	6,554	6,634	6,713	6,761	6,777	6,767	6,741	6,691	6,618	6,542	6,486	6,445	6,410	6,376	6,346	6,313	6,300	6,277	6,273
60-74	4,873	4,932	4,995	5,059	5,145	5,224	5,291	5,351	5,421	5,502	5,513	5,567	5,651	5,749	5,851	5,954	6,046	6,134	6,212	6,291	6,340
75 &over	2,977	3,007	3,055	3,100	3,134	3,188	3,267	3,360	3,450	3,544	3,720	3,862	3,980	4,086	4,180	4,268	4,358	4,447	4,530	4,619	4,715
All ages	32,390	32,556	32,747	32,940	33,143	33,342	33,544	33,742	33,940	34,136	34,330	34,522	34,711	34,896	35,078	35,256	35,429	35,598	35,762	35,922	36,078
Percentages																					
0-14	16.9	16.9	16.9	17.0	17.1	17.2	17.3	17.4	17.4	17.4	17.4	17.3	17.2	17.2	17.1	17.0	16.9	16.8	16.7	16.6	16.5
15-29	19.2	19.1	18.9	18.7	18.5	18.2	18.0	17.8	17.5	17.4	17.2	17.1	17.0	17.0	17.0	17.0	17.0	17.1	17.1	17.2	17.3
30-44	20.0	19.8	19.5	19.4	19.2	19.1	19.0	19.0	19.1	19.2	19.3	19.3	19.3	19.2	19.0	18.9	18.8	18.7	18.5	18.3	18.1
45-59	19.7	19.9	20.0	20.1	20.3	20.3	20.2	20.1	19.9	19.6	19.3	19.0	18.7	18.5	18.3	18.1	17.9	17.7	17.6	17.5	17.4
60-74	15.0	15.1	15.3	15.4	15.5	15.7	15.8	15.9	16.0	16.1	16.1	16.1	16.3	16.5	16.7	16.9	17.1	17.2	17.4	17.5	17.6
75 &over	9.2	9.2	9.3	9.4	9.5	9.6	9.7	10.0	10.2	10.4	10.8	11.2	11.5	11.7	11.9	12.1	12.3	12.5	12.7	12.9	13.1
All ages	100.0	100.0	100.0	100.0	100.0	100.0	100.0	100.0	100.0	100.0	100.0	100.0	100.0	100.0	100.0	100.0	100.0	100.0	100.0	100.0	100.0
Mean age	41.0	41.1	41.3	41.4	41.5	41.7	41.8	41.9	42.1	42.2	42.4	42.5	42.7	42.8	43.0	43.1	43.3	43.4	43.6	43.7	43.8
Median age	40.8	40.9	41.1	41.2	41.3	41.4	41.4	41.5	41.6	41.7	41.9	42.0	42.2	42.3	42.5	42.6	42.8	42.9	43.1	43.3	43.4

15.3b Population projections by the Office for National Statistics

United Kingdom
FEMALES, thousands

| | Projected populations at mid-years by age last birthday | | | | | | | | | | | Annual averages for longer-term projections | | | | | | | | |
Ages	2033	2034	2035	2036	2037	2041	2046	2051	2056	2061	2062	2066	2071	2076	2081	2086	2087	2092	2102	2112
Thousands																				
0-14	5,948	5,940	5,933	5,929	5,928	5,962	6,081	6,226	6,319	6,347	6,349	6,358	6,397	6,476	6,572	6,652	6,664	6,711	6,793	6,931
15-29	6,322	6,379	6,427	6,460	6,485	6,513	6,490	6,454	6,487	6,607	6,636	6,752	6,845	6,874	6,885	6,924	6,937	7,022	7,192	7,275
30-44	6,486	6,448	6,413	6,382	6,361	6,429	6,646	6,923	6,976	6,955	6,947	6,921	6,955	7,076	7,222	7,316	7,326	7,348	7,411	7,593
45-59	6,297	6,336	6,387	6,457	6,534	6,602	6,516	6,320	6,373	6,593	6,665	6,870	6,928	6,911	6,882	6,920	6,939	7,074	7,300	7,342
60-74	6,359	6,352	6,331	6,287	6,222	6,050	5,955	6,149	6,302	6,234	6,192	6,064	6,137	6,366	6,644	6,713	6,711	6,706	6,767	7,060
75 &over	4,817	4,923	5,030	5,147	5,272	5,786	6,299	6,516	6,675	6,898	6,944	7,170	7,414	7,568	7,691	7,999	8,073	8,423	9,137	9,746
All ages	36,229	36,377	36,522	36,663	36,802	37,341	37,987	38,588	39,132	39,634	39,732	40,134	40,676	41,271	41,896	42,525	42,651	43,283	44,600	45,948
Percentages																				
0-14	16.4	16.3	16.2	16.2	16.1	16.0	16.0	16.1	16.1	16.0	16.0	15.8	15.7	15.7	15.7	15.6	15.6	15.5	15.2	15.1
15-29	17.5	17.5	17.6	17.6	17.6	17.4	17.1	16.7	16.6	16.7	16.7	16.8	16.8	16.7	16.4	16.3	16.3	16.2	16.1	15.8
30-44	17.9	17.7	17.6	17.4	17.3	17.2	17.5	17.9	17.8	17.5	17.5	17.2	17.1	17.1	17.2	17.2	17.2	17.0	16.6	16.5
45-59	17.4	17.4	17.5	17.6	17.8	17.7	17.2	16.4	16.3	16.6	16.8	17.1	17.0	16.7	16.4	16.3	16.3	16.3	16.4	16.0
60-74	17.6	17.5	17.3	17.1	16.9	16.2	15.7	15.9	16.1	15.7	15.6	15.1	15.1	15.4	15.9	15.8	15.7	15.5	15.2	15.4
75 &over	13.3	13.5	13.8	14.0	14.3	15.5	16.6	16.9	17.1	17.4	17.5	17.9	18.2	18.3	18.4	18.8	18.9	19.5	20.5	21.2
All ages	100.0	100.0	100.0	100.0	100.0	100.0	100.0	100.0	100.0	100.0	100.0	100.0	100.0	100.0	100.0	100.0	100.0	100.0	100.0	100.0
Mean age	44.0	44.1	44.2	44.4	44.5	44.8	45.2	45.4	45.6	45.8	45.8	46.0	46.2	46.4	46.6	46.8	46.9	47.1	47.7	48.3
Median age	43.6	43.7	43.9	44.0	44.2	44.5	44.4	44.3	44.5	44.8	44.9	45.1	45.3	45.5	45.6	45.8	45.8	46.1	46.8	47.4

Note: Figures may not add exactly due to rounding.

* Children under 16. Working age and pensionable age populations based on state pension age (SPA) for given year.
Between 2012 and 2018, SPA will change from 65 years for men and 61 years for women, to 65 years for both sexes.
Then between 2019 and 2020, SPA will change from 65 years to 66 years for both men and women. Between 2034 and 2046,
SPA will increase in two stages from 66 years to 68 years for both sexes. This is based on SPA under the 2011 Pensions Act.

** This is consistent with the age-group definitions used in ONS Labour Market Statistics.

15.3c Mid-2012 Population Estimates: England and Wales; estimated resident population by single year of age and sex.

Thousands

Age	Persons	Males	Females	Age	Persons	Males	Females
All ages	**56,567.8**	**27,843.4**	**28,724.4**				
0-4	**3,573.2**	**1,829.1**	**1,744.1**	**45-49**	**4,142.3**	**2,047.6**	**2,094.7**
0	732.0	374.9	357.1	45	831.5	412.4	419.1
1	720.6	369.1	351.5	46	831.8	410.5	421.3
2	710.2	363.3	347.0	47	836.9	413.1	423.8
3	701.3	358.7	342.6	48	829.9	410.0	419.8
4	709.1	363.1	346.0	49	812.3	401.7	410.6
5-9	**3,251.1**	**1,664.4**	**1,586.8**	**50-54**	**3,730.5**	**1,850.1**	**1,880.4**
5	686.5	351.8	334.8	50	795.6	394.6	401.0
6	673.0	344.2	328.8	51	768.4	381.2	387.2
7	644.4	329.5	314.9	52	738.0	365.8	372.2
8	632.8	323.8	309.0	53	722.1	358.1	363.9
9	614.4	315.1	299.3	54	706.4	350.4	356.0
10-14	**3,179.1**	**1,627.8**	**1,551.3**	**55-59**	**3,242.1**	**1,602.2**	**1,639.9**
10	603.3	309.2	294.1	55	680.8	337.1	343.7
11	619.5	316.6	303.0	56	657.4	325.7	331.8
12	636.1	325.9	310.2	57	634.6	313.6	320.9
13	655.8	335.9	320.0	58	638.0	314.3	323.7
14	664.4	340.3	324.1	59	631.2	311.4	319.8
15-19	**3,482.6**	**1,786.4**	**1,696.2**	**60-64**	**3,208.4**	**1,572.3**	**1,636.0**
15	683.3	350.0	333.3	60	614.5	301.9	312.5
16	683.3	352.3	331.0	61	619.6	304.2	315.4
17	684.2	351.3	332.9	62	634.0	310.0	324.1
18	711.1	365.0	346.1	63	651.2	319.2	332.0
19	720.7	367.8	352.9	64	689.1	337.0	352.1
20-24	**3,837.7**	**1,944.1**	**1,893.6**	**65-69**	**2,973.3**	**1,447.3**	**1,526.0**
20	750.2	379.1	371.1	65	748.2	366.5	381.8
21	774.6	395.8	378.8	66	578.1	281.9	296.2
22	768.6	392.9	375.8	67	562.7	273.7	289.0
23	766.8	387.0	379.8	68	561.4	272.9	288.5
24	777.4	389.3	388.1	69	522.9	252.3	270.5
25-29	**3,845.7**	**1,919.7**	**1,926.0**	**70-74**	**2,189.4**	**1,038.2**	**1,151.2**
25	762.0	378.2	383.7	70	468.2	224.3	243.9
26	772.4	387.6	384.9	71	422.4	200.7	221.7
27	778.0	390.2	387.9	72	438.9	208.2	230.7
28	762.1	380.2	381.9	73	435.6	205.5	230.1
29	771.1	383.5	387.6	74	424.2	199.4	224.8
30-34	**3,784.9**	**1,886.5**	**1,898.4**	**75-79**	**1,814.5**	**827.6**	**986.9**
30	771.5	382.8	388.8	75	403.2	188.0	215.3
31	779.8	388.0	391.8	76	383.9	176.9	207.0
32	782.7	389.9	392.8	77	365.4	166.9	198.5
33	750.6	375.3	375.4	78	339.0	152.6	186.4
34	700.2	350.6	349.7	79	323.1	143.2	179.8
35-39	**3,596.1**	**1,792.7**	**1,803.4**	**80-84**	**1,367.8**	**572.0**	**795.8**
35	689.8	345.8	344.0	80	313.9	137.1	176.9
36	701.4	349.7	351.7	81	298.7	127.4	171.3
37	715.6	356.8	358.9	82	277.8	115.4	162.4
38	728.5	362.0	366.5	83	251.1	102.3	148.8
39	760.8	378.4	382.3	84	226.2	89.8	136.4
40-44	**4,051.7**	**2,003.7**	**2,048.0**	**85-89**	**831.9**	**303.4**	**528.6**
40	793.4	394.5	398.9	85	206.7	80.7	126.0
41	819.7	404.7	415.0	86	187.0	70.6	116.4
42	800.0	395.4	404.7	87	165.3	59.8	105.5
43	819.9	404.7	415.2	88	145.9	50.5	95.4
44	818.7	404.5	414.2	89	127.1	41.8	85.3
				90 and over	465.5	128.4	337.1

Note: Figures may not add exactly due to rounding.
Source: Office for National Statistics

15.3d Population projections by the Office for National Statistics

England
PERSONS, thousands

2012-based
Principal projection

Projected populations at mid-years by age last birthday

Ages	2012	2013	2014	2015	2016	2017	2018	2019	2020	2021	2022	2023	2024	2025	2026	2027	2028	2029	2030	2031	2032
Thousands																					
0-14	9,485	9,550	9,630	9,730	9,851	9,985	10,108	10,210	10,299	10,360	10,405	10,426	10,451	10,465	10,466	10,453	10,453	10,445	10,435	10,422	10,409
15-29	10,567	10,577	10,584	10,554	10,516	10,463	10,401	10,351	10,299	10,258	10,243	10,269	10,287	10,334	10,389	10,455	10,521	10,601	10,702	10,818	10,950
30-44	10,873	10,829	10,783	10,775	10,756	10,756	10,811	10,895	11,006	11,147	11,288	11,400	11,466	11,482	11,503	11,530	11,540	11,546	11,516	11,471	11,417
45-59	10,499	10,647	10,793	10,926	11,057	11,144	11,178	11,169	11,135	11,062	10,954	10,842	10,764	10,711	10,663	10,611	10,573	10,533	10,531	10,512	10,515
60-74	7,857	7,955	8,060	8,165	8,311	8,441	8,550	8,645	8,756	8,885	8,903	8,990	9,127	9,288	9,458	9,632	9,784	9,930	10,062	10,193	10,282
75 & over	4,212	4,285	4,377	4,464	4,528	4,626	4,765	4,929	5,086	5,250	5,546	5,781	5,977	6,150	6,303	6,444	6,589	6,730	6,861	7,001	7,151
All ages	53,494	53,844	54,228	54,613	55,020	55,414	55,812	56,198	56,582	56,962	57,338	57,708	58,073	58,430	58,781	59,124	59,459	59,787	60,107	60,419	60,724
Percentages																					
0-14	17.7	17.7	17.8	17.8	17.9	18.0	18.1	18.2	18.2	18.2	18.1	18.1	18.0	17.9	17.8	17.7	17.6	17.5	17.4	17.2	17.1
15-29	19.8	19.6	19.5	19.3	19.1	18.9	18.6	18.4	18.2	18.0	17.9	17.8	17.7	17.7	17.7	17.7	17.7	17.7	17.8	17.9	18.0
30-44	20.3	20.1	19.9	19.7	19.6	19.4	19.4	19.4	19.5	19.6	19.7	19.8	19.7	19.7	19.6	19.5	19.4	19.3	19.2	19.0	18.8
45-59	19.6	19.8	19.9	20.0	20.1	20.1	20.0	19.9	19.7	19.4	19.1	18.8	18.5	18.3	18.1	17.9	17.8	17.6	17.5	17.4	17.3
60-74	14.7	14.8	14.9	15.0	15.1	15.2	15.3	15.4	15.5	15.6	15.5	15.6	15.7	15.9	16.1	16.3	16.5	16.6	16.7	16.9	16.9
75 & over	7.9	8.0	8.1	8.2	8.2	8.3	8.5	8.8	9.0	9.2	9.7	10.0	10.3	10.5	10.7	10.9	11.1	11.3	11.4	11.6	11.8
All ages	100.0	100.0	100.0	100.0	100.0	100.0	100.0	100.0	100.0	100.0	100.0	100.0	100.0	100.0	100.0	100.0	100.0	100.0	100.0	100.0	100.0
Mean age	39.9	40.0	40.2	40.3	40.4	40.5	40.7	40.8	41.0	41.1	41.2	41.4	41.5	41.7	41.8	42.0	42.1	42.3	42.4	42.6	42.7
Median age	39.5	39.6	39.7	39.8	39.8	39.8	39.9	40.0	40.2	40.3	40.4	40.6	40.7	40.8	41.0	41.1	41.3	41.4	41.6	41.7	41.9

15.3d Population projections by the Office for National Statistics

England
PERSONS, thousands

Projected populations at mid-years by age last birthday / Annual averages for longer-term projections

Ages	2033	2034	2035	2036	2037	2041	2046	2051	2056	2061	2062	2066	2071	2076	2081	2086	2087	2092	2102	2112
Thousands																				
0-14	10,396	10,385	10,378	10,376	10,380	10,461	10,699	10,974	11,151	11,212	11,218	11,246	11,335	11,495	11,682	11,839	11,864	11,960	12,138	12,414
15-29	11,071	11,173	11,263	11,324	11,369	11,431	11,388	11,344	11,430	11,668	11,725	11,943	12,121	12,183	12,218	12,307	12,334	12,505	12,838	13,013
30-44	11,351	11,304	11,253	11,214	11,201	11,350	11,782	12,287	12,398	12,359	12,347	12,318	12,407	12,648	12,925	13,105	13,125	13,175	13,325	13,686
45-59	10,570	10,655	10,767	10,908	11,048	11,268	11,247	11,006	11,155	11,592	11,724	12,099	12,217	12,188	12,157	12,255	12,294	12,560	12,990	13,097
60-74	10,322	10,320	10,295	10,234	10,140	9,914	9,834	10,251	10,618	10,625	10,580	10,428	10,614	11,068	11,574	11,714	11,710	11,710	11,877	12,444
75 & over	7,312	7,477	7,646	7,831	8,029	8,840	9,655	10,022	10,318	10,733	10,817	11,274	11,796	12,162	12,471	13,079	13,224	13,901	15,209	16,311
All ages	61,022	61,315	61,603	61,886	62,166	63,265	64,606	65,883	67,070	68,189	68,411	69,308	70,490	71,744	73,027	74,299	74,552	75,811	78,377	80,965
Percentages																				
0-14	17.0	16.9	16.8	16.8	16.7	16.5	16.6	16.7	16.6	16.4	16.4	16.2	16.1	16.0	16.0	15.9	15.9	15.8	15.5	15.3
15-29	18.1	18.2	18.3	18.3	18.3	18.1	17.6	17.2	17.0	17.1	17.1	17.2	17.2	17.0	16.7	16.6	16.5	16.5	16.4	16.1
30-44	18.6	18.4	18.3	18.1	18.0	17.9	18.2	18.7	18.5	18.1	18.0	17.8	17.6	17.6	17.7	17.6	17.6	17.4	17.0	16.9
45-59	17.3	17.4	17.5	17.6	17.8	17.8	17.4	16.7	16.6	17.0	17.1	17.5	17.3	17.0	16.6	16.5	16.5	16.6	16.6	16.2
60-74	16.9	16.8	16.7	16.5	16.3	15.7	15.2	15.6	15.8	15.6	15.5	15.0	15.1	15.4	15.8	15.8	15.7	15.4	15.2	15.4
75 & over	12.0	12.2	12.4	12.7	12.9	14.0	14.9	15.2	15.4	15.7	15.8	16.3	16.7	17.0	17.1	17.6	17.7	18.3	19.4	20.1
All ages	100.0	100.0	100.0	100.0	100.0	100.0	100.0	100.0	100.0	100.0	100.0	100.0	100.0	100.0	100.0	100.0	100.0	100.0	100.0	100.0
Mean age	42.8	43.0	43.1	43.2	43.3	43.7	44.0	44.3	44.5	44.7	44.8	45.0	45.2	45.5	45.8	46.0	46.1	46.4	47.0	47.6
Median age	42.1	42.2	42.4	42.5	42.6	42.9	42.8	42.9	43.2	43.6	43.7	44.0	44.2	44.4	44.6	44.9	44.9	45.3	46.0	46.5

Note: Figures may not add exactly due to rounding.
* Children under 16. Working age and pensionable age populations based on state pension age (SPA) for given year.
Between 2012 and 2018, SPA will change from 65 years for men and 61 years for women, to 65 years for both sexes.
Then between 2019 and 2020, SPA will change from 65 years to 66 years for both men and women. Between 2034 and 2046,
SPA will increase in two stages from 66 years to 68 years for both sexes. This is based on SPA under the 2011 Pensions Act.
** This is consistent with the age-group definitions used in ONS Labour Market Statistics.

15.3d Population projections by the Office for National Statistics

England
MALES, thousands

2012-based
Principal projection

Projected populations at mid-years by age last birthday

Ages	2012	2013	2014	2015	2016	2017	2018	2019	2020	2021	2022	2023	2024	2025	2026	2027	2028	2029	2030	2031	2032
Thousands																					
0-14	4,855	4,889	4,931	4,982	5,045	5,114	5,177	5,229	5,276	5,308	5,331	5,342	5,355	5,363	5,364	5,357	5,357	5,353	5,347	5,341	5,334
15-29	5,345	5,363	5,379	5,373	5,363	5,349	5,327	5,307	5,280	5,260	5,257	5,272	5,280	5,304	5,330	5,365	5,399	5,441	5,493	5,554	5,621
30-44	5,407	5,384	5,364	5,365	5,363	5,364	5,397	5,448	5,516	5,600	5,678	5,744	5,790	5,813	5,839	5,868	5,887	5,903	5,897	5,883	5,867
45-59	5,198	5,268	5,337	5,399	5,460	5,501	5,516	5,509	5,491	5,454	5,401	5,347	5,311	5,285	5,262	5,234	5,216	5,199	5,203	5,201	5,204
60-74	3,807	3,856	3,907	3,959	4,031	4,095	4,149	4,195	4,250	4,313	4,323	4,366	4,432	4,511	4,593	4,679	4,752	4,822	4,885	4,946	4,989
75 &over	1,722	1,769	1,821	1,871	1,908	1,961	2,034	2,119	2,199	2,282	2,427	2,542	2,638	2,721	2,794	2,861	2,931	2,997	3,059	3,125	3,195
All ages	26,333	26,530	26,739	26,949	27,170	27,384	27,599	27,807	28,012	28,216	28,416	28,613	28,807	28,997	29,183	29,364	29,541	29,715	29,884	30,049	30,210
Percentages																					
0-14	18.4	18.4	18.4	18.5	18.6	18.7	18.8	18.8	18.8	18.8	18.8	18.7	18.6	18.5	18.4	18.2	18.1	18.0	17.9	17.8	17.7
15-29	20.3	20.2	20.1	19.9	19.7	19.5	19.3	19.1	18.8	18.6	18.5	18.4	18.3	18.3	18.3	18.3	18.3	18.3	18.4	18.5	18.6
30-44	20.5	20.3	20.1	19.9	19.7	19.6	19.6	19.6	19.7	19.8	20.0	20.1	20.1	20.0	20.0	20.0	19.9	19.9	19.7	19.6	19.4
45-59	19.7	19.9	20.0	20.0	20.1	20.1	20.0	19.8	19.6	19.3	19.0	18.7	18.4	18.2	18.0	17.8	17.7	17.5	17.4	17.3	17.2
60-74	14.5	14.5	14.6	14.7	14.8	15.0	15.0	15.1	15.2	15.3	15.2	15.3	15.4	15.6	15.7	15.9	16.1	16.2	16.3	16.5	16.5
75 &over	6.5	6.7	6.8	6.9	7.0	7.2	7.4	7.6	7.9	8.1	8.5	8.9	9.2	9.4	9.6	9.7	9.9	10.1	10.2	10.4	10.6
All ages	100.0	100.0	100.0	100.0	100.0	100.0	100.0	100.0	100.0	100.0	100.0	100.0	100.0	100.0	100.0	100.0	100.0	100.0	100.0	100.0	100.0
Mean age	38.9	39.0	39.2	39.3	39.4	39.6	39.7	39.9	40.0	40.1	40.3	40.4	40.6	40.7	40.9	41.0	41.2	41.3	41.4	41.6	41.7
Median age	38.5	38.5	38.6	38.6	38.6	38.7	38.8	38.9	39.0	39.1	39.2	39.4	39.5	39.6	39.7	39.9	40.0	40.2	40.3	40.5	40.7

15.3d Population projections by the Office for National Statistics

England
MALES, thousands

Projected populations at mid-years by age last birthday | | | | | | | | | | | | Annual averages for longer-term projections

Ages	2033	2034	2035	2036	2037	2041	2046	2051	2056	2061	2062	2066	2071	2076	2081	2086	2087	2092	2102	2112
Thousands																				
0-14	5,328	5,322	5,319	5,318	5,319	5,361	5,483	5,624	5,715	5,746	5,749	5,764	5,809	5,891	5,987	6,068	6,080	6,130	6,221	6,363
15-29	5,683	5,736	5,783	5,814	5,837	5,871	5,849	5,827	5,871	5,993	6,023	6,134	6,226	6,257	6,275	6,321	6,335	6,423	6,594	6,684
30-44	5,843	5,824	5,798	5,779	5,777	5,853	6,078	6,339	6,398	6,378	6,372	6,358	6,404	6,528	6,670	6,763	6,773	6,800	6,877	7,063
45-59	5,236	5,288	5,357	5,440	5,517	5,681	5,730	5,636	5,717	5,946	6,013	6,207	6,271	6,258	6,244	6,295	6,316	6,453	6,675	6,732
60-74	5,007	5,005	4,993	4,963	4,919	4,817	4,796	5,046	5,289	5,349	5,338	5,279	5,383	5,620	5,882	5,958	5,957	5,961	6,054	6,348
75 &over	3,270	3,348	3,426	3,513	3,605	3,980	4,354	4,520	4,660	4,868	4,911	5,171	5,483	5,710	5,901	6,233	6,310	6,670	7,345	7,906
All ages	30,368	30,523	30,676	30,826	30,976	31,565	32,291	32,991	33,650	34,281	34,406	34,914	35,576	36,265	36,959	37,638	37,772	38,435	39,766	41,095
Percentages																				
0-14	17.5	17.4	17.3	17.3	17.2	17.0	17.0	17.0	17.0	16.8	16.7	16.5	16.3	16.2	16.2	16.1	16.1	15.9	15.6	15.5
15-29	18.7	18.8	18.9	18.9	18.8	18.6	18.1	17.7	17.4	17.5	17.5	17.6	17.5	17.3	17.0	16.8	16.8	16.7	16.6	16.3
30-44	19.2	19.1	18.9	18.7	18.7	18.5	18.8	19.2	19.0	18.6	18.5	18.2	18.0	18.0	18.0	18.0	17.9	17.7	17.3	17.2
45-59	17.2	17.3	17.5	17.6	17.8	18.0	17.7	17.1	17.0	17.3	17.5	17.8	17.6	17.3	16.9	16.7	16.7	16.8	16.8	16.4
60-74	16.5	16.4	16.3	16.1	15.9	15.3	14.9	15.3	15.7	15.6	15.5	15.1	15.1	15.5	15.9	15.8	15.8	15.5	15.2	15.4
75 &over	10.8	11.0	11.2	11.4	11.6	12.6	13.5	13.7	13.8	14.2	14.3	14.8	15.4	15.7	16.0	16.6	16.7	17.4	18.5	19.2
All ages	100.0	100.0	100.0	100.0	100.0	100.0	100.0	100.0	100.0	100.0	100.0	100.0	100.0	100.0	100.0	100.0	100.0	100.0	100.0	100.0
Mean age	41.8	42.0	42.1	42.2	42.3	42.7	43.0	43.3	43.6	43.8	43.9	44.1	44.5	44.8	45.1	45.4	45.5	45.8	46.5	47.1
Median age	40.8	41.0	41.1	41.2	41.3	41.6	41.5	41.8	42.3	42.7	42.8	43.1	43.4	43.7	43.9	44.2	44.3	44.7	45.4	46.0

Note: Figures may not add exactly due to rounding.

* Children under 16. Working age and pensionable age populations based on state pension age (SPA) for given year. Between 2012 and 2018, SPA will change from 65 years for men and 61 years for women, to 65 years for both sexes. Then between 2019 and 2020, SPA will change from 65 years to 66 years for both men and women. Between 2034 and 2046, SPA will increase in two stages from 66 years to 68 years for both sexes. This is based on SPA under the 2011 Pensions Act.

** This is consistent with the age-group definitions used in ONS Labour Market Statistics.

15.3d Population projections by the Office for National Statistics

England
FEMALES, thousands

2012-based
Principal projection

Projected populations at mid-years by age last birthday

Ages	2012	2013	2014	2015	2016	2017	2018	2019	2020	2021	2022	2023	2024	2025	2026	2027	2028	2029	2030	2031	2032
Thousands																					
0-14	4,630	4,661	4,700	4,748	4,806	4,871	4,931	4,980	5,024	5,052	5,074	5,084	5,096	5,102	5,103	5,096	5,096	5,092	5,087	5,081	5,075
15-29	5,223	5,214	5,205	5,181	5,153	5,114	5,074	5,045	5,019	4,998	4,987	4,998	5,007	5,030	5,058	5,090	5,121	5,160	5,209	5,265	5,329
30-44	5,467	5,445	5,419	5,410	5,394	5,392	5,414	5,447	5,489	5,547	5,610	5,656	5,676	5,670	5,663	5,662	5,652	5,644	5,619	5,589	5,550
45-59	5,301	5,379	5,456	5,527	5,597	5,643	5,662	5,660	5,644	5,608	5,553	5,494	5,453	5,426	5,401	5,377	5,357	5,334	5,328	5,311	5,311
60-74	4,050	4,100	4,153	4,206	4,280	4,346	4,401	4,449	4,506	4,572	4,580	4,624	4,695	4,777	4,865	4,953	5,032	5,109	5,178	5,248	5,294
75 &over	2,490	2,516	2,556	2,594	2,620	2,665	2,731	2,810	2,887	2,968	3,118	3,239	3,339	3,429	3,509	3,582	3,658	3,733	3,803	3,877	3,957
All ages	27,160	27,314	27,489	27,665	27,849	28,030	28,213	28,392	28,570	28,747	28,922	29,095	29,266	29,434	29,598	29,760	29,918	30,072	30,223	30,370	30,514
Percentages																					
0-14	17.0	17.1	17.1	17.2	17.3	17.4	17.5	17.5	17.6	17.6	17.5	17.5	17.4	17.3	17.2	17.1	17.0	16.9	16.8	16.7	16.6
15-29	19.2	19.1	18.9	18.7	18.5	18.2	18.0	17.8	17.6	17.4	17.2	17.2	17.1	17.1	17.1	17.1	17.1	17.2	17.2	17.3	17.5
30-44	20.1	19.9	19.7	19.6	19.4	19.2	19.2	19.2	19.2	19.3	19.4	19.4	19.4	19.3	19.1	19.0	18.9	18.8	18.6	18.4	18.2
45-59	19.5	19.7	19.8	20.0	20.1	20.1	20.1	19.9	19.8	19.5	19.2	18.9	18.6	18.4	18.2	18.1	17.9	17.7	17.6	17.5	17.4
60-74	14.9	15.0	15.1	15.2	15.4	15.5	15.6	15.7	15.8	15.9	15.8	15.9	16.0	16.2	16.4	16.6	16.8	17.0	17.1	17.3	17.3
75 &over	9.2	9.2	9.3	9.4	9.4	9.5	9.7	9.9	10.1	10.3	10.8	11.1	11.4	11.7	11.9	12.0	12.2	12.4	12.6	12.8	13.0
All ages	100.0	100.0	100.0	100.0	100.0	100.0	100.0	100.0	100.0	100.0	100.0	100.0	100.0	100.0	100.0	100.0	100.0	100.0	100.0	100.0	100.0
Mean age	40.9	41.0	41.1	41.3	41.4	41.5	41.6	41.8	41.9	42.0	42.2	42.3	42.5	42.6	42.8	42.9	43.1	43.2	43.4	43.5	43.7
Median age	40.5	40.7	40.8	40.9	41.0	41.1	41.1	41.2	41.3	41.4	41.6	41.8	41.9	42.1	42.2	42.4	42.5	42.7	42.9	43.0	43.2

15.3d Population projections by the Office for National Statistics

England
FEMALES, thousands

Ages	Projected populations at mid-years by age last birthday												Annual averages for longer-term projections							
	2033	2034	2035	2036	2037	2041	2046	2051	2056	2061	2062	2066	2071	2076	2081	2086	2087	2092	2102	2112
Thousands																				
0-14	5,068	5,063	5,060	5,059	5,060	5,100	5,216	5,350	5,436	5,466	5,469	5,482	5,526	5,604	5,695	5,772	5,784	5,830	5,917	6,052
15-29	5,388	5,437	5,481	5,509	5,531	5,560	5,539	5,517	5,559	5,675	5,703	5,809	5,896	5,926	5,942	5,986	5,999	6,082	6,244	6,330
30-44	5,509	5,480	5,455	5,435	5,423	5,497	5,704	5,948	6,000	5,981	5,975	5,960	6,003	6,120	6,254	6,342	6,352	6,376	6,448	6,623
45-59	5,333	5,367	5,410	5,468	5,531	5,587	5,517	5,370	5,437	5,647	5,711	5,891	5,946	5,931	5,914	5,960	5,979	6,107	6,315	6,365
60-74	5,315	5,315	5,302	5,271	5,221	5,097	5,038	5,205	5,330	5,276	5,242	5,149	5,231	5,447	5,693	5,756	5,754	5,749	5,823	6,095
75 &over	4,042	4,130	4,220	4,318	4,424	4,860	5,301	5,502	5,658	5,865	5,906	6,103	6,313	6,452	6,570	6,846	6,913	7,231	7,864	8,405
All ages	30,654	30,792	30,927	31,060	31,190	31,700	32,314	32,892	33,420	33,909	34,005	34,395	34,915	35,479	36,068	36,662	36,780	37,376	38,612	39,870
Percentages																				
0-14	16.5	16.4	16.4	16.3	16.2	16.1	16.1	16.3	16.3	16.1	16.1	15.9	15.8	15.8	15.8	15.7	15.7	15.6	15.3	15.2
15-29	17.6	17.7	17.7	17.7	17.7	17.5	17.1	16.8	16.6	16.7	16.8	16.9	16.9	16.7	16.5	16.3	16.3	16.3	16.2	15.9
30-44	18.0	17.8	17.6	17.5	17.4	17.3	17.7	18.1	18.0	17.6	17.6	17.3	17.2	17.2	17.3	17.3	17.3	17.1	16.7	16.6
45-59	17.4	17.4	17.5	17.6	17.7	17.6	17.1	16.3	16.3	16.7	16.8	17.1	17.0	16.7	16.4	16.3	16.3	16.3	16.4	16.0
60-74	17.3	17.3	17.1	17.0	16.7	16.1	15.6	15.8	15.9	15.6	15.4	15.0	15.0	15.4	15.8	15.7	15.6	15.4	15.1	15.3
75 &over	13.2	13.4	13.6	13.9	14.2	15.3	16.4	16.7	16.9	17.3	17.4	17.7	18.1	18.2	18.2	18.7	18.8	19.3	20.4	21.1
All ages	100.0	100.0	100.0	100.0	100.0	100.0	100.0	100.0	100.0	100.0	100.0	100.0	100.0	100.0	100.0	100.0	100.0	100.0	100.0	100.0
Mean age	43.8	43.9	44.1	44.2	44.3	44.7	45.0	45.3	45.5	45.7	45.7	45.8	46.0	46.2	46.4	46.7	46.7	47.0	47.6	48.2
Median age	43.3	43.5	43.6	43.8	43.9	44.2	44.1	44.0	44.3	44.6	44.6	44.9	45.1	45.2	45.4	45.6	45.6	45.9	46.6	47.2

Note: Figures may not add exactly due to rounding.

* Children under 16. Working age and pensionable age populations based on state pension age (SPA) for given year. Between 2012 and 2018, SPA will change from 65 years for men and 61 years for women, to 65 years for both sexes. Then between 2019 and 2020, SPA will change from 65 years to 66 years for both men and women. Between 2034 and 2046, SPA will increase in two stages from 66 years to 68 years for both sexes. This is based on SPA under the 2011 Pensions Act.

** This is consistent with the age-group definitions used in ONS Labour Market Statistics.

15.3d Population projections by the Office for National Statistics

Wales
PERSONS, thousands

2012-based
Principal projection

Projected populations at mid-years by age last birthday

Ages	2012	2013	2014	2015	2016	2017	2018	2019	2020	2021	2022	2023	2024	2025	2026	2027	2028	2029	2030	2031	2032
Thousands																					
0-14	519	518	519	521	524	529	534	538	542	544	545	545	546	546	545	544	544	544	544	543	541
15-29	599	602	605	605	605	603	599	595	590	584	580	576	574	574	574	573	572	573	575	578	583
30-44	559	553	546	542	537	534	536	540	548	558	569	579	585	588	591	596	599	602	602	601	599
45-59	616	620	624	628	632	632	630	624	617	608	597	586	576	569	562	555	549	542	538	533	531
60-74	514	519	525	529	535	540	544	547	551	556	554	555	559	564	570	576	580	585	588	593	594
75 & over	268	271	276	282	287	293	302	312	322	331	349	364	376	387	396	405	413	421	428	435	442
All ages	3,074	3,083	3,095	3,107	3,119	3,132	3,144	3,157	3,169	3,181	3,193	3,205	3,216	3,227	3,238	3,248	3,258	3,267	3,275	3,283	3,291
Percentages																					
0-14	16.9	16.8	16.8	16.8	16.8	16.9	17.0	17.1	17.1	17.1	17.1	17.0	17.0	16.9	16.8	16.8	16.7	16.7	16.6	16.5	16.4
15-29	19.5	19.5	19.6	19.5	19.4	19.2	19.1	18.8	18.6	18.4	18.2	18.0	17.8	17.8	17.7	17.6	17.6	17.5	17.6	17.6	17.7
30-44	18.2	17.9	17.6	17.4	17.2	17.1	17.0	17.1	17.3	17.5	17.8	18.1	18.2	18.2	18.3	18.4	18.4	18.4	18.4	18.3	18.2
45-59	20.0	20.1	20.2	20.2	20.2	20.2	20.0	19.8	19.5	19.1	18.7	18.3	17.9	17.6	17.4	17.1	16.8	16.6	16.4	16.2	16.1
60-74	16.7	16.8	17.0	17.0	17.1	17.2	17.3	17.3	17.4	17.5	17.4	17.3	17.4	17.5	17.6	17.7	17.8	17.9	18.0	18.1	18.1
75 & over	8.7	8.8	8.9	9.1	9.2	9.4	9.6	9.9	10.2	10.4	10.9	11.4	11.7	12.0	12.2	12.5	12.7	12.9	13.1	13.2	13.4
All ages	100.0	100.0	100.0	100.0	100.0	100.0	100.0	100.0	100.0	100.0	100.0	100.0	100.0	100.0	100.0	100.0	100.0	100.0	100.0	100.0	100.0
Mean age	41.3	41.4	41.5	41.7	41.8	41.9	42.1	42.2	42.3	42.5	42.6	42.7	42.9	43.0	43.1	43.3	43.4	43.5	43.7	43.8	43.9
Median age	41.7	41.9	42.0	42.1	42.2	42.2	42.2	42.1	42.1	42.1	42.2	42.3	42.4	42.4	42.5	42.5	42.6	42.7	42.8	42.9	43.0

15.3d Population projections by the Office for National Statistics

Wales
PERSONS, thousands

Projected populations at mid-years by age last birthday

Annual averages for longer-term projections

Ages	2033	2034	2035	2036	2037	2041	2046	2051	2056	2061	2062	2066	2071	2076	2081	2086	2087	2092	2102	2112
Thousands																				
0-14	540	538	536	535	533	530	532	537	540	539	538	536	533	534	537	538	538	538	536	538
15-29	588	592	596	598	599	599	597	589	584	586	587	592	595	593	590	588	588	589	593	591
30-44	595	591	586	581	576	571	576	595	596	594	593	587	582	584	590	594	594	592	587	591
45-59	532	537	545	555	565	588	598	579	570	575	580	595	597	596	589	584	584	588	597	593
60-74	592	587	581	573	563	534	511	534	567	578	576	560	555	562	582	585	585	585	578	590
75 & over	450	458	466	475	484	520	552	553	549	555	557	579	612	634	646	671	676	699	750	792
All ages	3,298	3,304	3,310	3,316	3,321	3,342	3,365	3,387	3,407	3,427	3,431	3,449	3,475	3,504	3,533	3,561	3,566	3,591	3,641	3,694
Percentages																				
0-14	16.4	16.3	16.2	16.1	16.1	15.9	15.8	15.9	15.9	15.7	15.7	15.5	15.4	15.2	15.2	15.1	15.1	15.0	14.7	14.6
15-29	17.8	17.9	18.0	18.0	18.0	17.9	17.7	17.4	17.1	17.1	17.1	17.2	17.1	16.9	16.7	16.5	16.5	16.4	16.3	16.0
30-44	18.0	17.9	17.7	17.5	17.3	17.1	17.1	17.6	17.5	17.3	17.3	17.0	16.8	16.7	16.7	16.7	16.6	16.5	16.1	16.0
45-59	16.1	16.3	16.5	16.7	17.0	17.6	17.8	17.1	16.7	16.8	16.9	17.3	17.2	17.0	16.7	16.4	16.4	16.4	16.4	16.0
60-74	18.0	17.8	17.6	17.3	17.0	16.0	15.2	15.8	16.6	16.9	16.8	16.3	16.0	16.0	16.5	16.4	16.4	16.3	15.9	16.0
75 & over	13.7	13.9	14.1	14.3	14.6	15.6	16.4	16.3	16.1	16.2	16.2	16.8	17.6	18.1	18.3	18.8	19.0	19.5	20.6	21.4
All ages	100.0	100.0	100.0	100.0	100.0	100.0	100.0	100.0	100.0	100.0	100.0	100.0	100.0	100.0	100.0	100.0	100.0	100.0	100.0	100.0
Mean age	44.0	44.1	44.2	44.3	44.4	44.7	45.0	45.2	45.4	45.6	45.6	45.8	46.1	46.5	46.8	47.1	47.2	47.5	48.1	48.7
Median age	43.2	43.4	43.5	43.7	43.9	44.3	44.4	44.3	44.6	44.9	44.9	45.3	45.7	46.0	46.3	46.5	46.6	46.9	47.6	48.2

Note: Figures may not add exactly due to rounding.
* Children under 16. Working age and pensionable age populations based on state pension age (SPA) for given year.
Between 2012 and 2018, SPA will change from 65 years for men and 61 years for women, to 65 years for both sexes.
Then between 2019 and 2020, SPA will change from 65 years to 66 years for both men and women. Between 2034 and 2046,
SPA will increase in two stages from 66 years to 68 years for both sexes. This is based on SPA under the 2011 Pensions Act.
** This is consistent with the age-group definitions used in ONS Labour Market Statistics.

15.3d Population projections by the Office for National Statistics

Wales   2012-based
MALES, thousands   Principal projection

Projected populations at mid-years by age last birthday

Ages	2012	2013	2014	2015	2016	2017	2018	2019	2020	2021	2022	2023	2024	2025	2026	2027	2028	2029	2030	2031	2032
Thousands																					
0-14	266	266	266	268	269	272	274	276	278	279	280	280	280	280	280	280	280	280	279	279	278
15-29	306	309	312	313	314	314	313	311	308	306	304	302	301	301	301	301	300	301	302	304	306
30-44	276	273	270	269	267	266	268	272	277	283	289	296	301	304	307	311	314	316	318	318	318
45-59	302	304	305	307	309	309	307	305	301	297	291	286	281	278	275	271	268	265	264	263	262
60-74	250	253	255	257	260	262	263	264	266	268	267	267	269	271	274	276	278	280	282	284	285
75 &over	109	112	115	118	121	125	129	134	139	144	153	160	166	171	175	179	183	187	190	192	196
All ages	1,510	1,516	1,524	1,532	1,539	1,547	1,555	1,562	1,570	1,577	1,585	1,592	1,599	1,605	1,612	1,618	1,624	1,630	1,635	1,640	1,645
Percentages																					
0-14	17.6	17.5	17.5	17.5	17.5	17.6	17.6	17.7	17.7	17.7	17.7	17.6	17.5	17.5	17.4	17.3	17.2	17.2	17.1	17.0	16.9
15-29	20.2	20.4	20.4	20.4	20.4	20.3	20.1	19.9	19.7	19.4	19.2	19.0	18.9	18.8	18.7	18.6	18.5	18.5	18.5	18.5	18.6
30-44	18.3	18.0	17.7	17.6	17.4	17.2	17.2	17.4	17.6	18.0	18.3	18.6	18.8	18.9	19.0	19.2	19.3	19.4	19.4	19.4	19.4
45-59	20.0	20.0	20.0	20.0	20.0	20.0	19.8	19.5	19.2	18.8	18.4	18.0	17.6	17.3	17.1	16.8	16.5	16.3	16.2	16.0	15.9
60-74	16.6	16.7	16.8	16.8	16.9	16.9	16.9	16.9	16.9	17.0	16.9	16.8	16.8	16.9	17.0	17.1	17.1	17.2	17.3	17.3	17.3
75 &over	7.2	7.4	7.5	7.7	7.9	8.1	8.3	8.6	8.9	9.1	9.6	10.0	10.4	10.7	10.9	11.1	11.3	11.5	11.6	11.7	11.9
All ages	100.0	100.0	100.0	100.0	100.0	100.0	100.0	100.0	100.0	100.0	100.0	100.0	100.0	100.0	100.0	100.0	100.0	100.0	100.0	100.0	100.0
Mean age	40.2	40.3	40.4	40.5	40.7	40.8	40.9	41.0	41.2	41.3	41.4	41.6	41.7	41.8	41.9	42.0	42.2	42.3	42.4	42.5	42.6
Median age	40.5	40.5	40.6	40.5	40.5	40.4	40.3	40.3	40.3	40.4	40.4	40.4	40.4	40.4	40.5	40.5	40.6	40.7	40.9	41.0	41.2

15.3d Population projections by the Office for National Statistics

Wales
MALES, thousands

Projected populations at mid-years by age last birthday | Annual averages for longer-term projections

Ages	2033	2034	2035	2036	2037	2041	2046	2051	2056	2061	2062	2066	2071	2076	2081	2086	2087	2092	2102	2112
Thousands																				
0-14	277	277	276	275	274	272	273	276	278	277	277	275	274	275	276	277	277	277	276	276
15-29	309	311	313	314	315	314	313	309	307	308	309	311	313	312	310	309	309	310	312	311
30-44	317	316	313	310	309	306	309	319	320	319	319	315	313	314	317	319	319	318	316	318
45-59	264	267	272	279	285	302	314	307	303	306	309	317	318	317	314	312	312	314	319	317
60-74	284	281	279	275	270	257	248	265	287	299	299	293	291	295	306	308	308	308	305	312
75 &over	199	203	206	210	214	230	243	243	242	247	248	264	286	302	312	328	330	344	372	395
All ages	1,650	1,654	1,658	1,663	1,667	1,682	1,701	1,720	1,738	1,756	1,760	1,775	1,795	1,815	1,835	1,852	1,855	1,870	1,899	1,928
Percentages																				
0-14	16.8	16.7	16.6	16.5	16.4	16.2	16.1	16.1	16.0	15.8	15.7	15.5	15.3	15.1	15.0	14.9	14.9	14.8	14.5	14.3
15-29	18.7	18.8	18.8	18.9	18.9	18.7	18.4	18.0	17.7	17.5	17.5	17.5	17.4	17.2	16.9	16.7	16.7	16.6	16.4	16.1
30-44	19.2	19.1	18.9	18.7	18.5	18.2	18.2	18.6	18.4	18.2	18.1	17.8	17.4	17.3	17.3	17.2	17.2	17.0	16.6	16.5
45-59	16.0	16.2	16.4	16.8	17.1	18.0	18.5	17.8	17.4	17.4	17.5	17.8	17.7	17.5	17.1	16.8	16.8	16.8	16.8	16.4
60-74	17.2	17.0	16.8	16.5	16.2	15.3	14.6	15.4	16.5	17.0	17.0	16.5	16.2	16.3	16.7	16.6	16.6	16.5	16.1	16.2
75 &over	12.1	12.2	12.4	12.6	12.8	13.7	14.3	14.2	14.0	14.0	14.1	14.9	15.9	16.6	17.0	17.7	17.8	18.4	19.6	20.5
All ages	100.0	100.0	100.0	100.0	100.0	100.0	100.0	100.0	100.0	100.0	100.0	100.0	100.0	100.0	100.0	100.0	100.0	100.0	100.0	100.0
Mean age	42.7	42.8	42.9	43.0	43.1	43.4	43.7	43.9	44.2	44.5	44.6	44.9	45.3	45.8	46.2	46.6	46.7	47.0	47.6	48.3
Median age	41.4	41.6	41.8	41.9	42.1	42.5	42.6	42.8	43.3	43.8	43.9	44.3	44.9	45.3	45.7	46.0	46.1	46.4	47.2	47.8

Note: Figures may not add exactly due to rounding.

* Children under 16. Working age and pensionable age populations based on state pension age (SPA) for given year. Between 2012 and 2018, SPA will change from 65 years for men and 61 years for women, to 65 years for both sexes. Then between 2019 and 2020, SPA will change from 65 years for both men and women. Between 2034 and 2046, SPA will increase in two stages from 66 years to 68 years for both sexes. This is based on SPA under the 2011 Pensions Act.

** This is consistent with the age-group definitions used in ONS Labour Market Statistics.

15.3d Population projections by the Office for National Statistics

Wales
FEMALES, thousands

2012-based
Principal projection

Projected populations at mid-years by age last birthday

Ages	2012	2013	2014	2015	2016	2017	2018	2019	2020	2021	2022	2023	2024	2025	2026	2027	2028	2029	2030	2031	2032
Thousands																					
0-14	253	252	253	254	255	258	260	262	263	264	265	265	265	265	265	264	265	264	264	264	263
15-29	293	293	294	293	291	289	286	284	281	278	276	274	273	272	273	272	272	272	273	275	277
30-44	283	280	276	273	270	268	268	269	271	275	279	283	285	285	284	285	285	285	284	283	281
45-59	314	316	318	321	323	323	322	320	316	311	305	300	295	291	287	283	280	276	274	271	269
60-74	263	266	270	272	275	278	280	282	285	288	287	287	290	293	296	299	301	304	306	309	309
75 &over	158	159	161	163	166	169	173	178	183	187	196	204	210	216	221	225	230	235	238	242	247
All ages	1,564	1,567	1,571	1,576	1,580	1,585	1,590	1,594	1,599	1,604	1,609	1,613	1,618	1,622	1,626	1,630	1,634	1,637	1,640	1,643	1,645
Percentages																					
0-14	16.2	16.1	16.1	16.1	16.2	16.3	16.4	16.4	16.5	16.5	16.5	16.4	16.4	16.4	16.3	16.2	16.2	16.2	16.1	16.0	16.0
15-29	18.7	18.7	18.7	18.6	18.4	18.2	18.0	17.8	17.6	17.4	17.1	17.0	16.9	16.8	16.8	16.7	16.6	16.6	16.6	16.7	16.8
30-44	18.1	17.8	17.5	17.3	17.1	16.9	16.8	16.9	17.0	17.1	17.4	17.5	17.6	17.5	17.5	17.5	17.5	17.4	17.3	17.2	17.0
45-59	20.1	20.2	20.3	20.4	20.4	20.4	20.3	20.0	19.8	19.4	19.0	18.6	18.2	17.9	17.7	17.4	17.1	16.9	16.7	16.5	16.3
60-74	16.8	17.0	17.2	17.3	17.4	17.5	17.6	17.7	17.8	17.9	17.8	17.8	17.9	18.1	18.2	18.3	18.5	18.6	18.7	18.8	18.8
75 &over	10.1	10.2	10.3	10.4	10.5	10.7	10.9	11.2	11.4	11.7	12.2	12.7	13.0	13.3	13.6	13.8	14.1	14.3	14.5	14.8	15.0
All ages	100.0	100.0	100.0	100.0	100.0	100.0	100.0	100.0	100.0	100.0	100.0	100.0	100.0	100.0	100.0	100.0	100.0	100.0	100.0	100.0	100.0
Mean age	42.4	42.5	42.6	42.8	42.9	43.0	43.2	43.3	43.5	43.6	43.8	43.9	44.1	44.2	44.4	44.5	44.6	44.8	44.9	45.1	45.2
Median age	42.9	43.0	43.3	43.5	43.7	43.8	43.9	44.0	44.0	44.0	44.1	44.1	44.3	44.4	44.5	44.6	44.7	44.8	44.9	45.0	45.1

15.3d Population projections by the Office for National Statistics

Wales
FEMALES, thousands

	Projected populations at mid-years by age last birthday												Annual averages for longer-term projections								
Ages	2033	2034	2035	2036	2037	2041	2046	2051	2056	2061	2062	2066	2071	2076	2081	2086	2087	2092	2102	2112
Thousands																				
0-14	262	261	261	260	259	257	258	261	263	262	262	260	259	260	261	261	262	261	260	261
15-29	280	281	283	284	285	284	283	279	277	278	278	281	282	282	280	279	279	279	281	280
30-44	278	275	273	270	267	265	267	276	276	275	275	271	269	270	273	275	275	274	271	273
45-59	269	270	272	276	280	286	284	272	267	269	272	278	279	278	275	273	273	274	278	276
60-74	308	306	303	298	293	277	263	270	280	279	277	268	264	267	276	278	278	277	273	279
75 &over	251	256	260	265	270	290	308	309	307	308	309	315	326	332	334	344	346	355	378	397
All ages	1,648	1,650	1,652	1,653	1,655	1,660	1,664	1,667	1,669	1,671	1,671	1,674	1,680	1,688	1,699	1,709	1,711	1,721	1,742	1,766
Percentages																				
0-14	15.9	15.8	15.8	15.7	15.7	15.5	15.5	15.7	15.7	15.7	15.6	15.5	15.4	15.4	15.3	15.3	15.3	15.2	14.9	14.8
15-29	17.0	17.1	17.1	17.2	17.2	17.1	17.0	16.8	16.6	16.6	16.7	16.8	16.8	16.7	16.5	16.3	16.3	16.2	16.1	15.9
30-44	16.9	16.7	16.5	16.3	16.2	15.9	16.0	16.5	16.5	16.5	16.4	16.2	16.0	16.0	16.1	16.1	16.1	15.9	15.6	15.5
45-59	16.3	16.4	16.5	16.7	16.9	17.2	17.1	16.3	16.0	16.1	16.2	16.6	16.6	16.5	16.2	16.0	15.9	15.9	16.0	15.6
60-74	18.7	18.6	18.3	18.1	17.7	16.7	15.8	16.2	16.7	16.7	16.6	16.0	15.7	15.8	16.3	16.2	16.2	16.1	15.7	15.8
75 &over	15.2	15.5	15.8	16.0	16.3	17.5	18.5	18.6	18.4	18.4	18.5	18.8	19.4	19.7	19.7	20.1	20.2	20.6	21.7	22.5
All ages	100.0	100.0	100.0	100.0	100.0	100.0	100.0	100.0	100.0	100.0	100.0	100.0	100.0	100.0	100.0	100.0	100.0	100.0	100.0	100.0
Mean age	45.3	45.4	45.6	45.7	45.8	46.1	46.3	46.5	46.6	46.7	46.7	46.8	47.0	47.2	47.4	47.7	47.7	48.0	48.5	49.1
Median age	45.2	45.4	45.5	45.6	45.8	46.3	46.4	46.0	46.0	46.1	46.1	46.3	46.6	46.8	47.0	47.2	47.2	47.5	48.2	48.8

Note: Figures may not add exactly due to rounding.

* Children under 16. Working age and pensionable age populations based on state pension age (SPA) for given year.
Between 2012 and 2018, SPA will change from 65 years for men and 61 years for women, to 65 years for both sexes.
Then between 2019 and 2020, SPA will change from 65 years to 66 years for both men and women. Between 2034 and 2046, SPA will increase in two stages from 66 years to 68 years for both sexes. This is based on SPA under the 2011 Pensions Act.
** This is consistent with the age-group definitions used in ONS Labour Market Statistics.

15.3e Mid-2012 Population Estimates: Scotland; estimated resident population by single year of age and sex

Thousands

Age	Persons	Males	Females	Age	Persons	Males	Females
All ages	**5,313.6**	**2,577.1**	**2,736.5**				
0-4	**295.9**	**151.0**	**144.8**	**45-49**	**410.3**	**199.5**	**210.8**
0	58.7	30.2	28.5	45	81.2	39.7	41.4
1	60.6	31.0	29.6	46	80.6	39.1	41.5
2	57.8	29.4	28.4	47	83.5	40.7	42.8
3	59.5	30.2	29.3	48	82.6	39.9	42.7
4	59.3	30.2	29.1	49	82.4	40.1	42.3
5-9	**275.5**	**141.1**	**134.4**	**50-54**	**384.7**	**188.2**	**196.5**
5	57.0	29.2	27.8	50	80.6	39.6	41.0
6	55.9	28.5	27.4	51	78.8	38.5	40.3
7	55.5	28.5	26.9	52	76.0	37.4	38.7
8	54.5	28.1	26.4	53	75.7	36.9	38.8
9	52.8	26.9	25.9	54	73.7	35.9	37.7
10-14	**281.6**	**144.1**	**137.5**	**55-59**	**339.3**	**166.2**	**173.1**
10	52.6	26.8	25.8	55	71.8	35.2	36.6
11	54.8	27.8	27.0	56	69.7	34.2	35.5
12	56.2	28.9	27.2	57	66.8	32.6	34.2
13	58.4	30.0	28.4	58	66.1	32.4	33.7
14	59.6	30.5	29.1	59	64.9	31.8	33.1
15-19	**319.8**	**163.4**	**156.4**	**60-64**	**322.6**	**157.8**	**164.8**
15	61.7	31.7	30.0	60	62.7	30.6	32.0
16	61.5	31.8	29.7	61	63.5	31.0	32.5
17	62.3	32.1	30.2	62	63.6	31.3	32.3
18	65.6	33.4	32.1	63	65.5	32.0	33.5
19	68.7	34.4	34.4	64	67.4	32.9	34.5
20-24	**370.6**	**184.4**	**186.2**	**65-69**	**285.7**	**137.3**	**148.4**
20	74.6	37.0	37.6	65	73.2	35.5	37.6
21	76.4	38.1	38.3	66	55.4	27.0	28.4
22	73.8	36.7	37.1	67	52.4	25.1	27.3
23	72.8	36.3	36.5	68	53.3	25.6	27.7
24	73.1	36.4	36.7	69	51.4	24.1	27.3
25-29	**347.1**	**170.7**	**176.3**	**70-74**	**221.5**	**101.6**	**119.9**
25	70.9	34.9	36.0	70	47.3	22.0	25.3
26	70.3	34.9	35.4	71	43.9	20.1	23.7
27	69.9	34.3	35.5	72	44.6	20.4	24.2
28	67.5	33.1	34.3	73	43.5	19.8	23.7
29	68.5	33.5	35.0	74	42.3	19.2	23.1
30-34	**333.0**	**163.3**	**169.7**	**75-79**	**180.6**	**78.4**	**102.2**
30	69.5	33.8	35.7	75	40.1	17.7	22.4
31	69.2	34.0	35.2	76	38.5	16.9	21.6
32	67.8	33.2	34.6	77	36.5	15.9	20.6
33	65.5	32.5	33.0	78	33.9	14.6	19.3
34	61.0	29.8	31.2	79	31.6	13.4	18.2
35-39	**322.0**	**158.2**	**163.9**	**80-84**	**128.6**	**50.9**	**77.7**
35	59.8	29.6	30.2	80	30.9	12.7	18.2
36	63.6	31.3	32.3	81	28.4	11.6	16.9
37	64.1	31.2	32.9	82	25.6	10.0	15.6
38	65.3	32.1	33.1	83	23.3	9.0	14.3
39	69.2	34.0	35.3	84	20.4	7.6	12.8
40-44	**385.5**	**186.2**	**199.3**	**85-89**	**72.3**	**24.8**	**47.5**
40	73.7	35.7	38.0	85	18.5	6.7	11.8
41	76.7	36.9	39.8	86	16.7	5.9	10.8
42	75.8	36.6	39.2	87	14.3	4.9	9.4
43	78.8	38.1	40.7	88	12.5	4.1	8.4
44	80.4	38.8	41.6	89	10.3	3.2	7.1
				90 and over	**36.9**	**9.8**	**27.1**

Note: Figures may not add exactly due to rounding.
Source: National Records of Scotland.

15.3f Population projections by the Office for National Statistics

Scotland
PERSONS, thousands

2012-based
Principal projection

Projected populations at mid-years by age last birthday

Ages	2012	2013	2014	2015	2016	2017	2018	2019	2020	2021	2022	2023	2024	2025	2026	2027	2028	2029	2030	2031	2032
Thousands																					
0-14	853	851	851	854	859	866	874	881	887	893	897	899	901	904	904	906	909	911	913	913	913
15-29	1,037	1,038	1,039	1,035	1,029	1,020	1,010	1,001	991	979	968	963	959	956	957	955	954	954	957	962	970
30-44	1,040	1,028	1,017	1,012	1,007	1,005	1,011	1,020	1,033	1,049	1,069	1,084	1,094	1,099	1,102	1,104	1,106	1,108	1,105	1,100	1,092
45-59	1,134	1,146	1,155	1,161	1,165	1,164	1,158	1,146	1,133	1,117	1,097	1,075	1,059	1,044	1,033	1,022	1,012	1,002	998	993	992
60-74	830	839	850	861	877	891	905	919	935	951	955	965	978	994	1,007	1,022	1,034	1,044	1,051	1,056	1,057
75 & over	418	426	434	443	450	460	472	484	495	508	535	555	573	589	603	616	630	644	658	674	690
All ages	5,314	5,328	5,346	5,365	5,386	5,407	5,429	5,452	5,474	5,497	5,520	5,542	5,564	5,585	5,606	5,626	5,645	5,664	5,681	5,698	5,714
Percentages																					
0-14	16.1	16.0	15.9	15.9	15.9	16.0	16.1	16.2	16.2	16.2	16.3	16.2	16.2	16.2	16.1	16.1	16.1	16.1	16.1	16.0	16.0
15-29	19.5	19.5	19.4	19.3	19.1	18.9	18.6	18.4	18.1	17.8	17.5	17.4	17.2	17.1	17.1	17.0	16.9	16.8	16.8	16.9	17.0
30-44	19.6	19.3	19.0	18.9	18.7	18.6	18.6	18.7	18.9	19.1	19.4	19.6	19.7	19.7	19.7	19.6	19.6	19.6	19.4	19.3	19.1
45-59	21.3	21.5	21.6	21.6	21.6	21.5	21.3	21.0	20.7	20.3	19.9	19.4	19.0	18.7	18.4	18.2	17.9	17.7	17.6	17.4	17.4
60-74	15.6	15.7	15.9	16.0	16.3	16.5	16.7	16.9	17.1	17.3	17.3	17.4	17.6	17.8	18.0	18.2	18.3	18.4	18.5	18.5	18.5
75 & over	7.9	8.0	8.1	8.3	8.4	8.5	8.7	8.9	9.0	9.2	9.7	10.0	10.3	10.5	10.8	11.0	11.2	11.4	11.6	11.8	12.1
All ages	100.0	100.0	100.0	100.0	100.0	100.0	100.0	100.0	100.0	100.0	100.0	100.0	100.0	100.0	100.0	100.0	100.0	100.0	100.0	100.0	100.0
Mean age	41.0	41.2	41.3	41.5	41.7	41.8	42.0	42.1	42.2	42.4	42.5	42.7	42.8	42.9	43.1	43.2	43.3	43.4	43.6	43.7	43.8
Median age	41.5	41.7	41.9	42.0	42.1	42.2	42.2	42.2	42.2	42.2	42.3	42.4	42.5	42.6	42.7	42.8	42.9	43.0	43.1	43.3	43.4

15.3f Population projections by the Office for National Statistics

Scotland
PERSONS, thousands

Ages	Projected populations at mid-years by age last birthday											Annual averages for longer-term projections								
	2033	2034	2035	2036	2037	2041	2046	2051	2056	2061	2062	2066	2071	2076	2081	2086	2087	2092	2102	2112
Thousands																				
0–14	911	910	908	905	903	896	898	910	922	928	928	927	926	927	933	940	941	946	949	955
15–29	978	985	991	996	1,001	1,008	1,017	1,009	1,000	1,002	1,004	1,014	1,027	1,032	1,032	1,030	1,030	1,033	1,046	1,053
30–44	1,082	1,073	1,064	1,052	1,041	1,031	1,037	1,071	1,083	1,093	1,093	1,086	1,078	1,080	1,092	1,105	1,107	1,111	1,110	1,120
45–59	998	1,008	1,021	1,037	1,057	1,089	1,089	1,044	1,025	1,033	1,041	1,068	1,081	1,091	1,086	1,079	1,078	1,084	1,110	1,116
60–74	1,052	1,043	1,032	1,018	1,000	948	920	967	1,018	1,020	1,014	981	970	981	1,017	1,033	1,035	1,046	1,040	1,064
75 & over	707	724	741	760	779	853	916	925	923	943	950	993	1,045	1,077	1,094	1,132	1,140	1,176	1,277	1,366
All ages	5,728	5,742	5,756	5,768	5,780	5,826	5,877	5,925	5,972	6,019	6,029	6,069	6,126	6,188	6,254	6,319	6,332	6,396	6,532	6,674
Percentages																				
0–14	15.9	15.8	15.8	15.7	15.6	15.4	15.3	15.4	15.4	15.4	15.4	15.3	15.1	15.0	14.9	14.9	14.9	14.8	14.5	14.3
15–29	17.1	17.1	17.2	17.3	17.3	17.3	17.3	17.0	16.8	16.6	16.7	16.7	16.8	16.7	16.5	16.3	16.3	16.1	16.0	15.8
30–44	18.9	18.7	18.5	18.2	18.0	17.7	17.6	18.1	18.1	18.2	18.1	17.9	17.6	17.5	17.5	17.5	17.5	17.4	17.0	16.8
45–59	17.4	17.6	17.7	18.0	18.3	18.7	18.5	17.6	17.2	17.2	17.3	17.6	17.6	17.6	17.4	17.1	17.0	16.9	17.0	16.7
60–74	18.4	18.2	17.9	17.7	17.3	16.3	15.7	16.3	17.1	17.0	16.8	16.2	15.8	15.9	16.3	16.3	16.4	16.4	15.9	15.9
75 & over	12.3	12.6	12.9	13.2	13.5	14.6	15.6	15.6	15.4	15.7	15.8	16.4	17.1	17.4	17.5	17.9	18.0	18.4	19.5	20.5
All ages	100.0	100.0	100.0	100.0	100.0	100.0	100.0	100.0	100.0	100.0	100.0	100.0	100.0	100.0	100.0	100.0	100.0	100.0	100.0	100.0
Mean age	43.9	44.1	44.2	44.3	44.4	44.7	45.0	45.2	45.4	45.5	45.6	45.7	46.0	46.3	46.5	46.8	46.8	47.1	47.7	48.3
Median age	43.6	43.8	43.9	44.1	44.3	44.7	44.8	44.6	44.7	44.8	44.9	45.1	45.4	45.8	46.0	46.2	46.2	46.5	47.2	47.8

Note: Figures may not add exactly due to rounding.

* Children under 16. Working age and pensionable age populations based on state pension age (SPA) for given year.
Between 2012 and 2018, SPA will change from 65 years for men and 61 years for women, to 65 years for both sexes.
Then between 2019 and 2020, SPA will change from 65 years to 66 years for both men and women. Between 2034 and 2046,
SPA will increase in two stages from 66 years to 68 years for both sexes. This is based on SPA under the 2011 Pensions Act.
** This is consistent with the age-group definitions used in ONS Labour Market Statistics.

15.3f Population projections by the Office for National Statistics

Scotland
MALES, thousands

2012-based
Principal projection

Projected populations at mid-years by age last birthday

Ages	2012	2013	2014	2015	2016	2017	2018	2019	2020	2021	2022	2023	2024	2025	2026	2027	2028	2029	2030	2031	2032
Thousands																					
0-14	436	435	435	436	439	443	447	450	453	456	458	459	460	462	462	463	465	466	467	467	467
15-29	519	520	522	521	519	516	511	507	503	497	492	490	488	486	486	485	484	484	486	488	492
30-44	508	502	497	496	494	494	498	504	511	520	530	539	545	549	552	555	557	560	559	558	555
45-59	554	558	562	563	564	563	560	554	547	539	529	519	511	504	499	494	490	485	484	483	484
60-74	397	402	407	413	421	428	435	441	449	456	458	462	468	475	481	487	493	497	499	501	501
75 &over	164	168	173	178	181	186	192	199	205	211	224	235	244	252	259	265	272	278	285	292	300
All ages	2,577	2,586	2,596	2,607	2,619	2,630	2,643	2,655	2,667	2,680	2,692	2,704	2,716	2,728	2,739	2,750	2,760	2,770	2,780	2,789	2,798
Percentages																					
0-14	16.9	16.8	16.8	16.7	16.8	16.8	16.9	17.0	17.0	17.0	17.0	17.0	17.0	16.9	16.9	16.8	16.8	16.8	16.8	16.7	16.7
15-29	20.1	20.1	20.1	20.0	19.8	19.6	19.3	19.1	18.9	18.5	18.3	18.1	18.0	17.8	17.7	17.6	17.6	17.5	17.5	17.5	17.6
30-44	19.7	19.4	19.2	19.0	18.9	18.8	18.8	19.0	19.2	19.4	19.7	19.9	20.0	20.1	20.1	20.2	20.2	20.2	20.1	20.0	19.8
45-59	21.5	21.6	21.6	21.6	21.6	21.4	21.2	20.9	20.5	20.1	19.7	19.2	18.8	18.5	18.2	18.0	17.7	17.5	17.4	17.3	17.3
60-74	15.4	15.5	15.7	15.8	16.1	16.3	16.5	16.6	16.8	17.0	17.0	17.1	17.2	17.4	17.6	17.7	17.8	17.9	18.0	18.0	17.9
75 &over	6.4	6.5	6.7	6.8	6.9	7.1	7.3	7.5	7.7	7.9	8.3	8.7	9.0	9.2	9.4	9.6	9.8	10.1	10.2	10.5	10.7
All ages	100.0	100.0	100.0	100.0	100.0	100.0	100.0	100.0	100.0	100.0	100.0	100.0	100.0	100.0	100.0	100.0	100.0	100.0	100.0	100.0	100.0
Mean age	39.9	40.1	40.2	40.4	40.5	40.7	40.8	41.0	41.1	41.3	41.4	41.5	41.6	41.8	41.9	42.0	42.2	42.3	42.4	42.5	42.6
Median age	40.3	40.5	40.6	40.6	40.7	40.7	40.6	40.6	40.7	40.8	40.9	40.9	41.0	41.1	41.2	41.3	41.4	41.5	41.6	41.8	42.0

15.3f Population projections by the Office for National Statistics

Scotland
MALES, thousands

Ages	Projected populations at mid-years by age last birthday											Annual averages for longer-term projections								
	2033	2034	2035	2036	2037	2041	2046	2051	2056	2061	2062	2066	2071	2076	2081	2086	2087	2092	2102	2112
Thousands																				
0-14	466	465	464	463	462	458	459	465	471	474	474	474	473	474	477	481	481	484	485	488
15-29	497	500	503	506	508	512	517	513	508	509	510	516	522	525	525	524	524	525	532	535
30-44	550	546	543	537	532	527	530	547	554	559	559	555	551	552	559	565	566	569	568	573
45-59	488	493	501	510	520	541	548	529	520	524	528	542	549	555	552	549	549	552	566	569
60-74	499	494	488	482	473	450	440	468	499	506	504	490	485	491	510	519	520	526	524	537
75 &over	307	315	323	332	341	373	400	402	402	414	418	443	474	494	506	527	532	552	604	650
All ages	2,806	2,814	2,821	2,829	2,835	2,862	2,893	2,924	2,955	2,986	2,993	3,019	3,055	3,091	3,129	3,165	3,172	3,207	3,279	3,353
Percentages																				
0-14	16.6	16.5	16.4	16.4	16.3	16.0	15.9	15.9	16.0	15.9	15.9	15.7	15.5	15.3	15.2	15.2	15.2	15.1	14.8	14.6
15-29	17.7	17.8	17.8	17.9	17.9	17.9	17.9	17.5	17.2	17.1	17.0	17.1	17.1	17.0	16.8	16.6	16.5	16.4	16.2	16.0
30-44	19.6	19.4	19.2	19.0	18.8	18.4	18.3	18.7	18.7	18.7	18.7	18.4	18.0	17.9	17.9	17.9	17.9	17.7	17.3	17.1
45-59	17.4	17.5	17.7	18.0	18.3	18.9	18.9	18.1	17.6	17.5	17.6	17.9	18.0	17.9	17.6	17.3	17.3	17.2	17.2	17.0
60-74	17.8	17.6	17.3	17.0	16.7	15.7	15.2	16.0	16.9	16.9	16.8	16.2	15.9	15.9	16.3	16.4	16.4	16.4	16.0	16.0
75 &over	11.0	11.2	11.5	11.7	12.0	13.0	13.8	13.8	13.6	13.9	14.0	14.7	15.5	16.0	16.2	16.7	16.8	17.2	18.4	19.4
All ages	100.0	100.0	100.0	100.0	100.0	100.0	100.0	100.0	100.0	100.0	100.0	100.0	100.0	100.0	100.0	100.0	100.0	100.0	100.0	100.0
Mean age	42.8	42.9	43.0	43.1	43.2	43.5	43.8	44.0	44.2	44.4	44.5	44.7	45.1	45.4	45.7	46.0	46.1	46.4	47.0	47.7
Median age	42.2	42.3	42.5	42.7	42.8	43.2	43.2	43.2	43.4	43.7	43.7	44.1	44.5	44.8	45.1	45.3	45.4	45.7	46.4	47.1

Note: Figures may not add exactly due to rounding.

* Children under 16. Working age and pensionable age populations based on state pension age (SPA) for given year.
Between 2012 and 2018, SPA will change from 65 years for men and 61 years for women, to 65 years for both sexes.
Then between 2019 and 2020, SPA will change from 65 years to 66 years for both men and women. Between 2034 and 2046,
SPA will increase in two stages from 66 years to 68 years for both sexes. This is based on SPA under the 2011 Pensions Act.
** This is consistent with the age-group definitions used in ONS Labour Market Statistics.
SPA will increase in two stages from 66 years to 68 years for both sexes. This is based on SPA under the 2011 Pensions Act

15.3f Population projections by the Office for National Statistics

Scotland
FEMALES, thousands

2012-based
Principal projection

Projected populations at mid-years by age last birthday

Ages	2012	2013	2014	2015	2016	2017	2018	2019	2020	2021	2022	2023	2024	2025	2026	2027	2028	2029	2030	2031	2032
Thousands																					
0-14	417	416	416	418	420	424	428	431	434	437	439	440	440	442	442	443	444	445	446	446	446
15-29	519	518	517	513	510	505	499	494	488	482	476	473	471	470	471	470	469	470	471	474	477
30-44	533	526	520	516	512	511	513	517	522	529	539	545	549	550	550	549	549	548	545	542	537
45-59	580	587	593	597	600	601	598	592	586	578	567	557	547	539	533	528	522	517	513	510	509
60-74	433	437	443	448	456	463	470	478	486	495	497	503	510	519	526	534	541	547	552	555	556
75 & over	254	257	261	265	269	273	279	285	291	297	310	321	330	337	345	351	359	366	373	381	390
All ages	2,736	2,742	2,750	2,758	2,767	2,777	2,787	2,797	2,807	2,817	2,828	2,838	2,848	2,857	2,867	2,876	2,885	2,893	2,901	2,909	2,916
Percentages																					
0-14	15.2	15.2	15.1	15.1	15.2	15.3	15.3	15.4	15.5	15.5	15.5	15.5	15.5	15.5	15.4	15.4	15.4	15.4	15.4	15.3	15.3
15-29	19.0	18.9	18.8	18.6	18.4	18.2	17.9	17.7	17.4	17.1	16.8	16.7	16.5	16.5	16.4	16.3	16.3	16.2	16.2	16.3	16.4
30-44	19.5	19.2	18.9	18.7	18.5	18.4	18.4	18.5	18.6	18.8	19.1	19.2	19.3	19.2	19.2	19.1	19.0	19.0	18.8	18.6	18.4
45-59	21.2	21.4	21.6	21.6	21.7	21.6	21.5	21.2	20.9	20.5	20.1	19.6	19.2	18.9	18.6	18.4	18.1	17.9	17.7	17.5	17.4
60-74	15.8	16.0	16.1	16.2	16.5	16.7	16.9	17.1	17.3	17.6	17.6	17.7	17.9	18.2	18.4	18.6	18.8	18.9	19.0	19.1	19.1
75 & over	9.3	9.4	9.5	9.6	9.7	9.8	10.0	10.2	10.4	10.5	11.0	11.3	11.6	11.8	12.0	12.2	12.4	12.7	12.9	13.1	13.4
All ages	100.0	100.0	100.0	100.0	100.0	100.0	100.0	100.0	100.0	100.0	100.0	100.0	100.0	100.0	100.0	100.0	100.0	100.0	100.0	100.0	100.0
Mean age	42.1	42.2	42.4	42.6	42.7	42.9	43.0	43.2	43.3	43.5	43.6	43.7	43.9	44.0	44.2	44.3	44.4	44.6	44.7	44.8	45.0
Median age	42.5	42.8	43.0	43.2	43.4	43.5	43.6	43.7	43.7	43.7	43.8	43.8	43.9	44.1	44.2	44.3	44.4	44.5	44.7	44.8	44.9

15.3f Population projections by the Office for National Statistics

Scotland
FEMALES, thousands

Ages	Projected populations at mid-years by age last birthday					Annual averages for longer-term projections															
	2033	2034	2035	2036	2037	2041	2046	2051	2056	2061	2062	2066	2071	2076	2081	2086	2087	2092	2102	2112
Thousands																				
0-14	445	445	444	442	441	438	439	445	451	453	453	453	452	453	456	459	460	462	464	467
15-29	481	485	488	490	493	496	500	496	492	493	494	499	505	507	507	506	506	508	514	517
30-44	532	527	521	515	509	504	507	524	530	534	534	531	527	527	534	540	540	543	542	546
45-59	511	515	520	528	537	548	541	515	505	509	513	526	532	537	534	530	530	532	545	547
60-74	554	549	543	536	527	498	480	499	520	514	510	491	484	490	507	514	515	520	516	527
75 &over	399	409	418	428	438	480	517	522	520	529	532	550	572	583	588	604	608	624	672	716
All ages	2,922	2,928	2,934	2,940	2,945	2,964	2,984	3,002	3,017	3,033	3,036	3,050	3,071	3,097	3,125	3,154	3,160	3,189	3,253	3,321
Percentages																				
0-14	15.2	15.2	15.1	15.0	15.0	14.8	14.7	14.8	14.9	14.9	14.9	14.9	14.7	14.6	14.6	14.6	14.6	14.5	14.3	14.1
15-29	16.5	16.6	16.6	16.7	16.7	16.7	16.8	16.5	16.3	16.3	16.3	16.4	16.4	16.4	16.2	16.1	16.0	15.9	15.8	15.6
30-44	18.2	18.0	17.8	17.5	17.3	17.0	17.0	17.5	17.5	17.6	17.6	17.4	17.1	17.0	17.1	17.1	17.1	17.0	16.7	16.4
45-59	17.5	17.6	17.7	17.9	18.2	18.5	18.1	17.2	16.7	16.8	16.9	17.2	17.3	17.3	17.1	16.8	16.8	16.7	16.8	16.5
60-74	19.0	18.7	18.5	18.2	17.9	16.8	16.1	16.6	17.2	17.0	16.8	16.1	15.8	15.8	16.2	16.3	16.3	16.3	15.9	15.9
75 &over	13.7	14.0	14.2	14.6	14.9	16.2	17.3	17.4	17.2	17.4	17.5	18.0	18.6	18.8	18.8	19.2	19.2	19.6	20.7	21.6
All ages	100.0	100.0	100.0	100.0	100.0	100.0	100.0	100.0	100.0	100.0	100.0	100.0	100.0	100.0	100.0	100.0	100.0	100.0	100.0	100.0
Mean age	45.1	45.2	45.3	45.4	45.5	45.9	46.2	46.4	46.5	46.6	46.6	46.7	46.9	47.1	47.3	47.6	47.6	47.8	48.4	49.0
Median age	45.1	45.2	45.4	45.6	45.7	46.2	46.4	46.1	46.0	46.0	46.0	46.2	46.4	46.7	46.9	47.0	47.1	47.3	47.9	48.6

Note: Figures may not add exactly due to rounding.

* Children under 16. Working age and pensionable age populations based on state pension age (SPA) for given year.

Between 2012 and 2018, SPA will change from 65 years for men and 61 years for women, to 65 years for both sexes.
Then between 2019 and 2020, SPA will change from 65 years to 66 years for both men and women. Between 2034 and 2046, SPA will increase in two stages from 66 years to 68 years for both sexes. This is based on SPA under the 2011 Pensions Act.

** This is consistent with the age-group definitions used in ONS Labour Market Statistics.

15.3g Mid-2012 Population Estimates: Northern Ireland; estimated resident population by single year of age and sex

Thousands

Age	Persons	Males	Females	Age	Persons	Males	Females
All ages	1,823.6	894.5	929.1				
0-4	127.3	65.1	62.2	45-49	133.1	65.6	67.4
0	25.3	13.0	12.3	45	26.6	13.0	13.6
1	25.5	13.0	12.5	46	26.7	13.2	13.5
2	25.2	12.8	12.4	47	27.1	13.3	13.8
3	25.6	13.2	12.5	48	26.7	13.2	13.5
4	25.6	13.2	12.5	49	26.0	13.0	13.0
5-9	114.3	58.8	55.6	50-54	120.7	59.5	61.1
5	24.3	12.5	11.8	50	25.4	12.5	12.9
6	23.2	11.9	11.3	51	25.0	12.3	12.6
7	22.6	11.7	10.9	52	24.0	11.8	12.2
8	22.3	11.5	10.8	53	23.3	11.5	11.8
9	21.8	11.2	10.7	54	23.0	11.4	11.6
10-14	115.7	59.4	56.2	55-59	102.8	51.5	51.4
10	21.9	11.2	10.7	55	22.1	10.9	11.2
11	22.2	11.4	10.8	56	21.2	10.6	10.6
12	23.1	12.0	11.1	57	20.2	10.2	10.0
13	24.1	12.3	11.7	58	19.9	10.1	9.8
14	24.4	12.5	11.9	59	19.5	9.7	9.8
15-19	124.1	63.4	60.7	60-64	93.4	46.1	47.3
15	24.8	12.7	12.2	60	18.7	9.3	9.4
16	24.6	12.6	11.9	61	18.7	9.3	9.4
17	24.9	12.8	12.1	62	18.8	9.3	9.5
18	25.3	12.9	12.5	63	18.6	9.2	9.5
19	24.5	12.4	12.1	64	18.6	9.0	9.6
20-24	123.9	63.0	60.9	65-69	86.1	41.4	44.6
20	24.0	12.3	11.7	65	18.6	8.9	9.7
21	24.6	12.6	12.0	66	17.3	8.4	8.9
22	24.8	12.7	12.2	67	17.0	8.2	8.8
23	25.1	12.7	12.4	68	17.0	8.2	8.8
24	25.3	12.7	12.6	69	16.3	7.8	8.5
25-29	125.1	61.7	63.5	70-74	65.1	30.4	34.7
25	25.2	12.6	12.7	70	14.5	6.9	7.6
26	25.2	12.4	12.8	71	13.1	6.1	6.9
27	25.3	12.5	12.8	72	12.7	5.9	6.8
28	24.9	12.2	12.7	73	12.7	5.9	6.8
29	24.6	12.0	12.6	74	12.0	5.6	6.5
30-34	122.0	59.4	62.7	75-79	51.8	22.8	29.0
30	24.6	12.0	12.6	75	11.7	5.3	6.4
31	25.2	12.3	12.9	76	10.9	4.8	6.1
32	25.2	12.3	12.9	77	10.3	4.6	5.7
33	24.0	11.5	12.5	78	9.6	4.2	5.4
34	23.1	11.3	11.8	79	9.2	3.9	5.4
35-39	118.2	57.8	60.4	80-84	37.2	14.6	22.6
35	22.8	11.1	11.7	80	8.7	3.6	5.1
36	23.0	11.2	11.7	81	8.2	3.3	4.9
37	23.4	11.5	11.9	82	7.4	2.9	4.6
38	24.1	11.8	12.3	83	6.8	2.6	4.2
39	24.9	12.2	12.7	84	6.1	2.2	3.9
40-44	130.1	63.8	66.3	85-89	21.7	7.4	14.3
40	25.4	12.5	12.9	85	5.6	2.0	3.5
41	26.0	12.7	13.3	86	4.8	1.7	3.2
42	25.9	12.7	13.3	87	4.3	1.5	2.8
43	26.2	12.8	13.4	88	3.8	1.2	2.6
44	26.6	13.1	13.5	89	3.2	1.0	2.2
				90 and over	11.0	2.9	8.2

Note: Figures may not add exactly due to rounding.
Source: Northern Ireland Statistics and Research Agency.

15.3h Population projections by the Office for National Statistics

Northern Ireland
PERSONS, thousands

Projected populations at mid-years by age last birthday

2012-based
Principal projection

Ages	2012	2013	2014	2015	2016	2017	2018	2019	2020	2021	2022	2023	2024	2025	2026	2027	2028	2029	2030	2031	2032
Thousands																					
0-14	357	358	359	361	364	367	370	373	375	376	376	374	372	371	368	366	364	361	359	356	354
15-29	373	371	369	365	360	356	351	347	343	340	338	338	339	340	341	343	344	345	347	350	353
30-44	370	368	366	364	363	363	363	364	365	367	369	370	371	369	366	365	364	362	358	354	350
45-59	357	363	368	373	377	380	382	382	381	379	376	373	370	368	366	364	362	360	359	358	358
60-74	245	249	253	257	263	268	273	277	282	288	293	299	306	313	320	327	333	338	343	347	350
75 & over	122	124	128	130	134	138	143	149	154	159	166	172	177	183	188	193	198	203	208	214	220
All ages	1,824	1,832	1,842	1,852	1,861	1,871	1,881	1,891	1,900	1,910	1,918	1,927	1,935	1,943	1,950	1,957	1,963	1,969	1,975	1,980	1,985
Percentages																					
0-14	19.6	19.5	19.5	19.5	19.6	19.6	19.7	19.7	19.7	19.7	19.6	19.4	19.2	19.1	18.9	18.7	18.5	18.4	18.2	18.0	17.8
15-29	20.5	20.3	20.0	19.7	19.4	19.0	18.6	18.3	18.0	17.8	17.6	17.6	17.5	17.5	17.5	17.5	17.5	17.5	17.6	17.7	17.8
30-44	20.3	20.1	19.9	19.7	19.5	19.4	19.3	19.2	19.2	19.2	19.2	19.2	19.1	19.0	18.8	18.7	18.5	18.4	18.1	17.9	17.6
45-59	19.6	19.8	20.0	20.2	20.3	20.3	20.3	20.2	20.1	19.8	19.6	19.4	19.1	18.9	18.8	18.6	18.4	18.3	18.2	18.1	18.0
60-74	13.4	13.6	13.7	13.9	14.1	14.3	14.5	14.6	14.8	15.1	15.3	15.5	15.8	16.1	16.4	16.7	17.0	17.2	17.4	17.6	17.7
75 & over	6.7	6.8	6.9	7.0	7.2	7.4	7.6	7.9	8.1	8.4	8.6	8.9	9.2	9.4	9.6	9.8	10.1	10.3	10.5	10.8	11.1
All ages	100.0	100.0	100.0	100.0	100.0	100.0	100.0	100.0	100.0	100.0	100.0	100.0	100.0	100.0	100.0	100.0	100.0	100.0	100.0	100.0	100.0
Mean age	38.3	38.5	38.7	38.9	39.1	39.3	39.5	39.7	39.9	40.1	40.3	40.5	40.8	41.0	41.2	41.4	41.6	41.9	42.1	42.3	42.5
Median age	37.6	37.8	38.0	38.2	38.4	38.6	38.8	39.1	39.4	39.6	39.8	40.1	40.3	40.6	40.9	41.1	41.4	41.6	41.9	42.2	42.4

15.3h Population projections by the Office for National Statistics

Northern Ireland
PERSONS, thousands
Projected populations at mid-years by age last birthday

Annual averages for longer-term projections

Ages	2033	2034	2035	2036	2037	2041	2046	2051	2056	2061	2062	2066	2071	2076	2081	2086	2087	2092	2102	2112
Thousands																				
0-14	351	349	347	345	343	340	343	348	346	339	337	331	327	326	327	326	326	321	312	309
15-29	356	359	361	362	362	354	343	331	326	330	331	334	333	326	318	313	313	313	312	302
30-44	345	341	337	334	333	336	345	357	349	338	335	326	322	326	330	329	328	320	309	310
45-59	358	359	361	363	365	362	351	332	334	343	346	355	348	337	326	322	322	327	328	314
60-74	352	353	352	350	348	341	335	341	342	332	328	315	319	329	341	335	333	323	313	322
75 & over	226	233	240	247	254	284	315	331	342	354	356	367	374	377	376	390	393	406	430	440
All ages	1,989	1,993	1,997	2,001	2,005	2,018	2,032	2,039	2,040	2,035	2,034	2,028	2,023	2,020	2,017	2,014	2,014	2,010	2,004	1,998
Percentages																				
0-14	17.7	17.5	17.4	17.2	17.1	16.9	16.9	17.0	17.0	16.7	16.6	16.3	16.1	16.1	16.2	16.2	16.2	16.0	15.6	15.5
15-29	17.9	18.0	18.1	18.1	18.1	17.6	16.9	16.2	16.0	16.2	16.3	16.5	16.4	16.1	15.7	15.5	15.5	15.6	15.6	15.1
30-44	17.4	17.1	16.9	16.7	16.6	16.7	17.0	17.5	17.1	16.6	16.5	16.1	15.9	16.1	16.4	16.3	16.3	15.9	15.4	15.5
45-59	18.0	18.0	18.1	18.1	18.2	17.9	17.3	16.3	16.4	16.9	17.0	17.5	17.2	16.7	16.2	16.0	16.0	16.3	16.4	15.7
60-74	17.7	17.7	17.6	17.5	17.4	16.9	16.5	16.7	16.7	16.3	16.1	15.5	15.8	16.3	16.9	16.6	16.5	16.1	15.6	16.1
75 & over	11.4	11.7	12.0	12.3	12.7	14.1	15.5	16.2	16.8	17.4	17.5	18.1	18.5	18.7	18.6	19.3	19.5	20.2	21.4	22.0
All ages	100.0	100.0	100.0	100.0	100.0	100.0	100.0	100.0	100.0	100.0	100.0	100.0	100.0	100.0	100.0	100.0	100.0	100.0	100.0	100.0
Mean age	42.7	42.9	43.1	43.3	43.4	44.0	44.6	45.0	45.4	45.8	45.9	46.1	46.4	46.7	46.9	47.2	47.2	47.6	48.3	48.9
Median age	42.7	42.9	43.1	43.3	43.5	44.0	44.3	44.3	44.9	45.5	45.6	46.0	46.4	46.5	46.6	46.8	46.9	47.3	48.2	48.8

Note: Figures may not add exactly due to rounding.

* Children under 16. Working age and pensionable age populations based on state pension age (SPA) for given year.
Between 2012 and 2018, SPA will change from 65 years for men and 61 years for women, to 65 years for both sexes.
Then between 2019 and 2020, SPA will change from 65 years to 66 years for both men and women. Between 2034 and 2046,
SPA will increase in two stages from 66 years to 68 years for both sexes. This is based on SPA under the 2011 Pensions Act.
** This is consistent with the age-group definitions used in ONS Labour Market Statistics.

5.3h Population projections by the Office for National Statistics

Northern Ireland
MALES, thousands

2012-based
Principal projection

Projected populations at mid-years by age last birthday

Ages	2012	2013	2014	2015	2016	2017	2018	2019	2020	2021	2022	2023	2024	2025	2026	2027	2028	2029	2030	2031	2032
Thousands																					
0-14	183	184	184	185	186	188	190	191	192	192	192	191	190	189	188	187	186	185	183	182	181
15-29	188	188	187	186	184	182	180	178	176	174	174	174	174	175	175	176	177	177	178	180	181
30-44	181	179	178	178	177	177	178	179	180	181	183	184	185	185	184	184	184	183	182	181	179
45-59	177	179	182	184	185	187	187	187	186	185	183	181	180	178	177	176	175	174	174	173	173
60-74	118	120	123	125	128	131	133	135	138	141	143	147	150	153	156	159	162	164	166	168	170
75 &over	48	49	51	53	54	57	59	62	65	68	71	74	77	79	82	84	87	90	92	95	98
All ages	895	900	905	910	915	921	926	931	937	942	946	951	955	959	963	967	970	973	976	979	982
Percentages																					
0-14	20.5	20.4	20.4	20.3	20.4	20.4	20.5	20.5	20.5	20.4	20.3	20.1	19.9	19.7	19.5	19.3	19.1	19.0	18.8	18.6	18.4
15-29	21.0	20.9	20.7	20.4	20.1	19.7	19.4	19.1	18.8	18.5	18.4	18.3	18.2	18.2	18.2	18.2	18.2	18.2	18.2	18.3	18.4
30-44	20.2	20.0	19.7	19.6	19.4	19.3	19.2	19.2	19.2	19.3	19.3	19.4	19.4	19.2	19.1	19.0	19.0	18.8	18.7	18.5	18.2
45-59	19.7	19.9	20.1	20.2	20.2	20.3	20.2	20.1	19.9	19.7	19.4	19.1	18.8	18.6	18.4	18.2	18.0	17.9	17.8	17.7	17.7
60-74	13.2	13.4	13.5	13.8	14.0	14.2	14.4	14.5	14.7	15.0	15.2	15.4	15.7	16.0	16.2	16.5	16.7	16.9	17.0	17.2	17.3
75 &over	5.3	5.5	5.6	5.8	5.9	6.1	6.4	6.7	6.9	7.2	7.5	7.7	8.0	8.3	8.5	8.7	9.0	9.2	9.5	9.7	10.0
All ages	100.0	100.0	100.0	100.0	100.0	100.0	100.0	100.0	100.0	100.0	100.0	100.0	100.0	100.0	100.0	100.0	100.0	100.0	100.0	100.0	100.0
Mean age	37.3	37.5	37.7	37.9	38.1	38.3	38.5	38.7	38.9	39.1	39.4	39.6	39.8	40.0	40.2	40.5	40.7	40.9	41.1	41.3	41.5
Median age	36.5	36.7	36.8	37.0	37.2	37.4	37.7	37.9	38.1	38.3	38.5	38.8	39.0	39.2	39.5	39.7	40.0	40.3	40.5	40.8	41.0

5.3h Population projections by the Office for National Statistics

Northern Ireland
MALES, thousands

| | Projected populations at mid-years by age last birthday | | | | | | | | | | | Annual averages for longer-term projections | | | | | | | | |
Ages	2033	2034	2035	2036	2037	2041	2046	2051	2056	2061	2062	2066	2071	2076	2081	2086	2087	2092	2102	2112
Thousands																				
0-14	179	178	177	176	175	174	175	178	177	173	172	169	167	167	167	167	166	164	159	158
15-29	183	184	185	185	185	181	175	169	167	169	169	171	170	167	162	160	160	160	160	155
30-44	177	175	173	172	171	173	177	183	179	173	172	167	165	167	169	169	168	164	159	159
45-59	174	175	176	178	179	181	178	169	171	175	177	181	177	172	166	164	164	166	167	160
60-74	170	170	170	169	168	163	161	166	169	166	165	159	162	166	172	169	168	163	159	164
75 &over	101	104	107	111	114	128	142	148	152	158	159	166	171	175	176	185	186	194	206	212
All ages	984	986	988	990	992	1,000	1,007	1,013	1,014	1,014	1,014	1,013	1,012	1,013	1,014	1,013	1,013	1,012	1,010	1,008
Percentages																				
0-14	18.2	18.1	17.9	17.8	17.6	17.4	17.4	17.5	17.4	17.1	17.0	16.7	16.5	16.4	16.5	16.4	16.4	16.2	15.8	15.7
15-29	18.6	18.6	18.7	18.7	18.7	18.1	17.4	16.7	16.5	16.6	16.7	16.9	16.8	16.4	16.0	15.8	15.8	15.8	15.8	15.4
30-44	18.0	17.7	17.5	17.3	17.3	17.3	17.6	18.1	17.7	17.1	17.0	16.5	16.3	16.5	16.7	16.6	16.6	16.2	15.7	15.8
45-59	17.7	17.7	17.8	17.9	18.1	18.1	17.6	16.7	16.8	17.3	17.4	17.9	17.5	16.9	16.4	16.2	16.2	16.4	16.6	15.9
60-74	17.3	17.3	17.2	17.0	16.9	16.3	15.9	16.3	16.6	16.4	16.3	15.7	16.0	16.4	17.0	16.7	16.6	16.1	15.7	16.2
75 &over	10.3	10.6	10.9	11.2	11.5	12.8	14.1	14.6	15.0	15.5	15.7	16.3	16.9	17.3	17.4	18.2	18.4	19.2	20.4	21.0
All ages	100.0	100.0	100.0	100.0	100.0	100.0	100.0	100.0	100.0	100.0	100.0	100.0	100.0	100.0	100.0	100.0	100.0	100.0	100.0	100.0
Mean age	41.7	41.9	42.1	42.3	42.4	43.0	43.5	44.0	44.4	44.7	44.8	45.1	45.5	45.8	46.1	46.5	46.5	46.9	47.6	48.3
Median age	41.3	41.5	41.7	41.9	42.1	42.6	42.7	43.1	43.7	44.3	44.5	44.9	45.4	45.6	45.7	46.0	46.1	46.6	47.5	48.0

Note: Figures may not add exactly due to rounding.
* Children under 16. Working age and pensionable age populations based on state pension age (SPA) for given year.
Between 2012 and 2018, SPA will change from 65 years for men and 61 years for women, to 65 years for both sexes.
Then between 2019 and 2020, SPA will change from 65 years to 66 years for both men and women. Between 2034 and 2046,
SPA will increase in two stages from 66 years to 68 years for both sexes. This is based on SPA under the 2011 Pensions Act.
** This is consistent with the age-group definitions used in ONS Labour Market Statistics.

15.3h Population projections by the Office for National Statistics

Northern Ireland
FEMALES, thousands

2012-based
Principal projection

Projected populations at mid-years by age last birthday

Ages	2012	2013	2014	2015	2016	2017	2018	2019	2020	2021	2022	2023	2024	2025	2026	2027	2028	2029	2030	2031	2032
Thousands																					
0-14	174	174	175	176	178	179	181	182	183	184	184	183	182	181	180	179	178	177	176	174	173
15-29	185	183	182	179	176	174	171	169	167	165	165	164	164	165	166	167	167	168	169	171	172
30-44	189	188	187	186	186	185	185	185	185	186	186	186	186	184	182	181	180	178	176	173	171
45-59	180	183	187	190	192	194	195	195	195	194	193	192	190	190	189	188	187	186	185	185	184
60-74	127	128	130	132	135	137	140	142	144	147	150	153	156	160	164	167	171	174	177	179	181
75 &over	74	75	76	78	79	81	84	86	89	92	95	98	101	103	106	108	111	113	116	118	122
All ages	929	933	937	942	946	950	955	959	964	968	972	976	980	983	987	990	993	996	998	1,001	1,003
Percentages																					
0-14	18.7	18.7	18.7	18.7	18.8	18.9	18.9	19.0	19.0	19.0	18.9	18.8	18.6	18.4	18.3	18.1	17.9	17.8	17.6	17.4	17.3
15-29	19.9	19.7	19.4	19.0	18.7	18.3	17.9	17.6	17.3	17.1	16.9	16.8	16.8	16.8	16.8	16.8	16.8	16.8	16.9	17.0	17.2
30-44	20.4	20.2	20.0	19.8	19.6	19.5	19.4	19.3	19.2	19.2	19.1	19.1	19.0	18.7	18.5	18.3	18.1	17.9	17.6	17.3	17.0
45-59	19.4	19.7	19.9	20.1	20.3	20.4	20.4	20.3	20.2	20.0	19.8	19.6	19.4	19.3	19.1	19.0	18.8	18.7	18.6	18.4	18.4
60-74	13.6	13.8	13.9	14.0	14.2	14.4	14.6	14.8	15.0	15.2	15.4	15.7	15.9	16.3	16.6	16.9	17.2	17.5	17.7	17.9	18.0
75 &over	8.0	8.0	8.2	8.3	8.4	8.5	8.8	9.0	9.2	9.5	9.8	10.0	10.3	10.5	10.7	10.9	11.2	11.4	11.6	11.8	12.1
All ages	100.0	100.0	100.0	100.0	100.0	100.0	100.0	100.0	100.0	100.0	100.0	100.0	100.0	100.0	100.0	100.0	100.0	100.0	100.0	100.0	100.0
Mean age	39.3	39.5	39.7	39.9	40.1	40.3	40.5	40.7	40.9	41.1	41.3	41.5	41.7	41.9	42.2	42.4	42.6	42.8	43.0	43.3	43.5
Median age	38.6	38.9	39.1	39.3	39.5	39.8	40.0	40.2	40.5	40.8	41.1	41.4	41.6	41.9	42.2	42.5	42.7	43.0	43.3	43.6	43.8

Population and vital statistics

15.3h Population projections by the Office for National Statistics

Northern Ireland
FEMALES, thousands

	Projected populations at mid-years by age last birthday					Annual averages for longer-term projections														
Ages	2033	2034	2035	2036	2037	2041	2046	2051	2056	2061	2062	2066	2071	2076	2081	2086	2087	2092	2102	2112
Thousands																				
0-14	172	171	170	169	168	166	168	170	169	166	165	162	160	160	160	160	159	157	153	151
15-29	174	175	176	177	177	173	167	162	159	161	162	163	163	159	155	153	153	153	152	147
30-44	168	166	164	162	162	163	168	174	170	165	163	159	157	159	161	160	160	156	150	151
45-59	184	184	185	185	185	182	173	163	164	168	170	174	171	165	160	158	158	160	161	154
60-74	182	183	182	182	181	178	175	176	173	165	163	156	157	162	168	165	164	159	154	159
75 &over	125	128	132	136	140	156	173	183	190	196	197	201	203	202	199	205	206	212	223	228
All ages	1,005	1,007	1,009	1,011	1,012	1,018	1,024	1,027	1,026	1,021	1,020	1,016	1,010	1,007	1,004	1,001	1,000	998	994	990
Percentages																				
0-14	17.1	17.0	16.8	16.7	16.6	16.4	16.4	16.6	16.5	16.2	16.2	16.0	15.8	15.9	16.0	15.9	15.9	15.7	15.3	15.3
15-29	17.3	17.4	17.5	17.5	17.5	17.0	16.3	15.7	15.5	15.8	15.8	16.1	16.1	15.8	15.5	15.3	15.3	15.3	15.3	14.9
30-44	16.7	16.5	16.3	16.1	16.0	16.0	16.4	16.9	16.6	16.1	16.0	15.7	15.5	15.8	16.0	16.0	16.0	15.6	15.1	15.2
45-59	18.3	18.3	18.3	18.3	18.3	17.8	16.9	15.8	15.9	16.5	16.6	17.2	16.9	16.4	15.9	15.8	15.8	16.1	16.2	15.5
60-74	18.1	18.1	18.1	18.0	17.8	17.4	17.0	17.1	16.8	16.2	16.0	15.3	15.6	16.1	16.8	16.5	16.4	16.0	15.5	16.0
75 &over	12.4	12.8	13.1	13.5	13.8	15.3	16.9	17.8	18.5	19.2	19.3	19.8	20.1	20.1	19.9	20.5	20.6	21.3	22.5	23.1
All ages	100.0	100.0	100.0	100.0	100.0	100.0	100.0	100.0	100.0	100.0	100.0	100.0	100.0	100.0	100.0	100.0	100.0	100.0	100.0	100.0
Mean age	43.7	43.9	44.1	44.3	44.4	45.1	45.6	46.1	46.5	46.8	46.9	47.1	47.3	47.5	47.7	47.9	47.9	48.2	48.9	49.5
Median age	44.1	44.3	44.6	44.8	45.0	45.6	45.9	45.7	46.1	46.6	46.7	47.1	47.4	47.5	47.5	47.6	47.7	48.0	49.0	49.5

Note: Figures may not add exactly due to rounding.

* Children under 16. Working age and pensionable age populations based on state pension age (SPA) for given year.
Between 2012 and 2018, SPA will change from 65 years for men and 61 years for women, to 65 years for both sexes.
Then between 2019 and 2020, SPA will change from 65 years to 66 years for both men and women. Between 2034 and 2046, SPA will increase in two stages from 66 years to 68 years for both sexes. This is based on SPA under the 2011 Pensions Act.
** This is consistent with the age-group definitions used in ONS Labour Market Statistics.

15.4 Families by family type and presence of children

United Kingdom, 1996-2012

thousands

Number of families	1996 Estimate	1996 CI+/-	1997 Estimate	1997 CI+/-	1998 Estimate	1998 CI+/-	1999 Estimate	1999 CI+/-	2000 Estimate	2000 CI+/-	2001 Estimate	2001 CI+/-	2002 Estimate	2002 CI+/-	2003 Estimate	2003 CI+/-	2004 Estimate	2004 CI+/-	2005 Estimate	2005 CI+/-	2006 Estimate	2006 CI+/-	2007 Estimate	2007 CI+/-	2008 Estimate	2008 CI+/-	2009 Estimate	2009 CI+/-	2010 Estimate	2010 CI+/-	2011 Estimate	2011 CI+/-	2012 Estimate	2012 CI+/-
Married couple family	12,641	64	12,582	66	12,497	70	12,417	69	12,443	69	12,280	71	12,247	72	12,208	74	12,193	77	12,250	77	12,198	79	12,191	81	12,146	82	12,184	82	12,197	87	12,096	101	12,185	101
No children	5,746	63	5,840	63	5,871	65	5,880	65	5,977	66	5,892	67	5,957	67	5,972	69	5,913	71	5,992	71	6,024	72	5,971	73	6,010	74	5,924	74	5,995	78	5,934	91	5,936	90
Dependent children	5,223	50	5,126	51	5,013	52	4,936	52	4,918	53	4,833	54	4,776	54	4,743	56	4,684	57	4,721	58	4,663	59	4,657	60	4,599	60	4,655	63	4,643	64	4,567	65	4,610	66
Non-dependent children only	1,673	42	1,616	42	1,612	45	1,601	46	1,548	43	1,555	44	1,514	43	1,493	45	1,595	47	1,537	47	1,510	47	1,563	48	1,537	49	1,605	51	1,559	51	1,595	52	1,639	54
Civil partner couple family	N/A	N/A	N/A	N/A	N/A	N/A	N/A	N/A	N/A	N/A	N/A	N/A	N/A	N/A	N/A	N/A	N/A	N/A	N/A	N/A	13	5	32	9	40	9	40	9	44	10	59	12	66	12
No children or non-dependent children only	N/A	N/A	N/A	N/A	N/A	N/A	N/A	N/A	N/A	N/A	N/A	N/A	N/A	N/A	N/A	N/A	N/A	N/A	N/A	N/A	13	5	28	8	37	9	37	9	43	10	54	12	60	12
Dependent children	N/A	N/A	N/A	N/A	N/A	N/A	N/A	N/A	N/A	N/A	N/A	N/A	N/A	N/A	N/A	N/A	N/A	N/A	N/A	N/A	..		4	3	3	3	4	3	2	2	5	3	6	3
Opposite sex cohabiting couple family	1,459	43	1,674	47	1,728	52	1,855	53	1,984	52	2,129	55	2,151	55	2,232	58	2,285	60	2,372	61	2,433	63	2,520	65	2,624	67	2,659	69	2,727	70	2,853	75	2,893	75
No children	877	35	1,035	37	1,036	41	1,083	41	1,184	42	1,260	44	1,265	44	1,348	46	1,322	47	1,393	47	1,400	49	1,458	51	1,500	52	1,540	55	1,537	55	1,626	60	1,632	60
Dependent children	539	27	592	28	638	30	718	32	739	32	808	34	808	34	816	36	881	38	894	38	947	40	966	40	1,031	42	1,017	42	1,073	44	1,103	46	1,131	47
Non-dependent children only	43	8	46	8	54	8	54	9	61	10	61	10	79	12	68	11	82	11	85	13	86	13	96	14	93	14	102	15	117	17	124	17	130	18
Same sex cohabiting couple family	16	5	28	7	30	7	31	7	38	8	45	9	46	9	53	10	61	11	56	11	68	12	51	10	60	11	53	11	50	11	62	13	69	13
No children or non-dependent children only	15	5	27	7	29	7	30	7	37	8	44	9	45	9	52	10	60	11	54	11	65	12	47	10	57	11	50	11	48	11	60	13	64	13
Dependent children	..		..		..		1	1	..		..		..		..		..		3	2	..		4	3	3	3	3	2	2	2	3	2	6	3
Lone parent family	2,445	54	2,372	53	2,474	55	2,490	55	2,428	55	2,512	58	2,547	57	2,593	60	2,681	62	2,688	62	2,682	63	2,671	63	2,729	65	2,853	68	2,896	69	2,853	70	2,975	72
Dependent children	1,631	41	1,613	41	1,719	43	1,742	43	1,698	43	1,745	45	1,807	45	1,801	47	1,865	47	1,875	49	1,856	49	1,858	49	1,873	51	1,951	53	1,955	53	1,933	55	1,986	55
Non-dependent children only	814	34	759	33	755	34	748	34	731	34	767	35	739	35	792	37	816	38	814	39	826	39	814	39	856	41	902	43	940	44	920	45	989	47
Lone mother family	2,089	48	2,055	48	2,163	50	2,162	50	2,108	50	2,159	51	2,205	51	2,247	53	2,315	55	2,343	56	2,335	57	2,320	56	2,386	58	2,478	61	2,517	62	2,513	64	2,575	65
Dependent children	1,466	38	1,463	38	1,558	40	1,579	40	1,550	41	1,575	42	1,635	43	1,623	43	1,682	45	1,699	46	1,687	46	1,691	46	1,705	47	1,767	49	1,768	49	1,771	50	1,811	52
Non-dependent children only	623	29	592	29	605	30	583	29	558	29	584	30	570	30	624	32	633	33	644	34	648	34	629	34	680	36	711	37	748	39	741	40	764	41
Lone father family	356	22	317	21	311	21	328	22	320	22	353	24	341	24	346	24	366	26	345	25	347	26	352	26	344	26	375	27	379	28	341	27	400	30
Dependent children	164	15	150	15	161	15	163	16	147	15	170	16	173	17	178	17	183	17	175	18	169	18	167	18	168	18	183	18	187	19	162	19	176	19
Non-dependent children only	191	17	167	17	150	16	165	16	173	17	184	18	169	17	168	17	183	19	170	18	178	19	185	20	176	19	191	20	192	20	178	20	224	23
All families	16,560	57	16,655	58	16,729	73	16,793	71	16,893	59	16,966	61	16,991	62	17,087	64	17,219	67	17,367	67	17,393	68	17,466	70	17,599	71	17,789	71	17,914	74	17,923	89	18,188	88
No children	6,637	69	6,902	70	6,936	73	6,993	73	7,198	73	7,196	75	7,266	75	7,372	78	7,295	80	7,439	80	7,502	81	7,504	84	7,603	85	7,550	85	7,622	89	7,673	102	7,688	101
Dependent children	7,393	41	7,332	42	7,371	43	7,398	44	7,355	44	7,386	44	7,392	45	7,361	46	7,431	47	7,492	48	7,469	48	7,488	49	7,509	50	7,629	50	7,676	52	7,612	54	7,739	54
Non-dependent children only	2,530	50	2,421	50	2,421	55	2,403	56	2,339	52	2,383	53	2,332	53	2,353	54	2,493	57	2,436	57	2,422	58	2,474	59	2,487	60	2,610	62	2,616	64	2,639	65	2,761	66

Source: Labour Force Survey (LFS), Office for National Statistics
Produced by Demographic Analysis Unit, Office for National Statistics
families@ons.gsi.gov.uk

1. Totals may not sum due to rounding.
2. In the table .. indicates that the data are not sufficiently reliable to be published.
3. The robustness of an estimate is presented in two ways:

The coefficient of variation (CV) indicates the robustness of each estimate. It is defined as $CV = \dfrac{\text{standard error}}{\text{estimate}} \times 100$, where standard error is an estimate of the margin of error associated with a sample survey. The coloured shading on the table indicates the precision of each estimate as follows:

Statistical Robustness

0 ≤ CV < 5	Estimates are considered precise
5 ≤ CV < 10	Estimates are considered reasonably precise
10 ≤ CV < 20	Estimates are considered acceptable
CV ≥ 20	Estimates are not considered reliable for practical purposes

Confidence intervals are also presented. CI+/- is the upper(+) and lower(-) 95% confidence interval. It is defined as 1.96 x standard error. The confidence interval provides an estimated range of values in which an actual data value is likely to fall around 95 per cent of the time. For example, there were 12.

4. Civil partnerships were introduced in the UK in December 2005.
5. Families with no children and non-dependent children only have been added together for civil partner couple families and same sex cohabiting couple families to improve the robustness of the estimates.
6. A family is a married, civil partnered or cohabiting couple with or without children, or a lone parent with at least one child. Children may be dependent or non-dependent.
7. Dependent children are those living with their parent(s) and either (a) aged under 16, or (b) aged 16 to 18 in full-time education, excluding children aged 16 to 18 who have a spouse, partner or child living in the household.
8. Non-dependent children are those living with their parent(s), and either (a) aged 19 or over, or (b) aged 16 to 18 who are not in full-time education or who have a spouse, partner or child living in the household. Non-dependent children are sometimes called adult children.
9. Families with no children are families where there are no children currently living in the household. This does not necessarily indicate that the adult(s) in the household have never had children.

15.5 Geographical distribution of the population

		Mid-year population estimate[1]	
		2011	2012
United Kingdom	**K02000001**	**63,285,145**	**63,705,030**
Great Britain	**K03000001**	**61,470,827**	**61,881,396**
England and Wales	K04000001	56,170,927	56,567,796
England	E92000001	53,107,169	53,493,729
Wales	W92000004	3,063,758	3,074,067
Scotland	S92000003	5,299,900	5,313,600
Northern Ireland	N92000002	1,814,318	1,823,634
North East	E12000001	2,596,441	2,602,310
North West	E12000002	7,055,961	7,084,337
Yorkshire and The Humber	E12000003	5,288,212	5,316,691
East Midlands	E12000004	4,537,448	4,567,731
West Midlands	E12000005	5,608,667	5,642,569
East	E12000006	5,862,418	5,907,348
London	E12000007	8,204,407	8,308,369
South East	E12000008	8,652,784	8,724,737
South West	E12000009	5,300,831	5,339,637
Hartlepool UA	E06000001	92,088	92,238
Middlesbrough UA	E06000002	138,368	138,744
Redcar and Cleveland UA	E06000003	135,164	134,998
Stockton-on-Tees UA	E06000004	191,824	192,406
Darlington UA	E06000005	105,584	105,248
Halton UA	E06000006	125,722	125,692
Warrington UA	E06000007	202,709	203,652
Blackburn with Darwen UA	E06000008	147,657	147,713
Blackpool UA	E06000009	142,080	141,976
Kingston upon Hull, City of UA	E06000010	256,123	257,204
East Riding of Yorkshire UA	E06000011	334,673	335,887
North East Lincolnshire UA	E06000012	159,735	159,727
North Lincolnshire UA	E06000013	167,516	168,372
York UA	E06000014	197,783	200,018
Derby UA	E06000015	248,943	250,568
Leicester UA	E06000016	329,627	331,606
Rutland UA	E06000017	37,581	37,015
Nottingham UA	E06000018	303,899	308,735
Herefordshire UA	E06000019	183,619	184,932
Telford and Wrekin UA	E06000020	166,831	167,682
Stoke-on-Trent UA	E06000021	248,719	249,903
Bath and North East Somerset UA	E06000022	175,538	177,643
Bristol, City of UA	E06000023	428,074	432,451
North Somerset UA	E06000024	203,091	204,385
South Gloucestershire UA	E06000025	263,417	266,147
Plymouth UA	E06000026	256,589	258,026
Torbay UA	E06000027	131,193	131,492
Bournemouth UA	E06000028	183,450	186,744
Poole UA	E06000029	148,075	148,615
Swindon UA	E06000030	209,709	211,934
Peterborough UA	E06000031	184,457	186,372
Luton UA	E06000032	203,641	205,843
Southend-on-Sea UA	E06000033	174,274	174,838
Thurrock UA	E06000034	158,268	159,533
Medway UA	E06000035	264,885	268,218
Bracknell Forest UA	E06000036	113,696	115,058
West Berkshire UA	E06000037	154,148	154,486
Reading UA	E06000038	155,339	157,112
Slough UA	E06000039	140,713	141,838
Windsor and Maidenhead UA	E06000040	145,098	145,822
Wokingham UA	E06000041	154,943	156,663
Milton Keynes UA	E06000042	249,895	252,358
Brighton and Hove UA	E06000043	272,952	275,762

15.5 Geographical distribution of the population

		Mid-year population estimate[1]	
		2011	**2012**
Portsmouth UA	E06000044	205,433	206,836
Southampton UA	E06000045	235,870	239,428
Isle of Wight UA	E06000046	138,392	138,748
County Durham UA	E06000047	512,994	514,348
Northumberland UA	E06000048	316,278	316,116
Cheshire East UA	E06000049	370,736	372,146
Cheshire West and Chester UA	E06000050	329,526	330,200
Shropshire UA	E06000051	307,108	308,207
Cornwall UA	E06000052	533,760	537,914
Isles of Scilly UA	E06000053	2,224	2,264
Wiltshire UA	E06000054	474,319	476,816
Bedford UA	E06000055	157,840	159,207
Central Bedfordshire UA	E06000056	255,644	259,969
Isle of Anglesey UA	W06000001	69,913	70,049
Gwynedd UA	W06000002	121,523	122,142
Conwy UA	W06000003	115,326	115,515
Denbighshire UA	W06000004	93,919	94,066
Flintshire UA	W06000005	152,666	152,743
Wrexham UA	W06000006	135,070	135,919
Powys UA	W06000023	133,071	132,952
Ceredigion UA	W06000008	75,293	76,046
Pembrokeshire UA	W06000009	122,613	123,035
Carmarthenshire UA	W06000010	183,961	184,317
Swansea UA	W06000011	238,691	239,633
Neath Port Talbot UA	W06000012	139,880	140,108
Bridgend UA	W06000013	139,410	139,740
The Vale of Glamorgan UA	W06000014	126,679	126,831
Cardiff UA	W06000015	345,442	348,493
Rhondda, Cynon, Taf UA	W06000016	234,373	235,599
Merthyr Tydfil UA	W06000024	58,851	58,898
Caerphilly UA	W06000018	178,782	179,022
Blaenau Gwent UA	W06000019	69,812	69,822
Torfaen UA	W06000020	91,190	91,372
Monmouthshire UA	W06000021	91,508	91,659
Newport UA	W06000022	145,785	146,106
Greater London	E12000007	8,204,407	8,308,369
Greater Manchester (Met County)	E11000001	2,685,386	2,702,209
Merseyside (Met County)	E11000002	1,380,770	1,385,666
South Yorkshire (Met County)	E11000003	1,343,805	1,352,144
Tyne And Wear (Met County)	E11000004	1,104,141	1,108,212
West Midlands (Met County)	E11000005	2,739,733	2,762,716
West Yorkshire (Met County)	E11000006	2,227,371	2,240,711
Buckinghamshire	E10000002	506,550	511,488
Cambridgeshire	E10000003	622,312	628,339
Cumbria	E10000006	499,817	499,104
Derbyshire	E10000007	770,688	773,522
Devon	E10000008	747,709	753,157
Dorset	E10000009	413,813	414,940
East Sussex	E10000011	527,209	531,201
Essex	E10000012	1,396,599	1,406,517
Gloucestershire	E10000013	598,289	602,159
Hampshire	E10000014	1,322,118	1,330,153
Hertfordshire	E10000015	1,119,824	1,129,096
Kent	E10000016	1,466,466	1,480,166
Lancashire	E10000017	1,171,558	1,175,979
Leicestershire	E10000018	651,179	656,698
Lincolnshire	E10000019	714,768	718,838
Norfolk	E10000020	859,426	865,302
Northamptonshire	E10000021	693,967	700,576

15.5 Geographical distribution of the population

		Mid-year population estimate[1]	
		2011	**2012**
North Yorkshire	E10000023	601,206	602,628
Nottinghamshire	E10000024	786,796	790,173
Oxfordshire	E10000025	654,791	660,772
Somerset	E10000027	531,581	534,950
Staffordshire	E10000028	849,546	852,123
Suffolk	E10000029	730,133	732,332
Surrey	E10000030	1,135,367	1,143,509
Warwickshire	E10000031	546,554	547,974
West Sussex	E10000032	808,919	815,119
Worcestershire	E10000034	566,557	569,032
City of London	E09000001	7,412	7,604
Barking and Dagenham	E09000002	187,029	190,560
Barnet	E09000003	357,538	363,956
Bexley	E09000004	232,774	234,271
Brent	E09000005	312,245	314,660
Bromley	E09000006	310,554	314,036
Camden	E09000007	220,087	224,962
Croydon	E09000008	364,815	368,886
Ealing	E09000009	339,314	340,671
Enfield	E09000010	313,935	317,287
Greenwich	E09000011	255,483	260,068
Hackney	E09000012	247,182	252,119
Hammersmith and Fulham	E09000013	182,445	179,850
Haringey	E09000014	255,540	258,912
Harrow	E09000015	240,499	242,377
Havering	E09000016	237,927	239,733
Hillingdon	E09000017	275,499	281,756
Hounslow	E09000018	254,927	259,052
Islington	E09000019	206,285	211,047
Kensington and Chelsea	E09000020	158,251	155,930
Kingston upon Thames	E09000021	160,436	163,906
Lambeth	E09000022	304,481	310,200
Lewisham	E09000023	276,938	281,556
Merton	E09000024	200,543	202,225
Newham	E09000025	310,460	314,084
Redbridge	E09000026	281,395	284,617
Richmond upon Thames	E09000027	187,527	189,145
Southwark	E09000028	288,717	293,530
Sutton	E09000029	191,123	193,630
Tower Hamlets	E09000030	256,012	263,003
Waltham Forest	E09000031	259,742	262,566
Wandsworth	E09000032	307,710	308,312
Westminster	E09000033	219,582	223,858
Bolton	E08000001	277,296	278,984
Bury	E08000002	185,422	186,199
Manchester	E08000003	502,902	510,772
Oldham	E08000004	225,157	225,875
Rochdale	E08000005	211,929	212,020
Salford	E08000006	234,487	237,085
Stockport	E08000007	283,253	283,897
Tameside	E08000008	219,727	220,241
Trafford	E08000009	227,091	228,466
Wigan	E08000010	318,122	318,670
Knowsley	E08000011	145,903	145,936
Liverpool	E08000012	465,656	469,690
St. Helens	E08000013	175,405	176,114
Sefton	E08000014	273,969	273,697
Wirral	E08000015	319,837	320,229
Barnsley	E08000016	231,865	233,671
Doncaster	E08000017	302,468	302,739
Rotherham	E08000018	257,716	258,352

15.5 Geographical distribution of the population

		Mid-year population estimate[1]	
		2011	**2012**
Sheffield	E08000019	551,756	557,382
Gateshead	E08000020	200,349	200,153
Newcastle upon Tyne	E08000021	279,092	282,442
North Tyneside	E08000022	201,206	201,446
South Tyneside	E08000023	148,164	148,428
Sunderland	E08000024	275,330	275,743
Birmingham	E08000025	1,074,283	1,085,417
Coventry	E08000026	316,915	323,132
Dudley	E08000027	313,261	313,589
Sandwell	E08000028	309,042	311,304
Solihull	E08000029	206,856	207,380
Walsall	E08000030	269,524	270,924
Wolverhampton	E08000031	249,852	250,970
Bradford	E08000032	523,115	524,619
Calderdale	E08000033	204,170	205,293
Kirklees	E08000034	422,970	425,517
Leeds	E08000035	750,683	757,655
Wakefield	E08000036	326,433	327,627
Aylesbury Vale	E07000004	174,880	177,793
Chiltern	E07000005	92,652	92,954
South Bucks	E07000006	67,060	67,435
Wycombe	E07000007	171,958	173,306
Cambridge	E07000008	122,725	125,155
East Cambridgeshire	E07000009	84,245	85,097
Fenland	E07000010	95,461	95,996
Huntingdonshire	E07000011	170,039	171,023
South Cambridgeshire	E07000012	149,842	151,068
Allerdale	E07000026	96,444	96,268
Barrow-in-Furness	E07000027	69,056	68,446
Carlisle	E07000028	107,475	107,952
Copeland	E07000029	70,627	70,329
Eden	E07000030	52,502	52,656
South Lakeland	E07000031	103,713	103,453
Amber Valley	E07000032	122,521	122,746
Bolsover	E07000033	76,029	76,447
Chesterfield	E07000034	103,788	103,782
Derbyshire Dales	E07000035	71,104	71,336
Erewash	E07000036	112,249	112,809
High Peak	E07000037	90,982	91,118
North East Derbyshire	E07000038	99,100	99,325
South Derbyshire	E07000039	94,915	95,959
East Devon	E07000040	133,272	134,359
Exeter	E07000041	117,063	119,397
Mid Devon	E07000042	77,936	78,335
North Devon	E07000043	93,976	93,847
South Hams	E07000044	83,563	83,597
Teignbridge	E07000045	124,271	125,020
Torridge	E07000046	63,973	64,743
West Devon	E07000047	53,655	53,859
Christchurch	E07000048	47,916	47,987
East Dorset	E07000049	87,301	87,755
North Dorset	E07000050	69,002	69,348
Purbeck	E07000051	45,184	45,289
West Dorset	E07000052	99,275	99,532
Weymouth and Portland	E07000053	65,135	65,029
Eastbourne	E07000061	99,308	100,049
Hastings	E07000062	90,173	90,345
Lewes	E07000063	97,584	98,690
Rother	E07000064	90,729	91,088
Wealden	E07000065	149,415	151,029
Basildon	E07000066	174,971	176,474

15.5 Geographical distribution of the population

		Mid-year population estimate[1]	
		2011	2012
Braintree	E07000067	147,514	148,384
Brentwood	E07000068	73,841	74,020
Castle Point	E07000069	87,964	88,218
Chelmsford	E07000070	168,491	169,335
Colchester	E07000071	173,614	176,008
Epping Forest	E07000072	124,880	126,080
Harlow	E07000073	82,177	82,676
Maldon	E07000074	61,720	61,918
Rochford	E07000075	83,333	83,869
Tendring	E07000076	138,062	138,285
Uttlesford	E07000077	80,032	81,250
Cheltenham	E07000078	115,645	116,080
Cotswold	E07000079	83,180	83,562
Forest of Dean	E07000080	82,200	82,731
Gloucester	E07000081	121,921	123,439
Stroud	E07000082	113,074	113,363
Tewkesbury	E07000083	82,269	82,984
Basingstoke and Deane	E07000084	168,550	170,492
East Hampshire	E07000085	116,010	116,400
Eastleigh	E07000086	125,852	126,764
Fareham	E07000087	111,931	112,802
Gosport	E07000088	82,669	83,276
Hart	E07000089	91,662	92,162
Havant	E07000090	120,783	121,271
New Forest	E07000091	176,789	177,382
Rushmoor	E07000092	94,354	94,870
Test Valley	E07000093	116,698	117,032
Winchester	E07000094	116,820	117,702
Broxbourne	E07000095	93,702	94,497
Dacorum	E07000096	145,298	146,727
East Hertfordshire	E07000097	138,155	139,458
Hertsmere	E07000098	100,379	100,710
North Hertfordshire	E07000099	127,494	128,428
St Albans	E07000240	141,248	141,899
Stevenage	E07000101	84,247	84,798
Three Rivers	E07000102	87,921	88,801
Watford	E07000103	90,653	91,732
Welwyn Hatfield	E07000241	110,727	112,046
Ashford	E07000105	118,405	120,116
Canterbury	E07000106	150,600	153,399
Dartford	E07000107	97,604	98,940
Dover	E07000108	111,718	111,765
Gravesham	E07000109	101,766	102,764
Maidstone	E07000110	155,764	157,297
Sevenoaks	E07000111	115,351	116,400
Shepway	E07000112	108,199	108,700
Swale	E07000113	136,324	137,670
Thanet	E07000114	134,402	135,661
Tonbridge and Malling	E07000115	121,087	121,912
Tunbridge Wells	E07000116	115,246	115,542
Burnley	E07000117	87,032	87,127
Chorley	E07000118	107,591	109,077
Fylde	E07000119	76,098	76,020
Hyndburn	E07000120	80,549	80,190
Lancaster	E07000121	137,823	139,665
Pendle	E07000122	89,576	89,613
Preston	E07000123	140,054	140,540
Ribble Valley	E07000124	57,292	57,596
Rossendale	E07000125	68,053	68,366
South Ribble	E07000126	109,181	108,971
West Lancashire	E07000127	110,617	110,925

15.5 Geographical distribution of the population

		Mid-year population estimate[1]	
		2011	**2012**
Wyre	E07000128	107,692	107,889
Blaby	E07000129	94,132	94,593
Charnwood	E07000130	165,876	168,779
Harborough	E07000131	85,699	86,389
Hinckley and Bosworth	E07000132	105,328	106,046
Melton	E07000133	50,495	50,770
North West Leicestershire	E07000134	93,670	94,018
Oadby and Wigston	E07000135	55,979	56,103
Boston	E07000136	64,615	64,793
East Lindsey	E07000137	136,683	136,596
Lincoln	E07000138	93,085	94,588
North Kesteven	E07000139	108,518	109,263
South Holland	E07000140	88,390	88,518
South Kesteven	E07000141	134,125	135,033
West Lindsey	E07000142	89,352	90,047
Breckland	E07000143	131,009	131,857
Broadland	E07000144	124,740	125,215
Great Yarmouth	E07000145	97,424	97,570
King's Lynn and West Norfolk	E07000146	147,936	148,628
North Norfolk	E07000147	101,664	101,790
Norwich	E07000148	132,158	134,264
South Norfolk	E07000149	124,495	125,978
Corby	E07000150	61,607	63,073
Daventry	E07000151	78,070	78,281
East Northamptonshire	E07000152	86,869	87,365
Kettering	E07000153	93,846	94,841
Northampton	E07000154	212,492	214,566
South Northamptonshire	E07000155	85,446	86,350
Wellingborough	E07000156	75,637	76,100
Craven	E07000163	55,459	55,457
Hambleton	E07000164	89,602	89,748
Harrogate	E07000165	158,683	158,610
Richmondshire	E07000166	53,287	53,935
Ryedale	E07000167	51,893	52,102
Scarborough	E07000168	108,735	108,632
Selby	E07000169	83,547	84,144
Ashfield	E07000170	119,522	120,131
Bassetlaw	E07000171	113,003	113,178
Broxtowe	E07000172	109,749	110,716
Gedling	E07000173	113,741	114,052
Mansfield	E07000174	104,551	104,737
Newark and Sherwood	E07000175	114,982	115,761
Rushcliffe	E07000176	111,248	111,598
Cherwell	E07000177	142,252	142,822
Oxford	E07000178	150,245	152,527
South Oxfordshire	E07000179	134,961	135,541
Vale of White Horse	E07000180	121,891	122,764
West Oxfordshire	E07000181	105,442	107,118
Mendip	E07000187	109,406	109,938
Sedgemoor	E07000188	114,919	116,071
South Somerset	E07000189	162,113	163,012
Taunton Deane	E07000190	110,555	111,370
West Somerset	E07000191	34,588	34,559
Cannock Chase	E07000192	97,582	97,940
East Staffordshire	E07000193	113,858	114,388
Lichfield	E07000194	100,911	101,186
Newcastle-under-Lyme	E07000195	123,878	124,183
South Staffordshire	E07000196	108,318	108,441
Stafford	E07000197	130,895	131,630
Staffordshire Moorlands	E07000198	97,209	97,237
Tamworth	E07000199	76,895	77,118

15.5 Geographical distribution of the population

		Mid-year population estimate[1]	
		2011	**2012**
Babergh	E07000200	87,901	87,917
Forest Heath	E07000201	60,038	60,735
Ipswich	E07000202	133,729	134,466
Mid Suffolk	E07000203	97,076	97,611
St Edmundsbury	E07000204	111,443	111,610
Suffolk Coastal	E07000205	124,590	124,323
Waveney	E07000206	115,356	115,670
Elmbridge	E07000207	131,428	131,512
Epsom and Ewell	E07000208	75,191	76,052
Guildford	E07000209	137,580	139,710
Mole Valley	E07000210	85,637	85,846
Reigate and Banstead	E07000211	138,375	139,888
Runnymede	E07000212	80,501	82,189
Spelthorne	E07000213	95,852	96,744
Surrey Heath	E07000214	86,378	86,614
Tandridge	E07000215	83,178	83,693
Waverley	E07000216	121,754	121,884
Woking	E07000217	99,493	99,377
North Warwickshire	E07000218	62,089	62,200
Nuneaton and Bedworth	E07000219	125,409	125,805
Rugby	E07000220	100,496	100,751
Stratford-on-Avon	E07000221	120,824	120,578
Warwick	E07000222	137,736	138,640
Adur	E07000223	61,334	61,929
Arun	E07000224	149,811	151,384
Chichester	E07000225	113,995	114,521
Crawley	E07000226	107,053	108,302
Horsham	E07000227	131,540	132,160
Mid Sussex	E07000228	140,188	141,162
Worthing	E07000229	104,998	105,661
Bromsgrove	E07000234	93,732	94,285
Malvern Hills	E07000235	74,706	74,980
Redditch	E07000236	84,318	84,419
Worcester	E07000237	98,679	99,604
Wychavon	E07000238	117,074	117,670
Wyre Forest	E07000239	98,048	98,074
Aberdeen City	S12000033	222,460	224,970
Aberdeenshire	S12000034	253,650	255,540
Angus	S12000041	116,200	116,210
Argyll and Bute	S12000035	88,930	86,900
Clackmannanshire	S12000005	51,500	51,280
Dumfries and Galloway	S12000006	151,410	150,830
Dundee City	S12000042	147,200	147,800
East Ayrshire	S12000008	122,690	122,720
East Dunbartonshire	S12000045	105,000	105,880
East Lothian	S12000010	99,920	100,850
East Renfrewshire	S12000011	90,810	91,030
Edinburgh, City of	S12000036	477,940	482,640
Eilean Siar	S12000013	27,690	27,560
Falkirk	S12000014	156,250	156,800
Fife	S12000015	365,300	366,220
Glasgow City	S12000046	593,060	595,080
Highland	S12000017	232,730	232,910
Inverclyde	S12000018	81,220	80,680
Midlothian	S12000019	83,450	84,240
Moray	S12000020	93,470	92,910
North Ayrshire	S12000021	138,090	137,560
North Lanarkshire	S12000044	337,720	337,870
Orkney Islands	S12000023	21,420	21,530
Perth and Kinross	S12000024	146,850	147,740

15.5 Geographical distribution of the population

		Mid-year population estimate[1]	
		2011	**2012**
Renfrewshire	S12000038	174,700	174,310
Scottish Borders	S12000026	113,880	113,710
Shetland Islands	S12000027	23,240	23,210
South Ayrshire	S12000028	112,980	112,910
South Lanarkshire	S12000029	313,900	314,360
Stirling	S12000030	90,330	91,020
West Dunbartonshire	S12000039	90,610	90,340
West Lothian	S12000040	175,300	175,990
Antrim	95T	53,632	53,835
Ards	95X	78,047	78,550
Armagh	95O	59,651	60,147
Ballymena	95G	64,127	64,551
Ballymoney	95D	31,276	31,551
Banbridge	95Q	48,333	48,730
Belfast	95Z	280,922	280,537
Carrickfergus	95V	39,102	39,096
Castlereagh	95Y	67,418	67,716
Coleraine	95C	58,959	58,993
Cookstown	95I	37,098	37,411
Craigavon	95N	93,334	94,597
Derry	95A	108,261	108,586
Down	95R	69,934	70,440
Dungannon	95M	58,100	58,813
Fermanagh	95L	62,006	62,400
Larne	95F	32,136	32,191
Limavady	95B	33,610	33,761
Lisburn	95S	120,486	121,687
Magherafelt	95H	45,132	45,450
Moyle	95E	17,062	17,129
Newry and Mourne	95P	100,003	100,858
Newtownabbey	95U	85,019	85,322
North Down	95W	79,245	79,420
Omagh	95K	51,495	51,830
Strabane	95J	39,930	40,033

Source: Office for National Statistics

1. Estimated resident population by single year of age group for constituent countries; counties; London boroughs and districts in England; unitary authorities in Wales; council areas within Scotland and district council areas in Northern Ireland.

It is ONS policy to publish population estimates rounded to at least the nearest hundred persons. These unit-level estimates are provided to enable and encourage further calculations and analysis. However, the estimates cannot be guaranteed to be as exact as the level of detail implied by unit-level data.

The estimated resident population of an area includes all those people who usually live there, regardless of nationality. Arriving international migrants are included in the usually resident population if they remain in the UK for at least a year. Emigrants are excluded if they remain outside the UK for at least a year. This is consistent with the United Nations definition of a long-term migrant. Armed forces stationed outside of the UK are excluded. Students are taken to be usually resident at their term time address.

At a subnational level, the population estimates reflect boundaries that were in place on 1 April of the reference year.

Codes are those used by ONS from 1 January 2011, in line with the UK coding and naming policy for statistical geographies. A lookup for the previous codes is available via the ONS website

15.6 Comparing the Broad Ethnic groups for England and Wales

Percentage of total population

	Estimates		Differences	Percentages		Percentage point difference
	2011 Census	Mid-2010 PEEGs	Census - PEEGs	% 2011 Census	% mid-2010 PEEGs	% Census - PEEGs
White British	45,134,686	45,793,249	-658,563	80.5	82.9	-2.4
White Other	3,074,709	2,540,805	533,904	5.5	4.6	0.9
Mixed Ethnic Group	1,224,400	1,034,065	190,335	2.2	1.9	0.3
Asian/Asian British	4,213,531	3,812,176	401,355	7.5	6.9	0.6
Black/Black British	1,864,890	1,594,016	270,874	3.3	2.9	0.4
Other Ethnic Group	563,696	454,555	109,141	1.0	0.8	0.2
All Groups	56,075,912	55,228,865	847,047			

Note: Figures may not sum due to rounding.

Source:
ONS: Comparison of mid-2010 Population Estimates
by Ethnic Group against the 2011 Census

Important Note

The Population Estimates by Ethnic Group (PEEGs) methodology is currently being evaluated by external (outside ONS) experts and as such production of ethnic groups estimates is currently on hold until a new methodology is implemented. As such, no new estimates have been produced since the previous edition of Annual Abstract of Statistics.

15.7 Long-Term International Migration, 1991 to 2011

United Kingdom,
England and Wales

Citizenship

thousands

Year	2011 Census Revised Balance estimates[1]	All citizenships	British	Non British	European Union[2]	European Union EU15	European Union EU8	Non European Union[3] All	Commonwealth[4] All[4]	Old	New[4]	Other Foreign[5]
United Kingdom												
Inflow												
1991		**329**	110	219	53	53	z	167	85	26	59	82
1992		**268**	93	175	44	44	z	131	65	18	46	67
1993		**266**	86	179	44	44	z	135	70	23	47	65
1994		**315**	109	206	50	50	z	156	80	21	59	76
1995		**312**	84	228	61	61	z	167	85	27	58	82
1996		**318**	94	224	72	72	z	152	78	29	49	74
1997		**327**	90	237	71	71	z	166	90	31	59	76
1998		**391**	104	287	82	82	z	206	105	54	51	101
1999		**454**	115	338	66	66	z	272	123	55	68	150
2000		**479**	99	379	63	63	z	316	147	56	91	169
2001		**481**	110	370	58	58	z	313	149	65	84	164
2002		**516**	98	418	61	61	z	357	155	63	92	201
2003		**511**	100	411	66	66	z	344	167	62	105	177
2004		**589**	89	500	130	77	53	370	215	73	141	155
2005		**567**	98	469	152	73	76	317	180	62	117	137
2006		**596**	83	513	170	74	92	343	201	62	139	143
2007		**574**	74	500	195	77	112	305	174	45	129	131
2008		**590**	85	505	198	90	89	307	165	44	121	142
2009		**567**	96	471	167	82	68	303	171	30	141	132
2010		**591**	93	498	176	76	86	322	187	31	156	135
2011		**566**	78	488	174	83	77	314	179	29	151	135
Outflow												
1991		**285**	154	130	53	53	z	77	35	18	17	43
1992		**281**	155	126	38	38	z	88	31	18	13	57
1993		**266**	149	118	40	40	z	77	34	17	17	43
1994		**238**	125	113	42	42	z	71	31	14	17	40
1995		**236**	135	101	38	38	z	63	29	18	12	34
1996		**264**	156	108	44	44	z	64	32	17	14	32
1997		**279**	149	131	53	53	z	77	40	20	20	37
1998		**251**	126	126	49	49	z	77	33	20	13	44
1999		**291**	139	152	59	59	z	93	41	29	12	52
2000		**321**	161	160	57	57	z	103	47	32	15	55
2001		**309**	159	150	51	51	z	99	51	32	19	49
2002		**363**	186	177	54	54	z	122	58	42	16	64
2003		**363**	191	172	51	51	z	121	59	42	17	62
2004		**344**	196	148	43	39	3	104	53	33	19	52
2005		**361**	186	175	56	40	15	119	60	37	23	59
2006		**398**	207	192	66	44	22	126	66	42	24	60
2007		**341**	171	169	69	41	25	101	58	31	26	43
2008		**427**	173	255	134	54	69	120	66	35	31	55
2009		**368**	140	228	109	53	52	119	66	32	34	53
2010		**339**	136	203	99	58	37	104	52	22	30	52
2011		**351**	149	202	92	49	37	110	60	21	39	50
Balance												
1991		**+ 44**	- 44	+ 89	- 1	- 1	z	+ 89	+ 50	+ 8	+ 42	+ 39
1992		**- 13**	- 62	+ 49	+ 5	+ 5	z	+ 44	+ 34	0~	+ 33	+ 10
1993		**- 1**	- 62	+ 62	+ 4	+ 4	z	+ 58	+ 36	+ 6	+ 30	+ 22
1994		**+ 77**	- 16	+ 94	+ 9	+ 9	z	+ 85	+ 49	+ 7	+ 42	+ 36
1995		**+ 76**	- 51	+ 127	+ 23	+ 23	z	+ 104	+ 56	+ 9	+ 46	+ 48
1996		**+ 55**	- 62	+ 116	+ 28	+ 28	z	+ 88	+ 47	+ 12	+ 35	+ 41
1997		**+ 48**	- 59	+ 107	+ 18	+ 18	z	+ 88	+ 50	+ 11	+ 39	+ 38
1998		**+ 140**	- 22	+ 162	+ 33	+ 33	z	+ 129	+ 72	+ 34	+ 38	+ 57
1999		**+ 163**	- 24	+ 187	+ 8	+ 8	z	+ 179	+ 82	+ 26	+ 56	+ 98
2000		**+ 158**	- 62	+ 220	+ 6	+ 6	z	+ 214	+ 100	+ 24	+ 76	+ 114

15.7 Long-Term International Migration, 1991 to 2011

United Kingdom,
England and Wales
Citizenship

thousands

United Kingdom (net balance)

Year	2011 Census Revised Balance estimates[1]	All citizenships	British	Non British	European Union[2]	European Union EU15	European Union EU8	Non European Union[3] All	Commonwealth[4] All[4]	Old	New[4]	Other Foreign[5]
2001	+ 179	+ 171	- 48	+ 220	+ 7	+ 7	z	+ 213	+ 98	+ 33	+ 65	+ 115
2002	+ 172	+ 153	- 88	+ 241	+ 7	+ 7	z	+ 234	+ 97	+ 21	+ 77	+ 137
2003	+ 185	+ 148	- 91	+ 239	+ 15	+ 15	z	+ 224	+ 109	+ 20	+ 88	+ 115
2004	+ 268	+ 245	- 107	+ 352	+ 87	+ 38	+ 49	+ 266	+ 162	+ 40	+ 122	+ 104
2005	+ 267	+ 206	- 88	+ 294	+ 96	+ 33	+ 61	+ 198	+ 120	+ 25	+ 94	+ 78
2006	+ 265	+ 198	- 124	+ 322	+ 104	+ 30	+ 71	+ 218	+ 135	+ 20	+ 115	+ 83
2007	+ 273	+ 233	- 97	+ 330	+ 127	+ 36	+ 87	+ 204	+ 116	+ 13	+ 103	+ 88
2008	+ 229	+ 163	- 87	+ 251	+ 63	+ 37	+ 20	+ 187	+ 100	+ 9	+ 91	+ 87
2009	+ 229	+ 198	- 44	+ 242	+ 58	+ 29	+ 16	+ 184	+ 105	- 2	+ 107	+ 79
2010	+ 256	+ 252	- 43	+ 294	+ 77	+ 18	+ 49	+ 217	+ 135	+ 9	+ 126	+ 83
2011	+ 205	+ 215	- 70	+ 286	+ 82	+ 34	+ 40	+ 204	+ 119	+ 8	+ 111	+ 85

England and Wales

Inflow

Year	All citizenships	British	Non British	European Union[2]	European Union EU15	European Union EU8	Non European Union[3] All	Commonwealth[4] All[4]	Old	New[4]	Other Foreign[5]
1991	304	98	207	50	50	z	157	81	25	57	76
1992	251	87	164	42	42	z	123	60	18	42	63
1993	249	80	170	40	40	z	130	67	22	45	62
1994	292	94	199	47	47	z	151	78	21	58	73
1995	299	79	220	59	59	z	162	83	25	58	79
1996	300	86	214	67	67	z	147	77	29	48	70
1997	310	85	226	69	69	z	157	86	29	57	71
1998	370	96	274	76	76	z	198	101	53	48	97
1999	424	101	323	63	63	z	260	117	51	65	143
2000	446	95	351	53	53	z	298	140	51	89	158
2001	449	99	350	56	56	z	295	139	59	79	156
2002	485	92	394	57	57	z	337	149	61	89	188
2003	480	93	387	61	61	z	326	159	58	101	167
2004	549	82	467	122	72	50	345	199	70	129	146
2005	523	87	436	143	66	74	293	167	56	111	126
2006	549	78	471	149	67	78	322	186	55	131	136
2007	524	65	460	175	68	101	285	163	43	120	122
2008	528	67	461	178	75	84	283	157	40	117	126
2009	507	83	424	142	69	58	282	160	25	135	122
2010	532	80	451	151	68	72	300	175	28	147	124
2011	515	71	445	153	74	67	291	169	27	142	122

Outflow

Year	All citizenships	British	Non British	European Union[2]	European Union EU15	European Union EU8	Non European Union[3] All	Commonwealth[4] All[4]	Old	New[4]	Other Foreign[5]
1991	253	138	115	45	45	z	71	32	17	14	39
1992	248	135	113	34	34	z	79	29	17	12	49
1993	244	137	107	37	37	z	70	31	15	16	39
1994	216	113	103	36	36	z	67	29	13	16	38
1995	216	124	92	33	33	z	59	28	17	11	31
1996	238	141	97	39	39	z	58	28	16	12	30
1997	244	125	120	48	48	z	72	37	19	18	35
1998	223	107	116	44	44	z	72	31	19	12	41
1999	273	129	144	56	56	z	88	39	28	11	49
2000	291	141	151	55	55	z	96	44	30	14	52
2001	282	143	138	46	46	z	93	48	30	18	44
2002	328	168	159	47	47	z	112	52	38	14	60
2003	333	174	159	47	47	z	112	54	38	16	59
2004	311	175	135	41	37	3	94	48	31	17	46
2005	328	171	157	50	35	15	106	55	34	21	51
2006	369	192	177	60	38	22	117	62	39	22	55
2007	307	152	155	60	38	20	94	53	29	23	42
2008	393	157	235	126	49	65	110	59	32	27	50
2009	328	123	205	98	49	46	107	61	31	31	46
2010	308	123	184	89	54	32	95	48	21	27	47
2011	312	134	178	78	42	31	100	55	18	37	45

15.7 Long-Term International Migration, 1991 to 2011

United Kingdom,
England and Wales
Citizenship

thousands

Year	2011 Census Revised Balance estimates[1]	All citizenships	British	Non British	European Union[2]	European Union EU15	European Union EU8	Non European Union[3] All	Commonwealth[4] All[4]	Old	New[4]	Other Foreign[5]
Balance												
1991		+ 51	- 40	+ 91	+ 5	+ 5	z	+ 86	+ 50	+ 7	+ 42	+ 37
1992		+ 4	- 48	+ 51	+ 7	+ 7	z	+ 44	+ 30	+ 1	+ 29	+ 14
1993		+ 5	- 57	+ 62	+ 3	+ 3	z	+ 59	+ 36	+ 7	+ 30	+ 23
1994		+ 77	- 19	+ 96	+ 12	+ 12	z	+ 84	+ 49	+ 8	+ 42	+ 35
1995		+ 83	- 45	+ 129	+ 25	+ 25	z	+ 103	+ 55	+ 8	+ 47	+ 48
1996		+ 62	- 55	+ 117	+ 27	+ 27	z	+ 90	+ 49	+ 12	+ 37	+ 41
1997		+ 66	- 40	+ 106	+ 21	+ 21	z	+ 85	+ 49	+ 10	+ 39	+ 36
1998		+ 147	- 10	+ 157	+ 31	+ 31	z	+ 126	+ 70	+ 34	+ 36	+ 56
1999		+ 151	- 28	+ 179	+ 7	+ 7	z	+ 171	+ 77	+ 23	+ 54	+ 94
2000		+ 154	- 46	+ 200	- 2	- 2	z	+ 202	+ 96	+ 22	+ 74	+ 105
2001		+ 167	- 45	+ 212	+ 10	+ 10	z	+ 202	+ 90	+ 29	+ 61	+ 112
2002		+ 158	- 77	+ 234	+ 9	+ 9	z	+ 225	+ 97	+ 22	+ 75	+ 128
2003		+ 147	- 81	+ 228	+ 14	+ 14	z	+ 214	+ 105	+ 21	+ 84	+ 108
2004		+ 238	- 94	+ 332	+ 81	+ 35	+ 46	+ 251	+ 151	+ 38	+ 112	+ 100
2005		+ 195	- 84	+ 279	+ 92	+ 31	+ 59	+ 186	+ 112	+ 22	+ 90	+ 75
2006		+ 180	- 114	+ 294	+ 89	+ 29	+ 56	+ 205	+ 124	+ 16	+ 109	+ 81
2007		+ 217	- 88	+ 305	+ 115	+ 30	+ 81	+ 190	+ 110	+ 14	+ 97	+ 80
2008		+ 135	- 90	+ 225	+ 52	+ 26	+ 19	+ 173	+ 97	+ 8	+ 89	+ 76
2009		+ 179	- 40	+ 219	+ 44	+ 20	+ 12	+ 174	+ 99	- 5	+ 104	+ 76
2010		+ 224	- 43	+ 267	+ 62	+ 14	+ 39	+ 205	+ 127	+ 7	+ 120	+ 78
2011		+ 203	- 64	+ 267	+ 75	+ 32	+ 37	+ 192	+ 114	+ 8	+ 106	+ 77

Source: Office for National Statistics (ONS), Home Office, Central Statistics Office (CSO) Ireland, Northern Ireland Statistics and Research Agency (NISRA).

Totals may not sum due to rounding.

"z" - Not applicable, "0~" - Rounds to zero. Please see the Notes worksheet for more information.

1   Net migration ("Balance") figures for the United Kingdom for 2001 to 2011 have been revised in light of the results of the 2011 Census. These revisions are not reflected in the body of the table. Users should continue to use the estimates in the body of the table to analyse detailed breakdowns of inflows and outflows of long-term international migrants but, in doing so, should bear in mind that the headline net migration estimates have been revised.

2   European Union estimates are for the EU15 (Austria, Belgium, Denmark, Finland, France, Germany, Greece, Republic of Ireland, Italy, Luxembourg, Netherlands, Portugal, Spain and Sweden) up to 2003, the EU25 (the EU15 and the EU8 groupings plus Malta and Cyprus) from 2004 - 2006, and for the EU27 (the EU25 plus Bulgaria and Romania) from 2007. Estimates are also shown separately for the EU15 and the EU8 (Czech Republic, Estonia, Hungary, Latvia, Lithuania, Poland, Slovakia and Slovenia, formerly known collectively as the A8). British citizens are excluded from all citizenship groupings and are shown

3   Excludes British and other European Union citizens as defined in footnote 1.

4   From 2004 onwards, All and New Commonwealth exclude Malta and Cyprus.

5   From 2004 onwards, Other Foreign excludes the eight central and eastern European member states that joined the EU in May 2004 (the EU8). From 2007 onwards, Other Foreign excludes Bulgaria and Romania which joined the EU in January 2007.

15.8 Long-Term International Migration, 1991 to 2011

United Kingdom,
England and Wales
Country of Last or Next Residence

Year	2011 Census Revised Balance estimates[1]	All countries	European Union[2]	European Union EU15	European Union EU8	Non European Union[3] All	Commonwealth[4] All[4]	Old Commonwealth All	Australia	Canada	New Zealand	South Africa
United Kingdom												
Inflow												
1991		329	95	95	z	234	130	51	28	6	10	7
1992		268	89	89	z	179	96	38	20	4	8	6
1993		266	75	75	z	191	103	42	22	5	6	9
1994		315	95	95	z	220	112	42	19	6	8	9
1995		312	89	89	z	223	111	41	19	8	9	5
1996		318	98	98	z	220	112	48	22	7	9	11
1997		327	100	100	z	226	121	53	22	9	10	13
1998		391	109	109	z	282	148	84	38	9	16	20
1999		454	96	96	z	358	174	92	40	6	16	29
2000		479	89	89	z	389	189	85	35	10	18	22
2001		481	84	84	z	397	199	99	52	7	17	23
2002		516	90	90	z	426	188	86	38	8	13	28
2003		511	101	101	z	410	204	92	40	12	12	28
2004		589	153	98	54	436	249	96	39	7	13	37
2005		567	186	107	76	381	219	90	39	7	15	29
2006		596	210	110	93	386	219	80	40	7	12	21
2007		574	220	100	113	354	200	65	31	6	10	17
2008		590	224	114	89	366	196	68	29	10	9	20
2009		567	198	114	67	368	204	56	29	8	8	11
2010		591	208	110	81	383	219	57	30	9	11	7
2011		566	203	107	77	363	204	51	26	9	8	8
Outflow												
1991		285	95	95	z	189	101	68	38	15	9	7
1992		281	86	86	z	195	87	57	35	7	10	5
1993		266	88	88	z	178	92	61	38	9	10	4
1994		238	76	76	z	162	81	51	28	7	12	4
1995		236	76	76	z	161	81	58	33	7	12	6
1996		264	94	94	z	170	94	63	36	9	13	5
1997		279	92	92	z	187	100	65	35	9	13	8
1998		251	85	85	z	167	83	59	36	7	11	6
1999		291	103	103	z	188	101	80	53	8	12	7
2000		321	103	103	z	217	111	86	54	8	17	7
2001		309	95	95	z	214	114	88	54	10	16	8
2002		363	128	128	z	234	123	94	53	13	18	10
2003		363	123	123	z	240	131	104	62	7	21	14
2004		344	125	111	6	219	125	95	54	12	20	9
2005		361	138	118	17	223	128	99	51	12	22	13
2006		398	145	118	24	253	148	114	68	11	21	14
2007		341	131	98	25	210	127	94	58	8	17	11
2008		427	202	123	66	225	119	86	55	11	13	7
2009		368	144	88	50	224	127	88	57	11	14	6
2010		339	136	92	38	204	102	64	40	9	9	7
2011		351	124	80	36	226	124	74	48	8	14	3
Balance												
1991		+ 44	0~	0~	z	+ 44	+ 29	- 17	- 10	- 10	+ 2	+ 1
1992		- 13	+ 3	+ 3	z	- 16	+ 9	- 19	- 15	- 3	- 2	+ 1
1993		- 1	- 14	- 14	z	+ 13	+ 10	- 18	- 15	- 5	- 3	+ 5
1994		+ 77	+ 19	+ 19	z	+ 58	+ 31	- 9	- 9	- 2	- 4	+ 5
1995		+ 76	+ 13	+ 13	z	+ 63	+ 30	- 17	- 13	0~	- 3	- 1
1996		+ 55	+ 5	+ 5	z	+ 50	+ 17	- 15	- 14	- 2	- 4	+ 5
1997		+ 48	+ 9	+ 9	z	+ 39	+ 21	- 12	- 13	0~	- 4	+ 5
1998		+ 140	+ 24	+ 24	z	+ 116	+ 65	+ 25	+ 3	+ 2	+ 5	+ 15
1999		+ 163	- 7	- 7	z	+ 170	+ 73	+ 12	- 13	- 2	+ 5	+ 22
2000		+ 158	- 14	- 14	z	+ 172	+ 78	- 1	- 18	+ 2	+ 1	+ 15
2001	+ 179	+ 171	- 11	- 11	z	+ 183	+ 85	+ 11	- 1	- 3	+ 1	+ 14
2002	+ 172	+ 153	- 38	- 38	z	+ 191	+ 65	- 8	- 15	- 5	- 6	+ 17
2003	+ 185	+ 148	- 23	- 23	z	+ 170	+ 74	- 12	- 23	+ 5	- 8	+ 14
2004	+ 268	+ 245	+ 28	- 14	+ 47	+ 217	+ 123	+ 2	- 16	- 4	- 7	+ 28
2005	+ 267	+ 206	+ 48	- 11	+ 59	+ 158	+ 91	- 9	- 12	- 5	- 8	+ 15
2006	+ 265	+ 198	+ 65	- 8	+ 69	+ 133	+ 72	- 34	- 28	- 4	- 9	+ 7
2007	+ 273	+ 233	+ 88	+ 2	+ 88	+ 145	+ 73	- 29	- 27	- 2	- 7	+ 6
2008	+ 229	+ 163	+ 21	- 9	+ 23	+ 142	+ 76	- 18	- 26	- 1	- 4	+ 14
2009	+ 229	+ 198	+ 54	+ 26	+ 18	+ 144	+ 77	- 32	- 27	- 3	- 6	+ 4
2010	+ 256	+ 252	+ 73	+ 18	+ 43	+ 179	+ 117	- 7	- 10	0~	+ 2	+ 1
2011	+ 205	+ 215	+ 79	+ 27	+ 41	+ 137	+ 80	- 23	- 22	+ 1	- 6	+ 5

15.8 Long-Term International Migration, 1991 to 2011

United Kingdom,
England and Wales
Country of Last or Next Residence

Year	2011 Census Revised Balance estimates[1]	All countries	European Union[2]			Non European Union[3]						
			European Union[2]	European Union EU15	European Union EU8	All	Commonwealth[4] All[4]	Old Commonwealth				
								All	Australia	Canada	New Zealand	South Africa

England and Wales

Inflow

Year		All countries	EU[2]	EU15	EU8	Non-EU All	Commonwealth All[4]	Old Comm. All	Australia	Canada	New Zealand	South Africa
1991		304	89	89	z	215	120	44	25	5	10	4
1992		251	85	85	z	166	87	35	19	4	7	5
1993		249	67	67	z	183	98	40	22	5	6	8
1994		292	86	86	z	207	108	40	18	6	8	8
1995		299	85	85	z	214	107	37	18	6	9	4
1996		300	89	89	z	210	108	45	21	6	9	9
1997		310	99	99	z	212	116	50	21	7	9	13
1998		370	101	101	z	269	139	79	36	8	16	20
1999		424	92	92	z	332	162	83	37	6	13	27
2000		446	77	77	z	369	182	80	33	6	18	22
2001		449	80	80	z	369	183	89	45	5	17	22
2002		485	84	84	z	401	179	82	36	7	12	27
2003		480	93	93	z	387	192	83	37	9	11	27
2004		549	144	92	51	404	231	91	37	7	12	35
2005		523	175	98	74	348	202	80	35	6	12	28
2006		549	190	104	79	359	203	71	34	7	11	19
2007		524	195	86	102	330	187	60	29	6	10	15
2008		528	199	95	84	329	183	61	27	6	8	19
2009		507	168	95	58	339	188	46	25	7	6	7
2010		532	178	94	69	353	205	53	28	7	10	7
2011		515	179	95	68	336	191	46	24	8	7	7

Outflow

Year		All countries	EU[2]	EU15	EU8	Non-EU All	Commonwealth All[4]	Old Comm. All	Australia	Canada	New Zealand	South Africa
1991		253	87	87	z	166	89	58	34	11	8	5
1992		248	78	78	z	170	79	53	32	7	9	4
1993		244	82	82	z	162	85	56	36	8	9	3
1994		216	67	67	z	149	72	44	24	7	9	4
1995		216	69	69	z	147	74	54	30	7	11	6
1996		238	85	85	z	152	83	55	31	6	13	5
1997		244	78	78	z	166	90	58	32	6	12	8
1998		223	74	74	z	148	70	49	30	4	9	6
1999		273	96	96	z	177	95	75	49	7	11	7
2000		291	95	95	z	196	102	78	49	7	15	7
2001		282	89	89	z	193	104	79	48	8	15	8
2002		328	113	113	z	214	110	85	49	11	16	10
2003		333	115	115	z	218	117	92	56	5	18	13
2004		311	116	104	6	195	113	86	49	10	18	9
2005		328	126	106	17	202	116	90	47	10	20	13
2006		369	137	111	24	232	137	105	62	10	19	14
2007		307	119	90	20	188	112	83	50	7	15	11
2008		393	186	111	62	207	111	80	53	9	13	6
2009		328	128	78	43	201	115	79	50	10	13	6
2010		308	122	84	33	186	94	59	36	8	9	6
2011		312	108	71	30	204	112	66	43	8	13	3

Balance

Year		All countries	EU[2]	EU15	EU8	Non-EU All	Commonwealth All[4]	Old Comm. All	Australia	Canada	New Zealand	South Africa
1991		+ 51	+ 2	+ 2	z	+ 49	+ 32	- 14	- 9	- 6	+ 2	- 1
1992		+ 4	+ 8	+ 8	z	- 4	+ 8	- 18	- 13	- 3	- 2	+ 1
1993		+ 5	- 16	- 16	z	+ 21	+ 14	- 15	- 14	- 3	- 3	+ 5
1994		+ 77	+ 18	+ 18	z	+ 58	+ 36	- 4	- 6	- 1	- 2	+ 5
1995		+ 83	+ 16	+ 16	z	+ 67	+ 33	- 17	- 11	- 1	- 2	- 2
1996		+ 62	+ 4	+ 4	z	+ 58	+ 26	- 10	- 10	0~	- 4	+ 4
1997		+ 66	+ 21	+ 21	z	+ 45	+ 26	- 8	- 10	+ 1	- 3	+ 5
1998		+ 147	+ 26	+ 26	z	+ 120	+ 69	+ 30	+ 5	+ 3	+ 7	+ 14
1999		+ 151	- 4	- 4	z	+ 155	+ 68	+ 8	- 12	- 1	+ 2	+ 20
2000		+ 154	- 18	- 18	z	+ 172	+ 80	+ 2	- 16	0~	+ 3	+ 15
2001		+ 167	- 9	- 9	z	+ 176	+ 79	+ 10	- 3	- 3	+ 1	+ 14
2002		+ 158	- 29	- 29	z	+ 187	+ 69	- 4	- 13	- 4	+ 4	+ 18
2003		+ 147	- 23	- 23	z	+ 169	+ 75	- 9	- 19	+ 4	- 8	+ 13
2004		+ 238	+ 28	- 12	+ 45	+ 210	+ 118	+ 5	- 12	- 3	- 6	+ 26
2005		+ 195	+ 49	- 8	+ 57	+ 146	+ 85	- 10	- 12	- 4	- 8	+ 15
2006		+ 180	+ 52	- 7	+ 55	+ 127	+ 66	- 34	- 28	- 4	- 8	+ 6
2007		+ 217	+ 76	- 4	+ 82	+ 141	+ 75	- 23	- 21	- 1	- 5	+ 5
2008		+ 135	+ 12	- 16	+ 22	+ 123	+ 71	- 20	- 25	- 3	- 4	+ 13
2009		+ 179	+ 41	+ 17	+ 14	+ 138	+ 73	- 34	- 25	- 3	- 7	+ 1
2010		+ 224	+ 57	+ 10	+ 36	+ 167	+ 111	- 6	- 8	- 1	+ 2	+ 1
2011		+ 203	+ 71	+ 24	+ 38	+ 132	+ 79	- 20	- 18	0~	- 6	+ 5

15.8 Long-Term International Migration, 1991 to 2011

United Kingdom,
England and Wales
Country of Last or Next Residence

thousands

Year	New Commonwealth[4] All[3]	Other African	Indian Subcontinent	Other[3]	Other Foreign[5] All[5]	Remainder of Europe[5]	United States of America	Rest of America	Middle East	Other
United Kingdom										
Inflow										
1991	79	27	33	19	104	23	24	4	11	42
1992	57	17	23	17	84	21	18	5	8	32
1993	60	18	27	15	88	23	23	4	10	29
1994	71	23	27	20	108	26	29	5	12	36
1995	71	23	28	21	112	23	27	4	13	45
1996	64	19	27	18	109	20	32	4	14	39
1997	67	13	31	23	106	23	23	5	15	39
1998	64	20	27	17	134	32	37	4	13	48
1999	83	24	40	19	183	57	31	7	15	74
2000	104	30	50	24	200	50	24	12	30	85
2001	101	30	51	19	197	37	25	6	31	99
2002	102	41	46	15	237	47	29	7	33	122
2003	113	40	58	15	206	35	30	8	26	107
2004	152	45	90	17	187	18	27	9	29	104
2005	130	32	86	11	162	20	25	7	19	90
2006	139	23	102	14	167	21	23	8	21	93
2007	135	24	95	16	154	17	23	10	23	82
2008	128	31	80	17	171	14	28	12	30	87
2009	148	31	101	16	164	13	31	9	26	84
2010	162	23	121	19	163	14	22	10	24	94
2011	153	19	122	12	159	12	23	6	26	91
Outflow										
1991	33	9	10	14	88	12	35	5	14	23
1992	29	8	8	14	108	20	40	5	15	28
1993	31	8	9	14	86	12	36	5	11	22
1994	30	7	7	16	81	18	27	6	13	18
1995	23	5	6	12	80	12	30	3	10	25
1996	31	9	6	15	76	16	26	3	8	23
1997	35	7	9	18	88	21	28	2	13	22
1998	24	5	7	11	84	17	27	4	9	27
1999	21	3	5	14	87	16	33	4	10	24
2000	26	7	8	10	106	22	33	6	15	30
2001	26	5	11	10	100	24	28	4	9	34
2002	29	5	11	13	112	28	37	3	12	31
2003	27	6	11	10	109	35	27	6	7	34
2004	31	6	9	15	93	13	25	7	11	37
2005	29	6	16	7	95	17	24	8	11	34
2006	33	7	17	10	106	17	29	6	16	38
2007	33	5	18	9	83	15	18	7	11	31
2008	34	8	17	9	105	15	23	10	21	36
2009	39	8	23	8	97	11	27	5	15	39
2010	38	8	21	8	102	15	25	5	15	43
2011	50	7	29	13	103	17	24	4	17	41
Balance										
1991	+ 46	+ 18	+ 23	+ 5	+ 16	+ 11	- 10	- 1	- 3	+ 19
1992	+ 28	+ 9	+ 15	+ 3	- 25	0~	- 22	0~	- 7	+ 4
1993	+ 29	+ 10	+ 19	+ 1	+ 3	+ 12	- 13	- 1	- 1	+ 7
1994	+ 41	+ 16	+ 20	+ 4	+ 27	+ 9	+ 2	- 1	- 1	+ 18
1995	+ 47	+ 17	+ 22	+ 8	+ 32	+ 12	- 3	+ 1	+ 3	+ 20
1996	+ 33	+ 10	+ 20	+ 2	+ 33	+ 4	+ 7	+ 1	+ 5	+ 16
1997	+ 32	+ 6	+ 22	+ 5	+ 18	+ 2	- 5	+ 3	+ 2	+ 16
1998	+ 40	+ 14	+ 20	+ 6	+ 50	+ 15	+ 10	0~	+ 4	+ 21
1999	+ 62	+ 22	+ 35	+ 5	+ 97	+ 41	- 2	+ 3	+ 5	+ 50
2000	+ 79	+ 23	+ 42	+ 14	+ 94	+ 28	- 10	+ 6	+ 15	+ 55
2001	+ 74	+ 25	+ 40	+ 10	+ 98	+ 13	- 3	+ 2	+ 21	+ 65
2002	+ 73	+ 36	+ 36	+ 2	+ 126	+ 19	- 9	+ 4	+ 21	+ 91
2003	+ 86	+ 34	+ 47	+ 5	+ 97	0~	+ 3	+ 2	+ 19	+ 73
2004	+ 122	+ 39	+ 81	+ 2	+ 94	+ 5	+ 2	+ 2	+ 18	+ 68
2005	+ 101	+ 26	+ 70	+ 4	+ 67	+ 3	+ 1	- 1	+ 8	+ 56
2006	+ 106	+ 16	+ 85	+ 4	+ 61	+ 4	- 6	+ 3	+ 6	+ 55
2007	+ 103	+ 19	+ 77	+ 7	+ 72	+ 2	+ 4	+ 2	+ 12	+ 51
2008	+ 94	+ 23	+ 63	+ 8	+ 65	- 2	+ 5	+ 2	+ 9	+ 51
2009	+ 109	+ 23	+ 78	+ 8	+ 67	+ 2	+ 4	+ 4	+ 11	+ 46
2010	+ 124	+ 15	+ 99	+ 11	+ 62	- 1	- 3	+ 5	+ 10	+ 52
2011	+ 103	+ 12	+ 93	- 1	+ 56	- 5	- 1	+ 2	+ 9	+ 50

15.8 Long-Term International Migration, 1991 to 2011

United Kingdom,
England and Wales
Country of Last or Next Residence

thousands

| Year | New Commonwealth[4] | | | | Other Foreign[5] | | | | | |
	All[3]	Other African	Indian Subcontinent	Other[3]	All[5]	Remainder of Europe[5]	United States of America	Rest of America	Middle East	Other
England and Wales										
Inflow										
1991	76	26	32	18	95	20	21	4	10	39
1992	52	17	22	13	79	20	17	4	8	30
1993	58	17	27	14	84	22	21	3	10	28
1994	68	23	27	18	99	25	22	5	11	35
1995	70	22	27	20	107	23	23	4	13	44
1996	63	19	26	18	102	18	29	4	12	38
1997	66	13	30	23	96	22	20	5	14	35
1998	60	17	27	16	129	31	35	4	12	47
1999	79	23	38	18	170	56	25	7	14	68
2000	102	30	49	24	187	49	22	9	29	78
2001	94	28	48	17	187	35	22	6	29	95
2002	98	39	45	14	222	45	26	7	30	114
2003	108	39	55	15	196	32	29	7	25	102
2004	139	40	85	15	174	17	25	8	27	96
2005	121	30	81	10	147	18	21	7	17	83
2006	132	22	96	14	157	20	22	7	20	88
2007	126	23	88	16	143	15	21	9	21	77
2008	122	29	78	16	147	12	24	10	23	78
2009	143	30	97	16	150	12	26	9	24	79
2010	152	21	114	17	148	12	19	9	22	87
2011	145	18	116	11	145	12	20	6	24	84
Outflow										
1991	30	8	9	13	78	10	29	5	13	21
1992	27	7	7	12	91	17	31	5	13	25
1993	29	7	8	13	77	10	31	5	10	21
1994	28	7	6	15	77	16	26	6	12	17
1995	20	5	5	11	73	11	28	3	9	22
1996	27	8	5	14	70	14	25	3	7	21
1997	32	7	9	16	76	20	23	2	11	19
1998	21	4	7	10	78	14	25	4	8	27
1999	20	3	5	12	82	16	31	4	10	22
2000	24	6	8	10	95	21	29	5	12	28
2001	25	5	11	9	89	23	26	4	9	27
2002	24	5	10	10	104	27	34	3	11	30
2003	24	5	10	9	101	33	25	5	5	33
2004	27	6	9	12	82	12	22	7	8	33
2005	26	6	14	7	86	16	19	6	10	33
2006	32	6	16	10	95	16	25	5	15	33
2007	29	5	16	8	77	15	16	7	10	28
2008	31	8	15	8	95	15	20	9	19	31
2009	36	7	22	7	86	11	22	5	14	34
2010	35	8	20	8	92	14	23	5	13	38
2011	46	7	27	12	92	15	22	4	15	36
Balance										
1991	+ 45	+ 18	+ 23	+ 5	+ 17	+ 11	- 7	- 1	- 2	+ 17
1992	+ 25	+ 9	+ 15	+ 1	- 12	+ 3	- 14	- 1	- 5	+ 5
1993	+ 29	+ 10	+ 18	+ 1	+ 7	+ 12	- 10	- 1	0~	+ 7
1994	+ 40	+ 17	+ 20	+ 3	+ 22	+ 9	- 3	- 1	- 1	+ 18
1995	+ 49	+ 18	+ 22	+ 9	+ 34	+ 13	- 6	+ 1	+ 3	+ 23
1996	+ 36	+ 11	+ 21	+ 3	+ 32	+ 4	+ 4	+ 1	+ 5	+ 18
1997	+ 34	+ 6	+ 21	+ 7	+ 20	+ 2	- 3	+ 2	+ 3	+ 16
1998	+ 39	+ 13	+ 20	+ 7	+ 51	+ 17	+ 10	0~	+ 4	+ 20
1999	+ 59	+ 21	+ 33	+ 6	+ 88	+ 40	- 7	+ 3	+ 4	+ 47
2000	+ 79	+ 24	+ 41	+ 14	+ 92	+ 28	- 7	+ 4	+ 17	+ 50
2001	+ 69	+ 23	+ 38	+ 8	+ 98	+ 12	- 4	+ 2	+ 20	+ 68
2002	+ 73	+ 34	+ 35	+ 4	+ 118	+ 19	- 8	+ 4	+ 19	+ 84
2003	+ 84	+ 34	+ 44	+ 6	+ 94	- 1	+ 4	+ 3	+ 19	+ 70
2004	+ 112	+ 34	+ 76	+ 3	+ 92	+ 5	+ 3	+ 1	+ 19	+ 64
2005	+ 95	+ 24	+ 67	+ 3	+ 61	+ 1	+ 2	+ 1	+ 7	+ 50
2006	+ 100	+ 16	+ 80	+ 5	+ 62	+ 4	- 3	+ 1	+ 4	+ 55
2007	+ 97	+ 18	+ 72	+ 8	+ 66	0~	+ 5	+ 2	+ 11	+ 49
2008	+ 91	+ 21	+ 62	+ 8	+ 52	- 3	+ 3	0~	+ 4	+ 47
2009	+ 107	+ 22	+ 76	+ 9	+ 65	+ 2	+ 4	+ 4	+ 10	+ 45
2010	+ 117	+ 14	+ 94	+ 9	+ 56	- 3	- 4	+ 4	+ 9	+ 49
2011	+ 99	+ 11	+ 89	- 1	+ 53	- 3	- 2	+ 2	+ 9	+ 47

Source: Office for National Statistics (ONS), Home Office, Central Statistics Office (CSO) Ireland, Northern Ireland Statistics and Research Agency (NISRA).

Totals may not sum due to rounding.

"z" - Not applicable, "0~" - Rounds to zero. Please see the Notes worksheet for more information.

1 Net migration ("Balance") figures for the United Kingdom for 2001 to 2011 have been revised in light of the results of the 2011 Census. These revisions are not reflected in the body of the table. Users should continue to use the estimates in the body of the table to analyse detailed breakdowns of inflows and outflows of long-term international migrants but, in doing so, should bear in mind that the headline net migration estimates have been revised.

2 European Union estimates are for the EU15 (Austria, Belgium, Denmark, Finland, France, Germany, Greece, Republic of Ireland, Italy, Luxembourg, Netherlands, Portugal, Spain and Sweden) up to 2003, the EU25 (the EU15 and the EU8 groupings plus Malta and Cyprus) from 2004 - 2006, and for the EU27 (the EU25 plus Bulgaria and Romania) from 2007. Estimates are also shown separately for the EU15 and the EU8 (Czech Republic, Estonia, Hungary, Latvia, Lithuania, Poland, Slovakia and Slovenia, formerly known collectively as the A8).

3 Excludes migrants to and from European Union countries as defined in footnote 1.

4 From 2004 onwards, All, New and Other Commonwealth exclude Malta and Cyprus.

5 From 2004 onwards, Remainder of Europe and Other Foreign excludes the eight central and eastern European member states that joined the EU in May 2004 (the EU8). From 2007 onwards, Remainder of Europe and Other Foreign excludes Bulgaria and Romania which joined the EU in January 2007.

15.9 Grants of settlement by country of nationality and category and in-country refusals of settlement

Year	Geographical region	Country of nationality	Total grants of settlement
2012	*Total	*Total	129,749
2012	Africa	*Total Africa	30,826
2012	Americas	*Total Americas	11,037
2012	Asia	*Total Asia	70,612
2012	Europe	*Total Europe	6,953
2012	Middle East	*Total Middle East	4,607
2012	Oceania	*Total Oceania	5,497
2012	Other	*Total Other	217
2012	Asia	Afghanistan	2,260
2012	Europe	Albania	437
2012	Africa	Algeria	521
2012	Oceania	American Samoa	0
2012	Europe	Andorra	0
2012	Africa	Angola	103
2012	Americas	Anguilla (British)	0
2012	Americas	Antigua and Barbuda	17
2012	Americas	Argentina	106
2012	Europe	Armenia	39
2012	Americas	Aruba	0
2012	Oceania	Australia	3,690
2012	Europe	Austria	:
2012	Europe	Azerbaijan	148
2012	Americas	Bahamas, The	18
2012	Middle East	Bahrain	19
2012	Asia	Bangladesh	3,293
2012	Americas	Barbados	61
2012	Europe	Belarus	178
2012	Europe	Belgium	:
2012	Americas	Belize	18
2012	Africa	Benin	8
2012	Americas	Bermuda (British)	0
2012	Asia	Bhutan	296
2012	Americas	Bolivia	85
2012	Americas	Bonaire, Sint Eustatius and Saba	0
2012	Europe	Bosnia and Herzegovina	42
2012	Africa	Botswana	64
2012	Americas	Brazil	856
2012	Other	British overseas citizens	22
2012	Asia	Brunei	6
2012	Europe	Bulgaria	:
2012	Africa	Burkina	4
2012	Asia	Burma	371
2012	Africa	Burundi	46
2012	Asia	Cambodia	19
2012	Africa	Cameroon	409
2012	Americas	Canada	1,300
2012	Africa	Cape Verde	4
2012	Americas	Cayman Islands (British)	0
2012	Africa	Central African Republic	0
2012	Africa	Chad	16
2012	Americas	Chile	81
2012	Asia	China	6,298
2012	Oceania	Christmas Island	0
2012	Oceania	Cocos (Keeling) Islands	0
2012	Americas	Colombia	511
2012	Africa	Comoros	1
2012	Africa	Congo	52
2012	Africa	Congo (Democratic Republic)	836
2012	Oceania	Cook Islands	0
2012	Americas	Costa Rica	21
2012	Europe	Croatia	103
2012	Americas	Cuba	68
2012	Americas	Curacao	0
2012	Europe	Cyprus	:
2012	Europe	Cyprus (Northern part of)	21
2012	Europe	Czech Republic	:
2012	Europe	Denmark	:
2012	Africa	Djibouti	12
2012	Americas	Dominica	34
2012	Americas	Dominican Republic	40
2012	Asia	East Timor	0
2012	Americas	Ecuador	92
2012	Africa	Egypt	726
2012	Americas	El Salvador	8
2012	Africa	Equatorial Guinea	0

15.9 Grants of settlement by country of nationality and category and in-country refusals of settlement

Year	Geographical region	Country of nationality	Total grants of settlement
2012	Africa	Eritrea	1,765
2012	Europe	Estonia	:
2012	Africa	Ethiopia	1,003
2012	Americas	Falkland Islands (British)	0
2012	Europe	Faroe Islands	0
2012	Oceania	Fiji	137
2012	Europe	Finland	:
2012	Europe	Former Yugoslavia	13
2012	Europe	France	:
2012	Americas	French Guiana	0
2012	Oceania	French Polynesia	0
2012	Africa	Gabon	6
2012	Africa	Gambia, The	457
2012	Europe	Georgia	102
2012	Europe	Germany	:
2012	Africa	Ghana	2,250
2012	Europe	Gibraltar (British)	0
2012	Europe	Greece	:
2012	Europe	Greenland	0
2012	Americas	Grenada	42
2012	Americas	Guadeloupe	0
2012	Americas	Guam	0
2012	Americas	Guatemala	6
2012	Africa	Guinea	87
2012	Africa	Guinea-Bissau	1
2012	Americas	Guyana	110
2012	Americas	Haiti	3
2012	Oceania	Heard Island and McDonald Islands	0
2012	Americas	Honduras	18
2012	Asia	Hong Kong	316
2012	Europe	Hungary	:
2012	Europe	Iceland	:
2012	Asia	India	26,532
2012	Asia	Indonesia	240
2012	Middle East	Iran	1,507
2012	Middle East	Iraq	1,521
2012	Europe	Ireland	:
2012	Middle East	Israel	362
2012	Europe	Italy	:
2012	Africa	Ivory Coast	154
2012	Americas	Jamaica	1,668
2012	Asia	Japan	1,001
2012	Middle East	Jordan	176
2012	Europe	Kazakhstan	127
2012	Africa	Kenya	886
2012	Oceania	Kiribati	1
2012	Asia	Korea (North)	80
2012	Asia	Korea (South)	571
2012	Europe	Kosovo	308
2012	Middle East	Kuwait	88
2012	Europe	Kyrgyzstan	54
2012	Asia	Laos	14
2012	Europe	Latvia	:
2012	Middle East	Lebanon	270
2012	Africa	Lesotho	6
2012	Africa	Liberia	43
2012	Africa	Libya	239
2012	Europe	Liechtenstein	:
2012	Europe	Lithuania	:
2012	Europe	Luxembourg	:
2012	Asia	Macau	0
2012	Europe	Macedonia	56
2012	Africa	Madagascar	9
2012	Africa	Malawi	219
2012	Asia	Malaysia	1,342
2012	Asia	Maldives	26
2012	Africa	Mali	5
2012	Europe	Malta	:
2012	Oceania	Marshall Islands	0
2012	Americas	Martinique	0
2012	Africa	Mauritania	3
2012	Africa	Mauritius	660
2012	Africa	Mayotte	0
2012	Americas	Mexico	291
2012	Oceania	Micronesia	0

15.9 Grants of settlement by country of nationality and category and in-country refusals of settlement

Year	Geographical region	Country of nationality	Total grants of settlement
2012	Europe	Moldova	59
2012	Europe	Monaco	0
2012	Asia	Mongolia	56
2012	Europe	Montenegro	12
2012	Americas	Montserrat (British)	0
2012	Africa	Morocco	490
2012	Africa	Mozambique	14
2012	Africa	Namibia	39
2012	Oceania	Nauru	3
2012	Asia	Nepal	3,213
2012	Europe	Netherlands	:
2012	Americas	Netherlands Antilles	:
2012	Oceania	New Caledonia	0
2012	Oceania	New Zealand	1,647
2012	Americas	Nicaragua	14
2012	Africa	Niger	2
2012	Africa	Nigeria	6,538
2012	Oceania	Niue	0
2012	Oceania	Norfolk Island	0
2012	Oceania	Northern Mariana Islands	0
2012	Europe	Norway	:
2012	Middle East	Occupied Palestinian Territories	124
2012	Middle East	Oman	8
2012	Other	Other and unknown	35
2012	Asia	Pakistan	13,061
2012	Oceania	Palau	0
2012	Americas	Panama	5
2012	Oceania	Papua New Guinea	1
2012	Americas	Paraguay	8
2012	Americas	Peru	149
2012	Asia	Philippines	5,699
2012	Oceania	Pitcairn Islands (British)	0
2012	Europe	Poland	:
2012	Europe	Portugal	:
2012	Americas	Puerto Rico	0
2012	Middle East	Qatar	0
2012	Other	Refugee	118
2012	Africa	Reunion	0
2012	Europe	Romania	:
2012	Europe	Russia	1,713
2012	Africa	Rwanda	56
2012	Oceania	Samoa	1
2012	Europe	San Marino	0
2012	Africa	Sao Tome and Principe	2
2012	Middle East	Saudi Arabia	60
2012	Africa	Senegal	40
2012	Europe	Serbia	257
2012	Europe	Serbia and Montenegro	:
2012	Africa	Seychelles	25
2012	Africa	Sierra Leone	337
2012	Asia	Singapore	336
2012	Europe	Slovakia	:
2012	Europe	Slovenia	:
2012	Oceania	Solomon Islands	0
2012	Africa	Somalia	3,102
2012	Africa	South Africa	4,921
2012	Americas	South Georgia and South Sandwich Islands	0
2012	Europe	Spain	:
2012	Asia	Sri Lanka	2,814
2012	Africa	St. Helena (British)	0
2012	Americas	St. Kitts and Nevis	12
2012	Americas	St. Lucia	104
2012	Americas	St. Maarten (Dutch Part)	0
2012	Americas	St. Martin (French Part)	0
2012	Americas	St. Pierre and Miquelon	0
2012	Americas	St. Vincent and the Grenadines	76
2012	Other	Stateless	42
2012	Africa	Sudan	626
2012	Africa	Sudan (South)	0
2012	Americas	Surinam	0
2012	Europe	Svalbard and Jan Mayen	0
2012	Africa	Swaziland	16
2012	Europe	Sweden	:
2012	Europe	Switzerland	:
2012	Middle East	Syria	288

15.9 Grants of settlement by country of nationality and category and in-country refusals of settlement

Year	Geographical region	Country of nationality	Total grants of settlement
2012	Asia	Taiwan	238
2012	Europe	Tajikistan	5
2012	Africa	Tanzania	272
2012	Asia	Thailand	2,216
2012	Africa	Togo	24
2012	Oceania	Tokelau	0
2012	Oceania	Tonga	17
2012	Americas	Trinidad and Tobago	322
2012	Africa	Tunisia	204
2012	Europe	Turkey	2,376
2012	Europe	Turkmenistan	26
2012	Americas	Turks and Caicos Islands (British)	0
2012	Oceania	Tuvalu	0
2012	Africa	Uganda	514
2012	Europe	Ukraine	777
2012	Middle East	United Arab Emirates	7
2012	Americas	United States	4,660
2012	Americas	Uruguay	13
2012	Europe	Uzbekistan	100
2012	Oceania	Vanuatu	0
2012	Europe	Vatican City	0
2012	Americas	Venezuela	220
2012	Asia	Vietnam	314
2012	Americas	Virgin Islands (British)	0
2012	Americas	Virgin Islands (US)	0
2012	Oceania	Wallis and Futuna	0
2012	Africa	Western Sahara	0
2012	Middle East	Yemen	177
2012	Africa	Zambia	306
2012	Africa	Zimbabwe	2,703

: = Not applicable.
.. = Not available.

15.10 Asylum applications and initial decisions for main applicants, by country of nationality

Year	Geographical region	Country of nationality	Total applications
2012	*Total	*Total	21,843
2012	Africa	*Total Africa	6,111
2012	Americas	*Total Americas	249
2012	Asia	*Total Asia	9,561
2012	Europe	*Total Europe	1,344
2012	Middle East	*Total Middle East	4,313
2012	Oceania	*Total Oceania	6
2012	Other	*Total Other	259
2012	Asia	Afghanistan	1,008
2012	Europe	Albania	819
2012	Africa	Algeria	258
2012	Oceania	American Samoa	0
2012	Europe	Andorra	0
2012	Africa	Angola	32
2012	Americas	Anguilla (British)	0
2012	Americas	Antigua and Barbuda	2
2012	Americas	Argentina	4
2012	Europe	Armenia	8
2012	Americas	Aruba	0
2012	Oceania	Australia	2
2012	Europe	Austria	0
2012	Europe	Azerbaijan	13
2012	Americas	Bahamas, The	2
2012	Middle East	Bahrain	28
2012	Asia	Bangladesh	1,057
2012	Americas	Barbados	2
2012	Europe	Belarus	23
2012	Europe	Belgium	0
2012	Americas	Belize	0
2012	Africa	Benin	4
2012	Americas	Bermuda (British)	0
2012	Asia	Bhutan	9
2012	Americas	Bolivia	12
2012	Americas	Bonaire, Sint Eustatius and Saba	0
2012	Europe	Bosnia and Herzegovina	2
2012	Africa	Botswana	15
2012	Americas	Brazil	17
2012	Other	British overseas citizens	2
2012	Asia	Brunei	0
2012	Europe	Bulgaria	3
2012	Africa	Burkina	4
2012	Asia	Burma	73
2012	Africa	Burundi	4
2012	Asia	Cambodia	0
2012	Africa	Cameroon	119
2012	Americas	Canada	8
2012	Africa	Cape Verde	0
2012	Americas	Cayman Islands (British)	0
2012	Africa	Central African Republic	5
2012	Africa	Chad	10
2012	Americas	Chile	0
2012	Asia	China	696
2012	Oceania	Christmas Island	1
2012	Oceania	Cocos (Keeling) Islands	0
2012	Americas	Colombia	15
2012	Africa	Comoros	4
2012	Africa	Congo	27
2012	Africa	Congo (Democratic Republic)	217
2012	Oceania	Cook Islands	0
2012	Americas	Costa Rica	0
2012	Europe	Croatia	2
2012	Americas	Cuba	4
2012	Americas	Curacao	0
2012	Europe	Cyprus	0
2012	Europe	Cyprus (Northern part of)	1
2012	Europe	Czech Republic	0
2012	Europe	Denmark	0
2012	Africa	Djibouti	2
2012	Americas	Dominica	5
2012	Americas	Dominican Republic	0
2012	Asia	East Timor	0
2012	Americas	Ecuador	0
2012	Africa	Egypt	190
2012	Americas	El Salvador	3
2012	Africa	Equatorial Guinea	1
2012	Africa	Eritrea	728
2012	Europe	Estonia	1
2012	Africa	Ethiopia	143
2012	Americas	Falkland Islands (British)	0
2012	Europe	Faroe Islands	0

15.10 Asylum applications and initial decisions for main applicants, by country of nationality

Year	Geographical region	Country of nationality	Total applications
2012	Oceania	Fiji	3
2012	Europe	Finland	0
2012	Europe	Former Yugoslavia	0
2012	Europe	France	0
2012	Americas	French Guiana	0
2012	Oceania	French Polynesia	0
2012	Africa	Gabon	1
2012	Africa	Gambia, The	300
2012	Europe	Georgia	22
2012	Europe	Germany	0
2012	Africa	Ghana	184
2012	Europe	Gibraltar (British)	0
2012	Europe	Greece	1
2012	Europe	Greenland	0
2012	Americas	Grenada	3
2012	Americas	Guadeloupe	0
2012	Americas	Guam	0
2012	Americas	Guatemala	1
2012	Africa	Guinea	52
2012	Africa	Guinea-Bissau	3
2012	Americas	Guyana	6
2012	Americas	Haiti	1
2012	Oceania	Heard Island and McDonald Islands	0
2012	Americas	Honduras	8
2012	Asia	Hong Kong	6
2012	Europe	Hungary	5
2012	Europe	Iceland	0
2012	Asia	India	1,087
2012	Asia	Indonesia	2
2012	Middle East	Iran	2,659
2012	Middle East	Iraq	275
2012	Europe	Ireland	0
2012	Middle East	Israel	3
2012	Europe	Italy	1
2012	Africa	Ivory Coast	66
2012	Americas	Jamaica	104
2012	Asia	Japan	0
2012	Middle East	Jordan	20
2012	Europe	Kazakhstan	2
2012	Africa	Kenya	90
2012	Oceania	Kiribati	0
2012	Asia	Korea (North)	22
2012	Asia	Korea (South)	9
2012	Europe	Kosovo	22
2012	Middle East	Kuwait	82
2012	Europe	Kyrgyzstan	5
2012	Asia	Laos	1
2012	Europe	Latvia	2
2012	Middle East	Lebanon	40
2012	Africa	Lesotho	2
2012	Africa	Liberia	5
2012	Africa	Libya	218
2012	Europe	Liechtenstein	0
2012	Europe	Lithuania	7
2012	Europe	Luxembourg	0
2012	Asia	Macau	0
2012	Europe	Macedonia	3
2012	Africa	Madagascar	1
2012	Africa	Malawi	116
2012	Asia	Malaysia	49
2012	Asia	Maldives	2
2012	Africa	Mali	13
2012	Europe	Malta	0
2012	Oceania	Marshall Islands	0
2012	Americas	Martinique	0
2012	Africa	Mauritania	6
2012	Africa	Mauritius	40
2012	Africa	Mayotte	0
2012	Americas	Mexico	6
2012	Oceania	Micronesia	0
2012	Europe	Moldova	6
2012	Europe	Monaco	0
2012	Asia	Mongolia	20
2012	Europe	Montenegro	0
2012	Americas	Montserrat (British)	0
2012	Africa	Morocco	55
2012	Africa	Mozambique	1
2012	Africa	Namibia	16
2012	Oceania	Nauru	0
2012	Asia	Nepal	60

15.10 Asylum applications and initial decisions for main applicants, by country of nationality

Year	Geographical region	Country of nationality	Total applications
2012	Europe	Netherlands	1
2012	Americas	Netherlands Antilles	:
2012	Oceania	New Caledonia	0
2012	Oceania	New Zealand	0
2012	Americas	Nicaragua	0
2012	Africa	Niger	4
2012	Africa	Nigeria	959
2012	Oceania	Niue	0
2012	Oceania	Norfolk Island	0
2012	Oceania	Northern Mariana Islands	0
2012	Europe	Norway	1
2012	Middle East	Occupied Palestinian Territories	156
2012	Middle East	Oman	0
2012	Other	Other and unknown	4
2012	Asia	Pakistan	3,280
2012	Oceania	Palau	0
2012	Americas	Panama	0
2012	Oceania	Papua New Guinea	0
2012	Americas	Paraguay	0
2012	Americas	Peru	1
2012	Asia	Philippines	19
2012	Oceania	Pitcairn Islands (British)	0
2012	Europe	Poland	43
2012	Europe	Portugal	1
2012	Americas	Puerto Rico	0
2012	Middle East	Qatar	0
2012	Other	Refugee	112
2012	Africa	Reunion	0
2012	Europe	Romania	6
2012	Europe	Russia	97
2012	Africa	Rwanda	17
2012	Oceania	Samoa	0
2012	Europe	San Marino	0
2012	Africa	Sao Tome and Principe	0
2012	Middle East	Saudi Arabia	11
2012	Africa	Senegal	43
2012	Europe	Serbia	1
2012	Europe	Serbia and Montenegro	:
2012	Africa	Seychelles	0
2012	Africa	Sierra Leone	74
2012	Asia	Singapore	2
2012	Europe	Slovakia	2
2012	Europe	Slovenia	0
2012	Oceania	Solomon Islands	0
2012	Africa	Somalia	599
2012	Africa	South Africa	60
2012	Americas	South Georgia and South Sandwich Islands	0
2012	Europe	Spain	1
2012	Asia	Sri Lanka	1,744
2012	Africa	St. Helena (British)	0
2012	Americas	St. Kitts and Nevis	2
2012	Americas	St. Lucia	6
2012	Americas	St. Maarten (Dutch Part)	0
2012	Americas	St. Martin (French Part)	0
2012	Americas	St. Pierre and Miquelon	0
2012	Americas	St. Vincent and the Grenadines	4
2012	Other	Stateless	141
2012	Africa	Sudan	636
2012	Africa	Sudan (South)	0
2012	Americas	Surinam	0
2012	Europe	Svalbard and Jan Mayen	0
2012	Africa	Swaziland	6
2012	Europe	Sweden	0
2012	Europe	Switzerland	0
2012	Middle East	Syria	988
2012	Asia	Taiwan	3
2012	Europe	Tajikistan	0
2012	Africa	Tanzania	29
2012	Asia	Thailand	10
2012	Africa	Togo	11
2012	Oceania	Tokelau	0
2012	Oceania	Tonga	0
2012	Americas	Trinidad and Tobago	14
2012	Africa	Tunisia	26
2012	Europe	Turkey	190
2012	Europe	Turkmenistan	4
2012	Americas	Turks and Caicos Islands (British)	0
2012	Oceania	Tuvalu	0
2012	Africa	Uganda	263
2012	Europe	Ukraine	35

15.10 Asylum applications and initial decisions for main applicants, by country of nationality

Year	Geographical region	Country of nationality	Total applications
2012	Middle East	United Arab Emirates	1
2012	Americas	United States	14
2012	Americas	Uruguay	0
2012	Europe	Uzbekistan	14
2012	Oceania	Vanuatu	0
2012	Europe	Vatican City	0
2012	Americas	Venezuela	5
2012	Asia	Vietnam	402
2012	Americas	Virgin Islands (British)	0
2012	Americas	Virgin Islands (US)	0
2012	Oceania	Wallis and Futuna	0
2012	Africa	Western Sahara	7
2012	Middle East	Yemen	50
2012	Africa	Zambia	22
2012	Africa	Zimbabwe	423

: = Not applicable.
.. = Not available.

Fresh claims' are when a human rights or asylum claim has been refused, withdrawn or treated as withdrawn under paragraph 333C of Immigration Rule 353 and any appeal relating to that claim is no longer pending, the decision maker will consider any further submissions and, if rejected, will then determine whether they amount to a fresh claim. The submissions will amount to a fresh claim if they are significantly different from the material that has previously been considered. The submissions will only be significantly different if the content: had not already been considered; and taken together with the previously considered material, created a realistic prospect of success, not withstanding its rejection.

'Pending' cases are those asylum applications, including fresh claims, lodged since 1 April 2006 which are still under consideration at the end of the reference period.

15.11 Previous marital status and manner of solemnisation (numbers and percentages), 1981, 1991, 2001, 2002, 2007–2011

England and Wales

Year of marriage		Total marriages		Civil marriages		Religious marriages	
		Number	Percentage	Number	Percentage	Number	Percentage
2011	**Total marriages**	**249,133**	**100.0**	**174,681**	**70.1**	**74,452**	**29.9**
	First marriage for both	165,467	66.4	104,609	42.0	60,858	24.4
	First marriage for one	47,425	19.0	38,557	15.5	8,868	3.6
	Remarriage for both	36,241	14.5	31,515	12.6	4,726	1.9
2010	**Total marriages**	**243,808**	**100.0**	**165,680**	**68.0**	**78,128**	**32.0**
	First marriage for both	161,028	66.0	96,903	39.7	64,125	26.3
	First marriage for one	46,190	18.9	37,069	15.2	9,121	3.7
	Remarriage for both	36,590	15.0	31,708	13.0	4,882	2.0
2009	**Total marriages**	**232,443**	**100.0**	**155,950**	**67.1**	**76,493**	**32.9**
	First marriage for both	151,392	65.1	88,741	38.2	62,651	27.0
	First marriage for one	44,323	19.1	35,469	15.3	8,854	3.8
	Remarriage for both	36,728	15.8	31,740	13.7	4,988	2.1
2008	**Total marriages**	**235,794**	**100.0**	**157,296**	**66.7**	**78,498**	**33.3**
	First marriage for both	149,204	63.3	85,323	36.2	63,881	27.1
	First marriage for one	46,712	19.8	37,238	15.8	9,474	4.0
	Remarriage for both	39,878	16.9	34,735	14.7	5,143	2.2
2007	**Total marriages**	**235,367**	**100.0**	**156,198**	**66.4**	**79,169**	**33.6**
	First marriage for both	146,216	62.1	82,351	35.0	63,865	27.1
	First marriage for one	47,669	20.3	37,941	16.1	9,728	4.1
	Remarriage for both	41,482	17.6	35,906	15.3	5,576	2.4
2002	**Total marriages**	**255,596**	**100.0**	**169,210**	**66.2**	**86,386**	**33.8**
	First marriage for both	151,014	59.1	82,564	32.3	68,450	26.8
	First marriage for one	57,768	22.6	46,207	18.1	11,561	4.5
	Remarriage for both	46,814	18.3	40,439	15.8	6,375	2.5
2001	**Total marriages**	**249,227**	**100.0**	**160,238**	**64.3**	**88,989**	**35.7**
	First marriage for both	148,642	59.6	77,048	30.9	71,594	28.7
	First marriage for one	55,943	22.4	44,601	17.9	11,342	4.6
	Remarriage for both	44,642	17.9	38,589	15.5	6,053	2.4
1991	**Total marriages**	**306,756**	**100.0**	**151,333**	**49.3**	**155,423**	**50.7**
	First marriage for both	192,238	62.7	64,614	21.1	127,624	41.6
	First marriage for one	63,159	20.6	44,643	14.6	18,516	6.0
	Remarriage for both	51,359	16.7	42,076	13.7	9,283	3.0
1981	**Total marriages**	**351,973**	**100.0**	**172,514**	**49.0**	**179,459**	**51.0**
	First marriage for both	227,713	64.7	71,530	20.3	156,183	44.4
	First marriage for one	67,048	19.0	51,628	14.7	15,420	4.4
	Remarriage for both	57,212	16.3	49,356	14.0	7,856	2.2

Note:
Figures and percentages may not sum due to rounding.

Source: Office for National Statistics

15.12 Duration of marriage at divorce by age of wife at marriage, 1981-2011

England and Wales Numbers

Year of divorce	Age of wife at marriage	All durations	0-2 years	0 years	1 year	2 years	3 years	4 years	5-9 years	5 years	6 years
							Duration of marriage (completed years)				
2011	All ages	117,558	5,803	30	1,748	4,025	5,890	6,654	32,989	6,727	7,111
	Under 20	9,727	238	1	59	178	309	329	1,915	344	400
	20-24	38,327	1,392	10	416	966	1,535	1,681	8,320	1,745	1,751
	25-29	33,379	1,783	11	544	1,228	1,734	1,986	9,406	1,949	2,001
	30-44	31,999	1,924	4	576	1,344	1,931	2,246	11,736	2,332	2,604
	45 and over	4,126	466	4	153	309	381	412	1,612	357	355
2010	All ages	119,589	6,278	17	1,897	4,364	6,109	6,936	33,700	7,418	7,652
	Under 20	10,619	255	-	85	170	332	351	2,085	450	489
	20-24	39,963	1,528	4	429	1,095	1,551	1,849	8,624	1,895	2,072
	25-29	33,309	1,874	3	583	1,288	1,795	1,947	9,609	2,072	2,123
	30-44	31,660	2,134	8	624	1,502	2,009	2,404	11,834	2,597	2,607
	45 and over	4,038	487	2	176	309	422	385	1,548	404	361
2009	All ages	113,949	6,270	21	1,951	4,298	5,884	6,947	31,290	7,561	6,864
	Under 20	10,529	267	1	60	206	293	371	1,943	478	439
	20-24	39,231	1,540	1	472	1,067	1,516	1,813	8,350	2,065	1,889
	25-29	31,400	1,808	8	572	1,228	1,715	1,986	8,994	2,106	1,898
	30-44	29,021	2,184	7	683	1,494	1,981	2,389	10,610	2,554	2,307
	45 and over	3,768	471	4	164	303	379	388	1,393	358	331
2008	All ages	121,708	6,937	27	2,103	4,807	6,776	7,929	31,803	7,369	6,714
	Under 20	11,657	319	1	78	240	365	500	1,948	478	407
	20-24	42,578	1,685	10	463	1,212	1,798	2,103	8,401	2,043	1,879
	25-29	33,050	2,044	7	621	1,416	1,875	2,148	9,287	1,985	1,863
	30-44	30,642	2,379	7	741	1,631	2,349	2,751	10,819	2,512	2,304
	45 and over	3,781	510	2	200	308	389	427	1,348	351	261
2007	All ages	128,131	8,195	38	2,558	5,599	7,206	7,574	32,419	7,164	7,046
	Under 20	13,224	411	1	120	290	417	487	2,053	430	470
	20-24	45,806	2,039	7	623	1,409	1,905	1,977	8,481	1,928	1,814
	25-29	34,564	2,234	13	668	1,553	1,990	2,115	9,987	2,099	2,106
	30-44	30,808	2,942	11	929	2,002	2,521	2,591	10,617	2,403	2,366
	45 and over	3,729	569	6	218	345	373	404	1,281	304	290
2006	All ages	132,140	8,763	37	2,793	5,933	7,226	7,376	33,736	7,398	7,310
	Under 20	14,441	503	2	157	344	376	447	2,232	474	506
	20-24	48,396	2,240	9	668	1,563	1,975	1,997	8,954	1,967	1,901
	25-29	35,054	2,381	13	796	1,572	2,052	2,172	10,416	2,182	2,181
	30-44	30,613	3,087	6	966	2,115	2,441	2,424	10,858	2,473	2,437
	45 and over	3,636	552	7	206	339	382	336	1,276	302	285
2005	All ages	141,322	9,573	49	3,181	6,343	7,520	8,175	36,064	7,920	7,697
	Under 20	16,473	537	2	148	387	515	579	2,389	576	544
	20-24	52,884	2,469	15	783	1,671	2,025	2,203	9,961	2,083	2,016
	25-29	36,992	2,545	9	845	1,691	2,081	2,507	11,296	2,367	2,431
	30-44	31,213	3,413	17	1,171	2,225	2,540	2,554	11,025	2,545	2,406
	45 and over	3,760	609	6	234	369	359	332	1,393	349	300
2004	All ages	152,923	10,101	42	3,345	6,714	8,319	8,894	39,681	8,840	8,375
	Under 20	18,655	626	3	201	422	557	662	2,626	667	581
	20-24	59,356	2,662	7	854	1,801	2,361	2,494	11,818	2,477	2,359
	25-29	39,459	2,871	8	947	1,916	2,480	2,642	12,426	2,674	2,593
	30-44	31,631	3,353	15	1,122	2,216	2,542	2,724	11,356	2,679	2,515
	45 and over	3,822	589	9	221	359	379	372	1,455	343	327
2003	All ages	153,065	10,286	42	3,283	6,961	8,276	8,882	40,497	8,968	8,639
	Under 20	20,008	694	-	198	496	591	662	2,644	614	562
	20-24	60,883	2,735	11	825	1,899	2,352	2,587	12,944	2,636	2,564
	25-29	38,628	2,954	9	903	2,042	2,554	2,715	12,663	2,778	2,716
	30-44	29,873	3,304	10	1,131	2,163	2,444	2,554	10,865	2,600	2,468
	45 and over	3,673	599	12	226	361	335	364	1,381	340	329
2002	All ages	147,735	10,239	31	3,326	6,882	8,325	8,780	39,730	8,823	8,370
	Under 20	19,828	684	3	184	497	623	597	2,589	591	541
	20-24	60,353	2,833	6	878	1,949	2,411	2,696	13,727	2,739	2,754
	25-29	36,387	2,903	8	906	1,989	2,581	2,778	12,269	2,795	2,602
	30-44	27,803	3,250	7	1,132	2,111	2,366	2,387	9,865	2,374	2,171
	45 and over	3,364	569	7	226	336	344	322	1,280	324	302

15.12 Duration of marriage at divorce by age of wife at marriage, 1981-2011

England and Wales Numbers

Year of divorce	Age of wife at marriage	7 years	8 years	9 years	10-14 years	15-19 years	20-24 years	25-29 years	30 years and over	Not stated	Median duration
2011	All ages	7,263	6,389	5,499	22,126	15,547	12,228	7,712	8,609	-	11.5
	Under 20	487	384	300	1,276	901	1,111	1,130	2,518	-	..
	20-24	1,902	1,619	1,303	5,749	5,361	5,834	4,052	4,403	-	..
	25-29	2,042	1,756	1,658	7,097	5,198	3,370	1,644	1,161	-	..
	30-44	2,488	2,323	1,989	7,267	3,754	1,804	831	506	-	..
	45 and over	344	307	249	737	333	109	55	21	-	..
2010	All ages	7,101	5,995	5,534	22,105	15,772	12,412	7,639	8,638	-	11.4
	Under 20	432	381	333	1,280	1,012	1,305	1,366	2,633	-	..
	20-24	1,825	1,481	1,351	5,967	5,920	5,929	4,117	4,478	-	..
	25-29	2,018	1,690	1,706	7,163	5,134	3,369	1,351	1,067	-	..
	30-44	2,527	2,189	1,914	6,961	3,419	1,693	770	436	-	..
	45 and over	299	254	230	734	287	116	35	24	-	..
2009	All ages	5,968	5,634	5,263	20,591	15,390	11,855	7,490	8,225	7	11.4
	Under 20	355	357	314	1,177	1,092	1,337	1,484	2,565	-	..
	20-24	1,629	1,466	1,301	5,909	5,944	5,964	3,956	4,235	4	..
	25-29	1,679	1,648	1,663	6,704	4,926	2,983	1,299	985	-	..
	30-44	2,068	1,919	1,762	6,090	3,128	1,494	713	429	3	..
	45 and over	237	244	223	711	300	77	38	11	-	..
2008	All ages	6,365	6,034	5,321	21,561	16,945	12,706	8,136	8,907	8	11.5
	Under 20	358	363	342	1,174	1,274	1,526	1,749	2,800	2	..
	20-24	1,619	1,528	1,332	6,315	6,881	6,511	4,247	4,632	5	..
	25-29	1,880	1,862	1,697	7,075	5,204	2,945	1,389	1,082	1	..
	30-44	2,228	2,032	1,743	6,324	3,295	1,620	722	383	-	..
	45 and over	280	249	207	673	291	104	29	10	-	..
2007	All ages	6,560	6,072	5,577	23,427	18,203	13,117	8,701	9,282	7	11.7
	Under 20	423	395	335	1,240	1,542	1,929	2,099	3,045	1	..
	20-24	1,650	1,607	1,482	7,397	7,930	6,757	4,498	4,820	2	..
	25-29	2,021	1,953	1,808	7,777	5,240	2,802	1,377	1,039	3	..
	30-44	2,203	1,890	1,755	6,343	3,219	1,526	686	362	1	..
	45 and over	263	227	197	670	272	103	41	16	-	..
2006	All ages	6,769	6,249	6,010	24,606	18,735	13,472	8,764	9,449	13	11.6
	Under 20	490	397	365	1,491	1,831	2,191	2,241	3,128	1	..
	20-24	1,751	1,681	1,654	8,443	8,470	6,949	4,415	4,947	6	..
	25-29	2,159	2,004	1,890	7,708	5,157	2,745	1,365	1,053	5	..
	30-44	2,107	1,939	1,902	6,263	3,034	1,483	717	305	1	..
	45 and over	262	228	199	701	243	104	26	16	-	..
2005	All ages	7,343	6,801	6,303	26,310	20,310	14,268	9,241	9,852	9	11.6
	Under 20	478	429	362	1,722	2,299	2,605	2,571	3,255	1	..
	20-24	2,007	1,920	1,935	9,570	9,450	7,368	4,636	5,200	2	..
	25-29	2,291	2,173	2,034	8,364	5,146	2,683	1,310	1,058	2	..
	30-44	2,266	2,040	1,768	5,965	3,161	1,526	699	326	4	..
	45 and over	301	239	204	689	254	86	25	13	-	..
2004	All ages	7,900	7,683	6,883	28,984	21,515	15,431	9,705	10,293	-	11.5
	Under 20	498	485	395	2,133	2,737	3,103	2,804	3,407	-	..
	20-24	2,324	2,389	2,269	11,471	10,355	7,893	4,792	5,510	-	..
	25-29	2,517	2,436	2,206	8,671	5,082	2,823	1,427	1,037	-	..
	30-44	2,274	2,111	1,777	6,064	3,093	1,539	639	321	-	..
	45 and over	287	262	236	645	248	73	43	18	-	..
2003	All ages	8,228	7,686	6,976	29,751	20,863	14,974	9,627	9,907	2	11.3
	Under 20	551	495	422	2,613	2,911	3,559	2,985	3,349	-	..
	20-24	2,569	2,622	2,553	12,281	10,413	7,534	4,708	5,327	2	..
	25-29	2,594	2,361	2,214	8,537	4,508	2,409	1,333	955	-	..
	30-44	2,232	1,965	1,600	5,679	2,811	1,391	564	261	-	..
	45 and over	282	243	187	641	220	81	37	15	-	..
2002	All ages	8,020	7,564	6,953	28,592	19,784	13,989	9,106	9,190	-	11.1
	Under 20	481	517	459	2,774	3,160	3,439	2,891	3,071	-	..
	20-24	2,795	2,770	2,669	12,516	9,810	6,845	4,480	5,035	-	..
	25-29	2,514	2,265	2,093	7,524	4,032	2,279	1,175	846	-	..
	30-44	1,985	1,796	1,539	5,249	2,577	1,355	523	231	-	..
	45 and over	245	216	193	529	205	71	37	7	-	..

15.12 Duration of marriage at divorce by age of wife at marriage, 1981-2011

England and Wales   **Numbers**

Year of divorce	Age of wife at marriage	All durations	Duration of marriage (completed years)								
			0-2 years	0 years	1 year	2 years	3 years	4 years	5-9 years	5 years	6 years
2001	All ages	143,818	10,190	36	3,413	6,741	8,206	8,591	39,079	8,632	8,329
	Under 20	20,218	738	3	225	510	634	560	2,676	574	498
	20-24	60,211	2,809	12	870	1,927	2,472	2,711	14,418	2,900	2,938
	25-29	34,759	3,041	10	973	2,058	2,571	2,737	11,728	2,648	2,600
	30-44	25,405	3,054	6	1,116	1,932	2,177	2,246	9,059	2,202	2,028
	45 and over	3,225	548	5	229	314	352	337	1,198	308	265
2000	All ages	141,135	10,438	52	3,494	6,892	8,296	8,740	38,206	8,506	8,148
	Under 20	20,930	846	2	284	560	598	575	2,937	571	594
	20-24	59,874	2,954	8	925	2,021	2,631	2,978	14,663	3,014	3,021
	25-29	33,282	3,095	17	1,038	2,040	2,567	2,675	11,443	2,625	2,510
	30-44	23,912	2,971	14	1,012	1,945	2,159	2,179	8,082	2,032	1,779
	45 and over	3,137	572	11	235	326	341	333	1,081	264	244
1999	All ages	144,556	11,350	49	3,813	7,488	8,833	9,124	39,676	8,958	8,521
	Under 20	22,486	868	5	268	595	658	625	3,367	604	691
	20-24	62,853	3,445	15	1,125	2,305	2,965	3,366	16,221	3,440	3,404
	25-29	32,867	3,182	6	1,074	2,102	2,710	2,745	11,170	2,670	2,432
	30-44	23,270	3,197	14	1,082	2,101	2,147	2,076	7,898	1,982	1,735
	45 and over	3,080	658	9	264	385	353	312	1,020	262	259
1998	All ages	145,214	12,247	68	4,191	7,988	9,270	9,619	40,239	9,180	8,497
	Under 20	24,276	976	7	327	642	704	785	3,858	753	762
	20-24	64,453	4,000	16	1,303	2,681	3,475	3,737	17,413	3,800	3,586
	25-29	31,533	3,510	21	1,144	2,345	2,697	2,787	10,518	2,569	2,289
	30-44	22,076	3,162	18	1,140	2,004	2,062	2,027	7,478	1,801	1,631
	45 and over	2,876	599	6	277	316	332	283	972	257	229
1997	All ages	146,689	12,596	61	4,369	8,166	9,410	9,761	41,260	9,326	8,580
	Under 20	25,579	1,024	7	359	658	757	809	4,424	857	851
	20-24	66,167	4,412	10	1,449	2,953	3,773	4,114	18,226	3,917	3,736
	25-29	31,022	3,576	13	1,213	2,350	2,706	2,712	10,417	2,591	2,263
	30-44	21,017	2,958	20	1,073	1,865	1,879	1,818	7,241	1,719	1,513
	45 and over	2,904	626	11	275	340	295	308	952	242	217
1996	All ages	157,107	14,021	76	5,010	8,935	10,467	10,436	44,609	10,042	9,850
	Under 20	29,927	1,178	4	383	791	970	1,022	5,543	1,128	1,165
	20-24	71,123	5,289	20	1,744	3,525	4,236	4,392	20,221	4,408	4,417
	25-29	31,396	3,872	23	1,384	2,465	2,901	2,778	10,373	2,557	2,359
	30-44	21,640	3,018	15	1,197	1,806	2,008	1,919	7,480	1,702	1,691
	45 and over	3,021	664	14	302	348	352	325	992	247	218
1995	All ages	155,499	14,015	95	4,944	8,976	10,209	10,283	44,304	10,447	9,812
	Under 20	31,322	1,374	8	418	948	1,090	1,158	5,894	1,224	1,180
	20-24	71,360	5,634	28	1,948	3,658	4,375	4,477	20,360	4,748	4,457
	25-29	29,441	3,568	17	1,257	2,294	2,591	2,576	9,892	2,523	2,255
	30-44	20,506	2,817	26	1,034	1,757	1,842	1,792	7,208	1,684	1,707
	45 and over	2,870	622	16	287	319	311	280	950	268	213
1994	All ages	158,175	13,841	81	4,895	8,865	10,400	11,454	44,769	10,836	9,896
	Under 20	34,069	1,582	6	518	1,058	1,297	1,468	6,805	1,404	1,418
	20-24	73,291	5,689	19	1,956	3,714	4,518	5,106	21,102	4,975	4,681
	25-29	28,360	3,408	24	1,208	2,176	2,520	2,698	9,187	2,414	2,077
	30-44	19,686	2,574	17	959	1,598	1,749	1,838	6,807	1,806	1,523
	45 and over	2,769	588	15	254	319	316	344	868	237	197
1993	All ages	165,018	14,096	74	4,708	9,314	11,357	11,799	46,536	11,137	10,352
	Under 20	38,811	1,867	9	583	1,275	1,668	1,653	8,196	1,713	1,685
	20-24	76,853	6,163	12	2,045	4,106	5,066	5,470	21,731	5,194	4,901
	25-29	27,178	3,051	27	953	2,071	2,439	2,506	8,777	2,282	1,970
	30-44	19,357	2,419	18	878	1,523	1,832	1,827	6,920	1,722	1,562
	45 and over	2,819	596	8	249	339	352	343	912	226	234
1992	All ages	160,385	14,247	62	4,630	9,555	11,299	11,352	43,745	10,417	9,459
	Under 20	39,734	1,990	3	590	1,397	1,736	1,739	8,544	1,798	1,697
	20-24	74,701	6,208	19	1,949	4,240	5,159	5,510	20,464	4,952	4,469
	25-29	25,173	2,992	11	1,010	1,971	2,241	2,213	7,759	1,952	1,796
	30-44	18,011	2,430	16	832	1,582	1,822	1,631	6,054	1,476	1,275
	45 and over	2,766	627	13	249	365	341	259	924	239	222
1991	All ages	158,745	15,332	62	5,239	10,031	11,321	11,126	42,735	10,049	9,345
	Under 20	40,594	2,387	1	780	1,606	1,894	2,014	9,143	1,857	1,805
	20-24	74,050	6,863	17	2,271	4,575	5,308	5,292	19,926	4,808	4,493
	25-29	24,025	2,942	12	1,003	1,927	2,162	2,014	7,048	1,776	1,571
	30-44	17,359	2,486	16	892	1,578	1,640	1,556	5,765	1,390	1,269
	45 and over	2,717	654	16	293	345	317	250	853	218	207

15.12 Duration of marriage at divorce by age of wife at marriage, 1981-2011

England and Wales — Numbers

Year of divorce	Age of wife at marriage	7 years	8 years	9 years	10-14 years	15-19 years	20-24 years	25-29 years	30 years and over	Not stated	Median duration
2001	All ages	7,909	7,463	6,746	28,176	18,603	13,318	8,986	8,667	2	10.9
	Under 20	524	513	567	2,999	3,309	3,607	2,830	2,865	-	..
	20-24	2,925	2,943	2,712	12,875	9,251	6,432	4,505	4,736	2	..
	25-29	2,398	2,183	1,899	7,075	3,587	2,052	1,158	810	-	..
	30-44	1,810	1,612	1,407	4,721	2,270	1,157	475	246	-	..
	45 and over	252	212	161	506	186	70	18	10	-	..
2000	All ages	7,778	7,183	6,591	27,459	17,870	12,907	9,017	8,196	6	10.7
	Under 20	566	604	602	3,230	3,413	3,556	3,003	2,770	2	..
	20-24	2,959	2,909	2,760	12,720	8,839	6,142	4,479	4,465	3	..
	25-29	2,356	2,046	1,906	6,521	3,192	1,995	1,078	715	1	..
	30-44	1,665	1,429	1,177	4,461	2,250	1,145	433	232	-	..
	45 and over	232	195	146	527	176	69	24	14	-	..
1999	All ages	7,861	7,338	6,998	27,384	18,072	12,888	9,349	7,871	9	10.5
	Under 20	620	722	730	3,532	3,886	3,874	3,040	2,633	3	..
	20-24	3,217	3,111	3,049	12,984	8,729	5,960	4,871	4,308	4	..
	25-29	2,205	2,044	1,819	6,209	3,127	1,950	1,053	720	1	..
	30-44	1,622	1,312	1,247	4,191	2,156	1,037	362	205	1	..
	45 and over	197	149	153	468	174	67	23	5	-	..
1998	All ages	7,785	7,757	7,020	26,698	17,934	12,675	9,056	7,468	8	10.2
	Under 20	740	823	780	3,986	4,364	4,020	3,075	2,508	-	..
	20-24	3,435	3,413	3,179	12,757	8,469	5,833	4,738	4,028	3	..
	25-29	2,026	1,955	1,679	5,599	2,955	1,851	896	716	4	..
	30-44	1,398	1,419	1,229	3,907	1,993	911	325	210	1	..
	45 and over	186	147	153	449	153	60	22	6	-	..
1997	All ages	8,324	7,935	7,095	26,215	18,027	13,148	9,058	7,202	12	10.0
	Under 20	923	894	899	4,197	4,648	4,284	2,957	2,476	3	..
	20-24	3,750	3,540	3,283	12,447	8,298	6,082	4,971	3,837	7	..
	25-29	2,065	1,918	1,580	5,353	2,881	1,860	834	681	2	..
	30-44	1,409	1,400	1,200	3,776	2,006	869	274	196	-	..
	45 and over	177	183	133	442	194	53	22	12	-	..
1996	All ages	9,092	8,171	7,454	27,332	19,321	14,236	9,511	7,165	9	9.9
	Under 20	1,120	1,116	1,014	5,084	5,507	4,867	3,294	2,461	1	..
	20-24	4,029	3,776	3,591	12,921	8,558	6,549	5,112	3,841	4	..
	25-29	2,168	1,734	1,555	5,119	2,998	1,882	805	665	3	..
	30-44	1,549	1,375	1,163	3,765	2,087	887	285	190	1	..
	45 and over	226	170	131	443	171	51	15	8	-	..
1995	All ages	8,822	7,965	7,258	27,365	18,943	14,483	8,925	6,962	10	9.6
	Under 20	1,161	1,176	1,153	5,768	5,604	5,009	3,072	2,350	3	..
	20-24	4,051	3,668	3,436	12,640	8,476	6,815	4,860	3,718	5	..
	25-29	2,023	1,664	1,427	4,781	2,832	1,796	711	692	2	..
	30-44	1,426	1,275	1,116	3,727	1,868	795	268	189	-	..
	45 and over	161	182	126	449	163	68	14	13	-	..
1994	All ages	8,881	7,900	7,256	28,073	19,200	14,891	8,801	6,739	7	9.8
	Under 20	1,403	1,327	1,253	6,458	6,077	5,101	3,050	2,230	1	14.6
	20-24	4,222	3,727	3497	12,808	8,351	7,303	4,777	3,633	4	10.1
	25-29	1,774	1,559	1,363	4,733	2,804	1,663	675	670	2	7.6
	30-44	1,315	1,144	1,019	3,693	1,785	761	278	201	-	7.1
	45 and over	167	143	124	381	183	63	21	5	-	5.5
1993	All ages	9,029	8,475	7,543	30,156	20,233	15,503	8,426	6,907	5	9.8
	Under 20	1,593	1,621	1,584	7,812	6,830	5,452	3,065	2,267	1	13.9
	20-24	4,311	3,892	3,433	13,538	8,796	7,909	4,434	3,743	3	10.0
	25-29	1,624	1,627	1,274	4,753	2,808	1,497	671	675	1	7.8
	30-44	1,328	1,177	1,131	3,667	1,648	588	242	214	-	7.0
	45 and over	173	158	121	386	151	57	14	8	-	5.4
1992	All ages	8,708	7,914	7,247	29,285	20,160	15,488	8,098	6,704	7	9.9
	Under 20	1,708	1,670	1,671	8,192	6,920	5,395	3,090	2,125	3	13.5
	20-24	4,090	3,694	3,259	12,837	8,721	8,038	4,067	3,694	3	10.0
	25-29	1,513	1,340	1,158	4,401	2,791	1,448	633	694	1	7.9
	30-44	1,219	1,059	1,025	3,477	1,552	570	289	186	-	6.9
	45 and over	178	151	134	378	176	37	19	5	-	5.6
1991	All ages	8,423	7,797	7,121	28,791	20,127	14,957	7,845	6,492	19	9.8
	Under 20	1,808	1,883	1,790	8,295	6,988	5,112	2,825	1,930	6	12.7
	20-24	3,902	3,506	3,217	12,304	8,775	7,924	4,066	3,581	11	9.9
	25-29	1,438	1,228	1,035	4,417	2,686	1,318	685	751	2	8.1
	30-44	1,118	1,033	955	3,355	1,521	553	261	222	-	7.0
	45 and over	157	147	124	420	157	50	8	8	-	5.7

15.12 Duration of marriage at divorce by age of wife at marriage, 1981-2011

England and Wales   **Numbers**

Year of divorce	Age of wife at marriage	All durations	Duration of marriage (completed years)								
			0-2 years	0 years	1 year	2 years	3 years	4 years	5-9 years	5 years	6 years
1990	All ages	153,386	15,122	64	5,142	9,916	10,863	10,314	42,061	9,883	9,025
	Under 20	41,116	2,558	6	788	1,764	1,993	1,961	9,790	2,030	1,917
	20-24	71,489	6,919	20	2,312	4,587	5,115	4,981	19,248	4,702	4,265
	25-29	21,701	2,637	11	906	1,720	1,898	1,721	6,567	1,627	1,462
	30-44	16,387	2,378	16	866	1,496	1,533	1,386	5,608	1,297	1,214
	45 and over	2,693	630	11	270	349	324	265	848	227	167
1989	All ages	150,872	15,231	56	5,420	9,755	10,372	10,116	42,108	9,569	8,928
	Under 20	42,612	2,915	11	980	1,924	2,059	2,144	10,798	2,209	2,199
	20-24	69,424	6,956	18	2,424	4,514	4,886	4,783	18,725	4,377	4,042
	25-29	20,369	2,468	8	887	1,573	1,651	1,580	6,189	1,476	1,360
	30-44	15,774	2,272	12	853	1,407	1,487	1,338	5,535	1,286	1,118
	45 and over	2,693	620	7	276	337	289	271	861	221	209
1988	All ages	152,633	15,003	88	5,403	9,512	10,213	10,376	42,617	9,730	9,080
	Under 20	44,693	3,151	7	1,055	2,089	2,296	2,472	11,676	2,374	2,424
	20-24	69,489	6,676	31	2,339	4,306	4,751	4,777	18,310	4,378	3,936
	25-29	20,267	2,298	16	854	1,428	1,525	1,543	6,167	1,464	1,331
	30-44	15,472	2,207	17	852	1,338	1,328	1,368	5,584	1,302	1,182
	45 and over	2,712	671	17	303	351	313	216	880	212	207
1987	All ages	151,007	14,549	..	..	..	10,248	10,626	43,150	10,262	9,626
	Under 20	46,097	3,387	..	..	..	2,554	2,755	12,428	2,823	2,628
	20-24	68,345	6,393	..	..	..	4,643	4,751	18,180	4,461	4,190
	25-29	19,049	2,045	..	..	..	1,449	1,449	6,088	1,420	1,353
	30-44	14,802	2,085	..	..	..	1,293	1,405	5,549	1,327	1,242
	45 and over	2,714	639	..	..	..	309	266	905	231	213
1986	All ages	153,903	14,596	..	..	..	11,683	12,358	42,187	10,656	9,329
	Under 20	48,621	3,735	..	..	..	3,239	3,618	12,978	3,204	2,863
	20-24	68,387	6,216	..	..	..	5,020	5,257	17,059	4,446	3,713
	25-29	18,990	1,955	..	..	..	1,504	1,561	5,845	1,369	1,296
	30-44	15,064	2,068	..	..	..	1,553	1,583	5,369	1,387	1,248
	45 and over	2,841	622	..	..	..	367	339	936	250	209
1985	All ages	160,300	14,662	..	..	..	16,929	14,185	41,537	10,942	9,352
	Under 20	52,858	4,034	..	..	..	5,320	4,481	13,455	3,471	3,008
	20-24	69,663	5,927	..	..	..	6,983	5,735	16,294	4,374	3,607
	25-29	18,689	1,748	..	..	..	1,894	1,720	5,620	1,408	1,269
	30-44	15,765	2,160	..	..	..	2,187	1,827	5,181	1,403	1,249
	45 and over	3,325	793	..	..	..	545	422	987	286	219
1984	All ages	144,501	1,336	..	..	..	15,296	13,868	40,866	10,434	8,830
	Under 20	49,610	304	..	..	..	5,084	4,577	13,821	3,452	2,994
	20-24	62,642	427	..	..	..	6,107	5,443	15,716	4,020	3,371
	25-29	16,811	183	..	..	..	1,707	1,737	5,477	1,329	1,118
	30-44	12,944	289	..	..	..	1,921	1,739	4,895	1,362	1,126
	45 and over	2,494	133	..	..	..	477	372	957	271	221
1983	All ages	147,479	1,528	..	..	..	15,706	13,863	42,041	10,413	8,785
	Under 20	52,547	389	..	..	..	5,529	4,866	15,084	3,693	3,129
	20-24	63,382	477	..	..	..	6,054	5,228	15,887	3,942	3,294
	25-29	16,351	196	..	..	..	1,723	1,654	5,362	1,270	1,130
	30-44	12,675	326	..	..	..	1,904	1,725	4,726	1,253	1,027
	45 and over	2,524	140	..	..	..	496	390	982	255	205
1982	All ages	146,698	1,712	..	..	..	15,190	13,360	42,499	10,126	8,984
	Under 20	54,067	484	..	..	..	5,580	5,003	15,957	3,720	3,283
	20-24	62,955	491	..	..	..	5,746	4,874	16,225	3,862	3,444
	25-29	15,714	247	..	..	..	1,671	1,581	5,188	1,235	1,116
	30-44	11,604	325	..	..	..	1,707	1,556	4,248	1,076	933
	45 and over	2,358	165	..	..	..	486	346	881	233	208
1981	All ages	145,713	1,859	..	..	..	14,318	12,463	43,808	10,413	9,511
	Under 20	54,424	550	..	..	..	5,489	4,889	16,870	4,042	3,560
	20-24	63,034	506	..	..	..	5,343	4,579	16,951	3,874	3,630
	25-29	15,281	264	..	..	..	1,553	1,382	5,227	1,281	1,168
	30-44	10,661	354	..	..	..	1,517	1,283	3,855	980	939
	45 and over	2,313	185	..	..	..	416	330	905	236	214

Source: Office for National Statistics

15.12 Duration of marriage at divorce by age of wife at marriage, 1981-2011

England and Wales — Numbers

Year of divorce	Age of wife at marriage	7 years	8 years	9 years	10-14 years	15-19 years	20-24 years	25-29 years	30 years and over	Not stated	Median duration
1990	**All ages**	**8,289**	**7,634**	**7,230**	**27,310**	**19,819**	**14,186**	**7,479**	**6,216**	**16**	**9.8**
	Under 20	1,950	1,933	1,960	8,313	7,122	4,974	2,648	1,755	2	12.4
	20-24	3,767	3,380	3,134	11,542	8,786	7,500	3,897	3,490	11	9.8
	25-29	1,316	1,144	1,018	3,893	2,416	1,156	639	772	2	8.2
	30-44	1,101	1,016	980	3,163	1,330	514	283	191	1	7.0
	45 and over	155	161	138	399	165	42	12	8	-	6.0
1989	**All ages**	**8,392**	**7,887**	**7,332**	**26,281**	**19,418**	**13,575**	**7,333**	**6,419**	**19**	**9.7**
	Under 20	2,233	2,037	2,120	8,289	6,951	4,963	2,632	1,854	7	11.9
	20-24	3,698	3,538	3,070	10,775	8,890	7,051	3,758	3,590	10	9.8
	25-29	1,210	1,113	1,030	3,900	2,201	1,026	640	713	1	8.4
	30-44	1,094	1,054	983	2,885	1,226	491	286	253	1	7.0
	45 and over	157	145	129	432	150	44	17	9	-	5.8
1988	**All ages**	**8,784**	**7,906**	**7,117**	**26,545**	**20,132**	**13,723**	**7,476**	**6,548**	**-**	**9.7**
	Under 20	2,410	2,352	2,116	8,648	7,126	4,896	2,571	1,857	-	11.5
	20-24	3,813	3,247	2,936	10,753	9,646	7,074	3,915	3,587	-	10.1
	25-29	1,256	1,083	1,033	3,962	2,046	1,180	698	848	-	8.7
	30-44	1,137	1,069	894	2,787	1,149	527	274	248	-	7.0
	45 and over	168	155	138	395	165	46	18	8	-	5.7
1987	**All ages**	**8,781**	**7,827**	**6,654**	**26,194**	**19,576**	**12,970**	**7,314**	**6,380**	**-**	**9.5**
	Under 20	2,592	2,324	2,061	8,925	7,019	4,820	2,472	1,737	-	11.0
	20-24	3,652	3,212	2,665	10,656	9,671	6,602	3,861	3,588	-	10.1
	25-29	1,196	1,127	992	3,723	1,791	1,021	694	789	-	8.5
	30-44	1,163	993	824	2,475	975	488	276	256	-	6.8
	45 and over	178	171	112	415	120	39	11	10	-	5.1
1986	**All ages**	**8,457**	**7,465**	**6,280**	**26,718**	**19,547**	**12,909**	**7,357**	**6,539**	**9**	**9.4**
	Under 20	2,616	2,313	1,982	9,208	6,946	4,810	2,317	1,766	4	10.4
	20-24	3,410	2,981	2,509	10,953	9,857	6,376	3,986	3,661	2	10.3
	25-29	1,205	1,044	931	3,679	1,688	1,145	736	874	3	8.6
	30-44	1,034	969	731	2,477	940	541	301	232	-	6.4
	45 and over	192	158	127	401	116	37	17	6	-	5.4
1985	**All ages**	**7,932**	**6,884**	**6,427**	**27,087**	**19,460**	**12,463**	**7,388**	**6,576**	**13**	**8.9**
	Under 20	2,553	2,262	2,161	9,658	7,125	4,645	2,347	1,789	4	9.6
	20-24	3,114	2,705	2,494	11,276	9,665	6,122	4,016	3,638	7	10.0
	25-29	1,054	981	908	3,388	1,630	1,122	700	865	2	8.3
	30-44	1,015	781	733	2,348	935	538	315	274	-	6.0
	45 and over	196	155	131	417	105	36	10	10	-	4.8
1984	**All ages**	**7,854**	**7,105**	**6,643**	**27,336**	**19,108**	**12,516**	**7,528**	**6,637**	**10**	**10.1**
	Under 20	2,640	2,450	2,285	9,933	7,127	4,614	2,410	1,737	3	10.4
	20-24	3,060	2,687	2,578	11,723	9,412	6,154	3,942	3,711	7	11.5
	25-29	1,048	1,034	948	3,209	1,578	1,159	827	934	-	9.3
	30-44	911	793	703	2,093	884	545	328	250	-	6.8
	45 and over	195	141	129	378	107	44	21	5	-	6.0
1983	**All ages**	**8,072**	**7,662**	**7,109**	**28,432**	**19,103**	**12,579**	**7,529**	**6,661**	**37**	**10.1**
	Under 20	2,867	2,752	2,643	10,412	7,596	4,599	2,331	1,728	13	10.2
	20-24	3,111	2,916	2,624	12,764	8,987	6,227	4,045	3,699	14	11.6
	25-29	1,042	997	923	2,999	1,551	1,129	786	943	8	9.2
	30-44	846	825	775	1,899	865	587	355	286	2	7.1
	45 and over	206	172	144	358	104	37	12	5	-	5.9
1982	**All ages**	**8,444**	**7,747**	**7,198**	**28,737**	**18,855**	**12,585**	**7,199**	**6,517**	**44**	**10.1**
	Under 20	3,236	2,940	2,778	10,879	7,699	4,512	2,224	1,713	16	10.0
	20-24	3,188	2,936	2,795	13,312	8,606	6,298	3,821	3,559	23	11.5
	25-29	1,034	930	873	2,654	1,498	1,186	761	924	4	9.0
	30-44	817	803	619	1,586	940	552	375	314	1	7.3
	45 and over	169	138	133	306	112	37	18	7	-	5.8
1981	**All ages**	**8,522**	**8,098**	**7,264**	**28,242**	**18,499**	**12,435**	**7,301**	**6,763**	**25**	**10.1**
	Under 20	3,374	3,088	2,806	10,855	7,468	4,385	2,115	1,796	7	9.8
	20-24	3,186	3,196	3,065	13,263	8,477	6,332	3,932	3,635	16	11.5
	25-29	1,052	974	752	2,333	1,543	1,119	835	1,023	2	9.0
	30-44	726	669	541	1,479	902	559	409	303	-	7.4
	45 and over	184	171	100	312	109	40	10	6	-	6.0

Source: Office for National Statistics

15.13 Duration of marriage at divorce by age of husband at marriage, 2002-2011

England and Wales

Year of divorce	Age of husband at marriage	All durations	0-2 years	0 years	1 year	2 years	3 years	4 years	5-9 years	5 years	6 years
									Duration of marriage (completed years)			
2011	All ages	117,558	5,803	30	1,748	4,025	5,890	6,654	32,989	6,727	7,111
	Under 20	2,871	75	-	19	56	87	101	536	108	124
	20-24	27,934	813	4	213	596	910	1,034	5,343	1,092	1,135
	25-29	36,299	1,679	13	489	1,177	1,780	1,890	9,183	1,919	1,883
	30-44	43,304	2,547	6	793	1,748	2,493	2,965	15,209	3,022	3,345
	45 and over	7,150	689	7	234	448	620	664	2,718	586	624
2010	All ages	119,589	6,278	17	1,897	4,364	6,109	6,936	33,700	7,418	7,652
	Under 20	2,958	74	-	20	54	86	97	542	115	120
	20-24	29,661	909	2	251	656	951	1,145	5,437	1,240	1,247
	25-29	36,920	1,740	5	522	1,213	1,723	1,969	9,584	1,998	2,185
	30-44	43,027	2,763	8	829	1,926	2,697	3,070	15,439	3,380	3,468
	45 and over	7,023	792	2	275	515	652	655	2,698	685	632
2009	All ages	113,949	6,270	21	1,951	4,298	5,884	6,947	31,290	7,561	6,864
	Under 20	3,066	74	-	24	50	75	114	543	129	98
	20-24	29,150	883	1	246	636	894	1,193	5,281	1,305	1,221
	25-29	35,305	1,746	4	553	1,189	1,702	1,991	9,186	2,188	1,912
	30-44	39,984	2,810	9	856	1,945	2,623	3,032	13,948	3,370	3,104
	45 and over	6,444	757	7	272	478	590	617	2,332	569	529
2008	All ages	121,708	6,937	27	2,103	4,807	6,776	7,929	31,803	7,369	6,714
	Under 20	3,364	91	-	29	62	98	130	564	125	125
	20-24	32,151	1,006	4	236	766	1,090	1,319	5,161	1,281	1,132
	25-29	37,895	1,978	9	604	1,365	1,889	2,278	9,594	2,013	1,972
	30-44	41,529	3,051	9	941	2,101	3,040	3,544	14,089	3,345	2,979
	45 and over	6,769	811	5	293	513	659	658	2,395	605	506
2007	All ages	128,131	8,195	38	2,558	5,599	7,206	7,574	32,419	7,164	7,046
	Under 20	4,036	132	-	36	96	122	146	611	131	151
	20-24	35,408	1,238	4	364	870	1,214	1,275	5,430	1,198	1,153
	25-29	39,546	2,202	13	659	1,530	1,986	2,109	10,074	2,129	2,133
	30-44	42,408	3,736	12	1,171	2,553	3,279	3,351	13,960	3,163	3,085
	45 and over	6,733	887	9	328	550	605	693	2,344	543	524
2006	All ages	132,140	8,763	37	2,793	5,933	7,226	7,376	33,736	7,398	7,310
	Under 20	4,115	140	-	49	91	119	132	630	142	143
	20-24	38,096	1,400	4	411	985	1,192	1,239	5,727	1,211	1,204
	25-29	40,683	2,304	10	724	1,570	2,054	2,176	10,907	2,285	2,295
	30-44	42,417	4,002	14	1,287	2,701	3,234	3,238	14,093	3,209	3,146
	45 and over	6,829	917	9	322	586	627	591	2,379	551	522
2005	All ages	141,322	9,573	49	3,181	6,343	7,520	8,175	36,064	7,920	7,697
	Under 20	4,685	175	-	53	122	159	139	634	166	134
	20-24	42,354	1,516	5	497	1,014	1,308	1,415	6,526	1,328	1,309
	25-29	43,807	2,625	18	836	1,771	2,175	2,529	11,853	2,547	2,481
	30-44	43,631	4,287	13	1,472	2,802	3,250	3,466	14,547	3,270	3,219
	45 and over	6,845	970	13	323	634	628	626	2,504	609	554
2004	All ages	152,923	10,101	42	3,345	6,714	8,319	8,894	39,681	8,840	8,375
	Under 20	5,392	178	-	52	126	146	187	680	186	136
	20-24	47,794	1,680	7	552	1,121	1,475	1,538	7,762	1,572	1,540
	25-29	48,067	2,863	7	881	1,975	2,568	2,974	13,672	2,982	2,812
	30-44	44,701	4,428	19	1,507	2,902	3,468	3,531	15,035	3,505	3,299
	45 and over	6,969	952	9	353	590	662	664	2,532	595	588
2003	All ages	153,065	10,286	42	3,283	6,961	8,276	8,882	40,497	8,968	8,639
	Under 20	5,764	191	-	58	133	157	169	690	176	148
	20-24	50,015	1,720	4	483	1,233	1,484	1,658	8,685	1,675	1,718
	25-29	47,353	3,021	5	927	2,089	2,702	2,960	13,881	3,000	2,901
	30-44	43,173	4,386	17	1,456	2,913	3,362	3,459	14,702	3,519	3,328
	45 and over	6,760	968	16	359	593	571	636	2,539	598	544
2002	All ages	147,735	10,239	31	3,326	6,882	8,325	8,780	39,730	8,823	8,370
	Under 20	5,572	184	-	54	130	169	146	600	123	109
	20-24	50,028	1,739	5	481	1,253	1,529	1,717	9,494	1,814	1,928
	25-29	45,913	3,173	8	985	2,180	2,886	3,009	13,756	3,089	2,897
	30-44	39,977	4,218	9	1,460	2,749	3,125	3,349	13,589	3,216	2,930
	45 and over	6,245	925	9	346	570	616	559	2,291	581	506

Source: Office for National Statistics

15.13 Duration of marriage at divorce by age of husband at marriage, 2002-2011

England and Wales **Numbers**

Year of divorce	Age of husband at marriage	Duration of marriage (completed years)									Median duration
		7 years	8 years	9 years	10-14 years	15-19 years	20-24 years	25-29 years	30 years and over	Not stated	
2011	All ages	7,263	6,389	5,499	22,126	15,547	12,228	7,712	8,609	-	11.5
	Under 20	116	115	73	365	226	309	358	814	-	..
	20-24	1,228	1,024	864	3,599	3,622	4,365	3,444	4,804	-	..
	25-29	2,062	1,766	1,553	7,217	5,803	4,318	2,380	2,049	-	..
	30-44	3,264	2,997	2,581	9,549	5,252	2,962	1,434	893	-	..
	45 and over	593	487	428	1,396	644	274	96	49	-	..
2010	All ages	7,101	5,995	5,534	22,105	15,772	12,412	7,639	8,638	-	11.4
	Under 20	98	123	86	345	277	323	371	843	-	..
	20-24	1,167	904	879	3,769	4,147	4,715	3,596	4,992	-	..
	25-29	2,022	1,726	1,653	7,523	5,757	4,398	2,234	1,992	-	..
	30-44	3,269	2,801	2,521	9,150	5,021	2,738	1,373	776	-	..
	45 and over	545	441	395	1,318	570	238	65	35	-	..
2009	All ages	5,968	5,634	5,263	20,591	15,390	11,855	7,490	8,225	7	11.4
	Under 20	106	108	102	316	296	343	429	876	-	..
	20-24	1,004	912	839	3,716	4,298	4,673	3,545	4,665	2	..
	25-29	1,732	1,719	1,635	7,059	5,566	4,022	2,124	1,907	2	..
	30-44	2,690	2,458	2,326	8,270	4,620	2,617	1,306	755	3	..
	45 and over	436	437	361	1,230	610	200	86	22	-	..
2008	All ages	6,365	6,034	5,321	21,561	16,945	12,706	8,136	8,907	8	11.5
	Under 20	113	90	111	321	342	407	501	909	1	..
	20-24	987	922	839	4,134	4,924	5,257	3,993	5,265	2	..
	25-29	1,910	1,908	1,791	7,677	6,168	4,089	2,233	1,984	5	..
	30-44	2,860	2,697	2,208	8,147	4,911	2,701	1,317	729	-	..
	45 and over	495	417	372	1,282	600	252	92	20	-	..
2007	All ages	6,560	6,072	5,577	23,427	18,203	13,117	8,701	9,282	7	11.7
	Under 20	139	108	82	353	425	516	661	1,070	-	..
	20-24	1,045	1,077	957	4,993	5,878	5,654	4,230	5,494	2	..
	25-29	2,003	1,961	1,848	8,330	6,392	4,045	2,396	2,009	3	..
	30-44	2,892	2,522	2,298	8,441	4,939	2,695	1,332	673	2	..
	45 and over	481	404	392	1,310	569	207	82	36	-	..
2006	All ages	6,769	6,249	6,010	24,606	18,735	13,472	8,764	9,449	13	11.6
	Under 20	145	106	94	370	463	569	666	1,025	1	..
	20-24	1,130	1,099	1,083	5,866	6,495	5,991	4,431	5,752	3	..
	25-29	2,199	2,085	2,043	8,483	6,388	4,053	2,268	2,044	6	..
	30-44	2,783	2,571	2,384	8,503	4,814	2,615	1,317	598	3	..
	45 and over	512	388	406	1,384	575	244	82	30	-	..
2005	All ages	7,343	6,801	6,303	26,310	20,310	14,268	9,241	9,852	9	11.6
	Under 20	116	125	93	445	575	734	761	1,062	1	..
	20-24	1,303	1,317	1,269	6,815	7,425	6,596	4,831	5,921	1	..
	25-29	2,437	2,267	2,121	9,377	6,742	4,049	2,313	2,142	2	..
	30-44	2,951	2,651	2,456	8,448	4,979	2,672	1,274	703	5	..
	45 and over	536	441	364	1,225	589	217	62	24	-	..
2004	All ages	7,900	7,683	6,883	28,984	21,515	15,431	9,705	10,293	-	11.5
	Under 20	127	120	111	596	710	894	849	1,152	-	..
	20-24	1,543	1,585	1,522	8,361	8,403	7,232	5,081	6,262	-	..
	25-29	2,699	2,699	2,480	10,158	6,893	4,251	2,510	2,178	-	..
	30-44	3,016	2,851	2,364	8,605	4,924	2,838	1,200	672	-	..
	45 and over	515	428	406	1,264	585	216	65	29	-	..
2003	All ages	8,228	7,686	6,976	29,751	20,863	14,974	9,627	9,907	2	11.3
	Under 20	127	122	117	705	798	1,064	902	1,087	1	..
	20-24	1,751	1,760	1,781	9,169	8,627	7,216	5,204	6,251	1	..
	25-29	2,781	2,745	2,454	10,243	6,314	3,938	2,330	1,964	-	..
	30-44	3,015	2,616	2,224	8,378	4,617	2,573	1,119	577	-	..
	45 and over	554	443	400	1,256	507	183	72	28	-	..
2002	All ages	8,020	7,564	6,953	28,592	19,784	13,989	9,106	9,190	-	11.1
	Under 20	130	115	123	741	875	1,005	899	953	-	..
	20-24	1,927	1,896	1,929	9,648	8,300	6,801	4,968	5,832	-	..
	25-29	2,760	2,645	2,365	9,594	5,843	3,593	2,193	1,866	-	..
	30-44	2,741	2,509	2,193	7,511	4,281	2,395	983	526	-	..
	45 and over	462	399	343	1,098	485	195	63	13	-	..

Source: Office for National Statistics

15.14 Live births by local authority of usual residence of mother, numbers, sex, General Fertility Rates and Total Fertility Rates, 2012

England and Wales, regions (within England), unitary authorities/counties/districts & London boroughs [1]

Area of usual residence	Live births	Male	Female	GFR[2]	TFR[3]
ENGLAND, WALES AND ELSEWHERE	729,674	374,346	355,328	64.8	1.94
ENGLAND	694,241	356,251	337,990	64.9	1.94
WALES	35,238	17,992	17,246	61.2	1.88
NORTH EAST	30,291	15,568	14,723	60.6	1.83
County Durham UA	5,701	2,978	2,723	59.2	1.83
Darlington UA	1,359	681	678	68.6	2.10
Hartlepool UA	1,137	587	550	65.0	1.98
Middlesbrough UA	2,084	1,073	1,011	73.9	2.17
Northumberland UA	3,151	1,631	1,520	59.8	1.89
Redcar and Cleveland UA	1,600	824	776	65.9	2.03
Stockton-on-Tees UA	2,444	1,276	1,168	65.4	1.98
Tyne and Wear (Met County)	12,815	6,518	6,297	57.3	1.71
Gateshead	2,321	1,169	1,152	59.7	1.77
Newcastle upon Tyne	3,420	1,731	1,689	52.6	1.62
North Tyneside	2,315	1,192	1,123	60.1	1.82
South Tyneside	1,675	855	820	60.6	1.85
Sunderland	3,084	1,571	1,513	57.6	1.75
NORTH WEST	89,211	45,730	43,481	64.1	1.94
Blackburn with Darwen UA	2,300	1,177	1,123	75.9	2.26
Blackpool UA	1,770	911	859	68.2	2.09
Cheshire East UA	4,112	2,120	1,992	63.2	2.03
Cheshire West and Chester UA	3,700	1,956	1,744	60.4	1.89
Halton UA	1,661	866	795	68.0	2.06
Warrington UA	2,484	1,266	1,218	63.9	1.97
Cumbria	4,996	2,596	2,400	59.1	1.90
Allerdale	940	474	466	58.7	1.93
Barrow-in-Furness	762	383	379	62.2	1.99
Carlisle	1,222	634	588	60.3	1.85
Copeland	804	447	357	66.8	2.11
Eden	442	232	210	53.8	1.81
South Lakeland	826	426	400	52.6	1.75
Greater Manchester (Met County)	37,852	19,326	18,526	66.9	1.97
Bolton	3,975	1,993	1,982	72.1	2.19
Bury	2,514	1,321	1,193	69.7	2.14
Manchester	8,160	4,188	3,972	61.0	1.75
Oldham	3,288	1,655	1,633	73.7	2.22
Rochdale	3,020	1,586	1,434	70.5	2.13
Salford	3,608	1,797	1,811	69.5	1.97
Stockport	3,548	1,774	1,774	67.7	2.09
Tameside	3,098	1,578	1,520	71.2	2.15
Trafford	2,910	1,513	1,397	65.9	2.00
Wigan	3,731	1,921	1,810	60.5	1.87
Lancashire	13,681	6,997	6,684	61.8	1.93
Burnley	1,227	613	614	72.9	2.17
Chorley	1,229	619	610	61.5	1.93
Fylde	682	363	319	58.4	1.88
Hyndburn	1,121	575	546	72.1	2.20
Lancaster	1,584	808	776	54.5	1.78
Pendle	1,305	707	598	75.4	2.23
Preston	1,857	949	908	60.3	1.81
Ribble Valley	475	231	244	50.8	1.75
Rossendale	835	429	406	63.9	2.03
South Ribble	1,242	640	602	61.4	1.93
West Lancashire	1,168	592	576	57.6	1.92
Wyre	956	471	485	55.9	1.83
Merseyside (Met County)	16,655	8,515	8,140	60.7	1.83
Knowsley	1,971	1,032	939	67.0	2.03
Liverpool	5,942	3,028	2,914	55.6	1.65
Sefton	2,795	1,437	1,358	59.1	1.86
St. Helens	2,131	1,084	1,047	64.6	2.01
Wirral	3,816	1,934	1,882	66.0	2.05

15.14 Live births by local authority of usual residence of mother, numbers, sex, General Fertility Rates and Total Fertility Rates, 2012

England and Wales, regions (within England), unitary authorities/counties/districts & London boroughs [1]

Area of usual residence	Live births	Male	Female	GFR[2]	TFR[3]
YORKSHIRE AND THE HUMBER	**67,408**	**34,441**	**32,967**	**64.2**	**1.94**
East Riding of Yorkshire UA	**3,162**	**1,672**	**1,490**	**57.6**	**1.93**
Kingston upon Hull, City of UA	**3,871**	**2,001**	**1,870**	**70.2**	**1.99**
North East Lincolnshire UA	**1,990**	**1,018**	**972**	**66.5**	**2.01**
North Lincolnshire UA	**1,957**	**974**	**983**	**64.7**	**2.00**
York UA	**2,095**	**1,052**	**1,043**	**47.9**	**1.50**
North Yorkshire	**5,921**	**3,039**	**2,882**	**60.2**	**1.97**
Craven	458	237	221	53.7	1.84
Hambleton	890	468	422	64.3	2.16
Harrogate	1,606	828	778	60.0	1.94
Richmondshire	543	280	263	63.3	1.99
Ryedale	436	222	214	55.5	1.91
Scarborough	1,059	521	538	60.7	1.91
Selby	929	483	446	60.9	1.96
South Yorkshire (Met County)	**16,869**	**8,586**	**8,283**	**61.9**	**1.87**
Barnsley	2,961	1,486	1,475	67.1	2.07
Doncaster	3,752	1,907	1,845	66.0	2.00
Rotherham	3,264	1,660	1,604	67.4	2.08
Sheffield	6,892	3,533	3,359	56.0	1.73
West Yorkshire (Met County)	**31,543**	**16,099**	**15,444**	**67.9**	**2.02**
Bradford	8,322	4,139	4,183	77.3	2.27
Calderdale	2,753	1,409	1,344	70.8	2.21
Kirklees	5,725	2,875	2,850	67.8	2.06
Leeds	10,533	5,469	5,064	61.6	1.84
Wakefield	4,210	2,207	2,003	67.0	2.05
EAST MIDLANDS	**55,645**	**28,440**	**27,205**	**63.1**	**1.95**
Derby UA	**3,756**	**1,880**	**1,876**	**71.5**	**2.10**
Leicester UA	**5,273**	**2,732**	**2,541**	**66.8**	**1.92**
Nottingham UA	**4,408**	**2,248**	**2,160**	**57.3**	**1.76**
Rutland UA	**333**	**193**	**140**	**56.7**	**1.95**
Derbyshire	**8,361**	**4,323**	**4,038**	**60.2**	**1.93**
Amber Valley	1,296	666	630	58.9	1.89
Bolsover	940	456	484	65.6	2.09
Chesterfield	1,204	590	614	62.4	1.96
Derbyshire Dales	555	294	261	53.0	1.83
Erewash	1,348	719	629	62.6	1.96
High Peak	945	499	446	58.4	1.88
North East Derbyshire	949	504	445	57.0	1.86
South Derbyshire	1,124	595	529	61.2	1.93
Leicestershire	**7,147**	**3,655**	**3,492**	**58.8**	**1.87**
Blaby	1,078	578	500	62.3	1.98
Charnwood	1,854	961	893	54.1	1.73
Harborough	826	393	433	56.6	1.90
Hinckley and Bosworth	1,176	615	561	62.0	1.94
Melton	574	287	287	65.0	2.10
North West Leicestershire	1,023	514	509	59.9	1.92
Oadby and Wigston	616	307	309	58.1	1.92
Lincolnshire	**8,008**	**4,016**	**3,992**	**63.1**	**1.98**
Boston	913	454	459	77.1	2.28
East Lindsey	1,295	635	660	64.5	2.09
Lincoln	1,373	691	682	60.6	1.77
North Kesteven	1,114	562	552	60.1	1.98
South Holland	967	495	472	64.3	2.03
South Kesteven	1,409	714	695	59.1	1.91
West Lindsey	937	465	472	62.5	2.11
Northamptonshire	**9,288**	**4,709**	**4,579**	**68.6**	**2.11**
Corby	959	463	496	74.1	2.20
Daventry	836	448	388	62.8	2.13
East Northamptonshire	930	451	479	59.2	1.94
Kettering	1,271	624	647	69.8	2.18
Northampton	3,369	1,748	1,621	73.1	2.10
South Northamptonshire	880	457	423	59.0	1.96
Wellingborough	1,043	518	525	73.3	2.30

15.14 Live births by local authority of usual residence of mother, numbers, sex, General Fertility Rates and Total Fertility Rates, 2012

England and Wales, regions (within England), unitary authorities/counties/districts & London boroughs [1]

Area of usual residence	Live births	Male	Female	GFR[2]	TFR[3]
Nottinghamshire	**9,071**	**4,684**	**4,387**	62.9	1.98
Ashfield	1,557	795	762	67.7	2.11
Bassetlaw	1,237	641	596	62.8	2.04
Broxtowe	1,268	643	625	61.5	1.88
Gedling	1,256	646	610	60.1	1.88
Mansfield	1,345	674	671	67.5	2.04
Newark and Sherwood	1,312	708	604	65.1	2.11
Rushcliffe	1,096	577	519	55.3	1.74
WEST MIDLANDS	**73,940**	**38,090**	**35,850**	67.2	2.04
Herefordshire, County of UA	**1,906**	**964**	**942**	62.4	1.98
Shropshire UA	**2,912**	**1,483**	**1,429**	57.4	1.85
Stoke-on-Trent UA	**3,767**	**1,944**	**1,823**	74.6	2.18
Telford and Wrekin UA	**2,226**	**1,143**	**1,083**	67.8	2.10
Staffordshire	**9,060**	**4,662**	**4,398**	59.2	1.88
Cannock Chase	1,174	612	562	61.2	1.90
East Staffordshire	1,515	771	744	71.7	2.22
Lichfield	979	493	486	57.1	1.85
Newcastle-under-Lyme	1,262	648	614	53.5	1.68
South Staffordshire	933	486	447	52.4	1.76
Stafford	1,316	695	621	57.9	1.84
Staffordshire Moorlands	889	468	421	55.3	1.85
Tamworth	992	489	503	64.1	1.96
Warwickshire	**6,305**	**3,253**	**3,052**	62.1	1.91
North Warwickshire	688	363	325	62.6	2.01
Nuneaton and Bedworth	1,598	834	764	66.0	2.00
Rugby	1,261	653	608	66.6	2.04
Stratford-on-Avon	1,139	565	574	58.6	1.92
Warwick	1,619	838	781	58.0	1.76
West Midlands (Met County)	**41,237**	**21,310**	**19,927**	71.1	2.10
Birmingham	17,766	9,157	8,609	72.6	2.12
Coventry	4,731	2,446	2,285	66.4	1.97
Dudley	3,966	2,052	1,914	67.7	2.10
Sandwell	5,151	2,619	2,532	79.6	2.34
Solihull	2,268	1,172	1,096	61.0	1.96
Walsall	3,816	2,023	1,793	72.6	2.18
Wolverhampton	3,539	1,841	1,698	69.4	2.06
Worcestershire	**6,527**	**3,331**	**3,196**	64.3	2.03
Bromsgrove	929	507	422	58.4	1.94
Malvern Hills	657	318	339	57.6	1.98
Redditch	1,226	607	619	72.7	2.16
Worcester	1,425	751	674	66.5	1.99
Wychavon	1,179	600	579	61.5	2.04
Wyre Forest	1,111	548	563	66.1	2.10
EAST	**74,571**	**38,026**	**36,545**	66.5	2.02
Bedford UA	**2,116**	**1,088**	**1,028**	66.9	2.02
Central Bedfordshire UA	**3,295**	**1,699**	**1,596**	66.9	2.04
Luton UA	**3,578**	**1,829**	**1,749**	78.6	2.22
Peterborough UA	**3,270**	**1,693**	**1,577**	83.4	2.43
Southend-on-Sea UA	**2,345**	**1,205**	**1,140**	69.2	2.09
Thurrock UA	**2,476**	**1,284**	**1,192**	72.8	2.16
Cambridgeshire	**7,740**	**3,915**	**3,825**	62.2	1.87
Cambridge	1,511	797	714	47.1	1.48
East Cambridgeshire	1,105	577	528	69.1	2.09
Fenland	1,207	580	627	71.3	2.23
Huntingdonshire	2,143	1,071	1,072	67.3	2.10
South Cambridgeshire	1,774	890	884	64.1	1.96
Essex	**16,860**	**8,595**	**8,265**	64.9	2.02
Basildon	2,493	1,256	1,237	71.4	2.16
Braintree	1,788	916	872	64.6	2.02
Brentwood	808	459	349	60.5	1.86
Castle Point	849	420	429	57.6	1.90
Chelmsford	1,995	1,011	984	60.9	1.84
Colchester	2,353	1,204	1,149	64.7	1.94

517

15.14 Live births by local authority of usual residence of mother, numbers, sex, General Fertility Rates and Total Fertility Rates, 2012

England and Wales, regions (within England), unitary authorities/counties/districts & London boroughs [1]

Area of usual residence	Live births	Male	Female	GFR[2]	TFR[3]
Epping Forest	1,622	838	784	68.7	2.10
Harlow	1,363	720	643	80.1	2.35
Maldon	559	268	291	56.3	1.92
Rochford	767	383	384	53.2	1.81
Tendring	1,365	673	692	66.1	2.18
Uttlesford	898	447	451	63.0	2.08
Hertfordshire	**14,913**	**7,552**	**7,361**	**66.3**	**1.98**
Broxbourne	1,231	630	601	65.4	1.99
Dacorum	1,940	977	963	68.4	2.06
East Hertfordshire	1,589	804	785	59.9	1.85
Hertsmere	1,297	673	624	65.3	1.97
North Hertfordshire	1,663	871	792	68.2	2.06
St Albans	1,932	939	993	70.6	2.00
Stevenage	1,261	645	616	71.8	2.14
Three Rivers	1,078	568	510	64.0	1.95
Watford	1,544	740	804	74.1	2.05
Welwyn Hatfield	1,378	705	673	56.7	1.77
Norfolk	**9,662**	**4,917**	**4,745**	**63.6**	**1.97**
Breckland	1,451	727	724	65.5	2.06
Broadland	1,194	596	598	58.7	1.96
Great Yarmouth	1,143	595	548	67.6	2.09
King's Lynn and West Norfolk	1,713	891	822	69.5	2.18
North Norfolk	828	430	398	58.7	1.92
Norwich	2,008	1,019	989	61.6	1.76
South Norfolk	1,325	659	666	62.9	2.06
Suffolk	**8,316**	**4,249**	**4,067**	**65.3**	**2.03**
Babergh	790	406	384	56.6	1.93
Forest Heath	1,031	550	481	83.9	2.31
Ipswich	2,039	1,028	1,011	72.0	2.08
Mid Suffolk	942	476	466	59.7	1.97
St Edmundsbury	1,201	618	583	61.4	1.91
Suffolk Coastal	1,039	540	499	55.7	1.90
Waveney	1,274	631	643	67.7	2.14
LONDON	**134,186**	**68,811**	**65,375**	**67.0**	**1.84**
Inner London	**53,957**	**27,582**	**26,375**	**60.8**	**1.65**
Camden	2,944	1,519	1,425	48.2	1.35
Hackney and City of London	4,585	2,365	2,220	63.7	1.76
Hammersmith and Fulham	2,646	1,350	1,296	52.5	1.42
Haringey	4,209	2,134	2,075	64.7	1.79
Islington	2,988	1,546	1,442	49.5	1.39
Kensington and Chelsea	2,024	1,052	972	53.9	1.40
Lambeth	4,825	2,442	2,383	56.0	1.56
Lewisham	5,095	2,598	2,497	72.1	2.00
Newham	6,426	3,273	3,153	82.3	2.21
Southwark	5,030	2,557	2,473	62.7	1.72
Tower Hamlets	4,784	2,420	2,364	62.1	1.62
Wandsworth	5,451	2,807	2,644	59.8	1.59
Westminster	2,950	1,519	1,431	51.6	1.37
Outer London	**80,229**	**41,229**	**39,000**	**71.8**	**2.03**
Barking and Dagenham	3,957	2,080	1,877	90.0	2.58
Barnet	5,585	2,887	2,698	68.3	1.90
Bexley	3,076	1,564	1,512	64.9	1.99
Brent	5,340	2,710	2,630	72.1	1.97
Bromley	4,140	2,123	2,017	66.5	1.98
Croydon	5,884	2,955	2,929	73.0	2.12
Ealing	5,847	2,991	2,856	73.7	2.00
Enfield	5,094	2,588	2,506	71.9	2.07
Greenwich	4,624	2,388	2,236	74.6	2.08
Harrow	3,585	1,857	1,728	69.6	1.95
Havering	2,888	1,506	1,382	61.9	1.88
Hillingdon	4,536	2,395	2,141	72.5	2.08
Hounslow	4,621	2,325	2,296	76.2	2.07
Kingston upon Thames	2,328	1,182	1,146	60.6	1.74
Merton	3,476	1,783	1,693	72.6	1.94
Redbridge	4,792	2,445	2,347	75.5	2.11
Richmond upon Thames	2,916	1,500	1,416	72.1	1.88
Sutton	2,708	1,429	1,279	66.0	1.93
Waltham Forest	4,832	2,521	2,311	77.5	2.15

15.14 Live births by local authority of usual residence of mother, numbers, sex, General Fertility Rates and Total Fertility Rates, 2012

England and Wales, regions (within England), unitary authorities/counties/districts & London boroughs [1]

Area of usual residence	Live births	Male	Female	GFR[2]	TFR[3]
SOUTH EAST	107,858	55,622	52,236	64.5	1.97
Bracknell Forest UA	1,554	799	755	65.1	1.93
Brighton and Hove UA	3,166	1,630	1,536	47.8	1.45
Isle of Wight UA	1,329	667	662	61.0	2.00
Medway UA	3,693	1,897	1,796	67.2	2.03
Milton Keynes UA	3,887	2,019	1,868	72.5	2.12
Portsmouth UA	2,782	1,381	1,401	59.8	1.78
Reading UA	2,748	1,428	1,320	72.1	1.98
Slough UA	2,704	1,353	1,351	81.2	2.23
Southampton UA	3,420	1,743	1,677	60.2	1.74
West Berkshire UA	1,896	1,003	893	66.0	2.11
Windsor and Maidenhead UA	1,860	984	876	66.9	1.98
Wokingham UA	1,963	1,012	951	66.7	2.05
Buckinghamshire	6,197	3,179	3,018	65.5	2.04
Aylesbury Vale	2,299	1,165	1,134	68.4	2.12
Chiltern	918	474	444	60.9	1.97
South Bucks	753	395	358	64.6	2.01
Wycombe	2,227	1,145	1,082	65.0	1.99
East Sussex	5,451	2,823	2,628	62.6	2.01
Eastbourne	1,193	609	584	66.2	2.00
Hastings	1,208	632	576	70.5	2.14
Lewes	987	525	462	62.1	2.02
Rother	751	378	373	60.1	2.05
Wealden	1,312	679	633	55.8	1.88
Hampshire	15,400	7,934	7,466	64.1	2.02
Basingstoke and Deane	2,401	1,255	1,146	71.0	2.14
East Hampshire	1,214	655	559	62.3	2.08
Eastleigh	1,581	789	792	65.2	1.98
Fareham	1,121	554	567	58.3	1.92
Gosport	1,037	565	472	66.1	2.03
Hart	1,051	529	522	64.2	1.99
Havant	1,374	726	648	65.8	2.10
New Forest	1,709	918	791	62.5	2.04
Rushmoor	1,379	700	679	66.2	1.94
Test Valley	1,314	628	686	64.4	2.11
Winchester	1,219	615	604	55.5	1.80
Kent	18,147	9,410	8,737	65.7	2.05
Ashford	1,597	796	801	70.6	2.23
Canterbury	1,419	737	682	43.9	1.56
Dartford	1,560	810	750	74.9	2.21
Dover	1,257	650	607	66.7	2.12
Gravesham	1,472	771	701	72.4	2.20
Maidstone	2,040	1,068	972	68.7	2.10
Sevenoaks	1,383	711	672	68.2	2.17
Shepway	1,230	641	589	66.8	2.11
Swale	1,777	932	845	69.7	2.17
Thanet	1,654	858	796	69.7	2.15
Tonbridge and Malling	1,432	750	682	63.8	2.07
Tunbridge Wells	1,326	686	640	62.4	1.96
Oxfordshire	8,217	4,239	3,978	61.7	1.84
Cherwell	1,891	968	923	68.4	2.07
Oxford	2,006	1,060	946	49.1	1.54
South Oxfordshire	1,543	782	761	65.0	2.01
Vale of White Horse	1,465	746	719	67.3	2.06
West Oxfordshire	1,312	683	629	69.0	2.13
Surrey	14,237	7,319	6,918	65.7	1.99
Elmbridge	1,826	913	913	75.4	2.22
Epsom and Ewell	952	474	478	64.6	1.97
Guildford	1,677	877	800	57.3	1.76
Mole Valley	868	456	412	61.4	1.95
Reigate and Banstead	1,872	956	916	69.7	2.05
Runnymede	996	489	507	56.4	1.82
Spelthorne	1,224	633	591	65.6	1.95
Surrey Heath	940	494	446	60.2	1.90
Tandridge	966	487	479	64.9	2.07
Waverley	1,385	762	623	66.4	2.10

15.14 Live births by local authority of usual residence of mother, numbers, sex, General Fertility Rates and Total Fertility Rates, 2012

England and Wales, regions (within England), unitary authorities/counties/districts & London boroughs [1]

Area of usual residence	Live births	Male	Female	GFR[2]	TFR[3]
Woking	1,531	778	753	77.4	2.19
West Sussex	**9,207**	**4,802**	**4,405**	**64.1**	**1.98**
Adur	775	389	386	71.8	2.26
Arun	1,619	825	794	67.0	2.13
Chichester	1,136	614	522	62.3	2.00
Crawley	1,648	886	762	69.4	1.97
Horsham	1,290	693	597	58.1	1.86
Mid Sussex	1,545	787	758	61.3	1.89
Worthing	1,194	608	586	61.8	1.87
SOUTH WEST	**61,131**	**31,523**	**29,608**	**63.1**	**1.96**
Bath and North East Somerset UA	**1,867**	**939**	**928**	**52.2**	**1.77**
Bournemouth UA	**2,348**	**1,186**	**1,162**	**58.4**	**1.68**
Bristol, City of UA	**6,781**	**3,491**	**3,290**	**66.6**	**1.91**
Cornwall UA and Isles of Scilly UA	**5,721**	**2,950**	**2,771**	**62.7**	**2.01**
North Somerset UA	**2,363**	**1,220**	**1,143**	**68.3**	**2.16**
Plymouth UA	**3,418**	**1,746**	**1,672**	**63.7**	**1.90**
Poole UA	**1,670**	**860**	**810**	**62.9**	**1.93**
South Gloucestershire UA	**3,204**	**1,621**	**1,583**	**63.1**	**1.97**
Swindon UA	**3,073**	**1,612**	**1,461**	**70.7**	**2.10**
Torbay UA	**1,462**	**731**	**731**	**68.2**	**2.15**
Wiltshire UA	**5,378**	**2,849**	**2,529**	**64.1**	**2.08**
Devon	**7,585**	**3,994**	**3,591**	**60.8**	**1.95**
East Devon	1,169	624	545	60.8	2.06
Exeter	1,446	770	676	52.0	1.61
Mid Devon	896	458	438	68.8	2.24
North Devon	1,005	531	474	66.2	2.12
South Hams	685	361	324	56.9	1.91
Teignbridge	1,208	629	579	62.2	2.05
Torridge	669	373	296	67.0	2.21
West Devon	507	248	259	62.8	2.05
Dorset	**3,674**	**1,929**	**1,745**	**59.7**	**1.99**
Christchurch	418	221	197	60.4	2.00
East Dorset	649	321	328	53.4	1.84
North Dorset	697	356	341	63.6	2.11
Purbeck	401	227	174	59.4	1.95
West Dorset	827	435	392	58.4	2.01
Weymouth and Portland	682	369	313	64.3	2.03
Gloucestershire	**6,880**	**3,532**	**3,348**	**63.2**	**1.98**
Cheltenham	1,365	707	658	55.9	1.65
Cotswold	725	359	366	55.3	1.86
Forest of Dean	803	411	392	59.8	2.06
Gloucester	1,903	965	938	75.8	2.24
Stroud	1,138	597	541	61.1	2.06
Tewkesbury	946	493	453	66.9	2.09
Somerset	**5,707**	**2,863**	**2,844**	**63.5**	**2.05**
Mendip	1,174	561	613	62.7	2.10
Sedgemoor	1,272	618	654	65.0	2.10
South Somerset	1,712	881	831	63.6	2.05
Taunton Deane	1,260	648	612	63.6	1.99
West Somerset	289	155	134	60.5	1.91
WALES	**35,238**	**17,992**	**17,246**	**61.2**	**1.88**
Isle of Anglesey	835	415	420	73.3	2.29
Gwynedd	1,327	688	639	60.0	1.94
Conwy	1,178	622	556	64.9	2.10
Denbighshire	1,047	542	505	65.9	2.14
Flintshire	1,689	885	804	60.9	1.93
Wrexham	1,750	890	860	68.8	2.09
Powys	1,190	634	556	58.5	1.95
Ceredigion	676	346	330	47.5	1.81
Pembrokeshire	1,307	636	671	65.2	2.08
Carmarthenshire	1,995	1,033	962	63.2	1.97
Swansea	2,730	1,436	1,294	58.3	1.79
Neath Port Talbot	1,520	803	717	59.6	1.83
Bridgend	1,624	807	817	63.3	1.98
The Vale of Glamorgan	1,370	698	672	60.5	1.94

15.14 Live births by local authority of usual residence of mother, numbers, sex, General Fertility Rates and Total Fertility Rates, 2012

England and Wales, regions (within England), unitary authorities/counties/districts & London boroughs [1]

Area of usual residence	Live births	Male	Female	GFR[2]	TFR[3]
Cardiff	4,709	2,386	2,323	57.4	1.71
Rhondda, Cynon, Taff	2,788	1,391	1,397	60.6	1.83
Merthyr Tydfil	767	389	378	66.2	1.96
Caerphilly	2,114	1,061	1,053	60.8	1.86
Blaenau Gwent	781	379	402	57.9	1.75
Torfaen	1,126	576	550	65.7	2.02
Monmouthshire	821	423	398	56.4	1.92
Newport	1,894	952	942	65.2	1.96
Usual residence outside England and Wales	**195**	**103**	**92**	:	:

Notes: A birth to a mother whose usual residence is outside England and Wales is assigned to the country of residence. These births are included in total figures for England and Wales, but excluded from any sub-division of England and Wales.

To preserve confidentiality, counts for City of London and Isles of Scilly have been combined with those for Hackney LB and Cornwall UA respectively.

1 Rates for 2012 have been calculated using mid-2012 population estimates based on the 2011 Census.
2 The General Fertility Rate (GFR) is the number of live births per 1,000 women aged 15–44. The GFRs have been calculated using mid-2012 population estimates.
3 The Total Fertility Rate (TFR) is the average number of live children that a group of women would bear if they experienced the age-specific fertility rates of the calendar year in question throughout their childbearing lifespan.
   The national TFRs have been calculated using mid-2012 population estimates by single year of age.
   The sub-national TFRs have been calculated using mid-2012 population estimates by five year age group.

Source: Office for National Statistics (ONS)

15.15 Live births by age of mother and registration type[1], 1971-2011

England and Wales

Year	Type of Registration	Age of mother at birth							
		All ages	Under 20	20-24	25-29	30-34	35-39	40-44	45 and over
		Numbers of births							
2011	All	723,913	36,435	134,946	200,587	207,151	115,444	27,518	1,832
	Within Marriage/Civil Partnership[1]	382,574	1,410	31,785	107,383	143,519	79,951	17,388	1,138
	Outside Marriage/Civil Partnership[1]	341,339	35,025	103,161	93,204	63,632	35,493	10,130	694
	Joint Registrations same address	226,057	14,600	63,287	66,102	47,706	26,688	7,213	461
	Joint Registrations different address	73,464	12,960	26,826	17,379	9,489	5,093	1,603	114
	Sole Registrations	41,818	7,465	13,048	9,723	6,437	3,712	1,314	119
2010	All	723,165	40,591	137,312	199,233	202,457	115,841	25,973	1,758
	Within Marriage/Civil Partnership[1]	384,375	1,684	33,955	108,465	141,873	80,846	16,404	1,148
	Outside Marriage/Civil Partnership[1]	338,790	38,907	103,357	90,768	60,584	34,995	9,569	610
	Joint Registrations same address	224,001	16,401	63,816	64,656	45,498	26,453	6,769	408
	Joint Registrations different address	72,297	14,352	26,184	16,393	8,838	4,903	1,525	102
	Sole Registrations	42,492	8,154	13,357	9,719	6,248	3,639	1,275	100
2009	All	706,248	43,243	136,012	194,129	191,600	114,288	25,357	1,619
	Within Marriage/Civil Partnership[1]	380,069	2,334	35,920	108,499	135,802	80,156	16,318	1,040
	Outside Marriage/Civil Partnership[1]	326,179	40,909	100,092	85,630	55,798	34,132	9,039	579
	Joint Registrations same address	214,189	17,200	61,813	60,876	41,831	25,637	6,444	388
	Joint Registrations different address	68,251	14,778	24,376	14,811	7,991	4,790	1,420	85
	Sole Registrations	43,739	8,931	13,903	9,943	5,976	3,705	1,175	106
2008	All	708,711	44,691	135,971	192,960	192,450	116,220	24,991	1,428
	Within Marriage	387,930	2,739	38,239	110,353	138,066	81,602	15,991	940
	Outside Marriage	320,781	41,952	97,732	82,607	54,384	34,618	9,000	488
	Joint Registrations same address	210,076	17,231	59,913	59,104	41,178	26,036	6,289	325
	Joint Registrations different address	65,241	15,161	23,102	13,543	7,257	4,662	1,441	75
	Sole Registrations	45,464	9,560	14,717	9,960	5,949	3,920	1,270	88
2007	All	690,013	44,805	130,784	182,570	191,124	115,380	24,041	1,309
	Within Marriage	384,463	3,087	38,859	106,603	138,157	81,399	15,484	874
	Outside Marriage	305,550	41,718	91,925	75,967	52,967	33,981	8,557	435
	Joint Registrations same address	198,470	17,036	55,904	54,040	39,783	25,383	6,050	274
	Joint Registrations different address	61,379	14,714	21,415	12,204	7,024	4,587	1,359	76
	Sole Registrations	45,701	9,968	14,606	9,723	6,160	4,011	1,148	85
2006	All	669,601	45,509	127,828	172,642	189,407	110,509	22,512	1,194
	Within Marriage	378,225	3,199	40,126	103,348	137,996	78,269	14,511	776
	Outside Marriage	291,376	42,310	87,702	69,294	51,411	32,240	8,001	418
	Joint Registrations same address	185,461	17,061	52,162	48,474	38,133	23,897	5,469	265
	Joint Registrations different address	60,460	14,870	20,755	11,651	7,159	4,578	1,375	72
	Sole Registrations	45,455	10,379	14,785	9,169	6,119	3,765	1,157	81
2005	All	645,835	44,830	122,145	164,348	188,153	104,113	21,155	1,091
	Within Marriage	369,330	3,654	40,010	99,957	137,401	73,810	13,760	738
	Outside Marriage	276,505	41,176	82,135	64,391	50,752	30,303	7,395	353
	Joint Registrations same address	175,555	16,316	48,755	45,165	37,764	22,265	5,057	233
	Joint Registrations different address	55,780	14,108	18,909	10,320	6,801	4,289	1,287	66
	Sole Registrations	45,170	10,752	14,471	8,906	6,187	3,749	1,051	54
2004	All	639,721	45,094	121,072	159,984	190,550	102,228	19,884	909
	Within Marriage	369,997	4,063	41,285	98,539	139,838	72,555	13,098	619
	Outside Marriage	269,724	41,031	79,787	61,445	50,712	29,673	6,786	290
	Joint Registrations same address	171,498	16,262	47,793	43,038	37,820	21,758	4,648	179
	Joint Registrations different address	52,854	13,608	17,628	9,620	6,713	4,133	1,096	56
	Sole Registrations	45,372	11,161	14,366	8,787	6,179	3,782	1,042	55
2003	All	621,469	44,236	116,622	156,931	187,214	97,386	18,205	875
	Within Marriage	364,244	4,338	40,887	98,694	138,002	69,595	12,113	615
	Outside Marriage	257,225	39,898	75,735	58,237	49,212	27,791	6,092	260
	Joint Registrations same address	163,374	16,000	45,225	40,867	36,630	20,335	4,151	166
	Joint Registrations different address	48,976	12,706	16,076	8,815	6,488	3,831	1,014	46
	Sole Registrations	44,875	11,192	14,434	8,555	6,094	3,625	927	48

15.15 Live births by age of mother and registration type[1], 1971-2011

England and Wales

Year	Type of Registration	All ages	Under 20	20-24	25-29	30-34	35-39	40-44	45 and over
					Age of mother at birth				
2002	All	596,122	43,467	110,959	153,379	180,532	90,449	16,441	895
	Within Marriage	354,090	4,582	40,712	97,583	134,093	65,369	11,110	641
	Outside Marriage	242,032	38,885	70,247	55,796	46,439	25,080	5,331	254
	Joint Registrations same address	154,086	15,824	42,315	39,554	34,326	18,236	3,656	175
	Joint Registrations different address	44,817	11,832	14,333	8,109	6,164	3,471	866	42
	Sole Registrations	43,129	11,229	13,599	8,133	5,949	3,373	809	37
2001	All	594,634	44,189	108,844	159,926	178,920	86,495	15,499	761
	Within Marriage	356,548	4,640	40,736	103,131	133,710	63,202	10,582	547
	Outside Marriage	238,086	39,549	68,108	56,795	45,210	23,293	4,917	214
	Joint Registrations same address	150,421	16,215	40,843	39,797	33,306	16,790	3,341	129
	Joint Registrations different address	43,921	11,665	13,682	8,416	6,029	3,290	800	39
	Sole Registrations	43,744	11,669	13,583	8,582	5,875	3,213	776	46
2000	All	604,441	45,846	107,741	170,701	180,113	84,974	14,403	663
	Within Marriage	365,836	4,742	40,262	111,606	136,165	62,671	9,910	480
	Outside Marriage	238,605	41,104	67,479	59,095	43,948	22,303	4,493	183
	Joint Registrations same address	149,510	17,011	40,450	41,236	31,795	15,836	3,055	127
	Joint Registrations different address	43,322	11,634	13,110	8,646	6,037	3,158	706	31
	Sole Registrations	45,773	12,459	13,919	9,213	6,116	3,309	732	25
1999	All	621,872	48,375	110,722	181,931	185,311	81,281	13,617	635
	Within Marriage	379,983	5,333	43,190	120,716	140,330	60,470	9,466	478
	Outside Marriage	241,889	43,042	67,532	61,215	44,981	20,811	4,151	157
	Joint Registrations same address	149,584	17,833	40,190	42,126	32,152	14,455	2,725	103
	Joint Registrations different address	44,102	12,015	12,865	9,153	6,214	3,135	695	25
	Sole Registrations	48,203	13,194	14,477	9,936	6,615	3,221	731	29
1998	All	635,901	48,285	113,537	193,144	188,499	78,881	12,980	575
	Within Marriage	395,290	5,278	45,724	130,747	144,599	59,320	9,189	433
	Outside Marriage	240,611	43,007	67,813	62,397	43,900	19,561	3,791	142
	Joint Registrations same address	146,521	17,589	39,818	42,212	30,938	16,410	3,118	114
	Joint Registrations different address	44,130	11,588	13,157	9,513	6,194			
	Sole Registrations	49,960	13,830	14,838	10,672	6,768	3,151	673	28
1997	All	643,095	46,372	118,589	202,792	187,528	74,900	12,332	582
	Within Marriage	404,873	5,233	49,068	139,383	145,293	56,671	8,797	428
	Outside Marriage	238,222	41,139	69,521	63,409	42,235	18,229	3,535	154
	Joint Registrations same address	141,740	16,551	39,784	42,020	28,715	15,179	2,860	122
	Joint Registrations different address	45,900	11,365	14,147	10,374	6,523			
	Sole Registrations	50,582	13,223	15,590	11,015	6,997	3,050	675	32
1996	All	649,485	44,667	125,732	211,103	186,377	69,503	11,516	587
	Within Marriage	416,822	5,365	54,651	148,770	145,898	53,265	8,421	452
	Outside Marriage	232,663	39,302	71,081	62,333	40,479	16,238	3,095	135
	Joint Registrations same address	135,282	15,410	39,978	40,384	26,875	13,347	2,517	107
	Joint Registrations different address	46,365	10,946	14,858	10,599	6,626			
	Sole Registrations	51,016	12,946	16,245	11,350	6,978	2,891	578	28
1995	All	648,138	41,938	130,744	217,418	181,202	65,517	10,779	540
	Within Marriage	428,189	5,623	61,029	157,855	144,200	51,129	7,944	409
	Outside Marriage	219,949	36,315	69,715	59,563	37,002	14,388	2,835	131
	Joint Registrations same address	127,789	14,424	39,274	38,376	24,376	11,859	2,335	99
	Joint Registrations different address	44,244	10,011	14,815	10,323	6,141			
	Sole Registrations	47,916	11,880	15,626	10,864	6,485	2,529	500	32
1994	All	664,726	42,026	140,240	229,102	179,568	63,061	10,241	488
	Within Marriage	449,190	6,099	69,227	170,605	145,563	49,668	7,662	366
	Outside Marriage	215,536	35,927	71,013	58,497	34,005	13,393	2,579	122
	Joint Registrations same address	123,874	14,168	39,827	37,168	22,288	10,892	2,084	97
	Joint Registrations different address	42,632	9,752	14,778	9,939	5,513			
	Sole Registrations	49,030	12,007	16,408	11,390	6,204	2,501	495	25

15.15 Live births by age of mother and registration type[1], 1971-2011

England and Wales

Year	Type of Registration	All ages	Under 20	20-24	25-29	30-34	35-39	40-44	45 and over
1993	All	673,467	45,121	151,975	235,961	171,061	58,824	9,986	539
	Within Marriage	456,919	6,875	76,950	178,456	139,671	46,919	7,621	427
	Outside Marriage	216,548	38,246	75,025	57,505	31,390	11,905	2,365	112
	Joint Registrations same address	118,758	14,134	40,168	35,307	20,084	9,569	1,882	85
	Joint Registrations different address	47,548	11,577	17,381	10,780	5,339			
	Sole Registrations	50,242	12,535	17,476	11,418	5,967	2,336	483	27
1992	All	689,656	47,861	163,311	244,798	166,839	56,650	9,696	501
	Within Marriage	474,431	7,787	86,220	188,928	137,904	45,733	7,456	403
	Outside Marriage	215,225	40,074	77,091	55,870	28,935	10,917	2,240	98
	Joint Registrations same address	119,239	15,236	42,063	34,756	18,673	8,784	1,811	78
	Joint Registrations different address	44,514	11,381	16,658	9,693	4,620			
	Sole Registrations	51,472	13,457	18,370	11,421	5,642	2,133	429	20
1991	All	699,217	52,396	173,356	248,727	161,259	53,644	9,316	519
	Within Marriage	487,923	8,948	95,605	196,281	135,542	43,810	7,294	443
	Outside Marriage	211,294	43,448	77,751	52,446	25,717	9,834	2,022	76
	Joint Registrations same address	115,298	16,351	42,245	32,532	16,468	7,861	1,594	60
	Joint Registrations different address	41,865	11,848	15,835	8,518	3,851			
	Sole Registrations	54,131	15,249	19,671	11,396	5,398	1,973	428	16
1990	All	706,140	55,541	180,136	252,577	156,264	51,905	9,220	497
	Within Marriage	506,141	10,958	106,188	204,701	133,384	43,179	7,302	429
	Outside Marriage	199,999	44,583	73,948	47,876	22,880	8,726	1,918	68
	Joint Registrations same address	106,001	16,311	39,062	29,181	14,585	6,793	1,505	55
	Joint Registrations different address	39,167	12,081	14,751	7,555	3,289			
	Sole Registrations	54,831	16,191	20,135	11,140	5,006	1,933	413	13
1989	All	687,725	55,543	185,239	242,822	145,320	49,465	8,845	491
	Within Marriage	501,921	12,027	114,456	200,961	125,439	41,528	7,079	431
	Outside Marriage	185,804	43,516	70,783	41,861	19,881	7,937	1,766	60
	Joint Registrations same address	95,858	15,686	36,582	24,859	12,543	6,156	1,341	49
	Joint Registrations different address	36,409	11,688	14,022	6,603	2,738			
	Sole Registrations	53,537	16,142	20,179	10,399	4,600	1,781	425	11
1988	All	693,577	58,741	193,726	243,460	140,974	47,649	8,520	507
	Within Marriage	516,225	14,099	125,575	205,292	123,384	40,400	7,025	450
	Outside Marriage	177,352	44,642	68,151	38,168	17,590	7,249	1,495	57
	Joint Registrations same address	87,601	15,304	33,994	22,070	10,765	5,607	1,159	44
	Joint Registrations different address	35,807	12,240	13,807	5,913	2,505			
	Sole Registrations	53,944	17,098	20,350	10,185	4,320	1,642	336	13
1981[2]	All	634,492	56,570	194,500	215,760	126,590	34,210	6,170	690
	Within Marriage	553,509	30,140	165,690	201,460	118,720	31,480	5,340	680
	Outside Marriage	80,983	26,430	28,810	14,300	7,870	2,730	840	20
	Joint Registrations	47,140	12,750	16,820	9,520	5,530	1,940	550	20
	Sole Registrations	33,850	13,670	12,000	4,770	2,340	780	290	-
1971	All	783,155	82,641	285,703	247,239	109,616	45,224	11,915	817
	Within Marriage	717,477	61,086	263,660	235,701	103,366	42,073	10,848	743
	Outside Marriage	65,678	21,555	22,043	11,538	6,250	3,151	1,067	74

1. The Human Fertilisation and Embryology Act 2008 contained provisions enabling two females in a same-sex couple to register a birth from 1 September 2009 onwards. Due to the small numbers, births registered to a same-sex couple in a civil partnership (556 in 2012) are included with marital births while births registered to a same-sex couple outside a civil partnership (252 in 2012) are included with births outside marriage.
2. 1981 births for age-groups are based on a 10 per cent sample.

Source: Office for National Statistics

15.16 Legal abortions: by country of procedure (i) age, (ii) gestation weeks, (iii) procedure, (iv) parity, (v) previous abortions, (vi) grounds and (vii) principal medical condition for abortions performed under ground E, 2012

Country of abortion					numbers and percentages	
	England & Wales		Scotland p		Great Britain p	
All legal abortions	**190,972**	*100%*	**12,447**	*100%*	**203,419**	*100%*
(i) Age						
Under 16	2,996	*2*	249	*2*	3,245	*2*
16-17	10,128	*5*	788	*6*	10,916	*5*
18-19	18,873	*10*	1,460	*12*	20,333	*10*
20-24	56,077	*29*	3,809	*31*	59,886	*29*
25-29	43,269	*23*	2,730	*22*	45,999	*23*
30-34	31,482	*16*	1,786	*14*	33,268	*16*
35+	28,147	*15*	1,625	*13*	29,772	*15*
(ii) Gestation weeks						
3 - 9	147,211	*77*	9,762	*78*	156,973	*77*
10 - 12	25,986	*14*	1,752	*14*	27,738	*14*
13 - 19	14,577	*8*	867	*7*	15,444	*8*
20 and over	3,198	*2*	66	*1*	3,264	*2*
(iii) Procedure						
Surgical	100,796	*53*	1,780	*14*	102,576	*50*
Medical	90,176	*47*	10,667	*86*	100,843	*50*
(iv) Parity (number of previous pregnancies resulting in live or stillbirth)						
0	91,504	*48*	6,238	*50*	97,742	*48*
1+	99,468	*52*	6,209	*50*	105,677	*52*
(v) Number of previous pregnancies resulting in abortion under the Act						
0	121,896	*64*	8,627	*69*	130,523	*64*
1+	69,076	*36*	3,820	*31*	72,896	*36*
(vi) Grounds						
A (alone or with B, C or D) or F or G	62	*0*	*	.	*	.
B (alone or with C or D)	130	*0*	*	.	*	.
C (alone)	185,758	*97*	11,761	*94*	197,519	*97*
D (alone or with C)	2,193	*1*	519	*4*	2,712	*1*
E (alone one with A, B, C or D)	2,829	*1*	159	*1*	2,988	*1*
(vii) Principal medical condition for abortions performed under ground E						
Total Ground E	**2,692**	*100%*	**159** [1]	*100%*	**2,851**	*100%*
The nervous system (Q00 - Q007)	607	*23*	41	*26*	648	*23*
Other congenital malformations (Q10-Q89)	590	*22*	40	*25*	630	*22*
Chromosomal abnormalities	1,012	*38*	56	*35*	1,068	*37*
Other	483	*18*	22	*14*	505	*18*

p Provisional data
* Adhering to ISD Statistical Disclosure Control Protocol.
. Not available
[1] Some notifications record more than one Statutory Ground, therefore totals may not match with the numbers released by ISD Scotland.
Source: ISD Scotland, Department of Health
Note: percentages are rounded and may not add up to 100

15.17 Death rates per 1,000 population: by age and sex, 2012

England and Wales

Age	Males	Females	Age	Males	Females	Age	Males	Females
All ages	8.63	9.02						
0-4	1.10	0.87	35-39	1.09	0.64	70-74	24.94	16.39
0	4.62	3.69	35	0.93	0.52	70	20.01	13.18
1	0.34	0.26	36	0.94	0.52	71	23.06	14.48
2	0.18	0.11	37	1.11	0.64	72	25.11	16.44
3	0.11	0.12	38	1.19	0.68	73	27.18	18.04
4	0.11	0.09	39	1.29	0.82	74	29.90	20.04
5-9	0.09	0.08	40-44	1.68	1.00	75-79	41.23	28.42
5	0.11	0.10	40	1.53	0.82	75	33.76	22.33
6	0.09	0.09	41	1.48	0.87	76	37.09	25.11
7	0.07	0.08	42	1.57	1.02	77	40.86	28.27
8	0.10	0.06	43	1.81	1.08	78	46.54	31.90
9	0.08	0.07	44	1.99	1.19	79	50.91	36.09
10-14	0.11	0.08	45-49	2.42	1.61	80-84	73.23	53.61
10	0.09	0.08	45	2.08	1.38	80	56.81	41.81
11	0.11	*0.05*	46	2.23	1.41	81	66.28	46.95
12	0.11	0.10	47	2.47	1.61	82	74.03	52.23
13	0.11	0.09	48	2.57	1.70	83	84.35	61.29
14	0.11	0.10	49	2.78	1.93	84	94.45	70.53
15-19	0.32	0.15	50-54	3.62	2.50	85-89	129.67	100.49
15	0.14	0.12	50	3.01	2.05	85	104.55	78.89
16	0.17	0.11	51	3.27	2.31	86	121.04	90.86
17	0.32	0.17	52	3.51	2.55	87	133.52	100.02
18	0.50	0.15	53	4.01	2.73	88	147.68	114.00
19	0.43	0.19	54	4.40	2.93	89	165.41	131.05
20-24	0.48	0.20	55-59	5.87	4.04	90 and over	236.15	207.54
20	0.46	0.21	55	4.77	3.37			
21	0.44	0.21	56	5.38	3.59			
22	0.47	0.18	57	5.84	3.86			
23	0.55	0.21	58	6.35	4.38			
24	0.49	0.21	59	7.12	5.09			
25-29	0.57	0.27	60-64	9.47	6.24			
25	0.52	0.25	60	7.77	5.22			
26	0.55	0.21	61	8.78	5.72			
27	0.53	0.27	62	9.41	6.35			
28	0.61	0.33	63	10.09	6.57			
29	0.64	0.28	64	11.09	7.21			
30-34	0.76	0.41	65-69	14.55	9.57			
30	0.72	0.33	65	11.42	7.61			
31	0.74	0.40	66	13.55	8.95			
32	0.70	0.40	67	15.30	10.03			
33	0.84	0.44	68	15.64	10.35			
34	0.80	0.51	69	18.21	11.71			

Source: Office for National Statistics

15.18 Stillbirth[1,2] and infant death[3] rates: age at death, 1921-2012

England and Wales

Period	Infant mortality per 1,000 live births[3] at various ages										Stillbirths[2] and infant deaths per 1,000 total births			
	Under 1 year	Neonatal mortality					Postneonatal mortality				Still-births	Still-births plus deaths under 1 week	Still-births plus deaths under 4 weeks	Still-births plus deaths under 1 year
		Under 4 weeks	Early neonatal			Late neo-natal	4 weeks and under 1 year	4 weeks and under 3 months	3 months and under 6 months	6 months and under 1 year				
			Under 1 week	Under 1 day	1 day and under 1 week	1 week and under 4 weeks								
1921	82.8	35.3	22.4	10.8	11.6	12.9	47.5	14.8	14.0	18.6	..	..	..	..
1922	77.1	34.1	22.0	10.4	11.6	12.1	43.0	12.7	11.0	19.3	..	..	..	..
1923	69.4	31.9	21.1	10.2	10.9	10.8	37.5	11.3	10.0	16.1	..	..	..	..
1924	75.1	33.1	21.8	10.6	11.2	11.3	42.0	12.5	10.9	18.6	..	..	..	..
1925	75.0	32.3	21.2	10.1	11.1	11.1	42.7	12.6	11.3	18.8	..	..	..	..
1926	70.2	31.9	21.3	10.0	11.3	10.6	38.3	11.6	10.4	16.3	..	..	..	..
1927	69.7	32.3	22.2	10.6	11.6	10.1	37.4	10.7	9.7	16.9	38.8	59.6	69.3	105.3
1928	65.1	31.1	21.6	10.4	11.2	9.5	34.0	10.7	9.2	14.1	40.1	60.8	69.9	102.6
1929	74.4	32.8	22.3	10.4	11.9	10.6	41.5	11.6	10.7	19.3	40.0	61.4	71.6	111.4
1930	60.0	30.9	22.0	10.4	11.6	8.9	29.1	9.6	7.8	11.6	40.8	61.9	70.4	98.3
1931	65.7	31.5	22.1	10.4	11.7	9.5	34.2	10.8	9.2	14.2	40.9	62.1	71.2	104.5
1932	64.5	31.5	22.4	10.6	11.8	9.2	33.0	10.8	9.0	13.2	41.3	62.8	71.6	103.7
1933	62.7	32.1	22.9	11.0	11.8	9.3	30.6	9.8	8.6	12.2	41.4	63.4	72.3	102.5
1934	59.3	31.4	22.7	10.9	11.8	8.7	27.9	8.9	7.7	11.3	40.5	62.2	70.5	96.7
1935	57.0	30.4	22.0	10.7	11.3	8.4	26.6	9.1	7.7	9.8	40.7	61.9	69.9	95.4
1936	58.7	30.2	21.9	10.7	11.3	8.2	28.5	9.3	8.3	10.9	39.7	60.8	68.7	95.9
1937	57.7	29.7	22.0	10.8	11.2	7.8	28.0	9.4	8.3	10.3	39.0	60.2	67.6	94.4
1938	52.8	28.3	21.1	10.3	10.8	7.1	24.5	8.2	7.3	9.0	38.3	58.6	65.5	88.9
1939	50.6	28.3	21.2	10.3	10.9	7.1	22.2	7.9	7.0	7.3	38.1	58.5	65.3	86.9
1940	56.8	29.6	21.3	9.8	11.5	8.3	27.2	9.3	8.2	9.7	37.2	57.7	65.7	92.5
1941	60.0	29.0	20.7	10.1	10.6	8.3	31.1	11.3	9.7	10.1	34.8	54.7	62.7	92.4
1942	50.6	27.2	19.6	9.6	10.0	7.7	23.4	8.7	7.5	7.2	33.2	52.1	59.4	81.1
1943	49.1	25.2	18.3	9.1	9.2	6.9	23.9	8.8	7.8	7.3	30.1	47.9	54.6	77.5
1944	45.4	24.4	17.5	8.8	8.8	6.9	21.1	8.0	7.0	6.1	27.6	44.5	51.1	70.9
1945	46.0	24.8	18.0	9.0	9.0	6.8	21.3	8.2	7.0	6.1	27.6	45.2	51.8	73.4
1946	42.9	24.5	17.8	8.7	9.1	6.7	18.4	7.1	6.1	5.2	27.2	44.3	50.7	66.9
1947	41.4	22.7	16.5	7.8	8.7	6.2	18.6	6.9	6.0	5.7	24.1	40.3	46.4	65.0
1948	33.9	19.7	15.6	7.8	7.9	4.1	14.2	5.5	4.8	3.9	23.2	38.5	42.5	56.8
1949	32.4	19.3	15.6	7.6	8.0	3.7	13.0	4.8	4.4	3.8	22.7	38.0	41.5	54.6
1950	29.6	18.5	15.2	7.2	8.0	3.3	11.1	4.3	3.7	3.1	22.6	37.4	40.7	51.7
1951	29.7	18.8	15.5	7.5	8.0	3.3	10.9	4.1	3.6	3.2	23.0	38.2	41.5	52.2
1952	27.6	18.3	15.2	7.6	7.6	3.2	9.3	3.7	3.0	2.6	22.7	37.5	40.6	49.6
1953	26.8	17.7	14.8	7.4	7.4	2.9	9.1	3.4	3.0	2.7	22.4	36.9	39.7	48.6
1954	25.4	17.7	14.9	7.6	7.4	2.8	7.7	3.0	2.6	2.1	23.5	38.1	40.8	48.4
1955	24.9	17.3	14.6	7.6	7.0	2.6	7.6	2.9	2.6	2.1	23.2	37.4	40.0	47.5
1956	23.7	16.8	14.2	7.4	6.8	2.6	6.9	2.7	2.3	1.8	22.9	36.7	39.3	46.0
1957	23.1	16.5	14.1	7.6	6.5	2.4	6.7	2.6	2.1	1.9	22.5	36.2	38.5	45.1
1958	22.5	16.2	13.8	7.5	6.3	2.4	6.4	2.6	2.1	1.7	21.5	35.0	37.3	43.6
1959	22.2	15.9	13.6	7.6	6.0	2.3	6.3	2.4	2.1	1.8	20.8	34.1	36.3	42.6
1960	21.8	15.5	13.3	7.5	5.8	2.2	6.3	2.5	2.1	1.6	19.8	32.8	35.0	41.1
1961	21.4	15.3	13.3	7.6	5.7	2.1	6.1	2.4	2.0	1.7	19.0	32.0	34.1	40.0
1962	21.7	15.1	13.0	7.4	5.6	2.1	6.6	2.5	2.3	1.8	18.1	30.8	32.9	39.4
1963	21.1	14.3	12.3	7.2	5.1	2.0	6.9	2.7	2.4	1.8	17.2	29.3	31.3	38.0
1964	19.9	13.8	12.0	7.1	4.9	1.8	6.1	2.4	2.1	1.6	16.3	28.2	29.9	35.9
1965	19.0	13.0	11.3	6.6	4.7	1.7	6.0	2.4	2.1	1.6	15.8	26.9	28.6	34.5
1966	19.0	12.9	11.1	6.5	4.6	1.7	6.1	2.5	2.0	1.6	15.3	26.3	28.0	34.1
1967	18.3	12.5	10.7	6.3	4.4	1.8	5.8	2.4	2.0	1.4	14.8	25.4	27.2	32.9
1968	18.3	12.4	10.6	6.3	4.3	1.8	5.9	2.4	2.1	1.5	14.3	24.7	26.4	32.3
1969	18.0	12.0	10.3	6.0	4.3	1.7	6.0	2.5	2.1	1.5	13.2	23.4	25.1	31.0
1970	18.2	12.3	10.6	6.3	4.3	1.7	5.9	2.6	2.0	1.3	13.0	23.5	25.2	31.0
1971	17.5	11.6	9.9	6.0	3.9	1.7	5.9	2.6	2.0	1.3	12.5	22.3	24.0	29.8
1972	17.2	11.5	9.8	5.8	4.1	1.7	5.7	2.4	2.0	1.4	12.0	21.7	23.4	29.0
1973	16.9	11.1	9.5	5.5	4.0	1.6	5.7	2.5	1.9	1.3	11.6	21.0	22.6	28.3
1974	16.3	11.0	9.4	5.2	4.2	1.7	5.3	2.3	1.9	1.1	11.1	20.4	22.0	27.3
1975	15.7	10.7	9.1	5.0	4.1	1.7	5.0	2.2	1.7	1.1	10.3	19.3	20.9	25.9
1976	14.3	9.7	8.2	4.7	3.5	1.5	4.6	1.9	1.6	1.1	9.7	17.7	19.3	23.8

15.18 Stillbirth[1,2] and infant death[3] rates: age at death, 1921-2012

England and Wales

Period	Infant mortality per 1,000 live births[3] at various ages										Stillbirths[2] and infant deaths per 1,000 total births			
	Under 1 year	Neonatal mortality					Postneonatal mortality				Still-births	Still-births plus deaths under 1 week	Still-births plus deaths under 4 weeks	Still-births plus deaths under 1 year
		Under 4 weeks	Early neonatal			Late neo-natal	4 weeks and under 1 year	4 weeks and under 3 months	3 months and under 6 months	6 months and under 1 year				
			Under 1 week	Under 1 day	1 day and under 1 week	1 week and under 4 weeks								
1977	13.8	9.3	7.6	4.2	3.5	1.6	4.5	1.9	1.6	1.1	9.4	17.0	18.6	23.0
1978	13.2	8.7	7.1	3.7	3.4	1.6	4.5	1.9	1.6	1.0	8.5	15.5	17.1	21.6
1979	12.8	8.2	6.8	3.7	3.0	1.5	4.6	1.9	1.7	1.0	8.0	14.7	16.1	20.7
1980	12.0	7.7	6.2	3.4	2.8	1.5	4.4	1.8	1.5	1.1	7.2	13.3	14.8	19.2
1981	11.1	6.7	5.3	2.9	2.3	1.4	4.4	1.8	1.6	1.0	6.6	11.8	13.2	17.6
1982	10.8	6.3	5.0	2.8	2.2	1.2	4.6	1.9	1.6	1.1	6.3	11.3	12.5	17.0
1983	10.1	5.9	4.7	2.6	2.1	1.2	4.3	1.9	1.5	0.9	5.7	10.4	11.6	15.8
1984	9.5	5.6	4.4	2.6	1.9	1.1	3.9	1.6	1.3	0.9	5.7	10.1	11.2	15.1
1985	9.4	5.4	4.3	2.5	1.9	1.0	4.0	1.7	1.4	0.9	5.5	9.8	10.9	14.8
1986	9.6	5.3	4.3	2.4	1.8	1.0	4.3	1.8	1.5	1.0	5.3	9.6	10.6	14.8
1987	9.2	5.1	3.9	2.3	1.6	1.1	4.1	1.8	1.5	0.9	5.0	8.9	10.0	14.2
1988	9.0	4.9	3.9	2.2	1.7	1.0	4.1	1.7	1.5	0.9	4.9	8.7	9.8	13.8
1989	8.4	4.8	3.7	2.1	1.6	1.1	3.7	1.6	1.3	0.8	4.7	8.3	9.4	13.1
1990	7.9	4.6	3.5	2.0	1.5	1.0	3.3	1.3	1.2	0.7	4.6	8.1	9.1	12.4
1991	7.4	4.4	3.4	2.0	1.4	0.9	3.0	1.2	1.0	0.7	4.6	8.0	9.0	12.0
1992	6.6	4.3	3.3	2.0	1.4	1.0	2.3	1.0	0.8	0.6	4.3	7.6	8.5	10.8
1993	6.3	4.2	3.2	1.9	1.3	0.9	2.1	0.9	0.7	0.6	5.7	8.9	9.8	12.0
1994	6.2	4.1	3.2	1.9	1.4	0.9	2.1	0.8	0.7	0.6	5.7	8.9	9.8	11.9
1995	6.1	4.2	3.2	1.8	1.5	0.9	2.0	0.9	0.6	0.5	5.5	8.7	9.7	11.6
1996	6.1	4.1	3.2	1.9	1.3	0.9	2.0	0.9	0.6	0.5	5.4	8.6	9.5	11.5
1997	5.9	3.9	3.0	1.8	1.2	0.9	2.0	0.9	0.6	0.5	5.3	8.3	9.2	11.2
1998	5.7	3.8	2.9	1.7	1.2	0.9	1.9	0.9	0.6	0.4	5.3	8.2	9.1	11.0
1999	5.8	3.9	2.9	1.7	1.2	1.0	1.9	0.9	0.6	0.5	5.3	8.2	9.2	11.1
2000	5.6	3.9	2.9	1.7	1.2	1.0	1.7	0.8	0.5	0.4	5.3	8.2	9.1	10.8
2001	5.4	3.6	2.7	1.7	1.0	0.9	1.9	0.8	0.5	0.5	5.3	8.0	8.9	10.7
2002	5.2	3.6	2.7	1.7	1.0	1.0	1.7	0.8	0.0	0.0	5.6	8.0	9.0	11.0
2003	5.3	3.6	2.8	1.8	1.0	0.8	1.7	0.8	0.4	0.4	5.8	8.6	9.4	11.1
2004	5.0	3.5	2.7	1.7	1.0	0.8	1.6	0.8	0.4	0.4	5.7	8.4	9.2	10.7
2005	5.0	3.4	2.6	1.7	1.0	0.8	1.6	0.8	0.5	0.4	5.4	8.0	8.8	10.4
2006	5.0	3.5	2.6	1.7	0.9	0.9	1.5	0.7	0.4	0.3	5.4	8.0	8.8	10.3
2007	4.7	3.3	2.5	1.6	0.9	0.7	1.5	0.7	0.4	0.4	5.2	7.7	8.4	9.9
2008	4.6	3.2	2.4	1.6	0.8	0.7	1.4	0.7	0.4	0.3	5.1	7.5	8.3	9.7
2009	4.5	3.1	2.4	1.5	0.9	0.7	1.4	0.7	0.4	0.3	5.2	7.6	8.3	9.7
2010	4.3	2.9	2.3	1.5	0.8	0.6	1.3	0.7	0.3	0.3	5.1	7.4	8.0	9.3
2011	4.2	3.0	2.3	1.5	0.7	0.7	1.2	0.6	0.3	0.3	5.2	7.5	8.2	9.4
2012	4.0	2.8	2.2	1.5	0.6	0.6	1.2	0.6	0.3	0.3	4.9	7.0	7.6	8.8

1 Registration of stillbirths commenced on 1 July 1927. Annual figures for 1927 are estimated.

2 From 1927 to 30 September 1992 stillbirths relate to fetal deaths at or over 28 weeks gestation, and from 1 October 1992 at or over 24 weeks gestation.

3 Infant deaths are based on the live births occurring in the year, except in the years 1931-56 when they were based on related live births - that is, the combined live births of the associated and preceding years to which they relate.

Source: Office for National Statistics

15.19 Interim Life Tables, 2010-2012

United Kingdom

Age	Males		Females*	
x	l_x	e_x	l_x	e_x
0	100000.0	78.71	100000.0	82.58
5	99452.5	74.14	99557.5	77.94
10	99403.5	69.18	99518.9	72.97
15	99351.7	64.21	99477.5	68.00
20	99182.9	59.32	99390.9	63.06
25	98908.3	54.47	99279.6	58.13
30	98582.5	49.64	99128.9	53.21
35	98151.8	44.85	98906.5	48.33
40	97548.9	40.11	98566.1	43.48
45	96673.2	35.45	98034.3	38.71
50	95445.8	30.87	97217.7	34.01
55	93589.4	26.43	95913.0	29.43
60	90665.0	22.20	93921.2	25.00
65	86312.3	18.19	90953.6	20.73
70	79805.2	14.45	86442.4	16.67
75	69988.2	11.11	79363.5	12.92
80	56311.8	8.17	68353.4	9.57
85	38304.5	5.79	51715.8	6.80
90	19357.3	4.06	30891.9	4.67
95	6299.8	2.82	12307.0	3.20
100	1034.8	2.09	2644.8	2.27

England & Wales

Age	Males		Females	
x	l_x	e_x	l_x	e_x
0	100000.0	78.96	100000.0	82.79
5	99449.5	74.40	99554.3	78.16
10	99401.8	69.43	99515.6	73.19
15	99350.6	64.47	99473.8	68.22
20	99193.6	59.57	99391.7	63.27
25	98935.2	54.71	99285.4	58.34
30	98636.3	49.87	99142.6	53.42
35	98239.0	45.06	98929.0	48.53
40	97669.0	40.31	98600.2	43.68
45	96826.3	35.64	98084.5	38.89
50	95633.4	31.05	97290.8	34.19
55	93827.7	26.60	96027.3	29.60
60	90979.9	22.34	94080.4	25.16
65	86713.0	18.31	91184.9	20.88
70	80323.8	14.56	86787.0	16.80
75	70667.0	11.19	79872.9	13.02
80	57107.1	8.22	69044.3	9.64
85	39060.0	5.82	52505.6	6.84
90	19845.1	4.08	31538.0	4.71
95	6518.5	2.82	12692.0	3.22
100	1071.9	2.11	2772.5	2.29

Scotland

Age	Males		Females*	
x	l_x	e_x	l_x	e_x
0	100000.0	76.51	100000.0	80.75
5	99496.2	71.89	99609.5	76.06
10	99432.0	66.94	99573.4	71.09
15	99385.3	61.97	99535.6	66.11
20	99156.7	57.10	99409.5	61.19
25	98781.6	52.31	99258.8	56.28
30	98222.4	47.59	99027.2	51.41
35	97461.3	42.94	98700.1	46.57
40	96511.8	38.34	98231.8	41.78
45	95310.1	33.79	97548.8	37.05
50	93763.3	29.31	96535.8	32.41
55	91480.6	24.97	94880.1	27.93
60	87930.6	20.88	92519.5	23.58
65	82762.7	17.01	88867.2	19.44
70	75102.6	13.48	83275.6	15.56
75	63943.4	10.37	74752.3	12.03
80	49428.5	7.66	62239.2	8.92
85	31745.2	5.50	44857.9	6.37
90	15158.9	3.88	25333.0	4.35
95	4440.6	2.71	9034.5	2.95
100	697.5	1.85	1628.5	2.08

Northern Ireland

Age	Males		Females	
x	l_x	e_x	l_x	e_x
0	100000.0	77.69	100000.0	82.12
5	99439.8	73.13	99528.2	77.50
10	99388.0	68.16	99485.9	72.54
15	99311.6	63.22	99445.9	67.56
20	98965.5	58.43	99340.5	62.63
25	98487.6	53.70	99192.5	57.72
30	97972.4	48.97	99026.4	52.81
35	97394.3	44.24	98817.2	47.92
40	96732.4	39.53	98487.8	43.07
45	95794.6	34.89	97915.5	38.31
50	94494.5	30.33	97012.8	33.64
55	92470.6	25.94	95595.4	29.10
60	89253.7	21.77	93424.9	24.71
65	84851.7	17.76	90370.4	20.46
70	78327.0	14.02	85782.3	16.41
75	68006.6	10.75	78583.2	12.67
80	53598.0	7.95	67330.0	9.34
85	35797.9	5.62	50220.9	6.61
90	17558.9	3.96	29353.2	4.52
95	5337.7	2.91	11101.9	3.04
100			1983.8	2.14

Source: Office for National Statistics

*The female tables for Scotland, were corrected in June 2014 due to an error found in the calculation for infant mortality, This has increased the number of babies surviving from age 0 to age 1, thereby increasing life expectancy at birth by 0.06 years in this table.

*The female tables for the UK, were corrected in June 2014 due to an error found in the calculation of infant mortality for Scotland.This has increased the number of babies surviving from age 0 to age 1. This has not changed life expectancy figures in this table.

l_x is the number of survivors to exact age x of 100,000 live births of the same sex who are assumed to be subject throughout their lives to the mortality rates experienced in the three year period to which the National Life Table relates.

e_x is the average period expectation of life at exact age x, that is the average number of years that those aged x exact will live thereafter based on the mortality rates experienced in the three year period to which the National Life Table relates.

15.20a Adoptions by date of entry in Adopted Children Register (numbers and percentages): sex and age[1], 2001-2012

England and Wales

Year	All ages		Under 1		1-4		5-9		10-14		15-17	
	Number	Percentage	Number	Percentage	Number	Percentage	Number	Percentage	Number	Percentage	Number	Percentage
Total												
2001	**5,977**	100	246	4	2,644	44	1,847	31	983	16	257 [2]	4
2002	**5,671**	100	287	5	2,524	45	1,748	31	900	16	212	4
2003	**4,809**	100	183	4	2,255	47	1,499	31	683	14	189	4
2004	**5,555**	100	253	5	2,620	47	1,651	30	786	14	245	4
2005	**5,556**	100	222	4	2,900	52	1,552	28	683	12	199	4
2006	**4,978**	100	197	4	2,590	52	1,406	28	585	12	200 [4]	4
2007	**4,637**	100	151	3	2,511	54	1,206	26	575	12	194 [11]	4
2008	**5,065**	100	120	2	2,832	56	1,239	24	628	12	246 [12]	5
2009	**4,725**	100	91	2	2,783	59	1,184	25	480	10	187 [11]	4
2010	**4,550**	100	95	2	2,649	58	1,140	25	470	10	196 [13]	4
2011	**4,777**	100	76	2	2,953	62	1,117	23	467	10	164 [8]	3
2012	**5,053**	100	113	2	3,161	63	1,179	23	434	9	166 [5]	3
Males												
2001	**3,011**	100	124	4	1,370	45	906	30	494	16	117	4
2002	**2,866**	100	160	6	1,318	46	846	30	444	15	98	3
2003	**2,337**	100	91	4	1,114	48	736	31	301	13	95	4
2004	**2,773**	100	132	5	1,323	48	831	30	373	13	114	4
2005	**2,790**	100	112	4	1,461	52	807	29	320	11	90	3
2006	**2,445**	100	95	4	1,281	52	707	29	267	11	95 [2]	4
2007	**2,315**	100	77	3	1,253	54	618	27	270	12	97 [3]	4
2008	**2,522**	100	53	2	1,425	57	622	25	324	13	98 [4]	4
2009	**2,392**	100	46	2	1,448	61	599	25	214	9	85 [3]	4
2010	**2,302**	100	53	2	1,350	59	586	25	223	10	90 [5]	4
2011	**2,369**	100	47	2	1,472	62	555	23	222	9	73 [3]	3
2012	**2,558**	100	60	2	1,635	64	586	23	201	8	76 [3]	3
Females												
2001	**2,966**	100	122	4	1,274	43	941	32	489	16	140 [2]	5
2002	**2,805**	100	127	5	1,206	43	902	32	456	16	114	4
2003	**2,472**	100	92	4	1,141	46	763	31	382	15	94	4
2004	**2,782**	100	121	4	1,297	47	820	29	413	15	131	5
2005	**2,766**	100	110	4	1,439	52	745	27	363	13	109	4
2006	**2,533**	100	102	4	1,309	52	699	28	318	13	105 [6]	4
2007	**2,322**	100	74	3	1,258	54	588	25	305	13	97 [7]	4
2008	**2,543**	100	67	3	1,407	55	617	24	304	12	148 [8]	6
2009	**2,333**	100	45	2	1,335	57	585	25	266	11	102 [7]	4
2010	**2,248**	100	42	2	1,299	58	554	25	247	11	106 [9]	5
2011	**2,408**	100	29	1	1,481	62	562	23	245	10	91 [10]	4
2012	**2,495**	100	53	2	1,526	61	593	24	233	9	90 [3]	4

Percentages may not add precisely due to rounding.

1 Age is at date of court order.
2 Includes 1 case where age was greater than 17.
3 Includes 8 cases where age was greater than 17.
4 Includes 5 cases where age was greater than 17.
5 Includes 16 cases where age was greater than 17.
6 Includes 4 cases where age was greater than 17.
7 Includes 15 cases where age was greater than 17.
8 Includes 21 cases where age was greater than 17.
9 Includes 12 cases where age was greater than 17.
10 Includes 13 cases where age was greater than 17.
11 Includes 23 cases where age was greater than 17.
12 Includes 26 cases where age was greater than 17.
13 Includes 28 cases where age was greater than 17.

Source: Office for National Statistics

15.20b Adoptions by age of child and relationship of the adopter(s), 2012

Scotland

Age and sex of child		Total	Relationship of adopter(s)				
			Both parents	Step-parent	Grandparent(s)	Other relation(s)	No relation
All ages	P	495	-	138	4	20	333
	M	250	-	69	1	11	169
	F	245	-	69	3	9	164
Months							
less than 6	M	-	-	-	-	-	-
	F	1	-	1	-	-	-
6-8	M	5	-	3	-	-	2
	F	5	-	4	-	1	-
9-11	M	2	-	-	-	1	1
	F	4	-	-	-	-	4
12-17	M	15	-	3	-	2	10
	F	8	-	-	-	-	8
18-23	M	15	-	2	-	1	12
	F	17	-	1	-	-	16
Years							
2	M	35	-	1	-	3	31
	F	40	-	4	-	1	35
3-4	M	55	-	2	1	1	51
	F	61	-	7	1	5	48
5-9	M	77	-	25	-	2	50
	F	65	-	20	2	1	42
10-14	M	36	-	26	-	1	9
	F	32	-	24	-	1	7
15 and over	M	10	-	7	-	-	3
	F	12	-	8	-	-	4

© Crown Copyright 2013

Source: GRO-Scotland

15.20c Adoptions - Northern Ireland, 2009-2011

Year	All ages		Under 1		1-4		5-9		10-14		15-17	
	Numbers	Percentage	Numbers	Percentage	Numbers	Percentage	Numbers	Percentage	Numbers	Percentage	Numbers	Percentage
Persons	VOYS	VOYT	VOYU	VOYV	VOYW	VOYX	VOYY	VOYZ	VOZA	VOZB	VOZC	VOZD
2009	116	100%	1	1%	43	37%	46	40%	20	17%	6	5%
2010	116	100%	3	3%	46	40%	46	40%	17	15%	4	3%
2011	104	100%	3	3%	40	38%	40	38%	13	13%	8	8%

Year	All ages		Under 1		1-4		5-9		10-14		15-17	
	Numbers	Percentage	Numbers	Percentage	Numbers	Percentage	Numbers	Percentage	Numbers	Percentage	Numbers	Percentage
Males	VOYS	VOYT	VOYU	VOYV	VOYW	VOYX	VOYY	VOYZ	VOZA	VOZB	VOZC	VOZD
2009	55	100%	0	0%	24	44%	20	36%	10	18%	1	2%
2010	56	100%	2	4%	26	46%	21	38%	6	11%	1	2%
2011	47	100%	0	0%	19	40%	18	38%	6	13%	4	9%

Year	All ages		Under 1		1-4		5-9		10-14		15-17	
	Numbers	Percentage	Numbers	Percentage	Numbers	Percentage	Numbers	Percentage	Numbers	Percentage	Numbers	Percentage
Females	VOYS	VOYT	VOYU	VOYV	VOYW	VOYX	VOYY	VOYZ	VOZA	VOZB	VOZC	VOZD
2009	61	100%	1	2%	19	31%	26	43%	10	16%	5	8%
2010	60	100%	1	2%	20	33%	25	42%	11	18%	3	5%
2011	57	100%	3	5%	21	37%	22	39%	7	12%	4	7%

Source: NISRA Demography & Methodology Branches

this page is intentionally blank

Health

Chapter 16

Health

Deaths: analysed by cause (Table 16.6)

All figures in this table for England and Wales represent the number of deaths occurring in each calendar year. All data for Scotland and Northern Ireland relate to the number of deaths registered during each calendar year. From 2001, all three constituent countries of the UK are coding their causes of death using the latest, tenth, revision of the International Statistical Classification of Diseases and Related Health Problems (ICD-10). All cause of death information from 2001 (also for 2000 for Scotland) presented in this table is based on the revised classification.

To assist users in assessing any discontinuities arising from the introduction of the revised classification, bridge-coding exercises were carried out on all deaths registered in 1999 in England and Wales and also in Scotland. For further information about ICD-10 and the bridge-coding carried out by The Office for National Statistics (ONS), see the ONS Report: Results of the ICD-10 bridge-coding study, England and Wales, Statistics Quarterly 14 (2002), pages 75–83 or log on to the Office for National Statistics (ONS) website at: www.ons.gov.uk. For information on the Scottish bridge-coding exercise, consult the Annual Report of the General Register Office for Scotland or log on to their website at: www.gro-scotland.gov.uk. No bridge-coding exercise was conducted for Northern Ireland.

Neonatal deaths and homicide and assault

For England and Wales, neonatal deaths (those at age under 28 days) are included in the number of total deaths but excluded from the cause figures. This has particular impact on the totals shown for the chapters covered by the ranges P and Q, 'Conditions originating in the perinatal period' and 'Congenital malformations, deformations and chromosomal abnormalities'. These are considerably lower than the actual number of deaths because it is not possible to assign an underlying cause of death from the neonatal death certificate used in England and Wales.

Also, for England and Wales only, the total number shown for Homicide and assault, X85–Y09, will not be a true representation because the registration of these deaths is often delayed by adjourned inquests.

Occupational ill health (Tables 16.8 and 16.9)

There are a number of sources of data on the extent of occupational or work-related ill health in Great Britain. For some potentially severe lung diseases caused by exposures which are highly unlikely to be found in a non-occupational setting, it is useful to count the number of death certificates issued each year. This is also true for mesothelioma, a cancer affecting the lining of the lungs and stomach, for which the number of cases with non-occupational causes is likely to be larger (although still a minority). Table 16.9 shows the number of deaths for mesothelioma and asbestosis (linked to exposure to asbestos), pneumoconiosis (linked to coal dust or silica), byssinosis (linked to cotton dust) and some forms of allergic alveolitis (including farmer's lung). For asbestos-related diseases the figures are derived from a special register maintained by HSE.

Most conditions which can be caused or made worse by work can also arise from other factors. The remaining sources of data on work-related ill health rely on attribution of individual cases of illness to work causes. In The Health and Occupation Reporting Network (THOR), this is done by specialist doctors – either occupational physicians or those working in particular disease specialisms (covering musculoskeletal, psychological, respiratory, skin, audio logical and infectious disease). Table 16.8 presents data from THOR for the last three years. It should be noted that not all cases of occupational disease will be seen by participating specialists; for example, the number of deaths due to mesothelioma (shown in Table 16.9) is known to be greater than the number of cases reported to THOR.

Injuries at work (Table 16.10)

The Reporting of Injuries, Diseases and Dangerous Occurrences Regulations 1995 (RIDDOR) places a legal duty on employers to report injuries arising from work activity to the relevant enforcing authority, namely HSE, local authorities and the Office of Rail Regulation (ORR). These include injuries to employees, self-employed people and members of the public. From 12 September 2011 the reporting of all RIDDOR incidents will move to a predominantly online system.

While the enforcing authorities are informed about almost all relevant fatal workplace injuries, it is known that non-fatal injuries are substantially under-reported. Currently, it is estimated that just over half of all such injuries to employees are actually reported, with the self-employed reporting a much smaller proportion. These results are achieved by comparing reported non-fatal injuries (major as well as over-3-day), with results from the Labour Force Survey (LFS).

16.1a NHS Hospital and Community Health Services:
Qualified ambulance service staff and support to ambulance service staff

England as at September 2012	headcount
Ambulance service staff total	**32,076**
Qualified ambulance service staff	**18,645**
Manager	657
Emergency care practitioner	742
Paramedic	11,954
Ambulance technician	5,295
Ambulance personnel (old definition)	..
Support to ambulance service staff	**13,451**
Ambulance personnel (new definition)	6,290
Trainee ambulance technician	875
Trainee ambulance personnel	..
Clerical & administrative	4,382
Estates (maintenance & works)	237
Healthcare assistant	980
Support worker	695

Headcount totals are unlikely to equal the sum of components.
Further information on the headcount methodology is available in the Census publication.

16.1b NHS Labour Turnover and Stability Analysis
Welsh Ambulance Trust

		Headcount
As of 31 Dec 2012		
020 Welsh Ambulance Trust	**Ambulance Officer**	73
	Urgent Care Assistants	126
	Paramedic Practitioner	29
	Paramedic	968
	Ambulance Technician	404
	Staff Group Summary Total	1600

Source: Welsh Ambulance Service NHS Trust

16.1c Ambulance staff by Type: Scotland

As of December 2012

	Total	Under 20	20 - 24	25 - 29	30 - 34	35 - 39	40 - 44	45 - 49	50 - 54	55 - 59	60 - 64	65 +
Emergency services	**3,661.8**	**2.0**	**56.5**	**143.1**	**254.2**	**499.0**	**701.5**	**708.6**	**628.6**	**429.2**	**205.4**	**33.6**
Ambulance care assistant	812.1	-	2.0	4.5	20.5	75.8	126.8	147.8	153.0	142.9	111.3	27.3
Auxillary	-	-	-	-	-	-	-	-	-	-	-	-
Driver	56.7	-	-	-	0.8	1.7	3.1	5.7	10.1	12.5	16.5	6.3
EMDC / control	289.3	1.0	18.5	48.5	50.9	45.0	42.3	31.8	24.4	20.2	6.6	-
Paramedic [1]	1,399.4	-	4.0	21.0	82.3	219.2	318.1	342.5	260.2	131.6	20.5	-
Technician	1,011.6	1.0	32.0	68.0	93.7	148.3	200.2	171.7	153.8	97.0	45.9	-
Other	92.0	-	-	1.0	6.0	9.0	11.0	9.0	27.0	25.0	4.0	-
Not assimilated / not known	0.8	-	-	-	-	-	-	-	-	-	0.8	-

Source: Scottish Workforce Information Standard System (SWISS)

Note:
1. From the 1st April 2013 Paramedics have been reclassified from Emergency Services to Allied Health Professionals.

16.1d Ambulance Staff by Type: Northern Ireland

										Headcount
		2004	2005	2006	2007	2008	2009	2010	2011	2012
Northern Ireland										
Total Ambulance staff	JHQ9	867	911	989	1,007	1,025	1,036	1026	1045	1052
Emergency Medical Technicians and Paramedics	JHR2	567	576	637	659	625	629	598	610	618
Other/Patient care services	JHR3	176	211	220	219	231	227	244	240	231
Ambulance officers	JHR4	59	61	63	67	94	108	106	102	107
Manager	JHR5	65	63	69	62	75	72	78	93	96

Department of Health, Social Services and Public Safety Northern Ireland

16.2 Hospital and primary care services Scotland

			2000 /01	2001 /02	2002 /03	2003 /04	2004 /05	2005 /06
Hospital and community services In-patients:[1,2]								
Average available staffed beds	KDEA	Thousands	32.1	30.9	29.8	28.9	28.1	27.4
Average occupied beds:								
All departments	KDEB	"	25.8	25.1	24.2	23.2	22.5	22.1
Psychiatric and learning disability	KDEC	"	7.6	7.0	6.4	5.9	5.5	5.2
Discharges or deaths[3]	KDED	"	972	969	959	989	1,003	1,015
Outpatients:[2,4]								
New cases	KDEE	"	2,749	2,728	2,731	2,750	2,718	2,762
Total attendances	KDEF	"	6,382	6,254	6,193	6,147	5,981	6,060
Medical and dental staff:[5,6,22]	JYXO	Headcount	9,325	9,644	10,256	10,407	10,658	10,871
Whole-time	KDEG	"	7,216	7,530	8,115	8,349	8,612	8,796
Part-time	KDEH	"	1,648	1,681	1,697	1,636	1,630	1,670
Honorary	JYXN	"	495	468	468	437	431	418
Professional and technical staff:[6,7,22]								
Whole-time	KDEI	"	11,261	11,705	12,265	12,942	13,258	13,750
Part-time	KDEJ	"	5,483	5,852	6,273	6,708	6,968	7,440
Nursing and midwifery staff:[6,8,22]								
Whole-time	KDEK	"	32,401	33,334	34,294	34,939	35,338	36,093
Part-time	KDEL	"	29,131	29,004	29,015	29,354	29,484	29,688
Administrative and clerical staff:[6,9,22]								
Whole-time	KDEM	"	14,710	15,361	16,200	17,260	17,806	18,434
Part-time	KDEN	"	7,677	8,075	8,630	9,307	9,943	10,707
Domestic, transport, etc, staff:[6,10,22]								
Whole-time	KDEO		7,848	7,625	7,768	8,234	8,305	8,516
Part-time	KDEP		12 272	11 522	11 915	12 588	12 324	12 545
Primary care services								
Primary Medical services								
General medical practitioners (GPs):[11,23]	JX4B	Headcount	4,253	4,346	4,361	4,447	4,456	4,521
Performer[12,23]	KDET	"	3,710	3,761	3,770	3,805	3,782	3,763
Performer salaried[13,23]	KDEU	"	99	108	114	155	188	288
Performer registrar	JX4C	"	261	283	284	281	282	300
Performer retainee[14,23]	JX4D	"	184	196	194	209	208	176
Expenditure on Primary Medical Services[15,23]	KDEW	£million	405	430	468	519	628	701
Pharmaceutical services[16]								
Prescriptions dispensed	KDEX	Millions	63	66	70	72	75	77
Payments to pharmacists (gross)	KDEY	£million	..	..	887	963	984	1016
Average gross cost per prescription	KDEZ	£	11.7	12.2	12.8	13.3	12.6	12.5
Dental services								
Dentists on list[17]	KDFA	Headcount	1,808	1,844	1,869	1,882	1,900	1,936
Number of courses of treatment completed	KDFB	Thousands	3,389	3,359	3,420	3,359	3,375	3,348
Payments to dentists (gross)	KDFC	£million	163	165	172	170	174	179
Payments bypatients	KDFD	"	51	52	55	53	54	54
Payments out of public funds	KDFE	"	112	113	118	117	120	125
Average gross cost per course	KDFF	£	38	38	40	40	40	41
General ophthalmic services Number of Eye Exams given[18,19]	KDFG	Thousands	861	877	907	920	935	960
Number of pairs of supplied[20]	KDFH	"	439	463	458	450	457	457
Payments out of public funds forsight testing and dispensing[21]	KDFK	£ million	..	..	35	36	38	39

Sources: ISD Scotland, NHS National Services Scotland; 0131 275 7777

16.2 Hospital and primary care services Scotland

			2006 /07	2007 /08	2008 /09	2009 /10	2010 /11	2011 /12
Hospital and community services In-patients:[1,2]								
Average available staffed beds	KDEA	Thousands	26.9	26.3	25.8	24.9	23.9	23.3
Average occupied beds:								
All departments	KDEB	"	21.7	21.0	20.6	19.9	19.2	18.8
Psychiatric and learning disability	KDEC	"	4.9	4.6	4.3	4.1	3.8	3.6
Discharges or deaths[3]	KDED	"	1,037	1,066	1,091	1,090	1,096	1,114
Outpatients:[2,4]								
New cases	KDEE	"	2,827	2,894	3,003	3,026	3,044	3,021
Total attendances	KDEF	"	6,048	6,093	6,271	6,208	6,206	6,235
Medical and dental staff:[5,6,22]	JYXO	Headcount	11,201	11,822	12,534	12,619	12,757	13,336
Whole-time	KDEG	"	9,201	9,828	9,971	9,975	9,973	10,360
Part-time	KDEH	"	1,607	2,028	2,252	2,444	2,563	2,797
Honorary	JYXN	"	411	418	377	247	263	252
Professional and technical staff:[6,7,22]								
Whole-time	KDEI	"	14,323	13,642	14,567	15,403	15,590	15,021
Part-time	KDEJ	"	7,990	7,953	8,375	9,036	9,504	9,689
Nursing and midwifery staff:[6,8,22]								
Whole-time	KDEK	"	37,104	37,071	37,654	37,995	37,165	35,547
Part-time	KDEL	"	29,995	29,544	29,555	29,949	30,261	30,065
Administrative and clerical staff:[6,9,22]								
Whole-time	KDEM	"	18,907	18,181	18,158	19,007	18,686	17,639
Part-time	KDEN	"	11,375	10,836	11,231	11,679	11,703	11,345
Domestic, transport, etc, staff:[6,10,22]								
Whole-time	KDEO		8,697	10,205	10,623	11,037	10,927	10,522
Part-time	KDEP		12 675	12,819	12,874	13,138	12,576	12,042
Primary care services								
Primary Medical services								
General medical practitioners (GPs):[11,23]	JX4B	Headcount	4,597	4,686	4,890	4,907	4,905	4,888
Performer[12,23]	KDET	"	3,770	3,785	3,783	3,805	3,777	3,748
Performer salaried[13,23]	KDEU	"	354	418	460	487	482	523
Performer registrar	JX4C	"	308	325	490	465	497	478
Performer retainee[14,23]	JX4D	"	169	164	164	159	156	145
Expenditure on Primary Medical Services[15,23]	KDEW	£million	700	705	701	729	741	747
Pharmaceutical services[16]								
Prescriptions dispensed	KDEX	Millions	80	82	86	89	91	95
Payments to pharmacists (gross)	KDEY	£million	1045	1067	1107	1139	1160	1177
Average gross cost per prescription	KDEZ	£	12.1	11.7	11.4	11.1	11.0	10.7
Dental services								
Dentists on list[17]	KDFA	Headcount	2,009	2,099	2,204	2,313	2,354	2,486
Number of courses of treatment completed	KDFB	Thousands	3,387	3,401	3,548	3,686	3,830	4,100
Payments to dentists (gross)	KDFC	£million	188	199	220	231	243	255
Payments bypatients	KDFD	"	46	47	50	52	55	59
Payments out of public funds	KDFE	"	143	152	170	180	188	196
Average gross cost per course	KDFF	£	42	43	45			
General ophthalmic services Number of Eye Exams given[18,19]	KDFG	Thousands	1,573	1,626	1,728	1,775	1,805	1,914
Number of pairs of glasses supplied[20]	KDFH	"	443	451	468	474	466	489
Payments out of public funds forsight testing and dispensing[21]	KDFK	£ million	66	79	86	91	90	95

Sources: ISD Scotland, NHS National Services Scotland; 0131 275 7777

16.2   Hospital and primary care services Scotland

1 Excludes joint user and contractual hospitals.

2 In year to 31 March.

3 Includes transfers out and emergency inpatients treated in day bed units.

4 Including attendances at accident and emergency consultant clinics.

5 As at 30 September. Figures exclude officers holding honorary locum appointments. Part-time includes maximum part-time appointments. There is an element of double counting of "heads" in this table as doctors can hold more than one contract. For example, they may hold contracts of different type, eg part time and honorary. Doctors holding two or more contracts of the same type, eg part time, are not double counted. Doctors, whose sum of contracts amounts to whole time, are classed as such. Figures have been revised due to coding changes.

6 The change in both collection and presentation of workforce data due to changes to staff groupings under Agenda for Change has inevitably meant that the amount of historical trend analysis of data is limited, though still available for some high level groupings.

7 As at 30 September. Comprises Therapeutic, Healthcare science, Technical and Pharmacy staff.

8 As at 30 September. Includes Health Care Assistants. Figures post 2003 have been amended due to a coding error resulting in some staff previously in this group being moved to the admin and clerical group.

9 As at 30 September. Comprises Senior Management and Administrative and Clerical staff. Figures for 2003 onwards have been amended due to the inclusion of some staff previously in the nursing and midwifery staff group

10 As at 30 September.Comprises Ambulance, Works, Ancillary and Trades.

11 Contracted GP's in post in Scottish general practices, at 1 October up to 2003/04 and 30 Sept for 2004/05 onwards. Excludes GP locums and GPs working only in Out of Hours services. The total may not equal the sum of the figures for individual GP designations as some GPs hold more than one contract. Source: www.isdscotland.org/workforce

12 For 2004/05 onwards this group comprised mainly of Provider (partner) GPs. Known prior to 2004/05 as Principal GPs.

13 Up to 2003/04 this group comprises salaried GPs plus associates, assistants and 'other' GPs. Terminology changed with the introduction of the new GMS contract in April 2004.

14 Data on the number of GP retainees not available prior to 2000.

15 Total expenditure on General Medical Services/Primary Medical Services Source: NHS Scotland Costs Book "R390" tables, www.isdscotland.org/costs Note, the contractual arrangements for payments to many general practices changed with the introduction of the new GMS contract in April 2004.

16 For prescriptions dispensed in financial year by all community pharmacists (including stock orders), dispensing doctors and appliance suppliers. Gross total excludes patient charges.

17 Comprises of non-salaried GDS principal dentists only as at 31 March.

18 Figures represent sight tests paid for by health boards, hospital eye service referrals and GOD(s) ST (v) claimants.

19 Free NHS eye examinations were extended to all on 1st April 2006.

20 Does not include hospital eye service.

21 OPTIX, the electronic system for recording ophtalmic payment information, was introduced in 2002. Information for previous years is now not centrally available from ISD

22 In order to provide additional and more accurate information, ISD revised methodologies. These changes include the revision to the headcount measure. Headcount refers to the actual number of individuals (employees) working within the NHSS. This eliminates any double counting that may exist as a result of an employee holding more than one post. Please note due to revisions in the headcount measure, it is not possible to compare data prior to 2007. 23 Figures have been revised and differ from those previously published due to improvements in source data quality.

*** Figures not yet published.

16.3 Hospital and general health services
Northern Ireland

			2001	2002	2003	2004	2005	2006
Hospital services[1]								
In-patients:								
Beds available[2]	KDGA	Numbers	8,419	8,301	8,347	8,323	8,238	7,976
Average daily occupation of beds	KDGB	Percentages	83	84	84	84	84	83
Discharges or deaths[3]	KDGC	Thousands	328	327	332	337	296	295
Out-patients:[4]								
New cases	KDGD	"	997	992	1,014	1,027	1,040	1,081
Total attendances	KDGE	"	2,131	2,122	2,161	2,175	2,219	2,233
General health services								
Medical services[1]								
Doctors (principals) on the list[5,6]	KDGF	Numbers	1,073	1,076	1,076	1,078	1,084	1,100
Number of patients per doctor	KDGG	"	1,651	1,652	1,658	1,663	1,655	1,631
Gross Payments to doctors[7]	KDGH	£ thousand	84,664	88,194	96,894	..	..	..
Pharmaceutical services[8]								
Prescription forms dispensed	KDGI	Thousands	14,277	14,622	15,158	15,283	15,860	16,393
Number of prescriptions	KDGJ	"	24,705	25,501	26,656	27,401	28,417	29,599
Gross Cost[9]	KDGK	£ thousand	303,489	327,045	362,401	382,789	390,763	408,771
Charges[10]	KDGL	"	9,074	9,597	9,798	10,262	10,676	11,298
Net Cost[9]	KDGM	"	294,415	317,448	352,602	372,527	380,087	397,473
Average gross cost per prescription[9]	KDGN	£	12	13	14	14	14	14
Dental services[8,11]								
Dentists on the list[5]	KDGO	Numbers	673	689	696	720	722	751
Number of courses of paid treatment	KDGP	Thousands	1,126	1,123	1,107	1,086	1,084	1,064
Gross cost	KDGQ	£ thousand	64,454	66,201	66,910	67,294	69,480	65,172
Patients	KDGR	Thousands	16,041	930	919	907	910	900
Contributions (Net cost)	KDGS	£ thousand	48,413	49,376	50,282	50,498	52,308	50,068
Average gross cost per paid treatment	KDGT	£	57	59	60	62	64	61
Ophthalmic services[8]								
Number of sight tests given[12]	KDGU	Thousands	326	334	346	347	360	368
Number of optical appliances supplied[13]	KDGV	"	187	190	192	189	194	196
Cost of service (gross)[14]	KDGW	£ thousand	12,738	13,473	13,981	14,395	15,868	16,280
Health and social services[15]								
Medical and dental staff:								
Whole-time	KDGZ	Numbers	2,280	2,409	2,606	2,749	2,947	3,152
Part-time	KDHA	"	595	624	619	626	561	554
Nursing and midwifery staff:								
Whole-time	KDHB	"	9,804	10,221	10,709	11,116	11,395	11,454
Part-time	KDHC	"	7,774	8,354	8,665	8,850	9,015	9,072
Administrative and clerical staff:								
Whole-time	KDHD	"	7,447	7,820	8,188	8,676	8,878	8,938
Part-time	KDHE	"	3,112	3,349	3,579	3,828	4,160	4,221
Professional and technical staff:								
Whole-time	KDHF	"	3,752	3,968	4,155	4,518	4,685	4,758
Part-time	KDHG	"	1,362	1,491	1,605	1,724	1,822	2,021
Social services staff(excluding casual home helps):								
Whole-time	KDHH	"	3,120	3,280	3,454	3,709	3,773	3,889
Part-time	KDHI	"	906	978	1,093	1,197	1,289	1,417
Ancillary and other staff:								
Whole-time	KDHJ	"	3,467	3,421	3,413	3,469	3,722	3,833
Part-time	KDHK	"	4,917	5,118	5,410	5,580	5,486	5,892
Cost of services (gross)[14]	KDHL	£ thousand	1,639,283	1,868,538	2,113,453	..	..	..
Payments by recipients	KDHM	Thousands	78,478	88,860	87,999	..	..	..
Payments out of public funds	KDHN	£ thousand	1,560,805	1,779,678	2,025,454	..	..	..

16.3 Hospital and general health services
Northern Ireland

			2007	2008	2009	2010	2011	2012
Hospital services[1]								
In-patients:								
Beds available[2]	KDGA	Numbers	7,827	7,636	7274	6732	6439	6288
Average daily occupation of beds	KDGB	Percentages	83	82	82	83	84	84
Discharges or deaths[3]	KDGC	Thousands	306	311	300	295	295	301
Out-patients:[4]								
New cases	KDGD	"	1,115	1,149	1150	1148	1123	1124
Total attendances	KDGE	"	2,282	2,256	2231	2234	2239	2247
General health services								
Medical services[1]								
Doctors (principals) on the list[5,6]	KDGF	Numbers	1,127	1,148	1,156	1,160	1163	1170
Number of patients per doctor	KDGG	"	1,626	1,618	1,615	1,623	1631	1631
Gross Payments to doctors[7]	KDGH	£ thousand	..	..				
Pharmaceutical services[8]								
Prescription forms dispensed	KDGI	Thousands	17,280	17,910	19,241	20,411	20860	21416
Number of prescriptions	KDGJ	"	30,864	32,107	34,263	36,298	36916	38614
Gross Cost[9]	KDGK	£ thousand	425,440	445,184	470,049	490,670	462947	457492
Charges[10]	KDGL	"	11,943	10,243	4,447	0	0	0
Net Cost[9]	KDGM	"	413,497	434,940	465,603	490,670	462947	457492
Average gross cost per prescription[9]	KDGN	£	14	14	14	14	13	12
Dental services[8,11]								
Dentists on the list[5]	KDGO	Numbers	763	795	816	889	1010	1044
Number of courses of paid treatment	KDGP	Thousands	1,002	1,034	1,051	1,172	1231	1283
Gross cost	KDGQ	£ thousand	68,775	71,401	73,741	81,621	84659	90759
Patients	KDGR	Thousands	859	868	885	1,001	1119	1147
Contributions (Net cost)	KDGS	£ thousand	53,301	55,801	57,897	64,280	66533	69960
Average gross cost per paid treatment	KDGT	£	69	69	70	70	69	71
Ophthalmic services[8]								
Number of sight tests given[12]	KDGU	Thousands	385	404	413	425	435	438
Number of optical appliances supplied[13]	KDGV	"	200	210	212	219	226	233
Cost of service (gross)[14]	KDGW	£ thousand	16,970	18,468	19,638	19,823	20220	
Health and social services[15]								
Medical and dental staff:								
Whole-time	KDGZ	Numbers	3,250	3,278	3,301	3,294	3347	3415
Part-time	KDHA	"	587	603	599	618	649	677
Nursing and midwifery staff:								
Whole-time	KDHB	"	11,623	11,512	11,716	11,292	11171	11426
Part-time	KDHC	"	9,310	9,251	9,277	9,470	9356	9422
Administrative and clerical staff:								
Whole-time	KDHD	"	8,683	8,255	8,197	7,880	7795	8106
Part-time	KDHE	"	4,226	4,196	4,286	4,280	4304	4447
Professional and technical staff:								
Whole-time	KDHF	"	4,936	4,619	4,704	4,748	4807	5069
Part-time	KDHG	"	2,076	2,347	2,423	2,533	2639	2725
Social services staff(excluding casual home helps):								
Whole-time	KDHH	"	4,014	4,441	4,619	4,632	4581	4622
Part-time	KDHI	"	2,041	2,808	2,863	2,877	2896	2919
Ancillary and other staff:								
Whole-time	KDHJ	"	3,857	3,831	3,816	3,855	3814	3740
Part-time	KDHK	"	5,667	4,794	4,904	4,805	4582	4598
Cost of services (gross)[14]	KDHL	£ thousand	..	..	..	..		
Payments by recipients	KDHM	Thousands	..	..	..	..		
Payments out of public funds	KDHN	£ thousand	..	..	..	..		

Sources: Business Services Organisation (BSO) Northern Ireland: 028 9053 2975;
Dept. of Health, Social Services & Public Safety Northern Ireland: 028 9052 2509;
(Figures on Hospital Services: 028 9052 2800)

16.3 Hospital and general health services
Northern Ireland

1 Financial Year.

2 Average available beds in wards open overnight during the year.

3 Includes transfers to other hospitals. This figure also excludes day case admissions.

4 Includes consultant outpatient clinics and Accident and Emergency departments.

5 At beginning of period for Dentists. Doctors numbers at 2002 (Oct), 2003 (Nov), 2004, 2005 & 2006 (Oct).

6 From 2003 onwards (UPE's).

7 These costs refer to the majority of non-cash limited services: further expenditure under GMS is allocated through HSS Boards on a cash limited basis. Change between 2002 and 2003 is due to advance payments being made in relation to the new GMS contract introduced in April 2004.

8 From 1995 onwards figures are taken from financial year.

9 Gross cost is defined as net ingredient costs plus on-cost, fees and other payments.

10 Excludes amount paid by patients for pre-payment certificates.

11 Due to changes in the Dental Contract which came into force in October 1990 dentists are paid under a combination of headings relating to Capitation and Continuing Care patients. Prior to this, payment was simply on an item of service basis.

12 Excluding sight tests given in hospitals and under the school health service and in the home.

13 Relates to the number of vouchers supplied and excludes repair/replace spectacles.

14 Figures relate to the costs of the hospital, community health and personal social services,and have been estimated from financial year data.

15 Workforce figures are headcounts at 30th September and are taken from the HSC NI's Human Resources Management System.   All workforce figures have been revised and now exclude Home Helps, Bank staff, staff on career breaks, Chairperson / Members of Boards and staff with a whole-time equivalent equal to or less than 0.03. The Ancillary and Other staff category includes Ancillary & General/Support Services staff, Works & Maintenance/Estates staff and Ambulance staff for all years, and from 2008 also includes Generic staff who are multidisciplinary staff. Due to Agenda for Change, new grade codes were introduced (from 2007 onwards) which resulted in some staff moving between categories. Backward comparison of the workforce is therefore not advised due to variations in definitions.

Data used in this table can be found at - http://www.dhsspsni.gov.uk/index/stats_research/work_force/stats-hsc.htm

16.4 NHS Hospital & Community Health Service (HCHS) and General Practice workforce as at 30 September each specified year

England

Headcount

	2002	2003	2004	2005	2006	2007	2008	2009	2010 [1]	2011	2012
Total	**1,161,483**	**1,212,585**	**1,260,860**	**1,298,202**	**1,284,261**	**1,272,884**	**1,308,774**	**1,365,303**	**1,387,191**	**1,361,533**	**1,358,295**
Total HCHS medical and dental staff (incl HPCAs)	77,031	80,851	86,996	90,630	93,320	94,638	98,703	102,961	103,912	105,711	107,242
Total HCHS non-medical staff	949,748	992,530	1,030,800	1,063,121	1,038,368	1,027,299	1,060,629	1,110,138	1,109,195	1,083,637	1,075,035
Total GPs	32,292	33,564	34,855	35,944	36,008	36,420	37,720	40,269	39,409	39,780	40,265
Total GP Practice staff[6]	107,275	110,091	112,254	112,094	119,642	117,375	114,483	114,268	136,831	134,177	137,290
Professionally qualified clinical staff	**572,529**	**596,233**	**622,720**	**643,219**	**643,906**	**645,933**	**661,993**	**683,703**	**687,009**	**686,747**	**687,810**
All doctors [2]	**104,460**	**109,964**	**117,806**	**122,987**	**126,251**	**128,210**	**133,662**	**140,897**	**141,326**	**143,836**	**146,075**
Consultants (including Directors of public health)	27,070	28,750	30,650	31,993	32,874	33,674	34,910	36,950	37,752	39,088	40,394
Registrars	13,770	14,619	16,823	18,006	18,808	30,759	35,042	37,108	38,158	38,891	39,404
Other doctors in training and equivalents	21,145	22,701	24,874	26,305	27,461	16,024	14,136	14,394	14,034	14,018	13,952
Hospital practitioners and clinical assistants (non-dental specialties) [2]	4,863	4,451	4,045	3,587	3,077	2,848	2,761	2,333	2,148	1,782	1,547
Other medical and dental staff	10,183	10,330	10,604	10,739	11,100	11,333	11,854	12,176	12,223	12,292	12,302
GPs total	32,292	33,564	34,855	35,944	36,008	36,420	37,720	40,269	39,409	39,780	40,265
GP Providers	28,117	28,646	28,781	29,340	27,691	27,342	27,347	27,613	27,036	27,218	26,886
Other GPs	1,085	1,712	2,742	3,398	5,400	6,022	6,663	8,304	8,319	8,585	8,898
GP registrars [5]	1,980	2,235	2,562	2,564	2,278	2,491	3,203	3,881	3,880	4,013	4,426
GP retainers	1,110	971	770	642	639	565	507	471	419	365	321
Total qualified nursing staff [3]	**335,862**	**348,246**	**358,759**	**367,581**	**366,981**	**363,719**	**368,425**	**375,505**	**375,950**	**372,277**	**369,868**
Qualified nursing, midwifery & health visiting staff	314,879	326,579	336,615	344,677	343,184	340,859	346,377	353,570	352,104	348,693	346,410
GP practice nurses[6]	20,983	21,667	22,144	22,904	23,797	22,860	22,048	21,935	23,846	23,584	23,458
Total qualified scientific, therapeutic & technical staff	**116,598**	**122,066**	**128,883**	**134,534**	**134,498**	**136,976**	**142,455**	**149,379**	**151,607**	**152,216**	**153,472**
Qualified Allied Health Professions	59,415	62,189	65,515	67,841	67,483	68,687	71,301	73,953	74,374	74,647	74,902
Qualified Healthcare Scientists	23,824	25,649	28,242	30,046	30,453	30,158	30,925	32,161	31,972	31,481	31,173
Other qualified scientific, therapeutic & technical staff	33,359	34,228	35,126	36,647	36,562	38,131	40,229	43,265	45,337	46,167	47,490
Qualified ambulance staff [4]	**15,609**	**15,957**	**17,272**	**18,117**	**16,176**	**17,028**	**17,451**	**17,922**	**18,450**	**18,687**	**18,645**
Support to clinical staff	**312,731**	**327,463**	**336,044**	**344,971**	**334,713**	**324,249**	**334,929**	**352,800**	**356,410**	**347,064**	**343,927**
Support to doctors & nursing staff	255,305	265,549	271,389	279,193	267,934	259,547	266,070	278,390	279,522	271,384	269,714
Support to scientific, therapeutic & technical staff	48,030	52,230	55,025	55,715	54,307	53,259	55,792	60,048	62,726	62,057	61,345
Support to ambulance staff	9,396	9,684	9,630	10,063	12,472	11,443	13,067	14,362	14,738	14,238	13,451
NHS infrastructure support	**189,274**	**199,808**	**211,489**	**220,387**	**209,387**	**207,778**	**219,064**	**236,103**	**233,342**	**219,624**	**215,071**
Central functions	85,706	92,257	99,831	105,565	101,860	100,177	105,354	115,818	116,846	109,315	106,696
Hotel, property & estates	71,274	72,230	73,932	75,431	70,776	71,102	73,797	75,624	74,712	72,283	71,242
Manager & senior manager	32,294	35,321	37,726	39,391	36,751	36,499	39,913	44,661	41,962	38,214	37,314
Other non-medical staff or those with unknown classification	**657**	**657**	**497**	**435**	**410**	**409**	**353**	**364**	**356**	**266**	**237**
Other GP practice staff[6]	86,292	88,424	90,110	89,190	95,845	94,515	92,436	92,333	112,985	110,593	113,832

Notes:

1 The new headcount methodology is not fully comparable with data for years prior to 2010, due to improvements that make it a more stringent count of absolute staff numbers
  Headcount totals are unlikely to equal the sum of components. Further information on the headcount methodology is available in the Census publication.
2 In order to avoid double counting Hosptial Practitioners & Clinical Assistants (HPCAs) are excluded from the all doctors totals, as they are predominantly GPs that work part time in hospitals
  (applies to headcount data only).
3 Nursing and midwifery figures exclude students on training courses leading to a first qualification as a nurse or midwife.
4 In 2006 ambulance staff were collected under new, more detailed, occupation codes. As a result, qualified totals and support to ambulance staff totals are not directly comparable with previous years.
5 GP Registrar count from 2008 onwards represents an improvement in data collection processes and comparisons with previous years should be treated with caution
6 Practice staff counts for 2010 & 2011 have been revised to provide a 100% census, with estimated numbers for those practices with null returns. Further details can be found in the data quality
  statement/methodology. Note, this will affect any related totals and comparisons with years prior to 2010
From 2011 the bank staff return was suspended. All data (for all years) in these tables excludes bank staff

16.5 Staffing summary
Wales

	Unit (a)	2008	2009	2010	2011	2012
Directly employed NHS staff (b):						
Medical and dental staff (c):						
Hospital medical staff	Wte	5,272	5,237	5,330	5,468	5,525
Of which consultants	Wte	1,893	1,941	2,042	2,126	2,182
Community/Public health medical staff	Wte	102	81	75	78	82
Hospital dental staff	Wte	149	153	158	159	159
Of which consultants	Wte	40	41	45	45	48
Community/Public health dental staff	Wte	48	91	92	108	112
Total	**Wte**	**5,571**	**5,562**	**5,654**	**5,813**	**5,878**
Nursing, midwifery and health visiting staff (d)	Wte	27,806	28,199	28,168	27,999	28,080
of which qualified	Wte	21,426	21,585	21,823	21,733	21,779
Scientific, therapeutic and technical staff	Wte	10,843	11,202	11,483	11,450	11,542
Health care assistants and other support staff	Wte	9,488	9,920	10,049	9,711	9,796
Administration and estates staff	Wte	16,056	16,151	15,502	15,230	15,009
Ambulance staff	Wte	1,398	1,403	1,429	1,458	1,509
Other (e)	Wte	209	204	145	144	151
Unknown	Wte	96	96	14	13	4
Total	**Wte**	**71,467**	**72,737**	**72,444**	**71,817**	**71,969**
Family Practitioners:						
General medical practitioners (f)	Number	1,940	1,940	1,991	2,022	2,015
General dental practitioners (g)	Number	1,247	1,293	1,310	1,349	1,360
Ophthalmic medical practitioners (h)	Number	23	21	16	12	14
Ophthalmic opticians (h)	Number	711	690	740	756	795

(a) Wte = whole-time equivalent.

(b) At 30 September. The majority of the information on NHS staff has been obtained as a by-product of personnel systems. Some staff may be undergoing temporary regrading at the time and these staff are excluded from the figures.

(c) Excludes locum staff.

(d) Excludes pre-registration learners.

(e) Professional advisors and staff on general payments, eg Macmillan and Marie Curie nurses.

(f) At 30 September,except for 2009 which was counted at 1st October. All practitioners excluding GP registrars, GP Retainers and locums

(g) Number of dental performers who have any NHS activity recorded against them via FP17 claim forms at any time in the year ending 31 March.

(h) At 31 December.

16.6 Deaths[1]: underlying cause, sex and age-group, Summary

	England and Wales		2011		2012
ICD-10 code	Underlying cause (excludes deaths under 28 days for individual causes)		Age-group		Age-group
			All ages		All ages
A00-R99, U509, V01-Y89	All causes, all ages	M F	234,660 249,707	M F	240,238 259,093
	All causes, ages under 28 days	M F	1,288 915	M F	1,196 904
A00-R99, U509, V01-Y89	All causes, ages 28 days and over	M F	233,372 248,792	M F	239,042 258,189
A00-B99	I Certain infectious and parasitic diseases	M F	2,392 3,018	M F	2,271 2,838
C00-D48	II Neoplasms	M F	75,323 67,858	M F	76,695 68,700
D50-D89	III Diseases of the blood and blood-forming organs and certain disorders involving the immune mechanism	M F	442 557	M F	422 521
E00-E90	IV Endocrine, nutritional and metabolic diseases	M F	2,989 3,508	M F	3,132 3,578
F00-F99	V Mental and behavioural disorders	M F	10,088 20,960	M F	11,710 24,155
G00-G99	VI Diseases of the nervous system	M F	8,398 10,150	M F	9,499 11,674
H00-H59	VII Diseases of the eye and adnexa	M F	8 11	M F	11 9
H60-H95	VIII Diseases of the ear and mastoid process	M F	12 11	M F	14 7
I00-I99	IX Diseases of the circulatory system	M F	69,587 70,119	M F	69,516 71,846
J00-J99	X Diseases of the respiratory system	M F	32,033 35,657	M F	33,463 37,245
K00-K93	XI Diseases of the digestive system	M F	11,909 12,673	M F	11,766 12,807
L00-L99	XII Diseases of the skin and subcutaneous tissue	M F	553 1,106	M F	564 1,111
M00-M99	XIII Diseases of the musculoskeletal system and connective tissue	M F	1,391 2,789	M F	1,397 2,933
N00-N99	XIV Diseases of the genitourinary system	M F	3,935 5,565	M F	4,080 5,682
O00-O99	XV Pregnancy, childbirth and the puerperium	F	44	F	46
P00-P96	XVI Certain conditions originating in the perinatal period	M F	117 78	M F	114 91
Q00-Q99	XVII Congenital malformations, deformations and chromosomal abnormalities	M F	558 542	M F	595 554
R00-R99	XVIII Symptoms, signs and abnormal clinical and laboratory findings, not elsewhere classified	M F	2,624 7,569	M F	2,800 7,923
U509, V01-Y89	XX External causes of morbidity and mortality	M F	11,013 6,577	M F	10,993 6,469

1 Deaths registered in England and Wales

Source: Office for National Statistics

16.7a Notifications of infectious diseases

England and Wales

Year	1999	2000	2001	2002	2003	2004	2005	2006	2007	2008	2009	2010	2011	2012
Acute Meningitis	2094	2432	2623	1545	1472	1267	1381	1494	1251	1181	1219	922	538	522
Dysentery #	1538	1494	1388	1087	1047	1203	1237	1122	1217	1166	1218	267		
Enteric fever (typhoid or paratyphoid fever)												272	224	137
Food poisoning *	86316	86528	85468	72649	70895	70311	70407	70603	72382	68962	74974	57041	24384	20680
Malaria	1005	1128	1081	847	791	609	679	613	426	386	381	327	296	267
Measles	2438	2378	2250	3187	2488	2356	2089	3705	3670	5088	5191	2235	2355	4211
Meningococcal septicaemia	1822	1614	1238	842	732	691	721	657	673	528	495	367	261	301
Mumps	1691	2162	2741	1997	4204	16367	56256	12841	7196	7827	18629	10402	6888	7530
Ophthalmia neonatorum #	163	176	115	91	102	85	87	100	83	77	90	18		
Other												1068	611	670
Paratyphoid fever	125	79	129	84	99	134	119	185	126	170	130	33		
Rubella	1954	1653	1483	1660	1361	1287	1155	1221	1082	1096	1130	631	476	756
Scarlet fever	2086	1933	1756	2159	2553	2201	1678	2166	1948	2920	4176	2969	2719	4254
Tuberculosis x	6144	6572	6714	6753	6518	6723	7628	7621	6989	7319	7241	8333	9227	9101
Typhoid fever	151	125	121	91	176	146	179	201	208	240	210	68		
Viral hepatitis #	3424	3541	3388	3859	4004	3932	4109	4007	3857	4756	4979	1043		
Whooping cough	1139	712	888	883	409	504	594	550	1089	1512	1155	405	911	6557

No longer notifiable as from 6th April 2010, but may still be reported under Other disease

* Otherwise ascertained cases are no longer collected as from week 35 2010.

x Excludes chemoprophylaxis

16.7b Notifications of infectious diseases

Scotland

Notifiable Disease[1,2,3]	2001	2002	2003	2004	2005	2006	2007	2008	2009	2010	2011
Botulism	..	.. ..		.. ..	..		..	..	..	0	3
Anthrax	0	0	0	0	0	1	0	0	4	39	0
Brucellosis	..	..	..	..	..	..	..	..	..	1	1
Cholera	3	2	1	1	6	3	8	3	5	3	3
Clinical Syndrome E.coli O 157 infection	..	..	..	..	..	..	..	..	..	33	4
Diphtheria	0	0	0	0	0	0	1	0	0	0	0
Haemolytic Uraemic Syndrome (HUS)	..	..	..	..	..	..	..	..	..	5	3
Haemophilus influenzae type b (Hib)	..	..	..	..	..	..	..	..	..	3	6
Measles	315	399	181	257	186	259	168	219	172	93	82
Meningococcal disease	256	175	117	147	139	140	150	120	122	93	103
Mumps	155	259	181	3 595	5 698	2 917	2 741	720	1129	727	607
Necrotizing fasciitis	..	..	..	..	..	..	..	..	..	2	12
Paratyphoid	0	0	0	0	0	0	1	4	2	2	1
Pertussis (Whooping cough)	106	99	60	87	51	67	98	134	104	45	85
Poliomyelitis	0	0	0	0	0	0	0	0	0	0	0
Rabies	0	1	0	0	0	0	0	0	0	0	0
Rubella	234	292	130	222	141	153	146	106	93	39	21
Tetanus	0	1	1	1	1	0	0	0	0	0	0
Typhoid	3	4	2	2	1	3	3	3	1	6	3

.. Not available

1 Figures for all years are confirmed notifications

2 The following diseases were also notifiable but there were no cases in 2011: Plague, Severe Acute Respiratory Syndrome (SARS), Smallpox, Tularemia,

Viral haemorrhagic fevers, West Nile fever, Yellow fever

3 From 2010 the following diseases are no longer notifiable - Bacillary dysentery, Chickenpox, Erysipelas, Food poisoning, Legionellosis, Leptospirosis, Lyme disease, Malaria,

Puerperal fever, Scarlet fever, Toxoplasmosis, Typhus fever and Viral hepatitis

Source: HPS SIDSS2

Queries to: patriciacassels@nhs.net (tel 0141 300 1148)

16.7c Notifications of Infectious diseases
Northern Ireland

Description	2010	2011	2012
Acute Encephalitis/Meningitis Bacterial	49	28	37
Acute Encephalitis/Meningitis Viral	11	13	10
Anthrax	0	0	0
Chickenpox	2111	1566	2126
Cholera	0	0	0
Diphtheria	0	0	0
Dysentery	6	7	11
Food Poisoning	1550	1575	1777
Gastroenteritis (< 2years)	18089	661	799
Hepatitis A	4	0	4
Hepatitis B	90	129	130
Hepatitis Unspecified	0	0	0
Legionnaires' Disease	4	4	6
Leptospirosis	0	3	3
Malaria	6	1	5
Measles	72	27	43
Meningococcal Septicaemia	38	45	33
Mumps	212	123	298
Paratyphoid Fever	0	0	0
Plague	0	0	0
Poliomyelitis (Acute)	0	0	0
Poliomyelitis (Paralytic)	0	0	0
Rabies	0	0	0
Relapsing Fever	0	0	0
Rubella	18	18	13
Scarlet Fever	154	130	196
Smallpox	0	0	0
Tetanus	0	1	1
Tuberculosis (Non Pulmonary)	32	14	45
Tuberculosis (Pulmonary)	34	44	51
Typhoid	1	1	1
Typhus	0	0	0
Viral Haemorraghic Fever	0	0	2
Whooping Cough	18	18	394
Yellow Fever	0	0	0

Public Health Agency, Northern Ireland

16.8a Work-related and occupational respiratory disease: estimated number of cases reported by chest physicians to SWORD 2006-2011 and by occupational physicians to OPRA 2006-2010 by sex and diagnostic category

Sex	Diagnostic category	Chest physicians (SWORD)						Occupational Physicians (OPRA)				
		2006	2007	2008	2009	2010	2011	2006	2007	2008	2009	2010
All cases (b)	Allergic alveolitis	47	19	87	39	29	25	-	-	-	13	-
	Asthma	451	251	307	181	205	159	145	104	55	47	65
	Bronchitis/emphysema	65	15	18	69	18	52	-	2	12	-	-
	Infectious diseases	49	28	24	25	2	60	2	36	-	24	12
	Inhalation accidents	16	5	38	50	3	14	4	16	1	-	50
	Lung cancer	82	104	91	86	71	133	2	-	-	-	-
	Malignant mesothelioma	637	884	611	559	522	472	16	1	14	-	-
	Benign pleural disease	1281	1008	1114	893	790	831	12	-	-	12	1
	Pneumoconiosis	194	167	145	208	110	224	3	5	-	-	-
	Other	53	81	56	100	61	105	47	114	80	77	30
	Total diagnoses	2875	2562	2491	2210	1811	2075	231	278	162	173	158
	Total cases (a)	2829	2534	2442	2135	1760	2009	230	278	161	172	157

(a) Individuals may have more than one diagnosis.
(b) May not equal males plus females because sex is not recorded for some cases.
(c) The OPRA scheme is no longer running, therefore the latest figures shown are for 2010.
"-" means zero.
(p) Provisional data.

16.8b Work-related mental ill-health: estimated number of cases reported by psychiatrists to SOSMI and by occupational physicians to OPRA, by sex and diagnostic category, 2005-2009**

Sex	Diagnostic Category	Psychiatrists and Occupational Physicians (c)					Psychiatrists (SOSMI)					Occupational Physicians (OPRA)				
		2005	2006	2007	2008	2009(p)	2005	2006	2007	2008	2009(p)	2005	2006	2007	2008	2009(p)
All	Anxiety/Depression	3905	3515	3102	2843	2689	1607	1288	914	1005	857	2298	2227	2188	1838	1832
Cases	Post-traumatic stress disorder	381	299	287	93	212	264	246	184	61	158	117	53	103	32	54
(b)	Other work-related stress	2158	2133	2522	2029	1901	144	135	100	95	86	2014	1998	2422	1934	1815
	Alcohol or drug abuse	259	289	139	149	142	220	214	87	123	94	39	75	52	26	48
	Psychotic episode	64	15	86	50	49	63	15	86	50	37	1	-	-	-	12
	Other problems	208	305	294	302	178	155	185	150	163	121	53	120	144	139	57
	Total number of diagnoses	6975	6556	6430	5466	5171	2453	2083	1521	1497	1353	4522	4473	4909	3969	3818
	Total number of individuals (a)	6396	5916	5909	5196	4734	2223	1975	1421	1420	1274	4173	3941	4488	3776	3460

(a) Individuals may have more than one diagnosis.
(b) May not equal males plus females because sex is not recorded for some cases.
(c) Reports by psychiatrists to SOSMI began in January 1999.
"-" means zero.
(p) Provisional

The SOSMI and OPRA schemes are no longer running. The latest figures shown in the table were released in 2010.
** For 2010 data onwards, see THOR tables on the following page

16.8c Work-related skin disease: estimated number of cases reported by dermatologists to EPIDERM 2006 - 2011 and by occupational physicians to OPRA 2006 - 2010, by sex and diagnostic category

Sex	Diagnostic category	Dermatologists (EPIDERM)						Occupational physicians (OPRA) (c)				
		2006	2007	2008	2009	2010	2011	2006	2007	2008	2009	2010
All cases(b)	Contact dermatitis	1788	1386	1325	1423	1281	1208	596	488	322	373	342
	Contact urticaria	120	73	43	44	55	38	26	15	13	14	13
	Folliculitis /acne	16	11	17	3	-	1	-	-	1	-	-
	Infective skin disease	16	3	2	13	14	1	-	14	36	2	12
	Mechanical skin disease	82	8	9	18	18	14	1	-	1	12	-
	Nail conditions	3	25	13	13	1	-	-				-
	Skin neoplasia	759	622	418	492	390	231	-	-			-
	Other dermatoses	58	35	30	72	30	72	68	40	36	40	37
	Total number of diagnoses	2842	2163	1857	2078	1789	1565	691	557	409	441	404
	Total number of individuals[a]	2805	2137	1839	2015	1745	1550	679	556	409	440	392

(a) Individuals may have more than one diagnosis.
(b) May not equal males plus females because sex is not recorded for some cases.
(c) The OPRA scheme is no longer running, therefore the latest figures shown are for 2010.
"-" means zero.
(p) - provisional data.

16.8d Work-related musculoskeletal disorders: estimated number of cases reported by rheumatologists to MOSS and by occupational physicians to OPRA, by sex and diagnostic category, 2005-2009**

Sex	Diagnostic Category	Rheumatologists and Occupational					Rheumatologists (MOSS)					Occupational Physicians (OPRA)				
		2005	2006	2007	2008	2009(p)	2005	2006	2007	2008	2009(p)	2005	2006	2007	2008	2009(p)
All Cases (a)	Upper Limb disorders*	3654	3328	2391	2209	2044	1521	1503	1049	1121	734	2133	1825	1342	1088	1310
	Raynauds/HAV/VWF	633	622	290	266	621	129	139	62	66	29	504	483	228	200	592
	Other Hand/wrist/arm	1927	1652	1287	1336	830	923	809	663	784	418	1004	843	624	552	412
	Elbow	622	545	400	393	318	333	363	234	251	198	289	182	166	142	120
	Shoulder	528	543	524	258	328	168	213	174	63	129	360	330	350	195	199
	Spine/back disorders*	1761	1348	1243	1139	708	447	392	297	227	208	1314	956	946	912	500
	Neck/thoracic spine	562	407	427	355	201	253	225	165	86	121	309	182	262	269	80
	Lumbar spine/trunk	1247	968	830	796	521	219	169	132	141	101	1028	799	698	655	420
	Lower Limbs*	441	406	487	225	328	122	158	150	125	134	319	248	337	100	194
	Hip/knee/leg	284	258	370	168	167	85	82	102	76	61	199	176	268	92	106
	Ankle/foot	181	148	117	33	161	61	76	48	25	73	120	72	69	8	88
	Others	221	204	149	191	145	33	55	28	41	40	188	149	121	150	105
	Total number of diagnoses**	6205	5347	4394	3796	3292	2204	2131	1608	1533	1170	4001	3216	2786	2263	2122
	Total number of individuals	5932	5160	4226	3646	3154	2064	2036	1521	1469	1060	3868	3124	2705	2177	2094

*For each group of disorders, totals for main disease categories may be less than the sum of the disease subcategories. This is because an individual may have more than one (for example) upper limb disorder (diagnosis) which would only be counted once in the 'upper limb disorders' total.

** The total cases may be less than the sum of the major disease categories. This is because an individual may have more than one major category disorder (e.g. upper limb and spine/back) but this would only count once in the 'total cases'.

(a) May not equal males plus females because sex is not recorded for some cases

"-" Means zero

".." Denotes not available

(p) Provisional

The MOSS and OPRA schemes are no longer running. The latest figures shown in the table were released in 2010
** For 2010 data onwards, see THOR tables below

** THOR GP is a surveillance scheme in which general practitioners (GPs) are asked to report new cases of work-related ill health.

Work-related Mental ill-health cases reported to THOR-GP by diagnosis 2010 to 2012

Mental ill-health diagnoses	Estimated number* of cases reported to THOR-GP 2010 to 2012	% of all diagnoses
Anxiety/depression	1363	42
PTSD	36	1
Other stress	1664	51
Alcohol & drug abuse	36	1
Other diagnoses	24	1
Other stress symptoms	138	4
Total diagnoses	3261	100
Total cases	3225	

*Estimated cases without core:sample weighting

Work-related Musculoskeletal cases reported to THOR-GP by anatomical site 2010 to 2012

Anatomical site	Estimated number* of cases reported to THOR-GP 2010 to 2012	% of all diagnoses
Hand/wrist/arm	754	18
Elbow	481	11
Shoulder	413	10
Neck/thoracic spine	439	10
Lumbar spine/trunk	1375	33
Hip/knee	359	8
Ankle/foot	244	6
Other	160	4
Total diagnoses	4225	100
Total cases	4027	

*Estimated cases without core:sample weighting

16.9 Deaths due to occupationally related lung disease Great Britain

Numbers

		1998	1999	2000	2001	2002	2003	2004	2005	2006	2007	2008	2009	2010	2011(p)
Asbestosis (without mesothelioma)[1,3]	KADY	165	171	186	233	234	236	268	303	327	320	367	412	414	429
Mesothelioma[2]	KADZ	1,541	1,615	1,633	1,860	1,867	1,887	1,978	2,049	2,060	2,176	2,265	2336	2360	2291
Pneumoconiosis (other than asbestosis)	KAEA	268	321	279	240	271	231	214	194	167	149	139	149	134	152
Byssinosis	KAEB	5	6	4	2	-	3	4	3	5	2	1	2	2	1
Farmer's lung and other occupational allergic alveolitis	KAEC	8	9	7	7	6	7	5	13	10	5	7	7	8	9
Total	KAED	1,987	2,122	2,109	2,342	2,378	2,364	2,469	2,562	2,569	2,652	2,779	2,906	2,918	2882

(p) Provisional

Sources: Office for National Statistics;
Health and Safety Executive

1 By definition every case of asbestosis is due to asbestos; the association with mesothelioma is also very strong, though there is thought to be a low natural background incidence.

2 For the inclusion into the Mesothelioma register the cause of death on the death certificate must mention the word Mesothelioma.

3 For inclusion into the Asbestosis register the cause of death on the death certificate must mention the word Asbestosis.

Link used to obtain data: http://www.hse.gov.uk/statistics/tables/dc01.xls

This information has been extracted from the disease pages located at - http://www.hse.gov.uk/statistics/causdis/index.htm

To find the dates of the latest and upcoming publications for HSE - http://www.hse.gov.uk/statistics/index.

16.10 Reported injuries to employees and the self-employed in Great Britain, by detailed industry and severity of injury, 2011/12

Detailed industry description +	Section	Division	Employees								Self-employed			
			Fatal injuries	Non-fatal major injuries	Over-3-day injuries	Total injuries	Fatal injury rate per 100 000 employees	Major injury rate per 100 000 employees	Over-3-day injury rate per 100 000 employees	All reported injuries rate per 100 000 employees	Fatal injuries	Non-fatal major injuries	Over-3-day injuries	Total injuries
Agriculture, Forestry and Fishing (a)	A	01-03	13	376	734	1 123	8.7	250.3	488.7	747.7	22	58	19	99
Crop and animal production, hunting and related service activities	A	01	10	316	565	891	7.4	233.5	417.5	658.4	17	46	10	73
Forestry and logging	A	02	2	46	105	153	20.9	479.6	1 094.7	1 595.1	4	11	8	23
Fishing and aquaculture (a)	A	03	1	14	64	79	..	..	..	..	1	1	1	3
Mining and Quarrying	B	05-09	10	105	335	450	11.2	117.6	375.2	504.0	-	3	2	5
Mining of coal and lignite	B	05	5	33	197	235	..	..	..	..	-	-	-	-
Extraction of crude petroleum and natural gas	B	06	3	29	68	100	19.1	184.8	433.3	637.2	-	1	1	2
Mining of metal ores	B	07	-	-	1	1	-	-	..	..	-	-	-	-
Other mining and quarrying	B	08	2	34	53	89	10.5	179.0	279.1	468.7	-	2	-	2
Mining support service activities	B	09	-	9	16	25	-	19.2	34.2	53.4	-	-	1	1
Manufacturing	C	10-33	27	3 514	14 633	18 174	1.0	135.8	565.4	702.2	3	89	89	181
Manufacture of food products	C	10	5	695	3 776	4 476	1.6	216.5	1 176.3	1 394.3	2	11	16	29
Manufacture of beverages	C	11	-	56	317	373	-	102.1	577.8	679.9	-	5	3	8
Manufacture of tobacco products	C	12	-	2	7	9	-	..	..	..	-	-	-	-
Manufacture of textiles	C	13	1	72	241	314	2.2	161.7	541.1	705.1	-	1	4	5
Manufacture of wearing apparel	C	14	-	6	15	21	-	21.4	53.4	74.8	-	-	-	-
Manufacture of leather and related products	C	15	-	1	32	33	-	9.5	303.1	312.6	-	1	-	1
Manufacture of wood and of products of wood and cork, except furniture; manufacture of articles of straw and plaiting materials	C	16	1	160	493	654	1.9	305.0	939.9	1 246.8	-	8	7	15
Manufacture of paper and paper products	C	17	1	89	303	393	1.8	159.1	541.6	702.4	-	-	-	-
Printing and reproduction of recorded media	C	18	-	101	395	496	-	86.2	337.3	423.5	-	3	-	3
Manufacture of coke and refined petroleum products	C	19	-	19	28	47	-	58.2	85.8	144.0	-	-	-	-
Manufacture of chemicals and chemical products	C	20	-	96	329	425	-	88.6	303.6	392.2	-	1	2	3
Manufacture of basic pharmaceutical products and pharmaceutical preparations	C	21	-	36	171	207	-	36.2	172.0	208.2	-	1	-	1
Manufacture of rubber and plastic products	C	22	1	201	865	1 067	0.7	148.7	639.9	789.3	-	4	2	6
Manufacture of non-metallic mineral products	C	23	1	135	478	614	1.2	161.8	572.9	735.9	-	5	7	12
Manufacture of basic metals	C	24	3	232	735	970	3.5	269.7	854.6	1 127.8	-	3	4	7
Manufacture of fabricated metal products, except machinery and equipment	C	25	5	420	1 388	1 813	2.4	200.6	662.9	865.8	1	12	11	24
Manufacture of computer, electronic and optical products	C	26	-	33	109	142	-	17.9	59.1	77.0	-	1	-	1
Manufacture of electrical equipment	C	27	1	51	291	343	1.3	64.1	365.6	431.0	-	1	2	3
Manufacture of machinery and equipment not elsewhere classified	C	28	1	177	645	823	0.4	78.1	284.6	363.1	-	3	3	6
Manufacture of motor vehicles, trailers and semi-trailers	C	29	1	155	697	853	0.6	89.9	404.4	495.0	-	8	2	10
Manufacture of other transport equipment	C	30	3	113	488	604	1.9	71.0	306.5	379.4	-	1	3	4
Manufacture of furniture	C	31	-	79	349	428	-	110.3	487.2	597.5	-	4	3	7
Other manufacturing	C	32	-	455	1 983	2 438	-	568.1	2 475.9	3 044.0	-	11	13	24
Repair and installation of machinery and equipment	C	33	3	130	498	631	1.8	76.5	293.2	371.5	-	5	7	12
Electricity, Gas, Steam and Air Conditioning Supply	D	35	-	118	290	408	-	65.9	162.0	227.9	-	5	4	9
Water Supply; Sewerage; Waste Management and Remediation Activities	E	36-39	4	614	2 658	3 276	1.9	288.0	1 246.7	1 536.6	2	19	18	39
Water collection, treatment and supply	E	36	-	52	197	249	-	88.3	334.6	423.0	-	2	3	5
Sewerage	E	37	-	32	131	163	-	219.2	897.2	1 116.4	-	-	1	1
Waste collection, treatment and disposal activities; materials recovery	E	38	4	512	2 268	2 784	3.4	437.8	1 939.3	2 380.5	1	16	11	28
Remediation activities and other waste management services	E	39	-	18	62	80	-	79.0	272.2	351.3	1	1	3	5
Construction	F	41-43	25	2 124	5 014	7 163	1.9	163.7	386.4	552.0	23	638	740	1 401
Construction of buildings	F	41	8	624	1 495	2 127	1.6	127.3	304.9	433.8	8	297	422	727
Civil engineering	F	42	2	309	706	1 017	0.8	124.6	284.7	410.1	1	46	38	85
Specialised construction activities	F	43	15	1 191	2 813	4 019	2.7	212.9	502.9	718.6	14	295	280	589
Service industries	G-U	45-99	35	15 243	65 541	80 819	0.2	75.5	324.4	400.1	7	268	284	559
Wholesale and retail trade and repair of motor vehicles and motorcycles	G	45	3	368	1 025	1 396	0.8	103.4	288.0	392.2	3	6	9	18
Wholesale trade, except of motor vehicles and motorcycles	G	46	4	353	1 371	1 728	0.6	53.6	208.1	262.2	-	6	6	12
Retail trade, except of motor vehicles and motor-cycles	G	47	2	1 742	7 512	9 256	0.1	68.7	296.1	364.9	-	14	15	29
Land transport and transport via pipelines	H	49	5	959	4 534	5 498	1.0	183.0	865.0	1 049.0	1	10	11	22
Water transport (b)	H	50	-	46	209	255	-	130.1	591.1	721.2	-	-	1	1
Air transport	H	51	-	113	1 127	1 240	-	194.8	1 943.3	2 138.2	-	2	-	2
Warehousing and support actvities for transportation	H	52	2	813	4 927	5 742	0.7	268.1	1 624.7	1 893.5	-	21	48	69
Postal and courier activities	H	53	1	518	2 944	3 463	0.4	195.8	1 112.9	1 309.1	-	12	9	21
Accommodation	I	55	-	393	1 512	1 905	-	129.8	499.5	629.3	-	8	9	17
Food and beverage service activities	I	56	-	743	3 813	4 556	-	71.2	365.4	436.6	1	8	16	25
Publishing activities	J	58	-	13	47	60	-	7.8	28.1	35.8	-	1	-	1
Motion picture, video and television programme production, sound recording and music publishing activities	J	59	-	28	68	96	-	44.0	106.7	150.7	-	7	10	17
Programming and broadcasting activities	J	60	-	19	38	57	-	38.0	76.1	114.1	-	5	2	7
Telecommunications	J	61	-	87	491	578	-	53.6	302.3	355.8	-	3	2	5
Computer programming, consultancy and related activities	J	62	1	21	53	75	0.2	5.2	13.2	18.6	-	-	1	1
Information service activities	J	63	-	18	89	107	-	68.8	340.0	408.8	-	2	2	4
Financial service activities, except insurance and pension funding	K	64	-	152	475	627	-	28.3	88.4	116.7	-	1	2	3
Insurance, reinsurance and pension funding, except compulsory social security	K	65	-	24	76	100	-	10.7	34.0	44.7	-	-	-	-
Activities auxiliary to financial services and insurance activities	K	66	-	26	78	104	-	8.3	24.9	33.2	-	1	-	1
Real estate activities	L	68	1	185	725	911	0.4	77.3	303.1	380.8	-	7	2	9
Legal and accounting activities	M	69	-	35	82	117	-	9.7	22.7	32.4	-	2	-	2
Activities of head offices; management consultancy activities	M	70	-	32	52	84	-	11.3	18.4	29.7	-	-	2	2
Architectural and engineering activities; technical testing and analysis	M	71	2	101	215	318	0.5	27.1	57.7	85.4	-	5	3	8
Scientific research and development	M	72	-	23	67	90	-	22.4	65.4	87.8	-	-	1	1
Advertising and market research	M	73	-	6	38	44	-	4.4	27.7	32.1	-	2	-	2
Other professional, scientific and technical activities	M	74	-	40	66	106	-	34.0	56.1	90.1	-	2	1	3
Veterinary activities	M	75	-	50	77	127	-	125.2	192.8	318.0	-	-	1	1
Rental and leasing activities	N	77	1	152	376	529	1.0	155.0	383.5	539.6	-	7	3	10
Employment activities	N	78	2	306	672	980	1.0	158.9	348.9	508.8	-	10	22	32
Travel agency, tour operator and other reservation service and related activities	N	79	-	13	18	31	-	14.4	20.0	34.4	-	-	-	-
Security and investigation activities	N	80	1	148	593	742	0.6	88.0	352.5	441.1	-	4	6	10
Services to buildings and landscape activities	N	81	3	463	1 983	2 449	0.8	125.9	539.4	666.2	2	30	17	49
Office administrative, office support and other business support activities	N	82	1	151	547	699	0.6	86.7	314.0	401.3	-	6	5	11
Public administration and defence; compulsory social security	O	84	2	1 636	6 695	8 333	0.1	90.1	368.8	459.0	-	4	8	12
Education	P	85	1	1 854	5 015	6 870	..	64.3	174.1	238.4	-	19	13	32
Human health activities	Q	86	1	1 592	10 333	11 926	0.1	83.5	542.1	625.7	-	5	15	20
Residential care activities	Q	87	-	753	3 713	4 466	-	97.8	482.4	580.2	-	8	5	13
Social work activities without accommodation	Q	88	-	470	1 928	2 398	-	51.8	212.6	264.4	-	6	1	7
Creative, arts and entertainment activities	R	90	1	72	192	265	2.3	168.7	449.9	620.9	-	11	20	31
Libraries, archives, museums and other cultural activities	R	91	-	54	175	229	-	52.6	170.4	222.9	-	1	-	1
Gambling and betting activities	R	92	-	47	142	189	-	56.6	171.0	227.6	-	2	-	2
Sports activities and amusement and recreation activities	R	93	1	454	897	1 352	0.3	116.5	230.2	347.0	-	20	12	32
Activities of membership organisations	S	94	-	61	155	216	-	24.4	62.1	86.6	-	4	1	5
Repair of computers and personal and household goods	S	95	-	20	85	105	-	34.2	145.2	179.4	-	-	-	-
Other personal service activities	S	96	-	89	303	392	-	39.9	135.7	175.6	-	3	2	5
Activities of households as employers of domestic personnel	T	97	-	-	-	-	-	-	-	-	-	-	-	-
Undifferentiated goods- and services-producing activities of private households for own use	T	98	-	-	5	5	-	-	49.1	49.1	-	3	1	4
Activities of extraterritorial organisations and bodies	U	99	-	-	3	3	-	-	6.4	6.4	-	-	-	-
All industries	A-U	01-99	114	22 094	89 205	111 413	0.5	88.5	357.4	446.4	57	1 080	1 156	2 293

Source: RIDDOR - Reporting of Injuries, Diseases and Dangerous Occurrences Regulations 1995
From September 2011 reporting arrangements changed: Summary of the effects to statistics for 2011/12 onwards

+ HSE is now recording and publishing data in Standard Industrial Classification (SIC) 2007 format. Data from previous years which was collected in the SIC1992/2003 formats has been computer recoded to the SIC2007 coding to allow comparisons over time. However, there may be errors as a result of this recoding and care should be taken when interpreting trends over time. Inconsistencies are most likely to be visible in data between 2008/09 and 2009/10. For more information see: www.hse.gov.uk/statistics/industry/sic2007.htm

a) Excludes sea fishing.
b) Injuries arising from shore-based services only. Excludes incidents reported under merchant shipping legislation.
.. Employment numbers are too small to provide reliable rate estimates.

Employment data
The Annual Population Survey (APS) is the source of employment data for this document.
For more information please go to: www.hse.gov.uk/statistics/sources.htm#employment

this page is intentionally blank

Prices

Chapter 17

Prices

**Producer price index numbers
(Tables 17.1 and 17.2)**

The producer price indices (PPIs) were published for the first time in August 1983, replacing the former wholesale price indices. Full details of the differences between the two indices were given in an article published in British Business, 15 April 1983. The producer price indices are calculated using the same general methodology as that used by the wholesale price indices.

The high level index numbers in Tables 17.1 and 17.2 are constructed on a net sector basis. That is to say, they are intended to measure only transactions between the sector concerned and other sectors. Within-sector transactions are excluded. Index numbers for the whole of manufacturing are thus not weighted averages of sector index numbers.

The index numbers for selected industries in Tables 17.1 and 17.2 are constructed on a gross sector basis, that is, all transactions are included in deriving the weighting patterns, including sales within the same industry.

Producer Prices has implemented the change to the Standard Industrial Classification 2007 (SIC 2007). The most significant change to PPI output prices involves the reclassification of 'recovered secondary raw materials' and 'publishing'. These are no longer classified in the manufacturing sector, but are classified under services. In addition to this, a new SIC division, 'repair, installation and maintenance of machinery and equipment' has been created. Under SIC 2003 these activities were classified within the output of manufacturing, but as part of the specific industries where this activity took place.

Fundamental changes have been made to the classification of the PPI Trade surveys, Import Price indices (IPI) and Export Price Indices (EPI). As part of the reclassification project the classification of these trade surveys have become compliant with Eurostat's Short Term Statistics Regulation. The collection of IPI and EPI will now be on an SIC basis, a switch from the Standard International Trade Classification (SITC) and Combined Nomenclature (CN) previously used. PPI input prices are heavily dependant on IPI.

Further details are available from the Office for National Statistics website: www.ons.gov.uk.

Purchasing power of the pound
(Table 17.3)

Changes in the internal purchasing power of a currency may be defined as the 'inverse' of changes in the levels of prices; when prices go up, the amount which can be purchased with a given sum of money goes down. Movements in the internal purchasing power of the pound are based on the consumers' expenditure deflator (CED) prior to 1962 and on the general index of retail prices (RPI) from January 1962 onwards. The CED shows the movement in prices implied by the national accounts estimates of consumers' expenditure valued at current and at constant prices, while the RPI is constructed directly by weighting together monthly movements in prices according to a given pattern of household expenditure derived from the Expenditure and Food Survey. If the purchasing power of the pound is taken to be 100p in a particular month (quarter, year), the comparable purchasing power in a subsequent month (quarter, year) is:

$$100 \times \frac{\text{earlier period price index}}{\text{later period price index}}$$

where the price index used is the CED for years 1946–1961

Consumer prices index
(Table 17.4)

The CPI is the main UK domestic measure of consumer price inflation for macroeconomic purposes. It forms the basis for the Government's target for inflation that the Bank of England's Monetary Policy Committee (MPC) is required to achieve. From April 2011 the CPI is also being used for the indexation of benefits, tax credits and public service pensions. The uprating is based on the 12-month change in the September CPI.

Internationally, the CPI is known as the Harmonised Index of Consumer Prices (HICP). HICPs are calculated in each Member State of the European Union, according to rules specified in a series of European regulations developed by Eurostat in conjunction with the EU Member States. HICPs are used to compare inflation rates across the European Union. Since January 1999, the HICP has also been used by the European Central Bank (ECB) as the measure of price stability across the euro area.

The official CPI series starts in 1996 but estimates for earlier periods are available back to 1988. These estimates are broadly consistent with data from 1996 but should be treated with some caution.

A full description of how the CPI is compiled is given in the Consumer Price Indices Technical Manual at: www.ons.gov.uk/ons/guide-method/user-guidance/prices/cpi-and-rpi/index.html

Retail prices index
(Table 17.5)

The all items retail prices index (RPI) is the most long-standing general purpose measure of inflation in the UK. Historically the uses of the RPI include the indexation of various prices and incomes and the uprating of pensions, state benefits and index-linked gilts, as well as the revalorisation of excise duties. Please note, though, that from April 2011 the CPI is being used to uprate benefits, tax credits and public service pensions. RPI data are available back to 1947 but have been re-referenced on several occasions since then, generally accompanied by changes to the coverage and/or structure of the detailed sub-components.

A full description of how the RPI is compiled is given in the Consumer Price Indices Technical Manual at: www.ons.gov.uk/ons/guide-method/user-guidance/prices/cpi-and-rpi/index.html

Further details are available from the Office for National Statistics website: www.ons.gov.uk/ons/taxonomy/index.html?nscl=Price+Indices+and+Inflation

Tax and price index (TPI)
(Table 17.6)

The purpose and methodology of the TPI were described in an article in the August 1979 issue (No. 310) of Economic Trends. The TPI measures the change in gross taxable income needed for taxpayers to maintain their purchasing power, allowing for changes in retail prices. The TPI thus takes account of the changes to direct taxes (and employees' National Insurance (NI) contributions) faced by a representative cross-section of taxpayers as well as changes in the retail prices index (RPI).
When direct taxation or employees' NI contributions change, the TPI will rise by less than or more than the RPI according to the type of changes made. Between Budgets, the monthly increase in the TPI is normally slightly larger than that in the RPI, since all the extra income needed to offset any rise in retail prices is fully taxed.

Index numbers of agricultural prices
(Tables 17.7 and 17.8)

The indices of producer prices of agricultural products are currently based on the calendar year 2005. They are designed to provide short-term and medium-term indications of movements in these prices. All annual series are baseweighted Laspeyres type, using value weights derived from the Economic Accounts for Agriculture prepared for the Statistical Office of the European Union. Prices are measured exclusive of VAT. For Table 17.7, it has generally been necessary to measure the prices of materials (inputs) ex-supplier. For Table 17.8, it has generally been necessary to measure the prices received by producers (outputs) at the first marketing stage. The construction of the indices enables them to be combined with similar indices for other member countries of the EU to provide an overall indication of trends within the Union which appears in the Union's Eurostat series of publications.

Index numbers at a more detailed level and for earlier based series are available from the Department for Environment, Food and Rural Affairs, Room 309, Foss House, Kingspool 1–2 Peasholme Green, York, YO1 7PX, tel 01904 456561

17.1 Producer Price Index (2010=100, SIC2007)

Net Sector Input Price Indices of Materials & Fuel purchased

	6207000050: NSI - All Manufacturing including CCL	6207000010: NSI - All Manufacturing, materials only	6207000060: NSI - Fuel Purchased by Manufacturing Industry including CCL	6207990050: NSI - Materials & Fuels Purchased other than FBTP Industries, NSA	6207998950: NSI - All Manufacturing excl FBTP (incl CCL) - SA	6207990010: NSI - Materials Purchased other than FBTP Industries, NSA
	K646 NSA	K644 NSA	K647 NSA	K655 NSA	K658 SA	K653 NSA
2009	92.6	90.9	107.4	95.5	95.6	93.6
2010	100.0	100.0	100.0	100.0	100.0	100.0
2011	114.5	115.1	109.7	109.1	109.1	109.1
2012	116.0	115.9	117.6	108.9	108.9	107.5
2011 JAN	108.8	109.0	107.6	106.0	105.4	105.8
FEB	110.0	110.5	106.5	106.3	105.5	106.4
MAR	113.3	113.9	109.1	107.5	106.1	107.4
APR	116.5	117.5	107.9	108.9	108.3	109.2
MAY	115.2	116.1	108.1	109.4	109.0	109.7
JUN	115.4	116.5	107.3	109.5	109.9	110.0
JUL	116.0	117.1	107.8	110.0	110.7	110.5
AUG	114.3	115.2	107.3	110.0	111.0	110.5
SEP	116.4	117.7	106.2	110.6	111.6	111.4
OCT	115.8	116.2	112.9	110.3	110.9	110.0
NOV	116.2	116.3	116.7	110.4	110.8	109.5
DEC	115.8	115.6	118.8	110.0	110.0	108.7
2012 JAN	115.8	115.7	117.7	110.1	109.6	109.0
FEB	118.3	118.1	121.1	111.0	110.0	109.5
MAR	119.8	120.2	117.4	110.9	109.4	110.1
APR	118.3	118.5	117.4	110.1	109.3	109.0
MAY	115.5	115.6	115.3	108.9	108.6	107.9
JUN	113.4	113.3	114.4	108.4	108.8	107.5
JUL	113.1	113.1	113.3	107.3	108.0	106.4
AUG	115.1	115.5	112.3	107.1	108.0	106.3
SEP	115.0	115.0	116.1	107.2	108.2	105.8
OCT	115.6	115.3	119.5	108.0	108.6	106.2
NOV	116.0	115.3	122.8	108.6	108.9	106.3
DEC	116.3	115.4	124.5	108.7	108.9	106.2
2013 JAN	117.7	117.1	123.8	109.9	109.6	107.7
FEB	120.7	120.4	124.0	112.1	111.2	110.1
MAR	120.9	120.0	129.9	112.7	111.3	110.0
APR	118.6	117.6	127.3	111.1	110.4	108.6
MAY	117.1	116.6	121.9	109.3	109.2	107.2
JUN	116.8	116.4	120.4	108.4	108.9	106.4

17.1 Producer Price Index (2010=100, SIC2007)

Gross Sector Price Indices of Materials & Fuel purchased

	6107113140: GSI Sub-section - Inputs for Manuf of Textiles & Textile products	6107215000: GSI (excl. CCL) - Inputs for Manuf of Leather & Related products	6107216000: GSI (excl. CCL) - Inputs for Manuf of Wood & products of Wood/Cork	6107117180: GSI Sub-section - Inputs for Manuf of Pulp, Paper & Paper products	6107219000: GSI (excl. CCL) - Inputs for Manuf of Coke & Refined Petroleum products	6107120000: GSI Sub-section - Inputs for Manuf of Chemicals, Chemical products	6107222000: GSI (excl. CCL) - Inputs for Manufacture of Rubber/Plastic products
	MC36 NSA	MC3O NSA	MC3P NSA	MC39 NSA	MC3R NSA	MC3B NSA	MB4R NSA
2009	97.4	97.5	94.9	98.3	78.1	95.8	95.2
2010	100.0	100.0	100.0	100.0	100.0	100.0	100.0
2011	108.2	108.8	106.3	106.9	133.4	111.5	108.7
2012	110.4	110.7	108.5	107.4	136.9	111.8	108.9
2011 JAN	104.7	104.1	103.6	104.0	118.2	107.6	105.6
FEB	104.7	104.9	104.0	104.1	122.2	107.4	105.5
MAR	106.1	106.9	104.8	105.3	133.2	109.1	106.8
APR	107.5	109.4	105.7	106.2	142.3	111.2	108.6
MAY	108.1	109.8	106.4	106.6	133.9	112.0	109.7
JUN	108.9	110.2	106.8	107.4	134.7	112.6	110.2
JUL	109.1	110.5	107.2	108.1	137.8	113.0	110.5
AUG	108.9	110.0	107.1	108.1	131.2	113.9	110.5
SEP	109.9	110.4	107.4	108.1	138.3	114.1	110.6
OCT	110.2	110.1	107.4	108.4	136.5	112.8	109.4
NOV	110.1	109.8	107.6	108.5	137.6	112.5	109.0
DEC	109.8	109.8	107.5	108.4	135.4	111.3	108.3
2012 JAN	110.2	109.6	107.7	108.6	136.2	111.1	107.9
FEB	110.4	109.7	108.1	108.1	144.1	112.1	109.1
MAR	110.7	109.9	108.5	107.8	151.8	113.4	110.0
APR	109.9	111.1	108.9	107.9	146.1	113.9	110.4
MAY	109.9	111.2	108.6	107.5	136.6	113.3	110.2
JUN	109.5	110.7	108.4	107.4	123.3	111.4	108.9
JUL	110.0	110.3	108.4	107.0	127.3	109.5	107.1
AUG	110.3	110.2	108.6	106.6	137.7	110.7	108.0
SEP	110.7	110.8	108.8	106.6	137.1	111.3	108.5
OCT	111.2	111.4	108.7	106.9	136.4	111.6	108.9
NOV	111.3	111.5	108.6	107.1	134.2	111.6	109.0
DEC	110.4	111.5	108.5	107.2	132.5	111.5	109.1
2013 JAN	110.7	112.0	108.8	107.5	136.5	111.5	109.3
FEB	111.3	112.5	109.4	108.0	144.1	112.1	109.7
MAR	111.9	113.5	109.9	108.8	141.2	113.0	110.6
APR	111.4	114.1	110.0	108.4	132.9	111.6	109.6
MAY	111.3	114.1	109.4	107.9	131.7	110.2	108.5
JUN	111.1	114.3	109.4	107.8	130.0	109.7	108.3

17.1 Producer Price Index (2010=100, SIC2007)

Gross Sector Price Indices of Materials & Fuel purchased

	6107123000: GSI - Purchases of materials and fuels for Manufacture of Other Non-Metallic Mineral Products	6107124250: GSI Sub-section - Inputs of Manuf of Basic Metals & Fabricated products	6107126270: GSI Sub-section - Inputs for Manuf of Computer, Elect & Opt products	6107228000: GSI (excl. CCL) - Inputs for Manufacture of Machinery & Equipment	6107129300: GSI Sub-section - Inputs for Manufacture of Motor Vechicles	6107131330: GSI Sub-section - Inputs for Manuf of Other Manufactured Goods n.e.c
	MC3E	MC3F	MC3G	MB4U	MC3I	MC3J
		NSA	NSA	NSA	NSA	NSA
2009	98.0	92.5	97.0	96.8	97.4	96.4
2010	100.0	100.0	100.0	100.0	100.0	100.0
2011	109.1	110.1	103.3	105.3	104.1	104.5
2012	111.7	108.4	103.1	105.3	104.0	105.4
2011 JAN	105.0	106.4	102.1	103.0	102.5	102.9
FEB	104.4	107.7	102.2	103.5	102.7	103.1
MAR	106.4	109.8	102.7	104.3	103.2	103.4
APR	107.0	111.8	103.4	105.6	104.1	104.2
MAY	108.7	111.5	103.5	105.8	104.3	104.6
JUN	108.8	111.1	103.6	105.8	104.5	104.8
JUL	109.2	111.2	103.8	106.0	104.7	105.0
AUG	111.9	110.7	103.8	105.9	104.7	105.3
SEP	111.8	111.6	104.1	106.3	105.1	105.6
OCT	112.2	110.1	103.7	105.7	104.6	105.3
NOV	112.4	110.1	103.6	105.7	104.4	105.2
DEC	111.5	109.5	103.5	105.6	104.2	105.1
2012 JAN	111.9	109.4	103.3	105.6	104.2	105.3
FEB	112.7	111.2	103.7	106.2	104.8	105.8
MAR	113.1	111.6	103.9	106.3	104.9	106.0
APR	113.1	110.5	103.5	106.0	104.3	105.9
MAY	112.1	108.8	103.3	105.5	103.9	105.6
JUN	111.1	107.1	103.0	105.2	104.1	105.5
JUL	110.1	106.6	102.8	104.9	103.6	105.2
AUG	109.6	106.5	102.7	104.5	103.4	105.0
SEP	110.6	107.4	102.6	104.8	103.4	105.0
OCT	111.5	107.5	102.8	104.9	103.7	105.2
NOV	111.9	106.9	102.7	104.7	103.8	105.1
DEC	112.1	107.1	102.3	104.8	103.8	105.0
2013 JAN	112.3	108.0	102.7	105.5	104.6	105.8
FEB	113.1	109.9	103.6	106.7	105.4	106.8
MAR	114.1	110.2	104.2	107.0	105.3	107.2
APR	112.8	108.2	103.8	106.4	104.8	106.8
MAY	111.3	106.9	103.4	105.6	104.4	106.5
JUN	110.7	106.0	103.1	105.3	104.1	106.2

Source: Office for National Statistics

Climate change Levy was introduced in April 2001

Rebasing the Producer Price Index, including trade prices (PPI) and the Services Producer Price Index (SPPI) onto 2010=100 occurred at the end of 2013.
Further information can be found at: http://www.ons.gov.uk/ons/rel/ppi2/producer-price-index/ppi-rebasing-2010---100/index.html

Accuracy
Figures for the latest two months are provisional and the latest five months are subject to revisions in light of (a) late and revised respondent data and
(b), for the seasonally adjusted series; revisions to seasonal adjustment factors are re-estimated every month. A routine seasonal adjustment review is normally
conducted in the autumn each year.

Abreviations
NSI - Net Sector Input
FBTP - Food, Beverages and Tobacco Products
NSA - Not Seasonally Adjusted
SA - Seasonally Adjusted
GSI - Gross Sector Input
CCL - Climate Change Levy

17.2 Producer Price Index of Output (2010=100, SIC2007)

	Net Sector Output Price Indices of Materials & Fuel purchased		Gross Sector Output Price Indices of Materials & Fuel purchased (All Manufacturing & Selected Industries)				
	7200700000: Net Sector Output - Output of Manufactured products	7200799000: Net Sector Output - All Manufacturing excl Food, Beverages Tobacco	7111101280: Gross Sector Output - Food Products, Beverages & Tobacco incl duty	7112130000: Textiles	7112140000: Wearing Apparel	7112150000: Leather & related products	7112160000: Wood, Products of Wood & Cork, except Furniture; Articles of Straw
	JVZ7 NSA	K3BI NSA	K65A NSA	K37R NSA	K37S NSA	K37T NSA	K37U NSA
2008	96.9	97.1	95.7	95.6	99.6	98.7	94.8
2009	97.4	98.5	98.9	98.2	99.7	93.7	96.2
2010	100.0	100.0	100.0	100.0	100.0	100.0	100.0
2011	104.8	102.8	106.6	107.0	102.8	116.5	105.2
2012	107.0	103.9	110.9	110.6	106.1	119.0	109.0
2011 JAN	102.3	101.2	103.5	103.8	100.5	106.0	102.6
FEB	102.8	101.4	104.4	103.9	100.6	109.2	103.2
MAR	103.8	101.8	105.1	104.7	100.6	115.2	103.6
APR	104.8	102.6	105.9	106.1	102.8	120.8	103.9
MAY	104.9	102.7	106.5	106.3	103.3	119.9	105.1
JUN	105.1	102.9	107.0	107.3	103.1	120.6	105.5
JUL	105.4	103.2	107.4	107.4	103.8	120.6	105.9
AUG	105.4	103.5	107.3	107.3	103.8	117.7	106.1
SEP	105.6	103.6	107.7	108.9	103.8	117.8	106.2
OCT	105.6	103.5	108.0	109.7	103.9	117.2	106.8
NOV	105.8	103.4	108.2	109.6	104.0	116.0	106.8
DEC	105.7	103.5	108.3	109.6	104.0	116.4	107.0
2012 JAN	105.9	103.4	108.8	110.6	104.7	114.8	107.6
FEB	106.3	103.7	109.0	110.2	105.1	114.8	107.9
MAR	106.8	103.8	109.8	110.4	105.4	115.6	108.3
APR	107.2	104.0	110.4	108.8	105.7	119.4	108.9
MAY	107.0	104.0	110.8	109.1	106.5	119.6	108.9
JUN	106.6	103.9	110.9	109.2	105.9	120.1	109.1
JUL	106.8	104.0	111.0	111.2	106.7	119.6	109.4
AUG	107.2	104.0	111.3	111.4	106.6	118.9	109.4
SEP	107.5	104.1	111.7	111.9	106.7	119.7	109.6
OCT	107.6	104.1	111.8	112.1	106.7	121.2	109.5
NOV	107.4	104.1	112.5	112.3	106.4	122.2	109.4
DEC	107.2	103.9	112.7	110.5	106.5	122.3	109.6
2013 JAN	107.6	104.2	113.2	110.8	106.6	122.3	109.7
FEB	108.1	104.4	113.4	111.2	106.6	122.4	109.7
MAR	108.4	104.7	114.0	111.2	106.6	122.5	109.9
APR	108.3	104.8	114.7	111.1	106.6	123.6	110.1
MAY	108.3	104.8	115.0	111.8	107.3	124.4	109.7
JUN	108.4	104.8	115.3	111.8	107.3	124.5	109.9

17.2 Producer Price Index of Output (2010=100, SIC2007)

Gross Sector Output Price Indices of Materials & Fuel purchased (All Manufacturing & Selected Industries)

	7112170000: Paper & Paper products	7112180000: Printing & Recording Services	7112200000: Chemicals & Chemical products	7112220000: Rubber & Plastics products	7112230000: Other Non-Metallic Mineral products	7112240000: Basic Metals	7112260000: Computer, Electronic & Optical products
	K37V NSA	K37W NSA	K37Z NSA	K383 NSA	K384 NSA	K385 NSA	K387 NSA
2008	97.1	99.6	96.4	96.5	97.2	99.7	97.5
2009	97.4	100.6	98.8	97.8	99.5	90.8	98.3
2010	100	100	100	100	100	100	100
2011	107.7	100.4	107.8	105.4	102.7	108.8	98.2
2012	106.9	99.9	108.4	107	106.4	104.7	96.5
2011 JAN	104	100.4	105.5	102.2	101	105.5	98.2
FEB	104.4	99.9	105.3	103.1	101.5	107.2	98.2
MAR	105.6	100.1	106.1	103.9	101.8	109.1	98.1
APR	106.9	100.1	107.3	104.7	102.4	111.3	98.2
MAY	107.2	100.3	107.7	105.5	102.9	111.6	98
JUN	108.5	100.7	108.5	106.1	102.9	110.2	98
JUL	109.5	101	109	106.6	103.1	109	98
AUG	109.7	100.7	109.7	106.7	103.2	109.3	98.4
SEP	109.6	100.9	109.8	106.7	103.3	110.3	98.5
OCT	109.5	100	108.6	106.6	103.5	107.8	98.4
NOV	109	100	108.5	106.4	103.4	107.3	98.3
DEC	108.9	100.3	107.7	106.3	103.5	106.5	98.3
2012 JAN	109.3	100.4	107.7	106.2	105	106.1	97.2
FEB	107.6	100.4	108.6	106.1	105.9	107.6	97.2
MAR	107.5	100.1	109.6	106.5	106.3	107.5	97.2
APR	107.6	100.2	109.9	106.8	106.6	106.8	96.6
MAY	107.4	100.4	109.7	107	106.4	105.8	96.5
JUN	107.5	100.2	108.3	106.9	106.3	104.8	96.3
JUL	107.3	100.2	106.9	106.9	106.3	103.9	96.8
AUG	106.4	99.4	107.7	107.1	106.5	102.3	96.6
SEP	105.7	99.5	108.1	107.4	106.6	103.4	96.5
OCT	105.7	99.4	108	107.5	106.9	103.2	96.3
NOV	105.6	99.3	107.9	107.3	106.8	102.4	95.9
DEC	105.5	99.3	108.1	107.7	106.7	102.6	94.7
2013 JAN	105.7	99.5	108	108.4	107.5	103.3	94.9
FEB	105.6	99.3	107.9	108.3	107.7	104.3	95.1
MAR	106.2	99.2	108.4	108.3	107.7	104.3	95.9
APR	106.3	99.1	107.7	108.4	107.7	102.9	96.9
MAY	106.4	99	106.8	108.5	107.2	102.3	97.2
JUN	106.4	99.1	106.2	108.7	107.3	101.3	97.1

17.2 Producer Price Index of Output (2010=100, SIC2007)

Gross Sector Output Price Indices of Materials & Fuel purchased (All Manufacturing & Selected Industries)

	7112270000: Electrical Equipment	7112280000: Machinery & Equipment n.e.c.	7112290000: Motor Vehicles, Trailers & Semi-trailers	7112300000: Other Transport Equipment	7112310000: Furniture	7112320000: Other Manufactured Goods	Output in the Construction Industry All New Work *	Monthly index of average price of new dwellings - at mortgage completion stage
	K388 NSA	K389 NSA	K38A NSA	K38B NSA	K38C NSA	K38D NSA		
2008	94.3	97.5	96.2	97.1	96.7	97.2	106.9	164.4
2009	96.9	98.8	99.4	99.1	98.3	98.9	104.4	150.5
2010	100	100	100	100	100	100	100.0	158.1
2011	102.9	103.3	100.9	101.3	102.7	102	101.2	170.5
2012	102.8	105.5	101.5	102.9	105.1	104	104.5	177.2
2011 JAN	102.8	101	100.1	100.5	101.2	101.3	99.9	168.1
FEB	103.1	100.9	100.1	100.4	101.4	101.4	100.1	168.0
MAR	103.4	101.6	100.4	100.5	101.8	101.5	100.2	167.5
APR	103.2	103.2	100.7	101.2	102	101.3	100.6	168.5
MAY	103	103.4	100.8	101.4	102	101.8	100.9	167.2
JUN	102.9	103.6	101.1	101.4	102.2	101.9	101.1	167.9
JUL	102.8	104.1	101.2	101.6	103.2	102	101.3	172.5
AUG	103	104.3	101.5	101.6	103.4	102.1	101.5	170.7
SEP	102.6	104.4	101.6	101.6	103.4	102.3	101.6	172.8
OCT	102.6	104.2	101.5	101.6	103.5	102.3	102.1	172.4
NOV	102.6	104.7	101.1	101.7	103.8	102.5	102.4	172.0
DEC	102.7	104.7	101	101.8	103.9	103.5	102.8	178.6
2012 JAN	102.1	104.4	100.9	102	104.2	103.5	103.2	183.1
FEB	102.5	104.4	101.2	102	104.4	105.3	103.6	181.4
MAR	103	105.1	101.2	102.1	104.3	104.1	104.0	179.0
APR	102.9	105.4	101.6	102	105	104.1	104.0	176.9
MAY	102.8	105.5	101.4	102.5	105.3	104.1	104.2	177.5
JUN	102.6	105.7	101.5	102.9	105.3	104.1	104.4	177.4
JUL	102.8	105.5	101.3	103.9	105.4	104	104.7	174.1
AUG	102.9	105.4	101.3	103.8	105.4	103.8	105.1	175.9
SEP	102.8	105.8	101.8	102.9	105.6	103.6	105.3	169.3
OCT	103	105.9	101.9	103.5	105.6	103.6	105.3	171.4
NOV	103	106.1	101.7	103.7	105.5	103.8	105.5	174.8
DEC	103	106.2	101.9	103.7	105.4	104	105.8	185.7
2013 JAN	103.3	106.4	102.4	103.8	105.6	104.4	106.4	183.3
FEB	103.3	107.5	102.6	104.5	105.6	104.6	106.7	180.9
MAR	103.4	107.8	102.5	104.9	105.5	104.8	107.1	180.8
APR	103.4	108.2	102.2	105.1	105.6	104.9	107.4	184.8
MAY	103.3	108.2	102.2	105.2	105.7	104.9	107.7	180.1
JUN	103.3	108.3	102.3	105	105.6	105.5	108.0	183.3

Source: Office for National Statistics
ONS (JYYC): 01633 456662
CLG (FCBA): 0303 444 2345

Climate change Levy was introduced in April 2001
Rebasing the Producer Price Index, including trade prices (PPI) and the Services Producer Price Index (SPPI) onto

Accuracy
Figures for the latest two months are provisional and the latest five months are subject to revisions in light of (a) late and revised respondent data and (b), for the seasonally adjusted series; revisions to seasonal adjustment factors are re-estimated every month. A routine

Abreviations
NSI - Net Sector Input
FBTP - Food, Beverages and Tobacco Products
NSA - Not Seasonally Adjusted
SA - Seasonally Adjusted
GSI - Gross Sector Input
CCL - Climate Change Levy

*JYYC 'Quarterly construction output price index' was previously published in Annual Abstract of Statistics but has now been replaced by 'All New Work' from Output in the Construction Industry. This can be foun in Table 9a at the following address:
http://www.ons.gov.uk/ons/rel/construction/output-in-the-construction-industry/july-2014/rft-output-tables-july-2014.xls

17.3 Internal purchasing power of the pound (based on RPI) [1,2,3,4]: 1990 to 2012

pence	1990	1991	1992	1993	1994	1995	1996	1997	1998	1999	2000	2001	2002	2003	2004	2005	2006	2007	2008	2009	2010	2011	2012
	BAMW	BASX	CZVM	CBXX	DOFX	DOHR	DOLM	DTUL	CDQG	JKZZ	ZMHO	IKHI	FAUI	SEZH	C687	E9AO	GB4Y	HT4R	J5TL	JRT3	K9AD	KO2K	KVO5
1990	100	106	110	112	114	118	121	125	129	131	135	137	140	144	148	152	157	164	170	169	177	186	192
1991	94	100	104	105	108	112	114	118	122	124	128	130	132	136	140	144	148	155	161	160	167	176	182
1992	91	96	100	102	104	108	110	114	118	119	123	125	127	131	135	139	143	149	155	154	161	170	175
1993	90	95	98	100	102	106	109	112	116	118	121	123	125	129	133	136	141	147	153	152	159	167	173
1994	88	93	96	98	100	103	106	109	113	115	118	120	122	126	130	133	137	143	149	148	155	163	168
1995	85	90	93	94	97	100	102	106	109	111	114	116	118	122	125	129	133	139	144	143	150	158	163
1996	83	87	91	92	94	98	100	103	107	108	112	113	115	119	122	126	130	135	141	140	146	154	159
1997	80	85	88	89	92	95	97	100	103	105	108	110	112	115	119	122	126	131	136	136	142	149	154
1998	77	82	85	86	88	92	94	97	100	102	105	106	108	111	115	118	122	127	132	131	137	144	149
1999	76	81	84	85	87	90	92	95	98	100	103	105	107	110	113	116	120	125	130	129	135	142	147
2000	74	78	81	83	85	88	90	92	96	97	100	102	103	106	110	113	116	121	126	125	131	138	143
2001	73	77	80	81	83	86	88	91	94	95	98	100	102	105	108	111	114	119	124	123	129	136	140
2002	72	76	79	80	82	85	87	89	92	94	97	98	100	103	106	109	112	117	122	121	127	133	138
2003	70	74	76	78	79	82	84	87	90	91	94	96	97	100	103	106	109	114	118	118	123	130	134
2004	68	72	74	75	77	80	82	84	87	89	91	93	94	97	100	103	106	111	115	114	120	126	130
2005	66	70	72	73	75	78	80	82	85	86	89	90	92	94	97	100	103	108	112	111	116	123	126
2006	64	67	70	71	73	75	77	80	82	83	86	87	89	92	94	97	100	104	108	108	113	119	123
2007	61	65	67	68	70	72	74	76	79	80	82	84	85	88	90	93	96	100	104	103	108	114	117
2008	59	62	64	65	67	69	71	73	76	77	79	81	82	84	87	89	92	96	100	99	104	109	113
2009	59	62	65	66	67	70	71	74	76	77	80	81	82	85	87	90	93	97	101	100	105	110	114
2010	56	60	62	63	64	67	68	70	73	74	76	78	79	81	84	86	89	92	96	96	100	105	109
2011	54	57	59	60	61	63	65	67	69	70	72	74	75	77	79	82	84	88	91	91	95	100	103
2012	52	55	57	58	59	61	63	65	67	68	70	71	73	75	77	79	82	85	89	88	92	97	100

1. To find the purchasing power of the pound in 2001, given that it was 100 pence in 1990, select the column headed 1990 and look at the 2001 row. The result is 73 pence.

2. Changes in the internal purchasing power of a currency may be defined as the 'inverse' of changes in the levels of prices; when prices go up, the amount which can be purchased with a given sum of money goes down. The monthly figures of the all items RPI can be used to obtain estimates of the changes in prices or in purchasing power between any 2 months. To find the purchasing power of the pound in one month, given that it was 100p in a previous month the calculation is: 100p multiplied by the earlier month RPI then divided by the later month RPI

3. Comparisons between any 2 years may be made in the same way using the annual averages of the RPI found in table 5.3. These figure are reproduced in the above table.

4. In accordance with the *Statistics and Registration Service Act 2007* , the Retail Prices Index and its derivatives have been assessed against the Code of Practice for Official Statistics and found not to meet the required standards for designation as National Statistics. A full report can be found at: http://www.statisticsauthority.gov.uk/

Source:
Office for National Statistics
Prices Division
2.001 Cardiff Road
Newport
South Wales
NP10 8XG
Tel: +44 (0) 1633 456900

http://www.ons.gov.uk

17.4 CPI: Detailed figures by division [1, 3]

	Food and non-alcoholic beverages	Alcoholic beverages and tobacco	Clothing and footwear	Housing, water, electricity, gas & other fuels	Furniture, household equipment & routine maintenance	Health [2]	Transport	Communic-ation	Recreation and culture	Education [2]	Restaurants and hotels	Miscell-aneous goods and services [2]	CPI (overall index)
COICOP Division	1	2	3	4	5	6	7	8	9	10	11	12	
	CHZR	CHZS	CHZT	CHZU	CHZV	CHZW	CHZX	CHZY	CHZZ	CJUU	CJUV	CJUW	CHZQ
Weights 2012	112	42	65	144	61	24	162	27	134	19	114	96	1000
Index level (2005=100)													
	D7BU	D7BV	D7BW	D7BX	D7BY	D7BZ	D7C2	D7C3	D7C4	D7C5	D7C6	D7C7	D7BT
2010	127.4	121.7	78.8	130.3	110.0	115.7	122.1	99.9	100.4	154.5	116.9	113.7	114.5
2011	134.3	132.3	80.6	137.5	115.2	119.7	131.7	103.9	100.4	162.5	122.1	116.5	119.6
2012	138.7	140.3	81.3	144.4	118.5	123.2	134.7	108.1	100.6	176.7	125.9	119.1	123.0
Monthly indices (2005=100)													
	D7BU	D7BV	D7BW	D7BX	D7BY	D7BZ	D7C2	D7C3	D7C4	D7C5	D7C6	D7C7	D7BT
Jan 2012	136.8	135.5	78.4	143.3	116.2	121.7	132.4	106.0	100.4	168.3	123.5	117.9	121.1
Feb	138.5	136.7	80.7	142.9	118.0	121.8	133.2	106.6	100.3	168.3	124.0	118.7	121.8
Mar	137.8	136.9	82.4	142.7	119.6	121.8	134.2	107.2	100.2	168.3	124.3	118.7	122.2
Apr	137.6	140.9	82.6	144.0	118.1	123.1	135.8	107.6	100.6	168.3	125.5	118.8	122.9
May	138.0	140.8	82.5	143.8	118.9	123.1	134.7	108.5	100.2	168.3	126.0	118.9	122.8
Jun	138.0	140.1	79.0	143.6	118.9	123.6	134.1	108.4	100.3	168.3	126.1	118.5	122.3
Jul	138.2	141.1	76.9	144.2	117.7	123.5	135.5	108.8	100.4	168.3	126.3	118.7	122.5
Aug	138.5	141.4	79.1	144.4	118.6	123.6	137.2	108.8	100.2	168.3	126.5	119.0	123.1
Sep	138.5	142.9	82.8	144.6	119.2	123.8	135.4	108.8	100.8	169.1	126.8	119.9	123.5
Oct	139.1	143.4	83.8	144.8	118.5	124.0	135.3	109.0	101.2	201.5	126.8	119.9	124.2
Nov	140.7	142.7	84.3	145.7	118.4	124.0	133.9	108.8	101.2	201.5	127.5	120.3	124.4
Dec	142.4	141.1	83.1	148.6	119.9	124.2	134.9	108.7	101.1	201.5	127.5	120.4	125.0
Jan 2013	142.6	147.1	78.6	148.4	117.2	124.4	134.0	109.7	101.0	201.5	127.5	119.6	124.4
Feb	143.5	146.3	80.2	149.1	118.9	124.4	135.7	110.8	101.5	201.5	127.8	119.7	125.2
Mar	142.9	145.6	82.1	149.1	119.8	124.7	136.5	110.8	102.0	201.5	128.1	120.0	125.6
Apr	143.9	148.9	82.0	150.1	118.3	126.1	135.6	111.0	102.0	201.5	128.7	120.2	125.9
May	143.9	149.6	83.0	149.8	119.6	126.1	136.2	111.4	101.7	201.5	129.1	120.1	126.1
Jun	143.2	149.1	81.4	149.9	119.0	126.0	136.3	111.5	101.6	201.5	129.3	120.3	125.9
Jul	143.5	150.1	78.8	150.5	117.8	126.9	137.5	111.8	101.1	201.5	129.5	120.4	125.8
Aug	144.2	150.0	80.4	150.5	119.9	127.1	138.9	111.6	101.1	201.5	129.5	120.5	126.4

Percentage change on a year earlier

	D7G8	D7G9	D7GA	D7GB	D7GC	D7GD	D7GE	D7GF	D7GG	D7GH	D7GI	D7GJ	D7G7
2010	3.4	5.5	-1	0.4	3.1	2.9	8.3	4.9	1.9	5.3	2.9	2.4	3.3
2011	5.5	8.7	2.3	5.5	4.7	3.4	7.8	4.0	0.1	5.2	4.5	2.5	4.5
2012	3.3	6.1	0.9	5.0	2.9	3.0	2.3	4.1	0.2	8.6	3.1	2.3	2.8
Jan 2012	3.5	6.2	2.9	7.4	4.4	3.2	4.0	4.9	-0.5	5.1	3.1	2.9	3.6
Feb	3.7	8.3	2.2	6.8	4.6	3.5	3.7	4.1	-0.9	5.1	2.9	2.9	3.4
Mar	4.6	8.0	3.2	6.2	4.1	2.8	3.3	4.8	-0.6	5.1	2.9	2.7	3.5
Apr	4.3	5.5	2.1	6.2	3.7	3.1	1.7	4.2	-0.5	5.1	3.3	2.7	3.0
May	3.3	4.8	1.6	6.2	3.9	3.3	1.7	4.1	-0.7	5.1	3.3	2.1	2.8
Jun	2.3	4.8	-0.8	6.0	3.5	3.7	0.9	4.9	0.3	5.1	3.1	1.9	2.4
Jul	2.1	5.0	0.1	6.1	3.5	3.0	1.3	4.4	0.4	5.1	3.2	1.7	2.6
Aug	2.2	5.8	-0.7	5.6	2.3	2.6	1.7	4.3	0.6	5.1	3.1	1.6	2.5
Sep	2.0	6.1	-0.5	2.2	1.7	2.4	2.5	3.4	1.2	3.2	3.0	2.3	2.2
Oct	3.4	6.5	-0.1	1.7	1.7	2.5	3.1	3.7	0.8	19.7	2.9	1.9	2.7
Nov	3.9	5.7	-0.6	2.0	0.6	2.5	2.6	3.7	1.0	19.7	3.3	2.3	2.7
Dec	3.8	6.0	0.8	3.9	0.9	2.8	1.1	2.2	0.7	19.7	3.2	2.0	2.7
Jan 2013	4.2	8.5	0.2	3.5	0.8	2.2	1.3	3.5	0.5	19.7	3.2	1.4	2.7
Feb	3.7	7.1	-0.6	4.4	0.7	2.1	1.9	4.0	1.2	19.7	3.1	0.9	2.8
Mar	3.7	6.3	-0.4	4.5	0.2	2.3	1.7	3.3	1.8	19.7	3.1	1.1	2.8
Apr	4.6	5.7	-0.6	4.2	0.1	2.5	-0.1	3.2	1.4	19.7	2.5	1.1	2.4
May	4.3	6.2	0.7	4.2	0.6	2.4	1.1	2.7	1.6	19.7	2.5	1.0	2.7
Jun	3.8	6.4	3.1	4.4	-	2.0	1.7	2.9	1.3	19.7	2.5	1.5	2.9
Jul	3.9	6.3	2.5	4.3	0.1	2.7	1.5	2.8	0.7	19.7	2.5	1.5	2.8
Aug	4.1	6.0	1.6	4.2	1.1	2.9	1.2	2.5	0.9	19.7	2.4	1.2	2.7

Key: - zero or negligible

1) Inflation rates prior to 1997 and index levels prior to 1996 are estimated.
(Details are given in Economic Trends No. 541 December 1998 available on the Office for National Statistics website)
2) The coverage of these categories was extended in January 2000; further extensions to coverage came into effect in January 2001 for health and miscellaneous goods and services; the coverage of miscellaneous goods and services was further extended with effect from January 2002. (Details are given in a series of Economic Trends articles available on the National Statistics website)

3) More detailed CPI data are available at
http://www.ons.gov.uk
Source:
Office for National Statistics
Prices Division
2.001 Cardiff Road
Newport, South Wales
NP10 8XG, Tel: +44 (0) 1633 456900

17.5 Retail Prices Index[1] United Kingdom

	All items (RPI)	All items excluding mortgage interest payments (RPIX)	mortgage interest payments and depreci-ation	Housing	All items excluding Food	All items excluding Seasonal food[2]	Food and catering	Alcohol and tobacco	Housing and household expend-iture	Pesonal expend-iture	Travel and leisure	Consumer durables	All items excluding mortgage interest payments and indirect taxes (RPIY)[3]
Weights													
	CZGU	CZGY	DOGZ	CZGX	CZGV	CZGW	CBVV	CBVW	CBVX	CBVY	CBVZ	CBWA	
2001	1000	954	914	795	884	982	169	97	362	96	276	125	
2002	1000	964	924	801	886	980	166	99	363	94	278	126	
2003	1000	961	919	797	891	983	160	98	365	92	285	126	
2004	1000	961	914	791	889	981	160	97	367	93	283	121	
2005	1000	950	901	776	890	981	159	96	387	89	269	122	
2006	1000	950	906	778	895	983	155	96	392	90	267	117	
2007	1000	945	895	762	895	981	152	95	408	83	262	109	
2008	1000	940	885	746	889	980	158	86	417	83	256	104	
2009	1000	959	909	764	882	979	168	90	416	80	246	106	
2010	1000	966	911	763	888	981	159	91	403	81	266	105	
2011	1000	968	914	762	882	980	165	88	408	82	257	106	
2012	1000	971	915	763	886	981	161	85	412	84	258	100	
2013	1000	971	913	746	884	980	163	91	419	83	244	96	
Annual averages													
	CHAW	CHMK	CHON	CHAZ	CHAY	CHAX	CHBS	CHBT	CHBU	CHBV	CHBW	CHBY	CBZW
2001	173.3	171.3	169.5	163.7	178.0	174.3	162.2	216.9	180.0	135.7	172.0	105.0	163.7
2002	176.2	175.1	172.5	166.0	181.1	177.2	164.8	223.3	184.6	133.2	174.2	101.9	167.5
2003	181.3	180.0	176.2	168.9	186.7	182.4	167.9	228.0	194.3	133.2	177.0	99.8	172.0
2004	186.7	184.0	179.1	170.9	192.8	187.9	170.0	233.6	207.4	131.5	178.1	97.7	175.5
2005	192.0	188.2	182.6	173.7	198.7	193.3	172.9	239.8	219.4	131.0	179.2	95.3	179.4
2006	198.1	193.7	187.8	178.3	205.2	199.5	176.9	247.1	231.8	131.7	181.1	94.0	184.8
2007	206.6	199.9	193.3	183.2	213.9	207.9	184.3	256.2	248.1	132.9	183.8	93.3	190.8
2008	214.8	208.5	201.9	191.3	221.2	216.0	198.5	266.7	258.6	132.4	189.0	91.6	199.2
2009	213.7	212.6	207.2	196.3	218.3	214.6	207.6	276.7	247.4	131.4	191.2	90.7	204.8
2010	223.6	222.7	217	206.5	228.8	224.5	214.1	289.9	253.8	138.2	207.6	94.4	211.9
2011	235.2	234.5	229.3	219.6	240.5	236.3	225.6	311.3	262.5	149.8	220.1	99.7	220.4
2012	242.7	242.0	237.0	227.4	248.2	243.9	232.9	327.1	270.9	158.2	224.1	104.1	227.7
Monthly figures													
2012 Jan	238.0	237.3	232.2	222.6	243.2	239.1	229.8	317.6	266.8	149.3	220.8	98.4	223.4
Feb	239.9	239.3	234.2	224.8	245.0	241.0	231.8	319.3	267.7	155.3	221.9	102.4	225.3
Mar	240.8	240.2	235.3	226.0	246.2	242.0	231.3	320.4	268.2	158.4	223.1	105.1	226.3
Apr	242.5	241.9	237.0	227.4	248.1	243.7	231.3	327.7	269.0	159.4	225.7	104.7	227.2
May	242.4	241.8	237.0	227.3	248.0	243.7	232.1	328.1	269.4	159.4	224.6	105.0	227.2
June	241.8	241.1	236.2	226.4	247.3	243.0	232.0	327.4	270.1	155.9	223.3	103.8	226.5
July	242.1	241.3	236.3	226.4	247.5	243.3	232.6	329.1	270.3	154.1	224.2	101.6	226.8
Aug	243.0	242.3	237.2	227.4	248.6	244.3	232.7	329.5	270.9	157.0	225.2	103.1	227.8
Sep	244.2	243.5	238.4	228.8	250.0	245.5	233.1	331.5	271.8	161.5	225.5	106.0	229.0
Oct	245.6	244.7	239.7	230.2	251.4	246.9	234.1	332.2	274.6	162.5	225.6	106.6	230.3
Nov	245.6	244.9	239.9	230.4	251.1	246.8	236.0	331.9	274.5	163.4	224.2	106.2	230.5
Dec	246.8	246.0	241.1	231.7	252.1	247.8	237.8	330.0	277.2	162.2	224.8	106.7	231.9
2013 Jan	245.8	245.1	240.0	230.5	250.9	246.8	238.3	336.3	276.0	157.4	223.5	102.5	230.8
Feb	247.6	246.9	241.9	232.8	252.8	248.6	239.7	335.6	277.4	162.2	225.2	106.7	232.7
Mar	248.7	248.0	243.1	234.2	254.1	249.7	239.3	335.2	277.4	165.4	228.0	108.8	233.8
Apr	249.5	248.8	243.9	234.6	254.8	250.5	240.6	341.4	278.1	166.5	227.0	108.4	234.1
May	250.0	249.2	244.4	235.1	255.3	250.9	241.0	342.6	278.9	167.7	226.7	109.7	234.6
June	249.7	249.0	244.0	234.7	255.2	250.8	240.2	342.1	278.9	166.3	226.9	108.5	234.3
July	249.7	249.0	244.0	234.4	255.2	250.8	240.6	343.4	279.4	163.7	227.0	106.2	234.5

1 See chapter text.
2 Seasonal food is defined as items of food the prices of which show significant seasonal variations. These are fresh fruit and vegetables, fresh fish, eggs and home-killed lamb.
3 There are no weights available for RPIY.

Source: Office for National Statistics: 020 7533 5874

17.6 Tax and Price Index[1] United Kingdom

Indices and percentages

Tax and Price Index: (January 1988=100)
DQAB

	1998	1999	2000	2001	2002	2003	2004	2005	2006	2007	2008	2009	2010	2011	2012	2013
January	147.1	150.5	152.7	156.7	156.5	161.4	166.9	172.1	175.9	183.3	190.7	188.6	194.7	205.5	212.8	218.8
February	147.9	150.8	153.7	157.6	157.0	162.3	167.6	172.8	176.7	184.8	192.3	189.8	196.0	207.7	214.6	220.5
March	148.4	151.2	154.6	157.8	157.7	163.0	168.4	173.7	177.4	186.1	192.9	189.7	197.4	208.8	215.6	221.6
April	149.7	151.2	155.7	156.3	158.6	164.9	168.9	174.1	178.3	186.3	192.2	188.5	199.5	209.2	215.6	219.7
May	150.6	151.7	156.3	157.4	159.1	165.2	169.7	174.5	179.5	187.1	193.4	189.7	200.3	210.0	215.5	220.2
June	150.5	151.7	156.7	157.6	159.1	165.0	170.0	174.7	180.3	188.2	195.1	190.2	200.8	210.0	214.9	219.9
July	150.1	151.1	156.1	156.5	158.8	165.0	170.0	174.7	180.3	187.0	194.8	190.2	200.3	209.5	215.2	219.9
August	150.8	151.5	156.1	157.2	159.3	165.4	170.6	175.1	181.0	188.2	195.5	191.3	201.2	210.9	216.1	221.1
September	151.5	152.3	157.3	157.8	160.6	166.3	171.3	175.6	181.9	188.9	196.7	192.2	201.9	212.7	217.2	222.0
October	151.6	152.6	157.2	157.5	160.9	166.4	171.8	175.8	182.2	189.8	196.0	192.9	202.4	212.8	218.6	222.0
November	151.5	152.8	157.7	156.8	161.2	166.5	172.2	176.1	182.8	190.6	194.3	193.4	203.4	213.2	218.6	222.2
December	151.5	153.4	157.8	156.6	161.5	167.3	173.1	176.6	184.4	191.8	191.2	194.8	204.9	214.1	219.8	223.5

Retail Prices Index: (January 1988=100)
CHAW

	1998	1999	2000	2001	2002	2003	2004	2005	2006	2007	2008	2009	2010	2011	2012	2013
January	159.5	163.4	166.6	171.1	173.3	178.4	183.1	188.9	193.4	201.6	209.8	210.1	217.9	229.0	238.0	245.8
February	160.3	163.7	167.5	172.0	173.8	179.3	183.8	189.6	194.2	203.1	211.4	211.4	219.2	231.3	239.9	247.6
March	160.8	164.1	168.4	172.2	174.5	179.9	184.6	190.5	195.0	204.4	212.1	211.3	220.7	232.5	240.8	248.7
April	162.6	165.2	170.1	173.1	175.7	181.2	185.7	191.6	196.5	205.4	214.0	211.5	222.8	234.4	242.5	249.5
May	163.5	165.6	170.7	174.2	176.2	181.5	186.5	192.0	197.7	206.2	215.1	212.8	223.6	235.2	242.4	250
June	163.4	165.6	171.1	174.4	176.2	181.3	186.8	192.2	198.5	207.3	216.8	213.4	224.1	235.2	241.8	249.7
July	163.0	165.1	170.5	173.3	175.9	181.3	186.8	192.2	198.5	206.1	216.5	213.4	223.6	234.7	242.1	249.7
August	163.7	165.5	170.5	174.0	176.4	181.6	187.4	192.6	199.2	207.3	217.2	214.4	224.5	236.1	243.0	251
September	164.4	166.2	171.7	174.6	177.6	182.5	188.1	193.1	200.1	208.0	218.4	215.3	225.3	237.9	244.2	251.9
October	164.5	166.5	171.6	174.3	177.9	182.6	188.6	193.3	200.4	208.9	217.7	216.0	225.8	238.0	245.6	251.9
November	164.4	166.7	172.1	173.6	178.2	182.7	189.0	193.6	201.1	209.7	216.0	216.6	226.8	238.5	245.6	252.1
December	164.4	167.3	172.2	173.4	178.5	183.5	189.9	194.1	202.7	210.9	212.9	218.0	228.4	239.4	246.8	253.4

Percentage changes on one year earlier[1]
CZVL

	1998	1999	2000	2001	2002	2003	2004	2005	2006	2007	2008	2009	2010	2011	2012	2013
Tax and Price Index[1]																
January	2.4	2.3	1.5	2.6	−0.1	3.1	3.4	3.1	2.2	4.2	4.0	−1.1	3.2	5.5	3.6	2.8
February	2.6	2.0	1.9	2.5	−0.4	3.4	3.3	3.1	2.3	4.6	4.1	−1.3	3.3	6.0	3.3	2.7
March	2.6	1.9	2.2	2.1	−0.1	3.4	3.3	3.1	2.1	4.9	3.7	−1.7	4.1	5.8	3.3	2.8
April	4.1	1.0	3.0	0.4	1.5	4.0	2.4	3.1	2.4	4.5	3.2	−1.9	5.8	4.9	3.1	1.9
May	4.3	0.7	3.0	0.7	1.1	3.8	2.7	2.8	2.9	4.2	3.4	−1.9	5.6	4.8	2.6	2.2
June	3.8	0.8	3.3	0.6	1.0	3.7	3.0	2.8	3.2	4.4	3.7	−2.5	5.6	4.6	2.3	2.3
July	3.5	0.7	3.3	0.3	1.5	3.9	3.0	2.8	3.2	3.7	4.2	−2.4	5.3	4.6	2.7	2.2
August	3.3	0.5	3.0	0.7	1.3	3.8	3.1	2.6	3.4	4.0	3.9	−2.1	5.2	4.8	2.5	2.3
September	3.1	0.5	3.3	0.3	1.8	3.5	3.0	2.5	3.6	3.8	4.1	−2.3	5.0	5.3	2.1	2.2
October	3.1	0.7	3.0	0.2	2.2	3.4	3.2	2.3	3.6	4.2	3.3	−1.6	4.9	5.1	2.7	1.6
November	2.9	0.9	3.2	−0.6	2.8	3.3	3.4	2.3	3.8	4.3	1.9	−0.5	5.2	4.8	2.5	1.6
December	2.6	1.3	2.9	−0.8	3.1	3.6	3.5	2.0	4.4	4.0	−0.3	1.9	5.2	4.5	2.7	1.7
Retail Prices Index - CZBH																
January	3.3	2.4	2.0	2.7	1.3	2.9	2.6	3.2	2.4	4.2	4.1	0.1	3.7	5.1	3.9	3.3
February	3.4	2.1	2.3	2.7	1.0	3.2	2.5	3.2	2.4	4.6	4.1	0.0	3.7	5.5	3.7	3.2
March	3.5	2.1	2.6	2.3	1.3	3.1	2.6	3.2	2.4	4.8	3.8	−0.4	4.4	5.3	3.6	3.3
April	4.0	1.6	3.0	1.8	1.5	3.1	2.5	3.2	2.6	4.5	4.2	−1.2	5.3	5.2	3.5	2.9
May	4.2	1.3	3.1	2.1	1.1	3.0	2.8	2.9	3.0	4.3	4.3	−1.1	5.1	5.2	3.1	3.1
June	3.7	1.3	3.3	1.9	1.0	2.9	3.0	2.9	3.3	4.4	4.6	−1.6	5.0	5.0	2.8	3.3
July	3.5	1.3	3.3	1.6	1.5	3.1	3.0	2.9	3.3	3.8	5.0	−1.4	4.8	5.0	3.2	3.1
August	3.3	1.1	3.0	2.1	1.4	2.9	3.2	2.8	3.4	4.1	4.8	−1.3	4.7	5.2	2.9	3.3
September	3.2	1.1	3.3	1.7	1.7	2.8	3.1	2.7	3.6	3.9	5.0	−1.4	4.6	5.6	2.6	3.2
October	3.1	1.2	3.1	1.6	2.1	2.6	3.3	2.5	3.7	4.2	4.2	−0.8	4.5	5.4	3.2	2.6
November	3.0	1.4	3.2	0.9	2.6	2.5	3.4	2.4	3.9	4.3	3.0	0.3	4.7	5.2	3.0	2.6
December	2.8	1.8	2.9	0.7	2.9	2.8	3.5	2.2	4.4	4.0	0.9	2.4	4.8	4.8	3.1	2.7

1 See chapter text.

Source: Office for National Statistics: 020 7533 5874

17.7 Index of Producer Prices of Agricultural Products, UK (2005=100)

Annual Averages		2003	2004	2005	2006	2007	2008	2009	2010	2011	2012
Total Inputs	a	93.5	99.6	100.0	103.9	114.2	140.1	130.3	135.8	152.2	155.1
All goods and services currently consumed in agriculture	a	93.0	100.3	100.0	104.1	115.7	146.1	133.5	139.2	158.3	161.6
Seeds	a	104.0	130.1	100.0	92.5	104.3	111.6	121.2	108.8	121.3	118.9
Energy and lubricants	a	73.5	80.0	100.0	113.0	116.8	160.6	132.0	149.8	177.0	183.6
Electricity	a	85.0	90.3	100.0	122.8	130.0	154.9	157.5	154.1	167.7	174.7
Fuels for heating		65.8	74.5	100.0	116.5	127.9	173.1	138.9	170.7	188.9	204.9
Motor fuels		71.1	77.7	100.0	109.5	111.1	160.4	123.3	145.4	178.1	183.2
Fertilisers and soil improvers		82.0	91.0	100.0	105.7	119.8	272.5	189.8	182.4	229.3	220.3
Straight fertilisers		76.1	87.6	100.0	107.9	113.3	233.8	158.5	162.5	223.0	207.1
Straight fertilisers - nitrogenous		75.5	87.2	100.0	108.3	112.0	225.0	151.4	158.5	220.5	204.3
Straight fertilisers - phosphatic		87.4	94.1	100.0	100.0	147.3	390.1	220.0	211.5	274.5	249.3
Straight fertilisers - potassic		85.8	92.4	100.0	106.5	121.8	351.6	319.9	237.6	249.8	250.6
Compound fertilisers		87.1	94.2	100.0	103.4	128.1	330.0	231.8	211.5	247.1	244.9
Other fertilisers and soil improvers		99.8	99.8	100.0	103.5	108.4	113.6	113.9	107.6	107.6	109.8
Plant protection products	a	94.0	96.9	100.0	102.5	104.2	106.4	108.5	105.6	105.4	106.5
Fungicides		96.6	98.9	100.0	101.6	102.9	105.3	106.9	103.3	103.2	107.8
Insecticides		88.0	88.2	100.0	106.2	111.1	113.3	126.7	124.0	128.2	111.8
Herbicides	a	92.1	95.9	100.0	103.3	104.8	107.0	107.4	105.0	104.1	104.1
Other plant protection products		96.8544	99.9154	100	100.122	101.437	103.195	106.552	103.76	103.407	108.044
Veterinary services	a	97.8	100.7	100.0	107.0	108.7	104.3	104.8	119.1	121.5	123.5
Animal feedingstuffs	q	102.0	108.7	100.0	104.6	129.7	167.3	151.3	160.8	196.2	208.1
Straight feedingstuffs		104.9	112.2	100.0	106.4	142.9	184.0	153.2	173.4	217.1	235.5
Cereal and milling by products		107.5	118.8	100.0	113.3	159.7	206.6	148.6	167.2	247.2	252.0
Feed wheat		109.0	122.5	100.0	114.7	159.8	216.3	159.4	175.6	251.1	252.9
Feed barley		106.5	114.6	100.0	111.5	161.8	194.6	134.0	155.8	239.4	247.7
Feed oats		89.4	99.2	100.0	108.2	130.9	164.7	117.6	142.9	268.6	289.0
Oilcakes		107.5	109.4	100.0	99.2	126.8	184.2	173.0	193.3	188.3	239.3
Soya bean meal		107.7	112.2	100.0	95.8	116.4	174.7	186.7	192.3	188.0	242.2
Sunflower seed meal		97.2	99.4	100.0	98.4	133.1	180.9	141.7	182.6	167.2	207.0
Rape seed meal		126.6	117.8	100.0	107.9	144.2	195.2	158.1	201.2	188.9	257.7
Products of animal origin (incl. white fish meal)		102.0	95.0	100.0	144.2	137.2	138.6	159.0	236.5	241.1	244.9
Other straights		99.6	106.7	100.0	99.1	133.3	156.8	142.9	160.1	196.4	208.5
Field peas		103.3	114.9	100.0	94.9	167.9	207.1	160.0	170.3	216.9	238.4
Field beans		99.5	117.1	100.0	96.9	171.0	205.2	157.8	176.1	222.6	248.2
Soya beans		109.2	112.4	100.0	95.2	124.6	179.5	192.5	199.0	239.3	277.3
Compound feedingstuffs	q	99.7	106.1	100.0	103.2	119.7	154.6	149.8	151.2	180.2	187.2
Compound feedingstuffs for cattle and calves	q	98.6	104.2	100.0	101.4	116.4	151.6	147.3	145.0	171.0	182.7
Compound feedingstuffs for pigs	q	101.0	107.3	100.0	105.5	122.7	151.6	147.0	154.6	183.4	190.1
Compound feedingstuffs for poultry	q	100.6	108.0	100.0	104.9	123.6	162.2	155.7	159.7	193.0	193.7
Compound feedingstuffs for sheep	q	98.1	104.6	100.0	99.8	112.2	141.9	141.9	137.8	164.6	174.8
Maintenance of Materials		89.1	94.0	100.0	105.8	109.9	116.3	121.5	126.9	133.1	135.2
Maintenance of Buildings		91.4	95.9	100.0	106.3	114.1	122.3	122.0	130.1	139.8	142.6
Other goods and services	a	91.4	96.2	100.0	102.7	108.5	113.8	115.4	123.6	127.8	128.0
Goods and services contributing to investment	a	96.0	96.4	100.0	103.0	107.0	111.4	114.7	118.9	122.7	123.9
Materials	a	99.1	96.9	100.0	101.9	104.5	107.4	111.5	115.2	117.5	118.3
Machinery and other equipment	a	91.6	92.5	100.0	104.5	110.3	117.5	122.1	124.0	126.1	124.7
Plant and machinery for cultivation		90.2	94.8	100.0	101.4	106.3	113.6	117.1	117.6	123.1	118.5
Plant and machinery for harvesting		90.1	89.2	100.0	107.7	115.8	125.1	130.2	132.5	132.5	132.5
Farm machinery and installations	a	97.0	97.2	100.0	100.9	102.8	104.6	109.3	112.4	115.2	114.3
Transport Equipment		104.1	99.8	100.0	100.2	100.6	100.7	104.5	109.4	111.7	114.0
Tractors		102.7	97.6	100.0	101.4	102.9	105.5	110.7	115.5	119.7	123.6
Other vehicles		106.9	104.5	100.0	97.8	95.7	90.8	91.7	96.8	95.3	94.0
Buildings		90.7	95.5	100.0	105.9	113.0	120.3	120.6	126.7	134.1	136.2
Other (Engineering and soil improvement operations)		92.7	96.0	100.0	101.8	106.7	111.6	117.7	120.1	123.2	125.6

a:- Part or all of the series is made up of annual data
q:- Part or all of the series is made up of quarterly data

Enquiries Defra prices team. Tel: ++44(0)1904 455249 or email: prices@defra.gsi.gov.uk

Footnotes:
This table shows the API for main categories and selected primary items. Further detail is available on request.
© Crown copyright, 2013

17.8 Index of Producer Prices of Agricultural Products, UK (2005=100)

Table 3 Outputs annual series		2003	2004	2005	2006	2007	2008	2009	2010	2011	2012
Total Outputs	a	100.4	103.3	100.0	104.0	119.3	142.7	136.3	145.1	165.0	172.8
Crop products	a	102.9	107.2	100.0	108.8	134.2	155.6	133.1	152.4	182.0	190.3
Cereals	a	107.6	116.8	100.0	111.8	166.7	207.1	150.1	172.4	245.6	253.0
Wheat	a	109.2	121.5	100.0	112.8	166.6	213.0	158.6	179.1	249.8	255.5
Wheat - Feeding	a	108.4	122.9	100.0	114.3	158.2	216.2	159.8	174.8	252.5	250.3
Wheat - Breadmaking		109.5	117.0	100.0	106.7	176.6	210.3	162.1	182.8	236.2	253.5
Wheat - Other Milling		112.3	121.5	100.0	113.6	188.5	206.9	152.8	190.3	255.1	277.8
Barley	a	105.5	106.8	100.0	109.5	170.1	195.7	131.3	157.8	232.9	243.7
Barley - Feeding	a	106.6	112.7	100.0	111.3	162.7	189.9	133.1	158.6	239.4	247.0
Barley - Malting		105.8	98.4	100.0	109.5	187.6	205.7	128.9	162.7	237.6	241.9
Oats	a	88.0	96.7	100.0	109.6	134.6	167.7	119.8	145.8	266.2	281.8
Oats - Milling		87.1	92.7	100.0	111.7	141.6	167.3	125.0	155.2	261.5	278.4
Oats - Feeding	a	88.6	98.8	100.0	108.4	129.7	167.8	116.4	140.1	270.4	284.7
Potatoes		93.8	130.2	100.0	130.7	146.4	153.8	123.8	141.1	150.5	173.4
Potatoes - Earlies		91.8	127.3	100.0	134.5	104.2	142.1	106.8	144.5	107.8	221.8
Potatoes - Main Crop		94.1	131.0	100.0	130.9	149.1	155.0	124.4	141.0	153.2	171.5
Industrial Crops	a	111.5	109.2	100.0	98.7	112.0	162.4	139.6	149.5	187.8	186.9
Oilseed Rape (non set aside)		123.7	117.1	100.0	119.8	143.9	238.4	184.2	204.7	289.4	281.8
Sugar Beet	a	101.6	103.4	100.0	80.0	82.5	92.2	97.5	98.5	95.1	100.2
Forage plants		76.3	88.7	100.0	95.2	128.6	145.6	147.7	181.5	214.2	198.2
Hay and dried grass		86.6	99.2	100.0	102.0	128.3	121.0	129.2	186.1	254.8	186.9
Straw		67.7	78.7	100.0	93.9	115.3	129.4	146.1	182.5	207.3	183.6
Other forage plants		99.0	115.3	100.0	97.7	166.3	195.0	154.9	177.8	227.2	241.2
Fresh Vegetables		104.1	95.6	100.0	109.1	122.1	117.5	113.9	131.9	119.7	141.8
Cauliflowers		97.3	82.6	100.0	105.1	130.7	107.7	114.3	128.4	115.3	131.8
Tomatoes				158.4	120.6	98.7	106.7	100.5	100.5	170.4	148.2
Cabbages		95.5	92.0	100.0	103.8	139.6	124.6	124.0	131.3	130.0	150.2
Lettuce		108.4	93.9	100.0	109.4	107.1	119.1	107.9	129.9	116.4	144.0
Carrots		90.3	83.7	100.0	107.6	123.4	128.2	129.5	117.6	126.5	141.3
Onions		118.7	115.3	100.0	129.3	165.4	131.2	133.3	211.5	192.4	158.2
Beans (Green)							133.1	102.5	87.1	125.0	106.3
Mushrooms		119.2	112.5	100.0	95.7	84.5	84.6	87.2	127.1	83.9	120.7
Fresh Fruit		111.9	98.4	100.0	104.1	107.4	126.4	124.6	129.6	132.2	140.1
Dessert Apples		110.7	104.4	100.0	105.7	121.5	130.9	131.4	140.8	147.4	167.5
Cooking Apples		135.8	121.3	100.0	111.5	122.9	155.1	127.5	129.1	133.5	170.9
Dessert Pears		102.7	102.2	100.0	108.6	106.0	134.0	149.7	131.3	134.7	153.7
Strawberries		111.3	87.8	100.0	96.5	101.5	112.9	122.1	130.4	135.1	123.2
Raspberries		101.8	96.6	100.0	111.5	100.5	119.6	120.9	123.6	121.0	124.2
Flowers and plants	a	101.3	99.6	100.0	103.7	111.0	120.2	124.9	151.2	165.9	167.5
Other crop products	a	81.6	86.2	100.0	100.5	113.3	119.4	111.5	104.8	131.9	132.2
Seeds	a	73.8	80.4	100.0	100.2	118.3	126.4	114.7	104.4	143.4	143.4
Animals and animal products	a	98.6	100.5	100.0	100.6	108.9	133.8	138.6	140.1	153.3	160.6
Animals (for slaughter & export)		98.7	100.0	100.0	102.7	106.1	129.4	144.5	143.8	157.2	164.4
Cattle and calves		93.3	99.1	100.0	108.2	109.9	141.9	151.4	144.2	166.1	185.9
Cattle (clean)		93.1	99.0	100.0	108.3	109.9	141.7	151.2	144.0	165.8	185.8
Cows and Bulls		93.9	93.9	100.0	99.8	100.0	158.7	160.7	164.6	213.9	208.3
Calves		135.3	137.1	100.0	117.0	132.6	155.0	193.6	158.2	165.1	198.0
Pigs		98.9	99.6	100.0	101.0	103.4	121.6	140.2	135.9	138.7	144.6
Pigs (clean)		99.3	99.6	100.0	101.0	104.1	121.7	140.2	136.4	139.5	144.8
Sows and Boars		83.1	99.1	100.0	101.5	80.9	126.4	151.7	132.7	126.3	151.6
Sheep and lambs		109.7	108.7	100.0	102.4	91.8	116.4	147.4	162.2	181.4	170.7
Sheep and lambs (clean)		108.0	107.1	100.0	102.0	90.6	116.0	143.8	156.4	174.2	163.7
Ewes and Rams		127.1	125.1	100.0	106.6	104.2	120.5	183.7	221.6	254.9	242.1
All Poultry	a	98.4	97.0	100.0	96.2	109.2	122.3	133.9	134.5	138.8	141.8
Chickens	a	98.3	96.5	100.0	94.9	108.7	114.9	129.6	130.5	133.0	134.8
Turkeys		103.7	101.0	100.0	99.4	114.6	157.6	157.7	155.3	166.2	174.9
Animal products	a	98.5	101.3	100.0	97.6	112.7	140.0	130.2	134.8	147.7	155.3
Milk		97.6	100.0	100.0	97.2	112.3	140.4	128.4	133.5	148.1	152.0
Eggs	q	104.7	109.9	100.0	104.0	118.3	140.4	144.7	137.8	137.9	174.2
Intensive eggs	q	113.9	115.5	100.0	108.2	122.0	148.9	156.9	151.8	154.0	205.6
Free range eggs	q	95.9	104.6	100.0	100.0	114.7	132.3	133.0	124.3	122.5	144.0
Wool clip	a	117.5	116.3	100.0	36.4	77.7	71.0	103.2	219.4	266.7	266.7

a:- Part or all of the series is made up of annual data

q:- Part or all of the series is made up of quarterly data

Enquiries Defra prices team. Tel: ++44(0)1904 455249 or email: prices@defra.gsi.gov.uk

Footnotes:
This table shows the API for main categories and selected primary items. Further detail is available on request.
© Crown copyright, 2013

17.9 Harmonised Indices of Comsumer Prices (HICPs) - International comparisons: EU countries: 2009 to 2013 Percentage change over 12 months

per cent

	Austria	Belgium	Bulgaria	Cyprus	Czech Republic	Denmark	Estonia	Finland	France	Germany	Greece	Hungary	Ireland	Italy	Latvia
Annual average															
	D7SK	D7SL	GHY8	D7RO	D7RP	D7SM	D7RQ	D7SN	D7SO	D7SP	D7SQ	D7RR	D7SS	D7ST	D7RS
2009	0.4	-	2.5	0.2	0.6	1.1	0.2	1.6	0.1	0.2	1.3	4.0	-1.7	0.8	3.3
2010	1.7	2.3	3.0	2.6	1.2	2.2	2.7	1.7	1.7	1.2	4.7	4.7	-1.6	1.6	-1.2
2011	3.6	3.4	3.4	3.5	2.1	2.7	5.1	3.3	2.3	2.5	3.1	3.9	1.2	2.9	4.2
2012	2.6	2.6	2.4	3.1	3.5	2.4	4.2	3.2	2.2	2.1	1.0	5.7	1.9	3.3	2.3
Monthly															
Jul 2012	2.1	2.0	2.4	3.8	3.3	2.1	4.1	3.1	2.2	1.9	0.9	5.7	2.0	3.6	1.9
Aug	2.3	2.6	3.1	4.5	3.4	2.6	4.2	3.3	2.4	2.2	1.2	6.0	2.6	3.3	1.9
Sep	2.8	2.6	3.4	3.6	3.5	2.5	4.1	3.4	2.2	2.1	0.3	6.4	2.4	3.4	1.9
Oct	2.9	2.7	3.0	2.6	3.6	2.3	4.2	3.5	2.1	2.1	0.9	6.0	2.1	2.8	1.6
Nov	2.9	2.2	2.7	1.4	2.8	2.2	3.8	3.2	1.6	1.9	0.4	5.3	1.6	2.6	1.5
Dec	2.9	2.1	2.8	1.5	2.4	1.9	3.6	3.5	1.5	2.0	0.3	5.1	1.7	2.6	1.6
Jan 2013	2.8	1.5	2.6	2.0	1.8	1.0	3.7	2.6	1.4	1.9	0.0	2.8	1.5	2.4	0.6
Feb	2.6	1.4	2.2	1.8	1.8	1.0	4.0	2.5	1.2	1.8	0.1	2.9	1.2	2.0	0.3
Mar	2.4	1.3	1.6	1.3	1.5	0.7	3.8	2.5	1.1	1.8	-0.2	2.3	0.6	1.8	0.3
Apr	2.1	1.1	0.9	0.1	1.7	0.4	3.4	2.4	0.8	1.1	-0.6	1.8	0.5	1.3	-0.4
May	2.4	1.1	1.0	0.2	1.2	0.6	3.6	2.5	0.9	1.6	-0.3	1.8	0.5	1.3	-0.2
Jun	2.2	1.5	1.2	0.8	1.6	0.6	4.1	2.3	1.0	1.9	-0.3	2.0	0.7	1.4	0.2
Jul	2.1	1.6	0.0	0.7	1.4	0.4	3.9	2.5	1.2	1.9	-0.5	1.7	0.7	1.2	0.5

per cent

	Lithuania	Luxembourg	Malta	Netherlands	Poland	Portugal	Romania	Slovakia	Slovenia	Spain	Sweden	United Kingdom [1]	EICP [2] EU 25 average [3]	EICP [2] EU 27 average [3]	MUICP average [4]
Annual average															
	D7RT	D7SU	D7RU	D7SV	D7RV	D7SX	GHY7	D7RW	D7RX	D7SY	D7SZ	D7G7	D7RY	GJ2E	D7SR
2009	4.2	-	1.8	1.0	4.0	-0.9	5.6	0.9	0.9	-0.2	1.9	2.2	..	1.0	0.3
2010	1.2	2.8	2.0	0.9	2.7	1.4	6.1	0.7	2.1	2.0	1.9	3.3	..	2.1	1.6
2011	4.1	3.7	2.5	2.5	3.9	3.6	5.8	4.1	2.1	3.1	1.4	4.5	..	3.1	2.7
2012	3.2	2.9	3.2	2.8	3.7	2.8	3.4	3.7	2.8	2.4	0.9	2.8	..	2.6	2.5
Monthly															
Jul 2012	2.9	2.7	4.2	2.6	4.0	2.8	3.1	3.8	2.6	2.2	0.7	2.6	..	2.5	2.4
Aug	3.4	2.8	3.2	2.5	3.8	3.2	4.0	3.8	3.1	2.7	0.9	2.5	..	2.7	2.6
Sep	3.3	3.2	2.9	2.5	3.8	2.9	5.4	3.8	3.7	3.5	1.0	2.2	..	2.7	2.6
Oct	3.2	3.2	3.2	3.3	3.4	2.1	5.0	3.9	3.2	3.5	1.2	2.7	..	2.6	2.5
Nov	2.8	2.7	3.6	3.2	2.7	1.9	4.4	3.5	2.8	3.0	0.8	2.7	..	2.4	2.2
Dec	2.9	2.5	2.8	3.4	2.2	2.1	4.6	3.4	3.1	3.0	1.0	2.7	..	2.3	2.2
Jan 2013	2.7	2.1	2.4	3.2	1.6	0.4	5.1	2.5	2.8	2.8	0.7	2.7	..	2.1	2.0
Feb	2.3	2.4	1.8	3.2	1.2	0.2	4.8	2.2	2.9	2.9	0.5	2.8	..	2.0	1.8
Mar	1.6	2.0	1.4	3.2	1.0	0.7	4.4	1.9	2.2	2.6	0.5	2.8	..	1.9	1.7
Apr	1.4	1.7	0.9	2.8	0.8	0.4	4.4	1.7	1.6	1.5	0.0	2.4	..	1.4	1.2
May	1.5	1.4	0.8	3.1	0.5	0.9	4.4	1.8	1.6	1.8	0.3	2.7	..	1.6	1.4
Jun	1.3	2.0	0.6	3.2	0.2	1.2	4.5	1.7	2.2	2.2	0.5	2.9	..	1.7	1.6
Jul	0.6	1.8	0.9	3.1	0.9	0.8	3.4	1.6	2.8	1.9	0.8	2.8	..	1.7	1.6

Key: - zero or negligible   .. Not available   * Provisional

† Date of earliest revision   ⌀ Estimated

1 Published as the CPI in the UK.

2 The EICP (European Index of Consumer Prices) is the official EU aggregate. It covers 15 member states until April 2004, 25 member states from May 2004 to Dec 2006, and 27 member states from Jan 2007.
The EU 25 annual average for 2004 is calculated from the EU 15 average from January to April and the EU 25 average from May to December.

3 The coverage of the European Union was extended to include Cyprus, Czech Republic, Estonia, Hungary, Latvia, Lithuania, Malta, Poland, Slovakia and Slovenia with effect from 1 May 2004, and Bulgaria and Romania from 1 Jan 2007. Data for the EU 25 average is available from May 2004 and for the EU 27 average from Jan 2007.

4 The coverage of the Monetary Union Indices of Consumer Prices (MUICP) was extended to include Greece with effect from Jan 2001 and Slovakia from Jan 2009.

Source:
Office for National Statistics
Prices Division
2.001 Cardiff Road
Newport
South Wales
NP10 8XG
Tel: +44 (0) 1633 456900

http://www.ons.gov.uk

Eurostat
www.ec.europa.eu/eurostat

this page is intentionally blank

Production

Production

Annual Business Survey
(Table 18.1)

The Annual Business Survey (ABS) estimates cover all UK businesses registered for Value Added Tax (VAT) and/or Pay As You Earn (PAYE) classified to the 2007 Standard Industrial Classification (SIC (2007)) headings listed in the tables. The ABS obtains details on these businesses from the Office for National Statistics (ONS) Inter-Departmental Business Register (IDBR).

As with all its statistical inquiries, ONS is concerned to minimise the form-filling burden of individual contributors and as such the ABS is a sample inquiry. The sample was designed as a stratified random sample of about 66,300 businesses; the inquiry population is stratified by SIC (2007) and employment using the information from the register.

The inquiry results are grossed up to the total population so that they relate to all active UK businesses on the IDBR for the sectors covered.

The results meet a wide range of needs for government, economic analysts and the business community at large. In official statistics the inquiry is an important source for the national accounts and input-output tables, and also provides weights for the indices of production and producer prices. Inquiry results also enable the UK to meet statistical requirements of the European Union.

Revised ABS results down to SIC (2007) 4 digit class level for 2008-2009, giving both analysis and tabular detail, are available from the ONS website at: www.ons.gov.uk with further extracts and bespoke analyses available on request.

UK Manufacturer's Sales by Industry
(Table 18.2)

Table 18.2 lists total UK manufacturers' sales by industry.

Number of local units in manufacturing industries
(Table 18.3)

The table shows the number of local units (sites) in manufacturing by employment size band. The classification breakdown is at division level (two digit) as classified to SIC(2003) held on the Inter-Departmental Business Register (IDBR). This register became fully operational in 1995 and combines information on VAT traders and PAYE employers in a statistical register comprising 2.1 million enterprises (businesses) representing nearly 99 per cent of economic activity.
UK Business: Activity, Size and Location 2007 provides further details and contains detailed information regarding enterprises in the UK including size, classification, and local units in the UK including size, classification and location.

For further information on the IDBR see the ONS website at: www.ons.gov.uk/idbr

Production of primary fuels
(Table 18.4)

This table shows indigenous production of primary fuels. It includes the extraction or capture of primary commodities and the generation or manufacture of secondary commodities. Production is always gross; that is, it includes the quantities used during the extraction or manufacturing process. Primary fuels are coal, natural gas (including colliery methane), oil, primary electricity (that is, electricity generated by hydro, nuclear wind and tide stations and also electricity imported from France through the interconnector) and renewables (includes solid renewables such as wood, straw and waste and gaseous renewables such as landfill gas and sewage gas). The figures are presented on a common basis expressed in million tonnes of oil equivalent. Estimates of the gross calorific values used for converting the statistics for the various fuels to these are given in the Digest of UK Energy Statistics available at:
www.decc.gov.uk/en/content/cms/statistics/publications/dukes/dukes.aspx

Total inland energy consumption
(Table 18.5)

This table shows energy consumption by fuel and final energy consumption by fuel and class of consumer. Primary energy consumption covers consumption of all primary fuels (defined above) for energy purposes. This measure of energy consumption includes energy that is lost by converting primary fuels into secondary fuels (the energy lost burning coal to generate electricity or the energy used by refineries to separate crude oil into fractions) in addition to losses in distribution. The other common way of measuring energy consumption is to measure the energy content of the fuels supplied to consumers. This is called final energyconsumption. It is net of fuel used by the energy industries, conversion, transmission and distribution losses. The figures are presented on a common basis, measured as energy supplied and expressed in million tonnes of oil equivalent. Estimates of the gross calorific values used for converting the statistics for the various fuels to these are given in the Digest of UK Energy Statistics available at:
www.decc.gov.uk/ en/content/cms/statistics/publications/dukes/dukes.aspx

So far as practicable the user categories have been grouped on the basis of the SIC(2007) although the methods used by each of the supply industries to identify end users are slightly different. Chapter 1 of the Digest of UK Energy Statistics gives more information on these figures.

Coal
(Table 18.6)

Since 1995, aggregate data on coal production have been obtained from the Coal Authority. In addition, main coal producers provide data in response to an annual Department of Energy and Climate Change (DECC) inquiry which covers production (deepmined and opencast), trade, stocks and disposals. HM Revenue & Customs (HMRC) also provides trade data for solid fuels. DECC collects information on the use of coal from the UK Iron and Steel Statistics Bureau and consumption of coal for electricity generation is covered by data provided by the electricity generators.

Gas
(Table 18.7)

Production figures, covering the production of gas from the UK Continental Shelf offshore and onshore gas fields and gas obtained during the production of oil, are obtained from returns made under the DECC's Petroleum Production Reporting System. Additional information is used on imports and exports of gas and details from the operators of gas terminals in the UK to complete the picture.

It is no longer possible to present information on fuels input into the gas industry and gas output and sales in the same format as in previous editions of this table. As such, users are directed to Chapter 4 of the 2002 edition of the Digest of UK Energy Statistics, where more detailed information on gas production and consumption in the UK is available.

DECC carry out an annual survey of gas suppliers to obtain details of gas sales to the various categories of consumer. Estimates are included for the suppliers with the smallest market share, since the DECC inquiry covers only the largest suppliers (that is, those known to supply more than 1,750 GWh per year).

Electricity
(Tables 18.8–18.10)

Tables 18.8 to 18.10 cover all generators and suppliers of electricity in the UK. The relationship between generation, supply, availability and consumption is as follows:

Electricity generated

less electricity used on works

equals electricity supplied (gross)

less electricity used in pumping at pumped storage stations.

equals electricity supplied (net)

plus imports (net of exports) of electricity

equals electricity available

less losses and statistical differences

equals electricity consumed

In Table 18.8 'major power producers' are those generating companies corresponding to the old public sector supply system:
• AES Electric Ltd.
• Baglan Generation Ltd.
• Barking Power Ltd.
• British Energy plc
• Centrica Energy
• Coolkeeragh ESB Ltd.
• Corby Power Ltd.
• Coryton Energy Company Ltd.
• Derwent Cogeneration Ltd.
• Drax Power Ltd.
• EDF Energy plc
• E.ON UK plc
• Energy Power Resources Ltd.
• Gaz De France
• GDF Suez Teesside Power Ltd
• Immingham CHP
• International Power plc
• Magnox Electric Ltd.
• Premier Power Ltd.
• RGS Energy Ltd.
• Rocksavage Power Company Ltd.
• RWE Npower plc
• Scottish Power plc
• Scottish and Southern Energy plc
• Seabank Power Ltd.
• SELCHP Ltd.
• Spalding Energy Company Ltd.
• Uskmouth Power Company Ltd.
• Western Power Generation Ltd.

Additionally, from 2007, the following major wind farm companies are included as 'major power producers':

• Airtricity
• Cumbria Wind Farms
• Fred Olsen
• H G Capital
• Renewable Energy Systems
• Vattenfall Wind

In Table 18.10 all fuels are converted to the common unit of million tonnes of oil equivalent, that is, the amounts of oil which would be needed to produce the output of electricity generated from those fuels.

More detailed statistics on energy are given in the Digest of United Kingdom Energy Statistics 2009. Readers may wish to note that the production and consumption of fuels are presented using commodity balances. A commodity balance shows the flows of an individual fuel through from production to final consumption, showing its use in transformation and energy industry own use.

Oil and oil products
(Tables 18.11–18.13)

Data on the production of crude oil, condensates and natural gases given in Table 19.11 are collected by DECC direct from the operators of production facilities and terminals situated on UK territory, either onshore or offshore, that is, on the UK Continental Shelf. Data are also collected from the companies on their trade in oil and oil products. These data are used in preference to the foreign trade as recorded by HMRC in Overseas Trade Statistics.

Data on the internal UK oil industry (that is, on the supply, refining and distribution of oil and oil products in the UK) are collected by the UK Petroleum Industry Association. These data, reported by individual refining companies and wholesalers and supplemented where necessary by data from other sources, provide the contents of Tables 19.12 and 19.13. The data are presented in terms of deliveries to the inland UK market. This is regarded as an acceptable proxy for actual consumption of products. The main shortcoming is that, while changes in stocks held by companies in central storage areas are taken into account, changes in the levels of stocks further down the retail ladder (such as stocks held on petrol station forecourts) are not. This is not thought to result in a significant degree of difference in the data.

Iron and steel
(Tables 18.14–18.16)
Iron and steel industry
The general definition of the UK iron and steel industry is based on groups 271 'ECSC iron and steel', 272 'Tubes', and 273 'Primary Transformation' of the UK SIC(92), except those parts of groups 272 and 273 which cover cast iron pipes, drawn wire, cold formed sections and Ferro alloys.

The definition excludes certain products which may be made by works within the industry, such as refined iron, finished steel castings, steel tyres, wheels, axles and rolled rings, open and closed die forgings, colliery arches and springs. Iron foundries and steel stockholders are also considered to be outside of the industry.

Statistics

The statistics for the UK iron and steel industry are compiled by the Iron and Steel Statistics Bureau (ISSB) Ltd from data collected from UK steel producing companies, with the exception of trade data which is based on HMRC data.

'Crude steel' is the total of usable ingots, usable continuously cast semi-finished products and liquid steel for castings.

'Production of finished products' is the total production at the mill of that product after deduction of any material which is immediately scrapped

'Deliveries' are based on invoiced tonnages and will include deliveries made to steel stockholders and service centres by the UK steel industry.

For more detailed information on definitions etc please contact ISSB Ltd. on 020 7343 3900.

Fertilisers
(Table 18.17)

Table 18.17 gives the quantity of the fertiliser nutrients nitrogen (N), phosphate (P2O5) and potash (K2O) used by UK farmers during the growing season, or fertiliser year, which is taken as the year ending in June.

Minerals
(Table 18.18)

Table 18.18 gives, separately for Great Britain and Northern Ireland, the production of minerals extracted from the ground. The figures for chemicals and metals are estimated from the quality of the ore which is extracted. The data come from an annual census of the quarrying industry, which, for Great Britain, is conducted by ONS for Communities and Local Government and Business, Innovation and Skills (BIS) –formally known as Business, Enterprise and Regulatory Reform (BERR)

Building materials
(Table 18.19)

Table 18.19 gives the production and deliveries of a number of building materials, including bricks, concrete blocks, sand and gravel, slate, cement, concrete roofing tiles and ready mixed cement. This data comes from the Monthly Bulletin of Building Materials and Components.

Construction
(Tables 18.20–18.21)

Figures for the construction industry are based on SIC(2003).

The value of output represents the value of construction work done during the quarter in Great Britain and is derived from returns made by private contractors and public authorities with their own direct labour forces. The series (and the accompanying index of the volume of output) include estimates of the output of small firms and self-employed workers not recorded in the regular quarterly output inquiry.

The new orders statistics are collected from private contractors and analysed by the principal types of construction work involved. The series includes speculative work for eventual sale or lease undertaken on the initiative of the respondent where no formal contract or order is involved.

Engineering turnover and orders
(Tables 18.22–18.23)

The figures represent the output of UK-based manufacturers classified to Subsections DK and DL of the SIC(2003). They are derived from the monthly production inquiry (MPI) and include estimates for non-responders and for establishments which are not sampled.

Drink and tobacco
(Tables 18.24–18.25)

Data for these tables are derived by HMRC from the systems for collecting excise duties.
Alcoholic drinks and tobacco products become liable for duty when released for consumption in the
UK. Figures for releases include both home-produced products and commercial imports. Production
figures are also available for potable spirits distilled and beer brewed in the UK.

Alcoholic drink
(Table 18.24)

The figures for imported ad other spirits released for home consumption include gin and other
UK produced spirits for which a breakdown is not available.

Since June 1993 beer duty has been charged when the beer leaves the brewery or other registered
premises. Previously duty was chargeable at an earlier stage (the worts stage) in the brewing process
and an allowance was made for wastage. Figures for years prior to 1994 include adjustments to bring
them into line with current data. The change in June 1993 also led to the availability of data on the
strength; a series in hectolitres of pure alcohol is shown from 1994.

Made wine with alcoholic strength from 1.2 per cent to 5.5 per cent is termed 'coolers'. Included in
'coolers' are alcoholic lemonade and similar products of appropriate strength. From 28 April 2002
duty on spirit-based 'coolers' (ready to drink products) is charged at the same rate as spirits per litre
of alcohol. Made wine coolers include only wine based 'coolers' from this period.

Tobacco products
(Table 18.25)

Releases of cigarettes and other tobacco products tend to be higher in the period before a Budget.
Products may then be stocked, duty paid, before being sold.

The industries are now grouped according to the 2007 Standard Industrial Classification at 2-digit level.

18.1 PRODUCTION AND CONSTRUCTION INDUSTRIES

	Description	Year	Number of enterprises	Total turnover	Approximate gross value added at basic prices (aGVA)	Total purchases of goods, materials and services	Total employment - point in time [1]	Total employment - average during the year [1]
	Standard Industrial Classification (Revised 2007)		Number	£ million	£ million	£ million	Thousand	Thousand
Section	Division							
B-F	Production and Construction	2009	411,950	797,484	264,428	507,669	4,369	4,373
		2010	397,056	835,034	276,229	537,030	4,168	4,222
		2011	396,645	892,106	285,411	591,093	4,203	4,244
B-E	Production industries	2009	136,022	611,347	195,543	394,009	2,896	2,866
		2010	131,774	652,941	208,870	425,519	2,821	2,864
		2011	131,430	702,639	215,261	471,926	2,851	2,854
B	Mining and quarrying	2009	1,238	45,940	23,663	22,413	58	54
		2010	1,152	47,785	26,488	21,882	60	61
		2011	1,206	53,951	28,597	26,469	65	63
05	Mining of coal and lignite	2009	25	864	349	537	*	*
		2010	23	917	350	552	6	6
		2011	21	*	*	744	6	7
06	Extraction of crude petroleum and natural gas	2009	94	34,878	19,668	15,517	*	*
		2010	99	36,950	22,198	15,402	12	15
		2011	124	42,317	24,589	18,928	13	13
07	Mining of metal ores	2009	-	-	-	-	*	*
		2010	-	-	-	-	-	-
		2011	4	*	*	4	-	-
08	Other mining and quarrying	2009	751	3,379	1,031	2,185	19	19
		2010	708	3,394	927	2,327	17	17
		2011	718	4,097	1,205	2,793	*	*
09	Mining support service activities	2009	368	6,819	2,616	4,174	20	17
		2010	322	6,524	3,013	3,601	25	23
		2011	339	6,358	2,367	4,001	*	*
C	Manufacturing	2009	128,426	449,873	131,202	294,215	2,580	2,563
		2010	123,979	482,086	145,997	317,333	2,479	2,523
		2011	122,591	516,408	149,313	349,623	2,495	2,510
10	Manufacture of food products	2009	6,327	69,673	18,762	50,821	372	364
		2010	6,377	70,560	18,979	51,622	377	380
		2011	6,444	73,175	19,271	54,355	377	376
11	Manufacture of beverages	2009	935	18,198	5,694	9,519	*	*
		2010	975	17,795	5,627	8,952	*	*
		2011	1,034	17,635	*	*	*	*
12	Manufacture of tobacco products	2009	10	10,018	1,645	959	*	*
		2010	10	10,248	1,647	832	*	*
		2011	10	10,418	*	*	*	*
13	Manufacture of textiles	2009	4,068	5,047	1,887	3,115	61	59
		2010	3,935	5,304	1,934	3,463	*	*
		2011	3,871	5,473	1,847	3,668	54	54
14	Manufacture of wearing apparel	2009	3,572	2,561	651	1,862	31	32
		2010	3,389	2,816	885	1,928	38	40
		2011	3,378	2,834	831	2,009	29	30
15	Manufacture of leather and related products	2009	577	762	242	504	*	*
		2010	525	893	325	593	*	*
		2011	540	976	365	642	*	*
16	Manufacture of wood and of products of wood and cork, except furniture; manufacture of articles of straw and plaiting materials	2009	8,033	6,498	2,058	4,361	68	63
		2010	7,583	6,693	2,372	4,385	74	76
		2011	7,321	6,806	2,454	4,363	61	58

18.1 PRODUCTION AND CONSTRUCTION INDUSTRIES

Description	Year	Number of enterprises	Total turnover	Approximate gross value added at basic prices (aGVA)	Total purchases of goods, materials and services	Total employment - point in time [1]	Total employment - average during the year [1]
Standard Industrial Classification (Revised 2007)		Number	£ million	£ million	£ million	Thousand	Thousand
Section Division							
17 Manufacture of paper and paper products	2009	1,881	10,873	2,968	7,889	*	*
	2010	1,770	10,796	3,541	7,298	54	54
	2011	1,679	11,507	4,049	7,561	56	58
18 Printing and reproduction of recorded media	2009	15,433	11,383	5,068	6,275	131	118
	2010	14,465	11,388	5,087	6,300	134	139
	2011	13,923	11,411	5,337	6,113	121	127
19 Manufacture of coke and refined petroleum products	2009	208	32,798	1,418	20,725	*	*
	2010	174	39,300	2,248	26,597	*	*
	2011	164	49,895	2,232	38,281	10	9
20 Manufacture of chemicals and chemical products	2009	2,710	34,074	9,087	24,397	116	120
	2010	2,565	37,764	10,326	28,061	106	110
	2011	2,464	38,874	8,910	30,330	114	117
21 Manufacture of basic pharmaceutical products and pharmaceutical preparations	2009	465	16,071	7,824	8,325	46	39
	2010	444	18,716	9,629	9,163	44	48
	2011	448	17,248	7,417	9,863	44	45
22 Manufacture of rubber and plastic products	2009	6,264	20,064	6,845	13,095	164	155
	2010	5,994	19,789	7,118	12,824	153	148
	2011	5,809	22,182	7,881	14,478	156	154
23 Manufacture of other non-metallic mineral products	2009	4,150	13,241	3,693	9,196	104	103
	2010	3,958	14,164	4,502	9,568	93	90
	2011	3,799	14,248	3,987	10,187	96	96
24 Manufacture basic metals	2009	1,505	15,986	3,196	12,364	74	68
	2010	1,452	17,964	4,370	14,078	72	76
	2011	1,403	19,661	4,600	15,320	75	76
25 Manufacture of fabricated metal products, except machinery and equipment	2009	26,814	28,880	12,039	16,505	329	341
	2010	25,592	30,335	12,042	18,554	281	290
	2011	24,801	31,745	13,170	18,866	305	302
26 Manufacture of computer, electronic and optical products	2009	6,968	17,802	7,453	10,277	120	116
	2010	6,384	20,033	8,314	11,781	128	133
	2011	6,117	19,592	8,560	11,289	122	128
27 Manufacture of electrical equipment	2009	2,960	13,086	4,156	8,734	87	94
	2010	2,928	12,824	4,503	8,580	92	93
	2011	2,951	14,016	4,450	9,561	97	95
28 Manufacture of machinery and equipment n.e.c	2009	9,203	31,105	11,044	19,330	198	193
	2010	8,644	33,389	12,249	21,386	184	190
	2011	8,251	37,833	13,423	24,879	201	199
29 Manufacture of motor vehicles, trailers and semi-trailers	2009	2,999	38,556	5,989	32,063	142	158
	2010	2,794	46,500	10,045	36,799	134	135
	2011	2,703	54,375	11,253	43,546	131	129
30 Manufacture of other transport equipment	2009	1,867	26,003	8,206	18,123	145	157
	2010	1,856	26,819	8,081	18,631	137	141
	2011	1,817	28,208	9,605	18,436	139	134
31 Manufacture of furniture	2009	6,381	6,817	2,526	4,287	91	94
	2010	6,207	7,091	2,873	4,239	70	67
	2011	6,129	6,460	2,599	3,913	75	81
32 Other manufacturing	2009	9,820	8,322	3,618	4,604	90	86
	2010	9,732	8,712	3,938	4,760	89	88
	2011	9,838	9,502	3,987	5,615	88	95

18.1 PRODUCTION AND CONSTRUCTION INDUSTRIES

Description		Year	Number of enterprises	Total turnover	Approximate gross value added at basic prices (aGVA)	Total purchases of goods, materials and services	Total employment - point in time [1]	Total employment - average during the year [1]
Standard Industrial Classification (Revised 2007)			Number	£ million	£ million	£ million	Thousand	Thousand
Section	Division							
33	Repair and installation of machinery and equipment	2009	5,276	12,054	5,134	6,884	90	83
		2010	6,226	12,191	5,364	6,938	99	102
		2011	7,697	12,336	5,634	6,651	86	89
D	Electricity, gas, steam and air conditioning supply	2009	591	87,539	26,149	63,599	121	112
		2010	647	94,424	21,561	72,362	130	125
		2011	1,219	100,735	21,206	80,139	131	123
E	Water supply, sewerage, waste management, and remediation activities	2009	5,767	27,995	14,529	13,782	137	137
		2010	5,996	28,646	14,824	13,942	152	156
		2011	6,414	31,544	16,145	15,695	159	158
36	Water collection, treatment and supply	2009	137	11,290	8,059	3,615	*	*
		2010	118	10,138	7,623	2,754	*	*
		2011	119	10,246	8,024	2,485	*	*
37	Sewerage	2009	942	2,449	1,936	686	14	15
		2010	935	2,424	1,859	724	12	12
		2011	896	2,361	1,927	608	11	11
38	Waste collection, treatment and disposal activities; materials recovery	2009	4,443	14,158	4,477	9,432	85	83
		2010	4,596	15,895	5,245	10,373	102	104
		2011	4,940	18,789	6,098	12,546	111	110
39	Remediation activities and other waste management services	2009	245	99	57	49	*	*
		2010	347	189	97	90	*	*
		2011	459	148	96	55	*	*
F	Construction	2009	275,928	186,137	68,885	113,660	1,473	1,507
		2010	265,282	182,093	67,359	111,511	1,347	1,358
		2011	265,215	189,467	70,150	119,168	1,352	1,391
41	Construction of buildings	2009	82,181	76,254	25,221	48,097	410	457
		2010	76,980	71,933	22,624	46,489	385	384
		2011	73,696	71,561	23,440	47,483	393	403
42	Civil engineering	2009	22,956	41,529	12,686	28,641	226	217
		2010	21,430	36,935	12,033	24,691	208	214
		2011	20,093	39,332	12,446	27,322	200	202
43	Specialised construction activities	2009	170,791	68,355	30,978	36,922	836	832
		2010	166,872	73,225	32,702	40,331	755	760
		2011	171,426	78,575	34,264	44,362	759	786

Source: Annual Business Survey (ABS)

The following symbols and abbreviations are used throughout the ABS releases;

* Information suppressed to avoid disclosure

.. not available

- nil or less than half the level of rounding

The sum of constituent items in tables may not always agree exactly with the totals shown due to rounding.

Notes:

1. Total employment - point in time and Total employment - average during the year are from the Business Register and Employment Survey (BRES). Caution should be taken when combining financial data from the ABS with employment data from BRES due to differences in methodology. More information can be found in the ABS Technical Report.

18.1 PRODUCTION AND CONSTRUCTION INDUSTRIES

Description	Year	Total employment costs	Total net capital expenditure	Total capital expenditure- acquisitions	Total capital expenditure - disposals	Total stocks and work in progress - value at end of year	Total stocks and work in progress - value at beginning of year	Total stocks and work in progress - increase during year
Standard Industrial Classification (Revised 2007)		£ million	£ million	£ million	£ million	£ million	£ million	£ million
Section Division								
B-F Production and Construction	2009	124,923	32,348	38,816	6,468	103,636	107,201	-3,565
	2010	123,557	32,410	38,564	6,154	94,199	93,994	205
	2011	125,296	43,208	50,673	7,465	93,752	88,680	5,072
B-E Production industries	2009	89,035	29,026	32,212	3,186	54,244	54,454	-211
	2010	87,944	28,443	31,571	3,127	55,498	52,372	3,126
	2011	89,836	36,431	39,446	3,015	59,943	54,897	5,047
B Mining and quarrying	2009	3,831	5,590	5,889	299	1,453	1,403	50
	2010	4,275	5,988	6,311	323	1,570	1,467	103
	2011	4,681	8,910	9,184	274	1,970	1,774	195
05 Mining of coal and lignite	2009	313	116	*	*	117	93	24
	2010	313	107	*	*	103	118	-15
	2011	303	*	126	*	110	107	3
06 Extraction of crude petroleum and natural gas	2009	1,704	5,018	5,129	111	865	775	90
	2010	1,921	5,493	*	*	853	832	21
	2011	2,120	*	8,445	*	1,137	953	184
07 Mining of metal ores	2009	-	-	-	-	-	-	-
	2010	-	-	-	-	-	-	-
	2011	2	3	3	-	-	-	-
08 Other mining and quarrying	2009	576	116	153	36	273	307	-33
	2010	591	155	191	36	274	276	-2
	2011	705	202	256	54	321	328	-7
09 Mining support service activities	2009	1,237	340	478	138	198	229	-31
	2010	1,450	234	340	107	341	241	100
	2011	1,552	331	355	24	401	387	15
C Manufacturing	2009	76,151	9,342	11,609	2,267	47,831	50,074	-2,243
	2010	74,231	9,707	11,885	2,178	50,095	46,562	3,533
	2011	74,964	11,573	13,707	2,133	53,680	49,401	4,278
10 Manufacture of food products	2009	9,522	1,369	1,704	335	4,599	4,533	67
	2010	9,429	1,946	2,205	259	4,661	4,391	270
	2011	9,433	1,739	1,958	219	4,725	4,219	507
11 Manufacture of beverages	2009	1,953	616	*	*	5,133	4,790	343
	2010	1,719	533	664	131	5,092	4,890	203
	2011	1,820	659	*	*	5,406	5,047	359
12 Manufacture of tobacco products	2009	156	51	*	*	262	186	76
	2010	145	94	96	2	220	224	-4
	2011	132	50	*	*	175	222	-48
13 Manufacture of textiles	2009	1,163	78	107	29	618	655	-37
	2010	1,113	87	131	44	754	650	104
	2011	1,144	137	153	16	745	696	48
14 Manufacture of wearing apparel	2009	445	15	20	5	386	428	-42
	2010	450	24	28	4	482	476	6
	2011	479	49	52	3	369	352	18
15 Manufacture of leather and related products	2009	157	13	14	1	141	152	-11
	2010	156	26	28	1	133	105	28
	2011	186	25	25	1	179	146	34
16 Manufacture of wood and of products of wood and cork, except furniture; manufacture of articles of straw and plaiting materials	2009	1,332	185	209	23	520	597	-78
	2010	1,343	89	159	70	602	542	60
	2011	1,398	128	192	64	608	623	-15

18.1 PRODUCTION AND CONSTRUCTION INDUSTRIES

Description		Year	Total employment costs	Total net capital expenditure	Total capital expenditure- acquisitions	Total capital expenditure - disposals	Total stocks and work in progress - value at end of year	Total stocks and work in progress - value at beginning of year	Total stocks and work in progress - increase during year
Standard Industrial Classification (Revised 2007)			£ million	£ million	£ million	£ million	£ million	£ million	£ million
Section	Division								
17	Manufacture of paper and paper products	2009	1,829	134	232	98	772	793	-21
		2010	1,851	166	233	67	904	857	47
		2011	1,889	310	354	43	920	828	91
18	Printing and reproduction of recorded media	2009	3,407	352	488	137	451	493	-42
		2010	3,034	248	361	113	503	501	2
		2011	2,842	280	420	140	498	485	13
19	Manufacture of coke and refined petroleum products	2009	702	375	390	16	1,806	1,353	453
		2010	810	206	382	176	2,332	1,881	451
		2011	969	535	560	25	3,854	2,842	1,012
20	Manufacture of chemicals and chemical products	2009	4,507	711	883	173	3,420	3,980	-560
		2010	4,273	917	1,004	87	3,660	3,225	435
		2011	4,381	953	1,101	148	4,005	3,665	340
21	Manufacture of basic pharmaceutical products and pharmaceutical preparations	2009	2,692	550	617	67	1,994	1,919	75
		2010	2,191	505	553	48	1,937	1,876	61
		2011	1,847	438	465	27	1,893	1,878	14
22	Manufacture of rubber and plastic products	2009	4,365	423	537	113	1,787	1,916	-128
		2010	4,046	458	518	61	1,797	1,665	132
		2011	4,143	508	609	100	2,004	1,835	170
23	Manufacture of other non-metallic mineral products	2009	2,871	324	459	135	1,460	1,719	-258
		2010	2,789	292	392	100	1,661	1,615	46
		2011	2,732	347	423	76	1,504	1,431	73
24	Manufacture basic metals	2009	2,687	230	278	49	2,073	2,496	-423
		2010	2,811	258	287	29	2,649	2,166	483
		2011	2,863	431	489	58	2,728	2,460	268
25	Manufacture of fabricated metal products, except machinery and equipment	2009	7,658	546	675	129	2,849	3,210	-361
		2010	7,629	608	743	134	3,322	3,094	228
		2011	7,809	908	1,051	143	3,511	3,235	276
26	Manufacture of computer, electronic and optical products	2009	3,955	294	384	90	2,674	2,732	-58
		2010	4,037	416	492	75	2,441	2,356	85
		2011	4,168	480	553	73	2,601	2,338	263
27	Manufacture of electrical equipment	2009	2,742	161	241	80	1,428	1,605	-177
		2010	2,568	224	299	75	1,619	1,356	263
		2011	2,545	158	236	78	1,743	1,730	13
28	Manufacture of machinery and equipment n.e.c	2009	6,767	528	716	188	3,878	4,632	-754
		2010	6,870	537	752	215	3,875	3,620	255
		2011	7,016	471	847	376	4,409	3,927	482
29	Manufacture of motor vehicles, trailers and semi-trailers	2009	4,969	1,161	1,329	168	2,765	3,212	-446
		2010	4,922	1,001	1,128	127	3,196	2,771	425
		2011	5,077	1,662	1,715	53	3,770	3,277	492
30	Manufacture of other transport equipment	2009	5,450	616	701	85	5,666	5,356	310
		2010	5,572	672	794	122	5,193	5,363	-170
		2011	5,322	709	858	149	5,109	5,305	-196
31	Manufacture of furniture	2009	1,642	172	198	26	629	660	-31
		2010	1,634	116	140	25	608	587	21
		2011	1,663	124	168	44	587	533	54
32	Other manufacturing	2009	1,980	260	318	58	1,165	1,264	-99
		2010	1,986	196	276	79	1,163	1,175	-12
		2011	2,139	275	319	45	1,202	1,140	62

18.1 PRODUCTION AND CONSTRUCTION INDUSTRIES

Description	Year	Total employment costs	Total net capital expenditure	Total capital expenditure- acquisitions	Total capital expenditure - disposals	Total stocks and work in progress - value at end of year	Total stocks and work in progress - value at beginning of year	Total stocks and work in progress - increase during year
Standard Industrial Classification (Revised 2007)		£ million	£ million	£ million	£ million	£ million	£ million	£ million
Section Division								
33 Repair and installation of machinery and equipment	2009	3,201	178	258	81	1,353	1,395	-41
	2010	2,854	87	221	134	1,290	1,176	114
	2011	2,969	198	260	62	1,138	1,187	-50
D Electricity, gas, steam and air conditioning supply	2009	4,822	8,052	8,514	462	4,170	2,207	1,963
	2010	5,286	7,434	7,811	378	2,889	3,574	-685
	2011	5,765	9,801	10,256	455	3,381	2,935	446
E Water supply, sewerage, waste management, and remediation activities	2009	4,230	6,042	6,199	158	790	771	19
	2010	4,152	5,315	5,563	248	944	769	174
	2011	4,426	6,147	6,299	152	913	786	127
36 Water collection, treatment and supply	2009	1,605	4,245	4,273	27	137	171	-34
	2010	1,363	3,305	3,345	41	145	137	8
	2011	1,391	4,000	4,028	27	175	193	-17
37 Sewerage	2009	376	*	*	*	13	13	1
	2010	423	*	*	39	21	20	1
	2011	355	*	*	27	18	13	5
38 Waste collection, treatment and disposal activities; materials recovery	2009	2,202	*	*	*	635	585	50
	2010	2,331	*	*	167	774	607	167
	2011	2,611	*	*	98	715	579	137
39 Remediation activities and other waste management services	2009	47	17	18	2	5	2	3
	2010	34	10	12	1	3	5	-2
	2011	68	30	30	-	4	1	3
F Construction	2009	35,888	3,322	6,604	3,282	49,392	52,747	-3,355
	2010	35,612	3,966	6,993	3,027	38,701	41,622	-2,921
	2011	35,460	6,777	11,227	4,451	33,809	33,784	25
41 Construction of buildings	2009	10,002	2,250	4,777	2,527	43,734	46,576	-2,841
	2010	10,123	2,701	4,943	2,242	32,305	35,040	-2,734
	2011	10,463	4,902	8,474	3,572	27,601	28,156	-554
42 Civil engineering	2009	7,985	460	679	219	3,093	3,264	-172
	2010	7,836	352	658	307	3,028	3,193	-165
	2011	7,673	598	867	268	2,721	2,362	359
43 Specialised construction activities	2009	17,902	612	1,148	536	2,565	2,907	-342
	2010	17,653	914	1,392	478	3,368	3,389	-21
	2011	17,324	1,276	1,887	610	3,486	3,266	220

Source: Annual Business Survey (ABS)

The following symbols and abbreviations are used throughout the ABS releases;

* Information suppressed to avoid disclosure

.. not available

- nil or less than half the level of rounding

The sum of constituent items in tables may not always agree exactly with the totals shown due to rounding.

Notes:

1. Total employment - point in time and Total employment - average during the year are from the Business Register and Employment Survey (BRES). Caution should be taken when combining financial data from the ABS with employment data from BRES due to differences in methodology. More information can be found in the ABS Technical Report.

18.2 UK Manufacturer's Sales by Industry

S - Suppressed as disclosive

Industry	SIC(07)	2008	2009	2010	2011	£ million 2012
Other mining and quarrying						
Quarrying of ornamental and building stone, limestone, gypsum, chalk and slate	08110	12	9	S	12	12
Operation of gravel and sand pits; mining of clays and kaolin	08120	95	68	74	54	55
Mining of chemical and fertiliser minerals	08910	S	S	S	S	S
Extraction of salt	08930	S	S	S	S	S
Other mining and quarrying n.e.c.	08990	S	S	S	S	33
Manufacture of food products						
Processing and preserving of meat	10110	4,489	4,473	4,637	5,035	5,460
Processing and preserving of poultry meat	10120	2,618	2,682	2,732	2,894	S
Production of meat and poultry meat products	10130	5,084	5,222	5,383	5,318	5,459
Processing and preserving of fish, crustaceans and molluscs	10200	1,700	1,620	1,887	2,106	2,215
Processing and preserving of potatoes	10310	S	S	S	S	S
Manufacture of fruit and vegetable juice	10320	592	491	495	549	575
Other processing and preserving of fruit and vegetables	10390	2,580	2,720	2,841	2,910	2,850
Manufacture of oils and fats	10410	2,256	981	930	1,198	1,174
Manufacture of margarine and similar edible fats	10420	S	S	S	S	482
Operation of dairies and cheese making	10510	6,637	6,445	6,829	7,075	6,871
Manufacture of ice cream	10520	593	562	600	566	590
Manufacture of grain mill products	10610	3,583	3,506	3,410	3,770	3,779
Manufacture of starches and starch products	10620	437	374	304	S	S
Manufacture of bread; manufacture of fresh pastry goods and cakes	10710	5,581	5,282	S	S	5,735
Manufacture of rusks and biscuits; manufacture of preserved pastry goods and cakes	10720	3,229	S	3,695	S	4,068
Manufacture of macaroni, noodles, couscous and similar farinaceous products	10730	30	S	35	S	S
Manufacture of sugar	10810	1,108	1,128	1,076	S	1,267
Manufacture of cocoa, chocolate and sugar confectionery	10820	3,704	3,528	3,781	2,707	2,757
Processing of tea and coffee	10830	1,618	S	S	S	S
Manufacture of condiments and seasonings	10840	1,453	1,416	1,482	1,636	1,619
Manufacture of prepared meals and dishes	10850	1,781	2,302	2,477	2,546	S
Manufacture of homogenised food preparations and dietetic food	10860	S	30	29	33	31
Manufacture of other food products n.e.c.	10890	2,773	2,991	3,019	3,295	3,602
Manufacture of prepared feeds for farm animals	10910	3,173	3,002	3,278	3,811	3,775
Manufacture of prepared pet foods	10920	1,385	1,508	1,536	1,541	1,527
Manufacture of beverages						
Distilling, rectifying and blending of spirits	11010	2,662	2,502	S	S	3,709
Manufacture of wine from grape	11020	S	S	S	S	S
Manufacture of cider and other fruit wines	11030	608	641	574	760	768
Manufacture of other non-distilled fermented beverages	11040	0	0	0	0	0
Manufacture of beer	11050	3,753	4,766	3,914	4,081	3,604
Manufacture of malt	11060	S	418	S	377	S
Manufacture of soft drinks; production of mineral waters and other bottled waters	11070	S	3,538	3,963	S	4,103
Manufacture of tobacco products						
Manufacture of tobacco products	12000	1,735	1,912	1,626	1,673	1,793

18.2 UK Manufacturer's Sales by Industry

S - Suppressed as disclosive

Industry	SIC(07)	2008	2009	2010	2011	£ million 2012
Manufacture of textiles						
Preparation and spinning of textile fibres	13100	591	315	367	384	401
Weaving of textiles	13200	548	469	542	591	603
Finishing of textiles	13300	538	414	490	517	496
Manufacture of knitted and crocheted fabrics	13910	155	134	S	S	S
Manufacture of made-up textile articles, except apparel	13920	1,340	1,042	1,094	1,064	1,173
Manufacture of carpets and rugs	13930	735	691	675	S	676
Manufacture of cordage, rope, twine and netting	13940	88	64	46	52	57
Manufacture of non-wovens and articles made from non-wovens, except apparel	13950	S	S	S	172	S
Manufacture of other technical and industrial textiles	13960	S	S	279	309	299
Manufacture of other textiles n.e.c.	13990	129	102	108	108	109
Manufacture of wearing apparel						
Manufacture of leather clothes	14110	4	6	S	S	6
Manufacture of workwear	14120	255	214	191	171	156
Manufacture of other outerwear	14130	667	551	538	474	564
Manufacture of underwear	14140	448	397	S	388	413
Manufacture of other wearing apparel and accessories	14190	250	242	215	198	214
Manufacture of articles of fur	14200	S	0	S	S	1
Manufacture of knitted and crocheted hosiery	14310	110	S	108	95	86
Manufacture of other knitted and crocheted apparel	14390	138	113	124	159	161
Manufacture of leather and related products						
Tanning and dressing of leather; dressing and dyeing of fur	15110	183	150	228	263	244
Manufacture of luggage, handbags and the like, saddlery and harness	15120	130	111	134	119	138
Manufacture of footwear	15200	S	S	S	236	257
Manufacture of wood and of products of wood and cork; except furniture; manufacture of articles of straw and plaiting materials						
Sawmilling and planing of wood	16100	891	797	897	968	981
Manufacture of veneer sheets and wood-based panels	16210	959	801	836	856	881
Manufacture of assembled parquet floors	16220	2	S	S	2	S
Manufacture of other builders' carpentry and joinery	16230	3,588	2,803	3,212	3,014	2,936
Manufacture of wooden containers	16240	463	388	434	401	450
Manufacture of other products of wood; manufacture of articles of cork, straw and plaiting materials	16290	441	334	332	336	365
Manufacture of paper and paper products						
Manufacture of pulp	17110	S	S	S	S	S
Manufacture of paper and paperboard	17120	2,664	2,309	2,437	2,507	2,482
Manufacture of corrugated paper and paperboard and of containers of paper and paperboard	17210	3,551	3,097	3,399	3,815	3,948
Manufacture of household and sanitary goods and of toilet requisites	17220	1,985	2,201	S	2,302	S
Manufacture of paper stationery	17230	756	641	548	548	531
Manufacture of wallpaper	17240	S	113	136	132	136
Manufacture of other articles of paper and paperboard	17290	1,296	970	962	989	952
Printing and reproduction of recorded media						
Printing of newspapers	18110	304	217	218	219	S
Other printing	18120	7,726	7,478	7,659	7,965	7,849
Pre-press and pre-media services	18130	837	470	455	404	391
Binding and related services	18140	320	275	271	232	234
Reproduction of recorded media	18200	214	167	111	S	S

18.2 UK Manufacturer's Sales by Industry

Industry	SIC(07)	2008	2009	2010	2011	£ million 2012
Manufacture of coke and refined petroleum products						
Manufacture of coke oven products	19100	S	S	S	S	S
Manufacture of chemicals and chemical products						
Manufacture of industrial gases	20110	581	528	594	623	631
Manufacture of dyes and pigments	20120	1,124	930	1,001	1,066	839
Manufacture of other inorganic basic chemicals	20130	1,235	1,100	1187	1,209	958
Manufacture of other organic basic chemicals	20140	4,529	3,111	3,579	3,597	3,583
Manufacture of fertilisers and nitrogen compounds	20150	1,362	1,118	1,294	1,550	1,598
Manufacture of plastics in primary forms	20160	3,564	3,038	3,518	3,930	3,884
Manufacture of synthetic rubber in primary forms	20170	503	298	392	S	S
Manufacture of pesticides and other agrochemical products	20200	520	624	577	582	600
Manufacture of paints, varnishes and similar coatings, printing ink and mastics	20300	2,977	2,761	2,847	3,086	3,211
Manufacture of soap and detergents, cleaning and polishing preparations	20410	1,550	1,662	1,755	1,752	1,768
Manufacture of perfumes and toilet preparations	20420	2,267	2,243	2,380	2,356	2,384
Manufacture of explosives	20510	163	186	171	159	S
Manufacture of glues	20520	340	340	342	357	384
Manufacture of essential oils	20530	S	642	690	878	863
Manufacture of other chemical products n.e.c.	20590	2,681	2,645	2,612	2,606	2,550
Manufacture of man-made fibres	20600	287	211	208	256	216
Manufacture of basic pharmaceutical products and pharmaceutical preparations						
Manufacture of basic pharmaceutical products	21100	797	495	559	936	963
Manufacture of pharmaceutical preparations	21200	9,396	12,702	14,159	12,965	11,498
Manufacture of rubber and plastic products						
Manufacture of rubber tyres and tubes; retreading and rebuilding of rubber tyres	22110	S	S	S	S	S
Manufacture of other rubber products	22190	1,542	1,276	1,399	1,607	1,648
Manufacture of plastic plates, sheets, tubes and profiles	22210	4,613	4,065	4,471	4,574	4,590
Manufacture of plastic packing goods	22220	2,878	2,651	2,852	3,295	3,486
Manufacture of builders€™ ware of plastic	22230	4,104	3,634	3,795	3,478	3,385
Manufacture of other plastic products	22290	3,129	2,762	3,011	3,424	3,434
Manufacture of other non-metallic mineral products						
Manufacture of flat glass	23110	S	S	S	S	S
Shaping and processing of flat glass	23120	1,347	1,143	1,237	1,115	1,123
Manufacture of hollow glass	23130	585	635	654	694	S
Manufacture of glass fibres	23140	405	374	424	432	422
Manufacture and processing of other glass, including technical glassware	23190	153	119	125	172	S
Manufacture of refractory products	23200	247	237	234	276	276
Manufacture of ceramic tiles and flags	23310	91	88	76	74	78
Manufacture of bricks, tiles and construction products, in baked clay	23320	532	S	S	478	467
Manufacture of ceramic household and ornamental articles	23410	248	205	236	S	S
Manufacture of ceramic sanitary fixtures	23420	S	S	S	110	S
Manufacture of ceramic insulators and insulating fittings	23430	36	34	35	31	27
Manufacture of other technical ceramic products	23440	S	S	26	28	S
Manufacture of other ceramic products	23490	S	18	19	27	28
Manufacture of cement	23510	1,046	814	S	714	703
Manufacture of lime and plaster	23520	235	S	184	S	209
Manufacture of concrete products for construction purposes	23610	S	S	S	1,474	1,431
Manufacture of plaster products for construction purposes	23620	S	S	S	S	S
Manufacture of ready-mixed concrete	23630	1,384	1,208	1,095	1,127	1,082

18.2 UK Manufacturer's Sales by Industry

S - Suppressed as disclosive

Industry	SIC(07)	2008	2009	2010	2011	£ million 2012
Manufacture of mortars	23640	S	104	118	S	S
Manufacture of fibre cement	23650	89	S	S	S	S
Manufacture of other articles of concrete, plaster and cement	23690	163	134	S	146	156
Cutting, shaping and finishing of stone	23700	445	463	402	420	428
Production of abrasive products	23910	S	109	90	100	S
Manufacture of other non-metallic mineral products n.e.c.	23990	1,063	1,280	1,320	1,484	1,545

Manufacture of basic metals

Industry	SIC(07)	2008	2009	2010	2011	2012
Manufacture of basic iron and steel and of ferro-alloys	24100	188	76	127	97	123
Manufacture of tubes, pipes, hollow profiles and related fittings, of steel	24200	1,603	S	1,266	1,544	1,542
Cold drawing of bars	24310	153	76	128	190	168
Cold rolling of narrow strip	24320	98	31	S	S	S
Cold forming or folding	24330	S	S	S	S	S
Cold drawing of wire	24340	S	S	S	S	157
Precious metals production	24410	504	443	643	875	653
Aluminium production	24420	2,061	1,211	1,478	1,646	1,265
Lead, zinc and tin production	24430	461	S	541	529	513
Copper production	24440	735	454	637	727	618
Other non-ferrous metal production	24450	1,317	923	1,046	1,011	1,017
Casting of iron	24510	427	256	316	421	416
Casting of steel	24520	332	299	287	388	420
Casting of light metals	24530	421	294	362	388	356
Casting of other non-ferrous metals	24540	206	157	184	224	226

Manufacture of fabricated metal products; except machinery and equipment

Industry	SIC(07)	2008	2009	2010	2011	2012
Manufacture of metal structures and parts of structures	25110	6,944	5,801	5,418	5,682	5,724
Manufacture of doors and windows of metal	25120	1,597	1,278	1,235	1,217	1,350
Manufacture of central heating radiators and boilers	25210	832	S	787	798	807
Manufacture of other tanks, reservoirs and containers of metal	25290	455	379	324	395	414
Manufacture of steam generators, except central heating hot water boilers	25300	578	S	S	S	S
Manufacture of weapons and ammunition	25400	2,709	2,912	2,032	1,941	1,885
Forging, pressing, stamping and roll-forming of metal; powder metallurgy	25500	1,958	1,319	1,608	1,839	1,889
Treatment and coating of metals	25610	1,223	1,054	1,045	1,187	1,258
Machining	25620	4,098	3,383	3,629	4,243	4,586
Manufacture of cutlery	25710	S	21	20	23	25
Manufacture of locks and hinges	25720	573	491	537	561	571
Manufacture of tools	25730	857	730	796	799	831
Manufacture of steel drums and similar containers	25910	113	96	107	112	110
Manufacture of light metal packaging	25920	1,357	S	1,533	1,499	1,381
Manufacture of wire products, chain and springs	25930	937	768	857	904	784
Manufacture of fasteners and screw machine products	25940	412	340	364	454	476
Manufacture of other fabricated metal products n.e.c.	25990	1,836	1,386	1,595	1,747	1,801

Manufacture of computer; electronic and optical products

Industry	SIC(07)	2008	2009	2010	2011	2012
Manufacture of electronic components	26110	1,378	1,048	1,296	1,301	897
Manufacture of loaded electronic boards	26120	576	937	1,044	1,256	1,164
Manufacture of computers and peripheral equipment	26200	1,373	1,359	1,182	1,270	1,240
Manufacture of communication equipment	26300	2,085	1,754	1,736	1,691	1,516
Manufacture of consumer electronics	26400	1,382	S	S	404	395
Manufacture of instruments and appliances for measuring, testing and navigation	26510	4,838	4,817	5,112	5,544	5,724
Manufacture of watches and clocks	26520	31	S	34	30	31
Manufacture of irradiation, electromedical and electrotherapeutic equipment	26600	837	787	S	S	S
Manufacture of optical instruments and photographic equipment	26700	357	304	332	394	388
Manufacture of magnetic and optical media	26800	11	12	9	S	10

18.2 UK Manufacturer's Sales by Industry

S - Suppressed as disclosive

Industry	SIC(07)	2008	2009	2010	2011	£ million 2012
Manufacture of electrical equipment						
Manufacture of electric motors, generators and transformers	27110	2,749	2,187	2,602	3,153	3,049
Manufacture of electricity distribution and control apparatus	27120	1,664	1,465	1,891	2,086	2,207
Manufacture of batteries and accumulators	27200	S	224	247	S	259
Manufacture of fibre optic cables	27310	110	92	124	S	114
Manufacture of other electronic and electric wires and cables	27320	1,240	952	1,263	1,399	1,304
Manufacture of wiring devices	27330	656	423	576	601	593
Manufacture of electric lighting equipment	27400	1,324	1,020	1,142	1,293	1,294
Manufacture of electric domestic appliances	27510	1,424	1,272	1,277	1,268	1,331
Manufacture of non-electric domestic appliances	27520	S	406	427	463	408
Manufacture of other electrical equipment	27900	1,436	1,101	1,356	1,211	1,273
Manufacture of machinery and equipment n.e.c.						
Manufacture of engines and turbines, except aircraft, vehicle and cycle engines	28110	4,364	3,263	3,662	4,303	4,143
Manufacture of fluid power equipment	28120	887	606	791	977	1,086
Manufacture of other pumps and compressors	28130	2,282	1,984	2,175	2,447	2,212
Manufacture of other taps and valves	28140	1,141	1,063	1,103	1,303	1,428
Manufacture of bearings, gears, gearing and driving elements	28150	1,105	812	903	1,027	999
Manufacture of ovens, furnaces and furnace burners	28210	289	239	222	271	304
Manufacture of lifting and handling equipment	28220	2,684	1,965	1,842	2,132	2,337
Manufacture of office machinery and equipment (except computers and peripheral equipment)	28230	419	410	524	548	605
Manufacture of power-driven hand tools	28240	S	70	100	S	108
Manufacture of non-domestic cooling and ventilation equipment	28250	2,717	S	2,502	2,371	2,269
Manufacture of other general-purpose machinery n.e.c.	28290	2,246	1,969	1,990	2,090	2,083
Manufacture of agricultural and forestry machinery	28300	1,378	1,177	1,275	1,483	1,776
Manufacture of metal forming machinery	28410	488	334	389	554	678
Manufacture of other machine tools	28490	300	247	280	329	372
Manufacture of machinery for metallurgy	28910	S	60	76	97	84
Manufacture of machinery for mining, quarrying and construction	28920	4,108	2,171	2,894	4,087	4,336
Manufacture of machinery for food, beverage and tobacco processing	28930	481	424	467	461	425
Manufacture of machinery for textile, apparel and leather production	28940	91	77	67	82	67
Manufacture of machinery for paper and paperboard production	28950	126	109	134	135	127
Manufacture of plastics and rubber machinery	28960	107	51	68	86	104
Manufacture of other special-purpose machinery n.e.c.	28990	1,415	972	1,181	1,252	1,234
Manufacture of motor vehicles; trailers and semi-trailers						
Manufacture of motor vehicles	29100	24,382	18,506	25,590	27,516	28,043
Manufacture of bodies (coachwork) for motor vehicles; manufacture of trailers and semi-trailers	29200	2,634	1,890	2,097	2,165	2,204
Manufacture of electrical and electronic equipment for motor vehicles	29310	666	515	S	544	497
Manufacture of other parts and accessories for motor vehicles	29320	8,970	6,345	8,301	8,222	8,686
Manufacture of other transport equipment						
Building of ships and floating structures	30110	2,171	2,456	2,756	2,903	S
Building of pleasure and sporting boats	30120	945	842	850	792	858
Manufacture of railway locomotives and rolling stock	30200	S	S	S	1,366	S
Manufacture of air and spacecraft and related machinery	30300	14,283	15,815	15,378	15,853	16,919
Manufacture of motorcycles	30910	S	S	S	S	S
Manufacture of bicycles and invalid carriages	30920	101	115	115	113	133
Manufacture of other transport equipment n.e.c.	30990	72	51	41	S	S
Manufacture of furniture						
Manufacture of office and shop furniture	31010	1,452	1,032	1,011	1,100	1,196

18.2 UK Manufacturer's Sales by Industry

S - Suppressed as disclosive

Industry	SIC(07)	2008	2009	2010	2011	£ million 2012
Manufacture of kitchen furniture	31020	1,098	1,016	1,036	1,055	1,117
Manufacture of mattresses	31030	536	544	587	S	578
Manufacture of other furniture	31090	3,170	2,783	2,988	3,084	3,203
Other manufacturing						
Striking of coins	32110	S	184	206	S	S
Manufacture of jewellery and related articles	32120	370	S	411	437	466
Manufacture of imitation jewellery and related articles	32130	S	44	48	45	47
Manufacture of musical instruments	32200	27	24	16	18	19
Manufacture of sports goods	32300	293	S	324	369	350
Manufacture of games and toys	32400	205	210	171	162	155
Manufacture of medical and dental instruments and supplies	32500	2,753	2,783	2,667	2,541	2,591
Manufacture of brooms and brushes	32910	112	105	105	91	92
Other manufacturing n.e.c.	32990	606	589	531	572	596
Repair and installation of machinery and equipment						
Repair of fabricated metal products	33110	666	455	800	977	1,016
Repair of machinery	33120	3,251	3,130	2,759	2,983	3,092
Repair of electronic and optical equipment	33130	S	654	618	631	662
Repair of electrical equipment	33140	619	522	439	476	530
Repair and maintenance of ships and boats	33150	378	327	338	331	404
Repair and maintenance of aircraft and spacecraft	33160	2,767	2,904	2,557	S	3,318
Repair and maintenance of other transport equipment	33170	747	S	S	S	821
Repair of other equipment	33190	3	S	S	S	S
Installation of industrial machinery and equipment	33200	3,307	2,914	S	3,379	3,189

SUPPRESSION OF DATA

Statistical disclosure control methodology is applied to PRODCOM data. This ensures that information attributable to an individual or individual organisation is not identifiable in any published outputs. The Code of Practice for Official Statistics, and specifically the Principle on Confidentiality (P.C) set out practices for how ONS protects data from being disclosed. The P.C includes the statement that ONS outputs should "ensure that official statistics do not reveal the identity of an individual or organisation, or any private information relating to them, taking into account other relevant sources of information". More information can be found in National Statistician's Guidance: Confidentiality of Official Statistics and also on the statistical disclosure control methodology page of the ONS website.

S Suppressed as disclosive

Source: Office for National Statistics
PRODCOM Publications & Analysis
Room 1.362
Government Buildings
Cardiff Road
Newport
Gwent, Wales
NP10 8XG
Tel: +44 (0) 1633 456746
Email: prodcompublication@ons.gsi.gov.uk

18.3 UNITED KINGDOM - NUMBER OF LOCAL UNITS in VAT and/or PAYE BASED ENTERPRISES in 2012

STANDARD INDUSTRIAL CLASSIFICATION (UK SIC 2007) DIVISION by EMPLOYMENT SIZE BAND

Division		Employment size									
		0 - 4	5 - 9	10 - 19	20 - 49	50 - 99	100 - 249	250 - 499	500 - 999	1,000 +	TOTAL
01	Crop and animal production, hunting and related service activities Enterprises	118,615	11,650	3,040	885	225	95	30	5	0	134,545
02	Forestry and logging Enterprises	2,990	340	155	65	20	5	0	0	0	3,575
03	Fishing and aquaculture Enterprises	3,525	305	100	20	0	0	0	0	0	3,950
05	Mining of coal and lignite Enterprises	5	5	5	10	15	10	0	5	0	55
06	Extraction of crude petroleum and natural gas Enterprises	55	25	15	15	15	10	10	0	0	145
07	Mining of metal ores Enterprises	5	0	0	0	0	0	0	0	0	5
08	Other mining and quarrying Enterprises	780	350	240	140	35	20	0	0	0	1,565
09	Mining support service activities Enterprises	245	35	20	35	20	25	5	5	5	395
10	Manufacture of food products Enterprises	3,225	1,620	1,105	865	470	405	215	115	25	8,045
11	Manufacture of beverages Enterprises	730	180	145	105	55	50	20	10	0	1,295
12	Manufacture of tobacco products Enterprises	0	5	5	0	0	0	0	5	0	15
13	Manufacture of textiles Enterprises	2,345	735	465	320	120	80	20	0	0	4,085
14	Manufacture of wearing apparel Enterprises	2,320	695	370	195	50	20	5	0	0	3,655
15	Manufacture of leather and related products Enterprises	360	100	55	50	20	10	0	0	0	595
16	Manufacture of wood and of products of wood and cork, except furniture; manufacture of articles of straw and plaiting materials Enterprises	4,955	1,360	830	440	145	50	5	0	0	7,785
17	Manufacture of paper and paper products Enterprises	785	255	235	245	150	130	25	0	0	1,825
18	Printing and reproduction of recorded media Enterprises	9,610	2,360	1,250	745	250	130	25	5	0	14,375
19	Manufacture of coke and refined petroleum products Enterprises	90	20	25	10	15	5	5	10	0	180
20	Manufacture of chemicals and chemical products Enterprises	1,215	450	375	415	230	150	60	20	0	2,915
21	Manufacture of basic pharmaceutical products and pharmaceutical preparations Enterprises	310	65	40	90	50	40	40	15	0	650
22	Manufacture of rubber and plastic products Enterprises	2,480	1,280	1,025	835	425	260	50	10	5	6,370
23	Manufacture of other non-metallic mineral products Enterprises	2,865	910	620	430	210	115	35	5	0	5,190
24	Manufacture of basic metals Enterprises	645	230	205	260	110	85	20	15	5	1,575
25	Manufacture of fabricated metal products, except machinery and equipment Enterprises	15,235	4,745	3,305	2,145	690	275	35	10	5	26,445
26	Manufacture of computer, electronic and optical products Enterprises	3,740	945	695	565	280	160	60	15	5	6,465
27	Manufacture of electrical equipment Enterprises	1,395	465	480	460	205	135	30	15	0	3,185
28	Manufacture of machinery and equipment n.e.c. Enterprises	4,435	1,640	1,105	960	410	260	70	25	5	8,910
29	Manufacture of motor vehicles, trailers and semi-trailers Enterprises	1,505	445	295	285	165	130	55	20	15	2,915
30	Manufacture of other transport equipment Enterprises	1,360	245	145	130	95	95	45	25	20	2,160
31	Manufacture of furniture Enterprises	3,860	1,120	690	460	165	90	30	5	0	6,420

18.3 UNITED KINGDOM - NUMBER OF LOCAL UNITS in VAT and/or PAYE BASED ENTERPRISES in 2012

STANDARD INDUSTRIAL CLASSIFICATION (UK SIC 2007) DIVISION by EMPLOYMENT SIZE BAND

Division		0 - 4	5 - 9	10 - 19	20 - 49	50 - 99	100 - 249	250 - 499	500 - 999	1,000 +	TOTAL
32	Other manufacturing Enterprises	7,065	1,775	770	410	130	80	25	5	0	10,260
33	Repair and installation of machinery and equipment Enterprises	7,565	1,065	780	435	165	100	35	15	5	10,165
35	Electricity, gas, steam and air conditioning supply Enterprises	1,265	240	195	185	140	85	50	35	20	2,215
36	Water collection, treatment and supply Enterprises	435	170	150	115	60	35	10	5	0	980
37	Sewerage Enterprises	765	240	180	145	45	15	0	5	0	1,395
38	Waste collection, treatment and disposal activities; materials recovery Enterprises	3,915	1,310	940	840	345	175	25	10	0	7,560
39	Remediation activities and other waste management services Enterprises	400	85	50	20	5	0	0	0	0	560
41	Construction of buildings Enterprises	64,690	7,395	2,960	1,460	600	345	65	15	5	77,535
42	Civil engineering Enterprises	15,315	2,815	1,425	1,050	455	270	75	30	15	21,450
43	Specialised construction activities Enterprises	144,020	18,135	7,555	3,505	955	370	60	15	5	174,620
45	Wholesale and retail trade and repair of motor vehicles and motorcycles Enterprises	52,710	14,075	5,760	4,130	1,010	245	20	10	0	77,960
46	Wholesale trade, except of motor vehicles and motorcycles Enterprises	78,050	22,195	13,580	7,180	2,135	920	230	70	20	124,380
47	Retail trade, except of motor vehicles and motorcycles Enterprises	165,915	66,050	32,765	14,915	3,750	2,215	1,210	250	30	287,100
49	Land transport and transport via pipelines Enterprises	32,980	5,860	3,640	2,325	920	575	230	60	10	46,600
50	Water transport Enterprises	1,125	230	145	80	20	25	5	5	0	1,635
51	Air transport Enterprises	775	130	100	70	55	65	20	15	10	1,240
52	Warehousing and support activities for transportation Enterprises	8,730	2,695	1,935	1,615	700	435	155	80	20	16,365
53	Postal and courier activities Enterprises	12,305	1,620	965	1,125	730	360	70	35	15	17,225
55	Accommodation Enterprises	8,130	3,470	3,205	2,830	1,205	645	85	15	10	19,595
56	Food and beverage service activities Enterprises	70,100	39,105	22,835	13,515	2,135	480	65	35	15	148,285
58	Publishing activities Enterprises	7,770	1,295	800	515	210	110	65	20	15	10,800
59	Motion picture, video and television programme production, sound recording and music publishing activities Enterprises	16,225	905	595	470	225	60	15	10	5	18,510
60	Programming and broadcasting activities Enterprises	1,535	155	135	65	50	25	5	10	0	1,980
61	Telecommunications Enterprises	7,600	1,370	875	595	235	190	95	40	20	11,020
62	Computer programming, consultancy and related activities Enterprises	104,585	6,035	3,490	2,070	745	365	110	40	25	117,465
63	Information service activities Enterprises	6,135	600	350	195	80	65	30	10	5	7,470
64	Financial service activities, except insurance and pension funding Enterprises	15,480	6,495	4,160	2,140	430	255	140	115	75	29,290
65	Insurance, reinsurance and pension funding, except compulsory social security Enterprises	5,855	375	225	170	90	90	65	40	15	6,925
66	Activities auxiliary to financial services and insurance activities Enterprises	19,970	4,310	2,185	1,315	560	370	145	75	35	28,965
68	Real estate activities Enterprises	69,780	12,920	5,215	1,715	555	345	70	25	0	90,625

18.3 UNITED KINGDOM - NUMBER OF LOCAL UNITS in VAT and/or PAYE BASED ENTERPRISES in 2012

STANDARD INDUSTRIAL CLASSIFICATION (UK SIC 2007) DIVISION by EMPLOYMENT SIZE BAND

Division		Employment size									
		0 - 4	5 - 9	10 - 19	20 - 49	50 - 99	100 - 249	250 - 499	500 - 999	1,000 +	TOTAL
69	Legal and accounting activities										
	Enterprises	50,840	10,065	5,855	2,965	845	425	130	50	30	71,205
70	Activities of head offices; management consultancy activities										
	Enterprises	117,855	6,775	3,425	1,875	655	445	125	55	25	131,235
71	Architectural and engineering activities; technical testing and analysis										
	Enterprises	64,060	6,640	3,780	2,010	650	335	90	30	10	77,605
72	Scientific research and development										
	Enterprises	2,980	510	370	285	180	130	50	30	10	4,545
73	Advertising and market research										
	Enterprises	17,180	1,895	1,020	585	245	135	50	25	10	21,145
74	Other professional, scientific and technical activities										
	Enterprises	54,450	3,750	1,440	520	145	45	10	10	0	60,370
75	Veterinary activities										
	Enterprises	2,185	1,410	1,045	470	50	10	0	0	0	5,170
77	Rental and leasing activities										
	Enterprises	13,065	4,175	1,885	930	230	115	15	5	0	20,420
78	Employment activities										
	Enterprises	13,340	2,765	2,180	2,455	1,705	1,390	405	120	45	24,405
79	Travel agency, tour operator and other reservation service and related activities										
	Enterprises	5,870	3,040	1,065	420	185	85	25	5	0	10,695
80	Security and investigation activities										
	Enterprises	5,540	1,095	735	495	265	195	85	30	25	8,465
81	Services to buildings and landscape activities										
	Enterprises	36,025	7,500	3,855	2,035	795	440	175	80	70	50,975
82	Office administrative, office support and other business support activities										
	Enterprises	53,320	6,240	3,010	1,350	515	300	100	50	20	64,905
84	Public administration and defence; compulsory social security										
	Enterprises	8,725	3,865	4,025	4,010	2,155	1,705	835	350	160	25,830
85	Education										
	Enterprises	22,445	8,600	8,490	15,560	8,050	4,410	655	190	120	68,520
86	Human health activities										
	Enterprises	27,810	12,365	10,155	7,275	2,045	1,245	355	145	315	61,710
87	Residential care activities										
	Enterprises	8,740	4,640	6,255	7,485	3,195	615	45	15	5	30,995
88	Social work activities without accommodation										
	Enterprises	22,735	13,900	11,515	7,425	2,135	915	150	30	10	58,815
90	Creative, arts and entertainment activities										
	Enterprises	26,215	1,480	590	285	190	65	15	5	0	28,845
91	Libraries, archives, museums and other cultural activities										
	Enterprises	2,910	1,490	960	735	220	105	25	10	0	6,455
92	Gambling and betting activities										
	Enterprises	4,045	6,330	525	455	135	70	10	0	5	11,575
93	Sports activities and amusement and recreation activities										
	Enterprises	18,065	4,955	3,605	2,725	1,080	465	75	30	5	31,005
94	Activities of membership organisations										
	Enterprises	16,840	4,670	2,375	1,225	390	200	50	10	5	25,765
95	Repair of computers and personal and household goods										
	Enterprises	6,830	745	370	160	70	30	10	0	5	8,220
96	Other personal service activities										
	Enterprises	51,740	14,320	4,660	1,190	180	75	20	0	0	72,185
97	Activities of households as employers of domestic personnel										
	Enterprises	0	0	0	0	0	0	0	0	0	0
98	Undifferentiated goods- and services-producing activities of private households for own use										
	Enterprises	0	0	0	0	0	0	0	0	0	0
99	Activities of extraterritorial organisations and bodies										
	Enterprises	5	0	5	0	0	0	0	0	0	10
TOTAL ALL INDUSTRIES											
	Enterprises	1,774,690	388,920	218,200	141,305	49,690	26,105	7,575	2,710	1,340	2,610,535

18.4 Production of primary fuels

United Kingdom   **Million tonnes of oil equivalent**

	1997	1998	1999	2000	2001	2002	2003	2004	2005	2006	2007	2008	2009	2010	2011	2012
Coal	30.3	25.8	23.2	19.6	20.0	18.8	17.6	15.6	12.7	11.4	10.7	11.3	11.0	11.5	11.6	10.6
Petroleum	140.4	145.3	150.2	138.3	127.8	127.0	116.2	104.5	92.9	84.0	83.9	78.6	74.7	69.0	56.9	48.8
Natural Gas	85.9	90.2	99.1	108.4	105.9	103.6	103.0	96.4	88.2	80.0	72.1	69.7	59.7	57.2	45.3	38.9
Primary electricity	23.5	24.0	22.9	20.2	21.2	20.6	20.4	18.7	19.0	17.9	14.9	13.0	16.5	15.1	17.5	17.4
Renewable energy	1.9	2.1	2.2	2.3	2.5	2.8	3.0	3.1	3.7	4.0	4.3	4.5	4.9	5.2	5.6	6.4
Total Production	282.1	287.2	297.7	288.7	277.4	272.9	260.3	238.4	216.5	197.2	186.0	177.0	166.9	157.9	136.8	122.1

NB : See footnote in chapter table.   Source: Department of Energy and Climate Change

Datasource	Location
DUKES 1.1.2	https://www.gov.uk/government/publications/energy-chapter-1-digest-of-united-kingdom-energy-statistics-dukes

18.5 Total inland energy consumption

United Kingdom
Million tonnes of oil equivalent

	1997	1998	1999	2000	2001	2002	2003	2004	2005	2006	2007	2008	2009	2010	2011	2012
Inland energy consumption of primary fuels and equivalents	226.8	230.7	231.3	234.8	236.9	229.6	231.9	233.6	236.3	233.1	227.5	223.5	210.4	216.8	202.1	206.3
Coal	40.8	41.0	36.0	38.5	40.8	37.7	40.5	39.1	39.9	43.4	41.0	38.2	31.3	32.2	32.4	41.1
Petroleum	75.5	75.4	76.4	76.7	75.9	73.5	73.0	75.1	78.2	77.4	76.3	72.9	70.1	69.0	67.1	65.9
Primary electricity	25.0	25.0	24.2	21.4	22.1	21.3	20.6	19.4	19.8	18.5	15.4	13.9	16.7	15.3	18.0	18.5
Natural gas	83.5	87.3	92.5	95.9	95.6	94.3	94.6	96.6	94.3	89.4	90.2	93.2	86.1	93.3	77.3	73.1
Renewables and waste	1.9	2.1	2.2	2.3	2.5	2.8	3.1	3.5	4.2	4.4	4.7	5.4	6.2	6.9	7.3	7.8
less Energy used by fuel producers and losses in conversion and distribution	72.8	74.7	74.1	74.5	75.4	73.2	73.8	73.6	74.4	74.2	73.4	71.5	68.4	68.4	65.5	66.1
Total consumption by final users	153.9	155.9	156.5	159.4	160.9	156.5	158.1	159.9	159.6	157.0	154.2	151.7	142.4	148.6	137.3	140.6
Final energy consumption by type of fuel																
Coal (direct use)	4.3	3.7	3.5	2.7	2.7	2.2	2.1	2.0	1.7	1.6	1.8	1.8	1.7	1.7	1.7	1.6
Coke and breeze	0.8	0.9	0.9	0.8	0.8	0.7	0.7	0.6	0.6	0.5	0.5	0.5	0.4	0.3	0.3	0.4
Other solid fuel	0.7	0.7	0.6	0.6	0.5	0.5	0.4	0.4	0.4	0.4	0.4	0.4	0.4	0.4	0.4	0.3
Coke oven gas	0.5	0.4	0.2	0.2	0.2	0.1	0.1	0.1	0.1	0.1	0.1	0.1	0.0	0.1	0.1	0.1
Natural gas (direct use)	54.2	55.9	55.1	57.1	57.8	55.2	56.7	57.1	55.4	52.6	50.0	50.8	46.2	51.8	42.9	47.1
Electricity	26.8	27.1	27.8	28.3	28.6	28.7	28.9	29.1	30.0	29.7	29.4	29.4	27.7	28.3	27.3	27.3
Petroleum (direct use)	65.4	66.1	65.1	66.3	67.1	66.1	66.8	68.6	69.5	69.8	69.5	65.4	62.6	62.1	60.9	60.2
Renewables[6]	0.9	0.9	0.7	0.7	0.7	0.7	0.7	0.7	0.8	1.0	1.2	1.9	2.1	2.5	2.5	2.4
Heat	..	..	2.5	2.5	2.3	2.1	1.8	1.3	1.3	1.2	1.3	1.5	1.2	1.3	1.2	1.2
Final energy consumption by class of consumer																
Agriculture	1.3	1.4	1.3	1.2	1.3	1.2	0.9	0.9	1.0	0.9	0.9	1.0	0.9	1.0	1.0	0.9
Iron and steel industry	4.2	4.0	3.8	2.2	2.3	2.0	1.9	1.9	1.8	1.9	1.8	1.6	1.2	1.4	1.3	1.2
Other industries	30.4	30.5	30.5	33.3	33.2	31.8	32.1	31.0	30.5	29.6	28.7	28.6	25.0	25.5	24.6	24.0
Railways	1.2	1.3	1.4	1.4	1.4	1.4	1.4	1.0	1.0	1.0	1.0	1.0	1.0	1.0	1.1	1.0
Road transport	41.3	41.0	41.4	41.1	41.1	41.9	41.8	42.2	42.6	42.7	43.2	41.9	40.7	40.4	39.8	39.5
Water transport	1.3	1.2	1.1	1.0	0.8	0.7	1.2	1.2	1.4	1.8	1.6	0.4	0.4	0.4	0.4	0.3
Air transport	9.3	10.2	11.0	12.0	11.8	11.7	11.9	12.9	13.9	14.0	13.9	13.4	12.8	12.3	12.8	12.4
Domestic	44.8	46.1	46.1	46.9	48.2	47.5	48.3	49.3	47.8	46.6	44.9	45.4	43.0	48.5	38.9	43.2
Public administration	8.4	8.1	8.2	8.1	8.0	7.0	6.7	7.2	7.1	6.6	6.3	6.6	6.4	6.7	6.3	6.6
Commercial and other services	11.7	12.0	11.8	12.2	12.8	11.3	11.8	12.2	12.7	12.0	11.8	11.8	11.1	11.4	11.2	11.5

NB : See footnote in chapter tables.   Source: Department of Energy and Climate Change

Datasource	Location
DUKES 1.1.2	https://www.gov.uk/government/publications/energy-chapter-1-digest-of-united-kingdom-energy-statistics-dukes
DUKES 1.1.5	https://www.gov.uk/government/publications/energy-chapter-1-digest-of-united-kingdom-energy-statistics-dukes
DUKES 1.1-1.3	https://www.gov.uk/government/publications/energy-chapter-1-digest-of-united-kingdom-energy-statistics-dukes

((-Transformation in total column) + industry use + losses) in DUKES 1.1-1.3

18.6 Coal: supply and demand

United Kingdom   Million tonnes

	1997	1998	1999	2000	2001	2002	2003	2004	2005	2006	2007	2008	2009	2010	2011	2012
Supply																
Production of deep-mined coal	30.3	25.7	20.9	17.2	17.3	16.4	15.6	12.5	9.6	9.4	7.7	8.1	7.5	7.4	7.3	6.2
Production of opencast coal	16.7	14.3	15.3	13.4	14.2	13.1	12.1	12.0	10.4	8.6	8.9	9.5	9.9	10.4	10.6	10.1
Total	47.0	40.0	36.2	30.6	31.5	29.5	27.7	24.5	20.0	18.0	16.6	17.6	17.4	17.8	17.9	16.3
Recovered slurry, fines, etc	1.5	1.1	0.9	0.6	0.4	0.4	0.5	0.6	0.5	0.4	0.5	0.4	0.5	0.6	0.7	0.8
Imports	19.8	21.2	20.3	23.4	35.5	28.7	31.9	36.2	44.0	50.5	43.4	43.9	38.2	26.5	32.5	44.8
Total	68.3	62.3	57.4	54.6	67.4	58.6	60.1	61.3	64.5	68.9	60.5	61.9	56.1	44.9	51.1	61.9
Change in stocks at collieries and opencast sites	-0.6	0.2	-0.6	3.6	0.0	-0.9	0.9	0.4	0.1	0.3	0.1	-0.2	-0.5	-0.1	0.6	-0.2
Total supply	67.7	62.5	56.8	58.2	67.4	57.7	61.0	61.7	64.6	69.2	60.6	61.7	55.6	44.8	51.7	61.7
Home consumption																
Total home consumption	63.4	62.9	55.4	59.8	63.5	58.6	62.9	60.6	61.8	67.3	62.9	58.2	48.8	51.4	51.5	64.3
Overseas shipments and bunkers	1.1	1.0	0.8	0.7	0.5	0.5	0.5	0.6	0.5	0.4	0.5	0.6	0.6	0.7	0.5	0.5
Total consumption and shipments	64.5	63.9	56.2	60.5	64.0	59.1	63.4	61.2	62.3	67.7	63.4	58.8	49.4	52.1	52	64.8
Change in distributed stocks	-4.6	1.2	-0.6	2.4	-3.5	1.4	2.4	-0.5	-1.9	-1.9	3.0	-3.0	-6.2	7.2	0.3	3.2
Balance	0.3	-0.3	-0.3	-0.1	-0.3	0.1	-0.2	0.1	-0.1	-0.3	-0.1	-0.2	0	0	-0.1	0.1
Stocks at end of year																
Distributed	15.4	14.2	14.8	12.4	15.9	14.5	12.1	12.6	14.5	16.4	13.4	16.4	22.6	15.4	15.1	11.9
At collieries and opencast sites	4.8	4.6	5.2	1.6	1.6	2.5	1.6	1.2	1.1	0.8	0.7	0.9	1.4	1.5	0.9	1.1
Total stocks	20.2	18.8	19.9	14.1	17.5	17.0	13.7	13.8	15.6	17.2	14.2	17.2	24.1	16.9	16.0	13.0

NB : See footnote in chapter table.   Source: Department of Energy and Climate Change

Datasource: DUKES 2.4
location: https://www.gov.uk/government/publications/solid-fuels-and-derived-gases-chapter-2-digest-of-united-kingdom-energy-statistics-dukes

18.7 Fuel input and gas output: gas consumption

United Kingdom   Giga-watt hours

	1999	2000	2001	2002	2003	2004	2005	2006	2007	2008	2009	2010	2011	2012
Analysis of gas consumption														
Transformation sector	341,678	349,454	336,525	351,856	344,410	362,668	354,146	333,431	379,518	402,236	382,061	397,293	330,076	236,537
Electricity generation	315,493	324,563	312,939	329,847	324,580	340,824	331,658	311,408	355,878	376,810	359,303	373,586	307,140	214,146
Heat generation	26,185	24,891	23,586	22,009	19,830	21,844	22,488	22,023	23,640	25,426	22,758	23,707	22,936	22,392
Energy industry use total	76,973	77,941	91,451	91,260	88,907	88,468	87,161	81,859	76,025	72,280	69,182	69,048	59,287	55,709
Oil and gas extraction	64,634	65,555	78,457	79,364	76,837	77,753	73,372	69,252	64,230	61,292	61,110	61,124	53,163	48,461
Petroleum refineries	4,155	3,641	4,189	3,350	2,773	3,076	5,163	5,161	5,206	4,971	4,033	3,841	3,633	3,278
Coal extraction and coke manufacture	265	241	220	196	188	150	114	112	91	95	89	87	87	127
Blast furnaces	643	712	375	222	539	728	941	611	719	718	450	641	453	266
Other	7,276	7,792	8,210	8,128	8,570	6,761	7,572	6,723	5,779	5,204	3,499	3,355	1,951	3,578
Final consumption total	654,312	678,142	683,753	653,151	669,457	673,860	652,024	620,035	591,274	599,018	544,598	610,651	504,842	553,386
Iron and steel industry	21,622	8,953	8,502	8,791	10,327	9,715	8,453	8,391	7,323	6,920	5,037	5,827	5,569	4,854
Other industries	155,193	174,488	171,341	156,375	155,890	144,238	142,988	136,150	126,028	127,013	108,105	108,578	107,995	105,869
Domestic	358,066	369,909	379,426	376,372	386,486	396,411	381,879	366,928	352,868	359,554	332,499	389,595	293,400	339,080
Public administration	43,253	44,552	46,232	42,998	44,362	51,934	50,319	45,803	42,444	45,665	45,233	49,559	45,295	48,005
Commercial	36,622	36,216	37,098	36,224	39,537	37,595	38,197	34,273	33,098	38,448	34,791	36,369	34,609	37,045
Agriculture	1,155	1,522	2,329	2,346	2,324	2,355	2,261	2,013	1,998	2,161	1,760	1,969	1,778	1,536
Miscellaneous	25,457	28,166	27,452	19,265	20,510	21,591	20,014	18,564	17,286	11,052	10,285	10,665	10,247	11,048
Non energy use	12,944	14,336	11,373	10,780	10,021	10,021	7,913	7,913	10,228	8,206	6,887	8,089	5,949	5,949
Total gas consumption	1,072,963	1,105,537	1,111,729	1,096,267	1,102,774	1,124,996	1,093,331	1,035,325	1,046,817	1,073,535	995,840	1,076,992	894,205	845,633

NB : See footnote in chapter table   Source: Department of Energy and Climate Change

Data source
DUKES 4.2 - Supply and consumption of natural gas and colliery methane

Location
https://www.gov.uk/government/publications/natural-gas-chapter-4-digest-of-united-kingdom-energy-statistics-dukes

18.8 Electricity: generation, supply and consumption

United Kingdom   Gigawatt-hours

	2000	2001	2002	2003	2004	2005	2006	2007	2008	2009	2010	2011	2012
Electricity generated													
Major power producers: total	341783	353066	353994	362600	358313	362212	361232	361317	355209	342374	347785	332312	328106
Conventional thermal and other	131062	132744	126694	146382	139105	140405	156813	144596	128944	106939	111133	111270	148034
Combined cycle gas turbine stations	117935	123846	132016	121076	131182	130689	118495	139826	160109	151454	160518	131886	85647
Nuclear stations	85063	90093	87848	88686	79999	81618	75451	63028	52486	69098	62140	68980	70405
Hydro-electric stations:													
Natural flow	4331	3215	3927	2568	3908	3826	3693	4144	4224	4294	2703	4594	4169
Pumped storage	2694	2422	2652	2734	2649	2930	3853	3859	4089	3685	3150	2906	2966
Renewables other than hydro	698	738	856	1154	1471	2744	2928	5910	7966	9574	11832	17208	23041
Other generators: total	35285	31721	33252	35609	35616	36148	36050	35513	33663	34378	33974	35142	35730
Conventional thermal and other	19094	16621	15788	17244	14419	13407	12354	13865	19457	20218	20408	20406	20332
Combined cycle gas turbine stations	10859	8979	10577	10879	11852	11792	11561	11516	11522	10790	10609	10560	10392
Hydro-electric stations (natural flow)	755	840	860	660	936	1096	900	933	931	947	872	1096	1115
Renewables other than hydro	4577	5283	6028	6825	8408	9853	11235	8702	8680	10428	10430	11747	12932
All generating companies: total	377068	384787	387246	398209	393929	398360	397282	396830	388872	376753	381759	367454	363836
Conventional thermal and other[2]	150156	149365	142482	163626	153524	153812	169167	158461	148401	127157	131542	131676	168366
Combined cycle gas turbine stations	128794	132825	142593	131955	143034	142481	130056	151342	171631	162244	171126	142447	96039
Nuclear stations	85063	90093	87848	88686	79999	81618	75451	63028	52486	69098	62140	68980	70405
Hydro-electr ic stations:													
Natural flow	5086	4055	4787	3228	4844	4922	4593	5077	5155	5241	3575	5690	5284
Pumped storage	2694	2422	2652	2734	2649	2930	3853	3859	4089	3685	3150	2906	2966
Renewables other than hydro	5275	6021	6884	7979	9879	12597	14164	14612	16645	20002	22263	28955	35974
Electricity used on works: Total	16304	17394	17126	18136	17032	17873	18503	17694	16340	16571	16108	16427	18002
Major generating companies	14952	16066	15746	16747	15582	16265	17031	16090	14662	14750	14403	14480	15881
Other generators	1352	1328	1380	1389	1451	1608	1472	1605	1678	1821	1705	1947	2121
Electricity supplied (gross)													
Major power producers: total	326831	336999	338248	345854	342732	345947	344201	345227	340547	327624	333382	317832	312224
Conventional thermal and other	125468	127119	128795	140196	133607	135999	151866	138793	121816	101100	105148	105359	140073
Combined cycle gas turbine stations	116110	121344	121886	118546	128983	128179	115695	137657	157417	148907	157818	129669	84207
Nuclear stations	78334	82985	81090	81911	73682	75173	69237	57249	47673	62762	56442	62655	63949
Hydro-electric stations:													
Natural flow	4316	3203	3914	2559	3901	3821	3680	4114	4209	4279	2694	4578	4155
Pumped storage	2603	2340	2562	2641	2559	2776	3722	3846	4075	3672	3139	2895	2956
Renewables other than hydro	640	692	802	1059	1367	2486	2643	5675	7704	9306	11462	16753	22423
Other generators: total	33933	30393	31873	34220	34165	34539	34578	33908	31985	32558	32269	33195	33609
Conventional thermal and other	21926	20066	19716	21942	20046	19494	18598	19801	18371	18952	19248	19007	18750
Combined cycle gas turbine stations	10318	8531	10049	10336	11260	11204	10859	11471	10947	10251	10079	10033	9873
Hydro-electric stations (natural flow)	743	829	849	653	919	930	885	918	915	930	857	1075	1095
Renewables other than hydro	4374	5037	5764	6519	8000	9380	10702	8147	8000	9584	9688	10754	11752
All generating companies: total	360764	367392	370121	380074	376896	380486	378779	379136	372532	360182	365651	351026	345834
Conventional thermal and other	147394	147185	148511	162138	153653	155493	170464	158594	140186	120052	124396	124366	158824
Combined cycle gas turbine stations	126428	129875	131935	128882	140243	139382	126554	149127	168364	159159	167898	139702	94080
Nuclear stations	78334	82985	81090	81911	73682	75173	69237	57249	47673	62762	56442	62655	63949
Hydro-electr ic stations:													
Natural flow	5059	4032	4763	3212	4821	4750	4566	5032	5124	5209	3550	5653	5250
Pumped storage	2603	2340	2562	2641	2559	2776	3722	3846	4075	3672	3139	2895	2956
Renewables other than hydro	5014	5729	6566	7578	9367	11867	13345	13822	15704	18889	21149	27507	34175
Electricity used in pumping													
Major power producers	3499	3210	3463	3546	3497	3707	4918	5071	5371	4843	4212	3843	3978
Electricity supplied (net): Total	357266	364182	366657	376528	373399	376780	373861	374064	367161	355339	361439	347183	341856
Major power producers	323332	333789	334785	342308	339235	342240	339283	340156	335175	322781	329170	313988	308247
Other generators	33933	30393	31873	34220	34165	34539	34578	33908	31985	32558	32269	33195	33609
Net imports	14174	10399	8415	2160	7490	8321	7517	5215	11022	2861	2663	6222	12044
Electricity available	371440	374581	375072	378687	380889	385101	381378	379279	378183	358200	364102	353406	353900
Losses in transmission etc	29649	30902	29980	29862	30728	27674	27410	28223	27849	28043	27036	28143	28946
Electricity consumption: Total	340297	342504	344109	346618	347714	357199	353863	351448	350100	330018	337498	325920	325316
Fuel industries	10877	9783	10708	10400	8766	8525	8634	9792	8277	8270	8674	8046	7741
Final users: total	329420	332721	333401	336218	338948	348675	345229	341656	341822	321748	328824	317873	317575
Industrial sector	114112	111337	110168	109278	111467	116024	114896	112799	114151	99738	104522	102348	97820
Domestic sector	111842	115337	120014	123001	124200	125711	124704	123076	119800	118541	118836	111603	114698
Other sectors	103466	106047	103219	103939	103280	106939	105629	105781	107871	103469	105466	103922	105057

See footnote in chapter table   Source: Department of Energy and Climate Change

Datasource

Electricity fuel use, generation and supply (DUKES 5.6)

https://www.gov.uk/government/publications/electricity-chapter-5-digest-of-united-kingdom-energy-statistics-dukes

Electricity commodity balances : (DUKES 5.1)

https://www.gov.uk/government/publications/electricity-chapter-5-digest-of-united-kingdom-energy-statistics-dukes

Electricity supply, electricity supplied (net), electricity available, electricity consumption and electricity sales (DUKES 5.5)

https://www.gov.uk/government/publications/electricity-chapter-5-digest-of-united-kingdom-energy-statistics-dukes

DUKES 5.6 and DUKES 5.1.3   Contains formulae

https://www.gov.uk/government/publications/electricity-chapter-5-digest-of-united-kingdom-energy-statistics-dukes

18.9 Electricity: plant capacity and demand

United Kingdom
At end of December

Megawatts

	1999	2000	2001	2002	2003	2004	2005	2006	2007	2008	2009	2010	2011	2012
Major power producers														
Total declared net capability	70,245	72,193	73,382	70,369	71,471	73,293	73,941	74,996	75,979	76,993	77,810	83,426	81,783	81,742
Conventional steam stations	35,647	34,835	34,835	32,227	31,867	31,982	32,292	33,608	34,134	32,823	32,831	32,839	31,763	28,523
Combined cycle gas turbine stations	16,110	19,349	20,517	20,260	21,452	23,178	23,678	24,274	24,269	26,203	26,785	31,724	30,183	33,113
Nuclear stations	12,956	12,486	12,486	12,240	11,852	11,852	11,852	10,969	10,979	10,979	10,858	10,865	10,663	9,946
Gas turbines and oil engines	1,301	1,291	1,291	1,432	1,582	1,540	1,541	1,629	1,630	1,641	1,779	1,779	1,706	1,651
Hydro-electric stations:														
Natural flow	1,327	1,327	1,348	1,304	1,273	1,276	1,273	1,294	1,293	1,392	1,395	1,391	1,391	1,392
Pumped storage	2,788	2,788	2,788	2,788	2,788	2,788	2,788	2,726	2,744	2,744	2,744	2,744	2,744	2,744
Renewables other than hydro	117	117	117	117	117	117	117	96	929	1,210	1,418	2,083	3,332	4,373
Other generators:														
Total capacity of own generating plant	5,388	6,258	6,296	6,336	6,793	6,829	7,422	7,407	6,763	6,686	7,021	7,045	7,267	7,498
Conventional steam stations	3,315	3,544	3,464	3,325	3,480	3,275	3,269	3,059	2,924	2,749	2,828	3,196	2,407	2,446
Combined cycle gas turbine stations	1,243	1,709	1,777	1,854	1,927	1,968	2,182	2,106	2,076	1,988	1,846	1,581	2,206	2,207
Hydro-electric stations (natural flow)	150	158	160	162	129	132	127	123	126	126	128	130	154	157
Renewables other than hydro	680	847	895	995	1,257	1,454	1,852	2,118	1,637	1,822	2,218	2,138	2,500	2,687
All generating companies: Total capacity	75,633	78,451	79,678	76,705	78,264	80,122	81,363	82,403	82,742	83,678	84,831	90,471	89,050	89,241
Conventional steam stations	38,962	38,379	38,299	35,552	35,347	35,257	35,561	36,667	37,058	35,572	35,660	36,036	34,170	30,970
Combined cycle gas turbine stations	17,353	21,058	22,294	22,114	23,379	25,146	25,860	26,380	26,345	28,191	28,631	33,305	32,389	35,320
Nuclear stations	12,956	12,486	12,486	12,240	11,852	11,852	11,852	10,969	10,979	10,979	10,858	10,865	10,663	9,946
Gas turbines and oil engines	1,301	1,291	1,291	1,432	1,582	1,540	1,541	1,629	1,630	1,641	1,779	1,779	1,706	1,651
Hydro-electric stations:														
Natural flow	1,477	1,485	1,508	1,466	1,402	1,408	1,400	1,417	1,419	1,518	1,524	1,521	1,545	1,549
Pumped storage	2,788	2,788	2,788	2,788	2,788	2,788	2,788	2,726	2,744	2,744	2,744	2,744	2,744	2,744
Renewables other than hydro	797	964	1,012	1,112	1,374	1,571	1,969	2,214	2,566	3,032	3,636	4,221	5,832	7,060
Major power producers:														
Simultaneous maximum load met	57,849	58,452	58,589	61,717	60,501	61013 (5	61,697	59,071	61,527	60,289	60,231	60,893	57,086	57,490
System load factor (percentages)	67	67	69	65	67	67	66	69	66	68	64	65	67	66

NB : See footnote in chapter table   Source: Department of Energy and Climate Change

Data source
DUKES Table 5.7 - Plant capacity
DUKES Table 5.10 - Plant loads,
demand and efficiency

Location

https://www.gov.uk/government/publications/electricity-chapter-5-digest-of-united-kingdom-energy-statistics-dukes

https://www.gov.uk/government/publications/electricity-chapter-5-digest-of-united-kingdom-energy-statistics-dukes

18.10 Electricity: fuel used in generation

United Kingdom
At end of December

Million tonnes of oil equivalent

	1997	1998	1999	2000	2001	2002	2003	2004	2005	2006	2007	2008	2009	2010	2011	2012
Major power producers: total all fuels	71.5	74.9	73.6	74.4	77.4	75.8	77.5	76.8	78.2	78.7	76.0	74.2	70.2	70.9	68.2	69.6
Coal	27.1	28.7	24.5	27.8	30.6	28.6	31.6	30.4	31.7	35.0	32.0	29.0	23.8	24.8	25.2	33.7
Oil	1.2	0.8	0.8	0.8	0.8	0.7	0.7	0.6	0.9	1.0	0.7	1.1	1.0	0.6	0.3	0.4
Gas	19.3	20.3	24.2	24.4	23.8	25.0	24.5	26.2	25.4	23.9	27.5	29.6	28.2	29.4	23.7	15.7
Nuclear	22.0	23.4	22.2	19.6	20.8	20.1	20.0	18.2	18.4	17.1	14.0	11.9	15.2	13.9	15.6	15.2
Hydro (natural flow)	0.3	0.4	0.4	0.4	0.3	0.3	0.2	0.3	0.3	0.3	0.4	0.4	0.4	0.2	0.4	0.4
Wind							-	-	-		0.3	0.5	0.6	0.7	1.1	1.5
Other renewables	0.2	0.2	0.2	0.2	0.3	0.3	0.4	0.5	0.8	0.7	0.6	0.8	0.7	1.0	1.3	1.7
Net imports	1.4	1.1	1.2	1.2	0.9	0.7	0.2	0.6	0.7	0.6	0.4	0.9	0.2	0.2	0.5	1.0
Other generators: total all fuels	6.7	7.1	7.3	8.0	7.6	8.0	8.7	8.4	9.2	9.0	8.8	8.3	8.5	8.5	8.7	8.8
Transport under takings																
Gas	0.223	0.220	0.215	0.189	0.192	0.154	0.008	0.002	0.003	0.002	0.002	0.002	0.001	0.002	0.001	0.001
Under takings in industrial sector																
Coal	1.2	1.2	1.0	0.9	1.0	1.0	1.0	0.9	0.9	0.9	0.9	1.0	0.9	0.8	0.8	0.7
Oil	0.8	0.7	0.7	0.8	0.6	0.6	0.5	0.5	0.4	0.5	0.5	0.5	0.5	0.5	0.4	0.4
Gas	2.2	2.5	2.7	3.3	2.9	3.2	3.4	3.1	3.1	2.9	3.1	2.8	2.7	2.7	2.7	2.7
Hydro (natural flow)	0.1	0.1	0.1	0.1	0.1	0.1	0.1	0.1	0.1	0.1	0.1	0.1	0.1	0.1	0.1	0.1
Wind, wave and solar photovoltaics	0.1	0.1	0.1	0.1	0.1	0.1	0.1	0.2	0.3	0.4	0.1	0.2	0.2	0.2	0.3	0.3
Other renewables	0.7	1.0	1.2	1.3	1.6	1.8	2.0	2.2	2.5	2.7	2.8	2.7	3.2	3.4	3.4	3.5
Other fuels	1.4	1.4	1.4	1.4	1.0	1.1	1.5	1.4	1.9	1.6	1.3	1.1	1.0	0.8	1.0	1.1
All generating companies: total fuels	78.2	82.0	80.9	82.4	84.9	83.8	86.2	85.2	87.4	87.7	84.7	82.5	78.7	79.4	76.9	78.4
Coal	28.3	29.9	25.5	28.7	31.6	29.6	32.5	31.3	32.6	35.9	32.9	30.0	24.7	25.6	26.0	34.3
Oil	2.0	1.5	1.5	1.5	1.4	1.3	1.2	1.1	1.3	1.4	1.2	1.6	1.5	1.2	0.8	0.8
Gas	21.7	23.0	27.1	27.9	26.9	28.4	27.9	29.3	28.5	26.8	30.6	32.4	30.9	32.1	26.4	18.4
Nuclear	22.0	23.4	22.2	19.6	20.8	20.1	20.0	18.2	18.4	17.1	14.0	11.9	15.2	13.9	15.6	15.2
Hydro (natural flow)	0.4	0.4	0.5	0.4	0.3	0.4	0.3	0.4	0.4	0.4	0.4	0.4	0.5	0.3	0.5	0.5
Wind, wave and solar photovoltaics	0.1	0.1	0.1	0.1	0.1	0.1	0.1	0.2	0.3	0.4	0.5	0.6	0.8	0.9	1.4	1.8
Other renewables	0.9	1.1	1.4	1.6	1.9	2.1	2.4	2.8	3.4	3.5	3.4	3.5	4.0	4.4	4.7	5.3
Other fuels	1.4	1.4	1.4	1.4	1.0	1.1	1.5	1.4	1.9	1.6	1.3	1.1	1.0	0.8	1.0	1.1
Net imports	1.4	1.1	1.2	1.2	0.9	0.7	0.2	0.6	0.7	0.6	0.4	0.9	0.2	0.2	0.5	1.0

NB : See footnote in chapter table   Source: Department of Energy and Climate Change

Data source
DUKES 5.4 - Fuel used in generation

Location
https://www.gov.uk/government/publications/electricity-chapter-5-digest-of-united-kingdom-energy-statistics-dukes

18.11 Indigenous petroleum production, refinery receipts, imports and exports of oil

Thousand tonnes

	1998	1999	2000	2001	2002	2003	2004	2005	2006	2007	2008	2009	2010	2011	2012
Total indigenous petroleum production	132633	137099	126245	116678	115944	106073	95374	84721	76578	76575	71665	68199	62962	51972	44561
Crude petroleum:															
Refinery receipts total	93797	88286	88013	83343	84784	84585	89821	86134	83213	81477	81034	75604	73543	75080	68862
Foreign trade															
Imports	47958	44869	54386	53551	56968	54177	62517	58885	59443	57357	60335	55056	55064	58092	60559
Exports	84610	91797	92917	86930	87144	74898	64504	54099	50195	50999	48401	45444	42196	33745	33961
Net imports	-36652	-46928	-38531	-33378	-30176	-20720	-1987	4786	9249	6357	11934	9612	12868	24348	26598
Petroleum products															
Foreign trade															
Imports	11327	13896	14212	17234	14900	16472	18545	22481	26836	25110	23741	22172	23665	22656	25978
Exports	24375	21730	20677	19088	23444	23323	30495	29722	28945	29983	28803	25491	26065	27800	27083
Net imports	-12957	-7834	-6464	-1854	-8544	-6851	-11950	-7241	-2109	-4874	-5062	-3319	-2400	-5145	-1105
International marine bunkers	3080	2329	2079	2274	1913	1764	2085	2055	2348	2371	4012	3807	3351	3602	3126

NB : See footnote in chapter tables   Source: Department of Energy and Climate Change

Data source

DUKES 3.1 - Primary oil commodity balances
https://www.gov.uk/government/publications/petroleum-chapter-3-digest-of-united-kingdom-energy-statistics-dukes

DUKES 3.2-3.4 - Petroleum products commodity balances
https://www.gov.uk/government/publications/petroleum-chapter-3-digest-of-united-kingdom-energy-statistics-dukes

18.12 Throughput of crude and process oils and output of refined products from refineries

United Kingdom

Thousand tonnes

	1998	1999	2000	2001	2002	2003	2004	2005	2006	2007	2008	2009	2010	2011	2012
Throughput of crude and process oils	93797	88286	88014	83343	84784	84585	89821	86134	83213	81477	81034	75604	73543	75080	68862
less: Refinery fuel:	6177	5538	5252	5059	5677	5456	5417	5601	4879	4676	4706	4304	4378	4586	4255
Losses	1005	1553	1633	1233	788	56	-7	371	374	293	470	777	566	373	172
Total output of refined products	86615	81195	81130	77051	78319	79073	84411	80146	77961	76509	75858	70523	68599	70122	64435
Gases:															
Butane and propane	1961	1975	1917	1764	2139	2281	2152	2184	2104	2259	2250	2113	2247	2598	2512
Other petroleum	394	361	289	272	537	715	520	427	661	517	369	449	518	434	331
Naphtha and other feedstock	2316	2430	3082	3428	3153	3503	3168	3019	2734	2561	1863	1287	1596	1493	924
Aviation spirit	0	16	30	101	28	26	31	32	25	0	0	0	0	0	0
Motor spirit	27166	25230	23445	21455	22944	22627	24589	22604	21443	21313	20319	20404	19918	19856	17627
Industrial and white spirit	135	129	122	121	121	104	100	136	107	70	55	61	66	65	72
Kerosene:															
Aviation turbine fuel	7876	7249	6484	5910	5365	5277	5615	5167	6261	6176	6549	6022	5781	6411	5775
Burning oil	3442	3553	3078	3088	3506	3521	3613	3325	3374	2968	3092	2830	2570	2377	2268
DERV								19056	15821	16138	16350	15908	15332	16801	15772
Gas/diesel oil	27542	25755	28229	26748	28343	27380	28646	9430	10215	10165	10566	9487	9505	8683	8941
Fuel oil	11125	10446	10296	10179	8507	9495	11308	10155	11280	10433	10483	8043	7004	7432	6816
Lubr icating oil	1125	907	702	656	509	576	1136	936	617	547	514	530	412	430	457
Bitumen	2172	1644	1438	1707	1918	1925	2196	1912	1749	1628	1485	1338	1276	1476	1222
Petroleum coke	678	648	657	513	441	612	633	660	606	676	781	847	817	654	467
Other products	684	854	1363	1108	808	1030	702	1103	964	1058	1182	1204	1557	1412	1252

NB : See footnote in chapter table

Source: Department of Energy and Climate Change

Data source
DUKES 3.5 - Supply and disposal of petroleum
DUKES 3.2-3.4 - Petroleum product

18.13 Deliveries of petroleum products for inland consumption [1]

United Kingdom

	2000	2001	2002	2003	2004	2005	2006	2007	2008	2009	2010	2011	2012
Total (including refinery fuel)	77196	76413	76233	77154	79066	80736	79812	77424	74616	70744	69980	68290	66631
Total (excluding refinery fuel)	71944	71354	70557	71697	73649	75135	74933	72748	69911	66440	65602	63705	62376
Butane and propane	1978	2061	2553	3017	3115	3310	3123	2823	3386	3083	2833	2976	2392
Other Petroleum Gases (includes Ethane)	1707	1898	1953	1885	1737	1838	1714	1563	1459	1344	1199	1003	899
Naphtha	2344	1592	1592	2332	2029	1916	2278	1608	856	1011	1061	1046	1061
Aviation spirit	52	59	50	46	49	52	46	33	30	22	21	21	17
Motor spirit													
Retail deliveries													
Lead Replacement Petrol/Super premium	1865	1258	1107	1044	884	851	737	787	757	745	647	560	446
Premium unleaded	19008	19100	19167	18291	17795	17221	16615	16322	15250	14300	13435	12870	12357
Total retail deliveries	20873	20358	20274	19335	18679	18071	17351	17109	16007	15045	14082	13430	12803
Commercial consumers													
Lead Replacement Petrol/Super premium													
unleaded (6)	49	44	36	41	40	22	21	16	12	12	11	11	2
Premium unleaded	480	538	499	542	765	759	719	624	523	555	509	454	426
Total commercial consumers	530	581	535	583	805	781	739	641	535	567	520	465	428
Total motor spirit	21403	20939	20809	19918	19484	18852	18091	17750	16542	15613	14602	13895	13231
Industrial and white spirits	170	151	157	147	281	284	156	167	145	174	224	143	219
Kerosene													
Aviation turbine fuel	10806	10614	10519	10765	11637	12497	12641	12574	12142	11533	11116	11574	11221
Burning oil	3839	4236	3578	3569	3950	3870	4017	3629	3681	3732	4012	3288	3329
Gas/diesel oil													
DERV fuel													
Retail deliveries	7181	7846	8153	9057	9517	10532	11501	12685	12777	12669	13157	13549	13965
Commercial consumers	8451	8213	8774	8655	8997	8845	8660	8730	7724	7443	7583	7442	7573
Total DERV fuel	15632	16059	16927	17712	18514	19377	20161	21415	20501	20112	20740	20991	21538
Other gas/diesel oil (includes MDF)	7576	6959	6099	6325	6030	6243	6095	5712	4510	3970	3965	3650	3890
Fuel oil	2119	2578	1721	1539	2062	2206	2251	2209	2063	1625	1448	1042	761
Lubricating oils	801	846	829	868	914	750	713	672	510	510	580	491	412
Bitumen	1975	1935	2002	1959	1991	1906	1610	1563	1741	1381	1370	1621	1355
Petroleum coke	776	702	893	880	1145	1042	925	366	738	550	761	490	545
Miscellaneous products	495	508	647	506	526	556	437	338	590	573	671	592	541

Datasource

Supply and demand of petroleum (DUKES Table 3.5)

https://www.gov.uk/government/publications/petroleum-chapter-3-digest-of-united-kingdom-energy-statistics-dukes

Additional information on inland deliveries of selected products (DUKES 3.6)

https://www.gov.uk/government/publications/petroleum-chapter-3-digest-of-united-kingdom-energy-statistics-dukes

Additional information on inland deliveries for non-energy uses (DUKES 3.8)

https://www.gov.uk/government/publications/petroleum-chapter-3-digest-of-united-kingdom-energy-statistics-dukes

Inland deliveries of petroleum (DUKES 3.1.2)

https://www.gov.uk/government/publications/petroleum-chapter-3-digest-of-united-kingdom-energy-statistics-dukes

Commodity (DUKES 3.2-3.4)

https://www.gov.uk/government/publications/petroleum-chapter-3-digest-of-united-kingdom-energy-statistics-dukes

18.14 Iron and steel:[1] summary of steel supplies, deliveries and stocks
United Kingdom

		2010	2011	2012
Supply, disposal and consumption -(Finished product weight -Thousand tonnes)				
UK producers' home deliveries	**KLTA**	4685	4604	4256
Imports excluding steelworks receipts	**KLTB**	5168	5613	5554
Total deliveries to home market (a)	**KLTC**	9853	10217	9810
Total exports (producers, consumers, merchants)	**KLTD**	5830	5779	6185
Exports by UK producers	**KLTE**	4767	4614	4950
Derived consumers' and merchants' exports (b)	**KLTF**	1063	1165	1235
Net home disposals (a)-(b)	**KLTG**	8790	9052	8575
Estimated home consumption	**KLTI**	8790	9052	8575
Stocks -(Finished product weight - Thousand tonnes)				
Producers				
-ingots & semis	**KLTJ**	552	470	564
-finished steel	**KLTK**	704	632	632
Estimated home consumption -(Crude steel equivalent -Million tonnes)				
Crude steel production[2]	**KLTN**	9.71	9.48	9.58
Producers' stock change	**KLTO**	-0.18	-0.20	0.14
Re-usable material	**KLTP**	0.00	0.00	0.00
Total supply from home sources	**KLTQ**	9.89	9.68	9.44
Total imports3	**KLTR**	6.86	8.03	7.83
Total exports3	**KLTS**	6.67	6.66	7.02
Net home disposals	**KLTT**	10.08	11.05	10.25
Estimated home consumption	**KLTV**	10.08	11.05	10.25

1 See chapter text. The figures relate to periods of 52 weeks.
2 Includes liquid steel for castings only up to 2003.

Source: www.issb.co.uk

18.15 Iron and steel:[1] iron ore, manganese ore, pig iron and iron and steel scrap

United Kingdom   Thousand tonnes

		2010	2011	2012
Iron ore[2]	**KLOF**	10572	9735	10511
Manganese ore[2]	**KLOG**	0	0	0
Pig iron (and blast furnace ferro-alloys)				
Average number of furnaces in blast during period	**KLOH**	5	5	5
Production				
Steelmaking iron	**KLOI**	7233	6625	7183
In blast furnaces: total	**KLOL**	7233	6625	7183
In steel works	**KLOM**	7233	6625	7183
Consumption of pig iron: total	**KLOO**	7233	6625	7183
Iron and steel scrap				
Steelworks and steel foundries				
Circulating scrap	**KLOQ**	1256	1317	1413
Purchased receipts	**KLOR**	2507	2517	2384
Consumption	**KLOS**	3713	3890	3675
Stocks (end of period)	**KLOT**	179	123	245

1 See chapter text. The figures relate to periods of 52 weeks.   Source: www.issb.co.uk
2 Consumption.

18.16 Iron and steel:[1] furnaces and production of steel

United Kingdom   Number and thousand tonnes

		2010	2011	2012
Steel furnaces (numbers[2])	**KLPA**			
Oxygen converters	**KLPC**			
Electric	**KLPD**			
Production of crude steel	**KLPF**	9708	9478	9579
by process				
Oxygen converters	**KLPH**	7323	6946	7525
Electric	**KLPI**	2385	2532	2054
by cast method				
Cast to ingot	**KLPK**	153	205	189
Continuously cast	**KLPL**	9555	9273	9390
Steel for castings	**KLPM**			
by quality				
Non alloy steel	**KLPN**	9201	8835	8992
Stainless and other alloy steel	**KLPO**	508	643	587
Production of finished steel products (All quantities)				
Rods and bars for reinforcement (in coil and lengths)	**KLPP**	792	637	606
Wire rods and other rods and bars in coil	**KLPQ**	874	787	728
Hot rolled bars in lengths	**KLPR**	887	1002	849
Bright steel bars	**KLPS**	154	187	168
Light sections other than rails	**KLPT**	129	117	112
Heavy sections	**KGQZ**	1069	978	883
Hot rolled plates, sheets and strip in coil and lengths	**KLPW**	4733	4575	3962
Cold rolled plates and sheets in coil and lengths	**KLPX**	2200	2215	1939
Cold rolled strip	**KLPZ**	45	42	38
Tinplate	**KLQW**	468	411	411
Other coated sheet	**KLQX**	1278	1262	1161
Tubes and pipes	**KLQY**	702	803	799
Forged bars	**KLQZ**			

1 See chapter text. The figures relate to periods of 52 weeks.   Source: www.issb.co.uk
2 Includes steel furnaces at steel foundries, only up to 2003.

18.17 Fertilisers - UK consumption

Thousand tonnes

Years ending 30 June		1999	2000	2001	2002	2003	2004	2005	2006	2007	2008	2009	2010	2011	2012
Nutrient Content															
Nitrogen (N):	XXXX	1284	1268	1162	1197	1131	1125	1061	1003	1008	1001	948	1016	1022	1000
Straight	KGRM	819	819	714	751	664	662	691	631	656	744	733	771		
Compounds	KGRN	465	449	448	446	467	463	370	372	352	292	180	245		
Phosphate (P2O5)	KGRO	347	317	279	283	282	278	259	235	224	215	129	184	192	188
Potash (K2O)	KGRP	451	409	369	391	375	375	352	325	317	325	208	251	283	259
Compounds - total product	KGRQ	3,013	2,851	2,471	2,511	2,558	2,550	2,221	2,134	2,039	1,827	1,116	1,529		

Source: Agricultural Industries Confederation: 01733 385230 and British Survey of Fertiliser Practice (Defra)

Table 18.17 gives the quantity of the fertiliser nutrients nitrogen (N), phosphate (P2O5) and potash (K2O) used by UK farmers during the fertiliser year, which runs from 1st July to 30th June. The year shown in the table is the year in which the harvest takes place, at the end of each fertiliser year.

18.18a United Kingdom production of minerals 2006–2012

Thousand tonnes

Mineral	2006	2007	2008	2009	2010	2011
Coal:						
Deep-mined	9 444	7 674	8 096	7 520	7 390	7 312
Opencast	8 635	8 866	9 509	9 854	10 426	10 580
Other (a)	438	467	449	500	600	600
Natural gas and oil:						
Methane (oil equivalent)						
Colliery	65	62	63	67	63	58
Onshore	91	105	92	89	88	27
Offshore	79 856	71 957	69 525	59 581	57 036	45 204
Crude oil						
Onshore	1 379	1 271	1 248	1 181	941	678
Offshore	68 287	69 086	64 249	61 639	57 106	47 893
Condensates and other (c)						
Onshore	41	38	33	32	17	0
Offshore	6 872	6 180	6 135	5 346	4 898	3 401
Iron ore	0.4	0.3	0.1	—	—	—
Non-ferrous ores (metal content):						
Tin	—	—	—	—	—	—
Lead (h)	0.4	0.3	0.3	0.2	0.3	0.3
Gold (kg)	...	88	163	187	177	202
Silver (kg)	—	212	398	514	506	531
Chalk (e)	7 376	7 566	5 874	4 047	3 626	3 996
Clay and shale (e)	10 432	10 104	8 459	5 310	5 934	6 154
Igneous rock (j) (k)	53 954	58 909	53 489	44 618	44 876	44 490
Limestone (excluding dolomite)	80 228	83 491	74 143	60 110	60 207	57 930
Dolomite (excluding limestone)	12 101	7 622	5 509	3 164	4 540	4 490
Sand and gravel:						
Land	71 418	72 810	66 638	50 973	47 167	46 826
Marine (i)	20 689	20 426	18 833	15 253	14 533	17 287
Sandstone	18 038	16 806	12 255	12 335	11 556	12 477
Slate (g)	865	1 428	1 058	683	695	763
Ball clay (sales)	1 015	1 022	1 020	727	900 (h)	930 (h)
Barytes	48	53	43	36	34	31
Chert and flint	2	1	1	1	1	1
China clay (sales) (d)	1 762	1 671	1 355	1 060	(h) 1 140	(h) 1 290
China stone	1	1	0.5	0.0	0.0	0.0
Fireclay (e)	228	338	180	129	110	162
Fluorspar (h)	50	45	37	19	26	—
Gypsum (natural)	(h) 1 700	(h) 1 700	(h) 1 700	(h) 1 700	(h) 1 700	(h) 1 700
Lignite	...	...	...	...	...	...
Peat (000 m^3)	1 593	885	760	887	1 004	825
Potash (b)	716	712	673	700	700	770
Salt	5 499	5 600	5 565	6 166	6 666	6 060
Silica sand	5 174	4 909	4 777	3 755	4 070	3 969
Talc	4	3	2	3	3	4

(a) Slurry etc. recovered from dumps, ponds, rivers etc.
(b) Marketable product (KCI).
(c) Including ethane, propane and butane, in addition to condensates.
(d) Dry weight.
(e) Excluding a small production in Northern Ireland.
(f) BGS estimates based on data from producing companies.
(g) Slate figures include waste used for constructional fill and powder and granules used in industry.
(h) BGS estimate.
(i) Including marine-dredged landings at foreign ports (exports).
(j) Excluding a small production of granite in Northern Ireland.

(k) In addition, the following amounts of igneous rock were produced in Guernsey (thousand tonnes): 2006: 136; 2007: 160; 2008: 139; 2009: 120; 2010: 116; 2011: 156
and Jersey: 2006: 286; 2007: 295; 2008: 325; 2009: 249; 2010: 238; 2011: 220

Sources: Office for National Statistics, Department of Business, Innovation and Skills, Dept. of Enterprise, Trade & Investment (Northern Ireland), Crown Estate Commissioners (marine sand and gravel produced for export), and company data.

18.18b Minerals produced in Northern Ireland, the Isle of Man, Guernsey and Jersey 2007–2011

Thousand tonnes

		2007	2008	2009	2010	2011
Northern Ireland						
Gold (kg)		88	163	187	177	202
Silver (kg)		212	398	514	506	531
Lead		(c) 200	(c) 200	243	251	280
Limestone		5,904	3,739	3,972	3,689	...
Sand and gravel		8,086	7,134	4,856	2,178	...
Basalt and igneous rock (a)		8,225	6,481	5,758	5,438	...
Sandstone		4,828	2,697	3,793	2,768	...
Granite		...	...	...	...	...
Clay and shale		...	...	...	...	...
Others (b)		2,468	2,931	1,998	2,087	...
	Total	**29,511**	**22,982**	**20,377**	**16,160**	...
Isle of Man						
Limestone		112	113	352	71	82
Sand and gravel		206	197	171	145	141
Igneous rock		104	158	132	109	96
Slate		58	64	45	28	29
	Total	**480**	**532**	**701**	**353**	**347**
Guernsey						
Igneous rock		160	139	120	116	156
Jersey						
Igneous rock (c)		295	325	249	238	220
Sand and gravel		65	67	67	57	74

(a) Excluding granite.
(b) Including rock salt, chalk, dolomite, fireclay and granite.
(c) BGS estimates.

Sources: Department of Enterprise, Trade & Investment (Northern Ireland),
Department of Economic Development (Isle of Man),
Company data (Guernsey and Jersey).

18.19a : Building materials and components

Bricks - Production, Deliveries and Stocks

Great Britain

Millions

(a) Brick Type

	Production	Deliveries (from)	Stocks*	Production	Deliveries (from)	Stocks*	Production	Deliveries (from)	Stocks*	Production	Deliveries (from)	Stocks*
	All Types			Commons			Facings			Engineerings		
2008	1,929	1,796	1,105	246	242	151	1,514	1,386	895	170	168	58
2009	1,257	1,469	887	185	224	108	973	1,135	732	99	109	48
2010	1,430	1,606	702	182	194	94	1,124	1,280	570	124	132	39
2011	1,554	1,646	610	172	185	82	1,230	1,304	494	152	157	34
2012	1,459	1,551	515	137	166	52	1,172	1,239	425	150	146	38
2012 Q1	370	391	588	32	45	68	298	310	483	40	36	38
Q2	408	397	599	35	41	62	334	320	497	39	37	40
Q3	370	418	552	37	45	54	292	332	457	41	41	40
Q4	311	345	515	33	35	52	248	277	425	30	33	38
2013 Q1	344	343	518	33	36	50	274	273	426	37	34	41
2012 April	129	131	586	12	14	66	108	105	486	10	12	35
May	144	142	589	12	15	63	119	114	490	14	13	37
June	134	124	599	11	12	62	107	100	497	15	12	40
July	126	140	586	12	16	58	101	111	487	13	13	40
August	115	146	555	11	15	55	90	117	461	13	15	39
September	129	132	552	14	15	54	101	105	457	14	13	40
October	132	141	542	13	14	53	105	114	448	13	13	41
November	116	132	523	12	13	52	92	105	432	12	13	40
December	64	72	515	8	8	52	51	58	425	5	7	38
2013 January	101	96	520	10	11	51	77	75	428	13	10	41
February	114	116	519	11	12	51	92	93	427	10	11	40
March	130	131	518	12	13	50	104	106	426	14	13	41
April (P)	127	142	503	13	14	49	103	114	415	11	14	39

(b) Material Type

	Production	Deliveries (from)	Stocks*	Production	Deliveries (from)	Stocks*	Production	Deliveries (from)	Stocks*	Production	Deliveries (from)	Stocks*
	All Materials			Clay#			Sand-Lime#			Concrete		
2008	1,929	1,796	1,105	1,814	1,676	1,093	..	..	..	115	120	11
2009	1,257	1,469	887	..	..	..	..	..	..	..	..	..
2010	1,430	1,606	702	..	..	..	..	..	..	..	..	..
2011	1,554	1,646	610	..	..	..	..	..	..	..	..	..
2012	1,459	1,551	515	..	..	..	..	..	..	..	..	..
2012 Q1	370	391	588	..	..	..	..	..	..	..	..	..
Q2	408	397	599	..	..	..	..	..	..	..	..	..
Q3	370	418	552	..	..	..	..	..	..	..	..	..
Q4	311	345	515	..	..	..	..	..	..	..	..	..
2013 Q1	344	343	518	..	..	..	..	..	..	..	..	..
2012 April	129	131	586	..	..	..	..	..	..	..	..	..
May	144	142	589	..	..	..	..	..	..	..	..	..
June	134	124	599	..	..	..	..	..	..	..	..	..
July	126	140	586	..	..	..	..	..	..	..	..	..
August	115	146	555	..	..	..	..	..	..	..	..	..
September	129	132	552	..	..	..	..	..	..	..	..	..
October	132	141	542	..	..	..	..	..	..	..	..	..
November	116	132	523	..	..	..	..	..	..	..	..	..
December	64	72	515	..	..	..	..	..	..	..	..	..
2013 January	101	96	520	..	..	..	..	..	..	..	..	..
February	114	116	519	..	..	..	..	..	..	..	..	..
March	130	131	518	..	..	..	..	..	..	..	..	..
April (P)	127	142	503	..	..	..	..	..	..	..	..	..

* Refers to stocks at end of period

#Sand-lime bricks are included with clay bricks

Note: Data covering January 2009 to February 2011 were revised in the December 2011. These data are included in this table. For more information on revisions, see the 'Pre-announcements and Summary of Revisions to Monthly Statistics of Building Materials and Components Publication' document.

18.19b: Building materials and components

Concrete Blocks - Production, Deliveries and Stocks

Great Britain   Thousand square metres

	All Types			Dense			Lightweight			Aerated		
	Production	Deliveries (from)	Stocks*	Production	Deliveries (from)	Stocks*	Production	Deliveries (from)	Stocks*	Production	Deliveries (from)	Stocks*
2002	91,474	91,342	9,014	35,744	36,019	3,963	23,478	23,537	2,188	32,252	31,786	2,863
2003	95,675	96,383	8,513	36,775	37,175	3,684	24,991	25,161	2,107	33,909	34,047	2,721
2004	96,256	94,854	10,088	37,677	37,444	3,690	25,462	25,736	2,271	33,117	31,674	4,127
2005	89,997	89,551	9,680	36,188	36,473	3,465	25,561	25,673	2,173	28,248	27,405	4,042
2006	87,510	87,015	..	34,956	34,741	..	25,345	25,222	..	27,209	27,051	..
2007	89,951	88,746	..	36,686	35,396	..	25,965	25,667	..	27,300	27,682	..
2008	67,743	67,136	8,920	29,675	29,889	3,498	18,168	18,363	2,149	19,900	18,884	3,273
2009	50,394	50,639	8,320	22,607	22,748	3,291	13,421	13,989	1,522	14,367	13,903	3,507
2010	53,629	51,758	10,152	22,393	21,731	3,833	14,415	13,923	2,044	16,822	16,104	4,276
2011	54,583	52,901	10,810	22,940	22,101	4,486	15,153	14,821	1,728	16,490	15,978	4,596
2012	51,693	52,021	10,700	21,551	22,323	3,808	14,383	14,103	2,024	15,759	15,595	4,868
2008 Q1	21,131	18,855	11,749	8,564	7,853	5,075	5,580	5,389	2,633	6,988	5,612	4,041
Q2	20,231	19,714	11,977	8,767	8,677	5,107	5,421	5,405	2,549	6,043	5,632	4,321
Q3	14,894	16,309	10,224	7,131	7,576	4,479	4,110	4,309	2,338	3,653	4,424	3,406
Q4	11,487	12,259	8,920	5,214	5,783	3,498	3,057	3,260	2,149	3,216	3,216	3,273
2009 Q1	12,094	11,649	9,161	5,635	5,438	3,628	3,213	3,258	2,181	3,247	2,953	3,352
Q2	13,463	13,191	9,455	6,192	6,032	3,821	3,498	3,553	2,125	3,773	3,607	3,510
Q3	12,771	13,924	8,203	5,811	6,255	3,390	3,293	3,765	1,544	3,667	3,903	3,269
Q4	12,066	11,874	8,320	4,969	5,023	3,291	3,416	3,412	1,522	3,681	3,439	3,507
2010 Q1	12,614	12,072	8,740	5,033	4,896	3,333	3,344	3,252	1,601	4,238	3,924	3,806
Q2	14,956	14,753	8,990	6,343	6,176	3,513	4,031	3,950	1,692	4,582	4,627	3,785
Q3	15,172	14,343	9,832	6,477	6,125	3,837	4,208	3,899	2,023	4,487	4,319	3,971
Q4	10,887	10,590	10,152	4,541	4,534	3,833	2,832	2,822	2,044	3,515	3,234	4,276
2011 Q1	13,982	12,795	11,516	5,642	5,278	4,197	3,916	3,665	2,301	4,423	3,852	5,017
Q2	14,761	13,911	12,510	6,217	5,871	4,647	4,008	3,827	2,507	4,537	4,212	5,357
Q3	14,208	14,076	12,352	6,217	5,931	4,862	3,908	3,970	2,218	4,083	4,175	5,272
Q4	11,632	12,120	10,810	4,864	5,021	4,486	3,321	3,359	1,728	3,447	3,739	4,596
2012 Q1	13,323	12,642	11,493	5,374	5,426	4,456	3,559	3,314	1,964	4,389	3,903	5,074
Q2	13,268	13,235	11,595	5,535	5,824	4,209	3,487	3,437	2,006	4,245	3,973	5,380
Q3	12,584	13,795	10,471	5,360	5,773	3,773	3,756	3,887	1,904	3,467	4,135	4,794
Q4	12,519	12,349	10,700	5,281	5,300	3,808	3,580	3,465	2,024	3,658	3,584	4,868
2013 Q1	12,096	12,651	10,199	5,189	5,367	3,683	3,089	3,391	1,723	3,818	3,893	4,793
2011 April	4,415	4,308	..	1,867	1,811	..	1,188	1,201	..	1,361	1,296	..
May	5,037	4,690	..	2,119	2,019	..	1,401	1,316	..	1,517	1,355	..
June	5,309	4,912	12,510	2,231	2,041	4,647	1,420	1,311	2,507	1,658	1,561	5,357
July	4,805	4,574	..	2,088	1,935	..	1,335	1,291	..	1,383	1,348	..
August	4,413	4,675	..	2,073	1,987	..	1,306	1,327	..	1,034	1,361	..
September	4,990	4,826	12,352	2,056	2,009	4,862	1,267	1,352	2,218	1,666	1,466	5,272
October	4,515	4,582	..	1,863	1,904	..	1,166	1,265	..	1,487	1,414	..
November	4,244	4,375	..	1,776	1,795	..	1,386	1,271	..	1,082	1,308	..
December	2,873	3,163	10,810	1,225	1,322	4,486	769	823	1,728	878	1,017	4,596
2012 January	4,229	3,870	..	1,707	1,639	..	1,165	990	..	1,357	1,241	..
February	4,339	3,719	..	1,843	1,653	..	1,112	998	..	1,384	1,068	..
March	4,754	5,053	11,493	1,824	2,133	4,456	1,281	1,326	1,964	1,648	1,594	5,074
April	4,167	4,281	..	1,746	1,874	..	1,106	1,100	..	1,315	1,307	..
May	4,842	4,756	..	2,014	2,154	..	1,303	1,230	..	1,525	1,371	..
June	4,258	4,199	11,595	1,775	1,797	4,209	1,078	1,107	2,006	1,405	1,295	5,380
July	4,313	4,285	..	1,828	1,939	..	1,206	1,155	..	1,280	1,191	..
August	3,927	4,931	..	1,751	1,970	..	1,337	1,430	..	839	1,530	..
September	4,344	4,579	10,471	1,782	1,863	3,773	1,213	1,302	1,904	1,348	1,414	4,794
October	4,642	4,867	..	1,945	2,074	..	1,393	1,453	..	1,304	1,340	..
November	4,726	4,582	..	2,022	1,943	..	1,333	1,308	..	1,371	1,330	..
December	3,151	2,900	10,700	1,314	1,283	3,808	854	704	2,024	983	914	4,868
2013 January	3,742	3,415	..	1,689	1,482	..	928	927	..	1,125	1,006	..
February	3,785	4,409	..	1,499	1,863	..	1,047	1,212	..	1,239	1,334	..
March	4,569	4,827	10,199	2,001	2,021	3,683	1,115	1,252	1,723	1,454	1,553	4,793
April (P)	4,857	5,371	..	2,290	2,440	..	1,323	1,387	..	1,244	1,544	..

* Refers to stocks at end of period

Missing returns for provisional data (P) have been estimated using an improved methodology. See the 'pre-announcement of any major changes to samples or methodology' on the website

Data from December 2011 to June 2012 has been revised following receipt of corrected data. The period August 2007 to November 2011 may also be affected, but non-availability of a back-series of corrected data means that this period cannot be revised, and should be treated with caution. Full details are available in the 'Summary of revision to monthly statistics of building materials and components publication' document.

18.19c Building materials and components

Other Building Materials

		Great Britain			United Kingdom
		Concrete Roofing Tiles (Th.sq.m. of roof area covered)			**Ready-Mixed Concrete #** (Th.cu.m.)
		Production	Deliveries	Stocks *	Deliveries
2002		25,023	24,390	4,586	22,597
2003		21,437	21,401	2,982	22,289
2004		20,739	19,403	2,850	22,856
2005		25,719	24,489	4,902	22,432
2006		23,730	24,118	4,426	23,029
2007		23,551	23,812	3,646	23,548
2008		20,084	19,926	3,899	20,051
2009		14,079	15,612	2,344	14,069
2010		17,817	17,146	3,023	14,038
2011		17,712	17,684	3,126	15,121
2012		17,224	17,159	3,191	13,758
2004	Q1	5,498	4,294	3,787	5,334
	Q2	5,266	4,800	3,728	5,931
	Q3	4,920	5,134	3,048	6,038
	Q4	5,055	5,175	2,850	5,553
2005	Q1	5,787	4,779	3,732	5,137
	Q2	7,502	6,406	5,818	5,994
	Q3	6,135	7,103	4,850	5,920
	Q4	6,295	6,200	4,902	5,381
2006	Q1	6,792	6,252	5,418	5,445
	Q2	6,002	5,709	5,708	5,995
	Q3	5,448	6,371	4,688	6,047
	Q4	5,489	5,787	4,426	5,542
2007	Q1	6,618	5,629	5,368	5,554
	Q2	5,775	5,728	5,360	6,103
	Q3	5,129	6,541	3,929	6,205
	Q4	6,028	5,914	3,646	5,686
2008	Q1	5,708	5,421	3,922	5,193
	Q2	5,815	5,679	4,488	5,773
	Q3	4,657	4,977	3,840	4,902
	Q4	3,903	3,849	3,899	4,183
2009	Q1	3,664	3,281	4,273	3,583
	Q2	3,055	3,936	3,391	3,637
	Q3	3,580	4,447	2,522	3,628
	Q4	3,779	3,949	2,344	3,221
2010	Q1	4,129	3,505	2,967	3,328
	Q2	4,961	4,922	3,008	3,819
	Q3	4,783	4,824	2,967	3,831
	Q4	3,945	3,894	3,023	3,060
2011	Q1	4,820	4,079	3,858	3,827
	Q2	4,565	4,398	4,022	3,907
	Q3	4,210	4,901	3,316	3,908
	Q4	4,116	4,306	3,126	3,479
2012	Q1	4,673	3,928	3,872	3,463
	Q2	4,236	4,100	4,008	3,399
	Q3	3,971	4,885	3,093	3,556
	Q4	4,344	4,246	3,191	3,340
2013	Q1	4,319	3,876	3,634	3,325

* Refers to stocks at the end of the period.

In April 2012, the Mineral Products Association (who provide these figures), estimated that data understates UK deliveries by around 20-25%. Previously, they had estimated that figures understate UK deliveries by 14-18%.

Concrete roofing tiles data underwent imputation for a non-responder in each quarter of 2012.

18.19d Building materials and components

Slate - Production, Deliveries and Stocks

Great Britain   Tonnes

	Production			Deliveries			Stocks (a)			Deliveries
	Roofing (b)	Other (c)	Powder & Granules	Roofing (b)	Other (c)	Powder & Granules	Roofing (b)	Other (c)	Powder & Granules	Fill & Other Uses
2001	30,770	14,834	47,521	33,052	13,586	47,588	3,159	8,465	2,799	383,353
2002	32,182	18,348	44,424	32,653	19,069	43,947	2,674	7,850	3,275	498,212
2003	34,471	15,623	29,003	34,700	14,576	29,240	2,477	8,849	3,416	669,818
2004	..	..	..	..	..	..	..	..	..	..
2005	..	..	..	..	..	..	2,824	10,281	5,347	..
2006	..	61,612	22,967	..	64,037	22,719	..	6,454	4,274	860,395
2007	..	65,260	19,141	..	62,646	19,431	2,563	2,521	3,746	..
2008	..	59,644	16,915	..	58,129	18,402	..	2,749	2,253	..
2009	..	33,759	9,150	22,555	34,322	10,637	2,420	2,186	766	615,346
2010	..	28,001	..	..	27,355	..	..	3,063	..	582,111
2011	..	30,665	..	..	30,437	..	..	3,245	..	662,003
2012	..	29,634	..	..	28,083	..	..	3,262	..	607,127
2005 Q1	..	..	..	..	..	..	..	..	..	..
Q2	..	..	..	..	..	..	..	..	..	..
Q3	..	..	..	..	..	..	..	..	..	..
Q4	..	13,635	7,448	..	6,194	7,635	2,824	10,281	5,347	124,188
2006 Q1	..	11,594	6,575	..	12,879	6,406	3,170	8,967	5,440	195,762
Q2	..	14,804	5,051	..	14,983	5,257	3,079	7,424	3,990	223,696
Q3	..	16,170	5,194	..	16,803	5,094	..	6,792	4,090	251,314
Q4	..	19,044	6,147	..	19,372	5,962	..	6,454	4,274	189,623
2007 Q1	..	17,787	5,571	..	16,829	5,036	6,984	4,996	4,571	376,876
Q2	..	16,577	4,315	..	14,765	4,875	3,066	5,850	4,011	346,426
Q3	..	16,017	4,672	..	15,475	4,929	2,977	6,391	3,754	..
Q4	..	14,879	4,583	..	15,577	4,591	2,563	2,521	3,746	255,249
2008 Q1	..	18,608	4,282	..	18,071	4,414	..	3,059	3,594	246,495
Q2	..	15,465	4,738	..	14,457	4,862	..	3,801	3,484	..
Q3	..	13,811	3,843	..	13,841	5,511	3,851	2,749	1,816	..
Q4	..	11,760	4,052	..	11,760	3,615	..	2,749	2,253	..
2009 Q1	..	7,370	2,128	5,315	7,688	2,724	..	2,431	1,658	148,722
Q2	5,084	9,124	2,046	5,328	9,319	3,385	4,142	2,236	318	169,661
Q3	5,503	8,263	2,046	6,534	8,267	2,163	3,111	2,232	201	154,862
Q4	4,687	9,002	2,930	5,378	9,048	2,365	2,420	2,186	766	142,101
2010 Q1	..	6,772	..	..	6,662	..	..	2,296	..	88,805
Q2	..	7,517	..	..	7,388	..	2,049	3,284	683	175,098
Q3	..	7,335	..	..	7,184	..	1,326	3,332	281	159,574
Q4	4,907	6,377	..	4,909	6,121	..	..	3,063	..	158,634
2011 Q1	4,736	6,516	3,314	4,449	6,504	3,399	..	3,029	..	198,547
Q2	4,677	8,167	3,370	4,630	8,187	3,094	2,012	3,009	472	216,524
Q3	..	9,851	..	..	9,732	..	..	3,128	..	139,359
Q4	..	6,131	..	..	6,014	..	..	3,245	..	107,573
2012 Q1	..	9,247	..	..	8,829	..	..	2,646	..	131,311
Q2	..	8,216	..	..	9,677	..	..	1,154	..	177,748
Q3	..	6,219	..	..	6,167	..	..	1,206	..	146,152
Q4	..	5,952	..	..	3,410	..	..	3,262	..	151,916
2013 Q1	..	6,052	..	..	9,220	..	..	..	802	157,215

Note : 1) We have improved our sampling panel to include some new sites and have removed some non-pure slate sites. In line with the Code of Practice we have revised the data for Q2, Q3 and Q4 2010.

2) From Q1 1995, the coverage of 'powder & granules' has been extended to include non-quarry manufacture; and 'crude blocks' are included in 'other' maufacture slate.

(a)   Refers to stocks at the end of the period.

(b)   Consists of all slate tiles which could be used as roofing tiles.

(c)   Consists of all slate products for cladding and decorative uses

18.19e Building materials and components
Cement & Clinker - Production, Deliveries and Stocks

Great Britain   Thousand tonnes

		Cement								Clinker
		Production		Deliveries	Imports (into GB)		Cementitious Material			Production
			Exports	(into GB from	by	by				
		of which	(from GB)	GB production)	'Manuf.	Others**	other	total		
2007		11,887	74	11,638	255	1,121	2,769	15,783		10,227
2008		10,071	61	9,937	283	1,084	2,432	13,660		8,700
2009		7,623	21	7,474	99	1,085	1,680	10,338		6,421
2010		7,883	0	7,767	61	1,153	1,535	10,515		6,598
2011		8,529	0	8,318	86	1,173	1,736	11,312		7,096
2012		7,952	0	7,728	61	1,122	1,605	10,515		6,555
2007	Q2	3,188	22	3,061	59	297	701	4,117		2,812
	Q3	3,130	9	3,011	84	294	746	4,135		2,751
	Q4	2,891	16	2,787	69	259	681	3,796		2,643
2008	Q1	2,609	18	2,551	88	268	598	3,505		2,267
	Q2	2,803	18	2,816	94	327	682	3,917		2,366
	Q3	2,520	13	2,496	72	263	648	3,445		2,202
	Q4	2,139	12	2,074	29	226	505	2,793		1,865
2009	Q1	1,762	14	1,782	37	256	410	2,485		1,378
	Q2	2,004	1	1,970	21	279	451	2,721		1,587
	Q3	1,998	5	1,999	25	283	453	2,760		1,831
	Q4	1,859	1	1,723	17	268	366	2,373		1,624
2010	Q1	1,726	0	1,744	24	246	336	2,350		1,261
	Q2	2,157	0	2,154	8	345	416	2,923		1,745
	Q3	2,203	0	2,195	17	310	450	2,971		1,880
	Q4	1,796	0	1,674	12	252	332	2,270		1,713
2011	Q1	1,979	0	2,043	12	281	402	2,738		1,427
	Q2	2,245	0	2,165	25	319	448	2,956		1,791
	Q3	2,246	0	2,200	25	303	494	3,022		2,015
	Q4	2,059	0	1,909	24	270	392	2,595		1,863
2012	Q1	1,880	0	1,928	16	285	370	2,599		1,366
	Q2	2,073	0	1,974	13	277	389	2,653		1,736
	Q3	2,120	0	2,021	13	302	444	2,780		1,722
	Q4	1,879	0	1,805	20	257	400	2,483		1,731
2013	Q1	1,425	0	1,716	16	..	..	..		1,198
2012	Mar	765	0	757	8	..	..	..		661
	Apr	678	0	610	4	..	..	..		579
	May	726	0	741	4	..	..	..		563
	Jun	668	0	622	4	..	..	..		594
	Jul	736	0	692	4	..	..	..		630
	Aug	682	0	687	4	..	..	..		547
	Sep	701	0	642	4	..	..	..		545
	Oct	692	0	733	4	..	..	..		566
	Nov	674	0	668	8	..	..	..		536
	Dec	513	0	404	8	..	..	..		629
2013	Jan	355	0	470	4	..	..	..		291
	Feb	515	0	623	8	..	..	..		427
	Mar	555	0	623	4	..	..	..		480

NB   Where the coverage is for Great Britain, the figures for imports & exports are defined accordingly and have been estimated.

Cementitious material covers cement itself, fly ash to EN 450 Part 1 where used as part of the cement in concrete

(previously known as pulverised fuel ash (pfa) to BS 3892 Part 1) and ground granulated blast furnace slag (ggbs) to

EN 15167 Part 1 (previously BS 6699)   * Refers to stocks at end of period   ** Estimated

18.19f Building materials and components
Sales of Sand and Gravel in Great Britain

Great Britain   Thousand tonnes

	Sand		Gravel	Sand & Gravel	Sand, Gravel & Hoggin	Sand & Gravel	of which
	for Building	for Concreting	for Concreting & other uses	for Coating	for Fill	Total	Marine-Dredged
2002	11,152	30,334	35,642	2,106	6,279	85,513	12,833
2003	11,474	31,349	31,725	1,493	6,498	82,539	12,249
2004	11,017	32,366	30,184	1,380	6,399	81,346	12,996
2005	12,419	30,704	30,648	1,569	5,173	80,513	13,025
2006	9,499	29,893	31,963	2,346	4,195	77,896	13,974
2007	8,649	29,803	31,114	1,695	4,254	75,515	13,777
2008	8,864	28,922	28,297	..	..	74,651	12,582
2009	7,270	21,582	..	..	..	58,482	9,589
2010	6,074	19,887	..	..	..	54,530	9,341
2011	6,041	23,489	..	..	..	57,062	11,169
2012	6,499	21,994	23,077	..	..	57,972	10,320
2007 Q1	2,081	6,919	7,242	443	904	17,589	3,177
Q2	2,305	7,762	8,202	432	1,179	19,880	3,596
Q3	2,304	7,829	8,191	398	1,162	19,884	3,675
Q4	1,959	7,293	7,479	422	1,009	18,162	3,329
2008 Q1	2,151	7,156	7,286	379	1,180	18,152	3,035
Q2	2,385	7,724	7,668	456	2,041	20,274	3,541
Q3	2,279	7,644	7,091	..	..	19,341	3,337
Q4	2,049	6,398	6,252	490	1,695	16,884	2,669
2009 Q1	1,727	5,313	5,330	695	1,566	14,631	2,389
Q2	1,916	5,637	5,756	..	..	15,359	2,637
Q3	1,992	5,598	..	..	..	14,878	2,457
Q4	1,635	5,034	..	..	1,432	13,614	2,106
2010 Q1	1,539	4,952	..	..	..	13,711	2,131
Q2	1,585	4,983	..	..	..	13,940	2,444
Q3	1,584	5,268	..	..	..	14,112	2,592
Q4	1,366	4,684	..	..	..	12,767	2,174
2011 Q1	1,572	5,665	..	..	..	14,150	2,746
Q2	1,579	6,127	5,291	..	..	14,831	2,923
Q3	1,533	6,085	5,160	..	..	14,684	2,937
Q4	1,357	5,612	4,719	..	..	13,397	2,563
2012 Q1	1,481	5,635	5,039	..	..	13,894	2,675
Q2	1,712	5,608	5,633	..	..	14,474	2,609
Q3	1,778	5,612	6,259	..	..	15,192	2,749
Q4	1,528	5,139	6,146	..	..	14,412	2,287
2013 Q1 (P)	1,411	5,004	5,270	..	..	13,325	2,352

Note : The figures above are from a quarterly sample inquiry whereas those below are from the Annual Minerals Raised Inquiry, a census.

The two inquiries differ because some respondents are only able to provide estimated information for the quarterly inquiry.

1999	11,356	31,730	31,614	2,585	10,924	88,209	13,424
2000	11,758	31,167	31,797	2,461	12,051	89,234	14,356
2001	11,515	31,656	35,135	2,257	7,647	88,210	13,611
2002	11,190	31,224	32,434	2,031	5,842	82,721	12,832
2003	11,851	31,411	30,236	1,766	4,957	80,221	12,131
2004	10,688	32,529	32,346	2,437	8,058	86,057	12,996
2005	11,558	29,848	32,163	2,172	6,651	82,392	13,024
2006	9,907	29,815	31,002	2,648	6,869	80,242	13,974
2007	9,877	30,202	29,350	2,636	6,436	78,501	13,777
2008	8,527	26,885	23,388	2,222	11,106	72,127	12,621
2009	6,296	21,570	19,553	2,270	6,021	55,709	9,592
2010	6,110	20,947	18,540	2,112	6,621	54,330	9,341
2011	6,140	22,591	18,712	1,913	5,659	55,015	11,169

18.20: Volume of construction output in Great Britain: constant (2005) prices, seasonally adjusted index numbers - by sector

£ Million	New Housing			Other New Work				All New Work	Repair and Maintenance				All Repair and Maintenance	All Work	Period on Period Growths	Period on same period one year ago growths
	Public	Private	Infras-tructure	Excluding Infrastructure					Housing			Non Housing R&M				
				Public	Private Industrial	Private Commercial			Public	Private	Total					
2008 Q1	128.0	90.6	99.5	97.1	94.8	127.0		107.3	89.4	94.7	92.8	105.9	99.7	104.6	1.6%	1.1%
Q2	125.4	81.2	101.3	98.7	84.4	122.1		102.3	96.1	93.7	94.5	110.4	102.9	102.5	-2.0%	-0.6%
Q3	123.3	72.1	104.5	101.8	77.9	120.7		99.3	94.3	89.0	90.8	107.7	99.7	99.4	-3.0%	-2.4%
Q4	113.1	62.2	98.9	103.2	69.3	112.6		91.9	90.1	91.8	91.2	101.9	96.8	93.7	-5.8%	-9.0%
2009 Q1	107.8	55.4	100.7	106.9	60.6	102.8		86.1	86.3	86.2	86.2	97.5	92.1	88.3	-5.8%	-15.6%
Q2	111.3	52.5	107.1	114.1	54.9	95.8		83.9	89.7	80.5	83.7	94.7	89.5	85.9	-2.6%	-16.2%
Q3	131.9	50.2	116.7	124.6	54.3	84.7		82.2	97.2	83.9	88.6	95.9	92.4	85.8	-0.1%	-13.7%
Q4	150.8	52.3	139.8	139.1	59.1	78.6		85.8	90.2	72.9	79.0	94.5	87.2	86.3	0.5%	-7.9%
2010 Q1	168.1	55.7	147.3	148.1	61.2	83.3		91.2	98.3	79.0	85.8	80.9	83.2	88.3	2.3%	0.1%
Q2	188.9	60.2	150.6	160.9	64.5	87.9		97.0	97.5	85.4	89.7	87.4	88.5	93.9	6.3%	9.3%
Q3	208.7	63.9	146.8	165.6	73.2	93.1		101.4	96.7	90.5	92.7	84.1	88.1	96.6	2.9%	12.6%
Q4	208.4	66.6	137.7	162.5	57.0	90.1		98.3	96.8	88.9	91.7	86.0	88.7	94.9	-1.8%	9.9%
2011 Q1	203.6	66.6	150.7	158.6	59.1	86.7		98.1	92.1	87.3	89.0	89.2	89.1	94.9	0.0%	7.4%
Q2	204.0	67.2	163.5	151.9	60.0	89.9		100.3	89.3	86.8	87.7	89.5	88.6	96.1	1.3%	2.3%
Q3	193.0	68.4	158.5	146.7	56.5	93.5		100.1	87.9	85.9	86.6	91.3	89.1	96.2	0.1%	-0.5%
Q4	187.6	67.6	159.3	133.5	56.0	94.3		98.5	87.9	88.2	88.1	91.2	89.8	95.4	-0.8%	0.5%
2012 Q1 R	168.5	67.6	138.1	123.7	58.3	85.0		91.1	89.2	87.3	88.0	90.8	89.5	90.5	-5.1% R	-4.6%
Q2 R	161.0	64.1	129.4	118.3	59.2	84.4		88.1	88.8	82.9	85.0	91.7	88.5	88.3	-2.5%	-8.2%
Q3 R	162.0	61.8	138.8	115.2	59.6	78.2		85.9	91.5	80.7	84.5	88.7	86.7	86.2	-2.3%	-10.4%
Q4 R	159.5	65.9	141.9	108.2	61.5	78.8		86.9	90.7	78.6	82.8	90.5	86.8	86.9	0.8%	-8.9%
2013 Q1 R	154.1	63.4	136.0	99.4	62.0	77.7		84.0	88.2	78.3	81.8	90.4	86.3	84.8	-2.4%	-6.3%

Source: Output in the Construction Industry: April 2013

R Revised since March 2013 publication of Output in the Construction Industry

18.21 Value of orders for new construction obtained by main contractors in Great Britain: current prices - by sector

	New Housing			Other New Work					All New Work	Period on Period Growths
	Public & Housing Association	Private	All Housing	Infra-structure	Excluding Infrastructure			All Other New Work		
					Public	Private Industrial	Private Commercial			
2008	3,082	9,201	12,283	7,897	14,671	4,346	23,353	50,267	62,550	-17.8%
2009	3,107	6,393	9,500	11,032	14,709	2,653	12,886	41,280	50,780	-18.8%
2010	3,482	9,953	13,435	9,774	13,430	2,131	13,580	38,915	52,350	3.1%
2011	2,690	10,507	13,197	8,499	9,064	2,146	13,005	32,714	45,911	-12.3%
2012 R	2,450	10,804	13,254	12,509	8,028	2,659	11,973	35,169	48,424	5.5%
2008 Q1	992	3,217	4,210	2,220	3,588	1,267	7,066	14,141	18,351	6.3%
Q2	829	2,732	3,562	2,379	3,498	942	6,268	13,087	16,648	-9.3%
Q3	709	1,778	2,487	1,695	4,123	1,166	5,832	12,816	15,303	-8.1%
Q4	551	1,473	2,024	1,603	3,463	971	4,187	10,223	12,248	-20.0%
2009 Q1	765	1,422	2,186	2,474	2,793	554	3,297	9,117	11,303	-7.7%
Q2	638	1,668	2,306	3,265	4,091	738	3,433	11,527	13,833	22.4%
Q3	907	1,456	2,363	3,089	4,405	630	2,926	11,050	13,413	-3.0%
Q4	797	1,847	2,645	2,204	3,420	732	3,230	9,586	12,231	-8.8%
2010 Q1	1,333	2,294	3,627	3,350	3,712	492	3,348	10,902	14,529	18.8%
Q2	738	2,182	2,920	2,533	3,465	603	3,586	10,187	13,106	-9.8%
Q3	544	2,913	3,457	1,501	2,882	526	3,650	8,559	12,016	-8.3%
Q4	867	2,564	3,431	2,390	3,371	510	2,997	9,267	12,698	5.7%
2011 Q1	1,203	2,798	4,001	2,110	2,927	530	3,279	8,846	12,847	1.2%
Q2	535	2,594	3,129	1,461	2,141	551	3,225	7,379	10,508	-18.2%
Q3	533	2,573	3,105	1,726	2,355	537	3,928	8,546	11,652	10.9%
Q4	420	2,541	2,961	3,202	1,642	527	2,573	7,943	10,904	-6.4%
2012 Q1	736	2,524	3,260	3,347	1,709	778	3,550	9,383	12,643	15.9%
Q2	490	2,631	3,121	1,941	2,103	578	2,833	7,456	10,577	-16.3%
Q3	592	2,644	3,236	2,681	2,128	734	2,716	8,259	11,494	8.7%
Q4 R	632	3,006	3,638	4,541	2,088	569	2,874	10,071	13,709	19.3%
2013 Q1	1,032	3,240	4,272	2,022	2,572	627	3,277	8,497	12,769	-6.9%

Source: ONS - Orders for New Construction: 2013 Q1

R = Revised since Q4 2012 publication of Order for New Construction

18.22 Total engineering[1]

Values at current prices

£ million

	Turnover			New Orders		
	Export	Home	Total	Export	Home	Total
	JWO5	JWO6	JWO7	JWO8	JWO9	JWP2
2006	31,570.6	62,715.9	94,287.4	28,845.7	46,964.1	75,809.6
2007	33,202.3	67,167.5	100,370.1	32,938.0	52,618.8	85,556.6
2008	33,929.2	68,053.8	101,983.0	30,512.2	54,571.6	85,084.4
2009	29,994.1	56,556.9	86,550.6	26,189.2	44,661.1	70,850.7
2010	37,532.0	61,679.2	99,211.2	35,537.8	54,997.3	90,535.1
2011	40,021.3	63,718.0	103,739.3	38,364.0	53,445.6	91,809.6
2012	40,458.8	66,938.9	107,397.7	38,569.9	52,650.2	91,220.1
2007 Q1	8,282.8	16,603.9	24,886.4	8,726.8	12,596.4	21,323.2
Q2	8,491.7	16,349.6	24,841.6	8,693.7	12,280.6	20,974.2
Q3	8,064.4	17,149.3	25,213.8	8,108.5	13,463.0	21,571.4
Q4	8,363.4	17,064.7	25,428.3	7,409.0	14,278.8	21,687.8
2008 Q1	8,142.2	17,060.6	25,203.3	7,687.2	14,276.8	21,964.2
Q2	8,770.8	17,362.6	26,133.1	8,176.6	13,830.9	22,007.5
Q3	8,394.8	17,295.0	25,689.6	7,371.0	14,296.0	21,667.3
Q4	8,621.4	16,335.6	24,957.0	7,277.4	12,167.9	19,445.4
2009 Q1	7,396.6	14,414.2	21,810.7	6,415.1	10,982.5	17,398.1
Q2	7,065.8	13,824.1	20,889.9	6,452.2	10,589.0	17,041.3
Q3	7,094.7	14,005.9	21,100.4	6,328.2	11,271.4	17,599.5
Q4	8,437.0	14,312.7	22,749.6	6,993.7	11,818.2	18,811.8
2010 Q1	8,405.6	14,561.7	22,967.3	8,184.8	13,131.0	21,315.8
Q2	9,268.8	15,326.0	24,594.8	9,293.0	14,418.4	23,711.4
Q3	9,498.2	16,005.1	25,503.3	8,595.8	13,589.2	22,185.0
Q4	10,359.4	15,786.4	26,145.8	9,464.2	13,858.7	23,322.9
2011 Q1	10,003.1	15,286.3	25,289.4	10,198.5	12,874.7	23,073.2
2011 Q2	10,216.5	15,953.7	26,170.2	10,357.6	13,311.0	23,668.6
2011 Q3	9,737.5	16,471.0	26,208.5	8,777.4	13,159.5	21,936.9
2011 Q4	10,064.2	16,007.0	26,071.2	9,030.5	14,100.4	23,130.9
2012 Q1	9784.2	16486.3	26270.5	10167.2	13636.5	23803.7
2012 Q2	10224.1	17159.1	27383.2	9528.5	13034.2	22562.7
2012 Q3	9862.7	16861.3	26724	8794.5	12945.7	21740.2
2012 Q4	10587.8	16432.2	27020	10079.7	13033.8	23113.5
2011 Jan	3,049.6	4,618.7	7,668.3	3,456.5	4,027.5	7,484.0
Feb	3,161.8	4,795.4	7,957.2	3,027.1	4,060.1	7,087.2
Mar	3,791.7	5,872.2	9,663.9	3,714.9	4,787.1	8,502.0
Apr	3,152.8	4,769.6	7,922.4	3,448.7	4,040.4	7,489.1
May	3,350.6	5,280.3	8,630.9	3,568.5	3,907.4	7,475.9
June	3,713.1	5,903.8	9,616.9	3,340.4	5,363.2	8,703.6
July	3,110.8	5,177.1	8,287.9	2,966.0	4,319.1	7,285.1
August	3,052.7	5,375.4	8,428.1	2,661.0	4,206.1	6,867.1
September	3,574.0	5,918.5	9,492.5	3,150.4	4,634.3	7,784.7
October	3,286.2	5,366.3	8,652.5	3,026.8	4,282.0	7,308.8
November	3,427.0	5,639.9	9,066.9	2,875.6	4,704.2	7,579.8
December	3,351.0	5,000.8	8,351.8	3,128.1	5,114.2	8,242.3
2012 Jan	2897.7	5056.4	7954.1	3460.1	4114.6	7574.7
Feb	3152	5229	8381	3283.4	4555.9	7839.3
Mar	3734.5	6200.9	9935.4	3423.7	4966	8389.7
Apr	3262.3	5165.3	8427.6	3110.9	4509	7619.9
May	3490.6	5819	9309.6	3203.9	4294.2	7498.1
June	3471.2	6174.8	9646	3213.7	4231	7444.7
July	3275.6	5913.4	9189	2986.2	4677.5	7663.7
August	3101.7	5514.2	8615.9	2733.5	4078.9	6812.4
September	3485.4	5433.7	8919.1	3074.8	4189.3	7264.1
October	3567	5847.2	9414.2	3176.5	4528.9	7705.4
November	3591.7	5835.4	9427.1	3404.6	4414	7818.6
December	3429.1	4749.6	8178.7	3498.6	4090.9	7589.5

Source: Office for National Statistics : 01633 646659

1 The data for this table is based on SIC 2007 (the Industrial Classification for 2007). The change is a result of the SIC 2003 based MPI survey (which provided figures up to the April edition of the Monthly Digest) becoming part of the SIC 2007 based Monthly Business Survey (MBS). This is part of an ONS wide project to convert all data series to the latest SIC. This means that this table is now Total engineering (SIC 07 25-28) Please note this new table does not include Orders on Hand.

18.23 Manufacture of fabricated metal products and machinery and equipment n.e.c.[1]

Values at current prices

£ million

	Turnover			New Orders		
	Export	Home	Total	Export	Home	Total
	JWM9	JWN2	JWN3	JWN4	JWN5	JWN6
2006	17,288.6	40,598.9	57,887.9	14,977.7	29,110.8	44,088.3
2007	18,628.0	45,697.2	64,325.5	17,322.7	32,001.5	49,324.0
2008	20,022.2	46,615.9	66,638.5	16,445.4	36,125.6	52,571.6
2009	16,407.4	37,694.8	54,102.1	14,092.0	26,752.2	40,844.4
2010	22,257.5	42,731.1	64,988.6	21,727.5	34,866.8	56,594.3
2011	24,209.6	46,149.6	70,359.2	24,884.9	35,766.8	60,651.7
2012	24,794.0	47,704.2	72,498.2	24,489.3	34,234.2	58,723.5
2007 Q1	4,565.3	11,147.5	15,712.7	4,540.4	7,387.5	11,927.9
Q2	4,761.8	11,208.4	15,970.4	4,501.0	7,453.5	11,954.4
Q3	4,551.0	11,762.1	16,313.1	4,245.6	8,915.3	13,160.9
Q4	4,749.9	11,579.2	16,329.3	4,035.7	8,245.2	12,280.8
2008 Q1	4,920.2	11,586.7	16,507.3	4,337.7	9,049.0	13,386.9
Q2	5,340.0	11,958.4	17,298.4	4,470.1	9,120.8	13,591.0
Q3	4,968.4	12,009.0	16,977.3	4,004.0	10,027.5	14,031.7
Q4	4,793.6	11,061.8	15,855.5	3,633.6	7,928.3	11,562.0
2009 Q1	3,975.4	9,812.2	13,787.6	3,238.9	6,990.6	10,229.9
Q2	3,776.4	9,349.0	13,125.4	3,620.6	6,259.2	9,879.8
Q3	3,866.1	9,359.6	13,225.5	3,398.0	6,789.5	10,187.4
Q4	4,789.5	9,174.0	13,963.6	3,834.5	6,712.9	10,547.3
2010 Q1	4,838.8	9,902.9	14,741.7	4,810.6	8,203.9	13,014.5
Q2	5,567.2	10,577.9	16,145.1	5,852.1	9,155.6	15,007.7
Q3	5,622.2	11,313.3	16,935.5	5,113.6	8,520.7	13,634.3
Q4	6,229.3	10,937.0	17,166.3	5,951.2	8,986.6	14,937.8
2011 Q1	6033.3	10736	16769.3	6554.6	8407	14961.6
Q2	6110.9	11745.8	17856.7	6830.3	9006.5	15836.8
Q3	5978.8	12137.6	18116.4	5756.8	8804.5	14561.3
Q4	6086.6	11530.2	17616.8	5743.2	9548.8	15292
2012 Q1	5,995.6	11,728.6	17,724.2	6,493.8	8,721.4	15,215.2
Q2	6,327.4	12,382.9	18,710.3	6,089.3	8,674.9	14,764.2
Q3	6,095.4	12,006.9	18,102.3	5,459.0	8,355.3	13,814.3
Q4	6,375.6	11,585.8	17,961.4	6,447.2	8,482.6	14,929.8
2011 Jan	1813.3	3232.1	5045.4	2173.9	2618.9	4792.8
Feb	1925.7	3379.2	5304.9	2026.1	2646.6	4672.7
Mar	2294.3	4124.7	6419	2354.6	3141.5	5496.1
Apr	1872.9	3482.5	5355.4	2310.3	2762.9	5073.2
May	2058	3937.6	5995.6	2388	2590.3	4978.3
June	2180	4325.7	6505.7	2132	3653.3	5785.3
July	1935.9	3783.7	5719.6	1916.5	2831.8	4748.3
August	1827.7	3913.6	5741.3	1767	2832.2	4599.2
September	2215.2	4440.3	6655.5	2073.3	3140.5	5213.8
October	1983.8	3941	5924.8	1945.8	2870.1	4815.9
November	2083.3	4032.2	6115.5	1821.7	3002.5	4824.2
December	2019.5	3557	5576.5	1975.7	3676.2	5651.9
2012 Jan	1,752.4	3,643.4	5,395.8	2,278.6	2,645.7	4,924.3
Feb	1,942.9	3,701.6	5,644.5	2,036.8	2,968.6	5,005.4
Mar	2,300.3	4,383.6	6,683.9	2,178.4	3,107.1	5,285.5
Apr	2,011.2	3,659.0	5,670.2	1,953.1	3,175.2	5,128.3
May	2,204.1	4,150.0	6,354.1	2,142.6	2,826.0	4,968.6
June	2,112.1	4,573.9	6,686.0	1,993.6	2,673.7	4,667.3
July	2,080.5	4,274.4	6,354.9	1,821.7	3,096.4	4,918.1
August	1,869.3	3,909.3	5,778.6	1,746.4	2,605.7	4,352.1
September	2,145.6	3,823.2	5,968.8	1,890.9	2,653.2	4,544.1
October	2,122.9	4,126.2	6,249.1	2,101.6	2,871.7	4,973.3
November	2,211.1	4,162.6	6,373.7	2,092.9	2,851.4	4,944.3
December	2,041.6	3,297.0	5,338.6	2,252.7	2,759.5	5,012.2

Source: Office for National Statistics : 01633 646659

1 The data for this table is based on SIC 2007 (the Industrial Classification for 2007). The change is a result of the SIC 2003 based MPI survey (which provided figures up to the April edition of the Monthly Digest) becoming part of the SIC 2007 based Monthly Business Survey (MBS). This is part of an ONS wide project to convert all data series to the latest SIC. Manufacture of fabricated metal products and machinery and equipment n.e.c. (SIC 07 25, 28). Please note this new table does not include Orders on Hand.

18.24 Alcoholic drink

Calendar Year	Spirits					Beer			
	Production (hl of pure alcohol)	Whisky (hl of pure alcohol)	RTD (hl of pure alcohol)	Imported and other (hl of pure alcohol)	Total (hl of pure alcohol)	Production (thousand hl)	Released for home consumption (thousand hl)	Production (thousand hl of pure alcohol)	Clearances (thousand hl of pure alcohol)
2002	4508	321	105	689	1115	56672	59384	2352	2473
2003	4553	318	124	744	1187	58014	60301	2414	2515
2004	4081	319	114	792	1226	57461	59194	2433	2499
2005	4365	301	84	822	1206	56255	57572	2338	2398
2006	4485	283	65	767	1114	53768	55751	2250	2335
2007	5498	286	52	832	1170	51341	53465	2160	2247
2008	6072	289	42	817	1148	49611	51498	2062	2145
2009	5757	258	32	802	1091	45141	46817	1891	1957
2010	5074	267	35	842	1144	44997	45872	1905	1932
2011	5697	252	30	828	1111	45694	44844	1934	1888

Calendar Year	Wine of Fresh Grapes				Made Wine				Cider and Perry
	Fortified (hl)	Still table (hl)	Sparkling (hl)	Total (hl)	Still (hl)	Sparkling (hl)	Coolers (hl)	Total (hl)	Released for home consumption (thousand hl)
2002	325	10319	578	11222	366	2	1606	1974	5939
2003	296	10647	640	11584	338	1	423	762	5876
2004	298	11768	676	12742	351	1	508	859	6139
2005	306	12117	721	13143	334	0	597	931	6377
2006	302	11655	715	12672	316	1	528	844	7523
2007	305	12559	838	13702	343	5	720	1068	8046
2008	324	12402	757	13483	374	7	611	993	8412
2009	219	11729	731	12680	390	2	597	989	9404
2010	220	11870	810	12900	400	5	758	1162	9399
2011	220	11827	812	12860	440	7	828	1275	9280

Source: Her Majesty's Revenue and Customs
Published on the May 2013 Alcohol Bulletin
https://www.uktradeinfo.com/Statistics/Tax%20and%20Duty%20Bulletins/Alcohol0513.xls

HL = Hectolitres

18.25 Tobacco products: released for home consumption

Calendar Year	Cigarettes			Other			Overall Total (thousand kg)
	Home Produced (million sticks)	Imported (million sticks)	Total (million sticks)	Cigars (thousand kg)	HRT (thousand kg)	Other (thousand kg)	
2008	7005	579	7585	86	473	27	8171
2009	7473	578	8051	92	607	29	8779
2010	7590	662	8252	86	683	29	9051
2011	7899	657	8556	87	845	28	9517

Source: Her Majesty's Revenue and Customs
Published on the June 2013 Tobacco Bulletin
https://uktradeinfo.com/Statistics/Tax%20and%20Duty%20Bulletins/Tobacco0613.xls

this page is intentionally blank

National accounts

Chapter 19

National accounts

The tables are based on those in The Blue Book 2013 Edition. The Blue Book presents the full set of economic accounts for the United Kingdom. The accounts are based on the European System of Accounts 1995 (ESA 95), a system of national accounts that all European Union members have agreed to use. ESA 95 is fully compliant with the System of National Accounts 1993 (SNA93), which was unanimously approved by the Statistical Commission of the United Nations, and is used by statistical offices throughout the world.

The Blue Book contains an introduction which provides an overview of the accounts and an explanation of the underlying framework. A detailed description of the structure of the accounts and the methods used to derive the figures is provided in a separate Office for National Statistics (ONS) publication United Kingdom National Accounts: Concepts, Sources and Methods (TSO 1998). Further information on the financial accounts is given in the Financial Statistics Explanatory Handbook.

Brief definitions of some national accounting terms used in this chapter are included here. Current prices (or, more precisely, current price estimates) describe values during the period of the observation. Hence, in a time series, they will describe changes to price and to volume. Chain volume measures exclude the effects of price change. Basic prices do not include taxes and subsidies on products, whereas these are included in market prices.

Gross Domestic Product and Gross National Income
(Tables 19.1, 19.2, 19.3)

Table 19.1 shows three of the most important economic aggregates: Gross Domestic Product (GDP), Gross National Income (GNI) and Gross National Disposable Income (GNDI). In all three cases 'gross' denotes that depreciation (or consumption) of fixed capital is ignored. GDP is the total value of the UK's output. GNI is GDP plus primary incomes received from the rest of the world minus primary incomes paid to the rest of the world. Primary income comprises taxes on production and imports, property income and compensation of employees. These measures are given as current price estimates and chained volume measures. GNDI equals GNI plus net current transfers to the rest of the world. Transfers are unrequited payments such as taxes, social benefits and remittances.

There are three different approaches to measuring GDP: output, income and expenditure. Table 19.2 shows the various money flows which are used in these different approaches, and those that are used to measure GNI at current prices. The output approach to measuring GDP takes the gross value added for the entire economy (that is, the value of the UK's output minus the goods and services consumed in the productive process) to give gross value added at basic prices. This figure is then adjusted to include taxes and exclude subsidies on products. This gives gross value added at market prices for the UK, which is equivalent to GDP.

The expenditure approach to GDP shows consumption expenditure by households and government, gross capital formation and expenditure on UK exports. The sum of these items overstates the amount of income generated in the UK by the value of imported goods and services. This item is therefore subtracted to produce GDP at market prices.

The income approach to GDP shows gross operating surplus, mixed income and compensation of employees (previously known as income from employment). Production taxes less subsidies are added to produce the total of the income-based components at market prices.

Table 19.2 also shows the primary incomes received from the rest of the world, which are added to GDP, and primary incomes payable to non-resident units, which are deducted from GDP, to arrive at GNI. Primary income comprises compensation of employees, taxes less subsidies on production, and property and entrepreneurial income. The data in Table 19.2 are in current prices. This means that changes between years will be driven by a combination of price effects and changes in the volume of production. The second of these components is often referred to as 'real growth'.

Table 19.3 shows the expenditure approach to the chained volume measure of GDP, that is to say the effects of price change have been removed. In chained volume series, volume measures for each year are produced in prices of the previous year. These volume measures are then 'chain-linked' together to produce a continuous time series.

Industrial analysis
(Tables 19.4, 19.5)

The analysis of gross value added by industry at current prices shown in Table 19.4 reflects the estimates based on the 2007 Standard Industrial Classification (SIC2007). The table is based on current price data reconciled through the input–output process for 2002 to 2008.

Table 19.5 shows chained volume measures of gross value added by industry. These indices are based on basic price measures. Chained volume measures of gross value added provides a lead economic indicator. The analysis of gross value added is estimated in terms of change and expressed in index number form.

Sector analysis – Distribution of income accounts and capital account
(Tables 19.6 to 19.13)

The National Accounts accounting framework includes the sector accounts which provide, by institutional sector, a description of the different stages of the economic process, from the income generated by production and its distribution and re-distribution to different economic units, and finally, capital accumulation and financing. Tables 19.6 to 19.12 show the 'allocation of primary income account' and the 'secondary distribution of income account' for the non-financial corporations, financial corporations, government and households sectors. Additionally, Table 19.12 shows the 'use of income account' for the households sector and Table 19.13 provides a summary of the capital account. The full sequence of accounts is shown in The Blue Book.

The allocation of primary income account shows the resident units and institutional sectors as recipients rather than producers of primary income. The balancing item of this account is the gross balance of primary income (B.5g) for each sector and, if the gross balance is aggregated across all sectors of the economy, the result is Gross National Income.

The secondary distribution of income account describes how the balance of income for each sector is allocated by redistribution; through transfers such as taxes on income, social contributions and benefits, and other current transfers. The balancing item of this account is Gross Disposable Income (GDI). For the households sector, the chained volume measure of GDI is shown as real household disposable income.

Table 19.12 shows, for the household sector, the use of disposable income where the balancing item is saving (B.8g). For the non-financial corporations sector the balancing item of the secondary distribution of income account, gross disposable income (B.6g), is equal to saving (B.8g).

The summary capital account (Table 19.13) brings together the saving and investment of the sectors of the economy. It shows saving, capital transfers, gross capital formation and net acquisition of non-financial assets for each of these.

Households' and non-profit institutions serving households' consumption expenditure at current market prices and chained volume measures
(Tables 19.14 to 19.17)

Households' and non-profit institutions serving households' (NPISH) final consumption expenditure is a major component of the expenditure measure of GDP. In Table 19.2 this expenditure is given at current market prices, broken down by the type of good or service purchased. Table 19.3 supplies the same breakdown in chain volume measures. Household final consumption expenditure includes the value of income-in-kind and imputed rent of owner-occupied dwellings. It includes expenditure on durable goods (for instance motor cars) which, from the point of view of the individual might more appropriately be treated as capital expenditure. The purchase of land and dwellings (including costs incurred in connection with the transfer of their ownership) and expenditure on major improvements by occupiers are treated as personal capital expenditure. Other goods and services purchased by the household sector (with the exception of goods and services that are to be used in self-employment) are treated as final consumption expenditure. The most detailed figures are published quarterly in Consumer Trends

Change in inventories (previously known as value of physical increase in stocks and work in progres
(Table 19.18)

This table gives a broad analysis by industry of the value of entries less withdrawals and losses of inventories (stocks), and analysis by asset for manufacturing industry.

Gross fixed capital formation
(Table 19.19 to 19.22)

Gross fixed capital formation is the total value of the acquisition less disposal of fixed assets, and improvements to land.

19.1 UK national and domestic product
Main aggregates: index numbers and values
Current prices and chained volume measures (reference year 2010)

			1999	2000	2001	2002	2003	2004	2005
	INDICES (2010=100)								
	VALUES AT CURRENT PRICES								
B.1*g	Gross domestic product at current market prices ("money GDP")	YBEU	63.2	66.4	69.4	72.8	77.3	81.6	85.9
B.1g	Gross value added at current basic prices	YBEX	62.7	65.9	69.1	72.5	77.1	81.4	85.8
	CHAINED VOLUME MEASURES								
B.1*g	Gross domestic product at market prices	YBEZ	81.4	85.0	86.8	88.8	92.3	95.3	98.4
B.6*g	Gross national disposable income at market prices	YBFP	81.2	84.6	87.5	90.5	94.4	97.5	100.4
B.1g	Gross value added at basic prices	CGCE	81.7	85.4	86.9	88.7	92.3	95.1	98.5
	PRICES								
	Implied deflator of GDP at market prices	YBGB	77.6	78.2	80.0	81.9	83.7	85.7	87.4

VALUES AT CURRENT PRICES (£ million)

Gross measures (before deduction of fixed capital consumption) at current market prices

			1999	2000	2001	2002	2003	2004	2005
B.1*g	Gross domestic product ("money GDP")	YBHA	938 383	987 139	1 031 732	1 081 465	1 148 524	1 212 968	1 276 743
D.1+D.4	Employment, property and entrepreneurial income from the rest of the world (receipts *less* payments)	YBGG	−4 046	−285	5 831	15 566	16 534	18 413	23 766
-D.21+D.31	Subsidies (receipts) *less* taxes (payments) on products from/to the rest of the world	-QZOZ	−3 438	−4 098	−3 578	−2 359	−2 060	−1 102	−4 260
+D.29-D.39	Other subsidies on production from/to the rest of the world	-IBJL	338	335	582	519	592	592	3 408
B.5*g	**Gross national income (GNI)**	ABMX	931 237	983 091	1 034 567	1 095 191	1 163 590	1 230 871	1 299 657
D.5,6,7	Current transfers from the rest of the world (receipts *less* payments)	-YBGF	−4 224	−6 016	−3 401	−6 620	−8 105	−9 318	−10 949
B.6*g	**Gross national disposable income**	NQCO	927 013	977 075	1 031 166	1 088 571	1 155 485	1 221 553	1 288 708

Adjustment to current basic prices

			1999	2000	2001	2002	2003	2004	2005
B.1*g	Gross domestic product (at current market prices)	YBHA	938 383	987 139	1 031 732	1 081 465	1 148 524	1 212 968	1 276 743
-D.21 +D.31	Adjustment to current basic prices (*less* taxes *plus* subsidies on products)	-NQBU	−106 284	−112 399	−114 069	−118 158	−124 251	−131 954	−137 488
B.1g	**Gross value added (at current basic prices)**	ABML	832 099	874 740	917 663	963 307	1 024 273	1 081 014	1 139 255

			1999	2000	2001	2002	2003	2004	2005
-K.1	*Net measures (after deduction of fixed capital consumption) at current market prices*	-NQAE	−105 507	−111 251	−115 796	−121 914	−125 603	−135 067	−138 272
B.1*n	Net domestic product	NHRK	832 876	875 888	915 936	959 551	1 022 921	1 077 901	1 138 471
B.5*n	Net national income	NSRX	825 730	871 840	918 771	973 277	1 037 987	1 095 804	1 161 385
B.6*n	Net national disposable income	NQCP	821 506	865 824	915 370	966 657	1 029 882	1 086 486	1 150 436

CHAINED VOLUME MEASURES (reference year 2010, £ million)

Gross measures (before deduction of fixed capital consumption) at market prices

			1999	2000	2001	2002	2003	2004	2005
B.1*g	Gross domestic product	ABMI	1 209 852	1 262 629	1 290 216	1 319 829	1 371 948	1 415 482	1 461 270
TGL	Terms of trade effect ("Trading gain or loss")	YBGJ	4 702	1 684	4 736	9 548	14 543	15 886	9 822
GDI	Real gross domestic income	YBGL	1 214 554	1 264 313	1 294 952	1 329 377	1 386 491	1 431 368	1 471 092
D.1+D.4	Real employment, property and entrepreneurial income from the rest of the world (receipts *less* payments)	YBGI	−5 257	−364	7 316	19 147	19 970	21 765	27 413
-D.21+D.31	Subsidies (receipts) *less* taxes (payments) on products from/to the rest of the world	-QZPB	−4 042	−4 710	−4 255	−2 841	−2 429	−1 277	−4 760
+D.29-D.39	Other subsidies on production from/to the rest of the world	-IBJN	322	309	546	486	586	590	4 200
B.5*g	**Gross national income (GNI)**	YBGM	1 205 309	1 259 140	1 298 528	1 346 284	1 404 712	1 452 554	1 497 540
D.5,6,7	Real current transfers from the rest of the world (receipts *less* payments)	-YBGP	−5 464	−7 692	−4 268	−8 144	−9 790	−11 014	−12 628
B.6*g	**Gross national disposable income**	YBGO	1 199 838	1 251 440	1 294 258	1 338 136	1 394 919	1 441 538	1 484 912

Adjustment to basic prices

			1999	2000	2001	2002	2003	2004	2005
B.1*g	Gross domestic product (at market prices)	ABMI	1 209 852	1 262 629	1 290 216	1 319 829	1 371 948	1 415 482	1 461 270
-D.21 +D.31	Adjustment to basic prices (*less* taxes *plus* subsidies on products)	-NTAQ	−124 960	−129 175	−135 641	−142 305	−146 521	−152 936	−153 638
B.1g	**Gross value added (at basic prices)**	ABMM	1 085 239	1 133 951	1 154 616	1 177 360	1 225 278	1 262 366	1 307 478

			1999	2000	2001	2002	2003	2004	2005
-K.1	*Net measures (after deduction of fixed capital consumption) at market prices*	-CIHA	−124 782	−129 512	−133 294	−139 315	−141 688	−150 439	−151 256
B.5*n	Net national income at market prices	YBET	1 080 483	1 129 672	1 165 310	1 206 935	1 263 301	1 302 091	1 346 516
B.6*n	Net national disposable income at market prices	YBEY	1 075 063	1 122 003	1 161 116	1 198 826	1 253 538	1 291 098	1 333 903

19.1
continued

UK national and domestic product
Main aggregates: index numbers and values
Current prices and chained volume measures (reference year 2010)

			2006	2007	2008	2009	2010	2011	2012
	INDICES (2010=100)								
	VALUES AT CURRENT PRICES								
B.1*g	Gross domestic product at current market prices ("money GDP")	YBEU	90.8	96.1	98.4	95.4	100.0	103.5	105.2
B.1g	Gross value added at current basic prices	YBEX	90.7	96.0	98.8	96.4	100.0	102.5	104.2
	CHAINED VOLUME MEASURES								
B.1*g	Gross domestic product at market prices	YBEZ	101.1	104.5	103.7	98.4	100.0	101.1	101.3
B.6*g	Gross national disposable income at market prices	YBFP	101.8	106.0	105.9	99.2	100.0	101.2	99.6
B.1g	Gross value added at basic prices	CGCE	101.1	104.7	104.1	98.4	100.0	101.2	101.5
	PRICES								
	Implied deflator of GDP at market prices	YBGB	89.9	91.9	94.9	97.0	100.0	102.3	103.8

VALUES AT CURRENT PRICES (£ million)

Gross measures (before deduction of fixed capital consumption) at current market prices

			2006	2007	2008	2009	2010	2011	2012
B.1*g	Gross domestic product ("money GDP")	YBHA	1 349 483	1 427 889	1 462 070	1 417 359	1 485 615	1 536 937	1 562 263
D.1+D.4	Employment, property and entrepreneurial income from the rest of the world (receipts *less* payments)	YBGG	8 645	18 985	32 488	18 382	13 410	22 494	−2 254
-D.21+D.31	Subsidies (receipts) *less* taxes (payments) on products from/to the rest of the world	-QZOZ	−4 496	−4 731	−4 906	−4 238	−5 186	−5 122	−5 167
+D.29-D.39	Other subsidies on production from/to the rest of the world	-IBJL	3 221	2 952	3 051	3 411	3 059	3 166	2 661
B.5*g	Gross national income (GNI)	ABMX	1 356 853	1 445 095	1 492 703	1 434 914	1 496 898	1 557 475	1 557 503
D.5,6,7	Current transfers from the rest of the world (receipts *less* payments)	-YBGF	−10 522	−11 714	−11 844	−14 274	−18 452	−19 786	−20 756
B.6*g	Gross national disposable income	NQCO	1 346 331	1 433 381	1 480 859	1 420 640	1 478 446	1 537 689	1 536 747

Adjustment to current basic prices

			2006	2007	2008	2009	2010	2011	2012
B.1*g	Gross domestic product (at current market prices)	YBHA	1 349 483	1 427 889	1 462 070	1 417 359	1 485 615	1 536 937	1 562 263
-D.21 +D.31	Adjustment to current basic prices (*less* taxes *plus* subsidies on products)	-NQBU	−144 642	−153 012	−149 958	−137 098	−157 692	−176 012	−179 181
B.1g	Gross value added (at current basic prices)	ABML	1 204 841	1 274 877	1 312 112	1 280 261	1 327 923	1 360 925	1 383 082

			2006	2007	2008	2009	2010	2011	2012
-K.1	*Net measures (after deduction of fixed capital consumption) at current market prices*	-NQAE	−147 323	−154 297	−151 370	−159 862	−164 006	−170 986	−176 050
B.1*n	Net domestic product	NHRK	1 202 160	1 273 592	1 310 700	1 257 497	1 321 609	1 365 951	1 386 213
B.5*n	Net national income	NSRX	1 209 530	1 290 798	1 341 333	1 275 052	1 332 892	1 386 489	1 381 453
B.6*n	Net national disposable income	NQCP	1 199 008	1 279 084	1 329 489	1 260 778	1 314 440	1 366 703	1 360 697

CHAINED VOLUME MEASURES
(reference year 2010, £ million)

Gross measures (before deduction of fixed capital consumption) at market prices

			2006	2007	2008	2009	2010	2011	2012
B.1*g	Gross domestic product	ABMI	1 501 528	1 552 989	1 541 039	1 461 361	1 485 616	1 502 216	1 504 777
TGL	Terms of trade effect ("Trading gain or loss")	YBGJ	7 711	7 947	4 221	1 412	−1	−7 413	−8 242
GDI	Real gross domestic income	YBGL	1 509 239	1 560 936	1 545 260	1 462 773	1 485 615	1 494 803	1 496 535
D.1+D.4	Real employment, property and entrepreneurial income from the rest of the world (receipts *less* payments)	YBGI	9 681	20 794	34 342	18 971	13 410	21 859	−2 158
-D.21+D.31	Subsidies (receipts) *less* taxes (payments) on products from/to the rest of the world	-QZPB	−4 923	−5 037	−5 200	−4 773	−5 186	−5 212	−5 475
+D.29-D.39	Other subsidies on production from/to the rest of the world	-IBJN	3 881	3 519	3 531	4 027	3 059	3 311	3 075
B.5*g	Gross national income (GNI)	YBGM	1 517 528	1 579 805	1 577 639	1 480 890	1 496 898	1 514 761	1 491 977
D.5,6,7	Real current transfers from the rest of the world (receipts *less* payments)	-YBGP	−11 783	−12 831	−12 520	−14 730	−18 452	−19 229	−19 881
B.6*g	Gross national disposable income	YBGO	1 505 745	1 566 974	1 565 118	1 466 160	1 478 446	1 495 532	1 472 096

Adjustment to basic prices

			2006	2007	2008	2009	2010	2011	2012
B.1*g	Gross domestic product (at market prices)	ABMI	1 501 528	1 552 989	1 541 039	1 461 361	1 485 616	1 502 216	1 504 777
-D.21 +D.31	Adjustment to basic prices (*less* taxes *plus* subsidies on products)	-NTAQ	−158 391	−162 921	−158 946	−154 397	−157 692	−158 479	−157 351
B.1g	Gross value added (at basic prices)	ABMM	1 342 966	1 389 907	1 381 998	1 306 896	1 327 924	1 343 737	1 347 426

			2006	2007	2008	2009	2010	2011	2012
-K.1	*Net measures (after deduction of fixed capital consumption) at market prices*	-CIHA	−157 610	−161 813	−158 084	−159 860	−164 006	−167 706	−171 688
B.5*n	Net national income at market prices	YBET	1 359 894	1 418 083	1 419 813	1 321 116	1 332 892	1 347 055	1 320 289
B.6*n	Net national disposable income at market prices	YBEY	1 348 132	1 405 272	1 407 313	1 306 400	1 314 440	1 327 826	1 300 408

Source: Office for National Statistics, Blue Book 2013

19.2 UK gross domestic product and national income
Current prices

£ million

			1999	2000	2001	2002	2003	2004	2005
	GROSS DOMESTIC PRODUCT								
	Gross domestic product: production								
B.1g	Gross value added, at basic prices								
P.1	Output of goods and services	KN26	1 702 805	1 796 090	1 882 558	1 965 296	2 063 323	2 173 118	2 264 377
-P.2	*less* intermediate consumption	-KN25	-870 706	-921 350	-964 895	-1 001 989	-1 039 050	-1 092 104	-1 125 122
B.1g	**Total gross value added**	ABML	**832 099**	**874 740**	**917 663**	**963 307**	**1 024 273**	**1 081 014**	**1 139 255**
D.211	Value added taxes (VAT) on products	QYRC	61 524	64 202	67 100	71 066	77 343	81 544	83 425
D.212,4	Other taxes on products	NSUI	50 536	54 127	52 940	54 271	54 977	58 446	59 376
-D.31	*less* subsidies on products	-NZHC	-5 776	-5 930	-5 971	-7 179	-8 069	-8 036	-5 313
B.1*g	**Gross domestic product at market prices**	YBHA	**938 383**	**987 139**	**1 031 732**	**1 081 465**	**1 148 524**	**1 212 968**	**1 276 743**
	Gross domestic product: expenditure								
P.3	Final consumption expenditure								
P.41	Actual individual consumption								
P.3	Household final consumption expenditure	ABPB	588 911	624 205	652 852	683 268	718 238	754 867	794 537
P.3	Final consumption expenditure of NPISH	ABNV	22 150	23 510	24 994	26 516	27 785	29 289	30 962
P.31	Individual govt. final consumption expenditure	NNAQ	97 215	103 528	111 679	124 026	136 994	148 874	160 344
P.41	Total actual individual consumption	NQEO	708 276	751 243	789 525	833 810	883 017	933 030	985 843
P.32	Collective govt. final consumption expenditure	NQEP	71 644	77 332	82 497	88 663	95 709	102 850	107 754
P.3	Total final consumption expenditure	ABKW	779 920	828 575	872 022	922 473	978 726	1 035 880	1 093 597
P.3	Households and NPISH	NSSG	611 061	647 715	677 846	709 784	746 023	784 156	825 499
P.3	Central government	NMBJ	103 119	110 386	118 197	130 232	142 236	152 274	161 329
P.3	Local government	NMMT	65 740	70 474	75 979	82 457	90 467	99 450	106 769
P.5	Gross capital formation								
P.51	Gross fixed capital formation	NPQX	165 956	171 501	176 602	185 126	191 611	205 027	214 371
P.52	Changes in inventories	ABMP	6 060	5 271	6 189	2 909	3 983	4 886	4 472
P.53	Acquisitions less disposals of valuables	NPJO	125	56	266	237	160	137	-117
P.5	Total gross capital formation	NQFM	172 144	176 828	183 058	188 270	195 755	210 051	218 728
P.6	Exports of goods and services	KTMW	242 360	269 568	277 732	279 995	293 081	305 821	339 843
-P.7	*less* imports of goods and services	-KTMX	-256 038	-287 832	-301 079	-309 275	-319 037	-338 784	-375 423
B.11	External balance of goods and services	KTMY	-13 678	-18 264	-23 347	-29 280	-25 956	-32 963	-35 580
de	Statistical discrepancy between								
	expenditure components and GDP	RVFD	–	–	–	–	–	–	–
B.1*g	**Gross domestic product at market prices**	YBHA	**938 383**	**987 139**	**1 031 732**	**1 081 465**	**1 148 524**	**1 212 968**	**1 276 743**
	Gross domestic product: income								
B.2g	Operating surplus, gross								
	Non-financial corporations								
	Public non-financial corporations	NRJT	8 516	8 062	8 260	7 816	8 616	7 980	9 820
	Private non-financial corporations	NRJK	178 272	179 723	178 048	190 704	202 785	218 876	227 512
	Financial corporations	NQNV	18 392	13 201	18 074	22 806	29 702	32 349	42 527
	General government	NMXV	9 262	9 542	9 796	10 289	10 807	11 312	11 927
	Households and non-profit institutions serving households	QWLS	50 524	56 307	58 529	61 488	65 654	71 171	75 010
B.2g	Total operating surplus, gross	ABNF	264 966	266 835	272 707	293 103	317 564	341 688	366 796
B.3	Mixed income	QWLT	53 583	56 905	61 240	66 217	73 479	74 076	79 240
D.1	Compensation of employees	HAEA	498 364	534 618	567 182	586 982	616 552	648 465	679 357
D.2	Taxes on production and imports	NZGX	128 247	135 621	137 829	143 761	150 860	158 843	162 520
-D.3	*less* subsidies	-AAXJ	-6 777	-6 840	-7 226	-8 599	-9 932	-10 105	-11 170
di	Statistical discrepancy between								
	income components and GDP	RVFC	–	–	–	–	–	–	–
B.1*g	**Gross domestic product at market prices**	YBHA	**938 383**	**987 139**	**1 031 732**	**1 081 465**	**1 148 524**	**1 212 968**	**1 276 743**
	GROSS NATIONAL INCOME at market prices								
B.1*g	**Gross domestic product at market prices**	YBHA	**938 383**	**987 139**	**1 031 732**	**1 081 465**	**1 148 524**	**1 212 968**	**1 276 743**
D.1	Compensation of employees								
	receipts from the rest of the world (ROW)	KTMN	960	1 032	1 087	1 121	1 116	931	974
	less payments to the rest of the world (ROW)	-KTMO	-759	-882	-1 021	-1 054	-1 057	-1 425	-1 584
D.1	Total	KTMP	201	150	66	67	59	-494	-610
-D.21+D.31	*less* Taxes on products paid to the ROW *plus* Subsidies received from the ROW	-QZOZ	-3 438	-4 098	-3 578	-2 359	-2 060	-1 102	-4 260
+D.29-D.39	Other subsidies on production	-IBJL	338	335	582	519	592	592	3 408
D.4	Property and entrepreneurial income								
	receipts from the rest of the world	HMBN	100 733	131 902	137 447	120 543	121 974	137 548	186 115
	less payments to the rest of the world	-HMBO	-104 980	-132 337	-131 682	-105 044	-105 499	-118 641	-161 739
D.4	Total	HMBM	-4 247	-435	5 765	15 499	16 475	18 907	24 376
B.5*g	**Gross national income at market prices**	ABMX	**931 237**	**983 091**	**1 034 567**	**1 095 191**	**1 163 590**	**1 230 871**	**1 299 657**

19.2

UK gross domestic product and national income
Current prices

continued

£ million

			2006	2007	2008	2009	2010	2011	2012
	GROSS DOMESTIC PRODUCT								
	Gross domestic product: production								
B.1g	Gross value added, at basic prices								
P.1	Output of goods and services[1]	KN26	2 452 067	2 605 691	2 693 194	2 637 437	2 711 180	2 797 108	..
-P.2	*less* intermediate consumption[1]	-KN25	-1 247 226	-1 330 814	-1 381 082	-1 357 176	-1 383 257	-1 436 183	..
B.1g	**Total gross value added**	ABML	**1 204 841**	**1 274 877**	**1 312 112**	**1 280 261**	**1 327 923**	**1 360 925**	**1 383 082**
D.211	Value added taxes (VAT) on products	QYRC	87 758	92 025	92 002	79 900	95 888	111 449	113 856
D.212,4	Other taxes on products	NSUI	63 102	66 911	63 638	63 683	68 741	70 924	72 314
-D.31	*less* subsidies on products	-NZHC	-6 218	-5 924	-5 682	-6 485	-6 937	-6 361	-6 989
B.1*g	**Gross domestic product at market prices**	YBHA	**1 349 483**	**1 427 889**	**1 462 070**	**1 417 359**	**1 485 615**	**1 536 937**	**1 562 263**
	Gross domestic product: expenditure								
P.3	Final consumption expenditure								
P.41	Actual individual consumption								
P.3	Household final consumption expenditure	ABPB	828 839	873 591	892 696	876 553	921 034	953 882	991 091
P.3	Final consumption expenditure of NPISH	ABNV	32 948	34 956	35 892	35 762	37 562	38 457	37 665
P.31	Individual govt. final consumption expenditure	NNAQ	173 003	181 746	194 553	207 180	211 581	212 781	213 648
P.41	Total actual individual consumption	NQEO	1 034 790	1 090 293	1 123 141	1 119 495	1 170 177	1 205 120	1 242 404
P.32	Collective govt. final consumption expenditure	NQEP	112 534	114 007	120 987	121 639	124 957	124 389	127 264
P.3	Total final consumption expenditure	ABKW	1 147 324	1 204 300	1 244 128	1 241 134	1 295 134	1 329 509	1 369 668
P.3	Households and NPISH	NSSG	861 787	908 547	928 588	912 315	958 596	992 339	1 028 756
P.3	Central government	NMBJ	173 416	178 074	191 431	199 649	205 140	209 890	218 019
P.3	Local government	NMMT	112 121	117 679	124 109	129 170	131 398	127 280	122 893
P.5	Gross capital formation								
P.51	Gross fixed capital formation	NPQX	231 861	253 988	245 549	211 195	221 156	220 726	224 252
P.52	Changes in inventories	ABMP	5 212	5 815	4 343	-11 760	1 926	8 797	4 662
P.53	Acquisitions less disposals of valuables	NPJO	285	519	621	165	250	1 166	2 119
P.5	Total gross capital formation	NQFM	237 356	260 322	250 512	199 598	223 333	230 689	231 033
P.6	Exports of goods and services	KTMW	387 585	380 516	429 758	402 171	447 269	492 884	492 810
-P.7	*less* imports of goods and services	-KTMX	-422 784	-417 249	-462 330	-425 544	-480 121	-516 144	-526 711
B.11	External balance of goods and services	KTMY	-35 199	-36 733	-32 572	-23 373	-32 852	-23 260	-33 901
de	Statistical discrepancy between expenditure components and GDP	RVFD	–	–	–	–	–	–	-4 538
B.1*g	**Gross domestic product at market prices**	YBHA	**1 349 483**	**1 427 889**	**1 462 070**	**1 417 359**	**1 485 615**	**1 536 937**	**1 562 263**
	Gross domestic product: income								
B.2g	Operating surplus, gross								
	Non-financial corporations								
	Public non-financial corporations	NRJT	10 817	11 435	10 877	9 805	10 010	9 484	10 195
	Private non-financial corporations	NRJK	243 350	252 796	257 208	227 953	241 222	255 670	258 772
	Financial corporations	NQNV	41 941	51 767	65 256	74 050	61 007	53 731	39 804
	General government	NMXV	12 634	13 231	13 963	14 675	15 500	16 301	17 110
	Households and non-profit institutions serving households	QWLS	79 192	89 147	86 336	75 005	91 200	100 770	106 982
B.2g	Total operating surplus, gross	ABNF	387 934	418 376	433 640	401 488	418 939	435 956	432 863
B.3	Mixed income	QWLT	82 559	83 125	85 411	81 374	85 561	85 322	85 360
D.1	Compensation of employees	HAEA	719 872	758 387	776 962	780 145	801 796	820 157	842 386
D.2	Taxes on production and imports	NZGX	171 650	180 510	178 725	167 966	192 592	207 746	212 033
-D.3	*less* subsidies	-AAXJ	-12 532	-12 509	-12 668	-13 614	-13 271	-12 245	-12 693
di	Statistical discrepancy between income components and GDP	RVFC	–	–	–	–	–	–	2 314
B.1*g	**Gross domestic product at market prices**	YBHA	**1 349 483**	**1 427 889**	**1 462 070**	**1 417 359**	**1 485 615**	**1 536 937**	**1 562 263**
	GROSS NATIONAL INCOME at market prices								
B.1*g	**Gross domestic product at market prices**	YBHA	**1 349 483**	**1 427 889**	**1 462 070**	**1 417 359**	**1 485 615**	**1 536 937**	**1 562 263**
D.1	Compensation of employees								
	receipts from the rest of the world (ROW)	KTMN	938	984	1 046	1 176	1 097	1 121	1 124
	less payments to the rest of the world (ROW)	-KTMO	-1 896	-1 718	-1 761	-1 435	-1 486	-1 293	-1 272
D.1	Total	KTMP	-958	-734	-715	-259	-389	-172	-148
	less Taxes on products paid to the ROW								
-D.21+D.31	*plus* Subsidies received from the ROW	-QZOZ	-4 496	-4 731	-4 906	-4 238	-5 186	-5 122	-5 167
+D.29-D.39	Other subsidies on production	-IBJL	3 221	2 952	3 051	3 411	3 059	3 166	2 661
D.4	Property and entrepreneurial income								
	receipts from the rest of the world	HMBN	237 522	289 986	260 855	167 220	160 134	191 250	160 856
	less payments to the rest of the world	-HMBO	-227 919	-270 267	-227 652	-148 579	-146 335	-168 584	-162 962
D.4	Total	HMBM	9 603	19 719	33 203	18 641	13 799	22 666	-2 106
B.5*g	**Gross national income at market prices**	ABMX	**1 356 853**	**1 445 095**	**1 492 703**	**1 434 914**	**1 496 898**	**1 557 475**	**1 557 503**

1 These series are not available for the latest year

Source: Office for National Statistics, Blue Book 2013

19.3 UK gross domestic product
Chained volume measures (reference year 2010)

£ million

			1999	2000	2001	2002	2003	2004	2005
	GROSS DOMESTIC PRODUCT								
	Gross domestic product: expenditure approach								
P.3	Final consumption expenditure								
P.41	Actual individual consumption								
P.3	Household final consumption expenditure	ABPF	726 909	766 651	796 116	827 909	859 295	887 172	912 593
P.3	Final consumption expenditure of non-profit institutions serving households	ABNU	37 796	38 547	38 753	38 665	38 391	38 519	38 424
P.31	Individual government final consumption expenditure	NSZK	157 876	162 115	168 287	173 537	179 909	185 784	191 399
P.41	Total actual individual consumption	YBIO	920 163	965 956	1 002 033	1 039 472	1 077 206	1 111 201	1 142 235
P.32	Collective government final consumption expenditure	NSZL	99 305	103 798	107 373	113 041	118 123	123 594	124 979
P.3	Total final consumption expenditure	ABKX	1 019 486	1 069 799	1 109 464	1 152 536	1 195 333	1 234 782	1 267 216
P.5	Gross capital formation								
P.51	Gross fixed capital formation	NPQR	209 909	215 372	211 280	216 955	221 909	235 691	244 373
P.52	Changes in inventories	ABMQ	8 866	8 286	10 808	2 474	6 554	7 386	6 915
P.53	Acquisitions less disposals of valuables	NPJP	−410	−906	−689	−1 318	137	−110	−576
P.5	Total gross capital formation	NPQU	211 604	216 611	214 567	214 817	224 817	238 734	247 626
	Gross domestic final expenditure	YBIK	1 231 411	1 286 462	1 323 638	1 366 376	1 419 295	1 472 971	1 514 389
P.6	Exports of goods and services	KTMZ	308 564	337 563	345 551	352 106	362 118	379 680	414 063
	Gross final expenditure	ABME	1 541 510	1 625 836	1 671 020	1 720 338	1 783 399	1 854 649	1 929 622
-P.7	*less* imports of goods and services	-KTNB	−330 271	−361 753	−379 179	−398 897	−409 564	−438 049	−468 426
de	Statistical discrepancy between expenditure components and GDP	GIXS	–	–	–	–	–	–	–
B.1*g	**Gross domestic product at market prices**	ABMI	**1 209 852**	**1 262 629**	**1 290 216**	**1 319 829**	**1 371 948**	**1 415 482**	**1 461 270**
B.11	*of which* External balance of goods and services	KTNC	−21 707	−24 190	−33 628	−46 791	−47 446	−58 369	−54 363

continued

£ million

			2006	2007	2008	2009	2010	2011	2012
	GROSS DOMESTIC PRODUCT								
	Gross domestic product: expenditure approach								
P.3	Final consumption expenditure								
P.41	Actual individual consumption								
P.3	Household final consumption expenditure	ABPF	928 786	954 679	946 011	912 222	921 034	916 395	927 428
P.3	Final consumption expenditure of non-profit institutions serving households	ABNU	38 906	39 238	38 197	36 586	37 562	38 321	37 489
P.31	Individual government final consumption expenditure	NSZK	195 775	198 703	204 061	209 023	211 581	214 811	221 947
P.41	Total actual individual consumption	YBIO	1 163 267	1 192 467	1 188 138	1 157 812	1 170 177	1 169 527	1 186 864
P.32	Collective government final consumption expenditure	NSZL	127 630	127 054	128 460	125 880	124 957	121 565	123 786
P.3	Total final consumption expenditure	ABKX	1 290 899	1 319 553	1 316 599	1 283 691	1 295 134	1 291 092	1 310 650
P.5	Gross capital formation								
P.51	Gross fixed capital formation	NPQR	258 060	277 341	258 332	215 142	221 156	215 918	216 974
P.52	Changes in inventories	ABMQ	5 852	10 078	6 439	−16 265	1 927	8 444	3 240
P.53	Acquisitions less disposals of valuables	NPJP	172	845	877	195	251	1 049	1 895
P.5	Total gross capital formation	NPQU	260 613	284 992	263 659	203 824	223 334	225 411	222 109
	Gross domestic final expenditure	YBIK	1 551 212	1 604 616	1 580 312	1 487 322	1 518 468	1 516 503	1 532 759
P.6	Exports of goods and services	KTMZ	463 806	454 298	459 102	419 290	447 269	467 216	471 293
	Gross final expenditure	ABME	2 014 572	2 059 729	2 039 459	1 906 755	1 965 737	1 983 719	2 004 052
-P.7	*less* imports of goods and services	-KTNB	−515 289	−507 335	−498 617	−445 100	−480 121	−481 503	−494 906
de	Statistical discrepancy between expenditure components and GDP	GIXS	–	–	–	–	–	–	−4 369
B.1*g	**Gross domestic product at market prices**	ABMI	**1 501 528**	**1 552 989**	**1 541 039**	**1 461 361**	**1 485 616**	**1 502 216**	**1 504 777**
B.11	*of which* External balance of goods and services	KTNC	−51 483	−53 037	−39 515	−25 810	−32 852	−14 287	−23 613

Source: Office for National Statistics, Blue Book 2013

19.4 Output and capital formation: by industry [1,2]
Gross value added at current basic prices

£ million

			2005	2006	2007	2008	2009	2010	2011	2012
	Agriculture									
	Output									
D.1	Compensation of employees	KLR2	3 339	3 432	3 962	3 994	4 146	4 248	4 744	4 690
D.29-D.39	Taxes *less* subsidies on production other than those on products	KLR3	−3 219	−3 049	−2 845	−2 675	−3 512	−2 606	−2 552	−2 173
B.2g+B.3g	Operating surplus and mixed income, gross	KLR4	7 282	7 157	7 117	7 764	6 871	7 840	7 032	7 480
B.1g	Gross value added at basic prices	KLR5	7 402	7 540	8 234	9 083	7 505	9 482	9 224	9 997
P.2	Intermediate consumption at purchasers' prices	KLR6	10 987	11 470	13 194	13 723	15 550	14 861	16 115	15 813
P.1	Total output at basic prices	KLR7	18 389	19 010	21 428	22 806	23 055	24 343	25 339	25 810
P.5	Gross capital formation	KLR8	4 294	4 359	5 714	5 901	6 164	5 755	5 904	6 926
	Production									
	Output									
D.1	Compensation of employees	KLR9	110 385	116 696	118 735	119 577	115 376	118 671	121 723	126 438
D.29-D.39	Taxes *less* subsidies on production other than those on products	KLS4	3 758	3 971	3 850	4 190	4 238	4 204	4 254	4 375
B.2g+B.3g	Operating surplus and mixed income, gross	KLS3	79 322	83 082	82 273	88 937	81 243	82 704	84 876	82 393
B.1g	Gross value added at basic prices	KLS5	193 465	203 749	204 858	212 704	200 857	205 579	210 853	213 206
P.2	Intermediate consumption at purchasers' prices	KLS6	321 573	349 198	363 878	379 629	358 960	388 219	423 844	433 468
P.1	Total output at basic prices	KLS7	515 038	552 947	568 736	592 333	559 817	593 798	634 697	646 674
P.5	Gross capital formation	KLS8	48 899	37 540	40 289	42 394	33 335	36 748	47 539	54 690
	Construction									
	Output									
D.1	Compensation of employees	KLS9	37 212	40 993	46 678	45 824	44 292	44 922	45 543	46 871
D.29-D.39	Taxes *less* subsidies on production other than those on products	KLT3	672	750	819	924	968	1 015	926	1 137
B.2g+B.g	Operating surplus and mixed income, gross	KLT2	42 670	44 294	43 571	43 217	35 560	37 671	45 048	40 708
B.1g	Gross value added at basic prices	KLT4	80 554	86 037	91 068	89 965	80 820	83 608	91 517	88 716
P.2	Intermediate consumption at purchasers' prices	KLT5	111 243	119 415	134 456	135 736	116 656	117 775	119 182	119 411
P.1	Total output at basic prices	KLT6	191 797	205 452	225 524	225 701	197 476	201 383	210 699	208 127
P.5	Gross capital formation	KLT7	5 962	5 628	7 795	4 235	−4 478	1 592	3 089	3 280

1 The contribution of each industry to the gross domestic product before providing for consumption of fixed capital. The industrial composition in this table is consistent with the Supply-Use Tables in Table 2.1, which show data from 2009-2012.

2 Components may not sum to totals due to rounding.

19.4
Output and capital formation: by industry [1,2]
Gross value added at current basic prices

continued

£ million

			2005	2006	2007	2008	2009	2010	2011	2012
	Distribution, transport, hotels & restaurants									
	Output									
D.1	Compensation of employees	KLT8	144 451	152 022	160 627	167 070	164 146	167 529	169 422	176 072
D.29-D.39	Taxes *less* subsidies on production other than those on products	KLU2	8 848	8 881	8 806	9 810	10 907	11 001	11 781	12 027
B.2g+B.3g	Operating surplus and mixed income, gross	KLT9	76 159	76 426	80 012	76 322	72 242	79 115	80 300	79 363
B.1g	Gross value added at basic prices	KLU3	229 458	237 329	249 445	253 202	247 295	257 645	261 503	267 462
P.2	Intermediate consumption at purchasers' prices	KLU4	214 519	229 095	241 684	248 813	243 112	245 967	250 631	262 742
P.1	Total output at basic prices	KLU5	443 977	466 424	491 129	502 015	490 407	503 612	512 134	530 204
P.5	Gross capital formation	KLU6	32 342	35 556	38 494	40 424	31 829	44 216	38 394	36 580
	Information and communication									
	Output									
D.1	Compensation of employees	KLU7	47 709	47 768	51 408	52 915	50 000	51 345	54 170	57 040
D.29-D.39	Taxes *less* subsidies on production other than those on products	KLU9	1 118	1 204	1 264	1 195	1 129	1 177	1 189	1 112
B.2g+B.3g	Operating surplus and mixed income, gross	KLU8	29 945	31 918	32 344	34 113	32 307	33 913	33 999	34 062
B.1g	Gross value added at basic prices	KLV2	78 772	80 890	85 016	88 223	83 436	86 435	89 358	92 214
P.2	Intermediate consumption at purchasers' prices	KLV3	57 188	61 663	64 060	64 368	63 973	68 763	69 718	68 418
P.1	Total output at basic prices	KLV4	135 960	142 553	149 076	152 591	147 409	155 198	159 076	160 632
P.5	Gross capital formation	KLV5	18 622	20 069	19 344	19 884	18 043	17 319	17 607	16 826
	Financial and insurance									
	Output									
D.1	Compensation of employees	KLV6	48 281	59 115	65 679	58 944	61 197	63 941	61 445	59 698
D.29-D.39	Taxes *less* subsidies on production other than those on products	KLV8	1 471	1 566	1 667	1 803	1 790	5 475	1 870	2 701
B.2g+B.3g	Operating surplus and mixed income, gross	KLV7	45 704	43 536	52 394	47 658	62 708	50 615	55 425	57 362
B.1g	Gross value added at basic prices	KLV9	95 456	104 217	119 740	108 405	125 695	120 031	118 740	119 761
P.2	Intermediate consumption at purchasers' prices	KLW2	84 258	118 704	141 458	133 792	122 284	117 085	119 635	124 265
P.1	Total output at basic prices	KLW3	179 714	222 921	261 198	242 197	247 979	237 116	238 375	244 026
P.5	Gross capital formation	KLW4	7 628	6 629	7 499	8 202	6 451	8 313	8 024	9 627

1 The contribution of each industry to the gross domestic product before providing for consumption of fixed capital. The industrial composition in this table is consistent with the Supply-Use Tables in Table 2.1, which show data from 2009-2012.
2 Components may not sum to totals due to rounding.

19.4 Output and capital formation: by industry [1,2]
Gross value added at current basic prices

continued

£ million

			2005	2006	2007	2008	2009	2010	2011	2012
	Real estate									
	Output									
D.1	Compensation of employees	KLW5	7 807	8 574	9 334	9 955	9 025	9 547	9 677	11 082
	Taxes *less* subsidies on production other than									
D.29-D.39	those on products	KLW7	−799	−1 250	−1 052	−1 752	−1 088	−861	−386	−401
B.2g+B.3g	Operating surplus and mixed income, gross	KLW6	96 720	103 384	111 556	128 223	115 694	137 446	146 122	156 604
B.1g	Gross value added at basic prices	KLW8	103 728	110 708	119 838	136 426	123 631	146 132	155 413	167 285
P.2	Intermediate consumption at purchasers' prices	KLW9	35 960	39 673	42 513	34 485	61 547	65 504	62 176	60 116
P.1	Total output at basic prices	KLX2	139 688	150 381	162 351	170 911	185 178	211 636	217 589	227 401
P.5	Gross capital formation	KLX3	4 176	4 154	5 383	5 939	4 047	2 831	2 518	2 546
	Professional and support									
	Output									
D.1	Compensation of employees	KLX4	81 597	86 383	93 610	96 426	95 713	96 212	97 748	102 858
	Taxes *less* subsidies on production other than									
D.29-D.39	those on products	KLX6	923	1 181	1 325	1 325	1 225	1 250	1 617	1 578
B.2g+B.3g	Operating surplus and mixed income, gross	KLX5	50 200	58 814	60 271	63 937	59 680	63 141	68 928	71 341
B.1g	Gross value added at basic prices	KLX7	132 720	146 378	155 206	161 688	156 618	160 603	168 293	175 777
P.2	Intermediate consumption at purchasers' prices	KLX8	94 247	104 187	113 661	122 092	117 131	119 445	124 381	127 455
P.1	Total output at basic prices	KLX9	226 967	250 565	268 867	283 780	273 749	280 048	292 674	303 232
P.5	Gross capital formation	KLY2	15 901	16 958	19 137	16 575	13 886	16 451	20 186	20 109
	Government, health and education									
	Output									
D.1	Compensation of employees	KLY3	183 644	193 671	201 505	210 507	220 430	228 223	230 701	231 416
	Taxes *less* subsidies on production other than									
D.29-D.39	those on products	KLY5	298	344	340	408	375	456	436	509
B.2g+B.3g	Operating surplus and mixed income, gross	KLY4	37 617	40 667	43 138	45 830	46 606	46 146	48 069	49 952
B.1g	Gross value added at basic prices	KLY6	221 559	234 682	244 983	256 745	267 411	274 825	279 206	281 877
P.2	Intermediate consumption at purchasers' prices	KLY7	154 399	169 415	178 920	190 622	206 309	206 477	205 551	208 117
P.1	Total output at basic prices	KLY8	375 958	404 097	423 903	447 367	473 720	481 302	484 757	489 994
P.5	Gross capital formation	KLY9	18 668	36 909	39 197	47 424	48 806	48 549	45 527	45 125

1 The contribution of each industry to the gross domestic product before providing for consumption of fixed capital. The industrial composition in this
table is consistent with the Supply-Use Tables in Table 2.1, which show data from 2009-2012.
2 Components may not sum to totals due to rounding.

19.4 Output and capital formation: by industry [1,2]
Gross value added at current basic prices

continued

£ million

			2005	2006	2007	2008	2009	2010	2011	2012
	Other services									
	Output									
D.1	Compensation of employees	KLZ2	23 351	24 498	26 052	27 216	27 661	32 320	32 655	33 258
	Taxes *less* subsidies on production other									
D.29-D.39	than those on products	KLZ4	673	762	704	768	1 007	875	863	1 024
B.2g+B.3g	Operating surplus and mixed income, gross	KLZ3	22 034	22 294	22 800	24 292	23 110	23 149	23 973	25 371
B.1g	Gross value added at basic prices	KLZ5	46 058	47 554	49 556	52 276	51 778	56 344	57 491	59 653
	Intermediate consumption at									
P.2	purchasers' prices	KLZ6	29 238	32 341	33 130	35 970	35 186	32 628	33 057	32 384
P.1	Total output at basic prices	KLZ7	75 296	79 895	82 686	88 246	86 964	88 972	90 548	92 037
P.5	Gross capital formation	KLZ8	5 549	5 609	6 094	6 354	6 303	5 532	5 515	5 388
	Not allocated to industries									
P.5	Gross capital formation[3]	KN28	79 912	86 282	94 504	76 864	57 465	67 386	70 803	72 333
	All industries									
	Output									
D.1	Compensation of employees	HAEA	687 776	733 152	777 590	792 428	791 986	816 958	827 828	849 423
	Taxes *less* subsidies on production other									
D.29-D.39	than those on products	KN22	13 743	14 360	14 878	15 996	17 039	21 986	19 998	21 889
B.2g	Operating surplus, gross	ABNF	399 537	417 927	443 059	465 603	442 401	465 137	497 198	507 992
B.3g	Mixed income, gross	QWLT	88 116	93 645	92 417	94 690	93 620	96 603	96 574	96 644
	Statistical discrepancy between income									
di	and GDP	RVFC	–	–	–	–	–	–	–	–
B.1g	Gross value added at basic prices	ABML	1 189 172	1 259 084	1 327 944	1 368 717	1 345 046	1 400 684	1 441 598	1 475 948
	Intermediate consumption at									
P.2	purchasers' prices	KN25	1 113 612	1 235 161	1 326 954	1 359 230	1 340 708	1 376 724	1 424 290	1 452 189
P.1	Total output at basic prices	KN26	2 302 784	2 494 245	2 654 898	2 727 947	2 685 754	2 777 408	2 865 888	2 928 137
	Gross capital formation									
P.51g	Gross fixed capital formation	NPQX	238 837	254 926	273 750	272 516	239 078	250 198	260 779	268 823
P.52	Changes in inventories	ABMP	3 547	5 311	7 538	535	−16 039	4 285	2 751	1 767
P.53	Acquisitions less disposals of valuables	NPJO	−431	−544	2 162	1 145	−1 188	209	1 576	2 840
P.5	Total gross capital formation	NQFM	241 953	259 693	283 450	274 196	221 851	254 692	265 106	273 430

1 The contribution of each industry to the gross domestic product before providing for consumption of fixed capital. The industrial composition in this
table is consistent with the Supply-Use Tables in Table 2.1, which show data from 2009-2012.
2 Components may not sum to totals due to rounding.
3 GFCF of dwellings and costs associated with the transfer of non-produced
as and acquisitions less disposals of valuables.

19.5 Gross value added at basic prices: by industry[1,2,3]
Chained volume indices

Indices 2010=100

		Weight per 1000[1]		2004	2005	2006	2007	2008	2009	2010	2011	2012
		2010										
A	**Agriculture**	6.8	L2KL	100.1	106.0	102.5	98.6	108.2	100.7	100.0	110.6	106.9
B - F	**Production and Construction**											
B - E	Production											
B	Mining and quarrying	22.9	L2KR	142.5	132.1	124.3	120.8	113.4	102.5	100.0	85.2	77.0
C	Manufacturing											
CA	Food products, beverages and tobacco	16.5	KN3D	100.8	101.7	100.8	100.3	98.0	95.9	100.0	105.3	102.7
CB	Textiles, wearing apparel and leather products	3.1	KN3E	111.0	108.4	108.5	106.8	107.1	97.0	100.0	101.9	98.7
CC	Wood, paper products and printing	8.3	KN3F	116.4	114.6	113.2	112.8	108.4	100.5	100.0	94.0	88.8
CD	Coke and refined petroleum products	2.5	KN3G	125.4	117.8	111.0	110.2	108.7	102.2	100.0	101.9	92.0
CE	Chemicals and chemical products	6.4	KN3H	118.3	117.9	119.7	121.4	121.1	103.5	100.0	105.7	98.4
CF	Basic pharmaceutical products and preparations	9.7	KN3I	91.7	98.3	103.9	99.6	101.4	107.7	100.0	86.5	81.4
CG	Rubber, plastic and other non-metallic mineral products	8.6	KN3J	120.0	118.7	123.6	122.9	117.0	100.3	100.0	100.0	95.9
CH	Basic metals and metal products	11.7	KN3K	116.2	116.7	119.5	122.0	116.8	93.9	100.0	102.3	104.1
CI	Computer, electronic and optical products	6.6	KN3L	124.9	118.5	119.2	119.3	112.0	106.6	100.0	99.4	99.1
CJ	Electrical equipment	3.2	KN3M	114.4	112.2	117.2	119.6	116.9	90.8	100.0	95.7	106.3
CK	Machinery and equipment n. e. c.	7.6	KN3N	96.0	98.0	103.3	106.0	105.3	83.8	100.0	108.8	109.8
CL	Transport equipment	11.7	KN3O	94.9	94.7	97.2	100.6	97.3	82.5	100.0	109.7	115.8
CM	Other manufacturing and repair	8.2	KN3P	101.2	101.4	103.8	106.1	102.5	96.9	100.0	105.4	98.5
C	Total manufacturing	104.0	L2KX	107.3	107.1	109.0	109.9	106.9	96.0	100.0	101.8	100.1
D	Electricity, gas, steam and air conditioning supply	13.0	L2MW	100.3	100.1	99.9	100.6	101.1	96.2	100.0	94.1	93.8
E	Water supply, sewerage, waste mgmt and remediation	12.1	L2N2	106.9	111.9	108.9	112.7	110.5	101.3	100.0	104.1	104.0
B - E	Total production	152.0	L2KQ	110.9	110.0	110.3	110.7	107.5	97.2	100.0	98.8	96.4
F	Construction	63.2	L2N8	108.8	106.2	106.9	109.2	106.4	92.3	100.0	102.3	93.8
B - F	Total production and construction	215.2	L2KP	110.1	108.7	109.2	110.2	107.1	95.7	100.0	99.8	95.6

1 The weights shown are in proportion to total gross value added (GVA) in 2010 and are used to combine the industry output indices to calculate the totals. For 2009 and earlier, totals are calculated using the equivalent weights for the previous year (e.g. totals for 2008 use 2007 weights). Weights may not sum to totals due to rounding.

2 As GVA is expressed in index number form, it is inappropriate to show as a statistical adjustment any divergence from the other measures of GDP. Such an adjustment does, however, exist implicitly.

3 See footnote 2 to Table 19.4.

Source: Office for National Statistics, Blue Book 2013

19.5
continued

Gross value added at basic prices: by industry[1,2,3]
Chained volume indices

Indices 2010=100

		Weight per 1000[1]		2004	2005	2006	2007	2008	2009	2010	2011	2012
		2010										
G - T	**Services**											
G - I	Distribution, transport, hotels and restaurants											
G	Wholesale, retail, repair of motor vehicles and m/cycles	111.1	L2NE	100.4	100.0	103.6	108.7	105.5	99.3	100.0	100.4	100.9
H	Transportation and storage	44.3	L2NI	113.6	117.7	117.4	119.5	116.0	102.7	100.0	100.3	98.4
I	Accommodation and food service activities	26.7	L2NQ	93.4	97.8	102.4	106.1	103.9	98.1	100.0	101.9	104.6
G - I	Total distribution, transport, hotels and restaurants	182.1	L2ND	102.3	103.7	106.6	110.8	107.7	99.9	100.0	100.6	100.8
J	Information and communication											
JA	Publishing, audiovisual and broadcasting activities	17.6	L2NU	102.2	101.0	103.2	108.1	106.9	97.7	100.0	103.2	104.5
JB	Telecommunications	17.5	L2NZ	69.2	78.1	80.0	87.3	90.1	93.3	100.0	105.2	105.1
JC	IT and other information service activities	28.3	L2O3	78.2	84.5	88.1	95.9	97.6	91.4	100.0	100.2	103.2
J	Total information and communication	63.5	L2NT	81.1	86.6	89.4	96.3	97.6	93.6	100.0	102.4	104.1
K	Financial and insurance	95.4	L2O6	89.6	95.2	102.2	108.1	110.8	106.4	100.0	99.2	98.0
L	Real estate	96.9	L2OC	86.7	91.1	93.8	96.4	96.9	98.6	100.0	101.5	103.6
M - N	Professional and support											
M	Professional, scientific and technical activities											
MA	Legal, accounting, mgmt, architect, engineering etc	52.9	L2OJ	75.7	85.5	94.5	108.0	109.2	100.2	100.0	104.3	106.2
MB	Scientific research and development	3.1	L2OQ	77.8	86.1	92.8	96.5	94.2	90.4	100.0	93.0	96.4
MC	Other professional, scientific and technical activities	12.6	L2OS	99.0	107.2	104.9	107.5	105.1	93.3	100.0	115.6	117.1
M	Total professional, scientific and technical activities	68.6	L2OI	79.8	89.3	96.3	107.3	107.5	98.3	100.0	105.9	107.8
N	Administrative and support service activities	46.4	L2OX	83.9	90.9	95.8	104.8	104.0	90.0	100.0	106.5	113.7
M - N	Total professional and support	114.9	L2OH	81.3	89.8	95.9	106.1	105.9	94.7	100.0	106.1	110.2
O - Q	Government, health and education											
O	Public admin, defence, compulsory social security	53.5	L2P8	98.4	101.8	101.3	100.6	101.7	101.8	100.0	95.3	92.9
P	Education	62.4	L2PA	98.9	103.1	102.3	101.7	100.8	100.8	100.0	101.3	103.1
Q	Human health and social work activities											
QA	Human health activities	55.2	L2PD	78.0	84.4	87.5	90.3	94.2	98.4	100.0	102.9	108.1
QB	Residential care and social work activities	20.5	L2PF	92.7	96.9	98.7	99.8	95.9	94.5	100.0	101.3	102.0
Q	Total human health and social work activities	75.7	L2PC	81.7	87.5	90.3	92.7	94.6	97.3	100.0	102.5	106.4
O - Q	Total government, health and education	191.6	L2P7	91.5	96.2	97.0	97.7	98.5	99.7	100.0	100.1	101.6
R - T	Other services											
R	Arts, entertainment and recreation	14.6	L2PJ	103.9	108.1	107.1	110.4	109.5	99.9	100.0	103.4	110.3
S	Other service activities	14.3	L2PP	89.9	95.5	103.0	97.5	100.0	103.1	100.0	105.3	101.9
T	Activities of households as employers, undiff. goods	4.6	L2PT	97.1	101.0	98.5	96.2	99.8	90.1	100.0	95.3	99.1
R - T	Total other services	33.6	L2PI	96.9	101.7	104.0	103.0	104.1	99.8	100.0	103.1	105.2
G - T	Total service industries	778.0	L2NC	90.8	95.6	98.9	103.2	103.2	99.2	100.0	101.5	102.8
B.1g	**All industries**	1 000.0	CGCE	95.1	98.5	101.1	104.7	104.1	98.4	100.0	101.2	101.5

1 The weights shown are in proportion to total gross value added (GVA) in 2010 and are used to combine the industry output indices to calculate the totals. For 2009 and earlier, totals are calculated using the equivalent weights for the previous year (e.g. totals for 2008 use 2007 weights). Weights may not sum to totals due to rounding.

2 As GVA is expressed in index number form, it is inappropriate to show as a statistical adjustment any divergence from the other measures of GDP. Such an adjustment does, however, exist implicitly.

3 See footnote 2 to Table 19.4.

Source: Office for National Statistics, Blue Book 2013

19.6 Non-financial corporations
ESA95 sector S.11

£ million

			2004	2005	2006	2007	2008	2009	2010	2011	2012
II.1.2	ALLOCATION OF PRIMARY INCOME ACCOUNT before deduction of fixed capital consumption										
	Resources										
B.2g	Operating surplus, gross	NQBE	226 856	237 332	254 167	264 231	268 085	237 758	251 232	265 154	268 967
D.4	Property income, received										
D.41	Interest	EABC	12 539	12 712	16 460	19 297	16 191	4 597	4 073	4 035	3 781
D.42	Distributed income of corporations	EABD	42 964	46 687	43 893	38 953	47 124	62 564	57 887	67 102	54 615
D.43	Reinvested earnings on direct foreign investment	WEYD	22 868	33 354	36 725	50 760	37 714	12 505	26 240	27 737	23 595
D.44	Attributed property income of insurance policy-holders	FAOF	862	1 362	942	714	1 004	859	584	204	198
D.45	Rent	FAOG	122	122	124	123	126	132	130	132	132
D.4	Total	FAKY	79 355	94 237	98 144	109 847	102 159	80 657	88 914	99 210	82 321
Total	Total resources	FBXJ	306 211	331 569	352 311	374 078	370 244	318 415	340 146	364 364	351 288
	Uses										
D.4	Property income, paid										
D.41	Interest	EABG	33 518	36 376	39 786	50 188	49 708	30 864	21 313	19 224	17 768
D.42	Distributed income of corporations	NVCS	93 012	104 201	108 117	108 338	112 351	110 888	113 800	134 487	129 447
D.43	Reinvested earnings on direct foreign investment	HDVB	6 325	4 983	15 452	15 051	3 656	−4 535	161	−6 373	9 754
D.45	Rent	FBXO	177	224	220	229	160	168	168	174	258
D.4	Total	FBXK	133 032	145 784	163 575	173 806	165 875	137 385	135 442	147 512	157 227
B.5g	**Balance of primary incomes, gross**	NQBG	**173 179**	**185 785**	**188 736**	**200 272**	**204 369**	**181 030**	**204 704**	**216 852**	**194 061**
Total	Total uses	FBXJ	306 211	331 569	352 311	374 078	370 244	318 415	340 146	364 364	351 288
-K.1	After deduction of fixed capital consumption	-DBGF	−75 559	−77 277	−80 365	−83 243	−86 127	−90 888	−94 636	−97 887	−101 299
B.5n	Balance of primary incomes, net	FBXQ	97 620	108 508	108 371	117 029	118 242	90 142	110 068	118 965	92 762

Source: Office for National Statistics, Blue Book 2013

19.7 Non-financial corporations
ESA95 sector S.11

£ million

			2004	2005	2006	2007	2008	2009	2010	2011	2012
II.2	SECONDARY DISTRIBUTION OF INCOME ACCOUNT										
	Resources										
B.5g	**Balance of primary incomes, gross**	NQBG	**173 179**	**185 785**	**188 736**	**200 272**	**204 369**	**181 030**	**204 704**	**216 852**	**194 061**
D.61	Social contributions										
D.612	Imputed social contributions	NSTJ	4 123	4 394	4 561	4 830	5 754	6 699	5 293	4 126	4 498
D.7	Current transfers other than taxes, social contributions and benefits										
D.72	Non-life insurance claims	FCBP	6 877	6 631	5 361	5 595	5 230	4 030	4 366	5 756	5 534
D.75	Miscellaneous current transfers	CY8C	28	–	–	–	–	–	–	–	724
D.7	Total	NRJB	6 905	6 631	5 361	5 595	5 230	4 030	4 366	5 756	6 258
Total	Total resources	FCBR	184 207	196 810	198 658	210 697	215 353	191 759	214 363	226 734	204 817
	Uses										
D.5	Current taxes on income, wealth etc.										
D.51	Taxes on income	FCBS	27 366	33 594	37 204	38 309	40 826	33 946	35 844	38 291	35 171
D.62	Social benefits other than social transfers in kind	NSTJ	4 123	4 394	4 561	4 830	5 754	6 699	5 293	4 126	4 498
D.7	Current transfers other than taxes, social contributions and benefits										
D.71	Net non-life insurance premiums	FCBY	6 877	6 631	5 361	5 595	5 230	4 030	4 366	5 756	5 534
D.75	Miscellaneous current transfers	CY8B	451	488	477	488	488	488	488	488	488
D.7	Total, other current transfers	FCBX	7 328	7 119	5 838	6 083	5 718	4 518	4 854	6 244	6 022
B.6g	**Gross Disposable Income**	NRJD	**145 390**	**151 703**	**151 055**	**161 475**	**163 055**	**146 596**	**168 372**	**178 073**	**159 126**
Total	Total uses	FCBR	184 207	196 810	198 658	210 697	215 353	191 759	214 363	226 734	204 817
-K.1	After deduction of fixed capital consumption	-DBGF	−75 559	−77 277	−80 365	−83 243	−86 127	−90 888	−94 636	−97 887	−101 299
B.6n	Disposable income, net	FCCF	69 831	74 426	70 690	78 232	76 928	55 708	73 736	80 186	57 827

Source: Office for National Statistics, Blue Book 2013

19.8 Private non-financial corporations
ESA95 sectors S.11002 National controlled and S.11003 Foreign controlled

£ million

			2004	2005	2006	2007	2008	2009	2010	2011	2012
II.1.2	ALLOCATION OF PRIMARY INCOME ACCOUNT										
	before deduction of fixed capital consumption										
	Resources										
B.2g	Operating surplus, gross[1]	NRJK	218 876	227 512	243 350	252 796	257 208	227 953	241 222	255 670	258 772
D.4	Property income, received										
D.41	Interest	DSZR	11 314	10 962	15 600	18 560	15 361	4 353	3 832	3 820	3 585
D.42	Distributed income of corporations	DSZS	42 902	46 646	43 855	38 462	46 389	62 539	57 803	67 016	54 529
D.43	Reinvested earnings on direct foreign investment	HDVR	22 713	33 199	36 511	50 609	37 890	12 387	26 179	27 676	23 534
D.44	Property income attributed to insurance policy-holders	FCFP	862	1 362	942	714	1 004	859	584	204	198
D.45	Rent	FAOL	122	122	124	123	126	132	130	132	132
D.4	Total	FACV	77 913	92 291	97 032	108 468	100 770	80 270	88 528	98 848	81 978
Total	Total resources	FCFQ	296 789	319 803	340 382	361 264	357 978	308 223	329 750	354 518	340 750
	Uses										
D.4	Property income, paid										
D.41	Interest	DSZV	32 207	35 148	38 406	48 677	48 017	29 421	20 268	18 495	17 205
D.42	Distributed income of corporations	NVDC	92 214	103 406	107 439	107 712	111 820	110 192	113 228	133 898	127 599
	Of which: Dividend payments	NETZ	72 689	82 891	83 684	83 909	88 150	84 627	82 596	103 728	95 193
D.43	Reinvested earnings on direct foreign investment	HDVB	6 325	4 983	15 452	15 051	3 656	−4 535	161	−6 373	9 754
D.45	Rent	FCFU	177	224	220	229	160	168	168	174	258
D.4	Total	FCFR	130 923	143 761	161 517	171 669	163 653	135 246	133 825	146 194	154 816
B.5g	**Balance of primary incomes, gross**	NRJM	**165 866**	**176 042**	**178 865**	**189 595**	**194 325**	**172 977**	**195 925**	**208 324**	**185 934**
Total	Total uses	FCFQ	296 789	319 803	340 382	361 264	357 978	308 223	329 750	354 518	340 750
-K.1	After deduction of fixed capital consumption	-NSRK	−71 482	−72 990	−75 941	−78 715	−81 451	−86 079	−89 668	−92 837	−96 143
B.5n	Balance of primary incomes, net	FCFW	94 384	103 052	102 924	110 880	112 874	86 898	106 257	115 487	89 791

1 Companies gross trading profits and rental of buildings less holding gains of inventories, details of which are shown at Table C: The Sector Accounts Key Economic Indicators.

Source: Office for National Statistics, Blue Book 2013

19.9 Private non-financial corporations
ESA95 sectors S.11002 National controlled and S.11003 Foreign controlled

£ million

			2004	2005	2006	2007	2008	2009	2010	2011	2012
II.2	SECONDARY DISTRIBUTION OF INCOME ACCOUNT										
	Resources										
B.5g	**Balance of primary incomes, gross**	NRJM	165 866	176 042	178 865	189 595	194 325	172 977	195 925	208 324	185 934
D.61	Social contributions										
D.612	Imputed social contributions	EWRT	3 991	4 262	4 426	4 693	5 614	6 559	5 149	3 978	4 353
D.7	Current transfers other than taxes, social contributions and benefits										
D.72	Net non-life insurance claims	FDBA	6 877	6 631	5 361	5 595	5 230	4 030	4 366	5 756	5 534
Total	Total resources	FDBC	176 734	186 935	188 652	199 883	205 169	183 566	205 440	218 058	195 821
	Uses										
D.5	Current taxes on income, wealth etc.										
D.51	Taxes on income	FCCP	27 291	33 453	36 832	38 084	40 572	33 674	35 561	38 011	34 886
D.62	Social benefits other than social transfers in kind	EWRT	3 991	4 262	4 426	4 693	5 614	6 559	5 149	3 978	4 353
D.7	Current transfers other than taxes, social contributions and benefits										
D.71	Net non-life insurance premiums	FDBH	6 877	6 631	5 361	5 595	5 230	4 030	4 366	5 756	5 534
D.75	Miscellaneous current transfers	CY88	446	488	477	488	488	488	488	488	488
D.7	Total	FCCN	7 323	7 119	5 838	6 083	5 718	4 518	4 854	6 244	6 022
B.6g	**Gross Disposable Income**	NRJQ	**138 129**	**142 101**	**141 556**	**151 023**	**153 265**	**138 815**	**159 876**	**169 825**	**150 560**
Total	Total uses	FDBC	176 734	186 935	188 652	199 883	205 169	183 566	205 440	218 058	195 821
-K.1	After deduction of fixed capital consumption	-NSRK	−71 482	−72 990	−75 941	−78 715	−81 451	−86 079	−89 668	−92 837	−96 143
B.6n	Disposable income, net	FDBK	66 647	69 111	65 615	72 308	71 814	52 736	70 208	76 988	54 417

Source: Office for National Statistics, Blue Book 2013

19.10 Households and non-profit institutions serving households
ESA95 sectors S.14 and S.15

£ million

			2004	2005	2006	2007	2008	2009	2010	2011	2012
II.1.2	**ALLOCATION OF PRIMARY INCOME ACCOUNT** before deduction of fixed capital consumption										
	Resources										
B.2g	Operating surplus, gross	QWLS	71 171	75 010	79 192	89 147	86 336	75 005	91 200	100 770	106 982
B.3g	Mixed income, gross	QWLT	74 076	79 240	82 559	83 125	85 411	81 374	85 561	85 322	85 360
D.1	Compensation of employees										
D.11	Wages and salaries	QWLW	552 709	572 678	604 767	639 533	655 682	652 060	662 596	678 849	697 715
D.12	Employers' social contributions	QWLX	95 262	106 069	114 147	118 120	120 565	127 826	138 811	141 136	144 523
D.1	Total	QWLY	647 971	678 747	718 914	757 653	776 247	779 886	801 407	819 985	842 238
D.4	Property income, received										
D.41	Interest	QWLZ	34 823	40 373	43 720	54 889	50 584	9 728	9 402	9 836	9 321
D.42	Distributed income of corporations	QWMA	46 119	48 580	51 058	52 601	46 947	46 786	51 051	54 307	53 740
D.44	Attributed property income of insurance policy holders	QWMC	53 397	57 997	60 774	60 500	65 768	58 097	58 054	62 073	60 013
D.45	Rent	QWMD	110	110	110	110	115	115	118	123	127
D.4	Total	QWME	134 449	147 060	155 662	168 100	163 414	114 726	118 625	126 339	123 201
Total	Total resources	QWMF	927 667	980 057	1 036 327	1 098 025	1 111 408	1 050 991	1 096 793	1 132 416	1 157 781
	Uses										
D.4	Property income, paid										
D.41	Interest	QWMG	43 672	50 667	55 632	74 221	67 091	7 694	5 765	6 027	6 923
D.45	Rent	QWMH	224	224	226	225	233	239	239	243	247
D.4	Total	QWMI	43 896	50 891	55 858	74 446	67 324	7 933	6 004	6 270	7 170
B.5g	**Balance of primary incomes, gross**	QWMJ	**883 771**	**929 166**	**980 469**	**1 023 579**	**1 044 084**	**1 043 058**	**1 090 789**	**1 126 146**	**1 150 611**
Total	Total uses	QWMF	927 667	980 057	1 036 327	1 098 025	1 111 408	1 050 991	1 096 793	1 132 416	1 157 781
-K.1	After deduction of fixed capital consumption	-QWLL	−42 509	−43 257	−48 584	−51 904	−44 914	−47 375	−46 716	−49 363	−49 968
B.5n	Balance of primary incomes, net	QWMK	841 262	885 909	931 885	971 675	999 170	995 683	1 044 073	1 076 783	1 100 643

Source: Office for National Statistics, Blue Book 2013

19.11 Households and non-profit institutions serving households
ESA95 sectors S.14 and S.15

£ million

			2004	2005	2006	2007	2008	2009	2010	2011	2012
II.2	**SECONDARY DISTRIBUTION OF INCOME ACCOUNT**										
	Resources										
B.5g	**Balance of primary incomes, gross**	QWMJ	**883 771**	**929 166**	**980 469**	**1 023 579**	**1 044 084**	**1 043 058**	**1 090 789**	**1 126 146**	**1 150 611**
D.612	Imputed social contributions	RVFH	498	506	514	518	524	524	528	543	529
D.62	Social benefits other than social transfers in kind	QWML	199 101	212 542	226 996	227 935	252 207	277 604	288 545	296 593	313 593
D.7	Other current transfers										
D.72	Non-life insurance claims	QWMM	21 457	19 573	18 840	24 141	21 674	20 062	27 597	24 356	27 712
D.75	Miscellaneous current transfers	QWMN	34 845	37 841	38 729	40 518	39 651	41 651	43 129	41 777	45 474
D.7	Total	QWMO	56 302	57 414	57 569	64 659	61 325	61 713	70 726	66 133	73 186
	Total resources	QWMP	1 139 672	1 199 628	1 265 548	1 316 691	1 358 140	1 382 899	1 450 588	1 489 415	1 537 919
	Uses										
D.5	Current taxes on income, wealth, etc										
D.51	Taxes on income	QWMQ	119 482	129 986	139 215	150 948	154 602	145 672	146 847	152 627	150 044
D.59	Other current taxes	NVCO	26 972	28 387	29 831	31 586	32 931	33 776	34 603	36 411	36 999
D.5	Total	QWMS	146 454	158 373	169 046	182 534	187 533	179 448	181 450	189 038	187 043
D.61	Social contributions										
D.611	Actual social contributions										
D.6111	Employers' actual social contributions	QWMT	83 868	93 279	101 272	104 361	105 694	111 141	122 778	126 542	129 953
D.6112	Employees' social contributions	QWMU	70 959	78 278	83 202	83 412	89 235	83 509	85 055	89 794	92 592
D.6113	Social contributions by self- and non-employed	QWMV	2 727	2 825	2 930	2 860	3 053	2 850	2 720	2 641	2 458
D.611	Total	QWMW	157 554	174 382	187 404	190 633	197 982	197 500	210 553	218 977	225 003
D.612	Imputed social contributions	QWMX	11 394	12 790	12 875	13 759	14 871	16 685	16 033	14 594	14 570
D.61	Total	QWMY	168 948	187 172	200 279	204 392	212 853	214 185	226 586	233 571	239 573
D.62	Social benefits other than social transfers in kind	QWMZ	987	1 000	1 010	1 014	1 020	1 018	1 014	1 039	1 025
D.7	Other current transfers										
D.71	Net non-life insurance premiums	QWNA	21 457	19 573	18 840	24 141	21 674	20 062	27 597	24 355	27 712
D.75	Miscellaneous current transfers	QWNB	12 311	13 292	13 121	14 247	13 616	13 939	14 113	14 387	14 488
D.7	Total	QWNC	33 768	32 865	31 961	38 388	35 290	34 001	41 710	38 742	42 200
B.6g	**Gross Disposable Income**[1]	QWND	**789 515**	**820 218**	**863 252**	**890 363**	**921 444**	**954 247**	**999 828**	**1 027 025**	**1 068 078**
	Total uses	QWMP	1 139 672	1 199 628	1 265 548	1 316 691	1 358 140	1 382 899	1 450 588	1 489 415	1 537 919
-K.1	After deduction of fixed capital consumption	-QWLL	-42 509	-43 257	-48 584	-51 904	-44 914	-47 375	-46 716	-49 363	-49 968
B.6n	Disposable income, net	QWNE	747 006	776 961	814 668	838 459	876 530	906 872	953 112	977 662	1 018 110

1 Gross household disposable income revalued by the implied households
and NPISH's final consumption expenditure deflator is as follows:

		2004	2005	2006	2007	2008	2009	2010	2011	2012
Real household disposable income: (Chained volume measures)										
£ million (reference year 2010)	RVGK	931 821	944 857	969 272	973 995	976 624	992 407	999 828	988 087	1 001 799
Index (2010 = 100)	OSXR	93.2	94.5	96.9	97.4	97.7	99.3	100.0	98.8	100.2

19.12 Households and non-profit institutions serving households
ESA95 sectors S.14 and S.15

£ million

		2004	2005	2006	2007	2008	2009	2010	2011	2012
II.3	**REDISTRIBUTION OF INCOME IN KIND ACCOUNT**									
	Resources									
B.6g	Gross Disposable Income	QWND 789 515	820 218	863 252	890 363	921 444	954 247	999 828	1 027 025	1 068 078
D.63	Social transfers in kind									
D.631	Social benefits in kind									
D.6313	Social assistance benefits in kind	QWNH –	–	–	–	–	–	–	–	–
D.632	Transfers of individual non-market goods and services	NSSA 178 163	191 306	205 951	216 702	230 445	242 942	249 143	251 238	251 313
D.63	Total social transfers in kind	NSSB 178 163	191 306	205 951	216 702	230 445	242 942	249 143	251 238	251 313
Total	Total resources	NSSC 967 678	1 011 524	1 069 203	1 107 065	1 151 889	1 197 189	1 248 971	1 278 263	1 319 391
	Uses									
D.63	Social transfers in kind									
D.631	Social benefits in kind									
D.6313	Social assistance benefits in kind	HAEJ –	–	–	–	–	–	–	–	–
D.632	Transfers of individual non-market goods and services	HABK 29 289	30 962	32 948	34 956	35 892	35 762	37 562	38 457	37 665
D.63	Total social transfers in kind	HAEK 29 289	30 962	32 948	34 956	35 892	35 762	37 562	38 457	37 665
B.7g	Adjusted disposable income, gross	NSSD 938 389	980 562	1 036 255	1 072 109	1 115 997	1 161 427	1 211 409	1 239 806	1 281 726
Total	Total uses	NSSC 967 678	1 011 524	1 069 203	1 107 065	1 151 889	1 197 189	1 248 971	1 278 263	1 319 391

19.12 Households and non-profit institutions serving households
ESA95 sectors S.14 and S.15

£ million

		2004	2005	2006	2007	2008	2009	2010	2011	2012
II.4	**USE OF INCOME ACCOUNT**									
II.4.1	**USE OF DISPOSABLE INCOME ACCOUNT**									
	Resources									
B.6g	Gross Disposable Income	QWND 789 515	820 218	863 252	890 363	921 444	954 247	999 828	1 027 025	1 068 078
D.8	Adjustment for the change in net equity of households in pension funds	NSSE 25 591	30 022	28 482	37 980	27 858	26 549	34 384	36 554	34 792
Total	Total resources	NSSF 815 106	850 240	891 734	928 343	949 302	980 796	1 034 212	1 063 579	1 102 870
	Uses									
P.3	Final consumption expenditure									
P.31	Individual consumption expenditure	NSSG 784 156	825 499	861 787	908 547	928 588	912 315	958 596	992 339	1 028 756
B.8g	**Gross Saving**	NSSH 30 950	24 741	29 947	19 796	20 714	68 481	75 616	71 240	74 114
Total	Total uses	NSSF 815 106	850 240	891 734	928 343	949 302	980 796	1 034 212	1 063 579	1 102 870
-K.1	After deduction of fixed capital consumption	-QWLL -42 509	-43 257	-48 584	-51 904	-44 914	-47 375	-46 716	-49 363	-49 968
B.8n	Saving, net	NSSI -11 559	-18 516	-18 637	-32 108	-24 200	21 106	28 900	21 877	24 146
II.4.2	**USE OF ADJUSTED DISPOSABLE INCOME ACCOUNT**									
	Resources									
B.7g	Adjusted disposable income, gross	NSSD 938 389	980 562	1 036 255	1 072 109	1 115 997	1 161 427	1 211 409	1 239 806	1 281 726
D.8	Adjustment for the change in net equity of households in pension funds	NSSE 25 591	30 022	28 482	37 980	27 858	26 549	34 384	36 554	34 792
Total	Total resources	NSSJ 963 980	1 010 584	1 064 737	1 110 089	1 143 855	1 187 976	1 245 793	1 276 360	1 316 518
	Uses									
P.4	Actual final consumption									
P.41	Actual individual consumption	NQEO 933 030	985 843	1 034 790	1 090 293	1 123 141	1 119 495	1 170 177	1 205 120	1 242 404
B.8g	**Gross Saving**[1]	NSSH 30 950	24 741	29 947	19 796	20 714	68 481	75 616	71 240	74 114
Total	Total uses	NSSJ 963 980	1 010 584	1 064 737	1 110 089	1 143 855	1 187 976	1 245 793	1 276 360	1 316 518

1 Households' saving as a percentage of total available households' resources is as follows:

		2004	2005	2006	2007	2008	2009	2010	2011	2012
Households' saving ratio (per cent)	RVGL	3.8	2.9	3.4	2.1	2.2	7.0	7.3	6.7	6.7

Source: Office for National Statistics, Blue Book 2013

19.13 The sector accounts: Key economic indicators

£ million

			2004	2005	2006	2007	2008	2009	2010	2011	2012
	Net lending/borrowing by:										
B.9	Non-financial corporations	EABO	34 633	35 848	36 674	32 763	32 683	55 919	57 071	57 560	39 195
B.9	Financial corporations	NHCQ	18 806	25 603	15 978	47 312	74 555	60 138	30 811	30 914	−17 369
B.9	General government	NNBK	−42 773	−43 951	−38 631	−42 443	−74 022	−159 299	−148 083	−121 596	−98 830
B.9	Households and NPISH's	NSSZ	−32 970	−39 559	−51 386	−66 270	−43 754	26 828	24 052	14 665	14 731
B.9	Rest of the world	NHRB	22 303	22 057	37 367	28 638	10 540	16 414	36 151	18 455	55 422
	Private non-financial corporations										
	Gross trading profits										
	Continental shelf profits	CAGD	18 668	23 578	27 311	26 080	28 120	21 452	25 379	29 806	25 194
	Others	CAED	184 611	187 344	199 616	208 429	207 055	186 092	193 601	204 967	214 232
	Rental of buildings	DTWR	15 288	16 882	17 005	19 233	22 353	21 317	22 557	20 847	20 930
	less Holding gains of inventories	-DLRA	310	−292	−581	−946	−319	−907	−316	51	−1 584
B.2g	Gross operating surplus	CAER	218 877	227 512	243 351	252 796	257 209	227 954	241 221	255 671	258 772
	Households and NPISH										
B.6g	Household gross disposable income	QWND	789 515	820 218	863 252	890 363	921 444	954 247	999 828	1 027 025	1 068 078
	Implied deflator of household and NPISH individual consumption expenditure index (2010=100)[1]	YBFS	84.7	86.8	89.1	91.4	94.3	96.2	100.0	103.9	106.6
	Real household disposable income:										
	Chained volume measures (reference year 2010)	RVGK	931 821	944 857	969 272	973 995	976 624	992 407	999 828	988 087	1 001 799
	Index (2010=100)[1]	OSXR	93.2	94.5	96.9	97.4	97.7	99.3	100.0	98.8	100.2
B.8g	Gross saving	NSSH	30 950	24 741	29 947	19 796	20 714	68 481	75 616	71 240	74 114
	Households total resources	NSSJ	963 980	1 010 584	1 064 737	1 110 089	1 143 855	1 187 976	1 245 793	1 276 360	1 316 518
	Saving ratio, per cent	RVGL	3.8	2.9	3.4	2.1	2.2	7.0	7.3	6.7	6.7

1 Rounded to one decimal place

Source: Office for National Statistics, Blue Book 2013

19.14 Household final consumption expenditure: classified by purpose at current market prices

£ million

			2004	2005	2006	2007	2008	2009	2010	2011	2012
P.31	**FINAL CONSUMPTION EXPENDITURE OF HOUSEHOLDS**										
	Durable goods										
05.	Furnishings, household equipment and routine maintenance of the house	LLIJ	21 451	22 169	22 413	23 217	23 017	20 424	21 630	21 917	23 137
06.	Health	LLIK	2 557	2 463	2 834	2 952	3 069	3 171	2 980	3 055	3 212
07.	Transport	LLIL	37 443	37 330	37 433	39 699	35 912	35 543	36 473	37 151	41 824
08.	Communication	LLIM	728	770	792	716	803	873	758	684	599
09.	Recreation and culture	LLIN	20 156	21 199	22 610	22 649	24 248	23 138	23 214	21 735	22 353
12.	Miscellaneous goods and services	LLIO	5 094	5 043	5 556	5 376	5 532	5 323	5 742	6 830	6 807
D	Total durable goods	UTIA	87 429	88 974	91 638	94 609	92 581	88 472	90 797	91 372	97 932
	Semi-durable goods										
03.	Clothing and footwear	LLJL	42 300	43 576	45 133	46 639	48 361	48 131	50 409	54 342	56 777
05.	Furnishings, household equipment and routine maintenance of the house	LLJM	13 090	13 281	14 096	14 553	13 784	13 927	14 483	14 405	14 605
07.	Transport	LLJN	3 213	3 694	3 721	3 705	4 089	4 119	3 933	3 810	4 419
09.	Recreation and culture	LLJO	27 898	27 079	27 436	29 639	30 116	27 792	27 820	26 681	27 588
12.	Miscellaneous goods and services	LLJP	3 583	3 439	3 584	3 460	3 255	3 548	5 648	5 593	5 592
SD	Total semi-durable goods	UTIQ	90 084	91 069	93 970	97 996	99 605	97 517	102 293	104 831	108 981
	Non-durable goods										
01.	Food & drink	ABZV	65 527	67 895	70 334	73 372	78 147	79 851	82 917	86 599	90 486
02.	Alcohol & tobacco	ADFL	28 707	29 100	29 400	29 849	29 906	30 029	31 571	33 817	35 198
04.	Housing, water, electricity, gas and other fuels	LLIX	21 015	22 611	26 932	28 658	33 680	34 193	35 713	34 560	38 112
05.	Furnishings, household equipment and routine maintenance of the house	LLIY	3 545	3 640	3 873	3 881	3 887	4 279	4 254	4 224	4 269
06.	Health	LLIZ	4 005	4 126	4 438	4 627	4 644	4 763	5 026	5 180	5 239
07.	Transport	LLJA	20 927	23 248	24 855	26 624	29 522	25 379	28 665	31 319	30 827
09.	Recreation and culture	LLJB	14 191	14 576	15 476	15 678	15 908	15 165	15 131	14 915	14 848
12.	Miscellaneous goods and services	LLJC	13 822	14 415	15 367	16 080	15 871	16 026	15 921	16 586	17 569
ND	Total non-durable goods	UTII	171 739	179 611	190 675	198 769	211 565	209 685	219 198	227 200	236 548
	Total goods	UTIE	349 252	359 654	376 283	391 374	403 751	395 674	412 288	423 403	443 461
	Services										
03.	Clothing and footwear	LLJD	709	782	846	910	1 037	1 095	1 013	866	828
04.	Housing, water, electricity, gas and other fuels	LLJE	123 990	133 558	141 160	152 612	160 720	174 437	192 433	205 230	217 437
05.	Furnishings, household equipment and routine maintenance of the house	LLJF	5 622	5 896	5 952	6 041	6 460	5 959	6 770	6 665	6 798
06.	Health	LLJG	5 276	5 645	6 205	6 930	6 398	6 788	7 070	7 748	7 488
07.	Transport	LLJH	45 085	49 002	52 003	55 807	56 362	55 091	57 537	61 150	64 826
08.	Communication	LLJI	16 739	17 596	17 632	18 377	18 297	17 847	19 081	19 731	20 247
09.	Recreation and culture	LLJJ	27 009	29 359	30 952	33 101	34 285	33 588	35 309	37 676	39 462
10.	Education	ADIE	10 031	10 255	10 866	12 023	12 343	12 613	13 188	13 721	14 639
11.	Restaurants and hotels	ADIF	78 679	81 139	83 241	86 945	87 952	82 710	87 583	92 857	96 779
12.	Miscellaneous goods and services	LLJK	80 536	89 691	92 310	97 259	91 602	81 241	80 729	78 581	73 549
S	Total services	UTIM	393 676	422 923	441 167	470 005	475 456	471 369	500 713	524 225	542 053
0.	Final consumption expenditure in the UK by resident and non-resident households (domestic concept)	ABQI	742 928	782 577	817 450	861 379	879 207	867 043	913 001	947 628	985 514
P.33	Final consumption expenditure outside the UK by UK resident households	ABTA	27 547	29 026	30 388	31 701	33 286	29 062	29 202	28 343	28 958
-P.34	Less Final consumption expenditure in the UK by households resident in the rest of the world	CDFD	−15 608	−17 066	−18 999	−19 489	−19 797	−19 552	−21 169	−22 089	−23 381
P.31	Final consumption expenditure by UK resident households in the UK and abroad (national concept)	ABPB	754 867	794 537	828 839	873 591	892 696	876 553	921 034	953 882	991 091

Source: Office for National Statistics, Blue Book 2013

19.15 Household final consumption expenditure: classified by purpose
Chained volume measures (reference year 2010)

£ million

			2004	2005	2006	2007	2008	2009	2010	2011	2012
P.31	**FINAL CONSUMPTION EXPENDITURE OF HOUSEHOLDS**										
	Durable goods										
	Furnishings, household equipment and										
05.	routine maintenance of the house	LLME	23 744	24 477	24 896	25 386	24 573	21 076	21 630	21 239	21 915
06.	Health	LLMF	2 626	2 528	2 939	3 027	3 115	3 203	2 980	3 038	3 178
07.	Transport	LLMG	38 924	38 853	39 012	41 183	38 286	38 795	36 473	35 839	40 301
08.	Communication	LLMH	694	755	777	731	846	914	758	658	558
09.	Recreation and culture	LLMI	9 959	12 043	14 575	16 884	21 319	22 138	23 214	23 860	26 868
12.	Miscellaneous goods and services	LLMJ	6 465	6 464	6 826	6 382	6 216	5 683	5 742	6 353	5 905
D	Total durable goods	UTIC	76 644	80 835	86 007	91 436	93 824	91 605	90 797	90 987	98 725
	Semi-durable goods										
03.	Clothing and footwear	LLNG	31 556	34 281	37 011	39 754	44 206	47 684	50 409	53 184	55 171
	Furnishings, household equipment and										
05.	routine maintenance of the house	LLNH	12 809	13 468	14 632	15 146	14 391	14 293	14 483	13 541	13 352
07.	Transport	LLNI	3 704	4 181	4 106	4 074	4 399	4 293	3 933	3 666	4 210
09.	Recreation and culture	LLNJ	24 828	24 855	25 920	28 366	29 555	27 689	27 820	27 454	28 528
12.	Miscellaneous goods and services	LLNK	3 701	3 570	3 717	3 523	3 273	3 524	5 648	5 559	5 486
SD	Total semi-durable goods	UTIS	75 620	79 518	84 628	90 225	95 557	97 436	102 293	103 404	106 747
	Non-durable goods										
01.	Food & drink	ADIP	84 448	86 248	87 247	87 069	85 048	82 429	82 917	82 028	83 096
02.	Alcohol & tobacco	ADIS	35 350	35 257	34 564	34 065	32 829	31 451	31 571	30 695	29 909
	Housing, water, electricity, gas and										
04.	other fuels	LLMS	37 374	35 852	35 403	34 821	35 098	33 374	35 713	31 807	32 675
	Furnishings, household equipment and										
05.	routine maintenance of the house	LLMT	4 267	4 397	4 523	4 441	4 302	4 415	4 254	3 969	3 899
06.	Health	LLMU	4 160	4 331	4 675	4 817	4 794	4 838	5 026	5 120	4 934
07.	Transport	LLMV	31 495	32 267	32 792	34 133	32 833	30 558	28 665	28 021	27 362
09.	Recreation and culture	LLMW	16 598	16 964	17 606	17 600	17 257	15 830	15 131	14 332	13 942
12.	Miscellaneous goods and services	LLMX	15 185	15 991	16 789	17 203	16 705	16 426	15 921	16 158	16 972
ND	Total non-durable goods	UTIK	227 509	230 553	233 137	233 680	228 406	218 908	219 198	212 130	212 789
	Total goods	UTIG	372 870	385 385	399 913	413 138	417 124	407 795	412 288	406 521	418 261
	Services										
03.	Clothing and footwear	LLMY	844	895	938	976	1 079	1 116	1 013	835	787
	Housing, water, electricity, gas and										
04.	other fuels	LLMZ	175 167	178 729	182 430	185 333	187 926	190 551	192 433	195 138	197 139
	Furnishings, household equipment and										
05.	routine maintenance of the house	LLNA	6 950	6 984	6 777	6 562	6 715	6 080	6 770	6 549	6 563
06.	Health	LLNB	6 690	6 828	7 168	7 711	6 937	7 051	7 070	7 516	7 052
07.	Transport	LLNC	55 793	58 353	59 652	61 548	59 674	56 600	57 537	57 947	59 402
08.	Communication	LLND	16 372	17 644	17 628	18 987	19 390	18 719	19 081	18 985	18 670
09.	Recreation and culture	LLNE	33 770	35 415	35 747	36 799	37 010	34 898	35 309	35 921	36 474
10.	Education	ADMJ	16 264	15 849	15 680	15 246	14 018	13 288	13 188	13 049	12 822
11.	Restaurants and hotels	ADMK	95 611	95 017	93 923	94 628	92 093	84 548	87 583	88 774	88 053
12.	Miscellaneous goods and services	LLNF	85 404	90 360	88 281	90 691	85 448	81 425	80 729	79 284	75 515
S	Total services	UTIO	494 236	508 441	509 828	520 607	511 345	494 265	500 713	503 998	502 477
	Final consumption expenditure in the UK										
	by resident and non-resident households										
0.	(domestic concept)	ABQJ	865 515	892 353	909 128	933 341	928 371	902 069	913 001	910 519	920 738
	Final consumption expenditure outside the UK										
P.33	by UK resident households	ABTC	40 899	40 405	41 572	43 334	38 646	30 114	29 202	27 173	28 504
	Less Final consumption expenditure in the UK										
-P.34	by households resident in the rest of the world	CCHX	−17 683	−18 900	−20 507	−20 455	−20 368	−19 982	−21 169	−21 297	−21 814
	Final consumption expenditure by UK resident										
	households in the UK and abroad										
P.3	(national concept)	ABPF	887 172	912 593	928 786	954 679	946 011	912 222	921 034	916 395	927 428

Source: Office for National Statistics, Blue Book 2013

19.16 Individual consumption expenditure at current market prices by households, non-profit institutions serving households and general government

Classified by function (COICOP/COPNI/COFOG) [1]

£ million

		2004	2005	2006	2007	2008	2009	2010	2011	2012
P.31 FINAL CONSUMPTION EXPENDITURE OF HOUSEHOLDS										
01. Food and non-alcoholic beverages	ABZV	65 527	67 895	70 334	73 372	78 147	79 851	82 917	86 599	90 486
01.1 Food	ABZW	57 512	59 599	61 593	64 422	69 087	70 526	73 229	76 036	79 685
01.2 Non-alcoholic beverages	ADFK	8 015	8 296	8 741	8 950	9 060	9 325	9 688	10 563	10 801
02. Alcoholic beverages and tobacco	ADFL	28 707	29 100	29 400	29 849	29 906	30 029	31 571	33 817	35 198
02.1 Alcoholic beverages	ADFM	13 331	13 791	13 844	14 068	14 004	14 160	14 389	15 531	16 480
02.2 Tobacco	ADFN	15 376	15 309	15 556	15 781	15 902	15 869	17 182	18 286	18 718
03. Clothing and footwear	ADFP	43 009	44 358	45 979	47 549	49 398	49 226	51 422	55 208	57 605
03.1 Clothing	ADFQ	37 037	38 266	39 349	40 642	42 179	41 707	43 760	47 173	49 213
03.2 Footwear	ADFR	5 972	6 092	6 630	6 907	7 219	7 519	7 662	8 035	8 392
04. Housing, water, electricity, gas and other fuels	ADFS	145 005	156 169	168 092	181 270	194 400	208 630	228 146	239 790	255 549
04.1 Actual rentals for housing	ADFT	29 379	32 034	34 777	38 359	40 750	43 300	47 463	50 922	54 880
04.2 Imputed rentals for housing	ADFU	90 694	96 924	101 393	108 941	114 711	125 796	139 355	148 505	157 213
04.3 Maintenance and repair of the dwelling	ADFV	2 123	2 524	2 423	2 371	2 044	1 942	2 101	2 251	1 901
04.4 Water supply and miscellaneous dwelling services	ADFW	5 826	6 385	6 929	7 617	8 040	8 231	8 636	9 044	9 303
04.5 Electricity, gas and other fuels	ADFX	16 983	18 302	22 570	23 982	28 855	29 361	30 591	29 068	32 252
05. Furnishings, household equipment and routine maintenance of the house	ADFY	43 708	44 986	46 334	47 692	47 148	44 589	47 137	47 211	48 809
05.1 Furniture, furnishings, carpets and other floor coverings	ADFZ	16 854	17 064	17 411	18 186	17 540	15 696	15 717	16 318	17 261
05.2 Household textiles	ADGG	4 990	4 700	5 014	5 445	5 499	5 713	6 308	5 559	5 799
05.3 Household appliances	ADGL	5 794	6 102	6 114	5 961	6 078	5 698	7 028	7 052	7 004
05.4 Glassware, tableware and household utensils	ADGM	4 148	4 651	4 754	4 511	4 341	4 269	4 155	4 657	4 841
05.5 Tools and equipment for house and garden	ADGN	3 395	3 568	3 813	4 229	3 812	3 437	3 419	3 373	3 439
05.6 Goods and services for routine household maintenance	ADGO	8 527	8 901	9 228	9 360	9 878	9 776	10 510	10 252	10 465
06. Health	ADGP	11 838	12 234	13 477	14 509	14 111	14 722	15 076	15 983	15 939
06.1 Medical products, appliances and equipment	ADGQ	6 562	6 589	7 272	7 579	7 713	7 934	8 006	8 235	8 451
06.2 Out-patient services	ADGR	2 920	3 142	3 580	4 217	3 601	3 672	3 882	4 665	4 326
06.3 Hospital services	ADGS	2 356	2 503	2 625	2 713	2 797	3 116	3 188	3 083	3 162
07. Transport	ADGT	106 668	113 274	118 012	125 835	125 885	120 132	126 608	133 430	141 896
07.1 Purchase of vehicles	ADGU	37 443	37 330	37 433	39 699	35 912	35 543	36 473	37 151	41 824
07.2 Operation of personal transport equipment	ADGV	42 145	46 781	49 313	51 821	55 805	51 856	56 758	59 682	60 395
07.3 Transport services	ADGW	27 080	29 163	31 266	34 315	34 168	32 733	33 377	36 597	39 677
08. Communication	ADGX	17 467	18 366	18 424	19 093	19 100	18 720	19 839	20 415	20 846
08.1 Postal services	CDEF	970	1 039	1 041	1 076	1 013	1 051	1 017	1 069	1 292
08.2 Telephone & telefax equipment	ADWO	728	770	792	716	803	873	758	684	599
08.3 Telephone & telefax services	ADWP	15 769	16 557	16 591	17 301	17 284	16 796	18 064	18 662	18 955
09. Recreation and culture	ADGY	89 254	92 213	96 474	101 067	104 557	99 683	101 474	101 007	104 251
09.1 Audio-visual, photographic and information processing equipment	ADGZ	21 530	22 096	22 607	21 662	22 893	20 745	20 091	18 801	19 012
09.2 Other major durables for recreation and culture	ADHL	5 804	6 158	6 496	6 766	7 146	7 372	7 742	7 248	7 738
09.3 Other recreational items and equipment; flowers, garden and pets	ADHZ	25 601	25 163	25 905	29 304	30 308	29 019	29 913	28 713	30 521
09.4 Recreational and cultural services	ADIA	24 942	26 883	28 624	30 425	31 713	30 839	32 259	34 849	35 874
09.5 Newspapers, books and stationery	ADIC	11 377	11 913	12 842	12 910	12 497	11 708	11 469	11 396	11 106
09.6 Package holidays[2]	ADID	–	–	–	–	–	–	–	–	–
10. Education										
10. Education services	ADIE	10 031	10 255	10 866	12 023	12 343	12 613	13 188	13 721	14 639
11. Restaurants and hotels	ADIF	78 679	81 139	83 241	86 945	87 952	82 710	87 583	92 857	96 779
11.1 Catering services	ADIG	68 024	69 950	71 573	73 667	74 360	70 872	74 152	78 061	80 674
11.2 Accommodation services	ADIH	10 655	11 189	11 668	13 278	13 592	11 838	13 431	14 796	16 105
12. Miscellaneous goods and services	ADII	103 035	112 588	116 817	122 175	116 260	106 138	108 040	107 590	103 517
12.1 Personal care	ADIJ	20 125	20 831	21 793	22 513	22 270	22 705	23 434	23 956	24 963
12.3 Personal effects n.e.c.	ADIK	7 205	7 145	7 999	7 699	7 816	7 705	9 867	10 864	11 009
12.4 Social protection	ADIL	10 842	11 315	11 622	12 077	12 586	11 951	12 475	12 671	12 270
12.5 Insurance	ADIM	18 814	23 686	21 120	23 846	19 221	21 461	20 790	22 042	19 741
12.6 Financial services n.e.c.	ADIN	39 439	42 525	47 216	48 685	47 194	35 675	34 895	31 249	28 441
12.7 Other services n.e.c.	ADIO	6 610	7 086	7 067	7 355	7 173	6 641	6 579	6 808	7 093
Final consumption expenditure in the UK by resident and non-resident households										
0. (domestic concept)	ABQI	742 928	782 577	817 450	861 379	879 207	867 043	913 001	947 628	985 514
P.33 Final consumption expenditure outside the UK by UK resident households	ABTA	27 547	29 026	30 388	31 701	33 286	29 062	29 202	28 343	28 958
-P.34 less Final consumption expenditure in the UK by households resident in the rest of the world	CDFD	−15 608	−17 066	−18 999	−19 489	−19 797	−19 552	−21 169	−22 089	−23 381
P.31 Final consumption expenditure by UK resident households in the UK and abroad (national concept)	ABPB	754 867	794 537	828 839	873 591	892 696	876 553	921 034	953 882	991 091

Source: Office for National Statistics, Blue Book 2013

19.16
continued

Individual consumption expenditure at current market prices by households, non-profit institutions serving households and general government
Classified by function (COICOP/COPNI/COFOG) [1]

£ million

		2004	2005	2006	2007	2008	2009	2010	2011	2012
P.31 CONSUMPTION EXPENDITURE OF UK RESIDENT HOUSEHOLDS										
P.31 Final consumption expenditure of UK resident households in the UK and abroad	ABPB	754 867	794 537	828 839	873 591	892 696	876 553	921 034	953 882	991 091
13. FINAL INDIVIDUAL CONSUMPTION EXPENDITURE OF NPISH										
P.31 Final individual consumption expenditure of NPISH	ABNV	29 289	30 962	32 948	34 956	35 892	35 762	37 562	38 457	37 665
14. FINAL INDIVIDUAL CONSUMPTION EXPENDITURE OF GENERAL GOVERNMENT										
14.1 Health	IWX5	76 163	81 879	89 403	94 222	101 611	109 958	112 660	115 316	116 660
14.2 Recreation and culture	IWX6	5 221	5 591	5 813	6 186	6 122	6 225	6 071	6 140	6 224
14.3 Education	IWX7	42 466	46 045	49 065	51 648	55 327	58 483	60 140	59 419	59 644
14.4 Social protection	IWX8	25 024	26 829	28 722	29 690	31 493	32 514	32 710	31 906	31 120
P.31 Final individual consumption expenditure of general government	NNAQ	148 874	160 344	173 003	181 746	194 553	207 180	211 581	212 781	213 648
P.31 Total, individual consumption expenditure/ P.41 actual individual consumption	NQEO	933 030	985 843	1 034 790	1 090 293	1 123 141	1 119 495	1 170 177	1 205 120	1 242 404

1 "Purpose" or "function" classifications are designed to indicate the "socio-economic objectives" that institutional units aim to achieve through various kinds of outlays. COICOP is the Classification of Individual Consumption by Purpose and applies to households. COPNI is the Classification of the Purposes of Non-profit Institutions Serving Households and COFOG the Classification of the Functions of Government. The introduction of ESA95 coincides with the redefinition of these classifications and data will be available on a consistent basis for all European Union member states.
2 Package holidays data are dispersed between components (transport etc).

Source: Office for National Statistics, Blue Book 2013

19.17 Individual consumption expenditure by households, NPISH and general government chained volume measures (reference year 2010)

Classified by function (COICOP/COPNI/COFOG)[1]

£ million

			2004	2005	2006	2007	2008	2009	2010	2011	2012
P.31	**FINAL CONSUMPTION EXPENDITURE OF HOUSEHOLDS**										
01.	**Food and non-alcoholic beverages**	ADIP	84 448	86 248	87 247	87 069	85 048	82 429	82 917	82 028	83 096
01.1	Food	ADIQ	74 615	76 061	76 913	76 902	75 009	72 541	73 229	72 314	73 565
01.2	Non-alcoholic beverages	ADIR	9 844	10 191	10 336	10 178	10 045	9 896	9 688	9 714	9 531
02.	**Alcoholic beverages and tobacco**	ADIS	35 350	35 257	34 564	34 065	32 829	31 451	31 571	30 695	29 909
02.1	Alcoholic beverages	ADIT	14 615	15 392	15 266	15 494	15 044	14 427	14 389	14 160	14 151
02.2	Tobacco	ADIU	21 032	19 960	19 361	18 576	17 781	17 019	17 182	16 535	15 758
03.	**Clothing and footwear**	ADIW	32 371	35 153	37 932	40 721	45 276	48 795	51 422	54 019	55 958
03.1	Clothing	ADIX	27 400	29 824	31 916	34 350	38 354	41 335	43 760	45 725	47 284
03.2	Footwear	ADIY	4 971	5 320	6 039	6 385	6 923	7 461	7 662	8 294	8 674
04.	**Housing, water, electricity, gas and other fuels**	ADIZ	212 000	214 435	217 844	220 181	223 051	223 729	228 146	226 945	229 814
04.1	Actual rentals for housing	ADJA	38 918	40 891	43 165	44 808	46 615	47 404	47 463	48 942	49 290
04.2	Imputed rentals for housing	ADJB	131 287	132 259	133 439	134 619	135 813	137 822	139 355	140 540	142 899
04.3	Maintenance and repair of the dwelling	ADJC	2 619	3 039	2 846	2 673	2 190	2 018	2 101	2 151	1 752
04.4	Water supply and miscellaneous dwelling services	ADJD	8 233	8 206	8 336	8 623	8 553	8 325	8 636	8 745	8 523
04.5	Electricity, gas and other fuels	ADJE	31 823	30 292	30 120	29 441	29 858	28 388	30 591	26 567	27 350
05.	**Furnishings, household equipment and routine maintenance of the house**	ADJF	47 598	49 200	50 794	51 536	49 971	45 860	47 137	45 298	45 729
05.1	Furniture, furnishings, carpets and other floor coverings	ADJG	19 050	19 072	19 342	19 844	18 528	16 135	15 717	15 792	16 193
05.2	Household textiles	ADJH	4 414	4 337	4 849	5 411	5 582	5 783	6 308	5 265	5 400
05.3	Household appliances	ADJI	6 027	6 473	6 783	6 560	6 693	5 934	7 028	6 896	6 843
05.4	Glassware, tableware and household utensils	ADJJ	4 295	5 006	5 201	4 864	4 628	4 438	4 155	4 442	4 546
05.5	Tools and equipment for house and garden	ADJK	3 605	3 880	4 109	4 507	4 025	3 552	3 419	3 007	2 854
05.6	Goods and services for routine household maintenance	ADJL	10 473	10 674	10 647	10 397	10 548	10 017	10 510	9 896	9 893
06.	**Health**	ADJM	13 439	13 642	14 767	15 522	14 847	15 094	15 076	15 674	15 164
06.1	Medical products, appliances and equipment	ADJN	6 784	6 856	7 614	7 843	7 909	8 042	8 006	8 158	8 112
06.2	Out-patient services	ADJO	3 445	3 547	3 884	4 449	3 765	3 737	3 882	4 593	4 192
06.3	Hospital services	ADJP	3 283	3 315	3 291	3 227	3 172	3 320	3 188	2 923	2 860
07.	**Transport**	ADJQ	129 908	133 474	135 306	140 723	134 895	129 997	126 608	125 473	131 275
07.1	Purchase of vehicles	ADJR	38 924	38 853	39 012	41 183	38 286	38 795	36 473	35 839	40 301
07.2	Operation of personal transport equipment	ADJS	58 598	60 824	60 958	61 865	60 685	57 866	56 758	55 209	55 362
07.3	Transport services	ADJT	32 212	33 872	35 380	37 538	35 975	33 389	33 377	34 425	35 612
08.	**Communication**	ADJU	17 065	18 399	18 406	19 717	20 235	19 633	19 839	19 643	19 228
08.1	Postal services	CCGZ	1 482	1 530	1 411	1 323	1 170	1 113	1 017	978	996
08.2	Telephone & telefax equipment	ADQF	694	755	778	732	846	914	758	658	558
08.3	Telephone & telefax services	ADQG	15 024	16 234	16 298	17 697	18 223	17 607	18 064	18 007	17 674
09.	**Recreation and culture**	ADJV	79 969	85 235	91 191	97 881	104 733	100 484	101 474	101 567	105 812
09.1	Audio-visual, photographic and information processing equipment	ADJW	9 394	11 180	13 068	14 622	18 739	19 348	20 091	21 273	23 928
09.2	Other major durables for recreation and culture	ADJX	6 547	6 864	7 229	7 478	7 744	7 720	7 742	6 970	7 220
09.3	Other recreational items and equipment; flowers, gardens and pets	ADJY	24 836	24 880	26 196	29 892	31 120	29 275	29 913	29 033	30 886
09.4	Recreational and cultural services	ADJZ	31 180	32 409	33 009	33 739	34 207	32 039	32 259	33 233	33 133
09.5	Newspapers, books and stationery	ADKM	13 348	13 902	14 550	14 413	13 419	12 176	11 469	11 058	10 645
09.6	Package holidays[2]	ADMI	–	–	–	–	–	–	–	–	–
10.	**Education**										
10.	Education services	ADMJ	16 264	15 849	15 680	15 246	14 018	13 288	13 188	13 049	12 822
11.	**Restaurants and Hotels**	ADMK	95 611	95 017	93 923	94 628	92 093	84 548	87 583	88 774	88 053
11.1	Catering services	ADML	83 160	82 634	81 552	80 913	78 302	72 503	74 152	74 425	72 897
11.2	Accommodation services	ADMM	12 545	12 475	12 455	13 721	13 771	12 050	13 431	14 349	15 156
12.	**Miscellaneous goods and services**	ADMN	110 831	116 511	115 557	117 882	111 637	107 025	108 040	107 354	103 878
12.1	Personal care	ADMO	22 650	23 363	23 959	24 147	23 385	23 283	23 434	23 293	24 035
12.3	Personal effects n.e.c.	ADMP	8 432	8 426	9 177	8 581	8 356	7 937	9 867	10 392	10 046
12.4	Social protection	ADMQ	14 445	14 185	13 832	13 635	13 591	12 334	12 475	12 308	11 620
12.5	Insurance	ADMR	25 330	30 189	25 422	27 478	21 366	22 785	20 790	20 900	18 553
12.6	Financial services n.e.c.	ADMS	32 677	33 666	35 617	36 581	36 901	33 966	34 895	33 888	32 977
12.7	Other services n.e.c.	ADMT	9 070	9 089	8 407	8 264	7 541	6 834	6 579	6 573	6 647
0.	**Final consumption expenditure in the UK by resident and non-resident households** (domestic concept)	ABQJ	865 515	892 353	909 128	933 341	928 371	902 069	913 001	910 519	920 738
P.33	Final consumption expenditure outside the UK by UK resident households	ABTC	40 899	40 405	41 572	43 334	38 646	30 114	29 202	27 173	28 504
-P.34	*less* Final consumption expenditure in the UK by households resident in the rest of the world	CCHX	−17 683	−18 900	−20 507	−20 455	−20 368	−19 982	−21 169	−21 297	−21 814
P.31	**Final consumption expenditure by UK resident households in the UK and abroad (national concept)**	ABPF	887 172	912 593	928 786	954 679	946 011	912 222	921 034	916 395	927 428

Source: Office for National Statistics, Blue Book 2013

19.17 Individual consumption expenditure by households, NPISH and general government chained volume measures (reference year 2010)

Classified by function (COICOP/COPNI/COFOG)[1]

£ million

		2004	2005	2006	2007	2008	2009	2010	2011	2012
P.31 CONSUMPTION EXPENDITURE OF UK RESIDENT HOUSEHOLDS										
P.31 Final consumption expenditure of UK resident households in the UK and abroad	ABPF	887 172	912 593	928 786	954 679	946 011	912 222	921 034	916 395	927 428
13. FINAL INDIVIDUAL CONSUMPTION EXPENDITURE OF NPISH										
P.31 Final individual consumption expenditure of NPISH	ABNU	38 519	38 424	38 906	39 238	38 197	36 586	37 562	38 321	37 489
14. FINAL INDIVIDUAL CONSUMPTION EXPENDITURE OF GENERAL GOVERNMENT										
14.1 Health	K4CP	87 001	92 182	96 408	99 619	105 534	110 039	112 660	115 843	122 462
14.2 Recreation and culture	K4CQ	6 151	6 366	6 399	6 527	6 253	6 282	6 071	6 201	6 080
14.3 Education	K4CR	60 381	60 064	59 792	59 717	59 536	59 809	60 140	60 907	61 943
14.4 Social protection	K4CS	33 506	33 514	33 628	33 107	32 795	32 911	32 710	31 860	31 462
P.31 Final individual consumption expenditure of general government	NSZK	185 784	191 399	195 775	198 703	204 061	209 023	211 581	214 811	221 947
P.31 Total, individual consumption expenditure/ P.41 actual individual consumption	YBIO	1 111 201	1 142 235	1 163 267	1 192 467	1 188 138	1 157 812	1 170 177	1 169 527	1 186 864

1 "Purpose" or "function" classifications are designed to indicate the "socio-economic objectives" that institutional units aim to achieve through various kinds of outlays. COICOP is the Classification of Individual Consumption by Purpose and applies to households. COPNI is the Classification of the Purposes of Non-profit Institutions Serving Households and COFOG the Classification of the Functions of Government. The introduction of ESA95 coincides with the redefinition of these classifications and data will be available on a consistent basis for all European Union member states.

2 Package holidays data are dispersed between components (transport etc)

Source: Office for National Statistics, Blue Book 2013

19.18 Change in inventories at chained volume measures [1]

Reference year 2010, £ million

	Manufacturing industries					Distributive trades				
Level of inventories held at end-December 2011 [4]	Mining and quarrying	Materials and fuel	Work in progress	Finished goods	Total	Electricity, gas and water supply	Wholesale [2]	Retail [2]	Other industries	Changes in inventories [3]
	5 524	16 385	33 160	30 628	80 173	3 581	50 630	30 133	75 432	245 473
	FADO	FBID	FBIE	FBIF	DHBH	FADP	FAJM	FBYH	DLWV	ABMQ
Non-seasonally adjusted										
1997	3 659	2 384	1 144	35	1 568	- 1 364	- 85	156	2 258	9 915
1998	2 072	6 584	259	724	2 484	- 91	1 341	951	1 153	8 389
1999	3 449	- 683	- 98	882	1 023	- 1 389	1 590	- 24	903	8 866
2000	- 1 849	304	1 392	- 315	1 907	- 704	1 376	1 384	1 242	8 286
2001	4 299	- 4 498	2 211	- 205	1 231	522	2 547	1 798	1 788	10 808
2002	- 3 514	- 3 632	395	2 049	177	545	388	- 763	- 901	2 474
2003	- 1 508	- 3 616	707	433	1 174	134	489	1 200	970	6 554
2004	1 117	- 1 234	621	1 320	366	- 39	832	463	1 665	7 386
2005	93	2 311	2 006	- 508	1 705	32	2 726	- 2 500	1 110	6 915
2006	732	- 4 631	2 906	- 2 852	1 348	581	- 309	802	762	5 852
2007	4 680	1 987	666	- 5 215	2 863	106	- 333	- 182	2 442	10 078
2008	- 6 466	2 616	838	2 070	1 309	24	2 776	- 242	1 508	6 439
2009	- 4 459	- 3 516	- 925	9 085	- 4 523	114	- 3 642	- 95	- 3 732	- 16 265
2010	- 1	175	154	274	603	20	825	252	227	1 927
2011	- 447	146	963	596	1 705	289	2 288	309	4 300	8 444
2012	1 343	- 2 365	1 454	- 923	- 1 834	- 750	4 252	822	- 593	3 240

1 Estimates are given to the nearest £ million but cannot be regarded as accurate to this degree.
2 Wholesaling and retailing estimates exclude the motor trades.
3 Quarterly alignment adjustment included in this series.
4 Estimates of level based on previously available data.

19.19 Gross fixed capital formation at current purchasers' prices[1,2]
Analysis by broad sector and type of asset
Total economy

£ million

			2004	2005	2006	2007	2008	2009	2010	2011	2012
	Private sector										
	New dwellings, excluding land	L5ZQ	41 696	45 125	56 881	57 457	51 253	38 612	46 207	48 886	48 022
	Other buildings and structures	EQBU	30 325	33 729	36 384	46 046	51 977	45 424	40 606	50 030	46 016
	Transport equipment	EQBV	11 401	10 257	11 087	10 237	10 478	9 674	13 139	3 751	5 365
	Other machinery and equipment and cultivated assets	EQBW	34 634	33 633	33 043	37 871	38 464	30 781	32 908	33 714	38 526
	Intangible fixed assets	EQBX	28 848	28 869	26 092	28 320	30 575	27 693	30 290	31 675	33 571
	Costs associated with the transfer of ownership of non-produced assets	L5ZR	31 487	31 420	36 967	39 706	20 284	11 554	12 677	11 546	12 248
P.51	Total	EQBZ	178 393	183 032	200 451	219 638	203 029	163 736	175 827	179 601	183 746
S.11001	**Public non-financial corporations**										
	New dwellings, excluding land	L5YQ	8 154	5 277	5 725	5 182	4 522	4 102	4 248	4 098	3 017
	Other buildings and structures	DEES	−3 140	−14	161	331	1 054	1 793	1 102	551	335
	Transport equipment	DEEP	517	483	257	204	415	297	465	430	223
	Other machinery and equipment and cultivated assets	DEEQ	2 640	17 564	1 399	1 701	2 250	1 487	1 407	1 333	999
	Intangible fixed assets	DLXJ	4 984	2 886	2 840	2 778	2 261	1 931	1 954	1 988	1 987
	Costs associated with the transfer of ownership of non-produced assets	L5ZL	−8 260	−4 215	−3 562	−3 056	−1 637	−356	−390	−355	−378
P.51	Total	FCCJ	4 896	21 981	6 820	7 140	8 867	9 254	8 786	8 043	6 185
S.13	**General government**										
	New dwellings, excluding land	L5ZU	131	49	9	5	14	–	−5	−6	94
	Other buildings and structures	EQCH	12 787	20 188	21 739	23 525	27 125	28 573	25 472	22 748	23 592
	Transport equipment	EQCI	1 128	742	559	571	483	543	608	452	455
	Other machinery and equipment and cultivated assets	EQCJ	4 131	−11 393	2 876	3 170	3 711	4 791	5 638	5 191	5 072
	Intangible fixed assets	EQCK	292	308	466	414	300	292	438	696	863
	Costs associated with the transfer of ownership of non-produced assets	L5ZV	3 268	−536	−1 060	−474	2 017	4 004	4 393	4 002	4 246
P.51	Total	NNBF	21 738	9 359	24 589	27 210	33 652	38 203	36 544	33 082	34 321
P.51	Total gross fixed capital formation	NPQX	205 027	214 371	231 861	253 988	245 549	211 195	221 156	220 726	224 252

1 Components may not sum to totals due to rounding.
2 Please note that the annual current price and chained volume measures for some asset and sector breakdowns may not may not be equal in the reference year (2010) due to rounding. These differences are well within the range of uncertainty on the estimates.

Source: Office for National Statistics, Blue Book 2013

19.20 Gross fixed capital formation at current purchasers' prices[1,2]
Analysis by type of asset
Total economy

£ million

		2004	2005	2006	2007	2008	2009	2010	2011	2012
Tangible fixed assets										
New dwellings, excluding land	DFDK	49 982	50 450	62 614	62 645	55 788	42 712	50 450	52 977	51 135
Other buildings and structures	DLWS	39 972	53 902	58 286	69 901	80 156	75 790	67 179	73 330	69 942
Transport equipment	DLWZ	13 045	11 482	11 902	11 011	11 378	10 512	14 213	4 633	6 043
Other machinery and equipment and cultivated assets	DLXI	41 405	39 805	37 317	42 742	44 424	37 059	39 952	40 238	44 595
Total	EQCQ	144 404	155 640	170 120	186 299	191 747	166 075	171 795	171 176	171 714
Intangible fixed assets	DLXP	34 126	32 062	29 396	31 513	33 137	29 918	32 680	34 359	36 421
Costs associated with the transfer of ownership of non-produced assets	DFBH	26 497	26 669	32 345	36 176	20 664	15 202	16 681	15 191	16 116
P.51 Total gross fixed capital formation	NPQX	205 027	214 371	231 861	253 988	245 549	211 195	221 156	220 726	224 252

1 Components may not sum to totals due to rounding.
2 Please note that the annual current price and chained volume measures for some asset and sector breakdowns may not may not be equal in the reference year (2010) due to rounding. These differences are well within the range of uncertainty on the estimates.

Source: Office for National Statistics, Blue Book 2013

19.21 Gross fixed capital formation[1,2,3]
Chained volume measures (reference year 2010)
Total economy: Analysis by broad sector and type of asset

£ million

		2004	2005	2006	2007	2008	2009	2010	2011	2012
Private sector										
New dwellings, excluding land	L62K	57 573	57 710	67 848	65 050	55 391	39 999	46 204	47 859	46 233
Other buildings and structures	EQCU	33 757	36 098	37 009	45 345	48 775	43 142	40 709	49 315	45 206
Transport equipment	EQCV	11 772	10 922	11 927	10 918	11 057	9 975	13 075	3 538	5 121
Other machinery and equipment and cultivated assets	EQCW	38 123	37 633	38 181	45 229	43 671	32 176	32 860	32 341	36 422
Intangible fixed assets	EQCX	31 109	30 784	27 414	29 285	31 281	28 151	30 267	30 901	32 314
Costs associated with the transfer of ownership of non-produced assets	L62L	33 153	35 424	41 448	43 985	21 905	11 715	12 662	11 233	11 625
P.51 Total	EQCZ	205 549	210 613	225 915	243 211	217 154	168 723	175 777	175 188	176 922
S.11001 **Public non-financial corporations**										
New dwellings, excluding land	L62M	11 288	6 739	6 848	5 883	4 900	4 252	4 256	4 022	2 902
Other buildings and structures	DEEX	−3 441	−39	159	305	990	1 695	1 102	545	329
Transport equipment	DEEU	532	513	277	217	439	307	468	407	212
Other machinery and equipment and cultivated assets	DEEV	2 899	17 365	1 616	2 031	2 552	1 561	1 416	1 280	946
Intangible fixed assets	EQDE	5 375	3 077	2 986	2 875	2 312	1 964	1 955	1 940	1 913
Costs associated with the transfer of ownership of non-produced assets	L62N	−8 696	−4 752	−3 994	−3 386	−1 767	−360	−391	−346	−357
P.51 Total	EQDG	5 629	22 676	7 695	7 869	9 423	9 404	8 807	7 847	5 945
S.13 **General government**										
New dwellings, excluding landcosts	L62O	183	64	13	6	16	2	−16	−174	−246
Other buildings and structures	EQDI	14 171	21 661	22 151	23 332	25 397	27 056	25 483	22 932	24 005
Transport equipment	EQDJ	1 167	786	602	610	508	563	612	437	449
Other machinery and equipment and cultivated assets	EQDK	4 516	−10 571	3 321	3 775	4 200	5 020	5 643	5 067	4 929
Intangible fixed assets	EQDL	313	328	494	430	309	298	438	690	855
Costs associated with the transfer of ownership of non-produced assets	L62P	3 442	−603	−1 189	−524	2 178	4 059	4 410	3 932	4 116
P.51 Total	EQDN	25 051	9 064	25 572	27 353	32 566	36 932	36 572	32 883	34 107
P.51 Total gross fixed capital formation	NPQR	235 691	244 373	258 060	277 341	258 332	215 142	221 156	215 918	216 974

1 For the years before 2010, totals differ from the sum of their components.
2 Components may not sum to totals due to rounding.
3 Please note that the annual current price and chained volume measures for some asset and sector breakdowns may not may not be equal in the reference year (2010) due to rounding. These differences are well within the range of uncertainty on the estimates.

Source: Office for National Statistics, Blue Book 2013

19.22 Gross fixed capital formation[1,2,3]
Chained volume measures (reference year 2010)
Total economy: Analysis by type of asset

£ million

		2004	2005	2006	2007	2008	2009	2010	2011	2012
Tangible fixed assets										
New dwellings, excluding land	DFDV	69 044	64 513	74 709	70 939	60 307	44 253	50 444	51 707	48 889
Other buildings and structures	EQDP	44 486	57 720	59 321	68 982	75 163	71 893	67 295	72 793	69 542
Transport equipment	DLWJ	13 472	12 222	12 805	11 745	12 003	10 847	14 155	4 380	5 781
Other machinery and equipment and cultivated assets	DLWM	45 538	44 426	43 119	51 034	50 425	38 755	39 921	38 689	42 297
Total	EQDS	172 414	178 567	186 600	199 548	196 760	166 401	171 815	167 569	166 509
Intangible fixed assets	EQDT	36 799	34 190	30 894	32 590	33 901	30 411	32 660	33 530	35 081
Costs associated with the transfer of ownership of non-produced assets	DFDW	27 899	30 069	36 265	40 075	22 316	15 414	16 681	14 819	15 384
P.51 Total gross fixed capital formation	NPQR	235 691	244 373	258 060	277 341	258 332	215 142	221 156	215 918	216 974

1 For the years before 2010, totals differ from the sum of their components.
2 Components may not sum to totals due to rounding.
3 Please note that the annual current price and chained volume measures for some asset and sector breakdowns may not may not be equal in the reference year (2010) due to rounding. These differences are well within the range of uncertainty on the estimates.

Source: Office for National Statistics, Blue Book 2013

Education

Chapter 20

Education

Educational establishments in the UK are administered and financed in several ways. Most schools are controlled by local authorities, which are part of the structure of local government, but some are 'assisted', receiving grants direct from central government sources and being controlled by governing bodies who have a substantial degree of autonomy. Completely outside the public sector are non.maintained schools run by individuals, companies or charitable institutions.

For the purposes of UK education statistics, schools fall under the following broad categories:

Mainstream state schools
(In Northern Ireland, grant-aided mainstream schools)

These schools work in partnership with other schools and local authorities and they receive funding from local authorities. Since 1 September 1999, the categories (typically in England) are:

Community – schools formerly known as 'county' plus some former grant-maintained (GM) schools

Foundation – most former GM schools

Voluntary Aided – schools formerly known as 'aided' and some former GM schools

Voluntary Controlled – schools formerly known as 'controlled'

Non-maintained mainstream schools

These consist of:

(a) Independent schools

Schools which charge fees and may also be financed by individuals, companies or charitable institutions. These include Direct Grant schools, where the governing bodies are assisted by departmental grants and a proportion of the pupils attending them do so free or under an arrangement by which local authorities meet tuition fees. City Technology Colleges (CTCs) and Academies (applicable in England only) are also included as independent schools.

(b) Non-maintained schools
Run by voluntary bodies who may receive some grant from central government for capital work and for equipment, but their current expenditure is met primarily from the fees charged to local authorities for pupils placed in schools.

Special schools

Special schools provide education for children with Special Educational Needs (SEN) (in Scotland, Record of Needs or a Coordinated Support Plan), who cannot be educated satisfactorily in an ordinary school. Maintained special schools are run by local authorities, while non-maintained special schools are financed as described at (b) above.

Pupil Referral Units

Pupil Referral Units (PRUs) operate in England and Wales and provide education outside of a mainstream or special school setting, to meet the needs of difficult or disruptive children.

Schools in Scotland are categorised as Education Authority, Grant-aided, Opted-out/Self-governing (these three being grouped together as 'Publicly funded' schools), Independent schools and Partnership schools.

The home government departments dealing with education statistics are:

Department for Education (DfE)
Department for Business, Innovation and Skills (BIS)
Welsh Government (WG)
Scottish Government (SG)
Northern Ireland Department of Education (DENI)
Northern Ireland Department for Employment and Learning (DELNI)

Each of the home education departments in Great Britain, along with the Northern Ireland Department of Education, have overall responsibility for funding the schools sectors in their own country.

Up to March 2001, further education (FE) courses in FE sector colleges in England and in Wales were largely funded through grants from the respective FE funding councils. In April 2001, however, the Learning and Skills Council (LSC) took over the responsibility for funding the FE sector in England, and the National Council for Education and Training for Wales (part of Education and Learning Wales – ELWa) did so for Wales. The Apprenticeships, Skills, Children and Learning Act 2009 received Royal Assent on 12 November 2009 for the dissolution of the Learning and Skills Council by 2010 and the transfer of its functions on 1 April 2010 to local authorities and two new agencies: the Young People's Learning Agency (YPLA) and the Skills Funding Agency. The YPLA champions young people's learning by providing financial support to young learners; by funding academies, general FE and sixth form colleges and other 16 to 19 providers; and supporting local authorities to secure sufficient education and training places for all 16 to 19 year olds in England. The Skills Funding Agency funds further education colleges and training providers in England to deliver adult skills and apprenticeships. In Wales, the National Council – ELWa, funds FE provision made by FE institutions via a third party or sponsored arrangements. The Scottish Further Education Funding Council (SFEFC) funds FE colleges in Scotland, while the Department for Employment and Learning funds FE colleges in Northern Ireland.

From 1 April 2012, funding for the education and training of 3 to 19 year olds in England will become the responsibility of the Education Funding Agency (EFA), which will be a new executive agency of the Department for Education. The EFA will directly fund academies, free schools, university technology colleges, studio schools and 16 to 19 providers. It will distribute funding to local authorities for them to pass on to their maintained schools and it will also be responsible for the distribution of capital funding.

Higher education (HE) courses in higher education establishments are largely publicly funded through block grants from the HE funding councils in England and Scotland, the Higher Education Council – ELWa in Wales, and the Department for Employment and Learning in Northern Ireland. In addition, some designated HE (mainly HND/HNC Diplomas and Certificates of HE) is also funded by these sources. The FE sources mentioned above fund the remainder.

Statistics for the separate systems obtained in England, Wales, Scotland and Northern Ireland are collected and processed separately in accordance with the particular needs of the responsible departments. Since 1994/95 the Higher Education Statistics Agency (HESA) has undertaken the data collection for all higher education institutions (HEIs) in the UK. This includes the former Universities Funding Council (UFC) funded UK universities previously collected by the Universities Statistical Record. There are some structural differences in the information collected for schools, FE and HE in each of the four home countries and in some tables the GB/UK data presented are amalgamations from sources that are not entirely comparable.

Stages of education

There are five stages of education: early years, primary, secondary, FE and HE, and education is compulsory for all children between the ages of 5 (4 in Northern Ireland) and 16. The non-compulsory fourth stage, FE, covers non-advanced education, which can be taken at further (including tertiary) education colleges, HE institutions (HEIs) and increasingly in secondary schools. The fifth stage, HE, is study beyond GCE A levels and their equivalent which, for most full-time students, takes place in universities and other HEIs.

Early years education

Children under 5 attend a variety of settings including state nursery schools, nursery classes within primary schools and, in England and Wales, reception classes within primary schools, as well as s ettings outside the state sector such as voluntary pre-schools or privately run nurseries. In recent years there has been a major expansion of early years education, and the Education Act 2002 extended the National Curriculum for England to include the foundation stage. The foundation stage was introduced in September 2000, and covered children's education from the age of 3 to the end of the reception year, when most are just 5 and some almost 6 years old. The Early Years Foundation Stage (EYFS), came into force in September 2008, and is a single regulatory and quality framework for the provision of learning, development and care for children in all registered early years settings between birth and the academic year in which they turn 5.

Children born in Scotland between March and December are eligible for early years education at the time the Pre-School Education and Day Care Census is carried out. In Scotland, early years education is called ante-pre-school education for those aged 3 to 4 years old, and pre-school education for those aged 4.

Primary education

The primary stage covers three age ranges: nursery (under 5), infant (5 to 7 or 8) and junior (up to 11 or 12) but in Scotland and Northern Ireland there is generally no distinction between infant and junior schools. Most public sector primary schools take both boys and girls in mixed classes. It is usual to transfer straight to secondary school at age 11 (in England, Wales and Northern Ireland) or 12 (in Scotland), but in England some children make the transition via middle schools catering for various age ranges between 8 and 14. Depending on their individual age ranges middle schools are classified as either primary or secondary.

Secondary education

Public provision of secondary education in an area may consist of a combination of different types of school, the pattern reflecting historical circumstance and the policy adopted by the local authority. Comprehensive schools largely admit pupils without reference to ability or aptitude and cater for all the children in a neighbourhood, but in some areas they co.exist with grammar, secondary modern or technical schools. In 2005/06, 88 per cent of secondary pupils in England attended comprehensive schools while all secondary schools in Wales are comprehensive schools.

The majority of education authority secondary schools in Scotland are comprehensive in character and offer six years of secondary education; however, in remote areas there are several two-year and four-year secondary schools.

In Northern Ireland, post-primary education is provided by grammar schools and non-selective secondary schools.

In England, the Specialist Schools Programme helps schools, in partnership with private sector sponsors and supported by additional government funding, to establish distinctive identities through their chosen specialisms and achieve their targets to raise standards. Specialist schools have a special focus on their chosen subject area but must meet the National Curriculum requirements and deliver a broad and balanced education to all pupils. Any maintained secondary school in England can apply to be designated as a specialist school in one of ten specialist areas: arts, business & enterprise, engineering, humanities, languages, mathematics & computing, music, science, sports and technology. Schools can also combine any two specialisms.

Academies, operating in England, are publicly funded independent local schools that provide free education. They are all-ability schools established by sponsors from business, faith or voluntary groups working with partners from the local community.

Academies benefit from greater freedoms to help innovate and raise standards. These include freedom from local authority control, ability to set pay and conditions for staff, freedom from following the National Curriculum and the ability to change the lengths of terms and school days.

The Academies Programme was first introduced in March 2000 with the objective of replacing poorly performing schools. Academies were established and driven by external sponsors, to achieve a transformation in education performance.

The Academies Programme was expanded through legislation in the Academies Act 2010. This enables all maintained primary, secondary and special schools to apply to become an Academy. The early focus is on schools rated outstanding by Ofsted and the first of these new academies opened in September 2010. These schools do not have a sponsor but instead are expected to work with underperforming schools to help raise standards.

Special schools

Special schools (day or boarding) provide education for children who require specialist support to complete their education, for example because they have physical or other difficulties. Many pupils with special educational needs are educated in mainstream schools. All children attending special schools are offered a curriculum designed to overcome their learning difficulties and to enable them to become self-reliant. Since December 2005, special schools have also been able to apply for the Special Educational Needs (SEN) specialism, under the Specialist Schools Programme. They can apply for a curriculum specialism, but not for both the SEN and a curriculum specialism.

Further education

The term further education may be used in a general sense to cover all non.advanced courses taken after the period of compulsory education, but more commonly it excludes those staying on at secondary school and those in higher education, that is, courses in universities and colleges leading to qualifications above GCE A Level, Scottish Certificate of Education (SCE) Higher Grade, GNVQ/NVQ level 3, and their equivalents. Since 1 April 1993, sixth form colleges in England and Wales have been included in the further education sector.

Higher education

Higher education is defined as courses that are of a standard that is higher than GCE A level, the Higher Grade of the SCE/National Qualification, GNVQ/NVQ level 3 or the Edexcel (formerly BTEC) or SQA National Certificate/Diploma. There are three main levels of HE course:

(i) Postgraduate courses leading to higher degrees, diplomas and certificates (including postgraduate certificates of education (PGCE) and professional qualifications) which usually require a first degree as entry qualification.

(ii) Undergraduate courses which include first degrees, first degrees with qualified teacher status, enhanced first degrees, first degrees obtained concurrently with a diploma, and intercalated first degrees (where first degree students, usually in medicine, dentistry or veterinary medicine, interrupt their studies to complete a one-year course of advanced studies in a related topic).

(iii) Other undergraduate courses which include all other higher education courses, for example HNDs and Diplomas in HE.

As a result of the Further and Higher Education Act 1992, former polytechnics and some other HEIs were designated as universities in 1992/93. Students normally attend HE courses at HEIs, but some attend at FE colleges. Some also attend institutions which do not receive public grant (such as the University of Buckingham) and these numbers are excluded from the tables. However, the University of Buckingham is included in Tables 20.6 and 20.7.

20.1 Number of schools, by type of school - time series

United Kingdom   **Numbers**

	Academic years				
	1990/91	1995/96	2000/01	2010/11	2011/12
UNITED KINGDOM					
Public sector mainstream					
Nursery[1]	1,364	1,486	3,228	3,130	3,095
Primary	24,135	23,441	22,902	21,281	21,165
Middle [13]	.	.	.	.	.
Secondary[2,3,4]	4,797	4,478	4,352	4,121	4,072
of which Middle deemed secondary	491	400	316	225	196
Non-maintained mainstream	2,501	2,485	2,397	2,498	2,502
Special schools	1,830	1,560	1,498	1,293	1,281
of which state-funded	..	1,456	1,401	1,218	1,209
of which non-maintained	..	104	97	75	72
Pupil referral units	.	315	338	427	403
ALL SCHOOLS	34,627	33,765	34,715	32,750	32,518
ENGLAND					
Public sector mainstream					
Maintained nursery	566	547	506	423	423
State-funded primary[9]	19,047	18,480	18,069	16,884	16,818
State-funded secondary[2,3,4]	3,904	3,609	3,496	3,310	3,268
of which Middle deemed secondary	491	400	316	225	196
Non-maintained mainstream[10]	2,282	2,251	2,190	2,417	2,421
Special schools	1,380	1,263	1,175	1,046	1,039
of which state-funded[11]	..	1,191	1,113	971	967
of which non-maintained	..	72	62	75	72
Pupil referral units	.	291	308	427	403
ALL SCHOOLS	27,179	26,441	25,744	24,507	24,372
WALES					
Public sector mainstream					
Nursery	54	52	41	23	22
Primary	1,717	1,681	1,631	1,435	1,412
Middle [13]	.	.	.	.	.
Secondary[3,5]	230	228	229	222	221
Non-maintained mainstream	71	62	54	66	66
Special (maintained)	61	54	45	43	43
Pupil referral units	.	24	30	..	..
ALL SCHOOLS	2,133	2,101	2,030	1,789	1,764
SCOTLAND					
Public sector mainstream					
Nursery[1,12]	659	796	2,586	2,586	2,553
Primary	2,372	2,332	2,278	2,099	2,081
Secondary[5]	424	405	389	372	367
Non-maintained mainstream[8]	131	151	127	..	..
Special schools	343	196	230	163	158
of which maintained	343	164	195	163	158
of which non-maintained[8]	.	32	35	..	..
ALL SCHOOLS	3,929	3,880	5,610	5,220	5,159
NORTHERN IRELAND					
Grant aided mainstream					
Nursery[6]	85	91	95	98	97
Primary[7]	999	948	924	863	854
Secondary	239	236	238	217	216
Non-maintained mainstream	17	21	26	15	15
Special (maintained)	46	47	48	41	41
ALL SCHOOLS	1,386	1,343	1,331	1,234	1,223

Sources: Department for Education; Welsh Government; Scottish Government; Northern Ireland Department of Education

1 Nursery schools figures for Scotland prior to 1998/99 only include data for Local Authority pre-schools. Data thereafter include partnership pre-schools.
  From 2005/06, figures exclude pre-school education centres not in partnership with the local authority.
2 Time series revised to show State-funded secondary schools (i.e. including CTCs and Academies, previously included in the 'Non-maintained mainstream' category).
3 From 1993/94, excludes sixth form colleges in England and Wales which were reclassified as further education colleges on 1 April 1993.
  In 1990/91, there were 114 sixth form colleges in England and 2 in Wales.
4 In England includes secondary sponsor-led academies, secondary converter academies and secondary free schools.
5 All secondary schools are classed as Comprehensive.
6 Excludes voluntary and private pre-school education centres.
7 From 1995/96, includes Preparatory Departments in Grammar Schools.
8 Figures for non-maintained schools are not available as the relevant publication was discontinued in 2010.
9 In England includes middle deemed primary schools as well as primary sponsor-led academies, primary convertor academies and primary free schools
10 In England includes direct grant nurseries.
11 In England includes special converter academies. Excludes general hospital schools.
12 In Scotland, there was a change in the timing of the Pre-School Education Census in 2010 from January to September. Please note that due to changes in timing, figures for
  September 2010 (provided for 2010/11) may not be directly comparable with previously published January figures. For 2010/11, September 2010 census figure provided.
  For 2011/12, September 2011 census figure provided. For 2012/13, September 2012 census figure provided.

20.2 Full-time and part-time pupils by age, gender[1,2] and school type, 2012/13

United Kingdom   Thousands

| | Maintained schools[3] | | | | | | | | | Non-maintained[13] | | | |
| | Primary Schools[15,16,18] | | | | Middle Schools[19] | Secondary Schools[7,15] | Special schools[17] | Pupil Referral Units[8] | All maintained schools | Special schools | Other Schools[9] | All non-maintained schools | All schools |
	Nursery Schools[4,5,14,20]	Nursery Classes	Other Classes[6]	Total[16]									
Age at 31 August 2012[10]													
All													
2-4[11]	139.6	285.8	609.9	1,030.3	0.2	6.1	6.2	-	1,182.4	0.1	65.5	65.6	1,248.0
5[12]	4.4	-	641.7	718.3	0.1	3.3	4.3	-	730.5		29.4	29.4	759.9
6	-	0.0	625.7	699.9	0.1	3.0	4.7	-	707.7	0.1	29.8	29.9	737.5
7	0.0	0.0	609.0	683.9	0.1	2.7	5.4	0.1	692.2	0.1	31.7	31.8	724.0
8	0.0	0.0	597.0	670.0	0.1	2.6	5.7	0.1	678.5	0.1	34.2	34.3	712.8
9	0.0	0.0	565.5	636.1	0.1	17.3	6.2	0.2	659.9	0.1	35.2	35.4	695.3
10	0.0	0.0	542.5	610.8	0.1	20.4	6.6	0.2	638.1	0.2	35.6	35.7	673.9
11	0.0	0.0	53.9	54.0	0.5	574.6	9.6	0.2	638.8	0.3	42.6	42.9	681.7
12	0.0	0.0	5.2	5.2	0.5	635.0	10.3	0.6	651.6	0.4	43.9	44.2	695.8
13	0.0	0.0	0.2	0.2	0.4	656.1	11.1	1.2	669.0	0.4	47.4	47.8	716.9
14	0.0	0.0	0.2	0.2	0.5	662.9	11.6	2.6	677.7	0.5	49.4	49.9	727.5
15	0.0	0.0	0.2	0.2	0.5	672.0	12.0	6.3	691.0	0.5	52.0	52.5	743.5
16	0.0	0.0	-	-	0.2	297.5	5.9	0.1	303.8	0.4	41.5	42.0	345.8
17	0.0	0.0	-	-	0.2	240.0	4.7	0.1	245.0	0.4	39.9	40.4	285.4
18	0.0	0.0	-	-	-	27.0	3.6	-	30.7	0.3	7.8	8.1	38.8
19 and over	0.0	0.0	0.0	0.0	0.0	1.2	-	-	1.2	0.2	3.3	3.5	4.8
Total	**144.1**	**285.8**	**4,250.9**	**5,108.9**	**3.6**	**3,821.8**	**107.9**	**11.8**	**9,198.1**	**4.2**	**589.3**	**593.5**	**9,791.6**
of which													
England	38.7	277.1	3,720.9	4,306.0	.	3,191.3	92.0	11.8	7,639.7	4.2	579.7	584.0	8,223.7
Wales	1.4	..	..	264.2	3.6	191.3	4.3	..	464.9	0.0	8.9	8.9	473.7
Scotland	98.0	.	370.7	370.7	.	293.6	7.0	.	769.2	..	..	..	769.2
Northern Ireland	5.9	8.7	159.3	168.0	.	145.7	4.7	.	324.3	.	0.7	0.7	324.9
Males[1]													
2-4[11]	23.9	145.0	311.6	525.4	0.1	3.0	4.2	-	556.6	-	32.6	32.6	589.2
5[12]	-	-	327.6	366.6	-	1.7	3.1	-	371.6	-	14.9	14.9	386.5
6	-	0.0	319.5	357.4	-	1.5	3.3	-	362.3	-	15.0	15.0	377.3
7	0.0	0.0	310.6	348.9	0.1	1.4	3.9	0.1	354.3	0.1	16.2	16.3	370.5
8	0.0	0.0	304.8	342.1	-	1.3	4.1	0.1	347.7	0.1	17.5	17.6	365.3
9	0.0	0.0	288.4	324.4	0.1	8.9	4.5	0.2	338.1	0.1	18.3	18.4	356.5
10	0.0	0.0	276.0	311.0	0.1	10.4	4.9	0.2	326.5	0.1	18.2	18.4	344.9
11	0.0	0.0	27.6	27.7	0.2	291.8	6.9	0.1	326.7	0.2	21.8	22.0	348.7
12	0.0	0.0	3.2	3.2	0.2	321.8	7.5	0.5	333.3	0.3	22.5	22.8	356.1
13	0.0	0.0	0.1	0.1	0.2	333.2	8.1	0.9	342.5	0.3	24.3	24.6	367.2
14	0.0	0.0	0.1	0.1	0.2	336.2	8.4	1.8	346.7	0.4	25.4	25.8	372.4
15	0.0	0.0	0.1	0.1	0.2	339.8	8.7	4.2	353.0	0.4	26.6	26.9	379.9
16	0.0	0.0	0.0	0.0	0.1	144.3	3.8	0.1	148.3	0.3	21.6	21.9	170.1
17	0.0	0.0	-	-	0.1	112.7	3.0	-	115.8	0.3	20.4	20.7	136.5
18	0.0	0.0	-	-	-	14.4	2.3	-	16.7	0.2	4.5	4.7	21.4
19 and over	0.0	0.0	0.0	0.0	0.0	0.5	-	0.0	0.6	0.1	2.0	2.2	2.8
Total	**23.9**	**145.0**	**2,169.6**	**2,607.0**	**1.6**	**1,923.1**	**76.5**	**8.3**	**4,640.5**	**3.0**	**301.7**	**304.7**	**4,945.2**
of which													
England	20.1	140.6	1,898.9	2,196.6	.	1,605.9	65.5	8.3	3,896.4	3.0	296.7	299.7	4,196.1
Wales	0.7	..	..	135.3	1.6	96.7	3.0	..	237.4	0.0	4.6	4.6	242.1
Scotland	..	.	189.3	189.3	.	147.9	4.8	.	342.1	..	..	..	342.1
Northern Ireland	3.1	4.5	81.3	85.7	.	72.5	3.2	.	164.6	.	0.3	0.3	164.9
Females[1]													
2-4[11]	22.2	140.8	298.3	504.9	0.1	3.1	2.0	-	532.3	-	33.0	33.0	565.3
5[12]	-	-	314.1	351.7	-	1.6	1.2	-	354.5	-	14.5	14.5	369.0
6	-	0.0	306.3	342.5	0.1	1.5	1.4	-	345.4	-	14.8	14.8	360.2
7	0.0	0.0	298.3	335.0	-	1.3	1.5	-	337.9	-	15.5	15.6	353.5
8	0.0	0.0	292.2	327.8	0.1	1.3	1.6	-	330.8	-	16.7	16.7	347.5
9	0.0	0.0	277.1	311.7	-	8.4	1.7	-	321.8	-	16.9	17.0	338.8
10	0.0	0.0	266.5	299.8	0.1	10.0	1.8	-	311.6	-	17.3	17.4	329.0
11	0.0	0.0	26.2	26.3	0.2	282.9	2.7	-	312.1	0.1	20.8	20.9	333.0
12	0.0	0.0	2.0	2.0	0.2	313.1	2.8	0.1	318.3	0.1	21.4	21.5	339.8
13	0.0	0.0	0.1	0.1	0.2	322.9	3.0	0.3	326.5	0.1	23.1	23.2	349.7
14	0.0	0.0	0.1	0.1	0.3	326.7	3.2	0.8	331.0	0.1	24.0	24.1	355.1
15	0.0	0.0	0.1	0.1	0.3	332.2	3.3	2.1	338.0	0.1	25.5	25.6	363.6
16	0.0	0.0	-	-	0.1	153.2	2.1	0.1	155.5	0.1	20.0	20.1	175.6
17	0.0	0.0	0.0	0.0	0.1	127.3	1.7	0.1	129.2	0.1	19.5	19.7	148.9
18	0.0	0.0	-	-	-	12.6	1.4	-	14.0	0.1	3.3	3.4	17.4
19 and over	0.0	0.0	0.0	0.0	0.0	0.6	-	-	0.7	0.1	1.3	1.3	2.0
Total	**22.2**	**140.8**	**2,081.4**	**2,501.9**	**2.0**	**1,898.7**	**31.4**	**3.5**	**4,459.6**	**1.2**	**287.6**	**288.8**	**4,748.4**
of which													
England	18.7	136.5	1,822.0	2,109.4	.	1,585.3	26.5	3.5	3,743.4	1.2	283.0	284.2	4,027.6
Wales	0.7	..	..	128.9	2.0	94.6	1.3	..	227.4	0.0	4.2	4.2	231.7
Scotland	..	.	181.3	181.3	.	145.6	2.1	.	329.1	..	..	..	329.1
Northern Ireland	2.8	4.2	78.1	82.3	.	73.1	1.4	.	159.7	.	0.3	0.3	160.0

Sources: Department for Education; Welsh Government; Scottish Government; Northern Ireland Department of Education

1 In Scotland gender split is not collected by age but has been calculated according to figures collected in September each year. There are a small number of pupils for whom it has not been
possible to assign an age; these pupils are included in the Scotland total but excluded from the age breakdowns.

2 In Northern Ireland a gender split is not collected by age but is available by year group and so this is used as a proxy. For example pupils in Year 1 are counted as age 4, pupils in Year 2 are counted as age 5 etc.

3 Maintained school figures includes all state-funded schools (Grant-aided schools in Northern Ireland)

4 Excludes 8,410 children in total at voluntary and private pre-school centres in Northern Ireland in places funded under the Pre-School Expansion Programme which began in 1998/99.

5 For centres providing pre-school education in Scotland (this includes nursery classes within schools); children are counted once for each centre they are registered with. Only the
'All' figures are provided for pre-school education registrations in Scotland, as these cannot be split by gender.

6 Includes reception pupils in primary classes and, in Northern Ireland, pupils in preparatory departments of grammar schools.

7 Includes City Technology Colleges (CTCs) and Academies in England. Also includes secondary free schools, university technical colleges and studio schools.

8 England and Wales only. Figures exclude dually registered pupils. In PRUs also includes pupils registered with other providers and further education colleges. Includes alternative provision academies and
alternative provision free schools.

9 Includes pupils less than 2 years of age in England.

10 1 July for Northern Ireland, 28 February for maintained primary and secondary school pupils in Scotland and age at census date in January for pre-school education in Scotland.

11 Includes the so-called rising five's (i.e. those pupils who became 5 during the autumn term).

12 In Scotland, includes some 4-year-olds.

13 In Scotland figures for the Non-maintained sector have not been provided, the collection was discontinued in 2010.

14 In Scotland, there was a change in the timing of the Pre-School Education Census in 2010 from January to September. Please note that due to changes in timing, figures for
September 2010 (provided for 2010/11) may not be directly comparable with previously published January figures.   For 2010/11, September 2010 census figure provided.
For 2011/12, September 2011 census figure provided. For 2012/13, September 2012 census figure provided.

15 In England includes middle schools as deemed.

16 In England includes primary converter academies, primary sponsor led academies and primary free schools.

17 Includes general hospital schools. Also includes special converter academies, special sponsored academies and special free schools.   Hospital schools not included in Northern Ireland figures.

18 A Primary school breakdown by class type is not available in Wales.

19 In Wales, the Middle School for pupils of both primary and secondary school age was introduced in 2012/13.

20 In Scotland, from April 2012 funds were made available to allow local authorities to provide looked after two year olds with free early learning and childcare provision. This is the first year
information on under threes has been broken down to capture this data. The large increase in the number of under threes (from 4,290 in 2011 to 7,374 in 2012) suggests that some centres are
including children not recieving pre-school education and this figure is likely to be an overcount.

20.3 Pupil: teacher ratios (PTRs) and pupil: adult ratios (PARs) within schools, by type of school - time series

United Kingdom   **Numbers**

	Pupil: teacher ratio within schools[1]				Pupil: adult ratio within schools[2]		
	1995/96 [3]	2000/01	2010/11	2011/12	2000/01	2010/11	2011/12
United Kingdom							
Public sector mainstream							
Nursery schools[10]	21.3	23.1	17.2	17.7	..	..	..
Primary schools[5,12]	22.7	22.3	20.4	20.5	..	..	..
Middle[16]	.	.	.	.	..	..	..
Secondary schools[6,7]	16.1	16.5	15.3	15.3	..	..	..
Pupil Referral Units (PRUs)	..	..	3.5	3.1	.	.	.
Non-maintained mainstream schools	10.3	9.7	10.6	8.0	.	.	.
Special schools							
Maintained[15]	6.3	6.4	6.1	6.0	.	.	.
Non-maintained	.	.	..	..	.	.	.
All schools[8]	18.0	17.9	16.3	16.2	.	.	.
England[9,14]							
Public sector mainstream							
Nursery schools	19.2	17.7	16.1	16.7	6.8	..	4.9
State-funded primary schools[12]	23.2	22.9	20.9	21.0	15.7	..	11.9
State-funded secondary schools[6,7]	16.6	17.1	15.6	15.6	14.0	..	10.6
Pupil Referral Units (PRUs)	4.3	4.4	3.5	3.1	.	.	.
Non-maintained mainstream schools	10.2	9.7	10.6	8.0	.	.	.
Special schools							
State-funded[14]	6.7	6.7	6.4	6.3	.	.	.
Non-maintained	4.6	4.8	..	..	.	.	.
All schools	18.2	18.1	16.4	16.3	.	.	.
Wales							
Public sector mainstream							
Nursery schools	19.5	17.3	15.7	15.2	..	5.6	5.6
Primary schools	22.5	21.5	20.5	20.7	..	10.5	10.2
Middle[15]	.	.	.	.	..	.	.
Secondary schools[6]	16.0	16.6	16.6	16.7	..	12.0	11.9
Pupil Referral Units (PRUs)	..	..	..	..	.	.	.
Non-maintained mainstream schools	10.1	9.6	8.0	8.1	.	.	.
Special schools (maintained)	6.7	6.8	6.4	6.6	.	.	.
All schools[8]	18.7	18.4	17.8	17.9	.	.	.
Scotland							
Public sector mainstream							
Nursery schools[10]	24.3	28.5	..	..	..	..	..
Primary schools	19.5	19.0	15.8	16.0	..	11.4	11.7
Secondary schools	12.9	13.0	12.1	12.3	..	10.2	9.9
Non-maintained mainstream schools	11.0	10.1	..	..	..	.	.
Special schools							
Maintained	4.8	4.2	3.6	3.5	.	.	.
Non-maintained[13]	3.7	3.3	..	..	.	..	.
All schools	15.5	15.4	13.3	13.7	.	.	.
Northern Ireland[4]							
Grant-aided sector mainstream							
Nursery schools	24.1	24.4	25.9	26.1	..	..	..
Primary schools[5]	20.7	20.1	21.1	21.4	..	..	..
Secondary schools	14.8	14.5	15.0	15.2	..	..	..
Non-maintained mainstream schools	10.9	9.3	6.6	6.7	.	.	.
Special schools (maintained)	6.7	5.9	6.3	6.3	.	.	.
All schools	17.2	16.6	17.3	17.5	.	.	.

Sources: Department for Education; Welsh Government; Scottish Government; Northern Ireland Department of Education

1 The within-schools PTR is calculated by dividing the total full-time equivalent (FTE) number of pupils on roll in schools by the total FTE number of **qualified teachers** regularly employed in schools. The UK PTR excludes Pupil Referral Units and non-maintained special schools

2 The within-schools PAR is calculated by dividing the total FTE number of pupils on roll in schools by the total FTE number of **all teachers** and support staff employed in schools, excluding administrative and clerical staff

3 Nursery schools figures for Scotland exclude pre-school education centres and are not therefore directly comparable with figures from 1999/00

4 Since 2003/04, data on teacher numbers in Northern Ireland have been compiled on a new, improved basis. Pupil/teacher ratios in Northern Ireland from 2003/04 onward are not comparable with previous years.

5 Includes preparatory departments attached to grammar schools in Northern Ireland

6 Excludes sixth form colleges in England and Wales which were reclassified as further education colleges from 1 April 1993

7 From 2011/12, State-funded secondary schools (i.e. including City Technology Colleges (CTCs), secondary converter academies, secondary sponsor-led academies and secondary free schools in England, which were previously included under 'Non-maintained'). All through academies are included with secondary academies. Pupil adult ratio figure amended for 2011/12.

8 Excludes Pupil Referral Units as information on teachers is not collected for Wales

9 Teacher numbers up to and including 2009 are sourced from 'Form 618g' in January of each year. From 2010 onwards figures are derived from the 'School Workforce Census in November of each year and are not directly comparable with earlier data

10 Excluding pre-school education figures for Scotland as FTE pupil numbers are not available

11 The figures for Northern Ireland exclude temporary teachers i.e. teachers filling vacant posts, secondments or career breaks

12 Since 2011/12, includes primary converter academies, primary sponsor-led academies and primary free schools in England, previously included under 'Non-maintained

13 Figures on Non-maintained schools are not included, the collection was discontinued in 2010

14 Since 2011/12, includes special academies in England

20.4 Pupils with statements of Special Educational Needs (SEN) (1)

As at January each year: 2008-2012
England

	2008	2009	2010	2011	2012
ALL SCHOOLS					
Pupils with statements	227,315	225,400	223,945	224,210	226,125
Pupils on roll	8,121,955	8,092,280	8,098,360	8,123,865	8,178,200
Incidence (%) (2)	2.8	2.8	2.8	2.8	2.8
STATE-FUNDED SCHOOLS					
Maintained nursery					
Pupils with statements	265	285	265	250	305
Pupils on roll	37,440	37,285	37,575	38,830	39,395
Incidence (%) (2)	0.7	0.8	0.7	0.6	0.8
Placement (%) (3)	0.1	0.1	0.1	0.1	0.1
State-funded primary (4)(5)					
Pupils with statements	59,695	58,505	57,850	57,855	58,535
Pupils on roll	4,090,400	4,077,350	4,096,580	4,137,755	4,217,000
Incidence (%) (2)	1.5	1.4	1.4	1.4	1.4
Placement (%) (3)	26.3	26.0	25.8	25.8	25.9
State-funded secondary (4)(6)					
Pupils with statements	67,875	65,890	64,605	63,720	62,630
Pupils on roll	3,294,575	3,278,130	3,278,485	3,262,635	3,234,875
Incidence (%) (2)	2.1	2.0	2.0	2.0	1.9
Placement (%) (3)	29.9	29.2	28.8	28.4	27.7
Maintained special (7)					
Pupils with statements	83,600	84,295	85,445	86,660	88,230
Pupils on roll	87,135	87,615	88,690	89,860	91,590
Incidence (%) (2)	95.9	96.2	96.3	96.4	96.3
Placement (%) (3)	36.8	37.4	38.2	38.7	39.0
Pupil Referral Units (8)					
Pupils with statements	3,260	3,230	1,910	1,695	1,610
Pupils on roll	25,290	24,760	15,550	14,050	13,495
Incidence (%) (2)	12.9	13.0	12.3	12.1	11.9
Placement (%) (3)	1.4	1.4	0.9	0.8	0.7
OTHER SCHOOLS					
Independent (9)					
Pupils with statements	8,055	8,690	9,470	9,750	10,630
Pupils on roll	582,425	582,490	576,940	576,325	577,515
Incidence (%) (2)	1.4	1.5	1.6	1.7	1.8
Placement (%) (3)	3.5	3.9	4.2	4.3	4.7
Non-maintained special					
Pupils with statements	4,565	4,500	4,400	4,280	4,185
Pupils on roll	4,695	4,655	4,540	4,415	4,325
Incidence (%) (2)	97.3	96.7	97.0	97.0	96.7
Placement (%) (3)	2.0	2.0	2.0	1.9	1.9

Source: School Census

(1) Includes pupils who are sole or dual main registrations.

(2) Incidence of pupils - the number of pupils with statements expressed as a proportion of the number of pupils on roll.

(3) Placement of pupils - the number of pupils with statements expressed as a proportion of the number of pupils with statements in all schools.

(4) Includes middle schools as deemed.

(5) Includes all primary academies, including free schools.

(6) Includes city technology colleges and all secondary academies, including free schools. Includes all-through schools.

(7) Includes general hospital schools and special academies.

(8) Includes pupils registered with other providers and in further education colleges. Prior to 2010 includes dual subsidiary registered pupils.

(9) Includes direct grant nursery schools.

Totals may not appear to equal the sum of the component parts because numbers have been rounded to the nearest 5.

20.5 GCE, GCSE, SCE/NQ[1] and vocational qualifications obtained by pupils and students - time series

United Kingdom

Percentages and thousands

	1995/96	2000/01	2009/10	2010/11
All				
Pupils in their last year of compulsory education[2]				
England, Wales and Northern Ireland[8]				
Percentage achieving GCSE or equivalent				
5 or more grades A*-C[3]	45.5	51.0	73.6	78.7
5 or more grades A*-C incl English and Maths	..	..	52.9	58.5
Any Passes	..	..	98.9	99.1
Scotland[9]				
Percentage of pupils in S4, last year of compulsory education achieving				
5 or more qualifications at SCQF level 3 or better	..	90.7	92.4	92.7
5 or more qualifications at SCQF level 4 or better	..	76.8	78.3	78.8
5 or more qualifications at SCQF level 5 or better	..	33.8	36.1	36.4
Pupils/students in education[4,5]				
England, Wales and Northern Ireland[8]				
Percentage achieving GCE A Levels and equivalent[6,7]				
2 or more passes[9]	29.6	37.4	52.7	52.8
Population aged 17 (thousands)[11]	672.1	717.9	800.0	707.4
Scotland[10]				
Percentage of pupils from relevant S4 roll achieving				
3 or more qualifications at SCQF level 6 or better by end of S5	..	..	25	26.3
1 or more qualifications at SCQF level 7 or better by end of S6	..	..	14.6	15.8
Males				
Pupils in their last year of compulsory education[2]				
England, Wales and Northern Ireland[8]				
Percentage achieving GCSE or equivalent				
5 or more grades A*-C[3]	40.6	45.7	69.5	75
5 or more grades A*-C incl English and Maths	..	..	48.9	54.8
Any Passes	..	..	98.4	98.9
Scotland[9]				
Percentage of pupils in S4, last year of compulsory education achieving				
5 or more qualifications at SCQF level 3 or better	..	89.7	91.8	92.3
5 or more qualifications at SCQF level 4 or better	..	73.8	75.6	76.6
5 or more qualifications at SCQF level 5 or better	..	28.7	31.8	32.4
Pupils/students in education[4,5]				
England, Wales and Northern Ireland[8]				
Percentage achieving GCE A Levels and equivalent[6,7]				
2 or more passes[9]	26.7	33.4	47.3	48.0
Population aged 17 (thousands)[11]	345.8	366.6	411.0	364.0
Scotland[10]				
Percentage of pupils from relevant S4 roll achieving				
3 or more qualifications at SCQF level 6 or better by end of S5	..	..	21.6	22.6
1 or more qualifications at SCQF level 7 or better by end of S6	..	..	13.0	13.9
Females				
Pupils in their last year of compulsory education[2]				
England, Wales and Northern Ireland[8]				
Percentage achieving GCSE or equivalent				
5 or more grades A*-C[3]	50.5	56.5	77.9	82.6
5 or more grades A*-C incl English and Maths	..	..	57.1	62.4
Any Passes	..	..	99.4	99.4
Scotland[9]				
Percentage of pupils in S4, last year of compulsory education achieving				
5 or more qualifications at SCQF level 3 or better	..	91.7	92.9	93.1
5 or more qualifications at SCQF level 4 or better	..	79.9	81.1	81.1
5 or more qualifications at SCQF level 5 or better	..	39.1	40.5	40.6
Pupils/students in education[4,5]				
England, Wales and Northern Ireland[8]				
Percentage achieving GCE A Levels and equivalent[6,7]				
2 or more passes[9]	32.7	41.6	58.5	57.9
Population aged 17 (thousands)[11]	326.3	351.3	389.0	343.4
Scotland[10]				
Percentage of pupils from relevant S4 roll achieving				
3 or more qualifications at SCQF level 6 or better by end of S5	..	..	28.4	30
1 or more qualifications at SCQF level 7 or better by end of S6	..	..	16.3	17.7

Source: Department for Education; Welsh Government; Scottish Government; Northern Ireland Department of Education

1 National Qualifications (NQ) include Standard Grades, Intermediate 1 & 2 and Higher Grades. The figures for Higher Grades combine the new NQ Higher and the old SCE Higher and include Advanced Highers.

2 Pupils aged 15 at the start of the academic year; pupils in Year S4 in Scotland; Year 12 Pupils in Northern Ireland. From 2004/05, pupils at the end of Key Stage 4 in England.

3 Standard Grades 1-3/Intermediate 2 A-C/Intermediate 1 A in Scotland for 2009/10 and earlier.

4 Pupils in schools and students in further education institutions generally aged 16-18 at the start of the academic year in England, Wales and Northern Ireland as a percentage of the 17-year-old population. Data from 2002/03 for Wales and Northern Ireland, however, relate to schools only. Pupils in Scotland generally sit Highers one year earlier than those sitting A levels in the rest of the UK, and the figures relate to the results of pupils in Year S5/S6.

5 Figures, other than for Scotland, include Vocational Certificates of Education (VCE) and, previously, Advanced level GNVQ, which is equivalent to 2 GCE A levels or AS equivalents.   From 2005/06, figures included for England cover achievements in all Level 3 qualifications approved under Section 96 of the Learning and Skills Act (2000), therefore UK aggregates are not comparable with previous years.

6 2 AS levels or 2 Highers/1 Advanced Higher or 1 each in Scotland, count as 1 A level pass for 2009/10 and earlier.

7 3 or more SCE/NQ Higher Grades/2 or more Advanced Highers/1 Advanced Higher with 2 or more Higher Passes in Scotland for 2009/10 and earlier.

8 Also includes Scotland for 2009/10 and earlier.

9 In Scotland qualifications cover the Scottish Credit and Qualifications Framework (SCQF) levels 3-5. Standard Grades span SCQF levels 3-5 depending on the results, whereas Intermediate 1 is at SCQF level 4 and Intermediate 2 is at SCQF level 5

10 In Scotland, pupils stay on into S5 and S6 to take additional qualifications or qualifications at a higher level. Most pupils will take Highers, SCQF level 5 qualifications in S5. If pupils stay on into S6 they may take more highers and/or Advanced Higher qualifications (SCQF level 7). Not all schools offer advanced highers and pupils can enter university with Highers

11 For 2011/12, based on mid-2010 based population projections. These do not take into account the 2011 UK Census. Census-based estimates following the publication of mid-2012 will not be available until after the UK volume is published.

Notes on population data

1 National population estimates and projections are the responsibility of the Office for National Statistics.

2 It is ONS policy to publish population estimates rounded to at least the nearest hundred persons. Estimates are sometimes provided in units to facilitate further calculations. They cannot be guaranteed to be as exact as the level of detail implied by unit figures and should be re-rounded prior to further presentation or publication.

3 The data are Crown copyright. They may be reproduced freely within your organisation. They must not be used for sale or advertising purposes

Source: ONS mid-2010 based population projections adjusted within DfE to academic age at January. These will be superseded by ONS mid-2012 based population projections in November 2013.

Method: The age and count adjustment takes account of the actual distribution of births across the year, using monthly birth data for each nation.

The figures for UK are derived by summation of England, Wales, Northern Ireland and Scotland.

The figures for UK excluding Scotland are derived by summation of England, Wales and Northern Ireland.

This is an improvement to the method used in 2012, which only considered the distribution of births at a UK level.

Differences from the previous method are small - less than 10 persons at the UK level.

20.6 Qualifications obtained by students on HE courses at HEIs in the UK by gender, subject area and level of qualification obtained 2008/09 to 2012/13

	2008/09	2009/10	2010/11	2011/12							
				Postgraduate			Undergraduate				
	All levels	All levels	All levels	Postgraduate research	Postgraduate taught	Total postgraduate	First degree	Foundation degree	Other undergraduate	Total undergraduate	All levels
Female											
Medicine & dentistry	9340	9705	10145	1305	3495	4800	5515	0	330	5850	10650
Subjects allied to medicine	65345	65535	66695	950	11730	12680	30085	2125	23575	55785	68470
Biological sciences	29395	31155	33210	1990	6890	8880	22290	700	2580	25570	34450
Veterinary science	760	740	820	50	110	160	715	0	0	715	875
Agriculture & related subjects	3020	3215	3860	110	695	805	1730	715	385	2830	3635
Physical sciences	9815	10030	10840	1110	2345	3455	6590	235	825	7650	11110
Mathematical sciences	3735	3970	4445	180	780	965	3215	0	540	3755	4720
Computer science	5270	5445	5860	225	2025	2250	2635	190	675	3500	5750
Engineering & technology	6805	7545	8315	730	3510	4240	3680	205	470	4355	8595
Architecture, building & planning	6560	7315	7270	150	3065	3215	3195	195	730	4125	7340
Total - Science subject areas	**140050**	**144660**	**151465**	**6805**	**34645**	**41450**	**79655**	**4365**	**30115**	**114135**	**155590**
Percentage - Science subject areas	**36%**	**36%**	**35%**	**61%**	**26%**	**29%**	**36%**	**27%**	**46%**	**38%**	**35%**
Social studies	39800	42770	44920	1075	12700	13775	23495	2140	6845	32480	46255
Law	18150	18470	19080	235	6730	6965	10935	75	1610	12620	19585
Business & administrative studies	53375	58355	64445	415	29520	29935	30715	1970	7030	39715	69655
Mass communications & documentation	9370	9590	11125	85	4220	4305	6730	220	560	7510	11815
Languages	22435	22750	25035	875	4700	5570	16650	5	3120	19775	25345
Historical & philosophical studies	13265	13185	14110	705	2960	3665	9675	270	1395	11335	15000
Creative arts & design	30905	33150	35905	315	6650	6965	25705	2360	2725	30790	37755
Education	55580	58760	60335	680	29820	30500	15405	4990	10535	30930	61430
Combined	3775	4180	3870	0	70	70	2920	0	1115	4030	4100
Total - All subject areas	**386700**	**405865**	**430295**	**11190**	**132015**	**143205**	**221885**	**16390**	**65045**	**303320**	**446520**
Male											
Medicine & dentistry	6290	6760	7190	1040	2220	3260	4155	0	135	4290	7555
Subjects allied to medicine	15070	15480	16495	595	4510	5105	7200	875	4095	12175	17280
Biological sciences	16715	18215	19795	1275	3225	4500	13630	880	1960	16470	20970
Veterinary science	250	205	250	20	55	75	180	0	0	180	255
Agriculture & related subjects	2065	2135	2370	85	510	595	850	505	305	1660	2255
Physical sciences	13015	13565	15055	1840	2940	4780	8770	300	1255	10320	15100
Mathematical sciences	5590	6005	6415	425	1200	1625	4230	0	910	5140	6765
Computer science	21900	23675	25265	785	7420	8205	12590	885	3085	16560	24765
Engineering & technology	34725	38855	41230	2360	13585	15940	19915	1735	4490	26145	42085
Architecture, building & planning	13405	15385	15190	215	4420	4635	7405	445	1920	9770	14405
Total - Science subject areas	**129020**	**140285**	**149260**	**8645**	**40080**	**48725**	**78925**	**5635**	**18155**	**102715**	**151440**
Percentage - Science subject areas	**45%**	**45%**	**45%**	**67%**	**37%**	**40%**	**47%**	**52%**	**45%**	**47%**	**44%**
Social studies	23290	24440	26305	1075	8535	9610	14750	820	2310	17875	27485
Law	12795	12865	13295	220	5445	5665	6505	70	1245	7820	13480
Business & administrative studies	54655	61220	66825	600	32205	32805	28725	1860	6980	37565	70370
Mass communications & documentation	6390	7030	7855	90	1950	2040	5165	310	575	6050	8090
Languages	10015	10305	11390	600	1965	2565	6835	5	2095	8935	11495
Historical & philosophical studies	11760	11840	12720	970	2710	3680	8340	205	945	9490	13170
Creative arts & design	19645	20965	22300	360	4040	4400	15390	1465	2280	19135	23535
Education	17735	19515	19725	370	11010	11380	2495	380	4660	7535	18915
Combined	2400	2610	2565	0	25	30	1975	5	695	2675	2705
Total - All subject areas	**287710**	**311070**	**332245**	**12925**	**107960**	**120885**	**169105**	**10755**	**39940**	**219795**	**340685**

20.6 Qualifications obtained by students on HE courses at HEIs in the UK by gender, subject area and level of qualification obtained 2008/09 to 2012/13

	2008/09 All levels	2009/10 All levels	2010/11 All levels	2011/12							
				Postgraduate			Undergraduate				
				Postgraduate research	Postgraduate taught	Total postgraduate	First degree	Foundation degree	Other undergraduate	Total undergraduate	All levels
All sexes											
Medicine & dentistry	15630	16470	17335	2350	5715	8065	9670	0	465	10140	18200
Subjects allied to medicine	80415	81015	83190	1550	16240	17790	37290	3000	27675	67960	85750
Biological sciences	46110	49370	53000	3265	10115	13380	35920	1580	4540	42040	55420
Veterinary science	1010	945	1075	75	160	235	895	0	0	900	1135
Agriculture & related subjects	5085	5350	6235	190	1205	1395	2580	1220	690	4490	5885
Physical sciences	22830	23595	25895	2945	5285	8235	15360	535	2080	17975	26210
Mathematical sciences	9325	9975	10860	605	1980	2590	7445	0	1450	8895	11485
Computer science	27170	29120	31125	1010	9445	10455	15225	1075	3760	20060	30520
Engineering & technology	41530	46405	49550	3090	17090	20180	23595	1940	4960	30500	50680
Architecture, building & planning	19965	22700	22460	365	7485	7850	10600	640	2655	13895	21745
Total - Science subject areas	269075	284940	300725	15445	74730	90175	158580	9995	48275	216850	307025
Percentage - Science subject areas	40%	40%	39%	64%	31%	34%	41%	37%	46%	41%	39%
Social studies	63090	67210	71225	2145	21235	23380	38245	2960	9155	50355	73740
Law	30945	31335	32380	455	12170	12630	17440	145	2850	20440	33065
Business & administrative studies	108035	119575	131270	1015	61725	62740	59440	3830	14010	77280	140020
Mass communications & documentation	15760	16620	18980	175	6165	6340	11890	530	1140	13560	19905
Languages	32450	33050	36430	1475	6665	8135	23480	15	5210	28705	36845
Historical & philosophical studies	25030	25025	26830	1675	5670	7345	18015	470	2340	20825	28170
Creative arts & design	50545	54115	58205	675	10690	11365	41095	3825	5005	49920	61285
Education	73315	78280	80060	1050	40825	41875	17900	5370	15195	38465	80340
Combined	6175	6785	6435	0	95	100	4895	5	1810	6710	6810
Total - All subject areas(#2)	674415	716940	762540	24115	239975	264090	390990	27145	104985	523115	787205

20.6 Qualifications obtained by students on HE courses at HEIs in the UK by gender, subject area and level of qualification obtained 2008/09 to 2011/13

	2008/09 All levels	2009/10 All levels	2010/11 All levels	2012/13 Postgraduate research	Postgraduate taught	Total postgraduate	First degree	Foundation degree	Other undergraduate	Total undergraduate	All levels
Female											
Medicine & dentistry	9340	9705	10145	1330	3435	4765	5755	0	235	5990	10755
Subjects allied to medicine	65345	65535	66695	1075	12435	13510	31690	2080	23155	56930	70440
Biological sciences	29395	31155	33210	2165	7675	9840	23425	785	2640	26845	36685
Veterinary science	760	740	820	45	80	125	660	0	15	675	800
Agriculture & related subjects	3020	3215	3860	120	740	860	1840	830	390	3060	3920
Physical sciences	9815	10030	10840	1245	2325	3570	6790	255	785	7825	11395
Mathematical sciences	3735	3970	4445	205	910	1115	3490	0	405	3895	5015
Computer science	5270	5445	5860	255	1790	2045	2675	180	555	3410	5455
Engineering & technology	6805	7545	8315	735	3580	4315	3830	190	420	4440	8755
Architecture, building & planning	6560	7315	7270	140	3165	3305	3140	130	555	3820	7125
Total - Science subject areas	140050	144660	151465	7320	36130	43455	83290	4445	29150	116885	160340
Percentage - Science subject areas	36%	36%	35%	61%	27%	29%	37%	30%	49%	39%	36%
Social studies	39800	42770	44920	1095	13360	14455	24490	1870	5905	32265	46720
Law	18150	18470	19080	220	6790	7015	10995	55	1530	12580	19590
Business & administrative studies	53375	58355	64445	470	30450	30920	30700	1825	6390	38915	69835
Mass communications & documentation	9370	9590	11125	105	4385	4490	6455	200	500	7160	11645
Languages	22435	22750	25035	910	4845	5755	16980	10	2810	19800	25555
Historical & philosophical studies	13265	13185	14110	750	3150	3900	9490	200	1190	10880	14780
Creative arts & design	30905	33150	35905	365	7135	7500	26080	200	2400	30665	38165
Education	55580	58760	60335	800	29685	30485	15840	4230	8265	28335	58815
Combined	3775	4180	3870	0	55	55	2815	10	1145	3970	4025
Total - All subject areas	386700	405865	430295	12035	135990	148025	227130	15030	59285	301450	449470
Male											
Medicine & dentistry	6290	6760	7190	1055	2080	3135	4425	0	105	4530	7670
Subjects allied to medicine	15070	15480	16495	760	4005	4765	7790	860	4230	12875	17640
Biological sciences	16715	18215	19795	1345	3455	4795	15515	1040	2105	18660	23460
Veterinary science	250	205	250	30	45	70	190	0	0	190	260
Agriculture & related subjects	2065	2135	2370	110	520	630	935	540	275	1750	2380
Physical sciences	13015	13565	15055	2000	2715	4715	9610	240	1205	11055	15770
Mathematical sciences	5590	6005	6415	495	1305	1795	4940	0	695	5635	7430
Computer science	21900	23675	25265	785	5575	6360	12890	875	2755	16520	22880
Engineering & technology	34725	38855	41230	2495	11790	14285	20920	1685	4695	27300	41585
Architecture, building & planning	13405	15385	15190	215	4375	4590	6900	445	1665	9010	13600
Total - Science subject areas	129020	140285	149260	9285	35865	45150	84115	5680	17730	107520	152675
Percentage - Science subject areas	45%	45%	45%	67%	36%	40%	48%	56%	47%	48%	45%
Social studies	23290	24440	26305	1125	8500	9620	15615	530	2085	18230	27850
Law	12795	12865	13295	250	5200	5450	6500	40	1110	7650	13100
Business & administrative studies	54655	61220	66825	665	28890	29555	30190	1815	7090	39095	68650
Mass communications & documentation	6390	7030	7855	110	1810	1915	5155	280	515	5950	7870
Languages	10015	10305	11390	650	1980	2630	6790	5	1975	8770	11400
Historical & philosophical studies	11760	11840	12720	980	2750	3730	8655	160	895	9705	13440
Creative arts & design	19645	20965	22300	400	4045	4440	15410	1345	1805	18560	23000
Education	17735	19515	19725	400	11055	11455	2430	345	3730	6510	17965
Combined	2400	2610	2565	0	20	20	1740	5	645	2390	2410
Total - All subject areas	287710	311070	332245	13865	100110	113975	176595	10205	37580	224380	338355

20.6 Qualifications obtained by students on HE courses at HEIs in the UK by gender, subject area and level of qualification obtained 2008/09 to 2012/13

	2008/09 All levels	2009/10 All levels	2010/11 All levels	2012/13							
				Postgraduate			Undergraduate				
				Postgraduate research	Postgraduate taught	Total postgraduate	First degree	Foundation degree	Other undergraduate	Total undergraduate	All levels
All sexes											
Medicine & dentistry	15630	16470	17335	2385	5520	7900	10180	0	340	10520	18425
Subjects allied to medicine	80415	81015	83190	1840	16440	18275	39480	2940	27385	69805	88085
Biological sciences	46110	49370	53000	3510	11130	14635	38945	1825	4745	45515	60150
Veterinary science	1010	945	1075	75	120	195	845	0	15	865	1060
Agriculture & related subjects	5085	5350	6235	230	1260	1490	2775	1370	665	4810	6300
Physical sciences	22830	23595	25895	3250	5040	8285	16400	495	1990	18885	27170
Mathematical sciences	9325	9975	10860	700	2215	2915	8430	0	1095	9530	12445
Computer science	27170	29120	31125	1040	7370	8410	15565	1055	3310	19930	28340
Engineering & technology	41530	46405	49550	3230	15370	18600	24755	1875	5115	31740	50345
Architecture, building & planning	19965	22700	22460	355	7545	7900	10040	575	2215	12830	20730
Total - Science subject areas	**269075**	**284940**	**300725**	**16610**	**72000**	**88610**	**167420**	**10130**	**46885**	**224435**	**313045**
Percentage - Science subject areas	**40%**	**40%**	**39%**	**64%**	**30%**	**34%**	**41%**	**40%**	**48%**	**43%**	**40%**
Social studies	63090	67210	71225	2220	21865	24080	40115	2400	7990	50505	74585
Law	30945	31335	32380	470	11990	12465	17495	95	2645	20230	32695
Business & administrative studies	108035	119575	131270	1135	59345	60475	60890	3640	13480	78015	138490
Mass communications & documentation	15760	16620	18980	210	6195	6405	11615	480	1015	13110	19515
Languages	32450	33050	36430	1560	6825	8385	23770	15	4785	28670	36955
Historical & philosophical studies	25030	25025	26830	1730	5900	7635	18145	360	2085	20590	28220
Creative arts & design	50545	54115	58205	760	11180	11940	41495	3535	4210	49235	61175
Education	73315	78280	80060	1205	40740	41940	18270	4580	11995	34845	76785
Combined	6175	6785	6435	0	75	75	4555	15	1790	6355	6435
Total - All subject areas	**674415**	**716940**	**762540**	**25900**	**236115**	**262015**	**403770**	**25240**	**96875**	**525885**	**787900**

In this table 0,1, 2 are rounded up or down to the nearest multiple of 5. All other numbers are rounded up or down to the nearest multiple of 5.
Percentages are not subject to rounding. ".." represents a percentage calculated on a population of between 0 and 52 inclusive.

20.7 Qualifications obtained by students on HE courses at HEIs in the UK by gender, level of qualification obtained, mode of study and domicile 2008/09 to 2010/11

	2008/09 All modes	2009/10 All modes	2010/11 Full-time	Part-time	All modes
All UK HEIs					
Female					
Postgraduate research	9270	9820	8400	2040	**10440**
Postgraduate taught	101580	110510	79860	43015	**122880**
..of which Postgraduate Certificate in Education	14925	15690	13770	1125	**14895**
First degree	188925	198530	185740	23150	**208890**
Foundation degree	11590	15015	10010	6360	**16370**
Other undergraduate	75335	71990	27335	44380	**71715**
..of which Professional Graduate Certificate in Education	4540	4970	2935	1535	**4470**
Total female	**386700**	**405865**	**311345**	**118945**	**430295**
Male					
Postgraduate research	11300	11860	10450	2165	**12615**
Postgraduate taught	82410	94140	74265	31955	**106220**
..of which Postgraduate Certificate in Education	5780	6340	5850	470	**6320**
First degree	144795	152325	144980	15145	**160125**
Foundation degree	7260	9850	7590	3345	**10935**
Other undergraduate	41950	42895	19000	23350	**42350**
..of which Professional Graduate Certificate in Education	1975	2465	1410	780	**2185**
Total male	**287710**	**311070**	**256285**	**75960**	**332245**
All sexes					
Postgraduate research	20570	21680	18850	4205	**23055**
Postgraduate taught	183990	204650	154125	74975	**229100**
..of which Postgraduate Certificate in Education	20705	22030	19620	1595	**21215**
First degree	333720	350860	330715	38295	**369010**
Foundation degree	18850	24865	17600	9705	**27305**
Other undergraduate	117280	114885	46335	67730	**114070**
..of which Professional Graduate Certificate in Education	6515	7435	4345	2310	**6655**
Total all sexes	**674415**	**716940**	**567630**	**194910**	**762540**

In this table 0,1, 2 are rounded to 0. All other numbers are rounded up or down to the nearest multiple of 5.

Percentages are not subject to rounding. ".." represents a percentage calculated on a population of between 0 and 52 inclusive.

20.8: Students[1] in further[2] and higher[3] education - time series

United Kingdom

Further education	2007/08	2008/09	2009/10	2010/11	2011/12
All					
United Kingdom					
England - participation[4]	4,360.7	4,837.1	4,635.5	4264.9	4216.6
Wales[5]	223.5	218.1	187.3	212.7	211.3
Scotland	386.6	381.0	353.2	311	256.5
Northern Ireland	131.8	132.2	151.9	144.4	141.7
Males					
United Kingdom					
England - participation[4]	1,855.4	2,141.9	2,089.3	1941.2	1940.9
Wales[5]	91.9	83.2	79.6	94	92.1
Scotland	172.1	172.0	160.6	144.8	121.0
Northern Ireland	63.4	64.7	75.0	72.2	71.1
Females					
United Kingdom					
England - participation[4]	2,505.4	2,695.2	2,546.2	2323.7	2275.7
Wales[5]	131.7	117.8	107.7	118.7	119.3
Scotland	214.6	209.0	192.6	166.2	135.5
Northern Ireland	68.6	67.6	76.9	72.3	70.8

Higher education	2007/08		2008/09		2009/10		2010/11		2011/12	
	Full-time	Part-time	Full-time	Part-time	Full-time	Part-time	Full-time	Part-time	Full-time	Part-time
All										
Postgraduate	249.2	258.9	268.7	273.8	298.9	284.6	310.5	282.5	309.7	261.8
of which										
PhD & equivalent	58.2	22.8	58.6	23.1	61.4	23.9	65.5	24.5	69.5	25.5
Masters and Others	191.0	236.1	210.1	250.7	237.5	260.8	245	257.9	240.2	236.3
First Degree	1,117.1	205.0	1,154.0	214.6	1,215.9	222.7	1,258.0	224.7	1,319.8	241.3
Other Undergraduate	173.1	471.7	174.1	471.3	177.9	458.2	170.5	413.1	151.1	378.5
Total	**1,539.9**	**936.9**	**1,596.9**	**959.7**	**1,692.7**	**965.5**	**1,739.0**	**920.3**	**1,780.6**	**881.6**
Males										
Postgraduate	124.2	109.4	136.5	113.8	151.5	118.5	155.5	115.9	148.8	108.2
of which										
PhD & equivalent	31.9	11.5	32.1	11.6	33.4	11.7	35.7	12.0	38.0	12.4
Masters and Others	92.3	97.9	104.4	102.2	118.1	106.8	119.8	103.9	110.8	95.8
First Degree	507.2	82.3	524.7	86.5	553.3	91.2	573.9	92.9	601.9	100.0
Other Undergraduate	66.4	172.5	68.7	175.3	73.3	168.2	70.7	154	63.8	142.3
Total	**698.1**	**364.8**	**729.9**	**375.5**	**778.1**	**378.0**	**800.1**	**362.8**	**814.5**	**350.5**
Females										
Postgraduate	124.9	149.5	132.2	160.0	147.3	166.1	155	166.5	160.9	153.6
of which										
PhD & equivalent	26.3	11.3	26.5	11.5	27.9	12.2	29.8	12.6	31.5	13.1
Masters and Others	98.7	138.3	105.7	148.5	119.4	153.9	125.2	154	129.4	140.5
First Degree	609.9	122.7	629.3	128.1	662.6	131.4	684	131.8	717.9	141.3
Other Undergraduate	106.7	299.2	105.5	296.1	104.6	289.9	99.8	259.2	87.3	236.2
Total	**841.8**	**572.1**	**867.0**	**584.2**	**914.5**	**587.5**	**938.9**	**557.5**	**966.1**	**531.1**

Sources: Department for Business, Innovation and Skills; Welsh Government; Scottish Funding Council; Northern Ireland Department for Employment and Learning

1 Home and overseas students.

2 Further education (FE) institution figures are based on whole year enrolments (excluding England which are based on headcounts).

3 Higher education (HE) figures include Open University students. Part-time figures include dormant modes (up to 2003/04), those writing up at home and on sabbaticals. Full-time includes sandwich. Part-time comprises both day and evening, including block release and open/distance learning. In Scotland, full-time at HE level covers programmes of at least 480 hours of planned notional hours. Part-time includes short full-time, block/day release, evenings/weekends, assessment of work based learning, distance/locally based learning, college based private study, other open learning and flexible learning. In Wales, full-time learners are those with at least 450 guided contact hours in the academic year.

4 Learner Participation rate. Information on full-time and part-time learners in England is not available across all of the funding streams covered under Further Education.

5 From 2010/11, includes students in Wales FE colleges undertaking work based learning (WBL).

20.9 Students in higher[1] education by level, mode of study,[2] gender and subject group, 2011/12[3,4,5,9]

United Kingdom | Home and Overseas Students | Thousands

	PhD & equivalent[10]		Masters and Others[11]		Total Postgraduate		First degree[12]		Other Undergraduate[13]		Total higher education students	
	Full-time	Part-time	Full-time	Part-time	Full-time	Part-time	Full-time	Part-time	Full-time	Part-time	Full-time	Part-time
All												
Medicine & Dentistry	5.3	2.5	4.3	9.1	9.6	11.6	45.9	0.2	0.5	0.4	56.0	12.2
Subjects Allied to Medicine	3.5	2.4	11.7	39.6	15.2	41.9	116.7	25.3	37.3	65.2	169.2	132.4
Biological Sciences	10.4	2.3	11.0	9.3	21.4	11.6	131.6	23.5	5.0	7.0	157.9	42.0
Vet. Science, Agriculture & related	0.9	0.1	1.7	1.5	2.6	1.6	13.3	0.6	4.2	5.1	20.1	7.3
Physical Sciences	9.9	0.8	6.3	2.9	16.3	3.6	61.4	8.2	1.6	4.0	79.3	15.9
Mathematical and Computing Sciences	5.5	0.9	12.5	6.0	18.1	6.9	86.1	16.3	7.6	7.9	111.8	31.1
Engineering & Technology	10.6	1.4	19.1	10.9	29.7	12.3	89.9	13.1	9.2	14.6	128.8	40.1
Architecture, Building & Planning	1.2	0.5	7.4	6.2	8.6	6.7	28.9	6.9	3.6	5.4	41.0	19.1
Social Sciences (inc Law)	7.4	2.8	37.5	24.0	44.9	26.9	185.1	29.4	11.0	26.9	241.1	83.2
Business & Administrative Studies	3.5	2.4	65.1	43.1	68.6	45.5	181.3	23.7	19.1	39.3	269.0	108.5
Mass Communications & Documentation	0.5	0.3	7.0	3.2	7.5	3.5	40.0	1.4	2.7	1.0	50.2	5.9
Languages	3.7	1.3	8.1	4.5	11.8	5.8	82.4	12.6	2.6	20.9	96.8	39.4
Historical and Philosophical Studies	3.7	2.0	6.1	6.0	9.8	8.1	55.9	15.8	0.6	8.9	66.4	32.8
Creative Arts & Design	1.8	1.2	13.4	6.4	15.1	7.6	139.5	5.5	18.4	5.1	172.9	18.1
Education[6]	1.6	4.7	28.7	59.6	30.2	64.3	50.6	12.2	8.4	37.9	89.2	114.4
Other subjects[7]	-	-	0.1	1.4	0.1	1.4	4.5	35.9	3.1	52.5	7.7	89.8
Unknown[8]	-	-	0.3	2.6	0.3	2.6	6.6	10.6	16.4	76.3	23.3	89.5
All subjects	69.5	25.5	240.2	236.3	309.7	261.8	1,319.8	241.3	151.1	378.5	1,780.6	881.6
of which overseas students	32.9	5.8	143.7	27.3	176.6	33.1	189.5	9.2	10.6	16.8	376.8	59.0
Males												
Medicine & Dentistry	2.2	1.3	1.5	4.1	3.7	5.4	20.2	0.1	0.1	0.2	24.0	5.6
Subjects Allied to Medicine	1.5	0.8	3.3	10.2	4.8	11.0	25.1	4.9	5.6	10.3	35.4	26.2
Biological Sciences	3.8	0.8	3.8	2.9	7.6	3.7	53.1	6.9	3.2	2.2	63.8	12.7
Vet. Science, Agriculture & related	0.4	0.1	0.7	0.6	1.1	0.7	4.0	0.3	1.7	2.7	6.8	3.6
Physical Sciences	6.4	0.4	3.6	1.6	10.0	2.0	36.8	4.8	0.8	2.3	47.6	9.0
Mathematical and Computing Sciences	4.1	0.7	9.3	4.7	13.4	5.3	65.4	12.3	6.4	5.4	85.2	23.1
Engineering & Technology	8.0	1.1	14.9	8.8	22.9	9.9	76.4	11.9	8.1	13.4	107.5	35.2
Architecture, Building & Planning	0.7	0.3	4.3	4.0	5.0	4.3	19.4	5.5	2.7	4.0	27.1	13.8
Social Sciences (inc Law)	3.7	1.3	15.5	8.8	19.2	10.2	74.0	9.7	3.0	6.7	96.2	26.6
Business & Administrative Studies	2.0	1.5	32.9	23.4	34.9	24.9	93.0	11.4	8.9	18.4	136.8	54.8
Mass Communications & Documentation	0.3	0.1	2.1	1.1	2.4	1.2	17.7	0.6	1.6	0.5	21.7	2.3
Languages	1.5	0.5	2.5	1.4	4.0	1.9	24.5	3.5	1.3	8.5	29.8	13.9
Historical and Philosophical Studies	2.1	1.1	3.0	2.9	5.1	4.1	26.8	6.8	0.3	3.3	32.2	14.1
Creative Arts & Design	0.8	0.6	5.1	2.5	5.9	3.0	52.8	2.0	7.6	1.5	66.3	6.5
Education[6]	0.5	1.8	8.3	17.4	8.8	19.2	8.4	1.5	2.0	9.7	19.2	30.4
Other subjects[7]	-	-	-	0.6	-	0.6	1.7	13.9	1.9	19.9	3.7	34.4
Unknown[8]	-	-	0.1	0.9	0.1	0.9	2.5	4.1	8.8	33.3	11.3	38.2
All subjects	38.0	12.4	110.8	95.8	148.8	108.2	601.9	100.0	63.8	142.3	814.5	350.5
of which overseas students	18.8	3.1	70.2	15.5	89.0	18.6	94.4	5.3	5.8	7.9	189.2	31.7
Females												
Medicine & Dentistry	3.1	1.2	2.8	5.0	5.9	6.3	25.8	0.1	0.4	0.2	32.0	6.6
Subjects Allied to Medicine	2.1	1.5	8.4	29.4	10.5	30.9	91.6	20.4	31.7	54.9	133.8	106.2
Biological Sciences	6.6	1.5	7.2	6.4	13.8	7.9	78.5	16.6	1.8	4.8	94.1	29.3
Vet. Science, Agriculture & related	0.5	0.1	1.0	0.8	1.5	0.9	9.4	0.4	2.4	2.4	13.3	3.7
Physical Sciences	3.6	0.4	2.7	1.3	6.3	1.7	24.6	3.4	0.8	1.8	31.7	6.8
Mathematical and Computing Sciences	1.5	0.2	3.2	1.4	4.7	1.6	20.7	4.0	1.2	2.4	26.6	8.0
Engineering & Technology	2.5	0.3	4.2	2.2	6.7	2.5	13.5	1.2	1.1	1.3	21.3	4.9
Architecture, Building & Planning	0.5	0.2	3.1	2.2	3.6	2.4	9.5	1.5	0.9	1.4	13.9	5.3
Social Sciences (inc Law)	3.7	1.5	22.0	15.2	25.7	16.7	111.1	19.7	8.1	20.2	144.9	56.6
Business & Administrative Studies	1.5	0.9	32.2	19.7	33.7	20.6	88.3	12.3	10.2	20.9	132.2	53.7
Mass Communications & Documentation	0.3	0.1	4.8	2.1	5.1	2.3	22.2	0.8	1.1	0.5	28.5	3.6
Languages	2.2	0.8	5.6	3.2	7.7	3.9	57.9	9.2	1.3	12.4	66.9	25.5
Historical and Philosophical Studies	1.7	0.9	3.1	3.1	4.8	4.0	29.1	9.0	0.3	5.7	34.2	18.7
Creative Arts & Design	0.9	0.6	8.3	3.9	9.2	4.5	86.7	3.5	10.8	3.6	106.7	11.6
Education[6]	1.0	2.9	20.4	42.1	21.5	45.0	42.1	10.8	6.4	28.2	70.0	84.0
Other subjects[7]	-	-	0.1	0.8	0.1	0.8	2.7	22.1	1.2	32.6	4.0	55.4
Unknown[8]	-	-	0.2	1.7	0.2	1.7	4.1	6.6	7.6	43.0	12.0	51.2
All subjects	31.5	13.1	129.4	140.5	160.9	153.6	717.9	141.3	87.3	236.2	966.1	531.1
of which overseas students	14.2	2.6	73.5	12.0	87.7	14.6	95.3	4.5	5.9	10.3	188.9	29.4

Sources: Department for Business, Innovation and Skills; Welsh Government; Scottish Funding Council; Northern Ireland Department for Employment and Learning

1 Higher Education Statistics Agency (HESA) higher education institutions include Open University students.
The field "gender" has changed to be consistent with the MIAP common data definitions coding frame. Students of "indeterminate gender" are now included in total figures but not in separate breakdowns. "Indeterminate" means unable to be classified as either male or female and is not related in any way to trans-gender.
2 Full-time includes sandwich. Part-time comprises both day and evening, including block release and open/distance learning. In Scotland, full-time at HE level covers programmes of at least 480 hours of planned notional hours. Part-time includes short full-time, block/day release, evenings/weekends, assessment of work based learning, distance/locally based learning, college based private study, other open learning and flexible learning. In Wales, full-time learners are those with at least 450 guided contact hours in the academic year.
3 Figures for higher education (HE) institutions are based on the HESA 'standard registration' count. Figures for FE institutions and colleges are whole year enrolments.
4 Further education (FE) institution figures for England include Skills Funded Agency students only.
5 FE insititution figures for Wales are counts of unique learners. As a learner may pursue more than one course, only one subject per learner has been selected (based on the most recently started course of the learner where applicable). Students have been assigned a level on the basis of learning programme type. For the purpose of this table, HE learners are those pursuing a (non-WBL) overarching HE learning programme. (It excludes learners pursuing HE level activities within an FE or WBL programme.)
6 Including Initial Teacher Training (ITT) and In-Service Education and Training (INSET).
7 Includes Combined and general programmes and programmes not otherwise classified.
8 Includes data for higher education students in further education institutions in England, which cannot be split by subject group.
9 Figures for Northern Ireland further education colleges are professional and technical course enrolments rather than headcounts. Figures for Scotland do not include students with under 25% attendance rate.
10 Defined as 'Doctorate' in Scotland.
11 For Scotland includes masters (research/taught) and postgraduate diploma/certificate.
12 For Scotland includes first degree honours/ordinary
13 For Scotland includes 'SVQ or NVQ: Level 4 and Level 5,' 'Diploma (HNC/D level for diploma and degree holders),' and 'HND/C or equivalent.'

20.10 Qualified teachers by type of school and gender - time series

United Kingdom	(i) Full-time teachers									Thousands
	1990/91	1995/96[2]	2000/01[3,4]	2009/10	2010/11	2011/12				
						Total	of which			
							England[1]	Wales	Scotland[10,14]	Northern Ireland[11]
All										
Public sector mainstream										
Nursery[5,6] and Primary[15]	208.8	211.8	211.2	200.5	199.4	205.4	167.0	10.6	20.7	7.1
Secondary[7,12]	233.1	222.1	225.7	208.1	220.0	223.7	182.2	10.8	21.7	9.0
Non-maintained mainstream[13]	44.9	48.6	52.3	67.9	55.4	56.9	55.9	0.9	..	0.1
All Special[16]	19.0	17.2	16.5	15.0	14.8	15.4	12.5	0.6	1.7	0.6
All schools[9]	**505.7**	**499.7**	**505.7**	**491.5**	**489.6**	**501.4**	**417.7**	**22.8**	**44.1**	**16.8**
Males										
Public sector mainstream										
Nursery[5,6] and Primary[15]	37.7	35.5	32.1	29.9	30.2	31.9	26.9	2.0	1.7	1.2
Secondary[7,12]	120.7	107.9	102.9	86.1	90.4	91.2	74.9	4.3	8.7	3.3
Non-maintained mainstream[13]	20.6	21.1	21.3	27.6	22.3	22.8	22.4	0.4	..	0.0
All Special[16]	5.9	5.4	5.0	4.2	4.1	4.2	3.5	0.2	0.4	0.1
All schools[9]	**184.9**	**169.8**	**161.3**	**147.7**	**147.0**	**150.1**	**127.8**	**6.9**	**10.8**	**4.7**
Females										
Public sector mainstream										
Nursery[5,6] and Primary[15]	171.1	176.3	179.1	169.0	167.5	171.8	139.9	8.6	17.5	5.8
Secondary[7,12]	112.3	114.2	122.8	122.0	129.4	132.2	107.1	6.4	13.0	5.8
Non-maintained mainstream[13]	24.3	27.4	30.9	40.3	33.1	34.1	33.5	0.5	..	0.1
All Special[16]	13.1	11.8	11.6	10.8	10.7	11.2	9.0	0.4	1.3	0.5
All schools[9]	**320.8**	**329.9**	**344.4**	**342.2**	**340.7**	**349.3**	**289.5**	**16.0**	**31.8**	**12.2**

	(ii) Full-time equivalent (FTE) of part-time teachers									Thousands
	1990/91	1995/96[2]	2000/01[3,4]	2009/10	2010/11	2011/12				
						Total	of which			
							England[1]	Wales	Scotland	Northern Ireland[11]
All										
Public sector mainstream										
Nursery[5,6] and Primary[15]	..	19.1	21.9	37.8	39.3	40.1	32.9	2.9	3.5	0.8
Secondary[7,12]	..	17.7	16.7	25.3	27.2	27.7	22.7	1.9	2.4	0.6
Non-maintained mainstream[13]	..	8.9 [8]	10.2	13.0	13.0	12.7	12.3	0.4	..	0.0
All Special[16]	..	1.5	1.6	2.4	2.6	2.5	2.1	0.1	0.3	0.1
All schools[9]	**30.0**	**47.2**	**50.4**	**78.4**	**82.1**	**83.0**	**70.0**	**5.3**	**6.2**	**1.5**

Sources: Department for Education; Welsh Government; Scottish Government; Northern Ireland Department of Education

1 Teacher numbers up to and including 2009 are sourced from 'Form 618g' in January of each year and also from the 'Database of Teacher Records' in March of each year
 From 2010 onwards figures are derived from the 'School Workforce Census' in November of each year and are not directly comparable with earlier data. Totals include gender unspecified or not known, therefore totals may not equal the sum of component parts.

2 Includes 1994/95 data for Northern Ireland.

3 Includes 1999/00 pre-school data for Scotland.

4 Includes 2001/02 data for Northern Ireland.

5 From 2005/06, data for Scotland include only centres providing pre-school education as a local authority centre or in partnership with the local authority. Figures are not therefore directly comparable with previous years.

6 From 2005/06, for Scotland pre-school education centres, the total full-time equivalent (FTE) of General Teaching Council of Scotland (GTC) registered staff has been provided within the 'full-time' section only because information on full-time/part-time split is not available. Teachers are counted once for each centre they work for, so the number of teachers contains some double counting. However, as each centre calculates the teacher's FTE as the time they spend working in that centre, the FTE should not be double-counted. Full-time/part-time figures for 2004/05 are estimates based on the headcount of all GTC registered staff.

7 From 1993/94 excludes sixth form colleges in England and Wales which were reclassified as further education colleges on 1 April 1993.

8 Figures refer to Great Britain.

9 Excludes Pupil Referral Units (PRUs).

10 For Scotland pre-school education centres FTE staff, a gender split is not available. Gender figures for 2004/05 are estimates based on the headcount of all GTC registered staff.

11 The figures for Northern Ireland exclude temporary teachers i.e. teachers filling vacant posts, secondments or career breaks.

12 From 2010/11, State-funded secondary schools (i.e. including City Technology Colleges (CTCs), secondary converter academies, secondary sponsor-led academies and secondary free schools in England, which were previously included under 'Non-maintained'). All through academies are included with secondary academies.

13 For Scotland, figures on non-maintained schools are not included, the collection was discontinued in 2010.

14 For Scotland, due to the change in the timing of the Pre-school Education Census from January to September, nursery figures for September 2010 (provided for 2010/11) are not directly comparable with previously published January figures. This is because some centres may take on additional teachers, or teachers may have their hours increased, once new children become eligible and start receiving pre-school education from the start of the January term.

15 Since 2010/11, includes primary converter academies, primary sponsor-led academies and primary free schools in England, previously included under 'Non-maintained'.

16 From 2010/11, includes special academies in England.

this page is intentionally blank

Crime and Justice

Chapter 21

Crime and Justice

There are differences in the legal and judicial systems of England and Wales, Scotland and Northern Ireland which make it impossible to provide tables covering the UK as a whole in this section. These differences concern the classification of offences, the meaning of certain terms used in the statistics, the effects of the several Criminal Justice Acts and recording practices.

Recorded crime statistics
(Table 21.3)

Crimes recorded by the police provide a measure of the amount of crime committed. For a variety of reasons, many offences are either not reported to the police or not recorded by them. The changes in the number of offences recorded do not necessarily provide an accurate reflection of changes in the amount of crime committed.

The recorded crime statistics include all indictable and triable-either-way offences together with a few summary offences which are closely linked to these offences. The revised rules changed the emphasis of measurement more towards one crime per victim, and also increased the coverage of offences.

In order to further improve the consistency of recorded crime statistics and to take a more victim-oriented approach to crime recording, the National Crime Recording Standard (NCRS) was introduced across all forces in England, Wales and Northern Ireland from 1 April 2002. Some police forces implemented the principles of NCRS in advance of its introduction across all forces. The NCRS had the effect of increasing the number of offences recorded by the police and data before and after 2002/03 are not directly comparable.

For a variety of reasons many offences are either not reported to the police or not recorded by them. The changes in the number of offences recorded do not necessarily provide an accurate reflection of changes in the amount of crime committed.

Similarly, the Scottish Crime Recording Standard (SCRS) was introduced by the eight Scottish police forces with effect from 1 April 2004. This means that no corroborative evidence is required initially to record a crime-related incident as a crime if the victim perceived it as a crime. Again, the introduction of this new recording standard was expected to increase the numbers of minor crimes recorded by the police, such as minor crimes of vandalism and minor thefts and offences of petty assault and breach of the peace. However, it was expected that the SCRS would not have much impact on the figures for the more serious crimes such as serious assault, sexual assault, robbery or housebreaking.

The Sexual Offences Act 2003 introduced in May 2004 altered the definition and coverage of sexual offences. In particular, it redefined indecent exposure as a sexual offence, which is likely to account for much of the increase in sexual offences.

The Sexual Offences (Scotland) Act 2009 introduced in 1 December 2010 repealed a number of common law crimes including rape, clandestine injury to women and sodomy and replaced them with new statutory sexual offences. The Act created a number of new "protective" offences, which criminalise sexual activity with children and mentally disordered persons. Protective offences are placed into categories concerning young children (under 13) and older (13-15 years). The new legislation may result in some increases in Group 2 crimes. For example, the offences of voyeurism or indecent communication towards an adult would previously have been classified as breach of the peace. It is likely that the effect will be to change the distribution of these crimes among the sub classifications. For example, some crimes previously categorised as lewd and libidinous practices will now be classified as sexual assault. The standard breakdown provided in response to information requests on sexual offences has had to be revised to accommodate these changes. Details of changes are provided below.

Offences committed before 1 December 2010:

Rape & attempted rape includes:

- Rape
- Assault with intent to rape

Indecent assault includes:

- Indecent assault

Lewd and indecent behaviour includes:

- Public indecency

'Other' includes:
- Incest
- Unnatural crimes
- Prostitution
- Procuration and other sexual offences

Offences committed on or after 1 December 2010:

Rape & attempted rape includes:
- Rape
- Attempted rape

Sexual assault includes:

- Contact sexual assault (13-15 years old or adult 16+)

- other sexually coercive conduction (adult 16+)

- Sexual offences against children under 13

- Sexual activity with children aged 13-15

- Other sexual offences involving children aged 13-15

- Lewd and libidinous practices

Prostitution

- Offences relating to prostitution

'Other' includes:

- Incest
- Unnatural crimes
- Public indecency
- Sexual exposure
- Procuration and other sexual offences

Further information is available from Crime in England and Wales 2007/2008 (Home Office, Sian Nicholas, Chris Kershaw and Alison Walker, editors).

Court proceedings and police cautions
(Tables 21.4 to 21.8, 21.12 to 21.16, 21.19 to 21.20

The statistical basis of the tables of court proceedings is broadly similar in England and Wales, Scotland and Northern Ireland; the tables show the number of persons found guilty, recording a person under the heading of the principal offence of which they were found guilty, excluding additional findings of guilt at the same proceedings. A person found guilty at a number of separate court proceedings is included more than once.

The statistics on offenders cautioned in England and Wales cover only those who, on admission of guilt, were given a formal caution by, or on the instructions of, a senior police officer as an alternative to prosecution. Written warnings by the police for motor offences and persons paying fixed penalties for certain motoring offences are excluded. Formal cautions are not issued in Scotland. There are no statistics on cautioning available for Northern Ireland.

The Crime and Disorder Act 1998 created provisions in relation to reprimands and final warnings, new offences and orders which have been implemented nationally since 1 June 2000. They replace the system of cautioning for offenders aged under 18. Reprimands can be given to first-time offenders for minor offences. Any further offending results in either a final warning or a charge.

For persons proceeded against in Scotland, the statistics relate to the High Court of Justiciary, the sheriff courts and the district courts. The High Court deals with serious solemn (that is, jury) cases and has unlimited sentencing power. Sheriff courts are limited to imprisonment of 3 years for solemn cases, or 3 months (6 months when specified in legislation for second or subsequent offences and 12 months for certain statutory offences) for summary (that is, non-jury) cases. District courts deal only with summary cases and are limited to 60 days imprisonment and level 4 fines. Stipendiary magistrates sit in Glasgow District Court and have the summary sentencing powers of a sheriff.

In England and Wales, indictable offences are offences which are:

• triable only on indictment. These offences are the most serious breaches of the criminal law and must be tried at the Crown Court. 'Indictable-only' offences include murder, manslaughter, rape and robbery
• triable either way. These offences may be tried at the Crown Court or a magistrates' court

The Criminal Justice Act 1991 led to the following main changes in the sentences available to the courts in England and Wales:

• introduction of combination orders
• introduction of the 'unit fine scheme' at magistrates' courts
• abolishing the sentence of detention in a young offender institution for 14-year-old boys and changing the minimum and maximum sentence lengths for 15 to 17-year-olds to 10 and 12 months respectively, and
• abolishing partly suspended sentences of imprisonment and restricting the use of a fully suspended sentence

(The Criminal Justice Act 1993 abolished the 'unit fine scheme' in magistrates' courts, which had been introduced under the Criminal Justice Act 1991.

A charging standard for assault was introduced in England and Wales on 31 August 1994 with the aim of promoting consistency between the police and prosecution on the appropriate level of charge to be brought.

The Criminal Justice and Public Order Act 1994 created several new offences in England and Wales, mainly in the area of public order, but also including male rape (there is no statutory offence of male rape in Scotland, although such a crime may be charged as serious assault). The Act also:

• extended the provisions of section 53 of the Children and Young Persons Act 1993 for 10 to 13-year-olds
• increased the maximum sentence length for 15 to 17-year-olds to 2 years
• increased the upper limit from £2,000 to £5,000 for offences of criminal damage proceeded against as if triable only summarily
• introduced provisions for the reduction of sentences for early guilty pleas, and
• increased the maximum sentence length for certain firearm offences

Provisions within the Crime (Sentences) Act 1997 (as amended by the Powers of Criminal Courts Sentencing Act 2000) in England and Wales, and the Crime and Punishment (Scotland) Act 1997 in Scotland, included:

• an automatic life sentence for a second serious violent or sexual offence unless there are exceptional circumstances (this provision has not been enacted in Scotland)
• a minimum sentence of 7 years for an offender convicted for a third time of a class A drug trafficking offence unless the court considers this to be unjust in all the circumstances, and
• in England and Wales, the new section 38A of the Magistrates' Courts' Act 1980 extending the circumstances in which a magistrates' court may commit a person convicted of an offence triable-either-way to the Crown Court for sentence – it was implemented in conjunction with section 49 of the Criminal Procedure and Investigations Act 1996, which involves the magistrates' courts in asking defendants to indicate a plea before the mode of trial decision is taken and compels the court to sentence, or commit for sentence, any defendant who indicates a guilty plea.

Under the Criminal Justice and Court Service Act 2000 new terms were introduced for certain orders. Community rehabilitation order is the new name for a probation order. A community service order is now known as a community punishment order. Finally, the new term for a combination order is community punishment and rehabilitation order. In April 2000 the secure training order was replaced by the detention and training order. Section 53 of the Children and Young Persons Act 1993 was repealed on 25 August 2000 and its provisions were transferred to sections 90 to 92 of the Powers of Criminal Courts (Sentencing) Act 2000. Reparation and action plan orders were implemented nationally from 1 June 2000. The drug treatment and testing order was introduced in England, Scotland and Wales from October 2000. The referral order was introduced in England, Scotland and Wales from April 2000. Youth rehabilitation orders came into effect in November 2009 as part of the Criminal Justice and Immigration Act 2008. These changes are now reflected in Table 21.8.

Following the introduction of the Libra case management system during 2008, offenders at magistrates' courts can now be recorded as sex 'Not Stated'. In 2008 one per cent of offenders sentenced were recorded as sex 'Not Stated' as well as 'Male', 'Female', or 'Other'. Amendments to the data tables have been made to accommodate this new category.

The system of magistrates' courts and Crown courts in Northern Ireland operates in a similar way to that in England and Wales. A particularly significant statutory development, however, has been the Criminal Justice (NI) Order 1996 which introduced a new sentencing regime into Northern Ireland, largely replicating that which was introduced into England and Wales by the Criminal Justice Acts of 1991 and 1993. The order makes many changes to both community and custodial sentences, while introducing new orders such as the combination order, the custody probation order, and orders for release on licence of sexual offenders.

Abbreviations
(Tables 21.4a, 21.6a-c, 21.6d-f)

Every effort is made to ensure that the figures presented are accurate and complete. However, it is important to note that these data have been extracted from large administrative data systems generated by the police forces and courts.

As a consequence, care should be taken to ensure data collection processes and their inevitable limitations are taken into account when those data are used.

Abbreviation	Description
Total Proc Against	Total Proceeded Against
Proc Disc	Proceedings Discontinued
Proc Disc	Discharge Section 6 Magistrates' Courts Act 1980
Charge Wdrn	Charge Withdrawn
Charge Dism	Charge Dismissed
Comm For Trial	Committed for Trial
Comm For Sent	Committed for Sentence
Total For Sent	Total for Sentence
Abslt Disch	Absolute Discharge
Condl Disch	Conditional Discharge
CRO	Community Rehabilitation Order
YRO	Youth Rehabilitation Order
SO	Supervision Order
CPO	Community Punishment Order
ACO	Attendance Centre Order
CP & RO	Community Punishment Order and Rehabilitation Order
Curf Order	Curfew Order
Rep Order	Reparation Order
APO	Action Plan Order
DTTO	Drug Treatment and Test Order
Ref Order	Referral Order
Comm Order	Community Order
YRO	Youth Rehabilitation Order
SS	Suspended Sentence
DTO	Detention and Training Order
YOI	Young Offender Institution
Unsus Sent Impri	Unsuspended sentence of imprisonment
Imm Cust	Immediate Custody
ODW	Otherwise dealt with

21.1a Police officers in England and Wales, by police force area as at 31 March 2013

Police force	All officers (full-time equivalent)[1]			Officers available for duty (headcount)		
	Male	Female	Total	Male	Female	Total
Avon and Somerset	2,123	750	2,873	2,077	759	2,836
Bedfordshire	760	332	1,092	745	321	1,066
Cambridgeshire	1,004	379	1,384	997	368	1,365
Cheshire	1,451	562	2,013	1,420	544	1,964
Cleveland	1,132	331	1,463	931	255	1,186
Cumbria	728	392	1,121	720	387	1,107
Derbyshire	1,332	495	1,827	1,334	536	1,870
Devon and Cornwall	2,262	820	3,082	2,233	849	3,082
Dorset	984	317	1,301	962	327	1,289
Durham	975	386	1,362	950	381	1,331
Essex	2,353	958	3,311	2,296	961	3,257
Gloucestershire	851	348	1,198	841	349	1,190
Greater Manchester	5,228	1,974	7,202	5,111	1,859	6,970
Hampshire	2,391	1,005	3,397	2,312	985	3,297
Hertfordshire	1,347	606	1,953	1,322	599	1,921
Humberside	1,269	502	1,771	1,248	511	1,759
Kent	2,412	912	3,323	2,369	901	3,270
Lancashire	2,288	912	3,200	2,228	884	3,112
Leicestershire	1,544	545	2,089	1,519	542	2,061
Lincolnshire	832	299	1,130	813	290	1,103
London, City of	605	170	774	596	163	759
Merseyside	2,896	1,013	3,909	2,834	972	3,806
Metropolitan Police	22,856	7,542	30,398	22,439	7,344	29,783
Norfolk	1,145	399	1,544	1,130	409	1,539
Northamptonshire	893	375	1,268	884	388	1,272
Northumbria	2,716	1,034	3,750	2,662	1,009	3,671
North Yorkshire	989	381	1,370	966	381	1,347
Nottinghamshire	1,536	559	2,095	1,499	552	2,051
South Yorkshire	1,983	784	2,767	1,980	784	2,764
Staffordshire	1,343	487	1,829	1,331	481	1,812
Suffolk	874	320	1,195	863	330	1,193
Surrey	1,321	649	1,970	1,296	630	1,926
Sussex	1,999	848	2,847	1,976	862	2,838
Thames Valley	3,059	1,263	4,322	3,020	1,221	4,241
Warwickshire	585	220	805	575	208	783
West Mercia	1,498	590	2,087	1,453	570	2,023
West Midlands	5,363	2,252	7,615	5,296	2,233	7,529
West Yorkshire	3,564	1,498	5,062	3,517	1,488	5,005
Wiltshire	728	322	1,050	713	310	1,023
Dyfed-Powys	810	302	1,112	799	296	1,095
Gwent	979	398	1,377	963	385	1,348
North Wales	1,069	414	1,483	1,065	415	1,480
South Wales	2,106	756	2,862	2,088	750	2,838
Total 43 forces	94,182	35,401	129,584	92,373	34,789	127,162
Central service secondments	302	70	372	313	74	387
British Transport Police (BTP)	2,225	427	2,652	2,182	415	2,597
Total police officers	96,709	35,898	132,608	94,868	35,278	130,146
Total police officers (excluding BTP)	94,484	35,471	129,956	92,686	34,863	127,549

1. This and other tables contain full-time equivalent figures that have been rounded to the nearest whole number. Because of rounding, there may be an apparent discrepancy between totals and the sums of the constituent items.1

21.1b Special constables, as at 31 March 2013, and joiners/leavers in the 12 months to 31 March 2013, by police force area, gender and ethnicity

England and Wales

Police force	Total			Special constables Minority Ethnic			Joiners			Leavers		Number of staff[1]
	Male	Female	Total strength	Male	Female	Total	Male	Female	Total	Male	Female	Total
Avon and Somerset	385	183	568	10	2	12	39	32	71	75	46	121
Bedfordshire	136	60	196	6	3	9	19	16	35	25	12	37
Cambridgeshire	174	71	245	5	1	6	43	24	67	40	22	62
Cheshire	225	106	331	7	3	10	0	0	0	62	33	95
Cleveland	69	33	102	1	0	1	0	0	0	17	16	33
Cumbria	87	48	135	1	1	2	17	9	26	44	21	65
Derbyshire	209	82	291	8	1	9	14	10	24	61	25	86
Devon and Cornwall	368	230	598	3	2	5	58	53	111	48	26	74
Dorset	149	60	209	0	1	1	3	1	4	38	21	59
Durham	55	21	76	1	0	1	0	0	0	27	14	41
Essex	367	140	507	11	3	14	55	30	85	66	33	99
Gloucestershire	122	54	176	4	0	4	11	4	15	14	14	28
Greater Manchester	518	184	702	51	8	59	154	52	206	122	77	199
Hampshire	437	160	597	9	6	15	115	56	171	88	51	139
Hertfordshire	311	99	410	22	7	29	80	41	121	79	33	112
Humberside	212	139	351	3	3	6	55	46	101	44	45	89
Kent	282	82	364	13	3	16	53	24	77	67	39	106
Lancashire	287	114	401	12	2	14	87	49	136	67	28	95
Leicestershire	209	95	304	31	10	41	74	42	116	53	20	73
Lincolnshire	143	82	225	0	1	1	43	38	81	36	26	62
London, City of	56	25	81	6	1	7	0	0	0	14	2	16
Merseyside	361	205	566	11	3	14	85	65	150	91	78	169
Metropolitan Police	3,620	1,683	5,303	1,072	396	1,468	788	399	1,187	977	474	1,451
Norfolk	213	78	291	4	1	5	39	15	54	54	34	88
Northamptonshire	185	63	248	8	3	11	23	14	37	53	35	88
Northumbria	235	87	322	8	3	11	76	43	119	54	18	72
North Yorkshire	102	56	158	2	0	2	15	16	31	21	17	38
Nottinghamshire	252	129	381	16	7	23	67	46	113	75	42	117
South Yorkshire	189	117	306	6	6	12	26	19	45	36	31	67
Staffordshire	313	156	469	11	3	14	73	57	130	63	27	90
Suffolk	174	75	249	5	1	6	36	17	53	79	30	109
Surrey	199	74	273	8	4	12	10	7	17	51	28	79
Sussex	240	110	350	8	5	13	60	32	92	56	26	82
Thames Valley	530	211	741	31	10	41	149	62	211	137	52	189
Warwickshire	213	87	300	16	7	23	44	18	62	17	12	29
West Mercia	211	108	319	3	2	5	54	50	104	31	26	57
West Midlands	376	135	511	78	25	103	0	0	0	32	22	54
West Yorkshire	363	130	493	33	10	43	60	31	91	78	79	157
Wiltshire	185	111	296	5	2	7	35	21	56	35	18	53
Dyfed-Powys	132	61	193	1	0	1	15	8	23	11	9	20
Gwent	94	44	138	1	1	2	8	6	14	10	7	17
North Wales	89	47	136	0	1	1	6	3	9	22	8	30
South Wales	79	20	99	2	1	3	0	0	0	63	27	90
Total all 43 forces	13,156	5,855	19,011	1,533	549	2,082	2,589	1,456	4,045	3,133	1,704	4,837
British Transport Police (BTP)	196	27	223	21	1	22	43	9	52	54	9	63
Total special constables	13,352	5,882	19,234	1,554	550	2,104	2,632	1,465	4,097	3,187	1,713	4,900
Total special constables (excluding BTP)	13,156	5,855	19,011	1,533	549	2,082	2,589	1,456	4,045	3,133	1,704	4,837

1. Special constable figures are given as headcount measures.

21.1c Police forces strength:[1] by country and sex

As at 31 March

Numbers

		2000	2001	2002	2003	2004	2005	2006	2007	2008	2009	2010	2011	2012	2013
Northern Ireland															
Regular police[2,3]															
Strength:															
Men	**KERU**	6,844	6,227	6,057	6,171	6,108	6,016	5,992	5,949	5,761	5,669	5,548	5,371	5238	5085
Women	**KERV**	966	1,009	1,080	1,266	1,418	1,547	1,534	1,600	1,653	1,735	1,837	1,922	1907	1877
Reserve[4]															
Strength:															
Men	**KERW**	2,962	2,629	2,223	1,983	1,824	1,431	1,424	1,212	1,119	930	774	597	333	313
Women	**KERX**	607	556	510	453	485	410	402	400	382	345	311	283	247	222

1. All figures are full-time equivalent strength figures that have been rounded to the nearest whole

2 Does not include officers on secondment.

3 Also includes student officers.

3 As at 31/03/12 No longer any FTR in PSNI, As at 31/03/12 Reserve figures only include Con PT (Formerly known as PTR)

The Police Service of Northern Ireland: 0845 6008000 ext 24070

21.1d Number of Police Officers (Full-time Equivalent) in Scotland[1] by Police Force and Deployment, 31 March 2013

Deployment	Central Scotland Police	Dumfries and Galloway Constabulary	Fife Constabulary	Grampian Police	Lothian and Borders Police	Northern Constabulary	Strathclyde Police	Tayside Police	Police Service of Scotland[4]	Scotland[2]
Police Officers in Force	835	508	1,038	1,496	2,866	780	8,133	1,228	8	16,893
Central Service	5	3	8	8	58	7	214	2	0	305
SCDEA/SPSA	17	14	39	8	54	2	103	14	0	251
Secondments	17	1	25	0	4	0	0	1	0	48
Total[3]	874	526	1,109	1,512	2,983	789	8,449	1,245	8	17,496

1. All figures are expressed in terms of full-time equivalent (FTE) police officers, rounded to the nearest whole number.

2. Force and Scotland totals may not equal the sum of constituent parts due to rounding; other figures within the bulletin ar also calculated using un-rounded data.

3 Police Service of Scotland only includes police officers in posts filled between 1 October 2012 and 31 March 2013

21.2 Prison Population International Comparisons with other EU Countries

	Prison population total (no. in penal institutions incl. pre-trial detainees)	Date	Estimated national population	Prison population rate (per 100,000 of national population)	Source of prison population total
Northern Europe					
Denmark	4,091	1/9/13	5.61m	73	NPA
Estonia	3,186	30/9/13	1.34m	238	Ministry of Justice
Finland	3,134	1/1/13	5.43m	58	NPA
Iceland	152	1/9/13	321,400	47	NPA
Ireland	4,068	30/9/13	4.6m	88	NPA
Latvia	6,117	1/1/13	2.01m	304	NPA
Lithuania	9,729	1/1/13	2.96m	329	NPA
Norway	3,649	1/9/13	5.1m	72	NPA
Sweden	6,364	1/10/12	9.53m	67	NPA
United Kingdom					
– England & Wales	84,430	27/9/13	57.06m	148	Ministry of Justice
– Northern Ireland	1,851	27/9/13	1.84m	101	NPA
– Scotland	7,855	27/9/13	5.33m	147	NPA
Faeroe Is. (Denmark)	10	avrge 12	48,230	21	Danish NPA
Guernsey (UK)	97	4/13	65,800	147	Guernsey prison administration
Isle of Man (UK)	97	9/9/13	86,700	112	Isle of Man prison administration
Jersey (UK)	163	10/9/13	98,750	165	Jersey prison administration
Southern Europe					
Albania	4,505	1/1/13	2.85m	158	Council of Europe
Andorra	33	1/1/13	86,900	38	Council of Europe
Bosnia & Herzegovina					
– Federation	1,883	1/1/13	2.35m	80	Council of Europe
– Republika Srpska	1,027	31/12/12	1.4m	73	Rep. Srpska prison administration
Croatia	4,741	1/1/13	4.38m	108	Council of Europe
Cyprus	905*	1/9/11	854,700*	106	C of E Annual Penal Statistics

*Does not include the internationally unrecognised Turkish Republic of Northern Cyprus (TRNC).

Greece	12,479	1/1/12	11.29m	111	NPA
Italy	64,835	31/8/13	61.14m	106	Ministry of Justice
Kosovo/Kosova	1,691	31/12/12	1.82m	93	US State Dept human rights report
Macedonia (F Yug Rep)	2,515	1/9/11	2.06m	122	C of E Annual Penal Statistics
Malta	610	1/7/13	420,050	145	Ministry of Justice & Home Affairs
Montenegro	1,297	1/1/13	622,600	208	Council of Europe
Portugal	14,264	1/9/13	10.49m	136	NPA
San Marino	2*	1/9/11	32,100	6*	C of E Annual Penal Statistics

*By agreement with Italy, most persons imprisoned by San Marino are held in Italian prisons.

Serbia	10,226	31/12/12	7.21m	142	NPA
Slovenia	1,357	1/9/13	2.06m	66	NPA
Spain	68,220	23/8/13	46.27m	147	NPA
Gibraltar (UK)	70	avrge 11	29,450	238	Gibraltar prison administration
Western Europe					
Austria	8,273	1/1/13	8.48m	98	NPA
Belgium	12,126	1/1/13	11.19m	108	Council of Europe
France	62,443*	1/9/13	63.94m*	98	NPA

*Metropolitan France, excluding departments and territories in Africa, the Americas and Oceania.

Germany	64,379	31/3/13	81.96m	79	German Federal Statistical Office
Liechtenstein	9*	1/1/13	36,800	24*	Council of Europe

*By agreement with Austria, some persons imprisoned by Liechtenstein may be held in Austrian prisons.

Luxembourg	656	1/1/13	538,000	122	Council of Europe
Monaco	27*	1/1/13	36,900	73*	Council of Europe

*By agreement with France, some persons imprisoned by Monaco may be held in French prisons.

Netherlands	13,749	30/9/12	16.79m	82	NPA
Switzerland	6,599	5/9/12	8.01m	82	Swiss Federal Statistical Office
Europe/Asia					
Armenia	4,756	1/1/13	2.9m	164	Council of Europe
Azerbaijan	37,989*	1/9/11	9.19m	413*	C of E Annual Penal Statistics

*Includes pre-trial detainees not held in the prisons of the Ministry of Justice.

Georgia	10,202*	30/4/13	4.54m*	225	Ministry of Corrections and Legal Affairs

* Does not include Abkhazia and South Ossetia, which have declared independence from Georgia.

Russian Federation	681,600	1/9/13	143.4m	475	NPA
Turkey	137,133	17/9/13	76.43m	179	NPA

21.2 Prison Population International Comparisons with other EU Countries

	Prison population total (no. in penal institutions incl. pre-trial detainees)	Date	Estimated national population	Prison population rate (per 100,000 of national population)	Source of prison population total
Central and Eastern Europe					
Belarus	31,700	1/10/12	9.45m	335	NPA
Bulgaria	10,996	10/12	7.3m	151	US State Dep't human rights report
Czech Republic	16,257	30/8/13	10.54m	154	NPA
Hungary	18,388	13/6/13	9.9m	186	NPA
Moldova	6,710*	1/4/13	3.56m*	188	NPA
*Does not include the internationally unrecognised Transdniestria/Transnistria/Pridnestrovie.					
Poland	83,610	31/8/13	38.55m	217	NPA
Romania	33,015	24/9/13	21.25m	155	NPA
Slovakia	10,152	31/8/13	5.42m	187	NPA
Ukraine	137,965	1/9/13	45.21m	305	NPA

Abbreviations

C of E   Council of Europe

NPA   National prison administration

Source: International Centre for Prison Studies

21.3 Police recorded crime by offence, 2002/03 to 2013/14 and percentage change between 2012/13 and 2013/14

England and Wales

Offence	2002/03[1,2]	2003/04	2004/05	2005/06	2006/07	2007/08	2008/09	2009/10	2010/11	2011/12	2012/13	2013/14	% change between years
VICTIM BASED CRIME	**5,403,456**	**5,422,954**	**5,022,946**	**4,910,238**	**4,788,218**	**4,338,484**	**4,091,230**	**3,760,387**	**3,598,145**	**3,454,955**	**3,150,575**	**3,108,037**	**-1**
1 Murder													
4.1 Manslaughter													
4.10 Corporate manslaughter	1,047	904	868	764	758	775	664	620	639	553	558	537	-4
4.2 Infanticide													
Homicide [3,4]	**1,047**	**904**	**868**	**764**	**758**	**775**	**664**	**620**	**639**	**553**	**558**	**537**	**-4**
2 Attempted murder [4]	822	888	740	920	633	621	574	591	523	483	412	500	21
4.3 Intentional destruction of viable unborn child	2	8	4	5	5	4	2	3	3	3	1	4	-
4.4 Causing death by dangerous driving	:	:	:	:	:	:	373	296	213	200	174	282	62
4.6 Causing death by careless driving when under the influence of drink or drugs	:	:	:	:	:	:	29	36	25	24	14	23	-
4.8 Causing death by careless or inconsiderate driving	:	:	:	:	:	:	35	188	172	179	139	134	-4
4.4/6/8 Causing death by dangerous or careless driving	414	445	441	432	459	422	:	:	:	:	:	:	:
5 More serious wounding or other act endangering life [5]	18,016	19,528	19,612	18,825	17,276	15,118	:	:	:	:	:	:	:
5A Inflicting grievous bodily harm (GBH) with intent [5,6]	:	:	:	:	:	:	22,663	22,795	19,489	17,777	:	:	:
5B Use of substance or object to endanger life [5,6]	:	:	:	:	:	:	462	416	371	315	:	:	:
5C Possession of items to endanger life [5,6]	:	:	:	:	:	:	266	331	329	298	:	:	:
5D Assault with intent to cause serious harm [6]	:	:	:	:	:	:	:	:	:	:	17,006	17,913	5
5E Endangering life [6]	:	:	:	:	:	:	:	:	:	:	777	798	3
6 Endangering railway passengers [6]	1,164	811	718	646	484	402	320	231	257	214	:	:	:
7 Endangering life at sea [6]	2	2	3	13	5	10	8	6	4	6	:	:	:
8F Inflicting grievous bodily harm (GBH) without intent [7,8]	:	:	:	:	:	:	17,159	16,482	15,112	14,409	:	:	:
8H Racially or religiously aggravated inflicting GBH without intent [7,8]	:	:	:	:	:	:	384	224	188	169	:	:	:
37.1 Causing death by aggravated vehicle taking	55	63	40	24	18	18	14	5	14	7	8	4	-
4.7 Causing or allowing death of child or vulnerable person	:	:	:	5	3	3	7	3	5	6	8	22	-
4.9 Causing death by driving: unlicensed or disqualified or uninsured drivers	:	:	:	:	:	1	8	16	6	6	10	5	-
8A Less serious wounding [7]	347,353	431,056	488,135	516,523	481,822	430,818	:	:	:	:	:	:	:
8G Actual bodily harm (ABH) and other injury [7,8]	:	:	:	:	:	:	374,255	355,962	328,463	301,223	:	:	:
8D Racially or religiously aggravated less serious wounding [7]	4,415	4,930	5,426	6,107	5,620	4,830	:	:	:	:	:	:	:
8J Racially or religiously aggravated ABH or other injury [7,8]	:	:	:	:	:	:	3,921	3,521	2,985	2,688	:	:	:
8K Poisoning or female genital mutilation [7,8]	:	:	:	:	:	:	163	138	118	118	:	:	:
8N Assault with injury [8]	:	:	:	:	:	:	:	:	:	:	290,956	300,480	3
8P Racially or religiously aggravated assault with injury [8]	:	:	:	:	:	:	:	:	:	:	2,579	2,446	-5
Violence with injury	**372,243**	**457,731**	**515,119**	**543,500**	**506,325**	**452,247**	**420,643**	**401,244**	**368,277**	**338,125**	**312,084**	**322,611**	**3**
3 Threat or conspiracy to murder [9]	18,132	22,299	23,758	18,683	12,822	9,966	:	:	:	:	:	:	:
3A Conspiracy to murder [9]	:	:	:	:	:	:	56	45	36	36	28	30	:
3B Threats to kill [9]	:	:	:	:	:	:	9,448	9,523	9,480	7,643	7,347	8,528	16
8L Harassment [10]	31,249	38,434	49,815	54,644	55,493	52,107	48,363	52,959	51,173	48,141	54,532	61,248	12
8M Racially or religiously aggravated harassment [11]	1,753	2,088	2,302	2,548	2,657	2,424	2,395	2,370	1,971	1,625	1,500	1,446	-4
11 Cruelty to and neglect of children [12]	4,109	6,083	5,724	5,045	4,917	5,287	6,204	6,611	6,087	6,081	6,370	7,997	26
11A Cruelty to children/young persons [12]													
12 Abandoning a child under the age of two years [12]	59	49	49	49	23	19	23	9	6	12	:	:	:
13 Child abduction	846	930	1,035	919	696	595	567	560	548	532	513	569	11
14 Procuring illegal abortion	7	9	7	6	6	6	5	3	5	3	5	6	:
36 Kidnapping	3,198	3,141	2,814	2,799	2,367	1,991	2,035	1,860	1,717	1,516	1,387	1,727	25
104 Assault without injury on a constable	33,948	22,189	23,604	22,217	21,749	20,384	17,384	15,781	15,510	15,873	14,527	14,455	0
105A Assault without injury	237,549	241,229	216,712	183,555	202,701	198,653	197,035	203,098	205,975	202,509	198,390	211,334	7
105B Racially or religiously aggravated assault without injury	4,602	4,161	3,866	3,945	4,351	4,325	4,186	4,328	4,062	4,071	3,898	4,098	5
Violence without injury	**335,452**	**340,612**	**329,686**	**294,410**	**307,782**	**295,757**	**287,701**	**297,147**	**296,570**	**288,042**	**288,497**	**311,438**	**8**
TOTAL VIOLENCE AGAINST THE PERSON	**708,742**	**799,247**	**845,673**	**838,674**	**814,865**	**748,779**	**709,008**	**699,011**	**665,486**	**626,720**	**601,139**	**634,586**	**6**

21.3 Police recorded crime by offence, 2002/03 to 2013/14 and percentage change between 2012/13 and 2013/14

England and Wales

Offence		2002/03[1,2]	2003/04	2004/05	2005/06	2006/07	2007/08	2008/09	2009/10	2010/11	2011/12	2012/13	2013/14	% change between years
19A	Rape of a female [13,14]	11,445	12,378	693	61	25	145	170	..	..	..	..	..	..
19C	Rape of a female aged 16 or over [13]	..	..	8,192	8,725	8,222	7,610	7,768	9,027	9,469	9,773	9,633	12,299	28
19D	Rape of a female child under 16 [13]	..	..	3,014	3,153	2,853	2,422	2,537	2,908	2,877	2,777	2,797	3,396	21
19E	Rape of a female child under 13 [13]	..	..	970	1,388	1,524	1,487	1,658	1,967	2,243	2,212	2,371	2,833	19
19B	Rape of a male [13,14]	850	894	81	22	18	10	22	..	..	..	..	..	..
19F	Rape of a male aged 16 or over [13]	..	..	444	438	413	332	317	368	387	387	414	662	60
19G	Rape of a male child under 16 [13]	..	..	322	292	261	237	216	241	246	288	354	415	17
19H	Rape of a male child under 13 [13]	..	..	297	364	458	430	408	563	670	601	788	1,120	42
	Rape	12,295	13,272	14,013	14,443	13,774	12,673	13,096	15,074	15,892	16,038	16,357	20,725	27
16	Buggery [13,14]	287	247	73	39	35	49	36	..	..	..	..	..	..
17	Indecent assault on a male [13,14]	4,132	4,110	1,003	347	76	209	158	..	..	..	..	..	..
17A	Sexual assault on a male aged 13 and over [13]	..	..	1,316	1,428	1,450	1,323	1,161	1,208	1,285	1,261	1,400	1,961	40
17B	Sexual assault on a male child under 13 [13]	..	..	1,227	1,394	1,237	1,121	1,004	1,054	1,126	1,011	1,271	1,651	30
18	Gross indecency between males [13,14]	245	260	49	20	12	17	14	..	..	..	..	..	..
20	Indecent assault on a female [13,14]	25,275	27,240	5,152	1,215	267	768	575	..	..	..	..	..	..
20A	Sexual assault on a female aged 13 and over [13]	..	..	15,087	17,158	16,883	15,793	15,500	15,693	16,346	15,794	15,533	17,380	12
20B	Sexual assault on a female child under 13 [13]	..	..	4,391	4,647	4,245	3,984	3,665	4,148	4,298	3,991	4,175	5,119	23
21	Unlawful sexual intercourse with a girl under 13 [13]	183	212	..	..	..	..	..	..	..	..	..	..	..
21	Sexual activity involving a child under 13 [13]	..	..	1,510	1,950	1,936	1,836	1,650	1,817	1,769	1,808	2,176	2,887	33
22	Unlawful sexual intercourse with a girl under 16 [13,14]	1,515	1,911	436	138	67	33	51	..	..	..	..	..	..
22B	Sexual activity involving a child under 16 [13]	..	..	2,546	3,283	3,208	3,123	3,318	3,992	4,039	3,971	4,477	5,882	31
22A	Causing sexual activity without consent [13,15]	..	..	239	744	224	217	151	130	167	203	191	274	43
23	Incest or familial sexual offences [13]	99	105	713	966	1,344	1,125	1,041	1,111	803	637	510	491	-4
25	Abduction of female [13,14]	291	403	86	36	21	4	4	..	..	..	..	..	..
70	Sexual activity with a person with a mental disorder [13]	..	..	104	139	163	127	131	124	130	101	116	135	16
71	Abuse of children through prostitution and pornography [13]	..	..	99	124	101	108	116	134	153	159	176	290	65
72	Trafficking for sexual exploitation [13]	..	..	21	33	43	57	52	58	66	59	70	124	77
73	Abuse of position of trust of a sexual nature [13]	678	792	682	463	361	328	195	185	146	176	196	194	-1
74	Gross indecency with a child [13,14]	1,917	1,987	398	120	64	149	121	..	..	..	..	..	..
88A	Sexual grooming [13]	..	..	186	237	322	274	313	393	309	371	371	469	26
88B	Other miscellaneous sexual offences [13,16,17]	9,735	9,873	11,593	11,363	10,209	8,848	..	..	..	..	..	..	..
88C	Other miscellaneous sexual offences [13,17]	..	..	..	..	..	..	298	354	198	163	160	199	24
88D	Unnatural sexual offences [13,17]	..	..	..	..	..	..	5	15	12	11	16	17	-
88E	Exposure and voyeurism [13,17]	..	..	..	..	..	..	7,530	7,516	7,201	7,006	6,425	6,402	0
	Other sexual offences [13]	44,357	47,140	46,911	45,844	42,268	39,493	37,089	37,932	38,048	36,722	37,263	43,475	17
	TOTAL SEXUAL OFFENCES [13]	56,652	60,412	60,924	60,287	56,042	52,166	50,185	53,006	53,940	52,760	53,620	64,200	20
34A	Robbery of business property	11,066	10,110	7,934	8,760	9,454	9,173	9,350	8,182	7,729	6,770	6,120	5,786	-5
34B	Robbery of personal property	99,205	93,626	83,076	89,438	91,922	75,600	70,780	66,923	68,460	67,918	59,035	52,032	-12
	TOTAL ROBBERY	110,271	103,736	91,010	98,198	101,376	84,773	80,130	75,105	76,189	74,688	65,155	57,818	-11
28	Burglary in a dwelling	434,098	398,945	318,969	298,355	290,454	279,125	282,977	..	..	..	..	..	..
28A	Burglary in a dwelling	..	..	..	..	..	..	..	214,889	208,484	198,853	185,147	171,415	-7
28B	Attempted burglary in a dwelling	..	..	..	..	..	..	..	44,706	42,298	40,287	37,385	36,363	-3
28C	Distraction burglary in a dwelling	..	..	..	..	..	..	..	6,936	5,480	4,467	3,305	2,847	-14
28D	Attempted distraction burglary in a dwelling	..	..	..	..	..	..	..	722	543	368	257	192	-25
29	Aggravated burglary in a dwelling	3,485	3,400	2,538	2,162	1,806	1,571	1,454	1,353	1,360	1,337	1,181	1,177	0
	Domestic burglary	437,563	402,345	321,507	300,517	292,260	280,696	284,431	268,606	258,165	245,312	227,275	211,994	-7
	of which: distraction burglary	..	15,716	13,258	11,552	12,750	10,058	9,092	7,658	6,023	4,835	3,562	3,039	-15

21.3 Police recorded crime by offence, 2002/03 to 2013/14 and percentage change between 2012/13 and 2013/14

England and Wales

Offence		2002/03 [1,2]	2003/04	2004/05	2005/06	2006/07	2007/08	2008/09	2009/10	2010/11	2011/12	2012/13	2013/14	% change between years
30	Burglary in a building other than a dwelling	451,904	417,133	358,398	344,195	329,473	302,799	296,970	236,019	230,868	223,153	202,440	200,532	-1
30A	Burglary in a building other than a dwelling	..	..	..	..	..	..	..	35,868	33,515	32,473	29,960	30,552	2
30B	Attempted burglary in a building other than a dwelling	..	..	..	..	..	..	183	152	135	110	120	106	-12
31	Aggravated burglary in a building other than a dwelling	612	535	453	356	279	215	..	..	..	..	..	..	..
	Non-domestic burglary	*452,516*	*417,668*	*358,851*	*344,551*	*329,752*	*303,014*	*297,153*	*272,039*	*264,518*	*255,736*	*232,520*	*231,190*	*-1*
	Burglary	**890,099**	**820,013**	**680,358**	**645,068**	**622,012**	**583,710**	**581,584**	**540,645**	**522,683**	**501,048**	**459,795**	**443,184**	**-4**
37.2	Aggravated vehicle taking	11,560	11,570	11,409	10,943	10,920	10,334	9,730	8,000	6,954	6,253	5,652	5,252	-7
45	Theft from a vehicle	663,679	603,256	500,360	507,239	502,651	432,412	396,976	339,170	313,467	300,377	285,047	276,613	-3
48	Theft or unauthorised taking of a motor vehicle	306,947	280,288	231,323	203,239	182,464	159,704	137,508	109,684	99,208	85,803	74,169	70,078	-6
126	Vehicle interference [18]	92,473	89,892	77,004	71,400	68,980	54,003	47,639	38,019	29,987	25,009	22,492	20,364	-9
	Vehicle offences	**1,074,659**	**985,006**	**820,096**	**792,821**	**765,015**	**656,453**	**591,853**	**494,873**	**449,616**	**417,442**	**387,360**	**372,307**	**-4**
39	Theft from the person	148,488	137,154	122,081	123,867	114,852	101,660	89,652	92,247	92,902	100,588	109,757	98,305	-10
	Theft from the person	**148,488**	**137,154**	**122,081**	**123,867**	**114,852**	**101,660**	**89,652**	**92,247**	**92,902**	**100,588**	**109,757**	**98,305**	**-10**
44	Theft or unauthorised taking of a pedal cycle	97,755	105,467	105,953	113,192	110,526	104,000	104,169	109,847	108,962	115,902	97,286	97,686	0
	Bicycle theft	**97,755**	**105,467**	**105,953**	**113,192**	**110,526**	**104,000**	**104,169**	**109,847**	**108,962**	**115,902**	**97,286**	**97,686**	**0**
46	Shoplifting	310,881	303,235	281,127	295,999	294,282	290,653	320,739	307,823	305,896	308,326	300,623	321,008	7
	Shoplifting	**310,881**	**303,235**	**281,127**	**295,999**	**294,282**	**290,653**	**320,739**	**307,823**	**305,896**	**308,326**	**300,623**	**321,008**	**7**
35	Blackmail [20]	1,331	1,497	1,465	1,645	2,481	1,201	1,363	1,450	1,491	1,369	1,496	2,134	43
40	Theft in a dwelling other than from an automatic machine or meter	56,444	61,099	57,713	54,757	54,471	51,336	51,220	53,338	54,798	54,518	52,385	50,519	-4
41	Theft by an employee	17,530	17,700	17,251	17,048	16,323	15,864	15,467	13,169	12,141	11,589	10,446	10,321	-1
42	Theft of mail	13,458	20,537	22,509	9,351	4,740	3,051	3,724	3,098	2,792	2,447	2,878	2,162	-25
43	Dishonest use of electricity	1,413	1,309	1,296	1,299	1,497	2,024	1,785	1,736	1,860	1,948	2,007	2,228	11
47	Theft from automatic machine or meter [19]	24,311	29,515	35,918	42,049	33,721	11,932	7,651	7,753	6,215	6,692	6,394	4,953	-23
49	Other theft	647,827	634,491	589,189	554,368	536,603	526,949	472,325	436,244	481,585	491,559	419,688	388,797	-7
49A	Making off without payment [35]	129,123	132,624	102,906	87,767	82,261	73,895	80,048	70,397	66,505	61,351	50,833	51,639	2
	All other theft offences	**891,437**	**898,772**	**828,247**	**768,284**	**732,097**	**686,252**	**633,583**	**587,185**	**627,387**	**631,473**	**546,127**	**512,753**	**-6**
	TOTAL THEFT OFFENCES	**3,413,319**	**3,249,647**	**2,837,862**	**2,739,231**	**2,638,784**	**2,422,728**	**2,321,580**	**2,132,620**	**2,107,446**	**2,074,779**	**1,900,948**	**1,845,243**	**-3**
56	Arson [21]	53,552	57,546	48,368	45,731	43,100	39,327	..	..	..	..	..	..	..
56A	Arson endangering life [21]	..	..	..	..	..	..	3,629	3,623	3,325	3,100	2,588	2,571	-1
56B	Arson not endangering life [21]	..	..	..	..	..	..	31,198	28,957	25,791	24,119	16,717	16,008	-4
	Arson	**53,552**	**57,546**	**48,368**	**45,731**	**43,100**	**39,327**	**34,827**	**32,580**	**29,116**	**27,219**	**19,305**	**18,579**	**-4**
58A	Criminal damage to a dwelling [22]	291,999	321,613	308,973	297,579	288,285	256,804	235,424	198,623	172,916	155,982	131,158	121,560	-7
58B	Criminal damage to a building other than a dwelling [22]	176,702	186,784	174,489	161,436	160,207	131,146	109,440	88,887	75,677	67,329	57,631	52,622	-9
58C	Criminal damage to a vehicle [22]	434,270	457,950	461,346	468,143	483,237	425,632	389,719	336,927	289,045	259,871	222,770	218,061	-2
58D	Other criminal damage [22]	152,440	180,411	188,842	195,069	197,036	173,127	157,109	140,575	125,751	113,478	97,008	93,495	-4
58E	Racially or religiously aggravated criminal damage to a dwelling [22]	2,044	1,982	1,845	1,742	1,543	1,150	999	849	639	499	..	..	..
58F	Racially or religiously aggravated criminal damage to a building other than a dwelling [22]	1,160	1,185	1,137	1,274	1,079	833	778	663	534	431	..	..	..
58G	Racially or religiously aggravated criminal damage to a vehicle [22]	1,525	1,603	1,640	1,899	1,711	1,338	1,304	1,135	869	788	..	..	..
58H	Racially or religiously aggravated other criminal damage [22]	780	838	837	975	953	681	727	606	537	411	..	..	..
58J	Racially or religiously aggravated other criminal damage [22]	..	..	..	..	..	..	..	..	..	..	1,841	1,873	2
	Criminal damage	**1,060,920**	**1,152,366**	**1,139,109**	**1,128,117**	**1,134,051**	**990,711**	**895,500**	**768,065**	**665,968**	**598,789**	**510,408**	**487,611**	**-4**
	TOTAL CRIMINAL DAMAGE AND ARSON	**1,114,472**	**1,209,912**	**1,187,477**	**1,173,848**	**1,177,151**	**1,030,038**	**930,327**	**800,645**	**695,084**	**626,008**	**529,713**	**506,190**	**-4**

21.3 Police recorded crime by offence, 2002/03 to 2013/14 and percentage change between 2012/13 and 2013/14

England and Wales

Offence		2002/03[1,2]	2003/04	2004/05	2005/06	2006/07	2007/08	2008/09	2009/10	2010/11	2011/12	2012/13	2013/14	% change between years
OTHER CRIMES AGAINST SOCIETY		**387,821**	**420,595**	**453,825**	**515,453**	**534,159**	**542,656**	**539,153**	**504,649**	**480,330**	**448,626**	**402,616**	**398,662**	**-1**
Trafficking in controlled drugs	92A	22,435	24,628	24,190	25,276	26,550	28,323	29,885	33,223	32,336	31,316	29,745	29,461	-1
Trafficking of drugs		**22,435**	**24,628**	**24,190**	**25,276**	**26,550**	**28,323**	**29,885**	**33,223**	**32,336**	**31,316**	**29,745**	**29,461**	**-1**
Possession of controlled drugs	92B	119,896	118,006	..	..	..	..	..	..	..	..	..	..	..
Other drug offences	92C	989	877	781	601	680	817	1,123	1,122	1,142	1,127	1,034	1,200	16
Possession of controlled drugs (excluding cannabis)[23]	92D	..	..	32,603	32,685	36,608	42,519	44,578	38,439	38,711	36,453	34,596	33,986	-2
Possession of cannabis[23]	92E	..	..	88,263	119,917	130,395	158,254	167,950	162,800	160,733	160,203	142,627	133,529	-6
Possession of drugs		**120,885**	**118,883**	**121,647**	**153,203**	**167,683**	**201,590**	**213,651**	**202,361**	**200,586**	**197,783**	**178,257**	**168,715**	**-5**
TOTAL DRUG OFFENCES		**143,320**	**143,511**	**145,837**	**178,479**	**194,233**	**229,913**	**243,536**	**235,584**	**232,922**	**229,099**	**208,002**	**198,176**	**-5**
Possession of weapons[24]	8B	32,816	35,669	36,374	35,590	34,689	32,513	..	..	..	..	..	..	..
Possession of firearms with intent[24]	10A	..	..	..	..	..	..	1,973	1,587	1,385	1,151	998	1,077	8
Possession of firearms offences[25]	10B	..	..	..	..	..	..	4,460	4,070	3,650	3,402	3,052	2,926	-4
Possession of other weapons[24]	10C	..	..	..	..	..	..	14,944	11,950	10,564	9,138	7,274	7,334	1
Possession of article with blade or point[24]	10D	..	..	..	..	..	..	13,985	10,885	10,474	9,762	8,425	9,043	7
Other firearms offences[26]	81	3,522	3,322	4,210	4,106	4,239	4,560	293	253	254	229	160	238	49
Other knives offences	90	41	30	21	15	9	6	7	13	0	6	1	2	-
TOTAL POSSESSION OF WEAPONS OFFENCES		**36,379**	**39,021**	**40,605**	**39,711**	**38,937**	**37,079**	**35,662**	**28,758**	**26,327**	**23,688**	**19,910**	**20,620**	**4**
Public fear, alarm or distress[10]	9A	91,561	116,566	147,801	164,061	173,152	158,045	142,246	126,597	114,781	97,085	81,139	79,613	-2
Racially or religiously aggravated public fear, alarm or distress[11]	9B	15,157	18,887	21,061	24,057	25,828	24,086	23,355	23,226	20,967	20,188	20,420	21,679	6
Treason[27]	62	0	1	0	0	0	0	0	0	0	0	..	..	..
Violent disorder[27]	62A	..	..	..	..	..	..	..	..	..	..	656	640	-2
Treason felony[27]	63	0	0	0	0	0	0	0	0	0	0	..	..	..
Riot[27]	64	8	8	4	7	4	2	3	0	2	3	..	..	..
Violent disorder[27]	65	2,856	2,790	2,636	2,457	1,742	1,180	1,022	859	751	696	..	..	..
Other offences against the State or public order	66	19,935	19,926	20,370	31,999	35,935	35,067	37,663	37,572	36,580	32,886	29,989	32,501	8
TOTAL PUBLIC ORDER OFFENCES		**129,517**	**158,178**	**191,872**	**222,581**	**236,661**	**218,380**	**204,289**	**188,254**	**173,081**	**150,858**	**132,204**	**134,433**	**2**
Concealing an infant death close to birth	15	7	6	6	8	4	8	8	6	9	5	2	2	-
Exploitation of prostitution[13]	24	127	186	117	153	190	184	173	148	153	110	120	124	3
Bigamy	26	88	71	104	101	61	74	64	60	44	31	39	40	-
Soliciting for prostitution[13]	27	2,111	1,944	1,821	1,640	1,290	1,216	1,071	1,190	826	797	883	750	-15
Going equipped for stealing, etc.	33	5,792	5,706	4,567	4,382	4,253	3,781	3,791	3,647	4,129	3,765	3,473	3,477	0
Making, supplying or possessing articles for use in fraud[28]	33A	..	..	..	1,548	1,961	2,382	2,505	2,609	2,344	1,779	1,427	1,486	4
Profiting from or concealing proceeds of crime[28]	38	..	..	..	..	..	183	611	862	975	1,301	1,384	..	..
Making or supplying articles for use in fraud[29]	53H	..	..	..	..	..	1,108	1,466	1,564	1,559	1,366	1,287	..	..
Possession of articles for use in fraud[29]	53J	..	..	..	..	..	..	..	..	..	..	..	2,982	..
Handling stolen goods	54	18,817	17,308	14,157	12,714	11,826	11,335	10,766	9,448	9,184	9,769	8,134	8,532	5
Threat etc. to commit criminal damage	59	6,138	8,612	10,066	10,501	7,889	6,318	6,034	5,996	5,916	5,214	4,950	5,791	17
Forgery or use of drug prescription	60	881	805	747	693	593	440	446	343	298	361	379	412	9
Other forgery	61	8,793	7,992	10,249	10,627	8,479	4,211	4,241	2,526	1,632	2,124	2,984	2,896	-3
Possession of false documents	61A	..	..	..	..	..	2,301	2,646	2,263	1,770	1,378	962	934	-3
Perjury	67	186	206	265	245	197	193	177	184	339	151	134	96	-28
Libel[30]	68	2	0	0	1	1	0	1	0	4	0	..	..	..
Offender Management Act offences	69	..	..	..	..	..	..	533	533	518	583	1,024	1,110	8
Betting, gaming and lotteries[30]	75	5	1	12	6	13	11	22	21	14	12	..	..	-
Aiding suicide	76	8	11	6	11	13	9	7	17	7	10	11	12	-
Immigration offences[30]	78	433	451	550	935	792	661	573	411	445	344	..	..	-
Perverting the course of justice	79	11,346	11,894	11,567	12,712	11,114	9,131	8,396	7,997	6,890	5,698	4,948	5,373	9
Absconding from lawful custody	80	1,553	1,721	1,362	1,272	979	828	651	557	499	414	482	370	-23

21.3 Police recorded crime by offence, 2002/03 to 2013/14 and percentage change between 2012/13 and 2013/14

England and Wales

Offence	2002/03[1,2]	2003/04	2004/05	2005/06	2006/07	2007/08	2008/09	2009/10	2010/11	2011/12	2012/13	2013/14	% change between years
82 Customs and Revenue offences[30]	117	49	30	49	27	10	13	10	3	5	..	..	..
83 Bail offences	252	212	202	177	83	25	3	4	6	3	2	3	-
84 Trade descriptions, etc	195	513	1,344	1,360	1,353	1,321	1,143	809	486	263	..	..	..
85 Health and Safety offences	3	4	15	8	9	8	15	6	2	8	..	..	..
86 Obscene publications, etc and protected sexual material	2,106	2,881	2,861	2,592	2,378	2,672	2,775	3,215	3,342	3,335	3,506	4,577	31
87 Protection from eviction	63	75	70	75	69	81	71	81	73	68	..	..	..
89 Adulteration of food	80	34	29	45	32	44	13	4	9	0	..	..	..
91 Public health offences[30,31]	20	86	112	128	50	44	115	488	398	289	..	..	..
94 Planning laws	1	3	4	5	0	0	1	0	1	1	..	..	..
95 Disclosure, obstruction, false or misleading statements etc	16	22	144	368	266	425	506	426	348	363	294	356	21
99 Other indictable or triable-either-way offences	3,223	3,440	2,577	2,197	1,915	1,391	1,735	1,629	1,569	1,589	2,510	2,518	0
802 Dangerous driving	7,624	7,567	6,669	5,923	5,353	4,725	4,240	3,941	3,475	3,239	3,092	3,149	2
814 Fraud, forgery associated with vehicle driver records	8,618	8,016	5,420	4,206	3,138	2,164	1,387	1,058	733	606	473	443	-6
TOTAL MISCELLANEOUS CRIMES AGAINST SOCIETY	78,605	79,885	75,511	74,682	64,328	57,284	55,666	52,053	48,000	44,981	42,500	45,433	7
TOTAL RECORDED CRIME - ALL OFFENCES EXCLUDING FRAUD[32]	5,791,277	5,843,549	5,476,771	5,425,691	5,322,377	4,881,140	4,630,383	4,265,036	4,078,475	3,903,581	3,553,191	3,506,699	-1
FRAUD OFFENCES[33]													
51 Fraud by company director[34]	27	80	51	626	101	162	815	85	207	45	103	1	-
52 False accounting	880	721	541	487	462	251	146	155	108	75	59	3	-
53A Cheque and credit card fraud (pre Fraud Act 2006)[29]	142,249	131,022	121,376	87,860	59,011	..	..	..	..	..	..	..	..
53B Preserved other fraud and repealed fraud offences (pre-Fraud Act 2006)[29,35]	40,516	38,378	38,761	40,415	45,593	9,984	3,494	3,666	3,342	3,799	3,027	0	-
53C Fraud by false representation: cheque, plastic card and online bank accounts[29]	..	..	..	..	..	23,345	26,578	27,148	24,942	22,703	17,873	5	-
53D Fraud by false representation: other frauds[29]	..	..	..	..	..	34,544	38,884	39,626	42,460	44,719	40,333	8	-
53E Fraud by failing to disclose information[29]	..	..	..	..	..	265	304	364	339	246	163	1	-
53F Fraud by abuse of position[29]	..	..	..	..	..	675	926	1,160	1,033	1,170	927	1	-
53G Obtaining services dishonestly[29]	..	..	..	..	..	1,880	1,152	1,042	..	..	..	..	-
55 Bankruptcy and insolvency offences	11	9	11	93	14	31	15	13	10	11	12	46	-
TOTAL FRAUD OFFENCES RECORDED BY THE POLICE[29,33]	183,683	170,210	160,740	129,481	105,181	71,137	72,314	73,259	72,441	72,768	62,497	65	-
FRAUD OFFENCES RECORDED BY ACTION FRAUD[33]	..	..	..	..	..	..	..	..	..	46,658	117,402	211,279	80
TOTAL FRAUD OFFENCES	183,683	170,210	160,740	129,481	105,181	71,137	72,314	73,259	72,441	119,426	179,899	211,344	17
TOTAL RECORDED CRIME - ALL OFFENCES INCLUDING FRAUD[32]	5,974,960	6,013,759	5,637,511	5,555,172	5,427,558	4,952,277	4,702,697	4,338,295	4,150,916	4,023,007	3,733,090	3,718,043	0

Source: Police recorded crime, Home Office
Police recorded crime data are not designated as National Statistics.
See notes to accompany table 21.3

NOTES TO ACCOMPANY TABLE 21.3

1.   The National Crime Recording Standard (NCRS) was introduced in April 2002, although some forces adopted NCRS practices before the standard was formally introduced. Figures before and after that date are not directly comparable. The introduction of NCRS led to a rise in recording in 2002/03 and, particularly for violent crime, in the following years as forces continued to improve compliance with the new standard.

2.   Includes the British Transport Police from 2002/03 onwards.

3.   The homicide figure for 2002/03 includes 172 homicides attributed to Harold Shipman in previous years but coming to light in the official inquiry in 2002.

4.   The homicide figure in 2005/06 of 764 includes 52 homicide victims of the 7 July London bombings, which also accounted for approximately one-quarter of the total of 920 attempted murders.

5.   Offence classifications 5A, 5B and 5C were introduced from 1 April 2008 and replaced classification 5. Classification 5A was influenced by a clarification in recording rules that had the effect of significantly increasing levels of recording in some forces. Classification 5A also includes some other offences of endangering life as well as GBH with intent, though GBH with intent is the major part of this category.

6.   Offence classification 5D was introduced from 1 April 2012 and replaced classification 5A offences. Offence classification 5E was also introduced and replaced the remaining classification 5A offences. 5B. 5C. 6 and 7.

7.   Offence classifications 8F, 8G, 8H, 8J and 8K were introduced from 1 April 2008 and had previously been recorded as part of classifications 8A or 8D.

8.   Offence classification 8N was introduced from 1 April 2012 and replaced classifications 8F, 8G and 8K. Offence classification 8P was also introduced and replaced classifications 8H and 8J.

9.   Offence classifications 3A and 3B were introduced from 1 April 2008 and had previously been recorded as classification 3.

10.   Prior to 2008/09, the police sent combined figures for harassment (8L, 8M) and public fear, alarm and distress (9A, 9B) offences. For the years 2002/03 to 2007/08, figures for these offence groups are estimated based upon the proportionate split between the offences in 2008/09.

11.   Prior to 2008/09, the police sent combined figures for harassment (8L, 8M) and public fear, alarm and distress (9A, 9B) offences. For the years 2002/03 to 2007/08, figures for these offence groups are estimated based upon the proportionate split between the offences in 2008/09.

12.   Offence classification 11A was introduced from 1 April 2012 and replaced classifications 11 and 12.

13.   The Sexual Offences Act 2003, introduced in May 2004, altered the definition and coverage of sexual offences.

14.   Prior to 2009/10, a small number of offences continued to be recorded relating to offences repealed by the Sexual Offences Act 2003. While these may have been legitimately recorded for offences committed prior to May 2004 it is also possible that some may have been recorded in these old categories in error, so any changes based on small numbers should be interpreted with caution.

15.   The increase in 2005/06 was accounted for by a large number of offences that were dealt with by the Norfolk Constabulary.

16.   This offence consists solely of the former offence of 'Indecent Exposure' for years prior to 2004/05. This became the offence of 'Exposure' and was included within 'Other miscellaneous sexual offences' from May 2004.

17.   Offence classification 88B was split into 88C–E with effect from 2008/09. Since that time offences of exposure have been recorded as classification 88E.

18.   Includes tampering with a motor vehicle.

19.   The large increase in 2006/07 was due to the recording of threats made against shareholders of GlaxoSmithKline by animal rights activists.

20.   Following a change in the implementation of the Fraud Act 2006, offences involving theft from an automatic machine using a plastic card are now regarded as false representation and recorded under classification 53C.

21.   Offence classifications 56A and 56B were introduced from 1 April 2008 and had previously been recorded as classification 56.

22.   Offence classifications 58E-58H were amalgamated on 1 April 2012 to form classification 58J.

23.   Possession of controlled drugs offences were split with effect from April 2004 into possession of cannabis and possession of drugs other than cannabis.

24.   Offence classifications 10A, 10C and 10D were introduced from 1 April 2008 and had previously been recorded as classification 8B.

25.   These are offences under the Firearms Act 1968 and other Firearms Acts connected with licensing and certification of firearms. Such offences are not included in the firearms offences statistics.

26.   Offence classification 10B was introduced from 1 April 2008. Possession of firearms offences are those offences where the weapon has not been used during the commission of another offence.

27.   Offence classifications 62-65 were amalgamated on 1 April 2012 to form classification 62A.

28.   These offences were added to the series from 1 April 2003.

29.   New offences were introduced under the Fraud Act 2006, which came into force on 15 January 2007.

30.   Offence classifications 68, 75, 78, 82, 84, 85, 87, 89, 91 and 94 were included with classification 99 with effect from 1 April 2012.

31.   The large increase in this offence from 2008/09 is mainly due to the recording of fly-tipping by some forces following advice that this offence is notifiable.

32.   Some forces have revised their data and totals may therefore not agree with those previously published.

33.   Action Fraud have taken over the recording of fraud offences on behalf of individual police forces. This process began in April 2011 and was rolled out to all police forces by March 2013. Due to this change caution should be applied when comparing data over this transitional period and with earlier years. There were 65 cases in 2013/14 where police forces recorded a fraud offence after the transfer of responsibility to Action Fraud. These cases are due to the transition process, and are likely to be revised in future quarters. See the user Guide for more details including information on transfer date to Action Fraud for each force.

34.   The large increase in this offence in 2005/06 was due to one large-scale fraud recorded by the Cambridgeshire Constabulary. The increase in 2007/08 was due to a fraud recorded by North Yorkshire Police. The large increase in 2008/09 was due to large-scale frauds recorded by Gwent Police, Leicestershire Constabulary and the Metropolitan Police. The increase in 2010/11 was due to a large-scale fraud recorded by North Yorkshire Police.

35.   Offence classification 49A was introduced as a separate theft classification in 2013/14. Before this, it was recorded under the fraud offence classification 53B. Data for 49A are provided for all years following a special request to forces. In some cases, these have been estimated where forces were unable to provide data.

-    Indicates that data are not reported because the base number of offences is less than 50.

21.4 Offenders convicted and sentenced at all courts

England and Wales, 2012

Offence group	Description		Total Proc Against	Total found Guilty	Total For Sent	Absl Disch	Condl Disch	Fine	CRO	SO	CPO	ACO	CPO&RO	Curf Order	Rep Order	APO	DTTO	REFO	Comm Order	YRO (1)	Total Comm Sentences	SS	Sec 90-92	DTO	YOI	Unsus Sent Impr	Imm cust	ODW
Violence Against Person	1 Murder	M	494	324	324	-	-	-	-	-	-	-	-	-	-	-	-	-	-	-	-	-	19	-	35	270	324	-
		F	46	32	32	-	-	-	-	-	-	-	-	-	-	-	-	-	-	-	-	-	1	-	1	30	32	-
		NS	20	-	-	-	-	-	-	-	-	-	-	-	-	-	-	-	-	-	-	-	-	-	-	-	-	-
		T	560	356	356	-	-	-	-	-	-	-	-	-	-	-	-	-	-	-	-	-	20	-	36	300	356	-
	2 Attempted Murder	M	279	71	71	-	-	-	-	-	-	-	-	-	-	-	-	-	-	-	-	-	2	-	3	64	69	2
		F	27	4	4	-	-	-	-	-	-	-	-	-	-	-	-	-	-	-	-	-	-	-	-	2	2	2
		NS	2	-	-	-	-	-	-	-	-	-	-	-	-	-	-	-	-	-	-	-	-	-	-	-	-	-
		T	308	75	75	-	-	-	-	-	-	-	-	-	-	-	-	-	-	-	-	-	2	-	3	66	71	4
	3 Threat or Conspiracy to Murder	M	1,107	405	398	-	8	1	-	-	-	-	-	-	-	-	-	5	77	9	91	78	-	1	10	188	199	21
		F	74	41	36	-	2	-	-	-	-	-	-	-	-	-	-	2	6	1	9	7	-	-	2	14	16	2
		NS	9	3	2	-	-	-	-	-	-	-	-	-	-	-	-	1	-	-	1	-	-	1	-	1	1	-
		T	1,190	449	436	-	10	1	-	-	-	-	-	-	-	-	-	8	83	10	101	85	-	2	12	202	216	23
	4.1 Manslaughter	M	55	149	149	1	-	-	-	-	-	-	-	-	-	-	-	-	1	-	1	-	4	-	23	110	137	10
		F	8	17	17	-	-	-	-	-	-	-	-	-	-	-	-	-	-	-	-	-	-	-	2	14	16	-
		NS	3	-	-	-	-	-	-	-	-	-	-	-	-	-	-	-	-	-	-	-	-	-	-	-	-	-
		T	66	166	166	1	-	-	-	-	-	-	-	-	-	-	-	-	1	-	1	-	4	-	25	124	153	10
	4.2 Infanticide	F	-	1	1	1	-	-	-	-	-	-	-	-	-	-	-	-	-	-	-	-	-	-	-	-	-	-
		T	-	1	1	1	-	-	-	-	-	-	-	-	-	-	-	-	-	-	-	-	-	-	-	-	-	-
	4.4 Causing Death by Dangerous Driving	M	145	107	107	1	-	-	-	-	-	-	-	-	-	-	-	-	1	-	1	2	1	-	16	86	103	-
		F	17	9	9	-	-	-	-	-	-	-	-	-	-	-	-	-	-	-	-	1	-	-	-	7	8	-
		NS	1	-	-	-	-	-	-	-	-	-	-	-	-	-	-	-	-	-	-	-	-	-	-	-	-	-
		T	163	116	116	1	-	-	-	-	-	-	-	-	-	-	-	-	1	-	1	3	1	-	17	93	111	-
	4.5 Manslaughter Due to Diminished Responsibility	M	-	10	10	-	-	-	-	-	-	-	-	-	-	-	-	-	1	-	1	-	-	-	-	5	5	4
		F	-	3	3	-	-	-	-	-	-	-	-	-	-	-	-	-	1	-	1	1	-	-	-	1	1	-
		T	-	13	13	-	-	-	-	-	-	-	-	-	-	-	-	-	2	-	2	1	-	-	-	6	6	4
	4.6 Causing Death by Careless Driving when under the influence of Drink or Drugs	M	18	22	22	-	-	1	-	-	-	-	-	-	-	-	-	-	1	-	1	-	-	-	2	18	20	-
		F	1	-	-	-	-	-	-	-	-	-	-	-	-	-	-	-	-	-	-	-	-	-	-	-	-	-
		T	19	22	22	-	-	1	-	-	-	-	-	-	-	-	-	-	1	-	1	-	-	-	2	18	20	-
	4.7 Causing Death of a child or vulnerable person	M	4	4	4	-	-	-	-	-	-	-	-	-	-	-	-	-	1	-	1	-	-	-	-	3	3	-
		F	-	-	-	-	-	-	-	-	-	-	-	-	-	-	-	-	-	-	-	-	-	-	-	-	-	-
		T	4	4	4	-	-	-	-	-	-	-	-	-	-	-	-	-	1	-	1	-	-	-	-	3	3	-
	4.8 Causing Death by careless or inconsiderate driving	M	219	186	190	-	-	7	-	-	-	-	-	-	-	-	-	-	67	1	68	57	-	-	3	51	54	3
		F	38	34	33	-	-	1	-	-	-	-	-	-	-	-	-	-	20	-	20	7	-	-	-	4	5	-
		NS	1	1	1	-	-	-	-	-	-	-	-	-	-	-	-	-	-	-	-	1	-	-	-	-	-	-
		T	261	221	224	-	-	8	-	-	-	-	-	-	-	-	-	-	88	1	89	64	-	-	4	55	59	3
	4.9 Causing death by driving unlicensed, disqualified or uninsured drivers	M	13	12	13	-	-	1	-	-	-	-	-	-	-	-	-	1	5	-	6	4	-	-	-	2	2	1
		F	3	1	2	-	-	-	-	-	-	-	-	-	-	-	-	-	-	-	-	-	-	-	-	2	2	-
		T	16	13	15	-	-	1	-	-	-	-	-	-	-	-	-	1	5	-	6	4	-	-	-	4	4	1
	4.10 Applicable organisation causing death by gross breach of duty of care	O	-	1	1	-	-	1	-	-	-	-	-	-	-	-	-	-	-	-	-	-	-	-	-	-	-	-
		T	-	1	1	-	-	1	-	-	-	-	-	-	-	-	-	-	-	-	-	-	-	-	-	-	-	-
	4.12 Causing serious injury by dangerous driving	M	1	1	1	-	-	-	-	-	-	-	-	-	-	-	-	-	-	-	-	-	-	-	-	1	1	-
		T	1	1	1	-	-	-	-	-	-	-	-	-	-	-	-	-	-	-	-	-	-	-	-	1	1	-
	5 Wounding or other act Endangering Life	M	4,870	1,703	1,701	1	9	15	-	-	-	-	-	-	-	-	-	12	26	17	55	13	49	29	235	1,264	1,577	31
		F	556	125	124	1	1	1	-	-	-	-	-	-	-	-	-	1	5	3	9	2	4	3	15	85	107	3
		NS	40	-	-	-	-	-	-	-	-	-	-	-	-	-	-	-	-	-	-	-	-	-	-	-	-	-
		T	5,466	1,828	1,825	2	10	16	-	-	-	-	-	-	-	-	-	13	31	20	64	15	53	32	250	1,349	1,684	34
	6 Endangering Railway Passenger	M	14	14	14	-	-	2	-	-	-	-	-	-	-	-	-	-	6	-	6	3	-	-	1	2	3	-
		F	2	3	3	-	-	-	-	-	-	-	-	-	-	-	-	-	2	-	2	1	-	-	-	-	-	-
		NS	1	-	-	-	-	-	-	-	-	-	-	-	-	-	-	-	-	-	-	-	-	-	-	-	-	-
		T	17	17	17	-	-	2	-	-	-	-	-	-	-	-	-	-	8	-	8	4	-	-	1	2	3	-

21.4 Offenders convicted and sentenced at all courts

England and Wales, 2012

Offence group	Description		Total Proc Against	Total found Guilty	Total For Sent	Absit Disch	Condl Disch	Fine	CRO	SO	CPO	ACO	CPO&RO	Curf Order	Rep Order	APO	DTTO	REFO	Comm Order	YRO (1)	Total Comm Sentences	SS	Sec 90-92	DTO	YOI	Unsus Sent Impr	Imm cust	ODW
	7 Endangering Life at Sea	M	12	6	4	-	2	2	-	-	-	-	-	-	-	-	-	-	-	-	-	-	-	-	-	-	-	-
		T	12	6	4	-	2	2	-	-	-	-	-	-	-	-	-	-	-	-	-	-	-	-	-	-	-	-
	8 Malicious Wounding etc.	M	36,712	29,217	28,957	70	1,138	1,956	4	2	-	3	-	22	11	-	-	1,335	6,449	1,047	8,873	6,091	7	303	1,205	8,597	10,112	717
		F	4,434	3,414	3,393	14	279	279	-	-	-	-	-	3	4	-	-	221	947	167	1,343	778	-	26	81	430	537	163
		NS	242	124	107	-	4	10	-	-	-	-	-	-	-	-	-	10	32	12	54	9	-	5	1	21	27	3
		T	41,388	32,755	32,467	84	1,421	2,245	4	2	-	3	-	25	15	-	-	1,566	7,428	1,226	10,270	6,878	7	334	1,287	9,048	10,676	883
	11 Cruelty to or Neglect of Children	M	339	234	226	-	11	-	2	-	-	-	-	-	-	-	-	50	-	50	85	-	-	5	71	76	2
		F	505	380	378	-	17	-	-	-	-	-	-	-	-	-	-	1	156	-	157	134	-	-	3	63	66	4
		NS	7	1	1	-	-	-	-	-	-	-	-	-	-	-	-	-	-	-	-	1	-	-	-	-	-	-
		T	851	615	605	-	28	-	2	-	-	-	-	-	-	-	-	1	206	-	207	220	-	-	8	134	142	6
	12 Abandoning Child aged under Two Years	M	2	2	-	-	-	-	-	-	-	-	-	-	-	-	-	-	-	-	-	-	-	-	-	-	-
		F	1	1	-	-	-	-	-	-	-	-	-	-	-	-	-	-	-	-	-	-	-	-	-	-	-
		T	3	3	-	-	-	-	-	-	-	-	-	-	-	-	-	-	-	-	-	-	-	-	-	-	-
	13 Child Abduction	M	117	76	73	1	4	1	-	-	-	-	-	-	-	-	-	2	14	-	16	11	-	-	4	36	40	1
		F	23	17	17	-	1	-	-	-	-	-	-	-	-	-	-	-	8	-	8	2	-	-	-	5	5	-
		NS	1	-	-	-	-	-	-	-	-	-	-	-	-	-	-	-	-	-	-	-	-	-	-	-	-	-
		T	141	93	90	1	5	1	-	-	-	-	-	-	-	-	-	2	22	-	24	13	-	-	4	41	45	1
	14 Procuring Illegal Abortion	M	2	2	1	-	-	-	-	-	-	-	-	-	-	-	-	-	-	-	-	1	-	-	-	1	1	-
		F	1	1	1	-	-	-	-	-	-	-	-	-	-	-	-	-	-	-	-	-	-	-	-	1	1	-
		T	3	3	1	-	-	-	-	-	-	-	-	-	-	-	-	-	-	-	-	1	-	-	-	1	1	-
	37.1 Causing Death by Aggravated Vehicle Taking	M	6	4	4	-	-	-	-	-	-	-	-	-	-	-	-	-	-	1	1	-	-	1	1	-	3	-
		T	6	4	4	-	-	-	-	-	-	-	-	-	-	-	-	-	-	-	1	1	-	-	1	1	-	3	-
	Sub-total	M	44,405	32,541	32,264	74	1,173	1,988	4	2	-	3	-	22	11	-	-	1,355	6,696	1,076	9,169	6,345	82	334	1,543	10,766	12,725	790
		F	5,739	4,086	4,057	15	300	281	-	-	-	-	-	3	4	-	-	225	1,144	171	1,548	933	5	29	106	662	802	178
		NS	331	129	111	-	4	10	-	-	-	-	-	-	-	-	-	11	33	12	56	10	-	6	1	21	28	3
		O	1	-	-	-	-	-	-	-	-	-	-	-	-	-	-	-	-	-	-	-	-	-	-	-	-	-
		T	50,475	36,757	36,433	89	1,477	2,280	4	2	-	3	-	25	15	-	-	1,591	7,873	1,259	10,773	7,288	87	369	1,650	11,449	13,555	971
Sexual Offences	16 Buggery	M	59	48	48	-	-	-	-	2	-	-	-	-	-	-	-	-	-	-	2	2	-	-	-	-	46	46
		NS	3	-	-	-	-	-	-	-	-	-	-	-	-	-	-	-	-	-	-	-	-	-	-	-	-	-
		T	62	48	48	-	-	-	-	2	-	-	-	-	-	-	-	-	-	-	2	2	-	-	-	-	46	46
	17 Sexual Assault on a Male	M	210	212	212	-	3	3	-	1	-	-	-	-	1	-	-	7	26	5	40	20	-	3	2	136	141	5
		F	13	4	4	-	-	-	-	-	-	-	-	-	-	-	-	-	-	-	1	1	-	-	-	2	2	-
		NS	3	-	-	-	-	-	-	-	-	-	-	-	-	-	-	-	-	-	-	-	-	-	-	-	-	-
		T	226	216	216	-	3	3	-	1	-	-	-	-	1	-	-	7	26	5	41	21	-	3	2	138	143	5
	19 Rape of a Female	M	2,596	1,044	1,044	-	-	-	-	2	-	-	-	-	-	-	-	7	26	15	34	1	23	15	69	884	991	17
		F	14	11	11	-	-	-	-	-	-	-	-	-	-	-	-	-	9	-	9	-	2	-	-	9	11	-
		NS	28	-	-	-	-	-	-	-	-	-	-	-	-	-	-	-	-	-	-	-	-	-	-	-	-	-
		T	2,638	1,055	1,055	-	-	-	-	2	-	-	-	-	-	-	-	7	26	15	34	1	25	15	69	893	1,002	17
	19 Rape of a Male	M	182	90	88	-	-	-	-	2	-	-	-	-	-	-	-	3	3	4	12	5	5	2	5	62	74	2
		NS	1	-	-	-	-	-	-	-	-	-	-	-	-	-	-	-	-	-	-	-	-	-	-	-	-	-
		T	184	90	90	-	-	-	-	2	-	-	-	-	-	-	-	3	3	4	12	5	5	2	5	62	74	2
	20 Sexual Assault on a Female	M	3,498	2,081	2,078	4	38	39	-	2	-	-	-	-	-	-	-	66	540	61	673	240	5	21	38	958	1,022	62
		F	35	21	21	-	1	-	-	-	-	-	-	-	-	-	-	1	4	-	4	4	-	-	1	11	12	-
		NS	20	6	6	-	-	-	-	-	-	-	-	-	-	-	-	-	3	1	5	1	-	-	-	-	-	-
		T	3,553	2,108	2,105	4	39	39	-	2	-	-	-	-	-	-	-	67	547	62	682	245	5	21	39	969	1,034	62
	21 Sexual Activity with child under 13	M	425	230	225	1	2	-	-	2	-	1	-	1	-	-	-	15	40	20	76	15	5	3	10	110	123	8
		NS	2	-	-	-	-	-	-	-	-	-	-	-	-	-	-	-	-	-	-	-	-	-	-	-	-	-
		T	427	230	225	1	2	-	-	2	-	1	-	1	-	-	-	15	40	20	76	15	5	3	10	110	123	8
	22 Sexual Activity with child under 16	M	926	823	817	1	7	-	-	1	-	-	1	-	-	-	1	15	163	14	193	87	-	4	65	450	519	10
		NS	7	1	-	-	-	-	-	-	-	-	-	-	-	-	-	-	-	-	-	-	-	-	-	-	-	-
		T	933	824	817	1	7	-	-	1	-	-	1	-	-	-	1	15	163	14	193	87	-	4	65	450	519	10

21.4 Offenders convicted and sentenced at all courts

England and Wales, 2012

Offence group	Description	Sex	Total Proc Against	Total found Guilty	Total For Sent	Absit Disch	Condl Disch	Fine	CRO	SO	CPO	ACO	CPO&RO	Curf Order	Rep Order	APO	DTTO	REFO	Comm Order	YRO (1)	Total Comm Sentences	SS	Sec 90-92	DTO	YOI	Unsus Sent Impr	Imm cust	ODW
	23 Familial Sexual Offences (Incest)	M	122	104	104	-	1	-	-	-	-	-	-	-	-	-	-	1	19	2	22	5	-	-	1	75	76	-
		F	4	3	3	-	-	-	-	-	-	-	-	-	-	-	-	1	1	-	2	1	-	-	-	-	-	-
		NS	2	-	-	-	-	-	-	-	-	-	-	-	-	-	-	-	-	-	-	-	-	-	-	-	-	-
		T	128	107	107	-	1	-	-	-	-	-	-	-	-	-	-	2	20	2	24	6	-	-	1	75	76	-
	24 Exploitation of Prostitution	M	17	26	27	-	-	1	-	-	-	-	-	-	-	-	-	-	1	-	1	9	-	-	1	15	16	1
		F	19	16	15	-	-	-	-	-	-	-	-	-	-	-	-	1	1	-	1	2	-	-	-	11	11	1
		T	36	42	42	-	-	1	-	-	-	-	-	-	-	-	-	1	2	-	2	11	-	-	1	26	27	1
	70 Sexual activity etc. with a person with a mental disorder	M	40	28	27	-	-	-	-	-	-	-	-	-	-	-	-	1	2	-	3	1	-	-	1	22	23	1
		F	4	1	1	-	-	-	-	-	-	-	-	-	-	-	-	-	-	-	-	-	-	-	-	-	-	-
		T	44	29	28	-	-	-	-	-	-	-	-	-	-	-	-	1	2	-	3	1	-	-	1	23	24	1
	71 Abuse of children through prostitution and pornography	M	73	64	64	-	1	-	-	-	-	-	-	-	-	-	-	-	5	-	5	3	-	-	-	53	53	2
		F	7	2	2	-	-	-	-	-	-	-	-	-	-	-	-	-	-	-	-	-	-	-	-	2	2	2
		T	80	66	66	-	1	-	-	-	-	-	-	-	-	-	-	-	5	-	5	3	-	-	-	55	55	2
	72 Trafficking for sexual exploitation	M	12	7	7	-	-	-	-	-	-	-	-	-	-	-	-	-	-	-	-	-	-	-	1	6	7	-
		F	4	3	3	-	-	-	-	-	-	-	-	-	-	-	-	-	-	-	-	-	-	-	-	3	3	-
		T	16	10	10	-	-	-	-	-	-	-	-	-	-	-	-	-	-	-	-	-	-	-	1	9	10	1
	73 Abuse of trust- sexual offences	M	23	24	26	1	-	-	-	-	-	-	-	-	-	-	-	-	5	-	5	7	-	-	1	12	12	1
		F	5	6	6	-	-	-	-	-	-	-	-	-	-	-	-	-	1	-	1	2	-	-	-	3	3	-
		T	28	30	32	1	-	-	-	-	-	-	-	-	-	-	-	-	6	-	6	9	-	-	1	15	15	1
	74 Gross Indecency with Children	M	32	82	82	-	1	-	-	-	-	-	-	-	-	-	-	1	9	-	11	10	-	-	-	60	60	1
		F	2	2	2	-	-	-	-	2	-	-	-	-	-	-	-	-	-	-	-	-	-	-	-	-	-	-
		T	33	84	84	-	1	-	-	2	-	-	-	-	-	-	-	1	9	-	11	11	-	-	-	61	61	1
	88 Miscellaneous sexual offences	M	1,015	823	826	-	38	58	-	8	-	2	1	-	-	-	-	21	385	13	419	76	-	-	11	202	213	22
		F	4	1	1	-	-	-	-	-	-	-	-	-	-	-	-	-	-	-	1	-	-	-	-	-	-	-
		NS	6	6	6	-	-	-	-	-	-	-	-	-	-	-	-	-	4	-	4	-	-	-	-	-	-	-
		T	1,025	830	833	-	38	58	-	8	-	2	1	-	-	-	-	21	390	13	424	76	-	-	11	203	214	22
	Sub-total	M	9,230	5,686	5,675	8	91	59	6	8	-	3	1	-	-	-	-	136	1,207	134	1,494	476	33	48	204	3,091	3,376	129
		F	111	70	69	-	1	1	1	-	-	1	-	-	-	-	-	1	8	-	10	11	2	-	1	43	46	1
		NS	72	12	12	-	-	-	-	-	-	-	-	-	-	-	1	1	7	1	9	1	-	-	-	1	1	-
		T	9,413	5,769	5,756	8	92	102	7	8	-	4	1	-	-	-	1	138	1,222	135	1,513	488	35	48	205	3,135	3,423	130
Burglary	28 Burglary in a Dwelling	M	15,589	12,021	11,818	2	71	32	2	2	-	2	1	10	3	-	-	636	1,476	920	3,051	1,373	10	446	1,196	5,474	7,126	163
		F	1,041	685	671	-	9	2	1	-	-	-	-	-	-	-	-	54	161	38	254	120	-	9	34	229	272	14
		NS	125	66	-	-	1	1	1	-	-	-	-	-	-	-	-	7	5	7	19	-	-	10	2	-	14	-
		T	16,755	12,772	12,531	2	81	35	3	2	-	2	1	10	3	-	-	697	1,642	965	3,324	1,497	10	465	1,232	5,708	7,415	177
	29 Aggravated Burglary in a Dwelling	M	765	298	298	2	1	-	-	-	-	3	-	-	-	-	-	3	3	3	9	3	9	5	53	213	280	6
		F	45	14	14	-	-	-	-	-	-	1	-	-	-	-	-	-	-	-	1	-	-	1	3	9	13	-
		NS	7	-	-	-	-	-	-	-	-	-	-	-	-	-	-	-	-	-	-	-	-	-	-	1	-	-
		T	817	312	312	2	1	-	-	-	-	4	-	-	-	-	-	3	3	3	10	3	9	6	56	222	293	6
	30 Burglary in a Building Other than a Dwelling	M	11,056	8,954	8,848	10	245	228	2	-	-	3	1	5	4	-	-	445	2,431	560	3,450	1,054	1	108	341	3,141	3,591	270
		F	433	330	338	-	14	7	-	-	-	1	-	-	3	-	-	49	86	32	171	44	-	5	16	69	90	12
		NS	74	41	36	-	1	-	-	-	-	-	-	-	-	-	-	2	11	4	17	-	-	2	2	13	16	-
		T	11,563	9,325	9,222	10	260	235	2	-	-	4	1	5	7	-	-	496	2,528	596	3,638	1,100	1	115	358	3,223	3,697	282
	31 Aggravated Burglary in a Building not a Dwelling	M	44	18	18	-	-	-	-	-	-	-	-	-	-	-	-	1	-	-	1	-	2	-	1	14	17	-
		NS	1	-	-	-	-	-	-	-	-	-	-	-	-	-	-	-	-	-	-	-	-	-	-	-	-	-
		T	45	18	18	-	-	-	-	-	-	-	-	-	-	-	-	1	-	-	1	-	2	-	1	14	17	-
	Sub-total	M	27,454	21,291	20,982	12	316	260	4	-	-	5	-	15	7	-	-	1,085	3,910	1,483	6,511	2,430	22	559	1,591	8,842	11,014	439
		F	1,519	1,029	1,023	-	23	9	1	-	-	1	-	-	3	-	-	103	247	71	426	164	-	15	53	307	375	26
		NS	207	107	78	-	1	-	5	-	-	6	-	15	-	-	-	9	16	11	36	6	-	12	2	18	33	-
		T	29,180	22,427	22,083	12	341	270	5	2	-	6	1	15	10	-	-	1,197	4,173	1,565	6,973	2,600	22	586	1,647	9,167	11,422	465
Robbery	34 Robbery	M	11,176	7,641	7,640	1	15	-	5	3	-	5	-	1	10	-	-	1,076	178	994	2,270	474	131	568	1,233	2,784	4,716	164
		F	972	666	673	-	2	-	3	-	-	1	-	1	-	-	-	141	33	111	286	81	1	32	48	205	286	17
		NS	119	30	30	1	-	-	3	3	-	-	-	-	-	-	-	20	20	8	28	-	-	-	1	-	17	1

21.4 Offenders convicted and sentenced at all courts

England and Wales, 2012

Offence group	Description		Total Proc Against	Total found Guilty	Total For Sent	Absit Disch	Condl Disch	Fine	CRO	SO	CPO	ACO	CPO&RO	Curf Order	Rep Order	APO	DTTO	REFO	Comm Order	YRO (1)	Total Comm Sentences	SS	Sec 90-92	DTO	YOI	Unsus Sent Impr	Imm cust	ODW
	Sub-total	T	12,267	8,337	8,343	2	17	1	3	3	-	5	-	11	1	-	-	1,237	211	1,113	2,584	555	132	600	1,281	2,989	5,002	182
		M	11,176	7,641	7,640	1	15	-	3	3	-	5	-	10	1	-	-	1,076	178	994	2,270	474	131	568	1,233	2,784	4,716	164
		F	972	666	673	-	2	1	-	-	-	-	-	1	-	-	-	141	33	111	286	81	1	32	48	205	286	17
		NS	119	30	30	1	-	-	-	-	-	-	-	1	-	-	-	20	-	8	28	-	-	-	-	-	-	1
Theft and Handling	37.2 Aggravated Vehicle Taking	T	1,077	1,025	1,039	2	12	9	-	-	-	-	-	11	-	-	-	77	260	76	414	152	-	31	90	314	435	17
		M	1,018	971	984	2	10	7	-	-	-	-	-	10	-	-	-	74	235	73	383	142	-	31	89	308	428	17
		F	52	48	50	-	2	2	-	-	-	-	-	1	-	-	-	3	24	2	29	10	-	-	1	6	7	-
		NS	7	6	5	-	-	-	-	-	-	-	-	-	-	-	-	-	1	-	2	-	-	-	-	-	-	-
	38 Money laundering	T	1,136	1,079	1,094	-	14	11	-	-	-	-	-	1	1	-	-	81	285	78	445	162	-	34	91	320	445	17
		M	1,898	1,138	1,113	-	67	67	-	-	-	1	-	1	1	-	-	19	244	20	284	264	-	2	17	396	415	16
		F	548	274	270	-	27	6	-	-	-	-	-	1	-	-	-	5	68	2	76	112	-	-	1	44	45	4
		NS	59	10	6	-	1	-	-	-	-	-	-	-	-	-	-	-	2	-	3	-	-	-	-	1	-	-
	39 Theft from the Person of Another	T	2,505	1,422	1,389	-	95	73	1	-	-	1	-	1	1	-	-	24	314	23	363	377	-	2	18	441	461	20
		M	5,249	4,688	4,706	14	409	325	1	-	-	1	-	4	11	-	-	300	1,047	311	1,675	429	2	62	167	1,487	1,718	136
		F	1,336	1,182	1,181	3	120	57	-	-	-	-	-	-	2	-	-	64	252	70	388	198	-	14	19	344	377	38
		NS	114	83	77	-	5	7	-	-	-	-	-	-	-	-	-	6	12	8	26	6	-	2	2	28	32	1
	40 Theft in Dwelling not Automatic M/c or Meter	T	6,699	5,953	5,964	17	534	389	1	-	-	1	-	4	13	-	-	370	1,311	389	2,089	633	2	78	188	1,859	2,127	175
		M	2,308	1,996	1,987	4	201	106	1	-	-	1	-	3	6	-	-	112	604	133	860	188	-	24	71	440	535	93
		F	515	428	434	3	55	34	-	-	-	-	-	-	1	-	-	32	130	20	183	67	-	5	1	68	74	18
		NS	19	11	8	-	-	-	-	-	-	-	-	-	-	-	-	-	-	-	-	-	-	-	3	3	3	-
	41 Theft by an Employee	T	2,842	2,435	2,429	7	256	140	1	-	-	1	-	3	7	-	-	144	736	154	1,046	257	-	29	75	508	612	111
		M	1,879	1,668	1,686	1	99	179	-	-	-	1	-	-	-	-	-	11	752	5	768	415	-	2	2	200	202	22
		F	682	601	614	3	42	34	-	-	-	-	-	-	-	-	-	5	268	1	274	183	-	-	-	70	70	8
		NS	26	20	16	-	6	1	-	-	-	-	-	-	-	-	-	-	6	-	6	5	-	-	-	2	8	-
	42 Theft or Unauthorised Taking from Mail	T	2,587	2,289	2,316	4	143	214	1	-	-	1	-	4	13	-	-	16	1,026	6	1,048	603	2	2	188	272	274	30
		M	109	123	127	-	2	9	-	-	-	1	-	-	-	-	-	3	46	2	51	39	-	1	4	21	26	14
		F	11	13	13	2	2	-	-	-	-	-	-	1	-	-	-	-	7	-	7	2	-	-	2	2	2	2
		NS	14	9	9	-	-	-	-	-	-	-	-	-	-	-	-	-	1	-	1	6	-	-	-	2	2	-
	43 Abstracting Electricity	T	134	145	149	-	4	9	1	-	-	2	-	3	-	-	-	3	54	5	59	47	-	1	4	25	30	12
		M	330	332	379	-	75	58	-	-	-	2	-	28	68	-	-	105	752	5	107	109	-	1	4	18	12	2
		F	111	101	102	-	28	16	-	-	-	-	-	7	21	-	-	42	42	1	42	11	-	-	-	3	3	2
		NS	2	2	2	-	-	-	-	-	-	-	-	-	-	-	-	-	-	-	-	-	-	-	-	3	3	-
	44 Theft of Pedal Cycle	T	443	434	482	-	103	74	-	-	-	2	-	35	89	-	-	147	440	2	149	120	-	11	22	245	280	14
		M	2,157	1,815	1,804	18	303	191	-	-	-	2	-	1	10	-	-	159	440	214	824	100	-	11	24	245	280	88
		F	58	42	42	-	7	6	-	-	-	-	-	-	-	-	-	7	11	3	21	2	-	-	3	4	4	2
		NS	36	32	31	1	2	2	-	-	-	-	-	-	-	-	-	7	7	6	20	2	-	-	1	5	5	1
	45 Theft from Vehicle	T	2,251	1,889	1,877	19	312	197	1	-	-	1	-	1	10	-	-	173	458	223	865	104	-	11	27	251	289	91
		M	4,789	3,940	3,883	13	427	300	3	1	-	2	-	3	7	-	-	173	1,216	189	1,591	307	-	26	72	949	1,047	198
		F	119	83	83	1	15	4	-	-	-	-	-	1	-	-	-	6	30	5	41	7	-	-	6	11	11	4
		NS	15	12	11	-	-	1	-	-	-	-	-	-	-	-	-	1	-	-	5	-	-	-	-	3	-	-
	46 Theft from Shops	T	77,042	72,321	71,866	395	17,687	12,025	-	1	-	13	-	35	89	-	-	1,386	17,011	1,346	19,880	3,853	-	82	468	13,094	13,644	4,382
		M	56,980	53,663	53,302	311	12,041	9,296	-	1	-	2	-	3	7	-	-	180	1,250	194	1,637	314	-	26	72	963	1,061	202
		F	19,583	18,211	18,122	82	5,565	2,673	-	-	-	12	-	28	68	-	-	903	12,173	984	14,168	2,812	-	66	400	10,734	11,200	3,474
		NS	479	447	442	2	81	56	-	-	-	1	-	7	21	-	-	471	4,749	344	5,593	1,002	-	12	6	2,251	2,325	882
	47 Theft from Automatic Machine or Meter	T	313	304	306	-	30	28	-	-	-	1	-	-	1	-	-	12	89	18	119	39	-	4	109	251	119	26
		M	29	23	22	-	1	1	-	-	-	2	-	3	7	-	-	5	76	7	88	29	3	-	4	116	120	11
		F	4	3	3	-	1	-	-	-	-	-	-	-	-	-	-	1	10	-	10	3	-	-	-	8	8	8
		NS	-	-	-	-	-	-	-	-	-	-	-	-	-	-	-	-	-	-	-	-	-	-	-	-	-	-
	48 Theft or Unauthorised Taking of Motor Vehicle	T	346	330	331	-	32	28	-	-	-	1	-	-	-	-	-	5	87	7	99	32	-	13	4	125	129	11
		M	1,131	784	781	1	48	26	-	-	-	1	-	1	1	-	-	26	224	35	287	82	2	29	29	278	320	17
		F	28	22	22	-	5	1	-	-	-	-	-	-	-	-	-	5	5	-	6	6	-	-	-	3	3	3
		NS	8	5	4	-	-	-	-	-	-	-	-	-	-	-	-	2	2	-	2	7	-	-	-	2	2	2

21.4 Offenders convicted and sentenced at all courts

England and Wales, 2012

Offence group	Description		Total Proc Against	Total found Guilty	Total For Sent	Absl Disch	Cond Disch	Fine	CRO	SO	CPO	ACO	CPO&RO	Curf Order	Rep Order	APO	DTTO	REFO	Comm Order	YRO [1]	Total Comm Sentences	SS	Sec 90-92	DTO	YOI	Unsus Sent Impr	Imm cust	ODW
	(continued)	T	1,167	811	807	-	53	27	-	-	-	1	-	1	1	-	-	27	231	35	295	89	-	13	29	283	325	17
	49 Other Theft or Unauthorised Taking	M	12,063	9,819	9,760	40	1,751	1,478	-	-	1	1	-	11	25	-	-	460	2,766	471	3,737	701	-	34	124	1,531	1,689	364
		F	1,544	1,203	1,195	8	287	146	-	-	1	1	-	2	3	-	-	64	327	51	448	99	-	2	7	145	154	53
		NS	96	68	63	-	9	8	-	-	-	-	-	1	-	-	-	3	13	8	25	3	-	-	-	15	15	3
		T	13,703	11,090	11,018	48	2,047	1,632	-	-	1	3	-	14	28	-	-	527	3,106	530	4,210	803	-	36	131	1,691	1,858	420
	54 Handling Stolen Goods	M	7,904	6,539	6,441	20	579	860	-	-	1	6	-	5	10	-	-	282	1,928	431	2,663	710	-	38	188	1,262	1,488	121
		F	1,042	874	858	3	168	116	-	-	-	4	-	-	-	-	-	30	299	35	366	104	-	4	11	73	88	13
		NS	55	32	27	2	2	3	-	-	-	-	-	-	-	-	-	3	6	-	10	2	-	-	1	8	9	1
		T	9,001	7,445	7,326	23	749	979	-	-	1	6	-	5	12	-	-	315	2,233	467	3,039	816	-	42	200	1,343	1,585	135
	Sub-total	M	98,187	87,834	87,314	422	16,044	12,932	-	2	2	25	-	56	139	-	-	2,530	21,881	2,880	27,517	6,337	-	308	1,192	17,991	19,493	4,569
		F	25,658	23,105	23,008	103	6,324	3,095	-	-	2	2	-	10	29	-	-	688	6,222	533	7,484	1,807	-	37	105	3,029	3,171	1,024
		NS	934	739	703	3	105	76	-	-	-	-	-	1	-	-	-	33	146	43	223	66	2	9	12	177	198	32
		T	124,779	111,678	111,025	528	22,473	16,103	-	2	2	27	-	67	168	-	-	3,251	28,249	3,456	35,224	8,210	2	354	1,309	21,197	22,862	5,625
Fraud and Forgery	51 Fraud by Company Director etc.	M	43	23	22	-	1	2	-	-	-	-	-	-	-	-	-	-	-	-	4	4	-	-	-	15	15	-
		F	10	2	2	-	-	-	-	-	-	-	-	-	-	-	-	-	-	-	-	-	-	-	-	-	-	-
		NS	1	1	1	-	-	1	-	-	-	-	-	-	-	-	-	-	-	-	-	-	-	-	-	-	-	-
		O	-	-	-	-	-	-	-	-	-	-	-	-	-	-	-	-	-	-	-	-	-	-	-	-	-	-
		T	55	26	25	-	1	3	-	-	-	-	-	-	-	-	-	-	-	-	4	4	-	-	-	15	15	-
	52 False Accounting	M	63	81	84	-	3	2	-	-	-	-	-	-	-	-	-	-	13	-	13	5	-	-	-	16	16	-
		F	39	35	35	-	-	-	-	-	-	-	-	-	-	-	-	-	9	-	9	37	-	-	-	29	29	-
		NS	2	1	-	-	-	1	-	-	-	-	-	-	-	-	-	-	-	-	-	17	-	-	-	9	9	-
		O	-	-	-	-	-	-	-	-	-	-	-	-	-	-	-	-	-	-	-	-	-	-	-	-	-	-
		T	104	117	119	-	3	3	-	-	-	-	-	-	-	-	-	-	22	-	22	54	-	-	-	54	54	-
	53 Other Fraud	M	11,634	9,349	9,265	20	858	1,300	-	1	-	-	-	10	5	-	-	79	2,875	80	3,050	1,582	-	8	78	2,115	2,201	254
		F	5,250	4,134	4,114	16	582	379	-	-	-	-	-	6	1	-	-	51	1,363	37	1,459	1,134	-	2	8	461	471	73
		NS	860	443	379	-	53	66	-	-	-	-	-	-	-	-	-	-	152	2	154	85	-	-	1	18	19	2
		O	24	4	4	-	-	1	-	-	-	-	-	-	-	-	-	-	-	-	-	-	-	-	-	-	-	-
		T	17,768	13,930	13,761	36	1,493	1,746	-	1	1	-	-	16	6	-	-	130	4,390	119	4,663	2,801	-	10	87	2,594	2,691	331
	55 Bankruptcy Offence	M	112	112	113	-	5	7	-	-	-	-	-	-	-	-	-	-	25	-	25	48	-	-	-	28	28	-
		F	16	17	19	-	1	3	-	-	-	-	-	-	-	-	-	-	2	-	2	10	-	-	-	3	3	-
		NS	25	13	7	-	-	2	-	-	-	-	-	-	-	-	-	-	2	-	1	4	-	-	-	-	-	-
		O	-	-	-	-	-	-	-	-	-	-	-	-	-	-	-	-	-	-	-	-	-	-	-	-	-	-
		T	153	142	139	-	6	12	-	-	-	-	-	-	-	-	-	-	28	-	28	62	-	-	-	31	31	-
	60 Forgery etc. of Drug Prescription	M	30	32	31	-	10	2	-	-	-	-	-	-	-	-	-	-	10	-	10	5	-	-	-	4	4	-
		F	9	12	14	-	8	-	-	-	-	-	-	-	-	-	-	-	2	-	3	3	-	-	-	-	-	-
		NS	-	-	-	-	-	-	-	-	-	-	-	-	-	-	-	-	-	-	-	-	-	-	-	-	-	-
		O	-	-	-	-	-	-	-	-	-	-	-	-	-	-	-	-	-	-	-	-	-	-	-	-	-	2
		T	39	44	45	-	18	2	-	-	-	-	-	-	-	-	-	-	12	-	13	8	-	-	-	4	4	2
	61 Other Forgery etc.	M	1,764	1,552	1,538	3	34	74	-	-	-	-	-	-	1	-	-	10	148	13	172	237	-	6	47	951	1,004	14
		F	329	244	244	2	13	3	-	-	-	-	-	-	-	-	-	1	27	1	28	68	-	-	7	122	129	1
		NS	56	8	5	-	2	2	-	-	-	-	-	-	-	-	-	-	-	-	1	-	-	-	-	-	-	-
		O	4	-	-	-	-	-	-	-	-	-	-	-	-	-	-	-	-	-	-	-	-	-	-	-	-	-
		T	2,153	1,806	1,789	5	49	81	-	-	-	-	-	-	1	-	-	11	175	14	201	305	-	6	54	1,073	1,133	15
	814 Fraud, Forgery etc associated with Vehicle or Driver Records	M	430	311	304	1	14	224	-	-	-	-	-	-	-	-	-	1	37	-	38	15	-	6	54	8	9	3
		F	31	15	15	2	2	11	-	-	-	-	-	-	-	-	-	1	1	-	1	-	-	-	1	8	-	-
		NS	45	38	36	-	5	31	-	-	-	-	-	-	-	-	-	-	-	-	-	-	-	-	-	-	-	-
		O	-	-	-	-	-	-	-	-	-	-	-	-	-	-	-	-	-	-	-	-	-	-	-	-	-	-
		T	526	363	363	2	22	273	-	-	-	-	-	-	1	-	-	1	38	-	39	15	-	14	54	8	9	3
	Sub-total	M	14,076	11,460	11,357	24	925	1,611	-	1	-	-	-	6	6	-	-	90	3,108	93	3,308	1,928	-	14	126	3,150	3,290	271
		F	5,684	4,459	4,443	19	606	396	-	-	-	-	-	1	1	-	-	51	1,404	38	1,502	1,233	-	2	15	596	613	74
		NS	989	503	427	-	60	101	-	-	-	-	-	-	-	-	-	1	153	2	156	89	-	-	1	18	19	2
		O	49	15	14	-	1	11	-	-	-	-	-	-	-	-	-	-	-	-	-	-	-	-	-	-	-	-
		T	20,798	16,437	16,241	43	1,592	2,119	-	1	1	-	-	16	7	-	-	142	4,665	133	4,966	3,250	-	16	142	3,764	3,922	349
Criminal Damage	56 Arson	M	1,355	1,101	1,095	18	18	5	-	-	-	-	-	2	3	-	-	134	153	74	368	113	4	15	78	428	525	62
		F	321	251	252	1	12	-	1	-	-	-	-	2	1	-	-	24	58	13	95	28	-	5	10	78	93	23
		NS	12	2	2	-	-	-	-	1	-	-	-	-	-	-	-	2	2	-	2	-	-	-	-	-	-	-

[1] YRO — Youth Rehabilitation Order.

21.4 Offenders convicted and sentenced at all courts

England and Wales, 2012

Note: This is a very dense, multi-column statistical table. Rows are broken down by sex (M = male, F = female, NS = not stated, T = total). A dash (-) indicates nil/no cases. Column abbreviations: Proc = Total Proceeded Against; Guilty = Total found Guilty; ForSent = Total For Sentence; Abs = Absolute Discharge; Cond = Conditional Discharge; CRO = Community Rehabilitation Order; SO = Supervision Order; CPO = Community Punishment Order; ACO = Attendance Centre Order; CPO&RO = Community Punishment & Rehabilitation Order; Curf = Curfew Order; Rep = Reparation Order; APO = Action Plan Order; DTTO = Drug Treatment & Testing Order; REFO = Referral Order; Comm = Community Order; YRO = Youth Rehabilitation Order [1]; TotComm = Total Community Sentences; SS = Suspended Sentence; DTO = Detention & Training Order; YOI = Young Offender Institution; Unsus = Unsuspended Sentence of Imprisonment; Imm = Immediate custody; ODW = Otherwise Dealt With.

Description	Sex	Proc	Guilty	ForSent	Abs	Cond	Fine	CRO	SO	CPO	ACO	CPO&RO	Curf	Rep	APO	DTTO	REFO	Comm	YRO[1]	TotComm	SS	Sec 90-92	DTO	YOI	Unsus	Imm	ODW
(continued)	T	1,688	1,354	1,349	5	30	5	1	1	1	-	-	2	3	-	-	160	211	87	465	141	4	20	88	506	618	85
57 Criminal Damage Endangering Life	M	146	84	85	1	8	9	-	-	-	-	-	-	-	-	-	4	24	3	31	14	-	1	2	17	20	2
	F	18	11	11	-	-	1	-	-	-	-	-	-	-	-	-	4	3	-	7	2	-	-	-	1	1	-
	NS	11	5	5	-	1	1	-	-	-	-	-	-	-	-	-	-	2	-	2	-	-	-	-	1	1	-
	T	175	100	101	1	9	11	-	-	-	-	-	-	-	-	-	8	29	3	40	16	-	1	2	19	22	2
58 Other Criminal Damage	M	4,579	3,536	3,475	30	825	611	-	-	-	-	-	-	7	-	-	222	897	195	1,322	133	-	6	23	219	248	306
	F	566	432	425	11	129	44	-	-	-	-	-	-	3	-	-	53	87	37	180	9	-	1	1	7	9	43
	NS	34	25	24	-	5	3	-	-	-	-	-	-	-	-	-	3	6	2	11	1	-	-	1	1	2	2
	T	5,179	3,993	3,924	41	959	658	-	-	-	-	-	-	10	-	-	278	990	234	1,513	143	-	7	25	227	259	351
59 Threat etc., to commit Criminal Damage	M	831	512	499	2	107	58	-	-	-	-	-	-	3	-	-	15	137	17	172	45	-	1	5	82	88	27
	F	80	53	53	1	17	3	-	-	-	-	-	-	1	-	-	4	16	4	25	3	-	-	-	1	1	3
	NS	3	1	1	-	-	-	-	-	-	-	-	-	-	-	-	-	1	-	1	-	-	-	-	-	-	-
	T	914	566	553	3	124	61	-	-	-	-	-	-	4	-	-	19	154	21	198	48	-	1	5	83	89	30
Sub-total	M	6,911	5,233	5,154	37	958	683	1	1	-	-	-	3	13	-	-	375	1,211	289	1,893	305	4	23	108	746	881	397
	F	985	747	741	13	158	48	-	-	-	-	-	-	4	-	-	85	164	54	307	42	-	6	11	87	104	69
	NS	60	33	32	-	6	4	-	-	-	-	-	-	-	-	-	5	9	2	16	1	-	-	1	2	3	2
	T	7,956	6,013	5,927	50	1,122	735	1	1	-	-	-	3	17	-	-	465	1,384	345	2,216	348	4	29	120	835	988	468

Drug Offences

Description	Sex	Proc	Guilty	ForSent	Abs	Cond	Fine	CRO	SO	CPO	ACO	CPO&RO	Curf	Rep	APO	DTTO	REFO	Comm	YRO[1]	TotComm	SS	Sec 90-92	DTO	YOI	Unsus	Imm	ODW
92.1 Unlawful importation - Class unspecified	M	11	24	24	-	-	-	-	-	-	-	-	-	-	-	-	-	4	4	4	4	-	-	-	6	16	16
	F	-	5	6	-	-	-	-	-	-	-	-	-	-	-	-	-	-	-	-	-	-	-	-	-	6	-
	T	11	29	30	-	-	-	-	-	-	-	-	-	-	-	-	-	4	4	4	4	-	-	-	6	22	16
92.2 Unlawful exportation - Class unspecified	M	-	-	-	-	-	-	-	-	-	-	-	-	-	-	-	-	-	-	-	-	-	-	-	-	-	-
	F	-	-	-	-	-	-	-	-	-	-	-	-	-	-	-	-	-	-	-	-	-	-	-	-	-	-
	T	-	-	-	-	-	-	-	-	-	-	-	-	-	-	-	-	-	-	-	-	-	-	-	-	-	-
92.3 Unlawful importation - Class A	M	318	283	284	-	-	-	-	-	-	-	-	-	-	-	-	-	1	-	1	2	-	-	-	273	279	2
	F	76	59	61	-	-	-	-	-	-	-	-	-	-	-	-	-	-	-	-	-	-	-	-	58	61	-
	NS	33	6	-	-	-	-	-	-	-	-	-	-	-	-	-	-	-	-	-	-	-	-	-	-	-	-
	T	427	348	345	-	-	-	-	-	-	-	-	-	-	-	-	-	1	-	1	2	-	-	-	331	340	2
92.4 Unlawful importation - Class B	M	125	88	78	-	-	2	-	-	-	-	-	-	-	-	-	-	1	-	1	6	-	-	-	331	340	2
	F	30	21	20	-	-	1	-	-	-	-	-	-	-	-	-	-	2	-	2	4	-	-	-	66	67	1
	NS	10	4	-	-	-	-	-	-	-	-	-	-	-	-	-	-	-	-	-	-	-	-	-	13	14	-
	T	165	113	98	-	-	3	-	-	-	-	-	-	-	-	-	-	3	-	3	10	-	-	-	331	81	2
92.5 Unlawful importation - Class C	M	20	15	14	-	-	-	-	-	-	-	-	-	-	-	-	-	2	-	2	5	-	-	-	79	8	1
	F	2	-	-	-	-	-	-	-	-	-	-	-	-	-	-	-	-	-	-	-	-	-	-	8	8	-
	NS	2	-	-	-	-	-	-	-	-	-	-	-	-	-	-	-	-	-	-	-	-	-	-	-	-	-
	T	24	15	14	-	-	-	-	-	-	-	-	-	-	-	-	-	2	-	2	5	-	-	-	-	8	-
92.6 Unlawful exportation - Class A	M	3	-	-	-	-	-	-	-	-	-	-	-	-	-	-	-	-	-	-	-	-	-	-	8	8	-
	F	1	-	-	-	-	-	-	-	-	-	-	-	-	-	-	-	-	-	-	-	-	-	-	7	7	-
	T	4	-	-	-	-	-	-	-	-	-	-	-	1	-	-	-	-	-	-	1	-	-	-	5	5	-
92.7 Unlawful exportation - Class B	M	2	-	-	-	-	-	-	-	-	-	-	-	-	-	-	-	-	-	-	-	-	-	-	12	12	-
	F	2	-	-	-	-	-	-	-	-	-	-	-	-	-	-	-	1	-	1	1	-	-	-	18	18	1
	T	4	-	-	-	-	-	-	-	-	-	-	-	-	-	-	-	1	-	1	1	-	-	-	4	4	1
92.8 Unlawful exportation - Class C	M	2	-	-	-	-	-	-	-	-	-	-	-	-	-	-	-	1	-	1	1	-	-	-	22	22	-
	T	2	-	-	-	-	-	-	-	-	-	-	-	1	-	-	1	1	-	1	1	-	-	-	-	-	-
Inciting another to supply a controlled drug - Class A	M	1	-	-	-	-	-	-	-	-	-	-	-	-	-	-	-	-	-	-	1	-	-	-	-	-	-
	T	1	-	-	-	-	-	-	-	-	-	-	-	-	-	-	-	-	-	-	1	-	-	-	-	-	-
Inciting another to supply a controlled drug - Class B	M	1	-	-	-	-	-	-	-	-	-	-	-	-	-	-	-	-	-	-	1	-	-	-	-	-	-
	T	1	-	-	-	-	-	-	-	-	-	-	-	-	-	-	-	-	-	-	1	-	-	-	-	-	-
Other drug offences	M	459	423	422	1	42	92	-	-	-	-	-	-	-	-	-	1	132	7	140	85	-	-	3	48	51	11
	F	238	244	244	-	47	26	-	-	-	-	-	-	-	-	-	-	119	-	120	36	-	-	-	10	10	5
	NS	4	3	3	-	-	1	-	-	-	-	-	-	-	-	-	-	2	2	2	-	-	-	-	-	-	-
	T	701	670	669	1	89	119	-	-	-	-	-	1	-	-	-	1	253	7	262	121	-	-	3	58	61	16

21.4 Offenders convicted and sentenced at all courts

England and Wales, 2012

Offence group	Description		Total Proc Against	Total found Guilty	Total For Sent	Absl Disch	Condl Disch	Fine	CRO	SO	CPO	ACO	CPO&RO	Curf Order	Rep Order	APO	DTTO	REFO	Comm Order	YRO (1)	Total Comm Sentences	SS	Sec 90-92	DTO	YOI	Unsus Sent Impr	Imm cust	ODW
	Possession of a controlled drug - Class A	M	9,282	8,896	8,812	19	1,087	4,648	-	-	-	-	-	2	-	-	-	83	1,609	96	1,790	238	-	3	35	483	521	509
		F	913	849	849	2	196	326	-	-	-	-	-	1	-	-	-	2	147	7	157	34	-	-	3	46	49	85
		NS	54	48	46	1	6	25	-	-	-	-	-	-	-	-	-	3	4	2	9	-	-	-	-	3	3	2
		T	10,249	9,793	9,707	22	1,289	4,999	-	-	-	-	-	3	-	-	-	88	1,760	105	1,956	272	-	3	38	532	573	596
	Possession of a controlled drug - Class B	M	28,466	27,209	27,052	341	5,949	13,993	-	-	-	10	-	11	32	-	-	977	2,957	680	4,667	280	-	15	57	456	528	1,294
		F	1,662	1,531	1,531	20	524	597	-	-	-	-	-	-	-	-	-	55	204	24	283	24	-	-	-	24	24	59
		NS	143	130	127	2	29	53	-	-	-	-	-	-	-	-	-	7	16	7	30	1	-	-	1	4	5	7
		T	30,271	28,870	28,710	363	6,502	14,643	-	-	-	10	-	11	32	-	-	1,039	3,177	711	4,980	305	-	15	58	484	557	1,360
	Possession of a controlled drug - Class C	M	1,149	1,056	1,050	14	346	478	-	-	-	-	-	2	2	-	-	5	114	8	131	17	-	1	1	22	25	39
		F	123	111	111	2	46	31	-	-	-	-	-	-	-	-	-	1	16	1	17	2	-	-	-	6	6	7
		NS	7	6	6	-	1	5	-	-	-	-	-	-	-	-	-	-	-	-	-	-	-	-	-	-	-	-
		T	1,279	1,173	1,167	16	393	514	-	-	-	-	-	2	2	-	-	5	130	9	148	19	-	1	2	28	31	46
	Possession of a controlled drug - Class unspecified	T	-	-	-	-	-	-	-	-	-	-	-	-	-	-	-	-	-	-	-	-	-	-	-	-	-	-
	Production, supply and possession with intent to supply a controlled drug - Class A	M	6,441	4,946	4,910	3	7	8	1	-	-	-	-	3	-	-	-	51	304	61	420	486	5	71	521	3,348	3,945	41
		F	595	388	385	-	3	1	-	-	-	-	-	-	-	-	-	3	80	2	85	104	-	3	8	179	190	2
		NS	56	3	3	-	-	-	-	-	-	-	-	-	-	-	-	-	-	-	-	-	-	-	-	-	-	-
		T	7,092	5,337	5,295	3	10	9	1	-	-	-	-	3	-	-	-	54	384	63	505	590	5	74	529	3,527	4,135	43
	Production, supply and possession with intent to supply a controlled drug - Class B	M	11,777	10,265	10,106	2	442	932	-	-	-	-	-	12	2	-	-	143	2,954	103	3,214	2,549	3	24	162	2,573	2,762	205
		F	1,058	738	729	-	66	60	-	-	-	-	-	-	-	-	-	7	276	1	284	220	-	1	7	77	84	15
		NS	78	36	25	-	1	6	-	-	-	-	-	-	-	-	-	2	9	3	14	1	-	-	-	-	-	2
		T	12,913	11,039	10,860	2	509	998	-	-	-	-	-	12	2	-	-	152	3,239	107	3,512	2,770	3	25	169	2,650	2,847	222
	Production, supply and possession with intent to supply a controlled drug - Class C	M	419	369	341	-	20	56	-	-	-	1	-	-	-	-	-	3	97	4	105	88	-	-	5	61	66	6
		F	56	45	43	-	4	2	-	-	-	-	-	-	-	-	-	1	16	1	18	13	-	-	-	5	5	1
		NS	3	2	1	-	-	-	-	-	-	-	-	-	-	-	-	-	-	-	-	-	-	-	-	-	-	-
		T	478	416	385	-	24	58	-	-	-	1	-	-	-	-	-	4	114	5	124	101	-	-	5	66	71	7
	Production, supply and possession with intent to supply a controlled drug - Class unspecified	M	269	269	269	1	-	-	-	-	-	-	-	-	-	-	-	-	11	-	12	14	-	3	10	229	242	1
		F	-	13	13	-	-	-	-	-	-	-	-	-	-	-	-	-	12	-	13	3	-	-	1	8	9	-
		T	282	282	282	1	-	-	-	-	-	-	-	-	-	-	-	-	12	-	13	17	-	3	11	237	251	1
	Sub-total	M	58,474	53,873	53,391	380	7,893	20,210	2	-	-	11	-	30	36	-	-	1,263	8,191	959	10,492	3,772	8	117	802	7,608	8,535	2,109
		F	4,754	4,014	4,002	24	886	1,044	-	-	-	-	-	2	-	-	-	68	859	36	965	441	-	3	23	441	467	175
		NS	390	238	208	3	37	90	-	-	-	-	-	-	-	-	-	12	32	12	56	2	-	-	-	7	9	11
		T	63,618	58,125	57,601	407	8,816	21,344	2	-	-	11	-	32	36	-	-	1,343	9,082	1,007	11,513	4,215	8	121	826	8,056	9,011	2,295
Indictable Motoring	99 Dangerous Driving	M	2,815	2,577	2,629	-	11	83	-	-	-	-	-	-	-	-	-	39	587	32	660	765	-	20	144	922	1,086	24
		F	163	153	154	-	3	20	-	-	-	-	-	-	-	-	-	4	44	-	47	66	-	-	-	18	18	-
		NS	20	10	5	-	-	2	-	-	-	-	-	-	-	-	-	-	2	-	3	-	-	-	-	-	-	-
		T	2,998	2,740	2,788	-	14	105	-	-	-	-	-	1	-	-	-	43	633	32	710	831	-	20	144	940	1,104	24
	99A Driving licence related offences: Making false statements	M	10	6	5	-	-	4	-	-	-	-	-	-	-	-	-	-	6	-	6	-	-	-	-	-	-	-
		F	-	2	2	-	-	-	-	-	-	-	-	-	-	-	-	-	-	-	-	-	-	-	-	1	1	-
		T	11	8	7	-	1	4	-	-	-	-	-	1	-	-	-	-	6	-	6	1	-	-	-	1	1	1
	99C Vehicle insurance offences: Making false statements	M	220	174	174	-	8	104	-	-	-	-	-	-	-	-	-	-	39	-	39	9	-	-	-	10	10	10
		F	22	18	18	-	1	12	-	-	-	-	-	-	-	-	-	-	3	-	3	2	-	-	-	-	-	-
		NS	1	1	1	-	-	-	-	-	-	-	-	-	-	-	-	-	-	-	1	-	-	-	-	-	-	-
		T	243	193	193	-	9	116	-	-	-	-	-	-	-	-	-	-	43	-	43	11	-	-	-	10	10	10
	99D Vehicle registration and excise licence offences: Making false statements	M	-	1	1	-	-	-	-	-	-	-	-	-	-	-	-	-	1	-	1	1	-	-	-	-	-	-
		T	-	1	1	-	-	-	-	-	-	-	-	-	-	-	-	-	1	-	1	1	-	-	-	-	-	-
	99F Work record or employment offences	M	-	1	1	-	-	-	-	-	-	-	-	-	-	-	-	-	-	-	-	-	-	-	-	-	-	-
		T	-	1	1	-	-	-	-	-	-	-	-	-	-	-	-	-	-	-	-	-	-	-	-	-	-	-
	Sub-total	M	3,045	2,759	2,810	3	19	191	-	-	1	-	-	1	-	-	-	39	627	32	700	776	-	20	144	932	1,096	25

21.4 Offenders convicted and sentenced at all courts

England and Wales, 2012

Offence group	Description	Sex	Total Proc Against	Total found Guilty	Total For Sent	Absl Disch	Cond Disch	Fine	CRO	SO	CPO	ACO	CPO&RO	Curf Order	Rep Order	APO	DTTO	REFO	Comm Order	YRO(1)	Total Comm Sentences	SS	Sec 90-92	DTO	YOI	Unsus Sent Impr	Imm cust	ODW
Other Indictable (Not Motoring)		F	186	173	174	-	5	32	-	-	-	-	-	-	-	-	-	3	47	-	50	68	-	-	-	19	19	-
		NS	21	11	6	3	-	2	-	-	-	-	-	-	-	-	-	1	3	3	4	4	-	-	-	-	-	-
		T	3,252	2,943	2,990	3	24	225	-	-	-	-	-	-	-	-	-	43	677	32	754	844	-	20	144	951	1,115	25
	33 Going Equipped for Stealing, etc.	M	2,197	1,647	1,653	5	135	169	-	-	-	-	-	-	-	-	-	66	558	58	682	148	-	9	36	420	465	49
		F	201	148	149	-	13	28	-	-	-	-	-	-	-	-	-	-	55	-	56	9	-	-	2	32	34	9
		NS	25	16	16	-	1	1	-	-	-	-	-	-	-	-	-	1	6	-	6	3	-	-	1	3	4	1
		T	2,423	1,811	1,818	5	149	198	-	-	-	-	-	-	-	-	-	67	619	58	744	160	-	9	39	455	503	59
	35 Blackmail	M	281	145	145	5	1	-	-	-	-	-	-	-	-	-	-	3	3	10	16	11	-	1	9	106	116	1
		F	28	14	14	-	-	-	-	-	-	-	-	-	-	-	-	-	-	-	-	-	-	-	-	11	11	-
		NS	3	-	-	-	-	-	-	-	-	-	-	-	-	-	-	-	-	-	-	-	-	-	-	-	-	-
		T	312	159	159	5	1	-	-	-	-	-	-	-	-	-	-	3	3	10	16	11	-	1	9	117	127	1
	36 Kidnapping, etc.	M	832	309	309	-	1	-	-	-	-	-	-	-	-	-	-	2	17	5	24	32	2	2	39	202	245	7
		F	86	26	26	-	-	-	-	-	-	-	-	-	-	-	-	-	2	2	4	9	2	-	3	8	13	-
		NS	11	-	-	-	-	-	-	-	-	-	-	-	-	-	-	-	-	-	-	-	-	-	-	-	-	-
		T	929	335	335	-	1	-	-	-	-	-	-	-	-	-	-	2	19	7	28	41	4	2	42	210	258	7
	64 Rioting	M	18	20	20	-	-	-	-	-	-	-	-	-	-	-	-	-	-	-	-	-	-	-	4	14	20	7
		T	18	20	20	-	-	-	-	-	-	-	-	-	-	-	-	-	-	-	-	-	-	-	4	14	20	7
	65 Violent Disorder	M	568	522	534	1	3	3	-	-	-	-	-	-	-	-	-	34	24	40	99	62	-	41	118	199	359	7
		F	15	10	10	-	-	-	-	-	-	-	-	-	-	-	-	-	2	-	2	6	-	-	-	-	-	-
		NS	5	2	2	-	-	-	-	-	-	-	-	-	-	-	-	1	-	1	2	-	-	-	1	-	2	-
		T	588	534	546	1	3	3	-	-	-	-	-	-	-	-	-	35	26	41	103	68	-	41	119	199	361	7
	66 Other Offence against the State or Public Order	M	8,831	8,829	8,351	37	579	931	-	-	-	-	-	10	-	-	-	159	1,352	137	1,663	1,722	1	66	293	2,304	2,664	1,235
		F	603	562	614	5	37	56	-	-	-	-	-	2	-	-	-	17	171	21	211	125	-	1	15	84	100	69
		NS	43	46	78	-	3	4	-	-	-	-	-	-	-	-	-	-	3	4	7	3	-	1	2	11	14	12
		T	9,477	9,437	9,043	42	619	991	-	-	-	-	-	12	-	-	-	176	1,526	162	1,881	1,850	1	68	310	2,399	2,778	1,316
	67 Perjury	M	70	75	76	1	1	7	-	-	-	-	-	-	-	-	-	-	10	-	10	27	-	-	-	31	31	-
		F	23	21	21	-	-	2	-	-	-	-	-	-	-	-	-	-	4	-	4	-	-	-	-	6	6	-
		NS	2	1	-	-	-	-	-	-	-	-	-	-	-	-	-	-	-	-	-	-	-	-	-	-	-	-
		T	95	97	97	1	1	9	-	-	-	-	-	-	-	-	-	-	14	-	14	27	-	-	-	37	37	-
	75 Betting, Gaming and Lotteries	M	11	7	7	-	2	2	-	-	-	-	-	-	-	-	-	-	-	-	-	-	-	-	-	7	7	-
		T	11	7	7	-	2	2	-	-	-	-	-	-	-	-	-	-	-	-	-	-	-	-	-	7	7	-
	76 Aiding Suicide	M	1	1	1	-	-	-	-	-	-	-	-	-	-	-	-	-	-	-	-	-	-	-	-	1	1	-
		F	1	1	1	-	-	-	-	-	-	-	-	-	-	-	-	-	-	-	-	-	-	-	-	-	-	-
		T	2	1	1	-	-	-	-	-	-	-	-	-	-	-	-	-	-	-	-	-	-	-	-	1	1	-
	78 Assist Entry of Illegal Immigrant	M	323	244	244	-	1	2	-	-	-	-	-	-	-	-	-	-	5	-	5	27	-	-	2	206	208	2
		F	132	91	89	-	1	1	-	-	-	-	-	-	-	-	-	-	4	-	5	1	-	-	3	50	53	1
		NS	36	15	10	-	-	-	-	-	-	-	-	-	-	-	-	-	-	-	-	-	-	-	1	9	10	-
		T	491	350	343	-	1	3	-	-	-	-	-	-	-	-	-	-	9	-	10	28	-	-	6	265	271	3
	79 Perverting the Course of Justice	M	2,141	1,075	1,067	1	10	2	-	-	-	-	-	1	1	-	-	25	95	39	160	298	-	24	46	514	584	3
		F	564	311	309	-	5	-	-	-	-	-	-	-	-	-	-	16	40	3	60	150	-	-	15	74	91	12
		NS	30	-	-	-	-	-	-	-	-	-	-	-	-	-	-	-	-	-	-	-	-	-	-	-	-	-
		T	2,735	1,386	1,376	1	15	2	-	-	-	-	-	1	1	-	-	41	135	42	220	448	-	24	61	588	675	15
	80 Absconding from Lawful Custody	M	361	261	259	1	6	1	-	-	-	-	-	1	1	-	-	-	9	11	23	10	-	6	6	179	214	4
		F	4	4	4	-	-	-	-	-	-	-	-	-	-	-	-	-	-	-	-	-	-	-	-	-	-	-
		NS	5	1	1	-	-	-	-	-	-	-	-	-	-	-	-	-	-	-	-	-	-	-	-	-	-	-
		T	370	266	264	1	6	1	-	-	-	-	-	1	1	-	-	-	9	11	23	10	-	6	6	181	217	4
	81 Firearms Act Offence	M	1,430	1,275	1,277	5	125	152	-	-	-	-	-	1	1	-	-	36	302	30	368	181	2	8	44	372	426	20
		F	109	86	85	2	27	5	-	-	-	-	-	-	-	-	-	2	10	1	13	14	-	-	4	18	22	2
		NS	15	8	5	-	-	1	-	-	-	-	-	-	-	-	-	-	1	1	2	1	-	-	-	-	-	-
		O	1	1	1	-	-	-	-	-	-	-	-	-	-	-	-	-	-	-	-	-	-	-	-	-	1	-
		T	1,555	1,369	1,367	7	152	158	-	-	-	-	-	1	1	-	-	38	313	32	383	196	2	8	48	390	449	22
	82 Revenue Law Offence	M	48	34	37	-	-	-	-	-	-	-	-	1	-	-	-	4	-	-	4	15	2	9	-	18	18	22

21.4 Offenders convicted and sentenced at all courts

England and Wales, 2012

Offence group	Description	Sex	Total Proc Against	Total found Guilty	Total For Sent	Absl Disch	Cond Disch	Fine	CRO	SO	CPO	ACO	CPO&RO	Curf Order	Rep Order	APO	DTTO	REFO	Comm Order	YRO (1)	Total Comm Sentences	SS	Sec 90-92	DTO	YOI	Unsus Sent Impr	Imm cust	ODW
		F	20	21	21	-	-	-	-	-	-	-	-	-	-	-	-	-	2	-	2	14	-	-	-	4	4	-
		NS	6	2	1	-	-	-	-	-	-	-	-	-	-	-	-	-	-	-	-	1	-	-	-	-	-	-
		T	74	57	59	-	-	1	-	-	-	-	-	-	-	-	-	-	6	-	6	30	-	-	-	22	22	22
83 Failing to Surrender to Bail		M	19,071	11,242	11,355	234	823	5,031	-	-	-	-	-	3	4	-	-	52	921	120	1,100	177	-	5	112	1,052	1,169	2,821
		F	3,412	1,788	1,806	38	193	785	-	-	-	-	-	1	1	-	-	17	160	25	204	34	-	-	9	127	136	416
		NS	176	103	102	5	5	35	-	-	-	-	-	-	-	-	-	-	7	2	9	2	-	-	3	12	15	31
		T	22,659	13,133	13,263	277	1,021	5,851	-	-	-	-	-	4	5	-	-	69	1,088	147	1,313	213	-	5	124	1,191	1,320	3,268
84 Trade Descriptions Act and Similar Offences		M	578	495	493	-	33	166	-	-	-	-	-	-	-	-	-	2	119	4	125	82	-	-	2	76	78	9
		F	102	73	77	-	13	22	-	-	-	-	-	-	-	-	-	-	18	-	18	12	-	-	-	8	8	4
		NS	138	80	70	-	5	44	-	-	-	-	-	-	-	-	-	-	16	-	16	3	-	-	-	1	1	1
		O	117	71	72	-	1	67	-	-	-	-	-	-	-	-	-	2	-	-	-	-	-	-	-	-	-	4
		T	935	719	712	-	52	299	-	-	-	-	-	-	-	-	-	2	153	4	159	97	-	-	2	85	87	18
85 Health and Safety at Work etc. Act 1974		M	259	189	195	-	-	140	-	-	-	-	-	-	-	-	-	2	18	4	18	22	-	-	-	3	3	-
		F	34	18	20	-	-	17	-	-	-	-	-	-	-	-	-	-	2	-	2	-	-	-	-	-	-	-
		NS	70	39	36	-	-	29	-	-	-	-	-	-	-	-	-	-	4	-	4	-	-	-	-	-	-	2
		O	367	371	361	1	-	359	-	-	-	-	-	-	-	-	-	-	-	-	-	2	-	-	-	-	-	2
		T	730	617	612	1	-	545	-	-	-	-	-	-	-	-	-	2	24	4	24	24	-	-	-	3	3	17
86 Possession of Obscene Material etc.		M	1,791	1,651	1,618	1	14	29	-	-	-	-	-	-	-	-	-	19	717	5	741	344	-	1	5	454	460	17
		F	12	14	14	-	-	3	-	-	-	-	-	-	-	-	-	-	1	-	1	4	-	-	-	5	5	-
		NS	13	5	5	-	-	1	-	-	-	-	-	-	-	-	-	-	-	-	-	-	-	-	-	1	1	-
		O	3	3	3	-	-	3	-	-	-	-	-	-	-	-	-	-	-	-	-	-	-	-	-	-	-	-
		T	1,819	1,673	1,637	1	14	36	-	-	-	-	-	-	-	-	-	19	718	5	742	348	-	1	5	460	466	17
87 Protection from Eviction Act 1977.		M	30	16	16	-	-	9	-	-	-	-	-	-	-	-	-	19	4	5	4	3	-	1	5	3	3	-
		F	6	4	4	-	-	-	-	-	-	-	-	-	-	-	-	-	1	-	1	2	-	-	-	-	-	-
		NS	5	1	1	-	-	-	-	-	-	-	-	-	-	-	-	-	-	-	-	1	-	-	-	1	1	-
		O	1	1	1	-	-	1	-	-	-	-	-	-	-	-	-	-	-	-	-	-	-	-	-	-	-	-
		T	42	22	21	-	-	36	-	-	-	-	-	-	-	-	-	19	4	5	4	3	-	1	5	460	466	17
89 Adulteration of Food		M	33	26	28	-	-	23	-	-	-	-	-	-	-	-	-	-	4	-	4	-	-	-	-	-	-	2
		F	3	1	1	-	-	1	-	-	-	-	-	-	-	-	-	-	1	-	1	-	-	-	-	-	-	2
		NS	6	6	5	-	-	3	-	-	-	-	-	-	-	-	-	-	-	-	-	-	-	-	-	2	2	4
		O	12	11	11	-	-	9	-	-	-	-	-	-	-	-	-	-	-	-	-	-	-	-	-	-	-	-
		T	54	44	45	-	-	36	-	-	-	-	-	-	-	-	-	-	-	-	1	3	-	-	-	3	3	-
91 Public Health		M	1,327	994	991	2	152	726	9	-	-	-	-	-	-	-	-	-	55	-	55	17	-	-	8	18	26	13
		F	283	186	187	3	67	105	23	-	-	-	-	-	-	-	-	-	4	-	4	4	-	-	1	-	1	-
		NS	343	233	229	-	30	189	1	-	-	-	-	-	-	-	-	-	4	-	4	4	-	-	-	2	2	-
		O	297	200	201	2	3	193	3	-	-	-	-	-	-	-	-	-	1	-	1	-	-	-	-	-	-	4
		T	2,250	1,613	1,608	7	252	1,213	36	-	-	-	-	-	-	-	-	-	64	-	64	17	-	-	9	20	29	21
94 Town and Country Planning Act 1990		M	483	263	274	-	40	228	7	-	-	-	-	-	14	-	-	-	64	-	64	22	-	-	-	-	-	4
		F	166	73	73	2	17	54	2	-	-	-	-	-	2	-	-	-	2	-	2	2	-	-	-	-	-	-
		NS	189	82	79	2	8	68	2	-	-	-	-	-	-	-	-	-	-	-	-	-	-	-	-	-	-	1
		O	80	35	34	-	1	32	-	-	-	-	-	-	-	-	-	-	-	-	-	-	-	-	-	-	-	-
		T	918	453	460	4	66	382	11	-	-	-	-	-	16	-	-	-	64	-	64	22	-	-	-	-	-	4
95 Disclosure, obstruction, false or misleading statements		M	93	67	67	-	-	36	-	-	-	-	-	-	-	-	-	-	-	-	-	-	-	-	-	14	27	6
		F	6	3	3	-	-	3	-	-	-	-	-	-	-	-	-	-	-	-	-	-	-	-	-	-	-	-
		NS	17	14	13	-	-	7	-	-	-	-	-	-	-	-	-	-	-	-	-	-	-	-	-	-	-	-
		O	4	2	2	-	-	2	-	-	-	-	-	-	-	-	-	-	2	-	2	1	-	-	-	1	6	3
		T	120	86	85	-	2	48	2	-	-	-	-	-	-	-	-	-	2	-	2	1	-	-	-	15	33	3
99 Other (Excluding Motoring Offences)		M	5,684	5,157	5,119	95	163	1,142	48	-	-	-	-	-	14	-	-	42	191	240	488	336	1	63	96	1,686	1,846	1,049
		F	1,002	890	887	21	37	178	-	-	-	-	-	-	2	-	-	3	39	29	73	125	-	4	9	245	258	195
		NS	208	113	99	-	2	58	-	-	-	-	-	-	-	-	-	-	-	-	-	-	-	-	2	-	15	14
		O	179	111	113	1	5	107	-	-	1	-	-	-	-	-	-	-	2	-	2	4	-	-	-	-	18	1
		T	7,073	6,271	6,218	117	207	1,485	48	-	1	-	-	-	16	-	-	45	232	269	563	465	1	67	107	1,947	2,122	1,259

21.4 Offenders convicted and sentenced at all courts

England and Wales, 2012

Offence group / Description	Sex	Total Proc Against	Total found Guilty	Total For Sent	Abslt Disch	Condl Disch	Fine	CRO	SO	CPO	ACO	CPO&RO	Curf Order	Rep Order	APO	DTTO	REFO	Comm Order	YRO [1]	Total Comm Sentences	SS	Sec 90-92	DTO	YOI	Unsus Sent Impr	Imm cust	ODW
Sub-total	M	45,981	34,543	34,615	382	2,116	8,797	3	1	-	3	-	14	19	-	-	442	4,405	699	5,586	3,518	7	228	856	7,872	8,963	5,253
	F	6,823	4,344	4,403	71	412	1,262	1	-	-	-	-	4	3	-	-	56	516	81	661	549	2	8	62	674	746	702
	NS	1,381	767	714	8	56	441	-	-	-	-	-	-	-	-	-	1	43	8	52	18	-	3	14	56	73	66
	O	1,061	805	797	2	11	772	-	-	-	-	-	-	-	-	-	-	1	-	1	2	-	-	-	-	-	9
	T	55,246	40,459	40,529	463	2,595	11,272	4	1	-	3	-	18	22	-	-	499	4,965	788	6,300	4,087	9	239	932	8,602	9,782	6,030
Indictable excluding motoring	M	315,894	260,102	258,392	1,340	29,531	46,582	25	19	3	52	1	161	232	-	1	8,352	50,787	8,607	68,240	25,585	289	2,199	7,655	62,850	72,993	14,121
	F	52,245	42,520	42,419	245	8,712	6,136	5	-	-	3	-	26	44	-	1	1,418	10,597	1,095	13,189	5,261	10	132	424	6,044	6,610	2,266
	NS	4,483	2,559	2,315	15	270	724	-	-	-	-	-	1	-	-	-	93	439	99	632	193	-	31	33	300	364	117
	O	1,110	821	812	2	12	784	-	-	-	-	-	-	-	-	-	-	1	-	1	2	-	-	-	-	-	11
	T	373,732	306,002	303,938	1,602	38,525	54,226	30	19	3	55	1	188	276	-	2	9,863	61,824	9,801	82,062	31,041	299	2,362	8,112	69,194	79,967	16,515
Indictable motoring	M	3,045	2,759	2,810	3	19	191	-	-	-	-	-	1	-	-	-	39	627	32	700	776	-	20	144	932	1,096	25
	F	186	173	174	-	5	32	-	-	-	-	-	-	-	-	-	3	47	-	50	68	-	-	-	19	19	-
	NS	21	11	6	-	-	2	-	-	-	-	-	-	-	-	-	1	3	-	4	-	-	-	-	-	-	-
	O	-	-	-	-	-	-	-	-	-	-	-	-	-	-	-	-	-	-	-	-	-	-	-	-	-	-
	T	3,252	2,943	2,990	3	24	225	-	-	-	-	-	1	-	-	-	43	677	32	754	844	-	20	144	951	1,115	25
Indictable including motoring	M	318,939	262,861	261,202	1,343	29,550	46,773	25	19	4	52	1	162	232	-	1	8,391	51,414	8,639	68,940	26,361	289	2,219	7,799	63,782	74,089	14,146
	F	52,431	42,693	42,593	245	8,717	6,168	5	-	-	3	-	26	44	-	1	1,421	10,644	1,095	13,239	5,329	10	132	424	6,063	6,629	2,266
	NS	4,504	2,570	2,321	15	270	726	-	-	-	-	-	1	-	-	-	94	442	99	636	193	-	31	33	300	364	117
	O	1,110	821	812	2	12	784	-	-	-	-	-	-	-	-	-	-	1	-	1	2	-	-	-	-	-	11
	T	376,984	308,945	306,928	1,605	38,549	54,451	30	19	4	55	1	189	276	-	2	9,906	62,501	9,833	82,816	31,885	299	2,382	8,256	70,145	81,082	16,540
Summary Non-Motoring																											
101 Adulteration of Food, Drug, etc.	M	2	1	1	-	-	1	-	-	-	-	-	-	-	-	-	-	-	-	-	-	-	-	-	-	-	-
	O	1	-	-	-	-	-	-	-	-	-	-	-	-	-	-	-	-	-	-	-	-	-	-	-	-	-
	T	3	1	1	-	-	1	-	-	-	-	-	-	-	-	-	-	-	-	-	-	-	-	-	-	-	-
104 On Constable	M	11,896	9,696	9,684	37	1,481	3,435	-	-	-	3	-	6	8	-	-	270	2,413	254	2,954	454	-	26	86	890	1,002	321
	F	3,505	2,966	2,956	15	582	761	-	-	-	1	-	-	3	-	-	146	884	109	1,143	140	-	10	17	175	202	113
	NS	76	58	57	1	10	17	-	-	-	-	-	-	-	-	-	4	7	-	12	4	-	4	-	-	-	6
	T	15,477	12,720	12,697	53	2,073	4,213	-	-	-	4	-	6	11	-	-	420	3,304	364	4,109	598	-	36	103	1,072	1,211	440
105 Common, etc	M	64,885	43,973	44,079	124	5,664	5,619	1	1	1	5	-	25	58	-	-	1,818	16,490	1,657	20,056	4,639	-	176	562	5,919	6,657	1,320
	F	10,920	7,392	7,399	66	1,641	833	-	1	-	-	-	6	17	-	-	706	2,398	530	3,657	504	-	23	26	355	404	294
	NS	384	272	272	1	36	35	-	-	-	-	-	-	-	-	-	19	97	20	137	14	-	7	3	21	44	7
	T	76,189	51,637	51,750	191	7,341	6,487	1	1	1	5	-	31	76	-	-	2,543	18,985	2,207	23,850	5,157	-	206	591	6,308	7,105	1,619
106 Betting or Gaming Offence	M	183	156	154	-	11	27	-	-	-	-	-	-	-	-	-	34	34	-	34	9	-	-	6	63	69	4
	F	10	8	8	-	2	2	-	-	-	-	-	-	-	-	-	1	2	-	2	-	-	-	-	1	2	-
	NS	4	4	4	-	1	1	-	-	-	-	-	1	-	-	-	-	-	-	1	-	-	-	1	1	1	-
	T	197	168	166	-	14	30	-	-	-	-	-	1	-	-	-	36	36	-	37	9	-	-	7	65	72	4
107 Brothel Keeping	M	9	14	14	-	-	1	-	-	-	-	-	1	-	-	-	2	2	-	5	5	-	-	-	5	5	4
	F	11	22	22	-	-	-	-	-	-	-	-	-	-	-	-	6	6	-	7	7	-	-	-	3	3	1
	T	22	36	36	-	-	1	-	-	-	-	-	1	-	-	-	8	8	-	12	12	-	-	-	8	8	-
108 Cruelty to Animal	M	1,142	845	842	3	139	144	-	-	-	4	-	1	4	-	-	7	323	9	340	103	-	2	13	88	103	10
	F	738	575	576	-	125	113	-	-	-	-	-	2	-	-	-	4	246	-	252	57	-	1	-	21	22	7
	NS	198	152	152	-	24	42	-	-	-	-	-	-	-	-	-	-	47	-	47	25	-	-	-	10	10	3
	O	3	1	1	-	-	1	-	-	-	-	-	-	-	-	-	-	-	-	-	-	-	-	-	-	-	-
	T	2,081	1,573	1,571	4	288	300	-	-	-	4	-	3	4	-	-	11	616	9	639	185	-	3	13	119	135	20
110 Diseases of Animals Act	M	3	3	3	-	-	3	-	-	-	-	-	-	-	-	-	-	-	-	-	-	-	-	-	-	-	-
	NS	1	1	1	-	-	-	-	-	-	-	-	-	-	-	-	-	2	-	2	-	-	-	-	-	-	-
	O	1	-	-	-	-	-	-	-	-	-	-	-	-	-	-	-	-	-	-	-	-	-	-	-	-	-
	T	5	3	3	-	-	3	-	-	-	-	-	-	-	-	-	-	2	-	2	-	-	-	-	-	-	-
111 Offences Relating to Dogs	M	865	684	688	10	152	438	3	-	-	-	-	-	-	-	-	1	44	-	45	3	-	-	-	10	11	29
	F	454	324	324	5	82	213	-	-	-	-	-	-	-	-	-	1	12	-	13	1	-	-	-	-	-	10
	NS	81	53	53	1	4	48	-	-	-	-	-	-	-	-	-	-	-	-	-	-	-	-	1	-	-	-
	T	1,400	1,061	1,065	16	238	699	3	-	-	-	-	-	-	-	-	2	56	-	58	4	-	-	1	10	11	39
112 Education Acts	M	2,896	2,114	2,114	37	472	1,463	-	-	-	-	-	-	-	-	-	4	89	1	94	16	-	-	1	6	6	26

21.4 Offenders convicted and sentenced at all courts

England and Wales, 2012

Offence group / Description		Total Proc Against	Total found Guilty	Total For Sent	Absit Disch	Condl Disch	Fine	CRO	SO	CPO	ACO	CPO&RO	Curf Order	Rep Order	APO	DTTO	REFO	Comm Order	YRO (1)	Total Comm Sentences	SS	Sec 90-92	DTO	YOI	Unsus Sent Impr	Imm cust	ODW
	F	8,058	6,621	6,621	73	1,652	4,345	-	-	-	-	-	1	-	-	-	1	387	1	390	70	-	-	-	14	14	77
	NS	2,118	1,561	1,561	24	342	1,133	-	-	-	-	-	-	-	-	-	-	39	-	39	5	-	-	-	-	-	18
	O	1	-	-	-	-	-	-	-	-	-	-	-	-	-	-	-	-	-	-	-	-	-	-	-	-	-
	T	13,073	10,296	10,296	134	2,466	6,941	-	-	-	-	-	1	-	-	-	5	515	2	523	91	-	-	-	20	20	121
113 Explosives Acts	M	1	1	1	-	-	-	-	-	-	-	-	-	-	-	-	-	-	-	-	-	-	-	-	-	-	-
	T	1	1	1	-	-	-	-	-	-	-	-	-	-	-	-	-	-	-	-	-	-	-	-	-	-	-
115 Firearms Acts	M	287	227	226	5	32	71	-	-	-	-	-	1	-	-	-	16	65	12	94	7	-	1	-	13	13	3
	F	4	3	3	-	-	2	-	-	-	-	-	-	-	-	-	-	1	-	1	-	-	-	-	-	-	-
	T	291	230	229	5	32	73	-	-	-	-	-	1	-	-	-	16	66	12	95	7	-	1	-	13	14	3
116 Fishery Acts	M	2,137	2,019	2,019	23	55	1,933	-	-	-	-	-	-	-	-	-	-	5	-	5	-	-	-	-	-	-	3
	F	35	30	30	-	2	28	-	-	-	-	-	-	-	-	-	-	-	-	-	-	-	-	-	-	-	-
	NS	569	531	531	12	17	501	-	-	-	-	-	-	-	-	-	-	-	-	-	-	-	-	-	-	-	1
	O	1	1	1	-	-	1	-	-	-	-	-	-	-	-	-	-	-	-	-	-	-	-	-	-	-	-
	T	2,742	2,581	2,581	35	74	2,463	-	-	-	-	-	-	-	-	-	-	5	-	5	-	-	-	-	-	-	4
117 Friendly Societies Acts	NS	1	1	1	-	-	1	-	-	-	-	-	-	-	-	-	-	-	-	-	-	-	-	-	-	-	-
	O	20	17	17	-	-	17	-	-	-	-	-	-	-	-	-	-	-	-	-	-	-	-	-	-	-	-
	T	21	18	18	-	-	18	-	-	-	-	-	-	-	-	-	-	-	-	-	-	-	-	-	-	-	-
118 Night Poaching	M	50	35	35	1	6	28	-	-	-	-	-	-	-	-	-	-	-	-	-	-	-	-	-	-	-	-
	T	50	35	35	1	6	28	-	-	-	-	-	-	-	-	-	-	-	-	-	-	-	-	-	-	-	-
119 Day Poaching	M	244	196	196	4	7	181	-	-	-	-	-	-	-	-	-	-	1	-	1	-	-	-	-	-	-	3
	F	1	-	-	-	-	-	-	-	-	-	-	-	-	-	-	-	-	-	-	-	-	-	-	-	-	-
	NS	2	2	2	-	-	2	-	-	-	-	-	-	-	-	-	-	-	-	-	-	-	-	-	-	-	-
	T	247	198	198	4	7	183	-	-	-	-	-	-	-	-	-	-	1	-	1	-	-	-	-	-	-	3
120 Unlawful Possession of Game, etc.	M	9	9	9	-	2	6	-	-	-	-	-	-	-	-	-	-	1	-	1	-	-	-	-	-	-	-
	T	9	9	9	-	2	6	-	-	-	-	-	-	-	-	-	-	1	-	1	-	-	-	-	-	-	-
121 Other Offence against Game Law	M	88	53	53	3	3	47	-	-	-	-	-	-	-	-	-	-	-	-	-	-	-	-	-	-	-	-
	F	4	1	1	-	-	1	-	-	-	-	-	-	-	-	-	-	-	-	-	-	-	-	-	-	-	-
	O	3	2	2	-	-	2	-	-	-	-	-	-	-	-	-	-	-	-	-	-	-	-	-	-	-	-
	T	95	56	56	3	3	50	-	-	-	-	-	-	-	-	-	-	-	-	-	-	-	-	-	-	-	-
122 Obstruction Other than by Vehicle	M	113	69	69	3	9	56	-	-	-	-	-	-	-	-	-	-	-	-	-	1	-	-	-	-	-	-
	F	38	25	25	-	8	17	-	-	-	-	-	-	-	-	-	-	-	-	-	-	-	-	-	-	-	-
	NS	6	1	1	-	-	1	-	-	-	-	-	-	-	-	-	-	-	-	-	-	-	-	-	-	-	-
	O	9	5	5	-	1	4	-	-	-	-	-	-	-	-	-	-	-	-	-	-	-	-	-	-	-	-
	T	166	100	100	3	18	78	-	-	-	-	-	-	-	-	-	-	-	-	-	1	-	-	-	-	-	-
123 Nuisance Other than by Vehicle	M	43	32	32	3	5	17	-	-	-	-	-	-	-	-	-	4	1	2	7	-	-	-	-	-	-	-
	F	2	2	2	-	-	1	-	-	-	-	-	-	-	-	-	1	-	-	1	-	-	-	-	-	-	-
	O	1	1	1	-	-	1	-	-	-	-	-	-	-	-	-	-	-	-	-	-	-	-	-	-	-	-
	T	46	35	35	3	5	19	-	-	-	-	-	-	-	-	-	5	1	2	8	-	-	-	-	-	-	-
124 Other Highways Act Offence	M	17	13	13	-	-	13	-	-	-	-	-	-	-	-	-	-	-	-	-	-	-	-	-	-	-	-
	F	4	2	2	-	-	-	-	-	-	-	-	-	-	-	-	-	2	-	2	-	-	-	-	-	-	-
	NS	7	6	6	-	-	6	-	-	-	-	-	-	-	-	-	-	-	-	-	-	-	-	-	-	-	-
	O	75	56	56	-	-	54	-	-	-	-	-	-	-	-	-	-	2	-	2	-	-	-	-	-	-	-
	T	103	77	77	-	-	73	-	-	-	-	-	-	-	-	-	-	4	-	4	-	-	-	-	-	-	-
125 Public Order Act 1986	M	28,394	21,984	22,052	164	5,050	9,170	-	-	-	4	-	5	48	-	-	609	3,713	397	4,776	840	-	27	119	1,112	1,258	794
	F	4,150	3,020	3,022	43	1,055	1,138	-	-	-	1	-	-	4	-	-	159	314	74	552	67	-	2	7	53	62	105
	NS	274	193	193	3	40	85	-	-	-	-	-	-	-	-	-	9	22	6	37	2	-	-	1	12	13	13
	O	8	-	-	-	-	-	-	-	-	-	-	-	-	-	-	-	-	-	-	-	-	-	-	-	-	-
	T	32,826	25,197	25,267	210	6,145	10,393	-	-	-	5	-	5	52	-	-	777	4,049	477	5,365	909	-	29	127	1,177	1,333	912
126 Interference with Motor Vehicles	M	1,326	985	979	3	120	149	-	-	-	5	-	2	3	-	-	55	305	58	423	46	-	1	14	169	184	54
	F	27	15	14	-	-	4	-	-	-	-	-	-	-	-	-	-	7	1	8	-	-	-	-	-	1	1
	NS	5	4	4	-	2	1	-	-	-	-	-	-	-	-	-	-	-	-	-	1	-	-	-	-	-	1
	T	1,358	1,003	998	3	122	154	-	-	-	5	-	2	3	-	-	55	312	59	431	47	-	1	14	170	185	56

21.4 Offenders convicted and sentenced at all courts

England and Wales, 2012

Offence group / Description		Total Proc Against	Total found Guilty	Total For Sent	Absl Disch	Cond Disch	Fine	CRO	SO	CPO	ACO	CPO&RO	Curf Order	Rep Order	APO	DTTO	REFO	Comm Order	YRO(1)	Total Comm Sentences	SS	Sec 90-92	DTO	YOI	Unsus Sent Impr	Imm cust	ODW
130 Unauthorised Taking of a Conveyance	M	3,184	2,426	2,434	11	153	296	-	1	-	1	-	3	6	-	-	191	930	247	1,382	129	-	24	66	338	428	35
	F	171	112	113	1	19	21	-	-	-	-	-	-	-	-	-	12	38	8	58	4	-	-	6	6	6	4
	NS	15	12	12	-	1	2	-	-	-	-	-	-	3	-	-	1	3	3	7	1	-	-	1	-	1	-
	T	3,370	2,550	2,559	12	173	319	-	1	-	1	-	3	9	-	-	204	971	258	1,447	134	-	24	67	344	435	39
131 Summary Aggravated Vehicle Taking	M	1,772	1,575	1,575	2	28	48	-	-	-	-	-	3	1	-	-	177	696	146	1,023	150	-	29	67	185	281	43
	F	180	149	151	-	6	15	-	-	-	-	-	-	-	-	-	23	82	6	111	4	-	1	2	11	14	1
	NS	9	8	8	1	-	2	-	-	-	-	-	-	-	-	-	-	2	3	5	-	-	-	-	-	-	-
	T	1,961	1,722	1,734	3	34	65	-	-	-	-	-	3	1	-	-	200	780	155	1,139	154	-	30	69	196	295	44
135 Horsedrawn Vehicle	M	4	4	4	-	4	4	-	-	-	-	-	-	-	-	-	-	-	-	-	-	-	-	-	-	-	-
	T	4	4	4	-	4	4	-	-	-	-	-	-	-	-	-	-	-	-	-	-	-	-	-	-	-	-
137 Pedal Cycle	M	816	670	670	30	110	469	-	-	-	-	-	-	-	-	-	14	11	12	37	1	-	-	-	1	-	22
	F	52	45	45	3	2	40	-	-	-	-	-	-	-	-	-	-	-	-	-	-	-	-	-	-	-	-
	NS	3	2	2	-	1	1	-	-	-	-	-	-	-	-	-	-	-	-	-	-	-	-	-	-	-	-
	T	871	717	717	33	113	510	-	-	-	-	-	-	-	-	-	14	11	12	37	1	-	-	-	1	-	22
138 Offences involving impersonation	M	46	34	34	-	14	19	-	-	-	-	-	-	-	-	-	1	1	-	1	-	-	-	-	1	-	-
	F	15	11	11	-	-	11	-	-	-	-	-	-	-	-	-	-	-	-	-	-	-	-	-	-	-	-
	NS	4	3	3	-	-	2	-	-	-	-	-	-	-	-	-	-	-	-	-	-	-	-	-	-	-	-
	T	65	48	48	-	14	32	-	-	-	-	-	-	-	-	-	1	1	-	1	1	-	-	-	1	-	1
139 Indecent Exposure	M	1	1	1	-	1	-	-	-	-	-	-	-	-	-	-	-	-	-	-	-	-	-	-	-	-	-
	T	1	1	1	-	1	-	-	-	-	-	-	-	-	-	-	-	-	-	-	-	-	-	-	-	-	-
140 Drunkenness, Simple	M	728	650	649	15	155	428	-	-	-	-	-	-	-	-	-	1	2	2	3	-	-	-	-	-	-	48
	F	113	97	97	2	25	63	-	-	-	-	-	-	-	-	-	2	1	1	3	-	-	-	-	-	-	4
	NS	28	25	25	-	4	17	-	-	-	-	-	-	-	-	-	-	-	-	-	-	-	-	-	-	-	4
	T	869	772	771	17	184	508	-	-	-	-	-	-	-	-	-	3	3	3	6	-	-	-	-	-	-	56
141 Drunkenness, with Aggravation	M	15,116	13,508	13,506	435	3,793	8,401	-	-	-	-	-	2	7	-	-	67	49	30	155	5	-	-	-	4	4	713
	F	2,691	2,392	2,394	101	865	1,233	-	-	-	-	-	-	2	-	-	32	43	8	85	5	-	-	-	6	6	99
	NS	113	102	101	2	34	47	-	-	-	-	-	-	-	-	-	1	-	1	2	-	-	-	-	-	-	16
	T	17,920	16,002	16,001	538	4,692	9,681	-	-	-	-	-	2	9	-	-	100	92	39	242	10	-	-	-	10	10	828
142 Offence by Licenced Person, etc.	M	16	12	12	-	1	11	-	-	-	-	-	-	-	-	-	-	-	-	-	-	-	-	-	-	-	-
	F	2	2	2	-	-	2	-	-	-	-	-	-	-	-	-	-	-	-	-	-	-	-	-	-	-	-
	NS	5	4	4	-	-	4	-	-	-	-	-	-	-	-	-	-	-	-	-	-	-	-	-	-	-	-
	O	2	2	2	-	-	2	-	-	-	-	-	-	-	-	-	-	-	-	-	-	-	-	-	-	-	-
	T	25	20	20	-	1	19	-	-	-	-	-	-	-	-	-	-	-	-	-	-	-	-	-	-	-	-
143 Other Offence against the Liquor Law	M	2,050	1,699	1,701	62	453	1,103	-	-	-	-	-	-	1	-	-	14	13	3	31	-	-	-	3	1	1	51
	F	217	169	169	13	45	103	-	-	-	-	-	-	-	-	-	2	1	1	3	-	-	-	1	-	-	5
	NS	115	95	95	1	15	78	-	-	-	-	-	-	-	-	-	-	-	-	-	-	-	-	-	-	-	-
	O	37	24	24	-	1	22	-	-	-	-	-	-	-	-	-	-	-	-	-	-	-	-	-	-	-	1
	T	2,419	1,987	1,989	76	514	1,306	-	-	-	-	-	-	1	-	-	16	14	4	34	-	-	-	4	1	1	58
144 Selling Tobacco to Juvenile	M	64	55	55	-	7	48	-	-	-	-	-	-	-	-	-	-	-	-	-	-	-	-	-	-	-	-
	F	6	4	4	-	1	3	-	-	-	-	-	-	-	-	-	-	-	-	-	-	-	-	-	-	-	-
	NS	25	21	21	-	1	20	-	-	-	-	-	-	-	-	-	-	-	-	-	-	-	-	-	-	-	-
	O	19	13	13	-	1	12	-	-	-	-	-	-	-	-	-	-	-	-	-	-	-	-	-	-	-	-
	T	114	93	93	-	10	83	-	-	-	-	-	-	-	-	-	-	-	-	-	-	-	-	-	-	-	-
146 Shops Act	M	3	3	3	-	-	1	-	-	-	-	-	-	-	-	-	-	-	-	-	-	-	-	-	-	-	-
	F	3	2	2	-	-	-	-	-	-	-	-	-	-	-	-	-	-	-	-	-	-	-	-	-	-	-
	NS	19	17	17	-	3	12	-	-	-	-	-	-	-	-	-	-	-	-	-	-	-	-	-	-	-	-
	O	8	8	8	-	-	8	-	-	-	-	-	-	-	-	-	-	-	-	-	-	-	-	-	-	-	-
	T	33	30	30	-	4	21	-	-	-	-	-	-	-	-	-	-	-	-	-	-	-	-	-	-	-	-
148 Other Offence against the Labour Law	M	2	2	2	-	-	2	-	-	-	-	-	-	-	-	-	-	-	-	-	-	-	-	-	1	2	-
	NS	1	1	1	-	-	1	-	-	-	-	-	-	-	-	-	-	-	-	-	1	-	-	-	2	2	-
	T	3	3	3	-	-	3	-	-	-	-	-	-	1	-	-	-	-	-	-	1	-	-	-	4	4	1
149 Summary Criminal or Malicious Damage	M	29,551	24,333	24,330	205	7,118	4,792	-	1	-	11	-	13	98	-	-	1,223	5,978	930	8,254	483	-	-	132	1,097	1,229	2,249

21.4 Offenders convicted and sentenced at all courts

England and Wales, 2012

Offence group / Description	Sex	Total Proc Against	Total found Guilty	Total For Sent	Absl Disch	Condl Disch	Fine	CRO	SO	CPO	ACO	CPO&RO	Curf Order	Rep Order	APo	DTTO	REFO	Comm Order	YRO [1]	Total Comm Sentences	SS	Sec 90-92	DTO	YOI	Unsus Sent Impr	Imm cust	ODW
Offence	F	3,214	2,516	2,517	46	1,034	280	-	-	-	1	-	-	6	-	-	209	452	147	815	32	-	1	5	66	72	238
	NS	176	141	139	3	32	22	-	-	-	-	-	-	-	-	-	11	33	13	57	3	-	-	-	9	9	13
	T	32,941	26,990	26,986	254	8,184	5,094	-	-	-	12	-	13	104	-	-	1,443	6,463	1,090	9,126	518	-	1	137	1,172	1,310	2,500
150 Merchant Shipping Acts	M	5	5	5	-	-	3	-	-	-	-	-	-	-	-	-	-	-	1	1	-	-	-	-	-	1	-
	NS	1	1	1	-	-	1	-	-	-	-	-	-	-	-	-	-	-	-	-	-	-	-	-	-	-	-
	T	6	6	6	-	-	4	-	-	-	-	-	-	-	-	-	-	-	1	1	-	-	-	-	-	1	1
151 Social Security Offence	M	3,440	3,052	3,054	11	652	847	-	-	-	-	-	5	-	-	-	-	1,351	-	1,356	137	-	-	-	34	34	17
	F	3,823	3,408	3,422	9	983	755	-	-	-	-	-	3	-	-	-	-	1,457	-	1,460	187	-	-	-	20	20	8
	NS	1,248	1,071	1,055	5	265	290	-	-	-	-	-	-	-	-	-	-	445	-	445	43	-	-	-	3	3	4
	O	4	3	3	-	-	3	-	-	-	-	-	-	-	-	-	-	-	-	-	-	-	-	-	-	-	-
	T	8,515	7,534	7,534	25	1,900	1,895	-	-	-	-	-	8	-	-	-	-	3,253	-	3,261	367	-	-	-	57	57	29
155 Military Law - Air Force	M	50	39	39	-	5	27	-	-	-	-	-	-	-	-	-	4	1	1	6	1	-	-	-	-	-	-
	F	4	4	4	-	-	3	-	-	-	-	-	-	-	-	-	1	-	-	1	-	-	-	-	-	-	-
	NS	2	2	2	1	-	1	-	-	-	-	-	-	-	-	-	-	-	-	-	-	-	-	-	-	-	-
	O	2	2	2	-	-	2	-	-	-	-	-	-	-	-	-	-	-	-	-	-	-	-	-	-	-	-
	T	58	47	47	1	5	33	-	-	-	-	-	-	-	-	-	5	1	1	7	1	-	-	-	-	-	1
156 Park, Common or Other Open Space Offence	M	2	2	2	-	1	1	-	-	-	-	-	-	-	-	-	-	-	-	-	-	-	-	-	-	-	-
	T	2	2	2	-	1	1	-	-	-	-	-	-	-	-	-	-	-	-	-	-	-	-	-	-	-	-
158 Reporting Restrictions	NS	1	1	1	-	-	1	-	-	-	-	-	-	-	-	-	-	-	-	-	-	-	-	-	-	-	-
	T	1	1	1	-	-	1	-	-	-	-	-	-	-	-	-	-	-	-	-	-	-	-	-	-	-	-
160 Pedlars Act	M	142	128	128	3	7	118	-	-	-	-	-	-	-	-	-	-	-	-	-	-	-	-	-	-	-	-
	F	5	4	4	-	2	2	-	-	-	-	-	-	-	-	-	-	-	-	-	-	-	-	-	-	-	-
	NS	3	3	3	-	-	3	-	-	-	-	-	-	-	-	-	-	-	-	-	-	-	-	-	-	-	-
	T	150	135	135	3	9	123	-	-	-	-	-	-	-	-	-	-	-	-	-	-	-	-	-	-	-	-
161 Certain Local regulations - Allowing Chimney to be on Fire	NS	1	1	1	-	-	1	-	-	-	-	-	-	-	-	-	-	-	-	-	-	-	-	-	-	-	-
	T	1	1	1	-	-	1	-	-	-	-	-	-	-	-	-	-	-	-	-	-	-	-	-	-	-	-
162 Disorderly Behaviour	M	1,084	919	918	19	58	818	-	-	-	-	-	-	-	-	-	-	5	2	7	2	-	-	-	5	5	9
	F	59	49	49	4	7	36	-	-	-	-	-	-	-	-	-	-	-	-	-	-	-	-	-	1	1	1
	NS	100	71	71	-	5	66	-	-	-	-	-	-	-	-	-	-	-	-	-	-	-	-	-	-	-	-
	O	5	1	1	-	-	1	-	-	-	-	-	-	-	-	-	-	-	-	-	-	-	-	-	-	-	-
	T	1,248	1,040	1,039	23	70	921	-	-	-	-	-	-	-	-	-	-	5	2	7	2	-	-	-	6	6	10
163 Playing in Street	M	6	6	6	-	2	4	-	-	-	-	-	-	-	-	-	-	-	-	-	-	-	-	-	-	-	-
	NS	4	2	2	-	-	2	-	-	-	-	-	-	-	-	-	-	-	-	-	-	-	-	-	-	-	-
	T	10	8	8	-	2	6	-	-	-	-	-	-	-	-	-	-	-	-	-	-	-	-	-	-	-	-
164 Other Offence	M	144	107	108	3	17	65	-	-	-	-	-	-	-	-	-	1	5	-	6	3	-	-	-	3	3	11
	F	28	23	23	1	1	20	-	-	-	-	-	-	-	-	-	-	-	-	-	-	-	-	-	-	-	1
	NS	7	6	6	2	-	4	-	-	-	-	-	-	-	-	-	-	-	-	-	-	-	-	-	-	-	-
	T	179	136	137	6	18	89	-	-	-	-	-	-	-	-	-	1	5	-	6	3	-	-	-	3	3	11
165 Kerb Crawling	M	82	65	65	6	13	20	-	-	-	-	-	-	-	-	-	1	10	-	10	3	-	-	-	-	-	11
	F	2	2	2	-	1	1	-	-	-	-	-	-	-	-	-	-	-	-	-	-	-	-	-	-	-	-
	T	84	67	67	6	14	21	-	-	-	-	-	-	-	-	-	1	10	-	10	3	-	-	-	-	-	11
166 Offence by Prostitute	M	2	1	1	-	-	1	-	-	-	-	-	-	-	-	-	-	-	-	-	-	-	-	-	-	-	-
	F	387	275	275	4	70	103	-	-	-	-	-	-	-	-	-	-	2	-	2	-	-	-	-	-	-	96
	NS	6	3	3	-	-	1	-	-	-	-	-	-	-	-	-	-	-	-	-	-	-	-	-	-	-	2
	T	395	279	279	4	70	103	-	-	-	-	-	-	-	-	-	-	2	-	2	-	-	-	-	-	-	98
167 Aiding, etc. Offence by Prostitute	M	233	184	185	2	40	139	-	-	-	-	-	-	-	-	-	-	2	-	2	-	-	-	-	-	-	4
	F	5	2	2	-	-	-	-	-	-	-	-	-	-	-	-	-	-	-	-	-	-	-	-	-	-	1
	NS	3	2	2	-	1	1	-	-	-	-	-	-	-	-	-	-	-	-	-	-	-	-	-	-	-	-
	T	241	188	188	2	41	140	-	-	-	-	-	-	-	-	-	-	2	-	2	-	-	-	-	-	-	5
168 Public Health Offence	M	4,469	3,441	3,440	15	111	3,291	-	-	-	-	-	-	-	-	-	1	6	-	7	4	-	-	-	-	-	12
	F	2,372	1,868	1,868	4	63	1,790	-	-	-	-	-	-	-	-	-	-	-	-	1	1	-	-	-	-	-	9
	NS	1,939	1,482	1,482	7	33	1,442	-	-	-	-	-	-	-	-	-	-	-	-	-	-	-	-	-	-	-	-

21.4 Offenders convicted and sentenced at all courts

England and Wales, 2012

Offence group / Description		Total Proc Against	Total found Guilty	Total For Sent	Absl Disch	Cond Disch	Fine	CRO	SO	CPO	ACO	CPO&RO	Curf Order	Rep Order	APO	DTTO	REFO	Comm Order	YRO (1)	Total Comm Sentences	SS	Sec 90-92	DTO	YOI	Unsus Sent Impr	Imm cust	ODW
169 Railway Offence	O	170	65	64	-	2	58	-	-	-	-	-	-	-	-	-	-	-	-	-	-	-	-	-	-	-	4
	T	8,950	6,856	6,854	26	209	6,581	-	-	-	-	-	-	-	-	-	1	7	-	8	5	-	-	-	-	-	25
170 Motor Vehicle Licence	M	46,747	38,481	38,479	134	474	37,461	-	-	-	-	-	1	1	-	-	25	153	16	196	7	-	-	2	-	12	193
	F	12,434	9,663	9,663	37	110	9,460	-	-	-	-	-	-	-	-	-	6	19	1	26	-	-	-	-	-	-	30
	NS	9,309	7,494	7,494	15	60	7,384	-	-	-	-	-	-	-	-	-	4	2	4	10	-	-	-	-	-	1	24
	O	10	4	4	-	-	-	-	-	-	-	-	-	-	-	-	-	-	-	-	-	-	-	-	-	-	-
	T	68,500	55,642	55,640	186	644	54,309	-	-	-	-	-	1	1	-	-	35	174	21	232	7	-	-	2	-	13	247
172 Other Offence Against Revenue Law	M	18,220	15,127	15,127	65	55	14,991	-	-	-	-	-	-	-	-	-	-	-	-	-	-	-	-	-	-	-	16
	F	6,057	4,987	4,987	22	17	4,938	-	-	-	-	-	-	-	-	-	-	-	-	-	-	-	-	-	-	-	10
	NS	8,066	6,702	6,702	31	14	6,644	-	-	-	-	-	-	-	-	-	-	-	-	-	-	-	-	-	-	-	13
	O	357	252	252	-	3	249	-	-	-	-	-	-	-	-	-	-	-	-	-	-	-	-	-	-	-	-
	T	32,700	27,068	27,068	118	89	26,822	-	-	-	-	-	-	-	-	-	-	-	-	-	-	-	-	-	-	-	39
173 Stage Carriage or Public Service Vehicle Offence	M	19,500	17,006	17,006	96	125	16,757	-	-	-	-	-	-	-	-	-	-	-	-	-	-	-	-	-	-	-	28
	F	8,357	7,307	7,307	47	82	7,157	-	-	-	-	-	-	-	-	-	-	-	-	-	-	-	-	-	-	-	21
	NS	1,075	901	901	8	4	881	-	-	-	-	-	-	-	-	-	-	-	-	-	-	-	-	-	-	-	8
	O	106	66	66	-	-	66	-	-	-	-	-	-	-	-	-	-	-	-	-	-	-	-	-	-	-	-
	T	29,038	25,280	25,280	151	211	24,861	-	-	-	-	-	-	-	-	-	-	-	-	-	-	-	-	-	-	-	57
175 Sexual Offences - Miscellaneous	M	70	61	61	-	4	53	-	-	-	-	-	-	-	-	-	-	-	-	-	-	-	-	-	-	-	3
	F	25	22	22	-	2	19	-	-	-	-	-	-	-	-	-	-	-	-	-	-	-	-	-	-	-	-
	NS	15	12	12	-	2	10	-	-	-	-	-	-	-	-	-	-	-	-	-	-	-	-	-	-	-	-
	O	15	13	13	-	-	9	-	-	-	-	-	-	-	-	-	-	-	-	-	-	-	-	-	-	-	-
	T	125	108	108	-	8	91	-	-	-	-	-	-	-	-	-	-	3	-	3	1	-	-	-	-	-	3
176 Private security industry	M	24	18	18	-	3	11	-	-	-	-	-	-	-	-	-	-	-	-	-	-	-	-	-	-	-	1
	F	1	1	1	-	-	-	-	-	-	-	-	-	-	-	-	-	-	-	-	-	-	-	-	-	-	-
	T	25	19	19	-	3	11	-	-	-	-	-	-	-	-	-	-	3	-	3	1	-	-	-	-	-	1
179 Sunday Trading, etc.	M	14	10	12	-	4	6	-	-	-	-	-	-	-	-	-	-	-	-	-	-	-	-	-	-	-	1
	F	2	2	2	-	-	2	-	-	-	-	-	-	-	-	-	-	-	-	-	-	-	-	-	-	-	-
	NS	4	4	4	-	-	-	-	-	-	-	-	-	-	-	-	-	-	-	-	-	-	-	-	-	-	-
	T	20	16	18	-	4	8	-	-	-	-	-	-	-	-	-	-	-	-	-	1	-	-	-	-	-	1
180 Tram or Trolley Vehicle Offence	M	1	1	1	-	-	-	-	-	-	-	-	-	-	-	-	-	-	-	-	-	-	-	-	-	-	-
	F	2	2	2	-	-	1	-	-	-	-	-	-	-	-	-	-	-	-	-	-	-	-	-	-	-	-
	T	3	3	3	-	-	1	-	-	-	-	-	-	-	-	-	-	-	-	-	-	-	-	-	-	-	-
182 Begging	M	1,530	1,425	1,425	3	13	1,404	-	-	-	-	-	-	-	-	-	1	2	2	4	-	-	-	-	1	1	127
	F	623	574	574	2	1	571	-	-	-	-	-	-	-	-	-	1	2	2	5	-	-	-	-	-	1	48
	NS	104	97	97	-	-	97	-	-	-	-	-	-	-	-	-	1	-	-	1	-	-	-	-	-	-	1
	T	2,257	2,096	2,096	5	14	2,072	-	-	-	-	-	-	-	-	-	4	4	2	10	-	-	-	-	1	1	176
183 Sleeping Out	M	969	798	798	69	193	405	-	-	-	-	-	-	-	-	-	2	-	-	4	-	-	-	-	2	-	3
	F	232	194	194	10	54	76	-	-	-	-	-	-	-	-	-	1	1	-	1	-	-	-	-	1	-	-
	NS	28	18	18	1	5	10	-	-	-	-	-	-	-	-	-	-	1	-	-	-	-	-	-	-	-	1
	T	1,229	1,010	1,010	80	252	491	-	-	-	-	-	-	-	-	-	4	4	-	10	-	-	-	-	2	-	4
185 Found In Enclosed Premises	M	19	17	17	2	4	7	-	-	-	-	-	-	-	-	-	-	1	-	1	-	-	-	-	1	-	4
	F	2	2	2	-	1	-	-	-	-	-	-	-	-	-	-	-	-	-	-	-	-	-	-	-	-	-
	T	21	19	19	2	5	7	-	-	-	-	-	-	-	-	-	-	1	-	1	-	-	-	-	1	-	4
188 Other Vagrancy Offences	M	766	584	583	8	171	173	-	-	-	-	-	1	4	-	-	26	93	25	149	8	-	-	2	55	57	17
	F	11	8	8	-	3	3	-	-	-	-	-	-	-	-	-	1	1	-	2	-	-	-	-	2	2	-
	NS	2	1	1	-	-	-	-	-	-	-	-	-	-	-	-	-	-	-	-	-	-	-	-	-	-	-
	T	779	593	592	8	174	175	-	-	-	-	-	1	4	-	-	27	94	25	151	8	-	-	2	57	59	17
189 Weights and Measures Acts	M	2	2	2	-	-	4	-	-	-	-	-	-	-	-	-	-	-	-	-	-	-	-	-	-	-	-
	F	2	1	1	-	1	-	-	-	-	-	-	-	-	-	-	-	-	-	-	-	-	-	-	-	-	-
	NS	4	4	4	-	-	4	-	-	-	-	-	-	-	-	-	-	-	-	-	-	-	-	-	-	-	1
	O	4	1	1	-	-	-	-	-	-	-	-	-	-	-	-	-	-	-	-	-	-	-	-	-	-	-
	T	1	1	1	-	-	-	-	-	-	-	-	-	-	-	-	-	-	-	-	-	-	-	-	-	-	1

21.4 Offenders convicted and sentenced at all courts

England and Wales, 2012

Note: This is a rotated full-page statistical table. Abbreviated column headers are: Absl Disch = Absolute Discharge; Condl Disch = Conditional Discharge; CRO = Community Rehabilitation Order; SO = Supervision Order; CPO = Community Punishment Order; ACO = Attendance Centre Order; CPO&RO = Community Punishment and Rehabilitation Order; Curf Order = Curfew Order; Rep Order = Reparation Order; APO = Action Plan Order; DTTO = Drug Treatment and Testing Order; REFO = Referral Order; YRO = Youth Rehabilitation Order; SS = Suspended Sentence; Sec 90-92 = Section 90-92 detention; DTO = Detention and Training Order; YOI = Young Offender Institution; Unsus Sent Impr = Unsuspended Sentence of Imprisonment; Imm cust = Immediate custody; ODW = Otherwise dealt with.

Description	Sex	Total Proc Against	Total found Guilty	Total For Sent	Absl Disch	Condl Disch	Fine	CRO	SO	CPO	ACO	CPO&RO	Curf Order	Rep Order	APO	DTTO	REFO	Comm Order	YRO (1)	Total Comm Sentences	SS	Sec 90-92	DTO	YOI	Unsus Sent Impr	Imm cust	ODW
190 Wild Birds Protection Acts	M	2	2	2	-	-	2	-	-	-	-	-	-	-	-	-	-	-	-	-	-	-	-	-	-	-	-
	F	8	7	7	-	1	6	-	-	-	-	-	-	-	-	-	-	-	-	-	-	-	-	-	-	-	-
	NS	32	26	26	-	5	10	-	-	-	-	-	-	-	-	-	-	-	6	7	3	-	-	2	-	-	1
	O	2	2	2	-	-	-	-	-	-	-	-	-	-	-	-	-	-	-	-	2	-	-	-	-	-	-
	T	34	28	28	-	5	10	-	-	-	-	-	-	-	-	-	-	-	6	7	5	-	-	2	-	-	1
191 Wireless Telegraphy Acts	M	63,231	52,359	52,359	63	170	52,126	-	-	-	-	-	-	-	-	-	-	-	-	-	-	-	-	-	-	-	-
	F	129,351	112,237	112,237	169	360	111,706	-	-	-	-	-	-	-	-	-	-	-	-	-	-	-	-	-	-	-	2
	NS	450	322	322	-	1	321	-	-	-	-	-	-	-	-	-	-	-	-	-	-	-	-	-	-	-	-
	O	17	14	14	-	-	14	-	-	-	-	-	-	-	-	-	-	-	-	-	-	-	-	-	-	-	-
	T	193,049	164,932	164,932	232	531	164,167	-	-	-	-	-	-	-	-	-	-	-	-	-	-	-	-	-	-	-	2
192 Video Recording Act 1984	NS	1	1	1	-	-	1	-	-	-	-	-	-	-	-	-	-	-	-	-	-	-	-	-	-	-	-
	T	1	1	1	-	1	-	-	-	-	-	-	-	-	-	-	-	-	-	-	-	-	-	-	-	-	-
193 Drug Offence	M	1,518	1,447	1,446	45	343	678	-	-	-	-	-	-	-	-	-	-	18	-	18	15	-	-	-	65	67	280
	F	291	281	280	8	85	102	-	-	-	-	-	-	-	-	-	-	1	-	1	3	-	-	-	12	12	69
	NS	11	10	10	-	-	6	-	-	-	-	-	-	-	-	-	-	-	-	-	-	-	-	-	2	2	2
	T	1,820	1,738	1,736	53	428	786	-	-	-	-	-	-	-	-	-	-	19	-	19	18	-	-	-	79	81	351
194 Immigration Offence	M	17	23	23	-	3	1	-	-	-	-	-	-	-	-	-	-	1	1	1	3	-	-	2	13	15	-
	F	4	8	8	-	-	-	-	-	-	-	-	-	-	-	-	-	-	-	-	2	-	-	-	5	5	-
	NS	2	2	2	-	-	-	-	-	-	-	-	-	-	-	-	-	-	1	1	1	-	-	-	1	1	-
	T	23	33	33	-	3	1	-	-	-	-	-	-	-	-	-	-	2	2	2	6	-	-	2	19	21	-
Other Summary Offence (Excluding Motoring)	M	17,582	12,476	12,492	57	1,200	6,109	-	-	-	1	-	68	243	-	-	73	2,316	66	2,461	659	-	28	293	1,059	1,380	626
	F	3,714	2,255	2,266	12	256	1,383	-	-	-	3	-	13	34	-	-	28	259	14	305	77	-	2	28	91	121	112
	NS	3,450	2,057	2,053	5	51	1,884	-	-	-	-	-	-	1	-	-	1	16	-	18	5	-	3	22	23	48	42
	O	656	406	404	6	9	386	-	1	1	-	-	-	-	-	-	-	-	-	-	-	-	-	-	-	-	3
	T	25,402	17,194	17,215	80	1,516	9,762	1	1	1	1	-	81	278	-	-	102	2,591	80	2,784	741	-	33	343	1,173	1,549	783
Sub-total	M	347,848	275,882	276,066	1,772	28,719	173,950	-	3	1	25	-	68	243	-	-	4,607	35,137	3,869	43,954	7,737	-	314	1,368	11,156	12,838	7,096
	F	202,415	169,680	169,711	696	9,253	147,357	-	-	-	3	-	13	34	-	-	1,335	6,616	900	8,902	1,162	-	40	86	848	974	1,367
	NS	30,075	23,537	23,513	124	1,008	21,131	-	-	-	-	-	-	1	-	-	52	716	52	822	108	-	10	27	104	141	179
	O	1,536	960	957	8	18	920	2	1	-	-	-	-	-	-	-	-	-	-	-	-	-	-	-	-	-	11
	T	581,874	470,059	470,247	2,600	38,998	343,358	2	4	1	28	-	81	278	-	-	5,994	42,469	4,821	53,678	9,007	-	364	1,481	12,108	13,953	8,653
Summary Motoring — A Summary Motoring Offences	M	394,412	341,132	341,207	2,602	1,872	318,265	-	-	-	2	-	12	11	-	-	427	10,101	172	10,725	3,311	-	12	99	2,780	2,891	1,541
	F	93,760	82,090	82,088	638	416	78,196	-	-	-	2	-	12	11	-	-	51	1,999	2	2,057	427	-	-	-	106	106	248
	NS	31,110	24,554	24,551	61	62	24,270	-	-	-	-	-	-	-	-	-	4	46	-	52	14	-	-	2	13	15	77
	O	6,486	4,806	4,806	23	14	4,758	-	-	-	-	-	-	-	-	-	-	-	-	-	-	-	-	-	-	-	11
	T	525,768	452,582	452,652	3,324	2,364	425,489	-	-	-	2	-	12	11	-	-	482	12,146	181	12,834	3,752	-	12	101	2,899	3,012	1,877
Sub-total	M	394,412	341,132	341,207	2,602	1,872	318,265	-	-	-	2	-	12	11	-	-	427	10,101	172	10,725	3,311	-	12	99	2,780	2,891	1,541
	F	93,760	82,090	82,088	638	416	78,196	-	-	-	2	-	12	11	-	-	51	1,999	7	2,057	427	-	-	2	106	106	248
	NS	31,110	24,554	24,551	61	62	24,270	-	-	-	-	-	-	-	-	-	4	46	2	52	14	-	-	2	13	15	77
	O	6,486	4,806	4,806	23	14	4,758	-	-	-	-	-	-	-	-	-	-	-	-	-	-	-	-	-	-	-	11
	T	525,768	452,582	452,652	3,324	2,364	425,489	-	-	-	2	-	12	11	-	-	482	12,146	181	12,834	3,752	-	12	101	2,899	3,012	1,877
Total Summary	M	742,260	617,014	617,273	4,374	30,591	492,215	1	3	-	27	-	80	254	-	-	5,034	45,238	4,041	54,679	11,048	-	326	1,467	13,936	15,729	8,637
	F	296,175	251,770	251,799	1,334	9,669	225,553	1	-	-	3	-	13	34	-	-	1,386	8,615	907	10,959	1,589	-	40	86	954	1,080	1,615
	NS	61,185	48,091	48,064	185	1,070	45,401	-	1	-	-	-	-	1	-	-	56	762	54	874	122	-	10	29	117	156	256
	O	8,022	5,766	5,763	31	32	5,678	-	-	-	-	-	-	-	-	-	-	-	-	-	-	-	-	-	-	-	22
	T	1,107,642	922,641	922,899	5,924	41,362	768,847	1	3	-	30	-	93	289	-	-	6,476	54,615	5,002	66,512	12,759	-	376	1,582	15,007	16,965	10,530
All Offences	M	1,061,199	879,875	878,475	5,717	60,141	538,988	26	22	5	79	1	242	486	-	1	13,425	96,652	12,680	123,619	37,409	289	2,545	9,266	77,718	89,818	22,783
	F	348,606	294,463	294,392	1,579	18,386	231,721	6	1	-	6	-	39	78	-	1	2,807	19,259	2,002	24,198	6,918	-	172	510	7,017	7,709	3,881
	NS	65,689	50,661	50,385	33	1,340	46,127	-	-	-	-	-	1	1	-	-	150	1,204	153	1,510	315	10	41	62	417	520	373
	O	9,132	6,587	6,575	200	44	6,462	-	-	-	-	-	-	-	-	-	-	1	-	2	2	-	-	-	-	-	33
	T	1,484,626	1,231,586	1,229,827	7,529	79,911	823,298	32	23	5	85	1	282	565	-	2	16,382	117,116	14,835	149,328	44,644	299	2,758	9,838	85,152	98,047	27,070

(1) YRO = Youth Rehabilitation Order.

21.5 Persons cautioned for summary offences (excluding motoring) by offence, sex and age

England and Wales, 2012

Number of persons

Offence		Total	Aged 10 And Under 12	Aged 12 And Under 15	Aged 15 And Under 18	Aged 10 And Under 18	Aged 18 And Under 21	Aged 21 And Over
104 Assault: On Constable	M	2,011	2	43	230	275	421	1,315
	F	1,434	-	61	191	252	231	951
	NS	7	-	-	-	-	2	5
	T	3,452	2	104	421	527	654	2,271
105 Assault: Common, etc	M	35,280	171	1,304	2,143	3,618	4,180	27,482
	F	12,148	27	793	1,198	2,018	1,717	8,413
	NS	165	1	16	31	48	19	98
	T	47,593	199	2,113	3,372	5,684	5,916	35,993
106 Betting or Gaming Offence	M	26	-	-	2	2	6	18
	F	3	-	-	-	-	1	2
	T	29	-	-	2	2	7	20
107 Brothel Keeping	M	3	-	-	-	-	-	3
	F	16	-	-	-	-	2	14
	T	19	-	-	-	-	2	17
108 Cruelty to Animal	M	24	-	4	-	4	-	20
	F	6	-	2	-	2	-	4
	NS	1	-	-	-	-	-	1
	T	31	-	6	-	6	-	25
111 Offences Relating to Dogs	M	36	-	-	1	1	5	30
	F	40	-	1	-	1	2	37
	T	76	-	1	1	2	7	67
112 Education Acts	M	7	-	-	5	5	2	-
	F	1	-	1	-	1	-	-
	T	8	-	1	5	6	2	-
115 Firearms Acts	M	316	-	23	44	67	57	192
	F	4	-	-	-	-	1	3
	NS	2	-	-	2	2	-	-
	T	322	-	23	46	69	58	195
118 Game Law - Night Poaching	M	7	-	-	2	2	1	4
	T	7	-	-	2	2	1	4
119 Game Law - Day Poaching	M	13	-	-	2	2	2	9
	T	13	-	-	2	2	2	9
121 Other Offence against Game Law	M	4	-	-	2	2	1	1
	T	4	-	-	2	2	1	1
122 Highways Act - Obstruction Other than by Vehicle	M	2	-	-	1	1	-	1
	T	2	-	-	1	1	-	1
123 Highways Act - Nuisance Other than by Vehicle	M	4	1	-	-	1	-	3
	T	4	1	-	-	1	-	3
125 Offence against Public Order	M	8,921	15	321	986	1,322	1,694	5,905
	F	2,123	1	139	309	449	330	1,344
	NS	34	-	4	11	15	6	13
	T	11,078	16	464	1,306	1,786	2,030	7,262
126 Interference with Motor Vehicles	M	127	1	21	33	55	29	43
	F	4	-	-	1	1	2	1
	T	131	1	21	34	56	31	44
130 Unauthorised Taking of a Conveyance	M	1,001	-	56	312	368	272	361
	F	151	-	10	36	46	41	64
	NS	4	-	1	-	1	2	1
	T	1,156	-	67	348	415	315	426
131 Summary Aggravated Vehicle Taking	M	218	-	19	86	105	62	51
	F	38	-	6	13	19	14	5
	NS	1	-	-	1	1	-	-
	T	257	-	25	100	125	76	56
137 Highways Act - Pedal Cycle	M	76	-	8	12	20	27	29
	F	6	-	2	-	2	3	1
	T	82	-	10	12	22	30	30

21.5 Persons cautioned for summary offences (excluding motoring) by offence, sex and age

England and Wales, 2012   Number of persons

Offence		Total	Aged 10 And Under 12	Aged 12 And Under 15	Aged 15 And Under 18	Aged 10 And Under 18	Aged 18 And Under 21	Aged 21 And Over
138 Offences involving impersonation	M	1	-	-	-	-	1	-
	T	1	-	-	-	-	1	-
140 Drunkenness, Simple	M	338	-	1	13	14	30	294
	F	50	-	-	2	2	2	46
	NS	3	-	-	-	-	-	3
	T	391	-	1	15	16	32	343
141 Drunkenness, with Aggravation	M	3,467	-	22	352	374	586	2,507
	F	1,304	-	35	208	243	192	869
	NS	15	-	-	2	2	4	9
	T	4,786	-	57	562	619	782	3,385
142 Offence by Licenced Person, etc.	F	2	-	-	-	-	-	2
	T	2	-	-	-	-	-	2
143 Other Offence against the Liquor Law	M	198	-	-	4	4	16	178
	F	37	-	1	-	1	3	33
	T	235	-	1	4	5	19	211
149 Summary Criminal or Malicious Damage Offence	M	13,816	147	989	1,495	2,631	2,392	8,793
	F	2,779	6	242	366	614	402	1,763
	NS	58	1	12	12	25	11	22
	T	16,653	154	1,243	1,873	3,270	2,805	10,578
151 Social Security Offence	M	16	-	-	-	-	3	13
	F	6	-	-	1	1	-	5
	NS	1	-	-	-	-	-	1
	T	23	-	-	1	1	3	19
155 Naval, Military and Air Force Law - Air Force	M	8	-	-	1	1	2	5
	F	1	-	-	-	-	-	1
	T	9	-	-	1	1	2	6
160 Pedlars Act	M	12	-	-	1	1	1	10
	T	12	-	-	1	1	1	10
162 Disorderly Behaviour	M	12	-	-	1	1	3	8
	F	5	-	-	1	1	-	4
	T	17	-	-	2	2	3	12
164 Other Offence	M	14	-	1	4	5	2	7
	F	4	-	-	1	1	-	3
	T	18	-	1	5	6	2	10
165 Prostitution - Kerb Crawling	M	90	-	-	-	-	5	85
	F	21	-	-	-	-	1	20
	T	111	-	-	-	-	6	105
166 Prostitution - Offence by Prostitute	M	8	-	-	-	-	-	8
	F	34	-	-	-	-	2	32
	T	42	-	-	-	-	2	40
167 Prostitution - Aiding, etc. Offence by Prostitute	M	252	-	-	4	4	11	237
	NS	4	-	-	-	-	1	3
	T	256	-	-	4	4	12	240
168 Public Health Offence	M	6	-	-	-	-	-	6
	F	1	-	-	-	-	-	1
	T	7	-	-	-	-	-	7
169 Railway Offence	M	1,818	3	13	188	204	472	1,142
	F	286	-	7	52	59	96	131
	NS	33	-	1	8	9	9	15
	T	2,137	3	21	248	272	577	1,288
173 Stage Carriage or Public Service Vehicle Offence	M	280	-	-	-	-	3	277
	F	2	-	-	-	-	-	2
	T	282	-	-	-	-	3	279
175 Sexual Offences- Miscellaneous	M	29	-	-	1	1	-	28
	F	1	-	-	-	-	-	1
	T	30	-	-	1	1	-	29
176 Private security industry	M	13	-	-	-	-	-	13
	F	1	-	-	-	-	-	1
	T	14	-	-	-	-	-	14

21.5 Persons cautioned for summary offences (excluding motoring) by offence, sex and age

England and Wales, 2012   Number of persons

Offence		Total	Aged 10 And Under 12	Aged 12 And Under 15	Aged 15 And Under 18	Aged 10 And Under 18	Aged 18 And Under 21	Aged 21 And Over
182 Vagrancy Offences - Begging	M	214	-	-	-	-	2	212
	F	103	-	3	4	7	12	84
	T	317	-	3	4	7	14	296
183 Vagrancy Offences - Sleeping Out	M	1	-	-	-	-	-	1
	T	1	-	-	-	-	-	1
185 Vagrancy Offences - Found In Enclosed Premises	M	128	-	8	27	35	26	67
	F	6	-	2	1	3	-	3
	T	134	-	10	28	38	26	70
188 Other Vagrancy Offences	F	1	-	-	-	-	-	1
	T	1	-	-	-	-	-	1
190 Wild Birds Protection Acts	M	12	-	1	-	1	2	9
	T	12	-	1	-	1	2	9
193 Drug Offence	M	21	-	-	2	2	2	17
	F	8	-	1	-	1	-	7
	NS	1	-	-	-	-	-	1
	T	30	-	1	2	3	2	25
194 Immigration Offence	M	5	-	-	-	-	-	5
	F	1	-	-	-	-	-	1
	T	6	-	-	-	-	-	6
Other Summary Offence (Excluding Motoring)	M	4,388	2	61	187	250	454	3,684
	F	1,101	-	47	86	133	132	836
	NS	23	-	-	3	3	2	18
	T	5,512	2	108	276	386	588	4,538
Total Summary Offences (Exc Motoring)	M	73,223	342	2,895	6,141	9,378	10,772	53,073
	F	21,728	34	1,353	2,470	3,857	3,186	14,685
	NS	352	2	34	70	106	56	190
	T	95,303	378	4,282	8,681	13,341	14,014	67,948

21.6a Persons aged 10 to under 12 convicted and sentenced at all courts

England and Wales, 2012

Number of persons

Offence group	Description		Total Proc Against	Total found Guilty	Total For Sent	Absit Disch	Condi Disch	Fine	CRO	SO	CPO	ACO	CPO&RO	Curf Order	Rep Order	APO	DTTO	REFO	Comm Order	YRO (1)	Total Comm Sentences	SS	Sec 90-92	DTO	YOI	Unsus Sent Impr	Imm cust	ODW
Violence Against Person	5 Wounding or other act Endangering Life	M	1	1	1	-	-	-	-	-	-	-	-	-	-	-	-	1	-	-	1	-	-	-	-	-	-	-
		T	1	1	1	-	-	-	-	-	-	-	-	-	-	-	-	1	-	-	1	-	-	-	-	-	-	-
	8 Malicious Wounding etc.	M	16	11	11	-	-	-	-	-	-	-	-	-	-	-	-	10	-	1	11	-	-	-	-	-	-	-
		F	2	-	-	-	-	-	-	-	-	-	-	-	-	-	-	-	-	-	-	-	-	-	-	-	-	-
		T	18	11	11	-	-	-	-	-	-	-	-	-	-	-	-	10	-	1	11	-	-	-	-	-	-	-
	Sub-total	M	17	12	12	-	-	-	-	-	-	-	-	-	-	-	-	11	-	1	12	-	-	-	-	-	-	-
		F	2	-	-	-	-	-	-	-	-	-	-	-	-	-	-	-	-	-	-	-	-	-	-	-	-	-
		T	19	12	12	-	-	-	-	-	-	-	-	-	-	-	-	11	-	1	12	-	-	-	-	-	-	-
Sexual Offences	19 Rape of a Female	M	1	-	-	-	-	-	-	-	-	-	-	-	-	-	-	-	-	-	-	-	-	-	-	-	-	-
		T	1	-	-	-	-	-	-	-	-	-	-	-	-	-	-	-	-	-	-	-	-	-	-	-	-	-
	19 Rape of a Male	M	1	-	-	-	-	-	-	-	-	-	-	-	-	-	-	-	-	-	-	-	-	-	-	-	-	-
		T	1	-	-	-	-	-	-	-	-	-	-	-	-	-	-	-	-	-	-	-	-	-	-	-	-	-
	20 Sexual Assault on a Female	M	1	1	1	-	-	-	-	-	-	-	-	-	-	-	-	-	-	1	1	-	-	-	-	-	-	-
		T	1	1	1	-	-	-	-	-	-	-	-	-	-	-	-	-	-	1	1	-	-	-	-	-	-	-
	88 Miscellaneous sexual offences	M	1	1	1	-	-	-	-	-	-	-	-	-	-	-	-	1	-	-	1	-	-	-	-	-	-	-
		T	1	1	1	-	-	-	-	-	-	-	-	-	-	-	-	1	-	-	1	-	-	-	-	-	-	-
	Sub-total	M	4	2	2	-	-	-	-	-	-	-	-	-	-	-	-	1	-	1	2	-	-	-	-	-	-	-
		T	4	2	2	-	-	-	-	-	-	-	-	-	-	-	-	1	-	1	2	-	-	-	-	-	-	-
Burglary	28 Burglary in a Dwelling	M	11	7	7	-	-	-	-	-	-	-	-	-	-	-	-	7	-	-	7	-	-	-	-	-	-	-
		F	1	1	1	-	-	-	-	-	-	-	-	-	-	-	-	1	-	-	1	-	-	-	-	-	-	-
		NS	1	1	1	-	-	-	-	-	-	-	-	-	-	-	-	1	-	-	1	-	-	-	-	-	-	-
		T	13	9	9	-	-	-	-	-	-	-	-	-	-	-	-	9	-	-	9	-	-	-	-	-	-	-
	30 Burglary in a Building Other than a Dwelling	M	7	2	2	-	-	-	-	-	-	-	-	-	-	-	-	2	-	-	2	-	-	-	-	-	-	-
		F	1	-	-	-	-	-	-	-	-	-	-	-	-	-	-	-	-	-	-	-	-	-	-	-	-	-
		T	8	2	2	-	-	-	-	-	-	-	-	-	-	-	-	2	-	-	2	-	-	-	-	-	-	-
	Sub-total	M	18	9	9	-	-	-	-	-	-	-	-	-	-	-	-	9	-	-	9	-	-	-	-	-	-	-
		F	2	1	1	-	-	-	-	-	-	-	-	-	-	-	-	1	-	-	1	-	-	-	-	-	-	-
		NS	1	1	1	-	-	-	-	-	-	-	-	-	-	-	-	1	-	-	1	-	-	-	-	-	-	-
		T	21	11	11	-	-	-	-	-	-	-	-	-	-	-	-	11	-	-	11	-	-	-	-	-	-	-
Robbery	34 Robbery	M	20	12	12	-	-	-	-	-	-	-	-	-	-	-	-	10	-	2	12	-	-	-	-	-	-	-
		F	3	2	2	-	-	-	-	-	-	-	-	-	-	-	-	2	-	-	2	-	-	-	-	-	-	-
		T	23	14	14	-	-	-	-	-	-	-	-	-	-	-	-	12	-	2	14	-	-	-	-	-	-	-
	Sub-total	M	20	12	12	-	-	-	-	-	-	-	-	-	-	-	-	10	-	2	12	-	-	-	-	-	-	-
		F	3	2	2	-	-	-	-	-	-	-	-	-	-	-	-	2	-	-	2	-	-	-	-	-	-	-
		T	23	14	14	-	-	-	-	-	-	-	-	-	-	-	-	12	-	2	14	-	-	-	-	-	-	-
Theft and Handling	39 Theft from the Person of Another	M	4	2	2	-	-	-	-	-	-	-	-	-	-	-	-	2	-	-	2	-	-	-	-	-	-	-
		T	4	2	2	-	-	-	-	-	-	-	-	-	-	-	-	2	-	-	2	-	-	-	-	-	-	-
	40 Theft in Dwelling not Automatic M/c or Meter	M	1	1	1	-	-	-	-	-	-	-	-	-	-	-	-	1	-	-	1	-	-	-	-	-	-	-
		F	1	-	-	-	-	-	-	-	-	-	-	-	-	-	-	-	-	-	-	-	-	-	-	-	-	-
		T	2	1	1	-	-	-	-	-	-	-	-	-	-	-	-	1	-	-	1	-	-	-	-	-	-	-
	44 Theft of Pedal Cycle	M	2	2	2	-	-	-	-	-	-	-	-	-	-	-	-	2	-	-	2	-	-	-	-	-	-	-
		T	2	2	2	-	-	-	-	-	-	-	-	-	-	-	-	2	-	-	2	-	-	-	-	-	-	-
	46 Theft from Shops	M	13	8	8	2	-	-	-	-	-	-	-	-	-	-	-	6	-	-	6	-	-	-	-	-	-	-
		F	7	4	4	-	-	-	-	-	-	-	-	-	-	-	-	3	-	1	4	-	-	-	-	-	-	-
		T	20	12	12	2	-	-	-	-	-	-	-	-	-	-	-	9	-	1	10	-	-	-	-	-	-	-
	49 Other Theft or Unauthorised Taking	M	6	5	5	-	-	-	-	-	-	-	-	-	-	-	-	4	-	1	5	-	-	-	-	-	-	-
		F	1	-	-	-	-	-	-	-	-	-	-	-	-	-	-	-	-	-	-	-	-	-	-	-	-	-
		T	7	5	5	-	-	-	-	-	-	-	-	-	-	-	-	4	-	1	5	-	-	-	-	-	-	-
	54 Handling Stolen Goods	M	2	-	-	-	-	-	-	-	-	-	-	-	-	-	-	-	-	-	-	-	-	-	-	-	-	-
		T	2	-	-	-	-	-	-	-	-	-	-	-	-	-	-	-	-	-	-	-	-	-	-	-	-	-
	Sub-total	M	28	18	18	2	-	-	-	-	-	-	-	-	-	-	-	15	-	1	16	-	-	-	-	-	-	-
		F	9	4	4	-	-	-	-	-	-	-	-	-	-	-	-	3	-	1	4	-	-	-	-	-	-	-
		T	37	22	22	2	-	-	-	-	-	-	-	-	-	-	-	18	-	2	20	-	-	-	-	-	-	-
Fraud and Forgery	53 Other Fraud	F	1	1	1	-	-	-	-	-	-	-	-	-	-	-	-	1	-	-	1	-	-	-	-	-	-	-
		T	1	1	1	-	-	-	-	-	-	-	-	-	-	-	-	1	-	-	1	-	-	-	-	-	-	-
	Sub-total	F	1	1	1	-	-	-	-	-	-	-	-	-	-	-	-	1	-	-	1	-	-	-	-	-	-	-
		T	1	1	1	-	-	-	-	-	-	-	-	-	-	-	-	1	-	-	1	-	-	-	-	-	-	-
Criminal Damage	56 Arson	M	7	6	6	-	-	-	-	-	-	-	-	-	-	-	-	4	-	1	5	-	-	-	-	-	-	1
		T	7	6	6	-	-	-	-	-	-	-	-	-	-	-	-	4	-	1	5	-	-	-	-	-	-	1
	58 Other Criminal Damage	M	18	14	14	1	1	-	-	-	-	-	-	-	-	-	-	9	-	3	12	-	-	-	-	-	-	-
		T	18	14	14	1	1	-	-	-	-	-	-	-	-	-	-	9	-	3	12	-	-	-	-	-	-	-
	Sub-total	M	25	20	20	1	1	-	-	-	-	-	-	-	-	-	-	13	-	4	17	-	-	-	-	-	-	1
		T	25	20	20	1	1	-	-	-	-	-	-	-	-	-	-	13	-	4	17	-	-	-	-	-	-	1
Other Indictable (Not Motoring)	66 Other Offence against the State or Public Order	M	3	2	2	-	-	-	-	-	-	-	-	-	-	-	-	2	-	-	2	-	-	-	-	-	-	-
		T	3	2	2	-	-	-	-	-	-	-	-	-	-	-	-	2	-	-	2	-	-	-	-	-	-	-
	83 Failing to Surrender to Bail	M	2	-	-	-	-	-	-	-	-	-	-	-	-	-	-	-	-	-	-	-	-	-	-	-	-	-
		T	2	-	-	-	-	-	-	-	-	-	-	-	-	-	-	-	-	-	-	-	-	-	-	-	-	-
	99 Other (Excluding Motoring Offences)	M	1	1	1	-	-	-	-	-	-	-	-	-	-	-	-	1	-	-	1	-	-	-	-	-	-	-
		T	1	1	1	-	-	-	-	-	-	-	-	-	-	-	-	1	-	-	1	-	-	-	-	-	-	-
	Sub-total	M	6	3	3	-	-	-	-	-	-	-	-	-	-	-	-	3	-	-	3	-	-	-	-	-	-	-
		T	6	3	3	-	-	-	-	-	-	-	-	-	-	-	-	3	-	-	3	-	-	-	-	-	-	-
Indictable excluding motoring		M	118	76	76	3	1	-	-	-	-	-	-	-	-	-	-	62	-	9	71	-	-	-	-	-	-	1
		F	17	8	8	-	-	-	-	-	-	-	-	-	-	-	-	7	-	1	8	-	-	-	-	-	-	-
		NS	1	1	1	-	-	-	-	-	-	-	-	-	-	-	-	1	-	-	1	-	-	-	-	-	-	-
		T	136	85	85	3	1	-	-	-	-	-	-	-	-	-	-	70	-	10	80	-	-	-	-	-	-	1
Indictable including motoring		M	118	76	76	3	1	-	-	-	-	-	-	-	-	-	-	62	-	9	71	-	-	-	-	-	-	1
		F	17	8	8	-	-	-	-	-	-	-	-	-	-	-	-	7	-	1	8	-	-	-	-	-	-	-
		NS	1	1	1	-	-	-	-	-	-	-	-	-	-	-	-	1	-	-	1	-	-	-	-	-	-	-
		T	136	85	85	3	1	-	-	-	-	-	-	-	-	-	-	70	-	10	80	-	-	-	-	-	-	1

21.6a Persons aged 10 to under 12 convicted and sentenced at all courts

England and Wales, 2012

Number of persons

Offence group	Description		Total Proc Against	Total found Guilty	Total For Sent	Absl Disch	Condl Disch	Fine	CRO	SO	CPO	ACO	CPO&RO	Curf Order	Rep Order	APO	DTTO	REFO	Comm Order	YRO (1)	Total Comm Sentences	SS	Sec 90-92	DTO	YOI	Unsus Sent Impr	Imm cust	ODW
Summary Non-Motoring	105 Common, etc	M	60	45	45	6	1	-	-	-	-	-	-	-	-	-	-	33	-	5	38	-	-	-	-	-	-	-
		F	3	-	-	-	-	-	-	-	-	-	-	-	-	-	-	-	-	-	-	-	-	-	-	-	-	-
		T	63	45	45	6	1	-	-	-	-	-	-	-	-	-	-	33	-	5	38	-	-	-	-	-	-	-
	125 Public Order Act 1986	M	13	9	9	-	-	-	-	-	-	-	-	-	-	-	-	7	-	2	9	-	-	-	-	-	-	-
		F	1	-	-	-	-	-	-	-	-	-	-	-	-	-	-	-	-	-	-	-	-	-	-	-	-	-
		T	14	9	9	-	-	-	-	-	-	-	-	-	-	-	-	7	-	2	9	-	-	-	-	-	-	-
	131 Summary Aggravated Vehicle Taking	M	1	-	-	-	-	-	-	-	-	-	-	-	-	-	-	-	-	-	-	-	-	-	-	-	-	-
		T	1	-	-	-	-	-	-	-	-	-	-	-	-	-	-	-	-	-	-	-	-	-	-	-	-	-
	149 Summary Criminal or Malicious Damage Offence	M	36	25	25	3	4	-	-	-	-	-	-	-	-	-	-	18	-	-	18	-	-	-	-	-	-	-
		F	1	-	-	-	-	-	-	-	-	-	-	-	-	-	-	-	-	-	-	-	-	-	-	-	-	-
		T	37	25	25	3	4	-	-	-	-	-	-	-	-	-	-	18	-	-	18	-	-	-	-	-	-	-
	169 Railway Offence	M	4	-	-	-	-	-	-	-	-	-	-	-	-	-	-	-	-	-	-	-	-	-	-	-	-	-
		F	1	-	-	-	-	-	-	-	-	-	-	-	-	-	-	-	-	-	-	-	-	-	-	-	-	-
		T	5	-	-	-	-	-	-	-	-	-	-	-	-	-	-	-	-	-	-	-	-	-	-	-	-	-
	Other Summary Offence (Excluding Motoring)	M	1	1	1	-	-	-	-	-	-	-	-	-	-	-	-	1	-	-	1	-	-	-	-	-	-	-
		T	1	1	1	-	-	-	-	-	-	-	-	-	-	-	-	1	-	-	1	-	-	-	-	-	-	-
	Sub-total	M	115	80	80	9	5	-	-	-	-	-	-	-	-	-	-	59	-	7	66	-	-	-	-	-	-	-
		F	6	-	-	-	-	-	-	-	-	-	-	-	-	-	-	-	-	-	-	-	-	-	-	-	-	-
		T	121	80	80	9	5	-	-	-	-	-	-	-	-	-	-	59	-	7	66	-	-	-	-	-	-	-
Summary Motoring	A Summary Motoring Offences	M	4	3	3	-	-	2	-	-	-	-	-	-	-	-	-	1	-	-	1	-	-	-	-	-	-	-
		F	1	-	-	-	-	-	-	-	-	-	-	-	-	-	-	-	-	-	-	-	-	-	-	-	-	-
		T	5	3	3	-	-	2	-	-	-	-	-	-	-	-	-	1	-	-	1	-	-	-	-	-	-	-
	Sub-total	M	4	3	3	-	-	2	-	-	-	-	-	-	-	-	-	1	-	-	1	-	-	-	-	-	-	-
		F	1	-	-	-	-	-	-	-	-	-	-	-	-	-	-	-	-	-	-	-	-	-	-	-	-	-
		T	5	3	3	-	-	2	-	-	-	-	-	-	-	-	-	1	-	-	1	-	-	-	-	-	-	-
Total Summary		M	119	83	83	9	5	2	-	-	-	-	-	-	-	-	-	60	-	7	67	-	-	-	-	-	-	-
		F	7	-	-	-	-	-	-	-	-	-	-	-	-	-	-	-	-	-	-	-	-	-	-	-	-	-
		T	126	83	83	9	5	2	-	-	-	-	-	-	-	-	-	60	-	7	67	-	-	-	-	-	-	-
All Offences		M	237	159	159	12	6	2	-	-	-	-	-	-	-	-	-	122	-	16	138	-	-	-	-	-	-	1
		F	24	8	8	-	-	-	-	-	-	-	-	-	-	-	-	7	-	1	8	-	-	-	-	-	-	-
		NS	1	1	1	-	-	-	-	-	-	-	-	-	-	-	-	1	-	-	1	-	-	-	-	-	-	-
		T	262	168	168	12	6	2	-	-	-	-	-	-	-	-	-	130	-	17	147	-	-	-	-	-	-	1

(1) The Youth Rehabilitation Order came into effect on 30 November 2009. Figures prior to 2010 are recorded as community orders.

21.6b Persons aged 12 to under 15 convicted and sentenced at all courts

England and Wales, 2012

Number of persons

Offence group	Description		Total Proc Against	Total found Guilty	Total For Sent	Absl Disch	Condl Disch	Fine	CRO	SO	CPO	ACO	CPO&RO	Curf Order	Rep Order	APO	DTTO	REFO	Comm Order	YRO [1]	Total Comm Sentences	SS	Sec 90-92	DTO	YOI	Unsus Sent Impr	Imm cust	ODW
Violence Against Person	1 Murder	M	2	-	-	-	-	-	-	-	-	-	-	-	-	-	-	-	-	-	-	-	-	-	-	-	-	-
		F	1	-	-	-	-	-	-	-	-	-	-	-	-	-	-	-	-	-	-	-	-	-	-	-	-	-
		T	3	-	-	-	-	-	-	-	-	-	-	-	-	-	-	-	-	-	-	-	-	-	-	-	-	-
	2 Attempted Murder	F	1	-	-	-	-	-	-	-	-	-	-	-	-	-	-	-	-	-	-	-	-	-	-	-	-	-
		T	1	-	-	-	-	-	-	-	-	-	-	-	-	-	-	-	-	-	-	-	-	-	-	-	-	-
	3 Threat or Conspiracy to Murder	M	4	2	2	-	-	-	-	-	-	-	-	-	-	-	-	-	-	-	2	2	-	-	-	-	-	-	-
		F	1	1	1	-	-	-	-	-	-	-	-	-	-	-	-	1	-	-	1	-	-	-	-	-	-	-
		T	5	3	3	-	-	-	-	-	-	-	-	-	-	-	-	1	-	2	3	-	-	-	-	-	-	-
	4.1 Manslaughter	M	4	-	-	-	-	-	-	-	-	-	-	-	-	-	-	-	-	-	-	-	-	-	-	-	-	-
		T	4	-	-	-	-	-	-	-	-	-	-	-	-	-	-	-	-	-	-	-	-	-	-	-	-	-
	5 Wounding or other act Endangering Life	M	28	13	13	1	1	-	-	-	-	-	-	-	-	-	-	4	-	6	10	-	1	-	-	-	1	-
		F	5	1	1	-	-	-	-	-	-	-	-	-	-	-	-	-	-	1	1	-	-	-	-	-	-	-
		T	33	14	14	1	1	-	-	-	-	-	-	-	-	-	-	4	-	7	11	-	1	-	-	-	1	-
	8 Malicious Wounding etc.	M	569	431	431	4	10	-	-	-	-	-	-	-	1	-	-	273	-	123	397	-	-	12	-	-	12	8
		F	153	109	109	2	2	-	-	-	-	-	-	-	2	-	-	66	-	35	103	-	-	1	-	-	1	1
		NS	8	5	4	-	-	-	-	-	-	-	-	-	-	-	-	4	-	-	4	-	-	-	-	-	-	-
		T	730	545	544	6	12	-	-	-	-	-	-	-	3	-	-	343	-	158	504	-	-	13	-	-	13	9
	13 Child Abduction	M	1	1	1	-	-	-	-	-	-	-	-	-	-	-	-	1	-	-	1	-	-	-	-	-	-	-
		T	1	1	1	-	-	-	-	-	-	-	-	-	-	-	-	1	-	-	1	-	-	-	-	-	-	-
	Sub-total	M	608	447	447	5	11	-	-	-	-	-	-	-	1	-	-	278	-	131	410	-	1	12	-	-	13	8
		F	161	111	111	2	2	-	-	-	-	-	-	-	2	-	-	67	-	36	105	-	-	1	-	-	1	1
		NS	8	5	4	-	-	-	-	-	-	-	-	-	-	-	-	4	-	-	4	-	-	-	-	-	-	-
		T	777	563	562	7	13	-	-	-	-	-	-	-	3	-	-	349	-	167	519	-	1	13	-	-	14	9
Sexual Offences	17 Sexual Assault on a Male	M	7	4	4	-	-	-	-	1	-	-	-	-	-	-	-	1	-	2	4	-	-	-	-	-	-	-
		T	7	4	4	-	-	-	-	1	-	-	-	-	-	-	-	1	-	2	4	-	-	-	-	-	-	-
	19 Rape of a Female	M	36	15	15	-	-	-	-	1	-	-	-	-	-	-	-	3	-	6	10	-	3	-	-	2	5	-
		F	-	1	1	-	-	-	-	-	-	-	-	-	-	-	-	-	-	-	-	-	1	-	-	-	1	-
		NS	1	-	-	-	-	-	-	-	-	-	-	-	-	-	-	-	-	-	-	-	-	-	-	-	-	-
		T	37	16	16	-	-	-	-	1	-	-	-	-	-	-	-	3	-	6	10	-	4	-	-	2	6	-
	19 Rape of a Male	M	14	10	9	-	-	-	-	2	-	-	-	-	-	-	-	3	-	2	7	-	1	-	-	-	1	1
		T	14	10	9	-	-	-	-	2	-	-	-	-	-	-	-	3	-	2	7	-	1	-	-	-	1	1
	20 Sexual Assault on a Female	M	64	38	38	2	-	-	-	-	-	-	-	-	-	-	-	23	-	11	34	-	-	1	-	-	1	1
		F	2	-	-	-	-	-	-	-	-	-	-	-	-	-	-	-	-	-	-	-	-	-	-	-	-	-
		NS	1	1	1	-	-	-	-	-	-	-	-	-	-	-	-	-	-	1	1	-	-	-	-	-	-	-
		T	67	39	39	2	-	-	-	-	-	-	-	-	-	-	-	23	-	12	35	-	-	1	-	-	1	1
	21 Sexual Activity with child under 13	M	19	17	17	-	1	-	-	-	-	-	-	-	-	-	-	5	-	7	12	-	-	-	-	-	-	4
		T	19	17	17	-	1	-	-	-	-	-	-	-	-	-	-	5	-	7	12	-	-	-	-	-	-	4
	22 Sexual Activity with child under 16	M	2	2	2	-	-	-	-	-	-	-	-	-	-	-	-	1	-	1	2	-	-	-	-	-	-	-
		T	2	2	2	-	-	-	-	-	-	-	-	-	-	-	-	1	-	1	2	-	-	-	-	-	-	-
	23 Familial Sexual Offences (Incest)	M	2	1	1	-	-	-	-	-	-	-	-	-	-	-	-	-	-	1	1	-	-	-	-	-	-	-
		T	2	1	1	-	-	-	-	-	-	-	-	-	-	-	-	-	-	1	1	-	-	-	-	-	-	-
	70 Sexual activity etc. with a person with a mental disorder	M	1	1	1	-	-	-	-	-	-	-	-	-	-	-	-	1	-	-	1	-	-	-	-	-	-	-
		T	1	1	1	-	-	-	-	-	-	-	-	-	-	-	-	1	-	-	1	-	-	-	-	-	-	-
	88 Miscellaneous sexual offences	M	9	7	7	-	-	-	-	-	-	-	-	-	-	-	-	5	-	2	7	-	-	-	-	-	-	-
		T	9	7	7	-	-	-	-	-	-	-	-	-	-	-	-	5	-	2	7	-	-	-	-	-	-	-
	Sub-total	M	154	95	94	2	1	-	-	4	-	-	-	-	-	-	-	42	-	32	78	-	4	1	-	2	7	6
		F	2	1	1	-	-	-	-	-	-	-	-	-	-	-	-	-	-	-	-	-	1	-	-	-	1	-
		NS	2	1	1	-	-	-	-	-	-	-	-	-	-	-	-	-	-	1	1	-	-	-	-	-	-	-
		T	158	97	96	2	1	-	-	4	-	-	-	-	-	-	-	42	-	33	79	-	5	1	-	2	8	6
Burglary	28 Burglary in a Dwelling	M	397	307	307	-	5	-	-	1	-	-	-	-	-	-	-	152	-	114	267	-	-	26	-	-	26	9
		F	24	18	18	-	-	-	-	-	-	-	-	-	-	-	-	14	-	3	17	-	-	-	-	-	-	1
		NS	5	5	5	-	-	-	-	-	-	-	-	-	-	-	-	2	-	2	4	-	-	1	-	-	1	-
		T	426	330	330	-	5	-	-	1	-	-	-	-	-	-	-	168	-	119	288	-	-	27	-	-	27	10
	29 Aggravated Burglary in a Dwelling	M	7	1	1	-	-	-	-	-	-	-	-	-	-	-	-	-	-	1	1	-	-	-	-	-	-	-
		T	7	1	1	-	-	-	-	-	-	-	-	-	-	-	-	-	-	1	1	-	-	-	-	-	-	-
	30 Burglary in a Building Other than a Dwelling	M	299	220	219	2	4	-	-	-	-	-	-	-	3	-	-	109	-	87	199	-	-	7	-	-	7	7
		F	24	19	19	-	-	-	-	-	-	-	-	-	-	-	-	16	-	3	19	-	-	-	-	-	-	-
		NS	1	1	1	-	-	-	-	-	-	-	-	-	-	-	-	1	-	-	1	-	-	-	-	-	-	-
		T	324	240	239	2	4	-	-	-	-	-	-	-	3	-	-	126	-	90	219	-	-	7	-	-	7	7
	Sub-total	M	703	528	527	2	9	-	-	1	-	-	-	-	3	-	-	261	-	202	467	-	-	33	-	-	33	16
		F	48	37	37	-	-	-	-	-	-	-	-	-	-	-	-	30	-	6	36	-	-	-	-	-	-	1
		NS	6	6	6	-	-	-	-	-	-	-	-	-	-	-	-	3	-	2	5	-	-	1	-	-	1	-
		T	757	571	570	2	9	-	-	1	-	-	-	-	3	-	-	294	-	210	508	-	-	34	-	-	34	17
Robbery	34 Robbery	M	950	633	633	-	4	-	-	1	-	2	-	1	1	-	-	358	-	194	557	-	6	40	-	1	47	25
		F	112	80	80	-	-	-	-	-	-	-	-	-	-	-	-	45	-	32	77	-	-	-	-	-	-	3
		NS	11	10	10	1	-	-	-	-	-	-	-	-	-	-	-	7	-	2	9	-	-	-	-	-	-	-
		T	1,073	723	723	1	4	-	-	1	-	2	-	1	1	-	-	410	-	228	643	-	6	40	-	1	47	28
	Sub-total	M	950	633	633	-	4	-	-	1	-	2	-	1	1	-	-	358	-	194	557	-	6	40	-	1	47	25
		F	112	80	80	-	-	-	-	-	-	-	-	-	-	-	-	45	-	32	77	-	-	-	-	-	-	3
		NS	11	10	10	1	-	-	-	-	-	-	-	-	-	-	-	7	-	2	9	-	-	-	-	-	-	-
		T	1,073	723	723	1	4	-	-	1	-	2	-	1	1	-	-	410	-	228	643	-	6	40	-	1	47	28
Theft and Handling	37.2 Aggravated Vehicle Taking	M	25	20	20	-	-	-	-	-	-	-	-	-	-	-	-	10	-	7	17	-	-	3	-	-	3	-
		NS	1	1	1	-	-	-	-	-	-	-	-	-	-	-	-	-	-	-	-	-	-	1	-	-	1	-
		T	26	21	21	-	-	-	-	-	-	-	-	-	-	-	-	10	-	7	17	-	-	4	-	-	4	-
	38 Money laundering	M	6	3	3	-	-	-	-	-	-	-	-	-	-	-	-	3	-	-	3	-	-	-	-	-	-	-
		F	3	2	2	-	-	-	-	-	-	-	-	-	-	-	-	2	-	-	2	-	-	-	-	-	-	-
		T	9	5	5	-	-	-	-	-	-	-	-	-	-	-	-	5	-	-	5	-	-	-	-	-	-	-
	39 Theft from the Person of Another	M	200	161	160	1	7	-	-	-	1	-	-	6	-	-	-	88	-	51	146	-	-	-	-	-	-	6
		F	36	30	30	-	2	-	-	-	-	-	-	-	-	-	-	14	-	13	27	-	-	1	-	-	1	-
		NS	3	3	3	-	-	-	-	-	-	-	-	-	-	-	-	2	-	1	3	-	-	-	-	-	-	-
		T	239	194	193	1	9	-	-	-	1	-	-	6	-	-	-	104	-	65	176	-	-	1	-	-	1	6

21.6b Persons aged 12 to under 15 convicted and sentenced at all courts

England and Wales, 2012

Number of persons

Offence group	Description		Total Proc Against	Total found Guilty	Total For Sent	Abst Disch	Condl Disch	Fine	CRO	SO	CPO	ACO	CPO&RO	Curf Order	Rep Order	APO	DTTO	REFO	Comm Order	YRO (1)	Total Comm Sentences	SS	Sec 90-92	DTO	YOI	Unsus Sent Impr	Imm cust	ODW
	40 Theft in Dwelling not Automatic M/c or Meter	M	71	56	56	-	4	-	-	-	-	-	-	-	1	-	-	24	-	22	47	-	-	-	-	-	-	5
		F	13	12	12	2	-	-	-	-	-	-	-	-	1	-	-	6	-	3	10	-	-	-	-	-	-	-
		T	84	68	68	2	4	-	-	-	-	-	-	-	2	-	-	30	-	25	57	-	-	-	-	-	-	5
	41 Theft by an Employee	F	1	1	1	-	-	-	-	-	-	-	-	-	-	-	-	-	-	1	1	-	-	-	-	-	-	-
		T	1	1	1	-	-	-	-	-	-	-	-	-	-	-	-	-	-	1	1	-	-	-	-	-	-	-
	42 Theft or Unauthorised Taking	M	1	1	1	-	-	-	-	-	-	-	-	-	-	-	-	1	-	-	1	-	-	-	-	-	-	-
		T	1	1	1	-	-	-	-	-	-	-	-	-	-	-	-	1	-	-	1	-	-	-	-	-	-	-
	44 Theft of Pedal Cycle	M	112	91	91	3	6	1	-	-	-	-	-	-	2	-	-	42	-	36	80	-	-	-	-	-	-	1
		F	4	3	3	-	-	-	-	-	-	-	-	-	-	-	-	3	-	-	3	-	-	-	-	-	-	-
		NS	2	1	1	-	-	-	-	-	-	-	-	-	-	-	-	-	-	1	1	-	-	-	-	-	-	-
		T	118	95	95	3	6	1	-	-	-	-	-	-	2	-	-	45	-	37	84	-	-	-	-	-	-	1
	45 Theft from Vehicle	M	78	59	59	3	6	-	-	-	-	-	-	-	-	-	-	30	-	17	47	-	-	1	-	-	1	2
		F	3	2	2	1	-	-	-	-	-	-	-	-	-	-	-	1	-	-	1	-	-	-	-	-	-	-
		T	81	61	61	4	6	-	-	-	-	-	-	-	-	-	-	31	-	17	48	-	-	1	-	-	1	2
	46 Theft from Shops	M	548	478	478	31	69	6	-	-	-	1	-	-	10	-	-	194	-	144	349	-	-	10	-	-	10	13
		F	207	182	182	8	13	2	-	-	-	-	-	-	2	-	-	107	-	45	154	-	-	-	-	-	-	5
		NS	7	6	6	1	1	-	-	-	-	-	-	-	-	-	-	3	-	1	4	-	-	-	-	-	-	-
		T	762	666	666	40	83	8	-	-	-	1	-	-	12	-	-	304	-	190	507	-	-	10	-	-	10	18
	47 Theft from Automatic Machine or Meter	M	3	3	3	-	-	-	-	-	-	-	-	-	-	-	-	1	-	2	3	-	-	-	-	-	-	-
		F	1	-	-																								
		NS	1	1	1	-	1	-	-	-	-	-	-	-	-	-	-	-	-	-	-	-	-	-	-	-	-	-
		T	5	4	4	-	1	-	-	-	-	-	-	-	-	-	-	1	-	2	3	-	-	-	-	-	-	-
	48 Theft or Unauthorised Taking of Motor Vehicle	M	21	13	13	-	-	-	-	-	-	-	-	-	-	-	-	3	-	9	12	-	-	1	-	-	1	-
		T	21	13	13	-	-	-	-	-	-	-	-	-	-	-	-	3	-	9	12	-	-	1	-	-	1	-
	49 Other Theft or Unauthorised Taking	M	295	243	240	5	19	1	-	-	-	-	-	1	3	-	-	126	-	76	206	-	-	-	-	-	-	9
		F	34	25	25	1	1	-	-	-	-	-	-	-	-	-	-	15	-	8	23	-	-	-	-	-	-	-
		T	329	268	265	6	20	1	-	-	-	-	-	1	3	-	-	141	-	84	229	-	-	-	-	-	-	9
	54 Handling Stolen Goods	M	165	117	117	1	11	-	-	-	-	-	-	-	3	-	-	47	-	50	100	-	-	3	-	-	3	2
		F	12	8	8	-	1	-	-	-	-	-	-	-	-	-	-	5	-	2	7	-	-	-	-	-	-	-
		NS	1	1	1	-	-	-	-	-	-	-	-	-	-	-	-	1	-	-	1	-	-	-	-	-	-	-
		T	178	126	126	1	12	-	-	-	-	-	-	-	3	-	-	53	-	52	108	-	-	3	-	-	3	2
	Sub-total	M	1,525	1,245	1,241	44	122	8	-	-	-	2	-	1	25	-	-	569	-	414	1,011	-	-	18	-	-	18	38
		F	314	265	265	12	17	2	-	-	-	-	-	-	3	-	-	153	-	72	228	-	-	1	-	-	1	5
		NS	15	13	13	1	2	-	-	-	-	-	-	-	-	-	-	6	-	3	9	-	-	1	-	-	1	-
		T	1,854	1,523	1,519	57	141	10	-	-	-	2	-	1	28	-	-	728	-	489	1,248	-	-	20	-	-	20	43
Fraud and Forgery	53 Other Fraud	M	24	22	22	2	-	1	-	-	-	-	-	-	1	-	-	11	-	6	18	-	-	-	-	-	-	1
		F	14	12	12	-	-	-	-	-	-	-	-	-	-	-	-	10	-	2	12	-	-	-	-	-	-	-
		T	38	34	34	2	-	1	-	-	-	-	-	-	1	-	-	21	-	8	30	-	-	-	-	-	-	1
	61 Other Forgery etc.	M	5	4	4	-	1	-	-	-	-	-	-	-	-	-	-	-	-	2	2	-	-	1	-	-	1	-
		T	5	4	4	-	1	-	-	-	-	-	-	-	-	-	-	-	-	2	2	-	-	1	-	-	1	-
	Sub-total	M	29	26	26	2	1	1	-	-	-	-	-	-	1	-	-	11	-	8	20	-	-	1	-	-	1	1
		F	14	12	12	-	-	-	-	-	-	-	-	-	-	-	-	10	-	2	12	-	-	-	-	-	-	-
		T	43	38	38	2	1	1	-	-	-	-	-	-	1	-	-	21	-	10	32	-	-	1	-	-	1	1
Criminal Damage	56 Arson	M	100	78	79	-	1	-	-	-	-	-	-	-	-	-	-	58	-	17	75	-	-	1	-	-	1	2
		F	18	11	11	-	-	-	-	-	-	-	-	-	-	-	-	5	-	4	9	-	-	2	-	-	2	-
		NS	1	1	1	-	-	-	-	-	-	-	-	-	-	-	-	1	-	-	1	-	-	-	-	-	-	-
		T	119	90	91	-	1	-	-	-	-	-	-	-	-	-	-	64	-	21	85	-	-	3	-	-	3	2
	57 Criminal Damage Endangering Life	M	4	2	2	-	-	-	-	-	-	-	-	-	-	-	-	2	-	-	2	-	-	-	-	-	-	-
		F	2	1	1	-	-	-	-	-	-	-	-	-	-	-	-	1	-	-	1	-	-	-	-	-	-	-
		T	6	3	3	-	-	-	-	-	-	-	-	-	-	-	-	3	-	-	3	-	-	-	-	-	-	-
	58 Other Criminal Damage	M	154	112	112	5	10	-	-	-	-	-	-	-	-	-	-	63	-	31	94	-	-	-	-	-	-	3
		F	37	30	30	-	-	-	-	-	-	-	-	-	-	-	-	16	-	14	30	-	-	-	-	-	-	-
		NS	5	4	4	-	1	-	-	-	-	-	-	-	-	-	-	1	-	2	3	-	-	-	-	-	-	-
		T	196	146	146	5	11	-	-	-	-	-	-	-	-	-	-	80	-	47	127	-	-	-	-	-	-	3
	59 Threat etc., to commit Criminal Damage	M	15	8	8	-	2	-	-	-	-	-	-	-	2	-	-	2	-	2	6	-	-	-	-	-	-	-
		F	2	1	1	-	-	-	-	-	-	-	-	-	-	-	-	1	-	-	1	-	-	-	-	-	-	-
		T	17	9	9	-	2	-	-	-	-	-	-	-	2	-	-	3	-	2	7	-	-	-	-	-	-	-
	Sub-total	M	273	200	201	5	13	-	-	-	-	-	-	-	2	-	-	125	-	50	177	-	-	1	-	-	1	5
		F	59	43	43	-	-	-	-	-	-	-	-	-	-	-	-	23	-	18	41	-	-	2	-	-	2	-
		NS	6	5	5	-	1	-	-	-	-	-	-	-	-	-	-	2	-	2	4	-	-	-	-	-	-	-
		T	338	248	249	5	14	-	-	-	-	-	-	-	2	-	-	150	-	70	222	-	-	3	-	-	3	5
Drug Offences	Other drug offences	M	3	1	1	-	-	-	-	-	-	-	-	-	-	-	-	-	-	1	1	-	-	-	-	-	-	-
		T	3	1	1	-	-	-	-	-	-	-	-	-	-	-	-	-	-	1	1	-	-	-	-	-	-	-
	Possession of a controlled drug - Class A	M	9	8	8	-	1	-	-	-	-	-	-	-	-	-	-	2	-	3	5	-	-	1	-	-	1	1
		T	9	8	8	-	1	-	-	-	-	-	-	-	-	-	-	2	-	3	5	-	-	1	-	-	1	1
	Possession of a controlled drug - Class B	M	274	253	253	22	43	12	-	-	-	-	-	-	4	-	-	89	-	69	162	-	-	1	-	-	1	13
		F	16	15	15	1	1	1	-	-	-	-	-	-	-	-	-	8	-	4	12	-	-	-	-	-	-	-
		NS	1	1	1	1	-	-	-	-	-	-	-	-	-	-	-	-	-	-	-	-	-	-	-	-	-	-
		T	291	269	269	24	44	13	-	-	-	-	-	-	4	-	-	97	-	73	174	-	-	1	-	-	1	13
	Possession of a controlled drug - Class C	M	1	1	1	-	-	-	-	-	-	-	-	-	-	-	-	1	-	-	1	-	-	-	-	-	-	-
		T	1	1	1	-	-	-	-	-	-	-	-	-	-	-	-	1	-	-	1	-	-	-	-	-	-	-
	Production, supply and possession with intent to supply a controlled drug - Class A	M	16	10	10	2	-	-	-	-	-	-	-	-	-	-	-	4	-	3	7	-	-	-	-	-	-	1
		F	1	1	1	-	-	-	-	-	-	-	-	-	-	-	-	1	-	-	1	-	-	-	-	-	-	-
		T	17	11	11	2	-	-	-	-	-	-	-	-	-	-	-	5	-	3	8	-	-	-	-	-	-	1

21.6b Persons aged 12 to under 15 convicted and sentenced at all courts

England and Wales, 2012

Number of persons

Offence group	Description		Total Proc Against	Total found Guilty	Total For Sent	Abslt Disch	Condl Disch	Fine	CRO	SO	CPO	ACO	CPO&RO	Curf Order	Rep Order	APO	DTTO	REFO	Comm Order	YRO [1]	Total Comm Sentences	SS	Sec 90-92	DTO	YOI	Unsus Sent Impr	Imm cust	ODW
	Production, supply and possession with intent to supply a controlled drug - Class B	M	7	6	6	-	-	-	-	-	-	-	-	-	-	-	-	4	-	2	6	-	-	-	-	-	-	-
		F	1	-	-	-	-	-	-	-	-	-	-	-	-	-	-	-	-	-	-	-	-	-	-	-	-	-
		T	8	6	6	-	-	-	-	-	-	-	-	-	-	-	-	4	-	2	6	-	-	-	-	-	-	-
	Sub-total	M	310	279	279	24	44	12	-	-	-	-	-	-	4	-	-	100	-	78	182	-	-	2	-	-	2	15
		F	18	16	16	1	1	1	-	-	-	-	-	-	-	-	-	9	-	4	13	-	-	-	-	-	-	-
		NS	1	1	1	1	-	-	-	-	-	-	-	-	-	-	-	-	-	-	-	-	-	-	-	-	-	-
		T	329	296	296	26	45	13	-	-	-	-	-	-	4	-	-	109	-	82	195	-	-	2	-	-	2	15
Indictable Motoring	99 Dangerous Driving	M	7	6	6	-	-	-	-	-	-	-	-	-	-	-	-	2	-	4	6	-	-	-	-	-	-	-
		T	7	6	6	-	-	-	-	-	-	-	-	-	-	-	-	2	-	4	6	-	-	-	-	-	-	-
	Sub-total	M	7	6	6	-	-	-	-	-	-	-	-	-	-	-	-	2	-	4	6	-	-	-	-	-	-	-
		T	7	6	6	-	-	-	-	-	-	-	-	-	-	-	-	2	-	4	6	-	-	-	-	-	-	-
Indictable excluding motoring		M	4,893	3,680	3,675	99	215	28	-	6	-	4	-	2	40	-	-	1,820	-	1,199	3,071	-	11	122	-	3	136	126
		F	767	580	580	18	21	3	-	-	-	-	-	-	5	-	-	343	-	174	522	-	1	4	-	-	5	11
		NS	50	41	40	3	3	-	-	-	-	-	-	-	-	-	-	22	-	10	32	-	-	2	-	-	2	-
		T	5,710	4,301	4,295	120	239	31	-	6	-	4	-	2	45	-	-	2,185	-	1,383	3,625	-	12	128	-	3	143	137
Indictable motoring		M	7	6	6	-	-	-	-	-	-	-	-	-	-	-	-	2	-	4	6	-	-	-	-	-	-	-
		T	7	6	6	-	-	-	-	-	-	-	-	-	-	-	-	2	-	4	6	-	-	-	-	-	-	-
Indictable including motoring		M	4,900	3,686	3,681	99	215	28	-	6	-	4	-	2	40	-	-	1,822	-	1,203	3,077	-	11	122	-	3	136	126
		F	767	580	580	18	21	3	-	-	-	-	-	-	5	-	-	343	-	174	522	-	1	4	-	-	5	11
		NS	50	41	40	3	3	-	-	-	-	-	-	-	-	-	-	22	-	10	32	-	-	2	-	-	2	-
		T	5,717	4,307	4,301	120	239	31	-	6	-	4	-	2	45	-	-	2,187	-	1,387	3,631	-	12	128	-	3	143	137
Other Indictable (Not Motoring)	33 Going Equipped for Stealing, etc.	M	34	19	19	1	1	-	-	-	-	-	-	-	-	-	-	14	-	2	16	-	-	1	-	-	1	-
		T	34	19	19	1	1	-	-	-	-	-	-	-	-	-	-	14	-	2	16	-	-	1	-	-	1	-
	35 Blackmail	M	1	-	-	-	-	-	-	-	-	-	-	-	-	-	-	-	-	-	-	-	-	-	-	-	-	-
		T	1	-	-	-	-	-	-	-	-	-	-	-	-	-	-	-	-	-	-	-	-	-	-	-	-	-
	36 Kidnapping, etc.	M	3	1	1	-	-	-	-	-	-	-	-	-	-	-	-	1	-	-	1	-	-	-	-	-	-	-
		T	3	1	1	-	-	-	-	-	-	-	-	-	-	-	-	1	-	-	1	-	-	-	-	-	-	-
	65 Violent Disorder	M	6	6	7	-	-	-	-	-	-	-	-	-	-	-	-	5	-	2	7	-	-	-	-	-	-	-
		T	6	6	7	-	-	-	-	-	-	-	-	-	-	-	-	5	-	2	7	-	-	-	-	-	-	-
	66 Other Offence against the State or Public Order	M	64	35	35	-	1	-	-	-	-	-	-	-	-	-	-	23	-	9	32	-	-	2	-	-	2	-
		F	12	5	5	-	-	-	-	-	-	-	-	-	-	-	-	3	-	1	4	-	-	-	-	-	-	1
		NS	1	-	-	-	-	-	-	-	-	-	-	-	-	-	-	-	-	-	-	-	-	-	-	-	-	-
		T	77	40	40	-	1	-	-	-	-	-	-	-	-	-	-	26	-	10	36	-	-	2	-	-	2	1
	79 Perverting the Course of Justice	M	19	9	9	-	-	-	-	-	-	-	-	-	1	-	-	3	-	4	8	-	-	1	-	-	1	-
		F	6	4	4	-	-	-	-	-	-	-	-	-	-	-	-	3	-	1	4	-	-	-	-	-	-	-
		T	25	13	13	-	-	-	-	-	-	-	-	-	1	-	-	6	-	5	12	-	-	1	-	-	1	-
	80 Absconding from Lawful Custody	M	2	1	1	-	-	-	-	-	-	-	-	-	-	-	-	-	-	-	-	-	-	1	-	-	1	-
		T	2	1	1	-	-	-	-	-	-	-	-	-	-	-	-	-	-	-	-	-	-	1	-	-	1	-
	81 Firearms Act Offence	M	18	12	12	-	-	-	-	-	-	-	-	-	-	-	-	6	-	6	12	-	-	-	-	-	-	-
		F	1	1	1	-	1	-	-	-	-	-	-	-	-	-	-	-	-	-	-	-	-	-	-	-	-	-
		T	19	13	13	-	1	-	-	-	-	-	-	-	-	-	-	6	-	6	12	-	-	-	-	-	-	-
	83 Failing to Surrender to Bail	M	81	33	33	1	6	1	-	-	-	-	-	-	-	-	-	7	-	14	21	-	-	-	-	-	-	4
		F	18	3	3	2	-	-	-	-	-	-	-	-	-	-	-	-	-	1	1	-	-	-	-	-	-	-
		T	99	36	36	3	6	1	-	-	-	-	-	-	-	-	-	7	-	15	22	-	-	-	-	-	-	4
	86 Possession of Obscene Material etc.	M	1	1	1	-	-	-	-	-	-	-	-	-	-	-	-	1	-	-	1	-	-	-	-	-	-	-
		T	1	1	1	-	-	-	-	-	-	-	-	-	-	-	-	1	-	-	1	-	-	-	-	-	-	-
	91 Public Health	M	1	1	1	-	-	1	-	-	-	-	-	-	-	-	-	-	-	-	-	-	-	-	-	-	-	-
		T	1	1	1	-	-	1	-	-	-	-	-	-	-	-	-	-	-	-	-	-	-	-	-	-	-	-
	99 Other (Excluding Motoring Offences)	M	111	109	108	13	2	5	-	-	-	-	-	-	2	-	-	16	-	53	71	-	-	9	-	-	9	8
		F	2	2	2	1	-	-	-	-	-	-	-	-	-	-	-	-	-	1	1	-	-	-	-	-	-	-
		T	113	111	110	14	2	5	-	-	-	-	-	-	2	-	-	16	-	54	72	-	-	9	-	-	9	8
	Sub-total	M	341	227	227	15	10	7	-	-	-	-	-	-	3	-	-	76	-	90	169	-	-	14	-	-	14	12
		F	39	15	15	3	1	-	-	-	-	-	-	-	-	-	-	6	-	4	10	-	-	-	-	-	-	1
		NS	1	-	-	-	-	-	-	-	-	-	-	-	-	-	-	-	-	-	-	-	-	-	-	-	-	-
		T	381	242	242	18	11	7	-	-	-	-	-	-	3	-	-	82	-	94	179	-	-	14	-	-	14	13
Summary Non-Motoring	104 On Constable	M	103	67	67	3	7	-	-	-	2	-	-	-	-	-	-	30	-	24	56	-	-	1	-	-	1	-
		F	62	48	48	-	4	-	-	-	-	-	-	-	-	-	-	28	-	15	43	-	-	1	-	-	1	-
		T	165	115	115	3	11	-	-	-	2	-	-	-	-	-	-	58	-	39	99	-	-	2	-	-	2	-
	105 Common, etc	M	1,298	1,003	1,002	26	58	-	-	-	-	-	1	-	19	-	-	568	-	304	892	-	-	7	-	-	7	19
		F	510	380	380	21	22	-	-	-	-	-	1	-	4	-	-	227	-	91	323	-	-	2	-	-	2	12
		NS	16	9	9	-	-	-	-	-	-	-	-	-	-	-	-	6	-	3	9	-	-	-	-	-	-	-
		T	1,824	1,392	1,391	47	80	-	-	-	-	-	2	-	23	-	-	801	-	398	1,224	-	-	9	-	-	9	31
	108 Cruelty to Animal	M	3	3	3	-	-	-	-	-	-	-	-	-	-	-	-	3	-	-	3	-	-	-	-	-	-	-
		F	1	1	1	-	-	-	-	-	-	-	-	-	-	-	-	1	-	-	1	-	-	-	-	-	-	-
		T	4	4	4	-	-	-	-	-	-	-	-	-	-	-	-	4	-	-	4	-	-	-	-	-	-	-
	112 Education Acts	M	7	5	5	1	3	1	-	-	-	-	-	-	-	-	-	-	-	-	-	-	-	-	-	-	-	-
		T	7	5	5	1	3	1	-	-	-	-	-	-	-	-	-	-	-	-	-	-	-	-	-	-	-	-
	115 Firearms Acts	M	6	4	4	1	1	-	-	-	-	-	-	-	-	-	-	1	-	1	2	-	-	-	-	-	-	-
		T	6	4	4	1	1	-	-	-	-	-	-	-	-	-	-	1	-	1	2	-	-	-	-	-	-	-
	119 Day Poaching	M	3	2	2	2	-	-	-	-	-	-	-	-	-	-	-	-	-	-	-	-	-	-	-	-	-	-
		T	3	2	2	2	-	-	-	-	-	-	-	-	-	-	-	-	-	-	-	-	-	-	-	-	-	-
	121 Other Offence against Game Law	M	1	-	-	-	-	-	-	-	-	-	-	-	-	-	-	-	-	-	-	-	-	-	-	-	-	-
		T	1	-	-	-	-	-	-	-	-	-	-	-	-	-	-	-	-	-	-	-	-	-	-	-	-	-
	123 Nuisance Other than by Vehicle	M	5	4	4	-	-	-	-	-	-	-	-	-	-	-	-	1	-	1	2	-	-	-	-	-	-	2
		T	5	4	4	-	-	-	-	-	-	-	-	-	-	-	-	1	-	1	2	-	-	-	-	-	-	2
	125 Public Order Act 1986	M	401	263	262	15	56	8	-	-	-	-	1	-	10	-	-	116	-	49	176	-	-	3	-	-	3	4
		F	133	93	93	9	20	-	-	-	-	-	-	-	-	-	-	44	-	17	61	-	-	-	-	-	-	3
		NS	4	3	3	-	2	-	-	-	-	-	-	-	-	-	-	-	-	1	1	-	-	-	-	-	-	-
		T	538	359	358	24	78	8	-	-	-	-	1	-	10	-	-	160	-	67	238	-	-	3	-	-	3	7

21.6b Persons aged 12 to under 15 convicted and sentenced at all courts

England and Wales, 2012

Number of persons

Offence group	Description		Total Proc Against	Total found Guilty	Total For Sent	Abslt Disch	Condl Disch	Fine	CRO	SO	CPO	ACO	CPO&RO	Curf Order	Rep Order	APO	DTTO	REFO	Comm Order	YRO (1)	Total Comm Sentences	SS	Sec 90-92	DTO	YOI	Unsus Sent Impr	Imm cust	ODW
	126 Interference with Motor Vehicles	M	33	22	22	1	1	-	-	-	-	-	-	-	1	-	-	11	-	8	20	-	-	-	-	-	-	-
		F	1	-	-																							
		T	34	22	22	1	1	-	-	-	-	-	-	-	1	-	-	11	-	8	20	-	-	-	-	-	-	-
	130 Unauthorised Taking of a Conveyance	M	121	89	89	2	6	-	-	-	-	-	-	1	2	-	-	42	-	33	78	-	-	-	-	-	-	3
		F	7	4	4	-	1	-	-	-	-	-	-	-	-	-	-	3	-	-	3	-	-	-	-	-	-	-
		T	128	93	93	2	7	-	-	-	-	-	-	1	2	-	-	45	-	33	81	-	-	-	-	-	-	3
	131 Summary Aggravated Vehicle Taking	M	48	45	45	-	1	-	-	-	-	-	-	-	-	-	-	17	-	24	41	-	-	1	-	-	1	2
		F	2	2	2													2	-	-	2							
		NS	2	2	2													-	-	2	2							
		T	52	49	49	-	1	-	-	-	-	-	-	-	-	-	-	19	-	26	45	-	-	1	-	-	1	2
	137 Pedal Cycle	M	27	17	17	2	4	2	-	-	-	-	-	-	-	-	-	5	-	3	8	-	-	-	-	-	-	1
		NS	1	-																								
		T	28	17	17	2	4	2	-	-	-	-	-	-	-	-	-	5	-	3	8	-	-	-	-	-	-	1
	138 Offences involving impersonation	M	1	1	1	-	-	-	-	-	-	-	-	-	-	-	-	1	-	-	1	-	-	-	-	-	-	-
		F	1	1	1	-	-	1											-	-	-	-							
		T	2	2	2	-	-	1	-	-	-	-	-	-	-	-	-	1	-	-	1	-	-	-	-	-	-	-
	141 Drunkenness, with Aggravation	M	17	12	12	4	2	-	-	-	-	-	-	-	-	-	-	6	-	-	6	-	-	-	-	-	-	-
		F	16	11	11	3	3	-	-	-	-	-	-	-	-	-	-	4	-	1	5	-	-	-	-	-	-	-
		T	33	23	23	7	5	-	-	-	-	-	-	-	-	-	-	10	-	1	11	-	-	-	-	-	-	-
	143 Other Offence against the Liquor Law	M	1	1	1	-	1	-										-	-	-	-							
		F	1	-																								
		T	2	1	1	-	1	-	-	-	-	-	-	-	-	-	-	-	-	-	-	-	-	-	-	-	-	-
	149 Summary Criminal or Malicious Damage Offence	M	819	616	615	35	89	2	-	-	-	1	-	1	13	-	-	289	-	160	464	-	-	-	-	-	-	25
		F	149	105	105	7	18	-	-	-	-	-	-	-	-	-	-	52	-	26	78	-	-	-	-	-	-	2
		NS	1	1	1	-	-	-										-	-	1	1							
		T	969	722	721	42	107	2	-	-	-	1	-	1	13	-	-	341	-	187	543	-	-	-	-	-	-	27
	155 Military Law - Air Force	M	3	2	2	-	-	-	-	-	-	-	-	-	-	-	-	1	-	1	2	-	-	-	-	-	-	-
		T	3	2	2	-	-	-	-	-	-	-	-	-	-	-	-	1	-	1	2	-	-	-	-	-	-	-
	162 Disorderly Behaviour	M	3	3	3	-	2	-	-	-	-	-	-	-	-	-	-	-	-	1	1	-	-	-	-	-	-	-
		F	1	-																								
		T	4	3	3	-	2	-	-	-	-	-	-	-	-	-	-	-	-	1	1	-	-	-	-	-	-	-
	164 Other Offence	M	2	-																								
		F	1	-																								
		T	3	-																								
	168 Public Health Offence	M	2	-																								
		F	1	-																								
		NS	1	-																								
		T	4	-																								
	169 Railway Offence	M	48	24	24	3	9	2	-	-	-	-	-	-	-	-	-	6	-	3	9	-	-	-	-	-	-	1
		F	12	7	7	3	2	2	-	-	-	-	-	-	-	-	-	-	-	-	-	-	-	-	-	-	-	-
		NS	9	8	8	-	4	1	-	-	-	-	-	-	-	-	-	2	-	1	3	-	-	-	-	-	-	-
		T	69	39	39	6	15	5	-	-	-	-	-	-	-	-	-	8	-	4	12	-	-	-	-	-	-	1
	173 Stage Carriage or Public Service Vehicle Offence	M	1	-																								
		T	1	-																								
	180 Tram or Trolley Vehicle Offence	M	2	1	1	-	-	1	-	-	-	-	-	-	-	-	-	-	-	-	-	-	-	-	-	-	-	-
		T	2	1	1	-	-	1	-	-	-	-	-	-	-	-	-	-	-	-	-	-	-	-	-	-	-	-
	182 Begging	F	3	2	2	-	1	-	-	-	-	-	-	-	-	-	-	1	-	-	1	-	-	-	-	-	-	-
		T	3	2	2	-	1	-	-	-	-	-	-	-	-	-	-	1	-	-	1	-	-	-	-	-	-	-
	185 Found In Enclosed Premises	M	22	15	15	-	-	-	-	-	-	-	-	-	1	-	-	8	-	6	15	-	-	-	-	-	-	-
		T	22	15	15	-	-	-	-	-	-	-	-	-	1	-	-	8	-	6	15	-	-	-	-	-	-	-
	191 Wireless Telegraphy Acts	M	3	-																								
		F	2	1	1	-	-	1										-	-	-	-							
		T	5	1	1	-	-	1	-	-	-	-	-	-	-	-	-	-	-	-	-	-	-	-	-	-	-	-
	Other Summary Offence (Excluding Motoring)	M	69	48	48	-	2	11	-	-	-	-	-	-	1	-	-	13	-	9	23	-	-	-	-	-	-	12
		F	25	15	15	-	-	-	-	-	-	-	-	-	1	-	-	8	-	5	14	-	-	-	-	-	-	1
		NS	3	3	3	-	-	3	-	-	-	-	-	-	-	-	-	-	-	-	-	-	-	-	-	-	-	-
		T	97	66	66	-	2	14	-	-	-	-	-	-	2	-	-	21	-	14	37	-	-	-	-	-	-	13
	Sub-total	M	3,049	2,247	2,244	95	242	27	-	-	-	3	-	4	47	-	-	1,118	-	627	1,799	-	-	12	-	-	12	69
		F	928	670	670	43	71	4	-	-	-	-	-	1	5	-	-	370	-	155	531	-	-	3	-	-	3	18
		NS	37	26	26	-	6	4	-	-	-	-	-	-	-	-	-	8	-	8	16	-	-	-	-	-	-	-
		T	4,014	2,943	2,940	138	319	35	-	-	-	3	-	5	52	-	-	1,496	-	790	2,346	-	-	15	-	-	15	87
Summary Motoring	A Summary Motoring Offences	M	142	107	107	15	26	20	-	-	-	-	-	-	-	-	-	23	-	15	38	-	-	1	-	-	1	7
		F	7	4	4	-	1	1	-	-	-	-	-	-	-	-	-	1	-	-	1	-	-	-	-	-	-	1
		NS	4	3	3	-	1	2	-	-	-	-	-	-	-	-	-	-	-	-	-	-	-	-	-	-	-	-
		T	153	114	114	15	28	23	-	-	-	-	-	-	-	-	-	24	-	15	39	-	-	1	-	-	1	8
	Sub-total	M	142	107	107	15	26	20	-	-	-	-	-	-	-	-	-	23	-	15	38	-	-	1	-	-	1	7
		F	7	4	4	-	1	1	-	-	-	-	-	-	-	-	-	1	-	-	1	-	-	-	-	-	-	1
		NS	4	3	3	-	1	2	-	-	-	-	-	-	-	-	-	-	-	-	-	-	-	-	-	-	-	-
		T	153	114	114	15	28	23	-	-	-	-	-	-	-	-	-	24	-	15	39	-	-	1	-	-	1	8
Total Summary		M	3,191	2,354	2,351	110	268	47	-	-	-	3	-	4	47	-	-	1,141	-	642	1,837	-	-	13	-	-	13	76
		F	935	674	674	43	72	5	-	-	-	-	-	1	5	-	-	371	-	155	532	-	-	3	-	-	3	19
		NS	41	29	29	-	7	6	-	-	-	-	-	-	-	-	-	8	-	8	16	-	-	-	-	-	-	-
		T	4,167	3,057	3,054	153	347	58	-	-	-	3	-	5	52	-	-	1,520	-	805	2,385	-	-	16	-	-	16	95
All Offences		M	8,091	6,040	6,032	209	483	75	-	6	-	7	-	6	87	-	-	2,963	-	1,845	4,914	-	11	135	-	3	149	202
		F	1,702	1,254	1,254	61	93	8	-	-	-	-	-	1	10	-	-	714	-	329	1,054	-	1	7	-	-	8	30
		NS	91	70	69	3	10	6	-	-	-	-	-	-	-	-	-	30	-	18	48	-	-	2	-	-	2	-
		T	9,884	7,364	7,355	273	586	89	-	6	-	7	-	7	97	-	-	3,707	-	2,192	6,016	-	12	144	-	3	159	232

(1) The Youth Rehabilitation Order came into effect on 30 November 2009. Figures prior to 2010 are recorded as community orders.

21.6c Persons aged 15 to under 18 convicted and sentenced at all courts

England and Wales, 2012

Number of persons

Offence group	Description		Total Proc Against	Total found Guilty	Total For Sent	Absolt Disch	Condl Disch	Fine	CRO	SO	CPO	ACO	CPO&RO	Curf Order	Rep Order	APO	DTTO	REFO	Comm Order	YRO [1]	Total Comm Sentences	SS	Sec 90-92	DTO	YOI	Unsus Sent Impr	Imm cust	ODW
Violence Against Person	1 Murder	M	28	13	13	-	-	-	-	-	-	-	-	-	-	-	-	-	-	-	-	-	13	-	-	-	13	-
		F	-	1	1	-	-	-	-	-	-	-	-	-	-	-	-	-	-	-	-	-	1	-	-	-	1	-
		NS	2	-	-	-	-	-	-	-	-	-	-	-	-	-	-	-	-	-	-	-	-	-	-	-	-	-
		T	30	14	14	-	-	-	-	-	-	-	-	-	-	-	-	-	-	-	-	-	-	14	-	-	-	14	-
	2 Attempted Murder	M	12	5	5	-	-	-	-	-	-	-	-	-	-	-	-	-	-	-	-	-	2	-	3	-	5	-
		NS	1	-	-	-	-	-	-	-	-	-	-	-	-	-	-	-	-	-	-	-	-	-	-	-	-	-
		T	13	5	5	-	-	-	-	-	-	-	-	-	-	-	-	-	-	-	-	-	2	-	3	-	5	-
	3 Threat or Conspiracy to Murder	M	26	14	14	-	-	-	-	-	-	-	-	-	-	-	-	5	-	7	12	-	-	1	-	-	1	1
		F	5	2	2	-	-	-	-	-	-	-	-	-	-	-	-	1	-	1	2	-	-	-	-	-	-	-
		NS	2	2	2	-	-	-	-	-	-	-	-	-	-	-	-	1	-	-	1	-	-	1	-	-	1	-
		T	33	18	18	-	-	-	-	-	-	-	-	-	-	-	-	7	-	8	15	-	-	2	-	-	2	1
	4.1 Manslaughter	M	5	7	7	-	-	-	-	-	-	-	-	-	-	-	-	-	-	1	1	-	4	-	2	-	6	-
		NS	1	-	-	-	-	-	-	-	-	-	-	-	-	-	-	-	-	-	-	-	-	-	-	-	-	-
		T	6	7	7	-	-	-	-	-	-	-	-	-	-	-	-	-	-	1	1	-	4	-	2	-	6	-
	4.4 Causing Death by Dangerous Driving	M	3	1	1	-	-	-	-	-	-	-	-	-	-	-	-	-	-	-	-	-	1	-	-	-	1	-
		T	3	1	1	-	-	-	-	-	-	-	-	-	-	-	-	-	-	-	-	-	1	-	-	-	1	-
	4.8 Causing Death by careless or inconsiderate driving	M	1	1	1	-	-	-	-	-	-	-	-	-	-	-	-	-	-	1	1	-	-	-	-	-	-	-
		T	1	1	1	-	-	-	-	-	-	-	-	-	-	-	-	-	-	1	1	-	-	-	-	-	-	-
	4.9 Causing death by driving unlicensed, disqualified or uninsured drivers	M	1	1	1	-	-	-	-	-	-	-	-	-	-	-	-	1	-	-	1	-	-	-	-	-	-	-
		T	1	1	1	-	-	-	-	-	-	-	-	-	-	-	-	1	-	-	1	-	-	-	-	-	-	-
	5 Wounding or other act Endangering Life	M	380	106	108	-	1	1	-	-	-	-	-	-	-	-	-	7	-	11	18	-	47	29	10	-	86	2
		F	32	10	10	-	-	-	-	-	-	-	-	-	-	-	-	1	-	2	3	-	4	3	-	-	7	-
		NS	3	-	-	-	-	-	-	-	-	-	-	-	-	-	-	-	-	-	-	-	-	-	-	-	-	-
		T	415	116	118	-	1	1	-	-	-	-	-	-	-	-	-	8	-	13	21	-	51	32	10	-	93	2
	6 Endangering Railway Passenger	M	1	-	-	-	-	-	-	-	-	-	-	-	-	-	-	-	-	-	-	-	-	-	-	-	-	-
		T	1	-	-	-	-	-	-	-	-	-	-	-	-	-	-	-	-	-	-	-	-	-	-	-	-	-
	7 Endangering Life at Sea	M	2	-	-	-	-	-	-	-	-	-	-	-	-	-	-	-	-	-	-	-	-	-	-	-	-	-
		T	2	-	-	-	-	-	-	-	-	-	-	-	-	-	-	-	-	-	-	-	-	-	-	-	-	-
	8 Malicious Wounding etc.	M	3,193	2,467	2,467	17	61	6	1	2	-	2	-	2	10	-	-	1,052	-	923	1,992	-	7	291	-	-	298	93
		F	466	350	350	3	14	-	-	-	-	-	-	-	2	-	-	155	-	132	289	-	-	25	-	-	25	19
		NS	27	24	24	-	1	-	-	-	-	-	-	-	-	-	-	6	-	12	18	-	-	5	-	-	5	-
		T	3,686	2,841	2,841	20	76	6	1	2	-	2	-	2	12	-	-	1,213	-	1,067	2,299	-	7	321	-	-	328	112
	11 Cruelty to or Neglect of Children	F	2	1	1	-	-	-	-	-	-	-	-	-	-	-	-	1	-	-	1	-	-	-	-	-	-	-
		T	2	1	1	-	-	-	-	-	-	-	-	-	-	-	-	1	-	-	1	-	-	-	-	-	-	-
	13 Child Abduction	M	2	2	2	1	-	-	-	-	-	-	-	-	-	-	-	1	-	-	1	-	-	-	-	-	-	-
		T	2	2	2	1	-	-	-	-	-	-	-	-	-	-	-	1	-	-	1	-	-	-	-	-	-	-
	37.1 Causing Death by Aggravated Vehicle Taking	M	5	2	2	-	-	-	-	-	-	-	-	-	-	-	-	-	-	1	1	-	-	1	-	-	1	-
		T	5	2	2	-	-	-	-	-	-	-	-	-	-	-	-	-	-	1	1	-	-	1	-	-	1	-
	Sub-total	M	3,659	2,619	2,621	18	62	7	1	2	-	2	-	2	10	-	-	1,066	-	944	2,027	-	74	322	15	-	411	96
		F	505	364	364	3	14	-	-	-	-	-	-	-	2	-	-	158	-	135	295	-	5	28	-	-	33	19
		NS	36	26	26	-	1	-	-	-	-	-	-	-	-	-	-	7	-	12	19	-	-	6	-	-	6	-
		T	4,200	3,009	3,011	21	77	7	1	2	-	2	-	2	12	-	-	1,231	-	1,091	2,341	-	79	356	15	-	450	115
Sexual Offences	17 Sexual Assault on a Male	M	14	13	13	-	-	-	-	-	-	-	-	-	-	-	-	6	-	3	9	-	3	-	-	-	3	1
		F	2	-	-	-	-	-	-	-	-	-	-	-	-	-	-	-	-	-	-	-	-	-	-	-	-	-
		T	16	13	13	-	-	-	-	-	-	-	-	-	-	-	-	6	-	3	9	-	3	-	-	-	3	1
	19 Rape of a Female	M	153	58	58	1	-	-	1	1	-	-	-	-	-	-	-	4	-	9	15	-	10	25	3	-	38	4
		F	-	1	1	-	-	-	-	-	-	-	-	-	-	-	-	-	-	-	-	-	1	-	-	-	1	-
		NS	1	-	-	-	-	-	-	-	-	-	-	-	-	-	-	-	-	-	-	-	-	-	-	-	-	-
		T	154	59	59	1	-	-	1	1	-	-	-	-	-	-	-	4	-	9	15	-	11	25	3	-	39	4
	19 Rape of a Male	M	20	11	9	-	-	-	-	-	-	-	-	-	-	-	-	-	-	2	2	-	4	2	1	-	7	-
		T	20	11	9	-	-	-	-	-	-	-	-	-	-	-	-	-	-	2	2	-	4	2	1	-	7	-
	20 Sexual Assault on a Female	M	192	126	126	-	1	-	-	-	-	2	-	-	-	-	-	43	-	49	94	-	5	20	-	-	25	6
		F	2	1	1	-	1	-	-	-	-	-	-	-	-	-	-	-	-	-	-	-	-	-	-	-	-	-
		NS	2	1	1	-	-	-	-	-	-	-	-	-	-	-	-	1	-	-	1	-	-	-	-	-	-	-
		T	196	128	128	-	2	-	-	-	-	2	-	-	-	-	-	44	-	49	95	-	5	20	-	-	25	6
	21 Sexual Activity with child under 13	M	45	32	31	1	-	-	-	-	-	-	-	-	-	-	1	10	-	13	24	-	3	-	1	-	4	2
		T	45	32	31	1	-	-	-	-	-	-	-	-	-	-	1	10	-	13	24	-	3	-	1	-	4	2
	22 Sexual Activity with child under 16	M	40	36	36	-	1	-	-	1	-	-	-	-	-	-	-	14	-	13	28	-	4	-	1	-	5	2
		T	40	36	36	-	1	-	-	1	-	-	-	-	-	-	-	14	-	13	28	-	4	-	1	-	5	2
	23 Familial Sexual Offences (Incest)	M	1	2	2	-	-	-	-	-	-	-	-	-	-	-	-	1	-	1	2	-	-	-	-	-	-	-
		F	1	1	1	-	-	-	-	-	-	-	-	-	-	-	-	1	-	-	1	-	-	-	-	-	-	-
		T	2	3	3	-	-	-	-	-	-	-	-	-	-	-	-	2	-	1	3	-	-	-	-	-	-	-
	88 Miscellaneous sexual offences	M	37	28	28	-	1	-	-	-	-	-	-	-	-	-	-	15	-	11	26	-	-	-	-	-	-	1
		T	37	28	28	-	1	-	-	-	-	-	-	-	-	-	-	15	-	11	26	-	-	-	-	-	-	1
	Sub-total	M	502	306	303	2	3	-	-	1	-	4	-	-	-	-	1	93	-	101	200	-	29	47	6	-	82	16
		F	5	3	3	-	1	-	-	-	-	-	-	-	-	-	-	1	-	-	1	-	1	-	-	-	1	-
		NS	3	1	1	-	-	-	-	-	-	-	-	-	-	-	-	1	-	-	1	-	-	-	-	-	-	-
		T	510	310	307	2	4	-	-	1	-	4	-	-	-	-	1	95	-	101	202	-	30	47	6	-	83	16
Burglary	28 Burglary in a Dwelling	M	2,459	1,813	1,810	2	19	1	2	1	-	1	-	4	3	-	-	477	-	806	1,294	-	10	420	-	-	430	64
		F	138	86	85	-	-	-	-	1	-	-	-	-	-	-	-	39	-	35	75	-	-	9	-	-	9	1
		NS	21	18	18	-	-	-	-	-	-	-	-	-	-	-	-	4	-	5	9	-	-	9	-	-	9	-
		T	2,618	1,917	1,913	2	19	1	3	1	-	1	-	4	3	-	-	520	-	846	1,378	-	10	438	-	-	448	65
	29 Aggravated Burglary in a Dwelling	M	69	21	21	-	-	-	-	-	-	-	-	-	-	-	-	3	-	2	5	-	9	5	-	-	14	2
		F	3	2	2	-	-	-	-	-	-	-	-	-	-	-	-	-	-	1	1	-	-	1	-	-	1	-
		T	72	23	23	-	-	-	-	-	-	-	-	-	-	-	-	3	-	3	6	-	9	6	-	-	15	2
	30 Burglary in a Building Other than a Dwelling	M	1,311	975	971	5	26	1	1	-	-	2	-	2	1	-	-	334	-	473	813	-	1	101	-	-	102	24
		F	87	70	70	-	-	-	-	-	-	-	-	-	3	-	-	33	-	29	65	-	-	5	-	-	5	-
		NS	9	7	7	-	-	-	-	-	-	-	-	-	-	-	-	1	-	4	5	-	-	2	-	-	2	-
		T	1,407	1,052	1,048	5	26	1	1	-	-	2	-	2	4	-	-	368	-	506	883	-	1	108	-	-	109	24
	31 Aggravated Burglary in a Building not a Dwelling	M	7	3	3	-	-	-	-	-	-	-	-	-	-	-	-	1	-	-	1	-	2	-	-	-	2	-
		NS	1	-	-	-	-	-	-	-	-	-	-	-	-	-	-	-	-	-	-	-	-	-	-	-	-	-
		T	8	3	3	-	-	-	-	-	-	-	-	-	-	-	-	1	-	-	1	-	2	-	-	-	2	-
	Sub-total	M	3,846	2,812	2,805	7	45	2	3	1	-	3	-	6	4	-	-	815	-	1,281	2,113	-	22	526	-	-	548	90
		F	228	158	157	-	-	-	-	1	-	-	-	-	3	-	-	72	-	65	141	-	-	15	-	-	15	1
		NS	31	25	25	-	-	-	-	-	-	-	-	-	-	-	-	5	-	9	14	-	-	11	-	-	11	-
		T	4,105	2,995	2,987	7	45	2	4	1	-	3	-	6	7	-	-	892	-	1,355	2,268	-	22	552	-	-	574	91

21.6c Persons aged 15 to under 18 convicted and sentenced at all courts

England and Wales, 2012

Number of persons

Offence group	Description		Total Proc Against	Total found Guilty	Total For Sent	Abslt Disch	Condl Disch	Fine	CRO	SO	CPO	ACO	CPO&RO	Curf Order	Rep Order	APO	DTTO	REFO	Comm Order	YRO [1]	Total Comm Sentences	SS	Sec 90-92	DTO	YOI	Unsus Sent Impr	Imm cust	ODW
Robbery	34 Robbery	M	3,515	2,298	2,291	1	8	-	3	2	-	3	-	7	-	-	-	708	-	798	1,521	-	125	528	-	12	665	96
		F	334	217	218	-	1	-	-	-	-	-	-	1	-	-	-	94	-	79	174	-	1	32	-	-	33	10
		NS	38	20	20	-	-	-	-	-	-	-	-	-	-	-	-	13	-	6	19	-	-	-	-	-	-	1
		T	3,887	2,535	2,529	1	9	-	3	2	-	3	-	8	-	-	-	815	-	883	1,714	-	126	560	-	12	698	107
	Sub-total	M	3,515	2,298	2,291	1	8	-	3	2	-	3	-	7	-	-	-	708	-	798	1,521	-	125	528	-	12	665	96
		F	334	217	218	-	1	-	-	-	-	-	-	1	-	-	-	94	-	79	174	-	1	32	-	-	33	10
		NS	38	20	20	-	-	-	-	-	-	-	-	-	-	-	-	13	-	6	19	-	-	-	-	-	-	1
		T	3,887	2,535	2,529	1	9	-	3	2	-	3	-	8	-	-	-	815	-	883	1,714	-	126	560	-	12	698	107
Theft and Handling	37.2 Aggravated Vehicle Taking	M	194	173	173	-	2	-	-	-	-	-	-	1	-	-	-	67	-	69	137	-	-	28	-	-	28	6
		F	7	5	5	-	-	-	-	-	-	-	-	-	-	-	-	3	-	2	5	-	-	-	-	-	-	-
		NS	3	3	3	-	-	-	-	-	-	-	-	-	-	-	-	1	-	-	1	-	-	2	-	-	2	-
		T	204	181	181	-	2	-	-	-	-	-	-	1	-	-	-	71	-	71	143	-	-	30	-	-	30	6
	38 Money laundering	M	83	49	49	-	8	-	-	-	-	-	-	-	1	-	-	16	-	20	37	-	-	2	-	-	2	2
		F	10	7	7	-	2	-	-	-	-	-	-	-	-	-	-	3	-	2	5	-	-	-	-	-	-	-
		NS	1	1	1	-	-	-	-	-	-	-	-	-	-	-	-	-	-	1	1	-	-	-	-	-	-	-
		T	94	57	57	-	10	-	-	-	-	-	-	-	1	-	-	19	-	23	43	-	-	2	-	-	2	2
	39 Theft from the Person of Another	M	786	613	617	6	39	5	1	-	-	-	-	1	5	-	-	210	-	260	477	-	2	62	-	-	64	26
		F	172	142	142	3	5	1	-	-	-	-	-	-	2	-	-	50	-	57	109	-	-	13	-	-	13	11
		NS	16	14	14	-	-	-	-	-	-	-	-	-	-	-	-	4	-	7	11	-	-	2	-	-	2	1
		T	974	769	773	9	44	6	1	-	-	-	-	1	7	-	-	264	-	324	597	-	2	77	-	-	79	38
	40 Theft in Dwelling not Automatic M/c or Meter	M	345	272	271	2	27	2	1	-	-	-	-	1	5	-	-	87	-	111	205	-	-	24	-	-	24	11
		F	77	59	59	-	8	2	-	-	-	-	-	-	-	-	-	26	-	17	43	-	-	5	-	-	5	1
		NS	2	1	1	-	-	-	-	-	-	-	-	-	-	-	-	-	-	1	1	-	-	-	-	-	-	-
		T	424	332	331	2	35	4	1	-	-	-	-	1	5	-	-	113	-	129	249	-	-	29	-	-	29	12
	41 Theft by an Employee	M	19	16	16	-	-	-	-	-	-	-	-	-	-	-	-	11	-	5	16	-	-	-	-	-	-	-
		F	8	6	6	1	-	-	-	-	-	-	-	-	-	-	-	5	-	-	5	-	-	-	-	-	-	-
		T	27	22	22	1	-	-	-	-	-	-	-	-	-	-	-	16	-	5	21	-	-	-	-	-	-	-
	42 Theft or Unauthorised Taking from Mail	M	5	5	5	-	-	-	-	-	-	-	-	-	-	-	-	2	-	2	4	-	-	1	-	-	1	-
		F	1	-	-	-	-	-	-	-	-	-	-	-	-	-	-	-	-	-	-	-	-	-	-	-	-	-
		T	6	5	5	-	-	-	-	-	-	-	-	-	-	-	-	2	-	2	4	-	-	1	-	-	1	-
	43 Abstracting Electricity	M	5	2	2	-	-	-	-	-	-	-	-	-	-	-	-	-	-	2	2	-	-	-	-	-	-	-
		T	5	2	2	-	-	-	-	-	-	-	-	-	-	-	-	-	-	2	2	-	-	-	-	-	-	-
	44 Theft of Pedal Cycle	M	525	406	405	11	60	6	-	-	-	-	-	1	8	-	-	115	-	178	302	-	-	11	-	-	11	15
		F	13	11	11	-	2	-	-	-	-	-	-	-	-	-	-	4	-	3	7	-	-	-	-	-	-	2
		NS	13	13	13	1	-	-	-	-	-	-	-	-	-	-	-	7	-	5	12	-	-	-	-	-	-	-
		T	551	430	429	12	62	6	-	-	-	-	-	1	8	-	-	126	-	186	321	-	-	11	-	-	11	17
	45 Theft from Vehicle	M	539	414	413	3	42	3	-	1	-	2	-	1	7	-	-	143	-	172	326	-	-	25	-	-	25	14
		F	17	12	12	-	1	-	-	-	-	-	-	-	-	-	-	5	-	5	10	-	-	-	-	-	-	1
		NS	2	1	1	-	-	-	-	-	-	-	-	-	-	-	-	1	-	-	1	-	-	-	-	-	-	-
		T	558	427	426	3	43	3	-	1	-	2	-	1	7	-	-	149	-	177	337	-	-	25	-	-	25	15
	46 Theft from Shops	M	2,621	2,393	2,384	103	436	114	-	-	-	7	-	1	58	-	-	703	-	840	1,609	-	-	56	-	-	56	66
		F	1,015	895	895	30	130	22	-	-	-	-	-	-	19	-	-	361	-	298	678	-	-	12	-	-	12	23
		NS	43	38	38	-	6	-	-	-	-	-	-	-	-	-	-	9	-	17	26	-	-	4	-	-	4	2
		T	3,679	3,326	3,317	133	572	136	-	-	-	7	-	1	77	-	-	1,073	-	1,155	2,313	-	-	72	-	-	72	91
	47 Theft from Automatic Machine or Meter	M	12	9	9	-	-	-	-	-	-	-	-	-	-	-	-	4	-	5	9	-	-	-	-	-	-	-
		F	1	-	-	-	-	-	-	-	-	-	-	-	-	-	-	-	-	-	-	-	-	-	-	-	-	-
		T	13	9	9	-	-	-	-	-	-	-	-	-	-	-	-	4	-	5	9	-	-	-	-	-	-	-
	48 Theft or Unauthorised Taking of Motor Vehicle	M	133	78	78	-	8	3	-	-	-	-	-	-	1	-	-	23	-	26	50	-	-	12	-	-	12	5
		F	2	1	1	-	-	-	-	-	-	-	-	-	-	-	-	1	-	-	1	-	-	-	-	-	-	-
		T	135	79	79	-	8	3	-	-	-	-	-	-	1	-	-	24	-	26	51	-	-	12	-	-	12	5
	49 Other Theft or Unauthorised Taking	M	1,234	988	987	25	131	15	-	1	-	1	-	-	22	-	-	330	-	394	748	-	-	34	-	-	34	34
		F	152	123	123	3	17	-	-	-	-	1	-	-	3	-	-	49	-	43	96	-	-	2	-	-	2	5
		NS	15	14	14	-	3	-	-	-	-	-	-	-	-	-	-	3	-	8	11	-	-	-	-	-	-	-
		T	1,401	1,125	1,124	28	151	15	-	1	-	2	-	-	25	-	-	382	-	445	855	-	-	36	-	-	36	39
	54 Handling Stolen Goods	M	1,027	784	783	15	63	17	-	-	-	3	-	1	7	-	-	235	-	381	627	-	-	35	-	-	35	26
		F	102	83	83	3	11	2	-	-	-	-	-	-	2	-	-	25	-	33	60	-	-	4	-	-	4	3
		NS	6	5	5	-	1	-	-	-	-	-	-	-	-	-	-	2	-	1	3	-	-	-	-	-	-	1
		T	1,135	872	871	18	75	19	-	-	-	3	-	1	9	-	-	262	-	415	690	-	-	39	-	-	39	30
	Sub-total	M	7,528	6,202	6,192	165	816	165	2	2	-	13	-	7	114	-	-	1,946	-	2,465	4,549	-	2	290	-	-	292	205
		F	1,577	1,344	1,344	40	176	27	-	-	-	1	-	-	26	-	-	532	-	460	1,019	-	-	36	-	-	36	46
		NS	101	90	90	1	10	-	-	-	-	-	-	-	-	-	-	27	-	40	67	-	-	8	-	-	8	4
		T	9,206	7,636	7,626	206	1,002	192	2	2	-	14	-	7	140	-	-	2,505	-	2,965	5,635	-	2	334	-	-	336	255
Fraud and Forgery	53 Other Fraud	M	268	203	204	9	25	10	-	-	-	-	-	-	4	-	-	68	-	74	146	-	-	8	-	-	8	6
		F	121	99	98	5	12	2	-	-	-	-	-	-	1	-	-	40	-	35	76	-	-	2	-	-	2	1
		NS	3	3	3	-	1	-	-	-	-	-	-	-	-	-	-	-	-	2	2	-	-	-	-	-	-	-
		T	392	305	305	14	38	12	-	-	-	-	-	-	5	-	-	108	-	111	224	-	-	10	-	-	10	7
	61 Other Forgery etc.	M	38	33	33	1	3	2	-	-	-	-	-	-	1	-	-	10	-	11	22	-	-	5	-	-	5	-
		F	4	1	1	-	-	-	-	-	-	-	-	-	-	-	-	-	-	1	1	-	-	-	-	-	-	-
		NS	3	1	1	-	-	-	-	-	-	-	-	-	-	-	-	1	-	-	1	-	-	-	-	-	-	-
		T	45	35	35	1	3	2	-	-	-	-	-	-	1	-	-	11	-	12	24	-	-	5	-	-	5	-
	814 Fraud, Forgery etc associated with Vehicle or Driver Records	M	5	2	2	-	1	-	-	-	-	-	-	-	-	-	-	1	-	-	1	-	-	-	-	-	-	-
		T	5	2	2	-	1	-	-	-	-	-	-	-	-	-	-	1	-	-	1	-	-	-	-	-	-	-
	Sub-total	M	311	238	239	10	29	12	-	-	-	-	-	-	5	-	-	79	-	85	169	-	-	13	-	-	13	6
		F	125	100	99	5	12	2	-	-	-	-	-	-	1	-	-	40	-	36	77	-	-	2	-	-	2	1
		NS	6	4	4	-	1	-	-	-	-	-	-	-	-	-	-	1	-	2	3	-	-	-	-	-	-	-
		T	442	342	342	15	42	14	-	-	-	-	-	-	6	-	-	120	-	123	249	-	-	15	-	-	15	7
Criminal Damage	56 Arson	M	216	163	164	2	3	-	1	1	-	-	-	2	3	-	-	72	-	56	135	-	4	14	-	-	18	6
		F	60	36	36	1	2	-	-	-	-	-	-	-	-	-	-	19	-	9	28	-	-	3	-	-	3	2
		NS	2	1	1	-	-	-	-	-	-	-	-	-	-	-	-	1	-	-	1	-	-	-	-	-	-	-
		T	278	200	201	3	5	-	1	1	-	-	-	2	3	-	-	92	-	65	164	-	4	17	-	-	21	8
	57 Criminal Damage Endangering Life	M	13	6	6	-	-	-	-	-	-	-	-	-	-	-	-	2	-	3	5	-	-	1	-	-	1	-
		F	4	3	3	-	-	-	-	-	-	-	-	-	-	-	-	3	-	-	3	-	-	-	-	-	-	-
		T	17	9	9	-	-	-	-	-	-	-	-	-	-	-	-	5	-	3	8	-	-	1	-	-	1	-
	58 Other Criminal Damage	M	590	436	436	15	64	5	-	-	-	-	-	-	7	-	-	150	-	161	318	-	-	6	-	-	6	28
		F	109	83	83	9	6	-	-	-	-	-	-	-	3	-	-	37	-	23	63	-	-	1	-	-	1	4
		NS	3	3	3	-	-	-	-	-	-	-	-	-	-	-	-	2	-	-	2	-	-	-	-	-	-	1
		T	702	522	522	24	70	5	-	-	-	-	-	-	10	-	-	189	-	184	383	-	-	7	-	-	7	33
	59 Threat etc., to commit Criminal Damage	M	72	41	41	-	7	2	-	-	-	-	-	-	1	-	-	13	-	15	29	-	-	1	-	-	1	2
		F	17	14	14	1	2	-	-	-	-	-	-	-	1	-	-	3	-	4	8	-	-	-	-	-	-	3
		T	89	55	55	1	9	2	-	-	-	-	-	-	2	-	-	16	-	19	37	-	-	1	-	-	1	5

21.6c Persons aged 15 to under 18 convicted and sentenced at all courts

England and Wales, 2012

Number of persons

Offence group	Description		Total Proc Against	Total found Guilty	Total For Sent	Abslt Disch	Condl Disch	Fine	CRO	SO	CPO	ACO	CPO&RO	Curf Order	Rep Order	APO	DTTO	REFO	Comm Order	YRO [1]	Total Comm Sentences	SS	Sec 90-92	DTO	YOI	Unsus Sent Impr	Imm cust	ODW
	Sub-total	M	891	646	647	17	74	7	1	1	-	-	-	2	11	-	-	237	-	235	487	-	4	22	-	-	26	36
		F	190	136	136	11	10	-	-	-	-	-	-	-	4	-	-	62	-	36	102	-	-	4	-	-	4	9
		NS	5	4	4	-	-	-	-	-	-	-	-	-	-	-	-	3	-	-	3	-	-	-	-	-	-	1
		T	1,086	786	787	28	84	7	1	1	-	-	-	2	15	-	-	302	-	271	592	-	4	26	-	-	30	46
Drug Offences	92.3 Unlawful importation - Class A	F	1	-	-	-	-	-	-	-	-	-	-	-	-	-	-	-	-	-	-	-	-	-	-	-	-	-
		T	1	-	-	-	-	-	-	-	-	-	-	-	-	-	-	-	-	-	-	-	-	-	-	-	-	-
	Other drug offences	M	21	10	10	-	3	-	-	-	-	-	-	-	-	-	-	1	-	6	7	-	-	-	-	-	-	-
		T	21	10	10	-	3	-	-	-	-	-	-	-	-	-	-	1	-	6	7	-	-	-	-	-	-	-
	Possession of a controlled drug - Class A	M	252	221	221	4	20	16	-	-	-	-	-	1	-	-	-	81	-	93	175	-	-	2	-	-	2	4
		F	19	14	14	1	2	2	-	-	-	-	-	-	-	-	-	2	-	7	9	-	-	-	-	-	-	-
		NS	6	6	6	-	-	1	-	-	-	-	-	-	-	-	-	3	-	2	5	-	-	-	-	-	-	-
		T	277	241	241	5	22	19	-	-	-	-	-	1	-	-	-	86	-	102	189	-	-	2	-	-	2	4
	Possession of a controlled drug - Class B	M	3,423	3,128	3,125	197	771	530	-	-	-	6	-	-	28	-	-	888	-	611	1,533	-	-	14	-	-	14	80
		F	152	130	129	10	43	9	-	-	-	-	-	-	-	-	-	47	-	20	67	-	-	-	-	-	-	-
		NS	25	21	21	1	3	3	-	-	-	-	-	-	-	-	-	7	-	7	14	-	-	-	-	-	-	-
		T	3,600	3,279	3,275	208	817	542	-	-	-	6	-	-	28	-	-	942	-	638	1,614	-	-	14	-	-	14	80
	Possession of a controlled drug - Class C	M	30	27	27	2	4	5	-	-	-	-	-	-	2	-	-	4	-	8	14	-	-	1	-	-	1	1
		F	1	1	1	-	-	-	-	-	-	-	-	-	-	-	-	-	-	1	1	-	-	-	-	-	-	-
		NS	1	-	-	-	-	-	-	-	-	-	-	-	-	-	-	-	-	-	-	-	-	-	-	-	-	-
		T	32	28	28	2	4	5	-	-	-	-	-	-	2	-	-	4	-	9	15	-	-	1	-	-	1	1
	Production, supply and possession with intent to supply a controlled drug - Class A	M	317	206	205	-	-	-	1	-	-	-	-	3	-	-	-	47	-	58	109	-	5	71	-	-	76	20
		F	14	7	7	-	-	-	-	-	-	-	-	-	-	-	-	2	-	2	4	-	-	3	-	-	3	-
		NS	1	-	-	-	-	-	-	-	-	-	-	-	-	-	-	-	-	-	-	-	-	-	-	-	-	-
		T	332	213	212	-	-	-	1	-	-	-	-	3	-	-	-	49	-	60	113	-	5	74	-	-	79	20
	Production, supply and possession with intent to supply a controlled drug - Class B	M	365	296	297	1	10	3	-	-	-	-	-	1	2	-	-	139	-	101	243	-	3	24	-	-	27	13
		F	22	8	8	-	-	-	-	-	-	-	-	-	-	-	-	7	-	1	8	-	-	-	-	-	-	-
		NS	8	6	6	-	-	-	-	-	-	-	-	-	-	-	-	2	-	3	5	-	-	1	-	-	1	-
		T	395	310	311	1	10	3	-	-	-	-	-	1	2	-	-	148	-	105	256	-	3	25	-	-	28	13
	Production, supply and possession with intent to supply a controlled drug - Class C	M	12	8	8	-	-	-	-	-	-	-	-	-	-	-	-	3	-	4	7	-	-	-	-	-	-	1
		F	2	2	2	-	-	-	-	-	-	-	-	-	-	-	-	1	-	1	2	-	-	-	-	-	-	-
		T	14	10	10	-	-	-	-	-	-	-	-	-	-	-	-	4	-	5	9	-	-	-	-	-	-	1
	Production, supply and possession with intent to supply a controlled drug - Class unspecified	M	-	4	4	-	-	-	1	-	-	-	-	-	-	-	-	-	-	-	1	-	-	3	-	-	3	-
		T	-	4	4	-	-	-	1	-	-	-	-	-	-	-	-	-	-	-	1	-	-	3	-	-	3	-
	Sub-total	M	4,420	3,900	3,897	204	808	554	2	-	-	6	-	5	32	-	-	1,163	-	881	2,089	-	8	115	-	-	123	119
		F	211	162	161	11	45	11	-	-	-	-	-	-	-	-	-	59	-	32	91	-	-	3	-	-	3	-
		NS	41	33	33	1	3	4	-	-	-	-	-	-	-	-	-	12	-	12	24	-	-	1	-	-	1	-
		T	4,672	4,095	4,091	216	856	569	2	-	-	6	-	5	32	-	-	1,234	-	925	2,204	-	8	119	-	-	127	119
Indictable Motoring	99 Dangerous Driving	M	113	90	89	-	-	1	-	-	-	-	-	1	-	-	-	37	-	28	66	-	-	20	-	-	20	2
		F	3	3	3	-	-	-	-	-	-	-	-	-	-	-	-	3	-	-	3	-	-	-	-	-	-	-
		NS	1	1	1	-	-	-	-	-	-	-	-	-	-	-	-	1	-	-	1	-	-	-	-	-	-	-
		T	117	94	93	-	-	1	-	-	-	-	-	1	-	-	-	41	-	28	70	-	-	20	-	-	20	2
	Sub-total	M	113	90	89	-	-	1	-	-	-	-	-	1	-	-	-	37	-	28	66	-	-	20	-	-	20	2
		F	3	3	3	-	-	-	-	-	-	-	-	-	-	-	-	3	-	-	3	-	-	-	-	-	-	-
		NS	1	1	1	-	-	-	-	-	-	-	-	-	-	-	-	1	-	-	1	-	-	-	-	-	-	-
		T	117	94	93	-	-	1	-	-	-	-	-	1	-	-	-	41	-	28	70	-	-	20	-	-	20	2
Other Indictable (Not Motoring)	33 Going Equipped for Stealing, etc.	M	208	135	135	3	13	1	-	-	-	-	-	-	-	-	-	52	-	56	108	-	-	8	-	-	8	2
		F	1	1	1	-	-	-	-	-	-	-	-	-	-	-	-	1	-	-	1	-	-	-	-	-	-	-
		NS	2	-	-	-	-	-	-	-	-	-	-	-	-	-	-	-	-	-	-	-	-	-	-	-	-	-
		T	211	136	136	3	13	1	-	-	-	-	-	-	-	-	-	53	-	56	109	-	-	8	-	-	8	2
	35 Blackmail	M	26	14	14	-	-	-	-	-	-	-	-	-	-	-	-	3	-	10	13	-	-	1	-	-	1	-
		F	1	-	-	-	-	-	-	-	-	-	-	-	-	-	-	-	-	-	-	-	-	-	-	-	-	-
		T	27	14	14	-	-	-	-	-	-	-	-	-	-	-	-	3	-	10	13	-	-	1	-	-	1	-
	36 Kidnapping, etc.	M	33	10	10	-	-	-	-	-	-	-	-	-	-	-	-	1	-	5	6	-	2	2	-	-	4	-
		F	7	4	4	-	-	-	-	-	-	-	-	-	-	-	-	-	-	2	2	-	2	-	-	-	2	-
		NS	1	-	-	-	-	-	-	-	-	-	-	-	-	-	-	-	-	-	-	-	-	-	-	-	-	-
		T	41	14	14	-	-	-	-	-	-	-	-	-	-	-	-	1	-	7	8	-	4	2	-	-	6	-
	64 Rioting	M	-	2	2	-	-	-	-	-	-	-	-	-	-	-	-	-	-	-	-	-	-	2	-	-	2	-
		T	-	2	2	-	-	-	-	-	-	-	-	-	-	-	-	-	-	-	-	-	-	2	-	-	2	-
	65 Violent Disorder	M	150	114	114	-	-	1	1	-	-	-	-	-	-	-	-	29	-	38	68	-	1	41	-	-	42	3
		F	4	1	1	-	-	-	-	-	-	-	-	-	-	-	-	-	-	-	-	-	-	1	-	-	1	-
		NS	2	2	2	-	-	-	-	-	-	-	-	-	-	-	-	1	-	1	2	-	-	-	-	-	-	-
		T	156	117	117	-	-	1	1	-	-	-	-	-	-	-	-	30	-	39	70	-	1	42	-	-	43	3
	66 Other Offence against the State or Public Order	M	529	368	370	5	12	3	1	1	-	1	-	2	-	-	-	134	-	128	267	-	1	64	-	-	65	18
		F	49	41	41	-	2	-	-	-	-	-	-	-	-	-	-	14	-	20	34	-	-	1	-	-	1	4
		NS	8	5	5	-	-	-	-	-	-	-	-	-	-	-	-	-	-	4	4	-	-	1	-	-	1	-
		T	586	414	416	5	14	3	1	1	-	1	-	2	-	-	-	148	-	152	305	-	1	66	-	-	67	22
	79 Perverting the Course of Justice	M	163	84	83	1	1	-	-	-	-	-	-	-	-	-	-	22	-	35	57	-	-	23	-	-	23	1
		F	32	17	17	-	-	-	-	-	-	-	-	-	-	-	-	13	-	2	15	-	-	2	-	-	2	-
		T	195	101	100	1	1	-	-	-	-	-	-	-	-	-	-	35	-	37	72	-	-	25	-	-	25	1
	80 Absconding from Lawful Custody	M	31	24	24	1	3	-	-	-	-	-	-	1	-	-	-	2	-	11	14	-	-	5	-	-	5	1
		NS	1	1	1	-	-	-	-	-	-	-	-	-	-	-	-	-	-	-	-	-	-	1	-	-	1	-
		T	32	25	25	1	3	-	-	-	-	-	-	1	-	-	-	2	-	11	14	-	-	6	-	-	6	1
	81 Firearms Act Offence	M	102	72	72	2	2	-	-	-	-	-	-	-	-	-	-	30	-	24	54	-	1	8	-	-	9	5
		F	8	5	5	1	1	-	-	-	-	-	-	-	-	-	-	2	-	1	3	-	-	-	-	-	-	-
		NS	2	2	2	-	-	-	-	-	-	-	-	-	-	-	-	-	-	1	1	-	-	1	-	-	1	-
		T	112	79	79	3	3	-	-	-	-	-	-	-	-	-	-	32	-	26	58	-	1	9	-	-	10	5
	83 Failing to Surrender to Bail	M	883	398	394	42	62	65	-	-	-	-	-	-	4	-	-	45	-	106	155	-	-	5	-	-	5	65
		F	161	71	71	6	10	6	-	-	-	-	-	-	1	-	-	17	-	24	42	-	-	-	-	-	-	7
		NS	7	4	4	-	2	-	-	-	-	-	-	-	-	-	-	-	-	2	2	-	-	-	-	-	-	-
		T	1,051	473	469	48	74	71	-	-	-	-	-	-	5	-	-	62	-	132	199	-	-	5	-	-	5	72
	84 Trade Descriptions Act and Similar Offences	M	8	8	8	-	1	1	-	-	-	-	-	-	-	-	-	2	-	4	6	-	-	-	-	-	-	-
		NS	1	-	-	-	-	-	-	-	-	-	-	-	-	-	-	-	-	-	-	-	-	-	-	-	-	-
		T	9	8	8	-	1	1	-	-	-	-	-	-	-	-	-	2	-	4	6	-	-	-	-	-	-	-
	85 Health and Safety at Work etc. Act 1974	M	1	1	1	-	-	1	-	-	-	-	-	-	-	-	-	-	-	-	-	-	-	-	-	-	-	-
		T	1	1	1	-	-	1	-	-	-	-	-	-	-	-	-	-	-	-	-	-	-	-	-	-	-	-
	86 Possession of Obscene Material etc.	M	31	25	26	-	-	-	-	-	-	-	-	-	-	-	-	18	-	5	23	-	-	1	-	-	1	2
		F	2	-	-	-	-	-	-	-	-	-	-	-	-	-	-	-	-	-	-	-	-	-	-	-	-	-
		T	33	25	26	-	-	-	-	-	-	-	-	-	-	-	-	18	-	5	23	-	-	1	-	-	1	2

21.6c Persons aged 15 to under 18 convicted and sentenced at all courts

England and Wales, 2012

Number of persons

Offence group	Description		Total Proc Against	Total found Guilty	Total For Sent	Abslt Disch	Condl Disch	Fine	CRO	SO	CPO	ACO	CPO&RO	Curf Order	Rep Order	APO	DTTO	REFO	Comm Order	YRO [1]	Total Comm Sentences	SS	Sec 90-92	DTO	YOI	Unsus Sent Impr	Imm cust	ODW
	91 Public Health	M	8	4	3	-	1	2	-	-	-	-	-	-	-	-	-	-	-	-	-	-	-	-	-	-	-	-
		F	4	-	-	-	-	-	-	-	-	-	-	-	-	-	-	-	-	-	-	-	-	-	-	-	-	-
		T	12	4	3	-	1	2	-	-	-	-	-	-	-	-	-	-	-	-	-	-	-	-	-	-	-	-
	94 Town and Country Planning Act 1990	M	4	-	-	-	-	-	-	-	-	-	-	-	-	-	-	-	-	-	-	-	-	-	-	-	-	-
		F	2	1	1	-	-	1	-	-	-	-	-	-	-	-	-	-	-	-	-	-	-	-	-	-	-	-
		T	6	1	1	-	-	1	-	-	-	-	-	-	-	-	-	-	-	-	-	-	-	-	-	-	-	-
	95 Disclosure, obstruction, false or misleading statements	M	1	1	1	-	-	1	-	-	-	-	-	-	-	-	-	-	-	-	-	-	-	-	-	-	-	-
		T	1	1	1	-	-	1	-	-	-	-	-	-	-	-	-	-	-	-	-	-	-	-	-	-	-	-
	99 Other (Excluding Motoring Offences)	M	433	417	416	36	14	60	-	-	-	1	-	-	12	-	-	25	-	187	225	-	1	54	-	-	55	26
		F	59	58	58	10	4	4	-	-	-	-	-	-	2	-	-	3	-	28	33	-	-	4	-	-	4	3
		NS	1	1	1	-	1	-	-	-	-	-	-	-	-	-	-	-	-	-	-	-	-	-	-	-	-	-
		T	493	476	475	46	19	64	-	-	-	1	-	-	14	-	-	28	-	215	258	-	1	58	-	-	59	29
	Sub-total	M	2,611	1,677	1,673	90	109	135	2	1	-	2	-	3	16	-	-	363	-	609	996	-	6	214	-	-	220	123
		F	330	199	199	17	17	11	-	-	-	-	-	-	3	-	-	50	-	77	130	-	2	8	-	-	10	14
		NS	25	15	15	-	3	-	-	-	-	-	-	-	-	-	-	1	-	8	9	-	-	3	-	-	3	-
		T	2,966	1,891	1,887	107	129	146	2	1	-	2	-	3	19	-	-	414	-	694	1,135	-	8	225	-	-	233	137
Indictable excluding motoring		M	27,283	20,698	20,668	514	1,954	882	15	13	-	29	-	32	192	-	1	6,470	-	7,399	14,151	-	270	2,077	-	33	2,380	787
		F	3,505	2,683	2,681	87	276	51	1	-	-	1	-	1	39	-	-	1,068	-	920	2,030	-	9	128	-	-	137	100
		NS	286	218	218	2	18	4	-	-	-	-	-	-	-	-	-	70	-	89	159	-	-	29	-	-	29	6
		T	31,074	23,599	23,567	603	2,248	937	16	13	-	30	-	33	231	-	1	7,608	-	8,408	16,340	-	279	2,234	-	33	2,546	893
Indictable motoring		M	113	90	89	-	-	1	-	-	-	-	-	1	-	-	-	37	-	28	66	-	-	20	-	-	20	2
		F	3	3	3	-	-	-	-	-	-	-	-	-	-	-	-	3	-	-	3	-	-	-	-	-	-	-
		NS	1	1	1	-	-	-	-	-	-	-	-	-	-	-	-	1	-	-	1	-	-	-	-	-	-	-
		T	117	94	93	-	-	1	-	-	-	-	-	1	-	-	-	41	-	28	70	-	-	20	-	-	20	2
Indictable including motoring		M	27,396	20,788	20,757	514	1,954	883	15	13	-	29	-	33	192	-	1	6,507	-	7,427	14,217	-	270	2,097	-	33	2,400	789
		F	3,508	2,686	2,684	87	276	51	1	-	-	1	-	1	39	-	-	1,071	-	920	2,033	-	9	128	-	-	137	100
		NS	287	219	219	2	18	4	-	-	-	-	-	-	-	-	-	71	-	89	160	-	-	29	-	-	29	6
		T	31,191	23,693	23,660	603	2,248	938	16	13	-	30	-	34	231	-	1	7,649	-	8,436	16,410	-	279	2,254	-	33	2,566	895
Summary Non-Motoring	104 On Constable	M	904	670	668	16	105	27	-	-	-	1	-	1	8	-	-	240	-	230	480	-	-	25	-	-	25	15
		F	342	265	265	3	24	2	-	-	-	1	-	-	3	-	-	118	-	94	216	-	-	9	-	-	9	11
		NS	8	8	8	-	3	-	-	-	-	-	-	-	-	-	-	4	-	1	5	-	-	-	-	-	-	-
		T	1,254	943	941	19	132	29	-	-	-	2	-	1	11	-	-	362	-	325	701	-	-	34	-	-	34	26
	105 Common, etc	M	4,385	3,259	3,258	51	247	31	1	1	-	2	-	6	39	-	-	1,217	-	1,348	2,614	-	-	169	-	-	169	146
		F	1,489	1,109	1,109	21	101	3	-	-	-	-	-	2	13	-	-	479	-	439	933	-	-	21	-	-	21	30
		NS	56	44	44	1	5	-	-	-	-	-	-	-	1	-	-	13	-	17	31	-	-	7	-	-	7	-
		T	5,930	4,412	4,411	73	353	34	1	1	-	2	-	8	53	-	-	1,709	-	1,804	3,578	-	-	197	-	-	197	176
	106 Betting or Gaming Offence	F	1	1	1	-	-	-	-	-	-	-	-	-	-	-	-	1	-	-	1	-	-	-	-	-	-	-
		T	1	1	1	-	-	-	-	-	-	-	-	-	-	-	-	1	-	-	1	-	-	-	-	-	-	-
	108 Cruelty to Animal	M	34	19	19	1	2	1	-	-	-	-	-	-	-	-	-	4	-	9	13	-	-	2	-	-	2	-
		F	7	5	5	-	1	-	-	-	-	-	-	-	-	-	-	3	-	-	3	-	-	1	-	-	1	-
		NS	2	1	1	1	-	-	-	-	-	-	-	-	-	-	-	-	-	-	-	-	-	-	-	-	-	-
		T	43	25	25	2	3	1	-	-	-	-	-	-	-	-	-	7	-	9	16	-	-	3	-	-	3	-
	111 Offences Relating to Dogs	M	16	13	13	3	5	4	-	-	-	-	-	-	-	-	-	1	-	-	1	-	-	-	-	-	-	-
		F	4	4	4	1	1	1	-	-	-	-	-	-	-	-	-	1	-	-	1	-	-	-	-	-	-	-
		NS	1	1	1	-	-	1	-	-	-	-	-	-	-	-	-	-	-	-	-	-	-	-	-	-	-	-
		T	21	18	18	4	6	6	-	-	-	-	-	-	-	-	-	2	-	-	2	-	-	-	-	-	-	-
	112 Education Acts	M	37	27	27	1	14	7	-	-	-	-	-	-	-	-	-	4	-	1	5	-	-	-	-	-	-	-
		F	41	35	35	-	8	24	-	-	-	-	-	-	-	-	-	1	-	1	2	-	-	-	-	-	-	1
		T	78	62	62	1	22	31	-	-	-	-	-	-	-	-	-	5	-	2	7	-	-	-	-	-	-	1
	113 Explosives Acts	M	1	1	1	-	1	-	-	-	-	-	-	-	-	-	-	-	-	-	-	-	-	-	-	-	-	-
		T	1	1	1	-	1	-	-	-	-	-	-	-	-	-	-	-	-	-	-	-	-	-	-	-	-	-
	115 Firearms Acts	M	38	34	34	1	3	1	-	-	-	-	-	1	-	-	-	15	-	11	27	-	-	1	-	-	1	1
		T	38	34	34	1	3	1	-	-	-	-	-	1	-	-	-	15	-	11	27	-	-	1	-	-	1	1
	116 Fishery Acts	M	1	1	1	-	-	1	-	-	-	-	-	-	-	-	-	-	-	-	-	-	-	-	-	-	-	-
		T	1	1	1	-	-	1	-	-	-	-	-	-	-	-	-	-	-	-	-	-	-	-	-	-	-	-
	118 Night Poaching	M	2	1	1	1	-	-	-	-	-	-	-	-	-	-	-	-	-	-	-	-	-	-	-	-	-	-
		T	2	1	1	1	-	-	-	-	-	-	-	-	-	-	-	-	-	-	-	-	-	-	-	-	-	-
	119 Day Poaching	M	12	9	9	2	1	4	-	-	-	-	-	-	-	-	-	1	-	-	1	-	-	-	-	-	-	1
		T	12	9	9	2	1	4	-	-	-	-	-	-	-	-	-	1	-	-	1	-	-	-	-	-	-	1
	121 Other Offence against Game Law	M	7	2	2	-	-	1	-	-	-	-	-	-	-	-	-	1	-	-	1	-	-	-	-	-	-	-
		T	7	2	2	-	-	1	-	-	-	-	-	-	-	-	-	1	-	-	1	-	-	-	-	-	-	-
	122 Obstruction Other than by Vehicle	M	1	-	-	-	-	-	-	-	-	-	-	-	-	-	-	-	-	-	-	-	-	-	-	-	-	-
		F	2	1	1	-	-	1	-	-	-	-	-	-	-	-	-	-	-	-	-	-	-	-	-	-	-	-
		T	3	1	1	-	-	1	-	-	-	-	-	-	-	-	-	-	-	-	-	-	-	-	-	-	-	-
	123 Nuisance Other than by Vehicle	M	12	9	9	-	1	3	-	-	-	-	-	-	-	-	-	3	-	1	4	-	-	-	-	-	-	1
		F	1	1	1	-	-	-	-	-	-	-	-	-	-	-	-	1	-	-	1	-	-	-	-	-	-	-
		T	13	10	10	-	1	3	-	-	-	-	-	-	-	-	-	4	-	1	5	-	-	-	-	-	-	1
	125 Public Order Act 1986	M	2,258	1,573	1,572	70	412	155	-	-	-	-	-	-	38	-	-	486	-	346	870	-	-	24	-	-	24	41
		F	438	313	313	14	93	17	-	-	-	-	-	-	4	-	-	115	-	57	176	-	-	2	-	-	2	11
		NS	22	19	19	1	3	-	-	-	-	-	-	-	-	-	-	9	-	5	14	-	-	-	-	-	-	1
		T	2,718	1,905	1,904	85	508	172	-	-	-	-	-	-	42	-	-	610	-	408	1,060	-	-	26	-	-	26	53
	126 Interference with Motor Vehicles	M	201	135	133	-	23	5	-	-	-	-	-	1	2	-	-	44	-	50	97	-	-	1	-	-	1	7
		F	1	-	-	-	-	-	-	-	-	-	-	-	-	-	-	-	-	-	-	-	-	-	-	-	-	-
		NS	1	1	1	-	-	-	-	-	-	-	-	-	-	-	-	-	-	1	1	-	-	-	-	-	-	-
		T	203	136	134	-	23	5	-	-	-	-	-	1	2	-	-	44	-	51	98	-	-	1	-	-	1	7
	130 Unauthorised Taking of a Conveyance	M	633	458	454	8	31	8	-	1	-	1	-	-	7	-	-	149	-	214	372	-	-	24	-	-	24	11
		F	28	22	22	1	3	-	-	-	-	-	-	-	-	-	-	9	-	8	17	-	-	-	-	-	-	1
		NS	5	4	4	-	-	-	-	-	-	-	-	-	-	-	-	1	-	3	4	-	-	-	-	-	-	-
		T	666	484	480	9	34	8	-	1	-	1	-	-	7	-	-	159	-	225	393	-	-	24	-	-	24	12
	131 Summary Aggravated Vehicle Taking	M	376	329	330	1	3	1	-	-	-	-	-	2	1	-	-	160	-	122	285	-	-	28	-	-	28	12
		F	37	29	29	-	1	-	-	-	-	-	-	-	-	-	-	21	-	6	27	-	-	1	-	-	1	-
		NS	2	2	2	1	-	-	-	-	-	-	-	-	-	-	-	-	-	1	1	-	-	-	-	-	-	-
		T	415	360	361	2	4	1	-	-	-	-	-	2	1	-	-	181	-	129	313	-	-	29	-	-	29	12
	137 Pedal Cycle	M	123	87	87	9	28	30	-	-	-	-	-	-	-	-	-	9	-	9	18	-	-	-	-	-	-	2
		T	123	87	87	9	28	30	-	-	-	-	-	-	-	-	-	9	-	9	18	-	-	-	-	-	-	2
	138 Offences involving impersonation	M	5	4	4	-	3	1	-	-	-	-	-	-	-	-	-	-	-	-	-	-	-	-	-	-	-	-
		T	5	4	4	-	3	1	-	-	-	-	-	-	-	-	-	-	-	-	-	-	-	-	-	-	-	-
	140 Drunkenness, Simple	M	15	13	13	4	5	3	-	-	-	-	-	-	-	-	-	1	-	-	1	-	-	-	-	-	-	-
		F	6	6	6	1	3	-	-	-	-	-	-	-	-	-	-	2	-	-	2	-	-	-	-	-	-	-
		T	21	19	19	5	8	3	-	-	-	-	-	-	-	-	-	3	-	-	3	-	-	-	-	-	-	-
	141 Drunkenness, with	M	566	459	459	66	197	87	-	-	-	-	-	-	7	-	-	61	-	30	98	-	-	-	-	-	-	11

21.6c Persons aged 15 to under 18 convicted and sentenced at all courts

England and Wales, 2012

Number of persons

Offence group	Description		Total Proc Against	Total found Guilty	Total For Sent	Absl Disch	Condl Disch	Fine	CRO	SO	CPO	ACO	CPO&RO	Curf Order	Rep Order	APO	DTTO	REFO	Comm Order	YRO(1)	Total Comm Sentences	SS	Sec 90-92	DTO	YOI	Unsus Sent Impr	Imm cust	ODW
	Aggravation	F	169	138	138	26	56	16	-	-	-	-	-	-	2	-	-	28	-	7	37	-	-	-	-	-	-	3
		NS	7	6	6	-	3	1	-	-	-	-	-	-	-	-	-	1	-	1	2	-	-	-	-	-	-	-
		T	742	603	603	92	256	104	-	-	-	-	-	-	9	-	-	90	-	38	137	-	-	-	-	-	-	14
	143 Other Offence against the Liquor Law	M	90	71	71	11	25	16	-	-	-	-	-	-	1	-	-	14	-	3	18	-	-	-	-	-	-	1
		F	9	3	3	1	-	-	-	-	-	-	-	-	2	-	-	-	-	-	2	-	-	-	-	-	-	-
		NS	1	1	1	-	-	1	-	-	-	-	-	-	-	-	-	-	-	-	-	-	-	-	-	-	-	-
		T	100	75	75	12	25	17	-	-	-	-	-	-	1	-	-	16	-	3	20	-	-	-	-	-	-	1
	149 Summary Criminal or Malicious Damage Offence	M	3,294	2,580	2,579	100	501	33	-	1	-	5	-	2	85	-	-	916	-	770	1,779	-	-	-	-	-	-	166
		F	506	397	397	26	70	2	-	-	-	-	-	-	6	-	-	157	-	121	284	-	-	1	-	-	1	14
		NS	32	29	29	2	3	-	-	-	-	-	-	-	-	-	-	11	-	12	23	-	-	-	-	-	-	1
		T	3,832	3,006	3,005	128	574	35	-	1	-	5	-	2	91	-	-	1,084	-	903	2,086	-	-	1	-	-	1	181
	150 Merchant Shipping Acts	M	1	1	1	-	-	-	-	-	-	-	-	-	-	-	-	-	-	-	-	-	-	-	-	-	-	1
		T	1	1	1	-	-	-	-	-	-	-	-	-	-	-	-	-	-	-	-	-	-	-	-	-	-	1
	151 Social Security Offence	F	1	1	1	-	1	-	-	-	-	-	-	-	-	-	-	-	-	-	-	-	-	-	-	-	-	-
		T	1	1	1	-	1	-	-	-	-	-	-	-	-	-	-	-	-	-	-	-	-	-	-	-	-	-
	155 Military Law - Air Force	M	4	3	3	-	-	-	-	-	-	-	-	-	-	-	-	3	-	-	3	-	-	-	-	-	-	-
		NS	1	1	1	-	-	-	-	-	-	-	-	-	-	-	-	1	-	-	1	-	-	-	-	-	-	-
		T	5	4	4	-	-	-	-	-	-	-	-	-	-	-	-	4	-	-	4	-	-	-	-	-	-	-
	160 Pedlars Act	M	9	7	7	1	1	5	-	-	-	-	-	-	-	-	-	-	-	-	-	-	-	-	-	-	-	-
		T	9	7	7	1	1	5	-	-	-	-	-	-	-	-	-	-	-	-	-	-	-	-	-	-	-	-
	162 Disorderly Behaviour	M	17	11	11	4	5	-	-	-	-	-	-	-	-	-	-	-	-	1	1	-	-	-	-	-	-	1
		F	6	4	4	1	1	1	-	-	-	-	-	-	-	-	-	-	-	-	-	-	-	-	-	-	-	1
		T	23	15	15	5	6	1	-	-	-	-	-	-	-	-	-	-	-	1	1	-	-	-	-	-	-	2
	164 Other Offence	M	6	4	4	1	1	1	-	-	-	-	-	-	-	-	-	1	-	-	1	-	-	-	-	-	-	-
		T	6	4	4	1	1	1	-	-	-	-	-	-	-	-	-	1	-	-	1	-	-	-	-	-	-	-
	167 Aiding, etc. Offence by Prostitute	M	3	-	-	-	-	-	-	-	-	-	-	-	-	-	-	-	-	-	-	-	-	-	-	-	-	-
		T	3	-	-	-	-	-	-	-	-	-	-	-	-	-	-	-	-	-	-	-	-	-	-	-	-	-
	168 Public Health Offence	M	36	19	19	2	1	15	-	-	-	-	-	-	-	-	-	1	-	-	1	-	-	-	-	-	-	-
		F	13	7	7	1	-	6	-	-	-	-	-	-	-	-	-	-	-	-	-	-	-	-	-	-	-	-
		NS	1	1	1	-	-	1	-	-	-	-	-	-	-	-	-	-	-	-	-	-	-	-	-	-	-	-
		T	50	27	27	3	1	22	-	-	-	-	-	-	-	-	-	1	-	-	1	-	-	-	-	-	-	-
	169 Railway Offence	M	454	287	287	27	74	139	-	-	-	-	-	-	1	-	-	19	-	13	33	-	-	-	-	-	-	14
		F	77	49	49	4	9	27	-	-	-	-	-	-	-	-	-	6	-	1	7	-	-	-	-	-	-	2
		NS	53	31	31	2	5	17	-	-	-	-	-	-	-	-	-	2	-	3	5	-	-	-	-	-	-	2
		T	584	367	367	33	88	183	-	-	-	-	-	-	1	-	-	27	-	17	45	-	-	-	-	-	-	18
	170 Motor Vehicle Licence	M	19	12	12	-	-	12	-	-	-	-	-	-	-	-	-	-	-	-	-	-	-	-	-	-	-	-
		F	9	7	7	-	-	7	-	-	-	-	-	-	-	-	-	-	-	-	-	-	-	-	-	-	-	-
		NS	4	3	3	-	-	3	-	-	-	-	-	-	-	-	-	-	-	-	-	-	-	-	-	-	-	-
		T	32	22	22	-	-	22	-	-	-	-	-	-	-	-	-	-	-	-	-	-	-	-	-	-	-	-
	173 Stage Carriage or Public Service Vehicle Offence	M	10	3	3	-	2	1	-	-	-	-	-	-	-	-	-	-	-	-	-	-	-	-	-	-	-	-
		F	6	4	4	2	-	2	-	-	-	-	-	-	-	-	-	-	-	-	-	-	-	-	-	-	-	-
		T	16	7	7	2	2	3	-	-	-	-	-	-	-	-	-	-	-	-	-	-	-	-	-	-	-	-
	180 Tram or Trolley Vehicle Offence	M	8	4	4	-	1	2	-	-	-	-	-	-	-	-	-	1	-	-	1	-	-	-	-	-	-	-
		T	8	4	4	-	1	2	-	-	-	-	-	-	-	-	-	1	-	-	1	-	-	-	-	-	-	-
	182 Begging	M	2	2	2	-	-	-	-	-	-	-	-	-	-	-	-	2	-	-	2	-	-	-	-	-	-	-
		F	8	6	6	1	3	-	-	-	-	-	-	-	-	-	-	-	-	2	2	-	-	-	-	-	-	-
		NS	2	2	2	1	-	-	-	-	-	-	-	-	-	-	-	1	-	-	1	-	-	-	-	-	-	-
		T	12	10	10	2	3	-	-	-	-	-	-	-	-	-	-	3	-	2	5	-	-	-	-	-	-	-
	185 Found In Enclosed Premises	M	105	67	67	5	18	3	-	-	-	-	-	-	3	-	-	18	-	19	40	-	-	-	-	-	-	1
		F	2	1	1	-	-	-	-	-	-	-	-	-	-	-	-	1	-	-	1	-	-	-	-	-	-	-
		T	107	68	68	5	18	3	-	-	-	-	-	-	3	-	-	19	-	19	41	-	-	-	-	-	-	1
	190 Wild Birds Protection Acts	M	1	1	1	-	-	-	-	-	-	-	-	-	-	-	-	-	-	1	1	-	-	-	-	-	-	-
		T	1	1	1	-	-	-	-	-	-	-	-	-	-	-	-	-	-	1	1	-	-	-	-	-	-	-
	191 Wireless Telegraphy Acts	M	30	19	19	-	-	19	-	-	-	-	-	-	-	-	-	-	-	-	-	-	-	-	-	-	-	-
		F	43	20	20	-	-	20	-	-	-	-	-	-	-	-	-	-	-	-	-	-	-	-	-	-	-	-
		T	73	39	39	-	-	39	-	-	-	-	-	-	-	-	-	-	-	-	-	-	-	-	-	-	-	-
	Other Summary Offence (Excluding Motoring)	M	784	691	691	12	37	306	-	-	-	-	-	-	4	-	-	59	-	57	120	-	-	28	-	-	28	188
		F	122	90	90	1	8	24	-	-	-	-	-	-	1	-	-	20	-	9	30	-	-	2	-	-	2	25
		NS	52	50	50	-	-	24	-	1	-	-	-	-	-	-	-	1	-	-	2	-	-	3	-	-	3	21
		T	958	831	831	13	45	354	-	1	-	-	-	-	5	-	-	80	-	66	152	-	-	33	-	-	33	234
	Sub-total	M	14,500	10,885	10,875	397	1,747	922	1	3	-	9	-	13	196	-	-	3,430	-	3,235	6,887	-	-	302	-	-	302	620
		F	3,368	2,518	2,518	104	383	153	-	-	-	1	-	2	29	-	-	965	-	745	1,742	-	-	37	-	-	37	99
		NS	250	204	204	9	22	48	-	1	-	-	-	-	1	-	-	44	-	44	90	-	-	10	-	-	10	25
		T	18,118	13,607	13,597	510	2,152	1,123	1	4	-	10	-	15	226	-	-	4,439	-	4,024	8,719	-	-	349	-	-	349	744
Summary Motoring	A Summary Motoring Offences	M	3,075	2,520	2,519	149	274	1,439	-	-	-	1	-	-	11	-	-	403	-	157	572	-	-	11	-	-	11	74
		F	236	187	186	11	11	104	-	-	-	-	-	-	-	-	-	50	-	7	57	-	-	-	-	-	-	3
		NS	57	30	30	-	3	20	-	-	-	-	-	-	-	-	-	4	-	2	6	-	-	-	-	-	-	1
		T	3,368	2,737	2,735	160	288	1,563	-	-	-	1	-	-	11	-	-	457	-	166	635	-	-	11	-	-	11	78
	Sub-total	M	3,075	2,520	2,519	149	274	1,439	-	-	-	1	-	-	11	-	-	403	-	157	572	-	-	11	-	-	11	74
		F	236	187	186	11	11	104	-	-	-	-	-	-	-	-	-	50	-	7	57	-	-	-	-	-	-	3
		NS	57	30	30	-	3	20	-	-	-	-	-	-	-	-	-	4	-	2	6	-	-	-	-	-	-	1
		T	3,368	2,737	2,735	160	288	1,563	-	-	-	1	-	-	11	-	-	457	-	166	635	-	-	11	-	-	11	78
Total Summary		M	17,575	13,405	13,394	546	2,021	2,361	1	3	-	10	-	13	207	-	-	3,833	-	3,392	7,459	-	-	313	-	-	313	694
		F	3,604	2,705	2,704	115	394	257	-	-	-	1	-	2	29	-	-	1,015	-	752	1,799	-	-	37	-	-	37	102
		NS	307	234	234	9	25	68	-	1	-	-	-	-	1	-	-	48	-	46	96	-	-	10	-	-	10	26
		T	21,486	16,344	16,332	670	2,440	2,686	1	4	-	11	-	15	237	-	-	4,896	-	4,190	9,354	-	-	360	-	-	360	822
All Offences		M	44,971	34,193	34,151	1,060	3,975	3,244	16	16	-	39	-	46	399	-	1	10,340	-	10,819	21,676	-	270	2,410	-	33	2,713	1,483
		F	7,112	5,391	5,388	202	670	308	1	-	-	2	-	3	68	-	-	2,086	-	1,672	3,832	-	9	165	-	-	174	202
		NS	594	453	453	11	43	72	-	1	-	-	-	-	1	-	-	119	-	135	256	-	-	39	-	-	39	32
		T	52,677	40,037	39,992	1,273	4,688	3,624	17	17	-	41	-	49	468	-	1	12,545	-	12,626	25,764	-	279	2,614	-	33	2,926	1,717

(1) The Youth Rehabilitation Order came into effect on 30 November 2009. Figures prior to 2010 are recorded as community orders.

21.6d Persons aged 18 to under 21 convicted and sentenced at all courts

England and Wales, 2012

Number of persons

Offence group	Description		Total Proc Against	Total found Guilty	Total For Sent	Absit Disch	Condl Disch	Fine	CRO	SO	CPO	ACO	CPO&RO	Curf Order	Rep Order	APO	DTTO	REFO	Comm Order	YRO [1]	Total Comm Sentences	SS	Sec 90-92	DTO	YOI	Unsus Sent Impr	Imm cust	ODW
Violence Against Person	1 Murder	M	74	41	41	-	-	-	-	-	-	-	-	-	-	-	-	-	-	-	-	-	6	-	35	-	41	-
		F	4	1	1	-	-	-	-	-	-	-	-	-	-	-	-	-	-	-	-	-	-	-	1	-	1	-
		NS	4	-	-	-	-	-	-	-	-	-	-	-	-	-	-	-	-	-	-	-	-	-	-	-	-	-
		T	82	42	42	-	-	-	-	-	-	-	-	-	-	-	-	-	-	-	-	-	-	6	-	36	-	42	-
	2 Attempted Murder	M	28	5	5	-	-	-	-	-	-	-	-	-	-	-	-	-	-	-	-	-	-	-	3	2	5	-
		F	3	1	1	-	-	-	-	-	-	-	-	-	-	-	-	-	-	-	-	-	-	-	-	-	-	1
		T	31	6	6	-	-	-	-	-	-	-	-	-	-	-	-	-	-	-	-	-	-	-	3	2	5	1
	3 Threat or Conspiracy to Murder	M	78	27	24	-	-	-	-	-	-	-	-	-	-	-	-	-	6	-	6	7	-	-	10	-	10	1
		F	5	3	2	-	-	-	-	-	-	-	-	-	-	-	-	-	-	-	-	-	-	-	2	-	2	-
		T	83	30	26	-	-	-	-	-	-	-	-	-	-	-	-	-	6	-	6	7	-	-	12	-	12	1
	4.1 Manslaughter	M	4	26	26	-	-	-	-	-	-	-	-	-	-	-	-	-	-	-	-	-	-	-	23	2	25	1
		F	-	2	2	-	-	-	-	-	-	-	-	-	-	-	-	-	-	-	-	-	-	-	2	-	2	-
		T	4	28	28	-	-	-	-	-	-	-	-	-	-	-	-	-	-	-	-	-	-	-	25	2	27	1
	4.4 Causing Death by Dangerous Driving	M	20	17	17	1	-	-	-	-	-	-	-	-	-	-	-	-	-	-	-	-	-	-	16	-	16	-
		F	3	1	1	-	-	-	-	-	-	-	-	-	-	-	-	-	-	-	-	-	-	-	1	-	1	-
		T	23	18	18	1	-	-	-	-	-	-	-	-	-	-	-	-	-	-	-	-	-	-	17	-	17	-
	4.6 Causing Death by Careless Driving when under the influence of Drink or Drugs	M	6	2	2	-	-	-	-	-	-	-	-	-	-	-	-	-	-	-	-	-	-	-	2	-	2	-
		T	6	2	2	-	-	-	-	-	-	-	-	-	-	-	-	-	-	-	-	-	-	-	2	-	2	-
	4.7 Causing Death of a child or vulnerable person	M	-	-	-	-	-	-	-	-	-	-	-	-	-	-	-	-	-	-	-	-	-	-	-	-	-	-
		F	1	-	-	-	-	-	-	-	-	-	-	-	-	-	-	-	-	-	-	-	-	-	-	-	-	-
		T	1	-	-	-	-	-	-	-	-	-	-	-	-	-	-	-	-	-	-	-	-	-	-	-	-	-
	4.8 Causing Death by careless or inconsiderate driving	M	20	13	13	-	-	-	-	-	-	-	-	-	-	-	-	-	6	-	6	4	-	-	3	-	3	-
		F	4	4	4	-	-	-	-	-	-	-	-	-	-	-	-	-	3	-	3	-	-	-	1	-	1	-
		T	24	17	17	-	-	-	-	-	-	-	-	-	-	-	-	-	9	-	9	4	-	-	4	-	4	-
	4.9 Causing death by driving unlicensed, disqualified or uninsured drivers	M	1	2	2	-	-	-	-	-	-	-	-	-	-	-	-	-	1	-	1	1	-	-	-	-	-	-
		T	1	2	2	-	-	-	-	-	-	-	-	-	-	-	-	-	1	-	1	1	-	-	-	-	-	-
	5 Wounding or other act Endangering Life	M	862	293	293	-	-	1	-	-	-	-	-	-	-	-	-	-	11	-	11	4	1	-	235	41	277	-
		F	69	20	18	-	-	-	-	-	-	-	-	-	-	-	-	-	2	-	2	-	-	-	15	1	16	-
		NS	8	-	-	-	-	-	-	-	-	-	-	-	-	-	-	-	-	-	-	-	-	-	-	-	-	-
		T	939	313	311	-	-	1	-	-	-	-	-	-	-	-	-	-	13	-	13	4	1	-	250	42	293	-
	6 Endangering Railway Passenger	M	3	3	3	-	-	-	-	-	-	-	-	-	-	-	-	-	2	-	2	-	-	-	1	-	1	-
		F	-	1	1	-	-	-	-	-	-	-	-	-	-	-	-	-	1	-	1	-	-	-	-	-	-	-
		T	3	4	4	-	-	-	-	-	-	-	-	-	-	-	-	-	3	-	3	-	-	-	1	-	1	-
	7 Endangering Life at Sea	M	1	1	1	-	1	-	-	-	-	-	-	-	-	-	-	-	-	-	-	-	-	-	-	-	-	-
		T	1	1	1	-	1	-	-	-	-	-	-	-	-	-	-	-	-	-	-	-	-	-	-	-	-	-
	8 Malicious Wounding etc.	M	4,692	3,746	3,660	5	139	176	-	-	-	1	-	1	-	-	-	-	1,166	-	1,168	910	-	-	1,205	3	1,208	54
		F	518	427	426	1	20	16	-	-	-	-	-	1	-	-	-	-	174	-	175	115	-	-	81	-	81	18
		NS	37	13	8	-	2	1	-	-	-	-	-	-	-	-	-	-	4	-	4	-	-	-	1	-	1	-
		T	5,247	4,186	4,094	6	161	193	-	-	-	1	-	2	-	-	-	-	1,344	-	1,347	1,025	-	-	1,287	3	1,290	72
	11 Cruelty to or Neglect of Children	M	16	12	10	-	-	-	-	-	-	-	-	-	-	-	-	-	2	-	2	3	-	-	5	-	5	-
		F	24	12	12	-	-	-	-	-	-	-	-	-	-	-	-	-	5	-	5	4	-	-	3	-	3	-
		T	40	24	22	-	-	-	-	-	-	-	-	-	-	-	-	-	7	-	7	7	-	-	8	-	8	-
	13 Child Abduction	M	16	11	10	-	1	-	-	-	-	-	-	-	-	-	-	-	4	-	4	1	-	-	4	-	4	-
		F	3	1	1	-	-	-	-	-	-	-	-	-	-	-	-	-	1	-	1	-	-	-	-	-	-	-
		T	19	12	11	-	1	-	-	-	-	-	-	-	-	-	-	-	5	-	5	1	-	-	4	-	4	-
	37.1 Causing Death by Aggravated Vehicle Taking	M	-	1	1	-	-	-	-	-	-	-	-	-	-	-	-	-	-	-	-	-	-	-	-	1	-	1	-
		T	-	1	1	-	-	-	-	-	-	-	-	-	-	-	-	-	-	-	-	-	-	-	1	-	1	-
	Sub-total	M	5,821	4,200	4,108	6	141	177	-	-	-	1	-	1	-	-	-	-	1,198	-	1,200	930	7	-	1,543	48	1,598	56
		F	634	473	469	1	20	16	-	-	-	-	-	1	-	-	-	-	186	-	187	119	-	-	106	1	107	19
		NS	49	13	8	-	2	1	-	-	-	-	-	-	-	-	-	-	4	-	4	-	-	-	1	-	1	-
		T	6,504	4,686	4,585	7	163	194	-	-	-	1	-	2	-	-	-	-	1,388	-	1,391	1,049	7	-	1,650	49	1,706	75
Sexual Offences	17 Sexual Assault on a Male	M	12	5	5	-	-	-	-	-	-	-	-	-	-	-	-	-	3	-	3	-	-	-	2	-	2	-
		F	2	-	-	-	-	-	-	-	-	-	-	-	-	-	-	-	-	-	-	-	-	-	-	-	-	-
		T	14	5	5	-	-	-	-	-	-	-	-	-	-	-	-	-	3	-	3	-	-	-	2	-	2	-
	19 Rape of a Female	M	280	97	97	-	-	-	-	-	-	-	-	-	-	-	-	-	3	-	3	-	-	-	69	21	90	4
		NS	7	-	-	-	-	-	-	-	-	-	-	-	-	-	-	-	-	-	-	-	-	-	-	-	-	-
		T	287	97	97	-	-	-	-	-	-	-	-	-	-	-	-	-	3	-	3	-	-	-	69	21	90	4
	19 Rape of a Male	M	23	8	8	-	-	-	-	-	-	-	-	-	-	-	-	-	2	-	2	-	-	-	5	1	6	-
		NS	1	-	-	-	-	-	-	-	-	-	-	-	-	-	-	-	-	-	-	-	-	-	-	-	-	-
		T	24	8	8	-	-	-	-	-	-	-	-	-	-	-	-	-	2	-	2	-	-	-	5	1	6	-
	20 Sexual Assault on a Female	M	227	118	117	-	4	1	-	-	-	-	-	-	-	-	-	-	48	-	48	14	-	-	38	4	42	8
		F	4	3	3	-	-	-	-	-	-	-	-	-	-	-	-	-	1	-	1	-	-	-	1	1	2	-
		NS	1	-	-	-	-	-	-	-	-	-	-	-	-	-	-	-	-	-	-	-	-	-	-	-	-	-
		T	232	121	120	-	4	1	-	-	-	-	-	-	-	-	-	-	49	-	49	14	-	-	39	5	44	8
	21 Sexual Activity with child under 13	M	35	26	28	-	-	-	-	-	-	-	-	-	-	-	-	-	14	-	14	3	-	-	10	-	10	1
		T	35	26	28	-	-	-	-	-	-	-	-	-	-	-	-	-	14	-	14	3	-	-	10	-	10	1
	22 Sexual Activity with child under 16	M	157	137	137	-	5	-	-	-	-	-	-	-	-	-	-	-	40	-	40	22	-	-	65	2	67	3
		NS	1	-	-	-	-	-	-	-	-	-	-	-	-	-	-	-	-	-	-	-	-	-	-	-	-	-
		T	158	137	137	-	5	-	-	-	-	-	-	-	-	-	-	-	40	-	40	22	-	-	65	2	67	3
	23 Familial Sexual Offences (Incest)	M	2	6	6	-	-	-	-	-	-	-	-	-	-	-	-	-	4	-	4	1	-	-	1	-	1	-
		T	2	6	6	-	-	-	-	-	-	-	-	-	-	-	-	-	4	-	4	1	-	-	1	-	1	-
	24 Exploitation of Prostitution	M	1	1	1	-	-	-	-	-	-	-	-	-	-	-	-	-	-	-	-	-	-	-	1	-	1	-
		T	1	1	1	-	-	-	-	-	-	-	-	-	-	-	-	-	-	-	-	-	-	-	1	-	1	-
	70 Sexual activity etc. with a person with a mental disorder	M	2	1	1	-	-	-	-	-	-	-	-	-	-	-	-	-	-	-	-	-	-	-	1	-	1	-
		T	2	1	1	-	-	-	-	-	-	-	-	-	-	-	-	-	-	-	-	-	-	-	1	-	1	-
	71 Abuse of children through prostitution and pornography	M	5	2	2	-	1	-	-	-	-	-	-	-	-	-	-	-	-	-	-	-	-	-	-	1	1	-
		F	1	-	-	-	-	-	-	-	-	-	-	-	-	-	-	-	-	-	-	-	-	-	-	-	-	-
		T	6	2	2	-	1	-	-	-	-	-	-	-	-	-	-	-	-	-	-	-	-	-	-	1	1	-
	72 Trafficking for sexual exploitation	M	1	1	1	-	-	-	-	-	-	-	-	-	-	-	-	-	-	-	-	-	-	-	1	-	1	-
		F	1	-	-	-	-	-	-	-	-	-	-	-	-	-	-	-	-	-	-	-	-	-	-	-	-	-
		T	2	1	1	-	-	-	-	-	-	-	-	-	-	-	-	-	-	-	-	-	-	-	1	-	1	-

21.6d Persons aged 18 to under 21 convicted and sentenced at all courts

England and Wales, 2012

Number of persons

Offence group	Description		Total Proc Against	Total found Guilty	Total For Sent	Absit Disch	Condl Disch	Fine	CRO	SO	CPO	ACO	CPO&RO	Curf Order	Rep Order	APO	DTTO	REFO	Comm Order	YRO [1]	Total Comm Sentences	SS	Sec 90-92	DTO	YOI	Unsus Sent Impr	Imm cust	ODW
	88 Miscellaneous sexual offences	M	79	60	60	-	3	3	-	-	-	-	-	-	-	-	-	-	35	-	35	7	-	-	11	-	11	1
		F	1	1	1	-	-	-	-	-	-	-	-	-	-	-	-	-	1	-	1	-	-	-	-	-	-	-
		T	80	61	61	-	3	3	-	-	-	-	-	-	-	-	-	-	36	-	36	7	-	-	11	-	11	1
	Sub-total	M	824	462	463	-	13	4	-	-	-	-	-	-	-	-	-	-	149	-	149	47	-	-	204	29	233	17
		F	9	4	4	-	-	-	-	-	-	-	-	-	-	-	-	-	2	-	2	-	-	-	1	1	2	-
		NS	10	-	-	-	-	-	-	-	-	-	-	-	-	-	-	-	-	-	-	-	-	-	-	-	-	-
		T	843	466	467	-	13	4	-	-	-	-	-	-	-	-	-	-	151	-	151	47	-	-	205	30	235	17
Burglary	28 Burglary in a Dwelling	M	2,849	2,221	2,118	-	18	3	-	-	-	1	-	-	1	-	-	-	506	-	508	366	-	-	1,196	-	1,196	27
		F	146	101	99	-	2	-	-	-	-	-	-	-	-	-	-	-	45	-	45	16	-	-	34	-	34	2
		NS	22	15	9	-	-	1	-	-	-	-	-	-	-	-	-	-	2	-	2	4	-	-	2	-	2	-
		T	3,017	2,337	2,226	-	20	4	-	-	-	1	-	-	1	-	-	-	553	-	555	386	-	-	1,232	-	1,232	29
	29 Aggravated Burglary in a Dwelling	M	129	55	55	-	-	-	-	-	-	-	-	-	-	-	-	-	-	-	-	-	-	-	53	1	54	1
		F	7	3	3	-	-	-	-	-	-	-	-	-	-	-	-	-	-	-	-	-	-	-	3	-	3	-
		T	136	58	58	-	-	-	-	-	-	-	-	-	-	-	-	-	-	-	-	-	-	-	56	1	57	1
	30 Burglary in a Building Other than a Dwelling	M	1,447	1,164	1,141	2	47	50	1	-	-	1	-	-	1	-	-	-	535	-	538	131	-	-	341	-	341	32
		F	64	46	47	-	4	-	-	-	-	1	-	-	-	-	-	-	10	-	11	14	-	-	16	-	16	2
		NS	12	7	6	-	-	-	-	-	-	-	-	-	-	-	-	-	4	-	4	1	-	-	1	-	1	-
		T	1,523	1,217	1,194	2	51	50	1	-	-	2	-	-	1	-	-	-	549	-	553	146	-	-	358	-	358	34
	31 Aggravated Burglary in a Building not a Dwelling	M	9	1	1	-	-	-	-	-	-	-	-	-	-	-	-	-	-	-	-	-	-	-	1	-	1	-
		T	9	1	1	-	-	-	-	-	-	-	-	-	-	-	-	-	-	-	-	-	-	-	1	-	1	-
	Sub-total	M	4,434	3,441	3,315	2	65	53	1	-	-	2	-	-	2	-	-	-	1,041	-	1,046	497	-	-	1,591	1	1,592	60
		F	217	150	149	-	6	-	-	-	-	1	-	-	-	-	-	-	55	-	56	30	-	-	53	-	53	4
		NS	34	22	15	-	-	1	-	-	-	-	-	-	-	-	-	-	6	-	6	5	-	-	3	-	3	-
		T	4,685	3,613	3,479	2	71	54	1	-	-	3	-	-	2	-	-	-	1,102	-	1,108	532	-	-	1,647	1	1,648	64
Robbery	34 Robbery	M	2,252	1,628	1,628	-	1	-	-	-	-	-	-	2	-	-	-	-	106	-	108	249	-	-	1,233	27	1,260	10
		F	139	79	79	-	-	-	-	-	-	-	-	-	-	-	-	-	12	-	12	17	-	-	48	-	48	2
		NS	28	-	-	-	-	-	-	-	-	-	-	-	-	-	-	-	-	-	-	-	-	-	-	-	-	-
		T	2,419	1,707	1,707	-	1	-	-	-	-	-	-	2	-	-	-	-	118	-	120	266	-	-	1,281	27	1,308	12
	Sub-total	M	2,252	1,628	1,628	-	1	-	-	-	-	-	-	2	-	-	-	-	106	-	108	249	-	-	1,233	27	1,260	10
		F	139	79	79	-	-	-	-	-	-	-	-	-	-	-	-	-	12	-	12	17	-	-	48	-	48	2
		NS	28	-	-	-	-	-	-	-	-	-	-	-	-	-	-	-	-	-	-	-	-	-	-	-	-	-
		T	2,419	1,707	1,707	-	1	-	-	-	-	-	-	2	-	-	-	-	118	-	120	266	-	-	1,281	27	1,308	12
Theft and Handling	37.2 Aggravated Vehicle Taking	M	272	257	255	-	4	2	-	-	-	-	-	-	-	-	-	-	109	-	109	42	-	-	90	-	90	8
		F	11	11	12	-	1	-	-	-	-	-	-	-	-	-	-	-	6	-	6	4	-	-	1	-	1	-
		NS	1	1	-	-	-	-	-	-	-	-	-	-	-	-	-	-	-	-	-	-	-	-	-	-	-	-
		T	284	269	267	-	5	2	-	-	-	-	-	-	-	-	-	-	115	-	115	46	-	-	91	-	91	8
	38 Money laundering	M	163	119	115	-	14	14	-	-	-	-	-	-	-	-	-	-	55	-	55	14	-	-	17	-	17	1
		F	33	22	22	-	6	-	-	-	-	-	-	1	-	-	-	-	7	-	8	5	-	-	1	-	1	2
		NS	2	1	1	-	-	-	-	-	-	-	-	-	-	-	-	-	1	-	1	-	-	-	-	-	-	-
		T	198	142	138	-	20	14	-	-	-	-	-	1	-	-	-	-	63	-	64	19	-	-	18	-	18	3
	39 Theft from the Person of Another	M	656	602	605	1	69	46	-	-	-	-	-	-	-	-	-	-	242	-	242	60	-	-	167	-	167	20
		F	130	99	99	-	22	4	-	-	-	-	-	-	-	-	-	-	36	-	36	12	-	-	19	-	19	6
		NS	16	10	7	-	1	1	-	-	-	-	-	-	-	-	-	-	2	-	2	1	-	-	2	-	2	-
		T	802	711	711	1	92	51	-	-	-	-	-	-	-	-	-	-	280	-	280	73	-	-	188	-	188	26
	40 Theft in Dwelling not Automatic M/c or Meter	M	459	386	386	1	50	26	-	-	-	1	-	-	1	-	-	-	182	-	184	30	-	-	71	-	71	24
		F	71	58	58	-	4	7	-	-	-	-	-	-	-	-	-	-	40	-	40	5	-	-	1	-	1	1
		NS	6	6	5	-	-	-	-	-	-	-	-	-	-	-	-	-	1	-	1	1	-	-	3	-	3	-
		T	536	450	449	1	54	33	-	-	-	1	-	-	1	-	-	-	223	-	225	36	-	-	75	-	75	25
	41 Theft by an Employee	M	160	139	140	-	11	17	-	-	-	-	-	-	-	-	-	-	89	-	89	19	-	-	2	-	2	2
		F	71	65	64	-	8	1	-	-	-	-	-	-	-	-	-	-	46	-	46	8	-	-	-	-	-	1
		T	231	204	204	-	19	18	-	-	-	-	-	-	-	-	-	-	135	-	135	27	-	-	2	-	2	3
	42 Theft or Unauthorised Taking from Mail	M	4	9	9	-	-	-	-	-	-	-	-	-	-	-	-	-	3	-	3	2	-	-	4	-	4	-
		F	1	1	1	-	-	-	-	-	-	-	-	-	-	-	-	-	1	-	1	-	-	-	-	-	-	-
		T	5	10	10	-	-	-	-	-	-	-	-	-	-	-	-	-	4	-	4	2	-	-	4	-	4	-
	43 Abstracting Electricity	M	17	12	13	-	8	1	-	-	-	-	-	-	-	-	-	-	1	-	1	2	-	-	-	-	-	1
		F	5	5	5	-	1	2	-	-	-	-	-	-	-	-	-	-	1	-	1	-	-	-	-	-	-	1
		T	22	17	18	-	9	3	-	-	-	-	-	-	-	-	-	-	2	-	2	2	-	-	-	-	-	2
	44 Theft of Pedal Cycle	M	371	324	321	2	70	47	-	-	-	-	-	-	-	-	-	-	143	-	143	21	-	-	24	-	24	14
		F	9	7	7	-	3	1	-	-	-	-	-	-	-	-	-	-	-	-	-	-	-	-	3	-	3	-
		NS	3	3	3	-	2	-	-	-	-	-	-	-	-	-	-	-	1	-	1	-	-	-	-	-	-	-
		T	383	334	331	2	75	48	-	-	-	-	-	-	-	-	-	-	144	-	144	21	-	-	27	-	27	14
	45 Theft from Vehicle	M	649	528	521	3	76	55	-	-	-	-	-	1	-	-	-	-	258	-	259	42	-	-	72	-	72	14
		F	16	12	12	-	4	-	-	-	-	-	-	-	-	-	-	-	7	-	7	1	-	-	-	-	-	-
		NS	3	2	2	-	-	-	-	-	-	-	-	-	-	-	-	-	2	-	2	-	-	-	-	-	-	-
		T	668	542	535	3	80	55	-	-	-	-	-	1	-	-	-	-	267	-	268	43	-	-	72	-	72	14
	46 Theft from Shops	M	4,044	3,807	3,771	19	1,120	824	-	-	-	4	-	1	-	-	-	-	1,102	-	1,107	122	-	-	400	-	400	179
		F	1,287	1,213	1,208	5	436	227	-	-	-	1	-	-	-	-	-	-	378	-	379	49	-	-	62	-	62	50
		NS	41	39	38	-	5	9	-	-	-	-	-	-	-	-	-	-	13	-	13	3	-	-	6	-	6	2
		T	5,372	5,059	5,017	24	1,561	1,060	-	-	-	5	-	1	-	-	-	-	1,493	-	1,499	174	-	-	468	-	468	231
	47 Theft from Automatic Machine or Meter	M	29	23	22	-	6	1	-	-	-	-	-	-	-	-	-	-	9	-	9	2	-	-	4	-	4	-
		F	3	2	2	-	-	-	-	-	-	-	-	-	-	-	-	-	2	-	2	-	-	-	-	-	-	-
		NS	2	1	1	-	-	-	-	-	-	-	-	-	-	-	-	-	1	-	1	-	-	-	-	-	-	-
		T	34	26	25	-	6	1	-	-	-	-	-	-	-	-	-	-	12	-	12	2	-	-	4	-	4	-
	48 Theft or Unauthorised Taking of Motor Vehicle	M	179	122	121	-	10	6	-	-	-	1	-	-	-	-	-	-	62	-	63	12	-	-	29	-	29	1
		F	3	2	2	-	1	-	-	-	-	-	-	-	-	-	-	-	-	-	-	1	-	-	-	-	-	-
		NS	1	1	-	-	-	-	-	-	-	-	-	-	-	-	-	-	-	-	-	-	-	-	-	-	-	-
		T	183	125	123	-	11	6	-	-	-	1	-	-	-	-	-	-	62	-	63	13	-	-	29	-	29	1
	49 Other Theft or Unauthorised Taking	M	1,504	1,234	1,235	4	281	187	-	-	-	1	-	5	-	-	-	-	513	-	519	77	-	-	124	-	124	43
		F	153	115	112	-	30	14	-	-	-	-	-	-	-	-	-	-	50	-	50	6	-	-	7	-	7	5
		NS	12	7	5	-	1	-	-	-	-	-	-	-	-	-	-	-	2	-	2	-	-	-	-	-	-	1
		T	1,669	1,356	1,352	4	312	202	-	-	-	1	-	5	-	-	-	-	565	-	571	83	-	-	131	1	131	49
	54 Handling Stolen Goods	M	1,342	1,141	1,114	-	144	185	-	-	1	3	-	4	-	-	-	-	482	-	490	88	-	-	188	-	188	19
		F	139	128	125	-	37	22	-	-	-	-	-	-	-	-	-	-	46	-	46	8	-	-	11	-	11	1
		NS	7	4	3	-	1	1	-	-	-	-	-	-	-	-	-	-	1	-	1	-	-	-	-	-	-	-
		T	1,488	1,273	1,242	-	182	208	-	-	1	3	-	4	-	-	-	-	528	-	536	96	-	-	200	-	200	20

21.6d Persons aged 18 to under 21 convicted and sentenced at all courts

England and Wales, 2012

Number of persons

Offence group	Description		Total Proc Against	Total found Guilty	Total For Sent	Absit Disch	Condl Disch	Fine	CRO	SO	CPO	ACO	CPO&RO	Curf Order	Rep Order	APO	DTTO	REFO	Comm Order	YRO (1)	Total Comm Sentences	SS	Sec 90-92	DTO	YOI	Unsus Sent Impr	Imm cust	ODW
	Sub-total	M	9,849	8,703	8,628	30	1,863	1,411	-	-	1	10	-	12	-	-	-	-	3,250	-	3,273	533	-	-	1,192	-	1,192	326
		F	1,932	1,740	1,729	5	553	278	-	-	-	1	-	1	-	-	-	-	620	-	622	99	-	-	105	-	105	67
		NS	94	75	65	-	10	12	-	-	-	-	-	-	-	-	-	-	23	-	23	5	-	-	12	-	12	3
		T	11,875	10,518	10,422	35	2,426	1,701	-	-	1	11	-	13	-	-	-	-	3,893	-	3,918	637	-	-	1,309	-	1,309	396
Fraud and Forgery	53 Other Fraud	M	858	698	677	1	112	126	-	-	-	-	-	2	-	-	-	-	284	-	286	47	-	-	78	-	78	27
		F	311	246	239	-	64	36	-	-	-	-	-	1	-	-	-	-	93	-	94	25	-	-	8	-	8	11
		NS	13	10	10	-	1	3	-	-	-	-	-	-	-	-	-	-	2	-	2	2	-	-	1	-	1	1
		T	1,182	954	926	2	177	165	-	-	-	-	-	3	-	-	-	-	379	-	382	74	-	-	87	-	87	39
	60 Forgery etc. of Drug Prescription	M	2	2	2	-	-	-	-	-	-	-	-	-	-	-	-	-	2	-	2	-	-	-	-	-	-	-
		F	1	1	1	-	1	-	-	-	-	-	-	-	-	-	-	-	-	-	-	-	-	-	-	-	-	-
		T	3	3	3	-	1	-	-	-	-	-	-	-	-	-	-	-	2	-	2	-	-	-	-	-	-	-
	61 Other Forgery etc.	M	138	114	109	-	4	5	-	-	-	-	-	-	-	-	-	-	24	-	24	27	-	-	47	-	47	2
		F	20	12	12	-	-	-	-	-	-	-	-	-	-	-	-	-	4	-	4	-	-	-	7	-	7	1
		NS	2	1	1	-	1	-	-	-	-	-	-	-	-	-	-	-	-	-	-	-	-	-	-	-	-	-
		T	160	127	122	-	5	5	-	-	-	-	-	-	-	-	-	-	28	-	28	27	-	-	54	-	54	3
	814 Fraud, Forgery etc associated with Vehicle or Driver Records	M	20	16	16	-	1	11	-	-	-	-	-	-	-	-	-	-	3	-	3	-	-	-	1	-	1	-
		F	1	-	-	-	-	-	-	-	-	-	-	-	-	-	-	-	-	-	-	-	-	-	-	-	-	-
		T	21	16	16	-	1	11	-	-	-	-	-	-	-	-	-	-	3	-	3	-	-	-	1	-	1	-
	Sub-total	M	1,018	830	804	1	117	142	-	-	-	-	-	2	-	-	-	-	313	-	315	74	-	-	126	-	126	29
		F	333	259	252	1	65	36	-	-	-	-	-	1	-	-	-	-	97	-	98	25	-	-	15	-	15	12
		NS	15	11	11	-	2	3	-	-	-	-	-	-	-	-	-	-	2	-	2	2	-	-	1	-	1	1
		T	1,366	1,100	1,067	2	184	181	-	-	-	-	-	3	-	-	-	-	412	-	415	101	-	-	142	-	142	42
Criminal Damage	56 Arson	M	194	148	143	-	1	-	-	-	-	-	-	-	-	-	-	-	36	-	36	20	-	-	78	4	82	4
		F	33	24	25	-	-	-	-	-	-	-	-	-	-	-	-	-	10	-	10	2	-	-	10	-	10	3
		NS	1	-	-	-	-	-	-	-	-	-	-	-	-	-	-	-	-	-	-	-	-	-	-	-	-	-
		T	228	172	168	-	1	-	-	-	-	-	-	-	-	-	-	-	46	-	46	22	-	-	88	4	92	7
	57 Criminal Damage Endangering Life	M	18	10	11	-	1	1	-	-	-	-	-	-	-	-	-	-	5	-	5	2	-	-	2	-	2	-
		F	3	3	3	-	-	-	-	-	-	-	-	-	-	-	-	-	2	-	2	1	-	-	-	-	-	-
		NS	1	1	1	-	-	-	-	-	-	-	-	-	-	-	-	-	1	-	1	-	-	-	-	-	-	-
		T	22	14	15	-	1	1	-	-	-	-	-	-	-	-	-	-	8	-	8	3	-	-	2	-	2	-
	58 Other Criminal Damage	M	708	552	544	5	146	93	-	-	-	-	-	-	-	-	-	-	190	-	190	26	-	-	23	-	23	61
		F	76	67	66	1	22	13	-	-	-	-	-	-	-	-	-	-	22	-	22	2	-	-	1	-	1	5
		NS	5	3	3	-	-	-	-	-	-	-	-	-	-	-	-	-	2	-	2	-	-	-	1	-	1	-
		T	789	622	613	6	168	106	-	-	-	-	-	-	-	-	-	-	214	-	214	28	-	-	25	-	25	66
	59 Threat etc., to commit Criminal Damage	M	109	55	55	-	13	10	-	-	-	-	-	-	-	-	-	-	20	-	20	4	-	-	5	-	5	3
		F	9	5	5	-	3	-	-	-	-	-	-	-	-	-	-	-	2	-	2	-	-	-	-	-	-	-
		T	118	60	60	-	16	10	-	-	-	-	-	-	-	-	-	-	22	-	22	4	-	-	5	-	5	3
	Sub-total	M	1,029	765	753	5	161	104	-	-	-	-	-	-	-	-	-	-	251	-	251	52	-	-	108	4	112	68
		F	121	99	99	1	25	13	-	-	-	-	-	-	-	-	-	-	36	-	36	5	-	-	11	-	11	8
		NS	7	4	4	-	-	-	-	-	-	-	-	-	-	-	-	-	3	-	3	-	-	-	1	-	1	-
		T	1,157	868	856	6	186	117	-	-	-	-	-	-	-	-	-	-	290	-	290	57	-	-	120	4	124	76
Drug Offences	92.1 Unlawful importation - Class unspecified	M	-	2	2	-	-	-	-	-	-	-	-	-	-	-	-	-	1	-	1	1	-	-	-	-	-	-
		T	-	2	2	-	-	-	-	-	-	-	-	-	-	-	-	-	1	-	1	1	-	-	-	-	-	-
	92.3 Unlawful importation - Class A	M	6	5	7	-	-	-	-	-	-	-	-	-	-	-	-	-	-	-	-	1	-	-	6	-	6	-
		F	3	3	3	-	-	-	-	-	-	-	-	-	-	-	-	-	-	-	-	-	-	-	3	-	3	-
		NS	1	1	-	-	-	-	-	-	-	-	-	-	-	-	-	-	-	-	-	-	-	-	-	-	-	-
		T	10	9	10	-	-	-	-	-	-	-	-	-	-	-	-	-	-	-	-	1	-	-	9	-	9	-
	92.4 Unlawful importation - Class B	M	3	2	2	-	-	1	-	-	-	-	-	-	-	-	-	-	-	-	-	-	-	-	1	-	1	-
		F	1	2	2	-	-	1	-	-	-	-	-	-	-	-	-	-	-	-	-	-	-	-	1	-	1	-
		T	4	4	4	-	-	2	-	-	-	-	-	-	-	-	-	-	-	-	-	-	-	-	2	-	2	-
	92.6 Unlawful exportation - Class A	M	1	1	-	-	-	-	-	-	-	-	-	-	-	-	-	-	-	-	-	-	-	-	-	-	-	-
		T	1	1	-	-	-	-	-	-	-	-	-	-	-	-	-	-	-	-	-	-	-	-	-	-	-	-
	Inciting another to supply a controlled drug - Class B	M	1	1	1	-	-	1	-	-	-	-	-	-	-	-	-	-	-	-	-	-	-	-	-	-	-	-
		T	1	1	1	-	-	1	-	-	-	-	-	-	-	-	-	-	-	-	-	-	-	-	-	-	-	-
	Other drug offences	M	61	32	32	-	6	9	-	-	-	-	-	-	-	-	-	-	12	-	12	1	-	-	3	-	3	1
		F	12	9	9	-	2	2	-	-	-	-	-	-	-	-	-	-	2	-	2	3	-	-	-	-	-	-
		T	73	41	41	-	8	11	-	-	-	-	-	-	-	-	-	-	14	-	14	4	-	-	3	-	3	1
	Possession of a controlled drug - Class A	M	832	794	781	2	102	418	-	-	-	-	-	-	-	-	-	-	173	-	173	16	-	-	35	-	35	35
		F	57	51	49	-	13	12	-	-	-	1	-	-	-	-	-	-	13	-	14	2	-	-	3	-	3	5
		NS	4	4	4	-	1	2	-	-	-	-	-	-	-	-	-	-	1	-	1	-	-	-	-	-	-	-
		T	893	849	834	2	116	432	-	-	-	1	-	-	-	-	-	-	187	-	188	18	-	-	38	-	38	40
	Possession of a controlled drug - Class B	M	4,753	4,529	4,482	31	1,037	2,426	-	-	-	4	-	1	-	-	-	-	636	-	641	44	-	-	57	-	57	246
		F	147	123	119	1	46	47	-	-	-	-	-	-	-	-	-	-	18	-	18	1	-	-	-	-	-	6
		NS	16	15	15	-	3	6	-	-	-	-	-	-	-	-	-	-	3	-	3	-	-	-	1	-	1	2
		T	4,916	4,667	4,616	32	1,086	2,479	-	-	-	4	-	1	-	-	-	-	657	-	662	45	-	-	58	-	58	254
	Possession of a controlled drug - Class C	M	122	114	115	1	30	65	-	-	-	-	-	-	-	-	-	-	11	-	11	1	-	-	2	-	2	5
		F	11	10	10	-	2	6	-	-	-	-	-	-	-	-	-	-	1	-	1	-	-	-	-	-	-	1
		NS	1	1	1	-	-	1	-	-	-	-	-	-	-	-	-	-	-	-	-	-	-	-	-	-	-	-
		T	134	125	126	1	32	72	-	-	-	-	-	-	-	-	-	-	12	-	12	1	-	-	2	-	2	6
	Production, supply and possession with intent to supply a controlled drug - Class A	M	957	687	659	-	1	1	-	-	-	-	-	-	-	-	-	-	42	-	42	92	-	-	521	-	521	2
		F	48	26	21	-	-	-	-	-	-	-	-	-	-	-	-	-	5	-	5	8	-	-	8	-	8	-
		NS	7	-	-	-	-	-	-	-	-	-	-	-	-	-	-	-	-	-	-	-	-	-	-	-	-	-
		T	1,012	713	680	-	1	1	-	-	-	-	-	-	-	-	-	-	47	-	47	100	-	-	529	-	529	2
	Production, supply and possession with intent to supply a controlled drug - Class B	M	1,130	925	892	-	36	69	-	-	-	-	-	3	-	-	-	-	391	-	394	205	-	-	162	-	162	26
		F	65	43	44	-	6	2	-	-	-	-	-	-	-	-	-	-	22	-	22	6	-	-	7	-	7	1
		NS	4	1	1	-	-	-	-	-	-	-	-	-	-	-	-	-	1	-	1	-	-	-	-	-	-	-
		T	1,199	969	937	-	42	71	-	-	-	-	-	3	-	-	-	-	414	-	417	211	-	-	169	-	169	27
	Production, supply and possession with intent to supply a controlled drug - Class C	M	37	32	29	-	1	-	-	-	-	-	-	1	-	-	-	-	16	-	17	6	-	-	5	-	5	-
		F	4	1	1	-	-	-	-	-	-	-	-	-	-	-	-	-	1	-	1	-	-	-	-	-	-	-
		T	41	33	30	-	1	-	-	-	-	-	-	1	-	-	-	-	17	-	18	6	-	-	5	-	5	-

21.6d Persons aged 18 to under 21 convicted and sentenced at all courts

England and Wales, 2012

Number of persons

Offence group	Description		Total Proc Against	Total found Guilty	Total For Sent	Absl Disch	Condl Disch	Fine	CRO	SO	CPO	ACO	CPO&RO	Curf Order	Rep Order	APO	DTTO	REFO	Comm Order	YRO[1]	Total Comm Sentences	SS	Sec 90-92	DTO	YOI	Unsus Sent Impr	Imm cust	ODW
	Production, supply and possession with intent to supply a controlled drug - Class unspecified	M	-	11	11	-	-	-	-	-	-	-	-	-	-	-	-	-	-	-	-	1	-	-	10	-	10	-
		F	-	2	2	-	-	-	-	-	-	-	-	-	-	-	-	-	-	-	-	1	-	-	1	-	1	-
		T	-	13	13	-	-	-	-	-	-	-	-	-	-	-	-	-	-	-	-	2	-	-	11	-	11	-
	Sub-total	M	7,903	7,135	7,013	34	1,213	2,990	-	-	-	5	-	4	-	-	-	-	1,282	-	1,291	368	-	-	802	-	802	315
		F	348	270	260	1	69	70	-	-	-	-	-	1	-	-	-	-	62	-	63	21	-	-	23	-	23	13
		NS	33	22	21	-	4	9	-	-	-	-	-	-	-	-	-	-	5	-	5	-	-	-	1	-	1	2
		T	8,284	7,427	7,294	35	1,286	3,069	-	-	-	5	-	5	-	-	-	-	1,349	-	1,359	389	-	-	826	-	826	330
Indictable Motoring	99 Dangerous Driving	M	453	406	421	-	1	10	-	-	-	-	-	-	-	-	-	-	140	-	140	122	-	-	144	-	144	4
		F	18	13	13	-	-	-	-	-	-	-	-	-	-	-	-	-	9	-	9	4	-	-	-	-	-	-
		NS	2	1	-	-	-	-	-	-	-	-	-	-	-	-	-	-	-	-	-	-	-	-	-	-	-	-
		T	473	420	434	-	1	10	-	-	-	-	-	-	-	-	-	-	149	-	149	126	-	-	144	-	144	4
	99A Driving licence related offences: Making false statements	M	1	1	-	-	-	-	-	-	-	-	-	-	-	-	-	-	-	-	-	-	-	-	-	-	-	-
		T	1	1	-	-	-	-	-	-	-	-	-	-	-	-	-	-	-	-	-	-	-	-	-	-	-	-
	99C Vehicle insurance offences: Making false statements	M	20	14	14	-	-	8	-	-	-	-	-	-	-	-	-	-	6	-	6	-	-	-	-	-	-	-
		F	1	-	-	-	-	-	-	-	-	-	-	-	-	-	-	-	-	-	-	-	-	-	-	-	-	-
		T	21	14	14	-	-	8	-	-	-	-	-	-	-	-	-	-	6	-	6	-	-	-	-	-	-	-
	Sub-total	M	474	421	435	-	1	18	-	-	-	-	-	-	-	-	-	-	146	-	146	122	-	-	144	-	144	4
		F	19	13	13	-	-	-	-	-	-	-	-	-	-	-	-	-	9	-	9	4	-	-	-	-	-	-
		NS	2	1	-	-	-	-	-	-	-	-	-	-	-	-	-	-	-	-	-	-	-	-	-	-	-	-
		T	495	435	448	-	1	18	-	-	-	-	-	-	-	-	-	-	155	-	155	126	-	-	144	-	144	4
Other Indictable (Not Motoring)	33 Going Equipped for Stealing, etc.	M	238	168	168	-	17	28	-	-	-	-	-	-	-	-	-	-	72	-	72	11	-	-	36	-	36	4
		F	21	16	16	-	1	5	-	-	-	-	-	-	-	-	-	-	7	-	7	-	-	-	2	-	2	1
		NS	2	2	2	-	1	-	-	-	-	-	-	-	-	-	-	-	-	-	-	-	-	-	1	-	1	-
		T	261	186	186	-	19	33	-	-	-	-	-	-	-	-	-	-	79	-	79	11	-	-	39	-	39	5
	35 Blackmail	M	29	11	11	-	1	-	-	-	-	-	-	-	-	-	-	-	1	-	1	-	-	-	9	-	9	-
		F	3	-	-	-	-	-	-	-	-	-	-	-	-	-	-	-	-	-	-	-	-	-	-	-	-	-
		T	32	11	11	-	1	-	-	-	-	-	-	-	-	-	-	-	1	-	1	-	-	-	9	-	9	-
	36 Kidnapping, etc.	M	123	52	52	-	1	-	-	-	-	-	-	-	-	-	-	-	3	-	3	6	-	-	39	1	40	2
		F	13	4	4	-	-	-	-	-	-	-	-	-	-	-	-	-	-	-	-	1	-	-	3	-	3	-
		NS	2	-	-	-	-	-	-	-	-	-	-	-	-	-	-	-	-	-	-	-	-	-	-	-	-	-
		T	138	56	56	-	1	-	-	-	-	-	-	-	-	-	-	-	3	-	3	7	-	-	42	1	43	2
	64 Rioting	M	1	4	4	-	-	-	-	-	-	-	-	-	-	-	-	-	-	-	-	-	-	-	4	-	4	-
		T	1	4	4	-	-	-	-	-	-	-	-	-	-	-	-	-	-	-	-	-	-	-	4	-	4	-
	65 Violent Disorder	M	170	150	151	-	1	-	-	-	-	-	-	-	-	-	-	-	14	-	14	17	-	-	118	-	118	1
		F	3	2	2	-	-	-	-	-	-	-	-	-	-	-	-	-	1	-	1	-	-	-	1	-	1	-
		NS	2	-	-	-	-	-	-	-	-	-	-	-	-	-	-	-	-	-	-	-	-	-	-	-	-	-
		T	175	152	153	-	1	-	-	-	-	-	-	-	-	-	-	-	15	-	15	17	-	-	119	-	119	1
	66 Other Offence against the State or Public Order	M	919	976	982	6	39	47	1	-	-	1	-	1	-	-	-	-	257	-	260	254	-	-	293	1	294	82
		F	84	85	91	-	2	6	-	-	-	-	-	-	-	-	-	-	40	-	40	23	-	-	15	-	15	5
		NS	8	3	3	-	-	-	-	-	-	-	-	-	-	-	-	-	-	-	-	-	-	-	2	-	2	1
		T	1,011	1,064	1,076	6	41	53	1	-	-	1	-	1	-	-	-	-	297	-	300	277	-	-	310	1	311	88
	67 Perjury	M	3	1	1	-	-	1	-	-	-	-	-	-	-	-	-	-	-	-	-	-	-	-	-	-	-	-
		T	3	1	1	-	-	1	-	-	-	-	-	-	-	-	-	-	-	-	-	-	-	-	-	-	-	-
	78 Assist Entry of Illegal Immigrant	M	9	2	2	-	-	-	-	-	-	-	-	-	-	-	-	-	-	-	-	-	-	-	2	-	2	-
		F	6	5	4	-	-	-	-	-	-	-	-	-	-	-	-	-	1	-	1	-	-	-	3	-	3	-
		NS	1	1	1	-	-	-	-	-	-	-	-	-	-	-	-	-	-	-	-	-	-	-	1	-	1	-
		T	16	8	7	-	-	-	-	-	-	-	-	-	-	-	-	-	1	-	1	-	-	-	6	-	6	-
	79 Perverting the Course of Justice	M	239	102	102	-	1	-	-	-	-	-	-	-	-	-	-	-	22	-	22	32	-	-	46	-	46	1
		F	75	39	38	-	1	-	-	-	-	-	-	-	-	-	-	-	7	-	7	15	-	-	15	-	15	-
		NS	1	-	-	-	-	-	-	-	-	-	-	-	-	-	-	-	-	-	-	-	-	-	-	-	-	-
		T	315	141	140	-	2	-	-	-	-	-	-	-	-	-	-	-	29	-	29	47	-	-	61	-	61	1
	80 Absconding from Lawful Custody	M	62	37	37	-	1	-	-	-	-	-	-	-	-	-	-	-	3	-	3	2	-	-	29	-	29	2
		T	62	37	37	-	1	-	-	-	-	-	-	-	-	-	-	-	3	-	3	2	-	-	29	-	29	2
	81 Firearms Act Offence	M	180	147	148	-	22	10	-	-	-	-	-	-	-	-	-	-	43	-	43	25	1	-	44	-	45	3
		F	9	7	7	-	-	-	-	-	-	-	-	-	-	-	-	-	1	-	1	2	-	-	4	-	4	-
		T	189	154	155	-	22	10	-	-	-	-	-	-	-	-	-	-	44	-	44	27	1	-	48	-	49	3
	83 Failing to Surrender to Bail	M	2,441	1,522	1,551	30	125	720	-	-	-	-	-	-	-	-	-	-	188	-	188	19	-	-	112	-	112	357
		F	313	181	181	4	20	86	-	-	-	-	-	-	-	-	-	-	22	-	22	-	-	-	9	-	9	40
		NS	21	17	17	-	1	5	-	-	-	-	-	-	-	-	-	-	1	-	1	-	-	-	3	-	3	7
		T	2,775	1,720	1,749	34	146	811	-	-	-	-	-	-	-	-	-	-	211	-	211	19	-	-	124	-	124	404
	84 Trade Descriptions Act and Similar Offences	M	16	10	10	-	2	5	-	-	-	-	-	-	-	-	-	-	1	-	1	-	-	-	2	-	2	-
		NS	5	2	2	-	1	1	-	-	-	-	-	-	-	-	-	-	-	-	-	-	-	-	-	-	-	-
		T	21	12	12	-	3	6	-	-	-	-	-	-	-	-	-	-	1	-	1	-	-	-	2	-	2	-
	85 Health and Safety at Work etc. Act 1974	M	1	-	1	-	-	1	-	-	-	-	-	-	-	-	-	-	-	-	-	-	-	-	-	-	-	-
		T	1	-	1	-	-	1	-	-	-	-	-	-	-	-	-	-	-	-	-	-	-	-	-	-	-	-
	86 Possession of Obscene Material etc.	M	67	61	61	-	4	-	-	-	-	-	-	-	-	-	-	-	37	-	37	13	-	-	5	-	5	2
		F	1	1	1	-	-	-	-	-	-	-	-	-	-	-	-	-	-	-	-	1	-	-	-	-	-	-
		NS	1	1	-	-	-	-	-	-	-	-	-	-	-	-	-	-	-	-	-	-	-	-	-	-	-	-
		T	69	63	62	-	4	-	-	-	-	-	-	-	-	-	-	-	37	-	37	14	-	-	5	-	5	2
	91 Public Health	M	63	51	51	-	11	27	-	-	-	-	-	-	-	-	-	-	5	-	5	-	-	-	8	-	8	-
		F	12	10	10	-	3	5	-	-	-	-	-	-	-	-	-	-	-	-	-	-	-	-	1	-	1	1
		NS	10	8	8	-	2	4	-	-	-	-	-	-	-	-	-	-	-	-	-	-	-	-	-	-	-	2
		T	85	69	69	-	16	36	-	-	-	-	-	-	-	-	-	-	5	-	5	-	-	-	9	-	9	3
	94 Town and Country Planning Act 1990	F	1	-	-	-	-	-	-	-	-	-	-	-	-	-	-	-	-	-	-	-	-	-	-	-	-	-
		T	1	-	-	-	-	-	-	-	-	-	-	-	-	-	-	-	-	-	-	-	-	-	-	-	-	-
	95 Disclosure, obstruction, false or misleading statements	M	45	37	37	-	-	24	-	-	-	-	-	-	-	-	-	-	-	-	-	-	-	-	13	-	13	-
		F	2	-	-	-	-	-	-	-	-	-	-	-	-	-	-	-	-	-	-	-	-	-	-	-	-	-
		NS	12	10	10	-	-	5	-	-	-	-	-	-	-	-	-	-	-	-	-	-	-	-	5	-	5	-
		T	59	47	47	-	-	29	-	-	-	-	-	-	-	-	-	-	-	-	-	-	-	-	18	-	18	-
	99 Other (Excluding Motoring Offences)	M	462	454	440	4	18	108	-	-	-	-	-	-	-	-	-	-	23	-	23	44	-	-	96	-	96	147
		F	63	48	46	-	2	9	-	-	-	-	-	-	-	-	-	-	3	-	3	7	-	-	9	-	9	16
		NS	10	10	9	-	-	2	-	-	-	-	-	-	-	-	-	-	-	-	-	2	-	-	2	-	2	3
		T	535	512	495	4	20	119	-	-	-	-	-	-	-	-	-	-	26	-	26	53	-	-	107	-	107	166

21.6d Persons aged 18 to under 21 convicted and sentenced at all courts

England and Wales, 2012

Number of persons

Offence group	Description		Total Proc Against	Total found Guilty	Total For Sent	Absit Disch	Condl Disch	Fine	CRO	SO	CPO	ACO	CPO&RO	Curf Order	Rep Order	APO	DTTO	REFO	Comm Order	YRO [1]	Total Comm Sentences	SS	Sec 90-92	DTO	YOI	Unsus Sent Impr	Imm cust	ODW
	Sub-total	M	5,068	3,785	3,809	40	243	971	1	-	-	1	-	1	-	-	-	-	669	-	672	423	1	-	856	2	859	601
		F	606	398	400	4	29	111	-	-	-	-	-	-	-	-	-	-	82	-	82	49	-	-	62	-	62	63
		NS	75	54	52	-	5	17	-	-	-	-	-	-	-	-	-	-	1	-	1	2	-	-	14	-	14	13
		T	5,749	4,237	4,261	44	277	1,099	1	-	-	1	-	1	-	-	-	-	752	-	755	474	1	-	932	2	935	677
Indictable excluding motoring		M	38,198	30,949	30,521	118	3,817	5,852	2	-	1	19	-	24	-	-	-	-	8,259	-	8,305	3,173	8	-	7,655	111	7,774	1,482
		F	4,339	3,472	3,441	13	767	524	-	-	-	2	-	4	-	-	-	-	1,152	-	1,158	365	-	-	424	2	426	188
		NS	345	201	176	-	23	43	-	-	-	-	-	-	-	-	-	-	44	-	44	14	-	-	33	-	33	19
		T	42,882	34,622	34,138	131	4,607	6,419	2	-	1	21	-	28	-	-	-	-	9,455	-	9,507	3,552	8	-	8,112	113	8,233	1,689
Indictable motoring		M	474	421	435	-	1	18	-	-	-	-	-	-	-	-	-	-	146	-	146	122	-	-	144	-	144	4
		F	19	13	13	-	-	-	-	-	-	-	-	-	-	-	-	-	9	-	9	4	-	-	-	-	-	-
		NS	2	1	-	-	-	-	-	-	-	-	-	-	-	-	-	-	-	-	-	-	-	-	-	-	-	-
		T	495	435	448	-	1	18	-	-	-	-	-	-	-	-	-	-	155	-	155	126	-	-	144	-	144	4
Indictable including motoring		M	38,672	31,370	30,956	118	3,818	5,870	2	-	1	19	-	24	-	-	-	-	8,405	-	8,451	3,295	8	-	7,799	111	7,918	1,486
		F	4,358	3,485	3,454	13	767	524	-	-	-	2	-	4	-	-	-	-	1,161	-	1,167	369	-	-	424	2	426	188
		NS	347	202	176	-	23	43	-	-	-	-	-	-	-	-	-	-	44	-	44	14	-	-	33	-	33	19
		T	43,377	35,057	34,586	131	4,608	6,437	2	-	1	21	-	28	-	-	-	-	9,610	-	9,662	3,678	8	-	8,256	113	8,377	1,693
Summary Non-Motoring	104 On Constable	M	1,708	1,407	1,412	4	242	546	-	-	-	-	-	3	-	-	-	-	432	-	435	48	-	-	86	-	86	51
		F	480	416	414	2	81	120	-	-	-	-	-	-	-	-	-	-	162	-	162	17	-	-	17	-	17	15
		NS	10	7	6	-	1	3	-	-	-	-	-	-	-	-	-	-	1	-	1	1	-	-	-	-	-	-
		T	2,198	1,830	1,832	6	324	669	-	-	-	-	-	3	-	-	-	-	595	-	598	66	-	-	103	-	103	66
	105 Common, etc	M	6,655	4,740	4,756	10	687	556	-	-	-	3	-	5	-	-	-	-	2,291	-	2,299	481	-	-	562	-	562	161
		F	1,232	883	883	4	211	117	-	-	-	-	-	1	-	-	-	-	425	-	426	66	-	-	26	-	26	33
		NS	46	29	29	-	5	1	-	-	-	-	-	-	-	-	-	-	18	-	18	1	-	-	3	-	3	1
		T	7,933	5,652	5,668	14	903	674	-	-	-	3	-	6	-	-	-	-	2,734	-	2,743	548	-	-	591	-	591	195
	106 Betting or Gaming Offence	M	16	13	13	-	1	-	-	-	-	-	-	-	-	-	-	-	5	-	5	1	-	-	6	-	6	-
		F	2	2	2	-	1	-	-	-	-	-	-	-	-	-	-	-	-	-	-	-	-	-	1	-	1	-
		T	18	15	15	-	2	-	-	-	-	-	-	-	-	-	-	-	5	-	5	1	-	-	7	-	7	-
	108 Cruelty to Animal	M	69	51	51	-	6	8	-	-	-	-	-	-	-	-	-	-	20	-	20	4	-	-	13	-	13	-
		F	40	30	30	-	8	3	-	-	-	-	-	-	-	-	-	-	19	-	19	-	-	-	-	-	-	-
		NS	11	8	8	-	-	3	-	-	-	-	-	-	-	-	-	-	4	-	4	-	-	-	-	-	-	1
		T	120	89	89	-	14	14	-	-	-	-	-	-	-	-	-	-	43	-	43	4	-	-	13	-	13	1
	111 Offences Relating to Dogs	M	75	61	62	1	19	33	-	-	-	-	-	-	-	-	-	-	6	-	6	-	-	-	1	-	1	2
		F	20	15	15	-	4	10	-	-	-	-	-	-	-	-	-	-	-	-	-	-	-	-	-	-	-	1
		T	95	76	77	1	23	43	-	-	-	-	-	-	-	-	-	-	6	-	6	-	-	-	1	-	1	3
	112 Education Acts	M	9	6	6	-	3	3	-	-	-	-	-	-	-	-	-	-	-	-	-	-	-	-	-	-	-	-
		F	3	3	3	-	1	2	-	-	-	-	-	-	-	-	-	-	-	-	-	-	-	-	-	-	-	-
		NS	2	2	2	-	-	2	-	-	-	-	-	-	-	-	-	-	-	-	-	-	-	-	-	-	-	-
		T	14	11	11	-	4	7	-	-	-	-	-	-	-	-	-	-	-	-	-	-	-	-	-	-	-	-
	115 Firearms Acts	M	44	35	35	-	2	13	-	-	-	-	-	-	-	-	-	-	20	-	20	-	-	-	-	-	-	-
		F	2	2	2	-	-	1	-	-	-	-	-	-	-	-	-	-	1	-	1	-	-	-	-	-	-	-
		T	46	37	37	-	2	14	-	-	-	-	-	-	-	-	-	-	21	-	21	-	-	-	-	-	-	-
	116 Fishery Acts	M	168	161	161	1	2	158	-	-	-	-	-	-	-	-	-	-	-	-	-	-	-	-	-	-	-	-
		F	2	2	2	-	-	2	-	-	-	-	-	-	-	-	-	-	-	-	-	-	-	-	-	-	-	-
		NS	35	32	32	1	1	30	-	-	-	-	-	-	-	-	-	-	-	-	-	-	-	-	-	-	-	-
		T	205	195	195	2	3	190	-	-	-	-	-	-	-	-	-	-	-	-	-	-	-	-	-	-	-	-
	118 Night Poaching	M	8	7	7	-	2	5	-	-	-	-	-	-	-	-	-	-	-	-	-	-	-	-	-	-	-	-
		T	8	7	7	-	2	5	-	-	-	-	-	-	-	-	-	-	-	-	-	-	-	-	-	-	-	-
	119 Day Poaching	M	27	19	19	-	1	18	-	-	-	-	-	-	-	-	-	-	-	-	-	-	-	-	-	-	-	-
		T	27	19	19	-	1	18	-	-	-	-	-	-	-	-	-	-	-	-	-	-	-	-	-	-	-	-
	120 Unlawful Possession of Game, etc.	M	2	2	2	-	1	1	-	-	-	-	-	-	-	-	-	-	-	-	-	-	-	-	-	-	-	-
		T	2	2	2	-	1	1	-	-	-	-	-	-	-	-	-	-	-	-	-	-	-	-	-	-	-	-
	121 Other Offence against Game Law	M	7	4	4	-	-	4	-	-	-	-	-	-	-	-	-	-	-	-	-	-	-	-	-	-	-	-
		T	7	4	4	-	-	4	-	-	-	-	-	-	-	-	-	-	-	-	-	-	-	-	-	-	-	-
	122 Obstruction Other than by Vehicle	M	8	6	6	-	-	6	-	-	-	-	-	-	-	-	-	-	-	-	-	-	-	-	-	-	-	-
		F	1	-	-	-	-	-	-	-	-	-	-	-	-	-	-	-	-	-	-	-	-	-	-	-	-	-
		NS	1	1	1	-	-	1	-	-	-	-	-	-	-	-	-	-	-	-	-	-	-	-	-	-	-	-
		T	10	7	7	-	-	7	-	-	-	-	-	-	-	-	-	-	-	-	-	-	-	-	-	-	-	-
	123 Nuisance Other than by Vehicle	M	5	1	1	-	-	1	-	-	-	-	-	-	-	-	-	-	-	-	-	-	-	-	-	-	-	-
		F	1	1	1	-	-	1	-	-	-	-	-	-	-	-	-	-	-	-	-	-	-	-	-	-	-	-
		T	6	2	2	-	-	2	-	-	-	-	-	-	-	-	-	-	-	-	-	-	-	-	-	-	-	-
	125 Public Order Act 1986	M	3,903	3,114	3,116	14	780	1,222	-	-	-	4	-	3	-	-	-	-	775	-	782	122	-	-	119	-	119	77
		F	464	342	344	3	129	131	-	-	-	1	-	-	-	-	-	-	59	-	60	3	-	-	7	-	7	11
		NS	25	19	19	1	5	7	-	-	-	-	-	-	-	-	-	-	3	-	3	-	-	-	1	-	1	2
		T	4,392	3,475	3,479	18	914	1,360	-	-	-	5	-	3	-	-	-	-	837	-	845	125	-	-	127	-	127	90
	126 Interference with Motor Vehicles	M	222	161	156	1	31	22	-	-	-	-	-	-	-	-	-	-	71	-	71	9	-	-	14	-	14	8
		F	4	2	2	-	-	-	-	-	-	-	-	-	-	-	-	-	2	-	2	-	-	-	-	-	-	-
		T	226	163	158	1	31	22	-	-	-	-	-	-	-	-	-	-	73	-	73	9	-	-	14	-	14	8
	130 Unauthorised Taking of a Conveyance	M	685	546	551	-	52	84	-	-	-	-	-	-	-	-	-	-	312	-	312	32	-	-	66	-	66	5
		F	39	24	24	-	8	4	-	-	-	-	-	-	-	-	-	-	9	-	9	1	-	-	-	-	-	2
		NS	3	3	3	-	1	1	-	-	-	-	-	-	-	-	-	-	-	-	-	-	-	-	1	-	1	-
		T	727	573	578	-	61	89	-	-	-	-	-	-	-	-	-	-	321	-	321	33	-	-	67	-	67	7
	131 Summary Aggravated Vehicle Taking	M	513	465	469	1	17	17	-	-	-	-	-	-	-	-	-	-	304	-	304	50	-	-	67	-	67	13
		F	48	36	37	-	1	4	-	-	-	-	-	-	-	-	-	-	28	-	28	1	-	-	2	-	2	1
		NS	3	2	2	-	-	1	-	-	-	-	-	-	-	-	-	-	1	-	1	-	-	-	-	-	-	-
		T	564	503	508	1	18	22	-	-	-	-	-	-	-	-	-	-	333	-	333	51	-	-	69	-	69	14
	137 Pedal Cycle	M	128	103	103	3	20	73	-	-	-	-	-	-	-	-	-	-	2	-	2	-	-	-	-	-	-	5
		F	3	3	3	-	-	3	-	-	-	-	-	-	-	-	-	-	-	-	-	-	-	-	-	-	-	-
		T	131	106	106	3	20	76	-	-	-	-	-	-	-	-	-	-	2	-	2	-	-	-	-	-	-	5
	138 Offences involving impersonation	M	7	5	5	-	3	2	-	-	-	-	-	-	-	-	-	-	-	-	-	-	-	-	-	-	-	-
		F	1	1	1	-	-	1	-	-	-	-	-	-	-	-	-	-	-	-	-	-	-	-	-	-	-	-
		NS	1	-	-	-	-	-	-	-	-	-	-	-	-	-	-	-	-	-	-	-	-	-	-	-	-	-
		T	9	6	6	-	3	3	-	-	-	-	-	-	-	-	-	-	-	-	-	-	-	-	-	-	-	-
	140 Drunkenness, Simple	M	31	28	28	1	9	18	-	-	-	-	-	-	-	-	-	-	-	-	-	-	-	-	-	-	-	-
		F	2	2	2	-	1	1	-	-	-	-	-	-	-	-	-	-	-	-	-	-	-	-	-	-	-	-
		T	33	30	30	1	10	19	-	-	-	-	-	-	-	-	-	-	-	-	-	-	-	-	-	-	-	-

21.6d Persons aged 18 to under 21 convicted and sentenced at all courts

England and Wales, 2012

Number of persons

Offence group	Description		Total Proc Against	Total found Guilty	Total For Sent	Absl Disch	Condl Disch	Fine	CRO	SO	CPO	ACO	CPO&RO	Curf Order	Rep Order	APO	DTTO	REFO	Comm Order	YRO [1]	Total Comm Sentences	SS	Sec 90-92	DTO	YOI	Unsus Sent Impr	Imm cust	ODW
	141 Drunkenness, with Aggravation	M	1,676	1,534	1,534	26	479	1,000	-	-	-	-	-	-	-	-	-	-	4	-	4	-	-	-	-	-	-	25
		F	316	291	292	14	103	165	-	-	-	-	-	-	-	-	-	-	-	-	-	-	-	-	-	-	-	10
		NS	15	11	11	1	7	3	-	-	-	-	-	-	-	-	-	-	-	-	-	-	-	-	-	-	-	-
		T	2,007	1,836	1,837	41	589	1,168	-	-	-	-	-	-	-	-	-	-	4	-	4	-	-	-	-	-	-	35
	143 Other Offence against the Liquor Law	M	308	248	249	2	81	163	-	-	-	-	-	-	-	-	-	-	1	-	1	-	-	-	-	-	-	2
		F	19	11	11	1	3	7	-	-	-	-	-	-	-	-	-	-	-	-	-	-	-	-	-	-	-	-
		NS	1	-	-	-	-	-	-	-	-	-	-	-	-	-	-	-	-	-	-	-	-	-	-	-	-	-
		T	328	259	260	3	84	170	-	-	-	-	-	-	-	-	-	-	1	-	1	-	-	-	-	-	-	2
	144 Selling Tobacco to Juvenile	M	4	2	2	-	1	1	-	-	-	-	-	-	-	-	-	-	-	-	-	-	-	-	-	-	-	-
		T	4	2	2	-	1	1	-	-	-	-	-	-	-	-	-	-	-	-	-	-	-	-	-	-	-	-
	149 Summary Criminal or Malicious Damage Offence	M	4,527	3,792	3,789	14	1,216	674	-	-	-	5	-	3	-	-	-	-	1,291	-	1,299	84	-	-	132	-	132	370
		F	397	324	325	2	148	41	-	-	-	1	-	-	-	-	-	-	91	-	92	7	-	-	5	-	5	30
		NS	17	13	13	-	3	1	-	-	-	-	-	-	-	-	-	-	7	-	7	1	-	-	-	-	-	1
		T	4,941	4,129	4,127	16	1,367	716	-	-	-	6	-	3	-	-	-	-	1,389	-	1,398	92	-	-	137	-	137	401
	151 Social Security Offence	M	31	25	26	-	7	7	-	-	-	-	-	-	-	-	-	-	10	-	10	2	-	-	-	-	-	-
		F	35	29	29	-	9	12	-	-	-	-	-	-	-	-	-	-	8	-	8	-	-	-	-	-	-	-
		NS	10	10	10	-	1	5	-	-	-	-	-	-	-	-	-	-	4	-	4	-	-	-	-	-	-	-
		T	76	64	65	-	17	24	-	-	-	-	-	-	-	-	-	-	22	-	22	2	-	-	-	-	-	-
	155 Military Law - Air Force	M	16	9	9	-	2	6	-	-	-	-	-	-	-	-	-	-	-	-	-	1	-	-	-	-	-	-
		T	16	9	9	-	2	6	-	-	-	-	-	-	-	-	-	-	-	-	-	1	-	-	-	-	-	-
	160 Pedlars Act	M	24	22	22	-	-	22	-	-	-	-	-	-	-	-	-	-	-	-	-	-	-	-	-	-	-	-
		NS	1	1	1	-	-	1	-	-	-	-	-	-	-	-	-	-	-	-	-	-	-	-	-	-	-	-
		T	25	23	23	-	-	23	-	-	-	-	-	-	-	-	-	-	-	-	-	-	-	-	-	-	-	-
	162 Disorderly Behaviour	M	178	157	157	3	12	141	-	-	-	-	-	-	-	-	-	-	1	-	1	-	-	-	-	-	-	-
		F	10	10	10	-	-	10	-	-	-	-	-	-	-	-	-	-	-	-	-	-	-	-	-	-	-	-
		NS	3	1	1	-	-	1	-	-	-	-	-	-	-	-	-	-	-	-	-	-	-	-	-	-	-	-
		T	191	168	168	3	12	152	-	-	-	-	-	-	-	-	-	-	1	-	1	-	-	-	-	-	-	-
	163 Playing in Street	NS	1	-	-	-	-	-	-	-	-	-	-	-	-	-	-	-	-	-	-	-	-	-	-	-	-	-
		T	1	-	-	-	-	-	-	-	-	-	-	-	-	-	-	-	-	-	-	-	-	-	-	-	-	-
	164 Other Offence	M	12	7	7	-	2	4	-	-	-	-	-	-	-	-	-	-	1	-	1	-	-	-	-	-	-	-
		F	3	2	2	-	1	1	-	-	-	-	-	-	-	-	-	-	-	-	-	-	-	-	-	-	-	-
		NS	1	1	1	-	-	1	-	-	-	-	-	-	-	-	-	-	-	-	-	-	-	-	-	-	-	-
		T	16	10	10	-	3	6	-	-	-	-	-	-	-	-	-	-	1	-	1	-	-	-	-	-	-	-
	165 Kerb Crawling	M	7	5	5	-	2	-	-	-	-	-	-	-	-	-	-	-	-	-	-	-	-	-	1	-	1	2
		T	7	5	5	-	2	-	-	-	-	-	-	-	-	-	-	-	-	-	-	-	-	-	1	-	1	2
	166 Offence by Prostitute	F	25	22	22	-	4	11	-	-	-	-	-	-	-	-	-	-	-	-	-	-	-	-	-	-	-	7
		NS	1	-	-	-	-	-	-	-	-	-	-	-	-	-	-	-	-	-	-	-	-	-	-	-	-	-
		T	26	22	22	-	4	11	-	-	-	-	-	-	-	-	-	-	-	-	-	-	-	-	-	-	-	7
	167 Aiding, etc. Offence by Prostitute	M	9	6	6	-	-	6	-	-	-	-	-	-	-	-	-	-	-	-	-	-	-	-	-	-	-	-
		T	9	6	6	-	-	6	-	-	-	-	-	-	-	-	-	-	-	-	-	-	-	-	-	-	-	-
	168 Public Health Offence	M	305	250	250	-	3	247	-	-	-	-	-	-	-	-	-	-	-	-	-	-	-	-	-	-	-	-
		F	193	153	153	-	4	149	-	-	-	-	-	-	-	-	-	-	-	-	-	-	-	-	-	-	-	-
		NS	123	106	106	-	1	105	-	-	-	-	-	-	-	-	-	-	-	-	-	-	-	-	-	-	-	-
		T	621	509	509	-	8	501	-	-	-	-	-	-	-	-	-	-	-	-	-	-	-	-	-	-	-	-
	169 Railway Offence	M	9,053	7,373	7,373	24	93	7,180	-	-	-	-	-	-	-	-	-	-	44	-	44	-	-	-	2	-	2	30
		F	2,946	2,340	2,340	7	25	2,299	-	-	-	-	-	-	-	-	-	-	4	-	4	-	-	-	-	-	-	5
		NS	1,945	1,550	1,550	2	10	1,534	-	-	-	-	-	-	-	-	-	-	-	-	-	-	-	-	-	-	-	4
		T	13,944	11,263	11,263	33	128	11,013	-	-	-	-	-	-	-	-	-	-	48	-	48	-	-	-	2	-	2	39
	170 Motor Vehicle Licence	M	292	243	243	2	-	241	-	-	-	-	-	-	-	-	-	-	-	-	-	-	-	-	-	-	-	-
		F	95	79	79	-	-	79	-	-	-	-	-	-	-	-	-	-	-	-	-	-	-	-	-	-	-	-
		NS	100	85	85	1	2	82	-	-	-	-	-	-	-	-	-	-	-	-	-	-	-	-	-	-	-	-
		T	487	407	407	3	2	402	-	-	-	-	-	-	-	-	-	-	-	-	-	-	-	-	-	-	-	-
	172 Other Offence Against Revenue Law	M	2	1	1	-	-	1	-	-	-	-	-	-	-	-	-	-	-	-	-	-	-	-	-	-	-	-
		T	2	1	1	-	-	1	-	-	-	-	-	-	-	-	-	-	-	-	-	-	-	-	-	-	-	-
	173 Stage Carriage or Public Service Vehicle Offence	M	3,750	3,328	3,328	12	29	3,282	-	-	-	-	-	-	-	-	-	-	-	-	-	-	-	-	-	-	-	5
		F	2,124	1,904	1,904	5	21	1,874	-	-	-	-	-	-	-	-	-	-	-	-	-	-	-	-	-	-	-	4
		NS	219	188	188	1	-	187	-	-	-	-	-	-	-	-	-	-	-	-	-	-	-	-	-	-	-	-
		T	6,093	5,420	5,420	18	50	5,343	-	-	-	-	-	-	-	-	-	-	-	-	-	-	-	-	-	-	-	9
	175 Sexual Offences-Miscellaneous	M	1	-	-	-	-	-	-	-	-	-	-	-	-	-	-	-	-	-	-	-	-	-	-	-	-	-
		T	1	-	-	-	-	-	-	-	-	-	-	-	-	-	-	-	-	-	-	-	-	-	-	-	-	-
	180 Tram or Trolley Vehicle Offence	M	321	301	301	1	1	298	-	-	-	-	-	-	-	-	-	-	-	-	-	-	-	-	-	-	-	1
		F	167	151	151	-	-	151	-	-	-	-	-	-	-	-	-	-	-	-	-	-	-	-	-	-	-	-
		NS	19	19	19	-	-	19	-	-	-	-	-	-	-	-	-	-	-	-	-	-	-	-	-	-	-	-
		T	507	471	471	1	1	468	-	-	-	-	-	-	-	-	-	-	-	-	-	-	-	-	-	-	-	1
	182 Begging	M	18	13	13	4	2	4	-	-	-	-	-	-	-	-	-	-	-	-	-	-	-	-	-	-	-	3
		F	16	14	14	-	5	3	-	-	-	-	-	-	-	-	-	-	-	-	-	-	-	-	-	-	-	6
		NS	1	-	-	-	-	-	-	-	-	-	-	-	-	-	-	-	-	-	-	-	-	-	-	-	-	-
		T	35	27	27	4	7	7	-	-	-	-	-	-	-	-	-	-	-	-	-	-	-	-	-	-	-	9
	183 Sleeping Out	M	2	2	2	-	-	2	-	-	-	-	-	-	-	-	-	-	-	-	-	-	-	-	-	-	-	-
		T	2	2	2	-	-	2	-	-	-	-	-	-	-	-	-	-	-	-	-	-	-	-	-	-	-	-
	185 Found In Enclosed Premises	M	113	83	82	-	33	28	-	-	-	-	-	-	-	-	-	-	17	-	17	1	-	-	2	-	2	1
		F	3	2	2	-	1	-	-	-	-	-	-	-	-	-	-	-	1	-	1	-	-	-	-	-	-	-
		T	116	85	84	-	34	28	-	-	-	-	-	-	-	-	-	-	18	-	18	1	-	-	2	-	2	1
	190 Wild Birds Protection Acts	M	3	1	1	-	-	-	-	-	-	-	-	-	-	-	-	-	1	-	1	-	-	-	-	-	-	-
		T	3	1	1	-	-	-	-	-	-	-	-	-	-	-	-	-	1	-	1	-	-	-	-	-	-	-
	191 Wireless Telegraphy Acts	M	1,684	1,351	1,351	4	8	1,339	-	-	-	-	-	-	-	-	-	-	-	-	-	-	-	-	-	-	-	-
		F	4,296	3,557	3,557	4	19	3,534	-	-	-	-	-	-	-	-	-	-	-	-	-	-	-	-	-	-	-	-
		NS	11	6	6	-	-	6	-	-	-	-	-	-	-	-	-	-	-	-	-	-	-	-	-	-	-	-
		T	5,991	4,914	4,914	8	27	4,879	-	-	-	-	-	-	-	-	-	-	-	-	-	-	-	-	-	-	-	-
	193 Drug Offence	M	136	133	133	4	26	74	-	-	-	-	-	-	-	-	-	-	-	-	-	2	-	-	2	-	2	25
		F	19	18	18	-	5	7	-	-	-	-	-	-	-	-	-	-	-	-	-	-	-	-	-	-	-	6
		T	155	151	151	4	31	81	-	-	-	-	-	-	-	-	-	-	-	-	-	2	-	-	2	-	2	31
	194 Immigration Offence	M	-	2	2	-	-	-	-	-	-	-	-	-	-	-	-	-	-	-	-	-	-	-	2	-	2	-
		F	1	-	-	-	-	-	-	-	-	-	-	-	-	-	-	-	-	-	-	-	-	-	-	-	-	-
		T	1	2	2	-	-	-	-	-	-	-	-	-	-	-	-	-	-	-	-	-	-	-	2	-	2	-

21.6d Persons aged 18 to under 21 convicted and sentenced at all courts

England and Wales, 2012

Number of persons

Offence group	Description		Total Proc Against	Total found Guilty	Total For Sent	Absit Disch	Condl Disch	Fine	CRO	SO	CPO	ACO	CPO&RO	Curf Order	Rep Order	APO	DTTO	REFO	Comm Order	YRO (1)	Total Comm Sentences	SS	Sec 90-92	DTO	YOI	Unsus Sent Impr	Imm cust	ODW
	Other Summary Offence (Excluding Motoring)	M	1,898	1,473	1,471	4	90	737	-	-	-	1	-	-	-	-	-	-	201	-	202	47	-	-	293	-	293	98
		F	266	180	185	-	25	85	1	-	-	-	-	-	-	-	-	-	27	-	28	4	-	-	28	-	28	15
		NS	133	107	107	-	3	70	-	-	-	-	-	-	-	-	-	-	-	-	-	1	-	-	22	-	22	11
		T	2,297	1,760	1,763	4	118	892	1	-	-	1	-	-	-	-	-	-	228	-	230	52	-	-	343	-	343	124
	Sub-total	M	38,660	31,296	31,320	136	3,965	18,247	-	-	-	13	-	14	-	-	-	-	5,809	-	5,836	884	-	-	1,368	-	1,368	884
		F	13,275	10,851	10,859	42	818	8,828	1	-	-	2	-	1	-	-	-	-	836	-	840	99	-	-	86	-	86	146
		NS	2,738	2,201	2,200	7	40	2,064	-	-	-	-	-	-	-	-	-	-	38	-	38	4	-	-	27	-	27	20
		T	54,673	44,348	44,379	185	4,823	29,139	1	-	-	15	-	15	-	-	-	-	6,683	-	6,714	987	-	-	1,481	-	1,481	1,050
Summary Motoring	A Summary Motoring Offences	M	18,742	16,527	16,530	231	170	15,136	-	-	-	1	-	-	-	-	-	-	619	-	620	129	-	-	99	-	99	145
		F	3,086	2,790	2,788	46	17	2,642	-	-	-	-	-	-	-	-	-	-	71	-	71	3	-	-	-	-	-	9
		NS	506	379	379	2	2	370	-	-	-	-	-	-	-	-	-	-	1	-	1	1	-	-	2	-	2	1
		T	22,334	19,696	19,697	279	189	18,148	-	-	-	1	-	-	-	-	-	-	691	-	692	133	-	-	101	-	101	155
	Sub-total	M	18,742	16,527	16,530	231	170	15,136	-	-	-	1	-	-	-	-	-	-	619	-	620	129	-	-	99	-	99	145
		F	3,086	2,790	2,788	46	17	2,642	-	-	-	-	-	-	-	-	-	-	71	-	71	3	-	-	-	-	-	9
		NS	506	379	379	2	2	370	-	-	-	-	-	-	-	-	-	-	1	-	1	1	-	-	2	-	2	1
		T	22,334	19,696	19,697	279	189	18,148	-	-	-	1	-	-	-	-	-	-	691	-	692	133	-	-	101	-	101	155
Total Summary		M	57,402	47,823	47,850	367	4,135	33,383	-	-	-	14	-	14	-	-	-	-	6,428	-	6,456	1,013	-	-	1,467	-	1,467	1,029
		F	16,361	13,641	13,647	88	835	11,470	1	-	-	2	-	1	-	-	-	-	907	-	911	102	-	-	86	-	86	155
		NS	3,244	2,580	2,579	9	42	2,434	-	-	-	-	-	-	-	-	-	-	39	-	39	5	-	-	29	-	29	21
		T	77,007	64,044	64,076	464	5,012	47,287	1	-	-	16	-	15	-	-	-	-	7,374	-	7,406	1,120	-	-	1,582	-	1,582	1,205
All Offences		M	96,074	79,193	78,806	485	7,953	39,253	2	-	1	33	-	38	-	-	-	-	14,833	-	14,907	4,308	8	-	9,266	111	9,385	2,515
		F	20,719	17,126	17,101	101	1,602	11,994	1	-	-	4	-	5	-	-	-	-	2,068	-	2,078	471	-	-	510	2	512	343
		NS	3,591	2,782	2,755	9	65	2,477	-	-	-	-	-	-	-	-	-	-	83	-	83	19	-	-	62	-	62	40
		T	120,384	99,101	98,662	595	9,620	53,724	3	-	1	37	-	43	-	-	-	-	16,984	-	17,068	4,798	8	-	9,838	113	9,959	2,898

(1) The Youth Rehabilitation Order came into effect on 30 November 2009. Figures prior to 2010 are recorded as community orders.

21.6e Persons aged 21 or over convicted and sentenced at all courts

England and Wales, 2012

Number of persons

Offence group	Description		Total Proc Against	Total found Guilty	Total For Sent	Abslt Disch	Condl Disch	Fine	CRO	SO	CPO	ACO	CPO&RO	Curf Order	Rep Order	APO	DTTO	REFO	Comm Order	YRO [1]	Total Comm Sentences	SS	Sec 90-92	DTO	YOI	Unsus Sent Impr	Imm cust	ODW
Violence Against Person	1 Murder	M	390	270	270	-	-	-	-	-	-	-	-	-	-	-	-	-	-	-	-	-	-	-	-	270	270	-
		F	41	30	30	-	-	-	-	-	-	-	-	-	-	-	-	-	-	-	-	-	-	-	-	30	30	-
		NS	14	-	-	-	-	-	-	-	-	-	-	-	-	-	-	-	-	-	-	-	-	-	-	-	-	-
		T	445	300	300	-	-	-	-	-	-	-	-	-	-	-	-	-	-	-	-	-	-	-	-	300	300	-
	2 Attempted Murder	M	239	61	61	-	-	-	-	-	-	-	-	-	-	-	-	-	-	-	-	-	-	-	-	59	59	2
		F	23	3	3	-	-	-	-	-	-	-	-	-	-	-	-	-	-	-	-	-	-	-	-	2	2	1
		NS	1	-	-	-	-	-	-	-	-	-	-	-	-	-	-	-	-	-	-	-	-	-	-	-	-	-
		T	263	64	64	-	-	-	-	-	-	-	-	-	-	-	-	-	-	-	-	-	-	-	-	61	61	3
	3 Threat or Conspiracy to Murder	M	999	362	358	1	8	1	-	-	-	-	-	-	-	-	-	-	71	-	71	71	-	-	-	188	188	18
		F	63	35	31	-	2	-	-	-	-	-	-	-	-	-	-	-	6	-	6	7	-	-	-	14	14	2
		NS	7	1	-	-	-	-	-	-	-	-	-	-	-	-	-	-	-	-	-	-	-	-	-	-	-	-
		T	1,069	398	389	1	10	1	-	-	-	-	-	-	-	-	-	-	77	-	77	78	-	-	-	202	202	20
	4.1 Manslaughter	M	42	116	116	-	-	-	-	-	-	-	-	-	-	-	-	-	-	-	-	1	-	-	-	106	106	9
		F	8	15	15	-	-	-	-	-	-	-	-	-	-	-	-	-	-	-	-	1	-	-	-	14	14	-
		NS	2	-	-	-	-	-	-	-	-	-	-	-	-	-	-	-	-	-	-	-	-	-	-	-	-	-
		T	52	131	131	-	-	-	-	-	-	-	-	-	-	-	-	-	-	-	-	2	-	-	-	120	120	9
	4.2 Infanticide	F	-	1	1	-	-	-	-	-	-	-	-	-	-	-	-	-	-	-	-	-	-	-	-	-	-	1
		T	-	1	1	-	-	-	-	-	-	-	-	-	-	-	-	-	-	-	-	-	-	-	-	-	-	1
	4.4 Causing Death by Dangerous Driving	M	122	89	89	-	-	-	-	-	-	-	-	-	-	-	-	-	1	-	1	2	-	-	-	86	86	-
		F	14	8	8	-	-	-	-	-	-	-	-	-	-	-	-	-	-	-	-	1	-	-	-	7	7	-
		NS	1	-	-	-	-	-	-	-	-	-	-	-	-	-	-	-	-	-	-	-	-	-	-	-	-	-
		T	137	97	97	-	-	-	-	-	-	-	-	-	-	-	-	-	1	-	1	3	-	-	-	93	93	-
	4.5 Manslaughter Due to Diminished Responsibility	M	-	10	10	-	-	-	-	-	-	-	-	-	-	-	-	-	-	-	-	-	-	-	-	5	5	5
		F	-	3	3	-	-	-	-	-	-	-	-	-	-	-	-	-	-	-	-	-	-	-	-	1	1	2
		T	-	13	13	-	-	-	-	-	-	-	-	-	-	-	-	-	-	-	-	-	-	-	-	6	6	7
	4.6 Causing Death by Careless Driving when under the influence of Drink or Drugs	M	12	20	20	-	-	1	-	-	-	-	-	-	-	-	-	-	1	-	1	-	-	-	-	18	18	-
		F	1	1	1	-	-	-	-	-	-	-	-	-	-	-	-	-	-	-	-	-	-	-	-	1	1	-
		T	13	21	21	-	-	1	-	-	-	-	-	-	-	-	-	-	1	-	1	-	-	-	-	19	19	-
	4.7 Causing Death of a child or vulnerable person	M	-	-	-	-	-	-	-	-	-	-	-	-	-	-	-	-	-	-	-	-	-	-	-	-	-	-
		F	3	3	3	-	-	-	-	-	-	-	-	-	-	-	-	-	-	-	-	-	-	-	-	3	3	-
		T	3	3	3	-	-	-	-	-	-	-	-	-	-	-	-	-	-	-	-	-	-	-	-	3	3	-
	4.8 Causing Death by careless or inconsiderate driving	M	198	172	176	-	1	7	-	-	-	-	-	-	-	-	-	-	61	-	61	53	-	-	-	51	51	3
		F	34	30	29	-	-	1	-	-	-	-	-	-	-	-	-	-	17	-	17	7	-	-	-	4	4	-
		NS	4	1	1	-	-	-	-	-	-	-	-	-	-	-	-	-	1	-	1	-	-	-	-	-	-	-
		T	236	203	206	-	1	8	-	-	-	-	-	-	-	-	-	-	79	-	79	60	-	-	-	55	55	3
	4.9 Causing death by driving unlicensed, disqualified or uninsured drivers	M	11	9	10	-	-	1	-	-	-	-	-	-	-	-	-	-	4	-	4	3	-	-	-	2	2	-
		F	3	1	2	-	-	-	-	-	-	-	-	-	-	-	-	-	-	-	-	-	-	-	-	2	2	-
		T	14	10	12	-	-	1	-	-	-	-	-	-	-	-	-	-	4	-	4	3	-	-	-	4	4	-
	4.10 Applicable organisation causing death by gross breach of duty of care	O	-	1	1	-	-	1	-	-	-	-	-	-	-	-	-	-	-	-	-	-	-	-	-	-	-	-
		T	-	1	1	-	-	1	-	-	-	-	-	-	-	-	-	-	-	-	-	-	-	-	-	-	-	-
	4.12 Causing serious injury by dangerous driving	M	1	1	1	-	-	-	-	-	-	-	-	-	-	-	-	-	-	-	-	-	-	-	-	1	1	-
		T	1	1	1	-	-	-	-	-	-	-	-	-	-	-	-	-	-	-	-	-	-	-	-	1	1	-
	5 Wounding or other act Endangering Life	M	3,599	1,290	1,286	-	7	13	-	-	-	-	-	-	-	-	-	-	15	-	15	9	-	-	-	1,213	1,213	29
		F	450	94	95	1	1	1	-	-	-	-	-	-	-	-	-	-	3	-	3	2	-	-	-	84	84	3
		NS	29	-	-	-	-	-	-	-	-	-	-	-	-	-	-	-	-	-	-	-	-	-	-	-	-	-
		T	4,078	1,384	1,381	1	8	14	-	-	-	-	-	-	-	-	-	-	18	-	18	11	-	-	-	1,297	1,297	32
	6 Endangering Railway Passenger	M	10	11	11	-	-	2	-	-	-	-	-	-	-	-	-	-	4	-	4	3	-	-	-	2	2	-
		F	1	2	2	-	-	-	-	-	-	-	-	-	-	-	-	-	1	-	1	1	-	-	-	-	-	-
		NS	2	-	-	-	-	-	-	-	-	-	-	-	-	-	-	-	-	-	-	-	-	-	-	-	-	-
		T	13	13	13	-	-	2	-	-	-	-	-	-	-	-	-	-	5	-	5	4	-	-	-	2	2	-
	7 Endangering Life at Sea	M	9	5	3	-	1	2	-	-	-	-	-	-	-	-	-	-	-	-	-	-	-	-	-	-	-	-
		T	9	5	3	-	1	2	-	-	-	-	-	-	-	-	-	-	-	-	-	-	-	-	-	-	-	-
	8 Malicious Wounding etc.	M	28,242	22,562	22,388	44	928	1,774	3	-	-	-	-	19	-	-	-	-	5,283	-	5,305	5,181	-	-	-	8,594	8,594	562
		F	3,295	2,528	2,508	8	243	263	-	-	-	-	-	2	-	-	1	-	773	-	776	663	-	-	-	430	430	125
		NS	170	82	71	-	1	9	-	-	-	-	-	-	-	-	-	-	28	-	28	9	-	-	-	21	21	3
		T	31,707	25,172	24,967	52	1,172	2,046	3	-	-	-	-	21	-	-	1	-	6,084	-	6,109	5,853	-	-	-	9,045	9,045	690
	11 Cruelty to or Neglect of Children	M	323	222	216	-	11	2	-	-	-	-	-	-	-	-	-	-	48	-	48	82	-	-	-	71	71	2
		F	479	367	365	-	17	-	-	-	-	-	-	-	-	-	-	-	151	-	151	130	-	-	-	63	63	4
		NS	7	1	1	-	-	-	-	-	-	-	-	-	-	-	-	-	-	-	-	1	-	-	-	-	-	-
		T	809	590	582	-	28	2	-	-	-	-	-	-	-	-	-	-	199	-	199	213	-	-	-	134	134	6
	12 Abandoning Child aged under Two Years	M	2	-	-	-	-	-	-	-	-	-	-	-	-	-	-	-	-	-	-	-	-	-	-	-	-	-
		F	1	-	-	-	-	-	-	-	-	-	-	-	-	-	-	-	-	-	-	-	-	-	-	-	-	-
		T	3	-	-	-	-	-	-	-	-	-	-	-	-	-	-	-	-	-	-	-	-	-	-	-	-	-
	13 Child Abduction	M	98	62	60	-	3	1	-	-	-	-	-	-	-	-	-	-	10	-	10	10	-	-	-	36	36	-
		F	20	16	16	-	1	-	-	-	-	-	-	-	-	-	-	-	7	-	7	2	-	-	-	5	5	1
		NS	1	-	-	-	-	-	-	-	-	-	-	-	-	-	-	-	-	-	-	-	-	-	-	-	-	-
		T	119	78	76	-	4	1	-	-	-	-	-	-	-	-	-	-	17	-	17	12	-	-	-	41	41	1
	14 Procuring Illegal Abortion	M	2	-	-	-	-	-	-	-	-	-	-	-	-	-	-	-	-	-	-	-	-	-	-	-	-	-
		F	1	1	1	-	-	-	-	-	-	-	-	-	-	-	-	-	-	-	-	-	-	-	-	1	1	-
		T	3	1	1	-	-	-	-	-	-	-	-	-	-	-	-	-	-	-	-	-	-	-	-	1	1	-
	37.1 Causing Death by Aggravated Vehicle Taking	M	1	1	1	-	-	-	-	-	-	-	-	-	-	-	-	-	-	-	-	-	-	-	-	1	1	-
		T	1	1	1	-	-	-	-	-	-	-	-	-	-	-	-	-	-	-	-	-	-	-	-	1	1	-
	Sub-total	M	34,300	25,263	25,076	45	959	1,804	3	-	-	-	-	19	-	-	-	-	5,498	-	5,520	5,415	-	-	-	10,703	10,703	630
		F	4,437	3,138	3,113	9	264	265	-	-	-	-	-	2	-	-	1	-	958	-	961	814	-	-	-	661	661	139
		NS	238	85	73	-	1	9	-	-	-	-	-	-	-	-	-	-	29	-	29	10	-	-	-	21	21	3
		O	-	1	1	-	-	1	-	-	-	-	-	-	-	-	-	-	-	-	-	-	-	-	-	-	-	-
		T	38,975	28,487	28,263	54	1,224	2,079	3	-	-	-	-	21	-	-	1	-	6,485	-	6,510	6,239	-	-	-	11,385	11,385	772
Sexual Offences	16 Buggery	M	59	48	48	-	-	-	-	-	-	-	-	-	-	-	-	-	-	-	-	2	-	-	-	46	46	-
		NS	3	-	-	-	-	-	-	-	-	-	-	-	-	-	-	-	-	-	-	-	-	-	-	-	-	-
		T	62	48	48	-	-	-	-	-	-	-	-	-	-	-	-	-	-	-	-	2	-	-	-	46	46	-
	17 Sexual Assault on a Male	M	177	190	190	-	3	3	1	-	-	-	-	-	-	-	-	-	23	-	24	20	-	-	-	136	136	4
		F	9	4	4	-	-	-	1	-	-	-	-	-	-	-	-	-	-	-	1	1	-	-	-	2	2	-
		NS	3	-	-	-	-	-	-	-	-	-	-	-	-	-	-	-	-	-	-	-	-	-	-	-	-	-
		T	189	194	194	-	3	3	2	-	-	-	-	-	-	-	-	-	23	-	25	21	-	-	-	138	138	4
	19 Rape of a Female	M	2,126	874	874	-	-	-	-	-	-	-	-	-	-	-	-	-	6	-	6	1	-	-	-	858	858	9
		F	14	9	9	-	-	-	-	-	-	-	-	-	-	-	-	-	-	-	-	-	-	-	-	9	9	-
		NS	19	-	-	-	-	-	-	-	-	-	-	-	-	-	-	-	-	-	-	-	-	-	-	-	-	-
		T	2,159	883	883	-	-	-	-	-	-	-	-	-	-	-	-	-	6	-	6	1	-	-	-	867	867	9
	19 Rape of a Male	M	124	61	62	-	-	-	-	-	-	-	-	-	-	-	-	-	1	-	1	-	-	-	-	60	60	1
		F	1	-	-	-	-	-	-	-	-	-	-	-	-	-	-	-	-	-	-	-	-	-	-	-	-	-
		T	125	61	62	-	-	-	-	-	-	-	-	-	-	-	-	-	1	-	1	-	-	-	-	60	60	1
	20 Sexual Assault on a Female	M	3,014	1,798	1,796	2	33	38	2	-	-	-	1	1	-	-	-	-	492	-	496	226	-	-	-	954	954	47
		F	27	17	17	-	-	-	-	-	-	-	-	-	-	-	-	-	3	-	3	4	-	-	-	10	10	-
		NS	16	4	4	-	-	-	-	-	-	-	-	-	-	-	-	-	3	-	3	1	-	-	-	-	-	-
		T	3,057	1,819	1,817	2	33	38	2	-	-	-	1	1	-	-	-	-	498	-	502	231	-	-	-	964	964	47
	21 Sexual Activity with child under 13	M	326	155	149	-	1	-	-	-	-	-	-	-	-	-	-	-	26	-	26	12	-	-	-	109	109	1
		NS	2	-	-	-	-	-	-	-	-	-	-	-	-	-	-	-	-	-	-	-	-	-	-	-	-	-
		T	328	155	149	-	1	-	-	-	-	-	-	-	-	-	-	-	26	-	26	12	-	-	-	109	109	1
	22 Sexual Activity with child under 16	M	727	648	642	1	1	-	-	-	-	-	-	-	-	-	-	-	123	-	123	65	-	-	-	447	447	5
		NS	6	1	-	-	-	-	-	-	-	-	-	-	-	-	-	-	-	-	-	-	-	-	-	-	-	-
		T	733	649	642	1	1	-	-	-	-	-	-	-	-	-	-	-	123	-	123	65	-	-	-	447	447	5
	23 Familial Sexual Offences (Incest)	M	117	95	95	-	1	-	-	-	-	-	-	-	-	-	-	-	15	-	15	4	-	-	-	75	75	-
		F	3	2	2	-	-	-	-	-	-	-	-	-	-	-	-	-	1	-	1	1	-	-	-	-	-	-
		NS	2	-	-	-	-	-	-	-	-	-	-	-	-	-	-	-	-	-	-	-	-	-	-	-	-	-
		T	122	97	97	-	1	-	-	-	-	-	-	-	-	-	-	-	16	-	16	5	-	-	-	75	75	-
	24 Exploitation of Prostitution	M	16	25	26	-	-	1	-	-	-	-	-	-	-	-	-	-	1	-	1	9	-	-	-	15	15	-
		F	19	16	15	-	-	-	-	-	-	-	-	-	-	-	-	-	1	-	1	2	-	-	-	11	11	1
		T	35	41	41	-	-	1	-	-	-	-	-	-	-	-	-	-	2	-	2	11	-	-	-	26	26	1

21.6e Persons aged 21 or over convicted and sentenced at all courts

England and Wales, 2012

Number of persons

Offence group	Description		Total Proc Against	Total found Guilty	Total For Sent	Absit Disch	Condl Disch	Fine	CRO	SO	CPO	ACO	CPO&RO	Curf Order	Rep Order	APO	DTTO	REFO	Comm Order	YRO [1]	Total Comm Sentences	SS	Sec 90-92	DTO	YOI	Unsus Sent Impr	Imm cust	ODW
	70 Sexual activity etc. with a person with a mental disorder	M	37	26	25	-	-	-	-	-	-	-	-	-	-	-	-	-	2	-	2	1	-	-	-	22	22	-
		F	4	1	1	-	-	-	-	-	-	-	-	-	-	-	-	-	-	-	-	-	-	-	-	1	1	-
		T	41	27	26	-	-	-	-	-	-	-	-	-	-	-	-	-	2	-	2	1	-	-	-	23	23	-
	71 Abuse of children through prostitution and pornography	M	68	62	62	-	-	-	-	-	-	-	-	-	-	-	-	-	5	-	5	3	-	-	-	52	52	2
		F	6	2	2	-	-	-	-	-	-	-	-	-	-	-	-	-	-	-	-	-	-	-	-	2	2	-
		T	74	64	64	-	-	-	-	-	-	-	-	-	-	-	-	-	5	-	5	3	-	-	-	54	54	2
	72 Trafficking for sexual exploitation	M	11	6	6	-	-	-	-	-	-	-	-	-	-	-	-	-	-	-	-	-	-	-	-	6	6	-
		F	3	3	3	-	-	-	-	-	-	-	-	-	-	-	-	-	-	-	-	-	-	-	-	3	3	-
		T	14	9	9	-	-	-	-	-	-	-	-	-	-	-	-	-	-	-	-	-	-	-	-	9	9	-
	73 Abuse of trust- sexual offences	M	23	24	26	1	-	-	-	-	-	-	-	-	-	-	-	-	5	-	5	7	-	-	-	12	12	1
		F	5	6	6	-	-	-	-	-	-	-	-	-	-	-	-	-	1	-	1	2	-	-	-	3	3	-
		T	28	30	32	1	-	-	-	-	-	-	-	-	-	-	-	-	6	-	6	9	-	-	-	15	15	1
	74 Gross Indecency with Children	M	32	82	82	-	1	-	2	-	-	-	-	-	-	-	-	-	9	-	11	10	-	-	-	60	60	-
		F	1	2	2	-	-	-	-	-	-	-	-	-	-	-	-	-	-	-	-	1	-	-	-	1	1	-
		T	33	84	84	-	1	-	2	-	-	-	-	-	-	-	-	-	9	-	11	11	-	-	-	61	61	-
	88 Miscellaneous sexual offences	M	889	727	730	-	34	55	-	-	-	-	-	-	-	-	-	-	350	-	350	69	-	-	-	202	202	20
		F	3	-	-	-	-	-	-	-	-	-	-	-	-	-	-	-	-	-	-	-	-	-	-	-	-	-
		NS	6	6	6	-	-	1	-	-	-	-	-	-	-	-	-	-	4	-	4	-	-	-	-	1	1	-
		T	898	733	736	-	34	56	-	-	-	-	-	-	-	-	-	-	354	-	354	69	-	-	-	203	203	20
	Sub-total	M	7,746	4,821	4,813	4	74	97	5	-	-	-	1	1	-	-	-	-	1,058	-	1,065	429	-	-	-	3,054	3,054	90
		F	95	62	61	-	-	-	1	-	-	-	-	-	-	-	-	-	6	-	7	11	-	-	-	42	42	1
		NS	57	11	10	-	-	1	-	-	-	-	-	-	-	-	-	-	7	-	7	1	-	-	-	1	1	-
		T	7,898	4,894	4,884	4	74	98	6	-	-	-	1	1	-	-	-	-	1,071	-	1,079	441	-	-	-	3,097	3,097	91
Burglary	28 Burglary in a Dwelling	M	9,873	7,673	7,576	-	29	28	-	-	-	-	-	5	-	-	-	-	970	-	975	1,007	-	-	-	5,474	5,474	63
		F	732	479	468	-	7	2	-	-	-	-	-	-	-	-	-	-	116	-	116	104	-	-	-	229	229	10
		NS	76	27	9	-	1	-	-	-	-	-	-	-	-	-	-	-	3	-	3	-	-	-	-	5	5	-
		T	10,681	8,179	8,053	-	37	30	-	-	-	-	-	5	-	-	-	-	1,089	-	1,094	1,111	-	-	-	5,708	5,708	73
	29 Aggravated Burglary in a Dwelling	M	560	221	221	-	-	-	-	-	-	-	-	-	-	-	-	-	3	-	3	3	-	-	-	212	212	3
		F	35	9	9	-	-	-	-	-	-	-	-	-	-	-	-	-	-	-	-	-	-	-	-	9	9	-
		NS	7	-	-	-	-	-	-	-	-	-	-	-	-	-	-	-	-	-	-	-	-	-	-	-	-	-
		T	602	230	230	-	-	-	-	-	-	-	-	-	-	-	-	-	3	-	3	3	-	-	-	221	221	3
	30 Burglary in a Building Other than a Dwelling	M	7,992	6,593	6,515	1	168	177	-	-	-	-	-	2	-	-	-	-	1,896	-	1,898	923	-	-	-	3,141	3,141	207
		F	257	195	202	-	10	7	-	-	-	-	-	-	-	-	-	-	76	-	76	30	-	-	-	69	69	10
		NS	52	26	22	-	1	-	-	-	-	-	-	-	-	-	-	-	7	-	7	1	-	-	-	13	13	-
		T	8,301	6,814	6,739	1	179	184	-	-	-	-	-	2	-	-	-	-	1,979	-	1,981	954	-	-	-	3,223	3,223	217
	31 Aggravated Burglary in a Building not a Dwelling	M	28	14	14	-	-	-	-	-	-	-	-	-	-	-	-	-	-	-	-	-	-	-	-	14	14	-
		T	28	14	14	-	-	-	-	-	-	-	-	-	-	-	-	-	-	-	-	-	-	-	-	14	14	-
	Sub-total	M	18,453	14,501	14,326	1	197	205	-	-	-	-	-	7	-	-	-	-	2,869	-	2,876	1,933	-	-	-	8,841	8,841	273
		F	1,024	683	679	-	17	9	-	-	-	-	-	-	-	-	-	-	192	-	192	134	-	-	-	307	307	20
		NS	135	53	31	-	2	-	-	-	-	-	-	-	-	-	-	-	10	-	10	1	-	-	-	18	18	-
		T	19,612	15,237	15,036	1	216	214	-	-	-	-	-	7	-	-	-	-	3,071	-	3,078	2,068	-	-	-	9,166	9,166	293
Robbery	34 Robbery	M	4,439	3,070	3,076	-	2	-	-	-	-	-	-	-	-	-	-	-	72	-	72	225	-	-	-	2,744	2,744	33
		F	384	288	294	-	1	1	-	-	-	-	-	-	-	-	-	-	21	-	21	64	-	-	-	205	205	2
		NS	42	-	-	-	-	-	-	-	-	-	-	-	-	-	-	-	-	-	-	-	-	-	-	-	-	-
		T	4,865	3,358	3,370	-	3	1	-	-	-	-	-	-	-	-	-	-	93	-	93	289	-	-	-	2,949	2,949	35
	Sub-total	M	4,439	3,070	3,076	-	2	-	-	-	-	-	-	-	-	-	-	-	72	-	72	225	-	-	-	2,744	2,744	33
		F	384	288	294	-	1	1	-	-	-	-	-	-	-	-	-	-	21	-	21	64	-	-	-	205	205	2
		NS	42	-	-	-	-	-	-	-	-	-	-	-	-	-	-	-	-	-	-	-	-	-	-	-	-	-
		T	4,865	3,358	3,370	-	3	1	-	-	-	-	-	-	-	-	-	-	93	-	93	289	-	-	-	2,949	2,949	35
Theft and Handling	37.2 Aggravated Vehicle Taking	M	586	575	591	-	6	7	-	-	-	-	-	-	-	-	-	-	151	-	151	110	-	-	-	314	314	3
		F	34	32	33	-	1	2	-	-	-	-	-	-	-	-	-	-	18	-	18	6	-	-	-	6	6	-
		NS	2	1	1	-	-	-	-	-	-	-	-	-	-	-	-	-	1	-	1	-	-	-	-	-	-	-
		T	622	608	625	-	7	9	-	-	-	-	-	-	-	-	-	-	170	-	170	116	-	-	-	320	320	3
	38 Money laundering	M	1,646	967	946	-	45	53	-	-	-	-	-	-	-	-	-	-	189	-	189	250	-	-	-	396	396	13
		F	502	243	239	-	19	6	-	-	-	-	-	-	-	-	-	-	61	-	61	107	-	-	-	44	44	2
		NS	56	8	4	-	1	-	-	-	-	-	-	-	-	-	-	-	1	-	1	1	-	-	-	1	1	-
		T	2,204	1,218	1,189	-	65	59	-	-	-	-	-	-	-	-	-	-	251	-	251	358	-	-	-	441	441	15
	39 Theft from the Person of Another	M	3,603	3,310	3,322	6	294	274	-	-	-	-	-	3	-	-	-	-	805	-	808	369	-	-	-	1,487	1,487	84
		F	998	911	910	-	91	52	-	-	-	-	-	-	-	-	-	-	216	-	216	186	-	-	-	344	344	21
		NS	79	56	53	-	4	6	-	-	-	-	-	-	-	-	-	-	10	-	10	5	-	-	-	28	28	-
		T	4,680	4,277	4,285	6	389	332	-	-	-	-	-	3	-	-	-	-	1,031	-	1,034	560	-	-	-	1,859	1,859	105
	40 Theft in Dwelling not Automatic M/c or Meter	M	1,432	1,281	1,273	1	120	78	-	-	-	-	-	1	-	-	-	-	422	-	423	158	-	-	-	440	440	53
		F	353	299	305	1	43	25	-	-	-	-	-	-	-	-	-	-	90	-	90	62	-	-	-	68	68	16
		NS	11	4	2	-	-	-	-	-	-	-	-	-	-	-	-	-	1	-	1	1	-	-	-	-	-	-
		T	1,796	1,584	1,580	2	163	103	-	-	-	-	-	1	-	-	-	-	513	-	514	221	-	-	-	508	508	69
	41 Theft by an Employee	M	1,700	1,513	1,530	1	88	162	-	-	-	-	-	-	-	-	-	-	663	-	663	396	-	-	-	200	200	20
		F	602	529	543	2	34	33	-	-	-	-	-	-	-	-	-	-	222	-	222	175	-	-	-	70	70	7
		NS	26	20	16	-	2	1	-	-	-	-	-	-	-	-	-	-	6	-	6	5	-	-	-	2	2	-
		T	2,328	2,062	2,089	3	124	196	-	-	-	-	-	-	-	-	-	-	891	-	891	576	-	-	-	272	272	27
	42 Theft or Unauthorised Taking from Mail	M	99	108	112	-	2	9	-	-	-	-	-	-	-	-	-	-	43	-	43	37	-	-	-	21	21	-
		F	9	12	12	-	2	-	-	-	-	-	-	-	-	-	-	-	6	-	6	2	-	-	-	2	2	-
		NS	14	9	9	-	-	-	-	-	-	-	-	-	-	-	-	-	1	-	1	6	-	-	-	2	2	-
		T	122	129	133	-	4	9	-	-	-	-	-	-	-	-	-	-	50	-	50	45	-	-	-	25	25	-
	43 Abstracting Electricity	M	308	318	364	-	67	57	-	-	-	-	-	-	-	-	-	-	104	-	104	107	-	-	-	18	18	11
		F	106	96	97	-	27	14	-	-	-	-	-	-	-	-	-	-	41	-	41	11	-	-	-	3	3	1
		NS	2	1	1	-	-	-	-	-	-	-	-	-	-	-	-	-	-	-	-	-	-	-	-	1	1	-
		T	416	415	462	-	94	71	-	-	-	-	-	-	-	-	-	-	145	-	145	118	-	-	-	22	22	12
	44 Theft of Pedal Cycle	M	1,147	992	985	2	167	137	-	-	-	-	-	-	-	-	-	-	297	-	297	79	-	-	-	245	245	58
		F	32	21	21	-	2	5	-	-	-	-	-	-	-	-	-	-	11	-	11	2	-	-	-	1	1	-
		NS	18	15	14	-	-	-	-	-	-	-	-	-	-	-	-	-	6	-	6	2	-	-	-	5	5	1
		T	1,197	1,028	1,020	2	169	142	-	-	-	-	-	-	-	-	-	-	314	-	314	83	-	-	-	251	251	59
	45 Theft from Vehicle	M	3,523	2,939	2,890	4	303	242	-	-	-	-	-	1	-	-	-	-	958	-	959	265	-	-	-	949	949	168
		F	83	57	57	-	10	4	-	-	-	-	-	-	-	-	-	-	23	-	23	6	-	-	-	11	11	3
		NS	10	9	8	-	2	1	-	-	-	-	-	-	-	-	-	-	2	-	2	-	-	-	-	3	3	-
		T	3,616	3,005	2,955	4	315	247	-	-	-	-	-	1	-	-	-	-	983	-	984	271	-	-	-	963	963	171
	46 Theft from Shops	M	49,754	46,977	46,661	156	10,416	8,352	-	-	-	-	-	26	-	-	-	-	11,071	-	11,097	2,690	-	-	-	10,734	10,734	3,216
		F	17,067	15,917	15,833	39	4,986	2,422	-	-	-	-	-	7	-	-	-	-	4,371	-	4,378	953	-	-	-	2,251	2,251	804
		NS	388	364	360	1	69	47	-	-	-	-	-	-	-	-	-	-	76	-	76	36	-	-	-	109	109	22
		T	67,209	63,258	62,854	196	15,471	10,821	-	-	-	-	-	33	-	-	-	-	15,518	-	15,551	3,679	-	-	-	13,094	13,094	4,042
	47 Theft from Automatic Machine or Meter	M	269	269	272	-	24	27	-	-	-	-	-	-	-	-	-	-	67	-	67	27	-	-	-	116	116	11
		F	24	21	20	-	1	-	-	-	-	-	-	-	-	-	-	-	8	-	8	3	-	-	-	8	8	-
		NS	1	1	1	-	-	-	-	-	-	-	-	-	-	-	-	-	-	-	-	-	-	-	-	1	1	-
		T	294	291	293	-	25	27	-	-	-	-	-	-	-	-	-	-	75	-	75	30	-	-	-	125	125	11
	48 Theft or Unauthorised Taking of Motor Vehicle	M	798	571	569	1	30	17	-	-	-	-	-	-	-	-	-	-	162	-	162	70	-	-	-	278	278	11
		F	23	19	19	-	4	1	-	-	-	-	-	-	-	-	-	-	5	-	5	6	-	-	-	3	3	-
		NS	7	4	4	-	-	-	-	-	-	-	-	-	-	-	-	-	2	-	2	-	-	-	-	2	2	-
		T	828	594	592	1	34	18	-	-	-	-	-	-	-	-	-	-	169	-	169	76	-	-	-	283	283	11
	49 Other Theft or Unauthorised Taking	M	9,024	7,349	7,293	6	1,320	1,275	-	-	1	-	-	5	-	-	-	-	2,253	-	2,259	624	-	-	-	1,531	1,531	278
		F	1,204	940	935	4	239	132	-	-	-	-	-	2	-	-	-	-	277	-	279	93	-	-	-	145	145	43
		NS	69	47	44	-	5	7	-	-	-	-	-	1	-	-	-	-	11	-	12	3	-	-	-	15	15	2
		T	10,297	8,336	8,272	10	1,564	1,414	-	-	1	-	-	8	-	-	-	-	2,541	-	2,550	720	-	-	-	1,691	1,691	323
	54 Handling Stolen Goods	M	5,368	4,497	4,427	4	361	658	-	-	-	-	-	-	-	-	-	-	1,446	-	1,446	622	-	-	-	1,262	1,262	74
		F	789	655	642	-	119	92	-	-	-	-	-	-	-	-	-	-	253	-	253	96	-	-	-	73	73	9
		NS	41	22	18	-	-	2	-	-	-	-	-	-	-	-	-	-	6	-	6	2	-	-	-	8	8	-
		T	6,198	5,174	5,087	4	480	752	-	-	-	-	-	-	-	-	-	-	1,705	-	1,705	720	-	-	-	1,343	1,343	83
	Sub-total	M	79,257	71,666	71,235	181	13,243	11,348	-	-	1	-	-	36	-	-	-	-	18,631	-	18,668	5,804	-	-	-	17,991	17,991	4,000
		F	21,826	19,752	19,666	46	5,578	2,788	-	-	-	-	-	9	-	-	-	-	5,602	-	5,611	1,708	-	-	-	3,029	3,029	906
		NS	724	561	535	1	83	64	-	-	-	-	-	1	-	-	-	-	123	-	124	61	-	-	-	177	177	25
		T	101,807	91,979	91,436	228	18,904	14,200	-	-	1	-	-	46	-	-	-	-	24,356	-	24,403	7,573	-	-	-	21,197	21,197	4,931

21.6e Persons aged 21 or over convicted and sentenced at all courts

England and Wales, 2012

Number of persons

Offence group	Description		Total Proc Against	Total found Guilty	Total For Sent	Abslt Disch	Condl Disch	Fine	CRO	SO	CPO	ACO	CPO&RO	Curf Order	Rep Order	APO	DTTO	REFO	Comm Order	YRO (1)	Total Comm Sentences	SS	Sec 90-92	DTO	YOI	Unsus Sent Impr	Imm cust	ODW
Fraud and Forgery	51 Fraud by Company Director etc.	M	43	23	22	-	1	2	-	-	-	-	-	-	-	-	-	-	-	-	-	4	-	-	-	15	15	-
		F	10	2	2	-	-	-	-	-	-	-	-	-	-	-	-	-	-	-	-	1	-	-	-	1	1	-
		NS	1	-	-	-	-	-	-	-	-	-	-	-	-	-	-	-	-	-	-	-	-	-	-	-	-	-
		O	1	1	1	-	-	1	-	-	-	-	-	-	-	-	-	-	-	-	-	-	-	-	-	-	-	-
		T	55	26	25	-	1	3	-	-	-	-	-	-	-	-	-	-	-	-	-	5	-	-	-	16	16	-
	52 False Accounting	M	63	81	84	-	3	2	-	-	-	-	-	-	-	-	-	-	13	-	13	37	-	-	-	29	29	-
		F	39	35	35	-	-	-	-	-	-	-	-	-	-	-	-	-	9	-	9	17	-	-	-	9	9	-
		NS	2	1	-	-	-	-	-	-	-	-	-	-	-	-	-	-	-	-	-	-	-	-	-	-	-	-
		T	104	117	119	-	3	2	-	-	-	-	-	-	-	-	-	-	22	-	22	54	-	-	-	38	38	-
	53 Other Fraud	M	10,484	8,426	8,362	8	721	1,163	-	-	1	-	-	8	-	-	-	-	2,591	-	2,600	1,535	-	-	-	2,115	2,115	220
		F	4,803	3,776	3,764	10	506	341	1	-	-	-	-	5	-	-	-	-	1,270	-	1,276	1,109	-	-	-	461	461	61
		NS	844	430	366	-	51	63	-	-	-	-	-	-	-	-	-	-	150	-	150	83	-	-	-	18	18	1
		O	24	4	3	-	-	1	-	-	-	-	-	-	-	-	-	-	-	-	-	-	-	-	-	-	-	2
		T	16,155	12,636	12,495	18	1,278	1,568	1	-	1	-	-	13	-	-	-	-	4,011	-	4,026	2,727	-	-	-	2,594	2,594	284
	55 Bankruptcy Offence	M	112	112	113	-	5	7	-	-	-	-	-	-	-	-	-	-	25	-	25	48	-	-	-	28	28	-
		F	16	17	19	-	1	3	-	-	-	-	-	-	-	-	-	-	2	-	2	10	-	-	-	3	3	-
		NS	25	13	7	-	-	2	-	-	-	-	-	-	-	-	-	-	1	-	1	4	-	-	-	-	-	-
		T	153	142	139	-	6	12	-	-	-	-	-	-	-	-	-	-	28	-	28	62	-	-	-	31	31	-
	60 Forgery etc. of Drug Prescription	M	28	30	29	-	10	2	-	-	-	-	-	-	-	-	-	-	8	-	8	5	-	-	-	4	4	-
		F	8	11	13	-	7	-	1	-	-	-	-	-	-	-	-	-	2	-	3	3	-	-	-	-	-	-
		T	36	41	42	-	17	2	1	-	-	-	-	-	-	-	-	-	10	-	11	8	-	-	-	4	4	-
	61 Other Forgery etc.	M	1,583	1,401	1,392	2	26	67	-	-	-	-	-	-	-	-	-	-	124	-	124	210	-	-	-	951	951	12
		F	305	231	231	2	13	3	-	-	-	-	-	-	-	-	-	-	23	-	23	68	-	-	-	122	122	-
		NS	51	6	3	-	1	2	-	-	-	-	-	-	-	-	-	-	-	-	-	-	-	-	-	-	-	-
		O	4	2	2	-	-	2	-	-	-	-	-	-	-	-	-	-	-	-	-	-	-	-	-	-	-	-
		T	1,943	1,640	1,628	4	40	74	-	-	-	-	-	-	-	-	-	-	147	-	147	278	-	-	-	1,073	1,073	12
	814 Fraud, Forgery etc associated with Vehicle or Driver Records	M	405	293	286	1	12	213	-	-	-	-	-	-	-	-	-	-	34	-	34	15	-	-	-	8	8	3
		F	30	15	15	1	2	11	-	-	-	-	-	-	-	-	-	-	1	-	1	-	-	-	-	-	-	-
		NS	45	38	36	-	5	31	-	-	-	-	-	-	-	-	-	-	-	-	-	-	-	-	-	-	-	-
		O	20	8	8	-	1	7	-	-	-	-	-	-	-	-	-	-	-	-	-	-	-	-	-	-	-	-
		T	500	354	345	2	20	262	-	-	-	-	-	-	-	-	-	-	35	-	35	15	-	-	-	8	8	3
	Sub-total	M	12,718	10,366	10,288	11	778	1,456	-	-	1	-	-	8	-	-	-	-	2,795	-	2,804	1,854	-	-	-	3,150	3,150	235
		F	5,211	4,087	4,079	13	529	358	2	-	-	-	-	5	-	-	-	-	1,307	-	1,314	1,208	-	-	-	596	596	61
		NS	968	488	412	-	57	98	-	-	-	-	-	-	-	-	-	-	151	-	151	87	-	-	-	18	18	1
		O	49	15	14	-	1	11	-	-	-	-	-	-	-	-	-	-	-	-	-	-	-	-	-	-	-	2
		T	18,946	14,956	14,793	24	1,365	1,923	2	-	1	-	-	13	-	-	-	-	4,253	-	4,269	3,149	-	-	-	3,764	3,764	299
Criminal Damage	56 Arson	M	838	706	703	2	13	5	-	-	-	-	-	-	-	-	-	-	117	-	117	93	-	-	-	424	424	49
		F	210	180	180	-	10	-	-	-	-	-	-	-	-	-	-	-	48	-	48	26	-	-	-	78	78	18
		NS	8	-	-	-	-	-	-	-	-	-	-	-	-	-	-	-	-	-	-	-	-	-	-	-	-	-
		T	1,056	886	883	2	23	5	-	-	-	-	-	-	-	-	-	-	165	-	165	119	-	-	-	502	502	67
	57 Criminal Damage Endangering Life	M	111	66	66	1	7	8	-	-	-	-	-	-	-	-	-	-	19	-	19	12	-	-	-	17	17	2
		F	9	4	4	-	-	1	-	-	-	-	-	-	-	-	-	-	1	-	1	1	-	-	-	1	1	-
		NS	10	4	4	-	1	1	-	-	-	-	-	-	-	-	-	-	1	-	1	-	-	-	-	1	1	-
		T	130	74	74	1	8	10	-	-	-	-	-	-	-	-	-	-	21	-	21	13	-	-	-	19	19	2
	58 Other Criminal Damage	M	3,109	2,422	2,369	4	604	513	-	-	-	-	-	1	-	-	-	-	707	-	708	107	-	-	-	219	219	214
		F	344	252	246	1	101	31	-	-	-	-	-	-	-	-	-	-	65	-	65	7	-	-	-	7	7	34
		NS	21	15	14	-	4	3	-	-	-	-	-	-	-	-	-	-	4	-	4	1	-	-	-	1	1	1
		T	3,474	2,689	2,629	5	709	547	-	-	-	-	-	1	-	-	-	-	776	-	777	115	-	-	-	227	227	249
	59 Threat etc., to commit Criminal Damage	M	635	408	395	2	85	46	-	-	-	-	-	-	-	-	-	-	117	-	117	41	-	-	-	82	82	22
		F	52	33	33	-	12	3	-	-	-	-	-	-	-	-	-	-	14	-	14	3	-	-	-	1	1	-
		NS	3	1	1	-	-	-	-	-	-	-	-	-	-	-	-	-	1	-	1	-	-	-	-	-	-	-
		T	690	442	429	2	97	49	-	-	-	-	-	-	-	-	-	-	132	-	132	44	-	-	-	83	83	22
	Sub-total	M	4,693	3,602	3,533	9	709	572	-	-	-	-	-	1	-	-	-	-	960	-	961	253	-	-	-	742	742	287
		F	615	469	463	1	123	35	-	-	-	-	-	-	-	-	-	-	128	-	128	37	-	-	-	87	87	52
		NS	42	20	19	-	5	4	-	-	-	-	-	-	-	-	-	-	6	-	6	1	-	-	-	2	2	1
		T	5,350	4,091	4,015	10	837	611	-	-	-	-	-	1	-	-	-	-	1,094	-	1,095	291	-	-	-	831	831	340
Drug Offences	92.1 Unlawful importation - Class unspecified	M	11	22	22	-	-	-	-	-	-	-	-	-	-	-	-	-	3	-	3	3	-	-	-	16	16	-
		F	-	5	6	-	-	-	-	-	-	-	-	-	-	-	-	-	-	-	-	-	-	-	-	6	6	-
		T	11	27	28	-	-	-	-	-	-	-	-	-	-	-	-	-	3	-	3	3	-	-	-	22	22	-
	92.2 Unlawful exportation - Class unspecified	M	-	-	-	-	-	-	-	-	-	-	-	-	-	-	-	-	-	-	-	-	-	-	-	-	-	-
		F	-	-	-	-	-	-	-	-	-	-	-	-	-	-	-	-	-	-	-	-	-	-	-	-	-	-
		T	-	-	-	-	-	-	-	-	-	-	-	-	-	-	-	-	-	-	-	-	-	-	-	-	-	-
	92.3 Unlawful importation - Class A	M	312	278	277	-	-	-	-	-	-	-	-	-	-	-	-	-	1	-	1	1	-	-	-	273	273	2
		F	72	56	58	-	-	-	-	-	-	-	-	-	-	-	-	-	-	-	-	-	-	-	-	58	58	-
		NS	32	5	-	-	-	-	-	-	-	-	-	-	-	-	-	-	-	-	-	-	-	-	-	-	-	-
		T	416	339	335	-	-	-	-	-	-	-	-	-	-	-	-	-	1	-	1	1	-	-	-	331	331	2
	92.4 Unlawful importation - Class B	M	122	86	76	-	-	1	-	-	-	-	-	-	-	-	-	-	2	-	2	6	-	-	-	66	66	1
		F	29	19	18	-	-	-	-	-	-	-	-	-	-	-	-	-	-	-	-	4	-	-	-	13	13	1
		NS	10	4	-	-	-	-	-	-	-	-	-	-	-	-	-	-	-	-	-	-	-	-	-	-	-	-
		T	161	109	94	-	-	1	-	-	-	-	-	-	-	-	-	-	2	-	2	10	-	-	-	79	79	2
	92.5 Unlawful importation - Class C	M	20	15	14	-	-	-	-	-	-	-	-	-	-	-	-	-	5	-	5	1	-	-	-	8	8	-
		F	2	-	-	-	-	-	-	-	-	-	-	-	-	-	-	-	-	-	-	-	-	-	-	-	-	-
		NS	2	-	-	-	-	-	-	-	-	-	-	-	-	-	-	-	-	-	-	-	-	-	-	-	-	-
		T	24	15	14	-	-	-	-	-	-	-	-	-	-	-	-	-	5	-	5	1	-	-	-	8	8	-
	92.6 Unlawful exportation - Class A	M	2	8	7	-	-	-	-	-	-	-	-	-	-	-	-	-	-	-	-	-	-	-	-	7	7	-
		F	1	5	5	-	-	-	-	-	-	-	-	-	-	-	-	-	-	-	-	-	-	-	-	5	5	-
		T	3	13	12	-	-	-	-	-	-	-	-	-	-	-	-	-	-	-	-	-	-	-	-	12	12	-
	92.7 Unlawful exportation - Class B	M	2	18	19	-	-	-	-	-	-	-	-	-	-	-	-	-	1	-	1	-	-	-	-	18	18	-
		F	-	5	5	-	-	-	-	-	-	-	-	-	-	-	-	-	-	-	-	1	-	-	-	4	4	-
		T	2	23	24	-	-	-	-	-	-	-	-	-	-	-	-	-	1	-	1	1	-	-	-	22	22	-
	92.8 Unlawful exportation - Class C	M	1	1	1	-	-	-	-	-	-	-	-	-	-	-	-	-	-	-	-	1	-	-	-	-	-	-
		T	1	1	1	-	-	-	-	-	-	-	-	-	-	-	-	-	-	-	-	1	-	-	-	-	-	-
	Inciting another to supply a controlled drug - Class A	M	-	1	1	-	-	-	-	-	-	-	-	-	-	-	-	-	-	-	-	1	-	-	-	-	-	-
		T	-	1	1	-	-	-	-	-	-	-	-	-	-	-	-	-	-	-	-	1	-	-	-	-	-	-
	Other drug offences	M	374	380	379	1	33	83	-	-	-	-	-	-	-	-	-	-	120	-	120	84	-	-	-	48	48	10
		F	226	235	235	-	45	24	-	-	-	-	-	1	-	-	-	-	117	-	118	33	-	-	-	10	10	5
		NS	4	3	3	-	-	1	-	-	-	-	-	-	-	-	-	-	2	-	2	-	-	-	-	-	-	-
		T	604	618	617	1	78	108	-	-	-	-	-	1	-	-	-	-	239	-	240	117	-	-	-	58	58	15
	Possession of a controlled drug - Class A	M	8,189	7,873	7,802	13	964	4,214	-	-	-	-	-	1	-	-	-	-	1,436	-	1,437	222	-	-	-	483	483	469
		F	837	784	786	1	181	312	-	-	-	-	-	-	-	-	-	-	134	-	134	32	-	-	-	46	46	80
		NS	44	38	36	1	5	22	-	-	-	-	-	-	-	-	-	-	3	-	3	-	-	-	-	3	3	2
		T	9,070	8,695	8,624	15	1,150	4,548	-	-	-	-	-	1	-	-	-	-	1,573	-	1,574	254	-	-	-	532	532	551
	Possession of a controlled drug - Class B	M	20,016	19,299	19,192	91	4,098	11,025	-	-	-	-	-	10	-	-	-	-	2,321	-	2,331	236	-	-	-	456	456	955
		F	1,347	1,263	1,268	8	434	540	-	-	-	-	-	-	-	-	-	-	186	-	186	23	-	-	-	24	24	53
		NS	101	93	90	-	23	44	-	-	-	-	-	-	-	-	-	-	13	-	13	1	-	-	-	4	4	5
		T	21,464	20,655	20,550	99	4,555	11,609	-	-	-	-	-	10	-	-	-	-	2,520	-	2,530	260	-	-	-	484	484	1,013
	Possession of a controlled drug - Class C	M	996	914	907	11	312	408	-	-	-	-	-	2	-	-	-	-	103	-	105	16	-	-	-	22	22	33
		F	111	100	100	2	44	25	-	-	-	-	-	-	-	-	-	-	15	-	15	2	-	-	-	6	6	6
		NS	5	5	5	-	1	4	-	-	-	-	-	-	-	-	-	-	-	-	-	-	-	-	-	-	-	-
		T	1,112	1,019	1,012	13	357	437	-	-	-	-	-	2	-	-	-	-	118	-	120	18	-	-	-	28	28	39
	Possession of a controlled drug - Class unspecified	F	-	-	-	-	-	-	-	-	-	-	-	-	-	-	-	-	-	-	-	-	-	-	-	-	-	-
		T	-	-	-	-	-	-	-	-	-	-	-	-	-	-	-	-	-	-	-	-	-	-	-	-	-	-
	Production, supply and possession with intent to supply a controlled drug - Class A	M	5,151	4,043	4,036	1	6	7	-	-	-	-	-	-	-	-	-	-	262	-	262	394	-	-	-	3,348	3,348	18
		F	532	354	356	-	3	1	-	-	-	-	-	-	-	-	-	-	75	-	75	96	-	-	-	179	179	2
		NS	48	3	-	-	-	-	-	-	-	-	-	-	-	-	-	-	-	-	-	-	-	-	-	-	-	-
		T	5,731	4,400	4,392	1	9	8	-	-	-	-	-	-	-	-	-	-	337	-	337	490	-	-	-	3,527	3,527	20
	Production, supply and possession with intent to supply a controlled drug - Class B	M	10,275	9,038	8,911	1	396	860	-	-	-	-	-	8	-	-	-	-	2,563	-	2,571	2,344	-	-	-	2,573	2,573	166
		F	970	687	677	-	60	58	-	-	-	-	-	-	-	-	-	-	254	-	254	214	-	-	-	77	77	14
		NS	66	29	18	-	1	6	-	-	-	-	-	-	-	-	-	-	8	-	8	1	-	-	-	-	-	2
		T	11,311	9,754	9,606	1	457	924	-	-	-	-	-	8	-	-	-	-	2,825	-	2,833	2,559	-	-	-	2,650	2,650	182

21.6e Persons aged 21 or over convicted and sentenced at all courts

England and Wales, 2012

Number of persons

Offence group	Description		Total Proc Against	Total found Guilty	Total For Sent	Absit Disch	Condl Disch	Fine	CRO	SO	CPO	ACO	CPO&RO	Curf Order	Rep Order	APO	DTTO	REFO	Comm Order	YRO [1]	Total Comm Sentences	SS	Sec 90-92	DTO	YOI	Unsus Sent Impr	Imm cust	ODW
	Production, supply and possession with intent to supply a controlled drug - Class C	M	370	329	304	-	19	56	-	-	-	-	-	-	-	-	-	-	81	-	81	82	-	-	-	61	61	5
		F	50	42	40	-	4	2	-	-	-	-	-	-	-	-	-	-	15	-	15	13	-	-	-	5	5	1
		NS	3	2	1	-	-	-	-	-	-	-	-	-	-	-	-	-	1	-	1	-	-	-	-	-	-	-
		T	423	373	345	-	23	58	-	-	-	-	-	-	-	-	-	-	97	-	97	95	-	-	-	66	66	6
	Production, supply and possession with intent to supply a controlled drug - Class unspecified	M	-	254	254	-	-	-	-	-	-	-	-	-	-	-	-	-	11	-	11	13	-	-	-	229	229	1
		F	-	11	11	-	-	-	-	-	-	-	-	-	-	-	-	-	1	-	1	2	-	-	-	8	8	-
		T	-	265	265	-	-	-	-	-	-	-	-	-	-	-	-	-	12	-	12	15	-	-	-	237	237	1
	Sub-total	M	45,841	42,559	42,202	118	5,828	16,654	-	-	-	-	-	21	-	-	-	-	6,909	-	6,930	3,404	-	-	-	7,608	7,608	1,660
		F	4,177	3,566	3,565	11	771	962	-	-	-	-	-	1	-	-	-	-	797	-	798	420	-	-	-	441	441	162
		NS	315	182	153	1	30	77	-	-	-	-	-	-	-	-	-	-	27	-	27	2	-	-	-	7	7	9
		T	50,333	46,307	45,920	130	6,629	17,693	-	-	-	-	-	22	-	-	-	-	7,733	-	7,755	3,826	-	-	-	8,056	8,056	1,831
Indictable Motoring	99 Dangerous Driving	M	2,242	2,075	2,113	-	10	72	-	-	1	-	-	-	-	-	-	-	447	-	448	643	-	-	-	922	922	18
		F	142	137	138	-	3	20	-	-	-	-	-	-	-	-	-	-	35	-	35	62	-	-	-	18	18	-
		NS	17	8	4	-	-	2	-	-	-	-	-	-	-	-	-	-	2	-	2	-	-	-	-	-	-	-
		T	2,401	2,220	2,255	-	13	94	-	-	1	-	-	-	-	-	-	-	484	-	485	705	-	-	-	940	940	18
	99A Driving licence related offences: Making false statements	M	9	5	5	-	-	4	-	-	-	-	-	-	-	-	-	-	-	-	-	1	-	-	-	-	-	-
		F	1	2	2	-	1	-	-	-	-	-	-	-	-	-	-	-	-	-	-	-	-	-	-	1	1	-
		T	10	7	7	-	1	4	-	-	-	-	-	-	-	-	-	-	-	-	-	1	-	-	-	1	1	-
	99C Vehicle insurance offences: Making false statements	M	200	160	160	3	8	96	-	-	-	-	-	-	-	-	-	-	33	-	33	9	-	-	-	10	10	1
		F	21	18	18	-	1	12	-	-	-	-	-	-	-	-	-	-	3	-	3	2	-	-	-	-	-	-
		NS	1	1	1	-	-	-	-	-	-	-	-	-	-	-	-	-	1	-	1	-	-	-	-	-	-	-
		T	222	179	179	3	9	108	-	-	-	-	-	-	-	-	-	-	37	-	37	11	-	-	-	10	10	1
	99D Vehicle registration and excise licence offences: Making false statements	M	-	1	1	-	-	-	-	-	-	-	-	-	-	-	-	-	-	-	-	1	-	-	-	-	-	-
		T	-	1	1	-	-	-	-	-	-	-	-	-	-	-	-	-	-	-	-	1	-	-	-	-	-	-
	99F Work record or employment offences	M	-	1	1	-	-	-	-	-	-	-	-	-	-	-	-	-	1	-	1	-	-	-	-	-	-	-
		T	-	1	1	-	-	-	-	-	-	-	-	-	-	-	-	-	1	-	1	-	-	-	-	-	-	-
	Sub-total	M	2,451	2,242	2,280	3	18	172	-	-	1	-	-	-	-	-	-	-	481	-	482	654	-	-	-	932	932	19
		F	164	157	158	-	5	32	-	-	-	-	-	-	-	-	-	-	38	-	38	64	-	-	-	19	19	-
		NS	18	9	5	-	-	2	-	-	-	-	-	-	-	-	-	-	3	-	3	-	-	-	-	-	-	-
		T	2,633	2,408	2,443	3	23	206	-	-	1	-	-	-	-	-	-	-	522	-	523	718	-	-	-	951	951	19
Other Indictable (Not Motoring)	33 Going Equipped for Stealing, etc.	M	1,717	1,325	1,331	1	104	140	-	-	-	-	-	-	-	-	-	-	486	-	486	137	-	-	-	420	420	43
		F	179	131	132	-	12	23	-	-	-	-	-	-	-	-	-	-	48	-	48	9	-	-	-	32	32	8
		NS	21	14	14	-	-	1	-	-	-	-	-	-	-	-	-	-	6	-	6	3	-	-	-	3	3	1
		T	1,917	1,470	1,477	1	116	164	-	-	-	-	-	-	-	-	-	-	540	-	540	149	-	-	-	455	455	52
	35 Blackmail	M	225	120	120	-	-	-	-	-	-	-	-	-	-	-	-	-	2	-	2	11	-	-	-	106	106	1
		F	24	14	14	-	-	-	-	-	-	-	-	-	-	-	-	-	-	-	-	3	-	-	-	11	11	-
		NS	3	-	-	-	-	-	-	-	-	-	-	-	-	-	-	-	-	-	-	-	-	-	-	-	-	-
		T	252	134	134	-	-	-	-	-	-	-	-	-	-	-	-	-	2	-	2	14	-	-	-	117	117	1
	36 Kidnapping, etc.	M	673	246	246	-	-	-	-	-	-	-	-	-	-	-	-	-	14	-	14	26	-	-	-	201	201	5
		F	66	18	18	-	-	-	-	-	-	-	-	-	-	-	-	-	2	-	2	8	-	-	-	8	8	-
		NS	8	-	-	-	-	-	-	-	-	-	-	-	-	-	-	-	-	-	-	-	-	-	-	-	-	-
		T	747	264	264	-	-	-	-	-	-	-	-	-	-	-	-	-	16	-	16	34	-	-	-	209	209	5
	64 Rioting	M	17	14	14	-	-	-	-	-	-	-	-	-	-	-	-	-	-	-	-	-	-	-	-	14	14	-
		T	17	14	14	-	-	-	-	-	-	-	-	-	-	-	-	-	-	-	-	-	-	-	-	14	14	-
	65 Violent Disorder	M	242	252	262	1	2	2	-	-	-	-	-	-	-	-	-	-	10	-	10	45	-	-	-	199	199	3
		F	8	7	7	-	-	-	-	-	-	-	-	-	-	-	-	-	1	-	1	6	-	-	-	-	-	-
		NS	1	-	-	-	-	-	-	-	-	-	-	-	-	-	-	-	-	-	-	-	-	-	-	-	-	-
		T	251	259	269	1	2	2	-	-	-	-	-	-	-	-	-	-	11	-	11	51	-	-	-	199	199	3
	66 Other Offence against the State or Public Order	M	6,836	7,448	7,442	26	527	881	-	-	-	-	-	7	-	-	-	-	1,095	-	1,102	1,468	-	-	-	2,303	2,303	1,135
		F	469	431	466	5	33	50	-	-	-	-	-	2	-	-	-	-	131	-	133	102	-	-	-	84	84	59
		NS	61	38	35	-	3	4	-	-	-	-	-	-	-	-	-	-	3	-	3	3	-	-	-	11	11	11
		T	7,366	7,917	7,943	31	563	935	-	-	-	-	-	9	-	-	-	-	1,229	-	1,238	1,573	-	-	-	2,398	2,398	1,205
	67 Perjury	M	67	74	75	-	1	6	-	-	-	-	-	-	-	-	-	-	10	-	10	27	-	-	-	31	31	-
		F	23	21	21	-	1	2	-	-	-	-	-	-	-	-	-	-	4	-	4	8	-	-	-	6	6	-
		NS	2	1	-	-	-	-	-	-	-	-	-	-	-	-	-	-	-	-	-	-	-	-	-	-	-	-
		T	92	96	96	-	2	8	-	-	-	-	-	-	-	-	-	-	14	-	14	35	-	-	-	37	37	-
	75 Betting, Gaming and Lotteries	M	11	7	7	-	-	2	-	-	-	-	-	-	-	-	-	-	-	-	-	4	-	-	-	1	1	-
		T	11	7	7	-	-	2	-	-	-	-	-	-	-	-	-	-	-	-	-	4	-	-	-	1	1	-
	76 Aiding Suicide	M	1	-	-	-	-	-	-	-	-	-	-	-	-	-	-	-	-	-	-	-	-	-	-	-	-	-
		F	1	-	-	-	-	-	-	-	-	-	-	-	-	-	-	-	-	-	-	-	-	-	-	-	-	-
		T	2	-	-	-	-	-	-	-	-	-	-	-	-	-	-	-	-	-	-	-	-	-	-	-	-	-
	78 Assist Entry of Illegal Immigrant	M	314	242	242	-	-	2	-	-	-	-	-	-	-	-	-	-	5	-	5	27	-	-	-	206	206	2
		F	126	86	85	-	1	1	1	-	-	-	-	-	-	-	-	-	3	-	4	28	-	-	-	50	50	1
		NS	35	14	9	-	-	-	-	-	-	-	-	-	-	-	-	-	-	-	-	-	-	-	-	9	9	-
		T	475	342	336	-	1	3	1	-	-	-	-	-	-	-	-	-	8	-	9	55	-	-	-	265	265	3
	79 Perverting the Course of Justice	M	1,720	880	873	-	8	2	-	-	-	-	-	-	-	-	-	-	73	-	73	266	-	-	-	514	514	10
		F	451	251	250	-	4	-	-	-	-	-	-	1	-	-	-	-	33	-	34	135	-	-	-	74	74	3
		NS	29	-	-	-	-	-	-	-	-	-	-	-	-	-	-	-	-	-	-	-	-	-	-	-	-	-
		T	2,200	1,131	1,123	-	12	2	-	-	-	-	-	1	-	-	-	-	106	-	107	401	-	-	-	588	588	13
	80 Absconding from Lawful Custody	M	266	199	197	-	2	1	-	-	-	-	-	-	-	-	-	-	6	-	6	8	-	-	-	179	179	1
		F	4	4	4	-	-	-	-	-	-	-	-	-	-	-	-	-	-	-	-	2	-	-	-	2	2	-
		NS	4	-	-	-	-	-	-	-	-	-	-	-	-	-	-	-	-	-	-	-	-	-	-	-	-	-
		T	274	203	201	-	2	1	-	-	-	-	-	-	-	-	-	-	6	-	6	10	-	-	-	181	181	1
	81 Firearms Act Offence	M	1,130	1,044	1,045	3	101	142	-	-	-	-	-	-	-	-	-	-	259	-	259	156	-	-	-	372	372	12
		F	91	73	72	1	25	5	-	-	-	-	-	-	-	-	-	-	9	-	9	12	-	-	-	18	18	2
		NS	13	6	3	-	-	1	-	-	-	-	-	-	-	-	-	-	1	-	1	1	-	-	-	-	-	-
		O	1	-	-	-	-	-	-	-	-	-	-	-	-	-	-	-	-	-	-	-	-	-	-	-	-	-
		T	1,235	1,123	1,120	4	126	148	-	-	-	-	-	-	-	-	-	-	269	-	269	169	-	-	-	390	390	14
	82 Revenue Law Offence	M	48	34	37	-	-	-	-	-	-	-	-	-	-	-	-	-	4	-	4	15	-	-	-	18	18	-
		F	20	21	21	-	-	1	-	-	-	-	-	-	-	-	-	-	2	-	2	14	-	-	-	4	4	-
		NS	6	2	1	-	-	-	-	-	-	-	-	-	-	-	-	-	-	-	-	1	-	-	-	-	-	-
		T	74	57	59	-	-	1	-	-	-	-	-	-	-	-	-	-	6	-	6	30	-	-	-	22	22	-
	83 Failing to Surrender to Bail	M	15,664	9,289	9,377	161	630	4,245	-	-	-	-	-	3	-	-	-	-	733	-	736	158	-	-	-	1,052	1,052	2,395
		F	2,920	1,533	1,551	26	163	693	-	-	-	-	-	1	-	-	-	-	138	-	139	34	-	-	-	127	127	369
		NS	148	82	81	5	2	30	-	-	-	-	-	-	-	-	-	-	6	-	6	2	-	-	-	12	12	24
		T	18,732	10,904	11,009	192	795	4,968	-	-	-	-	-	4	-	-	-	-	877	-	881	194	-	-	-	1,191	1,191	2,788
	84 Trade Descriptions Act and Similar Offences	M	554	477	475	-	30	160	-	-	-	-	-	-	-	-	-	-	118	-	118	82	-	-	-	76	76	9
		F	102	73	77	-	13	22	-	-	-	-	-	-	-	-	-	-	18	-	18	12	-	-	-	8	8	4
		NS	132	78	68	-	4	43	-	-	-	-	-	-	-	-	-	-	16	-	16	3	-	-	-	1	1	1
		O	117	71	72	-	1	67	-	-	-	-	-	-	-	-	-	-	-	-	-	-	-	-	-	-	-	4
		T	905	699	692	-	48	292	-	-	-	-	-	-	-	-	-	-	152	-	152	97	-	-	-	85	85	18
	85 Health and Safety at Work etc. Act 1974	M	257	188	193	-	12	138	-	-	-	-	-	-	-	-	-	-	18	-	18	22	-	-	-	3	3	-
		F	34	18	20	-	-	17	-	-	-	-	-	-	-	-	-	-	2	-	2	1	-	-	-	-	-	-
		NS	70	39	36	-	2	29	-	-	-	-	-	-	-	-	-	-	4	-	4	1	-	-	-	-	-	-
		O	367	371	361	-	-	359	-	-	-	-	-	-	-	-	-	-	-	-	-	-	-	-	-	-	-	2
		T	728	616	610	-	14	543	-	-	-	-	-	-	-	-	-	-	24	-	24	24	-	-	-	3	3	2
	86 Possession of Obscene Material etc.	M	1,692	1,564	1,530	1	22	29	-	-	-	-	-	-	-	-	-	-	680	-	680	331	-	-	-	454	454	13
		F	9	13	13	-	1	3	-	-	-	-	-	-	-	-	-	-	1	-	1	3	-	-	-	5	5	-
		NS	12	4	2	-	-	1	-	-	-	-	-	-	-	-	-	-	-	-	-	-	-	-	-	1	1	-
		O	3	3	3	-	-	3	-	-	-	-	-	-	-	-	-	-	-	-	-	-	-	-	-	-	-	-
		T	1,716	1,584	1,548	1	23	36	-	-	-	-	-	-	-	-	-	-	681	-	681	334	-	-	-	460	460	13
	87 Protection from Eviction Act 1977.	M	30	16	16	-	2	7	-	-	-	-	-	-	-	-	-	-	2	-	2	2	-	-	-	3	3	-
		F	6	4	4	-	-	1	-	-	-	-	-	-	-	-	-	-	2	-	2	1	-	-	-	-	-	-
		NS	5	1	1	-	-	1	-	-	-	-	-	-	-	-	-	-	-	-	-	-	-	-	-	-	-	-
		O	1	1	-	-	-	-	-	-	-	-	-	-	-	-	-	-	-	-	-	-	-	-	-	-	-	-
		T	42	22	21	-	2	9	-	-	-	-	-	-	-	-	-	-	4	-	4	3	-	-	-	3	3	-

21.6e Persons aged 21 or over convicted and sentenced at all courts

England and Wales, 2012

Number of persons

Offence group	Description		Total Proc Against	Total found Guilty	Total For Sent	Abslt Disch	Condl Disch	Fine	CRO	SO	CPO	ACO	CPO&RO	Curf Order	Rep Order	APO	DTTO	REFO	Comm Order	YRO [1]	Total Comm Sentences	SS	Sec 90-92	DTO	YOI	Unsus Sent Impr	Imm cust	ODW
	89 Adulteration of Food	M	33	26	28	-	4	23	-	-	-	-	-	-	-	-	-	-	1	-	1	-	-	-	-	-	-	-
		F	3	1	1	-	-	1	-	-	-	-	-	-	-	-	-	-	-	-	-	-	-	-	-	-	-	-
		NS	6	6	5	-	-	3	-	-	-	-	-	-	-	-	-	-	-	-	-	-	-	-	-	-	-	2
		O	12	11	11	-	1	9	-	-	-	-	-	-	-	-	-	-	-	-	-	1	-	-	-	-	-	-
		T	54	44	45	-	5	36	-	-	-	-	-	-	-	-	-	-	1	-	1	1	-	-	-	-	-	2
	91 Public Health	M	1,255	938	936	2	140	696	-	-	-	-	-	-	-	-	-	-	50	-	50	17	-	-	-	18	18	13
		F	267	176	177	3	64	100	-	-	-	-	-	-	-	-	-	-	4	-	4	4	-	-	-	-	-	2
		NS	333	225	221	-	28	185	-	-	-	-	-	-	-	-	-	-	4	-	4	-	-	-	-	2	2	2
		O	297	200	201	2	3	193	-	-	-	-	-	-	-	-	-	-	1	-	1	1	-	-	-	-	-	1
		T	2,152	1,539	1,535	7	235	1,174	-	-	-	-	-	-	-	-	-	-	59	-	59	22	-	-	-	20	20	18
	94 Town and Country Planning Act 1990	M	479	263	274	-	40	228	-	-	-	-	-	-	-	-	-	-	2	-	2	-	-	-	-	-	-	4
		F	163	72	72	2	17	53	-	-	-	-	-	-	-	-	-	-	-	-	-	-	-	-	-	-	-	-
		NS	189	82	79	2	8	68	-	-	-	-	-	-	-	-	-	-	-	-	-	-	-	-	-	-	-	1
		O	80	35	34	-	1	32	-	-	-	-	-	-	-	-	-	-	-	-	-	-	-	-	-	-	-	1
		T	911	452	459	4	66	381	-	-	-	-	-	-	-	-	-	-	2	-	2	-	-	-	-	-	-	6
	95 Disclosure, obstruction, false or misleading statements	M	47	29	29	-	-	11	-	-	-	-	-	-	-	-	-	-	-	-	-	1	-	-	-	14	14	3
		F	4	3	3	-	-	3	-	-	-	-	-	-	-	-	-	-	-	-	-	-	-	-	-	-	-	-
		NS	5	4	3	-	-	2	-	-	-	-	-	-	-	-	-	-	-	-	-	-	-	-	-	1	1	-
		O	4	2	2	-	-	2	-	-	-	-	-	-	-	-	-	-	-	-	-	-	-	-	-	-	-	-
		T	60	38	37	-	-	18	-	-	-	-	-	-	-	-	-	-	-	-	-	1	-	-	-	15	15	3
	99 Other (Excluding Motoring Offences)	M	4,677	4,176	4,154	42	129	969	-	-	-	-	-	-	-	-	-	-	168	-	168	292	-	-	-	1,686	1,686	868
		F	878	782	781	10	31	165	-	-	-	-	-	-	-	-	-	-	36	-	36	118	-	-	-	245	245	176
		NS	197	102	89	1	1	56	-	-	-	-	-	-	-	-	-	-	2	-	2	2	-	-	-	16	16	11
		O	179	111	113	-	5	107	-	-	-	-	-	-	-	-	-	-	-	-	-	-	-	-	-	-	-	1
		T	5,931	5,171	5,137	53	166	1,297	-	-	-	-	-	-	-	-	-	-	206	-	206	412	-	-	-	1,947	1,947	1,056
	Sub-total	M	37,955	28,851	28,903	237	1,754	7,684	-	-	-	-	-	10	-	-	-	-	3,736	-	3,746	3,095	-	-	-	7,870	7,870	4,517
		F	5,848	3,732	3,789	47	365	1,140	1	-	-	-	-	4	-	-	-	-	434	-	439	500	-	-	-	674	674	624
		NS	1,280	698	647	8	48	424	-	-	-	-	-	-	-	-	-	-	42	-	42	16	-	-	-	56	56	53
		O	1,061	805	797	2	11	772	-	-	-	-	-	-	-	-	-	-	1	-	1	2	-	-	-	-	-	9
		T	46,144	34,086	34,136	294	2,178	10,020	1	-	-	-	-	14	-	-	-	-	4,213	-	4,228	3,613	-	-	-	8,600	8,600	5,203
	Indictable excluding motoring	M	245,402	204,699	203,452	606	23,544	39,820	8	-	2	-	1	103	-	-	-	-	42,528	-	42,642	22,412	-	-	-	62,703	62,703	11,725
		F	43,617	35,777	35,709	127	7,648	5,558	4	-	-	-	-	21	-	-	1	-	9,445	-	9,471	4,896	-	-	-	6,042	6,042	1,967
		NS	3,801	2,098	1,880	10	226	677	-	-	-	-	-	1	-	-	-	-	395	-	396	179	-	-	-	300	300	92
		O	1,110	821	812	2	12	784	-	-	-	-	-	-	-	-	-	-	1	-	1	2	-	-	-	-	-	11
		T	293,930	243,395	241,853	745	31,430	46,839	12	-	2	-	1	125	-	-	1	-	52,369	-	52,510	27,489	-	-	-	69,045	69,045	13,795
	Indictable motoring	M	2,451	2,242	2,280	3	18	172	-	-	1	-	-	-	-	-	-	-	481	-	482	654	-	-	-	932	932	19
		F	164	157	158	-	5	32	-	-	-	-	-	-	-	-	-	-	38	-	38	64	-	-	-	19	19	-
		NS	18	9	5	-	-	2	-	-	-	-	-	-	-	-	-	-	3	-	3	-	-	-	-	-	-	-
		T	2,633	2,408	2,443	3	23	206	-	-	1	-	-	-	-	-	-	-	522	-	523	718	-	-	-	951	951	19
	Indictable including motoring	M	247,853	206,941	205,732	609	23,562	39,992	8	-	3	-	1	103	-	-	-	-	43,009	-	43,124	23,066	-	-	-	63,635	63,635	11,744
		F	43,781	35,934	35,867	127	7,653	5,590	4	-	-	-	-	21	-	-	1	-	9,483	-	9,509	4,960	-	-	-	6,061	6,061	1,967
		NS	3,819	2,107	1,885	10	226	679	-	-	-	-	-	1	-	-	-	-	398	-	399	179	-	-	-	300	300	92
		O	1,110	821	812	2	12	784	-	-	-	-	-	-	-	-	-	-	1	-	1	2	-	-	-	-	-	11
		T	296,563	245,803	244,296	748	31,453	47,045	12	-	3	-	1	125	-	-	1	-	52,891	-	53,033	28,207	-	-	-	69,996	69,996	13,814
Summary Non-Motoring	101 Adulteration of Food, Drug, etc.	M	2	1	1	-	1	-	-	-	-	-	-	-	-	-	-	-	-	-	-	-	-	-	-	-	-	-
		O	1	-	-	-	-	-	-	-	-	-	-	-	-	-	-	-	-	-	-	-	-	-	-	-	-	-
		T	3	1	1	-	1	-	-	-	-	-	-	-	-	-	-	-	-	-	-	-	-	-	-	-	-	-
	104 On Constable	M	9,181	7,552	7,537	14	1,127	2,862	-	-	-	-	-	2	-	-	-	-	1,981	-	1,983	406	-	-	-	890	890	255
		F	2,621	2,237	2,229	10	473	639	-	-	-	-	-	-	-	-	-	-	722	-	722	123	-	-	-	175	175	87
		NS	58	43	43	1	6	14	-	-	-	-	-	-	-	-	-	-	6	-	6	3	-	-	-	7	7	6
		T	11,860	9,832	9,809	25	1,606	3,515	-	-	-	-	-	2	-	-	-	-	2,709	-	2,711	532	-	-	-	1,072	1,072	348
	105 Common, etc	M	52,487	34,926	35,018	31	4,671	5,032	-	-	1	-	-	13	-	-	-	-	14,199	-	14,213	4,158	-	-	-	5,919	5,919	994
		F	7,686	5,020	5,027	20	1,307	713	-	-	-	-	-	2	-	-	-	-	1,973	-	1,975	438	-	-	-	355	355	219
		NS	266	190	190	-	26	34	-	-	-	-	-	-	-	-	-	-	79	-	79	13	-	-	-	34	34	4
		T	60,439	40,136	40,235	51	6,004	5,779	-	-	1	-	-	15	-	-	-	-	16,251	-	16,267	4,609	-	-	-	6,308	6,308	1,217
	106 Betting or Gaming Offence	M	167	143	141	-	10	27	-	-	-	-	-	-	-	-	-	-	29	-	29	8	-	-	-	63	63	4
		F	7	5	5	-	1	2	-	-	-	-	-	-	-	-	-	-	1	-	1	-	-	-	-	1	1	-
		NS	4	4	4	-	1	1	-	-	-	-	-	-	-	-	-	-	1	-	1	-	-	-	-	1	1	-
		T	178	152	150	-	12	30	-	-	-	-	-	-	-	-	-	-	31	-	31	8	-	-	-	65	65	4
	107 Brothel Keeping	M	9	14	14	-	1	1	-	-	-	-	-	-	-	-	-	-	2	-	2	5	-	-	-	5	5	-
		F	11	22	22	-	4	1	-	-	-	-	-	-	-	-	-	-	6	-	6	7	-	-	-	3	3	1
		NS	1	-	-	-	-	-	-	-	-	-	-	-	-	-	-	-	-	-	-	-	-	-	-	-	-	-
		T	21	36	36	-	5	2	-	-	-	-	-	-	-	-	-	-	8	-	8	12	-	-	-	8	8	1
	108 Cruelty to Animal	M	1,036	772	769	2	131	135	-	-	-	-	-	1	-	-	-	-	303	-	304	99	-	-	-	88	88	10
		F	690	539	540	-	116	110	-	-	-	-	-	2	-	-	-	-	227	-	229	57	-	-	-	21	21	7
		NS	185	143	143	-	24	39	-	-	-	-	-	-	-	-	-	-	43	-	43	25	-	-	-	10	10	2
		O	3	1	1	-	-	1	-	-	-	-	-	-	-	-	-	-	-	-	-	-	-	-	-	-	-	-
		T	1,914	1,455	1,453	2	271	285	-	-	-	-	-	3	-	-	-	-	573	-	576	181	-	-	-	119	119	19
	110 Diseases of Animals Act	M	3	2	2	-	-	2	-	-	-	-	-	-	-	-	-	-	-	-	-	-	-	-	-	-	-	-
		NS	1	-	-	-	-	-	-	-	-	-	-	-	-	-	-	-	-	-	-	-	-	-	-	-	-	-
		O	1	1	1	-	-	1	-	-	-	-	-	-	-	-	-	-	-	-	-	-	-	-	-	-	-	-
		T	5	3	3	-	-	3	-	-	-	-	-	-	-	-	-	-	-	-	-	-	-	-	-	-	-	-
	111 Offences Relating to Dogs	M	774	610	613	6	128	401	-	-	-	-	-	-	-	-	-	-	38	-	38	3	-	-	-	10	10	27
		F	430	305	305	4	77	202	-	-	-	-	-	-	-	-	-	-	12	-	12	1	-	-	-	-	-	9
		NS	80	52	52	1	4	47	-	-	-	-	-	-	-	-	-	-	-	-	-	-	-	-	-	-	-	-
		T	1,284	967	970	11	209	650	-	-	-	-	-	-	-	-	-	-	50	-	50	4	-	-	-	10	10	36
	112 Education Acts	M	2,843	2,076	2,076	35	452	1,452	-	-	-	-	-	-	-	-	-	-	89	-	89	16	-	-	-	6	6	26
		F	8,014	6,583	6,583	73	1,643	4,319	-	-	-	-	-	1	-	-	-	-	387	-	388	70	-	-	-	14	14	76
		NS	2,116	1,559	1,559	24	342	1,131	-	-	-	-	-	-	-	-	-	-	39	-	39	5	-	-	-	-	-	18
		O	1	-	-	-	-	-	-	-	-	-	-	-	-	-	-	-	-	-	-	-	-	-	-	-	-	-
		T	12,974	10,218	10,218	132	2,437	6,902	-	-	-	-	-	1	-	-	-	-	515	-	516	91	-	-	-	20	20	120
	115 Firearms Acts	M	199	154	153	3	26	57	-	-	-	-	-	-	-	-	-	-	45	-	45	7	-	-	-	13	13	2
		F	2	1	1	-	-	1	-	-	-	-	-	-	-	-	-	-	-	-	-	-	-	-	-	-	-	-
		T	201	155	154	3	26	58	-	-	-	-	-	-	-	-	-	-	45	-	45	7	-	-	-	13	13	2
	116 Fishery Acts	M	1,968	1,857	1,857	22	53	1,774	-	-	-	-	-	-	-	-	-	-	5	-	5	-	-	-	-	-	-	3
		F	33	28	28	-	2	26	-	-	-	-	-	-	-	-	-	-	-	-	-	-	-	-	-	-	-	-
		NS	534	499	499	11	16	471	-	-	-	-	-	-	-	-	-	-	-	-	-	-	-	-	-	-	-	1
		O	1	1	1	-	-	1	-	-	-	-	-	-	-	-	-	-	-	-	-	-	-	-	-	-	-	-
		T	2,536	2,385	2,385	33	71	2,272	-	-	-	-	-	-	-	-	-	-	5	-	5	-	-	-	-	-	-	4
	117 Friendly Societies Acts	NS	1	1	1	-	-	1	-	-	-	-	-	-	-	-	-	-	-	-	-	-	-	-	-	-	-	-
		O	20	17	17	-	-	17	-	-	-	-	-	-	-	-	-	-	-	-	-	-	-	-	-	-	-	-
		T	21	18	18	-	-	18	-	-	-	-	-	-	-	-	-	-	-	-	-	-	-	-	-	-	-	-
	118 Night Poaching	M	40	27	27	-	4	23	-	-	-	-	-	-	-	-	-	-	-	-	-	-	-	-	-	-	-	-
		T	40	27	27	-	4	23	-	-	-	-	-	-	-	-	-	-	-	-	-	-	-	-	-	-	-	-
	119 Day Poaching	M	202	166	166	-	5	159	-	-	-	-	-	-	-	-	-	-	-	-	-	-	-	-	-	-	-	2
		F	1	-	-	-	-	-	-	-	-	-	-	-	-	-	-	-	-	-	-	-	-	-	-	-	-	-
		NS	2	2	2	-	-	2	-	-	-	-	-	-	-	-	-	-	-	-	-	-	-	-	-	-	-	-
		T	205	168	168	-	5	161	-	-	-	-	-	-	-	-	-	-	-	-	-	-	-	-	-	-	-	2
	120 Unlawful Possession of Game, etc.	M	7	7	7	-	1	5	-	-	-	-	-	-	-	-	-	-	-	-	-	-	-	-	-	-	-	1
		T	7	7	7	-	1	5	-	-	-	-	-	-	-	-	-	-	-	-	-	-	-	-	-	-	-	1
	121 Other Offence against Game Law	M	73	47	47	-	3	42	-	-	-	-	-	-	-	-	-	-	2	-	2	-	-	-	-	-	-	-
		F	4	1	1	-	-	1	-	-	-	-	-	-	-	-	-	-	-	-	-	-	-	-	-	-	-	-
		O	3	2	2	-	-	2	-	-	-	-	-	-	-	-	-	-	-	-	-	-	-	-	-	-	-	-
		T	80	50	50	-	3	45	-	-	-	-	-	-	-	-	-	-	2	-	2	-	-	-	-	-	-	-
	122 Obstruction Other than by Vehicle	M	104	63	63	3	9	50	-	-	-	-	-	-	-	-	-	-	-	-	-	1	-	-	-	-	-	-
		F	35	24	24	-	8	16	-	-	-	-	-	-	-	-	-	-	-	-	-	-	-	-	-	-	-	-
		NS	5	-	-	-	-	-	-	-	-	-	-	-	-	-	-	-	-	-	-	-	-	-	-	-	-	-
		O	9	5	5	-	1	4	-	-	-	-	-	-	-	-	-	-	-	-	-	-	-	-	-	-	-	-
		T	153	92	92	3	18	70	-	-	-	-	-	-	-	-	-	-	-	-	-	1	-	-	-	-	-	-

21.6e Persons aged 21 or over convicted and sentenced at all courts

England and Wales, 2012

Number of persons

Offence group	Description		Total Proc Against	Total found Guilty	Total For Sent	Absit Disch	Condl Disch	Fine	CRO	SO	CPO	ACO	CPO&RO	Curf Order	Rep Order	APO	DTTO	REFO	Comm Order	YRO [1]	Total Comm Sentences	SS	Sec 90-92	DTO	YOI	Unsus Sent Impr	Imm cust	ODW
	123 Nuisance Other than by Vehicle	M	21	18	18	-	4	13	-	-	-	-	-	-	-	-	-	-	1	-	1	-	-	-	-	-	-	-
		O	1	1	1	-	-	1	-	-	-	-	-	-	-	-	-	-	-	-	-	-	-	-	-	-	-	-
		T	22	19	19	-	4	14	-	-	-	-	-	-	-	-	-	-	1	-	1	-	-	-	-	-	-	-
	124 Other Highways Act Offence	M	17	13	13	1	-	12	-	-	-	-	-	-	-	-	-	-	-	-	-	-	-	-	-	-	-	-
		F	4	2	2	-	1	1	-	-	-	-	-	-	-	-	-	-	-	-	-	-	-	-	-	-	-	-
		NS	7	6	6	-	-	6	-	-	-	-	-	-	-	-	-	-	-	-	-	-	-	-	-	-	-	-
		O	75	56	56	1	1	54	-	-	-	-	-	-	-	-	-	-	-	-	-	-	-	-	-	-	-	-
		T	103	77	77	2	2	73	-	-	-	-	-	-	-	-	-	-	-	-	-	-	-	-	-	-	-	-
	125 Public Order Act 1986	M	21,819	17,025	17,093	65	3,802	7,785	-	-	-	-	-	1	-	-	-	-	2,938	-	2,939	718	-	-	-	1,112	1,112	672
		F	3,114	2,272	2,272	17	813	990	-	-	-	-	-	-	-	-	-	-	255	-	255	64	-	-	-	53	53	80
		NS	223	152	152	1	30	78	-	-	-	-	-	-	-	-	-	-	19	-	19	2	-	-	-	12	12	10
		O	8	-	-	-	-	-	-	-	-	-	-	-	-	-	-	-	-	-	-	-	-	-	-	-	-	-
		T	25,164	19,449	19,517	83	4,645	8,853	-	-	-	-	-	1	-	-	-	-	3,212	-	3,213	784	-	-	-	1,177	1,177	762
	126 Interference with Motor Vehicles	M	870	667	668	1	65	122	-	-	-	-	-	1	-	-	-	-	234	-	235	37	-	-	-	169	169	39
		F	21	12	13	-	2	4	-	-	-	-	-	-	-	-	-	-	5	-	5	-	-	-	-	1	1	1
		NS	4	3	3	-	-	1	-	-	-	-	-	-	-	-	-	-	-	-	-	1	-	-	-	-	-	1
		T	895	682	684	1	67	127	-	-	-	-	-	1	-	-	-	-	239	-	240	38	-	-	-	170	170	41
	130 Unauthorised Taking of a Conveyance	M	1,745	1,333	1,340	1	64	204	-	-	-	-	-	2	-	-	-	-	618	-	620	97	-	-	-	338	338	16
		F	97	62	63	-	7	17	-	-	-	-	-	-	-	-	-	-	29	-	29	3	-	-	-	6	6	1
		NS	7	5	5	-	-	1	-	-	-	-	-	-	-	-	-	-	3	-	3	1	-	-	-	-	-	-
		T	1,849	1,400	1,408	1	71	222	-	-	-	-	-	2	-	-	-	-	650	-	652	101	-	-	-	344	344	17
	131 Summary Aggravated Vehicle Taking	M	834	726	731	-	7	30	-	-	-	-	-	1	-	-	-	-	392	-	393	100	-	-	-	185	185	16
		F	93	82	83	-	4	11	-	-	-	-	-	-	-	-	-	-	54	-	54	3	-	-	-	11	11	-
		NS	2	2	2	-	-	1	-	-	-	-	-	-	-	-	-	-	1	-	1	-	-	-	-	-	-	-
		T	929	810	816	-	11	42	-	-	-	-	-	1	-	-	-	-	447	-	448	103	-	-	-	196	196	16
	135 Horsedrawn Vehicle	M	4	4	4	-	-	4	-	-	-	-	-	-	-	-	-	-	-	-	-	-	-	-	-	-	-	-
		T	4	4	4	-	-	4	-	-	-	-	-	-	-	-	-	-	-	-	-	-	-	-	-	-	-	-
	137 Pedal Cycle	M	538	463	463	16	58	364	-	-	-	-	-	-	-	-	-	-	9	-	9	1	-	-	-	1	1	14
		F	49	42	42	3	2	37	-	-	-	-	-	-	-	-	-	-	-	-	-	-	-	-	-	-	-	-
		NS	2	2	2	-	1	1	-	-	-	-	-	-	-	-	-	-	-	-	-	-	-	-	-	-	-	-
		T	589	507	507	19	61	402	-	-	-	-	-	-	-	-	-	-	9	-	9	1	-	-	-	1	1	14
	138 Offences involving impersonation	M	33	24	24	-	8	16	-	-	-	-	-	-	-	-	-	-	-	-	-	-	-	-	-	-	-	-
		F	13	9	9	-	-	9	-	-	-	-	-	-	-	-	-	-	-	-	-	-	-	-	-	-	-	-
		NS	3	3	3	-	-	2	-	-	-	-	-	-	-	-	-	-	-	-	-	-	-	-	-	-	-	1
		T	49	36	36	-	8	27	-	-	-	-	-	-	-	-	-	-	-	-	-	-	-	-	-	-	-	1
	139 Indecent Exposure	M	1	1	1	-	1	-	-	-	-	-	-	-	-	-	-	-	-	-	-	-	-	-	-	-	-	-
		T	1	1	1	-	1	-	-	-	-	-	-	-	-	-	-	-	-	-	-	-	-	-	-	-	-	-
	140 Drunkenness, Simple	M	682	609	608	10	141	407	-	-	-	-	-	-	-	-	-	-	2	-	2	-	-	-	-	-	-	48
		F	105	89	89	1	21	62	-	-	-	-	-	-	-	-	-	-	1	-	1	-	-	-	-	-	-	4
		NS	28	25	25	-	4	17	-	-	-	-	-	-	-	-	-	-	-	-	-	-	-	-	-	-	-	4
		T	815	723	722	11	166	486	-	-	-	-	-	-	-	-	-	-	3	-	3	-	-	-	-	-	-	56
	141 Drunkenness, with Aggravation	M	12,857	11,503	11,501	339	3,115	7,314	-	-	-	-	-	2	-	-	-	-	45	-	47	5	-	-	-	4	4	677
		F	2,190	1,952	1,953	58	703	1,052	-	-	-	-	-	-	-	-	-	-	43	-	43	5	-	-	-	6	6	86
		NS	91	85	84	1	24	43	-	-	-	-	-	-	-	-	-	-	-	-	-	-	-	-	-	-	-	16
		T	15,138	13,540	13,538	398	3,842	8,409	-	-	-	-	-	2	-	-	-	-	88	-	90	10	-	-	-	10	10	779
	142 Offence by Licenced Person, etc.	M	16	12	12	-	1	11	-	-	-	-	-	-	-	-	-	-	-	-	-	-	-	-	-	-	-	-
		F	2	2	2	-	-	2	-	-	-	-	-	-	-	-	-	-	-	-	-	-	-	-	-	-	-	-
		NS	5	4	4	-	-	4	-	-	-	-	-	-	-	-	-	-	-	-	-	-	-	-	-	-	-	-
		O	2	2	2	-	-	2	-	-	-	-	-	-	-	-	-	-	-	-	-	-	-	-	-	-	-	-
		T	25	20	20	-	1	19	-	-	-	-	-	-	-	-	-	-	-	-	-	-	-	-	-	-	-	-
	143 Other Offence against the Liquor Law	M	1,651	1,379	1,380	49	346	924	-	-	-	-	-	-	-	-	-	-	12	-	12	-	-	-	-	1	1	48
		F	188	155	155	11	42	96	-	-	-	-	-	-	-	-	-	-	1	-	1	-	-	-	-	-	-	5
		NS	113	94	94	1	15	77	-	-	-	-	-	-	-	-	-	-	-	-	-	-	-	-	-	-	-	1
		O	37	24	24	-	1	22	-	-	-	-	-	-	-	-	-	-	-	-	-	-	-	-	-	-	-	1
		T	1,989	1,652	1,653	61	404	1,119	-	-	-	-	-	-	-	-	-	-	13	-	13	-	-	-	-	1	1	55
	144 Selling Tobacco to Juvenile	M	60	53	53	-	6	47	-	-	-	-	-	-	-	-	-	-	-	-	-	-	-	-	-	-	-	-
		F	6	4	4	-	1	3	-	-	-	-	-	-	-	-	-	-	-	-	-	-	-	-	-	-	-	-
		NS	25	21	21	-	1	20	-	-	-	-	-	-	-	-	-	-	-	-	-	-	-	-	-	-	-	-
		O	19	13	13	-	1	12	-	-	-	-	-	-	-	-	-	-	-	-	-	-	-	-	-	-	-	-
		T	110	91	91	-	9	82	-	-	-	-	-	-	-	-	-	-	-	-	-	-	-	-	-	-	-	-
	146 Shops Act	M	3	3	3	-	1	1	-	-	-	-	-	-	-	-	-	-	-	-	-	-	-	-	-	1	1	-
		F	3	2	2	-	-	-	-	-	-	-	-	-	-	-	-	-	-	-	-	-	-	-	-	2	2	-
		NS	19	17	17	-	3	12	-	-	-	-	-	-	-	-	-	-	-	-	-	1	-	-	-	1	1	-
		O	8	8	8	-	-	8	-	-	-	-	-	-	-	-	-	-	-	-	-	-	-	-	-	-	-	-
		T	33	30	30	-	4	21	-	-	-	-	-	-	-	-	-	-	-	-	-	1	-	-	-	4	4	-
	148 Other Offence against the Labour Law	M	2	2	2	-	-	2	-	-	-	-	-	-	-	-	-	-	-	-	-	-	-	-	-	-	-	-
		NS	1	1	1	-	-	1	-	-	-	-	-	-	-	-	-	-	-	-	-	-	-	-	-	-	-	-
		T	3	3	3	-	-	3	-	-	-	-	-	-	-	-	-	-	-	-	-	-	-	-	-	-	-	-
	149 Summary Criminal or Malicious Damage Offence	M	20,875	17,320	17,322	53	5,308	4,083	-	-	-	-	-	7	-	-	-	-	4,687	-	4,694	399	-	-	-	1,097	1,097	1,688
		F	2,161	1,690	1,690	11	798	237	-	-	-	-	-	-	-	-	-	-	361	-	361	25	-	-	-	66	66	192
		NS	126	98	96	1	26	21	-	-	-	-	-	-	-	-	-	-	26	-	26	2	-	-	-	9	9	11
		T	23,162	19,108	19,108	65	6,132	4,341	-	-	-	-	-	7	-	-	-	-	5,074	-	5,081	426	-	-	-	1,172	1,172	1,891
	150 Merchant Shipping Acts	M	4	4	4	-	1	3	-	-	-	-	-	-	-	-	-	-	-	-	-	-	-	-	-	-	-	-
		NS	1	1	1	-	-	1	-	-	-	-	-	-	-	-	-	-	-	-	-	-	-	-	-	-	-	-
		T	5	5	5	-	1	4	-	-	-	-	-	-	-	-	-	-	-	-	-	-	-	-	-	-	-	-
	151 Social Security Offence	M	3,409	3,027	3,028	11	645	840	-	-	-	-	-	5	-	-	-	-	1,341	-	1,346	135	-	-	-	34	34	17
		F	3,787	3,378	3,392	9	973	743	-	-	-	-	-	3	-	-	-	-	1,449	-	1,452	187	-	-	-	20	20	8
		NS	1,238	1,061	1,045	5	264	285	-	-	-	-	-	-	-	-	-	-	441	-	441	43	-	-	-	3	3	4
		O	4	3	3	-	-	3	-	-	-	-	-	-	-	-	-	-	-	-	-	-	-	-	-	-	-	-
		T	8,438	7,469	7,468	25	1,882	1,871	-	-	-	-	-	8	-	-	-	-	3,231	-	3,239	365	-	-	-	57	57	29
	155 Military Law - Air Force	M	27	25	25	-	3	21	-	-	-	-	-	-	-	-	-	-	1	-	1	-	-	-	-	-	-	-
		F	4	4	4	-	-	3	-	-	-	-	-	-	-	-	-	-	-	-	-	-	-	-	-	-	-	1
		NS	1	1	1	-	-	1	-	-	-	-	-	-	-	-	-	-	-	-	-	-	-	-	-	-	-	-
		O	2	2	2	-	-	2	-	-	-	-	-	-	-	-	-	-	-	-	-	-	-	-	-	-	-	-
		T	34	32	32	-	3	27	-	-	-	-	-	-	-	-	-	-	1	-	1	-	-	-	-	-	-	1
	156 Park, Common or Other Open Space Offence	M	2	2	2	-	1	1	-	-	-	-	-	-	-	-	-	-	-	-	-	-	-	-	-	-	-	-
		T	2	2	2	-	1	1	-	-	-	-	-	-	-	-	-	-	-	-	-	-	-	-	-	-	-	-
	158 Reporting Restrictions	NS	1	1	1	-	-	1	-	-	-	-	-	-	-	-	-	-	-	-	-	-	-	-	-	-	-	-
		T	1	1	1	-	-	1	-	-	-	-	-	-	-	-	-	-	-	-	-	-	-	-	-	-	-	-
	160 Pedlars Act	M	109	99	99	2	6	91	-	-	-	-	-	-	-	-	-	-	-	-	-	-	-	-	-	-	-	-
		F	5	4	4	-	2	2	-	-	-	-	-	-	-	-	-	-	-	-	-	-	-	-	-	-	-	-
		NS	2	2	2	-	-	2	-	-	-	-	-	-	-	-	-	-	-	-	-	-	-	-	-	-	-	-
		T	116	105	105	2	8	95	-	-	-	-	-	-	-	-	-	-	-	-	-	-	-	-	-	-	-	-
	161 Certain Local regulations - Allowing Chimney to be on Fire	NS	1	1	1	-	-	1	-	-	-	-	-	-	-	-	-	-	-	-	-	-	-	-	-	-	-	-
		T	1	1	1	-	-	1	-	-	-	-	-	-	-	-	-	-	-	-	-	-	-	-	-	-	-	-
	162 Disorderly Behaviour	M	886	748	747	12	39	677	-	-	-	-	-	-	-	-	-	-	4	-	4	2	-	-	-	5	5	8
		F	42	35	35	3	6	25	-	-	-	-	-	-	-	-	-	-	-	-	-	-	-	-	-	1	1	-
		NS	97	70	70	-	5	65	-	-	-	-	-	-	-	-	-	-	-	-	-	-	-	-	-	-	-	-
		O	5	1	1	-	-	1	-	-	-	-	-	-	-	-	-	-	-	-	-	-	-	-	-	-	-	-
		T	1,030	854	853	15	50	768	-	-	-	-	-	-	-	-	-	-	4	-	4	2	-	-	-	6	6	8
	163 Playing in Street	M	6	6	6	-	2	4	-	-	-	-	-	-	-	-	-	-	-	-	-	-	-	-	-	-	-	-
		NS	3	2	2	-	-	2	-	-	-	-	-	-	-	-	-	-	-	-	-	-	-	-	-	-	-	-
		T	9	8	8	-	2	6	-	-	-	-	-	-	-	-	-	-	-	-	-	-	-	-	-	-	-	-
	164 Other Offence	M	124	96	97	2	14	60	-	-	-	-	-	-	-	-	-	-	4	-	4	3	-	-	-	3	3	11
		F	24	21	21	1	-	19	-	-	-	-	-	-	-	-	-	-	-	-	-	1	-	-	-	-	-	-
		NS	6	5	5	2	-	3	-	-	-	-	-	-	-	-	-	-	-	-	-	-	-	-	-	-	-	-
		T	154	122	123	5	14	82	-	-	-	-	-	-	-	-	-	-	4	-	4	4	-	-	-	3	3	11
	165 Kerb Crawling	M	75	60	60	-	11	20	-	-	-	-	-	-	-	-	-	-	10	-	10	3	-	-	-	8	8	8
		F	2	2	2	-	1	1	-	-	-	-	-	-	-	-	-	-	-	-	-	-	-	-	-	-	-	-
		T	77	62	62	-	12	21	-	-	-	-	-	-	-	-	-	-	10	-	10	3	-	-	-	8	8	8

21.6e Persons aged 21 or over convicted and sentenced at all courts

England and Wales, 2012

Number of persons

Offence group	Description		Total Proc Against	Total found Guilty	Total For Sent	Absit Disch	Condl Disch	Fine	CRO	SO	CPO	ACO	CPO&RO	Curf Order	Rep Order	APO	DTTO	REFO	Comm Order	YRO [1]	Total Comm Sentences	SS	Sec 90-92	DTO	YOI	Unsus Sent Impr	Imm cust	ODW
	166 Offence by Prostitute	M	2	1	1	-	1	-	-	-	-	-	-	-	-	-	-	-	-	-	-	-	-	-	-	-	-	-
		F	362	253	253	2	66	92	-	-	-	-	-	-	-	-	-	-	2	-	2	-	-	-	-	2	2	89
		NS	5	3	3	-	1	-	-	-	-	-	-	-	-	-	-	-	-	-	-	-	-	-	-	-	-	2
		T	369	257	257	2	68	92	-	-	-	-	-	-	-	-	-	-	2	-	2	-	-	-	-	2	2	91
	167 Aiding, etc. Offence by Prostitute	M	221	178	179	2	40	133	-	-	-	-	-	-	-	-	-	-	-	-	-	-	-	-	-	-	-	4
		F	5	1	1	-	-	1	-	-	-	-	-	-	-	-	-	-	-	-	-	-	-	-	-	-	-	-
		NS	3	2	2	-	1	-	-	-	-	-	-	-	-	-	-	-	-	-	-	-	-	-	-	-	-	1
		T	229	181	182	2	41	134	-	-	-	-	-	-	-	-	-	-	-	-	-	-	-	-	-	-	-	5
	168 Public Health Offence	M	4,126	3,172	3,171	13	107	3,029	-	-	-	-	-	-	-	-	-	-	6	-	6	4	-	-	-	-	-	12
		F	2,165	1,708	1,708	3	59	1,635	-	-	-	-	-	-	-	-	-	-	1	-	1	1	-	-	-	-	-	9
		NS	1,814	1,375	1,375	7	32	1,336	-	-	-	-	-	-	-	-	-	-	-	-	-	-	-	-	-	-	-	-
		O	170	65	64	-	2	58	-	-	-	-	-	-	-	-	-	-	-	-	-	-	-	-	-	-	-	4
		T	8,275	6,320	6,318	23	200	6,058	-	-	-	-	-	-	-	-	-	-	7	-	7	5	-	-	-	-	-	25
	169 Railway Offence	M	37,188	30,797	30,795	80	298	30,140	-	-	-	-	-	1	-	-	-	-	109	-	110	7	-	-	-	12	12	148
		F	9,398	7,267	7,267	23	74	7,132	-	-	-	-	-	-	-	-	-	-	15	-	15	-	-	-	-	-	-	23
		NS	7,302	5,905	5,905	11	41	5,832	-	-	-	-	-	-	-	-	-	-	2	-	2	-	-	-	-	1	1	18
		O	10	4	4	-	-	4	-	-	-	-	-	-	-	-	-	-	-	-	-	-	-	-	-	-	-	-
		T	53,898	43,973	43,971	114	413	43,108	-	-	-	-	-	1	-	-	-	-	126	-	127	7	-	-	-	13	13	189
	170 Motor Vehicle Licence	M	17,909	14,872	14,872	63	55	14,738	-	-	-	-	-	-	-	-	-	-	-	-	-	-	-	-	-	-	-	16
		F	5,953	4,901	4,901	22	17	4,852	-	-	-	-	-	-	-	-	-	-	-	-	-	-	-	-	-	-	-	10
		NS	7,962	6,614	6,614	30	12	6,559	-	-	-	-	-	-	-	-	-	-	-	-	-	-	-	-	-	-	-	13
		O	357	252	252	-	3	249	-	-	-	-	-	-	-	-	-	-	-	-	-	-	-	-	-	-	-	-
		T	32,181	26,639	26,639	115	87	26,398	-	-	-	-	-	-	-	-	-	-	-	-	-	-	-	-	-	-	-	39
	172 Other Offence Against Revenue Law	M	68	60	60	1	4	52	-	-	-	-	-	-	-	-	-	-	-	-	-	-	-	-	-	-	-	3
		F	25	22	22	1	2	19	-	-	-	-	-	-	-	-	-	-	-	-	-	-	-	-	-	-	-	-
		NS	15	12	12	-	2	10	-	-	-	-	-	-	-	-	-	-	-	-	-	-	-	-	-	-	-	-
		O	15	13	13	1	-	9	-	-	-	-	-	-	-	-	-	-	-	-	-	-	-	-	-	-	-	3
		T	123	107	107	3	8	90	-	-	-	-	-	-	-	-	-	-	-	-	-	-	-	-	-	-	-	6
	173 Stage Carriage or Public Service Vehicle Offence	M	15,739	13,675	13,675	84	94	13,474	-	-	-	-	-	-	-	-	-	-	-	-	-	-	-	-	-	-	-	23
		F	6,227	5,399	5,399	40	61	5,281	-	-	-	-	-	-	-	-	-	-	-	-	-	-	-	-	-	-	-	17
		NS	856	713	713	7	4	694	-	-	-	-	-	-	-	-	-	-	-	-	-	-	-	-	-	-	-	8
		O	106	66	66	-	-	66	-	-	-	-	-	-	-	-	-	-	-	-	-	-	-	-	-	-	-	-
		T	22,928	19,853	19,853	131	159	19,515	-	-	-	-	-	-	-	-	-	-	-	-	-	-	-	-	-	-	-	48
	175 Sexual Offences-Miscellaneous	M	23	18	18	-	3	11	-	-	-	-	-	-	-	-	-	-	3	-	3	-	-	-	-	-	-	1
		F	1	1	1	-	1	-	-	-	-	-	-	-	-	-	-	-	-	-	-	-	-	-	-	-	-	-
		T	24	19	19	-	4	11	-	-	-	-	-	-	-	-	-	-	3	-	3	-	-	-	-	-	-	1
	176 Private security industry	M	14	10	12	1	3	6	-	-	-	-	-	-	-	-	-	-	1	-	1	1	-	-	-	-	-	-
		F	2	2	2	-	-	2	-	-	-	-	-	-	-	-	-	-	-	-	-	-	-	-	-	-	-	-
		NS	4	4	4	-	1	-	-	-	-	-	-	-	-	-	-	-	2	-	2	1	-	-	-	-	-	-
		T	20	16	18	1	4	8	-	-	-	-	-	-	-	-	-	-	3	-	3	2	-	-	-	-	-	-
	179 Sunday Trading, etc.	M	1	-	-	-	-	-	-	-	-	-	-	-	-	-	-	-	-	-	-	-	-	-	-	-	-	-
		O	2	1	1	-	-	1	-	-	-	-	-	-	-	-	-	-	-	-	-	-	-	-	-	-	-	-
		T	3	1	1	-	-	1	-	-	-	-	-	-	-	-	-	-	-	-	-	-	-	-	-	-	-	-
	180 Tram or Trolley Vehicle Offence	M	1,199	1,119	1,119	2	11	1,103	-	-	-	-	-	-	-	-	-	-	-	-	-	-	-	-	-	-	-	3
		F	456	423	423	2	1	420	-	-	-	-	-	-	-	-	-	-	-	-	-	-	-	-	-	-	-	-
		NS	85	78	78	-	-	78	-	-	-	-	-	-	-	-	-	-	-	-	-	-	-	-	-	-	-	-
		T	1,740	1,620	1,620	4	12	1,601	-	-	-	-	-	-	-	-	-	-	-	-	-	-	-	-	-	-	-	3
	182 Begging	M	949	783	783	65	191	401	-	-	-	-	-	-	-	-	-	-	2	-	2	-	-	-	-	-	-	124
		F	205	172	172	9	45	73	-	-	-	-	-	-	-	-	-	-	2	-	2	-	-	-	-	1	1	42
		NS	25	16	16	-	5	10	-	-	-	-	-	-	-	-	-	-	-	-	-	-	-	-	-	-	-	1
		T	1,179	971	971	74	241	484	-	-	-	-	-	-	-	-	-	-	4	-	4	-	-	-	-	1	1	167
	183 Sleeping Out	M	17	15	15	2	4	5	-	-	-	-	-	-	-	-	-	-	1	-	1	-	-	-	-	-	-	3
		F	2	2	2	-	1	-	-	-	-	-	-	-	-	-	-	-	-	-	-	-	-	-	-	-	-	1
		T	19	17	17	2	5	5	-	-	-	-	-	-	-	-	-	-	1	-	1	-	-	-	-	-	-	4
	185 Found In Enclosed Premises	M	526	419	419	3	120	142	-	-	-	-	-	1	-	-	-	-	76	-	77	7	-	-	-	55	55	15
		F	6	5	5	-	2	1	-	-	-	-	-	-	-	-	-	-	-	-	-	-	-	-	-	2	2	-
		NS	2	1	1	-	-	1	-	-	-	-	-	-	-	-	-	-	-	-	-	-	-	-	-	-	-	-
		T	534	425	425	3	122	144	-	-	-	-	-	1	-	-	-	-	76	-	77	7	-	-	-	57	57	15
	188 Other Vagrancy Offences	M	2	1	1	-	-	-	-	-	-	-	-	-	-	-	-	-	-	-	-	-	-	-	-	-	-	1
		T	2	1	1	-	-	-	-	-	-	-	-	-	-	-	-	-	-	-	-	-	-	-	-	-	-	1
	189 Weights and Measures Acts	M	4	4	4	-	-	4	-	-	-	-	-	-	-	-	-	-	-	-	-	-	-	-	-	-	-	-
		F	1	1	1	-	1	-	-	-	-	-	-	-	-	-	-	-	-	-	-	-	-	-	-	-	-	-
		NS	1	-	-	-	-	-	-	-	-	-	-	-	-	-	-	-	-	-	-	-	-	-	-	-	-	-
		O	2	2	2	-	-	2	-	-	-	-	-	-	-	-	-	-	-	-	-	-	-	-	-	-	-	-
		T	8	7	7	-	1	6	-	-	-	-	-	-	-	-	-	-	-	-	-	-	-	-	-	-	-	-
	190 Wild Birds Protection Acts	M	28	24	24	-	5	10	-	-	-	-	-	-	-	-	-	-	5	-	5	3	-	-	-	-	-	1
		NS	2	2	2	-	-	-	-	-	-	-	-	-	-	-	-	-	-	-	-	2	-	-	-	-	-	-
		T	30	26	26	-	5	10	-	-	-	-	-	-	-	-	-	-	5	-	5	5	-	-	-	-	-	1
	191 Wireless Telegraphy Acts	M	61,514	50,989	50,989	59	162	50,768	-	-	-	-	-	-	-	-	-	-	-	-	-	-	-	-	-	-	-	-
		F	125,010	108,659	108,659	165	341	108,151	-	-	-	-	-	-	-	-	-	-	-	-	-	-	-	-	-	-	-	2
		NS	439	316	316	-	1	315	-	-	-	-	-	-	-	-	-	-	-	-	-	-	-	-	-	-	-	-
		O	17	14	14	-	-	14	-	-	-	-	-	-	-	-	-	-	-	-	-	-	-	-	-	-	-	-
		T	186,980	159,978	159,978	224	504	159,248	-	-	-	-	-	-	-	-	-	-	-	-	-	-	-	-	-	-	-	2
	192 Video Recording Act 1984	NS	1	1	1	-	-	1	-	-	-	-	-	-	-	-	-	-	-	-	-	-	-	-	-	-	-	-
		O	1	-	-	-	-	-	-	-	-	-	-	-	-	-	-	-	-	-	-	-	-	-	-	-	-	-
		T	2	1	1	-	-	1	-	-	-	-	-	-	-	-	-	-	-	-	-	-	-	-	-	-	-	-
	193 Drug Offence	M	1,382	1,314	1,313	41	317	604	-	-	-	-	-	-	-	-	-	-	18	-	18	13	-	-	-	65	65	255
		F	272	263	262	8	80	95	-	-	-	-	-	-	-	-	-	-	1	-	1	3	-	-	-	12	12	63
		NS	11	10	10	-	-	6	-	-	-	-	-	-	-	-	-	-	-	-	-	-	-	-	-	2	2	2
		T	1,665	1,587	1,585	49	397	705	-	-	-	-	-	-	-	-	-	-	19	-	19	16	-	-	-	79	79	320
	194 Immigration Offence	M	17	21	21	-	3	1	-	-	-	-	-	-	-	-	-	-	1	-	1	3	-	-	-	13	13	-
		F	3	8	8	-	-	-	-	-	-	-	-	-	-	-	-	-	1	-	1	2	-	-	-	5	5	-
		NS	2	2	2	-	-	-	-	-	-	-	-	-	-	-	-	-	-	-	-	1	-	-	-	1	1	-
		T	22	31	31	-	3	1	-	-	-	-	-	-	-	-	-	-	2	-	2	6	-	-	-	19	19	-
	Other Summary Offence (Excluding Motoring)	M	14,830	10,263	10,281	41	1,071	5,055	-	-	-	-	-	-	-	-	-	-	2,115	-	2,115	612	-	-	-	1,059	1,059	328
		F	3,301	1,970	1,976	11	223	1,274	-	-	-	-	-	1	-	-	-	-	232	-	233	73	-	-	-	91	91	71
		NS	3,262	1,897	1,893	5	48	1,787	-	-	-	-	-	-	-	-	-	-	16	-	16	4	-	-	-	23	23	10
		O	656	406	404	6	9	386	-	-	-	-	-	-	-	-	-	-	-	-	-	-	-	-	-	-	-	3
		T	22,049	14,536	14,554	63	1,351	8,502	-	-	-	-	-	1	-	-	-	-	2,363	-	2,364	689	-	-	-	1,173	1,173	412
	Sub-total	M	291,524	231,374	231,547	1,135	22,760	154,754	-	-	1	-	-	37	-	-	-	-	29,328	-	29,366	6,853	-	-	-	11,156	11,156	5,523
		F	184,838	155,641	155,664	507	7,981	138,372	-	-	-	-	-	9	-	-	-	-	5,780	-	5,789	1,063	-	-	-	848	848	1,104
		NS	27,050	21,106	21,083	108	940	19,015	-	-	-	-	-	-	-	-	-	-	678	-	678	104	-	-	-	104	104	134
		O	1,536	960	957	8	18	920	-	-	-	-	-	-	-	-	-	-	-	-	-	-	-	-	-	-	-	11
		T	504,948	409,081	409,251	1,758	31,699	313,061	-	-	1	-	-	46	-	-	-	-	35,786	-	35,833	8,020	-	-	-	12,108	12,108	6,772
Summary Motoring	A Summary Motoring Offences	M	372,449	321,975	322,048	2,207	1,402	301,668	-	-	-	-	-	12	-	-	-	-	9,482	-	9,494	3,182	-	-	-	2,780	2,780	1,315
		F	90,430	79,109	79,110	581	387	75,449	-	-	-	-	-	-	-	-	-	-	1,928	-	1,928	424	-	-	-	106	106	235
		NS	30,543	24,142	24,139	59	56	23,878	-	-	-	-	-	-	-	-	-	-	45	-	45	13	-	-	-	13	13	75
		O	6,486	4,806	4,806	23	14	4,758	-	-	-	-	-	-	-	-	-	-	-	-	-	-	-	-	-	-	-	11
		T	499,908	430,032	430,103	2,870	1,859	405,753	-	-	-	-	-	12	-	-	-	-	11,455	-	11,467	3,619	-	-	-	2,899	2,899	1,636
	Sub-total	M	372,449	321,975	322,048	2,207	1,402	301,668	-	-	-	-	-	12	-	-	-	-	9,482	-	9,494	3,182	-	-	-	2,780	2,780	1,315
		F	90,430	79,109	79,110	581	387	75,449	-	-	-	-	-	-	-	-	-	-	1,928	-	1,928	424	-	-	-	106	106	235
		NS	30,543	24,142	24,139	59	56	23,878	-	-	-	-	-	-	-	-	-	-	45	-	45	13	-	-	-	13	13	75
		O	6,486	4,806	4,806	23	14	4,758	-	-	-	-	-	-	-	-	-	-	-	-	-	-	-	-	-	-	-	11
		T	499,908	430,032	430,103	2,870	1,859	405,753	-	-	-	-	-	12	-	-	-	-	11,455	-	11,467	3,619	-	-	-	2,899	2,899	1,636
Total Summary		M	663,973	553,349	553,595	3,342	24,162	456,422	-	-	1	-	-	49	-	-	-	-	38,810	-	38,860	10,035	-	-	-	13,936	13,936	6,838
		F	275,268	234,750	234,774	1,088	8,368	213,821	-	-	-	-	-	9	-	-	-	-	7,708	-	7,717	1,487	-	-	-	954	954	1,339
		NS	57,593	45,248	45,222	167	996	42,893	-	-	-	-	-	-	-	-	-	-	723	-	723	117	-	-	-	117	117	209
		O	8,022	5,766	5,763	31	32	5,678	-	-	-	-	-	-	-	-	-	-	-	-	-	-	-	-	-	-	-	22
		T	1,004,856	839,113	839,354	4,628	33,558	718,814	-	-	1	-	-	58	-	-	-	-	47,241	-	47,300	11,639	-	-	-	15,007	15,007	8,408
All Offences		M	911,826	760,290	759,327	3,951	47,724	496,414	8	-	4	-	1	152	-	-	-	-	81,819	-	81,984	33,101	-	-	-	77,571	77,571	18,582
		F	319,049	270,684	270,641	1,215	16,021	219,411	4	-	-	-	-	30	-	-	1	-	17,191	-	17,226	6,447	-	-	-	7,015	7,015	3,306
		NS	61,412	47,355	47,107	177	1,222	43,572	-	-	-	-	-	1	-	-	-	-	1,121	-	1,122	296	-	-	-	417	417	301
		O	9,132	6,587	6,575	33	44	6,462	-	-	-	-	-	-	-	-	-	-	1	-	1	2	-	-	-	-	-	33
		T	1,301,419	1,084,916	1,083,650	5,376	65,011	765,859	12	-	4	-	1	183	-	-	1	-	100,132	-	100,333	39,846	-	-	-	85,003	85,003	22,222

(1) The Youth Rehabilitation Order came into effect on 30 November 2009. Figures prior to 2010 are recorded as community orders.

21.7 Persons cautioned for indictable offences by offences, sex and age

England and Wales, 2012

Offence		Total	Aged 10 And Under 12	Aged 12 And Under 15	Aged 15 And Under 18	Aged 10 And Under 18	Aged 18 And Under 21	Aged 21 And Over	Aged 21 And Under 25	Aged 25 And Under 30	Aged 30 And Under 40	Aged 40 And Under 50	Aged 50 And Under 60	Aged 60 And Over
Violence against person														
3 Threat or Conspiracy to Murder	M	91	-	6	6	12	3	76	9	9	20	25	9	4
	F	18	-	2	3	5	1	12	1	1	5	5	-	-
	NS	1	-	-	-	-	-	1	-	-	-	1	-	-
	T	110	-	8	9	17	4	89	10	10	25	31	9	4
5 Wounding or other act Endangering Life	M	73	1	12	17	30	11	32	13	5	4	6	1	3
	F	16	-	4	2	6	4	6	5	1	-	-	-	-
	NS	2	-	1	1	2	-	-	-	-	-	-	-	-
	T	91	1	17	20	38	15	38	18	6	4	6	1	3
6 Endangering Railway Passenger	M	14	1	3	2	6	3	5	2	-	1	2	-	1
	F	2	-	1	-	1	-	1	-	-	-	-	-	-
	T	16	1	4	2	7	3	6	2	-	1	2	-	1
8 Malicious Wounding etc.	M	8,817	90	722	1,114	1,926	1,267	5,624	1,244	1,093	1,352	1,156	525	254
	F	2,625	12	251	380	643	336	1,646	338	341	480	330	117	40
	NS	65	1	12	13	26	8	31	6	5	7	10	2	1
	T	11,507	103	985	1,507	2,595	1,611	7,301	1,588	1,439	1,839	1,496	644	295
11 Cruelty to or Neglect of Children	M	444	-	-	-	-	12	432	35	76	164	112	36	9
	F	1,116	-	-	4	4	48	1,064	175	244	436	175	28	6
	NS	4	-	-	-	-	-	4	1	-	2	1	-	-
	T	1,564	-	-	4	4	60	1,500	211	320	602	288	64	15
12 Abandoning Child aged under Two Years	M	1	-	-	-	-	-	1	-	-	1	-	-	-
	F	4	-	-	-	-	-	4	2	1	-	1	-	-
	T	5	-	-	-	-	-	5	2	1	1	1	-	-
13 Child Abduction	M	12	-	-	-	-	2	10	-	3	3	2	2	-
	F	12	-	-	1	1	2	9	1	-	3	4	1	-
	T	24	-	-	1	1	4	19	1	3	6	6	3	-
Sub-Total	M	9,452	92	743	1,139	1,974	1,298	6,180	1,303	1,186	1,545	1,303	573	270
	F	3,793	12	258	390	660	391	2,742	522	588	924	515	146	47
	NS	72	1	13	14	28	8	36	7	5	9	12	2	1
	T	13,317	105	1,014	1,543	2,662	1,697	8,958	1,832	1,779	2,478	1,830	721	318
Sexual offences														
17 Sexual Assault on a Male	M	50	1	15	4	20	4	26	4	2	7	3	5	5
	F	3	-	-	-	-	-	3	-	1	1	1	-	-
	T	53	1	15	4	20	4	29	4	3	8	4	5	5
19 Rape of a Female	M	11	-	4	6	10	-	1	1	-	-	-	-	-
	T	11	-	4	6	10	-	1	1	-	-	-	-	-
19 Rape of a Male	M	5	1	4	-	5	-	-	-	-	-	-	-	-
	T	5	1	4	-	5	-	-	-	-	-	-	-	-
20 Sexual Assault on a Female	M	491	5	69	54	128	39	324	48	49	66	57	35	69
	F	6	-	-	1	1	1	4	-	2	2	-	-	-
	NS	2	-	-	-	-	1	1	-	1	-	-	-	-
	T	499	5	69	55	129	41	329	48	52	68	57	35	69
21 Sexual Activity with child under 13	M	116	3	34	51	88	12	16	3	2	3	4	1	3
	F	5	-	2	1	3	-	2	1	-	1	-	-	-
	T	121	3	36	52	91	12	18	4	2	4	4	1	3

21.7 Persons cautioned for indictable offences by offences, sex and age

England and Wales, 2012

Offence		Total	Aged 10 And Under 12	Aged 12 And Under 15	Aged 15 And Under 18	Aged 10 And Under 18	Aged 18 And Under 21	Aged 21 And Over	Aged 21 And Under 25	Aged 25 And Under 30	Aged 30 And Under 40	Aged 40 And Under 50	Aged 50 And Under 60	Aged 60 And Over
22 Sexual Activity with child under 16	M	329	-	9	97	106	114	109	45	25	16	13	3	7
	F	13	-	1	3	4	-	9	-	3	2	2	-	-
	NS	1	-	-	-	-	-	1	1	-	-	-	-	-
	T	343	-	10	100	110	114	119	48	28	18	15	3	7
23 Familial Sexual Offences (Incest)	M	18	-	3	4	7	3	8	2	1	1	1	-	3
	F	3	-	-	-	-	-	3	-	1	2	-	-	-
	T	21	-	3	4	7	3	11	2	2	3	1	-	3
24 Exploitation of Prostitution	M	30	-	-	-	-	3	27	4	3	6	6	4	4
	F	22	-	-	-	-	2	20	4	4	2	6	4	-
	T	52	-	-	-	-	5	47	8	7	8	12	8	4
27 Soliciting of women by Men	M	12	-	-	-	-	-	12	2	4	4	-	1	1
	T	12	-	-	-	-	-	12	2	4	4	-	1	1
70 Sexual activity etc. with a person with a mental disorder	M	5	-	-	-	-	-	5	-	-	-	-	3	2
	F	1	-	-	-	-	-	1	-	1	-	-	-	-
	T	6	-	-	-	-	-	6	-	1	-	-	3	2
71 Abuse of children through prostitution and pornography	M	9	-	-	2	2	3	4	1	2	1	-	-	-
	T	9	-	-	2	2	3	4	1	2	1	-	-	-
73 Abuse of trust- sexual offences	M	17	-	-	-	-	4	13	3	4	2	1	1	2
	F	1	-	-	-	-	-	1	-	-	-	1	-	-
	T	18	-	-	-	-	4	14	3	4	2	2	1	2
74 Gross Indecency with Children	M	4	-	-	-	-	-	4	-	-	-	1	2	1
	T	4	-	-	-	-	-	4	-	-	-	1	2	1
88 Miscellaneous sexual offences	M	328	-	23	24	47	29	252	38	41	62	47	34	30
	F	1	-	-	-	-	-	1	-	-	-	-	1	-
	T	329	-	23	24	47	29	253	38	41	62	47	35	30
Sub-Total	M	1,425	10	161	242	413	211	801	151	133	168	133	89	127
	F	55	-	3	5	8	3	44	7	12	10	10	5	-
	NS	3	-	-	-	-	1	2	1	1	-	-	-	-
	T	1,483	10	164	247	421	215	847	159	146	178	143	94	127
Burglary														
28 Burglary in a Dwelling	M	878	19	142	269	430	170	278	87	63	65	40	20	3
	F	177	2	24	47	73	30	74	20	14	16	19	4	1
	NS	3	1	1	1	3	-	-	-	-	-	-	-	-
	T	1,058	22	167	317	506	200	352	107	77	81	59	24	4
29 Aggravated Burglary in a Dwelling	M	4	-	-	-	-	1	3	2	-	-	-	1	-
	T	4	-	-	-	-	1	3	2	-	-	-	1	-
30 Burglary in a Building Other than a Dwelling	M	1,357	31	263	434	728	236	393	155	79	101	50	5	3
	F	105	5	21	37	63	11	31	10	6	7	4	4	-
	NS	6	-	3	2	5	1	-	-	-	-	-	-	-
	T	1,468	36	287	473	796	248	424	165	85	108	54	9	3
31 Aggravated Burglary in a Building not a Dwelling	M	1	-	1	-	1	-	-	-	-	-	-	-	-
	T	1	-	1	-	1	-	-	-	-	-	-	-	-
Sub-Total	M	2,240	50	406	703	1,159	407	674	244	142	166	90	26	6
	F	282	7	45	84	136	41	105	30	20	23	23	8	1
	NS	9	1	4	3	8	1	-	-	-	-	-	-	-
	T	2,531	58	455	790	1,303	449	779	274	162	189	113	34	7

21.7 Persons cautioned for indictable offences by offences, sex and age

England and Wales, 2012

Offence	Sex	Total	Aged 10 And Under 12	Aged 12 And Under 15	Aged 15 And Under 18	Aged 10 And Under 18	Aged 18 And Under 21	Aged 21 And Over	Aged 21 And Under 25	Aged 25 And Under 30	Aged 30 And Under 40	Aged 40 And Under 50	Aged 50 And Under 60	Aged 60 And Over
Robbery														
34 Robbery	M	161	7	69	68	144	11	6	2	1	2	1	-	-
	F	26	-	7	12	19	3	4	1	1	2	1	-	-
	NS	1	-	-	1	1	-	-	-	-	-	-	-	-
	T	188	7	76	81	164	14	10	3	2	4	1	-	-
Sub-Total	M	161	7	69	68	144	11	6	2	1	2	1	-	-
	F	26	-	7	12	19	3	4	1	1	2	-	-	-
	NS	1	-	-	1	1	-	-	-	-	-	-	-	-
	T	188	7	76	81	164	14	10	3	2	4	1	-	-
Theft and handling														
37.2 Aggravated Vehicle Taking	M	58	1	9	24	34	14	10	7	2	1	-	-	-
	F	18	-	2	4	6	6	6	4	2	-	-	-	-
	NS	1	-	-	-	-	-	1	-	-	1	-	-	-
	T	77	1	11	28	40	20	17	11	4	2	-	-	-
38 Money laundering	M	53	-	1	4	5	13	35	14	5	8	6	1	1
	F	21	-	-	1	1	7	13	1	2	6	-	4	-
	NS	-	-	-	-	-	-	-	-	-	-	-	-	-
	T	74	-	1	5	6	20	48	15	7	14	6	5	1
39 Theft from the Person of Another	M	753	10	81	163	254	147	352	110	76	81	50	26	9
	F	306	1	40	47	88	54	164	48	32	39	25	15	5
	NS	5	-	-	2	2	1	2	-	1	1	-	1	-
	T	1,064	11	121	212	344	202	518	158	109	121	75	41	14
40 Theft in Dwelling not Automatic M/c or Meter	M	747	6	71	161	238	171	338	109	83	89	39	14	4
	F	357	1	27	82	110	73	174	54	33	28	43	13	3
	NS	11	-	2	3	5	2	4	1	-	3	-	-	-
	T	1,115	7	100	246	353	246	516	164	116	120	82	27	7
41 Theft by an Employee	M	1,385	-	-	49	49	242	1,094	290	232	266	173	97	36
	F	726	-	1	17	18	102	606	150	100	119	137	83	17
	NS	7	-	-	-	-	1	6	3	1	-	-	2	-
	T	2,118	-	1	66	67	345	1,706	443	333	385	310	182	53
42 Theft or Unauthorised Taking from Mail	M	11	-	-	-	-	3	8	3	-	3	1	-	1
	F	3	-	-	-	-	1	2	-	1	-	-	-	1
	T	14	-	-	-	-	4	10	3	1	3	1	-	2
43 Abstracting Electricity	M	126	-	-	1	1	14	111	14	20	27	24	24	2
	F	72	-	-	-	-	7	65	13	14	18	14	6	-
	NS	1	-	-	-	-	1	-	-	-	-	-	-	-
	T	199	-	-	1	1	22	176	27	34	45	38	30	2
44 Theft of Pedal Cycle	M	661	12	107	249	368	130	163	63	42	33	17	4	4
	F	20	-	3	4	7	5	8	4	2	1	1	-	-
	NS	3	-	1	1	2	1	-	-	-	-	-	-	-
	T	684	12	111	254	377	136	171	67	44	34	18	4	4
45 Theft from Vehicle	M	764	3	79	173	255	191	318	119	67	78	34	15	5
	F	45	-	3	3	6	12	27	7	7	5	4	2	2
	NS	5	-	-	2	2	1	2	-	-	1	1	-	-
	T	814	3	82	178	263	204	347	126	74	84	39	17	7
46 Theft from Shops	M	11,091	89	682	1,430	2,201	1,336	7,554	1,570	1,489	2,144	1,349	691	311
	F	8,810	39	744	1,276	2,059	1,012	5,739	1,138	1,144	1,393	1,087	649	328
	NS	81	1	12	15	28	11	42	5	5	21	6	2	3
	T	19,982	129	1,438	2,721	4,288	2,359	13,335	2,713	2,638	3,558	2,442	1,342	642

21.7 Persons cautioned for indictable offences by offences, sex and age

England and Wales, 2012

Offence	Sex	Total	Aged 10 And Under 12	Aged 12 And Under 15	Aged 15 And Under 18	Aged 10 And Under 18	Aged 18 And Under 21	Aged 21 And Over	Aged 21 And Under 25	Aged 25 And Under 30	Aged 30 And Under 40	Aged 40 And Under 50	Aged 50 And Under 60	Aged 60 And Over
47 Theft from Automatic Machine or Meter	M	45	1	1	9	11	7	27	9	5	5	4	4	-
	F	11	-	-	-	-	3	8	3	1	-	2	1	1
	T	56	1	1	9	11	10	35	12	6	5	6	5	1
48 Theft or Unauthorised Taking of Motor Vehicle	M	194	4	24	63	91	36	67	18	11	20	11	7	-
	F	23	-	2	2	4	4	15	3	3	4	2	3	-
	NS	1	-	-	-	-	-	1	-	-	1	-	-	-
	T	218	4	26	65	95	40	83	21	14	25	13	10	-
49 Other Theft or Unauthorised Taking	M	5,401	57	328	789	1,174	936	3,291	837	672	816	575	285	106
	F	1,497	4	79	191	274	213	1,010	228	199	248	196	102	37
	NS	33	-	6	4	10	5	18	1	1	6	5	4	1
	T	6,931	61	413	984	1,458	1,154	4,319	1,066	872	1,070	776	391	144
54 Handling Stolen Goods	M	1,248	7	109	256	372	255	621	158	136	165	101	40	21
	F	425	-	12	50	62	80	283	81	72	60	47	18	5
	NS	6	-	1	1	2	1	3	-	1	2	-	-	-
	T	1,679	7	122	307	436	336	907	239	209	227	148	58	26
Sub-Total	M	22,537	190	1,492	3,371	5,053	3,495	13,989	3,321	2,840	3,736	2,384	1,208	500
	F	12,334	45	913	1,677	2,635	1,579	8,120	1,734	1,612	1,921	1,558	896	399
	NS	154	1	22	28	51	24	79	10	9	36	12	8	4
	T	35,025	236	2,427	5,076	7,739	5,098	22,188	5,065	4,461	5,693	3,954	2,112	903
Fraud and forgery														
52 False Accounting	M	15	-	-	-	-	2	13	1	5	5	1	1	-
	F	5	-	-	-	-	-	5	-	-	2	-	2	1
	NS	1	-	-	-	-	-	1	-	-	1	-	-	-
	T	21	-	-	-	-	2	19	1	5	8	1	3	1
53 Other Fraud	M	2,850	-	28	119	147	432	2,271	551	513	645	345	160	57
	F	1,557	2	17	80	99	201	1,257	265	222	341	260	126	43
	NS	18	-	-	3	3	1	14	-	8	4	2	-	-
	T	4,425	2	45	202	249	634	3,542	816	743	990	607	286	100
60 Forgery etc. of Drug Prescription	M	17	-	-	-	-	-	17	-	2	10	4	1	-
	F	22	-	-	-	-	-	22	3	3	7	5	2	2
	T	39	-	-	-	-	-	39	3	5	17	9	3	2
61 Other Forgery etc.	M	270	-	2	44	46	55	169	48	39	41	26	11	4
	F	63	-	1	12	13	3	47	7	10	15	8	6	1
	T	333	-	3	56	59	58	216	55	49	56	34	17	5
Sub-Total	M	3,152	-	30	163	193	489	2,470	600	559	701	376	173	61
	F	1,647	2	18	92	112	204	1,331	275	235	365	273	136	47
	NS	19	-	-	3	3	1	15	-	8	5	2	-	-
	T	4,818	2	48	258	308	694	3,816	875	802	1,071	651	309	108
Criminal damage														
56 Arson	M	313	21	120	93	234	26	53	14	12	11	4	7	5
	F	69	2	21	16	39	4	26	4	2	7	6	6	1
	NS	3	-	1	2	3	-	-	-	-	-	-	-	-
	T	385	23	142	111	276	30	79	18	14	18	10	13	6
57 Criminal Damage Endangering Life	M	63	-	4	7	11	15	37	8	3	13	7	5	1
	F	12	-	-	-	-	1	11	4	-	2	3	1	1
	NS	1	-	-	-	-	-	1	-	-	-	1	-	-
	T	76	-	4	7	11	16	49	12	3	15	11	6	2
58 Other Criminal Damage	M	2,484	50	276	368	694	431	1,359	386	342	361	171	69	30
	F	528	5	61	88	154	67	307	62	43	92	77	22	11
	NS	13	-	1	5	6	2	5	1	2	-	-	-	2
	T	3,025	55	338	461	854	500	1,671	449	387	453	248	91	43

21.7 Persons cautioned for indictable offences by offences, sex and age

England and Wales, 2012

Offence	Sex	Total	Aged 10 And Under 12	Aged 12 And Under 15	Aged 15 And Under 18	Aged 10 And Under 18	Aged 18 And Under 21	Aged 21 And Over	Aged 21 And Under 25	Aged 25 And Under 30	Aged 30 And Under 40	Aged 40 And Under 50	Aged 50 And Under 60	Aged 60 And Over
59 Threat etc., to commit Criminal Damage	M	324	-	12	26	38	52	234	57	51	60	35	19	12
	F	51	-	-	2	2	7	42	8	2	14	13	2	3
	NS	2	-	-	1	1	-	1	-	-	1	-	-	-
	T	377	-	12	29	41	59	277	65	53	75	48	21	15
Sub-Total	M	3,184	71	412	494	977	524	1,683	465	408	445	217	100	48
	F	660	7	82	106	195	79	386	78	47	115	99	31	16
	NS	19	-	2	8	10	2	7	1	2	1	1	-	2
	T	3,863	78	496	608	1,182	605	2,076	544	457	561	317	131	66
Drug offences														
92.1 Unlawful importation - Class unspecified	M	2	-	-	-	-	-	2	-	-	2	-	-	-
	T	2	-	-	-	-	-	2	-	-	2	-	-	-
92.2 Unlawful exportation - Class unspecified	M	1	-	-	-	-	-	1	-	-	-	-	1	-
	T	1	-	-	-	-	-	1	-	-	-	-	1	-
92.3 Unlawful importation - Class A	M	1	-	-	-	-	1	-	-	-	-	-	-	-
	T	1	-	-	-	-	1	-	-	-	-	-	-	-
92.4 Unlawful importation - Class B	M	7	-	-	-	-	5	2	1	1	-	-	-	-
	T	7	-	-	-	-	5	2	1	1	-	-	-	-
92.5 Unlawful importation - Class C	M	2	-	-	-	-	-	2	-	-	1	-	-	1
	F	1	-	-	-	-	1	-	-	-	-	-	-	-
	T	3	-	-	-	-	1	2	-	-	1	-	-	1
Inciting another to supply a controlled drug - Class C	F	1	-	-	-	-	-	1	1	-	-	-	-	-
	T	1	-	-	-	-	-	1	1	-	-	-	-	-
Other drug offences	M	146	-	-	9	9	26	111	24	20	21	28	12	6
	F	162	-	-	-	-	12	150	20	37	34	37	19	3
	NS	1	-	-	-	-	-	1	-	-	-	-	-	1
	T	309	-	-	9	9	38	262	44	57	55	65	31	10
Possession of a controlled drug - Class A	M	10,045	-	7	174	181	1,560	8,304	2,547	2,310	2,354	899	173	21
	F	1,087	-	-	12	12	138	937	255	233	296	124	25	4
	NS	19	-	-	1	1	3	15	4	5	5	1	-	-
	T	11,151	-	7	187	194	1,701	9,256	2,806	2,548	2,655	1,024	198	25
Possession of a controlled drug - Class B	M	19,025	4	387	3,715	4,106	3,814	11,105	3,849	2,739	2,716	1,345	379	77
	F	2,552	-	77	345	422	345	1,785	417	375	538	359	82	14
	NS	71	-	2	26	28	17	26	10	5	6	2	3	-
	T	21,648	4	466	4,086	4,556	4,176	12,916	4,276	3,119	3,260	1,706	464	91
Possession of a controlled drug - Class C	M	1,046	-	5	67	72	216	758	277	198	178	80	21	4
	F	187	-	1	11	12	48	127	40	34	37	11	3	2
	NS	5	-	2	1	3	2	-	-	-	-	-	-	-
	T	1,238	-	8	79	87	266	885	317	232	215	91	24	6
Possession of a controlled drug - Class unspecified	M	49	-	-	1	1	11	37	12	9	13	3	-	-
	F	13	-	1	-	1	3	9	5	3	1	-	-	-
	NS	1	-	-	-	-	-	1	1	-	-	-	-	-
	T	63	-	1	1	2	14	47	18	12	14	3	-	-
Production, supply and possession with intent to supply a controlled drug - Class A	M	117	-	5	8	13	27	77	29	14	20	7	6	1
	F	29	-	-	1	1	6	22	7	5	5	5	-	-
	T	146	-	5	9	14	33	99	36	19	25	12	6	1

21.7 Persons cautioned for indictable offences by offences, sex and age

England and Wales, 2012

Offence	Sex	Total	Aged 10 And Under 12	Aged 12 And Under 15	Aged 15 And Under 18	Aged 10 And Under 18	Aged 18 And Under 21	Aged 21 And Over	Aged 21 And Under 25	Aged 25 And Under 30	Aged 30 And Under 40	Aged 40 And Under 50	Aged 50 And Under 60	Aged 60 And Over
Production, supply and possession with intent to supply a controlled drug - Class B	M	3,930	-	20	140	160	311	3,459	490	688	1,044	831	319	87
	F	717	-	3	17	20	44	653	97	118	178	176	63	21
	NS	9	-	-	1	1	1	7	1	1	1	2	1	1
	T	4,656	-	23	158	181	356	4,119	588	807	1,223	1,009	383	109
Production, supply and possession with intent to supply a controlled drug - Class C	M	94	-	2	3	5	8	81	16	14	25	13	8	5
	F	21	-	-	-	-	1	20	1	3	6	6	3	1
	T	115	-	2	3	5	9	101	17	17	31	19	11	6
Production, supply and possession with intent to supply a controlled drug - Class unspecified	M	2	-	-	-	-	1	1	1	-	-	-	-	-
	F	1	-	-	-	-	1	-	-	-	-	-	-	-
	T	3	-	-	-	-	2	1	1	-	-	-	-	-
Sub-Total	M	34,467	4	427	4,116	4,547	5,981	23,939	7,246	5,993	6,373	3,206	920	201
	F	4,771	-	81	387	468	598	3,705	843	808	1,096	718	195	45
	NS	106	-	4	29	33	23	50	16	11	12	5	4	2
	T	39,344	4	512	4,532	5,048	6,602	27,694	8,105	6,812	7,481	3,929	1,119	248
Other Indictable (Not Motoring)														
33 Going Equipped for Stealing, etc.	M	287	-	7	50	57	51	179	62	38	45	21	12	1
	F	36	-	-	1	1	8	27	5	7	15	-	-	-
	T	323	-	7	51	58	59	206	67	45	60	21	12	1
35 Blackmail	M	9	-	-	2	2	2	5	-	2	2	1	-	-
	F	2	-	-	-	-	-	2	-	2	-	-	-	-
	T	11	-	-	2	2	2	7	-	4	2	1	-	-
36 Kidnapping, etc.	M	10	-	1	-	1	-	9	4	-	2	1	2	-
	F	1	-	-	-	-	-	1	-	1	-	-	-	-
	T	11	-	1	-	1	-	10	4	1	2	1	2	-
65 Violent Disorder	M	11	-	-	2	2	2	7	-	2	3	1	1	-
	T	11	-	-	2	2	2	7	-	2	3	1	1	-
66 Other Offence against the State or Public Order	M	2,429	9	57	145	211	381	1,837	433	333	419	336	192	124
	F	392	2	23	38	63	62	267	64	55	73	47	24	4
	NS	7	-	2	1	3	-	4	1	1	-	1	1	-
	T	2,828	11	82	184	277	443	2,108	498	389	492	384	217	128
67 Perjury	M	15	-	-	-	-	3	12	1	-	4	5	1	1
	F	19	-	-	1	1	1	17	7	1	7	1	1	-
	T	34	-	-	1	1	4	29	8	1	11	6	2	1
75 Betting, Gaming and Lotteries	M	3	-	-	-	-	-	3	1	1	1	-	-	-
	T	3	-	-	-	-	-	3	1	1	1	-	-	-
78 Assist Entry of Illegal Immigrant	M	14	-	-	-	-	-	14	1	3	4	4	2	-
	F	9	-	-	-	-	2	7	-	5	1	1	-	-
	T	23	-	-	-	-	2	21	1	8	5	5	2	-
79 Perverting the Course of Justice	M	70	-	3	6	9	12	49	12	9	11	11	5	1
	F	71	1	4	13	18	13	40	13	10	5	7	4	1
	T	141	1	7	19	27	25	89	25	19	16	18	9	2
80 Absconding from Lawful Custody	M	21	-	1	3	4	8	9	5	2	2	-	-	-
	F	3	-	1	1	2	-	1	-	1	-	-	-	-
	T	24	-	2	4	6	8	10	5	3	2	-	-	-

21.7 Persons cautioned for indictable offences by offences, sex and age

England and Wales, 2012

Offence		Total	Aged 10 And Under 12	Aged 12 And Under 15	Aged 15 And Under 18	Aged 10 And Under 18	Aged 18 And Under 21	Aged 21 And Over	Aged 21 And Under 25	Aged 25 And Under 30	Aged 30 And Under 40	Aged 40 And Under 50	Aged 50 And Under 60	Aged 60 And Over
81 Firearms Act Offence	M	440	1	16	40	57	55	328	48	49	63	82	38	48
	F	175	-	-	4	4	24	147	59	38	27	16	5	2
	NS	1	-	-	-	-	-	1	1	-	-	-	-	-
	T	616	1	16	44	61	79	476	108	87	90	98	43	50
82 Revenue Law Offence	M	1	-	-	-	-	-	1	-	-	-	-	1	-
	T	1	-	-	-	-	-	1	-	-	-	-	1	-
83 Failing to Surrender to Bail	M	21	-	-	3	3	5	13	-	2	5	2	2	2
	F	6	-	1	1	2	2	2	-	-	-	-	1	1
	T	27	-	1	4	5	7	15	-	2	5	2	3	3
84 Trade Descriptions Act and Similar Offences	M	35	-	-	-	-	2	33	2	9	10	10	-	2
	F	13	-	-	-	-	-	13	2	1	3	4	2	1
	NS	1	-	-	-	-	-	1	-	-	1	-	-	-
	T	49	-	-	-	-	2	47	4	10	14	14	2	3
85 Health and Safety at Work etc. Act 1974	M	3	-	-	-	-	-	3	-	-	-	2	-	1
	T	3	-	-	-	-	-	3	-	-	-	2	-	1
86 Possession of Obscene Material etc.	M	568	-	8	30	38	58	472	45	46	108	97	91	85
	F	12	-	3	3	6	-	6	2	-	1	2	1	-
	NS	1	-	-	-	-	-	1	-	-	-	-	1	-
	T	581	-	11	33	44	58	479	47	46	109	99	93	85
87 Protection from Eviction Act 1977.	M	4	-	-	-	-	-	4	-	-	2	1	1	-
	T	4	-	-	-	-	-	4	-	-	2	1	1	-
91 Public Health	M	4	-	1	-	1	-	3	-	-	1	1	1	-
	F	1	-	-	-	-	-	1	-	-	-	1	-	-
	T	5	-	1	-	1	-	4	-	-	1	2	1	-
95 Disclosure, obstruction, false or misleading statements	M	1	-	-	-	-	1	-	-	-	-	-	-	-
	T	1	-	-	-	-	1	-	-	-	-	-	-	-
99 Other (Excluding Motoring Offences)	M	222	-	4	14	18	16	188	20	32	48	48	24	16
	F	143	-	-	2	2	13	128	36	22	20	29	14	7
	T	365	-	4	16	20	29	316	56	54	68	77	38	23
Sub-Total	M	4,168	10	98	295	403	596	3,169	637	529	730	624	371	278
	F	883	3	32	64	99	125	659	188	145	152	108	51	15
	NS	10	-	2	1	3	-	7	2	1	1	1	2	-
	T	5,061	13	132	360	505	721	3,835	827	675	883	733	424	293
Total Indictable Offences (Exc Motoring)	M	80,786	434	3,838	10,591	14,863	13,012	52,911	13,969	11,791	13,866	8,334	3,460	1,491
	F	24,451	76	1,439	2,817	4,332	3,023	17,096	3,678	3,468	4,608	3,304	1,468	570
	NS	393	3	47	87	137	60	196	37	37	64	33	16	9
	T	105,630	513	5,324	13,495	19,332	16,095	70,203	17,684	15,296	18,538	11,671	4,944	2,070

21.8 Persons sentenced to immediate custody at all courts by offence, sex, length of sentence and average sentence length

England and Wales 2012

Offence	Sex	Total	Length of sentence													Number of persons — Average sentence length in months (1)
			Up to and including 3 months	Over 3 months up to 6 months	Over 6 months and under 1 year	1 year	Over 1 year up to 18 months	Over 18 months up to 3 years	Over 3 years up to 4 years	4 years	Over 4 years up to 5 years	Over 5 years up to 10 years	Over 10 years and less than life	Life	Indeterminate	
1 Murder	M	324	-	-	-	-	-	-	-	-	-	-	-	324	-	-
	F	32	-	-	-	-	-	-	-	-	-	-	-	32	-	-
	T	356	-	-	-	-	-	-	-	-	-	-	-	356	-	-
2 Attempted Murder	M	69	-	-	-	-	-	1	-	-	1	4	33	12	18	200.6
	F	2	-	-	-	-	-	1	-	-	-	1	-	-	-	63.0
	T	71	-	-	-	-	-	2	-	-	1	5	33	12	18	193.9
3 Threat or Conspiracy to Murder	M	199	16	28	25	17	30	57	3	9	2	2	-	-	10	18.8
	F	16	3	2	1	1	-	3	2	1	1	-	-	-	2	21.4
	NS	1	-	1	-	-	-	-	-	-	-	-	-	-	-	6.0
	T	216	19	31	26	18	30	60	5	10	3	2	-	-	12	18.9
4.1 Manslaughter	M	137	-	-	-	-	-	14	5	6	15	59	20	2	16	89.0
	F	16	-	-	-	-	-	3	1	1	1	6	2	-	2	80.4
	T	153	-	-	-	-	-	17	6	7	16	65	22	2	18	88.1
4.4 Causing Death by Reckless Driving	M	103	-	-	-	1	5	33	12	10	15	26	-	-	1	50.9
	F	8	-	-	-	-	3	2	2	1	-	-	-	-	-	32.1
	T	111	-	-	-	1	8	35	14	11	15	26	-	-	1	49.5
4.5 Manslaughter Due to Diminished Responsibility	M	5	-	-	-	-	-	-	1	-	-	-	1	2	1	90.0
	F	1	-	-	-	-	-	-	-	-	-	-	1	-	-	144.0
	T	6	-	-	-	-	-	-	1	-	-	-	2	2	1	108.0
4.6 Causing Death by Careless Driving when under the influence of Drink or Drugs	M	20	-	-	-	-	-	7	-	1	5	7	-	-	-	54.0
	F	1	-	-	-	-	1	-	-	-	-	-	-	-	-	15.0
	T	21	-	-	-	-	1	7	-	1	5	7	-	-	-	52.1
4.7 Causing Death of a child or vulnerable person	F	3	-	-	-	-	-	-	3	-	-	-	-	-	-	48.0
	T	3	-	-	-	-	-	-	3	-	-	-	-	-	-	48.0
4.8 Causing Death by careless or inconsiderate driving	M	54	12	-	13	5	12	11	-	1	-	-	-	-	-	13.9
	F	5	1	-	-	4	-	-	-	-	-	-	-	-	-	10.8
	T	59	13	-	13	9	12	11	-	1	-	-	-	-	-	13.7
4.9 Causing death by driving unlicensed, disqualified or uninsured drivers	M	2	-	-	2	-	-	-	-	-	-	-	-	-	-	8.0
	F	2	-	1	1	-	-	-	-	-	-	-	-	-	-	6.0
	T	4	-	1	3	-	-	-	-	-	-	-	-	-	-	7.0
4.12 Causing serious injury by dangerous driving	M	1	1	-	-	-	-	-	-	-	-	-	-	-	-	2.8
	T	1	1	-	-	-	-	-	-	-	-	-	-	-	-	2.8
37.1 Causing Death by Aggravated Vehicle Taking	M	3	-	-	-	1	-	1	-	-	1	-	-	-	-	32.7
	T	3	-	-	-	1	-	1	-	-	1	-	-	-	-	32.7
5 Wounding or other act Endangering Life	M	1,577	2	7	7	2	18	200	102	165	217	581	106	11	159	70.2
	F	107	2	-	-	2	1	20	14	12	20	28	5	-	3	60.3
	T	1,684	4	7	7	4	19	220	116	177	237	609	111	11	162	69.5
6 Endangering Railway Passenger	M	3	1	-	2	-	-	-	-	-	-	-	-	-	-	4.2
	T	3	1	-	2	-	-	-	-	-	-	-	-	-	-	4.2
8 Other Wounding etc.	M	10,112	2,271	2,280	1,492	882	1,490	1,500	71	39	38	18	3	-	28	11.0
	F	537	132	127	75	54	78	66	2	3	-	-	-	-	-	9.9
	NS	27	10	15	1	1	-	-	-	-	-	-	-	-	-	4.0
	T	10,676	2,413	2,422	1,568	937	1,568	1,566	73	42	38	18	3	-	28	10.9
11 Cruelty to or Neglect of Children	M	76	4	12	8	4	15	17	4	2	4	4	-	-	2	22.2
	F	66	4	4	7	5	14	25	1	2	1	3	-	-	-	22.5
	T	142	8	16	15	9	29	42	5	4	5	7	-	-	2	22.3
13 Child Abduction	M	40	3	3	6	7	8	10	1	1	1	-	-	-	-	17.5
	F	5	-	-	1	1	1	2	-	-	-	-	-	-	-	16.6
	T	45	3	3	7	8	9	12	1	1	1	-	-	-	-	17.4

21.8 Persons sentenced to immediate custody at all courts by offence, sex, length of sentence and average sentence length

England and Wales 2012

Number of persons

Columns "Up to and including 3 months" through "Life" fall under the heading "Length of sentence".

Offence	Sex	Total	Up to and including 3 months	Over 3 months up to 6 months	Over 6 months and under 1 year	1 year	Over 1 year up to 18 months	Over 18 months up to 3 years	Over 3 years up to 4 years	4 years	Over 4 years up to 5 years	Over 5 years up to 10 years	Over 10 years and less than life	Life	Indeterminate	Average sentence length in months (1)
14 Procuring Illegal Abortion	F	1	-	-	-	-	-	-	-	-	-	1	-	-	-	96.0
	T	1	-	-	-	-	-	-	-	-	-	1	-	-	-	96.0
Total Violence Against the Person	M	12,725	2,298	2,344	1,554	918	1,578	1,850	198	235	298	702	164	351	235	19.9
	F	802	141	135	85	68	98	120	22	23	24	39	8	32	7	20.2
	NS	28	10	16	1	1	-	-	-	-	-	-	-	-	-	4.0
	T	13,555	2,449	2,495	1,640	987	1,676	1,970	220	258	322	741	172	383	242	19.9
16 Buggery	M	46	-	-	-	-	-	3	2	2	5	19	14	1	-	104.9
	T	46	-	-	-	-	-	3	2	2	5	19	14	1	-	104.9
17 Sexual Assault on a Male	M	141	2	11	7	10	20	41	8	8	11	16	-	1	6	33.3
	F	2	-	-	-	-	-	1	-	-	-	1	-	-	-	48.0
	T	143	2	11	7	10	20	42	8	8	11	17	-	1	6	33.5
19 Rape of a Female	M	991	-	1	-	5	10	38	24	38	97	403	231	16	128	104.3
	F	11	-	-	-	-	-	2	-	1	1	2	2	-	3	92.8
	T	1,002	-	1	-	5	10	40	24	39	98	405	233	16	131	104.2
19 Rape of a Male	M	74	-	-	-	-	-	10	-	2	8	19	19	1	15	101.0
	T	74	-	-	-	-	-	10	-	2	8	19	19	1	15	101.0
20 Sexual Assault on a Female	M	1,022	79	87	57	74	126	263	44	68	35	111	25	1	52	33.3
	F	12	-	1	-	1	-	5	1	-	-	3	-	-	1	40.9
	T	1,034	79	88	57	75	126	268	45	68	35	114	25	1	53	33.4
21 Sexual Activity with child under 13	M	123	3	3	5	7	17	36	6	11	8	8	3	-	16	36.9
	T	123	3	3	5	7	17	36	6	11	8	8	3	-	16	36.9
22 Sexual Activity with child under 16	M	519	3	16	23	23	69	186	42	43	43	39	-	-	32	34.3
	T	519	3	16	23	23	69	186	42	43	43	39	-	-	32	34.3
23 Familial Sexual Offences (Incest)	M	76	-	1	2	2	9	21	3	7	15	14	-	-	2	44.7
	T	76	-	1	2	2	9	21	3	7	15	14	-	-	2	44.7
24 Exploitation of Prostitution	M	16	-	2	5	1	3	2	1	1	1	-	-	-	-	19.5
	F	11	-	1	6	2	-	1	1	-	-	-	-	-	-	14.5
	T	27	-	3	11	3	3	3	2	1	1	-	-	-	-	17.5
70 Sexual activity etc. with a person with a mental disorder	M	23	-	-	-	2	4	6	1	1	1	3	4	-	1	60.4
	F	1	-	-	-	-	1	-	-	-	-	-	-	-	-	18.0
	T	24	-	-	-	2	5	6	1	1	1	3	4	-	1	58.5
71 Abuse of children through prostitution and pornography	M	53	-	1	2	3	2	21	4	8	3	7	-	-	2	39.6
	F	2	-	-	-	-	1	-	-	-	1	-	-	-	-	38.0
	T	55	-	1	2	3	3	21	4	8	4	7	-	-	2	39.5
72 Trafficking for sexual exploitation	M	7	-	-	-	-	-	3	-	-	1	1	2	-	-	71.1
	F	3	-	-	-	-	-	1	-	-	1	1	-	-	-	66.0
	T	10	-	-	-	-	-	4	-	-	2	2	2	-	-	69.6
73 Abuse of trust - sexual offences	M	12	2	-	-	1	4	5	-	-	-	-	-	-	-	16.4
	F	3	-	-	1	1	1	-	-	-	-	-	-	-	-	12.4
	T	15	2	-	1	2	5	5	-	-	-	-	-	-	-	15.6
74 Gross Indecency with Children	M	60	-	1	4	6	14	20	3	1	4	7	-	-	-	31.1
	F	1	-	-	-	-	-	-	-	1	-	-	-	-	-	48.0
	T	61	-	1	4	6	14	20	3	2	4	7	-	-	-	31.4
88 Miscellaneous sexual offences	M	213	51	48	24	20	31	23	1	3	2	-	-	-	10	10.7
	NS	1	-	1	-	-	-	-	-	-	-	-	-	-	-	3.7
	T	214	51	49	24	20	31	23	1	3	2	-	-	-	10	10.7

21.8 Persons sentenced to immediate custody at all courts by offence, sex, length of sentence and average sentence length
England and Wales 2012

Number of persons

Offence	Sex	Total	Up to and including 3 months	Over 3 months up to 6 months	Over 6 months and under 1 year	1 year	Over 1 year up to 18 months	Over 18 months up to 3 years	Over 3 years up to 4 years	4 years	Over 4 years up to 5 years	Over 5 years up to 10 years	Over 10 years and less than life	Life	Indeterminate	Average sentence length in months (1)
Total Sexual Offences	M	3,376	140	171	129	154	309	678	139	194	234	647	298	19	264	54.3
	F	46	-	3	6	3	4	10	2	2	3	7	2	-	4	43.4
	NS	1	-	1	-	-	-	-	-	-	-	-	-	-	-	3.7
	T	3,423	140	175	135	157	313	688	141	196	237	654	300	19	268	54.2
28 Burglary in a Dwelling	M	7,126	231	787	788	688	1,090	2,626	381	256	178	100	-	-	1	22.4
	F	272	15	32	32	32	51	88	6	10	2	4	-	-	-	19.5
	NS	17	3	7	4	3	-	-	-	-	-	-	-	-	-	6.3
	T	7,415	249	826	824	723	1,141	2,714	387	266	180	104	-	-	1	22.2
29 Aggravated Burglary in a Dwelling	M	280	-	1	3	1	3	27	9	23	36	139	17	1	20	72.7
	F	13	-	-	1	-	-	1	1	2	5	3	-	-	-	54.0
	T	293	-	1	4	1	3	28	10	25	41	142	17	1	20	71.8
30 Burglary in a Building Other than a Dwelling	M	3,591	1,007	1,191	366	243	343	345	36	23	17	20	-	-	-	9.3
	F	90	19	27	7	11	14	6	4	2	-	-	-	-	-	10.7
	NS	16	6	9	1	-	-	-	-	-	-	-	-	-	-	3.8
	T	3,697	1,032	1,227	374	254	357	351	40	25	17	20	-	-	-	9.4
31 Aggravated Burglary in a Building not a Dwelling	M	17	-	-	-	2	-	2	-	-	2	10	-	1	1	73.5
	T	17	-	-	-	2	-	2	-	-	2	10	-	1	1	73.5
Total Burglary Offences	M	11,014	1,238	1,979	1,157	934	1,436	3,000	426	302	233	269	-	1	22	19.4
	F	375	34	59	40	43	65	95	11	14	7	7	-	-	-	18.5
	NS	33	9	16	5	3	-	-	-	-	-	-	-	-	-	5.1
	T	11,422	1,281	2,054	1,202	980	1,501	3,095	437	316	240	276	-	1	22	19.3
34 Robbery	M	4,716	6	172	284	310	584	1,597	349	349	328	547	60	2	128	36.2
	F	286	-	16	15	37	46	105	15	14	14	22	1	-	1	29.4
	T	5,002	6	188	299	347	630	1,702	364	363	342	569	61	2	129	35.8
Total Robbery Offences	M	4,716	6	172	284	310	584	1,597	349	349	328	547	60	2	128	36.2
	F	286	-	16	15	37	46	105	15	14	14	22	1	-	1	29.4
	T	5,002	6	188	299	347	630	1,702	364	363	342	569	61	2	129	35.8
37.2 Aggravated Vehicle Taking	M	435	56	115	93	61	99	11	-	-	-	-	-	-	-	9.3
	F	7	3	1	3	-	-	-	-	-	-	-	-	-	-	5.7
	NS	3	-	2	-	1	-	-	-	-	-	-	-	-	-	8.0
	T	445	59	118	96	62	99	11	-	-	-	-	-	-	-	9.2
38 Money laundering offences	M	415	41	48	53	35	82	95	16	9	12	23	1	-	1	21.6
	F	45	6	4	4	5	15	8	1	1	-	1	-	-	-	16.3
	NS	1	1	-	-	-	-	-	-	-	-	-	-	-	-	0.9
	T	461	48	52	57	40	97	103	17	10	12	24	1	-	1	21.0
39 Theft from the Person of Another	M	1,718	629	628	144	96	89	113	6	2	4	7	-	-	-	7.0
	F	377	123	154	32	15	22	27	1	3	-	-	-	-	-	7.2
	NS	32	23	9	-	-	-	-	-	-	-	-	-	-	-	2.5
	T	2,127	775	791	176	111	111	140	7	5	4	7	-	-	-	7.0
40 Theft in Dwelling not Automatic Machine or Meter	M	535	247	155	39	19	28	34	6	4	3	-	-	-	-	7.0
	F	74	25	33	6	4	2	3	-	1	-	-	-	-	-	6.0
	NS	3	2	1	-	-	-	-	-	-	-	-	-	-	-	3.0
	T	612	274	189	45	23	30	37	6	5	3	-	-	-	-	6.9
41 Theft by an Employee	M	202	40	32	26	19	36	38	3	5	1	-	-	-	-	13.9
	F	70	8	7	13	4	12	23	3	7	-	-	-	-	-	16.3
	NS	2	2	-	-	-	-	-	-	-	-	-	-	-	-	1.9
	T	274	50	39	39	23	48	61	6	7	1	-	-	-	-	14.4

Length of sentence

21.8 Persons sentenced to immediate custody at all courts by offence, sex, length of sentence and average sentence length

England and Wales 2012

Number of persons

Offence		Total	Length of sentence													Average sentence length in months (1)
			Up to and including 3 months	Over 3 months up to 6 months	Over 6 months and under 1 year	1 year	Over 1 year up to 18 months	Over 18 months up to 3 years	Over 3 years up to 4 years	4 years	Over 4 years up to 5 years	Over 5 years up to 10 years	Over 10 years and less than life	Life	Indeterminate	
42 Theft or Unauthorised Taking from Mail	M	26	6	3	6	5	2	2	1	1	-	-	-	-	-	11.8
	F	2	-	-	1	1	-	-	-	-	-	-	-	-	-	11.0
	NS	2	1	-	1	-	-	-	-	-	-	-	-	-	-	5.3
	T	30	7	3	8	6	2	2	1	1	-	-	-	-	-	11.3
43 Abstracting Electricity	M	18	15	3	-	-	-	-	-	-	-	-	-	-	-	1.9
	F	3	3	-	-	-	-	-	-	-	-	-	-	-	-	1.1
	NS	1	1	-	-	-	-	-	-	-	-	-	-	-	-	2.0
	T	22	19	3	-	-	-	-	-	-	-	-	-	-	-	1.8
44 Theft of Pedal Cycle	M	280	217	59	-	1	2	1	-	-	-	-	-	-	-	2.3
	F	4	4	-	-	-	-	-	-	-	-	-	-	-	-	1.3
	NS	5	5	-	-	-	-	-	-	-	-	-	-	-	-	1.1
	T	289	226	59	-	1	2	1	-	-	-	-	-	-	-	2.3
45 Theft from Vehicle	M	1,047	688	308	14	11	10	15	1	1	-	-	-	-	-	3.2
	F	11	8	3	-	-	-	-	-	-	-	-	-	-	-	2.1
	NS	3	2	1	-	-	-	-	-	-	-	-	-	-	-	2.2
	T	1,061	698	312	14	11	10	15	1	1	-	-	-	-	-	3.2
46 Theft from Shops	M	11,200	9,534	1,516	81	27	24	17	1	-	-	-	-	-	-	1.9
	F	2,325	1,968	335	12	9	1	-	-	-	-	-	-	-	-	1.9
	NS	119	110	8	-	1	-	-	-	-	-	-	-	-	-	1.6
	T	13,644	11,612	1,859	93	37	25	17	1	-	-	-	-	-	-	1.9
47 Theft from Automatic Machine or Meter	M	120	36	29	9	9	8	25	1	1	2	-	-	-	-	11.3
	F	8	3	1	-	-	3	1	-	-	-	-	-	-	-	9.4
	NS	1	1	-	-	-	-	-	-	-	-	-	-	-	-	2.8
	T	129	40	30	9	9	11	26	1	1	2	-	-	-	-	11.1
48 Theft of Motor Vehicle	M	320	87	100	28	22	36	37	5	4	1	-	-	-	-	10.2
	F	3	3	-	-	-	-	-	-	-	-	-	-	-	-	1.9
	NS	2	1	1	-	-	-	-	-	-	-	-	-	-	-	4.4
	T	325	91	101	28	22	36	37	5	4	1	-	-	-	-	10.0
49 Other Theft or Unauthorised Taking	M	1,689	925	411	78	53	82	111	11	10	6	2	-	-	-	6.2
	F	154	78	43	8	6	7	11	1	-	-	-	-	-	-	6.0
	NS	15	12	3	-	-	-	-	-	-	-	-	-	-	-	2.0
	T	1,858	1,015	457	86	59	89	122	12	10	6	2	-	-	-	6.1
54 Handling Stolen Goods	M	1,488	638	330	212	97	123	75	5	3	2	3	-	-	-	7.0
	F	88	50	20	11	5	2	-	-	-	-	-	-	-	-	4.1
	NS	9	8	1	-	-	-	-	-	-	-	-	-	-	-	2.0
	T	1,585	696	351	223	102	125	75	5	3	2	3	-	-	-	6.8
Total Theft and Handling Stolen Goods	M	19,493	13,159	3,737	783	455	621	574	56	41	31	35	1	-	-	4.2
	F	3,171	2,282	602	89	48	65	73	6	5	-	1	-	-	-	3.4
	NS	198	168	28	-	2	-	-	-	-	-	-	-	-	-	2.0
	T	22,862	15,609	4,367	872	505	686	647	62	46	31	36	1	-	-	4.1
51 Fraud by Company Director etc.	M	15	-	-	1	3	3	7	-	1	-	-	-	-	-	23.3
	F	1	-	-	-	-	1	-	-	-	-	-	-	-	-	18.0
	T	16	-	-	1	3	4	7	-	1	-	-	-	-	-	22.9
52 False Accounting	M	29	-	3	5	2	6	10	-	1	2	-	-	-	-	20.8
	F	9	-	1	1	-	2	5	-	-	-	-	-	-	-	21.0
	T	38	-	4	6	2	8	15	-	1	2	-	-	-	-	20.8
53 Other Fraud	M	2,201	565	448	244	163	229	355	47	48	48	53	1	-	-	14.4
	F	471	107	115	67	34	67	64	4	3	6	3	1	-	-	12.0
	NS	19	17	2	-	-	-	-	-	-	-	-	-	-	-	2.1
	T	2,691	689	565	311	197	296	419	51	51	54	56	2	-	-	13.9

21.8 Persons sentenced to immediate custody at all courts by offence, sex, length of sentence and average sentence length

England and Wales 2012

Offence	Sex	Total	Up to and including 3 months	Over 3 months up to 6 months	Over 6 months and under 1 year	1 year	Over 1 year up to 18 months	Over 18 months up to 3 years	Over 3 years up to 4 years	4 years	Over 4 years up to 5 years	Over 5 years up to 10 years	Over 10 years and less than life	Life	Indeterminate	Average sentence length in months (1)
55 Bankruptcy Offence	M	28	3	10	7	3	4	1	-	-	-	-	-	-	-	9.0
	F	3	1	2	-	-	-	-	-	-	-	-	-	-	-	4.3
	T	31	4	12	7	3	4	1	-	-	-	-	-	-	-	8.5
60 Forgery etc. of Drug Prescription	M	4	2	-	1	-	-	-	-	-	-	1	-	-	-	21.9
	T	4	2	-	1	-	-	-	-	-	-	1	-	-	-	21.9
61 Other Forgery etc.	M	1,004	93	355	191	221	90	38	4	4	6	2	-	-	-	9.6
	F	129	8	58	34	23	4	1	1	-	-	-	-	-	-	7.9
	T	1,133	101	413	225	244	94	39	5	4	6	2	-	-	-	9.4
814 Fraud, Forgery etc associated with Vehicle or Driver Records	M	9	2	4	2	1	-	-	-	-	-	-	-	-	-	5.5
	T	9	2	4	2	1	-	-	-	-	-	-	-	-	-	5.5
Total Fraud and Forgery	M	3,290	665	820	451	393	332	411	51	54	56	56	1	1	-	13.0
	F	613	116	176	102	57	74	70	5	3	6	3	1	-	-	11.2
	NS	19	17	2	-	-	-	-	-	-	-	-	-	-	-	2.1
	T	3,922	798	998	553	450	406	481	56	57	62	59	2	1	-	12.7
56 Arson	M	525	34	20	12	20	52	175	46	45	34	42	2	1	42	33.3
	F	93	9	2	-	3	5	47	5	8	3	4	-	-	7	29.9
	T	618	43	22	12	23	57	222	51	53	37	46	2	1	49	32.7
57 Criminal Damage Endangering Life	M	20	3	2	1	-	4	7	1	1	-	-	-	-	1	19.2
	F	1	1	-	-	-	-	-	-	-	-	-	-	-	-	1.4
	NS	1	1	-	-	-	-	-	-	-	-	-	-	-	-	2.3
	T	22	5	2	1	-	4	7	1	1	-	-	-	-	1	17.6
58 Other Criminal Damage	M	248	184	26	10	6	9	13	-	-	-	-	-	-	-	4.0
	F	9	7	-	1	-	-	-	-	-	-	-	-	-	1	2.3
	NS	2	2	-	-	-	-	-	-	-	-	-	-	-	-	1.9
	T	259	193	26	11	6	9	13	-	-	-	-	-	-	1	4.0
59 Threat etc., to commit Criminal Damage	M	88	39	21	6	5	10	6	-	1	-	-	-	-	-	7.5
	F	1	1	-	-	-	-	-	-	-	-	-	-	-	-	0.2
	T	89	40	21	6	5	10	6	-	1	-	-	-	-	-	7.4
Total Criminal Damage	M	881	260	69	29	31	75	201	47	47	34	42	2	1	43	21.6
	F	104	18	2	1	3	5	47	5	8	3	4	-	-	8	27.0
	NS	3	3	-	-	-	-	-	-	-	-	-	-	-	-	2.0
	T	988	281	71	30	34	80	248	52	55	37	46	2	1	51	22.1
Unlawful importation - Class A	M	279	-	-	1	1	-	29	41	41	41	90	35	-	-	75.5
	F	61	-	-	-	-	2	13	8	7	11	18	2	-	-	57.9
	T	340	-	-	1	1	2	42	49	48	52	108	37	-	-	72.3
Unlawful importation - Class B	M	67	1	8	8	7	12	20	2	2	5	1	1	-	-	24.5
	F	14	-	-	-	-	4	6	2	2	-	-	-	-	-	20.2
	T	81	1	8	8	7	16	26	4	4	5	1	1	-	-	23.8
Unlawful importation - Class C	M	8	-	-	-	-	-	2	1	1	2	2	-	-	-	36.6
	F	8	-	-	-	-	-	2	1	1	2	2	-	-	-	36.6
	T	16	-	-	-	-	-	4	2	2	4	4	-	-	-	36.6
Unlawful importation - Class unspecified	M	16	-	-	1	1	-	1	-	2	5	3	3	-	-	76.4
	F	6	-	-	-	-	-	-	2	-	2	2	-	-	-	58.7
	T	22	-	-	1	1	-	1	2	2	7	5	3	-	-	71.5
Unlawful exportation - Class A	M	7	-	-	-	-	-	2	-	-	3	2	-	-	-	57.4
	F	5	-	-	-	-	-	-	1	1	1	2	-	-	-	60.6
	T	12	-	-	-	-	-	2	1	1	4	4	-	-	-	58.8

21.8 Persons sentenced to immediate custody at all courts by offence, sex, length of sentence and average sentence length

England and Wales 2012

Number of persons

Offence	Sex	Total	Up to and including 3 months	Over 3 months up to 6 months	Over 6 months and under 1 year	1 year	Over 1 year up to 18 months	Over 18 months up to 3 years	Over 3 years up to 4 years	4 years	Over 4 years up to 5 years	Over 5 years up to 10 years	Over 10 years and less than life	Life	Indeterminate	Average sentence length in months (1)
Unlawful exportation - Class B	M	18	-	1	1	2	5	9	-	-	-	-	-	-	-	20.9
	F	4	-	-	2	1	-	1	-	-	-	-	-	-	-	15.6
	T	22	-	1	3	3	5	10	-	-	-	-	-	-	-	20.0
Production, supply and possession with intent to supply a controlled drug - Class A	M	3,945	10	42	46	99	381	1,834	411	304	316	461	41	-	-	39.4
	F	190	1	1	6	10	22	116	10	4	12	8	-	-	-	30.0
	T	4,135	11	43	52	109	403	1,950	421	308	328	469	41	-	-	39.0
Production, supply and possession with intent to supply a controlled drug - Class B	M	2,762	162	366	513	342	501	710	62	32	31	42	1	-	-	17.1
	F	84	7	20	18	7	11	18	1	1	-	1	-	-	-	13.7
	NS	1	-	1	-	-	-	-	-	-	-	-	-	-	-	6.0
	T	2,847	169	387	531	349	512	728	63	33	31	43	1	-	-	17.0
Production, supply and possession with intent to supply a controlled drug - Class C	M	66	9	17	11	6	12	5	2	-	-	3	-	-	-	14.4
	F	5	-	3	-	1	-	1	-	-	-	-	-	-	-	11.3
	T	71	9	20	11	7	12	6	2	-	-	3	-	-	-	14.2
Production, supply and possession with intent to supply a controlled drug - Class unspecified	M	242	-	1	11	9	15	71	19	13	24	70	9	-	-	53.7
	F	9	-	-	2	1	1	2	1	1	-	1	-	-	-	32.4
	T	251	-	1	13	10	16	73	20	14	24	71	9	-	-	52.9
Possession of a controlled drug - Class A	M	521	380	77	13	7	3	21	4	5	2	9	-	-	-	5.7
	F	49	42	4	-	-	1	2	-	-	-	-	-	-	-	3.0
	NS	3	3	-	-	-	-	-	-	-	-	-	-	-	-	0.8
	T	573	425	81	13	7	4	23	5	5	2	9	-	-	-	5.4
Possession of a controlled drug - Class B	M	528	464	43	8	3	3	2	-	2	3	-	-	-	-	2.1
	F	24	21	3	-	-	-	-	-	-	-	-	-	-	-	1.6
	NS	5	5	-	-	-	-	-	-	-	-	-	-	-	-	1.0
	T	557	490	46	8	3	3	2	-	2	3	-	-	-	-	2.1
Possession of a controlled drug - Class C	M	25	21	4	-	-	-	-	-	-	-	-	-	-	-	1.5
	F	6	6	-	-	-	-	-	-	-	-	-	-	-	-	1.0
	T	31	27	4	-	-	-	-	-	-	-	-	-	-	-	1.4
Other drug offences	M	51	12	11	6	8	5	8	1	-	-	-	-	-	-	11.2
	F	10	-	3	1	2	3	-	-	1	-	-	-	-	-	13.5
	T	61	12	14	7	10	8	8	1	1	-	-	-	-	-	11.6
Total Drug Offences	M	8,535	1,059	571	618	485	942	2,713	543	400	431	683	90	-	-	28.8
	F	467	77	36	30	22	44	160	23	14	28	31	2	-	-	25.8
	NS	9	8	1	-	-	-	-	-	-	-	-	-	-	-	1.5
	T	9,011	1,144	608	648	507	986	2,873	566	414	459	714	92	-	-	28.7
33 Going Equipped for Stealing, etc.	M	465	278	132	22	16	11	6	-	-	-	-	-	-	-	3.9
	F	34	28	5	1	-	-	-	-	-	-	-	-	-	-	2.4
	NS	4	4	-	-	-	-	-	-	-	-	-	-	-	-	2.3
	T	503	310	137	23	16	11	6	-	-	-	-	-	-	-	3.8
35 Blackmail	M	116	-	-	5	5	21	53	8	8	7	8	-	-	1	31.3
	F	11	-	-	-	-	1	9	1	-	-	-	-	-	-	27.1
	T	127	-	-	5	5	22	62	9	8	7	8	-	-	1	30.9
36 Kidnapping, etc.	M	245	-	3	12	18	29	77	16	23	15	26	6	-	19	39.3
	F	13	-	-	2	-	-	8	1	1	-	-	-	-	-	27.3
	T	258	-	3	14	18	29	85	17	24	15	26	6	-	19	38.7
64 Rioting	M	20	-	-	-	2	-	1	1	2	3	11	-	-	-	65.1
	T	20	-	-	-	2	-	1	1	2	3	11	-	-	-	65.1

21.8 Persons sentenced to immediate custody at all courts by offence, sex, length of sentence and average sentence length

England and Wales 2012

Number of persons

Offence		Total	Up to and including 3 months	Over 3 months up to 6 months	Over 6 months and under 1 year	1 year	Over 1 year up to 18 months	Over 18 months up to 3 years	Over 3 years up to 4 years	4 years	Over 4 years up to 5 years	Over 5 years up to 10 years	Over 10 years and less than life	Life	Indeterminate	Average sentence length in months (1)
								Length of sentence								
65 Violent Disorder	M	359	1	20	42	54	88	146	6	1	1	-	-	-	-	18.9
	F	2	-	1	1	-	-	-	-	-	-	-	-	-	-	6.0
	T	361	1	21	43	54	88	146	6	1	1	-	-	-	-	18.8
66 Other Offence against the State or Public Order	M	2,664	717	672	492	280	298	189	-	4	2	1	5	-	4	8.5
	F	100	30	33	19	5	9	3	-	-	-	1	-	-	-	7.4
	NS	14	12	2	-	-	-	-	-	-	-	-	-	-	-	1.9
	T	2,778	759	707	511	285	307	192	-	4	2	2	5	-	4	8.5
67 Perjury	M	31	14	4	8	2	3	-	-	-	-	-	-	-	-	6.6
	F	6	-	2	2	2	-	-	-	-	-	-	-	-	-	9.0
	T	37	14	6	10	4	3	-	-	-	-	-	-	-	-	6.9
75 Betting, Gaming and Lotteries	M	1	-	-	1	-	-	-	-	-	-	-	-	-	-	8.0
	T	1	-	-	1	-	-	-	-	-	-	-	-	-	-	8.0
78 Assist Entry of Illegal Immigrant	M	208	24	37	30	26	45	30	4	2	3	7	-	-	-	15.9
	F	53	6	8	9	7	11	8	1	2	-	1	-	-	-	16.0
	NS	10	8	2	-	-	-	-	-	-	-	-	-	-	-	2.9
	T	271	38	47	39	33	56	38	5	4	3	8	-	-	-	15.4
79 Perverting the Course of Justice	M	584	81	175	128	63	77	45	6	4	1	4	-	-	-	10.6
	F	91	15	25	13	9	14	13	2	-	-	-	-	-	-	11.2
	T	675	96	200	141	72	91	58	8	4	1	4	-	-	-	10.7
80 Absconding from Lawful Custody	M	214	59	92	40	10	6	1	-	-	-	5	-	-	1	7.2
	F	2	1	1	-	-	-	-	-	-	-	-	-	-	-	4.5
	NS	1	-	1	-	-	-	-	-	-	-	-	-	-	-	4.0
	T	217	60	94	40	10	6	1	-	-	-	5	-	-	1	7.2
81 Firearms Act Offence	M	426	33	53	28	26	25	65	9	11	125	50	-	1	1	36.8
	F	22	2	1	1	1	-	4	-	1	11	1	-	-	-	43.0
	NS	1	-	1	-	-	-	-	-	-	-	-	-	-	-	6.0
	T	449	35	55	29	27	25	69	9	12	136	51	-	1	1	37.1
82 Revenue Law Offence	M	18	1	3	-	4	2	7	-	-	1	-	-	-	-	20.4
	F	4	-	1	-	-	1	1	-	1	-	-	-	-	-	16.9
	T	22	1	4	-	4	3	8	-	1	1	-	-	-	-	19.8
83 Failing to Surrender to Bail	M	1,169	1,151	15	2	1	-	-	-	-	-	-	-	-	-	0.8
	F	136	134	2	-	-	-	-	-	-	-	-	-	-	-	0.6
	NS	15	15	-	-	-	-	-	-	-	-	-	-	-	-	1.0
	T	1,320	1,300	17	2	1	-	-	-	-	-	-	-	-	-	0.8
84 Trade Descriptions Act and Similar Offences	M	78	26	13	12	7	10	9	-	1	-	-	-	-	-	9.5
	F	8	4	1	-	2	-	1	-	-	-	-	-	-	-	7.5
	NS	1	-	1	-	-	-	-	-	-	-	-	-	-	-	4.0
	T	87	30	15	12	9	10	10	-	1	-	-	-	-	-	9.3
85 Health and Safety at Work etc. Act 1974	M	3	-	3	-	-	-	-	-	-	-	-	-	-	-	5.3
	T	3	-	3	-	-	-	-	-	-	-	-	-	-	-	5.3
86 Possession of Obscene Material etc.	M	460	22	72	87	59	83	114	3	8	-	1	-	-	11	15.6
	F	5	1	-	1	1	1	1	1	-	-	-	-	-	-	18.8
	NS	1	1	-	-	-	-	-	-	-	-	-	-	-	-	4.0
	T	466	23	73	88	59	84	115	4	8	-	1	-	-	11	15.6
87 Protection from Eviction Act 1977.	M	3	1	1	1	-	-	-	-	-	-	-	-	-	-	6.0
	T	3	1	1	1	-	-	-	-	-	-	-	-	-	-	6.0
91 Public Health	M	26	19	3	-	2	1	1	-	-	-	-	-	-	-	4.0
	F	1	1	-	-	-	-	-	-	-	-	-	-	-	-	0.5
	NS	2	2	-	-	-	-	-	-	-	-	-	-	-	-	1.0
	T	29	22	3	-	2	1	1	-	-	-	-	-	-	-	3.7

21.8 Persons sentenced to immediate custody at all courts by offence, sex, length of sentence and average sentence length

England and Wales 2012

Number of persons

Offence	Sex	Total	Up to and including 3 months	Over 3 months up to 6 months	Over 6 months and under 1 year	1 year	Over 1 year up to 18 months	Over 18 months up to 3 years	Over 3 years up to 4 years	4 years	Over 4 years up to 5 years	Over 5 years up to 10 years	Over 10 years and less than life	Life	Indeterminate	Average sentence length in months (1)
95 Disclosure, obstruction, false or misleading statements	M	27	25	-	-	-	2	-	-	-	-	-	-	-	-	2.1
	NS	6	6	-	-	-	-	-	-	-	-	-	-	-	-	0.8
	T	33	31	-	-	-	2	-	-	-	-	-	-	-	-	1.9
99 Other (Excluding Motoring Offences)	M	1,846	1,021	470	87	40	62	92	15	14	14	26	3	-	2	7.3
	F	258	150	55	13	9	17	11	1	-	-	1	1	-	1	5.6
	NS	18	15	3	-	-	-	-	-	-	-	-	-	-	-	1.8
	T	2,122	1,186	528	100	49	79	103	16	14	14	27	3	-	3	7.0
Total Other Indictable Offences (Excl. Motoring)	M	8,963	3,473	1,768	997	615	763	836	68	78	172	139	14	2	38	10.6
	F	746	372	135	63	35	55	59	7	4	11	4	-	-	1	8.2
	NS	73	62	11	-	-	-	-	-	-	-	-	-	-	-	1.9
	T	9,782	3,907	1,914	1,060	650	818	895	75	82	183	143	14	2	39	10.4
Total Indictable Offences (Excluding Motoring)	M	72,993	22,298	11,631	6,002	4,295	6,640	11,860	1,877	1,700	1,817	3,120	647	376	730	17.7
	F	6,610	3,040	1,164	431	316	456	739	96	87	96	118	14	32	21	10.8
	NS	364	277	75	6	6	-	-	-	-	-	-	-	-	-	2.4
	T	79,967	25,615	12,870	6,439	4,617	7,096	12,599	1,973	1,787	1,913	3,238	661	408	751	17.1
99 Dangerous Driving	M	1,086	56	268	333	166	241	22	-	-	-	-	-	-	-	9.8
	F	18	-	-	6	5	2	-	-	-	-	-	-	-	-	9.4
	T	1,104	56	274	338	171	243	22	-	-	-	-	-	-	-	9.8
99A Driving licence related offences: Making false statements	F	1	-	-	1	-	-	-	-	-	-	-	-	-	-	10.0
	T	1	-	-	1	-	-	-	-	-	-	-	-	-	-	10.0
99C Vehicle insurance offences: Making false statements	M	10	8	2	-	-	-	-	-	-	-	-	-	-	-	2.5
	T	10	8	2	-	-	-	-	-	-	-	-	-	-	-	2.5
Total Indictable Motoring Offences	M	1,096	64	270	333	166	241	22	-	-	-	-	-	-	-	9.8
	F	19	-	6	6	5	2	-	-	-	-	-	-	-	-	9.4
	T	1,115	64	276	339	171	243	22	-	-	-	-	-	-	-	9.8
Total Indictable Offences (Including Motoring)	M	74,089	22,362	11,901	6,335	4,461	6,881	11,882	1,877	1,700	1,817	3,120	647	376	730	17.6
	F	6,629	3,040	1,170	437	321	458	739	96	87	96	118	14	32	21	10.8
	NS	364	277	75	6	6	-	-	-	-	-	-	-	-	-	2.4
	T	81,082	25,679	13,146	6,778	4,788	7,339	12,621	1,973	1,787	1,913	3,238	661	408	751	17.0
104 Assault: On Constable	M	1,002	754	248	-	-	-	-	-	-	-	-	-	-	-	2.2
	F	202	147	54	1	-	-	-	-	-	-	-	-	-	-	2.2
	NS	7	6	1	-	-	-	-	-	-	-	-	-	-	-	2.2
	T	1,211	907	303	1	-	-	-	-	-	-	-	-	-	-	2.2
105 Assault: Common, etc	M	6,657	3,500	3,154	2	1	-	-	-	-	-	-	-	-	-	3.1
	F	404	258	146	-	-	-	-	-	-	-	-	-	-	-	2.7
	NS	44	19	25	-	-	-	-	-	-	-	-	-	-	-	3.3
	T	7,105	3,777	3,325	2	1	-	-	-	-	-	-	-	-	-	3.0
106 Betting or Gaming Offence	M	69	51	18	-	-	-	-	-	-	-	-	-	-	-	2.4
	F	2	2	-	-	-	-	-	-	-	-	-	-	-	-	1.2
	NS	1	1	-	-	-	-	-	-	-	-	-	-	-	-	1.9
	T	72	54	18	-	-	-	-	-	-	-	-	-	-	-	2.3
107 Brothel Keeping	M	5	4	1	-	-	-	-	-	-	-	-	-	-	-	3.6
	F	3	1	2	-	-	-	-	-	-	-	-	-	-	-	4.3
	T	8	5	3	-	-	-	-	-	-	-	-	-	-	-	3.9
108 Cruelty to Animal	M	103	45	57	1	-	-	-	-	-	-	-	-	-	-	3.3
	F	22	8	14	-	-	-	-	-	-	-	-	-	-	-	3.4
	NS	10	2	8	-	-	-	-	-	-	-	-	-	-	-	3.8
	T	135	55	79	1	-	-	-	-	-	-	-	-	-	-	3.4

21.8 Persons sentenced to immediate custody at all courts by offence, sex, length of sentence and average sentence length

England and Wales 2012

Number of persons

Offence	Sex	Total	Up to and including 3 months	Over 3 months up to 6 months	Over 6 months and under 1 year	1 year	Over 1 year up to 18 months	Over 18 months up to 3 years	Over 3 years up to 4 years	4 years	Over 4 years up to 5 years	Over 5 years up to 10 years	Over 10 years and less than life	Life	Indeterminate	Average sentence length in months (1)
111 Offences Relating to Dogs	M	11	10	1	-	-	-	-	-	-	-	-	-	-	-	2.1
	T	11	10	1	-	-	-	-	-	-	-	-	-	-	-	2.1
112 Education Acts	M	6	6	-	-	-	-	-	-	-	-	-	-	-	-	1.1
	F	14	14	-	-	-	-	-	-	-	-	-	-	-	-	1.3
	T	20	20	-	-	-	-	-	-	-	-	-	-	-	-	1.2
115 Firearms Acts	M	14	7	7	-	-	-	-	-	-	-	-	-	-	-	3.0
	T	14	7	7	-	-	-	-	-	-	-	-	-	-	-	3.0
125 Offence against Public Order	M	1,258	931	327	-	-	-	-	-	-	-	-	-	-	-	2.4
	F	62	50	12	-	-	-	-	-	-	-	-	-	-	-	2.0
	NS	13	13	-	-	-	-	-	-	-	-	-	-	-	-	1.9
	T	1,333	994	339	-	-	-	-	-	-	-	-	-	-	-	2.4
126 Interference with Motor Vehicles	M	184	179	5	-	-	-	-	-	-	-	-	-	-	-	1.4
	F	1	1	-	-	-	-	-	-	-	-	-	-	-	-	0.2
	T	185	180	5	-	-	-	-	-	-	-	-	-	-	-	1.4
130 Unauthorised Taking of a Conveyance	M	428	264	164	-	-	-	-	-	-	-	-	-	-	-	2.7
	F	6	4	2	-	-	-	-	-	-	-	-	-	-	-	1.7
	NS	1	1	-	-	-	-	-	-	-	-	-	-	-	-	2.8
	T	435	269	166	-	-	-	-	-	-	-	-	-	-	-	2.7
131 Summary Aggravated Vehicle Taking	M	281	125	153	-	1	2	-	-	-	-	-	-	-	-	3.6
	F	14	4	10	-	-	-	-	-	-	-	-	-	-	-	3.5
	T	295	129	163	-	1	2	-	-	-	-	-	-	-	-	3.6
137 Highways Act - Pedal Cycle	M	1	1	-	-	-	-	-	-	-	-	-	-	-	-	0.9
	T	1	1	-	-	-	-	-	-	-	-	-	-	-	-	0.9
141 Drunkenness, with Aggravation	M	4	4	-	-	-	-	-	-	-	-	-	-	-	-	0.5
	F	6	6	-	-	-	-	-	-	-	-	-	-	-	-	0.8
	T	10	10	-	-	-	-	-	-	-	-	-	-	-	-	0.7
143 Other Offence against the Liquor Law	M	1	1	-	-	-	-	-	-	-	-	-	-	-	-	2.8
	T	1	1	-	-	-	-	-	-	-	-	-	-	-	-	2.8
146 Labour Law - Shops Act	M	1	1	-	-	-	-	-	-	-	-	-	-	-	-	1.4
	F	2	2	-	-	-	-	-	-	-	-	-	-	-	-	1.2
	NS	1	1	-	-	-	-	-	-	-	-	-	-	-	-	1.9
	T	4	4	-	-	-	-	-	-	-	-	-	-	-	-	1.4
149 Summary Criminal or Malicious Damage Offence	M	1,229	1,193	35	1	-	-	-	-	-	-	-	-	-	-	1.3
	F	72	69	3	-	-	-	-	-	-	-	-	-	-	-	1.6
	NS	9	9	-	-	-	-	-	-	-	-	-	-	-	-	1.3
	T	1,310	1,271	38	1	-	-	-	-	-	-	-	-	-	-	1.3
151 Social Security Offence	M	34	32	2	-	-	-	-	-	-	-	-	-	-	-	2.1
	F	20	17	3	-	-	-	-	-	-	-	-	-	-	-	2.3
	NS	3	3	-	-	-	-	-	-	-	-	-	-	-	-	2.1
	T	57	52	5	-	-	-	-	-	-	-	-	-	-	-	2.1
162 Disorderly Behaviour	M	5	5	-	-	-	-	-	-	-	-	-	-	-	-	0.4
	F	1	1	-	-	-	-	-	-	-	-	-	-	-	-	0.7
	T	6	6	-	-	-	-	-	-	-	-	-	-	-	-	0.5
164 Other Offence	M	3	3	-	-	-	-	-	-	-	-	-	-	-	-	1.2
	T	3	3	-	-	-	-	-	-	-	-	-	-	-	-	1.2
165 Prostitution - Kerb Crawling	M	9	9	-	-	-	-	-	-	-	-	-	-	-	-	0.9
	T	9	9	-	-	-	-	-	-	-	-	-	-	-	-	0.9
166 Prostitution - Offence by Prostitute	F	2	2	-	-	-	-	-	-	-	-	-	-	-	-	0.7
	T	2	2	-	-	-	-	-	-	-	-	-	-	-	-	0.7

21.8 Persons sentenced to immediate custody at all courts by offence, sex, length of sentence and average sentence length

England and Wales 2012

Number of persons

Offence		Total	Up to and including 3 months	Over 3 months up to 6 months	Over 6 months and under 1 year	1 year	Over 1 year up to 18 months	Over 18 months up to 3 years	Over 3 years up to 4 years	4 years	Over 4 years up to 5 years	Over 5 years up to 10 years	Over 10 years and less than life	Life	Indeterminate	Average sentence length in months (1)
169 Railway Offence	M	14	13	1	-	-	-	-	-	-	-	-	-	-	-	1.2
	NS	1	1	-	-	-	-	-	-	-	-	-	-	-	-	1.0
	T	15	14	1	-	-	-	-	-	-	-	-	-	-	-	1.2
182 Vagrancy Offences - Begging	F	1	1	-	-	-	-	-	-	-	-	-	-	-	-	1.0
	T	1	1	-	-	-	-	-	-	-	-	-	-	-	-	1.0
185 Vagrancy Offences - Found In Enclosed Premises	M	57	56	1	-	-	-	-	-	-	-	-	-	-	-	1.1
	F	2	2	-	-	-	-	-	-	-	-	-	-	-	-	0.6
	T	59	58	1	-	-	-	-	-	-	-	-	-	-	-	1.1
193 Drug Offence	M	67	67	-	-	-	-	-	-	-	-	-	-	-	-	0.9
	F	12	12	-	-	-	-	-	-	-	-	-	-	-	-	1.3
	NS	2	2	-	-	-	-	-	-	-	-	-	-	-	-	0.6
	T	81	81	-	-	-	-	-	-	-	-	-	-	-	-	0.9
194 Immigration Offence	M	15	5	10	-	-	-	-	-	-	-	-	-	-	-	3.7
	F	5	1	4	-	-	-	-	-	-	-	-	-	-	-	5.0
	NS	1	-	1	-	-	-	-	-	-	-	-	-	-	-	3.7
	T	21	6	15	-	-	-	-	-	-	-	-	-	-	-	4.0
Other Summary Offence (Excluding Motoring)	M	1,380	1,099	280	1	-	-	-	-	-	-	-	-	-	-	2.0
	F	121	89	32	-	-	-	-	-	-	-	-	-	-	-	2.2
	NS	48	42	6	-	-	-	-	-	-	-	-	-	-	-	1.5
	T	1,549	1,230	318	1	-	-	-	-	-	-	-	-	-	-	2.0
Total Summary Offences (Excluding Motoring)	M	12,838	8,365	4,464	5	2	2	-	-	-	-	-	-	-	-	2.6
	F	974	691	282	1	-	-	-	-	-	-	-	-	-	-	2.4
	NS	141	100	41	-	-	-	-	-	-	-	-	-	-	-	2.3
	T	13,953	9,156	4,787	6	2	2	-	-	-	-	-	-	-	-	2.6
Summary Motoring Offences	M	2,891	1,528	1,360	3	-	-	-	-	-	-	-	-	-	-	3.1
	F	106	72	34	-	-	-	-	-	-	-	-	-	-	-	2.7
	NS	15	9	6	-	-	-	-	-	-	-	-	-	-	-	2.7
	T	3,012	1,609	1,400	3	-	-	-	-	-	-	-	-	-	-	3.1
Total Summary Offences (Including Motoring)	M	15,729	9,893	5,824	8	2	2	-	-	-	-	-	-	-	-	2.7
	F	1,080	763	316	1	-	-	-	-	-	-	-	-	-	-	2.4
	NS	156	109	47	-	-	-	-	-	-	-	-	-	-	-	2.3
	T	16,965	10,765	6,187	9	2	2	-	-	-	-	-	-	-	-	2.7
Total All Offences	M	89,818	32,255	17,725	6,343	4,463	6,883	11,882	1,877	1,700	1,817	3,120	647	376	730	14.9
	F	7,709	3,803	1,486	438	321	458	739	96	87	96	118	14	32	21	9.6
	NS	520	386	122	6	6	-	-	-	-	-	-	-	-	-	2.4
	T	98,047	36,444	19,333	6,787	4,790	7,341	12,621	1,973	1,787	1,913	3,238	661	408	751	14.5

(1) Average sentence excludes life sentences

21.9a Persons sentenced to life imprisonment[1] by sex and age, 2002 to 2012

England and Wales   Number of persons

Sex and age	2002	2003	2004	2005	2006	2007	2008	2009	2010	2011	2012
Males											
Aged 10-17	21	11	15	27	16	23	24	22	17	13	13
Aged 18-20	21	47	24	50	46	70	54	57	39	30	47
Aged 21 and over	494	431	509	517	469	378	417	322	308	328	316
All ages	536	489	548	594	531	471	495	401	364	371	376
Females											
Aged 10-17	1	-	1	1	-	3	1	1	2	2	1
Aged 18-20	2	4	2	4	2	3	2	1	2	5	1
Aged 21 and over	16	20	19	26	14	15	25	18	16	17	30
All ages	19	24	22	31	16	21	28	20	20	24	32
All persons											
Aged 10-17	22	11	16	28	16	26	25	23	19	15	14
Aged 18-20	23	51	26	54	48	73	56	58	41	35	48
Aged 21 and over	510	451	528	543	483	393	442	340	324	345	346
All ages	555	513	570	625	547	492	523	421	384	395	408

(1) Includes detention under the Powers of Criminal Courts (Sentencing) Act 2000, Secs 90-92 (Children and Young Persons Act 1933, Secs 53(1) and (2) prior to August 2000) (persons aged 10-17), custody for life under the Powers of Criminal Courts (Sentencing) Act 2000, Secs 93 and 94(1) (persons aged 18-20), mandatory life sentences under the Powers of Criminal Courts (Sentencing) Act 2000, Sec 109 (persons aged 18 and over) and immediate imprisonment (persons aged 21 and over). Indeterminate sentences for public protection under the Criminal Justice Act 2003 are excluded.

Note: Excludes data for Cardiff magistrates' court for April, July and August 2008.

21.9b Persons sentenced to determinate and indeterminate custodial sentences by age group, sex and type of sentence, 2002 to 2012

England and Wales

Number of persons

Age, sex and year		Immediate custodial sentences					Total persons sentenced
		Determinate sentence	Extended sentence of imprisonment[1][2] (EPP)	Imprisonment[1] for public protection (IPP)	Life sentence	Total immediate custody	
Males							
Aged 10-17	2002	6,865	*	*	21	6,886	83,186
	2003	5,765	*	*	11	5,776	80,838
	2004	5,866	*	*	15	5,881	83,413
	2005	5,397	66	22	27	5,512	82,465
	2006	5,570	99	45	16	5,730	80,136
	2007	5,182	95	61	23	5,361	82,619
	2008	4,888	51	67	24	5,030	74,021
	2009	4,468	17	25	22	4,532	67,841
	2010	3,867	10	41	17	3,935	62,145
	2011	3,838	26	28	13	3,905	53,600
	2012	2,813	6	30	13	2,862	40,342
Aged 18-20	2002	16,269	*	*	21	16,290	140,914
	2003	14,418	*	*	47	14,465	143,365
	2004	13,793	*	*	24	13,817	137,732
	2005	13,123	114	64	50	13,351	127,302
	2006	12,648	154	198	46	13,046	123,660
	2007	12,977	149	291	70	13,487	120,770
	2008	12,242	112	214	54	12,622	114,580
	2009	12,919	59	120	57	13,155	115,684
	2010	12,238	58	107	39	12,442	107,657
	2011	11,461	94	70	30	11,655	96,565
	2012	9,227	35	76	47	9,385	78,806
Aged 21 and over	2002	78,662	444	*	494	79,600	927,810
	2003	77,329	859	*	431	78,619	994,992
	2004	76,177	1,184	*	509	77,870	1,036,195
	2005	71,973	1,281	321	517	74,092	980,894
	2006	66,755	1,013	1,160	469	69,397	931,432
	2007	66,023	859	1,303	378	68,563	913,894
	2008	71,043	490	1,210	417	73,160	856,622
	2009	72,611	346	835	322	74,114	863,513
	2010	75,121	370	845	308	76,644	843,968
	2011	80,315	502	703	328	81,848	809,441
	2012	76,347	284	624	316	77,571	759,327
All ages	2002	101,796	444	*	536	102,776	1,151,909
	2003	97,512	859	*	489	98,860	1,219,195
	2004	95,836	1,184	*	548	97,568	1,257,340
	2005	90,493	1,461	407	594	92,955	1,190,661
	2006	84,973	1,266	1,403	531	88,173	1,135,228
	2007	84,182	1,103	1,655	471	87,411	1,117,283
	2008	88,173	653	1,491	495	90,812	1,045,223
	2009	89,998	422	980	401	91,801	1,047,038
	2010	91,226	438	993	364	93,021	1,013,770
	2011	95,614	622	801	371	97,408	959,606
	2012	88,387	325	730	376	89,818	878,475

21.9b Persons sentenced to determinate and indeterminate custodial sentences by age group, sex and type of sentence, 2002 to 2012

England and Wales   Number of persons

Age, sex and year		Immediate custodial sentences					Total persons sentenced
		Determinate sentence	Extended sentence of imprisonment[1][2] (EPP)	Imprisonment[1] for public protection (IPP)	Life sentence	Total immediate custody	
Females							
Aged 10-17	2002	529	*	*	1	530	11,362
	2003	424	*	*	-	424	11,693
	2004	443	*	*	1	444	12,775
	2005	491	7	4	1	503	13,738
	2006	449	4	-	-	453	13,670
	2007	460	6	-	3	469	14,768
	2008	440	2	3	1	446	13,694
	2009	378	-	2	1	381	13,092
	2010	256	-	-	2	258	11,200
	2011	265	1	1	2	269	9,271
	2012	181	-	-	1	182	6,650
Aged 18-20	2002	1,071	*	*	2	1,073	18,470
	2003	969	*	*	4	973	18,702
	2004	817	*	*	2	819	18,667
	2005	872	3	1	4	880	18,749
	2006	832	9	8	2	851	19,034
	2007	790	3	8	3	804	19,506
	2008	781	1	5	2	789	21,130
	2009	801	2	2	1	806	23,328
	2010	734	-	3	2	739	21,119
	2011	579	3	-	5	587	20,157
	2012	509	-	2	1	512	17,101
Aged 21 and over	2002	7,205	7	*	16	7,228	228,763
	2003	7,378	15	*	20	7,413	230,222
	2004	7,462	10	*	19	7,491	248,043
	2005	6,836	22	14	26	6,898	250,127
	2006	6,469	20	37	14	6,540	245,008
	2007	6,445	18	44	15	6,522	255,231
	2008	7,045	15	39	25	7,124	253,514
	2009	6,868	10	17	18	6,913	278,395
	2010	7,145	15	23	16	7,199	272,775
	2011	7,506	22	17	17	7,562	270,437
	2012	6,954	12	19	30	7,015	270,641
All ages	2002	8,805	7	*	19	8,831	258,595
	2003	8,771	15	*	24	8,810	260,617
	2004	8,722	10	*	22	8,754	279,485
	2005	8,199	32	19	31	8,281	282,614
	2006	7,750	33	45	16	7,844	277,712
	2007	7,695	27	52	21	7,795	289,505
	2008	8,266	18	47	28	8,359	288,338
	2009	8,047	12	21	20	8,100	314,815
	2010	8,135	15	26	20	8,196	305,094
	2011	8,350	22	17	24	8,413	299,865
	2012	7,644	12	21	32	7,709	294,392

21.9b Persons sentenced to determinate and indeterminate custodial sentences by age group, sex and type of sentence, 2002 to 2012

England and Wales   Number of persons

Age, sex and year		Immediate custodial sentences					Total persons sentenced
		Determinate sentence	Extended sentence of imprisonment[1][2] (EPP)	Imprisonment[1] for public protection (IPP)	Life sentence	Total immediate custody	
All persons							
Aged 10-17	2002	7,394	*	*	22	7,416	94,548
	2003	6,189	*	*	11	6,200	92,531
	2004	6,309	*	*	16	6,325	96,188
	2005	5,888	73	26	28	6,015	96,203
	2006	6,019	103	45	16	6,183	93,806
	2007	5,642	101	61	26	5,830	97,387
	2008	5,350	53	70	25	5,498	88,375
	2009	4,873	17	27	23	4,940	81,544
	2010	4,149	10	41	19	4,219	73,866
	2011	4,134	27	29	15	4,205	63,424
	2012	3,035	6	30	14	3,085	47,515
Aged 18-20	2002	17,340	*	*	23	17,363	159,384
	2003	15,387	*	*	51	15,438	162,067
	2004	14,610	*	*	26	14,636	156,399
	2005	13,995	117	65	54	14,231	146,051
	2006	13,480	163	206	48	13,897	142,694
	2007	13,767	152	299	73	14,291	140,276
	2008	13,067	113	219	56	13,455	137,575
	2009	13,776	61	122	58	14,017	141,968
	2010	13,015	58	110	41	13,224	131,344
	2011	12,078	97	70	35	12,280	120,103
	2012	9,798	35	78	48	9,959	98,662
Aged 21 and over	2002	85,867	451	*	510	86,828	1,156,573
	2003	84,707	874	*	451	86,032	1,225,214
	2004	83,639	1,194	*	528	85,361	1,284,238
	2005	78,809	1,303	335	543	80,990	1,231,021
	2006	73,224	1,033	1,197	483	75,937	1,176,440
	2007	72,468	877	1,347	393	75,085	1,169,125
	2008	78,376	505	1,249	442	80,572	1,127,987
	2009	79,726	356	852	340	81,274	1,174,766
	2010	82,493	385	868	324	84,070	1,152,390
	2011	88,096	524	720	345	89,685	1,122,143
	2012	83,718	296	643	346	85,003	1,077,075
All ages	2002	110,601	451	*	555	111,607	1,410,504
	2003	106,283	874	*	513	107,670	1,479,812
	2004	104,558	1,194	*	570	106,322	1,536,825
	2005	98,692	1,493	426	625	101,236	1,473,275
	2006	92,723	1,299	1,448	547	96,017	1,412,940
	2007	91,877	1,130	1,707	492	95,206	1,406,788
	2008	96,793	671	1,538	523	99,525	1,353,937
	2009	98,375	434	1,001	421	100,231	1,398,278
	2010	99,657	453	1,019	384	101,513	1,357,600
	2011	104,308	648	819	395	106,170	1,305,670
	2012	96,551	337	751	408	98,047	1,223,252

(1) Detention for persons under 21.

(2) Persons whose offences were committed prior to 4 April 2005 will have been sentenced to an extended sentence under s85 of Powers of the Criminal Court (Sentencing) Act 2000.

Note: Excludes data for Cardiff magistrates' court for April, July and August 2008.

21.10 Prison receptions and population in custody

England and Wales

Numbers[1]

		2002	2003	2004	2005	2006	2007	2008	2009	2010	2011	2012
Receptions												
Type of inmate:												
Untried	KEDA	58,708	58,696	54,556	55,455	55,809	55,305	57,417	55,207	-	54,837	50,227
Convicted, unsentenced	KEDB	53,301	53,246	50,115	49,104	47,995	43,566	44,773	37,003	-	39,391	36,646
Sentenced	KEDE	94,807	93,495	95,161	92,452	90,038	91,736	100,348	94,964	-	90,955	86,437
Immediate custodial sentence	KEDF	93,615	92,245	93,326	90,414	88,134	90,261	98,820	93,621	-	89,822	85,322
Young offenders	KEDG	20,236	18,179	18,264	17,819	17,985	19,022	19,489	17,745	-	15,731	13,190
Up to 12 months	KEDH	12,891	11,850	11,855	11,610	11,526	12,295	12,654	11,097	-	9,145	7,319
12 months up to 4 years	KEDJ	6,355	5,412	5,426	5,243	5,317	5,530	5,573	5,475	-	5,462	4,818
4 years up to and including life	KEDL	990	917	983	966	1,142	1,197	1,262	1,173	-	1,124	1,053
Adults	KFBO	73,379	74,066	75,062	72,595	70,149	71,239	79,331	75,877	-	74,091	72,132
Up to 12 months	KEDV	47,870	48,962	49,814	48,190	45,768	46,706	52,331	48,540	-	44,272	42,267
12 months up to 4 years	KEDW	18,313	17,968	17,988	17,397	16,970	17,233	19,061	19,804	-	21,855	21,696
4 years up to and including life	KEDX	7,196	7,136	7,260	7,008	7,411	7,300	7,939	7,533	-	7,964	8,169
Committed in default of payment of a fine	KEDY	1,192	1,250	1,835	1,876	1,904	1,475	1,528	1,343	-	1,133	1,115
Young offenders	KEEA	110	116	155	162	118	92	101	73	-	54	45
Adults	KAFQ	1,082	1,134	1,680	1,714	1,786	1,383	1,427	1,270	-	1,079	1,070
Non-criminal prisoners	KEDM	2,674	3,142	3,669	3,668	4,734	3,888	3,836	4,282	-	2,565	2,495
Immigration Act 1971	KEDN	2,093	2,457	3,041	3,093	4,073	3,347	3,466	-	-	2,304	2,238
Others	KEDO	581	685	628	575	661	541	370	-	-	261	257
Population (30 June)[2]												
Total in prison service establishments	KFBQ	71,218	73,657	74,488	76,190	77,982	79,734	83,193	83,454	85,002	85,374	86,048
Untried	KEDQ	7,877	7,896	7,716	8,084	8,064	8,387	8,750	8,933	8,487	8,299	7,671
Convicted, unsentenced	KEDR	5,204	5,177	4,779	4,780	5,003	4,457	4,690	4,523	4,517	4,165	3,653
Total sentenced	KEDU	57,306	59,439	60,976	62,257	63,493	65,601	68,233	68,488	71,000	71,964	73,562
Total Immediate custodial sentence	KFBR	57,272	59,393	60,924	62,179	63,404	65,533	68,123	68,375	70,871	71,835	73,435
Young offenders	KFBS	8,267	7,823	7,644	7,700	7,852	8,518	8,689	8,405	7,808	7,305	6,846
Determinate sentence	I7IJ	8,143	7,679	7,498	7,541	7,533	7,936	7,984	7,781	6,877	6,442	6,125
Indeterminate sentence	I7IL	124	144	146	159	319	582	705	624	454	358	300
Recalls		0	0	0	0	0	0	0	0	477	505	421
Adults	KFCO	49,005	51,570	53,280	54,479	55,552	57,015	59,434	59,970	63,063	64,530	66,589
Determinate sentence	I7IK	43,982	46,293	47,832	48,756	48,596	48,116	48,757	48,073	45,510	46,103	48,139
Indeterminate sentence	I7IM	5,023	5,277	5,448	5,723	6,956	8,899	10,677	11,897	12,680	13,286	13,454
Recalls		0	0	0	0	0	0	0	0	4,873	5,141	4,996
Committed in default of payment of a fine	KFCS	34	46	52	78	89	68	110	113	129	129	127
Young offenders	KFEW	0	3	5	3	5	4	6	5	5	6	4
Adults	KFEX	34	43	47	75	84	64	104	108	124	123	123
Non-criminal prisoners	KEEB	831	1,145	1,017	1,069	1,422	1,289	1,520	1,510	998	946	1,162
Immigration Act 1971	KEEC	759	1,079	957	996	1,366	1,218	1,473	1,465	963	918	1,140
Others	KEED	72	66	60	73	56	71	47	45	35	28	22
Accommodation[2]	I7IQ	64,232	66,104	67,576	69,443	70,585	73,618	73,452	74,849	77,855	79,292	80,843

Source: Ministry of Justice

1 Due to the introduction of a new prison IT system the 2010 prison population data is now taken from a different source and recalls are shown separately (they were previously included in the relevant sentence length band). See OMCS 2010 for more details.

2 In use Certified Normal Accommodation at 30 June every year.

21.11 Prison population under immediate custodial sentence by age and offence (2005 to 2012)

England and Wales

Numbers

	Total	15 - 17	18 - 20	21 - 24	25 - 29	30 - 39	40 - 49	50 - 59	60 and over
					Age				
At 30 June 2005									
Offences									
Males									
Total	58,707	1,782	5,595	9,937	10,969	16,843	8,731	3,256	1,594
Violence against the person	14,541	366	1,493	2,553	2,553	4,015	2,402	840	319
Sexual offences	6,147	65	186	397	505	1,436	1,552	1,084	922
Robbery	8,035	422	1,307	1,819	1,705	2,035	649	83	15
Burglary	7,844	285	719	1,559	1,947	2,570	669	78	17
Theft, handling, fraud and forgery	4,997	240	433	858	1,074	1,449	650	238	55
Drugs offences	9,429	76	491	1,332	1,834	3,263	1,741	544	148
Other offences	7,079	310	870	1,306	1,245	1,902	987	360	99
Offence not known	635	18	96	113	106	173	81	29	19
Females									
Total	3,479	55	269	614	680	1,073	585	179	24
Violence against the person	638	23	68	109	85	190	114	40	9
Sexual offences	39	0	2	3	4	12	8	7	3
Robbery	343	16	59	61	82	102	20	3	0
Burglary	239	4	18	50	62	79	23	3	0
Theft, handling, fraud and forgery	583	4	35	105	119	202	88	27	3
Drugs offences	1,234	3	54	195	255	366	268	84	9
Other offences	374	5	30	84	68	117	56	14	0
Offence not known	29	0	3	7	5	5	8	1	0
At 30 June 2006									
Offences									
Males									
Total	59,898	1,814	5,716	9,612	11,349	16,828	9,349	3,511	1,719
Violence against the person	15,537	381	1,563	2,616	2,977	4,109	2,609	935	348
Sexual offences	6,561	67	213	452	560	1,497	1,683	1,118	971
Robbery	8,100	486	1,413	1,739	1,674	1,975	706	91	16
Burglary	7,563	275	707	1,363	1,838	2,554	715	97	15
Theft, handling, fraud and forgery	5,147	200	451	830	1,093	1,598	707	214	54
Drugs offences	9,484	68	492	1,232	1,913	3,153	1,829	623	174
Other offences	7,129	327	835	1,326	1,231	1,838	1,040	406	129
Offence not known	378	12	43	55	64	105	60	28	10
Females									
Total	3,506	50	271	551	707	1,094	604	189	39
Violence against the person	678	11	75	111	101	205	118	48	9
Sexual offences	37	1	3	2	2	8	13	5	3
Robbery	315	17	48	67	76	86	18	2	0
Burglary	228	7	13	39	63	80	24	2	0
Theft, handling, fraud and forgery	671	3	30	97	171	232	106	24	7
Drugs offences	1,163	4	62	168	217	354	253	88	17
Other offences	385	7	36	61	72	120	67	19	3
Offence not known	30	1	5	5	4	9	5	1	0
At 30 June 2007									
Offences									
Males									
Total	62,188	1,827	6,354	9,860	11,653	16,606	10,092	3,823	1,973
Violence against the person	16,929	402	1,772	2,927	3,183	4,337	2,846	1,063	399
Sexual offences	7,287	73	276	487	675	1,555	1,909	1,202	1,112
Robbery	8,437	495	1,558	1,855	1,716	1,928	774	96	14
Burglary	7,723	281	817	1,334	1,865	2,492	812	109	13
Theft, handling, fraud and forgery	4,844	194	426	677	1,044	1,478	711	246	67
Drugs offences	9,569	71	546	1,285	1,858	3,002	1,908	689	210
Other offences	7,051	294	908	1,237	1,242	1,731	1,087	401	152
Offence not known	348	17	51	59	69	83	47	18	5
Females									
Total	3,345	56	280	475	662	1,011	610	202	49
Violence against the person	687	20	99	113	111	170	117	47	11
Sexual offences	48	0	1	3	7	16	15	4	2
Robbery	311	13	54	53	78	82	27	2	1
Burglary	197	2	11	28	56	76	23	1	0
Theft, handling, fraud and forgery	601	7	29	68	128	211	111	37	10
Drugs offences	1,044	3	42	124	201	335	230	90	19
Other offences	423	9	45	75	76	115	77	20	6
Offence not known	35	2	0	10	5	6	10	2	0

21.11 Prison population under immediate custodial sentence by age and offence (2005 to 2012)

England and Wales

	Total	15 - 17	18 - 20	21 - 24	25 - 29	30 - 39	40 - 49	50 - 59	60 and over
					Age				
At 30 June 2008									
Offences									
Males									
Total	64,600	1,876	6,454	10,373	12,144	17,056	10,564	3,995	2,139
Violence against the person	18,159	486	1,843	3,162	3,405	4,603	3,078	1,130	452
Sexual offences	7,569	74	300	513	729	1,552	1,997	1,204	1,200
Robbery	8,437	472	1,517	1,904	1,760	1,883	783	106	12
Burglary	7,733	315	831	1,294	1,793	2,521	854	108	16
Theft, handling, fraud and forgery	5,098	151	379	663	1,107	1,681	780	256	80
Drugs offences	9,992	106	672	1,437	1,929	2,994	1,914	726	215
Other offences	7,380	264	878	1,360	1,370	1,772	1,119	453	162
Offence not known									
	232	8	34	40	51	49	38	11	3
Females									
Total	3,524	57	303	523	698	1,033	654	201	55
Violence against the person	771	19	99	139	129	188	140	45	12
Sexual offences	47	0	0	7	7	10	15	6	2
Robbery	295	13	43	46	83	89	20	1	1
Burglary	203	5	15	23	52	70	33	5	0
Theft, handling, fraud and forgery	757	6	39	96	167	252	133	50	14
Drugs offences	990	5	56	145	180	289	219	74	22
Other offences	438	9	51	66	75	127	88	19	4
Offence not known	24	1	1	2	5	7	6	2	0
At 30 June 2009									
Offences									
Males									
Total	64,993	1,517	6,593	10,798	12,004	16,779	10,930	4,091	2,281
Violence against the person	19,108	366	1,949	3,408	3,604	4,750	3,345	1,188	497
Sexual offences	7,919	77	295	572	830	1,498	2,096	1,279	1,272
Robbery	8,715	440	1,611	2,053	1,810	1,873	790	123	14
Burglary	7,678	248	909	1,370	1,650	2,498	865	122	15
Theft, handling, fraud and forgery	4,592	125	325	641	926	1,501	723	253	96
Drugs offences	9,803	82	643	1,437	1,881	2,937	1,924	693	208
Other offences	6,888	175	818	1,266	1,236	1,656	1,144	416	178
Offence not known	291	4	42	52	67	65	43	15	3
Females									
Total	3,382	42	253	478	676	981	653	237	63
Violence against the person	839	15	101	137	136	205	172	57	15
Sexual offences	54	0	3	7	5	14	16	7	1
Robbery	334	10	45	58	83	96	36	5	1
Burglary	207	3	13	31	66	56	35	3	0
Theft, handling, fraud and forgery	665	3	26	69	135	225	137	55	16
Drugs offences	893	4	42	110	183	270	177	85	23
Other offences	378	7	23	64	68	108	78	25	6
Offence not known	13	0	0	2	1	7	3	0	0
At 30 June 2010									
Offences									
Males									
Total	67,450	1,162	6,337	11,358	12,350	17,539	11,600	4,540	2,564
Violence against the person	19,349	306	1,820	3,479	3,721	4,864	3,376	1,284	499
Sexual offences	9,221	57	399	818	982	1,763	2,319	1,417	1,466
Robbery	8,562	283	1,451	2,113	1,787	1,923	843	141	21
Burglary	6,706	201	838	1,219	1,320	2,164	826	116	22
Theft, handling, fraud and forgery	4,771	80	323	629	963	1,560	794	297	125
Drugs offences	10,235	63	579	1,537	1,983	3,097	2,028	730	218
Other offences	7,805	167	829	1,428	1,422	1,959	1,294	517	189
Offence not known	801	5	98	135	172	209	120	38	24

21.11 Prison population under immediate custodial sentence by age and offence (2005 to 2012)

England and Wales   Numbers

					Age				
	Total	15 - 17	18 - 20	21 - 24	25 - 29	30 - 39	40 - 49	50 - 59	60 and over
Females									
Total	**3,421**	**23**	**286**	**480**	**665**	**992**	**661**	**260**	**54**
Violence against the person	898	10	114	138	147	228	171	75	15
Sexual offences	83	0	7	9	10	26	20	8	3
Robbery	272	5	40	41	74	87	21	4	0
Burglary	151	0	10	23	32	56	27	3	0
Theft, handling, fraud and forgery	623	1	23	75	137	189	135	51	12
Drugs offences	829	1	39	104	172	254	168	77	14
Other offences	479	4	39	85	77	124	101	41	8
Offence not known	86	2	14	5	16	28	18	1	2
At 30 June 2011									
Offences									
Males									
Total	**68,424**	**1,134**	**5,896**	**11,349**	**12,341**	**17,988**	**11,934**	**5,039**	**2,743**
Violence against the person	19,520	232	1,615	3,376	3,705	5,078	3,512	1,447	555
Sexual offences	9,767	47	399	913	1,005	1,798	2,369	1,657	1,579
Robbery	8,842	289	1,408	2,143	1,874	2,067	853	178	28
Burglary	6,931	204	840	1,262	1,332	2,211	921	139	22
Theft, handling, fraud and forgery	4949	87	317	695	951	1,574	887	331	107
Drugs offences	9,899	59	525	1,456	1,892	3,051	1,982	721	213
Other offences	8,043	202	751	1,405	1,506	2,090	1,331	533	225
Offence not known	475	14	41	99	76	119	79	33	14
Females									
Total	**3,411**	**16**	**259**	**460**	**646**	**1,036**	**682**	**258**	**54**
Violence against the person	911	7	81	149	151	228	195	83	17
Sexual offences	83	1	7	4	14	27	19	8	3
Robbery	301	4	42	53	80	95	23	3	1
Burglary	171	0	6	19	42	66	33	5	0
Theft, handling, fraud and forgery	625	1	20	80	125	204	127	56	12
Drugs offences	722	0	35	76	135	251	156	61	8
Other offences	553	3	61	75	96	150	117	40	11
Offence not known	45	0	7	4	3	15	12	2	2
At 30 June 2012									
Offences									
Males									
Total	**69,976**	**979**	**5,623**	**11,403**	**12,604**	**18,429**	**12,420**	**5,523**	**2,995**
Violence against the person	19,488	217	1,439	3,305	3,737	5,105	3,571	1,510	604
Sexual offences	10,390	47	376	948	1,068	1,897	2,470	1,833	1,751
Robbery	8,951	301	1,396	2,153	1,929	2,073	879	189	31
Burglary	7,137	150	800	1,331	1,324	2,373	972	165	22
Theft, handling, fraud and forgery	5,390	72	362	758	963	1,683	1,009	427	116
Drugs offences	10,108	32	506	1,489	1,958	3,122	2,043	755	203
Other offences	8,062	152	705	1,350	1,543	2,059	1,390	615	248
Offence not known	450	8	39	69	82	117	86	29	20
Females									
Total	**3,459**	**16**	**228**	**455**	**625**	**1,066**	**705**	**295**	**69**
Violence against the person	949	8	87	146	168	225	202	89	24
Sexual offences	83	0	6	6	11	25	23	8	4
Robbery	328	2	35	58	75	120	36	2	0
Burglary	208	1	15	27	46	79	30	9	1
Theft, handling, fraud and forgery	710	0	25	72	120	237	164	72	20
Drugs offences	574	2	18	72	95	196	123	60	8
Other offences	562	2	38	70	102	170	119	49	12
Offence not known	45	1	4	4	8	14	8	6	0

Source: Ministry of Justice

1 The data presented in this table are drawn from administrative IT systems. Where figures in the table have been rounded to the nearest whole number, the rounded components do not always add to the totals, which are calculated and rounded independently. Reconciliation exercises with published Home Office figures may demonstrate differences due to rounded components.

2 Excludes persons committed in default of payment of a fine.

21.12 Crimes recorded by the police, Scotland, 2003-04 to 2012-13

Number & Percentage

Crime group	2003-04	2004-05	2005-06	2006-07	2007-08	2008-09	2009-10	2010-11	2011-12	2012-13	% change 11-12 to 12-13
Total Crimes	414,214	438,123	417,785	419,257	385,509	377,433	338,124	323,247	314,188	273,053	-13
Non-sexual crimes of violence	15,187	14,728	13,726	14,099	12,874	12,612	11,228	11,438	9,533	7,530	-21
Homicide[1]	149	165	121	159	142	134	106	122	121	91	-25
Attempted murder & serious assault	7,365	7,603	7,030	7,345	6,711	6,472	5,621	5,493	4,693	3,643	-22
Robbery	4,161	3,736	3,553	3,578	3,064	2,963	2,496	2,557	2,244	1,832	-18
Other	3,512	3,224	3,022	3,017	2,957	3,043	3,005	3,266	2,475	1,964	-21
Sexual offences[2,3]	6,785	7,325	6,558	6,726	6,552	6,331	6,527	6,696	7,361	7,693	5
Rape & attempted rape	1,037	1,109	1,161	1,123	1,053	963	996	1,131	1,274	1,462	15
Sexual assault[3]	3,257	3,470	3,392	3,452	3,502	3,297	3,412	3,220	2,908	3,008	3
Offences associated with prostitution	1,249	1,458	730	779	682	765	661	576	567	534	-6
Other	1,242	1,288	1,275	1,372	1,315	1,306	1,458	1,769	2,612	2,689	3
Crimes of dishonesty	211,004	210,365	187,798	183,760	166,718	167,812	153,256	155,870	154,337	135,899	-12
Housebreaking[4]	36,432	34,959	31,319	30,580	25,443	25,496	23,774	25,017	24,222	21,515	-11
Theft by opening a lockfast place (OLP)	7,405	7,849	8,263	7,422	6,378	6,952	5,074	4,059	3,529	3,239	-8
Theft from a motor vehicle by OLP	26,839	20,403	16,453	16,060	15,217	13,649	10,173	9,495	8,988	6,159	-31
Theft of a motor vehicle	17,604	15,633	14,041	15,000	12,105	11,551	9,304	8,716	7,060	5,731	-19
Shoplifting	27,948	28,534	28,247	28,750	29,186	32,048	30,332	29,660	29,758	26,449	-11
Other theft	72,488	77,586	72,128	70,241	64,645	64,384	61,008	64,680	66,681	58,704	-12
Fraud	15,277	18,307	11,074	9,332	8,409	8,316	8,283	8,983	8,892	8,898	0
Other	7,011	7,094	6,273	6,375	5,335	5,416	5,308	5,260	5,207	5,204	0
Fire-raising, vandalism etc.	103,732	128,566	127,889	129,734	118,025	109,430	93,443	82,020	75,201	59,479	-21
Fire-raising	4,163	4,698	4,856	4,976	4,635	4,651	4,244	3,966	3,755	3,066	-18
Vandalism etc.	99,569	123,868	123,033	124,758	113,390	104,779	89,199	78,054	71,446	56,413	-21
Other crimes	77,506	77,139	81,814	84,938	81,340	81,248	73,670	67,223	67,756	62,452	-8
Crimes against public justice	25,756	25,616	27,668	32,052	31,353	29,493	26,885	26,294	26,635	23,401	-12
Handling an offensive weapon	9,278	9,545	9,628	10,110	8,989	8,980	7,042	6,283	5,631	4,015	-29
Drugs	42,275	41,823	44,247	42,422	40,746	42,509	39,408	34,347	35,157	34,688	-1
Other	197	155	271	354	252	266	335	299	333	348	5

Notes:

1. Includes Murder, and Culpable homicide, which includes Causing death by dangerous driving, Causing death by careless driving while under the influence of drink or drugs, Causing death by careless driving and Corporate homicide.
2. Implementation of Sexual Offences (Scotland) Act will have an effect on comparability of breakdown of Sexual offences over time.
3. The totals of these categories for 2011-12 have been revised following the submission of amended data from Grampian Police.
4. Includes dwellings, non-dwellings and other premises.

21.13 People with a charge proved by main crime/offence, 2003-04 to 2012-13 Scotland

Main Crime or Offence	2003-04	2004-05	2005-06	2006-07	2007-08	2008-09	2009-10[1]	2010-11	2011-12	2012-13[2]	% change 2011-12 to 2012-13	All offences proved 2012-13[2,3]
All Crimes and offences	128,520	129,733	128,204	134,413	133,608	125,895	121,042	115,576	108,378	100,964	-7	134,063
All crimes	43,314	44,713	43,299	46,998	46,858	45,160	42,176	40,973	39,192	35,628	-9	46,959
Non-sexual crimes of violence	2,596	2,429	2,459	2,461	2,749	2,658	2,462	2,538	2,432	2,125	-13	2,351
Homicide	131	143	111	121	136	116	118	117	111	113	2	118
Serious assault and attempted murder	1,476	1,376	1,561	1,496	1,731	1,709	1,511	1,417	1,349	1,276	-5	1,335
Robbery	689	610	512	529	548	562	532	526	593	513	-13	626
Other violence	300	300	275	315	334	271	301	478	379	223	-41	272
Sexual Crimes	678	839	864	855	727	915	830	756	783	866	11	1,352
Rape and attempted rape	59	70	61	60	49	42	57	36	49	77	57	119
Sexual assault	209	197	185	184	145	182	158	159	150	206	37	448
Offences associated with prostitution	130	229	292	306	254	335	250	245	200	12	-29	145
Other indecency	280	343	326	305	279	356	365	316	384	441	15	640
Crimes of dishonesty	19,825	19,610	17,997	18,381	17,728	17,429	15,951	15,614	14,772	13,236	-10	17,295
Housebreaking	2,508	2,372	2,074	2,025	1,867	1,860	1,604	1,540	1,498	1,365	-9	1,694
Theft by opening a lockfast place	504	458	366	398	389	349	312	284	291	246	-15	352
Theft from a motor vehicle	725	649	489	408	447	387	297	270	250	200	-20	307
Theft of a motor vehicle	1,086	942	847	851	776	733	572	484	450	372	-17	730
Shoplifting	8,123	8,427	8,162	8,548	8,457	8,287	8,098	7,853	7,267	6,491	-11	7,806
Other theft	3,652	3,668	3,289	3,430	3,260	3,113	2,768	2,871	2,961	2,719	-8	3,520
Fraud	1,636	1,537	1,457	1,355	1,337	1,438	1,142	1,065	811	623	-23	1,265
Other dishonesty	1,591	1,557	1,313	1,366	1,195	1,262	1,158	1,247	1,244	1,220	-2	1,621
Fire-raising, vandalism, etc	4,759	5,028	5,000	5,438	5,392	4,375	3,836	3,362	3,015	2,579	-14	3,327
Fire-raising	169	192	192	251	224	244	190	159	145	133	-8	150
Vandalism, etc	4,590	4,836	4,808	5,187	5,168	4,131	3,646	3,203	2,870	2,446	-15	3,177
Other crimes	15,456	16,807	16,979	19,863	20,262	19,783	19,097	18,703	18,190	16,822	-8	22,634
Crimes against public justice	5,293	5,774	5,764	7,218	8,043	8,704	8,351	8,494	8,720	8,421	-3	11,861
Handling an offensive weapon	2,875	3,447	3,500	3,550	3,422	3,539	2,863	2,465	2,278	1,733	-24	2,092
Drugs	7,258	7,555	7,606	8,892	8,529	7,302	7,694	7,525	6,979	6,457	-7	8,447
Other crime	30	31	109	203	268	238	189	219	213	211	-1	234
All offences	85,206	85,020	84,905	87,415	86,750	80,735	78,864	74,603	69,186	65,336	-6	87,104
Miscellaneous offences	34,523	37,463	39,666	42,301	41,394	35,804	32,884	30,496	30,902	29,911	-3	41,593
Common assault	12,378	13,644	14,502	15,517	15,616	15,292	14,361	13,927	14,207	13,039	-8	17,233
Breach of the peace, etc.	15,050	16,172	16,894	18,104	17,494	16,004	14,077	12,114	12,544	12,935	3	18,789
Drunkenness	418	311	293	261	235	129	146	160	124	102	-18	208
Other offences	6,677	7,336	7,977	8,419	8,049	4,379	4,300	4,295	4,027	3,835	-5	5,363
Motor vehicle offences	50,683	47,557	45,239	45,114	45,356	44,931	45,980	44,107	38,284	35,425	-7	45,511
Dangerous and careless driving	4,067	3,774	3,620	3,774	3,967	3,696	3,404	3,167	2,858	2,812	-2	3,362
Drink/drug driving	8,145	7,997	7,970	8,066	7,820	7,222	6,232	5,351	5,287	4,730	-11	5,226
Speeding	12,539	13,512	12,252	13,395	14,156	13,589	14,357	12,955	12,381	12,028	-3	12,338
Unlawful use of vehicle	19,334	16,592	14,703	13,450	13,609	12,741	12,175	11,053	9,002	7,842	-13	13,703
Vehicle defect offences	1,823	1,786	1,652	1,707	1,414	1,483	1,662	1,723	1,504	1,241	-17	2,204
Other vehicle	4,775	3,896	5,042	4,722	4,390	6,200	8,150	9,858	7,252	6,772	-7	8,678

1. Includes two cases with unknown crime.

2. Figures for some categories dealt with by the High Court - including homicide, rape and major drug cases - may be underestimated slightly due to late recording of disposals

3. Number of individual offences relating to people with a charge proved, whether or not the main crime/offence involved. Breaches of social work orders are not counted as individual offences.

21.14 People with a charge proved by type of court, 2003-04 to 2012-13
Scotland

Number

Type of court	2003-04	2004-05	2005-06	2006-07	2007-08	2008-09	2009-10	2010-11	2011-12	2012-13
All court types[1]	128,520	129,733	128,204	134,413	133,608	125,895	121,042	115,576	108,378	100,964
High court [2,3]	1,217	974	885	908	861	810	771	702	722	691
Sheriff solemn	3,535	3,670	3,967	4,682	5,195	4,532	4,222	4,021	4,138	4,298
Sheriff summary	76,621	77,196	75,989	80,503	79,981	73,898	65,585	61,572	60,677	56,339
Justice of the Peace court [4,5]	47,144	47,891	47,358	48,319	47,569	46,632	50,448	49,281	42,841	39,636

Per cent

Type of court	2003-04	2004-05	2005-06	2006-07	2007-08	2008-09	2009-10	2010-11	2011-12	2012-13
All court types[1]	100	100	100	100	100	100	100	100	100	100
High court [2,3]	1	1	1	1	1	1	1	1	1	1
Sheriff solemn	3	3	3	3	4	4	3	3	4	4
Sheriff summary	60	60	59	60	60	59	54	53	56	56
Justice of the Peace court [4,5]	37	37	37	36	36	37	42	43	40	39

Index: 2003-04=100

Type of court	2003-04	2004-05	2005-06	2006-07	2007-08	2008-09	2009-10	2010-11	2011-12	2012-13
All court types[1]	100	101	100	105	104	98	94	90	84	79
High court [2,3]	100	80	73	75	71	67	63	58	59	57
Sheriff solemn	100	104	112	132	147	128	119	114	117	122
Sheriff summary	100	101	99	105	104	96	86	80	79	74
Justice of the Peace court [4,5]	100	102	100	102	101	99	107	105	91	84

1. Includes court type unknown.
2. Includes cases remitted to the High court from the Sheriff court.
3. The figures for 2012-13, and to an extent earlier years, may be underestimates due to late recording of disposals.
4. Includes the stipendiary magistrates court in Glasgow.
5. Includes District courts up to 2009-10

21.15 People with a charge proved by main penalty, 2003-04 to 2012-13
Scotland

Number

Main penalty	2003-04	2004-05	2005-06	2006-07	2007-08	2008-09	2009-10	2010-11	2011-12	2012-13	% change 11-12 to 12-13
Total[1]	128,520	129,733	128,204	134,413	133,608	125,895	121,042	115,576	108,378	100,964	-7
Custody	14,784	15,011	15,082	16,758	16,761	16,944	15,801	15,313	15,911	14,758	-7
Prison	11,959	12,306	12,155	13,489	13,593	13,905	13,019	13,127	13,696	13,046	-5
Young offenders institution	2,801	2,685	2,903	3,245	3,142	3,017	2,753	2,168	2,202	1,688	-23
Other custody	24	20	24	24	26	21	22	12	6	10	67
Order for life-long restriction	-	-	-	-	-	1	7	6	7	14	100
Community sentence	13,943	15,316	15,973	16,077	16,709	17,922	16,350	15,617	16,934	17,254	2
Community payback order	-	-	-	-	-	-	-	461	10,380	14,924	44
Community service order	4,299	4,850	5,183	5,286	5,601	5,784	5,471	5,308	2,642	479	-82
Probation	8,137	8,623	8,785	8,614	9,002	9,912	8,893	7,935	2,305	295	-87
Restriction of liberty order	879	1,097	1,136	1,179	1,155	1,143	931	831	845	910	8
Drug treatment & testing order	610	713	758	865	822	885	808	806	642	621	-3
Supervised attendance order[2]	18	33	99	112	129	198	247	276	120	25	-79
Community reparation order	-	-	11	15	-	-	-	-	-	-	-
Anti-social behaviour order	-	-	1	6	-	-	-	-	-	-	-
Financial penalty	86,094	84,932	82,194	84,820	83,345	73,993	72,491	67,575	59,320	53,423	-10
Fine	84,327	83,237	80,723	83,445	82,020	72,840	71,452	66,491	58,395	52,654	-10
Compensation order	1,767	1,695	1,471	1,375	1,325	1,153	1,039	1,084	925	769	-17
Other sentence[1]	13,699	14,474	14,955	16,758	16,793	17,036	16,400	17,071	16,213	15,529	-4
Insanity, hospital, guardianship order	129	95	115	65	20	16	15	19	24	31	29
Admonition[3]	12,935	13,744	14,175	15,967	16,084	16,399	15,687	16,422	15,577	15,010	-4
Absolute discharge	435	403	401	413	430	412	523	460	472	358	-24
Remit to children's hearing	196	221	260	313	259	209	175	170	140	130	-7
Average amount of penalty[4]											
Custody (days)[5]	257	238	229	232	248	263	284	278	286	283	
Community service order (hours)	154	149	148	147	146	146	146	149	155	161	
Fine[6,7] (£)	208	217	211	213	219	229	217	215	241	245	
Compensation order[7,8] (£)	208	247	282	335	322	378	394	391	426	439	

1. Includes a small number of sentence unknown for the years 2003-04, 2004-05 and 2005-06.
2. Of first instance.
3. Includes a small number of court cautions and dog-related disposals.
4. Excludes indeterminate/not known sentences.
5. Figures for 2012-13 may be underestimates.
6. Excludes company fines.
7. Excludes a small number of large fines.
8. As main or secondary penalty.

Percentage

Main penalty	2003-04	2004-05	2005-06	2006-07	2007-08	2008-09	2009-10	2010-11	2011-12	2012-13
Total										
Custody	12	12	12	12	13	13	13	13	15	15
Prison	9	9	9	10	10	11	11	11	13	13
Young offenders institution	2	2	2	2	2	2	2	2	2	2
Other custody	*	*	*	*	*	*	*	*	*	*
Order for life-long restriction	-	-	-	-	-	*	*	*	*	*
Community sentence	11	12	12	12	13	14	14	14	16	17
Community payback order	-	-	-	-	-	-	-	*	10	15
Community service order	3	4	4	4	4	5	5	5	2	*
Probation	6	7	7	6	7	8	7	7	2	*
Restriction of liberty order	1	1	1	1	1	1	1	1	1	1
Drug treatment & testing order	*	1	1	1	1	1	1	1	1	1
Supervised attendance order	*	*	*	*	*	*	*	*	*	*
Financial penalty	67	65	64	63	62	59	60	58	55	53
Fine	66	64	63	62	61	58	59	58	54	52
Compensation order	1	1	1	1	1	1	1	1	1	1
Other sentence	11	11	12	12	13	14	14	15	15	15
Insanity, hospital, guardianship order	*	*	*	*	*	*	*	*	*	*
Admonition	10	11	11	12	12	13	13	14	14	15
Absolute discharge	*	*	*	*	*	*	*	*	*	*
Remit to children's hearing	*	*	*	*	*	*	*	*	*	*

21.16 People with a charge proved by main penalty, gender and age, 2003-04 to 2012-13
Scotland

		2003-04	2004-05	2005-06	2006-07	2007-08	2008-09	2009-10	2010-11	2011-12	2012-13	% change 11-12 -12-13
Total[1,2,3]		128,053	129,235	127,843	134,113	133,353	125,881	121,038	115,556	108,293	100,849	-7
Males	Total[4]	107,933	108,460	107,804	113,511	112,788	106,301	101,614	97,027	90,856	84,304	-7
	Under 21	23,550	23,205	24,185	25,639	24,525	20,535	17,328	15,144	13,130	10,351	-21
	21-30	40,053	39,337	38,079	40,404	41,222	38,899	37,315	35,174	32,735	30,332	-7
	Over 30	44,325	45,912	45,537	47,466	47,041	46,867	46,971	46,708	44,991	43,621	-3
Females	Total[4]	20,120	20,775	20,039	20,602	20,565	19,580	19,424	18,529	17,437	16,545	-5
	Under 21	2,944	2,909	2,937	3,264	3,306	2,830	2,511	2,228	1,952	1,615	-17
	21-30	7,494	7,652	7,387	7,401	7,387	7,313	7,010	6,572	5,989	5,866	-2
	Over 30	9,680	10,214	9,715	9,935	9,872	9,437	9,903	9,727	9,496	9,064	-5
Custody		14,784	15,010	15,082	16,758	16,761	16,944	15,801	15,312	15,911	14,758	-7
Males	Total[4]	13,684	13,809	13,939	15,583	15,486	15,591	14,521	14,010	14,543	13,474	-7
	Under 21	2,620	2,521	2,803	3,070	2,986	2,856	2,601	2,013	2,049	1,586	-23
	21-30	6,726	6,478	6,030	6,684	6,864	6,718	6,154	6,074	6,036	5,485	-9
	Over 30	4,338	4,809	5,106	5,829	5,636	6,017	5,766	5,923	6,458	6,403	-1
Females	Total[4]	1,100	1,201	1,143	1,175	1,275	1,353	1,280	1,302	1,368	1,284	-6
	Under 21	211	191	125	200	182	182	175	168	160	116	-28
	21-30	542	611	563	592	615	682	581	588	620	594	-4
	Over 30	347	399	455	383	478	489	524	546	588	574	-2
Community sentence		13,943	15,316	15,973	16,077	16,709	17,921	16,350	15,617	16,934	17,254	2
Males	Total[4]	11,624	12,821	13,355	13,566	13,886	14,955	13,484	12,979	14,087	14,386	2
	Under 21	3,583	3,914	4,158	4,486	4,471	4,608	3,640	3,446	3,292	2,741	-17
	21-30	4,435	4,832	4,920	4,878	4,935	5,303	5,037	4,697	5,246	5,585	6
	Over 30	3,606	4,075	4,277	4,202	4,480	5,044	4,807	4,836	5,549	6,060	9
Females	Total[4]	2,319	2,495	2,618	2,511	2,823	2,966	2,866	2,638	2,847	2,868	1
	Under 21	478	529	532	633	667	593	559	453	433	425	-2
	21-30	987	1,042	1,126	926	1,092	1,176	1,013	1,020	1,014	1,065	5
	Over 30	854	924	960	952	1,064	1,197	1,294	1,165	1,400	1,378	-2
Monetary		85,647	84,468	81,862	84,541	83,105	73,980	72,487	67,558	59,243	53,312	-10
Males	Total[4]	72,573	71,134	69,505	72,051	71,058	63,241	61,480	57,350	50,260	45,143	-10
	Under 21	14,389	13,765	14,029	14,646	13,597	9,886	8,462	7,070	5,365	4,060	-24
	21-30	25,771	24,840	23,884	25,214	25,791	23,102	22,258	20,357	17,798	15,818	-11
	Over 30	32,409	32,524	31,589	32,189	31,670	30,253	30,760	29,922	27,097	25,265	-7
Females	Total[4]	13,074	13,334	12,357	12,490	12,047	10,739	11,007	10,208	8,983	8,169	-9
	Under 21	1,549	1,494	1,507	1,572	1,569	1,206	1,061	909	746	533	-29
	21-30	4,572	4,611	4,254	4,253	4,140	3,754	3,818	3,381	2,907	2,702	-7
	Over 30	6,952	7,229	6,596	6,663	6,338	5,779	6,128	5,916	5,330	4,934	-7
Other sentence		13,679	14,441	14,926	16,737	16,778	17,036	16,400	17,069	16,205	15,525	-4
Males	Total[4]	10,052	10,696	11,005	12,311	12,358	12,514	12,129	12,688	11,966	11,301	-6
	Under 21	2,958	3,005	3,195	3,437	3,471	3,185	2,625	2,615	2,424	1,964	-19
	21-30	3,121	3,187	3,245	3,628	3,632	3,776	3,866	4,046	3,655	3,444	-6
	Over 30	3,972	4,504	4,565	5,246	5,255	5,553	5,638	6,027	5,887	5,893	0
Females	Total[4]	3,627	3,745	3,921	4,426	4,420	4,522	4,271	4,381	4,239	4,224	0
	Under 21	706	695	773	859	888	849	716	698	613	541	-12
	21-30	1,393	1,388	1,444	1,630	1,540	1,701	1,598	1,583	1,448	1,505	4
	Over 30	1,527	1,662	1,704	1,937	1,992	1,972	1,957	2,100	2,178	2,178	0

1.Includes people with sentence unknown.
2.Excludes people with gender unknown.
3. Excludes companies.
4.Includes people with age unknown.

21.17a Average daily population in penal establishments by type of custody: 2002-03 to 2011-12

	2002-03	2003-04	2004-05	2005-06	2006-07	2007-08	2008-09	2009-10	2010-11	2011-12	% change over past year
Total	**6,453**	**6,606**	**6,776**	**6,856**	**7,187**	**7,376**	**7,826**	**7,963**	**7,853**	**8,178**	*4*
Remand	1,207	1,237	1,223	1,250	1,572	1,561	1,679	1,522	1,474	1,600	*9*
Untried	1,055	1,075	1,036	1,032	1,329	1,306	1,415	1,170	1,112	1,237	*11*
Convicted awaiting sentence	152	163	188	218	243	255	264	352	362	363	*
Young offenders	273	256	261	285	361	355	334	305	262	258	*-1*
Adults	933	981	962	965	1,211	1,206	1,344	1,217	1,212	1,342	*11*
Sentenced	5,246	5,369	5,553	5,605	5,615	5,815	6,147	6,441	6,379	6,578	*3*
Young offenders (direct sentence)	569	539	544	607	621	658	657	690	576	534	*-7*
Adults (direct sentence)	4,379	4,474	4,599	4,553	4,433	4,518	4,879	5,120	5,111	5,332	*4*
Fine defaulters	56	55	51	47	46	28	11	9	9	9	*-4*
Recalls from supervision/licence	235	293	351	397	514	610	599	621	681	701	*3*
Others	6	7	5	1	*	*	-	-	-	*	-
Sentenced by court martial	*	*	1	-	-	*	1	-	1	1	-
Civil prisoners	1	1	1	1	1	1	*	1	*	1	-
Men	**6,171**	**6,293**	**6,444**	**6,521**	**6,833**	**7,005**	**7,414**	**7,539**	**7,419**	**7,710**	*4*
Remand	1,125	1,150	1,138	1,166	1,471	1,444	1,545	1,417	1,369	1,492	*9*
Untried	1,000	1,016	980	976	1,257	1,232	1,330	1,107	1,044	1,170	*12*
Convicted awaiting sentence	126	134	159	191	213	213	215	311	325	322	*-1*
Sentenced	5,046	5,143	5,306	5,355	5,363	5,561	5,869	6,122	6,050	6,218	*3*
Young offenders (direct sentence)	548	515	515	583	591	634	633	662	545	506	*-7*
Adults (direct sentence)	4,206	4,279	4,387	4,333	4,219	4,296	4,633	4,836	4,827	5,013	*4*
Fine defaulters	51	50	47	43	43	26	10	8	9	8	*-5*
Recalls from supervision/licence	235	291	350	395	510	603	592	614	669	689	*3*
Others	5	7	5	1	*	*	-	-	-	*	-
Sentenced by court martial	*	*	1	-	-	*	1	-	1	1	-
Civil prisoners	1	1	1	*	*	1	*	1	*	*	-
Women	**282**	**314**	**332**	**334**	**353**	**371**	**412**	**424**	**434**	**468**	*8*
Remand	81	88	85	84	101	117	133	105	105	108	*2*
Untried	55	59	56	57	72	74	85	63	68	67	*-1*
Convicted awaiting sentence	26	29	29	27	29	42	49	41	38	41	*8*
Sentenced	200	226	247	250	252	255	278	319	329	360	*9*
Young offenders (direct sentence)	20	24	30	24	30	24	25	28	32	28	*-12*
Adults (direct sentence)	173	196	212	221	215	222	246	284	284	319	*12*
Fine defaulters	5	4	4	4	3	2	1	1	*	*	-
Recalls from supervision/licence	1	2	1	2	4	7	7	6	13	13	-
Others	1	*	*	*	-	-	-	-	-	-	-
Sentenced by court martial	-	-	-	-	-	-	-	-	-	-	-
Civil prisoners	*	*	*	*	*	*	*	*	*	*	-

Source: Prison Statistics and Population Projections Scotland: 2011-12

Data for 2012-2013 not yet published expected 2015

21.17b Average daily population of sentenced offenders by sentence length: 2002-03 to 2011-12

	2002-03	2003-04	2004-05	2005-06	2006-07	2007-08	2008-09	2009-10	2010-11	2011-12	% change over past year
Total	**5,245**	**5,367**	**5,551**	**5,605**	**5,614**	**5,814**	**6,146**	**6,440**	**6,377**	**6,576**	*3*
Fine default	56	55	51	47	46	28	11	9	9	9	*-4*
Less than 3 months	88	68	81	101	124	116	98	89	78	50	*-36*
3 months - less than 6 months	433	403	450	442	444	426	402	350	347	383	*10*
6 months - less than 2 years	1,176	1,163	1,161	1,214	1,159	1,226	1,567	1,767	1,682	1,822	*8*
2 years - less than 4 years	814	857	884	913	959	1,058	1,099	1,211	1,183	1,172	*-1*
4 years or over (excluding life)	1,839	1,932	1,957	1,841	1,702	1,654	1,643	1,631	1,597	1,600	*
Life/Section 205/206 sentences	599	590	612	650	666	696	726	763	800	838	*5*
Persons recalled from supervision/licence	235	293	351	397	514	610	599	621	681	701	*3*
Others	6	7	5	1	*	*	-	-	-	-	*-*
Young offenders	**579**	**552**	**558**	**624**	**644**	**684**	**686**	**719**	**604**	**556**	*-8*
Fine default	7	6	5	5	5	2	1	1	1	1	*-*
Less than 3 months	13	9	9	14	13	13	11	8	6	3	*-56*
3 months - less than 6 months	63	51	55	57	58	59	50	45	37	34	*-8*
6 months - less than 2 years	231	216	212	241	241	243	267	307	242	246	*2*
2 years - less than 4 years	112	111	118	142	136	175	165	182	164	137	*-16*
4 years or over (excluding life)	131	132	130	127	143	136	134	126	103	94	*-9*
Life/Section 205/206 sentences	19	19	19	26	30	31	30	22	23	19	*-18*
Persons recalled from supervision/licence	3	7	8	11	19	25	28	28	26	22	*-19*
Others	*	1	1	*	-	-	-	-	-	-	*-*
Adults	**4,666**	**4,816**	**4,993**	**4,981**	**4,970**	**5,130**	**5,460**	**5,722**	**5,774**	**6,020**	*4*
Fine default	49	49	46	43	41	26	10	8	8	8	*-1*
Less than 3 months	76	59	71	87	111	102	88	81	72	47	*-35*
3 months - less than 6 months	370	353	395	386	386	367	352	305	310	349	*13*
6 months - less than 2 years	945	947	949	972	918	983	1,300	1,460	1,440	1,576	*9*
2 years - less than 4 years	702	746	766	771	823	883	935	1,029	1,019	1,035	*2*
4 years or over (excluding life)	1,708	1,799	1,827	1,713	1,559	1,518	1,510	1,505	1,493	1,507	*1*
Life/Section 205/206 sentences	579	571	592	623	637	664	696	741	776	819	*6*
Persons recalled from supervision/licence	233	286	343	385	495	585	571	593	655	680	*4*
Others	5	6	4	1	*	*	-	-	-	-	*-*
Men	**5,045**	**5,142**	**5,304**	**5,355**	**5,362**	**5,560**	**5,868**	**6,121**	**6,049**	**6,216**	*3*
Fine default	51	50	47	43	43	26	10	8	9	8	*-5*
Less than 3 months	83	62	75	94	116	108	91	83	73	45	*-38*
3 months - less than 6 months	407	378	421	415	419	402	375	324	319	352	*10*
6 months - less than 2 years	1,119	1,084	1,075	1,120	1,070	1,133	1,464	1,644	1,554	1,689	*9*
2 years - less than 4 years	766	817	831	862	904	1,002	1,035	1,128	1,114	1,096	*-2*
4 years or over (excluding life)	1,793	1,878	1,905	1,792	1,652	1,607	1,595	1,582	1,539	1,529	*-1*
Life/Section 205/206 sentences	586	573	595	633	649	678	707	739	773	807	*4*
Persons recalled from supervision/licence	235	291	350	395	510	603	592	614	669	689	*3*
Others	5	7	5	1	*	*	-	-	-	-	*-*
Women	**200**	**226**	**247**	**250**	**252**	**254**	**278**	**319**	**329**	**360**	*9*
Fine default	5	4	4	4	3	2	1	1	*	*	*-*
Less than 3 months	5	5	6	7	8	8	7	7	5	5	*-9*
3 months - less than 6 months	26	25	30	27	25	24	28	26	28	31	*10*
6 months - less than 2 years	57	79	86	94	90	92	103	123	129	133	*3*
2 years - less than 4 years	48	41	52	51	55	56	64	83	70	76	*9*
4 years or over (excluding life)	46	54	52	49	49	47	48	49	58	71	*23*
Life/Section 205/206 sentences	13	17	16	17	18	18	19	24	26	31	*18*
Persons recalled from supervision/licence	1	2	1	2	4	7	7	6	13	13	*1*
Others	1	*	*	*	-	-	-	-	-	-	*-*

Source: Prison Statistics and Population Projections Scotland: 2011-12

Civil and court martial prisoners are excluded from this table.

Data for 2012-2013 not yet published expected 2015

21.17c Receptions to penal establishments by type of custody: 2002-03 to 2011-12

	2002-03	2003-04	2004-05	2005-06	2006-07	2007-08	2008-09	2009-10	2010-11	2011-12	% change over past year
Total	**39,783**	**39,076**	**38,347**	**38,746**	**43,506**	**40,450**	**38,986**	**36,521**	**36,012**	**37,002**	*3*
Remand	18,595	18,385	18,539	19,105	22,812	22,136	22,303	20,637	21,023	21,659	*3*
Unruly certificate [1]	26	22	20	24	29	15	10	5	-	-	-
Sentenced	20,957	20,437	19,652	19,488	20,430	18,229	16,566	15,824	14,943	15,331	*3*
Young offenders	3,299	2,880	2,674	2,933	2,985	2,760	2,449	2,324	1,862	1,805	*-3*
Direct sentenced	2,225	2,004	1,948	2,162	2,287	2,357	2,264	2,144	1,709	1,688	*-1*
Fine defaulters	1,074	876	726	771	698	403	185	180	153	117	*-24*
Adults	17,438	17,293	16,708	16,209	16,977	15,057	13,696	13,060	12,560	13,035	*4*
Direct sentenced	10,604	10,517	10,627	10,759	11,705	11,846	12,374	11,907	11,461	11,989	*5*
Fine defaulters	6,834	6,776	6,081	5,450	5,272	3,211	1,322	1,153	1,099	1,046	*-5*
Recalls from supervision/licence	220	264	270	346	468	412	421	440	521	491	*-6*
Sentenced by court martial	3	1	6	-	-	2	1	-	2	-	*n/a*
Civil prisoners	11	12	6	4	4	11	4	12	22	12	*-45*
Legalised police cells [2]	191	219	124	125	231	57	102	43	n/a	n/a	*n/a*
Men	**36,674**	**35,856**	**35,201**	**35,692**	**40,089**	**37,059**	**35,603**	**33,545**	**32,980**	**33,902**	*3*
Remand	16,881	16,601	16,787	17,374	20,810	19,966	20,057	18,792	19,130	19,680	*3*
Unruly certificate [1]	24	21	19	24	26	14	10	5	-	-	-
Sentenced	19,569	19,020	18,265	18,171	19,042	17,013	15,433	14,699	13,828	14,210	*3*
Young offenders	3,126	2,707	2,520	2,818	2,811	2,629	2,321	2,193	1,725	1,697	*-2*
Direct sentenced	2,102	1,885	1,827	2,074	2,157	2,244	2,145	2,019	1,576	1,588	*1*
Fine defaulters	1,024	822	693	744	654	385	176	174	149	109	*-27*
Adults	16,224	16,053	15,479	15,012	15,775	13,982	12,701	12,079	11,592	12,032	*4*
Direct sentenced	10,014	9,858	9,897	10,015	10,902	11,017	11,468	11,010	10,568	11,045	*5*
Fine defaulters	6,210	6,195	5,582	4,997	4,873	2,965	1,233	1,069	1,024	987	*-4*
Recalls from supervision/licence	219	260	266	341	456	402	411	427	511	481	*-6*
Sentenced by court martial	3	1	6	-	-	2	1	-	2	-	*n/a*
Civil prisoners	11	12	6	4	3	10	3	11	20	12	*-40*
Legalised police cells [2]	186	201	118	119	208	54	99	38	n/a	n/a	*n/a*
Women	**3,109**	**3,220**	**3,146**	**3,054**	**3,417**	**3,391**	**3,383**	**2,976**	**3,010**	**3,100**	*3*
Remand	1,714	1,784	1,752	1,731	2,002	2,170	2,246	1,845	1,893	1,979	*5*
Unruly certificate [1]	2	1	1	-	3	1	-	-	-	-	-
Sentenced	1,388	1,417	1,387	1,317	1,388	1,216	1,133	1,125	1,115	1,121	*1*
Young offenders	173	173	154	115	174	131	128	131	137	108	*-21*
Direct sentenced	123	119	121	88	130	113	119	125	133	100	*-25*
Fine defaulters	50	54	33	27	44	18	9	6	4	8	*100*
Adults	1,214	1,240	1,229	1,197	1,202	1,075	995	981	968	1,003	*4*
Direct sentenced	590	659	730	744	803	829	906	897	893	944	*6*
Fine defaulters	624	581	499	453	399	246	89	84	75	59	*-21*
Recalls from supervision/licence	1	4	4	5	12	10	10	13	10	10	-
Sentenced by court martial	-	-	-	-	-	-	-	-	-	-	-
Civil prisoners	-	-	-	-	1	1	1	1	2	-	*n/a*
Legalised police cells [2]	5	18	6	6	23	3	3	5	n/a	n/a	*n/a*

Source: Prison Statistics and Population Projections Scotland: 2011-12

Notes: Receptions do not equate to persons received since someone receiving a custodial sentence after a period on remand, or several custodial sentences at different times or from different courts, will be counted more than once.
1. The legislation under which children may be remanded in custody on an unruly certificate was repealed in 2010.
2. Figures from 2010-11 onward are not available due to technical difficulties.

Data for 2012-2013 not yet published expected 2015

21.18 Scottish Police Service Statement of Comprehensive Net Expenditure

	2011-12	Restated 2010-11
	£000	£000
Income		
Income from all sources	-2,836	-2,916
Expenditure		
Staff costs	136,813	131,253
Running costs	129,515	124,592
Other current expenditure	26,208	24,359
Prisoner compensation and related costs	-5,331	4,104
Total Expenditure	287,205	284,308
Operating cost	284,369	281,392
Interest payable and similar charges	10,952	9,540
Net operating cost	295,321	290,932
Other comprehensive Expenditure		
Net (surplus)/loss on revaluation of property, plant and equipment	-48,767	8,187
Total comprenensive expenditure for the year ending 31 March 2012	246,554	299,119

Source: SPS Annual Accounts 2011-12

21.19 Number of recorded crimes 2012/13 and 2013/14 - Northern Ireland

Offence group	Recorded crime		Number and percentage changes	
	2012/13	2013/14	change between years	% change between years[1]
VICTIM-BASED CRIME				
VIOLENCE AGAINST THE PERSON	30,305	32,403	2,098	6.9
Homicide	*20*	*21*	*1*	*-*
Violence with injury	*14,854*	*14,136*	*-718*	*-4.8*
Violence without injury	*15,431*	*18,246*	*2,815*	*18.2*
SEXUAL OFFENCES	1,932	2,234	302	15.6
Rape	*533*	*550*	*17*	*3.2*
Other sexual offences	*1,399*	*1,684*	*285*	*20.4*
ROBBERY	1,014	958	-56	-5.5
Robbery of personal property	*711*	*715*	*4*	*0.6*
Robbery of business property	*303*	*243*	*-60*	*-19.8*
THEFT OFFENCES	35,611	36,023	412	1.2
Burglary	*9,581*	*9,067*	*-514*	*-5.4*
Domestic burglary	*5,945*	*5,753*	*-192*	*-3.2*
Non-domestic burglary	*3,636*	*3,314*	*-322*	*-8.9*
Theft from the person	*661*	*576*	*-85*	*-12.9*
Vehicle offences	*5,339*	*5,609*	*270*	*5.1*
Bicycle theft	*1,073*	*1,097*	*24*	*2.2*
Shoplifting	*5,890*	*6,372*	*482*	*8.2*
All other theft offences	*13,067*	*13,302*	*235*	*1.8*
CRIMINAL DAMAGE	20,959	19,889	-1,070	-5.1
OTHER CRIMES AGAINST SOCIETY				
DRUG OFFENCES	4,378	4,732	354	8.1
Trafficking of drugs	*890*	*968*	*78*	*8.8*
Possession of drugs	*3,488*	*3,764*	*276*	*7.9*
POSSESSION OF WEAPONS OFFENCES	651	727	76	11.7
PUBLIC ORDER OFFENCES	1,517	1,536	19	1.3
MISCELLANEOUS CRIMES AGAINST SOCIETY	2,191	2,415	224	10.2
OTHER FRAUD[2]	1,831	1,829	-2	-0.1
TOTAL RECORDED CRIME – ALL OFFENCES	**100,389**	**102,746**	**2,357**	**2.3**

[1] '-' indicates that for offences recorded a percentage change is not reported because the base number of offences is less than 50.
[2] In England & Wales offences such as fraud by false representation (deception) are reported to Action Fraud and from April 2013 these figures are no longer included in police recorded crime statistics. However in Northern Ireland these offences are still reported to the police and so continue to be included in the PSNI recorded crime statistics.

21.20 Average Northern Ireland prison population,by sex, prisoner type and age group 2002-2012

		2002	2003	2004	2005	2006	2007	2008	2009	2010	2011	2012
MALE PRISONERS	Aged under 21	81	97	105	101	117	106	96	83	86	91	60
	Aged 21 or over	250	280	328	330	393	403	388	398	404	480	466
	Age unknown	0	0	1	0	0	0	0	0	0	0	0
Remand	Total	331	377	434	431	509	509	483	480	490	571	526
	Aged under 21	3	4	5	4	7	5	3	3	4	5	3
	Aged 21 or over	13	15	17	20	20	19	17	18	23	26	28
Fine defaulter	Total	16	19	22	24	27	24	20	21	27	31	32
	YOC	73	80	86	80	72	70	59	66	63	80	75
	Young Prisoners	20	22	30	32	34	39	47	44	43	53	62
Immediate	Adult Prisoners	557	633	666	697	748	776	829	804	795	895	1022
Custody	Total	650	735	782	809	854	884	934	914	902	1028	1160
Non-Criminal		5	7	8	5	2	5	6	5	2	2	1
All Males		1002	1138	1246	1269	1393	1422	1443	1420	1421	1632	1719
FEMALE PRISONERS	Aged under 21	1	2	4	3	4	3	3	2	3	1	2
Remand	Aged 21 or over	9	6	8	10	16	13	21	21	14	18	17
	Total	11	8	12	13	20	16	24	24	17	19	19
	Aged under 21	0	0	0	0	0	0	0	0	0	0	0
	Aged 21 or over	1	1	2	1	2	2	1	2	2	3	3
Fine defaulter	Total	1	1	2	1	2	3	1	2	2	3	3
	YOC	3	2	2	1	2	2	1	0	2	2	2
	Young Prisoners	0	0	0	0	0	0	0	0	0	0	0
Immediate	Adult Prisoners	9	10	10	15	17	24	20	23	21	27	32
Custody	Total	11	12	12	17	19	25	21	24	23	29	34
Non-Criminal		1	1	1	1	0	0	0	0	0	0	0
All Females		24	22	27	32	41	44	46	49	43	50	56
ALL PRISONERS	Remand	341	385	446	444	529	525	507	504	508	590	545
	Fine defaulter	17	20	24	25	29	26	21	23	30	33	35
	Immed. Custody	662	747	794	826	873	909	955	937	925	1057	1193
	Non-Criminal	6	8	10	6	2	6	6	6	2	2	1
	Total	1026	1160	1274	1301	1433	1466	1490	1470	1465	1682	1774

The Northern Ireland Average Prison Population in 2012

Note:
(1) Components may not sum to totals due to rounding.
(2) Within the Immediate Custody category, 'YOC' refers to those prisoners aged under 21 at date of reception and given a sentence of 4 years or less. Likewise, 'Young Prisoners' refers to those prisoners aged under 21 at date of reception and given a sentence of more than 4 years.while 'Adult Prisoners' refers to those prisoners aged 21 or more at reception, irrespective of sentence length.

Transport and communications

Chapter 22

Transport and communication

Road data (Tables 22.4 & 22.5)

The Department for Transport has undertaken significant development work over the last two years to improve its traffic estimates and measurement of traffic flow on particular stretches of the road network. This work has previously been outlined in a number of publications (Road Traffic Statistics: 2001 SB(02)23, Traffic in Great Britain Q4 2002 Data SB(03)5 and Traffic in Great Britain Q1 2003 SB(03)6).

The main point to note is that figures for 1993 to 2004 have been calculated on a different basis from years prior to 1993. Therefore, figures prior to 1993 are not directly comparable with estimates for later years. Estimates on the new basis for 1993 and subsequent years were first published by the Department on 8 May 2003 in Traffic in Great Britain Q1 2003 SB(03)6. A summary of the main methodological changes to take place over the last couple of years appears below.

Traffic estimates are now disaggregated for roads in urban and rural areas rather than between built-up and non built-up roads. Built-up roads were defined as those with a speed limit of 40 mph or lower. This created difficulties in producing meaningful disaggregated traffic estimates because an increasing number of clearly rural roads were subject to a 40 mph speed limit for safety reasons. The urban/rural split of roads is largely determined by whether roads lie within the boundaries of urban areas with a population of 10,000 or more with adjustments in some cases for major roads at the boundary.

Traffic estimates are based on the results of many 12-hour manual counts in every year, which are grossed up to estimates of annual average daily flows using expansion factors based on data from automatic traffic counters on similar roads. These averages are needed so that traffic in off-peak times, at weekends and in the summer and winter months (when only special counts are undertaken) can be taken into account when assessing the traffic at each site. For this purpose roads are now sorted into 22 groupings (previously there were only seven) and this allows a better match of manual count sites with our automatic count sites. These groupings are based on a detailed analysis of the results from all the individual automatic count sites and take into account regional groupings, road category (that is, both the urban/rural classification of the road and the road class) and traffic flow levels. The groupings range from lightly trafficked, rural minor roads in holiday areas such as Cornwall and Devon, to major roads in central London.

With the increasing interest in sub-regional statistics, we have undertaken a detailed study of traffic counts on minor roads carried out in the last ten years. This has been done in conjunction with a Geographic Information System to enable us to establish general patterns of minor road traffic in each local authority. As a result of this, we have been able to produce more reliable estimate of traffic levels in each authority in our base year of 1999. This in turn has enabled us to produce better estimates of traffic levels back to 1993, as well as more reliable estimates for 1999 onwards.

The Department created a database for major roads based on a Geographic Information System and Ordnance Survey data. This was checked by local authorities and discussed with government regional offices and the Highways Agency to ensure that good local knowledge supplemented the available technical data.

Urban major and minor roads, from 1993 onwards, are defined as being within an urban area with a population of more than 10,000 people, based on the 2001 urban settlements. The definition for urban settlement can be found on the CLG web site at:
 www.communities.gov.uk/planningandbuilding/planningbuilding/planningstatistics/urbanrural.

Rural major and minor roads, from 1993 onwards, are defined as being outside an urban settlement.

New vehicle registrations (Table 22.8)

Special concession group
Various revisions to the vehicle taxation system were introduced on 1 July 1995 and on 29 November 1995. Separate taxation classes for farmers' goods vehicles were abolished on 1 July 1995; after this date new vehicles of this type were registered as Heavy Goods Vehicles (HGVs). The total includes 5,900 vehicles registered between 1 January and 30 June in the (now abolished) agricultural and special machines group in classes which were not eligible to register in the special concession group. The old agricultural and special machines taxation group was abolished at end June 1995. The group includes agricultural and mowing machines, snow ploughs and gritting vehicles. Electric vehicles are also included in this group and are no longer exempt from Vehicle Excise Duty (VED). Steam propelled vehicles were added to this group from November 1995.

Other licensed vehicles
Includes three wheelers, pedestrian controlled vehicles, general haulage and showmen's tractors and recovery vehicles. Recovery vehicle tax class introduced January 1988.

Special vehicles group
The special vehicles group was created on 1 July 1995 and consists of various vehicle types over 3.5 tonnes gross weight but not required to pay VED as heavy goods vehicles. The group includes mobile cranes, work trucks, digging machines, road rollers and vehicles previously taxed as showman's goods and haulage. The figure shown for 1995 covers the period from 1 July to 31 December only.

National Travel Survey data (Tables 22.1 & 22.11)
The National Travel Survey (NTS) is designed to provide a databank of personal travel information for Great Britain. It has been conducted as a continuous survey since July 1988, following ad hoc surveys since the mid-1960s. The survey is designed to identify long-term trends and is not suitable for monitoring short-term trends.

In 2006, a weighting strategy was introduced to the NTS and applied retrospectively to data back to 1995. The weighting methodology adjusts for non-response bias and also adjusts for the drop-off in the number of trips recorded by respondents during the course of the travel week. All results now published for 1995 onwards are based on weighted data, and direct comparisons cannot be made to earlier years or previous publications.

During 2008, over 8,000 households provided details of their personal travel by filling in travel diaries over the course of a week. The drawn sample size from 2002 was nearly trebled compared with previous years following recommendations in a National Statistics Review of the NTS. This enables most results to be presented on a single year basis from 2002.

Travel included in the NTS covers all trips by British residents within Great Britain for personal reasons, including travel in the course of work.

A trip is defined as a one-way course of travel having a single main purpose. It is the basic unit of personal travel defined in the survey.

A round trip is split into two trips, with the first ending at a convenient point about half-way round as a notional stopping point for the outward destination and return origin.

A stage is that portion of a trip defined by the use of a specific method of transport or of a specific ticket (a new stage being defined if either the mode or ticket changes). The main mode of a trip is that used for the longest stage of the trip. With stages of equal length, the mode of the latest stage is used. Walks of less than 50 yards are excluded.

Travel details provided by respondents include trip purpose, method of travel, time of day and trip length. The households also provided personal information, such as their age, sex, working status, driving licence holding, and details of the cars available for their use.

Because estimates made from a sample survey depend on the particular sample chosen, they generally differ from the true values of the population. This is not usually a problem when considering large samples (such as all car trips in Great Britain), but it may give misleading information when considering data from small samples even after weighting.

The most recent editions of all NTS publications are available on the DfT website at: www.dft.gov.uk/transtat/personaltravel. Bulletins of key results are published annually. The most recent bulletin is National Travel Survey: 2005.

Households with regular use of cars (Table 22.11)

The mid-year estimates of the percentage of households with regular use of a car or van are based on combined data from the NTS, the Expenditure and Food Survey (previously the Family Expenditure Survey) and the General Household Survey. The method for calculating these figures was changed slightly in 2006, to incorporate weighted data from the NTS and the GHS. Figures since have also been revised to incorporate weighted data. Results by area type are based on weighted data from the NTS only.

Continuing Survey of Road Goods Transport (Tables 22.2, 22.17 & 22.18)

The estimates are derived from the Continuing Survey of Road Goods Transport (CSRGT) which in 2005 was based on an average weekly returned sample of some 330 HGVs. The samples are drawn from the computerised vehicle licence records held by the Driver and Vehicle Licensing Agency. Questionnaires are sent to the registered keepers of the sampled vehicles asking for a description of the vehicle and its activity during the survey week. The estimates are grossed to the vehicle population,, and at the overall national level have a 2 per cent margin of error (at 95 per cent confidence level). Further details and results are published in Road Freight Statistics 2005, and previously in Transport of Goods by Road in Great Britain.

Methodological changes

A key component of National Statistics outputs is a programme of quality reviews carried out at least every five years to ensure that such statistics are fit for purpose and that their quality and value continue to improve. A quality review of the Department for Transport's road freight surveys, including the CSRGT, was carried out in 2003. A copy of the report can be accessed at: www.statistics.gov.uk/nsbase/methods_quality/quality_review/downloads/NSQR30FinalReport.doc

The quality review made a number of recommendations about the CSRGT. The main methodological recommendation was that, to improve the accuracy of survey estimates, the sample strata should be amended to reflect current trends in vehicle type, weight and legislative groups. These new strata are described more fully in Appendix C of the survey report. For practical and administrative reasons, changes were also made to the sample selection methodology (see Appendix B of the report). These changes have resulted in figures from 2004 not being fully comparable with those for 2003 and earlier years. Detailed comparisons should therefore be made with caution.

Railways: permanent way and rolling stock (Table 22.21)

1) Locomotives - locos owned by Northern Ireland Railways (NIR), does not include those from the Republic of Ireland Railway System.

2) Diesel electric etc rail motor vehicles - powered passenger carrying vehicles, includes diesel electric (DE) power cars and all Construcciones y Auxiliar de Ferocarriles (CAF) vehicles. (Note: only 16 of the CAF sets were delivered to NIR at the time.)

3) Loco hauled coaches - NIR owned De Dietrich plus Gatwick but not including gen van.

4) Rail car trailers - 80 class and 450 class trailers. Not CAF, they are all powered.

5) Rolling stock for maintenance and repair - a 'standalone' figure - may or may not be included in the above totals. Anything listed as 'repair' or 'workshop' in the motive power sheets is included. Also, those CAF vehicles not yet delivered at the time.

6) The information is a 'snapshot' taken from the motive power sheets at end of March, together with any other known information.

22.23 - 22.26

All data from Airline Statistics, Civil Aviation Authority

22.1 Average number of trips (trip rates) by purpose and main mode: Great Britain, 2012

Trips/thousands

Purpose	Walk	Bicycle	Car / van driver	Car / van passenger	Motorcycle	Other private transport[1]	Local bus	Rail[2]	Other public transport[3]	All modes
					Trips per person per year					
Commuting	16	5	84	13	2	-	11	12	2	146
Business	3	-	22	2	-	-	1	2	-	31
Education / escort education	44	2	26	27	-	3	11	2	1	116
Shopping	41	2	85	40	-	1	16	2	2	189
Other escort	9	-	50	24	-	-	2	-	1	87
Personal business	19	1	41	22	-	1	6	1	1	94
Leisure[4]	38	5	93	84	1	2	13	7	6	248
Other including just walk	43	0	-	-	0	0	-	0	0	43
All purposes	212	16	401	213	3	7	61	27	13	954
Unweighted sample size: trips ('000s)	76	5	142	75	1	3	20	8	4	335

Source: National Travel Survey

1 Mostly private hire bus (including school buses).
2 Surface rail and London underground.
3 Non-local bus, taxi/minicab and other public transport (air, ferries, light rail).
4 Visit friends at home and elsewhere, entertainment, sport, holiday and day trip.

Telephone: 020 7944 3097
Email: national.travelsurvey@dft.gsi.gov.uk

The figures in this table are National Statistics

Note: The results presented in this table are weighted. The base (unweighted sample size) is shown in the table for information. Weights are applied to adjust for non-response to ensure the characteristics of the achieved sample match the population of Great Britain and for the drop off in trip recording. The survey results are subject to sampling error.

22.2 Domestic freight transport[1]: by mode: 2000-2011

	2000	2001	2002	2003	2004	2005	2006	2007	2008	2009	2010	2011[2]
(a) Goods moved											Billion tonne kilometres/percentage	
Petroleum products												
Road [3]	6.4	5.8	5.2	5.5	5.7	5.5	5.5	5.0	6.2	4.5	6.0	..
Rail [4]	1.4	1.2	1.2	1.2	1.2	1.2	1.5	1.6	1.5	1.4	1.3	1.2
Water	52.7	43.5	51.7	46.9	46.9	47.2	37.8	36.4	36.4	36.4	28.3	29.6
ow: coastwise	26.0	23.1	24.2	23.3	26.6	30.3	22.8	25.1	26.5	27.1	20.6	22.6
Pipeline	11.4	11.5	10.9	10.5	10.7	10.8	10.4	10.2	10.2	10.2	10.3	10.1
All modes	71.9	62.0	69.0	64.1	64.5	64.7	55.2	53.2	54.3	52.5	45.9	..
Coal and coke												
Road [3]	1.5	2.1	1.5	1.5	1.2	1.5	1.3	1.5	1.0	0.9	1.4	..
Rail [4]	4.8	6.2	5.7	5.8	6.7	8.3	8.6	7.7	7.9	6.2	5.5	6.4
Water	0.2	0.5	0.3	0.5	0.3	0.4	0.5	0.5	0.5	0.3	1.0	0.4
All modes	6.5	8.8	7.5	7.9	8.2	10.2	10.4	9.7	9.4	7.5	7.9	..
Other freight												
Road [3]	151.5	150.6	152.7	154.7	155.6	156.4	156.6	162.3	150.2	131.3	143.1	..
Rail [4]	11.9	12.0	11.7	11.9	12.5	12.2	11.8	11.9	11.2	11.4	12.5	13.4
Water	14.6	14.8	15.2	13.5	12.2	13.3	13.5	13.9	12.7	11.9	12.6	13.1
All modes	178.1	177.4	179.6	180.0	180.3	181.9	182.0	188.1	174.1	154.6	168.2	..
All traffic												
Road [3]	159.4	158.5	159.4	161.7	162.5	163.4	163.4	168.8	157.4	136.8	150.5	..
Rail [4]	18.1	19.4	18.5	18.9	20.3	21.7	21.9	21.2	20.6	19.1	19.2	21.1
Water	67.4	58.8	67.2	60.9	59.4	60.9	51.8	50.8	49.7	48.6	41.9	43.0
Pipeline	11.4	11.5	10.9	10.5	10.7	10.8	10.4	10.2	10.2	10.2	10.3	10.1
All modes	256.3	248.2	256.0	252.0	253.0	256.8	247.6	251.0	237.8	214.6	221.9	..
Percentage of all traffic												
Road [3]	62	64	62	64	64	64	66	67	66	64	68	..
Rail [4]	7	8	7	7	8	8	9	8	9	9	9	..
Water	26	24	26	24	24	24	21	20	21	23	19	..
Pipeline	4	5	4	4	4	4	4	4	4	5	5	..
All modes	100	100	100	100	100	100	100	100	100	100	100	..
(b) Goods lifted											Million tonnes/percentage	
Petroleum products												
Road [3]	75	74	59	64	67	70	66	69	76	57	67	..
Rail [4]	..	..	..	..	..	..	..	..	..	..	..	..
Water	72	60	67	64	63	66	57	56	58	55	46	46
ow: coastwise	40	34	36	35	38	42	34	35	36	35	28	28
Pipeline	151	151	146	141	158	168	159	146	147	148	149	151
All modes	298	285	272	269	288	304	282	272	281	259	263	..
Coal and coke												
Road [3]	22	21	17	22	14	21	16	23	14	10	11	..
Rail [4]	35	39	34	35	44	48	49	43	47	38	39	44
Water	3	3	2	2	1	2	2	2	2	1	2	1
All modes	60	63	53	59	59	71	68	68	63	49	52	..
Other freight												
Road [3]	1,596	1,587	1,658	1,667	1,782	1,777	1,819	1,861	1,709	1,422	1,543	..
Rail [4]	60	54	53	54	57	58	59	59	56	49	51	57
Water [3]	62	68	70	67	63	65	66	68	63	54	57	57
All modes	1,718	1,709	1,781	1,788	1,902	1,900	1,945	1,988	1,828	1,525	1,651	..
All traffic												
Road [3]	1,693	1,682	1,734	1,753	1,863	1,868	1,901	1,953	1,800	1,488	1,621	..
Rail [4]	96	94	87	89	101	105	108	102	103	87	90	102
Water	137	131	139	133	127	133	126	126	123	110	106	104
Pipeline	151	151	146	141	158	168	159	146	147	148	149	151
All modes	2,077	2,058	2,106	2,116	2,249	2,275	2,294	2,328	2,173	1,833	1,966	..
Percentage of all traffic												
Road [3]	82	82	82	83	83	82	83	84	83	81	82	..
Rail [4]	5	5	4	4	4	5	5	4	5	5	5	..
Water	7	6	7	6	6	6	6	5	6	6	5	..
Pipeline	7	7	7	7	7	7	7	6	7	8	8	..
All modes	100	100	100	100	100	100	100	100	100	100	100	..

Sources: Road and water - DfT; Rail - ORR; Pipeline - DECC

Telephone:
Rail: 020 7944 2419
Road: 020 7944 3180
Pipeline: 020 7215 2718

1 Discontinuities in the series (denoted by lines) are described in detail in the Notes and Definitions.
2 Road freight data are not currently available for 2011.
3 Statistics for all goods vehicles, including those 3.5 tonnes gross vehicle weight or less.
4 Figures for rail are for financial years (e.g. 2011 will be 2011/12).

See Notes and Definitions
https://www.gov.uk/government/uploads/system/uploads/attachment_data/file/263891/TSGB_2013_Freight_notes_and_definitions.pdf

The rail figures in this table are outside the scope of National Statistics

22.3 Passenger transport: by mode, annual from 2000

Billion passenger kilometres/*percentage*

Year	Buses & coaches	%	Cars, vans & taxis	%	Motor cycles	%	Pedal cycles	%	All Road	%	Rail[1]	%	Air (UK)[2]	%	All modes [3]	%
2000	47	6	639	85	5	1	4	1	694	93	47	6	8	1.0	749	100
2001	47	6	651	85	5	1	4	1	707	93	48	6	8	1.0	763	100
2002 R	47	6	673	86	5	1	4	1	730	93	48	6	8	1.1	786	100
2003 R	47	6	668	85	6	1	4	1	726	93	50	6	9	1.2	785	100
2004 R	41	5	673	86	5	1	4	1	723	92	50	6	10	1.2	784	100
2005 R	42	5	667	85	6	1	4	1	719	92	52	7	10	1.3	781	100
2006 R	40	5	672	85	5	1	5	1	723	92	55	7	10	1.3	788	100
2007 R	41	5	674	85	6	1	4	1	724	91	59	7	10	1.2	792	100
2008 R	43	5	666	84	5	1	5	1	719	91	61	8	9	1.1	788	100
2009 R	44	6	661	84	5	1	5	1	715	91	61	8	8	1.1	785	100
2010 R	44	6	644	84	5	1	5	1	698	91	65	8	8	1.0	770	100
2011 R	42	5	641	83	5	1	5	1	694	90	68	9	8	1.1	770	100
2012 P	42	5	643	83	5	1	5	1	694	90	70	9	8	1.1	773	100

Sources: Road - DfT Traffic Estimates, National Travel Survey; Rail - ORR; Air - CAA

1 Financial years. National Rail (franchised operators only to 2008, franchised and non-franchised operators from 2009), urban metros and modern trams.
2 UK airlines, domestic passengers uplifted on scheduled and non-scheduled flights.
3 Excluding travel by water.

R Road figures have been revised from 2002 due to the re-processing of National Travel Survey data in the new database. See Notes and Definitions.

See Notes and Definitions for details of discontinuity in road passengers figures from 1993 and 1996 onwards.
https://www.gov.uk/government/publications/transport-statistics-great-britain-guidance

Telephone:
Road: 020-7944 3097
Rail: 020-7944 2419
Air: 020-7944 3088
Email: publicationgeneral.enq@dft.gsi.gov.uk

The Rail and Air figures in this table are outside the scope of National Statistics.

22.4 Motor vehicle traffic (vehicle kilometres) by road class in Great Britain, annual from 1999

Billion vehicle kilometres

	Major roads					Minor roads			
		'A' roads		All 'A' roads	All major roads			All minor roads	
	Motorway [1]	Rural	Urban [2]			Rural	Urban [2]		All roads
1999	87.8	130.7	81.9	212.6	300.4	61.3	105.3	166.6	467.0
2000	88.3	130.0	81.7	211.7	300.0	61.3	104.8	166.1	466.2
2001	90.8	133.3	81.8	215.1	305.9	61.2	105.5	166.7	472.6
2002	92.6	136.4	82.2	218.6	311.2	63.9	108.6	172.5	483.7
2003	93.0	139.3	81.8	221.0	314.0	63.6	109.0	172.6	486.7
2004	96.6	141.3	82.8	224.1	320.7	64.9	108.3	173.3	493.9
2005	97.0	141.4	81.8	223.1	320.2	65.6	108.1	173.7	493.9
2006	99.5	143.6	82.5	226.1	325.5	67.9	107.6	175.5	501.1
2007	100.6	143.5	81.3	224.9	325.4	70.3	109.7	180.0	505.4
2008	100.1	142.8	80.1	222.8	323.0	70.3	107.3	177.6	500.6
2009	99.5	142.0	80.4	222.4	321.9	68.3	105.7	174.0	495.8
2010	98.2	139.8	79.7	219.5	317.7	68.1	102.1	170.2	487.9
2011	99.5	141.2	79.3	220.4	319.9	66.3	102.7	169.0	488.9
2012	100.4	140.4	78.1	218.5	319.0	64.6	103.5	168.1	487.1

1 Includes trunk motorways and principal motorways
2 Urban roads: Major and minor roads within an urban area with a population of 10,000 or more. These are based on the 2001 urban settlements. The definition for 'urban settlement' is in 'Urban and rural area definitions: a user guide' which can be found on the Notes & definitions web page (see link below).

Source: DfT National Road Traffic Survey

Telephone: 020 7944 3095
Email: roadtraff.stats@dft.gsi.gov.uk
Notes & definitions (www.gov.uk/transport-statistics-notes-and-guidance-road-traffic)

The figures in this table are National Statistics.

22.5 Road lengths (kilometres) by road type in Great Britain, 1999 - 2012

Kilometres

Year	Motorways			'A' roads			major roads	Minor roads					All roads
	Trunk	Principal	Total	Trunk	Principal	Total		'B' road	'C' road	'U' road	'C' and 'U' roads	All minor roads	
1999	3,404	45	3,449	11,698	34,871	46,569	50,018	30,205	84,509	224,783	309,292	339,497	389,515
2000	3,422	45	3,467	11,701	34,906	46,607	50,074	30,200	84,624	225,339	309,963	340,163	390,237
2001 [1]	3,431	45	3,476	11,369	35,285	46,654	50,130	30,196	84,742	225,901	310,643	340,839	390,969
2002	3,433	45	3,478	10,679	35,995	46,674	50,152	30,192	84,858	226,462	311,320	341,512	391,663
2003	3,432	46	3,478	9,615	37,037	46,652	50,130	30,188	84,976	227,048	312,024	342,212	392,342
2004 [2]	3,478	46	3,523	9,147	37,521	46,668	50,192	30,178	84,223	223,082	307,305	337,483	387,674
2005	3,471	48	3,518	8,708	38,019	46,727	50,246	30,189	84,459	223,183	307,642	337,830	388,076
2006 [2]	3,508	48	3,555	8,706	38,030	46,735	50,291	30,018	84,469	229,605	314,074	344,092	394,383
2007	3,518	41	3,559	8,670	38,073	46,743	50,302	30,265	84,423	229,889	314,312	344,577	394,879
2008	3,518	41	3,559	8,634	38,057	46,691	50,249	30,161	84,574	229,482	314,056	344,217	394,467
2009	3,519	41	3,560	8,596	38,173	46,770	50,329	30,141	84,813	229,145	313,958	344,099	394,428
2010	3,517	41	3,558	8,489	38,218	46,707	50,265	30,192	84,827	228,970	313,797	343,989	394,253
2011	3,529	41	3,570	8,508	38,225	46,734	50,304	30,208	84,831	228,953	313,784	343,992	394,296
2012	3,576	41	3,617	8,507	38,235	46,742	50,359	30,214	84,903	229,414	314,317	344,531	394,890

Source: Department for Transport
Telephone: 020 7944 5032
Email: road.length@dft.gsi.gov.uk

1. Figures for trunk and principal 'A' roads in England, from 2001 onwards, are affected by the detrunking programme.
2. New information from 2004 and from 2006 enabled better estimates of road lengths to be made - see Notes and definitions.

.. Sufficient data unavailable.
See Notes and definitions at
https://www.gov.uk/government/uploads/system/uploads/attachment_data/file/230605/road-length-notes-definitions.pdf
The figures in this table are National Statistics

22.6 Road traffic (vehicle kilometres) by vehicle type in Great Britain, annual from 1999

Billion vehicle kilometres

	Cars and taxis	Light vans [1]	Goods vehicles [2]	Other Vehicles			All motor vehicles
				Motorcycles	Buses & Coaches	Total [3]	
1999	377.4	51.6	28.1	4.5	5.3	9.8	467.0
2000	376.0	52.2	28.2	4.6	5.1	9.7	466.2
2001	381.2	53.4	28.0	4.8	5.1	9.9	472.6
2002	390.6	54.7	28.3	5.0	5.2	10.2	483.7
2003	390.0	57.4	28.4	5.6	5.3	10.9	486.7
2004	394.2	60.2	29.3	5.1	5.1	10.2	493.9
2005	392.7	61.8	28.9	5.3	5.1	10.4	493.9
2006	397.4	64.3	29.0	5.1	5.3	10.4	501.1
2007	397.9	67.4	29.3	5.5	5.4	10.9	505.4
2008	395.0	66.9	28.6	5.0	5.0	10.1	500.6
2009	394.0	65.5	26.2	5.1	5.0	10.1	495.8
2010	385.9	66.1	26.3	4.6	5.0	9.6	487.9
2011	387.4	66.6	25.6	4.6	4.7	9.3	488.9
2012	386.7	66.4	25.0	4.6	4.4	8.9	487.1

Source: DfT National Road Traffic Survey
Telephone: 020 7944 3095
Email: roadtraff.stats@dft.gsi.gov.uk

1 Not exceeding 3,500 kgs gross vehicle weight, post 1982
2 Over 3,500 kgs gross vehicle weight, post 1982
3 Total of all other vehicles (i.e. motorcycles, buses, and coaches)
4 Data for 1993 onwards are not directly comparable with the figures for 1992 and earlier

Notes & definitions (www.gov.uk/transport-statistics-notes-and-guidance-road-traffic)

The figures in this table are National Statistics.

22.7 Cars licensed by propulsion / fuel type, Great Britain, annually: 1994 to 2011

Thousands/*Percentages*

Year	Petrol	Diesel	Hybrid Electric	Gas[1]	Electric	Other[2]	Total
Total number of cars							
1994	19,620.9	1,576.2	0.0	1.8	0.1	0.2	21,199.2
1995	19,499.8	1,891.3	0.0	2.9	0.1	0.1	21,394.1
1996	20,051.6	2,181.6	0.0	4.1	0.1	0.1	22,237.5
1997	20,384.7	2,440.5	0.0	6.2	0.1	0.1	22,831.7
1998	20,590.5	2,692.9	0.0	9.6	0.2	0.1	23,293.3
1999	21,031.0	2,929.9	0.0	13.8	0.2	0.1	23,974.9
2000	21,232.6	3,152.7	-	20.0	0.2	-	24,405.5
2001	21,641.1	3,459.5	0.6	24.4	0.3	0.1	25,125.9
2002	21,839.5	3,912.4	0.9	28.8	0.3	0.1	25,781.9
2003	21,805.5	4,399.6	1.2	33.7	0.3	0.1	26,240.4
2004	21,976.6	5,010.6	2.8	37.6	0.4	0.1	27,028.1
2005	21,876.0	5,596.1	8.1	39.5	0.6	0.1	27,520.4
2006	21,465.8	6,083.3	16.6	42.4	0.8	0.2	27,609.2
2007	21,264.4	6,657.4	31.8	45.1	1.2	0.3	28,000.3
2008	20,899.1	7,163.5	46.7	49.6	1.3	0.4	28,160.7
2009	20,491.2	7,641.4	61.1	50.9	1.5	0.4	28,246.5
2010	20,083.1	8,202.7	82.1	51.0	1.5	0.5	28,420.9
2011	19,548.5	8,763.5	102.3	50.0	2.6	0.4	28,467.3
Percentage of cars							
1994	92.6	7.4	0.0	-	-	-	100.0
1995	91.1	8.8	0.0	-	-	-	100.0
1996	90.2	9.8	0.0	-	-	-	100.0
1997	89.3	10.7	0.0	-	-	-	100.0
1998	88.4	11.6	0.0	-	-	-	100.0
1999	87.7	12.2	0.0	0.1	-	-	100.0
2000	87.0	12.9	-	0.1	-	-	100.0
2001	86.1	13.8	-	0.1	-	-	100.0
2002	84.7	15.2	-	0.1	-	-	100.0
2003	83.1	16.8	-	0.1	-	-	100.0
2004	81.3	18.5	-	0.1	-	-	100.0
2005	79.5	20.3	-	0.1	-	-	100.0
2006	77.7	22.0	0.1	0.2	-	-	100.0
2007	75.9	23.8	0.1	0.2	-	-	100.0
2008	74.2	25.4	0.2	0.2	-	-	100.0
2009	72.5	27.1	0.2	0.2	-	-	100.0
2010	70.7	28.9	0.3	0.2	-	-	100.0
2011	68.7	30.8	0.4	0.2	-	-	100.0

1. Includes gas, gas bi-fuel, petrol/gas and gas-diesel
2. Includes vehicles propelled by steam

Source: DVLA/DfT
Telephone: 020 7944 3077
Email : vehicles.stats@dft.gsi.gov.uk

Notes & definitions https://www.gov.uk/government/publications/vehicles-statistics-guidance)

22.8 Motor vehicles registered for the first time by tax class: Great Britain, annually: 1999 to 2011

Thousands

Year	Private and light goods [1]	Goods vehicles	Motor cycles, scooters and mopeds	Buses [2]	Special machines etc [5]	Other vehicles [3,4,5]	Total
1999	2,342.0	48.0	168.0	8.0	25.0	174.0	2,766.0
2000	2,430.0	50.0	183.0	8.0	24.0	176.0	2,871.0
2001	2,710.0	49.0	177.0	7.0	27.0	169.0	3,138.0
2002	2,816.0	45.0	162.0	8.0	.	199.0	3,229.0
2003	2,820.7	48.4	157.3	8.4	.	197.1	3,231.9
2004	2,784.7	48.0	133.7	8.3	.	210.7	3,185.4
2005	2,603.6	51.2	132.3	8.9	.	225.5	3,021.4
2006	2,499.1	47.9	131.9	7.6	.	227.1	2,913.6
2007	2,539.3	41.1	143.0	9.0	.	264.6	2,996.9
2008	2,188.3	47.0	138.4	8.3	.	290.2	2,672.2
2009	1,959.1	27.0	111.5	7.2	.	266.3	2,371.2
2010	1,994.6	27.0	97.1	6.4	.	292.7	2,417.8
2011	1,928.6	36.9	96.2	5.8	.	314.0	2,381.5

Source: DVLA/DfT

1. Figures for 1969 to 1979 are estimated using the October 1982 tax classes. Figures for 1951 to 1969 refer to earlier classes. From 1980 onwards figures refer to the October 1990 taxation classes. Figures for 1969 and 1980 are given twice, once for the tax regime before and once for the tax regime afterwards.
2. Prior to 1995 this tax class was called 'Public Transport' and taxis and Hackney Carriages were included. Prior to 1969, tram cars were also included.
3. Includes crown and exempt vehicles, three wheelers, pedestrian controlled vehicles and showmen's goods vehicles.
4. Excludes vehicles officially registered by the armed forces.
5. Special Machines became part of the 'Crown and Exempt' taxation class with effect from January 2002.

Telephone: 020 7944 3077
Email : **vehicles.stats@dft.gsi.gov.uk**
Notes & definitions (http://www.dft.gov.uk/statistics/series/vehicle-licensing/)

22.9a Practical car test[1] pass rates by gender, monthly, Great Britain

Numbers / *Per cent*

	Male tests			Female tests			Total tests[2]		
	Conducted	Passes	Pass rate (%)	Conducted	Passes	Pass rate (%)	Conducted	Passes	Pass rate (%)
Annually (financial years)									
2007/08	865,427	409,222	47.3	896,314	369,795	41.3	1,762,148	779,207	44.2
2008/09	849,757	413,014	48.6	888,917	374,466	42.1	1,738,992	787,618	45.3
2009/10	753,618	370,049	49.1	780,007	333,770	42.8	1,533,738	703,859	45.9
2010/11	772,551	383,417	49.6	833,040	360,639	43.3	1,605,599	744,058	46.3
2011/12	744,487	374,472	50.3	824,572	361,685	43.9	1,569,069	736,158	46.9
2012/13	682,699	345,599	50.6	753,774	331,653	44.0	1,436,481	677,255	47.1

1 Includes test categories B and B1

Source: DSA/DfT

2 Gender details about licence holders from other countries (such as Northern Ireland) are reliant upon information being captured accurately at the time of booking a test. In some cases, gender will not have been captured. Where gender has not been captured these candidates will only be recorded in total tests conducted. There will therefore be small anomalies where the gender totals do not match overall totals.

Please note that all statistics are provisional until information for the whole financial year is published. Until that point, data for months / quarters from within the current financial year can be revised.

Telephone: 020 7944 3077
Email : vehicles.stats@dft.gsi.gov.uk
Notes & definitions (https://www.gov.uk/government/organisations/department-for-transport/series/driving-tests-and-instructors-statistics)

22.9b Practical motorcycle test[1] (Module 1) pass rates by gender, monthly, Great Britain

Numbers / *Per cent*

	Male tests			Female tests			Total tests		
	Conducted	Passes	Pass rate (%)	Conducted	Passes	Pass rate (%)	Conducted	Passes	Pass rate (%)
Annually (financial years)									
2009/10[1]	44,165	28,123	*63.7*	6,655	2,765	*41.5*	50,823	30,891	*60.8*
2010/11	50,046	33,735	*67.4*	7,665	3,498	*45.6*	57,711	37,233	*64.5*
2011/12	52,726	38,325	*72.7*	6,868	3,706	*54.0*	59,594	42,031	*70.5*
2012/13	58,280	42,490	*72.9*	7,770	4,092	*52.7*	66,050	46,582	*70.5*

Source: DSA/DfT

1 All test data excludes mopeds.

2 The two-part modular motorcycle test was introduced on 27 April 2009. The figures for April 2009 only includes tests conducted between 27 and 30 April 2009.

Please note that all statistics are provisional until information for the whole financial year is published. Until that point, data for months / quarters from within the current financial year can be revised.

Telephone: 020 7944 3077
Email : vehicles.stats@dft.gsi.gov.uk
Notes & definitions (https://www.gov.uk/government/organisations/department-for-transport/series/driving-tests-and-instructors-statistics)

22.9c Practical motorcycle test[1] (Module 2) pass rates by gender, monthly, Great Britain

Numbers / *Per cent*

	Male tests			Female tests			Total tests		
	Conducted	Passes	Pass rate (%)	Conducted	Passes	Pass rate (%)	Conducted	Passes	Pass rate (%)
Annually (financial years)									
2009/10[1]	34,550	24,122	*69.8*	3,363	2,352	*69.9*	37,914	26,474	*69.8*
2010/11	44,991	31,236	*69.4*	4,654	3,249	*69.8*	49,645	34,485	*69.5*
2011/12	52,619	36,367	*69.1*	5,292	3,559	*67.3*	57,911	39,926	*68.9*
2012/13	59,237	40,871	*69.0*	5,891	4,018	*68.2*	65,128	44,889	*68.9*

Source: DSA/DfT

1 All test data excludes mopeds.

2 The two-part modular motorcycle test was introduced on 27 April 2009. The figures for April 2009 only includes tests conducted between 27 and 30 April 2009.

Please note that all statistics are provisional until information for the whole financial year is published. Until that point, data for months / quarters from within the current financial year can be revised.

Telephone: 020 7944 3077
Email : vehicles.stats@dft.gsi.gov.uk
Notes & definitions (https://www.gov.uk/government/organisations/department-for-transport/series/driving-tests-and-instructors-statistics)

22.9d Practical large goods vehicle (LGV) test[1] rates by gender, monthly, Great Britain

Numbers / *Per cent*

	Male tests			Female tests			Total tests		
	Conducted	Passes	Pass rate (%)	Conducted	Passes	Pass rate (%)	Conducted	Passes	Pass rate (%)
Annually (financial years)									
2007/08	66,445	30,693	*46.2*	4,305	2,077	*48.2*	70,766	32,779	*46.3*
2008/09	61,950	30,258	*48.8*	3,892	2,035	*52.3*	65,852	32,298	*49.0*
2009/10	43,119	22,058	*51.2*	3,305	1,816	*54.9*	46,426	23,876	*51.4*
2010/11	41,011	21,122	*51.5*	2,883	1,542	*53.5*	43,894	22,664	*51.6*
2011/12	43,525	22,762	*52.3*	3,024	1,639	*54.2*	46,549	24,401	*52.4*
2012/13	42,937	22,736	*53.0*	3,309	1,762	*53.2*	46,246	24,498	*53.0*

Source: DSA/DfT

1 Includes test categories C, C1, C+E, C1+E

Please note that all statistics are provisional until information for the whole financial year is published. Until that point, data for months / quarters from within the current financial year can be revised.

Telephone: 020 7944 3077
Email : vehicles.stats@dft.gsi.gov.uk
Notes & definitions (https://www.gov.uk/government/organisations/department-for-transport/series/driving-tests-and-instructors-statistics)

22.9e Practical passenger carrying vehicle (PCV) test[1] rates by gender, monthly, Great Britain

Numbers / *Per cent*

	Male tests			Female tests			Total tests		
	Conducted	Passes	Pass rate (%)	Conducted	Passes	Pass rate (%)	Conducted	Passes	Pass rate (%)
Annually (financial years)									
2007/08	8,629	4,291	*49.7*	1,699	910	*53.6*	10,331	5,203	*50.4*
2008/09	8,566	4,394	*51.3*	1,740	957	*55.0*	10,306	5,351	*51.9*
2009/10	7,692	3,964	*51.5*	1,566	905	*57.8*	9,258	4,869	*52.6*
2010/11	7,131	3,718	*52.1*	1,415	882	*62.3*	8,546	4,600	*53.8*
2011/12	7,056	3,724	*52.8*	1,400	821	*58.6*	8,456	4,545	*53.7*
2012/13	7,627	4,007	*52.5*	1,535	837	*54.5*	9,162	4,844	*52.9*

Source: DSA/DfT

1 Includes test categories D, D1, D+E and D1+E

Please note that all statistics are provisional until information for the whole financial year is published. Until that point, data for months / quarters from within the current financial year can be revised.

Telephone: 020 7944 3077

Email : vehicles.stats@dft.gsi.gov.uk

Notes & definitions (https://www.gov.uk/government/organisations/department-for-transport/series/driving-tests-and-instructors-statistics)

22.10 Full car driving licence holders by age and gender: England, 1975/76 to 2012

	Percentage								Estimated licence holders (millions)	Unweighted sample size (individuals aged 17+)
	All aged 17+	17-20	21-29	30-39	40-49	50-59	60-69	70+		
All adults:										
1975/76	48	28	59	67	60	50	35	15	19.4	17,064
1985/86	57	33	63	74	71	60	47	27	24.3	19,835
1989/91[1]	64	44	74	78	79	68	55	32	24.1	17,466
1992/94	67	48	75	82	80	74	59	33	25.4	16,401
1995/97[2]	69	44	74	82	82	76	64	39	26.3	16,716
1998/00	71	41	75	85	83	78	68	40	27.3	17,156
2002	71	32	67	83	83	81	70	45	27.6	13,836
2003	71	29	67	82	84	81	72	44	27.8	14,556
2004	70	27	65	82	83	81	73	46	27.8	14,228
2005	72	31	65	82	84	83	75	52	28.8	15,063
2006	72	35	67	82	84	82	76	51	29.3	14,815
2007	72	38	66	81	84	82	76	53	29.5	14,693
2008	73	36	64	83	84	83	78	53	30.0	14,290
2009	73	36	64	80	84	83	80	55	30.2	14,791
2010	73	33	63	81	85	83	80	57	30.6	14,118
2011	72	31	64	78	84	83	80	59	30.7	13,723
2012	73	36	64	78	85	82	80	59	31.1	14,578
Males:										
1975/76	69	36	78	85	83	75	58	32	13.4	8,113
1985/86	74	37	73	86	87	81	72	51	15.1	9,367
1989/91[1]	80	54	83	88	90	86	79	58	14.5	8,306
1992/94	82	55	83	90	89	88	82	59	14.8	7,652
1995/97[2]	82	51	81	90	89	89	83	65	14.9	7,934
1998/00	82	44	81	90	91	89	83	66	15.2	8,117
2002	80	34	72	89	89	89	85	68	15.2	6,586
2003	81	34	72	87	91	91	88	69	15.4	6,950
2004	80	29	69	87	89	90	87	72	15.3	6,723
2005	81	36	68	86	90	91	88	74	15.7	7,159
2006	81	37	71	87	88	90	90	77	15.9	7,078
2007	81	41	69	86	90	90	88	77	16.0	6,978
2008	81	36	67	88	90	91	90	75	16.2	6,818
2009	80	38	67	85	89	91	91	77	16.3	7,021
2010	80	34	66	86	90	89	90	78	16.4	6,769
2011	80	31	68	81	89	90	90	79	16.4	6,521
2012	80	40	67	81	88	89	90	80	16.6	6,981
Females:										
1975/76	29	20	43	48	37	24	15	4	6.0	8,951
1985/86	41	29	54	62	56	41	24	11	9.2	10,468
1989/91[1]	50	35	65	68	67	50	33	15	9.7	9,160
1992/94	55	42	69	74	71	59	38	16	10.8	8,749
1995/97[2]	58	36	68	74	74	63	46	22	11.4	8,781
1998/00	61	38	70	79	75	67	54	22	12.1	9,039
2002	61	30	62	77	77	74	55	28	12.5	7,250
2003	61	24	62	77	77	71	58	26	12.4	7,606
2004	61	24	61	77	77	71	60	28	12.5	7,505
2005	64	26	61	77	79	75	62	36	13.2	7,904
2006	64	32	62	78	80	74	64	32	13.4	7,737
2007	64	35	63	76	78	74	64	36	13.4	7,715
2008	65	35	61	78	80	76	67	37	13.8	7,472
2009	65	33	62	76	79	75	69	38	13.9	7,770
2010	66	32	60	77	80	77	70	41	14.2	7,349
2011	66	30	59	74	79	76	71	44	14.3	7,202
2012	66	31	62	75	81	75	71	43	14.5	7,597

Source: National Travel Survey
Telephone: 020 7944 3097
Email: national.travelsurvey@dft.gsi.gov.uk

1 Figures prior to 1989 for Great Britain, rather than England only.
2 Figures prior to 1995 are based on unweighted data.
Notes & definitions (https://www.gov.uk/government/uploads/system/uploads/attachment_data/file/337241/nts2013-notes.pdf)

The figures in this table are National Statistics

The results presented in this table are weighted. The base (unweighted sample size) is shown in the table for information.
Weights are applied to adjust for non-response to ensure the characteristics of the achieved sample match the population of Great Britain (1995-2012) or England (2013 onwards) and for the drop off in trip recording in diary data.
The survey results are subject to sampling error.

22.11a Household car availability: Great Britain, 2002 to 2012

Percentage /number

Year	No car / van	One car / van	Two or more cars / vans	All households	Cars / vans per household	Cars / vans per adult (17+)	Unweighted sample size (households)
2002[r]	27	44	29	100	1.08	0.58	8,847
2003[r]	27	43	31	100	1.10	0.59	9,196
2004[r]	26	44	30	100	1.10	0.59	8,991
2005[r]	25	43	32	100	1.15	0.61	9,453
2006[r]	25	44	32	100	1.15	0.61	9,261
2007[r]	25	43	32	100	1.14	0.60	9,278
2008[r]	25	43	32	100	1.15	0.60	8,924
2009[r]	25	43	32	100	1.14	0.60	9,127
2010[r]	25	42	33	100	1.16	0.61	8,775
2011[r]	25	43	32	100	1.14	0.60	8,460
2012	25	44	31	100	1.13	0.60	8,971

Source: National Travel Survey
Telephone: 020 7944 3097
Email: national.travelsurvey@dft.gsi.gov.uk

1 Figures from 1985/86 are from the National Travel Survey. Earlier years are derived from other household surveys.
2 Figures prior to 1995 are based on unweighted data.

Notes & definitions including information about revisions (https://www.gov.uk/government/uploads/system/uploads/attachment_data/file/226817/nts2012-notes.pdf)

The figures in this table are National Statistics

Note: The results presented in this table are weighted. The base (unweighted sample size) is shown in the table for information. Weights are applied to adjust for non-response to ensure the characteristics of the achieved sample match the population of Great Britain and for the drop off in trip recording. The survey results are subject to sampling error.

22.11b Household car ownership by region and Rural-Urban Classification: England, 2002/03 and 2012/13[1]

	No car / van		One car / van		Two or more cars / vans		Cars / vans per household		Unweighted sample size (households)	
	2002/03	2012/13	2002/03	2012/13	2002/03	2012/13	2002/03	2012/13	2002/03	2012/13
Region of residence:										
North East	37	31	44	42	20	27	0.86	1.02	847	878
North West	27	27	44	43	28	31	1.05	1.10	2,164	2,096
Yorkshire and The Humber	30	25	45	43	25	32	0.99	1.13	1,605	1,559
East Midlands	20	21	45	45	34	34	1.20	1.21	1,321	1,359
West Midlands	26	21	40	44	34	35	1.15	1.23	1,593	1,630
East of England	20	18	42	44	38	38	1.26	1.30	1,637	1,752
London	41	44	40	39	19	17	0.82	0.77	2,228	2,221
South East	18	17	43	46	39	38	1.30	1.30	2,332	2,478
South West	19	17	47	47	34	36	1.24	1.27	1,661	1,571
England excluding London	24	21	44	44	33	34	1.16	1.21	13,160	13,323
England	26	25	43	43	31	32	1.10	1.14	15,388	15,544
Rural-Urban Classification[2] of residence:										
Urban Conurbation	35	35	41	41	24	25	0.93	0.95	5,882	5,720
Urban City and Town	24	22	46	47	31	32	1.13	1.17	6,842	6,826
Rural Town and Fringe	17	14	42	44	41	41	1.32	1.37	1,440	1,532
Rural Village, Hamlet and Isolated Dwelling	7	7	39	38	53	55	1.63	1.67	1,224	1,466
All areas	26	25	43	43	31	32	1.10	1.14	15,388	15,544

Source: National Travel Survey

1 Two survey years combined, e.g. 2012 and 2013. A survey year runs from mid-January to mid-January.
2 For more information on Rural-Urban Classifications see:
https://www.gov.uk/government/collections/rural-urban-definition

Telephone: 020 7944 3097
Email: national.travelsurvey@dft.gsi.gov.uk
Notes & definitions (https://www.gov.uk/government/uploads/system/uploads/attachment_data/file/337241/nts2013-notes.pdf)

The figures in this table are National Statistics

The results presented in this table are weighted. The base (unweighted sample size) is shown in the table for information.
Weights are applied to adjust for non-response to ensure the characteristics of the achieved sample match the population of Great Britain (1995-2012) or England (2013 onwards) and for the drop off in trip recording in diary data.
The survey results are subject to sampling error.

22.12 Vehicles currently licensed by taxation group: 2008-2012

Number at 31 December

Taxation Group (Taxation Classes)	2008		2009		2010		2011		2012	
	No.	%	No.	%	No.	%	No.	%	No.	%
Private Light Goods (11, 36, 39, 48, 49, 59, 91, 92)	857,044	83.7	873,562	83.7	877,034	83.5	879,787	83.5	885,976	83.6
Motorcycles, Scooters & Mopeds (17, 18)	28,180	2.8	28,080	2.7	26,771	2.5	25,196	2.4	23,559	2.2
General (HGV) Goods (1, 2, 10, 23, 45, 46, 53)	25,136	2.5	24,534	2.4	23,863	2.3	23,084	2.2	22,114	2.1
Bus (34, 38)	2,951	0.3	2,987	0.3	3,035	0.3	3,015	0.3	3,094	0.3
Agricultural/Tractors (40 & 44)	14,326	1.4	15,526	1.5	17,059	1.6	18,555	1.8	19,775	1.9
Other (14-16, 19, 37, 47, 50, 55-58, 79, 81, 82)	2,232	0.2	2,244	0.2	2,180	0.2	2,159	0.2	2,154	0.2
Crown (60)	6,902	0.7	7,215	0.7	7,488	0.7	7,646	0.7	7,862	0.7
Exempt (>60 except 79, 81, 82, 91, 92)	87,625	8.6	89,757	8.6	93,051	8.9	93,896	8.9	95,794	9.0
All Vehicles	**1,024,396**	**100.0**	**1,043,905**	**100.0**	**1,050,481**	**100.0**	**1,053,338**	**100.0**	**1,060,328**	**100.0**

Source: Driver and Vehicle Agency (DVA)

2009 was the first year for there to be vehicles in Taxation classes 91 and 92. DVA advised that these vehicles should be included in the Private and Light Goods taxation group.

22.13 Motor vehicles registered for the first time in NI by vehicle type: 2008-2012

Number at 31 December

Vehicle type	2008	2009	2010	2011	2012
Private cars					
New cars	46,427	42,693	42,416	35,330	36,365
New cars exempt - Govt owned	13	12	8	29	3
New cars exempt - Non Govt owned	11,370	10,154	12,019	12,407	11,622
Used cars	32,437	32,901	29,422	29,070	30,625
Used cars exempt - Govt owned	1	1	1	0	1
Used cars exempt - Non Govt owned	1,199	1,182	1,027	1,059	975
All private cars	**91,447**	**86,943**	**84,893**	**77,895**	**79,591**
Buses	**677**	**477**	**486**	**319**	**411**
Light goods					
Light goods	11,451	9,139	7,807	8,645	8,179
Light goods exempt - Govt owned	63	34	38	24	74
Light goods exempt - Non Govt owned	210	208	213	315	356
All light goods	**11,724**	**9,381**	**8,058**	**8,984**	**8,609**
Heavy goods					
Heavy goods	2,923	2,797	2,546	2,462	2,453
Heavy goods exempt - Govt owned	41	46	17	5	24
Heavy goods exempt - Non Govt owned	28	77	43	42	54
All heavy goods	**2,992**	**2,920**	**2,606**	**2,509**	**2,531**
Tractors					
Tractors	1	3	0	2	1
Tractors exempt - Govt Owned	6	0	10	2	6
Tractors exempt - Non Govt owned	1,813	1,811	1,953	1,981	2,092
All tractors	**1,820**	**1,814**	**1,963**	**1,985**	**2,099**
Motorcycles					
Motorcycles	3,985	3,403	2,528	2,009	1,874
Motorcycles exempt - Govt owned	0	29	22	19	0
Motorcycles exempt - Non Govt owned	102	129	98	170	137
All motorcycles	**4,087**	**3,561**	**2,648**	**2,198**	**2,011**
Other exempt	**0**	**0**	**0**	**0**	**0**
Other non exempt	**0**	**0**	**0**	**0**	**0**
General Haulage and Special Types	**16**	**26**	**25**	**23**	**15**
All vehicles	**112,763**	**105,122**	**100,679**	**93,913**	**95,267**

Source: DVA

22.14 Vehicle kilometres on local bus services by metropolitan area status and country: Great Britain

Millions

Year	Estimation method[1]	London	English metropolitan areas	English non-metropolitan areas	England	Scotland	Wales	Great Britain	England outside London
2000/01		371	654	1,134	2,158	369	126	2,653	1,788
2001/02		381	646	1,102	2,129	368	126	2,622	1,748
2002/03		404	630	1,088	2,122	374	123	2,619	1,718
2003/04		444	596	1,069	2,109	369	113	2,590	1,665
2004/05	Old	..	575	1,077	2,122	357	116	2,594	1,652
2004/05 R	New	470	592	1,061	2,123	359	130	2,612	1,653
2005/06 R		461	589	1,071	2,121	374	128	2,623	1,660
2006/07 R		465	591	1,066	2,122	384	124	2,630	1,657
2007/08 R		465	597	1,068	2,130	397	124	2,650	1,665
2008/09 R		474	589	1,077	2,140	386	126	2,652	1,666
2009/10 R		479	569	1,071	2,118	377	125	2,620	1,640
2010/11 R		481	568	1,073	2,122	346	125	2,592	1,640
2011/12 R		485	563	1,053	2,102	338	118	2,557	1,616
2012/13		486	553	1,049	2,088	327	116	2,531	1,602

Source: DfT Public Service Vehicle Survey, Transport for London

1 Break in the local bus series (outside London) due to changes in the estimation methodology from 2004/05

2 Deregulation of the bus market took place in October 1986. For more information see the technical information (link below)

R Previously published figures have been revised. For details of the revisions (which include planned updates) please see the technical information (link below)

Telephone: 020 7944 3094

Email: bus.statistics@dft.gsi.gov.uk

Notes and definitions (available via: https://www.gov.uk/government/organisations/department-for-transport/series/bus-statistics)
The figures in this table are National Statistics

22.15 Local bus fares index (at current prices[2]) by metropolitan area status and country: Great Britain, annual from 2000

March 2005=100

Year[1]	All items Retail Prices Index[3]	Local bus fares index							England outside London
		London	English metropolitan areas	English non-metropolitan areas	England	Scotland	Wales	Great Britain	
2000	88.4	83.2	79.1	78.4	79.6	89.6	80.3	80.9	78.7
2001	90.4	83.9	83.3	82.7	82.9	92.2	84.7	84.1	82.9
2002	91.6	81.5	87.3	86.6	85.3	93.5	88.6	86.4	86.9
2003	94.4	81.8	90.3	90.8	88.0	96.1	91.6	89.2	90.6
2004	96.9	86.9	94.7	95.3	92.7	97.1	95.8	93.4	95.1
2005	100.0	100.0	100.0	100.0	100.0	100.0	100.0	100.0	100.0
2006	102.4	105.7	111.9	107.8	108.3	105.1	105.0	107.9	109.6
2007	107.3	116.6	113.6	102.0	110.2	111.4	111.5	110.4	106.9
2008	111.3	111.2	121.6	106.7	112.8	116.7	117.5	113.4	113.0
2009	110.9	120.0	136.5	113.9	122.5	126.5	125.3	123.1	123.2
2010	115.9	135.2	137.6	115.6	128.8	129.5	128.7	129.0	124.7
2011	122.0	144.5	146.4	119.4	135.7	132.2	130.1	135.2	130.3
2012	126.4	152.3	156.2	127.0	144.0	139.1	137.8	143.4	138.9
2013	130.6	159.4	161.3	134.3	150.8	145.1	147.2	150.1	145.4

1 Index as at March.
2 Not adjusted for inflation.
3 These figures are not National Statistics

Source: DfT Fares Survey, Office for National Statistics
Telephone: 020 7944 3094
Email: bus.statistics@dft.gsi.gov.uk

Bus Statistics - Notes & Definitions (https://www.gov.uk/government/publications/buses-statistics-guidance)
The figures in this table are National Statistics except where indicated

22.16 Reported road accident casualties by road user type and severity: 2000-2012

Number

	2000	2001	2002	2003	2004	2005	2006	2007	2008	2009	2010	2011	2012
Child pedestrians: [1]													
Killed	107	107	79	74	77	63	71	57	57	37	26	33	20
KSI[2]	3,226	3,144	2,828	2,381	2,339	2,134	2,025	1,899	1,784	1,660	1,646	1,602	1,545
All severities	16,184	15,819	14,231	12,544	12,234	11,250	10,131	9,527	8,648	7,983	7,929	7,807	6,999
Adult pedestrians: [3]													
Killed	750	712	688	695	589	604	602	585	515	463	379	420	400
KSI	6,112	5,745	5,644	5,422	5,005	4,847	4,894	4,900	4,724	4,295	3,874	4,227	4,374
All severities	24,481	23,463	23,258	22,531	21,404	20,725	19,774	19,676	19,013	18,248	17,320	17,802	17,689
Child pedal cyclists: [1]													
Killed	27	25	22	18	25	20	31	13	12	14	7	6	13
KSI	758	674	594	595	577	527	503	522	417	458	398	398	324
All severities	6,260	5,451	4,809	4,769	4,682	4,286	3,765	3,633	3,306	3,204	2,828	2,881	2,198
Adult pedal cyclists: [3]													
Killed	98	111	107	95	109	127	115	122	103	90	104	101	105
KSI	1,954	1,951	1,801	1,776	1,697	1,787	1,898	1,994	2,101	2,225	2,333	2,750	2,976
All severities	13,630	12,974	11,712	11,643	11,366	11,637	11,911	12,050	12,546	13,420	13,970	15,908	16,446
Motorcyclists [4] **and passengers**													
Killed	605	583	609	693	585	569	599	588	493	472	403	362	328
KSI	7,374	7,305	7,500	7,652	6,648	6,508	6,484	6,737	6,049	5,822	5,183	5,609	5,328
All severities	28,212	28,810	28,353	28,411	25,641	24,824	23,326	23,459	21,550	20,703	18,686	20,150	19,310
Car drivers and passengers													
Killed	1,665	1,749	1,747	1,769	1,671	1,675	1,612	1,432	1,257	1,059	835	883	801
KSI	19,719	19,424	18,728	17,291	16,144	14,617	14,254	12,967	11,968	11,112	9,749	9,225	9,033
All severities	206,799	202,802	197,425	188,342	183,858	178,302	171,000	161,433	149,188	143,412	133,205	124,924	119,708
Bus/coach drivers and passengers													
Killed	15	14	19	11	20	9	19	12	6	14	9	7	11
KSI	578	562	551	500	488	363	426	455	432	370	401	332	323
All severities	10,088	9,884	9,005	9,068	8,820	7,920	7,253	7,079	6,929	6,317	6,268	6,177	5,234
LGV drivers and passengers													
Killed	66	64	70	72	62	54	52	58	43	36	34	34	33
KSI	813	811	780	765	631	587	564	494	445	417	359	340	363
All severities	7,007	7,304	7,007	6,897	6,166	6,048	5,914	5,340	4,913	4,743	4,494	4,499	4,533
HGV drivers and passengers													
Killed	55	54	63	44	47	55	39	52	23	14	28	28	29
KSI	571	500	524	429	406	395	383	363	240	189	212	195	198
All severities	3,597	3,388	3,178	3,061	2,883	2,843	2,530	2,476	1,930	1,519	1,578	1,415	1,339
All road users: [5]													
Killed	3,409	3,450	3,431	3,508	3,221	3,201	3,172	2,946	2,538	2,222	1,850	1,901	1,754
KSI	41,564	40,560	39,407	37,215	34,351	32,155	31,845	30,720	28,572	26,912	24,510	25,023	24,793
All severities	320,283	313,309	302,605	290,607	280,840	271,017	258,404	247,780	230,905	222,146	208,648	203,950	195,723

Source: Department for Transport
Contact: 020-7944 6595
E-mail: roadacc.stats@dft.gsi.gov.uk

1. Casualties aged 0 -15.
2. Killed and seriously injured.
3. Casualties aged 16 and over.
4. Includes mopeds and scooters.
5. Includes other motor or non-motor vehicle users, and unknown road user type and casualty age.
The figures in this table are National Statistics

22.17a Goods lifted[1] and goods moved[2] by mode of working: by GB HGVs in the UK

| | Million tonnes | | | | | Billion tonne kilometres | | | | |
| | Goods lifted[1] | | | | | Goods moved[2] | | | | |
Year	Mainly public haulage	% of total	Mainly own account	% of total	All modes	Mainly public haulage	% of total	Mainly own account	% of total	All modes
1999	991	64	576	36	1,567	111	75	38	25	149
2000	1,038	65	556	35	1,593	113	75	37	25	150
2001	1,052	67	529	33	1,581	115	77	35	23	149
2002	1,019	63	608	37	1,627	111	74	39	26	150
2003	1,053	64	590	36	1,643	114	75	37	25	152
2004	1,101	63	643	37	1,744	111	73	41	27	152
2005	1,079	62	667	38	1,746	110	72	43	28	153
2006	1,104	62	671	38	1,776	110	72	43	28	152
2007	1,116	61	706	39	1,822	113	72	45	28	157
2008	948	57	720	43	1,668	99	68	47	32	146
2009	690	51	666	49	1,356	77	62	48	38	125
2010	800	54	689	46	1,489	89	64	50	36	139
2011 Q1 p	192	47	216	53	408	20	56	16	44	36

1. Weight of goods in tonnes
2. Weight of goods multiplied by distance in tonne kilometres
p Provisional

Source: Continuing Survey of Road Goods Transport, DfT

Telephone: 020 7944 4261
Email: roadfreight.stats@dft.gsi.gov.uk

The figures in this table are National Statistics

Figures shown for 2011 are provisional figures for Q1 only. Complete figures for 2011 will be released in January 2015

22.17b Goods moved[1] by type and weight of vehicle: by GB HGVs in the UK

| | | | | | | | Billion tonne kilometres | | | |
| | Rigid vehicles | | | | | Articulated vehicles | | | |
Year	Over 3.5t to 7.5t	Over 7.5t to 17t	Over 17t to 25t	Over 25t	All Rigids	Over 3.5t to 33t	Over 33t	All artics	All vehicles
1999	5	13	4	15	37	14	98	112	149
2000	5	11	5	15	36	14	100	114	150
2001	5	9	6	16	34	13	102	115	149
2002	5	7	6	17	36	10	104	114	150
2003	4	6	7	18	35	9	108	116	152
2004	4	5	7	19	36	7	109	116	152
2005	4	4	8	21	37	6	110	116	153
2006	4	3	8	20	36	6	111	117	152
2007	3	3	9	22	37	6	115	120	157
2008	3	2	8	20	33	5	108	113	146
2009	3	2	7	17	30	5	91	96	125
2010	3	2	7	18	31	4	104	108	139
2011 Q1 p	1	1	1			1	26	27	36

Source: Continuing Survey of Road Goods Transport, DfT

1. Weight of goods multiplied by distance in tonne kilometres
p Provisional

Telephone: 020 7944 4261

Email: roadfreight.stats@dft.gsi.gov.uk

The figures in this table are National Statistics

Figures shown for 2011 are provisional figures for Q1 only. Complete figures for 2011 will be released in January 2015

22.17c Goods moved by commodity[1]

Billion tonne kilometres

Commodity	2000	2001	2002	2003	2004	2005	2006[R]	2007[R]	2008[R]	2009[R]	2010
Food, drink and tobacco											
Agricultural products	13.4	11.5	12.8	11.3	12.4	11.6	11.4	11.5	11.8	9.6	10.3
Beverages	6.4	6.1	7.0	6.5	6.6	6.0	6.5	6.6	6.0	5.2	4.6
Other foodstuffs	24.5	23.8	23.3	24.4	22.7	22.9	23.3	25.8	24.1	26.5	29.1
Subtotal	**44.3**	**41.4**	**43.1**	**42.2**	**41.7**	**40.6**	**41.2**	**43.9**	**41.9**	**41.3**	**44.0**
Bulk products											
Wood, timber and cork	3.7	3.9	3.8	4.1	4.5	4.6	4.1	3.2	3.9	3.7	3.7
Crude minerals[2]	12.4	13.0	13.9	13.8	14.0	14.8	15.1	15.5	12.8	9.8	11.6
Ores	1.2	1.2	1.1	1.2	1.4	1.7	1.3	1.8	1.7	1.2	1.1
Crude materials	2.6	2.3	2.7	2.3	3.3	2.4	2.7	2.6	2.2	2.0	2.7
Coal and coke	1.5	2.1	1.5	1.5	1.2	1.5	1.3	1.5	1.0	0.9	1.4
Building materials[3]	10.6	11.7	10.9	12.0	12.1	10.9	11.3	11.3	10.6	8.2	8.9
Iron and steel products	6.8	5.7	5.3	5.4	5.4	5.2	4.6	6.2	3.9	3.2	3.3
Subtotal	**38.8**	**39.8**	**39.3**	**40.4**	**41.9**	**41.2**	**40.4**	**42.1**	**36.1**	**29.1**	**32.8**
Chemicals, petrol & fertiliser											
Fertiliser	1.2	1.2	1.2	1.2	0.8	1.1	0.8	0.9	1.3	1.6	1.9
Petrol and petroleum products	6.4	5.8	5.2	5.5	5.7	5.5	5.6	5.0	6.2	4.6	6.0
Chemicals	6.8	7.2	6.5	6.8	6.2	7.6	6.1	6.8	5.8	5.0	4.7
Subtotal	**14.4**	**14.2**	**12.9**	**13.5**	**12.8**	**14.3**	**12.5**	**12.7**	**13.4**	**11.1**	**12.6**
Miscellaneous products											
Other metal products n.e.s	1.7	1.4	1.5	1.5	1.9	2.1	2.1	2.0	1.8	1.7	1.7
Machinery and transport equipment	9.1	8.9	8.5	8.7	8.9	9.3	9.2	9.3	8.5	6.9	7.5
Miscellaneous manufactures n.e.s	15.1	15.4	16.2	15.8	16.3	15.5	16.0	16.0	12.1	10.6	11.0
Miscellaneous articles n.e.s[4]	27.1	28.2	28.4	29.5	28.7	29.7	31.1	31.4	31.9	24.5	29.3
Subtotal	**52.9**	**53.9**	**54.6**	**55.6**	**55.7**	**56.5**	**58.4**	**58.6**	**54.3**	**43.7**	**49.4**
All commodities	**150.5**	**149.4**	**149.8**	**151.7**	**152.1**	**152.6**	**152.4**	**157.3**	**145.8**	**125.2**	**138.9**

Source: Continuing Survey of Road Goods Transport, DfT

1. See https://www.gov.uk/government/uploads/system/uploads/attachment_data/file/8970/notes-and-definitions.pdf for definitions of commodity.

2. Comprises 'sand, gravel and clay' and 'other crude minerals'.

3. Comprises 'cement' and 'other building materials'.

4. Including 'commodity not known'.

Note: figures for 2006 to 2009 have been revised. See the Notes and Definitions for further information.

https://www.gov.uk/government/uploads/system/uploads/attachment_data/file/8970/notes-and-definitions.pdf

Telephone: 020 7944 4261

Email: roadfreight.stats@dft.gsi.gov.uk

The figures in this table are National Statistics

2011 figures due for release January 2015

22.18a Goods lifted[1] by type and weight of vehicle: by GB HGVs in UK

Million tonnes

Year	Rigids					Articulated vehicles			All vehicles
	Over 3.5t to 7.5t	Over 7.5t to 17t	Over 17t to 25t	Over 25t	All Rigids	Over 3.5t to 33t	Over 33t	All artics	
1999	81	173	86	408	748	113	706	819	1,567
2000	77	152	87	424	741	107	746	852	1,593
2001	80	123	86	443	733	97	751	848	1,581
2002	77	111	90	491	768	81	778	859	1,627
2003	70	89	100	506	765	69	809	878	1,643
2004	77	87	108	540	812	59	873	932	1,744
2005	70	70	110	562	812	51	883	934	1,746
2006	64	64	118	585	831	49	896	945	1,776
2007	54	52	127	614	848	49	926	975	1,822
2008	56	44	118	513	731	44	892	937	1,668
2009	56	37	102	377	572	38	746	785	1,356
2010	54	37	103	414	607	33	848	881	1,489
2011 Q1 p	14	14	24	130	181	9	218	227	408

1. Weight of goods in tonn   *Source: Continuing Survey of Road Goods Transport, DfT*

p Provisional

Telephone: 020 7944 4261

Email: roadfreight.stats@dft.gsi.gov.uk

The figures in this table are National Statistics

Figures shown for 2011 are provisional figures for Q1 only. Complete figures for 2011 will be released in January 2015

22.18b Goods lifted by commodity[1]

Million tonnes

Commodity	2000	2001	2002	2003	2004	2005	2006[R]	2007[R]	2008[R]	2009[R]	2010
Food, drink and tobacco											
Agricultural products	119	96	113	106	113	111	103	102	104	98	102
Beverages	47	51	51	48	59	45	55	56	46	38	37
Other foodstuffs	180	174	175	179	180	183	195	207	206	216	244
Subtotal	**346**	**321**	**339**	**333**	**351**	**339**	**353**	**364**	**355**	**352**	**382**
Bulk products											
Wood, timber and cork	26	28	28	32	42	36	29	29	34	31	31
Crude minerals[2]	308	298	333	327	364	370	372	381	306	208	235
Ores	16	16	17	21	22	23	19	21	23	15	16
Crude materials	18	20	21	19	25	22	22	22	19	15	23
Coal and coke	22	21	17	22	14	21	16	23	14	10	11
Building materials[3]	165	165	167	165	185	169	176	171	171	121	139
Iron and steel products	49	44	39	41	43	42	40	46	31	25	27
Subtotal	**604**	**592**	**622**	**627**	**694**	**681**	**675**	**693**	**598**	**425**	**482**
Chemicals, petrol & fertiliser											
Fertiliser	10	9	11	12	7	14	6	9	21	19	29
Petrol and petroleum products	75	74	59	64	67	70	68	69	77	58	68
Chemicals	49	50	41	47	46	53	48	47	43	36	34
Subtotal	**134**	**133**	**111**	**123**	**121**	**138**	**122**	**125**	**140**	**114**	**132**
Miscellaneous products											
Other metal products n.e.s	16	14	14	16	19	19	21	19	19	19	18
Machinery and transport equipment	69	70	68	66	70	76	78	81	72	65	68
Miscellaneous manufactures n.e.s	97	97	105	98	111	109	110	110	91	78	76
Miscellaneous articles n.e.s[4]	328	353	367	379	378	384	418	430	391	303	329
Subtotal	**510**	**534**	**554**	**559**	**577**	**588**	**626**	**640**	**574**	**466**	**492**
All commodities	**1,593**	**1,581**	**1,627**	**1,643**	**1,744**	**1,746**	**1,776**	**1,822**	**1,668**	**1,356**	**1,489**

Source: Continuing Survey of Road Goods Transport, DfT

1. See https://www.gov.uk/government/uploads/system/uploads/attachment_data/file/8970/notes-and-definitions.pdf for definitions of commodity.
2. Comprises 'sand, gravel and clay' and 'other crude minerals'.
3. Comprises 'cement' and 'other building materials'.
4. Including 'commodity not known'.

Note: figures for 2006 to 2009 have been revised. See the Notes and Definitions for further information.
https://www.gov.uk/government/uploads/system/uploads/attachment_data/file/8970/notes-and-definitions.pdf
Telephone: 020 7944 4261
Email: roadfreight.stats@dft.gsi.gov.uk

The figures in this table are National Statistics

2011 figures due for release January 2015

22.19a Passenger journeys by sector - National Rail Great Britain (millions)

Financial Year	Franchised long distance operators	Franchised London and SE operators	Franchised regional operators	Total franchised passenger journeys	Non franchised
2002-03	77.2	679.1	219.2	975.5	-
2003-04	81.5	690.0	240.2	1,011.7	-
2004-05	83.7	704.5	251.3	1,039.5	-
2005-06	89.5	719.7	267.3	1,076.5	-
2006-07	99.0	769.5	276.5	1,145.0	-
2007-08	103.9	828.4	285.8	1,218.1	-
2008-09	109.4	854.3	302.8	1,266.5	-
2009-10	111.6	842.2	304.0	1,257.9	1.4
2010-11	117.9	917.6	318.2	1,353.8	1.8
2011-12	125.3	993.8	340.9	1,460.0	1.5

Source: LENNON database and train operating companies

This is an official statistic. For more details please contact the statistics Head of Profession Jay Lindop at jay.lindop@orr.gsi.gov.uk or on 020 7282 3978.

Passenger journeys on light rail and trams by system[1]: England

Millions

Financial year	Docklands Light Railway	Croydon Tramlink	Nottingham Express Transit	Midland Metro	Sheffield Supertram	Tyne and Wear Metro	Manchester Metrolink[2]	Blackpool Tramway	England
1998/99	27.6	.	.	.	10.4	33.8	13.2	4.4	89.3
1999/00	31.3	.	.	4.8	10.9	32.7	14.2	4.3	98.2
2000/01	38.4	15.0	.	5.4	11.1	32.5	17.2	4.1	123.6
2001/02	41.3	18.2	.	4.8	11.4	33.4	18.2	4.9	132.2
2002/03	45.7	18.7	.	4.9	11.5	36.6	18.8	4.5	140.7
2003/04	48.5	19.8	0.4	5.1	12.3	37.9	18.9	3.7	146.5
2004/05	50.1	22.0	8.5	5.0	12.8	36.8	19.7	3.9	158.7
2005/06	53.5	22.5	9.8	5.1	13.1	35.8	19.9	3.6	163.4
2006/07	63.9	24.6	10.1	4.9	14.0	37.9	19.8	3.4	178.6
2007/08	66.6	27.2	10.2	4.8	14.8	39.8	20.0	2.9	186.2
2008/09	67.8	27.2	9.8	4.7	15.0	40.6	21.1	2.3	188.6
2009/10	69.4	25.8	9.0	4.7	14.7	40.8	19.6	2.2	186.2
2010/11	78.3	27.9	9.7	4.8	15.0	39.9	19.2	1.6	196.5
2011/12	86.1	28.6	9.0	4.9	15.0	37.9	22.3	1.1	204.8
2012/13	100.0	30.1	7.4	4.8	14.4	37.0	25.0	3.7	222.5

Source: DfT Light Rail and Tram Survey

1 For further information on these systems including network and infrastructure changes that may affect the figures, please refer to the technical information

2 Manchester Metrolink have revised their method for calculation of passenger boardings so the figures from 2010/11 are not directly comparable with previous years.

Telephone: 020 7944 3094
Email: bus.statistics@dft.gsi.gov.uk
Notes and Definitions (www.gov.uk/transport-statistics-notes-and-guidance-light-rail-and-tram-statistics)

The figures in this table are National Statistics

22.19b Passenger revenue by sector - National Rail

Great Britain (£ millions)

Financial Year	Franchised long distance operators	Franchised London and SE operators	Franchised regional operators	Total franchised passenger revenue	Non franchised
2002-03	1,279	1,848	535	3,663	-
2003-04	1,384	1,932	585	3,901	-
2004-05	1,465	2,059	634	4,158	-
2005-06	1,609	2,197	687	4,493	-
2006-07	1,842	2,437	733	5,012	-
2007-08	2,036	2,717	801	5,555	-
2008-09	2,168	2,963	872	6,004	-
2009-10	2,216	3,046	916	6,179	36.7
2010-11	2,366	3,264	990	6,620	45.5
2011-12	2,533	3,602	1,094	7,229	43.9

Source: LENNON database and train operating companies

This is an official statistic. For more details please contact the statistics Head of Profession Jay Lindop at jay.lindop@orr.gsi.gov.uk or on 020 7282 3978.

Passenger revenue at 2013/14 prices[1] on light rail and trams by system[2]: England

£ Millions

Financial year	Docklands Light Railway	Croydon Tramlink	Nottingham Express Transit	Midland Metro	Sheffield Supertram	Tyne and Wear Metro	Manchester Metrolink	Blackpool Tramway	England
1998/99	27.7	.	.	.	8.4	31.3	21.5	5.8	94.8
1999/00	28.5		.	3.4	9.2	31.6	23.1	5.8	101.6
2000/01	38.8	16.4	.	4.2	9.6	32.6	24.5	5.8	131.8
2001/02	42.3	17.0	.	5.1	10.0	32.9	26.5	6.2	139.9
2002/03	45.8	19.2	.	6.4	13.1	36.9	26.9	5.9	154.1
2003/04	46.9	20.3	.	6.5	11.6	39.6	26.4	5.0	156.2
2004/05	49.5	22.1	7.2	6.7	13.6	39.9	27.1	5.3	171.3
2005/06	55.5	22.7	8.8	7.1	12.6	41.4	27.2	5.2	180.6
2006/07	63.0	22.2	8.8	7.4	14.5	41.1	27.6	5.2	189.9
2007/08	72.0	23.8	9.0	7.2	15.7	42.6	25.6	4.5	200.4
2008/09	71.0	20.1	9.5	7.3	16.8	45.8	24.9	3.9	199.5
2009/10	80.9	17.5	8.6	7.0	16.3	44.1	25.3	3.2	202.9
2010/11	93.5	20.1	9.5	7.4	16.1	43.8	28.9	2.6	221.8
2011/12	108.5	21.8	8.7	7.6	15.8	43.4	34.7	1.8	242.3

1 Adjusted for inflation using the GDP market price deflator (as at 28 March 2014).   Source: DfT Light Rail and Tram Survey
2 For further information on these systems including infrastructure changes that may affect the figures, please refer to the technical information.

Telephone: 020 7944 3094
Email: bus.statistics@dft.gsi.gov.uk
Notes and Definitions (www.gov.uk/transport-statistics-notes-and-guidance-light-rail-and-tram-statistics)

The figures in this table are National Statistics

22.19c Passenger kilometres by sector - National Rail
Great Britain (billions)

Financial Year	Franchised long distance operators	Franchised London and SE operators	Franchised regional operators	Total franchised passenger kilometres	Non franchised
2002-03	12.9	19.8	6.9	39.7	-
2003-04	13.3	20.1	7.5	40.9	-
2004-05	13.4	20.5	7.8	41.7	-
2005-06	14.2	20.7	8.2	43.1	-
2006-07	15.6	22.2	8.4	46.2	-
2007-08	16.5	23.5	8.9	48.9	-
2008-09	17.0	24.2	9.4	50.6	-
2009-10	17.6	23.8	9.7	51.1	0.3
2010-11	18.6	25.0	10.4	54.1	0.4
2011-12	19.3	26.5	11.2	56.9	0.4

Source: LENNON database and train operating companies

This is an official statistic. For more details please contact the statistics Head of Profession Jay Lindop at jay.lindop@orr.gsi.gov.uk or on 020 7282 3978.

Passenger miles on light rail and trams by system[1]: England

Millions

Financial year	Docklands Light Railway	Croydon Tramlink	Nottingham Express Transit	Midland Metro	Sheffield Supertram	Tyne and Wear Metro	Manchester Metrolink[2]	Blackpool Tramway[3]	England
1998/99	89.7	.	.	.	45.0	147.8	72.7	8.3	363.4
1999/00	106.9	.	.	31.0	47.3	142.9	78.3	8.1	414.6
2000/01	124.3	59.7	.	34.7	48.1	142.4	94.6	7.8	511.6
2001/02	128.5	61.5	.	31.1	49.7	148.1	100.2	9.3	528.5
2002/03	144.2	62.1	.	31.1	50.0	170.8	103.5	8.5	570.3
2003/04	146.3	65.2	1.2	33.3	53.5	176.4	105.0	7.0	588.0
2004/05	152.5	69.7	23.0	32.5	55.7	176.0	126.8	7.4	643.7
2005/06	160.0	72.7	25.9	33.5	57.0	173.4	128.0	6.9	657.4
2006/07	186.8	79.5	26.9	31.9	60.9	183.2	129.0	6.5	704.7
2007/08	202.8	87.9	27.3	31.4	64.4	194.4	130.5	5.4	744.1
2008/09	197.5	89.2	26.1	31.0	65.2	198.5	137.1	4.4	749.0
2009/10	226.5	83.5	23.6	30.8	64.0	203.2	128.1	4.1	763.8
2010/11	257.2	90.0	25.7	31.3	60.5	195.8	124.8	3.1	788.4
2011/12	283.0	92.2	24.9	31.7	60.3	188.8	141.9	2.1	824.9

Source: DfT Light Rail and Tram Survey

1 For further information on these systems including infrastructure changes that may affect the figures, please refer to the technical information.

2 Manchester Metrolink have revised their approach calculation of passenger boardings so the figure for 2010-11 is not directly comparable with previous years.

3 1983/84 to 1998/99 Blackpool Tramway data are imputed. The figures use passenger journeys data and an assumed average distance.

Telephone: 020 7944 3094
Email: bus.statistics@dft.gsi.gov.uk
Notes and Definitions (www.gov.uk/transport-statistics-notes-and-guidance-light-rail-and-tram-statistics)

The figures in this table are National Statistics

22.19d Infrastructure on the railways - National Rail Network

Great Britain (route kilometres and number of stations)

Year	Route open for traffic	Of which electrified	Route Open for Passenger & Freight Traffic	Route Open for Freight Traffic Only	Passenger Stations
1986-87	16,670	4,156	14,304	2,366	2,405
1987-88	16,633	4,207	14,302	2,331	2,426
1988-89	16,599	4,376	14,309	2,290	2,470
1989-90	16,587	4,546	14,318	2,269	2,471
1990-91	16,584	4,912	14,317	2,267	2,488
1991-92	16,588	4,886	14,291	2,267	2,468
1992-93	16,528	4,910	14,317	2,211	2,468
1993-94	16,536	4,968	14,357	2,179	2,493
1994-95	16,542	4,970	14,359	2,183	2,489
1995-96	16,666	5,163	15,002	1,664	2,497
1996-97	16,666	5,176	15,034	1,632	2,498
1997-98	16,656	5,166	15,024	1,632	2,495
1998-99	16,659	5,166	15,038	1,621	2,499
1999-00	16,649	5,167	15,038	1,610	2,503
2000-01	16,652	5,167	15,042	1,610	2,508
2001-02	16,652	5,167	15,042	1,610	2,508
2002-03	16,670	5,167	15,042	1,610	2,508
2003-04	16,493	5,200	14,883	1,610	2,507
2004-05	16,116	5,200	14,328	1,788	2,508
2005-06	15,810	5,205	14,356	1,454	2,510
2006-07	15,795	5,250	14,353	1,442	2,520
2007-08	15,814	5,250	14,484	1,330	2,516
2008-09	15,814	5,250	14,494	1,320	2,516
2009-10	15,753	5,239	14,482	1,271	2,516
2010-11	15,777	5,262	14,506	1,271	2,532
2011-12	15,742	5,261	14,506	1,236	2,535

Source: Network Rail

This is an official statistic. For more details please contact the Statistics Head of Profession Jay Lindop at jay.lindop@orr.gsi.gov.uk or on 0207 282 3978

Data prior to 2005 may not sum due to differences in methodology and less developed capability measures. The quality of data has since improved.
The break in series between 1993-94 and 1994-95 is for passenger stations only.
The break in the series between 2003-04 and 2004-05 is due to a change in the methodology for collection of the route length. Up until 2003-04 data were collected on a semi-annual basis from various systems. From 2004-05 the principal track engineers' database, GEOGIS, has been used. The drop from 2004-05 to 2005-06 was caused by data cleansing of GEOGIS over the last 12 months.
There is a break in the time series between 2006-07 and 2007-08 due to a new methodology where the route classification reference data has been revamped.
The drop in total route kilometres between 2005-06 and 2006-07 is due to the formal closure between Stratford to North Woolwich plus data cleansing by Network Rail, e.g. 2 km electrified passenger and freight to Ebbsfleet. The variation of electrified track includes the aforementioned changes but is principally due to data cleansing. In 2010-11, the variation of electrified track is principally due to the opening of the Airdrie to Bathgate link.

For more details on revisions, please see the revisions log: http://www.rail-reg.gov.uk/upload/xls/stats-revisions-log.xls. There are no changes proposed to this dataset.

Vehicle miles on light rail and trams by system[1]: England

Millions

Financial year	Docklands Light Railway	Croydon Tramlink	Nottingham Express Transit	Midland Metro	Sheffield Supertram	Tyne and Wear Metro	Manchester Metrolink	Blackpool Tramway	England
1999/00	1.8	.	.	1.1	1.5	3.0	2.3	0.7	10.3
2000/01	1.8	1.3	.	1.2	1.5	2.9	2.7	0.8	12.2
2001/02	1.8	1.5	.	1.0	1.5	2.9	2.8	0.8	12.4
2002/03	2.0	1.5	.	1.1	1.6	3.9	2.9	0.7	13.7
2003/04	2.1	1.6	0.0	1.0	1.5	3.6	2.8	0.6	13.2
2004/05	2.0	1.5	0.6	1.0	1.5	3.5	2.8	0.5	13.5
2005/06	2.1	1.5	0.7	1.0	1.5	3.4	2.8	0.5	13.5
2006/07	2.7	1.6	0.7	1.0	1.5	3.6	2.3	0.6	14.1
2007/08	2.8	1.4	0.7	1.0	1.5	3.8	2.5	0.5	14.1
2008/09	2.5	1.4	0.7	1.0	1.5	3.5	2.4	0.5	13.5
2009/10	2.8	1.6	0.7	1.0	1.5	3.5	2.1	0.4	13.6
2010/11	2.9	1.6	0.7	1.0	1.5	3.5	2.3	0.3	13.9
2011/12	3.1	1.7	0.7	1.0	1.5	3.5	2.9	0.1	14.5

1 For further information on these systems including infrastructure changes that may affect the figures, please refer to the technical information.

Source: DfT Light Rail and Tram Survey
Telephone: 020 7944 3094
Email: bus.statistics@dft.gsi.gov.uk

2 Figures for Manchester Metrolink represent total mileage of each tram 'set'. Where two sets are joined to form one train, the vehicle miles run will therefore be counted twice. Based on information supplied by the operator, this affects approximately 7% of services to 2012, around 12% in 12/13 and 20% in 13/14, meaning that figures for later years are not directly comparable with earlier ones (or with other systems). We estimate that the increasing use of double sets to form trains contributes around a third of the overall increase in vehicle mileage shown for this system since 2011/12.
Notes and Definitions (www.gov.uk/transport-statistics-notes-and-guidance-light-rail-and-tram-statistics)
The figures in this table are National Statistics

22.19e Number of stations or stops on light rail and trams by system[1]: England - annual

Financial year	Docklands Light Railway	Croydon Tramlink	Nottingham Express Transit	Midland Metro	Sheffield Supertram	Tyne and Wear Metro	Manchester Metrolink	Blackpool Tramway[2,3]	England
1995/96	28	.	.	.	45	46	26	62	207
1996/97	28	.	.	.	45	46	26	62	207
1997/98	29	.	.	.	46	46	26	62	209
1998/99	29	.	.	.	47	46	26	62	210
1999/00	34	.	.	23	47	46	36	62	248
2000/01	34	38	.	23	47	46	36	62	286
2001/02	34	38	.	23	48	58	36	62	299
2002/03	34	38	.	23	48	58	37	62	300
2003/04	34	38	23	23	48	58	37	62	323
2004/05	34	38	23	23	48	58	37	62	323
2005/06	38	39	23	23	48	59	37	62	329
2006/07	34	39	23	23	48	59	37	61	324
2007/08	39	38	23	23	48	60	37	61	329
2008/09	40	39	23	23	48	60	37	61	331
2009/10	40	39	23	23	48	60	37	59	329
2010/11	40	39	23	23	48	60	38	59	330
2011/12	45	39	23	23	48	60	42	31	311

Source: DfT Light Rail and Tram Survey

1 For further information on these systems including infrastructure changes that may affect the figures, please refer to the technical information.
2 The number of stops has been shown for one direction of the route (as is the case with the other systems). In publications prior to 2011/12 the figures shown covered both directions.

Telephone: 020 7944 3094
Email: bus.statistics@dft.gsi.gov.uk
Notes and Definitions (www.gov.uk/transport-statistics-notes-and-guidance-light-rail-and-tram-statistics)

The figures in this table are National Statistics

22.19f London Underground statistics, annual

	Passenger Journeys (millions)								Receipts (£ million)						
	Ordinary[1]	Season ticket	All journeys	Passenger miles (millions)	Loaded train miles (millions)	Stations	Rail carriages	Route miles	Ordinary[1]	Season ticket	Traffic receipts	Traffic receipts at 2013/14 prices[2]	Receipts per journey (£)	Receipts per jny at 2013/14 prices[2]
2000/01	486	484	970	4,642	40	274	3,954	254	610	519	1,129	1,524	1.16	1.57
2001/02	491	462	953	4,630	40	274	3,954	254	636	515	1,151	1,512	1.21	1.59
2002/03	495	446	942	4,578	41	274	3,954	254	628	510	1,138	1,461	1.21	1.55
2003/04	491	457	948	4,561	43	274	3,959	254	625	536	1,161	1,462	1.22	1.54
2004/05	486	490	976	4,726	43	274	3,959	254	663	578	1,241	1,521	1.27	1.56
2005/06	460	510	970	4,714	43	274	4,070	254	678	630	1,308	1,575	1.35	1.62
2006/07	519	521	1,040	4,938	43	273	4,070	254	782	635	1,417	1,658	1.36	1.59
2007/08	581	515	1,096	5,190	43	268	4,070	254	880	645	1,525	1,741	1.39	1.59
2008/09	616	473	1,089	5,372	44	270	4,070	254	962	654	1,615	1,793	1.48	1.65
2009/10	634	425	1,059	5,255	43	270	4,078	249	840	612	1,635	1,767	1.54	1.67
2010/11	660	447	1,107	5,515	43	270	4,134	249	1,087	672	1,759	1,852	1.59	1.67
2011/12	685	486	1,171	5,915	45	270	4,127	249	1,208	774	1,982	2,041	1.69	1.74

1. Ordinary journeys include daily travelcards and those where concessionary fares apply.
2. Adjustment to values using the HM Treasury GDP Deflator (as at 28 March 2014). 'Other' income no longer available on the same basis as previously published.

Source: Transport for London

Telephone: 020 7944 3094
Email: bus.statistics@dft.gsi.gov.uk

The figures in this table are outside the scope of National Statistics

22.19g Glasgow Underground statistics, annual

	Passenger journeys (millions)	Passenger miles (millions)	Loaded train or tram miles [also referred to as vehicle miles] (millions) [1][R]	Stations or stops served	Passenger carriages or tramcars	Route miles open for passenger traffic	Passenger revenue at 2013/14 prices (£ millions)
1998/99	14.6	29.0	0.7	15	41	6.8	12.6
1999/00	14.7	29.2	0.7	15	41	6.8	13.3
2000/01	14.4	28.6	0.7	15	41	6.8	13.5
2001/02	13.8	27.4	0.7	15	41	6.8	13.2
2002/03	13.4	26.6	0.7	15	41	6.8	13.1
2003/04	13.3	26.5	0.6	15	41	6.8	13.0
2004/05	13.3	26.5	0.6	15	41	6.8	13.4
2005/06	13.2	26.2	0.6	15	41	6.5	13.5
2006/07	13.5	26.8	0.6	15	41	6.5	14.5
2007/08	14.5	28.8	0.6	15	41	6.5	14.7
2008/09	14.1	28.1	0.7	15	41	6.5	16.3
2009/10	13.1	26.0	0.6	15	41	6.5	15.2
2010/11	13.0	25.9	0.6	15	41	6.5	14.9
2011/12	12.9	25.6	0.7	15	41	6.5	14.7

Source: DfT Light Rail and Tram Survey

[1] Loaded tram kilometers are only available as rolling stock totals, to calculate vehicle kilometres the figure provided by Glasgow is divided by 3, as all trams run with three carriages.

[R] Figures for 1982/83 to 2012/13 have been revised due to changes in the calculation, as advised by the operator.

Telephone: 020 7944 3094
Email: bus.statistics@dft.gsi.gov.uk
Notes and Definitions (www.gov.uk/transport-statistics-notes-and-guidance-light-rail-and-tram-statistics)

The figures in this table are outside the scope of National Statistics

22.20a Freight moved

Great Britain annual (billion net tonne kilometres)

Financial year	Coal	Metals	Construction	Oil and petroleum	International	Domestic intermodal	Other	Total (1)	Infrastructure (2)
2002-03	5.66	2.64	2.51	1.15	0.46	3.38	2.72	18.52	1.18
2003-04	5.82	2.41	2.68	1.19	0.48	3.53	2.77	18.87	1.23
2004-05	6.66	2.59	2.86	1.22	0.54	3.96	2.53	20.35	1.29
2005-06	8.26	2.22	2.91	1.22	0.46	4.33	2.29	21.70	1.38
2006-07	8.56	2.04	2.70	1.53	0.44	4.72	1.89	21.88	1.36
2007-08	7.73	1.83	2.79	1.58	0.37	5.15	1.73	21.18	1.70
2008-09	7.91	1.53	2.70	1.52	0.42	5.17	1.38	20.63	1.55
2009-10	6.23	1.64	2.78	1.45	0.44	5.51	1.01	19.06	1.43
2010-11	5.46	2.23	3.19	1.32	0.42	5.68	0.94	19.23	1.54

(1) Infrastructure data are not included in the total.
(2) This series excludes some possession trains used during engineering works.

Data can be subject to revisions indicated by (R). For the latest information on data revisions, please see the revisions log: http://www.rail-reg.gov.uk/upload/xls/stats-revisions-log.xls

This dataset is used in the freight rail usage statistical release. To view or download the statistical release please see: http://www.rail-reg.gov.uk/server/show/nav.3016

The quality report relating to this dataset can be found at http://www.rail-reg.gov.uk/server/show/nav.3016

The quality report pulls together the key qualitative information on relevance, accuracy and reliability, timeliness and punctuality, accessibility and clarity and coherence and comparability. It also includes information on some additional quality principles on user needs and perceptions, confidentiality, transparency and security of data.

22.20b Freight lifted
Great Britain annual data (million tonnes)

Financial year	Coal	Other	Total
1999-00	35.9	60.6	96.5
2000-01	35.3	60.3	95.6
2001-02	39.5	54.5	93.9
2002-03	34.0	53.0	87.0
2003-04	35.2	53.7	88.9
2004-05	44.1	56.8	100.9
2005-06	47.6	57.7	105.3
2006-07	48.7	59.5	108.2
2007-08	43.3	59.1	102.4
2008-09	46.6	56.1	102.7
2009-10	37.9	49.3	87.2
2010-11	38.8	51.1	89.9

Source: Freight operating companies

Data can be subject to revisions indicated by (R). For the latest information on data revisions, please see the revisions log:
http://www.rail-reg.gov.uk/upload/xls/stats-revisions-log.xls

This dataset is used in the freight rail usage statistical release. To view or download the statistical release please see:
http://www.rail-reg.gov.uk/server/show/nav.3016

The quality report relating to this dataset can be found at http://www.rail-reg.gov.uk/server/show/nav.3016

The quality report pulls together the key qualitative information on relevance, accuracy and reliability, timeliness and punctuality, accessibility and clarity and coherence and comparability. It also includes information on some additional quality principles on user needs and perceptions, confidentiality, transparency and security of data.

22.21 Railways: permanent way and rolling stock
Northern Ireland
At end of year

Numbers

		1999	2000	2001	2002	2003	2004	2005	2006	2007	2008	2009/10	2010/11	2011/12
Length of road open for traffic[1] (Km)	KNRA	335	356	334	334	334	299	299	299	299	299	299	299	299
Length of track open for traffic (Km)														
Total	KNRB	526	547	480	480	480	445	445	445	445	445	445	445	445
Running lines	KNRC	484	505	464	464	464	427	427	427	427	427	427	427	427
Sidings (as single track)	KNRD	42	42	16	16	16	18	18	18	18	18	18	18	18
Locomotives														
Diesel-electrics	KNRE	6	6	6	6	5	6	5	5	5	5	5	5	5
Passenger carrying vehicles														
Total	KNRF	105	105	106	100	100	102	124	125	128	130	130	130	130
Rail motor vehicles:														
Diesel-electric,etc	KNRG	30	30	29	28	28	28	70	85	84	84	84	84	84
Trailer carriages:														
Total locomotive hauled	KNRH	21	21	25	22	22	22	22	22	22	22	22	22	22
Ordinary coaches	KNRI	19	19	23	20	20	20	20	20	20	20	20	20	20
Restaurant cars	KNRJ	2	2	2	2	2	2	2	2	2	2	2	2	2
Rail car trailers	KNRK	54	54	52	50	50	52	32	18	22	24	24	24	24
Rolling stock for maintenance and repair	KNRT	18	18	18	18	39	46	48	48	48	48	48	48	48

1 The total length of railroad open for traffic irrespective of the number of tracks comprising the road.

Sources: Department for Regional Development;
Northern Ireland: 02890 540981

22.22 Operating statistics of railways
Northern Ireland

		Unit	2000	2001	2002	2003	2004	2005	2006	2007	2008	2009	2010	2011	2012
Maintenance of way and works															
Material used:															
Ballast	KNSA	Thousand m^2	47.0	80.0	40.0	130.0	70.0	90.0	30.0	15.0	10.0	35.0	10.0	16.2	46.2
Rails	KNSB	Thousand tonnes	3.5	2.5	1.0	4.5	1.0	3.2	1.0	1.0	0.1	1.4	1.2	3.4	0.2
Sleepers	KNSC	Thousands	40.0	50.0	5.0	40.0	28.0	45.0	2.0	5.0	2.0	2.0	2.0	27.7	2.7
Track renewed	KNSD	Km	29.0	15.0	5.0	25.8	2.0	29.0	1.0	-	..	6.0	1.0	0.5	21.6
New Track laid	KPGD	Km	21.0	-	-	-	-	-	-	-	..	–	0.0	-	-
Engine kilometres															
Total[1]	KNSE	Thousand Km	4,100	4,056	4,056	4,170	4,110	4,618	4,677	5,108	5,047	4,899	5,088	5,082	5,258
Train kilometres:															
Total	KNSF	"	3,670	3,626	3,626	3,704	4,110	4,618	4,677	5,108	5,047	4,899	5,088	5,082	5,258
Coaching	KNSG	"	3,666	3,622	3,622	3,700	4,110	4,618	4,677	5,108	5,047	4,899	5,088	5,082	5,258
Freight	KNSH	"	4	4	4	4	-	-	-	-	-	-	-	-	-

1 Including shunting, assisting, light, departmental, maintenance and repair.

Sources: Department for Regional Development;
Northern Ireland: 02890 540981

22.23 Main Outputs of UK Airlines (1989 - 2012) in Tonne-kilometres Available and Used (a)

	Available Tonne-Kilometres						Tonne-Kilometres Used					
	Total (000 000)	Percentage growth on previous year	Scheduled services (000 000)	Percentage growth on previous year	Non-scheduled services (000 000)	Percentage growth on previous year	Total (000 000)	Percentage growth on previous year	Scheduled services (000 000)	Percentage growth on previous year	Non-scheduled services (000 000)	Percentage growth on previous year
1989	18 893	9.7	13 422	8.2	5 471	13.7	13 352	11.1	8 971	10.7	4 381	12.0
1990	20 361	7.8	15 268	13.7	5 094	-6.9	14 105	5.6	10 020	11.7	4 085	-6.8
1991 (b)	20 156	-1.0	15 188	-0.5	4 968	-2.5	13 633	-3.3	9 570	-4.5	4 063	-0.5
1992	23 136	14.8	17 065	12.4	6 072	22.2	15 906	16.7	10 940	14.3	4 965	22.2
1993	25 089	8.4	18 591	8.9	6 498	7.0	17 374	9.2	11 966	9.4	5 408	8.9
1994	27 713	10.5	20 359	9.5	7 354	13.2	19 350	11.4	13 314	11.3	6 035	11.6
1995	29 901	7.9	22 016	8.1	7 885	7.2	21 306	10.1	14 890	11.8	6 416	6.3
1996	32 214	7.7	23 795	8.1	8 419	6.8	23 001	8.0	16 198	8.8	6 803	6.0
1997	35 571	10.4	26 507	11.4	9 064	7.7	25 091	9.1	17 914	10.6	7 176	5.5
1998	40 022	12.5	29 762	12.3	10 261	13.2	27 552	9.8	19 598	9.4	7 954	10.8
1999	41 911	4.7	31 856	7.0	10 055	-2.0	28 530	3.5	20 596	5.1	7 934	-0.3
2000	43 393	3.5	32 950	3.4	10 443	3.9	29 989	5.1	21 846	6.1	8 143	2.6
2001	42 374	-2.3	31 864	-3.3	10 510	0.6	28 118	-6.2	19 907	-8.9	8 211	0.8
2002	40 550	-4.3	30 433	-4.5	10 117	-3.7	27 913	-0.7	20 032	0.6	7 881	-4.0
2003	42 784	5.5	31 513	3.6	11 271	11.4	29 325	5.1	20 671	3.2	8 654	9.8
2004	43 904	2.6	32 442	2.9	11 462	1.7	29 923	2.0	20 963	1.4	8 960	3.5
2005	48 294	10.0	36 937	13.9	11 357	-0.9	29 494	-1.4	21 133	0.8	8 362	-6.7
2006	50 396	4.4	38 590	4.5	11 806	4.0	30 932	4.9	22 404	6.0	8 528	2.0
2007	54 190	7.5	40 979	6.2	13 211	11.9	32 863	6.2	23 557	5.1	9 306	9.1
2008	53 392	-1.5	41 316	0.8	12 076	-8.6	32 509	-1.1	24 107	2.3	8 402	-9.7
2009	49 150	-7.9	39 207	-5.1	9 944	-17.7	30 411	-6.5	23 427	-2.8	6 984	-16.9
2010	47 168	-4.0	38 059	-2.9	9 109	-8.4	29 915	-1.6	23 263	-0.7	6 651	-4.8
2011	50 120	6.3	41 043	7.8	9 078	-0.3	31 405	5.0	24 796	6.6	6 609	-0.6
2012	50 331	0.4	41 692	1.6	8 639	-4.8	31 614	0.7	25 250	1.8	6 364	-3.7

(a) Excludes Small Airlines Public Transport Operation
(b) Excludes Air Europe Operation

22.24a Air Transport Movements(a) by Type and Nationality of Operator 2012

	Total	Scheduled Services			Charter Flights		
		UK Operators	Other EU Operators	Other Overseas Operators	UK Operators	Other EU Operators	Other Overseas Operators
London Area Airports							
GATWICK	240 447	170 144	24 074	23 024	21 216	1 758	231
HEATHROW	471 382	258 689	102 919	107 727	436	1 568	43
LONDON CITY	64 310	23 003	32 495	8 810	-	2	-
LUTON	71 725	37 359	27 710	547	3 709	2 191	209
SOUTHEND	7 268	4 647	2 516	-	34	71	-
STANSTED	131 297	27 325	88 909	2 435	7 143	368	5 117
Total London Area Airports	986 429	521 167	278 623	142 543	32 538	5 958	5 600
Other UK Airports							
ABERDEEN	98 783	40 572	10 351	3 840	43 832	128	60
BARRA	1 254	1 254	-	-	-	-	-
BELFAST CITY (GEORGE BEST)	35 921	32 640	3 140	-	137	4	-
BELFAST INTERNATIONAL	39 120	28 707	3 859	578	3 937	2 003	36
BENBECULA	2 420	2 420	-	-	-	-	-
BIRMINGHAM	84 062	38 332	30 770	5 779	7 848	802	531
BLACKPOOL	9 607	1 396	2 593	-	5 609	9	-
BOURNEMOUTH	7 182	643	3 344	-	3 149	46	-
BRISTOL	50 654	28 001	17 736	560	4 122	229	6
CAMBRIDGE	63	3	16	-	36	8	-
CAMPBELTOWN	953	953	-	-	-	-	-
CARDIFF WALES	13 965	5 774	4 457	252	3 245	199	38
CITY OF DERRY (EGLINTON)	3 114	-	3 042	-	34	38	-
COVENTRY	738	-	-	-	738	-	-
DONCASTER SHEFFIELD	4 379	201	1 852	-	2 267	52	7
DUNDEE	2 706	1 328	1 339	-	35	4	-
DURHAM TEES VALLEY	4 202	2 011	2 023	-	103	65	-
EAST MIDLANDS INTERNATIONAL	54 643	18 134	11 021	14	13 054	10 552	1 868
EDINBURGH	102 884	68 267	25 286	2 642	4 711	1 959	19
EXETER	12 080	9 784	2	38	2 116	115	25
GLASGOW	72 287	55 398	6 771	2 911	6 463	197	547
GLOUCESTERSHIRE	1 402	-	1 402	-	-	-	-
HUMBERSIDE	12 518	2 005	2 122	-	8 237	106	48
INVERNESS	10 377	10 237	36	-	34	36	34
ISLAY	1 353	1 353	-	-	-	-	-
ISLES OF SCILLY (ST.MARYS)	10 157	10 157	-	-	-	-	-
ISLES OF SCILLY (TRESCO)	1 560	1 560	-	-	-	-	-
KIRKWALL	9 728	9 663	-	-	63	2	-
LANDS END (ST JUST)	5 785	5 641	-	-	144	-	-
LEEDS BRADFORD	30 223	19 442	9 574	200	893	114	-
LERWICK (TINGWALL)	1 545	1 496	-	-	49	-	-
LIVERPOOL (JOHN LENNON)	35 853	21 381	14 319	1	101	39	12
LYDD	97	96	-	-	-	-	1
MANCHESTER	160 473	77 024	44 977	16 127	20 285	1 294	766
MANSTON (KENT INT)	687	91	14	5	11	388	178
NEWCASTLE	43 660	25 568	9 703	1 176	6 520	265	428
NEWQUAY	4 747	4 691	48	-	2	6	-
NORWICH	15 915	5 913	2 151	-	6 789	202	860
OXFORD (KIDLINGTON)	715	548	114	-	23	28	2
PENZANCE HELIPORT	3 444	3 436	-	-	8	-	-
PRESTWICK	8 152	14	8 067	-	10	12	49
SCATSTA	13 626	-	-	-	13 626	-	-
SHOREHAM	435	-	-	-	435	-	-
SOUTHAMPTON	38 639	38 353	83	-	171	29	3
STORNOWAY	6 446	6 434	-	-	8	4	-
SUMBURGH	7 072	6 167	-	-	852	22	31
TIREE	885	885	-	-	-	-	-
WICK JOHN O GROATS	2 152	1 871	-	-	90	189	2
Total Other UK Airports	1 028 663	589 844	220 212	34 123	159 787	19 146	5 551
Total All Reporting UK Airports	2 015 092	1 111 011	498 835	176 666	192 325	25 104	11 151
Non UK Reporting Airports							
ALDERNEY	6 652	6 652	-	-	-	-	-
GUERNSEY	33 957	31 860	126	-	1 911	15	45
ISLE OF MAN	22 995	14 281	8 129	-	573	12	-
JERSEY	36 931	34 149	642	-	1 920	211	9
Total Non UK Reporting Airports	100 535	86 942	8 897	-	4 404	238	54

(a) Excludes Air Taxi operations
(b) Plymouth Airport closed December 2011
(c) Penzance Heliport closed October 2012

22.24b Air Passengers by Type and Nationality of Operator 2012

	Total Terminal and Transit Passengers	Scheduled Services						Charter Flights					
		UK Operators		Other EU Operators		Other Overseas Operators		UK Operators		Other EU Operators		Other Overseas Operators	
		Terminal	Transit	Terminal	Transit	Terminal	Transit	Terminal	Transit	Terminal	Transit	Terminal	Transit
London Area Airports													
GATWICK	34 235 982	22 865 829	3 916	2 840 872	774	3 686 231	6 316	4 522 761	6 039	264 515	269	38 460	-
HEATHROW	70 037 417	36 863 530	261	11 649 076	842	21 407 938	53 175	57 527	-	3 956	-	1 112	-
LONDON CITY	3 016 664	1 185 738	-	1 282 816	-	548 047	-	-	-	63	-	-	-
LUTON	9 617 697	5 048 124	2 476	4 053 560	-	44 154	-	446 623	849	18 429	171	3 285	26
SOUTHEND	617 027	544 584	53	68 764	-	-	-	833	-	2 793	-	-	-
STANSTED	17 472 699	3 364 837	4 480	13 157 844	1 276	305 239	311	558 412	1 384	20 521	451	57 939	5
Total London Area Airports	134 997 486	69 872 642	11 186	33 052 932	2 892	25 991 609	59 802	5 586 156	8 272	310 277	891	100 796	31
Other UK Airports													
ABERDEEN	3 330 126	1 733 325	478	650 836	-	167 616	37	756 354	1 008	13 588	-	6 814	70
BARRA	11 415	11 414	1	-	-	-	-	-	-	-	-	-	-
BELFAST CITY (GEORGE BEST)	2 246 202	2 132 198	-	100 715	-	-	-	13 092	-	197	-	-	-
BELFAST INTERNATIONAL	4 313 685	3 423 337	-	440 772	167	83 607	-	325 742	1 025	34 950	32	4 033	20
BENBECULA	31 364	30 849	515	-	-	-	-	-	-	-	-	-	-
BIRMINGHAM	8 922 539	3 182 104	2 408	3 028 508	868	973 935	957	1 634 131	1 843	97 531	254	-	-
BLACKPOOL	235 238	173 624	-	38 871	47	-	-	22 046	-	650	-	-	-
BOURNEMOUTH	692 545	34 203	2 321	470 434	-	-	-	179 861	469	5 257	-	-	-
BRISTOL	5 921 530	3 340 802	400	1 734 079	319	9 141	3 708	803 603	424	28 558	421	75	-
CAMBRIDGE	2 130	66	-	247	-	-	-	1 080	-	737	-	-	-
CAMPBELTOWN	9 144	8 689	455	-	-	-	-	-	-	-	-	-	-
CARDIFF WALES	1 028 123	212 455	14 347	216 751	75	3 743	10	549 141	305	23 358	-	7 938	-
CITY OF DERRY (EGLINTON)	398 209	-	-	385 224	-	-	-	6 272	-	6 713	-	-	-
DONCASTER SHEFFIELD	693 661	10 012	402	275 788	-	-	-	400 726	98	6 487	32	116	-
DUNDEE	54 655	25 238	13	27 789	-	-	-	1 543	-	72	-	-	-
DURHAM TEES VALLEY	166 251	36 983	1 424	100 814	1	-	-	16 042	-	10 987	-	-	-
EAST MIDLANDS INTERNATIONAL	4 076 178	1 446 674	2 298	1 623 363	174	316	784	977 937	3 218	19 625	1 789	-	-
EDINBURGH	9 195 061	5 900 210	242	2 679 713	2	355 896	-	220 674	-	36 992	483	849	-
EXETER	701 743	475 972	4 178	79	-	4 316	1 989	196 189	340	14 261	273	4 146	-
GLASGOW	7 157 859	4 640 329	1 331	457 813	1 344	609 007	3 530	1 408 589	1 030	22 689	414	11 668	115
GLOUCESTERSHIRE	15 292	-	-	15 245	47	-	-	-	-	-	-	-	-
HUMBERSIDE	234 142	38 791	403	114 398	-	-	-	58 924	32	15 007	118	6 469	-
INVERNESS	604 098	593 312	2 488	1 576	-	-	-	1 378	-	2 775	60	2 509	-
ISLAY	21 609	21 230	379	-	-	-	-	-	-	-	-	-	-
ISLES OF SCILLY (ST.MARYS)	97 012	97 012	-	-	-	-	-	-	-	-	-	-	-
ISLES OF SCILLY (TRESCO)	25 563	24 175	1 388	-	-	-	-	-	-	-	-	-	-
KIRKWALL	140 683	131 956	8 283	-	-	-	-	264	165	15	-	-	-
LANDS END (ST JUST)	33 108	31 682	1 144	-	-	-	-	282	-	-	-	-	-
LEEDS BRADFORD	2 990 517	1 645 596	21 589	1 132 971	102	26 667	12	147 691	114	15 775	-	-	-
LERWICK (TINGWALL)	5 041	4 930	-	-	-	-	-	111	-	-	-	-	-
LIVERPOOL (JOHN LENNON)	4 463 257	2 518 032	1 980	1 930 353	858	75	-	4 306	1 774	4 826	145	908	-
LYDD	445	444	-	-	-	-	-	-	-	-	-	1	-
MANCHESTER	19 736 502	7 722 378	2 867	4 422 478	2 699	2 881 239	54 332	4 454 265	20 383	156 648	2 121	17 092	-
MANSTON (KENT INT)	8 595	3 445	333	269	-	-	-	156	-	4 392	-	-	-
NEWCASTLE	4 366 196	2 351 671	6 209	691 694	-	185 879	1 935	1 094 860	596	30 260	2 642	284	166
NEWQUAY	166 609	161 685	337	3 378	-	-	-	341	-	868	-	-	-
NORWICH	396 676	148 021	30	123 573	-	-	-	87 309	-	18 646	-	19 097	-

22.24b Air Passengers by Type and Nationality of Operator 2012

	Total Terminal and Transit Passengers	Scheduled Services						Charter Flights					
		UK Operators		Other EU Operators		Other Overseas Operators		UK Operators		Other EU Operators		Other Overseas Operators	
		Terminal	Transit	Terminal	Transit	Terminal	Transit	Terminal	Transit	Terminal	Transit	Terminal	Transit
Other UK Airports (Continued)													
OXFORD (KIDLINGTON)	7 223	5 190	515	1 075	131	-	-	112	-	116	-	84	-
PENZANCE HELIPORT	61 747	61 618	-	-	-	-	-	129	-	-	-	-	-
PRESTWICK	1 067 933	1 801	70	1 064 191	383	-	-	672	231	253	-	-	332
SCATSTA	304 480	-	-	-	-	-	-	304 426	54	-	-	-	-
SHOREHAM	480	-	-	-	-	-	-	480	-	-	-	-	-
SOUTHAMPTON	1 694 120	1 669 092	701	6 702	-	-	-	16 986	49	446	20	124	-
STORNOWAY	119 411	115 601	3 551	-	-	-	-	77	-	182	-	-	-
SUMBURGH	150 567	136 570	147	-	-	-	-	11 282	1 559	561	-	448	-
TIREE	7 545	7 317	228	-	-	-	-	-	-	-	-	-	-
WICK JOHN O GROATS	24 976	22 233	-	-	-	-	-	1 071	56	1 462	-	154	-
Total Other UK Airports	85 931 485	44 332 266	83 455	21 739 699	7 217	5 301 437	67 294	13 698 144	34 773	574 884	8 804	82 809	703
Total All Reporting UK Airports	220 928 971	114 204 908	94 641	54 792 631	10 109	31 293 046	127 096	19 284 300	43 045	885 161	9 695	183 605	734
Non UK Reporting Airports													
ALDERNEY	64 165	64 165	-	-	-	-	-	-	-	-	-	-	-
GUERNSEY	890 746	854 878	27 320	4 306	932	-	-	1 496	25	92	-	1 558	139
ISLE OF MAN	697 123	580 684	130	110 124	1 383	-	-	4 074	-	728	-	802	-
JERSEY	1 468 333	1 375 850	25 323	34 221	642	-	-	11 348	697	19 450	-	-	-
Total Non UK Reporting Airports	3 120 367	2 875 577	52 773	148 651	2 957	-	-	16 918	722	20 270	-	2 360	139

(a) Plymouth Airport closed December 2011
(b) Penzance Heliport closed October 2012

22.25 Scheduled and Non-Scheduled Services All Services 2012 (a)

	Aircraft -Km (000)	Stage Flights	A/C Hours	(b) Number of Passengers Uplifted	Seat-Km Available (000)	Seat-Km Used (000)	As % of Avail	(b) Cargo Uplifted Tonnes	Tonne-Km Available (000)	Tonne-Kilometres Used — Total (000)	Mail (000)	Freight (000)	Passenger (000)	As % of Avail
Passenger Services														
ACROPOLIS AVIATION LTD	327	127	476	792	6 215	2 675	43.0	-	3 925	211	-	-	211	5.4
ARAVCO LTD	65	13	82	87	790	460	58.2	-	93	38	-	-	38	40.9
AURIGNY AIR SERVICES	3 058	20 724	14 042	494 710	168 406	115 716	68.7	319	17 140	8 712	14	24	8 674	50.8
BA CITYFLYER LTD	16 973	21 745	33 884	1 184 810	1 504 676	981 149	65.2	2	150 982	81 451	-	-	81 451	53.9
BLUE ISLANDS LIMITED	2 596	12 480	7 499	211 958	85 393	48 079	56.3	-	7 470	4 086	-	-	4 086	54.7
BMI GROUP	47 333	39 024	85 799	2 764 834	7 071 400	4 739 176	67.0	11 649	885 376	419 518	2 293	47 433	369 792	47.4
BMI REGIONAL	16 218	27 062	37 026	382 037	757 798	449 055	59.3	36	86 192	35 357	-	114	35 243	41.0
BRITISH AIRWAYS (BA) LTD	3 019	814	4 260	12 050	96 830	67 354	69.6	-	9 731	3 348	-	-	3 348	34.4
BRITISH AIRWAYS PLC	650 810	271 335	962 676	35 627 978	153 894 209	123 499 855	80.2	591 347	22 352 719	12 785 701	122 603	3 828 468	8 834 630	57.2
BRITISH INTERNATIONAL HELICOPTER	215	3 436	1 189	60 719	5 392	3 809	70.6	164	420	298	-	-	298	71.0
CELLO AVIATION LTD	180	204	367	5 975	8 281	5 879	71.0	-	1 245	585	-	-	585	47.0
EASTERN AIRWAYS	11 626	29 142	30 029	543 872	453 889	233 163	51.4	-	46 450	17 163	-	-	17 163	36.9
EASYJET AIRLINE COMPANY LTD	401 656	369 526	709 450	50 521 678	65 273 227	56 998 248	87.3	-	5 548 220	4 500 524	-	-	4 500 524	81.1
EXECUTIVE JET CHARTER LTD	264	146	353	714	3 222	1 136	35.3	-	264	92	-	-	92	34.8
FLYBE LTD	61 092	135 108	127 718	7 069 043	5 405 902	3 433 278	63.5	1 187	596 577	291 840	-	299	291 541	48.9
GAMA AVIATION	209	112	289	405	3 033	981	32.3	-	240	90	-	-	90	37.5
ISLES OF SCILLY SKYBUS	677	7 447	3 034	59 465	10 632	6 123	57.6	-	868	450	-	-	450	51.8
JET2.COM LTD	57 721	32 520	93 044	4 776 257	10 572 344	9 404 809	89.0	20	1 068 752	799 504	28	47	799 429	74.8
LOGANAIR	7 999	36 567	29 673	588 758	254 789	157 394	61.8	940	22 184	13 558	12	189	13 357	61.1
MONARCH AIRLINES	75 769	35 328	113 305	6 299 187	17 353 065	14 853 628	85.6	2 646	1 766 911	1 173 213	-	7 631	1 165 582	66.4
OCEAN SKY (UK) LTD	389	178	579	675	4 769	1 486	31.2	-	599	142	-	-	142	23.7
ORYX JET LTD	20	10	31	45	194	76	39.2	-	33	7	-	-	7	21.2
TAG AVIATION (UK) LTD	2 598	1 698	3 318	6 900	33 713	10 106	30.0	-	10 125	867	-	-	867	8.6
THOMAS COOK AIRLINES LTD	96 916	32 109	137 978	6 783 661	23 700 587	22 298 388	94.1	3 371	2 536 442	1 920 583	-	24 924	1 895 659	75.7
THOMSON AIRWAYS LTD	155 067	54 372	223 179	10 703 338	34 851 594	32 073 181	92.0	6 634	2 916 171	2 409 792	-	43 113	2 366 679	82.6
TITAN AIRWAYS LTD	5 489	3 465	7 001	148 574	1 081 159	593 001	54.8	-	125 959	41 336	-	-	41 336	32.8
TRIAIR (BERMUDA) LTD	280	69	359	266	3 351	1 580	47.2	-	615	126	-	-	126	20.5
TWINJET AIRCRAFT	419	209	689	2 216	9 785	4 781	48.9	-	4 349	373	-	-	373	8.6
VIRGIN ATLANTIC AIRWAYS LTD	149 231	21 066	190 033	5 448 283	50 490 911	39 406 447	78.0	199 651	8 400 149	4 522 288	-	1 460 778	3 061 510	53.8
Total Passenger Services	1 768 216	1 156 036	2 817 360	133 699 287	373 105 556	309 391 013	82.9	817 964	46 560 200	29 031 253	124 950	5 413 020	23 493 283	62.4
Cargo Services														
ATLANTIC AIRLINES LTD	3 232	8 550	10 358	-	-	-	..	33 207	28 836	12 820	4 408	8 412	-	44.5
BRITISH AIRWAYS PLC	13 610	4 815	20 445	-	-	-	..	144 223	1 330 795	899 968	-	899 968	-	67.6
DHL AIR LTD	23 160	18 098	38 528	-	-	-	..	91 074	885 847	588 319	-	588 319	-	66.4
GLOBAL SUPPLY SYSTEMS LTD	11 401	2 546	14 726	-	-	-	..	35	1 471 711	1 059 863	-	1 059 863	-	72.0
JET2.COM LTD	1 761	4 661	4 589	-	-	-	..	35 548	28 227	12 581	12 555	26	-	44.6
THOMAS COOK AIRLINES LTD	85	12	110	-	-	-	..	46	3 379	339	-	339	-	10.0
TITAN AIRWAYS LTD	1 762	3 153	2 414	-	-	-	..	13 911	21 580	8 724	8 646	78	-	40.4
Total Cargo Services	55 011	41 835	91 171	-	-	-	..	318 043	3 770 375	2 582 614	25 609	2 557 005	-	68.5
Grand Total	1 823 227	1 197 871	2 908 530	133 699 287	373 105 556	309 391 013	82.9	1 136 007	50 330 575	31 613 867	150 559	7 970 025	23 493 283	62.8

(a) Excludes small airlines' public transport operations
(b) Excludes passengers and cargo uplifted on sub-charter operations

22.26a Aircraft Movements 2012

	Total	Commercial Movements				Non-Commercial Movements						Business Aviation
		Air Transport	Of Which Air Taxi	Positioning Flights	Local Movements	Test and Training	Other Flights by Air Transport Operators	Aero Club	Private	Official	Military	
London Area Airports												
GATWICK	246 987	240 494	47	4 106	-	77	218	-	38	38	7	2 009
HEATHROW	475 176	471 791	409	1 296	3	15	123	-	36	504	47	1 361
LONDON CITY	70 781	69 902	5 592	423	-	192	-	-	-	-	-	264
LUTON	96 797	75 783	4 058	5 150	2	210	411	1	82	95	8	15 055
SOUTHEND	27 715	8 086	818	658	139	1 947	322	10 170	4 651	396	183	1 163
STANSTED	143 511	132 920	1 623	4 148	1	135	121	-	415	309	69	5 393
Total London Area Airports	1 060 967	998 976	12 547	15 781	145	2 576	1 195	10 171	5 222	1 342	314	25 245
METRO LONDON HELIPORT	7 170	2 014	2 014	1 643	54	-	919	-	2 145	28	95	272
Other UK Airports												
ABERDEEN	115 013	104 227	5 444	4 619	1	2 764	62	1 839	342	1	59	1 099
BARRA	1 403	1 319	65	5	-	-	-	-	79	-	-	-
BELFAST CITY (GEORGE BEST)	37 189	36 711	790	138	30	32	12	-	199	31	11	25
BELFAST INTERNATIONAL	58 011	40 714	1 594	1 180	4 508	12	5	1 177	2 242	1	6 905	1 267
BENBECULA	4 478	3 958	1 538	317	6	70	-	2	75	-	50	-
BIGGIN HILL	44 264	6 455	6 455	278	-	14	66	24 419	7 655	-	108	5 335
BIRMINGHAM	92 632	84 769	707	2 626	2 308	135	66	-	395	-	214	2 119
BLACKPOOL	46 875	11 215	1 608	586	138	2 341	9	25 395	5 531	4	368	1 288
BOURNEMOUTH	51 089	7 261	79	1 007	6	24 013	8 409	4	4 618	-	512	5 259
BRISTOL	61 206	51 160	506	681	-	-	10	3 302	5 638	-	401	14
CAMBRIDGE	17 292	129	66	10	1 200	306	-	10 164	2 645	4	348	2 486
CAMPBELTOWN	1 527	1 105	152	89	-	-	-	18	94	-	221	-
CARDIFF WALES	26 842	14 008	43	790	-	178	10	4 965	6 776	4	114	1
CARLISLE	17 349	449	449	77	136	49	-	11 076	3 872	9	1 391	290
CITY OF DERRY (EGLINTON)	7 355	3 326	212	46	38	1 568	10	1 240	1 079	4	24	30
COVENTRY	39 964	1 730	992	658	2	29 009	22	1 683	6 844	2	14	-
DONCASTER SHEFFIELD	11 724	4 718	339	244	4	2 043	4	2 746	1 133	2	686	144
DUNDEE	40 926	2 872	166	352	244	896	101	35 118	764	8	44	527
DURHAM TEES VALLEY	17 938	5 340	1 138	68	1 541	254	3	4 684	5 630	101	317	-
EAST MIDLANDS INTERNATIONAL	74 602	58 556	3 913	3 102	20	1 239	5 985	1	1 005	-	139	4 555
EDINBURGH	110 288	106 958	4 074	1 758	-	47	44	509	117	9	216	630
EXETER	31 093	12 625	545	542	219	8 974	498	2 198	3 982	12	338	1 705
GLASGOW	80 472	74 615	2 328	1 869	2	100	57	2 663	198	3	128	837
GLOUCESTERSHIRE	73 762	1 597	195	368	1 051	8 996	490	46 102	13 821	4	300	1 033
HAWARDEN	18 550	-	-	7	1 816	400	2 400	7 716	3 043	16	760	2 392
HUMBERSIDE	25 636	12 847	329	3 226	28	2 178	1 625	-	5 200	1	40	491
INVERNESS	31 764	14 814	4 437	1 471	13	1 167	154	11 972	1 519	-	43	611
ISLAY	2 969	1 817	464	190	2	1	-	-	593	-	348	18
ISLES OF SCILLY (ST.MARYS)	11 425	10 345	188	19	-	-	-	-	936	-	125	-
ISLES OF SCILLY (TRESCO)	1 560	1 560	-	-	-	-	-	-	-	-	-	-
KIRKWALL	13 980	12 400	2 672	777	16	196	9	217	325	-	22	18
LANDS END (ST JUST)	7 460	6 183	398	77	78	404	20	682	-	2	14	-
LEEDS BRADFORD	47 311	30 951	728	1 440	1 193	4 322	34	5 973	3 180	14	75	129
LERWICK (TINGWALL)	1 924	1 783	238	59	28	22	2	8	22	-	-	-
LIVERPOOL (JOHN LENNON)	60 270	36 493	640	288	8	38	10	17 119	4 873	9	362	1 070
LYDD	17 397	625	528	199	204	1 128	-	4 352	10 668	13	106	102

22.26a Aircraft Movements 2012

Other UK Airports(Continued)

	Total	Air Transport	Air Taxi	Positioning Flights	Local Movements	Test and Training	Other Flights by Air Transport Operators	Aero Club	Private	Official	Military	Business Aviation
MANCHESTER	168 883	160 678	205	3 831	28	-	145	-	635	-	53	3 513
MANSTON (KENT INT)	14 688	1 004	317	1 035	10	1 138	-	5 153	5 879	-	467	2
NEWCASTLE	61 006	43 903	243	1 346	889	571	22	-	11 279	2 426	434	136
NEWQUAY	4 859	4 749	2	81	-	28	1	-	-	-	-	7
NORWICH	39 846	18 502	2 587	9 360	737	5 897	269	3 727	1 216	2	129	-
OXFORD (KIDLINGTON)	40 322	1 990	1 275	5 407	165	23 983	537	390	5 938	-	18	1 894
PENZANCE HELIPORT	3 573	3 444	-	9	22	98	-	-	-	-	-	-
PRESTWICK	25 670	8 166	14	348	-	2 923	2	7 847	2 346	-	4 038	-
SCATSTA	15 587	13 915	289	1 003	-	640	29	-	-	-	-	-
SHOREHAM	54 764	435	-	82	2 198	204	77	38 943	12 744	4	77	-
SOUTHAMPTON	43 284	39 146	507	1 188	17	50	105	4	509	2	120	2 143
STORNOWAY	11 564	9 367	2 921	383	261	1 095	1	4	330	-	117	6
SUMBURGH	14 045	10 963	3 891	1 066	217	1 682	-	-	91	-	26	-
SWANSEA	36 393	2 168	2 168	251	108	14	-	21 111	7 549	-	5 115	77
TIREE	1 224	1 121	236	5	-	-	-	-	98	-	-	-
WICK JOHN O GROATS	5 474	2 660	508	989	-	678	1	4	1 078	-	34	30
Total Other UK Airports	1 844 722	1 087 846	59 183	55 547	19 492	131 897	21 230	303 845	155 467	2 684	25 431	41 283
Total All Reporting UK Airports	2 912 859	2 088 836	73 744	72 971	19 691	134 473	23 344	314 016	162 834	4 054	25 840	66 800
Non UK Reporting Airports												
ALDERNEY	10 362	6 853	201	118	1 016	123	44	645	1 559	2	2	-
GUERNSEY	50 859	35 783	1 826	1 439	4 293	299	359	5 436	3 066	44	88	52
ISLE OF MAN	32 697	25 857	2 862	1 041	-	175	1	1 976	3 423	-	92	132
JERSEY	57 144	38 595	1 664	1 060	-	284	761	5 067	10 977	1	371	28
Total Non UK Reporting Airports	151 062	107 088	6 553	3 658	5 309	881	1 165	13 124	19 025	47	553	212

Note
Business Aviation was collected under a category in its own right with effect from June 2001 data. However, currently it is not possible for all airports to report using this category

22.26b Terminal and Transit Passengers 2012 Comparison with the Previous Year

	Terminal and Transit Passengers			Terminal Passengers			Transit Passengers		
	2012	2011	Percentage Change	2012	2011	Percentage Change	2012	2011	Percentage Change
London Area Airports									
GATWICK	34 235 982	33 674 264	2	34 218 668	33 643 989	2	17 314	30 275	-43
HEATHROW	70 037 417	69 433 230	1	69 983 139	69 390 591	1	54 278	42 639	27
LONDON CITY	3 016 664	2 992 847	1	3 016 664	2 992 847	1	-	-	..
LUTON	9 617 697	9 513 704	1	9 614 175	9 509 915	1	3 522	3 789	-7
SOUTHEND	617 027	42 439	1354	616 974	42 439	1354	53	-	..
STANSTED	17 472 699	18 052 843	-3	17 464 792	18 047 403	-3	7 907	5 440	45
Total London Area Airports	134 997 486	133 709 327	1	134 914 412	133 627 184	1	83 074	82 143	1
Other UK Airports									
ABERDEEN	3 330 126	3 082 816	8	3 328 533	3 082 575	8	1 593	241	561
BARRA	11 415	10 482	9	11 414	10 482	9	1	..	..
BELFAST CITY (GEORGE BEST)	2 246 202	2 397 312	-6	2 246 202	2 397 270	-6	-	42	..
BELFAST INTERNATIONAL	4 313 685	4 103 620	5	4 312 441	4 101 914	5	1 244	1 706	-27
BENBECULA	31 364	34 682	-10	30 849	34 240	-10	515	442	17
BIRMINGHAM	8 922 539	8 616 296	4	8 916 209	8 608 192	4	6 330	8 104	-22
BLACKPOOL	235 238	235 682	0	235 191	235 682	0	47	-	..
BOURNEMOUTH	692 545	613 755	13	689 755	612 547	13	2 790	1 208	131
BRISTOL	5 921 530	5 780 746	2	5 916 258	5 767 628	3	5 272	13 118	-60
CAMBRIDGE	2 130	597	257	2 130	597	257	-	-	..
CAMPBELTOWN	9 144	9 387	-3	8 689	9 201	-6	455	186	145
CARDIFF WALES	1 028 123	1 222 715	-16	1 013 386	1 208 268	-16	14 737	14 447	2
CITY OF DERRY (EGLINTON)	398 209	405 697	-2	398 209	405 568	-2	-	129	..
DONCASTER SHEFFIELD	693 661	822 877	-16	693 129	821 615	-16	532	1 262	-58
DUNDEE	54 655	61 674	-11	54 642	61 648	-11	13	26	-50
DURHAM TEES VALLEY	166 251	192 410	-14	164 826	190 284	-13	1 425	2 126	-33
EAST MIDLANDS INTERNATIONAL	4 076 178	4 215 192	-3	4 067 915	4 208 402	-3	8 263	6 790	22
EDINBURGH	9 195 061	9 385 245	-2	9 194 334	9 383 695	-2	727	1 550	-53
EXETER	701 743	717 694	-2	694 963	709 314	-2	6 780	8 380	-19
GLASGOW	7 157 859	6 880 217	4	7 150 095	6 858 268	4	7 764	21 949	-65
GLOUCESTERSHIRE	15 292	14 748	4	15 245	14 737	3	47	11	327
HUMBERSIDE	234 142	274 609	-15	233 589	273 096	-14	553	1 513	-63
INVERNESS	604 098	581 956	4	601 550	579 123	4	2 548	2 833	-10
ISLAY	21 609	25 956	-17	21 230	25 784	-18	379	172	120
ISLES OF SCILLY (ST.MARYS)	97 012	112 515	-14	97 012	112 218	-14	-	297	..
ISLES OF SCILLY (TRESCO)	25 563	42 064	-39	24 175	40 628	-40	1 388	1 436	-3
KIRKWALL	140 683	145 897	-4	132 235	133 930	-1	8 448	11 967	-29
LANDS END (ST JUST)	33 108	34 534	-4	31 964	33 098	-3	1 144	1 436	-20
LEEDS BRADFORD	2 990 517	2 976 881	0	2 968 700	2 936 988	1	21 817	39 893	-45
LERWICK (TINGWALL)	5 041	5 181	-3	5 041	5 181	-3	4 757	4 621	..
LIVERPOOL (JOHN LENNON)	4 463 257	5 251 161	-15	4 458 500	5 246 540	-15	-	-	3
LYDD	445	496	-10	445	496	-10	-	-	..
MANCHESTER	19 736 502	18 892 756	4	19 654 100	18 806 655	5	82 402	86 101	-4
MANSTON (KENT INT)	8 595	48 450	-82	8 262	37 169	-78	333	11 281	-97
NEWCASTLE	4 366 196	4 346 270	0	4 354 648	4 336 304	0	11 548	9 966	16
NEWQUAY	166 609	216 249	-23	166 272	209 574	-21	337	6 675	-95
NORWICH	396 676	413 896	-4	396 646	413 837	-4	30	59	-49

22.26b Terminal and Transit Passengers 2012 Comparison with the Previous Year

	Terminal and Transit Passengers			Terminal Passengers			Transit Passengers		
	2012	2011	Percentage Change	2012	2011	Percentage Change	2012	2011	Percentage Change
Other UK Airports (Continued)									
OXFORD (KIDLINGTON)	7 223	1 491	384	6 577	1 491	341	646	-	::
PENZANCE HELIPORT	61 747	75 206	-18	61 747	75 206	-18	-	-	::
PLYMOUTH	-	37 342	..		28 834	::		8 508	-37
PRESTWICK	1 067 933	1 297 119	-18	1 066 917	1 295 512	-18	1 016	1 607	38
SCATSTA	304 480	288 264	6	304 426	288 225	6	54	39	::
SHOREHAM	480	646	-26	480	634	-24	-	12	570
SOUTHAMPTON	1 694 120	1 762 076	-4	1 693 350	1 761 961	-4	770	115	13
STORNOWAY	119 411	125 582	-5	115 860	122 439	-5	3 551	3 143	53
SUMBURGH	150 567	143 731	5	148 861	142 615	4	1 706	1 116	36
TIREE	7 545	8 478	-11	7 317	8 310	-12	228	168	-87
WICK JOHN O GROATS	24 976	24 706	1	24 920	24 262	3	56	444	
Total Other UK Airports	85 931 485	85 937 356	-	85 729 239	85 662 237	-	202 246	275 119	-26
Total All Reporting UK Airports	220 928 971	219 646 683	1	220 643 651	219 289 421	1	285 320	357 262	-20
Non UK Reporting Airports									
ALDERNEY	64 165	69 546	-8	64 165	69 546	-8	-	-	::
GUERNSEY	890 746	933 721	-5	862 330	899 857	-4	28 416	33 864	-16
ISLE OF MAN	697 123	701 847	-1	695 610	700 547	-1	1 513	1 300	16
JERSEY	1 468 333	1 491 332	-2	1 441 671	1 460 911	-1	26 662	30 421	-12
Total Non UK Reporting Airports	3 120 367	3 196 446	-2	3 063 776	3 130 861	-2	56 591	65 585	-14

Notes

(a) Plymouth Airport closed December 2011
(b) Penzance Heliport closed October 2012

Please note that figures may change overtime as each new version is produced. Information relating to an airport that has ceased to handle regular traffic/closed will be excluded from this table completely. For data concerning historical years it is recommended that you use earlier produced versions of this table.

22.26c Freight by Type and Nationality of Operator 2012 Tonnes

Columns grouped as: Total; Scheduled Services — UK Operators (Set Down / Picked Up), Other EU Operators (Set Down / Picked Up), Other Overseas Operators (Set Down / Picked Up); Charter Flights — UK Operators (Set Down / Picked Up), Other EU Operators (Set Down / Picked Up), Other Overseas Operators (Set Down / Picked Up).

	Total	Sched. UK Set Down	Sched. UK Picked Up	Sched. Other EU Set Down	Sched. Other EU Picked Up	Sched. Other Overseas Set Down	Sched. Other Overseas Picked Up	Charter UK Set Down	Charter UK Picked Up	Charter Other EU Set Down	Charter Other EU Picked Up	Charter Other Overseas Set Down	Charter Other Overseas Picked Up
London Area Airports													
GATWICK	97 567	22 212	24 028	935	520	22 359	21 047	3 260	2 885	56	226	4	36
HEATHROW	1 464 390	350 104	344 431	10 238	7 996	374 329	339 409	58	39	19 254	17 795	394	344
LUTON	29 635	163	135	11	22	2 185	1 555	903	1 175	14 976	8 485	-	25
SOUTHEND	9	3	-	-	-	-	-	-	-	1	-	-	-
STANSTED	214 160	47 511	14 918	5 738	2 096	3 156	3 045	982	838	931	604	72 150	62 189
Total London Area Airports	1 805 761	419 994	383 511	16 922	10 635	402 028	365 056	5 203	4 937	35 219	27 114	72 548	62 594
Other UK Airports													
ABERDEEN	6 166	33	426	208	219	219	171	2 279	2 518	29	13	9	43
BARRA	26	26	-	-	-	-	-	-	-	-	-	-	-
BELFAST CITY (GEORGE BEST)	581	186	369	11	16	-	-	-	-	-	-	-	-
BELFAST INTERNATIONAL	29 095	-	-	-	-	141	5	192	-	17 429	11 267	-	61
BENBECULA	134	129	5	-	-	-	-	-	-	-	-	-	-
BIRMINGHAM	19 088	156	239	272	248	6 564	6 884	254	62	125	156	2 078	2 050
BOURNEMOUTH	1 121	-	-	-	-	-	-	-	1 121	-	-	-	-
CARDIFF WALES	66	-	-	-	1	-	-	59	6	-	-	-	-
COVENTRY	2 500	-	-	-	-	-	-	1 155	1 344	-	-	-	-
DONCASTER SHEFFIELD	276	-	-	-	-	-	-	4	1	5	1	132	134
EAST MIDLANDS INTERNATIONAL	264 292	8	20	-	-	21	19	17 663	17 862	90 983	87 048	27 855	22 813
EDINBURGH	19 115	31	202	35	114	28	33	33	31	10 173	8 435	-	-
EXETER	4	3	-	-	-	-	-	-	-	-	-	-	-
GLASGOW	9 497	262	730	33	64	2 450	5 174	14	142	-	-	239	389
HUMBERSIDE	621	82	20	-	-	-	-	141	336	-	-	109	15
ISLAY	168	79	86	-	-	-	-	-	-	-	-	-	-
ISLES OF SCILLY (ST.MARYS)	91	16	11	-	-	-	-	-	-	-	-	-	-
ISLES OF SCILLY (TRESCO)	19	-	2	-	-	-	-	-	-	-	-	-	-
KIRKWALL	33	8	25	-	-	-	-	-	-	-	-	-	-
LANDS END (ST JUST)	16	3	13	1	1	-	-	-	-	-	-	-	-
LEEDS BRADFORD	282	4	89	1	9	171	17	-	-	-	-	-	-
LIVERPOOL (JOHN LENNON)	130	26	94	-	-	-	-	-	-	-	-	-	-
MANCHESTER	96 822	4 195	2 755	981	846	43 337	31 866	2 377	2 019	2 181	2 426	1 237	2 603
MANSTON (KENT INT)	31 078	-	-	-	-	-	-	-	-	19 109	145	9 505	2 319
NEWCASTLE	2 956	2	2	11	4	934	1 703	-	-	-	-	155	144
NORWICH	213	-	-	-	-	-	-	49	164	-	-	-	-
PENZANCE HELIPORT	95	12	83	-	-	-	-	-	-	-	-	-	-
PRESTWICK	10 314	-	-	5 497	3 411	-	-	-	-	2	22	432	950
SCATSTA	873	-	-	-	-	-	-	403	470	-	-	-	-
SOUTHAMPTON	359	-	355	-	-	-	-	-	-	-	3	-	-
STORNOWAY	154	80	65	-	-	-	-	9	-	-	-	-	-
SUMBURGH	362	254	17	-	-	-	-	5	3	72	-	10	-
TIREE	19	18	1	-	-	-	-	-	-	-	-	-	-
Total Other UK Airports	496 567	5 614	5 609	7 049	4 933	53 865	45 872	24 638	26 080	140 109	109 515	41 761	31 521

22.26c Freight by Type and Nationality of Operator 2012 Tonnes

| | Total | Scheduled Services | | | | | | Charter Flights | | | | | |
| | | UK Operators | | Other EU Operators | | Other Overseas Operators | | UK Operators | | Other EU Operators | | Other Overseas Operators | |
		Set Down	Picked Up	Set Down	Picked Up	Set Down	Picked Up	Set Down	Picked Up	Set Down	Picked Up	Set Down	Picked Up
Other UK Airports (Continued)													
Total All Reporting UK Airports	2 302 328	425 608	389 121	23 971	15 567	455 893	410 929	29 841	31 017	175 328	136 629	114 308	94 116
Non UK Reporting Airports													
ALDERNEY	161	121	41	-	-	-	-	-	-	-	-	-	-
GUERNSEY	1 940	391	181	-	-	-	-	1 165	190	-	13	-	-
ISLE OF MAN	433	179	64	4	-	-	-	172	-	13	-	-	-
JERSEY	2 478	418	128	-	-	-	-	1 710	222	-	-	-	-
Total Non UK Reporting Airports	5 013	1 108	415	4	1	-	-	3 047	412	13	13	-	-

Notes

(a) Plymouth Airport closed December 2011
(b) Penzance Heliport closed October 2012

22.26d Mail by Type and Nationality of Operator 2012 Tonnes

	Total	Scheduled Services						Charter Flights					
		UK Operators		Other EU Operators		Other Overseas Operators		UK Operators		Other EU Operators		Other Overseas Operators	
		Set Down	Picked Up	Set Down	Picked Up	Set Down	Picked Up	Set Down	Picked Up	Set Down	Picked Up	Set Down	Picked Up
London Area Airports													
GATWICK	3 806	247	1 250	541	1 261	69	431	6	3	-	-	-	-
HEATHROW	91 590	9 459	16 241	5 590	6 551	22 002	31 734	-	-	-	-	-	13
STANSTED	26 965	314	19	-	1	-	-	10 795	15 414	-	1	268	152
Total London Area Airports	122 361	10 019	17 510	6 131	7 813	22 070	32 166	10 801	15 417	-	1	268	165
Other UK Airports													
ABERDEEN	799	6	49	-	-	-	-	462	274	6	1	-	-
BELFAST CITY (GEORGE BEST)	3	1	2	-	-	-	-	-	-	-	-	-	-
BELFAST INTERNATIONAL	15 710	-	-	-	-	-	-	8 993	6 662	35	20	-	-
BENBECULA	1	1	1	-	-	-	-	-	-	-	-	-	-
BIRMINGHAM	3	-	-	-	3	-	-	-	-	-	-	-	-
BOURNEMOUTH	9 171	2	-	-	-	-	-	3 773	5 396	-	-	-	-
CARDIFF WALES	919	-	-	-	-	-	-	919	-	-	-	-	-
EAST MIDLANDS INTERNATIONAL	35 702	3	301	-	-	-	-	14 455	18 128	1 361	1 453	-	-
EDINBURGH	23 823	3	-	-	1	-	-	13 234	10 082	256	249	-	-
EXETER	6 022	-	-	-	-	-	-	3 424	2 597	-	-	-	-
GLASGOW	70	4	64	-	-	-	-	-	-	-	-	2	-
INVERNESS	26	-	-	-	-	-	-	25	-	1	-	-	-
ISLAY	60	32	28	-	-	-	-	-	-	-	-	-	-
ISLES OF SCILLY (ST.MARYS)	169	108	61	-	-	-	-	-	-	-	-	-	-
ISLES OF SCILLY (TRESCO)	3	1	2	-	-	-	-	-	-	-	-	-	-
KIRKWALL	21	7	14	-	-	-	-	-	-	-	-	-	-
LANDS END (ST JUST)	90	36	54	-	-	-	-	-	-	-	-	-	-
MANCHESTER	1 449	1	2	2	13	2	1 420	-	8	-	-	-	-
NEWCASTLE	7 929	-	-	-	-	-	-	4 354	3 575	-	-	-	-
PENZANCE HELIPORT	67	23	44	-	-	-	-	-	-	-	-	-	-
SCATSTA	14	-	-	-	-	-	-	7	7	-	-	-	-
SUMBURGH	1	1	-	-	-	-	-	-	-	-	-	-	-
TIREE	27	22	5	-	-	-	-	-	-	-	-	-	-
Total Other UK Airports	102 079	248	627	3	17	3	1 420	49 648	46 729	1 659	1 722	2	-
Total All Reporting UK Airports	224 439	10 267	18 137	6 134	7 829	22 073	33 586	60 449	62 146	1 659	1 724	270	166
Non UK Reporting Airports													
ALDERNEY	196	101	95	-	-	-	-	-	-	-	-	-	-
GUERNSEY	2 920	96	107	-	-	-	-	1 627	1 089	-	-	-	-
ISLE OF MAN	2 656	7	-	-	-	-	-	1 564	1 086	-	-	-	-
JERSEY	2 260	5	-	-	-	-	-	1 648	606	-	-	-	-
Total Non UK Reporting Airports	8 032	208	203	-	-	-	-	4 839	2 782	-	-	-	-

Notes

(a) Plymouth Airport closed December 2011
(b) Penzance Heliport closed October 2012

Government
finance

Chapter 23

Government Finance

Public sector (Tables 23.1 to 23.3 and 23.6)

In Table 23.1 the term public sector describes the consolidation of central government, local government and public corporations. General government is the consolidated total of central government and local government. The table shows details of the key public sector finances' indicators, consistent with the European System of Accounts 1995 (ESA95), by sub-sector.

The concepts in Table 23.1 are consistent with the format for public finances in the Economic and Fiscal Strategy Report (EFSR), published by HM Treasury on 11 June 1998, and the Budget. The public sector current budget is equivalent to net saving in national accounts plus capital tax receipts. Net investment is gross capital formation, plus payments less receipts of investment grants, less depreciation. Net borrowing is net investment less current budget. Net borrowing differs from the net cash requirement (see below) in that it is measured on an accruals basis whereas the net cash requirement is mainly a cash measure which includes some financial transactions.

Table 23.2 shows the public sector key fiscal balances. The table shows the component detail of the public sector key fiscal balance by economic category. The tables are consistent with the Budget.

Table 23.3 shows public sector net debt. Public sector net debt consists of the public sector's financial liabilities at face value, minus its liquid assets – mainly foreign currency exchange reserves and bank deposits. General government gross debt (consolidated) in Table 23.3 is consistent with the definition of general government gross debt reported to the European Commission under the requirements of the Maastricht Treaty.

More information on the concepts in Table 23.1, 23.2 and 23.3 can be found in a guide to monthly public sector finance statistics, GSS Methodology Series No 12, the ONS First Releases Public Sector Finances and Financial Statistics Explanatory Handbook.

Table 23.6 shows the taxes and National Insurance contributions paid to central government, local government, and to the institutions of the European Union. The table is the same as Table 11.1 of the National Accounts Blue Book. More information on the data and concepts in the table can be found in Chapter 11 of the Blue Book.

Consolidated Fund and National Loans Fund (Tables 23.4, 23.5 and 23.7)

The central government embraces all bodies for whose activities a Minister of the Crown, or other responsible person, is accountable to Parliament. It includes, in addition to the ordinary government departments, a number of bodies administering public policy, but without the substantial degree of financial independence which characterises the public corporations. It also includes certain extra-budgetary funds and accounts controlled by departments.

The government's financial transactions are handled through a number of statutory funds or accounts. The most important of these is the Consolidated Fund, which is the government's main account with the Bank of England. Up to 31 March 1968 the Consolidated Fund was virtually synonymous with the term 'Exchequer', which was then the government's central cash account. From 1 April 1968 the National Loans Fund, with a separate account at the Bank of England, was set up by the National Loans Act 1968. The general effect of this Act was to remove from the Consolidated Fund most of the government's domestic lending and the whole of the government's borrowing transactions, and to provide for them to be brought to account in the National Loans Fund.

Revenue from taxation and miscellaneous receipts, including interest and dividends on loans made from votes, continue to be paid into the Consolidated Fund.

After meeting the ordinary expenditure on Supply Services and the Consolidated Fund Standing Services, the surplus or deficit of the Consolidated Fund (Table 23.4), is payable into or met by the National Loans Fund. Table 23.4 also provides a summary of the transactions of the National Loans Fund. The service of the National Debt, previously borne by the Consolidated Fund, is now met from the National Loans Fund which receives:

• interest payable on loans to the nationalised industries, local authorities and other bodies, whether the loans were made before or after 1 April 1968 and

• the profits of the Issue Department of the Bank of England, mainly derived from interest on government securities, which were formerly paid into the Exchange Equalisation Account.

The net cost of servicing the National Debt after applying these interest receipts and similar items is a charge on the Consolidated Fund as part of the standing services. Details of National Loans Fund loans outstanding are shown in Table 23.5. Details of borrowing and repayments of debt, other than loans from the National Loans Fund, are shown in Table 23.7.

Income tax (Table 23.10, 23.11)

Following the introduction of Independent Taxation from 1990/91, the Married Couple's Allowance was introduced. It is payable in addition to the Personal Allowance and between 1990/91 and 1992/93 went to the husband unless the transfer condition was met. The condition was that the husband was unable to make full use of the allowance himself and, in that case, he could transfer only part or all of the Married Couple's Allowance to his wife. In 1993/94 all or half of the allowance could be transferred to the wife if the couple had agreed beforehand. The wife has the right to claim half the allowance. The Married Couple's Allowance, and allowances linked to it, were restricted to 20 per cent in 1994/95 and to 15 per cent from 1995/96. From 2000/01 only people born before 6 April 1935 are entitled to Married Couple's Allowance.

The age allowance replaces the single allowance, provided the taxpayer's income is below the limits shown in the table. From 1989/90, for incomes in excess of the limits, the allowance is reduced by £1 for each additional £2 of income until the ordinary limit is reached (before it was £2 for each £3 of additional income). The relief is due where the taxpayer is aged 65 or over in the year of assessment.

The additional Personal Allowance could be claimed by a single parent (or by a married man if his wife was totally incapacitated) who maintained a resident child at his or her own expense. Widow's Bereavement Allowance was due to a widow in the year of her husband's death and in the following year provided the widow had not remarried before the beginning of that year. Both the additional Personal Allowance and the Widow's Bereavement Allowance were abolished from April 2000.

The Blind Person's Allowance may be claimed by blind persons (in England and Wales, registered as blind by a local authority) and surplus Blind Person's Allowance may be transferred to a husband or wife. Relief on life assurance premiums is given by deduction from the premium payable. From 1984/85, it is confined to policies made before 14 March 1984.

From 1993/94 until 1998/99 a number of taxpayers with taxable income in excess of the lower rate limit only paid tax at the lower rate. This was because it was only their dividend income and (from 1996/97) their savings income which took their taxable income above the lower rate limit but below the basic rate limit, and such income was chargeable to tax at the lower rate and not the basic rate.

In 1999/2000 the 10 per cent starting rate replaced the lower rate and taxpayers with savings or dividend income at the basic rate of tax are taxed at 20 per cent and 10 per cent respectively. Before 1999/2000 these people would have been classified as lower rate taxpayers.

Rateable values (Table 23.12)

Major changes to local government finance in England and Wales took effect from 1 April 1990. These included the abolition of domestic rating (replaced by the Community Charge, then replaced in 1993 by the Council Tax), the revaluation of all non-domestic properties, and the introduction of the Uniform Business Rate. Also in 1990, a new classification scheme was introduced which has resulted in differences in coverage. Further differences are caused by legislative changes which have changed the treatment of certain types of property. There was little change in the total rateable value of non-domestic properties when all these properties were re-valued in April 1995. Rateable values for offices fell and there was a rise for all other property types shown in the table.

With effect from 1 April 2000, all non-domestic properties were re-valued. Overall there was an increase in rateable values of over 25 per cent compared with the last year of the 1995 list. The largest proportionate increase was for offices and cinemas, with all property types given in the table showing rises.

The latest revaluation affecting all non-domestic properties took effect from 1 April 2010. In this revaluation the overall increase in rateable values between 1 April of the first year of the new list and the same day on the last year of the 2005 list was 21 per cent. The largest proportionate increase was for offices and educational properties, with all property types in the table showing rises.

Local authority capital expenditure and receipts (Table 23.16)

Authorities finance capital spending in a number of ways, including use of their own revenue funds, borrowing or grants and contributions from elsewhere. Until 31 March 2004, the capital finance system laid down in Part 4 of the Local Government and Housing Act 1989 (the '1989 Act') provided the framework within which authorities were permitted to finance capital spending from sources other than revenue - that is by the use of borrowing, long-term credit or capital receipts.

Until 31 March 2004, capital spending could be financed by:

• revenue resources – either the General Fund Revenue Account, the Housing Revenue Account (HRA) or the Major Repairs Reserve – but an authority could not charge council tenants for spending on general services, or spending on council houses to local taxpayers

• borrowing or long-term credit as authorised by the credit approvals issued by central government. Credit approvals were normally accompanied by an element of Revenue Support Grant (RSG) covering most of the costs of borrowing

• grants received from central government

• contributions or grants from elsewhere – including the National Lottery and non-departmental public bodies (NDPBs) such as Sport England, English Heritage and Natural England, as well as private sector partners, capital receipts (that is, proceeds from the sale of land, buildings or other fixed assets) and sums set aside as Provision for Credit Liabilities (PCL). This required the use of a credit approval, unless the authority was debt-free

From 1 April 2004, capital spending can be financed in the same ways, except that central government no longer issues credit approvals to allow authorities to finance capital spending by borrowing. However, it continues to provide financial support in the usual way, via RSG or HRA subsidy, towards some capital spending financed by borrowing that is Supported Capital Expenditure (Revenue). Authorities are now free to finance capital spending by self-financed borrowing within limits of affordability set, having regard to the 2003 Act and the CIPFA Prudential Code. The concept of PCL has not been carried forward into the new system, although authorities that were debt-free and had a negative credit ceiling at the end of the old system could still spend amounts of PCL built up under the old rules.

In 2009/10 capital receipts remained well below the 2007/08 level, at £1.4 billion. This reflects a drop in the sale of assets by local authorities. The in-year capital receipts of £1.4 billion were more than offset by the use of £1.6 billion of capital receipts to finance expenditure.

In 2009/10 capital expenditure of £5 billion (about 23 per cent) was financed by self-financed borrowing, an increase of 18 per cent from the amount financed in 2008/09.

In 2009/10 government grants accounted for 34 per cent of the total financing. Financing by government grant in 2007/08 was affected by the grant of £1.7 billion paid by the Department for Transport to the Greater London Authority (GLA) in respect of Metronet liabilities; this caused government grants to account for 34 per cent of the total financing for 2007/08.

Local authority financing for capital expenditure (Table 23.16, 23.17)

Capital spending by local authorities is mainly for buying, constructing or improving physical assets such as:
• buildings – schools, houses, libraries and museums, police and fire stations
• land – for development, roads, playing fields
• vehicles, plant and machinery – including street lighting and road signs

It also includes grants and advances made to the private sector or the rest of the public sector for capital purposes, such as advances to Registered Social Landlords Local authority capital expenditure more than doubled between 2001/02 and 2007/08.

The underlying trend in capital expenditure shows an increase of 8 per cent from 2008/09 to 2009/10. The exceptional event was the payment by the Greater London Authority (Transport for London) of £1.7 billion to Metronet in 2007/08.

New construction, conversion and renovation forms the major part of capital spending. The largest increases in capital expenditure in 2008/09 were in police (44 per cent), and education (22 per cent). Capital expenditure on transport increased by 14 per cent, allowing for the Greater London Authority's grant payment via TfL in respect of Metronet in 2007/08. Between 2004/05 and 2008/09 capital expenditure on transport had risen from 20 per cent to 24 per cent of the total, while capital expenditure on housing has fallen from 28 per cent to 25 per cent of the total.

The largest percentage increase in capital expenditure in 2009/10 was in transport (24 per cent). Capital expenditure on housing and police fell by 8 per cent and 11 per cent respectively. Between 2005/06 and 2009/10 capital expenditure on transport has risen from 21 per cent to 28 per cent of the total, while capital expenditure on housing has fallen from 27 per cent to 21 per cent of the total.

23.1 Sector analysis of key fiscal balances[1]
United Kingdom
Not seasonally adjusted

£ million[2]

		2000 /01	2001 /02	2002 /03	2003 /04	2004 /05	2005 /06	2006 /07	2007 /08	2008 /09	2009 /10	2010 /11	2011 /12	2012 /13
Surplus on current budget[3]														
Central Government	ANLV	29 710	16 964	−4 885	−13 593	−16 783	−11 146	−5 079	−6 456	−47 053	−101 456	−96 802	−86 657	−85 720
Local government	NMMX	−4 836	−4 333	−5 275	−3 276	−5 154	−6 889	−5 454	−5 149	−7 258	−8 044	−5 480	−4 024	−2 611
General Government	ANLW	24 874	12 631	−10 160	−16 869	−21 937	−18 035	−10 533	−11 605	−54 311	−109 500	−102 282	−90 681	−88 331
Public corporations	IL6M	−1 307	−193	−1 325	390	490	3 014	1 879	2 301	15 103	16 337	18 900	19 014	13 035
Public sector	ANMU	23 613	12 480	−11 452	−16 448	−21 410	−14 983	−8 571	−9 197	−38 431	−86 678	−75 408	−62 700	−71 880
Net investment[4]														
Central government	-ANNS	12 163	17 939	22 052	23 209	25 454	24 881	31 094	36 113	47 708	54 918	42 009	26 434	39 330
Local government	-ANNT	−1 646	−904	−2 670	−1 459	424	276	−742	−2 473	590	−1 666	−1 172	6 525	−1 961
General Government	-ANNV	10 517	17 035	19 382	21 750	25 878	25 157	30 352	33 640	48 298	53 252	40 837	32 959	37 369
Public corporations	-JSH6	−3 914	−3 967	−4 238	−6 747	−3 697	884	−2 585	−2 593	−8 773	−9 027	−985	−1 912	−1 907
Public sector	-ANNW	6 441	13 053	15 132	15 002	22 167	26 007	27 764	31 047	39 527	44 222	39 857	31 056	35 487
Net borrowing[5]														
Central government	-NMFJ	−17 547	975	26 937	36 802	42 237	36 027	36 173	42 569	94 761	156 374	138 811	113 091	125 050
Local government	-NMOE	3 190	3 429	2 605	1 817	5 578	7 165	4 712	2 676	7 848	6 378	4 308	10 549	650
General Government	-NNBK	−14 357	4 404	29 542	38 619	47 815	43 192	40 885	45 245	102 609	162 752	143 119	123 640	125 700
Public corporations	-IL6E	−2 607	−3 774	−2 913	−7 137	−4 187	−2 130	−4 464	−4 894	−23 875	−25 362	−19 885	−20 926	−14 942
Public sector	-ANNX	−17 172	573	26 584	31 450	43 577	40 990	36 335	40 244	77 959	130 902	115 265	93 756	107 367
Net cash requirement														
Central government[6]	RUUX	−37 251	3 366	24 214	42 717	40 033	38 135	37 264	30 301	163 909	197 488	132 069	108 644	94 596
Local government	ABEG	−611	−423	−2 715	−2 712	1 270	4 153	58	−723	4 401	4 958	773	8 816	1 647
General Government	RUUS	−37 862	2 943	21 499	40 005	41 303	42 288	37 322	29 578	168 310	202 446	132 842	117 460	96 243
Public corporations	IL6F	1 541	1 159	3 095	−1 539	−242	396	−1 792	−1 746	14 178	−105 654	−120 579	−164 127	−105 869
Public sector	RURQ	−36 521	4 014	24 535	38 421	41 018	42 603	35 405	27 659	181 599	92 507	4 883	−57 919	−22 205
Public sector debt														
Public sector net debt	BKQK	316 359	323 090	354 940	393 646	448 092	490 220	526 737	652 583	2 132 191	2 245 235	2 261 744	2 184 999	2 211 886
Public sector net debt (£ billion)	RUTN	316.4	323.1	354.9	393.6	448.1	490.2	526.7	652.6	2 132.2	2 245.2	2 261.7	2 185.0	2 211.9
Public sector net debt as a percentage of GDP	RUTO	30.1	29.3	30.3	31.7	34.3	35.4	36.0	42.9	144.1	145.6	141.1	132.6	130.7
Excluding financial interventions														
Net debt	HF6W	316.4	323.1	354.9	393.6	448.1	490.2	526.7	558.2	724.4	956.4	1 101.0	1 190.9	1 299.1
Net debt as a % GDP	HF6X	30.1	29.3	30.3	31.7	34.3	35.4	36.0	36.7	49.0	62.0	68.7	72.3	76.8

1 Consistent with the latest Public Sector Finances data, compliant with the European System of Accounts 2010 (ESA10)
2 Unless otherwise stated.
3 Net saving *plus* capital taxes.
4 Gross capital formation *plus* payments *less* receipts of investment grants *less* depreciation.

5 Net investment *less* surplus on current budget. A version of General government net borrowing is reported to the European Commision under the requirements of the Maastricht Treaty.
6 Central government net cash requirement (own account).

Source: Office for National Statistics: 020 7014 2124

23.2 Public sector transactions and fiscal balances[1]

United Kingdom

£ million

		2000/01	2001/02	2002/03	2003/04	2004/05	2005/06	2006/07	2007/08	2008/09	2009/10	2010/11	2011/12	2012/13
Current receipts														
Taxes on income and wealth	ANSO	144 085	145 087	143 160	145 328	160 227	179 458	193 328	207 094	205 537	183 261	196 409	197 534	195 607
Taxes on production	NMYE	133 473	136 859	142 726	151 928	156 983	162 053	172 000	178 916	170 151	172 282	193 998	206 818	211 809
Other current taxes[2]	MJBC	19 904	21 628	23 232	25 913	27 277	28 801	30 308	31 882	33 274	33 961	34 824	37 150	37 326
Taxes on capital	NMGI	2 236	2 383	2 370	2 521	2 931	3 276	3 618	3 890	26 552	2 431	2 722	2 955	3 150
Social contributions	ANBO	62 068	63 162	63 529	75 148	80 923	85 559	90 916	95 437	96 613	96 638	97 747	101 597	104 483
Gross operating surplus	ANBP	21 446	22 352	23 019	24 530	25 454	28 945	30 361	33 121	46 003	48 337	50 727	50 942	49 668
Interest and dividends from private sector and Rest of World	ANBQ	6 112	4 806	4 292	4 416	5 592	6 247	5 836	10 306	45 653	50 652	46 260	49 171	43 446
Rent and other current transfers[3]	ANBS	1 918	2 160	2 175	1 786	1 838	1 855	1 704	1 647	950	1 811	-135	-949	1 151
Total current receipts	ANBT	391 294	398 414	404 356	431 655	461 463	496 210	527 522	561 413	600 206	589 397	622 445	645 307	646 563
Current expenditure														
Current expeniture on goods and services[4]	GZSN	182 816	196 878	215 791	236 176	256 799	273 978	288 041	302 179	320 678	333 772	340 335	340 002	342 734
Subsides	NMRL	4 262	4 527	6 071	6 680	7 179	7 879	8 642	9 872	8 471	10 171	8 591	7 904	9 421
Social benefits	ANLY	110 265	117 747	123 178	130 337	136 848	142 370	147 429	157 958	172 205	188 693	196 453	205 872	217 514
Net current grants abroad[5]	GZSI	-534	-2 132	-964	-1 263	-834	-258	-73	-274	-1 610	739	2 873	2 435	2 608
Other current grants	NNAI	15 991	18 593	19 761	21 271	22 750	24 541	25 227	25 849	25 548	28 711	27 345	25 981	23 490
Interest and dividends paid to private sector and Rest of World	ANLO	35 307	29 965	29 731	32 607	35 986	37 168	39 983	47 187	82 719	81 573	88 431	90 733	86 382
Total current expenditure	ANLT	347 998	365 395	393 353	425 645	458 537	485 533	509 095	542 597	607 913	643 585	663 943	672 802	682 149
Saving, gross plus capital taxes	ANSP	43 296	33 019	11 003	6 010	2 926	10 677	18 427	18 816	-7 707	-54 207	-41 502	-27 417	-35 539
Depreciation	-ANNZ	-19 683	-20 539	-22 455	-22 458	-24 336	-25 660	-26 998	-28 013	-30 725	-32 475	-33 906	-35 283	-36 341
Surplus on current budget	ANMU	23 613	12 480	-11 452	-16 448	-21 410	-14 983	-8 571	-9 197	-38 431	-86 678	-75 408	-62 700	-71 880
Net investment														
Gross fixed capital formation[6]	ANSQ	21 354	25 860	29 588	27 706	37 176	40 713	42 729	46 768	56 626	60 886	60 159	55 389	52 938
Less depreciation	-ANNZ	-19 683	-20 539	-22 455	-22 458	-24 336	-25 660	-26 998	-28 013	-30 725	-32 475	-33 906	-35 283	-36 341
Increase in inventories and valuables	ANSR	72	76	82	-139	125	155	-73	-107	349	-16	83	4	12
Capital grants to private sector and Rest of World	ANSS	5 240	8 658	9 113	11 238	10 174	12 001	13 519	13 900	40 290	17 033	14 467	11 754	19 916
Capital grants from private sector and Rest of World	-ANST	-542	-1 002	-1 196	-1 345	-972	-1 202	-1 413	-1 501	-27 013	-1 206	-946	-808	-1 038
Total net investment	-ANNW	6 441	13 053	15 132	15 002	22 167	26 007	27 764	31 047	39 527	44 222	39 857	31 056	35 487
Net borrowing[7]	-ANNX	-17 172	573	26 584	31 450	43 577	40 990	36 335	40 244	77 959	130 902	115 265	93 756	107 367
Financial transactions determining net cash requirement														
Net lending to private sector and Rest of World	ANSU	-3 241	-2 385	-2 476	-1 505	-636	256	29	-13 551	-39 996	-46 317	-48 434	-27 167	-49 993
Net acquisition of UK company securities	ANSV	1 924	4 414	4 292	3 827	2 092	4 491	9 793	6 699	-20 837	-24 714	-27 602	-64 781	-34 624
Accounts receivable/payable	ANSW	-20 377	2 617	-2 396	5 140	2 197	3 662	12 210	-2 740	13 351	10 997	218	-8 244	-34 866
Adjustment for interest on gilts	ANSX	-2 631	-360	-1 224	-912	-2 400	-2 476	-1 385	-4 812	-4 884	1 817	-7 821	-2 291	-5 125
Other financial transactions[8]	ANSY	-13 778	5 195	4 411	-1 855	6 250	7 527	22 536	27 566	-106 590	-179 902	-10 391	-52 302	-33 148
Public sector net cash requirement	RURQ	-27 719	-336	20 369	39 855	38 580	39 396	34 446	20 580	183 212	91 902	5 916	-55 216	-15 180

1 See chapter text.
2 Includes domestic rates, council tax, community charge, motor vehicle duty paid by household and some licence fees.
3 ESA95 transactions D44, D45, D74, D75 and D72-D71: includes rent of land, oil royalties, other property income and fines.
4 Includes non-trading capital consumption.

5 Net of current grants received from abroad.
6 Including net acquisition of land.
7 Net investment *less* surplus on current budget.
8 Includes statistical discrepancy, finance leasing and similar borrowing, insurance technical reserves and some other minor adjustments.

Source: Office for National Statistics: 020 7014 2124

23.3 Public sector net debt[1]

United Kingdom

£ million

		2002 /03	2003 /04	2004 /05	2005 /06	2006 /07	2007 /08	2008 /09	2009 /10	2010 /11	2011 /12	2012 /13
Central government sterling gross debt												
British government stock												
Conventional gilts	BKPK	206 119	232 877	261 373	287 481	306 489	320 622	426 107	608 511	697 968	788 598	853 342
Index linked gilts	BKPL	75 966	78 982	86 749	98 654	113 090	132 404	154 038	178 170	220 631	253 779	289 100
Total	BKPM	282 085	311 859	348 122	386 135	419 579	453 026	580 145	786 681	918 599	1 042 347	1 142 442
Sterling Treasury bills	BKPJ	15 000	19 300	20 350	19 100	15 600	17 569	43 748	62 866	63 174	69 933	56 370
National savings	ACUA	63 087	66 522	68 504	73 365	78 885	84 764	97 231	98 804	98 886	102 903	102 238
Tax instruments	ACRV	376	407	350	308	353	428	1 121	819	679	638	633
Other sterling debt[2]	BKSK	34 115	40 121	37 555	42 868	47 945	47 561	64 612	39 934	34 068	42 506	34 275
Central government sterling gross debt total	BKSL	394 663	438 209	474 881	521 776	562 362	603 348	786 857	989 104	1 115 406	1 258 327	1 335 958
Central government foreign currency gross debt												
US$ bonds	BKPG	-	1 632	1 587	1 730	1 530	1 509	-	-	-	-	-
ECU bonds	EYSJ	-	-	-	-	-	-	-	-	-	-	-
ECU/Euro Treasury notes	EYSV	-	-	-	-	-	-	-	-	-	-	-
Other foreign currency debt	BKPH	172	105	57	1	-	-	-	-	-	-	-
Central government foreign currency gross debt total	BKPI	172	1 738	1 644	1 731	1 530	1 509	-	-	-	-	-
Central government gross debt total	BKPW	394 835	439 947	492 387	541 917	582 275	625 006	809 649	1 059 345	1 196 643	1 329 736	1 403 516
Local government gross debt total	EYKP	51 398	50 756	53 284	59 380	61 911	66 351	67 323	68 562	70 954	81 594	84 703
less												
Central government holdings of local government debt	-EYKZ	-44 836	-41 556	-42 339	-46 664	-47 460	-50 364	-50 508	-51 195	-53 246	-62 499	-64 307
Local government holdings of central government debt	-EYLA	-858	-788	-342	-826	-210	-286	-3 180	-2 943	-2 263	-3 639	-3 288
General government gross debt (consolidated)	BKPX	400 539	448 359	502 990	553 807	596 516	640 707	823 284	1 073 769	1 212 088	1 345 192	1 420 624
Public corporations gross debt	EYYD	18 660	13 895	14 875	14 687	14 430	13 804	13 669	10 518	10 405	10 820	10 127
less												
Central government holdings of public corporations debt	-EYXY	-4 171	-5 188	-5 740	-5 631	-4 984	-5 092	-4 879	-5 617	-5 604	-5 839	-5 480
Local government holdings of public coporations debt	-EYXZ	-239	-240	-241	-232	-223	-224	-227	-296	-276	-273	-276
Public corporations holdings of central government debt	-BKPZ	-4 928	-4 780	-5 080	-2 822	-2 255	-4 119	-3 947	-3 352	-3 301	-4 383	-3 382
Public corporations holdings of local government debt	-EYXV	621	587	533	591	474	631	639	620	521	562	603
Public sector gross debt (consolidated)	BKQA	410 482	452 633	507 337	560 400	603 958	743 730	2 806 678	2 870 207	2 889 375	2 872 241	2 802 178
Public sector liquid assets:												
Official reserves	AIPD	26 387	25 266	25 813	27 835	26 631	29 561	31 527	44 652	52 969	60 954	68 218
Central government deposits[3]	BKSM	2 900	3 879	3 868	5 212	6 171	5 439	5 242	4 351	5 783	6 672	6 034
Other central government	BKSN	8 141	7 077	3 072	8 529	11 562	15 377	39 075	48 143	21 204	45 634	31 813
Local government deposits[3]	BKSO	12 729	15 332	18 718	20 993	23 740	28 327	21 781	18 177	19 145	18 123	21 109
Other local government short term assets	BKQG	551	449	395	650	976	2 041	2 072	1 780	3 227	4 733	4 119
Public corporation deposits[3]	BKSP	2 133	2 813	3 411	2 375	3 746	2 366	1 781	2 203	1 923	2 910	2 701
Other public corporations short term assets	BKSQ	1 586	2 845	2 457	2 453	2 378	2 254	2 166	2 284	2 170	2 296	2280
Public sector liquid assets total	BKQJ	54 427	57 661	57 734	68 047	75 204	89 042	673 963	637 424	632 261	681 778	612 635
Public sector net debt	BKQK	354 940	393 646	448 092	490 220	526 737	652 583	2 132 191	2 245 235	2 261 744	2 184 999	2 211 886
as percentage of GDP[4]	RUTO	30.3	31.7	34.3	35.4	36	42.9	144.1	145.6	141.1	132.6	130.7

1 See chapter text.
2 Including overdraft with Bank of England.
3 Bank and building society deposits.
4 Gross domestic product at market prices from 12 months centred on the end
  of the month.

Source: Office for National Statistics: 020 7014 2124

23.4a Central government surplus on current budget and net borrowing

£ million

	Current receipts									
	Taxes on production	of which	Taxes on income and wealth				Compulsory social contributions	Interest and dividends	Other receipts[3]	Total
	Total	VAT	Total	Income and capital gains tax[1]	Other[2]	Other taxes				
	NMBY	NZGF	NMCU	LIBR	LIBP	LIQR	AIIH	LIQP	LIQQ	ANBV
2002	141 549	71 066	142 814	112 440	30 374	9 569	63 410	7 154	11 930	376 426
2003	148 641	77 343	144 119	113 594	30 525	10 118	71 540	7 697	12 713	394 828
2004	156 416	81 544	154 018	120 616	33 402	10 862	79 224	7 426	13 246	421 192
2005	159 958	83 425	172 281	131 472	40 809	11 481	84 459	7 125	14 013	449 317
2006	169 003	87 758	192 127	141 241	50 886	12 262	89 550	6 747	14 516	484 205
2007	177 720	92 025	199 268	152 706	46 562	13 213	93 210	7 970	14 927	506 308
2008	175 685	92 002	206 908	156 366	50 542	12 939	98 319	9 746	15 861	519 458
2009	164 831	79 900	184 782	146 859	37 923	12 295	94 445	9 085	16 476	481 914
2010	189 232	95 865	192 116	147 924	44 192	12 881	97 346	7 920	17 056	516 551
2011	204 550	111 437	199 739	154 099	45 640	14 798	101 441	8 073	17 919	546 520
2012	210 416	113 892	195 245	151 933	43 312	15 248	104 319	11 880	19 556	556 664
2002/03	142 550	71 604	143 256	112 373	30 883	9 588	63 529	7 735	12 503	379 161
2003/04	151 777	79 207	145 450	115 196	30 254	10 309	75 148	7 660	12 244	402 588
2004/05	156 816	81 864	160 354	124 341	36 013	10 950	80 923	7 054	13 615	429 712
2005/06	161 866	83 507	179 721	134 679	45 042	11 760	85 559	7 048	14 123	460 077
2006/07	171 793	90 008	193 646	145 926	47 720	12 520	90 916	6 779	14 601	490 255
2007/08	178 630	92 469	207 282	157 941	49 341	13 264	95 437	8 683	15 098	518 394
2008/09	169 840	87 805	200 169	153 095	47 074	12 717	96 613	9 681	16 109	505 129
2009/10	171 965	84 825	182 213	144 020	38 193	12 389	96 638	8 580	16 559	488 344
2010/11	193 649	99 523	196 523	151 311	45 212	12 882	97 747	8 011	17 320	526 132
2011/12	206 464	112 067	198 053	152 329	45 724	15 355	101 597	9 607	18 134	549 210
2012/13	211 449	114 465	195 977	153 232	42 745	15 361	104 483	16 659	19 989	563 918
2007 Q1	42 871	22 568	62 877	51 858	11 019	3 260	24 995	1 940	3 705	139 648
Q2	43 996	22 676	39 065	30 477	8 588	3 311	22 354	1 767	3 734	114 227
Q3	45 363	23 368	50 949	37 741	13 208	3 438	22 560	1 789	3 712	127 811
Q4	45 490	23 413	46 377	32 630	13 747	3 204	23 301	2 474	3 776	124 622
2008 Q1	43 781	23 012	70 891	57 093	13 798	3 311	27 222	2 653	3 876	151 734
Q2	45 596	24 683	39 337	30 216	9 121	3 315	23 784	2 113	3 918	118 063
Q3	43 837	22 938	52 924	38 533	14 391	3 293	23 597	2 427	4 039	130 117
Q4	42 471	21 369	43 756	30 524	13 232	3 020	23 716	2 553	4 028	119 544
2009 Q1	37 936	18 815	64 152	53 822	10 330	3 089	25 516	2 588	4 124	137 405
Q2	40 363	19 079	35 888	28 783	7 105	3 040	22 990	2 659	4 048	108 988
Q3	42 555	20 658	43 776	35 312	8 464	3 243	22 535	1 779	4 124	118 012
Q4	43 977	21 348	40 966	28 942	12 024	2 923	23 404	2 059	4 180	117 509
2010 Q1	45 070	23 740	61 583	50 983	10 600	3 183	27 709	2 083	4 207	143 835
Q2	49 602	23 810	37 324	29 634	7 690	3 202	23 115	1 591	4 216	119 050
Q3	46 910	24 090	49 326	36 992	12 334	3 391	22 983	2 256	4 284	129 150
Q4	47 650	24 225	43 883	30 315	13 568	3 105	23 539	1 990	4 349	124 516
2011 Q1	49 487	27 398	65 990	54 370	11 620	3 184	28 110	2 174	4 471	153 416
Q2	49 997	27 363	38 879	30 843	8 036	3 394	24 484	1 874	4 444	123 072
Q3	52 652	28 427	50 119	37 396	12 723	4 494	24 326	2 124	4 485	138 200
Q4	52 414	28 249	44 751	31 490	13 261	3 726	24 521	1 901	4 519	131 832
2012 Q1	51 401	28 028	64 304	52 600	11 704	3 741	28 266	3 708	4 686	156 106
Q2	51 085	28 143	38 699	30 715	7 984	3 684	25 631	4 244	4 886	128 229
Q3	53 041	28 038	48 495	37 537	10 958	4 046	25 201	1 976	4 956	137 715
Q4	54 889	29 683	43 747	31 081	12 666	3 777	25 221	1 952	5 028	134 614
2013 Q1	52 434	28 601	65 036	53 899	11 137	3 854	28 430	8 487	5 119	163 360

23.4a Central government surplus on current budget and net borrowing
continued

	Current expenditure				Saving, gross plus capital taxes	Depreciation	Current budget	Net investment	Net borrowing
	Interest	Net Social Benefits	Other	Total					
	NMFX	GZSJ	LIQS	ANLP	ANPM	NSRN	ANLV	-ANNS	-NMFJ
2002	20 912	107 799	238 563	367 274	9 152	9 834	−682	19 539	20 221
2003	21 837	114 768	262 624	399 229	−4 401	10 905	−15 306	24 214	39 520
2004	23 420	122 033	280 690	426 143	−4 951	11 494	−16 445	23 615	40 060
2005	26 259	126 132	300 192	452 583	−3 266	12 207	−15 473	25 113	40 586
2006	27 413	130 115	322 240	479 768	4 437	12 849	−8 412	29 857	38 269
2007	31 520	139 204	332 047	502 771	3 537	13 296	−9 759	30 811	40 570
2008	32 831	148 887	349 518	531 236	−11 778	14 289	−26 067	44 652	70 719
2009	27 698	165 197	368 980	561 875	−79 961	14 836	−94 797	57 075	151 872
2010	44 756	172 580	386 909	604 245	−87 694	15 488	−103 182	44 036	147 218
2011	51 160	178 672	383 012	612 844	−66 324	16 390	−82 714	36 193	118 907
2012	47 828	189 884	396 706	634 418	−77 754	17 123	−94 877	35 070	129 947
2002/03	20 726	109 144	243 711	373 581	5 580	10 465	−4 885	22 052	26 937
2003/04	22 025	116 926	266 638	405 589	−3 001	10 592	−13 593	23 209	36 802
2004/05	24 570	122 624	287 475	434 669	−4 957	11 826	−16 783	25 454	42 237
2005/06	26 293	127 304	305 298	458 895	1 182	12 328	−11 146	24 881	36 027
2006/07	28 579	131 346	322 470	482 395	7 860	12 939	−5 079	31 094	36 173
2007/08	31 220	140 868	339 263	511 351	7 043	13 499	−6 456	36 113	42 569
2008/09	31 520	153 654	352 467	537 641	−32 512	14 541	−47 053	47 708	94 761
2009/10	31 566	167 192	376 129	574 887	−86 543	14 895	−101 438	54 918	156 356
2010/11	46 609	173 285	387 246	607 140	−81 008	15 790	−96 798	42 009	138 807
2011/12	49 704	181 466	388 171	619 341	−70 131	16 607	−86 738	26 434	113 172
2012/13	48 856	191 786	391 835	632 477	−68 559	17 213	−85 772	39 330	125 102
2007 Q1	7 400	32 084	80 445	119 929	19 719	3 273	16 446	10 889	−5 557
Q2	7 912	34 273	84 632	126 817	−12 590	3 300	−15 890	4 929	20 819
Q3	7 164	35 285	83 586	126 035	1 776	3 328	−1 552	6 944	8 496
Q4	9 044	37 562	83 384	129 990	−5 368	3 395	−8 763	8 049	16 812
2008 Q1	7 100	33 748	87 661	128 509	23 225	3 476	19 749	16 191	−3 558
Q2	8 869	36 923	89 218	135 010	−16 947	3 551	−20 498	7 396	27 894
Q3	7 716	37 854	85 651	131 221	−1 104	3 613	−4 717	9 957	14 674
Q4	9 146	40 362	86 988	136 496	−16 952	3 649	−20 601	11 108	31 709
2009 Q1	5 789	38 515	90 610	134 914	2 491	3 728	−1 237	19 247	20 484
Q2	7 886	40 705	95 369	143 960	−34 972	3 661	−38 633	12 336	50 969
Q3	4 348	41 672	91 298	137 318	−19 306	3 701	−23 007	10 282	33 289
Q4	9 675	44 305	91 703	145 683	−28 174	3 746	−31 920	15 210	47 130
2010 Q1	9 657	40 510	97 759	147 926	−4 091	3 787	−7 878	17 090	24 968
Q2	12 259	42 278	98 107	152 644	−33 594	3 837	−37 431	7 808	45 239
Q3	10 092	43 520	94 518	148 130	−18 980	3 901	−22 881	9 376	32 257
Q4	12 748	46 272	96 525	155 545	−31 029	3 963	−34 992	9 762	44 754
2011 Q1	11 510	41 215	98 096	150 821	2 595	4 089	−1 494	15 063	16 557
Q2	14 081	44 311	99 487	157 879	−34 807	4 064	−38 871	6 015	44 886
Q3	11 147	45 965	92 863	149 975	−11 775	4 103	−15 878	7 305	23 183
Q4	14 422	47 181	92 566	154 169	−22 337	4 134	−26 471	7 810	34 281
2012 Q1	10 054	44 009	103 255	157 318	−1 212	4 306	−5 518	5 304	10 822
Q2	14 219	47 695	98 232	160 146	−31 917	4 209	−36 126	16 235	52 361
Q3	9 600	48 272	96 303	154 175	−16 460	4 270	−20 730	6 548	27 278
Q4	13 955	49 908	98 916	162 779	−28 165	4 338	−32 503	6 983	39 486
2013 Q1	11 082	45 911	98 384	155 377	7 983	4 396	3 587	9 564	5 977

1 Includes capital gains tax paid by households. Includes income tax and capital gains tax paid by corporations.

2 Mainly comprises corporation tax and petroleum revenue tax.

3 Includes receipts from the spectrum.

23.4b Central government surplus on current budget and net borrowing

£ million

	Taxes on production	of which	Taxes on income and wealth				Compulsory social contributions	Interest and dividends	Other receipts[3]	Total
	Total	VAT	Total	Income and capital gains tax[1]	Other[2]	Other taxes				
	NMBY	NZGF	NMCU	LIBR	LIBP	LIQR	AIIH	LIQP	LIQQ	ANBV
2011 Jan	15 922	8 948	33 091	24 600	8 491	960	8 518	537	1 492	60 520
Feb	15 766	8 819	17 767	16 428	1 339	1 064	9 192	522	1 492	45 803
Mar	17 799	9 631	15 132	13 342	1 790	1 160	10 400	1 115	1 487	47 093
Apr	16 404	9 038	15 423	9 578	5 845	1 232	7 897	569	1 480	43 005
May	16 387	8 938	11 714	10 409	1 305	965	8 033	668	1 481	39 248
Jun	17 206	9 387	11 742	10 856	886	1 197	8 554	637	1 483	40 819
Jul	17 355	9 300	24 892	16 108	8 784	1 695	8 270	587	1 494	54 293
Aug	17 504	9 489	13 082	11 613	1 469	1 452	7 936	614	1 494	42 082
Sep	17 793	9 638	12 145	9 675	2 470	1 347	8 120	923	1 497	41 825
Oct	17 880	9 540	18 592	9 687	8 905	1 294	8 058	637	1 507	47 968
Nov	16 995	9 151	11 834	10 504	1 330	1 290	7 921	642	1 506	40 188
Dec	17 539	9 558	14 325	11 299	3 026	1 142	8 542	622	1 506	43 676
2012 Jan	16 320	9 253	34 163	24 942	9 221	1 186	8 710	562	1 562	62 503
Feb	16 670	9 109	15 657	14 412	1 245	1 457	9 077	493	1 563	44 917
Mar	18 411	9 666	14 484	13 246	1 238	1 098	10 479	2 653	1 561	48 686
Apr	16 549	9 304	15 620	10 448	5 172	1 157	8 670	3 092	1 652	46 740
May	16 943	9 304	10 986	9 493	1 493	1 279	8 150	656	1 606	39 620
Jun	17 593	9 535	12 093	10 774	1 319	1 248	8 811	496	1 628	41 869
Jul	17 894	9 379	23 365	16 278	7 087	1 431	8 486	612	1 660	53 448
Aug	17 399	9 145	12 571	11 128	1 443	1 418	8 214	551	1 655	41 808
Sep	17 748	9 514	12 559	10 131	2 428	1 197	8 501	813	1 641	42 459
Oct	18 167	9 775	18 175	10 117	8 058	1 427	8 157	799	1 677	48 402
Nov	18 073	9 758	10 849	9 270	1 579	1 187	8 136	578	1 675	40 498
Dec	18 649	10 150	14 723	11 694	3 029	1 163	8 928	575	1 676	45 714
2013 Jan	16 984	9 621	34 250	26 224	8 026	1 209	8 716	4 270	1 731	67 160
Feb	16 872	9 287	16 140	14 550	1 590	1 228	8 995	3 117	1 745	48 097
Mar	18 578	9 693	14 646	13 125	1 521	1 417	10 719	1 100	1 643	48 103
Apr	17 280	9 613	16 821	11 905	4 916	1 274	9 175	4 651	1 752	50 953
May	17 886	9 639	11 848	10 384	1 464	2 292	8 503	4 522	1 707	46 758

	Current expenditure				Saving, gross plus capital taxes	Depreciation	budget	investment	borrowing
	Interest	Net Social Benefits	Other	Total					
	NMFX		LIQS	ANLP	ANPM	NSRN	ANLV	-ANNS	-NMFJ
2011 Jan	4 023	14 082	815	920	11 600	1 364	10 236	2 930	-7 306
Feb	4 208	12 965	508	681	-2 878	364	-4 242	765	8 007
Mar	3 279	14 168	773	220	-6 127	1 361	-7 488	8 368	15 856
Apr	4 938	14 804	299	041	-11 036	1 354	-12 390	1 739	14 129
May	4 227	14 613	029	869	-11 621	1 354	-12 975	1 991	14 966
Jun	4 916	14 894	159	969	-12 150	1 356	-13 506	2 285	15 791
Jul	4 267	15 031	688	986	6 307	1 367	4 940	2 310	-2 630
Aug	3 862	15 319	116	297	-9 215	1 367	-10 582	2 079	12 661
Sep	3 018	15 615	059	692	-8 867	369	-10 236	2 916	13 152
Oct	5 079	14 853	472	404	-1 436	1 378	-2 814	2 112	4 926
Nov	4 974	16 815	201	990	-11 802	1 378	-13 180	1 692	14 872
Dec	4 369	15 513	893	775	-9 099	378	-10 477	4 006	14 483
2012 Jan	4 075	14 726	374	175	12 328	1 434	10 894	2 842	-8 052
Feb	4 001	14 328	006	335	-6 418	1 434	-7 852	3 063	10 915
Mar	1 978	14 955	875	808	-7 122	438	-8 560	-601	7 959
Apr	5 363	15 873	393	629	-6 889	1 427	-8 316	3 343	11 659
May	4 752	16 416	151	319	-14 699	1 381	-16 080	2 031	18 111
Jun	4 104	15 406	688	198	-10 329	1 401	-11 730	10 861	22 591
Jul	3 665	16 116	793	574	3 874	1 431	2 443	2 521	78
Aug	2 908	16 209	407	524	-10 716	1 427	-12 143	1 693	13 836
Sep	3 027	15 947	103	077	-9 618	412	-11 030	2 334	13 364
Oct	4 487	16 101	860	448	-4 046	1 447	-5 493	2 386	7 879
Nov	4 455	17 731	767	953	-13 455	1 445	-14 900	1 765	16 665
Dec	5 013	16 076	289	378	-10 664	1 446	-12 110	2 832	14 942
2013 Jan	3 816	15 928	474	218	14 942	1 489	13 453	3 757	-9 696
Feb	4 669	14 260	224	153	-2 056	488	-3 544		4 422
Mar	2 597	15 723	686	006	-4 903	1 419	-6 322	4 929	11 251
Apr	5 212	15 927	717	856	-12 903	1 514	-14 417	2 394	16 811
May	4 692	16 437	722	851	-5 093	1 468	-6 561	1 498	8 059

1 Includes capital gains tax paid by households. Includes income tax and capital gains tax paid by corporations.

2 Mainly comprises corporation tax and petroleum revenue tax.
3 Includes receipts from the spectrum.

23.5 National Loans Fund: assets and liabilities

United Kingdom
as at 31 March each year

	At 31 March 2013 £m	At 31 March 2012 £m
Assets		
Advances	171,596	128,301
Loans	2,997	3,610
Other assets	76,429	67,510
IMF Quota Subscription & Lending	12,958	12,421
Total assets	263,980	211,842
Liabilities		
Gilt-edged stock	1,315,472	1,201,171
National Savings and Investments products	102,238	102,903
Liabilities to the IMF	7,244	6,819
Other debt payable in sterling:		
FLS Treasury Bills	35,259	–
Other	46,485	60,007
Total liabilities	1,506,698	1,370,900
Net liabilities	1,242,718	1,159,058
Liability of the Consolidated Fund to the National Loans Fund	1,242,718	1,159,058

Source: HM Treasury

Nick Macpherson   15 July 2013
Accounting Officer
HM Treasury

23.6a Taxes paid by UK residents to general government and the European Union

Total economy sector S.1

£ million

			2004	2005	2006	2007	2008	2009	2010	2011	2012
Part	**GENERATION OF INCOME**										
	Uses										
D.2	Taxes on production and imports										
D.21	Taxes on products and imports										
D.211	Value added tax (VAT)										
	Paid to central government	NZGF	79 755	81 426	85 591	89 706	89 732	78 307	93 635	109 252	111 574
	Paid to the European Union	FJKM	1 789	1 999	2 167	2 319	2 270	1 593	2 253	2 197	2 282
D.211	Total	QYRC	81 544	83 425	87 758	92 025	92 002	79 900	95 888	111 449	113 856
D.212	Taxes and duties on imports excluding VAT										
D.2121	Paid to CG: import duties[1]	NMXZ	–	–	–	–	–	–	–	–	–
D.2121	Paid to EU: import duties	FJWE	2 145	2 237	2 329	2 412	2 636	2 645	2 933	2 925	2 885
D.212	Total	QYRB	2 145	2 237	2 329	2 412	2 636	2 645	2 933	2 925	2 885
D.214	Taxes on products excluding VAT and import duties										
	Paid to central government										
	Customs & excise revenue										
	Beer	GTAM	3 111	3 072	3 065	3 042	3 140	3 189	3 278	3 429	3 425
	Wines, cider, perry & spirits	GTAN	4 761	4 802	4 779	5 008	5 533	5 728	6 075	6 439	6 775
	Tobacco	GTAO	8 132	8 036	8 072	7 862	8 203	9 056	9 076	9 361	9 897
	Hydrocarbon oils	GTAP	23 412	23 346	23 448	24 512	24 790	25 894	27 013	26 923	26 703
	Car tax	GTAT	–	–	–	–	–	–	–	–	–
	Betting, gaming & lottery	CJQY	872	864	958	959	989	1 013	1 092	1 206	1 207
	Air passenger duty	CWAA	856	896	961	1 883	1 876	1 800	2 094	2 605	2 766
	Insurance premium tax	CWAD	2 359	2 343	2 314	2 306	2 281	2 259	2 402	2 942	3 009
	Landfill tax	BKOF	672	733	804	877	954	842	1 065	1 090	1 092
	Other	ACDN	–	–	–	–	–	–	–	–	–
	Fossil fuel levy	CIQY	–	–	–	–	–	–	–	–	–
	Gas levy	GTAZ	–	–	–	–	–	–	–	–	–
	Stamp duties	GTBC	8 884	9 910	13 074	14 634	9 499	7 141	9 098	8 831	8 918
	Levies on exports (Third country trade)	CUDF	–	–	–	–	–	–	–	–	–
	Camelot payments to National Lottery Distribution Fund	LIYH	1 342	1 349	1 440	1 310	1 405	1 553	1 625	1 793	1 832
	Purchase Tax	EBDB	–	–	–	–	–	–	–	–	–
	Hydro-benefit	LITN	40	10	–	–	–	–	–	–	–
	Aggregates levy	MDUQ	328	327	321	339	334	275	289	289	266
	Milk super levy	DFT3	69	19	1	–	–	–	–	–	–
	Climate change levy	LSNT	756	747	711	690	717	693	666	675	630
	Channel 4 funding formula	EG9G	–	–	–	–	–	–	–	–	–
	Renewable energy obligations	EP89	477	563	700	833	996	1 099	1 243	1 423	1 634
	Rail franchise premia	LITT	205	98	125	244	285	496	792	993	1 275
	Other taxes and levies	GCSP	–	–	–	–	–	–	–	–	–
	Total paid to central government	NMYB	56 276	57 115	60 773	64 499	61 002	61 038	65 808	67 999	69 429
	Paid to the European Union										
	Sugar levy	GTBA	25	24	–	–	–	–	–	–	–
	European Coal & Steel Community levy	GTBB	–	–	–	–	–	–	–	–	–
	Total paid to the European Union	FJWG	25	24	–	–	–	–	–	–	–
D.214	Total taxes on products excluding VAT & import duties	QYRA	56 301	57 139	60 773	64 499	61 002	61 038	65 808	67 999	69 429
D.21	Total taxes on products and imports	NZGW	139 990	142 801	150 860	158 936	155 640	143 583	164 629	182 373	186 170
D.29	Production taxes other than on products										
	Paid to central government										
	Consumer Credit Act fees	CUDB	220	197	223	281	328	435	480	480	480
	National non-domestic rates	CUKY	17 099	17 932	18 878	19 455	20 710	21 576	21 780	22 668	23 039
	Northern Ireland non-domestic rates	NSEZ	263	286	318	353	328	325	361	368	366
	Levies paid to CG levy-funded bodies	LITK	214	235	232	261	459	746	569	508	600
	London regional transport levy	GTBE	–	–	–	–	–	–	–	–	–
	IBA levy	GTAL	–	–	–	–	–	–	–	–	–
	Motor vehicle duties paid by businesses	EKED	808	809	865	878	885	908	937	931	940
	Regulator fees	GCSQ	86	78	72	76	70	72	90	78	90
	Northern Ireland Driver Vehicle Agency	IY9N	–	–	–	3	4	4	4	4	4
	Bank Payroll Tax: Accrued receipts	JT2Q	–	–	–	–	–	–	3 413	–	–
	Total	NMBX	18 690	19 537	20 588	21 307	22 784	24 066	27 634	25 037	25 519
	Paid to local government										
	Non-domestic rates[2]	NMYH	163	182	202	267	301	317	329	336	344
D.29	Total production taxes other than on products	NMYD	18 853	19 719	20 790	21 574	23 085	24 383	27 963	25 373	25 863
D.2	Total taxes on production and imports, paid										
	Paid to central government	NMBY	154 721	158 078	166 952	175 512	173 518	163 411	187 077	202 288	206 522
	Paid to local government	NMYH	163	182	202	267	301	317	329	336	344
	Paid to the European Union	FJWB	3 959	4 260	4 496	4 731	4 906	4 238	5 186	5 122	5 167
D.2	Total	NZGX	158 843	162 520	171 650	180 510	178 725	167 966	192 592	207 746	212 033

1 These taxes existed before the UK's entry into the EEC in 1973
2 From 1990/1991 onwards these series only contain rates paid in Northern Ireland

23.6b Taxes paid by UK residents to general government and the European Union

Total economy sector S.1

£ million

Part				2004	2005	2006	2007	2008	2009	2010	2011	2012
Part	**SECONDARY DISTRIBUTION OF INCOME**											
	Uses											
D.5	Current taxes on income, wealth etc											
D.51	Taxes on income											
	Paid to central government											
	Household income taxes	DRWH		117 372	127 884	136 686	147 371	149 575	137 964	144 478	149 103	145 776
	Corporation Tax	ACCD		31 164	37 893	47 129	43 912	46 487	35 402	41 253	42 267	39 694
	Petroleum revenue tax	DBHA		1 166	1 799	2 546	1 387	2 663	1 047	1 349	1 775	2 106
	Windfall tax	EYNK		–	–	–	–	–	–	–	–	–
	Other taxes on income	BMNX		4 316	4 705	5 766	6 601	8 190	10 387	5 041	6 594	7 308
D.51	Total	NMCU		154 018	172 281	192 127	199 271	206 915	184 800	192 121	199 739	194 884
D.59	Other current taxes											
	Paid to central government											
	Motor vehicle duty paid by households	CDDZ		3 955	3 953	4 145	4 506	4 639	4 722	4 903	4 889	4 933
	Northern Ireland domestic rates	NSFA		225	233	244	265	329	355	335	391	416
	Boat licences	NSNP		–	–	–	–	–	–	–	–	–
	Fishing licences	NRQB		19	20	20	20	20	20	20	23	21
	National non-domestic rates paid by non-market sectors[1]	BMNY		1 082	1 191	1 260	1 304	1 354	1 423	1 481	1 637	1 649
	Passport fees	E8A6		220	279	322	377	376	351	400	368	362
	Television licence fee	DH7A		2 490	2 655	2 696	2 862	2 949	3 009	3 088	3 088	3 117
	Northern Ireland Driver Vehicle Agency	IY9O		–	–	–	12	15	14	12	12	12
	Bank levy	KIH3		–	–	–	–	–	–	–	1 454	1 609
	Total	NMCV		7 991	8 331	8 687	9 346	9 682	9 894	10 239	11 862	12 119
	Paid to local government											
	Domestic rates[2]	NMHK		139	147	155	127	122	131	146	157	164
	Community charge	NMHL		–	–	–	–	–	–	–	–	–
	Council tax	NMHM		19 766	20 931	22 064	23 224	24 274	24 940	25 454	25 748	26 105
	Total	NMIS		19 905	21 078	22 219	23 351	24 396	25 071	25 600	25 905	26 269
D.59	Total	NVCM		27 896	29 409	30 906	32 697	34 078	34 965	35 839	37 767	38 388
D.5	Total current taxes on income, wealth etc											
	Paid to central government	NMCP		162 009	180 612	200 814	208 617	216 597	194 694	202 360	211 601	207 003
	Paid to local government	NMIS		19 905	21 078	22 219	23 351	24 396	25 071	25 600	25 905	26 269
D.5	Total	NMZL		181 914	201 690	223 033	231 968	240 993	219 765	227 960	237 506	233 272
D.61	Social contributions											
D.611	Actual social contributions											
	Paid to central government											
	(National Insurance Contributions)											
D.61111	Employers' compulsory contributions	CEAN		43 692	46 475	49 568	53 765	57 080	54 411	56 130	58 640	60 830
D.61121	Employees' compulsory contributions	GCSE		32 805	35 159	37 052	36 585	38 186	37 184	38 496	40 160	41 194
D.61131	Self- and non-employed persons' compulsory contributions	NMDE		2 727	2 825	2 930	2 860	3 053	2 850	2 720	2 641	2 458
D.611	Total	AIIH		79 224	84 459	89 550	93 210	98 319	94 445	97 346	101 441	104 482
Part	**CAPITAL ACCOUNT**											
	Changes in liabilities and net worth											
D.91	Other capital taxes											
	Paid to central government											
	Inheritance tax	GILF		2 821	3 100	3 471	3 764	3 130	2 305	2 592	2 856	3 041
	Tax on other capital transfers	GILG		50	50	50	50	50	50	50	50	50
	Development land tax and other	GCSV		–	–	–	–	–	–	–	–	–
	Tax paid on LG equal pay settlements	C625		–	–	54	53	77	46	–	30	38
	FSCS levies on private sector[3]	HZQ4		–	–	–	–	21 816	1 805	–	–	–
D.91	Total	NMGI		2 871	3 150	3 575	3 867	25 073	4 206	2 642	2 936	3 129
	TOTAL TAXES AND COMPULSORY SOCIAL CONTRIBUTIONS											
	Paid to central government	GCSS		398 825	426 299	460 891	481 206	513 507	456 756	489 425	518 266	521 136
	Paid to local government	GCST		20 068	21 260	22 421	23 618	24 697	25 388	25 929	26 241	26 613
	Paid to the European Union	FJWB		3 959	4 260	4 496	4 731	4 906	4 238	5 186	5 122	5 167
	Total	GCSU		422 852	451 819	487 808	509 555	543 110	486 382	520 540	549 629	552 916

1 Up until 1995/96 these payments are included in national non-domestic rates under production taxes other than on products

2 From 1990/1991 onwards these series only contain rates paid in Northern Ireland

3 Financial Services Compensation Scheme

23.7 Central government borrowing and repayment of debt
ESA95 sector S.1311 Unconsolidated

£ million

			2004	2005	2006	2007	2008	2009	2010	2011	2012
III.2	**FINANCIAL ACCOUNT**										
F.A	**Net acquisition of financial assets**										
F.1	Monetary gold and special drawing rights (SDRs)	NWXM	−37	−8	47	−50	−24	−132	18	333	111
F.2	Currency and deposits										
F.22	Transferable deposits										
F.221	Sterling deposits with UK MFIs	NART	−1 633	493	1 993	2 183	17 018	6 809	−6 246	6 551	1 054
F.2212	o/w Foreign currency deposits	NARV	−92	−92	289	456	−1 208	−782	484	4 824	−273
F.229	Deposits with rest of the world monetary financial institutions	NARX	−1 407	−1 516	−671	−579	2 913	540	423	140	935
F.29	Other deposits National Savings & tax	RYWO	–	–	161	3 761	11 021	7 075	−1 248	7 583	−898
F.2	Total currency and deposits	NARQ	−3 040	−1 023	1 483	5 365	30 952	14 424	−7 071	14 274	1 091
F.3	Securities other than shares										
F.331	Short term: money market instruments										
F.3315	Issued by UK MFIs	NSUN	751	213	1 768	−2 038	1 974	−2 144	−400	–	–
F.3316	Issued by other UK residents	NSRI	–	–	1 192	−1 142	–	882	1 349	3 336	−3 404
F.3319	Issued by the rest of the world	NASM	106	1 465	1 363	2 125	−1 029	471	466	315	−967
F.332	Medium (1 to 5 year) and long term (over 5 year) bonds										
F.3325-6	Issued by UK MFIs and other UK residents	NASV	–	856	−601	−21	4 978	−5 236	–	–	–
F.3329	Long term bonds issued by the rest of the world	NASW	1 551	370	−854	2 155	−1 085	7 834	5 824	4 745	6 123
F.34	Financial derivatives	CFZG	−173	137	−419	−284	538	936	273	214	−22
F.3	Total securities other than shares	NARZ	2 235	3 041	2 449	795	5 376	2 743	7 512	8 610	1 730
F.4	Loans										
F.42	Long term loans										
F.422	Loans secured on dwellings	NATM	–	–	–	–	–	–	–	–	–
F.424	Other long-term loans by UK residents	NATR	2 543	4 680	4 145	5 565	6 382	3 753	9 171	5 928	17 525
F.429	Other long-term loans by the rest of the world	NATS	–	–	–	–	–	–	–	–	–
F.4	Total loans	NATB	2 543	4 680	4 145	5 565	6 382	3 753	9 171	5 928	17 525
F.5	Shares and other equity										
F.51	Shares and other equity, excluding mutual funds' shares										
F.514	Quoted UK shares	NATY	−283	−177	−755	−727	11 325	40 217	−1 257	−1 508	−1 170
F.515	Unquoted UK shares	NATZ	–	−550	–	−2 102	−1 548	−279	−260	−260	−260
F.516	Other UK equity (including direct investment in property)	NAUA	−117	−1 249	−1 356	−2 416	–	−4 421	–	–	–
F.517	UK shares and bonds issued by other UK residents	NSOX	–	–	–	–	–	–	–	–	–
F.519	Shares and other equity issued by the rest of the world	NAUD	283	656	792	693	949	1 107	1 305	1 556	1 218
F.5	Total shares and other equity	NATT	−117	−1 320	−1 319	−4 552	10 726	36 624	−212	−212	−212
F.7	Other accounts receivable	NAUN	2 484	5 288	2 207	−2 043	11 069	1 289	6 215	6 434	1 710
F.A	**Total net acquisition of financial assets**	NARM	4 068	10 658	9 012	5 080	64 481	58 701	15 633	35 367	21 955

Source: Office for National Statistics; The Blue Book 2013

23.7
continued

Central government borrowing and repayment of debt
ESA95 sector S.1311 Unconsolidated

£ million

			2004	2005	2006	2007	2008	2009	2010	2011	2012
III.2	**FINANCIAL ACCOUNT** continued										
F.L	**Net acquisition of financial liabilities**										
F.2	Currency and deposits										
F.21	Currency	NAUV	171	180	154	122	163	115	152	96	225
F.29	Non-transferable deposits	NAVC	2 467	5 604	5 219	7 970	21 013	8 236	−7 407	10 250	−3 094
F.2	Total currency and deposits	NAUU	2 638	5 784	5 373	8 092	21 176	8 351	−7 255	10 346	−2 869
F.3	Securities other than shares										
F.331	Short term: money market instruments										
F.3311	Issued by UK central government	NAVF	999	−3 902	−1 752	−1 367	13 494	25 975	−2 077	14 454	−18 729
F.332	Medium (1 to 5 year) and long term (over 5 year) bonds										
F.33211	British government securities	NAVT	34 224	39 716	40 970	39 095	97 323	195 725	171 105	121 483	129 283
F.33212	Other central government bonds	NAVU	14	17	13	25	−1 490	−7	27	11	83
F.3	Total securities other than shares	NAVD	35 237	35 831	39 231	37 753	109 327	221 693	169 055	135 948	110 637
F.4	Loans										
F.41	Short term loans										
F.411	Loans by UK monetary financial institutions, excluding loans secured on dwellings & financial leasing	NAWH	6 368	2 567	−3 277	−568	7 605	−19 414	−1 338	3 325	−602
F.419	Loans by rest of the world monetary financial institutions	NAWL	–	–	–	–	–	–	–	–	–
F.42	Long term loans										
F.423	Finance leasing	NAWU	450	502	299	410	86	50	145	–	–
F.424	Other long term loans by UK residents	NAWV	−14	−12	−7	−6	−7	−18	−9	−9	−5
F.429	Other long term loans by the rest of the world	NAWW	−46	−65	7	−3	32	5	−495	−1 834	36
F.4	Total loans	NAWF	6 758	2 992	−2 978	−167	7 716	−19 377	−1 697	1 482	−571
F.7	Other accounts payable	NAXR	−1 435	4 650	6 394	206	−3 767	1 638	1 960	7 321	7 967
F.L	**Total net acquisition of financial liabilities**	NAUQ	43 198	49 257	48 020	45 884	134 452	212 305	162 063	155 097	115 164
B.9	**Net lending / borrowing**										
F.A	Total net acquisition of financial assets	NARM	4 068	10 658	9 012	5 080	64 481	58 701	15 633	35 367	21 955
-F.L	*less* Total net acquisition of financial liabilities	-NAUQ	−43 198	−49 257	−48 020	−45 884	−134 452	−212 305	−162 063	−155 097	−115 164
B.9f	Net lending (+) / net borrowing (-), from financial account	NZDX	−39 130	−38 599	−39 008	−40 804	−69 971	−153 604	−146 430	−119 730	−93 209
dB.9f	Statistical discrepancy	NZDW	−288	−976	459	−361	104	299	−604	−650	−891
B.9g	**Net lending (+) / net borrowing (-), from capital account**	NMFJ	−39 418	−39 575	−38 549	−41 165	−69 867	−153 305	−147 034	−120 380	−94 100

Source: Office for National Statistics; The Blue Book 2013

23.8 Central government net cash requirement on own account (receipts and outlays on a cash basis)

£ million

	Cash receipts								Cash outlays				
	HM Revenue and Customs												
	Total paid over[1]	Income tax[2]	Corpora-tion tax[2]	NICs[3]	V.A.T.[4]	Interest and dividends	Other receipts[5]	Total	Interest payments	Net acquisition of company securities[6]	Net departmental outlays[7]	Total	Own account net cash requirement
	1	2	3	4	5	6	7	8	9	10	11	12	13
	MIZX	RURC	ACCD	ABLP	EYOO	RUUL	RUUM	RUUN	RUUO	ABIF	RUUP	RUUQ	RUUX
2001	316517	111874	33520	62973	60282	8611	24643	349771	23132	-661	324633	347104	-5654
2002	315987	111559	28866	63992	63000	6954	25310	348251	19343	0	347612	366955	-2485
2003	325138	113712	28489	69360	67525	7335	25329	357802	20348	-39	379418	399727	-39062
2004	347514	121493	31160	77026	71907	6855	25137	379506	21027	0	400631	421658	-2667
2005	372567	130818	37820	83612	73012	6549	26341	405457	22434	0	421021	443455	18704
2006	401362	140616	47108	87156	76103	6640	28115	436117	25834	-347	448131	473618	41925
2007	422465	149968	43912	96656	80301	8251	30083	460799	25537	-2340	470169	493366	42152
2008	428380	157500	46487	98504	80709	9354	30556	468290	26033	19714	544720	590467	37998
2009	384875	147425	35402	95053	68637	6666	31282	422823	29304	41809	548810	619923	37501
2010	411846	147659	41253	95860	80865	5274	34063	451183	34008	0	569599	603607	32567
2011	434438	152095	42267	101033	95208	5757	42235	482430	43923	0	557494	601417	122177
2012	436196	151091	39710	102232	98619	9806	38399	484401	39016	-14287	565882	590611	197100
2001 Q1	89134	37819	8274	16842	14585	2621	5221	96976	4463	22	80126	84611	975
2001 Q2	72882	24620	5966	15923	15008	2120	5587	80589	6969	0	80187	87156	6435
2001 Q3	77727	27340	7322	15800	14707	1958	6631	86316	4754	-683	76620	80691	8192
2001 Q4	76774	22095	11958	14408	15982	1912	7204	85890	6946	0	87700	94646	1882
2002 Q1	87576	36973	6795	17037	15329	1853	5579	95008	3457	0	85219	88676	-2016
2002 Q2	74585	24145	5793	16649	15779	1688	5472	81745	6254	0	84027	90281	-5307
2002 Q3	78319	27737	7138	15720	15171	1797	7516	87632	3682	0	85156	88838	6123
2002 Q4	75507	22704	9140	14586	16721	1616	6743	83866	5950	0	93210	99160	-1940
2003 Q1	88763	36516	7197	17598	15780	2324	4994	96081	3801	-39	91497	95259	-4530
2003 Q2	76531	25184	5869	17760	16529	1547	6240	84318	7053	0	95376	102429	-5997
2003 Q3	81637	28919	7262	17404	17047	1728	6901	90266	4167	0	93496	97663	4791
2003 Q4	78207	23093	8161	16598	18169	1736	7194	87137	5327	0	99049	104376	-2801
2004 Q1	94758	38998	6785	20695	17330	2161	5013	101932	4704	0	97198	101902	1522
2004 Q2	82029	25114	7110	20601	18039	1546	5791	89366	5140	0	98121	103261	-14176
2004 Q3	87673	31464	8045	18585	17707	1549	7474	96696	5192	0	98424	103616	-12488
2004 Q4	83054	25917	9220	17145	18831	1599	6859	91512	5991	0	106888	112879	-15909
2005 Q1	103161	42707	9266	21767	18449	1939	4950	110050	5487	0	99835	105322	3511
2005 Q2	86274	28884	7766	20941	17342	1469	6592	94335	5568	0	105729	111297	-12365
2005 Q3	94524	32042	9765	22007	18188	1611	7430	103565	5836	0	105215	111051	6567
2005 Q4	88608	27185	11023	18897	19033	1530	7369	97507	5543	0	110242	115785	-5625
2006 Q1	112661	45408	13275	23677	18293	1783	5631	120075	6174	-347	107430	113257	8756
2006 Q2	91224	30604	7882	22211	18021	1497	6459	99180	5298	0	117434	122732	-6332
2006 Q3	100664	35891	12958	20798	18731	1428	8403	110495	8628	0	108129	116757	8536
2006 Q4	96813	28713	12993	20470	21058	1932	7622	106367	5734	0	115138	120872	1206
2007 Q1	117636	51926	10475	23795	19550	1897	4875	124408	6619	0	110361	116980	15294
2007 Q2	96004	29417	8015	25932	20123	1864	8204	106072	5959	-2340	121026	124645	-822
2007 Q3	107134	37488	12465	24165	19301	1986	9934	119054	6486	0	114418	120904	18111
2007 Q4	101691	31137	12957	22764	21327	2504	7070	111265	6473	0	124364	130837	7397
2008 Q1	126971	54549	12946	27550	19850	2646	5997	135614	6472	0	118768	125240	17239
2008 Q2	97153	34333	8509	23517	20087	2252	8154	107559	6449	0	131441	137890	-30
2008 Q3	108990	39286	12742	24801	21235	2266	9143	120399	6566	-255	150477	156788	13895
2008 Q4	95266	29332	12290	22636	19537	2190	7262	104718	6546	19969	144034	170549	6920
2009 Q1	115103	52753	9536	25930	17580	2016	3449	120568	6386	12536	131608	150530	21367
2009 Q2	85699	31277	6362	22727	16102	1892	9626	97217	8534	-2021	145058	151571	-4728
2009 Q3	93410	35562	8049	23574	16847	1357	9721	104488	7577	0	133158	140735	16962
2009 Q4	90663	27833	11455	22822	18108	1401	8486	100550	6807	31294	138986	177087	7486
2010 Q1	112559	47102	9939	26393	19103	1551	4493	118603	9271	0	139909	149180	18278
2010 Q2	94699	34366	7173	22870	19886	1049	8868	104616	6956	0	147380	154336	-6818
2010 Q3	107569	37334	11294	23950	20564	1370	11557	120496	10782	0	136851	147633	23552
2010 Q4	97019	28857	12847	22647	21312	1304	9145	107468	6999	0	145459	152458	6262
2011 Q1	120293	50993	10807	27081	21737	1836	9019	131148	11840	0	135142	146982	14505
2011 Q2	99487	33246	7345	24283	24084	1229	10614	111330	7392	0	145667	153059	-7428
2011 Q3	110502	37608	11600	25861	23984	1506	13346	125354	17071	0	137097	154168	18573
2011 Q4	104156	30248	12515	23808	25403	1186	9256	114598	7620	0	139588	147208	1850
2012 Q1	123458	49463	10691	27665	24821	3331	6142	132931	12421	-747	135613	147287	19572
2012 Q2	100129	33526	7271	24669	24469	3547	11978	115654	7542	-11109	147450	143883	-10374
2012 Q3	109251	37934	9843	25873	24524	1462	10843	121556	12622	-1174	136553	148001	30331
2012 Q4	103358	30168	11905	24025	24805	1466	9436	114260	6431	-1257	146266	151440	36339
2013 Q1	124619	51345	10435	27470	26772	13219	12683	150521	12701	639	153613	166953	65831

Relationships between columns 1+6+7=8; 9+10+11=12; 12-8=13

Sources: HM Revenue & Customs; Office for National Statistics

1 Comprises payments into the Consolidated Fund and all payovers of NICS excluding those for Northern Ireland.

2 Income tax includes capital gains tax and is net of any tax credits treated by HM Revenue and Customs as tax deductions.

3 UK receipts net of personal pension rebates; gross of Statutory Maternity Pay and Statutory Sick Pay.

4 Payments into Consolidated Fund.

5 Including some elements of expenditure not separately identified.

6 Mainly comprises privatisation proceeds.

7 Net of certain receipts, and excluding on-lending to local authorities and public corporations.

23.9 HM Revenue and Customs receipts

Amounts: £ million

Year	Total Paid Over [1]	Total HMRC receipts [2,3,8]	Total Income Tax [4]	Of which: PAYE Income Tax	Of which: SA Income Tax	Of which: CGT	Of which: Tax Credits (Neg)	NICs	VAT	Corporation Tax [5]	Bank payroll tax	Petroleum Revenue Tax	Fuel duties	IHT [6]	Stamp Taxes	Of which: Shares	Of which: Stamp Tax Land	Tobacco duties
	MIZX			BKMR	LISB	BKLO	MDYL	ABLP	EYOO	ACCD	JT2R	ACCJ	ACDD	ACCH		BKST	BKSU	ACDE
2001-02	314,959	321,064	107,994	91,937	15,281	3,034		63,168	61,026	32,041		1,310	21,916	2,357	6,984	2,852	4,132	7,754
2002-03	317,174	323,712	109,506	94,243	16,059	1,596		64,553	63,451	29,268		958	22,147	2,375	7,549	2,538	5,011	8,054
2003-04	331,133	343,632	117,917	101,389	15,772	2,225	-3,948	72,457	69,075	28,077		1,179	22,786	2,521	7,545	2,559	4,986	8,091
2004-05	355,917	371,045	127,294	108,699	17,141	2,282	-4,373	78,098	73,026	33,641		1,284	23,313	2,929	8,966	2,715	6,251	8,100
2005-06	382,067	397,929	134,916	113,894	18,077	3,042	-4,437	85,522	72,856	41,829		2,016	23,438	3,277	10,918	3,465	7,454	7,959
2006-07	406,337	423,674	147,712	124,799	20,306	3,830	-4,402	87,274	77,360	44,308		2,155	23,585	3,558	13,392	3,757	9,635	8,149
2007-08	431,800	451,063	151,738	126,760	22,443	5,268	-4,414	100,410	80,599	46,383		1,680	24,905	3,834	14,124	4,167	9,958	8,094
2008-09	416,512	439,103	153,442	128,470	22,531	7,852	-5,586	96,882	78,439	43,077		2,567	24,615	2,848	7,999	3,203	4,796	8,219
2009-10	382,331	408,509	144,881	122,584	21,708	2,491	-5,600	95,517	70,160	35,805		923	26,197	2,396	7,903	3,017	4,886	8,813
2010-11	419,580	447,159	153,491	132,263	22,108	3,601	-5,542	96,548	83,502	42,121	3,416	1,458	27,256	2,723	8,932	2,971	5,961	9,144
2011-12	437,594	466,634	150,939	132,189	20,334	4,337	-4,712	101,617	98,292	43,763	-2	2,032	26,800	2,913	8,920	2,794	6,125	9,551
2012-13	437,372	469,777	152,030	132,433	20,550	3,927	-2,984	102,037	100,572	41,047	0	1,737	26,571	3,888	9,141	2,234	6,907	9,681
Apr-09	36,349	39,027	13,705	12,327	253	2	-409	8,842	7,064	4,616	0	140	2,235	185	484	231	253	682
May-09	26,355	27,755	8,786	9,840	18	2	-459	7,507	4,881	645	0	119	2,112	174	574	262	312	1,427
Jun-09	22,995	25,647	10,151	9,800	255	2	-504	6,378	4,157	1,101	0	108	2,195	197	563	230	333	205
Jul-09	39,550	42,489	16,056	10,192	5,455	1	-567	8,590	6,968	6,178	0	87	2,146	196	666	264	401	574
Aug-09	28,412	29,979	11,056	9,599	1,832	1	-472	7,573	5,356	489	0	144	2,247	190	612	212	400	771
Sep-09	25,448	27,825	9,915	9,578	112	2	-430	7,411	4,523	1,382	0	-165	2,269	233	701	225	475	726
Oct-09	36,573	38,332	10,247	9,697	-23	2	-454	7,637	8,012	7,201	0	57	2,198	217	705	292	413	843
Nov-09	26,712	29,192	9,315	9,647	-123	2	-440	7,514	5,461	1,338	0	81	2,261	189	705	243	462	714
Dec-09	27,378	29,938	9,668	9,755	297	2	-509	7,671	4,635	2,916	0	58	2,285	210	841	354	486	715
Jan-10	48,185	50,112	19,067	10,289	7,976	1,558	-423	8,829	8,233	7,296	0	59	1,949	181	737	240	497	987
Feb-10	35,836	37,294	14,957	10,310	5,124	877	-447	8,545	6,587	1,469	0	11	2,193	191	578	194	384	723
Mar-10	28,538	30,921	11,957	11,550	531	41	-486	9,019	4,283	1,174	0	224	2,107	234	738	269	469	446
Apr-10	43,631	45,749	15,679	15,578	97	4	-408	9,285	9,465	5,207	0	-4	2,378	216	729	265	464	1,331
May-10	26,282	28,254	9,905	10,191	8	3	-438	7,450	5,463	744	0	57	2,233	207	668	282	386	234
Jun-10	24,786	27,265	10,126	10,175	-8	4	-507	6,135	4,957	1,222	0	48	2,245	246	736	251	485	645
Jul-10	45,103	48,490	16,960	10,931	5,898	3	-531	8,499	8,447	8,515	0	30	2,304	283	923	276	647	1,275
Aug-10	35,405	36,618	11,534	10,060	1,503	3	-467	7,897	7,527	1,069	3,107	44	2,306	218	910	294	616	386
Sep-10	27,061	29,821	10,286	10,185	39	5	-461	7,554	4,591	1,710	295	560	2,307	216	688	163	525	731
Oct-10	40,076	41,955	10,644	10,158	-25	10	-440	7,542	8,689	9,298	0	82	2,367	206	795	268	527	1,035
Nov-10	29,608	31,669	9,395	10,273	-74	11	-463	7,595	7,623	1,260	0	115	2,381	210	775	256	519	581
Dec-10	27,335	30,148	10,204	10,123	305	4	-507	7,510	5,000	2,289	-50	123	2,243	233	821	282	539	677
Jan-11	52,321	56,309	21,996	10,873	10,860	2,696	-412	9,101	8,803	8,270	30	86	2,141	196	607	163	444	1,012

23.9 HM Revenue and Customs receipts

Amounts: £ million

Year	Total Paid Over [1]	Total HMRC receipts [2,3,8]	Total Income Tax [4]	Of which: PAYE Income Tax	Of which: SA Income Tax	Of which: CGT	Of which: Tax Credits (Neg)	NICs	VAT	Corporation Tax [5]	Bank payroll tax	Petroleum Revenue Tax	Fuel duties	IHT [6]	Stamp Taxes	Of which: Shares	Of which: Stamp Tax Land	Tobacco duties
	MIZX			BKMR	LISB	BKLO	MDYL	ABLP	EYOO	ACCD	JT2R	ACCJ	ACDD	ACCH		BKST	BKSU	ACDE
Feb-11	38,809	39,198	14,867	11,499	3,152	786	-431	8,832	8,384	1,141	43	64	2,203	231	591	217	374	797
Mar-11	29,163	31,682	11,894	12,216	352	72	-475	9,148	4,551	1,396	-9	253	2,148	259	688	253	435	440
Apr-11	44,592	46,148	13,440	13,709	85	7	-380	9,916	10,608	5,594	1	124	2,384	221	819	267	552	1,492
May-11	29,847	32,640	10,570	10,548	-61	5	-395	7,990	7,999	1,094	0	83	2,157	241	659	244	415	185
Jun-11	25,047	27,749	10,426	10,584	-72	9	-437	6,377	5,474	657	0	99	2,269	257	595	218	377	651
Jul-11	47,037	50,789	17,069	11,238	5,104	6	-438	9,484	9,960	8,603	0	63	2,254	254	862	289	573	805
Aug-11	34,904	36,633	12,220	10,803	1,723	6	-424	8,476	8,552	1,278	8	70	2,187	278	812	241	571	808
Sep-11	28,561	30,674	9,545	10,283	86	2	-379	7,901	5,470	1,761	0	577	2,311	275	833	252	581	878
Oct-11	42,782	44,470	10,224	10,421	-24	2	-390	8,017	10,560	9,756	-9	114	2,305	235	810	244	566	935
Nov-11	32,548	35,635	10,671	10,378	-64	6	-390	7,983	9,465	1,071	-3	117	2,302	240	749	201	548	1,037
Dec-11	28,818	31,699	10,540	10,157	441	4	-420	7,808	5,381	2,786	0	125	2,262	216	806	233	572	478
Jan-12	56,559	60,168	21,929	11,112	10,184	3,324	-358	9,693	10,343	9,511	0	67	2,100	223	600	140	461	855
Feb-12	37,279	38,168	13,112	11,291	2,650	868	-383	9,000	8,796	1,060	0	72	2,197	253	639	208	431	668
Mar-12	29,620	31,860	11,192	11,666	281	97	-320	8,972	5,684	592	0	521	2,070	219	735	257	478	760
Apr-12	44,065	46,549	14,148	14,179	19	11	-233	9,798	10,232	5,177	0	150	2,386	237	683	204	479	1,818
May-12	30,304	33,041	10,166	10,912	-103	4	-284	8,335	8,363	1,244	0	127	2,119	262	609	75	534	136
Jun-12	25,760	28,595	9,956	10,264	-67	3	-247	6,536	5,873	1,137	0	53	2,247	256	722	213	509	600
Jul-12	46,840	50,429	17,464	11,290	6,146	4	-284	9,699	10,058	7,386	0	101	2,212	289	855	189	666	759
Aug-12	33,976	36,699	11,443	10,648	977	4	-269	8,287	9,047	1,208	0	108	2,237	337	901	218	683	1,054
Sep-12	28,435	30,682	9,794	10,318	28	2	-222	7,887	5,420	1,774	0	533	2,260	236	754	166	588	680
Oct-12	41,068	43,706	11,030	10,772	-12	9	-250	8,259	10,248	8,171	0	126	2,220	283	798	174	624	979
Nov-12	31,900	33,771	9,265	10,301	-67	4	-239	7,890	8,756	1,304	0	141	2,324	257	842	231	611	769
Dec-12	30,404	32,753	10,596	10,204	409	4	-250	7,876	5,803	2,795	0	107	2,331	238	779	188	591	622
Jan-13	57,229	61,983	23,578	11,103	10,685	2,971	-233	9,926	11,210	8,233	0	75	2,008	222	782	159	623	1,052
Feb-13	36,473	38,912	13,588	11,018	2,347	820	-230	8,751	9,129	1,352	0	115	2,155	164	647	145	502	566
Mar-13	30,918	32,656	11,002	11,426	189	90	-241	8,793	6,434	1,265	0	101	2,072	338	767	271	496	648
Apr-13*	44,262	48,137	15,946	14,086	52	2	-211	9,795	10,177	5,023	0	77	2,258	313	882	222	660	1,725

23.9 HM Revenue and Customs receipts

Amounts: £ million

Year	Spirits duties ACDF	Beer duties ACDG	Wines duties ACDH	Cider duties ACDI	Betting & Gaming ACDJ	Air Passenger Duty ACDP	Insurance Premium Tax ACDO	Landfill Tax DOLC	Climate Change Levy LSNS	Aggregates Levy MDUP	Swiss Capital Tax	Misc	Customs Duties ADET	Child and Working Tax Credits Net payments	Negative tax (MDYL)	Payment of entitlement (MDYN)	Child Benefit[7] Net Payments
2001-02	1,919	2,899	1,982	155	1,439	806	1,861	502	555			-1	2,042				
2002-03	2,273	2,935	1,936	153	1,292	816	2,138	541	829	247		2	1,907				
2003-04	2,362	3,044	2,006	153	1,347	791	2,294	607	832	339		-8	1,941	13,361	3,948	9,411	9,425
2004-05	2,385	3,101	2,233	157	1,421	864	2,359	672	764	334		0	2,195	15,896	4,373	11,523	9,593
2005-06	2,309	3,076	2,308	168	1,421	905	2,343	733	744	326		1	2,258	17,332	4,437	12,895	9,770
2006-07	2,256	3,072	2,385	200	1,391	971	2,314	804	712	321		1	2,325	18,684	4,402	14,282	10,156
2007-08	2,374	3,067	2,641	220	1,481	1,994	2,306	877	688	339		0	2,456	20,030	4,414	15,617	10,603
2008-09	2,358	3,127	2,741	244	1,474	1,862	2,281	954	716	334		0	2,659	24,098	5,586	18,513	11,262
2009-10	2,570	3,182	2,949	311	1,439	1,856	2,259	842	695	275		0	2,646	27,601	5,600	22,001	11,824
2010-11	2,675	3,296	3,101	324	1,533	2,155	2,400	1,065	674	288		0	2,998	28,879	5,542	23,338	12,160
2011-12	2,889	3,463	3,356	329	1,633	2,607	2,941	1,090	676	290	0	0	2,912	29,830	4,712	25,118	12,177
2012-13	2,931	3,426	3,537	326	1,680	2,791	3,021	1,092	635	265	342	0	2,854	29,888	2,984	26,904	12,167
Apr-09	210	267	242	24	101	142	99	150	16	30		0	201	2,060	409	1,651	962
May-09	232	319	256	26	135	143	443	19	181	20		0	212	2,230	459	1,771	990
Jun-09	155	260	215	27	117	143	2	-43	9	15		0	194	2,431	504	1,927	987
Jul-09	187	273	248	34	106	156	110	188	40	39		0	213	2,702	567	2,135	1,023
Aug-09	189	296	247	30	158	184	481	49	130	21		0	226	2,292	472	1,820	993
Sep-09	191	280	236	29	106	162	-1	15	3	14		0	224	2,160	430	1,730	969
Oct-09	210	259	246	24	104	179	132	189	40	38		0	246	2,259	454	1,805	999
Nov-09	308	264	290	28	147	158	435	50	102	20		0	250	2,186	440	1,746	948
Dec-09	335	284	328	28	110	140	1	-25	2	14		0	229	2,505	509	1,996	1,033
Jan-10	213	300	253	26	108	154	97	189	49	33		0	217	2,133	423	1,710	991
Feb-10	132	177	194	15	142	85	454	45	120	20		0	225	2,205	447	1,758	917
Mar-10	208	203	194	20	105	210	6	16	3	11		0	209	2,438	486	1,952	1,012
Apr-10	330	300	311	36	120	156	108	181	61	31		0	232	2,178	408	1,770	932
May-10	116	285	212	21	139	106	436	44	141	20		0	212	2,265	438	1,826	1,012
Jun-10	170	380	255	42	124	190	2	3	1	15		0	226	2,591	507	2,084	1,014
Jul-10	217	273	274	38	142	180	121	185	53	42		0	256	2,711	531	2,180	1,052
Aug-10	170	250	259	28	159	214	500	105	115	24		0	258	2,400	467	1,933	1,093
Sep-10	196	288	237	27	99	201	2	9	1	14		0	265	2,398	461	1,937	1,024
Oct-10	219	254	261	23	129	183	120	182	40	41		0	274	2,297	440	1,856	993
Nov-10	306	267	291	24	155	185	485	87	93	23		0	274	2,423	463	1,960	960
Dec-10	363	295	343	22	106	188	0	0	3	14		0	267	2,689	507	2,181	1,061
Jan-11	238	306	255	28	132	196	114	202	41	36		0	235	2,149	412	1,738	955

23.9 HM Revenue and Customs receipts

Amounts: £ million

Year	Spirits duties ACDF	Beer duties ACDG	Wines duties ACDH	Cider duties ACDI	Betting & Gaming ACDJ	Air Passenger Duty ACDP	Insurance Premium Tax ACDO	Landfill Tax DOLC	Climate Change Levy LSNS	Aggregates Levy MDUP	Swiss Capital Tax	Misc	Customs Duties ADET	Child and Working Tax Credits Net payments	Child and Working Tax Credits Negative tax (MDYL)	Child and Working Tax Credits Payment of entitlement (MDYN)	Child Benefit[7] Net Payments
Feb-11	137	182	203	16	123	91	510	30	120	17		0	262	2,259	431	1,828	981
Mar-11	213	217	203	20	106	267	4	37	5	12		0	236	2,521	475	2,045	1,082
Apr-11	322	345	314	32	118	182	123	192	26	32		0	236	2,403	380	2,024	1,075
May-11	128	287	230	28	174	216	531	58	161	22		0	216	2,439	395	2,043	1,037
Jun-11	180	302	271	31	104	227	1	7	4	15		0	231	2,660	437	2,224	938
Jul-11	228	293	270	31	156	226	150	188	45	41		0	239	2,667	438	2,229	1,040
Aug-11	194	290	268	29	186	274	621	102	120	23		0	254	2,599	424	2,175	1,038
Sep-11	225	317	291	30	109	255	12	12	3	14		0	230	2,390	379	2,011	991
Oct-11	235	278	278	27	134	233	157	215	40	42		0	272	2,417	390	2,027	932
Nov-11	310	285	321	28	154	234	605	52	103	21		0	274	2,453	390	2,064	1,058
Dec-11	402	320	404	29	106	177	3	19	2	13		0	240	2,657	420	2,238	1,155
Jan-12	231	313	259	23	167	223	149	194	46	39		0	235	2,258	358	1,900	900
Feb-12	154	193	215	18	122	179	576	34	122	17		0	255	2,409	383	2,026	973
Mar-12	281	240	236	23	105	180	14	17	3	11		0	230	2,478	320	2,158	1,040
Apr-12	352	386	381	36	147	213	133	186	54	33	0	0	220	2,378	233	2,145	943
May-12	115	238	217	22	154	223	574	45	139	18	0	0	216	2,881	284	2,598	1,180
Jun-12	202	336	284	35	105	231	8	11	2	12	0	0	231	2,401	247	2,154	949
Jul-12	202	286	259	28	163	246	157	219	55	39	0	0	231	2,766	284	2,481	1,042
Aug-12	184	287	291	31	188	284	627	57	108	19	0	0	268	2,666	269	2,397	1,059
Sep-12	228	308	282	31	118	272	16	38	2	12	0	0	261	2,220	222	1,998	987
Oct-12	222	251	261	23	127	246	189	184	44	37	0	0	252	2,527	250	2,276	1,009
Nov-12	365	289	355	27	164	260	561	60	82	19	0	0	278	2,418	239	2,179	996
Dec-12	430	318	427	29	124	195	12	68	2	14	0	0	234	2,532	250	2,282	1,027
Jan-13	217	293	291	24	147	237	163	153	48	36	342	0	209	2,351	233	2,117	1,016
Feb-13	151	205	236	20	150	119	562	66	97	16	0	0	232	2,302	230	2,072	895
Mar-13	263	230	252	21	95	263	20	6	3	11	0	0	225	2,446	241	2,205	1,064
Apr-13*	387	283	370	33	161	242	171	198	57	30	0	0	217	2,394	211	2,183	886

Updated November 2013

[1] Comprises of payments into the Consolidated Fund and all payovers of NICs excluding those of Northern Ireland.
[2] Total HMRC Receipts includes payable tax credits, and all payments into the Consolidated Fund and all payovers of NICs including those of Northern Ireland.
[3] Consistent with the OBR definition published in the supplementary table 2.8 i.e. on a cash basis.
[4] Income tax excludes capital gains tax and is gross of any tax credits treated as tax deductions (negative). Also includes other smaller elements of income tax
[5] Gross of tax credits that offset tax liabilities and includes Bank Levy. See table 11.1a for an annual Bank Levy total (due to be updated on the 10th August).
[6] Includes non cash receipts
[7] From April 2011, the Child Benefit series has been revised to ensure consistency with HMRC Resource Accounts
[8] Total of columns D, G to AE
* Provisional

For any queries regarding this table, please email Karen Mason
Room 2/64, 100 Parliament Street, London, WC1A 2BQ

23.10 INCOME TAX PERSONAL ALLOWANCES AND RELIEFS, 1990-91 TO 2013-14

| | Non-aged allowances | | | Aged allowances | | | | |
| | | | | Personal | | Married couple's | | |
Financial years	Personal	Married couple's (1)	Blind person's (2)	65-74	75+	65-74	75+	Income limit (3)
1990-91	3,005	1,720	1,080	3,670	3,820	2,145	2,185	12,300
1991-92	3,295	1,720	1,080	4,020	4,180	2,355	2,395	13,500
1992-93	3,445	1,720	1,080	4,200	4,370	2,465	2,505	14,200
1993-94	3,445	1,720	1,080	4,200	4,370	2,465	2,505	14,200
1994-95	3,445	1,720 (4)	1,200	4,200	4,370	2,665 (4)	2,705 (4)	14,200
1995-96	3,525	1,720 (5)	1,200	4,630	4,800	2,995 (5)	3,035 (5)	14,600
1996-97	3,765	1,790 (5)	1,250	4,910	5,090	3,115 (5)	3,155 (5)	15,200
1997-98	4,045	1,830 (5)	1,280	5,220	5,400	3,185 (5)	3,225 (5)	15,600
1998-99	4,195	1,900 (5)	1,330	5,410	5,600	3,305 (5)	3,345 (5)	16,200
1999-00	4,335	1,970 (6)	1,380	5,720	5,980	5,125 (6)	5,195 (6)	16,800
2000-01	4,385	-	1,400	5,790	6,050	5,185 (6,7)	5,255 (6,7)	17,000
2001-02	4,535	-	1,450	5,990	6,260	5,365 (6,7)	5,435 (6,7)	17,600
2002-03	4,615	-	1,480	6,100	6,370	5,465 (6,7)	5,535 (6,7)	17,900
2003-04	4,615	-	1,510	6,610	6,720	5,565 (6,7)	5,635 (6,7)	18,300
2004-05	4,745	-	1,560	6,830	6,950	5,725 (6,7)	5,795 (6,7)	18,900
2005-06	4,895	-	1,610	7,090	7,220	5,905 (6,7)	5,975 (6,7)	19,500
2006-07	5,035	-	1,660	7,280	7,420	6,065 (6,7)	6,135 (6,7)	20,100
2007-08	5,225	-	1,730	7,550	7,690	6,285 (6,7)	6,365 (6,7)	20,900
2008-09	6,035	-	1,800	9,030	9,180	6,535 (6,7)	6,625 (6,7)	21,800
2009-10	6,475	-	1,890	9,490	9,640	- (6,7)	6,965 (6,7)	22,900
2010-11	6,475	-	1,890	9,490	9,640	- (6,7)	6,965 (6,7)	22,900
2011-12	7,475	-	1,980	9,940	10,090	- (6,7)	7,295 (6,7)	24,000
2012-13	8,105	-	2,100	10,500	10,660	- (6,7)	7,705 (6,7)	25,400
2013-14	9,440	-	2,160	10,500 (8)	10,660 (9)	- (6,7)	7,915 (6,7)	26,100

Table updated March 2013

(1) Given in addition to the personal allowance to married couples. The additional personal allowance and the widow's bereavement allowance have the same value as the married couple's allowance.
(2) Married couples where both spouses are blind get double the single amount.
(3) Where an individual's income exceeds the income limit, their personal allowance is reduced by £1 for every £2 above the income limit.
(4) Allowance available at a flat rate of 20%.
(5) Allowance available at a flat rate of 15%.
(6) Allowance available at a flat rate of 10%.
(7) At least one of the partners must have been born before 6 April 1935.
(8) Available to people born in the period 6 April 1938 to 5 April 1948.
(9) Available to people born on or before 5 April 1938.

23.11

RATES OF INCOME TAX: 1990-91 TO 2013-14

	1999-2000 Bands of taxable income(1) £	Rate of tax %	2000-01 Bands of taxable income(1) £	Rate of tax %	2001-02 Bands of taxable income(1) £	Rate of tax %
Starting rate	1-1,500	10	1-1,520	10	1-1,880	10
Basic rate	1,501-28,000	23 (5)	1,521-28,400	22 (5)	1,881-29,400	22 (5)
Higher rate	Over 28,000	40 (6)	Over 28,400	40 (6)	Over 29,400	40 (6)

	2002-03 Bands of taxable income(1) £	Rate of tax %	2003-04 Bands of taxable income(1) £	Rate of tax %	2004-05 Bands of taxable income(1) £	Rate of tax %
Starting rate	1-1,920	10	1-1,960	10	1-2,020.	10
Basic rate	1,921-29,900	22 (5)	1,961-30,500	22 (5)	2,021-31,400	22 (5)
Higher rate	Over 29,900	40 (6)	Over 30,500	40 (6)	Over 31,400	40 (6)

	2005-06 Bands of taxable income(1) £	Rate of tax %	2006-07 Bands of taxable income(1) £	Rate of tax %	2007-08 Bands of taxable income(1) £	Rate of tax %
Starting rate	1-2.090	10	1-2,150	10	1-2,230	10
Basic rate	2,091-32,400	22 (5)	2,151-33,300	22 (5)	2,231-34,600	22 (5)
Higher rate	Over 32,400	40 (6)	Over 33,300	40 (6)	Over 34,600	40 (6)

	2008-09 Bands of taxable income(1) £	Rate of tax %	2009-10 Bands of taxable income(1) £	Rate of tax %	2010-11 Bands of taxable income(1) £	Rate of tax %
Basic rate (7)	1-34,800	20 (8)	1-37,400	20 (8)	1-37,400	20 (8)
Higher rate	Over 34,800	40 (6)	Over 37,400	40 (6)	Over 37,400	40 (6)
Additional Rate	Not Applicable		Not Applicable		Over 150,000	50 (9)

	2011-12 Bands of taxable income(1) £	Rate of tax %	2012-13 Bands of taxable income(1) £	Rate of tax %	2013-14 Bands of taxable income(1) £	Rate of tax %
Basic rate (7)	1-35,000	20 (8)	1-34,370	20 (8)	1-32,010	20 (8)
Higher rate	Over 35,000	40 (6)	Over 34,370	40 (6)	Over 32,010	40 (6)
Additional Rate	Over 150,000	50 (9)	Over 150,000	50 (9)	Over 150,000	45 (9)

Table updated March 2013

(1) Taxable income is defined as gross income for income tax purposes less any allowances and reliefs available at the taxpayer's marginal rate.

(2) Applies to the income of discretionary and accumulation trusts. Prior to 1993-94 trusts paid tax at the basic rate, with an additional rate of 10%

(3) The basic rate of tax on dividend income is 20%.

(4) The basic rate of tax on dividends and savings income is 20%.

(5) The basic rate of tax on dividends is 10% and savings income is 20%.

(6) The higher rate of tax on dividends is 32.5%.

(7) From 2008-09 the starting rate is abolished for all non-savings income (e.g. employment, self-employed trading profits, pensions and property income), which is the first slice of income to be charged to income tax. The starting rate and the starting rate limit for savings is shown in the table below. Where taxable non-savings income does not fully occupy the starting rate limit the remainder of the starting rate limit is available for savings income.

(8) The basic rate of tax on dividends is 10%.

(9) The additional rate of tax on dividends is 42.5% for 2010-11 to 2012-13, and 37.5% thereafter.

23.12 Non-domestic rating in England & Wales

Analysis of 2010 rating lists as at 1 April 2013 by detailed property type by country

Numbers: thousands; Rateable values: £ million

	Country					
	England		Wales		England & Wales	
	Number of properties	Rateable value	Number of properties	Rateable value	Number of properties	Rateable value
Commercial						
Advertising rights	36	65	1	1	37	66
Holiday sites	6	187	1	27	7	214
Garages & petrol stations	38	1,086	3	51	41	1,137
Hotels etc.	49	1,454	5	57	54	1,511
Pubs & wine bars	55	1,615	5	86	59	1,701
Markets	2	39	0	2	2	40
Offices	337	13,225	15	270	353	13,495
Car parks	56	534	2	19	58	552
Restaurants & cafes	37	1,109	2	43	39	1,151
Shops	468	12,942	28	594	496	13,536
Warehouses & stores	207	7,902	12	351	218	8,253
Other commercial	31	777	2	22	34	799
All commercial	1,322	40,934	77	1,522	1,399	42,456
Educational, training & cultural						
Local authority schools & colleges	22	1,752	2	94	24	1,846
Libraries and museums	4	250	0	10	5	260
Private schools & colleges	3	386	0	4	3	390
Universities	1	430	0	23	1	453
Other educational, training and cultural	12	271	1	8	13	280
All educational, training & cultural	43	3,090	3	139	46	3,229
Utilities						
Docks	0	78	0	5	0	83
Electricity companies	0	1,282	0	152	1	1,433
British Gas - Transco	0	89	0	5	0	94
Railways	0	347	0	14	0	360
Telecommunications	0	231	0	8	0	239
Water companies	0	736	0	45	0	781
Bus stations, moorings etc.	2	46	0	1	2	47
Other utilities	5	1,051	1	54	6	1,105
All utilities	7	3,860	1	283	8	4,143
Industrial						
Factories, mills & workshops	223	5,159	14	339	237	5,498
Quarries, mines etc.	5	450	0	23	5	473
Other industrial	3	463	0	35	3	498
All industrial	231	6,072	15	397	246	6,470
Leisure						
Community centres & halls	32	592	3	29	35	621
Sports centres & stadia	1	177	0	11	1	188
Sports grounds, golf courses etc	10	249	1	13	11	262
Cinemas, theatres etc.	2	219	0	12	3	232
Other leisure	36	376	1	15	37	391
All leisure	81	1,613	5	80	87	1,693
Miscellaneous						
Cemeteries and crematoria	2	32	0	2	3	34
Medical facilities	26	1,291	2	67	28	1,358
Local government offices	2	199	0	17	2	215
Police stations & courts	2	389	0	18	3	407
Hostels & homes	1	22	0	2	2	25
Other properties	48	1,583	3	54	51	1,637
All miscellaneous	82	3,517	6	160	88	3,677
All properties	1,766	59,085	107	2,581	1,873	61,667

Notes on the Table

1. This table shows the number of properties and rateable values for the 2010 list as at 1 April 2013 by detailed property type by country,

2. The analysis by type of property has been derived from the property codes used by the Valuation Office Agency for the rating lists. The individual codes are grouped into broad classes, which have been used to provide six broad groupings. Within each grouping various categories are identified, with the remaining properties assigned to an 'other' category.

3. Local government offices are shown in the table under the 'Miscellaneous' category but are included in the figures for property type 'Offices' in all other tables.

23.13 Revenue expenditure of local authorities

£ million

	2007-08 [1] outturn	2008-09 [1] outturn	2009-10 [2] outturn	2010-11 [3] outturn	2011-12 [3] outturn	2012-13 [3] outturn	2013-14 [3] outturn	2013/14 [3] budget	2014/15 [3] budget
England									
Education [4,5]	40,135	42,148	44,471	45,283	40,219	37,134	35,878	38,793	35,835
Highways and Transport	5,634	5,679	6,541	5,669	5,381	4,823	4,775	5,129	4,814
Social care [6,7]	18,587	19,604	20,963	21,062	21,160	21,136	21,526	21,286	22,090
of which:									
Children Social Care				6,654	6,423	6,612	6,952	6,636	7,726
Adult Social Care				14,408	14,738	14,524	14,574	14,650	14,364
Public Health [8]							2,504	2,699	2,849
Housing (excluding HRA) [9]	15,841	16,964	20,022	21,032	21,868	22,744	22,983	22,596	22,945
Cultural, environmental and planning	10,143	10,474	11,083	10,676	9,742	9,407	9,193	9,345	9,029
of which:									
Cultural	3,188	3,297	3,465	3,278	3,022	2,940	2,836	2,789	2,614
Environmental	4,836	5,087	5,308	5,201	5,068	5,036	4,986	5,291	5,139
Planning and development	2,120	2,091	2,310	2,197	1,652	1,430	1,371	1,265	1,276
Police	11,704	11,555	12,022	11,948	11,650	11,337	10,920	11,166	11,121
Fire	2,233	2,104	2,177	2,165	2,118	2,119	2,099	2,174	2,123
Central services [10]	3,596	3,846	3,771	3,608	3,342	3,412	3,281	3,679	3,686
Other	369	643	9	-267	-267	-193	-256	229	224
Appropriations to (+) / from (-) accumulated absences account				64	6	22	39	-6	-4
Reversal of revenue expenditure funded from capital under statue (RECS) [11]			-1,883						
Net current expenditure	108,241	113,018	119,176	121,240	115,219	111,941	112,941	117,091	114,711
Capital financing	3,008	2,974	3,710	4,135	4,639	4,348	4,465	4,441	4,482
Capital Expenditure charged to Revenue Account	1,096	1,706	1,964	2,598	2,915	1,307	1,412	3,316	3,120
Interest receipts	-1,862	-1,926	-780	-663	-860	-815	-836	-417	-744
Pension Interest Costs and expected return on Pension assets	4,808	7,042							
Appropriation to/from Pension Reserves	-5,595	-6,395							
Other non-current expenditure [12,13]	3,449	3,459	4,163	4,136	3,907	4,195	-240	-37	-199
Specific grants outside Aggregate External Finance (AEF)	-20,762	-21,772	-24,958	-27,191	-26,542	-26,829	-22,810	22,229	22,617
Revenue expenditure	92,384	98,107	103,276	104,256	99,278	94,148	94,932	102,165	98,753
Specific and special grants inside AEF	-44,485	-42,920	-45,639	-45,750	-45,502	-41,820	-40,366	-43,917	-40,763
Area Based Grant (ABG)		-3,050	-3,314	-4,363					
Local Services Support Grant (LSSG)					-253	-223	-77	-66	-33
Net revenue expenditure	47,898	52,137	54,323	54,143	53,524	52,105	54,489	58,182	57,957
Appropriation to/from reserves (excluding pension reserves)	1,497	248	-308	1,261	2,553	2,592	2,320	-1,183	-2,107
Other adjustments	2	2	1	-23	0	0	-1	0	-1
Formula Grant [13,14]	-25,639	-27,495	-28,269	-29,012	-29,436	-27,802	-22,656	-33,504	-31,603
of which:									
Police grant	-4,028	-4,136	-4,253	-4,374	-4,546	-4,224	-7,565	-7,565	-7,784
Revenue support grant	-3,105	-2,854	-4,501	-3,122	-5,873	-448	-15,091	-15,175	-12,675
Redistributed non-domestic rates	-18,506	-20,506	-19,515	-21,517	-19,017	-23,129			
Retained income from Rate Retention Scheme							-10,554	-10,763	-11,144
General Greater London Authority Grant	-38	-48	-48	-48	-63	-50			
Other items	-112	-85	-65	-65	-126	-131	-167	-124	-281
Council tax requirement	23,608	24,759	25,633	26,254	26,451	26,715	23,431	23,371	23,965

1 Produced on a Financial Reporting Standard 17 (FRS17) basis

2 Produced on a non-FRS17 and PFI off balance sheet basis.

3 Produced on a non-International Accounting Standard 19 (IAS19) and PFI off balance sheet basis.

4 Education expenditure for 2011-12 and 2012-13 are not comparable to previous years due to a number of schools changing their status to become academies, which are centrally funded rather than funded by local authorities.

5 Includes mandatory student awards and inter-authority education recoupment.

6 Social Care expenditure for 2011-12 is not comparable to previous years due to a change in responsibility between NHS and local government for adults with learning disabilities, where from 1st April 2011 the transfer of funding was made directly from Department of Health to LAs, where they now receive a new non-ring fenced grant which amounts to £1.2 billion in 2011-12.

7 Includes supported employment.

8 There was a transfer of Public Health duties to local authorities in 2013-14, following the Health and Social Care Act 2012

9 Includes mandatory rent allowances and rent rebates.

10 Includes court services.

11 Net current expenditure estimates for 2009-10 are not fully comparable to 2010-11 figures owing to revenue expenditure funded from capital by statute (RECS) distributed across all services. Furthermore 2010-11 net current expenditure figures include liabilities for short term accumulated compensated absences (e.g. untaken annual leave entitlement), distributed across all the services, which makes comparisons against previous years not fully comparable. However total net current expenditure has been adjusted for both 2009-10 and 2010-11 so that they can be compared.

12 Includes:

(i) Gross expenditure on council tax benefit.

(ii) Expenditure on council tax reduction scheme.

(iii) Discretionary (non-domestic) rate relief.

(iv) Flood defence payments to the Environment Agency.

(v) Bad debt provision.

(vi) Appropriations to(+)/ from(-) financial instruments adjustment account

(vii) Appropriations to(+)/ from(-) unequal pay back pay account

(viii) Private Finance Initiative (PFI) schemes - difference from service charge

(ix) Business Rates Supplement

(x) Community Infrastructure Levy

(xi) Carbon Reduction Commitment

13 Localisation of council tax support; prior to 2013-14, local authorities were given a grant outside AEF by the Department for Work and Pensions (DWP) to cover the cost of council tax benefit in their area. In 2013-14, local authorities and local policing bodies in England will receive £3.7 billion towards the cost of local council tax support schemes. The funding is now provided as part of the revenue support grant system and reduces the council tax requirement to local authorities.

14 Business Rates; from April 2013 local authorities, except police authorities, now retain a share of business rates and keep the growth on that share, thereby giving them a significant financial incentive to help deliver growth locally. This will have a significant effect on the amount of Revenue Support Grant each authority receives in 2013-14. In addition, police authorities, which are not part of the rates retention scheme, will receive all of their funding through Police Grant from 2013-14 onwards.

23.13 Revenue expenditure of local authorities

	2007/08 outturn	2008/09 outturn	2009/10 outturn	2010/11 outturn	2011/12 outturn	2012/13 outturn	2013/14 provisional Outturn	2014/15 Budget Estimates
Scotland [21]								
Net revenue expenditure on general fund	11,023	11,981	12,369	12,600,847	12,361,278	12,476,636	11,341,511	11,418,220
Wales [15]								
Education	2,325.6	2,427.5	2,550.4	2,584.3	2,590.5	2,630	2,641 (r)	2,630
Personal social services	1,302.9	1,348.8	1,418.0	1,461.1	1,486.5	1,536	1,565	1,599
Housing [16]	759.4	878.2	985.3	999.5	1,058.6	1,110	1,098	1,140
Local environmental services [17]	356.4	393.0	419.6	423.9	419.4	432	420	413
Roads and transport	296.4	329.8	325.3	330.7	317.9	315	307	302
Libraries, culture, heritage, sport and recreation	267.4	285.8	296.0	288.2	284.2	283	263	243
Planning, economic development and community development	113.6	164.7	152.4	159.0	147.9	132	125	110
Council tax benefit and administration [18]	31.7	31.5	32.4	31.3	28.9	30	34	40
Debt financing costs: counties	289.0	320.5	316.4	321.3	314.1	321	334	337
Central administrative and other revenue expenditure: counties [19]	217.3	198.0	190.1	205.9	275.0	310	307	295
Total county and county borough council expenditure	5,959.8	6,377.8	6,685.8	6,805.3	6,923.2	7,099	7,093 (r)	7,109
Total police expenditure	623.3	642.6	670.9	666.6	655.9	656	698	668
Total fire expenditure	138.2	145.0	150.1	148.0	145.6	146	149	148
Total national park expenditure	17.8	18.3	16.1	16.0	16.0	18	17	15
Gross revenue expenditure	6,739.1	7,183.6	7,522.9	7,636.0	7,740.6	7,919	7,958 (r)	7,940
less specific and special government grants (except council tax benefit grant)	1,630.2	1,809.0	1,987.2	2,019.6	2,013.8	2,112	1,933 (r)	1,981
Net revenue expenditure	5,108.9	5,374.6	5,535.7	5,616.4	5,726.8	5,806	6,025	5,959
Putting to (+)/drawing from (-) reserves	97.0	14.0	23.9	135.8	28.3	-32	-66	-72
Council tax reduction scheme [20]	.	.	.	.	.	.	244	247
Budget requirement	5,205.9	5,388.6	5,559.6	5,752.2	5,755.1	5,774	6,203	6,134
Plus discretionary non-domestic rate relief	2.5	2.4	2.6	2.8	3.1	3	3	4
less revenue support grant	-3,061.6	3,104.6	3,191.7	3,282.4	3,382.1	3,257	3,489	3,363
council tax reduction scheme grant	.	.	.	.	.	.	22	.
less police grant	-225.0	230.5	236.3	242.2	245.7	228	240	236
less re-distributed non-domestic rates income	-791.0	868.0	894.0	935.0	787.0	911	1,032	1,041
Council tax requirement	1,130.8	1,187.9	1,240.2	1,295.4	1,343.3	1,381	1,423	1,497
of which:								
Paid by council tax reduction scheme grant. [20]	184.6	194.8	218.6	230.9	242.2	247	244	247
Paid directly by council tax payers	946.2	993.1	1,021.6	1,064.5	1,101.2	1,134	1,179	1,250

Sources: Communities and Local Government: 0303 444 1333
Scottish Government, Local Government Financial Statistics: 0131 245 7034
Welsh Government: 02920 825355

15 Service expenditure is shown excluding that financed by sales, fees and charges, but including that financed by specific and special government grants.

16 Includes housing benefit and private sector costs such as provision for the homeless. Includes rent rebates granted to HRA tenants which is 100% grant funded. Excludes council owned housing.

17 Includes cemeteries and crematoria, community safety, environmental health, consumer protection, waste collection/disposal and central services to the public such as birth registration and elections.

18 Excludes council tax benefit expenditure funded by the specific grant from the Department for Work and Pensions.

19 Includes agricultural services, coastal and flood defence and community councils.Also includes central administrative costs of corporate management,democratic representation and certain costs, such as those relating to back year or additional pension contributions which should not be allocated to individual services, capital expenditure charged to the revenue account and is net of any interest expected to accrue on balances.

20 In 2013-14 council tax reduction scheme, funded by the Welsh Government, replaced council tax benefit grant funded from the Department for Work & Pensions.

21 For consistency with previous year, figures exclude non -HRA Housing, trading services and local authority transport

(r) revised

Service expenditure for 2009-10 are not fully comparable to later years due to revenue expenditure funded from capital by statute (RECS) distributed across all services. 2008-09 years and earlier include FRS17 pension costs.

. Data not applicable

23.14 Financing of revenue expenditure England and Wales

England and Wales
Years ending 31 March

£ million

		2002/03	2003/04	2004/05	2005/06	2006/07	2007/08	20081/09	2009/10	2010/11	2011/12	2012/13	2013/14
England[2]													
Revenue expenditure[3]													
Cash £m	KRTN	65,898	75,244	79,303	84,422	88,172	92,384	98,107	103,276	104,256	99,278	94,148	94,932
Government grants													
Cash £m	KRTO	32,634	41,777	45,258	45,838	49,093	51,657	53,007	57,755	57,657	56,237	46,765	63,099
Percentage of revenue expenditure	KRTP	50	56	57	54	56	56	54	56	55	57	50	66
Redistributed business rates[4]													
Cash £m	KRTQ	16,639	15,611	15,004	18,004	17,506	18,506	20,506	19,515	21,517	19,017	23,129	-
Percentage of revenue expenditure	KRTR	25	21	19	21	20	20	21	19	21	19	25	-
Retained income from rate retention scheme													
Cash £m		-	-	-	-	-	-	-	-	-	-	-	10,554
Percentage of revenue expenditure		-	-	-	-	-	-	-	-	-	-	-	11
Council tax													
Cash £m	KRTS	16,648	18,946	20,299	21,315	22,453	23,608	24,759	25,633	26,254	26,451	26,715	23,431
Percentage of revenue expenditure	KRTT	25	25	26	25	25	26	25	25	25	27	28	25
Wales													
Gross revenue expenditure[5]	ZBXH	4,709	5,243	5,786	6,128	6,472	6,739	7,184	7,523	7,636	7,741	7,919	7,958 (r)
General government grants[6]	ZBXI	2,541	2,743	2,817	2,987	3,169	3,287	3,335	3,428	3,525	3,628	3,485	3,507
Specific government grants[7]	ZBXG	779	1,005	1,381	1,473	1,530	1,630	1,809	1,987	2,020	2,014	2,112	1,933 (r)
Share of redistributed business rates	ZBXJ	643	660	672	672	730	791	868	894	935	787	911	1,032
Council tax income[8]	ZBXK	776	861	924	1,012	1,071	1,131	1,188	1,240	1,295	1,343	1,381	1,423
Other[9]	ZBXL	-30	-25	-8	-16	-27	-99	-16	-26	-139	-31	29	63

Sources: Communities and Local Government: 0303 444 1333;
Welsh Government 02920 825355

1 Budget estimates.
2 Produced on a non-Financial Reporting Standard 17 (FRS17) basis.
3 The sum of government grants, business rates and local taxes does not normally equal revenue expenditure because of the use of reserve
4 1993-94 to 2003-04 includes City of London Offset.

5 Gross revenue expenditure is total local authority expenditure on services, plus capital charges, but net of any income from sales, fees, and charges and other non-grant sources. It includes expenditure funded by specific grants. The figures have been adjusted to account for FRS17 pension costs.
6 Includes all unhypothecated grants, namely revenue support grant, police grant, council tax reduction scheme grant, transitional grant and the adjustment to reverse the transfer.
7 Comprises specific and supplementary grants,excluding police grant.
8 This includes community council precepts, and income covered by charge/council tax benefit grant, but excludes council tax reduction scheme (2013-14).
9 Includes use of reserves and discretionary non-domestic rate relief charge/council tax benefit grant, but excludes council tax reduction scheme (2013-14).

23.15 Financing of capital expenditure

£ million

	2008-09	2009-10	2010-11	2011-12	2012-13	2013-14 (F)
Central government grants	5,733	7,494	8,063	7,170 [a]	8,481	8,600
EU structural funds grants	156	43	38	77	55	89
Grants and contributions from private developers and from leaseholders etc	1,176 [b]	502	634	747	693	761
Grants and contributions from NDPBs [c]	540	602	753	522	442	369
National lottery grants	106	119	104	121	67	77
Use of capital receipts	2,040	1,603	1,409	1,647	1,294	2,131
Revenue financing of capital expenditure	3,241	3,532	3,984	4,504 [a]	3,167	4,335
of which:						
Housing Revenue Account (CERA)	*228*	*247*	*235*	*324*	*466*	*994*
Major Repairs Reserve	*1,224*	*1,377*	*1,069*	*1,160*	*1,259*	*1,354*
General Fund (CERA)	*1,789*	*1,908*	*2,680*	*3,020*	*1,442*	*1,987*
Capital expenditure financed by borrowing/credit	7,241	7,931	8,399	18,819	4,842	7,492
of which:						
SCE(R) Single Capital Pot[d]	2,257	2,181	1,581	338	88	73
SCE(R) Separate Programme Element[d]	760	748	484	74	30	7
Other borrowing & credit arrangements not supported by central government [f]	4,224	5,002	6,335	18,406 [e]	4,724	7,411
Total	**20,233**	**21,826**	**23,385**	**33,606** [e]	**19,042**	**23,854**

(a) There is a discontinuity from 2010-11 owing to a change in the treatment of expenditure by GLA. Previously this was recorded as 'Central government grant' but for 2011-12 it has been recorded as CERA to align with figures received on the Revenue Outturn

(b) Includes RSL financing of £483 million for the transfer of Salford's housing stock.

(c) Non-Departmental Public Bodies, organisations that are not government departments but which have a role in the processes of national government, such as Sport England, English Heritage and the Natural England.

(d) Supported capital expenditure (SCE) financed by borrowing that is attracting central government support has been discontinued as of March 31 2011. This may have a bearing on the financing of capital expenditure. A residue of schemes in 2011-12 and 2012-13 will continue to be financed in reliance of supported borrowing from earlier years.

(e) It is estimated that approximately £13 billion is associated with the financing of the HRA self-financing determination payment.

(f) The Prudential System, which came into effect on 1 April 2004, allows local authorities to raise finance for capital expenditure - without Government consent - where they can afford to service the debt without extra Government support.

Source: Department for Communities and Local Government:
Local Government Financial Statistics England No. 24 2014 (Table 4.4a)

23.16a Capital receipts: all services: England 2011-12: 2nd provisional outturn

£ thousand

	Sales & disposal of tangible fixed assets (10)	Sales of intangible assets (11)	Repayments of grants loans & financial assistance (12)	Total receipts(a) (10+11+12)
Pre-primary & Primary Education	25,429	0	128	25,557
Secondary Education	34,374	0	1,614	35,988
Special Education	4,829	0	0	4,829
Non-school funding	14,216	2,000	32	16,248
Education	**78,848**	**2,000**	**1,774**	**82,622**
Roads, Street Lights & Safety	11,919	0	4	11,923
Parking of Vehicles	3,157	0	15	3,172
Public Passenger Transport-Bus	0	0	0	0
Public Passenger Transport-Rail & Other	6,884	0	266	7,150
Airports	0	0	394	394
Local Authority Ports and Piers	7	0	428	435
Tolled Road bridges,tunnels,ferries, public transport companies	6	20	0	26
Highways & transport	**21,973**	**20**	**1,107**	**23,100**
Social services	**61,656**	**0**	**217**	**61,873**
Housing	**820,119**	**12,563**	**24,716**	**857,398**
Culture and heritage	5,498	0	264	5,762
Recreation and sport	28,642	0	778	29,420
Open spaces	16,922	0	18	16,940
Tourism	160	490	0	650
Library Services	2,574	0	0	2,574
Total Culture and related services	**53,796**	**490**	**1,060**	**55,346**
Cemeteries, cremation and mortuary	5,005	0	0	5,005
Coast protection	48	0	0	48
Community safety	173	0	0	173
Community safety (CCTV)	0	0	0	0
Flood defence and land drainage	0	0	96	96
Agriculture and fisheries services	45,681	784	0	46,465
Regulatory services (environmental health)	936	0	67	1,003
Regulatory services (trading standards)	2	0	0	2
Street cleaning not chargeable to highways	148	0	0	148
Waste collection	2,804	0	225	3,029
Waste disposal	3,085	0	923	4,008
Trade waste	32	0	0	32
Recycling	203	0	301	504
Waste minimisation	0	0	0	0
Climate change costs	6,274	175	0	6,449
Total environmental and regulatory services	**64,391**	**959**	**1,612**	**66,962**
Planning and development services	**129,065**	**13**	**3,195**	**132,273**
Police	**104,341**	**744**	**834**	**105,919**
Fire and rescue services	**11,175**	**0**	**0**	**11,175**
Central services	**361,395**	**3,938**	**8,629**	**373,962**
Industrial and commercial trading	192,602	0	48	192,650
Other trading	23,174	0	52	23,226
Total Trading	**215,776**	**0**	**100**	**215,876**
Total all services	**1,922,535**	**20,727**	**43,244**	**1,986,506**

(a) Figures in this column do not include disposals of share and loan capital

23.16b Capital expenditure: all services: England 2011-12: 2nd provisional outturn

£ thousand

	Total expenditure on fixed & intangible assets (6) (1+2+3+4+5)	Expenditure on grants (7)	Expenditure on loans & other financial assistance (8)	Total Expenditure[a] (9) (6+7+8)
Pre-primary & Primary Education	2,000,419	107,616	22	2,108,057
Secondary Education	2,542,420	242,497	22,252	2,807,169
Special Education	284,700	1,725	770	287,195
Non-school funding	266,196	15,616	10,564	292,376
Education	**5,093,735**	**367,454**	**33,608**	**5,494,797**
Roads, Street Lights & Safety	2,442,905	10,360	1,476	2,454,741
Parking of Vehicles	58,167	248	1	58,416
Public Passenger Transport-Bus	157,425	56,426	19	213,870
Public Passenger Transport-Rail & Other	664,683	1,679,000	1,208,975	3,552,658
Airports	4,529	0	646	5,175
Local Authority Ports and Piers	15,261	0	0	15,261
Tolled Road bridges,tunnels,ferries, public transport companies	78,827	0	0	78,827
Highways & transport	**3,421,797**	**1,746,034**	**1,211,117**	**6,378,948**
Social services	**215,150**	**37,489**	**475**	**253,114**
Housing	**2,762,927**	**464,620**	**46,744**	**3,274,291**
Culture and heritage	223,850	18,760	2,799	245,409
Recreation and sport	469,127	17,692	1,565	488,384
Open spaces	176,502	21,489	435	198,426
Tourism	11,723	32	0	11,755
Library Services	157,865	422	0	158,287
Total Culture and related services	**1,039,067**	**58,395**	**4,799**	**1,102,261**
Cemeteries, cremation and mortuary	47,062	1,344	0	48,406
Coast protection	30,385	350	44	30,779
Community safety	7,131	1,036	0	8,167
Community safety (CCTV)	10,141	178	0	10,319
Flood defence and land drainage	21,855	1,266	0	23,121
Agriculture and fisheries	16,844	2,219	12	19,075
Regulatory services (environmental health)	17,876	1,256	188	19,320
Regulatory services (trading standards)	1,011	0	0	1,011
Street cleaning (not chargeable to highways)	10,270	0	6	10,276
Waste collection	95,689	1,743	41	97,473
Waste disposal	117,412	4,098	181	121,691
Trade waste	2,107	0	0	2,107
Recycling	58,855	5,029	35	63,919
Waste minimisation	3,075	0	0	3,075
Climate change costs	22,421	6,853	236	29,510
Total environmental services	**462,134**	**25,372**	**743**	**488,249**
Planning and development services	**554,817**	**91,149**	**6,634**	**652,600**
Police	**537,776**	**12**	**0**	**537,788**
Fire and rescue services	**136,390**	**89**	**0**	**136,479**
Central services	**1,090,251**	**22,193**	**45,374**	**1,157,818**
Industrial and commercial trading	292,383	3,894	0	296,277
Other trading	61,769	93	98	61,960
Total Trading	**354,152**	**3,987**	**98**	**358,237**
Total all services	**15,668,195**	**2,816,794**	**1,349,592**	**19,834,581**

(a) Figures in this column do not include acquisitions of share and loan capital

23.17 Capital outturn expenditure, by service (£ thousand)

	2000-01	2001-02	2002-03	2003-04 (4)	2004-05	2005-06	2006-07	2007-08	2008-09	2009-10	2010-11	2011-12
Total capital expenditure/receipts	546,267	595,279	638,698	741,074	860,323	982,266	1,076,976	1,145,862	1,128,396	934,126	997,663	1,036,262
Total all services	548,270	597,382	637,849	739,865	859,323	980,845	1,061,728	1,128,517	1,123,578	932,218	993,058	1,027,215
Total education	76,044	96,077	96,933	115,863	143,758	161,086	185,828	189,771	203,553	215,542	233,276	260,584
Personal social services (1)	8,415	9,842	10,800	13,954	16,831	20,460	18,731	18,521	22,119	21,897	22,326	18,777
Total transport	108,426	111,216	109,893	127,390	141,188	203,418	213,950	237,631	231,377	203,963	210,947	206,930
General administration (2)	18,354	23,173	36,369	49,085	51,932	56,311	74,540	66,957	61,669	47,411	50,619	42,580
Total housing	194,676	201,724	219,282	220,919	242,328	257,461	267,013	247,097	238,170	217,445	210,084	230,148
Planning and development (3)	39,404	45,645	34,608	48,793	71,611	77,999	79,607	111,585	95,585	56,520	73,903	94,657
Total other local services	82,244	84,072	102,226	124,651	148,258	162,569	185,515	213,851	209,474	124,854	138,743	272,915
Total law, order and protective services	20,707	25,633	27,738	39,210	43,418	41,542	36,543	43,104	61,632	44,585	53,161	37,861
Other transactions	-2,003	-2,103	849	1,209	1,000	1,421	15,248	17,345	4,818	1,908	4,605	9,046

Source: Local Government Finance Statistics, Welsh Government

Wales Capital Outturn forms

Contact: stats.finance@wales.gsi.gov.uk

1. Expenditure and receipts on sheltered employment and workshops. Excludes port health. Where premises are provided for both educational and personal social services for children under five, only the expenditure/receipts attributable to personal social services are included.

2. Expenditure on an authority's own properties, transportation, equipment and material generally, which can not properly be set against some other specific service.

3. Expenditure on planning departments' payments on development control, building regulations and planning implementation; direct expenditure on conservation, environmental improvements, conversion and commercial development; gypsy sites; advances and grants for industrial and commercial enterprises and industrial development; and tourism. Excludes expenditure in respect of industrial trading estates.

4. From 2003-04 onwards data was also collected from National park authorities.

23.18 Expenditure of local authorities

Scotland
Years ending 31 March

£ thousand

		2000 /01	2001 /02	2002 /03	2003 /04	2004 /05	2005 /06
Out of revenue:[1]**Total**	KQTA	10,951,402	11,558,721	9,324,680	13,658,834	14,527,867	15,746,429
General Fund Services:	KQTB	7,884,168	8,428,217	5,756,415	10,139,679	10,964,598	12,021,453
Education	KQTC	3,037,780	3,283,827	3533 853	3,872,786	4,180,675	4,406,876
Libraries,museums and galleries	KQTD	134,174	138,318	152,308	160,540	161,650	168,953
Social work	KQTE	1,632,843	1,793,732	2,173,752	2,400,652	2,621,134	2,808,040
Law, order and protectiveservices	KQTF	1,047,034	1,088,791	1,130,693	1,226,067	1,306,085	1,501,854
Roads and Transport[2]	KQTG	564,738	506,326	601,454	611,721	635,329	673,167
Environmental services	KQTH	393,333	414,975	484,177	525,556	581,220	635,475
Planning	KQTI	194,771	223,414	265,315	282,572	299,182	351,617
Leisure and recreation	KQTJ	387,115	401,904	426,495	472,120	494,237	520,612
Other services	KQTL	465,612	572,136	515,661	585,425	681,288	948,167
Other general fund expenditure[3]	KQTM	26,768	4,794	6,560	2,240	3,798	6,692
Housing	KQTN	1,886,189	1,954,444	2,224,209	2,295,005	2,459,146	2,609,228
Trading services:	KQTO	80,355	61,899	74,062	92,782	106,445	103,461
Passenger transport	KQTR	162	343	427	441	282	353
Ferries	KQTS	10,005	9,650	11,493	11,768	13,759	14,308
Harbours,docks and piers	KQTT	13,604	10,912	12,222	13,405	12,407	11,995
Road bridges	KQTV	8,606	6,914	7,267	11,235	13,276	12,366
Slaughterhouses	KQTW	..	..	..	..	..	..
Markets	KQTX	23,844	16,657	17,995	14,824	15,353	17,447
Other trading services	KQTY	24,134	17,423	24,658	41,109	51,368	46,992
Loan charges:[4]Total	KQTZ	1,100,690	1,114,161	1,269,994	1,131,368	997,678	1,012,287
Allocated to :							
General Fund services	KMHV	708,822	739,351	738,870	772,852	772,648	792,404
Housing	KMHW	386,512	369,943	525,201	348,180	212,440	210,856
Trading services	KMHX	5,356	4,867	5,923	10,336	12,590	9,027
On capital works:[4]Total	KQUA	802,672	929,631	972,049	1,052,310	1,264,031	1,572,281
General Fund Services:	KQUB	538,843	610,485	662,869	767,122	1,006,150	1,160,818
Education	KQUC	127,781	143,268	157,439	172,227	199,387	310,054
Libraries, museums and galleries	KQUD	5,834	8,683	19,018	12,043	24,796	22,762
Social work	KQUE	21,539	31,359	30,116	31,966	33,450	37,877
Law, order and protectiveservices	KQUF	35,761	39,901	53,268	65,477	65,154	51,146
Roads and Transport	KQUG	117,485	147,975	147,357	200,278	258,071	308,366
Environmental services	KQUH	17,944	16,396	17,957	20,567	40,773	55,020
Planning	KQUI	47,684	33,312	40,241	36,496	61,544	76,043
Leisure and recreation	KQUJ	44,516	39,240	50,558	71,486	74,116	83,681
Administrative buildings and equipment	KQUK	34,633	53,189	68,438	48,896	64,414	84,569
Other services	KQUL	85,666	97,162	78,477	107,686	184,445	131,300
Housing	KQUM	255,189	300,054	284,418	261,715	241,107	382,697
Trading Services:	KQUN	8,640	19,092	24,762	23,473	16,774	28,766
Ferries	KQUR	23	467	1	111	608	195
Harbours,docks and piers	KQUS	6,192	15,898	20,361	19,503	12,024	12,899
Airports	KQUT	607	663	1,031	609	572	663
Shipping, Airports, Transport piers & Ferry Terminals	J96X	..	..	..	..	..	..
Road bridges	KQUU	964	882	2,386	2,395	442	12,106
Slaughterhouses	KQUV	..	40	116	82	-	-
Other trading services	KMHY	854	1,142	867	773	3,128	2,903

1 Gross expenditure less inter-authority and inter-account transfers.
2 Including general fund support for transport (LA and NON-LA).
3 General fund contributions to Housing and Trading services (excluding transport),are also included in the expenditure figures for these services.
4 Expenditure out of loans, government grants and other capital receipts.
5 Figures for 2009-10 have been adjusted to exclude expenditure financed through PPP/PFI for past years.

Source: Scottish Government,Local Government Finance Statistics: 0131 244 7033

23.18 Expenditure of local authorities

Scotland
Years ending 31 March

£ thousand

		2006/07	2007/08	2008/09	2009/10[5]	2010/11	2011/12
Out of revenue:[1]Total	**KQTA**	15,986,751	16,578,249	17,403,497	18,139,334	**18,067,933**	**17,940,377**
General Fund Services:	KQTB	12,143,056	12,653,585	13,255,975	13,662,114	**13,569,349**	**13,217,350**
Education	KQTC	4,596,832	4,747,148	4,869,127	4,818,152	4,856,964	4,737,915
Libraries,museums and galleries	KQTD	164,976	163,185	170,177	171,315	170,970	165,298 3,665,002
Social work	KQTE	2,994,486	3,192,214	3,408,851	3,559,328	3,609,012	1,543,973
Law, order and protectiveservices	KQTF	1,469,644	1,506,432	1,631,037	1,646,531	1,600,004	641,843 785,301
Roads and Transport[2]	KQTG	625,341	633,828	678,922	674,525	682,414	473,079
Environmental services	KQTH	670,308	708,736	757,555	789,900	792,494	547,327
Planning	KQTI	366,803	372,445	437,261	514,080	512,608	682,334
Leisure and recreation	KQTJ	543,047	547,132	572,111	597,672	567,987	-24,722
Other services	KQTL	702,554	782,035	730,934	889,716	774,715	
Other general fund expenditure[3]	KQTM	9,065	430	0	895	2,181	3,131,708
Housing	KQTN	2,740,592	2,788,537	2,976,629	3,097,399	3,021,676	
Trading services:	KQTO	102,336	100,104	110,042	100,677	**101,853**	**87,396**
Passenger transport	KQTR	355	315	397	248	277	236
Ferries	KQTS	18,483	21,907	23,872	25,018	25,075	25,834
Harbours,docks and piers	KQTT	8,495	8,312	276	-1,013	-770	3,940
Road bridges	KQTV	16,279	22,005	17,189	16,894	15,719	6,085
Slaughterhouses	KQTW	..	..	..	..	..	..
Markets	KQTX	16,793	18,461	20,250	18,467	20,031	22,239
Other trading services	KQTY	41,931	29,104	48,058	41,063	41,521	29,062
Loan charges:[4]Total	KQTZ	1,000,767	1,036,023	1,060,851	1,279,144	**1,375,055**	**1,503,923**
Allocated to :							
General Fund services	KMHV	782,002	806,806	854,918	1,072,286	1,147,421	1,268,766
Housing	KMHW	214,395	201,297	197,776	199,196	227,634	235,157
Trading services	KMHX	4,370	27,920	8,157	7,662	..	..
On capital works:[4]Total	KQUA	1,952,249	2,182,509	2,554,081	2,424,018	**2,348,162**	**2,661,534**
General Fund Services:	KQUB	1,462,620	1,652,425	1,850,660	1,723,958	**1,614,955**	**1,902,524**
Education	KQUC	402,865	464,827	479,258	418,540	508,691	691,878
Libraries, museums and galleries	KQUD	24,210	29,963	39,583	42,579	29,684	22,654
Social work	KQUE	50,327	65,449	63,233	66,375	51,256	46,487
Law, order and protectiveservices	KQUF	60,287	68,680	101,062	83,779	56,224	74,044 482,554
Roads and Transport	KQUG	418,987	484,669	479,769	471,763	399,084	105,036
Environmental services	KQUH	43,104	101,325	121,267	121,342	102,458	113,476
Planning	KQUI	66,063	121,596	124,060	171,613	120,742	222,717
Leisure and recreation	KQUJ	98,275	136,029	167,505	173,766	166,330	
Administrative buildings and equipment	KQUK	113,896	..	..	..	..	..
Other services	KQUL	184,606	179,887	274,923	174,201	180,486	143,678
Housing	KQUM	454,838	507,905	680,657	678,125	**720,520**	**748,620**
Trading Services:	KQUN	34,791	22,179	22,764	21,935	**12,687**	**10,390**
Ferries	KQUR	547	..	..	..	..	..
Harbours,docks and piers	KQUS	5,855	..	..	..	..	..
Airports	KQUT	798	..	..	..	..	..
Shipping, Airports, Transport piers & Ferry Terminals	J96X	..	18,654	14,018	2,273	1,308	2,887
Road bridges	KQUU	22,865	-	0	0	0	0
Slaughterhouses	KQUV	-	-	..	..	..	..
Other trading services	KMHY	4,726	3,525	8,746	19,662	11,379	7,503

1 Gross expenditure less inter-authority and inter-account transfers.
2 Including general fund support for transport (LA and NON-LA).
3 General fund contributions to Housing and Trading services (excluding transport),are also included in the expenditure figures for these services.
4 Expenditure out of loans, government grants and other capital receipts.
5 Figures for 2009-10 have been adjusted to exclude expenditure financed through PPP/PFI for past years.

Source: Scottish Government,Local Government Finance Statistics: 0131 244 7033

23.19a - Local Government Revenue Income by Source, 2007-08 to 2011-12, Scotland

£ Millions

	2007-08	2008-09	2009-10	2010-11	2011-12
Revenue Income					
General Revenue Funding[1]	6,170	7,426	7,757	8,149	7,790
Council Tax	1,890	1,909	1,910	1,923	1,926
Council Tax Benefit Subsidy	354	351	368	375	376
Non Domestic Rates	1,860	1,963	2,165	2,068	2,182
Sales, Rents, Fees & Charges	2,132	2,262	2,287	2,179	2,298
Other income	4,163	3,363	3,390	3,348	3,305
Total revenue income	**16,569**	**17,274**	**17,877**	**18,043**	**17,877**

1. Prior to 2008-09 this was Revenue Support Grant
Sources: General Revenue Funding (Up to 2010-11) – Finance Circulars; Non-Domestic Rates – Non Domestic Rates Returns (NDRI); All Other Data – Local Financial Returns (LFRs)

Source: Scottish Local Government Financial Statistics 2011-12

23.19b - Total Capital Expenditure and Financing, 2007-08 to 2011-12

£ thousands

	2007-08	2008-09	2009-10	2010-11	2011-12
Scottish Government General Capital Grant	nc	364,039	462,640	352,652	565,541
Scottish Government Specific Capital Grants	nc	262,093	268,370	228,865	234,365
Grants from Scottish Government Agencies and NDPBs	94,655	141,590	160,281	115,726	82,764
Grants from Scottish Government Directorates	627,516	nc	nc	nc	nc
Other Grants and Contributions	132,287	115,871	104,575	94,486	85,714
Borrowing from Loans fund	710,474	1,206,318	1,091,548	1,113,929	1,261,468
Capital receipts used from asset sales/disposals	406,547	204,048	164,746	114,722	94,020
Capital Fund applied	34,440	40,609	28,616	14,916	21,653
Capital funded from current revenue	173,668	196,836	166,141	208,894	209,122
Assets acquired under credit arrangements (e.g. finance leases, PPP/PFI)	4,760	737	824,442	103,972	106,888
Total Financing	**2,184,347**	**2,532,141**	**3,271,359**	**2,348,162**	**2,661,534**

1. From 2009-10 onwards assets acquired through PPP/PFI are included. In addition, figures for 2009-10 include assets acquired through PPP/PFI for past years. (more information on the changes can be found here - http://www.scotland.gov.uk/Topics/Government/local-government/17999/LACapital/CapExReport200910)
Source: Capital Returns (CR Final)

nc=not collected

Source: Scottish Local Government Financial Statistics 2011-12

23.20 Subjective Analysis of General Fund Revenue Income, 2011-12

£ thousands

	Education Services	Culture and Related Services	Social Work Services	Police Service	Fire Service	Roads and Transport	Environmental Services	Planning and Development Services	Central Services	Housing Services (Non-HRA)	Trading with the Public	Total General Fund Services	HRA Housing Services	Total General Fund Services (inc HRA)
INCOME														
Government Grants														
Ring-fenced Revenue Grants	5,104	0	0	498,493	0	0	0	0	0	7,067	0	510,664	3,507	514,171
General Capital Grant used to fund grants to third parties	646	598	628	16,666	0	1,925	164	10,715	16,683	137,085	0	185,110	38,683	223,793
Other Central Government Grants (excl GRG)	30,937	3,296	102,927	107,833	18,902	9,431	3,274	17,263	73,595	1,436,939	1	1,804,398	10,242	1,814,640
Total Government Grants	36,687	3,894	103,555	622,992	18,902	11,356	3,438	27,978	90,278	1,581,091	1	2,500,172	52,432	2,552,604
Other Grants reimbursements and Contributions														
Contributions from Health Authorities			375,368									375,368		375,368
All other grants, reimbursements and contributions	38,650	13,369	45,219	4,253	25,330	11,595	8,562	34,464	29,884	243,054	28	454,408	17,168	471,576
Total Other Grants reimbursements and Contributions	38,650	13,369	420,587	4,253	25,330	11,595	8,562	34,464	29,884	243,054	28	829,776	17,168	846,944
Customer and Client Receipts														
Income from charges to service users	51,613	40,153	237,881	21,930	88	86,534	54,257	19,214	30,766	20,335	15,570	578,341	19,528	597,869
Rent Income	1,099	5,443	6,353	4,121	154	12,006	1,636	45,427	12,554	101,087	947	190,827	880,274	1,071,101
Other Sales, Fees and Charges	62,305	31,883	23,867	37,503	2,779	73,134	61,874	53,877	100,201	57,694	47,009	552,126	66,118	618,244
Total Customer and Client Receipts	115,017	77,479	268,101	63,554	3,021	171,674	117,767	118,518	143,521	179,116	63,526	1,321,294	965,920	2,287,214
Credits resulting from soft loans	0	11	3	0	0	0	0	1	0	0	0	15	0	15
Total Income	190,354	94,753	792,246	690,799	47,253	194,625	129,767	180,961	263,683	2,003,261	63,555	4,651,257	1,035,520	5,686,777

Source: Scottish Local Government Financial Statistics 2011-12

23.21 Expenditure of local authorities

Northern Ireland
Years ending 31 March

£ thousand

	1997 /98	1998 /99	1999 /00	2000 /01	2001 /02	2002 /03	2003 /04	2004 /05	2005 /06	2006 /07	2007 /08	2008 /09[1]	2009 /10	2010 /11	2011 /12
Libraries, museums and art galleries	13,928	14,571	19,900	23,097	24,181	32,728	30,062	30,481	33,516	28,655	31,557	36,527	35,549	37,163	40,321
Environmental health services:															
Refuse collection and disposal	56,246	56,360	62,226	65,289	73,336	90,148	94,715	102,633	113,768	121,879	136,181	142,071	151,332	155,540	159,518
Public baths	2,585	2,634	1,750	1,724	1,423	..	..	..	..	..	..	..	..	..	..
Parks, recreation grounds,etc	115,302	118,396	158,304	170,999	184,406	194,224	193,617	205,734	221,298	198,314	213,780	265,720	257,522	278,716	263,211
Other sanitary services	39,682	42,923	44,214	45,552	48,784	52,075	55,349	59,906	66,294	68,641	74,624	86,428	87,000	90,966	91,358
Housing (grants and small dwellings acquisition)	545	358	37	28	27	12	21	18	10	15	17	8	15	79	13,474
Trading services:															
Cemeteries	5,626	5,887	5,973	6,151	6,538	7,208	7,980	8,455	8,520	7,752	8,726	9,125	9,353	10,994	10,274
Other trading services (including markets, fairs and harbours)	7,016	10,779	9,366	7,209	7,769	18,281	17,489	18,776	19,596	15,240	17,498	27,711	21,115	15,610	13,222
Miscellaneous	63,375	161,790	86,649	89,881	98,244	79,645	114,971	105,031	128,304	141,717	160,606	263,230	183,563	107,841	129,889
Total expenditure	304,305	413,698	388,419	409,930	444,708	474,321	490,619	531,034	591,306	582,213	642,991	830,820	745,450	696,909	707,809
Total loan charges	34,823	26,413	..	..	..	..	..	..	..	..	..	..	..	..	..

Source: Department of the Environment for Northern Ireland: 028 9025 6086

1. The overall expenditure figure for 2008/2009 is much higher than 2009/2010 substantially due to the Capital Finance Reserve of one particular council.

Agriculture

Chapter 24

Agriculture

Input and Output (Tables 24.1 and 24.2)

For both tables, output is net of VAT collected on the sale of non-edible products. Figures for total output include subsidies on products, that is, payments that have the purpose of influencing production, their prices or remuneration of the factors of production. Unspecified crops include turf, other minor crops and arable area payments for fodder maize. Eggs include the value of duck eggs and exports of eggs for hatching. Landlords' expenses are included within farm maintenance, miscellaneous expenditure and depreciation of buildings and works. Also included within 'Other farming costs' are livestock and crop costs, water costs, insurance premia, bank charges, professional fees, rates, and other farming costs.

Non-subsidy payments
Payments other than subsidies on products from which farmers can benefit as a consequence of engaging in agriculture. This includes:
• environment and countryside management schemes
• organic farming schemes
• support schemes for less favoured areas
• Single Payment Scheme
• animal disease compensation attributable to income
• other payments

Compensation of employees and interest charges
Total compensation of employees excludes the value of work done by farm labour on own account capital formation in buildings and work. 'Interest' relates to interest charges on loans for current farming purposes and buildings, less interest on money held on short-term deposit.

Rent
Rent paid (after deductions) is the rent paid on all tenanted land including 'conacre' land in Northern Ireland, less landlords' expenses and the benefit value of dwellings on that land. Rent received (after deductions) is the rent received by farming landowners from renting of land to other farmers, less landlords' expenses and the benefit value of dwellings on that land. Total net rent is the net rent flowing out of the agricultural sector paid to non-farming landowners, including that part of tenanted land in Northern Ireland.

Agricultural censuses and surveys
(Tables 24.3, 24.5 and 24.13)

For tables 24.3 and 24.5, the coverage includes all main and minor holdings for each country up until 2008. From 2009 onwards, the data for England relate to commercial holdings only. The term 'commercial' covers all English holdings which have more than 5 hectares of agricultural land, 1 hectare of orchards, 0.5 hectares of vegetables or 0.1 hectares of protected crops, or more than 10 cows, 50 pigs, 20 sheep, 20 goats or 1,000 poultry. These thresholds are specified in the EU Farm Structure Survey Regulation EC 1166/2008. All data in table 24.13 relate to commercial holdings only for England.

Estimated quantity of crops and grass harvested
(Table 24.4)

The estimated yield of sugar beet is obtained from production figures supplied by British
Sugar plc in England and Wales. In Great Britain, potato yields are estimated in consultation with
the Potato Council Limited.

Forestry
(Table 24.6)

Statistics for state forestry are from Forestry Commission and Forest Service management
information systems. For private forestry in Great Britain, statistics on new planting and restocking
are based on records of grant aid and estimates of planting undertaken without grant aid, and
softwood production is estimated from a survey of the largest timber harvesting companies. Hardwood
production is estimated from deliveries of roundwood to primary wood processors and others, based
on surveys of the UK timber industry, data provided by trade associations and estimates provided by
the Expert Group on Timber and Trade Statistics.

Average weekly earnings and hours of agricultural and horticultural workers
(Tables 24.11 and 24.12)

Before 1998, data were collected from a monthly postal survey, which mainly covered male
full-time workers. Between 1998 and 2002 the survey collected information on an annual basis
via a telephone survey. The survey was reviewed in 2002 and it was concluded that the
frequency of the survey should be increased to four times per year to enable the production
of more representative annual estimates. The annual sample size has been retained and has
been split between four quarterly telephone surveys.

From April 2009, publication of quarterly results ceased. In 2009 results were published on an
annual basis, for the 12 months ending in September, using data from the four quarterly data
collections. In 2010 the intention was to run surveys in March and September with larger sample
sizes than the quarterly surveys. However, following the announcement of the intention to abolish
the Agricultural Wages Board (AWB) the September 2010 survey was subsequently cancelled so
all 2010 figures are point-in-time estimates as at March 2010. The minimum wage and other terms
and conditions of employment for workers employed in agriculture are set by the Agricultural Wages
Board.

The Agricultural Wages Board is an independent body with a statutory obligation to set minimum
wages for workers employed in agriculture in England and Wales. It was established by the Agricultural
Wages Act (1948).. The Board also has powers to decide other terms and conditions of employment,
e.g. holidays and sick pay. It produces a legally binding Order which is enforced by Defra. The Order
is made annually and normally comes into force on 1 October.

As at autumn 2011 the future of the Survey of Earnings and Hours of Agricultural and Horticultural
Workers is under review.

The survey covers seven main categories of workers and provides data which are used by the
AWB when considering wage claims and in considering the cost of labour in agriculture and horticulture.

Data on earnings represents the total earnings for workers aged 20 and over. Figures include all payments-in-kind, valued where applicable in accordance with the Agricultural Wages Order. Part-time workers are defined as those working less than 39 basic hours per week. Casual workers are those employed on a temporary basis.

Results can be found on the Department for Environment, Food and Rural Affairs (DEFRA) website at: www.defra.gov.uk/statistics/foodfarm/farmmanage/earningshours/

Fisheries
(Table 24.15)
Figures show the number of registered and licensed fishing vessels based on information provided by the Marine Management Organisation.

Estimated average household food consumption – 'Family Food' Expenditure and Food Survey
(Table 24.16)
In 2008 the Expenditure and Food Survey (EFS) was renamed as the Living Costs and Food Survey (LCFS) when it became part of the Integrated Household Survey (IHS). The Expenditure and Food Survey started in April 2001, having been preceded by the National Food Survey (NFS) and the Family Expenditure Survey (FES). Both surveys were brought into one to provide value for money without compromising data quality. The EFS was effectively a continuation of the FES extended to record quantities of purchases. This extension is now known as the Family Food Module of the LCFS. Estimates from the NFS prior to 2000 have been adjusted by aligning estimates for the year 2000 with corresponding estimates from the FES. From 2006 the survey moved onto a calendar year basis (from the previous financial year basis) in preparation for its integration to the Integrated Household Survey from January 2008.

The Living Costs and Food Survey is a voluntary sample survey of private households throughout the UK. The basic unit of the survey is the household which is defined as a group of people living at the same address and sharing common catering arrangements. The survey is continuous, interviews being spread evenly over the year to ensure that seasonal effects are covered. Each household member over the age of seven keeps a diary of all their expenditure over a two-week period. A simplified version of the diary is used by those aged between seven and 15. The diaries record expenditure and quantities of purchases of food and drink rather than consumption of food and drink. Items of food and drink are defined as either household or eating out and are recorded in the form the item was purchased not how it was consumed. 'Household' covers all food that is brought into the household. 'Eating out' covers all food that never enters the household, for example restaurant meals, school meals and snacks eaten away from home.

In 2008 the Living Costs and Food Survey collected the diaries of 13,890 people within 5,845 households across the UK. The response rate for 2008 was 51 per cent in Great Britain and 54 per cent in Northern Ireland.

24.1 Production and income account at current prices; United Kingdom

Enquiries: Helen Mason on +44 (0)1904 455096
Email: helen.mason@defra.gsi.gov.uk

£ million

	2001	2002	2003	2004	2005	2006	2007	2008	2009	2010	2011	2012
Output at market prices (a)												
1 Output of cereals	1 344	1 535	1 491	1 707	1 434	1 507	1 949	3 147	2 338	2 292	3 218	3 205
wheat	837	1 095	1 001	1 232	1 018	1 066	1 325	2 242	1 562	1 668	2 305	2 160
rye	2	1	1	2	1	1	2	2	2	2	3	3
barley	466	392	446	433	380	384	555	812	701	557	815	926
oats and summer cereal mixtures	40	45	43	40	34	54	65	90	72	63	93	114
other cereals	1	1	1	1	1	1	1	1	2	2	2	2
2 Output of industrial crops	569	612	719	683	679	597	702	1 010	904	1 051	1 524	1 356
oil seeds	177	220	314	266	278	318	431	641	493	697	1 137	1 002
oilseed rape	172	217	304	257	261	310	426	631	476	674	1 110	986
other oil seeds	6	3	10	9	17	8	4	10	17	23	27	16
Protein crops	104	80	93	109	94	72	81	131	136	127	103	98
sugar beet	258	285	283	280	278	178	162	208	246	197	251	227
other industrial crops	30	28	28	28	28	29	29	29	29	30	32	29
fibre plants	2	1	2	1	1	1	-	1	-	1	1	-
hops	9	7	6	6	5	4	4	4	4	4	4	4
other industrial crops (b)	19	20	20	21	22	24	24	24	24	25	26	24
3 Output of forage plants	121	116	141	142	155	167	132	143	190	189	186	146
4 Output of vegetables and horticultural products	1 608	1 586	1 662	1 613	1 682	1 738	1 822	1 907	1 964	2 260	2 264	2 304
fresh vegetables	921	837	898	834	912	1 001	1 054	1 088	1 085	1 263	1 218	1 253
plants and flowers	688	748	764	779	770	737	768	819	879	997	1 047	1 051
5 Output of potatoes (including seeds)	703	512	562	715	535	650	708	793	681	622	717	730
6 Output of fruit	239	251	310	318	390	377	459	535	570	585	604	573
7 Output of other crop products including seeds	330	345	206	241	268	249	186	331	379	436	471	640
Total crop output (sum 1 - 7)	4 914	4 957	5 091	5 419	5 144	5 284	5 958	7 866	7 027	7 435	8 984	8 954
8 Output of livestock	4 278	4 573	4 814	4 814	5 093	5 067	5 149	6 374	7 026	7 306	8 169	8 645
primarily for meat	3 651	3 866	4 084	4 157	4 299	4 364	4 432	5 504	5 846	6 108	6 904	7 242
cattle	955	1 146	1 227	1 279	1 466	1 561	1 623	2 071	2 131	2 154	2 573	2 792
pigs	748	687	671	680	677	685	736	866	968	978	1 070	1 139
sheep	438	613	696	726	686	709	641	798	967	979	1 149	1 020
poultry	1 355	1 262	1 328	1 306	1 300	1 233	1 249	1 579	1 590	1 799	1 904	2 075
other animals	155	158	161	166	171	176	183	190	189	198	208	215
gross fixed capital formation	627	707	730	657	794	703	716	870	1 180	1 198	1 265	1 404
cattle	371	392	448	337	545	419	410	577	750	714	631	877
pigs	5	7	7	8	6	8	5	6	8	8	8	8
sheep	123	178	146	176	112	146	153	125	238	295	413	316
poultry	127	129	129	136	131	131	149	162	185	181	213	203
9 Output of livestock products	3 088	2 834	3 031	3 038	3 009	2 918	3 286	4 019	3 711	3 973	4 387	4 486
milk	2 743	2 466	2 628	2 610	2 592	2 497	2 823	3 447	3 123	3 329	3 738	3 767
eggs	307	315	336	378	349	362	410	520	531	561	559	662
raw wool	17	19	21	20	20	11	12	10	14	30	38	25
other animal products	21	34	45	29	48	48	41	41	43	53	52	32
Total livestock output (8 + 9)	7 366	7 407	7 845	7 852	8 103	7 985	8 434	10 393	10 737	11 279	12 556	13 131
10 Other agricultural activities	628	642	632	717	638	622	680	790	868	927	1 039	1 039
agricultural services	600	599	592	635	629	621	679	789	868	927	1 039	1 039
leasing out quota	28	43	40	82	9	1	-	-	-	-	-	-
11 Inseparable non-agricultural activities	624	560	592	637	678	684	763	813	913	990	1 026	1 074
12 Output (at market prices) (sum 1 to 11)	13 531	13 565	14 160	14 624	14 563	14 576	15 835	19 861	19 545	20 630	23 605	24 198
of which:												
transactions within the agricultural industry												
feed wheat	41	42	70	104	86	83	100	133	108	80	71	139
feed barley	149	145	149	149	136	142	178	222	191	206	272	284
feed oats	13	12	12	13	12	15	19	23	20	17	26	31
fodder maize	98	92	119	118	131	143	104	118	164	160	150	114
seed potatoes	11	12	9	11	10	10	14	14	16	19	20	23
straw	291	306	177	209	210	191	137	267	302	354	372	531
contract work	600	599	592	635	629	621	679	789	868	927	1 039	1 039
leasing of quota	28	43	40	82	9	1	-	-	-	-	-	-
total capital formation in livestock	627	707	730	657	794	703	716	870	1 180	1 198	1 265	1 404
13 Total subsidies (less taxes) on product (c)	1 750	1 944	1 978	2 172	214	87	62	57	38	29	28	20
14 Gross output at basic prices (12 + 13)	15 281	15 510	16 137	16 797	14 777	14 663	15 897	19 919	19 583	20 659	23 633	24 218
Intermediate consumption												
15 Seeds	507	486	472	622	659	573	614	705	690	640	660	675
16 Energy	682	647	600	669	779	831	897	1 166	1 101	1 216	1 371	1 420
electricity and fuels for heating	239	235	204	209	235	258	274	340	344	357	369	386
motor and machinery fuels	443	412	395	460	544	573	623	826	758	859	1 002	1 033
17 Fertilisers	855	808	746	734	785	791	792	1 455	1 176	1 339	1 589	1 525
18 Plant protection products	526	531	501	576	547	518	571	690	717	762	809	933
19 Veterinary expenses	241	250	253	279	280	284	302	338	364	405	410	426
20 Animal feed (d)	2 509	2 361	2 512	2 677	2 450	2 558	2 949	3 843	3 693	4 072	4 481	4 868
compounds	1 398	1 377	1 348	1 450	1 318	1 426	1 702	2 186	2 088	2 255	2 614	2 876
straights	810	693	814	844	767	748	845	1 161	1 123	1 353	1 348	1 424
feed produced and used on farm or purchased from other farms	301	290	350	384	365	384	401	497	482	464	519	568
21 Total maintenance (e)	967	953	962	1 008	990	1 007	1 076	1 206	1 283	1 367	1 442	1 467
materials	647	629	633	654	644	645	687	734	789	846	900	903
buildings	320	325	329	353	346	362	389	472	494	520	541	564
22 Agricultural services	600	599	592	635	629	621	679	789	868	927	1 039	1 039
23 FISM	103	86	86	90	111	115	122	146	137	154	176	191

24.1 Production and income account at current prices; United Kingdom

Enquiries: Helen Mason on +44 (0)1904 455096
Email: helen.mason@defra.gsi.gov.uk

£ million

	2001	2002	2003	2004	2005	2006	2007	2008	2009	2010	Calendar years 2011	2012
24 Other goods and services (e)(f)	2 025	2 066	2 120	2 357	2 344	2 316	2 380	2 580	2 669	2 787	3 011	3 057
25 Total intermediate consumption (sum 15 to 24)	9 016	8 787	8 844	9 647	9 574	9 614	10 383	12 918	12 699	13 668	14 987	15 600
26 Gross value added at market prices (12 - 25)	4 516	4 779	5 316	4 978	4 988	4 961	5 452	6 943	6 847	6 962	8 618	8 598
27 Gross value added at basic prices (14 - 25)	6 265	6 723	7 294	7 150	5 203	5 049	5 514	7 001	6 884	6 991	8 645	8 618
28 Total consumption of Fixed Capital	2 616	2 686	2 782	2 677	2 874	2 905	2 947	3 341	3 487	3 430	3 815	4 007
equipment	1 271	1 275	1 231	1 185	1 195	1 188	1 197	1 257	1 352	1 445	1 589	1 698
buildings (e)(g)	694	778	802	825	900	920	941	993	962	840	865	906
livestock	651	633	750	667	779	798	809	1 091	1 173	1 145	1 362	1 403
cattle	348	353	441	364	490	499	503	743	731	679	791	875
pigs	6	8	8	9	7	7	6	7	8	8	8	8
sheep	170	141	173	167	151	162	157	188	269	291	358	300
poultry	127	130	128	127	132	129	142	153	164	167	205	220
29 Net value added at market prices (26 - 28)	1 900	2 093	2 534	2 300	2 115	2 056	2 505	3 602	3 360	3 532	4 803	4 590
30 Net value added at basic prices (27 - 28)	3 649	4 038	4 511	4 473	2 329	2 143	2 567	3 660	3 397	3 561	4 830	4 611
31 Other taxes on production	- 84	- 80	- 83	- 95	- 101	- 99	- 101	- 102	- 106	- 111	- 121	- 121
32 Other subsidies on production (c)	689	712	781	781	2 852	3 042	2 932	3 237	3 616	3 471	3 483	3 240
33 Net value added at factor cost (30 + 31 + 32)	4 254	4 669	5 210	5 159	5 080	5 087	5 398	6 794	6 908	6 920	8 192	7 729
34 Compensation of employees (h)	1 859	1 836	1 827	1 894	1 944	1 973	2 004	2 067	2 167	2 215	2 335	2 355
35 Rent	315	297	311	284	267	286	305	350	366	366	373	426
rent paid (i)	411	383	408	388	352	374	402	445	456	467	477	530
rent received (j)	- 96	- 86	- 97	- 104	- 85	- 87	- 97	- 95	- 89	- 102	- 104	- 105
36 Interest (k)	421	367	340	391	403	372	417	322	167	167	165	192
37 Total Income from Farming (33 - 34 - 35 - 36)	1 659	2 169	2 731	2 589	2 465	2 456	2 672	4 055	4 207	4 172	5 319	4 756

- means 'nil' or 'negligible' (less than half the last digit shown).
. . means 'not available' or 'not applicable'.

Source: Department for Environment, Food and Rural Affairs

(a) Output is net of VAT collected on the sale of non-edible products. Figures for output at market prices exclude subsidies on products.

(b) Includes straw and minor crops.

(c) "Subsidies (less taxes) on product": payments linked to the production of agricultural products. "Other subsidies on production": payments not linked to production from which agricultural producers can benefit as a consequence of engaging in agricultural activities e.g. Single Payment Scheme, agri-environment

(d) For years prior to 1992 the split between compounds and straights was derived from the split present in later years.

(e) Landlords' expenses are included within total maintenance, other goods and services and total consumption of fixed capital of buildings.

(f) Includes livestock and crop costs, water costs, insurance premiums, bank charges, professional fees, rates, and other farming costs.

(g) A more empirically based methodology for calculating landlords' consumption of fixed capital was introduced in 2000. The new series has been linked with the old one using a smoothing procedure for the transition year of 1996.

(h) Excludes the value of work done by farm labour on own account capital formation in buildings and works.

(i) Rent paid on all tenanted land (including 'conacre' land in Northern Ireland) less landlords' expenses, landlords' consumption of fixed capital and the benefit value of dwellings on that land.

(j) Rent received by farming landowners from renting of land to other farmers less landlords' expenses. This series starts in 1996 following a revision to the methodology of calculating net rent.

(k) Interest charges on loans for current farming purposes and buildings and works less interest on money held on short term deposit.

© Crown copyright, 2014

24.2 Output and input of volume indices; United Kingdom

Enquiries: Nick Olney on +44 (0)1904 455355

email: nick.olney@defra.gsi.gov.uk

Indices 2010 = 100

Calendar years

	2001	2002	2003	2004	2005	2006	2007	2008	2009	2010	2011	2012
Outputs at market prices												
1 Output of cereals	88.7	107.6	101.1	103.2	98.8	97.8	90.0	113.3	102.5	100.0	100.8	91.5
wheat	78.4	107.4	96.7	104.2	100.4	99.3	89.1	115.2	95.5	100.0	101.9	89.2
barley	118.8	109.6	114.3	103.6	98.6	94.3	91.9	109.5	122.5	100.0	98.9	97.7
2 Output of industrial crops (a)	81.8	91.5	98.4	93.9	100.0	90.9	89.3	93.9	98.4	100.0	118.3	105.7
oilseed rape	49.4	62.5	75.5	69.0	81.3	80.9	90.2	88.5	85.7	100.0	123.7	114.6
protein crops	132.1	114.7	121.6	119.2	125.9	102.5	71.1	93.0	117.2	100.0	76.0	55.5
sugar beet	127.7	146.4	140.5	138.5	133.1	113.4	103.2	117.1	129.6	100.0	130.3	111.7
3 Output of forage plants	97.0	94.2	92.2	91.8	100.4	99.8	89.6	83.5	106.7	100.0	96.0	77.2
4 Output of vegetables and horticultural products	104.5	103.9	101.2	103.3	103.4	97.6	96.6	98.4	96.3	100.0	97.6	97.4
fresh vegetables	99.8	91.4	91.0	91.8	95.8	94.2	89.8	92.1	96.2	100.0	98.1	93.9
plants and flowers	110.2	121.1	115.0	119.1	113.6	101.9	106.1	107.2	96.4	100.0	97.1	101.6
5 Output of potatoes (including seeds)	135.2	133.2	123.4	129.1	117.8	110.9	107.9	116.5	118.3	100.0	112.1	97.9
6 Output of fruit	56.8	53.6	58.9	70.0	80.0	78.2	91.7	94.6	99.9	100.0	101.3	93.0
7 Output of other crop products including seeds	121.9	129.3	121.8	123.7	102.2	98.6	62.2	101.9	104.7	100.0	99.3	140.6
Total crop output	95.3	101.8	99.3	101.6	100.3	96.0	91.9	103.9	101.4	100.0	103.1	97.9
8 Output of livestock	96.8	100.4	97.9	98.6	103.4	98.4	98.7	97.6	96.1	100.0	102.3	103.0
primarily for meat	95.1	99.2	98.0	98.5	102.5	100.0	100.6	99.7	96.7	100.0	102.9	102.8
cattle	75.8	87.8	90.6	89.4	101.7	97.5	99.8	98.1	95.4	100.0	102.8	101.7
pigs	112.4	107.4	95.0	95.9	95.3	95.1	100.1	99.0	95.6	100.0	107.1	108.9
sheep	92.3	105.2	107.2	113.9	115.6	115.4	114.8	111.7	108.1	100.0	105.9	101.1
poultry	100.5	100.7	100.1	100.0	100.4	99.9	100.1	99.9	100.0	100.0	100.0	100.0
gross fixed capital formation	108.1	108.2	98.3	100.0	110.2	90.8	89.4	87.2	92.8	100.0	99.1	103.9
cattle	116.3	111.1	109.6	102.2	132.3	93.5	85.8	90.3	90.7	100.0	88.5	106.4
pigs	86.9	129.2	103.2	95.4	81.4	98.5	90.3	101.8	90.1	100.0	108.8	124.5
sheep	111.5	124.3	85.6	106.2	83.3	98.9	109.8	77.1	96.1	100.0	119.5	100.7
poultry	79.9	79.6	78.8	81.7	78.4	77.3	82.7	84.6	96.6	100.0	104.1	97.8
9 Output of livestock products	101.7	103.0	104.2	101.7	101.9	100.6	98.3	97.0	96.2	100.0	101.3	98.9
milk	105.5	106.6	107.8	104.5	103.8	102.8	100.9	98.6	97.5	100.0	101.5	99.9
eggs	68.6	108.6	135.3	81.9	135.1	135.2	107.2	87.8	92.9	100.0	98.7	57.5
Total livestock output	98.7	101.4	100.3	99.8	102.9	99.3	98.6	97.4	96.1	100.0	101.9	101.6
10 Other agricultural activities	77.9	79.5	78.2	86.8	76.0	72.6	77.8	88.6	95.5	100.0	109.8	107.7
11 Inseparable non-agricultural activities	90.0	78.3	80.0	82.3	84.0	80.9	85.5	86.1	96.8	100.0	98.2	100.5
12 Output (at market prices)	95.8	99.1	97.6	98.8	99.5	95.6	94.3	98.8	98.0	100.0	102.5	100.4
13 Total subsidies (less taxes) on product	92.2	106.0	106.8	106.9	116.5	107.5	101.9	96.3	99.4	100.0	93.4	85.0
14 Gross output at basic prices	94.0	98.5	97.3	98.3	99.6	95.7	94.3	98.8	98.0	100.0	102.5	100.4
Intermediate consumption												
15 Seeds	97.5	83.1	81.8	75.2	90.6	97.6	112.4	107.0	104.4	100.0	104.5	109.3
16 Energy	118.4	117.4	99.7	102.0	95.0	90.0	94.1	89.9	102.6	100.0	95.6	95.7
electricity and fuels for heating	141.4	143.7	116.1	109.5	104.2	94.9	94.0	94.0	100.5	100.0	94.5	93.9
motor and machinery fuels	108.7	106.5	92.9	98.8	91.2	87.9	94.1	88.2	103.5	100.0	96.1	96.3
17 Fertilisers	126.9	128.3	126.8	123.2	115.1	108.4	109.7	97.6	88.4	100.0	103.2	97.9
18 Pesticides	76.5	78.0	73.7	82.3	75.7	69.9	75.8	89.8	91.5	100.0	106.4	126.2
19 Veterinary expenses	74.8	78.2	76.3	81.6	82.5	78.3	81.9	95.5	102.4	100.0	99.4	101.7
20 Animal feed	93.2	90.8	94.0	95.5	94.4	93.8	90.0	92.6	94.5	100.0	92.1	93.8
compounds	91.4	90.8	90.7	91.7	88.4	92.6	95.5	94.9	93.6	100.0	97.3	102.9
straights	95.3	88.0	96.6	98.5	99.4	90.6	78.9	88.0	90.9	100.0	85.6	81.4
feed produced and used on farm or purchased from other farms	97.6	99.5	104.1	106.9	111.0	107.9	94.9	94.6	109.1	100.0	85.6	86.4
21 Total maintenance (b)	108.9	103.0	99.0	98.8	91.7	88.3	90.3	95.2	98.7	100.0	99.7	99.5
materials	120.9	111.9	106.3	104.2	96.3	91.3	93.7	94.7	97.4	100.0	101.4	100.2
buildings	89.9	88.8	87.4	90.2	84.3	83.5	84.8	96.0	101.0	100.0	97.1	98.2
22 Agricultural services	74.4	74.2	73.4	77.1	75.0	72.5	77.8	88.6	95.5	100.0	109.8	107.8
23 FISM	86.1	93.8	92.1	89.5	98.5	93.1	92.9	95.9	94.4	100.0	95.7	96.4
24 Other goods and services (b) (c)	97.4	98.1	103.4	109.8	103.2	98.9	96.3	99.3	102.5	100.0	102.5	102.1
25 Total intermediate consumption	96.8	95.2	95.2	97.5	94.7	91.9	92.7	94.9	97.2	100.0	99.0	100.1
26 Gross value added at market prices	93.3	106.3	102.1	101.1	109.3	103.1	97.4	106.4	99.5	100.0	109.4	101.2
27 Gross value added at basic prices	91.4	104.4	101.6	100.9	109.4	103.1	97.4	106.4	99.5	100.0	109.3	101.1
28 Total consumption of Fixed Capital	111.6	105.5	104.4	103.0	103.4	100.3	100.1	103.1	98.0	100.0	106.2	107.0
equipment	100.4	98.5	96.7	95.7	94.3	92.5	92.3	94.3	97.0	100.0	106.6	110.6
buildings (b)	113.3	111.0	107.6	104.3	99.4	100.9	103.2	102.3	100.8	100.0	100.7	99.8
livestock	126.6	107.0	110.0	110.2	121.3	109.7	106.5	115.4	97.0	100.0	109.4	107.7
cattle	125.1	110.0	117.3	118.0	133.4	114.4	108.7	121.3	93.2	100.0	112.2	111.3
pigs	96.8	139.2	111.7	111.4	97.3	94.8	98.8	107.3	93.8	100.0	114.1	125.9
sheep	158.3	103.3	102.3	103.2	113.1	113.8	111.6	116.2	109.8	100.0	104.0	96.0
poultry	86.6	87.4	85.1	83.4	85.9	83.4	86.2	86.7	93.3	100.0	107.9	113.8
29 Net value added at market prices	72.6	107.8	99.9	99.2	118.4	107.4	94.4	109.8	101.2	100.0	112.2	96.7
30 Net value added at basic prices	80.4	105.0	101.2	100.8	118.2	107.4	94.6	109.6	101.1	100.0	112.1	96.6

- means 'nil' or 'negligible' (less than half the last digit shown).

.. means 'not available' or 'not applicable'.

(a) Includes straw and minor crops.

(b) Landlords' expenses are included within total maintenance, other goods and services and total consumption of fixed capital of buildings.

(c) Includes livestock and crop costs, water costs, insurance premiums, bank charges, professional fees, rates, and other farming costs.

Source: Department for Food, Environment and Rural Affairs

© Crown copyright, 2014

24.3 Agricultural land use (a)

Enquiries: Lisa Richardson on +44 (0)1904 455075
email: farming-statistics@defra.gsi.gov.uk
Thousand hectares

At June of each year

	2001	2002	2003	2004	2005	2006	2007	2008	2009	2010	2011	2012
Utilised agricultural area (UAA) (b)	17 755	17 701	17 644	17 606	17 614	17 897	17 737	17 703	17 325	17 234	17 172	17 190
UAA as a proportion of total UK area	73%	72%	72%	72%	72%	73%	73%	73%	71%	71%	70%	70%
Total agricultural area	18 557	18 507	18 465	18 431	18 486	18 770	18 692	18 697	18 296	18 282	18 263	18 349
Common rough grazing	1 232	1 234	1 236	1 237	1 236	1 241	1 238	1 238	1 237	1 228	1 199	1 200
Total area on agricultural holdings	17 324	17 272	17 228	17 194	17 250	17 529	17 453	17 459	17 060	17 054	17 064	17 149
Total croppable area	6 504	6 460	6 395	6 423	6 313	6 197	6 215	6 070	6 092	6 015	6 106	6 258
Total crops	4 456	4 574	4 476	4 589	4 421	4 397	4 440	4 735	4 607	4 610	4 673	4 748
Arable crops (c)	4 283	4 398	4 301	4 413	4 251	4 231	4 271	4 565	4 437	4 441	4 497	4 576
Cereals	3 014	3 245	3 057	3 130	2 919	2 864	2 885	3 274	3 076	3 013	3 075	3 142
Oilseeds (includes linseed and borage)	434	369	492	528	564	605	687	621	600	686	742	785
Potatoes	165	158	145	148	137	140	140	144	144	138	146	149
Other crops	670	625	607	607	631	623	559	527	616	604	534	500
Horticultural crops	173	176	176	175	170	166	169	170	170	169	175	172
Uncropped arable land (d)(e)	843	644	718	589	699	663	599	194	244	174	156	153
Temporary grass under 5 years old	1 205	1 243	1 200	1 246	1 193	1 137	1 176	1 141	1 241	1 232	1 278	1 357
Total permanent grassland	10 019	10 006	10 013	9 946	10 065	10 458	10 284	10 395	9 996	9 980	9 858	9 725
Grass over 5 years old	5 584	5 519	5 683	5 620	5 711	5 967	5 965	6 036	5 865	5 925	5 877	5 799
Sole right rough grazing (f)	4 435	4 488	4 329	4 326	4 354	4 491	4 319	4 359	4 131	4 055	3 981	3 926
Other land on agricultural holdings	801	806	821	825	872	874	954	994	972	1 059	1 100	1 166
Woodland	514	524	544	563	583	606	663	705	726	774	786	827
Land used for outdoor pigs	..	..	..	..	..	..	..	..		10	9	7
All other non-agricultural land	287	282	276	262	289	268	291	289	246	274	305	332

Source: Department for Environment, Food and Rural Affairs

Please note that totals may not add up to the sum of components due to rounding. Totals may not agree across tables for the same reason.

#: The 2011 UK totals for other arable crops and glasshouse crops were revised in May 2012 to account for calculation changes in the Scotland and Northern Ireland figures. As a result some subtotals have also been revised.

(a) Figures for England from 2009 onwards relate to commercial holdings only. More information on commercial holdings can be found in the introduction section of this chapter.
(b) UAA includes all arable and horticultural crops, uncropped arable land, common rough grazing, temporary and permanent grassland and land used for outdoor pigs (it excludes woodland and other non-agricultural land).
(c) Includes crops grown on previous set-aside land for England for 2007.
(d) Includes uncropped set-aside land for 2007.
(e) Includes all arable land not in production, including land managed in Good Agricultural and Environmental Condition (GAEC12), wild bird cover and game cover. In the 2009 form guidance notes for England, bird cover and game strips were for the first time explicitly stated as belonging in this category, so the 2009 figure may have captured more of this land than in previous years.
(f) Also includes mountains, hills, heathland or moorland.

- means 'nil' or 'negligible' (less than half the last digit shown).
.. means 'not available' or 'not applicable'.

24.4a Estimated quantity of crops and grass harvested

United Kingdom

Thousand tonnes

		2000	2001	2002	2003	2004	2005	2006	2007	2008	2009	2010	2011	2012
Agricultural crops														
Wheat	BADO	16,704	11,580	15,973	14,288	15,473	14,863	14,755	13,221	17,227	14,076	14,878	15,257	13,261
Barley (Winter and Spring)	BADP	6,492	6,660	6,128	6,370	5,816	5,495	5,239	5,079	6,144	6,668	5,252	5,494	5,522
Oats	BADQ	640	621	753	749	627	528	728	712	784	744	685	613	627
Sugar beet[1]	BADR	9,079	8,335	9,557	9,168	9,042	8,687	7,400	6,733	7,641	8,457	6,527	8,504	7,291
Potatoes	BADS	6,178	6,674	6,921	6,058	6,246	5,979	5,727	5,564	6,132	6,396	6,056	6,310	4,658

1 Figures are adjusted to constant 16% sugar content.

Source: Defra Statistics

24.4b Fruit: Home production marketed for the calendar year in the UK

(Thousand tonnes)

CALENDAR YEAR	2001	2002	2003	2004	2005	2006	2007	2008	2009	2010	2011	2012 Provisional
ORCHARD FRUIT												
Dessert Apples -												
Cox's Orange Pippin	61.0	41.4	34.5	46.6	60.1	64.0	39.2	50.8	46.5	46.4	45.9	32.0
Worcester Pearmain	2.6	2.5	2.0	2.6	2.6	2.3	1.8	1.9	2.3	2.1	1.9	1.6
Discovery	3.7	2.9	2.4	2.2	2.9	3.0	2.9	2.8	2.8	3.0	2.7	2.2
Early Season	1.3	1.0	0.9	1.7	1.9	2.3	2.2	2.0	2.0	2.2	2.0	1.7
Mid Season Desserts	7.0	7.1	6.8	7.3	7.8	7.7	7.4	6.7	7.5	7.2	6.8	5.7
Late Season Desserts	28.9	29.1	22.4	31.7	42.8	50.0	52.7	54.3	60.7	63.9	68.6	73.0
Total Dessert Apples :	104.4	84.0	69.0	92.2	118.0	129.3	106.2	118.4	121.7	124.9	127.9	116.2
Culinary Apples -												
Bramley's Seedling	105.4	94.0	73.3	76.6	98.5	109.9	135.3	123.0	105.9	109.0	110.8	85.8
Other Culinary (a)	1.9	1.3	1.6	1.2	1.2	1.1	1.0	1.1	1.2	1.1	1.0	0.9
Total Culinary Apples :	107.4	95.3	74.9	77.8	99.7	111.0	136.3	124.1	107.1	110.1	111.8	86.7
Pears -												
Conference	35.7	29.6	26.6	20.8	19.6	24.6	17.7	17.2	16.6	27.1	26.9	21.3
Williams Bon Chretien	0.1	0.1	0.1	n/a	n/a	n/a	n/a	n/a	n/a	n/a	n/a	n/a
Comice	2.2	3.8	1.6	n/a	n/a	n/a	n/a	n/a	n/a	n/a	n/a	n/a
Others (b)	0.5	0.7	1.3	1.9	3.8	3.9	2.9	2.5	3.9	4.3	5.3	4.5
Total Pears :	38.5	34.2	29.6	22.7	23.4	28.4	20.6	19.8	20.5	31.4	32.2	25.8
Plums -												
Victoria	7.6	6.0	7.1	8.1	7.3	6.9	6.8	1.1	6.2	6.1	6.0	2.5
Marjorie's Seedling	1.5	1.8	2.2	n/a	n/a	n/a	n/a	n/a	n/a	n/a	n/a	n/a
Pershore Yellow Egg (c)	n/a	n/a	n/a	n/a	n/a	n/a	n/a	n/a	n/a	n/a	n/a	n/a
Damsons (d)	0.7	0.5	0.7	n/a	n/a	n/a	n/a	n/a	n/a	n/a	n/a	n/a
Other Plums (e)	5.1	4.2	5.1	5.5	6.2	6.3	6.2	1.4	6.7	7.1	7.0	3.1
Total Plums :	14.8	12.6	15.1	13.6	13.5	13.2	13.0	2.5	13.0	13.2	12.9	5.6
Cherries (f):	1.4	1.3	1.0	1.1	1.1	1.1	1.2	n/a	n/a	n/a	n/a	n/a
Others & Mixed :	2.7	2.3	1.9	2.9	3.3	3.8	4.8	6.1	6.7	6.4	6.9	5.9
TOTAL ORCHARD FRUIT :	269.1	229.7	191.5	210.2	259.0	286.9	282.2	270.9	268.9	286.0	291.8	240.2
SOFT FRUIT												
Strawberries	36.6	41.4	47.1	52.5	68.6	67.5	83.1	94.0	98.5	95.7	101.9	95.7
Raspberries	7.7	7.3	8.5	10.0	12.2	12.2	14.8	15.5	15.6	15.9	15.5	15.1
Blackcurrants	15.4	13.0	19.1	18.2	19.7	15.6	12.3	13.7	15.8	17.7	11.7	11.6
Other Soft Fruit:	4.9	5.3	5.2	5.4	5.1	6.0	7.8	7.8	8.9	8.9	7.7	7.4
TOTAL SOFT FRUIT (g):	64.6	67.1	79.9	86.0	105.4	101.3	118.1	130.9	138.9	138.3	136.8	129.8
TOTAL FRUIT :	333.7	296.7	271.3	296.2	364.4	388.2	400.3	401.9	407.8	424.3	428.6	370.0

Source: Basic Horticultural Statistics 2013

(a)   Data for both 'Early' and 'Mid/Late Season Culinary' apples has been combined under 'Total Other Culinary'.
(b)   Data for 'other' includes Williams & Comice
(c)   Data for 'Pershore Yellow Egg' included in 'Other Plums' from 2000.
(d)   Data for 'Damsons' included in Other plums from 2004.
(e)   Other plums - Includes other varieties from 2004.
(f)   Data for 'Cherries' included in 'Others & Mixed' from 2008
(g)   Excludes Glasshouse Fruit.

24.4c Field Vegetables: Home production marketed f or the calendar year in the UK

(Thousand Tonnes)

CALENDAR YEAR	2001	2002	2003	2004	2005	2006	2007	2008	2009	2010	2011	2012 Provisional
Roots and Onions												
Beetroot	68.6	56.3	58.8	53.1	51.0	57.3	56.8	55.0	55.2	57.3	59.0	62.3
Carrots	760.0	718.4	602.4	676.1	710.0	711.9	726.7	710.7	695.3	768.0	687.9	663.7
Parsnips	92.5	101.5	91.8	77.4	72.3	83.6	85.6	90.1	86.1	90.5	86.6	82.5
Turnips and Swedes	141.8	103.9	96.5	96.9	103.1	114.9	100.9	106.2	109.0	113.1	101.6	87.1
Onions, Dry Bulb	374.9	283.4	373.6	340.9	413.6	358.8	303.8	349.2	354.9	364.5	313.2	373.6
Onions, Green	13.3	11.3	16.4	14.4	24.1	24.5	20.1	15.3	13.9	14.4	14.8	14.4
Total :	**1,451.0**	**1,274.7**	**1,239.4**	**1,258.8**	**1,374.0**	**1,351.1**	**1,293.8**	**1,326.6**	**1,314.3**	**1,407.8**	**1,263.1**	**1,283.7**
Brassicas												
Brussels Sprouts	54.8	42.7	55.8	44.1	46.1	49.7	41.1	43.3	43.6	42.8	46.8	44.4
Cabbage, Spring	25.0	21.9	29.2	34.1	31.5	35.8	34.8	29.4	27.0	25.7	23.3	23.3
Cabbage, Summer and Autumn	47.8	44.4	40.6	44.3	75.2	61.9	56.8	56.0	61.0	60.8	59.8	49.3
Cabbage, Winter	209.4	177.7	159.4	144.0	156.6	158.4	126.1	149.0	145.9	162.4	151.4	150.6
Cauliflower	107.4	116.5	126.3	168.3	133.2	123.7	122.1	116.0	108.5	109.4	102.4	89.6
Calabrese	59.6	53.0	61.7	65.5	86.9	71.8	68.3	72.9	77.7	79.0	77.7	66.6
Total :	**503.9**	**456.2**	**472.9**	**500.2**	**529.5**	**501.3**	**449.0**	**466.7**	**463.7**	**480.1**	**461.5**	**423.8**
Legumes												
Beans, Broad (d)	11.0	10.3	11.9	9.6	9.9	9.6	9.7	9.3	11.6	11.9	11.3	11.3
Beans, Runner and Dwarf (a)	18.7	19.3	20.4	23.1	20.7	18.1	16.9	15.8	15.2	15.6	15.3	14.2
Peas, Green for Market	6.2	7.2	5.9	5.9	5.9	5.9	5.9	5.9	5.9	5.9	5.9	5.9
Peas, Green for Processing (b,d)	161.0	169.3	167.6	131.1	130.1	124.4	97.8	152.5	168.4	156.3	178.5	126.6
Peas, Harvested Dry (e)	37.7	23.7	16.2	29.7	29.3	22.0	20.4	15.5	20.6	19.6	17.0	7.3
Total :	**234.5**	**229.8**	**221.9**	**199.4**	**196.0**	**180.0**	**150.7**	**199.0**	**221.7**	**209.2**	**227.9**	**165.2**
Others												
Asparagus	1.5	1.7	1.7	1.7	2.3	3.0	3.0	3.2	3.5	3.9	5.1	5.4
Celery	42.5	32.0	37.5	41.3	46.7	36.3	47.2	49.8	49.5	50.5	51.0	50.8
Leeks	44.3	38.0	35.9	40.7	51.8	46.9	50.3	42.5	37.2	42.4	40.6	37.1
Lettuce	123.9	109.9	125.6	142.3	133.0	126.0	108.2	116.8	127.4	126.7	125.5	115.5
Rhubarb (c)	17.4	19.0	18.2	20.9	19.2	17.5	15.7	15.9	19.3	20.5	20.5	21.2
Watercress	2.6	2.4	2.5	2.3	1.9	2.0	2.0	2.0	2.2	2.2	2.2	2.1
Others (f)	121.2	104.0	104.2	111.3	122.2	117.4	112.5	116.0	140.8	139.7	126.0	116.0
Total :	**353.4**	**306.9**	**325.4**	**360.4**	**377.2**	**349.1**	**339.0**	**346.2**	**379.9**	**386.0**	**370.9**	**348.1**
TOTAL FIELD VEGETABLES :	**2,542.8**	**2,267.7**	**2,259.7**	**2,318.7**	**2,476.7**	**2,381.6**	**2,232.5**	**2,338.5**	**2,379.6**	**2,483.0**	**2,323.4**	**2,220.8**

(a) Dwarf beans are sometimes called French beans.
(b) Vining peas.
(c) Including forced rhubarb grown in sheds.
(d) Shelled weight.
(e) Dried shelled weight, excluding factory waste; for human consumption only.
(f) Includes all smaller field grown crops.

Source: Basic Horticultural Statistics 2013

24.5 Crop areas and livestock numbers (a)

Enquiries: Lisa Richardson on +44 (0)1904 455075

email: farming-statistics@defra.gsi.gov.uk

At June of each year

	2001	2002	2003	2004	2005	2006	2007	2008	2009	2010	2011	2012
Crop areas (thousand hectares)												
Total area of arable crops (b)	4 283	4 398	4 301	4 413	4 251	4 231	4 271	4 565	4 437	4 441	4 497	4 576
of which: wheat	1 635	1 996	1 836	1 990	1 867	1 836	1 830	2 080	1 775	1 939	1 969	1 992
barley	1 245	1 101	1 076	1 007	938	881	898	1 032	1 143	921	970	1 002
oats	112	126	121	108	90	121	129	135	129	124	109	122
rye, mixed corn and triticale	..	..	..	..	..	25	27	27	28	29	27	26
oilseed rape	404	357	460	498	519	568	674	598	570	642	705	756
linseed	31	12	32	29	45	36	13	16	28	44	36	28
potatoes	165	158	145	148	137	140	140	144	144	138	146	149
sugar beet (not for stockfeeding)	177	169	162	154	148	130	125	120	114	118	113	120
peas for harvesting dry and field beans	276	249	235	242	239	231	161	148	228	210	155	120
maize	129	121	119	118	131	137	146	153	163	164	164	158
Total area of horticultural crops	173	176	176	175	170	166	169	170	170	169	175	172
of which: vegetables grown outdoors	120	124	125	125	121	119	121	122	125	121	129	123
orchard fruit (c)	28	26	25	24	23	23	23	24	22	24	24	24
soft fruit & wine grapes	9	9	9	9	9	10	10	10	10	10	10	9
outdoor plants and flowers	14	15	14	15	14	12	13	13	11	12	11	12
glasshouse crops	2	2	2	2	2	2	2	2	2	2	2	3
Livestock numbers (thousand head)												
Total cattle and calves (d)	10 602	10 345	10 508	10 588	10 770	10 579	10 304	10 107	10 025	10 112	9 933	9 900
of which: cows in the dairy herd (e)	2 251	2 227	2 191	2 129	1 998	1 979	1 954	1 909	1 857	1 847	1 814	1 812
cows in the beef herd (f)	1 708	1 657	1 698	1 736	1 751	1 737	1 698	1 670	1 626	1 657	1 675	1 657
Total sheep and lambs	36 716	35 834	35 812	35 817	35 416	34 722	33 946	33 131	31 445	31 084	31 634	32 215
of which: ewes and shearlings	17 921	17 630	17 580	17 630	16 935	16 637	16 064	15 616	14 636	14 740	14 868	15 229
lambs under one year old	17 769	17 310	17 322	17 238	17 488	17 058	16 855	16 574	15 892	15 431	15 990	16 229
Total pigs	5 845	5 588	5 046	5 159	4 862	4 933	4 834	4 714	4 540	4 460	4 441	4 481
of which: sows in pig and other sows for breeding	527	483	442	449	403	401	398	365	379	360	362	357
gilts in pig	71	74	73	66	67	67	57	55	48	67	70	69
Total poultry	179 880	168 996	178 800	181 759	173 909	173 081	167 667	166 200	152 753	163 867	162 551	160 061
of which: table fowl	112 531	105 137	116 738	119 888	111 475	110 672	109 794	109 859	98 754	105 309	102 461	102 558
laying and breeding fowl	51 345	49 869	48 547	47 936	49 034	47 530	47 719	44 321	42 663	47 107	48 610	46 633
turkeys, ducks, geese and all other poultry	16 004	13 991	13 514	13 935	13 400	14 879	10 154	12 019	11 335	11 451	11 481	10 870

Source: June Surveys/Census of Agriculture/SAF land data Scotland. Also Cattle Tracing System/APHIS (for cattle data).

Please note that totals may not add up to the sum of components due to rounding. Totals may not agree across tables for the same reason.

#: The 2011 UK totals for other arable crops and glasshouse crops were revised in May 2012 to account for calculation changes in the Scotland and Northern Ireland figures. As a result some subtotals have also been revised.
(a) Figures for England from 2009 onwards relate to commercial holdings only.
(b) Includes arable crops grown on set-aside land in 2007 for England only.
(c) Includes non-commercial orchards.
(d) Cattle figures in this table are based on all agricultural holdings.
(e) Dairy cows are defined as female dairy cows over 2 years old with offspring.
(f) Beef cows are defined as female beef cows over 2 years old with offspring.
- means 'nil' or 'negligible' (less than half the last digit shown).
.. means 'not available' or 'not applicable'.

© Crown copyright 2014

24.6 Forestry[1]

United Kingdom

Woodland area[2] - (Thousand hectares)

		1990	2000	2004	2005	2006	2007	2008	2009	2010	2011	2012	2013
United Kingdom	C5OF	2400	2793	2816	2825	2829	2837	2841	2841	3059	3067	3110	3125
England[3]	C5OG	958	1103	1114	1119	1121	1124	1127	1128	1290	1292	1298	1298
Wales[3]	C5OI	248	289	286	286	285	285	285	284	303	304	305	305
Scotland[3]	C5OH	1120	1318	1330	1334	1337	1341	1342	1341	1378	1383	1403	1411
Northern Ireland	C5OJ	74	83	86	85	86	87	87	88	88	88	105	111
Forestry Commission/Forest Service	C5OK	956	886	842	838	832	827	821	814	868	869	874	874
Other[5]	C5OL	1443	1907	1974	1987	1997	2010	2020	2027	2191	2199	2236	2252
Conifer	C5OM	1576	1663	1651	1647	1642	1640	1635	1628	1603	1604	1617	1619
Broadleaved[6]	C5ON	824	1131	1165	1178	1187	1197	1207	1213	1457	1463	1493	1508

		1999 /00	2000 /01	2001 /02	2002 /03	2003 /04	2004 /05	2005 /06	2006 /07	2007 /08	2008 /09	2009 /10	2010 /11	2011 /12	2012 /13
New Planting[7] - (Thousand hectares)															
United Kingdom	C5OO	17.9	18.7	14.4	13.7	12.4	12.0	8.8	10.8	7.5	6.4	5.4	8.2	12.7	10.8
England	C5OP	5.9	5.9	5.4	5.9	4.6	5.3	3.7	3.2	2.6	2.5	2.3	2.5	2.6	2.6
Wales	C5OR	0.7	0.5	0.3	0.5	0.4	0.6	0.5	0.6	0.2	0.2	0.2	0.3	0.8	0.9
Scotland	C5OQ	10.4	11.7	8.0	6.7	6.8	5.7	4.0	6.6	4.2	3.4	2.7	5.1	9.0	7.0
Nor thern Ireland	C5OS	0.8	0.7	0.7	0.6	0.5	0.4	0.6	0.5	0.6	0.3	0.2	0.3	0.3	0.3
Forestry Commission/Forest Service	C5OT	0.3	0.3	0.8	0.9	0.2	0.1	0.3	0.2	0.2	0.9	0.7	0.8	1.3	0.9
Other[8]	C5OU	17.6	18.4	13.6	12.8	12.1	11.9	8.5	10.6	7.4	5.5	4.7	7.3	11.4	9.9
Conifer	C5OV	6.5	4.9	3.9	3.8	2.9	2.1	1.1	2.1	0.9	1.2	0.5	1.5	3.5	1.9
Broadleaved	C5OW	11.4	13.8	10.5	9.9	9.4	9.9	7.7	8.7	6.7	5.2	4.9	6.6	9.2	8.9
Restocking[7] - (Thousand hectares)															
United Kingdom	C5OX	15.2	15.3	13.9	14.5	14.9	16.1	15.9	19.0	18.9	16.1	15.1	14.0	12.3	13.1
England	C5OY	3.9	4.0	3.4	3.4	3.2	2.8	3.2	2.8	3.5	3.5	2.8	4.0	3.6	4.0
Wales	C5P2	2.6	2.2	1.9	1.9	1.8	1.8	2.8	3.0	2.3	2.2	2.1	2.1	2.0	2.0
Scotland	C5OZ	8.0	8.0	7.8	8.5	8.9	10.4	9.0	12.4	12.6	9.6	9.5	6.9	5.7	6.0
Northern Ireland	C5P3	0.6	1.1	0.9	0.7	1.1	1.0	0.9	0.8	0.5	0.8	0.7	1.0	1.0	1.2
Forestry Commission/Forest Service	C5P4	8.8	8.9	9.2	9.1	9.9	10.6	10.4	11.0	10.4	9.2	7.1	10.0	8.9	9.3
Other[8]	C5P5	6.4	6.4	4.7	5.3	5.0	5.5	5.5	8.0	8.5	6.9	8.0	4.1	3.3	3.8
Conifer	C5P6	11.9	12.3	11.5	12.0	12.1	13.0	12.5	15.3	14.8	12.1	11.5	10.3	9.0	9.7
Broadleaved	C5P7	3.3	3.0	2.4	2.4	2.8	3.0	3.4	3.6	4.1	4.0	3.6	3.8	3.3	3.4

		2001	2002	2003	2004	2005	2006	2007	2008	2009	2010	2011	2012
Wood Production (volume - Thousand green tonnes[9])													
United Kingdom	C5P8	8120	8060	8470	8650	8670	8680	9180	8670	8930	9760	10540	10627
Softwood total	C5PA	7490	7440	7910	8140	8080	8240	8740	8240	8390	9220	10000	10095
Forestry Commission/Forest Service	C5PB	4750	4770	4940	5000	4680	4630	4690	4460	4460	5220	4700	4891
Non-Forestry Commission/Forest Service	C5PC	3380	3290	3540	3650	3990	4050	4480	4210	3720	5070	5600	5737
Hardwood[10]	C5PD	630	620	560	510	590	440	440	430	540	540	540	532

1 See chapter text.

2 Areas as at 31 March.

3 Figures for England, Wales and Scotland, 1980 woodland area figures are the published results from the 1979-1982 Census of Woodlands and Trees and figures for 1990 are adjusted to reflect subsequent changes. From 1998 to 2009 they are based on results from the 1995-1999 National Inventory of Woodlands and Trees, adjusted to reflect subsequent changes. Figures from 2010 on-wards are based on data obtained from the National Forest Inventory (NFI) and adjusted for new planting, but at present no adjustment is made for woodland recently converted to another land use. The NFI did not include Northern Ireland, figures for 2012 have been obtained from the Northern Ireland Woodland Register.

4 The apparent fall in woodland cover in 2001 is due to the reclassification of Forestry Commission open land within the forest.

5 Includes private woodland and non-Forestry Commission / Forest Service public woodland.

6 Broadleaved includes coppice. For data based on1979-82 Census, all scrub and other non-plantation woodland have been assumed to be broadleaved.

7 Figures shown are for the areas of new planting and restocking in the year to 31 March.

8 Includes grant aided planting on non-Forestry Commission/ Forest Service woodland and estimates for areas planted without the aid of grants.

9 Figures have been rounded to the nearest 10 thousand green tonnes.

10 Hardwood is timber from broadleaved species. Most hardwood production in the UK comes from non-FC/FS woodland; the figures are estimates based on reported deliveries to wood processing industries and others.

Source: Forest Service Agency; Forestry Commission: 0131 314 6171

24.7 Sales for food of agricultural produce and livestock

			2000	2001	2002	2003	2004 (e)	2005	2006	2007	2008	2009	2010 (e)	2011	2012
Milk:															
Utilised for liquid consumption	KCQO	Million litres	6 793	6 748	6 825	6 753	6 693	6 652	6 734	6 724	6 678	6 626	6 836	6 892	6 816
Utilised for manufacture	KCQP	"	6 532	6 752	6 883	7 140	6 724	6 490	6 266	6 085	5 840	5 699	6 112	6 260	6 089
Total available for domestic use (a)	KCQQ	"	13 730	13 940	14 100	14 290	13 765	13 478	13 325	13 146	12 816	12 777	13 131	13 292	13 113
Hen eggs in shell	KCQR	Million dozens	712	753	747	730	773	772	742	720	754	751	826	821	797
Cattle and calves:															
Cattle	KCQS	Thousands	2 275	2 072	2 184	2 188	2 290	2 302	2 593	2 616	2 588	2 470	2 698	2 757	2 607
Calves	KCQT	"	152	92	98	87	103	111	51	46	44	43	62	81	74
Total	KCQU	"	2 427	2 164	2 282	2 275	2 393	2 413	2 644	2 661	2 632	2 513	2 760	2 838	2 681
Sheep and lambs	KCQV	"	18 442	12 964	14 993	15 095	15 492	16 284	16 414	15 804	16 697	15 600	14 289	14 477	13 746
Pigs:															
Clean pigs	MBGD	"	12 370	10 446	10 260	9 133	9 150	8 971	8 900	9 274	9 192	8 824	9 411	9 813	10 035
Sows and boars (d)	KCQZ	"	321	180	314	241	240	202	196	210	235	207	c	c	265
Total (d)	KCRA	"	12 692	10 626	10 575	9 374	9 390	9 173	9 097	9 484	9 427	9 031	c	c	10 300
Poultry (b)	KCRB	Millions	844	867	862	882	881	903	886	874	862	868	933	931	952

(a) The totals of liquid consumption and milk used for manufacture may not add up to total available for domestic use because of adjustments for dairy wastage, stock changes and other uses such as farmhouse consumption, milk fed to stock and on farm waste.

(b) fowls, turkeys, ducks and geese

(c) provisional data

(d) data marked as "C" are confidential

(e) denotes a 53 week year for slaughter of livestock

Totals of categories may not agree due to rounding

(p) Provisional data

Source: Defra statistics, Agriculture in the UK 2012 and slaugher statistics: 01904 455096

24.8 Organic and In Conversion Livestock Numbers in the UK

Number of head

	2003	2004	2005	2006	2007	2008	2009	2010	2011	2012
Cattle	126 813	174 751	214 276	244 752	250 376	319 587	331 156	350 183	334 759	290 212
Sheep (a)	n/a	n/a	n/a	n/a	n/a	n/a	884 810	981 223	1 161 717	1 152 097
Pigs	48 803	43 733	29 995	32 926	50 435	71 229	49 398	47 387	52 640	34 648
Poultry	2 166 152	2 431 555	3 439 548	4 421 326	4 440 698	4 362 939	3 958 669	3 870 891	2 838 150	2 457 656
Other livestock (b)	1 714	1 696	2 030	4 903	3 954	4 781	3 404	4 509	4 983	4 150

(a) We are unable to provide full historical data for sheep as there are some inconsistencies in the historical data

(b) "Other Livestock" includes goats, farmed deer, horses, camelids and any livestock not recorded elsewhere.

Julian Groom, DEFRA, Tel ++44 (0)1904 455435, E-mail organic-stats@defra.gsi.gov.uk

Department for Environment, Food and Rural Affairs

24.9 Number of organic producers and/or processors time series

numbers

	2005	2006	2007	2008	2009	2010	2011	2012
UK	6 413	7 043	7 631	7 896	7 567	7 287	6 929	6 487
England	4 554	5 005	5 516	5 474	5 278	5 131	4 897	4 592
Wales	800	835	953	1 230	1 176	1 166	1 119	1 080
Scotland	792	911	860	889	820	737	679	611
Northern Ireland	267	292	302	303	293	253	234	204
North East	129	161	173	179	167	160	152	137
North West	311	332	367	367	333	315	301	273
Yorkshire & Humberside	279	319	356	330	308	302	278	262
East Midlands	416	446	487	449	422	408	383	366
West Midlands	478	520	556	555	507	494	476	442
Eastern	508	556	574	551	529	515	481	456
South East (Inc London)	901	939	1 042	1 041	1 024	984	975	950
South West	1 532	1 732	1 961	2 002	1 988	1 953	1 851	1 706

Sarah Harriss, DEFRA, Tel ++44 (0)1904 455407, E-mail organic-stats@defra.gsi.gov.uk
Department for Environment, Food and Rural Affairs

24.10a Organic and In-conversion Land

Thousand hectares

	2003	2004	2005	2006	2007	2008	2009	2010	2011	2012
In-conversion										
North East	7	5	7	7	5	10	7	4	3	3
North West	3	3	3	2	3	4	3	2	1	1
Yorkshire & Humberside	2	1	2	3	4	4	3	1	1	1
East Midlands	2	1	2	2	3	4	3	1	0	1
West Midlands	4	2	3	4	6	8	6	2	2	1
Eastern	3	2	3	4	5	5	4	1	1	1
South East (inc. London)	7	5	11	13	15	10	7	4	4	3
South West	11	9	22	32	48	47	35	14	14	9
England	37	29	53	67	89	91	68	30	25	19
Wales	8	9	13	15	31	49	37	4	2	1
Scotland	20	14	17	35	35	6	12	13	5	8
Northern Ireland	1	2	3	4	3	2	3	4	4	4
United Kingdom	66	53	86	121	158	149	119	51	37	32
Organic										
North East	20	25	29	23	26	26	27	31	28	27
North West	20	20	19	19	20	21	20	20	16	15
Yorkshire & Humberside	8	9	9	9	10	11	12	14	13	10
East Midlands	16	13	13	12	13	12	14	16	15	15
West Midlands	25	27	27	26	28	30	32	35	29	31
Eastern	10	10	12	11	13	13	14	17	16	14
South East (inc. London)	34	35	35	36	43	47	52	54	51	47
South West	86	91	94	93	106	124	140	175	157	146
England	220	230	238	230	259	284	311	362	326	305
Wales	50	56	58	64	65	75	89	119	120	118
Scotland	352	332	231	200	193	225	209	176	165	144
Northern Ireland	7	5	6	5	7	10	10	10	8	7
United Kingdom	629	622	534	499	524	594	619	668	619	573
Total (Organic + In-conversion)										
North East	27	30	36	30	31	35	33	35	31	30
North West	22	22	22	21	24	25	23	22	18	17
Yorkshire & Humberside	10	10	11	12	14	15	15	15	13	10
East Midlands	18	15	16	15	16	16	18	17	16	16
West Midlands	29	29	30	30	34	38	38	38	31	32
Eastern	13	13	14	14	18	18	18	19	17	15
South East (inc. London)	41	40	46	49	57	58	59	58	55	50
South West	97	100	116	125	154	170	175	188	171	154
England	257	258	292	296	348	375	379	392	351	324
Wales	58	64	71	79	96	125	125	123	123	120
Scotland	372	345	248	235	228	231	221	189	170	152
Northern Ireland	7	7	10	9	10	12	13	15	12	10
United Kingdom	695	675	620	620	682	744	739	718	656	606

Sarah Harriss, DEFRA, Tel ++44 (0)1904 455407, E-mail organic-stats@defra.gsi.gov.uk
Department for Environment, Food and Rural Affairs

24.10b Organic and In-conversion Land use in England

Hectares

	2003	2004	2005	2006	2007	2008	2009	2010	2011	2012
In-conversion										
Cereals	5 900	3 290	8 580	8 412	8 983	8 420	5 295	1 646	971	1 060
Other crops	1 693	2 480	3 166	2 915	2 880	1 969	1 490	540	387	221
Fruit & nuts	227	164	146	192	376	367	307	220	169	103
Vegetables (including potatoes)	1 655	1 190	1 043	1 636	2 042	1 739	1 224	431	239	208
Herbaceous & ornamentals	51	11	174	77	124	475	524	900	436	252
Temporary pasture	10 035	7 874	12 902	19 095	28 553	27 751	16 026	6 410	5 248	4 994
Permanent pasture (a)	14 353	10 634	21 337	27 948	37 929	45 951	38 615	16 828	14 117	10 203
Woodland	464	423	3 263	3 513	4 802	2 196	1 658	1 597	1 578	844
Unutilised land	2 409	2 766	2 613	2 738	3 349	2 208	2 450	1 198	2 274	1 296
Total	**36 786**	**28 832**	**53 223**	**66 525**	**89 037**	**91 074**	**67 588**	**29 769**	**25 418**	**19 181**
Organic										
Cereals	28 578	27 241	30 769	28 702	31 101	35 534	41 092	43 636	40 418	36 806
Other crops	6 004	8 778	6 043	5 285	6 004	5 659	6 412	7 244	6 569	5 741
Fruit & nuts	1 316	1 415	1 447	1 490	1 489	1 477	1 843	1 988	1 925	1 973
Vegetables (including potatoes)	9 227	9 879	10 254	10 775	11 438	13 447	13 228	13 230	11 932	9,504
Herbaceous & ornamentals	134	219	607	606	421	3 710	3 812	3 877	4 557	4 838
Temporary pasture	60 993	63 142	64 711	62 868	72 914	78 549	87 096	96 678	90 856	82 129
Permanent pasture (a)	105 801	112 156	118 833	114 184	126 955	138 952	148 158	182 561	159 047	152 870
Woodland	1 706	1 900	1 800	2 293	4 281	2 115	3 270	4 503	4 623	4 564
Unutilised land	6 439	4 896	3 892	3 658	4 140	4 550	6 263	8 276	5 639	6 334
Total	**220 197**	**229 626**	**238 355**	**229 861**	**258 744**	**283 993**	**311 176**	**361 992**	**325 566**	**304 758**
Total organic area (In-conversion & Organic)										
Cereals	34 477	30 531	39 349	37 114	40 084	43 954	46 387	45 282	41 389	37 866
Other crops	7 697	11 258	9 208	8 200	8 884	7 628	7 902	7 784	6 956	5 962
Fruit & nuts	1 543	1 580	1 593	1 683	1 865	1 844	2 150	2 207	2 094	2 077
Vegetables (inc potatoes)	10 882	11 070	11 297	12 410	13 481	15 185	14 452	13 661	12 171	9 712
Herbaceous & ornamentals	185	230	780	682	545	4 185	4 336	4 777	4 993	5 090
Temporary pasture	71 028	71 016	77 613	81 963	101 467	106 300	103 122	103 088	96 105	87 123
Permanent pasture	120 154	122 790	140 170	142 133	164 884	184 903	186 773	199 389	173 164	163 073
Woodland	2 169	2 323	5 063	5 805	9 082	4 310	4 928	6 100	6 200	5 407
Unutilised land	8 848	7 662	6 505	6 395	7 489	6 758	8 713	9 474	7 913	7 630
Total	**256 984**	**258 458**	**291 578**	**296 386**	**347 781**	**375 067**	**378 764**	**391 761**	**350 984**	**323 939**

Notes:
(a) Includes rough grazing.

Sarah Harriss, DEFRA, Tel ++44 (0)1904 455407, E-mail organic-stats@defra.gsi.gov.uk
Department for Environment, Food and Rural Affairs

24.11 Average weekly and hourly earnings and hours of full-time male agricultural workers
Coverage: England and Wales

	2004	2005	2006	2007	2008	2009	2010
Average Weekly earnings (£)	331.26	357.64	340.60	352.33	356.13	404.05	389.57
Average weeky hours	46.2	48.4	46.1	47	46.6	49.4	47.5
Average earnings/hour (£)	7.16	7.40	7.39	7.50	7.64	8.19	8.20

Source: Defra Earnings and Hours survey

Average weekly and hourly earnings and hours of full-time male agricultural workers
Coverage: UK

		2011	2012
	Median	370.90	372.20
Average weekly earnings (£)	Mean	401.70	390.20
Average (mean) weekly hours [1]		47.2	47.2
	Median	8.22	8.03
Average earnings/hour (£)	Mean	8.49	8.40

Source: Annual Survey of Hours and Earnings (ASHE, collected by the ONS)

[1] Average weekly hours is a constant based on the average number of hours between 2003 and 2010

24.12 Median weekly and hourly earnings and hours of agricultural workers by type
UK 2011

		Full-time		Part-time	
		Male	Female	Male	Female
	Median	370.90	303.60	123.80	x
Average weekly earnings (£)	Mean	401.70	306.10	128.10	96.50
Average (mean) weekly hours[1]		47.2	42.5	20.7	21.7
	Median	8.22	7.41	6.63	7.16
Average earnings per hour (£)	Mean	8.49	7.40	7.26	7.48

Source: Annual Survey of Hours and Earnings (ASHE, collected by the ONS)

[1] Average weekly hours is a constant based on the average number of hours between 2003 and 2010

x = unreliable

24.12 Median weekly and hourly earnings and hours of agricultural workers by type
UK 2012

		Full-time		Part-time	
		Male	Female	Male	Female
	Median	372.20	320.90	122.90	134.80
Average weekly earnings (£)	Mean	390.20	324.40	124.00	141.30
Average (mean) weekly hours [1]		47.2	42.5	20.7	21.7
	Median	8.03	7.39	6.22	7.07
Average earnings per hour (£)	Mean	8.40	7.53	6.82	7.71

Source: Annual Survey of Hours and Earnings (ONS)

[1] Average weekly hours is a constant based on the average number of hours between 2003 and 2010

x = unreliable

24.13 Agricultural labour force on commercial holdings (a)

Enquiries: Lisa Richardson on +44 (0)1904 455075
email: farming-statistics@defra.gsi.gov.uk

Thousands

At June of each year

	2001	2002	2003	2004	2005	2006	2007	2008	2009	2010	2011	2012
Total labour force on commercial holdings (incl. farmers and spouses) (a)	514	507	491	501	494	491	481	483	464	466	476	481
Farmers, business partners, directors and spouses	318	319	313	315	311	313	305	302	289	295	299	298
Full time	163	160	155	151	149	146	141	140	137	134	140	141
Part time (b)	155	160	158	164	162	167	165	161	152	161	159	158
Salaried managers	12	12	11	14	15	14	15	14	11	11	11	11
Other workers	184	175	166	171	169	164	161	167	164	160	166	172
Full time	81	76	69	66	66	63	61	64	63	64	64	65
Male	71	64	60	57	56	53	51	54	52	..	..	..
Female	10	11	10	9	10	10	10	11	11	..	..	..
Part time (b)	40	38	36	38	39	39	43	43	42	39	39	41
Male	22	21	20	22	23	23	27	27	27	..	..	..
Female	18	17	16	16	16	16	16	16	16	..	..	..
Seasonal, casual or gang labour	62	62	61	66	64	62	57	60	59	56	62	67
Male	45	45	44	48	45	43	40	42	42	40	44	48
Female	17	17	17	18	18	19	17	18	17	17	18	19

Source: June Surveys/Census of Agriculture.

Please note that totals may not add up to the sum of components due to rounding.

(a) Figures for England relate to commercial holdings only. More information on commercial holdings can be found in the introduction section
(b) Part time is defined as less than 39 hours per week in England and Wales, less than 38 hours per week in Scotland and less than 30 hours per week in Northern Ireland.

- means 'nil' or 'negligible' (less than half the last digit shown).
.. means 'not available' or 'not applicable'.

24.14 Summary of UK fishing industry: 2002 to 2012

£ million (unless otherwise specified)

	2002	2003	2004	2005	2006	2007	2008	2009	2010	2011	2012
Fleet size at end of year [a]											
(no. of vessels)	7,578	7,096	7,022	6,716	6,752	6,763	6,573	6,500	6,477	6,444	6,406
Employment											
(no. of fishermen)	14,205	13,122	13,453	12,831	12,934	12,871	12,614	12,212	12,703	12,405	12,445
Total landings by UK vessels [b]											
Quantity ('000 tonnes)	685.5	639.7	653.7	715.7	619.6	613.9	587.2 R	582.9 R	605.2 R	594.5 R	627.0
Value (£ million)	545.6	528.3	513.0	574.6	614.3	646.3	634.5 R	679.6 R	720.2 R	831.6 R	770.3
Imports											
Quantity ('000 tonnes)	621.4	631.5	671.3	720.4	753.3	747.9	781.7	720.6	703.8 R	720.2	754.3
Value (£ million) [c]	1,438.7	1,439.0	1,474.0	1,696.0	1,920.6	1,993.9	2,210.1	2,177.2	2,254.7 R	2,558.6	2,568.8
Exports											
Quantity ('000 tonnes)	389.1	479.5	477.8	461.4	415.6	466.9	415.8	479.7	516.7 R	436.1 R	466.3
Value (£ million) [c]	762.2	891.0	886.0	939.0	942.2	982.0	1,009.4	1,166.1	1,345.7 R	1,463.9 R	1,344.4
Total household consumption											
of fish ('000 tonnes) [d]	468 R	473 R	480 R	509 R	519 R	515 R	510 R	501 R	483 R	472 R	nd
Population ('000 persons) [j]	57,990 R	58,142 R	58,313 R	58,473 R	58,603 R	59,737 R	60,816 R	60,907 R	61,464 R	61,528 R	nd
Total consumer expenditure											
on fish (£ million)	2,806 R	2,848 R	3,011 R	3,179 R	3,410 R	3,599 R	3,650 R	3,711 R	3,742 R	3,866 R	nd
on food (£ million) [e]	66,433 R	68,728 R	70,085 R	71,833 R	74,193 R	77,716 R	67,635 R	70,143 R	72,587 R	73,744 R	nd
Fish as a % of food [e]	4.2%	4.1%	4.3%	4.4%	4.6%	4.6%	5.4%	5.3%	5.2%	5.2%	nd
Landed Price Index [f]	103.1	105.7	109.3	123.8	134.4	136.2	141.1	141.7	152.2	163.7	153.9
Retail Price Index [g]	104.8	103.5	101.7	102.3	108.5	115.7	123.9	130.3	138.2	151.0	157.4
Consumer Price Index [h]	104.8	103.3	101.6	103.2	111.4	120.7	126.7	131.5	140.1	153.0	158.4
GDP for Fishing [i]											
Current price gross value added at basic prices (KK37)	367	368	377	407	435	491	506	493	523	404	479
Output index (chain volume measures) (L2KO) (2009=100)	126.0	108.7	100.9	100.5	92.7	99.4	94.6	96.8	100.0	100.5	100.4
GDP for Agriculture, Forestry and Fishing											
Current price gross value added at basic prices (KKD5)	7,999	8,841	9,588	7,174	7,156	8,005	9,093	7,392	9,054	9,438	9,040
Output index (chain volume measures) (L2KL) (2010=100)	104.7	101.0	100.1	106.0	102.5	98.6	108.2	100.7	100.0	110.6	106.9
GDP at Market Prices											
Current price GDP at market prices (KKP5) (£ billion)	963	1,024	1,081	1,139	1,205	1,275	1,312	1,280	1,328	1,361	1,381
Chain volume measures index (YBEZ) (2010=100)	88.8	92.3	95.3	98.4	101.1	104.5	103.7	98.4	100.0	101.1	101.3
Percentage contribution of GVA from fishing to GVA for agriculture, hunting, forestry and fishing											
Current prices (%)	4.6%	4.2%	3.9%	5.7%	6.1%	6.1%	5.6%	6.7%	5.8%	4.3%	5.3%

Source: Fisheries Administrations in the UK, H.M. Customs and Excise, Expenditure and Food Survey, Office for National Statistics

(a) The number of vessels includes those registered in the Channel Islands and Isle of Man.

(b) The quantity of landed fish is expressed in terms of liveweight. The figures relate to landings both into the UK and abroad.

(c) Imports are valued at cost, including insurance and freight terms whereas exports are valued at free on board terms.

(d) Figures for 2001 to 2005 are based on financial year data.

(e) Including non-alcoholic beverages.

(f) The landed price index has been calculated on an annual basis with 2000 = 100.

(g) The fish component of the RPI which includes canned and processed fish. The index has been re-based such that 2000 = 100.

(h) The fish component of the CPI which includes canned and processed fish. The index has been re-based such that 2000 = 100.

(i) GDP for fishing includes landings abroad, according to the KK37 index.

(j) The population estimate has been updated to be consistent with the Living Costs and Food Survey figures, which provide the basis for the household consumption and consumers expenditure figures given in this table

24.15 UK Fishing Fleet[1]

AT 1st January each year

	2002	2003	2004	2005	2006 [2]	2007	2008	2009	2010	2011	2012
By Size											
10m and under	5606	5661	5498	5445	5210	5238	5280	5137	5078	5042	5038
10.01 - 11.99m	517	494	466	446	433	425	424	410	405	396	399
12.00 - 14.99m	292	284	295	304	303	306	310	312	307	304	299
15.00 - 17.99m	327	288	263	239	224	220	217	211	208	201	193
18.00 - 23.99m	446	371	315	300	296	284	283	287	286	274	252
24.00 - 39.99m	376	323	280	267	253	246	228	218	210	200	190
40m and over	72	69	74	70	69	62	62	57	57	57	57
By Segment (based on activity in previous year)											
Drift and/or fixed netters	160	178	177	229	214	468	618	678	665	676	719
Dredgers	182	176	181	169	243	244	219	235	246	245	274
Demersal trawlers and/or demersal seiners	1307	1135	1052	1037	985	1047	1076	1057	1005	926	886
Vessels using pots and/or traps	1058	1084	1100	1061	1073	2208	2186	2186	2031	2067	2083
Vessels using hooks	201	238	147	266	270	224	382	387	488	524	508
Vessels using polyvalent active gears only	10	13	11	20	14	11	16	14	14	19	37
Vessels using polyvalent passive gears only	12	18	18	23	20	68	71	83	85	65	82
Vessels using active and passive gears	3	6	3	5	7	12	9	6	5	14	7
Purse seiners	55	44	45	41	50	34	31	34	40	44	39
Beam trawlers	177	171	175	155	131	126	135	136	124	117	81
Pelagic trawlers	2	1	1	1	1	1	1	1		1	
Inactive during previous year	4469	4426	4281	4064	3780	2338	2060	1815	1848	1776	1712
Total UK Fleet	7636	7490	7191	7071	6788	6781	6804	6632	6551	6474	6428

Source: Marine Management Organisation

1 Includes Channel Islands and Isle of Man
2 Pre 2006 data on activity by under 10m vessels was collected as grouped landings - as such for a significant number of vessels did not have activity listed against them. From September 2005 sales notes were required for sales by individual vessels leading to a reduction in the number of vessels regarded as inactive each year from 2006 onwards.

24.16 Estimated household food consumption[1]

Grammes per person per week

		Great Britain					United Kingdom		
		1997	1998	1999	2000		2001 /02	2002 /03	2003 /04
Liquid wholemilk[2] (ml)	KPQM	712	693	634	664	VQEW	599	555	585
Fully skimmed (ml)	KZBH	158	164	167	164	VQEX	160	166	154
Semi skimmed (ml)	KZBI	978	945	958	975	VQEZ	931	919	926
Other milk and cream (ml)	KZBJ	248	243	248	278	VQFA	333	350	358
Cheese	KPQO	109	104	104	110	VQFB	112	112	113
Butter	KPQP	38	39	37	39	VQFC	41	37	35
Margarine	KPQQ	26	26	20	21	VQFD	13	13	12
Low and reduced fat spreads	KZBK	77	69	71	68	VQFE	72	70	71
All other oils and fats (ml for oils)	KPQR	62	62	58	58	VQFF	70	70	68
Eggs (number)	KPQS	2	2	2	2	VQFG	2	2	2
Preserves and honey	KPQT	41	38	33	33	VQFH	35	35	33
Sugar	KPQU	128	119	107	105	VQFI	112	111	102
Beef and veal	KPQV	110	109	110	124	VQFJ	118	118	119
Mutton and lamb	KPQW	56	59	57	55	VQFK	51	51	49
Pork	KPQX	75	76	69	68	VQFL	61	61	56
Bacon and ham, uncooked	KPQY	72	76	68	71	VQFM	68	69	70
Bacon and ham, cooked (including canned)	KPQZ	41	40	39	41	VQFN	45	45	47
Poultry uncooked	JZCH	221	218	201	214	VQFO	206	199	200
Cooked poultry (not purchased in cans)	KYBP	33	33	35	39	VQFQ	44	45	48
Other cooked and canned meats	KPRB	52	49	48	51	VQFR	54	58	60
Offals	KPRC	7	5	5	5	VQFS	6	6	7
Sausages, uncooked	KPRD	63	60	58	60	VQFT	66	66	70
Other meat products	KPRE	209	216	221	239	VQFU	313	319	335
Fish, fresh and processed (including shellfish)	KPRF	70	70	70	67				
Canned fish	KPRG	31	29	31	32				
Fish and fish products, frozen	KPRH	46	46	42	44				
Fish, fresh chilled or frozen						VQAI	51	48	45
Other fish and fish products						VQAJ	105	107	111
Potatoes (excluding processed)	KPRI	745	715	673	707	VQFY	647	617	600
Fresh green vegetables	KPRJ	251	246	245	240	VQAK	229	231	228
Other fresh vegetables	KPRK	497	486	500	492	VQAL	502	505	505
Frozen potato products	KYBQ	106	111	113	120				
Other frozen vegetables	KPRL	94	88	87	80				
Potato products not frozen	JZCF	90	89	86	82				
Canned beans	KPRM	122	118	112	114				
Other canned vegetables (excl. potatoes)	KPRN	104	99	92	97				
Other processed vegetables (excl. potatoes)	LQZH	52	54	59	54				
All processed vegetables						VQAM	628	621	611
Apples	KPRO	179	181	169	180	VQGN	175	172	171
Bananas	KPRP	195	198	202	206	VQGO	203	208	211
Oranges	KPRQ	62	63	50	54	VQGP	55	62	64
All other fresh fruit	KPRR	276	274	290	304	VQGS	318	351	343
Canned fruit	KPRS	44	37	38	38	VQGT	40	39	40
Dried fruit, nuts and fruit and nut products	KPRT	35	34	30	35	VQGU	39	41	40
Fruit juices (ml)	KPRU	277	304	284	303	VQGX	327	333	322
Flour	KPRV	54	55	56	67	VQGY	55	61	52
Bread	KPRW	746	742	717	720	VQGZ	770	757	728
Buns, scones and teacakes	KPRX	43	41	40	43	VQHA	37	41	44
Cakes and pastries	KPRY	93	88	87	89	VQHB	126	122	120
Biscuits	KPRZ	138	137	132	141	VQHC	166	174	163
Breakfast cereals	KPSA	135	136	134	143	VQHE	133	132	134
Oatmeal and oat products	KPSB	16	11	13	15	VQHF	12	13	12
Other cereals and cereal products	JZCG	293	270	284	291	VQHG	365	370	360
Tea	KPSC	36	35	32	34	VQHK	34	34	31
Instant coffee	KPSD	11	12	11	11	VQHL	13	12	13
Canned soups	KPSE	70	71	67	71	VQHM	79	80	77
Pickles and sauces	KPSF	92	96	91	107	VQHN	121	123	121

1 See chapter text.

2 Including also school and welfare milk (pre-2001-02)

24.16 Estimated household food consumption[1]

Grammes per person per week

United Kingdom	2004 /05	2005 /06	2006	2007	2008	2009	2010	2011	2012
Liquid wholemilk[2] (ml)	484	460	477	420	410	412	352	355	297
Fully skimmed (ml)	158	159	163	173	158	165	172	167	158
Semi skimmed (ml)	975	1008	974	982	987	991	985	984	1051
Other milk and cream (ml)	366	385	395	397	392	427	389	398	394
Cheese	110	116	116	119	111	116	118	118	114
Butter	35	38	40	41	40	39	40	40	41
Margarine	11	20	18	19	22	24	23	20	24
Low and reduced fat spreads	68	55	57	53	51	48	49	46	43
All other oils and fats (ml for oils)	68	70	69	68	72	71	71	63	71
Eggs (number)	2	2	2	2	2	2	2	2	2
Preserves and honey	34	35	34	33	34	35	36	33	32
Sugar	99	94	92	92	93	90	90	93	91
Beef and veal	123	120	128	126	111	112	114	112	104
Mutton and lamb	50	53	54	55	45	46	44	37	36
Pork	56	52	55	54	55	54	53	56	55
Bacon and ham, uncooked	70	68	66	64	63	68	70	69	68
Bacon and ham, cooked (including canned)	43	44	45	45	45	43	43	43	40
Poultry uncooked	197	212	207	208	207	205	201	206	214
Cooked poultry (not purchased in cans)	49	48	48	43	44	41	41	41	37
Other cooked and canned meats	58	56	53	50	51	51	48	46	44
Offals	5	5	5	5	5	6	5	7	6
Sausages, uncooked	67	64	65	65	62	65	66	64	67
Other meat products	330	323	315	316	311	309	331	318	317
Fish, fresh and processed (including shellfish)									
Canned fish									
Fish and fish products, frozen									
Fish, fresh chilled or frozen	42	45	47	43	43	41	38	34	37
Other fish and fish products	115	122	123	122	118	117	113	113	108
Potatoes (excluding processed)	570	587	565	537	535	514	501	496	478
Fresh green vegetables	225	235	221	224	203	201	192	189	183
Other fresh vegetables	536	567	566	566	557	552	565	550	551
Frozen potato products									
Other frozen vegetables									
Potato products not frozen									
Canned beans									
Other canned vegetables (excl. potatoes)									
Other processed vegetables (excl. potatoes)									
All processed vegetables	597	608	601	594	599	597	592	601	597
Apples	173	179	180	178	162	163	156	149	135
Bananas	217	225	226	230	219	205	204	220	214
Oranges	57	59	55	59	49	45	47	48	50
All other fresh fruit	358	392	394	389	360	348	348	347	346
Canned fruit	38	36	39	35	32	29	30	30	29
Dried fruit, nuts and fruit and nut products	46	51	53	51	52	51	52	49	51
Fruit juices (ml)	280	350	366	340	325	302	296	307	282
Flour	55	60	54	54	63	58	58	71	73
Bread	695	701	692	677	659	656	634	621	615
Buns, scones and teacakes	47	46	45	44	43	47	45	46	45
Cakes and pastries	117	122	120	115	111	111	108	105	105
Biscuits	165	165	165	163	170	169	162	164	160
Breakfast cereals	131	135	135	130	130	133	133	132	128
Oatmeal and oat products	14	19	17	19	20	21	21	20	22
Other cereals and cereal products	354	378	378	387	386	393	402	395	392
Tea	31	33	30	30	30	29	28	27	26
Instant coffee	13	13	14	13	14	15	15	14	13
Canned soups	76	82	79	79	76	78	76	75	85
Pickles and sauces	120	125	128	129	130	132	131	131	129

Sources: Living Costs and Food Survey;
Department for Environment Food and Rural Affairs;
Office for National Statistics.
Contact: 01904 455303
familyfood@defra.gsi.gov.uk

1 See chapter text.
2 Including also school and welfare milk (pre-2001-02)

this page is intentionally blank

Sources:

This index of sources gives the titles of official publications or other sources containing statistics allied to those in the tables of this Annual Abstract. These publications provide more detailed analyses than are shown in the Annual Abstract. This index includes publications to which reference should be made for short–term (monthly or quarterly) series.

Table number in Abstract	Government department or other organisation

Chapter 1: Area

1.1	Office for National Statistics - Standard Area Measurement for UK Local Authority Districts (SAM 2013)

Chapter 2: Parliamentary elections

2.1	British Electoral Facts 1832-2012 Plymouth University for the Electoral Commission
2.2	Plymouth University for the Electoral Commission
2.3	British Electoral Facts 1832-2012; Plymouth University for the Electoral Commission
2.4	Electoral Facts 1832-2012; Plymouth University for the Electoral Commission

Chapter 3 International Development

3.1a	Department for International Development
3.1b	Department for International Development
3.1c	Department for International Development
3.2a	Department for International Development
3.2b	Department for International Development
3.2c	Department for International Development
3.2d	Department for International Development
3.2e	Department for International Development
3.3	Department for International Development

Chapter 4 Labour Market

4.1	Labour Force Survey, Office for National Statistics
4.2	Labour Force Survey, Office for National Statistics
4.3	Labour Force Survey, Office for National Statistics
4.4	Labour Force Survey, Office for National Statistics
4.5a	Labour market statistics, Office for National Statistics; Eurostat
4.5b	Labour Disputes Inquiry, Office for National Statistics
4.6	Annual Civil Service Employment Survey, Office for National Statistics
4.7	Labour Force Survey, Office for National Statistics
4.8	Labour Force Survey, Office for National Statistics
4.9	Office for National Statistics
4.10	Jobcentre Plus administrative system, Office for National Statistics
4.11a	Annual Survey of Hours and Earnings, Office for National Statistics
4.11b	Annual Survey of Hours and Earnings, Office for National Statistics
4.12a	Annual Survey of Hours and Earnings, Office for National Statistics
4.12b	Annual Survey of Hours and Earnings, Office for National Statistics
4.13	Office for National Statistics EMP Employment and Earnings
4.14a	Monthly Wages & Salaries Survey, Office for National Statistics
4.14b	Monthly Wages & Salaries Survey, Office for National Statistics
4.14c	Monthly Wages & Salaries Survey, Office for National Statistics
4.14d	Monthly Wages & Salaries Survey, Office for National Statistics
4.15a	Annual Survey of Hours and Earnings, Office for National Statistics
4.15b	Annual Survey of Hours and Earnings, Office for National Statistics
4.16	Annual Survey of Hours and Earnings, Office for National Statistics
4.17	Certification Office

Chapter 5 Social Protection

5.1	HM Revenue and Customs; Department for Work and Pensions
5.2	HM Revenue and Customs; Department for Work and Pensions (Information Directorate)
5.3	HM Revenue and Customs
5.4	Department for Work and Pensions
5.5	Department for Work and Pensions
5.6	Department for Work and Pensions (Information Directorate)
5.7	Department for Work and Pensions (Information, Governance and Security Directorate)
5.8	Department for Work and Pensions (Information Directorate)
5.9a	HM Revenue and Customs
5.9b	HM Revenue and Customs
5.10	HM Treasury

Table number in Abstract	Government department or other organisation
5.11	HM Revenue and Customs
5.12	Department for Work and Pensions (Information, Governance and Security Directorate), Work and Pensions Longitudinal Study
5.13	Department for Work and Pensions (Information, Governance and Security Directorate), Work and Pensions Longitudinal Study
5.14	Department for Work and Pensions (Information, Governance and Security Directorate), Work and Pensions Longitudinal Study
5.15a	Ministry of Defence/DASA (Health Information)
5.15b	Ministry of Defence/DASA (Health Information)
5.16	Department for Work and Pensions (Information, Governance and Security Directorate), Work and Pensions Longitudinal Study
5.17	Department for Work and Pensions (Information, Governance and Security Directorate), Work and Pensions Longitudinal Study
5.18	Department for Work and Pensions (Information, Governance and Security Directorate), Work and Pensions Longitudinal Study
5.19	Department for Work and Pensions (Information, Governance and Security Directorate), Work and Pensions Longitudinal Study

Chapter 6 External Trade

6.1	Office for National Statistics
6.2a	Office for National Statistics
6.3	Office for National Statistics
6.4	Office for National Statistics
6.5	Office for National Statistics
6.6	Office for National Statistics
6.7	Office for National Statistics
6.8	Office for National Statistics
6.9	Pink Book 2012, Office for National Statistics
6.10	Pink Book 2012, Office for National Statistics
6.11	Pink Book 2012, Office for National Statistics
6.12	Pink Book 2012, Office for National Statistics
6.13	Foreign Direct Investments Surveys, Office for National Statistics
6.14	Foreign Direct Investments Surveys, Office for National Statistics
6.15	Foreign Direct Investments Surveys, Office for National Statistics
6.16	Foreign Direct Investments Surveys, Office for National Statistics
6.17	Foreign Direct Investments Surveys, Office for National Statistics
6.18	Foreign Direct Investments Surveys, Office for National Statistics

Chapter 7 Research and development

7.1a	Office for National Statistics
7.1b	Office for National Statistics
7.2	Office for National Statistics
7.3	Office for National Statistics
7.4	Office for National Statistics
7.5a	Office for National Statistics
7.5b	Office for National Statistics

Chapter 8 Personal income, expendiure & wealth

8.1	Survey of Personal Incomes
8.2	Office for National Statistics
8.3	Family Spending 2012, Office for National Statistics
8.4	Family Spending 2011, Office for National Statistics
8.5	Family Spending 2011, Office for National Statistics

Chapter 9 Lifestyles

9.1	Department for Culture, Media and Sport
9.2	National Readership Surveys Ltd.
9.3	Annual Population Survey 2012, Office for National Statistics
9.4	Taking Part: The National Survey of Culture, Leisure and Sport, Department for Culture, Media and Sport
9.5	BFI RSU Analysis; BVA; Official Charts Company; Attentional, IHS
9.6	Rentrak EDI, RSU analysis
9.7	International Passenger Survey, Office for National Statistics
9.8	International Passenger Survey, Office for National Statistics
9.9	International Passenger Survey, Office for National Statistics
9.10	Visit England
9.11	The GB Tourist 2012, Visit England
9.12	National Lottery Commission; Gambling Commission; Department for Culture, Media and Sport
9.13	Office for National Statistics
9.14a	Taking Part Survey, Department for Culture, Media and Sport
9.14b	Taking Part Survey, Department for Culture, Media and Sport
9.14c	Taking Part Survey, Department for Culture, Media and Sport
9.15	Department for Culture, Media and Sport
9.16	Community Life Survey, Department of Communities and Local Government
9.17	International Passenger Survey, Office for National Statistics
9.18	Office for National Statistics
9.19	RAJAR

Table number in Abstract	Government department or other organisation

Chapter 10 Environment

10.1	AEA Energy & Environment, Office for National Statistics
10.2	Ricardo-AEA, Office for National Statistics
10.3	Department for Energy and Climate Change
10.4	Ricardo-AEA, Department of Energy & Climate Change, Office for National Statistics
10.5	Department for Energy and Climate Change
10.6	Department for Energy and Climate Change
10.7	Department for Energy and Climate Change
10.8	Office for National Statistics
10.9	Met Office; National Hydrological Monitoring Programme, Centre for Ecology and Hydrology
10.10	Met Office
10.11	Environment Agency
10.12	Scottish Environment Protection Agency
10.13	Water PLCs; Environment Agency; National Hydrological Monitoring Programme, Centre for Ecology and Hydrology
10.14a	Office of Water Services (OFWAT)
10.14b	Office of Water Services (OFWAT)
10.15	Environment Agency
10.16a	Bathing Water, Department for Environment, Food and Rural Affairs
10.16b	Bathing Water, Department for Environment, Food and Rural Affairs
10.17	Environment Agency
10.18	Office for National Statistics; Department of Energy and Climate Change
10.19a	Department for Environment, Food and Rural Affairs
10.19b	WasteDataFlow, Department for Environment Food and Rural affairs
10.19c	Scottish Environment Protection Agency
10.19d	Northern Ireland Environment Agency, NISRA, DSD
10.20a	WasteDataFlow, Department for Environment Food and Rural affairs
10.20b	Stats Wales
10.20c	www.wastedataflow.org, Scottish Environment Protection Agency
10.20d	Northern Ireland Environment Agency
10.21	The Chartered Institute of Environmental Health
10.22	Office for National Statistics; Department for Energy and Climate Change

Chapter 11 Housing

11.1a	Department for Communities and Local Government
11.1b	Welsh Assembly Government
11.1c	Scottish Government
11.1d	Department for Social Development (NI)
11.2	General Lifestyle Survey, Office for National Statistics
11.3	Welsh Assembly Government; Scottish Government; Department for Social Development (NI); Northern Ireland Housing Executive; Local Authority Building Control (NI)
11.4a	Department for Communities and Local Government
11.4b	Communities and Local Government; Welsh Government
11.5	HM Courts and Tribunals Service CaseMan; Possession Claim OnLine (PCOL); Council of Mortgage Lenders (CML)
11.6	Compendium of Housing Finance Statistics & Housing Finance, Council of Mortgage Lenders; Janet Ford, Roof
11.7	P1E Homelessness returns (quarterly), Department for Communities and Local Government
11.8	Statutory Homelessness data collection from local authorities, Welsh Government
11.9	Scottish Government

Chapter 12 Banking and Finance

12.1a	Bank of England
12.1b	Bank of England
12.1c	Bank of England
12.1d	Bank of England
12.1e	Bank of England
12.1f	Bank of England
12.2a	UK Payments Administration Ltd
12.2b	UK Payments Administration Ltd
12.2c	UK Payments Administration Ltd
12.2d	UK Payments Administration Ltd
12.2e	UK Payments Administration Ltd
12.2f	UK Payments Administration Ltd
12.2g	UK Payments Administration Ltd
12.2h	UK Payments Administration Ltd
12.2i	UK Payments Administration Ltd
12.2j	UK Payments Administration Ltd
12.3a	Bank of England
12.3b	Bank of England
12.3c	Bank of England
12.3d	Bank of England
12.3e	Bank of England
12.3f	Bank of England

Table number in Abstract	Government department or other organisation
12.3g	Bank of England
12.3h	Bank of England
12.4a	Bank of England
12.4b	Bank of England
12.4c	Bank of England
12.4d	Bank of England
12.5a	Bank of England
12.5b	Bank of England
12.6a	Bank of England
12.6b	Bank of England
12.7	Bank of England
12.8	Bank of England
12.9	Bank of England
12.10	Bank of England
12.11	Bank of England
12.12	Bank of England
12.13a	Office for National Statistics
12.13b	Office for National Statistics
12.14	Office for National Statistics
12.15a	Office for National Statistics
12.15b	Office for National Statistics
12.16a	Insolvency Service
12.16b	Accountant in Bankruptcy (AiB), Companies House
12.16c	Department for Enterprise, Trade and Investment, Northern Ireland (DETINI); Companies House
12.17a	Insolvency Service
12.17b	Accountant in Bankruptcy (AiB), Companies House
12.17c	Department for Enterprise, Trade and Investment, Northern Ireland (DETINI); Companies House
12.18a	Bank of England
12.18b	Bank of England
12.18c	Bank of England
12.18d	Bank of England
12.19	Bank of England
12.20	Mergers and Acquisitions Surveys, Office for National Statistics

Chapter 13 Services

13.1a	Business Register Employment Survey, Office for National Statistics
13.1b	Annual Business Survey (ABS), Office for National Statistics
13.2	Office for National Statistics
13.3	Annual Business Survey (ABS), Office for National Statistics
13.4	Annual Business Survey (ABS), Office for National Statistics

Chapter 14 Defence

14.1	Defence Economics (Defence Expenditure Analysis) and Defence Resources, Ministry of Defence
14.2	DASA (Quad-Service), Ministry of Defence
14.3a	MOD Finance & Military Capability, Ministry of Defence
14.3b	Army General Staff, Ministry of Defence
14.3c	MOD Finance & Military Capability, Ministry of Defence
14.3d	MOD Finance & Military Capability, Ministry of Defence
14.4	DASA (Quad-Service), Ministry of Defence
14.5	DASA (Quad-Service), Ministry of Defence
14.6a	DASA (Quad-Service), Ministry of Defence
14.6b	DASA (Quad-Service), Ministry of Defence
14.7a	MOD Defence Infrastructure Organisation, Ministry of Defence
14.7b	MOD Defence Infrastructure Organisation, Ministry of Defence
14.8a	DASA (Quad-Service), Ministry of Defence
14.8b	DASA (Quad-Service), Ministry of Defence
14.9a	UK Defence Statistics 2014, Ministry of Defence
14.9b	UK Defence Statistics 2014, Ministry of Defence
14.10a	UK Defence Statistics 2014, Ministry of Defence
14.10b	DASA (Price Indices), ARCC Database, Ministry of Defence
14.10c	UK Defence Statistics, ARCC Database, Ministry of Defence
14.10d	DASA, HQ Surgeon General
14.11	Marine Management Organisation

Chapter 15 Population

15.1	Office for National Statistics; National Records of Scotland; Northern Ireland Statistics and Research Agency
15.2a	National Population Projections, Office for National Statistics
15.2b	National Population Projections, Office for National Statistics
15.2c	National Population Projections, Office for National Statistics
15.2d	National Population Projections, Office for National Statistics
15.3a	Office for National Statistics; National Records of Scotland; Northern Ireland Statistics and Research Agency

Table number in Abstract	Government department or other organisation
15.3b	National Population Projections, Office for National Statistics
15.3c	Office for National Statistics
15.3d	Office for National Statistics
15.3e	National Records of Scotland
15.3f	Office for National Statistics
15.3g	Northern Ireland Statistics and Research Agency
15.3h	Office for National Statistics
15.4	Labour Force Survey, Office for National Statistics
15.5	Office for National Statistics; National Records of Scotland; Northern Ireland Statistics and Research Agency
15.6	Comparison of mid-2010 Population Estimates, Office for National Statistics
15.7	ONS; Home Office; Central Statistics Office (CSO) Ireland; Northern Ireland Statistics and Research Agency (NISRA)
15.8	ONS; Home Office; Central Statistics Office (CSO) Ireland; Northern Ireland Statistics and Research Agency (NISRA)
15.9	Home Office
15.10	Home Office
15.11	Office for National Statistics
15.12	Office for National Statistics
15.13	Office for National Statistics
15.14	Office for National Statistics
15.15	Office for National Statistics
15.16	ISD Scotland; Department of Health
15.17	Office for National Statistics
15.18	Office for National Statistics
15.19	Office for National Statistics
15.20a	Office for National Statistics
15.20b	GRO-Scotland
15.20c	Northern Ireland Statistics and Research Agency (NISRA) Demography and Methodology Branches

Chapter 16 Health

16.1a	Health and Social Care Information Centre
16.1b	Welsh Ambulance Service NHS Trust
16.1c	Scottish Workforce Information Standard System (SWISS)
16.1d	Department of Health, Social Services and Public Safety Northern Ireland
16.2	ISD Scotland, NHS National Services Scotland
16.3	Business Services Organisation (BSO) Northern Ireland; Dept of Health, Social Services & Public Safety Northern Ireland
16.4	Health and Social Care Information Centre
16.5	Welsh Government
16.6	Office for National Statistics
16.7a	Public Health England
16.7b	Health Protection Scotland, NHS Scotland
16.7c	Public Health Agency, Northern Ireland
16.8a	Health and Safety Executive (HSE)
16.8b	Health and Safety Executive (HSE)
16.8c	Health and Safety Executive (HSE)
16.8d	Health and Safety Executive (HSE)
16.9	Office for National Statistics; Health and Safety Executive
16.10	RIDDOR - Reporting of Injuries, Diseases and Dangerous Occurrences Regulations 1995, Health and Safety Executive (HSE)

Chapter 17 Prices

17.1	Office for National Statistics
17.2	Office for National Statistics; ONS (JYYC); CLG (FCBA)
17.3	Office for National Statistics
17.4	Office for National Statistics
17.5	Office for National Statistics
17.6	Office for National Statistics
17.7	Department for Environment, Food and Rural Affairs
17.8	Department for Environment, Food and Rural Affairs
17.9	Eurostat; Office for National Statistics

Chapter 18 Production

18.1	Annual Business Survey (ABS), Office for National Statistics
18.2	PRODCOM Publications & Analysis, Office for National Statistics
18.3	Office for National Statistics
18.4	Department of Energy and Climate Change
18.5	Department of Energy and Climate Change
18.6	Department of Energy and Climate Change
18.7	Department of Energy and Climate Change
18.8	Department of Energy and Climate Change
18.9	Department of Energy and Climate Change
18.10	Department of Energy and Climate Change

Table number in Abstract	Government department or other organisation
18.11	Department of Energy and Climate Change
18.12	Department of Energy and Climate Change
18.13	Department of Energy and Climate Change
18.14	International Steel Statistics Bureau
18.15	International Steel Statistics Bureau
18.16	International Steel Statistics Bureau
18.17	Agricultural Industries Confederation; British Survey of Fertiliser Practice (Defra)
18.18a	Office for National Statistics, Department of Business, Innovation and Skills;
	Dept. of Enterprise, Trade & Investment (Northern Ireland); Crown Estate Commissioners
18.18b	Department of Enterprise, Trade & Investment (Northern Ireland);
	Department of Economic Development (Isle of Man), Company data (Guernsey and Jersey)
18.19a	Department for Business,Innovation and Skills (BIS)
18.19b	Department for Business,Innovation and Skills (BIS)
18.19c	Department for Business,Innovation and Skills (BIS)
18.19d	Department for Business,Innovation and Skills (BIS)
18.19e	Department for Business,Innovation and Skills (BIS)
18.19f	Department for Business,Innovation and Skills (BIS)
18.20	Output in the Construction Industry, Office for National Statistics
18.21	Orders for New Construction, Office for National Statistics
18.22	Office for National Statistics
18.23	Office for National Statistics
18.24	Her Majesty's Revenue and Customs
18.25	Her Majesty's Revenue and Customs

Chapter 19 National Accounts

19.1	Blue Book 2013, Office for National Statistics
19.2	Blue Book 2013, Office for National Statistics
19.3	Blue Book 2013, Office for National Statistics
19.4	Blue Book 2014, Office for National Statistics
19.5	Blue Book 2013, Office for National Statistics
19.6	Blue Book 2013, Office for National Statistics
19.7	Blue Book 2013, Office for National Statistics
19.8	Blue Book 2013, Office for National Statistics
19.9	Blue Book 2013, Office for National Statistics
19.10	Blue Book 2013, Office for National Statistics
19.11	Blue Book 2013, Office for National Statistics
19.12	Blue Book 2013, Office for National Statistics
19.13	Blue Book 2013, Office for National Statistics
19.14	Blue Book 2013, Office for National Statistics
19.15	Blue Book 2013, Office for National Statistics
19.16	Blue Book 2013, Office for National Statistics
19.17	Blue Book 2013, Office for National Statistics
19.18	Office for National Statistics
19.19	Blue Book 2013, Office for National Statistics
19.20	Blue Book 2013, Office for National Statistics
19.21	Blue Book 2013, Office for National Statistics
19.22	Blue Book 2013, Office for National Statistics

Chapter 20 Education

20.1	Department for Education; Welsh Government; Scottish Government; Northern Ireland Department of Education
20.2	Department for Education; Welsh Government; Scottish Government; Northern Ireland Department of Education
20.3	Department for Education; Welsh Government; Scottish Government; Northern Ireland Department of Education
20.4	School Census, Department for Education
20.5	Department for Education; Welsh Government; Scottish Government; Northern Ireland Department of Education
20.6	Higher Education Statistics Agency Limited
20.7	Higher Education Statistics Agency Limited
20.8	Department for Business, Innovation and Skills; Welsh Government;
	Scottish Funding Council; Northern Ireland Department for Employment and Learning
20.9	Department for Business, Innovation and Skills; Welsh Government;
	Scottish Funding Council; Northern Ireland Department for Employment and Learning
20.10	Department for Education; Welsh Government; Scottish Government; Northern Ireland Department of Education

Chapter 21 Crime and Justice

21.1a	Home Office
21.1b	Home Office
21.1c	The Police Service of Northern Ireland
21.1d	The Police Service of Northern Ireland
21.2	International Centre for Prison Studies
21.3	Police Recorded Crime, Home Office
21.4	Ministry of Justice
21.5	Ministry of Justice
21.6a	Ministry of Justice

Table number in Abstract	Government department or other organisation
21.6b	Ministry of Justice
21.6c	Ministry of Justice
21.6d	Ministry of Justice
21.6e	Ministry of Justice
21.7	Ministry of Justice
21.8	Ministry of Justice
21.9a	Ministry of Justice
21.9b	Ministry of Justice
21.10	Ministry of Justice
21.11	Ministry of Justice
21.12	Scottish Government
21.13	Scottish Government
21.14	Scottish Government
21.15	Scottish Government
21.16	Scottish Government
21.17a	Prison Statistics and Population Projections, Scottish Government
21.17b	Prison Statistics and Population Projections, Scottish Government
21.17c	Prison Statistics and Population Projections, Scottish Government
21.18	Scottish Prison Service
21.19	Department of Justice Northern Ireland
21.20	Department of Justice Northern Ireland

Chapter 22 Transport

22.1	National Travel Survey, Department for Transport
22.2	Department for Transport; Office of Rail Regulation; Department of Energy and Climate Change
22.3	Department for Transport; Office of Rail Regulation; Civil Aviation Authority
22.4	National Road Traffic Survey, Department for Transport
22.5	Department for Transport
22.6	National Road Traffic Survey, Department for Transport
22.7	Department for Transport
22.8	Department for Transport
22.9a	Driving Standards Agency; Department for Transport
22.9b	Driving Standards Agency; Department for Transport
22.9c	Driving Standards Agency; Department for Transport
22.9d	Driving Standards Agency; Department for Transport
22.9e	Driving Standards Agency; Department for Transport
22.10	National Travel Survey, Department for Transport
22.11a	National Travel Survey, Department for Transport
22.11b	National Travel Survey, Department for Transport
22.12	Driver and Vehicle Agency
22.13	Driver and Vehicle Agency
22.14	DfT Public Service Vehicle Survey, Transport for London
22.15	Dft Fares survey; Office for National Statistics
22.16	Department for Transport
22.17a	Continuing Survey of Road Goods Transport, Department for Transport
22.17b	Continuing Survey of Road Goods Transport, Department for Transport
22.17c	Continuing Survey of Road Goods Transport, Department for Transport
22.18a	Continuing Survey of Road Goods Transport, Department for Transport
22.18b	Continuing Survey of Road Goods Transport, Department for Transport
22.18c	Continuing Survey of Road Goods Transport, Department for Transport
22.19a	Light Rail and Tram Survey, Department for Transport
22.19b	Light Rail and Tram Survey, Department for Transport
22.19c	Light Rail and Tram Survey, Department for Transport
22.19d	Network Rail
22.19e	DfT Light Rail and Tram Survey
22.19f	Transport for London
22.19g	Light Rail and Tram Survey, Department for Transport
22.20a	Network Rail
22.20b	Freight operating companies
22.21	Department for Regional Development, Northern Ireland
22.22	Department for Regional Development, Northern Ireland
22.23	Civil Aviation Authority
22.24a	Civil Aviation Authority
22.24b	Civil Aviation Authority
22.25	Civil Aviation Authority
22.26a	Civil Aviation Authority
22.26b	Civil Aviation Authority
22.26c	Civil Aviation Authority
22.26d	Civil Aviation Authority

Chapter 23 Government Finance

23.1	Office for National Statistics
23.2	Office for National Statistics
23.3	Office for National Statistics

Table number in Abstract	Government department or other organisation
23.4a	Office for National Statistics; HM Treasury
23.4b	Office for National Statistics; HM Treasury
23.5	HM Treasury
23.6a	Blue Book, Office for National Statistics
23.6b	Blue Book, Office for National Statistics
23.7	Blue Book, Office for National Statistics
23.8	HM Revenue & Customs; Office for National Statistics
23.9	HM Revenue & Customs
23.10	HM Revenue & Customs
23.11	HM Revenue & Customs
23.12	HM Revenue & Customs
23.13	Communities and Local Government; Scottish Government, Local Government Financial Statistics; Welsh Government
23.14	Communities and Local Government; Welsh Government
23.15	Department for Communities and Local Government
23.16a	Department for Communities and Local Government
23.16b	Department for Communities and Local Government
23.17	Local Government Finance Statistics, Welsh Government, Wales Capital Outturn forms
23.18	Scottish Government, Local Government Finance Statistics
23.19a	Scottish Government, Local Government Finance Statistics
23.19a	Scottish Government, Local Government Finance Statistics
23.20	Scottish Government, Local Government Finance Statistics
23.21	Department of the Environment for Northern Ireland

Chapter 24 Agriculture

24.1	Department for Environment, Food and Rural Affairs
24.2	Department for Environment, Food and Rural Affairs
24.3	Department for Environment, Food and Rural Affairs
24.4a	Department for Environment, Food and Rural Affairs
24.4b	Basic Horticultural Statistics, Department for Environment, Food and Rural Affairs
24.4c	Basic Horticultural Statistics, Department for Environment, Food and Rural Affairs
24.5	Department for Environment, Food and Rural Affairs
24.6	Forest Service Agency; Forestry Commission
24.7	Agriculture in the UK 2012 and slaugher statistics, Department for Environment, Food and Rural Affairs
24.8	Department for Environment, Food and Rural Affairs
24.9	Department for Environment, Food and Rural Affairs
24.10a	Department for Environment, Food and Rural Affairs
24.10b	Department for Environment, Food and Rural Affairs
24.11	Earnings and Hours Survey, Department for Environment, Food and Rural Affairs
24.12	Annual Survey of Hours and Earnings, Office for National Statistics
24.13	Census of Agriculture, Department for Environment, Food and Rural Affairs
24.14	Fisheries Administrations in the UK; H.M. Customs and Excise; Expenditure and Food Survey; Office for National Statistics
24.15	Marine Management Organisation
24.16	Living Costs and Food Survey, Department for Environment Food and Rural Affairs; Office for National Statistics